CHASE'S
Calendar of Events
2004

Contemporary Books

Chicago   New York   San Francisco   Lisbon   London   Madrid   Mexico City
Milan   New Delhi   San Juan   Seoul   Singapore   Sydney   Toronto

The McGraw·Hill Companies

Copyright © 2004 by The McGraw-Hill Companies, Inc. All rights reserved. Printed in the United States of America. Except as permitted under the United States Copyright Act of 1976, no part of this publication may be reproduced or distributed in any form or by any means, or stored in a database or retrieval system, without the prior written permission of the publisher.

1 2 3 4 5 6 7 8 9 0   QPD/QPD   2 1 0 9 8 7 6 5 4 3

ISBN 0-07-142405-9
ISSN 0740-5286

Some interior art courtesy of Dover Publications, Inc.

McGraw-Hill books are available at special quantity discounts to use as premiums and sales promotions, or for use in corporate training programs. For more information, please write to the Director of Special Sales, Professional Publishing, McGraw-Hill, Two Penn Plaza, New York, NY 10121-2298. Or contact your local bookstore.

NOTICE
Events listed herein are not necessarily endorsed by the editors or publisher. Every effort has been made to assure the correctness of all entries, but neither the editors nor the publisher can warrant their accuracy. IT IS IMPERATIVE, IF FINANCIAL PLANS ARE TO BE MADE IN CONNECTION WITH DATES OR EVENTS LISTED HEREIN, THAT PRINCIPALS BE CONSULTED FOR FINAL INFORMATION.

This book is printed on acid-free paper.

☆ Chase's 2004 Calendar of Events ☆
TABLE OF CONTENTS

How To Use This Book .... Inside Front Cover
Welcome to *Chase's 2004 Calendar of Events* 4
Spotlight on 2004 Anniversaries and Events 5
Chronological Calendar of Events: Jan 1–Dec 31 65
    January 65
    February 111
    March 154
    April 199
    May 252
    June 304
    July 352
    August 403
    September 449
    October 508
    November 564
    December 606
Calendar Information for the Years 2004–2006 643
Perpetual Calendar 646
National Days of the World 650
Selected Special Years: 1972–2005 651
Chinese Calendar 651
Wedding Anniversary Gifts 651
World Map of Time Zones 652
Universal, Standard and Daylight Times 653
Leap Seconds 653
Astronomical Phenomena for the Years 2004–2006 654
The Naming of Hurricanes 655
Some Facts about the Presidents 656
Presidential Proclamations 658
Some Facts about the United States 660
State & Territory Abbreviations: United States 661
State Governors/US Senators/US Supreme Court 662
Some Facts about Canada 663
Province & Territory Abbreviations: Canada 663
Some Facts about Mexico 663
Broadcasting Hall of Fame 664
ATAS Television Hall of Fame 665
National Film Registry and National Recording Registry 666
Major Awards Presented in 2002–2003 667
    Tony Awards, Academy Awards, Sundance Film Festival Awards, Cannes Film Festival Awards, Golden Globe Awards, Prime-Time Emmy Awards, Daytime Emmy Awards, American Music Awards, Grammy Awards, Country Music Awards, Dove Awards, Nobel Prize Recipients, National Endowment Awards, National Book Awards, National Book Critics Circle Awards, PEN/Faulkner Award for Fiction, Book Sense Book of the Year, American Library Association Awards for Children's Books, Booker Prize, Orange Prize for Fiction, Whitbread Book Awards, Koret Jewish Book Awards, Lambda Literary Awards, Edgar Awards, Nebula Awards, Hugo Awards, James Beard Foundation/KitchenAid Book Awards, Pulitzer Prizes, George Polk Awards, Peabody Awards, Webby Awards
Glossary 678
Index 680
Order Form for *Chase's* Additional Copies 751
How to Submit a New Entry 752

☆ *Chase's 2004 Calendar of Events* ☆

WELCOME TO *CHASE'S* 2004 CALENDAR OF EVENTS

Chase's Calendar of Events was founded in the summer of 1957 by brothers William D. and the late Harrison V. Chase. They realized then that there was a need for a single reference source for calendar dates—and for authoritative and current information about the various observances throughout the year. Their first publication (for the year 1958) came out in December 1957, and that initial 32-page, 364-entry book has grown to a reference of 752 pages and more than 12,000 entries. *Chase's Calendar of Events* today is the most respected and comprehensive reference available on events and special days, weeks and months.

Process for Declaring Special Observances

How do special days, weeks and months get created? The President has the authority to declare any commemorative event by proclamation, but this is done infrequently. In 2000, for example, the President issued 127 proclamations. A good number of those were proclamations, such as Mother's Day and Bill of Rights Week, for which there was legislation giving continuing authority for a proclamation to be issued each year. The White House Clerk's Office initiates the issuing of these proclamations each year, since they are mandated by authorizing legislation.

Until January 1995, Congress had been active in seeing that special observances were commemorated. Members of the Senate and House could introduce legislation for a special observance to commemorate people, events and other activities they thought worthy of national recognition. Because these bills took up a disproportionate amount of time on the part of senators and representatives and their staffs, when Congress met in January 1995 to review and reform its rules and procedures, it was decided to discontinue this process. However, at times Congress still does issue commemorative resolutions, which do not have the force of law. Some state legislatures and governors proclaim special days, as do mayors of cities.

How do organizations promote awareness about an event or concern that they feel deserves recognition by the public? They can send their information to us for free listing in THE standard reference book for event and observance information—*Chase's Calendar of Events*.

Types of Events in Chase's

PRESIDENTIAL PROCLAMATIONS: In addition to the complete list of proclamations issued Mar 5, 2002–June 30, 2003, we have included in the day-by-day directory proclamations that have continuing authority and those that have been issued consistently since 1995. The most recent proclamations can be found on the World Wide Web at the Federal Register Online: www.access.gpo.gov. In our text, ★ indicates a presidential proclamation.

NATIONAL DAYS AND STATE DAYS: Public holidays of other nations are gleaned from United Nations documents and from information we obtain from tourism agencies. Technically, the United States has no national holidays. Those holidays proclaimed by the president only apply to federal employees and to the District of Columbia. Governors of the states proclaim holidays for their states. In practice, federal holidays are usually proclaimed as state holidays by the governors as well. Some governors also proclaim commemorative days that are unique to their states.

SPONSORED EVENTS: Events for which there is individual or organizational sponsorship are listed with the name of the event, inclusive dates and place of observance, brief description, approximate attendance and the sponsor's name and contact information. We obtain information for these events directly from the sponsors.

ASTRONOMICAL PHENOMENA: Information about eclipses, equinoxes and solstices, moon phases and other astronomical information is calculated largely from data prepared by the US Naval Observatory's Nautical Almanac Office and Her Majesty's Nautical Almanac Office.

HISTORIC ANNIVERSARIES, FOLKLORIC EVENTS AND BIRTHDAYS: Most birthdays here are for people who are deceased—living persons are listed under "Birthdays Today." Dates for historic events can be assumed to be Gregorian calendar (New Style) dates unless (OS) appears after the date. This means it is an Old Style or Julian date. Most of America's founding fathers were born before 1752, when Great Britain and its colonies adopted the Gregorian calendar. As an example of this, we list George Washington's birthday as Feb 22, 1732, the Gregorian or New Style date. However, when he was born Great Britain and its colonies began the year on March 25th, not January 1, so his Julian birthdate was Feb 11, 1731.

RELIGIOUS OBSERVANCES: Principal observances of the Christian, Jewish, Muslim and Baha'i faiths are presented with background information from their respective calendars. We include anticipated dates for Muslim holidays. When known, religious and secular events of China, India and Japan are also listed. There is no single Hindu calendar and different sects define the Hindu lunar month differently. There is no single lunar calendar that serves as a model for all Buddhists, either. Therefore, we are not able to provide the dates of many religious holidays for these faiths.

Omissions/Errors

The omission of an event usually means that information was not available in time for inclusion. Errors in dates are most often the result of tentative information that was later changed by the sponsoring organization.

We welcome the submission of new entries. Instructions for this are on page 752 (or at www.chases.com). Final selection and format of information included in *Chase's* is, of course, the decision of the editors.

Acknowledgments

Many people helped in the process of compiling this 2004 edition, and we are indebted to them. Bill and Helen Chase are a continued inspiration as we prepare each new edition. Former *Chase's* editors remain valuable resources: Sandy Whiteley and Mary Eley. Many thanks to Chris Sewell, who contributed fascinating "Spotlight" essays on Haiti, the Iranian Revolution, the GOP, the 1929 Stock Market Crash, *Brown vs. Board of Education* and Three Mile Island. Thank you to Steve Gietschier for sports info. The reference staffs at the Chicago, Evanston and Skokie public libraries have always been there when we needed them.

Special thanks to our colleagues at Contemporary Books, a division of The McGraw-Hill Companies: Marisa L'Heureux, Martha Best, Gigi Grajdura, Jason Hindo, Vilma Peña, Terry Stone, Jeanette Wojtyla and Denise Duffy-Fieldman.

July 2003   Holly McGuire, Editor in Chief
                                          Kathy Keil, Associate Editor

Spotlight 2004 Events & Anniversaries

The following section focuses on milestone anniversaries in 2004. In Spotlight on the Past we highlight eight different years, from 300 years ago to 25 years ago, and provide an overview of the historical, cultural, scientific, economic and sporting activities that were happening in the year in question. In Spotlight on the World and Spotlight on America, we give more detailed information on a selection of landmark anniversaries that are being commemorated in 2004. If observances are planned, addresses are included for further information. In Spotlight on Education, we offer brief histories of some colleges and universities that are celebrating important founding anniversaries. Spotlight on People concentrates on milestone birth or death anniversaries in 2004. Finally, Spotlight on 2004 Events highlights events taking place this year, such as the Athens Olympics and the continuing Lewis and Clark Bicentennial commemorations.

Spotlight Contents

Spotlight on the Past 6
1704 • 1754 • 1804 • 1854 • 1904 • 1929 • 1954 • 1979

Spotlight on the World 33
David Completed by Michelangelo, 500 years • Haiti's Independence, 200 years • The Iranian Revolution, 25 years

Spotlight on America 35
Birth of the Republican Party, 150 years • The Stock Market Crash of 1929, 75 years • Brown vs. Board of Education of Topeka, 50 years • "That's All Right!": Elvis Presley Arrives, 50 years

Spotlight on Education 38
Columbia University, 250 years • Lincoln University, 150 years • US Air Force Academy, 50 years

Spotlight on People 40
World History • American History • Literature • Children's Literature • Journalism • Education • Entertainment • Music • Art • Science and Technology • Exploration • Business and Commerce • Sports

Spotlight on 2004 Events 61
Lewis and Clark Expedition Bicentennial • Bloomsday • Games of the XXVIII Olympiad • Holy Year at Santiago de Campostela, Spain

Spotlight on the Past *milestone anniversary years*

1704 *300 years ago*

Landmark World Events

Feb 29 The English settlement at Deerfield, MA, was attacked by 300 French and Native American forces from Canada. The town was burned, with 49 persons killed and 111 captured and tortured during a 300-mile forced march. Some of the captives later adopted a Native American way of life. The object of the raid was to recover a bell that had been shipped from France for installation in an Indian village church in Canada. The Deerfield congregation had bought the bell without realizing its intended destination or that a privateer had taken it from a captured ship and offered it for sale in Boston. The Deerfield attack was just one instance of decades-long tensions between the French, the English and the Native American nations of the Atlantic northeast.

Apr 24 The first successful American newspaper, *The Boston News-Letter*, was published in Boston by John Campbell, postmaster of the city. Technically, *The Boston News-Letter* was the *second* newspaper of America, but the first, 1690's *Publick Ocurrences, Both Foreign and Domestick*, only lasted one issue before being shut down. *The Boston News-Letter* started out as a weekly printed on both sides of a single 6.25 by 10.5-inch page. It lasted through the 18th century.

Aug 13 In the War of the Spanish Succession (begun in 1701 after the 1700 death of the childless King Charles II of Spain), John Churchill, Duke of Marlborough, and Eugene of Savoy, leading allied English, Dutch and Savoy forces, were victorious in the Battle of Blenheim over French and Bavarian armies. The battling forces had 50,000 men each. Of the defeated, 12,000 died and 14,000 were taken captive. The allied forces lost 12,000 men.

Aug The British captured Gibraltar from Spain, valuing its strategic importance in controlling the Mediterranean. Gibraltar was ceded to Britain in 1713.

Culture

Publications

Nonfiction

- *Lexicon Technicum*, by John Harris, was an early encyclopedia.
- "Giving Alms No Charity and Employing the Poor A Grievance to the Nation, Being an

---

The Real Robinson Crusoe?

Poor Alexander Selkirk. At the turn of the 18th century, the veteran Scottish sailor threw in his lot with privateer Captain William Dampier's fleet for a voyage seeking riches from the Spanish American empire, but misfortune seemed the only fortune he would find. Scurvy took many men. Dampier showed a ruthless neglect toward his men. The captain of Selkirk's ship fell ill and the new commander constantly quarreled with him. Some of the crew mutinied.

Finally, in October 1704, at the remote island of Juan Fernandez (far off the coast of what is now Chile) the new captain, fed up with Selkirk's adamancy that the ships were not fit to travel, left him on the island, despite Selkirk's pleas. It was the start of a four-year adventure that inspired *The Life and Strange Surprizing Adventures of Robinson Crusoe* (1719) by Daniel Defoe.

Selkirk was able to rouse himself from a terrible depression at his lot and survive on the island with only goats, cats and a dog for company. He built a hut and hunted for food. Selkirk was rescued by the privateer crew of the English ship *Duke* in January of 1709. Unused to speaking, he could only utter "marooned" several times.

As European shipping became more adventurous and aggressive, sea sagas like Selkirk's became common—and were eagerly devoured by the public. Selkirk wasn't even the first person marooned on Juan Fernandez Island, but the fact that he faced all those years alone struck a chord with the public when several accounts of his rescue were published.

Spotlight on the Past *milestone anniversary years*

Essay Upon this Great Question, Whether Work-houses, Corporations, and Houses of Correction for Employing the Poor, as now practis'd in England; or Parish-Stocks, as propos'd in a late Pamphlet, Entituled, A Bill for the better Relief, Imployment and Settlement of the Poor, etc. Are not mischievous to the Nation, tending to the Destruction of our Trade, and to Encrease the Number and Misery of the Poor," a pamphlet (with colorful spelling) reprinting of a speech presented to the English Parliament by Daniel Defoe. The text was only a little longer than the title.

Satire
- *Tale of a Tub*, Jonathan Swift

Theater
- *The Careless Husband*, Colley Cibber

Music
- "La Bretagne," a dance piece composed by Louis-Guillaume Pécour

Art
- *Waves*, Ogata Korin

Science and Technology
- Sir Isaac Newton published *Optics*, which expanded on his theories of light and color. He theorized that light is complex and composed of rays that refract at different angles.

Passings
- Heinrich Biber, Bohemian composer and Baroque violin master
- Thomas Brown, English satirist ("I do not love thee, Dr. Fell")
- Marc-Antoine Charpentier, French composer
- Sir Roger L'Estrange, English translator of Aesop
- Isabella Leonarda, Ursuline nun and sacred music composer
- John Locke, English philosopher

1754 *250 years ago*

Landmark World Events
Jan 16 George Washington—after being shot at, almost drowning and almost freezing to death—returned to Williamsburg, VA, after delivering an English ultimatum to the French at Fort LeBoeuf to abandon their ambitions in the Ohio Valley. The French had rebuffed this ultimatum, and Washington's account of it was speedily printed up and sent to London as evidence of a French problem in America for the English.

Apr The 22-year-old George Washington, now lieutenant colonel, led an advance guard seeking to check French advancement beyond Fort Duquesne (near what is now Pittsburgh, PA) and established Fort Necessity about 40 miles away.

May 9 The first American political newspaper cartoon was published in Benjamin Franklin's *Pennsylvania Gazette*. "Join, or Die" depicted a snake cut into segments representing the colonies and illustrated concern for the French threat to the west.

May 28 Washington's forces made a surprise attack on a French squad and thus began the French and Indian War.

The Building Tension

Tensions between England and France as they jockeyed for global spheres of influence blew up first in the colonies with the French and Indian War (1754–1763) and then into the Seven Years' War in Europe (1756–1763). In America, the battle centered on the lucrative fur trade, and French settlement west of the eastern/Atlantic English settlements prevented English expansion into French fur-trading areas.

Spotlight on the Past *milestone anniversary years*

1754 *continued*

July 3 The French forces counterattacked and hemmed in Fort Necessity. Washington surrendered.
- King's College was founded in New York. It was renamed Columbia College after the American Revolution. *See* Spotlight on Education.
- An earthquake in Cairo, Egypt, caused the deaths of 40,000 people.
- England's Naturalization Act, a 1753 act of Parliament allowing Jewish naturalization, was repealed after anti-Semitic protests. It was reinstated in 1845.
- Human life expectancy was 30 years of age.

Culture

Publications

Fiction
- *The History of Sir Charles Grandison*, Samuel Richardson

Nonfiction
- *Inquiry into Freedom of the Will*, Jonathan Edwards
- *Discourse on the Inequalities of Men*, Jean-Jacques Rousseau
- *History of Great Britain, Vol. 1*, David Hume

Poetry
- "Ode on the Pleasure Arising from Vicissitude" (published in 1775) and "The Progress of Poesy," Thomas Gray

Theater
- Shakespeare's *King Lear* was performed for the first time in North America in New York City.

Music
- *Le cinesi*, an opera by Christoph Gluck, premiered at the imperial court in Vienna.
- *Eliza*, an opera by Thomas Arne, premiered in London.

Art
- *The Visit of Venus to Vulcan*, Antoine Watteau
- *Old Walton Bridge over the Thames*, Giovanni Antonio Canal, called Canaletto

Science and Technology
- Scottish surgeon James Lind proved that scurvy could be prevented and cured by drinking or eating citrus fruits.
- Scottish chemist Joseph Black discovered carbon dioxide, or what he called "fixed air."

Commerce and New Products
- Thomas Chippendale published an extensive pattern book of furniture styles entitled *Gentleman and Cabinet-Maker's Director*. It was to be an immensely influential book on design and style.

Sports
- The Society of St. Andrews Golfers was founded in Fife, Scotland, and later renamed the Royal and Ancient Golf Club of St. Andrews. This organization would become the most august and storied in the sport of golf. Since the 19th century it has been the deliberator of the rules of golf for Great Britain. The nine holes to and back to make the 18-hole standard was established there in 1764.

Passings
- Nivelle de la Chaussée, French playwright
- Philippe-Néricault Destouches, French playwright
- Henry Fielding, English novelist, author of *Tom Jones*
- Giovanni Battista Piazetta, Venetian artist

Spotlight on the Past *milestone anniversary years*

1804 *200 years ago*

Landmark World Events

JAN 1 Haiti became an independent nation—the first black republic of the Americas. *See* Spotlight on the World.

FEB 21 The first steam railway locomotive traveled ten miles in Penydaren, Wales. It was built by English mechanical engineer Richard Trevithick.

MAR 21 The Napoleonic Code was instituted. This French civil code was the most influential code of the 19th century.

MAY 28 France was proclaimed an empire.

DEC 2 Pope Pius VII traveled from Rome to Paris to crown Napoleon as Emperor of France only to have Napoleon take the crown in his own hands and place it on his head, a highly symbolic gesture.

DEC Spain declared war on Great Britain.

- In the struggle between the Wahhabis and the Ottomans, Sa'ud al-Aziz captured Medina from the Ottoman Turks.
- Russia's Alexander I established the first ministry of education in Europe.
- Life expectancy throughout the world was 37 years.

Landmark US Events

FEB 16 American naval Lieutenant Stephen Decatur commanded a raid in Tripoli harbor, burning the US ship *Philadelphia*, which was in enemy hands. (Tripoli had declared war on the US in 1801 for failing to pay off Barbary rulers to prevent pirate attacks on US ships.)

MAR Supreme Court Justice Samuel Chase was impeached by the House of Representatives at the instigation of President Thomas Jefferson in a politically motivated retaliation against Chase's recent arraignments against the administration. (Chase was acquitted of all charges in 1805.)

MAY 14 The Lewis and Clark Expedition—Jefferson's "Corps of Discovery"—headed out from St. Louis with a 33-member group skilled in botany, zoology, outdoor survival and other scientific skills.

JUNE 15 The 12th Amendment to the US Constitution was ratified. It changed the method of electing the president and vice president after a tie in the electoral college in 1800. Rather than each elector voting for two candidates with the candidate receiving the most votes elected president and the second-place candidate becoming vice president, each elector was now required to designate his choice for president and vice president, respectively.

JULY 4 The first July Fourth celebration was held west of the Mississippi: the Lewis and Clark Corps of Discovery saluted the 28th birthday of the US near what is now Atchison, KS. That night Clark wrote in his journal: "Passed a Creek which we called Independence creek, in honor of the day, which we could celebrate only by an evening gun, and an additional gill of whisky to the men."

JULY 11 US Vice President Aaron Burr shot and mortally wounded former Secretary of the Treasury (and primary author of *The Federalist Papers*) Alexander Hamilton in a duel at Weehawken, NJ. Hamilton had insulted Burr and refused to make a public apology. Hamilton died July 12. Burr's political career thus ended.

OCT Lewis and Clark established Fort Mandan in what is now South Dakota to overwinter. It was here that Toussaint Charbonneau and his slave Shoshone wife Sacagewea joined them.

NOV 6 President Thomas Jefferson was reelected to a second term. He was opposed by Federalist candidate Charles Pinkney.

- In its *Marbury vs. Madison* decision, the US Supreme Court found a piece of legislation (the Judiciary Act of 1789) unconstitutional—a first for the court. Through this decision, the Supreme Court became the third balancing power in US government—

Spotlight on the Past *milestone anniversary years*

1804 *continued*

along with the executive and legislative branches.
- Paul Revere petitioned Congress to award Deborah Sampson a military pension in recognition of her service during the Revolutionary War. Sampson had enlisted under the name Robert Shurtleff and engaged in combat for one year before being discovered a woman. Congress agreed to the petition and granted her four dollars per month.

Culture

PUBLICATIONS

Fiction
- *Tales from Shakespeare*, Charles and Mary Lamb

Nonfiction
- *Histoire Naturelle*, by Georges-Louis Leclerc de Buffon, was completed posthumously this year. It is considered a masterpiece of natural history.

Poetry
- *Jerusalem* and *Milton*, William Blake

Children's Literature
- *Original Poems for Infant Minds*, Ann and Jane Taylor

MUSIC
- Ludwig van Beethoven, *Symphony No. 3 in E-flat Major*, "The Eroica"

ART
- *John Randolph*, Gilbert Stuart
- *Baron Graham*, John Singleton Copley

Design
- The dawn of the Empire style in France.

Science and Technology

SEPT 16 Scientist Joseph Gay-Lussac made a solo balloon ascent to 23,000 feet—the record for 50 years. He lost consciousness from oxygen deprivation until the balloon descended.
- *Recherches chimiques sur la végétation* (*Chemical Research into Vegetation*), published by Nicolas-Théodore de Saussure, proved the theory that plants absorb water and carbon dioxide in sunlight.
- The Royal Horticultural Society was founded in England.
- The element iridium was discovered.

Commerce and New Products
- The mechanical loom was invented.
- Invention of the bouillon tablet.

Passings
- Alexander Hamilton, American founding father
- Immanuel Kant, German philosopher
- Jacques Necker, French banker and statesman—his dismissal as head of France's Department of Finance was the immediate cause of the storming of the Bastille on July 14, 1789.
- Joseph Priestley, English scientist, discoverer of oxygen
- George Walton, signer of the US Declaration of Independence

1854 *150 years ago*

Landmark World Events

MAR 1 In the "Plan de Ayutla," a liberal junta called for the ouster of Antonio López de Santa Anna, the "Napoleon of the West" and dictator of Mexico. Various states began to join the rebellion during 1854. (Santa Anna renounced his presidency early the next year.)

MAR 28 Great Britain and France declared war on Russia in support of the Ottoman Turks, as the Crimean War escalated.

MAR Justo José Urquiza was inaugurated as first president of the Republic of Argentina, a confederacy. The province of Buenos Aires (which included the powerful city of the same name), rejecting the 1853 constitution that set up the Argentine confederacy, proclaimed its own independence and drew up a separate constitution.

Spotlight on the Past *milestone anniversary years*

June 10 Reconstruction of Crystal Palace was finished in London's Sydenham Park, and this day marked the official opening by Queen Victoria. The ceremony was delayed a month due to several problems; one of them was that all statues of male nudes had to have drapery added so as not to upset the public.

Sept During the Crimean War, allied forces laid siege to the Russian stronghold of Sebastopol on the shores of the Black Sea. The siege lasted a year.

Oct 25 The Battle of Balaklava took place. Misunderstanding their orders, British light cavalry (the "Light Brigade") attempted to take a Russian position by charging through a valley, leaving them vulnerable to fire. They lost more than a third of their men. The battle inspired the Tennyson poem, "Charge of the Light Brigade."

- Florence Nightingale organized 38 women as nurses to aid the injured in the Crimean War.
- Pope Pius IX declared the doctrine of the immaculate conception of the Virgin Mary to be an article of faith.
- The National Institute for Blind Children in Paris, France, adopted the Braille system, a code using raised dots within a grid that enabled the blind to read. Its developer, Louis Braille, had taken inspiration from a similar military code for night reading. Braille had died in 1852 not knowing his system would be a success.

Landmark US Events

Feb–Mar The Treaty of Kanagawa with Japan opened up diplomatic relations with the US. Commodore Matthew Perry's naval flotilla had entered Japan's Uraga Harbour seeking relations the year before.

Mar Irish noble Sir St. George Gore organized a two-year hunting spree that eventually covered 6,000 miles of the Great Plains. He left St. Louis with an entourage of 40 servants, cooks, guides, dog handlers and various companions, plus 100 horses (16 alone to haul his luggage), 36 greyhounds and 18 foxhounds. The party traveled in six wagons and more than 20 carts that carried china, linen and crystal besides the needed weaponry. The hunters killed an estimated 2,000 buffalo,

Dawn of the Plains Indians Wars, August 1854

The Louisiana Purchase of 1803 began the expansion west by Anglo settlers. Caused in part by the Gold Rush of 1849, encroachment into Native American territory created extreme tension by the mid-1800s. Fort Laramie, a strategic settlement on the Oregon Trail in what is now Wyoming, was the locus of a key treaty in 1851 meant to ease these tensions. Representatives from the Sioux, Cheyenne, Arapaho, Crow, Assinaboine, Mandan, Gros Ventre and Arickaree met with US military officials to determine tribal boundaries, cede some tribal land and recognize Native American sovereignty. The Fort Laramie Treaty was to be the model for many future treaties.

Unfortunately, the treaty was violated on Aug 19, 1854, when Second Lieutenant John Grattan led 30 soldiers from Fort Laramie into a Lakota Sioux encampment to arrest a brave for shooting a Mormon settler's calf. By the terms of the 1851 treaty, Chief Conquering Bear offered restitution for the animal, but Grattan instead opened fire on the village, killing Conquering Bear. The Sioux counterattacked and killed Grattan and all his men.

For the tribes involved, the attack confirmed their mistrust of Americans; for Secretary of War Jefferson Davis, the counterattack was a deliberately hostile military action, and he authorized an expedition a year later against the Sioux led by General William S. Harney. On Sept 3, 1855, Harney's 600 men attacked the small Sioux village of 250, killed 85 and carried away 70 women and children.

The Plains Indians Wars had begun. The coming decades would see escalating bloodshed and counter reprisals.

Spotlight on the Past *milestone anniversary years*

1854 *continued*

1,500 deer and elk, more than 100 bears and other animals. Plains tribes complained to the US government to no avail.

MAY 30 Congress passed the controversial Kansas-Nebraska Act, which repealed the Missouri Compromise and allowed inhabitants of Kansas and Nebraska to determine their slave- or nonslave-holding status. The act ushered in a time of great violence in the two territories.

JULY 6 In opposition to the Kansas-Nebraska Act, the Republican Party was formally founded and named at a convention in Jackson, MI. The party had originated at a convention at Ripon, WI, on Feb 28 of this year. *See* Spotlight on America.

OCT 16 Abraham Lincoln, like other Whigs dismayed at the Kansas-Nebraska Act, made a speech at Peoria, IL, in which he declaimed, "I hate [slavery] because it deprives the republican example of its just influence in the world—enables the enemies of free institutions, with plausibility, to taunt us as hypocrites—causes the real friends of freedom to doubt our sincerity." (Lincoln would join the new Republican Party in 1856.)

- The first "orphan train" arrived in Dowagiak, MI, this year. Orphan trains took homeless and orphaned New York children to the Midwest for adoption and foster care (the first instance of foster care in the US). From 1854 to 1929, when the last train went west, it is estimated that 150,000 children were relocated.
- Suffragette Elizabeth Cady Stanton was invited to speak at the New York state legislature.

A DIFFERENT DRUMMER

On July 4, 1845, Henry David Thoreau moved into a cabin that he had built on the shore of Walden Pond in Massachusetts. For more than two years, Thoreau engaged in an experiment of living simply. While he was there he began work on what would be one of the great works of American literature, *Walden*—a description and meditation of Thoreau's time at the pond. At a time of hastening American industrialization and urbanization, *Walden* spoke of the nobility of the individual self and of being in tune with Nature. *Walden* was published on Aug 9, 1854.

Walden sold slowly—it was the second and last book that Thoreau wrote. Critics of the time attacked it as anarchic and pantheistic—John Greenleaf Whittier pronounced it "wicked and heathenish." Thoreau, who died in 1862, never was to see his work grow in popularity and touch a chord in generations of readers.

Here are just a few of the sage thoughts from *Walden*:
- Our life is frittered away by detail.
- Simplify, simplify.
- The mass of men lead lives of quiet desperation.
- Beware of all enterprises that require new clothes.
- Heaven is under our feet as well as over our heads.
- If a man does not keep pace with his companions, perhaps it is because he hears a different drummer. Let him step to the music which he hears, however measured or far away.

Culture

PUBLICATIONS

Fiction
- *Hard Times*, Charles Dickens
- *North and South*, Elizabeth Gaskell

Nonfiction
- AUG 9 *Walden*, by Henry David Thoreau, was published by Ticknor and Fields.
- *The Life of P.T. Barnum, Written by Himself*, by circus impresario P.T. Barnum
- *Boyhood*, Leo Tolstoy

Children's Literature
- *A Child's History of England*, Charles Dickens
- *Flower Fables*, Louisa May Alcott (Alcott's first book—written for Ralph Waldo Emerson's daughter)

Poetry
- "Charge of the Light Brigade," Alfred, Lord Tennyson

Spotlight on the Past *milestone anniversary years*

Note
- The Boston Public Library, established in 1848 and a prototype for all new public libraries in America, opened its doors in 1854.

Music

Feb 9 The winners of a contest to find the Mexican national anthem were announced on this date. Francisco González Bocanegra wrote the lyrics and Jaime Nunó composed the music. The "Himno Nacional Mexicano" was first performed on Sept 15, 1854, at the Santa Anna Theatre (later renamed the National Theatre) in Mexico City.

Popular Songs
- "Jeanie with the Light Brown Hair," Stephen Foster
- "Pop Goes the Weasel," a nursery rhyme/song of anonymous creation

Art

- *The Winnowers*, Gustave Courbet
- *John Ruskin*, John Everett Millais

Science and Technology

- During the Soho, London, cholera outbreak of August 1854 that killed 600 people, English scientist John Snow demonstrated that cholera is not airborne as many thought but is rather caused by ingestion. He didn't know the bacteria that caused the disease, but through meticulous and quick research, he traced it to a neighborhood water pump. When the pump was shut down, the number of cholera cases plummeted.
- Dr. Samuel D. Gross published *A Practical Treatise on Foreign Bodies in the Air Passages*—the first serious look at choking and how to save its victims. He advocated tracheotomies.

> ## Victorian Visions of Dinosaurs, June 10, 1854
>
> When Crystal Palace was reopened to the public in Sydenham Park, London, in 1854, among the attractions were the first full-size replicas of dinosaurs ever created. Sculptor Benjamin Waterhouse Hawkins, directed by Sir Richard Owen (who coined the term "dinosaur" in 1842), made iguanodons, pterodactyls, plesiosaurs and other prehistoric creatures of concrete, bricks and iron hoops. Since no complete dinosaur skeletons had been found at that point, the replicas were created out of conjecture but gave the public a way to imagine the "terrible lizards." (Later paleontology discoveries revealed that the replica iguanodon's "horn" should have been its thumb.)

Commerce and New Products

Dec 15 Philadelphia implemented a street-cleaning machine: a cart with rotating brooms.

Dec 30 The first US oil company was founded: Pennsylvania Rock Oil Company.

- Wood pulp paper was introduced.

Sports

- In baseball, the playing ball's weight was increased to 5.5 or 6.5 ounces and was enlarged to a diameter of 2.75 or 3.5 inches.

Passings

- Conquering Bear, Lakota Sioux chief, one of the signers of the Fort Laramie Treaty of 1851
- Nicolás Bravo, one of the founders and former president of the Republic of Mexico
- Thomas "Broken Hand" Fitzpatrick, Irish-born legendary mountain man, fur trapper, guide and Indian agent who helped negotiate many treaties between Plains Indians tribes and the US government
- Fanny Forester (Emily Chubbock Judson), American poet and author
- James Montgomery, Scottish poet and hymnist
- Friedrich Schelling, German philosopher
- Qa' ani, Iranian classical poet

Spotlight on the Past *milestone anniversary years*

1904 *100 years ago*

Landmark World Events

FEB The Russo-Japanese War began when the Japanese attacked Port Arthur, a Russian base in Manchuria. The Japanese previously had demanded that Russia abandon its occupation of Manchuria, which had begun in 1900 after the Boxer Rebellion, and Korea. The Russians had built the Trans-Siberian Railroad through Manchuria to reach Vladivostok. The Russo-Japanese War harkened an age of modern warfare with the introduction of torpedoes, land mines and other advanced weaponry that enabled the smaller Japanese army to soundly defeat the larger Russian one in several land and naval battles. The war ended in September 1905 through the intercession of American president Theodore Roosevelt.

MAY Construction began on the Panama Canal.

- US Army surgeon William Gorgas was sent to Panama to rid the area of yellow fever and malaria. In two years, his success led to the completion of the canal that proved to be a major aid to worldwide commerce. He was later knighted in Great Britain for his efforts.
- Life expectancy throughout the world was 48 years.

THE 1904 WORLD'S FAIR: THE LOUISIANA PURCHASE EXPOSITION

Grander in all ways than the Columbian Exposition in Chicago in 1893, this fair was meant to honor the centennial of the Louisiana Purchase of 1803, but construction delays pushed it into 1904. The fair covered two square miles and contained 200 buildings. More than 200,000 people attended the opening day on Apr 30, and by fair's end, some 20 million people had sampled its delights.

The fair introduced ice cream cones, hot dogs, iced tea (an emergency measure since hot tea wasn't selling in summer), Dr. Pepper (a health drink around for some years but popularized at the fair) and sugar floss—now known as cotton candy. Fair goers were thrilled with wireless telegraphy and moving picture demonstrations, air conditioning and more. Thomas Edison himself oversaw much of the electronic displays.

One young cowboy who displayed dashing Western rope tricks at the fair would later become a beloved American entertainer: Will Rogers. He was 25 years old.

Landmark US Events

APR 30 The St. Louis World's Fair opened. It closed on Dec 1.

JUNE 15 The excursion sidewheel steamboat *General Slocum*, chartered by St. Mark's Lutheran Church in New York City, caught fire in the East River. Of 1,331 passengers, 1,021 perished—affecting 600 households in the Little Germany neighborhood.

JUNE 28 Helen Keller graduated cum laude from Radcliffe College, the first deaf and blind person to earn a bachelor's degree.

OCT 27 After four years of digging and construction, the New York City subway began operation, running from City Hall to West 145th Street.

NOV 8 Theodore Roosevelt was elected president in his own right (he had become president in 1901 after the assassination of William McKinley). His opponent was Democrat Alton B. Parker. Roosevelt's promise to Americans was the "square deal." In a campaign speech he had stated, "We must treat each man on his worth and merits as a man. We must see that each is given a square deal, because he is entitled to no more and should receive no less."

DEC 6 In a message to Congress, President Roosevelt defended the right of the US to intervene on behalf of Western Hemisphere nations under pressure (and in danger of attack) from European ones (specifically at the time European nations seeking to collect debts). This defense became

Spotlight on the Past *milestone anniversary years*

known as the Roosevelt Corollary to the Monroe Doctrine (which challenged European interference in the Western Hemisphere), and it described the US's role as one of "international police power" in the Western Hemisphere to combat "chronic wrongdoing."
- The Explorer's Club was founded in 1904 for explorers and scientists. New York–based, it was (and is still today) dedicated "to the advancement of field research, scientific exploration, and the ideal that it is vital to preserve the instinct to explore."
- American Red Cross founder Clara Barton was forced to resign as its leader after heading it for more than 20 years. Mabel Boardman became the new head.
- The American Lung Association was founded.

Culture
Publications

Fiction
- *The Sea-Wolf*, Jack London
- *The Golden Bowl*, Henry James
- *Nostromo*, Joseph Conrad
- *Green Mansions*, William Henry Hudson
- *The Return of Sherlock Holmes*, Arthur Conan Doyle
- *Cabbages and Kings*, O. Henry

Nonfiction
- *Zur Psychopathologie des Alltagslebens* (*The Psychopathology of Everyday Life*) was published by Sigmund Freud. This book represented Freud's summation of the meaning behind verbal slip-ups—now referred to as "Freudian slips."
- *History of the Standard Oil Company*, Ida Tarbell—this two-volume history led to federal action to break up John D. Rockefeller's giant corporation.
- *The Protestant Ethic and the Birth of Capitalism*, Max Weber
- *Mont-Saint-Michel and Chartres*, Henry Adams

Children's Literature
- *Poems of Childhood*, by Eugene Field, illustrated by Maxfield Parrish

Notes
- Frédéric Mistral from France and José Echegaray y Eizaguirre from Spain shared the Nobel Prize for literature.
- On June 16, 1904, young Irish writer James Joyce "walked out" with Nora Barnacle. In 1922, Joyce memorialized this day in Dublin in *Ulysses*. See Spotlight on 2004 Events.

Theater
Feb 17 Giacomo Puccini's *Madama Butterfly* was performed for the first time in Milan. The sold-out crowd, restive at what they saw as Puccini's lack of originality, began catcalls, boos, moos, groans and heckling to the extent that the performers couldn't hear the orchestra. Rosina Storchio, the soprano portraying Madama Butterfly, began crying on stage. Puccini, enraged at the opera's reception (saying the opera was "daisies thrown to swine"), nevertheless revised the work, and it had a successful performance on May 24.

Dec 27 *Peter Pan*, a play by James Barrie, opened in London. Although the character of Peter Pan was introduced briefly in some of Barrie's prose fiction in 1900 and 1902, the play fully created the world of Never-Never-Land and such immortal characters as Wendy, Captain Hook, Tinker Bell and the Lost Boys. The London production involved complicated new mechanics to enable "flying" and a large "reducing lens" to make Tinker Bell appear smaller to the audience. Gerald du Maurier (father of novelist Daphne du Maurier) played Captain Hook and Nina Boucicault played Peter Pan. The play was a great success and has consistently been in production since 1904.
- *The Cherry Orchard*, by Anton Chekhov, premiered at the Moscow Art Theater in Russia.
- *Riders to the Sea,* J.M. Synge
- *Little Johnny Jones* opened on Broadway with book, music and lyrics by George M. Cohan and starring—George M. Cohan.

Notes
- In London, famed American actor and stage manager William Gillette was starring in a revival of his play *Sherlock Holmes* (1899). A teenaged Charlie Chaplin was in the cast.

Spotlight on the Past *milestone anniversary years*

1904 *continued*

- Lady Augusta Gregory became director of Ireland's Abbey Theatre.

Music

- The London Symphony Orchestra was established. It is now that city's oldest operating symphony.

Popular Songs

- "Give My Regards to Broadway," "Yankee Doodle Dandy," by George M. Cohan from *Little Johnny Jones*
- "Meet Me in St. Louis" and "St. Louis Rag," written for the 1904 World's Fair in St. Louis
- "The Chrysanthemum" and "Cascades," by Scott Joplin

Art

- *Le Repas Frugal* and *Meditation*, Pablo Picasso
- *Bassin des Nymphéas* (*Waterlily Pond*), Claude Monet

Notes

- Spanish artist Pablo Picasso moved permanently to France in 1904.

Science and Technology

- Dr. I.P. Pavlov received a Nobel Prize in medicine for his work on the "physiology of digestion," which led to his later study of conditioned reflexes.
- Japanese physicist Hantaro Nagaoka offered a "Saturnian" theory of an atomic model where electrons rotated around a nucleus. Nobel Prize laureate Ernest Rutherford would offer a more coherent theory in 1911.
- *Radio-activity* was published by Ernest Rutherford.
- Silicones were discovered.

Commerce and New Products

Mar Louis Cartier invented the wristwatch for Brazilian aviator Alberto Santos-Dumont, who needed a more effective timing device than a cumbersome pocket watch.
Aug 23 Snow chains for automobiles were patented by Harry D. Weed.
Nov 8 The electric power plug was patented.
Nov 22 The electric motor was patented by Mathias Pfatischer of Philadelphia.
- 22-year-old Chicago cobbler William Scholl invented a leather arch support (the "Foot-Eazer") and started a foot-care company that quickly became the world's source of products for the relief of corns, bunions and other woes.
- Bethlehem Steel was incorporated.
- Ambrose Fleming invented the diode vacuum tube.
- Photoelectric cell was invented.
- Offset printing became the new standard.
- Canada Dry ginger ale was a new beverage offering.
- The banana split made its first appearance this year at Strickler's Drug Store in Latrobe, PA. Pharmicist Dr. David Strickler was the creator who brought joy to millions of children and adults.

Sports

Baseball

May 5 The first perfect game in the American League was recorded. Denton T. "Cy" Young of the Boston Americans pitched, and he didn't allow a single opposing Philadelphia player to reach first base. Boston won 3–0. (Lee Richmond pitched the first perfect game on June 12, 1880.)

Football

Nov 24 University of Tennessee fullback Sam McAllester was *thrown* for a touchdown to give the Volunteers a 7–0 victory over the University of Alabama. McAllester wore a special leather belt with handgrips sewn on the sides. His team engineered a 50-yard touchdown drive by repeatedly throwing him over the line of scrimmage, including one toss for the game's only touchdown. Football's rules were later changed to prohibit abetting the ballcarrier.

Spotlight on the Past *milestone anniversary years*

The St. Louis Olympics

The third modern Olympic Games came to America in 1904 and were held in St. Louis, MO, from July 1 to Nov 23. (Chicago had been the original host city, but World's Fair officials, fearing a loss of customers, threatened to hold rival athletic games unless St. Louis was the site. Olympic officials deferred to President Theodore Roosevelt, who chose St. Louis.) These third Olympics, which introduced gold, silver and bronze medals to the top three finishers for the first time, were marred by controversy and mishap.

Held to honor amateur athletes, the Olympics did not feature national teams, so athletes had to pay their own way. Due to the expense of world travel then, only 12 other nations besides the US were represented. Of 689 participants, 533 were from America. Of 300 medals given, Americans won 244.

The marathon of the 1904 Olympics has come down as the most bizarre in sports history. As the crowd eagerly awaited (in 90-plus-degree heat and humidity) the winner, Fred Lorz entered the stadium after three hours. Just before President Roosevelt's daughter, Alice, placed the laurel crown on his head, it came out that Lorz had run 9 miles, then hitched a ride in a car for 11 miles until it broke down in the heat. Lorz then completed the race on foot. The proper winner was Thomas Hicks, who fell unconscious across the finish line. During the race his trainers had dosed him with strychnine and brandy to help him finish. Two South African students, who were part of the World's Fair "anthropological" exhibits depicting Zulu tribesmen, entered the race as a lark and thus became the first black Africans to compete in an Olympics. Len Taunyane and Jan Mashiani of Orange Free State finished 9th and 12th, respectively. Less than half the competitors finished the race.

Golf
- Willie Anderson was US Open champion in golf.

Horse Racing
- Elwood won the Kentucky Derby.

Soccer
- The world's governing body for soccer, the Fédération Internationale de Football Association (FIFA) was founded.

Tennis
- Dorothy Douglass was the women's victor at Wimbledon; Hugh Doherty was men's victor.

Passings
- Frederic Auguste Bartholdi, French sculptor who created *Liberty Enlightening the World* (better known as the Statue of Liberty)
- Louis-François Cartier, founder of the jewelry house of the same name
- Anton Chekhov, Russian playwright
- Kate Chopin, American author
- Olivia Clemons, Mark Twain's wife
- Antonin Dvorák, Bohemian composer
- Daniel Decatur Emmett, lyricist of "Dixie's Land" (often called "Dixie")
- Marcus Alonzo Hanna, American industrialist and "kingmaker" for President McKinley
- Martin Johnson Heade, American artist
- Lafcadio Hearn, writer who introduced Japanese culture to the West
- Theodor Herzl, Hungarian founder of the modern Zionist movement
- In-mut-too-yah-lat-lat, or Chief Joseph, of the Nez Percé tribe
- Paul Kruger, former president of the South African Republic and leader of the Boers
- Eadweard Muybridge, pioneering English photographer who studied motion
- Samuel Smiles, Scottish writer who penned "A place for everything, and everything in its place"
- Sir Henry Morton Stanley, discoverer of Livingstone in Africa, utterer of "Dr. Livingstone, I presume?"
- Sir Leslie Stephen, British man of letters, first editor of the *Dictionary of National Biography* and father of Virginia Woolf and artist Vanessa Bell

Spotlight on the Past *milestone anniversary years*

1929 *75 years ago*

Landmark World Events

- **Jan 31** Lenin's designated heir, Leon Trotsky, was expelled from Russia. Joseph Stalin was now absolutely in power.
- **Feb 11** The Lateran Treaty, signed by Pietro Cardinal Gasparri for the Roman Catholic Church and Benito Mussolini for Italy, guaranteed the independence of the State of Vatican City and recognized the sovereignty of the Holy See over it. The area concerned was 109 acres.
- **July 24** The Pact of Paris, or Kellogg-Briand Pact, was proclaimed (it had been signed on August 27, 1928). Sixty-four nations signed this multinational treaty that renounced war as an instrument of national policy.
- **Oct 18** The Judicial Committee of England's Privy Council declared women to be persons in Canada, overturning a 1928 decision by the Supreme Court of Canada. Prior to this ruling, English common law prevailed ("Women are persons in matters of pains and penalties, but are not persons in matters of rights and privileges").
- **Dec 2** The skull of Peking Man was discovered by Dr. W.C. Pei in a cave near Choukoutien, China. Peking Man was believed to be a "missing link" between humans and nonhuman ancestors.
- American Frank Billings Kellogg received the Nobel Peace Prize in recognition of his work on the Pact of Paris, or Kellogg-Briand Pact. Accepting the prize, Kellogg stated, "I know of no greater work for humanity than in the cause of peace, which can only be achieved by the earnest efforts of nations and peoples."
- The Partido Revolucionario Institucional (PRI) was formed in Mexico and was the monopoly party in Mexican government until 2000. Its original name was Partido Revolucionario Nacional.
- The National Socialist (Nazi) Party was now an important minority party in Germany.
- Construction of Maginot Line began in France. The brainchild of France's minister of war, André Maginot, the line was a massive concrete defensive fortification along the France-Germany border.

Landmark US Events

- **Jan 2** The US and Canada agreed to protect Niagara Falls together.
- **Jan 29** Dorothy Eustis incorporated The Seeing Eye in Nashville, TN—a school to train dogs to aid the blind. She had two students at the first class that Feb (the first seeing eye dog, Buddy, and his master were among them).
- **Feb 20** The US Congress formally recognized the annexation of Tutuila and Manu'a islands (American Samoa). The islands had been ceded to the US by their chiefs in July of 1904.
- **Mar 27** Herbert Hoover became the first president to have a telephone when one was installed at his desk.
- **July 10** The US Treasury reduced the dimensions of paper currency to 6.14" by 2.61" (from 7.42" by 3.13"). It remains that size today.

THE ST. VALENTINE'S DAY MASSACRE, FEB 14, 1929

At 10:30 AM, four men—two of them in police uniforms—walked into a Chicago garage and lined up seven men against the wall as if to arrest them. Instead, the fake lawmen opened fire with 100 rounds of ammunition and killed all seven. The garage was the lair of the Bugs Moran gang, and the shooters, led by "Machine Gun Jack" McGurn, were sent by mob boss Al Capone, who wanted Moran's territory. The brutal killings were front page news across the country and were called the St. Valentine's Day Massacre. Outcry over the killings prompted increased police vigilance of Capone and led to the creation by the US Treasury of a special investigative unit in August.

Spotlight on the Past *milestone anniversary years*

Aug 19 Popular aviatrix Marvel Crosson, who earlier in the spring had set a new altitude record for women, died when her plane crashed during the National Women's Air Derby competition.

Aug US Treasury Agent Eliot Ness led a special unit focusing on Al Capone's illicit brewery businesses in Chicago. Because the handpicked agents were resistant to bribery, they were dubbed "The Untouchables" by the Chicago media.

Oct 24 Black Thursday: investors began panic selling on Wall Street. *See* Spotlight on America.

Oct 29 Black Tuesday: prices on the New York Stock Exchange virtually collapsed. The Great Depression was beginning. *See* Spotlight on America.

Nov 29 Richard E. Byrd flew over the South Pole—the first person to do so.

Dec 5 Togo, first lead sled dog on the 1925 heroic diphtheria run to Nome, AK, died.

- The last orphan train pulled into Trenton, MO. Since 1854, various charitable organizations had sponsored sending orphaned and impoverished children from New York City and the East Coast to the Heartland. 1929 was the final year for the massive train relocations.
- The League of United Latin American Citizens (LULAC) was founded in Texas. Today it is the oldest and largest Hispanic civic organization.
- The "21" Club—a speakeasy—opened in New York City.

Culture

Publications

Fiction
- Frederic Dannay and Manfred B. Lee, cousins and friends, responded to a $7,500 contest advertised in *McCall's* magazine for a first novel and created the detective Ellery Queen in *The Roman Hat Mystery*. Dannay and Lee wrote under the pseudonym Ellery Queen for the rest of their lives and kept their identities secret for eight years.
- *All Quiet on the Western Front*, Erich Maria Remarque, was the number one bestseller.
- *Dodsworth*, Sinclair Lewis
- *A Farewell to Arms*, Ernest Hemingway
- *Look Homeward, Angel*, Thomas Wolfe
- *The Sound and the Fury*, William Faulkner
- *Red Harvest* and *The Dain Curse*, Dashiell Hammett
- *Steppenwolf*, Herman Hesse
- *Les Enfants Terribles*, Jean Cocteau
- *Little Caesar*, W.R. Burnett

Nonfiction
- *A Room of One's Own*, Virginia Woolf
- *Is Sex Necessary?*, James Thurber and E.B. White
- *Marriage and Morals*, Bertrand Russell
- *Believe It or Not!*, a compilation of Robert L. Ripley's syndicated newspaper cartoons, was a huge bestseller.
- *The Mansions of Philosophy*, by Will Durant, was another bestseller.
- *The Quest for Certainty*, John Dewey
- *Goodbye to All That*, Robert Graves

Poetry
- *The Winding Stair*, W.B. Yeats

Comics

Jan 17 In E.C. Segar's comic strip "Thimble Theatre," a new character, Popeye, appeared on the scene and was an immediate success. Olive Oyl quickly dumped her beau, Ham Gravy, for the colorful sailor. Popeye's signature line was, "Tha's all I can stands, 'cause I can't stands no more!"

Notes
- German author Thomas Mann received the Nobel Prize in literature.
- *John Brown's Body* (1928), by Stephen Vincent Benét, was a bestseller and winner of the 1929 Pulitzer Prize for poetry.
- Ernest Hemingway was quoted describing courage as "grace under pressure" in the Nov 30 issue of *The New Yorker*.

Theater

Nov 27 The Cole Porter musical *Fifty Million Frenchmen*, which featured the song "You Do Something to Me," premiered at Broadway's Lyric Theatre.

- Louis Armstrong appeared on Broadway in *Hot Chocolates*, where he introduced the hit, "Ain't Misbehavin'," a song written by Andy Razaf, Fats Waller and Harry Brooks.

Spotlight on the Past *milestone anniversary years*

1929 *continued*

Notes
- Sir James Barrie gave the copyright for *Peter Pan* and its characters to Great Ormond Street Hospital in London.

Film
May 16 The first Academy Awards ceremony was held at the Blossom Room of the Roosevelt Hotel in Hollywood, CA. The 250 attendees paid $10 each. (The awards had been given out since 1927.) For the years 1927–1928, *Wings* was recognized as Best Picture, while Emil Jannings and Janet Gaynor were honored for lead acting performances. For 1929, Best Picture was awarded to *The Broadway Melody*, while Warner Baxter and Mary Pickford took statues for the acting honors.
- The Marx Brothers made their film debut in *The Cocoanuts*.
- Seven-year-old Frances Gumm (later known as Judy Garland) made her screen debut in the short *The Big Revue* with the Meglin Kiddies.
- *Hollywood Revue of 1929* featured the stars of MGM.
- *Spite Marriage* starred comedian Buster Keaton.
- *Blackmail*, directed by Alfred Hitchcock, was reshot to add sound. It had been a silent film.

Music
Popular Songs
- "Let's Do It, Let's Fall in Love," by Cole Porter (appeared the year before in the musical *Paris*)
- "Happy Days Are Here Again," words by Jack Yellen, music by Milton Ager. This song would be adopted by Franklin Delano Roosevelt in 1932 as a campaign song.
- "Sunny Side Up," words by Lew Brown and Buddy De Sylva, music by Ray Henderson
- "Singin' in the Rain" and "Pagan Love Song," words by Arthur Freed, music by Nacio Herb Brown

Art
- Lizzie Bliss, Abby Rockefeller and Mary Quinn Sullivan started the Museum of Modern Art (MOMA) in New York City.
- *The Lighthouse at Two Lights*, Edward Hopper
- *Fog Horns*, Arthur Dove
- Diego Rivera began work on the mural *The Indigenous World* in Mexico City's Palacio Nacional. That August, he married fellow artist Frida Kahlo.
- Georgia O'Keeffe visited New Mexico for the first time and it profoundly affected her art forever.

Photography
- *Portrait of a Couple, Man with Walking Stick*, James Van Der Zee
- *James Joyce*, Berenice Abbott

Design
- Ludwig Mies van der Rohe presented the Barcelona chair, which is still in production today.

Science and Technology
Aug 8–29 The German airship *Graf Zeppelin* circled the world.
Sept Flying from Long Island, New York's Mitchell Field, Major James H. Doolittle made the first plane flight using only instruments. At the time it was called "blind flight." Doolittle was given aviation's prestigious Harmon Trophy for his accomplishment.
- Phoebus Levene discovered deoxyribonucleic acids, or DNA. (The structure of DNA was deciphered in 1953 by Watson and Crick.)
- The first rocket-powered flight took place.
- Inventions of the year included foam rubber and FM radio.

Commerce and New Products
- D.F. Duncan Sr bought the rights to a mass-produced toy he admired and trademarked the "Yo-Yo" name for it. Although the yo-yo had been around for thousands of years as a weapon and plaything, Duncan is credited with improving the technology and making it a tremendously successful fad through creative marketing.
- Ford's Model A was introduced.
- New food brands were Colombo yogurt, the Klondike bar, Lithiated Lemon (now 7-Up), Libby's canned pumpkin,

Spotlight on the Past *milestone anniversary years*

The Expanding Universe

Our conception of the universe changed forever because of the observation of American astronomer Edwin Hubble in 1929. When studying the light emitted from other galaxies, Hubble noted differences in light colors. These "redshifts" (where colors shifted to the red side of the color spectrum) indicated that the light was receding. In other words, other galaxies were moving away from Earth. The universe was not constant; it was expanding. The only constant was the ratio of the speed the galaxies were traveling to their distance—Hubble's Constant. Scientists using Hubble's Constant have then estimated that the universe has been growing for 10 to 20 billion years. Hubble's observations (which caused Albert Einstein to reexamine his earlier work) laid the groundwork for the Big Bang Theory of the creation of the universe.

Niblets corn and Oscar Mayer wieners.
- Bingo was invented by Edwin S. Lowe.

Sports

Baseball

Aug 11 Babe Ruth of the New York Yankees became the first player to hit 500 career home runs when he connected off Willis Hudlin of the Cleveland Indians (who defeated the Yankees that day 6–5). The homer was also the 30th of the year for Ruth.
- MLB champions were the Philadelphia Athletics.

Golf
- Bobby Jones won the US Open.

Hockey
- Stanley Cup champions were the Boston Bruins.

Horse Racing
- Clyde Van Dusen won the Kentucky Derby.

Swimming
- Johnny Weissmuller, winner of 52 championships and five Olympic gold medals, retired from swimming at age 25. He had never been beaten in a race.

Tennis
- Helen Wills won her third women's Wimbledon title; Henri Cochet was the men's champion.

Miscellaneous

May 6–July 24 The longest footrace in history began May 6 at New York City Hall and concluded July 24 in San Francisco—3,415 miles later. Abraham Lincoln Monteverde, a veteran of more than 100 marathons, not only won the race but also was the only competitor to finish. He was 60 years old at the time.

Passings
- Katherine Lee Bates, lyricist of "America the Beautiful"
- Marvel Crosson, American aviatrix
- Asa Griggs Candler, pharmacist and creator of Coca-Cola
- Wyatt Earp, Western legend
- Baseball great Joseph Jerome "Iron Joe" McGinty, the turn-of-the-century pitcher who never had a losing season
- Baseball great Lee Richmond, who pitched baseball's first perfect game on June 12, 1880
- Sir Baldwin Spencer, anthropologist
- Thorstein Veblen, American economist, coiner of the phrase "conspicuous consumption"

1954 *50 years ago*

Landmark World Events

Apr 27 Georgi Malenkov became premier of the USSR after the death of Stalin in 1953.

May 7 The Indochina War (which had begun Dec 19, 1946, in the aftermath of WWII) ended after the French were defeated by nationalist forces (led by the Vietminh, a communist-oriented organization) at Dien Bien Phu.

Spotlight on the Past *milestone anniversary years*

1954 *continued*

July 20 An international conference at Geneva, Switzerland, met to settle the ending of the Indochina War. The provisions were: French Indochina ceased to exist (the French would withdraw) and the states established upon its demise were Cambodia, Laos, North Vietnam (Democratic Republic of Vietnam) and South Vietnam (Republic of Vietnam).

Aug Forty thousand died in China when the Yangtze River flooded.

Oct 23 US, France, UK, USSR agreed to end postwar occupation of Germany.

- The Office of the United Nations High Commissioner for Refugees received the Nobel Peace Prize.
- The Buddhist Council convened in Rangoon to commemorate the 2,500th anniversary of the death of Buddha.
- Algeria rebelled against colonial parent France in what would become an eight-year war.
- Life expectancy was 66 years in developed countries and 41 years in less developed countries.

Landmark US Events

Jan 21 The *Nautilus,* the first nuclear-powered submarine, was launched by First Lady Mamie Eisenhower at Groton, CT.

Jan The Army-McCarthy trials began. Senator Joe McCarthy was seeking communist infiltrators in the US Army. McCarthy's attacks on decorated officers drew President Dwight David Eisenhower's wrath.

Mar 1 US exploded a 22-megaton thermonuclear hydrogen bomb (code-named *Bravo*) at Bikini Atoll. It remains the most powerful bomb the US has ever exploded. A Japanese fishing boat, the *Lucky Dragon*, was accidentally exposed to the radiative fallout, creating tensions between the US and Japan when one crew member died and the others became ill.

Apr 1 The US Air Force Academy was established. *See* Spotlight on Education.

May 13 President Eisenhower signed legislation authorizing US-Canadian construction of a waterway that would enable oceangoing ships to reach the Great Lakes.

May 17 In the *Brown vs. Board of Education of Topeka* decision, the US Supreme Court ruled unanimously that "separate educational facilities were inherently unequal." *See* Spotlight on America.

June Congress by resolution added the "under God" phrase to the Pledge of Allegiance (which had originally been written in 1892).

Oct Benjamin O. Davis, Jr, became the first African-American general in the US Air Force.

Nov 11 This day was formally designated as Veterans Day (it was previously named Armistice Day).

Dec 2 McCarthyism came to an end with the Senate's censure of Senator Joseph McCarthy of Wisconsin. The Senate, by a vote of 67–22, cited "conduct contrary to Senate traditions."

THE MARILYN SHEPPARD MURDER CASE

In what had been the longest criminal trial in US history, Cleveland doctor Sam Sheppard was found guilty of murder on Dec 21, 1954, in the bludgeoning death of his wife, Marilyn, on the past July 4. The murder investigation and trial had been a media circus. Sheppard had claimed a "bushy-haired" intruder killed his wife. In 1963, ABC aired a popular TV series based on the case, "The Fugitive," starring David Jansen. In 1964, the US Supreme Court ruled that Sheppard had not received a fair trial. Rising lawyer F. Lee Bailey represented Sheppard at his 1966 retrial, which found Sheppard innocent. DNA testing 45 years after the crime indicated the presence of a third party at the scene, and the murder and Sheppard's level (if any) of involvement in it have remained a source of controversy. No one has ever been convicted in the murder of Marilyn Sheppard.

Spotlight on the Past *milestone anniversary years*

The televised Army-McCarthy hearings had exposed McCarthy's bullying conduct to the nation.

Dec 23 The first successful kidney transplant took place in Boston, conducted by Dr. Peter Merrill. Richard Herrick received a kidney from his twin brother, Ronald.

- Ellis Island ceased operation as a detention station for aliens. It had operated as such since 1943. (It had stopped receiving immigrants in 1924.)
- The Church of Scientology was founded in Los Angeles, CA.

Culture

Publications

Fiction
- The first two parts of *The Lord of the Rings*, by J.R.R. Tolkein, were published by George Allen and Unwin in London, England.
- *The Ponder Heart*, Eudora Welty
- *Lucky Jim*, Kingsley Amis
- *Lord of the Flies*, William Golding

Nonfiction
- *My Several Worlds*, Pearl S. Buck
- *The Alice B. Toklas Cookbook*, Alice B. Toklas

Notes
- Ernest Hemingway received the Nobel Prize in literature.
- Fredric Wertham's *Seduction of the Innocent* attacked the comic book industry for causing juvenile delinquency and homosexuality. The book had such an impact that Congress held hearings about comics. Comic book publishers, in order to forestall government regulation, agreed to self-censor their books.
- The *Guinness World Records Book* was published. It was the idea of the managing director of the Guinness Brewery, Hugh Beaver, who realized the marketing value of a book that could settle bar and pub arguments over records. (In its 50 years of existence, the reference book has sold 95 million copies.)
- Charles Lindbergh's autobiography won a Pulitzer Prize.
- The Mystery Writers of America established the Edgar Allan Poe Awards for excellence in the literary genre of mystery. The 1954 winners were Ira Levin for best first novel (*A Kiss Before Dying*), Charlotte Jay for the best novel (*Beat Not the Bones*) and Roald Dahl for the best short story ("Someone Like You").

Theater
- *Under Milk Wood*, Dylan Thomas's "play for voices," was presented posthumously by the BBC.
- J.M. Barrie's play *Peter Pan* was revived on Broadway with Mary Martin in the title role. She would win a Tony for her performance as the boy who refused to grow up.

Film
Jan 14 Rising star Marilyn Monroe wed baseball great Joe DiMaggio in a small civil ceremony.

- 1954 Academy Awards (presented in March 1955) went to *On the Waterfront* (Best Picture), Marlon Brando (Best Actor, *On the Waterfront*) and Grace Kelly (Best Actress, *The Country Girl*).
- Alfred Hitchcock released two films in 1954, *Dial M for Murder* (which was in 3-D) and *Rear Window*.

Godzilla Turns 50

The atomic age spawned an unlikely artistic creation in 1954: Godzilla, the radioactive monster star of many Japanese horror movies. The March Bikini Atoll hydrogen bomb blast had inadvertantly rained fallout on the crew of the Japanese tuna boat *Lucky Dragon*. The crew fell ill and one member died six months later. Japan's tuna supply was destroyed. Tensions between Japan and the US grew. *Godzilla: King of All Monsters*, released later in 1954, was actually a B-movie allegory of the danger of radiation fallout. Godzilla was a fire-breathing dragon who destroyed Tokyo—a kind of angry resurrection of the *Lucky Dragon*. The movie proved popular and has had more than 25 sequels and brother monster films.

Spotlight on the Past *milestone anniversary years*

1954 *continued*

- Musicals of the year included *Brigadoon*, *Seven Brides for Seven Brothers* and *White Christmas*.
- Judy Garland made a film comeback in *A Star Is Born*, with James Mason.
- *La Strada*, directed by Federico Fellini, starred Anthony Quinn.

TELEVISION

JAN 1 NBC's broadcast of the Tournament of Roses parade was the first color TV broadcast.
FEB 1 "The Secret Storm," television's first soap opera, premiered.
MAR Journalist Edward R. Murrow aired a scathing and influential report on Senator Joe McCarthy.
SEPT 12 "Lassie" premiered.
SEPT 27 "The Tonight Show" made its debut with host Steve Allen.
OCT 27 "Disneyland" premiered—later titled "Walt Disney Presents." It aired until 1980 and was one of the longest running prime-time shows. (It has reappeared in recent years on ABC.)
NOV 7 "Face the Nation" premiered on CBS.
DEC 15 "Davy Crockett," TV's first miniseries, premiered on the "Disneyland" show.
- The live drama "Twelve Angry Men" was broadcast on CBS's "Studio One" series. It starred Robert Cummings (who received an Emmy for his performance) and Franchot Tone. A film version was made three years later starring Henry Fonda.
- Agent 007 made his first screen appearance in a television adaption of the first James Bond novel: *Casino Royale* (published in 1953)
- "Father Knows Best" premiered.

MUSIC

JULY 5–6 Elvis Presley recorded "That's All Right" for Sun Records in Memphis, TN. *See* Spotlight on America.
JULY 30 In Memphis, TN, Elvis Presley appeared in concert for the first time, coming third on a bill whose headliner was Slim Whitman.

Albums
- *Songs for Young Lovers*, Frank Sinatra

Popular Songs
- "The Man That Got Away," Harold Arlen and Ira Gershwin
- "Young at Heart," Frank Sinatra
- "That's Amore," Dean Martin
- "Hey There" and "Mambo Italiano," Rosemary Clooney
- "Papa Loves Mambo," Perry Como
- "Smile," Nat King Cole
- "Sh-Boom," Crew Cuts
- "Three Coins in the Fountain," Four Aces
- "Secret Love," Doris Day

ART

- *Light, Earth, and Blue*, Mark Rothko
- *White Light*, Jackson Pollock
- *Flag*, Jasper Johns
- *Marxism Will Give Health to the Sick*, Frida Kahlo

FASHION

- French designer Coco Chanel returned to the fashion world by reopening the House of Chanel. It was a resounding success. Her new creation would be the "Chanel suit," which featured a collarless boxy jacket with bias trim over an a-line skirt. She had closed her design house in 1938 on the eve of WWII.

Science and Technology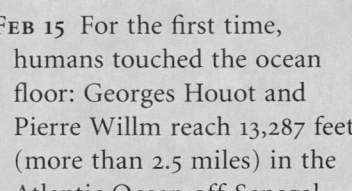

FEB 15 For the first time, humans touched the ocean floor: Georges Houot and Pierre Willm reach 13,287 feet (more than 2.5 miles) in the Atlantic Ocean off Senegal.
FEB The first vertical take-off and landing of an airplane, the Convair XFY-1 Pogo, took place in San Diego, CA.
JUNE 29 Physicist J. Robert Oppenheimer had his security access to classified information revoked by the Atomic Energy Commission, who accused him of having associations with Communists in the past.
NOV 30 A meteorite crashed through a frame house in Sylacauga, AL, and injured tenant Ann Hodges—the first recorded instance of a meteorite hitting a human. The US government, Hodges, her husband and their landlady began a court fight to see who would obtain ownership of the meteor. It wound up in a local museum.
- Linus Pauling was awarded the Novel Prize in chemistry.

Spotlight on the Past *milestone anniversary years*

- John Enders, Thomas Weller and Frederick Robbins of Boston's Children's Hospital's Research Laboratory received the Nobel Prize in physiology or medicine for their work on the poliomyelitis virus.
- Humans were discovered to have 46—not 48—chromosomes.
- Bell Labs created the photovoltaic cell (solar battery).
- The Fortran computer programming language was developed.

Commerce and New Products

Mar 25 RCA began production of color television sets.

Nov 19 The first automatic toll machine was put into use at New Jersey's Union Toll Plaza. Motorists dropped 25 cents into a wire mesh hopper and a green light would flash.

- The Burger King Corporation was founded in 1954 in Miami, FL, by James McLamore and David Edgerton. Today it is the major rival of the McDonald's chain.
- New food brands included Trix cereal, M&Ms candies, Butterball turkeys and Reddi-whip.
- General Electric introduced the first colored appliances.

Sports

Aug 16 The first issue of *Sports Illustrated* was published. The cover photograph showed Eddie Mathews of the Milwaukee Braves batting at Milwaukee County Stadium. The cover price was 25 cents.

Baseball

Apr 13 Hank Aaron made his major-league debut with the Milwaukee Braves (he was 0–for–5).

Apr 23 Aaron hit his first major-league home run off Vic Raschi of the St. Louis Cardinals. The Milwaukee Braves won 7–5.

May 2 Stan Musial of the St. Louis Cardinals hit five home runs in a doubleheader against the New York Giants, setting a major-league record.

- MLB champions were the New York Giants.

Basketball

Feb 2 Bevo Francis of Rio Grande College scored a small-college record 113 points in a 134–91 victory over Hillsdale.

Mar 7 The NBA experimented with baskets raised 12' instead of 10' in a game where the Minneapolis Lakers defeated the Milwaukee Hawks 65–63.

Four-minute Mile Shattered

Running the mile for the British Amateur Athletic Association team in a meet at Oxford University, 25-year-old medical student Roger Bannister broke the four-minute barrier with a time of 3:59.4 on May 6. Bannister shattered the existing record, set by Gunder Haag of Sweden in 1945, by a full two seconds. Four minutes (or one minute per quarter-mile) was at the time considered not only a physical barrier but also a psychological one.

In this epic race, Bannister relied on two teammates to pace him. Chris Brasher helped Bannister for the first two laps with times of 57.5 and 1:58.2. Christ Chataway sprang to the lead for the third quarter (3:00.5). Bannister followed Chataway around the curve and started his kick on the backstretch. He sprinted past Chataway and, as he broke the tape, into track history. But his record lasted little more than a month, until John Landy of Australia ran 3:58.0 on June 21.

"The Catch"

Willie Mays made a fabulous over-the-shoulder catch that many regard as the most famous in baseball history. It happened on Sept 29 in the first game of the World Series as the New York Giants were playing the Cleveland Indians. Vic Wertz of the Indians hit a long drive to deep center field in the Polo Grounds. Mays turned on the ball, caught it running full stride about 475 feet from home plate, wheeled and threw. The Giants won the game, 3–0, in 10 innings on Dusty Rhodes's pinch-hit home run and swept the Indians in the Series.

Spotlight on the Past *milestone anniversary years*

1954 *continued*

Apr 23 The NBA approved the 24-second clock rule in which the team controlling the ball must make an attempt to score within 24 seconds after gaining possession. This rule was proposed by Danny Biasone, owner of the Syracuse Nationals, who came up with 24 seconds by dividing the total number of shots taken in an average game by 48 minutes, the time played in a regulation game.
- NBA champions were the Minneapolis Lakers.
- Twenty-two-year-old Meadow George Lemon joined the Harlem Globetrotters (he later gained the nickname "Meadowlark").
- Heisman Trophy winner was Alan Ameche, Wisconsin.
- NFL champions were the Cleveland Browns.

Golf
- Ed Furgol was US Open champion; Babe Didrikson Zaharias was women's champion.
- US Amateur champion was Arnold Palmer.

Hockey

Mar 7 The USSR entered international hockey competition for the first time and came away with the world championship. The Soviets defeated Canada in the gold medal game, 7–2, played at Stockholm, Sweden.
- Stanley Cup champions were the Detroit Red Wings.

Horse Racing
- Determine won the Kentucky Derby.

Soccer
- World Cup victor was West Germany, which defeated Hungary.

Tennis
- Maureen Connolly won her third women's title at Wimbledon; Jaroslav Drobny was the men's champ.
- The Tennis Hall of Fame was established at the Newport Casino in Rhode Island.

Passings
- Lionel Barrymore, American actor
- Clyde Cessna, American aviation pioneer and designer
- Emilie Dionne, one of the Dionne Quintuplets (born 1934)
- David Fairchild, American botanist and explorer
- Enrico Fermi, nuclear physicist
- Miles Franklin, Australian novelist, author of *My Brilliant Career*
- Dr. James Herrick, discoverer of sickle-cell anemia and first describer of coronary thrombosis
- James Hilton, author of *Lost Horizon* and *Goodbye, Mr. Chips*
- Charles Ives, American composer
- Frida Kahlo, Mexican surrealist artist

Alan Turing

On June 7, 1954, Alan Turing dipped an apple into cyanide and ate it. At 42 years old, one of the 20th-century's most important thinkers was dead. He had earned degrees at Cambridge and Princeton in mathematics and mathematical logic. In 1936, he conceived the "Turing Machine," an abstract information-processing mathematical model that foreshadowed digital computers. During WWII, he was a member of the top-secret code-breaking team at England's Bletchley Park that created a machine that could decode Germany's "Enigma" machine, and their decoding saved incalculable Allied lives. Turing was honored by his country and made a member of the Order of the British Empire for his wartime service. In the 1950s, Turing turned his intellect to theories of artificial intelligence. He devised the "Turing Test" that would determine the success of an artificial intelligence machine (of whether it was thinking). In a devastating blow, Turing was stripped of his government security clearance after being convicted in 1952 for "gross indecency"—Turing was openly gay and homosexuality was a crime in England. This lack of security clearance disrupted his progress in computers. Nonetheless, his ideas continue to impact the field today.

Spotlight on the Past *milestone anniversary years*

- Auguste Lumière, film pioneer
- Henri Matisse, French artist
- Bill McGowan, considered the best umpire in baseball history
- Sportswriter Grantland Rice, who coined Notre Dame's "Four Horsemen" nickname
- Wilbur Shaw, American auto racer, three-time Indy 500 victor, president of the Indianapolis Speedway
- Alan Turing, British mathemetician and logician, WWII code-breaker
- Pop Warner, famed football coach
- Colette (Sidonie-Gabrielle Colette), French author

1979 *25 years ago*

Landmark World Events

Jan 7 Cambodian rebels and the Vietnamese army overthrew Pol Pot's Cambodian government.

Jan 16 Shah Mohammad Reza Pahlavi fled Iran in that country's revolution. *See* Spotlight on the World.

Feb 1 Ayatollah Khomeini returned to Iran from exile. *See* Spotlight on the World.

Feb 26 Solar eclipse was visible over much of North America.

Mar 8–15 Starting on International Women's Day, 20,000 Iranian women and 1,000 Iranian men took to the streets to protest the restriction of women's rights under Khomeini's rule.

Mar 26 Israel's Prime Minister Menachem Begin and Egypt's President Anwar al-Sadat signed the Camp David peace treaty in Washington, DC, ending 30 years of war between the two nations. Said Anwar al-Sadat, "Let there be no more war or bloodshed between Arabs and Israelis." The agreement was fostered by US President Jimmy Carter.

Apr 11 Ugandan dictator Idi Amin was driven from power after Tanzanian troops and Ugandan rebels took Kampala.

May 4 Margaret Thatcher became the first woman British prime minister. Her party, the Tories, dubbed her the "Iron Maiden" for her toughness.

June 2 Pope John Paul II made a seven-day tour of Poland, his homeland—the first time a pope had visited a communist country.

June 3 An oil rig blowout in Mexico's Gulf of Campeche caused a 400-mile slick after more than 500,000 tons of oil escaped.

July 5 The Isle of Man's parliament celebrated its 1,000th year—it was and is the world's oldest continuous parliament.

July 11 *Skylab I* crashed back to earth over the Australian outback and the Indian Ocean. There had been intense speculation as to where the 20–25 tons of debris would fall; it was calculated that the chance someone would be hit by *Skylab* was 1 in 152. There were no known casualties. This craft, the first US-manned orbiting laboratory, had been launched on May 14, 1973.

July 17 The Sandinistas ousted Nicaraguan dictator Anastasio Somoza Debayle, who fled the country.

July Saddam Hussein became president of Iraq upon his predecessor's stepping down. Hussein immediately executed 21 government officials of the old regime for treason and incarcerated many more.

Aug 27 An IRA bomb killed four on a boat in Ireland's Donegal Bay, including Lord Mountbatten, British hero and last viceroy of India, cousin of Queen Elizabeth II.

Sept Two East German families escaped their communist country by flying a patchwork hot air balloon over the border into West Germany in a 30-minute ride. The families used 60 pieces of canvas and bedsheets to construct their balloon.

Nov 4 The US Embassy in Tehran was seized by 500 Iranian students. There were 90 hostages, 60 of them Americans. The students demanded that the former Shah be returned to Iran for trial. *See* Spotlight on the World.

Spotlight on the Past *milestone anniversary years*

1979 *continued*

Nov 28 When New Zealand Flight 901 (a DC-10) crashed into Mount Erebus in Antarctica, 257 passengers were killed. This occurred almost exactly 50 years after Richard Byrd's historic first flight over the South Pole on Nov 29, 1929.

Nov Millions of Cambodians faced starvation as the world pondered how to intervene. From 1975 to 1979, four million Cambodians had died as the result of starvation or extermination—half the population.

Dec 24–27 The Soviet Union invaded Afghanistan and set up the government of Babrak Karmal.

- Mother Theresa received the Nobel Peace Prize. In accepting, Mother Theresa stated, "Love begins at home, and it is not how much we do, but how much love we put in that action."
- Southern Rhodesia became Zimbabwe.
- In El Salvador "death squads" were operating.
- South Korean leader Park Chung Hee was assassinated.
- In Britain, Sir Anthony Blunt was exposed publicly as a Soviet spy.
- Greenland gave its Inuit residents home rule.
- Life expectancy was 74 years in developed countries and 58 years in less developed countries.

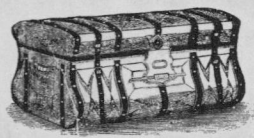

Landmark US Events

Jan–Oct The United Farm Workers' strike against lettuce and vegetable growers. The standoff grew violent when 35 strikers were injured and one was killed (Rufino Contreras). $10 million in lettuce and $1 million in carrots and broccoli rotted in the fields.

Feb Curtis "The Rock" Sliwa organized the "Magnificent 13," a weaponless civilian patrol, to travel on New York City's subways from 8 PM to 4 AM in order to protect patrons from muggers and attackers. This group later became known as the Guardian Angels.

Mar 29 The House Select Committee on Assassinations concluded that a conspiracy was possible in the cases of Martin Luther King, Jr, and Robert Kennedy and that President Kennedy's assassination was the result of a conspiracy and that acoustical evidence indicated two gunmen. In all cases, the committee pinpointed no suspects or organizations. (In December of 1980, the FBI refuted the two-gunmen theory in the assassination of President Kennedy.)

Apr 7 First Trident submarine launched, the *USS Ohio*, from Groton, CT.

May 25 In the worst air disaster in US history, an American

Three Mile Island

On Mar 28, 1979, Pennsylvania's Three Mile Island Nuclear Station experienced a partial core meltdown. Although no radiation injuries occurred, the incident frightened the public and further tarnished nuclear power's already controversial image.

The incident began at 4 AM when part of the water cooling system failed. Measures taken to correct the error caused a chain of events that led to radioactive water escaping from the core. Within hours, radiation had reached deadly levels.

Coolant water was restored that evening. But some experts argued that hydrogen generated during the partial meltdown could lead to an explosion. No such explosion occurred, but the media attention surrounding the threat had a lasting negative impact on public opinion and helped validate activists' concerns regarding nuclear power's safety.

Adding to the media circus and the public's fear was the fact that *The China Syndrome* had been released just weeks before. The film starred Jane Fonda as a television news reporter who works to uncover the dangers of a nuclear power plant. In one scene, a nuclear safety expert explains that a meltdown could result in having to evacuate an area "the size of Pennsylvania."

Spotlight on the Past *milestone anniversary years*

Airlines DC-10 lost an engine at takeoff and crashed seconds later at Chicago's O'Hare airport. 275 perished.

MAY In the largest award of punitive damages to date, the heirs of Karen Silkwood, the nuclear plant employee who was contaminated with plutonium (and who died in a mysterious car crash five years before), were given $10.5 million. Silkwood's employers, Kerr-McGee, argued that Silkwood contaminated herself with radiation "to embarrass the company."

MAY An estimated 70,000 protesters gathered in Washington, DC, to voice concern over nuclear power plants.

JUNE 18 President Jimmy Carter and Soviet General Secretary Leonid Brezhnev signed the SALT (Strategic Arms Limitations Talks) II treaty.

SEPT 27 The US Department of Education was established by Congress.

OCT 1 Panama was given control of the Panama Canal Zone by the US.

NOV 1 The oil tanker *Burmah Agate* collided with the freighter *Mimosa* and released 2.6 million gallons of oil into Texas's Galveston Bay. (Another 8 million gallons was consumed in the resulting fire.)

NOV 3 In Greensboro, NC, a shoot-out between KKK members and anti-KKK protesters resulted in four dead and nine wounded.

DEC 3 Eleven concert goers were killed and 28 wounded at a Who concert in Cincinnati, OH.

- The year was characterized by rampant inflation.
- Serial killer Ted Bundy was sentenced to death.
- Wichita Falls, TX, was devastated by a tornado. Sixty people died.
- Jane Byrne and Dianne Feinstein became the first women mayors of Chicago and San Francisco, respectively. The San Francisco mayoral election was the first in a major US city in which the homosexual vote was cited as a key factor.
- ABC TV reporter Bill Stewart was killed by Nicaraguan national guardsmen.

Culture

PUBLICATIONS

Fiction

FEB Danielle Steel's *The Promise* was selling 6,000 copies a week and was about to sell out its two-million-copy print run.

- *Burger's Daughter*, Nadine Gordimer
- *Sophie's Choice*, William Styron
- *A Bend in the River*, V.S. Naipaul
- *Jailbird*, Kurt Vonnegut
- *The Executioner's Song*, Norman Mailer
- *War and Remembrance*, Herman Wouk
- *Cruel Shoes*, Steve Martin

Nonfiction

- *The Power of Positive Thinking*, Norman Vincent Peale
- *The Pritiken Program for Diet and Exercise* and *The Complete Scarsdale Medical Diet* were bestsellers.
- *By Myself*, Lauren Bacall
- *The Right Stuff*, Tom Wolfe
- *Horoscopes for Dogs*, Jeane Dixon
- *Charmed Lives*, Michael Korda
- *Everyone's Money Book*, Jane Bryant Quinn
- *The Medusa and the Snail*, Lewis Thomas

Poetry

- *Field Work*, Seamus Heaney

Comics

- In Israel, the country's first comic book superhero, Sabraman, was a runaway bestseller. "Sabra" means prickly pear in Hebrew, and the Superman-like character wore a Star of David on his costume.

Notes

- Greek poet Odysseus Elytis received the Nobel Prize in literature.
- Robert Penn Warren won the Pulitzer Prize for poetry with *Now and Then: Poems 1976–1978*.
- John Cheever was awarded the Pulitzer Prize for fiction for *The Stories of John Cheever*.

PERFORMING ARTS

SEPT Alexander Godunov, star of Russia's Bolshoi Ballet, defected to the US.

- New York City's Lincoln Center celebrated its 20th anniversary.

THEATER

- Sam Shephard was awarded the Pulitzer Prize for drama for *Buried Child*.

Spotlight on the Past *milestone anniversary years*

1979 *continued*

- *Evita* opened on Broadway with stars Patti Lupone and Mandy Patinkin.
- *Sugar Babies* hit Broadway with stars Mickey Rooney and Ann Miller.
- *The Elephant Man* premiered.

Film

- The American Film Institute gave director Alfred Hitchcock its Life Achievement Award.
- The 1979 Academy Award for Best Picture went to *Kramer vs. Kramer*, and its star Dustin Hoffman won for Best Actor. Sally Field was honored as Best Actress for her performance in *Norma Rae*.
- Horror reigned in the theaters with *Alien*, *Amityville Horror* and *Invasion of the Body Snatchers*.
- *Breaking Away* was the sleeper hit of the year, a sensitive and funny film about a teenager's (Dennis Christopher) love of bicycling, Italy and a college coed one summer in Bloomington, IN.
- *All That Jazz*, starring Roy Scheider, was director/choreographer Bob Fosse's fictional film memoir.
- *Being There* starred Peter Stellars.
- *Manhattan* starred Woody Allen.
- *Moonraker* starred Roger Moore as Agent 007.
- *Apocalypse Now* starred Martin Sheen and Marlon Brando.
- *10* starred Dudley Moore and Bo Derek.

Television

- **Jan 26** "The Dukes of Hazzard" premiered.
- **Jan** *The Dallas Cowboys Cheerleaders* was a made-for-TV movie.
- **Apr 2** Nickelodeon, a cable TV channel for children, began operation.
- **Aug 24** "The Facts of Life" premiered.
- Other premieres included "Benson," "Knots Landing" and "Trapper John MD."

Notes

- A California court okayed making home tapes on "VTRs" (today called VCRs), creating a revolution in home video use.
- Kate Jackson was fired from the hit series "Charlie's Angels," prompting a search for a new "angel." Shelley Hack was hired. The program's producer, Aaron Spelling, assured viewers that each angel would have at least eight costume changes per show for the 1979–1980 season.
- "Point/Counterpoint" began its final year on "60 Minutes." For four years, Shana Alexander and James Kirkpatrick had debated the issues of the day on CBS's top-rated news program.

Radio

- **Feb 17** "A Prairie Home Companion," hosted by Garrison Keillor, debuted on Minnesota Public Radio.

Music

Albums

- Broadway star Ethel Merman gave in to the prevailing pop music style and recorded *The Ethel Merman Disco Album*, which featured up-tempo takes on such standards as "There's No Business Like Show Business."
- *Armed Forces*, Elvis Costello
- *Blondes Have More Fun*, Rod Stewart
- *Breakfast in America*, Supertramp

Popular Songs

- "I Will Survive," Gloria Gaynor
- "My Sharona," The Knack
- "Heartache Tonight," The Eagles
- "Fire," Pointer Sisters
- "Do Ya Think I'm Sexy," Rod Stewart
- "Knock on Wood," Amii Stewart

Art

- Chicago's Art Institute celebrated its 100th anniversary.
- *The Dinner Party*, by Judy Chicago, was presented at the San Francisco Museum of Modern Art. The large triangular installation celebrated 39 women from many different historical ages with beautifully designed place settings.

Fashion

- **Jan** Heiress Gloria Vanderbilt began promoting her line of blue jeans (which retailed for $36).

30

Spotlight on the Past *milestone anniversary years*

Science and Technology

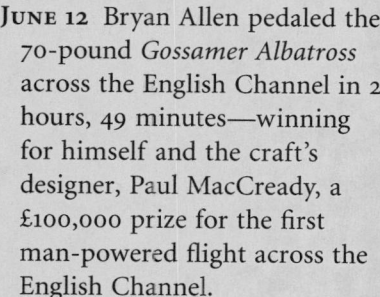

June 12 Bryan Allen pedaled the 70-pound *Gossamer Albatross* across the English Channel in 2 hours, 49 minutes—winning for himself and the craft's designer, Paul MacCready, a £100,000 prize for the first man-powered flight across the English Channel.

Aug 19 Cosmonauts Vladimir Lyakhov and Valery Ryumin returned from the *Salyut 6* space station after a then record 175 days in space.

Oct 1 President Jimmy Carter awarded the Congressional Space Medal of Honor to Neil Armstrong, Charles Conrad, Jr, John Glenn and Alan Shepard, Jr.

Dec 18 Fastest land speed by Budweiser Rocket was 739.666 mph—the only land vehicle to break the sound barrier.

- *Voyager I* discovered a ring around Saturn.
- Japanese magnetic-levitation train set a record speed of 321.2 mph.

Commerce and New Products

Dec The federal government bailed out the ailing Chrysler auto corporation, providing $1.5 billion in loan guarantees. Chrysler CEO Lee Iacocca was forced to cut 53,000 workers.

- Sony introduced the Walkman (then called the Soundabout) for $200.

Sports

Auto Racing
- Dale Earnhardt was NASCAR's Rookie of the Year.

Baseball
July 12 The Chicago White Sox staged "Disco Demolition Night" as a promotion between games of a doubleheader against the Detroit Tigers. Fans, encouraged to bring disco records to the ballpark so that they could be destroyed, surged onto the field and caused such destruction that the second game had to be forfeited to the Tigers.

Aug 2 Yankee catcher Thurmon Munson died when a small plane he was flying crashed at Canton, OH. He had three Golden Gloves and was Rookie of the Year as well as American League MVP in 1976.

Aug 9 Walter Francis O'Malley, perhaps the most vilified man in baseball history, died this day at Rochester, MN. He was the owner of the Brooklyn Dodgers when they left New York for Los Angeles in the 1958 season and was thus responsible for expanding the sport to the West Coast.

Aug 13 Outfielder Lou Brock of the St. Louis Cardinals got the 3,000th hit of his career. Brock finished his career that season with 3,023 hits.

Sept 12 Carl Yastrzemski of the Boston Red Sox got the 3,000th hit of his career. He became the first American Leaguer to record 3,000 hits and 400 home runs.

- MLB champions were the Pittsburgh Pirates. Willie Stargell was World Series MVP.

Basketball
Jan 9 New Orleans basketball player Daryl Moreau set a high school record by converting his 126th free throw in a row, a streak that lasted one year.

Mar 25 Chris Ford of the Boston Celtics made the first three-point field goal in NBA history in a game against the Houston Rockets.

Sept 9 Anne Meyers, All-American basketball player from UCLA, made history by signing a contract with the Indiana Pacers of the NBA, the first woman to do so. Meyers worked out with the team throughout training camp but was cut before the season began.

Oct 12 Indiana All-American Larry Bird made his professional debut with the Boston Celtics. He scored 14 points and had five assists in his 28 minutes of play. He would become the NBA's Rookie of the Year.

- NBA champions were the Seattle Supersonics.

Bullfighting
- The famous but controversial Spanish bullfighter El Cordobés (Manuel Benítez), began a comeback in the arena at age 43—after eight years of retirement. His notoriety stemmed from *aficionados'* claims that he picked weak bulls to fight.

Spotlight on the Past *milestone anniversary years*

1979 *continued*

Football
- Heisman Trophy winner was Charles White of USC.
- Pittsburgh Steelers defeated the Dallas Cowboys (this was their fifth Super Bowl) 35–31 in Super Bowl XIII.

Golf
- Hale Irwin was the US Open champion; Jerilyn Britz was the women's champion.
- Sam Snead shot a golf score below his age—the youngest Tour golfer ever to do so—at the Quad Cities Open in Coal City, IL. At 67 years of age he shot a 66.

Hockey
- Stanley Cup champions were the Montreal Canadiens.

Horse Racing
- Spectacular Bid won the Kentucky Derby.

Soccer
- North American Soccer League champions were the Vancouver Whitecaps.

Tennis
- Martina Navratilova repeated from 1978 as women's singles victor at Wimbledon; Björn Borg won his fourth men's title.
- Tracy Austin, at 16 years of age, became the youngest woman to win the US Open championship when she upset Chris Evert Lloyd.

Track and Field
July 17 Great Britain's Sebastian Coe broke the world record for the mile with a time of 3:49. His record would stand for a year. He would break the mile world record three times in his running career.

Passings
- Elizabeth Bishop, American poet
- Al Capp, American creator of the comic strip "Li'l Abner"
- Reverend Charles Coughlin, popular Depression-era American radio priest (1926–1940)
- Sonia Delaunay, modernist painter
- John Diefenbaker, former Canadian prime minister
- Mamie Eisenhower, former first lady
- Chick Evans, golfer who established the Chick Evans Caddie Foundation (later the Evans Scholarship Fund)
- James T. Farrell, American author (Studs Lonigan trilogy)
- Arthur Fiedler, beloved conductor of the Boston Pops
- Lowell George, of the rock band Little Feat
- Jon Hall, American actor
- Roy Harris, American composer
- Emmett Kelly, beloved American circus clown
- Herbert (Zeppo) Marx, vaudevillian and film star
- Don Miller, football player, member of Notre Dame's "Four Horsemen"
- Charles Mingus, jazz great
- Lord Mountbatten, last viceroy of India, British military hero
- Thurmon Munson, the decade's best baseball catcher
- Rachele Mussolini, widow of the Italian Fascist dictator
- Samuel Irving Newhouse, American media magnate
- Walter O'Malley, baseball executive
- S.J. Perelman, American writer and playwright
- Mary Pickford, American actress, the most popular star of the silent era, cofounder of United Artists
- Sally Rand, American entertainer and inventor of the fan dance
- Jean Renoir, French filmmaker
- I.A. Richards, English literary critic
- Eleanor Robson, Broadway star, at 100 years of age
- Nelson Rockefeller, former US vice president, former governor of New York
- Archbishop Fulton J. Sheen
- Charlie Smith, at 137 years old, the world's oldest man
- Jean Stafford, American author
- Dimitri Tiomkin, composer and three-time Oscar winner for film scores
- Alexandra Tolstoy, last surviving daughter of the great Russian author
- John Wayne, American actor
- Charles White, African-American artist
- Robert Burns Woodward, Nobel Prize–winning American scientist
- Darryl Zanuck, film executive at (and cofounder of) 20th Century-Fox

Spotlight on the World

David Completed by Michelangelo
1504 • 500 Years

On Sept 8, 1504, a statue was unveiled in Florence that was the largest marble nude sculpture created since classical times.

The 16-foot-10-inch *David* (with base) was sculpted by 29-year-old Michelangelo Buonarroti from a single colossal block of marble. In order to get the massive sculpture out of the studio where it had been carved, the studio door and wall above it had to be partially removed.

Cardinal Francesco Piccolomini commissioned the work in 1501, and Michelangelo chipped away from the block for three years. The biblical theme of David and Goliath was popular in the Renaissance, and David himself was a symbol for Florence, a small city-state surrounded by larger states. Some other Renaissance artists (notably Donatello) depicted David at the moment of victory, with Goliath's head at his feet. Michelangelo captured the youth tensely contemplating the coming fight.

David was erected in the Piazza della Signoria and stood there until 1873, when it was moved for protection into Florence's Galleria dell'Accademia (a copy was placed outside). In 2003 (for the first time in 129 years), the gallery gave him a more careful six-month cleaning—including carefully rubbing his ears with cotton swabs.

The statue is one of Western art's masterpieces.

For information:
Galleria dell'Accademia
Via Ricasoli, 58–60
Florence, Italy
Phone: (39) (055) 2388-609
E-mail: GalleriaAccademia@sbas.firenze.it
Open Tuesdays through Sundays. Closed Mondays, Dec 25 and Jan 1.

Haiti's Independence
Jan 1, 1804 • 200 Years

On Jan 1, 1804, Haiti became the first black-governed republic in the Western Hemisphere when it declared independence from France. The declaration ended a bloody slave revolt that spanned 12 years.

During the 18th century, Haiti—or Saint-Domingue as it was known at the time—was France's most lucrative colony. Thousands of plantations that produced coffee, sugar cane, cocoa and tobacco were established, and more than 500,000 slaves were imported from western Africa to drive agricultural production.

The French Revolution of 1789 spurred revolutionary fever in Haiti as well. With slaves outnumbering wealthy plantation owners ten to one, and a strong desire to end the brutality they endured at the hands of the white colonists, the stage was set for a violent conflict. In August 1791, a slave named Boukman led an uprising in which slaves everywhere burned plantations to the ground and used any weapons at their disposal to indiscriminately kill whites. The rebellion lost momentum, however, after only three weeks as infighting between slave factions weakened their position. White slave owners, meanwhile, regrouped and retaliated.

But the conflict was far from over. Pierre Toussaint—who was later given the nickname Toussaint L'Overture—emerged as a savvy military leader determined to organize and strengthen the slave forces. After several years and battles, by 1798 both France and Britain had been defeated. Toussaint and his army of more than 55,000 former slaves later secured the entire island when they defeated Spain in 1800. But French Emperor Napoleon Bonaparte felt Saint-Domingue was simply too valuable to relinquish, and under General Charles Leclerc, Napoleon sent 20,000 men to re-establish French rule. French soldiers arrived in January 1802, and Toussaint surrendered in May of that year.

Although France assured Toussaint that he would be permitted to retire peacefully after the war, he was betrayed, captured and imprisoned. He died in April 1803 after ten months in an ice-cold jail cell located high in the French Alps.

Following Toussaint's imprisonment, two of his lieutenants—Jean-Jacques Dessalines and Henri Christophe—resumed the fight against France. Napoleon's forces were defeated in the Battle of Vertières on Nov 18, 1803, and Dessalines declared the country's independence on the following

Spotlight on the World

New Year's Day, 1804. (They took the Taino-Arawak name "Haiti," which means "mountainous country.")

Haiti was in shambles. Most of the war-torn republic's plantations had been destroyed, and countries such as the United States, Spain and Britain—which still practiced slavery—did little to help foster the young nation's development. Evidence of despotic rule also began to surface early in the new republic. In October 1804, Dessalines crowned himself Jacques I, Emperor of Haiti. Many Haitians resisted his autocratic governing, which they likened to French rule. As a result, Dessalines was assassinated in October 1806.

Despite its post-independence hardships, Haiti's revolution inspired other uprisings abroad. In the United States, a slave rebellion led by Nat Turner in 1831 and another by white abolitionist John Brown in 1859 represented the belief that, much like Haiti's revolt, the fight to end slavery was not insurmountable.

The Iranian Revolution
1979 • 25 Years

On Jan 16, 1979, mounting pressure from revolutionary factions in Iran forced its hardline king, Shah Mohammed Reza Pahlavi, to flee the country. The overthrow of the Shah marked the beginning of an Islam-influenced theocracy in Iran and positioned Ayatollah Khomeini as the country's new leader.

The Shah's opponents included religious leaders and students who saw his iron-fisted monarchy as a threat to Islam and to Iran's constitution, which called for a representative government. Much of their frustration was also rooted in the Shah's friendly ties to the US government and the Western influence that was permeating Iran's culture.

The revolution gained enough momentum that in September 1978 the Shah declared martial law. On Sept 8, 1978, Iranian troops killed thousands of protestors in Iran's capital of Tehran—a day now known as "Black Friday." Khomeini returned from his 14-year exile on Feb 1, 1979, and those who championed his religion-based political views celebrated.

Khomeini, who had been exiled in 1964 for his criticisms of the Shah's policies, advocated a political system rooted in Islamic fundamentalism.

Hundreds of the Shah's supporters were executed shortly after Khomeini's return, and on Apr 1, 1979, a national referendum passed in a landslide that formed the Islamic Republic of Iran. The republic used Islam's moral codes as guiding principles for virtually every aspect of its culture and aimed to eliminate all Western influence.

Iranian women were particularly oppressed under the religion-driven policies of the postrevolution regime. In a speech delivered Mar 7, 1979, Khomeini announced that although women would be permitted to have jobs, they would have to cover their heads and faces with a veil while at work. The following day, thousands of Iranian women took to the streets to celebrate International Women's Day and to protest Khomeini's statements regarding the compulsory *chador*. Demonstrations continued for three days and on Mar 11, nearly 20,000 women marched in Tehran and gave speeches against the veil. But many women protesters were attacked or intimidated by armed men who supported Khomeini. As a result, protesters abandoned further demonstrations.

When President Jimmy Carter admitted the Shah to the US to receive medical treatment in September 1979, Iranian students stormed the US Embassy in Tehran on Nov 4, taking 66 American diplomats hostage. Fourteen hostages were released before the end of November, but the remaining 52 were held captive for more than a year. President Carter tried to win the hostages' release through diplomacy and by applying economic pressure on Iran, but he was unable to do so. A rescue mission in April 1980 that killed eight servicemen was unsuccessful. It wasn't until Jan 20, 1981—the same day that President Ronald Reagan was inaugurated—that the 52 American hostages were freed after 444 days in captivity.

Spotlight on America

Birth of the Republican Party

1854 • 150 Years

The political climate in the US during the mid-1800s was in turmoil as groups within existing parties were split on important issues—particularly the expansion of slavery to the west. As a result, the Republican Party, or Grand Old Party, was established in 1854 to unify members of various fractured parties who shared political ideologies.

The divisive slavery issue caused a rift among members of the two major political parties of the time, the Democrats and the Whigs. For northern and southern Democrats, slavery became a polarizing issue upon passage of the Kansas-Nebraska Act of 1854, which permitted individual territories to decide whether slavery would be legal.

The Kansas-Nebraska Act overturned the Missouri Compromise, which was a first step Congress took in 1821 toward halting the expansion of slavery to states entering the union. Southern Democrats who supported the act were predictably at odds with Democrats in the North who argued that slavery should be abolished.

The Whigs experienced similar upheaval. Northern Whigs—or Conscience Whigs—had embraced an antislavery position while so-called Cotton Whigs in the South believed slavery should remain intact. Conflicts around other issues also arose within smaller parties, and splinter groups emerged. For instance, the Free Soil Party—which combined Liberty Party members, Conscience Whigs and abolitionist Democrats—argued that settlers were entitled to land at no charge and spun off to push for government reform of homesteading legislation.

Disputes among these various parties had weakened the antislavery movement. As pro-slavery Whigs and others shifted their allegiance to southern Democrats, Conscience Whigs, Free Soil members and others had become a hodge-podge assortment of parties that shared common goals but were disorganized.

On Feb 28, 1854, Alvan E. Bovay held a meeting in Ripon, WI, to devise a plan for establishing a new political party that would challenge powerful southern Democrats. Together with disillusioned members of the Conscience Whigs, Free Soil Party and abolitionist Democrats, Bovay unified the fractured political movements by combining the slavery and land issues into a single movement's cause.

Calling themselves Republicans, the GOP held its first convention in Jackson, MI, on July 6, 1854. In 1856, John C. Frémont became the first Republican presidential candidate, running on the slogan, "Free soil, free labor, free speech, free men, Frémont." Although Frémont was defeated by Democratic nominee James Buchanan, he did capture one-third of the popular vote.

With slavery at the heart of growing tensions between the North and South, the Republican Party continued to gain momentum. The party rose quickly from third-party status to become a major political force. In 1860, the new party won the White House when Abraham Lincoln became the first Republican president.

For information:

Republican National Committee
310 First St SE
Washington, DC 20003
Phone: (202) 863-8500
E-mail: info@rnc.org
Web: www.rnc.org

The Stock Market Crash of 1929

October 24 and 29 • 75 Years

The financial exuberance and prosperity of the late 1920s ended on Thursday, Oct 24, 1929, when the bottom began to fall out of the seemingly invincible stock market. Dubbed "Black Thursday," the crash made a devastating impact on the global economy and sent much of the world spiraling into an economic depression.

Following WWI, the economy thrived as increased industrial and agricultural production spurred dramatic growth. Wages increased and consumer spending reflected the good times as many Americans used credit to purchase items such as homes, automobiles and household appliances. Americans also used credit to purchase stock. Between 1920 and 1929, the stock market

Spotlight on America

was considered a sure thing, and many borrowed heavily from banks or staked their life-savings to invest in the booming market. Although reasons for the crash are many, a major contributing factor was that many investors bought stock on margin, which meant they paid only 10 percent for a stock up front. The remaining balance was covered by a loan to be paid back.

With countless investors all buying on margin in the same companies, most stock prices increased due to the spike in sales. Ideally, the increased stock value would be enough to cover the loan amount, and all money beyond that would be profit. The only danger with the plan was if stock prices fell.

The combination of wild spending and easily obtainable credit created an unstable market that hinged on unsecured consumer debt. Investors were eager to borrow from banks, and banks obliged their enthusiasm. Many investors were working-class Americans who were not especially market savvy and jumped into the stock market headfirst to make a profit when they could. Many were caught up in the buying frenzy and did not recognize—or even consider—that the rapid growth would ever end. Stock values for some companies increased by as much as 450 percent as the buying craze continued. But when irrational market values were realized, panic selling ensued, and share prices fell sharply as millions pulled their holdings out of the market. On Oct 24, the market buckled. Then on Oct 29, 1929—known now as "Black Tuesday"—it broke completely, with the market losing 23 percent of its value.

By the end of 1929, stock values had plummeted by $15 billion and investors had lost $100 billion in assets. Consumer demand for goods declined as fewer Americans had disposable income, and production decreased as a result. Investor confidence in the market was predictably shaken, so sparking new growth through market investment was out of the question.

The crash left many families in financial ruin, and Black Tuesday is considered the beginning of the Great Depression. Unemployment in the US jumped from just 3 percent in 1929 to 25 percent by 1933, and it wasn't until the US entered WWII that the economy finally stabilized.

Brown vs. Board of Education of Topeka
May 17, 1954 • 50 Years

In a landmark decision that was a major step toward addressing US racial inequality, on May 17, 1954, the Supreme Court ruled unanimously in *Brown vs. Board of Education* that segregation in public schools was unconstitutional. The decision—considered one of the most important constitutional rulings in US history—overturned a "separate but equal" doctrine that had applied to blacks and whites.

On behalf of his seven-year-old daughter Linda, Oliver Brown was one of 13 families in Topeka, KS, who filed a lawsuit in 1951 against the Board of Education of the City of Topeka. The lawsuit represented 20 children who were required by law to attend racially segregated schools. McKinley Burnett, who was the Topeka chapter president of the National Association for the Advancement of Colored People (NAACP), recruited the families specifically to challenge the constitutionality of school segregation. Similar lawsuits in Delaware, South Carolina, Virginia and the District of Columbia were combined into a single case to be heard by the Supreme Court.

Thurgood Marshall, who at the time was the NAACP's legal counsel and was later appointed to the Supreme Court, argued the case for the plaintiffs. Arguments began in December 1952, but a decision wasn't reached until 1954.

During the Civil War Reconstruction era of the late 1800s, bitter divisions between races persisted, particularly in the South. Many states enacted so-called Jim Crow laws that prohibited blacks from using certain facilities reserved for whites such as theaters, restaurants, hotels, buses, public restrooms and public schools.

The Supreme Court's 1896 decision in *Plessy vs. Ferguson* upheld laws that segregated facilities, provided the facilities were of equal quality. The Court's "separate but equal" ruling made a distinction between segregation and discrimination, thus providing constitutional protec-

Spotlight on America

tion to segregation. The *Brown* case argued that "separate but equal" violated the 14th Amendment, which grants citizens equal protection under state law. In its 1954 decision, the Court ruled that segregating public schools was unconstitutional because it denied blacks those guaranteed rights. Chief Justice Earl Warren read the Court's opinion, which stated that, "Separate educational facilities are inherently unequal."

Brown vs. Board of Education was not the first case of its kind. A number of cases dating as far back as 1849 had challenged segregation in schools, but none prior to *Brown* was successful.

Although the ruling applied only to public schools, the implication was clear that "separate but equal" was to be erased from society altogether. But despite the *Brown* decision being hailed as a major victory for civil rights, implementing change in regions where segregation's roots ran deep proved difficult, and federally mandated desegregation of all facilities was not achieved until the Civil Rights Act of 1964.

"That's All Right!": Elvis Presley Arrives

July 1954 • 50 years

On July 1, 1954, Elvis Presley was a shy 19-year-old truck driver who loved to sing. By the end of that month, he had recorded his first commercial single, which was aired to immediate success in Memphis, he had been interviewed on the radio and he appeared in concert for the first time. It's hard to imagine a quicker rise to fame.

Born on Jan 8, 1935, at Tupelo, MS, to Vernon and Gladys Presley, Elvis showed an interest in gospel music and the singing stars of the day at an early age. The family moved to Memphis, TN, in 1948, and the boy was exposed to an exciting music scene of blues, country and rhythm and blues. In the summer of 1953, Presley first made song recordings at the Memphis Recording Service, where anyone could pay $3.98 to create their own raw recording. In January 1954, an employee at the studio spoke of him to owner Sam Phillips, who also ran the Sun Records label. Phillips saw potential and hooked Presley up with Scotty Moore, a talented guitarist, and Bill Black, who played standup bass. The trio began playing together, hoping they could find a hit for Sun Records.

The July 5-6, 1954, Sun recording sessions proved to be breakthrough ones. After the trio struggled through a few stilted takes of a popular country song, Presley spontaneously launched into a blues song entitled "That's All Right" and let it rip. The trio relaxed and created a raw and exciting song that Sam Phillips immediately recognized as a hit.

On July 7, Phillips took a rough version of the single to influential radio disc jockey Dewey Phillips at WHBQ, who immediately played it on his show, "Red, Hot, and Blue." The audience response to "That's All Right" was so strong that the song was played more than fourteen times just that night!

Memphis music promoters soon took notice, and Presley's band opened for Slim Whitman at Memphis' Overton Park Orchestra Shell on July 30. The shy young man with the two-tone shoes and ducktail haircut was suddenly thrust into the spotlight. His nervous stage tic would soon make him infamous all over the country: he began twitching his right leg and the girls went crazy. The band performed only "That's All Right" and "Blue Moon of Kentucky," but the crowd loved it.

By 1956, Elvis Presley was a hit RCA recording artist and a millionaire who was about to begin a movie career. He was 21 years old.

When Marion Keisker, the Memphis Recording Service employee who noted Presley's talent, asked him who he sounded like, he replied, "I don't sound like nobody." Presley had a unique voice and style that spoke to country, hillbilly, blues, R&B and gospel fans of many ages and backgrounds. He wouldn't have predicted that crazy month in July 1954, but his undeniable talent made it inevitable.

37

Spotlight on Education *founding anniversaries*

College and University Founding Anniversaries

The more than 3,500 colleges and universities across the US range from private to state-supported, small to large, liberal arts–based to technically oriented. The following is a selection of colleges and universities celebrating a founding anniversary in 2004.

Columbia University in the City of New York
1754 • 250 Years

The fifth oldest American university and oldest New York university was founded by Royal Charter of King George II as King's College in 1754. Its mandate was to "enlarge the Mind, improve the Understanding, polish the whole Man, and qualify them to support the brightest Characters in all the elevated stations in life." In 1767, it created the first American medical school to offer the MD degree. The Revolutionary War caused the closure of the school from 1776 to 1784. When it reopened, its name was changed to Columbia College. In 1896, the name became Columbia University, and today its official designation is Columbia University in the City of New York. In 1889, Columbia affiliated with Barnard College, an institution educating women. In 1983, women entered Columbia as the class of 1987.

As one of the oldest universities in America and due to its location in New York City, Columbia boasts many prominent alumni who emerged as leaders, among them founding fathers, state politicians and US presidents: Franklin Roosevelt, Theodore Roosevelt, John Jay, Benjamin Moore and Robert Livingston. Architect Robert A.M. Stern, anthropologist Margaret Mead, business leader Warren Buffet, television executive Roone Arledge, mystery author Amanda Cross, poet Allen Ginsberg, beat writer Jack Keroac, actor Paul Robeson, lyricist Ira Gershwin, pianist Emanuel Ax, actor James Cagney and baseball legend Lou Gehrig are only a few of the many notable Columbia graduates.

Columbia today is one of the world's premier research universities—one that embraces its urban milieu. Columbia's thrust is threefold: education, research and professional/community service; and Columbia graduates have made a difference in New York City and the nation. Many academic programs include community outreach elements. Enrollment (undergraduate and graduate) averages more than 20,000 students. The faculty of more than 3,000 has been awarded 64 Nobel Prizes, 20 MacArthur Foundation Awards and 10 National Medals of Science. Thirty-three faculty members belong to the National Academy of Sciences and 117 to the American Academy of Arts and Sciences. University scholarship in journalism, medicine, education, economics and law, among other disciplines, is world renowned.

The beautiful turn-of-the-century Italian Renaissance and Classical–style campus at Morningside Heights boasts the designs of architect Charles McKim of McKim, Mead and White. The campus comprises the largest collection of buildings in existence by this storied firm.

For information:

Columbia University in the
City of New York
Office of Public Affairs
535 W 116th St, MC 4321
New York, NY 10027
(212) 854-5573
Web: www.columbia.edu

Lincoln University
1854 • 150 Years

America's first historically black university was founded as the Ashmun Institute in Chester County, PA, in Apr 1854, by Presbyterian pastor John Miller Dickey and was renamed in 1866 in honor of slain president Abraham Lincoln. It was known as the "black Princeton" in its early years. Only men were admitted until 1952. In 1972 it joined Pennsylvania's Commonwealth System of Higher Education.

Lincoln has created community, national and international leaders in law, the sciences, human services and the arts. During Lincoln's first hundred

Spotlight on Education *founding anniversaries*

years, about 20 percent of all African-American physicians and 10 percent of all African-American jurists were Lincoln graduates. Today, about 2,000 students comprise the interracial student body, of which two-thirds are women. Lincoln is one of only 20 schools of higher learning in which 40 percent or more of its physics graduates are women. Lincoln is also a leader in community outreach. From 1963 to 1971, Lincoln was a major training site for the US Peace Corps.

Thurgood Marshall, first African-American Supreme Court justice, was a 1930 graduate from Lincoln. Other prominent graduates include Kwame Nkrumah, first president of Ghana; Nnamdi Asikiwe, first president of Nigeria; poet Langston Hughes (whose book collection helped form the Langston Hughes Memorial Library there); scientist Dr. Hildrus A. Poindexter; Rear Admiral (ret.) Lillian E. Fishburne, first African-American woman promoted to that rank in the US Navy, and acclaimed actor Roscoe Lee Browne.

To celebrate its sesquicentennial, Lincoln will be hosting several events with the theme "Advancing the Lincoln Legacy." Mar 10 is the Honors Convocation, Apr 29 is the Founder's Day celebration and May 2 is the 2004 commencement.

For information:

Lincoln University of the Commonwealth of Pennsylvania
1570 Old Baltimore Pike
P.O. Box 179
Lincoln University, PA 19352
(610) 932-8300
Web: www.lincoln.edu

US Air Force Academy
1954 • 50 Years

On Apr 1, 1954, President Dwight Eisenhower signed the bill establishing the US Air Force Academy at Colorado Springs, CO, to train officers for the Air Force. It is the youngest of the four service academies. Construction on the campus began July 11, 1955, and was completed in 1958. The academy was accredited in 1959, the same year it graduated its first class (207 cadets). Women were admitted in 1976.

The US Air Force Academy strives not only for academic success, but also to build leadership qualities in its students—qualities for service as officers in the Air Force and/or life beyond that. Student population is limited to 4,000. The academy offers 30 majors and a military and civilian faculty. The core curriculum is composed of the sciences, engineering, social sciences and the humanities. Besides their academic performance, cadets are also evaluated for their military performance. Athletics are an important component of academy life, and the campus has dozens of athletic fields that can accommodate 2,000 people at the same time.

The campus comprises 18,000 acres in a beautiful Rocky Mountain setting and boasts a breathtaking architectural masterpiece in the Cadet Chapel. Alluding to the mountains behind it, the chapel features 17 spires rising 150 feet up. The construction is of aluminum, steel and glass. The chapel, considered and created to be the symbolic heart of the campus, was designed by Walter A. Netsch, Jr, of the famed Skidmore, Owings and Merrill architecture firm and was completed in 1963.

For information:

US Air Force Academy
Public Affairs Office
2304 Cadet Drive, Suite 320
USAF Academy,
CO 80840-5016
(719) 333-2990
Web: www.usafa.edu

Spotlight on People

World History

SAINT AUGUSTINE OF CANTERBURY
Death • 604 • 1400 Years
Saint Augustine of Canterbury was one of the most important missionaries to travel across Europe following the collapse of the Roman Empire. He settled in Britain, preaching Christianity to the Saxons. He met with great success, converting thousands, including King Ethelbert. He quickly rose to the title of bishop of Canterbury, and in 601, Pope Gregory the Great appointed him archbishop of Canterbury, a position that gave him authority over all the churches in England, including the York and Celtic churches. The Celtic Church had not been previously under Roman jurisdiction, and Augustine met with church members in 603 or 604 in an attempt to resolve the differences between the Celtic people and the Saxon people. The plan failed, but nonetheless, Augustine definitely helped pave the way for the future unity. He died in 604 and was buried at Canterbury.

MARCO POLO
Birth • 1254 • 750 Years
The great Italian explorer Marco Polo was born to a leading Venice merchant and as early as his teenage years joined his father traveling across Asia. Polo soon set out on his own, following the fabled Silk Road, and his journey through Asia lasted 24 years. He reached farther than any of his predecessors, beyond Mongolia to China. He became a confidant of Kublai Khan and worked as an explorer for Khan for many years. Upon his return to Venice, Polo told stories of the wonders he had seen, describing items such as eyeglasses, ice cream, spaghetti and other various riches of Asia. He soon became the laughingstock of the townspeople, who did not believe his travel tales. When he was near death, a priest came to his room to ask him if he'd like to admit that his stories were false. His last words were reported to be: "I did not tell half of what I saw." Marco Polo died in 1324 and was buried in the Church of San Lorenzo in Venice.

PETRARCH
Birth • July 20, 1304 • 700 Years
Often called the "Father of Humanities," Francesco Petrarch was born at Arezzo, near what is now Florence, Italy. He was a poet during an era in which few people even learned to read or write, and he also studied law and the writings of Cicero. His studies of Cicero sparked an interest in reading and preserving other classical writings. He began to collect ancient manuscripts, traveling across Italy, France and Germany searching monastic and cathedral libraries for materials that he found significant enough to preserve. The resulting library became a model for scholars and educated gentlemen of the time. Petrarch's own poetry was considered superb, and in 1341, he was crowned poet laureate of Italy. His sonnets, mainly inspired by his unrequited love for a woman named Laura, were thought to influence the works of such English poets as Geoffrey Chaucer, William Shakespeare and Edmund Spenser. He died July 18, 1374, at Arquá, Padua, Italy.

WILLIAM BLIGH
Birth • Sept 24, 1754 • 250 Years
Popular history's favorite naval villain was born at Cornwall, England. He had a steady and competent career with the Royal Navy before undertaking command of the *HMS Bounty* on a voyage to Tahiti in 1787. In 1789, mate Fletcher Christian instigated the famous mutiny, and Bligh and 18 men were forced off the ship and put in the longboat. Bligh navigated an amazing journey back to civilization with limited means over 3,600 miles of open sea. Bligh later rose to the rank of vice admiral and was also governor of New South Wales, Australia. He was the victim of yet two more mutinies! Accused of being abusive in power and clearly an unpopular officer, Bligh at worst seems to have had a nasty tongue and some bad luck. He died Dec 7, 1817, at London, England.

LOUIS XVI
Birth • Aug 23, 1754 • 250 Years
The last Bourbon king of France was born at Versailles, France. In 1770, he married Marie-Antoinette, daughter of the Holy Roman Emperor Francis I, and in 1774, he ascended to the French throne upon the death of his grandfather, Louis XV. Louis XVI proved unable to master the

Spotlight on People

political turmoil around him that grew into the French Revolution. He threw his support to aristocratic factions and away from much-needed reform. His pursuit of kingly sport only fanned the flames of unrest higher. He and his family attempted to escape France in 1791 but were intercepted and sent to the Tuileries Palace, which a mob destroyed in June of 1792. The monarchy was abolished in September of 1792, and on Jan 18, 1793, "Citizen Capet" was found guilty of treason. On Jan 21, Louis XVI was guillotined.

WILLIAM BOOTH
Birth • Apr 10, 1829 • 175 Years

Born in Nottingham, England, William Booth spent his teenage years apprenticed to a pawnbroker, and his daily contact with the poor inspired him to dedicate his life to helping others. He became a Methodist minister, and later an evangelist, and traveled around England preaching to the destitute. In 1865 he founded the Christian Mission, a religious and social welfare organization designed to bring spiritual and material help to the needy in and around London. He changed the name of his organization to the Salvation Army in 1878, adopting a military structure: his volunteers had "ranks," his own being "General." Booth's seven children all "served" in his army, organizing units throughout the world. By the time Booth died on Aug 12, 1912, the Salvation Army was helping the poor in 58 countries. Today, there are chapters in 103 nations.

JOSEF STALIN
Birth • Dec 21, 1879 • 125 Years

Josef Stalin, the name assumed by the man whose family name was Dzhugashvili, was born at Gori, Georgia, in 1879. A devout student of the forbidden works of Karl Marx, he worked with various radical groups in Russia throughout his youth. He quickly rose through the ranks in underground Social-Democratic circles and was jailed for various offenses and spent many years in exile. He was a key figure in the 1917 revolution that toppled the czarist government. Stalin became secretary general of the Communist Party in 1922 and maneuvered to succeed Vladimir Ilyich Lenin as the leader of the Union of Soviet Socialist Republics. On Oct 1, 1928, he announced the first of a series of five-years plans that entailed the collectivization of farms and rapid industrialization. Farm collectivization had a devastating effect, bringing famine to the Ukraine. An estimated 8 million people perished. Stalin ruthlessly consolidated his power in purges of the 1930s and 1940s, having millions of Soviet citizens executed or imprisoned. During WWII, the Soviet Union defeated invading German forces, and after the war, Stalin shaped much of the political policies of communist Eastern Europe. Stalin was one of the most powerful and most feared men of the 20th century. He died (of a stroke) at the Kremlin, at Moscow, Mar 5, 1953.

LEON TROTSKY
Birth • Nov 7, 1879 • 125 Years

Born Lev Davidovich Bronstein at Yanovka in the Ukraine, Trotsky was first exposed to radical political ideas when he joined a radical student group, and he soon became enamored with ideas expressed by Karl Marx. He spent time in prison and in exile as a result of his political activities, before escaping Siberia in 1902 with a forged passport bearing the name "Trotsky." As a member of the Politburo and close associate of Lenin, Trotsky was an influential figure in foreign and military affairs and is largely credited both with the formation of the Red Army and its success during the Russian Civil War of 1918–1921. When Lenin suffered a stroke in 1922, Trotsky unsuccessfully attempted to prevent the ascension to power of Joseph Stalin. His continued criticism of Stalin resulted in Trotsky's gradual removal from positions of influence, and eventually he was expelled from the Communist Party and the Soviet Union itself. He continued to write and lived in various places during the late '20s and early '30s before settling with his family in Mexico City in 1936. He survived one assassination attempt but finally was killed in August of 1940 by a Spanish-born agent working on Stalin's behalf.

Spotlight on People

Deng Xiaopeng
Birth • Aug 22, 1904 • 100 Years

One of the most powerful political figures in modern Chinese history, Deng Xiaopeng restored economic growth and domestic stability to a nation reeling from the excesses of the Cultural Revolution. He became active in the communist movement in the 1920s and rose through the ranks of the Chinese Communist Party (CCP), becoming general secretary in 1954 and eventually deputy premier of China. Deng came into conflict with Mao Tse-Tung and his supporters during the Cultural Revolution and was stripped of power. However, following the death of Mao in 1976, he returned to a high-ranking post and began a series of reforms that affected all aspects of Chinese politics, economics and culture. Deng instituted radical population-control programs that included mandatory family planning and decentralized much of the industrial enterprises and agricultural productions. He strengthened China's trade and cultural ties with the West. He sided with the CCP during the student revolutions in Tiananmen Square in 1989 and was blamed for the considerable loss of life when the Chinese Army suppressed the demonstrators under the Party's orders. Deng Xiaopeng died at Peking on Feb 19, 1997.

Anne Frank
Birth • June 12, 1929 • 75 Years

Born at Frankfurt, Germany, Anne Frank with her family moved to Amsterdam to escape the Nazi regime. After Holland was invaded by Germany, Anne, her parents, Otto and Edith, and her sister, Margot, were forced into hiding, living in a secret "annex" that her father had constructed at his business. On her 13th birthday in 1942, Anne began to keep a diary. She wrote in the diary during the two years she was in hiding, until her family was discovered by the Nazis in August of 1944 and deported to concentration camps. Anne died of typhus at the Bergen-Belsen camp in 1945. After the war, her father published her diary in 1947, on which a stage play and movie were later based.

American History

John Eliot
Birth • 1604 • 400 Years

John Eliot, probably born at Widford, Hertfordshire, England, where he was baptized on Aug 5, 1604, emigrated to the New World in 1631. A Puritan, he became pastor of a church in Boston and began a mission to preach Christianity to the region's Native Americans in 1646. He learned the language of the Algonquin tribe, and translated pamphlets and a Bible into the language. Converts to Christianity were called "praying Indians," and Eliot helped this group form communities independent of the main tribes. Ultimately, there were fourteen towns with thousands of inhabitants, and he trained the Indians to become missionaries to their own people. The towns were severely damaged during King Philip's War in 1675, and the communities never fully recovered. Eliot died May 21, 1690, at Boston. The Native American Bible that he translated was most likely the first book to be printed in North America.

Pierre Charles L'Enfant
Birth • Aug 2, 1754 • 250 Years

Born at Paris, France, L'Enfant was trained as an architect and engineer. He volunteered as a soldier in the American Revolution; he was a commissioned officer and war hero and was discharged in 1784. He remained in the US, working as an architect, and in 1791 was commissioned by President Washington to design the new capital city along the banks of the Potomac River. His plan for the city was adopted, but L'Enfant antagonized the city commissioners. His attitude and demands led to his firing, and he was not permitted to oversee the plans through to completion. He struggled much throughout the rest of his career, and he was penniless when he died at Green Hill, MD, on June 14, 1825. In 1901 the Park Commission acknowledged L'Enfant's excellent plans and they were carried out in the development of the city. In 1909 his remains were moved to Arlington National Cemetery, which overlooks the city he designed—Washington, DC.

Spotlight on People

Molly Pitcher
Birth • Oct 13, 1754 • 250 Years

A heroine of the American Revolution, the woman known as Molly Pitcher was born Mary Ludwig near Trenton, NJ. She accompanied her husband, William Hays, as a camp follower during the Philadelphia campaign and spent the winter of 1777–78 with him at Valley Forge. At the Battle of Monmouth on June 28, 1778, she served as a water carrier, bringing pitchers of water to exhausted soldiers, thus earning her nickname. After her husband was wounded, she distinguished herself by loading and firing the cannon where he had fallen. She became affectionately known as "Sergeant Molly," and afterwards General Washington issued her a warrant as a noncommissioned officer. She was awarded a pension by the state of Pennsylvania, and she died at Carlisle, PA, Jan 22, 1832. In 1876, a marker noting her exemplary service was placed on her grave in Carlisle.

Franklin Pierce
Birth • Nov 23, 1804 • 200 Years

The 14th president of the US was born at Hillsboro, NH. The son of a Revolutionary War soldier and politician, he graduated from Bowdoin College, became a lawyer and was soon elected as a congressman and later a senator from New Hampshire. During the Democratic convention of 1852, there was no clear nominee, and finally, on the 49th ballot, Pierce was selected. Tragedy struck on the way to his inauguration when his 13-year-old son was killed during the train journey. Pierce's grieving overwhelmed the early days of his presidency. Politically, he was a supporter of slavery and under his leadership the controversial Kansas-Nebraska Act was passed, reopening the question of slavery in the western territories. Pierce was severely criticized for the resulting violence in Kansas and was refused his party's nomination in 1856 for a second term. He returned to New Hampshire, where he died at Concord, Oct 8, 1869.

Chester A. Arthur
Birth • Oct 5, 1829 • 175 Years

The 21st president of the US, Chester Alan Arthur, was born at Fairfield, VT. He worked as a labor leader and served as the collector for the Port of New York. During his tenure as collector, he became embroiled in controversy surrounding his Custom House employees; corruption and patronage played a large part in battles that Arthur fought with President Rutherford B. Hayes. Hayes fired Arthur, leading to a deep split in the Republican Party. James A. Garfield took Arthur on as his running mate in the 1880 presidential election, and Arthur succeeded to the presidency following Garfield's death Sept 19 (after being shot on July 2). Arthur served as president from Sept 20, 1881, to Mar 3, 1885, but was not successful in obtaining the Republican Party's nomination for the following term. He died at New York, NY, Nov 18, 1886.

Geronimo
Birth • June 1829 • 175 Years

A Native American of the Chiricahua (Apache) tribe, Geronimo was born in June 1829, probably in No-Doyohn Canyon in what is present-day New Mexico. His Indian name was Goyathlay ("One Who Yawns"), and he became a member of his tribe's warrior council in 1846. His tribe fought off colonization from both Mexicans and North Americans, and when they were forcibly moved by US authorities to a reservation in a barren section of Arizona, Geronimo became the leader of violent, bloody campaigns against the American military. His small band of warriors led devastating raids in Arizona, New Mexico and Mexico, and eventually the US Army sent 5,000 men to capture Geronimo. He was confined at Fort Sill, OK, where he died Feb 17, 1909, after dictating the story of his life for publication.

Margaret Sanger
Birth • Sept 14, 1879 • 125 Years

Growing up watching her mother cope with 18 pregnancies and 11 live births, Margaret Sanger became determined to help women get the medical care they needed and deserved. Born at Corning, NY, she worked as a practical nurse and midwife in New York City. She made it her mission to get women information regarding contraception, and it was she who coined the phrase "birth control." She published a newspaper called *The Woman Rebel* that offered

Spotlight on People

women options regarding their health care and ways to prevent pregnancies. She opened neighborhood women's health clinics and founded the American Birth Control League, which eventually became known as Planned Parenthood. The founder of the American birth control movement died at Tucson, AZ, Sept 6, 1966.

Ralph Johnson Bunche
Birth • Aug 7, 1904 • 100 Years
Born at Detroit, MI, Bunche was an educator, scholar, US State Department employee, supporter of Dr. Martin Luther King, Jr, United Nations official and Middle East peace ambassador. His parents died when he was 12, and his grandmother, a former slave, took him and his siblings to live in Los Angeles. He worked odd jobs to help support the family and attended college on scholarships. Eventually, armed with a doctorate in political science from Harvard, he took up the cause of civil rights. But it was in a different arena that Bunche would win the world's acclaim—as a diplomat seeking to ease Middle East fighting over Palestine. Beginning in Sept 1948 as acting UN mediator on Palestine, Bunche tirelessly mediated to obtain an armistice agreement between Israel and the Arab States. For his efforts Bunche received the NAACP Spingarn Medal in 1949 and numerous other honors and was given a ticker tape parade in New York. In 1950, Bunche became the first person of color to win a Nobel Peace Prize. He died Dec 9, 1971, at New York, NY.

Chief Joseph
Death • Sept 21, 1904 • 100 Years
Chief of the Nez Percé tribe, Joseph, whose Indian name was In-mut-too-yah-lat-lat, was born about 1840 at Wallowa Valley, Oregon Territory. In 1863, as the Gold Rush extended into the Nez Percé lands, the tribe was told by the US government to relocate to a small reservation in Idaho. Joseph's father, Chief Joseph the Elder, denounced the ruling and refused to budge, and tensions between Washington and the Nez Percé increased. When his father died in 1871, Joseph became chief. Faced with war or resettlement to a reservation, he led his people on a dramatic retreat from the US Calvary. After three months and more than 1,000 miles, he and his people were finally surrounded and sent to a reservation at Oklahoma. It was when they surrendered to US troops at Bear's Paw near Chinook, MT, Oct 5, 1877, that Chief Joseph made his famous speech of surrender, "From where the sun now stands, I will fight no more forever." Though the few survivors were later allowed to relocate to the Colville reservation in what is now Washington state, the Nez Percé never regained their ancestral lands. Chief Joseph died at Colville on Sept 21, 1904.

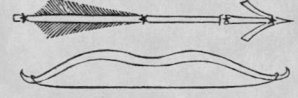

Pretty Boy Floyd
Birth • Feb 3, 1904 • 100 Years
Notorious gangster "Pretty Boy" Floyd was born Charles Arthur Floyd in Georgia and grew up as the son of poor farmers in Oklahoma. His early crimes were ones of desperation; after months of trying to find work to support his wife and young son, he held up a post office for $350, then stole $16,000 from a Kroger store. Floyd spent three years in prison and lost his wife in the process. He worked as a hired gun for bootleggers and rumrunners and received his nickname from a brothel owner named Beulah. He learned to use a machine gun and robbed at least 30 banks in a 12-year period. After the death of John Dillinger on July 22, 1934, Floyd was named Public Enemy No. 1, with a reward of $23,000 offered for his capture. A few months later, in October 1934, he was cornered by police in East Liverpool, OH, soon after robbing the Tiltonsville People's Bank. He was shot and killed Oct 22, 1934.

George Kennan
Birth • Feb 16, 1904 • 100 Years
US diplomat who coined the phrase "containment policy," Kennan was born at Milwaukee, WI. He joined the US Foreign Service in 1925, after graduating from Princeton. He served as a diplomat during WWII and was briefly arrested by the Nazis. After the war, while working as the director of the State Department's policy-planning staff, he wrote an article for *Foreign Affairs* magazine that had a great

Spotlight on People

influence on America's Cold War foreign policy. The article, entitled "The Sources of Soviet Conduct" and submitted under the pseudonym "Mr. X," called upon the US and its allies to prevent the territorial spread of communism, either by shows of military force or by economic and technological intervention in at-risk nations. Both the Marshall Plan and the Truman Doctrine were heavily influenced by the ideas expressed in Kennan's article. In 1952, President Truman appointed him ambassador to the Soviet Union. His term was cut short when the Soviet government took offense at unflattering statements Kennan made regarding Stalin. In later years, he emended his views on containment, no longer advocating direct conflict with the Soviet Union. From 1974 until the present, he has been Professor Emeritus at the Institute for Advanced Study, which is affiliated with Princeton.

John Sirica

Birth • Mar 19, 1904 • 100 Years

John Sirica, "the Watergate Judge," was born at Waterbury, CT. During two years of trials and hearings, federal judge Sirica relentlessly pushed for the names of those responsible for the June 17, 1972, burglary of the Democratic National Committee headquarters in Washington's Watergate complex. His unwavering search for the truth ultimately resulted in the toppling of the Nixon administration. Judge John Sirica died Aug 15, 1992, at Washington, DC.

Martin Luther King, Jr

Birth • Jan 29, 1929 • 75 Years

The great American civil rights leader and clergyman was born in Atlanta, GA. He followed in his father's footsteps: after receiving a doctorate from Boston University, King became pastor of the first of many congregations at Dexter Avenue Baptist Church in Montgomery, AL, in 1954. In 1957, he was elected president of the Southern Christian Leadership Conference. He believed in the nonviolent civil disobedience principles as articulated by Henry David Thoreau and Mohandas Gandhi, and he put them into practice during the 1950s and 1960s. To undermine segregation practices, he and his followers began with economic boycotts against bus, restaurant and other services that segregated black customers and then moved on to sit-ins and protest marches, culminating in the famous 1963 march to Washington, DC, where under the Lincoln Memorial Dr. King proclaimed, "I have a dream . . ." *Time* magazine named him man of the year for 1963. Congress passed the Civil Rights Act of 1964, and King received a Nobel Peace Prize. Dr. King became a beloved figure worldwide and a valued consultant to American presidents Kennedy and Johnson. He was assassinated by James Earl Ray at Memphis, TN, on Apr 3, 1968.

Literature

Sir Philip Sidney

Birth • Nov 30, 1554 • 450 Years

English poet, statesman and soldier was born at Penshurst, Kent. Sidney was the epitome of the Renaissance Man, possessing a questing intellect and artistic creativity. While serving in the Elizabethan court as a minor courtier, Sidney composed poetic verse that is still enjoyed today. His sonnet sequence *Astrophel and Stella* (1582) is rivaled only by Shakespeare's, and *Arcadia* (1584) is considered the most important work of prose romance of that time. He wrote *Defence of Poesie* in the same time period and it is the defining document of Elizabethan literary criticism. Sidney had ambitions to rise in the court and became involved in Queen Elizabeth's efforts to aid the Netherlands in a quarrel with Spain. Mortally wounded as he led an English detachment aiding the Dutch near Zutphen, Sept 22, 1586, Sidney died at Arnheim, Oct 17, 1586. All England mourned his death and every major poet contributed verses in his honor.

Joel Barlow

Birth • Mar 24, 1754 • 250 Years

Barlow, born in Redding, CT, to a farmer, was to be America's first best-selling author. After graduating from Yale, he was a lawyer, journalist and US diplomat who yearned to be a poet. With *The Vision of Columbus* (1787), he offered the young US its first epic poem, one

Spotlight on People

that extolled the glories of the Americas from ancient times to the 1780s. (Later revised as *The Columbiad* in 1807, it became ponderous and self-important.) Flush on the success of the poem and proclaimed America's bard, he traveled to Europe with a letter of recommendation from George Washington. Under the influence of the French Revolution, Barlow became a radical and honorary citizen of the French Republic. In Europe and homesick for Connecticut, he wrote *The Hasty Pudding* (1796), a mock-epic singing the praises of New England's cornmeal mush. "Come, dear bowl,/Glide o'er my palate, and inspire my soul." It is that work that seals his place in American literature. Barlow died of cold on Dec 24, 1812, in Poland while on a diplomatic mission for President James Madison to see Napoleon, whose army was retreating from Russia.

PHILLIS WHEATLEY
Birth • 1754 • 250 Years

Born at Senegal, West Africa, about 1753 or 1754, Phillis was brought to the US in 1761 and purchased as a slave by a Boston tailor named John Wheatley. She was allotted unusual privileges for a slave, including being allowed to learn to read and write. She wrote her first poetry at age 14, and her first work was published in 1770. Wheatley's fame as a poet spread throughout Europe as well as the US after her *Poems on Various Subjects, Religious and Moral* was published at England in 1773. She was invited to visit George Washington's army headquarters after he read a poem she had written about him in 1776. John Wheatley had freed her in 1773, but she stayed with his family until his death in 1778, when she married John Peters. Phillis Wheatley died Dec 5, 1784, at Boston, MA.

NATHANIEL HAWTHORNE
Birth • July 4, 1804 • 200 Years

The son of a sea captain, born to a Puritan family at Salem, MA, Nathaniel Hawthorne toiled many years as a writer before he achieved any kind of success. He published many stories, mostly anonymously, in the years after he finished college. (*Twice-Told Tales* is a collection of his early stories.) Still, Hawthorne had to take a job at the Boston Custom House to make ends meet. He married and settled in Concord, where his friends included Ralph Waldo Emerson, Henry David Thoreau and Herman Melville. He published *The Scarlet Letter* in 1850, which he wrote while working as a surveyor at Salem. His career as a writer was finally established with this groundbreaking book about adultery, guilt and moral responsibility set in 17th-century New England. This classic of American literature is often considered to be the first American psychological novel. Hawthorne followed with *The House of Seven Gables* in 1851 and the juvenile classics *The Wonder Book* (1852) and *The Tanglewood Tales* (1853). He wrote a campaign biography of his college friend Franklin Pierce, who appointed Hawthorne to a diplomatic position in England after he was elected president. Hawthorne died during a trip to the White Mountains with Pierce on May 19, 1864.

OSCAR WILDE
Birth • Oct 16, 1854 • 150 Years

Irish writer as beloved for his dramatic personal life as for his writing, Oscar Fingal O'Flahertie Wills Wilde was born at Dublin. He was an outstanding student, winning several scholarships and the Newdigate Prize for his poem "Ravenna" while still at Oxford. In 1881, his writing career began to take off: he published his first volume of poetry and sailed for the US to deliver a series of lectures on aestheticism, beauty for the sake of beauty, which was a frequent theme in his writings. Wilde was known for his flamboyant style, dressing outrageously for the times. He had great success both critically and financially; some of his best-known works include the fairy tales *The Happy Prince and Other Tales* (1888), *The Picture of Dorian Gray* (first published as a play in 1890 and later expanded to a novel) and the drama *The Importance of Being Earnest* (1893). He married and had children but also lived a secret life: in 1881 he was arrested, tried and jailed for "gross indecency," a result of his homosexual affair with Lord Alfred "Bosie" Douglas, son of the Marquis of Queensbury. Wilde served two years of hard labor, and his wife fled Great

Spotlight on People

Britain with the children in the face of the scandal. He moved to Paris after his release from prison and lived under a pseudonym. He died there, penniless, on Nov 30, 1900.

E.M. Forster
Birth • Jan 1, 1879 • 125 Years
Edward Morgan Forster, English author born at London, is remembered for his six novels: *Where Angels Fear to Tread* (1905), *The Longest Journey* (1907), *A Room with a View* (1908), *Howards End* (1910), *A Passage to India* (1924) and the posthumously published *Maurice* (1971). He also achieved eminence for his short stories and essays, and he collaborated on the libretto for an opera, Benjamin Britten's *Billy Budd* (1951). Forster died at Coventry, England, June 7, 1970.

Ding Ling
Birth • Oct 12, 1904 • 100 Years
Writer and political activist Ding Ling (the pseudonym of Jiang Wei) was born in the Hunan Province and raised by her independent-thinking mother following her father's death. In the years 1923–1957, she wrote and published dozens of controversial works of fiction, including 1928's *Diary of Miss Sophia* and 1940's *When I Was in Hsia Village*, that were explicit in their feminist leanings and hinted broadly at the incompetence and ineptness of the Communist Party. The party exiled her in 1957. During the Cultural Revolution, Ding Ling was persecuted for her right-leaning views and spent 1970–1975 in prison yet again. Her status was restored in 1979, and she began to write again. She continued writing until her death in 1986 in the Shanxi Province.

Graham Greene
Birth • Oct 2, 1904 • 100 Years
Graham Greene was one of the most widely read British novelists of the 20th century. Born at Berkhamsted, Hertfordshire, England, he began publishing poems and stories during his years at Oxford. During WWII, he worked in the British Foreign Office in an intelligence capacity, directly under his friend Kim Philby (who later defected to the Soviet Union). After the war, he traveled widely as a freelance journalist. His novels reflect the variety of his experiences: *The Quiet American* (1955) and *Our Man in Havana* (1958) both deal with characters working in the intelligence community, while 1951's *The End of the Affair* is presumed to be based on one of Greene's own affairs with a married woman. Several times nominated for the National Book Award, he also authored several screenplays, and many of his novels were adapted into highly successful films. He died Apr 3, 1991, at Vevey, Switzerland.

Christopher Isherwood
Birth • Aug 26, 1904 • 100 Years
Author of short stories, plays and novels, Christopher William Isherwood was born at High Lane, Cheshire, England. The play and motion picture *I Am a Camera* and the musical *Cabaret* were based on the short story "Sally Bowles" in his collection from the 1930s titled *Goodbye to Berlin*, which contained the line "I am a camera with its shutter open, quite passive, recording, not thinking." Isherwood died at Santa Monica, CA, Jan 4, 1986.

Pablo Neruda
Birth • July 12, 1904 • 100 Years
Born Neftalí Ricardo Reyes Basoalto at Parral, Chile, the poet better known as Pablo Neruda began writing poetry when he was ten years old. He published his first work at 13, and by 1920 was a contributor to several literary journals. Throughout his life he worked as a diplomat or politician, serving the Chilean government as a consul in several different nations and later elected to the Chilean Senate. Neruda's political career was rocky; he was frequently at odds with his own government's policies and spent many years in hiding. His poetry reflected his political views, including *Canto General* (1950) and *Estravagario*. He was not exclusively political, however; his *Cien Sonetos Del Amor* (1960) was a collection of love sonnets written to his second wife. Neruda had a prolific career, producing more than 40 volumes of verse, and he is the most widely read of all South American poets. In 1971, he was awarded the Nobel Prize for literature, and he died two years later at Santiago, Chile.

Spotlight on People

S.J. Perelman
Birth • Feb 1, 1904 • 100 Years

American humorist known for his mastery of language and irony, Sidney Joseph Perelman was born at Brooklyn, NY. He attended Brown University and edited its humor magazine. He began working with the Marx Brothers, writing the screenplays for *Monkey Business* (1931) and *Horse Feathers* (1932), both considered to be masterpieces of early American film comedy. He won an Academy Award for his screenplay for 1956's *Around the World in 80 Days*, but was best known for his satirical essays published in *The New Yorker* magazine. He poked fun at the commonality of everyday life, doing so with biting wit, outrageous puns and a pitch-perfect ability to mimic. Many volumes of his writings have been published. He died Oct 17, 1979, at New York, NY.

William Shirer
Birth • Feb 23, 1904 • 100 Years

American journalist and author William L. Shirer was born at Chicago, IL. As the European correspondent from 1927 to 1934 for the *Chicago Tribune*, he became a friend of Mohandas K. Gandhi, the leader of India's independence movement. As a result he published *Gandhi: A Memoir* in 1980. Shirer's best-known book is *The Rise and Fall of the Third Reich* (1960), in which he used his experiences in Europe with the *New York Herald Tribune*, the Universal News Service and CBS Radio. He died Dec 28, 1993, at Boston, MA.

Isaac Bashevis Singer
Birth • July 14, 1904 • 100 Years

Winner of the Nobel Prize for literature in 1978, Isaac Bashevis Singer was born at Radzymin, Poland. (His date of birth is uncertain; it has been published as July 14, Oct 26 and Nov 21.) The son of a Hasidic rabbi, he wrote almost exclusively in Yiddish and then personally oversaw English translations. He grew up in Warsaw before and during WWI, and his stories are full of images of the Polish Jewish community that vanished after the Holocaust. Jewish folklore, legends and mysticism are often themes, and many of his children's collections (especially *Zlatah the Goat and Other Stories* and *When Schlemiel Went to Warsaw and Other Stories*) are retellings of fables and legends of Eastern Europe. He emigrated to the US in 1935, and he died at Surfside, FL, on July 24, 1991.

Children's Literature

Theodor Geisel
Birth • Mar 2, 1904 • 100 Years

Theodor Seuss Geisel, the creator of *The Cat in the Hat* and *Oh, the Places You'll Go*, was born at Springfield, MA. Known to children and parents as Dr. Seuss, his books have sold more than 200 million copies and have been translated into 20 languages. His career began with *And to Think That I Saw It on Mulberry Street*, which was turned down by 27 publishing houses before being accepted by Vanguard Press in 1937. His titles intended for early readers, such as *Green Eggs and Ham*, *Hop on Pop* and *Fox in Socks*, revolutionized the way that millions of children learned to read. Later books included many messages, from environmental consciousness in *The Lorax* to the dangers of pacifism in *Horton Hatches the Egg*. He was awarded a Pulitzer Prize in 1984 "for his contribution over nearly half a century to the education and enjoyment of America's children and their parents." Several animated television specials were made of his books, including *How the Grinch Stole Christmas* and *Horton Hears a Who*. A short film that he wrote, *Gerald McBoing Boing*, won the Academy Award in 1951 for Best Short Subject. Other honors included a Peabody Award, three Caldecott Honors and the Laura Ingalls Wilder Medal for lifetime achievement. Geisel died Sept 24, 1991, at La Jolla, CA.

Sydney Taylor
Birth • Oct 31, 1904 • 100 Years

Born at New York, NY, Sydney Taylor was an actress and professional dancer with the Martha Graham Dance Company. She also wrote, choreographed and directed original plays in addition to writing books for children. Her beloved *All-of-a-Kind Family* (1951) was based on her own experiences growing up on the Lower East Side of Manhattan in the early 1900s.

Spotlight on People

This unique book about a loving Jewish family of five "step-and-stairs" sisters, their parents and baby brother won honors from the Jewish Book Council and the Association of Jewish Libraries. She authored several other books, such as the popular *Danny Loves a Holiday* and four "All-of-a-Kind" sequels. The Association of Jewish Libraries gives an annual award named for her to encourage the publication of outstanding books of positive Jewish content for children. Taylor died Feb 12, 1978, at Queens, NY.

Journalism
Louis Antoine Godey
Birth • June 6, 1804 • 200 Years
Born at New York, NY, Godey, a publisher based in Philadelphia, launched what is known as the first magazine specifically targeted at women, *Godey's Lady's Book*. For the first several years, it was comprised of reprints from British publications, but the tone changed when Godey hired Sarah J. Hale in 1836 to serve as editor. Soon the magazine was giving advice on everything from recipes, music, literature, equestrienne procedure, handcrafts and specifically fashion. Women all over the US relied on the color plate illustrations to learn the new styles of dress popular on the East Coast. *Godey's Lady's Book* was also an important literary magazine, publishing book reviews as well as original works by Harriet Beecher Stowe, Edgar Allen Poe, Nathaniel Hawthorne, Henry Wadsworth Longfellow and many other celebrated authors. By the mid-19th century, the magazine had a circulation of more than 150,000. Godey and Hale served as publisher and editor for over 40 years. Godey died Nov 28, 1878, and was buried at Philadelphia. Hale died in 1879, and the magazine ceased publication the following year. This magazine is considered one of the most important historic resources on life in 19th-century America.

Margaret Bourke-White
Birth • June 14, 1904 • 100 Years
Born at the Bronx, NY, Bourke-White began to study photography as a hobby while still a young girl. Her father, an inventor, engineer and camera enthusiast, believed in equality and education for women and encouraged his daughter in her pursuits. She became a pioneering photojournalist, hired as the first photographer for *Fortune* in 1929. She was the first female photojournalist to work for *Life* magazine, and one of her pictures graced the cover of the very first issue. Bourke-White had many other "first" accomplishments: first Western photographer allowed inside the Soviet Union, first female war correspondent and the first to be allowed into combat zones during WWII and one of the first photographers to be allowed inside the liberated death camps. She published several books, including *You Have Seen Their Faces* (1937) with her husband, Erskine Caldwell, about people living through the Depression years. Bourke-White died Aug 27, 1971, in Connecticut.

Marjorie Henderson Buell
Birth • Dec 11, 1904 • 100 Years
One of the first successful female cartoonists, Marjorie Henderson Buell (known as "Marge") was born at Philadelphia, PA, and began selling cartoons to local newspapers while still in high school. Her success grew, and by 1929 she was syndicated in publications such as *Life* magazine and *The Saturday Evening Post*. In 1935, the *Post* commissioned her to create a recurring character, and thus, Marge's Little Lulu was born. Buell was considered a pioneer for creating a female character who was resourceful, courageous and sometimes naughty, but who always managed to outsmart the neighborhood boys. The original newspaper strip was a single-panel cartoon but soon expanded into longer syndicated newspaper strips, books, dolls, merchandise and 28 animated cartoons. Lulu was a spokesperson for Kleenex tissues for many years! By the 1950s, other artists and writers were involved in producing the strip, and Buell sold her rights to Western Publishing in 1971. Little Lulu still makes occasional comebacks, appearing in her own TV show on HBO in the mid-1990s. Buell died May 30, 1993, at Elyria, OH.

Spotlight on People

A.J. LIEBLING
Birth • Oct 18, 1904 • 100 Years
American journalist and author who said "Freedom of the press belongs to those who own one," Abbott Joseph Liebling was born at New York, NY. He enrolled at Dartmouth at the age of 15 but was thrown out for missing compulsory chapel attendance. He finished his education at the Pulitzer School of Journalism at Columbia University and went on to write for the *Evening Post* in Providence, RI, and then later for *The New Yorker* magazine. He was known for his pieces on boxing, horse racing and food, his life's three passions. Liebling wrote a column for *The New Yorker* called "Wayward Press" from 1946 until his death in New York, Dec 28, 1963.

Education

PETER MARK ROGET
Birth • Jan 18, 1779 • 225 Years
Best known as author of Roget's *Thesaurus of English Words and Phrases*, Peter Mark Roget actually began his career as a physician. Born at London, England, he studied medicine at the University of Edinburgh and practiced full time until 1840, specializing in matters of the five senses. During this time, Roget invented the "log-log" slide rule, which calculated roots and powers of numbers. He also studied optical illusions, and his work in this area ultimately led to the development of moving pictures. He retired from medicine in 1840 to begin work on the *Thesaurus*, something he had been planning since 1805. An exhaustive collection of synonyms, the *Thesaurus of English Words and Phrases* has never been out of print since its publication in 1852. Roget died at West Malvern, Worcestershire, England, Sept 12, 1869.

ELIZABETH PALMER PEABODY
Birth • May 16, 1804 • 200 Years
Born at Billerica, MA, Peabody was an innovative educator, author and publisher. She opened her first school at Lancaster, MA, when only 16 years old. In 1839, Peabody opened a bookstore that quickly became the intellectuals' hangout. With her own printing press Peabody became the first woman publisher of Boston and possibly the US. She published three of her brother-in-law Nathaniel Hawthorne's books. For two years she printed and wrote for *The Dial*, the literary magazine and voice of the Transcendental movement. Peabody's enduring accomplishment was the establishment of the first kindergarten in the US—in 1860 at Boston. She created a magazine, *Kindergarten Messenger*, in 1873. Peabody died Jan 3, 1894, at Jamaica Plain, MA.

Entertainment

JOSEPH JEFFERSON
Birth • Feb 20, 1829 • 175 Years
Distinguished American actor, born at Philadelphia, PA, in a family of actors. Jefferson made his stage debut at the age of three in Kotzebue's *Pizarro*. After many successes, his search for a character both humorous and pathetic centered on Rip Van Winkle, about whom he wrote a short play. Later revised by Dion Boucicault, the play opened with Jefferson in the leading role at London, England, in 1865, and was an immediate success. Rip Van Winkle became the signature role for which Jefferson was known. He died at Palm Beach, FL, Apr 23, 1905. He is remembered each year in Chicago when the Joseph Jefferson (Jeff) Awards are presented to recognize excellence in theatrical productions.

WILL ROGERS
Birth • Nov 4, 1879 • 125 Years
William Penn Adair Rogers, born on a ranch in Indian Territory (now Oklahoma), got his show business start in 1902 doing rope tricks in a Wild West show. He moved on to vaudeville and, by 1916, was the wisecracking star of Florenz Ziegfeld's *Follies*. Part Cherokee Indian, Rogers once told a Boston audience, "My ancestors didn't come over on the Mayflower, but they met the boat." Such comments added to his huge success as a newspaper columnist and book author; he was famous for poking fun at important people and events and for his everyday philosophies of life. He was friendly with politicians all over the world, including Franklin D. Roosevelt. Rogers also met with great success as a motion picture actor, and his film credits

Spotlight on People

included *A Connecticut Yankee* in 1931 and *State Fair* in 1933. He was killed in an Alaska plane crash on Aug 15, 1935.

George Balanchine
Birth • Jan 22, 1904 • 100 Years

Born Georgi Militonovitch Balanchivadze at St. Petersburg, Russia, George Balanchine became one of the leading influences in 20th-century ballet. He choreographed more than 200 ballets including *Concerto Barocco*, *Apollo*, *Orpheus*, *Firebird*, *Swan Lake*, *Waltz Academy* and *The Nutcracker*. In 1933 he was invited to the US by Boston philanthropist Lincoln Kirstein to establish a school for American dancers. Together they founded the School of American Ballet in 1934 and then formed several ballet companies, including the New York City Ballet, which was led by Balanchine. He died at New York, NY, Apr 30, 1983.

Ralph Bellamy
Birth • June 17, 1904 • 100 Years

American actor Ralph Rexford Bellamy was born at Chicago, IL. He appeared in more than 100 films and was best known for his stage and film portrayals of President Franklin D. Roosevelt. He played Ellery Queen in a series of films in the 1940s and is also remembered for his roles in such films as *Lady on a Train* with Deanna Durbin and *Trading Places* with Eddie Murphy. He was a founder of the Screen Actors' Guild and president of Actors' Equity. Bellamy was awarded an honorary Academy Award in 1987. He died Nov 29, 1991, at Los Angeles, CA.

Joan Crawford
Birth • Mar 23, 1904 • 100 Years

Born Lucille Fay LeSueur at San Antonio, TX, Crawford became a Hollywood star with her performance in *Our Dancing Daughters*. She won an Oscar in 1945 for her role in *Mildred Pierce*. Events of Crawford's life are chronicled in *Mommie Dearest*, written by her adopted daughter Christina, who accused her of child abuse. Portions of the book were later disputed by her other children and by other Hollywood people who knew Crawford. She is also remembered for her style of dress, unique to Hollywood at the time. Her exaggerated eyebrows and lipstick, wide shoulder pads and ankle-strap high heels created a distinct look often imitated. Other films included *Grand Hotel*, *Dancing Lady*, *The Women* and *Whatever Happened to Baby Jane?* She died at New York, NY, May 10, 1977.

Sir John Gielgud
Birth • Apr 14, 1904 • 100 Years

Director and actor John Gielgud was born at London, England. Persuading his parents to let him train at the Royal Academy of Dramatic Arts, Gielgud promised them that if he had failed to make a stage career by the age of 25, he would become an architect. He found success on the London stage almost immediately and made his professional film debut in 1924 in *Who Is the Man?* Other film credits include *Murder on the Orient Express* and *Plenty*. He played the role of Hamlet more than 500 times. Gielgud won the Tony Award for best director in 1961 for *Big Fish Little Fish* and the Best Supporting Actor Oscar for 1981's *Arthur*. He was knighted in 1953, and on his 90th birthday the West End's Globe Theatre was renamed the Gielgud Theatre in his honor. He died at Buckinghamshire, England, May 21, 2000.

Cary Grant
Birth • Jan 18, 1904 • 100 Years

Known as a romantic leading actor, Cary Grant was born at Bristol, England, as Archibald Alexander Leach. His mother was institutionalized for mental problems when he was nine, and he fled Bristol at the age of 14, joining a vaudeville troupe where he worked as a stilt-walker. He arrived in Hollywood in the early 1930s, and his first big success on screen was as Mae West's leading man in 1933's *She Done Him Wrong*. He created his stage name from Gary Cooper's initials, and for the next three decades, Grant established his reputation as the most popular leading man in film history. His characters personified wit, charm and sophistication, always with a light comic touch and dashing good looks. Grant's films include *Topper*, *Arsenic and Old Lace*, *The Awful Truth*, *Bringing Up Baby*, *North by Northwest* and *Charade*. He died at Davenport, IA, on Nov 29, 1986.

Spotlight on People

Moss Hart
Birth • Oct 24, 1904 • 100 Years

Born at New York City, NY, playwright Moss Hart's life is a classic American rags-to-riches story. Escaping a miserable childhood, he worked odd jobs on the New York theater circuit while trying desperately to get his works produced. He met George S. Kaufman in 1929 and they collaborated on the script for *Once in a Lifetime*. It opened on Broadway in September, 1930, and, as they say, the rest was history. The play became one of the most successful of its time, and Hart and Kaufman would follow with seven more successful shows including *You Can't Take It with You* and *The Man Who Came to Dinner*. Hart went on to write any number of successful stage shows and film screenplays, including the 1954 film version of *A Star Is Born* and the Academy Award–winning *Gentleman's Agreement*. He also directed such plays as *My Fair Lady*. He and Kaufman remained lifelong friends and died within a few months of each other. Hart died at Palm Springs, CA, on Dec 20, 1961.

Peter Lorre
Birth • June 26, 1904 • 100 Years

Born László Löwenstein at what is now Ruzomberok, Slovakia (Austria-Hungary at the time), Peter Lorre ran away from home at a young age to become an actor. He made his debut in Austria and found moderate success in Germany in the late 1920s. His big break came when he was cast as the psychopathic child killer in Fritz Lang's *M* in 1931. He fled Nazi Europe and wound up in Hollywood by 1935. Lorre played villains and murderers in films such as *The Maltese Falcon*, *Casablanca*, *The Man Who Knew Too Much* and *Crime and Punishment*. He broke his stereotypical bad-guy roles by portraying Japanese detective Mr Moto in a series of mysteries during the late 1930s. He died at Los Angeles, CA, Mar 23, 1964.

Sally Rand
Birth • Apr 3, 1904 • 100 Years

Born Helen Gould Beck at Hickory County, MO, Sally got her show business start in chorus lines and vaudeville productions in the early 1920s. She worked for Ringling Bros as an acrobat and then formed a dance troupe that played Chicago's speakeasies during Prohibition. Rand shot to fame during the 1933 Chicago World's Fair, where she was arrested for public indecency when she performed her "fan dance," a form of striptease that she invented. She continued performing her fan dance for many years, rarely actually nude but usually wearing a body stocking that gave just subtle peeks of nudity. She died at Glendora, CA, Aug 31, 1979.

Music

Francis Scott Key
Birth • Aug 1, 1779 • 225 Years

American attorney, social worker, poet and author, Francis Scott Key wrote the poem that became the US national anthem. While on a legal mission, Key was detained on shipboard off Baltimore during the British bombardment of Fort McHenry on the night of Sept 13–14, 1814. Thrilled to see the American flag still flying over the fort at daybreak, Key wrote "The Star Spangled Banner." Printed in the *Baltimore American* on Sept 21, 1814, it was soon popularly sung to the music of an old English tune, "Anacreon in Heaven." It did not become the official US national anthem until 117 years later when, on Mar 3, 1931, President Herbert Hoover signed into law an act for that purpose. Key was born at Frederick County, MD, and died at Baltimore, MD, Jan 11, 1843.

Johann Strauss the Elder
Birth • Mar 14, 1804 • 200 Years

Born at Vienna, Johann Strauss could be called the first pop music idol. As a teenager, he played with various orchestras across Austria and quickly became known for his popular dance hall–style music. In 1834 he was appointed bandmaster to the 1st Vienna Militia Regiment, and the following year he became director of the imperial court balls. He toured throughout Europe, conducting his own compositions, and was extremely successful, affectionately called the "Austrian Napoleon." He is remembered for the waltz "Lorely-Rhein-Klänge" and the "Radetzky March." He died of scarlet fever at Vienna, Sept 25, 1849. His son, Johann II, followed in his

Spotlight on People

musical footsteps, composing such world-famous works as *The Blue Danube*. Two other sons, Josef and Eduard, were also conductors.

ENGLEBERT HUMPERDINCK
Birth • Sept 1, 1854 • 150 Years

Operatic composer born in the small town of Siegburg, near Bonn, Germany, Humperdinck's talent was evident early in his career. He won the Mendelssohn Prize of Berlin while still a student, and then became musical assistant to Richard Wagner for the first performance of *Parsifal*. He worked as a conservatory teacher, critic and composer, and is best remembered for his first opera, *Hänsel und Gretel*, based on the folktale by the Brothers Grimm. Other works include a religious mime play, *The Miracle*, and another fairy tale-based opera, *Königskinder*. He died at Neustrelitz, Germany, on Sept 27, 1921.

LEOŠ JANÁČEK
Birth • July 3, 1854 • 150 Years

Highly influential Czech composer Leoš Janáček was born at Hukvaldy, Moravia, in what was then the Austrian Empire. He enrolled at the Leipzig Conservatory to study composition and was soon composing his own operas, including *The Beginning of a Romance*, which was favorably received in 1894. He studied and collected folk music, eventually integrating the traditional melodies into his operatic compositions. He wrote music that could be performed following the inflections and often jagged rhythms of his native language. *Jenufa*, premiering in 1903, established his international reputation. Also remembered are 1925's *The Cunning Little Vixen* and *From the House of the Dead*, which did not premiere until two years after his death, at Moravska Ostrava, Czechoslovakia, on Aug 28, 1928.

JOHN PHILIP SOUSA
Birth • Nov 6, 1854 • 150 Years

A composer and bandleader born in Washington, DC, Sousa was known as the March King because of the popularity of the 136 marches he wrote. He commanded the US Marine Band from 1880 to 1892, when he left to form his own band, which became the most successful in the nation. He is remembered for such stirring marches as "Semper Fidelis," "El Capitan" and "The Washington Post March," which was associated with a new dance—the two-step. His most famous march, "The Stars and Stripes Forever," was first performed in Philadelphia on the occasion of the unveiling of a statue of George Washington on May 14, 1897. When the US entered WWI in 1917, Sousa reenlisted and this time led the Navy Band. He remained active in music almost until his death at Reading, PA, Mar 6, 1932.

SIR THOMAS BEECHAM
Birth • Apr 29, 1879 • 125 Years

Born the oldest son of the mayor of St. Helen's, Lancashire, England, Thomas Beecham was a self-taught conductor who took over the Hallé Orchestra at the age of 20. He went on to become perhaps the single most influential promoter of classical music for US and British audiences. He founded the Beecham Symphony Orchestra in 1909 and the Beecham Opera Company in 1915. Beecham became the conductor of the Royal Opera House, Covent Garden, where he conducted the UK premieres of Wagner's *Die Meistersinger* and Richard Strauss's *Der Rosenkavalier*. He founded the London Philharmonic Orchestra in 1932, and in 1946, the Royal Philharmonic Orchestra. He was knighted on Jan 1, 1916, for his services to music, and opera in particular. Hundreds of orchestral recordings that he conducted are still available. He died at London on Mar 8, 1961.

JIMMY DORSEY
Birth • Feb 29, 1904 • 100 Years

Born at Shenandoah, PA, to a coal miner-turned-music teacher, Jimmy Dorsey played a number of reed and brass instruments throughout his youth. Settling on clarinet and alto saxophone, he played in various bands, mostly with his younger brother Tommy. In 1934 they formed The Dorsey Brothers Orchestra, but the brothers frequently disagreed; and a year later, Tommy walked out, leaving Jimmy to run the group on his own. The renamed Jimmy Dorsey Orchestra became one of the most accomplished bands of the swing music era; it had a

Spotlight on People

strong jazz feel that kept popular music audiences listening. Jimmy was considered one of the finest jazz saxophonists of his era and made hundreds of recordings with various groups that remain in print today. He and Tommy reunited briefly in the 1950s, but the brothers died within a few months of each other, Tommy in 1956, and Jimmy on June 12, 1957, at New York, NY.

Vladimir Horowitz
Birth • Oct 1, 1904 • 100 Years

Born at Berdichev, Russia, Horowitz was widely hailed as one of the world's greatest pianists, renowned for his masterful technique. His debut was at Kiev in 1920; and at the age of 20, he played a series of 23 recitals at Leningrad, performing a total of more than 200 works with no duplications. He made his US debut in 1928 with the New York Philharmonic. Horowitz settled in the US in 1940 and became a citizen in 1944. His career swung full circle Apr 20, 1986, when he performed his first concert in his native Russia after a self-imposed absence of 60 years. He died Nov 5, 1989, at New York, NY.

Glenn Miller
Birth • Mar 1, 1904 • 100 Years

American bandleader and composer (Alton) Glenn Miller was born at Clarinda, IA. He and his big band orchestra enjoyed great popularity preceding and during World War II. His hit recordings included "Moonlight Serenade," "String of Pearls," "Jersey Bounce" and "Sleepy Lagoon." Major Miller, leader of the US Army Air Force band, disappeared Dec 15, 1944, over the English Channel on a flight to Paris where he was scheduled to give a show. There were many explanations of his disappearance, but 41 years later, in December 1985, crew members of an aborted RAF bombing said they believed they had seen Miller's plane go down, the victim of bombs being jettisoned by the RAF over the English Channel.

Fats Waller
Birth • May 21, 1904 • 100 Years

Born Thomas Wright Waller at New York, NY, Fats Waller was one of the few musicians of the Jazz Era to find commercial success. The son of a minister, he learned to play the organ at his father's church and became a professional piano player at age 15. By the late 1920s the songs that he wrote appeared frequently in Broadway reviews. He was known for the humor and slapstick in his music and for his own comedic talents on stage. He wrote such standards as "Ain't Misbehavin'" (first performed on Broadway by Louis Armstrong in 1929), "Honeysuckle Rose" and "Squeeze Me," the latter written with Clarence Williams. He died at Kansas City, MO, on Dec 15, 1943.

Art

Paul Klee
Birth • Dec 18, 1879 • 125 Years

Born at Münchenbuchsee, Switzerland into a family of musicians, Paul Klee as a child studied both art and the violin. Choosing art over music, he settled in Munich where he joined Der Blaue Reiter, an expressionist group that also included Wassily Kandinsky and Franz Marc. Their goal was to bring avant-garde and abstract art to the public eye. Klee taught at the Bauhaus School and the Düsseldorf Academy, but in the early 1930s, he was expelled from Germany by the Nazis, who considered his work "degenerate." He relocated to Switzerland where he continued to paint. He developed a progressive skin and muscular disease which caused him to modify his style as he had difficulty gripping a paintbrush. The disease eventually killed him on June 29, 1940, at Muralto-Locarno, Switzerland. Klee's work is considered highly influential to all later 20th-century surrealists and abstract expressionists.

Salvador Dalí
Birth • May 11, 1904 • 100 Years

A leading painter in the Surrealist movement, Salvador Dalí was equally well known for his baffling antics and attempts to shock his audiences. Born into a middle-class family in Figueras, Spain, he studied art in Barcelona and Madrid, experimenting with a variety of

Spotlight on People

painting styles. In the late 1920s, his work took a different direction. He began reading Sigmund Freud's writings on the erotic significance of subconscious imagery, which clearly began to influence his work. Dalí became affiliated with the Paris Surrealists, a group of artists and writers. His most famous paintings represent a kind of "dream world" with everyday objects deformed in often bizarre and irrational ways. *The Persistence of Memory* (1931) features a stark landscape of melting watches. The largest collection of his works resides in the Salvador Dalí Museum at St. Petersburg, FL. Dalí died Jan 23, 1989, at Figueras.

Willem de Kooning
Birth • Apr 24, 1904 • 100 Years

Born at Rotterdam, Netherlands, Willem de Kooning was apprenticed to a commercial art firm while studying at night at the Rotterdam Academy of Fine Arts and Techniques. He stowed away on a ship to the US in 1926 and eventually settled at New York City. He worked various commercial art jobs and became friends with painter Arshile Gorky and art critic John Graham. His art took on a more abstract focus, and in the 1930s he began experimenting with geometric shapes in his paintings. In 1935, he was hired by the Works Progress Administration (WPA) Federal Art Project and worked on murals. His first solo show took place in 1948 and his reputation as a major abstract artist was established. His primary works included the series *Women*, which explored female imagery in dramatic fashion. De Kooning died Mar 19, 1997 at Long Island, NY, and was honored with a retrospective at the Museum of Modern Art in New York that same year.

Science and Technology

Christiaan Huygens
Birth • Apr 14, 1629 • 375 Years

Dutch mathematician, astronomer and physicist, Christiaan Huygens was born at The Hague, Netherlands. Descartes was a family friend who took great interest in young Christiaan's mathematical education. Among his most significant accomplishments: he discovered the rings of Saturn, and in doing so, he developed a new method of polishing and grinding the lenses of telescopes, creating a much more accurate way of viewing the heavens. Huygens also studied and drew the first maps of Mars and calculated the length of the Martian day. The concept of time fascinated him, and he spent much of his career working on more accurate clocks and devices that could accurately calculate longitude. In 1656 he invented the pendulum clock. He also developed the wave or pulse theory of light. He died at The Hague, June 8, 1695.

Alvan Clark
Birth • Mar 8, 1804 • 200 Years

Alvan Clark was a moderately successful portrait painter born at Ashfield, MA, when he developed an interest in optics. His son George was studying engineering at the time, and together they founded Alvan Clark & Sons, manufacturers of the first optical lenses for telescopes. Their lenses were known for their unsurpassed quality and soon were installed at the US Naval Observatory at Washington, DC. Alvan's younger son, Alvan Graham Clark, used his father's lenses to discover 16 double stars, including the companion star of Sirius. The largest refracting telescope in the world, the 40-inch lens at Yerkes Observatory in Wisconsin, still uses lenses polished by Alvan Clark & Sons. Clark died in 1887.

Richard Owen
Birth • July 20, 1804 • 200 Years

Sir Richard Owen was the Victorian Age's preeminent academic, vertebrate anatomist and paleontologist. It was he who proposed that extinct animals be classed differently than living animals and finally gave these giant creatures a name—"dinosaurs" ("fearfully giant lizards")—in an April 1842 publication. Owen oversaw the first full-size dinosaur re-creations in 1854 in Sydenham Park, London, and was the first to describe the fossil bird archaeopteryx (although inaccurately). A friend of Charles Darwin, Owen later was heatedly opposed to Darwin's

Spotlight on People

theories of evolution and initiated anonymous attacks of *On the Origin of Species*. Born at Lancaster, England, Owen died Dec 18, 1892, at London.

ROBERT PARKER PARROTT
Birth • Oct 5, 1804 • 200 Years

Born in Lee, NH, Robert P. Parrott graduated from West Point Military Academy and served in the artillery. When he resigned from the military, he accepted the civilian position of superintendent of the West Point Foundry at Cold Spring, NY, which was responsible for providing the US Army with much of its weaponry. During his 41-year tenure, Parrott experimented with the manufacturing of artillery. He perfected a rifled cannon and its corresponding shells, as well as a sight and fuze, all of which bear his name. These weapons were used during the Civil War to great success. The Parrott rifle is known as the first machine gun. Parrott died Dec 24, 1877.

EMIL VON BEHRING
Birth • Mar 15, 1854 • 150 Years

Born in the village of Hansdorf, West Prussia, Germany, Emil von Behring studied medicine through a government grant and served as a military physician. He lived through the 1880's outbreak of diphtheria in Germany, which claimed thousands of lives. He was profoundly affected by this and dedicated himself to the treatment and prevention of infectious disease. Von Behring published groundbreaking research on serotherapy, the use of blood from immune animals in healing other species. Between 1893 and 1895 he conducted the first successful experiments on human patients with diphtheria, and in 1901 he was awarded the first Nobel Prize for medicine. His Behringwerke Company later developed the first successful tetanus immunization and also a tuberculosis vaccine. He died at Marburg, Germany, Mar 31, 1917.

WILLIAM CRAWFORD GORGAS
Birth • Oct 3, 1854 • 150 Years

Born at Toulminville, AL, Gorgas received his medical degree from Bellevue Medical College in New York. He had a brilliant military career, ultimately attaining the position of Surgeon General of the United States in 1914. He had been stricken with yellow fever while in the US Army medical corps but had recovered and remained immune from the disease. He became an expert in sanitation and insect control, and during the construction of the Panama Canal in the early 1900s, he worked to eradicate malaria and yellow fever by eliminating breeding places of mosquitoes and by isolating infected patients. The radical improvement of health conditions in Panama made the completion of the Canal possible. After a life of continued public service and honors from many countries, Gorgas died at London, England, July 4, 1920, and was given a funeral at St. Paul's Cathedral. He was then buried at Arlington National Cemetery.

ALBERT EINSTEIN
Birth • Mar 14, 1879 • 125 Years

Born at Ulm, Germany, Albert Einstein was educated in Italy and Switzerland but was unable to find a teaching position following his graduation in 1901. Thus, his first job was in the Swiss patent office while he worked towards his doctorate and produced many significant papers and writings on theoretical physics. He taught at various posts across Europe and emigrated to the US in 1933 for political reasons. Einstein took the post of Professor of Theoretical Physics at Princeton University and remained there for the rest of his career. His theory $E = mc^2$ revolutionized theories of energy, and he is best known for his theory of relativity, related in *General Theory of Relativity* and many other works published between 1905 and 1916. Einstein won the Nobel Prize in 1921. He died at Princeton, NJ, Apr 18, 1955.

CHARLES RICHARD DREW
Birth • June 3, 1904 • 100 Years

Charles Richard Drew was an African-American physician who developed an effective method for storing blood plasma. While working at Presbyterian Hospital in New York, NY, he discovered that by separating the liquid red blood cells from the near solid

Spotlight on People

plasma, the blood could be preserved and reconstituted at a later date. His blood plasma bank at Presbyterian served as the model for the widespread system of blood banks that the American Red Cross uses today. Drew also organized the first blood bank system in the US and UK during WWII. Born at Washington, DC, he was killed in an automobile accident near Burlington, NC, Apr 1, 1950.

George Gamow
Birth • Mar 4, 1904 • 100 Years
Nuclear physicist Gamow was born at Odessa in the Ukraine but left Europe in 1934 for the US, where he spent the remainder of his distinguished career. Although other scientists had theorized that the universe was expanding, Gamow put forth a more cohesive theory that he called the "big bang": a thermonuclear explosion created the universe—and as a result the universe was still expanding billions of years later. Besides his serious academic research and publications, Gamow published books for the layman to explain cosmology. He died at Boulder, CO, on Aug 19, 1968.

J. Robert Oppenheimer
Birth • Apr 22, 1904 • 100 Years
J. Robert Oppenheimer was a brilliant physicist born at New York, NY. He worked in the theoretical area of physics, and many of his hypotheses led to the discoveries of neutrons, positrons, mesons and neutron stars. In 1939, the US government learned that the Germans had split the atom, and concerned that this would lead to the development of powerful weaponry, President Roosevelt developed "The Manhattan Project," appointing Oppenheimer as director. He set up a research station at Los Alamos, NM, and by 1945, Oppenheimer's team had constructed the two atomic bombs dropped on Japan to effectively end WWII. After the war, Oppenheimer became the chairman of the US Atomic Energy Commission, where he vehemently opposed the development of more powerful hydrogen bombs. Oppenheimer became a victim of anti-Communist feeling during the McCarthy era and in 1953 was forced out of his governmental position. He died of throat cancer on Feb 18, 1967.

B.F. Skinner
Birth • Mar 20, 1904 • 100 Years
American psychologist Burrhus Frederic Skinner was born at Susquehanna, PA. As a child, he was known for experimenting and inventing things. Fascinated by psychology, he enrolled at Harvard but was impatient with studying introspective works that he considered unintelligent and found himself spending most of his time in the lab of an experimental biologist. He began working with experiments on relational behavior and became a pioneer in the field. He is best known for developing the "Skinner box" (an enclosed environment for testing). He died Aug 18, 1990, at Cambridge, MA.

Exploration
Amerigo Vespucci
Birth • Mar 9, 1454 • 550 Years
Italian navigator, merchant and explorer for whom the Americas were named born at Florence, Italy (some sources cite his birth year as 1451). He participated in at least two expeditions between 1499 and 1502 that took him to the coast of South America, where he discovered the Amazon and Plata rivers. Vespucci's expeditions were of great importance because he believed that he had discovered a new continent, not just a new route to the Orient. Neither Vespucci nor his exploits achieved the fame of Columbus, but the New World was to be named for Amerigo Vespucci by an obscure German geographer and mapmaker, Martin Waldseemuller. Ironically, in his work as an outfitter of ships, Vespucci had been personally acquainted with Christopher Columbus. Vespucci died at Seville, Spain, Feb 22, 1512.

Jim Bridger
Birth • Mar 17, 1804 • 200 Years
American fur trader, frontiersman and Army scout, born at Richmond, VA, Jim Bridger is believed to be the first white man to visit (in 1824) the Great Salt Lake. He was influential in plotting the course of the Oregon Trail, guiding pioneers across the South Pass. He also established Fort Bridger in southwestern Wyoming as a fur-trading post and as a way station for pioneers heading west. In 1865, Bridger guided General

Spotlight on People

Grenville Dodge and his surveyors through the Overland Stage routes across the mountains, determining the ultimate course of the Union Pacific railroad. After losing his eyesight, he retired in the 1870s to a farm near what is now Kansas City, MO, and he died there July 17, 1881. Bridger National Forest in western Wyoming is named for him.

SALOMON AUGUST ANDRÉE
Birth • Oct 18, 1854 • 150 Years

Swedish explorer and balloonist born at Grenna, Sweden, his North Pole expedition of 1897 attracted world attention but ended tragically. With two companions, Andrée left Spitzbergen, July 11, 1897, in a balloon, hoping to place the Swedish flag at the North Pole. The last message from Andrée, borne by carrier pigeons, was dated noon, July 13. The frozen bodies of the explorers were found 33 years later by another polar expedition. Diaries, maps and exposed photographic negatives also were retrieved. The photos were developed successfully, providing a pictorial record of the ill-fated expedition.

Business and Commerce

JOHN DEERE
Birth • Feb 7, 1804 • 200 Years

John Deere was born in Rutland, VT. During the depression of the mid-1830s, the blacksmith found it impossible to support his family and traveled west in search of work, settling in Grand Detour, IL, where he built plows and other farm equipment for the newly settled community. In 1837, he invented a plow that was more suitable to the rich Midwestern soil than those imported from the east and that would eventually revolutionize American farming. (His prototype had been fashioned from a discarded saw blade, steel and polished wrought iron.) Deere was a perfectionist, and every plow was produced with careful craftsmanship and high standards of quality. He began manufacturing plows before he had orders for them, taking a supply into the country to sell. Word spread quickly, and within 10 years, he was making 1,000 plows a year. In 1868, he incorporated as Deere & Company. His children and grandchildren helped build his company, known today as John Deere, from a one-man blacksmith shop into one of the most successful farm equipment companies in history, today doing business in more than 160 countries. Deere died May 17, 1886, at Moline, IL.

LEVI STRAUSS
Birth • Feb 26, 1829 • 175 Years

Born at Buttenheim, Bavaria, Germany, Levi Strauss came to the US in 1847 and joined with his half-brothers in running a dry goods business in New York. When the news of the California Gold Rush reached the East Coast, he moved to San Francisco to sell supplies to the miners. In March of 1853, he opened his first wholesale dry goods business at 90 Sacramento St. Recognizing the need for sturdier pants for the men working in the gold mines, Straus began making pants out of heavy canvas. In 1873, he and partner Jacob Davis received a patent for a process that used copper rivets to hold the pockets of the pants in place, making them much more durable. Thus, the world's first pair of jeans—sold as "waist overalls"—was born. The most popular style was one that is still manufactured today: Levi's 501 jeans. His nephews took over the business during the 1880s, and Levi Strauss died at San Francisco on Sept 23, 1902. His small dry goods business is now one of the world's largest brand-name apparel manufacturers.

GEORGE EASTMAN
Birth • July 12, 1854 • 150 Years

Born at Waterville, NY, George Eastman at a young age was forced to go to work selling insurance when his father died. After purchasing a camera for a vacation trip, he became engrossed in the hobby and began to experiment with photography, eventually developing and patenting dry plate formulas and a machine for preparing multiple plates simultaneously. He soon quit the insurance business and went to work manufacturing dry plates. Eastman wrote his own advertisements, named his business "Kodak" (a word he made up)

Spotlight on People

and began developing cameras that the everyday user could afford and operate. In 1900 he introduced the Brownie camera. His company grew and prospered, and by the 1920s his net worth was in the millions. Eastman was known for his generosity to his employees and for his philanthropy, donating millions to schools such as M.I.T. and the Tuskegee Institute and founding dental clinics nationwide. He never married, and, plagued in later years by a debilitating spinal disease, he committed suicide on Mar 14, 1932, at the age of 77.

Ottmar Mergenthaler
Birth • 1854 • 150 Years

Born in Württemberg, Germany, Ottmar Mergenthaler came to the US in 1872 and worked for the US government inspecting and repairing bells, clocks and signal apparatus in federal buildings. Later he worked as a mechanical engineer in Baltimore, where he invented the Linotype machine, which allowed lines of metal type to be set from a keyboard rather than by hand. Mergenthaler received the patent on this device in 1884, and it was first put into operation by the *New York Tribune* in 1886. This revolutionized the publishing industry; the speed at which type was set changed dramatically. Within a few years, hundreds of newspapers nationwide had replaced hand-set type with Linotype. It remained in use, virtually unchanged, for almost 100 years. Mergenthaler died in Baltimore in 1899.

Clyde Cessna
Birth • Dec 5, 1879 • 125 Years

Aviation pioneer Clyde Cessna was born at Hawthorne, IA. From an early age, he was fascinated with the idea of flying, and by 1911 had built his own monoplane and taught himself how to fly. His second plane, built in 1916 and named "The Comet," thrilled everyone who saw it fly, as Clyde performed exhibitions of twisting dives and steep banks, setting what was at the time an unbelievable speed record of 125 mph. Cessna's career as a designer of small aircraft was rocky because he was always determined to build single-wing planes that could outperform the more popular biplanes, and he also ran into great financial difficulties during the Depression. He eventually sold his business to his nephews and returned to his roots in farming. He died in 1954, and the company that he left behind is today one of the largest makers of small aircraft in the world.

Walter Diemer
Birth • 1904 • 100 Years

Walter Diemer was an accountant for the Fleer Chewing Gum Company in Philadelphia. In his spare time, he liked to experiment with new gum recipes, and in 1928 he unexpectedly came up with something different from most gums on the market. His was chewier and less sticky; it also stretched more easily. He added pink food coloring to his creation because it was the only color he had at hand and took five pounds to a nearby grocery. Diemer demonstrated how to blow bubbles with the gum, and it sold out that same afternoon. Almost immediately, the Fleer Company began marketing his product under the name "Double Bubble." Little is known about Diemer, other than he was the man who accidentally invented bubble gum. He died in 1998.

Forrest Edward Mars
Birth • 1904 • 100 Years

Born at Tacoma, WA, Forrest was the son of a candy maker. He did not get along with his father and set out on his own, running a successful pet-food business in the UK. He soon moved into candy-making himself, marketing a European version of his father's Milky Way bar, which he named the Mars Bar. He invented a procedure to candy-coat small nuggets of chocolate, and the phenomenally successful result was called M&M's. Ultimately, Forrest merged his business with his father's, creating M&M/Mars in 1964. The family-run corporation still produces many of America's most popular candy bars, including Snickers, Twix and Three Musketeers. Known as reclusive, difficult to work for and a stickler for punctuality, Forrest Mars turned his father's company into a multinational, multibillion-dollar corporation. He died July 1, 1999, at Miami, FL.

Spotlight on People

Sports

Dwight Filley Davis

Birth • July 5, 1879 • 125 Years

Born in St. Louis, MO, Davis graduated from Harvard and received a law degree from Washington University. He became active in civic affairs and exercised his special interest in recreational facilities by developing golf courses, baseball fields and the first municipal tennis courts in the US. Davis served in the military during WWI and later as Secretary of War under President Calvin Coolidge, during which time he superintended the Army's first experiments with a mechanized force. Before his government service, Davis had been a nationally prominent singles and doubles tennis player. His enduring contribution to the sport, however, was his creation of the Davis Cup international tennis competition. He purchased the cup from a Boston jeweler for $750 and helped win the first two competitions in 1900 and 1902. The Cup is still played today. He died at Washington, DC, on Nov 28, 1945.

Andrew "Rube" Foster

Birth • Sept 17, 1879 • 125 Years

Rube Foster's efforts in baseball earned him the title of "The Father of Negro Baseball." He was a manager and star pitcher, pitching 51 victories in one year. In 1919, he called a meeting of black baseball team owners and organized the first black baseball league, the Negro National League. He served as its president until his death. Foster was born at Calvert, TX, the son of a minister, and died Dec 9, 1930, at Kankakee, IL.

Ray Harroun

Birth • Jan 12, 1879 • 125 Years

Harroun was born at Spartanburg, PA, and was a mechanic for race cars before he began racing in 1906; in 1910 he won the national championship. He took a job as an automobile designer with Marmon but was coaxed into completing one more race. Driving a Marmon Wasp that he had designed, Harroun won the very first Indianapolis 500 in 1911, with his speed averaging 74.59 mph. Just before the race he bolted a massive 8" by 3" mirror to the hood of his car, thus inventing the first rearview mirror. Race cars of the period were usually heavy two-seaters that carried the driver and a mechanic to keep him informed about what was happening behind the car. Harroun designed a light, streamlined one-seater with a pointed tail and a stabilizer and was able to race without a mechanic watching his rear, the first driver to do so. The Indy 500 was his last race. Harroun later invented a carburetor that was a forerunner of modern fuel injection and also invented the automobile bumper. He died in Jan 19, 1968.

Rene Lacoste

Birth • July 2, 1904 • 100 Years

Jean Rene Lacoste, tennis player and clothier, was born at Paris, France. Lacoste, known as the Crocodile, was one-quarter of the great French tennis players in the 1920s known as the Four Musketeers. He won Wimbledon and the US championship twice each, the French Open three times and was ranked No. 1 in the world in 1926–27. Lacoste designed the first shirt specifically for tennis, a loose-fitting cotton polo shirt that soon became the standard. He adorned the Lacoste shirt with a small crocodile, the first apparel logo. He died at St. Jean-de-Luz, France, Oct 12, 1996.

Johnny Weissmuller

Birth • June 2, 1904 • 100 Years

Peter John (Johnny) Weissmuller, actor and Olympic gold medal swimmer, was born at Windber, PA. Sickly as a child, he took up swimming to improve his health, and by the time he entered the University of Chicago he was competing at national levels. He won three gold medals at the 1924 Olympics and two more at the 1928 games. He set 24 world records and in 1950 was voted the best swimmer of the first half of the 20th century. Weissmuller holds the unique distinction of never having been beaten in a race. After retiring from amateur swimming competition, he appeared as Tarzan in a dozen movies and was immensely popular. He did all his own stunts and created the trademark "Tarzan yell." He later appeared as "Jungle Jim" in the movies and on television. He retired to Acapulco, Mexico, where he died Jan 20, 1984.

Spotlight on 2004 Events

In a book that lists more than 6,000 events, it's difficult to spotlight any one. Here is a selection of four that will be of particular interest in 2004.

Lewis and Clark Expedition Bicentennial

2003–2006

The commemoration of the bicentennial of the Lewis and Clark expedition continues this year, with the 200th anniversary of the westward departure of the Corps of Discovery on May 14, 1804. Captain Meriwether Lewis and Lieutenant William Clark led an expedition force of 33 that trained in botany, zoology and outdoor survival in St. Louis while they stocked up on supplies. After leaving the city, they traveled up the Missouri River to what is now North Dakota and Montana. They picked up two valuable guides and translators in 1804: Toussaint Charbonneau and his slave wife, Sacagawea, who proved a valuable ambassador for the expedition to the Native American tribes they encountered. She didn't speak English, but she communicated to Charbonneau, and an expedition member translated Charbonneau's French.

Signature bicentennial events are sponsored by a variety of communities for 2004. Here is a selection:

Three Flags Ceremony
Mar 10–14
St. Louis, MO
Commemorates the transfer of Upper Louisiana from Spain to the US. A key event is the reenactment of the Discovery Expedition crossing the Mississippi from Illinois to the Gateway Arch grounds on March 14. Historical exhibits and music complete the celebration.

Expedition's Departure: Camp River Dubois
May 13–16
Lewis & Clark State Historic Site, Hartford, IL
This event celebrates the expedition's departure from its winter camp. Hartford features a Camp River Dubois replica; historical reenactors will bring history alive for their audience, showing what a frontier encampment was like 200 years ago. Music, period arts and crafts, dramatic presentations and more will be featured at this event.

25th Annual Lewis and Clark Heritage Days Festival
May 14–23
St. Charles, MO

In conjunction with the long-running festival, St. Charles will celebrate the expedition's departure west 200 years ago. The replica keel boat from Camp River Dubois will make its way to St. Charles and at the end of festivities will relaunch away from civilization. The historical village of St. Charles will be replicated as will a Native American encampment. Frontier boats will be on display. More than twenty-five drum and fife corps will be performing.

Heart of America: A Journey Fourth
July 3–4
Atchison and Leavenworth, KS, and Kansas City, MO
This event commemorates the first July 4th celebration in the American west when the Corps of Discovery observed Independence Day in 1804 by firing their cannon and enjoying an extra ration of whiskey. Events will include historical reenactments, an air show and a grand fireworks display.

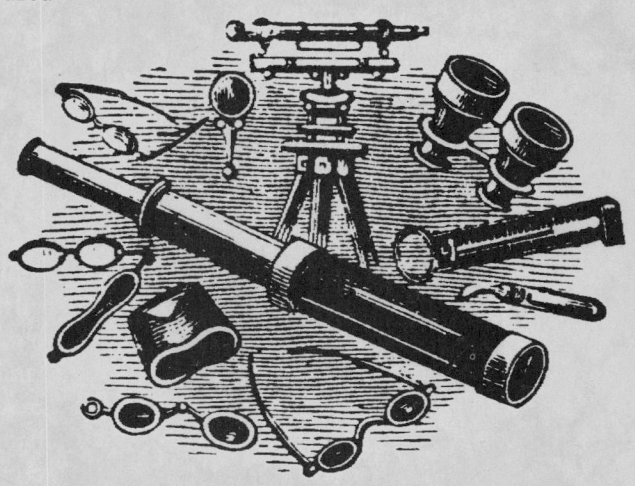

Spotlight on 2004 Events

First Tribal Council
July 31–Aug 3
Fort Calhoun and Omaha, NE
This event acknowledges the first council between Lewis and Clark's expedition team and the Otoe and Missouria tribes. This meeting of cultures will be reenacted at Fort Atchison State Historical Park. Renowned composer Philip Glass has been commissioned to write a Lewis and Clark piano concerto that will be an integral part of the event's evening performances. All tribes along the Lewis and Clark Trail are invited to participate.

Circle of Cultures, Time of Renewal and Exchange
Oct 22–31
North Dakota
As the Corps of Discovery searched for a winter encampment, they were welcomed by the "earth lodge" tribes of the Upper Missouri. This event commemorates and seeks to continue the friendship created 200 years ago with the Mandan, Hidatsa and Arikara. The public will be introduced to the culture of these tribes through a Mandan village replica.

For information:

The National Council of the Lewis & Clark Bicentennial
PO Box 11940
St. Louis, MO 63112-0040
Phone: (888) 999-1803
E-mail: bicentennial@lewis andclark200.org
Web: www.lewisandclark200 .org

Bloomsday
Dublin, Ireland, June 16

"I want to give a picture of Dublin so complete that if the city one day suddenly disappeared from the earth it could be reconstructed out of my book."
—James Joyce

On Feb 2, 1922, the novel *Ulysses* was published on its author's 40th birthday. It is considered the greatest novel of the 20th century. Its story is simple: a day in the life of three Dubliners on June 16, 1904—one hundred years ago.

James Joyce didn't pick June 16 at random: on that day in 1904, he took Nora Barnacle on a first date. He fell in love with her and eventually they lived a peripatetic life together in Europe, marrying in 1931 to appease their emotionally troubled daughter, Lucia. *Ulysses* was a lot of things: a reworking of Homer's *Odyssey*, a tribute to his relationship with Nora, a picture of Dublin on one day—meant to be accurate in every possible way.

Some decades after the book's controversial publication (it was denounced and banned by the Catholic Church and in America and Britain for some years), June 16 came to be celebrated by literary aficionados as "Bloomsday." On this day, there are readings and reenactments all over the world and, for the truly serious, a retracing of lead character Leopold Bloom's wanderings in Dublin (although current-day Dublin with all its changes makes following the actual route difficult).

Modern-day wanderers often don period clothing as they walk. Leopold Bloom's home at 7 Eccles Street is the usual starting point—except that it was torn down and replaced with a hospital (a plaque notes the address's significance, however). Lunch at Davy Byrne's pub (established 1889) is required: a gorgonzola sandwich and a glass of Burgundy—just as Bloom had.

Today, Bloomsday has become a week-long festival, but June 16 is still the major event day. The James Joyce Centre is the focal point of all celebrations, and guides conduct tours throughout Dublin all year.

For information:

The Irish Tourist Board
(Bord Fáilte)
Baggot Street Bridge
Baggot St
Dublin 2
Ireland
Phone: (00) (353) 1-602-4000
Fax: (00) (353) 1-602-4100
Web: www.ireland.travel.ie

The James Joyce Centre
35 North Great Georges's St
Dublin 1
Ireland
Phone: (00) (353) 1-878-8547
E-mail: joycecen@iol.ie
Web: www.jamesjoyce.ie

Davy Byrne's
21 Duke St
Dublin 2
Ireland
Phone: (00) (353) 1-677-5277

Spotlight on 2004 Events

Games of the XXVIII Olympiad

Athens, Greece, Aug 13-29

In 1896, the first modern Olympiad was held in its birthplace, Greece. The Olympic games of ancient times were first held in 776 BC. The 1896 Athens Olympics, featuring 43 events in nine sports, were a tremendous success, and the modern Olympics have been held in various cities around the world since then. In 1896, only men participated, but by the second Olympiad in Paris (1900), women were included. In 1911, the games were separated into winter and summer sessions. The only cancellations have been due to war: in 1916, 1940 and 1944.

The 2004 Athens games are the summer Olympics and will feature more than 300 events in 28 sports. It is estimated that 12,000 athletes and 3,000 officials will attend. The Torch Relay, the moving lead-up to the games, will begin in May of 2004, with the torch being carried from Olympia, Greece, to all five continents of the Olympic rings. The relay will take 35 days and visit 27 cities (including any city that has previously hosted an Olympiad). On Aug 13, the torch will arrive in Athens and the Olympic cauldron will be lighted—not to be extinguished until the conclusion of the games.

Paralympic Games Sept 17–28

Two weeks after the Olympics, the Paralympics will be held in the same venues. Some 4,000 athletes with disabilities and 2,000 officials will take part in these games.

For information:

International Olympic Committee
Château de Vidy
1007 Lausanne
Switzerland
Phone: (41) (21) 621-61-11
Fax: (41) (21) 621-62-16
Web: www.olympic.org

International Paralympic Committee
Adenauerallee 212–214
53113 Bonn
Germany
Phone: (49) (228) 209-7200
Fax: (49) (228) 209-7209
E-mail: info@paralympic.org
Web: www.paralympic.org

United States Olympic Committee
One Olympic Plaza
Colorado Springs, CO 80909
Phone: (719) 866-4500
E-mail: media@usoc.org
Web: www.usoc.org or www.olympic-usa.org
Official website with ticket information:
www.athens2004.com or www.athens.olympics.org

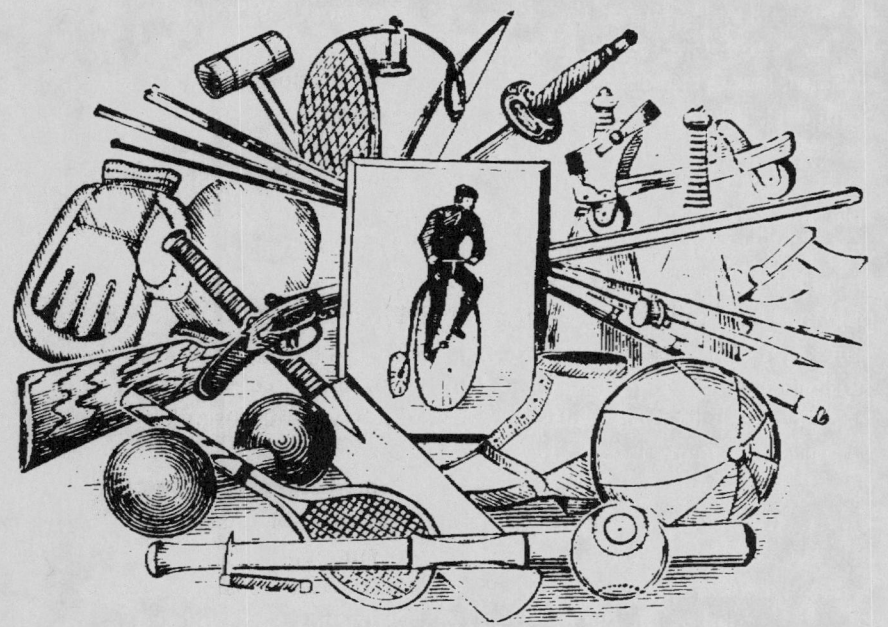

Spotlight on 2004 Events

Holy Year at Santiago de Campostela, Spain

The Way of St. James (Camino de Santiago)

St. James's Day, 2004

At midnight on Dec 31, 2003, the *Puerta Santa* ("Holy Door")—walled up since Dec 31, 1999—will be opened for the 2004 Holy Year at the beautiful Cathedral of Santiago de Campostela. The cathedral, consecrated in 1211, houses the relics of St. James the Apostle, the patron saint of Spain. Santiago de Campostela (the name means "St. James of the Starry Field"), an ancient city in Galicia on Spain's northwest coast, has been a pilgrimage destination since the ninth century. A Holy Year at the cathedral is declared when St. James's Day—July 25—falls on a Sunday, as it does in 2004. Although pilgrims travel to Santiago every year, a Holy Year has special significance—those Catholics who reach the cathedral in a Holy Year are granted a plenary indulgence and receive special blessings. The last Holy Year was 1999 (the last of that millennium) and the next will be 2010. At the close of the Holy Year the *Puerta Santa* will be walled in until Dec 31, 2009.

The European pilgrimage to Santiago is one of the most storied pilgrimages in the Catholic world—although many from different faiths and/or no religious background undertake the trip as well. It is a pilgrimage crossing the entire country of Spain from east to west, most often starting at one of four cities in France—Paris, Vezelay, Le Puy and Arles—or at the border with Spain (at the towns of Saint-Jean-Pied-de-Port or Somport). Pilgrims simply leave their doorstep—connecting with popular routes when they are able. Most walk, but some choose to bicycle or even to travel by horseback. And many pilgrims don scallop shells—the symbol of St. James—to distinguish themselves as pilgrims.

Since the pilgrimage dates to antiquity, many inns and conveniences for the traveler have evolved along the popular *caminos* ("ways" or "roads") for the up-to-five-week foot journey. The primary pilgrimage time is from Easter to October. While pilgrims number in the neighborhood of 50,000 for regular years, in a Holy Year that number triples to 150,000.

St. James's Day, July 25, is an awe-inspiring festival in Santiago de Campostela and one of the most important festivals in Spain. On the evening of July 24, spectacular fireworks in the main plaza, the Plaza del Obradoiro, fill the night. At the cathedral the next day is the magnificent religious service. One of the most storied elements of this service is the use of a huge incense burner (*Botafumeiro*) that swings over the congregation during the processional.

For information:

Tourist Office of Spain
666 Fifth Av
New York, NY 10103
Phone: (212) 265-8822
E-mail: fdbksp@eclipse.here-i.com

Confraternity of St. James
27 Blackfriars Rd
London SE1 8NY
England
Phone: (44) (20) 7928-9988
Fax: (44) (20) 7928-2844
E-mail: office@csj.org.uk
Web: www.csj.org.uk

American Association of Friends of the Road to Santiago
Web: www.geocities.com/friends_usa_santiago

☆ Chase's 2004 Calendar of Events ☆   Jan 1

Januarye.

JANUARY 1 — THURSDAY
Day 1 — 365 Remaining

THURSDAY, JANUARY ONE, 2004. Jan 1. First day of the first month of the Gregorian calendar year, Anno Domini 2004, being a Leap Year, and (until July 4th) 228th year of American independence. 2004 will be year 6717 of the Julian Period, a time frame consisting of 7,981 years that began at noon, universal [Greenwich] time, Jan 1, 4714 BC. Astronomers will note that Julian Day number 2,452,642 begins at noon, universal time (representing the number of days since the beginning of the Julian Period). New Year's Day is a public holiday in the US and in many other countries. Traditionally, it is a time for personal stocktaking, for making resolutions for the coming year and sometimes for recovering from the festivities of New Year's Eve. Financial accounting begins anew for businesses and individuals whose fiscal year is the calendar year. Jan 1 has been observed as the beginning of the year in most English-speaking countries since the British Calendar Act of 1751, prior to which the New Year began Mar 25 (approximating the vernal equinox). Earth begins another orbit of the sun, during which it, and we, will travel some 583,416,000 miles in 365.2422 days. New Year's Day has been called "Everyman's Birthday," and in some countries a year is added to everyone's age Jan 1 rather than on the anniversary of each person's birth.

ACADIA NATIONAL PARK ESTABLISHED: 85th ANNIVERSARY. Jan 1, 1919. Maine's Sieur de Monts National Monument, authorized in 1916, was established as Lafayette National Park in 1919. The name was changed to Acadia National Park by an act of Congress in 1929.

AUSTRALIA: COMMONWEALTH FORMED: ANNIVERSARY. Jan 1, 1901. On this day, the six colonies of Victoria, New South Wales, Queensland, South Australia, Western Australia and Northern Territory were united into one nation. The British Parliament had passed the Commonwealth Constitution Bill in the spring of 1900, and Queen Victoria signed the document Sept 17, 1900.

BILLIONAIRE BACHELOR BITES THE BULLET: 10th WEDDING ANNIVERSARY. Jan 1, 1994. America's most eligible billionaire, Bill "Mr Microsoft" Gates, married Melinda French, a marketing manager at Microsoft. Under tight security to protect privacy, the wedding took place at Lanai Island, HI.

BONZA BOTTLER DAY™. Jan 1 (also Feb 2, Mar 3, Apr 4, May 5, June 6, July 7, Aug 8, Sept 9, Oct 10, Nov 11 and Dec 12). To celebrate when the number of the day is the same as the number of the month. Bonza Bottler Day™ is an excuse to have a party at least once a month. Created by the late Elaine Fremont and continued by her family, Bonza Bottler Day is now celebrated in many countries. Logo buttons are available for $2 (includes postage and handling). For info: Gail M. Berger, Bonza Bottler Day, 14 Fernwood Dr, Taylors, SC 29687. Phone: (864) 609-9874. E-mail: gberger5@aol.com.

BOOK BLITZ MONTH. Jan 1–31. Focuses attention on improving authors' relationships with the media in order to create a best-selling book. Free book PR evaluation available. Annually, the month of January. For info: Barbara Gaughen, Media 21, 7456 Evergreen Dr, Santa Barbara, CA 93117. Phone: (805) 968-8567. Fax: (805) 968-5747. E-mail: bgaughenmu@aol.com.

BREAD MACHINE BAKING MONTH. Jan 1–31. Encourages the use of bread machines and accessories for use in the home to enjoy home-baked breads. For info: Glenna Vance, Bread Machine Industry Assn, PO Box 1832, Milwaukee, WI 53201. E-mail: bmiaorg@yahoo.com. Web: www.breadmachine.org.

BRYCE CANYON NATIONAL PARK ESTABLISHED: ANNIVERSARY. Jan 1, 1928. Utah's Bryce Canyon National Monument, created in 1923, was established as a national park and preserve.

CAPITAL ONE FLORIDA CITRUS BOWL. Jan 1. Florida Citrus Bowl Stadium, Orlando, FL. 58th annual. Postseason college football game matching two teams selected from the Big Ten and Southeastern conferences. Sponsors: Capital One and The Florida Department of Citrus. Est attendance: 70,000. For info: Florida Citrus Sports, One Citrus Bowl Place, Orlando, FL 32805. Phone: (407) 423-2476. Fax: (407) 425-8451. E-mail: fcsmedia@psinet.com. Web: www.fcsports.com.

CELEBRATION OF LIFE MONTH. Jan 1–31. The month of January, being the first month of the year, signifies the new year, a new beginning, a new life, a new happiness in many lives each year. Each community has a new hope to begin a new page in their lives. Remember always to value the gift of life for all Americans pursuing life, liberty, happiness and justice for all citizens. For info: Judith Natale, NCFA of America, 2091 Del Monte Ave, Monterey, CA 93940. Fax: (831) 655-4547. E-mail: childaware@aol.com.

CELEBRATION OF LIFE WEEK. Jan 1–7. The purpose of this week is to impress upon people all over the world the preciousness of life and the importance of all living things. For complete information and many famous quotations about life, send $5 to cover printing, handling and postage. For info: Dr. Stanley Drake, Pres, Intl Soc of Friendship and Good Will, 999 Hood Rd, Ste 127, Marietta, GA 30068. Phone: (770) 565-2322. E-mail: ISFGW@bellsouth.net.

CIRCUMCISION OF CHRIST. Jan 1. Holy day in many Christian churches. Celebrates Jesus's submission to Jewish law; on the octave day of Christmas. See also: "Solemnity of Mary, Mother of God" (Jan 1) for Roman Catholic observance since 1969 calendar reorganization.

COFFEE GOURMET INTERNATIONAL MONTH. Jan 1–31. From the first scent of its aroma when brewing to the last drop rolling off the palate, the pure joy that gourmet coffee evokes is something to be celebrated. This event is dedicated to introducing coffee lovers everywhere to the pleasures of truly gourmet coffee. For info: DiFrances Company, LLC, 208 E Oak Crest Dr, Ste 200, Wales, WI 53183-9700. Phone: (262) 968-9000. Fax: (262) 968-9854. E-mail: gourmetcoffee@difrancesco.com. Web: www.difrancesco.com.

COPYRIGHT REVISION LAW SIGNED: ANNIVERSARY. Jan 1, 1976. The first major revision since 1909 of laws governing intellectual property in the US was signed by President Ford. It took effect two years later on Jan 1, 1978. The act (Public Law 94-553) contains substantial revisions of the principles governing acquisition and duration of copyright and deals with issues that have been raised in recent years concerning photocopying and the use of copyrighted works by public broadcasting and cable television systems.

CUBA: 45th ANNIVERSARY OF THE REVOLUTION. Jan 1. National holiday celebrating the overthrow of the government of Fulgencio Batista in 1959 by the revolutionary forces of Fidel Castro, which had begun a civil war in 1956.

CUBA: LIBERATION DAY. Jan 1. A national holiday that celebrates the end of Spanish rule in 1899. Cuba, the largest island

65

of the West Indies, was a Spanish possession from its discovery by Columbus (Oct 27, 1492) until 1899. Under US military control 1899–1902 and 1906–09, a republican government took over Jan 28, 1909, and controlled the island until overthrown Jan 1, 1959, by Fidel Castro's revolutionary movement.

CZECH-SLOVAK DIVORCE: ANNIVERSARY. Jan 1, 1993. As Dec 31, 1992, gave way to Jan 1, 1993, the 74-year-old state of Czechoslovakia separated into two nations—the Czech and Slovak Republics. The Slovaks held a celebration through the night in the streets of Bratislava amid fireworks, bell ringing, singing of the new country's national anthem and the raising of the Slovak flag. In the new Czech Republic no official festivities took place, but later in the day the Czechs celebrated with a solemn oath by their parliament. The nation of Czechoslovakia ended peacefully though polls showed that most Slovaks and Czechs would have preferred that it survive. Before the split Czech Prime Minister Vaclav Klaus and Slovak Prime Minister Vladimir Meciar reached an agreement on dividing everything from army troops and gold reserves to the art on government building walls.

DAY OF MEDITATION: 24 HOURS OF LIVING MEDITATIVELY. Jan 1. In conjunction with the Universal Hour of Peace, the School of Metaphysics invites people all around the world to meditate as often as possible during the 24-hour period starting midnight Dec 31 through Jan 1. Meditation develops a spiritual consciousness that brings people together. Prayer, silence, contemplation and meditation promote peace, understanding and goodwill within self and among all people. For info: School of Metaphysics, 163 Moon Valley Rd, Windyville, MO 65783. Phone: (417) 345-8411. E-mail: som@som.org.

DIET RESOLUTION WEEK. Jan 1–7. This week emphasizes the importance of watching your weight by focusing on the type—not the amount—of food you put on your plate. Resolve to consume minimally processed, less-refined carbohydrate foods. Slim down permanently with whole grains, legumes, fresh fruits and vegetables. Eat more but weigh less for life. Delete meat and other animal foods to make miniscule meals and calorie counting obsolete. Start the year off right by eating light with every bite! For info: Vegetarian Awareness Network, Communications Center, PO Box 321, Knoxville, TN 37901-0321. Phone: (877) VEG-DIET.

ELLIS ISLAND OPENED: ANNIVERSARY. Jan 1, 1892. Ellis Island was opened on New Year's Day in 1892. Over the years more than 20 million individuals were processed through the stations. The island was used as a point of deportation as well: in 1932 alone, 20,000 people were deported from Ellis Island. When the US entered WWII in 1941, Ellis Island became a Coast Guard Station. It closed Nov 12, 1954, and was declared a national park in 1956. After years of disuse it was restored and in 1990 it was reopened as a museum.

EMANCIPATION PROCLAMATION TAKES EFFECT: ANNIVERSARY. Jan 1, 1863. Abraham Lincoln, by executive proclamation of Sept 22, 1862, declared that on this date ". . . all persons held as slaves within any state or designated part of a state, the people whereof shall then be in rebellion against the United States, shall be then, thenceforward, and forever, free. . ." Slaves in the four slave states that had not seceded from the Union (Delaware, Maryland, Kentucky and Missouri) were not freed until the passage of the 13th Amendment in 1865. See also: "Thirteenth Amendment to the Constitution Ratified" (Dec 6).

ENGLAND: THE NEW YEAR'S DAY PARADE—LONDON. Jan 1. London. The biggest parade of its kind in the world attracts a million people on the streets of the capital. The route starts at noon in Parliament Square, and goes along Whitehall, round Trafalgar Square and up Piccadilly. Dozens of the world's top marching bands, thousands of cheerleaders and the amazing eight-story-high cartoon character balloons all add to the fun. Est attendance: 1,000,000. For info: Mark Phillips, The New Year's Day Parade—London, Research House, Fraser Road, Greenford, Middlesex, England UB6 7AQ. Phone: (44) (20) 8566 8586. Fax: (44) (20) 8566 8494. E-mail: markp@london parade.co.uk. Web: www.londonparade.co.uk.

EURO INTRODUCED: 5th ANNIVERSARY. Jan 1, 1999. The euro, the common currency of members of the European Union, was introduced for use by financial institutions. The value of the currencies of the 11 nations (Austria, Belgium, Finland, France, Germany, Ireland, Italy, Luxembourg, the Netherlands, Portugal and Spain) was locked in at a permanent conversion rate to the euro. Greece joined the eurozone the following year. On Jan 1, 2002, euro bills and coins began circulating; other currencies were phased out as of February 28, 2002.

FAMILY FIT LIFESTYLE MONTH. Jan 1–31. Healthy living is achievable. Try for one month to reduce the fat, sugar and salt in your diet. Family Fit Lifestyle Inc is devoted to helping others add healthy foods in their place in the hope of preventing many of the diseases associated with high-fat/high-cholesterol diets. The first month of the New Year is the perfect time to change your life. For info: Family Fit Lifestyle, Inc, 15202 N 50th Pl, Scottsdale, AZ 85254. Phone: (866) 548-3348. E-mail: Jyl@Americas HealthiestMom.com. Web: www.AmericasHealthiestMom.com.

FEDEX ORANGE BOWL. Jan 1. Pro Player Stadium, Miami, FL. Part of the Bowl Championship Series. Game time is 8:30 PM, EST. Est attendance: 75,000. For info: Orange Bowl Committee, 703 Waterford Way, Ste 590, Miami, FL 33126. Phone: (305) 341-4700. E-mail: obie@orangebowl.org. Web: www.orange bowl.org.

FINANCIAL WELLNESS MONTH. Jan 1–31. For people to establish financial balance after credit card bills pour in from the holidays. This is a time to set new goals for financial freedom and moderation in spending. See a financial advisor. Create money management goals. Set up a savings plan. Figure out how to pay off old loans. Get out of debt. Spend less money. Give up a little luxury and donate the savings to charity. Buy in bulk, shop at discount stores, wait for sales and bargains. Shop garage sales, flea markets and online auctions. For info: Angela Brown, Words for Wellness, PO Box 49266, Charlotte, NC 28277. Phone: (704) 849-2900. Fax: (704) 845-3060. E-mail: angela@wordsofwellness .com. Web: www.wordsofwellness.com.

FIRST BABY BOOMER BORN: ANNIVERSARY. Jan 1, 1946. Kathleen Casey Wilkens, born at one minute after midnight at Philadelphia, PA, was the first of the almost 78 million Baby Boomers born between 1946 and 1964.

FORSTER, E.M.: 125th BIRTH ANNIVERSARY. Jan 1, 1879. Edward Morgan Forster, English author born at London, England, is remembered for his six novels: *Where Angels Fear to Tread* (1905), *The Longest Journey* (1907), *A Room with a View* (1908), *Howard's End* (1910), *A Passage to India* (1924) and the posthumously published *Maurice* (1971). He also achieved eminence for his short stories and essays, and he collaborated on the libretto for an opera, Benjamin Britten's *Billy Budd* (1951). Forster died at Coventry, England, June 7, 1970.

FRANCE: CELEBRATE FRANCE. Jan 1. Paris. The parade begins at 2 and its route takes in much of Montmartre and passes Sacre Coeur. International participation of marching bands, floats, vehicles, animals, etc. Est attendance: 100,000. For info: Mark Phillips, Celebrate France, Research House, Fraser Road, Perivale, Middlesex, England UB6 7AQ. Phone: (44) (20) 8566-8586. Fax: (44) (20) 8566-8494. E-mail: info@celebratefrance.com. Web: www.celebratefrance.com.

GREENBERG, HANK: BIRTH ANNIVERSARY. Jan 1, 1911. Henry Benjamin (Hank) Greenberg, Baseball Hall of Fame first baseman and outfielder, born at New York, NY. One of the game's most prodigious sluggers, Greenberg hit 331 home runs

January 2004

S	M	T	W	T	F	S
				1	2	3
4	5	6	7	8	9	10
11	12	13	14	15	16	17
18	19	20	21	22	23	24
25	26	27	28	29	30	31

☆ Chase's 2004 Calendar of Events ☆   Jan 1

and drove in 1,276 runs in only nine full seasons. Baseball's first Jewish superstar, Greenberg entered the army after playing just 19 games in 1941 and did not return to the Detroit Tigers until midway through the 1945 season. His grand slam on that season's last day won the pennant for the Tigers and propelled them toward a World Series triumph. Inducted into the Hall of Fame in 1956. Died at Beverly Hills, CA, Sept 4, 1986.

HAITI: INDEPENDENCE DAY: 200th ANNIVERSARY. Jan 1. A national holiday commemorating the proclamation of independence in 1804. Haiti, occupying the western third of the island Hispaniola (second largest of the West Indies), was a Spanish colony from the time of its discovery by Columbus in 1492 until 1697, then a French colony until the proclamation of independence in 1804.

HANGOVER HANDICAP RUN. Jan 1. Veteran's Park, Klamath Falls, OR. Two-mile fun run at 9 AM New Year's Day morning. The first-place male and female finishers each take home a beer can trophy. Est attendance: 100. For info: Hangover Handicap, 1800 Fairmont, Klamath Falls, OR 97601. Phone: (541) 882-6922. Fax: (541) 883-6481.

HOOVER, J. EDGAR: BIRTH ANNIVERSARY. Jan 1, 1895. John Edgar Hoover, born at Washington, DC. He led the Palmer Raids and was director of the FBI from 1924–1972. During his time as director, Hoover practiced modern investigative techniques, improved FBI agent training and increased FBI funding from Congress. He died May 2, 1972, at Washington, DC.

IMAGE IMPROVEMENT MONTH. Jan 1–31. Empowering others to look and feel better, while simplifying their lives. For info: Dana Mayeux, 160 N Coit Rd, PMB 407, Richardson, TX 75248. Phone: (972) 716-9970. E-mail: dana@internationalimagecoach.com. Web: www.internationalimagecoach.com or secretimagepolice.com

INTERNATIONAL BUSINESS SUCCESS RESOLUTIONS MONTH. Jan 1–31. Set in motion a successful year by focusing on PR and marketing efforts guaranteed to make your cash register ring and your bank statements sing. Resolve to get your business and message in front of your target market. For marketing and PR ideas: Raleigh Pinskey. Phone: (800) 249-7322. E-mail: raleigh@promoteyourself.com. Web: www.promoteyourself.com.

INTERNATIONAL CREATIVITY MONTH. Jan 1–31. A month to remind individuals and organizations around the globe to capitalize on the power of creativity. Unleashing creativity is vital for personal and business success in this age of accelerating change. The first month of the year provides an opportunity to take a fresh approach to problem solving and renew confidence in our creative capabilities. For info: Randall Munson, Pres, Creatively Speaking, 508 Meadow Run Dr SW, Rochester, MN 55902-2337. Phone: (507) 286-1331. Fax: (507) 286-1331. E-mail: Creativity@CreativelySpeaking.com. Web: www.CreativelySpeaking.com.

INTERNATIONAL LIFE BALANCE MONTH. Jan 1–31. Ever feel like a tumbleweed being blown about with no control because of all the demands put on your time? Overwhelmed by all your choices? Those choices can cause stress and isolation. This month is focused not on New Year's resolutions, but on making better strategic decisions yearlong to get your life in balance. Includes the importance of balancing time for self, family and friends. For info: Sheryl Nicholson, 23 Citrus Dr, Palm Harbor, FL 34684. Phone: (727) 937-3322. Fax: (727) 937-4722. Web: www.sheryl.com.

INTERNATIONAL QUALITY OF LIFE MONTH. Jan 1–31. An international recognition of the importance of the quality of life that encompasses family, community, education, work, finances, health, leisure and spirituality. Recognition and achievement of quality of life is a worldwide issue. For info: H. Stanley Jones, Dir, Quality of Life Institute, 590 Farrington, #210, Kapolei, HI 96707. Phone: (808) 672-0777. Fax: (808) 672-0775. E-mail: PRSpeakers@aol.com.

INTERNATIONAL WEALTH MENTALITY MONTH. Jan 1–31. The start of the New Year provides a great opportunity to examine your financial position and, more importantly, your beliefs and behavior regarding your financial goals. The International Center for Strategic Planning hosts this month-long effort each year to draw attention to the importance of having a wealth mentality (thoughts that encourage and support wealth building) and getting your personal finances in order. For info: Sherrin Ross Ingram, International Center for Strategic Planning, 104 W Chestnut St #101, Hinsdale, IL 60521. Phone: (800) 962-4750. Fax: (800) 962-0177. E-mail: info@wealthmentality.com. Web: www.wealthmentality.com.

JAPANESE ERA NEW YEAR. Jan 1–3. Celebration of the beginning of the year Heisei Sixteen, the 16th year of Emperor Akihito's reign.

KLIBAN, B(ERNARD): BIRTH ANNIVERSARY. Jan 1, 1935. Cartoonist B. Kliban was born at Norwalk, CT. He was known for his satirical drawings of cats engaged in human pursuits, which appeared in the books *Cat* (1975), *Never Eat Anything Bigger Than Your Head & Other Drawings* (1976) and *Whack Your Porcupine* (1977) and on T-shirts, greeting cards, calendars, bedsheets and other merchandise, creating a $50 million industry before his death at San Francisco, CA, Aug 12, 1990.

MEXICO: ZAPATISTA REBELLION: 10th ANNIVERSARY. Jan 1, 1994. Declaring war against the government of President Carlos Salinas de Gortari, the Zapatista National Liberation Army seized four towns in the state of Chiapas in southern Mexico in 1994. The rebel group, which took its name from the early 20th-century Mexican revolutionary Emiliano Zapata, issued a declaration stating that they were protesting discrimination against the Indian population of the region and against their severe poverty.

MUMMERS PARADE. Jan 1. Philadelphia, PA. World-famous New Year's Day parade of 20,000 spectacularly costumed mummers in a colorful parade that goes on all day. This celebration has taken place since the 1700s. Est attendance: 100,000. For info: Mummers Parade, 1100 S 2nd St, Philadelphia, PA 19147. Phone: (215) 636-1666. E-mail: parade@mummers.com. Web: www.mummers.com.

NATIONAL BE ON-PURPOSE MONTH. Jan 1–31. An observance to encourage us to start the new year by putting our good intentions into action, personally and professionally, and to trade confusion for clarity as we integrate our lives with more meaning and purpose. For info: Kevin W. McCarthy, CEO, The On-Purpose Partners, PO Box 1568, Winter Park, FL 32790-1568. Phone: (407) 657-6000. Fax: (407) 645-1345. E-mail: info@on-purpose.com.

NATIONAL CANCER PREVENTION MONTH. Jan 1–31. National Cancer Prevention Month was initiated by the Institute for Cancer Prevention (IFCP) as a public education initiative to remind Americans that 70% of all cancer deaths are preventable, and that they can modify their daily lifestyle to help prevent the disease. For info: Jessica Murphy, Savvy Partners, Inc, 104 W 29th St, 10th Fl, New York, NY 10001. Phone: (212) 813-3838. Fax: (212) 244-6875. E-mail: jessica@savvypartnersinc.com. Web: www.ifcp.us.

Jan 1 ☆ *Chase's 2004 Calendar of Events* ☆

NATIONAL CLEAN UP YOUR COMPUTER MONTH. Jan 1–31. Dedicated to the education of computer users with simple tips and methods to increase the efficiency of their systems. For info: Denise Hall, 24797 State St, PO Box 658, Elberta, AL 36530. Phone: (251) 986-6650. Fax: (251) 986-6652. E-mail: denise@specterweb.com. Web: specterweb.com.

NATIONAL ENVIRONMENTAL POLICY ACT: ANNIVERSARY. Jan 1, 1970. The National Environmental Policy Act of 1969 established the Council on Environmental Quality and made it federal government policy to protect the environment.

NATIONAL GET TO KNOW AN INDEPENDENT REAL ESTATE BROKER MONTH. Jan 1–31. January has been named "National Get to Know an Independent Real Estate Broker Month" by the National Association of Independent Real Estate Brokers. For info: Gary Bryce Conner, Dir, NAIREB, 7102 Mardyke Ln, Indianapolis, IN 46226. Phone: (317) 547-4679. Fax: (317) 547-4634. E-mail: director@IndependentRealEstate Brokers.com. Web: www.naireb.com.

NATIONAL GLAUCOMA AWARENESS MONTH. Jan 1–31. More than two million Americans age 40 and older suffer from glaucoma. Nearly half do not know they have the disease—it causes no early symptoms. Prevent Blindness America will provide valuable information about this "sneak thief of sight." Organizations are encouraged to educate the community through screenings, forums and programs. For info: Prevent Blindness America®, 500 E Remington Rd, Schaumburg, IL 60173. Phone: (800) 331-2020. Fax: (847) 843-8458. Web: www.preventblindness.org.

NATIONAL HIGH-TECH MONTH. Jan 1–31. Recognizing the dramatic effect high-tech products and services have had on the way we live now and how they will change the way we live in the 21st century. Promoting high-tech education and solutions in the home and in business. 2004 theme is "How today's technology would affect the outcome of yesterday's movie classics." E-mail or call us for sponsorship opportunities and educational materials. Annually, the month of January. For info: Kathleen Quinn, Founder, NHTM Foundation, PO Box 2373, Glenview, IL 60025. Phone: (847) 998-9950. Fax: (847) 998-9945. E-mail: NHTM 2000@aol.com. Web: www.nationalhightechmonth.com.

NATIONAL HOT TEA MONTH. Jan 1–31. To celebrate one of nature's most popular, soothing and relaxing beverages; the only beverage in America commonly served hot or iced, anytime, anywhere, for any occasion. For info: Joseph P. Simrany, Pres, The Tea Council of the USA, 420 Lexington Ave, Ste 825, New York, NY 10170. Phone: (212) 986-6998. Fax: (212) 697-8658. E-mail: info@teausa.org. Web: www.teausa.org.

January 2004

S	M	T	W	T	F	S
				1	2	3
4	5	6	7	8	9	10
11	12	13	14	15	16	17
18	19	20	21	22	23	24
25	26	27	28	29	30	31

NATIONAL LOSE WEIGHT/FEEL GREAT WEEK. Jan 1–8. To inspire individuals to incorporate fitness into their daily routine and make exercise a priority, whether it be to promote weight loss or maintain overall good health and physical condition. For info: Jana Angelakis, PEX Personalized Exercise, 924 Broadway, 3rd Fl, New York, NY 10010. Phone: (212) 254-1915. Fax: (212) 254-7912. E-mail: angelakisjana@cs.com. Web: www.pexinc.com.

NATIONAL MAILORDER GARDENING MONTH. Jan 1–31. There's no better way to beat the winter "blahs" than by curling up with a few colorful garden catalogs and spending some time dreaming and scheming about next spring's garden. Many catalogs offer tips and information on how to create a beautiful garden. For a listing of more than 135 garden catalogs and magazines, visit our website. For info: Camille Cimino, Exec Dir, Mailorder Gardening Assn, 5836 Rockburn Woods Way, Elkridge, MD 21075. Phone: (410) 730-9713. Fax: (410) 730-9619. E-mail: consumer@mailordergardening.com. Web: www.mailordergardening.com. Media contact: Randall Schultz, Schultz Communications. Phone: (505) 822-8222

NATIONAL MENTORING MONTH. Jan 1–31. Goals include raising awareness of mentoring in its various forms; recruiting individuals to mentor, especially in programs that have a waiting list of young people; and promoting the rapid growth of mentoring by recruiting organizations to help find mentors for young people. Each January, this month-long campaign will provide nationwide publicity and information about mentoring programs in various communities that need volunteers. For info: MENTOR/National Mentoring Partnership, 1600 Duke St, Ste 300, Alexandria, VA 22314. Phone: (703) 224-2200. Web: www.mentoring.org.

NATIONAL PERSONAL SELF-DEFENSE AWARENESS MONTH. Jan 1–31. To educate women and teens about realistic self-defense options that could very well save their lives. Sponsored by the National Self-Defense Institute, Inc, a not-for-profit 501(c)(3) corporation. NSDI/SAFE Program™ seminars and related events nationally emphasize being totally prepared by realizing that awareness + risk reduction = 90% of self-defense while the other 10% is physical and by waking up to the fact that the key to their own safety lies in themselves. For info: Natl Self-Defense Inst Inc, PO Box 398355, Miami Beach, FL 33239-8355. Phone: (305) 868-NSDI. Fax: (305) 867-6634. E-mail: nsdi@worldnet.att.net.

NATIONAL POVERTY IN AMERICA AWARENESS MONTH. Jan 1–31. To promote public awareness of the continuing existence of poverty and social injustice in America. Individuals are encouraged to support efforts to eradicate poverty by increasing their understanding of the causes and practical solutions and by active participation and support for antipoverty programs. Sponsored by the Catholic Campaign for Human Development, the largest private funder of self-help programs for the poor and disenfranchised in the US, regardless of religion, race or ethnic origin. For info: Barbara Stephenson, CCHD, US Conference of Catholic Bishops, 3211 Fourth St NE, Washington, DC 20017-1194. Phone: (202) 541-3364. Web: www.povertyusa.org.

NATIONAL RADON ACTION MONTH. Jan 1–31. To increase the public's awareness of the effects of radon. For info: Environmental Protection Agency, 1200 Pennsylvania Ave NW, Washington, DC 20460. Phone: (800) SOS-RADON. Web: www.epa.gov.

NATIONAL REACHING YOUR POTENTIAL MONTH. Jan 1–31. A time dedicated to encouraging and motivating people of all ages toward a happier and fuller life by realizing and reaching their full potential. For info: Dr. Clifford Lee, The Eagle Company, PO Box 150263, Longview, TX 75615. Phone: (903) 295-2149. E-mail: TheEagleCo@aol.com.

NATIONAL YOURS, MINE AND OURS MONTH. Jan 1–31. Blending families and creating positive step-relationships can be one of the most challenging aspects of a couple's remarriage. Each member of the family is affected in different ways. This observance focuses on what parents and children can expect as a step or blended family and offers tips for a smooth transition and enhanced long-term relationships. Annually, the month of January. For info send SASE to: Teresa Langston, Dir, Parenting Without Pressure, 1330 Boyer St, Longwood, FL 32750-6311. Phone: (407) 767-2524. Web: www.parentingwithoutpressure.com.

NEW YEAR'S DAY. Jan 1. Legal holiday in all states and territories of the US and in most other countries. The world's most widely celebrated holiday.

NEW YEAR'S DISHONOR LIST. Jan 1. Since 1976, America's dishonor list of words banished from the Queen's English. Overworked words and phrases (e.g., *uniquely unique, first time ever, safe sex, e-anything* and *dot.com*). Send nominations to following address. For info: PR Office, Lake Superior State University, Sault Ste. Marie, MI 49783. Phone: (906) 635-2315. Fax: (906) 635-2623. Web: www.lssu.edu/banished.

NEW YEAR'S RESOLUTIONS WEEK. Jan 1–7. To show people how, why and what resolutions/goals should be set and the necessary action steps to make this new year the best ever! For info: Gary Ryan Blair, The GoalsGuy, 36181 E Lake Rd, Ste 139, Palm Harbor, FL 34685. Phone: (877) GOALSGUY. Fax: (800) 731-GOAL. E-mail: nyrw@goalsguy.com. Web: www.goalsguy.com.

NOKIA SUGAR BOWL. Jan 1. Louisiana Superdome, New Orleans, LA. 70th annual. The Bowl Championship Series (BCS) National Championship Game. Game time is 7 PM, CST. The Sugar Bowl originated in 1935. Est attendance: 75,000. For info: Nokia Sugar Bowl, Louisiana Superdome, Mezzanine Level, 1500 Sugar Bowl Dr, New Orleans, LA 70112. Phone: (504) 525-8573. Fax: (504) 525-4867. E-mail: jeffh@sugrbowl.gs.net. Web: www.nokiasugarbowl.com.

OATMEAL MONTH. Jan 1–31. "Celebrate oatmeal, a low-fat, sodium-free, whole grain that when eaten daily as a part of a diet that's low in saturated fat and cholesterol may help reduce the risk of heart disease. Delicious recipes, helpful hints and tips from Quaker® Oats, The Oat Expert, will make enjoying the heart health benefits oatmeal has to offer easy, convenient and, above all, delicious." For info: The Oat Expert. Phone: (312) 629-1234. Email: oatexpert@aol.com

OUTBACK BOWL. Jan 1. Raymond James Stadium, Tampa, FL. The New Year's Day Outback Bowl Game brings together top college football teams from the SEC and the Big Ten. Game time is 11 AM, EST. In addition, the bowl is highlighted by a variety of special events, sports activities, concerts and private functions. Est attendance: 65,000. For info: Mike Schulze, Tampa Bay Bowl Assn, 4211 W Boy Scout Blvd, Ste 560, Tampa, FL 33607. Phone: (813) 874-2695. Fax: (813) 873-1959. Web: www.outbackbowl.com.

PENGUIN PLUNGE. Jan 1. Mackeral Cove, Jamestown, RI. Annual plunge into the icy waters of Narragansett Bay to benefit Rhode Island Special Olympics. Annually, Jan 1. Est attendance: 2,000. For info: Special Olympics Rhode Island, 33 College Hill Rd, Bldg 31, Warwick, RI 02886. Phone: (401) 823-7411. Fax: (401) 823-7415.

PHILIPPINES: BLACK NAZARENE FIESTA. Jan 1–9. Manila. This traditional nine-day fiesta honors Quiapo district's patron saint. Cultural events, fireworks and parades culminate in a procession with the life-size statue of the Black Nazarene. Procession begins at the historic Quiapo Church.

POETRY CONTEST. Jan 1–Apr 7. El Paso, TX. 14th annual. Every year the El Paso Public Library sponsors a poetry contest for children in grades 1–12. Entries may be submitted Jan 1–Feb 14. Judging will be held Feb 26–29. Award ceremonies will be held on Mar 31 for grades 1–6, Apr 7 for grades 7–12. There are three awards given for each grade in both English and Spanish. Each child receives a new book of poetry in English or Spanish. For info: Laurel Indalecio, El Paso Public Library, 501 N Oregon, El Paso, TX 79901. Phone/fax: (915) 543-5470. E-mail: indaleciol@ci.el-paso.tx.us. Web: www.geocities.com/epplkidszone.

POLAR BEAR SWIM. Jan 1. Sheboygan Armory, Sheboygan, WI. Each New Year's Day at 1 PM, more than 450 daring swimmers brave Lake Michigan's ice floes. Most are costumed, all are crazy. Refreshments and free live entertainment from 10 AM–6 PM. Sponsor: Sheboygan Polar Bear Club. Est attendance: 2,000. For info: Sheboygan Conv and Visitors Bureau, 712 Riverfront Dr, Ste 101, Sheboygan, WI 53081. Phone: (920) 467-8436.

PORTLAND CENTER STAGE. Jan 1–Apr 18. (Season began Sept 23, 2003.) Portland, OR. An eight-month season of plays by classical and contemporary playwrights in the Newmark Theatre of the Portland Center for the Performing Arts. Est attendance: 90,000. For info: Portland Center Stage, 1111 SW Broadway, Portland, OR 97205. Phone: (503) 274-6588. Fax: (503) 796-6509. Web: www.pcs.org.

THE PRESENT LOOKS AT THE PAST: MODERN VIEWS OF THE AMERICAN REVOLUTION. Jan 1–Mar 1. Yorktown Victory Center, Yorktown, VA. The American Revolution and national identity have been major themes of American folk art throughout the country's history. This exhibition presents an array of mostly 20th-century artistic interpretations, ranging from folk to commercial, of ideas, events and personalities of the Revolution and the new nation. Included are wood and metal sculpture, commemorative plates and medallions, needlework and paintings. Among the artists featured are Howard Finster and Oscar de Mejo. For info: Media Relations, Jamestown-Yorktown Fndn, PO Box 1607, Williamsburg, VA 23187. Phone: (757) 253-4838 or (888) 593-4682. Fax: (757) 253-5299. Web: www.historyisfun.org.

REVERE, PAUL: BIRTH ANNIVERSARY. Jan 1, 1735 (OS). American patriot, silversmith and engraver; maker of false teeth, eyeglasses, picture frames and surgical instruments. Best remembered for his famous ride Apr 18, 1775, celebrated in Longfellow's poem "The Midnight Ride of Paul Revere." Born at Boston, MA, died there May 10, 1818. See also: "Paul Revere's Ride: Anniversary" (Apr 18).

ROSE BOWL GAME PRESENTED BY ATT. Jan 1. Pasadena, CA. Part of the Bowl Championship Series. Football conference champions from Big Ten and Pacific-10 meet in the Rose Bowl game at 2 PM, EST. Tournament of Roses has been an annual New Year's event since 1890; Rose Bowl football game since 1902. Michigan defeated Stanford 49–0 in what was the first postseason football game. Called the Rose Bowl since 1923, it is preceded each year by the Tournament of Roses Parade. Est attendance: 100,000. For info: Program Coordinator, Tournament of Roses, 391 South Orange Grove Blvd, Pasadena, CA 91184. Phone: (626) 449-4100. Fax: (626) 449-9066. Web: www.tournamentofroses.com.

ROSS, BETSY: BIRTH ANNIVERSARY. Jan 1, 1752 (OS). According to legend based largely on her grandson's revelations in 1870, needleworker Betsy Ross created the first stars-and-stripes flag in 1775, under instructions from George Washington. Her sewing and her making of flags were well known, but there is little corroborative evidence of her role in making the first stars-and-stripes. The account is generally accepted, however, in the absence of any documented claims to the contrary. She was born Elizabeth Griscom at Philadelphia, PA, and died there Jan 30, 1836.

Jan 1 ☆ *Chase's 2004 Calendar of Events* ☆

RUSSIA: NEW YEAR'S DAY OBSERVANCE. Jan 1–2. National holiday. Modern tradition calls for setting up New Year's trees in homes, halls, clubs, palaces of culture and the hall of the Kremlin Palace. Children's parties with Granddad Frost and his granddaughter, Snow Girl. Games, songs, dancing, special foods, family gatherings and exchanges of gifts and New Year's cards.

SAINT BASIL'S DAY. Jan 1. St. Basil's or St. Vasily's feast day observed by Eastern Orthodox churches. Special traditions for the day include serving St. Basil cakes, each of which contains a coin. Feast day observed Jan 14 by those churches using Julian calendar.

SBC COTTON BOWL CLASSIC. Jan 1. Cotton Bowl Stadium, Dallas, TX. Since 1937. Postseason football game matching the #2 team from the Big 12 with the Southeastern Conference (SEC) division champion, division runner-up or a team with a comparable record. Game time is 1 PM, EST. Est attendance: 70,000. For info: Cotton Bowl Athletic Assn, Box 569420, Dallas, TX 75356-9420. Phone: (214) 634-7525. E-mail: mail@swbellcottonbowl.com. Web: www.swbellcottonbowl.com.

SENIOR WOMEN'S TRAVEL MONTH. Jan 1–31. A travel blueprint for the 50-plus woman. Safety strategies, solo dining, senior-friendly places, more. For info: Senior Women's Travel. Phone: (212) 838-4740. Fax: (212) 826-8710. E-mail: maryann @poshnosh.com. Web: www.poshnosh.com.

SILENT RECORD WEEK. Jan 1–7. To commemorate the anniversary of the invention of the silent record in 1960, which was played on Detroit jukeboxes. The following year a Silent Record Concert and Recording Session featured emcee Henry Morgan, Soupy Sales and the 120-piece Hush Symphonic Band. [Originated by the late W.T. Rabe of Sault Ste. Marie, MI.]

SOLEMNITY OF MARY, MOTHER OF GOD. Jan 1. Holy Day of Obligation in Roman Catholic Church since calendar reorganization of 1969, replacing the Feast of the Circumcision, which had been recognized for more than 14 centuries. See also: "Circumcision of Christ" (Jan 1).

STOCK EXCHANGE HOLIDAY (NEW YEAR'S DAY). Jan 1. The holiday schedules for the various exchanges are subject to change if relevant rules, regulations or exchange policies are revised. If you have questions, phone: American Stock Exchange (212) 306-1000; Chicago Board of Trade (312) 435-3500; Chicago Board of Options Exchange (312) 786-5600; New York Stock Exchange (212) 656-2065; Pacific Stock Exchange (415) 393-4000; Philadelphia Stock Exchange (215) 496-5000.

SUDAN: INDEPENDENCE DAY: ANNIVERSARY. Jan 1. National holiday. Sudan was proclaimed a sovereign independent republic in 1956, ending its status as an Anglo-Egyptian condominium (since 1899).

TAIWAN: FOUNDATION DAYS. Jan 1–2. Public holiday. Commemorates the founding of the Republic of China on Jan 1, 1912.

TAKE A NEW YEAR'S RESOLUTION TO STOP SMOKING (TANYRSS). Jan 1–Feb 10. 16th annual. To educate consumers/patients, healthcare professionals to take a New Year's resolution to stop smoking. Kit materials available for $15. For info: Fred Mayer, RPh, MPH, Pharmacists Planning Service Inc, c/o Pharmacy Council on Tobacco Dependence, 101 Lucas Valley Rd, Ste 210, San Rafael, CA 94903. E-mail: ppsi@aol.com. Web: www.ppsinc.org.

	S	M	T	W	T	F	S
January					1	2	3
2004	4	5	6	7	8	9	10
	11	12	13	14	15	16	17
	18	19	20	21	22	23	24
	25	26	27	28	29	30	31

TOURNAMENT OF ROSES PARADE. Jan 1. Pasadena, CA. 115th annual parade. Rose Parade starting at 8:00 AM, EST, includes floats, bands and equestrians. Est attendance: 1,000,000. For info: Pasadena Tournament of Roses Assn, 391 S Orange Grove Blvd, Pasadena, CA 91184. Phone: (626) 449-4100. Fax: (626) 449-9066. Web: www.tournamentofroses.com.

UNITED KINGDOM: NEW YEAR'S HOLIDAY. Jan 1.

UNITED NATIONS: DECADE FOR THE ERADICATION OF POVERTY: YEAR EIGHT. Jan 1–Dec 31. General Assembly, Dec 20, 1995 (Res 50/107 II), proclaimed 1997–2006 (the decade following the International Year for the Eradication of Poverty—1996) to be a time for governments and organizations to pursue implementation of the recommendations of the major UN conferences on this issue, particularly the World Summit for Social Development held at Copenhagen in March 1995. For info: United Nations, Dept of Public Info, New York, NY 10017. Web: www.un.org.

UNITED NATIONS: DECADE FOR HUMAN RIGHTS EDUCATION: YEAR TEN. Jan 1–Dec 31. On Dec 23, 1994, the General Assembly proclaimed this decade for 1995–2004 and welcomed the Plan of Action for the Decade submitted by the Secretary-General (Res 49/184). The Assembly expressed its conviction that human rights education should constitute a lifelong process, by which people learn respect for the dignity of others. For info: United Nations, Dept of Public Info, New York, NY 10017. Web: www.un.org.

UNITED NATIONS: DECADE TO ROLL BACK MALARIA IN DEVELOPING COUNTRIES, PARTICULARLY IN AFRICA: YEAR FOUR. Jan 1–Dec 31. On Sept 7, 2001, the United Nations General Assembly declared this decade for the years 2001–2010. Seeks to increase awareness of this deadly tropical disease—particularly in Africa where 9 in 10 cases occur. Calls for efforts to reach treatment goals by Africa and the international community. For info: United Nations, Dept of Public Info, New York, NY 10017. Web: www.un.org.

UNITED NATIONS: INTERNATIONAL DECADE FOR A CULTURE OF PEACE AND NONVIOLENCE FOR THE CHILDREN OF THE WORLD: YEAR FOUR. Jan 1–Dec 31. The General Assembly (Res 53/25) invites religious bodies, educational institutions, artists and the media to support this decade for the benefit of every child of the world. Member states are invited to ensure that the practice of peace and nonviolence is taught at all levels in their societies, including in educational institutions. Decade is 2001–2010. For info: United Nations, Dept of Public Info, New York, NY 10017. Web: www .un.org.

UNITED NATIONS: INTERNATIONAL DECADE OF THE WORLD'S INDIGENOUS PEOPLE: YEAR TEN. Jan 1–Dec 9. Proclaimed by the General Assembly, Dec 21, 1993 (Res 48/163), this decade (1994–2004) focuses international attention and cooperation on the problems of indigenous people in a range of areas, such as human rights, health,

☆ Chase's 2004 Calendar of Events ☆ Jan 1–2

education, development and environment. Governments are encouraged to include representatives of these people in planning and executing goals and activities for the decade. For info: United Nations, Dept of Public Info, New York, NY 10017. Web: www.un.org.

UNITED NATIONS: INTERNATIONAL YEAR TO COMMEMORATE THE STRUGGLE AGAINST SLAVERY AND ITS ABOLITION. Jan 1–Dec 31. The General Assembly, on Dec 18, 2002, proclaimed 2004 the International Year to Commemorate the Struggle against Slavery and Its Abolition (resolution 57/195). The Assembly reaffirmed its commitment to a global drive for the total elimination of racism, racial discrimination, xenophobia and related intolerance, and stressed the need to maintain political will and momentum at the national, regional and international levels. For info: United Nations, Dept of Public Info, New York, NY 10017. Web: www.un.org.

UNITED NATIONS: INTERNATIONAL YEAR OF RICE. Jan 1–Dec 31. Noting that rice is the staple food of more than half of the world's population, the Assembly, on Dec 16, 2002, declared 2004 as the International Year of Rice. In doing so, the Assembly affirmed the need to focus world attention on the role rice can play in attaining internationally agreed development goals. For info: United Nations, Dept of Public Info, New York, NY 10017. Web: www.un.org.

UNITED NATIONS LITERACY DECADE: EDUCATION FOR ALL: YEAR TWO. Jan 1–Dec 31. On Dec 19, 2001, the United Nations General Assembly proclaimed the ten years 2003–2012 the United Nations Literacy Decade: Education for All. This decade affirms that literacy is the bedrock of any universal basic education and that creating literate environments was essential to eradicating poverty, reaching gender equality and ensuring sustainable development. For info: United Nations, Dept of Public Info, New York, NY 10017. Web: www.un.org.

UNITED NATIONS: SECOND INTERNATIONAL DECADE FOR THE ERADICATION OF COLONIALISM: YEAR FOUR. Jan 1–Dec 31. On Nov 22, 1988, the General Assembly proclaimed 1990–2000 the International Decade for the Eradication of Colonialism. In December 1991 the Assembly declared the ultimate goal of the Decade to be the free exercise of the right of self-determination by the people of all remaining non-self-governing territories. In 2000, the General Assembly proclaimed the Second International Decade for the Eradication of Colonialism (2001–2010). For info: United Nations, Dept of Public Info, New York, NY 10017. Web: www.un.org.

UNIVERSAL HOUR OF PEACE. Jan 1. Begins at 11:30 PM on Dec 31, 2003, and ends at 12:30 AM on Jan 1, 2004. An hour dedicated to creating peace throughout our planet. Every man, woman and child is asked to spend the hour in meditation, prayer, conversation, listening to beautiful music or whatever helps them concentrate on peace. The simple truth is "living peaceably begins by thinking peacefully." To add your name to the "Millions for Peace" list, e-mail your name, city, state/country to peace@som.org. An hour-long cassette tape of the Universal Peace Covenant voiced in seven languages is available at no charge by contacting SOM. One hour of peace, a world of difference. For info: Dr. Barbara Condron, Intl Coord, School of Metaphysics, World HQ, 163 Moon Valley Rd, Windyville, MO 65783. Phone: (417) 345-8411. Fax: (417) 345-6668. E-mail: peace@som.org. Web: www.som.org.

WALK YOUR PET MONTH. Jan 1–31. New Year's resolutions are not just for humans. Most of our four-legged furry friends need to watch their weight and begin an exercise program, too. Grab that leash and walk! For info: Laurie Teague, PO Box 9315, Chico, CA 95927. Phone: (530) 342-1380. Fax: (530) 342-3870. E-mail: info@pethealthjournal.com. Web: www.PetHealthJournal.com.

WALKER, DOAK: BIRTH ANNIVERSARY. Jan 1, 1927. Ewell Doak Walker, Jr, Pro Football Hall of Fame and Heisman Trophy running back, born at Dallas, TX. Walker won the Heisman Trophy in 1948, playing for SMU, and went on to an outstanding pro career with the Detroit Lions. He was a handsome, humble player during a time when football players could become national heroes. Inducted into the Hall of Fame in 1986. Died at Steamboat Springs, CO, Sept 27, 1998.

WAYNE, "MAD ANTHONY": BIRTH ANNIVERSARY. Jan 1, 1745 (OS). American Revolutionary War general whose daring, sometimes reckless, conduct earned him the nickname "Mad Anthony" Wayne. His courage and shrewdness as a soldier made him a key figure in the capture of Stony Point, NY (1779), preventing Benedict Arnold's "delivery" of West Point to the British, and in subduing hostile Indians of the Northwest Territory (1794). He was born at Waynesboro, PA, and died at Presque Isle, PA, Dec 15, 1796.

WESTERN PACIFIC HURRICANE SEASON. Jan 1–Dec 31. Most hurricanes occur from June 1 through Oct 1, though the season lasts all year. (Western Pacific: West of International Dateline.) Info from: US Dept of Commerce, Natl Oceanic and Atmospheric Admin, Rockville, MD 20852.

Z DAY. Jan 1. To give recognition on the first day of the year to all persons and places whose names begin with the letter Z and who are always listed or thought of last in any alphabetized list. For info: Tom Zager, 4545 Kirkwood Dr, Sterling Heights, MI 48310. E-mail: tee_zee@excite.com.

ZWINGLI, ULRICH: BIRTH ANNIVERSARY. Jan 1, 1484. Swiss clergyman, theologian and reformer, born at Wildhaus, St. Gall, Switzerland. Ordained a Catholic priest, he converted to Protestantism. While serving as a military chaplain in the Second War of Kappel, Zwingli was killed on Oct 11, 1531. A monument marks the place where he fell during the battle.

BIRTHDAYS TODAY

Valentina Cortese, 79, actress (*The Barefoot Contessa, Juliet of the Spirits*), born Milan, Italy, Jan 1, 1925.
Jon Corzine, 57, US Senator (D, New Jersey), born Taylorville, IL, Jan 1, 1947.
Ernest F. Hollings, 82, US Senator (D, South Carolina), born Charleston, SC, Jan 1, 1922.
Helmut Jahn, 64, architect, born Nuremberg, Germany, Jan 1, 1940.
Frank Langella, 64, actor (*The Twelve Chairs, Lolita*), born Bayonne, NJ, Jan 1, 1940.
Don Novello, 61, actor, comedian ("The Smothers Brothers Show," "Saturday Night Live": Father Guido Sarducci), born Ashtabula, OH, Jan 1, 1943.
J.D. Salinger, 85, author (*Catcher in the Rye, Franny & Zooey, Seymour: An Introduction*), born New York, NY, Jan 1, 1919.

JANUARY 2 — FRIDAY
Day 2 — 364 Remaining

ASIMOV, ISAAC: BIRTH ANNIVERSARY. Jan 2, 1920. Although Isaac Asimov was one of the world's best-known writers of science fiction, his almost 500 books dealt with subjects as diverse as the Bible, works for preschoolers, college textbooks, mysteries, chemistry, biology, limericks, Shakespeare, Gilbert and Sullivan and modern history. During his prolific career he helped to elevate science fiction from pulp magazines to a more intellectual level. Some of his works include the *Foundation Trilogy, The Robots of Dawn, Robots and Empire, Nemesis, Murder at the A.B.A.* (in which he himself was a character), *The Gods Themselves* and *I, Robot*, in which he posited the famous Three Laws of Robotics. His *The Clock We Live On* is an accessible explanation of the origins of calendars. Asimov was born near Smolensk, Russia, and died at New York, NY, Apr 6, 1992.

CHICK-FIL-A PEACH BOWL. Jan 2. Georgia Dome, Atlanta, GA. Annual football matchup of ACC and SEC competitors. Est attendance: 72,000. For info: Chick-fil-A Peach Bowl, 235 Andrew Young International Blvd NW, Atlanta, GA 30303. Web: www.peachbowl.com.

Jan 2 ☆ Chase's 2004 Calendar of Events ☆

55-MPH SPEED LIMIT: 30th ANNIVERSARY. Jan 2, 1974. President Richard Nixon signed a bill requiring states to limit highway speeds to a maximum of 55 mph. This measure was meant to conserve energy during the crisis precipitated by the embargo imposed by the Arab oil-producing countries. A plan, used by some states, limited sale of gasoline on odd-numbered days for cars whose plates ended in odd numbers and even-numbered days for even-numbered plates. Some states limited purchases to $2–$3 per auto and lines as long as six miles resulted in some locations. See also: "Arab Oil Embargo Lifted: Anniversary" (Mar 13).

GEORGIA: RATIFICATION DAY. Jan 2, 1788. By unanimous vote, Georgia became the fourth state to ratify the Constitution.

GRAND AMERICAN COON HUNT. Jan 2–3. County Fairgrounds, Orangeburg, SC. Coon hunters and sportsmen from all over the US and Canada bring their dogs to compete for Grand American Champion. An ACHA qualifying event. Est attendance: 35,000. For info: Orangeburg County Chamber of Commerce, PO Box 328, Orangeburg, SC 29116-0328. Phone: (803) 534-6821 or (800) 545-6153. Fax: (803) 531-9435. Web: www.akc.org.

HAITI: ANCESTORS' DAY. Jan 2. Commemoration of the ancestors. Also known as Hero's Day. Public holiday.

HAPPY MEW YEAR FOR CATS DAY. Jan 2. Felines, ever above mere humans in the great chain of being, have a day unto themselves to celebrate the "mewness" of a new time. Annually, Jan 2. [©2003 by WH.] For info: Thomas & Ruth Roy, Wellcat Holidays, 2418 Long Ln, Lebanon, PA 17046. Phone: (717) 279-0184. E-mail: info@wellcat.com. Web: www.wellcat.com.

JAPAN: KAKIZOME. Jan 2. Traditional Japanese festival gets under way when the first strokes of the year are made on paper with the traditional brushes.

MILLER, ROGER: BIRTH ANNIVERSARY. Jan 2, 1936. Country and western singer, songwriter and musician "King of the Road" Roger Miller was born at Ft Worth, TX. Miller won 11 Grammy Awards and a Tony (1986 for the score to the Broadway play *Big River*). He died Oct 25, 1992, at Los Angeles, CA.

NATIONAL GEOGRAPHIC BEE 2004, SCHOOL LEVEL. Jan 2–16. (Began Nov 17, 2003. Principals must have registered their schools by Oct 15, 2003.) Nationwide contest involving millions of students at the school level. The Bee is designed to encourage the teaching and study of geography. There are three levels of competition. A student must win a school-level Bee in order to win the right to take a written exam. The written test determines the top 100 students in each state who are eligible to go on to the state level. National Geographic brings each state winner and a teacher from their school to Washington for the national level in May. Alex Trebek moderates the national level. For info: Natl Geographic Bee, Natl Geographic Soc, 1145 17th St NW, Washington, DC 20036. Phone: (202) 828-6659.

NEVADAPEX COIN AND STAMP EXPO. Jan 2–4 (also Apr 16–18 and Oct 22–24). River Palms Casino, Laughlin, NV. Est attendance: 5,000. For info: Intl Stamp Collectors Soc, PO Box 854, Van Nuys, CA 91408. Phone: (818) 997-6496. Fax: (818) 988-4337. E-mail: iibick@aol.com. Web: www.bick.net.

RUSSIA: PASSPORT PRESENTATION. Jan 2. A ceremony for 16-year-olds, who are recognized as citizens of the country. Always on the first working day of the New Year.

SCOTLAND: NEW YEAR'S BANK HOLIDAY. Jan 2. Public holiday. The day after New Year's Day.

SPACE MILESTONE: *LUNA 1* (USSR): 45th ANNIVERSARY. Jan 2, 1959. Launch of robotic moon probe that missed the moon and became the first spacecraft from Earth to orbit the sun.

SPAIN CAPTURES GRANADA: ANNIVERSARY. Jan 2, 1492. Spaniards took the city of Granada from the Moors, ending seven centuries of Muslim rule in Spain.

SWITZERLAND: BERCHTOLDSTAG. Jan 2. Holiday in many cantons. Commemorates the founding of the city of Berne by Duke Berchtold V in the 12th century. Now mainly a children's holiday.

TAFT, HELEN HERRON: BIRTH ANNIVERSARY. Jan 2, 1861. Wife of William Howard Taft, 27th president of the US, born at Cincinnati, OH. Died at Washington, DC, May 22, 1943.

THOMAS, MARTHA CAREY: BIRTH ANNIVERSARY. Jan 2, 1857. The second president of Bryn Mawr College, Martha Carey Thomas gained a reputation for her insistence that the education of women should be as rigorous as that of men. A zealous suffragist, she served as the first president of the National College Women's Equal Suffrage League. Thomas promoted Bryn Mawr's Summer School for Women in Industry (opened in 1921) to provide a liberal education for working women. Born at Baltimore, MD, she died at Philadelphia, PA, Dec 2, 1935.

TOSTITOS FIESTA BOWL. Jan 2. Sun Devil Stadium, Tempe, AZ. Part of the Bowl Championship Series. Game time is noon. Est attendance: 75,000. For info: Fiesta Bowl, 120 S Ash Ave, Tempe, AZ 85281. Phone: (480) 350-0900. Web: www.tostitosfiestabowl.com.

WOLFE, JAMES: BIRTH ANNIVERSARY. Jan 2, 1727. English general who commanded the British army's victory over Montcalm's French forces on the Plains of Abraham at Quebec City in 1759. As a result, France surrendered Canada to England. Wolfe was born at Westerham, Kent, England. He died at the Plains of Abraham of battle wounds, Sept 13, 1759.

BIRTHDAYS TODAY

Jim Bakker, 65, former TV evangelist, born James Orsen, Muskegon, MI, Jan 2, 1939.

Brian Boucher, 27, hockey player, born Woonsocket, RI, Jan 2, 1977.

Tia Carrere, 37, actress (*Wayne's World, True Lies*), born Honolulu, HI, Jan 2, 1967.

David Cone, 41, former baseball player, born Kansas City, MO, Jan 2, 1963.

Taye Diggs, 32, model, actor (*How Stella Got Her Groove Back*), born Rochester, NY, Jan 2, 1972.

Christopher Durang, 55, playwright, actor (*The Secret of My Success, Heaven Help Us*), born Montclair, NJ, Jan 2, 1949.

Cuba Gooding, Jr, 36, actor (*Jerry Maguire, As Good As It Gets*), born the Bronx, NY, Jan 2, 1968.

Dennis Hastert, 62, Speaker of the House, born Aurora, IL, Jan 2, 1942.

Edgar Martinez, 41, baseball player, born New York, NY, Jan 2, 1963.

January 2004

S	M	T	W	T	F	S
				1	2	3
4	5	6	7	8	9	10
11	12	13	14	15	16	17
18	19	20	21	22	23	24
25	26	27	28	29	30	31

☆ Chase's 2004 Calendar of Events ☆   Jan 2–3

Wendy Phillips, 52, actress ("Promised Land," "Homefront"), born Brooklyn, NY, Jan 2, 1952.
Renata Tebaldi, 82, opera singer, born Pesaro, Italy, Jan 2, 1922.
Christy Turlington, 35, model, born Walnut Creek, CA, Jan 2, 1969.

JANUARY 3 — SATURDAY
Day 3 — 363 Remaining

ALASKA: ADMISSION DAY: 45th ANNIVERSARY. Jan 3, 1959. Alaska, which had been purchased from Russia in 1867, became the 49th state. The area of Alaska is nearly one-fifth the size of the rest of the US.

"THE ARSENIO HALL SHOW" TV PREMIERE: 15th ANNIVERSARY. Jan 3, 1989. Arsenio Hall became the first African-American to host a successful syndicated late-night talk show. The show attracted a younger audience than that of Johnny Carson's "The Tonight Show" and effectively limited the impact of CBS's 1989 late-night entry, "The Pat Sajak Show." Hall was successful in booking soul and rap music acts that had rarely been seen on other shows. His was also the show on which presidential candidate Bill Clinton appeared, playing the saxophone in dark glasses. Hall was named by *TV Guide* (June 1990) as its first "TV Person of the Year."

ATTLEE, CLEMENT RICHARD: BIRTH ANNIVERSARY. Jan 3, 1883. English leader of the Labour Party and prime minister (July 1945–October 1951). Born at London, England; died there Oct 8, 1967.

COOLIDGE, GRACE ANNA GOODHUE: 125th BIRTH ANNIVERSARY. Jan 3, 1879. Wife of Calvin Coolidge, 30th president of the US, born at Burlington, VT. Died at Northampton, MA, July 8, 1957.

DAVIES, MARION: BIRTH ANNIVERSARY. Jan 3, 1897. Born at Brooklyn, NY, Marion Cecilia Douras became Marion Davies and made her first appearance on film in 1917. Her romantic and professional involvement with newspaper magnate William Randolph Hearst ensured the type of publicity that would launch her to stardom. Her films included *When Knighthood Was in Flower*, *The Patsy* and *Show People*. Davies died at Hollywood, Sept 23, 1961.

DRINKING STRAW PATENTED: ANNIVERSARY. Jan 3, 1888. A drinking straw made out of paraffin-covered paper was patented by Marvin Stone of Washington, DC. It replaced natural rye straws.

FIRST FEMALE CONGRESSIONAL PAGE: 65th ANNIVERSARY. Jan 3, 1939. Gene Cox, 13, served on the House floor as aide to her father, Representative Eugene Cox (D-GA), on opening day of the 76th Congress. She was paid $4 for three hours of work and there were no objections to her one-day service. More than 30 years later, however, there was much debate when Senator Jacob Javits (R-NY) nominated a female to be a real Senate page.

GREAT FRUITCAKE TOSS. Jan 3. Manitou Springs, CO. What do you do with leftover fruitcake? Toss, hurl, launch competitions. Annually, the first Saturday in January. Est attendance: 1,000. For info: Manitou Springs Chamber of Commerce, 354 Manitou Ave, Manitou Springs, CO 80829. Phone: (800) 642-2567. Web: www.manitousprings.org.

LENNON-ONO ALBUM CONFISCATION: 35th ANNIVERSARY. Jan 3, 1969. John Lennon and Yoko Ono posed nude for the cover of their album *Two Virgins*. On this day, a shipment of 30,000 of the albums was confiscated by police at Newark, NJ, as a violation of pornography statutes.

"LOOK UP AND LIVE" TV PREMIERE: 50th ANNIVERSARY. Jan 3, 1954. CBS broadcast this inspirational show on Sunday mornings for 24 years. The Reverend Lawrence McMasters appeared in the early years and Merv Griffin hosted the show in 1955. Pamela Ilott, executive producer, was also director of religious programming for CBS News.

MEMENTO MORI. Jan 3. "Memento, mori," Latin for "Remember, you die," is also the title of a novel by Muriel Spark. We suggest posting the words at home and at work, not to be morbid, but to remind us to cherish all that we have today . . . for tomorrow may never arrive. [©2003 by WH.] For info: Thomas and Ruth Roy, Wellcat Holidays, 2418 Long Ln, Lebanon, PA 17046. Phone: (717) 279-0184. E-mail: info@wellcat.com. Web: www.wellcat.com.

MOTT, LUCRETIA (COFFIN): BIRTH ANNIVERSARY. Jan 3, 1793. American teacher, minister, antislavery leader and (with Elizabeth Cady Stanton) one of the founders of the women's rights movement in the US. Born at Nantucket, MA, she died near Philadelphia, PA, Nov 11, 1880.

"QUEEN FOR A DAY" TV PREMIERE: ANNIVERSARY. Jan 3, 1956. Game show on which prizes were awarded to the contestant who evoked the most sympathy from the studio audience. The show began some 11 years earlier on the radio with Jack Bailey hosting. Five women were chosen from the audience to appear on stage. Each related her story of misfortune and explained what she needed to remedy the situation and the audience would vote by applause. The lucky winner was then given the royal treatment—crown, scepter and red robe—plus a prize to help with her problem. This soon became the top-rated daytime show. In 1969 the show went into syndication with Dick Curtis as host, but it didn't last long.

RAUH, JOSEPH L., JR: BIRTH ANNIVERSARY. Jan 3, 1911. Political activist Joseph L. Rauh, Jr, was born at Cincinnati, OH. In 1947 he cofounded Americans for Democratic Action (ADA), which supports liberal causes. Rauh helped create the minority civil rights plank at the 1948 Democratic National Convention—a foundation for the federal civil rights legislation in the 1960s. He served on the executive board of the NAACP and was general counsel to the Leadership Conference on Civil Rights. He died Sept 3, 1992, at Washington, DC.

STURGES, JOHN: BIRTH ANNIVERSARY. Jan 3, 1911. Motion picture director John Sturges, born at Oak Park, IL, was known for his action movies. He received an Academy Award nomination in 1955 for *Bad Day at Black Rock*. He also directed *Gunfight at the OK Corral* (1956), *The Magnificent Seven* (1960), *The Great Escape* (1963) and his last film *The Eagle Has Landed* (1977). He died Aug 18, 1992, at San Luis Obispo, CA.

TOLKIEN, J.R.R.: BIRTH ANNIVERSARY. Jan 3, 1892. John Ronald Reuel Tolkien, author of *The Hobbit* (1937) and the trilogy *The Lord of the Rings*. Though best known for his fantasies, Tolkien was also a serious philologist. Born at Bloemfontein, South Africa, he died at Bournemouth, England, Sept 2, 1973.

WIND CAVE NATIONAL PARK ESTABLISHED: ANNIVERSARY. Jan 3, 1903. President Theodore Roosevelt signed a bill on this date establishing South Dakota's Wind Cave a national park and preserve. It was the first national park established for the preservation of a cave.

BIRTHDAYS TODAY

Joan Walsh Anglund, 78, author, illustrator of children's books (*Crocus in the Snow*, *Bedtime Book*), born Hinsdale, IL, Jan 3, 1926.
Dabney Coleman, 72, actor ("Buffalo Bill," *Nine to Five*, *Tootsie*), born Austin, TX, Jan 3, 1932.
Mel Gibson, 48, actor (*Braveheart*, *Lethal Weapon*), born Peekskill, NY, Jan 3, 1956.
Robert Marvin (Bobby) Hull, 65, Hall of Fame hockey player, born Point Anne, ON, Canada, Jan 3, 1939.
Robert Loggia, 74, actor (*An Officer and a Gentleman*, *Scarface*), born Staten Island, NY, Jan 3, 1930.
Danica McKellar, 29, actress ("The Wonder Years," *Sidekicks*), born La Jolia, CA, Jan 3, 1975.
Victoria Principal, 54, actress ("Dallas"), born Fukuoka, Japan, Jan 3, 1950.
Stephen Stills, 59, musician, songwriter, born Dallas, TX, Jan 3, 1945.

Chase's 2004 Calendar of Events

JANUARY 4 — SUNDAY
Day 4 — 362 Remaining

AMNESTY FOR POLYGAMISTS: ANNIVERSARY. Jan 4, 1893. President Benjamin Harrison issued a proclamation granting full amnesty and pardon to all persons who had since Nov 1, 1890, abstained from unlawful cohabitation of a polygamous marriage. This was intended in the main for a specific group of elderly Mormons who had continued in the practice of contracting serial marriages. Amnesty was based on the condition that those pardoned must obey the law in the future or be "vigorously prosecuted." The practice of polygamy was a factor interfering with attainment of statehood for Utah.

ASARAH B'TEVET. Jan 4. Hebrew calendar date: Tevet 10, 5764. The Fast of the 10th of Tevet begins at first morning light and commemorates the beginning of the Babylonian siege of Jerusalem in the sixth century BC. Began at sunset Jan 3. Asarah B'Tevet falls on two dates in the 2004 calendar year.

BRAILLE, LOUIS: BIRTH ANNIVERSARY. Jan 4, 1809. The inventor of a widely used touch system of reading and writing for the blind was born at Coupvray, France. Permanently blinded at the age of three by a leatherworking awl in his father's saddlemaking shop, Braille developed a system of writing that used, ironically, an awl-like stylus to punch marks in paper that could be felt and interpreted by the blind. The system was largely ignored until after Braille died in poverty, suffering from tuberculosis, at Paris, Jan 6, 1852.

"THE CATHOLIC HOUR" TV PREMIERE: ANNIVERSARY. Jan 4, 1953. Produced in cooperation with the National Council of Catholic Men, this show ran for 17 years, alternating from week to week with "The Eternal Light" and "Frontiers of Faith."

CHRISTMAS EPIPHANY CELEBRATION. Jan 4. St. John's Lutheran Church, Isanti, MN. Celebrate the holiday season through lessons and carols all done in German. A traditional German Christmas tree graces the historic church on the National Register of Historic Sites. We'll heat up the wood stove, but dress warmly. Annually, the Sunday closest to the Epiphany. For info: Kathy McCully, Dir, Isanti County Historical Society, PO Box 525, Cambridge, MN 55008. Phone: (763) 689-4229. Fax: (763) 689-4229. E-mail: mccully@usfamily.net.

DIMPLED CHAD DAY. Jan 4. This is a day to commemorate all the dimpled chads of the world, left over from various and sundry contested elections. Chads, roasted in garlic, make an excellent sprinkle topping for salads. [©2003 by WH.] For info: Thomas & Ruth Roy, Wellcat Holidays, 2418 Long Ln, Lebanon, PA 17046. Phone: (717) 279-0184. E-mail: info@wellcat.com. Web: www.wellcat.com.

EARTH AT PERIHELION. Jan 4. At approximately 1 PM, EST, planet Earth will reach Perihelion, that point in its orbit when it is closest to the sun (about 91,400,000 miles). The Earth's mean distance from the sun (mean radius of its orbit) is reached early in the months of April and October. Note that Earth is closest to the sun during Northern Hemisphere winter. See also: "Earth at Aphelion" (July 5).

GENERAL TOM THUMB: BIRTH ANNIVERSARY. Jan 4, 1838. Charles Sherwood Stratton, perhaps the most famous midget in history, was born at Bridgeport, CT. He eventually reached a height of three feet, four inches and a weight of 70 pounds. Discovered by P.T. Barnum in 1842, Stratton, as "General Tom Thumb," became an internationally known entertainer and performed before Queen Victoria and other heads of state. On Feb 10, 1863, he married another midget, Lavinia Warren. Stratton died at Middleborough, MA, July 15, 1883.

GRIMM, JACOB: BIRTH ANNIVERSARY. Jan 4, 1785. Librarian, mythologist and philologist, born at Hanau, Germany. Best remembered for *Grimm's Fairy Tales* (in collaboration with his brother Wilhelm). Died at Berlin, Germany, Sept 20, 1863.

HOLLOWAY, STERLING: BIRTH ANNIVERSARY. Jan 4, 1905. Actor Sterling Holloway prospered in films and television, but he is probably best remembered as the voice of Winnie the Pooh. He provided the voices for characters in several full-length animated features, including *Alice in Wonderland* (the Cheshire Cat), *The Aristocats* and *The Jungle Book*. Born at Cedartown, GA, he died Nov 22, 1992, at Los Angeles, CA.

MYANMAR: INDEPENDENCE DAY. Jan 4. National Day. The British controlled the country from 1826 until 1948 when it was granted independence. The country's name was changed to the Union of Myanmar in 1989 to reflect that the population is made up not just of the Burmese but of many other ethnic groups as well.

NATIONAL JOYGERM DAY. Jan 4 Joygerms celebrate the gift of life and laughter by seeking to spread joy and cheer, kindness and courtesy, happiness and humor, sacredness and silliness on this day and every day. Free Joygerm membership cards available; somewhat disorderly quarterly newsletter available by subscription. Become a Joygerm Junkie and get high on happiness! For info: Joygerm Junkie Joan E. White, Founder, Joygerms Unlimited, PO Box 555, Eastwood Station, Syracuse, NY 13206-0555. Phone: (315) 472-2779.

NEWTON, ISAAC: BIRTH ANNIVERSARY. Jan 4, 1643. Sir Isaac Newton was the chief figure of the scientific revolution of the 17th century, a physicist and mathematician who laid the foundations of calculus, studied the mechanics of planetary motion and discovered the law of gravitation. Born at Woolsthorpe, England, he died at London, England, Mar 31, 1727. Newton was born before Great Britain adopted the Gregorian calendar. His Julian (Old Style) birth date is Dec 25, 1642.

"NIGHT COURT" TV PREMIERE: 20th ANNIVERSARY. Jan 4, 1984. NBC sitcom set in an urban courtroom. The cast included Harry Anderson as Judge Harry T. Stone, John Larroquette as prosecutor Dan Fielding, Richard Moll as court officer Bull Shannon and Selma Diamond as court officer Selma Hacker. Markie Post joined the cast in 1985 as PD Christine Sullivan. Mel Tormé made a few appearances as himself, Harry's idol. The last telecast was July 1, 1992.

NIXON'S REJECTION OF SENATE ORDER: 30th ANNIVERSARY. Jan 4, 1974. President Richard Nixon rejected the Senate Watergate Committee's subpoenas seeking White House tapes and documents.

POLISH-AMERICAN IN THE HOUSE: ANNIVERSARY. Jan 4, 1977. Maryland Democrat Barbara Mikulski took her seat in the US House of Representatives, the first Polish-American ever to do so. An able voice for female as well as working-class Baltimore constituents of the 3rd District, Ms Mikulski went on to be elected to the US Senate.

POP MUSIC CHART INTRODUCED: ANNIVERSARY. Jan 4, 1936. *Billboard* magazine published the first list of best-selling pop records, covering the week that ended Dec 30, 1935. On the list were recordings by the Tommy Dorsey and the Ozzie Nelson orchestras.

RUSH, BENJAMIN: BIRTH ANNIVERSARY. Jan 4, 1746. Physician, patriot and humanitarian of the American Revolution, born on a plantation at Byberry, PA. Rush was a signer of the Declaration of Independence, and his writings on mental illness earned him the title "Father of Psychiatry." His tract *Inquiry* attacked the common wisdom of the time that alcohol was a positive good. He was the first American to call alcoholism a chronic disease. Benjamin Rush died at Philadelphia, PA, Apr 19, 1813.

January 2004

S	M	T	W	T	F	S
				1	2	3
4	5	6	7	8	9	10
11	12	13	14	15	16	17
18	19	20	21	22	23	24
25	26	27	28	29	30	31

☆ Chase's 2004 Calendar of Events ☆ Jan 4–5

SETON, ELIZABETH ANN BAYLEY: FEAST DAY. Jan 4. First American-born saint (beatified Mar 17, 1963; canonized Sept 14, 1975). Born at New York, NY, Aug 28, 1774, Seton was the founder of the American Sisters of Charity, the first American order of Roman Catholic nuns. She died at Baltimore, MD, Jan 4, 1821.

"SOMEDAY WE'LL LAUGH ABOUT THIS" WEEK. Jan 4–10. We've all used the expression, "Someday we'll laugh about this!" Why wait? It usually takes less than seven days for people to violate 90 percent of their New Year's resolutions. This week helps us to remember the art of laughing at ourselves. This week tickles the yoke and joke of perfectionism while encouraging people to strive for excellence at the same time. This week is a great way to start the new year—laughing at the humorous human condition. For a free information packet on the positive power of humor send a stamped ($1.06) self-addressed envelope. For info: Dr. Joel Goodman, The Humor Project, Inc, 480 Broadway, Ste 210-C, Saratoga Springs, NY 12866-2288. Phone: (518) 587-8770. Fax: (518) 587-8771. E-mail: chase@HumorProject.com. Web: www.HumorProject.com.

TRIVIA DAY. Jan 4. In celebration of those who know all sorts of facts and/or have doctorates in uselessology. For info: Robert L. Birch, Puns Corps, Box 2364, Falls Church, VA 22042-0364. Phone: (703) 533-3668.

UTAH: ADMISSION DAY: ANNIVERSARY. Jan 4. Utah became the 45th state in 1896.

BIRTHDAYS TODAY

Dyan Cannon, 67, actress (Oscar nominations for *Heaven Can Wait, Bob and Carol and Ted and Alice*), born Tacoma, WA, Jan 4, 1937.
Patrick Cassidy, 42, actor ("Bay City Blues," *Longtime Companion*), born Los Angeles, CA, Jan 4, 1962.
Dave Foley, 42, actor ("NewsRadio"), born Toronto, ON, Canada, Jan 4, 1962.
Ann Magnuson, 48, actress, performance artist ("Anything but Love," *Clear and Present Danger*), born Charleston, WV, Jan 4, 1956.
Julia Ormond, 39, actress (*Legends of the Fall, Sabrina*), born Surrey, England, Jan 4, 1965.
Floyd Patterson, 69, former boxer, born Waco, NC, Jan 4, 1935.
Barbara Rush, 77, actress ("Peyton Place," *Magnificent Obsession, Hombre*), born Denver, CO, Jan 4, 1927.
Donald Francis (Don) Shula, 74, Hall of Fame football coach and player, born Paineville, OH, Jan 4, 1930.
Michael Stipe, 44, singer (REM), born Decatur, GA, Jan 4, 1960.
Jane Wyman, 90, actress ("Falcon Crest," *Magnificent Obsession*; Oscar for *Johnny Belinda*), born Sarah Jane Faulks, St. Joseph, MO, Jan 4, 1914.

JANUARY 5 — MONDAY
Day 5 — 361 Remaining

AILEY, ALVIN: BIRTH ANNIVERSARY. Jan 5, 1931. Born at Rogers, TX, Alvin Ailey began his noted career as a choreographer in the late 1950s after a successful career as a dancer. He founded the Alvin Ailey American Dance Theater, drawing from classical ballet, jazz, Afro-Caribbean and modern dance idioms to create the 79 ballets of the company's repertoire. He and his work played a central part in establishing a role for blacks in the world of modern dance. Ailey died Dec 1, 1989, at New York, NY.

"ALL MY CHILDREN" TV PREMIERE: ANNIVERSARY. Jan 5, 1970. This ABC show became TV's top-rated soap opera by the 1978–79 season and still keeps viewers glued to the screen. "All My Children" was created by Agnes Nixon, who had written for "Search for Tomorrow," "Another World" and "One Life to Live." Set in a place called Pine Valley, NY, the show focused on the Tyler and Martin families. The story includes the illegitimate child of Dr. Tyler, Erica Kane (played by Susan Lucci), who became one of daytime TV's most popular characters. Lucci had been nominated more than a dozen times for an Emmy, and finally won one in 1999. This serial has included in its cast Hugh Franklin as Dr. Charles Tyler and Ruth Warrick as his wife, Phoebe; son Lincoln has been played by James Karen, Paul Dumont, Nicholas Pryor and Peter White, daughter Ann by Diana De Vegh, Joanna Miles, Judith Barcroft and Gwyn Gilliss.

CARVER, GEORGE WASHINGTON: DEATH ANNIVERSARY. Jan 5, 1943. Black American agricultural scientist, author, inventor and teacher. Born into slavery at Diamond Grove, MO, probably in 1864. His research led to the creation of synthetic products made from peanuts, potatoes and wood. Carver died at Tuskegee, AL. His birthplace became a national monument in 1953.

CONGRESS ASSEMBLES. Jan 5. The Constitution provides that "the Congress shall assemble at least once in every year. . . ." and the 20th Amendment specifies "and such meeting shall begin at noon on the third day of January, unless they shall by law appoint a different day." If January 3 happens to fall on a weekend, Congress by resolution will meet on the following Monday or Tuesday.

DECATUR, STEPHEN: 225th BIRTH ANNIVERSARY. Jan 5, 1779. American naval officer (whose father and grandfather, both also named Stephen Decatur, were also seafaring men) born at Sinepuxent, MD. In a toast at a dinner in Norfolk in 1815, Decatur spoke his most famous words: "Our country! In her intercourse with foreign nations may she always be in the right; but our country, right or wrong." Mortally wounded in a duel with Commodore James Barron, at Bladensburg, MD, on the morning of Mar 22, 1820, Decatur was carried to his home in Washington where he died a few hours later.

FIVE-DOLLAR-A-DAY MINIMUM WAGE: 90th ANNIVERSARY. Jan 5, 1914. Henry Ford announced that all worthy Ford Motor Company employees would receive a minimum wage of $5 a day. Ford explained the policy as "profit sharing and efficiency engineering." The more cynical attributed it to an attempt to prevent unionization and to obtain a docile workforce that would accept job speedups. To obtain this minimum wage an employee had to be of "good personal habits." Whether an individual fit these criteria was determined by a new office created by Ford Motor Company—the Sociological Department.

ITALY: EPIPHANY FAIR. Jan 5. Piazza Navona, Rome, Italy. On the eve of Epiphany a fair of toys, sweets and presents takes place among the beautiful Bernini Fountains.

KIDFILM® FESTIVAL. Jan 5–18 (dates subject to change). Dallas, TX. 20th annual. Oldest and largest-attended international children's film festival in the world. Fifty shorts and features shown with filmmakers in attendance. Each year, a major figure in media (for all ages) is honored. Est attendance: 24,000. For info: USA Film Festival, 6116 N Central Expressway, Ste 105, Dallas, TX

75

Jan 5–6 ☆ Chase's 2004 Calendar of Events ☆

75206. Phone: (214) 821-6300 or (214) 821-FILM. Fax: (214) 821-6364. E-mail: info@usafilmfestival.com. Web: www.usafilmfestival.com.

NATIONAL THANK-YOUR-CUSTOMERS WEEK. Jan 5–9. Business owners should take some time each year to focus on thanking those who make their business possible. Thanking them each January, aside from what is done throughout the year, will strengthen relationships and lead to increased business. Event on Jan 7 at 10:00 AM, EST, at Radisson Hotel, Marlborough, MA, to share ideas and techniques, and to teach business owners how to say thank you to their customers. Annually, the first full week in January. For info: Robert Martel, JMB Marketing, 210 Cloverhill St, Marlborough, MA 01752. Phone: (508) 481-8383. Fax: (508) 481-8381. E-mail: bobmartel@jmbmarketing.com. Web: www.jmbmarketing.com.

ORGANIZE YOUR HOME DAY. Jan 5. Organize your life by clearing the clutter at home. Start today by organizing your kitchen, kid's room, closets or family room. Devote an entire day to your New Year's resolution of "getting it together!" Organized Times.com, the sponsor, will offer online chat sessions, free telephone seminars and giveaways. Annually, the first Monday in January. For info: Debbie Williams, OrganizedTimes.com, PO Box 590860, Houston, TX 77259. Phone: (281) 286-9512. E-mail: debbie@organizedtimes.com. Web: www.organizedtimes.com.

PICCARD, JEANNETTE RIDLON: BIRTH ANNIVERSARY. Jan 5, 1895. First American woman to qualify as free balloon pilot (1934). One of first women to be ordained as Episcopal priest (1976). Pilot for record-setting balloon ascent into stratosphere (from Dearborn, MI, Oct 23, 1934) (57,579 ft) with her husband, Jean Felix Piccard. Identical twin married to identical twin. See also: "Piccard, Jean Felix: Birth Anniversary" (Jan 28). Born at Chicago, IL. Died at Minneapolis, MN, May 17, 1981.

ROMAN CATHOLIC/EASTERN ORTHODOX MEETING: 40th ANNIVERSARY. Jan 5, 1964. Pope Paul VI and Patriarch Athenagoras of Jerusalem met in the Holy Land for the first meeting in five centuries between a Roman Catholic pontiff and an Eastern Orthodox patriarch.

RUFFIN, EDMUND: BIRTH ANNIVERSARY. Jan 5, 1794. Born at Prince George County, VA, Edmund Ruffin was an American agriculturist whose discoveries about crop rotation and fertilizer were influential in the early agrarian culture of the US. He published the *Farmer's Register* from 1833 to 1842, a journal that promoted scientific agriculture. A noted politician as well as a farmer, he was an early advocate of Southern secession whose views were widely circulated in pamphlets. As a member of the Palmetto Guards of Charleston, he was given the honor of firing the first shot on Fort Sumter Apr 12, 1861. According to legend, after the South's defeat he became despondent and, wrapping himself in the Confederate flag, took his own life on June 18, 1865, at Amelia County, VA.

TWELFTH NIGHT. Jan 5. Evening before Epiphany. Twelfth Night marks the end of medieval Christmas festivities and the end of Twelfthtide (the 12-day season after Christmas ending with Epiphany). Also called Twelfth Day Eve.

WOMEN'S SELF-EMPOWERMENT WEEK. Jan 5–11. Women wear many hats these days, and this week is a time to stop, take stock of your life and recognize all that you have accomplished. It's an occasion to pat yourself on the back and feel good about your role in society and the opportunities that have come your way through hard work and dedication. Let it inspire you to establish new goals and reach for the sky. For info: Robin Gorman Newman, The Love Coach, 44 Somerset Dr N, Great Neck, NY 11020. Phone: (516) 773-0911. Fax: (516) 773-0173. E-mail: robin@lovecoach.com. Web: www.ibwc.org.

WYOMING INAUGURATES FIRST WOMAN GOVERNOR IN US: ANNIVERSARY. Jan 5, 1925. Nellie Tayloe (Mrs William B.) Ross became the first woman to serve as governor upon her inauguration in Wyoming. She had previously finished out the term of her husband, who had died in office. In 1974 Ella Grasso of Connecticut became the first woman to be elected governor in her own right.

BIRTHDAYS TODAY

Suzy Amis, 42, actress (*Titanic, Judgement Day*), born Oklahoma City, OK, Jan 5, 1962.
Bradley Cooper, 29, actor ("Alias"), born Philadelphia, PA, Jan 5, 1975.
Mike DeWine, 57, US Senator (R, Ohio), born Springfield, OH, Jan 5, 1947.
Warrick Dunn, 29, football player, born Baton Rouge, LA, Jan 5, 1975.
Robert Duvall, 73, actor (*A Civil Action, The Godfather*), born San Diego, CA, Jan 5, 1931.
Umberto Eco, 72, author (*In the Name of the Rose*), born Alessandria, Italy, Jan 5, 1932.
Diane Keaton, 58, actress (Oscar for *Annie Hall; The First Wives Club, The Other Sister*), born Diane Hall, Los Angeles, CA, Jan 5, 1946.
Pamela Sue Martin, 50, actress (*The Poseidon Adventure*, "The Nancy Drew Mysteries," "Dynasty"), born Westport, CT, Jan 5, 1954.
Walter Frederick (Fritz) Mondale, 76, 42nd vice president of the US, former senator, born Ceylon, MN, Jan 5, 1928.
Ed Rendell, 60, Governor of Pennsylvania (D), born New York, NY, Jan 5, 1944.
Charlie Rose, 62, newscaster, TV host, born Henderson, NC, Jan 5, 1942.
W.D. Snodgrass, 78, poet, born Wilkinsburg, PA, Jan 5, 1926.

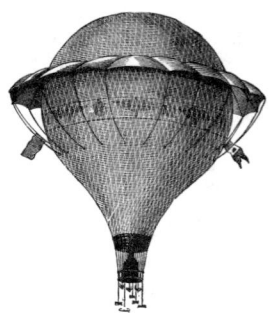

JANUARY 6 — TUESDAY
Day 6 — 360 Remaining

ARMENIAN CHRISTMAS. Jan 6. Christmas is observed in the Armenian Church, the oldest Christian national church.

CARNIVAL SEASON. Jan 6–Feb 24. A secular festival preceding Lent. A time of merrymaking and feasting before the austere days of Lenten fasting and penitence (40 weekdays between Ash Wednesday and Easter Sunday). The word *carnival* probably is derived from the Latin *carnem levare*, meaning "to remove meat." Depending on local custom, the carnival season may start any time between Nov 11 and Shrove Tuesday. Conclusion of the season is much less variable, being the close of Shrove Tuesday in most places. Celebrations vary considerably, but the festival often includes many theatrical aspects (masks, costumes and songs) and has given its name (in the US) to traveling amusement shows that may be seen throughout the year. Observed traditionally in Roman Catholic countries from Epiphany through Shrove Tuesday.

	S	M	T	W	T	F	S
January					1	2	3
2004	4	5	6	7	8	9	10
	11	12	13	14	15	16	17
	18	19	20	21	22	23	24
	25	26	27	28	29	30	31

76

EPIPHANY or TWELFTH DAY. Jan 6. Known also as Old Christmas Day and Twelfthtide. On the twelfth day after Christmas, Christians celebrate the visit of the Magi, the first Gentile recognition of Christ. Epiphany of Our Lord, one of the oldest Christian feasts, is observed in Roman Catholic churches in the US on a Sunday between Jan 2 and 8. Theophany of the Eastern Orthodox Church is observed in churches using the Gregorian calendar (Jan 19 in those churches using the Julian calendar). This feast day celebrates the manifestation of the divinity of Jesus at the time of his baptism in the Jordan River by John the Baptist.

GEORGE H.W. AND BARBARA BUSH WEDDING: ANNIVERSARY. Jan 6, 1945. George Herbert Walker Bush was 20 and Barbara Pierce was 19 when they married. They had four sons and two daughters (one of whom died in childhood). Bush served as the 41st president of the US. Their son George W. Bush became the 43rd president of the US.

GIBRAN, KAHLIL: BIRTH ANNIVERSARY. Jan 6, 1883. Lebanese-American poet (*The Prophet*) and artist. Born at Bsherri, Lebanon, he died Oct 10, 1931, at New York, NY.

"HALLMARK HALL OF FAME" TV PREMIERE: ANNIVERSARY. Jan 6, 1952. Carried at different times by ABC, CBS, NBC and PBS, this was a top-quality dramatic anthology series. Originally titled "Hallmark Television Playhouse," the program was sponsored by Hallmark Cards and hosted by Sarah Churchill until 1955. A few of the presentations were *Hamlet*, with Maurice Evans and Ruth Chatterton (Apr 26, 1953); *Moby Dick*, with Victor Jory (May 16, 1954); *Macbeth*, with Maurice Evans, Dame Judith Anderson and House Jameson (Nov 28, 1954); *Alice in Wonderland*, with Eva LeGallienne, Elsa Lanchester and Reginald Gardiner (Oct 23, 1955). The list goes on with splendid performances by many highly acclaimed actors and actresses.

ITALY: LA BEFANA. Jan 6. Epiphany festival in which the "Befana," a kindly witch, bestows gifts on children—toys and candy for those who have been good, but a lump of coal or a pebble for those who have been naughty. The festival begins on the night of Jan 5 with much noise and merrymaking (when the Befana is supposed to come down the chimneys on her broom, leaving gifts in children's stockings) and continues with joyous fairs, parades and other activities throughout Jan 6.

JAMAICA: MAROON FESTIVAL. Jan 6. Commemorates the 18th-century Treaty of Cudjoe. While Jamaica was a Spanish colony, its native inhabitants (Arawaks) were exterminated. The Spanish then imported African slaves to work their plantations. When the Spanish were driven out (1655), the black slaves fled to the mountains. The "Maroons" (fugitive slaves) were permitted to settle in the north of the island in 1738.

JOAN OF ARC: BIRTH ANNIVERSARY. Jan 6, 1412. Born at the village of Domrémy, in the Meuse River valley of France (probably in 1412). Turned over to an ecclesiastical court by the British, she was tried for heresy and burned to death at the stake May 30, 1431, at age 19; in reality, she was executed for the military action she'd taken against the British on behalf of Charles VII of France.

JOHNSON, BAN: BIRTH ANNIVERSARY. Jan 6, 1863. Byron Bancroft (Ban) Johnson, Baseball Hall of Fame executive, born at Cincinnati, OH. Johnson transformed the minor league Western League into the major league American League in 1901. He ruled as president with an iron hand and was eased out of power by the league's owners in 1927. Inducted into the Hall of Fame in 1937. Died at St. Louis, MO, Mar 28, 1931.

MALESKA, EUGENE T.: BIRTH ANNIVERSARY. Jan 6, 1916. *New York Times* crossword puzzle editor, Maleska was born at Jersey City, NJ. He invented new puzzle formats and clue styles for crossword puzzles in 1977 after a career in education. Maleska died Aug 3, 1993, at Daytona Beach, FL.

MIX, TOM: BIRTH ANNIVERSARY. Jan 6, 1880. American motion picture actor, especially remembered for western cowboy films. Born at Driftwood, PA. Died near Florence, AZ, Oct 12, 1940.

NATIONAL SMITH DAY. Jan 6. The commonest surname in the English-speaking world is Smith. There are an estimated 2,382,500 Smiths in the US. This special day honors the birthday in 1580 of Captain John Smith, the leader of the English colonists who settled at Jamestown, VA, in 1607, thus making him one of the first American Smiths. On this special day, all derivatives, such as Goldsmith, Blacksmith, Printsmith, etc., are invited to participate. To alleviate the escalating costs of Eventological® Literature, a charge of $7 must be assessed for each request. Checks are to be made payable to: Adrienne Sioux Koopersmith, 1437 W Rosemont, #1W, Chicago, IL 60660-1319. Phone: (773) 743-5341. Fax: (773) 743-5395. E-mail: la_koop @yahoo.com.

NEW MEXICO: ADMISSION DAY: ANNIVERSARY. Jan 6, 1912. Became 47th state in 1912.

PAN AM CIRCLES EARTH: ANNIVERSARY. Jan 6, 1942. A Pan American Airways plane arrived in New York to complete the first around-the-world trip by a commercial aircraft.

SALOMON, HAYM: DEATH ANNIVERSARY. Jan 6, 1785. American Revolutionary War patriot and financier was born at Lissa, Poland, in 1740 (exact date unknown). Salomon died at Philadelphia, PA.

SANDBURG, CARL: BIRTH ANNIVERSARY. Jan 6, 1878. American poet, biographer of Lincoln, historian and folklorist, born at Galesburg, IL. Died at Flat Rock, NC, July 22, 1967.

SMITH, JEDEDIAH STRONG: BIRTH ANNIVERSARY. Jan 6, 1799. Mountain man, fur trader and one of the first explorers of the American West, Smith helped develop the Oregon Trail. He was the first American to reach California by land and first to travel by land from San Diego, up the West Coast to the Canadian border. Smith was born at Jericho (now Bainbridge), NY, and was killed by Comanche Indians along the Santa Fe Trail in what is now Kansas on May 27, 1831.

SPACE MILESTONE: *LUNAR EXPLORER* (US). Jan 6, 1998. NASA headed back to the moon for the first time since the Apollo 17 flight 25 years before. This unmanned probe searched for evidence of frozen water on the moon and found evidence of ice in late 1998.

THOMAS, DANNY: BIRTH ANNIVERSARY. Jan 6, 1912. Comedian Danny Thomas was born Muzyad Yakhoob, later Amos Jacobs, at Deerfield, MI. Thomas began his entertainment career as a radio actor and nightclub comedian and then went on to movies in the late 1940s and early 1950s. His greatest fame came from his television show "Make Room for Daddy" (1953–64) and later as a television producer. He was also a tireless philanthropist who founded St. Jude's Children's Research Hospital at Memphis, TN. Thomas died Feb 6, 1991, at Los Angeles, CA.

THREE KINGS DAY. Jan 6. Major festival of Christian Church observed in many parts of the world with gifts, feasting, last lighting of Christmas lights and burning of Christmas greens. Twelfth and last day of the Feast of the Nativity. Commemorates visit of the Three Wise Men (Kings or Magi) to Bethlehem.

"WHEEL OF FORTUNE" TV PREMIERE: ANNIVERSARY. Jan 6, 1975. This daytime quiz show was originally hosted by Chuck Woolery. In 1981 Pat Sajak became host, assisted by Vanna White. A nighttime version was added in 1983. Not to be confused with the human interest show rewarding people who had done good deeds, hosted by Todd Russell, that premiered in 1952.

YOUNG, LORETTA: BIRTH ANNIVERSARY. Jan 6, 1913. Academy Award–winning actress, born at Salt Lake City, UT. She won an Oscar as Best Actress in 1947 for *The Farmer's Daughter* and several Emmys for her television show, "The Loretta Young Show," which ran from 1953 to 1961. She died Aug 12, 2000, at Los Angeles, CA.

BIRTHDAYS TODAY

Joey Lauren Adams, 33, actress (*Chasing Amy, Big Daddy*), born Little Rock, AR, Jan 6, 1971.
Rowan Atkinson, 49, British actor ("Mr Bean"), born Newcastle-upon-Tyne, England, Jan 6, 1955.
E.L. Doctorow, 73, writer (*Ragtime, Welcome to Hard Times*), born New York, NY, Jan 6, 1931.
Bonnie Franklin, 60, actress ("One Day at a Time," *The Kettles in the Ozarks*), born Santa Monica, CA, Jan 6, 1944.
Lou Harris, 83, public opinion analyst, author, born New Haven, CT, Jan 6, 1921.
Louis Leo (Lou) Holtz, 67, former Notre Dame football coach, born Follansbee, WV, Jan 6, 1937.
Howard M. (Howie) Long, 44, sportscaster, Hall of Fame football player, born Somerville, MA, Jan 6, 1960.
Nancy Lopez, 47, Hall of Fame golfer, born Torrance, CA, Jan 6, 1957.
Anthony Minghella, 50, director, writer (*The English Patient, The Talented Mr Ripley*), born Isle of Wight, England, Jan 6, 1954.
Gabrielle Reece, 34, pro volleyball player, born La Jolla, CA, Jan 6, 1970.
Earl Scruggs, 80, musician, born Flint Hill, NC, Jan 6, 1924.
John Singleton, 36, director, screenwriter (*Boyz N the Hood*), born Los Angeles, CA, Jan 6, 1968.
Bob Wise, 56, Governor of West Virginia (D), born Washington, DC, Jan 6, 1948.

JANUARY 7 — WEDNESDAY
Day 7 — 359 Remaining

ADDAMS, CHARLES: BIRTH ANNIVERSARY. Jan 7, 1912. The prolific cartoonist with a macabre sense of humor was born at Westfield, NJ. He became a full-time staff member of *The New Yorker* in 1935 and stayed there for his entire career, producing some 1,300 cartoons. His most famous creation was the ghoulish "Addams Family," who escaped print into television and film. Author of numerous bestselling cartoon collections and the *Charles Addams Mother Goose* (1967), Addams died Sept 29, 1988, at New York, NY. See also: " 'The Addams Family' TV Premiere: Anniversary" (Sept 18).

ALL STATES PICNIC (FOR SENIOR CITIZENS). Jan 7. Yuma, AZ. Seniors from all over the US and Canada gather for picnic lunch, entertainment and fun. Sponsor: City of Yuma Parks and Recreation Department. Est attendance: 1,000. For info: Yuma Civic and Conv Ctr, 1440 Desert Hills Dr, Yuma, AZ 85365. Phone: (928) 373-5043. Fax: (928) 344-9121.

ELVIS PRESLEY'S BIRTHDAY CELEBRATION. Jan 7–11. Graceland, Memphis, TN. Special birthday proclamation on Jan 8 as well as other Elvis birthday events at Graceland. For info: Graceland, 3734 Elvis Presley Blvd, Memphis, TN 38116. Phone: (800) 238-2000 or (901) 332-3322. Web: www.elvis.com.

EMPEROR HIROHITO: 15th DEATH ANNIVERSARY. Jan 7, 1989. After ruling Japan for 62 years as its longest-reigning ruler, Emperor Hirohito died at Tokyo of cancer at 6:33 AM on Jan 7, 1989. His only son, Crown Prince Akihito, succeeded him to the throne later that day.

FILLMORE, MILLARD: BIRTH ANNIVERSARY. Jan 7, 1800. 13th president of the US (July 10, 1850–Mar 3, 1853). Fillmore succeeded to the presidency upon the death of Zachary Taylor, but he did not get the hoped-for nomination from his party in 1852. He ran for president in 1856 as candidate of the "Know-Nothing Party," whose platform demanded, among other things, that every government employee (federal, state and local) should be a native-born citizen. Fillmore was born at Summerhill, NY, and died at Buffalo, NY, Mar 8, 1874. Now his birthday is often used as an occasion for parties for which there is no other reason.

FIRST BALLOON FLIGHT ACROSS ENGLISH CHANNEL: ANNIVERSARY. Jan 7, 1785. Dr. John Jeffries, a Boston physician, and Jean-Pierre Francois Blanchard, French aeronaut, crossed the English Channel from Dover, England, to Calais, France, landing in a forest after being forced to throw overboard all ballast, equipment and even most of their clothing to avoid a forced landing in the icy waters of the English Channel. Blanchard's trousers are said to have been the last article thrown overboard.

FIRST US COMMERCIAL BANK: ANNIVERSARY. Jan 7, 1782. The first commercial bank in the US, the Bank of North America, was opened at Philadelphia.

GARDENIA, VINCENT (VINCENT SCOGNAMIGLIO): BIRTH ANNIVERSARY. Jan 7, 1922. Stage, screen and television performer Vincent Gardenia was born at Naples, Italy. Gardenia once estimated he had played 500 parts in his lifetime. He received two Oscar nominations, one for playing a baseball manager in *Bang the Drum Slowly* and again for the role of patriarch of a goofy Brooklyn family in *Moonstruck*. He won a Tony for his part in *The Prisoner of Second Avenue* and an Emmy for his portrayal in *Age Old Friends*. Vincent Gardenia died Dec 9, 1992, at Philadelphia, PA.

GERMANY: MUNICH FASCHING CARNIVAL. Jan 7–Feb 24. Munich. From Jan 7 through Shrove Tuesday is Munich's famous carnival season. Costume balls are popular throughout carnival. "High points on Fasching Sunday (Feb 22) and Shrove Tuesday (Feb 24) with great carnival doings outside at the Viktualienmarkt and on Pedestrian Mall."

HARLEM GLOBETROTTERS PLAY FIRST GAME: ANNIVERSARY. Jan 7, 1927. Basketball promoter Abe Saperstein's "New York Globetrotters" took the floor on this date at Hinckley, IL. Despite the "New York" in their name, the Globetrotters (who included Inman Jackson, Lester Johnson and Walter Wright) hailed from Chicago's South Side. The talented African-American players—unable to play in white professional leagues—barnstormed the nation in serious basketball promotional events. They changed to "Harlem Globetrotters" in the 1930s and added humor to their games in the 1940s.

January 2004

S	M	T	W	T	F	S
				1	2	3
4	5	6	7	8	9	10
11	12	13	14	15	16	17
18	19	20	21	22	23	24
25	26	27	28	29	30	31

HURSTON, ZORA NEALE: BIRTH ANNIVERSARY. Jan 7, 1891. One of the most important African-American writers of the 20th century was born at Eatonville, FL, to a preacher and former schoolteacher. Hurston attended Barnard College and then became an integral part of the Harlem Renaissance of the 1920s and 1930s. Hurston published four novels in her lifetime, including the classic *Their Eyes Were Watching God* (1937), as well as important anthropological works, short stories, plays and a moving memoir. She was a trailblazer in collecting regional black folklore. Hurston died at Fort Pierce, FL, on Jan 28, 1960.

I'M NOT GOING TO TAKE IT ANYMORE DAY. Jan 7. A day to fight back and take control of all events that happen in one's life. Stand up for your rights—it's so easy to walk away. For info: Bob O'Brien, Consumer Advocate, 1061 Koelle Blvd, Secaucus, NJ 07094. Phone: (201) 860-1595. Fax: (201) 865-4775. E-mail: bobthebestthebest@yahoo.com. Web: www.consumeradvocateobrien.com.

JAPAN: NANAKUSA. Jan 7. Festival dates back to the 7th century and recalls the seven plants served to the emperor that are believed to have great medicinal value—shepherd's purse, chickweed, parsley, cottonweed, radish, hotoke-no-za and aona.

JAPAN: USOKAE (BULLFINCH EXCHANGE FESTIVAL). Jan 7. Dazaifu, Fukuoka Prefecture. "Good Luck" gilded wood bullfinches, mixed among many plain ones, are sought after by the throngs as priests of the Dazaifu Shrine pass them out in the dim light of a small bonfire.

MONTGOLFIER, JACQUES ETIENNE: BIRTH ANNIVERSARY. Jan 7, 1745. Merchant and inventor, born at Vidalon-lez Annonay, Ardèche, France. With his older brother, Joseph Michel, in November 1782, conducted experiments with paper and fabric bags filled with smoke and hot air, which led to the invention of the hot-air balloon and human's first flight. Died at Serrieres, France, Aug 2, 1799. See also: "First Balloon Flight: Anniversary" (June 5); "Aviation History Month" (Nov 1).

MOON PHASE: FULL MOON. Jan 7. Moon enters Full Moon phase at 10:40 AM, EST.

NATIONAL NO-TILLAGE CONFERENCE. Jan 7–10. Des Moines, IA. Attracts innovative farmers interested in reducing tillage to protect the environment and boost profits. Est attendance: 720. For info: Frank Lessiter, Natl No-Tillage Conference, PO Box 624, Brookfield, WI 53008-0624. Phone: (262) 782-4480. Fax: (262) 782-1252. E-mail: info@lesspub.com. Web: www.no-tillfarmer.com.

POL POT OVERTHROWN: 25th ANNIVERSARY. Jan 7, 1979. Pol Pot's Cambodian government fell to combined forces of Cambodian rebels and Vietnamese soldiers.

RUSSIA: CHRISTMAS OBSERVANCE. Jan 7. National holiday.

TRANSATLANTIC PHONING: ANNIVERSARY. Jan 7, 1927. Commercial transatlantic telephone service between New York and London was inaugurated. There were 31 calls made the first day.

BIRTHDAYS TODAY

William Blatty, 76, novelist (*The Exorcist*), screenwriter, born New York, NY, Jan 7, 1928.
Nicolas Cage, 40, actor (*Leaving Las Vegas, Con Air*), born Long Beach, CA, Jan 7, 1964.
David Caruso, 48, actor ("NYPD Blue," "CSI: Miami"), born Forest Hills, NY, Jan 7, 1956.
Katie Couric, 47, cohost ("The Today Show"), born Arlington, VA, Jan 7, 1957.
Dustin Diamond, 27, actor ("Saved by the Bell"), born San Jose, CA, Jan 7, 1977.
Eric Gagne, 28, baseball player, born Montreal, QC, Canada, Jan 7, 1976.
Erin Gray, 54, actress ("Buck Rogers in the 25th Century," "Silver Spoons"), born Honolulu, HI, Jan 7, 1950 (some sources say 1952).
Kenny Loggins, 56, singer (Loggins and Messina, "Your Mama Don't Dance"), songwriter ("What a Fool Believes" with Michael McDonald, won three Grammys), born Everett, WA, Jan 7, 1948.
Terry Moore, 75, actress ("Empire," *Gaslight, Come Back Little Sheba*), born Helen Koford, Los Angeles, CA, Jan 7, 1929.
Paul Revere, 66, singer, pianist (Paul Revere & the Raiders), born Harvard, NE, Jan 7, 1938.
Alfonso Soriano, 26, baseball player, born San Pedro de Macoris, Dominican Republic, Jan 7, 1978.
Jann Wenner, 57, journalist, publisher, *Rolling Stone* magazine, born New York, NY, Jan 7, 1947.

JANUARY 8 — THURSDAY
Day 8 — 358 Remaining

AMERICAN HISTORICAL ASSOCIATION: ANNUAL MEETING. Jan 8–11. Washington, DC. Approximately 180 sessions will be held covering a wide range of scholarly, professional and pedagogical topics dealing with world history. Est attendance: 4,700. For info: Sharon K. Tune, Convention Director, American Historical Assn, 400 A St SE, Washington, DC 20003. Phone: (202) 544-2422. Fax: (202) 544-8307. E-mail: aha@theaha.org. Web: www.theaha.org.

AT&T DIVESTITURE: ANNIVERSARY. Jan 8, 1982. In the most significant antitrust suit since the breakup of Standard Oil in 1911, American Telephone and Telegraph agreed to give up its 22 local Bell System companies ("Baby Bells"). These companies represented 80 percent of AT&T's assets. This ended the corporation's virtual monopoly on US telephone service.

BATTLE OF NEW ORLEANS: ANNIVERSARY. Jan 8, 1815. British forces suffered crushing losses (more than 2,000 casualties) in an attack on New Orleans, LA. Defending US troops were led by General Andrew Jackson, who became a popular hero as a result of the victory. Neither side knew that the War of 1812 had ended two weeks previously with the signing of the Treaty of Ghent, Dec 24, 1814. Battle of New Orleans Day is observed in Louisiana.

BIDDLE, NICHOLAS: BIRTH ANNIVERSARY. Jan 8, 1786. American lawyer, diplomat, statesman and financier who served as president of the Second Bank of the United States. Born at Philadelphia, PA, he died there Feb 27, 1844.

CHOU EN-LAI: DEATH ANNIVERSARY. Jan 8, 1976. Anniversary of the death of Chou En-Lai, premier of the State Council of the People's Republic of China. He was born in 1898 (exact date unknown).

COLLINS, WILLIAM WILKIE: BIRTH ANNIVERSARY. Jan 8, 1824. English novelist, author of *The Moonstone* (one of the first examples of detective fiction), *The Woman in White* and *The Dead Secret*. Born at London, England, he died there Sept 23, 1889.

EARTH'S ROTATION PROVED: ANNIVERSARY. Jan 8, 1851. Using a device now known as Foucault's pendulum in his Paris home, physicist Jean Foucault demonstrated that the Earth rotates on its axis.

ENGLAND: SCHRODERS LONDON INTERNATIONAL BOAT SHOW. Jan 8–18. ExCel, London. 50th show. One of the largest international boat shows in the world, displaying more than 1,000 craft, plus accessories for the marine enthusiast. Est attendance: 200,000. For info: British Marine Federation/Natl Boat Shows Ltd, Marine House, Thorpe Lea Rd, Egham, Surrey, England TW20 8BF. Phone: (44) (1784) 223600 or (44) (178) 447-3377. Fax: (44) (1784) 439678. E-mail: info@britishmarine.co.uk. Web: www.britishmarine.co.uk.

FERRER, JOSE: BIRTH ANNIVERSARY. Jan 8, 1912. Award-winning actor, producer, writer and director was born at Santurce, Puerto Rico. Nominated three times for an Academy Award, he won Best Actor for his role in *Cyrano de Bergerac*. In addition, Ferrer was awarded Tonys and Critics' Circle prizes during half a century in the entertainment world. He died Jan 26, 1992, at Coral Gables, FL.

FOURTEEN POINTS PROPOSED: ANNIVERSARY. Jan 8, 1918. In a speech before a hastily convened joint session of Congress, President Woodrow Wilson presented Fourteen Points for a just peace. The proposal called for reduction of armaments to the lowest point consistent with domestic safety, "open covenants openly arrived at," self-determination of governments and the creation of a League of Nations to preserve peace. Wilson was unable to obtain Allied agreement to his proposals.

GREECE: MIDWIFE'S DAY or WOMEN'S DAY. Jan 8. Midwife's Day or Women's Day is celebrated Jan 8 each year to honor midwives and all women. "On this day women stop their housework and spend their time in cafés, while the men do all the housework chores and look after the children." In some villages, men caught outside "will be stripped . . . and drenched with cold water."

PRESLEY, ELVIS AARON: BIRTH ANNIVERSARY. Jan 8, 1935. Popular American rock singer, born at Tupelo, MS. Although his middle name was spelled incorrectly as "Aron" on his birth certificate, Elvis had it legally changed to "Aaron," which is how it is spelled on his gravestone. Died at Memphis, TN, Aug 16, 1977.

SAINT GUDULA: FEAST DAY. Jan 8. Virgin, patron saint of the city of Brussels. Died Jan 8, probably in the year 712. Her relics were transferred to the church of St. Michael in Brussels.

SAN DIEGO BOAT SHOW. Jan 8–11. San Diego Convention Center, San Diego, CA. Annual show is largest one-stop nautical sports event on the West Coast and features a wide selection of boats and accessories, plus informative boating and fishing seminars. For info: Natl Marine Mfgrs Assn (NMMA), 4901 Morena Blvd, Ste 901, San Diego, CA 92117. Phone: (858) 274-9924. Web: www.boatshows.com or www.discoverboating.com/sandiego.

SHOW AND TELL DAY AT WORK. Jan 8. Since students have show and tell at school, adults should get to do the same. [©2003 by WH.] For info: Thomas & Ruth Roy, Wellcat Holidays, 2418 Long Ln, Lebanon, PA 17046. Phone: (717) 279-0184. E-mail: info@wellcat.com. Web: www.wellcat.com.

SIRANI, ELISABETTA: BIRTH ANNIVERSARY. Jan 8, 1638. Born at Bologna, Italy, Elisabetta Sirani was one of the few women Renaissance artists. Among the 190 pieces done by her during her short life was the 1663 *Virgin and Child*, which was chosen by the US Postal Service as the 1994 traditional holiday stamp. While in her 20s Sarani established a painting school for women. When she died at her native Bologna Aug 28, 1665, the entire city went into mourning for her.

UNIVERSAL LETTER-WRITING WEEK. Jan 8–14. The purpose of this week is for people all over the world to get the new year off to a good start by sending letters and cards to friends and acquaintances not only in their own country but to people throughout the world. For complete information and suggestions about writing good letters, send $5 to cover expense of printing, handling and postage. For info: Dr. Stanley Drake, Pres, Intl Soc of Friendship and Goodwill, 999 Hood Rd, Ste 127, Marietta, GA 30068. Phone: (770) 565-2322. E-mail: ISFGW@bellsouth.net.

WAR ON POVERTY: 40th ANNIVERSARY. Jan 8, 1964. President Lyndon Johnson declared a War on Poverty in his State of the Union address. He stressed improved education as one of the cornerstones of the program. The following Aug 20, he signed a $947.5 million antipoverty bill designed to assist more than 30 million citizens.

BIRTHDAYS TODAY

Shirley Bassey, 67, singer ("Goldfinger"), born Cardiff, Wales, Jan 8, 1937.
David Bowie, 57, musician, actor (*The Labyrinth*), born David Robert Jones, London, England, Jan 8, 1947.
Bob Eubanks, 67, game-show host ("The Newlywed Game"), born Flint, MI, Jan 8, 1937.
Vladimir Feltsman, 52, Russian pianist, born Moscow, USSR, Jan 8, 1952.
Jason Giambi, 33, baseball player, born West Covina, CA, Jan 8, 1971.
Stephen Hawking, 62, British physicist, author (*A Brief History of Time*), born Oxford, England, Jan 8, 1942.
Yvette Mimieux, 62, actress (*The Light in the Piazza*, "The Most Deadly Game"), born Hollywood, CA, Jan 8, 1942 (some sources say 1941).
Kathleen Noone, 58, actress ("Party of Five," "Sunset Beach"), born Hillsdale, NJ, Jan 8, 1946.
Charles Osgood, 71, CBS newsman, born New York, NY, Jan 8, 1933.
Soupy Sales, 78, comedian ("The Soupy Sales Show" may hold record for pies in the face), born Morton Supman, Wake Forest, NC, Jan 8, 1926.
Bob Taft, 62, Governor of Ohio (R), born Boston, MA, Jan 8, 1942.

JANUARY 9 — FRIDAY
Day 9 — 357 Remaining

AVIATION IN AMERICA: ANNIVERSARY. Jan 9, 1793. A Frenchman, Jean-Pierre François Blanchard, made the first manned free-balloon flight in America's history at Philadelphia, PA. The event was watched by President George Washington and many other high government officials. The hydrogen-filled balloon rose to a height of about 5,800 feet, traveled some 15 miles and landed 46 minutes later in New Jersey. Reportedly Blanchard had one passenger on the flight—a little black dog.

CATT, CARRIE LANE CHAPMAN: BIRTH ANNIVERSARY. Jan 9, 1859. American women's rights leader, founder (in 1919) of National League of Women Voters. Born at Ripon, WI, she died at New Rochelle, NY, Mar 9, 1947.

CONNECTICUT RATIFIES CONSTITUTION: ANNIVERSARY. Jan 9, 1788. By a vote of 128 to 40, Connecticut became the fifth state to ratify the Constitution.

	S	M	T	W	T	F	S
January 2004					1	2	3
	4	5	6	7	8	9	10
	11	12	13	14	15	16	17
	18	19	20	21	22	23	24
	25	26	27	28	29	30	31

☆ Chase's 2004 Calendar of Events ☆ Jan 9

FAKE HOWARD HUGHES BIOGRAPHY: ANNIVERSARY. Jan 9, 1972. Reclusive billionaire Howard Hughes held a telephone news conference to state that the biography about him written by Clifford Irving was a fake.

"IT TAKES A THIEF" TV PREMIERE: ANNIVERSARY. Jan 9, 1968. ABC's adventure series starred Robert Wagner as Alexander Mundy, an unlikely thief who agrees to conduct secret government missions instead of serving out his prison term. Malachi Throne costarred as Noah Bain, chief of the SIA and Mundy's employer. Fred Astaire sometimes made recurring cameo appearances as Mundy's father.

NC RV AND CAMPING SHOW. Jan 9–11. Special Events Center, Greensboro Coliseum Complex, Greensboro, NC. A display of the latest in recreation vehicles and accessories by various dealers. Est attendance: 11,000. For info: Apple Rock Advertising & Promotion, 1200 Eastchester Dr, High Point, NC 27265. Phone: (336) 881-7109. Fax: (336) 883-7198. E-mail: rvshows@applerock.com. Web: www.applerock.com.

NIXON, RICHARD MILHOUS: BIRTH ANNIVERSARY. Jan 9, 1913. Richard Nixon served as 36th vice president of the US (under President Dwight D. Eisenhower) Jan 20, 1953, to Jan 20. 1961. He was the 37th president of the US, serving Jan 20, 1969, to Aug 9, 1974, when he resigned the presidency while under the threat of impeachment. First US president to resign that office. He was born at Yorba Linda, CA, and died at New York, NY, Apr 22, 1994.

PANAMA: MARTYRS' DAY. Jan 9. Public holiday.

PHILIPPINES: FEAST OF THE BLACK NAZARENE. Jan 9. Culmination of a nine-day fiesta. Manila's largest procession takes place in the afternoon of Jan 9, in honor of the Black Nazarene, whose shrine is at the Quiapo Church.

"RAWHIDE" TV PREMIERE: 45th ANNIVERSARY. Jan 9, 1959. CBS western that kept them dogies [cattle] rollin' home from northern Texas to Sedalia, KS, for seven years. The series featured Eric Fleming as trail boss Gil Favor; Clint Eastwood as Rowdy Yates, ramrod and trail boss after Fleming's departure from the show; Jim Murdock as Mushy; Paul Brinegar as the cook, Wishbone; Steve Raines as Quince; Rocky Shahan as Joe Scarlet; Sheb Wooley as scout Pete Nolan; Robert Cabal as Hey Soos; John Ireland as Jed Colby; David Watson as Ian Cabot and Raymond St. Jacques as Simon Blake. (St. Jacques was the first African-American regular on the series.) Also remembered for its rollicking theme song.

RV WORKERS AND WORKAMPERS DAY. Jan 9. Idea exchange in conjunction with the Workamper Job Fair in Yuma, AZ. Est attendance: 2,500. For info: Jaimie Hall, 127 Rainbow Dr #2780, Livingston, TX 77399-1027. Phone: (928) 607-3181. Fax: (561) 892-2837. E-mail: calamityjaimie@escapees.com. Web: www.rvhometown.com.

"3rd ROCK FROM THE SUN" TV PREMIERE: ANNIVERSARY. Jan 9, 1996. In this comedy a quartet of space aliens who had taken on human form came to Earth to spy on its natives. They were led by Dick Solomon, played by John Lithgow, who fell in love with earthling Mary Albright, played by Jane Curtin. Other cast members included Kristen Johnston, French Stewart and Joseph Gordon-Levitt. Though it won a slew of Emmys, NBC bounced the series around to more than a dozen time slots, damaging the ratings, and finally pulled the show after six seasons.

US LANDING ON LUZON: ANNIVERSARY. Jan 9, 1945. US forces began the final push to retake the Philippines by attacking at the same location where the Japanese had begun their invasion nearly four years earlier. General Douglas MacArthur landed 67,000 troops in the Gulf of Lingayen on the western coast of the big island of Luzon. The Japanese offered little opposition to the landing itself but fought fiercely against Allied advancement, particularly around Clarke Field, the major air base in the islands.

VAN CLEEF, LEE: BIRTH ANNIVERSARY. Jan 9, 1925. Actor Lee Van Cleef was born at Somerville, NJ. He appeared in many westerns and action films including *High Noon* (1952), *The Man Who Shot Liberty Valance* (1962), *The Good, the Bad and the Ugly* (1967) and *Escape from New York* (1981). Van Cleef died on Dec 16, 1989, at Oxnard, CA.

YORBA LINDA, CALIFORNIA: NIXON BIRTHDAY HOLIDAY. Jan 9. Yorba Linda, the birthplace in 1913 of former president Richard M. Nixon, became the first community officially to declare his birth anniversary a public holiday. In announcing the declaration Sept 20, 1989, Mayor Henry Wedaa said, "We're not here to judge history—we're here to recognize it." The first observance by Yorba Linda's municipal employees took place in 1990.

YOUNG, MURAT BERNARD "CHIC": BIRTH ANNIVERSARY. Jan 9, 1901. The comic strip "Blondie" was created by Murat Bernard "Chic" Young in 1930. Originally about a jazz-age flapper who marries a playboy from a socially prominent family, "Blondie" soon changed its direction: two children and a dog were added to the cast, Dagwood became a working stiff and the strip focused on middle-class family situations and problems. "Blondie" introduced America to the "dagwood," an enormous sandwich made during Dagwood's late-night forays in the refrigerator. Chic Young was born at Chicago, IL, and died at St. Petersburg, FL, Mar 14, 1973.

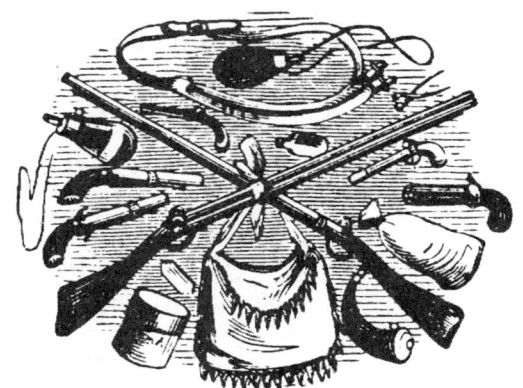

BIRTHDAYS TODAY

Joan Baez, 63, folksinger, born Staten Island, NY, Jan 9, 1941.
Tyrone Curtis ("Muggsy") Bogues, 39, former basketball player, born Baltimore, MD, Jan 9, 1965.
Bob Denver, 69, actor ("The Many Loves of Dobie Gillis," "Gilligan's Island"), born New Rochelle, NY, Jan 9, 1935.
Richard Allen (Dick) Enberg, 69, sportscaster, born Mount Clemens, MI, Jan 9, 1935.
Sergio Garcia, 24, golfer, born Borriol, Spain, Jan 9, 1980.
Crystal Gayle, 53, singer ("Don't It Make My Brown Eyes Blue"), born Brenda Gayle Webb, Paintsville, KY, Jan 9, 1951.
Mat Hoffman, 32, BMX bike racer, born Oklahoma City, OK, Jan 9, 1972.
Judith Krantz, 76, author (*Dazzle, Scruples*), born Judith Tarcher, New York, NY, Jan 9, 1928.
Dave Matthews, 37, singer, musician (The Dave Matthews Band), born Johannesburg, South Africa, Jan 9, 1967.
Joely Richardson, 39, actress (*101 Dalmatians*), born London, England, Jan 9, 1965.
J.K. Simmons, 49, actor ("Law & Order," *Spiderman*), born Detroit, MI, Jan 9, 1955.
Byron Bartlett (Bart) Starr, 70, Hall of Fame football player and former coach, born Montgomery, AL, Jan 9, 1934.
Susannah York, 63, actress (*Tom Jones; They Shoot Horses, Don't They?; Superman*), born London, England, Jan 9, 1941.

JANUARY 10 — SATURDAY
Day 10 — 356 Remaining

COMMON SENSE PUBLISHED: ANNIVERSARY. Jan 10, 1776. More than any other publication, *Common Sense* influenced the authors of the Declaration of Independence. Thomas Paine's 50-page pamphlet sold more than 500,000 copies within a few months of its first printing.

FIRST UNITED NATIONS GENERAL ASSEMBLY: ANNIVERSARY. Jan 10, 1946. On the 26th anniversary of the establishment of the unsuccessful League of Nations, delegates from 51 nations met at London, England, for the first meeting of the UN General Assembly.

HENRIED, PAUL: BIRTH ANNIVERSARY. Jan 10, 1908. Actor Paul Henried once estimated that he had played in or directed more than 300 films. Though a staunch anti-Nazi, his early film parts included a number of German roles, including those in *Goodbye Mr Chips* and *Night Train*. He eventually moved away from the German stereotype in such films as *Of Human Bondage*, *The Four Horsemen of the Apocalypse* and as Victor Laslo in *Casablanca*. His film career cut short by the anti-Communist blacklist in Hollywood during the 1940s, Henried found a second calling as a director, with more than 80 episodes of TV's "Alfred Hitchcock Presents" to his credit. Born at Trieste, Austria, he died Mar 29, 1992, at Pacific Palisades, CA.

JEFFERS, ROBINSON: BIRTH ANNIVERSARY. Jan 10, 1887. American poet and playwright. Born at Pittsburgh, PA, he died at Carmel, CA, Jan 20, 1962.

LEAGUE OF NATIONS FOUNDING: ANNIVERSARY. Jan 10, 1920. Through the Treaty of Versailles, the League of Nations came into existence. Fifty nations entered into a covenant designed to avoid war. The US never joined the League of Nations, which was dissolved Apr 18, 1946.

"MASTERPIECE THEATRE" TV PREMIERE: ANNIVERSARY. Jan 10, 1971. Television at its best, PBS's long-running anthology series consists of many highly acclaimed original and adapted dramatizations. Many are produced by the BBC. Alistair Cooke and Russell Baker have hosted the program. The first presentation was "The First Churchills." Other notable programs include: "Jude the Obscure," "The Six Wives of Henry VIII" and "Elizabeth R" (1972); "Upstairs Downstairs" (1974–77); "I, Claudius" (1978); "The Jewel in the Crown" (1984); "Bleak House" (1985); and "A Tale of Two Cities" (1989).

MONSTER TRUCK WINTER NATIONALS. Jan 10–11. MultiPurpose Events Center, Wichita Falls, TX. Monster truck racing, AMA-sanctioned motor cross racing. Est attendance: 8,000. For info: Wichita Falls CVB, 1000 5th St, Wichita Falls, TX 76301. Phone: (940) 716-5500. Fax: (940) 716-5509. E-mail: MPEC@wf.net. Web: www.wichitafalls.org or www.mpecwf.com.

NATIONAL WESTERN STOCK SHOW AND RODEO. Jan 10–25. Denver, CO. 98th annual. It's a rodeo and more! See horse shows, Colorado's largest trade show, Western art and educational displays and the Super Bowl of livestock shows. Est attendance: 640,000. For info: Natl Western Stock Show and Rodeo, 4655 Humboldt St, Denver, CO 80216. Phone: (303) 297-1166 or (800) 336-6977. Fax: (303) 292-1708. Web: www.nationalwestern.com.

PENNSYLVANIA FARM SHOW. Jan 10–17. Harrisburg, PA. The largest indoor agricultural event in America. For info: Pennsylvania Dept of Agriculture, State Farm Products Show Commission, 2301 N Cameron St, Harrisburg, PA 17110. Phone: (717) 783-3071. Web: www.agriculture.state.pa.us.

SPACE MILESTONE: *SOYUZ 17* (USSR). Jan 10, 1975. Launched on this date, cosmonauts A. Gubarev and G. Grechko completed a 30-day space flight, landing Feb 9. Cosmonauts spent 28 days aboard *Salyut 4*, orbiting space station. With the exception of *Soyuz 19*, the *Soyuz* craft were now used as ferries to the *Salyut* space stations. More than 20 more flights were made.

SPACE MILESTONE: *SOYUZ 27* (USSR). Jan 10, 1978. Launched on this date, cosmonauts Vladimir Dzhanibekov and Oleg Makarov linked with *Salyut 6* space station, which was already occupied by the crew of *Soyuz 26*. Returned to Earth Jan 16 in *Soyuz 26*.

US AND VATICAN REESTABLISH DIPLOMATIC RELATIONS: 20th ANNIVERSARY. Jan 10, 1984. The US and the Vatican established full diplomatic relations after a break of 117 years.

WELCOME BACK SNOWBIRDS PANCAKE BREAKFAST. Jan 10. El Centro, CA. Annually, the second Saturday in January. Est attendance: 2,500. For info: El Centro Chamber of Commerce, Box 3006, El Centro, CA 92244. Phone: (760) 352-3681. Fax: (760) 352-3246. Web: www.elcentrochamber.com.

WILDERNESS WILDLIFE WEEK OF NATURE. Jan 10–18. Music Road Hotel & Convention Center, Pigeon Forge, TN. 14th annual no-cost week of walks, talks and workshops led by experts in their various fields. Est attendance: 12,000. For info: Office of Special Events, Pigeon Forge Dept of Tourism, 3107 Parkway, PO Box 1390, Pigeon Forge, TN 37868-1390. Phone: (800) 251-9100 or (865) 429-7350. Fax: (865) 429-7392. E-mail: events@cityofpigeonforge.com. Web: www.mypigeonforge.com.

WOMEN'S SUFFRAGE AMENDMENT INTRODUCED IN CONGRESS: ANNIVERSARY. Jan 10, 1878. Senator A.A. Sargent of California, a close friend of Susan B. Anthony, introduced into the US Senate a women's suffrage amendment known as the Susan B. Anthony Amendment. It wasn't until Aug 26, 1920, 42 years later, that the amendment was signed into law.

BIRTHDAYS TODAY

Pat Benatar, 51, singer, born Patricia Andrejewski, Brooklyn, NY, Jan 10, 1953.
George Edward Foreman, 55, boxer, born Marshall, TX, Jan 10, 1949.
Gisele Mackenzie, 77, singer ("Hard to Get," regular on "Your Hit Parade"), born Winnipeg, MB, Canada, Jan 10, 1927.
Mark Pryor, 41, US Senator (D, Arkansas), born Fayetteville, AR, Jan 10, 1963.
Glenn Robinson, 31, basketball player, born Gary, IN, Jan 10, 1973.
Rod Stewart, 59, singer, musician ("Maggie May," "Do Ya Think I'm Sexy?"), born London, England, Jan 10, 1945.
William Anthony (Bill) Toomey, 65, Olympic gold medal decathlete, born Philadelphia, PA, Jan 10, 1939.

☆ Chase's 2004 Calendar of Events ☆   Jan 11

JANUARY 11 — SUNDAY
Day 11 — 355 Remaining

CUCKOO DANCING WEEK. Jan 11–17. To honor the memory of Laurel and Hardy, whose theme, "The Dancing Cuckoos," shall be heard throughout the land as their movies are seen and their antics greeted by laughter by old and new fans of these unique masters of comedy. [Originated by the late William T. Rabe of Sault Ste. Marie, MI.]

"DESIGNATED HITTER" RULE ADOPTED: ANNIVERSARY. Jan 11, 1973. American League adopted the "designated hitter" rule, whereby an additional player is used to bat for the pitcher.

FIRST BLACK SOUTHERN LIEUTENANT GOVERNOR: ANNIVERSARY. Jan 11, 1986. L. Douglas Wilder was sworn in as lieutenant governor of Virginia. He was the first black elected to statewide office in the South since Reconstruction. He later served as governor of Virginia.

HAMILTON, ALEXANDER: BIRTH ANNIVERSARY. Jan 11, 1755. American statesman, an author of *The Federalist* papers, first secretary of the treasury, born at British West Indies. Engaged in a duel with Aaron Burr the morning of July 11, 1804, at Weehawken, NJ. Mortally wounded there and died July 12, 1804.

HOME OFFICE SAFETY AND SECURITY WEEK. Jan 11–17. One week each year dedicated to ensuring that the more than 30 million American home offices are safeguarded and protected against break-ins, theft, workplace injury, computer virus and hacking, natural disaster and any other malady that can impact the at-home worker. For info: Jeff Zbar, PO Box 8263, Coral Springs, FL 33075. Phone: (954) 346-4393. Fax: (954) 346-0251. E-mail: jeff@chiefhomeofficer.com. Web: www.chiefhomeofficer.com.

HOSTOS, EUGENIO MARIA: BIRTH ANNIVERSARY. Jan 11, 1839. Puerto Rican patriot, scholar and author of more than 50 books. Born at Rio Canas, Puerto Rico, he died at Santo Domingo, Dominican Republic, Aug 11, 1903.

INTERNATIONAL PRINTING WEEK. Jan 11–17. To develop public awareness of the printing/graphic arts industry. Annually, the week including Ben Franklin's birthday, Jan 17. For info: Kevin P. Keane, Exec Dir, Intl Assn of Printing House Craftsmen, 7042 Brooklyn Blvd, Minneapolis, MN 55429-1370. Phone: (800) 466-4274. Web: www.iaphc.org.

INTERNATIONAL THANK YOU DAYS. Jan 11–18. An eight-day period in which to thank someone from your past or present who did something nice for you. Visit, write, call, fax or e-mail him or her and say thank you. [©1994] Because of the escalating costs of Eventological® Literature, a charge of $7 must be assessed for each request. Checks are to be made payable to: Adrienne Sioux Koopersmith, 1437 W Rosemont, #1W, Chicago, IL 60660-1319. Phone: (773) 743-5341. Fax: (773) 743-5395. E-mail: la_koop@yahoo.com.

JAMES, WILLIAM: BIRTH ANNIVERSARY. Jan 11, 1842. American psychologist and philosopher of distinguished family that included his brother, novelist Henry James. "There is no worse fear," he wrote in *Varieties of Religious Experience* (1902), "than a truth misunderstood by those who hear it." Born at New York City, he died at Chocorua, NH, Aug 26, 1910.

MacDONALD, JOHN A.: BIRTH ANNIVERSARY. Jan 11, 1815. Canadian statesman, first prime minister of Canada. Born at Glasgow, Scotland, he died June 6, 1891, at Ottawa. His birth anniversary is observed in Canada.

MOROCCO: INDEPENDENCE DAY. Jan 11. National holiday. Commemorates the date in 1944 when the Independence Party submitted a memo to the Allied authorities asking for independence under a constitutional regime. Morocco gained independence from France in 1956.

NEPAL: NATIONAL UNITY DAY. Jan 11. Celebration paying homage to King Prithvinarayan Shah (1723–75), founder of the present house of rulers of Nepal and creator of the unified Nepal of today.

PAUL, ALICE: BIRTH ANNIVERSARY. Jan 11, 1885. Women's rights leader and founder of the National Woman's Party in 1913, advocate of an equal rights amendment to the US Constitution. Born at Moorestown, NJ, she died there July 10, 1977.

SWITZERLAND: MEITLISUNNTIG. Jan 11. On Meitlisunntig, the second Sunday in January, the girls of Meisterschwanden and Fahrwangen, in the Seetal district of Aargau, Switzerland, stage a procession in historical uniforms and a military parade before a female General Staff. According to tradition, the custom dates from the Villmergen War of 1712, when the women of both communes gave vital help that led to victory. Popular festival follows the procession.

THEODOSIUS I: BIRTH ANNIVERSARY. Jan 11, 347. Roman emperor known as Theodosius the Great was born at Cauca, Gallaecia, in Spain. In 379 Theodosius was summoned by the emperor Gratian to become emperor of the east. On Feb 28, 380, without consulting religious authorities, he issued the edict that made the Nicene Creed (in which God the Father, the Son and the Holy Spirit are all of the same substance) binding on all subjects. Only those who accepted it would be considered Christians; this was the first recorded use of that designation. Theodosius engaged in a continuing struggle with the west for power. He prohibited pagan worship, but the emperors of the west had strong connections with pagan aristocracy. The two sides came to blows in 394. His final victory in September of that year was seen as a divine victory in which the Christian God had triumphed over the Roman gods. Theodosius died in January 395.

US SURGEON GENERAL DECLARES CIGARETTES HAZARDOUS: 40th ANNIVERSARY. Jan 11, 1964. US Surgeon General Luther Terry issued the first government report saying that smoking may be hazardous to one's health.

WARMEST YEAR ON RECORD DECLARED: ANNIVERSARY. Jan 11, 1999. NASA declared 1998 the warmest year on record. Global surface temperatures increased by 0.34 of a degree Fahrenheit. The average temperature of 58.496 degrees Fahrenheit eclipsed the previous record set in 1995. The 1998 warmth was associated partly with a strong El Niño, a periodic warming of the Pacific Ocean.

BIRTHDAYS TODAY

Mary J. Blige, 33, pop singer, born the Bronx, NY, Jan 11, 1971.
Jean Chretien, 70, 20th prime minister of Canada, born Shawinigan, QC, Canada, Jan 11, 1934.
Clarence Clemons, 62, musician, singer, born Norfolk, VA, Jan 11, 1942.
Ben Daniel Crenshaw, 52, golfer, born Austin, TX, Jan 11, 1952.
Jim Hightower, 61, radio host, author (*Hard Tomatoes, Hard Times; Eat Your Heart Out*), born Denison, TX, Jan 11, 1943.
Naomi Judd, 58, country singer ("Have Mercy," "Why Not Me"), born Ashland, KY, Jan 11, 1946.
Christine Kaufmann, 59, actress (*Taras Bulba, Bagdad Cafe*), born Lansdorf Graz, Austria, Jan 11, 1945.
Amanda Peet, 32, actress (*Saving Silverman*, "Jack & Jill"), born New York, NY, Jan 11, 1972.
Rod Taylor, 74, actor (*The Birds*, "Masquerade"), born Sydney, Australia, Jan 11, 1930.
Grant Tinker, 78, TV executive, born Stamford, CT, Jan 11, 1926.
Stanley Tucci, 44, actor (*Big Night*, "Murder One"), born Katonah, NY, Jan 11, 1960.

Jan 12 ☆ *Chase's 2004 Calendar of Events* ☆

JANUARY 12 — MONDAY
Day 12 — 354 Remaining

"ALL IN THE FAMILY" TV PREMIERE: ANNIVERSARY. Jan 12, 1971. Based on the success of the British comedy "Till Death Us Do Part," Norman Lear created CBS's controversial sitcom "All in the Family." The series was the first of its kind to realistically portray the prevailing issues and taboos of its time with a wickedly humorous bent. From bigotry to birth control, few topics were considered too sacred to discuss on air. Ultraconservative Archie Bunker (played by Carroll O'Connor) held court from his recliner, spewing invective at any who disagreed with him. Jean Stapleton portrayed Archie's dutiful wife, Edith. Sally Struthers and Rob Reiner rounded out the cast as Archie's liberal daughter and son-in-law, Gloria and Mike "Meathead" Stivic. All three characters often fell victim to Archie's zinging one-liners and insults. The series had a 12-year run.

"BATMAN" TV PREMIERE: ANNIVERSARY. Jan 12, 1966. ABC's crime-fighting show gained a place in Nielsen's top 10 ratings in its first season. The series was based on the DC Comics characters created by Bob Kane in 1939. Adam West starred as millionaire Bruce Wayne and superhero alter ego, Batman. Burt Ward costarred as Dick Grayson/Robin, the Boy Wonder. An assortment of villains guest-starring each week included: Cesar Romero as the Joker, Eartha Kitt and Julie Newmar as Catwoman, Burgess Meredith as the Penguin and Frank Gorshin as the Riddler. Some other stars making memorable appearances included Liberace, Vincent Price, Milton Berle, Tallulah Bankhead and Ethel Merman. The series played up its comic-strip roots with innovative and sharply skewed camera angles, bright bold colors and wild graphics. Although the last telecast was Mar 14, 1968, "Batman's" memorable theme song, composed by Neal Hefti, can be heard today with some 120 episodes in syndication.

"THE BELL TELEPHONE HOUR" TV PREMIERE: 45th ANNIVERSARY. Jan 12, 1959. NBC's musical series ran semi-regularly for nearly 10 seasons. The Bell Telephone Orchestra was conducted by Donald Voorhees.

BURKE, EDMUND: 275th BIRTH ANNIVERSARY. Jan 12, 1729. British orator, politician and philosopher, born at Dublin, Ireland. "Superstition is the religion of feeble minds," he wrote in 1790, but best remembered is "The only thing necessary for the triumph of evil is for good men to do nothing," not found in his writings but almost universally attributed to Burke. Died at Beaconsfield, England, July 9, 1797.

CONGRESS AUTHORIZED USE OF FORCE AGAINST IRAQ: ANNIVERSARY. Jan 12, 1991. The US Congress passed a resolution authorizing the president of the US to use force to expel Iraq from Kuwait. This was the sixth congressional vote in US history declaring war or authorizing force on another nation.

"DYNASTY" TV PREMIERE: ANNIVERSARY. Jan 12, 1981. The popular ABC prime-time serial focused on the high-flying exploits of the Denver-based Carrington family. The series had a weekly wardrobe budget of $10,000 with many elegant costumes designed by Nolan Miller. In addition to the juicy storylines, many tuned in worldwide to view the palatial mansions and lavish sets. John Forsythe played patriarch Blake Carrington with Linda Evans as his wife, Krystle. Joan Collins played Alexis, Blake's scheming ex-wife and arch business rival. Other cast members included Kathleen Beller, Pamela Bellwood, Diahann Carroll, Jack Coleman, John James, Heather Locklear, Pamela Sue Martin, Ted McGinley, Michael Nader, Catherine Oxenberg, Emma Samms and Gordon Thomson. Notable guest stars included William Campbell, James Farentino, George Hamilton, Charlton Heston, Rock Hudson, Billy Dee Williams and many others.

ENGLAND: PLOUGH MONDAY. Jan 12. Always the Monday after Twelfth Day. Work on the farm is resumed after the festivities of the 12 days of Christmas. On preceding Sunday ploughs may be blessed in churches. Celebrated with dances and plays.

FARMER, JAMES: BIRTH ANNIVERSARY. Jan 12, 1920. Civil Rights leader, born at Marshall, TX. Farmer was one of the founders of CORE, the Congress of Racial Equality, a volunteer organization established in 1942 to improve race relations and eliminate discriminatory practices. Farmer led the nonviolent fight to desegregate buses and terminals in 1961, known as the Freedom Rides. He received the Presidential Medal of Freedom in 1998. Died at Fredericksburg, VA, July 9, 1999.

FIRST ELECTED WOMAN SENATOR: ANNIVERSARY. Jan 12, 1932. Hattie W. Caraway, a Democrat from Arkansas, was the first woman elected to the US Senate. Born in 1878, Caraway was appointed to the Senate on Nov 13, 1931, to fill out the term of her husband, Senator Thaddeus Caraway, who had died a few days earlier. On Jan 12, 1932, she won a special election to fill the remaining months of his term. Subsequently elected to two more terms, she served in the Senate until January 1945. She was an adept and tireless legislator (once introducing 43 bills on the same day) who worked for women's rights (once cosponsoring an equal rights amendment) and supported New Deal policies. She died Dec 21, 1950, at Falls Church, VA. The first woman appointed to the Senate was Mrs W.H. Felton in 1922 who served for two days. The first woman to be elected to the Senate without having been appointed first was Margaret Chase Smith of Maine, who had served first in the House. She was elected to the Senate in 1948.

GRAVES' DISEASE AWARENESS WEEK. Jan 12–16. Graves' disease is an abnormality in the autoimmune system, causing production of antibodies that attach to the thyroid, enlargement of the gland and overproduction of thyroid hormone. Similar antibodies may also cause swelling of the eye muscles and swelling in the skin on the front of the lower leg. Graves' disease occurs in less than ¼ of 1 percent of the general population. Most people with Graves' disease are treated and then managed on hormone replacement. Because some people with Graves' disease are misdiagnosed and because it is an illness that occurs in all age groups, education and support continue to be vital. Annually, the second week in January. For info: Graves' Disease Foundation, PO Box 1969, Brevard, NC 28712. Phone: (828) 877-5251. Fax: (828) 885-7122. E-mail: ngdf@citcom.net. Web: www.ngdf.org.

HAYES, IRA HAMILTON: BIRTH ANNIVERSARY. Jan 12, 1922. Ira Hayes was one of six US Marines who raised the American flag on Iwo Jima's Mount Suribachi, Feb 23, 1945, following a US assault on the Japanese stronghold. The event was immortalized by AP photographer Joe Rosenthal's famous photo and later by a Marine War Memorial monument at Arlington, VA. Hayes was born on a Pima Indian Reservation at Arizona. He returned home after WWII a much celebrated hero but was unable to cope with fame. He was found dead of "exposure to freezing weather and overconsumption of alcohol" on the Sacaton Indian Reservation at Arizona, Jan 24, 1955.

January 2004	S	M	T	W	T	F	S
					1	2	3
	4	5	6	7	8	9	10
	11	12	13	14	15	16	17
	18	19	20	21	22	23	24
	25	26	27	28	29	30	31

☆ Chase's 2004 Calendar of Events ☆   Jan 12–13

INTIMATE APPAREL MARKET WEEK. Jan 12–16. (Also Mar 1–5, May 10–14, Aug 2–6 and Nov 1–5.) Market week dates for the intimate apparel industry. For info: Mary Howell, Dir of Specialty Markets, American Apparel & Footwear Assn, 1601 N Kent St, Ste 1200, Arlington, VA 22209. Phone: (703) 524-1864. Fax: (703) 522-6741. Web: www.apparelandfootwear.org.

JAPAN: COMING-OF-AGE DAY. Jan 12. National holiday for youth of the country who have reached adulthood during the preceding year. Annually, the second Monday in January.

LONDON, JACK: BIRTH ANNIVERSARY. Jan 12, 1876. American author of more than 50 books: short stories, novels and travel stories of the sea and of the far north, many marked by brutal realism. His most widely known work is *The Call of the Wild*, the great dog story published in 1903. London was born at San Francisco, CA. He died of gastrointestinal uremia on Nov 22, 1916, near Santa Rosa, CA.

MISSION SANTA CLARA DE ASIS: FOUNDING ANNIVERSARY. Jan 12, 1777. California mission built by followers of Father Junipero Serra to educate the Indians. In the 1850s, the mission became Santa Clara University, the oldest university in California. The current building, used by the University as its chapel, is a replica of an older building that was destroyed by fire in 1926.

NATIONAL CLEAN-OFF-YOUR-DESK DAY. Jan 12. To provide one day early each year for every desk worker to see the top of the desk and prepare for the following year's paperwork. Annually, the second Monday in January. For info: A.C. Moeller, Box 71, Clio, MI 48420-1042.

NATIONAL THANK GOD IT'S MONDAY! DAY. Jan 12. Besides holidays, such as President's Day, being celebrated on Mondays, people everywhere start new jobs, have birthdays, celebrate promotions and begin vacations on Mondays. A day in recognition of this first day of the week. For info: Dorothy Zjawin, 61 W Colfax Ave, Roselle Park, NJ 07204. Phone: (908) 241-6241.

TANZANIA: ZANZIBAR REVOLUTION DAY. Jan 12. National day. Zanzibar became independent in December 1963, under a sultan; the sultan was overthrown on this day in 1964.

WINTHROP, JOHN: BIRTH ANNIVERSARY. Jan 12, 1588 (OS). American colonial governor of Massachusetts Bay Colony, born at Edwardston, England. Governor Winthrop kept a diary of events in the Massachusetts Bay Colony, published nearly two centuries later (in 1825–26), titled *The History of New England from 1630 to 1649*. Died at Boston, MA, Mar 26, 1649 (OS).

WOMEN DENIED VOTE: ANNIVERSARY. Jan 12, 1915. The US House of Representatives rejected a proposal to give women the right to vote. Women gained the right to vote in 1920.

BIRTHDAYS TODAY

Kirstie Alley, 49, actress (Emmy for "Cheers"; *Look Who's Talking*, "Veronica's Closet"), born Wichita, KS, Jan 12, 1955.

Jeff Bezos, 40, founder (Amazon.com), born New Mexico, Jan 12, 1964.

Joe Frazier, 60, former boxer, born Beaufort, SC, Jan 12, 1944.

HAL, 12, computer in *2001: A Space Odyssey*, by Arthur C. Clarke, "born" Urbana, IL, Jan 12, 1992.

Marian Hossa, 25, hockey player, born Stara Lubovna, Czechoslovakia, Jan 12, 1979.

Rush Limbaugh, 53, talk-show host ("The Rush Limbaugh Show"), born Cape Girardeau, MO, Jan 12, 1951.

Ray Price, 78, country singer, born Perryville, TX, Jan 12, 1926.

Luise Rainer, 94, actress (Oscars for *The Great Ziegfeld* and *The Good Earth*), born Vienna, Austria, Jan 12, 1910 (some sources say 1912).

Howard Stern, 50, radio and TV personality ("The Howard Stern Show"), born Queens, NY, Jan 12, 1954.

JANUARY 13 — TUESDAY
Day 13 — 353 Remaining

ALGER, HORATIO, JR: BIRTH ANNIVERSARY. Jan 13, 1834. American clergyman and author of more than 100 popular books for boys (some 20 million copies sold). Honesty, frugality and hard work assured that the heroes of his books would find success, wealth and fame. Born at Revere, MA, he died at Natick, MA, July 18, 1899.

CHASE, SALMON PORTLAND: BIRTH ANNIVERSARY. Jan 13, 1808. American statesman, born at Cornish, NH. US senator, secretary of the treasury and chief justice of the Supreme Court. Salmon P. Chase spent much of his life fighting slavery (he was popularly known as "attorney general for runaway Negroes"). He was one of the founders of the Republican Party and his hopes for becoming candidate for president of the US in 1856 and 1860 were dashed because his unconcealed antislavery views made him unacceptable. Died at New York, NY, May 7, 1873.

FULLER, ALFRED CARL: BIRTH ANNIVERSARY. Jan 13, 1885. Founder of the Fuller Brush Company, born at Kings County, NS, Canada. In 1906 the young brush salesman went into business on his own, making brushes at a bench between the furnace and the coal bin in his sister's basement. Died at Hartford, CT, Dec 4, 1973.

NORWAY: TYVENDEDAGEN. Jan 13. "20th Day," the traditional end of the Christmas season. Also commemorated as St. Knut's Day (Tjugondag Knut or "The 20th Day of Knut") in Sweden.

RADIO BROADCASTING: ANNIVERSARY. Jan 13, 1910. Radio pioneer and electron tube inventor Lee De Forest arranged the world's first radio broadcast to the public at New York, NY. He succeeded in broadcasting the voice of Enrico Caruso along with other stars of the Metropolitan Opera to several receiving locations in the city where listeners with earphones marveled at wireless music from the air. Though only a few were equipped to listen, it was the first broadcast to reach the public and the beginning of a new era in which wireless radio communication became almost universal. See also: "First Scheduled Radio Broadcast: Anniv" (Nov 2).

RUSSIA: OLD NEW YEAR'S EVE. Jan 13. Although Jan 1 is the official New Year's Day in Russia, some Russians still celebrate on the old Julian date of Jan 13–14. Also celebrated in Belarus and Ukraine.

"THE SOPRANOS" TV PREMIERE: 5th ANNIVERSARY. Jan 13, 1999. The thinking viewer's mob drama, "The Sopranos" features James Gandolfini as Tony Soprano, whose panic attacks drive him to seek out a psychiatrist (Lorraine Bracco). The HBO drama revolves around Tony's home and crime lives. *TV Guide* has named the series one of the greatest TV shows of all time.

TOGO: LIBERATION DAY: ANNIVERSARY. Jan 13. National holiday. Commemorates 1967 uprising.

VERDON, GWEN: BIRTH ANNIVERSARY. Jan 13, 1926. One of Broadway's premier female dancers and actresses, many of her most successful roles were choreographed by her husband, Bob Fosse. She won Tony Awards for *Can-Can*, *Damn Yankees*, *New Girl in Town* and *Redhead*. She also acted in movies, including *Cocoon* and the film adaption of *Damn Yankees*. Born in Los Angeles, CA, she died Oct 18, 2000, at Woodstock, VT.

BIRTHDAYS TODAY

Kevin Anderson, 44, actor (*Hoffa*, *Rising Sun*), born Gurnee, IL, Jan 13, 1960.

Orlando Bloom, 27, actor (*The Lord of the Rings* trilogy), born Canterbury, Kent, England, Jan 13, 1977.

Keith Coogan, 34, actor (*Adventures in Babysitting*, *Cousins*), born Palm Springs, CA, Jan 13, 1970.

Patrick Dempsey, 38, actor (*Heaven Help Us, In the Mood*), born Lewiston, ME, Jan 13, 1966.
Nicole Eggert, 32, actress ("Baywatch," "Charles in Charge"), born Glendale, CA, Jan 13, 1972.
Frank Gallo, 71, artist, sculptor, born Toledo, OH, Jan 13, 1933.
Julia Louis-Dreyfus, 43, actress ("Seinfeld"), born New York, NY, Jan 13, 1961.
Jay McInerney, 49, writer (*Bright Lights, Big City*), born Hartford, CT, Jan 13, 1955.
Penelope Ann Miller, 40, actress (*Adventures in Babysitting, The Freshman, Carlito's Way*), born Los Angeles, CA, Jan 13, 1964.
Richard Moll, 61, actor ("Night Court," *Wicked Stepmother, The Flintstones*), born Pasadena, CA, Jan 13, 1943.
Charles Nelson Reilly, 73, director, actor ("The Ghost and Mrs Muir," "Match Game PM"), born New York, NY, Jan 13, 1931.
Frances Sternhagen, 74, actress (*The Tiger Makes Out, Misery*; stage: *The Good Doctor*), born Washington, DC, Jan 13, 1930.

JANUARY 14 — WEDNESDAY
Day 14 — 352 Remaining

ARNOLD, BENEDICT: BIRTH ANNIVERSARY. Jan 14, 1741 (OS). American officer who deserted to the British during the Revolutionary War and whose name has since become synonymous with treachery. Born at Norwich, CT. Died June 14, 1801, at London, England.

FIRST CAESAREAN SECTION: ANNIVERSARY. Jan 14, 1794. Dr. Jesse Bennett, of Edom, VA, performed the first successful Caesarean section. The patient was his wife.

ILLINOIS SNOW SCULPTING COMPETITION. Jan 14–17. Rockford, IL. Teams from around the state create enormous works of frozen art, as they compete to represent Illinois in national snow sculpting competition. In case of inclement weather, event may be postponed. Sponsor: Rockford Park District. Est attendance: 70,000. For info: Patricia Hayes, Rockford Park District, 1401 N Second St, Rockford, IL 61107-3086. Phone: (800) 521-0849 or (815) 987-8800. Fax: (815) 987-1631. E-mail: rpdmail@RockfordParkDistrict.org. Web: www.snowsculpting.org.

MAURY, MATTHEW FONTAINE: BIRTH ANNIVERSARY. Jan 14, 1806. Naval officer, born at Fredericksburg, VA. Maury established oceanography as a branch of science and revolutionized the recording of oceanographic data as a superintendent of the Naval Observatory. Died at Lexington, VA, Feb 1, 1873.

MOON PHASE: LAST QUARTER. Jan 14. Moon enters Last Quarter phase at 11:46 PM, EST.

NATIONAL SOCCER COACHES ASSOCIATION OF AMERICA NATIONAL CONVENTION. Jan 14–18. Kansas City Convention Center, Kansas City, MO. The NSCAA is the largest single-sport coaching organization in the US. The NSCAA convention is the largest annual gathering of soccer coaches in the world. The convention features clinics, lectures, exhibits and national awards. Est attendance: 5,800. For info: NSCAA, 6700 Squibb Rd, Ste 215, Mission, KS 66202. Phone: (800) 458-0678 or (913) 362-1747. Fax: (913) 362-3439. E-mail: info@nscaa.com. Web: www.nscaa.com.

OUTCAULT, RICHARD FELTON: BIRTH ANNIVERSARY. Jan 14, 1863. When Richard Felton Outcault was asked by the *New York World*'s Sunday editor to submit drawings for use with their new color printing process, the "funny papers" were born. Outcault's first color drawing, titled "Origin of a New Species," was published Nov 18, 1894. The first regular colored cartoon, "Hogan's Alley," drawn by Outcault, began appearing with its main character's blustery comments written across his yellow nightshirt—thus making him the "Yellow Kid." The term "yellow journalism" was coined for newspapers featuring the Kid. Outcault's strip "Buster Brown" brought him celebrity and fortune. Outcault was born at Lancaster, OH, and died Sept 25, 1928, at Flushing, NY.

RATIFICATION DAY. Jan 14, 1784. Anniversary of the act that officially ended the American Revolution and established the US as a sovereign power. On Jan 14, 1784, the Continental Congress, meeting at Annapolis, MD, ratified the Treaty of Paris, thus fulfilling the Declaration of Independence of July 4, 1776.

ROACH, HAL: BIRTH ANNIVERSARY. Jan 14, 1892. American film writer, director and producer Harold Eugene (Hal) Roach was born at Elmira, NY. He pioneered film comedy as chief of his own studio for nearly 40 years. During that time he produced, and sometimes directed and wrote, nearly 1,000 movies. Roach is noted for originating the *Our Gang* comedies in 1922 and for introducing Laurel and Hardy to film audiences. He won Academy Awards for the short films *The Music Box* (1931) and *Bored of Education* (1936). Roach produced the film version of Steinbeck's novel *Of Mice and Men* in 1939. In 1984 he won an honorary Academy Award for career achievement. Roach died Nov 2, 1992, at Los Angeles, CA.

"SANFORD AND SON" TV PREMIERE: ANNIVERSARY. Jan 14, 1972. NBC sitcom which gained immediate popularity depicting an African-American father and son engaged in the junkyard business. Norman Lear and Bud Yorkin developed the comedy series based on the British "Steptoe and Son." Comedian Redd Foxx played Fred Sanford. His son, Lamont, was played by Demond Wilson. Others appearing on the show were Whitman Mayo as Grady, Slappy White as Melvin, LaWanda Page as Aunt Esther, Gregory Sierra as Julio, Nathaniel Taylor as Rollo, Raymond Allen as Uncle Woody, Don Bexley as Bubba Bexley, Lynn Hamilton as Donna Harris, Howard Platt and Hal Williams as Hoppy and Smitty, Pat Morita as Ah Chew, Marlene Clark as Janet and Edward Crawford as Roger. The last telecast was Sept 2, 1977.

SCHWEITZER, ALBERT: BIRTH ANNIVERSARY. Jan 14, 1875. Alsatian philosopher, musician, physician and winner of the 1952 Nobel Peace Prize was born at Kayserberg, Upper Alsace, and died at Lambarene, Gabon, Sept 4, 1965.

SPACE MILESTONE: *SOYUZ 4* (USSR): 35th ANNIVERSARY. Jan 14, 1969. First docking of two manned spacecraft (with *Soyuz 5*) and first interchange of spaceship personnel in orbit by means of space walks.

"TODAY" TV PREMIERE: ANNIVERSARY. Jan 14, 1952. NBC program that started the morning news format we know today. Captained by Dave Garroway, the show was segmented with bits and pieces of news, sports, weather, interviews and other features that were repeated so that viewers did not have to stop their morning routine to watch. The segments were brief and to the point. Sylvester Weaver devised this concept to capitalize on television's unusual qualities. What used to take three hours to broadcast live across the country was done in two with videotape on a delayed basis. The addition of chimpanzee J. Fred Muggs in 1953 helped push ratings up. There have been a number of hosts over the years, from John Chancellor and Hugh Downs to Tom Brokaw, Bryant Gumbel and Matt Lauer. Female hosts (originally called "Today Girls") include Betsy Palmer, Florence Henderson, Barbara Walters, Jane Pauley and Katie Couric.

UZBEKISTAN: ARMY DAY. Jan 14. National holiday.

WHIPPLE, WILLIAM: BIRTH ANNIVERSARY. Jan 14, 1730. American patriot and signer of the Declaration of Independence. Born at Kittery, ME, he died at Portsmouth, NH, Nov 10, 1785.

January 2004

S	M	T	W	T	F	S
				1	2	3
4	5	6	7	8	9	10
11	12	13	14	15	16	17
18	19	20	21	22	23	24
25	26	27	28	29	30	31

☆ Chase's 2004 Calendar of Events ☆   Jan 14–15

BIRTHDAYS TODAY

Jason Bateman, 35, actor ("Chicago Sons," "The Hogan Family"), born Rye, NY, Jan 14, 1969.
Julian Bond, 64, legislator, civil rights leader, born Nashville, TN, Jan 14, 1940.
Faye Dunaway, 63, actress (Oscar for *Network*; *Bonnie and Clyde*, *Chinatown*), born Bascom, FL, Jan 14, 1941.
Marjoe Gortner, 59, ex-evangelist, actor, singer, born Long Beach, CA, Jan 14, 1945.
Lawrence Kasdan, 55, filmmaker (*The Bodyguard*, *The Big Chill*, *Mumford*), born Miami Beach, FL, Jan 14, 1949.
Shannon Lucid, 61, astronaut, born Shanghai, China, Jan 14, 1943.
Andy Rooney, 85, writer, columnist ("60 Minutes," *Pieces of My Mind*), born Albany, NY, Jan 14, 1919.
Steven Soderbergh, 41, filmmaker (Best Director Oscar for *Traffic*; *Ocean's Eleven*, *Erin Brockovich*), born Atlanta, GA, Jan 14, 1963.
Holland Taylor, 61, actress ("The Practice," *The Truman Show*), born Philadelphia, PA, Jan 14, 1943.
Nina Totenberg, 60, broadcast journalist, correspondent ("Nightline"), born New York, NY, Jan 14, 1944.
Emily Watson, 37, actress (*Angela's Ashes*, *The Boxer*), born London, England, Jan 14, 1967.
Carl Weathers, 56, actor (*Rocky*, *Happy Gilmore*), born New Orleans, LA, Jan 14, 1948.

JANUARY 15 — THURSDAY
Day 15 — 351 Remaining

ACE, GOODMAN: BIRTH ANNIVERSARY. Jan 15, 1899. Radio and TV writer, actor, columnist and humorist. With his wife, Jane, created and acted in the popular series of radio programs (1928–45) "Easy Aces." Called "America's greatest wit" by Fred Allen. Born at Kansas City, MO; died at New York, NY, Mar 25, 1982, soon after asking that his tombstone be inscribed "No flowers, please, I'm allergic."

ALPHA KAPPA ALPHA SORORITY FOUNDED: ANNIVERSARY. Jan 15, 1908. Founded at Howard University at Washington, DC, by Ethel Hedgeman Lyle, Alpha Kappa Alpha was the first organization of its type for black women. It was incorporated Jan 29, 1913.

BRITISH MUSEUM: ANNIVERSARY. Jan 15, 1759. On this date, the British Museum opened its doors at Montague House in London. Incorporated by an act of Parliament in 1753, following the death of British medical doctor and naturalist Sir Hans Sloane, who had bequeathed his personal collection of books, manuscripts, coins, medals and antiquities to Britain. As the national museum of the United Kingdom, the British Museum houses many of the world's most prized treasures. The national library moved to separate facilities in 1997.

CHAMPION OF THE MONTH. Jan 15. Recognize individuals who live their lives as Champions. Nominate your Champion at our website between the 15th and the 15th of each month. Each Champion of the Month will be recognized each month in our newsletter and on our radio show (NBC 1190 AM) in Phoenix. For info: Dan Kuschell, 3370 N Hayden, #123-146, Scottsdale, AZ 85251. Phone: (800) 211-4580. E-mail: dan@achampionvision.com. Web: www.achampionvision.com.

CUSTOMER SERVICE DAY. Jan 15. A day to reflect on the importance of providing good customer service—and to commit to learning new skills that will help you provide it. Annually, Jan 15. For info: Karen Leland, 180 Harbor Dr #221, Sausalito, CA 94965. Phone: (415) 331-5200. Fax: (415) 331-5272. E-mail: kleland@scgtraining.com. Web: www.scgtraining.com.

ENGLAND: WEST LONDON ANTIQUES AND FINE ART FAIR. Jan 15–18. Kensington Town Hall, London. 60 stands of authenticated antiques and art, 1600–2000. Established 1979. Est attendance: 4,000. For info: Penman Fairs, PO Box 114, Haywards Heath, Sussex, England RH16 2YU. Phone: (44) (870) 350-2442. Fax: (44) (870) 350-2443. E-mail: info@penman-fairs.co.uk.

FIRST SUPER BOWL: ANNIVERSARY. Jan 15, 1967. The Green Bay Packers won the first NFL–AFL World Championship Game, defeating the Kansas City Chiefs, 35–10, at the Los Angeles Memorial Coliseum. Packers quarterback Bart Starr was named the game's Most Valuable Player. Pro football's title game later became known as the Super Bowl and is now played on the last Sunday in January.

FLORIDA CITRUS FESTIVAL. Jan 15–25. Polk County Fairgrounds, Winter Haven, FL. Celebrating Diamond Jubilee featuring an industrywide fresh fruit competition, citrus fruit displays, an automated fresh fruit packing line and appearances by Miss Florida Citrus. FFA and 4-H exhibits, crafts and horticultural competitions, livestock exhibits, giant-sized midway and big-name country and western entertainers. Est attendance: 160,000. For info: Exec Dir, Florida Citrus Festival, PO Box 30, Winter Haven, FL 33882-0030. Phone: (863) 292-9810. Web: www.citrusfestival.com.

GET TO KNOW YOUR CUSTOMER DAY. Jan 15 (also Apr 15, July 15 and Oct 21). Set aside the third Thursday of each quarter to get to know your customers even better. For example, salespeople might plan to take a customer out to lunch, not to sell, but to learn more about their needs and why they like doing business with them. Executives could get out from behind the desk and go into the field. For info: Shep Hyken, Shepard Presentations, 711 Old Ballas Rd, Ste 215, St. Louis, MO 63141. Phone: (314) 692-2200. E-mail: Shep@hyken.com. Web: www.hyken.com.

"HAPPY DAYS" TV PREMIERE: 30th ANNIVERSARY. Jan 15, 1974. This nostalgic comedy set in Milwaukee in the 1950s starred Ron Howard as teenager Richie Cunningham with Anson Williams and Don Most as his friends "Potsie" Weber and Ralph Malph. Tom Bosley and Marion Ross played Richie's parents and his sister, Joanie, was played by Erin Moran. The most memorable character was The Fonz—Arthur "Fonzie" Fonzarelli—played by Henry Winkler. "Happy Days" remained on the air until July 12, 1984, and has been in syndication ever since. "Laverne and Shirley" was a spin-off.

"HILL STREET BLUES" TV PREMIERE: ANNIVERSARY. Jan 15, 1981. Immensely popular NBC police series created by Stephen Bochco and Michael Kozoll that focused more on police officers than on crime. The show was very realistic and highly praised by real policemen. It won a slew of Emmys and ran for seven seasons. Cast: Daniel J. Travanti as Captain Frank Furillo, Veronica Hamel as public defender Joyce Davenport, Michael Conrad as Sergeant Phil "Let's be careful out there" Esterhaus, Barbara Bosson as Fay Furillo, and as the wonderfully drawn cops, Bruce Weitz (Mick Belker), Taurean Blacque (Neal Washington), Kiel Martin (Johnny LaRue), Joe Spano (Henry Goldblume), James B. Sikking (Howard Hunter), René Enríquez (Ray Calletano), Michael Warren (Bobby Hill), Betty Thomas (Lucy Bates), Ed Marinaro (Joe Coffey) and Charles Haid (Andy Renko). The last telecast was on May 19, 1987.

ICEBOX DAYS XXIV. Jan 15–18. International Falls, MN. Smoosh racing, 10k and 5k "Freeze Yer Gizzard Blizzard Run," turkey bowling, ski races, mutt races and beach party. Est attendance: 5,000. For info: Kallie L. Briggs, Chamber of Commerce, 301 2nd Ave, International Falls, MN 56649. Phone: (800)

325-5766 or (218) 283-9400. Fax: (218) 283-3572. E-mail: intl fall@intlfalls.org. Web: www.internationalfallsmn.us.

KING, MARTIN LUTHER, JR: 75th BIRTH ANNIVERSARY. Jan 15, 1929. Black civil rights leader, minister, advocate of nonviolence and recipient of the Nobel Peace Prize (1964). Born at Atlanta, GA, he was assassinated at Memphis, TN, Apr 4, 1968. After his death many states and territories observed his birthday as a holiday. In 1983 the Congress approved HR 3706, "A bill to amend Title 5, United States Code, to make the birthday of Martin Luther King, Jr, a legal public holiday." Signed by the president on Nov 2, 1983, it became Public Law 98–144. The law sets the third Monday in January for observance of King's birthday. First observance was Jan 20, 1986. See also: "King, Martin Luther, Jr: Birthday Observed" (Jan 19).

LIVINGSTON, PHILIP: BIRTH ANNIVERSARY. Jan 15, 1716. Merchant and signer of the Declaration of Independence, born at Albany, NY. Died at York, PA, June 12, 1778.

MOLIERE DAY: BAPTISM ANNIVERSARY. Jan 15, 1622. Most celebrated of French authors and dramatists, Jean Baptiste Poquelin, baptized at Paris, France, Jan 15, 1622, took the stage name Molière when he was about 22 years old. While playing in a performance of his last play, *Le Malade Imaginaire* (about a hypochondriac afraid of death), Molière became ill and died within a few hours at Paris, Feb 17, 1673.

MONACO: INTERNATIONAL CIRCUS FESTIVAL OF MONTE CARLO. Jan 15–22. Espace de Fontvielle, Monte Carlo. 28th annual. The best circus acts and performers from five continents compete for the Golden Clown Award in this storied festival whose honorary ringmaster is Prince Rainier. For info: Monte Carlo Festivals, Avenue des Ligures, MC-98000 Monte Carlo, Monaco.

NATIONAL FRESH SQUEEZED JUICE WEEK. Jan 15–19. Drinking fresh squeezed juice is a great healthy way of living. For info: Bob O'Brien, Consumer Advocate, 1061 Koelle Blvd, Secaucus, NJ 07094. Phone: (201) 860-1595. Fax: (201) 865-4775. E-mail: bobthebestthebest@yahoo.com. Web: www.econsumeradvocate.com.

PENTAGON COMPLETED: ANNIVERSARY. Jan 15, 1943. The world's largest office building with 6.5 million square feet of usable space, the Pentagon is located in Virginia across the Potomac River from Washington, DC, and serves as headquarters for the Department of Defense.

QUARTERLY ESTIMATED FEDERAL INCOME TAX PAYERS' DUE DATE. Jan 15. For those individuals whose fiscal year is the calendar year and who make quarterly estimated federal income tax payments, today would be one of the due dates (Jan 15, Apr 15, June 15 and Sept 15, 2004).

SIEGMEISTER, ELIE: 95th BIRTH ANNIVERSARY. Jan 15, 1909. American composer Elie Siegmeister was born at New York, NY. He composed eight symphonies and eight operas and a number of other concertos, chamber pieces and orchestral works using folk, jazz and street songs to create a contemporary American classical music. He died Mar 10, 1991, at Manhasset, NY.

SUNDANCE FILM FESTIVAL. Jan 15–25. Park City, UT. "The premier US festival for independent filmmakers." More than 120 feature-length films and more than 80 short films screened. Est attendance: 30,000. For info: Sundance Institute, PO Box 3630, Salt Lake City, UT 84110. Phone: (801) 328-FILM. E-mail: festivalinfo@sundance.org. Web: www.sundance.org.

January 2004

S	M	T	W	T	F	S
				1	2	3
4	5	6	7	8	9	10
11	12	13	14	15	16	17
18	19	20	21	22	23	24
25	26	27	28	29	30	31

TRAIN FOR PARIS: ANNIVERSARY. Jan 15, 1945. The civilian populations of England and France had their first direct contact since May 1940 when a boat train left London's Victoria Station headed for Paris.

BIRTHDAYS TODAY

Chad Lowe, 36, actor ("Now and Again," "Life Goes On," *Nobody's Perfect*), born Dayton, OH, Jan 15, 1968.

Rod MacLeish, 78, broadcast journalist, born Bryn Mawr, PA, Jan 15, 1926.

Andrea Martin, 57, actress (*Wag the Dog, Anastasia*, "SCTV"), born Portland, ME, Jan 15, 1947.

Margaret O'Brien, 67, actress (*Little Women, Meet Me in St. Louis*), born San Diego, CA, Jan 15, 1937.

Edward Teller, 96, physicist, born Budapest, Hungary, Jan 15, 1908.

Mario Van Peebles, 47, actor (*Love Kills, Judgment Day*), born Mexico City, Mexico, Jan 15, 1957.

JANUARY 16 — FRIDAY
Day 16 — 350 Remaining

ARBOR DAY IN FLORIDA. Jan 16. The third Friday in January is Arbor Day in Florida, a ceremonial day.

ART DECO WEEKEND FESTIVAL. Jan 16–18. Miami Beach, FL. Features parade, arts and crafts displays, jazz entertainment and plenty of food. Includes art from local talent. 27th annual. Est attendance: 250,000. For info: Art Deco Weekend Festival, PO Box 190180, Miami Beach, FL 33119. Phone: (305) 672-2014. Fax: (305) 672-4319. Web: www.mdpl.org.

BALD EAGLE APPRECIATION DAYS. Jan 16–17. Riverfront, Keokuk, IA. Features trained personnel stationed at observation points for viewing the American bald eagle. Indoor exhibits at Keosippi Mall and live eagle demonstrations. Est attendance: 10,000. For info: Kirk Brandenberger, Dir of Tourism, Keokuk Area Conv and Tourism Bureau, 329 Main, Keokuk, IA 52632. Phone: (800) 383-1219 or (319) 524-5599. Fax: (319) 524-5016. E-mail: keokukia@interl.net. Web: www.keokuktourism.com.

BRITISH AIR RAID ON BERLIN: ANNIVERSARY. Jan 16, 1943. In the first bombing of Germany since the Casablanca Conference, the British Royal Air Force began heavy bombing of Germany by day and night to bring about "the progressive destruction and dislocation of the German military, industrial and economic system, and for the undermining of the morale of the German people." The RAF used their new "target indicator" bombs to mark targets for their bombers.

CIVIL SERVICE CREATED: ANNIVERSARY. Jan 16, 1883. The US Congress passed a bill creating the civil service.

COAL CONSERVATION ORDERED: ANNIVERSARY. Jan 16, 1918. In a precursor of things to come, 75 New York schools closed down for lack of coal on Jan 2, 1918. On Jan 16, by order of US Fuel Administrator Harry A. Garfield, all industry east of the Mississippi not crucial to the war effort was shut down. Factories remained closed for five days. In addition, the following nine Mondays became days of leisure for a large segment of the American workforce as further attempts were made to reserve coal for troop transport, ships and merchant vessels.

DEAN, DIZZY: BIRTH ANNIVERSARY. Jan 16, 1911. Jay Hanna "Dizzy" Dean, major league pitcher (St. Louis Cardinals) and Baseball Hall of Fame member was born at Lucas, AR. Following his baseball career, Dean established himself as a radio and TV sports announcer and commentator, becoming famous for his innovative delivery. "He slud into third," reported Dizzy, who on another occasion explained that "Me and Paul [baseball player brother Paul "Daffy" Dean] . . . didn't get much education." Died at Reno, NV, July 17, 1974.

DR. MARTIN LUTHER KING, JR, CELEBRATION. Jan 16–18. Hollywood, FL. Saturday Fun Fest features children's activities, DJ and basketball tournament. VIP evening dinner and a

☆ Chase's 2004 Calendar of Events ☆ — Jan 16

Sunday tribute. Est attendance: 3,000. For info: Cynthia Hancock, City of Hollywood, Department of Parks, Recreation & Cultural Arts, 1940 Harrison St, Ste 101, Hollywood, FL 33020. Phone: (954) 921-3404.

"DONNY AND MARIE" TV PREMIERE: ANNIVERSARY. Jan 16, 1976. ABC show hosted by brother-and-sister act Donny and Marie Osmond. There were seven other talented siblings in the Osmond family who appeared on the show at times along with regulars Jim Connell and Hank Garcia. The sister-and-brother team could sing, dance and perform on ice skates.

EISENHOWER ASSUMES COMMAND: 60th ANNIVERSARY. Jan 16, 1944. General Dwight D. Eisenhower arrived in London to assume command of the Supreme Headquarters Allied Expeditionary Forces in Europe (SHAEF). Having demonstrated his organizational abilities in North Africa as well as his strength as an arbitrator of inter-Allied rivalries, Eisenhower was charged with the most far-reaching push of the war—the invasion of France.

EL SALVADOR: NATIONAL DAY OF PEACE. Jan 16, 1992. A peace treaty was signed in Mexico City ending the 12-year civil war that had claimed 75,000 lives. On Feb 1, a cease-fire went into effect.

HABITAT FOR HUMANITY BUILDING ON THE DREAM. Jan 16–23. "Building on the Dream" honors the legacy of Dr. Martin Luther King, Jr, by encouraging people to volunteer with their local Habitat for Humanity affiliate and begin building houses or raising awareness of the need for adequate housing in their communities. "Building on the Dream" houses will stand as a tribute on Jan 19 to Dr. King. For info: Habitat for Humanity International, 121 Habitat St, Americus, GA 31709. Phone: (800) HABITAT or (229) 924-6935. E-mail: publicinfo@hfhi.org. Web: www.habitat.org.

JAPAN: HARU-NO-YABUIRI. Jan 16. Employees and servants who have been working over the holidays are given a day off.

LEE-JACKSON DAY IN VIRGINIA. Jan 16. Annually, the Friday in January that precedes Martin Luther King Day. To commemorate the January birthdays of Robert E. Lee and "Stonewall" Jackson.

MALAWI: JOHN CHILEMBWE DAY. Jan 16. National holiday. Honors a leader for independence who led an uprising against the British in 1915.

MERMAN, ETHEL: 95th BIRTH ANNIVERSARY. Jan 16, 1909. Musical comedy star famous for her belting voice and brassy style. Born Ethel Agnes Zimmerman on Jan 16, 1909 (or 1912—the date changed the older she got, but most sources say 1909) at Queens, NY. Died Feb 15, 1984, at New York, NY.

MICHELIN, ANDRE: BIRTH ANNIVERSARY. Jan 16, 1853. French industrialist who, along with his brother Edouard, started the Michelin Tire Company in 1888, manufacturing bicycle tires. They were the first to use demountable pneumatic tires on cars. Born at Paris, France; died there Apr 4, 1931.

NATIONAL NOTHING DAY: ANNIVERSARY. Jan 16. Anniversary of National Nothing Day, an event created by newspaperman Harold Pullman Coffin and first observed in 1973 "to provide Americans with one national day when they can just sit without celebrating, observing or honoring anything." Since 1975, though many other events have been listed on this day, lighthearted traditional observance of Coffin's idea has continued. Coffin, a native of Reno, NV, died at Capitola, CA, Sept 12, 1981, at the age of 76.

PERSIAN GULF WAR BEGINS: ANNIVERSARY. Jan 16, 1991. Allied forces launched a major air offensive against Iraq to begin the Gulf War. The strike was designed to destroy Iraqi air defenses, command, control and communication centers. As Desert Shield became Desert Storm, the world was able to see and hear for the first time an initial engagement of war as CNN broadcasters, stationed at Baghdad, covered the attack live.

PROHIBITION (EIGHTEENTH) AMENDMENT: 85th ANNIVERSARY. Jan 16, 1919. Nebraska became the 36th state to ratify the prohibition amendment and the 18th Amendment became part of the US Constitution. One year later, Jan 16, 1920, the 18th Amendment took effect and the sale of alcoholic beverages became illegal in the US with the Volstead Act providing for enforcement. This was the first time that an amendment to the Constitution dealt with a social issue. The 21st Amendment, repealing the 18th, went into effect Dec 6, 1933.

RELIGIOUS FREEDOM DAY. Jan 16, 1786. The legislature of Virginia adopted a religious freedom statute that protected Virginians against any requirement to attend or support any church and against discrimination. This statute, which had been drafted by Thomas Jefferson and introduced by James Madison, later was the model for the First Amendment to the US Constitution.

★ **RELIGIOUS FREEDOM DAY.** Jan 16. Commemorates the adoption of a religious freedom statute by the Virginia legislature in 1786.

SEATTLE BOAT SHOW. Jan 16–25. Stadium Exhibition Center, Seattle, WA. Huge display of new boats, accessories and services. Large boats (25 ft or longer) on display in Puget Sound with more than 70 accessories and 150 trailer boats dealers on land. Est attendance: 65,000. For info: NW Marine Trade Assn, 1900 N Northlake Way, #233, Seattle, WA 98103. Phone: (206) 634-0911. Fax: (206) 632-0078. Web: www.seattleboatshow.com.

SERVICE, ROBERT WILLIAM: BIRTH ANNIVERSARY. Jan 16, 1874. Canadian poet, born at Preston, England. Lived in the Canadian northwest for many years and perhaps is best remembered for such ballads as "The Shooting of Dan McGrew" and "The Cremation of Sam McGee" and for such books as *Songs of a Sourdough*, *Rhymes of a Rolling Stone* and *The Spell of the Yukon*. Died at France, Sept 11, 1958.

WINGS OVER WILLCOX/SANDHILL CRANE CELEBRATION. Jan 16–18. Willcox, AZ. Tours to the Willcox Playa and Wetlands to see Sandhill Cranes, Hawk Stalk tours, Plovers, Longspurs and much more. Visit Cochise Lake and see the waders. Workshops on wildlife. Seminars on birdwatching by various experts, a banquet, silent auction and a whole lot more. Est attendance: 1,000. For info: Willcox Chamber of Commerce. Phone: (800) 200-2272 or (520) 384-2272. Web: www.wingsoverwillcox.com or www.willcoxchamber.com.

BIRTHDAYS TODAY

Debbie Allen, 54, dancer, choreographer, singer, actress ("Fame"), born Houston, TX, Jan 16, 1950.

John Carpenter, 56, movie director (*Halloween*, *The Thing*), born Carthage, NY, Jan 16, 1948.

89

David Chokachi, 36, actor ("Baywatch"), born Plymouth, MA, Jan 16, 1968.
Anthony Joseph (A.J.) Foyt, Jr, 69, former auto racer, born Houston, TX, Jan 16, 1935.
Marilyn Horne, 70, opera singer, born Bradford, PA, Jan 16, 1934.
Jack Burns McDowell, 38, former baseball player, born Van Nuys, CA, Jan 16, 1966.
Ronnie Milsap, 60, singer ("[There's] No Gettin' Over Me"), born Robinsville, NC, Jan 16, 1944.
Albert Pujols, 24, baseball player, born Santo Domingo, Dominican Republic, Jan 16, 1980.
Francesco Scavullo, 75, fashion photographer, born Staten Island, NY, Jan 16, 1929.
Susan Sontag, 71, author (*Against Interpretation, The Volcano Lover: A Romance*), born New York, NY, Jan 16, 1933.

JANUARY 17 — SATURDAY
Day 17 — 349 Remaining

AFRMA FANCY RAT AND MOUSE ANNUAL SHOW. Jan 17 (tentative—or Jan 24). Riverside, CA. Annual show where trophies are awarded to the winners. Rats and mice are emerging as ideal pets: they provide all the pleasure and satisfaction of a warm, cuddly, intelligent and friendly pet companion. The American Fancy Rat and Mouse Association (AFRMA) was founded in 1983 to promote the breeding and exhibition of fancy rats and mice, to educate the public on their positive qualities as companion animals and to provide information on their proper care. Est attendance: 100. For info: AFRMA (CAE), PO Box 2589, Winnetka, CA 91396-2589. Phone: (909) 685-2350 or (818) 992-5564 or (626) 966-0350. Fax: (818) 592-6590. E-mail: afrma@afrma.org. Web: www.afrma.org.

"BARETTA" TV PREMIERE: ANNIVERSARY. Jan 17, 1975. CBS series starring Robert Blake as Baretta, a police detective who defied his superiors and solved his cases in a most unorthodox manner—usually by figuring it out while talking to his pet cockatoo, Fred, or his informant, Rooster (played by Michael D. Roberts). Commanding officer Lieutenant Hal Brubaker was played by Edward Grover. The last telecast aired on June 1, 1978.

THE BUSINESS OF AMERICA QUOTATION: ANNIVERSARY. Jan 17, 1925. President Calvin Coolidge, in a speech to the American Society of Newspaper Editors, described America in a way that was to define the country in the twentieth century and beyond—not just for the prosperous 1920s. "The chief business of the American people," he said, "is business."

CABLE CAR PATENT: ANNIVERSARY. Jan 17, 1871. Andrew Hallikie received a patent for a cable car system that began service in San Francisco in 1873.

CHINESE NEW YEAR FESTIVAL. Jan 17–Feb 8. San Francisco, CA. North America's largest Chinese community salutes the Year of the Horse. Activities include Chinatown Flower Fair (Jan 17–18); Miss Chinatown USA Pageant (Jan 31) with Coronation Ball (Feb 6); Chinese New Year Parade (Feb 7); Chinatown Community Street Fair (Feb 7–8). These events showcase the diversity of Chinese culture from Chinese opera and ballet, traditional dance and ancient dynastic costumes to martial arts. Booths feature cooking demonstrations, calligraphy and arts and crafts. Est attendance: 700,000. For info: Chinese Chamber of Commerce, New Year Festival, 730 Sacramento, San Francisco, CA 94108. Phone: (415) 391-9680. Fax: (415) 982-4720. Web: www.chineseparade.com.

DeSOTO'S WINTER ENCAMPMENT. Jan 17. Tallahassee, FL. Hernando DeSoto's Winter Camp at Apalachee Village Anhyca (present-day Tallahassee) interpreted with living history, craft demonstrations, exhibits, etc. Est attendance: 1,000. For info: DeSoto's Winter Encampment, 1022 DeSoto Park Dr, Tallahassee, FL 32301. Phone: (850) 922-6007. Fax: (850) 488-0366.

EAGLE DAYS. Jan 17–18. Milford Nature Center/Fish Hatchery, Junction City, KS. Learn more about the magnificent bird that is our national emblem. Meet both a live bald eagle and a golden eagle! Guides with spotting scopes and binoculars will be waiting to show you eagles as they roost and soar around Milford Lake. Sponsor: Kansas Wildlife and Parks; US Army Corps of Engineers. Est attendance: 700. For info: Milford Nature Center, 3115 Hatchery Dr, Junction City, KS 66441. Phone: (785) 238-5323. Fax: (785) 238-5775.

EAGLE DAYS IN SPRINGFIELD. Jan 17–18. Springfield Conservation Nature Center, Springfield, MO. Celebrate the return of bald eagles to Springfield through indoor programs with a live eagle and outdoor viewing opportunities. Est attendance: 1,000. For info: Springfield Conservation Nature Center, 4600 S Chrisman Ave, Springfield, MO 65804. Phone: (417) 888-4237. Fax: (417) 888-4241. Web: www.conservation.state.mo.us/areas/cnc/springfd/index.

FIRST NUCLEAR-POWERED SUBMARINE VOYAGE: ANNIVERSARY. Jan 17, 1955. At 11 AM, EST, the commanding officer of the world's first nuclear-powered submarine, the *Nautilus*, ordered all lines cast off and sent the historic message: "Under way on nuclear power." Highlights of the *Nautilus*: keel laid by President Harry S Truman June 14, 1952; christened and launched by Mrs Dwight D. Eisenhower Jan 21, 1954; commissioned to the US Navy Sept 30, 1954. It now forms part of the *Nautilus* Memorial Submarine Force Library and Museum at the Naval Submarine Base New London at Groton, CT.

FRANKLIN, BENJAMIN: BIRTH ANNIVERSARY. Jan 17, 1706. "Elder statesman of the American Revolution," oldest signer of both the Declaration of Independence and the Constitution, scientist, diplomat, author, printer, publisher, philosopher, philanthropist and self-made, self-educated man. Author, printer and publisher of *Poor Richard's Almanack* (1733–58). Born at Boston, MA, Franklin died at Philadelphia, PA, Apr 17, 1790. His birthday is commemorated each year by the Poor Richard Club of Philadelphia with graveside observance. In 1728 Franklin wrote a premature epitaph for himself. It first appeared in print in Ames's 1771 almanac: "The Body of BENJAMIN FRANKLIN/Printer/Like a Covering of an old Book/Its contents torn out/And stript of its Lettering and Gilding,/Lies here, Food for Worms;/But the work shall not be lost,/It will (as he believ'd) appear once more/In a New and more beautiful Edition/Corrected and amended/By the Author."

"FRONTLINE" TV PREMIERE: ANNIVERSARY. Jan 17, 1983. PBS hour-long independently produced documentaries initially hosted by Jessica Savitch. Judy Woodruff replaced Savitch, who was killed in an auto accident in the fall of 1983. The programs often create controversy, focusing on a variety of political, military and social issues.

FUN-IN-THE-SUN POSTCARD SALE. Jan 17–18 (tentative). Best Western Movieland, Orlando, FL. Sale of antique and modern postcards by 20 dealers. Est attendance: 300. For info: John H. McClintock, Dir, Postcard Soc, Inc, Box 1765, Manassas, VA 20108. Phone: (703) 368-2757.

"THE GOLDBERGS" TV PREMIERE: 55th ANNIVERSARY. Jan 17, 1949. Originally broadcast by CBS, this show was one of the earliest TV sitcoms. The show centered around a Jewish mother and her family living in the Bronx and later in the suburbs. Gertrude Berg created the hit radio show before she wrote, produced and starred as Molly Goldberg in the television version. Contributing actors and actresses included Philip Loeb, Arlene McQuade, Tom Taylor, Eli Mintz, Menasha Skulnik and Arnold Stang.

	S	M	T	W	T	F	S
January 2004					1	2	3
	4	5	6	7	8	9	10
	11	12	13	14	15	16	17
	18	19	20	21	22	23	24
	25	26	27	28	29	30	31

☆ Chase's 2004 Calendar of Events ☆ Jan 17

HULA BOWL MAUI ALL STAR CLASSIC. Jan 17. War Memorial Stadium, Kahului, Maui, HI. 58th annual. College senior all-star football classic. Televised on ESPN and Westwood One. Est attendance: 23,000. For info: Hula Bowl Maui Office, 300 Ohukai Rd, Ste C-324, Kihei, HI 96753. Phone: (808) 874-9500. Fax: (808) 874-9508. Web: www.hulabowlmaui.com.

HUTCHINS, ROBERT MAYNARD: BIRTH ANNIVERSARY. Jan 17, 1899. American educator, foundation executive and civil liberties activist, born at Brooklyn, NY. He was president and later chancellor of the University of Chicago, where he introduced many educational concepts, including the Great Books program. Died at Santa Barbara, CA, on May 14, 1977.

IKE'S FAREWELL: ANNIVERSARY. Jan 17, 1961. President Dwight D. Eisenhower, in his farewell address to the nation on national radio and television, spoke the sentences that would be the most quoted and remembered of his presidency. In a direct warning, he said, "In the councils of government, we must guard against the acquisition of unwarranted influence, whether sought or unsought, by the military-industrial complex. The potential for the disastrous rise of misplaced power exists and persists."

JAPAN SUFFERS MAJOR EARTHQUAKE: ANNIVERSARY. Jan 17, 1995. Japan suffered its second most deadly earthquake in the 20th century when a 20-second temblor left 5,500 dead and more than 21,600 people injured. The epicenter was six miles beneath Awaji Island at Osaka Bay. This was just 20 miles west of Kobe, Japan's sixth-largest city and a major port that accounted for 12 percent of the country's exports. Measuring 7.2 on the Richter scale, the quake collapsed or badly damaged more than 30,400 buildings and left 275,000 people homeless.

JUDGMENT DAY. Jan 17. No need to wait 'til it's too late. All you need to do to see how you measure up to the standards of your God is simple: look in the mirror. There's your judgment. [©2003 by WH.] For info: Thomas & Ruth Roy, Wellcat Holidays, 2418 Long Ln, Lebanon, PA 17046. Phone: (717) 279-0184. E-mail: info@wellcat.com. Web: www.wellcat.com.

LONGWOOD GARDENS WELCOME SPRING. Jan 17–Apr 2. Kennett Square, PA. Indoor conservatory display features thousands of colorful, fragrant spring bulbs, green lawns, orchids and roses. Est attendance: 90,000. For info: Elizabeth Sullivan, Publicity Director, Longwood Gardens, PO Box 501, Kennett Sq, PA 19348-0501. Phone: (610) 377-1000. Web: www.longwoodgardens.org.

MEXICO: BLESSING OF THE ANIMALS AT THE CATHEDRAL. Jan 17. Church of San Antonio at Mexico City or Xochimilco provide best sights of chickens, cows and household pets gaily decorated with flowers. (Saint's day for San Antonio Abad, patron saint of domestic animals.)

MINORITY SCIENTISTS SHOWCASE. Jan 17–19. St. Louis, MO. Open new doors to future science careers and interests during Martin Luther King, Jr, weekend with hands-on activities and information available as part of a free program. Meet and talk with African-Americans working in science-related fields throughout the St. Louis area. Annually, Martin Luther King, Jr, weekend. Est attendance: 3,000. For info: Bev Pfeifer-Harms, St. Louis Science Center, 5050 Oakland Ave, St. Louis, MO 63110. Phone: (314) 289-4419. Fax: (314) 533-8687. E-mail: bpharms@slsc.org. Web: www.slsc.org.

MODEL RAILROAD SHOW. Jan 17–18. Wilson Lodge, Oglebay, Wheeling, WV. Model train enthusiasts will find nearly 80 exhibitors displaying and selling their wide variety of model trains and accessories. Est attendance: 1,700. For info: Steve Mitch, Train Show Mgr, Oglebay Resort, Rt 88 N, Wheeling, WV 26003. Phone: (304) 243-4034. Fax: (304) 243-4110. E-mail: smitch@oglebay-resort.com. Web: www.oglebay-resort.com.

MUSEUM OF AMERICAN GLASS: MID-WINTER EXHIBIT. Jan 17–Mar 3. Wheaton Village, Millville, NJ. "Curator's Choice" exhibit of fine glass items. Est attendance: 6,000. For info: Wheaton Village, 1501 Glasstown Rd, Millville, NJ 08332-1566. Phone: (856) 825-6800 or (800) 998-4552. Fax: (856) 825-2410. E-mail: mail@wheatonvillage.org. Web: www.wheatonvillage.org.

PALOMARES HYDROGEN BOMB ACCIDENT: ANNIVERSARY. Jan 17, 1966. At 10:16 AM, according to villagers, fire fell from the sky over Palomares, Spain. An American B-52 bomber carrying four hydrogen bombs collided with its refueling plane, spilling the bombs (two of which had "chemical explosions," scattering radioactive plutonium over the area). In a cleanup, American soldiers burned crops, slaughtered animals and removed tons of topsoil (which was sent to South Carolina for burial). More than 19 years later, in November 1985, the Nuclear Energy Board permitted villagers to see their medical reports for the first time.

PAUL BUNYAN SLED DOG RACES, SKIJORING AND MUTT RACES. Jan 17–18. Belt City Fairgrounds, Bemidji, MN. 32nd annual competition. For info: Bemidji Area Chamber of Commerce, Box 850, Bemidji, MN 56619-0850. Phone: (800) 458-2223. Web: www.paulbunyan.net/paulbunyansleddograces.

PENGUIN AWARENESS DAY. Jan 17. Jenkinson's Aquarium, Point Pleasant Beach, NJ. Learn all about the African penguin families at Jenkinson's Aquarium and the status of penguins in the wild. Children will enjoy penguin storytelling as well as appearances by our mascot Perky the Penguin. Penguins are fed at 11 AM and 3:30 PM. Free arts and crafts from 1 PM to 4 PM. Est attendance: 800. For info: Jenkinson's Aquarium, 300 Ocean Ave, Point Pleasant Beach, NJ 08742. Phone: (732) 899-1212. Fax: (732) 899-1717. E-mail: aquarium@jenkinsons.com. Web: www.jenkinsons.com.

PGA OF AMERICA FOUNDED: ANNIVERSARY. Jan 17, 1916. Golf great Walter Hagen and some 30 other pro golfers met and formed the Professional Golfers' Association of America and also developed the idea for a national championship. Rodman Wanamaker provided the trophy and the $2,580 purse for the first PGA Championship, which was played Apr 10, 1916, at the Siwanoy course at Bronxville, NY. The winner was British golfer Jim Barnes, who also won the second competition—not held until 1919 because of World War I. In 1921 Walter Hagen became the first American to win, a feat he accomplished four more times—in 1924, '25, '26 and '27.

PHILIPPINES: ATI-ATIHAN FESTIVAL. Jan 17–18. Kalibo, Aklan. One of the most colorful celebrations in the Philippines, the Ati-Atihan Festival commemorates the peace pact between the Ati of Panay (pygmies) and the Malays, who were early migrants in the islands. The townspeople blacken their bodies with soot, don colorful and bizarre costumes and sing and dance in the streets. The festival also celebrates the Feast Day of Santo Niño (the infant Jesus). Annually, the third weekend in January.

POLAND: LIBERATION DAY. Jan 17, 1945. Celebration of liberation from Nazi oppression on this day of the city of Warsaw by Soviet troops. Special ceremonies at the Monument to the Unknown Soldier in Warsaw's Victory Square (which had been called Adolf Hitler Platz during the German occupation).

POPEYE DEBUTS: 75th ANNIVERSARY. Jan 17, 1929. In E.C. Segar's newspaper comic strip "Thimble Theatre," a new character, Popeye, appeared on the scene and was an immediate success. Olive Oyl quickly dumped her beau, Ham Gravy, for the colorful sailor. Popeye's signature line was to be "Thas' all I can stands, 'cause I can't stands no more!"

QUEEN LILIUOKALANI DEPOSED: ANNIVERSARY. Jan 17, 1893. Hawaiian Queen Liliuokalani, the last monarch of Hawaii, lost her throne when the monarchy was abolished by the "Committee of Safety," with the foreknowledge of US minister John L. Stevens, who encouraged the revolutionaries. The Queen's supporters were intimidated by the 300 US Marines sent to protect American lives and property. Judge Sanford B. Dole became president of the republic and later was Hawaii's first governor after the US annexed it by joint resolution of Congress on July 7, 1898. Hawaii held incorporated territory status for 60 years. President Dwight D. Eisenhower signed the proclamation making Hawaii the 50th state on Aug 21, 1959.

RUSH, WILLIAM: DEATH ANNIVERSARY. Jan 17, 1833. First American-born sculptor. William Rush's work in wood and clay included busts of many notables, American and European alike; carved wooden female figureheads for ships; the masks of Tragedy and Comedy seen at the Actor's House outside Philadelphia, PA; and the *Spirit of Schuylkill* in Fairmount Park in Philadelphia. In 1805 Rush and others founded the Pennsylvania Academy of the Fine Arts. Rush was born at Philadelphia in 1756.

SAINT ANTHONY'S DAY. Jan 17. Feast day honoring Egyptian hermit who became the first Christian monk and who established communities of hermits; patron saint of domestic animals and patriarch of all monks. Lived about AD 251–354.

SLAMDANCE 2004. Jan 17–24. Park City, Utah. 10th annual. Independent film festival "by filmmakers for filmmakers." Feature-length films and shorts. Numerous awards given. Screenplay competition during the year. For info: Slamdance, 5634 Melrose Ave, Los Angeles, CA 90038. Phone: (323) 466-1786. Fax: (323) 466-1784. E-mail: mail@slamdance.com. Web: www.slamdance.com.

SOUTHERN CALIFORNIA EARTHQUAKE: 10th ANNIVERSARY. Jan 17, 1994. An earthquake measuring 6.6 on the Richter scale struck the Los Angeles area about 4:20 AM. The epicenter was at Northridge in the San Fernando Valley, about 20 miles northwest of downtown Los Angeles. A death toll of 51 was announced Jan 20. Sixteen of the dead were killed in the collapse of one apartment building. More than 25,000 people were made homeless by the quake and 680,000 lost electric power. Many buildings were destroyed and others made uninhabitable due to structural damage. A section of the Santa Monica Freeway, part of the Simi Valley Freeway and three major overpasses collapsed. Hundreds of aftershocks occurred in the following several weeks. Costs to repair the damages were estimated at 15–30 billion dollars.

SOUTHWESTERN EXPOSITION LIVESTOCK SHOW AND RODEO. Jan 17–Feb 8. Fort Worth, TX. Western-flavored extravaganza. World's first indoor professional rodeo, began in 1918 (45 acres under roof). Ranch Rodeo, prize livestock (more than 22,000 head) displays, horse shows, midway, commercial exhibits and quality family-oriented entertainment. Est attendance: 930,000. For info: W.R. Watt, Jr, PO Box 150, Fort Worth, TX 76101-0150. Phone: (817) 877-2400. Fax: (817) 877-2499. Web: www.fwssr.com.

TIP-UP TOWN USA™. Jan 17–18 (also Jan 24–25). Houghton Lake, MI. 54th annual. Michigan's largest winter family festival featuring ice-fishing contests, softball on the ice, polar bear dip, parade, carnival, vendors, arts and crafts, fireworks, Poker Runs & Scavenger Hunts, Radar Runs and much more. Annually, the 3rd and 4th weekends of Jan. Est attendance: 35,000. For info: Chamber of Commerce, 1625 W Houghton Lake Dr, Houghton Lake, MI 48629. Phone: (800) 248-5253. E-mail: hlcc@iserv.net. Web: www.houghtonlakechamber.org.

WICHITA WEST BULLFEST. Jan 17. Multi-Purpose Events Center, J.S. Bridgewell Agricultural Center, Wichita Falls, TX. Bullriding at its best—local and area riders compete. Est attendance: 2,600. For info: Wichita Falls Conv & Visitors Bureau, 1000 5th St, Wichita Falls, TX 76301. Phone: (940) 716-5500 or (940) 691-2738. Fax: (940) 716-5509. E-mail: MPEC@wf.net. Web: www.wichitafalls.org or www.mpecwf.com.

WINTERFEST. Jan 17. Burton, MI. All kinds of cans and brewery memorabilia such as steins, coasters, signs, mirrors, bottles, neon signs, etc. $12 general admission includes display table if desired, available on first-come, first-served basis. Also includes food and beverages and door prize raffle tickets. Kids under eight free. Est attendance: 150. For info: Gene Goulet, Pres, Mid-Michigan Chapter, Beer Can Collectors of America, 5306 Lippincott, Burton, MI 48519. Phone: (810) 742-5353. E-mail: davevanh@aol.com. Web: www.bcca.com.

WISCONSIN DELLS FLAKE OUT FESTIVAL. Jan 17–18. Wisconsin Dells, WI. An exciting winter festival featuring Wisconsin's only state-sanctioned snow sculpting competition. Other activities include ice carving demonstrations, live entertainment, snowman making competition, totally tubular snow slide, turkey bowling, Eskimo Pie eating contest, pony rides, sleigh rides, glowing hot-air balloons, food, music and fireworks. Est attendance: 30,000. For info: Wisconsin Dells Visitors & Convention Bureau, PO Box 390, Wisconsin Dells, WI 53965. Phone: (800) 223-3557. E-mail: info@wisdells.com. Web: www.wisdells.com.

BIRTHDAYS TODAY

Muhammad Ali, 62, former heavyweight champion boxer, who changed his name after converting to Islam, born Cassius Marcellus Clay, Jr, Louisville, KY, Jan 17, 1942.

Jim Carrey, 42, actor (*Dumb and Dumber, The Truman Show, Ace Ventura*), comedian ("In Living Color"), born Newmarket, ON, Canada, Jan 17, 1962.

James Earl Jones, 73, actor (*The Great White Hope; Roots: The Next Generations*), born Arktabula, MS, Jan 17, 1931.

Eartha Kitt, 77, singer, actress, born North, SC, Jan 17, 1927.

Ruth Ann Minner, 69, Governor of Delaware (D), born Milford, DE, Jan 17, 1935.

Newton Minow, 78, former head of the Federal Communications Commission (1961–63), called television a "vast wasteland," born Milwaukee, WI, Jan 17, 1926.

Sheree North, 71, actress (*Marilyn; How to Be Very, Very Popular*), born Dawn Bethel, Los Angeles, CA, Jan 17, 1933.

Maury Povich, 65, talk-show host, born Washington, DC, Jan 17, 1939.

Vidal Sassoon, 76, hair stylist, born London, England, Jan 17, 1928.

Betty White, 80, actress ("Mary Tyler Moore," "The Golden Girls"), animal rights activist, born Oak Park, IL, Jan 17, 1924 (some sources say 1922).

Paul Young, 48, singer ("Every Time You Go Away"), born Luton, England, Jan 17, 1956.

Donald William (Don) Zimmer, 73, baseball manager and former player, born Cincinnati, OH, Jan 17, 1931.

JANUARY 18 — SUNDAY
Day 18 — 348 Remaining

FIRST BLACK US CABINET MEMBER: ANNIVERSARY. Jan 18, 1966. Robert Clifton Weaver was sworn in as Secretary of Housing and Urban Development, becoming the first black cabinet member in US history. He was nominated by President Lyndon Johnson. Weaver died at New York, NY, July 17, 1997.

FLOOD, CURT: BIRTH ANNIVERSARY. Jan 18, 1938. Curtis Charles (Curt) Flood, baseball player, born at Houston, TX. Flood was one of baseball's best center fielders in the 1960s, batting .293 over 15 seasons and playing spectacular defense. After the 1969 season, he refused to accept a trade from the St. Louis Cardinals to the Philadelphia Phillies. "I am not a piece of property to be bought and sold irrespective of my wishes," he said in a letter to Commissioner Bowie Kuhn. The resulting lawsuit went to the Supreme Court where Flood lost. But his stand, taken because he did not want to switch teams, paved the way for the end of baseball's reserve clause and the advent of free agency. Died at Los Angeles, CA, Jan 20, 1997.

GRANT, CARY: 100th BIRTH ANNIVERSARY. Jan 18, 1904. Known as a romantic leading actor, Grant was born at Bristol, England. For more than three decades Grant entertained with his wit, charm, sophistication and personality. His films include *Topper, The Awful Truth, Bringing Up Baby* and *Holiday*. Died at Davenport, IA, Nov 29, 1986.

HARDY, OLIVER: BIRTH ANNIVERSARY. Jan 18, 1892. Born at Atlanta, GA, Hardy teamed up with Stan Laurel in 1926 to form the comedy team of Laurel and Hardy. Among their most popular films: *From Soup to Nuts, Babes in Toyland, Swiss Miss*. Hardy died at Hollywood, Aug 7, 1957.

HEALTHY WEIGHT WEEK. Jan 18–24. 10th annual. People who diet the first week in January and binge the second are ready for better living by the third week: Healthy Weight Week. This is a week to promote healthy lifestyle habits that last a lifetime and prevent weight and eating problems (not cause them, as dieting does); a time to move on to Health at Any Size. News release, 2004 awards and consumer handouts available on website. For info: Francie M. Berg, Healthy Weight Network, 402 S 14th St, Hettinger, ND 58639. E-mail: fmberg@healthyweight.net. Web: www.healthyweight.net.

HOUSTON MARATHON AND HEALTH & FITNESS EXPO. Jan 18. Houston, TX. 32nd annual citywide race, sponsored by HP. Est attendance: 200,000. For info: Houston Marathon, 720 N Post Oak Rd, #335, Houston, TX 77024. Phone: (713) 957-3453. Fax: (713) 957-3406. E-mail: marathon@hphoustonmarathon.com. Web: www.hphoustonmarathon.com.

HUNT FOR HAPPINESS WEEK. Jan 18–24. Celebrate the 3rd annual Hunt for Happiness Week sponsored by the Secret Society of Happy People. Activities, suggestions and ideas for teachers, youth leaders and parents to encourage kids and teens to discover more happy moments are available on our website, or order your Hunt for Happiness Celebration Kit for $5. Annually, the third full week in January. For info: Secret Society of Happy People, 1315 Rivercháse Dr, #2316, Coppell, TX 75019. Phone: (972) 471-1485. E-mail: pjohnson@sohp.com. Web: www.sohp.com.

"THE JEFFERSONS" TV PREMIERE: ANNIVERSARY. Jan 18, 1975. CBS sitcom about an African-American family (formerly neighbors of the Bunkers on "All in the Family") who moved to Manhattan's East Side, thanks to the success of George Jefferson's chain of dry cleaning stores. Having a format similar to "All in the Family," the show featured a black bigot, George Jefferson. Particularly memorable were the racial slurs Jefferson used against the mixed-marriage neighbors, Tom and Helen Willis. The show was able to humorously introduce subjects such as mixed marriage on a prime-time series. Cast included Sherman Hemsley as George Jefferson, Isabel Sanford as Louise Jefferson, Mike Evans and Damon Evans as Lionel, Franklin Cover and Roxie Roker as the mixed couple and Berlinda Tolbert as their daughter, Jenny, and Paul Benedict as British bachelor neighbor Bentley. The last episode aired July 23, 1985.

KAYE, DANNY: BIRTH ANNIVERSARY. Jan 18, 1913. American entertainer Danny Kaye was born David Daniel Kaminski at Brooklyn, NY. Kaye became a star in films, international stage performances and television. His most notable films are *The Secret Life of Walter Mitty* (1947) and *Hans Christian Andersen* (1952), as well as the classic *White Christmas*. He hosted the television show *The Danny Kaye Show* in the 1960s. In addition, Kaye helped raise millions of dollars for the United Nations International Children's Emergency Fund (UNICEF) and musicians' pension plans. He died Mar 3, 1987, at Los Angeles, CA.

LEWIS AND CLARK EXPEDITION COMMISSIONED: ANNIVERSARY. Jan 18, 1803. Seeking information on what lay west of the young United States, President Thomas Jefferson sent a confidential letter to Congress on Jan 18, 1803, requesting funds for an exploratory expedition to be led by Captain Meriwether Lewis and Lieutenant William Clark. After the Louisiana Purchase was signed on April 30, 1803, the expedition's mission changed: it became a survey of new American land. The "Corps of Discovery" set off May 14 from St. Louis and returned with much information about the land, the peoples there and the flora and fauna on Sept 23, 1806. (See also May 14 and Sept 23.)

MUSICAL TRIBUTE TO DR. MARTIN LUTHER KING. Jan 18. Abraham Lincoln's Birthplace National Historical Site, Hodgenville, KY. Local Baptist and Methodist choirs present a selection of hymns and spirituals in commemoration of Dr. King's birthday. Est attendance: 150. For info: Patsy Cobb, 2995 Lincoln Farm Rd, Hodgenville, KY 42748. Phone: (502) 358-3137.

POOH DAY: A.A. MILNE: BIRTH ANNIVERSARY. Jan 18, 1882. Anniversary of the birth of A(lan) A(lexander) Milne, English author, especially remembered for his children's stories: *Winnie the Pooh* and *The House at Pooh Corner*. Also the author of *Mr Pim Passes By, When We Were Very Young* and *Now We Are Six*. Born at London, England, died at Hartfield, England, Jan 31, 1956.

ROGET, PETER MARK: 225th BIRTH ANNIVERSARY. Jan 18, 1779. English physician, best known as author of Roget's *Thesaurus of English Words and Phrases*, first published in 1852. Roget was also the inventor of the "log-log" slide rule. He was born at London, England, and died at West Malvern, Worcestershire, England, Sept 12, 1869.

RUFFIN, DAVIS ELI (DAVID): BIRTH ANNIVERSARY. Jan 18, 1941. American popular singer David Ruffin was born at Meridian, MS. He was one of the original members of the Motown singing group the Temptations, which began in Detroit in the 1960s. Ruffin left the group in 1968 to pursue a solo career. He and the other original members of the Temptations were inducted into the Rock and Roll Hall of Fame in 1989. Ruffin died June 1, 1991, at Philadelphia, PA.

SAN DIEGO MARATHON & HALF MARATHON. Jan 18. Plaza Camino Real, Carlsbad, CA. Race open to runners, walkers, race walkers and disabled. Post-race festival with refreshments, entertainment, massages and more. Jan 16–18 is the All About Fitness Expo under the Big Top at the Plaza Camino Real. Est attendance: 12,000. For info: San Diego Marathon, 511 S Cedros Ave, Solana Beach, CA 92075. Phone: (858) 792-2900. E-mail: imisdm@aol.com.

"TED MACK'S ORIGINAL AMATEUR HOUR" TV PREMIERE: ANNIVERSARY. Jan 18, 1948. This immensely popular show, featuring host Ted Mack, introduced amateurs performing their talents on live television. It debuted as a regularly scheduled broadcast on the Dumont network. The show had been a long-running success on radio as "Major Bowes' Original Amateur Hour" until the death of Edward Bowes. Mack became host of the radio show a year later. While a few episodes were televised in 1947, the show did not air weekly until this date. The program ran until 1970 and also continued on radio until 1952.

VERSAILLES PEACE CONFERENCE: 85th ANNIVERSARY. Jan 18, 1919. French President Raymond Poincare formally opened the (World War I) Peace Conference at Versailles, France. It proceeded under the chairmanship of Georges Clemenceau. In May the conference disposed of Germany's colonies and delivered a treaty to the German delegates on May 7, 1919, fourth anniversary of the sinking of the *Lusitania*. Final treaty-signing ceremonies were completed at the palace at Versailles, June 28, 1919.

WEBSTER, DANIEL: BIRTH ANNIVERSARY. Jan 18, 1782. American statesman and orator who said, on Apr 6, 1830, "The people's government, made for the people, made by the people, and answerable to the people." Born at Salisbury, NH; died at Marshfield, MA, Oct 24, 1852.

WEEK OF CHRISTIAN UNITY. Jan 18–25. From the Conversion of St. Peter (Jan 18) to the Conversion of St. Paul (Jan 25).

WORLD RELIGION DAY. Jan 18. To proclaim the oneness of religion and the belief that world religion will unify the peoples of the earth. Baha'i-sponsored observance established in 1950 by the Baha'is of the US. Annually, the third Sunday in January. For info: Baha'is of the US, Office of Public Information, 1320 Nineteenth St NW, Ste 350, Washington, DC 20036. Phone: (202) 466-9870. Fax: (202) 466-9873. E-mail: opi@usbnc.org. Web: www.us.bahai.org.

BIRTHDAYS TODAY

John Boorman, 71, filmmaker (*Deliverance, Excalibur*), born Shepperton, England, Jan 18, 1933.
Kevin Costner, 49, actor (*Field of Dreams, Dances with Wolves* [Oscar for directing], *Bull Durham*), born Lynwood, CA, Jan 18, 1955.
Ray Dolby, 71, inventor of the Dolby Sound System for sound recording, born Portland, OR, Jan 18, 1933.
Jane Horrocks, 40, actress (*Little Voice*, "Absolutely Fabulous"), born Lancashire, England, Jan 18, 1964.
Evelyn Lear, 73, opera singer, born New York, NY, Jan 18, 1931.
Jesse L. Martin, 35, actor ("Law & Order," "Ally McBeal"), born Rocky Mountain, VA, Jan 18, 1969.
Mark Messier, 43, hockey player, born Edmonton, AB, Canada, Jan 18, 1961.

JANUARY 19 — MONDAY
Day 19 — 347 Remaining

BOB HOPE CHRYSLER CLASSIC. Jan 19–25. La Quinta, CA. The nation's largest sports event for charity. It features PGA tour pros, celebrities and amateurs. Est attendance: 110,000. For info: Pat Bennett, PR and Production, Bob Hope Chrysler Classic, 39000 Bob Hope Dr, Rancho Mirage, CA 92270. Phone: (760) 346-8184. Fax: (760) 346-6329. E-mail: info@bhcc.com. Web: www.bhcc.com.

CÉZANNE, PAUL: BIRTH ANNIVERSARY. Jan 19, 1839. Post-impressionist painter, born at Aix-en-Provence, France. Still-lifes and landscapes were his preferred subjects. Cézanne died Oct 23, 1906, at Aix.

CONFEDERATE HEROES DAY. Jan 19. Observed on anniversary of Robert E. Lee's birthday. Official holiday in Texas.

ETHIOPIA: TIMKET. Jan 19. National holiday. Epiphany in the Ethiopian and Coptic churches. Occurs some years on Jan 20. Also a holiday in Eritrea.

"48 HOURS" TV PREMIERE: ANNIVERSARY. Jan 19, 1988. CBS prime-time newsmagazine program airing each week with first Dan Rather as host, then Leslie Stahl. Recently, the focus has been on crime mysteries.

HELMS, EDGAR J.: BIRTH ANNIVERSARY. Jan 19, 1863. Born near Malone, NY, Reverend Dr. Helms became a minister to a parish of poor immigrants in Boston's South End. In that capacity he developed the philosophy and organization that eventually became Goodwill Industries. Helms died Dec 23, 1942, at Boston.

JOPLIN, JANIS: BIRTH ANNIVERSARY. Jan 19, 1943. Possibly the most highly regarded white female blues singer of all time, Janis Joplin was born at Port Arthur, TX. Joplin's appearance with Big Brother and the Holding Company at the Monterey International Pop Festival in August 1967 launched her to superstar status. Among her recording hits were "Get It While You Can," "Piece of My Heart" and "Ball and Chain." She died of a heroin overdose Oct 4, 1970, at Hollywood, CA, at the age of 27.

KING, MARTIN LUTHER, JR: BIRTHDAY OBSERVED. Jan 19. Public Law 98-144 designates the third Monday in January as an annual legal public holiday observing the birth of Martin Luther King, Jr. First observed in 1986. In New Hampshire, this day is designated Civil Rights Day. See also: "King, Martin Luther, Jr: Birth Anniversary" (Jan 15).

LEE, ROBERT E.: BIRTH ANNIVERSARY. Jan 19, 1807. Greatest military leader of the Confederacy, son of Revolutionary War General Henry (Light Horse Harry) Lee. His surrender Apr 9, 1865, to Union General Ulysses S. Grant brought an end to the Civil War. Born at Westmoreland County, VA, he died at Lexington, VA, Oct 12, 1870. His birthday is observed in Florida, Kentucky, Louisiana, South Carolina and Tennessee. Observed on third Monday in January in Alabama, Arkansas and Mississippi.

★**MARTIN LUTHER KING, JR, FEDERAL HOLIDAY.** Jan 19. Presidential Proclamation has been issued without request each year for the third Monday in January since 1986.

"THE MILLIONAIRE" TV PREMIERE: ANNIVERSARY. Jan 19, 1955. The CBS drama that had all of America hoping to find Michael Anthony on their doorstep. Mr John Beresford Tipton was a millionaire who made a hobby of giving away million dollar checks anonymously to unknown people to see how they handled the sudden wealth. Michael Anthony, played by Marvin Miller, was Mr Tipton's personal secretary and the star of "The Millionaire." No one ever saw Mr Tipton but his voice would greet Anthony at the opening of each show and issue instructions for delivery of the next check. Anthony would then find the recipient and give him or her the check, explaining that the recipient had to agree never to divulge the amount or how it was acquired.

NATIONAL HANDWRITING ANALYSIS WEEK. Jan 19–23. To inform the public that handwriting is a form of behavior that can be analyzed for personality traits; that handwriting originates in the brain; that handwriting style, like personality, remains constant over a period of time while reflecting development; that personality traits can be changed by making changes in one's handwriting. Annually, a week in January to include National Handwriting Day (John Hancock's birthday, January 23, 1737 [NS]). Sponsor: American Handwriting Analysis Fdtn (AHAF), PO Box 6201, San Jose, CA 95150. Phone: (800) 447-2637. Web: www.handwritingfoundation.org. Additional contact: American Association of Handwriting Analysts, 820 W Maple St, Hinsdale, IL 60521. Phone: (708) 323-5647.

PEDDLER'S VILLAGE ANNUAL QUILT COMPETITION AND DISPLAY. Jan 19–Apr 4. Peddler's Village, Lahaska, PA. Handmade quilt entries compete for $1,500 in cash prizes in such categories as traditional, Amish, creative, clothing,

	S	M	T	W	T	F	S
January 2004					1	2	3
	4	5	6	7	8	9	10
	11	12	13	14	15	16	17
	18	19	20	21	22	23	24
	25	26	27	28	29	30	31

children's and amateur. A distinguished panel of judges chooses the winners, and quilts are displayed in the Village Gazebo. Open daily to public. Free admission. Est attendance: 250,000. For info: Peddler's Village, Routes 202 & 263, Lahaska, PA 18931. Phone: (215) 794-4000. Fax: (215) 794-4001. Web: www.peddlersvillage.com.

POE, EDGAR ALLAN: BIRTH ANNIVERSARY. Jan 19, 1809. American poet and story writer, called "America's most famous man of letters." Born at Boston, MA, he was orphaned in dire poverty in 1811 and was raised by Virginia merchant John Allan. In 1836 he married his 13-year-old cousin, Virginia Clemm. A magazine editor of note, he is best remembered for his poetry (especially "The Raven") and for his tales of suspense. Died at Baltimore, MD, Oct 7, 1849.

STOCK EXCHANGE HOLIDAY (MARTIN LUTHER KING DAY). Jan 19. The holiday schedules for the various exchanges are subject to change if relevant rules, regulations or exchange policies are revised. If you have questions, phone: American Stock Exchange (212) 306-1000; Chicago Board of Options Exchange (312) 786-5600; Chicago Board of Trade (312) 435-3500; New York Stock Exchange (212) 656-2065; Pacific Stock Exchange (415) 393-4000; Philadelphia Stock Exchange (215) 496-5000.

TIN CAN PATENT: ANNIVERSARY. Jan 19, 1825. Ezra Daggett and Thomas Kensett obtained a patent for a process for storing food in tin cans.

WATT, JAMES: BIRTH ANNIVERSARY. Jan 19, 1736 (OS). Scottish engineer and inventor, born at Greenock, Scotland. The modern steam engine grew out of his efficiency-improving inventions. Died at Heathfield, England, Aug 25, 1819.

BIRTHDAYS TODAY

Desi Arnaz, Jr, 51, singer, actor, born Los Angeles, CA, Jan 19, 1953.
Michael Crawford, 62, actor, singer (*Phantom of the Opera*), born Salisbury, Wiltshire, England, Jan 19, 1942.
Phil Everly, 65, singer, with brother Don (The Everly Brothers), born Chicago, IL, Jan 19, 1939.
Shelley Fabares, 62, actress ("The Donna Reed Show," "Coach," sang "Johnny Angel"), born Santa Monica, CA, Jan 19, 1942 (some sources say 1944).
Richard Lester, 72, director (*The Four Musketeers, Superman II & III*), born Philadelphia, PA, Jan 19, 1932.
Robert MacNeil, 73, broadcast journalist, born Montreal, QC, Canada, Jan 19, 1931.
Dolly Parton, 58, singer ("Jolene"), actress (*Nine to Five*), born Sevier County, TN, Jan 19, 1946.
William Ragsdale, 43, actor ("Brother's Keeper," "Herman's Head"), born El Dorado, AR, Jan 19, 1961.
Simon Rattle, 49, British orchestra conductor, born Liverpool, England, Jan 19, 1955.
Jean Stapleton, 81, actress (*Klute*; Emmy for "All in the Family"), born Jeanne Murray, New York, NY, Jan 19, 1923.
Jeff Van Gundy, 42, basketball coach, born Inkster, MI, Jan 19, 1962.
Shawn Wayans, 33, actor (*Scary Movie*, "In Living Color"), born New York, NY, Jan 19, 1971.
Fritz Weaver, 78, actor (*Holocaust, Marathon Man*), born Philadelphia, PA, Jan 19, 1926.

JANUARY 20 — TUESDAY
Day 20 — 346 Remaining

AQUARIUS, THE WATER CARRIER. Jan 20–Feb 19. In the astronomical/astrological zodiac, which divides the sun's apparent orbit into 12 segments, the period Jan 20–Feb 19 is identified, traditionally, as the sun-sign of Aquarius, the Water Carrier. The ruling planet is Uranus or Saturn.

AZERBAIJAN: MARTYRS' DAY. Jan 20. National holiday. Commemorates the Azeris killed by Soviet troops, Jan 20, 1990, as they fought for independence.

BRAZIL: NOSSO SENHOR DO BONFIM FESTIVAL. Jan 20–30. Salvador, Bahia, Brazil. Our Lord of the Happy Ending Festival is one of Salvador's most colorful religious feasts. Climax comes with people carrying water to pour over church stairs and sidewalks to cleanse them of impurities.

BRAZIL: SAN SEBASTIAN'S DAY. Jan 20. Patron Saint of Rio de Janeiro.

BURNS, GEORGE: BIRTH ANNIVERSARY. Jan 20, 1896. Comedian George Burns was born at New York City. He began in vaudeville without much success until he teamed up with Gracie Allen, who became his wife. As Burns and Allen, the two had a long career on radio, in film and with their hit TV show, "The George Burns and Gracie Allen Show." Later he played the role of God and the Devil in the *Oh, God!* movies. He lived to be 100, and died Mar 9, 1996, at Los Angeles, CA.

FELLINI, FEDERICO: BIRTH ANNIVERSARY. Jan 20, 1920. Director and screenwriter Federico Fellini was born at Rimini, Italy. Four of Fellini's movies won Oscars for best foreign-language film: *La Strada* (1956), *The Nights of Cabiria* (1957), *8½* (1963) and *Amarcord* (1974). He received an honorary Oscar in 1993 in recognition of his cinematic accomplishments. Fellini died Oct 31, 1993, at Rome.

GRAY, HAROLD LINCOLN: BIRTH ANNIVERSARY. Jan 20, 1894. The creator of *Little Orphan Annie* was born at Kankakee, IL. The comic strip featuring the 12-year-old Annie, her dog Sandy and her mentor and guardian Oliver "Daddy" Warbucks began appearing in the *Chicago Tribune* in 1924. While controversial for its strong conservative views, the strip was highly popular for its stories demonstrating the values of perseverance, independence and courage. Gray created the strip for 44 years until his death May 9, 1968, at La Jolla, CA, at age 74.

GUINEA-BISSAU: NATIONAL HEROES DAY. Jan 20. National holiday.

JOHN MARSHALL APPOINTED CHIEF JUSTICE: ANNIVERSARY. Jan 20, 1801. John Marshall was appointed the fourth chief justice of the US Supreme Court.

LEE, RICHARD HENRY: BIRTH ANNIVERSARY. Jan 20, 1732. Signer of the Declaration of Independence. Born at Westmoreland County, VA, he died June 19, 1794, at his birthplace.

LESOTHO: ARMY DAY. Jan 20. Lesotho.

RID THE WORLD OF FAD DIETS AND GIMMICKS DAY. Jan 20. The 15th annual Slim Chance Awards for the "worst" weight loss products of the year are announced. Diet quackery defrauds, disables and kills. Listing of 2004 awards, diet quackery information and consumer handouts available on website. For info: Francie M. Berg, Healthy Weight Network, 402 S 14th St, Hettinger, ND 58639. E-mail: fmberg@healthyweight.net. Web: www.healthyweight.net.

SONORA SHOWCASE. Jan 20–21 (tentative). Yuma, AZ. A fiesta to promote the state of Sonora, Mexico, features mariachis, folkloric dancers, food and beverage samples, vacation information and curios. Est attendance: 4,500. For info: Yuma Civic and Conv Ctr, 1440 Desert Hills Dr, Yuma, AZ 85365. Phone: (928) 373-5043. Fax: (928) 344-9121.

SOUTHWEST SENIOR INVITATIONAL GOLF CHAMPIONSHIP. Jan 20–23. Yuma Golf and Country Club, Yuma,

AZ. 28th annual. A 36-hole medal play tournament, limited to 120 players 50 and older. For info: Caballeros de Yuma, Inc, Box 5987, Yuma, AZ 85366-5987. Phone: (928) 343-1715. Fax: (928) 783-1609. Web: www.caballeros.org.

US REVOLUTIONARY WAR: CESSATION OF HOSTILITIES: ANNIVERSARY. Jan 20, 1783. The British and US Commissioners signed a preliminary "Cessation of Hostilities," which was ratified by England's King George III Feb 14 and led to the Treaties of Paris and Versailles, Sept 3, 1783, ending the war.

BIRTHDAYS TODAY

Edwin "Buzz" Aldrin, 74, former astronaut, one of first three men on moon, born Montclair, NJ, Jan 20, 1930.

Arte Johnson, 70, comedian, actor (Emmy for "Rowan & Martin's Laugh-In"), born Benton Harbor, MI, Jan 20, 1934 (some sources say 1929).

Lorenzo Lamas, 46, actor ("Falcon Crest," "Renegade"), born Los Angeles, CA, Jan 20, 1958.

David Lynch, 58, director ("Twin Peaks," *Blue Velvet*), writer, producer, born Missoula, MT, Jan 20, 1946.

Bill Maher, 48, comedian, TV host ("Politically Incorrect with Bill Maher"), born New York, NY, Jan 20, 1956.

Patricia Neal, 78, actress (*Breakfast at Tiffany's, Hud, The Subject Was Roses*), born Packard, KY, Jan 20, 1926.

Natan (Anatoly) Scharansky, 56, expatriate Soviet dissident, born Donetsk, USSR, Jan 20, 1948.

Skeet Ulrich, 34, actor (*Scream*), born New York, NY, Jan 20, 1970 (some sources say 1969).

Otis Dewey "Slim" Whitman, 80, singer (first country performer to play at the London Palladium), born Tampa, FL, Jan 20, 1924.

JANUARY 21 — WEDNESDAY
Day 21 — 345 Remaining

ALLEN, ETHAN: BIRTH ANNIVERSARY. Jan 21, 1738. Revolutionary War hero and leader of the Vermont "Green Mountain Boys." Born at Litchfield, CT, he died at Burlington, VT, Feb 12, 1789.

BALDWIN, ROGER NASH: BIRTH ANNIVERSARY. Jan 21, 1884. Founder of the American Civil Liberties Union, called the "country's unofficial agitator for, and defender of, its civil liberties." Born at Wellesley, MA, he died Aug 26, 1981, at Ridgewood, NJ.

BRECKINRIDGE, JOHN CABELL: BIRTH ANNIVERSARY. Jan 21, 1821. 14th vice president of the US (1857–61), serving under President James Buchanan. Born at Lexington, KY; died there May 17, 1875.

BROWNING, JOHN MOSES: BIRTH ANNIVERSARY. Jan 21, 1855. World-famous gunmaker and inventor who was taught gunsmithing by his Mormon pioneer father, Jonathan Browning, was born at Ogden, UT. Starting the J.M. & M.S. Browning Arms Company with his brother, he designed guns for Winchester, Remington, Stevens and Colt arms companies, as well as American and European armies. Browning had more gun patents than any other gunsmith in the world. He is best known for inventing the machine gun in 1890 and the automatic pistol in 1896. He died suddenly Nov 26, 1926, at age 71, while at Belgium on business. The company he founded, known now as Browning Arms Company, is located at Morgan, UT.

FIRST CONCORDE FLIGHT: ANNIVERSARY. Jan 21, 1976. The supersonic Concorde airplane was put into service by Britain and France.

JACKSON, THOMAS JONATHAN "STONEWALL": BIRTH ANNIVERSARY. Jan 21, 1824. Confederate general and one of the most famous soldiers of the American Civil War, best known as "Stonewall" Jackson. Born at Clarksburg, VA (now WV). He died of wounds received in battle near Chancellorsville, VA, May 10, 1863.

JUST DO IT DAY—MAKE THE CONNECTION. Jan 21. This is the day to honor "you" and to connect people and places. This is the day to plan a vacation or arrange to journey with a new travel companion rather than travel solo! This is the day to connect the "link," you select the "from" and "to." Annually, the third Wednesday in January. For info: Joy Babcock, JoyLinks—WeddingLinks, TraveLinks, SingleTravelersLinks, 666 Main St, Ste 210, Watertown, MA 02472. Phone: (617) 924-6840. E-mail: joy@joylinks.com. Web: joylinks.com.

KIWANIS INTERNATIONAL: ANNIVERSARY. Jan 21, 1915. First Kiwanis Club chartered at Detroit, MI.

MARGARET BRENT DEMANDS A POLITICAL VOICE: ANNIVERSARY. Jan 21, 1648. Margaret Brent made her claim as America's first feminist by demanding a voice and vote for herself in the Maryland colonial assembly. Brent came to America in 1638 and was the first woman to own property in Maryland. At the time of her demands she was serving as secretary to Governor Leonard Calvert. She was ejected from the meetings, but when Calvert died she became his executor and acting governor, presiding over the General Assembly.

MICHIGAN CAMPER, TRAVEL AND RV SHOW. Jan 21–25. Pontiac Silverdome, Pontiac, MI. This event brings together buyers and sellers of RVs, motor homes, campers and camping accessories, as well as buyers and sellers of camping vacations and travel destinations. Est attendance: 30,000. For info: Mike Wilbraham, ShowSpan, Inc, 2121 Celebration Dr NE, Grand Rapids, MI 49525. Phone: (616) 447-2860. Fax: (616) 447-2861. E-mail: events@showspan.com. Web: www.showspan.com.

MOON PHASE: NEW MOON. Jan 21. Moon enters New Moon phase at 4:05 PM, EST.

NATIONAL HUGGING DAY™. Jan 21. Since hugging is something everyone can do and since it is a healthful form of touching, this day should be spent hugging anyone who will accept a hug, especially family and friends. The most "Huggable People" of the year will be announced. Nominations accepted through Jan 10. For more info, please send SASE to: Kevin C. Zaborney, 2023 Vickory Rd, Caro, MI 48723. Phone: (989) 673-6696. E-mail: revkev@avci.net. Web: www.geocities.com/hugging_whining.

SOUTH FLORIDA SENIOR GAMES. Jan 21–Feb 5. Hollywood, FL. 14th annual. Hollywood observance includes paddleball, bocce, shuffleboard, golf and quilting. For info: Cynthia Hancock, City of Hollywood, Dept of Parks, Recreation & Cultural Arts, 1940 Harrison St, Ste 101, Hollywood, FL 33020. Phone: (954) 921-3404.

SQUIRREL APPRECIATION DAY. Jan 21. A day set aside each year to honor squirrels for being the wonderful little animals they are. For info: Christy Hargrove, 25 Jazaka Ridge Ln, Swan-

January 2004

S	M	T	W	T	F	S
				1	2	3
4	5	6	7	8	9	10
11	12	13	14	15	16	17
18	19	20	21	22	23	24
25	26	27	28	29	30	31

nanoa, NC 28778. Phone: (828) 686-4303. E-mail: christy@squirrelsrus.com. Web: www.squirrelsrus.com.

STONEWALL JACKSON'S BIRTHDAY CELEBRATION. Jan 21. Stonewall Jackson House, Lexington, VA. Celebrates the birthday of Stonewall Jackson. For info: Stonewall Jackson House, 8 E Washington St, Lexington, VA 24450. Phone: (540) 463-2552. E-mail: sjh1@rockbridge.net. Web: www.lexingtonvirginia.com.

TOPS CLUB, INC: ANNIVERSARY. Jan 21. Milwaukee, WI. TOPS (Take Off Pounds Sensibly) is the leading, international, nonprofit weight-loss support group. Founded in 1948 in Milwaukee, WI, by Esther Manz, a homemaker, TOPS has grown to almost 240,000 members in 11,000 chapters worldwide. It is dedicated to providing its members with information, motivation and fellowship in attaining and maintaining physician-prescribed weight-loss goals. For info: Melissa Baxter, TOPS Club Inc, 4575 S Fifth St, Milwaukee, WI 53207. Phone: (414) 482-4620 or (800) 932-8677. Web: www.tops.org.

WOLFMAN JACK: BIRTH ANNIVERSARY. Jan 21, 1938. Wolfman Jack was born Robert Smith at Brooklyn, NY. He became famous as a disc jockey for radio stations at Mexico in the 1960s. Wolfman Jack was influential as a border radio voice because the Mexican station broadcast at 250,000 watts, five times the legal limit for American stations at the time, and therefore he was heard over a vast part of the US. During his night shift he played blues, hillbilly and other black and white music that wasn't getting a lot of exposure. He later appeared on American radio, movies and television as an icon of 1960s radio. Wolfman Jack died July 1, 1995, at Belvidere, NC.

BIRTHDAYS TODAY

Robby Benson, 48, actor ("Search for Tomorrow," *Ode to Billie Joe*), born Robin Segal, Dallas, TX, Jan 21, 1956.
Geena Davis, 47, actress (Oscar for *The Accidental Tourist; Thelma and Louise*, "Buffalo Bill"), born Ware, MA, Jan 21, 1957.
Mac Davis, 62, actor, songwriter ("The Mac Davis Show," *North Dallas Forty*), born Lubbock, TX, Jan 21, 1942.
Placido Domingo, 63, opera singer, one of the "Three Tenors," born Madrid, Spain, Jan 21, 1941.
Jill Eikenberry, 57, actress ("LA Law"), born New Haven, CT, Jan 21, 1947.
Gary Locke, 54, Governor of Washington (D), born Seattle, WA, Jan 21, 1950.
Jack William Nicklaus, 64, golfer, born Columbus, OH, Jan 21, 1940.
Billy Ocean, 54, musician, songwriter, born Leslie Charles, Trinidad, West Indies, Jan 21, 1950.
Hakeem Abdul Olajuwon, 41, former basketball player, born Lagos, Nigeria, Jan 21, 1963.
Detlef Schrempf, 41, former basketball player, born Leverkusen, West Germany, Jan 21, 1963.
Paul Scofield, 82, actor (*A Man for All Seasons, Quiz Show*; stage: *A Man for All Seasons*), born Hurstpierpoint, England, Jan 21, 1922.

JANUARY 22 — THURSDAY
Day 22 — 344 Remaining

ALLIED LANDING AT ANZIO: 60th ANNIVERSARY. Jan 22, 1944. A predominately American Allied force of 36,000 men was landed at Anzio on Italy's western coast. Commanding officer John P. Lucas failed to take the initiative but instead fortified his original position and thus possibly missed an early opportunity to retake Rome. The Allies entered Rome, June 4, 1944.

ALLIES TAKE NEW GUINEA: ANNIVERSARY. Jan 22, 1943. In the first land victory over the Japanese in World War II, American and Australian soldiers overcame the last pockets of resistance west and south of Sanananda on New Guinea. Three thousand Allies were killed in the battle. The Japanese lost 7,000. Of the 350 prisoners taken, most were Chinese and Korean laborers attached to the Japanese forces. Almost no Japanese allowed themselves to be taken prisoner, preferring to commit hara-kiri.

AMPÈRE, ANDRE: BIRTH ANNIVERSARY. Jan 22, 1775. Physicist, student of electrical and magnetic phenomena, founder of the science of electrodynamics. Born at Lyons, France, from his early childhood, tragedy and depression pursued him. His father was executed during the French Revolution. Ampère died at Marseilles, France, June 10, 1836. The epitaph he selected for his tombstone was *tandem felix* ("happy at last"). The ampere, a unit of electrical current, is named for him.

ANSWER YOUR CAT'S QUESTION DAY. Jan 22. If you will stop what you are doing and take a look at your cat, you will observe that the cat is looking at you with a serious question. Meditate upon it, then answer the question! Annually, Jan 22. [©2003 by WH.] For info: Thomas & Ruth Roy, Wellcat Holidays, 2418 Long Ln, Lebanon, PA 17046. Phone: (717) 279-0184. E-mail: info@wellcat.com. Web: www.wellcat.com.

ANTIQUE VALENTINE EXHIBIT. Jan 22–Feb 15. Surratt House and Tavern, Clinton, MD. Display of 19th-century valentines and memorabilia. Est attendance: 800. For info: Surratt House Museum, PO Box 427, Clinton, MD 20735. Phone: (301) 868-1121. Fax: (301) 868-8177. Web: www.surratt.org.

AUGUSTA FUTURITY. Jan 22–31. Augusta, GA. Brings together the top cutting horses and riders in the world to compete for purse and awards of more than $880,000. Sponsors: Wrangler, John Deere, Ariat Boots, *Augusta Chronicle*, E-Z-Go Textron, Gist Silversmiths, COMCAST Cable, Circle R Custom Hat Works, Circle Y of Yoakum, Marsh Co., Horsecity.com, Dodge Trucks, INVESCO, CORTA-FLX, Bearing Point, Fort Dodge Animal Health, Carl Black Trailer Co, BellSouth and Augusta Metro Convention and Visitors Bureau. Est attendance: 42,000. For info: Skip Peterson, Dir of Mktg, Augusta Futurity, PO Box 936, Augusta, GA 30903. Phone: (706) 823-3370 or (706) 823-3417. Web: www.augustafuturity.com.

BACON, FRANCIS: BIRTH ANNIVERSARY. Jan 22, 1561 (OS). Statesman and essayist, born at London, England. One may guess that Bacon was of short stature as he wrote (*Apothegms*), "Wise nature did never put her precious jewels into a garret four stories high: and therefore . . . exceeding tall men had ever very empty heads." Died at London, Apr 9, 1626 (OS).

BALANCHINE, GEORGE: 100th BIRTH ANNIVERSARY. Jan 22, 1904. Born Georgi Militonovitch Balanchivadze at St. Petersburg, Russia, George Balanchine became one of the leading influences in 20th-century ballet. He choreographed more than 200 ballets including *Concerto Barocco, Apollo, Orpheus, Firebird, Swan Lake, Waltz Academy* and *The Nutcracker*. In 1933 he was invited to the US by Boston philanthropist Lincoln Kirstein to establish a school for American dancers. Together they founded the School of American Ballet in 1934 and then formed several ballet companies, including the New York City Ballet, which was led by Balanchine. Died at New York, NY, Apr 30, 1983.

Jan 22 ☆ *Chase's 2004 Calendar of Events* ☆

BYRON, GEORGE GORDON: BIRTH ANNIVERSARY. Jan 22, 1788. Romantic poet, born at London, England. Described as "Mad, bad, and dangerous to know." Died of fever at Missolonghi, Greece, Apr 19, 1824, while fighting for Greek independence.

CELEBRATION OF LIFE DAY. Jan 22. A time to honor our children and grandchildren in America. Each child and each life is to be held as a precious gift and should be treated with the highest respect and dignity of human life. For info: Judith Natale, Women of Freedom, USA, 2091 Del Monte Ave, Monterey, CA 93940. E-mail: childaware@aol.com.

CHINESE NEW YEAR. Jan 22. Traditional Chinese lunar year begins at sunset on the day of the second New Moon following the winter solstice. Outside China, the date of the New Year may differ by a day. The New Year can begin any time from Jan 21 through Feb 21. Begins the Year of the Monkey. Generally celebrated until the Lantern Festival 15 days later, but merchants usually reopen their stores and places of business on the fifth day of the first lunar month. This holiday is celebrated as Tet in Vietnam. See also: "China: Lantern Festival" (Feb 5).

"EMERGENCY!" TV PREMIERE: ANNIVERSARY. Jan 22, 1972. This NBC program was introduced in midseason up against "All in the Family." It surprised everyone by becoming quite popular. The fast-paced action of the fire department paramedics saving lives by giving victims emergency treatment and then taking them to the hospital demonstrated the steps taken during actual emergency situations. The last episode aired Sept 3, 1977.

GRIFFITH, DAVID (LEWELYN) WARK: BIRTH ANNIVERSARY. Jan 22, 1875. D.W. Griffith, pioneer producer-director in the American motion picture industry, best remembered for his film *Birth of a Nation* (1915). Born at LaGrange, KY. Died at Hollywood, CA, July 23, 1948.

"LAUGH-IN" TV PREMIERE: ANNIVERSARY. Jan 22, 1968. Actually the name of this NBC comedy was "Rowan and Martin's Laugh-In." Funny men Dan Rowan and Dick Martin hosted the show, but they seemed staid next to the show's other regulars, most of whom were young unknowns, including Dennis Allen, Chelsea Brown, Judy Carne, Ruth Buzzi, Ann Elder, Richard Dawson, Teresa Graves, Arte Johnson, Goldie Hawn, Alan Sues, Jo Anne Worley and Lily Tomlin. The show moved fast from gag to gag with heads popping out of bushes or doors in the big wall. The show brought a new energy to comedy as well as new phrases to our vocabulary ("You bet your sweet bippy," "Sock it to me"). The last telecast was May 14, 1973.

"OZARK JUBILEE" TV PREMIERE: ANNIVERSARY. Jan 22, 1955. ABC country and western music show hosted by Red Foley from Springfield, MO. Brenda "(Open Up Your Heart and Let the Sunshine In") Lee appeared on the show at age 10 as one of the regulars. Other regulars included Smiley Burnette, Bobby Lord, Wanda Jackson, Suzi Arden and Webb Pierce.

PONSELLE, ROSA: BIRTH ANNIVERSARY. Jan 22, 1897. Formerly Rosa Melba Ponzilla, soprano Ponselle was born at Meriden, CT. Her career changed direction from vaudeville to opera when she was discovered by Enrico Caruso at the age of 21. Ponselle made her operatic debut at the Met in Verdi's *La forza del destino*. Her career spanned 19 seasons at the Met and included performances at London and Florence. Ponselle died May 25, 1981, at Baltimore.

QUEEN VICTORIA: DEATH ANNIVERSARY. Jan 22, 1901. Queen Victoria died at age 82 after a reign of 64 years, the longest in British history. She had ruled over the one-quarter of the world that was the British Empire. Born May 24, 1819, at London, she died at Osborne, England.

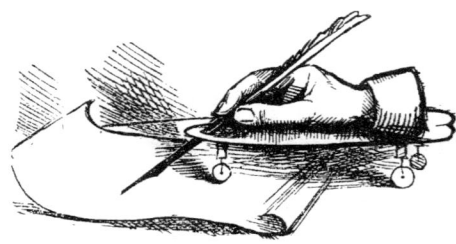

ROE v WADE DECISION: ANNIVERSARY. Jan 22, 1973. In the case of *Roe v Wade*, the US Supreme Court struck down state laws restricting abortions during the first six months of pregnancy. In the following two decades debate has continued to rage between those who believe a woman has a right to choose whether to continue a pregnancy and those who believe that aborting such a pregnancy is murder of an unborn child.

SAINT VINCENT: FEAST DAY. Jan 22. Spanish deacon and martyr who died AD 304. Patron saint of wine growers. Old weather lore says if there is sun on this day, good wine crops may be expected in the ensuing season.

STRINDBERG, AUGUST: BIRTH ANNIVERSARY. Jan 22, 1849. Swedish novelist and dramatist often called Sweden's greatest playwright. Born at Stockholm and died there of cancer on May 14, 1912, at age 63.

UKRAINE: UKRAINIAN DAY. Jan 22. National holiday. Commemorates the proclamation of the Ukrainian National Republic, Jan 22, 1918. Independence was short-lived, however; by 1921 Ukraine had become part of the Soviet Union. It gained its independence from the Soviet Union in 1991.

UPJOHN, RICHARD: BIRTH ANNIVERSARY. Jan 22, 1802. American architect and founder of the American Institute of Architects in 1857. A Gothic revivalist, he designed many churches. Among his works were Trinity Chapel, New York, NY; Corn Exchange Bank Building, New York, NY; Central Congregational Church, Boston, MA. Born at Shaftesbury, England, he died Aug 17, 1878, at Garrison, NY.

VINSON, FRED M.: BIRTH ANNIVERSARY. Jan 22, 1890. The 13th Chief Justice of the US, born at Louisa, KY. Served in the House of Representatives, appointed Director of War Mobilization during WWII and Secretary of the Treasury under Harry Truman. Nominated by Truman to succeed Harlan F. Stone as Chief Justice of the US Supreme Court. Died at Washington, DC, Sept 8, 1953.

WOMEN'S HEALTHY WEIGHT DAY. Jan 22. A day to honor American women of all sizes and confirm that beauty, talent and love cannot be weighed. Winners of the Women's Healthy Weight Day awards will be announced—businesses that portray size diversity and reject the national obsession with thinness that is shattering the lives of women, young girls and their families. News releases, 2004 awards and consumer handouts available on website. For info: Francie M. Berg, Healthy Weight Network, 402 S 14th St, Hettinger, ND 58639. E-mail: fmberg@healthyweight.net. Web: www.healthyweight.net.

BIRTHDAYS TODAY

Linda Blair, 45, actress (*The Exorcist, Airport*), born Westport, CT, Jan 22, 1959.
Seymour Cassel, 67, actor (*Faces, Dick Tracy, Honeymoon in Vegas*), born Detroit, MI, Jan 22, 1937.
Olivia D'Abo, 37, actress ("The Wonder Years," "The Single Guy"), born London, England, Jan 22, 1967.
Balthazar Getty, 29, actor (*Lost Highway*), born Los Angeles, CA, Jan 22, 1975.
John Hurt, 64, actor ("And the Band Played On," *The Elephant Man*), born Lincolnshire, England, Jan 22, 1940.

Diane Lane, 39, actress (*Unfaithful, A Walk on the Moon, A Little Romance*), born New York, NY, Jan 22, 1965.

Piper Laurie, 72, actress (*Fighting for My Daughter*, "Twin Peaks"), born Rosetta Jacobs, Detroit, MI, Jan 22, 1932.

Christopher Masterson, 24, actor ("Malcolm in the Middle," *My Best Friend's Wedding*), born Long Island, NY, Jan 22, 1980.

Steve Perry, 55, lead singer (Journey), born Hanford, CA, Jan 22, 1949.

Joseph Wambaugh, 67, ex-police officer, author (*The Blooding, Fugitive Nights*), born East Pittsburgh, PA, Jan 22, 1937.

JANUARY 23 — FRIDAY
Day 23 — 343 Remaining

"BARNEY MILLER" TV PREMIERE: ANNIVERSARY. Jan 23, 1975. ABC sitcom about a New York precinct captain starred Hal Linden as Captain Barney Miller. The 12th Precinct gang included Barbara Barrie as Miller's wife, Abe Vigoda as Detective Phil Fish, Max Gail as Sergeant Stan Wojciehowicz, Gregory Sierra as Sergeant Chano Amenguale, Jack Soo as Sergeant Nick Yemana, Ron Glass as Detective Ron Harris and a host of others. The last episode aired in 1982.

BIG BAND/SWING DANCE WEEKEND. Jan 23–25. Asheville, NC. 13th annual. Put on your dancing shoes and swing to two nights of great music. Enjoy our Saturday morning dance instruction, an afternoon tea dance and Big Band sounds. Est attendance: 1,400. For info: The Grove Park Inn Resort & Spa, 290 Macon Ave, Asheville, NC 28804. Phone: (800) 438-0050 or (828) 252-2711. Fax: (828) 252-6040. Web: www.grovepark inn.com.

BLACKWELL, ELIZABETH, AWARDED MD: ANNIVERSARY. Jan 23, 1849. Dr. Elizabeth Blackwell became the first woman to receive an MD degree. The native of Bristol, England, was awarded her degree by the Medical Institution of Geneva, NY.

BULGARIA: BABIN DEN. Jan 23. Celebrated throughout Bulgaria as Day of the Midwives or Grandmother's Day. Traditional festivities.

CARTER REINSTATES SELECTIVE SERVICE REGISTRATION: ANNIVERSARY. Jan 23, 1980. President Jimmy Carter, saying he planned to "revitalize" the Selective Service System, reinstated registration and pledged to use military force, if necessary, to protect the Persian Gulf from Soviet aggression.

EAGLES, ETC. Jan 23–25. Bismarck, AR. To see bald eagles in the wild and to learn about and observe birds of prey. Est attendance: 300. For info: Park Naturalist, DeGray Lake Resort State Park, 2027 State Park Entrance Rd, Bismarck, AR 71929-8194. Phone: (800) 737-8355. Fax: (501) 865-4436. E-mail: degray @arkansas.com. Web: www.degray.com.

HANCOCK, JOHN: BIRTH ANNIVERSARY. Jan 23, 1737. American patriot and statesman, first signer of the Declaration of Independence. Born at Braintree, MA, he died at Quincy, MA, Oct 8, 1793. Because of his conspicuous signature on the Declaration, Hancock's name has become part of the American language, referring to any handwritten signature, as in "Put your John Hancock on that!" (Some sources cite Hancock's Old Style birth date of January 12, 1736/7.)

HEWES, JOSEPH: BIRTH ANNIVERSARY. Jan 23, 1730. Signer of the Declaration of Independence. Born at Princeton, NJ, he died Nov 10, 1779, at Philadelphia, PA.

"THE KING FAMILY SHOW" TV PREMIERE: ANNIVERSARY. Jan 23, 1965. ABC musical variety show featuring the singing and playing of the King sisters and other descendents of William King Driggs, who organized the family musical group in the 1930s. Including spouses, children, grandchildren and great-grandchildren, some three dozen members of the King family have appeared on camera at one time.

KOVACS, ERNIE: 85th BIRTH ANNIVERSARY. Jan 23, 1919. Comedian and television pioneer, born at Trenton, NJ. Throughout the '40s and '50s Ernie Kovacs made a name for himself hosting his own shows including "The Ernie Kovacs Show" and "Ernie In Kovacsland" and a variety of quiz shows. He died in an automobile accident at Los Angeles, Jan 13, 1962.

LONGHORN WORLD CHAMPIONSHIP RODEO. Jan 23–25. Tulsa Convention Center, Tulsa, OK. 14th annual. More than 500 cowboys and cowgirls compete in six professional contests ranging from bronc riding to big, bad BONUS bull riding! Free beginners horsemanship clinic 40 minutes before performances. Qualifying rodeo for Longhorn's Championship Finals Rodeo in Nashville, TN. Featuring colorful opening and pageantry. Season opener for Longhorn rodeos nationally. Est attendance: 16,000. For info: W Bruce Lehrke, Pres, Longhorn World Chmpshp Rodeo Inc, PO Box 70159, Nashville, TN 37207. Phone: (615) 876-1016. Fax: (615) 876-4685. E-mail: info@long hornrodeo.com. Web: www.longhornrodeo.com.

MANET, ÉDOUARD: BIRTH ANNIVERSARY. Jan 23, 1832. Painter, born at Paris, France. Among his best-known paintings are *Olympia* and *Déjeuner sur l'herbe*. Manet died Apr 30, 1883, at Paris.

NATIONAL HANDWRITING DAY. Jan 23. Popularly observed on birthday of John Hancock to encourage more legible handwriting. (Some sources cite Hancock's Old Style birth date of January 12, 1736/7.)

SAINT PAUL WINTER CARNIVAL. Jan 23–Feb 8. St. Paul, MN. Minnesota's largest tourist attraction and the nation's oldest and largest winter festival. The 118-year-old St. Paul Winter Carnival provides 10 fun-filled days with more than 100 indoor and outdoor events celebrating the thrills and chills of wintertime fun. Est attendance: 275,000. For info: Saint Paul Festival and Heritage Foundation, 429 Landmark Ctr, 75 W 5th St, St. Paul, MN 55102. Phone: (651) 223-4700. Fax: (651) 223-4707. Web: www .winter-carnival.com.

SNOWPLOW MAILBOX HOCKEY DAY. Jan 23. It's wintertime and time for snowplow drivers everywhere to see how many rural mailboxes they can knock over. Twenty extra points for boosting one into the next township! [©2003 by WH.] For info: Thomas & Ruth Roy, Wellcat Holidays, 2418 Long Ln, Lebanon, PA 17046. Phone: (717) 279-0184. E-mail: info@wellcat .com. Web: www.wellcat.com.

STENDHAL: BIRTH ANNIVERSARY. Jan 23, 1783. French author Marie Henri Beyle, whose best-known pseudonym was Stendhal. Best remembered are his novels *The Red and the Black* (1831) and *The Charterhouse of Parma* (1839). Born at Grenoble, France, he died at Paris, Mar 23, 1842.

STEWART, POTTER: BIRTH ANNIVERSARY. Jan 23, 1915. Associate Justice of the Supreme Court of the US, nominated by President Eisenhower Jan 17, 1959. (Oath of office, May 15, 1959.) Born at Jackson, MI, he retired in July 1981 and died Dec 7, 1985, at Putney, VT, five days after suffering a stroke. Buried at Arlington National Cemetery.

TWENTIETH AMENDMENT TO US CONSTITUTION RATIFIED: ANNIVERSARY. Jan 23, 1933. The 20th Amendment was ratified, fixing the date of the presidential inauguration at the current Jan 20 instead of the previous Mar 4. It also specified that were the president-elect to die before taking office, the vice president-elect would succeed to the presidency. In addition, it set Jan 3 as the official opening date of Congress each year.

TWENTY-FOURTH AMENDMENT TO US CONSTITUTION RATIFIED: 40th ANNIVERSARY. Jan 23, 1964. Poll taxes and other taxes were eliminated as a prerequisite for voting in all federal elections by the 24th Amendment.

USS *PUEBLO* SEIZED BY NORTH KOREA: ANNIVERSARY. Jan 23, 1968. North Korea seized the USS *Pueblo* in the Sea of Japan, claiming the ship was on a spy mission. The crew was held for 11 months. The vessel was confiscated. Accompanying the crew when they were released—on Dec 22, 1968—was the body of Seaman Duane D. Hodges, the only crewman killed.

BIRTHDAYS TODAY

Richard Dean Anderson, 54, actor ("General Hospital," "MacGyver"), born Minneapolis, MN, Jan 23, 1950.
Princess Caroline, 47, born Monte Carlo, Monaco, Jan 23, 1957.
Tom Carper, 57, US Senator (D, Delaware), born Beckley, WV, Jan 23, 1947.
Gil Gerard, 61, actor ("Buck Rogers," "Sidekicks"), born Little Rock, AR, Jan 23, 1943.
Patrick Capper (Pat) Haden, 51, sportscaster, former football player, born Westbury, NY, Jan 23, 1953.
Mariska Hargitay, 40, actress ("Law & Order: Special Victims Unit"), born Los Angeles, CA, Jan 23, 1964.
Rutger Hauer, 60, actor (*Blade Runner*), born Breukelen, Netherlands, Jan 23, 1944.
Frank Lautenberg, 80, US Senator (D, New Jersey), born Paterson, NJ, Jan 23, 1924.
Jeanne Moreau, 76, actress (*Jules and Jim, Viva Maria*), born Paris, France, Jan 23, 1928.
Gail O'Grady, 41, actress ("NYPD Blue"), born Detroit, MI, Jan 23, 1963.
Chita Rivera, 71, singer, actress (*The Kiss of the Spider Woman*, "The New Dick Van Dyke Show"), born Conchita del Rivero, Washington, DC, Jan 23, 1933.
Tiffani-Amber Thiessen, 30, actress ("Beverly Hills 90210," "Saved by the Bell"), born Long Beach, CA, Jan 23, 1974.

JANUARY 24 — SATURDAY
Day 24 — 342 Remaining

ACHELIS, ELISABETH: BIRTH ANNIVERSARY. Jan 24, 1880. Calendar reform advocate, author of *The World Calendar*, born at Brooklyn, NY. Her proposed calendar made every year the same, with equal quarters, each year beginning on Sunday, Jan 1, and each date falling on same day of week every year. Died at New York, NY, Feb 11, 1973.

BELUSHI, JOHN: 55th BIRTH ANNIVERSARY. Jan 24, 1949. Actor, comedian ("Saturday Night Live," *Animal House, The Blues Brothers*), born at Chicago, IL. Died Mar 5, 1982, at Hollywood, CA.

BOLIVIA: ALACITIS FAIR. Jan 24–26. La Paz. Traditional annual celebration by Aymara Indians with prayers and offerings to god of prosperity.

BRICKHOUSE, JACK: BIRTH ANNIVERSARY. Jan 24, 1916. Born John Beasley Brickhouse at Peoria, IL. A legend in Chicago broadcasting, Brickhouse was the play-by-play voice for the first baseball game televised by WGN, an exhibition game between the Cubs and the White Sox on Apr 16, 1948. He broadcasted Cubs games for 40 years, Chicago Bears games for 24 years and some Chicago Bulls and White Sox games. In 1983, he received the Ford C. Frick Award. Died at Chicago, IL, Aug 6, 1998.

CALIFORNIA GOLD DISCOVERY: ANNIVERSARY. Jan 24, 1848. James W. Marshal, an employee of John Sutter, accidentally discovered gold while building a sawmill near Coloma, CA. Efforts to keep the discovery secret failed, and the gold rush of 1849 was under way.

CANADA: ROBBIE BURNS DINNER. Jan 24 (tentative). Bracebridge, ON. Dinner honoring Scottish poet Robert Burns with bagpipe music and haggis. For info: Royal Canadian Legion, c/o Pipe Band, Box 1252, Bracebridge, ON, Canada P1L 1V4. Phone: (705) 645-8500.

CHINESE NEW YEAR GOLDEN DRAGON PARADE. Jan 24. Chinatown, Los Angeles, CA. 105th annual. Traditional, colorful parade in celebration of the Chinese New Year. The most popular event of the New Year celebration activities. Jan 24–25 street fair, vendor booths, car show, carnival and stage show. Est attendance: 100,000. For info: Chinese Chamber of Commerce, 977 N Broadway, Ste E, Los Angeles, CA 90012. Phone: (213) 617-0396. Fax: (213) 617-2128. Web: www.lachinesechamber.org.

FARMERS MARKET. Jan 24 (also Feb 21, both dates tentative). El Centro, CA. Est attendance: 25,000. For info: El Centro Chamber of Commerce, Box 3006, El Centro, CA 92244. Phone: (760) 352-3681. Fax: (760) 352-3246. Web: www.elcentrochamber.com.

FDR's "UNCONDITIONAL SURRENDER" STATEMENT: ANNIVERSARY. Jan 24, 1943. At the end of the Casablanca Conference, 1943, Franklin D. Roosevelt and Winston Churchill held a press conference. Roosevelt stated, "Peace can come to the world only by the total elimination of German and Japanese war power. That means the unconditional surrender of Germany, Italy and Japan." This position calling for "unconditional surrender" has subsequently been criticized by some as having prolonged the war.

FIRST CANNED BEER: ANNIVERSARY. Jan 24, 1935. Canned beer went on sale for the first time at Richmond, VA.

GOODSON, MARK: BIRTH ANNIVERSARY. Jan 24, 1915. Producer and creator of TV game shows, Mark Goodson was born at Sacramento, CA. His career in entertainment began in radio where he created his first game show, "Pop the Question." He later teamed with Bill Todman and that partnership led to "What's My Line?" "I've Got a Secret," "Password," "The Price Is Right" and "Family Feud." He died Dec 18, 1992, at New York, NY.

ICE FEST. Jan 24–25. Ligonier, PA. A weekend of ice-carving demonstrations as blocks of ice are turned into works of art. Est attendance: 5,000. For info: Rachel Roehrig, Ligonier Chamber of Commerce, 120 E Main St, Ligonier, PA 15658. Phone: (724) 238-4200. Fax: (724) 238-4610. E-mail: ligonier@ligonier.com.

NATIONAL COWBOY POETRY GATHERING. Jan 24–31. Elko, NV. Soulful poetry and music performed by working cowboys. The event, which includes workshops, jam sessions, Western art and buckaroo trappings exhibits, attracts an international audience. For info: Western Folklife Center, 501 Railroad St, Elko, NV 89801. Phone: (775) 738-7508 for info or (888) 880-5885 for tickets. E-mail: wcf@westernfolklife.org. Web: www.westernfolklife.org.

ORANGE CITY BLUE SPRING MANATEE FESTIVAL. Jan 24–25. Valentine Park, Orange City, FL. Now in its 19th

☆ Chase's 2004 Calendar of Events ☆ Jan 24–25

year, this festival was created to raise awareness of the endangered West Indian manatee. It features more than 90 arts and crafts exhibitors, most of whom honor the manatee in a variety of mediums. Children's games, family entertainment, animal and environmental exhibits and food vendors round out the event. For info: Orange City Blue Spring Manatee Festival Office. Phone: (386) 775-9224. E-mail: info@themanateefestival.com. Web: www.themanateefestival.com.

SPACE MILESTONE: *COSMOS 954* (USSR) FALLS. Jan 24, 1978. Nuclear-equipped reconnaissance satellite launched Sept 18, 1977, fell into Earth's atmosphere and burned over northern Canada. Some radioactive debris reached ground on Jan 24, 1978.

SPACE MILESTONE: *DISCOVERY* (US). Jan 24, 1985. Space shuttle *Discovery* launched from and returned to Kennedy Space Center, FL, deploying eavesdropping satellite in secret, all-military mission, Jan 24–27, 1985.

TEXAS COLLECTORS' GUN & KNIFE SHOW. Jan 24–25. (Also May 15–16, Oct 2–4.) Multi-Purpose Events Center Exhibit Hall, Wichita Falls, TX. The largest gun, knife and shooting sports show and sale in the area. Buy, sell, swap. Est attendance: 5,000. For info: Wichita Falls CVB, 1000 5th St, Wichita Falls, TX 76301. Phone: (940) 716-5500. Fax: (940) 716-5509. E-mail: MPEC@wf.net. Web: www.wichitafalls.org.

WHARTON, EDITH: BIRTH ANNIVERSARY. Jan 24, 1862. American author (*The Age of Innocence, Ethan Frome*) and Pulitzer Prize winner. Born at New York, NY. Died at Pavillon Colombe, France, Aug 11, 1937, of a stroke.

BIRTHDAYS TODAY

Ernest Borgnine, 87, actor ("McHale's Navy," *Marty*), born Hamden, CT, Jan 24, 1917.
Neil Diamond, 63, singer, composer ("Cracklin' Rosie," "Song Sung Blue"), born Coney Island, NY, Jan 24, 1941.
Nastassja Kinski, 44, actress (*Tess, The Hotel New Hampshire*), born Berlin, Germany, Jan 24, 1960.
Matthew Lillard, 34, actor (*Scream, Scooby-Doo*), born Lansing, MI, Jan 24, 1970.
Aaron Neville, 63, singer, songwriter, born New Orleans, LA, Jan 24, 1941.
Michael Ontkean, 58, actor ("Twin Peaks," *Slap Shot*), born Vancouver, BC, Canada, Jan 24, 1946.
Mary Lou Retton, 36, Olympic gold medal gymnast, born Fairmont, WV, Jan 24, 1968.
Oral Roberts, 86, evangelist, born Tulsa, OK, Jan 24, 1918.
Yakov Smirnoff, 53, comedian ("What a Country," "Night Court"), born Odessa, USSR, Jan 24, 1951.
Maria Tallchief, 79, former ballet dancer, born Fairfax, OK, Jan 24, 1925.

JANUARY 25 — SUNDAY
Day 25 — 341 Remaining

BOYLE, ROBERT: BIRTH ANNIVERSARY. Jan 25, 1627 (OS). Irish physicist, chemist and author who formulated Boyle's Law in 1662. Born at Lismore, Ireland, he died at London, England, Dec 30, 1691 (OS).

BURNS, ROBERT: BIRTH ANNIVERSARY. Jan 25, 1759. Beloved Scottish poet ("Oh wad some power the giftie gie us/To see oursels as others see us!"). Born at Ayrshire, Scotland, he died at Dumfries, Scotland, July 21, 1796. His birthday is widely celebrated as Burns' Nights, especially in Scotland, England and Newfoundland.

CAPONE, AL: DEATH ANNIVERSARY. Jan 25, 1947. Gangster Alphonse ("Scarface") Capone, who dominated organized crime in Chicago throughout Prohibition, died at age 48 at Miami after suffering from syphilis. Capone was born Jan 17, 1899, at Naples, Italy, and moved with his family to Brooklyn, NY.

CATHOLIC SCHOOLS WEEK. Jan 25–31. A national celebration focusing on the uniqueness of Catholic schools. Many schools plan special activities celebrating their Catholic heritage. Jointly sponsored by the National Catholic Educational Association and the US Conference of Catholic Bishops. Annually, beginning on the last Sunday in January. For info: Natl Catholic Educational Assn, 1077 30th St NW, Ste 100, Washington, DC 20007-3852. Phone: (202) 337-6232. Web: www.catholicschoolsweek.org.

CHINESE LUNAR NEW YEAR FESTIVAL: YEAR OF THE MONKEY (MAH LO NIEN). Jan 25. Baltimore, MD. Chinese New Year (the Year of the Monkey) arrives on Jan 22. To celebrate, the annual Lunar New Year Festival will feature Dragon/Lion (Mo Tze) performance, Chinese culture, indoor program, evensong and traditions. Chinese dinner available by advance reservation. Est attendance: 500. For info: Lillian Lee Kim, Grace and St. Peter's Parish, 707 Park Ave, Baltimore, MD 21201. Phone: (410) 539-1395 or (410) 377-8143.

CURTIS, CHARLES: BIRTH ANNIVERSARY. Jan 25, 1860. The 31st vice president of the US (1929–33). Born at Topeka, KS, he died at Washington, DC, Feb 8, 1936.

FIRST SCHEDULED TRANSCONTINENTAL FLIGHT: 45th ANNIVERSARY. Jan 25, 1959. American Airlines opened the jet age in the US with the first scheduled transcontinental flight on a Boeing 707 nonstop from California to New York.

FIRST TELEVISED PRESIDENTIAL NEWS CONFERENCE: ANNIVERSARY. Jan 25, 1961. Beginning a tradition that survives to this day, John F. Kennedy held the first televised presidential news conference five days after being inaugurated the 35th president.

FIRST WINTER OLYMPICS: 80th ANNIVERSARY. Jan 25, 1924. The first Winter Olympic Games opened in Chamonix, France, with athletes representing 16 nations. The ski jump, previously unknown, thrilled spectators. The Olympics offered a boost to skiing, which would make enormous strides in the next decade.

GOLDEN GLOBE AWARDS. Jan 25. Beverly Hilton Hotel, Beverly Hills, CA. 61st annual. Sponsored by the Hollywood Foreign Press Association and honoring achievement in film and television. Begins at 8 PM, EST. Telecast live by NBC. For info: The Hollywood Foreign Press Assn, 646 N Robertson Blvd, West Hollywood, CA 90069. Phone: (310) 657-1731. Fax: (310) 657-5576. E-mail: info@hfpa.org. Web: www.goldenglobes.org or www.hfpa.org.

LEADERSHIP WEEK INTERNATIONAL. Jan 25–31. As leadership is foundational to all organizations, this week is dedicated to the development of leadership that is both great and morally good. Conference themes will include modeling, instructing and mentoring character traits necessary for effective leaders. For info: DiFrances & Assoc, LLC, 208 E Oak Crest Dr, Ste 200, Wales, WI 53183-9700. Phone: (262) 968-9850. Fax: (262) 968-9854. E-mail: leadership@difrances.com. Web: www.difrances.com/leadershipweek.

MACINTOSH DEBUTS: 20th ANNIVERSARY. Jan 25, 1984. Apple's Macintosh computer went on sale this day for $2,495. It wasn't until mid-1985, however, that sales began to take off and this computer began to replace the Apple II model.

MAUGHAM, W. SOMERSET: BIRTH ANNIVERSARY. Jan 25, 1874. English short story writer, novelist and playwright, born at Paris, France. Among his best-remembered books: *Of Human Bondage, Cakes and Ale* and *The Razor's Edge*. Died at Cap Ferrat, France, Dec 16, 1965.

MILLS, FLORENCE: BIRTH ANNIVERSARY. Jan 25, 1896. The leading black American singer and dancer of the Jazz Age and the Harlem Renaissance was born Florence Winfree at Washington, DC. She appeared in Langston Hughes's *Shuffle Along* in 1921 and *Plantation Review* on Broadway in 1922, then at the London Pavilion in *Dover Street to Dixie* in 1923. Offered a spot in the *Ziegfeld Follies*, she turned it down and joined in creating a rival show with an all-black cast. Mills was the first black woman to appear as a headliner at the Palace Theatre. She was so revered for her efforts to create opportunities for black entertainers and to bring the unique culture of blacks to Broadway that more than 150,000 people filled the streets of Harlem to mourn her when she died at New York City, Nov 1, 1927, at age 31.

NATIONAL CREATIVE FRUGALITY WEEK. Jan 25–31. Christmas has come and gone and for many Americans the credit card bills are now rolling in. Give your budget a break by participating in National Creative Frugality Week. Participants are encouraged to have fun as they experiment with frugality and resourcefulness. Whether you're new to frugal living or have been doing it for years, use this holiday to challenge yourself to learn a new skill or try a new money-saving technique. For info: Nancy Twigg, Editor, Counting the Cost Newsletter, 8715 Brucewood Ln, Knoxville, TN 37923. Phone: (865) 531-3947. E-mail: editor@countingthecost.com. Web: www.countingthecost.com/ncfw.htm.

NATIONAL NURSE ANESTHETISTS WEEK. Jan 25–31. To provide recognition for the nation's more than 30,000 certified registered nurse anesthetists (CRNAs), who have been providing safe anesthesia care for more than 100 years. CRNAs administer more than 65 percent of the anesthesia in the US each year. For info: Christopher Bettin, PR Dir, Amer Assn of Nurse Anesthetists, 222 S Prospect, Park Ridge, IL 60068. Phone: (847) 692-7050. Fax: (847) 692-6968. Web: www.aana.com.

A ROOM OF ONE'S OWN DAY. Jan 25. For anyone who knows or longs for the sheer bliss and rightness of having a private place, no matter how humble, to call one's own. [©2003 by WH.] For info: Thomas & Ruth Roy, Wellcat Holidays, 2418 Long Ln, Lebanon, PA 17046. Phone: (717) 279-0184. E-mail: info@wellcat.com. Web: www.wellcat.com.

SENIOR BOWL FOOTBALL GAME. Jan 25. Ladd-Peebles Stadium, Mobile, AL. 55th annual. All-star football game featuring the nation's top collegiate seniors on teams coached by National Football League coaching staffs. Proceeds go to charities. Est attendance: 40,700. For info: Vic Knight, PR Dir, Senior Bowl, 63 S Royal St, Ste 100, Mobile, AL 36602. Phone: (251) 438-2276. Fax: (251) 432-0409. E-mail: srbowl@seniorbowl.com. Web: www.seniorbowl.com.

SOCIETY FOR THE PRESERVATION & ENCOURAGEMENT OF BARBER SHOP QUARTET SINGING IN AMERICA (SPEBSQSA) MID-WINTER CONVENTION. Jan 25–Feb 1. Biloxi, MS. Members meet for administrative conferences, shows and contest to select national Seniors Quartet Champion. Est attendance: 1,200. For info: Reed Sampson, PR Dir, SPEBSQSA, Inc, 6315 Harmony Ln, Kenosha, WI 53143. Phone: (800) 876-SING. E-mail: info@spebsqsa.org. Web: www.spebsqsa.org.

SOLO–PRENEURING WEEK. Jan 25–31. Control your own destiny by taking charge of your work and your life. This week is set aside to plan and prepare for the work you were meant to do and to celebrate those who are following a path of their own choosing. Whether you are an employee, a business owner or just contemplating your place in the workforce, resolve to learn how you can do work that is satisfying and fulfilling, create your own job security, prepare for an uncertain future and have fun doing work you love. Free articles available for publishers and webmasters at IdeaLady.com/content.htm. For info: Cathy Stucker, Special Interests Publishing, 4646 Hwy 6, PMB 123, Sugar Land, TX 77478. Phone: (281) 265-7342. E-mail: cathy@idealady.com. Web: www.idealady.com.

WOOLF, VIRGINIA: BIRTH ANNIVERSARY. Jan 25, 1882. English writer, critic and novelist, author of *Jacob's Room* and *To the Lighthouse*. Born at London, England. After completing her last novel, *Between the Acts,* she collapsed under the strain and drowned herself in the River Ouse near Rodmell, England, on Mar 28, 1941.

BIRTHDAYS TODAY

Corazon "Cory" Aquino, 71, former president of the Philippines, born Tarlac Province, Philippine Islands, Jan 25, 1933.
Conrad Burns, 69, US Senator (R, Montana), born Gallatin, MO, Jan 25, 1935.
Vince Carter, 27, basketball player, born Daytona Beach, FL, Jan 25, 1977.
Chris Chelios, 42, hockey player, born Chicago, IL, Jan 25, 1962.
Ernie Harwell, 86, sportscaster, born Washington, GA, Jan 25, 1918.
Dean Jones, 73, actor (*Tea and Sympathy, The Love Bug, Beethoven*), born Decatur, AL, Jan 25, 1931 (some sources say 1935).
Alicia Keys, 23, musician, singer (*Songs in A Minor*), born Harlem, NY, Jan 25, 1981.
Dinah Manoff, 46, actress (stage: *I Ought to Be in Pictures* [Tony Award]; "Soap," "Empty Nest"), born New York, NY, Jan 25, 1958.
Edwin Newman, 85, journalist, author ("Comet," *A Civil Tongue*), born New York, NY, Jan 25, 1919.
Leigh Taylor-Young, 59, actress ("Peyton Place," "Dallas," *I Love You, Alice B. Toklas*), born Washington, DC, Jan 25, 1945.

JANUARY 26 — MONDAY
Day 26 — 340 Remaining

AUSTRALIA: AUSTRALIA DAY—FIRST BRITISH SETTLEMENT: ANNIVERSARY. Jan 26, 1788. A shipload of convicts arrived briefly at Botany Bay (which proved to be unsuitable) and then at Port Jackson (later the site of the city of Sydney). Establishment of an Australian prison colony was to relieve crowding of British prisons. Australia Day, formerly known as Foundation Day or Anniversary Day, has been observed since about 1817 and has been a public holiday since 1838.

BETTER BUSINESS COMMUNICATION DAY. Jan 26. This is a day set aside to encourage all workers to acknowledge the importance of effective communication in the workplace. Tips, workshops and seminars will be offered around this day to equip workers with the tools to demonstrate effective communication. Annually, the fourth Monday in January. For info: Katie Schwartz, 1826 Pine Needles Trail, Chattanooga, TN 37421. Phone: (423) 894-8024. Web: www.corspan.org or www.businessspeechimprovement.com.

BUBBLE WRAP® APPRECIATION DAY. Jan 26. A day to celebrate the joy that Bubble Wrap® brings to our lives. A day to learn the history and snapping etiquette and to gain a new appreciation of the country's favorite shipping material. Also, a day to snap and share Bubble Wrap® with coworkers, classmates and loved ones. For info: Wake-up Show WVNI with Todd & Denise, 2620 N Walnut, Bloomington, IN 47404. Phone: (812) 335-9500. Fax: (812) 335-8880. E-mail: spirit95@kiva.net. Web: www.SPIRIT95FM.com.

COLEMAN, BESSIE: BIRTH ANNIVERSARY. Jan 26, 1893. Born at Atlanta, TX, Bessie Coleman would not take no for an answer, especially where it concerned her dreams of flying. Because of her race and gender, she was denied admission to aviation school programs in the US. She therefore worked as a manicurist earning her way to Paris. There she received an international pilot's license from the Fédération Aéronautique Internationale in 1921. Upon return, "Queen Bess" took part in numerous acrobatic air exhibitions where her stunt-flying and "fig-

	S	M	T	W	T	F	S
January 2004					1	2	3
	4	5	6	7	8	9	10
	11	12	13	14	15	16	17
	18	19	20	21	22	23	24
	25	26	27	28	29	30	31

ure eights" won her many admirers. She avidly encouraged others to follow in her footsteps. Coleman, however, perished in a plane crash during a practice session, at Jacksonville, FL, Apr 30, 1926.

DENTAL DRILL PATENT: ANNIVERSARY. Jan 26, 1875. George F. Green, of Kalamazoo, MI, patented the electric dental drill.

DOMINICAN REPUBLIC: NATIONAL HOLIDAY. Jan 26. An official public holiday celebrates the birth anniversary of Juan Pablo Duarte, one of the fathers of the republic.

"THE DUKES OF HAZZARD" TV PREMIERE: 25th ANNIVERSARY. Jan 26, 1979. This comedy/action show ran for seven seasons and featured car chases. Brothers Bo Duke (John Schneider) and Luke Duke (Tom Wopat) were the good guys, fighting crooked law enforcement in their rural southern community. Other characters included Daisy Duke (Catherine Bach), Uncle Jesse Duke (Denver Pyle), Sheriff Roscoe P. Coltrane (James Best), Deputy Enos Strate (Sonny Shroyer) and Boss Hogg (Sorrell Booke).

FRANKLIN PREFERS TURKEY: ANNIVERSARY. Jan 26, 1784. In a letter to his daughter, Benjamin Franklin expressed his unhappiness over the choice of the eagle as the symbol of America. He preferred the turkey.

GRANT, JULIA DENT: BIRTH ANNIVERSARY. Jan 26, 1826. Wife of Ulysses Simpson Grant, 18th president of the US. Born at St. Louis, MO, died at Washington, DC, Dec 14, 1902.

HITLER YOUTH DEPLOYED: ANNIVERSARY. Jan 26, 1943. Due to the need for more men at the front, the Nazis began manning anti-aircraft batteries within Germany with members of the Hitler Youth who were aged 15 and up. This was 10 days after the British had begun the heavy bombing of Berlin and other German cities. See also: "British Air Raid on Berlin: Anniversary" (Jan 16).

INDIA: REPUBLIC DAY. Jan 26. National holiday. Anniversary of Proclamation of the Republic, Basant Panchmi. In 1929, Indian National Congress resolved to work for establishment of a sovereign republic, a goal that was realized Jan 26, 1950, when India became a democratic republic and its constitution went into effect.

INDIAN EARTHQUAKE: ANNIVERSARY. Jan 26, 2001. An earthquake that struck the state of Gujarat in India left more than 15,000 dead. The quake was estimated to be 7.7 on the Richter scale. India's largest port at Kandla suffered severe damage.

LOTUS 1-2-3 RELEASED: ANNIVERSARY. Jan 26, 1983. This spreadsheet software drove demand for the IBM PC, just as the introduction of VisiCalc had for the Apple II in 1979.

MacARTHUR, DOUGLAS: BIRTH ANNIVERSARY. Jan 26, 1880. US general and supreme commander of Allied forces in Southwest Pacific during World War II. Born at Little Rock, AR, he served as commander of the Rainbow Division's 84th Infantry Brigade in World War I, leading it in the St. Mihiel, Meuse-Argonne and Sedan offensives. Remembered for his "I shall return" prediction when forced out of the Philippines by the Japanese during WWII, a promise he fulfilled. Relieved of Far Eastern command by President Harry Truman on Apr 11, 1951, during the Korean War. MacArthur died at Washington, DC, Apr 5, 1964.

MICHIGAN: ADMISSION DAY: ANNIVERSARY. Jan 26. Became 26th state in 1837.

"MIKE HAMMER" TV PREMIERE: 20th ANNIVERSARY. Jan 26, 1984. Mike Hammer was a gritty, urban detective created by writer Mickey Spillane. Originally a TV series in the '50s, CBS revived the series with Stacy Keach as the hard-boiled detective. Production was stopped while Keach was briefly imprisoned for a drug charge in 1984 but the series returned in 1986. The series also featured Don Stroud as NYPD Captain Pat Chambers, Kent Williams as Assistant DA Barrington, Lindsay Bloom as Hammer's secretary Velda, Danny Goldman as "Ozzie the Answer," Donna Denton as "The Face" and Lee Benton as Jenny the bartender.

NATIONAL TAKE BACK YOUR TIME WEEK. Jan 26–30. Time is not the enemy! Good time management habits are not enough. You also need clear values to direct how you spend your time. Prioritize and say "no" to unwanted activities and demands. Annually, the last full week of January. For info: Jan Jasper. Phone: (212) 495-7472. Fax: (509) 356-2803. E-mail: jan@janjasper.com. Web: www.janjasper.com.

ROCKY MOUNTAIN NATIONAL PARK ESTABLISHED: ANNIVERSARY. Jan 26, 1915. Under President Woodrow Wilson, the area covering more than 1,000 square miles in Colorado became a national park.

TOAD HOLLOW DAY OF ENCOURAGEMENT. Jan 26. A day to give and receive a word of encouragement. For info: Ralph Morrison, Dir, Toad Hollow, PO Box 45, Vicksburg, MI 49097. Phone: (800) 574-8623.

VAN HEUSEN, JIMMY: BIRTH ANNIVERSARY. Jan 26, 1913. Jimmy Van Heusen was born Edward Chester Babcock at Syracuse, NY. He was a composer of many popular songs with his lyricist partners Johnny Burke and Sammy Cahn. One of his 76 songs that Frank Sinatra recorded was "My Kind of Town." Van Heusen won four Academy Awards for songs in movies such as *Going My Way* (1944). He was inducted into the Songwriters Hall of Fame when it was founded in 1971. Van Heusen died Feb 7, 1990, at Rancho Mirage, CA.

BIRTHDAYS TODAY

Anita Baker, 46, singer ("Sweet Love," "Rhythm of Love"), born Toledo, OH, Jan 26, 1958.
Father George Harold Clements, 72, Roman Catholic priest, civil rights leader, born Chicago, IL, Jan 26, 1932.
Angela Davis, 60, political activist, born Birmingham, AL, Jan 26, 1944.
Mark Dayton, 57, US Senator (D, Minnesota), born Minneapolis, MN, Jan 26, 1947.
Ellen DeGeneres, 46, comedienne, actress ("Ellen"), born New Orleans, LA, Jan 26, 1958.
Philip Jose Farmer, 86, science fiction writer, born Peoria, IL, Jan 26, 1918.
Jules Feiffer, 75, cartoonist, writer, born New York, NY, Jan 26, 1929.
Scott Glenn, 62, actor (*The Right Stuff, Silverado*), born Pittsburgh, PA, Jan 26, 1942.
Wayne Gretzky, 43, Hall of Fame hockey player, born Brantford, ON, Canada, Jan 26, 1961.
Paul Newman, 79, actor (Oscar for *The Color of Money; Cat on a Hot Tin Roof, Butch Cassidy and the Sundance Kid*), director (*Rachel, Rachel; The Glass Menagerie*), born Cleveland, OH, Jan 26, 1925.
Andrew Ridgeley, 41, musician, born Bushey, England, Jan 26, 1963.
David Strathairn, 54, actor (*LA Confidential*), born San Francisco, CA, Jan 26, 1950.
Robert George (Bob) Uecker, 69, sportscaster, former baseball player, actor ("Mr Belvedere"), born Milwaukee, WI, Jan 26, 1935.
Eddie Van Halen, 49, guitarist ("Jump," "Right Now"), born Nijmegen, Netherlands, Jan 26, 1955.

JANUARY 27 — TUESDAY
Day 27 — 339 Remaining

APOLLO I: SPACECRAFT FIRE: ANNIVERSARY. Jan 27, 1967. Three American astronauts, Virgil I. Grissom, Edward H. White and Roger B. Chaffee, died when fire suddenly broke out at 6:31 PM in *Apollo I* during a launching simulation test, as it stood on the ground at Cape Kennedy, FL. First launching in the Apollo program had been scheduled for Feb 27, 1967.

DODGSON, CHARLES LUTWIDGE (LEWIS CARROLL): BIRTH ANNIVERSARY. Jan 27, 1832. English mathematician and author, better known by his pseudonym, Lewis Carroll, creator of *Alice's Adventures in Wonderland*, was born at Cheshire, England. *Alice* was written for Alice Liddell, daughter of a friend, and first published in 1886. *Through the Looking-Glass*, a sequel, and *The Hunting of the Snark* followed. Dodgson's books for children proved equally enjoyable to adults, and they overshadowed his serious works on mathematics. Dodgson died at Guildford, Surrey, England, Jan 14, 1898.

GERMANY: DAY OF REMEMBRANCE FOR VICTIMS OF NAZISM. Jan 27. Since 1996 commemorated on this day, the date in 1945 that Soviet soldiers liberated the Auschwitz concentration camp in Poland.

GOMPERS, SAMUEL: BIRTH ANNIVERSARY. Jan 27, 1850. Labor leader, first president of the American Federation of Labor, born at London, England. Died Dec 13, 1924, at San Antonio, TX.

GUNPOWDER PLOT TRIAL: ANNIVERSARY. Jan 27, 1606. The surviving conspirators in the "Gunpowder Treason," a plot to blow up Parliament and the king of England on Nov 5, 1605, were brought to trial and convicted at London, Jan 27, 1606. Four days later they were executed. An inscription on a contemporary engraving states: "The heads of Percy and Catesby after they were dead, were cut off and set upon the ends of Parliament House. Friday the last of Jan, 1606, were executed in Parliament Yard: T. Winter, Rokenvood, Keys and Guido Fawkes, their quarters were placed over London gates and their heads upon London Bridge." See also: "Guy Fawkes Day" (Nov 5).

KERN, JEROME: BIRTH ANNIVERSARY. Jan 27, 1885. American composer born at New York City; died there Nov 11, 1945. In addition to scores for stage and screen, Kern wrote many memorable songs, including "Ol' Man River," "Smoke Gets in Your Eyes," "I Won't Dance," "The Way You Look Tonight," "All the Things You Are" and "The Last Time I Saw Paris."

"LAVERNE AND SHIRLEY" TV PREMIERE: ANNIVERSARY. Jan 27, 1976. This ABC sitcom was a spin-off of the popular TV show "Happy Days" that was also set during the late '50s in Milwaukee, WI. Penny Marshall (sister of series co-creator, Garry Marshall) starred as Laverne DeFazio with Cindy Williams as Shirley Feeney. The two friends worked at a brewery and shared a basement apartment. Also featured in the cast were: Phil Foster as Laverne's father, Frank DeFazio; David L. Lander as coworker Andrew "Squiggy" Squiggman; Michael McKean as coworker Lenny Kosnowski; Betty Garrett as landlady Edna Babish and Eddie Mekka as Carmine Ragusa, Shirley's sometime boyfriend.

LENINGRAD LIBERATED: 60th ANNIVERSARY. Jan 27, 1944. The seige of Leningrad began with German bombing of the city on Sept 4, 1941. The bombing continued for 430 hours. The suffering of the people of Leningrad during the 880-day seige was one of the greatest tragedies of World War II. More than half the population of Russia's second largest city died during the winter of 1942. The seige finally ended on Jan 27, 1944.

MOZART, WOLFGANG AMADEUS: BIRTH ANNIVERSARY. Jan 27, 1756. One of the world's greatest music makers. Born at Salzburg, Austria, into a gifted musical family, Mozart began performing at age three and composing at age five. Some of the best known of his more than 600 compositions include the operas *Marriage of Figaro*, *Don Giovanni*, *Cosi fan tutte* and *The Magic Flute*; his unfinished Requiem Mass; his C major symphony known as the "Jupiter" and many of his quartets and piano concertos. He died at Vienna, Dec 5, 1791.

NATIONAL SPEAK UP AND SUCCEED DAY. Jan 27. Fewer than 3 percent of Americans have no fear of public speaking or have never felt shy. Yet, the top-rated skill for success is effective communication skills. On National Speak Up and Succeed Day, face your fear of public speaking and speak out anyway—speak up at a committee meeting, voice your opinion to a group of colleagues, give the toast at a special event, volunteer to chair a program, join Toastmasters. You have nothing to lose and everything to gain. Annually, the fourth Tuesday in January. For info: Mary-Ellen Drummond, Polished Presentations Intl, PO Box 2104, Rancho Santa Fe, CA 92067. Phone: (858) 756-4248. Fax: (858) 756-9621. E-mail: medrummond@aol.com. Web: www.medrummond.com.

RICKOVER, HYMAN GEORGE: BIRTH ANNIVERSARY. Jan 27, 1900. American naval officer, known as the "Father of the Nuclear Navy." Admiral Rickover directed development of nuclear reactor-powered submarines, the first of which was the *Nautilus*, launched in 1954. Rickover was noted for his blunt remarks: "To increase the efficiency of the Department of Defense," he said, "you must first abolish it." The four-star admiral retired (unwillingly) at the age of 81, after 63 years in the navy. Born in Russia, Rickover died at Arlington, VA, July 9, 1986, and was buried at Arlington National Cemetery.

SCOTLAND: UP HELLY AA. Jan 27. Lerwick, Shetland Islands. Norse galley burned in impressive ceremony symbolizing sacrifice to the sun. Old Viking custom. A festival marking the end of Yule. Annually, the last Tuesday in January. For info: Tourist Information Centre, Market Cross, Lerwick, Shetland, Scotland ZE1 0LU. Phone: (44) (595) 693-434. Fax: (44) (595) 695-807. Web: www.visitshetland.com.

SIOUX EMPIRE FARM SHOW. Jan 27–31. Sioux Falls, SD. Winter farm and livestock show featuring all classes of livestock, commercial exhibits, horse pull, and a women's show. Est attendance: 30,000. For info: Sioux Empire Farm Show, Chamber of Commerce, 200 N Phillips Ave, #102, Sioux Falls, SD 57104. Phone: (605) 373-2016. Fax: (605) 336-6499. E-mail: cchristensen@siouxfalls.com.

THOMAS CRAPPER DAY. Jan 27, 1910. Born at Thorne, Yorkshire, England, in 1836 (exact date unknown), Crapper is often described as the prime developer of flush toilet mechanism as it is known today. The flush toilet had been in use for more than 100 years; Crapper perfected it. Founder, London, 1861, of Thomas Crapper & Co, later patentees and manufacturers of sanitary appliances. Died Jan 27, 1910. [Editor's Note: The date of Crapper's death has been revised based on info sent by Dr. Andy Gibbons of the International Thomas Crapper Society, who has viewed Crapper's gravestone and obtained a copy of his death certificate. Ken Grabowski sent further info.]

UNITED KINGDOM: HOLOCAUST MEMORIAL DAY. Jan 27. Commemorating the day in 1945 that Soviet troops liberated the Auschwitz concentration camp. For more info: www.holocaustmemorialday.gov.uk.

VIETNAM PEACE AGREEMENT SIGNED: ANNIVERSARY. Jan 27, 1973. US and North Vietnam, along with South Vietnam and the Viet Cong, signed an "Agreement on ending the war and restoring peace in Vietnam." Signed at Paris, France, to take effect Jan 28 at 8 AM Saigon time, thus ending US combat role in a war that had involved American personnel stationed in Vietnam since defeated French forces had departed under terms

January 2004

S	M	T	W	T	F	S
				1	2	3
4	5	6	7	8	9	10
11	12	13	14	15	16	17
18	19	20	21	22	23	24
25	26	27	28	29	30	31

of the Geneva Accords in 1954. This was the longest war in US history with more than one million combat deaths (US: 47,366). However, within weeks of the departure of American troops the war between North and South Vietnam resumed. For the Vietnamese, the war didn't end until Apr 30, 1975, when Saigon fell to Communist forces.

BIRTHDAYS TODAY

Mikhail Baryshnikov, 56, ballet dancer, actor (*White Nights, The Turning Point*), born Riga, Latvia, USSR, Jan 27, 1948.

(Anthony) Cris Collinsworth, 45, sportscaster, former football player, born Dayton, OH, Jan 27, 1959.

Mairead Corrigan, 60, pacifist, Nobel Peace Prize winner, born Belfast, Northern Ireland, Jan 27, 1944.

James Cromwell, 62, actor (*The People vs. Larry Flynt, Babe, LA Confidential*), born Los Angeles, CA, Jan 27, 1942.

Alan Cumming, 39, actor (Tony for *Cabaret; Spy Kids, The Anniversary Party, Emma*), director, born Perthshire, Scotland, Jan 27, 1965.

Bridget Fonda, 40, actress (*Single White Female, Lake Placid*), daughter of Peter Fonda, born Los Angeles, CA, Jan 27, 1964.

Julie Foudy, 33, soccer player, born San Diego, CA, Jan 27, 1971.

Skitch Henderson, 86, bandleader ("The Tonight Show"), born Halstad, MN, Jan 27, 1918.

Mimi Rogers, 48, actress (*The Doors, The Rapture*), born Coral Gables, FL, Jan 27, 1956.

JANUARY 28 — WEDNESDAY
Day 28 — 338 Remaining

"BARNABY JONES" TV PREMIERE: ANNIVERSARY. Jan 28, 1973. CBS drama about a mild-mannered, milk-drinking private eye who comes out of retirement following his son's murder. Cast included Buddy Ebsen as Barnaby Jones; Lee Meriwether as Barnaby's widowed daughter-in-law, Betty Jones; John Carter as Lieutenant Biddle and Mark Shera as Jedediah Jones. The last episode aired in 1980.

CHALLENGER SPACE SHUTTLE EXPLOSION: ANNIVERSARY. Jan 28, 1986. At 11:39 AM, EST, the Space Shuttle *Challenger STS-51L* exploded, 74 seconds into its flight and about 10 miles above the earth. Hundreds of millions around the world watched television replays of the horrifying event that killed seven people; destroyed the billion-dollar craft; suspended all shuttle flights and halted, at least temporarily, much of the US manned space flight program. Killed were teacher Christa McAuliffe (who was to have been the first ordinary citizen in space) and six crew members: Francis R. Scobee, Michael J. Smith, Judith A. Resnik, Ellison S. Onizuka, Ronald E. McNair and Gregory B. Jarvis.

"FANTASY ISLAND" TV PREMIERE: ANNIVERSARY. Jan 28, 1978. Ricardo Montalban starred as the prescient guide, Mr Roarke, with Hervé Villechaize as his faithful assistant, Tattoo; each week, guest stars played characters anxious to live out their fantasies in camp splendor. The show's run of 130 episodes, ending on Aug 18, 1984, was produced by Aaron Spelling and Leonard Goldberg. Who can forget Tattoo's opening line each week, "De plane, de plane!"

GREAT SEAL OF THE US: AUTHORIZATION ANNIVERSARY. Jan 28, 1782. Congress resolved that the secretary of the Congress should "keep the public seal, and cause the same to be affixed to every act, ordinance or paper, which Congress shall direct. . . ." Although the Great Seal did not exist yet, the Congress recognized the need for it. See also: "Great Seal of the United States: Anniversary" (July 4 and Sept 16).

ISRAELI SIEGE OF SUEZ CITY ENDS: 30th ANNIVERSARY. Jan 28, 1974. The Israeli army lifted its siege of Suez City, freed encircled Egyptian troops and turned over 300,000 square miles of Egyptian territory to the UN, thereby ending the occupation that started during the October 1973 war.

MacKENZIE, ALEXANDER: BIRTH ANNIVERSARY. Jan 28, 1822. The man who became the first Liberal prime minister of Canada (1873–78) was born at Logierait, Perth, Scotland. He died at Toronto, Apr 17, 1892.

MARTÍ, JOSÉ JULIAN: BIRTH ANNIVERSARY. Jan 28, 1853. Cuban author and political activist, born at Havana, Cuba, Martí was exiled to Spain, where he studied law before coming to the US in 1890. He was killed in battle at Dos Rios, Cuba, May 19, 1895.

NATIONAL COMPLIMENT DAY. Jan 28. This day is set aside to compliment at least five people. Not only are compliments appreciated by the receiver, they lift the spirit of the giver. Compliments provide a quick and easy way to connect positively with those you come in contact with. Giving compliments forges bonds, dispels loneliness and just plain feels good. Annually, the fourth Wednesday in January. For info: Debby Hoffman, Positive Results Seminars, PO Box 3478, Concord, NH 03303-3478. Phone: (603) 783-4446. E-mail: prseminars@compuserve.com. Or Kathy Chamberlin, Respectful Communication, 724 Park Ave, Contoocook, NH 03229-3089. Phone: (603) 746-6227. E-mail: Kathy Chamberlin@aol.com. Web: www.complimentday.com.

PICCARD, AUGUSTE: BIRTH ANNIVERSARY. Jan 28, 1884. Scientist and explorer, born at Basel, Switzerland. Made record-setting balloon ascent into the stratosphere on May 27, 1931, and also ocean depth descents and explorations. Twin brother of Jean Felix Piccard. Died at Lausanne, Switzerland, Mar 24, 1962. See also: "Piccard, Jean Felix: Birth Anniversary" (Jan 28).

PICCARD, JEAN FELIX: BIRTH ANNIVERSARY. Jan 28, 1884. Scientist, engineer, explorer, born at Basel, Switzerland. Noted for cosmic-ray research and record-setting balloon ascensions into stratosphere. Reached 57,579 ft in sealed gondola piloted by his wife, Jeannette, in 1934. Twin brother of Auguste Piccard. Died at Minneapolis, MN, Jan 28, 1963. See also: "Piccard, Jeannette Ridlon: Birth Anniversary" (Jan 5) and "Piccard, Auguste: Birth Anniversary" above.

STANLEY, HENRY MORTON: BIRTH ANNIVERSARY. Jan 28, 1841. Explorer, born at Wales, and leader of the expedition to find the missing missionary-explorer David Livingstone, who had not been heard from for more than two years. Stanley began the search in Africa on Mar 21, 1871, finally finding the explorer at Ujiji, near Lake Tanganyika, on Nov 10, 1871, whereupon he asked the now-famous question: "Dr. Livingstone, I presume?" Stanley died at London, England, May 10, 1904.

ZORA NEALE HURSTON FESTIVAL OF THE ARTS AND HUMANITIES. Jan 28–Feb 1. Eatonville, FL (10 miles east of Orlando). Festival celebrates Hurston, her work, her hometown, Eatonville (popularly known as the oldest incorporated African-American municipality in the country) and the cultural

Jan 28–29 ☆ Chase's 2004 Calendar of Events ☆

contributions Africa-descended people have made to the US and to world culture, with four days of arts and humanities programming highlighting theater, music, folklore and literature through seminars, symposia, master classes, intellectual conversations/dialogues, art exhibitions, workshops, self-tours, concert fare and performances. Festival attracts both "domestic and international travelers looking for 'the other Florida'—the Africa-descendant cultural matrix." Est attendance: 75,000. For info: Assn to Preserve Eatonville, Inc, 227 E Kennedy Blvd, Eatonville, FL 32751. Phone: (407) 647-3307. Fax: (407) 647-3959. E-mail: zora@cs.ucf.edu. Web: www.zoranealehurstonfestival.com.

BIRTHDAYS TODAY

Alan Alda, 68, actor (*Paper Lion, The Four Seasons*, "M*A*S*H"), director, born Alphonso D'Abruzzo, New York, NY, Jan 28, 1936.
John Beck, 61, actor ("Dallas," *Sleeper, The Big Bus*), born Chicago, IL, Jan 28, 1943.
Susan Howard, 61, actress ("Dallas"), born Jeri Lynn Mooney, Marshall, TX, Jan 28, 1943.
Harley Jane Kozak, 47, actress (*When Harry Met Sally . . ., Parenthood*), born Wilkes-Barre, PA, Jan 28, 1957.
Sarah McLachlan, 36, folksinger, born Halifax, NS, Canada, Jan 28, 1968.
Claes Oldenburg, 75, artist, sculptor (*Standing Trowel*), born Stockholm, Sweden, Jan 28, 1929.
Elijah Wood, 23, actor (the *Lord of the Rings* trilogy, *The Ice Storm*), born Cedar Rapids, IA, Jan 28, 1981.

JANUARY 29 — THURSDAY
Day 29 — 337 Remaining

CHEKHOV, ANTON PAVLOVICH: BIRTH ANNIVERSARY. Jan 29, 1860. Russian playwright and short story writer, especially remembered for *The Sea Gull, The Three Sisters* and *The Cherry Orchard*. Born at Taganrog, Russia; died July 15, 1904, at the Black Forest spa at Badenweiler, Germany.

FIELDS, W.C.: BIRTH ANNIVERSARY. Jan 29, 1880. Stage and motion picture actor (*My Little Chickadee*), screenwriter and expert juggler. Born Claude William Dukenfield at Philadelphia, PA; died Dec 25, 1946, at Pasadena, CA. He wrote his own epitaph: "On the whole, I'd rather be in Philadelphia."

FREETHINKER'S DAY. Jan 29. Annual celebration of the birth of Thomas Paine. For info: Truth Seeker Co, PO Box 28550, San Diego, CA 92198. Phone: (760) 489-5211 or (800) 551-5328. Fax: (760) 489-5311. E-mail: editor@truthseeker.com. Web: truthseeker.com.

KANSAS: ADMISSION DAY: ANNIVERSARY. Jan 29. Became the 34th state in 1861.

McKINLEY, WILLIAM: BIRTH ANNIVERSARY. Jan 29, 1843. 25th president of the US (1897–1901), born at Niles, OH. Died in office, at Buffalo, NY, Sept 14, 1901, as the result of a gunshot wound by an anarchist assassin Sept 6, 1901, while he was attending the Pan-American Exposition.

MILITARY BAN ON HOMOSEXUALS EASED: ANNIVERSARY. Jan 29, 1993. An interim policy on ending the ban on homosexuals in the US military was announced by President William Clinton. The policy ended the questioning of military recruits regarding their sexual orientation but allowed removal of openly homosexual members from active service. President Clinton's announced policy of "don't ask, don't tell, don't pursue" was intended to allow homosexuals to serve in the armed forces as long as they were discreet.

MOON PHASE: FIRST QUARTER. Jan 29. Moon enters First Quarter phase at 1:03 AM, EST.

MORMON BATTALION ARRIVAL IN CALIFORNIA: ANNIVERSARY. Jan 29, 1847. The 500 men of the US Mormon Battalion, along with 50 women and children, arrived at San Diego, CA, on this date, having marched 2,000 miles—the longest march in modern military history—since leaving Council Bluffs, IA, on July 16, 1846, to fight in the war against Mexico. In the course of their trek they established the first wagon route from Santa Fe to southern California. Their historic arrival is commemorated each year with a military parade in San Diego's Old Town.

PAINE, THOMAS: BIRTH ANNIVERSARY. Jan 29, 1737. American Revolutionary leader, a corset-maker by trade, author of *Common Sense, The Age of Reason* and many other influential works, was born at Thetford, England. "These are the times that try men's souls" are the well-known opening words of his inspirational tract *The Crisis*. Paine died at New York, NY, June 8, 1809, but 10 years later his remains were moved to England by William Cobbett for reburial there. Reburial was refused, however, and the location of Paine's bones, said to have been distributed, is unknown.

"THE RAVEN" PUBLISHED: ANNIVERSARY. Jan 29, 1845. One of the most famous poems in American literature was published on this date in New York's *Evening Mirror* newspaper. The author was anonymous, but the poem was such a sensation (it would be reprinted at least 16 times in various periodicals and books that year) that soon the author was revealed as literary critic and author Edgar Allan Poe. Despite the celebrity status Poe enjoyed as a result of "The Raven," it did not relieve his poverty: Poe received $15 for the poem. The classic lines, "Once upon a midnight dreary . . ." and "Quoth the Raven, 'Nevermore,'" resound in countless anthologies and dramatic readings as well as in parodies.

THE SEEING EYE ESTABLISHED: 75th ANNIVERSARY. Jan 29, 1929. The Seeing Eye, North America's first guide dog school, was incorporated on this date in Nashville, TN. The first class took place in February and included Buddy, the "seeing eye" dog brought from Europe. The Seeing Eye was the first program in the US that enabled people with a disability to be full participants in society. Its mission is to enhance the independence, self-confidence and dignity of people who are blind through the use of Seeing Eye dogs. Since its founding, The Seeing Eye has matched more than 13,000 specially bred dogs with blind people from the US and Canada. In 1931 the school moved to New Jersey, where it continues to breed, raise and train Seeing Eye dogs and instruct blind and visually impaired people in the use and care of their dogs. For info: Melissa Campbell, Mgr of Public Relations, The Seeing Eye, PO Box 375, Morristown, NJ 07963-0375. Phone: (973) 539-4425. Fax: (973) 539-0922. E-mail: info@seeingeye.org. Web: www.seeingeye.org.

SWEDENBORG, EMANUEL: BIRTH ANNIVERSARY. Jan 29, 1688 (OS). Born at Stockholm, Sweden, Swedenborg is remembered as a scientist, inventor, writer and religious leader. Swedenborg made plans for machine guns, submarines and airplanes and published Sweden's first scientific journal. His study of human anatomy and his search for the soul led him to begin thinking about religion. His writings interpreting the scriptures formed the basis of the Church of the New Jerusalem, which was established by his devotees soon after his death. He died at London, England, Mar 29, 1772.

	S	M	T	W	T	F	S
January					1	2	3
2004	4	5	6	7	8	9	10
	11	12	13	14	15	16	17
	18	19	20	21	22	23	24
	25	26	27	28	29	30	31

☆ Chase's 2004 Calendar of Events ☆ Jan 29–30

BIRTHDAYS TODAY

John Forsythe, 86, actor ("Bachelor Father," Charlie's voice on "Charlie's Angels," "Dynasty"), born John Freund, Penn's Grove, NJ, Jan 29, 1918.

Sara Gilbert, 29, actress ("Roseanne"), born Santa Monica, CA, Jan 29, 1975.

Heather Graham, 34, actress (*Lost in Space, Boogie Nights*), born Milwaukee, WI, Jan 29, 1970.

Germaine Greer, 65, author (*Daddy We Hardly Knew You, The Female Eunuch*), born Melbourne, Australia, Jan 29, 1939.

Dominik Hasek, 39, former hockey player, born Pardubice, Czech Republic, Jan 29, 1965.

Ann Jillian, 53, actress ("It's a Living," *The Ann Jillian Story*), born Cambridge, MA, Jan 29, 1951.

Andrew Keegan, 25, actor (*Independence Day*), born Los Angeles, CA, Jan 29, 1979.

Gregory Efthimios (Greg) Louganis, 44, actor, Olympic gold medal diver, born San Diego, CA, Jan 29, 1960.

Bobbie Phillips, 36, actress ("Murder One," *Red Shoe Diaries*), born Charleston, SC, Jan 29, 1968 (some sources say 1972).

Katharine Ross, 61, actress (*The Graduate*), born Los Angeles, CA, Jan 29, 1943.

Tom Selleck, 59, actor ("Magnum, PI," *Three Men and a Baby, Mr Baseball*), born Detroit, MI, Jan 29, 1945.

Nick Turturro, 42, actor ("NYPD Blue"), born Queens, NY, Jan 29, 1962.

Oprah Winfrey, 50, TV talk-show host (Emmys for "The Oprah Winfrey Show"), actress (*The Color Purple*), producer (owner of Harpo Studios), born Kosciusko, MS, Jan 29, 1954.

JANUARY 30 — FRIDAY
Day 30 — 336 Remaining

ALL THAT JAZZ WEEKEND. Jan 30–Feb 1. Asheville, NC. 12th annual. Delve into a world of music with evening and afternoon concerts in the Grand Ballroom and numerous jazz artists performing in the Great Hall all weekend. For info: The Grove Park Inn Resort & Spa, 290 Macon Ave, Asheville, NC 28804. Phone: (800) 438-5800 or (828) 252-2711. Web: www.grovepark inn.com.

BEATLES LAST CONCERT: 35th ANNIVERSARY. Jan 30, 1969. On this day the Beatles performed together in public for the last time. The show took place on the roof of their Apple Studios in London, England, but it was interrupted by police after they received complaints from the neighbors about the noise.

BLACK HILLS STOCK SHOW AND RODEO. Jan 30–Feb 8. Rapid City, SD. Events include PRCA rodeos, ranch rodeo, timed sheepdog trials, cattle cutting, livestock shows and sales, buffalo show and sale, team penning, bucking horse and bull sale, stockman banquet and ball and commercial exhibits. Est attendance: 250,000. For info: Black Hills Stock Show & Rodeo, 800 San Francisco, Rapid City, SD 57701. Phone: (605) 355-3861.

BLOODY SUNDAY: ANNIVERSARY. Jan 30, 1972. In Londonderry, Northern Ireland, 13 Roman Catholics were shot dead by British troops during a banned civil rights march. During 1972, the first year of British direct rule, 467 people were killed in the fighting.

CANADA: ONTARIO WINTER CARNIVAL BON SOO. Jan 30–Feb 8. Sault Ste. Marie, ON. One of Canada's largest winter carnivals features more than 125 festive indoor and hearty outdoor events for all ages during an annual 10-day winter extravaganza featuring winter sports, festive dances, entertainment, fireworks and the Fantasy Kingdom winter playground. Est attendance: 100,000. For info: Donna Gregg, Bon Soo Winter Carnival Inc, PO Box 781, Sault Ste. Marie, ON, Canada P6A 5N3. Phone: (705) 759-3000. Fax: (705) 759-6950. E-mail: mr bonsoo@bonsoo.on.ca. Web: www.bonsoo.on.ca.

CANADA: QUEBEC WINTER CARNIVAL. Jan 30–Feb 15. Québec City, QC. 50th edition of the world's biggest winter celebration. Snow-sculpture competition (many countries participating), two glittering night parades and a legendary international canoe race across the St. Lawrence River. Est attendance: 1,000,000. For info: Quebec Winter Carnival, 290 Joly St, Quebec, QC, Canada G1L 1N8. Phone: (418) 626-3716. E-mail: comm@carnaval.qc.ca. Web: www.carnaval.qc.ca.

CHARLES I EXECUTION: ANNIVERSARY. Jan 30, 1649. English king beheaded by order of Parliament under Oliver Cromwell on this date; considered a martyr by some.

CHENEY, RICHARD (DICK): BIRTHDAY. Jan 30, 1941. 46th vice president of the US, born at Lincoln, NE.

FIRST BRAWL IN THE US HOUSE OF REPRESENTATIVES: ANNIVERSARY. Jan 30, 1798. The first brawl to break out on the floor of the US House of Representatives occurred at Philadelphia, PA. The fight was precipitated by an argument between Matthew Lyon of Vermont and Roger Griswold of Connecticut. Lyon spat in Griswold's face. Although a resolution to expel Lyon was introduced, the measure failed and Lyon maintained his seat.

FLORIDA WILDLIFE AND WESTERN ART EXPO. Jan 30–Feb 1. The Lakeland Center, Historic Downtown Lakeland, FL. Featuring more than 200 of the nation's finest wildlife artists, wood sculptors, conservation groups and live wildlife exhibits. Est attendance: 8,000. For info: Michael E. Kessler, Pres, Florida Wildlife Exposition Inc, PO Box 15693, Sarasota, FL 34277. Phone: (941) 364-9453. Fax: (941) 364-9453. E-mail: fwexpo@comcast.net. Web: www.wildlifeartexpo.com.

FUN AT WORK DAY. Jan 30. Inject some laughter into your workplace by planning a fun and relaxing activity. Do something to encourage enthusiasm and openness, to help build rapport and release tension. When we enjoy our work, we are more productive and creative. Annually, the last Friday of January. For info: Diane C. Decker. Phone: (847) 394-0994. E-mail: dcdecker@msn.com. Web: www.qualitytransitions.com.

GANDHI ASSASSINATED: ANNIVERSARY. Jan 30, 1948. Indian religious and political leader, assassinated at New Delhi, India. The assassin was a Hindu extremist, Ram Naturam. See also: "Gandhi, Mohandas Karamchand (Mahatma): Birth Anniversary" (Oct 2).

INANE ANSWERING MESSAGE DAY. Jan 30. Annually, the day set aside to change, shorten, replace or delete those ridiculous and/or annoying answering machine messages that waste the time of anyone who must listen to them. [©2003 by WH.] For info: Thomas & Ruth Roy, Wellcat Holidays, 2418 Long Ln, Lebanon, PA 17046. Phone: (717) 279-0184. E-mail: info@wellcat.com. Web: www.wellcat.com.

JORDAN: KING'S BIRTHDAY. Jan 30. National holiday. Honors King Abdullah II, son of the late King Hussein, who was born Jan 30, 1962, and assumed the throne June 9, 1999.

LADIES' BLISS WEEKEND. Jan 30–31. Hall of the Great Lakes at the American Club, Kohler, WI. Bring your mom, your daughter or your best friend. Enjoy a weekend full of time just for you! Pamper yourself with a massage or facial, enjoy champagne and chocolates at the Saturday evening "It's All About Me" experience. For info: American Club, Highland Drive, Kohler, WI 53044. Phone: (800) 344-2838. Fax: (920) 457-6372. Web: www.destinationkohler.com.

107

Jan 30 ☆ *Chase's 2004 Calendar of Events* ☆

MARYLAND ADOPTS ARTICLES OF CONFEDERATION: ANNIVERSARY. Jan 30, 1781. Maryland became the last of the 13 original states to adopt the Articles of Confederation.

MOOSESTOMPERS WEEKEND. Jan 30–Feb 1 (tentative). Houlton, ME. Human curling, human dogsled racing, snow balls, giant sliding hill for children, snowmobiling activities, cross-country skiing, skating, bonfire, snowmobile light parade, MooseStompers ball, fireworks and much more. For info: Greater Houlton Chamber of Commerce, 109 Main St, Houlton, ME 04730. Phone: (207) 532-4216. E-mail: chamber@greaterhoulton.com. Web: www.greaterhoulton.com/moosestompers.

NATIONAL ADULT DAY SERVICES ASSOCIATION CONFERENCE. Jan 30–31. Astor Crowne Plaza Hotel, New Orleans, LA. 2nd annual conference. For info: National Adult Day Services Association, 8201 Greensboro Dr, Ste 300, McLean, VA 22102. Phone: (703) 610-9035 or (866) 890-7357. E-mail: info@nadsa.org. Web: www.nadsa.org.

NC RV AND CAMPING SHOW. Jan 30–Feb 1. Charlotte Merchandise Mart, Charlotte, NC. A display of the latest in recreation vehicles and accessories by various dealers. Est attendance: 11,000. For info: Apple Rock Advertising & Promotion, 1200 Eastchester Dr, High Point, NC 27265. Phone: (336) 881-7100. Fax: (336) 883-7198. E-mail: rvshows@applerock.com. Web: www.applerock.com.

OSCEOLA: DEATH ANNIVERSARY. Jan 30, 1838. Osceola was a leader during the Second Seminole War (1835–1842). During the first two years of the war, he led the fight against removal of the Florida Seminoles to Indian territory. He was captured under a flag of truce in 1837 and imprisoned at Fort Marion in St. Augustine, FL. He was moved to Fort Moultrie at Charleston Harbor, SC, where he died. He was born near present-day Tuskegee, AL, circa 1804.

RAF BOMBS HITLER CELEBRATION: ANNIVERSARY. Jan 30, 1943. British Royal Air Force Mosquito bombers ran a daylight raid on Berlin timed to coincide with a speech being given by Joseph Goebbels in honor of Hitler's 10th year in power.

ROOSEVELT, FRANKLIN DELANO: BIRTH ANNIVERSARY. Jan 30, 1882. 32nd president of the US (Mar 4, 1933–Apr 12, 1945). The only president to serve more than two terms, FDR was elected four times. He supported the Allies in WWII before the US entered the struggle by supplying them with war materials through the Lend-Lease Act; he became deeply involved in broad decision making after the Japanese attack on Pearl Harbor Dec 7, 1941. Born at Hyde Park, NY, he died a few months into his fourth term at Warm Springs, GA, Apr 12, 1945.

SUGARLOAF CRAFTS FESTIVAL. Jan 30–Feb 1. Dulles Expo Center, Chantilly, VA. This show, now in its 6th year, features more than 320 nationally recognized craft designers and fine artists displaying and selling their original creations. Includes craft demonstrations, live music, specialty foods, hourly gift certificate drawings and more. Est attendance: 26,000. For info: Sugarloaf Mountain Works, 200 Orchard Ridge Dr, #215, Gaithersburg, MD 20878. Phone: (800) 210-9900. Fax: (301) 253-9620. Web: www.sugarloafcrafts.com.

TET OFFENSIVE BEGINS: ANNIVERSARY. Jan 30, 1968. After calling for a cease-fire during the Tet holiday celebrations, North Vietnam and the National Liberation Front launched a major offensive throughout South Vietnam on that holiday. Attacks erupted in 36 of the 44 provincial capitals and five of the six major cities. In addition, the Viet Cong attacked the US embassy in Saigon, Tan Son Nhut Air Base, the presidential palace and South Vietnamese general staff headquarters. Costing as many as 40,000 battlefield deaths, the offensive was a tactical defeat for the Viet Cong and North Vietnam. The South Vietnamese held their ground and the US was able to airlift troops into the critical areas and quickly regain control. However, the offensive is credited as a strategic success in that it continued the demoralization of American public opinion. After Tet, American policy toward Vietnam shifted from winning the war to seeking an honorable way out.

THOMAS, ISAIAH: BIRTH ANNIVERSARY. Jan 30, 1749. American printer, editor, almanac publisher, historian and founder of the American Antiquarian Society. Born at Boston, MA; died Apr 4, 1831, at Worcester, MA.

TUCHMAN, BARBARA W.: BIRTH ANNIVERSARY. Jan 30, 1912. Historian and journalist Barbara Tuchman's most famous works were her Pulitzer Prize–winning books *The Guns of August* (1962) and *Stilwell and the American Experience in China, 1911–45* (1971). Tuchman was known for making history lively. Other well-known books included *The Proud Tower* (1966) and *The First Salute* (1988). Barbara Wertheim Tuchman was born at New York, NY, and died at Greenwich, CT, Feb 6, 1988.

WORLD OF WHEELS. Jan 30–Feb 1. Multi-Purpose Events Center Exhibit Hall, Wichita Falls, TX. Features spectacular customized, modified and restored vehicles of all sizes, shapes and colors. Famous television stars, exciting entertainment and fun for all ages. Est attendance: 12,000. For info: Wichita Falls Conv & Visitors Bureau, 1000 5th St, Wichita Falls, TX 76301. Phone: (940) 716-5500 or (940) 855-0499. Fax: (940) 716-5509. E-mail: MPEC@wf.net. Web: www.wichitafalls.org.

BIRTHDAYS TODAY

John Baldacci, 49, Governor of Maine (D), born Bangor, ME, Jan 30, 1955.

Christian Bale, 30, actor (*American Psycho, Little Women, Empire of the Sun*), born Pembrokeshire, West Wales, Jan 30, 1974.

Brett Butler, 46, comedienne, actress ("Grace Under Fire"), born Montgomery, AL, Jan 30, 1958.

Richard (Dick) Cheney, 63, 46th vice president of the US, born Lincoln, NE, Jan 30, 1941.

Phil Collins, 53, musician, singer, songwriter, born Chiswick, England, Jan 30, 1951.

Charles S. Dutton, 53, actor ("Roc," *Mississippi Masala, Menace II Society*), born Baltimore, MD, Jan 30, 1951.

Gene Hackman, 74, actor (*The French Connection, Bonnie and Clyde, Unforgiven*), born San Bernardino, CA, Jan 30, 1930.

Davey Johnson, 61, baseball manager and former player, born Orlando, FL, Jan 30, 1943.

Dorothy Malone, 79, actress ("Peyton Place"; Oscar for *Written on the Wind*), born Chicago, IL, Jan 30, 1925.

Dick Martin, 82, comedian, actor (Emmy for "Rowan & Martin's Laugh-In"), born Detroit, MI, Jan 30, 1922.

Frank O'Bannon, 74, Governor of Indiana (D), born Louisville, KY, Jan 30, 1930.

Vanessa Redgrave, 67, actress (*Mary, Queen of Scots; Julia*), born London, England, Jan 30, 1937.

Jalen Rose, 31, basketball player, born Detroit, MI, Jan 30, 1973.

	S	M	T	W	T	F	S
January					1	2	3
2004	4	5	6	7	8	9	10
	11	12	13	14	15	16	17
	18	19	20	21	22	23	24
	25	26	27	28	29	30	31

Louis Rukeyser, 70, financial commentator, host ("Wall Street Week"), born New York, NY, Jan 30, 1934.
Boris Spassky, 67, former chess player, journalist, born Leningrad, USSR, Jan 30, 1937.
Curtis Strange, 49, golfer, broadcaster, born Norfolk, VA, Jan 30, 1955.
Jody Watley, 45, singer, born Chicago, IL, Jan 30, 1959.

JANUARY 31 — SATURDAY
Day 31 — 335 Remaining

BROOKFIELD ICE HARVEST. Jan 31. Brookfield, VT. Demonstrations of ice harvesting using the original equipment near the Brookfield Floating Bridge, one of only two such bridges remaining in the US today. Annually, the last Saturday in January. Est attendance: 1,000. For info: Al Wilder, PO Box 405, Brookfield, VT 05036. Phone: (802) 276-3959. Fax: (802) 276-3023.

CANADAFEST. Jan 31–Feb 1. Hollywood, FL. Annual event held on the beach and boardwalk featuring Canadian and American entertainment, arts and crafts, community exhibits and international food. Est attendance: 100,000. For info: Roguey Doyle, City of Hollywood, Dept of Parks, Recreation & Cultural Arts, 1940 Harrison St, Ste 101, Hollywood, FL 33020. Phone: (954) 921-3404.

EINSTEIN ON WINE. Jan 31. Tampa, FL. 9th annual benefit. Taste wines from around the world and samples from local restauranteurs. Bid on Tampa's best during our fun and exciting silent auction. All proceeds benefit the Museum of Science & Industry's K+I+D+S education program. Musical entertainment. Sponsored by BEAM (Be Enthusiastic About MOSI) and ABC Fine Wine & Spirits. For tickets, please call (813) 978-6000. Est attendance: 1,500. For info: Museum of Science & Industry, 4801 E Fowler Ave, Tampa, FL 33617-2017. Phone: (813) 987-6000. Fax: (813) 987-6310.

FIRST SOCIAL SECURITY CHECK ISSUED: ANNIVERSARY. Jan 31, 1940. Ida May Fuller of Ludlow, VT, received the first monthly retirement check in the amount of $22.54. Ms Fuller had worked for three years under the Social Security program (which had been established by legislation in 1935). The accumulated taxes on her salary over those three years were $24.75. She lived to be 100 years old, collecting $22,888 in Social Security benefits. See also: "Social Security Act: Anniv" (Aug 14).

GREATER SPRINGFIELD GARAGE SALE. Jan 31–Feb 1. Ozark Empire Fairgrounds, Springfield, MO. Indoor garage sale featuring more than 400 booths of treasures for shoppers to seek out. For info: Nancy Bright, Ozark Empire Fair, PO Box 630, Springfield, MO 65801. Phone: (417) 833-2660. Fax: (417) 833-3769. E-mail: nancy@ozarkempirefair.com. Web: www.ozarkempirefair.com.

GREY, ZANE: BIRTH ANNIVERSARY. Jan 31, 1872. Zane Grey (original name Pearl Grey), American dentist and prolific author of tales of the Old West, was born at Zanesville, OH. Grey eventually wrote more than 80 books that were translated into many languages and sold more than 10 million copies. The novel *Riders of the Purple Sage* (1912) was the most popular. Grey died Oct 23, 1939, at Altadena, CA.

GROUNDHOG DAYS. Jan 31–Feb 2. Historic Woodstock Square, Woodstock, IL. Thanks to Bill Murray and the *Groundhog Day* movie, Woodstock celebrates with ice-sculpting demonstrations, walking tour of filming sites, breakfast and Woodstock Willie's prognostication. Est attendance: 500. For info: Woodstock Chamber of Commerce, 136 Cass St, Woodstock, IL 60098. Phone: (815) 338-2436. Fax: (815) 338-2927. E-mail: chamber@woodstockilchamber.com Web: www.woodstockilchamber.com.

INSPIRE YOUR HEART WITH ART DAY. Jan 31. A day to experience art in your life. "Food sustains you as a human; art inspires you to be divine." Go to an art museum, browse through an art book at the library, enroll in an art class or commission an artist. Inspire your heart with art! For info: Jayne Howard-Feldman, Angel Heights, PO Box 95, Upperco, MD 21155. Phone: (410) 833-6912. Fax: (410) 429-5425. E-mail: earthangel4peace@aol.com. Web: earthangel4peace.com.

KITES ON ICE. Jan 31–Feb 1. Monona Terrace designed by Frank Lloyd Wright, Lake Monona, Madison, WI. Kite flyers from around the world will hold demonstrations and shows on the ice and inside the Convention Center. Est attendance: 75,000. For info: Kristi Kent-Bracken, Director, Madison Festivals, Inc, PO Box 46427, Madison, WI 53744-6427. Phone: (608) 850-4900. Fax: (608) 850-4929. E-mail: globalcelebrations@tds.net. Web: www.madfest.org.

McDONALD'S INVADES THE SOVIET UNION: ANNIVERSARY. Jan 31, 1990. McDonald's Corporation opened its first fast-food restaurant in the Soviet Union.

MOORE, GARRY: BIRTH ANNIVERSARY. Jan 31, 1915. American television host Garry Moore was born Thomas Garrison Morfit at Baltimore, MD. His best-known shows were "I've Got a Secret" (1952–67) and "To Tell the Truth" (1969–76). He gave Carol Burnett her break on TV when he made her a regular on "The Garry Moore Show." He died Nov 28, 1993, at Hilton Head Island, SC.

MORRIS, ROBERT: BIRTH ANNIVERSARY. Jan 31, 1734. Signer of the Declaration of Independence, the Articles of Confederation and the Constitution. He was one of only two men who signed all three documents. He was born at Liverpool, England, and died May 7, 1806, at Philadelphia, PA.

NATIVE AMERICAN WHIPTOP CONTEST. Jan 31. Echo Lake, WI. A traditional Native American fast-action top game played in the winter on a frozen lake. Contest is followed by a Spinning Top Museum tour and top shows. Admission $8/person; children must be accompanied by an adult. For info: Spinning Top Museum, 533 Milwaukee Ave (Hwy 36), Burlington, WI 53105. Phone: (262) 763-3946.

NAURU: NATIONAL HOLIDAY. Jan 31. Republic of Nauru. Commemorates independence in 1968 from a UN trusteeship administered by Australia, New Zealand and the UK.

ORCHID SHOW. Jan 31–Mar 14. Missouri Botanical Garden, St. Louis, MO. Spectacular display of the Garden's vast orchid collection. For info: Missouri Botanical Garden, PO Box 299, St. Louis, MO 63166-0299. Phone: (314) 577-9400 or (800) 642-8842. Web: www.mobot.org.

ROBINSON, JACKIE: 85th BIRTH ANNIVERSARY. Jan 31, 1919. Jack Roosevelt Robinson, athlete and business executive, first black to enter professional major league baseball (Brooklyn Dodgers, 1947–56). Voted National League's Most Valuable Player in 1949 and elected to the Baseball Hall of Fame in 1962. Born at Cairo, GA, Jackson died at Stamford, CT, Oct 24, 1972.

ROLEX 24 AT DAYTONA GRAND-AM SERIES RACE. Jan 31–Feb 1. Daytona International Speedway, Daytona Beach, FL. 42nd annual running of the most prestigious endurance race in North America. For info: Daytona Intl Speedway, PO Box 2801, Daytona Beach, FL 32120-2801. Phone: (386) 253-7223. Fax: (386) 947-6791. Web: www.daytonainternationalspeedway.com.

SCHUBERT, FRANZ: BIRTH ANNIVERSARY. Jan 31, 1797. Composer, born at Vienna, Austria, and died there of typhus Nov 19, 1828, at age 31. Buried, at his request, near the grave of Beethoven. Schubert last worked on his "Unfinished Symphony" (No 8) in 1822. On the 100th anniversary of his death in 1928 a $10,000 prize was offered to "finish" the work. The protests were so great that the offer was withdrawn.

SLOVIK, EDDIE D.: EXECUTION ANNIVERSARY. Jan 31, 1945. Anniversary of execution by firing squad of 24-year-old Private Eddie D. Slovik. Born at Detroit, MI, Feb 18, 1920, Slovik was assigned to Company G, 109th Infantry, 28th Division, US Army. His death sentence, the first for desertion since the Civil War, has been a subject of controversy. First buried in France,

Jan 31 ☆ Chase's 2004 Calendar of Events ☆

Slovik's remains were exhumed in 1987 for reburial beside his wife, Antoinette, who died in 1979, after years of effort to clear Slovik's name and have his body returned to the US.

SPACE MILESTONE: *APOLLO 14* (US). Jan 31, 1971. Launch date of *Apollo 14*. Five days later on Feb 5 astronauts Alan B. Shepard, Jr, and Edgar D. Mitchell landed on the moon (Lunar Module *Antares*). Command Module *Kitty Hawk* was piloted by Stuart A. Roosa. Pacific splashdown on Feb 9.

SPACE MILESTONE: *EXPLORER 1* (US): ANNIVERSARY. Jan 31, 1958. The first successful US satellite. Although launched four months later than the Soviet Union's *Sputnik*, *Explorer* reached a higher altitude and detected a zone of intense radiation inside Earth's magnetic field. This was later named the Van Allen radiation belts. More than 65 subsequent *Explorer* satellites were launched through 1984.

SPACE MILESTONE: *LUNA 9* (USSR). Jan 31, 1966. Launch of unmanned mission that accomplished the first soft landing on the moon three days later on Feb 3. Relayed TV photos of the lunar surface.

SPACE MILESTONE: PROJECT MERCURY TEST (US). Jan 31, 1961. A test of Project Mercury spacecraft accomplished the first US recovery of a large animal from space. Ham, the chimpanzee, successfully performed simple tasks in space.

UNIVERSITY KIWANIS PANCAKE FESTIVAL. Jan 31. Multi-Purpose Events Center, J.S. Bridwell Center, Wichita Falls, TX. 47th annual. A day of food and fun, featuring the world's "best pancakes." Est attendance: 8,000. For info: Wichita Falls CVB, 1000 5th St, Wichita Falls, TX 76301. Phone: (940) 716-5500. Fax: (940) 716-5509. E-mail: MPEC@wf.net. Web: www.wichitafalls.org.

WORLD SHOVEL RACE CHAMPIONSHIPS. Jan 31–Feb 1. Angel Fire, NM. This famous event highlights thrilling competition in production and modified divisions for several age groups. "Modified" competition reaches speeds of 75 mph. Spectator competition on stock grain scoop shovels. Est attendance: 1,500. For info: Angel Fire Resort, PO Drawer B, Angel Fire, NM 87710. Phone: (800) 633-7463 or (505) 377-4224. Fax: (505) 377-4395. E-mail: events@angelfireresort.com. Web: www.angelfireresort.com.

YAWM ARAFAT: THE STANDING AT ARAFAT. Jan 31. Islamic calendar date: Dhu-Hijjah 9, 1424. The day when people on the Hajj (pilgrimage to Mecca) assemble for "the Standing" at the plain of Arafat at Mina, Saudi Arabia, near Mecca. This gathering is a foreshadowing of the Day of Judgment. Different methods for "anticipating" the visibility of the new moon crescent at Mecca are used by different Muslim groups. US date may vary. Began at sunset the preceding day.

BIRTHDAYS TODAY

Ernest (Ernie) Banks, 73, Hall of Fame baseball player, born Dallas, TX, Jan 31, 1931.

Queen Beatrix, 66, Queen of the Netherlands, born Sostdijk, Netherlands, Jan 31, 1938.

Carol Channing, 81, actress (stage: *Hello, Dolly!*; *Thoroughly Modern Millie*), born Carol Channing Lowe, Seattle, WA, Jan 31, 1923.

Minnie Driver, 33, actress (*Gross Pointe Blank*, *Good Will Hunting*), born London, England, Jan 31, 1971.

Philip Glass, 67, composer, born Baltimore, MD, Jan 31, 1937.

Johnny (Rotten) Lydon, 48, lead singer (Sex Pistols 1975–77), born near London, England, Jan 31, 1956.

Kelly Lynch, 45, actress (*Mr Magoo*, *Drugstore Cowboy*), born Minneapolis, MN, Jan 31, 1959.

Norman Mailer, 81, author (*The Executioner's Song*, *The Naked and the Dead*), born Long Branch, NJ, Jan 31, 1923.

Stuart Margolin, 64, actor, director, writer ("The Rockford Files" [Emmy Awards, 1979, 1980], *The Big Blue*, *S.O.B.*), born Davenport, IA, Jan 31, 1940.

Suzanne Pleshette, 67, actress ("The Bob Newhart Show"), born New York, NY, Jan 31, 1937.

(Lynn) Nolan Ryan, 57, Hall of Fame baseball player, born Refugio, TX, Jan 31, 1947.

Jean Simmons, 75, actress (*Black Narcissus*, *The Robe*, *Elmer Gantry*), born London, England, Jan 31, 1929.

Jessica Walter, 60, actress ("Amy Prentiss," *Play Misty for Me*, *The Flamingo Kid*), born Brooklyn, NY, Jan 31, 1944.

☆ *Chase's 2004 Calendar of Events* ☆   Feb 1

Februarie.

FEBRUARY 1 — SUNDAY
Day 32 — 334 Remaining

AMD/LOW VISION AWARENESS MONTH. Feb 1–29. Macular degeneration is a leading cause of vision loss. Low vision aids can make the most of remaining vision. Information on eye disease warning signs and on low vision aids will be available. For info: Prevent Blindness America, 500 E Remington Rd, Schaumburg, IL 60173. Phone: (800) 331-2020. Fax: (847) 843-8458. Web: www.preventblindness.org.

AMERICAN HEART MONTH. Feb 1–29. Volunteers across the country spend one to four weeks canvassing neighborhoods and providing educational information about heart disease and stroke. Know the warning signs of a heart attack. Call 911. Give CPR. For info: Call your local chapter of the American Heart Association or write us at American Heart Association, 7272 Greenville Ave, Dallas, TX 75231. Phone: (800) AHA-USA1. Fax: (214) 369-3685. Web: www.americanheart.org.

★**AMERICAN HEART MONTH.** Feb 1–29. Presidential Proclamation issued each year for February since 1964. (PL88–254 of Dec 30, 1963.)

BAKE FOR FAMILY FUN MONTH. Feb 1–29. The Home Baking Association has designated February as "Bake for Family Fun Month," dedicated to the great taste, good nutrition, economy and family fun of traditional home baking. For info: Charlene Patton, 2931 SW Gainsboro Road, Topeka, KS 66614. Phone: (785) 478-3283. Fax: (785) 478-3024. Web: www.homebaking.org.

BLACK HISTORY MONTH. Feb 1–29. Traditionally the month containing Abraham Lincoln's birthday (Feb 12) and Frederick Douglass's presumed birthday (Feb 14). Observance of a special period to recognize achievements and contributions by African Americans dates from February 1926, when it was launched by Dr. Carter G. Woodson. Variously designated Negro History, Black History, Afro-American History, African-American History, the observance period was initially one week, but since 1976 the entire month of February. For info: Assn for the Study of African American Life and History, Inc, 7961 Eastern Ave, #301, Silver Spring, MD 20910. Phone: (301) 587-5900. Fax: (301) 587-5915. E-mail: aslah@earthlink.net. Web: www.asalh.com.

BLACK MARIA STUDIO: ANNIVERSARY. Feb 1, 1893. The first moving picture studio was built at Thomas Edison's laboratory compound at West Orange, NJ, at a cost of less than $700. The wooden structure of irregular oblong shape was covered with black tar paper. It had a sharply sloping roof hinged at one edge so that half of it could be raised to admit sunlight. Fifty feet in length, it was mounted on a pivot enabling it to be swung around to follow the changing position of the sun. There was a stage draped in black at one end of the room. Though the structure was officially called a Kinetographic Theater, it was nicknamed the "Black Maria" because it resembled an old-fashioned police wagon.

CAMELLIA DAYS. Feb 1–29. Massee Lane Gardens, Fort Valley, GA. 10th annual celebration of the beautiful flower, the camellia. Events include garden tours and workshops, plant sale, Senior Citizen Day, fashion show and luncheon and more. Call for more details and ticket prices. Annually, the month of February. Sponsor: The American Camellia Society. Est attendance: 4,000. For info: Massee Lane Gardens, 100 Massee Lane, Fort Valley, GA 31030. Phone: (478) 967-2722. Fax: (478) 967-2083. Web: www.camellias-acs.com.

CAR INSURANCE FIRST ISSUED: ANNIVERSARY. Feb 1, 1898. Travelers Insurance Company issued the first car insurance against accidents with horses.

CARAWAY, HATTIE WYATT: BIRTH ANNIVERSARY. Feb 1, 1878. Born at Bakersville, TN, Hattie Caraway became a US Senator from Arkansas in 1931 when her husband died and she was appointed to fill out his term. The following year, she ran for the seat herself and became the first woman elected to the US Senate. She served 14 years there, becoming an adept and tireless legislator (once introducing 43 bills on the same day) who worked for women's rights (once cosponsoring an equal rights amendment), supported New Deal policies as well as Prohibition and opposed the increasing influence of lobbyists. Caraway died at Falls Church, VA, Dec 21, 1950.

CHILDREN'S AUTHORS & ILLUSTRATORS WEEK. Feb 1–7. To celebrate and recognize authors and illustrators who create books for young people and promote literacy by inspiring enjoyment of quality literature. During this week, members of the Children's Authors Network speak at schools, libraries and children's shelters. Motivate children to read and write: invite authors and illustrators to school and venues near you! Annually, the first week in February. For info: Children's Authors Network! (CAN!), 23291 Mobile St, West Hills, CA 91307. Phone: (818) 530-0300. Web: www.childrensauthorsnetwork.com.

EID-AL-ADHA: FEAST OF THE SACRIFICE. Feb 1. Islamic calendar date: Dhu-Hijja 10, 1424. Commemorates Abraham's willingness to sacrifice his son Ishmael in obedience to God. It is part of the Hajj (pilgrimage to Mecca). The day begins with the sacrifice of an animal in remembrance of the Angel Gabriel's substitution of a lamb as Abraham's offering. One-third of the meat is given to the poor and the rest is shared with friends and family. Celebrated with gifts and general merrymaking, the festival usually continues for several days. It is celebrated as Tabaski in Benin, Burkina Faso, Guinea, Guinea-Bissau, Ivory Coast, Mali, Niger and Senegal; as Hari Raya Hajj in South East Asia and as Kurban Bayram in Turkey and Bosnia. Different methods for "anticipating" the visibility of the moon crescent at Mecca are used by different Muslim groups. US date may vary. Began at sunset the preceding day.

FEBRUARY IS FABULOUS FLORIDA STRAWBERRY MONTH. Feb 1–29. Strawberries in February? You bet your snow boots! Though it's cold and dreary in many parts of the country, February is fabulous in Florida where strawberry growers are harvesting their winter crop and shipping handpicked fruit to key markets. Strawberries dipped in chocolate or champagne are a Valentine's Day delight. Consider using the ripe, luscious berry in a variety of recipes from salads to shortbread. For info: Florida Strawberry Growers Assn, PO Drawer 2550, Plant City, FL 33564. Phone: (813) 752-6822. Web: www.straw-berry.org.

Feb 1 ☆ Chase's 2004 Calendar of Events ☆

FESTIVAL OF THE NORTH. Feb 1–29. Ketchikan, AK. A cultural event encompassing an annual Wearable Art Show; performing, visual and literary arts, including a myriad of workshops. Annually, the month of February. Est attendance: 2,000. For info: Ketchikan Area Arts and Humanities Council, 716 Totem Way, Ketchikan, AK 99901. Phone: (907) 225-2211. Fax: (907) 225-4330. E-mail: ketchart@kpunet.net.

FIRST SESSION OF SUPREME COURT: ANNIVERSARY. Feb 1, 1790. The Supreme Court of the United States met for the first time in New York City with Chief Justice John Jay presiding.

FLAGSTAFF WINTERFEST. Feb 1–29. Flagstaff, AZ. This festival, now in its 18th year, celebrates the many facets of a Flagstaff winter. Family fun for everyone: concerts, performances, art shows, snow sports, wacky sports, winter workshops and much more. The fun will go on with or without snow. Est attendance: 20,000. For info: Heather Rogers, Winterfest Coordinator, Flagstaff Chamber of Commerce, 101 W Rte 66, Flagstaff, AZ 86001. Phone: (928) 774-4505. Fax: (928) 779-1209. E-mail: hrogers@flagstaff.az.us. Web: www.flagstaff.az.us.

FORD, JOHN: BIRTH ANNIVERSARY. Feb 1, 1895. Film director John Ford was born at Cape Elizabeth, ME, as Sean Aloysius O'Feeney; he changed his name after moving to Hollywood. Ford won his first Academy Award in 1935 for *The Informer*. Among his many other films: *Stagecoach, Young Mr Lincoln, The Grapes of Wrath, How Green Was My Valley, Rio Grande, What Price Glory?* and *Mister Roberts*. During World War II he served as chief of the Field Photographic Branch of the OSS. Two documentaries made during the war earned him Academy Awards. He died Aug 31, 1973, at Palm Desert, CA.

FREEDOM DAY: ANNIVERSARY. Feb 1, 1865. Anniversary of President Abraham Lincoln's approval of the 13th Amendment to the US Constitution (abolishing slavery): "1. Neither slavery nor involuntary servitude, except as a punishment for crime whereof the party shall have been duly convicted, shall exist within the United States or any place subject to their jurisdiction. 2. Congress shall have power to enforce this article by appropriate legislation." The amendment had been proposed by the Congress Jan 31, 1865; ratification was completed Dec 6, 1865.

GABLE, CLARK: BIRTH ANNIVERSARY. Feb 1, 1901. Actor William Clark Gable's first film was *The Painted Desert* in 1931, when talking films were replacing silent films. He won an Academy Award for his role in the comedy *It Happened One Night*, which established him as a romantic screen idol. Other films included *China Seas, Mutiny on the Bounty, Saratoga, Run Silent Run Deep* and *Gone with the Wind*, for which his casting as Rhett Butler seemed a foregone conclusion due to his popularity as the acknowledged "King of Movies." Gable was born at Cadiz, OH, and died Nov 16, 1960, at Hollywood, CA, shortly after completing his last film, Arthur Miller's *The Misfits*, in which he starred with Marilyn Monroe.

"GENERAL ELECTRIC THEATER" TV PREMIERE: ANNIVERSARY. Feb 1, 1953. CBS's half-hour dramatic anthology series was hosted by Ronald Reagan (in between his movie and political careers). Making their television debuts were Joseph Cotten (1954); Fred MacMurray, James Stewart and Myrna Loy (1955); Bette Davis, Anne Baxter, Tony Curtis and Fred Astaire (1957); Sammy Davis, Jr (1958); and Gene Tierney (1960). Other memorable stars who appeared on the series include: Joan Crawford, Harry Belafonte, Rosalind Russell, Ernie Kovacs, the Marx Brothers and Nancy Davis [Reagan], who starred with husband Ronald Reagan in an episode titled "A Turkey for the President" (1958).

February 2004

S	M	T	W	T	F	S
1	2	3	4	5	6	7
8	9	10	11	12	13	14
15	16	17	18	19	20	21
22	23	24	25	26	27	28
29						

GET PAID TO SHOP WEEK. Feb 1–7. Love to shop? Got those postholiday, maxed-out credit cards, can't go to the mall blues? Start getting paid to go shopping as a mystery shopper. Businesses use thousands of mystery shoppers to tell them what their customers won't—the truth about service, cleanliness and more. And if you work up an appetite shopping, mystery shoppers also get paid to eat out in restaurants. Free information and articles available for publishers and webmasters at IdeaLady.com/content.htm. Annually, the first full week in February. For info: Cathy Stucker, 4646 Hwy 6, PMB #123, Sugar Land, TX 77478. Phone: (281) 265-7342. E-mail: cathy@idealady.com. Web: www.idealady.com.

G.I. JOE INTRODUCED: 40th ANNIVERSARY. Feb 1, 1964. This toy action figure was introduced by Hasbro and sold for $2.49. It was the first mass-market doll intended for boys and was a great success. The figure's name came from a film, *The Story of G.I. Joe* (1945), that starred Robert Mitchum and Burgess Meredith.

"GOOD TIMES" TV PREMIERE: 30th ANNIVERSARY. Feb 1, 1974. A CBS spin-off from "Maude," which was a spin-off of "All in the Family." "Good Times" featured an African-American family living in the housing projects of Chicago. The series portrayed the Evans family's struggles to improve their lot. The cast featured Esther Rolle and John Amos as Florida and James Evans, Jimmie Walker as son J.J., BernNadette Stanis as daughter Thelma, Ralph Carter as son Michael, Johnny Brown as janitor Mr Bookman, Ja'Net DuBois as neighbor Willona Woods, Janet Jackson as Willona's adopted daughter Penny and Ben Powers as Thelma's husband Keith Anderson.

GREENSBORO SIT-IN: ANNIVERSARY. Feb 1, 1960. Commercial discrimination against blacks and other minorities provoked a nonviolent protest. At Greensboro, NC, four students from the Agricultural and Technical College (Ezell Blair, Jr; Franklin McCain; Joseph McNeill and David Richmond) sat down at a Woolworths store lunch counter and ordered coffee. Refused service, they remained all day. The following days similar sit-ins took place at the Woolworths' lunch counter. Before the week was over they were joined by a few white students. The protest spread rapidly, especially in southern states. More than 1,600 people were arrested before the year was over for participating in sit-ins. Civil rights for all became a cause for thousands of students and activists. In response, equal accommodation regardless of race became the rule at lunch counters, hotels and business establishments in thousands of places.

HUGHES, LANGSTON: BIRTH ANNIVERSARY. Feb 1, 1902. African-American poet and author, born at Joplin, MO. Among his works are the poetry collection *Montage of a Dream Deferred*, plays, a novel and short stories. Hughes died May 22, 1967, at New York, NY.

INTERNATIONAL BOOST SELF-ESTEEM MONTH. Feb 1–29. A month to focus on the importance of nurturing and cultivating self-esteem to beat the winter blahs, to boost morale and to inspire yourself and others to seize new challenges. For info: Valla Dana Fotiades, M.Ed., PO Box 8004, Cypress Gardens, FL 33884. E-mail: Valladana@cs.com.

INTERNATIONAL COACHING WEEK. Feb 1–7. To provide a week each year to educate the public about the value of working with a personal, business or executive coach and to provide an opportunity for coaches and their clients to acknowledge the results and progress made through the coaching process. Annually, the first week in February. For info: Jerri N. Udelson, MCC, Entrepreneurial Consulting Services, 72 Fresh Pond Parkway, Cambridge, MA 02138. Phone: (617) 876-5700. E-mail: JerriU@aol.com. Web: www.coachfederation.org or www.coachingweek.com.

INTERNATIONAL EXPECT SUCCESS MONTH. Feb 1–29. If you want good things to happen to you in the new year, you must "Expect Success . . . then work like there is no other option." For details and information on how to make this your most successful year yet by letting the power of positive expec-

☆ Chase's 2004 Calendar of Events ☆ — Feb 1

tation work for you, contact Life Power Dynamics. For info: Karla Brandau, Life Power Dynamics, 4985 Chartley Circle, Lilburn, GA 30047. Phone: (770) 923-0883. Fax: (770) 931-2530. E-mail: karla@karlaspeaks.com. Web: www.karlaspeaks.com.

"LATE NIGHT WITH DAVID LETTERMAN" TV PREMIERE: ANNIVERSARY. Feb 1, 1982. This is when it all began: the stupid pet tricks, the stupid human tricks and the legendary top ten lists. "Late Night" premiered on NBC as a talk/variety show appearing after "The Tonight Show with Johnny Carson." Host David Letterman was known for his irreverent sense of humor and daffy antics. The offbeat show attained cult status among college crowds and insomniacs, as many tuned in to see a Velcro-suited Letterman throw himself against a wall. The show also featured bandleader-sidekick Paul Shaffer, writer Chris Elliott and Calvert DeForest as geezer Larry "Bud" Melman. In 1993 Letterman made a highly publicized exit from NBC and began hosting "The Late Show" on CBS.

LIBERACE MEMORIAL MASS. Feb 1. Las Vegas, NV. To honor Liberace, a special memorial mass will be held. "Mr Showmanship" was known throughout the world for his beautiful music, his costumes and candelabra. He was honored with an astounding array of awards, including two Emmys, six gold albums and two stars on the Hollywood Walk of Fame. Annually, the first Sunday in February. For info: Jamie G. James, James Agency, PR, 3630 Coldwater Canyon Ave, Studio City, CA 91604. Phone: (818) 508-4902. Fax: (818) 508-0562. E-mail: Jjames@liberace.org.

LIBRARY LOVERS' MONTH. Feb 1–29. A month-long celebration of school, public and private libraries of all types. This is a time for everyone, especially library support groups, to recognize the value of libraries and to work to ensure that the nation's libraries will continue to serve. For info: Stephanie Stokes, Friends and Foundations for California Libraries, 11045 Wrightwood Pl, Studio City, CA 91604-3961. Phone: (818) 980-7476. E-mail: librarylovers@librarysupport.net. Web: www.librarysupport.net/librarylovers/.

MARFAN SYNDROME AWARENESS MONTH. Feb 1–29. Volunteers across the country distribute items with a heart theme and educational information about Marfan syndrome and related connective tissue disorders that can result in life-threatening cardiovascular problems as well as orthopedic and ophthalmologic handicaps; it affects about 200,000 Americans. Annually, the month of February. For info: Cathie Tsuchiya, National Marfan Foundation, 22 Manhasset Ave, Port Washington, NY 11050. Phone: (800) 862-7326 or (516) 883-8712. Fax: (516) 883-8040. E-mail: staff@marfan.org. Web: www.marfan.org.

★**NATIONAL AFRICAN AMERICAN HISTORY MONTH.** Feb 1–29.

NATIONAL BIRD FEEDING MONTH. Feb 1–29. To spread the word of how difficult it can be for birds to survive in North American winters, in 1993 the National Bird-Feeding Society named February National Bird Feeding Month. The widespread awareness generated by this event has contributed to the safe passage of winter for our feathered friends. Providing wild birds with food, water and shelter supplements their natural diet and helps them survive. For info: National Bird-Feeding Society, 507 Broad St PMB 143, Lake Geneva, WI 53147. Web: www.birdfeeding.org.

NATIONAL CHERRY MONTH. Feb 1–29. To publicize the colorful red tart cherry. Recipes, posters and table tents available. For info: Cherry Marketing Institute, PO Box 30285, Lansing, MI 48909-7785. Fax: (517) 669-3354. E-mail: info@cherrymkt.org. Web: www.usacherries.com.

NATIONAL CHILDREN'S DENTAL HEALTH MONTH. Feb 1–29. To increase dental awareness and stress the importance of regular dental care. For info: American Dental Assn, 211 E Chicago Ave, Chicago, IL 60611. Catalog sales: (800) 947-4746. Web: www.ada.org.

★**NATIONAL CONSUMER PROTECTION WEEK.** Feb 1–7 (tentative). Date varies.

NATIONAL HOT BREAKFAST MONTH. Feb 1–29. Take time out this month to start your day with a good hot breakfast. Sponsored by Jimmy Dean. For info: Sheryl Hudson, Sr Product Mgr, Sara Lee Foods, 10151 Carver Rd, Cincinnati, OH 45242-4719. Phone: (513) 936-2665. Fax: (513) 936-2170. E-mail: sheryl.hudson@saralee.com. Web: www.jimmydean.com.

NATIONAL PARENT LEADERSHIP MONTH. Feb 1–29. In order to recognize, honor and celebrate parents for their vital leadership roles in their homes and communities and in state, national and international arenas, Parents Anonymous® Inc has designated the month of February as National Parent Leadership Month. This annual event will acknowledge the strengths of parents as leaders and generate awareness about the important roles parents can play in shaping the lives of their families and communities. Founded in 1969, Parents Anonymous® Inc is dedicated to strengthening families by preventing child abuse and neglect all around the world. For info: Meryl Levine, Parents Anonymous® Inc, 675 W Foothill Blvd, Ste 220, Claremont, CA 91711. Phone: (909) 621-6184, ext 220. E-mail: mlevine@parentsanonymous.org. Web: www.parentsanonymous.org.

NATIONAL TIME MANAGEMENT MONTH. Feb 1–29. This is the month when those noble plans made in January start to go awry. This event is dedicated to renewing those best-laid plans; breaking open those new calendars that have yet to be opened; and reevaluating and reprioritizing harried, out-of-balance lives—making specific commitments to balance them. For info: Sylvia Henderson, Springboard Training, 18005 Lafayette Dr, Ste B, Olney, MD 20832. Phone: (301) 646-1668. Fax: (301) 856-8000. E-mail: admin@springboardtraining.com. Web: www.springboardtraining.com.

NATIONAL WEDDINGS MONTH. Feb 1–29. As the wedding season gets into high gear, this observance is to call attention to the fact that more than 2.5 million weddings are celebrated in the US each year. For info: Gerard J. Monaghan, Pres, Assn of Bridal Consultants, 200 Chestnutland Rd, New Milford, CT 06776-2521. Phone: (860) 355-0464. Fax: (860) 354-1404. E-mail: pres@bridalassn.com. Web: www.BridalAssn.com.

NORTH CAROLINA SWEETPOTATO MONTH. Feb 1–29. To educate the public about the nutritional benefits and versatility of sweet potatoes. North Carolina farmers want America to know that sweet potatoes aren't just for turkeys anymore. Available year-round, sweet potatoes are loaded with beta carotene and vitamin C. They can be boiled, baked, microwaved, grilled, broiled, fried, mashed, sauteed, candied or served raw. North Carolina produces more sweet potatoes than any other state. For info: Sue Johnson-Langdon, North Carolina SweetPotato Commission, 1327 N Brightleaf Blvd, Ste H, Smithfield, NC 27577. Phone: (919) 989-7323. Fax: (919) 989-3015. E-mail: ncsweetsue@aol.com. Web: www.ncsweetpotatoes.com.

Feb 1 ☆ ***Chase's 2004 Calendar of Events*** ☆

OCEAN COUNTY BLUEGRASS FESTIVAL. Feb 1. Waretown, NJ. An indoor bluegrass festival. No alcoholic beverages or smoking allowed. Est attendance: 400. For info: Albert Music Hall, PO Box 657, 125 Wells Mills Rd, Waretown, NJ 08758. Phone: (609) 971-1593. Web: www.alberthall.org.

PLANT THE SEEDS OF GREATNESS MONTH. Feb 1–29. Think globally—build for the future—Plant the Seeds of Greatness. If you're unhappy with your present situation, discover how you can remove the barriers and make a change in your life for the better. Use this month to put to use your own unique prosperity consciousness and plant the seeds for your new career, life objectives or goals. Make a difference for yourself, your family, your business or your community. Take a chance, help yourself or help another unlock the potential for success and plant the seeds of greatness. Get outside of your comfort zone and take action on your ideas and dreams. Info available for $2.00. For info: Lorrie Walters Marsiglio, Lorimar Communications, PO Box 284-CC, Wasco, IL 60183-0284. Phone: (630) 584-9368.

PUBLICITY FOR PROFIT WEEK. Feb 1–7. Harness the power of free publicity for yourself, your business or your organization. Spend each day this week getting free publicity by doing one task to promote whatever you deem important. For free and easy-to-follow publicity plans, see website or send SASE. For info: Tom Peric, Publicity for Profit, 2040 Fairfax Ave, Cherry Hill, NJ 08003. Phone: (856) 874-0049. Fax: (856) 874-0052. E-mail: tsperic@publicityforprofit.com. Web: www.publicityforprofit.com.

RELATIONSHIP WELLNESS MONTH. Feb 1–29. Recapture the spark and zeal of personal relationships. Rekindle the flame with your partner or spouse. Get close, communicate, laugh, love and live. This is a time of forgiveness, harmony and trust. Set new goals as a couple, and establish relationship priorities. Go out on a date once a week. Be irresistible. Be patient. Seek forgiveness. Avoid nagging and complaining. Give bear hugs and gentle kisses. For info: Angela Brown, Words of Wellness, PO Box 49266, Charlotte, NC 28277. Phone: (704) 849-2900. Fax: (704) 845-3060. E-mail: angela@WordsofWellness.com. Web: www.WordsofWellness.com.

RETURN SHOPPING CARTS TO THE SUPERMARKET MONTH. Feb 1–29. A month-long opportunity to return stolen shopping carts, milk crates, bread trays and ice cream baskets to supermarkets and to avoid the increased food prices that these thefts cause. Annually, the month of February. Sponsor: Illinois Food Retailers Association. For info: Anthony A. Dinolfo, Grocer-Retired, 163 Fairfield Dr, New Lenox, IL 60451-3523. Phone: (815) 463-9136.

ROBINSON CRUSOE DAY. Feb 1, 1709 (OS). Anniversary of the rescue of Alexander Selkirk, a Scottish sailor who had been put ashore (in September 1704) on the uninhabited island Juan Fernandez, at his own request, after a quarrel with his captain. His adventures formed the basis for Daniel Defoe's book *Robinson Crusoe*. A day to be adventurous and self-reliant.

ST. LAURENT, LOUIS STEPHEN: BIRTH ANNIVERSARY. Feb 1, 1882. Canadian lawyer and prime minister, born at Compton, QC. Died at Quebec City, July 25, 1973.

SANTA CRUZ BRIDAL EXPO. Feb 1. Cocoanut Grove, Santa Cruz, CA. Features more than 60 booths with every aspect needed for that perfect wedding, reception and honeymoon. Est attendance: 2,000. For info: Jan Bollwinkel-Smith, Communications Mgr, Santa Cruz Beach Boardwalk, 400 Beach St, Santa Cruz, CA 95060-5491. Phone: (831) 423-5590. Fax: (831) 460-3336. E-mail: publicity@scseaside.com. Web: www.cocoanutgrovesantacruz.com.

February 2004

S	M	T	W	T	F	S
1	2	3	4	5	6	7
8	9	10	11	12	13	14
15	16	17	18	19	20	21
22	23	24	25	26	27	28
29						

"THE SECRET STORM" TV PREMIERE: 50th ANNIVERSARY. Feb 1, 1954. "The Secret Storm" lathered up homes for 20 years. The first soap on television, it revolved around the Ames family in fictional Woodbridge and featured a variety of actors and actresses who have moved on to bigger things. Among them are Bibi Besch, Roy Scheider, Diana Muldaur, Nicolas Coster, Robert Loggia, Laurence Luckinbill, Christina Crawford, Diane Ladd, Troy Donahue and Frances Sternhagen.

SPACE SHUTTLE *COLUMBIA* DISASTER: ANNIVERSARY. Feb 1, 2003. Minutes before space shuttle *Columbia* was due to land after a successful 16-day scientific mission, it disintegrated 40 miles above the state of Texas, killing its seven-member crew. Commander Rick Husband, pilot William McCool, Michael Anderson, David Brown, Kalpana Chawla (first woman astronaut from India), Laurel Clark and Ilan Ramon (first Israeli astronaut) lost their lives and were mourned worldwide. *Columbia* was the first shuttle to fly in space (1981).

SPIRITUAL TEACHERS MONTH. Feb 1–29. Many people have dedicated their lives to practicing and teaching enlightenment throughout the ages. We can increase our awareness and show appreciation by commemorating these unique teachers. A newsletter with suggested activities is available. For info: Rev Margaret Allbritten, Light Paths, 211 Cherry St, Roseville, CA 95678. E-mail: goldenfire@mail.com.

SUPER BOWL XXXVIII. Feb 1. Reliant Stadium, Houston, TX. The battle between the NFC and AFC champions. For info: PR Dept, The Natl Football League, 280 Park Ave, New York, NY 10017. Phone: (212) 450-2000. Web: www.superbowl.com.

SWITZERLAND: HOMSTROM. Feb 1. Scuol. Burning of straw men on poles as a symbol of winter's imminent departure. Annually, the first Sunday in February.

WELLS FARGO WINTER GAMES OF IDAHO. Feb 1–29. Idaho Falls, Sun Valley, Boise, McCall, Salmon and Kellogg, ID. Idaho's official winter sports competition—four weekends of competition in ice hockey, figure skating, alpine skiing, telemark skiing, snowboarding and cross-country skiing with 3,000 participants. For info: Winter Games of Idaho, PO Box 9046, Boise, ID 83707. Phone: (800) 442-3794. Fax: (208) 343-6725. Web: www.idahowintergames.com.

WILLIE COVAN LOVED TO DANCE WEEK. Feb 1–7. To honor Willie Covan and his contribution to the unique American art form of tap dancing. Born in 1897 in Atlanta, GA, Covan danced during an era when black dancers weren't allowed in shows with white performers. However, prejudice did not hold him back; he spent 60 years in show business and became resident choreographer at MGM studios. There, he created innovative steps and styles for legendary screen stars Shirley Temple and Mickey Rooney. Celebrate his achievements with a dance marathon at your school or library! For info: Sherry Shahan, 2603 Richard Ave, Cayucos, CA 93430. Phone: (805) 995-1514. E-mail: kidbooks@thegrid.net.

WISE HEALTH CARE CONSUMER MONTH. Feb 1–29. Self-care is a proven way to reduce health care costs. For this reason, companies, hospitals and HMOs are offering more self-care programs. Wise Health Consumer Marketing packet available. For info: American Institute for Preventive Medicine, 30445 Northwestern Hwy, Ste 350, Farmington Hills, MI 48334. Phone: (248) 539-1800, ext 247. Fax: (248) 539-1808. E-mail: aipm@healthy.net. Web: www.HealthyLife.com.

WOMEN'S HEART HEALTH DAY. Feb 1. As American Heart Month begins, here is a day to promote awareness that heart disease is the number one killer of American women. For info: Charlotte Libov, Founder, Women's Health Hot Line, 28B Heritage Circle, Southbury, CT 06488. Phone: (203) 264-9704. Fax: (203) 264-9704. E-mail: char@libov.com. Web: www.libov.com.

WOMEN'S HEART WEEK. Feb 1–7. Raises awareness about heart disease—women's number one killer—and introduces fun activities to promote healthier living. See our own successful

☆ Chase's 2004 Calendar of Events ☆   Feb 1–2

piloted program with Focus Days at www.womensheartweek.org, a turnkey program for health centers to reciprocate! For assistance with your program, see our website's products page. For info: Women's Heart Foundation, PO Box 7827, West Trenton, NJ 08628. Phone: (609) 771-9600. Fax: (609) 771-9427. E-mail: admin@womensheartfoundation.org. Web: www.womensheartfoundation.org or www.womensheartweek.org.

"YOU ARE THERE" TV PREMIERE: ANNIVERSARY. Feb 1, 1953. The program began as an inventive radio show in 1947. News correspondents would comb the annals of history and "interview" the movers and shakers of times past. Walter Cronkite hosted the series on CBS for four seasons. The show's concept was revived for a season in 1971 with Cronkite gearing the program toward children.

YOUTH LEADERSHIP MONTH. Feb 1–29. This month is dedicated to celebrating young people who take on leadership roles in their lives. It is also dedicated to encouraging those who have not yet done so to consider doing so because they can. Programs that focus on youth leadership opportunities and effective leadership skill building are appropriate for this month. For info: Sylvia Henderson, Springboard Training, 18005 Lafayette Dr, Ste B, Olney, MD 20832. Phone: (301) 646-1668. Fax: (301) 856-8000. E-mail: admin@springboardtraining.com. Web: www.springboardtraining.com.

BIRTHDAYS TODAY

Michelle Akers, 38, soccer player, born Santa Clara, CA, Feb 1, 1966.
Michael B. Enzi, 60, US Senator (R, Wyoming), born Bremerton, WA, Feb 1, 1944.
Don Everly, 67, singer, musician ("Bye Bye Love"), with brother Phil (The Everly Brothers), born Brownie, KY, Feb 1, 1937.
Sherilyn Fenn, 39, actress ("Twin Peaks," *Wild at Heart*), born Detroit, MI, Feb 1, 1965.
Sherman Hemsley, 66, actor ("The Jeffersons," "Amen"), born Philadelphia, PA, Feb 1, 1938.
Rick James, 52, singer (King of Funk in the '80s, *Street Songs*), born James Johnson, Buffalo, NY, Feb 1, 1952.
Bob Jamieson, 61, broadcast journalist, born Streator, IL, Feb 1, 1943.
Terry Jones, 62, actor, director ("Monty Python's Flying Circus"), born Colwyn Bay, Wales, Feb 1, 1942.
Garrett Morris, 67, comedian ("Saturday Night Live"), born New Orleans, LA, Feb 1, 1937.
Bill Mumy, 50, actor (*Palm Springs Weekend*, *Twilight Zone—The Movie*, "The Rockford Files"), born El Centro, CA, Feb 1, 1954.
Lisa Marie Presley, 36, singer, daughter of Priscilla and Elvis, born Memphis, TN, Feb 1, 1968.
Pauly Shore, 34, actor ("Pauly," *What He's Got*), born Los Angeles, CA, Feb 1, 1970.
Stuart Whitman, 75, actor ("Cimarron Strip," *The Seekers*), born San Francisco, CA, Feb 1, 1929.

FEBRUARY 2 — MONDAY
Day 33 — 333 Remaining

AUDEN, W.H.: BIRTH ANNIVERSARY. Feb 2, 1907. Pulitzer Prize–winning Anglo-American poet was born Wystan Hugh Auden at York, England. "Some books," he wrote in *The Dyer's Hand* (1962), "are undeservedly forgotten; none are undeservedly remembered." Died at Vienna, Austria, Sept 28, 1973.

BAN ON AFRICAN NATIONAL CONGRESS LIFTED: ANNIVERSARY. Feb 2, 1990. The 30-year ban on the African National Congress was lifted by South African President F.W. de Klerk. De Klerk also vowed to free Nelson Mandela and lift restrictions on 33 other opposition groups.

BASEBALL HALL OF FAME'S CHARTER MEMBERS: ANNIVERSARY. Feb 2, 1936. The five charter members of the brand-new Baseball Hall of Fame at Cooperstown, NY, were announced. Of 226 ballots cast, Ty Cobb was named on 222, Babe Ruth on 215, Honus Wagner on 215, Christy Mathewson on 205 and Walter Johnson on 189. A total of 170 votes were necessary to be elected to the Hall of Fame.

BENET, WILLIAM ROSE: BIRTH ANNIVERSARY. Feb 2, 1886. American poet and critic. Born at Fort Hamilton, NY; died at New York, NY, May 4, 1950.

BONZA BOTTLER DAY™. Feb 2. To celebrate when the number of the day is the same as the number of the month. Bonza Bottler Day™ is an excuse to have a party at least once a month. For further information, see Jan 1. For info: Gail M. Berger, 14 Fernwood Dr, Taylors, SC 29687. Phone: (864) 609-9874. E-mail: gberger5@aol.com.

CANDLEMAS DAY or PRESENTATION OF THE LORD. Feb 2. Observed in the Roman Catholic Church. Commemorates presentation of Jesus in the Temple and the purification of Mary 40 days after his birth. Candles have been blessed since the 11th century. This marks the end of the Christmas liturgical season. Formerly called the Feast of Purification of the Blessed Virgin Mary. Old Scottish couplet proclaims: "If Candlemas is fair and clear/There'll be two winters in the year."

GERMAN SURRENDER AT STALINGRAD: ANNIVERSARY. Feb 2, 1943. Two pockets of starving German soldiers remained in Stalingrad on this date. They had received few supplies since Soviet soldiers had encircled the city the previous November. Friedrich von Paulus, whom Hitler had promoted to field marshal only the day before, was forced to seek surrender terms, thereby becoming the first German marshal to surrender. Hitler was furious with von Paulus, believing he should have preferred suicide to surrender. Approximately 160,000 Germans died in the Stalingrad Battle; 34,000 were evacuated by air. Of the 90,000 captured and sent to Siberia on foot, tens of thousands died on the way. This Allied victory is generally considered the psychological turning point of the war.

GETZ, STAN: BIRTH ANNIVERSARY. Feb 2, 1927. American jazz saxophonist Stan Getz was born at Philadelphia, PA. He introduced the cool-jazz style, which became a major movement in the 1950s, and the bossa nova (new wave) style of the 1960s. Getz received 11 Grammy Awards and was the first jazz musician to win the Grammy Award for Record of the Year (1965) for "The Girl from Ipanema." Died at Malibu, CA, June 6, 1991.

GROUNDHOG DAY. Feb 2. Old belief that if the sun shines on Candlemas Day, or if the groundhog sees his shadow when he emerges on this day, six weeks of winter will ensue.

GROUNDHOG DAY IN PUNXSUTAWNEY, PENNSYLVANIA. Feb 2. Widely observed traditional annual Candlemas Day event at which "Punxsutawney Phil, king of the weather prophets," is the object of a search. Tradition is said to have been established by early German settlers. The official trek (which began in 1887) is followed by a weather prediction for the next six weeks. [Phil made his dramatic film debut with Bill Murray in *Groundhog Day*.]

Feb 2

☆ Chase's 2004 Calendar of Events ☆

GROUNDHOG DAY IN SUN PRAIRIE, WISCONSIN. Feb 2. Sun Prairie, WI. To predict the weather for the balance of winter. Prognostication at 7:15 AM, EST, to see if Jimmy the Groundhog has seen his shadow. Persons born on this date are eligible for "official" groundhog birth certificate and/or groundhog club membership (for a small fee). Est attendance: 700. For info: Chamber of Commerce, 109 E Main St, Sun Prairie, WI 53590. Phone: (608) 837-4547. Fax: (608) 837-8765. Web: www.sunprairiechamber.com.

GROUNDHOG JOB SHADOW DAY. Feb 2. Students spend part of the day in the workplace "shadowing" an employee as he or she goes through a normal day on the job. Job Shadow Day demonstrates the connection between academics and careers and introduces students to the requirements of professions and industries. Local contacts can be found on the website. Planning kit available. For info: Groundhog Job Shadow Day. Phone: (800) 373-3174. Web: www.jobshadow.org.

HALAS, GEORGE: BIRTH ANNIVERSARY. Feb 2, 1895. George ("Papa Bear") Halas, Pro Football Hall of Fame coach and owner, born at Chicago, IL. After playing football at the University of Illinois and baseball with the New York Yankees, Halas helped to found the National Football League and the Chicago Bears in 1920. As coach of the Bears for 40 years, he compiled a record of 324 wins, 151 losses and 31 ties. Charter member of the Hall of Fame, 1963. Died at Chicago, IL, Oct 31, 1983.

IMBOLC. Feb 2. (Also called Imbolg, Candlemas, Lupercalia, Feast of Pan, Feast of Torches, Feast of Waxing Light, Brigit's Day and Oimelc.) One of the "Greater Sabbats" during the Wiccan year, Imbolc marks the recovery of the Goddess (after giving birth to the Sun, or the God, at Yule) and celebrates the anticipation of spring. Annually, Feb 2.

JOYCE, JAMES: BIRTH ANNIVERSARY. Feb 2, 1882. Irish novelist and poet, author of *Dubliners*, *A Portrait of the Artist as a Young Man*, *Ulysses* and *Finnegans Wake*, was born at Dublin, Ireland. "A man of genius," he wrote in *Ulysses*, "makes no mistakes. His errors are volitional and are portals of discovery." Of *Finnegans Wake* Joyce is reported to have replied to an academic whose letter had asked for clues to its meaning, "If I can throw any obscurity on the subject, let me know." Joyce died at the age of 58 of peritonitis at Zurich, Switzerland, Jan 13, 1941, and was buried there.

LINCOLN, ABRAHAM: OREGON BIRTHDAY OBSERVANCE. Feb 2. Observed annually in Oregon on the first Monday in February. See also: "Lincoln, Abraham: Birth Anniversary" (Feb 12).

LUXEMBOURG: CANDLEMAS. Feb 2. Traditional observance of Candlemas. At night children sing a customary song wishing health and prosperity to their neighbors and receive sweets in return. They carry special candles called *Lichtebengel* symbolizing the coming of spring.

MEXICO: DIA DE LA CANDELARIA. Feb 2. All Mexico celebrates. Dances, processions, bullfights.

NATIONAL SCHOOL COUNSELING WEEK. Feb 2–6. Promotes school counseling in the school and community. For info: American School Counselor Assn, 801 N Fairfax St, Ste 310, Alexandria, VA 22314. Phone: (800) 306-4722. Fax: (703) 683-1619. E-mail: asca@schoolcounselor.org. Web: www.schoolcounselor.org.

THE RECORD OF A SNEEZE: ANNIVERSARY. Feb 2, 1893. One day after Thomas Edison's "Black Maria" studio was completed at West Orange, NJ, a studio cameraman took the first "close-up" in film history. *The Record of a Sneeze*, starring Edison's assistant Fred P. Ott, was also the first motion picture to receive a copyright (1894). See also: "Black Maria Studio: Anniversary" (Feb 1).

SLED DOGS SAVE NOME: ANNIVERSARY. Feb 2, 1925. When a diphtheria outbreak was diagnosed in Nome, AK (population 1,500), on Jan 21, the nearest large amount of antitoxin serum was in Anchorage. Bitter winter temperatures made air delivery impossible, so a heroic dog sled relay was set up. 300,000 units of serum were delivered by train to Nenana, AK, and on Jan 27—in temperatures of 40–50 degrees below zero—20 mushers drove scores of dogs on a 674-mile journey to Nome in 127 hours. Togo was the lead dog for the first 350 miles, and Balto was the lead dog on the final 53 miles. The frozen serum arrived at 5:30 AM, and once thawed and administered, there were no more diphtheria deaths. Balto became a national hero, and a statue was erected in his honor in New York City's Central Park.

TREATY OF GUADALUPE HIDALGO: ANNIVERSARY. Feb 2, 1848. The war between Mexico and the US formally ended with the signing of the Treaty of Guadalupe Hidalgo, signed in the village for which it was named. The treaty provided for Mexico's cession to the US of the territory that became the states of California, Nevada, Utah, most of Arizona, and parts of New Mexico, Colorado and Wyoming, in exchange for $15 million from the US. In addition, Mexico relinquished all rights to Texas north of the Rio Grande. The Senate ratified the treaty Mar 10, 1848.

WALTON, GEORGE: 200th DEATH ANNIVERSARY. Feb 2, 1804. Signer of the Declaration of Independence. Born at Prince Edward County, VA, 1749 (exact date unknown). Died at Augusta, GA.

"WHAT'S MY LINE?" TV PREMIERE: ANNIVERSARY. Feb 2, 1950. This popular game show premiered on CBS and ran for 17 years in prime time. A panel of four celebrities figured out the professions of the contestants and the identities of the mystery guests by asking yes-or-no questions. The first panel consisted of poet Louis Untermeyer, columnist Dorothy Kilgallen, New Jersey Governor Harold Hoffman and psychiatrist Dr. Richard Hoffman. Yankee Phil Rizzuto was the first mystery guest. John Daly hosted.

BIRTHDAYS TODAY

Christie Brinkley, 51, model, born Monroe, MI, Feb 2, 1953.
John Cornyn, 52, US Senator (R, Texas), born Houston, TX, Feb 2, 1952.
Sean Michael Elliott, 36, former basketball player, born Tucson, AZ, Feb 2, 1968.
Farrah Fawcett, 57, actress, model ("Charlie's Angels," *The Burning Bed*), born Corpus Christi, TX, Feb 2, 1947.
Bo Hopkins, 62, actor ("The Rockford Files," "Dynasty," *American Graffiti*), born Greenwood, SC, Feb 2, 1942.
Robert Mandan, 72, actor ("Soap," "Days of Our Lives"), born Clever, MO, Feb 2, 1932.
Graham Nash, 62, musician, singer, born Blackpool, England, Feb 2, 1942.
Liz Smith, 81, journalist, author, born Fort Worth, TX, Feb 2, 1923.
Tom Smothers, 67, comedian, folksinger (brother of Dick Smothers, "The Smothers Brothers Comedy Hour"), born New York, NY, Feb 2, 1937.
Elaine Stritch, 79, actress (*Company*, sang "The Ladies Who Lunch"), born Birmingham, MI, Feb 2, 1925.
Michael T. Weiss, 42, actor ("The Pretender"), born Chicago, IL, Feb 2, 1962.

	February 2004
S	1 8 15 22 29
M	2 9 16 23
T	3 10 17 24
W	4 11 18 25
T	5 12 19 26
F	6 13 20 27
S	7 14 21 28

☆ Chase's 2004 Calendar of Events ☆   Feb 3

FEBRUARY 3 — TUESDAY
Day 34 — 332 Remaining

BLACKWELL, ELIZABETH: BIRTH ANNIVERSARY. Feb 3, 1821. First woman physician. Born near Bristol, England, she and several other members of her family were active abolitionists, women's suffrage advocates and pioneers in women's medicine. Her family moved to New York State in 1832, and she received a medical doctor's degree at Geneva, NY, in 1849. She established a hospital in New York City with an all-woman staff, where she recruited and trained nurses for service in the Civil War. Returning to England in 1869, she continued to teach and practice medicine until her death at Hastings, England, May 31, 1910.

CIVIL WAR PEACE TALKS: ANNIVERSARY. Feb 3, 1865. Abraham Lincoln and his Secretary of State, William Seward, met to discuss peace with Confederate Vice President Alexander Stephens and others at Hampton Roads, VA. The meeting, which took place on board the ship *River Queen*, lasted four hours and produced no positive results. The Confederates sought an armistice first and discussion of reunion later, while Lincoln was insistent that recognition of Federal authority must be the first step toward peace.

"THE DAY THE MUSIC DIED": 45th ANNIVERSARY. Feb 3, 1959. The anniversary of the death of rock-and-roll legend Charles Hardin "Buddy" Holly. "The Day the Music Died," so-called in singer Don McLean's song "American Pie," is the date on which Holly was killed in a plane crash in a cornfield near Mason City, IA, along with J.P. Richardson (otherwise known as "The Big Bopper") and Richie Valens. Holly was born Sept 7, 1936, at Lubbock, TX.

DUMP YOUR "SIGNIFICANT JERK" DAY. Feb 3. It's time to take out the garbage and get rid of that "Jerk" boyfriend or girlfriend. This year will be the 11th annual call to arms. Annually, the Tuesday of the week before Valentine's Day. For info: Marcus P. Meleton Jr, Sharkbait Press, PO Box 11300, Costa Mesa, CA 92627. Phone: (949) 413-3052. E-mail: mm@sharkbaitpress.com. Web: www.sharkbaitpress.com.

FIFTEENTH AMENDMENT TO US CONSTITUTION RATIFIED: ANNIVERSARY. Feb 3, 1870. The 15th Amendment granted that the right of citizens to vote shall not be denied on account of race, color or previous condition of servitude.

FOUR CHAPLAINS MEMORIAL DAY. Feb 3, 1943. Commemorates four chaplains (George Fox, Alexander Goode, Clark Poling, John Washington) who sacrificed their life belts and lives when the SS *Dorchester* was torpedoed off Greenland during WWII.

GREELEY, HORACE: BIRTH ANNIVERSARY. Feb 3, 1811. Newspaper editor, born at Amherst, NH. Founder of the *New York Tribune* and one of the organizers of the Republican Party, Greeley was an outspoken opponent of slavery. Best remembered for his saying, "Go West, young man." Died Nov 29, 1872, at New York City.

INCOME TAX BIRTHDAY: SIXTEENTH AMENDMENT TO US CONSTITUTION: RATIFICATION: ANNIVERSARY. Feb 3, 1913. The 16th Amendment was ratified, granting Congress the authority to levy taxes on income. (Church bells did not ring throughout the land and no dancing in the streets was reported.)

JAPAN: BEAN-THROWING FESTIVAL (SETSUBUN). Feb 3. Setsubun marks the last day of winter according to the lunar calendar. Throngs at temple grounds throw beans to drive away imaginary devils.

JOHNSTON, JOSEPH: BIRTH ANNIVERSARY. Feb 3, 1807. Born near Farmville, VA, and died Mar 21, 1891, at Washington, DC. Confederate general in the Civil War whose troops were never directly defeated. Longstanding differences with Jefferson Davis, president of the Confederacy, prevented him, however, from reaching his full potential.

MICHENER, JAMES: BIRTH ANNIVERSARY. Feb 3, 1907. American author, born at New York, NY. His *Tales of the South Pacific* was the basis for the popular musical *South Pacific*. A prolific author, his other works include *Sayonara, Iberia, Hawaii, Centennial* and *Texas*. Died at Austin, TX, Oct 17, 1997.

MOZAMBIQUE: HEROES' DAY. Feb 3. National holiday. Honors all heroic citizens, especially Eduardo Mondlane, leader of the fight for independence, assassinated on Feb 3, 1969.

NAUVOO LEGION CHARTERED: ANNIVERSARY. Feb 3, 1841. Created by Illinois Charter and composed of 5,000 Mormon men under the command of Lieutenant General Joseph Smith, the Nauvoo Legion was considered the "largest trained soldiery in the US" except for the US Army.

NORTH AMERICA'S COLDEST RECORDED TEMPERATURE: ANNIVERSARY. Feb 3, 1947. At Snag, in Canada's Yukon Territory, a temperature of 81 degrees below zero (Fahrenheit) was recorded on this date, a record low for all of North America.

ROCKWELL, NORMAN: BIRTH ANNIVERSARY. Feb 3, 1894. American artist and illustrator especially noted for his realistic and homey magazine cover art for the *Saturday Evening Post*. Born at New York, NY, he died at Stockbridge, MA, Nov 8, 1978.

SPACE MILESTONE: *CHALLENGER STS-10* (US): 20th ANNIVERSARY. Feb 3, 1984. Shuttle *Challenger* launched from Kennedy Space Center, FL, with a crew of five (Vance Brand, Robert Gibson, Ronald McNair, Bruce McCandless and Robert Stewart). On Feb 7 two astronauts became the first to fly freely in space (propelled by their backpack jets), untethered to any craft. Landed at Cape Canaveral, FL, Feb 11.

STEIN, GERTRUDE: BIRTH ANNIVERSARY. Feb 3, 1874. Avant-garde expatriate American writer, perhaps best remembered for her poetic declaration (in 1913): "Rose is a rose is a rose." Born at Allegheny, PA; died at Paris, France, July 27, 1946.

VIETNAM: NATIONAL HOLIDAY. Feb 3. National holiday. Anniversary of the founding of the Vietnamese Communist Party, Feb 3, 1930.

BIRTHDAYS TODAY

Shelley Berman, 78, comedian ("Mary Hartman, Mary Hartman"), born Chicago, IL, Feb 3, 1926.

Joey Bishop, 86, actor ("The Joey Bishop Show," "Liar's Club"), born Joseph Abraham Gottlieb, New York, NY, Feb 3, 1918.

Thomas Calabro, 45, actor ("Melrose Place"), born Brooklyn, NY, Feb 3, 1959.

Blythe Danner, 61, actress (*Butterflies Are Free, Brighton Beach Memoirs*), born Philadelphia, PA, Feb 3, 1943.

Vlade Divac, 36, basketball player, born Prijepolje, Yugoslavia, Feb 3, 1968.

Morgan Fairchild, 54, actress ("Dallas," "Falcon Crest," "Flamingo Road"), born Patsy McClenny, Dallas, TX, Feb 3, 1950.

Keith Gordon, 43, actor, director (*All That Jazz, Dressed to Kill, A Midnight Clear*), born New York, NY, Feb 3, 1961.
Robert Allen (Bob) Griese, 59, sportscaster, Hall of Fame football player, born Evansville, IN, Feb 3, 1945.
Nathan Lane, 48, actor (Tonys for *A Funny Thing Happened on the Way to the Forum, The Producers*; *The Birdcage*), born Jersey City, NJ, Feb 3, 1956.
Paul S. Sarbanes, 71, US Senator (D, Maryland), born Salisbury, MD, Feb 3, 1933.
Francis Asbury (Fran) Tarkenton, 64, Hall of Fame football player, born Richmond, VA, Feb 3, 1940.
Maura Tierney, 39, actress ("NewsRadio," "ER"), born Boston, MA, Feb 3, 1965.

FEBRUARY 4 — WEDNESDAY
Day 35 — 331 Remaining

AFRICAN AMERICAN COACHES DAY. Feb 4. To provide a day each year to educate the African-American community about the value of working with a personal or business coach and to provide an opportunity for coaches and their clients to acknowledge the results and progress made through the coaching process. For info: Monique Belton, Ph.D., 35 Dix Hills Rd, Huntington, NY 11743. Phone: (631) 549-7314. E-mail: drmonique @AfricanAmericanCoaches.com. Web: www.AfricanAmerican Coaches.com.

ANGOLA: ARMED STRUGGLE DAY. Feb 4. National holiday. Commemorates the beginning of the struggle for independence from Portugal in 1961.

APACHE WARS BEGAN: ANNIVERSARY. Feb 4, 1861. The period of conflict known as the Apache Wars began at Apache Pass, AZ, when Army Lieutenant George Bascom arrested Apache Chief Cochise for raiding a ranch. Cochise escaped and declared war. The wars lasted 25 years under the leadership of Cochise and, later, Geronimo.

CANADA: VANCOUVER INTERNATIONAL BOAT SHOW. Feb 4–8. British Columbia Place Stadium, Vancouver, BC. Sail- and powerboats, sailboards, inflatables, canoes, personal watercraft, marine electronics and accessories, marine services, charters, sailing schools, water skis, sporting goods, travel and resort destinations, fishing equipment and Marine Facts Stage. Est attendance: 38,000. For info: Canadian National Sportsmen's Shows, Ste 501, 4190 Lougheed Hwy, Burnaby, BC, Canada V5C 6A8. Phone: (604) 294-1313. Fax: (604) 294-4740. E-mail: mcgeachie@sportshows.ca. Web: www.sportshows.ca.

HALFWAY POINT OF WINTER. Feb 4. On this date, 44.5 days of winter will have elapsed and the equivalent remain before Mar 20, which is the spring equinox and the beginning of spring.

KOSCIUSKO, THADDEUS: BIRTH ANNIVERSARY. Feb 4, 1746. Polish patriot and American Revolutionary War figure. Born at Lithuania, he died at Solothurn, Switzerland, Oct 15, 1817.

LINDBERGH, CHARLES AUGUSTUS: BIRTH ANNIVERSARY. Feb 4, 1902. American aviator Charles "Lucky Lindy" Lindbergh was the first to fly solo and nonstop over the Atlantic Ocean, New York to Paris, May 20–21, 1927. Born at Detroit, MI; died at Kipahula, Maui, HI, Aug 27, 1974. See also: "Lindbergh Flight: Anniversary" (May 20).

NATIONAL GIRLS AND WOMEN IN SPORTS DAY. Feb 4. Celebrates and honors all girls and women participating in sports. Recognizes the passage of Title IX in 1972, the law that guarantees gender equity in federally funded school programs, including athletics. Sponsored by Girls Inc, the Girl Scouts, the National Association for Girls and Women in Sports, the Women's Sports Foundation and the YWCA. For info: Women's Sports Foundation, Eisenhower Park, East Meadow, NY 11554. Phone: (516) 542-4700 or (800) 227-3988. Web: www.NGWSDcentral .com.

NEW ORLEANS BOAT SHOW. Feb 4–8. Louisiana Superdome, New Orleans, LA. Annual show of boat and marine products, fishing equipment and resort info. Informative boating and fishing seminars. For info: Barbara Sclafani, Natl Marine Manufacturers Assn, 3925 N I-10 Service Rd, Ste 209, Metairie, LA 70002. Phone: (504) 780-1818. Fax: (504) 780-1813. E-mail: bsclafani@nmma.org. Web: www.discoverboating.com/neworleans.

SRI LANKA: INDEPENDENCE DAY: ANNIVERSARY. Feb 4. Democratic Socialist Republic of Sri Lanka observes National Day. Public holiday. On Feb 4, 1948, Ceylon (as it was then known) obtained independence from Great Britain. The country's name was changed to Sri Lanka in 1972.

TORTURE ABOLITION DAY: ANNIVERSARY. Feb 4, 1985. Twenty countries signed a UN document titled "Convention Against Torture and Other Cruel, Inhuman or Degrading Treatment or Punishment." Adopted Dec 10, 1984, by the UN General Assembly, it defined torture as any act "by which severe pain or suffering, whether physical or mental, is intentionally inflicted" to obtain information or a confession. While the US did sign the document, signing is only a preliminary stage that must be followed by ratification—which the US has never done.

US NATIONAL SNOW SCULPTING COMPETITION. Feb 4–8. Lake Geneva, WI. 9th annual. Snow sculpting competition where each 3-person team creates a work of art out of a 7-ft × 9-ft block of snow. Several awards given. For info: Lake Geneva Area Conv & Visitors Bureau, 201 Wrigley Dr, Lake Geneva, WI 53147-2004. Phone: (800) 345-1020 or (262) 248-4416. Web: www.usnationals.org.

USO: BIRTHDAY. Feb 4, 1941. To honor the civilian agency founded in 1941 that provides support worldwide for US service people and their families. The United Service Organizations (USO) centers have served as a home away from home for hundreds of thousands of Americans.

ZEHNDER'S SNOWFEST (WITH ICE CARVING AND STATE OF MICHIGAN SNOW SCULPTING COMPETITIONS). Feb 4–9. Frankenmuth, MI. Annual festival also includes ice demonstrations, snow exhibitions by international teams from 6–10 countries and many children's activities such as a petting zoo, rides and music. Est attendance: 200,000. For info: Linda Kelly, Zehnder's of Frankenmuth, 730 S Main St, Frankenmuth, MI 48734. Phone: (800) 863-7999. Fax: (517) 652-3544. Web: www.zehnders.com.

BIRTHDAYS TODAY

Gabrielle Anwar, 33, actress (*Scent of a Woman*), born Laleham, England, Feb 4, 1971.
Clint Black, 42, country singer, songwriter, born Katy, LA, Feb 4, 1962.
David Brenner, 59, comedian, born Philadelphia, PA, Feb 4, 1945.
Gary Conway, 68, actor ("Burke's Law," *I Was a Teenage Frankenstein*), born Boston, MA, Feb 4, 1936.
Alice Cooper, 56, singer, songwriter, born Vincent Damon Furnier, Detroit, MI, Feb 4, 1948.
Oscar de la Hoya, 31, boxer, born Los Angeles, CA, Feb 4, 1973.
Lisa Eichhorn, 52, actress (*The Vanishing, King of the Hill*), born Reading, PA, Feb 4, 1952.
Pamela Franklin, 54, actress (*The Prime of Miss Jean Brodie, The Legend of Hell House*), born Tokyo, Japan, Feb 4, 1950.
Betty Friedan, 83, author (*The Feminine Mystique*), founder, the National Organization for Women (NOW), born Peoria, IL, Feb 4, 1921.
Michael Goorjian, 33, actor ("Party of Five"), born San Francisco, CA, Feb 4, 1971.

☆ Chase's 2004 Calendar of Events ☆ Feb 4-5

Rosa Lee Parks, 91, civil rights leader who refused to give up her seat on the bus, born Tuskegee, AL, Feb 4, 1913.
J. Danforth (Dan) Quayle, 57, 44th vice president of US, born Indianapolis, IN, Feb 4, 1947.
John Schuck, 64, actor ("McMillan and Wife," *McCabe and Mrs Miller, Dick Tracy*), born Boston, MA, Feb 4, 1940.
Lawrence Taylor, 45, Hall of Fame football player, born Williamsburg, VA, Feb 4, 1959.

FEBRUARY 5 — THURSDAY
Day 36 — 330 Remaining

CARRADINE, JOHN: BIRTH ANNIVERSARY. Feb 5, 1906. American film actor John Carradine was born Richmond Reed Carradine at Greenwich Village, NY. He appeared in more than 200 films. Frequently observed wandering the streets in a velvet suit and satin cape while reciting Shakespeare, he became known as "the Bard of the Boulevard." Died Nov 27, 1988, at Milan, Italy.

CHINA: LANTERN FESTIVAL. Feb 5. Traditional Chinese festival falls on the 15th day of the first month of the Chinese lunar calendar year. Lantern processions mark the end of the Chinese New Year holiday season. Also celebrated in Taiwan and Korea. Date in other countries will differ from China's by up to one day. See also: "Chinese New Year" (Jan 22).

FAMILY-LEAVE BILL: ANNIVERSARY. Feb 5, 1993. President William Clinton signed legislation requiring companies with 50 or more employees (and all government agencies) to allow employees to take up to 12 weeks unpaid leave in a 12-month period to deal with the birth or adoption of a child or to care for a relative with a serious health problem. The bill became effective Aug 5, 1993.

FLORIDA STATE FAIR. Feb 5-16. Florida State Fairgrounds, Tampa, FL. The fair features the best arts, crafts, competitive exhibits, equestrian shows, livestock, entertainment and food found in Florida. Also not to be missed is "Cracker Country," where cultural and architectural history has been preserved. 2004 is the 100th anniversary of the fair. Est attendance: 545,000. For info: Sherry Powell, Mktg & Advertising Mgr, Florida State Fair, PO Box 11766, Tampa, FL 33680. Phone: (813) 621-7821 or (800) 345-FAIR. Web: www.floridastatefair.com.

GERMANY: BERLIN INTERNATIONAL FILM FESTIVAL. Feb 5-15. Potsdamer Platz, Berlin, Germany. The 54th festival. One of the premier international film festivals since its inaugural opening in 1951. Includes film competition, Children's Film Festival and other special programs. The awarding of Golden and Silver Bears by the International Jury marks the conclusion of the festival. Est attendance: 390,000. For info: Internationale Filmfestspiele Berlin, Potsdamer Strasse 5, D-10785 Berlin, Germany. Phone: (011) (49) (30) 25920. E-mail: info@berlinale.de. Web: www.berlinale.de.

HOBBY INDUSTRY ASSOCIATION ANNUAL CONVENTION AND TRADE SHOW. Feb 5-8 (classes begin Feb 4). Anaheim Convention Center, Anaheim, CA. 63rd annual showcase for wholesale and retail buyers to view and order craft and hobby products. Est attendance: 20,000. For info: Hobby Industry Association, 319 E 54th St, Elmwood Park, NJ 07407. Phone: (201) 794-1133. Fax: (201) 797-0657. E-mail: dcennimo @hobby.org. Web: www.hobby.org.

LONGEST WAR IN HISTORY: ENDING ANNIVERSARY. Feb 5, 1985. The Third Punic War, between Rome and Carthage, started in the year 149 BC. It culminated in the year 146 BC, when Roman soldiers led by Scipio razed Carthage to the ground. The desolated site was cursed and rebuilding forbidden. On this date, 2,131 years after the war began, Ugo Vetere, mayor of Rome, and Chedli Klibi, mayor of Carthage, met at Tunis to sign a treaty of friendship officially ending the Third Punic War.

MEXICO: CONSTITUTION DAY. Feb 5. National holiday. Present constitution, embracing major social reforms, adopted in 1917.

MILWAUKEE/NARI HOME IMPROVEMENT SHOW. Feb 5-8. Wisconsin State Fair Park, West Allis, WI. Cosponsored by Milwaukee/NARI Home Improvement Council and the *Milwaukee Journal Sentinel*, this show is of particular interest to homeowners planning a remodeling project for their home. More than 300 exhibitors in a no-pressure setting. Educational seminars by home improvement experts, a remodeler's showcase with the latest innovations plus guided tours and colorful garden areas. Annually, the second weekend in February. Est attendance: 30,000. For info: Mary Fox-Hagner, Exec Dir, Milwaukee/NARI Home Improvement Council, 11815 W Dearbourn Ave, PO Box 26788, Wauwatosa, WI 53226. Phone: (414) 771-4071. Fax: (414) 771-4077. E-mail: nari@execpc.com. Web: www.milwaukeenari.com.

MOVE HOLLYWOOD & BROADWAY TO LEBANON, PENNSYLVANIA DAY. Feb 5. There's lots of room, friendly folks and Amish farms. Lebanon is a safe haven for residents and tourists to serenely indulge in their world-famous bologna and the Wertz family homemade candies. [©2003 by WH.] For info: Thomas & Ruth Roy, Wellcat Holidays, 2418 Long Ln, Lebanon, PA 17046. Phone: (717) 279-0184. E-mail: info@wellcat.com. Web: www.wellcat.com.

OMAHA HOME & GARDEN EXPO. Feb 5-8. Omaha Convention Center, Omaha, NE. Held in conjunction with the Omaha Lawn, Flower & Patio Show. For info: Robert P. Mancuso, Pres, Mid-America Expositions, Inc, 7015 Spring St, Omaha, NE 68106-3518. Phone: (402) 346-8003 or (800) 475-SHOW. Fax: (402) 346-5412. E-mail: showoffice@aol.com. Web: www.showofficeonline.com.

OMAHA LAWN, FLOWER AND PATIO SHOW. Feb 5-8. Omaha Convention Center, Omaha, NE. For info: Robert P. Mancuso, Pres, Mid-America Expositions, Inc, 7015 Spring St, Omaha, NE 68106-3518. Phone: (402) 346-8003. Fax: (402) 346-5412. E-mail: showoffice@aol.com. Web: www.showofficeonline.com.

PEEL, ROBERT: BIRTH ANNIVERSARY. Feb 5, 1788. English statesman, established the Irish constabulary (known as the "Peelers"). Later, as England's Home Secretary, he reorganized the London police, thereafter known as "Bobbies." Born at Lancashire, England, he died July 2, 1850, at London from injuries received in a fall from his horse.

SMOKY MOUNTAINS STORYTELLING FESTIVAL. Feb 5-7. Pigeon Forge, TN. 13th annual. The region's finest yarn-spinners and folklore specialists. Est attendance: 2,500. For info: Office of Special Events, Pigeon Forge Dept of Tourism, 3107 Parkway, PO Box 1390, Pigeon Forge, TN 37868. Phone: (800) 251-9100 or (865) 429-7350. Fax: (865) 429-7392. E-mail: events @cityofpigeonforge.com. Web: www.mypigeonforge.com.

STEVENSON, ADLAI EWING: BIRTH ANNIVERSARY. Feb 5, 1900. American statesman, governor of Illinois, Democratic candidate for president in 1952 and 1956, US representative to the UN, 1961-65. Born at Los Angeles, CA. Died at London, England, July 14, 1965. Not to be confused with his grandfather, Vice President Adlai Ewing Stevenson. See also: "Stevenson, Adlai Ewing: Birth Anniversary" (Oct 23).

WEATHERMAN'S [WEATHERPERSON'S] DAY. Feb 5. Commemorates the birth of one of America's first weathermen, John Jeffries, a Boston physician who kept detailed records of weather conditions, 1774–1816. Born at Boston, Feb 5, 1744, and died there Sept 16, 1819. See also: "First Balloon Flight Across English Channel: Anniversary" (Jan 7).

WITHERSPOON, JOHN: BIRTH ANNIVERSARY. Feb 5, 1723. Clergyman, signer of the Declaration of Independence and reputed coiner of the word *Americanism* (in 1781). Born near Edinburgh, Scotland. Died at Princeton, NJ, Nov 15, 1794.

BIRTHDAYS TODAY

Henry Louis (Hank) Aaron, 70, Hall of Fame baseball player, baseball executive, all-time home run leader, born Mobile, AL, Feb 5, 1934.
Roberto Alomar, 36, baseball player, born Ponce, Puerto Rico, Feb 5, 1968.
Bobby Brown, 35, singer, dancer ("My Prerogative," "Every Little Step"), born Roxbury, MA, Feb 5, 1969.
Red Buttons, 85, actor ("The Red Buttons Show," "The Double Life of Henry Phyfe"), born Aaron Chwatt, the Bronx, NY, Feb 5, 1919.
Jennifer Granholm, 45, Governor of Michigan (D), born Vancouver, BC, Canada, Feb 5, 1955.
Father Andrew Greeley, 76, Roman Catholic priest and author (*Happy Are the Merciful, An Occasion of Sin*), born Oak Park, IL, Feb 5, 1928.
Christopher Guest, 56, writer, comedian (Emmy for writing *Lily Tomlin*; *Spinal Tap, Best in Show*), born New York, NY, Feb 5, 1948.
Barbara Hershey, 56, actress (*Hannah and Her Sisters*), born Barbara Hertzstein, Los Angeles, CA, Feb 5, 1948.
David Alan Ladd, 57, actor, producer (*A Dog of Flanders, The Day of the Locust*), born Los Angeles, CA, Feb 5, 1947.
Jennifer Jason Leigh (Morrow), 42, actress (*Miami Blues, Rush, Backdraft*), born Los Angeles, CA, Feb 5, 1962.
Laura Linney, 40, actress (*The Truman Show, You Can Count on Me*), born New York, NY, Feb 5, 1964.
Jane Bryant Quinn, 63, financial writer (*Everyone's Money Book*), born Niagara Falls, NY, Feb 5, 1941.
Charlotte Rampling, 58, actress (*Georgy Girl, Farewell My Lovely*), born Sturmer, England, Feb 5, 1946.
David Selby, 63, actor ("Falcon Crest," *Rich and Famous*), born Morgantown, WV, Feb 5, 1941.
Roger Thomas Staubach, 62, Hall of Fame football player, born Cincinnati, OH, Feb 5, 1942.
Darrell Waltrip, 57, auto racer, born Owensboro, KY, Feb 5, 1947.

February 2004

S	M	T	W	T	F	S
1	2	3	4	5	6	7
8	9	10	11	12	13	14
15	16	17	18	19	20	21
22	23	24	25	26	27	28
29						

FEBRUARY 6 — FRIDAY
Day 37 — 329 Remaining

ACCESSION OF QUEEN ELIZABETH II: ANNIVERSARY. Feb 6, 1952. Princess Elizabeth Alexandra Mary succeeded to the British throne (becoming Elizabeth II, Queen of the United Kingdom of Great Britain and Northern Ireland and Head of the Commonwealth) upon the death of her father, King George VI, Feb 6, 1952. Her coronation took place June 2, 1953, at Westminster Abbey at London.

BADGER STATE WINTER GAMES. Feb 6–8. Wausau, WI, and throughout Wisconsin. 16th annual sports festival for Wisconsin residents of all ages and abilities featuring 11 sports and opening ceremonies. More than 6,000 athletes in cross-country skiing, curling, downhill skiing, figure skating, ice hockey, ski jumping, freestyle snowboarding, speedskating and quadrathon. Major sponsors are American Family Insurance, Wisconsin Milk Marketing Board, Mobil, St. Joseph's Hospital. Est attendance: 10,000. For info: Badger State Games, PO Box 7788, Madison, WI 53707-7788. Phone: (608) 226-4780. Fax: (608) 226-9550. E-mail: info@SportsinWisconsin.com. Web: www.SportsinWisconsin.com.

BULLNANZA. Feb 6–7. Lazy E Arena, Guthrie, OK. Present and past champions, including the top 50 bull riders in the world, compete for the prestigious BULLNANZA Champion title. Annually, the first weekend in February. Est attendance: 14,000. For info: Lazy E Arena, 9600 Lazy E Dr, Guthrie, OK 73044. Phone: (800) 595-RIDE. Fax: (405) 282-3785. E-mail: arena@lazye.com. Web: www.lazye.com.

BURR, AARON: BIRTH ANNIVERSARY. Feb 6, 1756. 3rd vice president of the US (Mar 4, 1801–Mar 3, 1805). While vice president, Burr challenged political enemy Alexander Hamilton to a duel and mortally wounded him July 11, 1804, at Weehawken, NJ. Indicted for the challenge and for murder, he returned to Washington to complete his term of office (during which he presided over the impeachment trial of Supreme Court Justice Samuel Chase). In 1807 Burr was arrested, tried for treason (in an alleged scheme to invade Mexico and set up a new nation in the West) and acquitted. Born at Newark, NJ, he died at Staten Island, NY, Sept 14, 1836.

CANADA: WINTERLUDE. Feb 6–22. Ottawa, ON. Annual celebration of Canadian winter and traditions for the whole family. Skating on Rideau Canal, the world's longest skating rink; snow and ice sculptures; world-class figure skating; North America's largest snow playground and exciting Winter Triathlon. Est attendance: 700,000. For info: Natl Capital Commission, Capital Infocentre, 90 Wellington St, Ottawa, ON, Canada K1P 1C7. Phone: (613) 239-5000 or (800) 465-1867. Web: www.capcan.ca/winterlude.

DESERT FOOTHILLS MUSICFEST. Feb 6–Mar 14. Carefree/Cave Creek and North Scottsdale, AZ, in four venues. Arizona's premier winter classical music festival celebrates the music of the masters with 12 events over a 5-week period. Twelve concerts featuring the Festival Chamber Orchestra; prizewinning guest artists including the Quartetto Gelato, Timothy Dvikovic, Gian Riley and the Phoenix Symphony Orchestra. Est attendance: 5,000. For info: Desert Hills Musicfest, PO Box 5254, Carefree, AZ 85377. Phone: (480) 488-0806. Fax: (480) 488-1401. E-mail: info@azmusicfest.org. Web: www.azmusicfest.org.

ENGLAND: PETERSFIELD ANTIQUES FAIR. Feb 6–8 (also Sept 10–12). Festival Hall, Petersfield, Hampshire. Forty-three stands of good quality, but affordable, traditional antiques. Est attendance: 3,000. For info: Penman Fairs, PO Box 114, Haywards Heath, Sussex, England RH16 2YU. Phone: (44) (870) 350-2442. Fax: (44) (870) 350-2443. E-mail: info@penman-fairs.co.uk.

GREAT NORTHEAST HOME SHOW. Feb 6–8. Pepsi Arena and Empire State Plaza, Albany, NY. The annual kick-off to the home-building/remodeling season. Featuring more than 500 exhibits in two buildings and informative seminars. Annually, the first full weekend in February. Sponsor: The Times Union News-

☆ Chase's 2004 Calendar of Events ☆   Feb 6

paper. Est attendance: 30,000. For info: Cate Masterson, Ed Lewi Assoc, 6 Chelsea Pl, Clifton Park, NY 12065. Phone: (518) 383-6183. Fax: (518) 383-6755. Web: www.timesunion.com.

LONGHORN WORLD CHAMPIONSHIP RODEO. Feb 6–8. State Fair Coliseum, Columbus, OH. 30th annual. More than 350 cowboys and cowgirls compete in six professional contests ranging from bronc riding to big, bad BONUS bull riding. Free beginners horsemanship clinic 40 minutes before performances. Qualifying rodeo for Longhorn's Championship Finals Rodeo in Nashville, TN. Featuring colorful opening ceremonies. Est attendance: 18,000. For info: W. Bruce Lehrke, Pres, Longhorn World Championship Rodeo, Inc, PO Box 70159, Nashville, TN 37207. Phone: (615) 876-1016. Fax: (615) 876-4685. E-mail: info@longhornrodeo.com. Web: www.longhornrodeo.com.

MARLEY, BOB: BIRTH ANNIVERSARY. Feb 6, 1945. With his group, The Wailers, Bob Marley was one of the most popular and influential performers of reggae music, an "off-beat-accented Jamaican" music closely associated with the political/religious Rastafarian movement (admirers of the late Ethiopian emperor Haile Selassie, who was formerly called Ras Tafari). Marley was born at Rhoden Hall in northern Jamaica. Died of cancer at Miami, FL, May 11, 1981.

MASSACHUSETTS RATIFIES CONSTITUTION: ANNIVERSARY. Feb 6, 1788. By a vote of 187 to 168, Massachusetts became the sixth state to ratify the Constitution.

MERCEDES-BENZ FASHION WEEK FALL 04. Feb 6–13 (tentative). New York, NY. Fashion designers present their fall 2004 lines. For info: 7th on Sixth, 420 W 45th St, 6th Fl, New York, NY 10036. Phone: (212) 253-2692. E-mail: info@7thonsixth.com. Web: www.7thonsixth.com.

MIDWINTER'S DAY CELEBRATION. Feb 6. Ann Arbor, MI. To create euphoria by fiat in celebration that winter is half over. For info: Richard Ankli, The Fifth Wheel Tavern, 639 Fifth St, Ann Arbor, MI 48103.

MOON PHASE: FULL MOON. Feb 6. Moon enters Full Moon phase at 3:47 AM, EST.

NEW ZEALAND: WAITANGI DAY. Feb 6. National Day. Commemorates signing of the Treaty of Waitangi in 1840 (at Waitangi, Chatham Islands, New Zealand). The treaty, between the native Maori and the European peoples, provided for development of New Zealand under the British Crown.

PAY-A-COMPLIMENT DAY. Feb 6. Practice this simple act of premeditated kindness and pay a compliment to coworkers, family members or a stranger on the street or in the elevator in your office building. Go ahead, make someone feel special and see the difference a sincere compliment makes! (©1995) To alleviate the escalating costs of Eventological® Literature, a charge of $7 must be assessed for each request. Checks are to be made payable to: Adrienne Sioux Koopersmith, 1437 W Rosemont, #1W, Chicago, IL 60660-1319. Phone: (773) 743-5341. Fax: (773) 743-5395. E-mail: la_koop@yahoo.com.

REAGAN, RONALD WILSON: BIRTHDAY. Feb 6, 1911. 40th president of the US (1981–89). Former sportscaster, motion picture actor, governor of California (1967–74); he was the oldest and the first divorced person to become president. Born at Tampico, IL. Married actress Jane Wyman in 1940 (divorced in 1948); married actress Nancy Davis, Mar 4, 1952.

RUTH, "BABE": BIRTH ANNIVERSARY. Feb 6, 1895. One of baseball's greatest heroes, George Herman "Babe" Ruth was born at Baltimore, MD. The left-handed pitcher—"the Sultan of Swat"—hit 714 home runs in 22 major league seasons of play and played in 10 World Series. Died at New York, NY, Aug 16, 1948.

SARANAC LAKE WINTER CARNIVAL. Feb 6–15. Saranac Lake, NY. Come and join the family fun with fireworks and entertainment, food booths and much more. Annually, the first two full weekends in February. For info: Saranac Lake Winter Carnival, Saranac Lake Chamber of Commerce, 30 Main St, Saranac Lake, NY 12983. Phone: (518) 891-1990 or (800) 347-1992.

SITTER SCHOOL WEEK. Feb 6–14. Valentine's Day (Feb 14) is the biggest day of the year for babysitters. Sitter School Week encourages parents to certify their sitters and encourages sitters to take courses teaching consistent, safety-minded, competent child care. Annually, the week before Valentine's Day. For info: Karen Willson, 825 College Blvd, PBO 102-442, Oceanside, CA 92057. Phone: (760) 631-1498. Fax: (208) 475-7001. E-mail: administrator@babysittingclass.com. Web: www.babysittingclass.com.

TRUFFAUT, FRANÇOIS: BIRTH ANNIVERSARY. Feb 6, 1932. Born at Paris, France, Truffaut was the most popular and successful French film director of his time. His films include *The 400 Blows, Jules and Jim, The Last Metro* and *The Story of Adele H.* He died at Paris, Oct 21, 1984.

WELLS FARGO BANK CUP. Feb 6–8. Winter Park Resort, Winter Park, CO. Elite disabled skiers compete head to head on a dual giant slalom course in the World Disabled Invitational. Amateur races, silent auction and charity dinners benefit the National Sports Center for the Disabled. Est attendance: 10,000. For info: Winter Park Resort, PO Box 1290, Winter Park, CO 80482. Phone: (970) 726-1545. E-mail: sfeek@nscd.org. Web: www.nscd.org.

BIRTHDAYS TODAY

Sarah Brady, 62, handgun control activist, born Alexandria, VA, Feb 6, 1942.
Tom Brokaw, 64, journalist, born Yankton, SD, Feb 6, 1940.
Natalie Cole, 54, singer ("This Will Be," "Unforgettable"), born Los Angeles, CA, Feb 6, 1950.
Fabian, 61, singer, actor, born Fabian Forte, Philadelphia, PA, Feb 6, 1943.
Mike Farrell, 65, actor ("M*A*S*H," "Providence"), born St. Paul, MN, Feb 6, 1939.
Zsa Zsa (Sari) Gabor, 85, actress (*Ninotchka, Special Tonight*), born Budapest, Hungary, Feb 6, 1919.
Gayle Hunnicutt, 61, actress ("Dallas," *The Wild Angels, Marlowe*), born Fort Worth, TX, Feb 6, 1943.
Barry Miller, 46, actor (stage: *Biloxi Blues* [Tony Award]; *Saturday Night Fever, The Last Temptation of Christ*), born Los Angeles, CA, Feb 6, 1958.
Kathy Najimy, 47, actress ("Veronica's Closet," *Sister Act*), born San Diego, CA, Feb 6, 1957.
Gigi Perreau, 63, actress (*Bonzo Goes to College, Tammy Tell Me True*), born Los Angeles, CA, Feb 6, 1941.
Ronald Wilson Reagan, 93, 40th president of the US, former sportscaster and actor (*The Winning Team*), born Tampico, IL, Feb 6, 1911.
Rip Torn, 73, actor ("The Larry Sanders Show," *Men in Black*), born Elmore Torn, Jr, Temple, TX, Feb 6, 1931.
Robert Townsend, 47, actor, director (*The Five Heartbeats, The Mighty Quinn*), born Chicago, IL, Feb 6, 1957.
Michael Tucker, 60, actor ("LA Law"), born Baltimore, MD, Feb 6, 1944.
Mamie Van Doren, 71, actress (*High School Confidential, Three Nuts in Search of a Bolt*), born Rowena, SD, Feb 6, 1933.

Feb 7   ☆ *Chase's 2004 Calendar of Events* ☆

FEBRUARY 7 — SATURDAY
Day 38 — 328 Remaining

ARIZONA RENAISSANCE FESTIVAL. Feb 7–Mar 28. (Saturdays, Sundays and Presidents' Day [Feb 16] only.) Apache Junction, AZ. Enjoy your best day out in history. Find yourself surrounded by medieval merriment with knights, kings, maidens and minstrels. Stroll through acres of amusements, "shoppes" and nonstop revelry as you join our village celebration. The official sister event to the Robin Hood Festival in Sherwood Forest, England. Est attendance: 265,000. For info: Arizona Renaissance Festival, 12601 E Highway 60, Apache Junction, AZ 85219. Phone: (520) 463-2600. Web: www.royalfaires.com.

BALLET INTRODUCED TO THE US: ANNIVERSARY. Feb 7, 1827. Renowned French danseuse Mme Francisquy Hutin introduced ballet to the US with a performance of *The Deserter*, staged at the Bowery Theater, New York, NY. A minor scandal erupted when the ladies in the lower boxes left the theater upon viewing the light and scanty attire of Mme Hutin and her troupe.

BLAKE, EUBIE: BIRTH ANNIVERSARY. Feb 7, 1883. James Hubert "Eubie" Blake, American composer and pianist, writer of nearly 1,000 songs (including "I'm Just Wild About Harry" and "Memories of You"). Born at Baltimore, MD. Recipient of the Presidential Medal of Freedom in 1981. Last professional performance was in January 1982. Died at Brooklyn, NY, five days after his 100th birthday, Feb 12, 1983.

BUDWEISER SHOOTOUT AT DAYTONA WINSTON CUP SERIES RACE. Feb 7. Daytona International Speedway, Daytona Beach, FL. Dash for the cash featuring NASCAR Winston Cup stars. For info: Daytona International Speedway, PO Box 2801, Daytona Beach, FL 32120-2801. Phone: (386) 253-7223. Fax: (386) 947-6791. Web: www.daytonainternationalspeedway.com.

CHAPLIN'S "TRAMP" DEBUTS: ANNIVERSARY. Feb 7, 1914. Charlie Chaplin, vaudeville star–turned–comedic actor, debuted a new character in *Kid Auto Races at Venice*, a Keystone Studios short released on this date. The mischievous but innocent "Tramp," sporting a tiny mustache and twirling cane and wearing a little derby, tight-fitting jacket, baggy trousers and floppy shoes was an immediate success with audiences, and soon mass-produced Tramp dolls were selling all over the US and the world.

CHOCOLATE FESTIVAL. Feb 7–8. Galesburg Antiques Mall, Galesburg, IL. A chocolate lover's dream! Homemade and commercially made chocolates, tortes, cakes, pies and creams—all you can eat for a small admission fee. Annually, the weekend closest to Valentine's Day. Est attendance: 1,500. For info: Galesburg Area CVB, PO Box 60, Galesburg, IL 61402-0060. Phone: (309) 343-2485. Fax: (309) 343-2521. E-mail: visitors@visitgalesburg.com. Web: www.visitgalesburg.com.

CHOCOLATE FESTIVAL. Feb 7. Firehouse Art Center, Norman, OK. Tasting sessions, cooking competitions and tantalizing displays of chocolate as an art form are a treat for the eyes as well as the palate. Est attendance: 1,500. For info: The Firehouse Art Center, 444 S Flood, Norman, OK 73069. Phone: (405) 329-4523. Fax: (405) 292-9763. E-mail: firehouse@telepath.com.

CORVETTE AND HIGH PERFORMANCE MEET. Feb 7–8 (tentative). Puyallup, WA. 900-booth swap meet with new and used car parts and automobilia. Vehicles for sale, Corvette invitational display area. Est attendance: 10,000. For info: Larry Johnson, Show Organizer, PO Box 7753, Olympia, WA 98507. Phone: (360) 786-8844. Fax: (360) 754-1498. Web: www.corvhp.com.

February 2004

S	M	T	W	T	F	S
1	2	3	4	5	6	7
8	9	10	11	12	13	14
15	16	17	18	19	20	21
22	23	24	25	26	27	28
29						

COWBOY STATE GAMES SPORTS FESTIVAL. Feb 7–8. Also Feb 13–16, 21–22. Casper, WY. The festival features a variety of sporting events for athletes of all ages. Est attendance: 2,500. For info: Eileen Ford, Cowboy State Games, PO Box 3485, Casper, WY 82602. Phone: (307) 577-1125. Fax: (307) 577-8111. E-mail: csg@trib.com.

DICKENS, CHARLES: BIRTH ANNIVERSARY. Feb 7, 1812. English social critic and novelist, born at Portsmouth, England. Among his most successful books: *Oliver Twist*, *The Posthumous Papers of the Pickwick Club*, *A Tale of Two Cities*, *David Copperfield* and *A Christmas Carol*. Died at Gad's Hill, England, June 9, 1870, and was buried at Westminster Abbey.

ELEVENTH AMENDMENT TO US CONSTITUTION (SOVEREIGNTY OF THE STATES): RATIFICATION ANNIVERSARY. Feb 7, 1795. The 11th Amendment to the Constitution was ratified, curbing the powers of the federal judiciary in relation to the states. The amendment reaffirmed the sovereignty of the states by prohibiting suits against them.

ELGIN MARKET DAYS. Feb 7. Memorial Park, Elgin, TX. (Also Mar 6, Apr 3, May 1, June 5, July 3, Aug 7, Sept 4, Oct 2 and Nov 6.) First Saturday of every month, February–November. Buy and/or sell antiques, crafts and "junque." Vendors welcome. For info: Sharon McCall, 1462 Old Lytton Springs Rd, Lockhart, TX 78644. Phone: (512) 263-2512. E-mail: newcovenantpc@lycos.com.

GASPARILLA INVASION AND PARADE. Feb 7. Tampa, FL. As any Tampa resident can attest, "Gasparilla" means boats, pirates, parades, merriment and more. The city's illustrious festival celebration has 700 citizens, members of Ye Mystic Krewe, reenacting the 1904 invasion of Tampa by a band of pirates. Annually, in early February. For info: EventMakers Corp of Tampa, 3701 W Azeele St, Tampa, FL 33609. Phone: (813) 353-8108. E-mail: events@Eventmakers-FL.com. Web: www.gasparillapiratefest.com.

GRENADA: INDEPENDENCE DAY: 30th ANNIVERSARY. Feb 7. National Day. Commemorates independence from Great Britain in 1974.

HOGGETOWNE MEDIEVAL FAIRE. Feb 7–8 (also Feb 13–15). Alachua County Fairgrounds, Gainesville, FL. 18th annual faire features jousting, birds of prey, medieval arts and crafts, food and continuous entertainment on eight stages. Est attendance: 60,000. For info: Linda Piper, City of Gainesville, Dept of Cultural Affairs, PO Box 490 Sta. 30, Gainesville, FL 32602. Phone: (352) 334-5064. Fax: (352) 334-2249. E-mail: piperLr@ci.gainesville.fl.us.

JAMES DEAN BIRTHDAY CELEBRATION. Feb 7–8. Fairmount, IN. The town where James Dean grew up celebrates his birthday with a movie showing, exhibits, refreshments and more. *Rebel Without a Cause* will be screened on Feb 8 at 1 PM and the Fairmount Museum will be open all weekend. For info: Fairmount Historical Museum, Inc, 203 E Washington St, PO Box 92, Fairmount, IN 46928. Phone: (765) 948-4555. Web: www.jamesdeanartifacts.com.

JOHN DEERE'S 200th BIRTHDAY. Feb 7. Moline, IL. In celebration of John Deere's 200th birthday, his home, which is currently undergoing restoration, will be open to the public. For info: Joe Taylor, Quad Cities CVB, 2021 River Dr, Moline, IL

☆ Chase's 2004 Calendar of Events ☆   Feb 7

61265. Phone: (800) 747-7800. Fax: (309) 764-9443. E-mail: jtaylor@visitquadcities.com. Web: www.visitquadcities.com.

KISSIMMEE SLOUGH SHOOTOUT AND RENDEZVOUS. Feb 7–8. Ah-Tah-Thi-Ki Museum, Big Cypress Reservation, FL. Seminole War reenactment. Living history camps, Seminole dancing, Indian arts and crafts, pioneer traders and archery contest. Annually, the first weekend in February. Est attendance: 2,000. For info: Brian Zepeda, Ah-Tah-Thi-Ki Museum, HC-61, Box 21A, Clewiston, FL 33440. Phone: (863) 902-1113. Fax: (863) 902-1117. E-mail: bzepeda@semtribe.com. Web: www.seminoletribe.com/museum.

LAURA INGALLS WILDER GINGERBREAD SOCIABLE. Feb 7. Pomona, CA. The 37th annual event commemorates the birthday (Feb 7, 1867) of the renowned author of the Little House books. The library has on permanent display the handwritten manuscript of *Little Town on the Prairie* and other Wilder memorabilia. Entertainment by fiddlers, craft displays, apple cider and gingerbread. Annually, the first Saturday in February. Est attendance: 200. For info: Marguerite F. Raybould, Pomona Public Library, 625 S Garey Ave, Pomona, CA 91766. Phone: (909) 620-2043, ext 017. Fax: (909) 620-3713.

LEWIS, SINCLAIR: BIRTH ANNIVERSARY. Feb 7, 1885. American novelist and social critic. Recipient of Nobel Prize for Literature (1930). Among his novels: *Main Street, Babbitt* and *It Can't Happen Here*. Born Harry Sinclair Lewis at Sauk Center, MN. Died at Rome, Italy, Jan 10, 1951.

MID-WINTER ANTIQUES AND COLLECTIBLES SHOW AND SALE. Feb 7–8. Millville, NJ. Snow, rain or shine, the sale will go on. Est attendance: 2,000. For info: Wheaton Village, 1501 Glasstown Rd, Millville, NJ 08332. Phone: (800) 998-4552 or (856) 825-6800. Fax: (856) 825-2410. E-mail: mail@wheatonvillage.org. Web: www.wheatonvillage.org.

MORE, SIR THOMAS: BIRTH ANNIVERSARY. Feb 7, 1478. Anniversary of birth of lawyer, scholar, author, Lord Chancellor of England, martyr and saint at London, England. Refusing to recognize Henry VIII's divorce from Queen Catherine, the "Man for All Seasons" was found guilty of treason and imprisoned in the Tower of London, Apr 17, 1534. He was beheaded at Tower Hill on July 6, 1535, and his head displayed from Tower Bridge. Canonized in 1935. Memorial observed on June 22.

NATIONAL CITY CLEVELAND HOME AND GARDEN SHOW. Feb 7–15. I-X Center, Cleveland, OH. The largest show of its kind in the country with more than 35 feature gardens, 900 exhibitors and three fully decorated and landscaped walk-through model homes. Est attendance: 300,000. For info: Natl City Home and Garden Show, PO Box 550-Edgewater Branch, Cleveland, OH 44107. Phone: (216) 529-1300. Fax: (216) 529-0311. E-mail: expoinc@expoinc.com. Web: www.expoinc.com.

PERRY'S "BRR" (BIKE RIDE TO RIPPEY). Feb 7. Perry, IA. Winter bike riding. Twenty-two miles of frigid fun. Annually, the first Saturday in February. Est attendance: 2,000. For info: John Doyle, Chamber of Commerce, 1226 Second St, Perry, IA 50220. Phone: (515) 465-4601. Fax: (515) 465-2256. E-mail: perrychmbr@aol.com. Web: www.perryia.org.

RAILROAD AND HOBBY SHOW. Feb 7–8. West Springfield, MA. Now expanded to three buildings, nearly 5½ acres with more than 30 operating layouts; displays; art; railroads; Shortline, Tourist and Class 1 railroads; flea market, dealers and more. Est attendance: 25,000. For info: Amherst Railway Soc, PO Box 718, Warren, MA 01083-0718. Phone: (413) 436-0242. Fax: (413) 436-7013. E-mail: ars@samnet.net.

SHOW OF WHEELS. Feb 7–8. Lea County Fairgrounds, Lovington, NM. Car show presented by the Lovington Chamber of Commerce. Featuring antiques, classics, street rods, motorcycles and minitrucks. A swap meet, commercial exhibits and games will be an exciting part of the show. RV parking available. For info: Lovington Chamber of Commerce, 201 S Main St, Lovington, NM 88260. Phone: (505) 396-5311 or (505) 396-3661. Fax: (505) 396-2823. E-mail: visitus@leaconet.com. Web: www.leaco.net.

SPACE MILESTONE: *STARDUST* (US): 5th ANNIVERSARY. Feb 7, 1999. *Stardust* began its three billion-mile journey to collect comet dust on this date. The unmanned mission is to meet up with *Comet Wild-2* in January 2004 and the comet samples will reach Earth in January 2006. This is the first US mission devoted solely to a comet. NASA plans three more over a four-year period.

TU B'SHVAT. Feb 7. Hebrew calendar date: Shebat 15, 5764. The 15th day of the month of Shebat in the Hebrew calendar year is set aside as Hamishah Asar (New Year of the Trees or Jewish Arbor Day), a time to show respect and appreciation for trees and plants. Began at sundown on Feb 6.

WASHINGTON'S BIRTHDAY CELEBRATION. Feb 7–22. Laredo, TX. Founded in 1898, the event celebrates the cultures of both the US and Mexico with festivities ranging from the Jalapeño Festival to parades, fireworks and a carnival. The largest celebration of George Washington's birthday in the nation. Est attendance: 500,000. For info: Washington's Birthday Celebration Assn, 1819 E Hillside Rd, Laredo, TX 78041. Phone: (956) 722-0589. Fax: (956) 722-5528. E-mail: wbca@wbcalaredo.org.

WAVE ALL YOUR FINGERS AT YOUR NEIGHBORS DAY. Feb 7. After all the challenges our neighbors and we have faced, it's time to put it all aside for at least one day. Wave "hello" to everybody and mean it. Annually, Feb 7. [©2003 by WH.] For info: Thomas & Ruth Roy, Wellcat Holidays, 2419 Long Ln, Lebanon, PA 17046. Phone: (717) 279-0184. E-mail: info@wellcat.com. Web: www.wellcat.com.

WELLS FARGO BOULDER MOUNTAIN TOUR. Feb 7. Galena Lodge, Sun Valley, ID. A 32K cross-country ski race from Galena Lodge to the Sawtooth National Recreation Area (SNRA) headquarters. For info: Boulder Mountain Tour, PO Box 173, Sun Valley, ID 83353. Phone: (208) 788-1550. E-mail: bouldermttour@aol.com. Web: www.bouldermountaintour.com.

BIRTHDAYS TODAY

Hector Babenco, 58, director (*Ironweed, Kiss of the Spider Woman*), born Buenos Aires, Argentina, Feb 7, 1946.
Oscar Brand, 84, folksinger, born Winnipeg, MB, Canada, Feb 7, 1920.
Garth Brooks, 42, country singer ("Friends in Low Places"), born Tulsa, OK, Feb 7, 1962.
Miguel Ferrer, 50, actor ("Twin Peaks;" *Star Trek III; Hot Shots! Part Deux*), born Santa Monica, CA, Feb 7, 1954.
Juwan Howard, 31, basketball player, born Chicago, IL, Feb 7, 1973.
Herb Kohl, 69, US Senator (D, Wisconsin), born Milwaukee, WI, Feb 7, 1935.
Ashton Kutcher, 26, actor ("That 70s Show," *Hey Dude, Where's My Car?*), born Cedar Rapids, IA, Feb 7, 1978.
Pete Postlethwaite, 59, actor (*Amistad, The Lost World: Jurassic Park, Brassed Off*), born London, England, Feb 7, 1945.
Chris Rock, 38, actor, comedian ("Saturday Night Live," *Beverly Hills Ninja*), born Brooklyn, NY, Feb 7, 1966.
James Spader, 44, actor (*sex, lies, and videotape; Wolf*), born Boston, MA, Feb 7, 1960.
Gay Talese, 72, author (*The Kingdom and the Power, Unto the Sons*), born Ocean City, NJ, Feb 7, 1932.

FEBRUARY 8 — SUNDAY
Day 39 — 327 Remaining

BOY SCOUTS OF AMERICA FOUNDED: ANNIVERSARY. Feb 8, 1910. The Boy Scouts of America was founded at Washington, DC, by William Boyce, based on the work of Sir Robert Baden-Powell with the British Boy Scout Association.

BUD POLE DAY FOR THE DAYTONA 500. Feb 8. Daytona International Speedway, Daytona Beach, FL. Fastest qualifiers have the front row for the Daytona 500. For info: Daytona International Speedway, PO Box 2801, Daytona Beach, FL 32120-2801. Phone: (386) 253-7223. Fax: (386) 947-6791. Web: www.daytonainternationalspeedway.com.

CARDIAC REHABILITATION WEEK. Feb 8–14. For info: American Assn of Cardiovascular and Pulmonary Rehabilitation, 401 N Michigan Ave, Ste 2200, Chicago, IL 60611. Phone: (312) 321-5146. Fax: (312) 245-1085. E-mail: aacvpr@sba.com.

DEAN, JAMES: BIRTH ANNIVERSARY. Feb 8, 1931. American stage, film and television actor who achieved immense popularity during a brief career. Born at Fairmont, IN. Best remembered for his role in *Rebel Without a Cause*. Died in an automobile accident near Cholame, CA, Sept 30, 1955, at age 24.

THE GRAMMY AWARDS. Feb 8. Staples Center, Los Angeles, CA (site subject to change). 46th annual. Celebrating the best in recording arts and sciences, the Grammys cover 104 categories—from classical to jazz to pop and rock. Awarded by and to artists and technical professionals. (Also broadcast on CBS.) For info: National Academy of Recording Arts & Sciences, 3402 Pico Blvd, Santa Monica, CA 90405. Phone: (310) 392-3777. Fax: (310) 392-2778. Web: www.grammy.com.

GROUNDHOG RUN. Feb 8. Kansas City, MO. 22nd annual. The world's only 10K and 5K underground run takes place at the Hunt Midwest SubTropolis. Three thousand runners from across the country participate in this Grand Prix event to benefit Children's Therapeutic Learning Center. Est attendance: 3,000. For info: Children's TLC, 3101 Main St, Kansas City, MO 64111-1921. Phone: (816) 756-0780, ext 2104. Fax: (816) 756-1677. E-mail: jcollet@childrenstlc.org. Web: www.childrenstlc.org.

INTERNATIONAL TABLE MANNERS WEEK. Feb 8–14. This week encourages people to learn this important social and career skill so that good manners become second nature and dining becomes more pleasant. With good table manners, anyone can better participate in the global marketplace and cultures. Observing good manners will build self-confidence and self-esteem. Annually, the full week (Sunday through Saturday) that includes Valentine's Day. For info: Molly Miller-Davidson, 544 N Orange Dr, Los Angeles, CA 90036. Phone: (323) 936-2280. Fax: (323) 936-2239. E-mail: mollymd@mindspring.com. Web: imageinternational.ca.

JAPAN: HA-RI-KU-YO (NEEDLE MASS). Feb 8. Ha-Ri-Ku-Yo, a Needle Mass, may be observed on either Feb 8 or Dec 8. Girls do no needlework; instead they gather old and broken needles, which they dedicate to the Awashima Shrine at Wakayama. Girls pray to Awashima Myozin (their protecting deity) that their needlework, symbolic of love and marriage, will be good. Participation in the Needle Mass hopefully leads to a happy marriage.

JAPAN: SNOW FESTIVAL. Feb 8–12. Sapporo, Hokkaido. Huge, elaborate snow and ice sculptures are erected on the Odori-Koen Promenade.

JELL-O® WEEK IN UTAH. Feb 8–14. In January 2001 the Utah legislature passed a resolution declaring Jell-O® "the Official State Snack of Utah." The state will celebrate the designation annually with "Jell-O® Week" each February (the second full week). For info: Nora Bertucci, Hunter Public Relations, 41 Madison Ave, 5th Fl, New York, NY 10010. Phone: (212) 679-6600. Web: www.hunterpr.com.

LAUGH AND GET RICH DAY. Feb 8. Recognition of laughter's power to add to the bottom line. People are more effective and tend to remember things better, and laughter helps to lower the turnover rate. For info: Rick Segel, 1 Wheatland St, Burlington, MA 01803. Phone: (781) 272-9995. Fax: (781) 272-9996. E-mail: rick@ricksegel.com.

LEMMON, JACK: BIRTH ANNIVERSARY. Feb 8, 1925. Stage, screen and television actor, born John Uhler Lemmon III at Boston, MA. Often paired with actor Walter Matthau, he starred in such films as *The Odd Couple*, *The Fortune Cookie* and *The Front Page*. He was nominated for seven Academy Awards, winning in 1955 for his supporting role in *Mister Roberts* and in 1974 for his leading role in *Save the Tiger*. Other films included *Some Like It Hot*, *Days of Wine and Roses* and *Grumpy Old Men*. He also starred in television versions of *Inherit the Wind* and *Twelve Angry Men* and won an Emmy in 2000 for the TV movie *Tuesdays with Morrie*. He died at Los Angeles, CA, June 27, 2001.

LOVE MAY MAKE THE WORLD GO 'ROUND, BUT LAUGHTER KEEPS US FROM GETTING DIZZY WEEK. Feb 8–14. This week is dedicated to Victor Borge's notion that "Laughter is the shortest distance between two people" and Joel Goodman's notion that "Seven days without laughter makes one weak." This is a chance to lighten your relationships and to reinforce the connection between "heart" and "hearty laughter." Annually, the week leading up to and including Valentine's Day. To receive a free live-love-laugh info packet on the positive power of humor, send a ($1.06) SASE. For info: The HUMOR Project, Inc, 480 Broadway, Ste 210-C, Saratoga Springs, NY 12866-2288. Phone: (518) 587-8770. Fax: (518) 587-8771. E-mail: chase@HumorProject.com. Web: www.HumorProject.com.

MAN DAY. Feb 8. A day for celebration by friends, family and associates of the men of the world. Annually, the Sunday before Valentine's Day. [©2002 C. Daniel Rhodes.] For info: C. Daniel Rhodes, 1900 Crossvine Rd, Hoover, AL 35244. Phone: (205) 908-6781. Fax: (205) 987-2986. E-mail: drhodes2986@charter.net. Web: www.brothersdaymay24.com.

MARTHA GRIFFITHS SPEAKS OUT AGAINST SEX DISCRIMINATION: 40th ANNIVERSARY. Feb 8, 1964. During the congressional debate over the 1964 Civil Rights Act, Representative Martha Griffiths delivered a memorable speech advocating the prohibition of discrimination based on sex. Her efforts resulted in adding civil rights protection for women to the 1964 Act. She later successfully led the campaign for the Equal Rights Amendment in the House of Representatives.

MARY, QUEEN OF SCOTS: EXECUTION ANNIVERSARY. Feb 8, 1587. Mary Stuart, the queen regent of Scotland, was beheaded at Fotheringhay, England, her death warrant having been sealed by Queen Elizabeth I on Feb 1. Mary, the daughter of James V of Scotland by his second wife, Mary of Guise, was born Dec 7 or 8, 1542, at Linlithgow, Scotland, and became queen a week later upon the death of her father, although she did not begin governing until after the death of her mother in 1561. She was forced to abdicate in favor of her son (James VI) when the people turned against her after she married the Earl of Bothwell, who was believed to be the murderer with Mary's knowledge of her second husband (her cousin Henry Stewart, Lord Darnley). She fled to England for protection, only to find herself a prisoner for the rest of her life. She was tried and sentenced to death in 1586 because of her involvement in a plot to assassinate Elizabeth. She was buried at Peterborough, but in 1612 her body was moved to Henry VII's Chapel at Westminster, where a tomb was erected by her son. Essentially, Mary Stuart was a vic-

	S	M	T	W	T	F	S
February 2004	1	2	3	4	5	6	7
	8	9	10	11	12	13	14
	15	16	17	18	19	20	21
	22	23	24	25	26	27	28
	29						

tim of the political intrigue and Protestant–Roman Catholic conflicts that surrounded the Reformation and Henry VIII's ecclesiastical revolution.

MATERIALS TESTING WEEK. Feb 8–14. Recognition of the positive role material testing and inspection services provide in quality control and quality assurance for the construction industry. Focusing on the numerous tests, inspections and highly qualified technicians available to the construction industry for help in building a better quality of life for everyone—from bridges and smooth airport runways to sturdy steel high-rises and attractive multihousing developments. For info: Charlene Savoca, Materials Testing Inc, 180 Mill Rd, Edison, NJ 08817. Phone: (732) 248-3777. Fax: (732) 248-7979. Web: material-testing.com.

NATIONAL FAMILY, CAREER AND COMMUNITY LEADERS OF AMERICA WEEK. Feb 8–14. To call the nation's attention to the activities and goals of the FCCLA and to family and consumer sciences education. Theme: "FCCLA: Making the Leader." For info: Beth Carpenter, Communications Mgr, Family, Career and Community Leaders of America, 1910 Association Dr, Reston, VA 21091. Phone: (703) 476-4900. Fax: (703) 860-2713. E-mail: bcarpenter@fcclainc.org.

OPERA DEBUT IN THE COLONIES: ANNIVERSARY. Feb 8, 1735. The first opera produced in the colonies was performed at the Courtroom, at Charleston, SC. The opera was *Flora; or the Hob in the Well*, written by Colley Cibber.

REENACTMENT OF COWTOWN'S LAST OLD WEST GUNFIGHT. Feb 8. White Elephant Saloon, Fort Worth, TX. Annual reenactment of Fort Worth's last Old West gunfight, which took place on Feb 8, 1887, between White Elephant Saloon owner Luke Short and former Marshal T.I. "Longhaired Jim" Courtright. Annually, Feb 8. Est attendance: 400. For info: Tim Love, Owner, 108 E Exchange Ave, Fort Worth, TX 76106-8210. Phone: (817) 624-9712. Fax: (817) 625-9663. E-mail: whiteelephant@sbcglobal.net. Web: www.whiteelephantsaloon.com.

SHERMAN, WILLIAM TECUMSEH: BIRTH ANNIVERSARY. Feb 8, 1820. Born at Lancaster, OH, General Sherman is especially remembered for his devastating march through Georgia during the Civil War and his statement "War is hell." Died at New York, NY, Feb 14, 1891.

SLOVENIA: CULTURE DAY. Feb 8. National holiday. Honors France Preseren, Slovenia's national poet, who died Feb 8, 1849.

SPACE MILESTONE: *ARABSAT-1*. Feb 8, 1985. League of Arab States communications satellite launched into geosynchronous orbit from Kourou, French Guiana, by the European Space Agency.

SPACE MILESTONE: *BRASILSAT-1* (BRAZIL). Feb 8, 1985. Brazilian communications satellite launched into geosynchronous orbit from Kourou, French Guiana, by the European Space Agency.

VERNE, JULES: BIRTH ANNIVERSARY. Feb 8, 1828. French writer, sometimes called "the father of science fiction," born at Nantes, France. Author of *Around the World in Eighty Days*, *Twenty Thousand Leagues Under the Sea* and many other novels. Died at Amiens, France, Mar 24, 1905.

WORLD MARRIAGE DAY. Feb 8. World Marriage Day honors husband and wife as head of the family, the basic unit of society. It salutes the beauty of their faithfulness, sacrifice and joy in daily married life. Sponsored by WorldWide Marriage Encounter since 1981. Annually, second Sunday in February. For info: WorldWide Marriage Encounter, 2210 E Highland #106, San Bernardino, CA 92404. Phone: (301) 871-1595. Fax: (909) 863-9986. E-mail: irvinemj@earthlink.net. Web: wmd.wwme.org.

WSBA/WARM 103 EASTER CRAFT SHOW. Feb 8. York, PA. More than 175 quality craft displays will be presented with everything from country to contemporary dolls, jewelry, pottery and much more. Admission fee. Est attendance: 4,000. For info: Joe Alfano, Asst Promo Dir, PO Box 910, York, PA 17402-0910. Phone: (717) 764-1155. Fax: (717) 252-4708. E-mail: jalfano@suscom.com. Web: www.warm103.com.

BIRTHDAYS TODAY

Brooke Adams, 55, actress (*Days of Heaven, Gas Food Lodging*), born New York, NY, Feb 8, 1949.
Gary Coleman, 36, actor ("Diff'rent Strokes," *The Kid from Left Field*), born Zion, IL, Feb 8, 1968.
Seth Green, 30, actor ("Family Guy," "Greg the Bunny," *Austin Powers*), born Overbrook Park, PA, Feb 8, 1974.
John Grisham, 49, author (*The Firm, The Client*), born Jonesboro, AR, Feb 8, 1955.
Robert Klein, 62, comedian, actor ("Comedy Tonight," *They're Playing Our Song*), born New York, NY, Feb 8, 1942.
Ted Koppel, 64, journalist (anchor of "Nightline"), born Lancashire, England, Feb 8, 1940.
Alonzo Mourning, 34, basketball player, born Chesapeake, VA, Feb 8, 1970.
Nick Nolte, 63, actor (*Affliction, Prince of Tides*, "Rich Man, Poor Man"), born Omaha, NE, Feb 8, 1941.
Mary Steenburgen, 51, actress (*Melvin and Howard, Parenthood, Back to the Future Part III*), born Newport, AR, Feb 8, 1953.
John Williams, 72, pianist, conductor (formerly with Boston Pops), composer (scores for *Jaws, Star Wars, Jurassic Park, Schindler's List*), born New York, NY, Feb 8, 1932.

FEBRUARY 9 — MONDAY
Day 40 — 326 Remaining

ALLIES RETAKE GUADALCANAL: ANNIVERSARY. Feb 9, 1943. In a major strategic victory, the American 161st and 132nd Regiments retook Guadalcanal in the Solomon Islands on this date after a six-month-long battle. More than 9,000 Japanese and 2,000 Americans were killed. The fierce resistance by the Japanese was an indication to the Allies of things to come. Guadalcanal put the Allies within striking distance of Rabaul, the major Japanese base in the area.

THE BEATLES APPEAR ON "THE ED SULLIVAN SHOW": 40th ANNIVERSARY. Feb 9, 1964. British pop phenomenons The Beatles began the "British Invasion" of America with their appearance on America's top television variety show. They performed five songs before a screaming studio audience of 728. The estimated viewership for that night's show was 73 million people—making it the most viewed US TV program in history up to that time. See also: "Beatles Take Over Music Charts" (Apr 4).

BEHAN, BRENDAN: BIRTH ANNIVERSARY. Feb 9, 1923. Irish playwright and poet, born at Dublin, Ireland. Died there Mar 20, 1964.

CELEBRATION OF LOVE WEEK. Feb 9–15. To stress the importance and value of love in making the world a much better place in which to live. For complete info, send $5 to cover expense of printing, handling and postage. Annually, the second full week of February. For info: Dr. Stanley Drake, Pres, Intl Soc of Friendship and Good Will, 999 Hood Rd, Ste 127, Marietta, GA 30068. Phone: (770) 565-2322. E-mail: ISFGW@bellsouth.net.

Feb 9–10 ☆ Chase's 2004 Calendar of Events ☆

FREELANCE WRITERS APPRECIATION WEEK. Feb 9–14. Freelance writers do more than query editors and write and submit articles and books (nonfiction and fiction). They provide overworked editors with material, as well as inform and entertain readers. Annually, the second week of February. For info: Dorothy Zjawin, Dir, 61 W Colfax Ave, Roselle Park, NJ 07204. Phone: (908) 241-6241.

GYPSY ROSE LEE: 90th BIRTH ANNIVERSARY. Feb 9, 1914. American ecdysiast and author whose real name was Rose Louise Hovick, born at Seattle, WA. Her autobiography, *Gypsy*, was made into a Broadway musical and a motion picture. Died at Los Angeles, CA, Apr 26, 1970.

HARRISON, WILLIAM HENRY: BIRTH ANNIVERSARY. Feb 9, 1773. 9th president of the US (Mar 4–Apr 4, 1841). His term of office was the shortest in our nation's history—32 days. He was the first president to die in office (of pneumonia contracted during inaugural ceremonies). Born at Berkeley, VA, he died at Washington, DC, Apr 4, 1841. His grandson, Benjamin Harrison, was the 23rd president of the US.

INTERNATIONAL FLIRTING WEEK. Feb 9–15. Celebrating the ancient art of flirting and recognizing the role it plays in the lives of singles seeking a mate, couples looking to sustain their love and those simply exchanging a playful glance with a stranger, acquaintance, colleague, etc. For info: Robin Gorman Newman, 44 Somerset Dr, N, Great Neck, NY 11020. Phone: (516) 773-0911. E-mail: robin@lovecoach.com. Web: www.lovecoach.com.

LEBANON: ST. MARON'S DAY. Feb 9. Holiday of Lebanon's Maronite Christian community. St. Maron was a Syrian hermit of the 4th–5th centuries.

LOWELL, AMY: BIRTH ANNIVERSARY. Feb 9, 1874. American poet born at Brookline, MA. Died there May 12, 1925.

NATIONAL "DAV" DAY. Feb 9. "DAV" stands for Develop Alternative Vices. A day to change your habits, improve yourself and become your own person so that things you do today will affect you positively tomorrow. Annually, Feb 9. For info send an SASE to: Kevin Davenport, 5304 Regency Way, Rockford, IL 61114.

NATIONAL FIELD TRIAL CHAMPIONSHIP. Feb 9–20. (Monday–Friday only.) Ames Plantation, Grand Junction, TN. To select the national champion all-age bird dog. Est attendance: 6,000. For info: R.J. Carlisle, Secy/Treas, Natl Field Trial Champion Assn, Box 389, Grand Junction, TN 38039. Phone: (901) 878-1067. Fax: (901) 878-1068. E-mail: amesplantation@lunaweb.net. Web: www.amesplantation.com.

RUSK, (DAVID) DEAN: 95th BIRTH ANNIVERSARY. Feb 9, 1909. US diplomat Dean Rusk was born at Cherokee County, GA. He served as US secretary of state from 1961 to 1969, during which time he supported US involvement in the Vietnam War. He died Dec 20, 1994, at Athens, GA.

TUBB, ERNEST: 90th BIRTH ANNIVERSARY. Feb 9, 1914. Country and western singer, born at Crisp, TX. Ernest Tubb was the sixth member to be elected to the Country Music Hall of Fame and the headliner on the first country music show ever to be presented at Carnegie Hall. His first major hit, "Walking the Floor Over You," gained him his first appearance at the Grand Ole Opry in 1942, and he attained regular membership in 1943. He died Sept 6, 1984, at Nashville, TN.

UNION OFFICERS ESCAPE LIBBY PRISON: ANNIVERSARY. Feb 9, 1864. On this date 109 Union officers escaped from Libby Prison in Richmond, VA, in the largest and most dramatic prisoner of war escape of the Civil War. The Libby Prison was the former Libby and Sons candle factory. Forty-eight of the men were recaptured, two drowned and fifty-nine successfully made it back to Federal lines.

VEECK, BILL: 90th BIRTH ANNIVERSARY. Feb 9, 1914. William Louis (Bill) Veeck, Jr, Baseball Hall of Fame executive born at Chicago, IL. Veeck was baseball's premier promoter and showman as an owner of several teams. He integrated the American League, sent a midget to the plate to start a game and, in general, sought to provide fans with entertainment in addition to baseball. Inducted into the Hall of Fame in 1991. Died at Chicago, IL, Jan 2, 1986.

WAR TIME: ANNIVERSARY. Feb 9, 1942. US clocks were advanced one hour at 2 AM as the nation went on War Time to conserve electricity. President Roosevelt had signed this daylight savings bill on Jan 20.

WESTMINSTER KENNEL CLUB DOG SHOW. Feb 9–10. Madison Square Garden, New York, NY. 128th annual. For info: Westminster Kennel Club, 149 Madison Ave, Ste 803, New York, NY 10016. Web: westminsterkennelclub.org.

BIRTHDAYS TODAY

Mia Farrow, 59, actress ("Peyton Place," *Rosemary's Baby, Hannah and Her Sisters*), born Maria de Lourdes Villers, Los Angeles, CA, Feb 9, 1945.

Kathryn Grayson, 81, actress (*Kiss Me Kate, The Kissing Bandit*), born Zelma Hedrick, Winston-Salem, NC, Feb 9, 1923.

Vladimir Guerrero, 28, baseball player, born Nizao Bani, Dominican Republic, Feb 9, 1976.

Carole King, 62, singer, songwriter, born Brooklyn, NY, Feb 9, 1942.

Judith Light, 55, actress ("One Life to Live," "Who's the Boss?"), born Trenton, NJ, Feb 9, 1949.

Roger Mudd, 76, journalist (former anchorman "ABC Evening News"), born Washington, DC, Feb 9, 1928.

Joe Pesci, 61, actor (*Raging Bull, Goodfellas, My Cousin Vinny*), born Newark, NJ, Feb 9, 1943.

Shakira, 27, singer, born Shakira Isabelle Mebarak Ripoll, Barranquilla, Colombia, Feb 9, 1977.

Charles Shaughnessy, 49, actor ("Days of Our Lives," "The Nanny"), born London, England, Feb 9, 1955.

Mena Suvari, 25, actress (*American Beauty, Loser*), born Newport, RI, Feb 9, 1979.

Janet Suzman, 65, actress (*Nicholas and Alexandra, A Dry White Season*), born Johannesburg, South Africa, Feb 9, 1939.

Travis Tritt, 41, country and western singer (*Country Club*), born Marietta, GA, Feb 9, 1963.

Alice Walker, 60, author (*The Color Purple, Possessing the Secret of Joy, Meridian*), born Eatonton, GA, Feb 9, 1944.

FEBRUARY 10 — TUESDAY
Day 41 — 325 Remaining

"ALL THE NEWS THAT'S FIT TO PRINT": ANNIVERSARY. Feb 10, 1897. The familiar slogan "All the News That's Fit to Print" has appeared on page one of *The New York Times* since Feb 10, 1897. It had first appeared on the editorial page on Oct 25, 1896. Although in 1896 a $100 prize was offered for a slogan, owner Adolph S. Ochs concluded that his own slogan was best.

ANDERSON, DAME JUDITH: BIRTH ANNIVERSARY. Feb 10, 1898. Film and stage actress Dame Judith Anderson was born Frances Margaret Anderson at Adelaide, Australia. She was nominated for an Academy Award in 1941 for her role in Alfred Hitchcock's film *Rebecca*. In 1960 she was made Dame Commander of the British Empire by Queen Elizabeth II. She died Jan 3, 1992, at Santa Barbara, CA.

BRECHT, BERTOLT: BIRTH ANNIVERSARY. Feb 10, 1898. German playwright born at Augsburg, Germany. His plays, such as *Mother Courage*, reflect his Marxist and antimilitary world

February 2004

S	M	T	W	T	F	S
1	2	3	4	5	6	7
8	9	10	11	12	13	14
15	16	17	18	19	20	21
22	23	24	25	26	27	28
29						

☆ Chase's 2004 Calendar of Events ☆   Feb 10

view. Also wrote *The Threepenny Opera* in collaboration with composer Kurt Weill. Died at East Berlin, Aug 14, 1956.

DURANTE, JIMMY: BIRTH ANNIVERSARY. Feb 10, 1893. "The Schnozz," Jimmy Durante, was born at New York City. His first break into show biz came when he was 17 and got a regular job playing ragtime at a saloon at Coney Island. Later his friend Eddie Cantor urged him to try comedy. Durante developed a unique comedic style as a short-tempered but lovable personage. His shtick included slamming down his hat and flapping his arms. His clothing, enormous nose, craggy face, gravelly singing voice and mispronunciations were all part of the persona. Durante, whose career spanned six decades, appeared on TV, stage and screen. His television sign-off, "Good night, Mrs Calabash, wherever you are!" became a trademark. Jimmy Durante died at Santa Monica, CA, Jan 29, 1980.

FIRST ACTOR TO PERFORM IN TWO CITIES ON THE SAME DAY: ANNIVERSARY. Feb 10, 1887. Nathaniel Carr Goodwin performed at an 11:30 AM matinee of *Turned Up* at Boston, MA, then, following the closing curtain, he returned to New York City on the 1 PM train and that evening performed in *The Mascot* at the Bijou Theatre at 8 PM.

FIRST COMPUTER CHESS VICTORY OVER HUMAN: ANNIVERSARY. Feb 10, 1996. IBM's Deep Blue computer defeated world champion Garry Kasparov in 34 moves on this date in Philadelphia, PA—the first such victory by a computer in tournament conditions. Kasparov, however, went on to win the tournament, defeating the computer three times (the other two matches were draws). In May 1997, in a six-game rematch, Deep Blue emerged the overall victor. Deep Blue, an RS/6000 supercomputer, can evaluate 200 million chess positions a second, but is not capable of using artificial intelligence to "learn." Kasparov was reigning World Chess Champion from 1985 to 2000.

FIRST WORLD WAR II MEDAL OF HONOR: ANNIVERSARY. Feb 10, 1942. Second Lieutenant Alexander Ramsey ("Sandy") Nininger, Jr, was posthumously awarded World War II's first Medal of Honor for heroism at the Battle of Bataan. He had graduated from West Point in 1941 and was on his first assignment after being commissioned.

LAMB, CHARLES: BIRTH ANNIVERSARY. Feb 10, 1775. Literary critic, poet and essayist, born at London, England. "The greatest pleasure I know," he wrote in 1834, "is to do a good action by stealth, and to have it found out by accident." Died at Edmonton, England, Dec 27, 1834.

LEADERSHIP SUCCESS DAY. Feb 10. Honors the CEOs of companies with sales over $20 million where more than 60 percent of company employees voted in the past year that their CEO did not just pay lip service to the statement that "People are our greatest asset." These CEOs demonstrated through their actions on no less than 10 occasions throughout the year that people are their greatest asset. For info: Denis Orme, Leadership Success Institute, Ste 132, 2a Byron Ave, Takapuna, Auckland 1309, New Zealand. E-mail: principal@leader-success.com. Web: www.leader-success.com.

MALTA: FEAST OF ST. PAUL'S SHIPWRECK. Feb 10. Valletta. Holy day of obligation. Commemorates the shipwreck of St. Paul on the north coast of Malta in AD 60.

"MY FRIEND FLICKA" TV PREMIERE: ANNIVERSARY. Feb 10, 1956. CBS series about a boy and his horse based on the children's book by Mary O'Hara. The series was set in the early 1900s on the Goose Bar Ranch in Montana. Johnny Washbrook starred as Ken McLaughlin; Gene Evans as Ken's father, Rob; Anita Louise as Ken's mother, Nell; Frank Ferguson as Gus, the ranch hand; and Wahama, the beautiful Arabian horse, as Flicka.

PASTERNAK, BORIS LEONIDOVICH: BIRTH ANNIVERSARY. Feb 10, 1890. Russian poet and novelist, born at Moscow, Russia. Best-known work: *Doctor Zhivago*. Died at Moscow, May 30, 1960.

PLIMSOLL DAY. Feb 10, 1824. A day to remember Samuel Plimsoll, "The Sailor's Friend," a coal merchant turned reformer and politician, who was elected to the British Parliament in 1868. He attacked the practice of overloading heavily insured ships, calling them "coffin ships." His persistence brought about amendment of Britain's Merchant Shipping Act. The Plimsoll Line, named for him, is a line on the side of ships marking maximum load allowed by law. Born at Bristol, England, Feb 10, 1824. Died at Folkestone, England, June 3, 1898.

TEXOMA FARM AND RANCH SHOW. Feb 10–11. Multi-Purpose Events Center Exhibit Hall, Wichita Falls, TX. Farmers and ranchers from North Texas and Oklahoma come to see the latest in equipment. Seminars and information in new farming and ranching techniques. Est attendance: 8,000. For info: Wichita Falls CVB, 1000 5th St, Wichita Falls, TX 76301. Phone: (940) 716-5500. Fax: (940) 716-5509. E-mail: MPEC@wf.net. Web: www.wichitafalls.org.

TILDEN, BILL: BIRTH ANNIVERSARY. Feb 10, 1893. William Tatem (Bill) Tilden, Jr, tennis player, born at Philadelphia, PA. Generally considered one of the greatest players of all time, Tilden won more tournaments than the record books can count. A nearly flawless player, he was also an egotistical showman on the court with an interest in show business. He turned pro in 1930 and continued to win regularly. Died at Hollywood, CA, June 5, 1953.

TREATY OF PARIS ENDS FRENCH AND INDIAN WAR: ANNIVERSARY. Feb 10, 1763. Known in Europe as the Seven Years' War, this conflict ranged from North America to India, with many European nations involved. In North America French expansion in the Ohio River Valley in the 1750s led to conflict with Great Britain. Some Indians fought alongside the French; a young George Washington fought for the British. As a result of the signing of the Treaty of Paris, France lost all claims to Canada and had to cede Louisiana to Spain. Fifteen years later French bitterness over the loss of its North American colonies to Britain contributed to its supporting the colonists in the American Revolution.

TWENTY-FIFTH AMENDMENT TO US CONSTITUTION RATIFIED (PRESIDENTIAL SUCCESSION, DISABILITY): ANNIVERSARY. Feb 10, 1967. Procedures for presidential succession were further clarified by the 25th Amendment, along with provisions for continuity of power in the event of a disability or illness of the president.

WORLD AG EXPO. Feb 10–12. Tulare, CA. The largest farm equipment show in North America. For info: Intl Agri-Center, PO Box 1475, 4450 S Laspina, Tulare, CA 93275. Phone: (800) 999-9186 or (559) 688-1751. Fax: (559) 686-5065. E-mail: info@farmshow.org. Web: www.farmshow.org.

BIRTHDAYS TODAY

Laura Dern, 37, actress (*Blue Velvet*, *Rambling Rose*), born Los Angeles, CA, Feb 10, 1967.
Donovan, 58, singer, songwriter, born Donovan P. Leitch, Glasgow, Scotland, Feb 10, 1946.
Leonard Kyle (Lenny) Dykstra, 41, former baseball player, born Santa Ana, CA, Feb 10, 1963.
Roberta Flack, 65, singer, born Black Mountain, NC, Feb 10, 1939.
Frances Moore Lappe, 60, author (*Diet for a Small Planet*, *Rediscovering America's Values*), born Pendleton, OR, Feb 10, 1944.
Gregory John (Greg) Norman, 49, golfer, born Melbourne, Australia, Feb 10, 1955.
Leontyne Price, 77, opera singer, born Laurel, MS, Feb 10, 1927.
Mark Andrew Spitz, 54, Olympic gold medal swimmer, born Modesto, CA, Feb 10, 1950.
Robert Wagner, 74, actor ("It Takes a Thief," "Hart to Hart"), born Detroit, MI, Feb 10, 1930.

FEBRUARY 11 — WEDNESDAY
Day 42 — 324 Remaining

BE ELECTRIFIC DAY. Feb 11. A day to honor the birth of Thomas Alva Edison and recognize his electrical inventions, including the light bulb. It is also the day to discover our own "body electricity." For information on lectures, demonstrations and packets of information, contact: Carolyn Finch, Electrific Solutions, 51 Cedar Dr, Danbury, CT 06811. Phone: (800) 864-1022 or (203) 792-4833. Fax: (203) 743-5675. E-mail: Carolynf@electrific.com. Web: www.electrific.com.

CAMEROON: YOUTH DAY. Feb 11. Public holiday.

CHILD, LYDIA MARIA: BIRTH ANNIVERSARY. Feb 11, 1802. Born at Medford, MA. As a writer her works included *Hobomok*, about early Salem and Plymouth life, and *The Rebels*, which described pre-Revolutionary Boston. In addition, she produced several practical works including *The Frugal Housewife*, which enjoyed 21 editions, and *The Mother's Book*. In 1833 she and her husband, David Lee Child, published the controversial abolitionist document "An Appeal in Favor of That Class of Americans Called Africans," which called for educating the slaves. Their work for abolition continued with the weekly newspaper *The National Anti-Slavery Standard*, which they published at New York City from 1840–44. Lydia died Oct 20, 1880, at Wayland, MA.

DUNNE, PHILIP: BIRTH ANNIVERSARY. Feb 11, 1908. American screenwriter and director Philip Dunne was born at New York, NY. In 1947 he joined directors John Huston and William Wyler to found the Committee for the First Amendment, which campaigned against the "blacklisting" in Hollywood of anyone suspected of being a communist by the House Un-American Activities Committee. He was also a founder of the Screen Writers Guild. Dunne died June 2, 1992, at Malibu, CA.

EDISON, THOMAS ALVA: BIRTH ANNIVERSARY. Feb 11, 1847. American inventive genius and holder of more than 1,200 patents (including the incandescent electric lamp, phonograph, electric dynamo and key parts of many now-familiar devices such as the movie camera, telephone transmitter, etc). Edison said, "Genius is 1 percent inspiration and 99 percent perspiration." His birthday is now widely observed as Inventor's Day. Born at Milan, OH, and died at Menlo Park, NJ, Oct 18, 1931.

FIRST WOMAN EPISCOPAL BISHOP: 15th ANNIVERSARY. Feb 11, 1989. The presiding bishop of the Episcopal Church, Bishop Edmond L. Browning, consecrated the Reverend Barbara Clementine Harris as a bishop of the Episcopal Church.

FULLER, MELVILLE WESTON: BIRTH ANNIVERSARY. Feb 11, 1833. 8th chief justice of the US Supreme Court. Born at Augusta, ME, he died at Sorrento, ME, July 4, 1910.

IRAN: NATIONAL DAY. Feb 11. National holiday. Commemorates the revolution that overthrew the Shah in 1979.

ISLAND FALLS WINTERFEST. Feb 11–15. Island Falls, ME. Home of the Log Drivers Cookout, and featuring the "World's Largest Coffee Pot." Radar races, snowmobiling fun, dances, fireworks and fishing derby. Est attendance: 1,500. For info: Northern Katahdin Valley Chamber of Commerce. Phone: (207) 463-2077.

JAPAN: NATIONAL FOUNDATION DAY: ANNIVERSARY. Feb 11. Marks the founding of the Japanese nation. In 1872 the government officially set Feb 11, 660 BC, as the date of accession to the throne of the Emperor Jimmu (said to be Japan's first emperor) and designated the day a national holiday by the name of Empire Day. The holiday was abolished after WWII, but was revived as National Foundation Day in 1966. Ceremonies are held with Their Imperial Majesties the Emperor and Empress, the Prime Minister and other dignitaries attending. National holiday.

MANDELA, NELSON: PRISON RELEASE: ANNIVERSARY. Feb 11, 1990. After serving more than 27½ years of a life sentence (convicted, with eight others, of sabotage and conspiracy to overthrow the government), South Africa's Nelson Mandela, 71 years old, walked away from the Victor Verster prison farm at Paarl, South Africa, a free man. He had survived the governmental system of apartheid. Mandela greeted a cheering throng of well-wishers, along with hundreds of millions of television viewers worldwide, with demands for an intensification of the struggle for equality for blacks, who make up nearly 75 percent of South Africa's population.

MANKIEWICZ, JOSEPH L.: BIRTH ANNIVERSARY. Feb 11, 1909. Oscar-winning American film writer, director and producer was born at Wilkes-Barre, PA. He coined the famous W.C. Fields phrase "my little chickadee" in his screenplay for the 1932 film *If I Had a Million*. In 1935 he turned to producing and subsequently made *The Philadelphia Story* and *Woman of the Year*. He began directing in 1946 and his stature grew with such films as *The Late George Apley, The Ghost and Mrs Muir, A Letter to Three Wives, All About Eve, Guys and Dolls, Cleopatra* and *Sleuth*. Mankiewicz won four Academy Awards for directing and screenwriting. He died Feb 5, 1993, at Mount Kisco, NY.

MILWAUKEE BOAT SHOW & WISCONSIN SPORTFISHING EXPO. Feb 11–15. Midwest Airlines Center, Milwaukee, WI. This event brings together buyers and sellers of sail- and powerboats, including fishing boats, pontoons and boating accessories, as well as vacation property and travel destinations. Est attendance: 25,000. For info: Adam Starr, ShowSpan, Inc, 2121 Celebration Dr NE, Grand Rapids, MI 49525. Phone: (616) 447-2860. Fax: (616) 447-2861. E-mail: events@showspan.com. Web: www.showspan.com.

NATIONAL SHUT-IN VISITATION DAY. Feb 11. Visit and entertain shut-ins. For info: Natl Shut-In Visitation Day, 237 Franklin St, Reading, PA 19602. Phone: (610) 373-5579.

SATISFIED STAYING SINGLE DAY. Feb 11. As Valentine's Day approaches, some single folks would like to point out that they're quite content buying candy and flowers for no one but themselves. Live it up. Shadow dance! [©2003 by WH.] For info: Thomas & Ruth Roy, Wellcat Holidays, 2418 Long Ln, Lebanon, PA 17046. Phone: (717) 279-0184. E-mail: info@wellcat.com. Web: www.wellcat.com.

SPACE MILESTONE: *ENDEAVOUR* MAPPING MISSION (US). Feb 11, 2000. This manned flight spent 11 days in space creating a 3-D map of more than 70 percent of the Earth's surface. It will be the most accurate and complete topographic map of Earth ever produced.

SPACE MILESTONE: FIRST SOVIET COMMERCIAL SATELLITE MISSION. Feb 11, 1990. Anatoly Solovyov and

Aleksandr Balandin departed the Baikonur launching site on the Soviet Union's first satellite mission designed for profit—by producing industrial crystals in the weightlessness of space. The craft arrived at the *Mir* orbital space station on Feb 13. Launching of the *Soyuz TM-9* capsule was witnessed by four American astronauts and televised live. The mission was hailed as initiating a new level of openness of information about Soviet space projects.

SPACE MILESTONE: OSUMI (JAPAN). Feb 11, 1970. First Japanese satellite launched. Japan became the fourth nation to send a satellite into space.

VATICAN CITY: 75th INDEPENDENCE ANNIVERSARY. Feb 11, 1929. The Lateran Treaty, signed by Pietro Cardinal Gasparri and Benito Mussolini, guaranteed the independence of the State of Vatican City and recognized the sovereignty of the Holy See over it. Area is about 109 acres.

WHITE SHIRT DAY: ANNIVERSARY. Feb 11, 1937. Anniversary of UAW-GM agreement following 44-day sit-down strike at General Motors' Flint, MI, factories. Blue-collar workers traditionally wear white shirts to work on this day, symbolic of workingman's dignity won. Has been observed by proclamation at Flint, MI.

YALTA AGREEMENT SIGNED: ANNIVERSARY. Feb 11, 1945. President Franklin D. Roosevelt, British Prime Minister Winston Churchill and Soviet leader Joseph Stalin signed an agreement at Yalta, a Soviet city on the Black Sea in the Crimea. The agreement contained plans for new blows at the heart of Germany and for occupying Germany at the end of the war. It also called for a meeting in San Francisco to draft a charter for the United Nations.

BIRTHDAYS TODAY

Jennifer Aniston, 35, actress ("Friends," *Picture Perfect*), born Sherman Oaks, CA, Feb 11, 1969.
Paul Bocuse, 78, chef, born Collonges-au-Mont-d'Or, France, Feb 11, 1926.
Brandy (Norwood), 25, singer, actress ("Cinderella," "Moesha"), born Macomb, MS, Feb 11, 1979.
Jeb Bush, 51, Governor of Florida (R), born Midland, TX, Feb 11, 1953.
Sheryl Crow, 42, singer, musician, born Kennett, MO, Feb 11, 1962.
Virginia Johnson, 79, psychologist, born Springfield, MO, Feb 11, 1925.
Mike Leavitt, 53, Governor of Utah (R), born Cedar City, UT, Feb 11, 1951.
Tina Louise, 70, actress ("Gilligan's Island," *The Stepford Wives*), born New York, NY, Feb 11, 1934.
Carey Lowell, 43, actress ("Law & Order"), born New York, NY, Feb 11, 1961.
Sergio Mendes, 63, musician, bandleader, born Niteroi, Brazil, Feb 11, 1941.
Leslie Nielsen, 82, actor (*Naked Gun* films, *Airplane!*, "Peyton Place"), born Regina, SK, Canada, Feb 11, 1922.
Burt Reynolds, 68, actor (*Hooper, Deliverance, Cannonball Run*, "Evening Shade"), born Waycross, GA, Feb 11, 1936.
Sidney Sheldon, 87, author (*Bloodline, The Doomsday Conspiracy*), born Chicago, IL, Feb 11, 1917.

FEBRUARY 12 — THURSDAY
Day 43 — 323 Remaining

ADAMS, LOUISA CATHERINE JOHNSON: BIRTH ANNIVERSARY. Feb 12, 1775. Wife of John Quincy Adams, 6th president of the US. Born at London, England. Died at Washington, DC, May 14, 1852.

CANADA: CALGARY BOAT AND SPORTSMEN'S SHOW. Feb 12–15. Roundup Centre, Stampede Park, Calgary, AB. Sail-, power- and fishing boats; hunting, fishing and camping supplies; resort destinations and outdoor recreation; four-wheel-drive vehicles; family entertainment. Est attendance: 25,000. For info: Canadian Natl Sportsmen's Shows, 703 Evans Ave, Ste 202, Toronto, ON, Canada M9C 5E9. Phone: (416) 695-0311. Fax: (416) 695-0381. Web: www.sportsmenshows.com.

DARWIN, CHARLES ROBERT: BIRTH ANNIVERSARY. Feb 12, 1809. Author and naturalist, born at Shrewsbury, England. Best remembered for his books *On the Origin of Species by Means of Natural Selection, or the Preservation of Favoured Races in the Struggle for Life* and *The Descent of Man and Selection in Relation to Sex*. Died at Down, Kent, England, Apr 19, 1882.

DARWIN DAY. Feb 12. Darwin Day is an international celebration of science and humanity. Events are coordinated around the world to commemorate the life and work of Charles Darwin and the theory of evolution by natural selection, and to recognize the contributions and achievements of science and reason. On a broad scale, the program is an effort to advance science literacy, champion the efforts to humanize science and celebrate the adventurous spirit. Events are held on the anniversary of Darwin's birth. For info: Darwin's Bulldogs, PO Box 92762, Albuquerque, NM 87199. E-mail: a.human@mindspring.com. Web: www.darwinday.org.

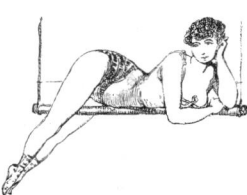

ENGLAND: CHESTER ANTIQUES AND FINE ART SHOW. Feb 12–15 (also Oct 21–24). Chester Racecourse, Cheshire. Sixty stands on three floors where all items have been vetted for authenticity and age. Est attendance: 3,500. For info: Penman Fairs, PO Box 114, Haywards Heath, Sussex, England RH16 2YU. Phone: (44) (870) 350-2442. Fax: (44) (870) 350-2443. E-mail: info@penman-fairs.co.uk.

GATORADE 125-MILE QUALIFYING RACES FOR THE DAYTONA 500. Feb 12. Daytona International Speedway, Daytona Beach, FL. 46th annual running. Drivers battle to set the Daytona 500 field. For info: Daytona Intl Speedway, PO Box 2801, Daytona Beach, FL 32120-2801. Phone: (386) 253-7223. Fax: (386) 947-6791. Web: www.daytonainternationalspeedway.com.

HARRIS, ROY: BIRTH ANNIVERSARY. Feb 12, 1898. Born at Chandler, OK, Harris was one of the most important composers of this century. He was known for his use of Anglo-American folk tunes. He composed more than 200 works, including 13 symphonies, several ballet scores and much chamber and choral music. His best-known work is his *Third Symphony* (1939). He died at Santa Monica, CA, Oct 1, 1979.

LEWIS, JOHN LLEWELLYN: BIRTH ANNIVERSARY. Feb 12, 1889. American labor leader born near Lucas, IA. His parents came to the US from Welsh mining towns, and Lewis left school in the seventh grade to become a miner himself. Became leader of United Mine Workers of America and champion of all miners' causes. Died at Washington, DC, June 11, 1969.

LINCOLN, ABRAHAM: BIRTH ANNIVERSARY. Feb 12, 1809. 16th president of the US (Mar 4, 1861–Apr 15, 1865) and the first to be assassinated (on Good Friday, Apr 14, 1865, at Ford's Theatre at Washington, DC). His presidency encompassed the tragic Civil War. Especially remembered are his Emancipation Proclamation (Jan 1, 1863), his Gettysburg Address (Nov 19, 1863) and his proclamation establishing the last Thursday of November as Thanksgiving Day. Born at Hardin County, KY, he died at Washington, DC, Apr 15, 1865. Lincoln's birthday is observed as part of Presidents' Day in most states, but is a legal holiday in Illinois and an optional bank holiday in Iowa, Maryland, Michigan, Pennsylvania, Washington and West Virginia. See also: "Presidents' Day" (Feb 16).

Feb 12 ☆ Chase's 2004 Calendar of Events ☆

LINCOLN'S BIRTHPLACE CABIN WREATH LAYING. Feb 12. Abraham Lincoln's Birthplace National Historic Site, Hodgenville, KY. A wreath is placed at the door of the symbolic "Birthplace Cabin" in commemoration of the birth of Abraham Lincoln. Refreshments are also served to park visitors. Est attendance: 75. For info: Patsy Cobb, 2995 Lincoln Farm Rd, Hodgenville, KY 42748. Phone: (502) 358-3137.

LOST PENNY DAY. Feb 12. Today is set aside to put all of those pennies stashed in candy dishes, coffee cans, bowls and jars back into circulation. Take those pennies and give them to a shelter or agency that assists the homeless or your local Humane Society. Annually, on President Abraham Lincoln's birthday, the man depicted on the copper penny. [©1995] To alleviate the escalating costs of Eventological® Literature, a charge of $7 must be assessed to each request. Checks are to be made payable to: Adrienne Sioux Koopersmith, 1437 W Rosemont, #1W, Chicago, IL 60660-1319. Phone: (773) 743-5341. Fax: (773) 743-5395. E-mail: la_koop@yahoo.com.

MIAMI INTERNATIONAL BOAT SHOW AND STRICTLY SAIL®. Feb 12–17. Miami Beach Convention Center, Miami Beach, FL. 63rd annual boat show, the biggest in the US and considered the main event for product introductions. With more than 3,000 boats, this show offers an unparalleled opportunity to view the sport's latest products. Est attendance: 175,000. For info: NMMA, 200 E Randolph St, Ste 5100, Chicago, IL 60601. Phone: (312) 946-6200. Fax: (312) 946-0388. Web: www.discoverboating.com.

MYANMAR: UNION DAY. Feb 12. National holiday. Commemorates the founding of the Union of Burma, Feb 12, 1947. The country changed its name to Union of Myanmar in 1989.

NAACP FOUNDED: 95th ANNIVERSARY. Feb 12, 1909. The National Association for the Advancement of Colored People was founded by W.E.B. Dubois and Ida Wells-Barnett, among others, to wage a militant campaign against lynching and other forms of racial oppression. Its legal wing brought many lawsuits that successfully challenged segregation in the 1950s and '60s.

NEW MEXICO: EXTRATERRESTRIAL CULTURE DAY. Feb 12. New Mexico. A day "to celebrate and honor all past, present and future extraterrestrial visitors in ways to enhance relationships among all citizens of the cosmos, known and unknown." Passed as a memorial (not law) by the New Mexico state legislature in acknowledgment that ever since the Roswell UFO incident of 1947, New Mexico is recognized worldwide as a nexus of sightings and unexplained mysteries. Annually, the second Thursday of February.

OGLETHORPE DAY. Feb 12. General James Edward Oglethorpe (born at London, England, Dec 22, 1696), with some 100 other Englishmen, landed at what is now Savannah, GA, on Feb 12, 1733. Naming the new colony Georgia for England's King George II, Oglethorpe was organizer and first governor of the colony and founder of the city of Savannah. Oglethorpe Day and Georgia Day observed on this date.

PAVLOVA, ANNA: BIRTH ANNIVERSARY. Feb 12, 1881. Russian ballerina Anna Pavlova, thought by some to have been the greatest dancer of all time, was born at St. Petersburg, Russia. After performing with great success with the Ballet Russe and other companies, she formed her own company in 1910 and performed on tour for enthusiastic audiences in nearly every country in the world. Pavlova died at The Hague, Netherlands, Jan 23, 1931.

SAFETYPUP'S® BIRTHDAY. Feb 12. This year Safetypup®, created by the National Child Safety Council, joyously celebrates his birthday by bringing safety awareness/education messages to children and their parents in a positive, nonthreatening manner. Age-appropriate materials available through local law enforcement departments on topics including bike safety, drug abuse prevention, child abduction prevention, farm safety, and more. For info: Barbara Handley Huggett, Dir, NCSC, R & D, Box 1368, Jackson, MI 49204-1368. Phone: (517) 764-6070. E-mail: bhuggett@nfed.org.

SEMINOLE TRIBE FESTIVAL, POWWOW AND PRCA RODEO. Feb 12–15. Hollywood Reservation, Hollywood, FL. The Seminole Tribe of Florida hosts dancers representative of more than 100 tribes from across North America. Featured events include Seminole art show, all-Indian rodeo and seldom seen deep-water alligator wrestling. Annually, the second weekend in February. Est attendance: 30,000. For info: Buster Baxley, Seminole Tribe of Florida, 5845 S State Rd 7, Fort Lauderdale, FL 33314. Phone: (954) 583-3404. Fax: (954) 583-3951. E-mail: bbaxley@semtribe.com. Web: www.seminoletribe.com.

SENATE ACQUITS CLINTON: 5th ANNIVERSARY. Feb 12, 1999. After President Bill Clinton was impeached by the US House of Representatives, the Senate began a January trial on the charges of perjury and obstruction of justice. On this date, the Senate acquitted Clinton. See also: "Clinton Impeachment Proceedings: Anniversary" (Dec 20).

UTAH WOMEN GIVEN THE VOTE: ANNIVERSARY. Feb 12, 1870. The women in the Utah Territory were granted the right to vote in political elections—50 years before the 19th Amendment was ratified.

BIRTHDAYS TODAY

Maud Adams, 59, actress (*Killer Force, Octopussy*), born Lulea, Sweden, Feb 12, 1945.

Joe Don Baker, 68, actor (*Charlie Varrick, Cool Hand Luke*), born Groesbeck, TX, Feb 12, 1936.

Ehud Barak, 62, former Israeli prime minister, born Mishmar, Hasharon, Israel, Feb 12, 1942.

Judy Blume, 66, author (*Blubber, Superfudge*), born Elizabeth, NJ, Feb 12, 1938.

Josh Brolin, 36, actor (*The Mod Squad, Best Laid Plans*), born Los Angeles, CA, Feb 12, 1968.

Cliff De Young, 57, actor (*Blue Collar, F/X*), born Inglewood, CA, Feb 12, 1947.

Joseph Henry (Joe) Garagiola, 78, sportscaster, former baseball player, born St. Louis, MO, Feb 12, 1926.

Arsenio Hall, 49, comedian, actor (*Coming to America*), former TV talk-show host, born Cleveland, OH, Feb 12, 1955.

Joanna Kerns, 51, actress ("Growing Pains"), former national-caliber gymnast, born San Francisco, CA, Feb 12, 1953.

Simon MacCorkindale, 52, actor, producer, screenwriter ("Falcon Crest," *Death on the Nile, Jaws 3-D*), born Isle-of-Ely, England, Feb 12, 1952.

Chynna Phillips, 36, singer (Wilson Phillips), born Los Angeles, CA, Feb 12, 1968.

Christina Ricci, 24, actress (*Sleepy Hollow, Ice Storm*), born Santa Monica, CA, Feb 12, 1980.

William Felton (Bill) Russell, 70, Hall of Fame baseball player and former coach, born Monroe, LA, Feb 12, 1934.

Arlen Specter, 74, US Senator (R, Pennsylvania), born Wichita, KS, Feb 12, 1930.

Franco Zeffirelli, 81, film director (*Otello, Romeo and Juliet*), born Florence, Italy, Feb 12, 1923.

February 2004	S	M	T	W	T	F	S
	1	2	3	4	5	6	7
	8	9	10	11	12	13	14
	15	16	17	18	19	20	21
	22	23	24	25	26	27	28
	29						

★ Chase's 2004 Calendar of Events ★   Feb 13

FEBRUARY 13 — FRIDAY
Day 44 — 322 Remaining

AMERICAN ASSOCIATION FOR THE ADVANCEMENT OF SCIENCE ANNUAL MEETING. Feb 13–18. Denver, CO. 169th annual meeting and science innovation exposition. Est attendance: 5,000. For info: AAAS, 1200 New York Ave NW, Washington, DC 20005. Phone: (202) 326-6450. Fax: (202) 289-4021. Web: www.aaas.org/meetings.

BLACK LOVE DAY. Feb 13. A national, commemorative holiday of observance, celebration, reconciliation and demonstration of love within and for the black community, conceived by Ayo-Handy Kendi in 1993. On this day blacks should perform five specific acts of love—toward the Creator, toward oneself, within the family, in the community and for the race—and whites are encouraged to demonstrate love through acts of service and self-inventory of their attitudes and behavior toward blacks. Annually, Feb 13. For info: African American Holiday Assn, 1305 Emerson St NW, Washington, DC 20011. E-mail: aaha@aaha-info.org. Web: aaha-info.org.

BLAME SOMEONE ELSE DAY. Feb 13. To share the responsibility and the guilt for the mess we're in. Blame someone else! Annually, the first Friday the 13th of the year. For info: A.C. Moeller, Box 71, Clio, MI 48420-1042.

"BRAVEHEART" SCOTTISH WEEKEND. Feb 13–15. Moultrie, GA. Honoring all Scottish organizations that have declared the Odom Library "home." A gathering of Scots and Scottish Americans from all around the country and abroad. Includes seminars, talks, banquet and Ceilidh with top Scottish entertainers. Sponsored by the Odom Library, an archival and genealogical home to 115+ Scottish clans and groups, and *The Family Tree*, the largest Scottish publication in the US and also the largest genealogical publication in the US. For info: Beth Gay, PO Box 2828, Moultrie, GA 31776-2828. Phone: (229) 985-6540.

CHURCHILL, RANDOLPH HENRY SPENCER: BIRTH ANNIVERSARY. Feb 13, 1849. English politician and the father of Winston Churchill. Born at Blenheim, Woodstock, Oxfordshire, England, he died at London, Jan 24, 1895.

CSICOP ANNUAL SUPERSTITION BASH. Feb 13. Amherst, NY. The Committee for Scientific Investigation of Claims of the Paranormal (CSICOP) and *Skeptical Inquirer* magazine hold an annual Superstition Bash on the first Friday the 13th of each year. Skeptic and science groups across the world also participate by holding their own events. The celebration works to educate people about the dangers and absurdities of superstitious belief and to champion skepticism and critical inquiry. For info: CSICOP/Skeptical Inquirer, PO Box 703, Amherst, NY 14226. E-mail: skeptinq@aol.com. Web: www.csicop.org/superstition.

DRESDEN FIREBOMBING: ANNIVERSARY. Feb 13, 1945. Dresden, Germany. Allied firebombing caused a firestorm that destroyed the city and killed 135,000 people.

FIRST MAGAZINE PUBLISHED IN AMERICA: ANNIVERSARY. Feb 13, 1741 (OS). Andrew Bradford published *The American Magazine* just three days ahead of Benjamin Franklin's *General Magazine*.

FLORIDA DODGE DEALERS 250 NASCAR CRAFTSMAN TRUCK SERIES RACE. Feb 13. Daytona International Speedway, Daytona, FL. NASCAR trucks on the Superspeedway. 5th annual. For info: Daytona International Speedway, PO Box 2801, Daytona Beach, FL 32120-2801. Phone: (386) 253-7223. Fax: (386) 947-6791. Web: www.daytonainternationalspeedway.com.

FRANCE: NICE CARNIVAL. Feb 13–24. Dates from the 14th century and is celebrated each year during the 12 days ending with Shrove Tuesday. Derived from ancient rites of spring, the carnival offers parades, floats, battles of flowers and confetti, a fireworks display lighting up the entire Baie des Anges. King Carnival is burned on his pyre at the end of the event.

FRIDAY THE THIRTEENTH. Feb 13. Variously believed to be a lucky or an unlucky day. Every year has at least one Friday the 13th, but never more than three. Two Fridays fall on the 13th in 2004: in February and August. Fear of the number 13 is known as triskaidekaphobia.

GET A DIFFERENT NAME DAY. Feb 13. For the pity of the millions of us who hate our birth names. On this day we may change our names to whatever we wish and have the right to expect colleagues, family and friends to so address us. [©2003 by WH.] For info: Thomas & Ruth Roy, Wellcat Holidays, 2418 Long Ln, Lebanon, PA 17046. Phone: (717) 279-0184. E-mail: info@wellcat.com. Web: www.wellcat.com.

GOLD RUSH DAYS. Feb 13–15. Wickenburg, AZ. 56th annual communitywide celebration of the Old West: rodeo, parade, carnival, gold panning. Named one of the top 100 events in North America by the American Bus Association. Annually, the second full weekend in February. Est attendance: 45,000. For info: Chamber of Commerce, 216 N Frontier St, Wickenburg, AZ 85390. Phone: (928) 684-5479 or (928) 684-0977. Fax: (928) 684-5470. E-mail: info@wickenburgchamber.com. Web: www.wickenburgchamber.com.

GREAT BACKYARD BIRD COUNT. Feb 13–16. Thousands of volunteers nationwide track the number and types of birds that live near their homes. Results help researchers monitor species in trouble. Cosponsored by the National Audubon Society and the Cornell University Lab of Ornithology. For info: National Audubon Society, 700 Broadway, New York, NY 10003. Phone: (212) 979-3000. Web: www.birdsource.org/gbbc.

INTERNATIONAL RACE OF CHAMPIONS XXVIII. Feb 13. Daytona International Speedway, Daytona Beach, FL. Best drivers from top stock and open wheel series. For info: Daytona Intl Speedway, PO Box 2801, Daytona Beach, FL 32120-2801. Phone: (386) 253-7223. Fax: (386) 947-6791. Web: www.daytonainternationalspeedway.com.

INTERNATIONAL SKEPTICS' DAY. Feb 13 (also Aug 13). International celebration of the fine art of skepticism. Today, examine those issues which you are most skeptical about. A day to collectively put these issues under a microscope and cut away those attachments that stand in your way of gaining greater success, freedom and independence. Annually, on Friday the 13th. [©1996.] Because of the escalating costs of Eventological® Literature, a charge of $7 must be assessed for each request. Checks are to be made payable to: Adrienne Sioux Koopersmith, 1437 W Rosemont, #1W, Chicago, IL 60660-1319. Phone: (773) 743-5341. Fax: (773) 743-5395. E-mail: la_koop@yahoo.com.

IRWIN WINS FIRST MEDAL OF HONOR: ANNIVERSARY. Feb 13, 1861. Colonel Bernard Irwin distinguished himself while leading troops in a battle with Chiricahua Apache Indians at Apache Pass, AZ (at the time part of the territory of New Mexico). For those actions Irwin later became the first person awarded the new US Medal of Honor, although he didn't actually receive it until three years later (Jan 24, 1864).

LONGHORN WORLD CHAMPIONSHIP RODEO. Feb 13–15. The Palace of Auburn Hills, Auburn Hills, MI. 40th annual. More than 250 cowboys and cowgirls compete in six professional contests ranging from bronc riding to big, bad BONUS bull riding! Free beginners horsemanship clinic 40 minutes before performances. Qualifying rodeo for Longhorn's Championship Finals Rodeo in Nashville, TN. Featuring colorful opening ceremonies. Est attendance: 32,000. For info: W. Bruce Lehrke, Pres, Longhorn World Chmpshp Rodeo, Inc, PO Box 70159, Nashville, TN 37207. Phone: (615) 876-1016. Fax: (615) 876-4685. E-mail: info@longhornrodeo.com. Web: www.longhornrodeo.com.

MOON PHASE: LAST QUARTER. Feb 13. Moon enters Last Quarter phase at 8:39 AM, EST.

NATIONAL DATE FESTIVAL. Feb 13–22. Indio, CA. America's most exotic county fair features Arabian Nights theme, camel and ostrich races, satellite horse wagering, nightly musical pageant, date exhibits and sampling, thousands of competitive exhib-

Feb 13–14 ☆ *Chase's 2004 Calendar of Events* ☆

its and carnival. Est attendance: 300,000. For info: Riverside County Fair/Natl Date Fest, 46-350 Arabia St, Indio, CA 92201-9990. Phone: (760) 863-8247 or (800) 811-FAIR. Web: www.datefest.org.

NBA ALL-STAR WEEKEND. Feb 13–15. Los Angeles, CA. For info: Brian McIntyre, Sr VP, Basketball Communications, Natl Basketball Assn, Olympic Tower, 645 Fifth Ave, New York, NY 10022. Phone: (212) 407-8000. Web: www.nba.com.

NC RV AND CAMPING SHOW. Feb 13–15. NC State Fairgrounds, Raleigh, NC. A display of the latest in recreational vehicles and accessories by various dealers. Est attendance: 12,000. For info: Apple Rock Advertising & Promotions, 1200 Eastchester Dr, High Point, NC 27265. Phone: (336) 881-7100. Fax: (336) 883-7198. E-mail: rvshows@applerock.com. Web: www.applerock.com.

NEWPORT WINTER FESTIVAL. Feb 13–22. Newport, RI. More than 160 individual events from food, music and entertainment to skating, hayrides, snow sculptures, ice carving, scavenger hunt and even winter polo demonstrations—fun for all ages. Est attendance: 25,000. For info: Mktg & Events, Inc, 28 Pelham St, Newport, RI 02840. Phone: (401) 847-7666. Web: www.newportevents.com.

NRA/NWRA RODEO FINALS. Feb 13–15. MetraPark Arena, Billings, MT. Rodeo action at its best—29th annual finals. A fun-filled rodeo weekend in cowboy country! Est attendance: 16,000. For info: Northern Rodeo Assn, PO Box 1122, Billings, MT 59103. Phone: (406) 252-1122. Fax: (406) 252-0300.

PIAZZETTA, GIOVANNI BATTISTA: BIRTH ANNIVERSARY. Feb 13, 1682. Prominent 18th-century Venetian painter. Notable among his works are the *Ecstasy of St. Francis* and *Fortune Teller*. Born at Venice, Italy, and died there Apr 28, 1754.

SOUTH COAST WRITER'S CONFERENCE. Feb 13–14. Event Center on the Beach and Gold Beach High School, Gold Beach, OR. Keynote speaker followed by a series of workshops and roundtable discussions concerning writing techniques, publishing guidelines and editorial commentary. Fireman's Fish Fry will take place on Feb 14. Est attendance: 350. For info: Southwestern Oregon Community College, PO Box 590, Gold Beach, OR 97444. Phone: (541) 247-2741. Fax: (541) 247-6247. E-mail: scwc@socc.edu.

SOUTHEASTERN WILDLIFE EXPOSITION. Feb 13–15. Charleston, SC. Spectacular wildlife and nature art exposition showcasing original paintings, prints, sculpture, photography, carvings, collectibles and crafts. Eleven exhibition sites throughout historic Charleston. Est attendance: 43,000. For info: Southeastern Wildlife Exposition, 211 Meeting St, Charleston, SC 29401. Phone: (843) 723-1748. E-mail: sewe@sewe.com.

STAMP EXPO/USA. Feb 13–15. Radisson Hotel, Anaheim, CA. Annual expo. Est attendance: 5,000. For info: Intl Stamp Collectors Soc, PO Box 854, Van Nuys, CA 91408. Phone: (818) 997-6496. Fax: (818) 988-4337. E-mail: iibick@aol.com. Web: www.bick.net.

TRUMAN, BESS (ELIZABETH) VIRGINIA WALLACE: BIRTH ANNIVERSARY. Feb 13, 1885. Wife of Harry S Truman, 33rd president of the US. Born at Independence, MO, and died there Oct 18, 1982.

WHISKEY FLAT DAYS. Feb 13–16. Kernville, CA. Whiskey Flat Days commemorates the old Kernville that was called Whiskey Flat until 1860. We turn back the clock as the parade, stores and residents go back to the 1860s. Frog races, craft booths, rodeo, parade, games for small children, carnival, street dances, puppet shows, costume and whiskerino contests, melodrama and much more. Est attendance: 25,000. For info: Kernville Chamber of Commerce, PO Box 397, Kernville, CA 93238. Phone: (760) 376-2629 or toll-free (866) KERNVILLE. Fax: (760) 376-4371. E-mail: kernvillechamber@lightspeed.net. Web: www.kernvillechamber.org.

WOOD, GRANT: BIRTH ANNIVERSARY. Feb 13, 1892. American artist, especially noted for his powerful realism and satirical paintings of the American scene, was born near Anamosa, IA. He was a printer, sculptor, woodworker and high school and college teacher. Among his best-remembered works are *American Gothic, Fall Plowing* and *Stone City*. Died at Iowa City, IA, Feb 12, 1942.

BIRTHDAYS TODAY

Stockard Channing, 60, actress (*Six Degrees of Separation, The House of Blue Leaves*, "The West Wing"), born Susan Stockard, New York, NY, Feb 13, 1944.
Peter Gabriel, 54, singer, songwriter, born London, England, Feb 13, 1950.
Kelly Hu, 37, actress ("Martial Law," "Nash Bridges"), born Honolulu, HI, Feb 13, 1967.
Carol Lynley, 62, actress (*Harlow, Bunny Lake Is Missing*), born New York, NY, Feb 13, 1942.
Randy Moss, 27, football player, born Rand, WV, Feb 13, 1977.
David Naughton, 53, singer, actor (*An American Werewolf in London, Overexposed*), born Hartford, CT, Feb 13, 1951.
Kim Novak, 71, actress (*Bell, Book and Candle, Vertigo*), born Marilyn Novak, Chicago, IL, Feb 13, 1933.
Eddie Robinson, 85, former college football coach, born Jackson, LA, Feb 13, 1919.
George Segal, 70, actor (*A Touch of Class*, "Just Shoot Me"), born Great Neck, NY, Feb 13, 1934.
Jerry Springer, 60, TV host ("The Jerry Springer Show"), born London, England, Feb 13, 1944.
Bo Svenson, 63, actor (*North Dallas Forty, Heartbreak Ridge*), born Goteborg, Sweden, Feb 13, 1941.
Peter Tork, 60, actor, singer (The Monkees), born Peter Thorkelson, Washington, DC, Feb 13, 1944 (some sources say 1942).
Chuck Yeager, 81, pilot who broke sound barrier, born Myra, WV, Feb 13, 1923.

FEBRUARY 14 — SATURDAY
Day 45 — 321 Remaining

AMERICAN BOWLING CONGRESS CHAMPIONSHIPS TOURNAMENT. Feb 14–June 6. Reno, NV. 101st tournament. The largest participatory sporting event in the world features more than 75,000 bowlers from around the US and the world. Bowlers compete for titles in singles, doubles, five-player team and all-events categories in arena setting. Lanes are specially built for the tournament in convention centers around the US each year. Every three years the tournament is held in Reno's National Bowling Stadium. Opening ceremonies include celebrities, traditional "Joe Bowler" selection and recognition of dignitaries. Est attendance: 100,000. For info: American Bowling Congress, 5301 S 76th St, Greendale, WI 53129-0500. Phone: (414) 423-3227. Fax: (414) 421-1194. Web: www.abctournament.com.

ARIZONA: ADMISSION DAY. Feb 14. Became 48th state in 1912.

	S	M	T	W	T	F	S
February 2004	1	2	3	4	5	6	7
	8	9	10	11	12	13	14
	15	16	17	18	19	20	21
	22	23	24	25	26	27	28
	29						

☆ Chase's 2004 Calendar of Events ☆   Feb 14

BENNY, JACK: BIRTH ANNIVERSARY. Feb 14, 1894. American comedian. Born Benjamin Kubelsky, Jack Benny entered vaudeville at Waukegan, IL, at age 17, using the violin as a comic stage prop. His radio show first aired in 1932 and continued for 20 years with little change in format. He also had a long-running television show. One of his most well-known comic gimmicks was his purported stinginess. Benny was born at Chicago, IL, and died Dec 26, 1974, at Beverly Hills, CA.

BLACKPOWDER HISTORICAL FAIR. Feb 14–15. Northbridge Mall, Albert Lea, MN. Reenactors and craftsmen from seven states dress in full costume and sell their colonial period items. Entertainment, kettle korn, food and drink, workshops and demonstrations. Est attendance: 3,000. For info: Big Island Rendezvous Inc, 143 W Clark St, Albert Lea, MN 56007. Phone: (800) 658-2526. Fax: (507) 373-0344. E-mail: bigisland@albertalea.org.

BULGARIA: VITICULTURISTS' DAY (TRIFON ZAREZAN). Feb 14. Celebrated since Thracian times. Festivities are based on cult of Dionysus, god of merriment and wine.

CANADA: BANCROFT FROSTY FROLICS. Feb 14–22. "Old Station" and Legion Hall, Bancroft, ON. Events throughout the week include skating, snowmobiling and various community events. The main attraction is the Bancroft Sled Dog Races, a two-day mid-distance race on Feb 21–22 that brings mushers from all over Ontario and the northeastern US. Sprint races, craft show and horse-drawn sleigh rides also round out the final weekend. For info: Bancroft & District Chamber of Commerce, Box 539, 8 Hastings Heritage Way, Unit #1, Bancroft, ON, K0L 1C0, Canada. Phone: (613) 332-1513. Fax: (613) 332-2119. E-mail: chamber@commerce.bancroft.on.ca. Web: www.BancroftDistrict.com.

CANADA: YUKON QUEST INTERNATIONAL 1,000-MILE SLED DOG RACE. Feb 14–28. Fairbanks, AK and Whitehorse, YT. The 21st annual running of the "Toughest Sled Dog Race in the World." Two weeks and 1,000 miles through true northern wilderness in the depths of Arctic winter, from Fairbanks, AK, USA, to Whitehorse, Yukon Territories, Canada. Top mushers from North America and around the world compete for the $125,000 purse. Est attendance: 10,000. For info: Yukon Quest Intl Canada, 1109 First Ave #2, Whitehorse, Yukon Y1A 5G4, Canada. Phone: (867) 668-4711. Fax: (867) 668-6674. E-mail: yukonquest@polarcom.com. Web: www.yukonquest.yk.ca.

CONGENITAL HEART DEFECT AWARENESS DAY. Feb 14. Public relations/media campaign, special events in cities throughout the United States. For info: Mona Barmash, Congenital Heart Information Network, 1561 Clark Dr, Yardley, PA 19067. Phone: (215) 493-3068. E-mail: mb@tchin.org. Web: www.tchin.org.

ENIAC COMPUTER INTRODUCED: ANNIVERSARY. Feb 14, 1946. J. Presper Eckert and John W. Mauchly demonstrated the Electronic Numerical Integrator and Computer (ENIAC) for the first time at the University of Pennsylvania. This was the first electronic digital computer. It occupied a room the size of a gymnasium and contained nearly 18,000 vacuum tubes. The army commissioned the computer to speed the calculation of firing tables for artillery. By the time the computer was ready, World War II was over. However, ENIAC prepared the way for future generations of computers.

FARM TOY SHOW AND AUCTION. Feb 14. Sauk Centre, MN. More than 30 vendors display farm toy equipment from 9 AM to 4:30 PM, with a consignment auction starting at 5:30 PM. Est attendance: 800. For info: Sauk Centre Chamber of Commerce, PO Box 222, Sauk Centre, MN 56378. Phone: (320) 352-5201. Fax: (320) 352-5202. Web: www.saukcentrechamber.com.

FERRIS WHEEL DAY. Feb 14, 1859. Anniversary of the birth of George Washington Gale Ferris, American engineer and inventor, at Galesburg, IL. Among his many accomplishments as a civil engineer, Ferris is best remembered as the inventor of the Ferris wheel, which he developed for the World's Columbian Exposition at Chicago, IL, in 1893. Built on the Midway Plaisance, the 250-feet-in-diameter Ferris wheel (with 36 coaches, each capable of carrying 40 passengers), proved one of the greatest attractions of the fair. It was America's answer to the Eiffel Tower of the Paris International Exposition of 1889. Ferris died at Pittsburgh, PA, Nov 22, 1896.

FIRST PRESIDENTIAL PHOTOGRAPH: ANNIVERSARY. Feb 14, 1849. President James Polk became the first US president to be photographed while in office. The photographer was Mathew B. Brady, who would become famous for his photography during the American Civil War.

HANCOCK, WINFIELD SCOTT: BIRTH ANNIVERSARY. Feb 14, 1824. Born at Montgomery, PA, died Feb 9, 1886, at Governor's Island, NY. After serving as Union general in the Civil War, his command of the military division of Texas and Louisiana won him much favor from the Democratic Party because he allowed local civil authorities to retain their power. He pleased the Democrats so well they made him their presidential candidate in 1880. He lost to James A. Garfield by a narrow margin.

KLONDIKE DAYS. Feb 14–15. Eagle River Derby Track, Eagle River, WI. A re-creation of primitive camps used by early buckskinners, pioneers, trappers and traders, complete with tomahawk throwing and black powder musket shoot. Additional attractions include a two-day horse weight-pull reminiscent of Wisconsin's logging days, a chain saw carving competition, a Native American cultural presentation including a ceremonial dance exhibition, lumberjack competition, craft show, dog weight-pull, snow-sculpting competition, northwoods wildlife art and Amish craft show and sale and much more. Wisconsin's premiere multifaceted winter festival. Est attendance: 12,000. For info: Eagle River Chamber of Commerce, PO Box 1917, Eagle River, WI 54521. Phone: (800) 359-6315. Web: www.eagleriver.org.

KOOLERZ 300 NASCAR BUSCH SERIES RACE. Feb 14. Daytona International Speedway, Daytona Beach, FL. 46th annual race. Busch Series' richest and most competitive event. For info: Daytona Intl Speedway, PO Box 2801, Daytona Beach, FL 32120-2801. Phone: (386) 253-7223. Fax: (386) 947-6791. Web: www.daytonainternationalspeedway.com.

LEAGUE OF WOMEN VOTERS FORMED: ANNIVERSARY. Feb 14, 1920. While meeting in Chicago to celebrate the imminent ratification of the 19th Amendment to the Constitution, leaders of the National American Woman Suffrage Association (NAWSA) approved the formation of a new organization—the League of Women Voters. With the vote for women just a few months away, the new organization was created to help American women exercise their new political rights and responsibilities. For info: League of Women Voters of Illinois, 332 S Michigan Ave, Ste 1142, Chicago, IL 60604. Phone: (312) 939-5935. Web: www.lwv.org.

NATIONAL CONDOM WEEK. Feb 14–21. To educate consumers, patients, students and professionals on the prevention of sexually transmitted diseases, AIDS and teenage pregnancies. For info: Frederick S. Mayer, Pres, Pharmacists Planning Service, Inc, 101 Lucas Valley Rd, #210, San Rafael, CA 94903. Phone: (415) 479-8628. Fax: (415) 479-8608. E-mail: ppsi@aol.com. Web: www.ppsinc.org.

NATIONAL HAVE-A-HEART DAY. Feb 14. The goal of this celebration of life is to create a new consciousness concerning the impact of our food choices on the environment, world hunger, animal welfare and human health—especially heart health. A vegetarian lifestyle increases longevity and helps prevent—and even reverse—heart disease. Vegetarians live about 15 years longer than nonvegetarians and they suffer less than one-tenth the heart disease death rate of nonvegetarians. For info: Vegetarian Awareness Network, Communications Center, PO Box 321, Knoxville, TN 37901-0321. Phone: (800) USA-VEGE.

OCEAN COUNTY WILDFOWL ART AND DECOY SHOW. Feb 14–15. Brick High School, Brick, NJ. 140 artists and carvers, decoy-carving competitions, decorative and gunning decoys, junior competition; free seminars on decoy carving, decoy

133

painting and flat art painting; etc. Est attendance: 4,000. For info: Janet Sellitto, Show Coord, Ocean County YMCA, 1088 Whitty Rd, Toms River, NJ 08755. Phone: (732) 341-9622. Fax: (732) 341-1629. E-mail: jsellitto@ocymca.org. Web: www.ocymca.org.

OREGON: ADMISSION DAY: ANNIVERSARY. Feb 14. Became 33rd state in 1859.

PRE-WILL HAYES MOVIE DAY. Feb 14. A day to watch movies made before the Hayes Code was established in the early 1930s. These were movies in which people actually slept in the same bed, bad guys were the heroes, and salty language and partial nudity were the norm. For info: Gary Olszewski, 828 Arrowhead Trail, Henderson, NV 89015. Phone: (702) 565-3961. E-mail: gmzewski@aol.com.

PROUT, MARY ANN ("AUNT MARY PROUT"): BIRTH ANNIVERSARY. Feb 14, 1801. It is believed most likely that Mary Prout—social activist, humanitarian, educator—was born free on this date at Baltimore, MD. Prout became a teacher and in 1830 founded a day school. Actively involved in her church, she founded a secret society that became the Independent Order of St. Luke to help with the cost of medical care and burial services for needy blacks, an organization that grew to have 1,500 chapters across the nation by 1900. Prout died at Baltimore in 1884.

RACE RELATIONS DAY. Feb 14. A day designated by some churches to recognize the importance of interracial relations. Formerly was observed on Abraham Lincoln's birthday or on the Sunday preceding it. Since 1970 observance has generally been Feb 14.

ROMANCE & REMEMBRANCE. Feb 14. Indianapolis, IN. Share a romantic evening with your Valentine by immersing yourselves in the beauty of Harrison's historical home. You will be treated to readings from Victorian and contemporary literature written by Indiana authors and interpreted by readers dressed in period costumes. You will then enjoy a candlelight dinner in the museum's Centennial Room. Est attendance: 80. For info: PR Dept, President Benjamin Harrison Home, 1230 N Delaware St, Indianapolis, IN 46202. Phone: (317) 631-1888. Fax: (317) 632-5488.

SALMAN RUSHDIE'S DEATH SENTENCE: 15th ANNIVERSARY. Feb 14, 1989. Iranian leader Ayatollah Ruholla Khomeini, offended by *The Satanic Verses*, called on Muslims to kill the book's British author, Salman Rushdie. On the following day the Ayatollah offered a $1 million reward for execution of his sentence. Rushdie, fearful for his life, went into hiding. Worldwide protests against the efforts to abridge academic and literary freedoms, countered by protests of Muslim and other religious fundamentalists, stimulated the sales of *The Satanic Verses*, but Rushdie remained virtually a prisoner, unable to resume a public life. In 1998 the Iranian government rescinded the death sentence.

SPACE MILESTONE: *NEAR* ORBITS ASTEROID. Feb 14, 2000. The robot spacecraft *Near Earth Asteroid Rendezvous* (now called *NEAR Shoemaker*) finished circling the asteroid Eros for the first time on this day. Eros is called a near-Earth asteroid because its orbit crosses that of Earth and poses a potential collision danger. *NEAR* continued orbiting the asteroid for a year, moving closer to the surface to make more precise measurements and thousands of pictures. In October 2000 it passed within three miles of Eros. Though it was never designed for landing, on Feb 12, 2001, *NEAR* touched down on Eros, history's first landing of an object on an asteroid. *NEAR* was launched from Cape Canaveral, FL, Feb 17, 1996.

SPACE MILESTONE: 100th SPACEWALK. Feb 14, 2001. Two astronauts from the space shuttle *Atlantis* took the 100th spacewalk; the first had been taken by American Edward White in 1965. On their excursion Thomas Jones and Robert Curbeam, Jr, put the finishing touches on the International Space Station's new science lab *Destiny*. See also: "Space Milestone: *Gemini 4*" (June 3).

SPACE MILESTONE: SMM (US). Feb 14, 1980. Unmanned Delta rocket, a "Solar Maximum Mission Observatory," launched on this date. Intended to study solar flares.

TWIN CITIES' KREWE OF JANUS MARDI GRAS PARADE. Feb 14. Monroe, LA. Festive parade to celebrate Mardi Gras. For info: Tourism Sales Mgr, 601 Constitution Dr, West Monroe, LA 71292. Phone: (800) 843-1872. Fax: (318) 324-1752. E-mail: mwmcvb@monroe-westmonroe.org. Web: www.monroe-westmonroe.org.

VALENTINE'S DAY. Feb 14. St. Valentine's Day celebrates the feasts of two Christian martyrs of this name. One, a priest and physician, was beaten and beheaded on the Flaminian Way at Rome, Italy, Feb 14, AD 269, during the reign of Emperor Claudius II. Another Valentine, the Bishop of Terni, is said to have been beheaded, also on the Flaminian Way at Rome, Feb 14 (possibly in a later year). Both history and legend are vague and contradictory about details of the Valentines and some say that Feb 14 was selected for the celebration of Christian martyrs as a diversion from the ancient pagan observance of Lupercalia. An old legend has it that birds choose their mates on Valentine's Day. Now it is one of the most widely observed unofficial holidays. It is an occasion for the exchange of gifts (usually books, flowers or sweets) and greeting cards with affectionate or humorous messages. See also: "Lupercalia" (Feb 15).

VALENTINE'S DAY MASSACRE: 75th ANNIVERSARY. Feb 14, 1929. Anniversary of Chicago gangland executions, when gunmen posing as police shot seven members of the George "Bugs" Moran gang.

WALLET, SKEEZIX: "BIRTHDAY." Feb 14. Comic strip character in "Gasoline Alley" by Frank King. First cartoon character to grow and age with the years of publication. Foundling child of Walt and Phyllis Wallet, discovered on doorstep Feb 14, 1921. Skeezix grew through childhood, marriage, military service in WWII, returning home to parenthood and business after the war. Comic strip began in the *Chicago Tribune*, Aug 23, 1919.

WMAS 94.7 FM VALENTINE'S BALL. Feb 14. Springfield, MA. A formal affair for both couples and singles. An evening of music, dancing and prizes. Est attendance: 900. For info: Dina McMahon, PO Box 9500, Springfield, MA 01102. Phone: (413) 737-1414. Fax: (413) 737-1488.

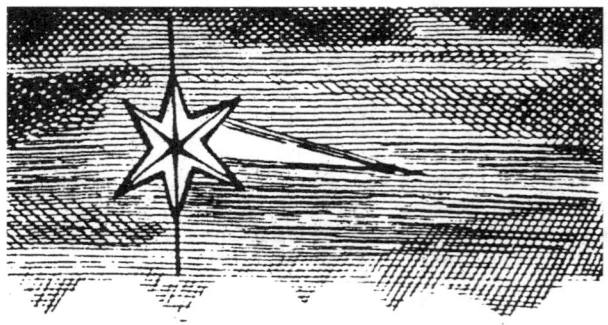

February 2004	S	M	T	W	T	F	S
	1	2	3	4	5	6	7
	8	9	10	11	12	13	14
	15	16	17	18	19	20	21
	22	23	24	25	26	27	28
	29						

☆ Chase's 2004 Calendar of Events ☆   Feb 14–15

BIRTHDAYS TODAY

Carl Bernstein, 60, journalist, author (investigated Watergate story with Bob Woodward), born Washington, DC, Feb 14, 1944.
Drew Bledsoe, 32, football player, born Ellensburg, WA, Feb 14, 1972.
Michael Bloomberg, 62, mayor of New York City (R), born Brighton, MA, Feb 14, 1942.
Enrico Colantoni, 41, actor ("Just Shoot Me"), born Toronto, ON, Canada, Feb 14, 1963.
Hugh Downs, 83, broadcaster ("Today," "20/20"), born Akron, OH, Feb 14, 1921.
Zach Galligan, 40, actor (Gremlins, Gremlins II), born New York, NY, Feb 14, 1964.
Judd Gregg, 57, US Senator (R, New Hampshire), born Nashua, NH, Feb 14, 1947.
Milan Hejduk, 28, hockey player, born Usti-nad-Labem, Czechoslovakia, Feb 14, 1976.
Florence Henderson, 70, singer, actress ("The Brady Bunch"), born Dale, IN, Feb 14, 1934.
Andrew Prine, 68, actor (The Miracle Worker, Chisum), born Jennings, FL, Feb 14, 1936.
Teller, 56, magician (Penn and Teller), name legally changed to Teller, born Philadelphia, PA, Feb 14, 1948.
Meg Tilly, 44, actress (Agnes of God, Two Jakes), born Long Beach, CA, Feb 14, 1960.
Jessica Yu, 38, filmmaker (Oscar for Breathing Lessons: The Life and Work of Mark O'Brien), born Los Altos Hills, CA, Feb 14, 1966.

FEBRUARY 15 — SUNDAY
Day 46 — 320 Remaining

AFGHANISTAN: SOVIET TROOP WITHDRAWAL: 15th ANNIVERSARY. Feb 15, 1989. The USSR's target of withdrawal of all Soviet troops from Afghanistan by this date was essentially met, ending more than nine years of intervention in a civil war.

ARLEN, HAROLD: BIRTH ANNIVERSARY. Feb 15, 1905. American composer and songwriter, born at Buffalo, NY. Arlen wrote many popular songs including "Over the Rainbow" (for which he won the 1939 Oscar for Best Song), "That Old Black Magic," "Blues in the Night" and "Stormy Weather." Died at New York, NY, Apr 23, 1986.

BARRYMORE, JOHN: BIRTH ANNIVERSARY. Feb 15, 1882. American actor of famous acting family, brother of Ethel and Lionel. Born John Blythe at Philadelphia, PA, and died at Los Angeles, CA, May 29, 1942.

BUILD A BETTER TRADE SHOW IMAGE WEEK. Feb 15–21. For companies that exhibit at trade shows, this week is set aside to evaluate and improve exhibit strategies for the upcoming trade show season. For "10 Steps to a Better Trade Show Image" tip sheet, send #10 SASE. Annually, the third full week of February. For info: Marlys K. Arnold, ImageSpecialist, 7885 NW Roanridge Rd, Ste A, Kansas City, MO 64151. Phone: (816) 746-7888. E-mail: marnold@imagespecialist.com. Web: www.imagespecialist.com.

CANADA: MAPLE LEAF FLAG ADOPTED: ANNIVERSARY. Feb 15, 1965. The new Canadian national flag was raised in Ottawa, Canada's capital, on this day. The red-and-white flag with a red maple leaf in the center replaced the Red Ensign flag which had the British Union Jack in the upper left-hand corner.

CERMAK, ANTON J.: ASSASSINATION ANNIVERSARY. Feb 15, 1933. At Bay Front Park, Miami, FL, an assassin aiming at President-elect Franklin D. Roosevelt had his aim deflected by a spectator. Cermak, mayor of Chicago, IL, born May 9, 1873, at Kladno, Bohemia, Czechoslovakia, was struck and killed instead. Giuseppe (Joe) Zangara, the 32-year-old assassin, who had emigrated from Italy in 1923, was electrocuted at the Raiford, FL, state prison Mar 20, 1933.

CLARK, ABRAHAM: BIRTH ANNIVERSARY. Feb 15, 1726. Signer of the Declaration of Independence, farmer and lawyer. Born at Elizabethtown, NJ, and died there Sept 15, 1794.

DAYTONA 500 NASCAR WINSTON CUP SERIES RACE. Feb 15. Daytona International Speedway, Daytona Beach, FL. 46th annual running of the "world's greatest race." For info: Daytona Intl Speedway, PO Box 2801, Daytona Beach, FL 32120-2801. Phone: (386) 253-7223. Fax: (386) 947-6791. Web: www.daytonainternationalspeedway.com.

GALILEI, GALILEO: BIRTH ANNIVERSARY. Feb 15, 1564. Physicist and astronomer who helped overthrow medieval concepts of the world, born at Pisa, Italy. He proved the theory that all bodies, large and small, descend at equal speed and gathered evidence to support Copernicus's theory that the Earth and other planets revolve around the sun. Galileo died at Florence, Italy, Jan 8, 1642.

HEART FAILURE AWARENESS WEEK. Feb 15–21. To raise awareness and educate health care providers, patients, family members and individuals at risk about heart failure, one of America's silent epidemics. For information visit the Heart Failure Society of America website at www.abouthf.org. For info: Cheryl Yano, HFSA, Court Intl, Ste 240 South, 2550 University Ave West, St. Paul, MN 55114. Phone: (651) 642-1633. E-mail: info@hfsa.org. Web: www.abouthf.org.

LUPERCALIA. Feb 15. Anniversary of ancient Roman fertility festival. Thought by some to have been established by Romulus and Remus who, legend says, were suckled by a she-wolf at Lupercal (a cave in Palestine). Goats and dogs were sacrificed. Lupercalia celebration persisted until the fifth century of the Christian era. Possibly a forerunner of Valentine's Day customs.

McCORMICK, CYRUS H.: BIRTH ANNIVERSARY. Feb 15, 1809. Inventor of the reaper, born at Rockbridge County, VA. It is said that Cyrus McCormick's invention of the reaper rates second only to the railroad in the development of the US. Continuing the dream of his father, McCormick constructed a horse-operated reaper which was demonstrated for the first time in a Virginia wheat field in July 1831. He moved his operation to Chicago, IL, in 1847 in order to be closer to the Midwest's expanding wheat fields. His business prospered despite two decades of constant litigation over patent rights. He died May 13, 1884, at Chicago, IL. In 1902–03, his McCormick Harvesting Machine Company was consolidated with other firms to become the International Harvester Company.

MENENDEZ DE AVILES, PEDRO: BIRTH ANNIVERSARY. Feb 15, 1519. Spanish explorer and naval adventurer. Explored Florida coastal regions for the king of Spain and established a fort at St. Augustine in September 1565. Died Sept 17, 1574, at Santander, Spain.

Feb 15–16 ☆ Chase's 2004 Calendar of Events ☆

NATIONAL I WANT BUTTERSCOTCH DAY. Feb 15. Celebrated the day after Valentine's Day each year, National I Want Butterscotch Day is for the legions of butterscotch fans who wish they had received butterscotch goodies, rather than chocolates, on Valentine's Day. This is the day for butterscotch lovers everywhere to declare their preference for this flavor and ask family and friends to remember their fondness for butterscotch the next time they choose edible gifts. For info: Diana Dalsass, 321 Rutland Ave, Teaneck, NJ 07666. Phone: (201) 837-9511. E-mail: ButtercupPress@cs.com.

ORTHODOX MEATFARE SUNDAY. Feb 15. Meatfare Sunday begins Meatfare Week, a time of abstaining from meat in preparation for Lent. Some Orthodox communities call this Butterweek.

REMEMBER THE *MAINE* DAY: ANNIVERSARY. Feb 15, 1898. American battleship *Maine* was blown up while at anchor in Havana Harbor, at 9:40 PM, on this day in 1898. The ship, under the command of Captain Charles G. Sigsbee, sank quickly, and 260 members of its crew were lost. Inflamed public opinion in the US ignored the lack of evidence to establish responsibility for the explosion. "Remember the *Maine*" became the war cry, and a formal declaration of war against Spain followed on Apr 25, 1898.

SHACKLETON, ERNEST: BIRTH ANNIVERSARY. Feb 15, 1874. The Antarctic explorer was born at Kilkea, Ireland. His fame rests not on reaching the South Pole (he tried three times), but on his leadership and bravery. During the British Imperial Trans-Arctic expedition of 1914, the icy seas crushed their ship, *Endurance*, but Shackleton protected his men and buoyed their morale for the two years they were marooned. In 1916 he led a six-man team in a lifeboat in a 17-day, 600-mile journey (without sleep) in search of help. Upon arrival at South Georgia Island, he rounded up a rescue effort and three months later all his men were rescued without a death. Shackleton died Jan 5, 1922, at Grytviken, South Georgia Island, while beginning a fourth expedition to the South Pole.

SPANISH WAR MEMORIAL DAY AND *MAINE* MEMORIAL DAY. Feb 15. Massachusetts.

SUSAN B. ANTHONY DAY. Feb 15. Honors one of the first women's rights advocates, working especially for the right to vote. Anthony was born on this day in 1820 at Adams, MA. She died Mar 13, 1906, at Rochester, NY.

SUTTER, JOHN AUGUSTUS: BIRTH ANNIVERSARY. Feb 15, 1803. Born at Kandern, Germany, Sutter established the first white settlement on the site of Sacramento, CA, in 1839, and owned a large tract of land there, which he named New Helvetia. The first great gold strike in the US was on his property, at Sutter's Mill, Jan 24, 1848. His land was soon overrun by gold seekers who, he claimed, slaughtered his cattle and stole or destroyed his property. Sutter was bankrupt by 1852. Died at Washington, DC, June 18, 1880.

TIFFANY, CHARLES LEWIS: BIRTH ANNIVERSARY. Feb 15, 1812. American jeweler whose name became synonymous with high standards of quality. Born at Killingly, CT, and died at New York, NY, Feb 18, 1902. Father of artist Louis Comfort Tiffany. See also: "Tiffany, Louis Comfort: Birth Anniversary" (Feb 18).

WINGS OVER THE PLATTE SPRING MIGRATION SEASON. Feb 15–Apr 15. Grand Island, NE. Celebrate the arrival of the world's largest concentration of sandhill cranes. Each spring up to 500,000 cranes gather along the Platte River during their northward migration. Seminars, tours, nature hikes, films. Est attendance: 100,000. For info: Renee Seifert, Grand Island/Hall County Conv and Visitors Bureau, PO Box 1486, Grand Island, NE 68802. Phone: (800) 658-3178 or (308) 382-4400. Fax: (308) 382-1154. E-mail: info@visitgrandisland.com. Web: www.visitgrandisland.com.

BIRTHDAYS TODAY

Adolfo, 71, fashion designer, born Adolfo F. Sardina, Havana, Cuba, Feb 15, 1933.
Marisa Berenson, 56, actress (*Cabaret, Barry Lyndon*), model, born New York, NY, Feb 15, 1948.
Claire Bloom, 73, actress (*A Doll's House, The Spy Who Came In from the Cold*), born London, England, Feb 15, 1931.
Susan Brownmiller, 69, author, feminist (*Against Our Will, Femininity*), born Brooklyn, NY, Feb 15, 1935.
Matt Groening, 50, cartoonist ("The Simpsons"), born Portland, OR, Feb 15, 1954.
Jaromir Jagr, 32, hockey player, born Kladno, Czechoslovakia, Feb 15, 1972.
Harvey Korman, 77, actor, comedian (two Emmys for "The Carol Burnett Show"; *High Anxiety*), born Chicago, IL, Feb 15, 1927.
Melissa Manchester, 53, singer ("Don't Cry Out Loud"), born the Bronx, NY, Feb 15, 1951.
Kevin McCarthy, 90, actor (*Invasion of the Body Snatchers, Buffalo Bill and the Indians*), born Seattle, WA, Feb 15, 1914.
William Mark Price, 40, former basketball player, born Bartlesville, OK, Feb 15, 1964.
Jane Seymour, 53, actress (Emmy for "East of Eden"; "Dr. Quinn: Medicine Woman"), born Hillingdon, England, Feb 15, 1951.

FEBRUARY 16 — MONDAY
Day 47 — 319 Remaining

BERGEN, EDGAR: BIRTH ANNIVERSARY. Feb 16, 1903. Actor, radio entertainer and ventriloquist, voice of Charlie McCarthy, Mortimer Snerd and Effie Klinker. Father of Emmy Award–winning actress Candice Bergen. Born at Chicago, IL; died at Las Vegas, NV, Sept 30, 1978.

CANADA: FAMILY DAY IN ALBERTA. Feb 16. Annually, the third Monday in February.

FLAHERTY, ROBERT JOSEPH: BIRTH ANNIVERSARY. Feb 16, 1884. American filmmaker, explorer and author, called "father of the documentary film." Born at Iron Mountain, MI; died at Dunnerston, VT, July 23, 1951. Films included *Nanook of the North, Moana* and *Man of Aran*.

GEORGE WASHINGTON BIRTHDAY CELEBRATION PARADE. Feb 16. Alexandria, VA. Nation's largest parade honoring George Washington, staged by his hometown. More than 200 units. Floats, bands, antique cars, equestrian units and bagpipers. Route through historic district. Sponsor: George Washington Birthday Celebration Committee. Free admission. Est attendance: 50,000. For info: Alexandria Conv and Visitors Assoc, 221 King St, Alexandria, VA 22314. Phone: (703) 838-4200. Fax: (703) 838-4683. E-mail: acva@FunSide.com. Web: www.FunSide.com.

KING, WAYNE: BIRTH ANNIVERSARY. Feb 16, 1901. American saxophonist and bandleader, widely known as "the Waltz King," born at Savannah, IL. His own composition, "The Waltz You Save for Me," was his theme song. Died at Paradise Valley, AZ, July 16, 1985.

KROGER ST. JUDE TENNIS INTERNATIONAL. Feb 16–22. Racquet Club of Memphis, Memphis, TN. The world's finest tennis players compete in one of the most prestigious tour events of the year. Est attendance: 63,000. For info: Tom Buford, Kroger St. Jude, Racquet Club of Memphis, 5111 Sanderlin, Memphis, TN 38117. Phone: (901) 765-4400.

	S	M	T	W	T	F	S
February 2004		1	2	3	4	5	6	7
	8	9	10	11	12	13	14
	15	16	17	18	19	20	21
	22	23	24	25	26	27	28
	29						

☆ Chase's 2004 Calendar of Events ☆ Feb 16–17

LITHUANIA: INDEPENDENCE DAY. Feb 16. National Day. The anniversary of Lithuania's declaration of independence in 1918 is observed as the Baltic state's Independence Day. In 1940 Lithuania became a part of the Soviet Union under an agreement between Joseph Stalin and Adolf Hitler. On Mar 11, 1990, Lithuania declared its independence from the Soviet Union, the first of the Soviet republics to do so. After demanding independence, Lithuania set up a border police force and aided young men in efforts to avoid the Soviet military draft, prompting then Soviet leader Mikhail Gorbachev to send tanks into the capital of Vilnius and impose oil and gas embargoes. In the wake of the failed coup attempt in Moscow on Aug 19, 1991, Lithuanian independence finally was recognized.

LIVE TO GIVE WEEK. Feb 16–22. This national week of community service is sponsored by the Dream-On Foundation. Volunteer projects that take place during this week are eligible for plaques and/or reward funds. Their goal is to raise $1 million in donations for charity. For info: Angel McCormick, President, Dream-On Foundation, PO Box 867, Seahurst, WA 98062. Phone: (888) 546-2357. Fax: (206) 241-2055. E-mail: Dream 98062@aol.com. Web: www.dreamonfoundation.com.

PRESIDENTS' DAY. Feb 16. Presidents' Day observes the birthdays of George Washington (Feb 22) and Abraham Lincoln (Feb 12). With the adoption of the Monday Holiday Law (which moved the observance of George Washington's birthday from Feb 22 to the third Monday in February), some of the specific significance of the event was lost and added impetus was given to the popular description of that holiday as Presidents' Day. Present usage often regards Presidents' Day as a day to honor all former presidents of the US, though the federal holiday is still Washington's Birthday. Annually, the third Monday in February. See also "Washington, George: Birthday Observance" below.

PRESIDENTS' DAY: LIVE FROM DELAWARE STREET. Feb 16. Indianapolis, IN. Visit President Benjamin Harrison Home and listen to the conversations and gossip of the day as you enter each room and speak with family members and household staff, whose roles are re-created by actors. For info: PR Dept, President Benjamin Harrison Home, 1230 N Delaware St, Indianapolis, IN 46202. Phone: (317) 631-1888. Fax: (317) 632-5488. Web: www.presidentbenjaminharrison.org.

STOCK EXCHANGE HOLIDAY (WASHINGTON'S BIRTHDAY). Feb 16. The holiday schedules for the various exchanges are subject to change if relevant rules, regulations or exchange policies are revised. If you have questions, phone American Stock Exchange (212) 306-1000; Chicago Board of Trade (312) 435-3500; Chicago Board of Options Exchange (312) 786-5600; New York Stock Exchange (212) 656-2065; Pacific Stock Exchange (415) 393-4000; Philadelphia Stock Exchange (215) 496-5000.

SURRENDER OF FORT DONELSON: ANNIVERSARY. Feb 16, 1862. With Confederate troops evacuating Bowling Green, KY, and other points along the Kentucky line, General Ulysses S. Grant's forces encircled Fort Donelson, KY. After hard fighting on land and on the Cumberland River, Grant requested surrender of Fort Donelson, stating that "No terms except unconditional and immediate surrender can be accepted." This earned him the nickname Unconditional Surrender Grant. Confederate General Simon Buckner surrendered the fort, in essence giving the Union army control of Tennessee and Kentucky and the Tennessee and Cumberland rivers. Disruption ensued and civilians attempted to flee the area occupied by Federal troops.

WASHINGTON, GEORGE: BIRTHDAY OBSERVANCE (LEGAL HOLIDAY). Feb 16. Legal public holiday (Public Law 90-363 sets Washington's birthday observance on the third Monday in February each year—applicable to federal employees and to the District of Columbia). Observed in all states. See also: "Washington, George: Birth Anniversary" (Feb 22).

WILSON, HENRY: BIRTH ANNIVERSARY. Feb 16, 1812. 18th vice president of the US (1873–75). Born at Farmington, NH; died at Washington, DC, Nov 22, 1875.

BIRTHDAYS TODAY

Jerome Bettis, 32, football player, born Detroit, MI, Feb 16, 1972.
LeVar Burton, 47, actor, host ("Roots," "Star Trek: The Next Generation," "Reading Rainbow"), born Landsthul, Germany, Feb 16, 1957.
Ice T, 45, rap singer, born Tracy Morrow, Newark, NJ, Feb 16, 1959.
James Ingram, 48, singer ("Baby, Come to Me" [with Patti Austin]), songwriter, born Akron, OH, Feb 16, 1956.
William Katt, 54, actor ("The Greatest American Hero," *Perry Mason Returns, Carrie*), born Los Angeles, CA, Feb 16, 1950 (some sources say 1955 or 1951).
George Frost Kennan, 100, historian, diplomat, born Milwaukee, WI, Feb 16, 1904.
John Patrick McEnroe, Jr, 45, former tennis player, born Wiesbaden, West Germany, Feb 16, 1959.
Barry Primus, 66, actor ("Cagney and Lacey," *Absence of Malice, Down and Out in Beverly Hills*), born New York, NY, Feb 16, 1938.

FEBRUARY 17 — TUESDAY
Day 48 — 318 Remaining

BARBER, WALTER LANIER "RED": BIRTH ANNIVERSARY. Feb 17, 1908. One of the first broadcasters inducted into the Baseball Hall of Fame, "Red" Barber was born at Columbus, MS. Barber's first professional play-by-play experience was announcing the Cincinnati Reds opening day on radio in 1934. That game was also the first major league game he had ever seen. He broadcast baseball's first night game (in Brooklyn) on Aug 26, 1939, the 1947 game in which Jackie Robinson broke the color barrier and Roger Maris's 61st home run in 1961. "Red" Barber died Oct 22, 1992, at Tallahassee, FL.

CHICAGO FLAG EXHIBIT CONTROVERSY: 15th ANNIVERSARY. Feb 17, 1989. An exhibit at the School of the Art Institute of Chicago, titled *What is the Proper Way to Display a US Flag?*, consisted of a ledger for viewers to write their impressions but required the viewers to stand on a US flag mounted on the floor to reach the ledger. The exhibit by art student Scott Tyler prompted protests from veterans' groups, a failed lawsuit and an introduction of legislation by Senator Bob Dole to make displaying a US flag on the floor or ground a crime. Although that legislation didn't pass, Congress continues to introduce legislation against flag desecration, most recently in 1999.

CORELLI, ARCANGELO: BIRTH ANNIVERSARY. Feb 17, 1653. Italian composer and virtuoso violinist, born at Fusignano, Italy. From his home in Rome, Corelli made extensive and popular concert tours throughout much of Europe. Died at Rome, Italy, Jan 8, 1713.

137

Feb 17 ☆ *Chase's 2004 Calendar of Events* ☆

FORT SUMTER RETURNED TO UNION CONTROL: ANNIVERSARY. Feb 17, 1865. After a siege that lasted almost a year and a half, Fort Sumter in South Carolina returned to Union hands on this date. The site of the first shots fired in the American Civil War on Apr 12, 1861, the fort had become a symbol for both sides. As Union attempts to retake it by shelling diminished the fort's capacity with large bombardments, Southern forces managed to hold out with few casualties.

GERONIMO: 95th DEATH ANNIVERSARY. Feb 17, 1909. American Indian of the Chiricahua (Apache) tribe was born about 1829 in Arizona. He was the leader of a small band of warriors whose devastating raids in Arizona, New Mexico and Mexico caused the US Army to send 5,000 men to recapture him after his first escape. He was confined at Fort Sill, OK, where he died Feb 17, 1909, after dictating the story of his life for publication.

GRAND RAPIDS BOAT SHOW. Feb 17–22. DeVos Place, Grand Rapids, MI. This event brings together buyers and sellers of power- and sailboats, boating accessories, docks, dockominiums and vacation properties. Est attendance: 32,000. For info: Henri Boucher, ShowSpan, Inc, 2121 Celebration Dr NE, Grand Rapids, MI 49525. Phone: (616) 447-2860. Fax: (616) 447-2861. E-mail: events@showspan.com. Web: www.showspan.com.

LAENNEC, RENE THEOPHILE HYACINTHE: BIRTH ANNIVERSARY. Feb 17, 1781. Famed French physician, author and inventor of the stethoscope, called "father of chest medicine." He wrote extensively about respiratory and heart ailments. Born at Quimper, France, he died there Aug 13, 1826.

LEAGUE OF UNITED LATIN AMERICAN CITIZENS (LULAC) FOUNDED: 75th ANNIVERSARY. Feb 17, 1929. Delegates from the Corpus Christi Order of the Sons of America, Knights of America of San Antonio and the League of Latin America Citizens from the Rio Grande Valley met at Obreros Hall, Corpus Christi, TX, to form LULAC. It is now the oldest and largest Hispanic civic organization.

MADAMA BUTTERFLY PREMIERE: 100th ANNIVERSARY. Feb 17, 1904. Giacomo Puccini's *Madama Butterfly* was performed for the first time in Milan. The sold-out crowd, restive at what they saw as Puccini's lack of originality, gave boos, moos, groans and heckling to the extent that the performers couldn't hear the orchestra. Rosina Storchio, the soprano portraying Madame Butterfly, began crying on stage. Puccini, enraged at the opera's reception (saying the opera was "daisies thrown to swine"), nevertheless revised the work, and it had a successful performance on May 24.

MALTHUS, THOMAS: BIRTH ANNIVERSARY. Feb 17, 1766. English economist, author and demographer, born near Dorking, England. Malthusian population theories (especially that population growth exceeds growth of production) provoked great controversy when published in 1798. Died near Bath, England, Dec 23, 1834.

MY WAY DAY. Feb 17. Hundreds of people have their opinions as to who we are. Today is the day we decide who's right. Today we determine our identities all by ourselves. [©2003 by WH.] For info: Thomas & Ruth Roy, Wellcat Holidays, 2418 Long Ln, Lebanon, PA 17046. Phone: (717) 279-0184. E-mail: info@wellcat.com. Web: www.wellcat.com.

NATIONAL PTA FOUNDERS' DAY: ANNIVERSARY. Feb 17, 1897. Celebrates the PTA's founding by Phoebe Apperson Hearst and Alice McLellan Birney. For info: Natl PTA, 330 N Wabash, Ste 2100, Chicago, IL 60611. Phone: (312) 670-6782. Fax: (312) 670-6783. E-mail: info@pta.org. Web: www.pta.org.

February 2004

S	M	T	W	T	F	S
1	2	3	4	5	6	7
8	9	10	11	12	13	14
15	16	17	18	19	20	21
22	23	24	25	26	27	28
29						

"A PRAIRIE HOME COMPANION" PREMIERE: 25th ANNIVERSARY. Feb 17, 1979. This popular live variety show debuted locally on Minnesota Public Radio in 1974 and was first broadcast nationally on Feb 17, 1979, as part of National Public Radio's Folk Festival USA. It became a regular Saturday night program in early 1980. Host Garrison Keillor's monologues about the mythical Lake Wobegon and his humorous ads for local businesses such as Bertha's Kitty Boutique, Powdermilk Biscuits and the Chatterbox Cafe were accompanied by various musical groups. Broadcast from the World Theater in St. Paul, MN, the show went off the air in 1986. A series of programs were done for cable TV, and Keillor continues to write works of fiction (*Lake Wobegon Days*). In 1994, "A Prairie Home Companion" went back on the air on Public Radio International.

WORLD HUMAN SPIRIT DAY. Feb 17. Fort Lauderdale, FL. At 3:00 PM, EST, we will hold two minutes of silent meditation throughout the world and beyond, to focus on the true spirit that flows through everything. Please join us in silence to bring the energy of universal healing and peace into the hearts and minds of all humanity. For info: Michael Levy, Point of Life Foundation, PO Box 7, 3032 E Commercial Blvd, Fort Lauderdale, FL 33308. Phone: (954) 785-8439. Fax: (954) 785-8439. E-mail: mikmikl@aol.com. Web: www.pointoflife.com or www.polfoundation.org.

BIRTHDAYS TODAY

Vanessa Atler, 22, gymnast, born Valencia, CA, Feb 17, 1982.
Alan Bates, 70, actor (*An Unmarried Woman, Women in Love*), born Arthur Bates, Derbyshire, England, Feb 17, 1934.
James Nathaniel (Jim) Brown, 68, Hall of Fame football player, activist, actor, born St. Simons Island, GA, Feb 17, 1936.
Ronald DeVoe, 37, singer (Bell Biv DeVoe), born Boston, MA, Feb 17, 1967.
Michelle Forbes, 37, actress ("Homicide: Life On the Street"), born Austin, TX, Feb 17, 1967.
Brenda Fricker, 59, actress (Oscar for *My Left Foot; The Field*), born Dublin, Ireland, Feb 17, 1945.
Joseph Gordon-Levitt, 23, actor ("3rd Rock from the Sun," *Halloween H20*), born Los Angeles, CA, Feb 17, 1981.
Lee Hoiby, 78, composer, concert pianist, born Madison, WI, Feb 17, 1926.
Hal Holbrook, 79, actor (*Magnum Force, All the President's Men*), born Harold Rowe, Jr, Cleveland, OH, Feb 17, 1925.
Barry Humphries, 70, actor, comedian, aka Dame Edna Everidge (*Spiceworld*), born Melbourne, Australia, Feb 17, 1934.
Michael Jeffrey Jordan, 41, former basketball player, former minor league baseball player, born Brooklyn, NY, Feb 17, 1963.
Richard Karn, 45, actor ("Home Improvement"), game-show host ("Family Feud"), born Seattle, WA, Feb 17, 1959.
Lou Diamond Phillips, 42, actor (*La Bamba, Stand and Deliver*), born Corpus Christi, TX, Feb 17, 1962.
Rene Russo, 50, actress (*Lethal Weapon 3, Ransom*), born Burbank, CA, Feb 17, 1954.
Craig Thomas, 71, US Senator (R, Wyoming), born Cody, WY, Feb 17, 1933.

138

☆ Chase's 2004 Calendar of Events ☆   Feb 18

FEBRUARY 18 — WEDNESDAY
Day 49 — 317 Remaining

ALEICHEM, SHOLEM: BIRTH ANNIVERSARY. Feb 18, 1859 (OS). Pen name of Russian-born author and humorist Solomon Rabinowitz. Affectionately known in the US as the "Jewish Mark Twain." Died at New York, NY, May 13, 1916.

BIG TEN WOMEN'S SWIMMING AND DIVING CHAMPIONSHIP. Feb 18–21. University of Minnesota, Minneapolis, MN. Est attendance: 1,500. For info: Sue Lister, Big Ten Conference, 1500 W Higgins Rd, Park Ridge, IL 60068-6300. Phone: (847) 696-1010. Fax: (847) 696-1110. Web: www.bigten.org.

CARNIVAL DE PONCE. Feb 18–24. Ponce, PR. Carnival, artisans, parade with floats and colorfully dressed people with papier-mâché masks (vejigantes). Annually, the week before Ash Wednesday. Est attendance: 100,000. For info: Elma Santiago, Tourism Dir, Municipality of Ponce, PO Box 331709, Ponce, PR 00733. Phone: (787) 841-8044. Fax: (787) 259-1316. E-mail: munponce@coqui.net. Web: ponceweb.org.

COW MILKED WHILE FLYING IN AN AIRPLANE: ANNIVERSARY. Feb 18, 1930. Elm Farm Ollie became the first cow to fly in an airplane. During the flight, which was attended by reporters, she was milked and the milk was sealed in paper containers and parachuted over St. Louis, MO.

DAVIS, JEFFERSON: INAUGURATION ANNIVERSARY. Feb 18, 1861. In the years before the Civil War, Senator Jefferson Davis was the acknowledged leader of the Southern bloc and a champion of states' rights, but he had little to do with the secessionist movement until after his home state of Mississippi joined the Confederacy Jan 9, 1861. Davis withdrew from the Senate that same day. He was unanimously chosen as president of the Confederacy's provisional government and was inaugurated at Montgomery, AL, Feb 18. Within the next year he was elected to a six-year term by popular vote and inaugurated a second time Feb 22, 1862, at Richmond, VA.

GAMBIA: INDEPENDENCE DAY. Feb 18, 1965. National holiday. Independence from Britain granted. Referendum in April 1970 established Gambia as a republic within the Commonwealth.

NEPAL: NATIONAL DEMOCRACY DAY. Feb 18. National holiday. Anniversary of the 1952 Constitution.

PEABODY, GEORGE: BIRTH ANNIVERSARY. Feb 18, 1795. American merchant and philanthropist, born at South Danvers, MA. He endowed the Peabody Institute in Baltimore, museums at Harvard and Yale and the George Peabody College for Teachers at Nashville, TN. Died at London, England, Nov 4, 1869.

PLANET PLUTO DISCOVERY: ANNIVERSARY. Feb 18, 1930. Pluto, the ninth planet, was discovered by astronomer Clyde Tombaugh at the Lowell Observatory at Flagstaff, AZ. It was given the name of the Roman god of the underworld. Some astronomers don't accept Pluto as a planet.

TIFFANY, LOUIS COMFORT: BIRTH ANNIVERSARY. Feb 18, 1848. American artist, son of famed jeweler Charles L. Tiffany. Best remembered for his remarkable work with decorative iridescent "favrile" glass. Born at New York, NY; died there Jan 17, 1933. See also: "Tiffany, Charles Lewis: Birth Anniversary" (Feb 15).

WASHINGTON BOAT SHOW. Feb 18–22. The New Washington Convention Center, Washington, DC. Biggest indoor boat show in the mid-Atlantic region: 400+ boats—power and sail—from express cruisers to daysailers to motor yachts to dinghies. Also hundreds of booths with every possible accessory, from electronics and foul-weather gear to marinas and destinations. For info: Gail Stafford, Washington Boat Show, 6017 Tower Ct, Alexandria, VA 22304. Phone: (703) 823-7960. E-mail: tjsevents@aol.com.

WILLKIE, WENDELL LEWIS: BIRTH ANNIVERSARY. Feb 18, 1892. American lawyer, author, public utility executive and politician, born at Elwood, IN. Presidential nominee of the Republican Party in 1940. Remembered for his book, *One World*, published in 1943. Died at New York, NY, Oct 8, 1944.

BIRTHDAYS TODAY

Helen Gurley Brown, 82, author (*Sex and the Single Girl*), publisher (*Cosmopolitan*), born Green Forest, AR, Feb 18, 1922.
Aldo Ceccato, 70, conductor, born Milan, Italy, Feb 18, 1934.
Matt Dillon, 40, actor (*My Bodyguard, Drugstore Cowboy*), born Westchester, NY, Feb 18, 1964.
Milos Forman, 72, film director (Oscars for *Amadeus* and *One Flew Over the Cuckoo's Nest*), born Caslaz, Czechoslovakia, Feb 18, 1932.
John Hughes, 54, producer, director (*Home Alone, National Lampoon's Christmas Vacation*), born Lansing, MI, Feb 18, 1950.
George Kennedy, 77, actor (Oscar for *Cool Hand Luke*; "The Blue Knight"), born New York, NY, Feb 18, 1927.
Allan Melvin, 81, actor ("The Brady Bunch," "All in the Family"), born Kansas City, MO, Feb 18, 1923.
Toni Morrison, 73, Nobel Prize–winning novelist (*Beloved, Jazz, Tar Baby, Sula*), born Lorain, OH, Feb 18, 1931.
Juice Newton, 52, singer (*Juice, Quiet Lives*), born Judy Cohen, Virginia Beach, VA, Feb 18, 1952.
Yoko Ono, 71, artist, musician, widow of John Lennon, born Tokyo, Japan, Feb 18, 1933.
Jack Palance, 84, actor (Oscar for *City Slickers*; "Bronk," "Ripley's Believe It or Not"), born Lattimer, PA, Feb 18, 1920.
Molly Ringwald, 36, actress (*Sixteen Candles, The Breakfast Club, Pretty in Pink*), born Roseville, CA, Feb 18, 1968.
Greta Scacchi, 44, actress (*White Mischief, Presumed Innocent*), born Milan, Italy, Feb 18, 1960.
Cybill Shepherd, 54, actress (*The Last Picture Show*, "Moonlighting," "Cybill"), born Memphis, TN, Feb 18, 1950.
John Travolta, 49, actor (*Pulp Fiction, Urban Cowboy, Saturday Night Fever*, "Welcome Back Kotter"), born Englewood, NJ, Feb 18, 1955.
John William Warner, 77, US Senator (R, Virginia), born Washington, DC, Feb 18, 1927.
Vanna White, 47, TV personality ("Wheel of Fortune"), born Conway, SC, Feb 18, 1957.

139

FEBRUARY 19 — THURSDAY
Day 50 — 316 Remaining

AMERICAN BIRKEBEINER RACE. Feb 19–21. Cable to Hayward, WI. The largest and most prestigious cross-country ski marathon in North America attracts more than 5,000 participants for the 51K trek. Starting off with the Birkie, skiers of the 23K Kortelopet finish at Telemark Lodge. A Nordic festival of related ski events and activities begins Feb 19. Est attendance: 25,000. For info: American Birkebeiner Ski Foundation, Inc, Box 911, Hayward, WI 54843. Phone: (715) 634-5025. Fax: (715) 634-5663. E-mail: birkie@birkie.com. Web: www.birkie.com.

BOLLINGEN PRIZE: 55th ANNIVERSARY. Feb 19, 1949. On this date, the first Bollingen Prize for poetry was awarded to Ezra Pound for his collection *The Pisan Cantos*. This first award was steeped in controversy because Pound had been charged with treason after making pro-Fascist broadcasts in Italy during World War II.

COPERNICUS, NICOLAUS: BIRTH ANNIVERSARY. Feb 19, 1473. Polish astronomer and priest who revolutionized scientific thought with what came to be called the Copernican theory that placed the sun instead of the earth at the center of our planetary system. Born at Torun, Poland, he died at East Prussia, May 24, 1543.

***THE FEMININE MYSTIQUE* PUBLISHED: ANNIVERSARY.** Feb 19, 1963. Betty Friedan published *The Feminine Mystique* this month, a call for women to achieve their full potential. Her book generated enormous response and revitalized the women's movement in the US.

GARRICK, DAVID: BIRTH ANNIVERSARY. Feb 19, 1717. English actor, theater manager and playwright. Born at Hereford, England; died Jan 20, 1779, at London.

HEDIN, SVEN: BIRTH ANNIVERSARY. Feb 19, 1865. Explorer and scientist, Sven Anders Hedin was born at Stockholm, Sweden, and died there Nov 26, 1952. His Tibetan explorations provided the first substantial knowledge of that region to the rest of the world.

ITALY: FEAST OF THE INCAPPUCCIATI. Feb 19. Gradoli (near Viterbo). On the Thursday before Ash Wednesday the members of the Confraternity of Purgatory make the rounds of the town dressed in traditional hooded robes, bearing a banner and walking to the beat of a drum. They stop at every house to collect foodstuffs in the name of the souls in purgatory; the food is then served at the banquet on Ash Wednesday.

JAPANESE INTERNMENT: ANNIVERSARY. Feb 19, 1942. As a result of President Franklin Roosevelt's Executive Order 9066, some 110,000 Japanese Americans living in coastal Pacific areas were placed in concentration camps in remote areas of Arizona, Arkansas, inland California, Colorado, Idaho, Utah and Wyoming. The interned Japanese Americans (two-thirds were US citizens) lost an estimated $400 million in property. They were allowed to return to their homes Jan 2, 1945.

KNIGHTS OF PYTHIAS: FOUNDING ANNIVERSARY. Feb 19, 1864. The social and fraternal order of the Knights of Pythias was founded at Washington, DC.

MAYMONT FLOWER & GARDEN SHOW. Feb 19–22. Greater Richmond Convention Center, Richmond, VA. At the 15th annual Maymont Flower and Garden Show, garden lovers will find breathtaking full-scale landscape exhibits, numerous associated shows and the "Great Garden Marketplace." Expert speakers give advice and provide insight into a variety of garden topics. Please contact us for ticket info and a free brochure. Est attendance: 31,000. For info: Maymont Foundation, 1700 Hampton St, Richmond, VA 23220. Phone: (804) 358-7166. E-mail: flowershow@maymont.org. Web: www.maymont.org.

SIMPLOT GAMES. Feb 19–21. Holt Arena, Idaho State University, Pocatello, ID. One of the nation's largest indoor high school track and field events, featuring 2,000 top high school athletes from the US and Canada. Est attendance: 20,000. For info: Carol Lish, Exec Dir, Simplot Games, PO Box 912, Pocatello, ID 83204. Phone: (800) 635-9444. Fax: (208) 235-5669. E-mail: clish@simplot.com. Web: www.simplotgames.com.

US LANDING ON IWO JIMA: ANNIVERSARY. Feb 19, 1945. Beginning at dawn, the landing of 30,000 American troops took place on the barren 12-square-mile island of Iwo Jima. Initially there was little resistance, but 21,500 Japanese stood ready underground to fight to the last man to protect massive strategic fortifications linked by tunnels. See also: "Iwo Jima Day: Anniversary" (Feb 23).

BIRTHDAYS TODAY

Prince Andrew, 44, Duke of York, born London, England, Feb 19, 1960.
Justine Bateman, 38, actress ("Family Ties," "Men Behaving Badly"), born Rye, NY, Feb 19, 1966.
Lou Christie, 61, singer ("Lightnin' Strikes Again"), born Glen Willard, PA, Feb 19, 1943.
Jeff Daniels, 49, actor (*The Purple Rose of Cairo, Something Wild, Dumb and Dumber*), born Chelsea, MI, Feb 19, 1955.
Benicio Del Toro, 37, actor (*Traffic, The Usual Suspects*), born Santurce, Puerto Rico, Feb 19, 1967.
Stephen Nichols, 53, actor ("Days of Our Lives," "General Hospital"), born Cincinnati, OH, Feb 19, 1951.
Smokey Robinson, 64, singer, songwriter ("Cruisin'," "Being With You"), born William Robinson, Jr, Detroit, MI, Feb 19, 1940.
Seal, 41, singer-songwriter ("Prayer for the Dying"), born Sealhenry Samuel, London, England, Feb 19, 1963.
Andrew Shue, 37, actor ("Melrose Place"), born South Orange, NJ, Feb 19, 1967.
Amy Tan, 52, author (*The Joy Luck Club*), born Oakland, CA, Feb 19, 1952.

FEBRUARY 20 — FRIDAY
Day 51 — 315 Remaining

ADAMS, ANSEL: BIRTH ANNIVERSARY. Feb 20, 1902. American photographer, known for his photographs of Yosemite National Park, born at San Francisco, CA. Adams died at Monterey, CA, Apr 22, 1984.

CLOSEST APPROACH OF A COMET TO EARTH: ANNIVERSARY. Feb 20, 1491. An unnamed comet came within 860,000 miles (.0094 AU) of Earth on this date in 1491. By comparison, the closest approach that Halley's Comet made to Earth was on Apr 10, 837, at 3 million miles.

DOUGLASS, FREDERICK: DEATH ANNIVERSARY. Feb 20, 1895. American journalist, orator and antislavery leader. Born at Tuckahoe, MD, probably in February 1817. Died at Anacostia Heights, DC. His original name before his escape from slavery was Frederick Augustus Washington Bailey.

JEFFERSON, JOSEPH: 175th BIRTH ANNIVERSARY. Feb 20, 1829. Distinguished American actor, born at Philadelphia, PA, in a family of actors. Jefferson made his stage debut at the age of three in Kotzebue's *Pizarro*. After many successes, his search for a character both humorous and pathetic centered on Rip Van Winkle, about whom he wrote a short play. Later revised by Dion Boucicault, the play opened with Jefferson in the leading role at London, England, in 1865 and was an immediate success. Rip Van Winkle became the signature role for which he was known. Jefferson died at Palm Beach, FL, Apr 23, 1905. He is remembered each year in Chicago when the Joseph Jefferson (Jeff) Awards are presented to recognize excellence in theatrical productions.

LONGHORN WORLD CHAMPIONSHIP RODEO. Feb 20–22. Cincinnati Gardens, Cincinnati, OH. More than 200 cowboys and cowgirls compete in six professional contests ranging from bronc riding to big, bad BONUS bull riding. Free beginners horsemanship clinic 40 minutes before performances. Qualifying rodeo for Longhorn's Championship Finals Rodeo in Nashville, TN. Featuring colorful opening and pageantry. 29th annual. Est attendance: 20,000. For info: W. Bruce Lehrke, Pres, Longhorn World Championship Rodeo, Inc, PO Box 70159, Nashville, TN 37207. Phone: (615) 876-1016. Fax: (615) 876-4685. E-mail: info@longhornrodeo.com. Web: www.longhornrodeo.com.

MOBIUS ADVERTISING AWARDS. Feb 20. Los Angeles, CA. Selection and recognition of the world's most outstanding television and radio commercials, print advertising and package designs. Founded in 1971. Est attendance: 500. For info: Lee W. Gluckman, The Mobius Advertising Awards, 713 S Pacific Coast Hwy, Ste A, Redondo Beach, CA 90277-4233. Phone: (310) 540-0959. Fax: (310) 316-8905. E-mail: mobiusinfo@mobiusawards.com. Web: www.mobiusawards.com.

MOON PHASE: NEW MOON. Feb 20. Moon enters New Moon phase at 4:18 AM, EST.

NORTHERN HEMISPHERE HOODIE-HOO DAY. Feb 20. At high noon (local time) citizens are asked to go outdoors and yell "Hoodie-Hoo" to chase away winter and make ready for spring, one month away. [©2003 by WH.] For info: Thomas & Ruth Roy, Wellcat Holidays, 2418 Long Ln, Lebanon, PA 17046. Phone: (717) 279-0184. E-mail: info@wellcat.com. Web: www.wellcat.com.

PISCES, THE FISH. Feb 20–Mar 20. In the astronomical/astrological zodiac, which divides the sun's apparent orbit into 12 segments, the period Feb 20–Mar 20 is identified, traditionally, as the sun sign of Pisces, the Fish. The ruling planet is Neptune.

PRESCOTT, WILLIAM: BIRTH ANNIVERSARY. Feb 20, 1726. American Revolutionary soldier, born at Groton, MA. Died at Pepperell, MA, Oct 13, 1795. Credited with the order, "Don't fire until you see the whites of their eyes," at the Battle of Bunker Hill, June 17, 1775.

RECREATIONAL VEHICLE SHOW. Feb 20–22 (also Feb 27–29, tentative). Timonium State Fairgrounds, Timonium, MD. Mid-Atlantic's oldest, largest and best-attended RV show with exhibitors to display all the latest in motor homes, camping and RV accessories. Est attendance: 20,000. For info: Maryland Recreational Vehicle Assn, 8332 Pulaski Hwy, Baltimore, MD 21237. Phone: (410) 987-6300. Web: www.mdrv.com.

SECOND HONEYMOON WEEKEND. Feb 20–22. This weekend is set aside for all couples to spend some quality time together away from the routine of their everyday lives. Take your significant other away and experience fun, joy and closeness together. Annually, the weekend immediately after Valentine's Day. [©1996] To alleviate the escalating costs of Eventological® Literature, a charge of $7 must be assessed for each request. Checks are to be made payable to: Adrienne Sioux Koopersmith, 1437 W Rosemont, #1W, Chicago, IL 60660-1319. Phone: (773) 743-5341. Fax: (773) 743-5395. E-mail: la_koop@yahoo.com.

SOUTH TEXAS RANCHING HERITAGE FESTIVAL. Feb 20–22. Kingsville, TX. Cowboy storytelling, craftsmen, ranching rodeo, chuckwagon cook-off and camp cooking. Est attendance: 10,000. For info: Kingsville CVB, 1501 N Hwy 77, Kingsville, TX 78363. Phone: (800) 333-5032. Fax: (361) 592-3227. E-mail: visitors@kingsvilletexas.com. Web: www.kingsvilletexas.com.

SPACE MILESTONE: *FRIENDSHIP 7* (US): FIRST AMERICAN TO ORBIT EARTH. Feb 20, 1962. John Herschel Glenn, Jr, became the first American, and the third person, to orbit Earth. Aboard the capsule *Friendship 7*, he made three orbits of Earth. Spacecraft was *Mercury-Atlas 6*. In 1998 the 77-year-old Glenn went into space again on the space shuttle *Discovery* to test the effects of aging.

SPACE MILESTONE: *MIR* SPACE STATION (USSR). Feb 20, 1986. A "third-generation" orbiting space station, *Mir* (Peace), was launched without crew from the Baikonur space center at Leninsk, Kazakhstan. Believed to be 40 feet long, weigh 47 tons and have six docking ports. Both Russian and American crews have used the station. After many equipment failures and financial problems, the Russians took *Mir* out of service Mar 23, 2001. See also: "Space Milestone: *Mir* Abandoned (USSR)" (Mar 23).

STAMP EXPO. Feb 20–22 (also Aug 27–29 and Nov 26–28). Pasadena Convention Center, Pasadena, CA. Est attendance: 5,000. For info: Intl Stamp Collectors Soc, PO Box 854, Van Nuys, CA 91408. Phone: (818) 997-6496. Fax: (818) 988-4337. E-mail: iibick@aol.com. Web: www.bick.net.

STOTZ, CARL E.: BIRTH ANNIVERSARY. Feb 20, 1920. Carl E. Stotz shaped the summers of millions of kids as the founder of Little League baseball. Born at Williamsport, PA, he organized the first three-team league there in 1939. Died at Williamsport, June 4, 1992.

BIRTHDAYS TODAY

Edward Albert, 53, actor (*Butterflies Are Free, Terminal Entry, Guarding Tess*), born Los Angeles, CA, Feb 20, 1951.
Robert Altman, 79, film director (*M*A*S*H, Nashville*), born Kansas City, MO, Feb 20, 1925.
Charles Barkley, 41, former basketball player, born Leeds, AL, Feb 20, 1963.
Brenda Blethyn, 58, actress (*Secrets and Lies, A River Runs Through It*), born Ramsgate, England, Feb 20, 1946.
Cindy Crawford, 38, model, actress, born DeKalb, IL, Feb 20, 1966.
Sandy Duncan, 58, actress (*Funny Face*, "The Hogan Family," *Peter Pan*), born Henderson, TX, Feb 20, 1946.
Ron Eldard, 41, actor ("Men Behaving Badly," "ER"), born Long Island, NY, Feb 20, 1963.
Philip Anthony (Phil) Esposito, 62, hockey executive, former coach and Hall of Fame hockey player, born Sault Ste. Marie, ON, Canada, Feb 20, 1942.
Stephon Marbury, 27, basketball player, born New York, NY, Feb 20, 1977.
Mitch McConnell, 62, US Senator (R, Kentucky), born Colbert County, AL, Feb 20, 1942.
Jennifer O'Neill, 56, actress (*The Summer of '42*, "Cover-Up"), born Rio de Janeiro, Brazil, Feb 20, 1948.
Sidney Poitier, 77, actor (*In the Heat of the Night*; Oscar for *Lilies of the Field*), born Miami, FL, Feb 20, 1927.
Buffy Sainte-Marie, 63, Native American folksinger ("Mister Can't You See," "He's an Indian Cowboy in the Rodeo"), born Craven, SK, Canada, Feb 20, 1941.
Patty Hearst Shaw, 50, newspaper heiress who was kidnapped by radical group Symbionese Liberation Army; actress (*Cry-Baby*), born San Francisco, CA, Feb 20, 1954.
French Stewart, 40, actor ("3rd Rock From the Sun"), born Albuquerque, NM, Feb 20, 1964.
Peter Strauss, 57, actor ("Rich Man, Poor Man," *Soldier Blue*), born Croton-on-Hudson, NY, Feb 20, 1947.

Feb 20–21 ☆ Chase's 2004 Calendar of Events ☆

Lili Taylor, 37, actress (*I Shot Andy Warhol, Mrs Parker and the Vicious Circle, Mystic Pizza*), born Glencoe, IL, Feb 20, 1967.
Robert William (Bobby) Unser, 70, auto racer, born Albuquerque, NM, Feb 20, 1934.
Gloria Vanderbilt, 80, fashion designer, artist, born New York, NY, Feb 20, 1924.
James Wilby, 46, actor (*DreamChild, Howard's End*), born Rangoon, Burma, Feb 20, 1958.
Nancy Wilson, 67, singer ("Yesterday's Love Songs/Today's Blues"), born Chillicothe, OH, Feb 20, 1937.

FEBRUARY 21 — SATURDAY
Day 52 — 314 Remaining

AMERICAN CLUB'S TEDDY BEAR AND DOLL CLASSIC. Feb 21–22. The American Club, Kohler, WI. The creations of 60 teddy bear artists and doll makers from across the country on display—dolls, bears, accessories, clothes, supplies, gifts and demonstrations. Est attendance: 3,500. For info: The American Club, Highland Dr, Kohler, WI 53044. Phone: (800) 344-2838. Fax: (920) 457-4441. Web: www.destinationkohler.com.

BANGLADESH: MARTYRS DAY. Feb 21. National mourning day in memory of martyrs of the Bengali Language Movement in 1952. Mourners gather at the Azimpur graveyard.

BATTLE OF VERDUN: ANNIVERSARY. Feb 21, 1916. The German High Command launched an offensive on the Western Front at Verdun, France, which became WWI's single longest battle. An estimated one million men were killed, decimating both the German and French armies, before the battle ended on Dec 15, 1916.

BOMBECK, ERMA: BIRTH ANNIVERSARY. Feb 21, 1927. Humorist and writer, born at Dayton, OH. Authored many books, including *The Grass Is Always Greener Over the Septic Tank*. Bombeck died at San Francisco, CA, Apr 22, 1996.

BRAZIL: CARNIVAL. Feb 21–24. Especially in Rio de Janeiro, this carnival is said to be one of the last great folk festivals and the big annual event in the life of Brazilians. Begins on Saturday night before Ash Wednesday and continues through Shrove Tuesday.

CIA AGENT ARRESTED AS SPY: 10th ANNIVERSARY. Feb 21, 1994. Aldrich Hazen Ames and his wife, Maria del Rosario Casas Ames, were arrested on charges they had spied for the Soviet Union beginning in 1985 and had continued to spy for Russia after the Soviet collapse in 1991. Ames had worked as a counterintelligence officer for the CIA at its headquarters at Langley, VA. Prosecutors said that the pair had been paid about $2.5 million for their activities and were probably responsible for the deaths of at least 10 CIA agents whom Ames had identified for the Soviets. The government considered this to be one of the most serious spy cases ever uncovered in the US. On Apr 28 Aldrich Ames was sentenced to life in prison. Rosario Ames was sentenced to a 63-month prison term in return for her husband's promise to cooperate with authorities.

	S	M	T	W	T	F	S
February 2004	1	2	3	4	5	6	7
	8	9	10	11	12	13	14
	15	16	17	18	19	20	21
	22	23	24	25	26	27	28
	29						

CLAM CHOWDER COOKOFF. Feb 21. Santa Cruz Beach Boardwalk, Santa Cruz, CA. Who makes the world's greatest clam chowder? Up to 60 teams compete to find out. Prizes for best booth encourage wacky costumes and elaborate props! Separate categories for restaurants, fire stations, media and individuals, Boston and Manhattan style chowder. Free admission. Est attendance: 15,000. For info: Jan Bollwinkel-Smith, Communications Mgr, Santa Cruz Beach Boardwalk, 400 Beach St, Santa Cruz, CA 95060-5491. Phone: (831) 423-5590. Fax: (831) 460-3336. E-mail: publicity@scseaside.com. Web: www.beachboardwalk.com.

DEEP CREEK DUNK. Feb 21. McHenry, MD. More than 360 dunkers will take the brisk dip into Deep Creek Lake to raise funds for the athletes of Special Olympics Maryland. Dunkers gather pledges to participate. Est attendance: 1,500. For info: Maria Hiewsky, 8300 Guilford Rd, Ste A, Columbia, MD 21046. Phone: (800) 541-7544 or (410) 290-7611 x3021. Fax: (410) 381-4483. E-mail: mhiewsky@somd.org. Web: www.somd.org.

FIRST WOMAN TO GRADUATE FROM DENTAL SCHOOL: ANNIVERSARY. Feb 21, 1866. Lucy Hobbs became the first woman to graduate from a dental school at Cincinnati, OH.

FRENCH WEST INDIES: CARNIVAL. Feb 21–25. Martinique. For four days, business comes to a halt. Streets spill over with parties and parades. A Carnival Queen is elected. On Dimanche Gras, or Fat Sunday, revelers dressed as red devils parade in the streets. King Carnival is "buried" on Ash Wednesday.

MALCOLM X: ASSASSINATION ANNIVERSARY. Feb 21, 1965. Malcolm X, a black leader who renounced the Black Muslim sect to form the Organization of Afro-American Unity and to practice a more orthodox form of Islam, was shot and killed as he spoke to a rally at the Audubon Ballroom at New York, NY. Three men were convicted of the murder in 1966 and sentenced to life in prison. Born Malcolm Little, the son of a Baptist preacher, at Omaha, NE, May 19, 1925.

MALTA: CARNIVAL. Feb 21–24. Valletta. Festival dates from 1535 when Knights of St. John of Jerusalem introduced Carnival at Malta. Dancing (featuring the sword dance, or "Parata," and other national dances), bands, decorated trucks and grotesque masks. Annually, the Saturday through Tuesday before Ash Wednesday.

MARRIAGE OF THE PORT CEREMONY. Feb 21. Bryan, TX. Old Portuguese ceremonial tradition in which a superb hearty red wine is fortified by adding brandy to the barrel. After considerable aging the result is gold medal–winning Papa Paulo Port. The ceremony takes place during each $5 tour of the winery and guests are treated to tastings of port and wedding cake. (From Feb 1–21, there are special tours of the winery and demonstrations of the port-making process.) For info: Julie Diefenthal, PR Dir, Messina Hof Wine Cellars, 4545 Old Reliance Rd, Bryan, TX 77808. Phone: (979) 778-9463 x30. Fax: (979) 778-1729.

142

☆ Chase's 2004 Calendar of Events ☆ Feb 21–22

NATIONAL FFA WEEK. Feb 21–28. More than 455,000 Future Farmers of America members in more than 7,200 chapters across the US, Puerto Rico and the Virgin Islands organize events and activities fostering and supporting agricultural education and the FFA. FFA is the organization for high school students studying the business, science and technology of agriculture. Annually, the week of Washington's Birthday. For info: Natl FFA Organization. Phone: (800) 772-0939. E-mail: aboutffa@ffa.org. Web: www.ffa.org.

NEW ENGLAND HOME SHOW. Feb 21–29. World Trade Center, Boston, MA. 54th annual. The oldest and largest home show of its kind in the region. More than 600 exhibits offer the latest ideas for remodeling and redecorating; the most up-to-date information; and product and creative ideas for both home and garden. Est attendance: 150,000. For info: Rich Castiglione, Show Mgr, New England Home Show, 45 Braintree Hill Office Park, Ste 102, Braintree, MA 02184. Phone: (781) 849-0990. Fax: (781) 849-7544. E-mail: richcastiglione@us.dmgworldmedia.com. Web: www.newenglandhomeshows.com.

NEW ENGLAND MID-WINTER SURFING CHAMPIONSHIP. Feb 21. Narragansett Town Beach, Narragansett, RI. 36th annual. Competition in all age categories and specialty events with prizes and trophies. Est attendance: 125. For info: Peter Panagiotis, ESA Dir, 126 Sayles Ave, Pawtucket, RI 02860.

***NEW YORKER* PUBLISHED: ANNIVERSARY.** Feb 21, 1925. First issue of the magazine published on this date.

NIXON'S TRIP TO CHINA: ANNIVERSARY. Feb 21, 1972. Richard Nixon became the first US president to visit any country not diplomatically recognized by the US when he went to the People's Republic of China for meetings with Chairman Mao Tse-tung and Premier Chou En-lai. Nixon arrived at Peking on this date and departed China on Feb 28. The "Shanghai Communique" was issued Feb 27. See also: "Shanghai Communique Anniversary" (Feb 27).

PALMER, ALICE FREEMAN: BIRTH ANNIVERSARY. Feb 21, 1855. Born at Colesville, NY, Alice Freeman Palmer became president of Wellesley College at the age of 27. Under her leadership the school grew into one of the leading women's colleges. She was also instrumental in bringing the women's school Radcliffe College into its association with Harvard University. One of the organizers of the American Association of University Women, she served as its president for two terms. She was appointed the first dean of women at the University of Chicago when it opened in 1892. Palmer died Dec 6, 1902, at Paris.

SANDINO, CESAR AUGUSTO: 70th ASSASSINATION ANNIVERSARY. Feb 21, 1934. Nicaraguan guerrilla leader after whom the Sandinistas of the present day are named. Sandino, born in 1893 (exact date unknown), was murdered along with his brother and several aides at Managua on Feb 21, 1934. He and his followers had eluded the occupying force of US Marines as well as the Nicaraguan National Guard from 1927 until 1933. Regarded by the US as an outlaw and a bandit, he is revered as a martyred patriot hero by many Nicaraguans. His successful resistance and the resulting widespread anti-US feeling were largely responsible for inauguration of a US counteraction—the "Good Neighbor Policy"—toward Latin American nations during the administration of President Franklin D. Roosevelt.

SIMONE, NINA: BIRTH ANNIVERSARY. Feb 21, 1933. The blues and jazz singer was born Eunice Waymon at Tryon, NC. Initially determined to become a concert pianist, Simone instead found a career as a singer of a wide range of musical genres where she could put her uniquely raw and emotional voice on display. She was an ardent supporter of the 1950s and '60s civil rights movement. She died at Carry-le-Rouet, France, on Apr 21, 2003.

UNITED NATIONS: INTERNATIONAL MOTHER LANGUAGE DAY. Feb 21. To help raise awareness among all peoples of the distinct and enduring value of their languages. Annually, on Feb 21. For info: United Nations, Dept of Public Info, New York, NY 10017. Web: www.un.org.

WASHINGTON MONUMENT DEDICATED: ANNIVERSARY. Feb 21, 1885. Monument to the first president was dedicated at Washington, DC.

BIRTHDAYS TODAY

Christopher Atkins, 43, actor ("Dallas," *The Blue Lagoon*), born Rye, NY, Feb 21, 1961.
William Baldwin, 41, actor (*Born on the Fourth of July*, *Backdraft*), born Massapequa, NY, Feb 21, 1963.
Mary Chapin Carpenter, 46, singer, musician ("Stones in the Road," "Hometown Girl"), born Princeton, NJ, Feb 21, 1958.
Charlotte Church, 18, singer (*Voice of an Angel*), born Cardiff, Wales, Feb 21, 1986.
Tyne Daly, 57, actress ("Judging Amy," Emmy for "Cagney and Lacey"; *Gypsy*), born Madison, WI, Feb 21, 1947.
Christine Ebersole, 51, actress (*Richie Rich*, *Amadeus*, "Saturday Night Live"), born Chicago, IL, Feb 21, 1953.
David Geffen, 60, record company executive (Geffen Records), born New York, NY, Feb 21, 1944.
Hubert de Givenchy, 77, fashion designer, born Beauvais, France, Feb 21, 1927.
Kelsey Grammer, 49, actor ("Cheers," "Frasier"), born St. Thomas, US Virgin Islands, Feb 21, 1955.
Jennifer Love Hewitt, 25, actress ("Party of Five," "Time of My Life"), born Waco, TX, Feb 21, 1979.
Gary Lockwood, 67, actor (*Splendor in the Grass*, *2001: A Space Odyssey*), born Van Nuys, CA, Feb 21, 1937.
Rue McClanahan, 70, actress ("Maude," "The Golden Girls"), born Healdton, OK, Feb 21, 1934.
William Petersen, 51, actor ("C.S.I.", *Manhunter*, *To Live and Die in LA*), born Evanston, IL, Feb 21, 1953.
Olympia J. Snowe, 57, US Senator (R, Maine), born Augusta, ME, Feb 21, 1947.

FEBRUARY 22 — SUNDAY
Day 53 — 313 Remaining

BADEN-POWELL, ROBERT: BIRTH ANNIVERSARY. Feb 22, 1857. British army officer who founded the Boy Scouts and Girl Guides. Born at London, England, he died at Kenya, Africa, Jan 8, 1941.

FASCHING SUNDAY. Feb 22. Germany and Austria. The last Sunday before Lent.

FLORIDA ACQUIRED BY US: ANNIVERSARY. Feb 22, 1819. Secretary of State John Quincy Adams signed the Florida Purchase Treaty under which Spain ceded Florida to the US. As payment, the US assumed $5 million of claims by US citizens against Spain. Florida became a state in 1845.

INTERNATIONAL FRIENDSHIP WEEK. Feb 22–28. Promotion of international friendship and the international language Esperanto. For complete information, send $5 to cover expense of printing, handling and postage. Annually, the last full week in February. For info: Dr. Stanley Drake, Pres, Intl Society of Friendship & Good Will, 999 Hood Rd, Suite 127, Marietta, GA 30068. Phone: (770) 565-2322. E-mail: ISFGW@bellsouth.net.

Feb 22 ☆ Chase's 2004 Calendar of Events ☆

ISLAMIC NEW YEAR. Feb 22. Islamic calendar date: Muharram 1, 1425. The first day of the first month of the Islamic calendar. Different methods for "anticipating" the visibility of the new moon crescent at Mecca are used by different groups. US date may vary. Began at sunset the preceding day.

ITALY: CARNIVAL WEEK. Feb 22–28. Milan. Carnival week is held according to local tradition, with shows and festive events for children on Tuesday and Thursday. Parades of floats, figures in the costume of local folk characters Meneghin and Cecca, parties and more traditional events are held on Saturday. Annually, the Sunday–Saturday of Ash Wednesday week.

JOE CAIN PROCESSION. Feb 22. Mobile, AL. Led by Slacabamorinico IV, it honors the man who revived the Mardi Gras in Mobile in 1866 following the War Between the States. Annually, the Sunday before Shrove Tuesday. Est attendance: 100,000. For info: The Rev Wayne Dean, Sr, VP, Joe Cain Society, 1064 Palmetto St, Mobile, AL 36604-3041. Phone: (251) 432-3960. E-mail: revchief@yahoo.com.

LOWELL, JAMES RUSSELL: BIRTH ANNIVERSARY. Feb 22, 1819. American essayist, poet and diplomat. Born at Cambridge, MA, he died there Aug 12, 1891.

MILLAY, EDNA ST. VINCENT: BIRTH ANNIVERSARY. Feb 22, 1892. American poet ("My candle burns at both ends . . ."), born at Rockland, ME. She died Oct 19, 1950, at Austerlitz, NY.

MONTGOMERY BOYCOTT ARRESTS: ANNIVERSARY. Feb 22, 1956. On Feb 20 white city leaders of Montgomery, AL, issued an ultimatum to black organizers of the three-month-old Montgomery bus boycott. They said if the boycott ended immediately there would be "no retaliation whatsoever." If it did not end, it was made clear they would begin arresting black leaders. Two days later, 80 well-known boycotters, including Rosa Parks, Martin Luther King, Jr and E.D. Nixon marched to the sheriff's office in the county courthouse, where they gave themselves up for arrest. They were booked, fingerprinted and photographed. The next day the story was carried by newspapers all over the world.

NATIONAL EATING DISORDERS AWARENESS WEEK. Feb 22–29. Provides opportunities for eating disorders organizations, mental health professionals, families and concerned individuals around the world to join together to distribute information and plan events relating to eating disorders. For info: National Eating Disorders Association, 603 Stewart St, Ste 803, Seattle, WA 98101. Phone: (206) 382-3587. E-mail: info@nationaleatingdisorders.org. Web: www.nationaleatingdisorders.org.

NATIONAL ENGINEERS WEEK. Feb 22–28. The 53rd annual observance, cosponsored by more than 140 national engineering societies, federal agencies and major corporations, will feature classroom programs in elementary and secondary schools throughout the US, hands-on activities in science centers and museums, engineering workplace tours, the Future City Competition (see www.furturecity.org) and the annual "Introduce a Girl to Engineering Day." Honorary Chair for 2004 is Alan Boeckman, Chairman and CEO of Fluor Corporation; Chair is IEEE-USA. For more info call: Natl Engineers Week Headquarters, 1420 King St, Alexandria, VA 22314. Phone: (703) 684-2852. E-mail: eweek@nspe.org. Web: www.eweek.org.

NATIONAL PANCAKE WEEK. Feb 22–28. Traditional celebration surrounding Shrove, or Pancake, Tuesday to recognize the history and continuing popularity of pancakes. For info: Shelly Dvorak, Bisquick Baking Mix, General Mills, Inc, #1 General Mills Blvd, Minneapolis, MN 55426. Phone: (763) 764-6451. Fax: (763) 764-4090.

ORTHODOX CHEESEFARE SUNDAY. Feb 22. The last day for dairy and fish before Clean Monday, which begins Great Lent in the Eastern Orthodox churches.

PEALE, REMBRANDT: BIRTH ANNIVERSARY. Feb 22, 1778. American portrait and historical painter, son of artist Charles Willson Peale, born at Bucks County, PA. Died at Philadelphia, PA, Oct 3, 1860.

SAINT LUCIA: INDEPENDENCE DAY: 25th ANNIVERSARY. Feb 22. National holiday. Commemorates independence of the island in the West Indies from Britain in 1979.

SCHOPENHAUER, ARTHUR: BIRTH ANNIVERSARY. Feb 22, 1788. Philosopher and author, born at Danzig, Germany, and died at Frankfurt am Main, Germany, Sept 21, 1860. Generally regarded as a misanthrope, the never-married Schopenhauer wrote in 1819, "To marry is to halve your rights and double your duties."

SHROVETIDE. Feb 22–24. The three days before Ash Wednesday: Shrove Sunday, Monday and Tuesday—a time for confession and for festivity before the beginning of Lent.

SPECIAL OLYMPICS MARYLAND WINTER GAMES. Feb 22–24. Wisp Ski Resort, McHenry, MD. More than 200 Special Olympics athletes throughout Maryland compete in alpine, cross-country and modified alpine skiing. The three-day festivities include an elaborate opening and closing ceremony featuring the traditional lighting of the Special Olympics cauldron. The Tubes of Fire Reggae Fest on Feb 20 and the Deep Creek Dunk on Feb 21 are fund-raising events that kick off all festivities. For info: Kelley Wallace, Sr Dir, Special Olympics Maryland, 8300 Guilford Rd, Ste A, Columbia, MD 21046. Phone: (800) 541-7544 or (410) 290-7611. Fax: (410) 381-4483. E-mail: somdmail@somd.org. Web: www.somd.org.

WADLOW, ROBERT PERSHING: BIRTH ANNIVERSARY. Feb 22, 1918. Tallest man in recorded history, born at Alton, IL. Though only 9 lbs at birth, by age 10 Wadlow already stood over 6 feet tall and weighed 210 lbs. When Wadlow died at age 22, he was a remarkable 8 feet 11.1 inches tall, 490 lbs. His gentle, friendly manner in the face of constant public attention earned him the name "Gentle Giant." Wadlow died July 15, 1940, at Manistee, MI, of complications resulting from a foot infection.

WASHINGTON, GEORGE: BIRTH ANNIVERSARY. Feb 22, 1732. First president of the US ("First in war, first in peace and first in the hearts of his countrymen" in the words of Henry "Light-Horse Harry" Lee). Born at Westmoreland County, VA, Feb 22, 1732 (New Style). However, the Julian (Old Style) calendar was still in use in the colonies when he was born and the year began in March, so the date on the calendar when he was born was Feb 11, 1731. He died at Mount Vernon, VA, Dec 14, 1799. See also: "Washington, George: Birthday Observance (Legal Holiday)" (Feb 16 in 2004).

WOOLWORTHS FIRST OPENED: 125th ANNIVERSARY. Feb 22, 1879. First chain store, Woolworths, opened at Utica, NY. In 1997 the closing of the chain was announced.

	S	M	T	W	T	F	S
February 2004	1	2	3	4	5	6	7
	8	9	10	11	12	13	14
	15	16	17	18	19	20	21
	22	23	24	25	26	27	28
	29						

☆ Chase's 2004 Calendar of Events ☆ Feb 22–23

BIRTHDAYS TODAY

Amy Strum Alcott, 48, golfer, born Kansas City, MO, Feb 22, 1956.

George Lee ("Sparky") Anderson, 70, Hall of Fame baseball manager and player, born Bridgewater, SD, Feb 22, 1934.

Drew Barrymore, 29, actress (*Charlie's Angels, E.T. The Extra-Terrestrial*), born Los Angeles, CA, Feb 22, 1975.

Michael Te Pei Chang, 32, tennis player, born Hoboken, NJ, Feb 22, 1972.

Jonathan Demme, 60, director (*Silence of the Lambs*), born Centre, MD, Feb 22, 1944.

Paul Dooley, 76, actor (*Slap Shot, Breaking Away, The Player*), born Parkersburg, WV, Feb 22, 1928.

Julius Winfield ("Dr. J") Erving, 54, Hall of Fame basketball player, born Roosevelt, NY, Feb 22, 1950.

William Frist, 52, US Senator (R, Tennessee), born Nashville, TN, Feb 22, 1952.

Steve Irwin, 42, naturalist, television personality ("The Crocodile Hunter"), born Victoria, Australia, Feb 22, 1962.

Edward Moore (Ted) Kennedy, 72, US Senator (D, Massachusetts), born Boston, MA, Feb 22, 1932.

Kyle MacLachlan, 45, actor ("Twin Peaks," *Blue Velvet, The Flintstones*), born Yakima, WA, Feb 22, 1959.

Miou-Miou, 54, actress (*Entre Nous, La Lectrice*), born Paris, France, Feb 22, 1950.

Jeri Ryan, 36, actress ("Star Trek: Voyager"), born Munich, Germany, Feb 22, 1968.

Kazuhiro Sasaki, 36, baseball player, born Sendai, Japan, Feb 22, 1968.

Vijay Singh, 41, golfer, born Lautoka, Fiji, Feb 22, 1963.

Julie Walters, 54, actress (*Educating Rita, Prick Up Your Ears*), born Birmingham, England, Feb 22, 1950.

Jayson Williams, 36, former basketball player, born Ritter, SC, Feb 22, 1968.

FEBRUARY 23 — MONDAY
Day 54 — 312 Remaining

BRUNEI DARUSSALAM: NATIONAL DAY: 20th ANNIVERSARY. Feb 23. National holiday observed in Brunei Darussalam, located on the island of Borneo. Commemorates independence from Britain, Feb 23, 1984.

CARNIVAL. Feb 23–24. Period of festivities, feasts, foolishness and gaiety immediately before Lent begins on Ash Wednesday. Ordinarily Carnival includes only Fasching (the Feast of Fools), being the Monday and Tuesday immediately preceding Ash Wednesday. The period of Carnival may also be extended to include longer periods in some areas.

CURLING IS COOL DAY. Feb 23. Offer up a worldwide embrace for an Olympic sport the entire family can play! If you don't get it, you ain't cool. [©2003 by WH.] For info: Thomas & Ruth Roy, Wellcat Holidays, 2418 Long Lane, Lebanon, PA 17046. Phone: (717) 279-0184. Fax: (240) 332-4886. E-mail: info@wellcat.com. Web: www.wellcat.com.

CYPRUS: GREEN MONDAY. Feb 23. Green, or Clean, Monday is the first Monday of Lent on the Orthodox Christian calendar. Lunch in the fields, with bread, olives and uncooked vegetables and no meat or dairy products.

DENMARK: STREET URCHINS' CARNIVAL. Feb 23. Observed on Shrove Monday.

DIESEL ENGINE PATENTED: ANNIVERSARY. Feb 23, 1893. Rudolf Diesel received a patent in Germany for the engine that bears his name. The diesel engine burns fuel oil rather than gasoline and is used in trucks and heavy industrial machinery.

Du BOIS, W.E.B.: BIRTH ANNIVERSARY. Feb 23, 1868. William Edward Burghardt Du Bois, American educator and leader of the movement for black equality. Born at Great Barrington, MA, he died at Accra, Ghana, Aug 27, 1963. "The cost of liberty," he wrote in 1909, "is less than the price of repression."

FASCHING. Feb 23–24. In Germany and Austria, Fasching, also called Fasnacht, Fasnet or Feast of Fools, is a Shrovetide festival with processions of masked figures, both beautiful and grotesque. Always the two days (Rose Monday and Shrove Tuesday) between Fasching Sunday and Ash Wednesday.

FIRST CLONING OF AN ADULT ANIMAL: ANNIVERSARY. Feb 23, 1997. Researchers in Scotland announced the first cloning of an adult animal, a lamb they named Dolly with a genetic makeup identical to that of her mother. This led to worldwide speculation about the possibility of human cloning. On Mar 4, President Clinton imposed a ban on the federal funding of human cloning research.

GROUND WAR AGAINST IRAQ BEGINS: ANNIVERSARY. Feb 23, 1991. After an air campaign lasting slightly more than a month, Allied forces launched the ground offensive against Iraqi forces as part of Desert Storm. The relentless air attacks had devastated troops and targets in both Iraq and Kuwait. A world that had watched and anticipated "the mother of all battles" was surprised at the swiftness and ease with which Allied forces were able to subdue Iraqi forces in 100 hours.

GUYANA: ANNIVERSARY OF REPUBLIC. Feb 23. National holiday. Guyana in South America became a republic within the British Commonwealth, Feb 23, 1970.

HANDEL, GEORGE FREDERICK: BIRTH ANNIVERSARY. Feb 23, 1685 (OS). Born at Halle, Saxony, Germany. Handel and Bach, born the same year, were perhaps the greatest masters of Baroque music. Handel's most frequently performed work is the oratorio *Messiah*, which was first heard in 1742. He died at London, England, Apr 14, 1759. See also: "Bach, Johann Sebastian: Birth Anniversary" (Mar 21).

ICELAND: BUN DAY. Feb 23. Children invade homes in the morning with colorful sticks and receive gifts of whipped cream buns (on Shrove Monday).

INTERNATIONAL WEEK AT TEXAS A&M. Feb 23–27. Memorial Student Center, Texas A&M University, College Station, TX. Texas A&M's more than 2,600 international students from some 100 countries introduce their cultures to the university and community during this 21st annual International Week. Cultural displays, an international buffet, talent show and traditional dress parade are some of the week's highlights. Annually, the last week in February. Est attendance: 5,000. For info: Intl Student Services, Texas A&M University, 1st Flr Bizzell Hall East, College Station, TX 77843-1226. Phone: (979) 845-1825. Fax: (979) 862-4633. E-mail: iss@iss.tamu.edu. Web: www.international.tamu.edu/iss.

IWO JIMA DAY: ANNIVERSARY. Feb 23, 1945. Anniversary of the day that the US flag was raised on the Pacific island of Iwo Jima by US Marines. Almost 20,000 American soldiers lost their lives before the island was finally taken from the Japanese on Mar 16, 1945.

JAPANESE ATTACK US MAINLAND: ANNIVERSARY. Feb 23, 1942. In the first attack on the US mainland, a Japanese submarine fired 25 shells at an oil refinery at the edge of Ellwood Oil Field 12 miles west of Santa Barbara, CA. One shell made a direct hit of the rigging, causing minor damage. President Roosevelt was giving a fireside chat at the time of the attack.

145

Feb 23-24 ☆ Chase's 2004 Calendar of Events ☆

ORTHODOX LENT. Feb 23–Apr 3. Great Lent or Easter Lent, observed by Eastern Orthodox churches, lasts until Holy Week begins on Orthodox Palm Sunday (Apr 4). The first day is known as Clean Monday which begins the Great Fast when Orthodox Christians abstain from eating meat, dairy and fish.

PEPYS, SAMUEL: BIRTH ANNIVERSARY. Feb 23, 1633 (OS). Diarist, born at London, England. Wrote Pepys in his diary (Mar 10, 1666): "The truth is, I do indulge myself a little the more in pleasure, knowing that this is the proper age of my life to do it; and, out of my observation that most men that do thrive in the world do forget to take pleasure during the time that they are getting their estate, but reserve that till they have got one, and then it is too late for them to enjoy it." Died at London, England, May 26, 1703 (OS).

RUSSIA: ARMY AND NAVY DAY. Feb 23. Also known as Defender of the Fatherland Day. Wreaths are laid at the Tomb of the Unknown Soldier. Commemorates a 1918 clash with German troops that went down in history as the birthday of the Red Army.

SHIRER, WILLIAM L.: 100th BIRTH ANNIVERSARY. Feb 23, 1904. American journalist and author William L. Shirer was born at Chicago, IL. As the European correspondent from 1927 to 1934 for the *Chicago Tribune* he became a friend of Mohandas K. Gandhi, the leader of India's independence movement. As a result of this he published *Gandhi: A Memoir* in 1980. His best-known book is *The Rise and Fall of the Third Reich* (1960), in which he used his experiences in Europe with the *New York Herald Tribune*, the Universal News Service and CBS Radio. He died Dec 28, 1993, at Boston, MA.

SHROVE MONDAY. Feb 23. The Monday before Ash Wednesday. In Germany and Austria, this is called Rose Monday.

TAYLOR, GEORGE: DEATH ANNIVERSARY. Feb 23, 1781. Signer of the Declaration of Independence. Born 1716 at British Isles (exact date unknown). Died at Easton, PA.

TRINIDAD AND TOBAGO: CARNIVAL. Feb 23–24. Port of Spain. Called by islanders "the mother of all carnivals," a special tradition that brings together people from all over the world in an incredibly colorful setting that includes the world's most celebrated calypsonians, steel band players, costume designers and masqueraders. Annually, the two days before Ash Wednesday. For info: Natl Carnival Commission, Tourism and Industrial Development Co, Administration Bldg, Queen Park Savannah, Port of Spain, Trinidad and Tobago, West Indies. Phone: (809) 623-1932. Fax: (809) 623-3848.

WILLARD, EMMA HART: BIRTH ANNIVERSARY. Feb 23, 1787. Pioneer in higher education for women, born at Berlin, CT. Intent on improving educational opportunities for women, she sent her *Plan for Improving Female Education* to the governor of New York. In it she described her ideal for a girls' school, including the instruction usually offered the girls of her day (music, drawing, penmanship, dancing), as well as adding religious and moral instruction, natural philosophy and domestic science. The New York legislature granted her a charter for the Waterford Academy for Young Ladies. The school later moved to Troy, NY, where it was first named the Troy Female Seminary and later the Emma Willard School. She assisted in the founding of a teachers' training school for girls at Athens, Greece, in 1832. She began the Willard Association for the Mutual Improvement of Female Teachers in 1837, and she authored several textbooks on geography, history and astronomy. Willard died at Troy, NY, Apr 15, 1870.

★ ★ ★

February 2004	S	M	T	W	T	F	S
	1	2	3	4	5	6	7
	8	9	10	11	12	13	14
	15	16	17	18	19	20	21
	22	23	24	25	26	27	28
	29						

BIRTHDAYS TODAY
Roberto Martin Antonio (Bobby) Bonilla, 41, former baseball player, born New York, NY, Feb 23, 1963.
Sylvia Chase, 66, newscaster, born Northfield, MN, Feb 23, 1938.
Peter Fonda, 65, actor (*Easy Rider, Ulee's Gold*), born New York, NY, Feb 23, 1939.
Edward Lee ("Too Tall") Jones, 53, former football player and boxer, born Jackson, TN, Feb 23, 1951.
Howard Jones, 49, singer (*Dream into Action*), born Southampton, England, Feb 23, 1955.
Patricia Richardson, 53, actress ("Double Trouble," "Home Improvement"), born Bethesda, MD, Feb 23, 1951.
Johnny Winter, 60, singer, musician, born John Dawson III, Beaumont, TX, Feb 23, 1944.

FEBRUARY 24 — TUESDAY
Day 55 — 311 Remaining

ENGLAND: SHROVETIDE PANCAKE RACE. Feb 24. Olney, Buckinghamshire. The pancake race at Olney has been run since 1445. Competitors must be women over 16 years of age, wearing traditional housewife's costume, including apron and head covering. With a toss and flip of the pancake on the griddle that each must carry, the women dash from the marketplace to the parish church, where the winner receives a kiss from the ringer of the Pancake Bell. Shriving service follows. Annually, on Shrove Tuesday.

ESTONIA: INDEPENDENCE DAY. Feb 24. National holiday. Commemorates declaration of independence from Soviet Union in 1918. Independence was brief, however; Estonia was again under Soviet control until 1991.

GREGORIAN CALENDAR DAY: ANNIVERSARY. Feb 24, 1582. Pope Gregory XIII, enlisting the expertise of distinguished astronomers and mathematicians, issued a bull correcting the Julian calendar that was then 10 days in error. The correction was a minor one, changing the rule about leap years. The new calendar named for him, the Gregorian calendar, became effective Oct 4, 1582, in most Catholic countries, in 1752 in Britain and the American colonies, in 1918 in Russia and in 1923 in Greece. It is the most widely used calendar in the world today. See also: "Calendar Adjustment Day: Anniversary" (Sept 2) and "Gregorian Calendar Adjustment: Anniversary" (Oct 4).

GRIMM, WILHELM CARL: BIRTH ANNIVERSARY. Feb 24, 1786. Mythologist and author, born at Hanau, Germany. Best remembered for *Grimm's Fairy Tales*, in collaboration with his brother, Jacob. Died at Berlin, Germany, Dec 16, 1859. See also: "Grimm, Jacob: Birth Anniversary" (Jan 4).

HADASSAH: ANNIVERSARY. Feb 24, 1912. Twelve members of the Daughters of Zion Study Circle met at New York City under the leadership of Henrietta Szold. A constitution was drafted to expand the study group into a national organization called Hadassah (Hebrew for "myrtle" and the biblical name of Queen Esther) to foster Jewish education in America and to create public health nursing and nurses training in Palestine. Hadassah is now the largest women's volunteer organization in the US with 1,500 chapters rooted in health care delivery, education and vocational training, children's villages and services and land reclamation in Israel.

HOMER, WINSLOW: BIRTH ANNIVERSARY. Feb 24, 1836. American artist, born at Boston, MA. Noted for the realism of his work, from the Civil War reportage to the highly regarded rugged outdoor scenes of hunting and fishing. Died at his home in Prout's Neck, ME, Sept 29, 1910.

ICELAND: BURSTING DAY. Feb 24. Feasts with salted mutton and thick pea soup. (Shrove Tuesday.)

INTERNATIONAL PANCAKE DAY. Feb 24. Liberal, KS. The 2004 International Pancake Race will be the 55th annual competition between the women of Liberal, KS, and Olney, Bucks, England. The women, wearing the traditional dress, apron and scarf, run a 415-yard S-shaped course, carrying a pancake in a skillet. Other events include a breakfast, parade, talent show, eating and flipping contests and the Miss Liberal scholarship pageant. Annually on Shrove Tuesday, the day before Ash Wednesday. Est attendance: 5,000. For info: JoAnn Combs, Exec Secy, PO Box 665, Liberal, KS 67905. Phone: (620) 624-6423. Web: www.pancakeday.com.

JOHNSON IMPEACHMENT PROCEEDINGS: ANNIVERSARY. Feb 24, 1867. In a showdown over reconstruction policy following the Civil War, the House of Representatives voted to impeach President Andrew Johnson. During the two years following the end of the war, the Republican-controlled Congress had sought to severely punish the South. Congress passed the Reconstruction Act that divided the South into five military districts headed by officers who were to take their orders from General Grant, the head of the army, instead of from President Johnson. In addition, Congress passed the Tenure of Office Act, which required Senate approval before Johnson could remove any official whose appointment was originally approved by the Senate. Johnson vetoed this act but the veto was overridden by Congress. To test the constitutionality of the act, Johnson dismissed Secretary of War Edwin Stanton, triggering the impeachment vote. On Mar 5, 1868, the Senate convened as a court to hear the charges against the president. The Senate vote of 35–19 fell one vote short of the two-thirds majority needed for impeachment.

MARDI GRAS. Feb 24. Celebrated especially at New Orleans, LA, Mobile, AL, and certain Mississippi and Florida cities. Last feast before Lent. Although Mardi Gras (Fat Tuesday, literally) is properly limited to Shrove Tuesday, it has come to be popularly applied to the preceding two weeks of celebration.

MEXICO: FLAG DAY. Feb 24. *El Día de la Bandera.* National holiday honoring the Mexican flag, which was created in 1821 after Mexico achieved independence.

NIMITZ, CHESTER: BIRTH ANNIVERSARY. Feb 24, 1885. Commander of all Allied naval, land and air forces in the southwest Pacific during a portion of WWII, Admiral Chester William Nimitz was born at Fredericksburg, TX. During the final assault on Japan in April 1945, Nimitz resumed command of the entire naval operation in the Pacific which he had shared with MacArthur for some time. Nimitz was one of the signers of the Japanese document of surrender Sept 2, 1945, aboard the USS *Missouri* in Tokyo Bay. Nimitz died Feb 20, 1966, at Treasure Island, San Francisco Bay, CA. The USS *Nimitz* was named in his honor.

PACZKI DAY. Feb 24. Food lovers pick this day to enjoy these round, sugar-coated, fruit-filled Polish pre-Lenten pastries, pronounced "poonch-kee," available in bakeries nationwide. Paczki Day coincides with Shrove Tuesday or Fat Tuesday, the day before Ash Wednesday. Sponsors: RBA (The Retailer's Bakery Association) and RBA National Paczki Promotion Board. For info: RBA—The Retailer's Bakery Assoc, 14239 Park Center Dr, Laurel, MD 20707. Phone: (301) 725-2149 or (800) 884-1500. E-mail: rba@rbanet.com.

SHROVE TUESDAY. Feb 24. Always the day before Ash Wednesday. Sometimes called Pancake Tuesday. This day is a legal holiday in some counties in Florida.

SPAY DAY USA. Feb 24. An annual, nationwide campaign to end the tragedy of pet overpopulation by encouraging every humane American to take responsibility for having at least one cat or dog spayed or neutered, be that pet theirs, a neighbor's or a shelter animal. Veterinary clinics, humane societies/shelters, businesses and individuals are encouraged to participate. For info: Doris Day Animal Foundation, Spay Day USA, 227 Massachusetts Ave NE, Ste 100, Washington, DC 20002. Phone: (202) 546-1761. Fax: (202) 546-2193. E-mail: info@ddaf.org. Web: www.ddaf.org/spayday.

WAGNER, HONUS: BIRTH ANNIVERSARY. Feb 24, 1874. American baseball great, born John Peter Wagner at Carnegie, PA. Nicknamed the "Flying Dutchman," Wagner was among the first five players elected to the Baseball Hall of Fame in 1936. Died at Carnegie, Dec 6, 1955.

BIRTHDAYS TODAY

Barry Bostwick, 59, actor (*The Rocky Horror Picture Show*, "Spin City"), born San Mateo, CA, Feb 24, 1945.

James Farentino, 66, actor ("Dynasty," "Cool Million," *The Story of a Woman*), born New York, NY, Feb 24, 1938.

Jeff Garcia, 34, football player, born Gilroy, CA, Feb 24, 1970.

Lleyton Hewitt, 23, tennis player, born Adelaide, Australia, Feb 24, 1981.

Steven Hill, 82, actor ("Law & Order"), born Seattle, WA, Feb 24, 1922.

Rupert Holmes, 57, musician, songwriter ("Escape"), born Tenafly, NJ, Feb 24, 1947.

Steven Jobs, 49, founder of Apple computer company, born Los Altos, CA, Feb 24, 1955.

Mark Lane, 77, lawyer, author (*Rush to Judgment, Eyewitness Chicago*), assassination buff, born New York, NY, Feb 24, 1927.

Michel Legrand, 72, composer, conductor, born Paris, France, Feb 24, 1932.

Joseph I. Lieberman, 62, US Senator (D, Connecticut), born Stamford, CT, Feb 24, 1942.

Zell Miller, 72, US Senator (D, Georgia), born Young Harris, GA, Feb 24, 1932.

Eddie Clarence Murray, 48, former baseball player, born Los Angeles, CA, Feb 24, 1956.

Edward James Olmos, 57, actor (*Stand and Deliver;* Emmy for "Miami Vice"), born East Los Angeles, CA, Feb 24, 1947.

Renata Scotto, 68, soprano, born Savona, Italy, Feb 24, 1936.

Helen Shaver, 53, actress (*Desert Hearts, The Color of Money*), born St. Thomas, ON, Canada, Feb 24, 1951.

John Vernon, 72, actor (*Point Blank, Dirty Harry, I'm Gonna Git You Sucka*), born Montreal, QC, Canada, Feb 24, 1932.

Abe Vigoda, 83, actor ("Barney Miller," "Fish"), born New York, NY, Feb 24, 1921.

Paula Zahn, 48, TV newscaster, born Naperville, IL, Feb 24, 1956.

Billy Zane, 38, actor (*Titanic, The Phantom*), born Chicago, IL, Feb 24, 1966.

FEBRUARY 25 — WEDNESDAY

Day 56 — 310 Remaining

ASH WEDNESDAY. Feb 25. Marks the beginning of Lent. Forty weekdays and six Sundays (Saturday considered a weekday) remain until Easter Sunday. Named for use of ashes in ceremonial penance.

BACKUS, JIM: BIRTH ANNIVERSARY. Feb 25, 1913. Born James Gilmore Backus at Cleveland, OH. An actor whose career encompassed radio, television and film, Jim Backus is most remembered as the voice behind the near-sighted bumbler, Mr Magoo, and for his portrayal of Thurston Howell III on the popular TV show, "Gilligan's Island." Backus died July 3, 1989, at Santa Monica, CA.

Feb 25 ☆ Chase's 2004 Calendar of Events ☆

BASCOM, "TEXAS ROSE": BIRTH ANNIVERSARY. Feb 25, 1922. A Cherokee-Choctaw Indian born at Covington County, MS, Rose Flynt married rodeo cowboy Earl Bascom and learned trick roping, becoming known as the greatest female trick roper in the world. She appeared on stage, in movies and on early TV. She toured with the USO during WWII, performing at every military base and military hospital in the US. After the war she entertained servicemen stationed overseas. In 1981 she was inducted into the National Cowgirl Hall of Fame (located at Hereford, TX). She died Sept 23, 1993, at St. George, UT.

BIG 12 MEN'S AND WOMEN'S SWIMMING AND DIVING CHAMPIONSHIPS. Feb 25–28. Austin, TX. Est attendance: 3,000. For info: Big 12 Conference, 2201 Stemmons Frwy, 28th Fl, Dallas, TX 75207. Phone: (214) 742-1212. Fax: (214) 753-0145. Web: www.big12sports.com.

BURGESS, ANTHONY: BIRTH ANNIVERSARY. Feb 25, 1917. Author (*A Clockwork Orange*). Born at Manchester, England. Died Nov 25, 1993, at London.

CARUSO, ENRICO: BIRTH ANNIVERSARY. Feb 25, 1873. Operatic tenor of legendary voice and fame, born at Naples, Italy. Died there Aug 2, 1921.

CLAY BECOMES HEAVYWEIGHT CHAMP: 40th ANNIVERSARY. Feb 25, 1964. Twenty-two-year-old Cassius Clay (later Muhammad Ali) became world heavyweight boxing champion by defeating Sonny Liston. At the height of his athletic career Ali was well known for both his fighting ability and personal style. His most famous saying was "I am the greatest!" In 1967 he was convicted of violating the Selective Service Act and was stripped of his title for refusing to be inducted into the armed services during the Vietnam War. Ali cited religious convictions as his reason for refusal. In 1971 the Supreme Court reversed the conviction. Ali is the only fighter to win the heavyweight fighting title three separate times. He defended that title nine times.

FENWICK, MILLICENT HAMMOND: BIRTH ANNIVERSARY. Feb 25, 1910. Former fashion model, author, member NJ General Assembly and US congresswoman, Millicent Fenwick was born at New York, NY. A champion of liberal causes, Fenwick pointed to her sponsorship of the resolution creating the commission to monitor the 1975 Helsinki accords on human rights as her proudest achievement. She fought for civil rights, peace in Vietnam, aid for the poor, reduction of military programs, gun control and restrictions on capital punishment. Fenwick, the inspiration for Garry Trudeau's "Doonesbury" character Lacey Davenport, died at Bernardsville, NJ, Sept 16, 1992.

LA FIESTA DE LOS VAQUEROS. Feb 25–29. Tucson, AZ. Tucson celebrates its Old West heritage with a parade, the PRCA rodeo and other related rodeo events, including Women's Championship Rodeo. Est attendance: 55,000. For info: Tucson Rodeo Committee, Inc, PO Box 11006, Tucson, AZ 85734. Phone: (520) 741-2233 or (800) 964-5662. Fax: (520) 741-7273. Web: www.tucsonrodeo.com.

FIRST NATIONAL BANK CHARTERED BY CONGRESS: ANNIVERSARY. Feb 25, 1791. The First Bank of the US at Philadelphia, PA, was chartered. Proposed as a national bank by Alexander Hamilton, it lost its charter in 1811. The Second Bank of the US received a charter in 1816 which expired in 1836. Since that time, the US has had no central bank. Central banking functions are carried out by the Federal Reserve System, established in 1913. See also: "Federal Reserve System: Anniversary" (Dec 23).

February 2004

S	M	T	W	T	F	S
1	2	3	4	5	6	7
8	9	10	11	12	13	14
15	16	17	18	19	20	21
22	23	24	25	26	27	28
29						

FREER, CHARLES LANG: BIRTH ANNIVERSARY. Feb 25, 1856. American art collector who built and endowed the Freer Gallery, which was presented to the Smithsonian Institution in 1906. Born at Kingston, NY, he died at New York, NY, Sept 25, 1919.

HARRISON, GEORGE: BIRTH ANNIVERSARY. Feb 25, 1945. Musician and singer born Liverpool, England, he was the guitarist and co-songwriter for the Beatles, alongside John Lennon, Paul McCartney and Ringo Starr. The band is considered to be the most influential rock-and-roll group of all time. Harrison is credited with introducing Eastern musical styles and instrumentation to Western pop. After the breakup of the Beatles, Harrison embarked on a successful solo career, became an independent film producer (*Time Bandits*) and created one of the first charity rock concerts with his Concert for Bangladesh, which brought relief to flood victims of that country. He died at Los Angeles, CA, on Nov 29, 2001.

HEBRON MASSACRE: 10th ANNIVERSARY. Feb 25, 1994. An American-born Jewish settler in Hebron, Israel, Baruch Goldstein, opened fire with an assault rifle in a crowded mosque, part of a complex sacred to both Jews and Muslims because it is believed to contain the tomb of Abraham and his wife Sarah. Of the more than 400 Muslims gathered for early morning prayers during the holy month of Ramadan, 29 were killed immediately and 150 were wounded. Others, including Goldstein, were crushed in the panic to flee or during subsequent rioting.

ITALY: PURGATORY BANQUET. Feb 25. Gradoli (near Viterbo). On Ash Wednesday, gourmands are on hand for the banquet of penitence for the souls in purgatory, held on the premises of the cooperative winery.

KUWAIT: NATIONAL DAY. Feb 25. National holiday. Commemorates the 1978 accession of King Shaykh Sir 'abdullah Al-Salim al-Sabah.

LENT. Feb 25–Apr 10. Most Christian churches observe a period of fasting and penitence (40 weekdays and six Sundays—Saturday considered a weekday) beginning on Ash Wednesday and ending on the Saturday before Easter. The word *Lent* comes from "lengthen," referring to the lengthening of the day that occurs in the spring.

RENOIR, PIERRE AUGUSTE: BIRTH ANNIVERSARY. Feb 25, 1841. Impressionist painter, born at Limoges, France. Renoir's paintings are known for their joy and sensuousness as well as the light techniques he employed in them. In his later years he was crippled with arthritis and would paint with the brush strapped to his hand. He died at Cagnes-sur-Mer, Provence, France, Dec 17, 1919.

SPACE MILESTONE: *SOYUZ 32* (USSR): 25th ANNIVERSARY. Feb 25, 1979. Launched from Baikonur space center in Soviet Central Asia. Cosmonauts Vladimir Lyakhov and Valery Ryumin aboard, docked at *Salyut 6* space station Feb 26. Returned to Earth in *Soyuz 34* after what was then a record 175 days in space Aug 19, 1979.

UI LIONEL HAMPTON JAZZ FESTIVAL. Feb 25–28. University of Idaho, Moscow, ID. Each year, college, high school, junior high school and elementary school vocal and instrumental jazz ensembles come from all over the US to compete in the festival and attend concerts and clinics given by the world's greatest jazz artists. Annually, Wednesday–Saturday the last full week of February. Est attendance: 40,000. For info: Dr. Lynn J. Skinner, Exec Dir, UI Lionel Hampton Jazz Fest, PO Box 444257, Moscow, ID 83844-4257. Phone: (208) 885-6765. Fax: (208) 885-6513. E-mail: jazzinfo@uidaho.edu.

"YOUR SHOW OF SHOWS" TV PREMIERE: ANNIVERSARY. Feb 25, 1950. Sid Caesar and Imogene Coca starred in the NBC 90-minute variety program along with Carl Reiner and Howard Morris. The show included monologues, improvisations, parodies, pantomimes and sketches of varying length. Some of its writers were Mel Tolkin, Lucille Kallen, Mel Brooks, Larry Gelbart, Neil Simon and Woody Allen.

☆ Chase's 2004 Calendar of Events ☆ Feb 25–26

BIRTHDAYS TODAY

Sean Astin, 33, actor (the *Lord of the Rings* trilogy, *Rudy, Courage Under Fire*), son of John Astin and Patty Duke, born Santa Monica, CA, Feb 25, 1971.

Diane Baker, 66, actress (*Silence of the Lambs*), born Hollywood, CA, Feb 25, 1938.

Tom Courtenay, 67, actor (*The Dresser, The Loneliness of the Long Distance Runner, Otley*), born Hull, England, Feb 25, 1937.

Larry Gelbart, 76, writer, producer ("M*A*S*H"), born Chicago, IL, Feb 25, 1928.

Karen Grassle, 60, actress ("Little House on the Prairie"), born Berkeley, CA, Feb 25, 1944.

Neil Jordan, 54, director, writer (*The Crying Game, Interview with the Vampire*), born County Sligo, Ireland, Feb 25, 1950.

Tea Leoni, 38, actress (*Jurassic Park III, Deep Impact, Flirting with Disaster*), born New York, NY, Feb 25, 1966.

Sally Jessy Raphael, 61, talk-show host, born Easton, PA, Feb 25, 1943.

Bob Schieffer, 67, TV newscaster, born Austin, TX, Feb 25, 1937.

Josh Wolff, 27, soccer player, born Stone Mountain, GA, Feb 25, 1977.

FEBRUARY 26 — THURSDAY
Day 57 — 309 Remaining

BELGIUM: CAT FESTIVAL. Feb 26. Traditional cultural observance. Annually, on the second day of Lent.

BIG TEN MEN'S SWIMMING AND DIVING CHAMPIONSHIP. Feb 26–28. Purdue University, West Lafayette, IN. Est attendance: 2,000. For info: Sue Lister, Big Ten Conference, 1500 W Higgins Rd, Park Ridge, IL 60068-6300. Phone: (847) 696-1010. Fax: (847) 696-1110. Web: www.bigten.org.

CANADA: MONTREAL SPORTSMEN'S SHOW. Feb 26–29. Place Bonaventure, Montreal, QC. Manufacturers' representatives, distributors and retailers of the outdoors, including camping, fishing, hunting, marine (fishing boats, canoes, kayaks, etc), tourism offices, outfitters (lodges), RVs and entertainment. Est attendance: 37,000. For info: Canadian National Sportsmen's Shows, 980 St-Antoine St W, Ste 222, Montreal, QC, Canada, H3C 1A8. Phone: (514) 866-5409. Fax: (514) 866-4092. Web: www.sportshows.ca or www.saloncamping.ca.

CANADA: OTTAWA BOAT, SPORTSMEN'S AND COTTAGE SHOW. Feb 26–29. Civic Centre, Coliseum and Aberdeen Pavilion, Lansdowne Park, Ottawa, ON. Boating, hunting, fishing and archery information. Products displayed: powerboats, runabouts, inflatables, personal watercraft, fishing tackle, travel info, cottage products, canoes, kayaks, camping and family entertainment. Est attendance: 30,000. For info: Canadian Natl Sportsmen's Shows, 703 Evans Ave, Ste 202, Toronto, ON, Canada M9C 5E9. Phone: (416) 695-0311. Fax: (416) 695-0381. Web: www.sportshows.ca.

CANADA: YUKON SOURDOUGH RENDEZVOUS. Feb 26–29. Whitehorse, YT. Mad trapper competitions, flour packing, beard-growing contests, old-time fiddle show, sourdough pancake breakfasts, can-can dancers, talent shows, etc. Also, many family-oriented activities. Visitors welcome to participate. Est attendance: 20,000. For info: Yukon Sourdough Rendezvous, Box 31721, Whitehorse, YT, Canada Y1A 6L3. Phone: (867) 667-2148 or (888) FUN-N-SNO. Fax: (867) 668-6755. E-mail: ysr@yukon.net. Web: www.yukonrendezvous.com.

CHARRO DAYS. Feb 26–29. Brownsville, TX. Two Nations—Twin Cultures, a true example of international harmony and cooperation between Brownsville, Texas, and Matamoros, Mexico. Starts the last Thursday in February. Colorful celebration of the charro horsemen of Mexico, men of great riding skills. Dances, parades and carnival. Est attendance: 150,000. For info: Charro Days, Inc, PO Box 3247, Brownsville, TX 78523-3247. Phone: (956) 542-4245. Fax: (956) 542-6771. Web: www.charrodays.org.

CODY, WILLIAM FREDERIC "BUFFALO BILL": BIRTH ANNIVERSARY. Feb 26, 1846. American frontiersman born at Scott County, IA, who claimed to have killed more than 4,000 buffaloes. Subject of many heroic Wild West yarns, Cody became successful as a showman, taking his acts across the US and to Europe. Died Jan 10, 1917, at Denver, CO.

COMMUNIST MANIFESTO PUBLISHED: ANNIVERSARY. Feb 26, 1848. Written by Karl Marx and Friedrich Engels on the eve of the revolutions of 1848, the *Manifesto* provided ideas for socialist and communist movements.

DAUMIER, HONORE: BIRTH ANNIVERSARY. Feb 26, 1808. French painter and caricaturist famous for his satirical and comic lithographs. Once spent six months in prison for a caricature of Louis Philippe shown as Gargantua consuming the heavy taxes of the citizens. Born at Marseilles, France, he died Feb 11, 1879, at Volmondois, France.

FEDERAL COMMUNICATIONS COMMISSION CREATED: 70th ANNIVERSARY. Feb 26, 1934. President Franklin D. Roosevelt ordered the creation of a Communications Commission, which became the FCC. It was created by Congress June 19, 1934, to oversee communication by radio, wire or cable. TV and satellite communication later became part of its charge.

FLORIDA STRAWBERRY FESTIVAL. Feb 26–Mar 7. Plant City, FL. Celebration of winter strawberry harvest. Est attendance: 725,000. For info: Patsy Brooks, Gen Mgr, Florida Strawberry Fest, PO Drawer 1869, Plant City, FL 33564-1869. Phone: (813) 752-9194 or (813) 754-1996. Fax: (813) 754-4297. Web: www.flstrawberryfestival.com.

FOR PETE'S SAKE DAY. Feb 26. A world wonders: after all these years, who is Pete and why do we do or not do things for his sake? [©2003 by WH.] For info: Thomas & Ruth Roy, Wellcat Holidays, 2418 Long Ln, Lebanon, PA 17046. Phone: (717) 279-0184. E-mail: info@wellcat.com. Web: www.wellcat.com.

GLEASON, JACKIE: BIRTH ANNIVERSARY. Feb 26, 1916. American musician, comedian and actor, Herbert John "Jackie" Gleason was born at Brooklyn, NY. Best known for his role as Ralph Kramden in the long-running television series "The Honeymooners." Died at Fort Lauderdale, FL, June 24, 1987.

GRAND CANYON NATIONAL PARK ESTABLISHED: 85th ANNIVERSARY. Feb 26, 1919. By an act of Congress, Grand Canyon National Park was established. An immense gorge cut through the high plateaus of northwest Arizona by the raging Colorado River and covering 1,218,375 acres, Grand Canyon National Park is considered one of the most spectacular natural phenomena in the world.

HOUSTON LIVESTOCK SHOW AND RODEO™. Feb 26–Mar 20 (tentative). Reliant Park, Houston, TX. Livestock show with more than 32,000 entries. Rodeo action and top-name musical entertainment. Est attendance: 1,700,000. For info: Marketing Dept, Houston Livestock Show and Rodeo, Box 20070, Houston, TX 77225-0070. Phone: (832) 667-1000. Fax: (832) 667-1134. Web: www.rodeohouston.com and hlsr.com.

HUGO, VICTOR: BIRTH ANNIVERSARY. Feb 26, 1802. French author, born at Besançon, France. "An invasion of armies can be resisted," he wrote in 1852, "but not an idea whose time has come." His most well-known work was the novel *Les Misérables*. Died at Paris, May 22, 1885.

INTRODUCE A GIRL TO ENGINEERING DAY. Feb 26. 5th annual. During National Engineers Week, the engineering community is asked to mobilize women and men engineers to reach more than one million girls and encourage them to pursue the fields that lead to engineering careers. Website includes links for teachers. For info: Natl Engineers Week Headquarters, 1420 King St, Alexandria, VA 22314. Phone: (703) 684-2852. E-mail: eweek@nspe.org. Web: www.eweek.org/site/News/Eweek/girlsday.shtml.

Feb 26–27 ☆ Chase's 2004 Calendar of Events ☆

STRAUSS, LEVI: 175th BIRTH ANNIVERSARY. Feb 26, 1829. Bavarian immigrant Levi Strauss created the world's first pair of jeans—Levi's 501 jeans—for California's gold miners in 1850. Born at Buttenheim, Bavaria, Germany, he died in 1902.

VERCORS, JEAN: BIRTH ANNIVERSARY. Feb 26, 1902. Jean Vercors was the author of the first clandestine novel published during the Nazi occupation of France. Vercors, whose real name was Jean-Marcel de Bruller, was best known for his novel *Silence of the Sea*, which he published with Pierre de Lescure for their publishing house, Les Editions de Minuit, after the Nazis occupied France in 1941. Vercors was born at Paris, France, and died there June 10, 1991.

WORLD TRADE CENTER BOMBING OF 1993: ANNIVERSARY. Feb 26, 1993. A 1,210-lb bomb packed in a van exploded in the underground parking garage of the World Trade Center in New York City, killing six people and injuring more than 1,000 (mostly from smoke inhalation). The powerful blast left a crater 200 feet wide and several stories deep. The cost for damage to the building and disruption of business for the 350 companies with offices in the Center exceeded more than $591 million. Fifteen people—the fundamentalist Moslem cleric Sheik Omar Abdul Rahman and fourteen of his followers—were indicted for the bombing. Rahman was given a life sentence and the others received prison terms of up to 240 years each.

BIRTHDAYS TODAY

Mason Adams, 85, actor ("Lou Grant," "Morningstar/Eveningstar"), born New York, NY, Feb 26, 1919.

Erykah Badu, 32, pop singer, born Dallas, TX, Feb 26, 1972.

Johnny Cash, 72, singer ("Guess Things Happen That Way," "Ring of Fire"), born Kingsland, AR, Feb 26, 1932.

Fats Domino, 76, singer, songwriter ("Ain't That a Shame," "I'm in Love Again," "Blueberry Hill"), born Antoine Domino, New Orleans, LA, Feb 26, 1928.

Marshall Faulk, 31, football player, born New Orleans, LA, Feb 26, 1973.

Jennifer Grant, 38, actress (*The Evening Star*), born Burbank, CA, Feb 26, 1966.

Betty Hutton, 83, singer, actress (*Annie Get Your Gun*, "The Betty Hutton Show"), born Elizabeth June Thornberg, Battle Creek, MI, Feb 26, 1921.

Tony Randall, 84, actor (*Pillow Talk*, "The Odd Couple"), born Leonard Rosenberg, Tulsa, OK, Feb 26, 1920.

FEBRUARY 27 — FRIDAY
Day 58 — 308 Remaining

ANDERSON, MARIAN: BIRTH ANNIVERSARY. Feb 27, 1897. Born at Philadelphia (some sources say in 1899 or 1902), Anderson's talent was evident at an early age. Her career stonewalled by the prejudice she encountered in the US, she moved to Europe where the magnificence of her voice and her versatility as a performer began to establish her as one of the world's finest contraltos. Preventing Anderson's performance at Washington's Constitution Hall in 1939 on the basis of her color, the Daughters of the American Revolution secured for her the publicity that would lay the foundation for her success in the States. Her performance was rescheduled, and on Apr 9 (Easter Sunday) 75,000 people showed up to hear her sing from the steps of the Lincoln Memorial and the performance was simultaneously broadcast by radio. In 1957 Anderson became the first African American to perform with the New York Metropolitan Opera. The following year President Eisenhower named her a delegate to the United Nations. She performed at President Kennedy's inauguration and in 1963 received the Presidential Medal of Freedom. Anderson died Apr 8, 1993, at Portland, OR.

BENNETT, JOAN: BIRTH ANNIVERSARY. Feb 27, 1910. American film and television actress was born at Palisades, NJ. Her film career was mostly during the 1930s and 1940s in such films as *Father of the Bride* (1950), after which she became a star of the television cult hit "Dark Shadows" (originally broadcast 1966–71). Died Dec 7, 1990, at Scarsdale, NY.

BIG 12 MEN'S AND WOMEN'S INDOOR TRACK CHAMPIONSHIPS. Feb 27–28. Lincoln, NE. Est attendance: 3,000. For info: Big 12 Conference, 2201 Stemmons Freeway, 28th Fl, Dallas, TX 75207. Phone: (214) 774-1212. Fax: (214) 753-0145. Web: www.big12sports.com.

CAMEX. Feb 27–Mar 2. San Antonio, TX. The only national conference and trade exhibit designed exclusively for collegiate retailers. College store buyers and suppliers gather at CAMEX to preview products to be seen on college campuses in the coming year. Est attendance: 7,000. For info: Laura Nakoneczny, Dir of PR, Natl Assn of College Stores (NACS), 500 E Lorain St, Oberlin, OH 44074. Phone: (440) 775-7777 x2351 or (800) 622-7498 x2351. E-mail: lnakoneczny@nacs.org. Web: www.nacs.org.

DOMINICAN REPUBLIC: INDEPENDENCE DAY. Feb 27. National Day. Independence gained in 1844 with the withdrawal of Haitians, who had controlled the area for 22 years.

FAITH CITY KENNEL CLUB DOG SHOW. Feb 27–29. Multi-Purpose Events Center, Wichita Falls, TX. More than 1,000 dogs in competition in the two-day event. Est attendance: 3,600. For info: Wichita Falls CVB, 1000 5th St, Wichita Falls, TX 76301. Phone: (940) 716-5500. Fax: (940) 716-5509. E-mail: MPEC@wf.net. Web: www.wichitafalls.org.

FARRELL, JAMES THOMAS: 100th BIRTH ANNIVERSARY. Feb 27, 1904. American author, novelist and short story writer, best known for his Studs Lonigan trilogy. Born at Chicago, IL, he died at New York, NY, Aug 22, 1979.

HAMILTON, ALICE: BIRTH ANNIVERSARY. Feb 27, 1869. American pathologist Alice Hamilton was born at New York, NY. She contributed to the workmen's compensation laws by reporting on the dangers to workers of industrial toxic substances. She taught at Harvard Medical School from 1919 until 1935. Hamilton died Sept 22, 1970, at Hadlyme, CT.

KUWAIT LIBERATED AND 100-HOUR WAR ENDS: ANNIVERSARY. Feb 27, 1991. Allied troops entered Kuwait City, Kuwait, four days after launching a ground offensive. President George Bush declared Kuwait to be liberated and ceased all offensive military operations in the Gulf War. The end of military operations at midnight EST came 100 hours after the beginning of the land attack. Feb 26 is commemorated as Liberation Day in Kuwait.

LONGFELLOW, HENRY WADSWORTH: BIRTH ANNIVERSARY. Feb 27, 1807. American poet and writer, born at Portland, ME. He is best remembered for his classic narrative poems, such as *The Song of Hiawatha*, *Paul Revere's Ride* and *The Wreck of the Hesperus*. Died at Cambridge, MA, Mar 24, 1882.

LONGHORN WORLD CHAMPIONSHIP RODEO. Feb 27–29. Lawrence-Joel Veterans Memorial Coliseum, Winston-Salem, NC. 33rd annual. More than 200 cowboys and cowgirls compete in six professional contests ranging from bronc riding to big, bad BONUS bull riding! Free beginners horsemanship clinic 40 minutes before performances. Qualifying rodeo for Longhorn's Championship Finals Rodeo in Nashville, TN. Featuring colorful opening and pageantry. Est attendance: 16,000. For info:

February 2004	S	M	T	W	T	F	S
	1	2	3	4	5	6	7
	8	9	10	11	12	13	14
	15	16	17	18	19	20	21
	22	23	24	25	26	27	28
	29						

☆ Chase's 2004 Calendar of Events ☆   Feb 27–28

W. Bruce Lehrke, Pres, Longhorn World Chmpshp Rodeo, Inc, PO Box 70159, Nashville, TN 37207. Phone: (615) 876-1016. Fax: (615) 876-4685. E-mail: info@longhornrodeo.com. Web: www.longhornrodeo.com.

LOST DUTCHMAN DAYS. Feb 27–29. Apache Junction, AZ. Arts and crafts show and sale. Three-day rodeo competiton, dance, carnival, parade, business vendors in celebration of the legend of the Superstition Mountains and the Lost Dutchman Mine. Annually, the last full weekend in February. Est attendance: 30,000. For info: Apache Junction Chamber of Commerce, PO Box 1747, Apache Junction, AZ 85217-1747. Phone: (800) 252-3141. Fax: (480) 982-3234. Web: www.apachejunctioncoc.com.

MOON PHASE: FIRST QUARTER. Feb 27. Moon enters First Quarter phase at 10:24 PM, EST.

NEWPORT SEAFOOD AND WINE FESTIVAL. Feb 27–29. Newport, OR. Central coastal festival featuring seafood and wines from Oregon, Washington, California and Idaho. Arts and crafts exhibits as well. Est attendance: 15,000. For info: Colleen Cockrell, Events Mgr, Greater Newport Chamber of Commerce, 555 SW Coast Hwy, Newport, OR 97365. Phone: (541) 265-5883. Fax: (541) 265-5589. Web: www.newportchamber.org/swf.

OREGON SHAKESPEARE FESTIVAL. Feb 27–Oct 31. An eight-month season of 11 plays by Shakespeare, classic and contemporary playwrights on three stages: the outdoor Elizabethan Stage, the versatile Angus Bowmer Theatre and the intimate New Theatre. Est attendance: 370,000. For info: Oregon Shakespeare Festival, Box 158, Ashland, OR 97520. Phone: (541) 482-4331. Web: www.osfashland.org.

OUR TOWN AMERICA FESTIVAL. Feb 27–29 (tentative). Sportsplex Park, Coral Springs, FL. Car and bike show, amusement rides, beauty pageants and local and professional entertainment. Est attendance: 100,000. For info: Fran Cunningham, Our Town America Festival, PO Box 770971, Coral Springs, FL 33077. Phone: (954) 752-0126. E-mail: rckcpa@bellsouth.net. Web: www.ourtownamerica.org.

SARAZEN, GENE: BIRTH ANNIVERSARY. Feb 27, 1902. Gene Sarazen, golfer, born Eugenio Saraceni at Harrison, NY. Sarazen was one of the game's greatest players and in his later years one of its greatest goodwill ambassadors. The inventor of the sand wedge, Sarazen was also the first to win the modern grand slam (the Masters, US Open, British Open and PGA), although not in the same year. During the 1935 Masters, he hit one of golf's most famous shots, a four-wood for a double eagle on the par-5 15th hole of the final round. The shot enabled him to tie Craig Wood for the lead and defeat him in a playoff. Sarazen's last shot was the traditional ceremonial tee shot to open the 1999 Masters. Died at Marco Island, FL, May 13, 1999.

SHANGHAI COMMUNIQUE: ANNIVERSARY. Feb 27, 1972. On this day, President Richard Nixon and Premier Chou En-Lai released a joint communique (the Shanghai Communique) after Nixon's weeklong visit to the People's Republic of China. The two nations agreed to work toward normalizing relations. Stopping short of establishing diplomatic relations, this was the first step in that direction. The two nations entered full diplomatic relations on Jan 1, 1979, during the Carter administration.

TERRY, ELLEN: BIRTH ANNIVERSARY. Feb 27, 1847. Popular English actress (Alice) Ellen Terry was born at Coventry, Warwickshire, Feb 27, 1847. Terry was best known for her portrayal of Shakespeare's heroines, especially Portia, and as theatrical partner of English actor Henry Irving. Together she and Irving dominated both the British and American theater of their day. She died at Small Hythe, Kent, July 21, 1928.

TWENTY-SECOND AMENDMENT TO US CONSTITUTION (TWO-TERM LIMIT): RATIFICATION ANNIVERSARY. Feb 27, 1950. After the four successive presidential terms of Franklin Roosevelt, the 22nd Amendment limited the tenure of presidential office to two terms.

BIRTHDAYS TODAY

Adam Baldwin, 42, actor (*My Bodyguard, Full Metal Jacket*), born Chicago, IL, Feb 27, 1962.
Michael Bolton, 51, singer ("How Am I Supposed to Live Without You"), born New Haven, CT, Feb 27, 1953.
Alan Guth, 57, physicist, born New Brunswick, NJ, Feb 27, 1947.
Howard Hesseman, 64, actor ("WKRP in Cincinnati," "Head of the Class"), born Salem, OR, Feb 27, 1940.
Charlayne Hunter-Gault, 62, broadcast journalist, born Due West, SC, Feb 27, 1942.
Ralph Nader, 70, consumer advocate, lawyer, born Winsted, CT, Feb 27, 1934.
Denise Richards, 33, actress (*Wild Things, The World is Not Enough*), born Downers Grove, IL, Feb 17, 1971.
Grant Show, 41, actor ("Melrose Place," "Ryan's Hope"), born Detroit, MI, Feb 27, 1963.
Elizabeth Taylor, 72, actress (Oscar for *Who's Afraid of Virginia Woolf?*; *National Velvet, Cleopatra, Cat on a Hot Tin Roof*), AIDS activist, born London, England, Feb 27, 1932.
Joanne Woodward, 74, actress (Oscar for *The Three Faces of Eve; Mr and Mrs Bridge*), born Thomasville, GA, Feb 27, 1930.
James Ager Worthy, 43, former basketball player, born Gastonia, NC, Feb 27, 1961.

FEBRUARY 28 — SATURDAY
Day 59 — 307 Remaining

AMERICAN COUNCIL ON EDUCATION ANNUAL MEETING. Feb 28–Mar 2. Miami Beach, FL. Est attendance: 1,300. For info: Stephanie Marshall, Amer Council on Educ, One Dupont Circle, Washington, DC 20036. Phone: (202) 939-9410. Fax: (202) 833-4760. E-mail: stephanie_marshall@ace.nche.edu. Web: www.acenet.edu.

BIG TEN MEN'S INDOOR TRACK AND FIELD CHAMPIONSHIP. Feb 28–29. University of Michigan, Ann Arbor, MI. Est attendance: 1,500. For info: Sue Lister, Assoc Commissioner, Big Ten Conference, 1500 W Higgins Rd, Park Ridge, IL 60068-6300. Phone: (847) 696-1010. Fax: (847) 696-1110. Web: www.bigten.org.

BIG TEN WOMEN'S INDOOR TRACK AND FIELD CHAMPIONSHIP. Feb 28–29. University of Iowa, Iowa City, IA. Est attendance: 1,500. For info: Sue Lister, Assoc Commissioner, Big Ten Conference, 1500 W Higgins Rd, Park Ridge, IL 60068-6300. Phone: (847) 696-1010. Fax: (847) 696-1110. Web: www.bigten.org.

BLONDIN, CHARLES: BIRTH ANNIVERSARY. Feb 28, 1824. Daring French acrobat and aerialist (whose real name was Jean Francois Gravelet), born at St. Omer, France. Especially remembered for his conquest of Niagara Falls on a tightrope. Died Feb 19, 1897, at London. See also: "Charles Blondin's Conquest of Niagara Falls: Anniversary" (June 30).

CANIFF, MILTON: BIRTH ANNIVERSARY. Feb 28, 1907. Creator of the comic strips "Terry and the Pirates®" and "Steve Canyon," Milton Caniff was born at Hillsboro, OH. His strips were noted for their fine draftsmanship and action/adventure story lines. Caniff died Apr 3, 1988, at New York City.

FLORAL DESIGN DAY. Feb 28. A day to commemorate floral designing as an art form. Annually, on Feb 28. For info: Dr. Stephen Rittner, Rittners School of Floral Design, 345 Marlborough St, Boston, MA 02115. Phone: (617) 267-3824. E-mail: stevrt@tiac.net. Web: www.floralschool.com.

GRANT SEAFOOD FESTIVAL. Feb 28–29. Grant, FL. 38th annual. Festival promotes Indian River seafood, environmental awareness and conservation. Est attendance: 85,000. For info: Robin Tibbitts, Grant Community Club, Inc, PO Box 44, Grant, FL 32949. Phone: (321) 723-8687. Web: www.grantseafoodfestival.com.

HATSUME FAIR. Feb 28–29. Morikami Museum and Japanese Gradens, Delray Beach, FL. Celebrates the coming of spring with

Feb 28 ☆ Chase's 2004 Calendar of Events ☆

demonstrations and performances of Japanese taiko drums, folk dancing, martial arts, plants, orchids and bonsai exhibits. Annually, the last weekend in February. Est attendance: 16,000. For info: Public Relations, The Morikami Museum and Japanese Gardens, 4000 Morikami Park Rd, Delray Beach, FL 33446. Phone: (561) 495-0233. Fax: (561) 499-2557. Web: www.morikami.org.

HECHT, BEN: BIRTH ANNIVERSARY. Feb 28, 1894. In the course of his career Ben Hecht wrote in many genres. His newspaper column, "1001 Afternoons in Chicago," popularized human interest sketches. His play *The Front Page*, written with Charles MacArthur, was a hit on Broadway (1928) and on film (1931). He was a successful reporter and his first novel *Eric Dorn*, resulted partly from his time reporting from Berlin after World War I. Hecht wrote or cowrote a number of successful movie scripts, including *Notorious* and *Wuthering Heights*. Born at New York City, he died there Apr 18, 1964.

HOME AND GARDEN FESTIVAL. Feb 28–29. Multi-Purpose Events Center, Wichita Falls, TX. More than 100 exhibitors providing seminars and demonstrations, home and garden needs and antiques. Est attendance: 15,000. For info: Wichita Falls CVB, 1000 5th St, Wichita Falls, TX 76301. Phone: (940) 716-5500. Fax: (940) 716-5509. E-mail: MPEC@wf.net. Web: www.wichitafalls.org.

LYON, MARY: BIRTH ANNIVERSARY. Feb 28, 1797. Mary Lyon, born near Buckland, MA, became a pioneer in the field of higher education for women. She founded Mount Holyoke Seminary (forerunner of Mount Holyoke College) in South Hadley, MA, in 1837 at a time when American women were educated primarily by ministers in classes held in their homes. Mount Holyoke was one of the first permanent women's colleges. She died Mar 5, 1849, at South Hadley.

"M*A*S*H": THE FINAL EPISODE: ANNIVERSARY. Feb 28, 1983. Concluding a run of 255 episodes, this 2½-hour finale was the most-watched television show at that time—77 percent of the viewing public was tuned in. The show premiered in 1972. See also: "M*A*S*H TV Premiere: Anniversary" (Sept 17).

MONTAIGNE, MICHEL DE: BIRTH ANNIVERSARY. Feb 28, 1533. French essayist and philosopher, born at Perigord, France. "And if you have lived a day," he wrote in Book I of his *Essays*, "you have seen everything. One day is equal to all days. There is no other light, no other night. This sun, this moon, these stars, the way they are arranged, all is the very same your ancestors enjoyed and that will entertain your grandchildren. . . ." Died at Montaigne, France, Sept 13, 1592.

NATO PLANES DOWN SERB JETS: 10th ANNIVERSARY. Feb 28, 1994. In the first military action by the North Atlantic Treaty Organization (NATO) in the two-year-old Bosnian civil war and the first combat action by NATO in its 45-year history, UN-designated American fighter planes shot down four of six Bosnian Serb jets operating in a no-fly zone.

ORANGE HISTORICAL SOCIETY ANNUAL ANTIQUE SHOW. Feb 28–29. Amity Jr High School, Orange, CT. More than 30 antique dealers displaying quality collections. Catered luncheon served until 3 PM both days. Saturday 10–5; Sunday 10–4. Admission $4.50. Annually, the last weekend in February. Est attendance: 1,000. For info: Show Coord, Orange Historical Society, PO Box 784, Orange, CT 06477. Phone: (203) 795-6465. Web: www.orangehistory.org.

PALME, OLOF: ASSASSINATION ANNIVERSARY. Feb 28, 1986. The popular prime minister of Sweden was shot to death as he left a movie theater in Stockholm with his wife. A courageous and dominant figure in Swedish politics, Palme, an aristocrat turned socialist, had earned international respect. On the day of his death he had signed (with five other world leaders) an appeal to the leaders of the United States and the Soviet Union to forgo nuclear testing until the next summit meeting. Born on Jan 30, 1927, Palme was the third European head of government to be assassinated since the beginning of World War II (the others: Prime Minister Armand Calinescu of Romania in 1939 and Prime Minister Luis Carrero Blanco of Spain in 1973).

PARKE COUNTY MAPLE FAIR. Feb 28–29 (also Mar 6–7). Rockville, IN. Headquarters at the 4-H Fairgrounds, one mile north of Rockville on US 41. Pancakes, sausage and maple syrup meals. Largest indoor craft and art show. Farmers' market, butcher shop, tours to the Sugar Camps featuring the unique process of making maple syrup. Annually, the last weekend in February and the first weekend in March. Est attendance: 50,000. For info: Anne Lynk, Covered Bridge Capital, PO Box 165, Rockville, IN 47872. Phone: (765) 569-5226. Fax: (765) 569-3900. E-mail: pci@ticz.com. Web: www.coverbridges.com.

SAINT OSWALD OF WORCESTER FEAST DAY. Feb 28. Bishop of Worcester, England, from 961, and Archbishop of York from 972. Oswald died Feb 29, 992, but Feb 28 is generally celebrated as his feast day.

"SMOKELESS" CIGARETTE WITHDRAWN: 15th ANNIVERSARY. Feb 28, 1989. The R.J. Reynolds Tobacco Company stopped marketing Premier, the "smokeless" cigarette, due to poor sales.

TENNIEL, JOHN: BIRTH ANNIVERSARY. Feb 28, 1820. Illustrator and cartoonist, born at London, England. Best remembered for his illustrations for Lewis Carroll's *Alice's Adventures in Wonderland*. Died at London, Feb 25, 1914.

USS *PRINCETON* EXPLOSION: ANNIVERSARY. Feb 28, 1844. The newly built "war steamer," USS *Princeton*, cruising on the Potomac River with top government officials as its passengers, fired one of its guns (known, ironically, as the "Peacemaker") to demonstrate the latest in naval armament. The gun exploded, killing Abel P. Upshur, Secretary of State; Thomas W. Gilmer, Secretary of the Navy; David Gardiner, of Gardiners Island, NY; and several others. Many were injured. The president of the US, John Tyler, was on board and narrowly escaped death.

BIRTHDAYS TODAY

Svetlana Allilueva, 78, daughter of Joseph Stalin, author (*The Faraway Music*), born Moscow, USSR, Feb 28, 1926.
Mario Gabrielle Andretti, 64, former auto racer, born Montana, Trieste, Italy, Feb 28, 1940.
Charles Durning, 81, actor (*Dog Day Afternoon*, "Evening Shade"), born Highland Falls, NY, Feb 28, 1923.
Frank Gehry, 75, architect, born Toronto, ON, Canada, Feb 28, 1929.
Robert Sean Leonard, 35, actor (*The Manhattan Project, Dead Poets Society*), born Westwood, NJ, Feb 28, 1969.
Eric Lindros, 31, hockey player, born London, ON, Canada, Feb 28, 1973.
Bernadette Peters, 60, singer, actress (*Dames at Sea, Annie Get Your Gun*), born Queens, NY, Feb 28, 1944.
Charles Aaron ("Bubba") Smith, 59, actor, former football player, born Beaumont, TX, Feb 28, 1945.
Jamaal Tinsley, 26, basketball player, born Brooklyn, NY, Feb 28, 1978.
Tommy Tune, 65, actor, singer, dancer (Tony for *My One and Only*; *Will Rogers Follies*, "Dean Martin Presents . . ."), musical theater director, born Wichita Falls, TX, Feb 28, 1939.
John Turturro, 47, actor (*Desperately Seeking Susan, Quiz Show*), born Brooklyn, NY, Feb 28, 1957.

	S	M	T	W	T	F	S
February 2004	1	2	3	4	5	6	7
	8	9	10	11	12	13	14
	15	16	17	18	19	20	21
	22	23	24	25	26	27	28
	29						

☆ Chase's 2004 Calendar of Events ☆   Feb 29

FEBRUARY 29 — SUNDAY
Day 60 — 306 Remaining

ACADEMY AWARDS PRESENTATION. Feb 29. Kodak Theatre, Los Angeles, CA. 76th annual. Honoring film achievements of the previous year. Begins at 5:30 PM, PST. Also televised live by ABC. The Scientific and Technical Awards Presentation takes place Feb 14 (location TBA). For info: Academy of Motion Picture Arts and Sciences, 8949 Wilshire Blvd, Beverly Hills, CA 90211-1972. Phone: (310) 247-3000. E-mail: www.oscars.org.

BACHELORS DAY. Feb 29. Observed only in Leap Years. A day of supposed immunity for unmarried men during Leap Year, a year during which bachelors are traditionally regarded as "fair game" for dates and proposals of marriage by women.

DEERFIELD MASSACRE: 300th ANNIVERSARY. Feb 29, 1704. The garrison at Deerfield, MA, was surprised by French and Indians from Canada on this date. The town was burned, with 47 persons killed and 120 captured. The object of the raid was to recover a bell that had been shipped from France intended for an Indian village church in Canada. The Deerfield congregation had bought the bell without knowing of its intended destination or that a privateer had taken it from a captured ship and offered it for sale in Boston. The bell was installed in the Indian church where, it is said, it still hangs.

FIRST SALEM WITCHES ARRESTED: ANNIVERSARY. Feb 29, 1692. After several Salem girls exhibited strange behavior and accused three women witches of causing their ailments, arrest warrants were issued for Sarah Good, Sarah Osborne and Tituba, a West Indian slave. The next day, Tituba broke down under examination and admitted to witchcraft—and that there were other witches in the Massachusetts Bay Colony village. Tituba's testimony and that of the afflicted girls sparked hysteria that claimed 24 lives. Good was hung, Osborne died in jail and Tituba was imprisoned for one year. Upon her release, she continued life as a slave. See also: "Salem Witch Hysteria Begins: Anniversary" (Mar 1).

GRAND TETON NATIONAL PARK ESTABLISHED: 75th ANNIVERSARY. Feb 29, 1929. Grand Teton, in Wyoming, was established as a national park and preserve by Congress. On Sept 14, 1950, Congress authorized enlarging the park to include areas of Jackson Hole National Monument.

LEAP YEAR DAY. Feb 29. In 2004 we add one day, Feb 29, to bring our calendar more nearly into accord with the seasons. Under the Julian calendar of 46 BC every fourth year was a leap year, on the assumption that it took the earth 365.25 days to orbit the sun. However, the earth's orbital period is actually 365.24219 days. For the more than 1,600 years that the Julian calendar was used the calendar got out of sync with the seasons. The Gregorian calendar made just one small change: a leap day is added to the calendar once every four years except for century years which are not exactly divisible by 400. Traditionally leap year is a time during which women may propose marriage to men. COMMON YEARS AND LEAP YEARS: A "common year" (any year that is not a leap year) comprises an exact number of weeks (52) plus one day. That extra day means that if a given date of the year, say your birthday, falls on a Monday in one common year, it will fall on a Tuesday the next common year, and so on—one extra day per year, as long as the years are common. However, the rule changes for leap years. A leap year is 52 weeks plus two days. So a date, such as your birthday, that fell on Monday the previous year, in a leap year falls not on Tuesday but on Wednesday. It has leaped over a day of the week. That is why the year is called a "leap year." The "leap" occurs throughout the period from Mar 1 through the following Feb 28—in this instance, from Mar 1, 2004 through Feb 28, 2005.

LEE, ANN: BIRTH ANNIVERSARY. Feb 29, 1736. The founder of Shakerism in America was born at Manchester, England. Joined the Shaking Quakers, or Shakers, in 1758, and came to the US in 1774, forming a Shaker group near Albany. Became known for the gift of tongues and ability to work miracles and to cure diseases. Pacifists, the Shakers refused to bear arms in the American Revolution. Branded a British sympathizer, Lee was charged with high treason and jailed for 4½ months. Known as "Ann the Word" or "Mother Ann," she died at Watervliet, NY, Sept 8, 1784, at age 48.

LUXEMBOURG: BÜRGSONNDEG. Feb 29. Young people build a huge bonfire on a hill to celebrate the victorious sun, marking the end of winter. A tradition dating to pre-Christian times. On the Sunday after Ash Wednesday.

NEMEROV, HOWARD: BIRTH ANNIVERSARY. Feb 29, 1920. Howard Nemerov was the third poet laureate of the US, from 1988 to 1990. Among his works are 26 books, including five novels. He won a Pulitzer Prize and the National Book Award for his *Collected Works* in 1978. He was also a recipient of the National Medal of the Arts. As poet laureate he penned verses commemorating the 200th anniversary of the US Congress and the launch of the space shuttle *Atlantis*. Nemerov was born at New York, NY, and died July 5, 1991, at St. Louis, MO.

TELECOMMUTER APPRECIATION WEEK. Feb 29–Mar 6. Sponsored by the American Telecommuting Association, this week is designed to call attention to the benefits of telecommuting: the individual and family as well as the employer and society benefit in a win-win situation. For info: American Telecommuting Assn, 1220 L St, NW, Ste 100, Washington, DC 20005. Phone: (800) ATA-4-YOU. Fax: (800) 465-8638. E-mail: YourATA@knowledgetree.com.

US LANDING ON THE ADMIRALTY ISLANDS: ANNIVERSARY. Feb 29, 1944. General Douglas MacArthur accompanied the first units to land on Los Negros Island, in the Admiralty Islands. The Momote airfield was taken with little resistance but was not held, and the beachhead was reduced overnight. MacArthur visited the fields personally and gave orders that the position had to be held. In spite of a Japanese counterattack the beachhead was maintained.

BIRTHDAYS TODAY

Joss Ackland, 76, actor (*The Hunt for Red October, The Sicilian*), born London, England, Feb 29, 1928.
Dennis Farina, 60, actor ("Buddy Faro," *Get Shorty*), born Chicago, IL, Feb 29, 1944.
Arthur Franz, 84, actor (*Sands of Iwo Jima, Caine Mutiny, That Championship Season*), born Perth Amboy, NJ, Feb 29, 1920.
Phyllis Frelich, 60, actress (Tony for *Children of a Lesser God; Love Is Never Silent*), born Devil's Lake, ND, Feb 29, 1944.
Simon Gagne, 24, hockey player, born Ste-Foy, QC, Canada, Feb 29, 1980.
Jack Lousma, 68, astronaut, born Grand Rapids, MI, Feb 29, 1936.
James Mitchell, 84, actor ("All My Children"), born Sacramento, CA, Feb 29, 1920.
Michèle Morgan, 84, actress (*The Fallen Idol*), born Simone Roussel, Neuilly, France, Feb 29, 1920.
Alex Rocco, 68, actor ("The Famous Teddy Z," *The Godfather, The Stunt Man*), born Cambridge, MA, Feb 29, 1936.
Antonio Sabato, Jr, 32, actor ("Earth 2"), born Rome, Italy, Feb 29, 1972.
Taylor Twellman, 24, soccer player, born St. Louis, MO, Feb 29, 1980.

Mar 1 ☆ *Chase's 2004 Calendar of Events* ☆

MARCH 1 — MONDAY
Day 61 — 305 Remaining

AHRMA VINTAGE MOTORCYCLE RACES. Mar 1–2. Daytona Speedway, Daytona Beach, FL. Pre-1973 motorcycles visit the Superspeedway. For info: Daytona International Speedway, PO Box 2801, Daytona Beach, FL 32120-2801. Phone: (386) 253-7223. Fax: (386) 947-6791. Web: www.daytonainternationalspeedway.com.

★**AMERICAN RED CROSS MONTH.** Mar 1–31. Presidential Proclamation for Red Cross Month issued each year for March since 1943. Issued as American Red Cross Month since 1987.

THE ARRIVAL OF MARTIN PINZON: ANNIVERSARY. Mar 1, 1493. Martin Alonzo Pinzon (1440–1493), Spanish shipbuilder and navigator (and co-owner of the *Niña* and the *Pinta*), accompanied Christopher Columbus on his first voyage, as commander of the *Pinta*. Storms separated the ships on their return voyage, and the *Pinta* first touched land at Bayona, Spain, where Pinzon gave Europe its first news of the discovery of the New World (before Columbus's landing at Palos). Pinzon's brother, Vicente Yanez Pinzon, was commander of the third caravel of the expedition, the *Niña*.

ARTICLES OF CONFEDERATION RATIFIED: ANNIVERSARY. Mar 1, 1781. This compact made among the original 13 states had been adopted by the Congress Nov 15, 1777, and submitted to the states for ratification Nov 17, 1777. Maryland was the last state to approve, Feb 27, 1781, but Congress named Mar 1, 1781, as the day of formal ratification. The Articles of Confederation remained the supreme law of the nation until Mar 4, 1789, when the US Constitution went into effect.

AUSTRALIA: EIGHT HOUR DAY or LABOR DAY. Mar 1. Western Australia and Tasmania. Parades and celebrations commemorate trade union efforts during the 19th century to limit working hours. Their slogan: "Eight hours labor, eight hours recreation, eight hours rest!" Annually, the first Monday in March.

"BELIEVE IT OR NOT" TV PREMIERE: 55th ANNIVERSARY. Mar 1, 1949. The series was originally a radio show based on Robert L. Ripley's comic strips describing curiosities. Both the radio program and the NBC TV show were hosted by Robert Ripley until his death in 1949. Robert St. John became Ripley's successor. ABC re-created the show in 1982 with Jack Palance as host.

	S	M	T	W	T	F	S
March		1	2	3	4	5	6
2004	7	8	9	10	11	12	13
	14	15	16	17	18	19	20
	21	22	23	24	25	26	27
	28	29	30	31			

BOSNIA AND HERZEGOVINA: INDEPENDENCE DAY. Mar 1. Commemorates independence in 1992.

CRANE WATCH '04. Mar 1–Apr 15. Kearney, NE. "World's Largest Concentration of Cranes." Each spring some 500,000 sandhill cranes (80 percent of the world's population of this species) gather on the Platte River "staging area" during their northward migration. For info: Kearney Visitors Bureau, PO Box 607, Kearney, NE 68848-0607. Phone: (800) 652-9435. Web: www.kearneycoc.org.

ELLISON, RALPH WALDO: 90th BIRTH ANNIVERSARY. Mar 1, 1914. American writer and educator, born at Oklahoma City, OK. Author of the acclaimed novel *Invisible Man* (1952), the story of a young black man's struggle for his own identity in the face of rejection from both whites and blacks. Quickly recognized as a classic of 20th-century literature, it won the National Book Award in 1953. While only one of his novels was published, Ellison published collections of his essays, reviews and stories in *Shadow and Act* (1964) and *Going to the Territory* (1986). He died Apr 16, 1994, at New York City.

FORD CHAMPIONSHIP AT DORAL. Mar 1–7. Doral Golf Resort and Spa, Miami, FL. A PGA TOUR golf tournament with a full week of events, including a free outdoor concert, two celebrity pro-ams and the four-day tournament, which features 144 of the top golfers in the world. More than $9 million raised to date for various South Florida charities. Est attendance: 120,000. For info: Mkg Dir, South Florida Golf Fndn, 4400 NW 87 Ave, Lodge 8, Miami, FL 33178. Phone: (305) 477-4653. Fax: (305) 477-4914. E-mail: dehrich@sfgf.net.

GAINES, WILLIAM M.: BIRTH ANNIVERSARY. Mar 1, 1922. The magazine *Mad*, especially popular in the 1960s and 1970s, was founded and published by William Gaines. Alfred E. Neuman, the loony, freckle-faced mascot of the publication, became a pop-culture hero. The magazine, known for its parodies of movies, comic strips and celebrities as well as its satire of politics and social mores, greatly influenced dozens of humorists. Gaines was born at the Bronx, NY. He died June 3, 1992, at New York City.

GUAM: DISCOVERY DAY or MAGELLAN DAY. Mar 1. Commemorates discovery of Guam in 1521 by Magellan. Annually, the first Monday in March.

HABITAT FOR HUMANITY INTERNATIONAL MARCH GLADNESS. Mar 1–31. The Habitat for Humanity Collegiate Challenge program and the RV Care-A-Vanner program are partnering to build houses together with affiliates across the US during the month of March. Plans are being made for the first Habitat for Humanity Intergenerational builds to take place during this "March Gladness." For info: Habitat for Humanity Intl, 121 Habitat St, Americus, GA 31709. Phone: (800) HAB-ITAT or (229) 924-6935. E-mail: mkitterman@hfhi.org. Web: www.habitat.org.

HEALTH CARE DIVERSITY MONTH. Mar 1–31. To increase awareness and respect for the wide range of cost-effective health care choices available to people for chronic and life-threatening illnesses. For info: Nan Andrews Amish, Big Picture Healthcare, PO Box 2555, El Granada, CA 94018. Phone: (650) 560-9800. Fax: (650) 560-9900. E-mail: nan@bigpicturehealthcare.com. Web: www.bigpicturehealthcare.com.

HONOR SOCIETY AWARENESS MONTH. Mar 1–31. Promote the students of honor societies and recognize superior scholarship, promote intelligent learning and living and promote equal opportunities for all people. Support the staff, faculty and advisers of honor societies and professional fraternities through the exchange of meaningful ideas, celebration of diversity, understanding and service. For info: Anne Englert, 6900 N Loop 1604 West, San Antonio, TX 78249. Phone: (210) 458-4155. E-mail: aenglert@utsa.edu.

HUMORISTS ARE ARTISTS MONTH (HAAM). Mar 1–31. To recognize the important contributions made by various types of humorists to the high art of living. For info: Lone Star Publications of Humor, 8452 Fredericksburg Rd, PMB 103, San

154

☆ Chase's 2004 Calendar of Events ☆

Antonio, TX 78229. E-mail: lspubs@aol.com. Web: members.aol.com/lspubs/lsindex.html.

ICELAND: BEER DAY. Mar 1. Reykjavik. This event began on Mar 1, 1989, when a 75-year-long prohibition of beer was lifted. Features celebrations in pubs and restaurants all over Reykjavik.

INTERNATIONAL IDEAS MONTH. Mar 1–31. Everybody has ideas! Many people need to be encouraged or motivated or need to build skills in order to communicate and get their ideas out in the open for consideration and/or action. This month is dedicated to all ideas—large, small, great, not-so-great, past, current and ideas yet to come. Without constant new ideas, progress and people stagnate. For info: Sylvia Henderson, Springboard Training, 18005 Lafayette Dr, Ste B, Olney, MD 20832. Phone: (301) 646-1668. Fax: (301) 856-8000. E-mail: admin@springboardtraining.com. Web: www.springboardtraining.com.

INTERNATIONAL LISTENING AWARENESS MONTH. Mar 1–31. Dedicated to learning more about the impact that listening has on all human activity. To promote the study, development and teaching of effective listening in all settings. For info: James Pratt, PO Box 744, River Falls, WI 54022. Phone: (800) 452-4505 or (715) 425-3377. Fax: (715) 425-9533. E-mail: ilistening@aol.com. Web: www.listen.org.

INTERNATIONAL MIRTH MONTH. Mar 1–31. The merry month of March is set aside to encourage more mirthful moments. Its focus is to show people how to use humor to deal with not-so-funny stuff. Mirth month was founded by Allen Klein, professional speaker. Free monthly mirth e-mail memo available; request through e-mail listed. For info: Allen Klein, 1034 Page St, San Francisco, CA 94117. Phone: (415) 431-1913. Fax: (415) 431-8600. E-mail: mirth@allenklein.com. Web: www.allenklein.com.

★ **IRISH-AMERICAN HERITAGE MONTH.** Mar 1–31. Presidential Proclamation called for by House Joint Resolution 401 (PL 103–379).

JAPAN: OMIZUTORI (WATER-DRAWING FESTIVAL). Mar 1–14. Todaiji, Nara. At midnight, a solemn rite is performed in the flickering light of pine torches. People rush for sparks from the torches, which are believed to have magic power against evil. Most spectacular on the night of Mar 12. The ceremony of drawing water is observed at 2 AM on Mar 13, to the accompaniment of ancient Japanese music.

KOKOSCHKA, OSKAR: BIRTH ANNIVERSARY. Mar 1, 1886. Born at Pochlarn, Austria. Avant-garde artist, playwright, teacher and humanitarian, his work evoked violent reaction. After viewing a 1911 exhibition of Kokoschka's work, the Archduke Franz Ferdinand is reported to have declared, "This man deserves to have every bone in his body broken." Kokoschka's work was featured in a 1937 Nazi exhibit of "Degenerate Art." Died at Montreux, Switzerland, Feb 22, 1980.

KOREA: SAMILJOL or INDEPENDENCE MOVEMENT DAY. Mar 1. Koreans observe the anniversary of the independence movement against Japanese colonial rule in 1919.

LAND MINE BAN: 5th ANNIVERSARY. Mar 1, 1999. A United Nations treaty banning land mines took effect on this date. More than 130 nations signed the treaty; the US, Russia and China did not.

LINDBERGH KIDNAPPING: ANNIVERSARY. Mar 1, 1932. Twenty-month-old Charles A. Lindbergh, Jr, the son of Charles A. and Anne Morrow Lindbergh, was kidnapped from their home at Hopewell, NJ. Even though the Lindberghs paid a $50,000 ransom, their child's body was found in a wooded area less than five miles from the family home on May 12. Bruno Richard Hauptmann was charged with the murder and kidnapping. He was executed in the electric chair Apr 3, 1936. As a result of the kidnapping and murder of the Lindbergh baby, the Crime Control Act was passed on May 18, 1934. It authorized the death penalty for kidnappers who take their victims across state lines.

MENTAL RETARDATION AWARENESS MONTH. Mar 1–31. To educate the public about the needs of this nation's more than seven million citizens with mental retardation and about ways to prevent retardation. The Arc is a national organization on mental retardation, formerly the Association for Retarded Citizens. For info: The Arc, 1010 Wayne Ave, Ste 650, Silver Spring, MD 20910. Phone: (301) 565-3842. Fax: (301) 565-3542. Web: www.thearc.org.

MILLER, GLENN: 100th BIRTH ANNIVERSARY. Mar 1, 1904. American bandleader and composer (Alton) Glenn Miller was born at Clarinda, IA. He enjoyed great popularity preceding and during World War II. His hit recordings included "Moonlight Serenade," "String of Pearls," "Jersey Bounce" and "Sleepy Lagoon." Major Miller, leader of the US Army Air Force band, disappeared Dec 15, 1944, over the English Channel, on a flight to Paris where he was scheduled to give a show. There were many explanations of his disappearance, but 41 years later, in December 1985, crew members of an aborted RAF bombing said they believed they had seen Miller's plane go down, the victim of bombs being jettisoned by the RAF over the English Channel.

MUSIC IN OUR SCHOOLS MONTH. Mar 1–31. To increase public awareness of the importance of music education as part of a balanced curriculum. Additional information and awareness items are available. For info: Music Educators Natl Conference, 1806 Robert Fulton Dr, Reston, VA 20191. Phone: (800) 336-3768. Web: www.menc.org.

NATIONAL ATHLETIC TRAINING MONTH. Mar 1–31. This month, Certified Athletic Trainers (ATCs) across the nation will be recognized for their dedication and commitment to providing quality health care for athletes at all levels. ATCs are highly educated and can be found everywhere in sports—from high schools to professional ranks. Annually, the month of March. For info: Ellen Satlof, National Athletic Trainers' Assoc, 2952 Stemmons Freeway, Dallas, TX 75247. Phone: (214) 637-6282, ext 159. E-mail: ellen@nata.org. Web: www.nata.org.

NATIONAL CAFFEINE AWARENESS MONTH. Mar 1–31. Reduce dependency on caffeine through education. Seminars and other events focus on coffee alternatives and the harm caffeine causes. For info: CaffeineAwareness.org, PO Box 144, Brooklyn, NY 11224. Phone: (718) 670-7263. E-mail: info@caffeineawareness.org. Web: www.caffeineawareness.org.

NATIONAL CHEERLEADING WEEK. Mar 1–7. Various cheer activites conducted on a daily basis throughout the week. Annually, the first full week in March. For info: Linda Lundy, 59 County Rd 3474, Cleveland, TX 77327. Phone: (281) 399-8357. E-mail: linda@unitedcheer.com.

NATIONAL CHRONIC FATIGUE SYNDROME AWARENESS MONTH. Mar 1–31. To educate patients, their families, the public and the medical profession about the nature and impact of CFS, "the Thief of Vitality," and related disorders, as well as to encourage and provide research funding. Annually, the month of March. For info: Natl Chronic Fatigue Syndrome and Fibromyalgia Assn, PO Box 18426, Kansas City, MO 64133. Phone: (816) 313-2000 (24-hour info line). Fax: (816) 524-6782. E-mail: information@ncfsfa.org.

NATIONAL COLLISION AWARENESS MONTH. Mar 1–31. A month of vehicle safety awareness to promote the use of seatbelts, child safety seats, safe driving in inclement weather, obeying speed limits and other safety tips for drivers. For info: Nathan Hostetler, Accurate Autobody, 5550 S Garnett, Ste A, Tulsa, OK 74146. Phone: (918) 270-0100. Fax: (918) 270-0102. E-mail: nathan@44fixit.com.

NATIONAL COLORECTAL CANCER AWARENESS MONTH. Mar 1–31. To generate widespread awareness about colorectal cancer and to encourage people to learn more about how to prevent the disease through a healthy lifestyle and regular screening. Founding partners include the Cancer Research and Prevention Foundation, the American Society for Gastrointestinal Endoscopy, the National Colorectal Cancer Roundtable and The Foundation for Digestive Health and Nutrition. For info: Enica Lewis, Cancer Research and Prevention Foundation, 1600 Duke St, Alexandria, VA 22314. Phone: (703) 836-4412. Fax:

Mar 1 ☆ *Chase's 2004 Calendar of Events* ☆

(703) 836-4413. E-mail: enica.lewis@preventcancer.org. Web: www.preventcancer.org/colorectal.

★**NATIONAL COLORECTAL CANCER AWARENESS MONTH.** Mar 1–31.

NATIONAL CRAFT MONTH. Mar 1–31. Promoting the fun and creativity of hobbies and crafts. For info: Hobby Industry Association, National Craft Month, PO Box 348, Elmwood Park, NJ 07407. Phone: (201) 794-1133. Fax: (201) 797-0657. E-mail: hia@hobby.org. Web: www.hobby.org or www.i-craft.com.

NATIONAL EYE DONOR MONTH. Mar 1–31. For info: Eye Bank Association of America, 1015 18th St NW, Ste 1010, Washington, DC 20036. Phone: (202) 775-4999. Web: www.restoresight.org.

NATIONAL FROZEN FOOD MONTH. Mar 1–31. Promotes national awareness of the economical and nutritional benefits of frozen foods. Annually, the month of March. For info: Julie Henderson, VP Communications, Natl Frozen & Refrigerated Foods Assn, 4755 Linglestown Rd, Ste 300, Harrisburg, PA 17112. Phone: (717) 657-8601. Fax: (717) 657-9862. E-mail: info@nfraweb.org. Web: www.nfraweb.org.

NATIONAL GHOSTWRITERS MONTH. Mar 1–31. Almost 50% of all books are written by ghostwriters. This month honors those people who do the work but don't get the credit. One way to celebrate is to do something nice for someone and don't let them know you did it. For info: Mahesh Grossman, 209 Marnell Ave, Santa Cruz, CA 95062. Phone: (831) 458-1550. Fax: (831) 458-1501. E-mail: GetPublished@AuthorsTeam.com. Web: www.AuthorsTeam.com.

NATIONAL KIDNEY MONTH. Mar 1–31. Kidney disease may often be silent for many years until it has reached an advanced stage. The National Kidney Foundation urges everyone to get regular checkups that include tests for blood pressure, blood sugar, urine protein and kidney function. For info: Ellie Schlam, National Kidney Foundation, 30 E 33rd St, New York, NY 10016. Phone: (800) 622-9010 or (212) 889-2210. Web: www.kidney.org.

NATIONAL LAWNMOWER TUNE-UP MONTH. Mar 1–31. Regular maintenance and repair of your lawnmower saves the environment by reducing emissions and fuel consumption. Also increases the life of the mower and the horsepower. For info: Sara Grant, c/o Briggs & Stratton, 733 N Van Buren St, Milwaukee, WI 53202. Phone: (414) 227-3584. Fax: (414) 227-1530. E-mail: sgrant@ckpr.biz. Web: www.tuneupmonth.com.

NATIONAL MARCH TO COLLEGE DAY. Mar 1–31. A day when middle school students are invited to spend a day on a college campus as the guests of campus chapters of The National Society of Collegiate Scholars. During the day students will tour campus, hear a lecture, meet other college students and tour residence halls. The day is designed to expose students to college as a viable option for their future. Annually, any day in March (various on different campuses). For info: The Natl Soc of Collegiate Scholars, 1900 K Street NW, Ste 890, Washington, DC 20006. Phone: (202) 265-9000. Fax: (202) 265-9200. E-mail: pfcs@nscs.org. Web: www.nscs.org.

NATIONAL MULTIPLE SCLEROSIS EDUCATION AND AWARENESS MONTH. Mar 1–31. This month focuses on raising awareness of and compassion for those diagnosed with multiple sclerosis. A series of national events take place and educational materials and publications are circulated upon request from the Multiple Sclerosis Foundation. For info: Maggie Sherman, MS Foundation, 6350 N Andrews Ave, Fort Lauderdale, FL 33309. Phone: (954) 776-6805. Fax: (954) 938-8708. E-mail: maggies@msfocus.org. Web: www.msfocus.org.

NATIONAL NUTRITION MONTH®. Mar 1–31. To educate consumers about the importance of good nutrition by providing the latest practical information on how simple it can be to eat healthfully. For info: American Dietetic Assn, 120 S Riverside Plaza, Ste 2000, Chicago, IL 60606-6995. Phone: (312) 899-0040. Fax: (312) 899-4739. E-mail: knowledge@eatright.org. Web: www.eatright.org.

NATIONAL ON-HOLD MONTH. Mar 1–31. A month to recognize everyone who has been placed "on hold" after calling a place of business, and to honor those businesses who make this hold time more enjoyable by supplying informative messages and music for their callers waiting on hold. For info: Audiomax, 470 Sentry Pkwy East, Blue Bell, PA 19422. Phone: (800) 284-4653 or (610) 825-9100. Fax: (610) 825-0703. E-mail: kkesler@audiomax.com. Web: www.audiomax.com.

NATIONAL PIG DAY. Mar 1. To accord to the pig its rightful, though generally unrecognized, place as one of man's most intelligent and useful domesticated animals. Annually, Mar 1. For further information send SASE to: Ellen Stanley, 7006 Miami, Lubbock, TX 79413.

NATIONAL PREPARE YOUR HOME TO BE SOLD MONTH. Mar 1–31. March has been declared to be "National Prepare Your Home to be Sold Month" by the National Association of Independent Real Estate Brokers. For info: Gary Bryce Conner, NAIREB, 7102 Mardyke Ln, Indianapolis, IN 46226. Phone: (317) 547-4679. Fax: (317) 547-4634. E-mail: GaryConner@NationalRealEstateBrokers.com. Web: www.NationalRealEstateBrokers.com.

NATIONAL PROCRASTINATION WEEK. Mar 1–7. To promote the benefits of relaxing through putting off until tomorrow everything that needn't be done today. For info: Les Waas, Pres, Procrastinators' Club of America Inc, PO Box 712, Bryn Athyn, PA 19009. Phone: (215) 947-9020. Fax: (215) 947-7210. E-mail: procrastinators_club_of_america@yahoo.com.

NATIONAL PROFESSIONAL SOCIAL WORK MONTH. Mar 1–31. To honor the social work profession and to recognize the contributions social workers and concerned citizens make within their communities. "Social Worker of the Year" and "Public Citizen of the Year" awards are announced and each winner receives a plaque. For info: Natl Assn of Social Workers, Inc, 750 First St NW, Ste 700, Washington, DC 20002-4241. Phone: (202) 408-8600. Web: www.socialworkers.org.

NATIONAL TALK WITH YOUR TEEN ABOUT SEX MONTH. Mar 1–31. The importance of frank talk with teenagers about sex is emphasized. Parents are encouraged to provide their teenage children with current, accurate information and open lines for communication, as well as to support their self-esteem, reduce misinformation and guide teenagers toward making responsible decisions regarding sex. Annually, the month of March. For info send SASE to: Teresa Langston, Dir, Parenting Without Pressure (PWOP), 1330 Boyer St, Longwood, FL 32750-6311. Phone: (407) 767-2524. Web: www.parentingwithoutpressure.com.

	S	M	T	W	T	F	S
March		1	2	3	4	5	6
	7	8	9	10	11	12	13
2004	14	15	16	17	18	19	20
	21	22	23	24	25	26	27
	28	29	30	31			

☆ Chase's 2004 Calendar of Events ☆   Mar 1

NATIONAL UMBRELLA MONTH. Mar 1–31. In honor of one of the most versatile and underrated inventions of the human race, this month is dedicated to the purchase of, use of and conversation about umbrellas. Annually, the month of March. Media: please call at least 24 hrs in advance for interviews. For info: Thomas Edward Knibb, 1654 Colonial Way, Frederick, MD 21702-3919. Phone: (301) 695-7351. E-mail: tomknibb@valley alley.com.

NATIONAL WOMEN'S HISTORY MONTH. Mar 1–31. A time for reexamining and celebrating the wide range of women's contributions and achievements that are too often overlooked in the telling of US history. Information catalog available. For info: Natl Women's History Project, 3343 Industrial Dr, Ste 4, Santa Rosa, CA 95403. Phone: (707) 636-2888. Fax: (707) 636-2909. E-mail: nwhp@aol.com. Web: www.nwhp.org.

NATIONAL WRITE A LETTER OF APPRECIATION WEEK. Mar 1–7. Send a letter expressing your gratitude to others, acknowledging the goodness that we find all around us. For info: Larry McManus, 1504 N Richmond Rd, McHenry, IL 60050-1410. Phone: (815) 344-4934. Fax: (815) 344-4824. E-mail: faithhealer@ameritech.net. Web: www.appreciationweek.org.

NEBRASKA: ADMISSION DAY: ANNIVERSARY. Mar 1. Became 37th state in 1867.

NEWSPAPER IN EDUCATION WEEK. Mar 1–5. A weeklong celebration of using newspapers in the classroom as living textbooks. Annually, the first full week in March (weekdays). For info: Mgr Education Programs, Newspaper Assn of America Foundation, 1921 Gallows Rd, Ste 600, Vienna, VA 22182-3900. Phone: (703) 902-1730. E-mail: abboj@naa.org. Web: www.naa.org.

OHIO: ADMISSION DAY: ANNIVERSARY. Mar 1. Became 17th state in 1803.

OPTIMISM MONTH. Mar 1–31. To encourage people to boost their optimism. Research proves optimists achieve more health, prosperity and happiness than pessimists. Use this monthlong celebration to practice optimism and turn optimism into a delightful, permanent habit. Free "Tip Sheets" available. For info: Dr. Michael Mercer & Dr. Maryann Troiani, The Mercer Group, Inc, 25597 Drake Rd, Barrington, IL 60010. For media interviews, Victoria Sterling. Phone: (847) 382-0690. E-mail: drmercer@mercersystems.com.

PARAGUAY: NATIONAL HEROES' DAY. Mar 1. National holiday. Honors those who have died for the country, especially Mariscal Francisco Solano López, who died Mar 1, 1870.

PEACE CORPS FOUNDED: ANNIVERSARY. Mar 1, 1961. Official establishment of the Peace Corps by President John F. Kennedy's signing of executive order. The Peace Corps has sent more than 169,000 volunteers to 136 countries to help people help themselves. The volunteers assist in projects such as health, education, water sanitation, agriculture, nutrition and forestry. For info: Peace Corps, 1111 20th St NW, Washington, DC 20526. Web: www.peacecorps.gov.

PLAY-THE-RECORDER MONTH. Mar 1–31. American Recorder Society members all over the continent will celebrate the organization's annual Play-the-Recorder Month by performing in public places such as libraries, bookstores, museums and shopping malls. Some will offer workshops on playing the recorder or demonstrations in schools. Founded in 1939, the ARS is the membership organization for all recorder players, including amateurs to leading professionals. Annually, the month of March. For info: American Recorder Soc, PO Box 631, Littleton, CO 80160-0631. Phone: (303) 347-1120. E-mail: recorder@compuserve.com. Web: www.americanrecorder.org.

POISON PREVENTION AWARENESS MONTH. Mar 1–31. To educate parents, grandparents, schoolchildren and PTAs about accidental poisoning and how to prevent it. PPSI is a non-profit organization. There is a $15 charge for kit materials. Annually, the month of March. For info: Frederick Mayer, Pres, Pharmacists Planning Service, Inc, 101 Lucas Valley Rd, #210, San Rafael, CA 94903. Phone: (415) 479-8628. Fax: (415) 479-8608. E-mail: ppsi@aol.com. Web: www.ppsinc.org.

RAID ON RICHMOND: ANNIVERSARY. Mar 1, 1864. Believing the Confederate capital of Richmond, VA, to be lightly fortified, President Abraham Lincoln ordered a surprise raid to capture the city and free Union prisoners. Federal troops under General Judson Kilpatrick and Colonel Ulric Dahlgren led the attack on this date, but failed when the plan was discovered by Southern forces. In the wake of their retreat, Dahlgren was killed, and two documents were discovered on his body. The incriminating documents contained plans to burn the city and kill Confederate President Jefferson Davis and his cabinet. Confederate General Robert E. Lee complained to the Union commander, George Meade, but a Federal investigation was inconclusive.

READ ME WEEK. Mar 1–5 (tentative). National and local celebrities and other volunteers read in classrooms wearing readable clothing with school appropriate messages. For info: Melanie Grand, Program Coord, Book 'Em!, 501 Metroplex Dr, Ste 205, Nashville, TN 37211. Phone: (615) 834-7323. Fax: (615) 834-7323.

RED CROSS MONTH. Mar 1–31. To make the public aware of American Red Cross service in the community. There are nearly 1,000 Red Cross offices nationwide; each local office plans its own activities. For info on activities in your area, contact your local Red Cross office. For info: American Red Cross Natl HQ, Office of Public Inquiry, 431 18th St NW, Washington, DC 20006. Phone: (202) 639-3520. E-mail: info@usa.redcross.org. Web: www.redcross.org.

RETURN THE BORROWED BOOKS WEEK. Mar 1–7. To remind you to make room for those precious old volumes that will be returned to you by cleaning out all that worthless trash that your friends are waiting for. Annually, the first seven days of March. For info: Inter-Global Society for Prevention of Cruelty to Cartoonists, Al Kaelin, Secy, 3119 Chadwick Dr, Los Angeles, CA 90032. Phone: (323) 221-7909 or (323) 222-7944.

ROSACEA AWARENESS MONTH. Mar 1–31. Rosacea Awareness Month has been designated by the National Rosacea Society to raise awareness and understanding of this increasingly common disease. Rosacea is a facial skin condition that can cause permanent physical and psychological damage if it is not diagnosed and treated. For info: Natl Rosacea Soc, 800 S Northwest Hwy, Ste 200, Barrington, IL 60010. Phone: (847) 382-8971 or (888) NO-BLUSH. Fax: (847) 382-5567. E-mail: rosaceas@aol.com. Web: www.rosacea.org.

ROZELLE, PETE: BIRTH ANNIVERSARY. Mar 1, 1926. Alvin Ray ("Pete") Rozelle, Commissioner of the National Football League, born at South Gate, CA. Rozelle began his career in the public relations department of the Los Angeles Rams, became general manager and was elected commissioner in 1960. He built the NFL into a sporting power through the use of television. He helped engineer the NFL's merger with the American Football League, created the Super Bowl as America's greatest sports extravaganza, conceived the idea for Monday Night Football and persuaded NFL owners to accept revenue sharing. Died at Rancho Santa Fe, CA, Dec 6, 1996.

SAINT-GAUDENS, AUGUSTUS: BIRTH ANNIVERSARY. Mar 1, 1848. Sculptor, born at Dublin, Ireland. His works include the statue of Lincoln in Lincoln Park, Chicago, and of Admiral Farragut in Madison Square, New York. Saint-Gaudens died at Cornish, NH, Aug 3, 1907.

SALEM WITCH HYSTERIA BEGINS: ANNIVERSARY. Mar 1, 1692. The Massachusetts Bay Colony village of Salem had experienced a strange February in which several teenaged girls exhibited bizarre behavior and attributed their ailments to witches. Three women were then arrested on Feb 29. One of the accused, Tituba, a West Indian slave, broke down under questioning on Mar 1 and admitted to being a witch. Soon the teenaged girls accused four other residents, and by the end of April, 19 women had been accused of witchcraft and were languishing in jail—including a four-year-old child. Massachusetts governor Sir William

Mar 1 ☆ Chase's 2004 Calendar of Events ☆

Phips, seeking to control the growing terror, ordered trials held. In October, the special court was dissolved after growing protests of the trials' unjust proceedings. By then, 19 people had been hung, 5 had died in jail, 1 had been tortured to death and more than 150 had been imprisoned. Two dogs were also executed. On Jan 14, 1697, Judge Samuel Sewall publicly apologized and a court-ordered day of atonement began. In 1711, all those accused of witchcraft were pardoned by the colony's legislature. See also: "Salem Witch Trials Begin: Anniversary" (June 2).

SAVE YOUR VISION MONTH. Mar 1–31. To remind Americans of the importance of eye health and regular exams. For info: American Optometric Assn, 243 N Lindbergh Blvd, St. Louis, MO 63141. Phone: (314) 991-4100. Fax: (314) 991-4101. E-mail: slthomas@aoa.org. Web: www.aoa.org.

SHORE, DINAH: BIRTH ANNIVERSARY. Mar 1, 1917. American radio and television personality Dinah Shore was born Frances Rose Shore at Winchester, TN. In addition to recording many hit songs in the 1930s and 1940s, she was one of the first women to be successful as a television host, beginning in the 1950s with the "Dinah Shore Chevy Show." She received 10 Emmys before she died Feb 24, 1994, at Beverly Hills, CA.

SLAYTON, DONALD "DEKE" K.: 80th BIRTH ANNIVERSARY. Mar 1, 1924. "Deke" Slayton, longtime chief of flight operations at the Johnson Space Center, was born at Sparta, WI. Slayton was a member of Mercury Seven, the original group of young military aviators chosen to inaugurate America's sojourn into space. Unfortunately, a heart problem prevented him from participating in any of the Mercury flights. When in 1971 the heart condition mysteriously went away, Slayton flew on the last Apollo mission. The July 1975 flight, involving a docking with a Soviet Soyuz spacecraft, symbolized a momentary thaw in relations between the two nations. During his years as chief of flight operations, Slayton directed astronaut training and selected the crews for nearly all missions. He died June 13, 1993, at League City, TX.

SPIRITUAL WELLNESS MONTH. Mar 1–31. As spring approaches, this is a time for a new beginning, a time for spiritual renewal and inner peace. Discover a new you as you focus on telling the truth, being honest in all endeavors. Be true to yourself and build your character. Make a list of the values you cherish and work toward incorporating them in your life. Create a life of order, prayer, fasting, faith, learning and respect. For info: Angela Brown, Words of Wellness, PO Box 49266, Charlotte, NC 28277. Phone: (704) 849-2900. Fax: (704) 845-3060. E-mail: Angela@WordsofWellness.com. Web: www.WordsofWellness.com.

SWITZERLAND: CHALANDRA MARZ. Mar 1. Engadine. Springtime traditional event when costumed young people, ringing bells and cracking whips, drive away the demons of winter.

UNIVERSAL HUMAN BEINGS WEEK. Mar 1–7. The purpose of this observance is to inspire men and women to become Universal Human Beings in a world that is rapidly becoming a "global village." Annually, Mar 1–7. For complete info send $5 to cover printing, handling and postage. For info: Dr. Stanley Drake, Pres, Intl Soc of Friendship and Good Will, 999 Hood Rd, Ste 127, Marietta, GA 30068. Phone: (770) 565-2322. E-mail: ISFGW@bellsouth.net.

VULVAR HEALTH AWARENESS MONTH. Mar 1–31. Annual. Become aware of this often misunderstood area of women's health. Learn about self-examination, disorders and vulvar cancer. For info: VHAM, PO Box 6762, Bloomington, IN 47407. E-mail: vulvarhealth@yahoo.com. Web: www.vulvarhealth.org.

	S	M	T	W	T	F	S
March		1	2	3	4	5	6
	7	8	9	10	11	12	13
2004	14	15	16	17	18	19	20
	21	22	23	24	25	26	27
	28	29	30	31			

WALES: SAINT DAVID'S DAY. Mar 1. Celebrates patron saint of Wales (Dewi Sant). Welsh tradition calls for the wearing of a leek on this day.

★**WOMEN'S HISTORY MONTH.** Mar 1–31.

WORKPLACE EYE HEALTH AND SAFETY MONTH. Mar 1–31. Can you see the dangers at your workplace? Accidents at work are a major cause of preventable blindness. Find out more about Prevent Blindness America®'s workplace safety program, The Wise Owl Club, and find out how to make your work environment easier on your eyes. For info: Prevent Blindness America®, 500 Remington Rd, Schaumburg, IL 60173. Phone: (800) 331-2020. Fax: (847) 843-8458. Web: www.preventblindness.org.

YELLOWSTONE NATIONAL PARK ESTABLISHED: ANNIVERSARY. Mar 1, 1872. The first area in the world to be designated a national park, most of Yellowstone is in Wyoming, with small sections in Montana and Idaho. It was established by an act of Congress.

YOUTH ART MONTH. Mar 1–31. To emphasize the value and importance of participation in art in the development of all children and youth. For info: Council for Art Education, Inc, 1280 Main St, PO Box 479, Hanson, MA 02341. Phone: (781) 293-4100. Fax: (781) 294-0808. Web: acminet.org/youthart month.

BIRTHDAYS TODAY

Catherine Bach, 50, actress ("The Dukes of Hazzard"), born Warren, OH, Mar 1, 1954.
Harry Belafonte, 77, singer ("Mary's Boy Child," "Island in the Sun," "Banana Boat Song"), born New York, NY, Mar 1, 1927.
John B. Breaux, 60, US Senator (D, Louisiana), born Crowley, LA, Mar 1, 1944.
Robert Conrad, 69, actor ("The Wild Wild West"), born Chicago, IL, Mar 1, 1935.
Roger Daltrey, 60, lead singer (The Who), born London, England, Mar 1, 1944.
Timothy Daly, 48, actor (Diner, "Wings"), born New York, NY, Mar 1, 1956.
George Eads, 37, actor ("CSI"), born Fort Worth, TX, Mar 1, 1967.
Ron Francis, 41, hockey player, born Sault Ste. Marie, ON, Canada, Mar 1, 1963.
Mark-Paul Gosselaar, 30, actor ("NYPD Blue," "Saved by the Bell"), born Panorama City, CA, Mar 1, 1974.
Yolanda Griffith, 34, former basketball player, born Chicago, IL, Mar 1, 1970.
Ron Howard, 50, actor ("The Andy Griffith Show," "Happy Days"); director (A Beautiful Mind, Apollo 13), born Duncan, OK, Mar 1, 1954.
Judith Rossner, 69, novelist (Looking for Mr Goodbar), born New York, NY, Mar 1, 1935.
Alan Thicke, 57, actor ("Thicke of the Night," "Growing Pains"), born Kirkland Lake, ON, Canada, Mar 1, 1947.
Chris Webber, 31, basketball player, born Detroit, MI, Mar 1, 1973.
Richard (Purdy) Wilbur, 83, former poet laureate of the US, born New York, NY, Mar 1, 1921.

☆ Chase's 2004 Calendar of Events ☆

MARCH 2 — TUESDAY
Day 62 — 304 Remaining

ARNAZ, DESI: BIRTH ANNIVERSARY. Mar 2, 1917. Born at Santiago, Cuba, as Desidero Alberto Arnaz y Acha III, to a wealthy family. The 1933 revolution sent them (now impoverished) to Miami, FL, and the young Arnaz sought a music career. Arnaz led his own band and introduced the conga line to America. He had several musical hits including "Babalu." He moved into acting, meeting his future wife, Lucille Ball, at RKO. Ball and Arnaz created one of the great TV comedies, "I Love Lucy" (1951–1957), and started the innovative Desilu TV production company. Ball and Arnaz divorced in 1960. Arnaz died on Dec 2, 1986, at Del Mar, CA.

ASHURA: TENTH DAY. Mar 2. Islamic calendar date: Muharram 10, 1425. For Shia Muslims, commemorates death of Muhammad's grandson at the Battle of Karbala. A time of fasting, reflection and meditation. Jews of Medina fasted on the tenth day in remembrance of their salvation from Pharoah. Different methods for "anticipating" the visibility of the new moon crescent at Mecca are used by different groups. US date may vary. Began at sunset the preceding day.

BATTLE OF BISMARCK SEA: ANNIVERSARY. Mar 2–4, 1943. Protected by American and Australian fighters, 137 American Flying Fortress and Liberator bombers attacked a Japanese convoy en route from its base at Rabaul to New Guinea on Mar 2, 1943. In the convoy were eight transports carrying 7,000 reinforcements, which were escorted by eight destroyers. All the transports and four of the destroyers were sunk and 3,500 Japanese troops were drowned. Of the 150 Japanese aircraft involved in the fighting, 102 were shot down. The Battle of Bismarck Sea was a major victory for the Allies, ending any efforts by the Japanese to send reinforcements to New Guinea.

CORAY, MELISSA BURTON: BIRTH ANNIVERSARY. Mar 2, 1828. Coray was born at Mersey, Ontario, Canada. At the age of 18 she accompanied her Mormon Battalion soldier husband, William Coray, on a 2,000-mile military march on foot from Council Bluffs, IA, to San Diego, CA, and then 1,500 more miles across the Sierra Nevada Mountains and the Nevada desert to Salt Lake City, UT, the only woman to make the entire trip. On July 30, 1994, a mountain peak near Carson Pass was named for her, the second peak in California to be named for a woman.

ETHIOPIA: ADWA DAY. Mar 2. Ethiopian forces under Menelik II inflicted a crushing defeat on the invading Italians at Adwa in 1896.

GEISEL, THEODOR "DR. SEUSS": 100th BIRTH ANNIVERSARY. Mar 2, 1904. Theodor Seuss Geisel, the creator of *The Cat in the Hat* and *How the Grinch Stole Christmas*, was born at Springfield, MA. Known to children and parents as Dr. Seuss, his books have sold more than 200 million copies and have been translated into 20 languages. His career began with *And to Think That I Saw It on Mulberry Street*, which was turned down by 27 publishing houses before being published by Vanguard Press. His books included many messages, from environmental consciousness in *The Lorax* to the dangers of pacifism in *Horton Hatches the Egg* and *Yertle the Turtle*'s thinly veiled references to Hitler as the title character. He was awarded a Pulitzer Prize in 1984 "for his contribution over nearly half a century to the education and enjoyment of America's children and their parents." He died Sept 24, 1991, at La Jolla, CA.

HIGHWAY NUMBERS INTRODUCED: ANNIVERSARY. Mar 2, 1925. A joint board of state and federal highway officials created the first system of interstate highway numbering in the US. Standardized road signs identifying the routes were also introduced. Later the system would be improved with the use of odd and even numbers that distinguish between north-south and east-west routes respectively.

HOUSTON, SAM: BIRTH ANNIVERSARY. Mar 2, 1793. American soldier and politician, born at Rockbridge County, VA, is remembered for his role in Texas history. Houston was a congressman (1823–27) and governor (1827–29) of Tennessee. He resigned his office as governor in 1829 and rejoined the Cherokee Indians (with whom he had lived for several years as a teenage runaway), who accepted him as a member of their tribe. Houston went to Texas in 1832 and became commander of the Texan army in the War for Texan Independence, which was secured when Houston routed the much larger Mexican forces led by Santa Anna, Apr 21, 1836, at the Battle of San Jacinto. After Texas's admission to the Union, Houston served as US senator and later as governor of the state. He was deposed in 1861 when he refused to swear allegiance to the Confederacy. Houston, the only person to have been elected governor of two different states, failed to serve his full term of office in either. The city of Houston, TX, was named for him. He died July 26, 1863, at Huntsville, TX.

MOUNT RAINIER NATIONAL PARK ESTABLISHED: ANNIVERSARY. Mar 2, 1899. Located in the Cascade Mountains of Washington State, this is the fourth oldest national park.

NEA'S READ ACROSS AMERICA DAY. Mar 2. A national reading campaign that advocates that all children read a book on Mar 2. Celebrated on Dr. Seuss's birthday. For info: Natl Education Assn, 1201 16th St NW, Washington, DC 20036. Phone: (202) 822-7387. E-mail: readacross@nea.org. Web: www.nea.org/readacross.

OTT, MELVIN (MEL): 95th BIRTH ANNIVERSARY. Mar 2, 1909. Baseball Hall of Fame outfielder, born at Gretna, LA. Playing for the New York Giants, Ott hit 511 home runs, a National League record until Willie Mays surpassed it in 1966. Inducted into the Hall of Fame in 1951. Died at New Orleans, LA, Nov 21, 1958.

PEACE CORPS DAY. Mar 2. Commemorates the founding of the Peace Corps on Mar 1, 1961, by President John F. Kennedy. Observed on the first Tuesday in March.

POPE PIUS XII: BIRTH ANNIVERSARY. Mar 2, 1876. Eugenio Maria Giovanni Pacelli, 260th pope of the Roman Catholic Church, born at Rome, Italy. Elected pope Mar 2, 1939. Died at Castel Gandolfo, near Rome, Oct 9, 1958.

RITT, MARTIN: 90th BIRTH ANNIVERSARY. Mar 2, 1914. American film and television director Martin Ritt was born at New York, NY. His best-known films are *Hud* (1963), *Sounder* (1972) and *Norma Rae* (1979). During the 1950s he was blacklisted by McCarthy's anti-Communist crusade. Died Dec 8, 1990, at Santa Monica, CA.

SCHURZ, CARL: 175th BIRTH ANNIVERSARY. Mar 2, 1829. American journalist, political reformer and army officer in Civil War. Born near Cologne, Germany, he died at New York, NY, May 14, 1906.

SPACE MILESTONE: *PIONEER 10* (US). Mar 2, 1972. This unmanned probe began a journey on which it passed and photographed Jupiter and its moons, 620 million miles from Earth, in December 1973. It crossed the orbit of Pluto, and then in 1983 become the first known Earth object to leave our solar system. On Sept 22, 1987, *Pioneer 10* reached another space milestone at 4:19 PM, when it reached a distance 50 times farther from the sun than the sun is from Earth.

SPACE MILESTONE: *SOYUZ 28* (USSR): ANNIVERSARY. Mar 2, 1978. Cosmonauts Alexi Gubarev and Vladimir Remek linked with *Salyut 6* space station Mar 3, visiting crew of *Soyuz 26*. Returned to Earth Mar 10. Remek, from Czechoslovakia, was the first person in space from a country other than the US or USSR. Launched Mar 2, 1978.

TASTE OF THE TOWN. Mar 2. Multi-Purpose Events Center Exhibit Hall, Wichita Falls, TX. More than 50 restaurants and vendors gather together to show off the best food in town. Benefits the Wichita County Chapter of the Red Cross. Est attendance: 2,000. For info: Wichita Falls Conv & Visitors Bureau, 1000 Fifth St, Wichita Falls, TX 76301. Phone: (940) 716-5500. Fax: (940) 716-5509. Web: www.wichitafalls.org.

Mar 2-3 ☆ Chase's 2004 Calendar of Events ☆

TEXAS INDEPENDENCE DAY. Mar 2, 1836. Texas adopted Declaration of Independence from Mexico.

TOWN MEETING DAY. Mar 2. Vermont. The first Tuesday in March is an official state holiday in Vermont. Nearly every town elects officers, approves budget items and deals with a multitude of other items in a daylong public meeting of the voters.

BIRTHDAYS TODAY

Jon Bon Jovi, 42, singer, songwriter, actor, born John Bongiovi, Sayreville, NJ, Mar 2, 1962.

John Cullum, 74, actor (stage: *Shenandoah, On the Twentieth Century*; "Northern Exposure"), born Knoxville, TN, Mar 2, 1930.

Russell D. Feingold, 51, US Senator (D, Wisconsin), born Janesville, WI, Mar 2, 1953.

Mikhail Sergeyvich Gorbachev, 73, former Soviet political leader, born Privolnoye, Stavropol, Russia, Mar 2, 1931.

John Irving, 62, author (*Cider House Rules, The World According to Garp*), born Exeter, NH, Mar 2, 1942.

Jennifer Jones, 85, actress (Oscar for *The Song of Bernadette*), born Phyllis Isley, Tulsa, OK, Mar 2, 1919.

Eddie Money, 55, musician, born Brooklyn, NY, Mar 2, 1949.

Laraine Newman, 52, comedienne ("Saturday Night Live"), born Los Angeles, CA, Mar 2, 1952.

Doc Watson, 81, singer, musician (*Riding the Midnight Train, Then and Now*), born Deep Gap, NC, Mar 2, 1923.

Tom Wolfe, 73, author, journalist (*The Bonfire of the Vanities, The Right Stuff*), born Richmond, VA, Mar 2, 1931.

MARCH 3 — WEDNESDAY
Day 63 — 303 Remaining

BELL, ALEXANDER GRAHAM: BIRTH ANNIVERSARY. Mar 3, 1847. Inventor of the telephone, born at Edinburgh, Scotland. Bell acquired his interest in the transmission of sound from his father, Melville Bell, a teacher of the deaf. Bell's use of visual devices to teach articulation to the deaf contributed to the theory from which he derived the principle of the vibrating membrane used in the telephone. On Mar 10, 1876, Bell spoke the first electrically transmitted sentence to his assistant in the next room: "Mr Watson, come here, I want you." Bell's other accomplishments include a refinement of Edison's phonograph, the first successful phonograph record and the audiometer, and he continued exploring the nature and causes of deafness. He died near Baddeck, Nova Scotia, Canada, Aug 2, 1922.

BETHUNE, NORMAN: BIRTH ANNIVERSARY. Mar 3, 1890. Canadian physician who worked in the front lines during World War I, the Spanish Civil War and the Chinese Revolution. Bethune was born at Gravenhurst, Ontario; he died at age 49 at China while treating a soldier of Mao's Eighth Route Army, Nov 11, 1939. He is said to be the only Western man recognized as a hero of the Chinese Revolution.

BONZA BOTTLER DAY™. Mar 3. To celebrate when the number of the day is the same as the number of the month. Bonza Bottler Day™ is an excuse to have a party at least once a month. For more information, see Jan 1. For info: Gail M. Berger, 14 Fernwood Dr, Taylors, SC 29687. Phone: (864) 609-9874. E-mail: gberger5@aol.com.

BULGARIA: LIBERATION DAY. Mar 3. Grateful tribute to the Russian, Romanian and Finnish soldiers and Bulgarian volunteers who, in the Russo-Turkish War, 1877–78, liberated Bulgaria from five centuries of Ottoman rule.

FLORIDA: ADMISSION DAY: ANNIVERSARY. Mar 3. Became 27th state in 1845.

I WANT YOU TO BE HAPPY DAY. Mar 3. A day dedicated to reminding people to be thoughtful of others by showing love and concern, even if things are not going well for them. For info: Harriette W. Grimes, Grandmother, PO Box 545, Winter Garden, FL 34777-0545. Fax: (407) 656-2790. E-mail: lgrimes@cybr.net.

JAPAN: HINAMATSURI (DOLL FESTIVAL). Mar 3. This special festival for girls is observed throughout Japan. Annually, Mar 3.

LOUISIANA SPORTSMEN'S SHOW. Mar 3–7. Louisiana Superdome, New Orleans, LA. 25th annual. Louisiana's original sportfishing, hunting and boat show also covering Baton Rouge and the Gulf Coast. Est attendance: 100,000. For info: Bob Del Giorno. Phone: (504) 464-7363. Fax: (504) 835-8692. Web: www.sportsmensshow.com.

MALAWI: MARTYR'S DAY. Mar 3. Public holiday in Malawi.

MICHIGAN BOAT, SPORT AND FISHING SHOW. Mar 3–7. Ford Field, Detroit, MI. This event brings together buyers and sellers of boating, fishing and outdoor sporting products. US and Canadian hunting and fishing trips, as well as other vacation travel destinations, are featured. Est attendance: 35,000. For info: Adam Starr, ShowSpan, Inc, 2121 Celebration Dr NE, Grand Rapids, MI 49525. Phone: (616) 447-2860. Fax: (616) 447-2861. E-mail: events@showspan.com. Web: www.showspan.com.

MISSOURI COMPROMISE: ANNIVERSARY. Mar 3, 1820. In February of 1819 a bill was introduced into Congress that would admit Missouri to the Union as a state that prohibited slavery. At the time there were 11 free states and 10 slave states. Southern congressmen feared this would upset the balance of power between North and South. As a compromise, on this date Missouri was admitted as a slave state but slavery was forever prohibited in the northern part of the Louisiana Purchase. In 1854 this act was repealed when Kansas and Nebraska were allowed to decide on slave or free status by popular vote.

"MR WIZARD" TV PREMIERE: ANNIVERSARY. Mar 3, 1951. Don Herbert as Mr Wizard explained the mysteries of science while performing experiments in front of wide-eyed children. The series ran on NBC for 14 continuous years. In 1983 Herbert returned to host "Mr Wizard's World" on Nickelodeon.

"MOONLIGHTING" TV PREMIERE: ANNIVERSARY. Mar 3, 1985. Cybill Shepherd and Bruce Willis starred in ABC's comedy-adventure hour with Allyce Beasley as rhyming receptionist Agnes DiPesto. The premise: former model Maddie Hayes (Shepherd) discovers that the Blue Moon Detective Agency is her only remaining asset after her business manager embezzled her wealth. After deciding to keep the agency, she and her sparring partner, wisecracking detective David Addison (Willis), go off on a series of madcap adventures. The show frequently broke with formula by using the show-within-a-show technique, having characters directly address the camera, shooting sequences in black and white or by going completely off-concept (as in an episode based on Shakespeare's "The Taming of the Shrew"). Last telecast on May 14, 1989, the show foundered due to personality conflicts and production delays.

NAIA MEN'S AND WOMEN'S SWIMMING AND DIVING NATIONAL CHAMPIONSHIPS. Mar 3–6. Lawrence Aquatic Center, Lawrence, KS. Individuals compete for the national championship. 24th annual for women; 48th annual for men. For info: Natl Assoc of Intercollegiate Athletics, 23500 W 105th St, PO Box 1325, Olathe, KS 66051-1325. Phone: (913) 791-0044. Fax: (913) 791-9555. E-mail: knoonan@naia.org. Web: www.naia.org.

	S	M	T	W	T	F	S
March		1	2	3	4	5	6
2004	7	8	9	10	11	12	13
	14	15	16	17	18	19	20
	21	22	23	24	25	26	27
	28	29	30	31			

☆ Chase's 2004 Calendar of Events ☆   Mar 3–4

NATIONAL ANTHEM DAY: ANNIVERSARY. Mar 3, 1931. The bill designating "The Star-Spangled Banner" as our national anthem was adopted by the US Senate and went to President Herbert Hoover for signature. The president signed it the same day.

PULLMAN, GEORGE: BIRTH ANNIVERSARY. Mar 3, 1831. Born at Brocton, NY, George Mortimer Pullman was an inventor and industrialist who became famous for his design and production of the "Pullman" railroad sleeping car. His first attempt at improving railroad sleeping accommodations began in 1858, while working as a contractor for the Chicago & Alton Railroad at Chicago, IL. His initial model was not adopted, but in 1863 a new design was enthusiastically received. He secured a patent for the folding upper berth design in 1864 and one for the lower berth design in 1865. By 1867 Pullman and his partner organized the Pullman Palace Car Company, which became the greatest railroad car-building organization in the world. In 1881 the town of Pullman, IL, south of Chicago, was formed by Pullman to house his employees. Because rents were not lowered when wages were cut, a strike was initiated against Pullman's company in May 1894. Pullman was eventually forced to give up control of all property in the town not directly required for manufacturing. Pullman died Oct 19, 1897, at Chicago, IL.

RIDGWAY, MATTHEW BUNKER: BIRTH ANNIVERSARY. Mar 3, 1895. American Army officer Matthew Bunker Ridgway was born at Fort Monroe, VA. As major general commanding the newly formed 82nd Airborne Division, he led it in the invasion of Sicily in July 1943 and the invasion of the Italian mainland in 1944. Ridgway replaced MacArthur as commander of the US Eighth Army in Korea in 1951 and succeeded Eisenhower as Supreme Allied Commander of the North Atlantic Treaty Organization in 1952. He became US Army Chief of Staff in 1953. Ridgway died at Fox Chapel, PA, July 26, 1993.

STOP THE BS (BAD SERVICE) DAY. Mar 3. Celebrates those companies that give exceptional service. Contest for consumers who submit excellent customer service stories. Details at the website. Annually, the first Wednesday of March. For info: Margo Chevers, PO Box 281, Wales, MA 01081. Phone: (413) 267-4500. Fax: (413) 267-4501. E-mail: margo@margochevers.com. Web: www.margochevers.com.

3-A-DAY WEEK. Mar 3–9. 3-A-Day Week begins on the third day of the third month of the third millennium. It's a call to action for families to start eating 3-A-Day of dairy: three servings of milk, cheese and yogurt is a deliciously easy way to build stronger bones and better bodies. Research shows that most Americans are eating only half the recommended three servings of dairy each day. Eating 3-A-Day of calcium-rich milk, cheese and yogurt is the easiest and most wholesome way for families to meet their calcium needs. Try it every day this week! For info: American Dairy Assn/Natl Dairy Council. Phone: (312) 240-2835. Fax: (312) 240-9382. Email: 3aday@rosedmi.com. Web: www.3aday.org.

TIME MAGAZINE FIRST PUBLISHED: ANNIVERSARY. Mar 3, 1923. The first issue of *Time* bore this date. The magazine was founded by Henry Luce and Briton Hadden.

TRIUMPH OF AGRICULTURE EXPO. Mar 3–4. Omaha Convention Center, Omaha, NE. Est attendance: 30,000. For info: Robert P. Mancuso, Mid-America Expositions, Inc, 7015 Spring St, Omaha, NE 68106-3518. Phone: (402) 346-8003. Fax: (402) 346-5412. E-mail: showoffice@aol.com. Web: www.showofficeonline.com.

WHAT IF CATS AND DOGS HAD OPPOSABLE THUMBS DAY. Mar 3. We are grateful today that the infinite wisdom of the universe has not allowed cats and dogs to have thumbs. Imagine the cat, able to operate the can opener! Imagine the dog, able to open the refrigerator door! [©2003 by WH.] For info: Thomas & Ruth Roy, Wellcat Holidays, 2418 Long Ln, Lebanon, PA 17046. Phone: (717) 279-0184. E-mail: info@wellcat.com. Web: www.wellcat.com.

WOMAN SUFFRAGE PARADE ATTACKED: ANNIVERSARY. Mar 3, 1913. A parade held by the National American Woman Suffrage Association at Washington, DC, on the day before Woodrow Wilson's inauguration turned into a near riot when people in the crowd began jeering and shoving the marchers. The 5,000 women and their supporters were spit upon, struck in the face and pelted with burning cigar stubs while police looked on and made no effort to intervene. Secretary of War Henry Stimson was forced to send soldiers from Fort Myer to restore order.

BIRTHDAYS TODAY

Jessica Biel, 22, actress ("7th Heaven"), born Ely, MN, Mar 3, 1982.
Julie Bowen, 34, actress (*Joe Somebody*, "Ed"), born Baltimore, MD, Mar 3, 1970.
David Faustino, 30, actor ("Married . . . With Children"), born Los Angeles, CA, Mar 3, 1974.
Ira Glass, 45, radio host ("This American Life"), born Baltimore, MD, Mar 3, 1959.
Jacqueline (Jackie) Joyner-Kersee, 42, Olympic gold medal heptathlete, born East St. Louis, IL, Mar 3, 1962.
Tim Kazurinsky, 54, actor, comedian, writer ("Saturday Night Live"), born Johnstown, PA, Mar 3, 1950.
Brian Leetch, 36, hockey player, born Corpus Christi, TX, Mar 3, 1968.
Princess Radziwill, 71, sister of the late Jackie Kennedy Onassis, born Caroline Lee Bouvier, New York, NY, Mar 3, 1933.
Miranda Richardson, 46, actress (*The Crying Game, Enchanted April*), born Lancashire, England, Mar 3, 1958.
Herschel Walker, 42, former football player, born Wrightsville, GA, Mar 3, 1962.

MARCH 4 — THURSDAY
Day 64 — 302 Remaining

ADAMS, JOHN QUINCY: RETURN TO CONGRESS ANNIVERSARY. Mar 4, 1830. On this day, John Quincy Adams returned to the House of Representatives to represent the district of Plymouth, MA. He was the first former president to do so and served for eight consecutive terms.

BIG TEN WOMEN'S BASKETBALL TOURNAMENT. Mar 4–8. Canseco Fieldhouse, Indianapolis, IN. Est attendance: 2,500. For info: Sue Lister, Big Ten Conference, 1500 W Higgins Rd, Park Ridge, IL 60068-6300. Phone: (847) 696-1010. Fax: (847) 696-1110. Web: www.bigten.org.

CONGRESS: ANNIVERSARY OF FIRST MEETING UNDER CONSTITUTION. Mar 4, 1789. The first Congress met at New York, NY. A quorum was obtained in the House Apr 1 and in the Senate Apr 5, and the first Congress was formally organized Apr 6. Electoral votes were counted, and George Washington was declared president (69 votes) and John Adams vice president (34 votes).

COURAGEOUS FOLLOWER DAY. Mar 4. We are a country built on the myth of "rugged individualism," in love with the concept of leadership. But all leaders require followers and, in fact, virtually all of us are followers at some times and leaders at others. This day honors the too-often disparaged role of follower. Its purpose is to dispel the myth that followers are passive and to raise awareness that good followership is energetic and at times

Mar 4 ☆ *Chase's 2004 Calendar of Events* ☆

courageous. In fact, only through active and courageous followership can leaders be counted on to use their power wisely and well. For info: Ira Chaleff, Exec Coaching & Consulting Assoc. Phone: (301) 933-3752. Web: www.exe-coach.com.

DAYTONA 200 BY ARAI QUALIFYING DAY. Mar 4. Daytona International Speedway, Daytona Beach, FL. For info: Daytona International Speedway, PO Box 2801, Daytona Beach, FL 32120-2801. Phone: (386) 253-7223. Fax: (386) 947-6791. Web: www.daytonainternationalspeedway.com.

"THE DICK CAVETT SHOW" TV PREMIERE: ANNIVERSARY. Mar 4, 1968. Dick Cavett began his television career on ABC with a daytime talk show that subsequently became a late-night program competing with Johnny Carson. Cavett, with his Yale background, had a reputation as an "intellectual" host and was particularly adept at the one-man interview. He has since appeared on the CBS, PBS and USA networks hosting a variety of shows.

DING LING: DEATH ANNIVERSARY. Mar 4, 1986. Writer and champion of women's rights, born at Hunan Province, China, in 1904. Ding was a prolific author, having written nearly 300 novels as well as plays, short stories and essays. She received the 1951 Stalin Prize for Literature for her novel *The Sun Shines Over the Sanggan River* (1949). She fell from favor in the 1950s, was exiled and in 1970 was imprisoned. After the death of Chairman Mao she was freed and during her last years she enjoyed renewed attention and favor. Died at age 82 at Beijing, China.

ENGLAND: CRUFTS DOG SHOW. Mar 4–7. National Exhibition Centre, Birmingham, West Midlands. The World's Greatest Dog Show where more than 21,000 top pedigree dogs compete to achieve the title of "Best in Show," the most prestigious award in the world of dogs. Held since 1891. Est attendance: 115,000. For info: Events Department, The Kennel Club, 1 Clarges St, London, England W1J 8AB. Phone: (44) (870) 606-6750. Fax: (44) (207) 5181050. Web: www.crufts.org.uk.

FULTON OYSTERFEST. Mar 4–7. Fulton Navigation Park, Fulton, TX. This salute to the oyster industry features oyster-shucking, raw oyster-eating contests, more than 100 arts and crafts booths, food and fun, live bands and other entertainment. Annually, the first full weekend in March. Est attendance: 30,000. For info: Fulton Oysterfest, PO Box 393, Fulton, TX 78358. Phone: (361) 729-2388. Fax: (361) 729-3248.

GREENWOOD, JOAN: BIRTH ANNIVERSARY. Mar 4, 1921. British stage and screen actress Joan Greenwood was born at Chelsea, London. With her husky voice she became best known for playing the roles of coquettes. She died Feb 27, 1987, at London.

GROVER CLEVELAND'S SECOND PRESIDENTIAL INAUGURATION: ANNIVERSARY. Mar 4, 1893. Grover Cleveland was inaugurated for a second but nonconsecutive term as president. In 1885 he had become 22nd president of the US and in 1893 the 24th. Originally a source of some controversy, the Congressional Directory for some time listed him only as the 22nd president. The Directory now lists him as both the 22nd and 24th presidents though some historians continue to argue that one person cannot be both. Benjamin Harrison served during the intervening term, defeating Cleveland in electoral votes, though not in the popular vote.

HOT SPRINGS NATIONAL PARK ESTABLISHED: ANNIVERSARY. Mar 4, 1921. To protect the Hot Springs of Arkansas the government set aside Hot Springs Reservation on Apr 20, 1832. In 1921 the area became a national park.

	S	M	T	W	T	F	S
March 2004		1	2	3	4	5	6
	7	8	9	10	11	12	13
	14	15	16	17	18	19	20
	21	22	23	24	25	26	27
	28	29	30	31			

HUG A GI DAY. Mar 4. Today is the only calendrical date which is a military command—March Fourth. Therefore, today we honor all of the gallant men and women who serve in all branches of the military. We acknowledge and salute the sacrifices they make to keep this the land of the free and the home of the brave. [©1996] To alleviate the escalating costs of Eventological® Literature, a charge of $7 must be assessed to each request. Checks are to be made payable to: Adrienne Sioux Koopersmith, 1437 W Rosemont, 1W, Chicago, IL 60660-1319. Phone: (773) 743-5341. Fax: (773) 743-5395. E-mail: la_koop@yahoo.com.

INTERNATIONAL SCRAPBOOKING INDUSTRY DAY. Mar 4. On this day, we celebrate the growth of the scrapbooking industry and the dedicated entrepreneurs who have worked so hard to make it happen. We seek to increase awareness of the scrapbooking industry and to reflect on the ways we can advance this industry to share the gift of scrapbooking with everyone. For info: Sue DiFranco, Fun Facts Publishing, 808 West End Ave, #811, New York, NY 10025. Phone: (212) 604-4562. Fax: (646) 349-3375. E-mail: info@funfactspublishing.com. Web: www.funfactspublishing.com.

KENNEDY CENTER IMAGINATION CELEBRATION. Mar 4–May 28. Colorado Springs, CO. A national festival program of the John F. Kennedy Center for the Performing Arts, this three-month-long communitywide celebration has something for everyone: from hundreds of lively performances that delight the senses to friendly, small-town happenings that warm the heart. Most events are free; a nominal fee is charged for those that are not. Est attendance: 231,000. For info: Mary Mashburn, Exec Dir, 1515 N Academy Blvd, Ste 200, Colorado Springs, CO 80909. Phone: (719) 597-3344. Fax: (719) 597-3343. E-mail: mary@imaginationcelebration.org. Web: imaginationcelebration.org.

MICHIGAN HOME AND GARDEN SHOW. Mar 4–7. Pontiac Silverdome, Pontiac, MI. Products and services for home building/remodeling, home furnishings and interior design, lawn and garden and related areas. On-site constructions, theme gardens, seminars and demonstrations, plus The Standard Flower Show sponsored by The Federated Garden Clubs of Michigan, District 1. Est attendance: 45,000. For info: Mike Wilbraham, ShowSpan, Inc, 2121 Celebration Dr NE, Grand Rapids, MI 49525. Phone: (616) 447-2860. Fax: (616) 447-2861. E-mail: events@showspan.com. Web: www.showspan.com.

NAIA MEN'S AND WOMEN'S INDOOR TRACK AND FIELD NATIONAL CHAMPIONSHIPS. Mar 4–6. Memorial Center, Johnson City, TN. Individuals compete for All-America honors while teams compete for the national championship. 39th annual competition for men; 24th annual for women. Est attendance: 2,500. For info: Natl Assn Intercollegiate Athletics, 23500 W 105th St, PO Box 1325, Olathe, KS 66051-1325. Phone: (913) 791-0044. Fax: (913) 791-9555. E-mail: thasseltine@naia.org. Web: www.naia.org.

OLD INAUGURATION DAY. Mar 4. Anniversary of the date set for beginning the US presidential term of office, 1789–1933. Although the Continental Congress had set the first Wednesday of March 1789 as the date for the new government to convene, a quorum was not present to count the electoral votes until Apr 6. Though George Washington's term of office began on Mar 4, he did not take the oath of office until Apr 30, 1789. All subsequent presidential terms (except successions following the death of an incumbent), until Franklin D. Roosevelt's second term, began Mar 4. The 20th Amendment (ratified Jan 23, 1933) provided that "the terms of the President and Vice President shall end at noon on the 20th day of January . . . and the terms of their successors shall then begin."

PENNSYLVANIA DEEDED TO WILLIAM PENN: ANNIVERSARY. Mar 4, 1681. To satisfy a debt of £16,000, King Charles II of England granted a royal charter, deed and governorship of Pennsylvania to William Penn.

☆ Chase's 2004 Calendar of Events ☆ Mar 4–5

PEOPLE MAGAZINE: 30th ANNIVERSARY. Mar 4, 1974. The popular magazine highlighting celebrities was officially launched with the Mar 4, 1974, issue featuring a cover photo of Mia Farrow.

PERKINS, FRANCES: CABINET APPOINTMENT ANNIVERSARY. Mar 4, 1933. Frances Perkins became the first woman appointed to the president's cabinet when she was appointed Secretary of Labor by President Franklin D. Roosevelt.

PULASKI, CASIMIR: BIRTH ANNIVERSARY. Mar 4, 1747. American Revolutionary hero, General Kazimierz (Casimir) Pulaski, born at Winiary, Mazovia, Poland, the son of a count. He was a patriot and military leader in Poland's fight against Russia of 1770–71 and went into exile at the partition of Poland in 1772. He came to America in 1777 to join the Revolution, fighting with General Washington at Brandywine and also serving at Germantown and Valley Forge. He organized the Pulaski Legion to wage guerrilla warfare against the British. Mortally wounded in a heroic charge at the siege of Savannah, GA, he died aboard the warship *Wasp* Oct 11, 1779. Pulaski Day is celebrated on the first Monday of March in Illinois.

ROCKNE, KNUTE: BIRTH ANNIVERSARY. Mar 4, 1888. Legendary Notre Dame football coach, born at Voss, Norway. Known for such sayings as "Win one for the Gipper," he died at Cottonwood Falls, KS, Mar 31, 1931.

RONALD AND NANCY REAGAN: WEDDING ANNIVERSARY. Mar 4, 1952. Little Brown Church in the San Fernando Valley, CA. Ronald Reagan was 41 and Nancy Davis (born Anne Frances Robbins) was 30. They were both actors; William Holden served as best man. This was Reagan's second marriage. His first marriage to actress Jane Wyman in 1940 produced daughter Maureen Elizabeth Reagan in 1941, adopted son Michael Edward Reagan (born 1942) in 1945 and daughter Christina Reagan in 1947, who was born prematurely and died within a few days. Nancy and Ronald have two children: Patricia Ann Reagan (Patti Davis), born in 1952, and Ronald Prescott Reagan, in 1958. Reagan was the first US president who had been divorced.

SPACE MILESTONE: OGO 5 (US): ANNIVERSARY. Mar 4, 1968. Orbiting Geophysical Observatory (OGO) collected data on the sun's influence on Earth. Launched Mar 4, 1968. Six OGOs were launched in all.

TA'ANIT ESTHER (FAST OF ESTHER). Mar 4. Hebrew calendar date: Adar 11, 5764. Ordinarily observed Adar 13, the Fast of Esther is observed on the previous Thursday (Adar 11) when Adar 13 falls on a Sabbath—as it does in 2004. Commemorates Queen Esther's fast, in the sixth century BC, to save the Jews of ancient Persia. Began at sundown Mar 3.

TELEVISION ACADEMY HALL OF FAME: FIRST INDUCTEES ANNOUNCED: 20th ANNIVERSARY. Mar 4, 1984. The Television Academy of Arts and Sciences announced the formation of the Television Academy Hall of Fame at Burbank, CA. The first inductees were Lucille Ball, Milton Berle, Paddy Chayefsky, Norman Lear, Edward R. Murrow, William S. Paley and David Sarnoff.

VERMONT: ADMISSION DAY: ANNIVERSARY. Mar 4. Became 14th state in 1791.

BIRTHDAYS TODAY

Landon Donovan, 22, soccer player, born Redlands, CA, Mar 4, 1982.
Emilio Estefan, 51, percussionist for the Miami Sound Machine ("Anything for You"), born Havana, Cuba, Mar 4, 1953.
Patricia Heaton, 45, actress ("Everybody Loves Raymond"), born Bay Village, OH, Mar 4, 1959.
Kevin Johnson, 38, former basketball player, born Sacramento, CA, Mar 4, 1966.
Patsy Kensit, 36, actress (*The Great Gatsby, Blame It on the Bellboy*), born London, England, Mar 4, 1968.
Kay Lenz, 51, actress (*Rich Man, Poor Man*), born Los Angeles, CA, Mar 4, 1953.
Miriam Makeba, 72, actress, singer, anti-apartheid activist, born Johannesburg, South Africa, Mar 4, 1932.
Barbara McNair, 70, singer, actress ("The Barbara McNair Show"), born Racine, WI, Mar 4, 1934.
Catherine O'Hara, 50, comedienne, writer ("SCTV Network 90"), actress (*Home Alone*), born Toronto, ON, Canada, Mar 4, 1954.
Rick Perry, 54, Governor of Texas (R), born Haskell, TX, Mar 4, 1950.
Paula Prentiss, 65, actress ("He & She," *What's New Pussycat?*), born Paula Ragusa, San Antonio, TX, Mar 4, 1939.
Steven Weber, 43, actor ("Wings"), born Queens, NY, Mar 4, 1961.
Mary Wilson, 60, singer (original member of the Supremes with Diana Ross and Florence Ballard), born Detroit, MI, Mar 4, 1944.

MARCH 5 — FRIDAY
Day 65 — 301 Remaining

ALL-NORTHWEST BARBERSHOP BALLAD CONTEST. Mar 5–6. Pacific University, Forest Grove, OR. Barbershop quartets from throughout the Pacific Northwest compete in an 1890s setting. Est attendance: 3,000. For info: Forest Grove Chamber of Commerce, 2417 Pacific Ave, Forest Grove, OR 97116. Phone: (503) 357-3006 or (503) 292-5673. Fax: (503) 357-2367. E-mail: fgchamber@groveweb.net.

AMA NATIONAL HOT SHOE DIRT TRACK RACE. Mar 5. Daytona Beach Municipal Stadium, Daytona Beach, FL. Dirt track series race. For info: Daytona Intl Speedway, Box 2801, Daytona Beach, FL 32120-2801. Phone: (386) 253-7223. Fax: (386) 947-6791. Web: www.daytonainternationalspeedway.com.

BLACKSTONE, WILLIAM: BIRTH ANNIVERSARY. Mar 5, 1595. William Blackstone, born at Durham County, England, was the first settler in what is now Boston, MA, and also the first in what is now Rhode Island. Blackstone came to New England with the Captain Robert Gorges expedition in 1623. When the expedition failed and most returned to England, he stayed and settled on what later became Beacon Hill. In 1634, he sold most of his Boston property and moved to the shores of the river that now bears his name. He died there at what is now Cumberland, RI, May 26, 1675.

BOSTON MASSACRE: ANNIVERSARY. Mar 5, 1770. A skirmish between British troops and a crowd at Boston, MA, became widely publicized and contributed to the unpopularity of the British regime in America before the American Revolution. Five men were killed and six more were injured by British troops commanded by Captain Thomas Preston.

CARNAVAL MIAMI. Mar 5–14. Little Havana, Miami, FL. Ten-day celebration includes 8K run (Mar 5), Carnaval Night (Mar 6), Sun Day on the Mile (Mar 7), Cooking Contest (Mar 9), Domino Tournament (Mar 10), Golf Classic (Mar 11), Carnaval Miami Internacional (Mar 13) culminating with Calle Ocho (Mar 14), the world's largest street party. Carnaval Miami extends an open invitation to locals and tourists to partake in events suitable for the entire family. Est attendance: 1,000,000. For info: Kiwanis Club of Little Havana, 701 SW 27th Ave, #900, Miami, FL 33155. Phone: (305) 644-8888. Fax: (305) 644-8693. Web: www.carnavalmiami.org.

Chase's 2004 Calendar of Events

CHALO NITKA. Mar 5–7 (tentative). Moore Haven, FL. To promote Lake Okeechobee bass fishing and bring the community together for a celebration. *Chalo Nitka* means Bass (Chalo) Day (Nitka) in the Seminole language. Annually, the first three-day weekend in March. Est attendance: 4,000. For info: Exec Dir, Glades County Chamber of Commerce, Box 490, Moore Haven, FL 33471. Phone: (863) 946-0440. Fax: (863) 946-2282. E-mail: gccommerce@ictransnet.com. Web: www.gladesonline.com.

CHANNEL ISLANDS NATIONAL PARK ESTABLISHED: ANNIVERSARY. Mar 5, 1980. California's Channel Islands Monument, authorized in 1938 by President Franklin D. Roosevelt, consisted of the islands of Anacapa and Santa Barbara. In 1980 President Jimmy Carter signed a bill establishing the Channel Islands National Park consisting of the islands Anacapa, San Miguel, Santa Barbara, Santa Cruz and Santa Rosa.

CRAFTSMEN'S CLASSIC ARTS & CRAFTS FESTIVAL. Mar 5–7. South Carolina State Fairgrounds, Columbia, SC. 21st annual. Features work from more than 300 talented artists and craftspeople. All juried exhibitors' work has been handmade by the exhibitors and must be their own original design and creation. See the creative process in action with several exhibitors demonstrating their craft. Something for every style, taste, and budget with items from the most contemporary to the most traditional. Est attendance: 20,000. For info: Gilmore Enterprises, 1240 Oakland Ave, Greensboro, NC 27403. Phone: (336) 274-5550. E-mail: gilmoreshows@triad.rr.com.

CRISPUS ATTUCKS DAY: DEATH ANNIVERSARY. Mar 5, 1770. Honors Crispus Attucks, possibly a runaway slave, who was the first to die in the Boston Massacre.

CULLIGAN, EMMETT J.: BIRTH ANNIVERSARY. Mar 5, 1893. Emmett J. Culligan, founder of world's largest water treatment organization, was born at Yankton, SD. Culligan first experimented with a water-softening device in the early 1920s—to soften water used to wash his baby's diapers. In 1936 he launched the company from a Northbrook, IL, blacksmith shop. Recipient of Horatio Alger Award in 1969, Culligan died at San Bernardino, CA, June 3, 1970.

GERMAN 16-YEAR-OLDS DRAFTED: ANNIVERSARY. Mar 5, 1945. The Nazis began inducting German boys of the Hilter Youth born in or before 1929 into the regular German army, thereby lowering the draft age to 16.

HARRISON, REX: BIRTH ANNIVERSARY. Mar 5, 1908. Born Reginald Carey at Huyton, England. Rex Harrison's career as an actor encompassed more than 40 films and scores of plays. He won both a Tony and an Oscar for the role of Henry Higgins in *My Fair Lady*, perhaps his most famous role. Among other films, he appeared in *Dr. Dolittle, Cleopatra, Blithe Spirit* and *Major Barbara*. He claimed he would never retire from acting, and he was appearing in a Broadway revival of Somerset Maugham's *The Circle* three weeks before his death June 2, 1990, at his home at New York, NY.

"IRON CURTAIN" SPEECH: ANNIVERSARY. Mar 5, 1946. Winston Churchill, speaking at Westminster College, Fulton, MO, established the cold war boundary with these words: "From Stettin in the Baltic to Trieste in the Adriatic an iron curtain has descended across the continent." Though Churchill was not the first to use the phrase *iron curtain*, his speech gave it a new currency and its usage persisted.

LONGHORN WORLD CHAMPIONSHIP RODEO. Mar 5–7. UTC Arena, Chattanooga, TN. 22nd annual. More than 250 cowboys and cowgirls compete in six professional contests ranging from bronc riding to big, bad BONUS bull riding! Free beginners horsemanship clinic 40 minutes before performances. Qualifying rodeo for Longhorn's Championship Finals Rodeo. Featuring colorful opening and pageantry. Est attendance: 16,000. For info: W. Bruce Lehrke, Pres, Longhorn World Championship Rodeo, Inc, PO Box 70159, Nashville, TN 37207. Phone: (615) 876-1016. Fax: (615) 876-4685. E-mail: info@longhornrodeo.com. Web: www.longhornrodeo.com.

MARYLAND HOME AND GARDEN SHOW. Mar 5–7 (also Mar 12–14). Timonium Fairgrounds, Baltimore, MD. The largest display of home building, remodeling and home decorating exhibits in the Baltimore area. Includes educational exhibits, crafts, plant marketplace and displays of landscaped gardens and floral arrangements. Est attendance: 72,000. For info: S & L Productions Inc, Crain Overlook, 1916 Crain Hwy, Ste 16, Glen Burnie, MD 21061. Phone: (410) 863-1180. Fax: (410) 863-1187. E-mail: showinfo@slprod.com.

MERCATOR, GERHARDUS: BIRTH ANNIVERSARY. Mar 5, 1512. Cartographer-geographer Mercator was born at Rupelmonde, Belgium. His Mercator projection for maps provided an accurate ratio of latitude to longitude and is still used today. He also introduced the term *atlas* for a collection of maps. He died at Duisberg, Germany, Dec 2, 1594.

MIDNIGHT AT THE OASIS. Mar 5–7. Ray Kroc Complex/Desert Sun Stadium, Yuma, AZ. 12th annual. Stroll down memory lane at an incredible nostalgic festival featuring the cars and music of the '50s and '60s. Limited to 850 '72 and older American cars and trucks and foreign classics. Show & Shine, rock 'n' roll concerts and dances, vendors, activities and entertainment for the whole family. Est attendance: 50,000. For info: Caballeros de Yuma, PO Box 5987, Yuma, AZ 85366. Phone: (928) 343-1715. Fax: (928) 783-1609. Web: www.caballeros.org.

MIDWEST REGIONAL LAWN, GARDEN AND FLOWER SHOW. Mar 5–7. RiverCenter, Davenport, IA. "Symphony in Bloom." An extraordinary array of landscape gardens, vignettes, special events, seminars, hands-on workshops and music. Room and patio settings, floral arrangements, and array of lawn and garden products and home accessories. Children's Activity Garden, speakers, silent auction and much more! For info: Phone: (563) 322-0931. Web: www.qcsymphony.com. For info on the Quad Cities: Quad Cities CVB, 102 S Harrison St, Davenport, IA 52801. Phone: (800) 747-7800. Web: www.visitquadcities.com.

NAIA WRESTLING NATIONAL CHAMPIONSHIPS. Mar 5–6. Great Falls, MT. Individuals compete for All-America honors in 12 weight divisions, while teams compete for the national championship. 47th annual competition. Est attendance: 4,000. For info: Natl Assn of Intercollegiate Athletics, 23500 W 105th St, PO Box 1325, Olathe, KS 66051-1325. E-mail: smcclure@naia.org. Web: www.naia.org.

NATIONAL SALESPERSON'S DAY. Mar 5. Salespeople are essential resources for customers today. The talented salesperson filters the vast amount of information that is available to customers and helps businesspeople make the best purchasing decisions. Salespeople also help consumers make better, quicker decisions with the counsel they offer. With the impact of new technologies, the role of the salesperson continually evolves. Annually, first Friday of March. For info: Maura Schreier-Fleming, Best@Selling, 7028 Judi, Dallas, TX 75252. Phone: (972) 380-0200. Fax: (972) 733-0126. E-mail: Maura@BestAtSelling.com. Web: www.BestAtSelling.com.

NETHERLANDS: THE EUROPEAN FINE ART FAIR. Mar 5–14. MECC, Maastricht. Old Master paintings, antiques, textile arts, modern paintings and sculptures, antiquities, books and prints. Annually, in March. Est attendance: 75,000. For info: The European Fine Art Fdtn, Broekwal 64, 5268 HD Helvoirt, The Netherlands. Phone: (31) 411 645090. Fax: (31) 411 645091. E-mail: info@tefaf.com. Web: www.tefaf.com.

NORTH DAKOTA WINTER SHOW. Mar 5–14. Valley City, ND. Ten-day agricultural expo featuring world's largest crop show,

	S	M	T	W	T	F	S
March 2004		1	2	3	4	5	6
	7	8	9	10	11	12	13
	14	15	16	17	18	19	20
	21	22	23	24	25	26	27
	28	29	30	31			

☆ Chase's 2004 Calendar of Events ☆   Mar 5–6

eight-breed cattle show, culinary arts show and competition, style and needlework show and competition, children's area, four-performance PRCA Rodeo, draft horse pulls, old-time tractor pull (tractors built prior to 1955), 80-vendor farm toy show and single performance headliner country concert. Annually, beginning the first Friday in March. Est attendance: 72,000. For info: Tom Langemo, Mgr, ND Winter Show, PO Box 846, Valley City, ND 58072. Phone: (701) 845-1401 or (800) 437-0218. Fax: (701) 845-3914. E-mail: ndws@valleycity.net. Web: www.ndws.org.

SAINT PIRAN'S DAY. Mar 5. Celebrates the birthday of St. Piran, the patron saint of Cornish tinners. Cornish worldwide celebrate this day. For info: The Cornish American Heritage Society, 5 Hampton Court, Neptune, NJ 07753. E-mail: nheydt@monmouth.com.

TEXAS COWBOY POETRY GATHERING. Mar 5–7. Sul Ross State University, Alpine, TX. 18th annual. Cowboys from Texas and neighboring states gather for poetry readings and music. Includes Trappings of Texas Art and gear show. Est attendance: 5,000. For info: J.J. Tucker, Texas Cowboy Poetry Gathering Committee, PO Box 395, Alpine, TX 79831. Phone: (432) 837-1071 or (432) 837-3237. Fax: (432) 837-8195. E-mail: jjtucker@llnet.net. Web: www.cowboypoetry.org.

US BANK HOLIDAY: ANNIVERSARY. Mar 5, 1933. On his first full day in office (Sunday, Mar 5, 1933), President Roosevelt proclaimed a national "Bank Holiday" to help save the nation's faltering banking system. Most banks were able to reopen after the 10-day "holiday" (Mar 4–14), but in the meantime, "scrip" had temporarily replaced money in many American households.

USA INDOOR TRACK & FIELD CHAMPIONSHIPS. Mar 5–7. Boston, MA. Annually, the first weekend in March. Est attendance: 12,000. For info: USA Track & Field, 1 RCA Dome, Ste 140, Indianapolis, IN 46225. Phone: (317) 261-0500. Fax: (317) 261-0481. Web: www.usatf.org.

VICTORIAN SHERLOCK HOLMES WEEKEND. Mar 5–7 (also Nov 5–7). Cape May, NJ. A weekend of mystery and intrigue awaits amateur sleuths when Cape May celebrates the works of Sir Arthur Conan Doyle, creator of Sherlock Holmes. Offered twice annually. Est attendance: 200. For info: Mid-Atlantic Center for the Arts, PO Box 340, 1048 Washington St, Cape May, NJ 08204. Phone: (609) 884-5404 or (800) 275-4278. Fax: (609) 884-0574. Web: www.capemaymac.org.

WORLD DAY OF PRAYER. Mar 5. An ecumenical event that reinforces bonds between peoples of the world as they join in a global circle of prayer. Annually, the first Friday in March. Sponsor: International Committee for World Day of Prayer. Church Women United is the National World Day of Prayer Committee for the US. For info: Church Women United, 475 Riverside Dr, Ste 1626, New York, NY 10115. Phone: (212) 870-3339 or (800) 298-5551. Fax: (212) 870-2338. Web: www.churchwomen.org.

BIRTHDAYS TODAY

Samantha Eggar, 65, actress ("Samantha and the King," *The Collector*), born London, England, Mar 5, 1939.
Penn Jillette, 49, magician, born Greenfield, MA, Mar 5, 1955.
Paul Sand, 60, actor ("St. Elsewhere"; Tony Award for *Story Theatre*), born Paul Sanchez, Los Angeles, CA, Mar 5, 1944.
Dean Stockwell, 68, actor (*The Boy with Green Hair*, "Quantum Leap"), born Los Angeles, CA, Mar 5, 1936.
Laurence Tisch, 81, broadcasting executive, born New York, NY, Mar 5, 1923.

Marsha Warfield, 50, actress ("Night Court," "Empty Nest"), born Chicago, IL, Mar 5, 1954.
Michael Warren, 58, actor ("Paris," "Hill Street Blues"), born South Bend, IN, Mar 5, 1946.
Fred Williamson, 66, actor ("Julia," "Half Nelson"), former professional football player, born Gary, IN, Mar 5, 1938.

MARCH 6 — SATURDAY
Day 66 — 300 Remaining

AMA GRAND NATIONAL KICKOFF. Mar 6. Daytona Beach Municipal Stadium, Daytona Beach, FL. Dirt track series race. For info: Daytona International Speedway, PO Box 2801, Daytona Beach, FL 32120-2801. Phone: (386) 253-7223. Fax: (386) 947-6791. Web: www.daytonainternationalspeedway.com.

ANTIQUE SHOW AND SALE. Mar 6–7. West Platte High School Auditorium, Weston, MO. 30–40 selected dealers from several states display a variety of antiques (including furniture) and collectibles for sale to the general public. For info: Weston Development Co, 502 Main, Weston, MO 64098. Phone: (816) 640-2909 or (888) 635-7457. E-mail: westonmo@kc.rr.com. Web: ci.weston.mo.us.

ANTIQUES IN SCHOHARIE. Mar 6–7 (also Sept 18–19). Schoharie, NY. Est attendance: 2,000. For info: Ruth Anne Keese, Schoharie Colonial Heritage Assn, PO Box 554, Schoharie, NY 12157. Phone: (518) 295-7505. E-mail: scha@midtel.net.

BABYSITTER SAFETY DAY. Mar 6. Darien, CT. Special events to promote babysitter safety will include local police sponsors and fire department participation to educate the community. For info: Suzanne Stillwell, The Sitting Service, 980 Post Rd, Darien, CT 06820. Phone: (203) 655-9783. E-mail: sitserve@aol.com. Web: www.thesittingservice.com.

BIG TEN WRESTLING CHAMPIONSHIP. Mar 6–7. Ohio State University, Columbus, OH. Est attendance: 1,000. For info: Sue Lister, Assoc Commissioner, Big Ten Conference, 1500 W Higgins Rd, Park Ridge, IL 60068-6300. Phone: (847) 696-1010. Fax: (847) 696-1110. Web: www.bigten.org.

BIG 12 WRESTLING CHAMPIONSHIP. Mar 6. Ames, IA. Est attendance: 6,000. For info: Big 12 Conference, 2201 Stemmons Freeway, 28th Fl, Dallas, TX 75207. Phone: (214) 742-1212. Fax: (214) 753-0145. Web: www.big12sports.com.

BROWNING, ELIZABETH BARRETT: BIRTH ANNIVERSARY. Mar 6, 1806. English poet, author of *Sonnets from the Portuguese*, wife of poet Robert Browning and subject of the play *The Barretts of Wimpole Street*, was born near Durham, England. She died at Florence, Italy, June 29, 1861.

DAYTONA SUPERCROSS BY HONDA. Mar 6. Daytona International Speedway, Daytona Beach, FL. One of the most famous and toughest supercross races in the world. For info: Daytona Intl Speedway, PO Box 2801, Daytona Beach, FL 32120-2801. Phone: (386) 253-7223. Fax: (386) 947-6791. Web: www.daytonainternationalspeedway.com.

DRED SCOTT DECISION: ANNIVERSARY. Mar 6, 1857. This was the most famous US Supreme Court decision during the prewar slavery controversy. Dred Scott, a slave, had successfully petitioned for his freedom based on his previous residence in a free state and territory. On this date, the Supreme Court overturned Missouri's Supreme Court decision and declared the 1820 Missouri Compromise unconstitutional. Chief Justice Roger Taney wrote that slaves were property, not citizens, and that Congress had no power to restrict slavery in the territories.

FALL OF THE ALAMO: ANNIVERSARY. Mar 6, 1836. Anniversary of the fall of the Texan fort, the Alamo. The siege, led by Mexican general Santa Anna, began Feb 23 and reached its climax Mar 6, when the last of the defenders was slain. Texans, under General Sam Houston, rallied with the war cry "Remember the Alamo" and, at the Battle of San Jacinto, Apr 21, defeated and captured Santa Anna, who signed a treaty recognizing Texas's independence.

165

Mar 6 ☆ Chase's 2004 Calendar of Events ☆

GHANA: INDEPENDENCE DAY. Mar 6. National holiday. Commemorates independence from Great Britain in 1957.

IDITAROD TRAIL SLED DOG RACE. Mar 6–21. 32nd running of "The Last Great Race on Earth" (first run on Mar 3, 1973). 1,150 miles through Alaskan wilderness from Anchorage to Nome, AK, along the historic Iditarod Trail. More than 60 16-dog teams competing. Awards ceremony on Sunday, Mar 21. Est attendance: 25,000. For info: Iditarod Trail Committee, PO Box 870800, Wasilla, AK 99687. Phone: (907) 376-5155. Fax: (907) 373-6998. Web: www.iditarod.com.

"IN THE HEAT OF THE NIGHT" TV PREMIERE: ANNIVERSARY. Mar 6, 1988. NBC's police drama was based on the 1967 movie with the same name. Carroll O'Connor played Mississippi police chief Bill Gillespie who, along with Howard Rollins as Detective Virgil Tibbs, investigated crimes in the rural South. The cast featured Alan Autry as Sergeant Bubba Skinner; Anne-Marie Johnson as Virgil's wife, Althea; David Hart as Deputy Parker William; Hugh O'Connor as Deputy Lonnie Jamison; Christian LeBlanc as Deputy Junior Abernathy; Geoffrey Thorne as Deputy Sweet and Crystal Fox as dispatcher Luanne Corbin. The last telecast aired July 28, 1994, but the program remains popular in reruns.

LARDNER, RING: BIRTH ANNIVERSARY. Mar 6, 1885. Ringgold Wilmer (Ring) Lardner, sportswriter, born at Niles, MI. Lardner wrote about sports for a variety of newspapers, mostly in Chicago. In both his columns and his short stories, he reproduced ballplayers' vernacular speech patterns with great success, thereby laying the groundwork for generations of baseball fiction to come. Lardner abandoned baseball after the Black Sox scandal was exposed. He wrote songs, plays and magazine articles but never the novel that some of his friends thought he should. Taciturn and solemn with a biting sense of humor, Lardner drank and smoked to excess, even after contracting tuberculosis in 1926. Given the J.G. Taylor Spink Award in 1963. Died at East Hampton, NY, Sept 25, 1933.

MICHELANGELO: BIRTH ANNIVERSARY. Mar 6, 1475. Anniversary of the birth, at Caprese, Italy, of Michelangelo di Lodovico Buonarroti Simoni, a prolific Renaissance painter, sculptor, architect and poet who had a profound impact on Western art. Michelangelo's fresco painting on the ceiling of the Sistine Chapel at the Vatican at Rome, Italy, is often considered the pinnacle of his achievement in painting, as well as the highest achievement of the Renaissance. Also among his works were the sculptures *David* and *The Pieta*. Appointed architect of St. Peter's in 1542, a post he held until his death Feb 18, 1564, at Rome.

MOON PHASE: FULL MOON. Mar 6. Moon enters Full Moon phase at 6:14 PM, EST.

NATIONAL WEEK OF THE OCEAN FESTIVAL SEASON. Mar 6–June 12. Fort Lauderdale, FL. This 15-week celebration includes sea chanty concerts, school marine fair, marine flea market, waterway cleanup, a seafood festival, a regatta, Mother Ocean Day, Earth Day and a Reef Sweep. Est attendance: 350,000. For info: Cynthia Hancock, Pres, Natl Week of the Ocean, Inc, PO Box 179, Ft Lauderdale, FL 33302. Phone: (954) 462-5573. Web: www.national-week-of-the-ocean.org.

NATURAL BRIDGE BATTLE REENACTMENT. Mar 6–7. Tallahassee, FL. Reenactment of the Confederate army's victory at the Natural Bridge site, which kept Tallahassee (the state capital) from falling into Union hands. Annually, the first weekend in March. Est attendance: 2,500. For info: Natural Bridge Battlefield Historic State Park, 1022 DeSoto Park Dr, Tallahassee, FL 32301. Phone: (850) 922-6007. Fax: (850) 488-0366.

	S	M	T	W	T	F	S
March		1	2	3	4	5	6
	7	8	9	10	11	12	13
2004	14	15	16	17	18	19	20
	21	22	23	24	25	26	27
	28	29	30	31			

NENANA TRIPOD RAISING FESTIVAL. Mar 6–7. Nenana, AK. Festival centers around the guessing of the exact time of the ice breakup on the Tanana River. Highlights include the raising of the tripod, Nenana Banana Eating, Weight-Pull Contest (humans and dogs), sled dog races, arm wrestling, turkey shoot, craft bazaar and much more. Est attendance: 2,500. For info: Nenana Ice Classic, Box 272, Nenana, AK 99760. Phone: (907) 832-5446. Fax: (907) 832-5888. E-mail: classic@mtaonline.net. Web: www.nenanaakiceclassic.com.

PEALE, ANNA CLAYPOOLE: BIRTH ANNIVERSARY. Mar 6, 1791. American painter of miniatures and a member of the famous Peale family of artists. Born at Philadelphia, PA; died Dec 25, 1878.

SAINT PIRAN'S DAY CELEBRATION. Mar 6. Location available after Jan 1. Celebration in honor of St. Piran, patron saint of Cornwall and Cornish peoples. Held to help preserve history and culture of the Cornish (Celtic). Annually, the Saturday nearest Mar 5. For info: Donald Whitman, Ed, Greater Kansas City Cornish Society, 24 E 68th St, Kansas City, MO 64113-2414. Phone: (816) 444-1963. E-mail: dandpwhit@aol.com.

SOUTHEAST FLORIDA SCOTTISH FESTIVAL AND GAMES. Mar 6. C.B. Smith Park, Pembroke Pines, FL. Est attendance: 8,000. For info: Scottish-American Soc of Southeast Florida, 5901 NE 21 Rd, Fort Lauderdale, FL 33308. Phone: (954) 776-5675.

WILLS, BOB: BIRTH ANNIVERSARY. Mar 6, 1905. The Father of Western Swing was born in Kosse, TX. Originally a performer (fiddler) with the Light Crust Doughboys, Wills later formed the popular Texas Playboys. Bob Wills and the Texas Playboys appeared on film and at the Grand Ole Opry and made western swing popular with such hits as "San Antonio Rose." Wills died May 13, 1975, at Fort Worth, TX.

WINTER CARNIVAL. Mar 6–7. Red Lodge, MT. Winter Carnival features parades, snow sculptures, King and Queen contest, Snow Ball, costume contest, Cardboard Classic Race (for which teams design crafts of cardboard for downhill races), live music and prizes. Torchlight parade and spaghetti dinner. Annually, the first weekend in March. Est attendance: 2,000. For info: Red Lodge Area Chamber of Commerce, PO Box 988, Red Lodge, MT 59068. Phone: (888) 281-0625. Fax: (406) 446-1718. E-mail: information@redlodge.com. Web: www.redlodge.com.

BIRTHDAYS TODAY

Tom Arnold, 45, actor ("Roseanne," *McHale's Navy, True Lies*), born Ottumwa, IA, Mar 6, 1959.

Christopher Samuel Bond, 65, US Senator (R, Missouri), born St. Louis, MO, Mar 6, 1939.

Sarah Caldwell, 80, conductor, born Maryville, MO, Mar 6, 1924.

L. Gordon Cooper, 77, astronaut, born Shawnee, OK, Mar 6, 1927.

Gabriel Garcia-Marquez, 76, Nobel Prize–winning author (*A Hundred Years of Solitude, Love in the Time of Cholera*), born Aracaracca, Colombia, Mar 6, 1928.

Dave Gilmour, 60, singer, musician (member Pink Floyd, *The Dark Side of the Moon*), born Cambridge, England, Mar 6, 1944.

Alan Greenspan, 78, economist, Chairman of the Federal Reserve Board, born New York, NY, Mar 6, 1926.

D.L. Hughley, 41, comedian, actor ("The Hughleys," *The Original Kings of Comedy*), born Los Angeles, CA, Mar 6, 1963.

Kiri Te Kanawa, 60, opera singer, born Gisborne, New Zealand, Mar 6, 1944.

Ed McMahon, 81, actor, TV host ("The Tonight Show," "Star Search"), born Detroit, MI, Mar 6, 1923.

Ben Murphy, 62, actor ("Alias Smith and Jones," *Yours, Mine and Ours*), born Jonesboro, AR, Mar 6, 1942.
Ryan Nyquist, 25, BMX bike racer, born Los Gatos, CA, Mar 6, 1979.
Shaquille Rashan O'Neal, 32, basketball player, born Newark, NJ, Mar 6, 1972.
Amy Pietz, 35, actress ("Caroline in the City"), born Oakcreek, WI, Mar 6, 1969.
Rob Reiner, 59, actor ("All in the Family"), director (*When Harry Met Sally. . ., This Is Spinal Tap*), born New York, NY, Mar 6, 1945 (some sources say 1947).
Valentina Tereshkova-Nikolaeva, 67, cosmonaut, born Maslennikovo, USSR, Mar 6, 1937.

MARCH 7 — SUNDAY
Day 67 — 299 Remaining

BURBANK, LUTHER: BIRTH ANNIVERSARY. Mar 7, 1849. Anniversary of the birth of American naturalist and author, creator and developer of many new varieties of flowers, fruits, vegetables and trees. Luther Burbank's birthday is observed in California as Bird and Arbor Day. Born at Lancaster, MA, he died at Santa Rosa, CA, Apr 11, 1926.

CELEBRATE YOUR NAME WEEK!. Mar 7–13. Who would you be if you didn't have a name? Your name identifies you to the world. "Celebrate Your Name Week" is about not neglecting your name. It's about making sure your name isn't an ignored part of your personhood. Use this week to become connected to your name! See also related events each day this week. Annually, the first full week in March. For info: E-mail: anotherjerryhill@angelfire.com. Web: www.jerryhill.com.

DAYTONA 200 BY ARAI SUPERBIKE CLASSIC. Mar 7. Daytona International Speedway, Daytona Beach, FL. Premier AMA pro division race. 63rd annual. Sponsor: Arai Helmets. For info: Daytona Intl Speedway, PO Box 2801, Daytona Beach, FL 32120-2801. Phone: (386) 253-7223. Fax: (386) 947-6791. Web: www.daytonainternationalspeedway.com.

DISTINGUISHED SERVICE MEDAL: ANNIVERSARY. Mar 7, 1918. With US troops fighting in the trenches in France during the First World War, President Woodrow Wilson authorized the creation of a new bronze, beribboned medal to be given to US Army personnel who performed "exceptionally meritorious service."

GIRL SCOUT SUNDAY. Mar 7. Girl Scouts worship together in the place of their choice. For info: Media Services, Girl Scouts of the USA, 420 Fifth Ave, New York, NY 10018. Phone: (212) 852-8000. Fax: (212) 852-6514. Web: www.girlscouts.org.

GIRL SCOUT WEEK. Mar 7–13. To observe the anniversary of the founding of the Girl Scouts of the USA, the largest voluntary organization for girls and women in the world, which began Mar 12, 1912. Special observances include Girl Scout Sunday, Mar 7, and Girl Scout Sabbath, Mar 13, when Girl Scouts gather to attend religious services together, and Girl Scout Birthday, Mar 12. For info: Media Services, Girl Scouts of the USA, 420 Fifth Ave, New York, NY 10018. Phone: (212) 852-8000. Fax: (212) 852-6514. Web: www.girlscouts.org.

HELP SOMEONE SEE WEEK. Mar 7–14. Rockford, OH. Residents and staff at the Laurels of Shane Hill and Maplewood of Shanes Village help the Rockford Lions Club collect used eyeglasses, frames, lenses and cases to be refurbished and distributed to those in need. Residents learn about the guide dog program and diseases and treatments of the eye. More than 400 pairs of glasses and cases were collected in 2003. For info: Brooke Reyman, Activities Dir, Laurels of Shane Hill Nursing Home, 10731 State Rte 118, Rockford, OH 45882-8947. Phone: (419) 363-2620.

HOPKINS, STEPHEN: BIRTH ANNIVERSARY. Mar 7, 1707. Colonial governor (Rhode Island) and signer of the Declaration of Independence. Born at Providence, RI, and died there July 13, 1785.

MONOPOLY INVENTED: ANNIVERSARY. Mar 7, 1933. While unemployed during the Depression, Charles Darrow devised this game and he sold it himself for two years. Monopoly was mass marketed by Parker Brothers beginning in 1935. Darrow died a millionaire in 1967.

NAMESAKE DAY. Mar 7. Today is for more than just pondering the existence of your namesakes (people with the same name as you). Consult a telephone directory and/or go online to find namesakes. Make polite, sincere, gentle contact with any namesake(s) you locate. Annually, the Sunday of Celebrate Your Name Week. For info: E-mail: anotherjerryhill@angelfire.com. Web: www.jerryhill.com.

NATIONAL PROFESSIONAL PET SITTERS WEEK. Mar 7–13. A week to show appreciation for the pet sitters who work 365 days a year for customers. Annually, the first full week (Sunday through Saturday) in March. For info: Pet Sitters Intl (PSI), 201 E King St, King, NC 27021. Phone: (336) 983-9222. Fax: (336) 983-5266. E-mail: info@petsit.com. Web: www.petsit.com.

PHILADELPHIA FLOWER SHOW. Mar 7–14. PA Convention Center, Philadelphia, PA. The largest flower show in the US. The premier event of its kind in the world. Est attendance: 250,000. For info: Pennsylvania Horticultural Society, 100 N 20th St, 5th Fl, Philadelphia, PA 19103-1495. Phone: (215) 988-8800 or (215) 988-8899. Fax: (215) 988-8810. Web: www.theflowershow.com.

PURIM. Mar 7. Hebrew calendar date: Adar 14, 5764. Feasts, gifts, charity and the reading of the Book of Esther mark this joyous commemoration of Queen Esther's intervention, in the sixth century BC, to save the Jews of ancient Persia. Haman's plot to exterminate the Jews was thwarted, and he was hanged on the very day he had set for execution of the Jews. Began at sundown Mar 6.

READ AN E-BOOK WEEK. Mar 7–13. A week set aside to learn about and/or read an electronic book (e-book). For info: Rita Toews, 9 Esker Pl, East St Paul, MB, Canada, R2E 0K2. Phone: (204) 661-2734. E-mail: r.toews@shaw.ca. Web: www.domokos.com.

REMAGEN BRIDGE CAPTURE: ANNIVERSARY. Mar 7, 1945. On this date in 1945, a small advance force of the US First Army captured the Ludendorff railway bridge across the Rhine River at Remagen (between Bonn and Coblenz)—the only bridge across the Rhine that had not been blown up by the German defenders—thus acquiring the first bridgehead onto the east bank and the beginning of the Allied advance into Germany, a turning point in World War II.

SAINT PATRICK'S DAY PARADE & FESTIVAL. Mar 7. Hollywood, FL. Traditional parade with pipes and drums, floats, etc, on downtown streets and festival in the park with entertainment stage, Irish food and wares. Est attendance: 10,000. For info: Roguey Doyle, City of Hollywood Dept of Parks, 1940 Harrison St, Ste 101, Hollywood, FL 33020. Phone: (954) 921-3404.

★**SAVE YOUR VISION WEEK.** Mar 7–13 (tentative). Presidential Proclamation issued for the first week of March since 1964, except 1971 and 1982 when issued for the second week of March. (PL88–1942, of Dec 30, 1963.)

SUEZ CANAL OPENS: ANNIVERSARY. Mar 7, 1869. This waterway across Egypt connecting the Mediterranean and Red seas was built by the French. In 1956 Egyptian president Nasser nationalized the canal, prompting an invasion by the British, French and Israelis. The Six-Day War in 1967 shut down the canal for eight years.

Mar 7–8 ☆ Chase's 2004 Calendar of Events ☆

BIRTHDAYS TODAY

Anthony Armstrong-Jones (Lord Snowdon), 74, photographer, born London, England, Mar 7, 1930.
Bryan Cranston, 48, actor ("Malcolm in the Middle"), born San Fernando Valley, CA, Mar 7, 1956.
Taylor Dayne, 42, singer ("Love Will Send You Back"), born Long Island, NY, Mar 7, 1962.
Michael Eisner, 62, Disney executive, born Mount Kisco, NY, Mar 7, 1942.
Janet Guthrie, 66, former auto racer, born Iowa City, IA, Mar 7, 1938.
Franco Harris, 54, Hall of Fame football player, born Fort Dix, NJ, Mar 7, 1950.
John Heard, 58, actor (*The Milagro Beanfield War, Rambling Rose, The Pelican Brief*), born Washington, DC, Mar 7, 1946.
Jeff Kent, 36, baseball player, born Bellflower, CA, Mar 7, 1968.
Ivan Lendl, 44, former tennis player, born Ostrava, Czechoslovakia, Mar 7, 1960.
Willard Herman Scott, 70, weatherman ("The Today Show"), friend of centenarians, born Alexandria, VA, Mar 7, 1934.
Daniel J. Travanti, 64, actor ("Hill Street Blues"), born Kenosha, WI, Mar 7, 1940.
Rachel Weisz, 33, actress (*The Mummy, The Mummy Returns*), born London, England, Mar 7, 1971.
Peter Wolf, 58, lead singer (J. Geils Band, "Centerfold"), born Boston, MA, Mar 7, 1946.

MARCH 8 — MONDAY
Day 68 — 298 Remaining

BEAVERS, LOUISE: BIRTH ANNIVERSARY. Mar 8, 1902. The Hollywood career of Louise Beavers spanned 30 years and more than 125 films. Though she was forced to play stereotypical roles, such as those of maids, her authentic talent was always apparent. Her starring role in the film *Imitation of Life* earned her high praise. Beavers was a member of the Black Filmmakers Hall of Fame. She also played the title role in the TV series "Beulah" (1951–53). Born at Cincinnati, OH; died at Los Angeles, Oct 26, 1962.

CAXTON'S *MIRROR OF THE WORLD* TRANSLATION: ANNIVERSARY. Mar 8, 1481. William Caxton, England's first printer, completed the translation from French into English of *The Mirror of the World*, a popular account of astronomy and other sciences. In print soon afterward, *Mirror of the World* became the first illustrated book printed in England.

CHASE'S DEADLINE APPROACHING. Mar 8. Time to plan ahead. Schedule 2005 celebrations and observances and submit information to *Chase's 2005 Calendar of Events* by Apr 15, 2004. Sponsors/information suppliers of events in this book should have received confirmation/revision forms for the 2005 edition by this time. To submit new entries for consideration, use a copy of the form on the last page of this book. Send to: Editor, Chase's Calendar of Events, The McGraw-Hill Companies, Contemporary Books, 130 E Randolph St, Ste 900, Chicago, IL 60601.

FUN FACTS ABOUT NAMES DAY. Mar 8. Celebrate names today by finding (at a library or online) fun facts about names. Does the doll we call "Barbie" have a last name? Does the dog game piece from Monopoly have a name? What was the name of the White House before it was renamed the White House? Annually, the Monday of Celebrate Your Name Week. For info: E-mail: anotherjerryhill@angelfire.com. Web: www.jerryhill.com.

GRAHAME, KENNETH: BIRTH ANNIVERSARY. Mar 8, 1859. Scottish author, born at Edinburgh. His children's book, *The Wind in the Willows*, has as its main characters a mole, a rat, a badger and a toad. He died July 6, 1932, at Pangbourne, Berkshire.

INTERNATIONAL (WORKING) WOMEN'S DAY. Mar 8. A day to honor women, especially working women. Said to commemorate an 1857 march and demonstration at New York, NY, by female garment and textile workers. Believed to have been first proclaimed for this date at an international conference of women held at Helsinki, Finland, in 1910, "that henceforth Mar 8 should be declared International Women's Day." The 50th anniversary observance, at Peking, China, in 1960, cited Clara Zetkin (1857–1933) as "initiator of Women's Day on Mar 8." This is perhaps the most widely observed holiday of recent origin and is unusual among holidays originating in the US in having been widely adopted and observed in other nations, including socialist countries. In Russia it is a national holiday, and flowers or gifts are presented to women workers.

NATIONAL SCHOOL BREAKFAST WEEK. Mar 8–12. To focus on the importance of a nutritious breakfast served in the schools, giving children a good start to their day. Annually, the first full week in March (weekdays). For info: American School Food Service Association, 700 S Washington St, Ste 300, Alexandria, VA 22314. Phone: (703) 739-3900. Fax: (703) 739-3915. E-mail: asfsa@asfsa.org. Web: www.asfsa.org.

RUSSIA: INTERNATIONAL WOMEN'S DAY. Mar 8. National holiday.

SYRIAN ARAB REPUBLIC: REVOLUTION DAY: ANNIVERSARY. Mar 8, 1963. Official public holiday commemorating assumption of power by Revolutionary National Council.

UNITED KINGDOM: COMMONWEALTH DAY. Mar 8. Replaces Empire Day observance recognized until 1958. Observed on second Monday in March. Also observed in the British Virgin Islands, Gibraltar and Newfoundland, Canada.

UNITED NATIONS: DAY FOR WOMEN'S RIGHTS AND INTERNATIONAL PEACE. Mar 8. An international day observed by the organizations of the United Nations system. In some years, known as International Women's Day. For info: United Nations, Dept of Public Info, New York, NY 10017. Web: www.un.org.

UNIVERSAL WOMEN'S WEEK. Mar 8–14. To remind ourselves and others of the value of women of all ages and classes and of their rights and dignity, and to honor outstanding women in the fields of government, business, industry, science, health, education, social work and the cultural arts by election to Universal Hall of Fame. Please send $5 to cover expense of printing, handling and postage. Annually, Mar 8–14. For info: Dr. Stanley Drake, Pres, Intl Soc of Friendship and Good Will, 999 Hood Rd, Ste 127, Marietta, GA 30068. Phone: (770) 565-2322. E-mail: ISFGW@bellsouth.net.

UPPITY WOMEN DAY. Mar 8. 4th annual. A day that will live in impudence! Make your mark on Uppity Women Day by celebrating your wild and uppity side—and by honoring our hell-raisers of the past. Outrageous women around the world, act! For info: Conari Press, 368 Congress St, Boston, MA 02210. Phone: (617) 542-1324 x 112 or (800) 423-7087. E-mail: vickleena@uppitywomenrule.com or lkasbarian@redwheelweiser.com. Web: www.conari.com or www.uppitywomenrule.com.

US INCOME TAX: ANNIVERSARY. Mar 8, 1913. The Internal Revenue Service began to levy and collect income taxes. The 16th Amendment to the Constitution, ratified Feb 3, 1913, gave Congress the authority to tax income. The US had also levied an income tax during the Civil War. See also: "Lincoln Signs Income Tax" (July 1).

VAN BUREN, HANNAH HOES: BIRTH ANNIVERSARY. Mar 8, 1783. Wife of Martin Van Buren, 8th president of the US. Born at Kinderhook, NY, she died at Albany, NY, Feb 5, 1819.

March 2004

S	M	T	W	T	F	S
	1	2	3	4	5	6
7	8	9	10	11	12	13
14	15	16	17	18	19	20
21	22	23	24	25	26	27
28	29	30	31			

☆ Chase's 2004 Calendar of Events ☆   Mar 8–9

BIRTHDAYS TODAY

George Allen, 52, US Senator (R, Virginia), born Whittier, CA, Mar 8, 1952.

Cyd Charisse, 81, actress (*Silk Stockings*), dancer (*Grand Hotel, Singin' in the Rain*), born Tula Finklea, Amarillo, TX, Mar 8, 1923.

Susan Clark, 64, actress ("Webster," *Babe*), born Sarnia, ON, Canada, Mar 8, 1940.

Micky Dolenz, 59, singer, actor ("The Monkees"), director, born Los Angeles, CA, Mar 8, 1945.

Kathy Ireland, 41, model, born Santa Barbara, CA, Mar 8, 1963.

Camryn Manheim, 43, actress ("The Practice"), born Caldwell, NJ, Mar 8, 1961.

Marcia Newby, 16, gymnast, born Virginia Beach, VA, Mar 8, 1988.

Freddie Prinze, Jr, 28, actor (*Scooby-Doo, She's All That*), born Albuquerque, NM, Mar 8, 1976.

Aidan Quinn, 45, actor (*Desperately Seeking Susan*; stage: *A Streetcar Named Desire*), born Chicago, IL, Mar 8, 1959.

Lynn Redgrave, 61, actress (*Georgy Girl*, "House Calls"), born London, England, Mar 8, 1943.

James Edward (Jim) Rice, 51, former baseball player, born Anderson, SC, Mar 8, 1953.

Carole Bayer Sager, 57, singer, songwriter ("That's What Friends Are For," with Burt Bacharach), born New York, NY, Mar 8, 1947.

Raynoma (Mayberry Liles) Gordy Singleton, 67, cofounder of Motown, born Detroit, MI, Mar 8, 1937.

James Van Der Beek, 27, actor ("Dawson's Creek"), born Cheshire, CT, Mar 8, 1977.

MARCH 9 — TUESDAY
Day 69 — 297 Remaining

BARBIE DEBUTS: 45th ANNIVERSARY. Mar 9, 1959. The popular girls' doll debuted in stores. More than 800 million dolls have been sold.

BELIZE: BARON BLISS DAY. Mar 9. Official public holiday. Celebrated in honor of Sir Henry Edward Ernest Victor Bliss, a great benefactor of Belize.

BIG 12 WOMEN'S BASKETBALL TOURNAMENT. Mar 9–11, 13. Reunion Arena, Dallas, TX. Est attendance: 35,000. For info: Big 12 Conference, 2201 Stemmons Freeway, 28th Fl, Dallas, TX 75207. Phone: (214) 742-1212. Fax: (214) 753-0145. Web: www.big12sports.com.

ENGLAND: WORDS BY THE WATER: A CUMBRIAN LITERATURE FESTIVAL. Mar 9–14. Lake District. The Theatre by the Lake at Keswick, sitting on the banks of Derwentwater, is the perfect setting for a lively literature festival. Young peoples' events during the school day complement a stimulating evening and weekend adult program. Program available October 2003. For info: Box Office, Ways With Words Lit Festival, Dorridge Farm, Dartington, Totnes, Devon, England TQ9 6JQ. Phone: (44) (180) 386-7373. E-mail: admin@wayswithwords.co.uk. Web: www.wayswithwords.co.uk.

GAGARIN, YURI ALEXSEYEVICH: 70th BIRTH ANNIVERSARY. Mar 9, 1934. Russian cosmonaut Yuri Gagarin, the first person to travel in space, was born at Gzhatsk, USSR. The 27-year-old Soviet Air Force major made his flight Apr 12, 1961, lasting 108 minutes and orbiting earth in a rocket-propelled, five-ton space capsule, 187 miles above the earth's surface. Gagarin was killed in an airplane crash near Moscow, USSR, Mar 27, 1968. After his death the town in which he was born was renamed Gagarin, and the Gagarin Museum was established in the frame house where he spent his childhood.

GRANT COMMISSIONED COMMANDER OF ALL UNION ARMIES: ANNIVERSARY. Mar 9, 1864. At Washington, DC, Ulysses S. Grant accepted his commission as Lieutenant General, becoming the commander of all the Union armies.

JOE FRANKLIN DAY. Mar 9. A day to honor the king of radio, television and entertainment for all his contributions on the anniversary of his birth. Franklin appeared on late-night television in New York from 1950–1993 and continues to entertain people today. For info: Bob O'Brien, Consumer Advocate, 1061 Koelle Ave, Secaucus, NJ 07094. Phone: (201) 860-1595. Fax: (201) 865-4775. E-mail: bobthebestthebest@yahoo.com.

JOHN DEERE MEMORABILIA CONFERENCE. Mar 9–10. John Deere Collectors Center, Moline, IL. 3rd annual. A two-day conference for collectors and enthusiasts of John Deere memorabilia. For info: Sarah Johnson, John Deere Pavillion, 320 16th St, Moline, IL 61265. Phone: (800) 240-5265. Fax: (309) 748-7946. E-mail: JohnsonSarah@johndeere.com. Web: www.johndeerecollectorsctr.com.

JULIA, RAUL: BIRTH ANNIVERSARY. Mar 9, 1940. Born at San Juan, Puerto Rico, Julia won acclaim and four Tony nominations for roles he played on Broadway ranging from Shakespeare's *Proteus* to *Mack the Knife*. Most widely known of his many film roles are Gomez in *The Addams Family* and Valentín in *Kiss of the Spider Woman*. Julia died Oct 24, 1994, at Manhasset, NY.

ORGANIZE YOUR HOME OFFICE DAY. Mar 9. One day each year for the more than 34 million home office households to find files, purge papers and tackle to-do lists. Annually, the second Tuesday in March. For info: Lisa Kanarek, HomeOfficeLife.com, 660 Preston Forest Ctr, #120, Dallas, TX 75230. Phone: (214) 361-0556. Web: www.homeofficelife.com.

PANIC DAY. Mar 9. Run around all day in a panic, telling others you can't handle it anymore. [©2003 by WH.] For info: Thomas & Ruth Roy, Wellcat Holidays, 2418 Long Ln, Lebanon, PA 17046. Phone: (717) 279-0184. E-mail: info@wellcat.com. Web: www.wellcat.com.

SAINT FRANCES OF ROME: FEAST DAY. Mar 9. Patron of motorists and model for housewives and widows (1384–1440). After 40 years of marriage she was widowed in 1436 and later joined the community of Benedictine Oblates. Canonized in 1608.

TAIWAN: BIRTHDAY OF KUAN YIN, GODDESS OF MERCY. Mar 9. A Buddhist deity, Kuan Yin is also the patron goddess of Taiwan. Nineteenth day of Second Moon of the lunar calendar, celebrated at Taipei's Lungshan (Dragon Mountain) and other temples.

TOKYO BLANKET BOMBING: ANNIVERSARY. Mar 9, 1945. The Japanese capital of Tokyo was bombed by 343 Superfortresses carrying all the incendiary bombs they could hold. Within the targeted areas of the city, population densities were four times greater than those of most American cities, and homes were made primarily of wood and paper. Carried by the wind, the fires leveled 16 sq miles. More than a quarter million buildings were destroyed, including 18% of the industrial area. The death toll was 83,000; 41,000 were injured. For the balance of WWII American strategic bombing followed this pattern.

Mar 9–10 ☆ Chase's 2004 Calendar of Events ☆

UNIQUE NAMES DAY. Mar 9. This is a day for all people to appreciate friends, acquaintances and loved ones who have a unique name. This is an opportunity for those of us who can buy mass-produced name items to celebrate the beauty of unique names. Annually, the Tuesday of Celebrate Your Name Week. For info: E-mail: anotherjerryhill@angelfire.com. Web: www.jerryhill.com.

VESPUCCI, AMERIGO: 550th BIRTH ANNIVERSARY. Mar 9, 1454. Italian navigator, merchant and explorer for whom the Americas were named. Born at Florence, Italy (some sources cite his birth year as 1451). He participated in at least two expeditions between 1499 and 1502 which took him to the coast of South America, where he discovered the Amazon and Plata rivers. Vespucci's expeditions were of great importance because he believed that he had discovered a new continent, not just a new route to the Orient. Neither Vespucci nor his exploits achieved the fame of Columbus, but the New World was to be named for Amerigo Vespucci by an obscure German geographer and mapmaker, Martin Waldseemuller. Ironically, in his work as an outfitter of ships, Vespucci had been personally acquainted with Christopher Columbus. Vespucci died at Seville, Spain, Feb 22, 1512. See also: "Waldseemuller, Martin: Remembrance Day" (Apr 25).

BIRTHDAYS TODAY

Juliette Binoche, 40, actress (*The English Patient, Chocolat*), born Paris, France, Mar 9, 1964.
Linda Fiorentino, 44, actress (*Men in Black*), born Philadelphia, PA, Mar 9, 1960.
Robert James (Bobby) Fischer, 61, World Chess Champion (1972), born Chicago, IL, Mar 9, 1943.
Mickey Gilley, 68, singer, musician ("City Lights," "Stand by Me"), cousin of Jerry Lee Lewis, born Natchez, MS, Mar 9, 1936.
Marty Ingels, 68, actor ("I'm Dickens . . . He's Fenster," *A Guide for the Married Man*), born Brooklyn, NY, Mar 9, 1936.
David Hume Kennerly, 57, photographer, born Rosenburg, OR, Mar 9, 1947.
Emmanuel Lewis, 33, actor ("Webster"), born Brooklyn, NY, Mar 9, 1971.
Terence John (Terry) Mulholland, 41, baseball player, born St. Paul, MN, Mar 9, 1963.
Jeffrey Osborne, 56, musician, songwriter, born Providence, RI, Mar 9, 1948.
Benito Santiago, 39, baseball player, born Ponce, Puerto Rico, Mar 9, 1965.
Mickey Spillane, 86, author (*The Killing Man, Vengeance Is Mine*), born Frank Spillane, Brooklyn, NY, Mar 9, 1918.
Trish Van Devere, 61, actress (*Where's Poppa?, One Is a Lonely Number*), born Tenafly, NJ, Mar 9, 1943.
Joyce Van Patten, 70, actress (*Monkey Shines*, "The Goodbye Guys"), born Queens, NY, Mar 9, 1934.

	S	M	T	W	T	F	S
March 2004		1	2	3	4	5	6
	7	8	9	10	11	12	13
	14	15	16	17	18	19	20
	21	22	23	24	25	26	27
	28	29	30	31			

MARCH 10 — WEDNESDAY
Day 70 — 296 Remaining

"BUFFY THE VAMPIRE SLAYER" TV PREMIERE: ANNIVERSARY. Mar 10, 1997. The popular WB show mixed B-movie horror with teen drama. Buffy Summers, played by Sarah Michelle Gellar, is a chosen slayer of vampires, but she still has to get through high school. The witty series was a spin-off of the 1992 film of the same name. After changing networks, the series ended in May 2003.

"THE INCREDIBLE HULK" TV PREMIERE: ANNIVERSARY. Mar 10, 1978. A wonderfully campy action series based on the popular Marvel comic books as well as a modern-day Jekyll and Hyde story. Bill Bixby played the erudite scientist, Dr. David Banner, who accidentally exposed himself to gamma radiation. When provoked, Banner metamorphosed into the shirt-shredding, body-baring, green-skinned, snarling neanderthal Hulk. The 6'5", 275-lb former Mr Universe, Lou Ferrigno, played the largely nonspeaking part of the Hulk.

JUPITER EFFECT: ANNIVERSARY. Mar 10, 1982. The much-talked-about and sometimes-feared planetary configuration of a semi-alignment of the planets on the same side of the sun occurred on this date without causing any of the disasters or unusual natural phenomena that some had predicted.

LEARN WHAT YOUR NAME MEANS DAY. Mar 10. Celebrate your name today by looking up (online or at a library) its meaning. Annually, the Wednesday of Celebrate Your Name Week. For info: E-mail: anotherjerryhill@angelfire.com. Web: www.jerryhill.com.

LUCE, CLARE BOOTHE: BIRTH ANNIVERSARY. Mar 10, 1903. Playwright and politician Clare Boothe Luce was born at New York City. Luce wrote for and edited *Vogue* and *Vanity Fair* as well as writing plays, three of which were later adapted into motion pictures—*The Women* (1936), *Kiss the Boys Goodbye* (1938) and *Margin of Error* (1939). She served in the US House of Representatives (1943–47) and as ambassador to Italy (1953–56)—the first woman appointed ambassador to a major country. Luce died Oct 9, 1987, at Washington, DC.

MARIO DAY. Mar 10. A day for all persons named Mario. Using the abbreviation for the month of March, i.e., MAR, with the day, i.e., 10, you get the name spelled out: MAR10. Annually, Mar 10. For info: Mario Fascitelli, 8800 Natalie NE, Albuquerque, NM 87111. Phone: (505) 293-2634. Fax: (505) 323-6333. E-mail: C21Allied@aol.com.

A MOUNTAIN QUILTFEST™. Mar 10–14. Smoky Mountain Convention Center, Pigeon Forge, TN. 10th annual show. The Piecemakers and the Sevier Valley Quilters join forces with some world-renowned instructors. Show free; fees for lessons. Est attendance: 9,000. For info: Office of Special Events, Pigeon Forge Dept of Tourism, 3107 Parkway, PO Box 1390, Pigeon Forge, TN 37868. Phone: (800) 251-9100 or (865) 429-7350. Fax: (865) 429-7392. E-mail: events@cityofpigeonforge.com. Web: www.mypigeonforge.com.

NAIA MEN'S DIVISION II BASKETBALL NATIONAL CHAMPIONSHIP TOURNAMENT. Mar 10–16. Branson, MO. 32-team field competes for the national championship. 13th annual. Est attendance: 30,000. For info: Natl Assn of Intercollegiate Athletics, 23500 W 105th St, PO Box 1325, Olathe, KS 66051-1325. Phone: (913) 791-0044. Fax: (913) 791-9555. E-mail: smcclure@naia.org. Web: www.naia.org.

NAIA WOMEN'S DIVISION II BASKETBALL NATIONAL CHAMPIONSHIP TOURNAMENT. Mar 10–16. Sioux City, IA. 32-team field competes for the national championship. 13th annual. Est attendance: 12,500. For info: Natl Assn of Intercollegiate Athletics, 23500 W 105th St, PO Box 1325, Olathe, KS 66051-1325. Phone: (913) 791-0044. Fax: (913) 791-9555. E-mail: lthomas@naia.org. Web: www.naia.org.

NCAA MEN'S AND WOMEN'S SKIING CHAMPIONSHIPS. Mar 10–13. Sugar Bowl Ski Resort and Auburn Ski

☆ Chase's 2004 Calendar of Events ☆   Mar 10–11

Club, Norden and Soda Springs, CA. Hosted by the University of Nevada. Est attendance: 1,500. For info: Natl Collegiate Athletic Assn, 700 W Washington St, PO Box 6222, Indianapolis, IN 46206-6222. Phone: (317) 917-6222. Fax: (317) 917-6888. Web: www.ncaa.org.

SALVATION ARMY IN THE US: ANNIVERSARY. Mar 10, 1880. Commissioner George Scott Railton and seven women officers landed at New York to officially begin the work of the Salvation Army in the US.

TELEPHONE INVENTION: ANNIVERSARY. Mar 10, 1876. Alexander Graham Bell transmitted the first telephone message to his assistant in the next room: "Mr Watson, come here, I want you," at Cambridge, MA. See also: "Bell, Alexander Graham: Birth Anniversary" (Mar 3).

THREE FLAGS CEREMONY (LEWIS AND CLARK BICENTENNIAL EVENT). Mar 10–14. Gateway Arch, St. Louis, MO. Commemorates the 200th anniversary of the transfer of Upper Louisiana from Spain to France to the US. A key event of the commemoration is the reenactment of Meriwether Lewis and members of the Discovery Expedition crossing the Mississippi River from Illinois to the ceremony site on Gateway Arch grounds on Mar 14. Historical exhibits and music complete the commemoration. Sponsored by the National Louisiana Purchase Bicentennial Committee and the National Park Service. For info: Dr. Wendell Smith, 401 Woods Hall, University of Missouri-St. Louis, 1001 Natural Bridge Rd, St. Louis, MO 63121. Phone: (314) 516-5255. E-mail: wsmith@umsl.edu. Web: louisianapurchase.umsl.edu.

TUBMAN, HARRIET: DEATH ANNIVERSARY. Mar 10, 1913. American abolitionist, Underground Railroad leader, born a slave at Bucktown, Dorchester County, MD, about 1820 or 1821. She escaped from a Maryland plantation in 1849 and later helped more than 300 slaves reach freedom. Died at Auburn, NY.

US PAPER MONEY ISSUED: ANNIVERSARY. Mar 10, 1862. The first paper money was issued in the US on this date. The denominations were $5 (Hamilton), $10 (Lincoln) and $20 (Liberty). They became legal tender by Act of Mar 17, 1862.

WALD, LILLIAN D.: BIRTH ANNIVERSARY. Mar 10, 1867. American sociologist, founder of the Henry Street Settlement at New York City and of the first nonsectarian public health nursing service. Born at Cincinnati, OH; died at Westport, CT, Sept 1, 1940.

BIRTHDAYS TODAY

Edie Brickell, 38, folksinger (New Bohemians), born Oak Cliff, TX, Mar 10, 1966.
Kim Campbell, 57, first woman prime minister of Canada (for five months in 1993), born Vancouver Island, BC, Canada, Mar 10, 1947.
Prince Edward, 40, son of Queen Elizabeth II, born London, England, Mar 10, 1964.
Bob Greene, 57, journalist, born Columbus, OH, Mar 10, 1947.
Jasmine Guy, 40, singer, actress ("A Different World"), born Boston, MA, Mar 10, 1964.
Shannon Miller, 27, Olympic gymnast, born Rolla, MO, Mar 10, 1977.
Chuck Norris, 64, actor (*Missing in Action*, "Walker, Texas Ranger"), born Ryan, OK, Mar 10, 1940.
David Rabe, 64, playwright, born Dubuque, IA, Mar 10, 1940.
Sharon Stone, 46, actress (*Basic Instinct, The Specialist, Casino*), born Meadville, PA, Mar 10, 1958.
Shannon Tweed, 47, actress ("Pacific Blue," *Detroit Rock City*), born St. John's, NF, Canada, Mar 10, 1957.

MARCH 11 — THURSDAY
Day 71 — 295 Remaining

BIG TEN MEN'S BASKETBALL TOURNAMENT. Mar 11–14. Canseco Fieldhouse, Indianapolis, IN. For info: Sue Lister, Big Ten Conference, 1500 W Higgins Rd, Park Ridge, IL 60068-6300. Phone: (847) 696-1010. Fax: (847) 696-1110. Web: www.bigten.org.

BIG 12 MEN'S BASKETBALL CHAMPIONSHIP. Mar 11–14. American Airlines Center, Dallas, TX. Est attendance: 95,000. For info: Big 12 Conference, 2201 Stemmons Freeway, 28th Fl, Dallas, TX 75207. Phone: (214) 742-1212. Fax: (214) 753-0145. Web: www.big12sports.com.

BUREAU OF INDIAN AFFAIRS ESTABLISHED: ANNIVERSARY. Mar 11, 1824. The US War Department created the Bureau of Indian Affairs.

CAMPBELL, MALCOLM: BIRTH ANNIVERSARY. Mar 11, 1885. Record-making British auto racer, the first man to travel five miles a minute (300 mph) in an automobile. Born at Chislehurst, Kent, England, Mar 11, 1885. Died at his home at Surrey, England, Dec 31, 1948.

CANADA: QUEBEC CITY SPORTSMEN'S SHOW. Mar 11–14. Centre de Foires, Quebec City. Major manufacturers, distributors and retailers of the outdoors, including camping, fishing and hunting, marine (fishing boats, canoes, kayaks and other craft), tourism offices, outfitters (lodges), and entertainment. Est attendance: 27,500. For info: Canadian National Sportsmen's Shows, 980 St-Antoine West, Ste 222, Montreal, QB, Canada H3C 1A8. Phone: (514) 866-5409. Fax: (514) 866-4092. Web: www.sportsmensshows.com.

DREAM 2004 DAY. Mar 11. To focus attention on the new millennium—so that all humans, nations and institutions devote 2004 to unparalleled dreams for a better world and thinking, action, inspiration, determination and love to solve the remaining problems and to achieve a peaceful, united human family on Earth. As envisioned by Robert Muller, called the Millennium Man. For info: Barbara Gaughen-Muller, Pres, Gaughen Global Public Relations, 7456 Evergreen Dr, Santa Barbara, CA 93117. Phone: (805) 968-8567. Fax: (805) 968-5747. E-mail: robert@robertmuller.org. Web: www.robertmuller.org.

JOHNNY APPLESEED DAY (JOHN CHAPMAN DEATH ANNIVERSARY). Mar 11, 1845. Anniversary of the death of John Chapman, better known as Johnny Appleseed, believed to have been born at Leominster, MA, Sept 26, 1774. The planter of orchards and friend of wild animals was regarded by the Indians as a great medicine man. He died at Allen County, IN. See also: "Johnny Appleseed: Birth Anniversary" (Sept 26).

LITHUANIA: RESTITUTION OF INDEPENDENCE DAY. Mar 11. National holiday. Commemorates independence from the Soviet Union in 1990. Lithuania had initially declared its independence in 1918 but lost it to the Soviet Union in 1940.

NAMETAG DAY. Mar 11. Today's celebration of names stipulates that wherever you are, whatever you're doing, you wear a "Hello, I'm [your name here]" nametag. (Note: this event is not for children.) Annually, the Thursday of Celebrate Your Name Week. For info: E-mail: anotherjerryhill@angelfire.com. Web: www.jerryhill.com.

PAINE, ROBERT TREAT: BIRTH ANNIVERSARY. Mar 11, 1731. Jurist and signer of the Declaration of Independence. Born at Boston, MA; died there May 11, 1814.

PANDEMIC OF 1918 HITS US: ANNIVERSARY. Mar 11, 1918. The first cases of the "Spanish" influenza were reported in the US when 107 soldiers became sick at Fort Riley, KS. By the end of 1920 nearly 25 percent of the US population had had it. As many as 500,000 civilians died from the virus, exceeding the number of US troops killed abroad in WWI. Worldwide, more than 1 percent of the global population, or 22 million people, had died by 1920. The origin of the virus was never determined absolutely, though it was probably somewhere in Asia. The name

171

"Spanish" influenza came from the relatively high number of cases in that country early in the epidemic. Due to the panic, cancellation of public events was common and many public service workers wore masks on the job. Emergency tent hospitals were set up in some locations due to overcrowding.

TASSO, TORQUATO: BIRTH ANNIVERSARY. Mar 11, 1544. Poet of the late Renaissance, born at Sorrento, Italy. His violent outbursts and acute sensitivity to criticism led to his imprisonment for seven years, during which the "misunderstood genius" continued his literary creativity. Died at Rome, Italy, Apr 25, 1595.

TURKEY VULTURES RETURN TO THE LIVING SIGN. Mar 11–17. Entire Canisteo Valley, Canisteo, NY. Traditionally turkey vultures return on St. Pat's Day to their roosting sites in and around the world-famous living sign. For info: Bill Berry, 6950 Lain Rd, Hornell, NY 14843-9419.

VIRGINIA SPRING SHOW. Mar 11–14. Showplace Exhibition Center, Richmond, VA. 17th annual. Features hundreds of artisans and craftspeople, food shops, spring entertainment. Holiday Cooking Theatre. Est attendance: 25,000. For info: Virginia Show Productions, PO Box 305, Chase City, VA 23924. Phone: (434) 372-3996. Fax: (434) 372-3410. E-mail: vashowsinc@aol.com

WELK, LAWRENCE: BIRTH ANNIVERSARY. Mar 11, 1903. Bandleader Lawrence Welk was born at Strasburg, ND. He learned to play the accordion and at 17 formed his first band. After playing all over the Midwest, he moved to Los Angeles where in 1955 his show began its nationwide television broadcast of "Champagne Music." The longest-running program in TV history, "The Lawrence Welk Show" played each Saturday on ABC from 1955 until 1971 when it was dropped because sponsors thought its audience was too old. Welk kept the show on a network of more than 250 independent stations for 11 more years and it still can be seen in reruns. Welk's entertainment empire included the purchase of royalty rights to songs, including the entire collection of songs by Jerome Kern. Welk died at Santa Monica, CA, May 17, 1992.

WILSON, HAROLD: BIRTH ANNIVERSARY. Mar 11, 1916. British statesman and twice prime minister (1964–70 and 1974–76), leader of the Labour Party. Born at Huddersfield, Yorkshire. He died May 24, 1995, at London.

WORLD'S LARGEST CONCERT. Mar 11 (tentative). To celebrate Music In Our Schools Month, the World's Largest Concert is broadcast on PBS stations nationwide and the Armed Forces Television Network overseas. Theme for the 2004 concert is "Connect with Music." Lesson plans, activities and awareness items are available. For info: WLC Coordinator, MENC: The Natl Assn for Music Education, 1806 Robert Fulton Dr, Reston, VA 20191. Phone: (800) 336-3768. Web: www.menc.org.

BIRTHDAYS TODAY

Elton Brand, 25, basketball player, born Peekskill, NY, Mar 11, 1979.
Curtis Brown, Jr, 48, astronaut, born Elizabethtown, NC, Mar 11, 1956.
Sam Donaldson, 70, journalist, born El Paso, TX, Mar 11, 1934.
Alex Kingston, 41, actress ("ER"), born London, England, Mar 11, 1963.
Bobby McFerrin, 54, jazz musician, singer, songwriter, conductor, born New York, NY, Mar 11, 1950.
Rupert Murdoch, 73, newspaper publisher (*New York Post, The Boston Herald*), born Melbourne, Australia, Mar 11, 1931.

March 2004

S	M	T	W	T	F	S
	1	2	3	4	5	6
7	8	9	10	11	12	13
14	15	16	17	18	19	20
21	22	23	24	25	26	27
28	29	30	31			

Gale Norton, 50, US Secretary of the Interior, born Wichita, KS, Mar 11, 1954.
Dominique Sanda, 53, actress (*The Garden of the Finzi-Continis, 1900*), born Paris, France, Mar 11, 1951 (some sources say 1948).
Antonin Scalia, 68, Associate Justice of the US Supreme Court, born Trenton, NJ, Mar 11, 1936.
Jerry Zucker, 54, writer (*Naked Gun* movies with brother David), producer (*Airplane!*), born Milwaukee, WI, Mar 11, 1950.

MARCH 12 — FRIDAY
Day 72 — 294 Remaining

AMERICAN CROSSWORD PUZZLE TOURNAMENT AND CONVENTION. Mar 12–14. Stamford Marriott Hotel, Stamford, CT. 500 solvers from the US and Canada compete on eight puzzles during this 27th annual event. Points are awarded for accuracy and speed. The final puzzle is played on giant white boards for everyone to watch. Prizes are awarded in 21 skill, age and geographical categories and the grand prize is $2,000. The weekend also includes group word games, guest speakers and appearances by celebrity crossword solvers. Solvers can compete at home by mail for fun and receive a ranking in all their solving categories. Est attendance: 600. For info: Will Shortz, Dir, American Crossword Puzzle Tournament, 55 Great Oak Lane, Pleasantville, NY 10570. Phone: (212) 556-7435. Web: www.crosswordtournament.com.

ATATÜRK, MUSTAFA KEMAL: BIRTH ANNIVERSARY. Mar 12, 1881. The founder of modern Turkey was born at Salonika, Greece (then part of the Ottoman Empire). After a distinguished army career, he led the Turkish revolution after World War I and was elected Turkey's first president. He died at Istanbul, Nov 10, 1938.

AUSTRIA INVADED BY NAZI GERMANY: ANNIVERSARY. Mar 12, 1938. As a test of its own war readiness and of the response of the other major powers, Germany occupied Austria. A year later Germany invaded Czechoslovakia and, in September 1939, Poland, beginning World War II.

BERMUDA COLONIZED BY ENGLISH: ANNIVERSARY. Mar 12, 1609. The ship of Admiral Sir George Somers, taking settlers to Virginia, was wrecked on the reefs of Bermuda. The islands had been discovered in the early 1500s but were uninhabited until 1609.

BOYCOTT, CHARLES CUNNINGHAM: BIRTH ANNIVERSARY. Mar 12, 1832. Charles Cunningham Boycott, born at Norfolk, England, has been immortalized by having his name become part of the English language. In County Mayo, Ireland, the Tenants' "Land League" in 1880 asked Boycott, an estate agent, to reduce rents (because of poor harvest and dire economic conditions). Boycott responded by serving eviction notices on the tenants, who retaliated by refusing to have any dealings with him. Charles Stewart Parnell, then President of the National Land League and agrarian agitator, retaliated against Boycott by formulating and implementing the method of economic and social ostracism that came to be called a "boycott." Boycott died at Suffolk, England, June 19, 1897.

CHURCH OF ENGLAND ORDAINS WOMEN PRIESTS: 10th ANNIVERSARY. Mar 12, 1994. The Church of England for the first time ordained 32 women at Bristol Cathedral. About 700 male members of the clergy and unknown thousands of members indicated they would leave the Church of England and join the Roman Catholic Church. The Catholic Church responded to the ordination by saying that it "constitutes a profound obstacle to every hope of reunion between the Catholic Church and the Anglican Communion." This day's ordinations were not the first. In early 1994 about 1,380 women priests were ordained in churches of the Anglican Communion outside of Great Britain.

CRAFTSMEN'S CLASSIC ARTS & CRAFTS FESTIVAL. Mar 12–14. Richmond Raceway Complex (formerly Virginia State Fairgrounds), Richmond, VA. 20th annual. Features

☆ Chase's 2004 Calendar of Events ☆   Mar 12

work from more than 410 talented artists and craftspeople. All juried exhibitors' work has been handmade by the exhibitors and must be their own original design and creation. See the creative process in action with several exhibitors demonstrating their craft. Something for every style, taste, and budget with items from the most contemporary to the most traditional. Est attendance: 20,000. For info: Gilmore Enterprises, Inc, 1240 Oakland Ave, Greensboro, NC 27403. Phone: (336) 274-5550. E-mail: gilmoreshows@triad.rr.com.

FDR'S FIRST FIRESIDE CHAT: ANNIVERSARY. Mar 12, 1933. President Franklin Delano Roosevelt made the first of his Sunday evening "fireside chats" to the American people. Speaking by radio from the White House, he reported rather informally on the economic problems of the nation and on his actions to deal with them.

GIRL SCOUTS OF THE USA FOUNDING: ANNIVERSARY. Mar 12, 1912. Juliet Low founded the Girl Scouts of the USA at Savannah, GA.

GREAT BLIZZARD OF '88: ANNIVERSARY. Mar 12, 1888. One of the most devastating blizzards to hit the northeastern US began in the early hours of Monday, Mar 12, 1888. A snowfall of 40–50 inches, accompanied by gale-force winds, left drifts as high as 30–40 feet. More than 400 persons died in the storm (200 at New York City alone). Some survivors of the storm, "The Blizzard Men of 1888," held annual meetings at New York City as late as 1941 to recount personal recollections of the event.

KEROUAC, JACK: BIRTH ANNIVERSARY. Mar 12, 1922. American poet and novelist Jack (Jean-Louis) Kerouac, leader and spokesman for the Beat movement, was born at Lowell, MA. Kerouac is best known for his novel *On the Road*, published in 1957, which celebrates the Beat ideal of nonconformity. Kerouac published *The Dharma Bums* in 1958, followed by *The Subterraneans* the same year, *Doctor Sax* and its sequel *Maggie Cassidy* in 1959, *Lonesome Traveler* in 1960, *Big Sur* in 1962 and *Desolation Angels* in 1965. Kerouac died at St. Petersburg, FL, at age 47, Oct 21, 1969. A previously unpublished part of *On the Road* called *Visions of Cody* was published posthumously in 1972.

LESOTHO: MOSHOESHOE'S DAY. Mar 12. National holiday. Commemorates the great leader Chief Moshoeshoe I, who unified the Basotho people, beginning in 1820.

LONGHORN WORLD CHAMPIONSHIP RODEO. Mar 12–14. Von Braun Civic Center, Huntsville, AL. 25th annual. More than 275 cowboys and cowgirls compete in six professional contests ranging from bronco riding to big, bad BONUS bull riding! Free beginners horsemanship clinic 40 minutes before performances. Qualifying rodeo for Longhorn's Championship Finals Rodeo in Nashville, TN. Est attendance: 16,000. For info: W. Bruce Lehrke, Pres, Longhorn World Chmpshp Rodeo, Inc, PO Box 70159, Nashville, TN 37207. Phone: (615) 876-1016. Fax: (615) 876-4685. E-mail: info@longhornrodeo.com. Web: www.longhornrodeo.com.

MAURITIUS: INDEPENDENCE DAY: ANNIVERSARY. Mar 12, 1968. National holiday commemorates attainment of independent nationhood (within the British Commonwealth).

MIDDLE NAME PRIDE DAY. Mar 12. Today's name celebration requires honesty and boldness. Tell three people who don't already know it what your middle name is (even if it's Egbert). Annually, the Friday of Celebrate Your Name Week. For info: E-mail: anotherjerryhill@angelfire.com. Web: www.jerryhill.com.

MILWAUKEE JOURNAL SENTINEL SPORTS SHOW. Mar 12–21. Milwaukee, WI. Travel and resort exhibits, hunting, fishing, boating, family travel, outdoor recreation. Largest outdoor show in Wisconsin. Est attendance: 150,000. For info: Great Outdoors, LLC, 113 McHenry Rd, #268, Buffalo Grove, IL 60089. Phone: (847) 419-0700. Fax: (847) 419-0701.

NCAA DIVISION I MEN'S & WOMEN'S INDOOR TRACK AND FIELD CHAMPIONSHIPS. Mar 12–13. University of Arkansas, Fayetteville, AR. Annually, the second weekend in March. Est attendance: 7,000. For info: Natl Collegiate Athletic Assn, 700 W Washington Ave, PO Box 6222, Indianapolis, IN 46206-6222. Phone: (317) 917-6222. Fax: (317) 917-6825. Web: www.ncaasports.com.

NEWCOMB, SIMON: BIRTH ANNIVERSARY. Mar 12, 1835. Astronomer, born at Wallace, NS, Canada. Newcomb investigated the orbits of Uranus, Neptune and the inner planets and devised planetary tables that were used universally by observatories. Died at Washington, DC, July 11, 1909.

PIERCE, JANE MEANS APPLETON: BIRTH ANNIVERSARY. Mar 12, 1806. Wife of Franklin Pierce, 14th president of the US. Born at Hampton, NH. Died at Concord, NH, Dec 2, 1863.

SHABBAT ACROSS AMERICA. Mar 12. More than 600 participating synagogues (Conservative, Orthodox, Reform and Reconstructionist) encourage Jews to observe the Sabbath on this Friday night. Est attendance: 60,000. For info: Natl Jewish Outreach Program, 989 Sixth Ave, 10th Fl, New York, NY 10018. Phone: (888) SHABBAT or (646) 871-4444. Web: www.njop.org.

SOUTH BY SOUTHWEST (SXSW). Mar 12–21. Austin, TX. Annual, internationally recognized music, new media and film conference. Hundreds of music, film and interactive events and panels. Est attendance: 25,000. For info: SXSW Headquarters, Box 4999, Austin, TX 78765. Phone: (512) 467-7979. Fax: (512) 451-0754. E-mail: sxsw@sxsw.com. Web: www.sxsw.com.

SPAIN: FIESTA DE LAS FALLAS. Mar 12–19. Valencia, Spain. This festival of burning effigies and fireworks has been celebrated for more than 150 years.

SUGARLOAF CRAFTS FESTIVAL. Mar 12–14. Garden State Exhibit Center, Somerset, NJ. This show, now in its 11th year, features 250 nationally recognized craft designers and fine artists displaying and selling their original creations. Includes craft demonstrations, live music, specialty foods, hourly gift certificate drawings and more! Est attendance: 18,500. For info: Sugarloaf Mountain Works, 200 Orchard Ridge Dr, #215, Gaithersburg, MD 20878. Phone: (800) 210-9900. Fax: (301) 253-9620. Web: www.SugarloafCrafts.com.

SUN YAT-SEN: DEATH ANNIVERSARY. Mar 12, 1925. The heroic leader of China's 1911 revolution is remembered on the anniversary of his death at Peking, China. Observed as Arbor Day in Taiwan.

WORLD'S LARGEST RATTLESNAKE ROUNDUP. Mar 12–14. Sweetwater, TX. Educational programs about rattlesnakes; flea market; gun, knife and coin show; large cookoff; dances; numerous pounds of live rattlesnakes on display; snake meat available to eat and snake articles for sale. Snake hunts and bus tours available. More than 750 booth spaces are available. Annually, the second weekend in March. Est attendance: 30,000. For info: Sweetwater Chamber of Commerce, PO Box 1148, Sweetwater, TX 79556. Phone: (325) 235-5488 or (800) 658-6757. Fax: (325) 235-1026. E-mail: chamber@sweetwatertexas.org. Web: www.sweetwatertexas.org or www.rattlesnakeroundup.com.

BIRTHDAYS TODAY

Edward Albee, 76, playwright, born Washington, DC, Mar 12, 1928.

Rob Cohen, 55, producer (*Bird on a Wire*), director (*Dragonheart*), born Cornwall-on-Hudson, NY, Mar 12, 1949.

Mar 12–13 ☆ Chase's 2004 Calendar of Events ☆

Kent Conrad, 56, US Senator (D, North Dakota), born Bismarck, ND, Mar 12, 1948.
Barbara Feldon, 63, actress ("Get Smart," *Smile*), born Pittsburgh, PA, Mar 12, 1941.
Marlon Jackson, 47, singer (Jackson 5), born Gary, IN, Mar 12, 1957.
Al (Alwin) Jarreau, 64, singer, songwriter, born Milwaukee, WI, Mar 12, 1940.
Liza Minnelli, 58, singer, actress (Oscar for *Cabaret; The Sterile Cuckoo, Arthur*), born Los Angeles, CA, Mar 12, 1946.
Raul Mondesi, 33, baseball player, born San Cristobal, Dominican Republic, Mar 12, 1971.
Dale Bryan Murphy, 48, former baseball player, born Portland, OR, Mar 12, 1956.
Mitt Romney, 57, Governor of Massachusetts (R), born Detroit, MI, Mar 12, 1947.
Wally Schirra, 81, former astronaut, born Hackensack, NJ, Mar 12, 1923.
Darryl Eugene Strawberry, 42, former baseball player, born Los Angeles, CA, Mar 12, 1962.
James Taylor, 56, singer, musician ("You've Got a Friend," "Handy Man"), born Boston, MA, Mar 12, 1948.
Andrew Young, 72, civil rights leader, former mayor of Atlanta, GA, born New Orleans, LA, Mar 12, 1932.

MARCH 13 — SATURDAY
Day 73 — 293 Remaining

ANNENBERG, WALTER: BIRTH ANNIVERSARY. Mar 13, 1908. Magazine publisher, philanthropist and ambassador, Walter Annenberg was born in Milwaukee, WI. The only son in a family of ten children, he inherited *The Philadelphia Inquirer* from his father and built the newspaper into the cornerstone of a publishing empire that included newspapers, magazines, and radio and television stations. He founded many enduring publications during his tenure with Triangle Publications, including *Seventeen* (1944) and *TV Guide* (1953). He served as US ambassador to the United Kingdom from 1969–76 and later became known for his philanthropy, giving billions to charities like the United Negro College Fund, many hospitals, and universities including Harvard, University of Pennsylvania and University of Southern California. He died at Wynnewood, PA on Oct 1, 2002.

ARAB OIL EMBARGO LIFTED: 30th ANNIVERSARY. Mar 13, 1974. The oil-producing Arab countries agreed to lift their five-month embargo on petroleum sales to the US. During the embargo prices went up 300 percent and a ban was imposed on Sunday gasoline sales. The embargo was in retaliation for US support of Israel during the October 1973 Middle East War.

ARTS AND ANTIQUES AT THE AMERICAN CLUB. Mar 13–14. The American Club's Grand Hall of the Great Lakes, Kohler, WI. Discover a wide variety of antiques, furniture, silver and jewelry from fine antique dealers. Carole Carter's Appraisal Service will appraise one item per paid admission daily. For info: The American Club, Highland Drive, Kohler, WI 53044. Phone: (800) 344-2838. Fax: (920) 457-4441. Web: www.destinationkohler.com.

BEACH PARTY. Mar 13. Deadwood, SD. 18th annual. Forget Ft Lauderdale for spring break! Head to the beach at the #10. Sand, hot tub, beach hats, music, limbo and wet T-shirt contests. Est attendance: 400. For info: Old Style Saloon #10, 657 Main St, Deadwood, SD 57732. Phone: (605) 578-3346 or (800) 952-9398. Fax: (605) 578-1944. E-mail: saloon10@deadwood.net. Web: www.saloon10.com.

March 2004

S	M	T	W	T	F	S
	1	2	3	4	5	6
7	8	9	10	11	12	13
14	15	16	17	18	19	20
21	22	23	24	25	26	27
28	29	30	31			

CLARENCE DARROW DEATH COMMEMORATION. Mar 13. Jackson Park, Chicago, IL. Annually, on the anniversary of his death, a wreath is tossed from the Jackson Park Clarence Darrow Bridge, named in honor of the famed lawyer and civil libertarian at 10 AM. At 11 AM a discussion follows in the Columbian Room of the Museum of Science and Industry, 57th St and South Lake Shore Dr, Chicago. Est attendance: 100. For info: Herb Kraus, 333 N Michigan, Ste 2032, Chicago, IL 60601. Phone: (312) 578-9114. Fax: (312) 726-9520.

DEAF HISTORY MONTH. Mar 13–Apr 15. Observance of three of the most important anniversaries for deaf Americans: Apr 15, 1817, establishment of the first public school for the deaf in America, later known as The American School for the Deaf; Apr 8, 1864, charter signed by President Lincoln authorizing the Board of Directors of the Columbia Institution (now Gallaudet University) to grant college degrees to deaf students; Mar 13, 1988, the victory of the Deaf President Now movement at Gallaudet. For info: Library for Deaf Action, 2930 Craiglawn Rd, Silver Spring, MD 20904-1816. Phone: (301) 572-5168 (TTY). Fax: (301) 572-4134. E-mail: alicehagemeyer@aol.com.

DELMONICO, LORENZO: BIRTH ANNIVERSARY. Mar 13, 1813. Famed restaurateur and gastronomic authority. Born at Marengo, Switzerland. Operated a number of restaurants at New York, NY, where he died, Sept 3, 1881.

EARMUFFS PATENTED: ANNIVERSARY. Mar 13, 1887. Chester Greenwood of Maine received a patent for earmuffs.

FILLMORE, ABIGAIL POWERS: BIRTH ANNIVERSARY. Mar 13, 1798. First wife of Millard Fillmore, 13th president of the US. Born at Stillwater, NY. It is said that the White House was without any books until Abigail Fillmore, formerly a teacher, made a room on the second floor into a library. Within a year, Congress appropriated $250 for the president to spend on books for the White House. Died at Washington, DC, Mar 30, 1853.

GENEALOGY DAY. Mar 13. Join in on one of the world's fastest growing hobbies and celebrate names at the same time. Get genealogy tips, hints and ideas, then begin the journey to knowing your heritage name by name, one ancestor at a time. Annually, the Saturday of Celebrate Your Name Week. For info: E-mail: anotherjerryhill@angelfire.com. Web: www.jerryhill.com.

GIRL SCOUT SABBATH. Mar 13. Girl Scouts of Jewish faith worship together in the temple of their choice. For info: Media Services, Girl Scouts of the USA, 420 Fifth Ave, New York, NY 10018. Phone: (212) 852-8000. Fax: (212) 852-6514. Web: www.girlscouts.org.

GOOD SAMARITAN INVOLVEMENT DAY. Mar 13. A day to emphasize the importance of unselfish aid to those who need it. Recognized on the anniversary of the killing of Catherine (Kitty) Genovese, Mar 13, 1964, in the Kew Gardens community, Queens, NY. Reportedly no fewer than 38 of her neighbors, not wanting "to get involved," witnessed and watched for nearly 30 minutes as the fleeing girl was pursued and repeatedly stabbed by her 29-year-old attacker.

GREENLAWN ANTIQUES SHOW. Mar 13–14. Greenlawn, NY. An annual antiques show that benefits the Greenlawn Centerport Historical Association. Sixty-seven outstanding quality dealers featuring country and formal furniture, decorative accessories, folk art and jewelry. For info: Michelle Athanas, Dir, Greenlawn Centerport Historical Assn, PO Box 354, Greenlawn, NY 11740. Phone: (631) 754-1180. Fax: (631) 757-7216. E-mail: gcha-info@usa.net. Web: gcha.suffolk.lib.ny.us.

HIGHLAND COUNTY MAPLE FESTIVAL. Mar 13–14 (also Mar 20–21). Highland County, VA. To welcome visitors to view the process of syrup making. Large craft shows. Est attendance: 60,000. For info: Highland County Chamber of Commerce, PO Box 223, Monterey, VA 24465. Phone: (540) 468-2550. Fax: (540) 468-2551. E-mail: highcc@cfw.com. Web: www.highlandcounty.org.

☆ Chase's 2004 Calendar of Events ☆ Mar 13

HUBBARD, L. RON: BIRTH ANNIVERSARY. Mar 13, 1911. Lafayette Ronald Hubbard, science fiction writer, recluse and founder of the Church of Scientology, was born at Tilden, NE. His best-known book was *Dianetics: The Modern Science of Mental Health*. Died at San Luis Obispo County, CA, Jan 24, 1986.

INDIANA FLOWER AND PATIO SHOW. Mar 13–21. Indiana State Fairgrounds Event Center, Indianapolis, IN. The oldest show of its kind in the Midwest, featuring more than 30 landscaped gardens and products and services for home, yard and patio. Est attendance: 106,000. For info: Donell Heberer Walton, Show Mgr, HSI Show Productions, Box 502797, Indianapolis, IN 46250. Phone: (317) 576-9933. Fax: (317) 576-9955. Web: www.hsishows.com.

"THE LARRY KING SHOW" TV PREMIERE: ANNIVERSARY. Mar 13, 1983. Radio talk-show host Larry King brought his topical interview program to syndicated TV in 1983. Using a telephone hookup, viewers called in to speak to particular guests. King has been appearing on CNN since 1985 interviewing a variety of newsmakers and celebrities.

LOWELL, PERCIVAL: BIRTH ANNIVERSARY. Mar 13, 1855. American astronomer, founder of the Lowell Observatory at Flagstaff, AZ. Born at Boston, MA, he died at Flagstaff, Nov 12, 1916. Lowell was initiator of the search that resulted (25 years after the search began and 14 years after his death) in discovery of the planet Pluto. The discovery was announced on Lowell's birthday, Mar 13, 1930, by the Lowell Observatory.

MOON PHASE: LAST QUARTER. Mar 13. Moon enters Last Quarter phase at 4:01 PM, EST.

NATCHEZ SPRING PILGRIMAGE. Mar 13–Apr 17. Natchez, MS. 73rd annual tour of 31 antebellum mansions furnished with period antiques, set in formal gardens. Exciting Confederate Pageant "Southern Exposure" and Southern Road to Freedom performances. Carriage and bus sight-seeing tours daily. Est attendance: 35,000. For info: Natchez Pilgrimage Tours, PO Box 347, Natchez, MS 39121. Phone: (800) 647-6742 or (601) 446-6631. Fax: (601) 446-8687. E-mail: tours@natchezpilgrimage.com. Web: www.natchezpilgrimage.com.

NATIONAL OPEN AN UMBRELLA INDOORS DAY. Mar 13. The purpose of this day is for people to open umbrellas indoors and note whether they have any bad luck. To arrange for an interview, call 24 hours in advance. Annually, Mar 13. For info: Thomas Edward Knibb, 1654 Colonial Way, Frederick, MD 21702-3919. Phone: (301) 695-7351. E-mail: tomknibb@valleyalley.com.

NATIONAL SKI-JORING FINALS. Mar 13–14. Red Lodge Rodeo Grounds, Red Lodge, MT. Horsemen and skiers provide action entertainment. Derived from the Scandinavian sport of pulling a skier behind a horse, ski-joring has evolved from a leisure winter diversion into lively, regulated competition. Annually, the second weekend in March. Est attendance: 4,000. For info: Red Lodge Chamber of Commerce, Box 988, Red Lodge, MT 59068. Phone: (888) 281-0625. Fax: (406) 446-1718. E-mail: information@redlodge.com. Web: www.redlodge.com.

OPERATION FLASH: ANNIVERSARY. Mar 13, 1943. Disillusioned German officers planned to take the life of Adolf Hitler on this date. Hitler was to stop at Smolensk on his way to his headquarters and an officer who was not involved in the plot had been commissioned to deliver a package to Hitler's plane which he was told contained two bottles of liquor for a friend in Rastenburg. A bomb in the package was timed to go off over Minsk, but it reached Rastenburg without detonating. The package was later recovered and a defective detonator was found. See also: "Gersdorff Hitler Assassination Attempt: Anniversary" (Mar 21).

PLANET URANUS DISCOVERY: ANNIVERSARY. Mar 13, 1781. German-born English astronomer Sir William Herschel discovered the seventh planet from the sun, Uranus.

PRIESTLY, JOSEPH: BIRTH ANNIVERSARY. Mar 13, 1733 (OS). English clergyman and scientist, discoverer of oxygen, born at Fieldhead, England. He and his family narrowly escaped an angry mob attacking their home because of his religious and political views. They moved to the US in 1794. Died at Northumberland, PA, Feb 6, 1804.

SAINT AUBIN, HELEN "CALLAGHAN" CANDAELE: 75th BIRTH ANNIVERSARY. Mar 13, 1929. Helen Candaele Saint Aubin, known as Helen Callaghan during her baseball days, was born at Vancouver, BC, Canada. Saint Aubin and her sister, Margaret Maxwell, were recruited for the All-American Girls Professional Baseball League, which flourished in the 1940s when many major league players were off fighting WWII. She first played at age 15 for the Minneapolis Millerettes, an expansion team that moved to Indiana and became the Fort Wayne Daisies. For the 1945 season the left-handed outfielder led the league with a .299 average and 24 extra base hits. In 1946 she stole 114 bases in 111 games. Her son Kelly Candaele's documentary on the women's baseball league inspired the film *A League of Their Own*. Saint Aubin, who was known as the "Ted Williams of women's baseball," died Dec 8, 1992, at Santa Barbara, CA.

SAINT PATRICK'S DAY PARADE. Mar 13. Downtown Hornell, NY. 17th annual. It's a "come as you are" line of march, open to anyone, with no entry fee, no judges, no prizes. Hornell's parade is designed as purely a fun affair, especially for those people who've always wanted to be in a parade but never had the opportunity. It has gotten larger and longer every year, with more and more "would-be Irish" strolling down Main Street. Annually, the Saturday before Saint Patrick's Day except when Saint Patrick's Day is a Thursday or Friday, then, the following Saturday. Est attendance: 4,000. For info: Wolf Berry, 6950 Lain Rd, Hornell, NY 14843-9419. Phone: (607) 324-1086. Fax: (607) 324-2001. E-mail: sales@wkpq.com. Web: www.wkpq.com.

SAINT PATRICK'S DAY PARADE & CELTIC FESTIVAL. Mar 13. Roanoke, VA. Sponsors: The Roanoke Special Events Committee. Est attendance: 20,000. For info: City of Roanoke, 210 Reserve Ave SW, Roanoke, VA 24016. Phone: (540) 342-2640. E-mail: katie@RoanokeSpecialEvents.org. Web: www.RoanokeSpecialEvents.org.

SAINT PATRICK'S DAY PARADE: "THE WEARIN' OF THE GREEN." Mar 13. Baton Rouge, LA. Includes floats, precision marching bands, bagpipers and more. Largest St. Patrick's Day celebration in the region. Est attendance: 150,000. For info: Parade Group, 6906 Moniteau Ct, Baton Rouge, LA 70809. Phone: (225) 925-8295. Fax: (225) 925-8295. E-mail: mabyn@futurebound.com. Web: www.paradegroup.com.

BIRTHDAYS TODAY

Thomas Andrew (Andy) Bean, 51, golfer, born Lafayette, GA, Mar 13, 1953.
Charo, 53, singer, actress ("Chico and the Man"), born Maria Martinez, Murcia, Spain, Mar 13, 1951.
Adam Clayton, 44, musician (U2), born Dublin, Ireland, Mar 13, 1960.
Dana Delany, 48, actress ("China Beach," *Moon Over Parador*), born New York, NY, Mar 13, 1956.

Mar 13–14 ☆ Chase's 2004 Calendar of Events ☆

Glenne Headly, 47, actress (*The Purple Rose of Cairo, Dick Tracy, Mortal Thoughts*), born New London, CT, Mar 13, 1957 (some sources say 1955).

John Hoeven, 47, Governor of North Dakota (R), born Bismarck, ND, Mar 13, 1957.

William H. Macy, 54, actor (*Fargo, Boogie Nights,* "ER"), born Miami, FL, Mar 13, 1950.

Deborah Raffin, 51, actress ("Foul Play"), born Los Angeles, CA, Mar 13, 1953.

Neil Sedaka, 65, singer, songwriter ("Breaking Up Is Hard to Do" with Howard Greenfield), born Brooklyn, NY, Mar 13, 1939.

MARCH 14 — SUNDAY
Day 74 — 292 Remaining

AMERICAN BOWLING CONGRESS CONVENTION & HALL OF FAME INDUCTION CEREMONIES. Mar 14–20. Reno, NV. Local, state and national bowling leaders gather to decide the rules of the game and the future of bowling in a democratic setting. The week features board of directors' meetings, special seminars, dinners honoring top leaders, Hall of Fame induction ceremonies (Mar 18) and workshops. Est attendance: 5,000. For info: American Bowling Congress, 5301 S 76th St, Greendale, WI 53129-0500. Phone: (414) 423-3309. Fax: (414) 421-3013. Web: www.abctournament.com or www.bowl.com.

ASSOCIATION OF AMERICAN GEOGRAPHERS ANNUAL MEETING. Mar 14–19. Philadelphia, PA. 100th annual national meeting of members with workshops, paper and poster sessions and field trips. Est attendance: 3,000. For info: Assn of American Geographers, 1710 16th St NW, Washington, DC 20009-3198. Phone: (202) 234-1450. E-mail: meeting@aag.org. Web: www.aag.org.

CARAY, HARRY: 90th BIRTH ANNIVERSARY. Mar 14, 1914. Born Harry Christopher Carabini at St. Louis, MO (some sources say Mar 1, 1920). Caray began his baseball broadcasting career with the St. Louis Cardinals in 1945. He then was the announcer for the Oakland A's, the Chicago White Sox and finally the Chicago Cubs. He became a legend at Wrigley Field with his 7th-inning stretch "Take Me out to the Ball Game" and his quirky phrase "Holy Cow." Caray was inducted into the Broadcasters Hall of Fame in 1989. Died at Rancho Mirage, CA, Feb 18, 1998.

EINSTEIN, ALBERT: 125th BIRTH ANNIVERSARY. Mar 14, 1879. Theoretical physicist best known for his theory of relativity. Born at Ulm, Germany, he won the Nobel Prize in 1921. Died at Princeton, NJ, Apr 18, 1955.

ENGLAND: LONDON BOOK FAIR. Mar 14–16. One of the world's most important publishing events. For info: London Book Fair, Oriel House, 26 The Quadrant, Richmond, Surrey, England TW9 1DL. Phone: (44) (20) 8910-7815. Web: www.lbf-virtual.com.

JONES, CASEY: BIRTH ANNIVERSARY. Mar 14, 1864. Railroad engineer and hero of ballad, whose real name was John Luther Jones. Born near Cayce, KY, he died in a railroad wreck near Vaughn, MS, Apr 30, 1900.

MARSHALL, THOMAS RILEY: 150th BIRTH ANNIVERSARY. Mar 14, 1854. 28th vice president of the US (1913–21). Born at North Manchester, IN, he died at Washington, DC, June 1, 1925.

	S	M	T	W	T	F	S
March 2004		1	2	3	4	5	6
	7	8	9	10	11	12	13
	14	15	16	17	18	19	20
	21	22	23	24	25	26	27
	28	29	30	31			

MOTH-ER DAY. Mar 14. A day set aside to honor moth collectors and specialists. Celebrated in museums or libraries with moth collections. For info: Bob Birch, Puns Corps Grand Punscorpion, Box 2364, Falls Church, VA 22042-0364. Phone: (703) 533-3668.

NATIONAL AGRICULTURE WEEK. Mar 14–20. "America's Largest Classroom on Agriculture." To honor America's providers of food and fiber and to educate future generations about the US agricultural system. Annually, the week that includes the first day of spring. For info: Agriculture Council of America, 11020 King St, Ste 205, Overland Park, KS 66210. Phone: (913) 491-1895. Fax: (913) 491-6502. E-mail: info@agday.org. Web: www.agday.org.

NATIONAL ANIMAL POISON PREVENTION WEEK. Mar 14–20. In conjunction with National Poison Prevention Week, the ASPCA sponsors this important week to educate Americans about common household products, plants and foods that can be dangerous or even deadly to pets. For info: Media Relations, ASPCA, 424 E 92nd St, New York, NY 10128. Phone: (212) 876-7700 x 4655. E-mail: press@aspca.org. Web: www.aspca.org.

NATIONAL CHILDREN'S CRAFT DAY. Mar 14. To encourage children's creativity through crafts. Celebrate by painting, sculpting or creating arts and crafts projects. For info: Hy Schwartz, 75 Mill St, Colchester, CT 06415. Phone: (800) 243-9232. E-mail: hjs@ssww.com. Web: www.ssww.com.

NATIONAL SAFE PLACE WEEK. Mar 14–20. The third week of March (for four years now). The US Senate has actually proclaimed this three of those years. Please see our website for more information about Safe Place, a national youth outreach program to help youth at risk of running away. For info: Janine Linder, YMCA Natl Safe Place, 1410 S First St, Louisville, KY 40208. Phone: (502) 635-5233. Fax: (502) 635-1443. Web: www.safeplaceservices.org.

NATIONAL SPRING FEVER WEEK. Mar 14–20. Annually, including the first day of spring. Recognizing the special socialization rites single people face during this season of revitalization. For info: Robin Gorman Newman, 44 Somerset Dr N, Great Neck, NY 11020. Phone: (516) 773-0911. E-mail: robin@lovecoach.com. Web: www.lovecoach.com.

NATIONAL TOAD HOLLOW WEEK. Mar 14–21. A community outreach program encouraging people to nourish their imagination, pursue their dreams and practice old-fashioned values in their relationships with others. For info: Ralph Morrison, Dir, Toad Hollow, PO Box 45, Vicksburg, MI 49097. Phone: (800) 574-8623.

PULMONARY REHABILITATION WEEK. Mar 14–20. For info: American Assn of Cardiovascular and Pulmonary Rehabilitation, 401 N Michigan Ave, Ste 2200, Chicago, IL 60611. Phone: (312) 321-5146. Fax: (312) 245-1085. E-mail: aacvpr@sba.com.

SEOUL RECAPTURED BY UN FORCES: ANNIVERSARY. Mar 14, 1951. Seoul, Korea, which had fallen to Chinese forces in January 1951, was retaken by United Nations troops during the Korean War.

TAYLOR, LUCY HOBBS: BIRTH ANNIVERSARY. Mar 14, 1833. Lucy Beaman Hobbs, first woman in America to receive

176

a degree in dentistry (Ohio College of Dental Surgery, 1866) and to be admitted to membership in a state dental association. Born at Franklin County, NY. In 1867 she married James M. Taylor, who also became a dentist (after she instructed him in the essentials). Active women's rights advocate. Died at Lawrence, KS, Oct 3, 1910.

"10 MOST WANTED" LIST DEBUTS: ANNIVERSARY. Mar 14, 1950. The Federal Bureau of Investigation instituted the "10 Most Wanted Fugitives" list in an effort to publicize particularly dangerous criminals who were at large. From 1950 to 1998, 454 fugitives appeared on the list; 130 were captured. Generally, the only way to get off the list is to die or be captured. The FBI cooperates with the producers of TV's "America's Most Wanted" to further publicize these fugitives.

BIRTHDAYS TODAY

Frank Borman, 76, former astronaut, airline executive, born Gary, IN, Mar 14, 1928.
Michael Caine, 71, actor (Best Supporting Actor Oscars for *The Cider House Rules* and *Hannah and Her Sisters*), born Maurice Micklewhite, London, England, Mar 14, 1933.
Billy Crystal, 57, actor ("Soap," *When Harry Met Sally . . ., City Slickers*), born Long Beach, NY, Mar 14, 1947.
Rick Dees, 53, disc jockey, comedian, born Jacksonville, FL, Mar 14, 1951.
Quincy Jones, 71, composer, producer ("We Are the World"), born Chicago, IL, Mar 14, 1933.
Kirby Puckett, 43, Hall of Fame baseball player, born Chicago, IL, Mar 14, 1961.
Tamara Tunie, 45, actress ("24," "Law & Order: SVU," "As the World Turns"), born McKeesport, PA, Mar 14, 1959.
Rita Tushingham, 62, actress (*Dr. Zhivago, A Taste of Honey*), born Liverpool, England, Mar 14, 1942.

MARCH 15 — MONDAY
Day 75 — 291 Remaining

ACT HAPPY DAY. Mar 15. Method acting techniques are prescribed by physicians to release chemicals in the body which aid health, wealth and friendship. Annually, the third Monday in March. For info: Dale L Anderson, MD, 2982 W Owasso Blvd, St Paul, MN 55113. Phone: (651) 484-5162. Fax: (651) 486-8860. E-mail: drdla@acthappy.com. Web: www.acthappy.com.

AUSTRALIA: CANBERRA DAY. Mar 15. Australian Capital Territory. Public holiday the third Monday in March.

BELARUS: CONSTITUTION DAY. Mar 15. National holiday. Commemorates the adoption of the constitution on Mar 15, 1994.

BRUTUS DAY. Mar 15. No matter where you work, you must admit there's as much intrigue, plotting and back-stabbing as was found in ancient Rome or is found today inside the Washington Beltway. [©2003 by WH.] For info: Thomas & Ruth Roy, Wellcat Holidays, 2418 Long Ln, Lebanon, PA 17046. Phone: (717) 279-0184. E-mail: info@wellcat.com. Web: www.wellcat.com.

CAMP FIRE USA BIRTHDAY WEEK. Mar 15–21. To celebrate the 94th anniversary of Camp Fire USA (founded in 1910 as Camp Fire Girls). For info: Camp Fire USA, 4601 Madison Ave, Kansas City, MO 64112. Phone: (816) 756-1950. Fax: (816) 756-2650. E-mail: info@campfireusa.org. Web: www.campfireusa.org.

"EIGHT IS ENOUGH" TV PREMIERE: ANNIVERSARY. Mar 15, 1977. This one-hour comedy-drama was set in Sacramento and starred Dick Van Patten as Tom Bradford, a columnist for a local paper and a widower with eight children. Diana Hyland played his wife, Joan; she died from cancer after filming five shows. The children were played by Grant Goodeve, Lani O'Grady, Laurie Walters, Susan Richardson, Dianne Kay, Connie Needham, Willie Aames and Adam Rich. In the fall of 1977 Betty Buckley joined the cast as tutor Abby Abbott, who later married Tom. Most of the cast was reunited for Tom's 50th birthday on "Eight Is Enough: A Family Reunion" shown on Oct 18, 1987.

HUNGARY: ANNIVERSARY OF THE 1848 REVOLUTION. Mar 15. National day. Commemorates when the country briefly attained autonomy from Austria.

IDES OF MARCH. Mar 15. In the Roman calendar the days of the month were not numbered sequentially. Instead, each month had three division days: kalends, nones and ides. Days were numbered from these divisions: e.g., IV Nones or III Ides. The ides occurred on the 15th of the month (or on the 13th in months that had less than 31 days). Julius Caesar was assassinated on this day in 44 BC. This system was used in Europe well into the Renaissance. When Shakespeare wrote "Beware the ides of March" in *Julius Caesar* his audience knew what he meant.

INTERNATIONAL BRAIN AWARENESS WEEK. Mar 15–21. Brain Awareness Week is an international effort to advance public awareness about the progress, promise, and benefits of brain research. The Dana Alliance is joined in the campaign by partners in the US and around the world, including medical and research organizations; patient advocacy groups; the National Institutes of Health and other government agencies; service groups; hospitals and universities; K–12 schools and professional organizations. For info: Dana Alliance for Brain Initiatives, 745 Fifth Ave, Ste 900, New York, NY 10151. Phone: (212) 401-1680. Fax: (212) 593-7623. E-mail: bawinfo@dana.org. Web: www.dana.org/brainweek.

JACKSON, ANDREW: BIRTH ANNIVERSARY. Mar 15, 1767. 7th president of the US (Mar 4, 1829–Mar 3, 1837) was born in a log cabin at Waxhaw, SC. Jackson was the first president since George Washington who had not attended college. He was a military hero in the War of 1812. His presidency reflected his democratic and egalitarian values. Died at Nashville, TN, June 8, 1845. His birthday is observed as a holiday in Tennessee.

LIBERIA: J.J. ROBERTS DAY. Mar 15. National holiday. Commemorates the birth in 1809 of the country's first president.

MAINE: ADMISSION DAY: ANNIVERSARY. Mar 15. Became 23rd state in 1820. Prior to this date, Maine had been part of Massachusetts.

"THREE'S COMPANY" TV PREMIERE: ANNIVERSARY. Mar 15, 1977. This half-hour comedy featured two girls and a guy sharing an apartment. In order for the landlord to go along with the living arrangements, Jack Tripper, played by John Ritter, had to pretend he was gay. Cast included Joyce DeWitt, Suzanne Somers, Norman Fell, Audra Findley, Richard Kline, Don Knotts and Priscilla Barnes. The last telecast aired on Sept 18, 1984.

TRUE CONFESSIONS DAY. Mar 15. Confession is good for the soul. Go into work today and tell all. If you plan to stay home, make an appointment with your mirror. [©2003 by WH.] For info: Thomas & Ruth Roy, Wellcat Holidays, 2418 Long Ln, Lebanon, PA 17046. Phone: (717) 279-0184. E-mail: info@wellcat.com. Web: www.wellcat.com.

VAN BROCKLIN, NORM: BIRTH ANIVERSARY. Mar 15, 1926. Norman Van Brocklin, Pro Football Hall of Fame quarterback and coach, born at Eagle Butte, SD. Van Brocklin played college football at Oregon and then signed with the Los Angeles Rams. He helped the Rams win their only NFL title in 1951. After finishing his playing career with the Philadelphia Eagles, he coached the Minnesota Vikings and the Atlanta Falcons. Inducted into the Pro Football Hall of Fame in 1979. Died at Social Circle, GA, May 2, 1983.

WASHINGTON'S ADDRESS TO CONTINENTAL ARMY OFFICERS: ANNIVERSARY. Mar 15, 1783. George Washington addressed a meeting at Newburgh, NY, of Continental army officers who were dissatisfied and rebellious for want of back pay, food, clothing and pensions. General Washington called for patience, opening his speech with the words "I have grown gray in your service. . . ." Congress later acted to satisfy most of the demands.

☆ Chase's 2004 Calendar of Events ☆
Mar 15–16

WELLDERLY DAY. Mar 15. Celebration and recognition of senior citizens who never act their age. Annually, the third Monday in March. For info: Dale L. Anderson, MD, 2982 W Owasso Blvd, St. Paul, MN 55113. Phone: (651) 484-5162. Fax: (651) 486-8860. E-mail: drdla@acthappy.com. Web: www.acthappy.com.

"THE WONDER YEARS" TV PREMIERE: ANNIVERSARY. Mar 15, 1988. A coming-of-age tale set in suburbia in the 1960s and 1970s. This drama/comedy starred Fred Savage as Kevin Arnold; Josh Saviano as his best friend, Paul and Danica McKellar as girlfriend Winnie. Kevin's dad was played by Dan Lauria, his homemaker mom by Alley Mills, his hippie sister by Olivia d'Abo and his bully brother by Jason Hervey. Narrator Daniel Stern was the voice of the grown-up Kevin. The last episode ran Sept 1, 1993, but it remains popular in syndication.

BIRTHDAYS TODAY

Harold Douglas Baines, 45, former baseball player, born St. Michael's, MD, Mar 15, 1959.
Alan Bean, 72, former astronaut, born Wheeler, TX, Mar 15, 1932.
Robert Terrell (Terry) Cummings, 43, former basketball player, born Chicago, IL, Mar 15, 1961.
Fabio, 43, model, born Fabio Lanzoni, Milan, Italy, Mar 15, 1961.
Ruth Bader Ginsburg, 71, Associate Justice of the US Supreme Court, born Brooklyn, NY, Mar 15, 1933.
Judd Hirsch, 69, actor (Emmy for "Taxi"; *Ordinary People*), born New York, NY, Mar 15, 1935.
Mike Love, 63, singer, musician (Beach Boys), born Los Angeles, CA, Mar 15, 1941.
Mark McGrath, 36, singer (Sugar Ray), born Newport Beach, CA, Mar 15, 1968.
Park Overall, 47, actress ("Empty Nest," *Mississippi Burning*), born Nashville, TN, Mar 15, 1957.
Dee Snider, 49, singer (Twisted Sister), composer, born Massapequa, NY, Mar 15, 1955.
Sly Stone, 60, singer, musician (Sly & the Family Stone), born Sylvester Stewart, Dallas, TX, Mar 15, 1944.
Craig Wasson, 50, actor ("Phyllis," *Body Double, Malcolm X*), born Ontario, OR, Mar 15, 1954.

MARCH 16 — TUESDAY
Day 76 — 290 Remaining

ANN ARBOR FILM FESTIVAL. Mar 16–21. Ann Arbor, MI. Independent 16mm and 35mm film festival in its 42nd year. Genres represented include experimental, animation, documentary, narrative, avant-garde. Entry deadline: Nov 15, 2003. $16,000 awarded in prizes. Est attendance: 5,000. For info: Chrisstina Hamilton, Ann Arbor Film Festival, PO Box 8232, Ann Arbor, MI 48107. Phone: (734) 995-5356. Fax: (734) 995-5396. E-mail: info@aafilmfest.org. Web: aafilmfest.org.

BLACK PRESS DAY: ANNIVERSARY OF THE FIRST BLACK NEWSPAPER. Mar 16, 1827. Anniversary of the founding of the first black newspaper in the US, *Freedom's Journal*, on Varick Street at New York, NY.

BONHEUR, ROSA: BIRTH ANNIVERSARY. Mar 16, 1822. French painter and sculptor best known for her paintings of animals, Rosa (Marie-Rosalie) Bonheur was born at Bordeaux. With the income from the sale of her art she purchased the castle of By near Fontainebleau at Melun, France, where she died May 25, 1899. Bonheur's *The Horse Fair*, which she painted in 1853, was purchased by the American millionaire Cornelius Vanderbilt for $53,600, a record price at the time. In 1865 Bonheur was awarded the Grand Cross of the Légion d'Honneur, the first woman so honored. An early Bohemian and feminist, Bonheur defied female convention of the day by dressing in pants and smoking cigarettes.

CLYMER, GEORGE: BIRTH ANNIVERSARY. Mar 16, 1739. Signer of the Declaration of Independence and of the US Constitution. Born at Philadelphia, PA, and died there Jan 24, 1813.

CURLEW DAY. Mar 16. Traditional arrival date for the long-billed curlew at the Umatilla (Oregon) National Wildlife Refuge. More than 500 of the long-billed curlews have been reported at this location during their nesting season.

ENGLAND: CHELTENHAM HUNT FESTIVAL. Mar 16–18. Cheltenham Racecourse, Prestbury, Cheltenham, Gloucestershire. "The Olympics of steeplechasing." Est attendance: 150,000. For info: Cheltenham Racecourse, Prestbury Park, Cheltenham, Gloucestershire, England GL50 4SH. Phone: (44) (1242) 513014 or (44) (1242) 226226. Fax: (44) (1242) 224227. Web: www.cheltenham.co.uk.

FREEDOM OF INFORMATION DAY. Mar 16. The American Library Association supports free and open access to government information created at taxpayer expense. On or near the birthday of James Madison (Mar 16), ALA urges libraries and librarians to join in celebrating the public's "right to know" by sponsoring activities to educate their communities about the importance of promoting and protecting freedom of information. Sponsored by the Freedom Forum and the American Library Association. For info: American Library Assn Washington Office, 1301 Pennsylvania Ave NW, Ste 403, Washington, DC 20004. Phone: (202) 628-8410. E-mail: alawash@alawash.org. Web: www.ala.org.

GODDARD DAY: ANNIVERSARY. Mar 16, 1926. Commemorates first liquid-fuel-powered rocket flight launched by Robert Hutchings Goddard (1882–1945) at Auburn, MA.

"THE GUMBY SHOW" TV PREMIERE: ANNIVERSARY. Mar 16, 1957. This kids' show was a spin-off from "Howdy Doody," where the character of Gumby was first introduced in 1956. Gumby and his horse, Pokey, were clay figures whose adventures were filmed using the process of "claymation." "The Gumby Show," created by Art Clokey, was first hosted by Bobby Nicholson and later by Pinky Lee. It was syndicated in 1966 and again in 1988.

LIPS APPRECIATION DAY. Mar 16. Where would all those lovely teeth we paid a bundle for be without a lovely frame? Do something nice for your lips today. Buy a lip balm. Better yet, kiss somebody! [©2003 by WH.] For info: Thomas & Ruth Roy, Wellcat Holidays, 2418 Long Ln, Lebanon, PA 17046. Phone: (717) 279-0184. E-mail: info@wellcat.com. Web: www.wellcat.com.

MADISON, JAMES: BIRTH ANNIVERSARY. Mar 16, 1751. 4th president of the US (Mar 4, 1809–Mar 3, 1817), born at Port Conway, VA. He was president when British forces invaded Washington, DC, requiring Madison and other high officials to flee while the British burned the Capitol, the president's residence and most other public buildings (Aug 24–25, 1814). Died at Montpelier, VA, June 28, 1836.

MY LAI MASSACRE: ANNIVERSARY. Mar 16, 1968. Most-publicized atrocity of Vietnam War. According to findings of US Army's investigating team, approximately 300 noncombatant Vietnamese villagers (at My Lai and Mykhe, near the South China Sea) were killed by infantrymen of the American Division.

NIXON, THELMA CATHERINE PATRICIA ("PAT") RYAN: BIRTH ANNIVERSARY. Mar 16, 1912. Wife of Richard Milhous Nixon, 37th president of the US. Born at Ely, NV, she died at Park Ridge, NJ, June 22, 1993.

POPE, JOHN: BIRTH ANNIVERSARY. Mar 16, 1822. Pope, a Union general in the Civil War, was born at Louisville, KY, graduated from West Point in 1842 and fought in the Mexican War. During the Civil War President Lincoln put Pope in charge of the Army of Virginia. He led the Union forces at the second Battle of Bull Run (August 1862) to a disastrous defeat, losing about 15,000 troops. He was immediately relieved of his command and sent to Minnesota to handle rioting Sioux Indians. Pope continued to deal with Indian matters until 1883 and eventually espoused the goal of assimilation into white culture. He died at Ohio, Sept 23, 1892.

SAINT URHO'S DAY. Mar 16. Hood River, OR. Join the parade and party to honor the tongue-in-cheek patron saint (invented in 1956) who drove the grasshoppers out of the vineyards of Finland. Est attendance: 150. For info: Camille Hukari, 3009 Dethman Ridge, Hood River, OR 97031. Phone: (541) 386-5785. Fax: (541) 387-4657.

SPACE MILESTONE: *GEMINI 8* (US). Mar 16, 1966. Executed (with *Agena*) first docking of orbiting spacecraft. Safe emergency landing after malfunction. Launched Mar 16, 1966.

US MILITARY ACADEMY FOUNDED: ANNIVERSARY. Mar 16, 1802. President Thomas Jefferson signed legislation establishing the US Military Academy to train officers for the army. The college is located at West Point, NY, on the site of the oldest continuously occupied military post in America. Women were admitted to West Point in 1976. The Academy's motto is "Duty, Honor, Country." For more info: www.usma.edu.

BIRTHDAYS TODAY

Bernardo Bertolucci, 63, filmmaker (Oscar for *The Last Emperor*; *Last Tango in Paris*), born Parma, Italy, Mar 16, 1941.
Erik Estrada, 55, actor ("CHiPS," *Honey Boy*), born New York, NY, Mar 16, 1949.
Lauren Graham, 37, actress (*Sweet November*, "The Gilmore Girls"), born Honolulu, HI, Mar 16, 1967.
Isabelle Huppert, 49, actress (*Violette*, *Story of Women*), born Paris, France, Mar 16, 1955.
Jerry Lewis, 79, comedian, actor (*My Friend Irma*); director (*The Bellboy*), born Newark, NJ, Mar 16, 1925.
Kate Nelligan, 53, actress (*Eye of the Needle*, *Frankie and Johnny*, *The Prince of Tides*), born London, ON, Canada, Mar 16, 1951.
Chuck Woolery, 62, game-show host ("Love Connection," "Scrabble"), born Ashland, KY, Mar 16, 1942.

MARCH 17 — WEDNESDAY
Day 77 — 289 Remaining

BRIDGER, JIM: 200th BIRTH ANNIVERSARY. Mar 17, 1804. American fur trader, frontiersman and scout, born at Richmond, VA, and died July 17, 1881, near Kansas City, MO. Believed to be the first white man to visit (in 1824) the Great Salt Lake, he also established Fort Bridger in southwestern Wyoming as a fur-trading post and as a way station for pioneers heading west on the Oregon Trail. Bridger National Forest in western Wyoming is named for him.

CAMP FIRE USA: ANNIVERSARY. Mar 17. To commemorate the anniversary of the founding of Camp Fire USA and the service given to children and youth across the nation. Founded in 1910 as Camp Fire Girls. For info: Camp Fire USA, 4601 Madison Ave, Kansas City, MO 64112. Phone: (816) 756-1950. Fax: (816) 756-2650. E-mail: info@campfireusa.org. Web: www.campfireusa.org.

CANADA: TORONTO SPORTSMEN'S SHOW. Mar 17–21. National Trade Center, Exhibition Place, Toronto, ON. Fishing manufacturers and retailers, fishing seminars, travel/vacation exhibits, cottages, camping products, boats and marine accessories, wildlife art, pet products and breeders, conservation and outdoor organizations, sporting goods, retriever trials, arena show and family entertainment. Est attendance: 125,000. For info: Harley Austin, Canadian Natl Sportsmen's Shows, 703 Evans Ave, Ste 202, Toronto, ON, Canada M9C 5E9. Phone: (416) 695-0311. Fax: (416) 695-0381. Web: www.sportshows.ca.

C.M. RUSSELL AUCTION OF ORIGINAL WESTERN ART. Mar 17–20. Heritage Inn, Great Falls, MT. Western art event features auctions, free seminars, 102 free display/sale rooms with thousands of artworks for sale, entertainment, elegant receptions and the best of Montana hospitality. Annually, a Wednesday–Saturday in March. Est attendance: 6,000. For info: Donna Madison, Exec Dir, Great Falls Adv Fed, PO Box 634, Great Falls, MT 59403-0634. Phone: (800) 803-3351 or (406) 761-6453. E-mail: gfaf@gfaf.com.

COLE, NAT "KING" (NATHANIEL ADAMS COLE): 85th BIRTH ANNIVERSARY. Mar 17, 1919. Nat "King" Cole was born at Montgomery, AL, and began his musical career at an early age, playing the piano at age four. He was the first black entertainer to host a national television show. His many songs included "The Christmas Song," "Nature Boy," "Mona Lisa," "Ramblin' Rose" and "Unforgettable." Although he was dogged by racial discrimination throughout his career, including the cancellation of his television show because opposition from southern white viewers decreased advertising revenue, Cole was criticized by prominent black newspapers for not joining other black entertainers in the civil rights struggle. Cole contributed more than $50,000 to civil rights organizations in response to the criticism. Nat "King" Cole died Feb 25, 1965, at Santa Monica, CA.

CORBETT-FITZSIMMONS TITLE FIGHT: ANNIVERSARY. Mar 17, 1897. In one of boxing's greatest fights—and the first heavyweight title fight to be filmed—"Gentleman Jim" Corbett lost the world title to "Ruby Robert" Fitzsimmons at Carson City, NV. Fitzsimmons, seemingly a long shot at 34 years of age, hung on for 13 rounds before landing the "solar plexus punch" that felled Corbett. Western legends in attendance were Bat Masterson (overseeing security) and Wyatt Earp.

DOCTOR-PATIENT TRUST DAY. Mar 17. To rekindle the once-revered sanctity of the doctor-patient relationship. For info: Dr. Frank H. Boehm, Vanderbilt Medical Center, B-1000 Medical Center North, Nashville, TN 37232. Phone: (615) 322-2071. E-mail: frank.boehm@vanderbilt.edu. Web: www.dr-boehm.com.

ENGLAND: CHELSEA ANTIQUES FAIR. Mar 17–22 (tentative; also Sept 17–26, tentative). Chelsea Old Town Hall, King's Rd, London. Traditional, prestigious event now modernizing its style, but retaining top-quality items. Est attendance: 6,000. For info: Penman Antiques Fair, PO Box 114, Haywards Heath, West Sussex, England RH16 2YU. Phone: (44) (870) 350-2442. Fax: (44) (870) 350-2443. E-mail: info@penman-fairs.co.uk.

EVACUATION DAY: ANNIVERSARY. Mar 17, 1776. A public holiday at Boston and Suffolk County, MA, celebrates anniversary of the evacuation from Boston of British troops.

FEMALE RELIEF SOCIETY OF NAUVOO ORGANIZED: ANNIVERSARY. Mar 17, 1842. Twenty Mormon women formally initiated this organization at Nauvoo, IL, which is now known as the Relief Society and has grown to almost four million members. Information furnished by Church of Jesus Christ of Latter-day Saints, Public Affairs Department.

IRELAND: NATIONAL DAY. Mar 17. St. Patrick's Day is observed in the Republic of Ireland as a legal national holiday.

JONES, BOBBY: BIRTH ANNIVERSARY. Mar 17, 1902. Golfing great Robert Tyre Jones, Jr, first golfer to win the grand slam (the four major British and American tournaments in one year). Born at Atlanta, GA, he died there Dec 18, 1971.

LEARNING DISABILITIES ASSOCIATION OF AMERICA INTERNATIONAL CONFERENCE. Mar 17–20. Atlanta Hilton, Atlanta, GA. 41st annual. Est attendance: 3,000. For info: Learning Disabilities Assn of America, 4156 Library Rd, Pittsburgh, PA 15234. Phone: (412) 341-1515. Fax: (412) 344-0224. E-mail: info@ldaamerica.org. Web: www.ldaamerica.org.

NAIA WOMEN'S DIVISION I NATIONAL BASKETBALL CHAMPIONSHIP TOURNAMENT. Mar 17–23. Jackson, TN. 32-team field competes for the national championship. 24th annual competition. Est attendance: 38,000. For info: Natl Assn of Intercollegiate Athletics, 23500 W 105th St, PO Box 1325, Olathe, KS 66051-1325. Phone: (913) 791-0044. Fax: (913) 791-9555. E-mail: ncronkhite@naia.org. Web: www.naia.org.

NATIONAL COMMON COURTESY DAY. Mar 17. Citizens of our country reflect on what it means to demonstrate common courtesy. We live in a society where it seems that we have forgotten how to display such behaviors in our everyday lives, be it at work, home or simply driving down the highway. On National Common Courtesy Day, stories will be collected from individuals who have demonstrated common courtesy or who have been the recipents of such acts. For info: Lefiest H. Galimore, 3139 Plymouth Rd, Ann Arbor, MI 48105. Phone: (734) 995-6816 or (734) 502-5775. Fax: (734) 995-6861. E-mail: Lefiest@familylearninginstitute.org.

NJCAA DIVISION II MEN'S BASKETBALL NATIONAL FINALS. Mar 17–20. Danville, IL. Junior College Division II national men's basketball finals tournament. Est attendance: 8,000. For info: Jeanie Cooke, Exec Dir, Danville Area Conv/Visitors Bureau, PO Box 992, Danville, IL 61834. Phone: (800) 383-4386. E-mail: dacub@cooktech.net.

NORTHERN IRELAND: SAINT PATRICK'S DAY HOLIDAY. Mar 17. National holiday.

NUREYEV, RUDOLF HAMETOVICH: BIRTH ANNIVERSARY. Mar 17, 1938. Rudolf Nureyev, one of the most charismatic ballet stars of the 20th century, was born on a train in southeastern Siberia. Nureyev's defection from the Soviet Union on June 17, 1961, while on tour with the Kirov Ballet, made headlines worldwide. The dancer was known for his ability to combine passion with a high level of perfectionism. His long partnership with Dame Margot Fonteyn of the Royal Ballet was legendary, and he also performed frequently with the Martha Graham Dance Company. Nureyev also choreographed and restaged many classics and served as the Paris Opera Ballet's artistic director. He died Jan 6, 1993, at Levallois, France, a suburb of Paris.

PARKER, GEORGE: DEATH ANNIVERSARY. Mar 17, 1764. George Parker, the second Earl of Macclesfield, was born in 1697 (exact date unknown). The eminent English astronomer was president of the Royal Society from 1752 until his death. He was one of the principal authors of the Bill for Regulating the Commencement of the Year (British Calendar Act of 1751), which was introduced in Parliament by Lord Chesterfield. That act caused the adoption, in 1752, of the "New Style" Gregorian calendar, which is still in use today. Parker died at Shirburn Castle, England.

RUSTIN, BAYARD: BIRTH ANNIVERSARY. Mar 17, 1910. Black pacifist and civil rights leader, Bayard Rustin was an organizer and participant in many of the great social protest marches—for jobs, freedom and nuclear disarmament. He was arrested and imprisoned more than 20 times for his civil rights and pacifist activities. Born at West Chester, PA, Rustin died at New York, NY, Aug 24, 1987.

SAINT PATRICK'S DAY. Mar 17. Commemorates the patron saint of Ireland, Bishop Patrick (AD 389–461) who, about AD 432, left his home in the Severn Valley, England, and introduced Christianity into Ireland. Feast day in the Roman Catholic Church. A national holiday in Ireland and Northern Ireland.

SAINT PATRICK'S DAY PARADE. Mar 17. Fifth Avenue, New York, NY. Held since 1762, the parade of 200,000 begins the two-mile march at 11:00 AM and lasts about six hours. Starts on 44th St and 5th Ave and ends at 86th St and First Ave. Est attendance: 700,000. For info: NYC & Company, 810 7th Ave, 3rd Fl, New York, NY 10019. Phone: (800) NYC-VISIT or (212) 484-1222.

SEVERE WEATHER AWARENESS WEEK. Mar 17–23 (varies). To remind the public of the danger of thunderstorms, tornadoes and flooding. Individual states sponsor this week on different dates—anywhere from February through April.

SOUTH AFRICAN WHITES VOTE TO END MINORITY RULE: ANNIVERSARY. Mar 17, 1992. A referendum proposing ending white minority rule through negotiations was supported by a whites-only ballot. The vote of 1,924,186 (68.6 percent) whites in support of President F.W. de Klerk's reform policies was greater than expected.

SPACE MILESTONE: *VANGUARD 1* (US): ANNIVERSARY. Mar 17, 1958. Established "pear shape" of Earth. At only three pounds it was the first solar-powered satellite.

TANEY, ROGER B.: BIRTH ANNIVERSARY. Mar 17, 1777. Fifth Chief Justice of the Supreme Court, born at Calvert County, MD. Served as Attorney General under President Andrew Jackson. Nominated as Secretary of the Treasury, he became the first presidential nominee to be rejected by the Senate. His rejection centered on his strong stance against the Bank of the United States as a central bank and his role in urging President Jackson to veto the congressional bill extending its charter. A year later, he was nominated to the Supreme Court as an associate justice by Jackson, but his nomination was stalled until the death of Chief Justice John Marshall July 6, 1835. Taney was nominated to fill Marshall's place on the bench and after much resistance he was sworn in as Chief Justice in March 1836. His tenure on the Supreme Court is most remembered for the Dred Scott decision. He died at Washington, DC, Oct 12, 1864.

BIRTHDAYS TODAY

Daniel Ray (Danny) Ainge, 45, basketball coach, former basketball and baseball player, born Eugene, OR, Mar 17, 1959.

Susie Allanson, 52, singer ("Baby Don't Keep Me Hangin' On"), born Minneapolis, MN, Mar 17, 1952.

Lesley-Anne Down, 50, actress ("Upstairs, Downstairs," *The Pink Panther Strikes Again*), born London, England, Mar 17, 1954.

Patrick Duffy, 55, actor ("Step by Step," "Dallas"), born Townsend, MT, Mar 17, 1949.

Paul Horn, 74, composer, musician, born New York, NY, Mar 17, 1930.

Vicki Lewis, 44, actress ("NewsRadio," *Godzilla*), born Cincinnati, OH, Mar 17, 1960.

Rob Lowe, 40, actor (*St. Elmo's Fire, About Last Night . . .*, "The West Wing"), born Charlottesville, VA, Mar 17, 1964.

Mercedes McCambridge, 86, actress (voice of Satan in *The Exorcist*; Oscar for *All the King's Men*), born Joliet, IL, Mar 17, 1918.

Kurt Russell, 53, actor (*Backdraft, Elvis*), born Springfield, MA, Mar 17, 1951.

Gary Sinise, 49, stage and screen actor (*Forrest Gump, Apollo 13*), born Chicago, IL, Mar 17, 1955.

March 2004

S	M	T	W	T	F	S
	1	2	3	4	5	6
7	8	9	10	11	12	13
14	15	16	17	18	19	20
21	22	23	24	25	26	27
28	29	30	31			

☆ Chase's 2004 Calendar of Events ☆   Mar 18

MARCH 18 — THURSDAY
Day 78 — 288 Remaining

ABSOLUTELY INCREDIBLE KID DAY. Mar 18. Camp Fire USA, one of the nation's oldest and largest youth development organizations, sponsors this day of appreciation for America's youth. Celebrate by writing letters of love and encouragement to the absolutely incredible children in your life. For info: Camp Fire USA, 4601 Madison Ave, Kansas City, MO 64112. Phone: (816) 756-1950. Fax: (816) 756-2650. E-mail: kidday@campfireusa.org. Web: www.campfireusa.org.

ARUBA: FLAG DAY. Mar 18. Aruba national holiday. Display of flags, national music and folkloric events.

AWKWARD MOMENTS DAY. Mar 18. Celebrate the humor in life's uncomfortable situations. Recognize those moments that make us feel unsure and embarrassed, then harness the power of humor, laughter and fun to cope with them. For info: Wayne & Laura Gignac, 30 Slater Ave, Norwich, CT 06360. Phone: (860) 887-7054. Fax: (860) 892-1951. E-mail: wayne@theshowworks.com. Web: www.theshowworks.com.

CALHOUN, JOHN CALDWELL: BIRTH ANNIVERSARY. Mar 18, 1782. American statesman and first vice president of the US to resign that office (Dec 28, 1832). Born at Abbeville District, SC, died at Washington, DC, Mar 31, 1850.

CLEVELAND, GROVER: BIRTH ANNIVERSARY. Mar 18, 1837. The 22nd and 24th president of the US was born Stephen Grover Cleveland at Caldwell, NJ. Terms of office as president: Mar 4, 1885–Mar 3, 1889, and Mar 4, 1893–Mar 3, 1897. He ran for president for the intervening term and received a plurality of votes cast but failed to win electoral college victory. Only president to serve two nonconsecutive terms. Also the only president to be married in the White House. He married 21-year-old Frances Folsom, his ward. Their daughter, Esther, was the first child of a president to be born in the White House. Died at Princeton, NJ, June 24, 1908.

COMPANIES THAT CARE DAY. Mar 18. An annual event, celebrated by companies that prize employees and are committed to community service. This day encourages employers to highlight and expand their staff and community initiatives as well as recognize the people who make their companies successful. Examples of how companies have celebrated the day can be found at our website. For info: Marci Koblenz, Companies That Care, 500 N Dearborn St, 2nd Fl, Chicago, IL 60610. Phone: (312) 286-1547. Fax: (847) 869-2465. E-mail: info@companies-that-care.org. Web: www.companies-that-care.org.

FESTIVAL OF HOUSES AND GARDENS. Mar 18–Apr 17. Charleston, SC. Held annually since 1947. Provides a rare opportunity to explore the private dwellings and gardens of historic Charleston. Est attendance: 14,000. For info: Dir of Tours & Special Events, Historic Charleston Fdtn, PO Box 1120, Charleston, SC 29402. Phone: (843) 722-3405. Fax: (843) 577-2067.

FIRST ELECTRIC RAZOR MARKETED: ANNIVERSARY. Mar 18, 1931. The first electric razor was marketed by Schick, Inc.

FORGIVE MOM & DAD DAY. Mar 18. Is there a parent alive who has not made mistakes? It's time to let Mom and Dad down off the wedding cake and into the world of mere humans. Besides, you're an alleged grown-up now, and it's time to stop living your life as a reaction to what used to be. [©2003 by WH.] For info: Thomas & Ruth Roy, Wellcat Holidays, 2418 Long Ln, Lebanon, PA 17046. Phone: (717) 279-0184. E-mail: info@wellcat.com. Web: www.wellcat.com.

GRAND RAPIDS SPORT, FISHING AND TRAVEL SHOW. Mar 18–21. DeVos Place, Grand Rapids, MI. This event brings together buyers and sellers of fishing boats and equipment, RVs, campers and their accessories, as well as other outdoor sporting goods. US and Canadian hunting and fishing trips and other vacation travel destinations are featured. All aspects of fishing, including tackle boats, seminars, demonstrations and displays are emphasized. Est attendance: 45,000. For info: Adam Starr, ShowSpan, Inc, 2121 Celebration Dr NE, Grand Rapids, MI 49525. Phone: (616) 447-2860. Fax: (616) 447-2861. E-mail: events@showspan.com. Web: www.showspan.com.

JAPANESE SUICIDE WEAPON INTRODUCED: ANNIVERSARY. Mar 18, 1945. The Japanese released mechanized flying bombs piloted by young Japanese men. These suicide bombs, directed against the US aircraft carrier fleet attacking the Japanese fleet in the Kure-Kobe area, inflicted serious damage on the *Enterprise*, *Intrepid* and *Wasp*.

JOHNSON, WILLIAM H.: BIRTH ANNIVERSARY. Mar 18, 1901. African-American artist, born at Florence, SC; died Apr 13, 1970, at Islip, NY. Johnson spent many years in Europe painting expressionist works. He was strongly influenced by the vivid styles and brushstrokes of Henry O. Tanner, Vincent van Gogh, Paul Gauguin, Edvard Munch and Otto Dix. He left Europe when Hitler began destroying art that had primitivist or African themes. Back in the US, Johnson developed a new, flatter style and delved into subjects of his own experience as well as historical African-American figures and events. *Going to Church* (1940–41) and *Mom and Dad* (1944) are examples of his later work.

MICHIGAN'S GRANDPARENTS AND GRANDCHILDREN DAY. Mar 18. During this annual observance grandparents are invited into schools across Michigan to join with the children in special programs and events. For info: Luella Davison, Grandparents Anonymous, 900 N Cass Lake Rd, Waterford, MI 48328. Phone: (800) 4A-CHILD or (248) 682-8384.

NATIONAL BIODIESEL DAY. Mar 18. Birthday of Rudolph Diesel, who invented the diesel engine and unveiled it at the World Fair in 1900. Diesel originally designed the engine to run on peanut oil and was a big believer in the role vegetable oils could play in fueling America. Biodiesel is a cleaner burning petroleum-free alternative to diesel that can be made from any fat or vegatable oil, most commonly soybean oil. This day honors the man whose vision comes full circle as biodiesel becomes an increasingly popular fuel. For info: Jenna Higgins, National Biodiesel Board, PO Box 104898, Jefferson City, MO 65110-4898. Phone: (573) 635-3893. Fax: (573) 635-7913. E-mail: jhiggins@biodiesel.org. Web: www.biodiesel.org.

NATIONAL FESTIVAL OF THE WEST. Mar 18–21. WestWorld, Scottsdale, AZ. Four days of pure cowboy fun including Western film celebrities, music and movies, cowboy poetry, costume contests, arena events including mounted shooting competitions, chuck wagon cookin' competition, historical reenactments, and a huge retail show including Western art, cowboy collectibles and anything Western. It's a fun event for the whole family with plenty to see and do. Est attendance: 70,000. For info: Mary Brown, Festival of the West, PO Box 12966, Scottsdale, AZ 85267. Phone: (602) 996-4387. Fax: (602) 867-4887. E-mail: mary@festivalofthewest.com. Web: www.festivalofthewest.com.

NCAA DIVISION I WOMEN'S SWIMMING AND DIVING CHAMPIONSHIPS. Mar 18–20. Student Recreation Center Natatorium, College Station, TX. Est attendance: 3,000. For info: NCAA, 700 W Washington St, PO Box 6222, Indianapolis, IN 46206-6222. Phone: (317) 917-6222. Fax: (317) 917-6888. Web: www.ncaa.org.

NCAA DIVISION I WRESTLING CHAMPIONSHIPS. Mar 18–20. Sawis Center, St. Louis, MO. For info: Natl Collegiate Athletic Assn, 700 W Washington St, PO Box 6222, Indianapolis, IN 46206-6222. Phone: (317) 917-6222. Web: www.ncaa.org.

SPACE MILESTONE: *VOSKHOD 2* (USSR). Mar 18, 1965. Colonel Leonov stepped out of the capsule for 20 minutes in a special space suit, the first man to leave a spaceship. It was two months prior to the first US space walk. See also: "Space Milestone: *Gemini 4* US" (June 3).

SUWANNEE SPRING FEST. Mar 18–21. Live Oak, FL. Outstanding festival. Previous artists have included Nitty Gritty Dirt Band, Earl Scruggs, Rhonda Vicent, Donna the Buffalo, Peter Rowan and more. Also available are vendors and activities for children. Est attendance: 8,000. For info: Spirit of the Suwannee Music Park, 3076 95th Dr, Live Oak, FL 32060. Phone: (386) 364-1683. Fax: (386) 364-2998. E-mail: spirit@musicliveshere.com. Web: www.musicliveshere.com.

"TALES OF WELLS FARGO" TV PREMIERE: ANNIVERSARY. Mar 18, 1957. This half-hour western starred Dale Robertson as Jim Hardie, agent for Wells Fargo transport company. In the fall of 1961, the show expanded to an hour. Hardie bought a ranch, and new cast members were added including Jack Ging as Beau McCloud, another agent; Virginia Christine as Ovie, a widow owning a nearby ranch; Lory Patrick and Mary Jane Saunders as Ovie's daughters and William Demarest as Jeb, Hardie's ranch foreman. Jack Nicholson appeared in one of his first major TV roles in the episode "The Washburn Girl."

BIRTHDAYS TODAY

Bonnie Blair, 40, Olympic gold medal speed skater, born Cornwall, NY, Mar 18, 1964.
Irene Cara, 45, singer ("Fame," "The Dream"), actress (*Ain't Misbehavin'*), born the Bronx, NY, Mar 18, 1959.
Frederik Willem de Klerk, 68, former president of South Africa, born Johannesburg, South Africa, Mar 18, 1936.
Kevin Dobson, 60, actor ("Kojak," "Knots Landing"), born New York, NY, Mar 18, 1944.
Brad Dourif, 54, actor (*One Flew Over the Cuckoo's Nest, Blue Velvet, Jungle Fever*), born Huntington, WV, Mar 18, 1950.
Peter Graves, 78, actor ("Mission: Impossible," "The Winds of War"), born Minneapolis, MN, Mar 18, 1926.
John Kander, 77, composer (*Cabaret, Chicago*), born Kansas City, MO, Mar 18, 1927.
Shashi Kapoor, 66, actor (*Heat and Dust, Sammy and Rosie Get Laid*), born Calcutta, India, Mar 18, 1938.
Queen Latifah, 34, rap artist, actress (*Chicago*, "Living Single"), born Dana Owens, East Orange, NJ, Mar 18, 1970.
Wilson Pickett, 63, singer, songwriter ("The Midnight Hour," "It's Too Late"), born Prattville, AL, Mar 18, 1941.
George Plimpton, 77, author (*Paper Lion, Shadow Box*), TV host, editor, born New York, NY, Mar 18, 1927.
Charley Pride, 66, singer, former minor league baseball player, born Sledge, MS, Mar 18, 1938.
John Updike, 72, author (*Rabbit Run, The Witches of Eastwick*), born Shillington, PA, Mar 18, 1932.
Vanessa Williams, 41, singer, actress (*Bye, Bye Birdie; Kiss of the Spider Woman*), born New York, NY, Mar 18, 1963.
Alexei Yagudin, 24, figure skater, born Leningrad, Russia, Mar 18, 1980.

	S	M	T	W	T	F	S
March		1	2	3	4	5	6
	7	8	9	10	11	12	13
2004	14	15	16	17	18	19	20
	21	22	23	24	25	26	27
	28	29	30	31			

MARCH 19 — FRIDAY
Day 79 — 287 Remaining

BIG TEN MEN'S GYMNASTICS CHAMPIONSHIP. Mar 19–20. University of Illinois, Champaign, IL. For info: Sue Lister, Assoc Commissioner, Big Ten Conference, 1500 W Higgins Rd, Park Ridge, IL 60068-6300. Phone: (847) 696-1010. Fax: (847) 696-1110. Web: www.bigten.org.

BRADFORD, WILLIAM: BIRTH ANNIVERSARY. Mar 19, 1589 (OS). Pilgrim father, governor of Plymouth Colony. Born at Yorkshire, England, and baptized Mar 19, 1589. Sailed from Southampton, England, on the *Mayflower* in 1620. Died at Plymouth, MA, May 9, 1657 (OS).

BRYAN, WILLIAM JENNINGS: BIRTH ANNIVERSARY. Mar 19, 1860. American political leader, member of Congress, Democratic presidential nominee (1896), "free silver" advocate, assisted in prosecution at Scopes trial, known as "the Silver-Tongued Orator." Born at Salem, IL, he died at Dayton, TN, July 26, 1925.

DAYTONA BEACH SPRING CAR SHOW & SWAP MEET. Mar 19–21. Daytona International Speedway, Daytona Beach, FL. 17th annual car show of all makes and models of collector vehicles. Many car clubs make this their largest annual event. Show includes display of antiques, classics, sportscars, muscle cars, race cars, customs, street rods and special trucks on the speedway infield, with a large swap meet of auto parts and accessories. Collector car sales corral and crafts sale. Annually, the last or next to the last weekend in March. Est attendance: 50,000. For info: Ron Baynton, Mgr of Show Operations, Daytona Beach Racing and Recreational Facilities District, PO Box 1958, Daytona Beach, FL 32115-1958. Phone: (386) 255-7355. Web: www.carshows.org.

EARP, WYATT: BIRTH ANNIVERSARY. Mar 19, 1848. Born at Monmouth, IL, and died Jan 13, 1929, at Los Angeles, CA. A legendary figure of the Old West, Earp worked as a railroad hand, saloon keeper, gambler, lawman, gunslinger, miner and real estate investor at various times. Best known for the gunfight at the OK Corral Oct 26, 1881, at Tombstone, AZ.

IRAN: NATIONAL DAY OF OIL. Mar 19. National holiday. Commemorates the nationalization of Iran's oil fields in 1963.

LIVINGSTONE, DAVID: BIRTH ANNIVERSARY. Mar 19, 1813. Scottish physician, missionary and explorer, born at Blantyre, Scotland. Subject of a famous search by Henry M. Stanley, who found him at Ujiji, near Lake Tanganyika in Africa, on Nov 10, 1871. Dr. Livingstone died at Africa, May 1, 1873. See also: "Stanley, Henry Morton: Birth Anniversary" (Jan 28).

MACON, GEORGIA'S 2004 INTERNATIONAL CHERRY BLOSSOM FESTIVAL. Mar 19–28. Macon, GA. 22nd annual Cherry Blossom Festival features concerts, exhibits, parades, children's events, hot-air balloons, street party, fireworks, food, fun and family entertainment. 275,000 Yoshino cherry trees. Est attendance: 700,000. For info: Mary Huff, Macon Cherry Blossom Fest, 794 Cherry St, Macon, GA 31201. Phone: (478) 751-7429. Fax: (478) 751-7408. Web: www.cherryblossom.com.

McKEAN, THOMAS: BIRTH ANNIVERSARY. Mar 19, 1734. Signer of the Declaration of Independence and governor of Pennsylvania. Born at Chester County, PA, he died June 24, 1817.

MURDER AT FORD'S THEATER: 5th ANNUAL CONFERENCE. Mar 19–21. Clinton, MD. Annual Civil War symposium focusing on the Lincoln assassination and its aftermath. Est attendance: 300. For info: Surratt House Museum, PO Box 427, Clinton, MD 20735. Phone: (301) 868-1121. Fax: (301) 868-8177. Web: www.surratt.org.

NORTHEAST GREAT OUTDOORS SHOW. Mar 19–21. Empire State Plaza, Albany, NY. Featuring fishing, hunting, camping and more. Attractions include informative seminars, fly casting pond, archery tournament, turkey and deer calling contests, deer scoring session, bass and other fishing boats, live predatory animals and much more. Annually, the third full weekend in March. Est attendance: 20,000. For info: Cate Masterson, Show Dir, Ed Lewi Assoc, 6 Chelsea Pl, Clifton Park, NY 12065. Phone: (518) 383-6183. Fax: (518) 383-6755. Web: www.edlewi.com.

OPERATION IRAQI FREEDOM: ANNIVERSARY. Mar 19, 2003. At 9:30 PM, EST, two hours past a deadline for Iraqi dictator Saddam Hussein to step down from power, US and British forces began air strikes against his regime. A ground campaign (adding Australian forces) followed quickly, and by Apr 9, Baghdad was in allied control and Hussein had disappeared. On May 1, President George W. Bush announced the end of major military operations in Iraq, although a peacekeeping force remained.

RENAISSANCE FEST. Mar 19–20 (also Mar 26–27, Apr 3–4). Live Oak, FL. Sixteenth-century reality experience of royal and peasant life. Events include human chess match and jousting knights on horseback. For info: Spirit of the Suwanee Music Park, 3076 95th Dr, Live Oak, FL 32060. Phone: (386) 364-1683. Fax: (386) 364-2998. E-mail: spirit@musicliveshere.com. Web: www.musicliveshere.com.

ROGERS, EDITH NOURSE: BIRTH ANNIVERSARY. Mar 19, 1881. Edith Nourse Rogers was a YMCA and Red Cross volunteer in France during World War I. In 1925 she was elected to the US Congress to fill the vacancy left by the death of her husband. An able legislator, she was reelected to the House of Representatives 17 times and became the first woman to have her name attached to major legislation. She was a major force in the legislation creating the Women's Army Auxiliary Corps (May 14, 1942) during World War II. Rogers was born at Saco, ME, and died Sept 10, 1960, at Boston.

RUSSELL, CHARLES M.: BIRTH ANNIVERSARY. Mar 19, 1864. Born at St. Louis, MO, Charles M. Russell moved to Montana at about age 16 and became a cowboy. Considered one of the greatest Western artists, he recorded the life of the cowboy in his artwork. He died Oct 26, 1926, at Great Falls, MT.

RYDER, ALBERT PINKHAM: BIRTH ANNIVERSARY. Mar 19, 1847. Painter Albert Pinkham Ryder was born at New Bedford, MA, where he gained a great love for the sea, the subject of many of his works. Ryder was a misanthrope and recluse. He dedicated himself to his painting, working slowly and piling layer after layer of paint on his canvases until he achieved the look he was after. In his lifetime Ryder created only 150 paintings. Three of his best-known works are *The Race Track*, *Toilers of the Sea* and *Siegfried and the Rhine Maidens*. Ryder died Mar 28, 1917, at Elmhurst, NY. Because of his method of painting, many of his works have deteriorated since their creation.

SIRICA, JOHN JOSEPH: 100th BIRTH ANNIVERSARY. Mar 19, 1904. John Sirica, "the Watergate Judge," was born at Waterbury, CT. During two years of trials and hearings, Sirica relentlessly pushed for the names of those responsible for the June 17, 1972, burglary of the Democratic National Committee headquarters in Washington's Watergate Complex. His unwavering search for the truth ultimately resulted in the toppling of the Nixon administration. Judge John Sirica died Aug 15, 1992, at Washington, DC.

SNOWMAN BURNING. Mar 19. Reading of poetry heralding the end of winter and the arrival of spring, followed by sacrifice in effigy, toasts and cheers. Annually, on or near the first day of spring. Est attendance: 300. For info: Public Relations Office, Lake Superior State University, Sault Ste. Marie, MI 49783. Phone: (906) 635-2315. Fax: (906) 635-2623. Web: www.lssu.edu.

SUGARLOAF CRAFTS FESTIVAL. Mar 19–21. Fort Washington Expo Center, Fort Washington, PA. Now in its 10th year, this show features 350 nationally recognized craft designers and fine artists displaying and selling their original creations. Includes craft demonstrations, live music, specialty foods, hourly gift certificate drawings and more. Est attendance: 24,500. For info: Sugarloaf Mountain Works, 200 Orchard Ridge Dr, #215, Gaithersburg, MD 20878. Phone: (800) 210-9900. Fax: (301) 253-9620. Web: www.SugarloafCrafts.com.

SWALLOWS RETURN TO SAN JUAN CAPISTRANO. Mar 19. Traditional date (St. Joseph's Day), since 1776, for swallows to return to old mission of San Juan Capistrano, CA. See also: "St. John of Capistrano: Death Anniversary" (Oct 23).

US STANDARD TIME ACT: ANNIVERSARY. Mar 19, 1918. Anniversary of passage by Congress of the Standard Time Act, which authorized the Interstate Commerce Commission to establish standard time zones for the US. The Act also established "daylight saving time" to save fuel and to promote other economies in a country at war. Daylight saving time first went into operation on Easter Sunday, Mar 31, 1918. The Uniform Time Act of 1966, as amended in 1986, by Public Law 99-359, now governs standard time in the US. See also: "US: Daylight Saving Time Begins" (Apr 4).

WARREN, EARL: BIRTH ANNIVERSARY. Mar 19, 1891. American jurist, 14th Chief Justice of the US Supreme Court. Born at Los Angeles, CA; died at Washington, DC, July 9, 1974.

BIRTHDAYS TODAY

Ursula Andress, 68, actress (*Dr. No*, *What's New Pussycat?*), born Bern, Switzerland, Mar 19, 1936.
Michael Bergin, 35, actor ("Baywatch"), born Naugatuck, CT, Mar 19, 1969.
Glenn Close, 57, actress (*The Big Chill*, *Fatal Attraction*; stage: *Sunset Boulevard*), born Greenwich, CT, Mar 19, 1947.
Ornette Coleman, 74, composer, saxophonist, born Fort Worth, TX, Mar 19, 1930.
Patrick McGoohan, 76, director, actor ("The Prisoner"), born New York, NY, Mar 19, 1928.
Philip Roth, 71, author (*The Great American Novel*, *Portnoy's Complaint*), born Newark, NJ, Mar 19, 1933.
Brent Scowcroft, 79, business executive, consultant, born Ogden, UT, Mar 19, 1925.
Renee Taylor, 69, actress, writer (Emmy for "Acts of Love and Other Comedies"; "Mary Hartman, Mary Hartman," *The Producers*, *A New Leaf*), born New York, NY, Mar 19, 1935.
Hedo Turkoglu, 25, basketball player, born Hiyadet Turkoglu at Istanbul, Turkey, Mar 19, 1979.
Bruce Willis, 49, actor ("Moonlighting," *The Sixth Sense*, *Die Hard*), born Idar-Oberstein, West Germany, Mar 19, 1955.

MARCH 20 — SATURDAY
Day 80 — 286 Remaining

ANONYMOUS GIVING WEEK. Mar 20–27. A time to celebrate the true spirit of giving. Experience the joy in random acts of kindness. Leave a legacy of anonymous contribution. Perfect for a one-time or all-week adventure designed to share time, talent and treasure. For info: Janna Krammer, Legacy Institute, 42747 Blackhawk Rd, Harris, MN 55032. Phone: (877) 646-9200. Fax: (651) 674-0228. E-mail: info@legacyinstitute.com.

BIG TEN WOMEN'S GYMNASTICS CHAMPIONSHIP. Mar 20. University of Minnesota, Minneapolis, MN. For info: Sue Lister, Assoc Commissioner, Big Ten Conference, 1500 W Higgins Rd, Park Ridge, IL 60068-6300. Phone: (847) 696-1010. Fax: (847) 696-1110. Web: www.bigten.org.

BIG 12 WOMEN'S GYMNASTICS CHAMPIONSHIP. Mar 20. Columbia, MO. Est attendance: 2,000. For info: Big 12 Conference, 2201 Stemmons Freeway, 28th Fl, Dallas, TX 75207. Phone: (214) 742-1212. Fax: (214) 753-0145. Web: www.big12sports.com.

CANADA: MAPLE FESTIVAL OF NOVA SCOTIA. Mar 20–Apr 17 (Saturdays only). Northern Nova Scotia. Promotion of the maple industry. Pancake suppers with entertainment, industry equipment displays and crafts displays. Est attendance: 5,000. For info: Lorna A. Crowe, RR1, Southampton, Cumberland County, NS, Canada B0M 1W0. Phone: (902) 546-2844. Web: www.novascotiamaplesyrup.com.

Mar 20 ☆ *Chase's 2004 Calendar of Events* ☆

ENGLAND: HEAD OF THE RIVER RACE. Mar 20. Mortlake to Putney, River Thames, London. At 3:30 PM. Processional race for 420 eight-oared crews, starting at 10-second intervals. Est attendance: 7,000. For info: Mr A. Ruddle, 59 Berkeley Ct, Oaklands Dr, Weybridge, Surrey, UK KT13 9HY. Phone: (44) (1932) 220401.

GREAT AMERICAN MEATOUT. Mar 20. America's foremost celebration of meatless eating asks consumers to "kick the meat habit, at least for the day" at 2,000 events across the country. 40 governors and mayors have issued supportive proclamations. For info: Farm Animal Reform Movement, Box 30654, Bethesda, MD 20824. Phone: (301) 530-1737 or (800) MEATOUT. Fax: (301) 530-5747. E-mail: info@meatout.org. Web: www.meatout.com.

IBSEN, HENRIK: BIRTH ANNIVERSARY. Mar 20, 1828. Norwegian playwright born at Skien, Norway. Among his best-remembered plays: *Peer Gynt, The Pillars of Society, The Wild Duck, An Enemy of the People* and *Hedda Gabler*. Died at Oslo, Norway, May 23, 1906.

INTERNATIONAL BRAIN BEE. Mar 20. Baltimore, MD. A Q&A competition about the human brain for high school students. The students are quizzed about intelligence, memory, emotions, sensations, movement, stress, aging, sleep and brain disorders. Thirty cities throughout North America conduct local bees during January and February, the winners of which are invited to the championship at the University of Maryland in Baltimore during Brain Awareness Week. The competitors are recognized at ceremonies at the National Institutes of Health in Washington. Thousands of dollars in scholarships are awarded. Est attendance: 200. For info: Norbert Myslinski, University of Maryland, 666 W Baltimore St, Baltimore, MD 21201. Phone: (410) 706-7258. Fax: (410) 706-0193. E-mail: nrm001@dental.umaryland.edu. Web: www.sfn.org/BAW/bee.

INTERNATIONAL DAY OF THE SEAL CELEBRATION. Mar 20. Jenkinson's Aquarium, Point Pleasant Beach, NJ. Learn all about seals and help us celebrate our seals' birthdays! A special artifact cart and seal stories for children will be presented throughout the day. Seals are fed at 10 AM, 1 PM and 4 PM. Free arts and crafts from 1–4 PM. Est attendance: 600. For info: Jenkinson's Aquarium, 300 Ocean Ave, Point Pleasant Beach, NJ 08742. Phone: (732) 899-1212. Fax: (732) 899-1717. E-mail: aquarium@jenkinsons.com. Web: www.jenkinsons.com.

JAPAN: VERNAL EQUINOX DAY. Mar 20. National holiday in Japan.

MAPLE SYRUP SATURDAY. Mar 20. Gordon Bubolz Nature Preserve, Appleton, WI. Find out how to make maple syrup. Est attendance: 1,000. For info: Mike Brandel, Exec Dir, Gordon Bubolz Nature Preserve, 4815 N Lynndale Dr, Appleton, WI 54913. Phone: (920) 731-6041. Fax: (920) 731-9593. E-mail: bubolz@dataex.com.

MILITARY THROUGH THE AGES. Mar 20–21. Jamestown Settlement, Williamsburg, VA. Reenactment groups depicting soldiers and military encounters throughout history join forces with modern-day veterans and active units to demonstrate camp life, tactics and weaponry. For info: Jamestown-Yorktown Fdtn, Box 1607, Williamsburg, VA 23187. Phone: (757) 253-4838 or toll-free (888) 593-4682. Fax: (757) 253-5299. Web: www.historyisfun.org.

MOON PHASE: NEW MOON. Mar 20. Moon enters New Moon phase at 5:41 PM, EST.

NATIONAL AGRICULTURE DAY. Mar 20. A day to honor America's providers of food and fiber and to educate the general public about the US agricultural system. Week of celebration: Mar 17–23. Annually, the first day of spring. For info: Agriculture Council of America, 11020 King St, Ste 205, Overland Park, KS 66210. Phone: (913) 491-1895. Fax: (913) 491-6502. E-mail: info@agday.org. Web: www.agday.org.

NATIONAL QUILTING DAY. Mar 20. Celebrated since 1992, this day is a grassroots effort to unite quilters and quilt lovers everywhere, not only in this country, but also around the world. Individuals, groups of quilters, shop owners, publishers and the entire community of quiltmaking are invited to join NQA in recognizing and promoting the tradition of quiltmaking. Annually, the third Saturday in March. For info: The Natl Quilting Assn, Inc, PO Box 393, Ellicott City, MD 21041-0393. Phone: (410) 461-5733. Fax: (410) 461-3693. E-mail: nqa@erols.com. Web: www.NQAQuilts.org.

NERVE-GAS ATTACK ON JAPANESE SUBWAY: ANNIVERSARY. Mar 20, 1995. Twelve people were killed and 5,000 injured in a nerve gas attack on the Tokyo subway system during rush hour. Suspected in the attack was the Japanese religious sect Aum Shinrikyo, founded and led by Shoko Asahara (real name Chizuo Matsumoto). The group, which professes belief in a hybrid of Buddhist-Hindu teachings, predicts an apocalypse. In a raid conducted against the sect's main compound in Kamikuishiki on Mar 25, police seized literature that predicted 90 percent of the people in the world would be killed by poison gas. Also seized were two tons of chemicals for making sarin, the poison used in the Mar 20 attack. This cache was reported to contain enough material to kill five million people. In a second raid, Asahara was arrested.

OSTARA. Mar 20. (Also called Alban Eilir.) One of the "Lesser Sabbats" during the Wiccan year, Ostara is a fire and fertility festival that marks the beginning of spring. Annually, on the spring equinox.

PROPOSAL DAY! ®. Mar 20 (also Sept 22). A holiday for those who seek marriage. Single adults who are ready to marry are encouraged to propose marriage to their true love on the days of the vernal equinox and the autumnal equinox. Thousands of men and women are married today as a result of a marriage proposal made on a "Proposal Day!"®, including the creator of the holiday. For info: John Michael O'Loughlin, 3124 Chisolm Trail, Irving, TX 75062. Phone: (972) 258-4996. E-mail: lldjohn@aol.com.

RAPPAHANNOCK RIVER WATERFOWL SHOW. Mar 20–21. White Stone, VA. Preview Night Gala, Mar 19, advance tickets required. 90 nationally recognized artists display their wildfowl art, including sculptures, paintings, photography, prints and carvings. Weekend admission $5. Sponsored by the White Stone Volunteer Fire Dept. Est attendance: 3,000. For info: William Bruce, Waterfowl Show, 151 Bruce Ln, White Stone, VA 22578. Phone: (804) 435-6355.

RIO GRANDE VALLEY LIVESTOCK SHOW. Mar 20–28. Mercedes, TX. Rodeo, open cattle show and carnival. For the youth of the four counties in the valley to exhibit their projects. Est attendance: 195,000. For info: Jim Beale, Rio Grande Valley Livestock Show Inc, Box 867, Mercedes, TX 78570. Phone: (956) 565-2456. Fax: (956) 565-3005. E-mail: info@rgvlivestockshow.com. Web: www.rgvlivestockshow.com.

ROGERS, FRED: BIRTH ANNIVERSARY. Mar 20, 1928. Born Fred McFeely Rogers at LaTrobe, PA, Rogers first began producing television for children in 1953. His first program, "The Children's Hour," was the precursor to "Mister Rogers' Neighborhood," which premiered in Canada in 1966 and the US in 1968. The show ran on public television until Rogers' death, and he became known worldwide for his dedication to the well-being of children and for his demonstrations of the importance of kindness, compassion and learning. He authored a number of books for parents and children, wrote more than 200 songs and won dozens of awards, including Emmys, Peabodys and the Presidential Medal of Freedom. He died Feb 27, 2003, at his home in Pittsburgh, PA.

	S	M	T	W	T	F	S
March 2004		1	2	3	4	5	6
	7	8	9	10	11	12	13
	14	15	16	17	18	19	20
	21	22	23	24	25	26	27
	28	29	30	31			

☆ Chase's 2004 Calendar of Events ☆   Mar 20–21

SAVE THE FLORIDA PANTHER DAY. Mar 20. Florida. A ceremonial holiday on the third Saturday in March.

SHEEP TO SHAWL FESTIVAL. Mar 20. Oatland Island Education Center, Savannah, GA. This is a popular annual event held at our Heritage Home site where visitors can observe and participate in the creation of a shawl—from sheep shearing to carding, spinning, dying and weaving the wool. Children's activities and refreshments will be available and the Native Animal Nature Trail will be open. Est attendance: 1,900. For info: Oatland Island Education Ctr, 711 Sandtown Rd, Savannah, GA 31410. Phone: (912) 898-3980. Fax: (912) 898-3983. Web: www.oatlandisland.org.

SKINNER, B.F.: 100th BIRTH ANNIVERSARY. Mar 20, 1904. American psychologist Burrhus Frederic Skinner was born at Susquehanna, PA. He was a pioneer in behaviorism, and is best known for developing the "Skinner box" (an enclosed experimental environment). He died Aug 18, 1990, at Cambridge, MA.

SONGWRITER'S SHOW. Mar 20. Waretown, NJ. Original music written and performed by musicians. No alcoholic beverages or smoking allowed. Est attendance: 400. For info: Songwriter's Show, Albert Music Hall, 125 Wells Mills Rd, PO Box 657, Waretown, NJ 08758. Phone: (609) 971-1593. Web: www.alberthall.org.

SPRING. Mar 20–June 20. In the Northern Hemisphere spring begins today with the vernal equinox, at 1:49 AM, EST. Note that in the Southern Hemisphere today is the beginning of autumn. Sun rises due east and sets due west everywhere on Earth (except near poles) and the daylight length (interval between sunrise and sunset) is virtually the same everywhere today: 12 hours, 8 minutes.

TUNISIA: INDEPENDENCE DAY. Mar 20. Commemorates treaty in 1956 by which France recognized Tunisian autonomy.

¡VIVA EL MARIACHI! FESTIVAL. Mar 20–21. Fresno Convention Center–Selland Arena. Fresno, CA. The most traditional mariachi festival in the US. Includes workshops, vendor booths and a concert featuring international, state and local mariachis and danzantes. Annually, the third weekend in March. Est attendance: 10,000. For info: Radio Bilingüe, 5005 E Belmont Ave, Fresno, CA 93727. Phone: (559) 455-5777. Web: www.radiobilingue.org.

BIRTHDAYS TODAY

Holly Hunter, 46, actress (Oscar for *The Piano*; *Broadcast News*, *The Firm*), born Conyers, GA, Mar 20, 1958.
William Hurt, 54, actor (*The Accidental Tourist*, *Broadcast News*), born Washington, DC, Mar 20, 1950.
Spike Lee, 47, director, producer, writer, actor (*She's Gotta Have It*, *Do the Right Thing*, *Malcolm X*), born Atlanta, GA, Mar 20, 1957.
Hal Linden, 73, actor ("Barney Miller," "Blacke's Magic"), born Harold Lipshitz, the Bronx, NY, Mar 20, 1931.
Marian McPartland, 84, jazz pianist (*After Hours, Personal Choice, In My Life*), born Slough, England, Mar 20, 1920.
Brian Mulroney, 65, Canadian statesman and 18th prime minister of Canada, born Baie Comeau, QC, Canada, Mar 20, 1939.
Robert Gordon (Bobby) Orr, 56, Hall of Fame hockey player, born Parry Sound, ON, Canada, Mar 20, 1948.
Jerry Reed, 67, singer, songwriter ("When You're Hot, You're Hot"), born Jerry Hubbard, Atlanta, GA, Mar 20, 1937.
Carl Reiner, 82, actor ("The Dick Van Dyke Show," "Your Show of Shows"), writer, director, born the Bronx, NY, Mar 20, 1922.
Patrick James (Pat) Riley, 59, basketball coach and former player, born Schenectady, NY, Mar 20, 1945.
Theresa Russell, 47, actress (*Straight Time, Black Widow*), born San Diego, CA, Mar 20, 1957.
David Thewlis, 41, actor ("Dinotopia"), born Blackpool, Lancashire, England, Mar 20, 1963.
Paul Junger Witt, 61, producer (*Three Kings*, "Everything's Relative"), director, born New York, NY, Mar 20, 1943.

MARCH 21 — SUNDAY
Day 81 — 285 Remaining

ARIES, THE RAM. Mar 21–Apr 19. In the astronomical/astrological zodiac, which divides the sun's apparent orbit into 12 segments, the period Mar 21–Apr 19 is identified, traditionally, as the sun sign of Aries, the Ram. The ruling planet is Mars.

BACH, JOHANN SEBASTIAN: BIRTH ANNIVERSARY. Mar 21, 1685 (OS). Organist and composer, one of the most influential composers in musical history. Born at Eisenach, Germany; he died at Leipzig, Germany, July 28, 1750.

ENGLAND: MOTHERING SUNDAY. Mar 21. Fourth Sunday of Lent, formerly occasion for attending services at Mother Church, family gatherings and visits to parents. Now popularly known as Mother's Day and a time for visiting and taking gifts to mothers.

FIRST ROUND-THE-WORLD BALLOON FLIGHT: 5th ANNIVERSARY. Mar 21, 1999. Swiss psychiatrist Bertrand Piccard and British copilot Brian Jones landed in the Egyptian desert on this date, having flown 29,056 miles nonstop around the world in a hot-air balloon. Leaving from Chateau d'Oex in the Swiss Alps on Mar 1, the trip took 19 days, 21 hours and 55 minutes. Piccard is the grandson of balloonist Auguste Piccard, who was the first to ascend into the stratosphere in a balloon. See also: "First Solo Round-the-World Balloon Flight: Anniversary" (July 2) and "Piccard, Auguste: Birth Anniversary" (Jan 28).

GALLO, JULIO: BIRTH ANNIVERSARY. Mar 21, 1910. American vintner Julio Gallo was born at Oakland, CA. He is best known for his role in the Ernest and Julio Gallo Winery, of Modesto, CA, which at one time claimed about 26 percent of the US wine industry. He died May 2, 1993, near Tracy, CA.

GERSDORFF HITLER ASSASSINATION ATTEMPT: ANNIVERSARY. Mar 21, 1943. In a suicide/assassination attempt planned for this date, Major General Baron von Gersdorff was to carry a bomb in the pocket of his greatcoat to the "Heroes Memorial Day" annual dedication to the dead of the First World War. Hitler was to attend this event to inspect some weaponry taken from captured Russian soldiers. The bomb was to go off within 10 minutes of Hitler's arrival at the event as he was not expected to be there for very long. The conspirators were unable to locate the necessary short time fuse and the attempt had to be called off. This was the second serious plan to assassinate Hitler in 1943.

INDIA: NEW YEAR'S DAY. Mar 21. This is the first day of the New Year on the Saka calendar adopted by India after independence from Great Britain. The Saka calendar is a solar calendar with the same Leap Year schedule as the Gregorian calendar. In non-Leap Years, the New Year falls on Mar 22.

IRANIAN NEW YEAR: NORUZ. Mar 21. National celebration for all Iranians, this is the traditional Persian New Year. (In Iran spring comes Mar 20 or 21.) It is a celebration of nature's rebirth. Every household spreads a special cover with symbols for the seven good angels on it. These symbols are sprouts, wheat germ, apples, hyacinth, fruit of the jujube, garlic and sumac heralding life, rebirth, health, happiness, prosperity, joy and beauty. A fishbowl is also customary, representing the end of the astrological year and wild rue is burnt to drive away evil and bring about a happy New Year. This pre-Islamic holiday, a legacy of Zoroas-

185

Mar 21 ☆ Chase's 2004 Calendar of Events ☆

trianism, is also celebrated as Navruz, Nau-Roz or Noo Roz in Afghanistan, Albania, Azerbaijan, Kazakhstan, Kyrgyzstan, Tajikistan, Turkmenistan and Uzbekistan. For info: Mahvash Tafreshi, Librarian, Farmingdale Public Library, 116 Merritts Rd, Farmingdale, NY 11735. Phone: (516) 249-9090. Fax: (516) 694-9697 or Yassaman Djalali, Librarian, West Valley Branch Library, 1243 San Tomas Aquino Rd, San Jose, CA 95117. Phone: (408) 244-4766.

LESOTHO: NATIONAL TREE PLANTING DAY. Mar 21. Lesotho.

LEWIS, FRANCIS: BIRTH ANNIVERSARY. Mar 21, 1713. Signer of the Declaration of Independence, born at Wales. Died Dec 31, 1802, at Long Island, NY.

LUNSFORD, BASCOM LAMAR: BIRTH ANNIVERSARY. Mar 21, 1882. Folk song writer and folklorist who authored the folk song "Mountain Dew," Lunsford started the first folk music festival in 1928 at Asheville, NC. This event, which led to the formation of the National Clogging and Hoedown Council, is held to this day. He was known as the "father of clogging dance" and the "king of folk music." He recorded some 320 folk songs, tunes and stories for the Library of Congress. Born at Mars Hill, NC, Lunsford died Sept 4, 1973, at South Turkey Creek, NC.

LUXEMBOURG: BRETZELSONNDEG. Mar 21. The fourth Sunday in Lent is an occasion for boys to give pretzel-shaped cakes to sweethearts who may respond, on Easter Sunday, with a gift of a decorated egg or sweet.

MARYLAND DAY. Mar 21. Historic St. Mary's City, MD. Celebrate Maryland's 370th birthday with pageantry and ceremonies marking the founding of the state in 1634. Est attendance: 1,500. For info: Visitors Services, Historic St. Mary's City, PO Box 39, St. Mary's City, MD 20686. Phone: (240) 895-4990 or (800) SMC-1634. Fax: (240) 895-4968. Web: www.stmaryscity.org.

MEMORY DAY. Mar 21. To encourage awareness of traditional memory system using pattern t,d = 1; n = 2; m = 3; r = 4; l = 5; j,ch = 6; k,q,g-hard = 7; f,v = 8; b,p = 9. Study historic examples of the use of the memory system in the writings of Milton, Thomas Gray, Longfellow, Lincoln and others. For info: Robert L. Birch, Coord, Puns Corps, Box 2364, Falls Church, VA 22042-0364. Phone: (703) 533-3668.

MEXICO: BENITO JUAREZ' BIRTH ANNIVERSARY. Mar 21. A full-blooded Zapotec Indian, Benito Pablo Juarez was born at Oaxaca, Mexico, in 1806 and grew up to become the president of Mexico. He learned Spanish at age 12. Juarez became judge of the civil court in Oaxaca in 1842, a member of congress in 1846 and governor in 1847. In 1858, following a rebellion against the constitution, the presidency was passed to Juarez. He died at Mexico City, July 18, 1872. A symbol of liberation and of Mexican resistance to foreign intervention, his birthday is a public holiday in Mexico.

NAMIBIA: INDEPENDENCE DAY. Mar 21. National Day. Commemorates independence from South Africa in 1990.

NATIONAL DANCE DAY. Mar 21. Participants across the country will organize events in every community to celebrate the spirit and diversity of dance of all kinds. For info: Sharon Hoge, 480 Park Ave, New York, NY 10022. Phone: (212) 759-6168. Fax: (212) 750-4979. E-mail: skinghoge@aol.com. Web: www.nationaldanceday.org.

★**NATIONAL POISON PREVENTION WEEK.** Mar 21-27 (tentative). Presidential Proclamation issued each year for the third week of March since 1962. (PL87-319 of Sept 26, 1961.)

	S	M	T	W	T	F	S
March		1	2	3	4	5	6
	7	8	9	10	11	12	13
2004	14	15	16	17	18	19	20
	21	22	23	24	25	26	27
	28	29	30	31			

NATIONAL POISON PREVENTION WEEK. Mar 21-27. To aid in encouraging the American people to learn of the dangers of accidental poisoning and to take preventive measures against it. Annually, the third full week in March. For info: Kim Dulic, Secy, Poison Prevention Week Council, Box 1543, Washington, DC 20013. E-mail: kdulic@cpsc.gov. Web: www.cpsc.gov or www.poisonprevention.org.

NAW-RUZ. Mar 21. Baha'i New Year's Day. Astronomically fixed to commence the year. One of the nine days of the year when Baha'is suspend work. For info: Baha'is of the US, Office of Public Info, 1320 Nineteenth St NW, Ste 350, Washington, DC 20036. Phone: (202) 466-9870. Fax: (202) 466-9873. E-mail: opi@usbnc.org. Web: www.us.bahai.org.

PEDIATRIC NURSE PRACTITIONER WEEK. Mar 21-27. The National Association of Pediatric Nurse Practitioners, an association of more than 6,700 pediatric nurse practitioners and specialty nurses in advanced practice providing primary health care to infants, children, adolescents and young adults, proclaims this week in honor of nearly 11,000 practitioners dedicated to improving children's health. For info: Joe Casey, Dir of Membership and Communications, NAPNAP, 20 Brace Rd, Ste 200, Cherry Hill, NJ 08034. Phone: (856) 857-9700. Fax: (856) 857-1600. E-mail: info@napnap.org. Web: www.napnap.org.

POCAHONTAS (REBECCA ROLFE): DEATH ANNIVERSARY. Mar 21, 1617. Pocahontas, daughter of Powhatan, born about 1595, near Jamestown, VA, leader of the Indian union of Algonkin nations, helped to foster goodwill between the colonists of the Jamestown settlement and her people. Pocahontas converted to Christianity, was baptized with the name Rebecca and married John Rolfe Apr 5, 1614. In 1616, she accompanied Rolfe on a trip to his native England, where she was regarded as an overseas "ambassador." Pocahontas's stay in England drew so much attention to the Virginia Company's Jamestown settlement that lotteries were held to help support the colony. Shortly before she was scheduled to return to Jamestown, Pocahontas died at Gravesend, Kent, England, of either smallpox or pneumonia.

RV LIFESTYLE WEEK. Mar 21-27. Celebrate and raise awareness about the RV lifestyle. Celebrations are planned in Yuma, AZ, and other locations. For info: Jaimie Hall, RV Hometown, 127 Rainbow Dr, #2780, Livingston, TX 77399. Phone: (928) 607-3181. Fax: (561) 892-2837. E-mail: calamityjaimie@escapees.com. Web: www.rvhometown.com.

SECOND BATTLE OF SOMME: ANNIVERSARY. Mar 21-Apr 4, 1918. General Erich Ludendorff launched the Michael offensive, the biggest German offensive of 1918, on Mar 21 with a five-hour artillery barrage. The Central Powers' objective was to drive a wedge between the British and French forces and drive the British to the sea. Although they did not accomplish this objective, in the south they captured Montdidier and advanced to a depth of 40 miles. They managed to create a bulge in the front south of Somme and end what had effectively been a stalemate. The Allies lost nearly 230,000 men and the Germans almost as many in the Battle of Somme.

SELMA CIVIL RIGHTS MARCH: ANNIVERSARY. Mar 21, 1965. More than 3,000 civil rights demonstrators led by Dr. Martin Luther King, Jr, began a four-day march from Selma, AL, to Montgomery, AL, to demand federal protection of voting rights. There were violent attempts by local police, using fire hoses and dogs, to suppress the march. A march two weeks before on Mar 7, 1965, was called "Bloody Sunday" because of the use of nightsticks, chains and electric cattle prods against the marchers by the police.

SOUTH AFRICA: HUMAN RIGHTS DAY. Mar 21. National holiday. Commemorates the Mar 21, 1960, massacre at Sharpeville and all those who lost their lives in the struggle for equal rights as citizens of South Africa.

☆ Chase's 2004 Calendar of Events ☆   Mar 21–22

STRANG, JAMES JESSE (KING STRANG): BIRTH ANNIVERSARY. Mar 21, 1813. Perhaps America's only crowned king was born at Scipio, NY, and christened Jesse James Strang (which he later changed to James Jesse Strang). He was crowned king of Mormons at Beaver Island, MI, July 8, 1850, and ruled his kingdom until his death. Elected to Michigan legislature in 1852 and 1854. Wounded by assassins June 16, 1856, at Beaver Island, he died June 19, 1856, at Voree, WI.

UNITED NATIONS: INTERNATIONAL DAY FOR THE ELIMINATION OF RACIAL DISCRIMINATION. Mar 21. Initiated by the United Nations General Assembly in 1966 to be observed annually Mar 21, the anniversary of the killing of 69 African demonstrators at Sharpeville, South Africa, in 1960, as a day to remember "the victims of Sharpeville and those countless others in different parts of the world who have fallen victim to racial injustice" and to promote efforts to eradicate racial discrimination worldwide. For info: United Nations, Dept of Public Info, New York, NY 10017. Web: www.un.org.

UNITED NATIONS: WEEK OF SOLIDARITY WITH THE PEOPLES STRUGGLING AGAINST RACISM AND RACIAL DISCRIMINATION. Mar 21–27. Annual observance initiated by United Nations General Assembly as part of its program of the Decade for Action to Combat Racism and Racial Discrimination. For info: United Nations, Dept of Public Info, New York, NY 10017. Web: www.un.org.

BIRTHDAYS TODAY

Matthew Broderick, 42, actor (*Godzilla, Inspector Gadget, Election*, stage: *The Producers*), born New York, NY, Mar 21, 1962.
Peter Brook, 79, theater director, born London, England, Mar 21, 1925.
Timothy Dalton, 58, actor (*Centennial*, James Bond movies), born Colwyn Bay, Wales, Mar 21, 1946.
Al Freeman, Jr, 70, actor (*A Patch of Blue; Roots: The Next Generations*), born San Antonio, TX, Mar 21, 1934.
Rosie O'Donnell, 42, actress (*A League of Their Own*), host ("The Rosie O'Donnell Show"), born Commack, NY, Mar 21, 1962.
Gary Oldman, 46, actor (*Sid and Nancy, JFK*), born South London, England, Mar 21, 1958.

MARCH 22 — MONDAY
Day 82 — 284 Remaining

AS YOUNG AS YOU FEEL DAY. Mar 22. Now more than ever you are as young as you feel. So stop acting your chronological age and get out there and start feeling peppy! [©2003 by WH.] For info: Thomas & Ruth Roy, Wellcat Holidays, 2418 Long Ln, Lebanon, PA 17046. Phone: (717) 279-0184. E-mail: info@wellcat.com. Web: www.wellcat.com.

EQUAL RIGHTS AMENDMENT SENT TO STATES FOR RATIFICATION: ANNIVERSARY. Mar 22, 1972. The Senate passed the 27th Amendment, prohibiting discrimination on the basis of sex, sending it to the states for ratification. Hawaii led the way as the first state to ratify and by the end of the year 22 states had ratified it. On Oct 6, 1978, the deadline for ratification was extended to June 30, 1982, by Congress. The amendment still lacked three of the required 38 states for ratification. This was the first extension granted since Congress set seven years as the limit for ratification. The amendment failed to achieve ratification as the deadline came and passed and no additional states ratified the measure.

FIRST WOMEN'S COLLEGIATE BASKETBALL GAME: ANNIVERSARY. Mar 22, 1893. The first women's collegiate basketball game was played at Smith College at Northampton, MA. Senda Berenson, then Smith's director of physical education and "mother of women's basketball," supervised the game, in which Smith's sophomore team beat the freshman team 5–4. For info: Dir of Media Relations, Smith College, Office of College Relations, Northampton, MA 01063. Phone: (413) 585-2190. Fax: (413) 585-2174. E-mail: lfenlason@smith.edu. Web: www.smith.edu.

INTERNATIONAL DAY OF THE SEAL. Mar 22. In 1982 Congress declared an International Day of the Seal to draw attention to the cruelty of seal hunts and the virtual inevitability of these creatures' extinction. Zoos and aquariums around the world observe this day with special programs and activities; contact your local affiliate for a schedule of activities.

INTERNATIONAL GOOF-OFF DAY. Mar 22. A day of relaxation and a time to be oneself; a day for some good-humored fun and some good-natured silliness. Everyone needs one special day each year to goof off.

LASER PATENTED: ANNIVERSARY. Mar 22, 1960. The first patent for a laser (light amplification by stimulated emission of radiation) granted to Arthur Schawlow and Charles Townes.

NABISCO CHAMPIONSHIP. Mar 22–28. Mission Hills Country Club, Rancho Mirage, CA. Held since 1972, this tournament is often called the Master's of women's professional golf. For info: Nabisco Championship. Phone: (760) 324-4546. Web: www.nabiscodinahshore.com.

PUERTO RICO: EMANCIPATION DAY. Mar 22. Holiday commemorates the end of slavery on Mar 22, 1873.

SPACE MILESTONE: RECORD TIME IN SPACE. Mar 22, 1995. Russian cosmonaut Valery Polyakov returned to Earth after setting a record of 438 days in space aboard *Mir*. Previous records include three Soviet cosmonauts who spent 237 days in space at *Salyut 7* space station in 1984, a Soviet cosmonaut who spent 326 days aboard *Mir* in 1987 and two Soviets who spent 366 days aboard *Mir* in 1988. The US space endurance record was set by Carl Walz and Daniel Bursch, who stayed 196 days in space aboard *Endeavor*, completing their mission on June 19, 2002. US astronaut Shannon Lucid set the record for women in space with her 188-day stay on *Mir* in 1996.

TUSKEGEE AIRMEN ACTIVATED: ANNIVERSARY. Mar 22, 1941. This pioneering and highly decorated WWII African-American aviator unit gained their name during training at the US Army airfield near Tuskegee, AL, and at the Tuskegee Institute. They were activated as the 99th Pursuit Squadron and later formed the 332nd Fighter Group (with the 100th, 301st and 302nd squadrons). 992 black pilots emerged from training to fly P-39, P-40, P-47 and P-51 aircraft in more than 15,000 sorties in North Africa, Sicily and Europe. On escort missions, they were the only unit that never lost a US bomber. They shot down 111 enemy planes and destroyed 273 planes on the ground. Lieutenant Colonel Benjamin O. Davis, Jr—later the US Air Force's first black general—was their commander. When President Harry Truman integrated the US military, the all-black group was deactivated. See also: "Davis, Benjamin O., Jr: Birth Anniversary" (Dec 18).

UNITED NATIONS: WORLD DAY FOR WATER. Mar 22. The General Assembly declared this observance (Res 47/193) to promote public awareness of how water resource development contributes to economic productivity and social well-being. Annually, on Mar 22.

BIRTHDAYS TODAY

George Benson, 61, singer, guitarist ("On Broadway," "Give Me the Night"), born Pittsburgh, PA, Mar 22, 1943.
Robert Quinlan (Bob) Costas, 52, sportscaster, born New York, NY, Mar 22, 1952.
Bruno Ganz, 63, actor (*The American Friend, Wings of Desire*), born Zurich, Switzerland, Mar 22, 1941.
Orrin Grant Hatch, 70, US Senator (R, Utah), born Pittsburgh, PA, Mar 22, 1934.
Andrew Lloyd Webber, 56, composer (*Cats, Phantom of the Opera*), born London, England, Mar 22, 1948.
Karl Malden, 90, actor (*A Streetcar Named Desire*, "The Streets of San Francisco"), born Mladen Sekulovich, Gary, IN, Mar 22, 1914 (some sources say 1912 or 1913).

Marcel Marceau, 81, actor, pantomimist (had the only speaking part in *Silent Movie*), born Strasbourg, France, Mar 22, 1923.
Matthew Modine, 45, actor (*Married to the Mob*, "And the Band Played On"), born Loma Linda, CA, Mar 22, 1959.
Allen Neuharth, 80, founder of *USA Today*, born Eureka, SD, Mar 22, 1924.
Cristen Powell, 25, race car driver, born Portland, OR, Mar 22, 1979.
Pat Robertson, 74, TV evangelist, born Lexington, VA, Mar 22, 1930.
William Shatner, 73, actor ("Star Trek," "TJ Hooker"), author (*Tek* novels), born Montreal, QC, Canada, Mar 22, 1931.
Stephen Sondheim, 74, composer (*A Little Night Music*), born New York, NY, Mar 22, 1930.
Elvis Stojko, 32, skater, born Newmarket, ON, Canada, Mar 22, 1972.
M. Emmet Walsh, 69, actor (*Serpico, Blood Simple, Raising Arizona*), born Ogdensburg, NY, Mar 22, 1935.
Reese Witherspoon, 28, actress (*The Importance of Being Earnest, Legally Blonde, Election*), born Nashville, TN, Mar 22, 1976.

MARCH 23 — TUESDAY
Day 83 — 283 Remaining

AMERICAN DIABETES ASSOCIATION ALERT DAY. Mar 23. A one-day "wake-up call" to raise awareness about the seriousness of diabetes and its risk factors. The centerpiece of the Alert is the diabetes risk test, which is distributed and promoted through national and local media. Annually, the fourth Tuesday in March. For info: 800-DIABETES (342-2383) or www.diabetes.org/alert.

"BEAT THE CLOCK" TV PREMIERE: ANNIVERSARY. Mar 23, 1950. On this game show from the team of Mark Goodson and Bill Todman, couples performed stunts within a specified time period with the winners being given a chance to try a special stunt. Special stunts were very difficult, and the same one was attempted every week until a couple got it right. In 1952, James Dean got his first TV job testing stunts and warming up the audience. Bud Collyer was the host, assisted by Roxanne (real name Dolores Rosedale). A 1969 syndicated version hosted by Jack Narz and then by Gene Wood had celebrities to help the contestants. A 1979 revival was hosted by Monty Hall.

"BIG BERTHA" PARIS GUN: ANNIVERSARY. Mar 23, 1918. Germany initiated use of a terrifying new weapon—the Paris Gun—so called because it was first used against that city. The great gun, with a 25-foot carriage, was first used in combat when it was fired from a wooded location near Laon on Mar 23, 1918. It took 176 seconds for a shell to reach the city from a distance of 75 miles. On that first day 15 shots killed 16 individuals. Ridiculing the designers and manufacturers of the weapon, Parisians nicknamed it "Big Bertha" after the wife of the head of the munitions corporation. On Good Friday, Mar 29, a shell from the armament struck the church of Saint Gervais, which was crowded with worshipers. The casualty toll was 88 dead and 68 injured.

"THE BOLD AND THE BEAUTIFUL" TV PREMIERE: ANNIVERSARY. Mar 23, 1987. A continuing daytime serial created by William Bell and Lee Phillip Bell to be "young and hip." It is set in the fashion industry of Los Angeles with two central families, the Logans and the Forresters. The cast has included, as the Forresters: John McCook, Susan Flannery, Clayton Norcross, Jeff Trachta, Ronn Moss, Teri Ann Linn, Colleen Dion and as the Logans: Robert Pine, Judith Baldwin, Nancy Burnette, Nancy Sloan, Carrie Mitchum (granddaughter of Robert), Ethan Wayne (son of John), Brian Patrick Clarke, Katherine Kelly Lang and Lesley Woods. Other cast members have included Jeff Conaway, Tippi Hedren and Hunter Tylo.

CLARK, BARNEY: DEATH ANNIVERSARY. Mar 23, 1983. Barney Clark died after living almost 112 days with an artificial heart. The heart, made of polyurethane plastic and aluminum, was implanted in Clark at the University of Utah Medical Center, Salt Lake City, Dec 2, 1982. Clark was the first person ever to receive a permanent artificial heart. Born at Provo, UT, Jan 21, 1921, Clark was 62 when he died.

COLFAX, SCHUYLER: BIRTH ANNIVERSARY. Mar 23, 1823. 17th vice president of the US (1869–73). Born at New York, NY. Died Jan 13, 1885, at Mankato, MN.

CRAWFORD, JOAN: 100th BIRTH ANNIVERSARY. Mar 23, 1904. Actress, born Lucille Fay LeSueur at San Antonio, TX. Crawford became a Hollywood star with her performance in *Our Dancing Daughters*. She won an Oscar in 1945 for her role in *Mildred Pierce*. Events of Crawford's life are chronicled in *Mommie Dearest*. Other films included *The Women, Whatever Happened to Baby Jane?* and *Twelve Miles Out*. She died at New York, NY, May 10, 1977.

DICK CLARK RETIRES FROM "AMERICAN BANDSTAND": 15th ANNIVERSARY. Mar 23, 1989. After 33 years, 59-year-old Dick Clark retired from hosting the television program "American Bandstand."

KUROSAWA, AKIRA: BIRTH ANNIVERSARY. Mar 23, 1910. Filmmaker (*Rashomon, The Seven Samurai*), born at Tokyo, Japan. Died at Tokyo, Sept 6, 1998.

LIBERTY DAY: ANNIVERSARY. Mar 23, 1775. Anniversary of Patrick Henry's speech for arming the Virginia militia at St. John's Church, Richmond, VA. "I know not what course others may take, but as for me, give me liberty or give me death."

NEAR MISS DAY: 15th ANNIVERSARY. Mar 23, 1989. A mountain-sized asteroid passed within 500,000 miles of Earth, a very close call according to NASA. Impact would have equaled the strength of 40,000 hydrogen bombs, created a crater the size of the District of Columbia and devastated everything for 100 miles in all directions.

NEW ZEALAND: OTAGO AND SOUTHLAND PROVINCIAL ANNIVERSARY. Mar 23. In addition to the statutory public holidays of New Zealand, there is in each provincial district a holiday for the provincial anniversary. This day is observed in Otago and Southland.

NURSING CONFERENCE ON PEDIATRIC PRIMARY CARE. Mar 23–27. Dallas, TX. Offers continuing education on clinical practice, professional development and legislative issues relevant to the nursing profession. Est attendance: 1,200. For info: Natl Assn of Pediatric Nurse Practitioners, 20 Brace Rd, Ste 200, Cherry Hill, NJ 08034-2633. Phone: (856) 857-9700. Fax: (856) 857-1600. E-mail: info@napnap.org. Web: www.napnap.org.

"O.K." FIRST APPEARANCE IN PRINT: ANNIVERSARY. Mar 23, 1839. *The Boston Morning Post* printed the first known "o.k." on this day in 1839. It derived from a jovial misspelling of "all correct"—"oll korrect." Etymologist Allen Read doggedly tracked down the word's origin in the 1960s. "O.K." is now used in most languages.

PAKISTAN: REPUBLIC DAY. Mar 23, 1940. National holiday. In 1940 the All-India-Muslim League adopted a resolution calling for a Muslim homeland. On the same day in 1956 Pakistan declared itself a republic.

RALLY FOR DECENCY: 35th ANNIVERSARY. Mar 23, 1969. Anita Bryant, Jackie Gleason and Kate Smith rallied with 30,000 others in Miami on this day in reaction to Jim Morrison's arrest for indecent exposure.

SPACE MILESTONE: *MIR* ABANDONED (USSR). Mar 23, 2001. The 140-ton *Mir* space station, launched in 1986, was

☆ Chase's 2004 Calendar of Events ☆   Mar 23–24

brought down into the South Pacific near Fiji, about 1,800 miles east of New Zealand, just before 1 AM, EST. Two-thirds of the station burned up during its controlled descent. *Mir's* core component had been aloft for more than 15 years and orbited Earth 86,330 times. Nearly 100 people, seven of them American, had spent some time on *Mir*. See also: "Space Milestone: *Mir* Space Station (USSR)" (Feb 20).

UNITED NATIONS: WORLD METEOROLOGICAL DAY. Mar 23. An international day observed by meteorological services throughout the world and by the organizations of the UN system. Annually, on Mar 23. For info: United Nations, Dept of Public Info, New York, NY 10017. Web: www.un.org.

BIRTHDAYS TODAY

Louie Anderson, 51, comedian, actor ("Life with Louie"), former game-show host ("Family Feud"), born Minneapolis, MN, Mar 23, 1953.

Dr. Roger Bannister, 75, distance runner, broke the 4-minute-mile record in 1954, born Harrow, Middlesex, England, Mar 23, 1929.

Mike Easley, 54, Governor of North Carolina (D), born Nash County, NC, Mar 23, 1950.

Richard Grieco, 39, actor (*Ultimate Deception, Blackheart*), born Watertown, NY, Mar 23, 1965.

Chaka Khan, 51, singer ("Tell Me Something Good," "You Got the Love"), born Yvette Marie Stevens, Chicago, IL, Mar 23, 1953.

Jason Kidd, 31, basketball player, born San Francisco, CA, Mar 23, 1973.

Moses Eugene Malone, 50, Hall of Fame basketball player, born Petersburg, VA, Mar 23, 1954.

Amanda Plummer, 47, actress (Tony for *Agnes of God*; *The Fisher King*), born New York, NY, Mar 23, 1957.

Keri Russell, 28, actress ("Felicity"), born Fountain Valley, CA, Mar 23, 1976.

MARCH 24 — WEDNESDAY
Day 84 — 282 Remaining

EXXON VALDEZ OIL SPILL: 15th ANNIVERSARY. Mar 24, 1989. The tanker *Exxon Valdez* ran aground at Prince William Sound, leaking 11 million gallons of oil into one of nature's richest habitats.

HOUDINI, HARRY: BIRTH ANNIVERSARY. Mar 24, 1874. Magician and escape artist. Born at Budapest, Hungary, died at Detroit, MI, Oct 31, 1926. Lecturer, athlete, author, expert on history of magic, exposer of fraudulent mediums and motion picture actor. Was best known for his ability to escape from locked restraints (handcuffs, straitjackets, coffins, boxes and milk cans). Anniversary of his death (Halloween) has been the occasion for meetings of magicians and attempts at communication by mediums.

MELLON, ANDREW W.: BIRTH ANNIVERSARY. Mar 24, 1855. American financier, industrialist, government official (Secretary of the Treasury), art and book collector, born at Pittsburgh, PA. Died Aug 26, 1937, at Southampton, NY.

MORRIS, WILLIAM: BIRTH ANNIVERSARY. Mar 24, 1834. English poet, artist and social reformer. Born at Walthamstow, England; died at Hammersmith, London, Oct 3, 1896.

NAIA MEN'S DIVISION I NATIONAL BASKETBALL CHAMPIONSHIP. Mar 24–30. Municipal Auditorium, Kansas City, MO. 67th annual tournament. Est attendance: 45,000. For info: Natl Assn of Intercollegiate Athletics, 23500 W 105th St, PO Box 1325, Olathe, KS 66051-1325. Phone: (913) 791-0044. Fax: (913) 791-9555. E-mail: kdee@naia.org. Web: www.naia.org.

"ORIGINAL" WESTERN MASSACHUSETTS HOME AND GARDEN SHOW. Mar 24–28. West Springfield, MA. The largest home show in New England with more than 700 booths and a large outside area covering more than six acres of exhibits. Annually, third or fourth week of March. Est attendance: 87,500. For info: Brad Campbell, Home Builders Assn of Western Massachusetts, 240 Cadwell Dr, Springfield, MA 01104. Phone: (413) 733-3126. Fax: (413) 781-8416. E-mail: bcampbell @hbawm.com. Web: www.hbawm.com.

PHILIPPINE INDEPENDENCE: 70th ANNIVERSARY. Mar 24, 1934. President Franklin Roosevelt signed a bill granting independence to the Philippines. The bill, which took effect July 4, 1946, brought to a close almost half a century of US control of the islands.

POWELL, JOHN WESLEY: BIRTH ANNIVERSARY. Mar 24, 1834. American geologist, explorer, ethnologist. He is best known for his explorations of the Grand Canyon by boat on the Colorado River. Born at Mount Morris, NY, he died at Haven, ME, Sept 23, 1902.

RHODE ISLAND VOTERS REJECT CONSTITUTION: ANNIVERSARY. Mar 24, 1788. In a popular referendum, Rhode Island rejected the new Constitution by a vote of 2,708 to 237. The state later ratified the Constitution (May 29, 1790) and the Bill of Rights (June 7, 1790).

SAINT GABRIEL: FEAST DAY. Mar 24. Saint Gabriel the Archangel, patron saint of postal, telephone and telegraph workers.

STRATTON, DOROTHY CONSTANCE: BIRTH ANNIVERSARY. Mar 24, 1898. Dorothy Constance Stratton, born at Brookfield, MO, was instrumental during WWII in organizing the SPARS, the women's branch of the US Coast Guard (authorized Nov 23, 1942). Under Lieutenant Commander Stratton's command some 10,000 women were trained for supportive noncombat roles in the Coast Guard. SPARS was dissolved in 1946 after the war had ended. Stratton worked with many women's organizations, including the Girl Scouts as national executive director in the '50s.

BIRTHDAYS TODAY

Lara Flynn Boyle, 34, actress ("Twin Peaks," "The Practice," *Dead Poets Society*), born Davenport, IA, Mar 24, 1970.

R. Lee Ermey, 60, actor (*Full Metal Jacket, Mississippi Burning*), born Emporia, KS, Mar 24, 1944.

Lawrence Ferlinghetti, 85, "Beat" poet, author (*Coney Island of the Mind*), born Yonkers, NY, Mar 24, 1919.

Byron Janis, 76, pianist, born McKeesport, PA, Mar 24, 1928.

Bob Mackie, 64, costume and fashion designer, born Monterey Park, CA, Mar 24, 1940.

Peyton Manning, 28, football player, born New Orleans, LA, Mar 24, 1976.

Donna Pescow, 50, actress (*Saturday Night Fever*, "Angie"), born Brooklyn, NY, Mar 24, 1954.

Annabella Sciorra, 40, actress (*The Hand That Rocks the Cradle, Jungle Fever*), born Wethersfield, CT, Mar 24, 1964.

MARCH 25 — THURSDAY
Day 85 — 281 Remaining

BARTOK, BELA: BIRTH ANNIVERSARY. Mar 25, 1881. Hungarian composer, born at Nagyszentmiklos (now in Romania). Died at New York, NY, Sept 26, 1945.

BED-IN FOR PEACE: 35th ANNIVERSARY. Mar 25–31, 1969. After their Mar 20 wedding, John Lennon (of The Beatles) and Yoko Ono celebrated their honeymoon with a "happening": a bed-in for peace at their hotel room. In Room 902 of the Hilton Hotel in Amsterdam, pajama-clad Lennon and Ono received the world's print, radio and TV media while sitting up in bed: singing and talking for seven days encouraging the world to choose peace. The couple held another bed-in May 26–June 2 in Montreal, during which "Give Peace a Chance" was recorded.

BLACK AWARENESS 365™. Mar 25, 2004–Mar 24, 2005. A year-long celebration aimed at the uplift of the fallen mentality, challenging everyone to renew and reassess the purpose and power of their minds. It begins Mar 25, as the earth makes its complete orbit of the sun—the true new year—and continues through the next complete orbit. Black Awareness 365™ is a holiyear encouraging us to cerebrate and boldly know what the ancient minds knew. For info: James Louis, PO Box 475, Mt Morris, MI 48458. Phone: (810) 787-7314. E-mail: lewisljr@aol.com. Web: www.blackawareness365.com.

BORGLUM, GUTZON: BIRTH ANNIVERSARY. Mar 25, 1867. American sculptor who created the huge sculpture of four American presidents (Washington, Jefferson, Lincoln and Theodore Roosevelt) at Mount Rushmore National Memorial in the Black Hills of South Dakota. Born John Gutzon de la Mothe Borglum at Bear Lake, ID, the son of Mormon pioneers, he worked the last 14 years of his life on the Mount Rushmore sculpture. He died at Chicago, IL, Mar 6, 1941.

"CAGNEY & LACEY" TV PREMIERE: ANNIVERSARY. Mar 25, 1982. "Cagney & Lacey" broke new ground as the first TV crime show in which the central characters were both female. The series was based on a made-for-TV movie that aired Oct 8, 1981, starring Loretta Swit and Tyne Daly. Meg Foster played Swit's character, Chris Cagney, but after one season she was replaced by Sharon Gless. Daly and Gless won six Emmys together for their roles. The last telecast aired on Aug 25, 1988.

CHARLIE PARKER AT THE LA PHILHARMONIC: ANNIVERSARY. Mar 25, 1946. One of the most influential solos of jazz alto saxophonist Charlie ("Bird") Parker's career was his rendition of "Lady Be Good," performed at the Los Angeles Philharmonic Auditorium. Every aspect of the performance became part of the language of modern jazz.

CHURCHILL ENTERS GERMANY: ANNIVERSARY. Mar 25, 1945. Winston Churchill briefly crossed to the eastern bank of the Rhine, the first British leader to enter Germany since Chamberlain signed the Munich Pact in September 1938. Churchill later wrote to Montgomery, "The Rhine and all its fortress lines lie behind the 21st Group of Armies. A beaten army, not long ago Master of Europe, retreats before its pursuers."

COSELL, HOWARD: BIRTH ANNIVERSARY. Mar 25, 1918. Howard Cosell, broadcaster, born at New York, NY. After earning a law degree, Cosell began his broadcasting career as the host of "Howard Cosell Speaking of Sports." He achieved national prominence and a great deal of notoriety for his support of Muhammad Ali's stand against the Vietnam War and then as cohost of ABC's "Monday Night Football." Died at New York, Apr 23, 1994.

March 2004

S	M	T	W	T	F	S
	1	2	3	4	5	6
7	8	9	10	11	12	13
14	15	16	17	18	19	20
21	22	23	24	25	26	27
28	29	30	31			

FEAST OF ANNUNCIATION. Mar 25. Celebrated in the Roman Catholic Church in commemoration of the message of the Angel Gabriel to Mary that she was to be the Mother of Christ.

GREECE: INDEPENDENCE DAY. Mar 25. National holiday. Celebrates the beginning of the Greek revolt for independence from the Ottoman Empire, Mar 25, 1821 (OS). Greece attained independence in 1829.

★**GREEK INDEPENDENCE DAY: A NATIONAL DAY OF CELEBRATION OF GREEK AND AMERICAN DEMOCRACY.** Mar 25.

LEAN, SIR DAVID: BIRTH ANNIVERSARY. Mar 25, 1908. British film director Sir David Lean was born at London. He directed 16 films and won two Best Director Academy Awards. His films include *Bridge on the River Kwai* (1957), *Lawrence of Arabia* (1962) and *Dr. Zhivago* (1965). He died Apr 16, 1991, at London.

MARYLAND DAY. Mar 25. Commemorates arrival of Lord Baltimore's first settlers in Maryland in 1634.

MIAEYC EARLY CHILDHOOD CONFERENCE. Mar 25–27. Amway Grand Plaza Hotel and Grand Rapids Convention Center, Grand Rapids, MI. This three-day conference sponsored by the Michigan Association for the Education of the Young Child (MIAEYC) focuses on issues affecting children from birth to age 8. Invited are educators, students, advocates and parents; participants can attend 1, 2 or all 3 days. Each day includes a keynote address, 2 full-day focus sessions and 75+ workshops. For info: Laurie Nickson, MiAEYC, Beacon Pl, 4572 S Hagadorn Rd, Ste 1-D, East Lansing, MI 48823. Phone: (800) 336-6424. Fax: (517) 336-9790. E-mail: MiAEYC@MiAEYC.org. Web: www.MiAEYC.org.

NATO FORCES ATTACK YUGOSLAVIA: 5th ANNIVERSARY. Mar 25, 1999. After many weeks of unsuccessful negotiations with Serb leader Slobodan Milosevic over the treatment of ethnic Albanians by Serb forces in the Kosovo Province of Yugoslavia, NATO forces began bombing Serbia and Kosovo. In response, the Serb army forced hundreds of thousands of ethnic Albanians to flee Kosovo for neighboring Albania, Macedonia and Montenegro. On June 10, 1999, NATO and Yugoslav officials signed an agreement providing for withdrawal of Serb troops from Kosovo, the end of Allied air strikes and the return of Kosovo refugees.

NCAA DIVISION I MEN'S SWIMMING AND DIVING CHAMPIONSHIPS. Mar 25–27. Goodwill Games Aquatic Center, East Meadow, NY. For info: NCAA, 700 W Washington St, PO Box 6222, Indianapolis, IN 46206-6222. Phone: (317) 917-6222. Fax: (317) 917-6888. Web: www.ncaa.org.

OLD NEW YEAR'S DAY. Mar 25. In Great Britain and its North American colonies this was the beginning of the new year up through 1751, when with the adoption of the Gregorian calendar the beginning of the year was changed to Jan 1.

PECAN DAY. Mar 25, 1775. Anniversary of the planting by George Washington of pecan trees (some of which still survive) at Mount Vernon. The trees were a gift to Washington from Thomas Jefferson, who had planted a few pecan trees from the southern US at Monticello, VA. The pecan, native to southern North America, is sometimes called "America's own nut." First cultivated by American Indians, it has been transplanted to other continents but has failed to achieve wide use or popularity outside the US.

ROME EXECUTIONS: 60th ANNIVERSARY. Mar 25, 1944. Nazis occupying Rome during World War II executed 300 Italian priests, Jews, women and two 14-year-old boys in retaliation for the deaths of 33 German soldiers who had been killed by Italian partisans. Hitler demanded 50 Italian lives for each German life that had been taken, but German officials in Italy lowered the number.

THE SAVANNAH TOUR OF HOMES AND GARDENS. Mar 25–28. Savannah, GA. Residents of Savannah open their homes to visitors to view 18th- and 19th-century architecture. The beauty of spring makes this tour of homes and gardens even more breathtaking. Est attendance: 4,000. For info: The Savannah Tour of Homes and Gardens, 18 Abercorn St, Savannah, GA 31401. Phone: (912) 234-8054. Fax: (912) 234-2123. E-mail: inforequest @savannahtourofhomes.org. Web: www.savannahtourofhomes.org.

SLAVE TRADE ABOLISHED BY ENGLAND: ANNIVERSARY. Mar 25, 1807. The English Parliament abolished the slave trade after a long campaign against it.

TOSCANINI, ARTURO: BIRTH ANNIVERSARY. Mar 25, 1867. Italian opera and symphony conductor Arturo Toscanini was born at Parma, Italy. He had an all-encompassing repertoire but was famous primarily for the operas of Verdi and the symphonies of Beethoven. Toscanini died at New York City, Jan 16, 1957.

TRIANGLE SHIRTWAIST FIRE: ANNIVERSARY. Mar 25, 1911. At about 4:30 PM, fire broke out at the Triangle Shirtwaist Company at New York, NY, minutes before the seamstresses were to go home. Some workers were fatally burned while others leaped to their deaths from the windows of the 10-story building. The fire lasted only 18 minutes but left 146 workers dead, most of them young immigrant women. Some of the deaths were a direct result of workers being trapped on the ninth floor by a locked door. Labor law forbade locking factory doors while employees were at work, and owners of the company were indicted on charges of first- and second-degree manslaughter. The tragic fire became a turning point in labor history, bringing about reforms in health and safety laws.

WASHINGTON HOME & GARDEN SHOW. Mar 25–28. The New Washington Convention Center, Washington, DC. Six acres of everything for the home and garden including full-size blooming gardens created by the area's best landscapers. The show also has demonstrations, lectures and a Spring Marketplace where visitors can purchase anything from orchids to a whole new kitchen. For info: Gail Stafford, Washington Home & Garden Show, 6017 Tower Ct, Alexandria, VA 22304. Phone: (703) 823-7960. E-mail: tjsevents@aol.com.

BIRTHDAYS TODAY

Bonnie Bedelia, 58, actress (*My Sweet Charlie, Die Hard, Die Hard 2*), born New York, NY, Mar 25, 1946 (some sources say 1952).

Anita Bryant, 64, singer ("The George Gobel Show"; hit song "Paper Roses"), Miss America ('58), born Barnsdall, OK, Mar 25, 1940.

John Ensign, 46, US Senator (R, Nevada), born Roseville, CA, Mar 25, 1958.

Eileen Ford, 82, model agency executive, born New York, NY, Mar 25, 1922.

Aretha Franklin, 62, singer ("Respect," "Think"), born Memphis, TN, Mar 25, 1942.

Paul Michael Glaser, 61, actor ("Starsky and Hutch"), director (*Butterflies Are Free*), born Cambridge, MA, Mar 25, 1943.

Tom Glavine, 38, baseball player, born Concord, MA, Mar 25, 1966.

Cammi Granato, 33, former hockey player, member of the 1998 Olympic team, born Maywood, IL, Mar 25, 1971.

Mary Gross, 51, comedienne, actress ("Saturday Night Live"), born Chicago, IL, Mar 25, 1953.

Elton John, 57, musician, singer, songwriter, born Reginald Kenneth Dwight, Pinner, England, Mar 25, 1947.

James Lovell, 76, astronaut, born Cleveland, OH, Mar 25, 1928.

Sarah Jessica Parker, 39, actress (*LA Story, Honeymoon in Vegas*, "Sex and the City"), born Nelsonville, OH, Mar 25, 1965.

Gloria Steinem, 69, feminist (original publisher of *Ms* magazine), journalist, born Toledo, OH, Mar 25, 1935.

John Stockwell, 43, actor, writer, director (*Top Gun, Under Cover*), born Galveston, TX, Mar 25, 1961.

Sheryl Swoopes, 33, basketball player, US Olympic Basketball Team, born Brownfield, TX, Mar 25, 1971.

MARCH 26 — FRIDAY
Day 86 — 280 Remaining

BANGLADESH: INDEPENDENCE DAY. Mar 26. Commemorates East Pakistan's independence in 1971 as the state of Bangladesh. Celebrated with parades, youth festivals and symposia.

BOWDITCH, NATHANIEL: BIRTH ANNIVERSARY. Mar 26, 1773. American mathematician and astronomer, author of the *New American Practical Navigator*. Born at Salem, MA, he died at Boston, MA, Mar 16, 1838.

CAMP DAVID ACCORD SIGNED: 25th ANNIVERSARY. Mar 26, 1979. Israeli Prime Minister Menachem Begin and Egyptian President Anwar Sadat signed the Camp David peace treaty, ending 30 years of war between their two countries. The agreement was fostered by President Jimmy Carter.

CRAFTSMEN'S CLASSIC ARTS & CRAFTS FESTIVAL. Mar 26–28. Dulles Expo and Convention Center, Chantilly, VA. 8th annual. Features work from more than 375 talented artists and craftspeople. All juried exhibitors' work has been handmade by the exhibitors and must be their own original design and creation. See the creative process in action with several exhibitors demonstrating their craft. Something for every style, taste and budget with items from the most contemporary to the most traditional. Est attendance: 20,000. For info: Gilmore Enterprises, Inc, 1240 Oakland Ave, Greensboro, NC 27403. Phone: (336) 274-5550. E-mail: gilmoreshows@triad.rr.com.

DELANO, JANE: BIRTH ANNIVERSARY. Mar 26, 1858. Jane Arminda Delano, dedicated American nurse and teacher, superintendent of the US Army Nurse Corps, chairman of the American Red Cross Nursing Service and recipient (posthumously) of the Distinguished Service Medal of the US, was born near Townsend, NY. While on an official visit to review Red Cross activities, she died Apr 15, 1919, in an army hospital at Savenay, France. Her last words: "What about my work? I must get back to my work." Buried at Loire, France, her remains were reinterred at Arlington National Cemetery in 1920.

FROST, ROBERT LEE: BIRTH ANNIVERSARY. Mar 26, 1874. American poet who tried his hand at farming, teaching, shoemaking and editing before winning acclaim as a poet. Pulitzer Prize winner. Born at San Francisco, CA, he died at Boston, MA, Jan 29, 1963.

LEGAL ASSISTANTS DAY. Mar 26. A day recognizing the many contributions made to the legal profession by legal assistants. For info: Claudia A. Evart, 30 Park Ave, #2-P, New York, NY 10016. Phone: (212) 779-2227. E-mail: paralegalcaevart @earthlink.net.

MAKE UP YOUR OWN HOLIDAY DAY. Mar 26. This day is a day you may name for whatever you wish. Reach for the stars! Make up a holiday! Annually, Mar 26. [©2003 by WH.] For info: Thomas & Ruth Roy, Wellcat Holidays, 2418 Long Ln, Lebanon, PA 17046. Phone: (717) 279-0184. E-mail: info@wellcat.com. Web: www.wellcat.com.

PALMETTO SPORTSMEN'S CLASSIC. Mar 26–28. South Carolina State Fairgrounds, Columbia, SC. Largest family-oriented wildlife show in the Carolinas with information on natural resources education and conservation, hunting, fishing and outdoor recreation. You will find activities for kids and adults throughout the show. Est attendance: 35,000. For info: Jim Goller or Mary Pugh, Palmetto Sportsmen's Classic, PO Box 167, Columbia, SC 29202. Phone: (803) 734-4008. E-mail: gollerj@scdnr.state.sc.us or maryp@scdnr.state.sc.us.

Mar 26–27 ☆ *Chase's 2004 Calendar of Events* ☆

PITTSBURGH ARTS & CRAFTS SPRING FEVER FESTIVAL. Mar 26–28. Greensburg, PA. Approximately 200 booths, including pottery, flowers, jewelry, quilts, furniture, tole and decorative painting, leather, toys and much more. Find that perfect gift. Est attendance: 16,000. For info: Debbie & Steve Stoner, Family Festivals Assn, PO Box 166, Irwin, PA 15642. Phone: (724) 863-4577. Fax: (724) 863-4577. E-mail: familyfestivals@hotmail.com. Web: www.familyfestivals.com.

PRINCE JONAH KUHIO KALANIANOLE DAY. Mar 26. Hawaii. Commemorates the man who, as Hawaii's delegate to the US Congress, introduced the first bill for statehood in 1919. Not until 1959 did Hawaii become a state.

SOVIET COSMONAUT RETURNS TO NEW COUNTRY: ANNIVERSARY. Mar 26, 1992. After spending 313 days in space in the Soviet *Mir* space station, cosmonaut Serge Krikalev returned to Earth and to what was for him a new country. He left Earth May 18, 1991, a citizen of the Soviet Union, but during his stay aboard the space station, the Soviet Union crumbled and became the Commonwealth of Independent States. Originally scheduled to return in October 1991, Krikalev's return was delayed by five months due to his country's disintegration and the ensuing monetary problems.

TEMPE SPRING FESTIVAL OF THE ARTS. Mar 26–28 (tentative). Downtown Tempe, AZ. Features 500 artists and craftspeople, continuous entertainment and children's activity area. Est attendance: 240,000. For info: Gary Sanders, Exec Dir, Mill Avenue Merchants Assn, PO Box 3084, Tempe, AZ 85281. Phone: (480) 967-4877. Fax: (480) 967-6638. E-mail: info@millavenue.org. Web: www.millavenue.org.

WILLIAMS, TENNESSEE: BIRTH ANNIVERSARY. Mar 26, 1911. Tennessee Williams was born at Columbus, MS. He was one of America's most prolific playwrights, producing such works as *The Glass Menagerie*; *A Streetcar Named Desire*, which won a Pulitzer Prize; *Cat on a Hot Tin Roof*, which won a second Pulitzer; *Night of the Iguana*; *Summer and Smoke*; *The Rose Tattoo* and *Sweet Bird of Youth*, among others. Williams died at New York, NY, Feb 25, 1983.

"THE YOUNG AND THE RESTLESS" TV PREMIERE: ANNIVERSARY. Mar 26, 1973. This daytime serial is generally thought of as TV's most artistic soap and has won numerous Emmys for outstanding daytime drama series. Its original storylines revolved around the Brooks and Foster families, but by the early '80s most of them were gone and the Abbott and Williams families were highlighted. The serial's very large and changing cast has included now-famous actors David Hasselhoff, Tom Selleck, Wings Hauser, Deidre Hall and Michael Damian. In 1980, "Y&R" expanded from a half-hour to an hour. Its theme music is well known as "Nadia's Theme," as it was played during Nadia Comaneci's routine at the 1976 Olympics.

BIRTHDAYS TODAY

Marcus Allen, 44, former football player, TV commentator, born San Diego, CA, Mar 26, 1960.
Alan Arkin, 70, actor (*Catch-22*); director (*Little Murders*), born New York, NY, Mar 26, 1934.
Pierre Boulez, 79, composer, conductor, born Montbrison, France, Mar 26, 1925.
James Caan, 64, actor (*Rabbit Run, The Godfather*), director, born New York, NY, Mar 26, 1940.
Lincoln Chafee, 51, US Senator (R, Rhode Island), born Warwick, RI, Mar 26, 1953.
Elaine Lan Chao, 51, US Secretary of Labor, born Taipei, Taiwan, Mar 26, 1953.
Leeza Gibbons, 47, TV hostess, born Hartsville, SC, Mar 26, 1957.
Jennifer Grey, 44, actress (*Dirty Dancing*, "It's Like, You Know. . ."), born New York, NY, Mar 26, 1960.
Erica Jong, 62, author, poet (*Fear of Flying, Becoming Light, How to Save Your Own Life*), born New York, NY, Mar 26, 1942.
Vicki Lawrence, 55, singer, actress ("The Carol Burnett Show," "Mama's Family"), born Inglewood, CA, Mar 26, 1949.
Josh Lucas, 32, actor (*Sweet Home Alabama, American Psycho*), born in Arkansas, Mar 26, 1972.
Leonard Nimoy, 73, actor ("Star Trek"), director (*Three Men and a Baby*), writer, born Boston, MA, Mar 26, 1931.
Sandra Day O'Connor, 74, Associate Justice of the US Supreme Court, born El Paso, TX, Mar 26, 1930.
Teddy Pendergrass, 54, singer, born Philadelphia, PA, Mar 26, 1950.
Diana Ross, 60, singer ("Keep Me Hangin' On," "Ain't No Mountain High Enough"); actress (*Lady Sings the Blues, The Wiz*), born Detroit, MI, Mar 26, 1944.
Martin Short, 54, actor (*The Three Amigos, Inner Space*), comedian ("SCTV Network 90," "Saturday Night Live"), born Hamilton, ON, Canada, Mar 26, 1950.
John Stockton, 42, former basketball player, born Spokane, WA, Mar 26, 1962.
Bob Woodward, 61, journalist (investigated Watergate with Carl Bernstein), born Geneva, IL, Mar 26, 1943.

MARCH 27 — SATURDAY
Day 87 — 279 Remaining

ANN ARBOR SPRING ART FAIR. Mar 27–28. Ann Arbor, MI. To give the public the opportunity to view and invest in the finest arts and crafts. 26th annual. Est attendance: 7,000. For info: Audree Levy, 1809 Morning Glory, Carrollton, TX 75007. Phone: (972) 394-5236. Fax: (972) 394-6236. E-mail: audree@levyartfairs.com. Web: www.levyartfairs.com.

CANARY ISLANDS PLANE DISASTER: ANNIVERSARY. Mar 27, 1977. The worst accident in the history of civil aviation. Two Boeing 747s collided on the ground; 570 people lost their lives—249 on the KLM Airlines plane and 321 on the Pan Am plane.

CELEBRATE EXCHANGE: NATIONAL EXCHANGE CLUB: BIRTHDAY. Mar 27, 1911. Anniversary of the day when the first Exchange Club was founded at Detroit, MI, by Charles A. Berkey. Since 1911, Exchange clubs have been working to improve their communities through service projects, by promoting patriotism and pride of country and through their national project, Child Abuse Prevention. Celebrated annually by nearly 32,000 Exchangites in the US and Puerto Rico. For info: The Natl Exchange Club, 3050 Central Ave, Toledo, OH 43606-1700. Phone: (800) 924-2643. Fax: (419) 535-1989. E-mail: nechq@aol.com. Web: www.nationalexchangeclub.org.

CHERRY BLOSSOM FESTIVAL. Mar 27–Apr 12. Various sites in Washington, DC. See more than 6,000 Japanese cherry trees in blossom. Festivities include the crowning of the Cherry Blossom Festival Queen, a 10-mile race, golf and rugby tournaments, arts and crafts show and the festival parade on Apr 3. For info: Cherry Blossom Fest, 1250 H St NW, Ste 1000, Washington, DC 20005. Phone: (202) 547-1500. Web: www.nationalcherryblossomfestival.org.

DELAND OUTDOOR ART FESTIVAL. Mar 27–28. Earl Brown Park, DeLand, FL. In its 38th year, the festival features more than 240 artists and craftsmen from around the US. Among the works featured are oil and acrylic paintings, watercolors, photography, pottery, sculpture and jewelry. A variety of entertainment runs throughout the festival featuring everything from jazz to original Irish music, classical to folk, strolling musicians and more. For info: DeLand Outdoor Art Festival. Phone: (386) 734-3243. Web: www.delandoutdoorartfest.com

EARTHQUAKE STRIKES ALASKA: 40th ANNIVERSARY. Mar 27, 1964. The strongest earthquake in North Amer-

March 2004	S	M	T	W	T	F	S
		1	2	3	4	5	6
	7	8	9	10	11	12	13
	14	15	16	17	18	19	20
	21	22	23	24	25	26	27
	28	29	30	31			

ican history (8.4 on the Richter scale) struck Alaska, east of Anchorage; 117 people were killed. This was the world's second worst earthquake of the 20th century in terms of magnitude.

★EDUCATION AND SHARING DAY. Mar 27. Proclaimed for the last week in March or the first week in April.

EGGSIBIT. Mar 27–28. Firth Youth Center, Phillipsburg, NJ. 34th annual show to encourage the art of decorating eggshells. Annually, the weekend prior to Palm Sunday. Est attendance: 2,000. For info: Dawn Slifer, Firth Youth Center, 108 Anderson St, Phillipsburg, NJ 08865. Phone: (908) 454-7281.

FUNKY WINKERBEAN: ANNIVERSARY. Mar 27, 1972. Anniversary of the nationally syndicated comic strip. For info: Tom Batiuk, Creator, 2750 Substation Rd, Medina, OH 44256. Phone: (330) 722-8755.

HILL, PATTY SMITH: BIRTH ANNIVERSARY. Mar 27, 1868. Patty Smith Hill, schoolteacher, author and education specialist, was born at Anchorage (suburb of Louisville), KY. She was author of the lyrics of the song "Good Morning to All," which later became known as "Happy Birthday to You." Her older sister, Mildred J. Hill, composed the melody for the song which was first published in 1893 as a classroom greeting in the book *Song Stories for the Sunday School*. A stanza beginning "Happy Birthday to You" was added in 1924, and the song became arguably the most frequently sung song in the world. Hill died at New York, NY, May 25, 1946. See also: "Happy Birthday to 'Happy Birthday to You'" (June 27).

LUXEMBOURG: OSWEILER. Mar 27. Blessing of horses, tractors and cars.

MYANMAR: RESISTANCE DAY. Mar 27. National holiday. Commemorates the day in 1945 when Burma officially joined the Allies in World War II. Also called Armed Forces Day.

NATCHEZ POWWOW. Mar 27–28. Natchez, MS. Native American dancing and crafts. Est attendance: 4,000. For info: Grand Village of the Natchez Indians, 400 Jefferson Davis Blvd, Natchez, MS 39120. Phone: (601) 446-6502. Fax: (601) 446-6503. E-mail: gvni@bkbank.com.

NORTH SEA OIL RIG DISASTER: ANNIVERSARY. Mar 27, 1980. The Alexander L. Keilland Oil Rig capsized during a heavy storm in the Norwegian sector of the North Sea. The pentagon-type, French-built oil rig had about 200 persons aboard, and 123 lives were lost.

NORTH TEXAS ARTS & CRAFTS SHOW. Mar 27–28. Multi-Purpose Events Center Exhibit Hall, Wichita Falls, TX. Come shop with some of America's finest artisans. Free admission. Est attendance: 4,500. For info: Wichita Falls CVB, 1000 5th St, Wichita Falls, TX 76301. Phone: (940) 716-5500. Fax: (940) 716-5509. E-mail: MPEC@wf.net. Web: www.wichitafalls.org.

QUIRKY COUNTRY MUSIC SONG TITLES DAY. Mar 27. We love those old country music quirky song titles, and it's time to create some new ones. How about "Put me out at the curb darlin', 'cause the recycling truck's a-comin', and you done throwed me out" for starters? [©2003 by WH.] For info: Thomas & Ruth Roy, Wellcat Holidays, 2418 Long Lane, Lebanon, PA 17046. Phone: (717) 279-0184. E-mail: info@wellcat.com. Web: www.wellcat.com.

ROENTGEN, WILHELM KONRAD: BIRTH ANNIVERSARY. Mar 27, 1845. German scientist who discovered X-rays (1895) and won a Nobel Prize in 1901. Born at Lennep, Prussia, he died at Munich, Germany, Feb 10, 1923.

SMITH, THORNE: BIRTH ANNIVERSARY. Mar 27, 1892. Perhaps the most critically neglected popular author of the 20th century, he was born James Thorne Smith, Jr, at Annapolis, MD, educated at Dartmouth, and died at Sarasota, Florida, June 20, 1934. Author of numerous humorous supernatural fantasy novels, including *Rain in the Doorway*, *The Stray Lamb* and *Topper*, he was the master of the pointless conversation. The "Thorne Smith" touch has inspired several motion pictures and television series, including "Bewitched." For info: George H. Scheetz, Exec Secy, The Thorne Smith Soc, 1409 Country Lake Dr, Champaign, IL 61821-6436. E-mail: scheetz@soltec.net.

SPACE MILESTONE: *VENERA 8* (USSR). Mar 27, 1972. Launched on this date, this unmanned probe made a soft landing on Venus July 22 and sent back radio transmissions of surface data.

STEICHEN, EDWARD: 125th BIRTH ANNIVERSARY. Mar 27, 1879. Celebrated American photographer. Born at Luxembourg, Germany, and died Mar 25, 1973, at West Redding, CT.

SWANSON, GLORIA: BIRTH ANNIVERSARY. Mar 27, 1899. American film actress (*Sunset Boulevard*) and businesswoman. Born Gloria May Josephine Svensson at Chicago. Author of an autobiography, *Swanson on Swanson*, published in 1980. Died at New York, NY, Apr 4, 1983.

SWITZERLAND: LUCERNE FESTIVAL, OSTERN (EASTER). Mar 27–Apr 4. Lucerne. Ostern bridges the gap between sacred music and concert music, including chamber music. About half the concerts take place in the most beautiful churches of Lucerne, the Jesuit and Franciscan, the other half at the Concert Hall of the Culture and Convention Centre. For info: Sheila Huber, Lucerne Festival, PO Box CH-6002, Lucerne, Switzerland. Phone: (41) 226-44-00. Fax: (41) 226-44-60. E-mail: info@lucernefestival.ch. Web: www.lucernefestival.ch.

VAUGHAN, SARAH: 80th BIRTH ANNIVERSARY. Mar 27, 1924. Legendary jazz singer, born at Newark, NJ, renowned for her melodic improvising, wide vocal range and extraordinary technique. She began her career by winning an amateur contest at New York's Apollo Theater in 1943. She was hired by Earl Hines to accompany his band as his relief pianist as well as singer. She was given the nickname "The Divine One" by Chicago disc jockey Dave Garroway, a moniker that would remain with her the rest of her life. Died at Los Angeles, CA, Apr 3, 1990.

BIRTHDAYS TODAY

Mariah Carey, 34, singer ("Vision of Love," "I'll Be There"), born Long Island, NY, Mar 27, 1970.

Randall Cunningham, 41, former football player, born Santa Barbara, CA, Mar 27, 1963.

Anthony Lewis, 77, journalist, author (*Gideon's Trumpet, Make No Law: The Sullivan Case and the First Amendment*), born New York, NY, Mar 27, 1927.

Austin Pendleton, 64, actor (*Mr and Mrs Bridge, Guarding Tess*), born Warren, OH, Mar 27, 1940.

Mstislav Leopoldovich Rostropovich, 77, musician, born Baku, USSR, Mar 27, 1927.

Maria Schneider, 52, actress (*Last Tango in Paris*), born Paris, France, Mar 27, 1952.

Quentin Tarantino, 41, actor, director (*Pulp Fiction, Jackie Brown*), born Knoxville, TN, Mar 27, 1963.

William Caleb (Cale) Yarborough, 64, former auto racer, born Timmonsville, SC, Mar 27, 1940.

Michael York, 62, actor (*Cabaret, The Three Musketeers*), born Fulmer, England, Mar 27, 1942.

MARCH 28 — SUNDAY
Day 88 — 278 Remaining

BARTHOLOMEW, FREDDIE: 80th BIRTH ANNIVERSARY. Mar 28, 1924. Child star of the 1930s, Freddie Bartholomew was born Frederick Llewellyn at Great Britain. He appeared in 24 films and became the second-highest paid child star after Shirley Temple. He died Jan 23, 1992, at Sarasota, FL.

BATTLE OF LA GLORIETTA PASS: ANNIVERSARY. Mar 28, 1862. At Pigeon's Ranch, a stagecoach stop on the Santa Fe Trail (about 19 miles southeast of Santa Fe, NM), Confederate forces briefly prevailed over Union troops in what some have called the most important battle of the Civil War in the Southwest. It was feared that if Union troops failed to hold here, the Confederate forces would proceed to Fort Union and on to control the rich gold fields of Colorado and California.

CONSIDER CHRISTIANITY WEEK. Mar 28–Apr 3. A week to encourage Christians to examine the evidence and reasons for their faith and for non-Christians to take another look at the faith that has played such an important role in shaping the history and culture in which we live. Annually, beginning two Sundays before Easter. For info: Hanna Hushbeck, PR, Aletheia, 936 N Lincoln St, Redlands, CA 92374. Phone: (909) 794-8941. Fax: (909) 794-8941. E-mail: elgin@consider.org. Web: www.consider.org.

CZECH REPUBLIC: TEACHERS' DAY. Mar 28. Celebrates birth on this day of Jan Amos Komensky (Comenius), Moravian educational reformer (1592–1671).

ENGLAND: CARE SUNDAY. Mar 28. The fifth Sunday of Lent, also known as Carling Sunday and Passion Sunday. First day of Passiontide, remembering the sorrow and passion of Christ.

EUROPE: SUMMER DAYLIGHT SAVING TIME. Mar 28–Oct 31. All members of the European Union observe daylight saving (summer) time from the last Sunday in March until the last Sunday in October.

"GREATEST SHOW ON EARTH" FORMED: ANNIVERSARY. Mar 28, 1881. P.T. Barnum and James A. Bailey merged their circuses to form the "Greatest Show on Earth."

GREECE: DUMB WEEK. Mar 28–Apr 3. The week preceding Holy Week on the Orthodox calendar is known as Dumb Week, as no services are held in churches throughout this period except on Friday, eve of the Saturday of Lazarus.

***HAIR* BROADWAY OPENING: ANNIVERSARY.** Mar 28, 1968. The controversial rock musical *Hair*, produced by Michael Butler, opened at the Biltmore Theatre at New York City, after playing off-Broadway. For those who opposed the Vietnam War and the "Establishment," this was a defining piece of work—as evidenced by some of its songs, such as "Aquarius," "Hair" and "Let the Sunshine In."

INDIA: HOLI. Mar 28. In this spring festival people run through the streets smearing each other with brightly hued powders and colored water. This is observed by Indians without regard to caste. Huge bonfires are built on the eve of Holi. Because there is no one universally accepted Hindu calendar, this holiday may be celebrated on a different date in some parts of India but it always falls in February or March.

LAZAR, IRVING ("SWIFTY"): BIRTH ANNIVERSARY. Mar 28, 1907. Hollywood talent agent whose clients included Ernest Hemingway, Lillian Hellman, Cole Porter, Richard Nixon and Humphrey Bogart (who nicknamed him "Swifty" after Lazar met Bogart's challenge to make him five film deals in one day in 1955). He died Dec 30, 1993, at Beverly Hills, CA.

LIBYA: BRITISH BASES EVACUATION DAY. Mar 28. National holiday. Commemorates the closing of British bases on this day in 1970.

MOON PHASE: FIRST QUARTER. Mar 28. Moon enters First Quarter phase at 6:48 PM, EST.

NATIONAL CLEANING WEEK. Mar 28–Apr 3. Established by Monica Nassif, founder and president of The Caldrea Company, the manufacturer of upscale cleaning products and cleaning accessories, National Cleaning Week serves as a reminder to tackle spring cleaning. Each day will be dedicated to a specific chore. Annually, the last week in March. For info: Monica Nassif, The Caldrea Company, 420 N 5th St, Ford Centre, Ste 600, Minneapolis, MN 55401. Phone: (612) 371-0003 or (877) 576-8808. Fax: (612) 371-9995. Web: www.caldrea.com.

PASSION WEEK. Mar 28–Apr 3. The week beginning on the fifth Sunday in Lent; the week before Holy Week.

PASSIONTIDE. Mar 28–Apr 10. The last two weeks of Lent (Passion Week and Holy Week), beginning with the fifth Sunday of Lent (Passion Sunday) and continuing through the day before Easter (Holy Saturday or Easter Even).

SAINT JOHN NEPOMUCENE NEUMANN: BIRTH ANNIVERSARY. Mar 28, 1811. First male saint of the US. Born at Prachatice, Bohemia, came to the US in 1836. As Bishop of Philadelphia, he was affectionately known as the "Little Bishop." Died at Philadelphia, PA, Jan 5, 1860. Beatified Oct 13, 1963. Canonized June 19, 1977.

SPACE MILESTONE: *NOAA 8* (US): ANNIVERSARY. Mar 28, 1983. Search and Rescue Satellite (SARSAT) launched from Vandenburg Air Force Base, CA, to aid in locating ships and aircraft in distress. *Kosmos 1383*, launched July 1, 1982, by the USSR, in a cooperative rescue effort, is credited with saving more than 20 lives.

THREE MILE ISLAND NUCLEAR POWER PLANT ACCIDENT: 25th ANNIVERSARY. Mar 28, 1979. A series of accidents beginning at 4 AM, EST, at Three Mile Island on the Susquehanna River about 10 miles southeast of Harrisburg, PA, was responsible for extensive reevaluation of the safety of existing nuclear power generating operations. Equipment and other failures reportedly brought Three Mile Island close to a meltdown of the uranium core, threatening extensive radiation contamination.

VIETNAM MORATORIUM CONCERT: ANNIVERSARY. Mar 28, 1970. A seven-hour concert at Madison Square Garden at New York City featured many stars who donated their services for the antiwar cause. Among them were Jimi Hendrix; Dave Brubeck; Harry Belafonte; Peter, Paul and Mary; Judy Collins; the Rascals; Blood, Sweat and Tears and the Broadway cast of *Hair*.

BIRTHDAYS TODAY

Conchata Ferrell, 61, actress ("LA Law," "Hearts Afire," *Edward Scissorhands*), born Charleston, WV, Mar 28, 1943.

Ken Howard, 60, actor ("Crossing Jordan," "The White Shadow"), born El Centro, CA, Mar 28, 1944.

Reba McEntire, 50, singer ("For My Broken Heart"), actress, born Chockie, OK, Mar 28, 1954.

Frank Hughes Murkowski, 71, Governor of Alaska (R), former US Senator (R, Alaska), born Seattle, WA, Mar 28, 1933.

Earnie Stewart, 35, soccer player, born Veghal, Holland, Mar 28, 1969.

Julia Stiles, 23, actress (*Save the Last Dance, O, 10 Things I Hate About You*), born New York, NY, Mar 28, 1981.

Keith Tkachuk, 32, hockey player, born Melrose, MA, Mar 28, 1972.

Dianne Wiest, 56, actress (Oscars for *Hannah and Her Sisters* and *Bullets Over Broadway*; "Law & Order"), born Kansas City, MO, Mar 28, 1948.

March 2004

S	M	T	W	T	F	S
	1	2	3	4	5	6
7	8	9	10	11	12	13
14	15	16	17	18	19	20
21	22	23	24	25	26	27
28	29	30	31			

☆ Chase's 2004 Calendar of Events ☆   Mar 29

MARCH 29 — MONDAY
Day 89 — 277 Remaining

"AMERICA'S SUBWAY" DAY: ANNIVERSARY. Mar 29, 1976. The Washington (DC) Metropolitan Area Transit Authority (WMATA) ran its first Metrorail passenger train 28 years ago. The Metro system consisted of only five stations and 4.6 miles on the Red Line Route. The Metro now consists of 83 stations and 103 miles on the Red, Blue, Orange, Yellow and Green Line routes. More stations are planned. Passengers take approximately 625,000 trips each weekday in the nation's capital and the greater Washington area. Many of these are made by tourists from across the country and around the world—hence the moniker "America's Subway." For info: Cheryl Johnson, WMATA, 600 Fifth St NW, Washington, DC 20001. Phone: (202) 962-1051. Fax: (202) 962-2897. Web: www.metroopensdoors.com.

BAILEY, PEARL MAE: BIRTH ANNIVERSARY. Mar 29, 1918. American singer and Broadway musical star Pearl Bailey was born at Newport News, VA. She began her career in vaudeville and won a special Tony Award in 1968 and the Presidential Medal of Freedom in 1988. Bailey died Aug 17, 1990, at Philadelphia, PA.

BIGGS, E. POWER: BIRTH ANNIVERSARY. Mar 29, 1906. Baroque organist who helped establish the organ as a concert instrument. Biggs refused to perform on electronic organs, but sought out and recorded on organs surviving from the era of Johann Sebastian Bach and George Frederick Handel. After arthritis forced him to retire, he published early organ music. Biggs was born at Westcliff-on-Sea, Essex, England, and came to the US in 1930 at the age of 24. He died Mar 10, 1977, at Boston.

CANADA: BRITISH NORTH AMERICA ACT: ANNIVERSARY. Mar 29, 1867. This act of the British Parliament established the Dominion of Canada, uniting Ontario, Quebec, Nova Scotia and New Brunswick. The remaining colonies in Canada were still ruled directly by Great Britain until Manitoba joined the Dominion in 1870, British Columbia in 1871, Prince Edward Island in 1873, Alberta and Saskatchewan in 1905 and Newfoundland in 1949. Union was proclaimed July 1, 1867. See also: "Canada: Canada Day" (July 1).

CENTRAL AFRICAN REPUBLIC: BOGANDA DAY. Mar 29. National holiday. Commemorates the death of Barthelemy Boganda, the first president, in 1959.

COMMITTEE ON ASSASSINATIONS REPORT: 25th ANNIVERSARY. Mar 29, 1979. The House Select Committee on Assassinations released the final report on its investigation into the assassinations of President John F. Kennedy, Martin Luther King, Jr, and Robert Kennedy on this day. Based on available evidence, the committee concluded that President Kennedy was assassinated as a result of a conspiracy, although no trail of a conspiracy could be established. They also concluded that on the basis of scientific acoustical evidence two gunmen fired at the President, although no second gunman could be identified. [Note: In December 1980, the FBI released a report discounting the two-gunman theory, stating that the distinguishable sounds of two separate guns were not proven scientifically.] In addition the committee concluded that the possibility of conspiracy did exist in the cases of Dr. King and Robert Kennedy, although no specific individuals or organizations could be pinpointed as being involved. See also: "Warren Commission Report: Anniversary" (Sept 27).

DOW-JONES TOPS 10,000: 5th ANNIVERSARY. Mar 29, 1999. The Dow-Jones Index of 30 major industrial stocks topped the 10,000 mark for the first time.

HOOVER, LOU HENRY: BIRTH ANNIVERSARY. Mar 29, 1875. Wife of Herbert Clark Hoover, 31st president of the US. Born at Waterloo, IA, she died at Palo Alto, CA, Jan 7, 1944.

JOHN PARTRIDGE "DEATH" HOAX: ANNIVERSARY. Mar 29, 1708. English astrologer John Partridge (real name: John Hewson) so offended readers by his foolish predictions that he became the target of parodies and jokes, most serious of which was that of the satirist Jonathan Swift. Under the pseudonym Isaac Bickerstaff, Swift published his own almanac for the year 1708, in which he predicted that Partridge would die at 11 PM, Mar 29, 1708, "of a raging fever." Poor Partridge made the mistake of trying to prove he was still alive, only to find writers, citizens and even the court were more amused by continuing the fiction of his death.

KNIGHTS OF COLUMBUS FOUNDER'S DAY. Mar 29. The first Knights of Columbus charter was granted in 1882 by the state of Connecticut. This Catholic, family, fraternal service organization has grown into a volunteer force of Knights and family members totaling nearly six million who annually donate tens of millions of dollars and volunteer hours to countless charitable projects. For info: Robert A. Goossens, Director, Fraternal Services, Knights of Columbus, 1 Columbus Plaza, New Haven, CT 06514.

MADAGASCAR: COMMEMORATION DAY. Mar 29. Memorial Day for the victims of the rebellion in 1947 against French colonization.

NATIONAL MOM AND POP BUSINESS OWNERS DAY. Mar 29. A day recognizing those very special husband-and-wife business owner teams that work and commune together. Take this day to strike a balance between business and love. For info: Rick/Margie Segel, 1 Wheatland St, Burlington, MA 01803. Phone: (781) 272-9995. Fax: (781) 272-9996. E-mail: rick@ricksegel.com.

NATIONAL SLEEP AWARENESS WEEK. Mar 29–Apr 4. All Americans are urged to recognize the importance of proper sleep to their health, safety and productivity and the dangers of untreated sleep disorders. For info: Natl Sleep Foundation, 1522 K St NW, Ste 500, Washington, DC 20005. Web: www.sleepfoundation.org.

QUINLAN, KAREN ANN: 50th BIRTH ANNIVERSARY. Mar 29, 1954. Born at Scranton, PA, Karen Ann Quinlan became the center of a legal, medical and ethical controversy over the right to die. She became irreversibly comatose on Apr 14, 1975. A petition filed by her adoptive parents in New Jersey's Superior Court, Sept 12, 1975, sought permission to discontinue use of a respirator, allowing her to die "with grace and dignity." In 1976 the petition was upheld by New Jersey's Supreme Court. Quinlan lived nearly a decade without the respirator, until June 11, 1985. Her plight brought into focus the ethical dilemmas of advancing medical technology—the need for a new understanding of life and death; the right to die; the role of judges, doctors and hospital committees in deciding when not to prolong life.

SEWARD'S DAY: ANNIVERSARY OF THE ACQUISITION OF ALASKA. Mar 29. Observed in Alaska near anniversary of its acquisition from Russia in 1867. The treaty of purchase was signed between the Russians and the Americans Mar 30, 1867, and ratified by the Senate May 28, 1867. The territory was formally transferred Oct 18, 1867. Annually, the last Monday in March.

TAIWAN: YOUTH DAY. Mar 29.

TEXAS LOVE THE CHILDREN DAY. Mar 29. A day recognizing every child's right and need to be loved. Promoting the hope that one day all children will live in loving, safe environments and will be given proper health care and equal learning opportunities. Precedes the start of National Child Abuse Prevention Month (April). For info: Patty Murphy, 1101 Lynda Lane, Arlington, TX 76013. Phone: (817) 498-5840. E-mail: MURPH0@swbell.net.

TWENTY-THIRD AMENDMENT TO US CONSTITUTION RATIFIED: ANNIVERSARY. Mar 29, 1961. District of Columbia residents were given the right to vote in presidential elections under the 23rd Amendment.

TYLER, JOHN: BIRTH ANNIVERSARY. Mar 29, 1790. Tenth president of the US (Apr 6, 1841–Mar 3, 1845). Born at Charles City County, VA, Tyler succeeded to the presidency upon the death of William Henry Harrison. Tyler's first wife died while he was president, and he remarried before the end of his term in office, becoming the first president to marry while in office. Fifteen children were born of the two marriages. In 1861 he was elected to the Congress of the Confederate States but died at Richmond, VA, Jan 18, 1862, before being seated. His death received no official tribute from the US government.

UNITED KINGDOM: SUMMER TIME. Mar 29–Oct 31. "Summer Time" (one hour in advance of Standard Time), similar to daylight saving time, is observed from the last Monday in March until the last Sunday in October.

WALTON, SAM: BIRTH ANNIVERSARY. Mar 29, 1918. Founder of Wal-Mart discount stores, born at Kingfisher, OK. One of the wealthiest men in America, he died at Little Rock, AR, Apr 5, 1992.

YOUNG, DENTON TRUE (CY): BIRTH ANNIVERSARY. Mar 29, 1867. Baseball Hall of Fame pitcher, born at Gilmore, OH. Young is baseball's all-time winningest pitcher, having accumulated 511 victories in his 22-year career. The Cy Young Award is given each year in his honor to the Major League's best pitcher. Inducted into the Hall of Fame in 1937. Died at Peoli, OH, Nov 4, 1955.

BIRTHDAYS TODAY

Earl Christian Campbell, 49, Hall of Fame football player, born Tyler, TX, Mar 29, 1955.
Jennifer Capriati, 28, tennis player, born New York, NY, Mar 29, 1976.
Bud Cort, 54, actor (*Harold and Maude, Brewster McCloud*), born New Rochelle, NY, Mar 29, 1950 (some sources say 1948).
Eric Idle, 61, actor ("Monty Python's Flying Circus," "Suddenly Susan"), author, born Durham, England, Mar 29, 1943.
Christopher Lambert, 47, actor (*Greystoke: The Legend of Tarzan, Lord of the Apes; To Kill a Priest*), born New York, NY, Mar 29, 1957.
Lucy Lawless, 36, actress ("Xena"), born Mount Albert, Auckland, New Zealand, Mar 29, 1968.
Elle Macpherson, 40, model, actress (*Sirens*), born Sydney, Australia, Mar 29, 1964.
John Major, 61, former British prime minister, born Brixton, England, Mar 29, 1943.
Eugene McCarthy, 88, former US Senator (anti-Vietnam War presidential hopeful in '68), born Watkins, MN, Mar 29, 1916.
John Joseph McLaughlin, 77, editor, columnist, TV host, born Providence, RI, Mar 29, 1927.
Kurt Thomas, 48, former gymnast, born Miami, FL, Mar 29, 1956.

March 2004	S	M	T	W	T	F	S
		1	2	3	4	5	6
	7	8	9	10	11	12	13
	14	15	16	17	18	19	20
	21	22	23	24	25	26	27
	28	29	30	31			

MARCH 30 — TUESDAY
Day 90 — 276 Remaining

ANESTHETIC FIRST USED IN SURGERY: ANNIVERSARY. Mar 30, 1842. Dr. Crawford W. Long, having seen the use of nitrous oxide and sulfuric ether at "laughing gas" parties, observed that individuals under their influence felt no pain. On this date, he removed a tumor from the neck of a man who was under the influence of ether.

DOCTORS' DAY. Mar 30. Traditional annual observance since 1933 to honor America's physicians on the anniversary of the occasion when Dr. Crawford W. Long became the first acclaimed physician to use ether as an anesthetic agent in a surgical technique, Mar 30, 1842. The red carnation has been designated the official flower of Doctors' Day.

GOYA, FRANCISCO JOSE de: BIRTH ANNIVERSARY. Mar 30, 1746. Spanish painter and etcher. It is estimated that he executed more than 1,800 paintings, drawings and lithographs during his lifetime. Born at Aragon, Spain; died at Bordeaux, France, Apr 16, 1828.

"I AM IN CONTROL" DAY: ANNIVERSARY. Mar 30, 1981. Anniversary of former Secretary of State Alexander Haig's televised announcement (while President Ronald Reagan was undergoing surgery after being shot by a would-be assassin): "As of now, I am in control here in the White House. . . ." Haig continued to say, "Constitutionally, gentlemen, you have the president, the vice president and the secretary of state in that order. . . ."

"JEOPARDY" TV PREMIERE: 40th ANNIVERSARY. Mar 30, 1964. The "thinking person's" game show, "Jeopardy" has a reputation as an intelligent and classy program. Art Fleming was the original host of the show, in which three contestants won cash by attempting to give the correct question to an answer in six different categories. Contestants go through two rounds and "final jeopardy," where they can wager up to all their earnings on one question. The series returned in 1984 with Alex Trebek as the popular host.

MERCEDES-BENZ SHOWS LA. Mar 30–Apr 2 (tentative). Los Angeles, CA. Fashion designers present their fall 2004 lines. For info: 7th on Sixth, 420 W 45th St, 6th Fl, New York, NY 10036. Phone: (212) 253-2692. E-mail: info@7thonsixth.com. Web: www.7thonsixth.com.

NICKERSON, CAMILLE ("THE LOUISIANA LADY"): BIRTH ANNIVERSARY. Mar 30, 1888. Camille Nickerson, music arranger, composer, musician and educator, is remembered for her musical talent and her work as a music collector who gathered and transcribed Creole music. Born at the French Quarter, New Orleans. Of Creole extraction herself, Nickerson performed for a time in the US and Europe using the stage name "The Louisiana Lady." She died at Washington, DC, at age 94.

O'CASEY, SEAN: BIRTH ANNIVERSARY. Mar 30, 1880. Irish playwright (*Juno and the Paycock*). Born at Dublin, Ireland, he died at Torquay, England, Sept 18, 1964.

PENCIL PATENTED: ANNIVERSARY. Mar 30, 1858. First pencil with the eraser top was patented by Hyman Lipman.

REAGAN, RONALD: ASSASSINATION ATTEMPT: ANNIVERSARY. Mar 30, 1981. President Ronald Reagan was shot in the chest by a 25-year-old gunman at Washington, DC. Three other persons were wounded. John W. Hinckley, Jr, the accused attacker, was arrested at the scene. On June 21, 1982, a federal jury in the District of Columbia found Hinckley not guilty by reason of insanity and he was committed to St. Elizabeth's Hospital at Washington, DC, for an indefinite time.

196

☆ Chase's 2004 Calendar of Events ☆   Mar 30–31

SPRING PILGRIMAGE TO ANTEBELLUM HOMES. Mar 30–Apr 11 (tentative). Columbus, MS. Tours of pre–Civil War homes for visiting public. Est attendance: 5,000. For info: Columbus Historic Foundation, PO Box 46, Columbus, MS 39703. Phone: (800) 327-2686 or (662) 329-3533. Fax: (662) 329-1027. E-mail: chf@historic-columbus.org or ccvb@columbus-ms.org. Web: www.columbus-ms.org.

TRINIDAD AND TOBAGO: SPIRITUAL BAPTIST LIBERATION SHOUTER DAY. Mar 30. Public holiday. For info: Information Dept, Tourism Div, Tourism and Industrial Development Co, 10-14 Phillips St, Port of Spain, Trinidad, West Indies.

VAN GOGH, VINCENT: BIRTH ANNIVERSARY. Mar 30, 1853. Dutch post-Impressionist painter, especially known for his bold and powerful use of color. Born at Groot Zundert, Holland, he died at Auvers-sur-Oise, France, July 29, 1890.

BIRTHDAYS TODAY

John Astin, 74, actor ("The Addams Family"; stage: *The Three Penny Opera*), director, born Baltimore, MD, Mar 30, 1930.
Brooke Astor, 102, philanthropist, author, 1996 Medal of Freedom recipient, born New York, NY, Mar 30, 1902.
Warren Beatty, 66, actor (*Bonnie and Clyde*); director (*Reds, Dick Tracy*), producer, born Richmond, VA, Mar 30, 1938.
Tracy Chapman, 40, singer ("Fast Car"), born Cleveland, OH, Mar 30, 1964.
Eric Clapton, 59, singer (with Yardbirds, Cream), songwriter ("Layla," with Jim Gordon), born Ripley, England, Mar 30, 1945.
Robbie Coltrane, 54, actor (*GoldenEye*, the Harry Potter films), born Rutherglen, Scotland, Mar 30, 1950 (some sources say Mar 31).
Celine Dion, 36, pop singer, Grammy winner, born Charlemagne, QC, Canada, Mar 30, 1968.
Richard Dysart, 75, actor ("LA Law"), born Augusta, ME, Mar 30, 1929.
M.C. Hammer, 41, rapper, born Stanley Kirk Burrell, Oakland, CA, Mar 30, 1963.
Frankie Laine, 91, actor, singer ("Frankie Laine Time," *Viva Las Vegas*), born Chicago, IL, Mar 30, 1913.
Peter Marshall, 77, TV host, actor, born Huntington, WV, Mar 30, 1927.
Paul Reiser, 47, actor (*Diner*, "Mad About You"), born New York, NY, Mar 30, 1957.

MARCH 31 — WEDNESDAY
Day 91 — 275 Remaining

BUNSEN BURNER DAY. Mar 31. A day to honor the inventor of the Bunsen burner, Robert Wilhelm Eberhard von Bunsen, who provided chemists and chemistry students with one of their most indispensable instruments. The Bunsen burner allows the user to regulate the proportions of flammable gas and air to create the most efficient flame. Bunsen was born at Gottingen, Germany, Mar 31, 1811, and was a professor of chemistry at the universities at Kassel, Marburg, Breslau and Heidelberg. He died at Heidelberg, Germany, Aug 16, 1899.

CHAVEZ, CESAR ESTRADA: BIRTH ANNIVERSARY. Mar 31, 1927. Labor leader who organized migrant farm workers in support of better working conditions. Chavez initiated the National Farm Workers Association in 1962, attracting attention to the migrant farm workers' plight by organizing boycotts of products including grapes and lettuce. He was born at Yuma, AZ, and died Apr 23, 1993, at San Luis, AZ. His birthday is a holiday in California.

CHESNUT, MARY BOYKIN MILLER: BIRTH ANNIVERSARY. Mar 31, 1823. Born at Pleasant Hill, SC, and died Nov 22, 1886, at Camden, SC. During the Civil War Chesnut accompanied her husband, a Confederate staff officer, on military missions. She kept a journal of her experiences and observations, which was published posthumously as *A Diary from Dixie*, a perceptive portrait of Confederate military and political leaders and insightful view of Southern life during the Civil War.

DALAI LAMA FLEES TIBET: 45th ANNIVERSARY. Mar 31, 1959. The Dalai Lama fled Chinese suppression and was granted political asylum in India. In 1950 Tibet had been invaded by China and in 1951 an agreement was signed under which Tibet became a "national autonomous region" of China. Tibetans suffered under China's persecution of Buddhism, and after years of scattered protest a full-scale revolt broke out in 1959. The Dalai Lama fled and with the beginning of the Chinese Cultural Revolution the Chinese took brutal repressive measures against the Tibetans, with the practice of religion banned and thousands of monasteries destroyed. The ban was lifted in 1976 with the end of the Cultural Revolution. The Dalai Lama received the Nobel Peace Prize in 1989 for his commitment to the nonviolent liberation of his country.

DESCARTES, RENE: BIRTH ANNIVERSARY. Mar 31, 1596. French philosopher and mathematician, known as the "father of modern philosophy," born at La Haye, Touraine, France. Cartesian philosophical precepts are often remembered because of his famous proposition "I think, therefore I am" (*Cogito ergo sum . . .*). Died of pneumonia at Stockholm, Sweden, Feb 11, 1650.

EIFFEL TOWER: ANNIVERSARY. Mar 31, 1889. Built for the Paris Exhibition of 1889, the tower was named for its architect, Alexandre Gustave Eiffel, and is one of the world's best-known landmarks.

FITZGERALD, EDWARD: BIRTH ANNIVERSARY. Mar 31, 1809. English author, born at Bredfield, England, perhaps best known for his translation of Omar Khayyam's *Rubaiyat*. Died at Merton, Norfolk, June 14, 1883.

GOGOL, NIKOLAI VASILEVICH: BIRTH ANNIVERSARY. Mar 31, 1809. Russian author of plays, novels and short stories. Born at Sorochinsk, Russia, he died at Moscow, Russia, Mar 4, 1852. Gogol's most famous work was the novel *Dead Souls*.

HAYDN, FRANZ JOSEPH: BIRTH ANNIVERSARY. Mar 31, 1732. "Father of the symphony," born at Rohrau, Austria-Hungary. Composed about 120 symphonies, more than a hundred works for chamber groups, a dozen operas and hundreds of other musical works. Died at Vienna, Austria, May 31, 1809.

JOHNSON, JOHN (JACK) ARTHUR: BIRTH ANNIVERSARY. Mar 31, 1878. In 1908 Jack Johnson became the first black to win the heavyweight boxing championship when he defeated Tommy Burns at Sydney, Australia. Unable to accept a black man's triumph, the boxing world tried to find a white challenger. Jim Jeffries, former heavyweight title holder, was badgered out of retirement. On July 4, 1919, at Reno, NV, the "battle of the century" proved to be a farce when Johnson handily defeated Jeffries. Race riots swept the US, and plans to exhibit the film of the fight were canceled. Johnson was born at Galveston, TX, and died in an automobile accident June 10, 1946, at Raleigh, NC. He was inducted into the Boxing Hall of Fame in 1990. The film *The Great White Hope* is based on his life.

MARVELL, ANDREW: BIRTH ANNIVERSARY. Mar 31, 1621. English poet. Born at Winestead, Yorkshire, England. From his poem "To His Coy Mistress": "Had we but world enough and time/this coyness, lady, were no crime. . . . But at my back I always hear/time's winged chariot drawing near. . . ." Died at London, England, Aug 18, 1678.

NATIONAL "SHE'S FUNNY THAT WAY" DAY. Mar 31. On this day, individuals will pay tribute to the humorous nature of women, by listing the top five ways in which women in our lives make us laugh. For info: Brenda Meridith, Dahomey Publishing Company, 50 Hall Rd, Winchendon, MA 01475. Phone: (978) 297-1820. Fax: (978) 297-2519. E-mail: BMeridith@aol.com. Web: www.DahomeyPublishing.com.

Mar 31 ☆ Chase's 2004 Calendar of Events ☆

PEARSE, RICHARD: ANNIVERSARY OF MONOPLANE FLIGHT. Mar 31, 1903. Richard Pearse, a farmer and inventor, flew a monoplane of his own design several hundred yards along a road near Temuka, New Zealand, and then landed it on top of a 12-foot-high hedge. Pearse had built the craft, which consisted of a steerable tricycle undercarriage and an internal combustion engine. A Pearse commemorative medal was issued on Sept 19, 1971, by the Museum of Transport and Technology, Auckland, New Zealand.

SOVIET GEORGIA VOTES FOR INDEPENDENCE: ANNIVERSARY. Mar 31, 1991. On this date the Soviet Republic of Georgia voted to declare its independence from the Soviet Union. Georgia followed the Baltic States of Lithuania, Estonia and Latvia by becoming the fourth republic to reject Mikhail Gorbachev's new vision of the Soviet Union as espoused in a new Union Treaty. Totals revealed that 98.9 percent of those voting favored independence from Moscow. Hours after the election, troops were dispatched from Moscow to Georgia under a state of emergency.

US VIRGIN ISLANDS: TRANSFER DAY. Mar 31. Commemorates transfer resulting from purchase of the Virgin Islands by the US from Denmark, Mar 31, 1917, for $25 million.

BIRTHDAYS TODAY

Herb Alpert, 69, musician (Tijuana Brass), born Los Angeles, CA, Mar 31, 1935.
Pavel Bure, 33, hockey player, born Moscow, USSR, Mar 31, 1971.
Richard Chamberlain, 69, actor ("Dr. Kildare," *Shogun*), born Los Angeles, CA, Mar 31, 1935.
Thomas Haden Church, 44, actor ("Wings," "Ned & Stacey"), born El Paso, TX, Mar 31, 1960 (some sources say June 17, 1961).
Liz Claiborne, 75, fashion designer, born Brussels, Belgium, Mar 31, 1929.
William Daniels, 77, actor (Emmy for "St. Elsewhere"; "Boy Meets World"), born Brooklyn, NY, Mar 31, 1927.
Al Gore, 56, 45th vice president of the US, born Albert Gore, Jr, Washington, DC, Mar 31, 1948.
Gordon (Gordie) Howe, 76, Hall of Fame hockey player, born Floral, SK, Canada, Mar 31, 1928.
John Jakes, 72, author (*California Gold, In the Big Country*), born Chicago, IL, Mar 31, 1932.
James Earl (Jimmy) Johnson, 66, Hall of Fame football player, born Dallas, TX, Mar 31, 1938.
Shirley Jones, 70, singer, actress ("The Partridge Family," *Elmer Gantry, Oklahoma!*), born Smithton, PA, Mar 31, 1934.
Gabe Kaplan, 58, actor ("Welcome Back Kotter"), born Brooklyn, NY, Mar 31, 1946.
Patrick J. Leahy, 64, US Senator (D, Vermont), born Montpelier, VT, Mar 31, 1940.
Edward Francis (Ed) Marinaro, 54, actor ("Hill Street Blues," "Sisters"), former football player, born New York, NY, Mar 31, 1950.
Marc McClure, 47, actor (*Freaky Friday, Back to the Future*), born San Mateo, CA, Mar 31, 1957.
Ewan McGregor, 33, actor (*Trainspotting, Emma,* Star Wars films), born Crieff, Scotland, Mar 31, 1971.
Rhea Perlman, 56, actress ("Cheers" [three Emmy Awards]; *Carpool*), born Brooklyn, NY, Mar 31, 1948.
Steve Smith, 35, basketball player, born Highland Park, MI, Mar 31, 1969.
Christopher Walken, 61, actor (*The Deer Hunter, Batman Returns*), born Queens, NY, Mar 31, 1943.

☆ Chase's 2004 Calendar of Events ☆   Apr 1

Aprill.

APRIL 1 — THURSDAY
Day 92 — 274 Remaining

ALCOHOL AWARENESS MONTH. Apr 1–30. To help raise awareness among community prevention leaders and citizens about the problem of underage drinking. Concentrates on community grassroots activities. For info: Public Info Dept, Natl Council on Alcoholism and Drug Dependence, Inc, 20 Exchange Pl, New York, NY 10005. Phone: (212) 269-7797. Fax: (212) 269-7510. E-mail: national@ncadd.org. Web: www.ncadd.org.

APRIL FOOLS' or ALL FOOLS' DAY. Apr 1. April Fools' Day seems to have begun in France in 1564. Apr 1 used to be New Year's Day but the New Year was changed to Jan 1 that year. People who insisted on celebrating the "old" New Year became known as April fools and it became common to play jokes and tricks on them. The general concept of a feast of fools is, however, an ancient one. The Romans had such a day and medieval monasteries also had days when the abbot or bishop was replaced for a day by a common monk, who would order his superiors to do the most menial or ridiculous tasks. "The joke of the day is to deceive persons by sending them upon frivolous and nonsensical errands; to pretend they are wanted when they are not, or, in fact, any way to betray them into some supposed ludicrous situation, so as to enable you to call them 'An April Fool.' "—Brady's *Clavis Calendaria*, 1812.

AZALEA FESTIVAL. Apr 1–30. Muskogee, OK. One of the oldest and most celebrated public parks in the southwest: 122 acres, 40 acres of manicured gardens with 30,000 azaleas of 625 varieties. Ranked in the top 100 events by the National Bus Association. Annually in April since 1967. Many related events take place during the month, including a parade and a chili cookoff. Contact Muskogee Convention and Tourism for specific dates and events. Est attendance: 300,000. For info: Ervalene Jenkins, Muskogee Conv and Tourism, PO Box 2361, Muskogee, OK 74402. Phone: (888) 687-6137. Fax: (918) 684-6364. E-mail: tourism@ok.azalea.net.

BATTLE OF OKINAWA BEGINS: ANNIVERSARY. Apr 1, 1945. On Easter Sunday, the US 10th Army began operation *Iceberg*, the invasion of the Ryukyu Islands of Okinawa. Ground troops numbering 180,000 plus 368,000 men in support services made a total of 548,000 troops involved—the biggest amphibious operation of the Pacific war.

BECOME A YARDNERD™ MONTH. Apr 1–30. YardNerds™ everywhere celebrate the benefits of yardening this month. YardNerds™ know that it isn't about being or even becoming an expert but rather about enjoying yourself while creating the yard of your dreams. It's about tending to your yard as a way of tending to your soul—almost like planting hope. For info: Merrell Stevenson, PO Box 373, Columbia, SC 29202. Phone: (803) 782-7225. Fax: (803) 782-4427. Web: www.yardnerd.com.

BOOMER BONUS DAY. Apr 1. Aging Baby Boomers do not look forward to birthdays. This is a non-threatening (no extra years added) day to celebrate for the over-50 crowd only! On Apr 1 because the whole thing gets to be a joke—the body goes . . . but the mind still thinks it's 21! For info: Gaye Andersen, Davenport University, 8200 Georgia St, Merrillville, IN 46410. Phone: (219) 650-5218. Fax: (219) 756-8911. E-mail: gaye.andersen@davenport.edu.

BRIDGE OVER THE NEPONSET: ANNIVERSARY. Apr 1, 1634. The first bridge built in the US spanned the Neponset River between Milton and Dorchester, MA. The authority to build the bridge and an adjoining mill was issued to Israel Stoughton on this date by the Massachusetts General Court.

BULGARIA: SAINT LASARUS'S DAY. Apr 1. Ancient Slavic holiday of young girls, in honor of the goddess of spring and love.

CALIFORNIA EARTHQUAKE PREPAREDNESS MONTH. Apr 1–30. 21st annual. Earthquakes are a constant concern in California. For the Los Angeles area, television station KTLA has a "Care & Prepare" earthquake readiness campaign. For info: Southern California Earthquake Center, USC, 3651 Trousdale Parkway, Ste 169, Los Angeles, CA 90089-0742. Phone: (213) 740-5843. E-mail: SCECinfo@usc.edu. Web: www.scec.org or ktla.trb.com/news/local/earthquake.

CANADA: NUNAVUT INDEPENDENCE: 5th ANNIVERSARY. Apr 1, 1999. Nunavut became Canada's third independent territory. This self-governing territory with an Inuit majority was created from the eastern half of the Northwest Territories.

★ **CANCER CONTROL MONTH.** Apr 1–30.

CHILD ABUSE PREVENTION MONTH. Apr 1–30. In 1979 The National Exchange Club adopted the prevention of child abuse as its national project and established The National Exchange Club Foundation. The Foundation is a chartered nonprofit corporation in Ohio. The Foundation has established nearly 100 Exchange Club Child Abuse Prevention Centers throughout the United States. More than 140,000 families and 190,000 children have received services from the Exchange Club Child Abuse Prevention network. For info: The Natl Exchange Club Foundation, 3050 Central Ave, Toledo, OH 43606-1700. Phone: (419) 535-3232 or (800) 760-3413. Fax: (419) 535-1989. E-mail: info@preventchildabuse.com. Web: www.preventchildabuse.com.

CIGARETTE ADVERTISING BANNED: ANNIVERSARY. Apr 1, 1970. Radio and television ads for cigarettes were banned by legislation signed by President Nixon on this date. The ban went into effect Jan 1, 1971.

COMMUNITY SPIRIT DAYS. Apr 1–30. During the 30 days of April each community collects items at a central point for distribution to local charities, conducts special projects to help the local populace, congregates the town's nonprofit groups and businesses, thanks all participants and presents the community's Spirit of America Foundation Awards for outstanding volunteerism. For info: Daniel R. Mower, Spirit of America Foundation, PO Box 5637, Augusta, ME 04332. Phone: (207) 622-8870.

COUPLE APPRECIATION MONTH. Apr 1–30. To show thanks for each other's love and emotional support. Do something special to reinforce and celebrate your relationship. Annually, the month of April. For info: Donald Etkes, PhD, PMB 148, 112 Harvard Ave, Claremont, CA 91711. Phone: (909) 981-7333.

DEFEAT AT FIVE FORKS: ANNIVERSARY. Apr 1, 1865. After withdrawing to Five Forks, VA, Confederate troops under George Pickett were defeated and cut off by Union troops. This defeat, according to many military historians, sealed the immediate fate of Robert E. Lee's armies at Petersburg and Richmond. On Apr 2, Lee informed Confederate President Jefferson Davis that he would have to evacuate Richmond. Davis and his cabinet fled by train to Danville, VA.

"THE DOCTORS" TV PREMIERE: ANNIVERSARY. Apr 1, 1963. "The Doctors" premiered on NBC on the same day as ABC's long-running soap "General Hospital," providing viewers with a double dose of medical drama. The show was set at Hope Memorial Hospital and began as an anthology series that was subsequently transformed into a serial in 1964. "The Doctors" ran for 19 years. Ellen Burstyn, Anna Stuart, Nancy Pinkerton, Jonathan Hogan, Julia Duffy and Alec Baldwin are some of its famous alums.

EMPOWERED WOMEN ENTREPRENEURS DAY. Apr 1. This event is for women entrepreneurs who are dedicated to igniting their business and fueling their souls. Powerful and visionary women can gain strength and inspiration from each other. For info: Christine Kloser, Network for Empowering Women Entrepreneurs, 3811 Lyceum Ave, Los Angeles, CA 90066. Phone: (310) 745-0794. E-mail: ck@newentrepreneurs.com. Web: www.newentrepreneurs.com.

FRESH FLORIDA TOMATO MONTH. Apr 1–30. To publicize the Florida tomato as a versatile, nutritious, flavorful food. For info: Anita Fial, Lewis & Neale, Inc, 49 E 21st St, 8th Flr, New York, NY 10010. Phone: (212) 420-8808. Fax: (212) 254-2452. E-mail: info@lewis-neale.com.

"GENERAL HOSPITAL" TV PREMIERE: ANNIVERSARY. Apr 1, 1963. "General Hospital," ABC's longest-running soap, revolves around the denizens of fictional Port Charles, NY. "GH" was created by Doris and Frank Hursley. John Beradino, who was with the show from the beginning until his death in May 1996, played the role of Dr. Steve Hardy, upstanding director of medicine and pillar of the community. In the '80s, story lines became unusual with plots involving international espionage, mob activity and aliens. The wedding of supercouple Luke and Laura (Anthony Geary and Genie Francis) was a ratings topper. By the '90s, stories moved away from high-powered action to more conventional romance. Many actors received their big break on the show, including Demi Moore, Janine Turner, Jack Wagner, Richard Dean Anderson, Rick Springfield, John Stamos, Emma Samms, Mark Hamill, Finola Hughes, Ricky Martin and Tia Carrere.

GOLDEN RULE WEEK. Apr 1–7. The purpose of this week is to remind everyone of the importance of the Golden Rule in making this a better world in which we all may live. For a copy of the Golden Rule of 10 religions, send $5 to cover printing and postage. For info: Dr. S.J. Drake, Pres, Intl Society of Friendship and Goodwill, 999 Hood Rd, Ste 127, Marietta, GA 30068. Phone: (770) 565-2322. E-mail: ISFGW@bellsouth.net.

GRANGE MONTH. Apr 1–30. State and local recognition for Grange's contribution to rural/urban America. Celebrated at National Headquarters at Washington, DC, and in all states with local, county and state Granges. Begun in 1867, the National Grange is the oldest US rural community service, family-oriented organization with a special interest in agriculture. Annually, the month of April. Est attendance: 3,000. For info: Clyde Berry, The Natl Grange, 1616 H St NW, Washington, DC 20006. Phone: (202) 628-3507 or (888) 4-GRANGE. Fax: (202) 347-1091. E-mail: program_resource@nationalgrange.org. Web: www.nationalgrange.org

HARVEY, WILLIAM: BIRTH ANNIVERSARY. Apr 1, 1578 (OS). Physician, born at Folkestone, England. The first to discover the mechanics of the circulation of the blood. Died at Roehampton, England, June 3, 1657 (OS).

HOLY HUMOR MONTH. Apr 1–30. To recognize the healing power of Christian joy, humor and celebration; to be "Fools for Christ" on April Fools' Day (Apr 1); to celebrate "Holy Humor Sunday," the Sunday after Easter (Apr 18). Churches and prayer groups nationwide participate. For info: Rev. C. Alan Harvey, The Fellowship of Merry Christians, PO Box 895, Portage, MI 49081-0895. Phone: (863) 294-3121. Fax: (269) 324-3984. E-mail: joyfulnz@aol.com. Web: www.joyfulnoiseletter.com.

```
                S   M   T   W   T   F   S
   April                        1   2   3
                4   5   6   7   8   9  10
   2004        11  12  13  14  15  16  17
               18  19  20  21  22  23  24
               25  26  27  28  29  30
```

HOME IMPROVEMENT TIME. Apr 1–Sept 30. To explain the investment advantages of spending disposable income for home improvement to create better family living and improved community environment. Editorial package includes approximately 100 camera-ready stories and photos free to editors. Also available on disk. (May is a promotion focal point.) For info: James A. Stewart, Jr, Home Improvement Time, PO Box 247, Oakdale, PA 15071-0247. Phone: (412) 787-2881. Fax: (412) 787-3233. E-mail: hitdirect@aol.com. Web: homeimprovementtime.com.

INFORMED WOMAN MONTH. Apr 1–30. You owe it to yourself to feel happy and fulfilled. To have confidence that you're in charge of your life and you're guiding it in the right direction. You can have whatever you want, but you need to determine what you need to know, where to go and whom to contact. Discover how to enjoy better living today and learn how to become a more informed and aware individual for the future. Ideas and tips for the month available for $2.50. For info: Lorrie Marsiglio, PO Box 284-CC, Wasco, IL 60183-0284. Phone: (630) 584-9368.

INTERNATIONAL CUSTOMER LOYALTY MONTH. Apr 1–30. We highlight this month to honor and generate customer loyalty! Even though building customer loyalty should be a year-round thing, not just a month, take this month to strategize on how you can improve on relationships with your customers through better service, higher quality, etc. For info: Shep Hyken, Shepard Presentations, 711 Old Ballas Rd, #215, St. Louis, MO 63141. Phone: (314) 696-2200. E-mail: Shep@hyken.com. Web: www.hyken.com.

INTERNATIONAL LEGACY MONTH. Apr 1–30. A month to focus on the legacy you are leaving for your family, friends, colleagues, career and community. What you have to be remembered for depends on what you do today. Let this month be the opportunity you've been waiting for, inspire yourself and others to leave enduring gifts and create yesterdays worth remembering. For info: Janna Krammer, Legacy Institute, 42747 Blackhawk Rd, Harris, MN 55032. Phone: (877) 646-9100. Fax: (651) 674-0228. E-mail: info@legacyinstitute.com.

INTERNATIONAL TWIT AWARD MONTH. Apr 1–30. Any famous name (celebrity with the worst sense of humor) is eligible for most Tiresome Wit (TWIT) of 2004. For info: Lauren Barnett, Lone Star Publications of Humor, 8452 Fredericksburg Rd, #103, San Antonio, TX 78229. E-mail: lspubs@aol.com. Web: members.aol.com/lspubs/lsindex.html.

INTERNATIONAL WORK LIFE ENRICHMENT MONTH. Apr 1–30. Take the next 30 days to focus on improving the quality of your life and work. Also, use this month to activate and celebrate improvements in your workplace. Individuals will gain more work satisfaction. Employers will gain more productive employees. For info: Gloria Dunn, Pres, Wiser Ways to Work®, PO Box 150869, San Rafael, CA 94915. Phone: (415) 479-8226. E-mail: gloria@wiserwaystowork.com. Web: www.wiserwaystowork.com.

IRAN: ISLAMIC REPUBLIC DAY. Apr 1. National holiday. Commemorates the approval of the new consitution of the Islamic Republic of Iran in 1979.

KINGSVILLE INTERNATIONAL YOUNG PERFORMERS' COMPETITIONS WITH THE ISABEL SCIONTI PIANO SOLO COMPETITIONS. Apr 1–3. Texas A&M University–Kingsville, TX. 23rd annual international music competition for performers of classical music. Prodigies and aspiring concert artists under age 26 compete in separate contests for piano solo and orchestral instruments. Cash prizes total about $25,000. Performance awards with orchestra and in recital offered. All contest events—including string, woodwind and brass master classes given by concert artist–contest judges—are free and open to the public. Contestant's entry fee $35; deadline Jan 21, 2004. Sponsor: Music Club of Kingsville, Inc (affiliate of National Federation and Texas Federation of Music Clubs). Est attendance: 1,500. For info: Mary or James Tryer, 1222 W Lee,

☆ Chase's 2004 Calendar of Events ☆   Apr 1

Kingsville, TX 78363. Phone: (361) 592-2374. E-mail: youngperf @hotmail.com. Web: www.kingsvillemusic.com.

LAUGH AT WORK WEEK. Apr 1–7. Laughter and humor are an important part of the workplace. Benefits of laughing at work include improved productivity, teamwork, communication, stress relief, job satisfaction and employee retention. This week, which begins on April Fools' Day, focuses on the very serious business of humor. For info: Randall Munson, Creatively Speaking®, 508 Meadow Run Dr SW, Rochester, MN 55902-2337. Phone: (507) 286-1331. Fax: (507) 286-1331. E-mail: humor@creativelyspeaking.com. Web: www.CreativelySpeaking.com.

LUPUS ALERT DAY. Apr 1. Don't be fooled by lupus! To call attention to the confusing characteristics of this potentially fatal autoimmune disease that mimics other, less serious illnesses. For info: Duane Peters, VP of Communications and Advocacy, Lupus Foundation of America, 2000 L St NW, Ste 710, Washington, DC 20036. Phone: (202) 349-1145. Fax: (202) 349-1156. E-mail: peters@lupus.org. Web: www.lupus.org.

MEDICATION SAFETY WEEK. Apr 1–7. Seven focus days to raise awareness about medication safety and offer strategies to reduce risk, including Cards4Life self-management system, free on our website. Brown-bag your medicine bottles and herbals that you are taking and have your questions or concerns answered by a pharmacist. A Medication Safety PowerPoint program is available on our website's Health Library page. For info: Women's Heart Foundation, PO Box 7827, West Trenton, NJ 08628. Phone: (609) 771-9600. Fax: (609) 771-9427. E-mail: admin@womensheartfoundation.org. Web: www.womensheartfoundation.org.

MONTH OF THE YOUNG CHILD®. Apr 1–30. Michigan. To promote awareness of the importance of young children and their specific needs in today's society. Many communities celebrate with special events for children and families. For info: Michigan Assn for Education of Young Children, Beacon Pl, Ste 1-D, 4572 S Hagadorn Rd, East Lansing, MI 48823-5385. Phone: (800) 336-6424 or (517) 336-9700. Fax: (517) 336-9790. E-mail: moyc@miaeyc.org. Web: www.miaeyc.org.

MULE DAY. Apr 1–4. Columbia, TN. Started in 1934 as Breeders Day when mules were brought into town to be sold and traded. Today this homecoming is celebrated with arts and crafts, flea market, knife show and a huge parade. Est attendance: 250,000. For info: Mule Day, PO Box 66, Columbia, TN 38402. Phone: (931) 381-9557. E-mail: muleday@bellsouth.net.

NATIONAL AUTISM AWARENESS MONTH. Apr 1–30. A month filled with autism awareness events such as conferences, presentations, displays and media attention. Contact the NJ Center for Outreach & Services for the Autism Community for information on how you can become an "Autism Awareness Ambassador." For info: Courtney Knox, COSAC, 1450 Parkside Ave, Ste 22, Ewing, NJ 08638. Phone: (609) 863-8100. Fax: (609) 883-5509. E-mail: information@njcosac.org. Web: www.njcosac.org.

NATIONAL CAR CARE MONTH. Apr 1–30. To educate motorists about the importance of maintaining their cars in an effort to improve air quality, highway safety and fuel conservation. For info: Car Care Council, 4600 East-West Hwy, Ste 300, Bethesda, MD 20814. Phone: (240) 333-1088. Fax: (301) 654-3299. E-mail: info@carcare.org. Web: www.carcare.org.

★**NATIONAL CHILD ABUSE PREVENTION MONTH.** Apr 1–30.

NATIONAL CHILD ABUSE PREVENTION MONTH. Apr 1–30. For info: Natl Committee to Prevent Child Abuse, 200 S Michigan Ave, 17th Fl, Chicago, IL 60604. Phone: (312) 663-3520. Web: www.preventchildabuse.org.

NATIONAL DONATE LIFE MONTH. Apr 1–30. Formerly known as National Organ and Tissue Donor Awareness Week, this observance expanded to a full month in 2003. The purpose is to encourage Americans to consider organ and tissue donation and to sign donor cards when getting a driver's license. For info: US Dept of Health and Human Services, 200 Independence Av SW, Washington, DC 20201. Phone: (877) 696-6775 or (202) 619-0257. Web: www.organdonor.gov.

NATIONAL FUN AT WORK DAY. Apr 1. Today and every day the workplace should be spiced with fun, laughter and a playful attitude. Morale will increase, productivity will soar and the bottom line will improve. For info: Matt Weinstein, Playfair, 2207 Oregon St, Berkeley, CA 94705. Phone: (510) 540-8768. Fax: (510) 540-7638. E-mail: playfair1@aol.com. Web: www.playfair.com.

NATIONAL HUMOR MONTH. Apr 1–30. 28th anniversary. Focuses on the joy and therapeutic value of laughter and how it can reduce stress, improve job performance and enrich the quality of life. For info send 68 cent SASE to: Larry Wilde, Dir, The Carmel Institute of Humor, 25470 Canada Dr, Carmel, CA 93923-8926. Web: www.larrywilde.com.

NATIONAL KITE MONTH. Apr 1–May 2. Celebrates kiting with more than 600 events throughout the country, including kite festivals, kitemaking classes for kids and adults, kitemaking classes in schools, kite displays in museums and public libraries and "fun flys" at local parks and beaches. For info: Jim M. Miller, Program Mgr, Kite Trade Assn Intl, 36467 Sandsu Circle, Rancho Mirage, CA 92270. Phone: (760) 202-9391. Fax: (760) 324-5636. E-mail: Admin@NationalKiteMonth.org. Web: www.NationalKiteMonth.org.

NATIONAL KNUCKLES DOWN MONTH. Apr 1–30. To recognize and revive the American tradition of playing and collecting marbles and keep it rolling along. Please send SASE with inquiries. For info: Cathy C. Runyan-Svacina, The Marble Lady, 7812 NW Hampton Rd, Kansas City, MO 64152. Phone: (816) 587-8687. Fax: (816) 587-8687. Web: www.themarblelady.com.

NATIONAL LANDSCAPE ARCHITECTURE MONTH. April 1–30. Investigate what landscapers do to beautify our grounds—both personal and public. Many architects will have site tours, exhibits, school visits and community projects this week. Annually, during April, as Apr 26 is the birth anniversary of Frederick Law Olmsted. Olmsted is widely regarded as the founder of the profession of landscape architecture in North America. For info: Jeffrey Lofton, APR, ASLA, 636 I Street NW, Washington, DC 20001. Phone: (202) 216-2331. Fax: (202) 898-1187. E-mail: jlofton@asla.org. Web: www.asla.org/lamonth/index.html.

NATIONAL LAWN AND GARDEN MONTH. Apr 1–30. National celebration highlighting the benefits of landscape and lawn care in the new millennium. Annually, the month of April. For info: Vicki Bendure, Associated Landscape Contractors of America (ALCA), 150 Elden St, Ste 270, Herndon, VA 20170. Phone: (703) 736-9666. Fax: (703) 736-9668. Web: www.alca.org.

NATIONAL OCCUPATIONAL THERAPY MONTH. Apr 1–30. To recognize the services and accomplishments of occupational therapy practitioners and promote awareness of the benefits of occupational therapy. For info: The American Occupational Therapy Assn, Inc, 4720 Montgomery Lane, PO Box 31220, Bethesda, MD 20824-1220. Phone: (301) 652-2682. TDD (800) 377-8555. Fax: (301) 652-7711. E-mail: praota@aota.org. Web: www.aota.org.

Apr 1 ☆ *Chase's 2004 Calendar of Events* ☆

NATIONAL PARKINSON'S AWARENESS MONTH. Apr 1–30. To help enhance the public education and awareness about Parkinson's disease by providing information on treatment, medication, support and research, as well as providing these resources to patients with the disease and their caregivers, helping to improve the quality of life for both. For info: National Parkinson Foundation, 1501 NW 9th Ave, Miami, FL 33136. Phone: (800) 327-4545. Web: www.parkinson.org.

NATIONAL PECAN MONTH. Apr 1–30. A celebration of the great taste, health benefits and versatility of pecans. This delicious tree nut native to North America adds unmistakable flavor, crunch and texture to just about any meal or snack. Pecans have proven cholesterol-lowering properties and contain more than 19 important vitamins and minerals. Almost 90 percent of the fats in pecans are of the heart-healthy, unsaturated variety. For info: Natl Pecan Shellers Assn, 5775 Peachtree-Dunwoody Rd, Ste 500, Bldg G, Atlanta, GA 30342. Phone: (404) 252-3663. Fax: (404) 252-0774. E-mail: npsa@assnhq.com. Web: www.ilovepecans.org.

NATIONAL PET FIRST AID AWARENESS MONTH. Apr 1–30. Sponsored by Pet Tech, Inc, the first national training center for pet first aid & care. To help pet owners everywhere in understanding the importance of knowing the skills and techniques of pet first aid, CPR & care for their pet. For info: Pet Tech, Inc, 5800 Severin Dr, La Mesa, CA 91942. Phone: (619) 589-7475. E-mail: info@pettech.net. Web: www.pettech.net.

NATIONAL POETRY MONTH. Apr 1–30. Annual observance to pay tribute to the great legacy and ongoing achievement of American poets and the vital place of poetry in American culture. In a proclamation issued in honor of the first observance, President Bill Clinton called it "a welcome opportunity to celebrate not only the unsurpassed body of literature produced by our poets in the past, but also the vitality and diversity of voices reflected in the works of today's American poets. . . . Their creativity and wealth of language enrich our culture and inspire a new generation of Americans to learn the power of reading and writing at its best." Spearheaded by the Academy of American Poets, this is the largest and most extensive celebration of poetry in American history. For info: Academy of American Poets, 588 Broadway, Ste 1203, New York, NY 10012-3210. Phone: (212) 274-0343. Web: www.poets.org.

NATIONAL PREPARE TO BUY A HOME MONTH. Apr 1–30. The National Association of Independent Real Estate Brokers would like to encourage prospective home buyers to consult with an independent real estate broker for information about the best ways to buy your new home. For info: Gary Bryce Conner, NAIREB, 7102 Mardyke Ln, Indianapolis, IN 46226. Phone: (317) 547-4679. Fax: (317) 547-4634. E-mail: GaryConner@NationalRealEstateBrokers.org. Web: www.NationalRealEstateBrokers.org.

NATIONAL SEXUAL ASSAULT AWARENESS AND PREVENTION MONTH. Apr 1–30. Every two minutes, somewhere in America, another person is sexually assaulted. During this month, efforts are focused on raising awareness of sexual assault, promoting legislative efforts to address sexual violence, lauding efforts of more than 10,000 volunteers across the US who assist in crisis services and related areas, promoting resources for victims such as the National Sexual Assault Hotline (800-656-HOPE) and, above all, demonstrating solidarity with victims of sexual assault. Celebrated nationally by RAINN, state sexual assault coalitions, local rape crisis centers and other similar organizations. Passed by US Senate Joint Resolution (SJRes 8). For info: Rape, Abuse & Incest National Network (RAINN), 635-B Pennsylvania Ave SE, Washington, DC 20003. Phone: (202) 544-1034 or (800) 656-HOPE (hotline). Fax: (202) 544-3556. E-mail: info@rainn.org. Web: www.rainn.org.

NATIONAL SEXUALLY TRANSMITTED DISEASES (STDs) EDUCATION AND AWARENESS MONTH. Apr 1–30. To educate consumers, patients, students and professionals about the prevention of sexually transmitted diseases. Kit of materials available for $15. For info: Frederick Mayer, Pharmacists Planning Service, Inc, 101 Lucas Valley Rd, #210, San Rafael, CA 94903. E-mail: ppsi@aol.com. Web: www.ppsinc.org.

NATIONAL SOFT PRETZEL MONTH. Apr 1–30. Recognizes and celebrates soft pretzels as one of America's favorite snack foods—Americans eat more than 700 million soft pretzels a year! Sponsored by J&J Snack Foods Corp, manufacturers of SUPERPRETZEL®, the #1 selling soft pretzel brand in the world. Special promotional emphasis is placed on SUPERPRETZEL® during the month of April. For info: J&J Snack Foods, 6000 Central Highway, Pennsauken, NJ 08109. Phone: (856) 665-9533. Web: www.jjsnack.com.

NATIONAL WOODWORKING MONTH™. Apr 1–30. To focus attention on the beauty and satisfaction of working with wood. To help motivate Americans to undertake woodworking projects to improve their home and general surroundings. To increase consumers' knowledge and skill in woodworking and wood-finishing endeavors. For info: Donna Wisecup, VP Account Supervisor, Brushfire Marketing Communications, Minwax® Natl Woodworking Month™ Program, 110 S Jefferson Rd, Whippany, NJ 07981.

NATIONAL YOUTH SPORTS SAFETY MONTH. Apr 1–30. Bringing public attention to the prevalent problem of injuries in youth sports. This event promotes safety in sports activities and is supported by more than 60 national sports and medical organizations. Resource material available on website. For info: Exec Dir, Natl Youth Sports Safety Fdtn, One Beacon St, Ste 3333, Boston, MA 02108. Phone: (617) 367-6677. Fax: (617) 722-9999. E-mail: NYSSF@aol.com. Web: www.nyssf.org.

PHARMACISTS WAR ON DIABETES. Apr 1–30. Educate consumers, patients and healthcare professionals about prevention of diabetes, especially focusing on "Know Your Numbers for Diabetes" and screening along with awareness and interest in the diabetes epidemic. Kits available for $15. For info: Fred Mayer, Pharmacists Planning Service, Inc (PPSI), c/o the Pharmacy Council on Diabetes Education (PCDE), 101 Lucas Valley Rd; Ste 210, San Rafael, CA 94903. E-mail: ppsi@aol.com. Web: www.ppsinc.org.

PHYSICAL WELLNESS MONTH. Apr 1–30. Time to get in shape for summer! Shed those winter clothes and extra pounds, and rejuvenate your body with healthy eating, restful sleep, vigorous exercise and a new look. Jog, swim, bike, rollerskate, play tennis, go hiking or backpacking. Spend time daily outdoor breathing in fresh air, and take time to relax. Retire to bed early for restful sleep and wake up early feeling refreshed and energized. For info: Angela Brown, Words of Wellness, PO Box 49266, Charlotte, NC 28277. Phone: (704) 849-2900. Fax: (704) 845-3060. E-mail: Angela@WordsofWellness.com. Web: www.WordsofWellness.com.

PREVENT INJURIES AMERICA! Apr 1–30. Move Better, Play Better, Live Better. Learn about preventing orthopaedic injuries and conditions. Throughout the month, orthopaedic surgeons will provide injury prevention information on topics such as preventing playground and sports injuries, osteoporosis, workplace injuries, low back pain and proper shoewear tips. For info: American Academy of Orthopaedic Surgeons, 6300 N River Rd, Rosemont, IL 60018. Phone: (847) 823-7186. Fax: (847) 823-7268. Web: www.aaos.org.

April 2004	S	M	T	W	T	F	S
					1	2	3
	4	5	6	7	8	9	10
	11	12	13	14	15	16	17
	18	19	20	21	22	23	24
	25	26	27	28	29	30	

☆ Chase's 2004 Calendar of Events ☆   Apr 1

PREVENTION OF ANIMAL CRUELTY MONTH. Apr 1–30. The ASPCA sponsors this crucial month which is designed to educate Americans about animal cruelty and to urge them to report any instances of violence toward animals. For info: ASPCA Media Relations Dept, 424 E 92nd St, New York, NY 10128. Phone: (212) 876-7700 x 4655. E-mail: press@aspca.org. Web: www.aspca.org.

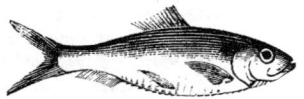

PRO-AM SNIPE EXCURSION AND HUNT. Apr 1. Moultrie, GA. Celebrating the time-honored custom of snipe hunting. The denim snipe has come back from the brink of extinction and will be honored at the 2003 event which will include a Snipe Parade, a Snipe Ball and festivities at the Denim Wing of the Snipe Museum at New Elm, GA. New Snipe-O-Rama racing oval open! Annually, Apr 1. For info: Beth Gay, PO Box 2828, Moultrie, GA 31776. Phone: (229) 985-6540.

RAM, JAGJIVAN: BIRTH ANNIVERSARY. Apr 1, 1908. Indian political leader and coworker with Mohandas K. Gandhi and Jawaharlal Nehru in the fight for Indian independence. Born into a family of "untouchables" at the village of Chandwa, Bihar, India, Ram was one of the first of that class to attend school and university. Known as the champion and spokesman for India's 100 million untouchables, he overcame most of the handicaps of caste. He served in a number of ministerial cabinet posts and twice was a candidate for prime minister. Ram died at New Delhi, India, July 6, 1986.

ROBERT THE HERMIT: DEATH ANNIVERSARY. Apr 1, 1832. One of the most famous hermits in American history died in his hermitage at Seekonk, MA. Robert was a bonded slave, the son of an African mother and probably an Anglo-Saxon father. After obtaining his freedom, he was swindled out of it and shipped to a foreign slave market, then later escaped to America. He was separated from his first wife by force and rejected by his second wife after a long sea voyage, before withdrawing from society.

SCHMECKFEST. Apr 1–3. Freeman, SD. Sausage and sauerkraut, kuchen and pluma moos. These are just a few of the dishes served at this German "festival of tasting" where visitors can also watch cooking and craft demonstrations and an evening musical. Est attendance: 4,000. For info: Kathy Kleinsasser, Schmeckfest, 43639 277th St, Freeman, SD 57029. Phone: (605) 925-7952.

SCHOOL LIBRARY MEDIA MONTH. Apr 1–30. Celebrates the work of school library media specialists in our nation's elementary and secondary schools. For info: American Assn of School Librarians, American Library Assn, 50 E Huron St, Chicago, IL 60611. Phone: (800) 545-2433. E-mail: AASL@ala.org. Web: www.ala.org/aasl.

SKAGIT VALLEY TULIP FESTIVAL. Apr 1–30. Skagit County, La Conner, Mount Vernon, Burlington, WA. To celebrate and share the spectacular beauty of more than 1,000 acres of blooming daffodils and tulips that herald the arrival of spring in the Skagit Valley of Washington state. Est attendance: 500,000. For info: Cindy Verge, SVTF Exec Dir, PO Box 1784, Mount Vernon, WA 98273. Phone: (360) 428-5959. Fax: (360) 428-6753. E-mail: info@tulipfestival.org. Web: www.tulipfestival.org.

SORRY CHARLIE DAY. Apr 1. To honor Charlie the Tuna, who has been rejected for 42 years and still keeps his spunk. A day to recognize anyone who has been rejected and lived through it. Join the "Sorry Charlie, No-Fan-Club-for-You Club" by sending in your best rejection story. Please send SASE with inquiries. For info: Cathy Runyan-Svacina, 7812 NW Hampton Rd, Kansas City, MO 64152. Phone: (816) 587-8687. Fax: (816) 587-8687.

SOYFOODS MONTH. Apr 1–30. Soyfoods Month is a key time to provide up-to-date, exciting information on new soy products, soy and health research, soyfood sales, and the soyfoods industry to retailers, consumers, and members of the press. For info: Soyfoods Assn of North America, 1001 Connecticut Ave NW, Ste 1120, Washington, DC 20036. Phone: (202) 659-3520. Fax: (202) 659-3522. E-mail: info@soyfoods.org. Web: www.soyfoods.org.

SPORTS EYE SAFETY MONTH. Apr 1–30. From major league stadiums to small town courts, America's favorite pastimes are great memories for many, but for many athletes those memories are ruined by preventable eye injuries. Sports Eye Safety Month seeks to inform the public that whatever their game, whatever their age, they need to protect their vision by wearing sport-specific protective eyewear while playing. With protective eyewear, 90% of sports eye injuries can be prevented. For info: American Academy of Opthalmology, PO Box 7424, San Francisco, CA 94120. Phone: (415) 561-8525. Fax: (415) 561-8533. E-mail: eyemd@aao.org. Web: www.medem.com/eyemd.

STRAW HAT MONTH. Apr 1–30. A month of celebration during which the felt hat is put aside in favor of the straw or fabric hat by both men and women. Local businesses and the media are encouraged to plan hat-related activities. Annually, coordinated with Easter. For info: Casey Bush, Exec Dir, Headwear Info Bureau, 302 W 12 St, PH-C, New York, NY 10014. Phone: (212) 627-8333. E-mail: milicase@aol.com. Web: www.hatsny.com/hib.

STRESS AWARENESS MONTH. Apr 1–30. To promote public awareness of what stress is, what causes it to occur and what can be done about it. A monthlong focus on the dangers of stress, successful coping strategies and the myths about stress that are prevalent in our society. For info: Morton C. Orman, MD, Dir, The Health Resource Network, 908 Cold Bottom Rd, Sparks, MD 21152. Web: www.stresscure.com.

SWITZERLAND: NAFELS PILGRIMAGE. Apr 1. Canton Glarus. Commemoration of the Battle of Nafels, fought on Apr 9, 1388. Observed annually on first Thursday in April, with processions, prayers, sermon and a reading out of the names of those killed in the battle.

TACKLE YOUR CLUTTER MONTH. Apr 1–30. Sponsored by ClosetMaid to encourage people to "tackle their clutter and bring order back into their homes." This means tackling clutter in every room in the house including the garage, basement, kitchen, bedrooms and closets; eliminating items you don't need (such as clothes that don't fit, clothes you don't wear, worn out shoes) and organizing what you keep. Please donate gently worn clothes or working condition appliances to charity. (If you have any doubts, call ahead to see if the charitable organization you have in mind can use your donation.) For info: ClosetMaid, PO Box 4400, Ocala, FL 34478. Web: www.closetmaid.com.

TESTICULAR CANCER AWARENESS WEEK. Apr 1–7. This public awareness and education program was conceived in 1997 to create a better public understanding of the dangers of undetected testicular cancer in young men ages 15–34. The campaign is designed to promote the importance of early detection, which saves hundreds of young men's lives each year. A free self-exam reminder is available at menstuff-testicular-exam-subscribe@topica.com, so that a monthly self-exam becomes a habit for health. Information is made available to high school and college health centers to ensure correct diagnosis. For info: National Men's Resource Center, PO Box 800-CH, San Anselmo, CA 94979. E-mail: tcaw@tcaw.org. Web: www.tcaw.org.

TOUR de CURE. Apr 1–June 30. Thousands of cyclists participate in the American Diabetes Association's annual cycling event to raise money to help find a cure for diabetes and to provide information and resources to improve the lives of all people affected by diabetes. Tours are held in more than 90 communities across America and participants are asked to raise a minimum of $75 in pledges. Contact your local affiliate for the date in your area. For info: (888) 342-2383 or www.diabetes.org.

US AIR FORCE ACADEMY ESTABLISHED: 50th ANNIVERSARY. Apr 1, 1954. President Dwight Eisenhower signed the bill this day that created the US Air Force Academy to train officers for the Air Force. Construction on the Colorado Springs, CO, academy began July 11, 1955, and ended in 1958. The academy was accredited in 1959. Women were admitted in 1976. For more info: www.usafa.edu.

Apr 1–2 ☆ *Chase's 2004 Calendar of Events* ☆

US HOUSE OF REPRESENTATIVES ACHIEVES A QUORUM: ANNIVERSARY. Apr 1, 1789. First session of Congress was held Mar 4, 1789, but not enough representatives arrived to achieve a quorum until Apr 1.

WOMEN'S EYE HEALTH AND SAFETY MONTH. Apr 1–30. Women often manage family health concerns. Do you know how to protect your sight? Hormonal changes, age and even the sun can endanger sight. Information on women's and family eye-health issues will be provided. For info: Prevent Blindness America®, 500 E Remington Rd, Schaumburg, IL 60173. Phone: (800) 331-2020. Fax: (847) 843-8458. Web: www.preventblindness.org.

WORLD HABITAT AWARENESS MONTH. Apr 1–30. A worldwide observance for the need to protect the habitat of all Earth's creatures, to make a conscious effort to preserve nature's ecosystems. Annually, the entire month of April. For info: Teresa Evans, ARK (Animalkind Rescue Kids), PO Box 1271, San Luis Obispo, CA 93406. Phone: (805) 544-0984. Web: www.ark.mailme.org.

BIRTHDAYS TODAY

David Eisenhower, 57, author (*Eisenhower at War*), lawyer, grandson of former president Dwight Eisenhower, born West Point, NY, Apr 1, 1947.

Ali MacGraw, 65, actress (*Goodbye, Columbus; Love Story*), born Pound Ridge, NY, Apr 1, 1939.

Annette O'Toole, 51, actress (*Smile, 48Hrs*), born Houston, TX, Apr 1, 1953.

Jane Powell, 75, actress (*Seven Brides for Seven Brothers*), born Suzanne Burce, Portland, OR, Apr 1, 1929.

Debbie Reynolds, 72, actress (*Singin' in the Rain, Mother*), born El Paso, TX, Apr 1, 1932.

Libby Riddles, 48, first woman to win the 1,135-mile Iditarod Alaskan dogsled race, born Madison, WI, Apr 1, 1956.

Glenn Edward ("Bo") Schembechler, Jr, 75, former baseball executive and football coach, born Barberton, OH, Apr 1, 1929.

Daniel Joseph ("Rusty") Staub, 60, former baseball player, born New Orleans, LA, Apr 1, 1944.

APRIL 2 — FRIDAY
Day 93 — 273 Remaining

AFRMA DISPLAY AT AMERICA'S FAMILY PET EXPO. Apr 2–4 (tentative). Costa Mesa, CA. Rats and mice are emerging as ideal pets: they provide all the pleasure and satisfaction of a warm, cuddly, intelligent and friendly pet companion. The American Fancy Rat and Mouse Association (AFRMA) was founded in 1983 to promote the breeding and exhibition of fancy rats and mice, to educate the public on their positive qualities as companion animals and to provide information on their proper care. For info: AFRMA (CAE), PO Box 2589, Winnetka, CA 91396-2589. Phone: (909) 685-2350 or (818) 992-5564 or (626) 966-0350. Fax: (818) 592-6590. E-mail: afrma@afrma.org. Web: www.afrma.org.

	S	M	T	W	T	F	S
April					1	2	3
2004	4	5	6	7	8	9	10
	11	12	13	14	15	16	17
	18	19	20	21	22	23	24
	25	26	27	28	29	30	

ALCOHOL-FREE WEEKEND. Apr 2–4. Observance to increase public awareness of the problems associated with drinking alcoholic beverages by asking Americans to refrain from drinking them for this weekend. For info: Public Info Office, Natl Council on Alcoholism and Drug Dependence, Inc, 20 Exchange Pl, New York, NY 10005. Phone: (212) 269-7797. Fax: (212) 269-7510. E-mail: national@ncadd.org. Web: www.ncadd.org.

ANDERSEN, HANS CHRISTIAN: BIRTH ANNIVERSARY. Apr 2, 1805. Author chiefly remembered for his more than 150 fairy tales, many of which are regarded as classics of children's literature. Andersen was born at Odense, Denmark, and died at Copenhagen, Denmark, Aug 4, 1875.

"AS THE WORLD TURNS" TV PREMIERE: ANNIVERSARY. Apr 2, 1956. One of the longest-running soaps currently on the air, "ATWT" premiered on CBS. The series is set in midwestern Oakdale and revolves around the Hughes family and their neighbors. Irma Phillips was the show's creator and head writer. Some of its cast members who made it big are: Meg Ryan, Julianne Moore, Michael Nader, Steven Weber and Swoosie Kurtz.

BARTHOLDI, FREDERIC AUGUSTE: BIRTH ANNIVERSARY. Apr 2, 1834. French sculptor who created *Liberty Enlightening the World* (better known as the Statue of Liberty), which stands at New York Harbor. Also remembered for the *Lion of Belfort* at Belfort, France. Born at Colman, at Alsace, France. Died at Paris, France, Oct 4, 1904.

BIG MUDDY FOLK MUSIC FESTIVAL. Apr 2–3. Thespian Hall, Boonville, MO. Performing folk festival with instructional workshop by artists appearing. Est attendance: 3,000. For info: Maryellen McVicker, Friends of Historic Boonville, PO Box 1776, Boonville, MO 65233. Phone: (660) 882-7977. Fax: (660) 882-9194. E-mail: friendsart@mid-mo.net.

BREAD RIOT AT RICHMOND: ANNIVERSARY. Apr 2, 1863. Indicative of conditions in the Confederate capital of Richmond, VA, an angry mob's demands for bread from a bakery wagon escalated into the destruction of nearby shops. Confederate president Jefferson Davis, in a bold move, stepped into the angry crowd and stated, "We do not desire to injure anyone, but this lawlessness must stop. I will give you five minutes to disperse, otherwise you will be fired upon." The mob dispersed without bloodshed.

CASANOVA, GIOVANNI GIACOMO GIROLAMO: BIRTH ANNIVERSARY. Apr 2, 1725. Celebrated Italian writer-librarian and, by his own account, philanderer, adventurer, rogue, seminarian, soldier and spy, was born at Venice, Italy. As the Chevalier de Seingalt, he died at Dux, Bohemia, June 4, 1798, while serving as librarian and working on his lively and frank *History of My Life*, a brilliant picture of 18th-century life.

CRAFTSMEN'S CLASSIC ARTS & CRAFTS FESTIVAL. Apr 2–4 (tentative). Greensboro Coliseum Complex Special Events Center, Greensboro, NC. 21st annual. Features work from more than 300 talented artists and craftspeople. All juried exhibitors' work has been handmade by the exhibitors and must be their own original design and creation. See the creative process in action with several exhibitors demonstrating their craft. Something for every style, taste, and budget with items from the most contemporary to the most traditional. Est attendance: 20,000. For info: Gilmore Enterprises, Inc, 1240 Oakland Ave, Greensboro, NC 27403. Phone: (336) 274-5550.

"DALLAS" TV PREMIERE: ANNIVERSARY. Apr 2, 1978. Oil tycoons battled for money, power and prestige in this prime-time CBS drama that ran for nearly 13 years. The Ewings and Barneses were Texas's modern-day Hatfields and McCoys. Larry Hagman starred as the devious, scheming womanizer J.R. Ewing. When J.R. was shot in the 1980 season-ending cliffhanger, the revelation of the mystery shooter was the single-most watched episode of its time (it was Kristin, J.R.'s sister-in-law, played by Mary Crosby). Cast members included Jim Davis, Barbara Bel Geddes, Donna Reed, Ted Shackelford, Joan Van Ark (who, along with Shackelford, starred in the spin-off "Knots Landing"), Patrick

Duffy, Linda Gray, Charlene Tilton, David Wayne, Keenan Wynn, Ken Kercheval, Victoria Principal and Steve Kanaly.

DOGWOOD FESTIVAL. Apr 2–25. Lewiston, ID. Art show, arts and crafts fair, wine and beer tasting, concerts and plays. Many sports and recreational events. Est attendance: 40,000. For info: Dogwood Festival, 415 Main, Lewiston, ID 83501. Phone: (208) 792-2243. Fax: (208) 792-2850.

DOLLY'S MUSIC ON PARADE. Apr 2. Pigeon Forge, TN. Dolly Parton serves as grand marshal in the 19th annual parade. Theme-based parade kicks off the spring season. Est attendance: 40,000. For info: Office of Special Events, Pigeon Forge Dept of Tourism, 2450 Parkway, PO Box 3107, Pigeon Forge, TN 37868. Phone: (800) 251-9100 or (865) 429-7350. Web: www.mypigeonforge.com.

EBSEN, BUDDY: BIRTH ANNIVERSARY. Apr 2, 1908. Born Christian Rudolph Ebsen, Jr, at Belleville, IL. Buddy Ebsen started his career as a vaudeville "song-and-dance" man, then was popular throughout the 1930s on film as well. He almost played the Tin Man in *The Wizard of Oz*, (1939), but had a serious allergic reaction to the makeup and was forced to stop filming. In the 1950s, he played Davy Crockett's sidekick on television and film. He played Jed Clampett in "The Beverly Hillbillies" from 1962–1971, and starred as "Barnaby Jones" from 1973–1980. He died at Torrance, CA, July 6, 2003.

"THE EDGE OF NIGHT" TV PREMIERE: ANNIVERSARY. Apr 2, 1956. "The Edge of Night" premiered on CBS along with "As The World Turns." Though the plots initially revolved around crime and courtroom drama, the serial's format soon developed along more conventional soap story lines of romance. The soap shifted to ABC in 1975 but was cancelled in 1984. Larry Hagman, Dixie Carter, Lori Loughlin, Willie Aames and Amanda Blake were some of the show's most prominent players.

FALKLAND ISLANDS WAR: ANNIVERSARY. Apr 2–June 15, 1982. Argentina, claiming sovereignty over the nearby Falkland Islands (called by them the Malvinas), invaded and occupied the British Crown Colony on Apr 2, 1982. British forces defeated the Argentinians on June 15, 1982. About 250 British and 600 Argentine lives were lost in the conflict. In 1986, three military officers, including General Leopoldo Galtieri (who was president of Argentina at the time of the invasion), were convicted and sentenced for the military crime of negligence. Commemorative ceremonies are observed as Malvinas Day on June 13 in Argentina.

FIRST WHITE HOUSE EASTER EGG ROLL: ANNIVERSARY. Apr 2, 1877. The first White House Easter Egg Roll took place during the administration of Rutherford B. Hayes. The traditional event was discontinued by President Franklin D. Roosevelt in 1942 and reinstated Apr 6, 1953, by President Dwight D. Eisenhower.

GUINNESS, SIR ALEC: 90th BIRTH ANNIVERSARY. Apr 2, 1914. Academy Award–winning actor (for *The Bridge on the River Kwai*), born at London, England. An active performer on both stage and screen, his film roles included *Star Wars, A Passage to India* and *Kind Hearts and Coronets*. He died at West Sussex, England, Aug 5, 2000.

HOSPITAL ADMITTING CLERKS DAY. Apr 2. A day set aside to recognize the worthwhile contribution made by Admitting Clerks in hospitals across the United States and Canada. Annually, first Friday in April. For info: Shannon Ouwendyk, 705-6 Ave SE, High River, AB, T1V 1K7 Canada. Phone: (403) 652-4892. E-mail: solo99@shaw.ca.

INTERNATIONAL CHILDREN'S BOOK DAY. Apr 2. Observes Hans Christian Andersen's birthday and commemorates the international aspects of children's literature. Sponsor: International Board on Books for Young People, Nonnenweg 12, Postfach, CH-4003 Basel, Switzerland. For info: USBBY Secretariat, PO Box 8139, Newark, DE 19714-8139. Phone: (302) 731-1600. E-mail: usbby@reading.org.

INTERNATIONAL SING-OUT DAY™. Apr 2. Break out in song today like they do in the musicals. After all, it is better to break OUT than to break up. Sing out (loud and strong) your words in conversations instead of speaking them. You can even add a few dance steps if you like. To alleviate the escalating costs of Eventological® Literature, a charge of $7 must be assessed for each request. Checks are to be made payable to: Adrienne Sioux Koopersmith, 1437 W Rosemont, #1W, Chicago, IL 60660. Phone: (773) 743-5341. Fax: (773) 743-5395. E-mail: la_koop@yahoo.com.

MEDIEVAL FAIR. Apr 2–4. Reaves Park, Norman, OK. Arts and crafts and living history fair. The Middle Ages come alive with dancers, music, theater, jousting, knights in combat and a human chess match. Feasts and follies include games and food "fit for a king." Meet such characters as King Arthur, Sir Lancelot and Merlin. Admission is free. Est attendance: 150,000. For info: Linda Linn, 1700 Asp, Norman, OK 73072. Phone: (405) 288-2536. Fax: (405) 325-7698. E-mail: llinn@ou.edu. Web: www.occe.ou.edu/medievalfair.

MOUNT HOOD RAILROAD: A SEASON OF FUN. Apr 2–Dec 21. Hood River, OR. 95-year-old historic railroad offers 44-mile round-trip excursions through natural beauty of the northwest Columbia River Gorge and foothills of Mount Hood, Oregon's highest peak. Special holiday events, murder mystery, dinner trains and harrowing train robberies throughout the season. For info: Mt Hood Railroad, 110 Railroad Ave, Hood River, OR 97031. Phone: (800) TRAIN-61 or (541) 386-3556. Fax: (541) 386-2140. Web: www.mthoodrr.com.

NATCHITOCHES JAZZ FESTIVAL. Apr 2–3. Natchitoches, LA. The event features numerous bands, continuous music from 11 AM til 9 PM. Annually, the first weekend of April. Est attendance: 25,000. For info: Calendar of Events, Natchitoches Parish Tourism Commission, 781 Front St, Natchitoches, LA 71457. Phone: (318) 352-8072 or (800) 259-1714. Fax: (318) 352-2415. Web: www.natchitoches.net.

NATIONAL GEOGRAPHIC BEE, STATE LEVEL. Apr 2. Site is different in each state—many are in the state capital. Winners of school-level competitions who scored in the top 100 in their state on a written test compete in the State Geographic Bees. The winner of each state bee will go to Washington, DC, for the national level in May. Est attendance: 400. For info: Natl Geographic Bee, Natl Geographic Soc, 1145 17th St NW, Washington, DC 20036. Phone: (202) 828-6659.

NICKELODEON PREMIERE: 25th ANNIVERSARY. Apr 2, 1979. Nickelodeon, the cable TV channel for kids owned by MTV Networks, debuted on this date.

PASCUA FLORIDA DAY. Apr 2. A legal holiday in Florida, designated as State Day. When it falls on a Saturday or Sunday, the governor may declare either the preceding Friday or the following Monday as State Day. Florida also observes Pascua Florida Week from Mar 27–Apr 2. Commemorates the sighting of Florida by Ponce de Leon in 1513. He named the land Pascua Florida because of its discovery at Easter, the "Feast of the Flowers."

PONCE DE LEON DISCOVERS FLORIDA: ANNIVERSARY. Apr 2, 1513. Juan Ponce de Leon discovered Florida, landing at the site that became the city of St. Augustine. He claimed the land for the King of Spain.

POTEET STRAWBERRY FESTIVAL. Apr 2–4. Poteet, TX. One of the oldest and largest festivals in Texas established to promote Poteet's crop—strawberries. Great food and family entertainment. Est attendance: 130,000. For info: Nita Harvey, Festival Coord, Poteet Strawberry Festival Assn, PO Box 227, Poteet, TX 78065. Phone: (830) 742-8144. Fax: (830) 742-3608. E-mail: nharvey@texas.net. Web: www.strawberryfestival.com.

Apr 2–3 ☆ Chase's 2004 Calendar of Events ☆

RECONCILIATION DAY. Apr 2. Columnist Ann Landers wrote, "Since 1989, I have suggested that April 2 be set aside to write that letter or make that phone call and mend a broken relationship. Life is too short to hold grudges. To forgive can be enormously life-enhancing. . . ."

SAINT PETERSBURG FESTIVAL OF STATES. Apr 2–11. To salute civic endeavors. Band field shows, art show, parades, open car show, blues festival, kids' art festival plus concert entertainment, 5K run, fireworks. Est attendance: 250,000. For info: St. Petersburg Festival of States, 663 6th Av S, St. Petersburg, FL 33701. Phone: (727) 898-3654. E-mail: festivalofstates@ij.net. Web: festivalofstates.com.

SCOTLAND: EDINBURGH INTERNATIONAL SCIENCE FESTIVAL. Apr 2–13. Edinburgh. A massive public celebration of science and technology, with more than 200 events at 25 venues. Includes workshops, talks, tours and exhibitions. Est attendance: 150,000. For info: Media Officer, Edinburgh Intl Science Festival, Roxburgh's Court, off 323 High St, Edinburgh, Scotland EH1 PW. Phone: (44) 131 220 1882. Fax: (44) 131 226 1771. E-mail: esf@scifest.demon.co.uk. Web: www.sciencefestival.co.uk.

STAMP EXPO. Apr 2–4. Wilshire Ebell Convention Complex, Los Angeles, CA. Est attendance: 4,000. For info: Intl Stamp Collectors Society, PO Box 854, Van Nuys, CA 91408. Phone: (818) 997-6496. Fax: (818) 988-4337. E-mail: iibick@aol.com. Web: www.bick.net.

STUDENT GOVERNMENT DAY IN MASSACHUSETTS. Apr 2. Annually, the first Friday of April.

SUGARLOAF CRAFTS FESTIVAL. Apr 2–4. Montgomery County Fairgrounds, Gaithersburg, MD. This show, now in its 29th year, features more than 475 nationally recognized craft designers and fine artists displaying and selling their original creations. Craft demonstrations, live music, hourly gift certificate drawings, specialty foods and more! Est attendance: 28,000. For info: Sugarloaf Mountain Works, Inc, 200 Orchard Ridge Dr, #215, Gaithersburg, MD 20878. Phone: (800) 210-9900. Fax: (310) 253-9620. Web: www.sugarloafcrafts.com.

US MINT: ANNIVERSARY. Apr 2, 1792. The first US Mint was established at Philadelphia, PA, as authorized by an act of Congress.

WHITE, CHARLES: BIRTH ANNIVERSARY. Apr 2, 1918. Renowned African American artist, born at Chicago, IL; died Oct 3, 1979. Charles White began his professional career by painting murals for the WPA during the Depression. He was influenced by Mexican muralists Diego Rivera and David Alfaro Siquieros. Among his most notable creations are: *J'Accuse* (1966), a series of charcoal drawings depicting a variety of African Americans from all ages and walks of life; the *Wanted* posters (c. 1969), a series of paintings based on old runaway slave posters; and *Homage to Langston Hughes* (1971).

ZOLA, EMILE: BIRTH ANNIVERSARY. Apr 2, 1840. Prolific French novelist of the naturalist school, remembered especially for his role in the Dreyfus case (resulting in retrial and vindication of Alfred Dreyfus). Emile Edouard Charles Antoine Zola was born at Paris, France. Defective venting of a stove flue in his bedroom (which some believed to be the work of political enemies) resulted in his death from carbon monoxide poisoning at Paris, Sept 28, 1902.

	S	M	T	W	T	F	S
April					1	2	3
2004	4	5	6	7	8	9	10
	11	12	13	14	15	16	17
	18	19	20	21	22	23	24
	25	26	27	28	29	30	

BIRTHDAYS TODAY

Emmylou Harris, 57, singer ("Amarillo," "Till I Gain Control Again"), born Birmingham, AL, Apr 2, 1947.
Linda Hunt, 59, actress ("The Flying Nun"; Oscar for *The Year of Living Dangerously*), born Morristown, NJ, Apr 2, 1945.
Christopher Meloni, 43, actor (*Runaway Bride*, "Law & Order: SVU"), born Washington, DC, Apr 2, 1961.
Camille Paglia, 57, literature professor and literary and cultural critic, born Endicott, NY, Apr 2, 1947.
Pamela Reed, 51, actress (*The Right Stuff*, *Bob Roberts*; stage: *Getting Out* [Drama Desk Award]), born Tacoma, WA, Apr 2, 1953 (some sources say 1949).
Leon Russell, 63, musician, born Lawton, OK, Apr 2, 1941.

APRIL 3 — SATURDAY
Day 94 — 272 Remaining

BIRMINGHAM RESISTANCE: ANNIVERSARY. Apr 3, 1962. In retaliation against a black boycott of downtown stores, the Birmingham, AL, City Commission voted not to pay the city's $45,000 share of a $100,000 county program which supplied surplus food to the needy. More than 90 percent of the recipients of aid were black. When the NAACP protested the Commission's decision, Birmingham Mayor Arthur J. Hanes dismissed their complaint as a "typical reaction from New York Socialist radicals."

BLACKS RULED ELIGIBLE TO VOTE: 60th ANNIVERSARY. Apr 3, 1944. The US Supreme Court, in an 8–1 ruling, declared that blacks could not be barred from voting in the Texas Democratic primaries. The high court repudiated the contention that political parties are private associations and held that discrimination against blacks violated the 15th Amendment.

BOSTON PUBLIC LIBRARY: ANNIVERSARY. Apr 3, 1848. The Massachusetts legislature passed legislation enabling Boston to levy a tax for a public library. This created the funding model for all public libraries in the US. The Boston Public Library opened its doors in 1854.

BURROUGHS, JOHN: BIRTH ANNIVERSARY. Apr 3, 1837. American naturalist and author, born at Roxbury, NY. "Time does not become sacred to us until we have lived it," he wrote in 1877. Died en route from California to New York, Mar 29, 1921.

CANADA: ELMIRA MAPLE SYRUP FESTIVAL. Apr 3. Elmira, ON. Tours of maple bush by hay wagon, sugaring-off shanty in operation, Pennsylvania Dutch cuisine, handcrafted goods, arts and crafts and antiques. Est attendance: 60,000. For info: Woolwich Visitor Services, 5 First St E, Elmira, ON, Canada N3B 2E3. Phone: (519) 669-2605. Fax: (519) 669-0503. Web: www.elmiramaplesyrup.com.

CLEAR LAKE CRAWFISH FESTIVAL. Apr 3. Landolt Pavilion, Clear Lake Park, Seabrook, TX. 9th annual. The festival will have crawfish-eating contests, food, games, silent auction and live zydeco music. Sponsored by the Clear Lake Area Chamber of Commerce. Proceeds fund the annual July 4th fireworks on Clear Lake. Est attendance: 3,000. For info: Shari Sweeney, Clear Lake Area Chamber of Commerce, 1201 Nasa Rd One, Houston, TX 77058. Phone: (281) 488-7676. Fax: (281) 488-8981. Web: www.clearlakearea.com.

CYPRUS: THE PROCESSION OF ICON OF SAINT LAZARUS. Apr 3. Larnaca, Cyprus. The tomb of Lazarus (the man raised from the dead by Christ) resides in the Ayios Lazaros Church—built by Emperor Leo VI in the ninth century. Eight days before the Orthodox Easter Sunday, his icon is taken through the streets of Lanarca.

DESOTO CAVERNS PARK INDIAN DANCE FESTIVAL. Apr 3–4 (tentative). DeSoto Caverns Park, Childersburg, AL. 29th annual festival. Artists and craftspeople from across the US. Native American dancing includes hoop, traditional, fine, fancy and many more. Est attendance: 10,000. For info: DeSoto

Caverns Park, 5181 DeSoto Caverns Pkwy, Childersburg, AL 35044. Phone: (800) 933-2283. E-mail: fun@desotocavernspark.com. Web: www.DeSotoCavernsPark.com.

EASTER FETE. Apr 3. Austin, TX. Spring celebration with Easter egg hunt, Egg Olympics, wine and cheese tasting, musical entertainment and games at the beautiful grounds of the historic French Legation Museum. For info: Jack Hinson, Dir, French Legation Museum, 802 San Marcos St, Austin, TX 78702. Phone: (512) 472-8180. Web: www.FrenchLegationMuseum.org.

FALL OF RICHMOND: ANNIVERSARY. Apr 3, 1865. After the withdrawal of Robert E. Lee's troops, the Confederate capital of Richmond and nearby Petersburg surrendered to Union forces on this day. Richmond had survived four years of continuous threats from the North. On Apr 4, the city was toured by President Abraham Lincoln.

GRAHAM, CALVIN "BABY VET": BIRTH ANNIVERSARY. Apr 3, 1930. The man who became known as World War II's "baby vet," Calvin Graham was born at Canton, TX, and enlisted in the Navy at the age of 12. As a gunner on the USS *South Dakota*, he was struck by shrapnel during the battle of Guadalcanal in 1942 but still helped pull fellow crew members to safety. The Navy gave Graham a dishonorable discharge, revoked his disability benefits and stripped him of his decorations, including a Purple Heart and Bronze Star, after discovering his age. Eventually, through congressional efforts, he was granted an honorable discharge and won back all but the Purple Heart. His benefits were restored in 1988. Graham died Nov 6, 1992, at Fort Worth, TX.

GUINEA: ANNIVERSARY OF THE SECOND REPUBLIC. Apr 3. National holiday. Commemorates the establishment of the Second Republic in 1984.

HISTORIC PENDLETON SPRING JUBILEE. Apr 3–4. Pendleton, SC. 27th annual. Come and join the fun in historic Pendleton with arts and crafts displays, food booths, entertainment and much more. Annually, the first full weekend in April. Est attendance: 30,000. For info: Historic Pendleton Spring Jubilee, PO Box 565, Pendleton, SC 29670. Phone: (864) 646-3782 or (800) 862-1795. Fax: (864) 646-2506. E-mail: jomc@innova.net. Web: www.pendleton-district.org.

HOWARD, LESLIE: BIRTH ANNIVERSARY. Apr 3, 1893. During the return trip from a British government-sponsored tour of Spain, a plane transporting 50-year-old actor Leslie Howard was shot down by German raiders. Rumors that he was serving on a spy mission for his government circulated at the time. In her biography about her father (*A Quite Remarkable Father*) his daughter expressed doubt that her father was the sort to get involved in espionage. Howard's most-remembered film role is that of Ashley Wilkes in *Gone with the Wind*. Born at London, England; died at sea June 1, 1943.

INAUGURATION OF PONY EXPRESS: ANNIVERSARY. Apr 3, 1860. The Pony Express began when the first rider left St. Joseph, MO. The following day another rider headed east from Sacramento, CA. For $5 an ounce letters were delivered within 10 days. There were 190 way stations between 10 and 15 miles apart, and each rider had a "run" of between 75 and 100 miles. The Pony Express lasted less than two years, ceasing operation in October 1861, when the overland telegraph was completed.

INTO THE WOOD SHOW. Apr 3–4. Wheaton Village, Millville, NJ. Demonstrations, exhibits and sales of handcrafted items made from wood: carvings, wood turnings, wood baskets, furniture, etc. For info: Wheaton Village, 1501 Glasstown Rd, Millville, NJ 08332. Phone: (856) 825-6800. Fax: (856) 825-2410. E-mail: mail@wheatonvillage.org. Web: www.wheatonvillage.org.

IRVING, WASHINGTON: BIRTH ANNIVERSARY. Apr 3, 1783. American author, attorney and one-time US Minister to Spain, Irving was born at New York, NY. Creator of *Rip Van Winkle* and *The Legend of Sleepy Hollow*, he was also the author of many historical and biographical works, including *A History of the Life and Voyages of Christopher Columbus* and the *Life of Washington*. Died at Tarrytown, NY, Nov 28, 1859.

ISLE ROYALE NATIONAL PARK ESTABLISHED: ANNIVERSARY. Apr 3, 1940. Isle Royale is the largest of a group of more than 200 islands that make up this national park preserve. To preserve upper Michigan's flora and fauna, Congress authorized a national park in 1931 and it was established in 1940.

LAZARUS SATURDAY. Apr 3. Orthodox celebration of Christ raising Lazarus from the dead. Only time the resurrection liturgy is used on a day other than Sunday.

LONGWOOD GARDENS EASTER DISPLAY. Apr 3–16. Kennett Square, PA. Fragrant Easter lilies trumpet the season, while brilliant tulips, daffodils, freesias and other colorful plants fill acres of indoor gardens. Est attendance: 40,000. For info: Elizabeth Sullivan, Publicity Director, Longwood Gardens, PO Box 501, Kennett Square, PA 19348-0501. Phone: (610) 388-1000. Web: www.longwoodgardens.org.

LUCE, HENRY: BIRTH ANNIVERSARY. Apr 3, 1898. American editor and publisher, born to missionary parents at Penglai, China. He built his publishing empire with *Time, Fortune, Life* and *Sports Illustrated*. Luce also was involved in broadcasting. Died at Phoenix, AZ, Feb 28, 1967.

MAPLE SYRUP FESTIVAL. Apr 3–4. Bradys Run County Park, Fallston, PA. Demonstrates the maple-tree-tapping process and builds a 19th-century arts, crafts and educational festival around it. Est attendance: 40,000. For info: Beaver County Conservation District, 1000 Third St, Ste 202, Beaver, PA 15009-2026. Phone: (724) 774-7090. Fax: (724) 774-9421.

MARSHALL PLAN: ANNIVERSARY. Apr 3, 1948. Suggested by Secretary of State George C. Marshall in a speech at Harvard, June 5, 1947, the legislation for the European Recovery Program, popularly known as the Marshall Plan, was signed by President Truman on Apr 3, 1948. After distributing more than $12 billion, the program ended in 1952.

NCAA DIVISION I MEN'S BASKETBALL CHAMPIONSHIP. Apr 3 & 5. Alamodome, San Antonio, TX. For info: Natl Collegiate Athletic Assn, 700 W Washington Ave, PO Box 6222, Indianapolis, IN 46206-6222. Phone: (317) 917-6222. Fax: (317) 917-6827. Web: www.ncaasports.com.

PRAIRIE DOG CHILI COOKOFF AND WORLD CHAMPIONSHIP OF PICKLED QUAIL-EGG EATING. Apr 3–4. Traders Village, Grand Prairie, TX. Tongue-in-cheek salute to the official state dish of Texas, chili con carne, or "Texas Red." World championship of pickled quail-egg eating featuring contestants devouring as many of these gourmet delights as possible in the 60-second time limit. Est attendance: 85,000. For info: Allan Hughes, Traders Village, 2602 Mayfield Rd, Grand Prairie, TX 75052-7246. Phone: (972) 647-2331. E-mail: tvgp@flash.net. Web: www.tradersvillage.com.

RAINEY, MA (GERTRUDE BRIDGET): BIRTH ANNIVERSARY. Apr 3, 1888. Known as the "Mother of the Blues," Gertrude "Ma" Rainey was born at Columbus, GA. She made her stage debut at the Columbus Opera House in 1900 in a talent show called "The Bunch of Blackberries." After touring together as "Rainey and Rainey, the Assassinators of the Blues," she and her husband eventually separated and she toured on her own. She made her first recording in 1923 and her last on Dec 28, 1928, after being told that the rural southern blues she sang had gone out of style. She died Dec 22, 1939, at Columbus, GA.

RAND, SALLY: 100th BIRTH ANNIVERSARY. Apr 3, 1904. American actress, ecdysiast and inventor of the fan dance, which gained fame at the 1933 Chicago World's Fair. Born Helen Gould Beck at Hickory County, MO. Died at Glendora, CA, Aug 31, 1979.

SPRING SWING CITY ELECTRA-QUANAH-WIDE GARAGE SALE. Apr 3. Electra, TX. Sales throughout the Electra area. 50 miles of garage sales. Chamber of Commerce will provide free coffee and maps at 7 AM; sales start at 8 AM. The Chamber of Commerce office will close at 8 AM so that we too may enjoy all of the bargains. Est attendance: 500. For info: Sherry Strange, Electra Chamber of Commerce, 112 W Cleveland, Electra, TX 76360. Phone: (940) 495-3577. E-mail: ElectraCoC@aol.com. Web: www.electratexas.org.

TARPON SPRINGS ARTS AND CRAFTS FESTIVAL. Apr 3–4. Tarpon Springs, FL. Est attendance: 30,000. For info: Tarpon Springs Chamber of Commerce, 11 E Orange St, Tarpon Springs, FL 34689. Phone: (727) 937-6109. Fax: (727) 937-2879. E-mail: chamber@tarponsprings.com. Web: www.TarponSprings.com.

TWEED DAY: ANNIVERSARY. Apr 3, 1823. Day to consider the cost of political corruption. Birthday of William March Tweed, New York City political boss, whose "Tweed Ring" is said to have stolen $30 million to $200 million from the city. Born at New York, NY, Apr 3, 1823, he died in his cell at New York's Ludlow Street Jail, Apr 12, 1878. Cartoonist Thomas Nast deserves much credit for Tweed's arrests and convictions.

***2001: A SPACE ODYSSEY* PREMIERE: ANNIVERSARY.** Apr 3, 1968. Directed by Stanley Kubrick, this influential film has elicited many different interpretations. Sci-fi novelist Arthur C. Clarke based the screenplay on his 1966 book which was prescient in several ways. Written before men had landed on the moon, Clarke describes an expedition launched to Jupiter to track a mysterious signal emanating from the moon. Clarke gave the world's population as six billion (achieved in 1999) and described a space station (the US is currently building one with Russia). During flight, a character reads the news on his electronic newspad. The film starred Keir Dullea, William Sylvester, Gary Lockwood, Daniel Richter and HAL 9000, the creepy computer that had human emotions. The theme music was Richard Strauss's *Also Sprach Zarathrustra*.

WOMAN PRESIDES OVER US SUPREME COURT: ANNIVERSARY. Apr 3, 1995. Supreme Court Justice Sandra Day O'Connor became the first woman to preside over the US high court when she sat in for Chief Justice William H. Rehnquist and second in seniority Justice John Paul Stevens when both were out of town.

YO-YO CONVENTION. Apr 3–4. Spinning Top Museum, Burlington, WI. 9th annual. Yo-yo exhibits, workshops, demonstrations, challenges, yo-yo shows, sales and trading, $1,000 worth of prizes and champions to meet. Participate in a world record challenge, enter the "oddest yo-yo," longest sleeper and longest walk-the-dog contests. Yo-yos galore, plus juggling, diabolos and paddleballs. Plus Big Wisconsin State Yo-Yo Contest. Admission charges per event. For info: Spinning Top Museum, 533 Milwaukee Ave (Hwy 36), Burlington, WI 53105. Phone: (262) 763-3946.

BIRTHDAYS TODAY

Alec Baldwin, 46, actor (*The Hunt for Red October, The Getaway, Miami Blues*), born Massapequa, NY, Apr 3, 1958.

Marlon Brando, 80, actor (Oscars for *On the Waterfront, The Godfather*; Emmy for *Roots: The Next Generations*), born Omaha, NE, Apr 3, 1924.

Doris Day, 80, actress, singer ("Young at Heart," *The Man Who Knew Too Much, Pillow Talk*, "The Doris Day Show"), born Doris Von Kappelhoff, Cincinnati, OH, Apr 3, 1924.

Max Frankel, 74, journalist, born Gera, Germany, Apr 3, 1930.

Jennie Garth, 32, actress ("Beverly Hills 90210"), born Champaign, IL, Apr 3, 1972.

Jane Goodall (Baroness Van Lawick-Goodall), 70, anthropologist known for study of chimpanzees, born London, England, Apr 3, 1934.

Jonathan Lynn, 61, writer, actor, director (*Into the Night, Nuns on the Run, My Cousin Vinny*), born Bath, England, Apr 3, 1943.

Marsha Mason, 62, actress (*The Goodbye Girl, Cinderella Liberty*), born St. Louis, MO, Apr 3, 1942.

Eddie Murphy, 43, comedian ("Saturday Night Live"), actor (*Dr. Dolittle, Trading Places, Beverly Hills Cop*), born Brooklyn, NY, Apr 3, 1961.

Wayne Newton, 62, singer ("Danke Schoen," "Daddy Don't You Walk So Fast"), born Norfolk, VA, Apr 3, 1942.

Michael Olowokandi, 29, basketball player, born Lagos, Nigeria, Apr 3, 1975.

Tony Orlando, 60, singer (Tony Orlando and Dawn, "Tie a Yellow Ribbon Round the Old Oak Tree"), born Michael Orlando Cassivitis, New York, NY, Apr 3, 1944.

Bernie Parent, 59, Hall of Fame hockey player, born Montreal, QC, Canada, Apr 3, 1945.

David Hyde Pierce, 45, actor ("Frasier"), born Albany, NY, Apr 3, 1959.

Picabo Street, 33, Olympic skier, born Triumph, ID, Apr 3, 1971.

APRIL 4 — SUNDAY
Day 95 — 271 Remaining

BEATLES TAKE OVER MUSIC CHARTS: 40th ANNIVERSARY. Apr 4, 1964. On this date The Beatles held the top five positions of the Billboard Hot 100 chart: "Can't Buy Me Love" was number one, followed by (in order) "Twist and Shout," "She Loves You," "I Want To Hold Your Hand" and "Please, Please Me." The Beatles had made their first US appearance barely two months before. In the same week they held the top six places on the Australian music chart.

BONZA BOTTLER DAY™. Apr 4. To celebrate when the number of the day is the same as the number of the month. Bonza Bottler Day™ is an excuse to have a party at least once a month. For more information, see Jan 1. For info: Gail M. Berger, 14 Fernwood Dr, Taylors, SC 29687. Phone: (864) 609-9874. E-mail: gberger5@aol.com.

CHECK YOUR BATTERIES DAY. Apr 4. A day set aside for checking the batteries in your smoke detector, carbon monoxide detector, HVAC thermostat, audio/visual remote controls and other electronic devices. This could save your life! Annually, the first Sunday in April.

	S	M	T	W	T	F	S
April 2004					1	2	3
	4	5	6	7	8	9	10
	11	12	13	14	15	16	17
	18	19	20	21	22	23	24
	25	26	27	28	29	30	

☆ Chase's 2004 Calendar of Events ☆ Apr 4

CHINA: QING MING FESTIVAL OR TOMB SWEEPING DAY. Apr 4. This Confucian festival was traditionally celebrated on the fourth or fifth day of the third month but is now on fixed dates (Apr 3, 4 or 5) in China. It is observed by the maintenance of ancestral graves, the presentation of food, wine and flowers as offerings and the burning of paper money at gravesides to help ancestors in the afterworld. People also picnic and gather for family meals. Also observed in Taiwan.

CURTIS EASTER PAGEANT. Apr 4. Medicine Valley High School Auditorium, Curtis, NE. "Truly an unforgettable, inspirational, touching spiritual experience!" A choir, acting cast and supporting cast of more than 200 people depict the last week in the life of Christ through music and narration. Seventeen magnificent "Living Pictures." Curtis is Nebraska's official "Easter City." Annually, 3 PM Palm Sunday afternoon. Sponsor: Curtis Community. Est attendance: 2,000. For info: Cathy Nutt, President, Easter Pageant Committee, PO Box 275, Curtis, NE 69025.

DALLAS CUP. Apr 4–11. Lake Highlands Stadium, Dallas, TX. 25th annual. International invitation-only boys' (under 12 to under 19) soccer competition, sanctioned by the USSF and FIFA. In past years, more than 98 countries and all 6 continents have been represented. Many of the world's premier teams participate. Super Group Final match to be televised. Annually, from Palm Sunday to Easter Sunday. Est attendance: 40,000. For info: Dallas Cup, 11551 Forest Central Drive, Ste 250, Dallas, TX 75243. Phone: (214) 228-3534. Fax: (214) 221-4636. E-mail: randy@dallascup.com. Web: www.dallascup.com.

DAYLIGHT SAVING TIME BEGINS. Apr 4–Oct 31. Daylight Saving Time begins at 2 AM in the US and Canada. The Uniform Time Act of 1966 (as amended in 1986 by Public Law 99–359), administered by the US Dept of Transportation, provides that Standard Time in each zone be advanced one hour from 2 AM on the first Sunday in April until 2 AM on the last Sunday in October (except where state legislatures provide exemption, as in Hawaii and parts of Arizona and Indiana). Prior to 1986, Daylight Saving Time began on the last Sunday in April. Many use the popular rule "spring forward, fall back" to remember which way to turn their clocks. See also: "Standard Time" (Oct 31).

DIX, DOROTHEA LYNDE: BIRTH ANNIVERSARY. Apr 4, 1802. American social reformer and author, born at Hampden, ME. Left home at age 10, was teaching at age 14 and founded a home for girls at Boston while still in her teens. In spite of frail health, she was a vigorous crusader for humane conditions in insane asylums, jails and almshouses and for the establishment of state-supported institutions to serve those needs. Named superintendent of women nurses during the Civil War. Died at Trenton, NJ, July 17, 1887.

FLAG ACT OF 1818: ANNIVERSARY. Apr 4, 1818. Congress approved the first flag of the US.

GIAMATTI, ANGELO BARTLETT: BIRTH ANNIVERSARY. Apr 4, 1938. Baseball Commissioner and former president of Yale University. Born at Boston, MA, Giamatti was the youngest person to be named president of Yale, at the age of 39, in 1978. He became the president of Major League Baseball's National League in 1986 and served in that capacity until he was appointed Commissioner of Baseball Apr 1, 1989. An accomplished author, he moved freely between the worlds of literature and baseball, often linking the two in the many articles he wrote. One week prior to his death, he suspended Pete Rose for life for betting on baseball games. Giamatti died at Martha's Vineyard, MA, Sept 1, 1989.

HATE WEEK. Apr 4–10. Recognizes the day on which the fictional character Winston Smith started his secret diary and wrote the words "DOWN WITH BIG BROTHER," Wednesday, Apr 4, 1984. From George Orwell's dystopian novel, *1984*, portraying the end of human privacy and the destruction of the individual in a totalitarian state (first published in 1949). "Hates" varied from the daily two-minute concentrated hate to the grand culmination observed during Hate Week.

HOLY WEEK. Apr 4–10. Christian observance dating from the fourth century, known also as Great Week. The seven days beginning on the sixth and final Sunday in Lent (Palm Sunday), consisting of: Palm Sunday, Monday of Holy Week, Tuesday of Holy Week, Spy Wednesday (or Wednesday of Holy Week), Maundy Thursday, Good Friday and Holy Saturday (or Great Sabbath or Easter Even). A time of solemn devotion to and memorializing of the suffering (passion), death and burial of Christ. Formerly a time of strict fasting.

KING, MARTIN LUTHER, JR: ASSASSINATION: ANNIVERSARY. Apr 4, 1968. The Reverend Dr. Martin Luther King, Jr, was shot at Memphis, TN. James Earl Ray was serving a 99-year sentence for the crime at the time of his death in 1998. See also: "King, Martin Luther, Jr: Birth Anniversary" (Jan 15).

KING OPPOSES VIETNAM WAR: ANNIVERSARY. Apr 4, 1967. Speaking before the Overseas Press Club at New York City, Reverend Dr. Martin Luther King, Jr, announced his opposition to the Vietnam War. That same day, at the Riverside Church at Harlem, King suggested that those who saw the war as dishonorable and unjust should avoid military service. He proposed that the US take new initiatives to conclude the war.

***LADY BE GOOD* LOST: ANNIVERSARY.** Apr 4, 1943. The nine-man crew of the World War II American Liberator bomber *Lady Be Good* bailed out 200 miles off course over the Sahara Desert and disappeared. They were returning to their base in Libya after a raid over southern Italy. On Nov 9, 1958, 15 years after the plane went down and more than 13 years after the war had ended, a pilot flying across the Sahara south of Tobruck sighted wreckage of an aircraft in the sand. Eight skeletons and a diary describing the final days of the crew were recovered near the wreckage. The radio, guns and ammunition in the plane were in working order.

NATIONAL BLUE RIBBON WEEK. Apr 4–10. National Blue Ribbon Week encourages all National Exchange Club members to wear and distribute Blue Ribbon pins or cut-outs in a national effort to raise awareness and funds for child abuse prevention. The Blue Ribbon symbolizes more than 3.2 million abused children reported each year to Child Protective Services. For info: The Natl Exchange Club Fndn for the Prevention of Child Abuse, 3050 Central Ave, Toledo, OH 43606-1700. Phone: (800) 924-2643. E-mail: info@preventchildabuse.com. Web: www.preventchildabuse.com.

NATIONAL REPOT YOUR PLANT DAY. Apr 4. The Scotts Company would like to remind people to repot their plants when they reset their clocks. When your prized plants starts to lose their vigor and color, the problem is usually due to growing pains below the surface. Over time, potting soil becomes tired and lacks essential nutrients and plants' roots continue to grow, taking up more space than the pots allow for, leaving plants root-bound. This combination of decomposing pot medium and cramped quarters inevitably leads to an unhealthy environment. Annually, on Daylight Saving Day. For info: Adam Rossow, Dan Klores Communications, 386 Park Ave South, 10th Fl, New York, NY 10016. Phone: (212) 981-5144. Fax: (212) 981-5344. E-mail: adam_rossow@dkcnews.com. Web: www.Scottsco.com.

NATIONAL WEEK OF THE OCEAN. Apr 4–10. A week focusing on humanity's interdependence with the ocean, asking each of us to appreciate, protect and use the ocean wisely. 21st annual. For info: Pres/Co-Founder, Cynthia Hancock, Natl Week of the Ocean, Inc, PO Box 179, Ft Lauderdale, FL 33302. Phone: (954) 462-5573. Web: www.national-week-of-the-ocean.org.

Apr 4 — Chase's 2004 Calendar of Events

NORTH ATLANTIC TREATY RATIFIED: 55th ANNIVERSARY. Apr 4, 1949. The North Atlantic Treaty Organization was created by this treaty, which was signed by 12 nations, including the US. (Other countries joined later.) The NATO member nations are united for common defense. The treaty went into effect Apr 24, 1949, and the first session of the North Atlantic Council was held Sept 17, 1949.

ORTHODOX PALM SUNDAY. Apr 4. Celebration of Christ's entry into Jerusalem, when His way was covered with palms by the multitudes. Beginning of Holy Week in the Orthodox Church.

PALM SUNDAY. Apr 4. Commemorates Christ's last entry into Jerusalem, when His way was covered with palms by the multitudes. Beginning of Holy (or Great) Week in Western Christian churches.

PERKINS, ANTHONY: BIRTH ANNIVERSARY. Apr 4, 1932. American actor Anthony Perkins was born at New York, NY. Best known for his movie role as homicidal innkeeper Norman Bates in the film *Psycho* (1960), Perkins appeared in many Broadway plays in addition to his numerous film roles. He received an Oscar nomination for his supporting role in *Friendly Persuasion* (1956). Perkins died Sept 12, 1992, at Hollywood, CA.

PHILIPPINES: HOLY WEEK. Apr 4–10. National observance. Flagellants in the streets, *cenaculos* (passion plays) and other colorful and solemn rituals mark the country's observance of Holy Week.

SALTER ELECTED FIRST WOMAN MAYOR IN US: ANNIVERSARY. Apr 4, 1887. The first woman elected mayor in the US was Susanna Medora Salter, who was elected mayor of Argonia, KS. Her name had been submitted for election without her knowledge by the Women's Christian Temperance Union, and she did not know she was a candidate until she went to the polls to vote. She received a two-thirds majority vote and served one year for the salary of $1.

SENEGAL: INDEPENDENCE DAY. Apr 4. National holiday. Commemorates independence from France in 1960.

SMOTHERS BROTHERS FIRED: 35th ANNIVERSARY. Apr 4, 1969. CBS canceled this popular comedy series on this date. The hour-long show strongly influenced television humor during the two years it aired. Tom and Dick, however, frequently found themselves at odds with the censors over material that would be considered tame today. Guests and cast members frequently knocked the Vietnam War and the Nixon Administration. Acts featuring antiwar protesters such as Harry Belafonte were often cut.

SPACE MILESTONE: *CHALLENGER* STS-6 (US): ANNIVERSARY. Apr 4, 1983. Shuttle *Challenger* launched from Kennedy Space Center, FL, with four astronauts (Paul Weitz, Karol Bobko, Storey Musgrave and Donald Peterson). Four-hour spacewalk by Musgrave and Peterson. Landed at Edwards Air Force Base, CA, Apr 9.

SUNDAY ARCHITREK TOURS. Apr 4–Nov 7 (first Sunday of each month). Oak Park, IL. The Frank Lloyd Wright Preservation Trust sponsors entertaining tours that focus on the historically significant architectural features and styles found in the Oak Park/River Forest communities just west of Chicago. Tours include a Victorian Walking Tour (Apr, Oct), River Forest Walking Tour (May, Sept), Prairie Bicycle Tour (June, Aug) and Oak Park Walking Tour (July, Nov). For info: Frank Lloyd Wright Preservation Trust, 931 Chicago Ave, Oak Park, IL 60302. Phone: (708) 848-1976. Web: www.wrightplus.org.

April 2004

S	M	T	W	T	F	S
				1	2	3
4	5	6	7	8	9	10
11	12	13	14	15	16	17
18	19	20	21	22	23	24
25	26	27	28	29	30	

VITAMIN C ISOLATED: ANNIVERSARY. Apr 4, 1932. Vitamin C was first isolated by C.C. King at the University of Pittsburgh.

WATERS, MUDDY: BIRTH ANNIVERSARY. Apr 4, 1915. Born McKinley Morganfield at Rolling Fork, MS, American blues guitarist and singer Muddy Waters played a significant part in developing modern rhythm and blues that came to be known as Chicago or urban blues. It was predominately from this music that later forms such as rock and roll and soul sprang. Muddy Waters died at Westmont, IL, Apr 30, 1983.

WISCONSIN STATE YO-YO CONTEST. Apr 4. Burlington, WI. Sanctioned by the American Yo-Yo Association. Divisions for tricks and free-style section. Participants can be from anywhere in the world. The winners receive traditional patches and accolades from the audience. For info: Spinning Top Museum, 533 Milwaukee Ave (Hwy 36), Burlington, WI 53105. Phone: (262) 763-3946.

YALE, LINUS: BIRTH ANNIVERSARY. Apr 4, 1821. American portrait painter and inventor of the lock that is named for him was born at Salisbury, NY. He was creator of the Yale Infallible Bank Lock and developer of the cylinder lock. Yale died at New York, NY, Dec 25, 1868.

YAMAMOTO, ISOROKU: BIRTH ANNIVERSARY. Apr 4, 1884. Considered Japan's greatest naval strategist, Admiral Isoroku Yamamoto, who planned the attack on Pearl Harbor, was born at Nagaoko, Honshu. Yamamoto also devised the complex attack on Midway Island which ended in defeat for the Japanese because the Allies had the key to the Imperial fleet code and were prepared for the June 4, 1942, attack. The US intercepted reports of Yamamoto's proposed 1943 tour of the Western Solomons and shot down his plane Apr 18, while he was touring Japanese installations in the area.

BIRTHDAYS TODAY

Maya Angelou, 76, poet, author (*I Know Why the Caged Bird Sings*), born St. Louis, MO, Apr 4, 1928.

Elmer Bernstein, 82, composer of dozens of movie soundtracks, born New York, NY, Apr 4, 1922.

David Blaine, 31, magician, born Brooklyn, NY, Apr 4, 1973.

Robert Downey, Jr, 39, actor (*Chaplin, Short Cuts, Natural Born Killers*), born New York, NY, Apr 4, 1965.

Kitty Kelley, 62, author (*Jackie Oh!, Nancy Reagan*), born Hartford, CT, Apr 4, 1942.

Christine Lahti, 54, actress ("The Harvey Korman Show," "Chicago Hope," *Swing Shift*), born Birmingham, MI, Apr 4, 1950.

Heath Ledger, 25, actor (*The Patriot*), born Perth, Australia, Apr 4, 1979.

Richard G. Lugar, 72, US Senator (R, Indiana), born Indianapolis, IN, Apr 4, 1932.

William Manchester, 82, author (*The Last Lion, A World Lit Only by Fire*), born Attleboro, MA, Apr 4, 1922.

Nancy McKeon, 38, actress ("The Facts of Life," "The Division"), born Westbury, NY, Apr 4, 1966.

Dave Mirra, 32, BMX bike racer, born Syracuse, NY, Apr 4, 1972.

Craig T. Nelson, 58, actor ("Coach," *Private Benjamin, Poltergeist, The Killing Fields*), born Spokane, WA, Apr 4, 1946.

Michael Parks, 66, actor ("Then Came Bronson," "Twin Peaks," *The Happening*), born Corona, CA, Apr 4, 1938.

Barry Pepper, 34, actor (*Saving Private Ryan, Enemy of the State*), born Campbell River, BC, Canada, Apr 4, 1970.

Scott Rolen, 29, baseball player, born Evansville, IN, Apr 4, 1975.

Elizabeth Wilson, 79, actress (*The Prisoner of Second Avenue, The Addams Family*; stage: *Taken in Marriage*), born Grand Rapids, MI, Apr 4, 1925.

APRIL 5 — MONDAY
Day 96 — 270 Remaining

DAVIS, BETTE: BIRTH ANNIVERSARY. Apr 5, 1908. American actress Bette Davis was born Ruth Elizabeth Davis at Lowell, MA. In addition to acting in more than 80 films, earning 10 Academy Award nominations and winning the best actress Academy Award twice, for *Dangerous* (1935) and *Jezebel* (1938), Davis also claimed to have nicknamed the Academy Award "Oscar" after her first husband, Harmon Oscar Nelson, Jr. She died Oct 6, 1989, at Neuilly-sur-Seine, France.

DISCOTHEQUE BOMBING: ANNIVERSARY. Apr 5, 1986. A bomb exploded at a popular discotheque in West Berlin, Germany, killing two American soldiers and a Turkish woman. Although three groups claimed responsibility for the bombing, American intelligence organizations attributed it to orders from Libyan head-of-state Muammar el-Qaddafi, and President Reagan ordered a retaliatory air strike on Libya. On Apr 14, 1986 (Apr 15, Libyan time), American forces launched a bombing attack on the cities of Tripoli and Benghazi, reportedly killing 37 (including a daughter of Qaddafi). Nearly two years later, on Jan 11, 1988, West German authorities arrested 27-year-old Christine Gabriele Endrigkeit, charging her with the bombing, citing "clues" that it might have been ordered by Syrian agents.

"FIRESIDE THEATRE" TV PREMIERE: 55th ANNIVERSARY. Apr 5, 1949. Gene Raymond and later Jane Wyman hosted this NBC anthology program consisting of 15- and 30-minute dramas. One of its most acclaimed presentations was "The Reign of Amelika Jo" on Oct 12, 1954. It was set in the South Pacific during World War II and had a mostly black and Asian cast.

FIRST US CHAMBER OF COMMERCE FOUNDED: ANNIVERSARY. Apr 5, 1768. The first Chamber of Commerce in the US was founded at New York City.

GRADUATE AND PROFESSIONAL STUDENT APPRECIATION WEEK. Apr 5–9. Graduate and professional students at universities around the country select a week in early April (varies from institution to institution) to honor the contribution these students make to higher education. For info: Natl Assn of Graduate and Professional Students, 209 Pennsylvania Ave SE, Washington, DC 20003-1107. Phone: 888-88-NAGPS. Web: www.nagps.org.

LISTER, JOSEPH: BIRTH ANNIVERSARY. Apr 5, 1827. English physician who was the founder of aseptic surgery, born at Upton, Essex, England. Died at Walmer, England, Feb 10, 1912.

"MARRIED . . . WITH CHILDREN" TV PREMIERE: ANNIVERSARY. Apr 5, 1987. This raunchy Fox TV show premiered as the antidote to Cosby-style family shows. Ed O'Neill starred as boorish, luckless shoe salesman Al Bundy, Katey Sagal portrayed Al's big-haired, spandex-clad, sex-starved wife Peggy, Christina Applegate played airheaded bombshell daughter Kelly and David Faustino played hormone-driven son Bud. The Bundys' neighbors were portrayed by Amanda Bearse as Marcy Rhoades, David Garrison as husband #1, Steve Rhoades and Ted McGinley as husband #2, Jefferson D'Arcy. The last episode aired Apr 20, 1997.

MOON PHASE: FULL MOON. Apr 5. Moon enters Full Moon phase at 7:03 AM, EDT.

NATIONAL MEDICAL PATIENT ADVOCACY WEEK. Apr 5–9. As the medical community continues to grow and get more complex, this one week is intended to create awareness about patient responsibility. The medical consumer has the option to educate him or herself regarding the physical, emotional, legal and financial concerns that are always encountered before, during and after hospital treatment. Patients no longer need to be passive bystanders in dealing with their healthcare issues, but can be active participants—defining how they receive treatment. Annually, the first full week in April, Monday through Friday. For info: Mark S. Vass, 617 N Keller Smithfield Rd, Keller, TX 76248-4229. Phone: (817) 379-5372. E-mail: l.ladybugs@verizon.net. Web: www.medicalselfhelpbooks.com.

NATIONAL PUBLIC HEALTH WEEK. Apr 5–11. Annually, the first full week in April. For info: American Public Health Assn, 800 I Street NW, Washington, DC 20001-3710. Phone: (202) 777-APHA. E-mail: comments@apha.org. Web: www.apha.org.

NATIONAL WORKPLACE NAPPING DAY. Apr 5. This is a day for employees to "lie down and be counted" in support of napping at the workplace. This day occurs on the Monday following the advent of daylight savings time. For info: The Napping Co. Inc, 26 Orchard Park Dr, Reading, MA 01867. Phone: (781) 944-3506. Fax: (781) 944-6856. E-mail: www.napping.com. Web: info@napping.com.

PASSOVER BEGINS AT SUNDOWN. April 5. See "Pesach" (April 6).

PECK, GREGORY: BIRTH ANNIVERSARY. Apr 5, 1916. Born Eldred Gregory Peck at La Jolla, CA, Gregory Peck was one of Hollywood's most popular and likeable leading men. Nominated five times for best actor, he finally won the Oscar for his role as Atticus Finch in 1962's *To Kill a Mockingbird*. Other popular films included *Roman Holiday*, *Gentleman's Agreement* and Alfred Hitchcock's *Spellbound*. He also founded the La Jolla Playhouse with Dorothy McGuire and Mel Ferrer in 1947, and appeared there throughout his career. He died at his home in La Jolla on June 11, 2003.

RESNIK, JUDITH A.: 55th BIRTH ANNIVERSARY. Apr 5, 1949. Dr. Judith A. Resnik, the second American woman in space (1984), was born at Akron, OH. The 36-year-old electrical engineer was mission specialist on Space Shuttle *Challenger*. She perished with all others aboard when *Challenger* exploded Jan 28, 1986. See also: "*Challenger* Space Shuttle Explosion: Anniversary" (Jan 28).

"SECRET AGENT" TV PREMIERE: ANNIVERSARY. Apr 5, 1961. Before Patrick McGoohan became "The Prisoner," he played the role of intelligence agent John Drake on this CBS adventure series. Produced in England by ATV, it also aired there as "Danger Man."

SPALDING UNIVERSITY RUNNING OF THE RODENTS. Apr 5–7. Louisville, KY. To celebrate the pre-final exams "Rat Race" that occurs each year, to develop community spirit and to unofficially kick off the Kentucky Derby festivities. Est attendance: 300. For info: Student Life Office, Spalding University, 851 S Fourth St, Louisville, KY 40203. Phone: (502) 585-9911. Web: www.spalding.edu.

TAIWAN: NATIONAL TOMB-SWEEPING DAY. Apr 5. National holiday since 1972. According to Chinese custom, the tombs of ancestors are swept "clear and bright" and rites honoring ancestors are held. Tomb-Sweeping Day is observed Apr 5, which is also the anniversary of the death of Chiang Kai-Shek.

"THE TRACEY ULLMAN SHOW" TV PREMIERE: ANNIVERSARY. Apr 5, 1987. This Emmy award-winning comedy-variety show was one of the Fox network's early critical hits. Tracey Ullman starred with Julie Kavner, Dan Castellaneta, Joe Malone and Sam McMurray. The show, produced by James L. Brooks, contained sketches, songs and satire. Animated snippets in between segments introduced us to the Simpsons, executed by Matt Groening, creator of the "Life in Hell" comic strip. "The Simpsons" spun off from the show in 1990 with Castellaneta and Kavner speaking the voices of Homer and Marge Simpson.

TRACY, SPENCER: BIRTH ANNIVERSARY. Apr 5, 1900. Born at Milwaukee, WI, Spencer Tracy was one of the most respected actors in film history. He won Academy Awards for best actor for 1937's *Captains Courageous* and 1938's *Boys Town*, and was nominated seven other times. In 1942, he met actress Katharine Hepburn, and they shared a relationship that lasted until his death, although they never married. Together, they starred in nine films, including *Adam's Rib* in 1949 and *Guess Who's Coming to Dinner* in 1967. Tracy died June 10, 1967, at Hollywood Hills, CA.

Apr 5–6 ☆ Chase's 2004 Calendar of Events ☆

TUTOR APPRECIATION DAY. Apr 5. A day to express appreciation for the volunteer and paid tutors who help us all be better students and wiser people. For info: Sharon Huntington, 3321 S 7700 W, Magna, UT 84044. Phone: (801) 250-6574. E-mail: SHuntington@helpuwrite.com. Web: www.helpuwrite.com.

WASHINGTON, BOOKER TALIAFERRO: BIRTH ANNIVERSARY. Apr 5, 1856. Black educator and leader born at Franklin County, VA. "No race can prosper," he wrote in *Up from Slavery*, "till it learns that there is as much dignity in tilling a field as in writing a poem." Died at Tuskegee, AL, Nov 14, 1915.

BIRTHDAYS TODAY

Jane Asher, 58, actress (*DreamChild, Brideshead Revisited*), born London, England, Apr 5, 1946.

Eric Burdon, 63, singer (*Eric Burdon Declares War, Black Man's Burdon*), songwriter, born Walker-on-Tyne, England, Apr 5, 1941.

Roger Corman, 78, filmmaker (king of B horror movies), born Detroit, MI, Apr 5, 1926.

Max Gail, 61, actor ("Barney Miller," *Pearl*), born Grosse Point, MI, Apr 5, 1943.

Arthur Hailey, 84, author (*Airport, The Final Diagnosis*), born Luton, England, Apr 5, 1920.

Michael Moriarty, 62, actor (*The Last Detail, Bang the Drum Slowly*, "Law & Order"), born Detroit, MI, Apr 5, 1942.

Mitch Pileggi, 52, actor ("The X-Files"), born Portland, OR, Apr 5, 1952.

Colin Luther Powell, 67, US Secretary of State, general, former Chairman US Joint Chiefs of Staff, born New York, NY, Apr 5, 1937.

Gale Storm, 82, actress ("My Little Margie," "NBC Comedy Hour," "The Gale Storm Show"), born Bloomington, TX, Apr 5, 1922.

APRIL 6 — TUESDAY
Day 97 — 269 Remaining

"BARNEY & FRIENDS" TV PREMIERE: ANNIVERSARY. Apr 6, 1992. Although most adults find it hopelessly saccharine, this PBS program is hugely popular with preschoolers. Purple dinosaur Barney, his pals, dinosaurs Baby Bop and B.J. and a multi-ethnic group of children sing, play games and learn simple lessons about getting along with one another. "Bedtime with Barney" was a 1994 prime-time special.

BATTLE OF SHILOH: ANNIVERSARY. Apr 6, 1862. General Ulysess S. Grant's Union forces at Shiloh, or Pittsburgh Landing, TN, were attacked by a large force under General Albert Sidney Johnston on this date. After heavy fighting, the first day of the battle ended without a conclusive victory for either side. Grant was reinforced before the Confederates on the second day and Confederate General Beauregard, in command after Johnston's death the previous day, ordered a retreat back to Corinth, MS, leaving the Federal troops in a stronger position in Tennessee than before the battle. Losses on both sides totaled more than 23,000.

BRANSON FEST. Apr 6–10 (tentative). Branson, MO. The Branson area's kick-off to a new season of great entertainment! The celebration of Ozarks food, arts and culture features some of Branson's best known performers and a taste of all the Branson area has to offer. For info: Branson/Lakes Area Chamber of Commerce, PO Box 1897, Branson, MO 65616. Phone: (800) 296-0529. Fax: (417) 334-4139. E-mail: info@bransoncvb.com. Web: www.explorebranson.com.

BRIGHAM YOUNG'S LAST MARRIAGE: ANNIVERSARY. Apr 6, 1868. Brigham Young, Mormon Church leader, married his 27th, and last, wife on this day.

CHURCH OF JESUS CHRIST OF LATTER-DAY SAINTS: ANNIVERSARY. Apr 6, 1830. Under the leadership of Joseph Smith, Jr, The Church of Jesus Christ of Latter-day Saints was founded with six members in a log cabin at Fayette, NY. For info: Church of Jesus Christ of Latter-day Saints, Public Affairs Dept, 15 E South Temple St, Salt Lake City, UT 84150. Phone: (801) 240-4395. Fax: (801) 240-1167.

ELECTION OFFICIALS DAY. Apr 6. Many people think of election administration as a one-day-a-year operation. Nothing could be further from the truth. From updating voter registration lists, securing poll locations and workers, to preparing the actual ballot and tallying the results, over 17,000 election officials work hard year-round to ensure the most fundamental right of our democracy: the right to vote. This day will spotlight the work of those dedicated public servants. For info: Patrick J. McNally, Essex County Clerk, Hall of Records, PO Box 690, Newark, NJ 07102. Phone: (973) 621-4929. Fax: (973) 621-5178. E-mail: essexclerk@nac.net. Web: www.essexclerk.com.

FIRST MODERN OLYMPICS: ANNIVERSARY. Apr 6, 1896. The first modern Olympics formally opened at Athens, Greece, after a 1,500-year hiatus. Thirteen nations participated, represented by 235 male athletes.

FIRST TONY AWARDS PRESENTED: ANNIVERSARY. Apr 6, 1947. The American Theatre Wing bestowed the first annual Tony awards for distinguished service to the theater.

FIRST US CREDIT UNION LAW: 95th ANNIVERSARY. Apr 6, 1909. The St. Canadian credit union of Manchester, NH, was chartered with the help of Alphonse Desjardins, Canadian credit union pioneer.

MULLIGAN, GERRY: BIRTH ANNIVERSARY. Apr 6, 1927. American jazz saxophonist Gerry Mulligan was born at New York, NY. He performed with many great jazz musicians including Miles Davis, Dave Brubeck, Chet Baker and Duke Ellington, and is credited with helping create the cool-jazz movement with Miles Davis. Mulligan died Jan 20, 1996, at Darien, CT.

NEW YORK STATE MISSING PERSONS DAY. Apr 6. Albany, NY. Missing Persons Memorial Site. As proclaimed by Gov. Pataki. The Center for HOPE sponsors this event for family members and friends of adults and children who have gone missing. Family members participate in a ceremony to remember their missing loved ones, listen to words of hope, comfort and support from other survivors, and share their stories with each other. For info: Doug & Mary Lyall, The Center for HOPE, 20 Prospect St, Ste 103, Chocolate Factory, Ballston Spa, NY 12020. Phone: (518) 884-8761. Web: www.hope4themissing.org.

NORTH POLE DISCOVERED: 95th ANNIVERSARY. Apr 6, 1909. Robert E. Peary reached the North Pole after several failed attempts. The team consisted of Peary, leader of the expedition; Matthew A. Henson, a black man who had served with Peary since 1886 as ship's cook, carpenter and blacksmith, and then as Peary's co-explorer and valuable assistant; and four Eskimo guides—Coquesh, Ootah, Eginwah and Seegloo. They sailed July 17, 1908, on the ship *Roosevelt*, wintering on Ellesmere Island. After a grueling trek with dwindling food supplies, Henson and two of the Eskimos were first to reach the Pole. An

April 2004

S	M	T	W	T	F	S
				1	2	3
4	5	6	7	8	9	10
11	12	13	14	15	16	17
18	19	20	21	22	23	24
25	26	27	28	29	30	

exhausted Peary arrived 45 minutes later and confirmed their location. Dr. Frederick A. Cook, surgeon on an earlier expedition with Peary, claimed to have reached the Pole first, but that could not be substantiated and the National Geographic Society credited the Peary expedition.

OPERATION FLOATING CHRYSANTHEMUM: ANNIVERSARY. Apr 6, 1945. Two US destroyers, two ammunition ships and a tank-landing ship were sunk off the coast of Okinawa when the Japanese Air Force launched 355 kamikaze (suicide) pilots against the Allied fleet in Operation Floating Chrysanthemum.

PESACH or PASSOVER. Apr 6–13. Hebrew calendar dates: Nisan 15–22, 5764. April 6, the first day of Passover, begins an eight-day celebration of the delivery of the Jews from slavery in Egypt. Unleavened bread (matzoh) is eaten at this time. Began at sundown Apr 5.

PORTLAND, OREGON: BIRTHDAY. Apr 6, 1851. "The City of Roses" adds a year today.

RAPHAEL: BIRTH ANNIVERSARY. Apr 6, 1483. Raffaello Santi (Sanzio), Italian painter and architect. Probably born Apr 6, 1483, at Urbino, Italy. Died on his birthday, at Rome, Italy, Apr 6, 1520.

SCHNEIDERMAN, ROSE: BIRTH ANNIVERSARY. Apr 6, 1882. A pioneer in the battle to increase wages and improve working conditions for women, Rose Schneiderman was born at Saven, Poland, and her family immigrated to the US six years later. At age 16 she began factory work in New York City's garment district and quickly became a union organizer. Opposed to the open-shop policy, which permitted nonunion members to work in a unionized shop, Schneiderman organized a 1913 strike of 25,000 women shirtwaist makers. She worked as an organizer for the International Ladies Garment Workers Union (ILGWU) and for the Women's Trade Union League (WTUL), serving as president for more than 20 years. During the Great Depression President Roosevelt appointed her to his Labor Advisory Board—the only woman member. Died Aug 11, 1972, at New York, NY.

SCOTTSBORO TRIAL: ANNIVERSARY. Apr 6, 1931. In what became a *cause célèbre*, nine black youths went on trial at Scottsboro, AL, accused of raping two white women on a freight train. All were convicted in a hasty trial, but by 1950 were free by parole, appeal or escape.

TARTAN DAY. Apr 6. Groups and societies throughout North America take the anniversary of the Declaration of Arbroath (1320) as the day to celebrate their Scottish roots. For more info: www.tartanday.com.

TEFLON INVENTED: ANNIVERSARY. Apr 6, 1938. Polytetraflouroethylene resin was invented by Roy J. Plunkett while he was employed by E.I. Du Pont de Nemours & Co. Commonly known as Teflon, it revolutionized the cookware industry. This substance or something similar coated three-quarters of the pots and pans in America at the time of Plunkett's death in 1994.

THAILAND: CHAKRI DAY. Apr 6. Commemorates foundation of present dynasty by King Rama I (1782–1809), who also established Bangkok as capital.

THOMAS, LOWELL: BIRTH ANNIVERSARY. Apr 6, 1892. World traveler, reporter, editor and radio newscaster, whose broadcasts spanned more than half a century, 1925–76. His radio sign-off, "So long until tomorrow," was known to millions of listeners and he is said to have been the first to broadcast from a ship, an airplane, a submarine and a coal mine. Born at Woodington, OH, he died at Pawling, NY, Aug 29, 1981.

TRAGEDY IN RWANDA: 10th ANNIVERSARY. Apr 6, 1994. A plane carrying the presidents of Rwanda and Burundi was shot down near Kigali, the Rwandan capital, exacerbating a brutal ethnic war that led to the massacre of hundreds of thousands. Presidents Juvenal Habyarimana of Rwanda and Cyprien Ntaryamira of Burundi were returning from a summit in Tanzania where they discussed ways of ending the killing in their countries sparked by ethnic rivalries between the Hutu and Tutsi tribes. Following the attack on the two leaders, Rwanda descended into chaos as the two tribes began killing each other in a genocidal battle for power, leading to a mass exodus of civilians caught in the maelstrom.

US ENTERS WORLD WAR I: ANNIVERSARY. Apr 6, 1917. Congress approved a declaration of war against Germany and the US entered WWI, which had begun in 1914. The first US "doughboys" landed in France June 27, 1917.

US SENATE ACHIEVES A QUORUM: ANNIVERSARY. Apr 6, 1789. The US Senate was formally organized after achieving a quorum.

WORLD'S LARGEST EASTER EGG HUNT. Apr 6. Garrison Homes, Homer, GA. Approximately 150,000 hidden eggs and 100 prize eggs. Begins at 2 PM. Free and open to all—no age limit. Est attendance: 10,000. For info: Banks County Chamber of Commerce, PO Box 57, Homer, GA 30547. Phone: (706) 677-2108 or (800) 638-5004. E-mail: bankscountychamber@alltel.net. Web: www.bankscountyga.org.

BIRTHDAYS TODAY

Bret Boone, 35, baseball player, born El Cajon, CA, Apr 6, 1969.
Candace Cameron Bure, 28, actress ("Full House"), born Canoga Park, CA, Apr 6, 1976.
Merle Haggard, 67, singer, songwriter ("Okie from Muskogee"), born Bakersfield, CA, Apr 6, 1937.
Marilu Henner, 52, actress ("Taxi," "Evening Shade"), born Chicago, IL, Apr 6, 1952.
Olaf Kolzig, 34, former hockey player, born Johannesburg, South Africa, Apr 6, 1970.
Barry Levinson, 62, director, producer, writer, actor ("The Carol Burnett Show" [writer; Emmy Awards 1974, 1975], *Rain Man, Avalon, Bugsy*), born Baltimore, MD, Apr 6, 1942.
Andre Previn, 75, composer, conductor, born Berlin, Germany, Apr 6, 1929.
John Ratzenberger, 57, actor ("Cheers"), born Bridgeport, CT, Apr 6, 1947.
Paul Rudd, 35, actor (*The Object of My Affection, Clueless*), born Passaic, NJ, Apr 6, 1969.
Roy Thinnes, 66, actor ("The Invaders," "The Outer Limits"), born Chicago, IL, Apr 6, 1938.
James Watson, 76, discoverer (with Francis Crick) of the structure of DNA, born Chicago, IL, Apr 6, 1928.
Billy Dee Williams, 67, actor (*Brian's Song, Lady Sings the Blues, Return of the Jedi*), born New York, NY, Apr 6, 1937.

APRIL 7 — WEDNESDAY
Day 98 — 268 Remaining

BATTLE OF LYS RIVER: ANNIVERSARY. Apr 7, 1918. Having failed to break through Allied lines at Somme in March, General Erich Ludendorff made another attempt by attacking Flanders along the Lys River. On the hot, misty, sticky mornings of Apr 7 and 8, 1918, the Germans released mustard gas. On Apr 9 the Central Powers began a high explosive bombardment along the 12-mile front from LaBasse to Armentieres. The British managed to avoid a break in their line, and finally Ferdinand Foch sent nine French divisions to take over a portion of it. On Apr 30, realizing that "further attacks promised no success," Ludendorff ended the offensive. As a result of this battle the British were unable to initiate an offensive for three months. The Allies suffered 240,000 casualties while the German losses exceeded 348,000.

213

CAMP, WALTER: BIRTH ANNIVERSARY. Apr 7, 1859. Walter Chauncey Camp, college athlete, coach and administrator, born at New Britain, CT. Camp played football and several other sports at Yale, but he gained prominence for helping to reshape the rules of rugby football into American football. Among his innovations were reducing the number of players on a side from 15 to 11, introducing the scrimmage, giving one team definite possession of the ball and proposing the downs system. He served as a volunteer coach at Yale and became a national figure as a promoter of football. He selected an All-American team from 1889 to his death. Died at New York, NY, Mar 14, 1925.

CHANNING, WILLIAM ELLERY: BIRTH ANNIVERSARY. Apr 7, 1780. Well-known abolitionist and leader of the Unitarian movement in the US, born at Newport, RI. He stood for religious liberalism and influenced such people as Longfellow, Bryant, Emerson, Lowell and Holmes. Died at Bennington, VT, Oct 2, 1842.

FAIRCHILD, DAVID GRANDISON: BIRTH ANNIVERSARY. Apr 7, 1869. American botanist, government official and explorer, born at East Lansing, MI. Noted for scientific studies on importation of tropical plant species such as avocados and mangoes. Died at Miami, FL, Aug 6, 1954.

HOLIDAY, BILLIE: BIRTH ANNIVERSARY. Apr 7, 1915. Billie Holiday (born Eleanora Fagan, nicknamed "Lady Day") is considered by many jazz critics to have been the greatest jazz singer ever recorded. In her 26-year career, despite having received no formal training, she demonstrated a unique style with sophisticated and dramatic phrasing. Among her best-known songs are "Lover Man," "God Bless the Child," "Don't Explain" and "Strange Fruit." Holiday was born at Philadelphia, PA. She died at New York, NY, July 17, 1959.

KING, WILLIAM RUFUS DEVANE: BIRTH ANNIVERSARY. Apr 7, 1786. 13th vice president of the US died on the 46th day after taking the Oath of Office, of tuberculosis, at Cahaba, AL, Apr 18, 1853. The Oath of Office had been administered to King at Havana, Cuba, as authorized by a special act of Congress (the only presidential or vice presidential oath to be administered outside the US). Born on this day at Sampson County, NY, King was the only vice president who had served in both the House of Representatives and the Senate. King's term as vice president was Mar 4–Apr 18, 1853.

McGRAW, JOHN: BIRTH ANNIVERSARY. Apr 7, 1873. John Joseph McGraw, Baseball Hall of Fame third baseman and manager, born at Truxton, NY. Generally regarded as the best manager ever or close to it, McGraw ran the New York Giants with an iron hand from 1902 to 1932. A scrappy ballplayer with the Baltimore Orioles in the 1890s, McGraw demanded and got total effort from his players. Inducted into the Hall of Fame in 1937. Died at New Rochelle, NY, Feb 25, 1934.

METRIC SYSTEM: ANNIVERSARY. Apr 7, 1795. The metric system was adopted in France, where it had been developed.

NEW YORK SLAVE REVOLT: ANNIVERSARY. Apr 7, 1712. Nine whites were killed in a slave revolt in New York City. Planned by 27 slaves, the rebellion was begun by setting fire to an outhouse; as whites came to put the fire out, they were shot. The state militia was called out to capture the rebels and the city of New York responded to the event by strengthening its slave codes. Twenty-one blacks were executed as participants, and six alleged participants committed suicide. New York outlawed slavery in 1799, though the last slaves were not freed until 1827.

NO HOUSEWORK DAY. Apr 7. No trash. No dishes. No making of beds or washing of laundry. And no guilt. Give it a rest. [©2003 by WH.] For info: Thomas & Ruth Roy, Wellcat Holidays, 2418 Long Ln, Lebanon, PA 17046. Phone: (717) 279-0184. E-mail: info@wellcat.com. Web: www.wellcat.com.

PARAPROFESSIONAL APPRECIATION DAY. Apr 7. Established several years ago by the Governor of Missouri, this holiday honors the contributions of paraprofessionals, especially in education. Annually, the first Wednesday in April. For info: Valerie Pennington, McQuerry Elementary School, 607 S Third St, Odessa, MO 64076. Phone: (816) 230-5334.

RWANDA: GENOCIDE REMEMBRANCE DAY. Apr 7. National holiday. Commemorates massacres of 1994.

SPACE MILESTONE: *MARS ODYSSEY* (US). Apr 7, 2001. *Odyssey* was launched on this day and successfully entered Mars's orbit on Oct 23, 2001. The one-way trip is 286 million miles. The two-and-one-half year mission will monitor space radiation, seek out underground water and identify minerals on the Red Planet.

UNITED NATIONS: WORLD HEALTH DAY: ANNIVERSARY. Apr 7. A United Nations observance commemorating the establishment of the World Health Organization in 1948. For info: United Nations, Dept of Public Info, New York, NY 10017. Web: www.un.org.

WAYNE STATE UNIVERSITY: FUNERAL FOR OL' MAN WINTER. Apr 7. Detroit, MI. Events include a New Orleans–style procession with band playing Dixieland music. "Miss Spring" and a local TV personality conduct an irreverent burial ceremony. Est attendance: 100. For info: Wayne State Dept of Music, 1321 Old Main, Detroit, MI 48202. Phone: (313) 577-1795. Fax: (313) 577-5420.

WINCHELL, WALTER: BIRTH ANNIVERSARY. Apr 7, 1897. Journalist, broadcaster, reporter and gossip columnist Walter Winchell was born at New York, NY, and died at Los Angeles, CA, Feb 20, 1972. He was admired for his way with turning a phrase. His show business columns were voraciously read by millions of Americans between 1924–63.

WORDSWORTH, WILLIAM: BIRTH ANNIVERSARY. Apr 7, 1770. English Lake Poet and philosopher, born at Cumberland, England. "Poetry," he said, "is the spontaneous overflow of powerful feelings: it takes its origin from emotion recollected in tranquility." Wordsworth died Apr 23, 1850, at Rydal Mount, Westmorland.

WORLD HEALTH ORGANIZATION: ANNIVERSARY. Apr 7, 1948. This agency of the UN was founded to coordinate international health systems. It is headquartered at Geneva. Among its achievements is the elimination of smallpox.

BIRTHDAYS TODAY

(William) Hodding Carter III, 69, television and newspaper journalist, born New Orleans, LA, Apr 7, 1935.

Jackie Chan, 50, martial artist, actor (*Rush Hour, Shanghai Noon, Project A*), born Hong Kong, Apr 7, 1954.

Francis Ford Coppola, 65, filmmaker (*Godfather* movies, *Apocalypse Now*), born Detroit, MI, Apr 7, 1939.

Russell Crowe, 40, actor (*LA Confidential, Gladiator* [Oscar for Best Actor], *A Beautiful Mind*), born Auckland, New Zealand, Apr 7, 1964.

☆ Chase's 2004 Calendar of Events ☆   Apr 7–8

Anthony Drew (Tony) Dorsett, 50, Hall of Fame football player, born Rochester, PA, Apr 7, 1954.
Daniel Ellsberg, 73, author (released the "Pentagon Papers" to *The New York Times*), born Chicago, IL, Apr 7, 1931.
David Frost, 65, entertainer ("That Was the Week That Was"), interviewer, born Tenterden, England, Apr 7, 1939.
James Garner, 76, actor (*Space Cowboys*, "Maverick," "The Rockford Files"), born James Baumgardner, Norman, OK, Apr 7, 1928.
John Oates, 56, singer ("Maneater" with Daryl Hall), songwriter, born New York, NY, Apr 7, 1948.
Wayne Rogers, 71, actor ("M*A*S*H," "House Calls"), born Birmingham, AL, Apr 7, 1933.
Gerhard Schroeder, 60, chancellor of Germany, born Mossenberg, Germany, Apr 7, 1944.

APRIL 8 — THURSDAY
Day 99 — 267 Remaining

BIRTHDAY OF THE BUDDHA: BIRTH ANNIVERSARY. Apr 8. Among Buddhist holidays, this day is the most important as it commemorates the birthday of the Buddha. It is also known as the Day of Vesak. The founder of Buddhism had the given name Siddhartha, the family name Gautama and the clan name Shaka. He is commonly called the Buddha, meaning in Sanskrit "the enlightened one." He is thought to have lived in India from c. 563 BC to 483 BC. Some countries celebrate this holiday on the lunar calendar, so the date changes from year to year but it always occurs in either April or May. This day is a holiday in Indonesia, Korea, Singapore and Thailand.

BLACK SENATE PAGE APPOINTED: ANNIVERSARY. Apr 8, 1965. Sixteen-year-old Lawrence Bradford of New York City was the first black page appointed to the US Senate.

DOGWOOD ARTS FESTIVAL. Apr 8–25. Knoxville, TN. The South's premier celebration with more than 60 miles of dogwood trails and more than 100 events featuring arts, crafts, parades, musical performances and much more. Est attendance: 250,000. For info: Dogwood Arts Festival, 601 W Summit Hill Dr, Knoxville, TN 37902. Phone: (865) 637-4561. Web: www.dogwoodarts.com.

FEDERAL GOVERNMENT SEIZURE OF STEEL MILLS: ANNIVERSARY. Apr 8, 1952. On this date President Harry S. Truman seized control of the nation's steel mills by presidential order in an attempt to prevent a shutdown by strikers. On Apr 29, a US District Court declared the seizure unconstitutional and workers immediately walked out. Production dropped from 300,000 tons a day to less than 20,000. After 53 days the strike ended on July 24, with steelworkers receiving a 16¢ hourly wage raise plus a 5.4¢ hourly increase in fringe benefits.

FIRST INTERCOLLEGIATE RODEO: 65th ANNIVERSARY. Apr 8, 1939. The first Intercollegiate Rodeo was held at historic Godshall Ranch, Apple Valley, CA. The student cowboys and cowgirls, who hailed from California and Arizona colleges and universities, were assisted by world champion professional cowboys including Harry Carey, Dick Foran, Curley Fletcher, Tex Ritter and Errol Flynn from Hollywood. Collegiate rodeos had been held since 1919 at Texas A&M University. College cowboys and cowgirls organized a national association in Texas in 1949 named National Intercollegiate Rodeo Association, which continues today as the only national college rodeo organization.

FISCUS, KATHY: 55th DEATH ANNIVERSARY. Apr 8, 1949. While playing, three-year-old Kathy Fiscus of San Marino, CA, fell into an abandoned well pipe 14 inches wide and 120 feet deep. Rescue workers toiled for two days while national attention was focused on the tragedy. Her body was recovered Apr 10, 1949. An alarmed nation suddenly became attentive to other abandoned wells and similar hazards, and "Kathy Fiscus laws" were enacted in a number of places requiring new safety measures to prevent recurrence of such an accident.

HENIE, SONJA: BIRTH ANNIVERSARY. Apr 8, 1912. Sonja Henie, Olympic gold medal figure skater, born at Oslo, Norway. Henie competed in the 1924 Winter Olympics when she was just 11, but finished last in ladies' singles. She won gold medals at the Winter Games of 1928, 1932 and 1936. She became a professional skater and an actress (*Sun Valley Serenade*). Died Oct 13, 1969.

HOME RUN RECORD SET BY HANK AARON: 30th ANNIVERSARY. Apr 8, 1974. Henry ("Hammerin' Hank") Aaron hit the 715th home run of his career, breaking the record set by Babe Ruth in 1935. Playing for the Atlanta Braves, Aaron broke the record at Atlanta in a game against the Los Angeles Dodgers. He finished his career in 1976 with a total of 755 home runs. This record remains unbroken. At the time of his retirement, Aaron also held records for first in RBIs, second in at-bats and runs scored and third in base hits.

HUNTER, "CATFISH": BIRTH ANNIVERSARY. Apr 8, 1946. James Augustus ("Catfish") Hunter, Baseball Hall of Fame pitcher, born at Hertford, NC. Died Sept 9, 1999, at Hertford.

INTERNATIONAL FENG SHUI AWARENESS DAY. Apr 8. To foster a better understanding of the principles and benefits of feng shui, the oriental art of placement. This ancient art/science promotes better health, success and well-being on all levels through proper alignment and coordination of one's property, home, furniture, pathways with universal forms and flow patterns to the natural landforms, local plant/animal life, waterways and general vibration of the area. The overall goal of feng shui is to help blend human creations with those of nature to attain and maintain the inherent harmony of the universe. For info: Bob or Celeste Longacre. Phone: (603) 756-4152. Fax: (603) 756-3196. E-mail: bob@bobsfengshui.com. Web: www.bobsfengshui.com.

ITALY: PROCESSION OF THE ADDOLORATA AND PROCESSION OF THE MYSTERIES. Apr 8–9. Taranto. Procession of the Addolorata is held on Holy Thursday, while the Procession of the Mysteries takes place on Good Friday. Both processions have in common the very slow pace of the participants and their unusual costumes.

JAPAN: FLOWER FESTIVAL (HANA MATSURI). Apr 8. Commemorates Buddha's birthday. Ceremonies in all temples.

KNIGHT, O. RAYMOND: BIRTH ANNIVERSARY. Apr 8, 1872. The "Father of Canadian Rodeo," O. Raymond Knight was born at Payson, UT. His father, the Utah mining magnate Jesse Knight, founded the town of Raymond, Alberta, in 1901. In 1902 Raymond produced Canada's first rodeo, "Raymond Stampede." He also built rodeo's first grandstand and first chute in 1903. O. Raymond Knight died Feb 7, 1947.

MAUNDY THURSDAY or HOLY THURSDAY. Apr 8. The Thursday before Easter, originally "dies mandate," celebrates Christ's injunction to love one another, "Mandatus novum do vobis. . . ." ("A new commandment I give to you. . . .")

McRAE, CARMEN: BIRTH ANNIVERSARY. Apr 8, 1920. After winning an amateur contest at Harlem's legendary Apollo Theatre in her hometown New York City, McRae went on to become a noted jazz singer, singing with the Earl Hines, Mercer Ellington and Benny Carter bands among others and recording more than 20 albums. She died Nov 10, 1994, at Beverly Hills, CA.

MORRIS, LEWIS: BIRTH ANNIVERSARY. Apr 8, 1726. Signer of the Declaration of Independence, born at Westchester County, NY. Died Jan 22, 1798, at Morrisania Manor at NY.

Apr 8–9 ☆ Chase's 2004 Calendar of Events ☆

NATIONAL ALCOHOL SCREENING DAY. Apr 8. To increase awareness of alcohol's effect on health and connect people with alcohol problems to treatment. Free, anonymous, nationwide. For info: Screening for Mental Health, One Washington St, Ste 304, Wellesley Hills, MA 02481-1706. Phone: (781) 239-0071. Fax: (781) 431-7447. Web: www.mentalhealthscreening.org.

NCAA DIVISION I MEN'S ICE HOCKEY CHAMPIONSHIP. Apr 8 & 10. FleetCenter, Boston, MA. For info: NCAA, PO Box 6222, Indianapolis, IN 46206-6222. Web: www.ncaasports.com.

PHILIPPINES: MORIONE'S FESTIVAL. Apr 8–11. Marinduque Island. Provincewide masquerade, Lenten plays and celebrations. Annually, Holy Thursday through Easter Sunday.

POLL TAX OUTLAWED: ANNIVERSARY. Apr 8, 1966. In the last of a series of moves to abolish poll taxes, a three-judge federal court at Jackson, MS, outlawed Mississippi's $2 poll tax as a voting requirement for state and local elections.

SEVENTEENTH AMENDMENT TO US CONSTITUTION RATIFIED: ANNIVERSARY. Apr 8, 1913. Prior to the 17th Amendment, members of the Senate were elected by each state's respective legislature. The advent and popularity of primary elections during the last decade of the 19th century and the early 20th century and a string of senatorial scandals, most notably a scandal involving William Lorimer, an Illinois political boss in 1909, forced the Senate to end its resistance to a constitutional amendment requiring direct popular election of senators.

SPRING BLUEGRASS FESTIVAL. Apr 8–10. Live Oak, FL. Three days of extraordinary music. Previous artists have included The Marksmen, Nothin' Fancy, White Sands, Gary Waldrep Band, Smokey Green and more. Est attendance: 7,000. For info: James Cornett, Spirit of the Suwannee Music Park, 3076 95th Dr, Live Oak, FL 32060. Phone: (386) 364-1683. Fax: (386) 364-2998. E-mail: spirit@musicliveshere.com. Web: www.musicliveshere.com.

VOTE LAWYERS OUT OF OFFICE DAY. Apr 8. This is a day prior to tax deadlines when voters renew their pledge never to vote for a lawyer for public office. A cleansing effort. Annually, the second Thursday in April. Sponsor: Sharkbait Press. For info: Marcus P. Meleton, Jr, Sharkbait Press, PO Box 11300, Costa Mesa, CA 92627-0300. Phone: (949) 413-3052. E-mail: mm@sharkbaitpress.com. Web: www.sharkbaitpress.com.

VOYAGEURS NATIONAL PARK ESTABLISHED: ANNIVERSARY. Apr 8, 1975. Minnesota's Voyageurs land was preserved by Congress on Jan 8, 1971. Four years later, it became the 36th US national park.

WHITE, RYAN: DEATH ANNIVERSARY. Apr 8, 1990. This young man, born Dec 6, 1971, at Kokomo, IN, put the face of a child on AIDS and helped promote greater understanding of the disease. Ryan, a hemophiliac, contracted AIDS from a blood transfusion. Banned from the public school system in Central Indiana at the age of 10, he moved with his mother and sister to Cicero, IN, where he was accepted by students and faculty alike. Ryan once stated that he only wanted to be treated as a normal teenager, but that was not to be as media attention made him a celebrity. A few days after attending the Academy Awards in 1990, 18-year-old Ryan was hospitalized and on Palm Sunday lost his valiant fight at Indianapolis, IN. His funeral was attended by many celebrities.

WILLIAMS, WILLIAM: BIRTH ANNIVERSARY. Apr 8, 1731. Signer of the Declaration of Independence, born at Lebanon, CT. Died there Aug 2, 1811.

April 2004	S	M	T	W	T	F	S
					1	2	3
	4	5	6	7	8	9	10
	11	12	13	14	15	16	17
	18	19	20	21	22	23	24
	25	26	27	28	29	30	

BIRTHDAYS TODAY

Kofi Annan, 66, UN Secretary General, born Kumasi, Ghana, Apr 8, 1938.
Patricia Arquette, 36, actress (*Lost Highway, Flirting with Disaster*), born Chicago, IL, Apr 8, 1968.
Gary Edmund Carter, 50, sportscaster, former baseball player, born Culver City, CA, Apr 8, 1954.
William D. Chase, 82, librarian and chronicler of contemporary civilization as cofounder and coeditor of *Chase's Annual Events*, born Lakeview, MI, Apr 8, 1922.
Elizabeth (Betty) Ford, 86, former First Lady, wife of Gerald Ford, 38th president of the US, born Chicago, IL, Apr 8, 1918.
Shecky Greene, 79, comedian, actor, born Chicago, IL, Apr 8, 1925.
John J. Havlicek, 64, Hall of Fame basketball player, born Lansing, OH, Apr 8, 1940.
Seymour Hersh, 67, journalist, born Chicago, IL, Apr 8, 1937.
Julian Lennon, 41, musician, singer, son of John Lennon, born Liverpool, England, Apr 8, 1963.
Stuart Pankin, 58, actor ("Not Necessarily the News," *Irreconcilable Differences, Arachnophobia*), born Philadelphia, PA, Apr 8, 1946.
Terry Porter, 41, basketball player, born Milwaukee, WI, Apr 8, 1963.
John Schneider, 50, actor ("Dukes of Hazzard," *Smokey and the Bandit*), born Mount Kisco, NY, Apr 8, 1954 (some sources say 1960).
Taran Noah Smith, 20, actor ("Home Improvement"), born San Francisco, CA, Apr 8, 1984.
Robin Wright, 38, actress (*Message in a Bottle, Forrest Gump*), born Dallas, TX, Apr 8, 1966.

APRIL 9 — FRIDAY
Day 100 — 266 Remaining

AFRICAN METHODIST EPISCOPAL CHURCH ORGANIZED: ANNIVERSARY. Apr 9, 1816. The first all-black US religious denomination, the AME church was organized at Philadelphia with Richard Allen, a former slave who had bought his freedom, as the first bishop.

BLACK PAGE APPOINTED TO US HOUSE OF REPRESENTATIVES: ANNIVERSARY. Apr 9, 1965. Fifteen-year-old Frank Mitchell of Springfield, IL, was the first black page appointed to the US House of Representatives.

CHINCOTEAGUE ISLAND EASTER DECOY SHOW. Apr 9–10. Chincoteague Island, VA. Wildfowl carving and wildlife art exhibits. Annually, Easter weekend. Est attendance: 5,000. For info: Chincoteague Chamber of Commerce, Box 258, Chincoteague Island, VA 23336. Phone: (757) 336-6161. Fax: (757) 336-1242. E-mail: pony@intercom.net. Web: www.chincoteaguechamber.com.

CIVIL RIGHTS BILL OF 1866: ANNIVERSARY. Apr 9, 1866. The Civil Rights Bill of 1866, passed by Congress over the veto of President Andrew Johnson, granted blacks the rights and privileges of American citizenship and formed the basis for the Fourteenth Amendment to the US Constitution.

CIVIL WAR ENDING: ANNIVERSARY. Apr 9, 1865. At 1:30 PM General Robert E. Lee, commander of the Army of Northern Virginia, surrendered to General Ulysses S. Grant, commander-in-chief of the Union Army, ending four years of civil war. The meeting took place in the house of Wilmer McLean at the

☆ Chase's 2004 Calendar of Events ☆   Apr 9

village of Appomattox Court House, VA. Confederate soldiers were permitted to keep their horses and go free to their homes, while Confederate officers were allowed to retain their swords and side arms as well. Grant wrote the terms of surrender. Formal surrender took place at the Courthouse on Apr 12. Death toll for the Civil War is estimated at 500,000 men.

ECKERT, J(OHN) PRESPER, JR: 85th BIRTH ANNIVERSARY. Apr 9, 1919. Co-inventor with John W. Mauchly of ENIAC (Electronic Numerical Integrator and Computer), which was first demonstrated at the Moore School of Electrical Engineering at the University of Pennsylvania at Philadelphia Feb 14, 1946. This is generally considered the birth of the computer age. Originally designed to process artillery calculations for the Army, ENIAC was also used in the Manhattan Project. Eckert and Mauchly formed Electronic Control Company, which later became Unisys Corporation. Eckert was born at Philadelphia and died at Bryn Mawr, PA, June 3, 1995.

ENGLAND: DEVIZES TO WESTMINSTER INTERNATIONAL CANOE RACE. Apr 9–12. 56th year. Starts from Wharf Car Park, Wharf St, Devizes, Wiltshire. Canoes race along 125 miles of the Kennet and Avon canals and the River Thames, ending at County Hall Steps, Westminster Bridge Rd, London. Annually, Good Friday to Easter Monday. Est attendance: 6,000. For info: Competition Secretary, Boscombe Forge, Church Road, Bookham, Surrey, England KT23 3JG. Phone: (44) (020) 7620-0298. Web: www.dwrace.org.uk.

GOOD FRIDAY. Apr 9. Observed in commemoration of the crucifixion. Oldest Christian celebration. Possible corruption of "God's Friday." Observed in some manner by most Christian sects and as a public holiday or part holiday in Canada and in Delaware, Florida, Hawaii, Illinois, Indiana, New Jersey, North Carolina, Pennsylvania and Tennessee.

IRAQ: NATIONAL DAY. Apr 9. National holiday commemorating anniversary of dictator Saddam Hussein's fall from power in 2003.

JENKINS'S EAR DAY: ANNIVERSARY. Apr 9, 1731. Spanish *guardacosta* boarded and plundered the British ship *Rebecca* off Jamaica, and, among other outrages, cut off the ear of English master mariner Robert Jenkins. Little notice was taken until seven years later, when Jenkins exhibited the detached ear and described the atrocity to a committee of the House of Commons. In consequence, Britain declared war on Spain in October 1739, a war that lasted until 1743 and is still known as the "War of Jenkins's Ear." Nothing else is known of him.

KING, FRANK: BIRTH ANNIVERSARY. Apr 9, 1883. Created by Frank King in 1919 as a comic strip about men's interest in autos, *Gasoline Alley* had a tremendous jump in popularity in 1921 when its main character Walt adopted a foundling called Skeezix. Devoid of melodrama, this strip sympathetically described the day-to-day lives of Walt, Skeezix and their friends and family, and it was the first American cartoon in which the characters actually aged. Frank King was born at Cashon, WI, and died at Winter Park, FL, June 24, 1969.

LUDENDORFF, ERICK: BIRTH ANNIVERSARY. Apr 9, 1865. German general who, during the last years of World War I, was chiefly responsible for military policy and strategy. Born near Pozen, Prussia, and died at Tutzing, Dec 20, 1937.

MARIAN ANDERSON EASTER CONCERT: 65th ANNIVERSARY. Apr 9, 1939. On this Easter Sunday, black American contralto Marian Anderson sang an open-air concert from the steps of the Lincoln Memorial at Washington, DC, to an audience of 75,000, after having been denied use of the Daughters of the American Revolution (DAR) Constitution Hall. The event became an American antidiscrimination *cause célèbre* and led First Lady Eleanor Roosevelt to resign from the DAR.

MUYBRIDGE, EADWEARD: BIRTH ANNIVERSARY. Apr 9, 1830. English photographer famed for his studies of animals in motion. Born Edward James Muggeridge, at Kingston-on-Thames, England. Died there May 8, 1904.

★**NATIONAL FORMER PRISONER OF WAR RECOGNITION DAY.** Apr 9.

OZARK UFO CONFERENCE. Apr 9–11. Inn of the Ozarks Conference Center, Eureka Springs, AR. 16th annual meeting of researchers from various states and foreign countries to inform the public of the latest news concerning UFOs. Speakers include authors of books on the subject and people who have investigated UFO cases; program includes audiovisual presentations of UFO evidence. Est attendance: 500. For info: Lucius Farish, Ozark UFO Conference, #2 Caney Valley Drive, Plumerville, AR 72127-8725. Phone: (501) 354-2558. E-mail: ozarkufo@webtv.net.

PHILIPPINES: ARAW NG KAGITINGAN. Apr 9, 1942. Day of Valor. National observance to commemorate the fall of Bataan. The infamous "Death March" is reenacted at the Mount Samat Shrine, the Dambana ng Kagitingan.

ROBESON, PAUL BUSTILL: BIRTH ANNIVERSARY. Apr 9, 1898. Paul Robeson, born at Princeton, NJ, was an All-American football player at Rutgers University and received his law degree from Columbia University in 1923. After being seen by Eugene O'Neill in an amateur stage production, he was offered a part in O'Neill's play *The Emperor Jones*. His performance in that play with the Provincetown Players established him as an actor. Without ever having taken a voice lesson, he also became a popular singer. His stage credits include *Show Boat, Porgy and Bess, The Hairy Ape* and *Othello*, which enjoyed the longest Broadway run of a Shakespeare play. In 1950 he was denied a passport by the US for refusing to sign an affidavit stating whether he was or ever had been a member of the Communist Party. The action was overturned by the Supreme Court in 1958. His film credits include *Emperor Jones, Show Boat, King Solomon's Mines* and *Song of Freedom*, among others. Robeson died at Philadelphia, PA, Jan 23, 1976.

SELF DAY. April 9 (tentative). A day devoted to bettering oneself mentally, physically and spiritually. Self Day originated in 2000 after a national survey by *Self* magazine found that only 3% of women say taking care of themselves is a top priority. For info: SELF, 4 Times Square 17th Floor, New York, NY 10036. Phone: (212) 286-8237. Fax: (212) 286-8110. Web: www.self.com.

SPACE MILESTONE: *SOYUZ 35* (USSR). Apr 9, 1980. Two cosmonauts (Valery Ryumin and Leonid Popov) were launched from Baikonur space center at Kazakhstan, USSR. Docked at *Salyut 6* Apr 10. Ryumin and Popov returned to Earth Oct 11, 1980, after setting a new space endurance record of 185 days.

STOCK EXCHANGE HOLIDAY (GOOD FRIDAY). Apr 9. The holiday schedules for the various exchanges are subject to change if relevant rules, regulations or exchange policies are revised. If you have questions, phone: American Stock Exchange (212) 306-1000; Chicago Board of Trade (312) 435-3500; Chicago Board of Options Exchange (312) 786-5600; New York Stock Exchange (212) 656-2065; Pacific Stock Exchange (415) 393-4000; Philadelphia Stock Exchange (215) 496-5000.

TEXAS PANHANDLE TORNADO: ANNIVERSARY. Apr 9, 1947. A monster tornado clearing a 1.5-mile-long path struck through at least 12 towns in Texas, Oklahoma and Kansas, killing 169 people and causing more than $15 million in damage. The tornado traveled 221 miles across the three states.

TUNISIA: MARTYRS' DAY. Apr 9.

UNITED KINGDOM: GOOD FRIDAY BANK HOLIDAY. Apr 9. Bank and public holiday in England, Wales, Scotland and Northern Ireland.

217

Apr 9–10 ☆ Chase's 2004 Calendar of Events ☆

WINSTON CHURCHILL DAY. Apr 9. Anniversary of enactment of legislation in 1963 that made the late British statesman an honorary citizen of the US.

THE WRESTLING PRESIDENT: 100th ANNIVERSARY. Apr 9, 1904. In a letter to his son Kermit, President Theodore Roosevelt wrote, "I am wrestling with two Japanese wrestlers three times a week. I am not the age or build one would think to be whirled lightly over an opponent's head and batted down on a mattress without damage. But they are so skillful that I have not been hurt at all." Roosevelt was 46 years old. An avid sportsman, he had given up boxing because "it seems rather absurd for a President to appear with a black eye or a swollen nose or a cut lip."

BIRTHDAYS TODAY

Severiano (Seve) Ballesteros, 47, golfer, born Pedrena, Spain, Apr 9, 1957.

Jean-Paul Belmondo, 71, actor (*Breathless, The Man from Rio, Is Paris Burning?*), born Neuilly-sur-Seine, France, Apr 9, 1933.

Hugh Hefner, 78, founder of *Playboy*, born Chicago, IL, Apr 9, 1926.

Paul Krassner, 72, editor, journalist, born Brooklyn, NY, Apr 9, 1932.

Michael Learned, 65, actress (*The Waltons, Nurses*; stage: *The Sisters Rosenzweig*), born Washington, DC, Apr 9, 1939.

Tom Lehrer, 76, songwriter ("Vatican Rag," "New Math"), pianist, mathematician, born New York, NY, Apr 9, 1928.

Cynthia Nixon, 38, actress ("Sex and the City," *Amadeus*), born New York, NY, Apr 9, 1966.

Keshia Knight Pulliam, 25, actress ("The Cosby Show"), born Newark, NJ, Apr 9, 1979.

Dennis Quaid, 50, actor (*The Rookie, Everybody's All-American*), born Houston, TX, Apr 9, 1954.

Jacques Villeneueve, 33, race car driver, winner of 1995 Indianapolis 500, born St. Jean d'Iberville, QC, Canada, Apr 9, 1971.

APRIL 10 — SATURDAY
Day 101 — 265 Remaining

BATAAN DEATH MARCH: ANNIVERSARY. Apr 10, 1942. On this morning American and Filipino prisoners were herded together by Japanese soldiers on Mariveles Airfield on Bataan (in the Philippine islands) and began the Death March to Camp O'Donnell, near Cabanatuan. During the six-day march they were given only one bowl of rice. More than 5,200 Americans and many more Filipinos lost their lives in the course of the march.

BOOTH, WILLIAM: 175th BIRTH ANNIVERSARY. Apr 10, 1829. General William Booth, founder of the movement that became known, in 1878, as the Salvation Army, was born at Nottingham, England. Apprenticed to a pawnbroker at the age of 13, Booth experienced firsthand the misery of poverty. He broke with conventional church religion and established a quasi-military religious organization with military uniforms and ranks. Recruiting from the poor, from converted criminals and from many other social outcasts, his organization grew rapidly and its influence spread from England to the US and to other countries. At revivals in slum areas the itinerant evangelist offered help for the poor, homes for the homeless, sobriety for alcoholics, rescue homes for women and girls, training centers and legal aid. Booth died at London, England, Aug 20, 1912. See also: "Salvation Army Founder's Day" (Apr 10).

BRAHMS "REQUIEM" PREMIERE: ANNIVERSARY. Apr 10, 1868. Composer Johannes Brahms fortified his reputation as one of the leading figures in 19th-century German Romantic music with the success of his *Requiem*, which premiered at Bremen Cathedral on this date. The choral piece, at turns both melancholy and exuberant, is one of the more recognized and often-sung funerary works in the musical canon.

CIMARRON TERRITORY CELEBRATION. Apr 10–17. Beaver, OK. Shoot-out, parade, talent show, Cow Chip Chili Cook-Off, 35th annual "World Cow Chip Throwing Championship®" Contest. Antiques, coins, guns and crafts show. Est attendance: 4,500. For info: Kim Hardin, Secy, Beaver County Chamber of Commerce, PO Box 878, Beaver, OK 73932. Phone: (580) 625-4726.

COMMODORE PERRY DAY. Apr 10, 1794. Birth anniversary of Matthew Calbraith Perry, commodore in the US Navy, negotiator of first treaty between US and Japan (Mar 31, 1854). Born at South Kingston, RI. Died Mar 4, 1858, at New York, NY.

CONNORS, CHUCK (KEVIN JOSEPH): BIRTH ANNIVERSARY. Apr 10, 1921. "The Rifleman" of television fame, Chuck Connors played that role from 1958 to 1963. His portrayal of a slave owner in the miniseries *Roots* won him an Emmy nomination. Connors acted in more than 45 films and appeared on many TV series and specials. He played professional basketball and baseball before becoming an actor. Born at Brooklyn, NY; died Nov 10, 1992, at Los Angeles, CA.

EASTER BEACH RUN. Apr 10. Daytona Beach, FL. The 36th annual beach run on "the world's most famous beach" includes a four-mile run for 28 age divisions and a two-mile run for youth 11 years old and younger. Est attendance: 1,000. For info: Easter Beach Run, Daytona Beach Leisure Services Dept, PO Box 2451, Daytona Beach, FL 32115-2451. Phone: (386) 671-3402 or (386) 322-0835 (Daytona Track Club). Fax: (386) 671-3410.

EASTER BUNNY BOP AND HOP. Apr 10. Aiken, SC. The Easter Bunny Bop and Hop is a noncompetitive Easter egg hunt with carnival rides and games at Virginia Acres Soccer Field. Annually, the Saturday before Easter. Est attendance: 700. For info: Easter Bunny Bop and Hop, City of Aiken Parks and Recreation, Odell Weeks Center, PO Box 1177, Aiken, SC 29803. Phone: (803) 642-7631. Fax: (803) 642-7639. E-mail: howeeks @aiken.net.

EASTER EGG HUNT. Apr 10. The Laurels of Shane Hill Nursing Home, and Maplewood of Shanes Village Assisted Living Center, Rockford, OH. Residents color 80 dozen Easter eggs to hide for the Egg Hunt held the Saturday before Easter for children and grandchildren of residents, staff and the surrounding community. Prizes are given in various catagories. Pictures with the Easter Bunny are offered for participants. Est attendance: 100. For info: Brooke Reyman, Activities Dir, The Laurels of Shane Hill Nursing Home, 10731 State Rte 118, Rockford, OH 45882-0159. Phone: (419) 363-2620.

EASTER EVEN. Apr 10. The Saturday before Easter. Last day of Holy Week and of Lent.

FIRST PGA CHAMPIONSHIP: ANNIVERSARY. Apr 10, 1916. The then-recently formed Professional Golfer's Association of America held its first championship at Siwanoy golf course at Bronxville, NY. The trophy and the lion's share of the $2,580 purse were won by British golfer Jim Barnes.

April 2004	S	M	T	W	T	F	S
					1	2	3
	4	5	6	7	8	9	10
	11	12	13	14	15	16	17
	18	19	20	21	22	23	24
	25	26	27	28	29	30	

☆ Chase's 2004 Calendar of Events ☆   Apr 10

GOOD FRIDAY PEACE AGREEMENT IN NORTHERN IRELAND: ANNIVERSARY. Apr 10, 1998. Protestant and Catholic factions agreed to a power-sharing agreement on Good Friday, 1998. It was endorsed by referenda in Northern Ireland and the Republic of Ireland on May 22, 1998. As a result, a provincial government was established in Northern Ireland to replace direct rule by Britain. The Northern Ireland Assembly met for the first time June 5, 2000. However, the peace remains strained and paramilitaries have yet to be disarmed. The 30-year-old conflict in Northern Ireland has taken more than 3,200 lives.

GREAT EGG CAPER AT AUDUBON ACRES. Apr 10. Audubon Acres, Chattanooga, TN. Children color eggs with natural dyes, play egg games, hunt eggs along the trails and meadows of Audubon Acres, then stroll to the swinging bridge and observe the beauty of wildflowers. Sponsor: Chattanooga Audubon Society. Annually, the Saturday before Easter. Est attendance: 250. For info: Lynda Logan, Audubon Acres, 900 N Sanctuary Rd, Chattanooga, TN 37421. Phone: (423) 892-1499. Fax: (423) 892-6376. E-mail: caudubons@aol.com. Web: www.audubonchattanooga.org.

GROTIUS, HUGO: BIRTH ANNIVERSARY. Apr 10, 1583 (OS). Anniversary of the birth of Hugo Grotius, the Dutch theologian, attorney, scholar and statesman whose beliefs profoundly influenced American thinking, especially with regard to the conscience of humanity. Born at Delft, Holland, he died at Rostock, Germany, Aug 28, 1645 (OS).

MEGGA HUNT. Apr 10. Lively Park, Springfield, OR. Hunt for 25,000 eggs, play carnival games, enjoy onstage entertainment and ride the Willamalane Train. The valley's biggest egg hunt! Est attendance: 3,500. For info: Willamalane Park and Recreation District, 765 A St, Springfield, OR 97477. Phone: (541) 736-4544. Web: www.willamalane.org.

★**NATIONAL D.A.R.E. DAY.** Apr 10. The Drug Abuse Resistance Education (D.A.R.E.) Program, founded in 1983 by the Los Angeles Police Department and the Los Angeles Unified School District, helps give children in grades K–12 the skills they need to avoid involvement in drugs, gangs and violence. Nearly 75 percent of American school districts offer D.A.R.E. training.

NATIONAL SIBLINGS DAY. Apr 10. A commemorative day to honor all brothers and sisters who are living and memorialize those who have died. Recognizing the bond between a brother and sister for the special gift it is. Created by Claudia A. Evart of New York City through her nonprofit charity, Siblings Day Foundation, in memory of her sister Lisette and brother Alan; they both died from accidents early in their lives. Annually, Apr 10. For info: Claudia A. Evart, Siblings Day Foundation, Inc, 30 Park Ave, Ste 2-P, New York, NY 10016-3833. Phone: (212) 779-2227. E-mail: siblingsday@earthlink.net. Web: www.siblingsday.org.

ODESSA RETAKEN: 60th ANNIVERSARY. Apr 10, 1944. The Red Army retook the Ukrainian city of Odessa, the port on the northwest coast of the Black Sea that had been in the hands of the Nazis since October 1941.

PERKINS, FRANCES: BIRTH ANNIVERSARY. Apr 10, 1880. First woman member of a US presidential cabinet. Born at Boston, MA, she was married in 1915 to Paul Caldwell Wilson, but used her maiden name in public life. She was appointed secretary of labor by President Franklin D. Roosevelt in 1933, a post in which she served until 1945. Died at New York, NY, May 14, 1965.

PULITZER, JOSEPH: BIRTH ANNIVERSARY. Apr 10, 1847. American journalist and newspaper publisher, founder of the Pulitzer Prizes, born at Budapest, Hungary. Died at Charleston, SC, Oct 29, 1911. Pulitzer Prizes awarded annually since 1917. Write for entry and deadline info. (Please specify Book, Journalism, Drama or Music Competition.) For info: Pulitzer Prize Bd, 709 Journalism, Columbia Univ, New York, NY 10027. Phone: (212) 854-3841. Web: www.pulitzer.org

ROBERT GRAY BECOMES FIRST AMERICAN TO CIRCUMNAVIGATE THE EARTH: ANNIVERSARY. Apr 10, 1790. When Robert Gray docked the *Columbia* at Boston Harbor, he became the first American to circumnavigate the earth. He sailed from Boston, MA, in September 1787, to trade with Indians of the Pacific Northwest. From there he sailed to China and then continued around the world. His 42,000-mile journey opened trade between New England and the Pacific Northwest and helped the US establish claims to the Oregon Territory.

SAFETY PIN PATENTED: ANNIVERSARY. Apr 10, 1849. Walter Hunt of New York patented the first safety pin.

SALVATION ARMY FOUNDER'S DAY. Apr 10, 1829. Birth anniversary of William Booth, a Methodist minister who began an evangelical ministry in the East End of London in 1865 and established mission stations to feed and house the poor. In 1878 he changed the name of the organization to the Salvation Army. Booth was born at Nottingham, England; he died at London, Aug 20, 1912. See also: "Booth, William: Birth Anniversary" (Apr 10).

STRAWBERRY HILL RACES. Apr 10. Colonial Downs, New Kent, VA. Annual steeplechase featuring a week of festivities leading up to the event. Elegant, yet fun, pre-race entertainment and tailgate competition on race day. $64,000 in purses. Sponsored by Atlantic Rural Exposition, Inc. Est attendance: 20,000. For info: Sue Mullins, Race Dir, Strawberry Hill Races, PO Box 26805, Richmond, VA 23261. Phone: (804) 569-3238. Fax: (804) 569-3252. E-mail: smullins@AREevents.com.

WELLS FARGO GOLDEN BUNNY EGG HUNT AND RACE. Apr 10. Winter Park Resort, Winter Park, CO. Winter Park Willie and the Easter Bunny give kids some holiday fun with an on-mountain egg hunt and traditional fun race for children 10 and under. Est attendance: 500. For info: Winter Park Resort, PO Box 36, Winter Park, CO 80482. Phone: (970) 726-1564. Fax: (970) 726-1572. E-mail: wpinfo@mail.skiwinterpark.com. Web: winterparkresort.com.

WICHITA WEST SPRING ARTS AND CRAFTS SHOW. Apr 10–11. Wichita Falls, TX. Artists/craftsmen from the area display and sell their quality arts and crafts. Free admission to the public. Est attendance: 3,000. For info: Wichita Falls Conv & Visitors Bureau, 1000 5th St, Wichita Falls, TX 76301. Phone: (940) 716-5500 or (940) 691-2738. Fax: (940) 716-5509. E-mail: MPEC@wf.net. Web: www.wichitafalls.org.

WOODWARD, ROBERT BURNS: BIRTH ANNIVERSARY. Apr 10, 1917. Nobel Prize–winning (1965) Harvard University science professor whose special field of study was molecular structure of complex organic compounds. Called "one of the most outstanding scientific minds of the century." Born at Boston, MA, he died at Cambridge, MA, July 8, 1979.

BIRTHDAYS TODAY

Kenneth ("Babyface") Edmonds, 47, pop performer and songwriter, born Indianapolis, IN, Apr 10, 1957.

David Halberstam, 70, author (*The Best and the Brightest, The Summer of Forty-Nine*), born New York, NY, Apr 10, 1934.

Dolores Huerta, 74, cofounder, with Cesar Chavez, of the United Farm Workers Union, born Dawson, NM, Apr 10, 1930.

Peter MacNicol, 50, actor ("Ally McBeal," *Ghostbusters II*), born Dallas, TX, Apr 10, 1954.

John Earl Madden, 68, sportscaster, former football coach, born Austin, MN, Apr 10, 1936.

Joe Don Meredith, 66, former sportscaster, actor and football player, born Mount Vernon, TX, Apr 10, 1938.

Harry Morgan, 89, actor (Emmy for "M*A*S*H"; "Dragnet"), born Harry Bratsburg, Detroit, MI, Apr 10, 1915.
Haley Joel Osment, 16, actor (*The Sixth Sense, Bogus*), born Los Angeles, CA, Apr 10, 1988.
Steven Seagal, 53, actor, producer (*Hard to Kill, On Deadly Ground*), born Lansing, MI, Apr 10, 1951.
Omar Sharif, 72, actor (*Lawrence of Arabia, Dr. Zhivago*), born Michael Shalhoub, Alexandria, Egypt, Apr 10, 1932.
Paul Edward Theroux, 63, author (*The Mosquito Coast, Millroy the Magician*), born Medford, MS, Apr 10, 1941.
Max Von Sydow, 75, actor (*The Seventh Seal, The Emigrants*), born Lund, Sweden, Apr 10, 1929.

APRIL 11 — SUNDAY
Day 102 — 264 Remaining

BARBERSHOP QUARTET DAY. Apr 11. Commemorates the gathering of some 26 persons at Tulsa, OK, Apr 11, 1938, and the founding there of the Society for the Preservation and Encouragement of Barbershop Quartet Singing in America.

BLISS, LIZZIE "LILLIE": BIRTH ANNIVERSARY. Apr 11, 1864. Lizzie "Lillie" Bliss was born at Boston, MA. She was one of the three founders (all women) of the Museum of Modern Art at New York City in 1929. She died Mar 12, 1931, at New York City.

BOLIN, JANE MATILDA: BIRTHDAY. Apr 11, 1908. Jane Matilda Bolin, born at Poughkeepsie, NY, was the first black woman to graduate from the Yale School of Law (1931) and went on to become the first black woman judge in the US. She served as assistant corporation counsel for the city of New York before being appointed to the city's Domestic Relations Court and the Family Court of the State of New York.

CIVIL RIGHTS ACT OF 1968: ANNIVERSARY. Apr 11, 1968. Exactly one week after the assassination of Martin Luther King, Jr, the Civil Rights Act of 1968 (protecting civil rights workers, expanding the rights of Native Americans and providing antidiscrimination measures in housing) was signed into law by President Lyndon B. Johnson, who said: "[T]he proudest moments of my presidency have been times such as this when I have signed into law the promises of a century."

COSTA RICA: JUAN SANTAMARÍA DAY. Apr 11. National holiday. Commemorates the 1856 Battle of Rivas.

DOLE SPRING SPLASH. Apr 11. Winter Park Resort, Winter Park, CO. One of Winter Park's most anticipated events, the wet and wild Spring Splash celebrates the joy of spring skiing. Spectators cheer as skiers and snowboarders struggle through a hilarious and challenging obstacle course that includes skimming across a pond of icy water to cross the finish line. Est attendance: 2,000. For info: Winter Park Resort, PO Box 36, Winter Park, CO 80482. Phone: (970) 726-1564. Fax: (970) 726-1572. E-mail: wpinfo@mail.skiwinterpark.com. Web: winterparkresort.com.

EASTER SUNDAY. Apr 11. Commemorates the Resurrection of Christ. Most joyous festival of the Christian year. The date of Easter, a movable feast, is derived from the lunar calendar: the first Sunday following the first ecclesiastical full moon on or after Mar 21—always between Mar 22 and Apr 25. The Council of Nicaea (AD 325) prescribed that Easter be celebrated on the Sunday after Passover, as that feast's date had been established in Jesus' time. After 1582, when Pope Gregory XIII introduced the Gregorian calendar, Orthodox Christians continued to use the Julian calendar, so Easter can sometimes be as much as five weeks apart in the Western and Eastern churches. Easter in 2005 will be Mar 27; in 2006 it will be Apr 16; in 2007 it will be Apr 8. Many other dates in the Christian year are derived from the date of Easter. See also: "Orthodox Easter Sunday or Pascha."

EASTER SUNRISE SERVICE. Apr 11. Chimney Rock Park, Chimney Rock, NC. Celebrate the glory of Easter at this 49th annual nondenominational community worship service overlooking beautiful Lake Lure. Gates open at 5:00 AM and close at 6:00 AM for the 6:30 AM service. No admission charge. Est attendance: 1,500. For info: Melinda Massey, PR, PO Box 39, Chimney Rock, NC 28720. Phone: (800) 277-9611 or (828) 625-9611. Fax: (828) 625-9610. E-mail: visit@chimneyrockpark.com. Web: www.chimneyrockpark.com.

HAROLD WASHINGTON ELECTED FIRST BLACK MAYOR OF CHICAGO: ANNIVERSARY. Apr 11, 1983. Harold Washington defeated Bernard Epton and became the first black mayor of Chicago. Of the city's 1.6 million voters a record 82 percent voted. Washington won 51 percent of the votes, which split along racial lines. He was reelected in April 1987, but died suddenly seven months later at his office, Nov 25, 1987.

HAUTE DOG CHARITY EASTER PARADE. Apr 11. Belmont Shore, Long Beach, CA. Just about every breed from bulldog to poodle will take over Belmont Shore for this annual parade. The event has raised thousands of dollars for animal shelters and rescue organizations. About 400 pooches—some colorfully costumed in Easter attire—are expected to pack Livingston Park for a Yappy Hour before beginning their parade down Second Street. Prizes awarded for best outfits and canine bonnets. Annually, Easter Sunday. Est attendance: 3,000. For info: Justin Rudd. Phone: (562) 439-3316. E-mail: justinrudd@aol.com. Web: www.hautedogs.org.

HUGHES, CHARLES EVANS: BIRTH ANNIVERSARY. Apr 11, 1862. 11th chief justice of US Supreme Court. Born at Glens Falls, NY. Died at Osterville, MA, Aug 27, 1948.

ITALY: EXPLOSION OF THE CART. Apr 11. Florence. At noon on Easter Sunday in Piazza del Duomo a cart full of fireworks is exploded, perpetuating a ceremony of ancient origin and recalling the fire that used to be kindled during the *Gloria* at Easter mass, and was then distributed to all of Florence's households. The tradition is held to date back to the time of the First Crusade, when the valorous Pazzino dei Pazzi was awarded some pieces of flint from the Holy Sepulcher. After his return to Florence the holy fire was kindled with these flints, now preserved in the church of Santi Apostoli.

JULIAN, PERCY: BIRTH ANNIVERSARY. Apr 11, 1899. Percy Julian, producer of a synthetic progesterone using soybeans, was born at Montgomery, AL. He also developed a cheaper method of producing cortisone, a drug to treat glaucoma and a chemical foam to fight petroleum fires. Julian died Apr 19, 1975, at Waukegan, IL.

LIBERATION OF BUCHENWALD CONCENTRATION CAMP: ANNIVERSARY. Apr 11, 1945. Buchenwald, north of Weimar, Germany, was entered by Allied troops. It was the first of the Nazi concentration camps to be liberated. It had been established in 1937, and about 56,000 people died there.

MARKSVILLE EASTER EGG KNOCKING CONTEST. Apr 11. Marksville, LA. Competition among owners of chicken and guinea eggs which have been boiled and dyed. Annually, on Easter Sunday 9 AM–noon. Est attendance: 500. For info: Chamber of Commerce, Box 767, Marksville, LA 71351. Phone: (318) 253-9222 or (318) 253-0284.

MERRIE MONARCH FESTIVAL (WITH WORLD'S LARGEST HULA COMPETITION). Apr 11–17. Hilo, HI. Cultural event honoring King David Kalakaua. Festival culminates with the world's largest hula competition. Hawaii's finest hula schools compete in ancient and modern divisions. Annually, beginning on Easter Sunday. Est attendance: 6,000. For info: Dorothy Thompson, Hawaii Naniloa Hotel, Merrie Monarch Office, 93 Banyan Dr, Hilo, HI 96720. Phone: (808) 935-9168.

April 2004

S	M	T	W	T	F	S
				1	2	3
4	5	6	7	8	9	10
11	12	13	14	15	16	17
18	19	20	21	22	23	24
25	26	27	28	29	30	

☆ Chase's 2004 Calendar of Events ☆   Apr 11–12

MOON PHASE: LAST QUARTER. Apr 11. Moon enters Last Quarter phase at 11:46 PM, EDT.

MORAVIAN EASTER RESURRECTION SERVICE. Apr 11. Winston-Salem, NC. Outdoor religious service featuring Moravian brass bands playing in streets to awaken sleepers. Service begins in Salem Square, and concludes in God's Acre, the Moravian Graveyard, at daybreak. Est attendance: 8,000. For info: Salem Congregation, 459 S Church St, Winston-Salem, NC 27101-5314. Phone: (336) 722-6504. Fax: (336) 725-2514. E-mail: facilitiesmgr@mcsp.org.

NATIONAL GARDEN WEEK. Apr 11–17. To recognize and honor the 78 million Americans who eagerly garden each year. These American gardeners enhance and improve the environment with their efforts. Annually, the second full week of April. For info: Natl Garden Bureau, 1311 Butterfield Rd, Ste 310, Downers Grove, IL 60515.

NATIONAL WOMEN'S NUTRITION WEEK. Apr 11–17. To recognize the importance and value of health in all phases of a woman's life. A woman's biochemistry needs nutritional support when on the pill, during pregnancy, during lactation, when she is under stress and going through menopause. This week is designed to educate women about the importance of nutrition for their ongoing health and well-being. For info: Dr. Lois M Vanderhoof, Applied Nutrition Concepts, 2828 W Parker Rd, #A205, Plano, TX 75075. Phone: (972) 612-5505. E-mail: drlois@appliednutritionconcepts.com. Web: www.appliednutritionconcepts.com.

ORTHODOX EASTER SUNDAY OR PASCHA. Apr 11. Observed by Eastern Orthodox Churches on this date. Normally Easter falls on different Sundays in the Eastern and Western churches. See also: "Easter Sunday" (Apr 11).

★**PAN AMERICAN WEEK.** Apr 11–17. Presidential Proclamation customarily issued as "Pan American Day and Pan American Week." Always issued for the week including Apr 14, except in 1965, from 1946 through 1948, 1955 through 1977, and 1979.

PYRAMID FESTIVALS. Apr 11–17 (also June 21–27). This time will be dedicated to all those who were involved in planning, prepartation and actual building of the pyramids all over the world. More information and a newsletter are available. For info: Rev Margaret Allbritten, LightPaths, 211 Cherry St, Roseville, CA 95678. Phone: (916) 446-4961. E-mail: goldenfire@mail.com.

SPACE MILESTONE: *APOLLO 13* (US). Apr 11, 1970. Astronauts Lovell, Haise and Swigert endangered when oxygen tank ruptured. Planned moon landing canceled. Details of accident made public and world shared concern for crew who splashed down successfully in the Pacific Apr 17.

SPELMAN COLLEGE ESTABLISHED: ANNIVERSARY. Apr 11, 1881. Spelman College, with funding from the Rockefeller family, opened its doors for the first time with the purpose of educating young African American women. The institution, located at Atlanta, GA, was dubbed "the Radcliffe for Negro women."

THETA NU XI MULTICULTURAL SORORITY FOUNDING DAY. Apr 11. Anniversary of the founding of the Multicultural Sorority. For info: Cori Ahrens, 3001 Park Center Dr #200, Alexandria, VA 22302. Phone: (703) 725-5419. E-mail: cori_ahrens@hotmail.com. Web: www.thetanuxi.org.

UGANDA: LIBERATION DAY: 25th ANNIVERSARY. Apr 11. Republic of Uganda celebrates anniversary of overthrow of Idi Amin's dictatorship in 1979.

WRITE YOUR MEMOIRS DAY. Apr 11. A day to encourage everyone to begin to write down their life stories, which will forge bonds from the past to the present, provide historical and cultural documentation, serve as cathartic healing and increase self-validation. Stories that make up a memoir are a wonderful way to celebrate our lives. For info: Sherry Tucker, 9524 Kearny Villa Rd #105H, San Diego, CA 92126. Phone: (858) 693-4056. Fax: (858) 271-5226. E-mail: sherry@yourmemories.net. Web: www.yourmemories.net.

BIRTHDAYS TODAY

Tony Brown, 71, journalist, host of "Tony Brown," born Charleston, WV, Apr 11, 1933.
Oleg Cassini, 91, fashion designer, born Paris, France, Apr 11, 1913.
Ellen Goodman, 56, Pulitzer Prize–winning columnist, born Newton, MA, Apr 11, 1948.
Joel Grey, 72, actor (Oscar for *Cabaret*; *The Seven Per Cent Solution*), born Joe Katz, Cleveland, OH, Apr 11, 1932.
Bill Irwin, 54, actor, choreographer (*The Regard of Flight*), born Santa Monica, CA, Apr 11, 1950.
Ethel Kennedy, 76, widow of Robert Kennedy, born Greenwich, CT, Apr 11, 1928.
Louise Lasser, 65, actress ("Mary Hartman, Mary Hartman"), born New York, NY, Apr 11, 1939.
Peter Riegert, 57, actor (*Local Hero, Crossing Delancey*), born New York, NY, Apr 11, 1947.
Bret William Saberhagen, 40, former baseball player, born Chicago Heights, IL, Apr 11, 1964.
Jean-Claude Servan-Schreiber, 86, journalist, author (*The Chosen and the Choice*), born Paris, France, Apr 11, 1918.
Meshach Taylor, 57, actor ("Dave's World," "Designing Women"), born Boston, MA, Apr 11, 1947.

APRIL 12 — MONDAY
Day 103 — 263 Remaining

ATTACK ON FORT SUMTER: ANNIVERSARY. Apr 12, 1861. After months of escalating tension, Major Robert Anderson refused to evacuate Fort Sumter at Charleston, SC. Confederate troops under the command of General P.T. Beauregard opened fire on the harbor fort at 4:30 AM and continued until Major Anderson surrendered on Apr 13. No lives were lost despite the firing of some 40,000 shells in the first major engagement of the American Civil War.

THE BIG WIND: 70th ANNIVERSARY. Apr 12, 1934. The highest-velocity natural wind ever recorded occurred in the morning at the Mount Washington, NH, Observatory. Three weather observers, Wendell Stephenson, Alexander McKenzie and Salvatore Pagliuca, observed and recorded the phenomenon in which gusts reached 231 miles per hour—"the strongest natural wind ever recorded on the earth's surface." The 50th anniversary was observed at the site in 1984, with the three original observers participating in the ceremony.

BILLINGS, JOHN SHAW: BIRTH ANNIVERSARY. Apr 12, 1838. American medical librarian and army physician. Born at Switzerland County, IN. Died at New York, NY, Mar 11, 1913.

CLAY, HENRY: BIRTH ANNIVERSARY. Apr 12, 1777. Statesman, born at Hanover County, VA. Served as the Speaker of the House of Representatives and later became the leader of the new Whig party. He was defeated for the presidency three times. Clay died at Washington, DC, June 29, 1852.

EASTER MONDAY. Apr 12. Holiday or bank holiday in many places, including England, Northern Ireland, Wales, Canada and North Carolina in the US.

EGG SALAD WEEK. Apr 12–18. Dedicated to the many delicious uses for all of the Easter eggs that have been cooked, colored, hidden and found. Annually, the full week after Easter. For info: Linda Braun, Consumer Serv Dir, American Egg Bd, 1460 Renaissance Dr, Park Ridge, IL 60068. Web: www.aeb.org.

Apr 12

EGYPT: SHAM EL-NESSIM. Apr 12. This festival ("The Smelling of the Breeze") has been celebrated by all Egyptians since pharaonic times as a day to celebrate the beginning of spring. Egyptians rise early to enjoy the day in parks and gardens, along the Nile's banks and at the beaches of the Mediterranean and Red Sea. Annually, the Monday after Coptic Easter. For info: Egyptian Tourist Authority, 645 N Michigan Ave, Ste 829, Chicago, IL 60611. Phone: (312) 280-4666 or (312) 280-4666. Web: www.visitegypt.gov.eg.

ELECTRONIC COMMUNICATIONS WEEK. Apr 12–18. A week dedicated to more effective use of electronic communications devices, with a special focus on etiquette for e-mail, voicemail and cell phone use. Annually, the second week of April. For info: Karen Leland, 180 Harbor Dr #221, Sausalito, CA 94965. Phone: (415) 331-5200. Fax: (415) 331-5272. E-mail: kleland@scgtraining.com. Web: www.scgtraining.com.

ENGLAND: HALLATON BOTTLE KICKING. Apr 12. Hallaton, Leicestershire. Ancient custom dating back at least 600 years. Annually, Easter Monday.

EXPLORE YOUR CAREER OPTIONS WEEK. Apr 12–17. Maybe you're aspiring to a new career or merely interested in more opportunities in your present career. Get a fresh start by taking stock of all available options. For info: Dorothy Zjawin, Dir, 61 W Colfax Ave, Roselle Park, NJ 07204. Phone: (908) 241-6241.

FDR COMMEMORATIVE CEREMONY. Apr 12. Little White House, Warm Springs, GA. Annual ceremony honoring Franklin Delano Roosevelt on the anniversary of his death in Warm Springs. Keynote speaker; Marine color guard highlight this impressive ceremony. For the 2004 ceremony, the new FDR Memorial Museum will be dedicated. Est attendance: 1,000. For info: Mgr, Little White House, 401 Little White House Rd, Warm Springs, GA 31830. Phone: (706) 655-5870.

HALIFAX INDEPENDENCE DAY: ANNIVERSARY. Apr 12, 1776. North Carolina. Anniversary of the resolution adopted by the Provincial Congress of North Carolina at Halifax, NC, authorizing the delegates from North Carolina to the Continental Congress to vote for a Declaration of Independence.

HALL, LYMAN: BIRTH ANNIVERSARY. Apr 12, 1724. Signer of the Declaration of Independence. Born at Wallingford, CT, he died at Burke County, GA, Oct 19, 1790.

LUXEMBOURG: EMAISHEN. Apr 12. Luxembourg (city). Popular traditional market and festival at the "Marche-aux-Poissons." Young lovers present each other with earthenware articles, sold only on this day. Annually, Easter Monday.

MASSACRE AT FORT PILLOW: ANNIVERSARY. Apr 12, 1864. After surrounding Fort Pillow, TN, Confederate General Nathan Bedford Forrest attacked the stronghold on this date. The ensuing Confederate victory led to many casualties, many of them black Union soldiers. Although Forrest claimed that the large amount of casualties was a result of the Fort's refusal to surrender, most believe that Forrest's men massacred the defenseless troops after the Fort was surrendered. The action inflamed Northern sentiments and is considered one of the most controversial events of the Civil War.

POLIO VACCINE: ANNIVERSARY. Apr 12, 1955. Anniversary of announcement that the polio vaccine developed by American physician Dr. Jonas E. Salk was "safe, potent and effective." Incidence of the dreaded infantile paralysis, or poliomyelitis, declined by 95 percent following introduction of preventive vaccines. The first mass innoculations of children with the Salk vaccine had begun in Pittsburgh, Feb 23, 1954.

April 2004	S	M	T	W	T	F	S
					1	2	3
	4	5	6	7	8	9	10
	11	12	13	14	15	16	17
	18	19	20	21	22	23	24
	25	26	27	28	29	30	

ROOSEVELT, FRANKLIN DELANO: DEATH ANNIVERSARY. Apr 12, 1945. With the end of WWII only months away, the nation and the world were stunned by the sudden death of the president shortly into his fourth term of office. Roosevelt, 32nd president of the US (Mar 4, 1933–Apr 12, 1945), was the only president to serve more than two terms—he was elected to four consecutive terms. He died at Warm Springs, GA.

SOUTH AFRICA: FAMILY DAY. Apr 12. National holiday. Annually, Easter Monday.

SPACE MILESTONE: *COLUMBIA* STS-1 (US) FIRST SHUTTLE FLIGHT. Apr 12, 1981. First flight of shuttle *Columbia*. Two astronauts (John Young and Robert Crippen), on first manned US space mission since *Apollo-Soyuz* in July 1976, spent 54 hours in space (36 orbits of Earth) before landing at Edwards Air Force Base, CA, Apr 14.

SPACE MILESTONE: *DISCOVERY* (US). Apr 12, 1985. On its 16th mission (from Kennedy Space Center, FL) shuttle *Discovery* was launched carrying US Senator Jake Garn as a member of its crew of seven.

SPACE MILESTONE: *VOSTOK I*, FIRST MAN IN SPACE. Apr 12, 1961. Yuri Gagarin became the first man in space when he made a 108-minute voyage, orbiting Earth in a 10,395-lb vehicle, *Vostok I*, launched by the USSR.

SWITZERLAND: EGG RACES. Apr 12. Rural northwest Swiss Easter Monday custom. Race among competitors carrying large numbers of eggs while running to neighboring villages.

TRUANCY LAW: ANNIVERSARY. Apr 12, 1853. The first truancy law was enacted at New York. A $50 fine was charged against parents whose children between the ages of five and 15 were absent from school.

"21 JUMP STREET" TV PREMIERE: ANNIVERSARY. Apr 12, 1987. Youthful big city cops busted crime in the local schools and colleges in this Fox police drama. Starred Johnny Depp as Tom Hanson, Holly Robinson Peete as Judy Hoffs, Dustin Nguyen as H.T. Ioki, Peter DeLuise as Doug Penhall, Frederic Forrest as Captain Jenko, Steven Williams as Captain Adam Fuller and Richard Grieco as Dennis Booker. It was one of the Fox network's early hits.

UNITED KINGDOM: EASTER MONDAY BANK HOLIDAY. Apr 12. Bank and public holiday in England, Wales and Northern Ireland. (Scotland not included.)

WALK ON YOUR WILD SIDE DAY. Apr 12. Time's wasting, friends. It's high time you went out and did some things no one expects you to do. Be unpredictable for once. Go to work dressed like a gorilla, get a master's degree—do something "they" said you'd never ever do. [©2003 by WH.] For info: Thomas & Ruth Roy, Wellcat Holidays, 2418 Long Lane, Lebanon, PA 17046. Phone: (717) 279-0184. E-mail: info@wellcat.com. Web: www.wellcat.com.

WHITE HOUSE EASTER EGG ROLL. Apr 12. Traditionally held at executive mansion's south lawn on Easter Monday. Custom said to have started at Capitol grounds about 1810. Transferred to White House lawn in 1870s.

YOUNG PEOPLE'S POETRY WEEK. Apr 12–18. An annual event, sponsored by The Children's Book Council, that highlights poetry for children and young adults and encourages everyone to celebrate poetry—read it, enjoy it, write it—in their homes, child-care centers, classrooms, libraries and bookstores. The CBC is coordinating its promotional efforts with the Academy of American Poets, the sponsor of National Poetry Month in April, and The Center for the Book in the Library of Congress. For info: The Children's Book Council, 12 W 37th St, 2nd Fl, New York, NY 10018-7480. Phone: (800) 999-2160. Fax: (888) 807-9355. E-mail: paula.quint@cbcbooks.org. Web: www.cbcbooks.org/html/poetry_week.html.

"YOUR HIT PARADE" RADIO PREMIERE: ANNIVERSARY. Apr 12, 1935. This program debuted on radio in 1935 with its countdown of the week's top songs. In 1950 it became a TV program. See also: "Your Hit Parade TV Premiere: Anniversary" (Oct 7).

BIRTHDAYS TODAY

David Cassidy, 54, singer ("Cherish"), actor ("The Partridge Family"), born New York, NY, Apr 12, 1950.
Tom Clancy, 57, author (*The Hunt for Red October, Red Storm Rising*), born Baltimore, MD, Apr 12, 1947.
Beverly Cleary, 88, author (*Ramona* series for children; winner of the Newbery Medal for *Dear Mr Henshaw*), born McMinnville, OR, Apr 12, 1916.
Claire Danes, 25, actress (*The Rainmaker*), born New York, NY, Apr 12, 1979.
Shannen Doherty, 33, actress ("Beverly Hills 90210," *Night Shift, Heathers*), born Memphis, TN, Apr 12, 1971.
Andy Garcia, 48, actor (*The Untouchables; The Godfather, Part III*), born Havana, Cuba, Apr 12, 1956.
Herbie Hancock, 64, musician, born Chicago, IL, Apr 12, 1940.
Dan Lauria, 57, actor ("The Wonder Years," *Stakeout*), born Brooklyn, NY, Apr 12, 1947.
David Letterman, 57, comedian, TV talk-show host ("Late Show with David Letterman"), born Indianapolis, IN, Apr 12, 1947.
Ann Miller, 85, actress (*Sugar Babies, You Can't Take It with You, Easter Parade*), born Lucille Ann Collier, Chireno, TX, Apr 12, 1919.
Ed O'Neill, 58, actor ("Married . . . With Children," *Deliverance, Wayne's World*), born Youngstown, OH, Apr 12, 1946.
Scott Turow, 55, writer (*Presumed Innocent, Burden of Proof*), born Chicago, IL, Apr 12, 1949.

APRIL 13 — TUESDAY
Day 104 — 262 Remaining

BECKETT, SAMUEL: BIRTH ANNIVERSARY. Apr 13, 1906. Author, critic and playwright, born at Foxrock, County Dublin, Ireland. Writing in both French and English, Samuel Beckett is best remembered for his plays, including *Waiting for Godot, Endgame, Krapp's Last Tape* and *Happy Days*. Beckett settled at Paris, France, in 1937 and served with an underground resistance group during the early years of World War II. In the years following the war he entered a period of intense creativity, producing among others the novels *Molloy, Malone Dies* and *The Unnamable* and two plays, *Eleutheria* and *Waiting for Godot*. *Waiting for Godot* received an acclaimed production at the Theatre de Babylone in Paris in January 1953, and with it Beckett achieved worldwide renown. He died Dec 22, 1989, at Paris, France.

BUTTS, ALFRED M.: BIRTH ANNIVERSARY. Apr 13, 1899. Alfred Butts was a jobless architect in the Depression when he invented the board game Scrabble. The game was just a fad for Butts's friends until a Macy's executive saw the game being played at a resort in 1952, and the world's largest store began carrying it. Manufacturing of the game was turned over to Selchow & Righter when 35 workers were producing 6,000 sets a week. Butts received three cents per set for years. He said, "One-third went to taxes. I gave one-third away, and the other third enabled me to have an enjoyable life." Butts was born at Poughkeepsie, NY. He died Apr 4, 1993, at Rhinebeck, NY.

CASSIDY, BUTCH: BIRTH ANNIVERSARY. Apr 13, 1866. Born Robert Leroy Parker at Beaver, UT, son of Mormon pioneer Maximillian Parker, he became a notorious outlaw of the Old West and leader of The Wild Bunch gang. Some believed he died in a gun battle at Bolivia in 1909, while others are certain he returned and died in the USA.

CHILDREN'S DAY IN FLORIDA. Apr 13. A legal holiday in Florida commemorated on the second Tuesday in April.

FIRST BASEBALL STRIKE ENDS: ANNIVERSARY. Apr 13, 1972. Major league baseball players and owners agreed on a settlement in which owners added an additional $500,000 to the players' pension fund. This ended the first baseball strike, which had begun Apr 5 when the season opener was canceled.

GREAT CHICAGO FLOOD: ANNIVERSARY. Apr 13, 1992. On this morning Chicagoans awoke to one of the most unusual disasters of modern times: the Chicago River broke through a rupture in an old underground freight tunnel wall, sending millions of gallons of water flooding into the tunnel system beneath the downtown business district. The water poured into basements of buildings that previously had been connected to the tunnel system. The greater Loop area had to be evacuated as electricity was cut off ahead of the rising water. A hectic effort mounted to plug the leak in the river eventually succeeded. Once the flow of water had stopped, the city began the slow and expensive process of draining the water.

INDIA: BAISAKHI. Apr 13. Sikh holiday that commemorates the founding of the brotherhood of the Khalsa in 1699. A large fair is held at the Golden Temple at Amritsar, the central shrine of Sikhism. While the date may vary in different parts of India, this holiday always falls in April or May.

JEFFERSON, THOMAS: BIRTH ANNIVERSARY. Apr 13, 1743. 3rd president of the US (Mar 4, 1801–Mar 3, 1809), 2nd vice-president (1797–1801), born at Albermarle County, VA. Jefferson, who died at Charlottesville, VA, July 4, 1826, wrote his own epitaph: "Here was buried Thomas Jefferson, author of the Declaration of American Independence, of the statute of Virginia for religious freedom, and father of the University of Virginia." A holiday in Alabama and Oklahoma. See also: "Adams, John, and Jefferson, Thomas: Death Anniversary" (July 4).

★**JEFFERSON, THOMAS: BIRTH ANNIVERSARY.** Apr 13. Presidential Proclamation 2276, of Mar 21, 1938, covers all succeeding years. (Pub Res No. 60 of Aug 16, 1937.)

NATIONAL CATHOLIC EDUCATIONAL ASSOCIATION CONVENTION AND EXPOSITION. Apr 13–16. Hynes Convention Center, Boston, MA. Annual meeting for NCEA members and anyone working in, or interested in, the welfare of Catholic education. Est attendance: 12,000. For info: Sue Arvo, Conv Dir, Natl Catholic Educational Assn, 1077 30th St NW, Ste 100, Washington, DC 20007. Phone: (202) 337-6232. Fax: (202) 333-6706.

***SILENT SPRING* PUBLICATION: ANNIVERSARY.** Apr 13, 1962. Rachel Carson's *Silent Spring* warned humankind that for the first time in history every person is subjected to contact with dangerous chemicals from conception until death. Carson painted a vivid picture of how chemicals—used in many ways but particularly in pesticides—have upset the balance of nature, undermining the survival of countless species. This enormously popular and influential book was a soft-spoken battle cry to protect our natural surroundings. Its publication signaled the beginning of the environmental movement.

SRI LANKA: SINHALA AND TAMIL NEW YEAR. April 13–14. This New Year festival includes traditional games, the wearing of new clothes in auspicious colors and special foods. Public holiday.

THAILAND: SONGKRAN FESTIVAL. Apr 13–15. Public holiday. Thai water festival. To welcome the new year the image of Buddha is bathed with holy or fragrant water and lustral water is sprinkled on celebrants. Joyous event, especially observed at Buddhist temples.

Apr 13–14 ☆ *Chase's 2004 Calendar of Events* ☆

BIRTHDAYS TODAY

Peabo Bryson, 53, singer ("Just Another Day," "I Can Make It Better"), born Greenville, SC, Apr 13, 1951.
Ben Nighthorse Campbell, 71, US Senator (R, Colorado), born Auburn, CA, Apr 13, 1933.
Jack Casady, 60, musician, born Washington, DC, Apr 13, 1944.
Bill Conti, 62, composer (Oscar for *The Right Stuff*; "Falcon Crest," "Inside Edition"), born Providence, RI, Apr 13, 1942.
Tony Dow, 59, actor ("Leave It to Beaver"), born Hollywood, CA, Apr 13, 1945.
Edward Fox, 67, actor (*The Day of the Jackal, Gandhi, The Dresser*), born London, England, Apr 13, 1937.
Al Green, 58, singer ("Let's Stay Together," "You Ought to Be with Me"), born Forrest City, AR, Apr 13, 1946.
Howard Keel, 85, actor (*Annie Get Your Gun, Seven Brides for Seven Brothers*), born Howard Leek, Gillespie, IL, Apr 13, 1919.
Davis Love, III, 40, golfer, born Charlotte, NC, Apr 13, 1964.
Ron Perlman, 54, actor ("Beauty and the Beast," *The Name of the Rose*), born New York, NY, Apr 13, 1950.
Saundra Santiago, 47, actress ("Miami Vice"), born the Bronx, NY, Apr 13, 1957.
Rick Schroder, 34, actor ("Silver Spoons," "NYPD Blue," *The Champ*), born Staten Island, NY, Apr 13, 1970.
Paul Sorvino, 65, actor ("Law & Order"), born Brooklyn, NY, Apr 13, 1939.
Lyle Waggoner, 69, actor ("The Carol Burnett Show," "Wonder Woman"), born Kansas City, KS, Apr 13, 1935.
Max M. Weinberg, 53, musician, bandleader ("Late Night with Conan O'Brien"), born South Orange, NJ, Apr 13, 1951.

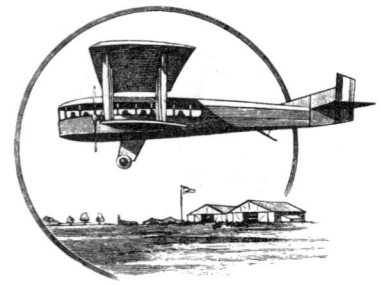

APRIL 14 — WEDNESDAY
Day 105 — 261 Remaining

CAMPBELL BECOMES FIRST AMERICAN AIR ACE: ANNIVERSARY. Apr 14, 1918. Lieutenant Douglas Campbell became the first American pilot to achieve the designation of ACE when he shot down his fifth German aircraft.

FIRST AMERICAN ABOLITION SOCIETY FOUNDED: ANNIVERSARY. Apr 14, 1775. The first abolition organization formed in the US was The Society for the Relief of Free Negroes Unlawfully Held in Bondage, founded at Philadelphia, PA.

FIRST DICTIONARY OF AMERICAN ENGLISH PUBLISHED: ANNIVERSARY. Apr 14, 1828. Noah Webster published his *American Dictionary of the English Language*.

GIELGUD, SIR JOHN: 100th BIRTH ANNIVERSARY. Apr 14, 1904. Director and actor, born at London, England. He made his professional film debut in 1924 in *Who Is the Man?*. Other film credits include *Arthur, Murder on the Orient Express* and *Plenty*. He played the role of Hamlet more than 500 times. He won the Tony Award for best director in 1961 for *Big Fish Little Fish*. He died at Buckinghamshire, England, May 21, 2000.

GRAPES OF WRATH PUBLISHED: 65th ANNIVERSARY. Apr 14, 1939. John Steinbeck's novel of the Great Depression, *Grapes of Wrath*, won the 1940 Pulitzer Prize. It chronicled the mass migration to California of dispossessed farmers from the Dust Bowl region of the Great Plains.

HONDURAS: DIA DE LAS AMERICAS. Apr 14. Honduras. Pan-American Day, a national holiday.

HUYGENS, CHRISTIAAN: 375th BIRTH ANNIVERSARY. Apr 14, 1629. Scientist, born at The Hague, Netherlands. He discovered the rings of Saturn and the wave or pulse theory of light. In 1656 he invented the pendulum clock. He died at The Hague, June 8, 1695.

INTERNATIONAL MOMENT OF LAUGHTER DAY. Apr 14. Laughter is a potent and powerful way to deal with the difficulties of modern living. Since the physical, emotional and spiritual benefits of laughter are widely accepted, this day is set aside for everyone to take the necessary time to experience the power of laughter. For info: Izzy Gesell, Head Honcho of Wide Angle Humor, PO Box 962, Northampton, MA 01061. Phone: (413) 586-2634. E-mail: izzy@izzyg.com. Web: www.izzyg.com.

LINCOLN, ABRAHAM: ASSASSINATION ANNIVERSARY. Apr 14, 1865. President Abraham Lincoln was shot while watching a performance of *Our American Cousin* at Ford's Theatre, Washington, DC. He died the following day. Assassin was John Wilkes Booth, a young actor.

★**PAN AMERICAN DAY.** Apr 14. Presidential Proclamation 1912, of May 28, 1930, covers every Apr 14 (required by Governing Board of Pan-American Union). Proclamation issued each year since 1948. Commemorates the first International Conference of American States in 1890.

PAN-AMERICAN DAY IN FLORIDA. Apr 14. A ceremonial day in Florida which is observed in the public schools as a day honoring the republics of Latin America. When Apr 14 does not fall on a school day, the governor may designate the preceding Friday or the following Monday as Pan-American Day.

PRESIDENT TAFT OPENS BASEBALL SEASON: ANNIVERSARY. Apr 14, 1910. President William Howard Taft began a sports tradition by throwing out the first baseball of the season at an American League game between Washington and Philadelphia. Washington won 3–0.

SCOTTSDALE CULINARY FESTIVAL™. Apr 14–18. Scottsdale, AZ. Ten spectacular culinary events including Le Tour Culinaire, a progressive black-tie dinner; Best of the Fest featuring 10 of the valley's best chefs; Great Arizona Picnic featuring 50 of the Valley's best restaurants; and more. Proceeds benefit arts education programs for youth in the community. Est attendance: 60,000. For info: Scottsdale Culinary Festival, 7375 E 6th Ave, #9, Scottsdale, AZ 85251. Phone: (480) 945-7193. Fax: (480) 945-6967. E-mail: karolyn@scottsdaleculinaryfestival.org. Web: www.scottsdaleculinaryfestival.org.

SULLIVAN, ANNE: BIRTH ANNIVERSARY. Apr 14, 1866. Anne Sullivan, born at Feeding Hills, MA, became well known for "working miracles" with Helen Keller, who was blind and deaf. Nearly blind herself, Sullivan used a manual alphabet communicated by the sense of touch to teach Keller to read, write and speak and then to help her go on to higher education. Anne Sullivan died Oct 20, 1936, at Forest Hills, NY.

TOYNBEE, ARNOLD JOSEPH: BIRTH ANNIVERSARY. Apr 14, 1889. English historian, author of monumental *Study of History*. Born at London, England; died at York, England, Oct 22, 1975.

	S	M	T	W	T	F	S
April 2004					1	2	3
	4	5	6	7	8	9	10
	11	12	13	14	15	16	17
	18	19	20	21	22	23	24
	25	26	27	28	29	30	

☆ Chase's 2004 Calendar of Events ☆ Apr 14–15

BIRTHDAYS TODAY

Adrien Brody, 31, actor (Oscar for *The Pianist*), born New York, NY, Apr 14, 1973.
Robert Carlyle, 43, actor (*Angela's Ashes, The Full Monty*), born Glasgow, Scotland, Apr 14, 1961.
Julie Christie, 64, actress (*Dr. Zhivago, Petulia, Shampoo*), born Chukua, India, Apr 14, 1940.
Cynthia Cooper, 41, basketball player, born Chicago, IL, Apr 14, 1963.
Bradford Dillman, 74, actor (*Compulsion*, "Falcon Crest"), born San Francisco, CA, Apr 14, 1930.
Brad Garrett, 44, comedian, actor ("Everybody Loves Raymond"), born Woodland Hills, CA, Apr 14, 1960.
Sarah Michelle Gellar, 27, actress (*Scooby-Doo*, "Buffy the Vampire Slayer"), born New York, NY, Apr 14, 1977.
Anthony Michael Hall, 36, actor, comedian ("Saturday Night Live," *Sixteen Candles, The Breakfast Club*), born Boston, MA, Apr 14, 1968.
David Christopher Justice, 38, baseball player, born Cincinnati, OH, Apr 14, 1966.
Loretta Lynn, 69, singer/songwriter ("Coal Miner's Daughter," "The Pill"), born Butcher's Hollow, KY, Apr 14, 1935.
Gregory Alan (Greg) Maddux, 38, baseball player, born San Angelo, TX, Apr 14, 1966.
Peter Edward (Pete) Rose, 63, former baseball manager and player, born Cincinnati, OH, Apr 14, 1941.
Emma Thompson, 45, actress (*Howard's End, Sense and Sensibility*), born London, England, Apr 14, 1959.

APRIL 15 — THURSDAY
Day 106 — 260 Remaining

ASTRONOMERS FIND NEW SOLAR SYSTEM: 5th ANNIVERSARY. Apr 15, 1999. Astronomers from San Francisco State University working at an observatory in Arizona announced the discovery of the first multi-planet system ever found orbiting around a star other than our own. Three planets orbit the star Upsilon Andromedae, which can be seen with the naked eye. This suggests that the Milky Way probably teems with similar planetary systems.

BENTON, THOMAS HART: BIRTH ANNIVERSARY. Apr 15, 1889. Thomas Hart Benton was an artist whose work was indicative of the American style of painting known as Regionalism. His works of life in the Midwest and South were not always flattering to their subjects, but his style became known as a truly American style of painting. He was born at Neosho, MO, and died at Kansas City, MO, Jan 19, 1975.

"BUCK ROGERS" TV PREMIERE: ANNIVERSARY. Apr 15, 1950. At first a radio show, "Buck Rogers" premiered on ABC with Kem Dibbs. Buck was an average American who woke up from a cave behind Niagara Falls to find himself in the year 2430. The show featured Lou Prentis as Lieutenant Wilma Deering; Harry Sothern as Dr. Huer and Harry Kingston as Black Barney Wade. Buck was later played by Robert Pastene.

CHINA: CANTON SPRING TRADE FAIR. Apr 15–May 15. The Guangzhou (Canton) Spring Trade Fair is held on the same dates each year.

DOGWOOD FESTIVAL. Apr 15–18. Camdenton, MO. This annual rite of spring features music, carnival, food, parade, arts and crafts, art exhibitions and more. For info: Bruce Mitchell, Exec Dir, Camdenton Area Chamber of Commerce, PO Box 1375, Camdenton, MO 65020. Phone: (573) 346-2227 or (800) 769-1004. Fax: (573) 346-3496. E-mail: cchamber@thelake.net.

FIRST MCDONALD'S OPENS: ANNIVERSARY. Apr 15, 1955. The first franchised McDonald's was opened at Des Plaines, IL, by Ray Kroc, who had gotten the idea from a hamburger joint at San Bernardino, CA, run by the McDonald brothers. On opening day a hamburger was 15 cents. The Big Mac was introduced in 1968 for 49 cents and the Quarter Pounder in 1971 for 53 cents. By the late 1990s, there were more than 25,000 McDonald's in 115 countries.

FIRST SCHOOL FOR DEAF FOUNDED: ANNIVERSARY. Apr 15, 1817. Thomas Hopkins Gallaudet and Laurent Clerc founded the first US public school for the deaf, Connecticut Asylum for the Education and Instruction of Deaf and Dumb Persons (now the American School for the Deaf), at Hartford, CT.

"IN LIVING COLOR" TV PREMIERE: ANNIVERSARY. Apr 15, 1990. Fox's sketch comedy series, created by Keenen Ivory Wayans, was modeled after "Saturday Night Live." Between skits, the Fly Girls would entertain the studio audience with hip-hop dance (choreographed by soon-to-be film actress Rosie Perez). The show featured Wayans, his brothers Damon, Marlon and Shawn, his sister Kim, Tommy Davidson, David Alan Grier, T'Keyah "Crystal" Keymáh, Kelly Coffield, Kim Coles and Jim Carrey before he was Ace Ventura. Some of the most popular recurring characters were Homey, the embittered clown, the flammable Fire Marshall Bill and the effeminate movie critics of "Men on Film."

INCOME TAX PAY DAY. Apr 15. A day all Americans need to know—the day by which taxpayers are supposed to make their accounting of the previous year and pay their share of the cost of government. The US Internal Revenue Service provides free forms.

JAMES, HENRY: BIRTH ANNIVERSARY. Apr 15, 1843. Novelist and critic, born at New York, NY. Among his best-known works are *The Portrait of a Lady, Washington Square* and *The Ambassadors*. James died Feb 28, 1916, at London, England.

LONGYEAR, JOHN MUNROE: BIRTH ANNIVERSARY. Apr 15, 1850. American capitalist, landowner, philanthropist, one-time mayor of Marquette, MI. Disapproving of a railway route through Marquette, he caused his home, a stone castle-like showplace, to be torn down in 1903 and moved, stone by stone and stick by stick, in more than 190 freight cars and re-erected at Brookline, MA. Born at Lansing, MI, he died May 28, 1922.

MUSTANG 40th ANNIVERSARY CELEBRATION. Apr 15–18. Nashville Superspeedway, Nashville, TN. Car show, track events, concerts, seminars and other events for Ford Mustang enthusiasts from the entire world. Est attendance: 50,000. For info: Jim Chism, Mustang 40th Anniversary Celebration, PO Box 51505, Bowling Green, KY 42102. Phone: (615) 799-8300. Fax: (615) 799-8477. E-mail: TradWnd@aol.com. Web: www.mustang.org.

NCAA DIVISION I WOMEN'S GYMNASTICS. Apr 15–17. University of California, Los Angeles, CA. For info: NCAA, PO Box 6222, Indianapolis, IN 46206-6222. Phone: (317) 917-6222. Fax: (317) 917-6888. Web: www.ncaasports.com.

PEALE, CHARLES WILLSON: BIRTH ANNIVERSARY. Apr 15, 1741 (OS). American portrait painter (best known for his many portraits of colonial and American Revolutionary War figures) was born at Queen Anne County, MD. His children Raphaelle, Rembrandt, Titian, Rubens and his niece Sarah were also artists. Died at Philadelphia, PA, Feb 22, 1827.

PUYALLUP SPRING FAIR. Apr 15–18. Puyallup Fairgrounds, Puyallup, WA. Fair to celebrate spring, including exhibits, animals, flowers, rides, demonstrations, gardening, Kid Zone, recycling, lots of entertainment, food and much more. Est attendance: 105,000. For info: Puyallup Spring Fair, PO Box 430, Puyallup, WA 98371-0162. Phone: (253) 841-5045. Fax: (253) 841-5390. E-mail: info@thefair.com. Web: www.thefair.com.

QUARTERLY ESTIMATED FEDERAL INCOME TAX PAYERS' DUE DATE. Apr 15. For those individuals whose fiscal year is the calendar year and who make quarterly estimated federal income tax payments, today is one of the due dates (Jan 15, Apr 15, June 15 and Sept 15, 2004).

ROBINSON BREAKS BASEBALL COLOR LINE: ANNIVERSARY. Apr 15, 1947. Jackie Robinson became the first African American to play in the major leagues in the 20th century when he made his debut for the Brooklyn Dodgers against the Boston Braves. Robinson went 0-for-3 but scored the deciding run as the Dodgers prevailed, 5–3. He was later voted 1947's Rookie of the Year.

SIMMS, HILDA: BIRTH ANNIVERSARY. Apr 15, 1920. American stage and film actress, born Hilda Moses at Minneapolis, MN. She joined the American Negro Theater at Harlem, NY, in 1943 and was given the title role in *Anna Lucasta*. When the production moved to Broadway in 1944, it became the first all-black production to be performed on Broadway without a racial theme. Simms was the creative arts director of New York State's human rights division, through which she was instrumental in bringing discrimination against black actors to public attention during the 1960s. She died at Buffalo, NY, Feb 6, 1994.

SINKING OF THE *TITANIC*: ANNIVERSARY. Apr 15, 1912. The "unsinkable" luxury liner *Titanic* on its maiden voyage from Southampton, England, to New York, NY, struck an iceberg just before midnight Apr 14, and sank at 2:27 AM, Apr 15. The *Titanic* had 2,224 persons aboard. Of these, more than 1,500 were lost. About 700 people were rescued from the icy waters off Newfoundland by the liner *Carpathia*, which reached the scene about two hours after the *Titanic* went down. See also: "Titanic Discovered: Anniversary" (Sept 1).

SMITH, BESSIE: BIRTH ANNIVERSARY. Apr 15, 1894. The "Empress of the Blues," Bessie Smith, was born at Chattanooga, TN (year varies as late as 1900). She was assisted in her efforts to break into show business by Ma Rainey, the first great blues singer. Her first recording was made in February 1923. Smith died of injuries she sustained in an automobile accident at Clarksdale, MS, Sept 26, 1937.

WASHINGTON, HAROLD: BIRTH ANNIVERSARY. Apr 15, 1922. Illinois legislator and Mayor of Chicago (1983–87). Born at Chicago, IL, and died there Nov 25, 1987. Harold Washington was one of the first African Americans to head a major US city. He was instrumental in tearing down Chicago's famed Democratic machine, a holdover from the many decades of domination by the Richard J. Daley administration.

BIRTHDAYS TODAY

Evelyn Ashford, 47, Olympic gold medal track athlete, born Shreveport, LA, Apr 15, 1957.
Linda Bloodworth-Thomason, 57, producer, writer ("Designing Women," "Evening Shade"), born Poplar Bluff, MO, Apr 15, 1947.
Claudia Cardinale, 66, actress (*The Pink Panther, Once Upon a Time in the West*), born Tunis, Tunisia, Apr 15, 1938.
Roy Clark, 71, singer and guitarist ("Yesterday, When I Was Young," regular on "Hee Haw"), born Meherrin, VA, Apr 15, 1933.
Heloise Cruse Evans, 53, newspaper columnist ("Hints from Heloise"), born Waco, TX, Apr 15, 1951.
Jason Sehorn, 33, football player, born Mt Shasta, CA, Apr 15, 1971.
Emma Watson, 14, actress (the Harry Potter films), born Oxford, England, Apr 15, 1990.
Amy Wright, 54, actress (*Breaking Away, Wise Blood, The Accidental Tourist*), born Chicago, IL, Apr 15, 1950.

	S	M	T	W	T	F	S
April 2004					1	2	3
	4	5	6	7	8	9	10
	11	12	13	14	15	16	17
	18	19	20	21	22	23	24
	25	26	27	28	29	30	

APRIL 16 — FRIDAY
Day 107 — 259 Remaining

AMIS, KINGSLEY: BIRTH ANNIVERSARY. Apr 16, 1922. Author (*The Old Devils, Lucky Jim*), born at London, England, and died there Oct 22, 1995.

CHAPLIN, CHARLES SPENCER: BIRTH ANNIVERSARY. Apr 16, 1889. Celebrated film comedian who portrayed "The Little Tramp" was born at London, England. Film debut in 1914. Knighted in 1975. Died at Vevey, Switzerland, Dec 25, 1977. In his autobiography Chaplin wrote: "There are more valid facts and details in works of art than there are in history books."

CONSUMER AWARENESS WEEK. Apr 16–20. Consumer advocate Bob O'Brien kicks off a weeklong event aimed at advising and helping consumers with their rights. For info: Bob O'Brien, Consumer Advocate, 1061 Koelle Blvd, Secaucus, NJ 07094. Phone: (201) 860-1595. Fax: (201) 865-4775. E-mail: bobthebestthebest@yahoo.com. Web: www.econsumeradvocate.com.

DENMARK: QUEEN MARGRETHE II'S BIRTHDAY. Apr 16. Thousands of children gather to cheer the queen (born 1940) at Amalienborg Palace and the Royal Guard wears scarlet gala uniforms.

DIEGO, JOSE de: BIRTH ANNIVERSARY. Apr 16, 1866. Puerto Rican patriot and political leader Jose de Diego was born at Aguadilla, PR. His birthday is a holiday in Puerto Rico. He died July 16, 1918, at New York, NY.

FIESTA SAN ANTONIO. Apr 16–25. San Antonio, TX. Ten days of culture, heritage, beauty and remembrance. Parades, carnivals, sports, fireworks, music, ethnic feasts, art exhibits, dances—more than 150 events. This colorful fiesta originated in 1891 with the Battle of Flowers parade honoring the memory of Texas heroes who fought against General Santa Anna for Texan independence at the Alamo and San Jacinto. Est attendance: 3,500,000. For info: Fiesta San Antonio Commission, Inc, 2611 Broadway, San Antonio, TX 78215-1022. Phone: (210) 227-5191 or (877) 723-4378. Fax: (210) 227-1139. Web: www.fiesta-sa.org.

FRENCH QUARTER FESTIVAL. Apr 16–18. New Orleans, LA. 21st annual. This festival focuses on all that makes the Quarter special—art, antiques, food, music, shopping, lifestyles and the people. Free concerts on 14 stages, historic patio tours, parade, children's activities, fireworks, 5K race and other family activities. Est attendance: 300,000. For info: French Quarter Festivals, Inc, 400 N Peters St #205, New Orleans, LA 70130. Phone: (504) 522-5730 or (800) 673-5725. Fax: (504) 522-5711. E-mail: feedback@fqfi.org. Web: www.fqfi.org.

HISTORY MEETS THE ARTS. Apr 16–18. Gettysburg, PA. More than 75 historical artists, authors and artisans with original artwork, special tours, historical films, book and print signings. Annually in April. Est attendance: 25,000. For info: Gettysburg CVB, PO Box 4117, Gettysburg, PA 17325. Phone: (717) 334-6274. Fax: (717) 334-1166. E-mail: gettysburgcvb@dejazzd.com. Web: www.gettysburgcvb.org.

HOLIDAY IN DIXIE. Apr 16–25. Shreveport and Bossier City, LA. Ten days in April celebrating the beginning of spring with more than 50 events including carnival, tournaments, a treasure hunt, parades; also Barksdale AFB Open House. Takes place throughout both cities. Est attendance: 300,000. For info: Susan Loftus, Exec. Dir., Holiday in Dixie, 220 Carroll St, Ste C-2, Shreveport, LA 71105. Phone: (318) 865-5555. Fax: (318) 868-9577. E-mail: sloftus55@aol.com. Web: www.holidayindixie.com.

KENTUCKY DERBY FESTIVAL. Apr 16–May 2. Louisville, KY. Civic celebration as Louisville warms up for the Kentucky Derby. About 70 events, two-thirds of which are free to the public. Est attendance: 1,500,000. For info: Kentucky Derby Festival, Inc, 1001 S Third St, Louisville, KY 40203. Phone: (502) 584-6383. Fax: (502) 589-4674. E-mail: info@kdf.org. Web: www.kdf.org.

☆ Chase's 2004 Calendar of Events ☆   Apr 16

MANCINI, HENRY: 80th BIRTH ANNIVERSARY. Apr 16, 1924. Born at Cleveland, OH, Mancini made his mark in Hollywood composing film scores and songs. He won 20 Grammy Awards and four Oscars (song "Moon River" and score for *Breakfast at Tiffany's*; song "Days of Wine and Roses" for the film; score for *Victor/Victoria*). He also composed *The Pink Panther*, "Peter Gunn" and "Mr Lucky" themes. Died June 14, 1994, at Beverly Hills, CA.

MASIH, IQBAL: DEATH ANNIVERSARY. Apr 16, 1995. Twelve-year-old Iqbal Masih, born at Pakistan in 1982, who reportedly had received death threats after speaking out against Pakistan's child labor practices, was shot to death, at Muridke Village, Punjab Province. Masih, who was sold into labor as a carpet weaver at the age of four, spent the next six years of his life shackled to a loom. He began speaking out against child labor after escaping from servitude at the age of 10. In November 1994 he spoke at an international labor conference in Sweden and he received a $15,000 Reebok Youth in Action Award a month later. There were reports after the shooting that Masih's death was arranged by a "carpet mafia."

MENNONITE RELIEF SALE. Apr 16–17. Kansas State Fair Grounds, Hutchinson, KS. More than 70 Mennonite, Brethren in Christ and Amish congregations in Kansas sponsor this annual festival and benefit auction for the worldwide hunger relief and community aid programs of the Mennonite Central Committee. Auctions of quilts, grandfather clocks, furniture, tools and crafts. Great food and lots more. No vendors. Est attendance: 24,000. For info: Rod Chrystie, 6113 S Shadeacres Rd, Hutchinson, KS 67501. Phone: (620) 665-7406. Web: www.mccsale.org/kansas.

NATIONAL STRESS AWARENESS DAY. Apr 16. To focus public awareness on one of the leading health problems in the world today. Health-related organizations throughout the country are encouraged to sponsor stress education programs and events. Annually, the first day after income taxes due. For info: Morton C. Orman, MD, Dir, The Health Resource Network, 908 Cold Bottom Rd, Sparks, MD 21152. Web: www.stresscure.com.

NATIONAL WEAR YOUR PAJAMAS TO WORK DAY. Apr 16. Relieve that stress and relax after staying up late working on your taxes! Annually, following the day income taxes are due. Sponsored by The PajamaGram Company. For info: Nicole L'Huillier, 6655 Shelburne Rd, Shelburne, VT 05482. Phone: (802) 985-1362. Fax: (802) 985-1382. E-mail: nicolel@vtbear.com. Web: www.pajamagram.com.

NATIONAL YOUTH SERVICE DAYS. Apr 16–18. This 16th annual observance offers thousands of volunteer opportunities in all 50 states for young people, kindergarten and up. More than three million young Americans will serve in 3,000 communities. This is the world's largest volunteer event. More than 55 national organizations serve as partners for this event, which runs in conjunction with Global Youth Service Day. For info: Youth Service America, 1101 15th St NW, Ste 200, Washington, DC 20005-5002. Phone: (202) 296-2992. Web: www.ysa.org/nysd/.

NATURAL BRIDGES NATIONAL MONUMENT: ANNIVERSARY. Apr 16, 1908. Utah. Natural Bridges National Monument was established on this date.

POSITIVE POWER OF HUMOR, HOPE & HEALING CONFERENCE. Apr 16–18. Saratoga Springs, NY. 19th annual. Participants will enjoy themselves while learning practical ideas they can apply both personally and on the job. Conferences have featured Jay Leno, Victor Borge, Steve Allen, Sid Caesar, David Hyde Pierce and The Smothers Brothers. More than 17,000 attendees from all 50 states and abroad. To receive a conference brochure and free Humor Sourcebook, send SASE ($1.06) to The Humor Project, 480 Broadway, Ste 210-C, Saratoga Springs, NY 12866-2288. Phone: (518) 587-8770. Fax: (518) 587-8771. E-mail: chase@HumorProject.com. Web: www.humorproject.com.

REKINDLE YOUR ROMANTIC SELF DAY. Apr 16. A day for men and women alike to take the time out to be more romantic to their partner or revitalize their romantic inner self. Individuals without a partner can spend this day with friends or family at places that bring the best out of them while rekindling their romantic self. Try spas, salons, retreats, mini-vacations, etc. For info: Victoria Pericon. Phone: (917) 826-3360. E-mail: LoveVictoria@aol.com. Web: www.LoveVictoria.com.

SELENA: BIRTH ANNIVERSARY. Apr 16, 1971. Tejana singer, born Selena Quintanilla at Lake Jackson, TX. Died Mar 31, 1995, at Corpus Christi, TX, murdered by the president of her fan club.

SLAVERY ABOLISHED IN DISTRICT OF COLUMBIA: ANNIVERSARY. Apr 16, 1862. Congress abolished slavery in the District of Columbia. One million dollars was appropriated to compensate owners of freed slaves, and $100,000 was set aside to pay district slaves who wished to emigrate to Haiti, Liberia or any other country outside the US.

SLOANE, HANS: BIRTH ANNIVERSARY. Apr 16, 1660. British medical doctor and naturalist whose personal collection became the nucleus of the British Museum, born at County Down, Ireland. Upon his death at Chelsea, England, Jan 11, 1753, his collections of books, manuscripts, medals and antiquities were bequeathed to Britain and accepted by an act of Parliament that incorporated the British Museum. It was opened to the public at London, England, Jan 15, 1759. It is the national museum of the United Kingdom.

SPACE MILESTONE: *APOLLO 16* (US). Apr 16, 1972. Astronauts John W. Young, Charles M. Duke, Jr and Thomas K. Mattingly II (command module pilot) began an 11-day mission that included 71-hour exploration of moon (Apr 20–23). Landing module (LM) named *Orion*. Splashdown in Pacific Ocean within a mile of target, Apr 27.

SPRING POLKA FEST. Apr 16–18. Wisconsin Dells, WI. Several Midwest polka bands will be playing all your Polka favorites. Be prepared to dance the night away! Est attendance: 1,500. For info: Howard Johnson Hotel & Conference Center and Antiqua Bay Waterpark, PO Box 236, Wisconsin Dells, WI, 53965. Phone: (800) 54-DELLS. E-mail: info@antiquabay.com.

STAMP EXPO: SOUTH. Apr 16–18. Radisson Hotel, Anaheim, CA. Est attendance: 4,000. For info: Intl Stamp Collectors Society, PO Box 854, Van Nuys, CA 91408. Phone: (818) 997-6496. Fax: (818) 988-4337. E-mail: iibick@aol.com. Web: www.bick.net.

SUGARLOAF ART FAIR. Apr 16–18. Novi Expo Center, Novi, MI. This show, now in its 10th year, features more than 325 nationally recognized craft designers and fine artists displaying and selling their original creations. Includes craft demonstrations, live music, specialty foods, hourly gift certificate drawings, and more. Est attendance: 22,500. For info: Sugarloaf Mountain Works, 200 Orchard Ridge Dr, #215, Gaithersburg, MD 20878. Phone: (800) 210-9900. Fax: (310) 253-9620. Web: www.sugarloafcrafts.com.

SYNGE, JOHN MILLINGTON: BIRTH ANNIVERSARY. Apr 16, 1871. Irish dramatist and poet, most of whose plays were written in the brief span of six years before his death at age 37 of lymphatic sarcoma. His best-known work was *The Playboy of the Western World* (1907), which caused protests and rioting at early performances. Synge (pronounced "Sing") was born near Dublin, Ireland, and died there Mar 24, 1909.

Apr 16–17   ☆ Chase's 2004 Calendar of Events ☆

TEXAS CITY DISASTER: ANNIVERSARY. Apr 16–17, 1947. The worst industrial disaster in US history. The French-owned *Grandcamp*, docked at the oil and port town of Texas City and carrying a load of ammonium nitrate, was discovered to have a smoldering fire in her hold. At 9:12 AM, as onlookers gathered and a small firefighting team attempted to extinguish the blaze, the ship exploded with tremendous force, immediately killing everyone at the dock area. The resulting fires destroyed the nearby Monsanto Chemical Company and spread through oil pipelines into the city. At 1:00 AM, another ship, the *High Flyer* exploded. The city was left defenseless due to the deaths of almost the entire fire department. There were 576 known casualties, but most estimate that at least 100 more died in the conflagrations. Thousands were injured. The fires burned for a week. The disaster prompted new regulations on handling chemicals. With thousands of lawsuits, the US Congress passed a special act to settle claims in 1956.

WORLD'S LARGEST TRIVIA CONTEST. Apr 16–18. Stevens Point, WI. More than 12,000 players including more than 500 teams compete to answer eight questions every hour for 54 hours straight. Prize: Oscar-like trophy. Est attendance: 12,000. For info: Jim Oliva, University of Wisconsin, Rm 101 CAC, WWSP-Radio (89.9 FM), Stevens Point, WI 54481. Phone: (715) 346-3755. E-mail: theoz@dwave.net. Web: www.momsfamilies.com/trivia.

WRIGHT, WILBUR: BIRTH ANNIVERSARY. Apr 16, 1867. Aviation pioneer, born at Millville, IN. Died at Dayton, OH, May 30, 1912. See also: "Wright Brothers First Powered Flight" (Dec 17).

BIRTHDAYS TODAY

Kareem Abdul-Jabbar, 57, Hall of Fame basketball player, born Lewis Ferdinand Alcindor, Jr, New York, NY, Apr 16, 1947.
Edie Adams, 73, singer, actress, born Elizabeth Edith Enke, Kingston, PA, Apr 16, 1931.
Ellen Barkin, 49, actress (*Tender Mercies, Diner*), born New York, NY, Apr 16, 1955.
Jon Cryer, 39, actor ("Partners," *Pretty in Pink, Hot Shots!*), born New York, NY, Apr 16, 1965.
Merce Cunningham, 85, dancer, choreographer, born Centralia, WA, Apr 16, 1919.
Lukas Haas, 28, actor (*Witness, Rambling Rose*), born West Hollywood, CA, Apr 16, 1976.
Martin Lawrence, 39, actor ("Martin," *Bad Boys*), born Frankfurt, Germany, Apr 16, 1965.
Barry Nelson, 84, actor (*Pete 'n Tillie, The Shining*), born San Francisco, CA, Apr 16, 1920.
Anthony Principi, 60, US Secretary of Veteran's Affairs, born New York, NY, Apr 16, 1944.
Jay O. Sanders, 51, actor ("Crime Story," *Tucker: The Man and His Dream*), born Austin, TX, Apr 16, 1953.
Peter Ustinov, 83, actor (Oscars for *Spartacus, Topkapi*), born London, England, Apr 16, 1921.
Bobby Vinton, 69, singer ("Mr Lonely," "Roses Are Red [My Love]"), born Canonsburg, PA, Apr 16, 1935.

April 2004

S	M	T	W	T	F	S
				1	2	3
4	5	6	7	8	9	10
11	12	13	14	15	16	17
18	19	20	21	22	23	24
25	26	27	28	29	30	

APRIL 17 — SATURDAY
Day 108 — 258 Remaining

AMERICAN SAMOA: FLAG DAY: ANNIVERSARY. Apr 17. National holiday commemorating first raising of American flag in what was formerly Eastern Samoa in 1900. Public holiday with singing, dancing, costumes and parades.

ANSON, CAP: BIRTH ANNIVERSARY. Apr 17, 1852. Adrian Constantine ("Cap") Anson, Baseball Hall of Fame player and manager, born at Marshalltown, IA. Anson played professional baseball from 1871 through 1897 and is considered one of the game's greatest first basemen. As a manager, he piloted the Chicago White Stockings (today's Cubs) to five National League pennants and a .575 winning percentage. Inducted into the Hall of Fame in 1939. Died at Chicago, IL, Apr 18, 1922.

BAY OF PIGS INVASION LAUNCHED: ANNIVERSARY. Apr 17, 1961. More than 1,500 Cuban exiles invaded Cuba in an ill-fated attempt to overthrow Fidel Castro.

BLAH BLAH BLAH DAY. Apr 17. Today's the day to do any of the following, or whatever. Stop smoking, take out the trash, empty the cat litter, lose weight, pick up your clothes, put dirty dishes in the sink, get a job or quit your job. Annually, Apr 17. [©2003 by WH.] For info: Thomas & Ruth Roy, Wellcat Holidays, 2418 Long Ln, Lebanon, PA 17046. Phone: (717) 279-0184. E-mail: info@wellcat.com. Web: www.wellcat.com.

BLOCK HOUSE STEEPLECHASE RACES. Apr 17. Foothills Equestrian Nature Center, Tryon, NC. 58th annual running of the Block House Steeplechase. Est attendance: 20,000. For info: Mitzi Lindsey, Tryon Riding & Hunt Club, PO Box 1095, Tryon, NC 28782. Phone: (800) 438-3681. Fax: (828) 859-5598. E-mail: trhc@teleplex.net. Web: www.trhcevents.com.

CALIFORNIA POPPY FESTIVAL. Apr 17–18. Lancaster, CA. Celebrating the golden poppy as the state flower of California, the California Poppy Festival features unique homemade crafts, a variety of musical entertainers, delicious food booths and a flower and garden market. Visitors can stop by the Poppy Pavilion to see dazzling displays of poppies or visit the Wildflower Information Center to get maps of the best poppy fields. Both kids and adults will enjoy the carnival, games and rides. Est attendance: 60,000. For info: Anne Aldrich, Public Information Officer, City of Lancaster, 44933 Fern Ave, Lancaster, CA 93534. Phone: (661) 723-6053. Fax: (661) 723-6141. Web: cityoflancasterca.org.

CAMBODIA FALLS TO THE KHMER ROUGE: ANNIVERSARY. Apr 17, 1975. Cambodia fell when its capital, Phnom Penh, was captured by the Khmer Rouge. The Pol Pot regime inaugurated "Year One," and the wholesale slaughter of intellectuals, political enemies and peasants began. As many as two million Cambodians perished. See also: "Pol Pot Overthrown: Anniversary" (Jan 7).

CELEBRATE EARTH DAY. Apr 17. Jenkinson's Aquarium, Point Pleasant Beach, NJ. Celebrate Earth Day in a positive way—learn what you can do to help the environment. Take part in environmental games and stop by for storytelling. Free arts and crafts from 1–4 PM. Stories, demonstrations and more throughout the day. Est attendance: 1,200. For info: Jenkinson's Aquarium, 300 Ocean Ave, Point Pleasant Beach, NJ 08742. Phone: (732) 899-1212. Fax: (732) 899-1717. E-mail: aquarium@jenkinsons.com. Web: www.jenkinsons.com.

CHASE, SAMUEL: BIRTH ANNIVERSARY. Apr 17, 1741. Signer of the Declaration of Independence. Born at Somerset County, MD, he died June 19, 1811.

ELLIS ISLAND FAMILY HISTORY DAY. Apr 17. Ellis Island, New York, NY. By official proclamation of our nation's governors, April 17 has been designated as "Ellis Island Family History Day." Sponsored by The Statue of Liberty–Ellis Island Foundation, Inc and the National Genealogical Society, this annual day recognizes the achievements and contributions made to America by Ellis Island immigrants and their descendants. Historically, April 17 marks the day in 1907 when more immigrants were processed through the island than on any other day in its colorful history: 11,747 people. In addition, the Foundation has established the "Ellis Island Family Heritage Awards," which are given annually to a select number of Ellis Island immigrants or their descendants who have made a significant contribution to the American experience. For info: Maria Antenorcruz, Statue of Liberty-Ellis Island Foundation, Inc, 292 Madison Ave, 14th Fl, New York, NY 10017. Phone: (212) 561-4542. Fax: (212) 779-1990. E-mail: mantenorcruz@ellisisland.org. Web: www.ellisisland.org.

FEAST OF THE RAMSON. Apr 17. Richwood, WV. A dinner dedicated to the ramp, a wild leek that grows in the mountains. Arts and crafts; mountain song and dance. Est attendance: 2,000. For info: Richwood Area Chamber of Commerce, PO Box 267, Richwood, WV 26261. Phone: (304) 846-6790. E-mail: rwdchamber@richwoodwv.com. Web: www.richwoodwv.com.

"THE FRED WARING SHOW" TV PREMIERE: 55th ANNIVERSARY. Apr 17, 1949. Fred Waring was leader of the big band called the Pennsylvanians, which featured about 65 musicians and singers. The show aired on Sunday nights until 1954.

GEORGIA RENAISSANCE SPRING FESTIVAL. Apr 17-May 30. (Saturdays, Sundays and Memorial Day.) Atlanta, GA. A rollicking rendition of a 16th-century English faire. Jousting knights, jugglers, Shakespearean parodies and more than 100 shows daily. Feast like a king and shop like royalty. Est attendance: 200,000. For info: Sarah Rutledge, Georgia Renaissance Festival, PO Box 986, Fairburn, GA 30213. Phone: (770) 964-8575. Fax: (770) 964-1477.

HISTORIC GARDEN WEEK IN VIRGINIA. Apr 17-25. This annual statewide event, celebrating its 71st anniversary, is billed as "America's Largest Open House." Showcases more than 250 of Virginia's finest homes, gardens, plantations and landmark properties on more than 30 separate tours on different days of the week. A 225-page guidebook will be available in February 2004. Please mail a contribution of $5 to cover postage and handling. Est attendance: 40,000. For info: Historic Garden Week, Garden Club of Virginia, 12 E Franklin St, Richmond, VA 23219. Phone: (804) 644-7776. Fax: (804) 644-7778. E-mail: gdnweek@erols.com. Web: www.VAGardenweek.org.

HOLDEN, WILLIAM: BIRTH ANNIVERSARY. Apr 17, 1918. William Holden's first starring role was in *Golden Boy*. The actor, born at O'Fallon, IL, won an Oscar for his role in *Stalag 17* in 1953. He was found dead at Los Angeles, CA, Nov 16, 1981.

HOOD RIVER VALLEY BLOSSOM FESTIVAL. Apr 17-18. Hood River, OR. Breathtaking views of the Hood River Valley's orchards in bloom. Arts and crafts, dinners, seasonal opening of the Mount Hood Railroad. Est attendance: 20,000. For info: Hood River County Chamber of Commerce, 405 Portway Ave, Hood River, OR 97031. Phone: (800) 366-3530. E-mail: hrccc@hoodriver.org. Web: www.hoodriver.org.

HUSBAND APPRECIATION DAY. April 17. Wives, show your husbands how much you love and appreciate them. Communicate the difference your husband makes in your life. Annually, the third Saturday in April. For info: Brooke Espinoza, PO Box 1054, Arcadia, CA 91007. Phone: (626) 574-7571. E-mail: brookeespinoza@equipyourmarriage.com. Web: www.equipyourmarriage.com.

INTERNATIONAL FORD MUSTANG DAY. Apr 17. Ford Mustang enthusiasts are encouraged to have car shows, cruises, parties and other events to celebrate the birthday of the Mustang automobile. For info: Bill Johnson, Mustang Club of America, 4051 Barrancas Ave, PMB 102, Pensacola, FL 32507. Phone: (360) 468-4343. Fax: (360) 468-4348. E-mail: tapemover@rockisland.com. Web: www.mustang.org.

JOHN WILKES BOOTH ESCAPE ROUTE TOUR. Apr 17 and 24. (also May 8, Sept 11, Sept 25 and Oct 9.) Clinton, MD. A 12-hour bus tour over the route used by Lincoln's assassin. Est attendance: 270. For info: Surratt House Museum, Box 427, Clinton, MD 20735. Phone: (301) 868-1121. Fax: (301) 868-8177. Web: www.surratt.org.

JUST PRAY NO: WORLDWIDE WEEKEND PRAYER. Apr 17-18. 14th annual. Churches throughout the world. Concerts of prayer, fasting, street rallies and marches to gain media attention. Bible studies and sermons concerning alcoholism and drug abuse and revival meetings aimed at those bound by addiction. For info: "Just Pray No," Ltd, 1380 Killie Ct, #102, Dunedin, FL 34698. Phone: (727) 738-0178. E-mail: justprayno@aol.com. Web: www.justprayno.org.

LONGWOOD GARDENS ACRES OF SPRING. Apr 17-May 28. Kennett Square, PA. Thousands of spring bulbs, flowering shrubs and trees bloom throughout 1,050 acres of formal gardens, woodlands and meadows. Est attendance: 150,000. For info: Elizabeth Sullivan, PR Dir, Longwood Gardens, PO Box 501, Kennett Square, PA 19348-0501. Phone: (610) 388-1000. Web: www.longwoodgardens.org.

MORGAN, JOHN PIERPONT: BIRTH ANNIVERSARY. Apr 17, 1837. American financier and corporation director, born at Hartford, CT. Morgan died Mar 31, 1913, at Rome, Italy, leaving an estate valued at more than $70 million.

MOSSY CREEK BARNYARD FESTIVAL. Apr 17-18 (also Oct 16-17). Warner Robins, GA. Arts and crafts chosen from best in the nation; heritage crafts, country and folk music and folk tales in relaxed atmosphere. Semiannually, the third weekend of April (usually) and of October. Est attendance: 25,000. For info: Carolyn Chester, Mossy Creek Barnyard Festival, Inc, 106 Anne Dr, Warner Robins, GA 31093. Phone: (478) 922-8265. E-mail: echester@bellsouth.net. Web: www.mossycreekfestival.com.

MS WALK. April 17-18. San Jose, CA. Looking for a fun family activity? Join the Silicon Valley chapter of the National Multiple Sclerosis Society for the annual MS Walk along the beautiful Los Gatos Creek Trail. Enjoy a delicious breakfast, make new friends and help end the devastating effects of multiple sclerosis. For info: Carolyn Wellsfry, Natl MS Society, 2589 Scott Blvd, Santa Clara, CA 95050. Phone: (408) 988-7557 or (800) FIGHT-MS. Fax: (408) 988-1816. E-mail: cau@nmss.org. Web: www.nationalmssociety.org.

NAB 2004/NATIONAL BROADCASTERS CONVENTION. Apr 17-22. Las Vegas, NV. World's largest convention of radio, television and other types of multimedia. The awards for the National Broadcasting Hall of Fame are also awarded at the convention. For info: Natl Assn of Broadcasters, 1771 N St NW, Washington, DC 20036-2891. Phone: (800) 342-2460 or (202) 429-4194. Fax: (202) 429-5343. E-mail: register@nab.org. Web: www.nab.org/conventions.

NATIONAL AUCTIONEERS DAY. April 17. Recognize the auction profession, and its contribution to American commerce. Annually, the third Saturday in April. For info: Tammy Dodderidge, 8880 Ballentine, Overland Park, KS 66214. Phone: (913) 541-8084. Fax: (913) 894-5281. E-mail: publicrelations@auctioneers.org. Web: www.auctioneers.org.

NATIONAL HEADACHE FOUNDATION FUNDRAISER. Apr 17. New York, NY. Annual black tie silent auction and dinner serves as the major fundraiser for the National Headache Foundation. Proceeds from the evening are used for research, education and service. Est attendance: 300. For info: Suzanne E. Simons, Exec Dir, Natl Headache Fdtn, 820 N Orleans, Ste 217,

Chicago, IL 60610-3132. Phone: (312) 640-5399. Fax: (312) 640-9049.

NATIONAL SENSE OF SMELL DAY. Apr 17 (tentative). A day when museums and science centers across the country, supported by a grant from the Sense of Smell Institute, host a variety of interactive educational activities. This day was created to educate the public about this mysterious fifth sense and explore the many ways it can positively impact our quality of life. For info: Sense of Smell Institute, 145 E 32nd St, New York, NY 10016. Phone: (212) 725-2755. Web: www.senseofsmell.org.

NETHERLANDS AND SCILLY ISLES PEACE: ANNIVERSARY. Apr 17, 1986. The 335-year "state of war" that had existed between the Netherlands and the Scilly Isles came to an end on this date when Dutch ambassador Jonkheer Huydecoper flew to the Scilly Isles to deliver a proclamation terminating the war that had started in 1651. Though hostilities had ceased three centuries earlier, a standing joke in the islands was that no one had bothered to declare an end to the war.

NEW ENGLAND CONFERENCE ON STORYTELLING FOR CHILDREN. Apr 17. Arts Center, Keene State College, Keene, NH. Warm, supportive one-day conference for teachers and others interested in learning about storytelling. Keynote speaker, plus workshops and a performance. Children may attend if capable. Resources will be available. Est attendance: 100. For info: Mary Mayshark-Stavely, Keene State College, Keene, NH 03435-2503. Phone: (603) 358-2232. E-mail: mmayshar@keene.edu.

REASONER, HARRY: BIRTH ANNIVERSARY. Apr 17, 1923. American television journalist Harry Reasoner was born at Dakota City, IA. In 1956 Reasoner joined CBS News, where he anchored the "CBS Sunday News" (1963–70) and was one of the two original anchors, along with Mike Wallace, of the news magazine show "60 Minutes." He was co-anchor of the "ABC Evening News" from 1970 until 1978, when he returned to CBS and "60 Minutes." He died Aug 6, 1991, at Norwalk, CT.

SAINT LOUIS VARIETY CLUB TELETHON AND DINNER WITH THE STARS. Apr 17–18. Chase Park Plaza Hotel, St. Louis, MO. A 10-hour telethon and dinner to raise funds for disabled and disadvantaged children in the greater St. Louis area. Televised on St. Louis KMOV, Channel 4 (CBS). Est attendance: 1,900. For info: St. Louis Variety Club, 2200 Westport Plaza Dr, St. Louis, MO 63146. Phone: (314) 453-0453. Fax: (314) 453-0488.

SFCC SPRING ARTS FESTIVAL. Apr 17–18. Gainesville, FL. Artists and craftsmen from all areas of the US display their work. Also, Kids Art Jungle—a complete art fest for kids. Est attendance: 129,000. For info: Santa Fe Community College, Spring Arts Fest, 3000 NW 83rd St, Gainesville, FL 32606. Phone: (352) 395-5355. Fax: (352) 395-5918. E-mail: kathryn.lehman@santafe.cc.fl.us.

SOLIDARITY GRANTED LEGAL STATUS: 15th ANNIVERSARY. Apr 17, 1989. After nearly a decade of struggle and suppression the Polish labor union Solidarity was granted legal status, clearing the way for the downfall of the Polish Communist Party. Solidarity and the Polish people surprised the government by winning 99 of the 100 parliamentary seats in the election. General Wojciech Jaruzelski was elected president on July 19 and nominated Czelaw Kiszczak prime minister, enraging the Lech Walesa–led Solidarity. On Aug 7 Walesa swayed the traditional allies of the Communist Party—the United Peasant and Democratic Parties—to switch sides. Kiszczak resigned as prime minister a week later after failing to form a government, forcing Jaruzelski to accept the principle of a government led by Solidarity.

SPACE MILESTONE: COLUMBIA NEUROLAB (US). Apr 17, 1998. Seven astronauts and scientists were launched with 2,000 animals (crickets, mice, snails and fish) to study the nervous system in space.

SPACE MILESTONE: SURVEYOR 3 (US). Apr 17, 1967. Launch date of lunar probe vehicle, which made soft landing on Moon on Apr 20 and with its digging apparatus established surface qualities.

STEIGER, ROD: BIRTH ANNIVERSARY. Apr 17, 1925. The magnetic character actor was born at Westhampton, NY. In a 50-year career, Steiger played a wide range of roles for some of the best directors of the day. He won a Best Actor Oscar for *In the Heat of the Night*, and was also nominated for *On the Waterfront* and *The Pawnbroker*. He died at Los Angeles, CA, July 9, 2002.

SYRIAN ARAB REPUBLIC: INDEPENDENCE DAY. Apr 17. Official holiday. Proclaimed independence from League of Nations mandate under French administration in 1946.

VERRAZANO DAY: ANNIVERSARY. Apr 17, 1524. Celebrates discovery of New York harbor by Giovanni Verrazano, Florentine navigator, 1485–1527.

WILDER, THORNTON: BIRTH ANNIVERSARY. Apr 17, 1897. Pulitzer Prize–winning American playwright (*Our Town*) and novelist, born at Madison, WI. Died at Hamden, CT, Dec 7, 1975.

WINE AND GARDEN FESTIVAL. Apr 17. Bryan, TX. This event features the 21st annual Texas Artists Competition. The winning painting becomes the focal point for the next year's Private Reserve wine label. Team grape-stomping competition, dozens of food and craft booths, hot air balloons, winery tours, wine tastings, vineyard hayrides plus a variety of live music performances. Hours are 11–6. Est attendance: 9,000. For info: Julie Diefenthal, PR Dir, Messina Hof Wine Cellars, 4545 Old Reliance Rd, Bryan, TX 77808. Phone: (979) 778-9463 x30.

WISCONSIN SPRING GARDEN MARKET. Apr 17–18. The American Club, Kohler, WI. Spring plants, garden ornaments, herbs and unusual varieties of annuals and perennials fill the Grand Hall of the Great Lakes. Lending counsel and a helping hand with seminars, demonstrations and an array of products are more than 70 plant and gardening specialists, landscape designers and architects. Est attendance: 5,000. For info: The American Club, Highland Dr, Kohler, WI 53044. Phone: (800) 344-2838. Fax: (920) 457-6372. Web: www.destinationkohler.com.

WORLD COW CHIP–THROWING CHAMPIONSHIP® CONTEST. Apr 17. Beaver, OK. 35th annual. A highly specialized international organic sporting event which draws dung flingers from around the world. A special division of this competition is held for politicians, who are known to be highly practiced in this area. Est attendance: 4,500. For info: Beaver County Chamber of Commerce, PO Box 878, Beaver, OK 73932-0878. Phone: (580) 625-4726.

BIRTHDAYS TODAY

Sean Bean, 46, actor (*Lord of the Rings: Fellowship of the Ring, Stormy Monday, Patriot Games*), born Sheffield, Yorkshire, England, Apr 17, 1958.

Victoria Adams Beckham, 29, actress, singer (Posh Spice of Spice Girls), born Hertfordshire, England, Apr 17, 1975.

Norman Julius ("Boomer") Esiason, 43, broadcaster and former football player, born West Islip, NY, Apr 17, 1961.

Jennifer Garner, 32, actress ("Alias," "Felicity"), born Houston, TX, Apr 17, 1972.

Olivia Hussey, 53, actress (*Romeo and Juliet*), born Buenos Aires, Argentina, Apr 17, 1951.

Don Kirshner, 70, music publisher, promoter, born the Bronx, NY, Apr 17, 1934.

☆ Chase's 2004 Calendar of Events ☆   Apr 17–18

Cynthia Ozick, 76, feminist, writer, born New York, NY, Apr 17, 1928.
Liz Phair, 37, rock singer/songwriter, born New Haven, CT, Apr 17, 1967.
Lela Rochon, 38, actress (*Waiting to Exhale, Boomerang*), born Los Angeles, CA, Apr 17, 1966.

APRIL 18 — SUNDAY
Day 109 — 257 Remaining

ADMINISTRATIVE PROFESSIONALS WEEK. Apr 18–24. Acknowledgment of the contributions of all administrative professionals and their vital roles in business, industry, education and government. Annually, the last full week (from Sunday–Saturday) in April. Administrative Professionals Day is observed on Wednesday of this week (Apr 21 in 2004). For info: Rick Stroud, Communications Dir, Intl Assn of Administrative Professionals, 10502 NW Ambassador Dr, PO Box 20404, Kansas City, MO 64195-0404. Phone: (816) 891-6600 x 2239. Fax: (816) 891-9118. E-mail: rstroud@iaap-hq.org. Web: www.iaap-hq.org.

CANADA: CANADA BOOK WEEK. Apr 18–24. To celebrate the important role of literature in Canada's past, present and future; to nurture a love of reading in Canada's youth; to celebrate the international success of Canadian literature and honor Canada's literary heroes; to promote Canadian books and the people who write them and to encourage Canadians from all walks of life to buy Canadian books. For info: The Writers' Trust of Canada, 40 Wellington St East, Ste 300, Toronto, ON, Canada M5E 1C7. Phone: (416) 504-8222. Web: www.canadabookday.com.

CANADA: CONSTITUTION ACT OF 1982: ANNIVERSARY. Apr 18, 1982. Replacing the British North America Act of 1867, the Canadian Constitution Act of 1982 provides Canada with a new set of fundamental laws and civil rights. Signed by Queen Elizabeth II, at Parliament Hill, Ottawa, Canada, it went into effect at 12:01 AM, Sunday, Apr 19, 1982.

CRAWFORD, SAMUEL EARL "WAHOO SAM": BIRTH ANNIVERSARY. Apr 18, 1880. Major league baseball player with the Detroit Tigers, born at Wahoo, NE. Wahoo Sam played pro ball for 20 years, racking up a career batting average of .309. His record of 312 career triples still stands. He was inducted into the Baseball Hall of Fame in 1957. Crawford died June 15, 1968, at Hollywood, CA.

DARROW, CLARENCE SEWARD: BIRTH ANNIVERSARY. Apr 18, 1857. American attorney often associated with unpopular causes, from the Pullman strike in 1894 to the Scottsboro case in 1932, born at Kinsman, OH. At the Scopes trial, July 13, 1925, Darrow said: "I do not consider it an insult, but rather a compliment, to be called an agnostic. I do not pretend to know where many ignorant men are sure—that is all that agnosticism means." Darrow died at Chicago, IL, Mar 13, 1938.

THE HOUSE THAT RUTH BUILT: ANNIVERSARY. Apr 18, 1923. More than 74,000 fans attended Opening Day festivities as the New York Yankees inaugurated their new stadium. Babe Ruth christened it with a game-winning three-run homer into the right-field bleachers. In his coverage of the game for the *New York Evening Telegram* sportswriter Fred Lieb described Yankee Stadium as "The House That Ruth Built," and the name stuck.

ISRAEL: HOLOCAUST DAY (YOM HASHOAH). Apr 18. Hebrew calendar date: Nisan 27, 5764. A day established by Israel's Knesset as a memorial to the Jewish dead of WWII. Anniversary in Jewish calendar of Nisan 27, 5705 (corresponding to Apr 10, 1945, in the Gregorian calendar), the day on which Allied troops liberated the first Nazi concentration camp, Buchenwald, north of Weimar, Germany, where about 56,000 prisoners, many of them Jewish, perished. Began at sundown Apr 17.

JAPAN BOMBED: ANNIVERSARY. Apr 18, 1942. For the first time during WWII, the mainland of Japan was bombed. Brigade General James Doolittle led a squadron of B-25s from the US carrier *Hornet*. Cities bombed included Tokyo, Yokohama, Kobe and Nagoya. Doolittle said they flew so low that "one of our party observed a ball game in progress." Although the bombers did little damage, the psychological victory was enormous.

JIMMY STEWART RELAY MARATHON. Apr 18 (tentative). Griffith Park, Los Angeles, CA. 23rd annual marathon. Team relay with five people, each running 5.2 miles. Funds raised go to benefit the Saint John's Child and Family Development Center. Est attendance: 35,000. For info: Jimmy Stewart Relay Marathon, 1328 22nd Street, Santa Monica, CA 90404. Phone: (310) 829-8968. Fax: (310) 829-8911. E-mail: marathon@stjohns.org. Web: www.stjohns.org.

NATIONAL COIN WEEK. Apr 18–24. To promote the history and lore of numismatics and the hobby of coin collecting. For info: Gail Baker, Dir of Educ, American Numismatic Assn, 818 N Cascade Ave, Colorado Springs, CO 80903. Phone: (719) 632-2646 or (800) 367-9723. Fax: (719) 634-4085. E-mail: Education@money.org. Web: www.money.org.

★**NATIONAL CRIME VICTIMS' RIGHTS WEEK.** Apr 18–24 (tentative). Date varies—a week in April.

NATIONAL KARAOKE WEEK. Apr 18–24. Karaoke has grown by leaps and bounds in the US. Once thought to be a fad, more and more people are recognizing the benefits of karaoke—increased self-esteem, confidence and stress release. Annually, the fourth week in April. For info: Visual Perspectives, 1083 W 124th Dr, Westminster, CO 80234-1757. Phone/fax: (303) 452-5140.

NATIONAL LIBRARY WEEK. Apr 18–24. A nationwide observance sponsored by the American Library Association. Celebrates libraries and librarians, the pleasures and importance of reading and invites library use and support. For info: American Library Assn, Public Info Office, 50 E Huron St, Chicago, IL 60611. Phone: (312) 280-5044. Fax: (312) 944-8520. E-mail: pio@ala.org. Web: www.ala.org.

★**NATIONAL ORGAN AND TISSUE DONOR AWARENESS WEEK.** Apr 18–24.

★**NATIONAL PARK WEEK.** Apr 18–24.

NATIONAL VOLUNTEER WEEK. Apr 18–24. National Volunteer Week honors those who reach out to others through volunteer community service and calls attention to the need for more community services for individuals, groups and families to help solve serious social problems that affect our communities. For info: Customer Information Center, Points of Light Foundation, 1400 I St NW, Ste 800, Washington, DC 20005. Phone: (202) 729-8168. Fax: (202) 729-8103. E-mail: volunteerweek@pointsoflight.org. Web: www.pointsoflight.org.

★**NATIONAL VOLUNTEER WEEK.** Apr 18–24.

NATIONAL WINDOW SAFETY WEEK. April 18–24. Designed to inform parents and caregivers about the critical role played by windows in the safety plans of their homes. Also, to address issues of children falling out windows and using windows as emergency escapes. For info: Alan Campbell, 1400 E Touhy Ave, Ste 470, Des Plaines, IL 60018. Phone: (847) 299-5200. Fax: (847) 299-1286. E-mail: acampbell@wdma.com. Web: www.wdma.com.

Apr 18 ☆ Chase's 2004 Calendar of Events ☆

PAUL REVERE'S RIDE: ANNIVERSARY. Apr 18, 1775. The "Midnight Ride" of Paul Revere and William Dawes started at about 10 PM, to warn American patriots between Boston, MA, and Concord, MA, of the approaching British.

PET OWNERS INDEPENDENCE DAY. Apr 18. Dog and cat owners take the day off from work and the pets go to work in their place, since most pets are jobless, sleep all day and do not even take out the trash. [©2003 by WH.] For info: Thomas & Ruth Roy, Wellcat Holidays, 2418 Long Ln, Lebanon, PA 17046. Phone: (717) 279-0184. E-mail: info@wellcat.com. Web: www.wellcat.com.

"REAL PEOPLE" TV PREMIERE: 25th ANNIVERSARY. Apr 18, 1979. Real people do the darndest things—from making paintings out of lint to making houses out of aluminum cans. NBC developed the program to spotlight the achievements, funny inventions and extraordinary stunts of ordinary Americans. Hosts of the show included Fred Willard, Sarah Purcell, John Barbour, Skip Stephenson, Byron Allen and Peter Billingsley.

SAN FRANCISCO 1906 EARTHQUAKE: ANNIVERSARY. Apr 18, 1906. Business section of San Francisco, some 10,000 acres, destroyed by earthquake. First quake at 5:13 AM, followed by fire. Nearly 4,000 lives lost.

SKY AWARENESS WEEK. Apr 18–24. A celebration of the sky and an opportunity to appreciate its natural beauty, to understand sky and weather processes and to work together to protect the sky as a natural resource (it's the only one we have). Events are held at schools, nature centers, etc, all across the US. For info: Barbara G. Levine, How The Weatherworks, 301 Creek Valley Ln, Rockville, MD 20850. Phone: (301) 527-9339. Fax: (301) 990-9324. E-mail: skyweek@weatherworks.com. Web: www.weatherworks.com.

SPACE MILESTONE: *TITAN 34-D* ROCKET FAILURE. Apr 18, 1986. Launched from Vandenburg Air Force Base, CA, the $65 million *Titan* exploded when it was only a few hundred feet into flight, destroying the $500 million KH-11 reconnaissance satellite payload. Poisonous fumes were released by the explosion, causing concern for the safety of people in nearby communities.

SURRENDER AT DURHAM STATION: ANNIVERSARY. Apr 18, 1865. Union General William Tecumseh Sherman and Confederate General Joseph Johnston signed a broad political peace agreement at Durham Station, NC. The agreement promised a general amnesty for all Southerners and pledged federal recognition of all Southern state governments after their officials took an oath of allegiance to the US. Sherman was roundly criticized for his role in drawing up the agreement, although he based it on an earlier conversation with Lincoln and Grant. The agreement was rejected by President Andrew Johnson, and Sherman and Johnston were forced to reach a new agreement with terms virtually the same as those given Robert E. Lee.

"THIRD WORLD" DAY: ANNIVERSARY. Apr 18, 1955. Anniversary of the first use of the phrase "third world," which was by Indonesia's President Sukarno in his opening speech at the Bandung Conference. Representatives of nearly 30 African and Asian countries (2,000 attendees) heard Sukarno praise the American war of independence, "the first successful anticolonial war in history." More than half the world's population, he said, was represented at this "first intercontinental conference of the so-called colored peoples, in the history of mankind." The phrase and the idea of a "third world" rapidly gained currency, generally signifying the aggregate of nonaligned peoples and nations—the nonwhite and underdeveloped portion of the world.

WEEK OF THE YOUNG CHILD. Apr 18–24. To focus on the importance of quality early childhood education. For info: Natl Assn for the Educ of Young Children, 1509 16th St NW, Washington, DC 20036. Phone: (800) 424-2460. Fax: (202) 328-1846. E-mail: naeyc@naeyc.org. Web: www.naeyc.org.

WORLD'S BIGGEST FISH FRY. Apr 18–24. Paris, TN. Since 1953. More than 10,000 pounds of catfish will be served. Includes parades, arts and crafts show, auto shows and more. All-you-can-eat dinners are served at the fairgrounds. For info: Paris Chamber of Commerce, 2508 E Wood Rd, PO Box 8, Paris, TN 38242. Phone: (731) 642-3431. E-mail: pariscoc@charterbn.com. Web: paris.tn.org.

WSBA/WARM 103 SPRING CRAFT SHOW. Apr 18. York Fairgrounds, York, PA. More than 200 craft displays, from country to contemporary, Victorian and southwestern, handcrafted furniture, wood carvings, dolls, jewelry, pottery, collectibles, quilts, baskets, garden needs and much more. Admission fee. Est attendance: 4,000. For info: Joe Alfano, Asst Promo Dir, PO Box 910, York, PA 17402-0910. Phone: (717) 764-1155. Fax: (717) 252-4708. E-mail: jalfano@suscom.com. Web: www.warm103.com.

ZIMBABWE: INDEPENDENCE DAY: ANNIVERSARY. Apr 18. National holiday commemorates the recognition by Great Britain of Zimbabwean independence on this day in 1980. Prior to this, the country had been the British colony of Southern Rhodesia.

BIRTHDAYS TODAY

Barbara Hale, 83, actress ("Perry Mason"), born DeKalb, IL, Apr 18, 1921.
Melissa Joan Hart, 28, actress ("Sabrina the Teenage Witch"), born Long Island, NY, Apr 18, 1976.
Cheryl Ann Haworth, 21, weightlifter, born Savannah, GA, Apr 18, 1983.
Robert Hooks, 67, actor, director, producer (*Star Trek III: The Search for Spock*; stage: *Day of Absence, Where's Daddy?* [Theatre World Awards for both]), born Washington, DC, Apr 18, 1937.
John James, 48, actor ("Search for Tomorrow," "Dynasty"), born Minneapolis, MN, Apr 18, 1956.
Jane Leeves, 43, actress ("Murphy Brown," "Frasier"), born East Grinstead, England, Apr 18, 1961.
Dorothy Lyman, 57, actress ("All My Children," "Mama's Family"), director, born Minneapolis, MN, Apr 18, 1947.
Eric McCormack, 41, actor ("Lonesome Dove," "Will & Grace"), born Toronto, ON, Canada, Apr 18, 1963.
Hayley Mills, 58, actress (*Pollyana, The Parent Trap, The Moon Spinners*), born London, England, Apr 18, 1946.
Rick Moranis, 50, actor, writer (*Ghostbusters, Honey I Shrunk the Kids*), born Toronto, ON, Canada, Apr 18, 1954.
Conan O'Brien, 41, host ("Late Night with Conan O'Brien"), born Brookline, MA, Apr 18, 1963.
John Pankow, 50, actor ("Mad About You"), born St. Louis, MO, Apr 18, 1954.
Eric Roberts, 48, actor (*Runaway Train, Star 80*), born Biloxi, MS, Apr 18, 1956.
James Woods, 57, actor (*Holocaust, The Onion Field*), born Vernal, UT, Apr 18, 1947.

April 2004

S	M	T	W	T	F	S
				1	2	3
4	5	6	7	8	9	10
11	12	13	14	15	16	17
18	19	20	21	22	23	24
25	26	27	28	29	30	

APRIL 19 — MONDAY
Day 110 — 256 Remaining

ASTRONOMY WEEK. Apr 19–25. To take astronomy to the people. Astronomy Week is observed during the calendar week in which Astronomy Day falls. See also: "Astronomy Day" (Apr 24).

BATTLE OF LEXINGTON AND CONCORD: ANNIVERSARY. Apr 19, 1775. Massachusetts. Start of the American Revolution as the British fired the "shot heard 'round the world."

BOSTON MARATHON—108th RUNNING. Apr 19. Boston, MA. The marathon begins in the rural New England town of Hopkinton, winds through eight cities and towns and finishes near downtown Boston. Always the third Monday in April. 2004 will be the 108th year of this historic running event. 20,000 participants. Athletes qualify by meeting time standards which correspond to age. Est attendance: 500,000. For info: Boston Athletic Assn, Boston Marathon, One Ash St, Hopkinton, MA 01748-1897. Phone: (508) 435-6905. E-mail: mile27@baa.org. Web: www.baa.org.

BRANCH DAVIDIAN FIRE AT WACO: ANNIVERSARY. Apr 19, 1993. After a 51-day standoff between the Branch Davidians and law-enforcement groups, the compound of the religious cult burned to the ground with 86 of its members inside, near Waco, TX, after federal agents began battering the compound with armored vehicles. Nine people escaped, but the 86 that perished included 17 children and the cult's leader, David Koresh.

EXPLOSION ON THE USS *IOWA*: 15th ANNIVERSARY. Apr 19, 1989. In one of the worst naval disasters since the war in Vietnam, a freak explosion rocked the battleship USS *Iowa*, killing 47 sailors. The explosion occurred in the No. 2 gun turret as the *Iowa* was participating in gunnery exercises about 300 miles northeast of Puerto Rico.

FORDYCE ON THE COTTON BELT FESTIVAL. Apr 19–24. Fordyce, AR. 24th annual railroad event includes arts and crafts, quilt show and sale, train rides, musical entertainment, rodeo, parade, railroad displays, beauty pageants, gospel singing and more. Est attendance: 10,000. For info: Chamber of Commerce, PO Box 588, Fordyce, AR 71742. Phone: (870) 352-5125 or (870) 352-3520. Fax: (870) 352-8090. E-mail: fordyce@ipa.net.

GARFIELD, LUCRETIA RUDOLPH: BIRTH ANNIVERSARY. Apr 19, 1832. Wife of James Abram Garfield, 20th president of the US, born at Hiram, OH. Died at Pasadena, CA, Mar 14, 1918.

HERITAGE WEEK. Apr 19–24. New Harmony, IN. Head to this historic village and watch crafters create 19th-century-style candles, baskets and pottery. Annually, Monday through Saturday of the third week in April. Est attendance: 5,000. For info: Special Projects Coord, Historic New Harmony, PO Box 579, New Harmony, IN 47631. Phone: (812) 682-4488. Fax: (812) 682-4313. E-mail: klinderm@usi.edu.

JOHN PARKER DAY. Apr 19. Remembering John Parker's order, at Lexington Green, Apr 19, 1775: "Stand your ground. Don't fire unless fired upon; but if they mean to have a war, let it begin here." Parker, revolutionary soldier, captain of minutemen, born at Lexington, MA, July 13, 1729. Died Sept 17, 1775.

MOON PHASE: NEW MOON. Apr 19. Moon enters New Moon phase at 9:21 AM, EDT.

MOORE, DUDLEY: BIRTH ANNIVERSARY. April 19, 1935. British comedian, actor and classically trained pianist born at Dagenham, near London, England. Initially pursuing a career as a concert and jazz pianist, Moore was invited by Peter Cook to join the comedy revue *Beyond the Fringe*. Moore was best known for his movies *10* and *Arthur*, for which he was nominated for an Oscar. Moore died at New Jersey on Mar 27, 2002.

NATIONAL CREDIT EDUCATION WEEK. Apr 19–24. A week during which members of the ACA International (The Association of Credit and Collection Professionals) put on seminars, contests and other events to educate consumers about the importance of financial responsibility and maintaining a good credit rating. Annually, the third week in April. For info: ACA Intl, PO Box 390106, Minneapolis, MN 55439-0106. Phone: (952) 926-6547. Fax: (952) 926-1624. E-mail: schaffer@collector.com. Web: www.collector.com.

NATIONAL TV TURNOFF WEEK. Apr 19–25. Encourages Americans to voluntarily turn off their TVs for seven days in order to promote richer, healthier and more connected lives, families and communities. Organizer's kit available. For info: TV-Turnoff Network, 1601 Connecticut Ave, Ste 303, Washington, DC 20009. Phone: (800) 939-6737. Web: www.tvturnoff.org.

NATIONAL WILDLIFE WEEK. Apr 19–25. In 1938 the National Wildlife Federation created National Wildlife Week, a celebration to alert the public to the needs of wildlife and NWF's efforts to preserve wildlife and their habitats. NWF educates students, families and adults about wildlife conservation issues and encourages them to become environmental stewards. For info: National Wildlife Federation, 11100 Wildlife Ctr Dr, Reston, VA 20190. Phone: (703) 438-6000. E-mail: wildlife@nwf.org. Web: www.nwf.org.

NETHERLANDS–US DIPLOMATIC RELATIONS: ANNIVERSARY. Apr 19, 1782. Anniversary of establishment of America's oldest continuously peaceful diplomatic relations. On this date, the States General of the Netherlands United Provinces admitted John Adams (later to become second president of the US) as minister plenipotentiary of the young American republic. This was the second diplomatic recognition of the US as an independent nation. Within six months Adams had succeeded in bringing about the signing of the first Treaty of Amity and Commerce between the two countries (Oct 8, 1782).

NICARAGUA: CIVIL WAR TRUCE: ANNIVERSARY. Apr 19, 1990. The Contra guerrillas, the leftist Sandinistas and the incoming Chamorro government agreed to a truce, ending a nine-year civil war.

OKLAHOMA CITY BOMBING: ANNIVERSARY. Apr 19, 1995. A car bomb exploded outside the Alfred P. Murrah Federal Building at Oklahoma City, OK, at 9:02 AM, killing 168 people, 19 of them children at a day-care center; a nurse died of head injuries sustained while helping in rescue efforts. The bomb, estimated to have weighed 5,000 pounds, had been placed in a rented truck. The blast ripped off the north face of the nine-story building, leaving a 20-foot-wide crater and debris two stories high. Structurally unsound and increasingly dangerous, the bombed building was razed May 23. Timothy J. McVeigh, a decorated Gulf War army vet who is alleged to have been angered by the Bureau of Alcohol, Tobacco and Firearms (ATF) attack on the Branch Davidian compound at Waco, TX, exactly two years before, was convicted of the bombing and was executed June 11, 2001. The ATF had offices in the OK federal building. Terry L. Nichols, an army buddy of McVeigh, was convicted of lesser charges.

PATRIOT'S DAY IN FLORIDA. Apr 19. A ceremonial day to commemorate the first blood shed in the American Revolution at Lexington and Concord in 1775.

PATRIOT'S DAY IN MASSACHUSETTS AND MAINE. Apr 19. Commemorates Battles of Lexington and Concord, 1775. Annually, the third Monday in April.

RICARDO, DAVID: BIRTH ANNIVERSARY. Apr 19, 1772. Economist David Ricardo, whose writings greatly influenced later economic theory, was born at London, England. He is recognized as the man who first systematized economics. In his best-known work, *Principles of Political Economy and Taxation* (1817), he discussed wages and rent and the economic relationships among landlords, workers and owners of capital. In 1819 Ricardo purchased his own seat in the House of Commons and became a member of Parliament. He died Sept 11, 1823, at Gatcombe Park, Gloucestershire.

Apr 19–20 ☆ Chase's 2004 Calendar of Events ☆

SHERMAN, ROGER: BIRTH ANNIVERSARY. Apr 19, 1721 (OS). American statesman, member of the Continental Congress (1774–81 and 1783–84), signer of the Declaration of Independence and of the Constitution, was born at Newton, MA. He also calculated astronomical and calendar information for an almanac. Sherman died at New Haven, CT, July 23, 1793.

SIERRA LEONE: NATIONAL HOLIDAY. Apr 19. Sierra Leone became a republic in 1971.

SOLAR ECLIPSE. Apr 19. Partial eclipse of the sun. Eclipse begins at 7:29 AM, EDT, reaches greatest eclipse at 9:33 AM and ends at 11:38 AM. Visible in Antarctica, southeast Atlantic Ocean and southern halves of Africa and Madagascar.

SPACE MILESTONE: *SALYUT* (USSR). Apr 19, 1971. The Soviet Union launched *Salyut*, the first manned orbiting space laboratory. It was replaced in 1986 by *Mir*, a manned space station and laboratory.

SWAZILAND: KING'S BIRTHDAY. Apr 19. National holiday. Commemorates the birth of King Mswati III, born Apr 19, 1968.

URUGUAY: LANDING OF THE 33 PATRIOTS DAY. Apr 19. National holiday. Commemorates the arrival in 1825 of exiles that resulted in independence from Brazil in 1828.

WARSAW GHETTO REVOLT: ANNIVERSARY. Apr 19, 1943. A prolonged revolt began at Warsaw, Poland, when German troops tried to resume deportation of Jewish residents of the Warsaw Ghetto to the Treblinka concentration camp. With only 17 rifles and handmade grenades, for almost a month 1,200 Jewish fighters resisted 2,100 German troops who were armed with machine guns. When the uprising ended on May 16, 300 Germans and 7,000 Jews had died and the Warsaw Ghetto lay in ruins.

BIRTHDAYS TODAY

Don Adams, 77, actor (Emmy for "Get Smart"), born New York, NY, Apr 19, 1927 (some sources say Apr 13).
Hayden Christensen, 23, actor (*The Virgin Suicides, Star Wars: Episode II — Attack of the Clones*), born Vancouver, BC, Canada, Apr 19, 1981.
Tim Curry, 58, actor (*The Rocky Horror Picture Show*; stage: *Hair, Amadeus, My Favorite Year*), born Cheshire, England, Apr 19, 1946.
Elinor Donahue, 67, actress ("Father Knows Best," "The Andy Griffith Show"), born Tacoma, WA, Apr 19, 1937.
James Franco, 26, actor (*Spider-Man*), born Palo Alto, CA, Apr 19, 1978.
Kate Hudson, 25, actress (*Almost Famous, 200 Cigarettes*), born Los Angeles, CA, Apr 19, 1979.
Ashley Judd, 36, actress (*Double Jeopardy, Kiss the Girls*), born Los Angeles, CA, Apr 19, 1968.
Hugh O'Brian, 74, actor ("The Life and Legend of Wyatt Earp," *Broken Lance, Ten Little Indians*), born Rochester, NY, Apr 19, 1930.
Alan Price, 62, singer, songwriter, born Fairfield, England, Apr 19, 1942.
Al Unser, Jr, 42, auto racer, Indy Car national champion, born Albuquerque, NM, Apr 19, 1962.

	S	M	T	W	T	F	S
April 2004					1	2	3
	4	5	6	7	8	9	10
	11	12	13	14	15	16	17
	18	19	20	21	22	23	24
	25	26	27	28	29	30	

APRIL 20 — TUESDAY
Day 111 — 255 Remaining

COLUMBINE HIGH SCHOOL KILLINGS: 5th ANNIVERSARY. Apr 20, 1999. At this high school at Littleton, CO, students Eric Harris and Dylan Klebold killed 12 other students, a teacher and then themselves.

EIGHTY-NINER CELEBRATION. Apr 20–25. Guthrie, OK. In celebration of its heritage, this historically restored town features Old West gunfights, chuckwagon feed, professional rodeo and Oklahoma's largest parade of bands, floats and roundup clubs from across the state. Est attendance: 30,000. For info: American Legion, Post 58, 123 N 21st St, Guthrie, OK 73044. Phone: (405) 282-2589.

FREDERICKSBURG DAY. Apr 20. Fredericksburg, VA. Spring tour of historic homes and gardens. To fund one historic garden restoration in Virginia per year. Est attendance: 2,000. For info: Visitor Center, 706 Caroline St, Fredericksburg, VA 22401. Phone: (800) 678-4748. Fax: (540) 372-6587. E-mail: gboswell@fburg.city.state.va.us.

FRENCH, DANIEL CHESTER: BIRTH ANNIVERSARY. Apr 20, 1850. American sculptor, born at Exeter, NH. One of the most important artists of the 19th and early 20th centuries as a sculptor of public monuments, French is best known for his 1875 "Minute Man" statue at Concord, MA, and his 1922 statue of the seated Abraham Lincoln in the Lincoln Memorial at Washington, DC. French died at Stockbridge, MA, Oct 7, 1931. His home and studio at Stockbridge, MA, were donated to the National Trust for Historic Preservation and are open to the public. For info: Chesterwood, PO Box 827, Stockbridge, MA 01262-0827.

HAMPTON, LIONEL: BIRTH ANNIVERSARY. Apr 20, 1908. The jazz great was born at Louisville, KY. Hampton started out on piano and drums, but Louis Armstrong urged him to take up the vibraphone in 1930. Hampton went on to make that his signature instrument. He recorded and played with Armstrong, Benny Goodman, Dizzy Gillespie, Benny Carter and other legends before becoming a bandleader himself. He played almost up until his death on Aug 31, 2002, at New York, NY.

HITLER, ADOLF: BIRTH ANNIVERSARY. Apr 20, 1889. German dictator, frustrated artist, obsessed with superiority of the "Aryan race" and the evil of Marxism (which he saw as a Jewish plot). Hitler was born at Braunau am Inn, Austria. Turning to politics, despite a five-year prison sentence (writing *Mein Kampf* during the nine months he served), his rise was predictable and, Aug 19, 1934, a German plebiscite vested sole executive power in Führer Adolf Hitler. Facing certain defeat by the Allied Forces, he shot himself, Apr 30, 1945, while his mistress, Eva Braun, took poison in a Berlin bunker where they had been hiding for more than three months.

LLOYD, HAROLD: BIRTH ANNIVERSARY. Apr 20, 1893. A comic genius of early American film, Harold Lloyd began acting at 20 years of age, and his career took off when he teamed with producer Hal Roach in the comic "Lonesome Luke" shorts (1916–1917). Lloyd then created the "glasses" character: the boy-next-door whose distinguishing feature was his round horn spectacles. This character thrilled audiences in "daredevil" comedy featuring dangerous stunts (Lloyd never used a double). Lloyd's hits included *Safety Last* (1923), where he dangled from a building's clock face, *The Freshman* (1925) and *Speedy* (1928). The biggest box-office star of the 1920s, Lloyd survived with lesser success in the talkie 1930s. He was given an honorary Oscar in 1953 for being a "master comedian and good citizen." Born at Burchard, NE, Lloyd died on Mar 8, 1971, at Hollywood, CA.

LUDLOW MINE INCIDENT: 90th ANNIVERSARY. Apr 20, 1914. Miners struggling for recognition of their United Mine Workers Union were attacked at Ludlow, CO, by National Guard troops. The Guardsmen were paid by the mining company. A tent colony was destroyed, five men and one boy were killed by machine-gun fire and eleven children and two women were burned to death.

234

☆ Chase's 2004 Calendar of Events ☆ Apr 20–21

NEWSPAPER ASSOCIATION OF AMERICA ANNUAL CONFERENCE. Apr 20–23. Washington, DC. For info: Newspaper Association of America, 1921 Gallows Rd, Ste 600, Vienna, VA 22182. Phone: (703) 902-1600. Web: www.naa.org.

PUENTE, TITO: BIRTH ANNIVERSARY. Apr 20, 1923. The King of the Mambo—or "El Rey"—was born Ernesto Antonio Puente, Jr, at Spanish Harlem, New York City, to Puerto Rican parents. The legendary Puente had a career that spanned more than six decades, starting in 1937. He popularized the timbale, but played many percussion instruments and was also a composer, arranger and bandleader. His album *Dance Mania* (1958) was an international bestseller, and he released more than 100 albums. His song "Oye Como Va" was covered by Carlos Santana and has become a classic. Puente won five Grammys, was inducted in the Jazz and Hispanic halls of fame and received a Smithsonian Lifetime Achievement Award. President Jimmy Carter pronounced him "The Goodwill Ambassador of Latin American Music." Puente died on May 31, 2000, at New York, NY.

SMITH, HOLLAND: BIRTH ANNIVERSARY. Apr 20, 1882. Considered the father of amphibious warfare, Holland "Howling Mad" Smith was born at Hatchechubie, AL. Smith developed techniques for amphibious assaults that involved coordination of land, sea and air forces. During WWII he led troops in assaults in the Marshall and Mariana Islands and also directed forces at Guam, Iwo Jima and Okinawa. Smith died Jan 12, 1967, at San Diego, CA.

TAURUS, THE BULL. Apr 20–May 20. In the astronomical/astrological zodiac that divides the sun's apparent orbit into 12 segments, the period Apr 20–May 20 is identified, traditionally, as the sun sign of Taurus, the Bull. The ruling planet is Venus.

BIRTHDAYS TODAY

Carmen Electra, 31, actress ("Baywatch," "Singled Out"), born Cincinnati, OH, Apr 20, 1973.
Nina Foch, 80, actress (*Scaramouche*), born Leyden, Holland, Apr 20, 1924.
Crispin Glover, 40, actor (*Back to the Future, The People vs. Larry Flynt*), born New York, NY, Apr 20, 1964.
Jessica Lange, 55, actress (Oscars for *Tootsie* and *Blue Skies*; *Frances, Sweet Dreams*), born Cloquet, MN, Apr 20, 1949.
Joey Lawrence, 28, actor ("Blossom," "Brotherly Love"), born Strawbridge, PA, Apr 20, 1976.
David Leland, 57, actor (*Time Bandits*); writer, director (*Mona Lisa, Wish You Were Here*), born Cambridge, England, Apr 20, 1947.
Donald Arthur (Don) Mattingly, 43, former baseball player, born Evansville, IN, Apr 20, 1961.
Shemar Moore, 34, actor ("The Young and the Restless"), host ("Soul Train"), born Oakland, CA, Apr 20, 1970.
Ryan O'Neal, 63, actor ("Peyton Place," *Love Story, Paper Moon*), born Los Angeles, CA, Apr 20, 1941.
Pat Roberts, 68, US Senator (R, Kansas), born Topeka, KS, Apr 20, 1936.
Steve Spurrier, 59, football player and Heisman Trophy quarterback, born Miami Beach, FL, Apr 20, 1945.
John Paul Stevens, 84, Associate Justice of the US Supreme Court, born Chicago, IL, Apr 20, 1920.
Luther Vandross, 53, singer, songwriter ("Never Too Much"), born New York, NY, Apr 20, 1951.

APRIL 21 — WEDNESDAY
Day 112 — 254 Remaining

ADMINISTRATIVE PROFESSIONALS DAY. Apr 21. Annually, the Wednesday of Administrative Professionals Week. For info: Rick Stroud, Communications Dir, Intl Assn of Administrative Professionals, 10502 NW Ambassador Dr, PO Box 20404, Kansas City, MO 64195-0404. Phone: (816) 891-6600 x 2239. E-mail: rstroud@iaap-hq.org. Web: www.iaap-hq.org.

AGGIE MUSTER. Apr 21. Texas A&M University, College Station, TX, and around the world. Ceremony where current and former students (Aggies) of Texas A&M University gather together to celebrate their days at the school and to honor those who have died in the past year. During the ceremony, a Roll Call for the Absent is read and a comrade answers "here" for the deceased. The school's most sacred and time-honored tradition. First held in 1883, but in 1903 the Muster date was moved to April 21—San Jacinto Day. Celebrated on the school campus and at more than 400 locations around the world. Annually, April 21. Est attendance: 100,000. For info: The Association of Former Students, 505 George Bush Dr, College Station, TX 77840-2918. Phone: (979) 845-7514. Fax: (979) 845-9263. E-mail: afs@aggienetwork.com. Web: www.aggienetwork.com.

AMERICAN QUILTER'S SOCIETY QUILT SHOW. Apr 21–24. Paducah, KY. More than 400 quilts are exhibited with $100,000 awarded in prizes. Seminars, workshops. Est attendance: 30,000. For info: American Quilter's Society, PO Box 3290, Paducah, KY 42002. Phone: (270) 898-7903. Web: www.AQSquilt.com.

BRAZIL: TIRADENTES DAY. Apr 21. National holiday commemorating execution of national hero, dentist Jose da Silva Xavier, nicknamed Tiradentes (tooth-puller), a conspirator in revolt against the Portuguese in 1789.

BRONTË, CHARLOTTE: BIRTH ANNIVERSARY. Apr 21, 1816. English novelist, born at Hartshead, Yorkshire, England. "Conventionality," she wrote in the preface to *Jane Eyre*, "is not morality. Self-righteousness is not religion. To attack the first is not to assail the last." She died Mar 31, 1855, at Haworth, Yorkshire, England.

FESTIVAL OF RIDVAN. Apr 21–May 2. Annual Baha'i festival commemorating the 12 days (Apr 21–May 2, 1863) when Baha'u'llah, the prophet-founder of the Baha'i faith, resided in a garden called Ridvan (Paradise) in Baghdad, at which time He publicly proclaimed His mission as God's messenger for this age. The first, ninth (Apr 29) and twelfth days are celebrated as holy days and are three of the nine days of the year when Baha'is suspend work. For info: Baha'is of the US, Office of Public Information, 1320 Nineteenth St NW, Ste 350, Washington, DC 20036. Phone: (202) 466-9870. Fax: (202) 466-9873. E-mail: opi@usbnc.org. Web: www.us.bahai.org.

FROEBEL, FRIEDRICH: BIRTH ANNIVERSARY. Apr 21, 1782. German educator and author Friedrich Froebel, who believed that play is an important part of a child's education, was born at Oberwiessbach, Thuringia. Froebel invented the kindergarten, founding the first one at Blankenburg, Germany, in 1837. Froebel also invented a series of toys which he intended to stimulate learning. (The American architect Frank Lloyd Wright as a child received these toys [maplewood blocks] from his mother and spoke throughout his life of their value.) Froebel's ideas about the role of directed play, toys and music in children's education had a profound influence in England and the US, where the nursery school became a further extension of his ideas. Froebel died at Marienthal, Germany, June 21, 1852.

INDONESIA: KARTINI DAY. Apr 21. Republic of Indonesia. Honors the birth in 1879 of Raden Adjeng Kartini, pioneer in the emancipation of the women of Indonesia.

INTERNATIONAL WHISTLERS CONVENTION. Apr 21–25. Louisburg, NC. Music festival. Assemblage and contest of professional and amateur whistlers and whistle collectors. Contests for children, teens and adults. Est attendance: 2,500. For info:

Allen de Hart, Dir, Franklin County Arts Council, Inc, PO Box 758, Louisburg, NC 27549. Phone: (919) 496-4771. Fax: (919) 496-1191.

ITALY: BIRTHDAY OF ROME. Apr 21. Celebration of the founding of Rome, traditionally thought to be in 753 BC.

KINDERGARTEN DAY. Apr 21. A day to recognize the importance of play, games and "creative self-activity" in children's education and to note the history of the kindergarten. Observed on the anniversary of the birth of Friedrich Froebel, in 1782, who established the first kindergarten in 1837. German immigrants brought Froebel's ideas to the US in the 1840s. The first kindergarten in a public school in the US was started in 1873, at St. Louis, MO.

MANGANO, SILVANA: BIRTH ANNIVERSARY. Apr 21, 1930. Italian actress Silvana Mangano was born at Rome, Italy. She is best known for her role in the film *Bitter Rice* (1948). Mangano died Dec 16, 1989, at Madrid, Spain.

MUIR, JOHN: BIRTH ANNIVERSARY. Apr 21, 1838. American naturalist, explorer, conservationist and author for whom the 550-acre Muir Woods National Monument (near San Francisco, CA) is named. Muir, born at Dunbar, Scotland, emigrated to the US in 1849, where he urged establishment of national parks and profoundly influenced US forest conservation. Died at Los Angeles, CA, Dec 24, 1914.

QUINN, ANTHONY: BIRTH ANNIVERSARY. Apr 21, 1915. Actor, sculptor and painter, Anthony Rudolf Oaxaca Quinn was born at Chihuahua, Mexico, and moved to the US as a child. He became a US citizen in 1947. He won Academy Awards for Best Supporting Actor in 1952 for *Viva Zapata!* and in 1956 for *Lust for Life*. His best-remembered role was that of *Zorba the Greek*, for which he was nominated for Best Actor in 1964. He died at Boston, MA, on June 3, 2001.

RABI' I: THE MONTH OF THE MIGRATION. Apr 21. Begins on Islamic calendar date Rabi' I 1, 1425. The third month of the Islamic calendar, the month of the migration of the Prophet Muhammad from Mecca to Medina in AD 622, the event that was used as the starting year of the Islamic lunar calendar. Different methods for "anticipating" the visibility of the new moon crescent at Mecca are used by different Muslim groups. US date may vary. Began at sunset the preceding day.

RED BARON SHOT DOWN: ANNIVERSARY. Apr 21, 1918. German flying ace Baron Manfred von Richtofen was shot down and killed during the battle of the Somme. The "Red Baron," so named for the color of his Fokker triplane, was credited with 80 kills in less than two years. Royal Flying Corps pilots recovered his body and the Allies buried him with full military honors. Asked about his fighting philosophy he was quoted as saying, "I am a hunter. My brother Lothar is a butcher. When I have shot down an Englishman, my hunting passion is satisfied for a quarter of an hour."

ROGER EBERT'S OVERLOOKED FILM FESTIVAL. Apr 21–25. Virginia Theatre, Champaign, IL. Spring film festival hosted by Roger Ebert, University of Illinois journalism graduate and Pulitzer Prize–winning film critic. Ebert selects 14 films representing a cross-section of important cinematic works that have been "overlooked" by audiences, critics and distributors. He introduces each film and leads a discussion on stage afterwards for general audiences, distributors and international critics. Often in attendance are the films' producers, writers, actors or directors. Festival includes academic panel discussions. Sponsored by the College of Communications, Univ of IL. Est attendance: 21,000. For info: Mary Susan Britt, University of Illinois, College of Communications, 119 Gregory Hall, MC-462, 810 S Wright St, Urbana, IL 61801. Phone: (217) 244-0552. Fax: (217) 333-9882. E-mail: marsue@uiuc.edu. Web: www.ebertfest.com.

SAN JACINTO DAY. Apr 21. Texas. Commemorates Battle of San Jacinto in 1836, in which Texas won independence from Mexico. A 570-foot monument, dedicated on the 101st anniversary of the battle, marks the site on the banks of the San Jacinto River, about 20 miles from present city of Houston, TX, where General Sam Houston's Texans decisively defeated the Mexican forces led by Santa Ana in the final battle between Texas and Mexico.

SPACE MILESTONE: *COPERNICUS*, OAO 4 (US). Apr 21, 1972. Launch of Orbiting Astronomical Observer, named in honor of the Polish astronomer.

STORIES DAY. Apr 21. A day to share stories with young children and to celebrate the benefits storytelling and reading provide for children and families. The Child Care Coalition of Lake County, IL, and local libraries declare this day for sharing stories and promoting activities that lead to children's literacy. Events will be held at libraries, child care centers, preschools, schools and many people's homes. Groups and people everywhere are encouraged to share stories with children. Annually, the Wednesday of the Week of the Young Child. For info: The Child Care Coalition of Lake County, 655 Rockland Rd, Lake Bluff, IL 60004. Web: www.childcarecoaltion.org.

THANK YOU, SCHOOL LIBRARIAN DAY. Apr 21. Recognizes the unique contribution made by school librarians who are resource people extraordinaire, supporting the myriad educational needs of faculty, staff, students and parents *all year long!* Three cheers to all the public, private and parochial school infomaniacs whose true love of reading and lifelong learning make them great role models for kids of all ages. To help celebrate, take your school librarian to lunch, donate a book in his/her honor to the library, tell your librarian what a difference he/she has made in your life. Sponsor: "Carpe Libris" (Seize the Book), a loosely knit group of underappreciated librarians. For info: Judyth Lessee, Organizer, Carpe Libris, 3645 E Pima St, Tucson, AZ 85716. Phone: (520) 232-8424. E-mail: judyth.lessee@tusd.k12.az.us.

BIRTHDAYS TODAY

Ed Belfour, 39, hockey player, born Carman, MB, Canada, Apr 21, 1964.
Tony Danza, 53, actor ("Taxi," "Who's the Boss?"), born Brooklyn, NY, Apr 21, 1951.
Queen Elizabeth II, 78, Queen of the United Kingdom, born London, England, Apr 21, 1926.
Charles Grodin, 69, actor (*Midnight Run, Beethoven*); director, host ("The Charles Grodin Show"), born Pittsburgh, PA, Apr 21, 1935.
Patti LuPone, 55, actress (stage: *Evita*; "Life Goes On"), born Northport, NY, Apr 21, 1949.
Andie MacDowell, 46, actress (*sex, lies, and videotape, Groundhog Day*), born Gaffney, SC, Apr 21, 1958.
Elaine May, 72, actress, writer (comedy with Mike Nichols), director (*A New Leaf*), born Philadelphia, PA, Apr 21, 1932.
Iggy Pop, 57, singer, born Ann Arbor, MI, Apr 21, 1947.

April 2004	S	M	T	W	T	F	S
					1	2	3
	4	5	6	7	8	9	10
	11	12	13	14	15	16	17
	18	19	20	21	22	23	24
	25	26	27	28	29	30	

APRIL 22 — THURSDAY
Day 113 — 253 Remaining

BABE RUTH'S PITCHING DEBUT: 90th ANNIVERSARY. Apr 22, 1914. Babe Ruth made his professional pitching debut, playing for the Baltimore Orioles in his own hometown. Allowing just six hits and contributing two singles himself, Ruth shut out the Buffalo Bisons, 6–0.

BLUEBERRY HILL OPEN DART TOURNAMENT. Apr 22–25. St. Louis, MO. America's oldest (32nd annual) and largest pub dart tournament open to everyone. Est attendance: 500. For info: Joe Edwards, Blueberry Hill, 6504 Delmar, St. Louis, MO 63130. Phone: (314) 727-0880. Web: www.blueberryhill.com.

BRAZIL: DISCOVERY OF BRAZIL DAY: ANNIVERSARY. Apr 22. Commemorates discovery by Pedro Alvarez Cabral in 1500.

COINS STAMPED "IN GOD WE TRUST": ANNIVERSARY. Apr 22, 1864. By Act of Congress, the phrase "In God We Trust" began to be stamped on all US coins.

ENGLAND: HARROGATE SPRING FLOWER SHOW. Apr 22–25. Great Yorkshire Showground, Harrogate, North Yorkshire. Spectacular exhibits and displays at Britain's premier spring show. Est attendance: 60,000. For info: Roger Brownbridge, Show Dir, North of England Horticultural Society, 4A South Park Rd, Harrogate, North Yorkshire, England HG1 5QU. Phone: (44) (1423) 561049. Fax: (44) (1423) 536880. E-mail: info@flowershow.org.uk. Web: www.flowershow.org.uk.

FIRST SOLO TRIP TO NORTH POLE: 10th ANNIVERSARY. Apr 22, 1994. Norwegian explorer Borge Ousland became the first person to make the trip to the North Pole alone. The trip took 52 days, during which he pulled a 265-pound sled. Departing from Cape Atkticheskiy at Siberia Mar 2, he averaged about 18½ miles per day over the 630-mile journey. Ousland had traveled to the Pole on skis with Erling Kagge in 1990.

ICELAND: "FIRST DAY OF SUMMER." Apr 22. A national public holiday, *Sumardagurinn fyrsti*, with general festivities, processions and much street dancing, especially at Reykjavik, greets the coming of summer. Flags are flown. Annually, the Thursday between April 19 and 25.

INTERNATIONAL HOME FURNISHINGS MARKET. Apr 22–28 (also Oct 14–20). High Point and Thomasville, NC. The largest wholesale home furnishings market in the world. (Not open to the general public.) Est attendance: 82,000. For info: Intl Home Furnishings Market Authority, 101 S Main St, High Point, NC 27260. Phone: (336) 869-1000. Fax: (336) 869-6999. Web: www.furnituremarket.org.

LENIN, NIKOLAI: BIRTH ANNIVERSARY. Apr 22, 1870. Russian socialist and revolutionary leader (real name: Vladimir Ilyich Ulyanov), ideological follower of Karl Marx, born at Simbirst, on the Volga, Russia. Leader of the Great October Socialist Revolution of 1917. Died at Gorky, near Moscow, Jan 21, 1924. His embalmed body, in a glass coffin at the Lenin Mausoleum, has been viewed by millions of visitors to Moscow's Red Square.

NATIONAL TEACH CHILDREN TO SAVE DAY. Apr 22. Thousands of bankers visit classrooms across America to teach children of all ages the importance of saving and making fiscal fitness a lifetime habit. For info: American Bankers Association, 1120 Connecticut Ave NW, Washington, DC 20036. Phone: (202) 663-5473. Fax: (202) 663-5464. E-mail: jhall@aba.com. Web: www.aba.com.

NEW ORLEANS JAZZ & HERITAGE FESTIVAL. Apr 22–May 2. New Orleans, LA. A two-weekend festival with hundreds of musicians playing. Evening concerts, outdoor daytime activities, Louisiana specialty foods and handmade crafts. Est attendance: 500,000. For info: New Orleans Jazz & Heritage Festival, 1205 N Rampart St, New Orleans, LA 70116. Phone: (504) 522-4786. Web: www.nojazzfest.com.

OKLAHOMA DAY. Apr 22. Oklahoma.

OKLAHOMA LAND RUSH: ANNIVERSARY. Apr 22, 1889. At noon a gunshot signaled the start of the Oklahoma land rush as thousands of settlers rushed into the territory to claim land. Under pressure from cattlemen, the federal government opened 1,900,000 acres of central Oklahoma that had been bought from the Creek and Seminole tribes.

TAKE OUR DAUGHTERS AND SONS TO WORK DAY. Apr 22. A national public education campaign sponsored by the Ms Foundation for Women in which children aged 8–12 go to work with adult hosts—parents, grandparents, cousins, aunts, uncles, friends. Annually, the fourth Thursday in April. Est attendance: 11,000,000. For info: Take Our Daughters and Sons to Work Day, Ms. Foundation for Women, 120 Wall St, 33rd Fl, New York, NY 10005. Phone: (800) 676-7780. Fax: (212) 742-1531. E-mail: tods@ms.foundation.org. Web: www.DaughtersandSonstoWork.org.

USA FILM FESTIVAL. Apr 22–29. Dallas, TX. 34th annual. Major showcase of new studio and independent films (features and shorts), filmmaker discussions with audience, Master Screen Artist, Great Director and other tributes and retrospectives. Festival is noncompetitive except for Annual National Short Film and Video Competition with cash awards in multiple categories. Est attendance: 15,000. For info: USA Film Festival, 6116 N Central Expressway, Ste 105, Dallas, TX 75206. Phone: (214) 821-6300 or (214) 821-FILM (for 24-hour updates of film programming). Fax: (214) 821-6364. E-mail: info@usafilmfestival.com. Web: www.usafilmfestival.com.

BIRTHDAYS TODAY

Eddie Albert, 96, actor ("Green Acres," *Roman Holiday*), born Edward Albert Heimberger, Rock Island, IL, Apr 22, 1908.
Byron Allen, 43, comedian, TV host ("Byron Allen Show," "Real People"), actor (*Case Closed*), born Detroit, MI, Apr 22, 1961.
Glen Campbell, 69, singer ("Gentle on My Mind," "By the Time I Get to Phoenix"), born Billstown, AR, Apr 22, 1935.
Peter Frampton, 54, singer ("Show Me the Way," "Do You Feel Like We Do"), born Beckenham, England, Apr 22, 1950.
Chris Makepeace, 40, actor (*My Bodyguard*), born Montreal, QC, Canada, Apr 22, 1964.
Jack Nicholson, 68, actor (Oscars for *One Flew Over the Cuckoo's Nest*, *Terms of Endearment* and *As Good As It Gets*), born Neptune, NJ, Apr 22, 1936.
Charlotte Rae, 78, actress ("Diff'rent Strokes," "Facts of Life"), born Milwaukee, WI, Apr 22, 1926.
Aaron Spelling, 76, writer, producer ("Fantasy Island," "Melrose Place"), born Dallas, TX, Apr 22, 1928.
Ryan Stiles, 45, actor ("The Drew Carey Show," "Whose Line Is It Anyway?"), born Seattle, WA, Apr 22, 1959.
John Waters, 58, filmmaker (*Pink Flamingoes*), born Baltimore, MD, Apr 22, 1946.

APRIL 23 — FRIDAY
Day 114 — 252 Remaining

"BAYWATCH" TV PREMIERE: 15th ANNIVERSARY. Apr 23, 1989. Set on a California beach, this program starred David Hasselhoff and a changing cast of nubile young men and women as lifeguards. Later the program was moved to Hawaii; the last episode was made in 2001. The most widely viewed TV series in the world, the program aired in 142 countries with an estimated weekly audience of 1.1 billion.

BERMUDA: PEPPERCORN CEREMONY: ANNIVERSARY. Apr 23. St. George. Commemorates the payment of one peppercorn in 1816 to the governor of Bermuda for rental of Old State House by the Masonic Lodge.

BIG TEN WOMEN'S GOLF CHAMPIONSHIP. Apr 23–25. Ohio State University, Columbus, OH. For info: Sue Lister, Assoc Commissioner, Big Ten Conference, 1500 W Higgins Rd, Park Ridge, IL 60068-6300. Phone: (847) 696-1010. Fax: (847) 696-1110. Web: www.bigten.org.

Apr 23 ☆ Chase's 2004 Calendar of Events ☆

BIG 12 WOMEN'S GOLF CHAMPIONSHIP. Apr 23–25. Pebble Creek Country Club, College Station, TX. Est attendance: 1,000. For info: Big 12 Conference, 2201 Stemmons Freeway, 28th Fl, Dallas, TX 75207. Phone: (214) 742-1212. Fax: (214) 742-2046. Web: www.big12sports.com.

BUCHANAN, JAMES: BIRTH ANNIVERSARY. Apr 23, 1791. 15th president of the US, born at Cove Gap, PA, was the only president who never married. He served one term in office, Mar 4, 1857–Mar 3, 1861, and died at Lancaster, PA, June 1, 1868.

CERVANTES SAAVEDRA, MIGUEL DE: DEATH ANNIVERSARY. Apr 23, 1616. Spanish poet, playwright and novelist, died at Madrid, Spain. The exact date of his birth at Alcala de Henares is unknown, but he was baptized Oct 9, 1547. As soldier and tax collector, Cervantes traveled widely. He spent more than five years in prisons in Spain, Italy and North Africa. His greatest creation was Don Quixote, the immortal Knight of La Mancha whose profession was chivalry. Riding his nag, Rozinante, and accompanied by Squire Sancho Panza, Don Quixote tilts at windmills of the mind in the world's best-known novel. Nearly a thousand editions of Don Quixote (a bestseller since its first appearance in 1605) have been published, and it has been translated into more languages than any other book except the Bible.

CIVIL WAR REENACTMENT. Apr 23–25. Rand Park, Keokuk, IA. Battle reenactment, military ball, historic encampment, ladies' tea and style show and historic dinner/theater. Est attendance: 20,000. For info: Kirk Brandenberger, Keokuk Area Conv and Tourism Bureau, 329 Main, Keokuk, IA 52632. Phone: (800) 383-1219 or (319) 524-5599. Fax: (319) 524-5016. E-mail: keokukia@interl.net. Web: www.keokuktourism.com.

CONNECTICUT STORYTELLING FESTIVAL. Apr 23–25. Connecticut College, New London, CT. 23rd annual festival features performances for families and adults, plus workshops and story-sharing by Connecticut and nationally renowned storytellers. Annually, in April. Est attendance: 500. For info: Ann Shapiro, Adm, Connecticut Storytelling Center, Connecticut College Box 5295, 270 Mohegan Ave, New London, CT 06320. Phone: (860) 439-2764. Fax: (860) 439-2895. E-mail: csc@conncoll.edu. Web: www.connstorycenter.org.

DAFFODIL FESTIVAL WEEKEND. Apr 23–25. Nantucket Island, MA. Nantucket's traditional welcome to spring, when more than three million daffodils bloom and turn the countryside into a vivid, yellow tapestry. Events include the annual antique car parade, tailgate picnic and activities such as hiking, fishing, bird watching and seal cruises. Est attendance: 1,000. For info: Nantucket Island Chamber of Commerce, 48 Main St, Nantucket, MA 02554-3595. Phone: (508) 228-1700. Web: www.nantucketchamber.org.

DISCOVERY WALK FESTIVAL. Apr 23–25. Red Lion Inn at the Quay, Vancouver, WA. International multi-day walking event, non-competitive. Sanctioned by the International Marching League and American Volkssport Association. Distances of 5K, 10K, 21K and 42K. Est attendance: 3,000. For info: Discovery Walk Festival, PO Box 2009, Vancouver, WA 98668. Phone: (877) 269-2009. E-mail: info@discoverywalk.org. Web: www.discoverywalk.org.

FIDDLER'S FROLICS. Apr 23–25. Knights of Columbus Hall, Hallettsville, TX. Competition to determine the Texas state champion fiddler and inductees to the Texas Fiddlers Hall of Fame. Est attendance: 15,000. For info: Kenneth Henneke, Co-chair, PO Box 46, Hallettsville, TX 77964. Phone: (361) 798-5934 or (361) 798-2311. Fax: (361) 798-4365. Web: www.kchall.com.

April 2004	S	M	T	W	T	F	S
					1	2	3
	4	5	6	7	8	9	10
	11	12	13	14	15	16	17
	18	19	20	21	22	23	24
	25	26	27	28	29	30	

FIRST MOVIE THEATER OPENS: ANNIVERSARY. Apr 23, 1896. The first movie was shown at Koster and Bials Music Hall at New York City. Up until this time, people saw films individually by looking into a Kinetoscope, a box-like "peep show." This was the first time in the US that an audience sat in a theater and watched a movie together.

FIRST PUBLIC SCHOOL IN AMERICA: ANNIVERSARY. Apr 23, 1635 (NS). The Boston Latin School opened—America's oldest public school.

HUG A PROM SPONSOR DAY. Apr 23. A day honoring all the teachers across the US who successfully help to organize, promote and chaperone their high school's prom. Annually, the fourth Friday in April. For info: Crystal Leighty, Stumps, One Party Place, South Whitley, IN 46787. Phone: (219) 723-5171 or (800) 22-PARTY. Fax: (219) 723-6976. Web: www.stumpsparty.com.

NATIONAL DREAM HOTLINE®. Apr 23–25. Now in its 16th year, the National Dream Hotline® is sponsored by the School of Metaphysics as an educational service to people throughout the world. Faculty and staff of the College and Schools of Metaphysics throughout the Midwest will offer the benefits of 30 years of research into the significance and meaning of dreams by manning the hotline phones from 6 PM EDT, Friday until midnight Sunday. Annually, the last weekend in April. For info: Christine Madar, School of Metaphysics, World Headquarters, 163 Moon Valley Rd, Windyville, MO 65783. Phone: (417) 345-8411. Fax: (417) 345-6668. E-mail: som@som.org. Web: www.som.org or www.dreamschool.org.

NEW BEGINNING FESTIVAL. Apr 23–24. Coffeyville, KS. A multistate arts and crafts festival, cheese festival, carnival, entertainment, 5K run, car show, kite festival. Est attendance: 10,000. For info: Chamber of Commerce, Box 457, Coffeyville, KS 67337. Phone: (620) 251-2550. Fax: (620) 251-5448. E-mail: chamber@coffeyville.com.

PANOPLY® 2004. Apr 23–25. Big Spring International Park, Huntsville, AL. Comprehensive arts festival celebrating its 23rd year. Showcases the performing arts through a variety of music, theatre and dance. The festival includes five performance stages, family hands-on activities, juried art show and choreography competition. Est attendance: 100,000. For info: The Arts Council, 700 Monroe St, Ste 2, Huntsville, AL 35801. Phone: (256) 519-ARTS. Fax: (256) 533-3811. Web: www.panoply.org.

PEARSON, LESTER B.: BIRTH ANNIVERSARY. Apr 23, 1897. 14th prime minister of Canada, born at Toronto, Canada. He was Canada's chief delegate at the San Francisco conference where the UN charter was drawn up and later served as president of the General Assembly. He wrote the proposal that resulted in the formation of the North Atlantic Treaty Organization (NATO). He was awarded the Nobel Peace Prize. Died at Rockcliffe, Canada, Dec 27, 1972.

PHYSICISTS DISCOVER TOP QUARK: 10th ANNIVERSARY. Apr 23, 1994. Physicists at the Department of Energy's Fermi National Accelerator Laboratory found evidence for the existence of the subatomic particle called the top quark, the last undiscovered quark of the six predicted to exist by current scientific theory. The discovery provides strong support for the quark theory of the structure of matter. Quarks are subatomic particles that make up protons and neutrons found in the nuclei of atoms. The five other quark types that had already been proven to exist are the up quark, down quark, strange quark, charm quark and bottom quark. Further experimentation over many months confirmed the discovery and it was publicly announced Mar 2, 1995.

PLANCK, MAX: BIRTH ANNIVERSARY. Apr 23, 1858. Formulator of the quantum theory which revolutionized physics, born at Kiel, Germany. Einstein's application of quantum theory to light led to the theories of relativity. Planck died at Gottingen, Germany, Oct 3, 1947.

POMPANO BEACH SEAFOOD FESTIVAL. Apr 23–25. Pompano Beach, FL. Fresh seafood prepared by Broward's finest restaurants plus live music and arts and crafts. Annually, the last full weekend of April. Est attendance: 100,000. For info: Pompano Beach Chamber of Commerce, 2200 E Atlantic Blvd, Pompano Beach, FL 33062. Phone: (954) 941-2940.

RATTLESNAKE DERBY. Apr 23–25. Mangum, OK. Hunters stalk these wily reptiles and attempt to bring in the most snakes and the longest snake. Snakeskins and meat will be sold, and entertainment will include live music, a carnival and flea market. A herpetologist will be on hand to educate festival-goers. Annually, the last full weekend in April. Est attendance: 40,000. For info: Shortgrass Rattlesnake Assn. Phone: (580) 782-2434.

RIVERFEST WEEKEND. Apr 23–25. Columbus, GA. Features fine arts and crafts, children's interactive area, olympigs, hot air balloons, Native American skills demonstrators, carnival, cornbread cook-off, Riverfest 10K, 5K and 1 Mile Fun Run and a fine arts and folk art show and sale. Also features the Folklife Village with demonstrations by blacksmiths, quilters, basket weavers and potters and the South's most famous barbeque cook-off, the Greater Columbus Pig Jig, an MIM-sanctioned event. Live entertainment on three stages. Annually, the last full weekend in April at the Historic South Commons along the Columbus Riverwalk. Est attendance: 100,000. For info: Riverfest, PO Box 5128, Columbus, GA 31906. Phone: (706) 324-7417. Web: www.columbusriverfest.com.

SAINT GEORGE: FEAST DAY. Apr 23. Martyr and patron saint of England, who died Apr 23, AD 303. Hero of the St. George and the dragon legend. The story says that his faith helped him slay a vicious dragon that demanded daily sacrifice after the king's daughter became the intended victim.

SHAKESPEARE, WILLIAM: BIRTH AND DEATH ANNIVERSARY. Apr 23. England's most famous and most revered poet and playwright. He was born at Stratford-on-Avon, England, Apr 23, 1564 (OS), baptized there three days later and died there on his birthday, Apr 23, 1616 (OS). Author of at least 36 plays and 154 sonnets, Shakespeare created the most influential and lasting body of work in the English language, an extraordinary exploration of human nature. His epitaph: "Good frend for Jesus sake forbeare, To digg the dust enclosed heare. Blese be ye man that spares thes stones, And curst be he that moves my bones."

SOUTH CAROLINA FESTIVAL OF ROSES. Apr 23–25. Edisto Memorial Gardens, Orangeburg, SC. To celebrate the beauty of the roses and the gardens. Est attendance: 45,000. For info: Orangeburg County Chamber of Commerce, PO Box 328, Orangeburg, SC 29116-0328. Phone: (803) 534-6821 or (800) 545-6153. Fax: (803) 531-9435. E-mail: chamber@orangeburgsc.net. Web: www.festivalofroses.com.

SPACE MILESTONE: *SOYUZ 10* (USSR). Apr 23, 1971. Launch date of Soviet mission in which cosmonauts V.A. Shatalov, A.S. Yeliseyev and N.N. Rukavishnikov docked Apr 24 with *Salyut 1* orbital space station. The crew did not enter the space station. Return Earth landing at Kazakhstan, USSR, Apr 24.

SPAIN: BOOK DAY AND LOVER'S DAY. Apr 23. Barcelona. Saint George's Day and the anniversary of the death of Spanish writer Miguel de Cervantes have been observed with special ceremonies in the Palacio de la Disputacion and throughout the city since 1714. Book stands are set up in the plazas and on street corners. This is Spain's equivalent of Valentine's Day. Women give books to men; men give roses to women.

SPRING FEST. Apr 23–24. Rebel State Park Outdoor Amphitheater, Marthaville, LA. Includes entertainment, food, state harmonica competition and Louisiana Fiddler's Championship. Admission. Est attendance: 1,500. For info: Natchitoches Parish Tourist Commission. Phone: (318) 472-6255 or (800) 259-1714. Web: www.natchitoches.net.

SPRING FESTIVAL. Apr 23–May 2. Cape May, NJ. Experience and appreciate the Victorian lifestyle with two weekends of spring activities at America's first seashore resort. Special events include a Vintage Dance Weekend, Victorian Murder Mystery Dinners, outdoor crafts, anitques and collectibles shows, free glassblowing demonstrations on the lawn of Cape May's only Victorian House Museum, the 1879 Emlen Physick Estate and much more. Annually, the third week in April. Est attendance: 15,000. For info: Mid-Atlantic Center for the Arts, 1048 Washington St, PO Box 340, Cape May, NJ 08204. Phone: (609) 884-5404. Fax: (609) 884-0574. E-mail: mac4arts@capemaymac.org. Web: www.capemaymac.org.

STAMP & COIN EXPO. Apr 23–25 (also Oct 29–31). Hotel Pennsylvania, New York, NY. Annual expo. Est attendance: 10,000. For info: Intl Stamp Collectors Society, PO Box 854, Van Nuys, CA 91408. Phone: (818) 997-6496. Fax: (818) 988-4337. E-mail: iibick@aol.com. Web: www.bick.net.

STARMAN FAMILY-CON 2004. Apr 23–25 (tentative). Hollywood, CA. Eighth biennial international "family reunion" of the people who created/appreciated the TV series "Starman" (and the movie on which it was based). A convention unlike any you've ever attended. Though it lasted only one season, this TV show touched many souls and helped people change their lives in positive ways. See also: "International Starman Month (Oct 1)." For info: Vicki Werkley, 16563 Ellen Springs Dr, Lower Lake, CA 95457-9477. Phone: (707) 995-1228. E-mail: spotlight_starman@bigfoot.com. Web: www.starmanet.com.

SUGARLOAF CRAFTS FESTIVAL. Apr 23–25. Maryland State Fairgrounds, Timonium, MD. This show, now in its 26th year, features more than 350 nationally recognized craft designers and fine artists displaying and selling their original creations. Includes craft demonstrations, live music, specialty food, hourly gift certificate drawings and more. Est attendance: 21,000. For info: Sugarloaf Mountain Works, Inc, 200 Orchard Ridge Dr, #215, Gaithersburg, MD 20878. Phone: (800) 210-9900. Fax: (310) 253-9620. Web: www.sugarloafcrafts.com.

TURKEY: NATIONAL SOVEREIGNTY AND CHILDREN'S DAY: ANNIVERSARY. Apr 23, 1923. Commemorates Grand National Assembly's inauguration.

UNITED NATIONS: WORLD BOOK AND COPYRIGHT DAY. Apr 23. Observed throughout the United Nations system. For info: United Nations, Dept of Public Info, New York, NY 10017. Web: www.un.org.

VERMONT MAPLE FESTIVAL. Apr 23–25. St. Albans, VT. The 38th annual festival includes carnival, talent show, entertainment, arts & crafts, antiques, maple exhibits and demonstrations, sugar house tours and sap run. For info: Vermont Maple Festival, PO Box 255, St. Albans, VT 05478. Phone: (802) 524-5800. Web: www.vtmaplefestival.org.

WARD WORLD CHAMPIONSHIP WILDFOWL CARVING COMPETITION. Apr 23–25. Roland E. Powell Convention Center, Ocean City, MD. 34th annual. Judging of contemporary decoys and wildlife sculpture, fish carvings and paintings. Est attendance: 10,000. For info: Kevan Collins, Events Coord, Ward Museum of Waterfowl Art, 909 S Schumaker Dr, Salisbury, MD 21804. Phone: (410) 742-4988. Fax: (410) 742-3107. E-mail: ward@wardmuseum.org. Web: www.wardmuseum.org.

WOODS, GRANVILLE T.: BIRTH ANNIVERSARY. Apr 23, 1856. Granville T. Woods was born at Columbus, OH. He invented the Synchronous Multiplex Railway Telegraph which allowed communication between dispatchers and trains while the trains were in motion, which decreased the number of train accidents. In addition, Woods is credited with a number of other electrical inventions. Died Jan 30, 1910, at New York, NY.

BIRTHDAYS TODAY

Valerie Bertinelli, 44, actress ("One Day at a Time," *Silent Witness*), born Wilmington, DE, Apr 23, 1960.
David Birney, 64, actor ("Love Is a Many Splendored Thing," "Bridget Loves Bernie"), born Washington, DC, Apr 23, 1940.
Shirley Temple Black, 76, former ambassador to Ghana, child actress (*Heidi, Curly Top, Little Miss Marker*), TV hostess ("Shirley Temple's Storybook" and "Shirley Temple Theatre"), born Santa Monica, CA, Apr 23, 1928.
Judy Davis, 49, actress (*A Passage to India, Deconstructing Harry*), born Perth, Australia, Apr 23, 1955.
Sandra Dee, 62, actress (*Imitation of Life, A Summer Place, Gidget*), born Alexandra Zuck, Bayonne, NJ, Apr 23, 1942.
Joyce Dewitt, 55, actress ("Three's Company"), born Wheeling, WV, Apr 23, 1949.
Jan Hooks, 47, actress ("Saturday Night Live," "Designing Women"), born Atlanta, GA, Apr 23, 1957.
Andruw Jones, 27, baseball player, born Wellemstad, Curacao, Netherlands Antilles, Apr 23, 1977.
Melina Kanakaredes, 37, actress ("Providence," "Guiding Light"), born Akron, OH, Apr 23, 1967.
Lee Majors, 64, actor ("The Six Million Dollar Man," "The Fall Guy"), born Wyandotte, MI, Apr 23, 1940.
Bernadette Devlin McAliskey, 57, political activist, born Cookstown, Northern Ireland, Apr 23, 1947.
Warren Edward Spahn, 83, Hall of Fame baseball player, born Buffalo, NY, Apr 23, 1921.
Narada Michael Walden, 52, drummer (Mahavishnu Orchestra), singer, songwriter, born Kalamazoo, MI, Apr 23, 1952.

APRIL 24 — SATURDAY
Day 115 — 251 Remaining

ANTIQUE AND COLLECTIBLE FLEA MARKET. Apr 24–25. Weston, MO. 22nd annual flea market sponsored by the Weston Lions Club, with antiques, collectibles and food available. Est attendance: 2,000. For info: Ernest "Bill" Williams, 209 Thomas, Weston, MO 64098. Phone: (816) 640-2348.

ARMENIA: ARMENIAN MARTYRS DAY. Apr 24. Commemorates the massacre of Armenians under the Ottoman Turks in 1915. Deportations from Turkey began. Also called Armenian Genocide Memorial Day. Adolf Hitler, in a speech at Obersalzberg, Aug 22, 1939, is reported to have said, "Who today remembers the Armenian extermination?" in an apparent justification of the Nazis' use of genocide.

ART IN THE PARK PLUS. Apr 24. Oakland Park Library, Oakland Park, FL. Annual celebration of National Library Week, features a juried fine arts and crafts show with cash awards. Free activities for all ages, including "Create Your Own Book," professional storytelling, face painting and sidewalk chalk art contest for children, plant displays, used book sale, live music and more. Annually, the Saturday before or after National Library Week. For info: Joanne Fischer, Art In The Park Plus Coord, Oakland Park Library, 1298 NE 37 St, Oakland Park, FL 33334-4576. Phone: (954) 561-6289. Fax: (954) 561-6146. E-mail: jo annef@oaklandparkfl.org.

ASTRONOMY DAY. Apr 24. To take astronomy to the people. International Astronomy Day is observed on a Saturday near the first quarter moon between mid-April and mid-May. Co-sponsored by 15 astronomical organizations. See also: "Astronomy Week" (Apr 19–25). For info: Gary E. Tomlinson, Coord, Astronomy Day Headquarters, c/o Chaffee Planetarium, 272 Pearl NW, Grand Rapids, MI 49504. Phone: (616) 456-3532. E-mail: gtom lins@triton.net. Web: www.astroleague.org.

BASCOM, GEORGE N.: BIRTH ANNIVERSARY. Apr 24, 1836. West Point Graduate Lieutenant George N. Bascom was assigned to search out Apache chief Cochise, believed to be responsible for an 1861 raid on an Arizona ranch. He arrested Cochise at Apache Pass, but the chief escaped and declared war, launching a reign of terror known as the Apache Wars. Bascom was born at Owingsville, KY, and died the year following his Apache adventure when he became a casualty of the Civil War battle at Fort Craig, Valverde, NM, Feb 21, 1862.

BOB WILLS DAY. Apr 24. Turkey, TX. Celebration of the creator of western swing, with music, fiddlers contest, parade and barbeque lunch. Appearances by his former band, the Texas Playboys. Annually, last Saturday in April. Est attendance: 10,000. For info: Bob Wills Foundation, PO Box 306, Turkey, TX 79261. Phone: (806) 423-1253. E-mail: turkey@caprock-spur.com. Web: www.turkeytexas.com.

CARTWRIGHT, EDMUND: BIRTH ANNIVERSARY. Apr 24, 1743. English cleric and inventor (developed the power loom and other weaving inventions) was born at Nottinghamshire, England. He died at Hastings, Sussex, England, Oct 30, 1823.

DÍA DE LOS NIÑOS/DÍA DE LOS LIBROS. Apr 24. Washington Park, El Paso, TX. An all-day celebration of children, family and reading. The event features storytelling, hands-on activities, performances, cultural and recreational activities and a parade. Each child will receive a free book. Annually, the last Saturday in April. Est attendance: 15,000. For info: Jack Galindo, El Paso Public Library, 501 N Oregon, El Paso, TX 79901. Phone: (915) 543-5468. Fax: (915) 543-5410. E-mail: galindojw@ci. el-paso.tx.us.

FORT MOORE ESTABLISHED: ANNIVERSARY. Apr 24, 1847. At the conclusion of the Mexican War, the Mormon Battalion of the Army of the West established Fort Moore overseeing the pueblo of Los Angeles. The fort was named in honor of their captain who had perished in the Battle of San Pascual.

FOXFIELD RACES. Apr 24 (also Sept 26). Charlottesville, VA. Steeplechase horse racing. Est attendance: 20,000. For info: W. Patrick Butterfield, Racing Mgr, Foxfield Racing Assn, PO Box 5187, Charlottesville, VA 22905. Phone: (804) 293-9501. Fax: (804) 293-8169.

HERB FESTIVAL. Apr 24. Mattoon, IL. Fresh herbs, everlasting plants, scented geraniums and lots of perennials. Annually, the last Saturday in April. Est attendance: 7,000. For info: The Picket Fence, 901 Broadway, Mattoon, IL 61938. Phone: (217) 258-6364.

IRELAND: EASTER RISING: ANNIVERSARY. Apr 24, 1916. Irish nationalists seized key buildings in Dublin and proclaimed an Irish republic. The rebellion collapsed, however, and it wasn't until 1922 that the Irish Free State, the predecessor of the Republic of Ireland, was established.

KECHI REDBUD & GARDEN FESTIVAL. Apr 24. Kechi, KS. 5th annual festival includes small redbud seedling trees for the area (donations accepted), vendors' display, new garden decor ideas and other ideas. 9 AM to 5 PM. Free admission. Enjoy shopping in Kechi's small-town atmosphere. Motel accomodations available within 2 miles. Est attendance: 800. For info: Rick Eberhard, Kechi KS Chamber of Commerce, 205 Heritage Ct, Kechi, KS 67067-8710. Phone: (316) 744-1337. E-mail: kechichamber @kechiksoc.com. Web: www.kechiksoc.com.

	S	M	T	W	T	F	S
April 2004					1	2	3
	4	5	6	7	8	9	10
	11	12	13	14	15	16	17
	18	19	20	21	22	23	24
	25	26	27	28	29	30	

KUUMBA FESTIVAL. Apr 24. Hollywood, FL. This ethnic festival celebrating creativity features gospel, rap, rhythm and blues, reggae, African dance, storytelling and poetry. African-Caribbean Marketplace with ethnic cuisine; crafts and children's hands-on activities. Est attendance: 5,000. For info: Roguey Doyle, City of Hollywood, Dept of Parks, Recreation and Cultural Arts, 1940 Harrison St, Ste 101, Hollywood, FL 33020. Phone: (954) 921-3404.

LIBRARY OF CONGRESS: ANNIVERSARY. Apr 24, 1800. Congress approved an act providing "for the purchase of such books as may be necessary for the use of Congress . . . and for fitting up a suitable apartment for containing them." Thus began one of the world's greatest libraries.

MAIN STREET FESTIVAL. Apr 24–25. Downtown Franklin, TN. 21st annual festival features more than 220 of the South's leading craftspersons. Food, entertainment (blues, pop, country, classical and rock), children's area and carnival. Showcases historical downtown. Est attendance: 155,000. For info: Shelly Spragins, Main Street Festival, PO Box 807, Franklin, TN 37065. Phone: (615) 595-1239. Fax: (615) 591-8502. E-mail: sspragins@historicfranklin.com. Web: www.historicfranklin.com.

MARCH FOR PARKS. Apr 24. Diamond, MO. The nations' largest walking event for parks. Environmental educational programs all day long. For info: George Washington Carver National Monument, 5646 Carver Rd, Diamond, MO 64840. Phone: (417) 325-4151. Fax: (417) 325-4231. E-mail: superintendent@nps.gov. Web: www.nps.gov/gwca.

MAYMONT'S HERBS GALORE. Apr 24. Richmond, VA. Discover new ways to use herbs in recipes and remedies at the 20th annual Herbs Galore, the popular festival centered around Maymont's celebrated Herb Garden. Enjoy cooking demonstrations, garden walks and seminars and shop the Marketplace on the Lawn featuring more than 40 plant and craft vendors. Free admission; fees and registration required for the seminars. Est attendance: 5,000. For info: Maymont Foundation, 1700 Hampton St, Richmond, VA 23220. Phone: (804) 358-7166. Web: www.maymont.org.

MISSISSIPPI RIVER VALLEY SCENIC DRIVE. Apr 24–25. Mississippi River valley of southeast Missouri. Homemade goodies, quilt shows, history and tours, entertainment, demonstrations; several small towns participate. For info: Frank Nickell, One University Plaza, Southeast Missouri State University, Cape Girardeau, MO 63701. Phone: (573) 651-2555. Fax: (573) 651-5114. E-mail: fnickell@semo.edu.

NATIONAL REBUILDING DAY. Apr 24. 240,000 volunteers come together to rehabilitate the homes of low-income, elderly or disabled people and nonprofit facilities. Annually, the last Saturday in April. For info: Rebuilding Together with Christmas in April, 1536 16th St NW, Washington, DC 20036-1402. Phone: (202) 483-9083 or (800) 4-REHAB-9. Fax: (202) 483-9081. Web: www.rebuildingtogether.org.

NATIONAL SCOOP THE POOP WEEK. Apr 24–30. Between the snowy storms of winter and the backyard barbecues of summer, now is the perfect time for dog-owners to catch up on all those "canine calling cards" that have accumulated during the cold months. Besides creating a nasty mess in your yard, it's a health hazard, it pollutes the groundwater and it annoys the neighbors. It doesn't go away by itself, so get it cleaned up this week. And remind your dog-owning friends! Your family, neighbors and dog will love you for it. Annually, last week of April. For info: Matthew Osborn, 2893 Brownlee Av, Columbus, OH 43209. Phone: (614) 237-8548. E-mail: matthew@pooper-scooper.com. Web: www.pooper-scooper.com.

NATIVE AMERICAN HERITAGE DAY. Apr 24. Stately Oaks Plantation, Jonesboro, GA. Native American folktales, food and crafts demonstrations. Visitors get a chance to learn Native American dances and can learn to shoot a blowgun. Est attendance: 1,000. For info: Historical Jonesboro, PO Box 922, Jonesboro, GA 30237. Phone: (770) 473-0197. E-mail: statelyoaks@historicaljonesboro.org.

POLK COUNTY RAMP TRAMP FESTIVAL. Apr 24. Polk County 4-H Camp, Camp McCroy, near Benton, TN. A tribute to the ramp, a wild onionlike plant that grows only in the Appalachian Mountains. Bluegrass music and feast of the ramps. Est attendance: 2,500. For info: Polk Co Ramp Fest, Box 189, Benton, TN 37307. Phone: (423) 338-4503.

REDBUD TRAIL RENDEZVOUS. Apr 24–25. Rochester, IN. Reenactment of a pre-1840 gathering to trade furs on the Tippecanoe River, featuring tepee village, traditional music and crafts, pioneer and Indian dances, foods cooked over wood fires. Museum, round barn and Living History Village at north end of grounds. For frontier fun, follow the redbuds blooming along the Tippecanoe River. Est attendance: 2,000. For info: Fulton County Historical Soc, 37 E 375 N, Rochester, IN 46975. Phone: (574) 223-4436. E-mail: fchs@rtcol.com. Web: www.icss.net/~fchs.

SOUTHERN MARYLAND CELTIC FESTIVAL. Apr 24. Jefferson Patterson Park, St. Leonard, MD. Scottish fiddling championship, bagpipe competition, Scottish heptathlon, Highland dancing competition, Celtic marketplace and crafts, parade of clans and nations, Celtic harp competition, Celtic folk music, demonstrations and Celtic foods. Annually, the last Saturday in April. Est attendance: 15,000. For info: Celtic Society of Southern Maryland, PO Box 209, Prince Frederick, MD 20678. Phone: (443) 404-7319. Web: www.cssm.org.

SPACE MILESTONE: *CHINA 1* (PEOPLE'S REPUBLIC OF CHINA). Apr 24, 1970. China became the fifth nation to orbit a satellite with launch of its own rocket. Broadcast Chinese song "Tang Fang Hung" ("The East Is Red") and telemetric signals.

SPRING FLING. Apr 24–25. Wichita Falls, TX. A celebration of the arts. Artists from all over the US display their art. Food booths, demonstrations and entertainment. Est attendance: 10,000. For info: Wichita Falls Conv and Visitors Bureau, PO Box 1860, Wichita Falls, TX 76307. Phone: (940) 716-5500 or (940) 692-0923. Fax: (940) 716-5509. Web: www.wichitafalls.org.

THOMAS, ROBERT BAILEY: BIRTH ANNIVERSARY. Apr 24, 1766. Founder and editor of *The Farmer's Almanac* (first issue for 1793) was born at Grafton, MA. Thomas died May 19, 1846, while working on the 1847 edition.

TROLLOPE, ANTHONY: BIRTH ANNIVERSARY. Apr 24, 1815. English novelist (*Barchester Towers*), born at London, England, and died there Dec 6, 1882. "Of the needs a book has," he wrote in his autobiography, "the chief need is that it be readable."

WARREN, ROBERT PENN: BIRTH ANNIVERSARY. Apr 24, 1905. American poet, novelist, essayist and critic. America's first official poet laureate, 1986–88, Robert Penn Warren was born at Guthrie, KY. Warren was awarded the Pulitzer Prize for his novel *All the King's Men*, as well as for his poetry in 1958 and 1979. He died of cancer Sept 15, 1989, at Stratton, VT.

Chase's 2004 Calendar of Events

BIRTHDAYS TODAY

Eric Balfour, 27, actor (*Rescue Me, No One Would Tell*), musician, born Los Angeles, CA, Apr 24, 1977.

Eric Bogosian, 51, actor (*Under Siege 2*), playwright, performance artist, born Boston, MA, Apr 24, 1953.

A. Paul Cellucci, 56, US ambassador to Canada, former Governor of Massachusetts (R), born Hudson, MA, Apr 24, 1948.

Richard M. Daley, 62, Mayor of Chicago, born Chicago, IL, Apr 24, 1942.

Sue Grafton, 64, author (*L Is for Lawless, M Is for Malice*), born Louisville, KY, Apr 24, 1940.

Chipper Jones, 32, baseball player, born DeLand, FL, Apr 24, 1972.

Stanley J. Kauffmann, 88, critic, born New York, NY, Apr 24, 1916.

Shirley MacLaine, 70, author, actress (Oscar for *Terms of Endearment; The Turning Point, Being There*), born Richmond, VA, Apr 24, 1934.

Michael O'Keefe, 49, actor (*The Great Santini, Caddyshack*; stage: *Mass Appeal*), born Larchmont, NY, Apr 24, 1955.

Barbra Streisand, 62, singer, actress (Oscar for *Funny Girl; The Way We Were, Yentl*); director (*Prince of Tides*), born Brooklyn, NY, Apr 24, 1942.

APRIL 25 — SUNDAY
Day 116 — 250 Remaining

ABORTION FIRST LEGALIZED: ANNIVERSARY. Apr 25, 1967. The first law legalizing abortion in the US was signed by Colorado Governor John Arthur Love. The law allowed therapeutic abortions in cases in which a three-doctor panel unanimously agreed.

ANZAC DAY. Apr 25. Australia, New Zealand and Samoa. Memorial day and veterans' observance, especially to mark WWI Anzac landing at Gallipoli, Turkey, in 1915 (ANZAC: Australia and New Zealand Army Corps).

BATTLE OF GALLIPOLI: ANNIVERSARY. Apr 25, 1915–Jan 1916. During World War I the Gallipoli Expedition, or the Dardanelles Campaign, combined Allied naval and military forces tried to capture the Gallipoli peninsula in Turkey in order to effect an open route to Russia via the Black Sea. One French and four British divisions were forced back by a strong Turkish-German defense after almost nine months of fighting. The Australian–New Zealand Army Corps took much of the brunt of the battle.

EARTH DAY: ANNIVERSARY. Apr 25. Earth Day, first observed Apr 22, 1970, with message "New Energy for a New Era" and attention to accelerating the transition to renewable energy worldwide. Earth Day 1990 was a global event with more than 200 million participating in 142 countries. Note: Earth Day activities are held by many groups on various dates, often on the weekends before and after Apr 22. Search for events online. For info: Earth Day Network, PO Box 9827, San Diego, CA 92169. Phone: (858) 272-7370. Fax: (858) 272-2933. E-mail: earthday@earthdayweb.org. Web: www.earthdayweb.org.

EARTH DAY COMMUNITY FESTIVAL. Apr 25 (tentative). St. Louis, MO. An educational event with hundreds of exhibitors related to environmental issues and their solutions. Est attendance: 5,000. For info: St. Louis Earth Day, PO Box 11454, St. Louis, MO 63105. Phone: (314) 962-5838. E-mail: info@stlouisearthday.org. Web: www.stlouisearthday.org.

EARTHFAIR. Apr 25. Balboa Park, San Diego, CA. A free public Earth Day event featuring more than 200 exhibitors representing nonprofit organizations, government agencies and earth-friendly businesses. Events foster public education and awareness of contemporary environmental issues. Included are five stages of live entertainment, a special edition "Earth Times" newspaper, speakers, natural food and a popular Kids Area. Hours are 10 AM to 5 PM. Est attendance: 65,000. For info: San Diego EarthWorks, PO Box 9827, San Diego, CA 92169-9827. Phone: (858) 496-6666. Fax: (858) 272-2933. E-mail: earthworks@earthdayweb.org. Web: www.earthdayweb.org.

EGYPT: SINAI DAY. Apr 25. National holiday celebrating the return of Sinai to Egypt in 1982 after the peace treaty between Egypt and Israel.

FARRAGUT CAPTURES NEW ORLEANS: ANNIVERSARY. Apr 25, 1862. Union forces under the command of Flag Officer David Farragut seized the city of New Orleans, LA, resulting in the surrender of several Confederate forts along the Mississippi in subsequent days. This action removed any Confederate resistance to Northern action on the Mississippi River as far north as New Orleans. General Benjamin Butler arrived on Apr 27 and took command of the management of the captured city.

FIRST LICENSE PLATES: ANNIVERSARY. Apr 25, 1901. New York began requiring license plates on automobiles, the first state to do so.

FITZGERALD, ELLA: BIRTH ANNIVERSARY. Apr 25, 1917. "First Lady of Song," born at Newport News, VA. Jazz singer known for her treatments of Rogers and Hart, Gershwin, Irving Berlin, Cole Porter and Duke Ellington. Fitzgerald died at Beverly Hills, CA, June 15, 1996.

GOSPEL SING—BLACK AND WHITE/NOW AND THEN. Apr 25. Stolberg-Jackson Community Center, Arrow Rock, MO. A celebration of gospel music with mid-Missouri choirs, quartets, duets and soloists performing music from black and spiritual traditions all the way to contemporary songs of praise. Est attendance: 200. For info: HARC, PO Box 121, Arrow Rock, MO 65320. Phone: (660) 837-3306. E-mail: garlin@mid-mo.net.

HELENA RAILROAD FAIR. Apr 25. Civic Center, Helena, MT. Largest railroad hobby event in Montana features a mix of scale and tin-plate trains; railroad memorabilia and collectibles; real-life train watching at the MRL Helena depot. Est attendance: 2,500. For info: Helena Railroad Fair, PO Box 4914, Helena, MT 59604-4914. Phone: (406) 442-2364 or (406) 443-1578. E-mail: rrfair@mt.net.

INDUSTRY DAY. Apr 25. Beatrice, NE. Features early industries of Gage County and their products. Antique gas engine demonstrations, exhibits of stationary engine equipment. Est attendance: 300. For info: Lesa Arterburn, Dir, Gage County Historical Society, PO Box 793, Beatrice, NE 68310. Phone: (402) 228-1679. E-mail: gagecountymuseum@beatriceNE.com. Web: www.beatriceNE.com/gagecountymuseum.

INNOVATION WEEK INTERNATIONAL. Apr 25–May 1. Innovation raises the standard in every area of human endeavor, whether in products, services or personal performance. Conference themes will focus on how to encourage and nurture innovation at each level of the organization in order to consistently achieve breakthrough results. For info: DiFrances & Assoc., LLC, 208 E Oak Crest Dr, Ste 200, Wales, WI 53187-9700. Phone: (262) 968-9850. Fax: (262) 968-9854. E-mail: innovation@difrances.com. Web: www.difrances.com/innovationweek.

ISRAEL: REMEMBRANCE DAY (YOM HA'ZIKKARON). Apr 25. Hebrew calendar date: Iyar 4, 5764. Honors the more than 20,000 soldiers killed in battle since the start of the nation's war for independence in 1947. Began at sundown Apr 24.

ITALY: LIBERATION DAY. Apr 25. National holiday. Commemorates the liberation of Italy from German troops in 1945.

★**JEWISH HERITAGE WEEK.** Apr 25–May 1.

☆ Chase's 2004 Calendar of Events ☆ Apr 25–26

LEWIS, ROBERT Q.: BIRTH ANNIVERSARY. Apr 25, 1920. American comedian Robert Q. Lewis was born at New York, NY. He is best known for his many appearances on television quiz shows such as "What's My Line," "To Tell the Truth" and "Call My Bluff." He died Dec 11, 1991, at Los Angeles, CA.

MARCONI, GUGLIELMO: BIRTH ANNIVERSARY. Apr 25, 1874. Inventor of wireless telegraphy (1895), born at Bologna, Italy. Died at Rome, Italy, July 20, 1937.

MOTHER, FATHER DEAF DAY. Apr 25. A day to honor deaf parents and recognize the gifts of culture and language they give to their hearing children. Annually, the last Sunday of April. Sponsored by Children of Deaf Adults International Inc (CODA). For info: Francine Stern, Deaf Awareness Events. E-mail: ocodasister@yahoo.com.

NO EXCUSE SUNDAY. Apr 25. The last Sunday in April is "No Excuse Sunday." For all those "once in a blue moon" attenders, this is an opportunity to use the Easter visit as a springboard to even more appearances. The motivation is from the Psalmist: "Blessed are those who dwell in your house." Remember: you can sit around depressing on your perch, or receive a wondrous blessing at your church. Annually, last Sunday in April. For info: Jim Bassett, CReative Outreach ServiceS (CROSS), PO Box 1600, Oakwood, GA 30566. Phone: (770) 538-2927. Fax: (770) 538-2927. E-mail: jkbcross@att.net.

PORTUGAL: LIBERTY DAY. Apr 25. Portugal. Public holiday. Anniversary of the 1974 revolution.

SPACE MILESTONE: HUBBLE SPACE TELESCOPE DEPLOYED (US). Apr 25, 1990. Deployed by *Discovery*, the telescope is the largest on-orbit observatory to date and is capable of imaging objects up to 14 billion light-years away. The resolution of images was expected to be seven to ten times greater than images from Earth-based telescopes, since the Hubble Space Telescope is not hampered by Earth's atmospheric distortion. Launched Apr 12, 1990, from Kennedy Space Center, FL. Unfortunately, the telescope's lenses were defective, so the anticipated high quality of imaging was not possible. In 1993, however, the world watched as a shuttle crew successfully retrieved the Hubble from orbit, executed the needed repair and replacement work and released it into orbit once more. In December 1999 the space shuttle *Discovery* was launched to do extensive repairs on the telescope.

SWAZILAND: NATIONAL FLAG DAY. Apr 25. National holiday.

THEODORE ROOSEVELT NATIONAL PARK ESTABLISHED: ANNIVERSARY. Apr 25, 1947. Located in North Dakota, the Theodore Roosevelt National Park includes two sections of the Badlands on the Missouri River as well as Theodore Roosevelt's Elkhorn Ranch.

WALDSEEMULLER, MARTIN: REMEMBRANCE DAY. Apr 25, 1507. Little is known about the obscure scholar now called the "godfather of America," the German geographer and mapmaker Martin Waldseemuller, who gave America its name. In a book titled *Cosmographiae Introductio*, published Apr 25, 1507, Waldseemuller wrote: "Inasmuch as both Europe and Asia received their names from women, I see no reason why any one should justly object to calling this part Amerige, i.e., the land of Amerigo, or America, after Amerigo, its discoverer, a man of great ability." Believing it was the Italian navigator and merchant Amerigo Vespucci who had discovered the new continent, Waldseemuller sought to honor Vespucci by placing his name on his map of the world, published in 1507. First applied only to the South American continent, it soon was used for both the American continents. Waldseemuller did not learn about the voyage of Christopher Columbus until several years later. Of the thousand copies of his map that were printed, only one is known to have survived. Waldseemuller probably was born at Radolfzell, Germany, about 1470. He died at St. Die, France, about 1517–20. See also: "Vespucci, Amerigo: Birth Anniversary" (Mar 9).

WWII: EAST MEETS WEST: ANNIVERSARY. Apr 25, 1945. US Army Lieutenant Albert Kotzebue encountered a single Soviet soldier near the German village of Lechwitz, 75 miles south of Berlin. Patrols of General Leonard Gerow's V Corps saluted the advance guard of Marshall Ivan Konev's Soviet 58th Guards Division. Soldiers of both nations embraced and exchanged toasts. The Allied armies of East and West had finally met.

BIRTHDAYS TODAY

Hank Azaria, 40, actor (*The Birdcage*, many voices on "The Simpsons"), born Forest Hills, NY, Apr 25, 1964.
Jeffrey DeMunn, 57, actor (*Ragtime, Frances*), born Buffalo, NY, Apr 25, 1947.
Tim Duncan, 28, basketball player, born St. Croix, Virgin Islands, Apr 25, 1976.
Jon Kyl, 62, US Senator (R, Arizona), born Oakland, NE, Apr 25, 1942.
Meadow George ("Meadowlark") Lemon III, 72, Hall of Fame basketball player, born Lexington, SC, Apr 25, 1932.
Paul Mazursky, 74, director (*Harry and Tonto, An Unmarried Woman, Scenes from a Mall*), born Brooklyn, NY, Apr 25, 1930.
Al Pacino, 64, actor (Oscar for *Scent of a Woman; Dog Day Afternoon, Godfather* movies), born New York, NY, Apr 25, 1940.
Talia Shire, 58, actress (the *Godfather* movies, the *Rocky* movies), born Jamaica, NY, Apr 25, 1946.
Renee Zellweger, 35, actress (*Jerry Maguire, Nurse Betty, Bridget Jones's Diary*), born Katy, TX, Apr 25, 1969.

APRIL 26 — MONDAY
Day 117 — 249 Remaining

AUDUBON, JOHN JAMES: BIRTH ANNIVERSARY. Apr 26, 1785. American artist and naturalist, best known for his *Birds of America*, born at Haiti. Died Jan 27, 1851, at New York, NY.

BIG 12 MEN'S GOLF CHAMPIONSHIP. Apr 26–27. Prairie Dunes Golf Course, Hutchinson, KS. Est attendance: 1,000. For info: Big 12 Conference, 2201 Stemmons Freeway, 28th Fl, Dallas, TX 75207. Phone: (214) 742-1212. Fax: (214) 753-0145. Web: www.big12sports.com.

CANADA: NEWFOUNDLAND: SAINT GEORGE'S DAY. Apr 26. Holiday observed at Newfoundland on Monday nearest Feast Day (Apr 23) of Saint George.

CHERNOBYL NUCLEAR REACTOR DISASTER: ANNIVERSARY. Apr 26, 1986. At 1:23 AM, local time, an explosion occurred at the Chernobyl atomic power station at Pripyat in the Ukraine. The resulting fire burned for days, sending radioactive material into the atmosphere. More than 100,000 persons were evacuated from a 300-square-mile area around the plant. Three months later 31 people were reported to have died and thousands exposed to dangerous levels of radiation. Estimates projected an additional 1,000 cancer cases in nations downwind of the radioactive discharge. The plant was encased in a concrete tomb in an effort to prevent the still-hot reactor from overheating again and to minimize further release of radiation.

"CHINA BEACH" TV PREMIERE: ANNIVERSARY. Apr 26, 1988. The stories of "China Beach" revolved around the lives of the women serving at a Da Nang armed forces hospital during the Vietnam War. The theme and background music of the series evoked plenty of nostalgia from the turbulent era. The ABC drama was created by William Boyles, Jr, and John Sacret Young. The cast featured Dana Delany, Michael Boatman, Nancy Giles, Jeff Kober, Robert Picardo, Concetta Tomei, Brian Wimmer, Marg Helgenberger, Chloe Webb, Nan Woods, Megan Gallagher, Ned Vaughn and Ricki Lake.

CONFEDERATE MEMORIAL DAY IN ALABAMA. Apr 26. On the fourth Monday in April.

Apr 26 ☆ Chase's 2004 Calendar of Events ☆

CONFEDERATE MEMORIAL DAY IN FLORIDA AND GEORGIA. Apr 26. See also: Confederate Memorial Day entries for May 10 and June 3.

CONFEDERATE MEMORIAL DAY IN MISSISSIPPI. Apr 26. Annually, last Monday in April. Observed on other dates in some states: the fourth Monday in April in Alabama, Apr 26 in Florida and Georgia, May 10 in North and South Carolina and on Jefferson Davis's birthday (June 3) in Kentucky, Louisiana and Tennessee.

FAUSET, JESSIE REDMON: BIRTH ANNIVERSARY. Apr 26, 1882. African American poet, editor and novelist, born at Fredericksville, NJ, and died in 1961. Fauset, as literary editor of *Crisis* (a publication of the NAACP), was a patron to so many writers of the Harlem Renaissance that her efforts prompted Langston Hughes to dub her the "midwife of the so-called New Negro Literature." Along with W.E.B. Du Bois, Fauset also published and edited the children's magazine *The Brownie Book*. Her novels about the African American middle-class experience dealt with issues of identity, autonomy and struggles for fulfillment. Her most recognized works include *The Chinaberry Tree* (1931) and *Comedy, American Style* (1933).

GUERNICA MASSACRE: ANNIVERSARY. Apr 26, 1937. Late in the afternoon, the ancient Basque town of Guernica, in northern Spain, was attacked without warning by German-made airplanes. Three hours of intensive bombing left the town in flames, and citizens who fled to the fields and ditches around Guernica were machine-gunned from the air. This atrocity inspired Pablo Picasso's mural *Guernica*. Responsibility for the bombing was never officially established, but the suffering and anger of the victims and their survivors are still evident at anniversary demonstrations. Intervention by Nazi Germany in the Spanish Civil War has been described as practice for WWII.

HESS, RUDOLF: BIRTH ANNIVERSARY. Apr 26, 1894. One of the most bizarre figures of World War II Germany, Walter Richard Rudolf Hess was born at Alexandria, Egypt. He was a close friend, confidant and personal secretary to Adolf Hitler who had dictated much of *Mein Kampf* to Hess while both were prisoners at Landsberg Prison. Third in command in Nazi Germany, Hess surprised the world on May 10, 1941, by flying alone to Scotland and parachuting from his plane on what he called a "mission of humanity": offering peace to Britain if she would join Germany in attacking the Soviet Union. He was immediately taken prisoner of war. At the Nuremberg Trials (1946), after questions about his sanity, he was convicted and sentenced to life imprisonment at Spandau Allied War Crimes Prison at Berlin, Germany. Outliving all other prisoners there, he was the only inmate from 1955 until he succeeded (in his fourth attempt) in committing suicide. He died at West Berlin, Germany, Aug 17, 1987.

HUG AN AUSTRALIAN DAY. Apr 26. To show our great appreciation for all the love and support the Aussies have given us over the years. [©2003 by WH.] For info: Thomas & Ruth Roy, Wellcat Holidays, 2418 Long Ln, Lebanon, PA 17046. Phone: (717) 279-0184. E-mail: info@wellcat.com. Web: www.wellcat.com.

ISRAEL: INDEPENDENCE DAY (YOM HA'ATZMA'UT): ANNIVERSARY. Apr 26. Hebrew calendar date: Iyar 5, 5764. Celebrates proclamation of independence from British mandatory rule by Palestinian Jews and establishment of the state of Israel and the provisional government May 14, 1948 (Hebrew calendar date: Iyar 5, 5708). Dates in the Hebrew calendar vary from their Gregorian equivalents from year to year, so, while Iyar 5 in 1948 was May 14, in 2004 it is Apr 26. Began at sundown Apr 25.

LOOS, ANITA: BIRTH ANNIVERSARY. Apr 26, 1893. American author and playwright, born at Sisson, CA. She is best remembered for her book *Gentlemen Prefer Blondes*, published in 1925. Loos, a brunette, died at New York, NY, Aug 18, 1981.

MONTGOMERY WARD SEIZED: 60th ANNIVERSARY. Apr 26, 1944. Montgomery Ward Chairman Sewell Avery was physically removed from his office when federal troops seized Ward's Chicago offices after the company refused to obey President Franklin D. Roosevelt's order to recognize a CIO union. Government control ended May 9, shortly before the National Labor Relations Board announced the United Mail Order Warehouse and Retail Employees Union had won an election to represent the company's workers.

NATIONAL PLAYGROUND SAFETY WEEK. Apr 26–30. An opportunity for families, community parks, schools and childcare facilities to focus on preventing public playground-related injuries. Sponsored by the National Program for Playground Safety (NPPS), this event helps educate the public about the more than 200,000 children (that's one child every 2½ minutes) that require emergency-room treatment for playground-related injuries each year. For info: Natl Program for Playground Safety, School of HPELS, UNI, Cedar Falls, IA 50614-0618. Phone: (800) 554-PLAY. Fax: (319) 273-7308. Web: www.uni.edu/playground.

OLMSTED, FREDERICK LAW: BIRTH ANNIVERSARY. Apr 26, 1822. Known as the "father of landscape architecture in America," Olmsted participated in the designing of Yosemite National Park, New York City's Central Park and parks for Boston, Hartford and Louisville. Born at Hartford, CT, died at Waverly, MA, Aug 28, 1903. Olmsted's home and studio, Fairsted Estate outside of Boston, is now preserved as a National Historic Site and is open to the public: 99 Warren St, Brookline, MA 02146.

RICHTER SCALE DAY. Apr 26. A day to recognize the importance of Charles Francis Richter's research and his work in development of the earthquake magnitude scale that is known as the Richter scale. Richter, an American author, physicist and seismologist, was born Apr 26, 1900, near Hamilton, OH. An Earthquake Awareness Week was observed in recognition of his work. Richter died at Pasadena, CA, Sept 30, 1985.

SIRK, DOUGLAS: BIRTH ANNIVERSARY. Apr 26, 1900. Film director Douglas Sirk was born Detlef Sierck at Hamburg, Germany. His films include *Magnificent Obsession* (1954), *Written on the Wind* (1956) and *Imitation of Life* (1959). He died Jan 14, 1987, at Lugano, Switzerland.

SOUTH AFRICAN MULTIRACIAL ELECTIONS: 10th ANNIVERSARY. Apr 26–29, 1994. For the first time in the history of South Africa, the nation's approximately 18 million blacks voted in multiparty elections. This event marked the definitive end of apartheid, the system of racial separation that had kept blacks and other minorities out of the political process. The election resulted in Nelson Mandela of the African National Congress being elected president and F.W. de Klerk (incumbent president) of the National Party vice president.

April 2004	S	M	T	W	T	F	S
					1	2	3
	4	5	6	7	8	9	10
	11	12	13	14	15	16	17
	18	19	20	21	22	23	24
	25	26	27	28	29	30	

☆ Chase's 2004 Calendar of Events ☆ Apr 26–27

TANZANIA: UNION DAY. Apr 26. Celebrates union between mainland Tanzania (formerly Tanganyika) and the islands of Zanzibar and Pemba, in 1964.

US HOLOCAUST MUSEUM OPENS: ANNIVERSARY. Apr 26, 1993. Washington, DC. After the Museum opened to the public on this day, more than two million visitors toured the permanent exhibition during its first year of operation.

BIRTHDAYS TODAY

Carol Burnett, 68, actress ("Garry Moore Show," "Carol Burnett Show," *The Four Seasons*), born San Antonio, TX, Apr 26, 1936.
Joan Chen, 43, actress ("Twin Peaks," "Golden Gate"), born Shanghai, China, Apr 26, 1961.
Michael Damian, 42, actor ("Young and the Restless"; stage: *Joseph and the Amazing Technicolor Dreamcoat*), born San Diego, CA, Apr 26, 1962.
Duane Eddy, 66, musician, born Corning, NY, Apr 26, 1938.
Giancarlo Esposito, 46, actor (*Do the Right Thing, Twilight*), born Copenhagen, Denmark, Apr 26, 1958.
Kevin James, 39, actor ("The King of Queens"), born Stony Brook, NY, Apr 26, 1965.
Jet Li, 41, actor (*Romeo Must Die, Once Upon a Time in China*), former martial arts champion, born Li Lian Jie at Beijing, China, Apr 26, 1963.
Boyd Matson, 57, TV journalist (host of "National Geographic Explorer"), born Oklahoma City, OK, Apr 26, 1947.
Bobby Rydell, 62, singer ("Wild One," "Volare"), born Philadelphia, PA, Apr 26, 1942.
Tom Welling, 27, actor ("Smallville"), born New York, NY, Apr 26, 1977.
Gary Wright, 61, musician, born Englewood, NJ, Apr 26, 1943.

APRIL 27 — TUESDAY
Day 118 — 248 Remaining

BABE RUTH DAY: ANNIVERSARY. Apr 27, 1947. Babe Ruth Day was celebrated in every ballpark in organized baseball in the US as well as Japan. Mortally ill with throat cancer, Ruth appeared at Yankee Stadium to thank his former club for the honor.

CONTRABAND DAYS (PIRATE FESTIVAL). Apr 27–May 9. Lake Charles, LA. A major 13-day festival celebrating Jean Lafitte, "The Gentleman Pirate," and the contraband treasures he is supposed to have hidden along the shores of Lake Charles. Events include a mock invasion by pirates, a night boat parade, concerts, fireworks, water events, children's area. Est attendance: 150,000. For info: Marlene C. Hobbs, Exec Dir, Contraband Days, Inc, PO Box 679, Lake Charles, LA 70602. Phone: (337) 436-5508. Fax: (337) 436-1126. E-mail: contraband@cox-internet.com. Web: www.contrabanddays.com.

DENNIS, SANDY: BIRTH ANNIVERSARY. Apr 27, 1937. American actress Sandy Dennis was born Sandra Dale Dennis at Hastings, NE. In addition to two Tony Awards, she won an Academy Award for her supporting role in *Who's Afraid of Virginia Woolf* (1966). She died Mar 2, 1992, at Westport, CT.

GIBBON, EDWARD: BIRTH ANNIVERSARY. Apr 27, 1737 (OS). English historian and author. His *History of the Decline and Fall of the Roman Empire* remains a model of historical writing. From his description of the Roman emperor Gordianus II: "Twenty-two acknowledged concubines, and a library of sixty-two thousand volumes, attested the variety of his inclinations; and from the productions which he left behind him, it appears that the former as well as the latter were designed for use rather than for ostentation." Born at Putney, Surrey, England, Gibbon died at London, Jan 6, 1794.

GODWIN, MARY WOLLSTONECRAFT: BIRTH ANNIVERSARY. Apr 27, 1759. English writer whose best-known book was *Vindication of the Rights of Women*, published in 1792. Born at London, England, and died there Sept 10, 1797. Her daughter, Mary, was the wife of poet Percy Bysshe Shelley but is best remembered as the author of *Frankenstein*, published in 1818.

GRANT, ULYSSES SIMPSON: BIRTH ANNIVERSARY. Apr 27, 1822. 18th president of the US (Mar 4, 1869–Mar 3, 1877), born Hiram Ulysses Grant at Point Pleasant, OH. He graduated from the US Military Academy in 1843. President Lincoln promoted Grant to lieutenant general in command of all the Union armies Mar 9, 1864. On Apr 9, 1865, Grant received General Robert E. Lee's surrender, at Appomattox Court House, VA, which he announced to the Secretary of War as follows: "General Lee surrendered the Army of Northern Virginia this afternoon on terms proposed by myself. The accompanying additional correspondence will show the conditions fully." Nicknamed "Unconditional Surrender Grant," he died at Mount McGregor, NY, July 23, 1885, just four days after completing his memoirs. He was buried at Riverside Park, New York, NY, where Grant's Tomb was dedicated in 1897.

LANTZ, WALTER: BIRTH ANNIVERSARY. Apr 27, 1900. Originator of Universal Studios' animated opening sequence for their first major musical film, *The King of Jazz*. Walter Lantz is best remembered as the creator of Woody Woodpecker, the bird with the wacky laugh and the taunting ways. Lantz received a lifetime achievement Academy Award for his animation in 1979. He was born at New Rochelle, NY, and died Mar 22, 1994, at Burbank, CA.

MAGELLAN, FERDINAND: DEATH ANNIVERSARY. Apr 27, 1521. Portuguese explorer Ferdinand Magellan was probably born near Oporto, Portugal, about 1480, but neither the place nor the date is certain. Usually thought of as the first man to circumnavigate the earth, he died before completing the voyage; thus his co-leader, Basque navigator Juan Sebastian de Elcano, became the world's circumnavigator. The westward, 'round-the-world expedition began Sept 20, 1519, with five ships and about 250 men. Magellan was killed by natives of the Philippine island of Mactan.

MATANZAS MULE DAY. Apr 27, 1898. In one of the first naval actions of the Spanish-American War, US naval forces bombarded the Cuban village of Matanzas. It was widely reported that the only casualty of the bombardment was one mule. "The Matanzas Mule" became instantly famous and remains a footnote in the history of the Spanish-American War.

MOON PHASE: FIRST QUARTER. Apr 27. Moon enters First Quarter phase at 1:32 PM, EDT.

MORSE, SAMUEL FINLEY BREESE: BIRTH ANNIVERSARY. Apr 27, 1791. American artist and inventor, after whom the Morse code is named, was born at Charlestown, MA, and died at New York, NY, Apr 2, 1872. Graduating from Yale University in 1810, he went to the Royal Academy of London to study painting. After returning to America he achieved success as a portraitist. Morse conceived the idea of an electromagnetic telegraph while on shipboard, returning from art instruction in Europe in 1832, and he proceeded to develop his idea. With financial assistance approved by Congress, the first telegraph line in the US was constructed, between Washington, DC, and Baltimore, MD. The first message tapped out by Morse from the Supreme Court Chamber at the US Capitol building on May 24, 1844, was: "What hath God wrought?"

NATIONAL CONVENTION OF AMERICAN MOTHERS, INC. Apr 27–May 2. Caribe Hotel, San Juan, Puerto Rico. Annual convention. Included is the announcement of National Mother of the Year®. For info: American Mothers, Inc®, National Headquarters, 15 Dupont Circle, Washington, DC 20036. Phone: (202) 234-7375 or (877) 242-4AMI. E-mail: info@americanmothers.org. Web: www.americanmothers.org.

Apr 27–28 ☆ Chase's 2004 Calendar of Events ☆

SIERRA LEONE: INDEPENDENCE DAY. Apr 27. National Day. Commemorates independence from Britain in 1961.

SLOVENIA: INSURRECTION DAY. Apr 27. National holiday. Commemorates the founding of the Liberation Front in 1941 to resist Slovenia's occupation by the Axis powers.

SOUTH AFRICA: FREEDOM DAY. Apr 27. National holiday. Commemorates the day in 1994 when, for the first time, all South Africans had the opportunity to vote.

SULTANA STEAMSHIP EXPLOSION: ANNIVERSARY. Apr 27, 1865. Early in the morning on this day, America's worst steamship disaster occurred. The Sultana, heavily overloaded with an estimated 2,300 passengers, exploded in the Mississippi River, just north of Memphis, en route to Cairo, IL. Most of the passengers were Union soldiers who had been prisoners of war and were eagerly returning to their homes. Although there was never an accurate accounting of the dead, estimates range from 1,450 to nearly 2,000. Cause of the explosion was not determined, but the little-known event is unparalleled in US history.

TOGO: INDEPENDENCE DAY. Apr 27. National holiday. In 1960 Togo gained its independence from French administration under a UN trusteeship.

YUGOSLAVIA: NATIONAL DAY. Apr 27. Commemorates the formation of the Yugoslav Federation (consisting of Serbia and Montenegro) by the adoption of a constitution in 1992.

BIRTHDAYS TODAY

Anouk Aimee, 70, actress (*A Man and a Woman, The Golden Salamander*), born Paris, France, Apr 27, 1934.
Sheena Easton, 45, singer ("Morning Train"), born Sheena Shirley Orr, Bellshill, Scotland, Apr 27, 1959.
Casey Kasem, 72, radio, TV host ("America's Top 40"), born Detroit, MI, Apr 27, 1932.
Coretta Scott King, 77, lecturer, writer, widow of Martin Luther King, Jr, born Marion, AL, Apr 27, 1927.
Jack Klugman, 82, actor ("The Odd Couple," "Quincy, ME"), born Philadelphia, PA, Apr 27, 1922.
August Wilson, 59, playwright (*Fences, Joe Turner's Come and Gone*), born Pittsburgh, PA, Apr 27, 1945.

APRIL 28 — WEDNESDAY
Day 119 — 247 Remaining

BARRYMORE, LIONEL: BIRTH ANNIVERSARY. Apr 28, 1878. Famed American actor of celebrated acting family, Lionel Barrymore was born Lionel Blythe, at Philadelphia, PA. Brother of Ethel and John Barrymore. He died at Van Nuys, CA, Nov 15, 1954.

BIOLOGICAL CLOCK GENE DISCOVERED: 10th ANNIVERSARY. Apr 28, 1994. Northwestern University announced that the so-called biological clock, that gene governing the daily cycle of waking and sleeping called the circadian rhythm, had been found in mice. Never before pinpointed in a mammal, the biological clock gene was found on mouse chromosome #5.

CANADA: NATIONAL DAY OF MOURNING. Apr 28. A national day of mourning for workers killed or injured on the job in Canada. The Canadian Labour Congress first officially recognized the day in 1986. Pointing to the nearly one million workplace injuries each year in Canada, the CLC has called for stricter health and safety regulations and for annual recognition of this day throughout Canada. Federal legislation (Bill D-223) first recognized this day in 1991.

	S	M	T	W	T	F	S
April					1	2	3
2004	4	5	6	7	8	9	10
	11	12	13	14	15	16	17
	18	19	20	21	22	23	24
	25	26	27	28	29	30	

ETHNIC AWARENESS PROGRAM. Apr 28–May 1. Macon, GA. To unite, educate and draw this diverse country together and to help its citizens understand one another's cultures, respect one another's differences and share one another's likenesses. Program will include informative films, racial discussions, skits, talent showcases, social events and the 6th annual Ethnic Awards Gala & Film Exposure Feast. For info: Betty Jean Slater, Willis-Slater Productions, 2806 Kent, Macon, GA 31206. Phone: (478) 788-5419.

GIBBS, MIFFLIN WISTER: BIRTH ANNIVERSARY. Apr 28, 1828. Mifflin Wister Gibbs was born at Philadelphia, PA. In 1873 he became the first black man to be elected a judge in the US, winning an election for City Judge at Little Rock, AR.

HOMER, LOUISE DILWORTH: BIRTH ANNIVERSARY. Apr 28, 1871. The mesmerizing Louise Dilworth Homer was one of the most formidable contraltos of her time. Her plum roles in *Aïda, Tristan und Isolde, Hänsel und Gretel* and *Samson et Dalilah* (with the legendary Caruso), brought her tremendous acclaim. She was born at Sewickley, PA, and died at Winter Park, FL, May 6, 1947.

JAMES MONROE BIRTHDAY CELEBRATION. Apr 28. Ash Lawn-Highland, home of James Monroe, Charlottesville, VA. Cookies prepared from Monroe family recipe. For info: Ash Lawn-Highland, 1000 James Monroe Pkwy, Charlottesville, VA 22902. Phone: (434) 293-9539. Fax: (434) 293-8000. E-mail: info@ashlawnhighland.org. Web: www.ashlawnhighland.org.

MARYLAND CONSTITUTION RATIFICATION: ANNIVERSARY. Apr 28, 1788. Maryland became the seventh state to ratify the Constitution, by a vote of 63 to 11.

MONROE, JAMES: BIRTH ANNIVERSARY. Apr 28, 1758. 5th president of the US was born at Westmoreland County, VA, and served two terms in that office (Mar 4, 1817–Mar 3, 1825). Monrovia, the capital city of Liberia, is named after him, as is the Monroe Doctrine, which he enunciated at Washington, DC, Dec 2, 1823. Last of three presidents to die on US Independence Day, Monroe died at New York, NY, July 4, 1831.

MUSSOLINI EXECUTED: ANNIVERSARY. Apr 28, 1945. Italian partisans shot Benito Mussolini near the lakeside village of Dongo. Leaders of the Fascist Party, several of his friends and his mistress Clara Petacci also were executed. The 23-year-long Fascist rule of Italy was ended.

MUTINY ON THE *BOUNTY*: ANNIVERSARY. Apr 28, 1789. The most famous of all naval mutinies occurred on board HMS *Bounty*. Captain of the *Bounty* was Lieutenant William Bligh, an able seaman and a mean-tempered disciplinarian. The ship, with a load of breadfruit tree plants from Tahiti, was bound for Jamaica. Fletcher Christian, leader of the mutiny, put Bligh and 18 of his loyal followers adrift in a 23-foot open boat. Miraculously Bligh and all of his supporters survived a 47-day voyage of more than 3,600 miles, before landing on the island of Timor, June 14, 1789. In the meantime, Christian had put all of the remaining crew (excepting 8 men and himself) ashore at Tahiti where he picked up 18 Tahitians (6 men and 12 women) and set sail again. Landing at Pitcairn Island in 1790 (probably uninhabited at the time), they burned the *Bounty* and remained undiscovered for 18 years, when an American whaler, the *Topaz*, called at the island (1808) and found only one member of the mutinous crew surviving. However, the little colony had thrived and, when counted by the British in 1856, numbered 194 persons.

SPACE MILESTONE: FIRST TOURIST IN SPACE. Apr 28, 2001. Millionaire US businessman Dennis Tito reportedly paid the Russian space agency $20 million to accompany *Soyuz TM* to the International Space Station. The rocket with Tito and two Russian cosmonauts was launched this day from the Baikonur launch in Kazakhstan and arrived at the ISS on Apr 30, 2001. The crew returned to Earth in a week. NASA initially objected to the inclusion of the 60-year-old tycoon on the mission but dropped its opposition.

SUNFEST. Apr 28–May 2. West Palm Beach, FL. Florida's largest music, art and waterfront festival features some of the best acts in jazz, pop, blues and more. Family-oriented event includes a juried art show, handmade crafts, fireworks, water and youth park activities and fabulous foods. Annually, the first weekend in May. Est attendance: 300,000. For info: SunFest of Palm Beach County, Inc, 525 Clematis St, West Palm Beach, FL 33401. Phone: (561) 659-5980. Fax: (561) 659-3567. E-mail: sunfest@sunfest.org. Web: www.sunfest.org.

WORKERS MEMORIAL DAY. Apr 28. To commemorate the Occupational Safety and Health Act of Apr 28, 1989. In some places observed on the fourth Friday of April.

BIRTHDAYS TODAY

Jessica Alba, 23, actress ("Dark Angel"), born Pomona, CA, Apr 28, 1981.
Ann-Margret, 63, actress (*Carnal Knowledge, Tommy*), born Ann-Margaret Olsson, Stockholm, Sweden, Apr 28, 1941.
Penelope Cruz, 30, actress (*All the Pretty Horses*), born Madrid, Spain, Apr 28, 1974.
John Daly, 38, golfer, born Carmichael, CA, Apr 28, 1966.
Saddam Hussein, 67, former Iraqi dictator, born Tikrit, Iraq, Apr 28, 1937.
Bruno Kirby, 55, actor (*When Harry Met Sally. . ., City Slickers*), born New York, NY, Apr 28, 1949.
Barry Louis Larkin, 40, baseball player, born Cincinnati, OH, Apr 28, 1964.
Harper Lee, 78, author (*To Kill a Mockingbird*), born Nelle Harper, Monroeville, AL, Apr 28, 1926.
Jay Leno, 54, TV talk-show host ("The Tonight Show"), comedian, born New Rochelle, NY, Apr 28, 1950.
Marcia Strassman, 56, actress ("Welcome Back Kotter," *Honey, I Shrunk the Kids*), born New York, NY, Apr, 28, 1948.
Chris Young, 33, actor ("Falcon Crest," *The Great Outdoors*), born Chambersburg, PA, Apr 28, 1971.

APRIL 29 — THURSDAY
Day 120 — 246 Remaining

BIG TEN MEN'S TENNIS CHAMPIONSHIP. Apr 29–May 2. Site TBD. For info: Sue Lister, Big Ten Conference, 1500 W Higgins Rd, Park Ridge, IL 60068-6300. Phone: (847) 696-1010. Fax: (847) 696-1110. Web: www.bigten.org.

BIG TEN WOMEN'S TENNIS CHAMPIONSHIP. Apr 29–May 2. Northwestern University, Evanston, IL. For info: Big Ten Conference, 1500 W Higgins Rd, Park Ridge, IL 60068-6300. Phone: (847) 696-1010. Fax: (847) 696-1150. Web: www.bigten.org.

BIG 12 MEN'S AND WOMEN'S OUTDOOR TRACK AND FIELD CHAMPIONSHIPS. Apr 29–May 1. Norman, OK. For info: Big 12 Conference, 2201 Stemmons Frwy, 28th FL, Dallas, TX 75207. Phone: (214) 742-1212. Fax: (214) 753-0145. Web: www.big12sports.com.

BIG 12 MEN'S AND WOMEN'S TENNIS CHAMPIONSHIP. Apr 29–May 2. Oklahoma Headington Family Tennis Center, Norman, OK. Est attendance: 3,000. For info: Big 12 Conference, 2201 Stemmons Freeway, 28th Fl, Dallas, TX 75207. Phone: (214) 742-1212. Fax: (214) 753-0145. Web: www.big12sports.com.

BIG 12 WOMEN'S SOFTBALL CHAMPIONSHIPS. Apr 29–May 2. Oklahoma City, OK. For info: Big 12 Conference, 2201 Stemmons Frwy, 28th Fl, Dallas, TX 75207. Phone: (214) 742-1212. Fax: (214) 753-0145. Web: www.big12sports.com.

EARNHARDT, DALE: BIRTH ANNIVERSARY. Apr 29, 1952. Stock car racer, born Kannapolis, NC. He was one of NASCAR's most popular personalities, winning the Winston Cup seven times. He was killed while driving in the Daytona 500 at Daytona Beach, FL, Feb 18, 2001.

ELLINGTON, "DUKE" (EDWARD KENNEDY): BIRTH ANNIVERSARY. Apr 29, 1899. "Duke" Ellington, one of the most influential individuals in jazz history, was born at Washington, DC. Ellington's professional career began when he was 17, and by 1923 he was leading a small group of musicians at the Kentucky Club at New York City who became the core of his big band. Ellington is credited with being one of the founders of big band jazz. He used his band as an instrument for composition and orchestration to create big band pieces, film scores, operas, ballets, Broadway shows and religious music. Ellington was responsible for more than 1,000 musical pieces. He drew together instruments from different sections of the orchestra to develop unique and haunting sounds such as that of his famous "Mood Indigo." "Duke" Ellington died May 24, 1974, at New York City.

ELLSWORTH, OLIVER: BIRTH ANNIVERSARY. Apr 29, 1745 (OS). Third chief justice of the US Supreme Court, born at Windsor, CT. Died there, Nov 26, 1807.

EMMETT KELLY CLOWN FESTIVAL. Apr 29–May 1. Downtown Houston, MO. Carnival, clown school, parade on Saturday, arts & crafts, Big Top performances, souvenir sales. Appearance by Emmett Kelly, Jr and Joey Kelly. Est attendance: 5,000. For info: Houston Area Chamber of Commerce, PO Box 374, Houston, MO 65483. Phone: (417) 967-2220. Fax: (417) 967-2178.

ENGLAND: MITSUBISHI MOTORS BADMINTON HORSE TRIALS. Apr 29–May 2 (scheduled). Badminton, Glos. Famous international horse trials consisting of show jumping, cross country and dressage. Est attendance: 200,000. For info: Box Office, Badminton Horse Trials, Badminton, Glos, England GL9 1DF. Phone: (44) (1454) 21-8375. Fax: (44) (1454) 21-8702. E-mail: boxoffice@badminton-horse.co.uk. Web: www.badminton-horse.co.uk.

EWELL, TOM: 95th BIRTH ANNIVERSARY. Apr 29, 1909. Born Samuel Yewell Tompkins at Owensboro, KY, Ewell acted in many films and TV series. He won a Tony Award for his Broadway role as the husband in *The Seven Year Itch*, a role he reprised in the film version costarring Marilyn Monroe. In the '60s he starred in his own TV show, "The Tom Ewell Show." He died Sept 12, 1994, at Woodland Hills, CA.

FESTIVAL OF NATIONS. Apr 29–May 2. River Centre, St. Paul, MN. Celebration by 90 ethnic groups, each presenting cultural exhibits, food specialties, folk dances and folk arts to the public. Est attendance: 85,000. For info: Intl Institute of Minnesota, 1694 Como Ave, St. Paul, MN 55108. Phone: (651) 647-0191. Fax: (651) 647-9268. Web: www.festivalofnations.com.

HEARST, WILLIAM RANDOLPH: BIRTH ANNIVERSARY. Apr 29, 1863. American newspaper editor and publisher, born at San Francisco, CA. Died at Beverly Hills, CA, Aug 14, 1951.

Apr 29 ☆ *Chase's 2004 Calendar of Events* ☆

HIROHITO MICHI-NO-MIYA, EMPEROR: BIRTH ANNIVERSARY. Apr 29, 1901. Former Emperor of Japan, born at Tokyo. Hirohito's death, Jan 7, 1989, ended the reign of the world's longest ruling monarch. He became the 124th in a line of monarchs when he ascended to the Chrysanthemum Throne in 1926. Hirohito presided over perhaps the most eventful years in the 2,500 years of recorded Japanese history, including the attempted military conquest of Asia; the attack on the US that brought that country into WWII, leading to Japan's ultimate defeat after the US dropped atomic bombs on Hiroshima and Nagasaki; and the amazing economic restoration following the war that led Japan to a preeminent position of economic strength.

JAPAN: GOLDEN WEEK HOLIDAYS. Apr 29–May 5. National holiday. This period includes Greenery Day (Apr 29), Constitution Memorial Day (May 3) and Children's Day (May 5). When a day is between two holidays, like May 4, it becomes a holiday, too.

JAPAN: GREENERY DAY. Apr 29. National holiday. To commemorate the birth of Emperor Hirohito in 1901.

KANSAS BARBED WIRE SWAP/SELL. Apr 29–May 1. LaCrosse, KS. Barbed Wire Collectors Association show and meeting. Est attendance: 200. For info: Kansas Barbed Wire Collectors Assn, PO Box 578, LaCrosse, KS 67548. Phone: (785) 222-9900.

LOS ANGELES RIOTS: ANNIVERSARY. Apr 29, 1992. A jury in Simi Valley, CA, failed to convict four Los Angeles police officers accused in the videotaped beating of Rodney King, providing the spark that set off rioting, looting and burning at South Central Los Angeles, CA, and other areas across the country. The anger unleashed during and after the violence was attributed to widespread racism, lack of job opportunities and the resulting hopelessness of inner-city poverty.

LOYALTY DAYS AND SEAFAIR FESTIVAL. Apr 29–May 2. Newport, OR. Celebration of loyalty to America. Parade, queen and court, Navy ships in port and other activities. Est attendance: 5,000. For info: Chamber of Commerce, 555 SW Coast Hwy, Newport, OR 97365. Phone: (541) 265-8801 or (800) 262-7844. Fax: (541) 265-5589. E-mail: chamber@newport.com.

PEACE ROSE INTRODUCED TO WORLD: ANNIVERSARY. Apr 29, 1945. The 20th-century's most popular rose was publicly released by the Pacific Rose Society in Pasadena, CA, just as Berlin was falling to the Allies. Peace's history is interwoven with events of WWII, and for many the Hybrid Tea rose has symbolized the hope that grew out of terrible conflict. French rose grower Frances Meilland bred the cream and pink rose (then called Mme A. Meilland) in the late 1930s and knew he had something extraordinary. A seedling was smuggled out of France in an American diplomatic pouch on one of the last planes to leave that country before Nazi occupation. American rose company Conrad-Pyle carefully cultivated it. To note Germany's surrender, Peace blooms were presented to all delegates during the first United Nations Conference that May of 1945.

POLICE OFFICERS WHO GAVE THEIR LIVES IN THE LINE OF DUTY WEEK. Apr 29–May 5. A week of events remembering all police officers nationwide who gave their lives to protect others. In addition, lectures on how famous crimes were solved. For info: Thomas A. Phelan, (201) 387-9066 or Bob O'Brien, Consumer Advocate, 1061 Koelle Blvd, Secaucus, NJ 07094. Phone: (201) 860-1595. Email: bobthebestthebest@yahoo.com.

SAINT CATHERINE OF SIENA: FEAST DAY. Apr 29, 1347. St. Catherine of Siena was born at Tuscany, Italy. Patron saint of Italy. She died Apr 29, 1380, at Rome, Italy.

SPACE MILESTONE: *CHALLENGER* STS-51B (US). Apr 29, 1985. *Challenger* launched from Kennedy Space Center, FL, with crew of seven and animal menagerie including monkeys and rats. Landed after 111 orbits of Earth on May 6, 1985, at Edwards Air Force Base, CA.

TAIWAN: CHENG CHENG KUNG LANDING DAY. Apr 29. Commemorates landing in Taiwan in 1661 of Ming Dynasty loyalist Cheng Cheng Kung (Koxinga), who ousted Dutch colonists who had occupied Taiwan for 37 years. Main ceremonies held at Tainan, in south Taiwan, where Dutch had their headquarters and where Cheng is buried.

WASHINGTON STATE APPLE BLOSSOM FESTIVAL. Apr 29–May 9. Wenatchee, WA. To showcase the greater Wenatchee Valley, its people and heritage by producing an ongoing community celebration. Parades, arts and crafts, gem and mineral show, theatrical productions, Youth Day and carnival. More than 40 events. Annually, the last weekend in April through the first weekend in May. Est attendance: 100,000. For info: Washington State Apple Blossom Festival, Box 2836, Wenatchee, WA 98807. Phone: (509) 662-3616. Fax: (509) 665-0347. E-mail: festival@appleblossom.org. Web: www.appleblossom.org.

ZIPPER PATENTED: ANNIVERSARY. Apr 29, 1913. Gideon Sundbach of Hoboken, NJ, received a patent for the zipper.

BIRTHDAYS TODAY

Andre Kirk Agassi, 34, tennis player, born Las Vegas, NV, Apr 29, 1970.
Daniel Day-Lewis, 47, actor (Oscar for *My Left Foot*; *The Unbearable Lightness of Being*), born London, England, Apr 29, 1957.
Nora Dunn, 52, actress (*Passion Fish*, "Saturday Night Live"), born Chicago, IL, Apr 29, 1952.
Robert Gottlieb, 73, editor, born New York, NY, Apr 29, 1931.
Celeste Holm, 85, actress (*All About Eve*; Oscar for *Gentleman's Agreement*), born New York, NY, Apr 29, 1919.
Rod McKuen, 71, poet, singer, born San Francisco, CA, Apr 29, 1933.
Zubin Mehta, 68, conductor, born Bombay, India, Apr 29, 1936.
Kate Mulgrew, 49, actress ("Star Trek: Voyager," "Ryan's Hope"), born Dubuque, IA, Apr 29, 1955.
Michelle Pfeiffer, 46, actress (*Batman Returns*, *Dangerous Liaisons*, *The Fabulous Baker Boys*), born Santa Ana, CA, Apr 29, 1958.
Eve Plumb, 46, actress ("The Brady Bunch," "Fudge"), born Burbank, CA, Apr 29, 1958.
Jerry Seinfeld, 50, comedian, actor ("Seinfeld"), born Brooklyn, NY, Apr 29, 1954.
Debbie Stabenow, 54, US Senator (D, Michigan), born Clare, MI, Apr 29, 1950.
Uma Thurman, 34, actress (*Henry and June*, *Pulp Fiction*), born Boston, MA, Apr 29, 1970.

April 2004

S	M	T	W	T	F	S
				1	2	3
4	5	6	7	8	9	10
11	12	13	14	15	16	17
18	19	20	21	22	23	24
25	26	27	28	29	30	

☆ Chase's 2004 Calendar of Events ☆   Apr 30

APRIL 30 — FRIDAY
Day 121 — 245 Remaining

ARBOR DAY FESTIVAL. Apr 30–May 2. Arbor Day Farm, Nebraska City, NE. To celebrate Arbor Day, the tree planters' holiday, in the hometown of J. Sterling Morton, the founder of Arbor Day. Events include more than 50 artists' and craftsmen's booths, children's environmental festival, parade; tree seedling giveaway, musicians, magicians and tree-planting demonstrations. Est attendance: 20,000. For info: Tourism and Events, 806 1st Ave, Nebraska City, NE 68410. Phone: (800) 514-9113. Fax: (402) 873-6701. E-mail: tourism@nebraskacity.com. Web: www.nebraskacity.com.

ARBOR DAY IN ARIZONA. Apr 30. The last Friday in April is proclaimed as Arbor Day in Arizona. It is not a legal holiday.

BELTANE. Apr 30. (Also called Bealtaine, May Eve, Walpurgis Night, Cyntefyn, Roodmass and Cethsamhain.) One of the "Greater Sabbats" during the Wiccan year, it celebrates the union or marriage of the Goddess and God. In Scotland Beltane was one of the quarter days or terms when rents were due and debts settled. On the eve of Beltane, two fires were built close together and cattle driven between them to ward off disease prior to putting them out to pasture for the new season. Annually, on Apr 30.

CAMBODIA INVADED BY US: ANNIVERSARY. Apr 30, 1970. President Nixon announced the US was sending troops into Cambodia in an attempt to destroy the "sanctuaries" from which men and materiel were infiltrated into South Vietnam. This sparked widespread protests on the homefront, including a march on Washington and the closure of many American colleges and universities. See also: "Kent State Students' Memorial Day: Anniversary" (May 4).

CANADA: GUELPH SPRING FESTIVAL. Apr 30–May 2 (also May 5–9 and May 14–16). Guelph, ON. Classical and contemporary music featuring outstanding musicians from across Canada and around the world. Est attendance: 5,000. For info: Guelph Spring Festival, 100 Crimea St, Unit B2, Guelph, ON, Canada N1H 2Y6. Phone: (519) 821-3210. Fax: (519) 821-5271. E-mail: info@guelphspringfestival.org. Web: www.guelphspringfestival.org.

FIRST PRESIDENTIAL TELECAST: 65th ANNIVERSARY. Apr 30, 1939. Franklin D. Roosevelt became the first president to appear on television when he was televised at the New York World's Fair. However, the appearance was only beamed to 200 TV sets in a 40-mile radius. See also: "First Regular TV Broadcasts: Anniversary" (July 1).

HAIRSTYLIST APPRECIATION DAY. Apr 30. The personalized service of hairstylists makes customers look great and feel great about themselves. Hairstyling is the art of creating a self-image to help boost self-esteem while lending an ear to customers' problems, thereby lessening their stress. For info: Anne Camilleri, 1220 Arroyo St, San Carlos, CA 94070. Phone: (650) 593-3733 or (650) 568-0565.

HARRISON, MARY SCOTT LORD DIMMICK: BIRTH ANNIVERSARY. Apr 30, 1858. Second wife of Benjamin Harrison, twenty-third president of the US, born at Honesdale, PA. Died at New York, NY, Jan 5, 1948.

INTERNATIONAL SCHOOL SPIRIT SEASON. Apr 30–Sept 30. To recognize everyone who has helped to make school spirit better and to provide time to plan improved spirit ideas for the coming school year. For info: Jim Hawkins, Chairman, Pepsters, Committee for More School Spirit, PO Box 122652, San Diego, CA 92112. Phone: (619) 280-0999.

INTERNATIONAL WALK DAYS. Apr 30 (also Dec 26). Today is the day to get primal, leave the magic carpet at home and whenever possible walk to your destination. Touted as the best exercise, walking is an undertaking that is not only aerobically correct, vital for workouts and a great method to pass the time, but it enables a person to get out and enjoy the weather and surroundings. [©1994] To alleviate the escalating costs of Eventological® Literature, a charge of $7 must be assessed to each request. Checks are to be made payable to: Adrienne Sioux Koopersmith, 1437 W Rosemont, #1W, Chicago, IL 60660-1319. Phone: (773) 743-5341. Fax: (773) 743-5395. E-mail: la_koop@yahoo.com.

ISLE OF EIGHT FLAGS SHRIMP FESTIVAL. Apr 30–May 2. Fernandina Beach, FL, on beautiful Amelia Island. Commemorates Fernandina's role as the birthplace of the modern shrimping industry. Multi-event festival includes juried fine arts and crafts show, entertainment, antiques, pirates, fun zone and food. Est attendance: 150,000. For info: Isle of Eight Flags Shrimp Festival, PO Box 6146, Fernandina Beach, FL 32035. Phone: (904) 261-3248 or toll-free (866) 4AMELIA. Web: www.shrimpfestival.com.

JOSEY'S WORLD CHAMPION JUNIOR BARREL RACE. Apr 30–May 2. Josey's Ranch, Marshall, TX. Youth barrel-racing competition. Annually, the first weekend in May. Est attendance: 4,000. For info: Patsy Dreesen, Dir of Conv and Visitor Development, Marshall Chamber of Commerce, PO Box 520, Marshall, TX 75671. Phone: (903) 935-7868. Fax: (903) 935-9982. E-mail: marshallcvd@hotmail.com. Web: www.marshalltxchamber.com.

LANDON AZALEA GARDEN FESTIVAL AND ANTIQUE SHOW. Apr 30–May 2. Bethesda, MD. Garden stroll amid 15,000 blooming azaleas. Plant sale, flower show, historic farmhouse tour, lunch, musical entertainment and tons of unique boutique shops and gift vendors. Est attendance: 30,000. For info: Landon School, 6101 Wilson Ln, Bethesda, MD 20817. Phone: (301) 320-3200. Fax: (301) 320-2787. E-mail: jeanne_hamrick@landon.net. Web: www.landon.net.

LILLY, WILLIAM: BIRTH ANNIVERSARY. Apr 30, 1602 (OS). English astrologer, author and almanac compiler, born at Diseworth, Leicestershire. His almanacs were among the most popular in Britain from 1644 until his death, June 9, 1681 (OS), at Hersham, Surrey, England.

LONG GROVE CHOCOLATE FESTIVAL. Apr 30–May 2 (tentative). Long Grove, IL. Restaurants and outdoor food booths serve up chocolate creations galore. Demonstrations by chocolate artists and chefs, contests, displays and free samples and tastings. Admission and parking free. 10 AM–6 PM. Est attendance: 30,000. For info: Long Grove Merchants Assn, Rtes 53 & 83, Long Grove, IL 60047. Phone: (847) 634-0888. Web: www.longgroveonline.com.

LOUISIANA: ADMISSION DAY: ANNIVERSARY. Apr 30. Became 18th state in 1812.

LOUISIANA PURCHASE DAY: ANNIVERSARY. Apr 30, 1803. One of the greatest real estate deals in history was completed in 1803, when more than 820,000 square miles of the Louisiana Territory were turned over to the US by France, for $15 million. This almost doubled the size of the US, extending its western border to the Rocky Mountains.

MAGIC DRAGON STREET MEET NATIONALS CAR SHOW. Apr 30–May 2. Lake Ozark, MO. 16th annual meet features more than 700 street rods, customs, trucks, street machines and motorcycles from throughout the United States. Always the first weekend in May. Est attendance: 7,000. For info:

Lake Area Chamber of Commerce, PO Box 1570, Lake Ozark, MO 65049. Phone: (800) 451-4117 or (573) 964-1008. E-mail: info@lakeareachamber.com.

MUHAMMAD ALI STRIPPED OF TITLE: ANNIVERSARY. Apr 30, 1967. Muhammad Ali was stripped of his world heavyweight boxing championship when he refused to be inducted into military service. Said Ali, "I have searched my conscience, and I find I cannot be true to my belief in my religion by accepting such a call." He had claimed exemption as a minister of the Black Muslim religion. He was convicted of violating the Selective Service Act but the Supreme Court reversed this decision in 1971.

NATIONAL ARBOR DAY. Apr 30. Since 1872, a day to honor and plant trees. Observed the last Friday in April (although some states have different dates), which is generally a good planting date throughout the country. First observance of Arbor Day was in Nebraska, Apr 10, 1872, where it is still a state holiday. Internationally it is Dec 22. For info: Natl Arbor Day Foundation, 100 Arbor Ave, Nebraska City, NE 68410. Web: www.arborday.org.

NATIONAL HAIRBALL AWARENESS DAY. Apr 30. A day to recognize hairballs in cats—the inconvenience created for owners and the discomfort suffered by our feline friends—and offer solutions to the problem while raising awareness. Annually, the last Friday in April. For info: Blake Hawley, PO Box 148, Topeka, KS 66601-0148. Phone: 785368-5614. Fax: (785) 368-5566. E-mail: blake_hawley@hillspet.com. Web: www.ScienceDiet.com.

NATIONAL HONESTY DAY (WITH HONEST ABE AWARDS). Apr 30. To celebrate honesty and those who are honest and honorable in their dealings with others. Nominations accepted for most honest people and companies. Winners to be awarded "Honest Abe" awards and given "Abies" on National Honesty Day. Also presented are dishonorable mentions for notables who have been less than honest. Annually, Apr 30. For info: M. Hirsh Goldberg, 3103 Szold Dr, Baltimore, MD 21208. Phone: (410) 486-4150.

NETHERLANDS: QUEEN'S BIRTHDAY. Apr 30. A public holiday in celebration of the birthday of former Queen Juliana and the Dutch National Day. The whole country parties as young and old participate in festivities such as markets, theater, music and games. The current monarch is Queen Beatrix.

ORGANIZATION OF AMERICAN STATES FOUNDED: ANNIVERSARY. Apr 30, 1948. This regional alliance was founded by 21 nations of the Americas at Bogota, Colombia. Its purpose is to further economic development and integration among nations of the Western hemisphere, to promote representative democracy and to help overcome poverty. The Pan-American Union, with offices at Washington, DC, serves as the General Secretariat for the OAS.

RICHMOND'S MUSHROOM FESTIVAL. Apr 30–May 1. Richmond, MO. Parade, arts and crafts, carnival, bands and stage shows. Est attendance: 5,000. For info: Exec Dir, Chamber of Commerce, 107 N Thornton, Richmond, MO 64085. Phone: (816) 776-6916. Fax: (816) 776-6917. Web: www.richmondchamber.org.

SEQUIM IRRIGATION FESTIVAL. Apr 30–May 9. Sequim, WA. Come and join the fun at this unique festival. Includes amusement rides, a parade, arts and crafts displays, entertainment, food booths and much more. Est attendance: 20,000. For info: Sequim Chamber of Commerce, Sequim Irrigation Festival, PO Box 2073, Sequim, WA 98382. Phone: (360) 683-6197. Fax: (360) 683-6349. Web: www.irrigationfestival.com.

April 2004	S	M	T	W	T	F	S
					1	2	3
	4	5	6	7	8	9	10
	11	12	13	14	15	16	17
	18	19	20	21	22	23	24
	25	26	27	28	29	30	

SMITH, MICHAEL J.: BIRTH ANNIVERSARY. Apr 30, 1945. Michael J. Smith, 40-year-old pilot of the Space Shuttle *Challenger* on Jan 28, 1986. It was to have been Commander Smith's first space flight. Born at Beaufort, NC, Smith perished with all others on board when the Space Shuttle *Challenger* exploded on Jan 28, 1986. See also: "*Challenger* Space Shuttle Explosion Anniversary" (Jan 28).

SOUTH VIETNAM FALLS TO VIETCONG: ANNIVERSARY. Apr 30, 1975. The president of South Vietnam announced the country's unconditional surrender to the Vietcong. Communist troops moved into Saigon and 1,000 Americans in the city were hastily evacuated. Thousands of South Vietnamese also tried to flee. The surrender announcement came 21 years after the 1954 Geneva agreements divided Vietnam into North and South. The last American troops had left South Vietnam in March 1973.

SPANK OUT DAY USA. Apr 30. A day on which all caretakers of children—parents, teachers and daycare workers—are asked not to use corporal punishment as discipline and to become acquainted with positive, effective disciplinary alternatives. For info: Nadine Block, EPOCH-USA, 155 W Main St, Ste 1603, Columbus, OH 43215. Phone: (614) 221-8829. E-mail: nblock@infinet.com. Web: www.stophitting.org.

SUGARLOAF CRAFTS FESTIVAL. Apr 30–May 2. Dulles Expo Center, Chantilly, VA. This show, now in its 4th year, features more than 300 nationally recognized craft designers and fine artists displaying and selling their original creations. Includes craft demonstrations, live music, specialty food, hourly gift certificate drawings and more. Est attendance: 14,500. For info: Sugarloaf Mountain Works, 200 Orchard Ridge Dr, #215, Gaithersburg, MD 20878. Phone: (800) 210-9900. Fax: (301) 253-9620. Web: www.sugarloafcrafts.com.

SWEDEN: FEAST OF VALBORG. Apr 30. An evening celebration in which Sweden "sings in the spring" by listening to traditional hymns to the spring, often around community bonfires. Also known as Walpurgis Night, the Feast of Valborg occurs annually Apr 30.

THEATER IN NORTH AMERICA FIRST PERFORMANCE: ANNIVERSARY. Apr 30, 1598. On the banks of the Rio Grande, near present day El Paso, TX, the first North American theatrical performance was acted. The play was a Spanish commedia featuring an expedition of soldiers. On July 10 of the same year, the same group produced *Moros y Los Cristianos* (*Moors and Christians*), an anonymous play.

TOAD SUCK DAZE. Apr 30–May 2. Downtown, Conway, AR. 23rd annual event features toad jumping contests, concerts, parade, street dancing, carnival, softball tournament, 5K and 10K runs, arts and crafts and more. Annually, the first weekend in May. Est attendance: 160,000. For info: Mary Margaret Satterfield, c/o Conway Chamber of Commerce, 900 Oak St, Conway, AR 72032. Phone: (501) 327-7788. Fax: (501) 327-7790. Web: www.toadsuck.org.

VIETNAM: LIBERATION DAY. Apr 30. National holiday. Commemorates the fall of Saigon to the Communists in 1975, ending the Vietnam War.

WALPURGIS NIGHT. Apr 30. The eve of May Day, which is the feast day of St. Walpurgis, the protectress against the magic arts. According to German legend, witches gather this night and celebrate their sabbath on the highest peak in the Harz Mountains. Celebrated particularly by university students in northern Europe.

WASHINGTON, GEORGE: PRESIDENTIAL INAUGURATION ANNIVERSARY. Apr 30, 1789. George Washington was inaugurated as the first president of the US under the new Constitution at New York, NY. Robert R. Livingston administered the oath of office to Washington on the balcony of Federal Hall, at the corner of Wall and Broad streets.

WILSON, ELLIS: BIRTH ANNIVERSARY. Apr 30, 1899. African American artist born at Mayfield, KY, and died at New York, NY, Jan 1, 1977. Wilson painted realistic portrayals of African Americans at work and at play. In 1944 he was awarded a Guggenheim fellowship. He visited South Carolina, painting city scenes and fishing towns. In the 1950s, Wilson took a revelatory trip to Haiti which changed the way he painted. Unable to note any facial features on the Haitians he painted from a distance, Wilson began painting flat, stylized silhouettes. *Haitian Funeral Procession* remains Wilson's most popular and accessible painting.

BIRTHDAYS TODAY

Jane Campion, 50, film director (*The Piano*), born Wellington, New Zealand, Apr 30, 1954.

Jill Clayburgh, 60, actress (*Fools Rush In, Luna*), born New York, NY, Apr 30, 1944.

Gary Collins, 66, actor, talk-show host, born Boston, MA, Apr 30, 1938.

Kirsten Dunst, 22, actress (*Spider-Man, Little Women, Interview With the Vampire*), born Point Pleasant, NJ, Apr 30, 1982.

Johnny Galecki, 29, actor ("Roseanne," *Suicide Kings*), born Bree, Belgium, Apr 30, 1975.

Perry King, 56, actor (*Slaughterhouse Five, The Lords of Flatbush, Switch*), born Alliance, OH, Apr 30, 1948.

Cloris Leachman, 74, actress (Oscar for *The Last Picture Show*; "Phyllis"), born Des Moines, IA, Apr 30, 1930.

Willie Nelson, 71, singer ("Always on My Mind," "On the Road Again"); actor (*Honeysuckle Rose, The Electric Horseman*), born Abbott, TX, Apr 30, 1933.

Isiah Thomas, 43, Hall of Fame basketball player, basketball coach, born Chicago, IL, Apr 30, 1961.

Burt Young, 64, writer, actor (*Chinatown, Rocky, Once Upon a Time in America*), born New York, NY, Apr 30, 1940.

May 1 ☆ *Chase's 2004 Calendar of Events* ☆

Maye.

MAY 1 — SATURDAY
Day 122 — 244 Remaining

ADDISON, JOSEPH: BIRTH ANNIVERSARY. May 1, 1672 (OS). English essayist born at Milston, Wiltshire, England. Died at London, June 17, 1719 (OS). "We are," he wrote in *The Spectator*, "always doing something for Posterity, but I would fain see Posterity do something for us."

AMTRAK: ANNIVERSARY. May 1, 1971. Amtrak, the national rail service which combined the operations of 18 passenger railroads, went into service.

APPLE BLOSSOM FESTIVAL. May 1–2. Gettysburg, PA. An annual event held the first weekend in May at the South Mountain Fairgrounds. Est attendance: 25,000. For info: Gettysburg CVB, PO Box 4117, Gettysburg, PA 17325. Phone: (717) 334-6274. Fax: (717) 334-1166. E-mail: gettysburgcvb@dejazzd.com. Web: www.gettysburgcvb.org.

★ **ASIAN PACIFIC AMERICAN HERITAGE MONTH.** May 1–31. Presidential Proclamation issued honoring Asian Pacific Americans each year since 1979. Public Law 102-450 of Oct 28, 1992, designated the observance for the month of May each year.

BARK IN THE PARK. May 1. Lincoln Park, Chicago, IL. In recognition of Be Kind to Animals Week, thousands of paws and feet will hit the ground walking for this 5K event. Entrance fee. Est attendance: 3,500. For info: The Anti-Cruelty Society, 157 W Grand Ave, Chicago, IL 60610. Phone: (312) 329-8726. E-mail: info@anticruelty.org. Web: www.barkinthepark.org.

BELGIUM: PLAY OF SAINT EVERMAAR. May 1. Annual performance (for more than 1,000 years) of a mystery play, in its original form, by the village inhabitants.

BETTER HEARING AND SPEECH MONTH. May 1–31. A nationwide public information campaign held each May to inform the 41 million Americans with hearing and speech problems that help is available. Annually, the month of May. For info: American Speech–Language–Hearing Assn, 10801 Rockville Pike, Rockville, MD 20852-3279. Phone: (301) 897-5700. Web: www.professional.asha.org.

BIG TEN WOMEN'S ROWING CHAMPIONSHIP. May 1. University of Iowa, Iowa City, IA. For info: Sue Lister, Assoc Commissioner, Big Ten Conference, 1500 W Higgins Rd, Park Ridge, IL 60068-6300. Phone: (847) 696-1010. Fax: (847) 696-1150. Web: www.bigten.org.

May 2004

S	M	T	W	T	F	S
						1
2	3	4	5	6	7	8
9	10	11	12	13	14	15
16	17	18	19	20	21	22
23	24	25	26	27	28	29
30	31					

BORNEO RHINO CHALLENGE. May 1–14. Borneo, Malaysia. Fundraising event to protect the Sumatran rhino. Biathlon consisting of a mountain trek and biking in Borneo. For info: Maggie Heydt, SOS Rhino, 680 N Lake Shore Dr, Ste 807, Chicago, IL 60611. Phone: (312) 222-0440. Fax: (312) 222-0990. E-mail: maggie@sosrhino.org. Web: www.sosrhino.org.

BREAD PUDDING RECIPE EXCHANGE. May 1–7. A week dedicated to the exchange of creative bread pudding recipes. For sample recipes send SASE. For info: Bread Pudding Update, PO Box 416, Denver, CO 80201. Phone: (303) 575-5676. E-mail: mail@breadpudding.net. Web: www.breadpudding.net.

***CITIZEN KANE* PREMIERE: ANNIVERSARY.** May 1, 1941. Orson Welles' directorial masterpiece premiered at New York City's RKO Palace. The premiere had been delayed almost three months due to studio jitters about what media magnate William Randolph Hearst's reaction would be—since the film was a thinly disguised version of his life. The film's multiple points of view, deep focus photography and witty script made it a favorite with critics at the time: John O'Hara in *Newsweek* said, "[Y]our faithful bystander reports that he has just seen a picture which he thinks must be the best picture he ever saw. . . ." Nominated for nine Academy Awards, *Citizen Kane* won for best original screenplay by Herman J. Mankiewicz and Welles. The film did not perform well commercially (due in part to Hearst's influence), but is now regarded as the greatest American film.

CLAM CHOWDER FESTIVAL, SPRING FLOWER & ART SHOW. May 1–2. Event Center on the Beach, Gold Beach, OR. The Curry County Historical Society, Innominata Garden Club and Curry Arts Association put together a weekend of food, fun, flowers and fine art. Curry Animal Shelter will be sponsoring the Clam Chowder Feed and also an auction on Sunday. Est attendance: 1,000. For info: Gold Beach Chamber of Commerce, 29279 Ellensburg Ave, #3, Gold Beach, OR 97444. Phone: (800) 525-2334. Fax: (541) 247-0188. E-mail: gbchamber@wave.net. Web: www.goldbeachchamber.com.

CLARK, MARK: BIRTH ANNIVERSARY. May 1, 1896. US general who served in both World Wars, Mark Clark was born at Madison Barracks, NY. In November 1942, he commanded the US forces taking part in the invasion of North Africa, and in January 1943, he became commander of the US Fifth Army, which invaded Italy in September 1943, taking Rome in June of 1944. After the Germans capitulated in Italy, Clark was appointed commander of US occupation forces in Austria. He died at Charleston, SC, Apr 17, 1984.

CLEAN AIR MONTH. May 1–31. The American Lung Association releases its annual air quality report, "State of the Air," on May 1. And during this month, local Lung Associations focus on other clean air issues, programs and events. For info: American Lung Assn, 1740 Broadway, New York, NY 10019. Phone: (800) LUNG-USA. E-mail: info@lungusa.org. Web: www.lungusa.org.

COLUMBIAN EXPOSITION OPENING: ANNIVERSARY. May 1, 1893. At 12:08 PM President Grover Cleveland, in the presence of nearly a quarter of a million people, placed his finger on a golden key opening the Columbian Exposition at Chicago, IL. Amid the unfurling of thousands of flags, sounding of trumpets and booming of cannons, the key activated an electromagnetic valve, steam rushed into great cylinders and the immense pump began its enormous burden of pumping 15,000,000 gallons of water a day to supply the 685-acre fair and its visitors with an ample water supply.

COMMUNITYWIDE GARAGE SALE. May 1. Elgin, TX. Bargains abound in Elgin. More than 100 garage sales held on the same day. Downtown businesses have sidewalk sales. Visitors and locals can seek out treasures in an historic setting. Annually, the first Saturday in May. Est attendance: 3,000. For info: Sharon McCall, 1462 Old Lytton Springs Rd, Lockhart, TX 78644. Phone: (512) 263-2512. E-mail: newcovenantpc@lycos.com.

CONNECTICUT TEEN DAY. May 1. An annual event, proclaimed by the Connecticut State Legislature in 1999, to celebrate the lives of all teenagers, to make them feel special and

☆ Chase's 2004 Calendar of Events ☆ May 1

appreciated. It provides any community with the opportunity to reach out and support their teenagers without comparisons. Est attendance: 800. For info on starting a Teen Day celebration in your town, contact: Veronica Diaz Esposito, Founder. E-mail: teendayismay1@yahoo.com or teendaymay1@hotmail.com.

COTTON PICKIN' FAIR. May 1–2 (also Oct 2–3). Gay, GA. At the old cotton gin complex, this award-winning festival features 300 exhibitors of antiques and arts and crafts, ongoing entertainment, great country cooking, children's activities and demonstrations by craftspeople. Biannually, the first weekend of May and October. Est attendance: 30,000. For info: Cotton Pickin' Fair, PO Box 1, Gay, GA 30218. Phone: (706) 538-6814. Web: www.cpfair.com.

CREATIVE BEGINNINGS MONTH. May 1–31. How are you creative? Have you tapped into your full potential? Enjoy the budding month of May while discovering something new about yourself. Enroll in a course, write a poem, plant a garden, coordinate a social event. While developing your gifts, encourage others to also cultivate their own creative beginnings. For info: Christina Bergenholtz, PO Box 301, Grafton, MA 01519. Phone: (508) 839-5139. Fax: (508) 887-9556. E-mail: chrismhb@aol.com.

DENMARK: TIVOLI GARDENS SEASON. May 1–Sept 19. Copenhagen. World famous for its variety of entertainment, symphony concerts, pantomime and ballet. Beautiful flower arrangements and excellent restaurants. Traditional season: May 1 until the third Sunday in September.

EAT DESSERT FIRST MONTH. May 1–31. Forget what your mother told you about eating your dinner before you eat dessert. In May each year, Rowena's, Inc, of Norfolk, VA, encourages you to eat dessert first and enjoy life to its fullest. Life is meant to be lived with gusto. Enjoy! For info: Cameron Foster, Rowena's, Inc, 758 W 22nd St, Norfolk, VA 23517. Phone: (757) 627-8699. Fax: (757) 627-1505. E-mail: cameron@rowenas.com. Web: www.rowenas.com.

FAMILY SUPPORT MONTH. May 1–31 (kicks off May 3). The purpose of this annual observance is to support families with children during both divorce and after, along with separation and custody issues. Promotes respect for mother/child relationships. Projects include lobbying for law changes regarding divorce/custody. The focus for 2004 is "Taking Time for Family." For info or to buy a parent resource guide: Children Hurt in Legal Disputes (CHILD), 1939 Waukegan Rd, Ste LL2, Glenview, IL 60025. Phone: (847) 998-9950. Fax: (847) 998-9945. E-mail: proquest2020@aol.com.

FAMILY WELLNESS MONTH. May 1–31. Spend more time with family and appreciate those closest to you. Hold a family meeting and resolve differences and disputes. Set family goals, and share dreams. Call up estranged family and reunite. Remember that your family members are just human, not superhuman, and tell your family members that you love them. For info: Angela Brown, Words of Wellness, PO Box 49266, Charlotte, NC 28277. Phone: (704) 289-2900. Fax: (704) 845-3060. E-mail: Angela@WordsofWellness.com. Web: www.WordsofWellness.com.

FIBROMYALGIA EDUCATION AND AWARENESS MONTH. May 1–31. To promote education and awareness of the dangers of fibromyalgia which is also known as the fibromyalgia syndrome (FSM), fibrositis or chronic muscle pain syndrome. Fibromyalgia affects more than 10 million American women. Kit of materials available for $15. For info: PPSI, c/o Fibromyalgia Council of America, 101 Lucas Valley Rd, San Rafael, CA 94903. Phone: (415) 479-8628. Fax: (415) 479-8608. E-mail: ppsi@aol.com. Web: www.ppsinc.org.

FIRST SKYSCRAPER: ANNIVERSARY. May 1, 1884. Construction was begun on the Home Insurance Company building on this date in Chicago. The 10-story building was completed in 1885. Designed by William Le Baron Jenney, it had a steel frame which carried the weight of the building. The walls provided no support but hung like curtains on the metal frame. This method of construction revolutionized American architecture and allowed architects to build taller and taller buildings. The Home Insurance Building was demolished in 1931.

FISHING CONTEST. May 1. Lake Shenandoah County Park, Lakewood, NJ. Catch the longest fish of a specific species. Novice or expert. Prizes awarded. Bait and Tackle Shop on premises. Picnic area. Rain or shine. Children $1, Adults $3. Est attendance: 500. For info: Mickey Coen, Coord, Wells Mills County Park, 905 Wells Mills Rd, Waretown, NJ 08758. Phone: (609) 971-3085. Fax: (609) 971-9540. Web: www.co.ocean.nj.us/parks/default.htm.

FREEDOM SHRINE MONTH. May 1–31. The Freedom Shrine is an exclusive program of the National Exchange Club, est 1911. It is a collection of 30 original historic documents photographically reproduced and attractively displayed in thousands of locations across the nation. The purpose of the Freedom Shrine is to remind all Americans that the freedoms, which they enjoy today, are gifts from the past—forged from idealism, determination and the sacrifice of the many courageous men and women who preceded us. It also serves to remind us that so precious a gift as freedom must be continually guarded and protected. For info: The Natl Exchange Club, 3050 Central Ave, Toledo, OH 43606-1700. Phone: (800) 924-2643. E-mail: nechq@aol.com. Web: www.nationalexchangeclub.com.

FREQUENT FLYER PROGRAM DEBUTS: ANNIVERSARY. May 1, 1981. American Airlines began the first frequent flyer program on this date. Now most airlines offer a frequent flyer program but American is still the industry leader with 45 million members. Today 40 percent of all miles are earned on the ground with affiliated businesses that pay the airlines for the miles, such as hotels, car rental companies, credit card companies, phone companies and retailers.

GALVESTON HISTORIC HOMES TOUR. May 1–2 (also May 8–9). Galveston Island, TX. Discover Galveston Island's great treasures of Victorian and post-Victorian architecture as privately owned homes are open to the public for tours. Annually, the first two full weekends in May. For info: Galveston Historical Foundation, 502 20th St, Galveston, TX 77550. Phone: (409) 765-7834. Fax: (409) 765-7851. Web: www.galvestonhistory.org.

GET CAUGHT READING MONTH. May 1–31. Celebrities appear in ads appealing to people of all ages to remind them of the joys of reading. Events will be held throughout the country to celebrate reading. For info: Assn of American Publishers, 71 Fifth Ave, New York, NY 10003. Phone: (212) 255-0200. Web: www.publishers.org or www.getcaughtreading.org.

GREAT BRITAIN FORMED: ANNIVERSARY. May 1, 1707 (OS). A union between England and Scotland resulted in the formation of Great Britain. (Wales had been part of England since the 1500s.) Today's United Kingdom consists of Great Britain and Northern Ireland.

HAITIAN HERITAGE MONTH. May 1–31. Boston, MA. A series of events are organized throughout the month of May in the Boston Haitian American community featuring exhibits, flag raisings, concerts, games, parades and presentations. The events are organized to honor Haitian General Toussaint Louverture, to

May 1 ☆ *Chase's 2004 Calendar of Events* ☆

remember the consensus reached by black and mulatto officers to fight for Haitian independence in 1803 and to celebrate the Haitian flag created that same year. The flag-raising ceremony will take place on May 14, and the Haitian-American Unity Day Parade will take place on May 16. For info: Haitian-Americans United, Inc, 10 Fairway St, PO Box 260440, Mattapan, MA 02126. Phone: (617) 298-2976. E-mail: unity@hauinc.org. Web: www.hauinc.org.

HEALTHY VISION MONTH. May 1–31. Although it is believed that half of all blindness can be prevented, the number of people in the United States who suffer from vision loss continues to increase. Healthy Vision Month informs the public that preventative eye care is important because eye conditions, diseases and injuries that can rob a person's vision can strike at any time in life, from newborn to old age. For info: American Academy of Ophthalmology, PO Box 7424, San Francisco, CA 9120-7424. Phone: (415) 561-8525. Fax: (415) 561-8533. E-mail: eyemd@aao.org. Web: www.medem.com/eyemd.

HOLLAND TULIP TIME FESTIVAL. May 1–8. Holland, MI. To celebrate the tulip blooms and to preserve the Dutch cultural heritage in the city of Holland. Est attendance: 1,000,000. For info: Holland Tulip Time Festival, Inc, 171 Lincoln Ave, Holland, MI 49423. Phone: (616) 396-4221 or (800) 822-2770. Fax: (616) 396-4545. E-mail: tulip@tuliptime.org. Web: www.tuliptime.org.

HUNTINGTON'S DISEASE AWARENESS MONTH. May 1–31. For info: Huntington's Disease Society of America, 158 W 29th St, 7th Fl, New York, NY 10001-5300. Phone: (800) 345-4372 or (212) 242-1968. Web: www.hdsa.org.

INTERNATIONAL BUSINESS IMAGE IMPROVEMENT MONTH. May 1–31. The image of your business sets the tone to how successful your company will be. Just as we judge others within the first few seconds of meeting, we do the same for a business. Receive more information on how to improve your business image and a free online business card evaluation. For info: Debbie Allen, Pres, Allen & Associates Consulting, Inc, PO Box 27946, Scottsdale, AZ 85255-0149. Phone: (800) 359-4544. Fax: (480) 634-7692. E-mail: debbie@debbieallen.com. Web: www.debbieallen.com.

INTERNATIONAL DENTAL AWARENESS MONTH. May 1–31. Smiling can change your life, which is why the American Academy of Cosmetic Dentistry® (AACD) reminds you to smile all throughout International Dental Awareness Month. Ninety-two percent of Americans say an attractive smile is an important social asset. It has the power to give you more confidence in your job, in your personal relationships, and in virtually everything you do. Annually, every May. For info: American Academy of Cosmetic Dentistry, 5401 World Dairy Drive, Madison, WI 53718. Phone: (608) 222-8583 or (800) 543-9220. Fax: (608) 222-9540. E-mail: pr@aacd.com. Web: www.aacd.com.

INTERNATIONAL INTERNAL AUDIT AWARENESS MONTH. May 1–31. This celebration promotes awareness of the internal audit process and its important role in organizational effectiveness and efficiency, internal control, risk management and corporate governance. For info: The Institute of Internal Auditors (IIA), Global Headquarters, 247 Maitland Ave, Altamonte Springs, FL 32701. Phone: (407) 937-1245. E-mail: tharris@theiia.org. Web: www.theiia.org.

INTERNATIONAL WILDLIFE FILM FESTIVAL. May 1–8. Missoula, MT. 27th annual juried international wildlife film festival. This eight-day gathering will involve the world's top wildlife filmmakers and producers sharing their ideas, techniques and products to interested members of the public and filmmaking profession. The festival provides films for viewing by people of all ages with special sections for children. Community celebrations such as a wildlife parade, workshops and panel discussions are also part of this annual festival. Festival venues are located at various locations in downtown Missoula. Est attendance: 12,000. For info: Exec Dir, Intl Wildlife Film Festival, 718 S Higgins, Missoula, MT 59801. Phone: (406) 728-9380. Fax: (406) 728-2881. E-mail: iwff@wildlifefilms.org. Web: www.wildlifefilms.org.

ITALY: FESTIVAL OF SAINT EFISIO. May 1–4. Cagliari. Said to be one of the biggest and most colorful processions in the world. Several thousand pilgrims on foot, in carts and on horseback wearing costumes dating from the 17th century accompany the statue of the saint through the streets.

JOIN HANDS DAY. May 1. To bring youth and adults together to improve their own communities. Sponsored by America's fraternal benefit societies and the Points of Light Foundation. Annually, the first Saturday in May. For info: Points of Light Foundation, 1400 I St NW, Ste 800, Washington, DC 20005. Phone: (202) 729-8168. Fax: (202) 729-8103. Web: www.joinhandsday.org.

JONES, MARY HARRIS (MOTHER JONES): BIRTH ANNIVERSARY. May 1, 1830. Irish-born American labor leader. After the death of her husband and four children (during the Memphis yellow fever epidemic of 1867) and loss of her belongings in the Chicago Fire in 1871, Jones devoted her energies and her life to organizing and advancing the cause of labor. It seemed she was present wherever there were labor troubles. She gave her last speech on her 100th birthday. Born at Cork, Ireland, she died Nov 30, 1930, at Silver Spring, MD.

KECHI SPRING "OUTDOOR" ANTIQUE SWAP MEET AND FLEA MARKET. May 1–2. Kechi, KS. Antique dealers come to Kechi and display their goods in between our current antique and specialty shops. Kechi is the official "Antique Capital of Kansas." Enjoy shopping in Kechi's small-town atmosphere. Hours 8 AM to 5 PM. Free admission. Est attendance: 1,200. For info: Kechi KS Chamber of Commerce, Kechi, KS 67067-8710. Phone: (316) 744-1337. For vendor booths call (316) 744-8710. E-mail: kechichamber@kechikscoc.com. Web: www.kechikscoc.com.

KENTUCKY DERBY. May 1. Churchill Downs, Louisville, KY. The running of America's premier thoroughbred horse race, inaugurated in 1875. First jewel in the "Triple Crown," traditionally followed by the Preakness (the second Saturday after Derby) and the Belmont Stakes (the fifth Saturday after Derby). Annually, the first Saturday in May. Est attendance: 140,000. For info: Churchill Downs, 700 Central Ave, Louisville, KY 40208. Phone: (502) 636-4400. Web: kentuckyderby.com.

★**LAW DAY, USA.** May 1. Presidential Proclamation issued each year for May 1 since 1958 at request. (PL87–20 of Apr 7, 1961.)

LAW ENFORCEMENT APPRECIATION MONTH IN FLORIDA. May 1–31. Law Enforcement Appreciation Day is May 15 in Florida, a ceremonial day.

LEI DAY. May 1. Hawaii. On this special day—the Hawaiian version of May Day—leis are made, worn, given, displayed and entered in lei-making contests. One of the most popular Lei Day celebrations takes place at Honolulu at Kapiolani Park at Waikiki. Includes the state's largest lei contest, the crowning of the Lei Day Queen, Hawaiian music, hula and flowers galore.

May 2004

S	M	T	W	T	F	S
						1
2	3	4	5	6	7	8
9	10	11	12	13	14	15
16	17	18	19	20	21	22
23	24	25	26	27	28	29
30	31					

☆ Chase's 2004 Calendar of Events ☆   May 1

LIGHT THE NIGHT FOR SIGHT™. May 1–July 31. Celebrate sight and safety with this national walkathon organized to raise awareness of consumer fireworks dangers and to celebrate the gift of sight. Safe celebrations will be promoted. For info: Prevent Blindness America®, 500 E Remington Rd, Schaumburg, IL 60173. Phone: (800) 331-2020. Fax: (847) 843-8458. Web: www.preventblindness.org.

LINDA DOMINIQUE GROSVENOR NATIONAL READ FOR LEISURE WEEK. May 1–7. Started by the author to encourage leisurely reading among high school and college students, and adults who are not members of book clubs. During the first week of May, teachers and librarians recommend her work, and the author donates copies of her books to libraries, schools and senior citizen centers. She also makes appearances and schedules interviews to promote reading and starting your own book club. Annually, first seven days in May. For info: Linda Dominique Grosvenor, PO Box 2443, Durham, NC 27715. E-mail: dom@lindadominiquegrosvenor.com. Web: www.lindadominiquegrosvenor.com.

LOW COUNTRY SHRIMP FESTIVAL. May 1. McClellanville, SC. Seafood, arts, crafts, civic display, entertainment and Blessing of the Fleet. Annually, the first Saturday in May. Est attendance: 8,000. For info: The Archibald Rutledge Academy, 1011 Old Cemetery Rd, McClellanville, SC 29458. Phone: (843) 887-3323.

★**LOYALTY DAY.** May 1. Presidential Proclamation issued annually for May 1 since 1959 at request. (PL85–529 of July 18, 1958.) Note that an earlier proclamation was issued in 1955.

LUCY STONE MARRIED: ANNIVERSARY. May 1, 1855. When nationally known public speaker and feminist Lucy Stone married Henry Blackwell, a marriage contract written by the bride and groom was read at the wedding that disavowed the gross inequity married women suffered under American law, and the word "obey" was omitted from their marriage vows. A year after the ceremony the bride further shocked society by taking back her maiden name, which she kept for the rest of her life.

MAINE STATE PARADE. May 1. Lewiston, ME. Maine's largest parade with floats, food, music and fun. Airs the next day on WCSH-TV (Ch 6) and WLBZ-TV (Ch 2) statewide. Annually, the first Saturday in May. Est attendance: 30,000. For info: WCSH-TV, One Congress Square, Portland, ME 04101. Phone: (207) 828-6666. Fax: (207) 828-6620. E-mail: communityrelations@wcsh6.com. Web: www.wcsh6.com.

MARSHALL ISLANDS, REPUBLIC OF THE: CONSTITUTION DAY. May 1. National holiday.

MARYLAND SHEEP AND WOOL FESTIVAL. May 1–2. Howard County Fairgrounds, West Friendship, MD. Sheep and Fleece show plus more than 200 craftspeople, shearing, sheepdog herding and cooking demonstrations. Free admission and parking. Annually, the first full weekend in May. Est attendance: 35,000. For info: Maryland Sheep & Wool Festival, PO Box 99, Glenwood, MD 21738. Phone: (410) 531-3647. E-mail: info@sheepandwool.org. Web: www.sheepandwoolfestival.org.

MAY DAY. May 1. The first day of May has been observed as a holiday since ancient times. Spring festivals, maypoles and maying are still common, but the political importance of May Day has grown since the 1880s, when it became a workers' day in the US. Now widely observed in countries as a workers' holiday or as Labor Day. (The US and Canada observe Labor Day in September.) In most European countries, when May Day falls on Saturday or Sunday, the Monday following is observed as a holiday, with bank and store closings, parades and other festivities.

MAY IN MONTCLAIR. May 1–31. Montclair Township, NJ. 26th annual month-long festival celebrating the wealth of cultural, artistic, historic and recreational opportunities in Montclair for residents, merchants and visitors. Est attendance: 4,000. For info: Jean H. Kidd, Chair, May in Montclair, 91 Central Ave, Montclair, NJ 07042. Phone: (973) 746-3762.

MEDICAL ORPHANS MONTH. May 1–31. A month dedicated to the awareness of medical orphans—rare disorders/diseases. Includes "Adopt a Medical Orphan" in AmericaCares AmericaCan Project; "Unsolved Cases" spotlighting real stories; publishing of "Hope and Healing" from submissions sent in by the public; and encourages and sponsors internship/study/volunteer programs for credit or noncredit. For info: The ForGoodnessSake! Center, 427 E 7th St, Michigan City, IN 46360. E-mail: ForGood@adsnet.com.

MELANOMA/SKIN CANCER DETECTION AND PREVENTION MONTH. May 1–31. For info: American Academy of Dermatology, 930 E Woodfield Rd, Schaumburg, IL 60173. Phone: (847) 330-0230 or (888) 462-DERM. Web: www.aad.org.

MEMPHIS IN MAY INTERNATIONAL FESTIVAL. May 1–31. Memphis, TN. North America's largest month-long international festival, celebrating the culture of a different country each year, as well as the city's own unique indigenous culture and heritage. Events include International Week, Beale Street Musical Festival, the World Championship Barbeque Cooking Contest and more. For info: Memphis in May Intl Festival, 245 Wagner Pl, Ste 220, Memphis, TN 38103. Phone: (901) 525-4611. Web: www.MemphisinMay.org.

MORE THAN JUST A PRETTY FACE MONTH. May 1–31. Great skin ranges from the scalp down to the soles of the feet. May is a perfect time to begin to prepare skin for the summer. A sun protection cream with an SPF of 15 or higher is to be applied all over the skin daily. Did you know that on average we receive approximately 24 hours a week of accidental sun? This is gathered via windshields, office windows, walking to and from the office or store. For tips on "saving face" and great skin ideas, ask for our free booklet. Annually, the month of May. For info: Susie Galvez, Beauty at Your Fingertips, 8502 Patterson Ave, Richmond, VA 23229. Phone: (804) 740-5665. Fax: (804) 741-7203. Web: www.beautyatyourfingertips.com.

MOTHER GOOSE DAY. May 1. To re-appreciate the old nursery rhymes. Motto: "Either alone or in sharing, read childhood nursery favorites and feel the warmth of Mother Goose's embrace." Website has ideas for celebrating, including recipes. Annually, May 1. For info: Gloria T. Delamar, Founder, Mother Goose Society. E-mail: mother.goose.society@juno.com. Web: www.delamar.org/mothergoosesociety.

MOTORCYCLE SAFETY MONTH. May 1–31. This month is dedicated to encouraging safe motorcycle riding practices. Learn safe riding practices through state and local motorcycle safety courses and continue improving skills through advanced riding courses. Set a safe environment this month to prepare for a safe riding season. For info: Sylvia Henderson, Springboard Training, 18005 Lafayette Dr, Ste B, Olney, MD 20832. Phone: (301) 646-1668. Fax: (301) 856-8000. E-mail: admin@v-twinvalues.com. Web: www.v-twinvalues.com.

NATIONAL ALLERGY/ASTHMA AWARENESS MONTH. May 1–31. Kit of materials available for $15 from this nonprofit organization. For info: Frederick S. Mayer, Pres, Pharmacist Planning Services, Inc, c/o Allergy Council of America (ACA), 101 Lucas Valley Rd, #210, San Rafael, CA 94903. Phone: (415) 479-8628. Fax: (415) 479-8608. E-mail: ppsi@aol.com. Web: www.ppsinc.org.

May 1 ☆ Chase's 2004 Calendar of Events ☆

NATIONAL ARTHRITIS MONTH. May 1–31. Increases awareness of the more than 100 forms of arthritis and related diseases and increases support for the 70 million Americans with arthritis. For info: Arthritis Foundation, 1330 W Peachtree St NW, Atlanta, GA 30309. Phone: (800) 283-7800. Fax: (404) 872-8694. Web: www.arthritis.org.

NATIONAL BARBECUE MONTH. May 1–31. To encourage people to start enjoying barbecuing early in the season when Daylight Saving Time lengthens the day. Annually, the month of May. Sponsor: Hearth, Patio & Barbecue Association. For info: NBM, DHM Group, Inc, 9 Professional Circle, Ste 101, Colts Neck, NJ 07722. Fax: (732) 866-4466.

NATIONAL BIKE MONTH. May 1–31. 48th annual celebration of bicycling for fun, fitness and transportation. Local activities sponsored by bicycling organizations, environmental groups, PTAs, police departments, health organizations and civic groups. About five million participants nationwide. Annually, the month of May. For info: Patrick McCormick, Communications Dir, League of American Bicyclists, 1612 K St, Ste 800, Washington, DC 20006. Phone: (202) 822-1333. Fax: (202) 822-1334. E-mail: bikeleague@bikeleague.org. Web: www.bikeleague.org.

NATIONAL BOOK MONTH. May 1–31. When the world demands more and more of our time, National Book Month invites everyone in America to take time out to treat themselves to a unique pleasure: reading a good book. Readers participate in National Book Month annually through literary events held at schools, bookstores, libraries, community centers and arts organizations. The organization also sponsors the annual National Book Awards. For info: Natl Book Foundation, 95 Madison Ave, Ste 709, New York, NY 10016. Phone: (212) 685-0261. Fax: (212) 235-6570. E-mail: nationalbook@nationalbook.org. Web: www.nationalbook.org.

NATIONAL CORRECT POSTURE MONTH. May 1–31. For info: American Chiropractic Assn, 1701 Clarendon Blvd, Arlington, VA 22209. Phone: (800) 986-4636. E-mail: memberinfo@amerchiro.org. Web: www.acatoday.com.

NATIONAL EGG MONTH. May 1–31. Dedicated to the versatility, convenience, economy and good nutrition of "The incredible edible egg™." Annually, the month of May. For info: Linda Braun, Consumer Serv Dir, American Egg Board, 1460 Renaissance Dr, Park Ridge, IL 60068. Web: www.aeb.org.

NATIONAL GARAGE SALE MONTH. May 1–31. Reap the benefits of living a more simplified, uncluttered life. Devote this month to freeing your household of unwanted possessions by hosting a garage sale. Increase your awareness of successful garage sale hosting techniques and have an outstanding sale! For info: Clutter MD. Phone: (260) 403-2226. Web: www.cluttermd.com.

NATIONAL GOOD CAR-KEEPING MONTH. May 1–31. To promote increased safety and value through good car maintenance. For info: Sander Allen, Good Car-Keeping Institute, 990 N Lake Shore Dr, Ste 11-A, Chicago, IL 60611.

NATIONAL HAMBURGER MONTH. May 1–31. Sponsored by White Castle, the original fast-food hamburger chain (founded in 1921), to pay tribute to one of America's favorite foods. With or without condiments, on or off a bun or bread, hamburgers have grown in popularity since the early 1920s and are now an American meal mainstay. For info: White Castle Management Co, Marketing Dept, 555 W Goodale St, Columbus, OH 43215-1171. Phone: (614) 228-5781. Fax: (614) 228-8841. Web: www.whitecastle.com.

	S	M	T	W	T	F	S
May 2004							1
	2	3	4	5	6	7	8
	9	10	11	12	13	14	15
	16	17	18	19	20	21	22
	23	24	25	26	27	28	29
	30	31					

NATIONAL HEPATITIS AWARENESS MONTH. May 1–31. For info: Hepatitis Foundation Intl, 504 Blick Dr, Silver Spring, MD 20904. Phone: (800) 891-0707. E-mail: HFI@comcast.net. Web: www.HepatitisFoundation.org.

NATIONAL MENTAL HEALTH MONTH. May 1–31. For info: Natl Mental Health Assn, 2001 Beauregard St, 12th Floor, Alexandria, VA 22311. Phone: (800) 969-NMHA or (703) 684-7722. E-mail: infoctr@nmha.org. Web: www.nmha.org.

NATIONAL MOVING MONTH. May 1–31. Recognizing America's mobile roots and kicking off the busiest moving season of the year. Each year more than 21 million Americans move between Memorial Day and Labor Day, with the average American moving every seven years. During this month moving experts will be educating Americans on how to plan a successful move, to pack efficiently and handle the uncertainties and questions that moving children may have. For info: Allied Van Lines, PO Box 9569, Downers Grove, IL 60515. Phone: (630) 932-4242. Fax: (630) 932-1418. Web: www.alliedvan.com.

NATIONAL NEUROFIBROMATOSIS AWARENESS MONTH. May 1–31. For info: John Radziejewski, Dir of Communications, Natl Neurofibromatosis Foundation, 95 Pine St, 16th Fl, New York, NY 10005. Phone: (800) 323-7938 or (212) 344-6633. E-mail: nnff@nf.org. Web: www.nf.org.

★**NATIONAL OLDER AMERICANS MONTH.** May 1–31. Presidential Proclamation; from 1963 through 1973 this was called "Senior Citizens Month." In May 1974 it became Older Americans Month. In 1980 the title included Senior Citizens Day, which was observed May 8, 1980. Issued annually since 1963.

NATIONAL OSTEOPOROSIS AWARENESS MONTH. May 1–31. Osteoporosis is not a natural part of aging but is a preventable disease for most people. For info: Natl Osteoporosis Foundation, 1232 22nd St NW, Washington, DC 20037. Phone: (202) 223-2226. Fax: (202) 223-2237. E-mail: nofmail@nof.org. Web: www.nof.org.

NATIONAL PEACE OF MIND WEEK. May 1–7. Achieving peace of mind means gaining "The Inside Advantage"—an acceptance of what is, a realization that we can act to create a better world for ourselves and those around us, and having faith that the future will bring the highest good for all concerned. It is knowing that there is meaning and purpose in our lives, and believing that each of us is truly extraordinary. For info: Cathy W. Lauro. Phone: (800) 215-3644. E-mail: mind@CWLauro.com. Web: www.CWLauro.com.

NATIONAL PHYSICAL FITNESS AND SPORTS MONTH. May 1–31. Encourages individuals and organizations to promote fitness activities and programs. Popularly known as "May Month," it was established by the President's Council on Physical Fitness and Sports in 1983. For info: President's Council on Physical Fitness and Sports, HHH Building, 200 Independence Ave SW, Room 738H, Washington, DC 20201-0004. Phone: (202) 690-9000. Fax: (202) 690-5211. Web: www.fitness.gov or www.presidentschallenge.org.

NATIONAL SAFE KIDS WEEK. May 1–8. Mission is to prevent the number one killer of children—unintentional injury. For info: National SAFE KIDS Campaign, 1301 Pennsylvania Ave NW, Ste 1000, Washington, DC 20004. Phone: (202) 662-0600. Web: www.safekids.org.

☆ Chase's 2004 Calendar of Events ☆   May 1

NATIONAL SALSA MONTH. May 1–31. Recognizing salsa as America's favorite way to add flavor to all kinds of food, such as eggs, burgers, chicken, tacos, chips, potatoes, rice and much more. Celebrates more than 50 years of picante sauce, a salsa created in 1947, and celebrates Cinco de Mayo, a major Mexican holiday now recognized across North America. For info: Pace Foods, c/o Dublin & Associates, 1017 N Main, Ste 201, San Antonio, TX 78212. Phone: (210) 227-0221. Web: www.pacefoods.com.

NATIONAL SCHOLARSHIP MONTH. May 1–31. To recognize organizations, businesses, individuals and communities that have helped and continue to help students with scholarships; to increase awareness of the need for more private sector aid for students; and to focus attention on the impact made by scholarships on students seeking postsecondary educational opportunities. May 7 is the official kick-off date, with a luncheon at the National Press Club in Washington, DC. An initiative of Scholarship America (formerly Citizens' Scholarship Foundation of America). For info: Barbara E. Arnold, VP, Office of Public Affairs & Communications, Scholarship America, 7703 Normandale Rd, Ste 110, Minneapolis, MN 55435-5314. Phone: (800) 642-7207. Fax: (952) 830-1929. E-mail: nsm@csfa.org. Web: www.nationalscholarshipmonth.org.

NATIONAL SCRAPBOOK DAY. May 1. This is a day designated for people in several countries around the world to gather together and create scrapbook photo albums that preserve precious memories. National Scrapbook Day began in 1995 to encourage the value of making and completing photo albums. Annually, the first Saturday in May. For info: Heidi Everett, Creative Memories, 2815 Clearwater Rd, PO Box 1839, St. Cloud, MN 56302. Phone: (320) 529-5807. Fax: (320) 529-5863. E-mail: heidieverett@antioch.com. Web: www.creativememories.com.

NATIONAL SHOES FOR ORPHANS MONTH. May 1–31. A month to create awareness of the basic needs of millions of orphans around the world. Buckner Orphan Care International kicks offs its Celebrity Shoes for Orphans campaign this month and culminates in the summer with a charity auction. All proceeds will go toward the purchase and distribution of shoes in the United States and more than 25 other countries. For info: Buckner Orphan Care Intl, 600 N Pearl St, Ste 1900, Dallas, TX 75201. Phone: (877) ORPHAN. Fax: (214) 758-8155. E-mail: orphancare@buckner.org. Web: www.celebrityshoesfororphans.org.

NATIONAL SIGHT-SAVING/ULTRAVIOLET AWARENESS MONTH. May 1–31. While the damage ultraviolet (UV) causes to skin is obvious, the damage it can do to eyes may not be. Not enough attention is paid to the damage UV can do to the eyes. Exposure to UV can burn delicate eye tissue and raise the risk of developing cataracts and cancers of the eye. For info: Prevent Blindness America®, 500 E Remington Rd, Schaumburg, IL 60173. Phone: (800) 331-2020. Fax: (847) 843-8458. Web: www.preventblindness.org.

NATIONAL STROKE AWARENESS MONTH. May 1–31. For info: Natl Stroke Assn, 9707 E Easter Ln, Englewood, CO 80112. Phone: (800) STROKES or (800) 787-6537. Web: www.stroke.org.

NATIONAL TUBEROUS SCLEROSIS AWARENESS MONTH. May 1–31. Following a presidential proclamation in 1974, the Tuberous Sclerosis Alliance (TS Alliance) dedicated the month of May to creating awareness about the many aspects of the genetic disorder tuberous sclerosis complex (TSC). Join the TS Alliance, the only national voluntary health organization for TSC, each May in its letter-writing campaign *Stamp Out Tuberous Sclerosis*. For info: Tuberous Sclerosis Alliance, 801 Roeder Rd, Ste 750, Silver Spring, MD 20910. Phone: (800) 225-6872. Fax: (301) 562-9870. E-mail: info@tsalliance.org. Web: www.tsalliance.org.

NEW HOMEOWNER'S DAY. May 1. You have faced all the challenges—now take the time as a new homeowner to stand back and reflect on your new home and savor the feeling. For info: Dorothy Zjawin, Dir, 61 W Colfax Ave, Roselle Park, NJ 07204. Phone: (908) 241-6241.

O. HENRY PUN-OFF (WORLD CHAMPIONSHIP). May 1 (tentative). The O. Henry Museum, Austin, TX. Pundits and punographers match wits for a wordy cause in two separate pun-filled competitions (Punniest of Show and High Lies & Low Puns). Sponsors: The City of Austin Parks and Recreation Dept, Friends of the O. Henry Museum and Punsters United Nearly Yearly (PUNY). Est attendance: 2,000. For info: Valerie Bennett, Curator, O. Henry Museum, 409 E Fifth St, Austin, TX 78701. Phone: (512) 472-1903. Fax: (512) 472-7102. Web: www.ci.austin.tx.us/parks/ohenry.htm OR www.ohenryfriends.com

PEN-FRIENDS WEEK INTERNATIONAL. May 1–7. To encourage everyone to have one or more pen-friends not only in their own country but in other countries. For complete information on how to become a good pen-friend and information about how to write good letters, send $5 to cover expense of printing, handling and postage. Annually, May 1–7. For info: Dr. Stanley J. Drake, Pres, Intl Society of Friendship and Good Will, 999 Hood Rd, Ste 127, Marietta, GA 30068. Phone: (770) 565-2322. E-mail: ISFGW@bellsouth.net.

PHILIPPINES: FEAST OF OUR LADY OF PEACE AND GOOD VOYAGE. May 1–31. Pilgrimage to the shrine of Nuestra Sra de la Paz y Buen Viaje at Antipolo, Rizal.

PHILIPPINES: SANTACRUZAN. May 1–31. Maytime pageant-procession that recalls the quest of Queen Helena and Prince Constantine for the Holy Cross.

REVISE YOUR WORK SCHEDULE MONTH. May 1–31. To increase awareness, exploration and implementation of nontraditional work schedules such as flextime, telecommuting, job sharing and compressed work weeks. Annually, the month of May. For info: Center for WorkTime Options, 1286 University Ave, #192, San Diego, CA 92103-3312. Phone: (619) 232-0404. E-mail: info@worktimeoptions.com.

RUSSIA: INTERNATIONAL LABOR DAY. May 1–2. Public holiday in Russian Federation. "Official May Day demonstrations of working people."

SAVE THE RHINO DAY. May 1. A new century. An old problem. Rhinos still in danger! Help save the world's remaining rhinos on the verge of extinction! Get involved with local, national and international conservation efforts to stop the senseless slaughter of these gentle pachyderms. Call your local zoo or write Really, Rhinos! For info: Judyth Lessee, Founder, Really, Rhinos!, PO Box 40503, Tucson, AZ 85717-0503. Phone: (520) 327-9048. E-mail: rinophyl@azstarnet.com.

SCHOOL PRINCIPALS' DAY. May 1. A day of recognition for all elementary, middle and high school principals for their leadership and dedication to providing the best education possible for their students. Annually, May 1. For info: Janet M. Dellaria, 202 N Bennett St, Geneva, IL 60134. Phone: (630) 232-0425.

SEND A KID TO KAMP RADIOTHON. May 1. Masterson Station Park, Lexington, KY. Annually, the first Saturday in May. Est attendance: 15,000. For info: Dennis Smith, 770 AM, WCGW, 3270 Blazer Parkway, Ste 101, Lexington, KY 40509-1847. Phone: (606) 264-9700. Fax: (606) 264-9705. E-mail: info@kidtokamp.com. Web: www.kidtokamp.com.

SENIOR CITIZENS MONTH. May 1–31. Massachusetts.

SMITH, KATE: 95th BIRTH ANNIVERSARY. May 1, 1909. One of America's most popular singers. Kate Smith, who never took a formal music lesson, recorded more songs than any other performer (more than 3,000), made more than 15,000 radio broadcasts and received more than 25 million fan letters. On Nov 11, 1938, she introduced a new song during her regular radio broadcast, written especially for her by Irving Berlin: "God Bless America." It soon became the unofficial national anthem. Born Kathryn Elizabeth Smith at Greenville, VA, she began her radio career May 1, 1931, with "When the Moon Comes Over the Mountain," a song identified with her throughout her career. She died at Raleigh, NC, June 17, 1986.

May 1 ☆ Chase's 2004 Calendar of Events ☆

SOUTHERN APPALACHIAN DULCIMER FESTIVAL. May 1. Tannehill Historical State Park, McCalla, AL. Festival highlighting old-time dulcimer music. Est attendance: 2,000. For info: Tannehill Historical State Park, 12632 Confederate Parkway, McCalla, AL 35111. Phone: (205) 477-5711. Fax: (205) 477-9400.

SOWERBY, LEO: BIRTH ANNIVERSARY. May 1, 1895. Pulitzer prize-winning composer of more than 550 compositions, born at Grand Rapids, MI, and died July 7, 1968, at Port Clinton, OH.

SPRING GALA. May 1–2. Lovington, NM. Arts and crafts show at the Lea County Fairgrounds. For info: Andra Conner, Dir, Lovington Chamber of Commerce, 201 S Main St, Lovington, NM 88260. Phone: (505) 396-5311. Fax: (505) 396-2823. E-mail: visitus@leaconet.com. Web: visitus.leaco.net.

STEPMOTHERS DAY. May 1. A day to honor stepmothers who care! Annually, May 1. For info: Susan Wilkins-Hubley, 4 Westwood Blvd Unit 14, Ste 113, Upper Tantallon, NS, B3Z 1H3, Canada. Phone: (902) 446-9028. E-mail: susan@secondwivesclub.com. Web: www.secondwivesclub.com.

STRAWBERRY FESTIVAL. May 1–2. Lahaska, PA. Strawberries served up in various forms—dipped in chocolate, in assorted pastries and shortcake, in jams, in fritters, and fresh and unadorned. Craftspeople gather to show their wares and demonstrate their skills. Live entertainment and pie-eating contests add to the festivities of this traditional spring celebration. Free admission. Est attendance: 18,000. For info: Peddler's Village, Routes 202 & 263, Lahaska, PA 18931. Phone: (215) 794-4000. Fax: (215) 794-4001. Web: www.peddlersvillage.com.

STRIKE OUT STROKES MONTH. May 1–31. Dedicated to the prevention of strokes. Factors resulting from heredity or natural processes can't be changed but with proper medical treatment and healthful lifestyle adjustments, some risk factors can be eliminated. Kit materials available for $15. For info: Pharmacy Council on Stroke Prevention, c/o PPSI, 101 Lucas Valley Rd, #210, San Rafael, CA 94903. Phone: (415) 479-8628. Fax: (415) 479-8608. E-mail: ppsi@aol.com. Web: www.ppsinc.org.

TEEN DAY. May 1. An annual event proclaimed by the Connecticut state legislature in 1999 to celebrate the lives of all teenagers—to make them feel special and appreciated. It provides any community with an opportunity to reach out and support their teenagers. Annually, May 1. For information on starting a Teen Day celebration in your community: Veronica Diaz Esposito (Founder). E-mail: teendayismay1@yahoo.com or teendaymay1@hotmail.com.

TEILHARD DE CHARDIN, PIERRE: BIRTH ANNIVERSARY. May 1, 1881. French Jesuit author, paleontologist and philosopher, born at Sarcenat, France. He died at New York, NY, Apr 10, 1955.

TOWSONTOWN SPRING FESTIVAL. May 1–2. Towson, MD. Five stages with continuous entertainment. 400 food, craft and display vendors on the street. Art and photography exhibit and antique auto display. Annually, the first Saturday and Sunday in May. Est attendance: 250,000. For info: Towsontown Spring Fest, PO Box 10115, Towson, MD 21285-0115. Phone: (410) 825-1144. Fax: (410) 832-5863. Web: www.towsontownspringfestival.com.

UNITY IN DIVERSITY DAY (UIDD). May 1. A national commemorative holiday to spiritually connect and celebrate the human race. This holiday was envisioned and proclaimed in 1998 by Ayo Handy Kendi, founder and director of the African American Holiday Association as a day to focus attention on the need for respect of people's differences and appreciation of all that they have in common. Annually, the first Saturday in May. For info: African American Holiday Assn, PO Box 43255, Washington, DC 20010. E-mail: aaha@aaha-info.org. Web: www.aaha-info.org.

U-2 INCIDENT: ANNIVERSARY. May 1, 1960. On the eve of a summit meeting between US President Dwight D. Eisenhower and Soviet Premier Nikita Khrushchev, a U-2 espionage plane flying at about 60,000 feet was shot down over Sverdlovsk, in central USSR. The pilot, CIA agent Francis Gary Powers, survived the crash, as did large parts of the aircraft, a suicide kit and sophisticated surveillance equipment. The sensational event, which US officials described as a weather reconnaissance flight gone astray, resulted in cancellation of the summit meeting. Powers was tried, convicted and sentenced to 10 years in prison by a Moscow court. In 1962 he was returned to the US in exchange for an imprisoned Soviet spy. He died in a helicopter crash in 1977. See also: "Powers, Francis Gary: Birth Anniversary" (Aug 17).

VEGETARIAN RESOURCE GROUP'S ESSAY CONTEST FOR KIDS. May 1. Children ages 18 and under are encouraged to submit a two–three-page essay on topics related to vegetarianism. Essays accepted up to May 1. Winners announced Sept 15 and will receive a $50 savings bond. For info: The Vegetarian Resource Group, PO Box 1463, Baltimore, MD 21203. Phone: (410) 366-8343. E-mail: vrg@vrg.org. Web: www.vrg.org.

VIRGINIA GOLD CUP. May 1. Great Meadow, The Plains, VA. Steeplechasing began in Ireland in 1762 when two horsemen held a cross-country match race to a far away church steeple. Great Meadow is the largest steeplechase course in the country with a spectacular hillside amphitheater. The $50,000 Virginia Gold Cup race is run over a challenging 4-mile post and rail course of 23 fences. Advance tickets only. Annually, the first Saturday in May. Est attendance: 45,000. For info: Virginia Gold Cup Assn, PO Box 840, Warrenton, VA 20188. Phone: (540) 347-2612. Fax: (540) 349-1829. Web: www.vagoldcup.com.

WILLIAMS, ARCHIE: BIRTH ANNIVERSARY. May 1, 1915. Archie Williams, along with Jesse Owens and others, debunked Hitler's theory of the superiority of Aryan athletes at the 1936 Berlin Olympics. As a black member of the US team Williams won a gold medal by running the 400-meter in 46.5 seconds (.4 second slower than his own record of earlier that year). Williams, who was born at Oakland, CA, earned a degree in mechanical engineering from the University of California–Berkeley in 1939 but had to dig ditches for a time because they weren't hiring black engineers. He became an airplane pilot and for 22 years trained Tuskegee Institute pilots, including the black air corps of WWII. When asked during a 1981 interview about his treatment by the Nazis during the 1936 Olympics, he replied, "Well, over there at least we didn't have to ride in the back of the bus." Archie Williams died June 24, 1993, at Fairfax, CA.

WOMEN'S HEALTH CARE MONTH. May 1–31. To initiate a public education campaign devoted to increasing awareness of

	S	M	T	W	T	F	S
May 2004							1
	2	3	4	5	6	7	8
	9	10	11	12	13	14	15
	16	17	18	19	20	21	22
	23	24	25	26	27	28	29
	30	31					

the many health concerns unique to women. Focus will be on the prevention of the major causes of death and poor health among women—heart disease, cancer, arthritis, osteoporosis and bone fractures, as well as on depression and alcoholism in women. There is a $15 charge for kit materials. Annually, the month of May. For info: Pharmacists Planning Service, Inc, c/o Pharmacists Council for Women's Health, 101 Lucas Valley Rd, #210, San Rafael, CA 94903. Phone: (415) 479-8628. Fax: (415) 479-8608. E-mail: ppsi@aol.com. Web: www.ppsinc.org.

YOUNG ACHIEVERS MONTH. May 1–31. International Leadership Network's Young Achievers Program recognizes and encourages leaders of tomorrow. Motivates positive behavior, leadership and accomplishment. Community recognition events honor student leaders in grades 5–12. Annually, the month of May. For info: Barbara Eichhorst, 1750 S Brentwood Blvd, Ste 502, St Louis, MO 63144. Phone: (314) 961-5978. Fax: (314) 961-8716. E-mail: inleadnet@aol.com. Web: www.iln-futurebound.org.

BIRTHDAYS TODAY

Wes Anderson, 35, film director/screenwriter (*The Royal Tenenbaums, Rushmore, Bottle Rocket*), born Houston, TX, May 1, 1969.
Charles (Chuck) Bednarik, 79, Hall of Fame football player, born Bethlehem, PA, May 1, 1925.
Steve Cauthen, 44, former jockey, born Walton, KY, May 1, 1960.
Judy Collins, 65, singer ("Both Sides Now," "Send In the Clowns"), born Seattle, WA, May 1, 1939.
Rita Coolidge, 59, singer ("[Your Love Has Lifted Me] Higher and Higher," "We're All Alone"), born Nashville, TN, May 1, 1945.
Glenn Ford, 88, actor (*The Blackboard Jungle, The Fastest Gun Alive*, "The Family Holvak"), born Sainte-Christine, QC, Canada, May 1, 1916.
Sonny James, 75, singer ("Young Love"), born Jimmy Loden, Hackleburg, AL, May 1, 1929.
Curtis Martin, 31, football player, born Pittsburgh, PA, May 1, 1973.
Bobbie Ann Mason, 64, writer (*In Country, Spence and Lila*), born Mayfield, KY, May 1, 1940.
Tim McGraw, 37, country singer, born Delhi, LA, May 1, 1967.
Jack Paar, 87, early host of "The Tonight Show," born Canton, OH, May 1, 1917.
Charlie Schlatter, 38, actor ("Diagnosis Murder"), born Englewood, NJ, May 1, 1966.

MAY 2 — SUNDAY
Day 123 — 243 Remaining

BE KIND TO ANIMALS WEEK®. May 2–8. To promote kindness and humane care toward animals. Annually, the first full week of May. Features "Be Kind to Animals Kid Contest" with college scholarship as grand prize. For info: American Humane, 63 Inverness Dr E, Englewood, CO 80112. Phone: (800) 227-4645 or (303) 792-9900. Fax: (303) 792-5333. E-mail: info@americanhumane.org. Web: www.americanhumane.org.

FLEXIBLE WORK ARRANGEMENTS WEEK. May 2–8. To promote experimentation with alternate work schedules and working at home. Annually, the week beginning with the first Sunday in May. For info: Center for WorkTime Options, 1286 University Ave, #192, San Diego, CA 92103-3312. Phone: (619) 232-0404. E-mail: info@worktimeoptions.com.

FRANKENMUTH SKYFEST. May 2 (tentative). Frankenmuth, MI. 23rd annual. To encourage family participation in a healthy outdoor sport that adapts to all age groups. Annually, the first Sunday in May. Est attendance: 4,500. For info: Audrey Fischer, Kite Kraft, 618 S Main St, Frankenmuth, MI 48734. Phone: (989) 652-2961.

GARDEN FESTIVAL. May 2. Chestnut Hill, PA. Lively street festival in charming urban village. Garden-related merchandise and handcrafts, live entertainment, food court and children's activities. Annually, the first Sunday in May. Est attendance: 40,000. For info: Chestnut Hill Business Assn, 8426 Germantown Ave, Philadelphia, PA 19118. Phone: (215) 247-6696. E-mail: info@chestnuthillpa.com. Web: www.chestnuthillpa.com.

GOODWILL INDUSTRIES WEEK. May 2–8. To call international attention to Goodwill Industries as a leader in job training and employment services for people with disabilities and other barriers to employment. Annually, the first full week in May. For info: Goodwill Industries Intl, Communications Dept, 9200 Rockville Pike, Bethesda, MD 20814-3896. Phone: (301) 530-6500. Fax: (301) 530-1516. E-mail: contactus@goodwill.org. Web: www.goodwill.org.

KING JAMES BIBLE PUBLISHED: ANNIVERSARY. May 2, 1611. King James I had appointed a committee of learned men to produce a new translation of the Bible in English. This version, popularly called the King James Version, is known in England as the Authorized Version.

LEE, PINKY (PINCUS LEFF): BIRTH ANNIVERSARY. May 2, 1907. Born at St. Paul, MN. When young, Leff had dreams of becoming an attorney, but abandoned the idea when classmates laughed at his lisp. His show business debut was in burlesque in the 1930s. He is best remembered for "The Pinky Lee Show" which telecast from Los Angeles in the early 1950s. Pinky Lee died Apr 3, 1993, at Mission Viejo, CA.

LEONARDO DA VINCI: DEATH ANNIVERSARY. May 2, 1519. Italian artist, scientist and inventor. Painter of the famed *Last Supper*, perhaps the first painting of the High Renaissance, and of the *Mona Lisa*. Inventor of the first parachute. Born at Vinci, Italy, in 1452 (exact date unknown), he died at Amboise, France.

MAWLID AL NABI: THE BIRTHDAY OF THE PROPHET MUHAMMAD. May 2. Mawlid al-Nabi (Birth of the Prophet Muhammad) is observed on Muslim calendar date Rabi al-Awal 12, 1425. Different methods for calculating the visibility of the new moon crescent at Mecca are used by different Muslim groups. US date may vary. Began at sunset the preceding day.

NATIONAL FAMILY WEEK. May 2–8. Traditionally the first Sunday and the first full week in May are observed as National Family Week in many Christian churches.

NATIONAL HUG HOLIDAY WEEK. May 2–8. Huggers of all ages are invited to make a difference one hug at a time! The Hugs 4 Health movement needs your help to increase hugs, friendship and volunteer support for the elderly living in senior centers and residential communities. Send $10 for a "Hugger's Package" that includes an "Official Hugger" button, a Daily Hug Prescription with Proper Hug Etiquette, Hug Tally Sheet, Hugger's Contest registration and more information about this movement. (Include your name, complete address and e-mail to the following address.) For info: Hugs 4 Health—NHHW2004, PO Box 896, Seal Beach, CA 90740-0896. Web: www.hugs4health.org.

NATIONAL INFERTILITY SURVIVAL DAY. May 2. A day for promoting awareness of infertility and related issues. Infertility survivors are encouraged to reach out to those struggling to find resolution to their challenges, through friendship, fundraising and other supportive and creative endeavors. Infertility Survival Day is for those who want to use their experiences to attain positive outcomes for themselves and others. Annually, the first Sunday in May. For info: Beverly Barna, 7640 Santee Terrace, Lake Worth, FL 33467. Phone: (561) 632-2152. E-mail: infertilitysucks@aol.com. Web: www.infertilitysucks-thebook.com.

NATIONAL PET WEEK. May 2–8. To promote responsible pet ownership and public awareness of veterinary medical service for animal health and care. Annually, the first full week in May. For info: The American Veterinary Medical Assn, 1931 N Meacham Rd, Schaumburg, IL 60173. Phone: (847) 285-6667. Web: www.avma.org.

☆ Chase's 2004 Calendar of Events ☆

May 2–3

NATIONAL POSTCARD WEEK. May 2–8. To advertise use of picture postcards for correspondence and collecting. Annually, the first full week of May since 1984. For info: Jim Ward, Publisher, Journal of the Postcard History Society, 1795 Kleinfeltersville Rd, Stevens, PA 17578-9669. Phone: (717) 721-9273. E-mail: midcreek@ptd.net.

NATIONAL SUICIDE AWARENESS WEEK. May 2–8. Annually, the first full week in May beginning on Sunday. For info: American Assn of Suicidology, 4201 Connecticut Ave NW, Ste 408, Washington, DC 20009. Phone: (202) 237-2280. Web: www.suicidology.org.

NATIONAL WILDFLOWER WEEK. May 2–8. A week "to encourage the observation, cultivation and study of native wildflowers as a means of deepening humankind's relationship, responsibility and commitment to protect and care for the ecological integrity of Mother Earth." Co-sponsors: National Council of Women, Environmental Alliance for Senior Involvement, The Groundwater Foundation, Center for Plant Conservation, Franciscans International/North America, North American Coalition on Religion and Ecology, Religious Campaign for Forest Conservation, Penn State University Urban Extension, Eastern Native Tree Society and Tree of Peace Society. Annually, the first full week in May. For info: Damon Waitt, Ph.D., Lady Bird Johnson Wildflower Center, 4801 La Crosse Ave, Austin, TX 78739-1702. Phone: (512) 292-4200. E-mail: wildflower@wildflower.org. Web: www.wildflower.org.

RAY, SATYAJIT: BIRTH ANNIVERSARY. May 2, 1921. Film director Satyajit Ray was born at Calcutta, India. Possibly India's best known film director, he made more than 30 films and won numerous international awards, including an Academy Award for lifetime achievement. His films include the trilogy *Pather Panchali* (1956), *Aparajito* (1956) and *The World of Apu* (1959). Ray died Apr 23, 1992, at Calcutta.

READING IS FUN WEEK. May 2–9. To highlight the importance and fun of reading. For info: Jill S. Colby, CMP, Special Events and Conference Coord, Reading Is Fundamental, Inc, 1825 Connecticut Ave NW, Ste 400, Washington, DC 20009. Phone: (202) 673-1613. Fax: (202) 287-3196. E-mail: jcolby@rif.org. Web: www.rif.org.

ROBERT'S RULES DAY. May 2, 1837. Anniversary of the birth of Henry M. Robert (General, US Army), author of *Robert's Rules of Order*, a standard parliamentary guide. Born at Robertville, SC. Died at Hornell, NY, May 11, 1923.

SIBLING APPRECIATION DAY. May 2. This is a day to let your brothers and sisters know you care. If you're not speaking to them, make an exception today. If they are mean and pick on you, tell them you love them anyway. If you think they already know you care, make sure by telling them how you feel and doing something extra nice. If you're lucky, you'll have them around for years to share your joys and sorrows with, to play practical jokes on and to remember when you were young. For info: Keri Mertens, 1819 Fidelity, Lansing, MI 48910. E-mail: kazu@att.net.

SPOCK, BENJAMIN: BIRTH ANNIVERSARY. May 2, 1903. Pediatrician and author, born at New Haven, CT. His book on childrearing, *Common Sense Book of Baby and Child Care* (later called *Baby and Child Care*), has sold more than 30 million copies. In 1955 he became professor of child development at Western Reserve University at Cleveland, OH. He resigned from this position in 1967 to devote his time to the pacifist movement. Spock died at San Diego, CA, Mar 15, 1998.

★ ★ ★

May 2004	S	M	T	W	T	F	S
							1
	2	3	4	5	6	7	8
	9	10	11	12	13	14	15
	16	17	18	19	20	21	22
	23	24	25	26	27	28	29
	30	31					

TAKE A SMART RISK WEEK. May 2–8. A week to encourage individuals and organizations to take smart, calculated risks to improve work results and life satisfaction. For a brochure, "How To Improve Your Work & Life with Smart Risks," send $3.00. For info: Peace Talks, 117 Marco Ln, Centreville, OH 45458. Phone: (937) 433-0053. E-mail: peacetalks@msn.com.

TEACHER APPRECIATION WEEK. May 2–8. A day for elementary through high school students to show appreciation to their teachers. Students are urged to thank their teachers for their care and concerned effort, to be extra cooperative with them. For info: Ann Thompson, Natl Education Assn, 1201 16th St NW, Washington, DC 20036. Phone: (202) 822-7205. Fax: (202) 822-7292. Web: www.nea.org.

TRADITIONAL PLOWING MATCH. May 2. Woodstock, VT. This annual event features a horse- and oxen-drawn plowing competition as well as demonstrations of different plowing techniques. Est attendance: 1,050. For info: Billings Farm and Museum, Rt 12 N and River Rd, Woodstock, VT 05091. Phone: (802) 457-2355. Fax: (802) 457-4663. E-mail: billings.farm@valley.net. Web: www.billingsfarm.org.

WINTERTHUR POINT-TO-POINT. May 2. Winterthur Museum, Garden and Library, Wilmington, DE. Steeplechase races, antique carriage parade, canine agility competition, kids' activities, tailgating plus much more! Call for pricing. Rain or shine event. Est attendance: 26,000. For info: Greater Wilmington CVB, 100 W 10th St, Ste 20, Wilmington, DE 19801-1661. Phone: (800) 422-1181 or (302) 652-4088. E-mail: info@wilmcvb.org. Web: www.visitwilmingtonde.com.

BIRTHDAYS TODAY

Christine Baranski, 52, actress ("Cybill"), born Buffalo, NY, May 2, 1952.
David Beckham, 29, soccer player, born Leytonstone, London, England, May 2, 1975.
Elizabeth Berridge, 42, actress ("The John Larroquette Show"), born Westchester, NY, May 2, 1962.
Theodore Bikel, 80, singer, actor (*Man On the Run, My Fair Lady*), born Vienna, Austria, May 2, 1924.
Larry Gatlin, 55, singer, songwriter ("Broken Lady," "All the Gold in California"), born Odessa, TX, May 2, 1949.
Lesley Gore, 58, singer ("I'll Cry If I Want To"), born Tenafly, NJ, May 2, 1946.
Sarah Hughes, 19, Olympic figure skater, born Manhasset, NY, May 2, 1985.
Bianca Jagger, 59, actress, political activist, ex-wife of Mick Jagger, born Managua, Nicaragua, May 2, 1945.
David Suchet, 58, actor ("The Way We Live Now," "Hercule Poirot Mysteries"), born London, England, May 2, 1946.
Jenna Von Oy, 27, actress ("Blossom"), born Newtown, CT, May 2, 1977.

MAY 3 — MONDAY
Day 124 — 242 Remaining

"CBS EVENING NEWS" TV PREMIERE: ANNIVERSARY. May 3, 1948. The news program began as a 15-minute telecast with Douglas Edwards as anchor. Walter Cronkite succeeded him in 1962 and expanded the show to 30 minutes; Eric Sevareid served as commentator. Dan Rather anchored the newscasts upon Cronkite's retirement in 1981. At one point, to boost sagging ratings, Connie Chung was added to the newscast as Rather's co-anchor, but she left in 1995 in a well-publicized dispute. Rather remains solo, and, as Cronkite would say, "[T]hat's the way it is."

260

☆ Chase's 2004 Calendar of Events ☆   May 3

CROSBY, HARRY LILLIS "BING": BIRTH ANNIVERSARY. May 3, 1903. American singer, composer and actor (*White Christmas, High Society*, various *Road* movies, Oscar for *Going My Way*), born at Tacoma, WA. Died while playing golf near Madrid, Spain, Oct 14, 1977.

DOW-JONES TOPS 11,000: ANNIVERSARY. May 3, 1999. The Dow-Jones Index of 30 major industrial stocks topped the 11,000 mark for the first time.

JAPAN: CONSTITUTION MEMORIAL DAY. May 3. National holiday commemorating adoption of constitution in 1947.

LABOR DAY. May 3. In 140 countries, May 1 is observed as a workers' holiday. When it falls on a Saturday or Sunday, the following Monday is observed as a holiday. Bermuda, Canada and the US are the only countries that observe Labor Day in September.

LUMPY RUG DAY. May 3. To encourage the custom of teasing bigots and trigots for shoving unwelcome facts under the rug. When many cans of worms have been shoved under the rug, the defenders of the status quo obtain a new rug high enough to cover the unwanted facts. For info: Robert L. Birch, Coord, Puns Corps, Box 2364, Falls Church, VA 22042-0364. Phone: (703) 533-3668.

MACHIAVELLI, NICCOLO: BIRTH ANNIVERSARY. May 3, 1469. Italian writer and statesman, born at Florence, Italy. Author of *The Prince*, a book of advice for a ruler that prescribes strong, absolute government. Died at Florence, June 22, 1527.

MEIR, GOLDA: BIRTH ANNIVERSARY. May 3, 1898. Born at Kiev, Russia, Meir was prime minister of Israel from 1969 to 1974. She died at Jerusalem, Dec 8, 1978.

MELANOMA MONDAY. May 3. Also known as National Self-Examination Day. People are encouraged to examine their skin for skin cancer. Annually, the first Monday in May. For info: American Academy of Dermatology, 930 E Woodfield Rd, Schaumburg, IL 60173. Phone: (847) 330-0230 or (888) 462-DERM. Web: www.aad.org.

MEXICO: DAY OF THE HOLY CROSS. May 3. Celebrated especially by construction workers and miners, a festive day during which anyone who is building must give a party for the workers. A flower-decorated cross is placed on every piece of new construction in the country.

NATIONAL HISTORIC PRESERVATION WEEK. May 3–9. To draw public attention to historic preservation including neighborhoods, districts, landmark buildings, open space and maritime heritage. Annually, the second full week in May. For info: Gary Kozel, Natl Trust for Historic Preservation, 1785 Massachusetts Ave NW, Washington, DC 20036. Phone: (202) 588-6000. Fax: (202) 588-6299. E-mail: pr@nthp.org. Web: www.nationaltrust.org.

NATIONAL MEETING PLANNERS APPRECIATION DAY. May 3. To recognize the important role that meeting and convention planners play in promoting tourism in local communities. Annually, the first Monday in May. For info: Beth Williams, Classic Basket, PO Box 36305, Birmingham, AL 35236. Phone: (205) 424-2275. Fax: (205) 428-3469. E-mail: gift4u@bellsouth.net. Web: www.classicbasket.com.

NATIONAL MUFFIN WEEK. May 3–7. Recognizing a famous American breakfast food. Annually, the first week (Monday through Friday) of May. For info: Marilyn Rosica, Rosica Mulhern Inc, 95 Route 17 S, Ste 109, Paramus, NJ 07652. Phone: (201) 843-5600. Fax: (201) 843-5680. E-mail: marilyn@rosica.com. Web: www.unclewallys.com.

NATIONAL ORGANIZING WEEK. May 3–7. Week-long celebration designed to educate the public about the importance of getting organized and how professional organizers can assist them in this process. Annually, the first full week in May. For info: Estelle Gee, Professional Organizers in Canada, PO Box 21073, Cambridge, ON, N3C 4B1, Canada. Phone: (416) 461-8018. Fax: (416) 461-1280. E-mail: info@orderlylives.net. Web: www.organizersincanada.com.

NATIONAL PTA TEACHER APPRECIATION WEEK. May 3–9. PTAs across the country conduct activities to strengthen respect and support for teachers and the teaching profession. For info: Natl PTA, 330 N Wabash Ave, Ste 2100, Chicago, IL 60611. Phone: (312) 670-6782. Fax: (312) 670-6783. E-mail: info@pta.org. Web: www.pta.org.

NATIONAL PUBLIC RADIO FIRST BROADCAST: ANNIVERSARY. May 3, 1971. National noncommercial radio network, financed by Corporation for Public Broadcasting, began programming.

PARANORMAL DAY. May 3. A day for all paranormal enthusiasts to get together and share their unique experiences with each other. Seminars, radio broadcasts and readings will take place worldwide. For info: Bob O'Brien, Consumer Advocate, 1061 Koelle Blvd, Secaucus, NJ 07094. Phone: (201) 860-1595. Fax: (201) 865-4775. E-mail: bobthebestthebest@yahoo.com.

POLAND: CONSTITUTION DAY (SWIETO TRZECIEGO MAJO). May 3. National Day. Celebrates ratification of Poland's first constitution, 1791.

ROBINSON, SUGAR RAY: BIRTH ANNIVERSARY. May 3, 1921. Ray ("Sugar Ray") Robinson, boxer, born Walker Smith, Jr, at Detroit, MI. Generally considered "pound for pound the greatest boxer of all time," Robinson was a welterweight and middleweight champion who won 175 professional fights and lost only 19. A smooth and precise boxer, he fought until he was 45, dabbled in show business and established the Sugar Ray Robinson Youth Foundation to counter juvenile delinquency. To this day, his name connotes class, style and dignity. Died at Los Angeles, CA, Apr 12, 1989.

SPACE MILESTONE: *DELTA 3914* ROCKET FAILURE. May 3, 1986. Launched from Cape Canaveral, FL, the rocket failed, flew out of control and was intentionally destroyed by explosives 90 seconds after launch to avoid the risk of having it land in a populated area.

TAX FREEDOM DAY. May 3. According to the Tax Freedom Foundation, the average American had to work until this day in 2004 to pay federal, state and local taxes. Because state and local taxes vary, this date can vary by almost a whole month depending on the state you live in, ranging from May 18 (Connecticut) to April 23 (Alabama, Alaska, Kentucky, Mississippi, Oklahoma, Tennessee).

UNITED KINGDOM: MAY DAY BANK HOLIDAY. May 3. Bank and public holiday in England, Wales, Scotland and Northern Ireland. Annually, the first Monday in May.

UNITED NATIONS: WORLD PRESS FREEDOM DAY. May 3. A day to recognize that a free, pluralistic and independent press is an essential component of any democratic society and to promote press freedom in the world. For info: United Nations, Dept of Public Info, New York, NY 10017. Web: www.un.org.

UPDATE YOUR REFERENCES WEEK. May 3–9. A reminder to all career professionals to update their references annually, because people are always moving or changing jobs. Additionally, it reminds former supervisors, etc, of who you are. Keeping an updated list of references means job seekers can be ready when the opportunity presents itself. For info: Susan Geary, Professional Resume Writing & Research Assoc, 1106 Coolidge

Ave, Lafayette, LA 70503. Phone: (800) 225-8688. Fax: (337) 233-1871. E-mail: sgeary@prwra.com. Web: www.prwra.com.

WORDSMITH DAY. May 3. A day dedicated to those who write the promotional prose that markets our goods and services, from copywriters to marketing writers to all-around wordsmiths. For info: We Know Words, 825 Reiten Rd, Kent, WA 98030. Phone: (253) 859-3275. Web: www.weknowwords.com.

BIRTHDAYS TODAY

James Brown, 71, singer, songwriter ("Papa's Got a Brand New Bag"), born Augusta, GA, May 3, 1933.
Greg Gumbel, 58, TV personality, sportscaster, born New Orleans, LA, May 3, 1946.
Dulé Hill, 30, actor ("The West Wing"), born Orange, NJ, May 3, 1974.
Jeffrey John Hornacek, 41, former basketball player, born Elmhurst, IL, May 3, 1963.
Engelbert Humperdinck, 68, singer ("Release Me," "After the Lovin'"), born Gerry Dorsey, Madras, India, May 3, 1936.
Pete Seeger, 85, folksinger, songwriter ("Where Have All the Flowers Gone?"), born New York, NY, May 3, 1919.
Frankie Valli, 67, singer ("Can't Take My Eyes Off You," "Grease"), born Newark, NJ, May 3, 1937.
Ron Wyden, 55, US Senator (D, Oregon), born Wichita, KS, May 3, 1949.

MAY 4 — TUESDAY
Day 125 — 241 Remaining

"ANOTHER WORLD" TV PREMIERE: 40th ANNIVERSARY. May 4, 1964. Created by Irna Phillips and sponsored by P&G, this soap was set in fictional Bay City. It was the first soap to air for a full hour and the first to beget two spin-offs ("Somerset" and "Texas"). Charles Durning, Ted Shackelford, Eric Roberts, Ray Liotta, Kyra Sedgwick, Faith Ford, Morgan Freeman, Jackée Harry, Victoria Wyndham and Valarie Pettiford are some of its well-known alums. The show was cancelled in 1999 and the last episode aired June 25, 1999.

CHILDHOOD DEPRESSION AWARENESS DAY. May 4. Also known as Green Ribbon Day. Annually, the Tuesday of the first full week in May. For info: Natl Mental Heath Assn, 2001 Beauregard St, 12th Floor, Alexandria, VA 22311. Phone: (800) 969-6642 or (703) 684-7722. Web: www.nmha.org.

CHINA: YOUTH DAY. May 4. Annual public holiday "recalls the demonstration on May 4, 1919, by thousands of patriotic students in Beijing's Tiananmen Square to protest imperialist aggression in China."

CURACAO: MEMORIAL DAY. May 4. Victims of WWII are honored on this day. Military ceremonies at the War Monument. Not an official public holiday.

DISCOVERY OF JAMAICA BY CHRISTOPHER COLUMBUS: ANNIVERSARY. May 4, 1494. Christopher Columbus discovered Jamaica. The Arawak Indians were its first inhabitants.

FIRST WOMAN BRITISH PRIME MINISTER: 25th ANNIVERSARY. May 4, 1979. With the Conservative Party victory in the British election of May 3, 1979, Margaret Thatcher accepted Queen Elizabeth's appointment as prime minister on May 4. She thus became the first woman prime minister in 700 years of English parliamentary history. Thatcher, dubbed by her party as the "Iron Maiden" for her toughness, held the office until forced to resign on Nov 22, 1990.

May 2004	S	M	T	W	T	F	S
							1
	2	3	4	5	6	7	8
	9	10	11	12	13	14	15
	16	17	18	19	20	21	22
	23	24	25	26	27	28	29
	30	31					

FREEDOM RIDERS: ANNIVERSARY. May 4, 1961. Militant students joined James Farmer of the Congress of Racial Equality (CORE) to conduct "freedom rides" on public transportation from Washington, DC, across the deep South to New Orleans. The trips were intended to test Supreme Court decisions and Interstate Commerce Commission regulations prohibiting discrimination in interstate travel. In several places riders were brutally beaten by local people and policemen. On May 14, members of the Ku Klux Klan attacked the Freedom Riders in Birmingham, AL, while local police watched. In Mississippi, Freedom Riders were jailed. They never made it to New Orleans. The rides were patterned after a similar challenge to segregation, the 1947 Journey of Reconciliation, which tested the US Supreme Court's June 3, 1946, ban against segregation in interstate bus travel.

HAYMARKET SQUARE RIOT: ANNIVERSARY. May 4, 1886. Labor union unrest at Chicago led to violence when a crowd of unemployed men tried to enter the McCormick Reaper Works, where a strike was underway. Although no one was killed, anarchist groups called a mass meeting in Haymarket Square to avenge the "massacre." When the police advanced on the demonstrators, a bomb was thrown and several policemen were killed. Four leaders of the demonstration were hanged and another committed suicide in jail. Three others were given jail terms. The case aroused considerable controversy around the world. See also: "Haymarket Pardon: Anniversary" (June 26).

HEPBURN, AUDREY: 75th BIRTH ANNIVERSARY. May 4, 1929. Audrey Hepburn, whose first major movie role in *Roman Holiday* (1953) won her an Academy Award as best actress, was born Edda Van Heemstra Hepburn-Rusten near Brussels, Belgium. She made 26 movies during her career and received four additional Oscar nominations. During the latter years of her life Hepburn served as spokesperson for the United Nations Children's Fund, traveling worldwide raising money for the organization. Audrey Hepburn died Jan 20, 1993, at Tolochenaz, Switzerland.

KENT STATE STUDENTS' MEMORIAL DAY: ANNIVERSARY. May 4, 1970. Four students (Allison Krause, 19; Sandra Lee Scheuer, 20; Jeffrey Glenn Miller, 20 and William K. Schroeder, 19) were killed by the National Guard during demonstrations against the Vietnam War at Kent (Ohio) State University.

LIBRARY LEGISLATIVE DAY. May 4. Librarians go to Washington and to their state capitals to talk to legislators about important library issues. For info: Public Information Office, American Library Assn, 1301 Pennsylvania Ave NW, Ste 403, Washington, DC 20004. Phone: (202) 628-8410. E-mail: alawash@alawash.org. Web: ww.ala.org.

LUNAR ECLIPSE. May 4. Total eclipse of the moon. Moon enters penumbra at approximately 1:50 PM EDT, reaches the midpoint at 4:30 PM, and leaves penumbra at 7:09 PM. Visible in Europe, eastern South America, Antarctica, Africa, Australasia (except New Zealand), Asia (except northeast), southern Japan and Indian Ocean.

MANN, HORACE: BIRTH ANNIVERSARY. May 4, 1796. American educator, author, public servant, known as the "father of public education in the US," was born at Franklin, MA. Founder of Westfield (MA) State College, president of Antioch College and editor of the influential *Common School Journal*. Mann died at Yellow Springs, OH, Aug 2, 1859.

☆ Chase's 2004 Calendar of Events ☆   May 4–5

MOON PHASE: FULL MOON. May 4. Moon enters Full Moon phase at 4:33 PM, EDT.

NATIONAL TEACHER DAY. May 4. To pay tribute to American educators, sponsored by the National Education Association, Teacher Day falls during the National PTA's Teacher Appreciation Week. Local communities and organizations are encouraged to use this opportunity to honor those who influence and inspire the next generation through their work. Annually, the Tuesday of the first full week in May. For info: Natl Education Assn (NEA), 1201 16th St NW, Washington, DC 20036. Phone: (202) 833-4000. Web: www.nea.org.

RELATIONSHIP RENEWAL DAY. May 4. To salute and strengthen committed couples who value change and acceptance in the context of an ongoing relationship. Celebrants will mutually cite the challenges and changes met in the past year and offer each other well-deserved congratulations. For info: Peter Rosenzweig, PhD, Cheerleader, Nondisposable Relationships, 8 S Michigan Ave, Ste 1405, Chicago, IL 60601. Phone: (847) 677-3560.

RHODE ISLAND: INDEPENDENCE DAY. May 4. Rhode Island abandoned allegiance to Great Britain in 1776.

SPACE MILESTONE: *ATLANTIS* (US): 15th ANNIVERSARY. May 4, 1989. First American planetary expedition in 11 years. Space shuttle *Atlantis* was launched, its major objective to deploy the *Magellan* spacecraft on its way to Venus to map the planet's surface. The shuttle was on its 65th orbit when it landed May 8, mission accomplished.

TYLER, JULIA GARDINER: BIRTH ANNIVERSARY. May 4, 1820. Second wife of John Tyler, tenth president of the US, born at Gardiners Island, NY. Died at Richmond, VA, July 10, 1889.

WADE-DAVIS RECONSTRUCTION BILL PASSES THE HOUSE: ANNIVERSARY. May 4, 1864. Over the objections of President Lincoln, the House of Representatives on this date passed the Wade-Davis Reconstruction bill, containing stiff punitive measures against the South that if put into law would have destroyed Lincoln's more moderate reconstruction aims. The bill was also adamantly opposed by Radical Republicans, led by Thaddeus Stevens for whom it was insufficiently severe in its treatment of the Southern rebels. Lincoln eventually killed the bill by using the pocket veto.

BIRTHDAYS TODAY

Nickolas Ashford, 62, singer, songwriter ("Ain't No Mountain High Enough"), born Fairfield, SC, May 4, 1942.
Maynard Ferguson, 76, bandleader, born Verdun, QC, Canada, May 4, 1928.
Ben Grieve, 28, baseball player, born Arlington, TX, May 4, 1976.
David Guterson, 48, author (*Snow Falling on Cedars*), born Seattle, WA, May 4, 1956.
Jackie Jackson, 53, singer (Jackson 5), born Sigmund Esco Jackson, Gary, IN, May 4, 1951.
Roberta Peters, 74, opera singer (retired), born the Bronx, NY, May 4, 1930.
Dawn Staley, 34, basketball player, born Philadelphia, PA, May 4, 1970.
Randy Travis, 45, country and western musician ("Forever and Ever, Amen"), born Marshville, NC, May 4, 1959.
George F. Will, 63, editor, columnist, baseball executive, born Champaign, IL, May 4, 1941.
Pia Zadora, 48, actress, singer, dancer, born Hoboken, NJ, May 4, 1956.

MAY 5 — WEDNESDAY
Day 126 — 240 Remaining

AMERICAN LEAGUE'S FIRST PERFECT GAME: 100th ANNIVERSARY. May 5, 1904. Denton T. "Cy" Young pitched the American League's first perfect game, not allowing a single opposing player to reach first base. Young's outstanding performance led the Boston Americans to a 3–0 victory over Philadelphia in the American League. The Cy Young Award for pitching was named in his honor. See also "Baseball's First Perfect Game" (June 12).

AMERICAN MEDICAL ASSOCIATION FOUNDED: ANNIVERSARY. May 5, 1847. The American Medical Association was organized at a meeting at Philadelphia attended by 250 delegates. This was the first national medical convention in the US.

AMERICAN ROSE SOCIETY SPRING NATIONAL CONVENTION. May 5–12. San Diego, CA. Amateur rose growers from all over the US display thousands of their roses in this major competition. Hobbyists from all over the country come together to talk shop, attend seminars and show their roses. For info: Sue Streeper: Phone: (619) 448-0321. E-mail: streeper@cox.net. Also: American Rose Society, PO Box 30000, Shreveport, LA 71130. Phone: (800) 637-6534. E-mail: ars@ars-hq.org. Web: www.ars.org.

BATTLE OF THE WILDERNESS: ANNIVERSARY. May 5, 1864. The Battle of the Wilderness was the first major encounter between opposing troops under Robert E. Lee and Ulysses S. Grant. So named for the area of dense forest and underbrush of northern Virginia where the battle occurred, the fighting was especially fierce with opposing armies often fighting at point-blank range as the battle lines became obscured in the smoke-filled forest. Both sides suffered heavy casualties totaling more than 28,000, and after the fighting had ceased on the second day, more than 200 wounded Federal troops were trapped and killed by the flames of fires started by the battle.

BEARD, JAMES: BIRTH ANNIVERSARY. May 5, 1903. The Father of American Cooking was born at Portland, OR. In a long and busy culinary career, he penned more than 20 classic cookbooks, appeared on television's first cooking show in 1946 and was an enthusiastic ambassador for the American style of cooking. He died Jan 21, 1985. His Greenwich Village brownstone is America's only culinary historic landmark and serves as the headquarters of the James Beard Foundation.

BLY, NELLIE: BIRTH ANNIVERSARY. May 5, 1867. Born at Cochran's Mills, PA. Nellie Bly was the pseudonym used by pioneering American journalist Elizabeth Cochrane Seaman. Like her namesake in a Stephen Foster song, Nellie Bly was a social reformer and human rights advocate. As a journalist, she is best known for her exposé of conditions in what were then known as "insane asylums," where she posed as an "inmate." As an adventurer, she is best known for her 1889–90 tour around-the-world in 72 days, in which she bettered the time of Jules Verne's fictional character Phileas Fogg by eight days. She died at New York, NY, Jan 27, 1922.

BONNIE BLUE NATIONAL HORSE SHOW. May 5–8. Virginia Horse Center, Lexington, VA. Major all-breed event, "A"-rated show of the American Horse Show Association. For info: Lexington Visitors Bureau, 106 E Washington St, Lexington, VA 24450. Phone: (540) 463-3777. Fax: (540) 463-1105. E-mail: lexington@rockbridge.net. Web: www.horsecenter.org.

263

May 5 ☆ Chase's 2004 Calendar of Events ☆

BONZA BOTTLER DAY™. May 5. To celebrate when the number of the day is the same as the number of the month. Bonza Bottler Day™ is an excuse to have a party at least once a month. For more information, see Jan 1. For info: Gail M. Berger, 14 Fernwood Dr, Taylors, SC 29687. Phone: (864) 609-9874. E-mail: gberger5@aol.com.

CARTOONISTS DAY. May 5. To honor all cartoonists in the industry: animation, magazines, comic strips, etc. For info: Ken Alvine, Creative Comic Syndicate, 1608 S Dakota Ave, Sioux Falls, SD 57105. Phone: (605) 336-9434. Fax: (605) 338-3501. E-mail: KAI1303567@aol.com.

CINCO DE MAYO FIESTA. May 5–9. Tom McCall Waterfront Park. Portland, OR. A Mexican celebration with ethnic foods, continuous entertainment, dancing, arts and crafts booths. Part of Portland's Sister City program with Guadalajara, Mexico. Est attendance: 300,000. For info: Portland-Guadalajara Sister City Assn, PO Box 728, Portland, OR 97207. Phone: (503) 222-9807. Fax: (503) 579-8388. Web: www.cincodemayo.org.

ETHIOPIA: PATRIOTS VICTORY DAY. May 5. National holiday. Commemorates the 1941 liberation of Addis Ababa by British and Ethiopian forces.

HALFWAY POINT OF SPRING. May 5. On this date, 46 days, 9 hours and 4 minutes of spring will have elapsed, and the equivalent will remain before June 20, 2004, which is the summer solstice and the beginning of summer.

JAPAN: CHILDREN'S DAY. May 5. National holiday. Observed on the fifth day of the fifth month each year.

JOHNSON, AMY: FLIGHT ANNIVERSARY. May 5, 1930. Yorkshire-born Amy Johnson began the first successful solo flight by a woman from England to Australia. Leaving Croydon Airport in a de Havilland Tiger Moth named *Jason*, she flew 9,960 miles to Port Darwin, Australia, arriving May 28. The song "Amy, Wonderful Amy" celebrated the fame of this "wonder girl of the air," who became a legend in her own lifetime. Serving as an air ferry pilot during WWII, she was lost over the Thames Estuary in 1941.

MARX, KARL: BIRTH ANNIVERSARY. May 5, 1818. German socialist, founder and father of modern communism, author of *Das Kapital* and (with Friedrich Engels) the *Communist Manifesto*. Born at Treves, Germany, he died at London, England, Mar 14, 1883, at age 64.

MEXICO: BATTLE OF PUEBLA: ANNIVERSARY. May 5, 1862. The Mexican Army defeated French troops at the city of Puebla. This day is commemorated as a national holiday in Mexico.

	S	M	T	W	T	F	S
May							1
	2	3	4	5	6	7	8
2004	9	10	11	12	13	14	15
	16	17	18	19	20	21	22
	23	24	25	26	27	28	29
	30	31					

MEXICO: CINCO DE MAYO: ANNIVERSARY. May 5. Mexican national holiday recognizing the anniversary of the Battle of Puebla in 1862, in which Mexican troops under General Ignacio Zaragoza, outnumbered three to one, defeated invading French forces of Napoleon III. Anniversary is observed by Mexicans everywhere with parades, festivals, dances and speeches.

NATIONAL ANXIETY DISORDERS SCREENING DAY. May 5. Screenings for anxiety and depressive disorders. For info: NADSD, 308 Seaview Ave, Staten Island, NY 10305. Phone: (718) 351-1717 or (888) 442-2022 for screening locations. Fax: (718) 667-8893. E-mail: fffnadsd@aol.com. Web: freedomfromfear.org.

NETHERLANDS: LIBERATION DAY. May 5. Marks liberation of the Netherlands from Nazi Germany in 1945.

POWER, TYRONE: BIRTH ANNIVERSARY. May 5, 1913. American actor, best known for his motion picture action-adventure roles, Tyrone Power was born at Cincinnati, OH. He died Nov 15, 1958, at Madrid, Spain.

SOUTH KOREA: CHILDREN'S DAY. May 5. A time for families to take their children on excursions. Parks and children's centers throughout the country are packed with excited and colorfully dressed children. A national holiday since 1975.

SPACE MILESTONE: *FREEDOM 7* (US). May 5, 1961. First US astronaut in space, second man in space, Alan Shepard, Jr, projected 115 miles into space in suborbital flight reaching a speed of more than 5,000 miles per hour. This was the first piloted Mercury mission.

STOCK MARKET CRASH OF 1893: ANNIVERSARY. May 5, 1893. Wall Street stock prices took a sudden drop. By the end of the year 600 banks had closed. The Philadelphia and Reading, the Erie, the Northern Pacific, the Union Pacific and the Atchison, Topeka and Santa Fe railroads had gone into receivership; 15,000 other businesses went into bankruptcy. Other than the "Great Depression" of the 1930s, this was the worst economic crisis in US history; 15–20 percent of the workforce was unemployed.

THAILAND: CORONATION DAY. May 5. National holiday. Commemorates the crowning of the current king in 1946.

TOTALLY CHIPOTLE DAY. May 5. To help trumpet what is proving to be one of the most popular "new" flavors in the United States. Totally Chipotle Day helps familiarize the uninitiated with the delectable chipotle—a smoked jalapeño pepper—and its somewhat difficult pronunciation. Celebrated alongside Cinco De Mayo to honor its Mexican-Indian heritage. For info: Martin Larkin, Rock & Roll Chef Productions, 1924 W Montrose Ave, #117, Chicago, IL 60613. Phone: (866) 868-6559 (toll-free). E-mail: chef@RnRChef.com. Web: www.TotallyChipotle.com.

BIRTHDAYS TODAY

Pat Carroll, 77, actress (Emmy for "Caesar's Hour"; "The Ted Knight Show"), born Shreveport, LA, May 5, 1927.

Richard E. Grant, 47, actor (*Henry and June, LA Story, The Age of Innocence*), born Mbabane, Swaziland, May 5, 1957.

Lance Henriksen, 61, actor (*Dog Day Afternoon, The Terminator, Near Dark*), born New York, NY, May 5, 1943 (some sources say 1940).

Jean-Pierre Leaud, 60, actor (Truffaut's *The 400 Blows, Love at 20, Stolen Kisses, Bed and Board*), born Paris, France, May 5, 1944.

Michael Murphy, 66, actor (*Nashville, Manhattan, Salvador*), born Los Angeles, CA, May 5, 1938.

Ziggy Palffy, 32, hockey player, born Skalica, Czechoslovakia, May 5, 1972.

Michael Palin, 61, actor, comedian ("Monty Python's Flying Circus," *Life of Brian*), born Sheffield, Yorkshire, England, May 5, 1943.

Tina Yothers, 31, singer, actress ("Family Ties"), born Whittier, CA, May 5, 1973.

MAY 6 — THURSDAY
Day 127 — 239 Remaining

BABE RUTH'S FIRST MAJOR LEAGUE HOME RUN: ANNIVERSARY. May 6, 1915. George Herman "Babe" Ruth of the Boston Red Sox hit his first major league home run in a game against the New York Yankees in New York.

BANNISTER BREAKS FOUR-MINUTE MILE: 50th ANNIVERSARY. May 6, 1954. Running for the British Amateur Athletic Association in a meet at Oxford University, Roger Bannister broke the four-minute barrier with a time of 3:59.4. Four minutes for a mile at the time was considered not only a physical barrier but also a psychological one.

BIRDS & BLOSSOMS SPRING NATURE FESTIVAL. May 6–9. Norfolk Botanical Garden, Norfolk, VA. For beginning to experienced birders and naturalists of all ages. Special guests and keynote speakers, waterfowl boat tours, sunrise birding walks, bird clinics, lectures, butterfly tours and nature walks. For info: Norfolk Botanical Garden, 6700 Azalea Garden Rd, Norfolk, VA 23518-5337. Phone: (757) 441-5838. Fax: (757) 853-8294. Web: www.norfolkbotanicalgarden.org.

CANADA: CANADIAN TULIP FESTIVAL. May 6–24. Ottawa, ON. The world's largest tulip festival with more than three million tulips in bloom. See a parade of decorated boats, floral sculptures, non-stop entertainment and fireworks. This event grew out of a thank-you gift of bulbs for providing refuge to the Dutch Royal Family. Est attendance: 750,000. For info: Canadian Tulip Festival, 112 Nelson St, Ste 106, Ottawa, ON, Canada K1N 7R5. Phone: (613) 567-5757. Fax: (613) 567-6216. Web: www.tulipfestival.ca.

FARMERS MARKET. May 6–Oct 23 (Thursdays and Saturdays only). Historic Woodstock Square, Woodstock, IL. Authentic farmers markets featuring locally grown produce, flowers, baked goods, potpourri and other items. 8 AM to 1:30 PM. For info: Woodstock Chamber of Commerce, 136 Cass St, Woodstock, IL 60098. Phone: (815) 338-2436. Fax: (815) 338-2927. E-mail: chamber@woodstockilchamber.com. Web: www.woodstockilchamber.com.

FREUD, SIGMUND: BIRTH ANNIVERSARY. May 6, 1856. Austrian physician, born at Freiberg, Moravia. Founder of psychoanalysis. Freud died at London, England, Sept 23, 1939.

HINDENBURG DISASTER: ANNIVERSARY. May 6, 1937. At 7:20 PM, the dirigible *Hindenburg* exploded as it approached the mooring mast at Lakehurst, NJ, after a transatlantic voyage. Of its 97 passengers and crew, 36 died in the accident, which ended the dream of mass transportation via dirigible.

IRELAND: MAY DAY BANK HOLIDAY. May 6. Bank holiday in the Republic of Ireland.

JOSEPH BRACKETT DAY. May 6. Day honoring the Shaker religious leader, born May 6, 1797, in Cumberland, ME. In 1848 he composed the popular Shaker song "Simple Gifts" (also known as "Tis the Gift To Be Simple") while at the Shaker Community in Alfred, ME. This Shaker dance song became known worldwide after Aaron Copland used it in his score for the ballet "Appalachian Spring" in 1944. Elder Joseph Brackett died at New Gloucester, ME, July 4, 1882. For info: PineTree Productions, 235 Prospect St, Stoughton, MA 02072. E-mail: tunes1342@aol.com. Web: hometown.aol.com/tunes1342/index.htm.

MARTIN Z. MOLLUSK DAY. May 6. Moorlyn Terrace Beach, Ocean City, NJ. If Martin Z. Mollusk, a hermit crab, sees his shadow at 11 AM, EST, summer comes a week early—if he doesn't, summer begins on time. Est attendance: 300. For info: Mark Soifer, City Hall, 9th St and Asbury Ave, Ocean City, NJ 08226. Phone: (609) 525-9300 or (609) 399-0272. Fax: (609) 399-0374. E-mail: mtsoifer@aol.com.

★**NATIONAL DAY OF PRAYER.** May 6. Presidential Proclamation always issued for the first Thursday in May since 1981. (PL100-307 of May 5, 1988.) Beginning in 1957, a day in October was designated, except in 1972 and 1975 through 1977.

NATIONAL DAY OF REASON. May 6. The event is used to promote reason and critical thought. Participants across the world are encouraged to celebrate the life of the thoughtful mind and inject rational thought into their actions and behaviors. Annually, the first Thursday in May. For info: American Humanist Assn, 1777 T St NW, Washington, DC 20009-7125. Phone: (202) 238-9088. Fax: (202) 238-9003. E-mail: aha@americanhumanist.org. Web: www.nationaldayofreason.org.

NATIONAL NURSES DAY AND WEEK. May 6–12. A week to honor the outstanding efforts of nurses everywhere to strengthen the health of the nation. Annually, beginning May 6, National Nurses Day, and ending May 12, Florence Nightingale's birthday. Call or write for a free catalog. For info: American Nurses Assn, 600 Maryland Ave SW, Ste 100W, Washington, DC 20024. Phone: (800) 274-4262. Fax: (202) 651-7003. E-mail: dpope@ana.org. Web: www.nursingworld.org.

NO DIET DAY. May 6. A day to stop dieting, stop hazardous weight-loss attempts. International No Diet Day celebrates a paradigm shift to the nondiet Health at Any Size approach to health and well-being, to acceptance and respect for oneself and others. Discover the Top 10 Reasons Not to Diet and the Risks of Weight Loss on website and in the book *Women Afraid to Eat*. For info: Francie M. Berg, Healthy Weight Network, 402 S 14th St, Hettinger, ND 58639. E-mail: fmberg@healthyweight.net. Web: www.healthyweight.net.

NO HOMEWORK DAY. May 6. Millions of kids, all of them overloaded with homework, get a much-needed night off tonight. Give 'em a break, teachers! These young folks are working harder than Mom 'n' Dad. [©2003 by WH.] For info: Thomas & Ruth Roy, Wellcat Holidays, 2418 Long Lane, Lebanon, PA 17046. Phone: (717) 279-0184. Fax: (240) 332-4886. E-mail: info@wellcat.com. Web: www.wellcat.com.

PEARY, ROBERT E.: BIRTH ANNIVERSARY. May 6, 1856. Born at Cresson, PA. Peary served as a cartographic draftsman in the US Coast and Geodetic Survey for two years, then joined the US Navy's Corps of Civil Engineers in 1881. He first worked as an explorer in tropical climates as he served as subchief of the Inter-Ocean Canal Survey in Nicaragua. After reading of the inland ice of Greenland, Peary became attracted to the Arctic. He organized and led eight Arctic expeditions and is credited with the verification of Greenland's island formation, proving that the polar ice cap extended beyond 82° north latitude, and the discovery of the Melville meteorite on Melville Bay, in addition to his famous discovery of the North Pole, Apr 6, 1909. Peary died Feb 20, 1920, at Washington, DC.

PELLA TULIP TIME FESTIVAL. May 6–8. Pella, IA. To pay homage to the founders of this predominately Dutch community. Activities include coronation of queen, parades, flowers, Dutch singing and dancing. Est attendance: 100,000. For info: Pella Historical Society, 507 Franklin, Pella, IA 50219. Phone: (641) 628-4311. Fax: (641) 628-9192. E-mail: pellatt@kdsi.net. Web: www.pellatuliptime.com.

PENN, JOHN: BIRTH ANNIVERSARY. May 6, 1740. Signer of the Declaration of Independence, born at Caroline County, VA. Died Sept 14, 1788.

PRIMARY DAY: LIVE FROM DELAWARE STREET. May 6. Indianapolis, IN. Visit President Benjamin Harrison Home and listen to the conversations and gossip of the day as you enter each room and meet and speak with all the family members and household staff, whose roles are recreated by exceptional actors. Est attendance: 500. For info: PR Dept, President Benjamin Harrison Home, 1230 N Delaware St, Indianapolis, IN 46202. Phone: (317) 631-1888. Fax: (317) 632-5488. Web: www.presidentbenjaminharrison.org.

SACK OF ROME: ANNIVERSARY. May 6, 1527. The Renaissance ended with the Sack of Rome which began on this date. As part of a series of wars between the Hapsburg Empire and the French monarchy, German troops killed some 4,000 inhabitants of Rome and looted works of art and libraries. Pope Clement VII, who supported the French, was imprisoned at the

Castel St. Angelo. Nearly a year passed before order could be restored in the city.

TAGORE, RABINDRANATH: BIRTH ANNIVERSARY. May 6, 1861. Hindu poet, mystic and musical composer was born at Calcutta, India. Received Nobel Prize (literature) in 1913. Died at Calcutta, Aug 7, 1941. His birthday is observed in Bangladesh on the 25th day of the Bengali month of Baishakha (second week of May), when the poet laureate is honored with songs, dances and discussions of his works.

VALENTINO, RUDOLPH: BIRTH ANNIVERSARY. May 6, 1895. Rodolpho Alfonzo Rafaello Pietro Filiberto Guglielmi Di Valentina D'Antonguolla, whose professional name was Rudolph Valentino, was born at Castellaneta, Italy. Popular cinema actor. For years press reports claimed that "at least one weeping veiled woman in black brought flowers to his tomb" (at Hollywood Memorial Park) every year on the anniversary of his death at New York, NY, Aug 23, 1926.

WELLES, ORSON: BIRTH ANNIVERSARY. May 6, 1915. Actor and director born at Kenosha, WI. *Citizen Kane*, which he directed and in which he played the title role, is one of the most influential films ever made. Other films in which he had a role include *The Third Man* and *The Magnificent Ambersons*. Welles died at Los Angeles, CA, Oct 10, 1985.

BIRTHDAYS TODAY

Tom Bergeron, 49, host ("Hollywood Squares"), born Haverhill, MA, May 6, 1955.
Tony Blair, 51, British prime minister, born Edinburgh, Scotland, May 6, 1953.
Martin Brodeur, 32, hockey player, born Montreal, QC, Canada, May 6, 1972.
George Clooney, 43, actor ("ER," *Ocean's Eleven, Three Kings, Batman and Robin*), born Lexington, KY, May 6, 1961.
Roma Downey, 40, actress ("Touched By an Angel"), born Derry, Northern Ireland, May 6, 1964.
Leslie Hope, 39, actress ("24," *Talk Radio*), born Halifax, NS, Canada, May 6, 1965.
Ben Masters, 57, actor (*All That Jazz, Making Mr Right*), born Corvallis, OR, May 6, 1947.
Willie Mays, 73, Hall of Fame baseball player, born Westfield, AL, May 6, 1931.
Bob Seger, 59, musician, singer ("Night Moves," "Travelin' Man"), born Ann Arbor, MI, May 6, 1945.
Richard C. Shelby, 70, US Senator (R, Alabama), born Birmingham, AL, May 6, 1934.
Lynn Whitfield, 51, actress (*Stepmom, Eve's Bayou*), born Baton Rouge, LA, May 6, 1953.

May 2004	S	M	T	W	T	F	S
							1
	2	3	4	5	6	7	8
	9	10	11	12	13	14	15
	16	17	18	19	20	21	22
	23	24	25	26	27	28	29
	30	31					

MAY 7 — FRIDAY
Day 128 — 238 Remaining

ALBANY TULIP FESTIVAL. May 7–9. Washington Park, Albany, NY. A celebration of spring, the Tulip Festival features thousands of tulips abloom throughout the city and honors Albany's Dutch heritage. Events include crowning of a Tulip Queen, arts and crafts vendors, food vendors, entertainment on three stages, children's activities and Dutch dancers in costume. Est attendance: 100,000. For info: City of Albany Office of Special Events, Eagle Street, Albany, NY 12207. Phone: (518) 434-2032. Web: www.albanyevents.org.

BEAUFORT SCALE DAY (FRANCIS BEAUFORT BIRTH ANNIVERSARY). May 7, 1774. A day to honor the British naval officer, Sir Francis Beaufort, who devised in 1805 a scale of wind force from 0 (calm) to 12 (hurricane) that was based on observation, not requiring any special instruments. The scale was adopted for international use in 1874 and has since been enlarged and refined. Beaufort was born at Flower Hill, Meath, Ireland, and died at Brighton, England, Dec 17, 1857.

BEETHOVEN'S NINTH SYMPHONY PREMIERE: ANNIVERSARY. May 7, 1824. Beethoven's Ninth Symphony in D Minor was performed for the first time at Vienna, Austria. Known as the *Choral* because of his use of voices in symphonic form for the first time, the Ninth was his musical interpretation of Schiller's *Ode to Joy*. Beethoven was completely deaf when he composed it, and it was said a soloist had to tug on his sleeve when the performance was over to get him to turn around and see the enthusiastic response he could not hear.

BIG TEN MEN'S GOLF CHAMPIONSHIP. May 7–9. University of Michigan, Ann Arbor, MI. For info: Sue Lister, Big Ten Conference, 1500 W Higgins Rd, Park Ridge, IL 60068-6300. Phone: (847) 696-1010. Fax: (847) 696-1110. Web: www.bigten.org.

BLUEGRASS FESTIVAL. May 7–8. Hope, AR. The 8th annual Hope/Hempstead County Chamber of Commerce Free Bluegrass Festival is the only free bluegrass festival in the state of Arkansas. Features local, regional and nationally known bluegrass acts. Est attendance: 3,000. For info: Hope/Hempstead Chamber of Commerce, PO Box 250, Hope, AR 71802. Phone: (870) 777-3640. Fax: (870) 722-6154. E-mail: hopeark@arkansas.net. Web: www.hopemelonfest.com.

BROWNING, ROBERT: BIRTH ANNIVERSARY. May 7, 1812. English poet and husband of poet Elizabeth Barrett Browning, born at Camberwell, near London. Known for his dramatic monologues. Died at Venice, Italy, Dec 12, 1889.

COOPER, GARY: BIRTH ANNIVERSARY. May 7, 1901. Frank James Cooper was born at Helena, MT. He changed his name to Gary at the start of his movie career. He is best known by baseball fans for his portrayal of Lou Gehrig in *The Pride of the Yankees*. Other films included *Wings, The Virginian, The Plainsman, Beau Geste, Sergeant York* (for which he won his first Academy Award), *High Noon* (winning his second Oscar for best actor), *The Court Martial of Billy Mitchell* and *Friendly Persuasion*. He died May 13, 1961, at Hollywood, CA.

COSAC ANNUAL CONFERENCE: ISSUES IN AUTISM 2004. May 7–8. The NJ Center for Outreach & Services for the Autism Community (COSAC) holds its annual autism conference—one of the largest in the nation—featuring educational workshops, exhibitions and an awards reception. Est attendance: 1,300. For info: Madelyn Schiering, Conf Dir, COSAC, 1450 Parkside Ave, Ste 22, Ewing, NJ 08638. Phone: (609) 883-8100. Fax: (609) 883-5509. E-mail: information@njcosac.org. Web: www.njcosac.org.

DANDELION MAY FEST. May 7–8. Der Marktplatz, Dover, OH. Old-fashioned festival includes finals in a nationwide dandelion recipe contest, live entertainment, slides and presentations about dandelions and food booths featuring dishes made from dandelions, including dandelion coffee ice cream, dandelion pizza, dandelion bread and dandelion omelettes. Also, dandelion wine

☆ Chase's 2004 Calendar of Events ☆ May 7

and jelly tasting, family entertainment and 5K fun run. Festival includes 11th National Dandelion Cook-Off; for entry forms for cook-off call: (800) 697-4858. Est attendance: 15,000. For info: Anita Davis, Coord, Der Marktplatz-Breitenbach Wine Cellars, 5934 Old Route 39 NW, Dover, OH 44622. Phone: (330) 343-3603. Fax: (330) 343-8290. E-mail: amishwine@tusco.net. Web: www.breitenbachwine.com.

DENMARK: COMMON PRAYER DAY. May 7. Public holiday. The fourth Friday after Easter, known as "Store Bededag," is a day for prayer and festivity.

DIEN BIEN PHU FALLS: 50th ANNIVERSARY. May 7, 1954. Vietnam's victory over France at Dien Bien Phu ended the Indochina War.

EL SALVADOR: DAY OF THE SOLDIER. May 7. National holiday. Anniversary of the founding of the country's armed forces in 1824.

ELECTRA GOAT BBQ COOK-OFF & ARTS AND CRAFTS SHOW. May 7–8. Electra Goat Grounds, Electra, TX. Goat brisket, pork ribs, chicken cook-off, Cow Patty Drop, live band, Jackpot Steak & Beans Competition, tug-o-war, eating contest, children's games and crafts. Little Mr and Miss Goat Competition, Friday night dance. Est attendance: 2,000. For info: Sherry Strange, Electra Chamber of Commerce, 112 W Cleveland, Electra, TX 76360. Phone: (940) 495-3577. E-mail: electracoc@aol.com. Web: www.electratexas.org.

FIRST PRESIDENTIAL INAUGURAL BALL: ANNIVERSARY. May 7, 1789. Celebrating the inauguration of George Washington, the first Presidential Inaugural Ball was held at New York, NY.

GERMANY: HAMBURG HARBOR BIRTHDAY. May 7, 1189. "Hafengeburtstag" celebrates establishment of Hamburg as a free city.

GERMANY'S FIRST SURRENDER: ANNIVERSARY. May 7, 1945. Russian, American, British and French ranking officers crowded into a second-floor recreation room of a small redbrick schoolhouse (which served as Eisenhower's headquarters) at Reims, Germany. Representing Germany, Field Marshall Alfred Jodl signed an unconditional surrender of all German fighting forces. After a signing that took almost 40 minutes, Jodl was ushered into Eisenhower's presence. The American general asked the German if he fully understood what he had signed and informed Jodl that he would be held personally responsible for any deviation from the terms of the surrender, including the requirement that German commanders sign a formal surrender to the USSR at a time and place determined by that government.

"KRAFT TELEVISION THEATRE" TV PREMIERE: ANNIVERSARY. May 7, 1947. Live theatrical programs appearing on both the NBC and ABC networks. The show was a gold mine for discovering new talent. Among the playwrights getting their big breaks were: Rod Serling, Paddy Chayefsky and Tad Mosel. Some of the show's most notable plays included: "The Easy Mark" (1951) with Jack Lemmon, "Double in Ivory" (1953) with Lee Remick, "To Live in Peace" (1953) with Anne Bancroft, "The Missing Years" (1954) with Anthony Perkins and Mary Astor and "A Profile in Courage" (1956) with James Whitmore. The last play was based on a book by Senator John F. Kennedy who appeared on the program to introduce the drama.

LUSITANIA SINKING: ANNIVERSARY. May 7, 1915. British passenger liner *Lusitania*, on its return trip from New York to Liverpool, carrying nearly 2,000 passengers, was torpedoed by a German submarine off the coast of Ireland, sinking within minutes; 1,198 lives were lost. US President Wilson sent note of protest to Berlin on May 13, but Germany, which had issued warning in advance, pointed to *Lusitania*'s cargo of ammunition for Britain. US maintained "neutrality," for the time being.

MacLEISH, ARCHIBALD: BIRTH ANNIVERSARY. May 7, 1892. American poet and Librarian of Congress (1939–44), born at Glencoe, IL. MacLeish, who was also a playwright, Pulitzer Prize winner, editor, lawyer, professor and farmer, died at Boston, MA, Apr 20, 1982.

MAY DAY. May 7. Lumpkin, GA. Celebration of the planting season with traditional May Day activities and the Maypole Dance. Est attendance: 800. For info: Patty Cannington, PR Dir, Westville Village, PO Box 1850, Lumpkin, GA 31815. Phone: (229) 838-6310 or (888) 733-1850. Web: www.westville.org.

RHODODENDRON FESTIVAL. May 7–9 (also May 14–16). Georgia Mountain Fairgrounds, Hiawassee, GA. Arts & crafts. Est attendance: 15,000. For info: Rhododendron Festival, PO Box 444, Hiawassee, GA 30546. Phone: (706) 896-4191.

"STRIKE IT RICH" TV PREMIERE: ANNIVERSARY. May 7, 1951. The downtrodden and the poverty-stricken showed up on this game show to tell their sob stories. Whoever received the most votes from the studio audience was declared the winner. The losers were able to receive help from sympathetic viewers through a telephone "heart line." The show got in trouble with the New York City Welfare Department in 1954 when 55 of the show's hopeful contestants remained in New York and went on welfare.

TCHAIKOVSKY, PETER ILICH: BIRTH ANNIVERSARY. May 7, 1840. Ranked among the outstanding composers of all time, Peter Ilich Tchaikovsky was born at Vatkinsk, Russia. His musical talent was not encouraged and he embarked upon a career in jurisprudence, not studying music seriously until 1861. Among his famous works are the three-act ballet *Sleeping Beauty*, two-act ballet *The Nutcracker* and the symphony *Pathetique*. Mystery surrounds Tchaikovsky's death. It was believed he had caught cholera from contaminated water, but today's scholars believe he probably committed suicide to avoid his homosexuality being revealed. He died at St. Petersburg, Nov 6, 1893.

TWENTY-SEVENTH AMENDMENT RATIFIED: ANNIVERSARY. May 7, 1992. The 27th amendment to the Constitution was ratified, prohibiting Congress from giving itself midterm pay raises.

UNITAS, JOHNNY: BIRTH ANNIVERSARY. May 7, 1933. Born at Pittsburgh, PA, Johnny Unitas played football for University of Louisville. After college, he went to work as a construction worker, but continued to play football (for $6 per game) for the Bloomfield Rams, a semipro team that played on dirt, not grass. Based on a fan's letter, the Baltimore Colts gave him a conditional contract and soon he was a star. He played 17 seasons for the Colts, was the MVP three times, went to 10 Pro Bowls, and led his team to three NFL championships. He was inducted into the Pro Football Hall of Fame in 1979, and has often been called the greatest quarterback ever to play the game. He died at Baltimore, MD, Sept 11, 2002.

BIRTHDAYS TODAY

Theresa Brewer, 73, singer ("[Open Up Your Heart and] Let the Sun Shine In"), born Toledo, OH, May 7, 1931.

Pete V. Domenici, 72, US Senator (R, New Mexico), born Albuquerque, NM, May 7, 1932.

Amy Heckerling, 50, filmmaker (*Fast Times at Ridgemont High*, *Look Who's Talking*), born New York, NY, May 7, 1954.

Darren McGavin, 82, actor (*A Christmas Story*, *The Man with the Golden Arm*), born Spokane, WA, May 7, 1922.

Peter Reckell, 49, actor ("Days of Our Lives"), born Elkhart, IN, May 7, 1955.

Tim Russert, 54, TV news talk-show moderator ("Meet the Press"), born Buffalo, NY, May 7, 1950.

MAY 8 — SATURDAY
Day 129 — 237 Remaining

BATTLE OF THE CORAL SEA: ANNIVERSARY. May 8, 1942. Beginning on this date, the Battle of the Coral Sea impeded Japanese expansion and introduced a new form of naval warfare. None of the surface vessels exchanged fire—the entire battle was waged by aircraft. The US lost a carrier, destroyer and tanker. The Japanese lost seven warships, including a carrier.

CZECH REPUBLIC: LIBERATION DAY. May 8. Commemorates the liberation of Czechoslovakia from the Germans in 1945.

DO DAH DAY. May 8. Birmingham, AL. Free music, arts and crafts festival and more to raise funds for the local animal shelters in Birmingham. A mile-long parade kicks off the event. Annually, the first Saturday in May. Est attendance: 50,000. For info: Betsy Stout-Jones, Do Dah Day Committee, 900 Essex Rd, Birmingham, AL 35222. Phone: (205) 595-3771. Web: www.dodahday.org.

DUNANT, JEAN HENRI: BIRTH ANNIVERSARY. May 8, 1828. Author and philanthropist, founder of the Red Cross Society, was born at Geneva, Switzerland. Nobel Prize winner in 1901. Died at Heiden, Switzerland, Oct 30, 1910.

ENGLAND: HELSTON FURRY DANCE. May 8. The world-famous Helston Furry Dance is held each year on May 8 (except when the 8th is a Sunday or Monday, in which case it is held on the previous Saturday). Dancing around the streets of Helston, Cornwall, begins early in the morning and continues throughout the day. The "Furry" dance leaves Guildhall at the stroke of noon and winds its way in and out of many of the larger buildings.

4-WHEEL DRIVE JAMBOREE. May 8–9. Ozark Empire Fairgrounds, Springfield, MO. 4-wheel drive truck show, monster trucks, thunder drags, mud races and more. For info: Nancy Bright, Ozark Empire Fair, PO Box 630, Springfield, MO 65801. Phone: (417) 833-2660. Fax: (417) 833-3769. E-mail: nancy@ozarkempirefair.com. Web: www.ozarkempirefair.com.

FRANCE: VICTORY DAY. May 8. Commemorates the surrender of Germany to Allied forces and the cessation of hostilities in 1945.

GERMANY'S SECOND SURRENDER: ANNIVERSARY. May 8, 1945. Stalin refused to recognize the document of unconditional surrender signed at Reims the previous day, so a second signing was held at Berlin. The event was turned into an elaborate formal ceremony by the Soviets who had lost some 20 million lives during the war. As in the Reims document, the end of hostilities was set for 12:01 AM local time on May 9.

GOTTSCHALK, LOUIS MOREAU: 175th BIRTH ANNIVERSARY. May 8, 1829. American pianist of international fame who toured the US during the Civil War. Gottschalk composed for the piano combining American and Creole folk themes and rhythms in his work. Born at New Orleans, LA, he died Dec 18, 1869, at Rio de Janeiro, Brazil.

GUM TREE FESTIVAL. May 8–9. Tupelo, MS. A juried art show with arts, crafts and live entertainment. 10K run. Annually, the second weekend in May. Est attendance: 15,000. For info: Tupelo Conv and Visitors Bureau, PO Drawer 47, Tupelo, MS 38802. Phone: (800) 533-0611 or (662) 844-2787. Fax: (662) 844-2787.

INTERNATIONAL MIGRATORY BIRD CELEBRATION. May 8–9. Chincoteague, VA. Three days of walks, talks, workshops, boat tours, children's activities and an art celebration all conducted outdoors with the birds. Annually, Mother's Day weekend. Est attendance: 10,000. For info: Chincoteague Chamber of Commerce, 6733 Maddox Blvd, Chincoteague, VA 23336. Phone: (757) 336-6161. Fax: (757) 336-1242. E-mail: pony@intercom.net. Web: www.chincoteaguechamber.com.

INTERNATIONAL MIGRATORY BIRD DAY. May 8. To educate the public about migratory birds and the preservation of their habitats in the US and Central America. The second Saturday in May.

INTERNATIONAL MIGRATORY BIRD DAY AND DORIS MAGER, "THE EAGLE LADY." May 8. Savannah, GA. Many birds stop to rest and feed here while on their long migratory journey north. Enjoy an early morning bird walk and Birder's Breakfast and learn about our migratory birds and how you can help them survive. Then join in on a thrilling performance from this region's foremost authority on our magnificent birds of prey, Doris Mager. Ms. Mager travels with her birds teaching audiences around the country about the plight of these spectacular animals. There will be two shows plus children's activities and Oatland's Native Animal Nature Trail will be open. The bird walk and Birder's Breakfast admission is $5 per person. For info: Oatland Island Education Center, 711 Sandtown Rd, Savannah, GA 31410. Phone: (912) 898-3980. Web: www.oatlandisland.org.

IROQUOIS STEEPLECHASE. May 8. Percy Warner Park, Nashville, TN. Nashville's original "Rite of Spring." This event is the oldest continuously run, weight-for-age steeplechase in the US. The steeplechase has a seven-race card with the featured Iroquois Memorial. Annually, the second Saturday in May. Est attendance: 20,000. For info: Steeplechase Office, 2424 Garland Ave, Nashville, TN 37212. Phone: (615) 343-4231. Fax: (615) 322-6453. Web: www.iroquoissteeplechase.org.

JOHNSON, ROBERT: BIRTH ANNIVERSARY. May 8, 1911. Born at Hazelhurst, MS, and murdered at age 27, Aug 16, 1938, at Greenwood, MS (poisoned by a jealous husband), in his short life Johnson was a master blues guitarist, a singer and songwriter of great influence. He developed a unique guitar style of such skill that it was said he acquired his ability by selling his soul to the Devil—the film *Crossroads* is based very loosely on this myth. Johnson's only two recording sessions captured the classics "Sweet Home Chicago," "Cross Road Blues," "Me and the Devil Blues" and others. Johnson was inducted posthumously into the Blues Hall of Fame in 1980 and the Rock & Roll Hall of Fame in 1986.

JUBILEE. May 8. Bennettsville, SC. Arts and crafts festival with entertainment, children's events and juried art show. Annually, the Saturday before Mother's Day. Est attendance: 6,000. For info: Ivy McLaurin, PO Box 765, Bennettsville, SC 29512. Phone: (843) 479-6982.

LAVOISIER, ANTOINE LAURENT: EXECUTION ANNIVERSARY. May 8, 1794. French chemist and the "father of modern chemistry." Especially noted for having first explained the real nature of combustion and for showing that matter is not destroyed in chemical reactions. Born at Paris, France, Aug 26, 1743, Lavoisier was guillotined at the Place de la Revolution for his former position as a tax collector. The Revolutionary Tribunal is reported to have responded to a plea to spare his life with the statement: "We need no more scientists in France."

LISTON, SONNY: BIRTH ANNIVERSARY. May 8, 1932. Charles ("Sonny") Liston, boxer born at St. Francis County, AR. Liston rose above a record of criminal activity to defeat Floyd Patterson for the heavyweight title on Sept 25, 1962. He defeated Patterson in a rematch but then lost the title to Cassius Clay, who later changed his name to Muhammad Ali. In a rematch Ali knocked out Liston with a punch few observers saw. Died at Las Vegas, NV, Dec 30, 1970.

MOTHER OCEAN DAY. May 8. To celebrate the wonder, vastness and beauty of the ocean. Casting of roses into the sea from the beach and from the water. Annually, on the day before Mother's Day. For info: Cynthia Hancock, Pres, Natl Week of the

☆ Chase's 2004 Calendar of Events ☆   May 8

Ocean, Inc, PO Box 179, Ft Lauderdale, FL 33302. Phone: (954) 462-5573. Web: www.national-week-of-the-ocean.org.

MOTHER'S DAY ANNUAL RHODODENDRON SHOW. May 8–9. Crystal Springs Rhododendron Gardens, Portland, OR. Spectacular display of rhododendron and azalea blooms and plant sale. Est attendance: 6,000. For info: Ted Van Veen, Garden Chair, American Rhododendron Society, Portland Chapter, PO Box 86424, Portland, OR 97286. Phone: (503) 777-1734.

MOUNT PELÉE ERUPTION: ANNIVERSARY. May 8, 1902. In the worst volcanic disaster of the 20th century, Mount Pelée erupted on the tiny French Caribbean island of Martinique. In minutes, a cloud of ashes, gases and rocks destroyed the thriving port city of Saint-Pierre, killing all but one of its 30,000 inhabitants.

NATIONAL BABYSITTERS DAY. May 8. To give babysitters across the nation appreciation and special recognition for their quality child care. Annually, the Saturday before Mother's Day. For info: Barbara Baldwin RN, Safety Whys, PO Box 1177, Helotes, TX 78023-1177. Phone: (210) 695-9838. Fax: (210) 695-5673. E-mail: bbaldwin@satx.rr.com.

NATIONAL TOURISM WEEK. May 8–16. 21st annual week promoting and enhancing awareness of travel and tourism's importance to the economic, social and cultural well-being of the US. The week begins with National Traveler's Appreciation Day on May 10. For info: Travel Industry Assn of America, 1100 New York Ave NW, Ste 450, Washington, DC 20005-3934. Phone: (202) 408-2182. E-mail: dminic@tia.org. Web: www.tia.org.

NATIVE AMERICAN ARTS FESTIVAL AND MOTHER'S DAY POW WOW. May 8–9. Riverside Park, Grants Pass, OR. Annually, on Mother's Day weekend. Est attendance: 2,500. For info: American Indian Traditional Preservation Committee, 773 Hitching Post Rd, Grants Pass, OR 97526. Phone: (541) 474-6394 or (541) 839-6704.

NETHERLANDS: NATIONAL WINDMILL DAY. May 8. About 950 windmills still survive, and some 300 still are used occasionally and have been designated national monuments by the government. As many windmills as possible are in operation on National Windmill Day for the benefit of tourists. Annually, the second Saturday in May.

NO SOCKS DAY. May 8. If we give up wearing socks for one day, it will mean a little less laundry, thereby contributing to the betterment of the environment. Besides, we will all feel a bit freer, at least for one day. Annually, May 8. [©2003 by WH.] For info: Thomas & Ruth Roy, Wellcat Holidays, 2418 Long Ln, Lebanon, PA 17046. Phone: (717) 279-0184. E-mail: info@wellcat.com. Web: www.wellcat.com.

OUIMET, FRANCIS DESALES: BIRTH ANNIVERSARY. May 8, 1893. American amateur golfer who is credited with establishing the popularity of golf in the US. Born at Brookline, MA, his golfing career began as a caddy. In 1913, at age 20, he generated national enthusiasm for the game when he became the first American and first amateur to win the US Open Golf Championship. He won the US Amateur Championship in 1914 and 1931, and was a member of the US Walker Cup team from its first tournament in 1922 until 1949, serving as its nonplaying captain for six of those years. In 1951 he became the first American to be elected Captain of the Royal and Ancient Golf Club of St. Andrews, Scotland. Ouimet died at Newton, MA, Sept 2, 1967.

SLOVAKIA: LIBERATION DAY. May 8. Commemorates the liberation of Czechoslovakia from the Germans in 1945.

SPRING GARDENER'S MARKET AND PLANT SALE. May 8–9. Norfolk Botanical Garden, Norfolk, VA. Gardening enthusiasts can shop from more than 30 specialty growers, plant societies and wholesalers for the best selection of plants, garden art, accessories, furniture and wildlife supplies. Annually, Mother's Day weekend. Est attendance: 4,000. For info: Norfolk Botanical Garden, 6700 Azalea Garden Rd, Norfolk, VA 23518. Phone: (757) 441-5830. Fax: (757) 853-8294. Web: www.norfolkbotanicalgarden.org.

TRUMAN, HARRY S: BIRTH ANNIVERSARY. May 8, 1884. The 33rd president of the US, succeeded to that office upon the death of Franklin D. Roosevelt, Apr 12, 1945, and served until Jan 20, 1953. Born at Lamar, MO, Truman was the last of the nine US presidents who did not attend college. Affectionately nicknamed "Give 'em Hell Harry" by admirers. Truman died at Kansas City, MO, Dec 26, 1972. His birthday is a holiday in Missouri.

V-E DAY: ANNIVERSARY. May 8, 1945. Victory in Europe Day commemorates unconditional surrender of Germany to Allied Forces. The surrender document was signed by German representatives at General Dwight D. Eisenhower's headquarters at Reims to become effective, and hostilities to end, at one minute past midnight May 9, 1945, which was 9:01 PM EDT on May 8 in the US. President Harry S. Truman on May 8 declared May 9, 1945, to be "V-E Day," but it later came to be observed on May 8. A separate German surrender to the USSR was signed at Karlshorst, near Berlin, May 8. See also: "Russia: Victory Day" (May 9).

VIRGINIA STATE CHAMPIONSHIP CHILI COOK-OFF. May 8. Historic Market area, Roanoke, VA. Live entertainment, pepper-eating contest, children's festival area and the best chili samples from across the US and the Commonwealth of Virginia. All compete for the state title. Est attendance: 55,000. For info: Sandra Carroll, Greenvale School, 627 Westwood Blvd, Roanoke, VA 24017. Phone: (540) 342-4716. Fax: (540) 344-0876. E-mail: scgns@aol.com. Web: downtown.roanoke.org.

WORLD CHAMPIONSHIP GOLD PANNING COMPETITION. May 8–9. Consolidated Gold Mine, Dahlonega, GA. Competitions for the quickest gold panner. For info: Dahlonega-Lumpkin Co Chamber of Commerce, 13 S Park St, Dahlonega, GA 30533. Phone: (706) 864-3513 or (800) 231-5543. Fax: (706) 864-7917. E-mail: dahlonega@alltel.net. Web: www.dahlonega.org.

WORLD FAIR TRADE DAY. May 8. A day to promote fair trade as an alternative economic model. "Fair trade" means that trading partnerships are based on reciprocal benefits and mutual respect; that prices paid to producers reflect the work they do; that workers have the right to organize; that national health, safety and wage laws are enforced; and that products are environmentally sustainable and conserve natural resources. Celebrated worldwide in 50 countries with a variety of events: from live music to symposia. For info: International Federation for Alternative Trade, 30 Murdock Rd, Bicester, Oxon, United Kingdom OX26 4RF. Phone: (44) (1869) 249-819. Fax: (44) (1869) 246-381. Web: www.ifat.org or www.wftday.org.

WORLD RED CROSS DAY. May 8. A day for commemorating the birth of Jean Henry Dunant, the Swiss founder of the International Red Cross Movement in 1863, and for recognizing the humanitarian work of the Red Cross around the world. For info on activities in your area, contact your local Red Cross chapter. For info: American Red Cross Natl Headquarters, 2025 E St NW, Washington, DC 20006. Web: www.redcross.org.

May 8–9 ☆ Chase's 2004 Calendar of Events ☆

BIRTHDAYS TODAY

David Attenborough, 78, author, naturalist (*Life on Earth, Trials of Life*), born London, England, May 8, 1926.
Peter Benchley, 64, author, journalist (*Rummies, Jaws*), born New York, NY, May 8, 1940.
Bill Cowher, 47, football coach and former player, born Pittsburgh, PA, May 8, 1957.
Melissa Gilbert, 40, actress ("Little House on the Prairie," *The Miracle Worker*), born Los Angeles, CA, May 8, 1964.
Enrique Iglesias, 29, singer, son of Julio Iglesias, born Madrid, Spain, May 8, 1975.
David Keith, 50, actor (*The Great Santini, An Officer and a Gentleman*), director, born Knoxville, TN, May 8, 1954.
Bobby Labonte, 40, race car driver, born Corpus Christi, TX, May 8, 1964.
Ronald Mandel (Ronnie) Lott, 45, Hall of Fame football player, born Albuquerque, NM, May 8, 1959.
Janet McTeer, 43, actress (*Tumbleweeds*), born Newcastle, England, May 8, 1961.
Thomas Pynchon, 67, writer (*V, Gravity's Rainbow*), born Glen Cove, NY, May 8, 1937.
Don Rickles, 78, comedian, actor (*Blazing Saddles*, "The Dean Martin Show"), born New York, NY, May 8, 1926.
Toni Tennille, 61, singer (with husband Daryl Dragon made up Captain and Tennille), born Montgomery, AL, May 8, 1943.

MAY 9 — SUNDAY
Day 130 — 236 Remaining

BOYD, BELLE: BIRTH ANNIVERSARY. May 9, 1843. Notorious Confederate spy who later became an actress and lecturer was born at Martinsburg, VA. Author of the book *Belle Boyd in Camp and Prison*, she died June 11, 1900, at Kilbourne, WI.

BRITISH CAPTURE ENIGMA MACHINE: ANNIVERSARY. May 9, 1941. During World War II, when a German *U-110* submarine attacked a British convoy, two British vessels, the *Bulldog* and *Aubretia*, were able to retaliate so quickly with depth charges that the submarine was disabled and unable to dive. With the submarine captured, British sailors investigated the radio room and discovered the typewriter-like Enigma, a ciphering machine that enabled safe German communication, and documents of tables that helped explain how it worked. *U-110*'s capture was kept secret, and British cryptographers used this break to begin unraveling German code during the war.

BROWN, JOHN: BIRTH ANNIVERSARY. May 9, 1800. Abolitionist leader born at Torrington, CT, and hanged Dec 2, 1859, at Charles Town, WV. Leader of attack on Harpers Ferry, Oct 16, 1859, which was intended to give impetus to movement for escape and freedom for slaves. His aim was frustrated and in fact resulted in increased polarization and sectional animosity. Legendary martyr of the abolitionist movement.

EUROPEAN UNION: ANNIVERSARY OBSERVANCE. May 9, 1950. Member countries of the European Union commemorate the announcement by French statesman Robert Schuman of the "Schuman Plan" for establishing a single authority for production of coal, iron and steel in France and Germany. The European Coal and Steel Community was founded in 1952. This organization was a forerunner of the European Economic Community, founded in 1958, which later became the European Union. At the European Summit at Milan in 1985, this day was proclaimed the Day of Europe.

	S	M	T	W	T	F	S
May 2004							1
	2	3	4	5	6	7	8
	9	10	11	12	13	14	15
	16	17	18	19	20	21	22
	23	24	25	26	27	28	29
	30	31					

GONZALES, PANCHO: BIRTH ANNIVERSARY. May 9, 1928. Richard Alonzo ("Pancho") Gonzales, tennis player born at Los Angeles, CA. A self-taught player, Gonzales won the 1948 US National Singles Championship and repeated in 1949. He turned pro and won the world's championship from 1954 through 1962. Gonzales was an aggressive, temperamental player who rarely trained. Died at Las Vegas, NV, July 3, 1995.

HUNTER FREES THE SLAVES: ANNIVERSARY. May 9, 1862. At Hilton Head, SC, General David Hunter, commander of the Department of the South, issued orders freeing slaves in South Carolina, Florida and Georgia. Not having congressional or presidential approval, the orders were countermanded by President Lincoln on May 19.

KIWANIS PRAYER WEEK. May 9–15. Encourages Kiwanis Clubs to promote religious activities throughout their communities and to recognize individuals for their contributions to spiritual welfare. Annually, the second full week in May. For info: Kiwanis Intl, Member Services, 3636 Woodview Trace, Indianapolis, IN 46268. Web: www.kiwanis.org.

LAG B'OMER. May 9. Hebrew calendar date: Iyar 18, 5764. Literally, the 33rd day of the omer (harvest time), the 33rd day after the beginning of Passover. Traditionally a joyous day for weddings, picnics and outdoor activities. Began at sundown May 8.

MOTHER'S DAY. May 9. Observed first in 1907 at the request of Anna Jarvis of Philadelphia, PA, who asked her church to hold service in memory of all mothers on the anniversary of her mother's death. In 1909, two years after her mother's death, Jarvis and friends began a letter-writing campaign to create a Mother's Day observance. Congress passed legislation in 1914 designating the second Sunday in May as Mother's Day. Some say the predecessor of Mother's Day was the ancient spring festival dedicated to mother godesses: Rhea (Greek) and Cybele (Roman).

★**MOTHER'S DAY.** May 9. Presidential Proclamation always issued for the second Sunday in May. (Pub Res No. 2 of May 8, 1914.)

MOTHER'S DAY CELEBRATION. May 9. Jenkinson's Aquarium, Point Pleasant Beach, NJ. Calling all kids! Bring your mom for a special day to learn about the roles of mothers in the marine environment. One mother admitted free with each paid child's admission. Est attendance: 800. For info: Jenkinson's Aquarium, 300 Ocean Ave, Point Pleasant Beach, NJ 08742. Phone: (732) 899-1212. Fax: (732) 899-1717. E-mail: aquarium@jenkinsons.com. Web: www.jenkinsons.com.

MOTHER'S DAY HOUSEWALK. May 9. Evanston, IL. 29th annual tour of historic homes as a fund-raiser for the Evanston Historical Society. Annually, on Mother's Day. Est attendance:

☆ Chase's 2004 Calendar of Events ☆ May 9–10

2,000. For info: Evanston Historical Society, 225 Greenwood St, Evanston, IL 60201. Phone: (847) 475-3410.

NATIONAL ALCOHOL AND OTHER DRUG-RELATED BIRTH DEFECTS WEEK. May 9–15. For info: National Council on Alcoholism and Drug Dependence, 20 Exchange Place, Ste 2902, New York, NY 10005. Phone: (212) 269-7797. E-mail: national@ncadd.org. Web: www.ncadd.org.

NATIONAL FAMILY MONTH®. May 9–June 20. A month-long national observance to celebrate and promote strong, supportive families. Sponsored by KidsPeace®, a private children's charity that helps kids overcome crisis. Annually, Mother's Day through Father's Day. For info: KidsPeace, 5300 KidsPeace Dr, Orefield, PA 18069. Phone: (800) 25P-EACE. E-mail: jvallone@kidspeace.org. Web: www.familymonth.net.

NATIONAL NURSING HOME WEEK. May 9–15. A community outreach program designed to familiarize the public with long-term care facilities and the services they provide. Activities are conducted locally by individual long-term care facilities. Annually, Mother's Day through the following Saturday. For info: American Health Care Assn, Natl Nursing Home Week, 1201 L St NW, Washington, DC 20005. Phone: (202) 842-4444. Fax: (202) 842-3860.

NATIONAL POLICE WEEK. May 9–15. See also: "Peace Officer Memorial Day" (May 15). For info: American Police Hall of Fame and Museum, 6350 Horizon Dr, Titusville, FL 32780. Phone: (321) 264-0911. E-mail: policeinfo@aphf.org. Web: www.aphf.org.

NATIONAL STUTTERING AWARENESS WEEK. May 9–15. Annually, the second full week of May. For info: Stuttering Foundation of America, 3100 Walnut Grove Rd, Ste 603, Memphis, TN 38111-0749. Phone: (800) 992-9392 or (901) 452-7343. E-mail: info@stutteringhelp.org. Web: www.stutteringhelp.org.

PENINSULA CAMPAIGN INTENSIFIED: ANNIVERSARY. May 9, 1862. Confederate forces at Norfolk, VA, evacuated the city in a costly move, leaving valuable materiel for the Union army. Norfolk and Portsmouth were occupied on May 10 and the naval yard at Gosport, VA, was burned. President Abraham Lincoln was personally involved in this action, supervising the Federal expeditionary force.

★ **POLICE WEEK.** May 9–15. Presidential Proclamation 3537 of May 4, 1963, covers all succeeding years. (PL87-726 of Oct 1, 1962.) Always the week including May 15 since 1962.

PREPARING TOMORROW'S PARENTS MONTH. May 9–June 20. To celebrate mothers and fathers, do at least one activity between Mother's Day and Father's Day to help prepare a child or teen to become a better parent in the future. To get ideas for parenting preparation activities for this month and year-round, visit www.parentingproject.org which posts easy, fun steps to take at home as well as classroom-ready learning experiences for teachers, parents and youth organization leaders. For info: The Parenting Project, 454 NE 3rd St, Boca Raton, FL 33432. Phone: (561) 620-0256 or (888) PARENTS. E-mail: info@parentingproject.org. Web: www.parentingproject.org.

RACE FOR THE CURE®. May 9. Pittsburgh, PA. 5K walk/run and one-mile fun walk to raise awareness of breast cancer and help fund research for a cure. One of 116 races around the country founded by the Susan G. Komen Breast Cancer Foundation. Annually, on Mother's Day. Est attendance: 38,000. For info: Race for the Cure®, 1620 Murray Ave, Pittsburgh, PA 15217. Phone: (412) 521-2873. Fax: (412) 421-1121. E-mail: info@pittsburghraceforthecure.org. Web: www.pittsburghraceforthecure.org.

RENO, NEVADA: BIRTHDAY. May 9, 1868. First known as Fullers Crossing, then Lakes Crossing, on this date it officially became Reno, known today as "The Biggest Little City in the World." Its six-week residency requirement for divorce became law on May 1, 1931.

RUSSIA: VICTORY DAY. May 9. National holiday observed annually to commemorate the 1945 Allied Forces defeat of Nazi Germany in WWII and to honor the 20 million Soviet people who died in that war. Hostilities ceased and the German surrender became effective at one minute after midnight on May 9, 1945. See also: "V-E Day: Anniversary" (May 8).

UZBEKISTAN: DAY OF MEMORY AND HONOR. May 9. Honors Uzbek citizens killed in World War II. Formerly Victory Day when Uzbekistan was part of the Soviet Union.

"VAST WASTELAND" SPEECH: ANNIVERSARY. May 9, 1961. Speaking before the bigwigs of network TV at the annual convention of the National Association of Broadcasters, Newton Minow, the new chairman of the Federal Communications Commission, exhorted those executives to sit through an entire day of their own programming. He suggested that they "will observe a vast wasteland." Further, he urged them to try for "imagination in programming, not sterility; creativity, not imitation; experimentation, not conformity; excellence, not mediocrity."

BIRTHDAYS TODAY

John D. Ashcroft, 62, US Attorney General, born Chicago, IL, May 9, 1942.

Candice Bergen, 58, actress (*Starting Over, The Group*, "Murphy Brown"), daughter of ventriloquist Edgar Bergen, born Beverly Hills, CA, May 9, 1946.

James L. Brooks, 64, screenwriter, producer ("Taxi," "The Mary Tyler Moore Show"), born Brooklyn, NY, May 9, 1940.

Albert Finney, 68, actor (*Tom Jones, Shoot the Moon, Annie, The Dresser*), born Salford, England, May 9, 1936.

Anthony Keith (Tony) Gwynn, 44, former baseball player, born Los Angeles, CA, May 9, 1960.

Glenda Jackson, 67, actress (Oscars for *Women in Love* and *Touch of Class*), born Cheshire, England, May 9, 1937.

Billy Joel, 55, singer, composer ("It's Still Rock and Roll to Me," "Just the Way You Are"), born Hicksville, NY, May 9, 1949.

Mike Wallace, 86, TV journalist ("60 Minutes"), born Brookline, MA, May 9, 1918.

Steve Yzerman, 39, hockey player, born Cranbrook, BC, Canada, May 9, 1965.

MAY 10 — MONDAY
Day 131 — 235 Remaining

ASTAIRE, FRED: BIRTH ANNIVERSARY. May 10, 1899. Actor, dancer and choreographer, born at Omaha, NE. Astaire began dancing with his sister Adele and in the mid-1930s began dancing with Ginger Rogers. After Astaire's first Hollywood screen test, a producer noted of him: "Can't act. Slightly bald. Can dance a little." Despite this, Astaire starred in more than 40 films including *Holiday Inn, The Gay Divorcee, Silk Stockings* and *Easter Parade*. Died at Los Angeles, CA, June 22, 1987.

ASTOR PLACE RIOT: ANNIVERSARY. May 10, 1849. A riot erupted outside the Astor Place Opera House at New York, NY, where the British actor William Charles Macready was performing. Led by the American actor Edwin Forrest, angry crowds revolted against dress requirements for admission and against Macready's public statements on the vulgarity of American life. On May 8, Macready's performance of *Macbeth* was stopped by Forrest's followers. Two days later, a mob led by Ned Buntline shattered the windows of the theater during a performance. Troops were summoned and they were ordered to fire, killing 22 and wounding 26.

CONFEDERATE MEMORIAL DAY IN NORTH AND SOUTH CAROLINA. May 10. See also: Apr 26 and June 3 for Confederate Memorial Day observances in other Southern states.

GOLDEN SPIKE DRIVING: ANNIVERSARY. May 10, 1869. Anniversary of the meeting of Union Pacific and Central Pacific railways, at Promontory Point, UT. On that day a golden spike was driven by Leland Stanford, president of the Central Pacific, to celebrate the linkage. The golden spike was promptly removed for preservation. Long called the final link in the ocean-to-ocean railroad, this event cannot be accurately described as completing the transcontinental railroad, but it did complete continuous rail tracks between Omaha and Sacramento. See also: "Transcontinental US Railway Completion: Anniversary" (Aug 15).

JAMES BEARD AWARDS CEREMONY. May 10. New York, NY. The James Beard Foundation celebrates the highest standards of culinary excellence all through the year, but most particularly at the James Beard Foundation Awards ceremony. The Awards—considered the "Oscars of the food industry"—honor the finest chefs, restaurants, journalists, cookbook authors, restaurant designers and electronic media professionals in America. For info: The James Beard Foundation, 167 W 12th St, New York, NY 10011. Phone: (212) 675-4984 or (800) 36-BEARD. Web: www.jamesbeard.org.

LIFE COACH RECOGNITION WEEK. May 10–16. Coaches love to help people lead joyful, purposeful, successful lives. Whether the goals be to find love, pursue passions, embrace challenges, cultivate a career or achieve personal gratification, a coach's job is to empower, guide and inform. This week is a time to recognize the contributions life coaches make to the well-being of society. For info: Robin Gorman Newman, 44 Somerset Dr N, Great Neck, NY 10020. Phone: (516) 773-0911. Fax: (516) 773-0173. E-mail: robin@lovecoach.com. Web: www.lovecoach.com.

MANDELA INAUGURATION: 10th ANNIVERSARY. May 10, 1994. In a dramatic and historic exchange of power, former political prisoner Nelson Mandela was inaugurated as President of South Africa. Long the focal point of apartheid foes' attempts to end the enforced policy of discrimination in South Africa, Mandela handily won the first free election in South Africa despite many attempts by various political factions to either stop the electoral process or alter the outcome.

MICRONESIA, FEDERATED STATES OF: NATIONAL HOLIDAY. May 10. Proclamation of the Federated States of Micronesia in 1979.

NATIONAL SMALL BUSINESS DAY. May 10. To honor entrepreneurs and small businesses in the US. Tips for promoting your small business will be provided. For info: Nancy Michaels, Impression Impact, 60 Thoreau St, Ste 308, Concord, MA 01742. Phone: (781) 866-8881. Fax: (781) 860-8818. E-mail: nmichaels@impressionimpact.com.

"THE REST OF THE STORY" RADIO PREMIERE: ANNIVERSARY. May 10, 1976. Radio legend Paul Harvey, whose "News and Comment" radio program had been on the air since 1951, spun off a popular segment into its own show on this date. "The Rest of the Story" looks at the story behind the story of famous people and events.

ROSS, GEORGE: BIRTH ANNIVERSARY. May 10, 1730. Signer of the Declaration of Independence. Born at New Castle, DE, he died July 14, 1779, at Philadelphia.

SINGAPORE: VESAK DAY. May 10. Public holiday. Monks commemorate their Lord Buddha's entry into Nirvana by chanting holy sutras and freeing captive birds.

TRUST YOUR INTUITION DAY. May 10. Today is the day we pay homage to the wonderful gift of sixth sense, "gut" feelings or that still small voice that is sometimes the only clue we have to go on in this ever-changing world. [©1994] Because of the escalating costs of Eventological® Literature, a charge of $7 must be assessed for each request. Checks are to be made payable to: Adrienne Sioux Kooperosmith, 1437 W Rosemont, #1W, Chicago, IL 60660-1319. Phone: (773) 743-5341. Fax: (773) 743-5395. E-mail: la_koop@yahoo.com.

BIRTHDAYS TODAY

Bono, 44, singer (U2), humanitarian activist, born Paul Hewson, Dublin, Ireland, May 10, 1960.
T. Berry Brazleton, 86, pediatrician, author, born Waco, TX, May 10, 1918.
Jason Brooks, 38, actor ("Days of Our Lives"), born Colorado Springs, CO, May 10, 1966.
Judith Jamison, 60, dancer and choreographer, born Philadelphia, PA, May 10, 1944.
Dave Mason, 58, singer, musician, songwriter ("We Just Disagree," "So High"), born Worcester, England, May 10, 1946.
Gary Owens, 68, actor ("Rowan & Martin's Laugh-In," "The Gong Show"), born Mitchell, SD, May 10, 1936.
Ara Raoul Parseghian, 81, former football coach and sportscaster, born Akron, OH, May 10, 1923.
Marie-France Pisier, 60, actress (*Cousin Cousine, French Postcards*), born Dalat, Vietnam, May 10, 1944.
Rick Santorum, 46, US Senator (R, Pennsylvania), born Winchester, VA, May 10, 1958.
Ronald F. (Rony) Seikaly, 39, former basketball player, born Beirut, Lebanon, May 10, 1965.

MAY 11 — TUESDAY

Day 132 — 234 Remaining

BATTLE OF HAMBURGER HILL: 35th ANNIVERSARY. May 11, 1969. Beginning of one of the most infamous battles that signified the growing frustration with America's involvement in the Vietnam war. Attempting to seize Dong Ap Bia mountain, American troops repeatedly scaled the hill over a 10-day period, often engaging in bloody hand-to-hand combat with the North Vietnamese. After finally securing the objective, American military decision makers chose to abandon it and the North Vietnamese retook it shortly thereafter. The heavy casualties in the struggle to take the hill inspired the name "Hamburger Hill."

BERLIN, IRVING: BIRTH ANNIVERSARY. May 11, 1888. Songwriter born Israel Isidore Baline at Tyumen, Russia. Irving Berlin moved to New York, NY, with his family when he was four years old. After the death of his father, he began singing in saloons and on street corners in order to help his family and worked as a singing waiter as a teenager. Berlin became one of America's most prolific songwriters, authoring such songs as "Alexander's Ragtime Band," "White Christmas," "God Bless America," "There's No Business Like Show Business," "Doin' What Comes Naturally," "Puttin' On the Ritz," "Blue Skies" and "Oh! How I Hate to Get Up in the Morning" among others. He could neither read nor write musical notation. Berlin died Sept 22, 1989, at New York, NY.

DALI, SALVADOR: 100th BIRTH ANNIVERSARY. May 11, 1904. A leading painter in the Surrealist movement, Salvador Dali was equally well known for his baffling antics and attempts to shock his audiences. The largest collection of his works resides in the Salvador Dali Museum at St. Petersburg, FL. Born at Figueras, Spain, Dali died there Jan 23, 1989.

EAT WHAT YOU WANT DAY. May 11. Here's a day you may actually enjoy yourself. Ignore all those on-again/off-again warn-

S	M	T	W	T	F	S
						1
2	3	4	5	6	7	8
9	10	11	12	13	14	15
16	17	18	19	20	21	22
23	24	25	26	27	28	29
30	31					

May 2004

☆ Chase's 2004 Calendar of Events ☆   May 11–12

ings. [©2003 by WH.] For info: Thomas & Ruth Roy, Wellcat Holidays, 2418 Long Ln, Lebanon, PA 17046. Phone: (717) 279-0184. E-mail: info@wellcat.com. Web: www.wellcat.com.

ELKIN, STANLEY: BIRTH ANNIVERSARY. May 11, 1930. Born at Brooklyn, NY, Stanley Elkin became a professor at Washington University at St. Louis, MO, where he lectured on fiction writing for more than 30 years. In addition to his teaching, Elkin was a novelist of particular acclaim. Author of 17 books, he was awarded the National Book Critics Circle Award in 1983 for his novel *George Mills*. Elkin died at St. Louis, MO, May 31, 1995.

FAIRBANKS, CHARLES WARREN: BIRTH ANNIVERSARY. May 11, 1852. 26th vice president of the US (1905–09) born at Unionville Center, OH. Died at Indianapolis, IN, June 4, 1918.

GLACIER NATIONAL PARK ESTABLISHED: ANNIVERSARY. May 11, 1910. Located in northwest Montana on the Canadian border. In 1932 Glacier and Waterton Lakes National Park in Alberta were joined together by the governments of the US and Canada as Waterton-Glacier International Peace Park.

GRAHAM, MARTHA: BIRTH ANNIVERSARY. May 11, 1894. Martha Graham was born at Allegheny, PA, and became one of the giants of the modern dance movement in the US. She began her dance career at the comparatively late age of 22 and joined the Greenwich Village Follies in 1923. Her new ideas began to surface in the late '20s and '30s, and by the mid-1930s she was incorporating the rituals of the southwestern American Indians in her work. She is credited with bringing a new psychological depth to modern dance by exploring primal emotions and ancient rituals in her work. She performed until the age of 75, and premiered in her 180th ballet, *The Maple Leaf Rag,* in the fall of 1990. Died Apr 1, 1991, at New York, NY.

HART, JOHN: 225th DEATH ANNIVERSARY. May 11, 1779. Signer of the Declaration of Independence, farmer and legislator, born about 1711 (exact date unknown), at Stonington, CT, died at Hopewell, NJ.

JAPAN: CORMORANT FISHING FESTIVAL. May 11–Oct 15. Cormorant fishing on the Nagara River, Gifu. "This ancient method of catching Ayu, a troutlike fish, with trained cormorants, takes place nightly under the light of blazing torches."

MERRIMAC DESTROYED: ANNIVERSARY. May 11, 1862. After a standoff with the Union ironclad *Monitor* on Mar 9, the Confederate ironclad *Merrimac* was destroyed by the Confederate navy on May 11. In the wake of advancing Union troops in the Peninsular Campaign, the South was forced to destroy the valuable vessel to prevent its capture by Union forces. See also: "Battle of the *Monitor* and the *Merrimac*: Anniv" (Mar 9).

MINNESOTA: ADMISSION DAY: ANNIVERSARY. May 11. Became 32nd state in 1858.

MOON PHASE: LAST QUARTER. May 11. Moon enters Last Quarter phase at 7:04 AM, EDT.

SEATTLE BLACKOUT: ANNIVERSARY. May 11, 1942. Seattle, WA, became the first US city to institute outside blackout control during WWII. All outdoor lighting became subject to permit. By June 1942 cities on both coasts had blackout restrictions.

UNIVERSAL FAMILY WEEK. May 11–17. To stress the importance of the fundamental role of good families in strengthening humankind. For complete info, send $5 to cover expense of printing, handling and postage. For info: Dr. Stanley Drake, Pres, Intl Society of Friendship and Goodwill, 999 Hood Rd, Ste 127, Marietta, GA 30068. Phone: (770) 565-2322. E-mail: ISFGW@bellsouth.net.

BIRTHDAYS TODAY

Louis Farrakhan, 71, Nation of Islam leader, born New York, NY, May 11, 1933.
Bernard Fox, 77, actor ("Bewitched," *Titanic*), born Portalbot, South Wales, May 11, 1927.
Jonathan Jackson, 22, actor (*The Deep End of the Ocean*, "General Hospital"), born Orlando, FL, May 11, 1982.
Robert Jarvik, 58, physician, inventor of artificial heart that went into Barney Clark, born Midland, MI, May 11, 1946.
James M. Jeffords, 70, US Senator (I, Vermont), born Rutland, VT, May 11, 1934.
Natasha Richardson, 41, actress (*The Handmaid's Tale, Nell*), born London, England, May 11, 1963.
Mort Sahl, 77, comic actor (*Don't Make Waves, Doctor You've Got to Be Kidding*), born Montreal, QC, Canada, May 11, 1927.

MAY 12 — WEDNESDAY
Day 133 — 233 Remaining

BATTLE OF SPOTSYLVANIA: ANNIVERSARY. May 12, 1864. After the Battle of the Wilderness, Grant and Lee next engaged at the Battle of Spotsylvania (VA). Lee had positioned his troops in breastworks along a horseshoe formation utilizing the natural features of the landscape. During Grant's attack on this strong defensive position both sides suffered losses of more than 12,000 in what became known as "The Bloody Angle." Lee was forced to use every available man in order to protect the position and so ordered his troops to pull back during the night.

CANNES FILM FESTIVAL. May 12–23. Cannes, France. 57th annual. Premier international film festival, with hundreds of screenings (in competition and out), critical panels, director spotlights, Cannes Market for film distribution, and numerous other cultural and artistic activities. Palme d'Or, Caméra d'Or, Grand Prix, and other awards presented on the last day of the festival. The festival was first held in September 1946, and there have been only 3 cancellations since then, in 1948, 1950 and 1968. For info: Assoc Française du Festival Intl du Film, 99 boulevard Malesherbes, 75 008 Paris, France. Phone: 33 (0) 1-45-61-66-00. E-mail: festival@festival-cannes.fr. Web: www.festival-cannes.org.

DONATE A DAY'S WAGES TO CHARITY DAY. May 12. All working people are asked to donate the money they make on May 12, 2004, to charity. If unable to afford the donation, they are then asked to take the day off of work and donate their time to charity. For info: E-mail: donatetocharity@yahoo.com.

ENGLAND: ROYAL WINDSOR HORSE SHOW. May 12–16. Home Park, Windsor, Berkshire. Major annual show jumping event with royal pageantry and color. Est attendance: 60,000. For info: Penelope Henderson, Sec'y, Royal Windsor Horse Show, The Royal Mews, Windsor Castle, Windsor, Berkshire, England SL4 1NG. Phone: (44) (175) 386-0633. Fax: (44) (175) 383-1074. Web: www.royal-windsor-horse-show.co.uk.

GEORGE VI'S CORONATION: ANNIVERSARY. May 12, 1937. George VI was crowned at Westminster Abbey at London, following the abdication of his brother, Edward VIII. Born Dec 14, 1895, King George died Feb 6, 1952. He was succeeded by his daughter Elizabeth, the current reigning monarch.

HEPBURN, KATHARINE: BIRTH ANNIVERSARY. May 12, 1907. American actress Katharine Houghton Hepburn was born at Hartford, CT. Nominated for 12 Oscars over the course of her career, she won four times: for 1933's *Morning Glory,* 1967's *Guess Who's Coming to Dinner,* 1968's *The Lion in Winter* and 1981's *On Golden Pond*. She is best remembered for her on-and-off-screen pairing with Spencer Tracy. Together, they made 9 films, including *Adam's Rib* and *Woman of the Year,* and enjoyed a 27-year personal relationship. There is often confusion regarding her date of birth; however, in her 1991 autobiography *Me: Stories of My Life,* she confirmed the May date and admitted often giving out her brother's birth date as her own. She died at Old Saybrook, CT, on June 29, 2003.

May 12 ☆ Chase's 2004 Calendar of Events ☆

INPEX®—AMERICA'S LARGEST INVENTION TRADE SHOW AND INVENTORS CONFERENCE. May 12–15. Monroeville ExpoMart, Pittsburgh, PA. INPEX is The Invention/New Product Exposition. Features fascinating inventions, new products and innovations. For info: Nicole Mike, 217 Ninth St, Pittsburgh, PA 15222. Phone: (412) 288-2136. Fax: (412) 288-2513. E-mail: nmike@isc-online.com. Web: www.inventionshow.com.

LEAR, EDWARD: BIRTH ANNIVERSARY. May 12, 1812. English artist and author, best remembered for his light verse and limericks. Lear was born at Highgate, England, and died at San Remo, Italy, Jan 29, 1888. See also: "Limerick Day" (May 12).

LIMERICK DAY. May 12. Observed on the birthday of one of its champions, Edward Lear. The limerick, which dates from the early 18th century, has been described as the "only fixed verse form indigenous to the English language." It gained its greatest popularity following the publication of Edward Lear's *Book of Nonsense* (and its sequels). Write a limerick today! Example: There was a young poet named Lear/Who said, it is just as I fear/Five lines are enough/For this kind of stuff/Make a limerick each day of the year. See also: "Lear, Edward: Birth Anniversary" (May 12).

NATIONAL NIGHTSHIFT WORKERS DAY. May 12. To honor those workers who reverse their natural circadian rhythm to keep business running 24 hours a day. Annually, the second Wednesday of May. For info: Velcea Kae, 3 Chester Rd, Springfield, VT 05156.

NATIONAL THIRD SHIFT WORKERS DAY. May 12. To show appreciation for and to honor those often-forgotten workers who toil through the night to keep countless companies and businesses running smoothly. Annually, the second Wednesday in May. For info: Jeff Corbett, PO Box 2, Statesville, NC 28687.

NIGHTINGALE, FLORENCE: BIRTH ANNIVERSARY. May 12, 1820. English nurse and public health activist who, through her unselfish devotion to nursing, contributed perhaps more than any other single person to the development of modern nursing procedures and dignity of nursing as a profession. Founder of the Nightingale training school for nurses. Author of *Notes on Nursing*. Born at Florence, Italy. Died at London, England, Aug 13, 1910.

NORTHERN IRELAND: ROYAL ULSTER AGRICULTURAL SOCIETY BALMORAL SHOW. May 12–14. The Showgrounds, Balmoral, Belfast. The premier agricultural show on Northern Ireland's calendar. Est attendance: 60,000. For info: Mr Philip Rees, Royal Ulster Agricultural Society, Balmoral Showgrounds, Belfast, Northern Ireland BT9 6GW. Phone: (44) (28) 9066 5225. Fax: (44) (28) 9066 1264. E-mail: prees@kingshall.co.uk. Web: www.balmoralshow.co.uk.

ODOMETER INVENTED: ANNIVERSARY. May 12, 1847. Anniversary of the invention of the first odometer, invented by Mormon pioneer William Clayton while crossing the plains in a covered wagon. Previous to this, mileage was calculated by counting the revolutions of a rag tied to a spoke of a wagon wheel. For info: Museum of Church History and Art, 45 North West Temple, Salt Lake City, UT 84150. Phone: (801) 240-4604.

PORTUGAL: PILGRIMAGE TO FATIMA: ANNIVERSARY. May 12–13. Commemorates first appearance of the Virgin of the Rosary to little shepherd children May 13, 1917. Pilgrims come to Cova da Iria, religious center, candlelit procession, Mass of the sick, for annual observance.

SEDONA CHAMBER MUSIC FESTIVAL. May 12–16. Sedona, AZ. 21st annual festival features internationally acclaimed ensembles and artists in 12–14 concerts. For info: Chamber Music Sedona, PO Box 153, Sedona, AZ 86339-0153. Phone: (928) 204-2415. E-mail: SedonaCMS@aol.com. Web: www.chambermusicsedona.org.

SMALL BUSINESS WEEK. May 12–14 (tentative). To honor the 22 million small businesses in the US. Previously commemorated in June. For info: Small Business Administration, Info Services, 409 3rd St SW, 7th Fl, Washington, DC 20416. Phone: (202) 205-6531. Web: www.sba.gov.

BIRTHDAYS TODAY

MacKenzie Astin, 31, actor ("The Long Island Incident"), son of John Astin and Patty Duke, born Los Angeles, CA, May 12, 1973.
Burt Bacharach, 75, composer ("Walk On By," "Close to You," "Raindrops Keep Fallin' on My Head"); many film scores, born Kansas City, MO, May 12, 1929.
Stephen Baldwin, 38, actor (*The Usual Suspects*), born Massapequa, NY, May 12, 1966.
Lawrence Peter ("Yogi") Berra, 79, Hall of Fame baseball player, former baseball coach and manager, born St. Louis, MO, May 12, 1925.
Jason Biggs, 26, actor (*American Pie, Loser*), born Pompton Plains, NJ, May 12, 1978.
Bruce Boxleitner, 53, actor (*How the West Was Won*, "Scarecrow and Mrs King"), born Elgin, IL, May 12, 1951.
Gabriel Byrne, 54, actor (*The Usual Suspects*), born Dublin, Ireland, May 12, 1950.
Christian Campbell, 32, actor ("Malibu Shores," *Cold Hearts*), born Toronto, ON, Canada, May 12, 1972.
George Carlin, 67, comedian ("That Girl," "The George Carlin Show"), born New York, NY, May 12, 1937.
Lindsay Crouse, 56, actress (*Slap Shot, The Verdict, Places in the Heart*), born New York, NY, May 12, 1948.
Emilio Estevez, 42, actor (*Breakfast Club, Repo Man*), born New York, NY, May 12, 1962.
Kim Fields, 35, actress ("The Facts of Life," "Living Single"), born Los Angeles, CA, May 12, 1969.
Kim Greist, 46, actress (*Brazil, Throw Momma from the Train*), born Stamford, CT, May 12, 1958.
Tony Hawk, 35, skateboarder, born Carlsbad, CA, May 12, 1969.
Jamie Luner, 33, actress ("Melrose Place," "Profiler"), born Los Angeles, CA, May 12, 1971.
Millie Perkins, 66, actress ("Knots Landing," *The Diary of Anne Frank, Wall Street*), born Passaic, NJ, May 12, 1938.
Ving Rhames, 43, actor (*Pulp Fiction*), born New York, NY, May 12, 1961.
Tom Snyder, 68, broadcast journalist, TV personality, born Milwaukee, WI, May 12, 1936.
Frank Stella, 68, artist (*Empress of India*), born Malden, MA, May 12, 1936.
Steve Winwood, 56, musician, singer, born Birmingham, England, May 12, 1948.

	S	M	T	W	T	F	S
May 2004							1
	2	3	4	5	6	7	8
	9	10	11	12	13	14	15
	16	17	18	19	20	21	22
	23	24	25	26	27	28	29
	30	31					

★ Chase's 2004 Calendar of Events ★   May 13

MAY 13 — THURSDAY
Day 134 — 232 Remaining

ATTEMPTED ASSASSINATION OF POPE JOHN PAUL II: ANNIVERSARY. May 13, 1981. Pope John Paul II was shot twice at close range while riding in an open automobile at St. Peter's Square at Rome, Italy. Two other persons also were wounded. An escaped terrorist, Mehmet Ali Agca (already under sentence of death for the murder of a Turkish journalist), was arrested immediately and was convicted July 22, 1981, of attempted murder of the pope. After convalescence Pope John Paul II was pronounced recovered by his doctors Aug 14, 1981. In 2000 Agca was released from prison and extradited to Turkey.

BIG TEN SOFTBALL TOURNAMENT. May 13–15. Site of conference champion. Est attendance: 1,500. For info: Sue Lister, Big Ten Conference, 1500 W Higgins Rd, Park Ridge, IL 60068-6300. Phone: (847) 696-1010. Fax: (847) 696-1110. Web: www.bigten.org.

CALAVERAS COUNTY FAIR AND JUMPING FROG JUBILEE. May 13–16. Calaveras Fairgrounds, Angels Camp, CA. County fair and reenactment of Mark Twain's "Celebrated Jumping Frog of Calaveras County." This "Superbowl" of the sport of frog jumping attracts more than 3,000 frogs annually from around the world. Est attendance: 45,000. For info: 39th District Agricultural Assn, S Highway 49, PO Box 489, Angels Camp, CA 95222. Phone: (209) 736-2561. Fax: (209) 736-2476. E-mail: info@frogtown.org. Web: www.frogtown.org.

CANADA: THUNDER BAY CHAMBER OF COMMERCE TRADE SHOW. May 13–15. Thunder Bay, ON. For info: Thunder Bay Chamber of Commerce, 857 May St North, Thunder Bay, ON, Canada P7C 3S2. Phone: (807) 624-2621. Fax: (807) 622-7752. E-mail: chamber@tb-chamber.on.ca. Web: tb-chamber.on.ca.

CORPS OF DISCOVERY DEPARTURE: CAMP RIVER DUBOIS (LEWIS AND CLARK BICENTENNIAL EVENT). May 13–16. Hartfood and Wood River, IL. Commemorates 200th anniversary of the Lewis and Clark Expedition's departure on May 14, 1804, from its winter encampment at Camp River Dubois for its journey west. Event will feature historical re-enactment of departure, musical and dramatic entertainment and period heritage craft and skill demonstrations. For info: Mr. Brian Widaman, Alden Hall #109, Godfrey, IL 62035. Phone: (618) 467-2288. E-mail: bwidaman@lc.cc.il.us. Web: www.lewisandclarkillinois.org.

DOUGLAS, VIRGINIA O'HANLON: DEATH ANNIVERSARY. May 13, 1971. Virginia O'Hanlon Douglas lived a long and productive life as an educator and a loving mother. However, to the reading public she is re-introduced year after year at Christmas time, as the disheartened eight-year-old who asked the staff of The New York Sun whether Santa Claus exists. In a famous 1897 editorial Francis P. Church answered her question and reassured Virginia that yes, indeed " . . . there is a Santa Claus." Douglas died at Valatie, NY, at the age of 81.

GETTYSBURG BLUEGRASS FESTIVAL. May 13–16. Gettysburg, PA. Granite Hill Campground on Rt 116. Est attendance: 5,000. For info: Gettysburg CVB, PO Box 4117, Gettysburg, PA 17325. Phone: (717) 334-6274. Fax: (717) 334-1166. E-mail: gettysburgcvb@dejazzd.com. Web: www.gettysburgcvb.org.

LOUIS, JOE: 90th BIRTH ANNIVERSARY. May 13, 1914. World heavyweight boxing champion, 1937–49, nicknamed the "Brown Bomber." Joseph Louis Barrow was born near Lafayette, AL. He died Apr 12, 1981, at Las Vegas, NV. Burial at Arlington National Cemetery. (Louis's burial there, by presidential waiver, was the 39th exception ever to the eligibility rules for burial in Arlington National Cemetery.)

MAGNOLIA BLOSSOM FESTIVAL. May 13–15. Magnolia, AR. 16th annual. The week's events include old-fashioned chicken supper, arts and crafts, entertainment and activities for all. World Championship Steak Cookoff (May 15) dinner served under fragrant magnolia trees. Est attendance: 20,000. For info: Magnolia-Columbia County Chamber of Commerce, 202 N Pine, PO Box 866, Magnolia, AR 71754-0866. Phone: (800) 482-3330. E-mail: magcoc@arkansas.net. Web: www.magblossom.org.

MEXICAN WAR DECLARED: ANNIVERSARY. May 13, 1846. Although fighting had begun days earlier, Congress officially declared war on Mexico on this date. The struggle cost the lives of 11,300 American soldiers and resulted in the annexation by the US of land that became parts of Oklahoma, New Mexico, Arizona, Nevada, California, Utah and Colorado. The war ended in 1848. See also: "Treaty of Guadalupe Hidalgo" (Feb 2).

PHILADELPHIA POLICE BOMBING: ANNIVERSARY. May 13, 1985. During the siege of the radical group MOVE at Philadelphia, PA, police in a helicopter reportedly dropped a bomb containing the powerful military plastic explosive C-4 on the building in which the group was housed. The bomb and the resulting fire left 11 persons dead (including four children) and destroyed 61 homes.

SAINT LAWRENCE SEAWAY ACT: 50th ANNIVERSARY. May 13, 1954. President Dwight D. Eisenhower signed legislation authorizing US–Canadian construction of a waterway that would make it possible for oceangoing ships to reach the Great Lakes.

SPACE MILESTONE: *ENDEAVOUR* (US). May 13, 1992. Three astronauts from the shuttle *Endeavour* simultaneously walked in space for the first time.

SULLIVAN, ARTHUR: BIRTH ANNIVERSARY. May 13, 1842. English composer best known for light operas (with Sir William Gilbert), born at London, England. Died there Nov 22, 1900.

TUNIS CAMPAIGN VICTORY: ANNIVERSARY. May 13, 1943. General Sir Harold Alexander telegraphed Winston Churchill, who was in Washington attending a conference, "It is my duty to report that the Tunis campaign is over. All enemy resistance has ceased. We are masters of the North African shores." About 250,000 Germans and Italians surrendered in the last few days of the campaign. This Allied victory in North Africa helped open Mediterranean shipping lanes.

WELLS, MARY: BIRTH ANNIVERSARY. May 13, 1943. Motown's first big star, Mary Wells was born at Detroit, MI. She was known for such hits as "You Beat Me to the Punch," "Two Lovers" and her signature song, "My Guy." She was one of a group of black artists of the '60s who helped end musical segregation by being played on white radio stations. Mary Wells died July 26, 1992, at Los Angeles, CA.

BIRTHDAYS TODAY

Franklyn Ajaye, 55, actor ("Keep on Truckin'," *Car Wash*), born Brooklyn, NY, May 13, 1949.

Beatrice Arthur, 78, actress (*Mame*, "Maude," "Golden Girls"), born Bernice Frankel, New York, NY, May 13, 1926.

Frances Barber, 47, actress (*Sammy and Rosie Get Laid*, *We Think the World of You*), born Wolverhampton, England, May 13, 1957.

Clive Barnes, 77, critic, born London, England, May 13, 1927.

Mike Bibby, 26, basketball player, born Cherry Hill, NJ, May 13, 1978.

Harvey Keitel, 65, actor (*Mean Streets*, *Blue Collar*, *Bugsy*, *The Piano*), born Brooklyn, NY, May 13, 1939.

Julianne Phillips, 42, actress (*Allie & Me*, "Sisters"), born Lake Oswego, OR, May 13, 1962.

Tim Pigott-Smith, 58, actor ("The Jewel in the Crown," *Remains of the Day*), born Rugby, England, May 13, 1946.

Dennis ("Worm") Rodman, 43, former basketball player, born Trenton, NJ, May 13, 1961.

Darius Rucker, 36, lead singer (Hootie and the Blowfish), born Charleston, SC, May 13, 1968.

Bobby Valentine, 54, baseball manager and former player, born Stamford, CT, May 13, 1950.

Stevie Wonder, 54, singer, musician (16 Grammy Awards; "I Just Called to Say I Love You"), born Steveland Morris Hardaway, Saginaw, MI, May 13, 1950.

MAY 14 — FRIDAY
Day 135 — 231 Remaining

BALANCHINE-GRAHAM COLLABORATION: 45th ANNIVERSARY. May 14, 1959. In a melding of classical ballet and modern dance, George Balanchine's and Martha Graham's *Episodes* premiered. A new experience for ballet enthusiasts, half of the program was choreographed by Balanchine and the other half by Graham.

BARABOO CIRCUS HERITAGE. May 14–16. Sauk County Fairgrounds, Baraboo, WI. A weekend of circus fun for Boy Scouts, Girl Scouts, 4-H, church youth groups and other organized youth groups. Hiking, camping, team skills competition, Pinewood Derby race, and the Circus World Museum. Annually, the weekend after Mother's Day. Est attendance: 2,000. For info: Baraboo Circus Heritage, Boy Scouts of America, Four Lakes Council, 34 Schroeder Ct, Madison, WI 53711-6222. Phone: (608) 273-1005.

BAY TO BREAKERS RACE. May 14–16. San Francisco, CA. Largest footrace in the world attracts 80,000 runners each year, from world-class athletes to fun runners; post-race festival, live concert, food and beverages. Est attendance: 75,000. For info: Bay to Breakers, 1213 Evans Ave, San Francisco, CA 94124. Phone: (415) 359-2800. E-mail: registration@baytobreakers.com. Web: www.baytobreakers.com.

BIG TEN MEN'S/WOMEN'S OUTDOOR TRACK AND FIELD CHAMPIONSHIPS. May 14–16. Site TBD. Est attendance: 1,500. For info: Sue Lister, Assoc Commissioner, Big Ten Conference, 1500 W Higgins Rd, Park Ridge, IL 60068-6300. Phone: (847) 696-1010. Fax: (847) 696-1110. Web: www.bigten.org.

CARLSBAD CAVERNS NATIONAL PARK ESTABLISHED: ANNIVERSARY. May 14, 1930. Located in southwestern New Mexico, Carlsbad Caverns was proclaimed a national monument, Oct 25, 1923, and later established as national park and preserve.

DERMOTT'S ANNUAL CRAWFISH FESTIVAL. May 14–15. Dermott, AR. 19th annual. To publicize and popularize crawfish as a delicacy, to promote the area and to raise funds for industrial expansion. Family fun, arts, crafts, exotic foods, carnival, live music and street dances. Annually, the third weekend in May. Est attendance: 20,000. For info: Dermott Area Chamber of Commerce, Box 147, Dermott, AR 71638. Phone: (870) 538-5656.

DULCIMER DAYS. May 14–16. Coshocton, OH. Dulcimer competition, workshops, exhibits, open stage, jam sessions, Saturday evening concert and more. Annually, the third weekend of May. Est attendance: 1,400. For info: Roscoe Village, 381 Hill St, Coshocton, OH 43812. Phone: (800) 877-1830 or (740) 622-9310. Fax: (740) 623-6555. E-mail: rvmarketing@roscoevillage.com. Web: www.roscoevillage.com.

"ERNIE KOVACS" TV PREMIERE: ANNIVERSARY. May 14, 1951. Comedian Ernie Kovacs first hosted "It's Time for Ernie," a 15-minute afternoon program on NBC in May of 1951 before replacing the "Kukla, Fran and Ollie Show" with "Ernie in Kovacsland." "The Ernie Kovacs Show" debuted on Dec 30, 1952. Kovacs also appeared on a variety of daytime and prime-time series and was a fill-in for Steve Allen on the "Tonight!" show. His early shows featured his wife, Edie Adams.

★ ★ ★

FAHRENHEIT, GABRIEL DANIEL: BIRTH ANNIVERSARY. May 14, 1686. German physicist whose name is attached to one of the major temperature measurement scales. He introduced the use of mercury in thermometers and greatly improved their accuracy. Born at Danzig, Germany, he died at Amsterdam, Holland, Sept 16, 1736.

FASHION SHOW. May 14. Mount Mary College, Milwaukee, WI. Student designer fashion show. Est attendance: 1,200. For info: Mary Cain, Mount Mary College, 2900 N Menomonee River Parkway, Milwaukee, WI 53222-4597. Phone: (414) 256-1210. Fax: (414) 256-1239. E-mail: mktg@mtmary.edu. Web: www.mtmary.edu.

FIRST FORMAL FEMALE HOUSE PAGE APPOINTMENT: ANNIVERSARY. May 14, 1973. The House of Representatives received formal approval of the appointment of female pages in 1972. On May 14, 1973, in the 93rd Congress, Felda Looper was appointed as the successor to Gene Cox who, for three hours, had served as the first female page 34 years earlier.

FISHING HAS NO BOUNDARIES—HAYWARD EVENT. May 14–16. Lake Chippewa Campgrounds, Hayward, WI. A three-day fishing experience for disabled persons. Any disability, age, sex, race, etc, eligible. Fishing with experienced guides on one of the best fishing waters in Wisconsin, attended by 200 participants and 500 volunteers. Advance registration by Apr 16. Est attendance: 2,400. For info: Fishing Has No Boundaries, PO Box 375, Hayward, WI 54843. Phone: (715) 634-3185. Fax: (715) 634-1305. E-mail: hayfhnb@juno.com.

GAINSBOROUGH, THOMAS: BIRTH ANNIVERSARY. May 14, 1727 (OS). English landscape and portrait painter. Among his most remembered works: *The Blue Boy*, *The Watering Place* and *The Market Cart*. Born at Sudbury, Suffolk, England, he was baptized on May 14, 1727 (OS), and he died at London, Aug 2, 1788.

JAMESTOWN, VIRGINIA: FOUNDING ANNIVERSARY. May 14, 1607 (OS). The first permanent English settlement in what is now the US took place at Jamestown, VA (named for England's King James I), on this date. Captains John Smith and Christopher Newport were among the leaders of the group of royally chartered Virginia Company settlers who had traveled from Plymouth, England, in three small ships: *Susan Constant*, *Godspeed* and *Discovery*.

LEWIS AND CLARK EXPEDITION SETS OUT: 200th ANNIVERSARY. May 14, 1804. Charged by President Thomas Jefferson with finding a route to the Pacific, Captain Meriwether Lewis and Lieutenant William Clark left St. Louis with a 33-member group skilled in botany, zoology, outdoor survival and other scientific skills. They arrived at the Pacific coast of Oregon in November 1805 and returned to St. Louis, Sept 23, 1806. (See also Jan 18 and Sept 23.)

LEWIS AND CLARK ST. CHARLES BICENTENNIAL NATIONAL SIGNATURE EVENT. May 14–23. St. Charles, MO. The Corps of Discovery's arrival in St. Charles kicks off a week-long event featuring a historical reenactment of Lewis and Clark's encampment in 1804 prior to embarking on the exploration of the Louisiana Purchase. Activities include parades with fife and drum corps, church service and 19th-century crafts, music, food and demonstrations. The fun concludes when St. Charles bids adieu to the expedition's replica keelboats and pirouges as they head up the Mississippi River. Est attendance: 25,000. For info: St. Charles Conv and Visitors Bureau, 230 S Main, St. Charles, MO 63301. Phone: (800) 366-2427 or (636) 946-7776. Web: www.lewisandclarkstcharles.com.

LILAC FESTIVAL. May 14–23. Highland Park, Rochester, NY. Developed by renowned park designer Frederick Law Olmsted, Highland Park is the site of the Lilac Festival, the largest celebration of its kind in North America. In addition to the spectacle of more than 500 varieties of lilacs in bloom, the festival provides free admission, free entertainment, free children's activities and entertainment, a parade, a 10K race, two juried art shows, a

May 2004	S	M	T	W	T	F	S
							1
	2	3	4	5	6	7	8
	9	10	11	12	13	14	15
	16	17	18	19	20	21	22
	23	24	25	26	27	28	29
	30	31					

☆ Chase's 2004 Calendar of Events ☆ May 14

senior citizens' day and music festivals. Est attendance: 400,000. For info: Susan LeBeau, Lilac Festival, 171 Reservoir Ave, Rochester, NY 14620. Phone: (716) 256-4960. Fax: (716) 256-4968. E-mail: info@lilacfestival.com. Web: www.lilacfestival.com.

LOST IN THE '50s. May 14–16. Sandpoint, ID. Dance and show with '50s & '60s stars, vintage car parade, car show, car rally and 5K run. Est attendance: 10,000. For info: Lost in the 50s, Carolyn Gleason, Chair, 215 S 2nd Ave, Sandpoint, ID 83864. Phone: (208) 263-9321 or (208) 265-LOST. E-mail: lost50s@sandpoint.net.

MAIFEST. May 14–16. MainStrasse Village, Covington, KY. MainStrasse celebrates the German tradition of welcoming the first spring wines and the beginning of the festival season. Artist and craftsman exhibits, food and drink, live music and entertainment. Est attendance: 175,000. For info: Donna Kremer, Admin Coord, MainStrasse Village, 605 Philadelphia St, Covington, KY 41011. Phone: (859) 491-0458 or (513) 357-MAIN. Fax: (859) 655-7932. Web: www.mainstrasse.org.

MILLION MOM MARCH: ANNIVERSARY. May 14, 2000. Women rallied in Washington, DC, and 60 other US cities to urge Congress to "get serious about common sense gun legislation." For info: Million Mom March, 1225 Eye St NW, Ste 1100, Washington, DC 20005. Phone: (202) 898-0792. E-mail: national@millionmommarch.org. Web: www.millionmommarch.com.

MOREL MUSHROOM FESTIVAL. May 14–16. Muscoda, Wisconsin's "Morel Mushroom Capital," celebrates the end of the morel mushroom's two-week peak season. The 22nd annual celebration includes the buying and selling of morels, slow-pitch softball tournament, arts & crafts, custom car show, antique tractor pull, helicopter rides and many fun activities for the whole family. Saturday evening is the annual Fireman's steak feed followed by music and fireworks, Sunday brings a huge parade. Annually, the weekend after Mother's Day. Est attendance: 2,000. For info: Village of Muscoda, Morel Mushroom Fest, PO Box 206, Muscoda, WI 53573-0206. Phone: (608) 739-3182. Fax: (608) 739-3183. E-mail: cljohnson@wppisys.org. Web: www.muscoda.com.

NATIONAL CHILDREN AND POLICE DAY. May 14. A day set aside for the interaction of the local police with school children so as to build relationships that will increase children's appreciation for the police and other authority figures. Also a day for school children throughout the US to say "Thank You" to the police for all the services rendered throughout the year. Annually, the Friday of National Police Week. For info: BJ Woods, 5126 La Vista Court, Granbury, TX 76049. Phone: (817) 910-2307. Fax: (817) 326-5927. E-mail: bjwoods@granbury.com.

NATIONAL RECEPTIONISTS DAY. May 14. Day of recognition for our nation's frontline personnel in business, because you only get one chance to make a good first impression. Receptionists may go by other names such as host/hostess, maitre d', front desk clerk, operator, customer service representative, information desk personnel or anyone responsible for creating or maintaining a favorable image for the company by greeting clients and guests. There are some 892,000 receptionists in the US. Annually, May 14 or the following Monday if May 14 falls on Saturday or Sunday. For info: Jennifer Alexander, Natl Receptionists Society, 180 Broad St #1216, Stamford, CT 06901. Phone: (203) 323-1480. E-mail: jennifer@nationalreceptionists.com. Web: www.nationalreceptionists.com.

NORWAY: MIDNIGHT SUN AT NORTH CAPE. May 14–July 30. North Cape. First day of the season with around-the-clock sunshine. At North Cape, the sun never dips below the horizon from May 14 to July 30, but the night is bright long before and after these dates.

OWEN, ROBERT: BIRTH ANNIVERSARY. May 14, 1771. English progressive owner of spinning works, philanthropist, Utopian socialist, founder of New Harmony, IN, born at Newtown, Wales. Died there Nov 17, 1858.

PHILIPPINES: CARABAO FESTIVAL. May 14–15. Pulilan, Bulacan; Nueva Ecija; Angono, Rizal. Parade of farmers to honor their patron saint, San Isidro, with hundreds of "dressed up" carabaos participating.

SMALLPOX VACCINE DISCOVERED: ANNIVERSARY. May 14, 1796. In the 18th century, smallpox was a widespread and often fatal disease. Edward Jenner, a physician in rural England, heard reports of dairy farmers who apparently became immune to smallpox as a result of exposure to cowpox, a related but milder disease. After two decades of studying the phenomenon, Jenner injected cowpox into a healthy eight-year-old boy, who subsequently developed cowpox. Six weeks later, Jenner inoculated the boy with smallpox. He remained healthy. Jenner called this new procedure *vaccination*, from *vaccinia*, another term for cowpox. Within 18 months, 12,000 people in England had been vaccinated and the number of smallpox deaths dropped by two-thirds.

SPACE MILESTONE: *SKYLAB* (US): ANNIVERSARY. May 14, 1973. The US launched *Skylab*, its first manned orbiting laboratory.

STAMP EXPO. May 14–16. Radisson Hotel, Anaheim, CA. Est attendance: 4,000. For info: Intl Stamp Collectors Society, PO Box 854, Van Nuys, CA 91408. Phone: (818) 997-6496. Fax: (818) 988-4337. E-mail: iibick@aol.com. Web: www.bick.net.

"THE STARS AND STRIPES FOREVER" DAY: ANNIVERSARY. May 14, 1897. Anniversary of the first public performance of John Philip Sousa's march "The Stars and Stripes Forever," at Philadelphia, PA. The occasion was the unveiling of a statue of George Washington, and President William McKinley was present.

UNDERGROUND AMERICA DAY. May 14. Underground America Day is one man's (Malcolm Wells) attempt to get others to think of designing and building structures underground. Mr Wells publishes illustrations and humorous suggestions for celebrating Underground America Day. 30th anniversary. Annually, May 14. For info: Malcolm Wells, 673 Satucket Rd, Brewster, MA 02631. Phone: (508) 896-6850. Fax: (508) 896-5116.

VIKING FEST. May 14–16. Poulsbo, WA. Celebrating Poulsbo's Norwegian heritage, festival features Scandinavian luncheon, pancake breakfast, road race, car show, food booths, parade, entertainment, crafts, outdoor concerts and carnival. Coincides with "Syttende Mai" (17th of May)—Norwegian Constitution Day. Est attendance: 50,000. For info: Viking Fest, PO Box 1125, Poulsbo, WA 98370. Phone: (360) 779-3378. E-mail: marketing@vikingfest.org. Web: www.VikingFest.org.

WAAC: ANNIVERSARY. May 14, 1942. During WWII women became eligible to enlist for noncombat duties in the Women's Auxiliary Army Corps (WAAC) by an act of Congress. Women also served as Women Appointed for Voluntary Emergency Service (WAVES), Women's Auxiliary Ferrying Squadron (WAFS), and Coast Guard or Semper Paratus Always Ready Service (SPARS), the Women's Reserve of the Marine Corp.

BIRTHDAYS TODAY

Cate Blanchett, 35, actress (*Elizabeth, Lord of the Rings*), born Melbourne, Australia, May 14, 1969.
David Byrne, 52, singer (Talking Heads), composer (songs, film scores), born Dumbarton, Scotland, May 14, 1952.
Byron L. Dorgan, 62, US Senator (D, North Dakota), born Dickinson, ND, May 14, 1942.

Meg Foster, 56, actress ("Cagney & Lacey," *The Emerald Forest, They Live*), born Reading, PA, May 14, 1948.
George Lucas, 60, filmmaker (*Star Wars* films, *American Graffiti*), born Modesto, CA, May 14, 1944.
Jose Dennis Martinez, 49, former baseball player, born Granada, Nicaragua, May 14, 1955.
Patrice Munsel, 79, opera singer, born Spokane, WA, May 14, 1925.
Ralph Neas, 58, president, People for the American Way, born Brookline, MA, May 14, 1946.
Atanasio (Tony) Perez, 62, Hall of Fame baseball player, born Camaguey, Cuba, May 14, 1942.
Tim Roth, 43, actor (*Pulp Fiction*), born London, England, May 14, 1961.
Valerie Still, 43, basketball player, born Lexington, KY, May 14, 1961.
Robert Zemeckis, 52, director (*Forrest Gump, Back to the Future*), born Chicago, IL, May 14, 1952.

MAY 15 — SATURDAY
Day 136 — 230 Remaining

★**ARMED FORCES DAY.** May 15. Presidential Proclamation 5983, of May 17, 1989, covers the third Saturday in May in all succeeding years. Originally proclaimed as "Army Day" for Apr 6, beginning in 1936 (S.Con.Res. 30 of Apr 2, 1936). S.Con.Res. 5 of Mar 16, 1937, requested annual Apr 6 issuance, which was done through 1949. Always the third Saturday in May since 1950. Traditionally issued once by each Administration.

BAUM, LYMAN FRANK: BIRTH ANNIVERSARY. May 15, 1856. American newspaperman who wrote the Wizard of Oz stories was born at Chittenango, NY. Although *The Wonderful Wizard of Oz* is the most famous, Baum also wrote many other books for children, including more than a dozen about Oz. He died at Hollywood, CA, May 6, 1919.

BEVERLY HILLS: AFFAIRE IN THE GARDENS. May 15–16 (also Oct 16–17). Beverly Gardens Park at Rodeo Drive, Beverly Hills, CA. To foster an appreciation of arts in the community. Juried show; only fine arts and crafts considered. Garden setting. Biannually, the third weekends in May and October. Est attendance: 40,000. For info: Karen McLean, Art Show Coordinator, Beverly Hills Recreation and Parks Dept, 501 Doheny Rd, Beverly Hills, CA 90210. Phone: (310) 550-4796. Fax: (310) 858-9238.

CHEROKEE ROSE FESTIVAL. May 15. Gilmer, TX. Car show, turtle race, children's games, ice cream crank-off, quilt show and much more. For info: Gilmer Area Chamber of Commerce, PO Box 854, Gilmer, TX 75644. Phone: (903) 843-2413 or (903) 843-3981. Fax: (903) 843-3759. E-mail: upchamber@aol.com. Web: www.gilmerareachamber.com.

COTTEN, JOSEPH: BIRTH ANNIVERSARY. May 15, 1905. Stage and screen star Joseph Cotten was born at Petersburg, VA. Among Cotten's movie credits were *Citizen Kane, The Magnificent Ambersons* and *The Third Man*. Among his most noted performances on Broadway were *The Philadelphia Story* and *Once More With Feeling*. Joseph Cotten died Feb 6, 1994, at Los Angeles.

EASTERN PACIFIC HURRICANE SEASON. May 15–Nov 30. Eastern Pacific defined as: Coast to 140 degrees west longitude. Info from: US Dept of Commerce, Natl Oceanic and Atmospheric Admin, Rockville, MD 20852.

	S	M	T	W	T	F	S
May 2004							1
	2	3	4	5	6	7	8
	9	10	11	12	13	14	15
	16	17	18	19	20	21	22
	23	24	25	26	27	28	29
	30	31					

FIRST FLIGHT ATTENDANT: ANNIVERSARY. May 15, 1930. Ellen Church became the first airline stewardess (today's flight attendant), flying on a United Airlines flight from San Francisco to Cheyenne, WY.

FISHING HAS NO BOUNDARIES. May 15–16. Freeman Lake, Monticello, IN. A two-day event for disabled persons to experience fishing on the lake. Any disability, sex, age, race, etc, are eligible. For info: FHNB, 7805 N Harrison, PO Box 325, Battle Ground, IN 47920. Phone: (765) 567-2567. E-mail: smlinder2000@yahoo.com.

FRISCH, MAX: BIRTH ANNIVERSARY. May 15, 1911. Max Frisch was one of Europe's leading post–World War II literary figures. His work includes the novels *Homo Faber, I'm Not Stiller, Juerg Reinhardt* and plays *The Firebugs, Andorra*. In addition to his writing, he was a controversial critic of his native Switzerland. Born at Zurich, he died there Apr 4, 1991.

GASOLINE RATIONING: ANNIVERSARY. May 15, 1942. Seventeen eastern states initiated gasoline rationing as part of the war effort. By Sept 25, rationing was nationwide. A limit of three gallons a week for nonessential purposes was set and a 35 mph speed limit was imposed.

GEORGE WALLACE SHOT: ANNIVERSARY. May 15, 1972. George Wallace, a former governor of Alabama and a symbol of segregation, was shot by Arthur Bremer while Wallace was at Laurel, MD, campaigning for the US presidency. For the remainder of his life (until he died in 1998), Wallace was paralyzed from the waist down. On Aug 4, 1972, Bremer was sentenced to 67 years in prison for the shooting.

HUMANATEE/ST. MARKS FESTIVAL. May 15 (tentative). San Marcos de Apalache State Historic Site, St. Marks, FL. Celebrate and welcome manatees back to St. Marks and Wakulla Rivers. Food, displays, music, walk and much more. Annually, the third Saturday in May. Est attendance: 1,500. For info: HuManatee, PO Box 52, St. Marks, FL 32355. Phone: (850) 925-6412 or San Marcos Fort at (850) 922-6007.

JAMESTOWN LANDING DAY. May 15. Jamestown Settlement, Williamsburg, VA. Maritime demonstrations and interpretative activities exploring contact between European and Virginia Indian cultures mark the 397th anniversary of the founding of America's first permanent English colony. Special programs and events are also held at Historic Jamestowne, administered by the Colonial National Historical Park and the Association for the Preservation of Virginia Antiquities. For info: Jamestown-Yorktown Foundation, PO Box 1607, Williamsburg, VA 23187. Phone: (757) 253-4838 or toll-free (888) 593-4682. Fax: (757) 253-5299. Web: www.historyisfun.org.

JAPAN: AOI MATSURI (HOLLYHOCK FESTIVAL). May 15. Kyoto. The festival features a pageant reproducing imperial processions of ancient times that paid homage to the shrine of Shimogamo and Kamigamo.

LIBERACE BIRTHDAY CELEBRATION AND LIBERACE PLAY-A-LIKE COMPETITION. May 15. The Liberace Museum, Las Vegas, NV. To celebrate Liberace's birthday, the museum will host the annual Liberace "Play-a-Like" Competition. Judges pianists on keyboard technique, costume and presentation in two divisions: professional and non-professional. Winners receive commemorative awards. Annually, the Saturday before May 16 (Liberace's birthday). Est attendance: 1,000. For info: Jamie G. James, The James Agency, 3630 Coldwater Canyon Ave, Studio City, CA 91604. Phone: (818) 508-4902. Fax: (818) 508-0562. E-mail: jjames@liberace.org.

LIBERTY SPRING ON THE SQUARE FESTIVAL. May 15. Historic Downtown Square, Liberty, MO. Handmade crafts, antiques, art and food booths. Annually, the third Saturday in May. Est attendance: 10,000. For info: Wendy Adams-Webb, 1600 S Withers Rd, Liberty, MO 64068. Phone: (816) 792-6009 x 3337. Fax: (816) 792-6148. E-mail: wwebb@ci.liberty.mo.us. Web: ci.liberty.mo.us.

☆ Chase's 2004 Calendar of Events ☆ May 15

MAIFEST. May 15–16. Hermann, MO. A German celebration of spring. Winery tours and wine tasting, stage show, volksplatz (craft area), parade, museum tours, children's activities, great German food, beer and wine gardens and German bands and dancing. Annually, the third full weekend of May. For info: Hermann Welcome Center, Market St, Hermann, MO 65041. Phone: (800) 932-8687. Fax: (573) 486-8995. Web: www.hermannmo.com.

MEET THE ARTISTS AND ARTISANS SHOW. May 15–16. Milford Green, CT. 42nd annual. More than 200 juried, award-winning artists and crafters from throughout the nation. For info: Meet the Artists & Artisans Show. Phone: (203) 874-5672. Web: www.meettheartistsandartisans.com. For additional info: Greater New Haven Conv & Visitors Bureau, 59 Elm St, New Haven, CT 06510. Phone: (203) 777-8550 or (800) 332-STAY.

MEXICO: SAN ISIDRO DAY. May 15. Day of San Isidro Labrador celebrated widely in farming regions to honor St. Isidore, the Plowman. Livestock gaily decorated with flowers. Celebrations usually begin about May 13 and continue for about a week.

MINT JULEP SCALE MEET. May 15–16. Rough River Dam State Resort Park, Falls of Rough, KY. A weekend for radio-controlled airplane enthusiasts. Est attendance: 450. For info: Tom DeHaven, Rec Supervisor, Rough River Dam State Resort Park, 450 Lodge Rd, Falls of Rough, KY 40119. Phone: (270) 257-2311.

NYLON STOCKINGS: ANNIVERSARY. May 15, 1940. Nylon hose went on sale at stores throughout the country. Competing producers bought their nylon yarn from E.J. du Pont de Nemours. W.H. Carothers of Du Pont developed nylon, called "Polymer 66," in 1935. It was the first totally man-made fiber and over time substituted for other materials and came to have widespread application.

OCONALUFTEE INDIAN VILLAGE. May 15–Oct 15. Cherokee Indian Reservation, Cherokee, NC. To portray the Cherokee lifestyle of the 1750 period. Also featuring *Unto These Hills* (mid-June–late-August), a drama portraying history of eastern band of Cherokees. Est attendance: 125,000. For info: Margie Douthit, PR, Cherokee Historical Assn, PO Box 398, Cherokee, NC 28719. Phone: (828) 497-2111. Fax: (828) 497-6987. Web: www.oconalufteevillage.com.

PARAGUAY: INDEPENDENCE DAY. May 15. Commemorates independence from Spain, attained 1811.

★**PEACE OFFICER MEMORIAL DAY.** May 15. Presidential Proclamation 3537, of May 4, 1963, covers all succeeding years. (PL87–726 of Oct 1, 1961.) Always May 15 of each year since 1963; however, first issued in 1962 for May 14.

PEACE OFFICER MEMORIAL DAY. May 15. An event honored by some 21,000 police departments nationwide. Memorial ceremonies at 10 AM in American Police Hall of Fame and Museum, Titusville, FL. See also: "National Police Week" (May 9–15). Sponsor: National Association of Chiefs of Police. Est attendance: 200. For info: American Police Hall of Fame and Museum, 6350 Horizon Dr, Titusville, FL 32780. Phone: (321) 264-0911. E-mail: policeinfo@aphf.org. Web: www.aphf.org.

PEC THING. May 15–16 (also Sept 18–19). Pecatonica, IL. Semiannual antique show with more than 400 exhibitors. Est attendance: 20,000. For info: Lisa Rosenkrans, Winnebago Country Fair Assn, PO Box 810, Pecatonica, IL 61063-0670. Phone: (815) 239-1641 or (800) 238-3587. Fax: (815) 239-1653. E-mail: pecthing@winnebagocountyfair.com.

PINCHOT LAKE FESTIVAL AND CRAFT SHOW. May 15. Pinchot Park, Wellsville, PA. More than 70 craft displays, from country to contemporary. Free admission. Sponsored by WSBA/WARM 103. Est attendance: 14,000. For info: Joe Alfano, Asst Promo Dir, WARM 103, PO Box 910, York, PA 17402-0910. Phone: (717) 764-1155. Fax: (717) 252-4708. Web: www.warm103.com.

PORTER, KATHERINE ANNE: BIRTH ANNIVERSARY. May 15, 1890. American prose writer Katherine Anne Porter was born at Indian Creek, TX. Her one long novel, *Ship of Fools* (1962), is considered by some to be one of the greatest allegorical works in English. She won the Pulitzer Prize and the National Book Award in 1965 for *Collected Short Stories*. Died Sept 18, 1980, at Silver Spring, MD.

PREAKNESS STAKES. May 15. Pimlico Race Course, Baltimore, MD. Preakness Stakes, middle jewel in the Visa Triple Crown, was inaugurated in 1873. Annually, the third Saturday in May—two Saturdays after the Kentucky Derby—and followed, three Saturdays later, by the Belmont Stakes. Est attendance: 100,000. For info: Maryland Jockey Club, Pimlico Race Course, Baltimore, MD 21215. Phone: (410) 542-9400. Web: www.marylandracing.com.

ROAD CHURCH MISSIONARY FAIR. May 15. Road Congregational Church, Pequot Trail, Stonington, CT. Bake sale, crafts, white elephants and more. Homemade luncheon available at noon. 10 AM–2 PM. For info: Libby Kennedy, 21 Roosevelt Ave, Mystic, CT 06355. Phone: (860) 536-1514. E-mail: roadchurch@juno.com. Web: www.roadchurch.org.

SCHNITZLER, ARTHUR: BIRTH ANNIVERSARY. May 15, 1862. Austrian playwright, novelist and medical doctor, Arthur Schnitzler was born at Vienna. Noted for his psychoanalytical examination of Viennese society. Died at Vienna, Oct 21, 1931.

SPACE MILESTONE: *FAITH 7* (US). May 15, 1963. Launched with Major Gordon Leroy Cooper and orbited the Earth 22 times.

SPRING CRAFT CELEBRATION. May 15–16 (tentative). Tyler State Park, Richboro, PA. High quality juried craft show featuring the work of 175 members of the Pennsylvania Guild of Craftsmen. Demonstrations, seminars, Crafts and Antiques Road Show, festival food, children's activites, musical entertainment. For information about tickets, or how to become a member of the PA Guild, contact: Est attendance: 15,000. Pennsylvania Guild of Craftsmen, 10 Stable Mill Trail, Richboro, PA 18954-1702. Phone: (800) 684-7440. E-mail: pacraft@comcat.com. Web: www.pacrafts.com.

STAGECOACH DAYS. May 15–16. Marshall, TX. Festival dedicated to transportation during the stagecoach era. Parade, arts and crafts booths, historic home tours and other entertainment. Annually, the third weekend in May. Est attendance: 15,000. For info: Patsy Dreesen, Dir, Convention & Visitor Development, PO Box 520, Marshall, TX 75670. Phone: (903) 935-7868 or (800) 953-7868. Fax: (903) 935-9982. E-mail: marshallcvd@hotmail.com. Web: www.marshalltxchamber.com.

STORYTELLING HISTORICAL WALK AROUND WASHINGTON. May 15–16. Washington, PA. Sponsored by Washington County Historical Society. Free admission. Est attendance: 180. For info: Washington County Historical Society, 49 E Maiden St, Washington County, PA 15301. Phone: (724) 225-6740. Fax: (724) 225-8495. E-mail: info@wchspa.org. Web: www.wchspa.org.

SUPER SCOUT SUNDAY. May 15 (tentative). Springfield, MO. Scouts earn nature-oriented badges by visiting programs and sta-

279

tions designed exclusively for scout groups. For info: Linda Chorice, Springfield Conservation Nature Center, 4600 S Chrisman Ave, Springfield, MO 65804. Phone: (417) 888-4237. Fax: (417) 888-4241. E-mail: choril@mdc.state.mo.us. Web: www.conservation.state.mo.us.

UNITED NATIONS: INTERNATIONAL DAY OF FAMILIES. May 15. The general assembly (res 47/237) Sept 20, 1993, voted this as an annual observance beginning in 1994. For info: United Nations, Dept of Public Info, New York, NY 10017. Web: www.un.org.

VIRGINIA WINE FESTIVAL. May 15–16. Ash Lawn-Highland, Home of James Monroe, Charlottesville, VA. Eight wineries offering tastings and sales. Commemorative wine glasses as gifts, crafts for sale, children's games, food and picnicking, live entertainment and tours of Monroe house and grounds. Est attendance: 2,000. For info: Ash Lawn-Highland, 1000 James Monroe Pkwy, Charlottesville, VA 22902. Phone: (434) 293-9539. Fax: (434) 293-8000. E-mail: info@ashlawnhighland.org. Web: www.ashlawnhighland.org.

WILDFLOWER FESTIVAL OF THE ARTS. May 15–16. Historic Square, Dahlonega, GA. Springtime in the North Georgia Mountains in a historic 1800s mining town. Visual and performing artists, programs and exhibits on wildflowers of the area, children's art area where children can create their own art. Annually, the third weekend in May. Est attendance: 25,000. For info: Dahlonega–Lumpkin County Chamber of Commerce, 13 S Park St, Dahlonega, GA 30533. Phone: (706) 864-3711. Fax: (706) 864-7917. E-mail: dahlonega@alltel.net. Web: www.dahlonega.org/wildflower/.

WILSON, ELLEN LOUISE AXSON: BIRTH ANNIVERSARY. May 15, 1860. First wife of Woodrow Wilson, 28th president of the US, born at Savannah, GA. Died at Washington, DC, Aug 6, 1914.

WORLD CHAMPIONSHIP STEAK COOK-OFF. May 15. Magnolia, AR. Held on the last day of the Magnolia Blossom Festival (May 13–15). Teams prepare and grill more than 2,500 ribeye steaks to win $2,000 first place and Governor's Silver Cup. Cash prizes for best pit, parade and showmanship. Steak dinners sold to public. Annually, the third Saturday of May. Est attendance: 20,000. For info: Magnolia-Columbia County Chamber of Commerce, 202 N Pine, PO Box 866, Magnolia, AR 71754-0866. Phone: (800) 482-3330. Fax: (870) 234-7937. E-mail: magcoc@arkansas.net.

WRIGHT PLUS. May 15. Oak Park, IL. The Frank Lloyd Wright Preservation Trust's annual housewalk features guided tours of the interiors of 10 buildings designed by Frank Lloyd Wright and his architectural contemporaries, including Wright's own home and studio. Reservations are required. Tickets limited. (Tickets available Mar 1.) Annually, third Saturday in May. Est attendance: 2,500. For info: Director of Public Relations, Frank Lloyd Wright Preservation Trust, 951 Chicago Ave, Oak Park, IL 60302. Phone: (708) 848-1976 or (708) 848-9518. Fax: (708) 848-1248. Web: www.wrightplus.org.

YOU GOTTA HAVE PARK. May 15–16. Prospect Park, Brooklyn, NY. This annual weekend-long celebration of Brooklyn's Prospect Park is dedicated to cleaning, greening and bringing the Park's neighbors and volunteers together. Annually, the third weekend in May. Est attendance: 2,000. For info: Prospect Park Alliance, Public Info Office, External Affairs, Litchfield Villa, 95 Prospect Park W, Brooklyn, NY 11215. Phone: (718) 965-8954 or (718) 965-8951. Fax: (718) 965-8926. E-mail: cmark@prospectpark.org. Web: www.prospectpark.org.

BIRTHDAYS TODAY

Anna Maria Alberghetti, 68, singer, actress (*Cinderfella, Carnival*), born Pesaro, Italy, May 15, 1936.
Madeleine Albright, 67, former US Secretary of State (Clinton administration), born Prague, Czechoslovakia, May 15, 1937.
Eddy Arnold, 86, country singer ("Make the World Go Away"), born Henderson, TN, May 15, 1918.
Richard Avedon, 81, photographer, born New York, NY, May 15, 1923.
George Howard Brett, 51, Hall of Fame baseball player, executive, born Glen Dale, WV, May 15, 1953.
David Charvet, 32, actor ("Melrose Place," "Baywatch"), born Lyon, France, May 15, 1972.
David Cronenberg, 61, filmmaker (*The Fly, Naked Lunch*), born Toronto, ON, Canada, May 15, 1943.
Brian Eno, 56, avant-garde musician, born Woodbridge, England, May 15, 1948.
Giselle Fernandez, 43, TV host, actress, born Mexico City, Mexico, May 15, 1961.
Lee Horsley, 49, actor ("Nero Wolfe," "Matt Houston"), born Muleshoe, TN, May 15, 1955.
Jasper Johns, 74, artist (Neo-Dada Encaustic and collage composition *Flag*), born Augusta, GA, May 15, 1930.
Lainie Kazan, 62, singer, actress (*My Favorite Year, Beaches*), born New York, NY, May 15, 1942.
Trini Lopez, 67, actor, singer (*Marriage on the Rocks, The Dirty Dozen*), born Dallas, TX, May 15, 1937.
Chazz Palminteri, 53, actor (*Bullets Over Broadway*), playwright, screenwriter (*A Bronx Tale*), born the Bronx, NY, May 15, 1951.
Dan Patrick, 48, sportcaster (ESPN's "SportsCenter"), radio personality, born Zanesville, OH, May 15, 1956.
Kathleen Sibelius, 56, Governor of Kansas (D), born Cincinatti, OH, May 15, 1948.
Emmitt Smith, 35, football player, born Pensacola, FL, May 15, 1969.
John Smoltz, 37, baseball player, born Warren, MI, May 15, 1967.

MAY 16 — SUNDAY

Day 137 — 229 Remaining

AFRMA FANCY RAT & MOUSE DISPLAY. May 16. Wm. S. Hart Park, Newhall, CA. American Fancy Rat and Mouse Association exhibits rats and mice of "fancy" species that make good pets. For info: AFRMA, PO Box 2589, Winnetka, CA 91396-2589. Phone: (909) 685-2350 or (818) 992-5564 or (626) 966-0350. Fax: (818) 592-6590. E-mail: afrma@afrma.org. Web: www.afrma.org.

BIOGRAPHERS DAY. May 16. Anniversary of the meeting, at London, England, May 16, 1763, of James Boswell and Samuel Johnson, beginning history's most famous biographer-biographee relationship. Boswell's *Journal of a Tour to the Hebrides* (1785) and his *Life of Samuel Johnson* (1791) are regarded as models of biographical writing. Thus, this day is recommended as one on which to start reading or writing a biography.

BUTLER ISSUES "WOMAN ORDER": ANNIVERSARY. May 16, 1862. General Benjamin Butler, military governor of New Orleans, issued what became known as the "Woman Order." The text of General Order Number 28 read, in part, "As the officers and soldiers of the United States have been subjected to repeated insults from women (calling themselves ladies) of New Orleans . . . when any female shall . . . show contempt for the United States, she shall be regarded as a woman of the town plying her avocation." This order typified Butler's attitude toward the captured city and its populace and, along with other controversial acts, set the stage for his dismissal as military governor in December of 1862.

D.C. BOOTH DAY (WITH FISH CULTURE HALL OF FAME). May 16. D.C. Booth Historic Fish Hatchery, Spearfish, SD. Antique auto show, musical entertainment, free tours of the historic Booth home and installation of new members into the

May 2004	S	M	T	W	T	F	S
							1
	2	3	4	5	6	7	8
	9	10	11	12	13	14	15
	16	17	18	19	20	21	22
	23	24	25	26	27	28	29
	30	31					

Fish Culture Hall of Fame. Est attendance: 1,200. For info: Roger Blunk, D.C. Booth Historic Fish Hatchery, 423 Hatchery Circle, Spearfish, SD 57783. Phone: (605) 642-7730.

FIRST ACADEMY AWARDS: 75th ANNIVERSARY. May 16, 1929. About 270 people attended a dinner at the Hollywood Roosevelt Hotel at which the first Academy Awards were given in 12 categories. The silent film *Wings* won Best Picture. A committee of only 20 members selected the winners that year. By the third year, the entire membership of the Academy voted. The Academy Awards were first televised in 1953.

FIRST WOMAN TO CLIMB MOUNT EVEREST: ANNIVERSARY. May 16, 1975. Japanese climber Junko Tabei, leading an all-woman expedition to Mount Everest, became the first woman to reach the summit on this date in 1975. Taking the South-East Ridge route, Tabei was delayed by an avalanche before her last leg up the mountain. "Even after reaching the peak," she later recalled, "instead of shouting with excitement I was simply happy that I didn't have to go any higher!"

FONDA, HENRY: BIRTH ANNIVERSARY. May 16, 1905. American stage, TV and screen actor (*The Grapes of Wrath, Mister Roberts*), Academy Award winner, born Henry Jaynes Fonda at Grand Island, NE. Began his acting career at the Omaha (NE) Playhouse. Fonda died at Los Angeles, CA, Aug 12, 1982.

GWINNETT, BUTTON: DEATH ANNIVERSARY. May 16, 1777. Signer of the Declaration of Independence, born at Down Hatherley, Gloucestershire, England, about 1735 (exact date unknown). Died following a duel at St. Catherine's Island, off of Savannah, GA.

LIBERACE: 85th BIRTH ANNIVERSARY. May 16, 1919. Wladziu Valentino Liberace, concert pianist who began with a piano, a candelabra, a brother named George and a huge engaging smile, threw in extravagant clothes and jewels and became a Las Vegas headliner and the winner of two Emmy Awards, six gold albums and two stars on the Hollywood Walk of Fame. Liberace was born at West Allis, WI; he died Feb 4, 1987, at Palm Springs, CA.

MARTIN, BILLY: BIRTH ANNIVERSARY. May 16, 1928. Baseball player and manager born at Berkeley, CA. Billy Martin's baseball career included managerial stints with five major league teams: the New York Yankees, Minnesota Twins, Detroit Tigers, Texas Rangers and the Oakland Athletics. After a successful playing career, he compiled a record of 1,258 victories to 1,018 losses in his 16 seasons as a manager. His combative style both on and off the field kept him in the headlines, and he will long be remembered for his on-again/off-again relationship with Yankees owner George Steinbrenner, for whom he managed the Yankees five different times. Martin died in an auto accident near Fenton, NY, Dec 25, 1989.

MORTON, LEVI PARSONS: BIRTH ANNIVERSARY. May 16, 1824. 22nd vice president of the US (1889–93) born at Shoreham, VT. Died at Rhinebeck, NY, May 16, 1920.

NATIONAL DOG BITE PREVENTION WEEK. May 16–22. To promote safety with dogs—especially among children, who are the #1 victims of dog bites. National Association for Humane and Environmental Education (NAHEE), youth education division of The Humane Society of the United States, has developed a dog bite prevention program for kids. Annually, third full week in May. For info: Heidi O'Brien, NAHEE, PO Box 362, East Haddam, CT 06423. Phone: (860) 434-8666 x17. Fax: (860) 434-9579. E-mail: obrien@nahee.org. Web: www.nahee.org or www.nodogbites.org.

NATIONAL EMERGENCY MEDICAL SERVICES (EMS) WEEK. May 16–22. Honoring EMS providers nationwide who provide life-saving care in a multitude of circumstances. Also a time for the public to learn about injury prevention, safety awareness and emergency preparedness. Annually, the third full week in May. For info: American College of Emergency Physicians, PO Box 619911, Dallas, TX 75261-9911. Phone: (800) 798-1822. E-mail: emsweek@acep.org. Web: www.acep.org.

NATIONAL ETIQUETTE WEEK. May 16–22. A national recognition of proper etiquette in all areas of American life (business, social, dining, international, wedding, computer, etc.). A self-assessment on the current status of civility in the US. Annually, the third week in May starting on Sunday. For info: Sandra Morisset, Protocol Training Services, PO Box 4981, New York, NY 10185. Phone: (212) 802-9098. Web: www.zyworld.com/etiquette.

NATIONAL NEW FRIENDS, OLD FRIENDS WEEK. May 16–22. A week to celebrate old friends and new friends and remember how vital friends are for our emotional and physical health and well-being and even professional or career success. Friendshifts® is the word coined by author and sociologist Jan Yager to denote the way our ideas about friendships as well as who our friends are change as we go through different stages of life. But at every stage, friendship is crucial, for children, for teenagers, for young adults, singles, couples, new mothers, the middle-aged and especially for those who are older, retired or widowed. For info: Jan Yager, PhD, PO Box 8038, Stamford, CT 06905-8038. Fax: (203) 968-0193. E-mail: jyager@aol.com. Web: www.JanYager.com/friendship.

NATIONAL RUNNING AND FITNESS WEEK. May 16–22. Educational campaign designed to introduce more Americans to the pleasures and benefits of participating in a regular exercise program. For info: Barbara Baldwin, American Running Assn, 4405 East-West Hwy, Ste 405, Bethesda, MD 20814. Phone: (800) 776-2732. Fax: (301) 913-9520. E-mail: run@americanrunning.org. Web: www.americanrunning.org.

NATIONAL SEA MONKEY DAY. May 16. A day on which we remember our briny friends, the Sea Monkeys. Annually, May 16 (formerly Feb 15). For info: Susan Barclay, 7520 Queen St, Chilliwack, BC, Canada V2R1B7. Phone: (604) 824-0678. Fax: (604) 858-5817. E-mail: drseamonkey@telus.net or sjbarclay@telus.net. Web: www.seamonkeyworship.com.

NATIONAL SPORTING GOODS ASSOCIATION MANAGEMENT CONFERENCE. May 16–19. Hilton Head Marriott Beach & Golf Resort, Hilton Head Island, SC. 40th annual management conference and 6th annual Team Dealer Summit. The premier educational and networking event for the sporting goods industry. Attracts leading retailers, dealers, manufacturers, agents, media and industry associations. Est attendance: 350. For info: Larry Weindruch, Dir of Communications, Natl Sporting Goods Assn, 1601 Feehanville Dr, Ste 300, Mt Prospect, IL 60056-6035. Phone: (847) 296-6742. Fax: (847) 391-9827. E-mail: info@nsga.org. Web: www.nsga.org.

NATIONAL STATIONERY SHOW. May 16–19. Javits Center, New York, NY. For info: George Little Management, 10 Bank St, White Plains, NY 10606. Phone: (914) 421-3200. Fax: (914) 948-6088. Web: www.glmshows.com or www.nationalstationeryshow.com.

★**NATIONAL TRANSPORTATION WEEK.** May 16–22. Presidential Proclamation issued for week including third Friday in May since 1960. (PL86–475 of May 20, 1960, first requested; PL87–449 of May 14, 1962, requested an annual proclamation.)

May 16-17 ☆ Chase's 2004 Calendar of Events ☆

PEABODY, ELIZABETH PALMER: 200th BIRTH ANNIVERSARY. May 16, 1804. Born at Billerica, MA, Peabody was an innovative educator, author and publisher. She opened her first school at Lancaster, MA, when only 16. In 1839 Peabody opened a bookstore that quickly became the intellectuals' hangout. With her own printing press Peabody became the first woman publisher of Boston and possibly the US. She published three of her brother-in-law Nathaniel Hawthorne's books. For two years she published and wrote for *The Dial*, the literary magazine and voice of the Transcendental movement. Peabody's enduring accomplishment was the establishment of the first kindergarten in the US, in 1860 at Boston. She created a magazine, *Kindergarten Messenger*, in 1873. Died Jan 3, 1894, at Jamaica Plain, MA.

PUBLIC SAFETY AND TECHNOLOGY AWARENESS WEEK. May 16-22. To bring awareness of the positive impact and role technology plays in public safety and homeland security: law enforcement, police, fire, military and government security agencies. For sponsorship and educational materials, contact us. Annually, the third week in May. For info: National High Tech Fndn, Phone: (847) 998-9950. E-mail: nhtm2000@aol.com. Web: www.nationalhightechmonth.com.

RAF BOMBS RUHR DAMS: ANNIVERSARY. May 16-17, 1943. Over these two days, Royal Air Force Lancasters attacked three dams in the German Ruhr Valley. They dropped 4.5-ton bombs designed specifically for this mission. The Mohne and the Eder (the largest dam in Europe at the time) were both damaged. These two dams provided drinking water for four million people and supplied 75 percent of the electrical power for industry. Widespread flooding and many deaths resulted.

ROGATION SUNDAY. May 16. The fifth Sunday after Easter is the beginning of Rogationtide (Rogation Sunday and the following three days before Ascension Day). Rogation Day rituals date from the 5th century.

RURAL LIFE SUNDAY OR SOIL STEWARDSHIP SUNDAY. May 16. With an increase in ecological and environmental concerns, Rural Life Sunday emphasizes the concept that Earth belongs to God, who has granted humanity the use of it, along with the responsibility of caring for it wisely. At the suggestion of the International Association of Agricultural Missions, Rural Life Sunday was first observed in 1929. The day is observed annually by churches of many Christian denominations and includes pulpit exchanges by rural and urban pastors. Under the auspices of the National Association of Soil and Water Conservation Districts, the week beginning with Rural Life Sunday is now widely observed as Soil Stewardship Week, with the Sunday itself alternatively termed Soil Stewardship Sunday. Traditionally, Rural Life Sunday is Rogation Sunday, the Sunday preceding Ascension Day.

SAINT LOUIS WALK OF FAME INDUCTION CEREMONY. May 16. St. Louis, MO. Outdoor free-admission ceremony with ragtime band. Famous St. Louisans are honored. Nonprofit organization provides a showcase for the cultural heritage of St. Louis. In addition to stars in the sidewalks are plaques describing the achievements and contributions each creative St. Louisan made to our country's culture (Chuck Berry, Miles Davis, Bob Costas, Betty Grable, Vincent Price, Tennessee Williams, Scott Joplin, Charles Lindbergh, John Goodman, etc). Annually, the third Sunday in May. Est attendance: 700. For info: Joe Edwards, Chair, St. Louis Walk of Fame, 6504 Delmar, St. Louis, MO 63130. Phone: (314) 727-STAR. Web: www.stlouiswalkoffame.org.

★**WORLD TRADE WEEK.** May 16-22. Presidential Proclamation has been issued each year since 1948 for the third week of May with three exceptions: 1949, 1955 and 1966.

BIRTHDAYS TODAY

David Boreanaz, 33, actor ("Angel," "Buffy the Vampire Slayer"), born Philadelphia, PA, May 16, 1971.
Pierce Brosnan, 52, actor ("Remington Steele," James Bond in *GoldenEye*), born County Meath, Ireland, May 16, 1952.
Jean-Sebastien Giguere, 27, hockey player, born Montreal, QC, Canada, May 16, 1977.
Tracey Gold, 35, actress ("Shirley," "Goodnight Beantown," "Growing Pains"), born New York, NY, May 16, 1969.
Janet Jackson, 38, singer ("What Have You Done for Me Lately"), born Gary, IN, May 16, 1966.
Olga Korbut, 49, Olympic gold medal gymnast, born Grodno, USSR, May 16, 1955.
John Scott (Jack) Morris, 49, former baseball player, born St. Paul, MN, May 16, 1955.
Gabriela Sabatini, 34, former tennis player, born Buenos Aires, Argentina, May 16, 1970.
Joan (Benoit) Samuelson, 47, Olympic gold medal runner, born Cape Elizabeth, ME, May 16, 1957.
Bill Smitrovich, 57, actor ("Crime Story," *Splash, Manhunter*), born Bridgeport, CT, May 16, 1947.
Tori Spelling, 31, actress ("Beverly Hills 90210"), born Beverly Hills, CA, May 16, 1973.
Studs Terkel, 92, author, journalist (*Hard Times, Working*), born Louis Terkel, New York, NY, May 16, 1912.
Mare Winningham, 45, actress (*The Thornbirds, St. Elmo's Fire*), born Phoenix, AZ, May 16, 1959.

MAY 17 — MONDAY
Day 138 — 228 Remaining

BELL, JAMES (COOL PAPA): BIRTH ANNIVERSARY. May 17, 1903. Negro League baseball player James "Cool Papa" Bell was born at Starkville, MS. He played 25 seasons from 1922 to 1946 (one year before Jackie Robinson broke the "color barrier" in major league baseball) with a career average of .338. Regarded as the fastest man ever to play the game—he could round the bases in 13 seconds—he was inducted into the Baseball Hall of Fame in 1974. Bell died Mar 7, 1991, at St. Louis, MO.

BROWN v BOARD OF EDUCATION DECISION: 50th ANNIVERSARY. May 17, 1954. The US Supreme Court ruled unanimously that segregation of public schools "solely on the basis of race" denied black children "equal educational opportunity" even though "physical facilities and other 'tangible' factors may have been equal. Separate educational facilities are inherently unequal." The case was argued before the Court by Thurgood Marshall, who would go on to become the first black appointed to the Supreme Court.

FIRST KENTUCKY DERBY: ANNIVERSARY. May 17, 1875. The first running of the Kentucky Derby took place at Churchill Downs, Louisville, KY. Jockey Oliver Lewis rode the horse Aristides to a winning time of 2:37.25.

☆ Chase's 2004 Calendar of Events ☆   May 17-18

JENNER, EDWARD: BIRTH ANNIVERSARY. May 17, 1749. English physician, born at Berkeley, England. He was the first to establish a scientific basis for vaccination with his work on smallpox. Jenner died at Berkeley, England, Jan 26, 1823.

NAIA MEN'S & WOMEN'S TENNIS NATIONAL CHAMPIONSHIPS. May 17-21. Peachtree City, GA. 53rd annual for men, 24th annual for women. Individuals compete for All-America honors, while teams compete for the national championship. Est attendance: 500. For info: Natl Assn of Intercollegiate Athletics, 23500 W 105th St, PO Box 1325, Olathe, KS 66051-1325. Phone: (913) 791-0044. Fax: (913) 791-9555. E-mail: lthomas@naia.org. Web: www.naia.org.

NATIONAL EFFECTIVENESS WEEK. May 17-21. Neatness and tidiness do not make you effective. On the other hand, messiness does not make you ineffective. What matters is that you get the important things done with a minimum of stress. This week, promote tolerance of different styles of getting things done. Annually, the third full week in May. For info: Jan Jasper. Phone: (212) 465-7472. Fax: (509) 356-2803. E-mail: jan@janjasper.com. Web: www.janjasper.com.

NEW YORK STOCK EXCHANGE ESTABLISHED: ANNIVERSARY. May 17, 1792. Some two dozen merchants and brokers agreed to establish what is now known as the New York Stock Exchange. In fair weather they operated under a buttonwood tree on Wall Street, at New York, NY. In bad weather they moved to the shelter of a coffeehouse to conduct their business.

NORWAY: CONSTITUTION DAY OR INDEPENDENCE DAY. May 17. National holiday. Constitution signed and Norway separated from Denmark in 1814. Parades and children's festivities.

SANTA CRUZ BEACH BOARDWALK GIANT DIPPER: 80th ANNIVERSARY. May 17, 1924. The Giant Dipper roller coaster opened at Santa Cruz Beach Boardwalk at Santa Cruz, CA, and quickly became the park's most popular ride. The Dipper was built by Arthur Looff, the son of master carousel-horse carver Charles I.D. Looff. In June 1987 the Giant Dipper and the Looff carousel were designated National Historic Landmarks by the US National Park Service.

SWITZERLAND: PACING THE BOUNDS. May 17. Liestal. Citizens set off at 8 AM and march along boundaries to the beating of drums and firing of pistols and muskets. Occasion for fetes. Annually, the Monday before Ascension Day.

UNITED NATIONS: WORLD TELECOMMUNICATION DAY. May 17. A day to draw attention to the necessity and importance of further development of telecommunications in the global community. For info: United Nations, Dept of Public Info, New York, NY 10017. Web: www.un.org.

USS *STARK* ATTACKED: ANNIVERSARY. May 17, 1987. The US Navy's guided missile frigate *Stark*, sailing off the Iranian coast in the Persian Gulf, was struck and set afire by two Exocet sea-skimming missiles fired from an Iraqi warplane at 2:10 PM, EDT. Also struck was a Cypriot flag tanker. At least 28 American naval personnel were killed. Only hours earlier a Soviet oil tanker in the Gulf had struck a mine.

BIRTHDAYS TODAY

Mia Hamm, 32, soccer player (US National Soccer Team), born Selma, AL, May 17, 1972.
Dennis Hopper, 68, actor (*Easy Rider, Giant, Rebel Without a Cause*), born Dodge City, KS, May 17, 1936.
Christian Lacroix, 54, French couturier, born Arles, France, May 17, 1950.
Ray Charles ("Sugar Ray") Leonard, 48, former boxer, born Washington, DC, May 17, 1956.
Daniel Ricardo (Danny) Manning, 38, former basketball player, born Hattiesburg, MS, May 17, 1966.
Ben Nelson, 63, US Senator (D, Nebraska), born McCook, NE, May 17, 1941.
Tony Parker, 22, basketball player, born Bruges, Belgium, May 17, 1982.
Bill Paxton, 49, actor (*Aliens, One False Move, Twister*), born Fort Worth, TX, May 17, 1955.
Trent Reznor, 39, singer (Nine Inch Nails), born Mercer, PA, May 17, 1965.
Bob Saget, 48, actor ("Full House"), host ("America's Funniest Home Videos"), born Philadelphia, PA, May 17, 1956.
Debra Winger, 49, actress (*Terms of Endearment, Shadowlands*), born Columbus, OH, May 17, 1955.

MAY 18 — TUESDAY
Day 139 — 227 Remaining

ALLIES CAPTURE MONTE CASSINO: 60th ANNIVERSARY. May 18, 1944. Between Oct 12, 1943, and Jan 17, 1944, there were five Allied attempts to take the German position at the Benedictine abbey at Monte Cassino. Although the abbey had been reduced to rubble, it served as a bunker for the Germans. In the spring of 1944 Marshal Alphonse Pierre Juin devised an operation that crossed the mountainous regions behind the fortresslike structure, using Moroccan troops of the French Expeditionary Force. Specially trained for mountain operations, they climbed 4,850 feet to locate a pass. On May 15, 1944, they attacked the Germans from behind. On May 18, Polish troops attached to this force took Monte Cassino.

BIRTHDAY OF MOTHER'S WHISTLER. May 18. Birthday of the world's most melodious human whistler, who not only duplicates the songs of rare, exotic and extinct birds, but in many cases, does so better than the birds themselves. For info: Mother's Whistler, Warfield and Twin Silo Lanes, Huntingdon Valley, PA 19006. Phone: (215) 947-0500. Fax: (215) 947-7210. E-mail: motherswhistler1@yahoo.com.

CAPRA, FRANK: BIRTH ANNIVERSARY. May 18, 1897. The Academy Award–winning filmmaker whose movies were suffused with affectionate portrayals of the common man and the strengths and foibles of American democracy. Capra was born at Palermo, Sicily. He bluffed his way into silent movies in 1922 and, despite total ignorance of movie-making, directed and produced a profitable one-reeler. He was the first to win three directorial Oscars—for *It Happened One Night* (1934), *Mr Deeds Goes to Town* (1936) and *You Can't Take It with You* (1938). The motion picture academy voted the first and third of these as best picture. Capra said his favorite of the films he made was *It's a Wonderful Life* (1946). He died at La Quinta, CA, Sept 3, 1991.

FONTEYN, MARGOT: 85th BIRTH ANNIVERSARY. May 18, 1919. Born Margaret Hookman at Reigate, Surrey, England, Dame Margot Fonteyn thrilled ballet audiences for 45 years. She emerged from the Sadler's Wells company during the 1930s and 1940s as a solo artist and followed those successes by partnering with Soviet exile Rudolph Nureyev in the 1960s. She died Feb 21, 1991, at Panama City, Panama.

HAITI: FLAG AND UNIVERSITY DAY. May 18. Public holiday.

INTERNATIONAL MUSEUM DAY. May 18. To pay tribute to museums of the world. "Museums are an important means of cultural exchange, enrichment of cultures and development of mutual

May 18–19 ☆ Chase's 2004 Calendar of Events ☆

understanding, cooperation and peace among people." Annually, May 18. Sponsor: International Council of Museums, Paris, France. For info: AAM/ICOM, 1575 Eye St NW, Ste 400, Washington, DC 20005. Phone: (202) 289-9115. Fax: (202) 289-6578. E-mail: aam-icom@aam-us.org.

MOUNT SAINT HELENS ERUPTION: ANNIVERSARY. May 18, 1980. A major eruption of Mount Saint Helens volcano, in southwestern Washington, blew steam and ash more than 11 miles into the sky. First major eruption of Mount Saint Helens since 1857, though on Mar 26, 1980, there had been a warning eruption of smaller magnitude.

NAIA MEN'S GOLF NATIONAL CHAMPIONSHIPS. May 18–21. Site TBD. 53rd annual. Est attendance: 500. For info: Natl Assn of Intercollegiate Athletics, 23500 W 105th St, PO Box 1325, Olathe, KS 66051-1325. Phone: (913) 791-0044. Fax: (913) 791-9555. E-mail: smcclure@naia.org. Web: www.naia.org.

NCAA DIVISION I WOMEN'S GOLF CHAMPIONSHIPS. May 18–21. Auburn University, Auburn, AL. For info: NCAA, 700 W Washington Ave, PO Box 6222, Indianapolis, IN 46206-6222. Phone: (317) 917-6222. Fax: (317) 917-6825. Web: www.ncaasports.com.

POPE JOHN PAUL II: BIRTHDAY. May 18, 1920. Karol Wojtyla, 264th pope of the Roman Catholic Church, born at Wadowice, Poland. Elected pope Oct 16, 1978. He was the first non-Italian to be elected pope in 456 years (since the election of Pope Adrian VI, in 1522) and the first Polish pope.

SPACE MILESTONE: APOLLO 10 (US): 35th ANNIVERSARY. May 18, 1969. Launched with astronauts Colonel Thomas Stafford and Commander Eugene Cernan, who brought lunar module (LM) "Snoopy" within nine miles of the moon's surface on May 22. Apollo 10 circled moon 31 times and returned to Earth May 26.

TURKMENISTAN: REVIVAL AND UNITY DAY. May 18. National holiday. Commemorates the 1992 adoption of the constitution.

URUGUAY: BATTLE OF LAS PIEDRAS DAY. May 18. National holiday. Commemorates battle fought for independence from Spain in 1811.

VISIT YOUR RELATIVES DAY. May 18. A day to renew family ties and joys by visiting often-thought-of-seldom-seen relatives. Annually, May 18. For info: A.C. Moeller, Box 71, Clio, MI 48420-1042.

WILLSON, MEREDITH: BIRTH ANNIVERSARY. May 18, 1902. American musician, playwright and composer best known for *The Music Man*. Born at Mason City, IA, Willson received Oscar nominations for *The Little Foxes* and *The Great Dictator*. Many of his songs, including "It's Beginning to Look a Lot Like Christmas," "Seventy-six Trombones" and "Till There Was You" have become standards. Willson died at Santa Monica, CA, June 15, 1984.

WOMAN INDUCTED INTO NATIONAL INVENTORS HALL OF FAME: ANNIVERSARY. May 18, 1991. Gertrude Belle Elion, co-recipient of the 1988 Nobel Prize in Medicine, became the first woman inducted as a member of the National Inventors Hall of Fame. Elion's research led to the development of leukemia-fighting drugs and immunosuppressant Imuran, which is used in kidney transplants.

	S	M	T	W	T	F	S
May							1
2004	2	3	4	5	6	7	8
	9	10	11	12	13	14	15
	16	17	18	19	20	21	22
	23	24	25	26	27	28	29
	30	31					

BIRTHDAYS TODAY

Chow Yun-Fat, 49, actor (*Crouching Tiger, Hidden Dragon; Anna and the King; The Killer*), born Lamma Island, Hong Kong, May 18, 1955.
Brad Friedel, 33, soccer player, born Lakewood, OH, May 18, 1971.
Reginald Martinez (Reggie) Jackson, 58, Hall of Fame baseball player, born Wyncote, PA, May 18, 1946.
Jari Kurri, 44, Hall of Fame hockey player, born Helsinki, Finland, May 18, 1960.
Robert Morse, 73, actor (*The Loved One, A Guide for the Married Man*; stage: *How to Succeed in Business Without Really Trying* [Tony Award]), born Newton, MA, May 18, 1931.
Yannick Noah, 44, former tennis player, born Sedan, France, May 18, 1960.
Pope John Paul II, 84, Roman Catholic leader, born Karol Wojtyla at Wadowice, Poland, May 18, 1920.
Pernell Roberts, 76, actor (*Ride Lonesome*, "Bonanza," "Trapper John, MD"), born Waycross, GA, May 18, 1928.
Brooks Robinson, 67, Hall of Fame baseball player, born Little Rock, AR, May 18, 1937.
James Stephens, 53, actor ("The Paper Chase"), born Mount Kisco, NY, May 18, 1951.
George Strait, 52, country singer, musician, born Poteet, TX, May 18, 1952.

MAY 19 — WEDNESDAY
Day 140 — 226 Remaining

ARMED FORCES DAY MILITARY VEHICLE RALLY. May 19–21. Hawthorne, NV. 54th annual rally and swap meet of military vehicles from WW II to the present. Always the third weekend in May. For local info: Mineral County Chamber of Commerce, PO Box 2250, Hawthorne, NV 89415. Phone: (775) 945-2507. Fax: (775) 945-2633.

BOYS' CLUBS FOUNDED: ANNIVERSARY. May 19, 1906. The Federated Boys' Clubs, which later became the Boys' and Girls' Clubs of America, was founded.

DARK DAY IN NEW ENGLAND: ANNIVERSARY. May 19, 1780. At midday near-total darkness unaccountably descended on much of New England. Candles were lit, fowls went to roost and many fearful persons believed that doomsday had arrived. At New Haven, CT, Colonel Abraham Davenport opposed adjournment of the town council in these words: "I am against adjournment. The day of judgment is either approaching or it is not. If it is not, there is no cause for an adjournment. If it is, I choose to be found doing my duty. I wish therefore that candles may be brought." No scientifically verifiable cause for this widespread phenomenon was ever discovered.

FLEET WEEK NEW YORK 2004. May 19–26. New York, NY. 17th annual. Week-long event honoring the US's maritime heritage. More than 20 vessels from the US Navy, US Coast Guard, international navies and the Military Sealife Command take part, sailing up the Hudson River from the Verrazano Narrows Bridge. Numerous demonstrations throughout the week, including ship tours, flyover, Marine Corps martial arts displays, parachute jump teams, equipment displays, Coast Guard drug dog exhibits and more. More than 6,000 sailors, Marines and soldiers participate. For info: Director of Fleet Support, US Coast

☆ Chase's 2004 Calendar of Events ☆ May 19–20

Guard Building, Battery Park, 1 South St, New York, NY 10004. Web: www.fleetweek.navy.mil.

GONE WITH THE WIND PUBLISHED: ANNIVERSARY. May 19, 1936. Margaret Mitchell's epic novel of the Civil War South was published on this date in 1936. It would be awarded the Pulitzer Prize and National Book Award as best novel of 1936. It has been a bestseller since publication, and forty countries have published translations. See also: "Gone with the Wind Film Premiere: Anniversary" (Dec 15).

HANSBERRY, LORRAINE: BIRTH ANNIVERSARY. May 19, 1930. American playwright Lorraine Hansberry was born at Chicago, IL. For her now classic play *A Raisin in the Sun*, she became the youngest American and first black to win the Best Play Award from the New York Critics' Circle. The play, titled after the Langston Hughes poem, deals with issues such as racism, cultural pride and self-respect and was the first stage production written by a black woman to appear on Broadway (1959). *To Be Young, Gifted, and Black*, a book of excerpts from her journals, letters, speeches and plays, was published posthumously in 1969. Lorraine Hansberry died of cancer Jan 12, 1965, at New York, NY.

HO CHI MINH: BIRTH ANNIVERSARY. May 19, 1890. Vietnamese leader and first president of the Democratic Republic of Vietnam, born at Kim Lien, a central Vietnamese village (Nghe An Province), probably May 19, 1890. His original name was Nguyen That Thanh. Died at Hanoi, Vietnam, Sept 3, 1969. The anniversary of his birth is a national holiday in Vietnam as is the anniversary of his death.

ISRAEL: JERUSALEM DAY (YOM YERUSHALAYIM). May 19. Hebrew calendar date: Iyar 28, 5764. Commemorates the liberation of the old city, June 7, 1967. Began at sundown May 18.

MALCOLM X: BIRTH ANNIVERSARY. May 19, 1925. Black nationalist and civil rights activist Malcolm X was born Malcolm Little at Omaha, NE. While serving a prison term he resolved to transform his life. On his release in 1952 he changed his name to Malcolm X and worked for the Nation of Islam until he was suspended by Black Muslim leader Elijah Muhammed Dec 4, 1963. Malcolm X later made the pilgrimage to Mecca and became an orthodox Muslim. He was assassinated as he spoke to a meeting at the Audubon Ballroom at New York, NY, Feb 21, 1965.

MAY RAY DAY. May 19. To celebrate the beginning of the warm outside days the sun gives us. Also, a day for people named Ray. Annually, May 19. For info: Richard Ankli, The Fifth Wheel Tavern, 639 Fifth St, Ann Arbor, MI 48103.

MOON PHASE: NEW MOON. May 19. Moon enters New Moon phase at 12:52 AM, EDT.

SCOBEE, FRANCIS R.: 65th BIRTH ANNIVERSARY. May 19, 1939. Commander of the ill-fated space shuttle *Challenger*, 46-year-old pilot Francis R. Scobee had been in the astronaut program since 1978 and had been named pilot of the *Challenger* in 1984. Born at Cle Elum, WA, Scobee perished with all others on board when the shuttle exploded on Jan 28, 1986. See also: "*Challenger* Space Shuttle Explosion Anniversary" (Jan 28).

SIMPLON TUNNEL OPENING: ANNIVERSARY. May 19, 1906. Tunnel from Brig, Switzerland to Iselle, Italy officially opened on this day. Construction started in 1898.

SPACE MILESTONE: *MARS 2* AND *MARS 3* (USSR). May 19 and 28, 1971. Entered Martian orbits on Nov 27 and Dec 2, respectively. *Mars 3* sent down a TV-equipped capsule that soft-landed and transmitted pictures for 20 seconds. Launch dates: May 19 and 28, 1971.

TURKEY: YOUTH AND SPORTS DAY. May 19. Public holiday commemorating the beginning of a national movement for independence in 1919, led by Mustafa Kemal Ataturk.

TURN BEAUTY INSIDE OUT DAY. May 19. Is beauty only skin-deep? Not if you turn it inside out. This day serves as a reminder that inner beauty is more important than outer beauty. On this day, people challenge the usual definition of beauty as portrayed in popular media and advertising by recognizing the wonderful actions and attitudes of people who are beautiful on the inside. Annually, the third Wednesday in May. For info: Mind on the Media, 505 Kimble Ct, Northfield, MN 55057. Phone: (952) 210-1625. Web: www.mindonthemedia.org.

BIRTHDAYS TODAY

Nora Ephron, 63, writer (*Heartburn*), director, born New York, NY, May 19, 1941.
James Fox, 65, actor (*A Passage to India, The Russia House, Patriot Games*), born London, England, May 19, 1939.
Kevin Garnett, 28, basketball player, born Mauldin, SC, May 19, 1976.
David Hartman, 67, actor (Emmy for "Good Morning America"; *Hello Dolly*), born Pawtucket, RI, May 19, 1937.
Grace Jones, 52, model, singer, actress (*A View to a Kill*), born Spanishtown, Jamaica, May 19, 1952.
William (Bill) Laimbeer, Jr, 47, former basketball player, born Boston, MA, May 19, 1957.
James Lehrer, 70, journalist, anchor ("The Newshour with Jim Lehrer"), born Wichita, KS, May 19, 1934.
Eric Lloyd, 18, actor ("Jesse," *Dunston Checks In*), born Glendale, CA, May 19, 1986.
Pete Townshend, 59, musician (The Who), born London, England, May 19, 1945.

MAY 20 — THURSDAY
Day 141 — 225 Remaining

AMELIA EARHART ATLANTIC CROSSING: ANNIVERSARY. May 20, 1932. Leaving Harbor Grace, Newfoundland, Canada at 7 PM, Amelia Earhart landed near Londonderry, Ireland. The 2,026-mile flight took 13 hours and 30 minutes. She was the first woman to fly solo across the Atlantic. Earhart, along with her navigator Fred Noonan, disappeared on July 2, 1937, between Lae, New Guinea, and Howland Island while trying to fly her Lockheed twin-engine plane around the equator to gather scientific data.

ASCENSION DAY. May 20. Commemorates Christ's ascension into heaven. Observed since AD 68. Ascension Day is the 40th day after the Resurrection, counting Easter as the first day.

ASPENCASH MOTORCYCLE RALLY. May 20–23. Ruidoso, NM. $10,000 cash poker run, trade show, poker run pin. Est attendance: 12,000. For info: Golden Aspen Rally Assn, PO Box 1467, Ruidoso, NM 88355. Phone: (800) 452-8045. E-mail: gara@zianet.com. Web: www.motorcyclerally.com.

BALZAC, HONORE DE: BIRTH ANNIVERSARY. May 20, 1799. French author of a huge cycle of stories and novels known as *The Human Comedy*, born at Tours, France. "It is easier," Balzac wrote in 1829, "to be a lover than a husband for the simple reason that it is more difficult to be witty every day than to say pretty things from time to time." Died at Paris, Aug 18, 1850.

BELGIUM: PROCESSION OF THE HOLY BLOOD. May 20. Religious historical procession. Recalls adventurous crusaders, including Count Thierry of Alsace, who carried back relics of the Holy Blood. Always on Ascension Day.

CAMEROON: NATIONAL HOLIDAY. May 20. Republic of Cameroon. Commemorates adoption of constitution in 1972.

COUNCIL OF NICAEA I: ANNIVERSARY. May 20–Aug 25, 325. First ecumenical council of Christian Church, called by Constantine I, first Christian emperor of Roman Empire. Nearly

300 bishops are said to have attended this first of 21 ecumenical councils (latest, Vatican II, began Sept 11, 1962), which was held at Nicaea, in Asia Minor (today's Turkey). The council condemned Arianism (which denied divinity of Christ), formulated the Nicene Creed and fixed the day of Easter—always on a Sunday.

EAST TIMOR: INDEPENDENCE DAY: ANNIVERSARY. May 20, 2002. East Timor became fully independent from Indonesia on this day. Indonesia had controlled the tiny nation since 1975. It had previously been a colony of Portugal for 450 years.

ELIZA DOOLITTLE DAY. May 20. To honor Miss Doolittle (heroine of Bernard Shaw's *Pygmalion*) for demonstrating the importance and the advantage of speaking one's native language properly. For info: H.M. Chase, Doolittle Day Committee, 2460 Devonshire Rd, Ann Arbor, MI 48104-2706.

HERZL, THEODOR: BIRTH ANNIVERSARY. May 20, 1860. Founder of the modern Zionist movement, born at Budapest, Hungary. Herzl died at Edlach, Austria, July 3, 1904.

HOMESTEAD ACT: ANNIVERSARY. May 20, 1862. President Lincoln signed the Homestead Act opening millions of acres of government-owned land in the West to settlers or "homesteaders," who had to reside on the land and cultivate it for five years.

LINDBERGH FLIGHT: ANNIVERSARY. May 20–21, 1927. Anniversary of the first solo trans-Atlantic flight. Captain Charles Augustus Lindbergh, 25-year-old aviator, departed from rainy, muddy Roosevelt Field, Long Island, NY, alone at 7:52 AM, May 20, 1927, in a Ryan monoplane named *Spirit of St. Louis*. He landed at Le Bourget airfield, Paris, at 10:24 PM Paris time (5:24 PM, NY time), May 21, winning a $25,000 prize offered by Raymond Orteig for the first nonstop flight between New York City and Paris, France (3,600 miles). The "flying fool" as he had been dubbed by some doubters became "Lucky Lindy," an instant world hero. See also: "Lindbergh, Charles Augustus: Birth Anniversary" (Feb 4).

MADISON, DOLLY (DOROTHEA) DANDRIDGE PAYNE TODD: BIRTH ANNIVERSARY. May 20, 1768. Wife of James Madison, 4th president of the US, born at Guilford County, NC. Died at Washington, DC, July 12, 1849.

MECKLENBURG DAY. May 20. North Carolina. Commemorates claimed signing of a declaration of independence from England by citizens of Mecklenburg County on this day, 1775.

MOTOR VOTER BILL SIGNED: ANNIVERSARY. May 20, 1993. The latest effort to remove barriers to voter registration resulted in the passage of the Motor Voter Bill, which was signed into law by President William Clinton. This bill requires the states to allow voter registration by mail or when a citizen applies for or renews a driver's license.

NCAA DIVISION I WOMEN'S TENNIS CHAMPIONSHIPS. May 20–29. Dan Magill Tennis Complex, University of Georgia, Athens, GA. For info: Natl Collegiate Athletic Assn, PO Box 6222, Indianapolis, IN 46206-6222. Web: www.NCAAsports.com.

NORMAN ROCKWELL'S FIRST *SATURDAY EVENING POST* COVER: ANNIVERSARY. May 20, 1916. Norman Rockwell's first cover for the *Post*, depicting a boy having to care for his infant sibling—pushing the baby carriage while his buddies set off to play ball—appeared on the May 20 edition. His last *Post* cover appeared in 1963.

ORTHODOX ASCENSION DAY. May 20. Observed by Eastern Orthodox Churches.

PENNSYLVANIA AVENUE CLOSED: ANNIVERSARY. May 20, 1995. Barricades were erected to close off a two-block stretch of Pennsylvania Avenue, a six-lane street with a sidewalk that passes within 150 feet of the north face of the White House. A review of security procedures had been initiated after an attempt by an unemployed truck driver to land a small airplane on the South Lawn in September of 1994, but the closing of Pennsylvania Avenue was a direct response to the bombing of the Alfred P. Murrah Federal Building at Oklahoma City, OK, Apr 19, 1995.

ROUSSEAU, HENRI JULIEN FELIX: BIRTH ANNIVERSARY. May 20, 1844. Henri Rousseau, nicknamed Le Douanier because of his one-time post as customs toll-keeper, was a celebrated French painter born at Laval, Mayenne, France. Painted deceptively "primitive" pictures of exotic foliage, flowers and fruit of the jungle, with stilted human and animal figures. Died at Hospital Necker, Paris, Sept 4, 1910.

SPACE MILESTONE: *PIONEER VENUS I* (US): ANNIVERSARY. May 20, 1978. Launched this date, became first Venus orbiter the following Dec 4.

STEWART, JIMMY: BIRTH ANNIVERSARY. May 20, 1908. Film actor born James Stewart at Indiana, PA. Best known for his roles in *Mr Smith Goes to Washington* and the Christmas classic *It's a Wonderful Life*, he won an Oscar for *The Philadelphia Story*. Died July 2, 1997 at Beverly Hills, CA.

WEIGHTS AND MEASURES DAY: ANNIVERSARY. May 20. Anniversary of international treaty, signed May 20, 1875, providing for the establishment of an International Bureau of Weights and Measures. The bureau was founded on international territory at Sevres, France.

BIRTHDAYS TODAY

Cher, 58, singer ("Believe"), actress (*Moonstruck*), born Cherilyn Sarkisian, El Centro, CA, May 20, 1946.

Joe Cocker, 60, singer ("You Are So Beautiful"), born Sheffield, England, May 20, 1944.

Michael Crapo, 53, US Senator (R, Idaho), born Idaho Falls, ID, May 20, 1951.

Tony Goldwyn, 44, actor (*Ghost, Kiss the Girls*), born Los Angeles, CA, May 20, 1960.

Stan Mikita, 64, Hall of Fame hockey player, born Sokolce, Czechoslovakia, May 20, 1940.

Bronson Pinchot, 45, actor ("Perfect Strangers," "Step By Step"), born New York, NY, May 20, 1959.

Ronald Prescott Reagan, 46, dancer, talk-show host, son of former President Ronald Reagan, born Los Angeles, CA, May 20, 1958.

Anthony Zerbe, 68, actor ("Harry-O," *Cool Hand Luke, Papillon*), born Long Beach, CA, May 20, 1936.

☆ Chase's 2004 Calendar of Events ☆ May 21

MAY 21 — FRIDAY
Day 142 — 224 Remaining

AMERICAN RED CROSS: FOUNDING ANNIVERSARY. May 21, 1881. Commemorates the founding of the American Red Cross by Clara Barton, its first president. The Red Cross had been founded in Switzerland in 1864 by representatives from 16 European nations. The organization is a voluntary, not-for-profit organization governed and directed by volunteers and provides disaster relief at home and abroad. 1.1 million volunteers are involved in community services such as collecting and distributing donated blood and blood products, teaching health and safety classes and acting as a medium for emergency communication between Americans and their armed forces.

ART FAIR AND WINEFEST. May 21–23. Washington, MO. The largest Missouri wine tasting of state wines as well as a juried art show featuring 60 midwestern artists. Art fair is free. Admission to the wine pavilion includes a commemorative wine glass. For info: Downtown Washington Inc, PO Box 144, Washington, MO 63090. Phone: (636) 239-1743. Fax: (636) 239-4832. E-mail: dwinc@yhti.net. Web: downtownwashmo.org.

BURR, RAYMOND WILLIAM STACY: BIRTH ANNIVERSARY. May 21, 1917. Stage, film and TV actor best known for the role of Perry Mason in the series of the same name. He was born at New Westminster, British Columbia, and died near Healdsburg, CA, Sept 12, 1993.

CHILE: BATTLE OF IQUIQUE DAY. May 21. Commemorates a naval battle in 1879, part of the War of the Pacific with Peru and Bolivia.

CURTISS, GLENN HAMMOND: BIRTH ANNIVERSARY. May 21, 1878. American inventor and aviator, born at Hammondsport, NY. The aviation pioneer died at Buffalo, NY, July 23, 1930.

DURER, ALBRECHT: BIRTH ANNIVERSARY. May 21, 1471. German painter and engraver, one of the greatest artists of the Renaissance, was born at Nuremberg, Germany, and died there Apr 6, 1528.

FRY, ELIZABETH GURNEY: BIRTH ANNIVERSARY. May 21, 1780. English reformer who dedicated her life to improving the condition of the poor and especially of women in prison, born at Earlham, Norfolk, England. Died at Ramsgate, Oct 12, 1845.

GEMINI, THE TWINS. May 21–June 20. In the astronomical/astrological zodiac, which divides the sun's apparent orbit into 12 segments, the period May 21–June 20 is traditionally identified as the sun sign period of Gemini, the Twins. The ruling planet is Mercury.

GUTHRIE JAZZ BANJO FESTIVAL. May 21–23. Downtown Guthrie, OK. Jazz banjo bands and soloists from all over the US perform music from the gay '90s, as well as the roaring '20s and contemporary selections at various venues around historic Guthrie. Also antique autos on parade. Est attendance: 10,000. For info: National Four String Banjo Museum, 116 E Oklahoma, Guthrie, OK 73044. Phone: (405) 282-1948 or (800) 299-1889 or (800) OK-BANJO. Fax: (405) 282-0061.

HAMMER, ARMAND: BIRTH ANNIVERSARY. May 21, 1898. American industrialist Armand Hammer was born at New York, NY. He built the Occidental Petroleum Company into a $20 billion conglomerate after he invested $100,000 in it in 1956 and it was awarded two oil concessions in Libya. He was a trained physician who was sympathetic to the Soviet people and gave away millions of dollars through philanthropy to cancer research. Hammer died Dec 10, 1990, at Los Angeles, CA.

HUMMEL, SISTER MARIA INNOCENTIA: 95th BIRTH ANNIVERSARY. May 21, 1909. Born at Massing, Bavaria, Sister Maria Innocentia Hummel attended Munich's Academy of Fine Arts. She entered Siessen Convent run by the Sisters of the Third Order of St. Francis and began teaching art to kindergarten children. In 1934 Franz Goebel obtained an exclusive license to translate her drawings into three-dimensional figurines. The first M.I. Hummel figurines were displayed at the Leipzig Trade Fair in 1935; they made their first appearance in the American market in May 1935. She died Nov 6, 1946, at Siessen, Germany. Many M.I. Hummel Clubs across the country commemorate her birthdate with special events and fundraisers for local charities.

"I NEED A PATCH FOR THAT" DAY. May 21. They have patches for nicotine and they have patches for heart patients. How about a patch for runny noses or bad hair? [©2003 by WH.] For info: Thomas & Ruth Roy, Wellcat Holidays, 2418 Long Lane, Lebanon, PA 17046. Phone: (717) 279-0184. E-mail: info@wellcat.com. Web: www.wellcat.com.

INTERNATIONAL PICKLE WEEK. May 21–30. To give national recognition to the world's most humorous vegetable. Sponsor: Pickle Packers International, Inc. For info: IPW, DHM Group Inc, 9 Professional Circle, Ste 101, Colts Neck, NJ 07722. Fax: (732) 866-4466.

MICHIGAN MAGIC DAY. May 21–23. Gilmore Theatre Complex, Kalamazoo, MI. If you want to learn, perform, watch or teach magic, then this is the event that you've been waiting for. There will be magic dealers, close-up and stage magic shows, junior and senior competitions, lectures and concessions. Three days of magic, magic, and more magic. This 35th annual event is sponsored by IBM Ring 333, The Timid Rabbit Magic & Masquerade Shop, Gerard Enterprises and The Kalamazoo Magic Society. For info: Antony Gerard, The Timid Rabbit Magic & Masquerade Shop, 2011 W Main St, Kalamazoo, MI 49006. Phone: (269) 343-7777. Fax: (269) 383-2948. E-mail: antonygerard@msn.com. Web: www.gerardenterprises.com.

MILES CITY BUCKING HORSE SALE. May 21–23. Miles City, MT. Miles City is real "Lonesome Dove" country and its annual bucking horse sale is where rodeo stock operators from around the nation and Canada come to purchase their bucking horses for the coming rodeo season. A festive event, the sale not only involves cowboys trying to ride some of the wildest horses in the country, but Western artists displaying and creating works in a weekend art show, a Western trade show featuring practical and gift items, a Saturday morning parade and Miles City's Western attractions like the Range Riders Museum. (Miles City is the community featured in the novel and two television miniseries about "Lonesome Dove.") Est attendance: 10,000. For info: Miles City Chamber of Commerce, 901 Main St, Miles City, MT 59301. Phone: (406) 234-2890.

NAIA SOFTBALL NATIONAL CHAMPIONSHIP. May 21–26. Decatur, AL. 24th annual competition. Est attendance: 2,000. For info: Natl Assn of Intercollegiate Athletics, 23500 W 105th St, PO Box 1325, Olathe, KS 66051-1325. E-mail: ncronkhite@naia.org. Web: www.naia.org.

NATIONAL BIKE TO WORK DAY. May 21. At the state or local level, Bike to Work events are conducted by small and large businesses, city governments, bicycle clubs and environmental groups. About two million participants nationwide. Annually, the third Friday in May. Est attendance: 2,000,000. For info: Patrick McCormick, Communications Dir, League of American Bicyclists, 1612 K St NW, Ste 800, Washington, DC 20006. Phone: (202) 822-1333. Fax: (202) 822-1334. E-mail: bikeleague@bikeleague.org. Web: www.bikeleague.org.

★**NATIONAL DEFENSE TRANSPORTATION DAY.** May 21. Presidential Proclamation customarily issued as "National Defense Transportation Day and National Transportation Week." Issued each year for the third Friday in May since 1957. (PL85-32 of May 16, 1957.)

May 21–22 ☆ Chase's 2004 Calendar of Events ☆

NATIONAL WAITSTAFF DAY. May 21. A day for restaurant managers and patrons to recognize and to express their appreciation for the many fine and dedicated waitresses and waiters. For info: Gaylord F. Ward, Promotion Dir, 1505 E Bristol Rd, Burton, MI 48529-2214.

PICKLEFEST. May 21–22. Atkins, AR (home of the fried dill pickle). Festivities include World's Champion Pickle Juice Drinking Contest, World's Champion Pickle Eating Contest, a pickle-tasting booth, the Pickle Pageant and pickle contest, arts and crafts and live entertainment. Est attendance: 7,000. For info: Picklefest, People for a Better Atkins, PO Box 474, Atkins, AR 72823. Phone: (501) 641-1147 (fest info) or (501) 641-1993 (PR and sales).

POPE, ALEXANDER: BIRTH ANNIVERSARY. May 21, 1688 (OS). English poet born at London, England. "A man," Pope wrote in 1727, "should never be ashamed to own he has been in the wrong, which is but saying, in other words, that he is wiser today than he was yesterday." Died at Twickenham, May 30, 1744 (OS).

RAJIV GANDHI ASSASSINATED: ANNIVERSARY. May 21, 1991. Former Indian Prime Minister Rajiv Gandhi was assassinated in the midst of an election campaign. He was killed when a bomb, hidden in a bouquet of flowers given by admirers, exploded as he approached a dais to begin a campaign rally. He had served as prime minister between 1984 and 1989 after succeeding his mother, Indira Gandhi, who was assassinated in 1984.

RHODODENDRON FESTIVAL. May 21–23. Florence, OR. Abundance of springtime rhododendron blooms celebrated with a Grand Floral Parade, arts and crafts show, dance, kite festival, show & shine, car cruise and carnival. Held annually since 1908. Est attendance: 35,000. For info: Florence Chamber of Commerce, 270 Hwy 101, Florence, OR 97439. Phone: (541) 997-3128 or (800) 524-4864. E-mail: florence@oregonfast.net. Web: www.florencechamber.com.

RHUBARB FESTIVAL. May 21–22. Intercourse, PA. A lighthearted celebration honoring rhubarb, which grows abundantly in the Pennsylvania Dutch country. Food, games and contests all featuring rhubarb—pie baking contest, rhubarb derby, rhubarb pick-up sticks and more—plus entertainment. Est attendance: 10,000. For info: Lisa Horn, Kitchen Kettle Village, Box 380, Intercourse, PA 17534. Phone: (800) 732-3538 or (717) 768-8261. Web: www.kitchenkettle.com.

SAKHAROV, ANDREI DMITRIYEVICH: BIRTH ANNIVERSARY. May 21, 1921. Soviet physicist, human rights activist and environmentalist Andrei Sakharov was born at Moscow, Russia. A collaborator in producing the first Soviet atomic bomb, and later the hydrogen bomb, Sakharov later denounced shortcomings of his country's government and was exiled to Gorky, Russia, 1980–86. He was a formulator of the reform and restructuring concept known as *perestroika* and of *glasnost* (freedom). He was named to the Soviet Congress of Peoples Deputies eight months before his death at Moscow on Dec 14, 1989. As a physicist, he was the developer of destructive weapons; as a humanitarian, he was courageous as a dissident from militarism and an advocate of human rights.

SEVEN DAYS IN MAY. May 21–23 (also May 28–31). Chapel Hill, NC. Unique architectural antiques, featuring an extensive collection of period wrought iron artifacts (especially iron gates, garden art and home embellishments). Annually, last two weekends in May. For info: Gaines Steer, The Last Unicorn, 536 Edwards Ridge Road, Chapel Hill, NC 27517. Phone: (919) 968-8440. E-mail: info@thelastunicorn.com. Web: www.thelastunicorn.com.

STAMP EXPO. May 21–23. Pasadena Convention Center, Pasadena, CA. Annual expo. Est attendance: 5,000. For info: Intl Stamp Collectors Society, Box 854, Van Nuys, CA 91408. Phone: (818) 997-6496. Fax: (818) 988-4337. E-mail: iibick@aol.com. Web: www.bick.net.

TEACHER'S DAY IN FLORIDA. May 21. A ceremonial day on the third Friday in May.

VEGASPEX. May 21–23 (also Dec 10–12). Las Vegas, NV. Coin, stamp, antique watch, jewelry and collectibles expo. Est attendance: 10,000. For info: Intl Coin & Stamp Collectors Society, PO Box 854, Van Nuys, CA 91408. Phone: (818) 997-6496. Fax: (818) 988-4337. E-mail: iibick@aol.com. Web: www.bick.net.

WILLAMETTE VALLEY FOLK FESTIVAL. May 21–23. Eugene, OR. 34th annual folk festival with multiple stages of musical performances, workshops, food and craft booths. Sponsor: UO Cultural Forum. Free. Annually, the Fri–Sun before Memorial Day weekend. Est attendance: 10,000. For info: Heritage Music Coord, EMU Cultural Forum, University of Oregon, Eugene, OR 97403. Phone: (541) 346-4373. Fax: (541) 346-4400. Web: culturalforum.uoregon.edu.

BIRTHDAYS TODAY

Bobby Cox, 63, baseball manager, former executive and player, born Tulsa, OK, May 21, 1941.
Robert Creeley, 78, author, poet (*Have a Heart, Windows*), born Arlington, MA, May 21, 1926.
Janet Dailey, 60, romance novelist (*Tangled Vines*), born Storm Lake, IA, May 21, 1944.
Al Franken, 53, comedian, writer (*Rush Limbaugh Is a Big Fat Idiot and Other Observations*), actor ("Saturday Night Live"), born New York, NY, May 21, 1951.
Heinz Holliger, 65, oboist, composer, conductor, born Langenthal, Switzerland, May 21, 1939.
William "Spike" O'Dell, 51, Chicago radio personality, born Moline, IL, May 21, 1953.
Judge Reinhold, 47, actor (*Beverly Hills Cop*), born Wilmington, DE, May 21, 1957.
Leo Sayer, 56, singer ("You Make Me Feel Like Dancing"), songwriter, born Shoreham, England, May 21, 1948.
Mr T, 52, actor (*Rocky III*, "The A-Team"), born Lawrence Tero or Tureaud, Chicago, IL, May 21, 1952.

MAY 22 — SATURDAY
Day 143 — 223 Remaining

CANADA: IMMIGRANTS' DAY. May 22. A day to celebrate and recognize the contributions made by immigrants to Canada and to discuss the Canadian Immigration policy and experience. For info: Sergio R. Karas, BA, LLB, Barrister and Solicitor, Karas & Assoc, 1 First Canadian Place, 100 King St W, Ste 2640, Toronto, ON, Canada M5X 1E4. Phone: (416) 506-1800. Fax: (416) 506-1305. E-mail: karas@karas.ca. Web: www.karas.ca.

CASSATT, MARY: BIRTH ANNIVERSARY. May 22, 1844. Leading American artist of the Impressionist school, Mary Cassatt was born May 22, 1844 (some sources give 1845), at Allegheny City, PA (now part of Pittsburgh). She settled in Paris in 1874 where she was influenced by Degas and the Impressionists. She was later instrumental in their works becoming well known in the US. The majority of her paintings and pastels were based on the theme of mother and child. After 1900 her eyesight began to fail, and by 1914 she was no longer able to paint. Cassatt died at Chateau de Beaufresne near Paris, France, June 14, 1926.

	S	M	T	W	T	F	S
May							1
	2	3	4	5	6	7	8
2004	9	10	11	12	13	14	15
	16	17	18	19	20	21	22
	23	24	25	26	27	28	29
	30	31					

☆ Chase's 2004 Calendar of Events ☆   May 22

CRATER LAKE NATIONAL PARK ESTABLISHED: ANNIVERSARY. May 22, 1902. One of the world's deepest lakes, Crater Lake was first discovered in 1853. In 1885 William Gladstone Steele saw the Oregon lake and made it his personal goal to establish the lake and surrounding areas as a national park. His goal was attained 17 years later.

DOYLE, SIR ARTHUR CONAN: BIRTH ANNIVERSARY. May 22, 1859. British physician Sir Arthur Conan Doyle is best remembered as a detective story writer, especially for the creation of Sherlock Holmes and Dr. Watson. Doyle was born at Edinburgh, Scotland. He was deeply interested in and lectured on the subject of spiritualism. Died at Crowborough, Sussex, England, July 7, 1930.

FIDDLE FEST AT AUDUBON ACRES. May 22. Audubon Acres, Chattanooga, TN. Fund-raising event cosponsored by Chattanooga Area Friends of Folk Music. Several local musicians including Tom Morgan will play music on the patio of Walker Hall. Guided tours of Spring Frog Cabin and eagle aviary will be available. Many other activities and crafts geared toward pioneer skills will be available, including the River Bend Fiber Arts Guilde. Sponsored by the Chattanooga Audubon Society. Est attendance: 1,000. For info: Lynda Logan, Audubon Acres, 900 N Sanctuary Rd, Chattanooga, TN 37421. Phone: (423) 892-1499. Fax: (423) 892-6376. E-mail: caudubons@aol.com. Web: www.audubonchattanooga.org.

FIND YOUR SOUL MATE DAY. May 22. Find Your Soul Mate Day is a day to put on your best suit, nicest dress and sweetest smile! Mr. Right and Miss Right are walking around out there somewhere, and you don't want them to pass you by! For info: Victoria Pericon. Phone: (917) 826-3360. E-mail: LoveVictoria @aol.com. Web: www.LoveVictoria.com.

FLORIDA FOLK FESTIVAL. May 22–24. Stephen Foster Folk Culture Center State Park, White Springs, FL. To celebrate Florida's folk heritage with music, song, dance and stories. Est attendance: 30,000. For info: Stephen Foster Folk Culture Center State Park, Post Office Drawer G, White Springs, FL 32096. Phone: (386) 397-2733 or (877) 6FL-FOLK.

GETTYSBURG OUTDOOR ANTIQUE SHOW. May 22. Gettysburg, PA. Features 150 dealers in antiques with exhibits and displays. Annually, a Saturday in May. Est attendance: 25,000. For info: Gettysburg CVB, PO Box 4117, Gettysburg, PA 17325. Phone: (717) 334-6274. Fax: (717) 334-1166. E-mail: gettysburgcvb@dejazzd.com. Web: www.gettysburgcvb.org.

JOHNNY CARSON'S FINAL SHOW: ANNIVERSARY. May 22, 1992. After almost 30 years as host of the "Tonight" show, Johnny Carson hosted his last show. Carson became host of the late-night talk show, which began as a local New York program hosted by Steve Allen, Oct 1, 1962. Over the years Carson occasionally made headlines with such extravaganzas as the marriage of Tiny Tim and Miss Vicki. Johnny received Emmys for his work four years in a row, 1976–79. Ed McMahon, his sidekick of 30 years, and Doc Severinsen, longtime bandleader, left the show with Carson. Jay Leno, the show's exclusive guest host, became the new regular host.

MIFFLIN-JUNIATA ARTS FESTIVAL. May 22–23. Lewistown Rec Park, Lewistown, PA. More than 75 juried arts and craft vendors; professional and amateur performances; free children's crafts and special exhibits. Admission free. Est attendance: 15,000. For info: Paul Olbrich, c/o Mifflin-Juniata Arts Council, 507 Lindbergh Way, Lewistown, PA 17044. Phone: (717) 248-0582. E-mail: thiry@acsworld.net.

"MISTER ROGERS' NEIGHBORHOOD" TV PREMIERE: ANNIVERSARY. May 22, 1967. Presbyterian minister Fred Rogers hosted this long-running PBS children's program. Puppets and human characters interacted in the neighborhood of make-believe. Rogers played the voices of many of the puppets and educated young viewers on a variety of important subjects. The last episodes of the program were made in 2001. Almost 1,000 episodes were produced over the show's history.

MUSEUM OPEN HOUSE. May 22–23 (also Nov 13–14). Clinton, MD. Annual open house at historic site features free tours, special activities and gift shop sales. Est attendance: 500. For info: Surratt House Museum, PO Box 427, Clinton, MD 20735. Phone: (301) 868-1121. Fax: (301) 868-8177. Web: www.surratt.org.

★**NATIONAL MARITIME DAY.** May 22. Presidential Proclamation always issued for May 22 since 1933. (Pub Res No 7 of May 20, 1933.)

NATIONAL MARITIME DAY. May 22. Anniversary of departure for first steamship crossing of Atlantic from Savannah, GA. to Liverpool, England, by steamship *Savannah* in 1819.

★**NATIONAL SAFE BOATING WEEK.** May 22–28. Presidential Proclamation during May since 1995. From 1958 through 1977, issued for a week including July 4 (PL85–445 of June 4, 1958). From 1981 through 1994, issued for the first week in June (PL96–376 of Oct 3, 1980). From 1995, issued for a seven-day period ending on the Friday before Memorial Day. Not issued from 1978 through 1980.

NATIONAL SAFE BOATING WEEK. May 22–28. Brings boating safety to the public's attention, decreases the number of boating fatalities and makes the waterways safer for all boaters. Sponsors: National Safe Boating Council and US Coast Guard. For info: Natl Safe Boating Council. E-mail: nsbcdirect@safeboatingcouncil.org. Web: www.safeboatingcouncil.org.

NCAA DIVISION I MEN'S TENNIS CHAMPIONSHIP. May 22–31. University of Tulsa, Tulsa, OK. For info: Natl Collegiate Athletic Assn, 700 W Washington Ave, PO Box 6222, Indianapolis, IN 46206-6222. Phone: (317) 917-6222. Fax: (317) 917-6825. Web: www.ncaasports.com.

NIXON FIRST AMERICAN PRESIDENT TO VISIT MOSCOW: ANNIVERSARY. May 22, 1972. President Richard Nixon became the first American president to visit Moscow. Four days later on May 26, Nixon and Soviet leader Leonid Brezhnev signed a treaty on antiballistic missile systems and an interim agreement on limitation of strategic missiles.

OLIVIER, LAURENCE: BIRTH ANNIVERSARY. May 22, 1907. Actor, director and theater manager, born at Dorking, England. Thought by many to be the most influential actor of this century, Olivier's theatrical and film career shaped the art forms in which he participated. Honored with nine Academy Award nominations, three Oscars and five Emmy awards, his repertoire included most of the prime Shakespearean roles and roles in such films as *Rebecca, Pride and Prejudice, Marathon Man* and *Wuthering Heights*. Olivier was an innovative theater manager with London's Old Vic company and the National Theatre of Great Britain. The National Theatre's largest auditorium and Britain's equivalent of Broadway's Tony awards carry his name. He was knighted in 1947 and made a peer of the throne in 1970. Olivier died at Ashurst, England, July 11, 1989.

ORIGINAL RAGGEDY ANN & ANDY FESTIVAL. May 22–23. Arcola, IL. The whole town celebrates Raggedy Ann & Andy with a parade, arts & crafts, collectibles, food court and entertainment. Est attendance: 10,000. For info: Arcola Chamber of Commerce, PO Box 274, Arcola, IL 61910. Phone: (800) 336-5456. Web: www.arcola-il.org.

☆ Chase's 2004 Calendar of Events ☆

May 22–23

RA, SUN: 90th BIRTH ANNIVERSARY. May 22, 1914. Born Herman (Sonny) Blount, Sun Ra was a pioneering and innovative jazz musician whose avant garde performances mixed elements of theater with his surreal composition and performance style. Ra was born at Birmingham, AL, and died there May 30, 1993.

SRI LANKA: NATIONAL HEROES DAY. May 22. Commemorates the struggle of the leaders of the National Independence Movement to liberate the country from colonial rule in 1971. Public holiday.

TRUMAN DOCTRINE: ANNIVERSARY. May 22, 1947. Congress approved the Truman Doctrine on this day. In order to contain Communism after World War II, it provided for US aid to Greece and Turkey. A corollary of this doctrine was the Marshall Plan, which began sending aid to war-torn European countries in 1948.

UNITED NATIONS: INTERNATIONAL DAY FOR BIOLOGICAL DIVERSITY. May 22. On Dec 19, 1994, the General Assembly proclaimed this observance for Dec 29, the date of entry into force of the Convention on Biological Diversity (Res 49/119). In 2000 the date was changed to May 22. This day is an opportunity to strengthen people's commitment and actions for the conservation of the world's biological diversity. For info: United Nations, Dept of Public Info, New York, NY 10017. Web: www.un.org.

WAGNER, RICHARD: BIRTH ANNIVERSARY. May 22, 1813. German composer born at Leipzig who made revolutionary changes in the structure of opera. Best known for his Ring Cycle (*Der Ring des Nibelungen*). Died at Italy, Feb 13, 1883.

WISCONSIN DELLS AUTOMOTION. May 22–23. Noah's Ark Waterpark, Wisconsin Dells, WI. A showcase of more than 700 cars, including street machines, classics and antiques. Show features swap meet, motorcycle classes, live entertainment, car cruise, car corral, four $500 cash drawings, eight getaway packages valued at approximately $500 each, and a car-themed movie at Big Sky Drive-In Theatre on Saturday night. Clowns, mini-tractor pull and model car contests for the kids. For auto buffs and visitors alike. Est attendance: 45,000. For info: Wisconsin Dells Visitor & Convention Bureau, Box 390, Wisconsin Dells, WI 53965. Phone: (800) 223-3557. E-mail: info@wisdells.com. Web: www.wisdells.com.

WORST EARTHQUAKE OF THE 20th CENTURY: ANNIVERSARY. May 22, 1960. An earthquake of a magnitude 9.5 struck southern Chile, killing 2,000 people and leaving 2,000,000 homeless. The earthquake also caused damage in Hawaii, Japan and the Philippines. While 20th-century earthquakes in Mexico City, Japan and Turkey resulted in far more deaths, this earthquake in Chile was of the highest magnitude.

YEMEN: NATIONAL DAY. May 22. Public holiday. Commemorates the reunification of Yemen in 1990.

BIRTHDAYS TODAY

Charles Aznavour, 80, singer, songwriter, actor (*Shoot the Piano Player, Candy, The Tin Drum*), born Paris, France, May 22, 1924.
Richard Benjamin, 66, actor (*Goodbye Columbus, Diary of a Mad Housewife*, "He & She"), born New York, NY, May 22, 1938.
Naomi Campbell, 34, model, born London, England, May 22, 1970.
Frank Converse, 66, actor ("Movin' On," *Hurry Sundown*), born St. Louis, MO, May 22, 1938.
Judith Crist, 82, critic, born New York, NY, May 22, 1922.
Thomas Edward (Tommy) John, 61, former baseball player, born Terre Haute, IN, May 22, 1943.
A.J. Langer, 30, actress ("My So-Called Life," "Brooklyn South"), born Columbus, OH, May 22, 1974.
Lisa Murkowski, 47, US Senator (R, Alaska), born Ketchikan, AK, May 22, 1957.
Barbara Parkins, 61, actress ("Peyton Place," *Valley of the Dolls*), born Vancouver, BC, Canada, May 22, 1943.
Michael Sarrazin, 64, actor (*The Flim Flam Man, The Reincarnation of Peter Proud*), born Quebec City, QC, Canada, May 22, 1940.
Garry Wills, 70, author (*John Wayne's America, Lincoln at Gettysburg*), born Atlanta, GA, May 22, 1934.
Paul Winfield, 64, actor (*Sounder, Star Trek II: The Wrath of Khan, Presumed Innocent*), born Los Angeles, CA, May 22, 1940.

MAY 23 — SUNDAY

Day 144 — 222 Remaining

CAPE MAY MUSIC FESTIVAL. May 23–June 27. Cape May, NJ. Enjoy world-class orchestral and chamber music performances along with internationally acclaimed guest artists. Est attendance: 10,000. For info: Mid-Atlantic Center for the Arts, 1048 Washington St, Cape May, NJ 08204. Phone: (800) 275-4278 or (609) 884-5404. Fax: (609) 884-0574. E-mail: mac4arts@capemaymac.org. Web: www.capemaymac.org.

CLOONEY, ROSEMARY: BIRTH ANNIVERSARY. May 23, 1928. The beloved pop and jazz singer was born at Maysville, KY. She became popular in the 1950s for singing the novelty song "Come-on-a-My House" and pop standards. She also starred in the holiday film *White Christmas* (1954). She died June 29, 2002, at Beverly Hills, CA.

DECLARATION OF THE BAB. May 23. Baha'i commemoration of May 23, 1844, when the Bab, the prophet-herald of the Baha'i Faith, announced in Shiraz, Persia, that he was the herald of a new messenger of God. One of the nine days of the year when Baha'is suspend work. For info: Baha'is of the US, Office of Public Information, 1320 Nineteenth St NW, Ste 350, Washington, DC 20036. Phone: (202) 466-9870. Fax: (202) 466-9873. E-mail: opi@usbnc.org. Web: www.us.bahai.org.

FAIRBANKS, DOUGLAS ELTON: BIRTH ANNIVERSARY. May 23, 1883. Douglas Fairbanks was born at Denver, CO. He made his professional debut as an actor at Richmond, VA, Sept 10, 1900, in *The Duke's Jester*. His theatrical career turned to Hollywood, and he became a movie idol appearing in such films as *The Mark of Zorro, The Three Musketeers, Robin Hood, The Thief of Bagdad, The Black Pirate* and *The Gaucho*. He married "America's Sweetheart," Mary Pickford, in 1918, and in 1919 they joined with D.W. Griffith and Charlie Chaplin to form the production company United Artists. He died at Santa Monica, CA, Dec 12, 1939.

FIRST BLACK RECEIVES CONGRESSIONAL MEDAL OF HONOR: ANNIVERSARY. May 23, 1900. Sergeant William H. Carney, of the 54th Massachusetts Colored Infantry, was the first black to win the Congressional Medal of Honor. He was cited for his efforts, although wounded twice, during the Battle of Fort Wagner, SC, June 18, 1863.

FULLER, MARGARET: BIRTH ANNIVERSARY. May 23, 1810. Journalist and author Sarah Margaret Fuller, born at Cambridgeport, MA, began reading Virgil at age six. Her conversa-

May 2004	S	M	T	W	T	F	S
							1
	2	3	4	5	6	7	8
	9	10	11	12	13	14	15
	16	17	18	19	20	21	22
	23	24	25	26	27	28	29
	30	31					

✫ Chase's 2004 Calendar of Events ✫ May 23-24

tional powers won her the admiration of students at Harvard University, and she was befriended by Ralph Waldo Emerson. She shared editorial duties with Emerson on the Transcendentalist quarterly *The Dial*, and was hired by Horace Greeley as literary critic for the *New York Tribune*. Her book *Women in the Nineteenth Century*, the first feminist statement by an American writer, brought her international acclaim. In 1846, as a foreign correspondent for the *Tribune*, she became caught up in the Italian revolutionary movement and secretly married a young Roman nobleman, the Marquis Giovanni Angelo Ossoli. En route to the US, Fuller and her husband and child died July 19, 1850, when their ship was wrecked off Fire Island near New York, NY.

ITALY: WEDDING OF THE SEA. May 23. Venice. The feast of the Ascension is the occasion of the ceremony recalling the "Wedding of the Sea" performed by Venice's Doge, who cast his ring into the sea from the ceremonial ship known as the *Bucintoro* to symbolize eternal dominion. Annually, on the Sunday following Ascension.

MANSFIELD, ARABELLA: BIRTH ANNIVERSARY. May 23, 1846. Arabella Mansfield, born Belle Aurelia Babb near Burlington, IA, was the first woman admitted to the legal profession in the US. In 1869 while teaching at Iowa Wesleyan College, Mansfield was certified as an attorney and admitted to the Iowa bar. According to the examiners, "she gave the very best rebuke possible to the imputation that ladies cannot qualify for the practice of law." Mansfield never did practice law, however, continuing her career as an educator. She joined the faculty of DePauw University, at Greencastle, IN, where she became dean of the schools of art and music. One of the first woman college professors and administrators in the US, Mansfield was also instrumental in the founding of the Iowa Woman Suffrage Society in 1870. She died Aug 2, 1911, at Aurora, IL.

MESMER, FRIEDRICH ANTON: BIRTH ANNIVERSARY. May 23, 1734. German physician after whom Mesmerism was named. Magnetism and hypnotism were used by him in treating disease. Born at Iznang, Swabia, Germany. Died Mar 5, 1815, at Meersburg, Swabia, Germany.

MOROCCO: NATIONAL DAY. May 23. National holiday. Commemorates referendum on the majority of the king in 1980.

NEIGHBOR DAY. May 23. A "Day of Special Observance" in Rhode Island, declared by the General Assembly. Annually, the Sunday prior to Memorial Day weekend. For info: Mary Jane DiMaio, Westerly Town Councilor, 15 Windward Dr, Westerly, RI 02891. Web: townofwesterly.com.

NEW YORK PUBLIC LIBRARY: ANNIVERSARY. May 23, 1895. New York's then-governor Samuel J. Tilden was the driving force that resulted in the combining of the private Astor and Lenox libraries with a $2 million endowment and 15,000 volumes from the Tilden Trust to become the New York Public Library. The main branch of the library opened to the public on this day in 1911.

SLOVO, JOE: BIRTH ANNIVERSARY. May 23, 1926. South African Communist Party leader Joe Slovo was a longtime friend and ally of Nelson Mandela. The first white to become a member of the African National Congress Executive Committee, he lived in exile from 1963 to 1990, serving as head of the military arm of the ANC during that period. Born at Obelai, Lithuania, he died Jan 6, 1995, at Johannesburg.

SOUTH CAROLINA CONSTITUTION RATIFICATION: ANNIVERSARY. May 23, 1788. By a vote of 149 to 73, South Carolina became the eighth state to ratify the Constitution.

SUPREME COURT UPHOLDS BAN ON ABORTION COUNSELING: ANNIVERSARY. May 23, 1991. In the case *Rust v Sullivan*, the Supreme Court, in a 5–4 ruling, upheld federal regulations that barred federally funded family planning clinics from providing any information about abortion.

SWEDEN: LINNAEUS DAY. May 23. Stenbrohult. Commemorates birth of Carolus Linnaeus (Carl von Linne), Swedish naturalist, born May 23, 1707 (OS) and who died at Uppsala, Sweden, Jan 10, 1778.

WORLD TURTLE DAY. May 23. An observance sponsored by American Tortoise Rescue to help people celebrate and protect turtles and tortoises, as well as their habitat around the world. For info: Susan Tellem, American Tortoise Rescue, 23852 Pacific Coast Highway, Malibu, CA 90265. Phone: (800) 938-3553. E-mail: info@tortoise.com. Web: www.tortoise.com.

BIRTHDAYS TODAY

Barbara Barrie, 73, actress ("Suddenly Susan," *One Potato, Two Potato; Breaking Away*), born Chicago, IL, May 23, 1931.
Drew Carey, 43, actor ("The Drew Carey Show"), born Cleveland, OH, May 23, 1961 (some sources say 1958).
Joan Collins, 71, actress ("Dynasty"), born London, England, May 23, 1933.
Marvelous Marvin Hagler, 50, former boxer, born Newark, NJ, May 23, 1954.
Jewel, 30, singer, born Jewel Kilcher, Payson, UT, May 23, 1974.
Charles Kimbrough, 68, actor ("Murphy Brown"), born St. Paul, MN, May 23, 1936.
Robert Moog, 70, inventor of first commercially viable keyboard synthesizer, born Flushing, NY, May 23, 1934.
Artie Shaw, 94, musician, bandleader, born New York, NY, May 23, 1910.

MAY 24 — MONDAY
Day 145 — 221 Remaining

ANCESTOR HONOR DAY. May 24. A national, commemorative observance to honor the nonmilitary contributions of the many nationalities and cultures that worked and died for freedom, justice and equality. This holiday was envisioned and proclaimed in 1998 by Ayo Handy Kendi, founder and director of the African American Holiday Association (AAHA). Annually, the Monday before Memorial Day. For info: African American Holiday Assn, PO Box 43255, Washington, DC 20010. E-mail: aaha@aaha-info.org. Web: www.aaha-info.org.

ANTI-SALOON LEAGUE FOUNDED: ANNIVERSARY. May 24, 1893. The Anti-Saloon League was founded by Howard H. Russell at Oberlin, OH. Efforts in that state were so successful that the Anti-Saloon League of America was organized in 1895. The League's permanent home became Otterbein College at Westerville, OH, in 1909.

BASEBALL FIRST PLAYED UNDER LIGHTS: ANNIVERSARY. May 24, 1935. The Cincinnati Reds defeated the Philadelphia Phillies by a score of 2–1, as more than 20,000 fans enjoyed the first night baseball game in the major leagues. The game was played at Crosley Field, Cincinnati, OH.

BELIZE: COMMONWEALTH DAY. May 24. Public holiday.

BROOKLYN BRIDGE OPENED: ANNIVERSARY. May 24, 1883. Nearly 14 years in construction, the $16 million Brooklyn Bridge over the East River opened. Designed by John A. Roebling, the steel suspension bridge has a span of 1,595 feet.

BROTHER'S DAY. May 24. Celebration of brotherhood for biological brothers, fraternity brothers, brothers bonded by union affiliation or lifetime experiences. Annually, May 24. [©2001 C. Daniel Rhodes.] For info: C. Daniel Rhodes, 1900 Crossvine Rd, Hoover, AL 35244. Phone: (205) 908-6781. Fax: (205) 987-2986. E-mail: drhodes2986@charter.net.

May 24-25 ☆ Chase's 2004 Calendar of Events ☆

BULGARIA: CULTURE DAY. May 24. National holiday festively celebrated by schoolchildren, students, people of science and art.

CANADA: VICTORIA DAY. May 24. Commemorates the birth of Queen Victoria May 24, 1819. Observed annually on the first Monday preceding May 25.

ECUADOR: BATTLE OF PICHINCHA. May 24. National holiday. Commemorates battle in 1822 that marked the final defeat of Spain in Ecuador.

ERITREA: INDEPENDENCE DAY: ANNIVERSARY. May 24. National Day. Gained independence from Ethiopia in 1993 after 30-year civil war.

GREAT FLOOD OF 1889 COMMEMORATIVE WEEKEND. May 24–31 (tentative). Johnstown Flood Museum, Johnstown, PA. The Johnstown Flood Museum recreates the catastrophe in which 2,209 people died, tens of thousands were left homeless and a prospering city was left a wasteland. "The Johnstown Flood," a 1989 Academy Award–winning documentary, is shown hourly. For info: Johnstown Flood Museum, PO Box 1889, Johnstown, PA 15907-1889. Phone: (814) 539-1889 or (888) 222-1889. Fax: (814) 535-1931. Web: www.jaha.org.

LEUTZE, EMANUEL: BIRTH ANNIVERSARY. May 24, 1816. Obscure itinerant painter, born at Wurttemberg, Germany, came to the US when he was nine years old, began painting by age 15. Painted some of the most famous of American scenes, such as *Washington Crossing the Delaware, Washington Rallying the Troops at Monmouth* and *Columbus Before the Queen.* Died July 18, 1868, at Washington, DC.

MORSE OPENS FIRST US TELEGRAPH LINE: ANNIVERSARY. May 24, 1844. The first US telegraph line was formally opened between Baltimore, MD, and Washington, DC. Samuel F.B. Morse sent the first officially telegraphed words "What hath God wrought?" from the Capitol building to Baltimore. Earlier messages had been sent along the historic line during testing, and one, sent May 1, contained the news that Henry Clay had been nominated as president by the Whig party, from a meeting in Baltimore. This message reached Washington one hour prior to a train carrying the same news.

NATIONAL BACKYARD GAMES WEEK. May 24–31. Observance to celebrate the unofficial start of summer by fostering social interaction and family togetherness through backyard games. Get outside and be both physically and mentally stimulated, playing classic games of the past while discovering and creating new ways to be active and interact with friends and neighbors. For info: Frank Beres, Patch Products, PO Box 268, Beloit, WI 53511. Phone: (608) 362-6896. Fax: (608) 362-8178. E-mail: patch@patchproducts.com. Web: www.patchproducts.com.

NEWHOUSE, SAMUEL I.: BIRTH ANNIVERSARY. May 24, 1895. Multimillionaire businessman who built family publishing and communications empire. Born to immigrant parents in a New York City tenement, Newhouse became "America's most profitable publisher." He accumulated 31 newspapers, seven magazines, six television stations, five radio stations and 20 cable television systems. He died at New York, NY, Aug 29, 1979.

PALMER, LILLI: 90th BIRTH ANNIVERSARY. May 24, 1914. Stage, screen and television actress Lilli Palmer was born Lillie Marie Peiser, at Poznan, Poland. She also painted and was the author of several novels and an autobiography titled *Change Lobsters—And Dance.* She died at Los Angeles, CA, Jan 27, 1986.

PGA SENIORS' CHAMPIONSHIP. May 24–30. Valhalla Golf Club, Louisville, KY. 65th competition for the oldest major championship in senior golf. Conducted by the Professional Golfers' Association of America. For info: Jamie Carbone, PR Manager, PGA of America, 100 Avenue of the Champions, Palm Beach Gardens, FL 33418. Phone: (561) 624-8400. Fax: (561) 624-8448. Web: www.pgaonline.com.

SPACE MILESTONE: *AURORA 7* MERCURY SPACE CAPSULE (US). May 24, 1962. With this launch Scott Carpenter became second American to orbit Earth, circling it three times.

BIRTHDAYS TODAY

DaMarcus Beasley, 22, soccer player, born Fort Wayne, IN, May 24, 1982.
Jim Broadbent, 55, actor (*Moulin Rouge, Topsy-Turvy,* Oscar for *Iris*), born Lincoln, Lincolnshire, England, May 24, 1949.
Gary Burghoff, 61, actor (Emmy for "M*A*S*H"), born Bristol, CT, May 24, 1943.
Tommy Chong, 66, actor (*Up in Smoke, The Corsican Brothers* [also wrote screenplay and directed]), born Edmonton, AB, Canada, May 24, 1938.
Joe Dumars III, 41, former basketball player, born Shreveport, LA, May 24, 1963.
Bob Dylan, 63, composer, singer, born Robert Zimmerman, Duluth, MN, May 24, 1941.
Patti LaBelle, 60, singer ("Since I Don't Have You"), born Patricia Louise Holte, Philadelphia, PA, May 24, 1944.
Tracy McGrady, 25, basketball player, born Bartow, FL, May 24, 1979.
Alfred Molina, 51, actor (*Chocolat, Letter to Brezhnev*), born London, England, May 24, 1953.
Frank Oz, 60, puppeteer, director, born Hereford, England, May 24, 1944.
Priscilla Beaulieu Presley, 59, actress ("Dallas," *Naked Gun* movies), ex-wife of Elvis, born Brooklyn, NY, May 24, 1945.
John Rowland, 47, Governor of Connecticut (R), born Waterbury, CT, May 24, 1957.
Kristin Scott Thomas, 44, actress (*The English Patient, The Horse Whisperer*), born Cornwall, England, May 24, 1960.

MAY 25 — TUESDAY
Day 146 — 220 Remaining

AFRICAN FREEDOM DAY: ANNIVERSARY. May 25. Public holiday in Chad, Zambia and some other African states. Members of the Organization for African Unity (formed May 25, 1963) commemorate their independence from colonial rule. Sports contests, political rallies and tribal dances.

AMERICAN FLIGHT CRASHES AT O'HARE: 25th ANNIVERSARY. May 25, 1979. An American Airlines DC-10 lost an engine upon takeoff and crashed seconds later, killing all 272 aboard and three people on the ground. This is the worst US air disaster in history.

ARGENTINA: REVOLUTION DAY. May 25. National holiday. Commemoration of revolt against Spanish rule in 1810.

CARVER, RAYMOND: BIRTH ANNIVERSARY. May 25, 1938. American poet and short story writer who chronicled the lives of America's working poor. Born at Clatskanie, OR, he died Aug 2, 1988, at his home at Port Angeles, WA, soon after finishing a book of poetry titled *A New Path to the Waterfall.*

CONSTITUTIONAL CONVENTION: ANNIVERSARY. May 25, 1787. At Philadelphia, PA, delegates from seven states, forming a quorum, opened the Constitutional Convention, which had been proposed by the Annapolis Convention Sept 11–14, 1786. Among those who were in attendance: George Washington, Benjamin Franklin, James Madison, Alexander Hamilton and Elbridge Gerry. See also: "Annapolis Convention: Anniversary" (Sept 11).

	S	M	T	W	T	F	S
May 2004							1
	2	3	4	5	6	7	8
	9	10	11	12	13	14	15
	16	17	18	19	20	21	22
	23	24	25	26	27	28	29
	30	31					

☆ Chase's 2004 Calendar of Events ☆   May 25

DAVIS, MILES: BIRTH ANNIVERSARY. May 25, 1926. Jazz trumpeter Miles Davis was born at Alton, IL. He was influenced by the be-bop music style of Charlie Parker and Dizzy Gillespie and ended up leaving the Juilliard School of Music to join Parker's quintet in 1945. He experimented with different styles throughout his career, exploring new voicings in jazz with arranger Gil Evans and musicians John Coltrane and Red Garland, delving into "modal" music with Tony Williams and Wayne Shorter and moving into a fusion sound in the '60s. His career was beset with bouts of drug addiction, but in the 1970s his return to the music scene found him creating a sound that melded his be-bop origins, modal chord progressions and driving rock rhythms. He died Sept 28, 1991, at Santa Monica, CA.

DOWIE, JOHN ALEXANDER: BIRTH ANNIVERSARY. May 25, 1847. Evangelist and claimant of the title "Elijah the Restorer" was born at Edinburgh, Scotland. He established the Christian Catholic Church at Zion, IL, where some 5,000 followers created a unique community without pharmacies, physicians, theaters or dance halls and where smoking, drinking and the eating of pork were prohibited. Dowie's ostentatiously expensive personal lifestyle and his unsuccessful attempt to convert New York City were partially responsible for the falling away of his followers. He was expelled from the church in 1906 and died at Chicago, IL, Mar 9, 1907.

EMERSON, RALPH WALDO: BIRTH ANNIVERSARY. May 25, 1803. American author and philosopher born at Boston, MA, and died there Apr 27, 1882. It was Emerson who wrote (in his essay "Self-Reliance," 1841), "A foolish consistency is the hobgoblin of little minds, adored by little statesmen and philosophers and divines. With consistency a great soul has simply nothing to do."

ENGLAND: CHELSEA FLOWER SHOW. May 25–28. Royal Hospital, Chelsea, London. The world's best flower show with specially designed gardens and spectacular floral displays. Est attendance: 158,000. For info: Shows Dept, Royal Horticultural Society, 80 Vincent Sq, London, England SW1P 2PE. Phone: (44) (20) 7630-7422. Fax: (44) (20) 7233-9525. Web: www.rhs.org.uk/chelsea.

JORDAN: INDEPENDENCE DAY. May 25. National holiday. Commemorates treaty in 1946, proclaiming independence from Britain and establishing monarchy.

MURRAY, PHILIP: BIRTH ANNIVERSARY. May 25, 1886. American labor leader and founder of the Congress of Industrial Organizations, also active in and a leader of the United Mine Workers, was born near Blantyre, Scotland. Murray died at San Francisco, CA, Nov 9, 1952.

NATIONAL GEOGRAPHIC BEE: NATIONAL FINALS. May 25–26. National Geographic Society Headquarters, Washington, DC. The first place winner from each state-level competition (that took place on Apr 2) advances to the national level. Alex Trebek of "Jeopardy!" fame moderates the finals which are televised on the National Geographic Channel and public television stations. They compete for scholarships and prizes totaling more than $50,000. Est attendance: 400. For info: Natl Geographic Bee, Natl Geographic Society, 1145 17th St NW, Washington, DC 20036. Phone: (202) 828-6659.

NATIONAL MISSING CHILDREN'S DAY. May 25. To promote awareness of the problem of missing children, to offer a forum for change and to offer safety information for children in school and community. Annually, May 25. For info: Child Find of America, Inc, PO Box 277, New Paltz, NY 12561-0277. Phone: (845) 255-1848. National toll-free hotline phone numbers: (800) I-AM-LOST or (800) A-WAY-OUT.

NATIONAL TAP DANCE DAY. May 25. To celebrate this unique American art form that represents a fusion of African and European cultures and to transmit tap to succeeding generations through documentation and archival and performance support. Held on the anniversary of the birth of Bill "Bojangles" Robinson to honor his outstanding contribution to the art of tap dancing on stage and in films through the unification of diverse stylistic and racial elements.

POETRY DAY IN FLORIDA. May 25. In 1947 the Legislature decreed this day to be "Poetry Day in all of the public schools of Florida."

ROBINSON, BILL "BOJANGLES": BIRTH ANNIVERSARY. May 25, 1878. Born at Richmond, VA, the grandson of a slave, Robinson is considered one of the greatest tap dancers. He is best known for a routine in which he tap-danced up and down a staircase. He appeared in several films with Shirley Temple and starred in *Stormy Weather*. Died at New York City, Nov 25, 1949.

SHAVUOT BEGINS AT SUNDOWN. May 25. Jewish Pentecost. See also: "Shavuot" (May 26).

SIKORSKY, IGOR: BIRTH ANNIVERSARY. May 25, 1889. Aeronautical engineer best remembered for his development of the first successful helicopter in 1939. Also pioneered in multi-engine airplanes and large flying boats that made transoceanic air transportation possible. Born at Kiev, Russia, he died Oct 26, 1972, at Easton, CT.

SOLZHENITSYN GOES HOME: 10th ANNIVERSARY. May 25, 1994. After 20 years living in exile, mostly in the US, Russian author Alexander Solzhenitsyn returned to his homeland. The author had been expelled from the Soviet Union in 1974 after his three-volume work exposing the Soviet prison camp system, *The Gulag Archipelago*, was published in the West. After the collapse of the Soviet Union late in 1991, he announced his intention to go back.

SPACE MILESTONE: *SKYLAB 2* (US): ANNIVERSARY. May 25, 1973. Joseph P. Kerwin, Paul J. Weitz and Charles (Pete) Conrad, Jr, spent 28 days in experimentation on this space station which had been launched May 14. Pacific splashdown occurred June 22. Launched May 25, 1973.

***STAR WARS* RELEASED: ANNIVERSARY.** May 25, 1977. "May the Force be with you" entered the modern lexicon as a new kind of science fiction film opened at 32 theaters. George Lucas' space epic, starring Mark Hamill as Luke Skywalker, Harrison Ford as Han Solo and Carrie Fisher as Princess Leia, featured stunning special effects and was a smash hit worldwide. It went on to win six Academy Awards out of ten nominations—plus an additional special Academy Award for sound effects. The film was part of a larger saga, and in later years was retitled *Star Wars—Episode IV: A New Hope* as prequels were released.

TITO (JOSIP BROZ): BIRTH ANNIVERSARY. May 25, 1892. Josip Broz, Yugoslavian soldier and political leader, born near Zagreb, Yugoslavia. Died May 4, 1980, at Ljubljana, Yugoslavia (now Slovenia), and was interred in the garden of his home at Belgrade. Tito, a Croat, had managed to keep the many nationalities and religions that made up Yugoslavia in one state, but in the early 1990s the nation broke up as Croats, Serbs and others went to war against each other.

TUNNEY, JAMES JOSEPH (GENE): BIRTH ANNIVERSARY. May 25, 1898. Heavyweight boxing champion, business executive. The famous "long count" occurred in the seventh round of the Jack Dempsey–Gene Tunney world championship fight, Sept 22, 1927, at Soldier Field, Chicago, IL. Tunney was born at New York, NY, and died at Greenwich, CT, Nov 7, 1978.

May 25–26 ☆ Chase's 2004 Calendar of Events ☆

UNITED NATIONS: WEEK OF SOLIDARITY WITH THE PEOPLE OF NON-SELF-GOVERNING TERRITORIES. May 25–31. On Dec 6, 1999 (res 54/91) the General Assembly requested the Special Committee on Decolonization to observe this week beginning on May 25, Africa Liberation Day. For info: United Nations, Dept of Public Info, New York, NY 10017. Web: www.un.org.

BIRTHDAYS TODAY

Dixie Carter, 65, actress ("Designing Women," "Family Law"), born McLemoresville, TN, May 25, 1939.
Jessi Colter, 57, singer, songwriter, born Miriam Johnson, Phoenix, AZ, May 25, 1947.
Tom T. Hall, 68, singer ("P.S. I Love You"), songwriter ("Harper Valley PTA"), born Olive Hill, KY, May 25, 1936.
Anne Heche, 35, actress (*Volcano; Six Days, Seven Nights*), born Aurora, OH, May 25, 1969.
Justin Henry, 33, actor (*Kramer v Kramer, Sixteen Candles*), born Rye, NY, May 25, 1971.
Lauryn Hill, 29, singer, actress (*Sister Act 2*), born South Orange, NJ, May 25, 1975.
K.C. Jones, 72, Hall of Fame basketball player, former coach, born Tyler, TX, May 25, 1932.
Jamie Kennedy, 34, actor ("JKX: The Jamie Kennedy Experiment," *Malibu's Most Wanted*), born Upper Darby, PA, May 25, 1970.
Sir Ian McKellen, 65, actor (stage: *Amadeus* [Tony Award]; *Lord of the Rings* trilogy, *Gods and Monsters*), born Burnley, England, May 25, 1939.
Mike Myers, 41, comedian, actor ("Saturday Night Live," *Wayne's World, Austin Powers: International Man of Mystery*), born Scarsborough, ON, Canada, May 25, 1963.
Connie Sellecca, 49, actress ("Hotel," *While My Pretty One Sleeps*), born the Bronx, NY, May 25, 1955.
Beverly Sills, 75, opera singer (retired), born Brooklyn, NY, May 25, 1929.
Gordon Smith, 52, US Senator (R, Oregon), born Pendleton, OR, May 25, 1952.
Leslie Uggams, 61, singer ("Sing Along with Mitch"), actress, born New York, NY, May 25, 1943.
Brian Urlacher, 26, football player, born Lovington, NM, May 25, 1978.
Karen Valentine, 57, actress ("Room 222"), born Sebastopol, CA, May 25, 1947.

MAY 26 — WEDNESDAY

Day 147 — 219 Remaining

AUSTRALIA: SORRY DAY. May 26. A day to express sorrow for the forced removal of Aboriginal children from their families. For info: www.acn.net.au/articles/sorry.

BIG TEN BASEBALL TOURNAMENT. May 26–29. Site of conference champion. Est attendance: 1,500. For info: Sue Lister, Big Ten Conference, 1500 W Higgins Rd, Park Ridge, IL 60068-6300. Phone: (847) 696-1010. Fax: (847) 696-1110. Web: www.bigten.org.

CANADA: ANNAPOLIS VALLEY APPLE BLOSSOM FESTIVAL. May 26–31. Windsor to Digby, NS. Annual festival with barbecues, sports events, art show, Princess Tea, coronation ceremonies, dances, concerts, fireworks, craft fair, children's parade, Grand Street Parade and "Sunday in the Park" (family entertainment). Annually, since 1933. Est attendance: 125,000. For info: Mrs Frances Anderson, Annapolis Valley Apple Blossom Fest, 57 Webster St, Ste 203, Kentville, NS, Canada B4N 1H6. Phone: (902) 678-8322. Fax: (902) 678-3710. E-mail: appleblossom@ns.sympatico.ca. Web: www.appleblossom.com.

CHINA: BIRTHDAY OF LORD BUDDHA. May 26. Religious observances are held in Buddhist temples and Buddha's statue is bathed. Annually, the eighth day of fourth lunar month. Date in other countries will differ from China's (in North America, expected date is May 25).

DUNKIRK EVACUATED: ANNIVERSARY. May 26, 1940. The British Expeditionary Force had become trapped by advancing German armies near this port on the northern coast of France. On this date, the evacuation of 200,000 British and 140,000 French and Belgian soldiers began. Sailing on every kind of transport available, including fishing boats and recreational craft, these men were safely across the English Channel by June 2.

FEAST OF SAINT AUGUSTINE OF CANTERBURY. May 26. Pope Gregory sent Augustine to convert the pagan English. Augustine became the first archbishop of Canterbury. He died May 26, 604 AD.

GEORGIA: INDEPENDENCE DAY. May 26. National Day. Commemorates declaration of independence from Russia in 1918. Was absorbed by the Soviet Union in 1922.

GREAT AMERICAN GRUMP OUT. May 26. We are asking America to go 24 hours without being grumpy or crabby. Can YOU meet the challenge? School children, parents, businesses and the community will be involved in promoting peace, harmony and light-hearted humor on this day. For info: Janice Hathy, Smile Mania, 1300 N River Rd, C-100, Venice, FL 34293. E-mail: grumpout@smilemania.com. Web: www.smilemania.com.

JOLSON, AL: BIRTH ANNIVERSARY. May 26, 1886. Actor (*The Jazz Singer*) singer, born Asa Yoelson at St. Petersburg, Russia. Died at San Francisco, CA, Oct 23, 1950.

LEE, PEGGY: BIRTH ANNIVERSARY. May 26, 1920. Singer, songwriter and actress Peggy Lee was born Norma Deloris Egstrom at Jamestown, ND. She got her start singing on a Fargo, ND, radio station, and was soon hired by Benny Goodman to sing with his band. Known for her simple, jazzy style as well as her sex appeal, her biggest hits were 1958's "Fever" and 1969's "Is That All There Is?"—both of which are now considered standards. She is perhaps best remembered for the songs that she co-wrote and performed in Disney's *Lady and the Tramp*. She continued to perform until the 1990s, when poor health forced her to retire. She died Jan 21, 2002, at Los Angeles, CA.

MORLEY, ROBERT: BIRTH ANNIVERSARY. May 26, 1908. British actor Robert Morley was born at Semley, England. Among his best known film credits are *Major Barbara* (1939) and *The African Queen* (1951). He died June 3, 1992, at Reading, England.

NAIA WOMEN'S GOLF NATIONAL CHAMPIONSHIPS. May 26–29. Location TBD. 10th annual. Est attendance: 300. For info: Natl Assn of Intercollegiate Athletics, 23500 W 105th St, PO Box 1325, Olathe, KS 66051-1325. Phone: (913) 791-0044. Fax: (913) 791-9555. E-mail: smcclure@naia.org. Web: www.naia.org.

	S	M	T	W	T	F	S
May 2004							1
	2	3	4	5	6	7	8
	9	10	11	12	13	14	15
	16	17	18	19	20	21	22
	23	24	25	26	27	28	29
	30	31					

☆ Chase's 2004 Calendar of Events ☆   May 26–27

NATIONAL SENIOR HEALTH AND FITNESS DAY. May 26. 1,500 local events held on the same day in all 50 states. 11th annual event to promote the value of fitness and exercise for older adults. During this day—as part of Older Americans Month activities—seniors across the country are involved in locally organized health promotion activities. Call the toll-free number for further info and a list of local sites. Annually, the last Wednesday in May. In 2003 more than 120,000 older adults participated in fitness activities at more than 1,000 events nationwide. Est attendance: 150,000. For info: Tina Godin, Program Mgr, Mature Market Resource Center, 1850 W Winchester Rd, Ste 213, Libertyville, IL 60048. Phone: (800) 828-8225. Fax: (847) 816-8662. E-mail: fitnessday@aol.com. Web: www.fitnessday.com.

RIDE, SALLY KRISTEN: BIRTHDAY. May 26, 1951. Dr. Sally Ride, one of the first women in the US astronaut corps and the first American woman in space, was born at Encino, CA. Her flight aboard the space shuttle *Challenger* was launched from Cape Canaveral, FL, June 18 and landed at Edwards Air Force Base, CA, June 24, 1983. The six-day flight was termed "nearly a perfect mission."

SHAVUOT or FEAST OF WEEKS. May 26–27. Jewish Pentecost holy days. Hebrew dates, Sivan 6–7, 5764. Celebrates giving of Torah (the Law) to Moses on Mount Sinai. Began at sundown May 25.

VIETNAM AND US RESUME RELATIONS: 10th ANNIVERSARY. May 26, 1994. Nearly 20 years after the end of the Vietnam War, the US and Vietnam agreed to resume diplomatic relations. In the early 1990s Vietnam had become one of the fastest growing economies in Asia after giving up Communist controls and allowing economic reform. Earlier in 1994 President Bill Clinton had lifted the American embargo that hindered Americans from doing business in Vietnam.

WAYNE, JOHN: BIRTH ANNIVERSARY. May 26, 1907. American motion picture actor, born Marion Michael Morrison, at Winterset, IA. He died at Los Angeles, CA, June 11, 1979. "Talk low, talk slow and don't say too much" was his advice on acting.

BIRTHDAYS TODAY

James Arness, 81, actor ("Gunsmoke," "How the West Was Won"), born Minneapolis, MN, May 26, 1923.
Helena Bonham Carter, 38, actress (*A Room With a View, Howard's End*), born London, England, May 26, 1966.
Genie Francis, 42, actress ("General Hospital"), born Englewood, NJ, May 26, 1962.
Pam Grier, 55, actress (*Jackie Brown, Mars Attacks, Something Wicked This Way Comes*), born Winston-Salem, NC, May 26, 1949.
Lenny Kravitz, 40, singer ("Circus"), musician, songwriter ("Justify My Love"), born New York, NY, May 26, 1964.
Brent Musburger, 65, sportscaster, born Portland, OR, May 26, 1939.
Stevie Nicks, 56, singer (with Fleetwood Mac, "Don't Stop"), songwriter ("Edge of Seventeen"), born Phoenix, AZ, May 26, 1948.
Paul E. Patton, 67, Governor of Kentucky (D), born Fallsburg, KY, May 26, 1937.
Sally K. Ride, 53, astronaut, first American woman in space, born Los Angeles, CA, May 26, 1951.
Philip Michael Thomas, 55, actor ("Miami Vice," *Hair*), born Los Angeles, CA, May 26, 1949.
Hank Williams, Jr, 55, singer ("All for the Love of Sunshine," "I Fought the Law"), born Shreveport, LA, May 26, 1949.

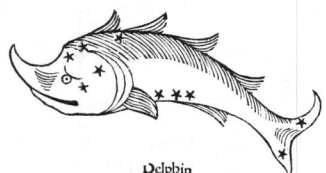
Delphin

MAY 27 — THURSDAY
Day 148 — 218 Remaining

BENNETT, ARNOLD: BIRTH ANNIVERSARY. May 27, 1867. English novelist, playwright and critic (Enoch) Arnold Bennett was born at Hanley, in the pottery-manufacturing district of North Staffordshire, England. Best known of his novels is *The Old Wives' Tale* (1908). His *Journals* from 1896 until near the time of his death in 1931 provide insight into Bennett's thought. "The price of justice," Arnold wrote, "is eternal publicity." He contracted typhoid fever in France and died at London, May 27, 1931.

BLOOMER, AMELIA JENKS: BIRTH ANNIVERSARY. May 27, 1818. American social reformer and women's rights advocate, born at Homer, NY. Her name is remembered especially because of her work for more sensible dress for women and her recommendation of a costume that had been introduced about 1849 by Elizabeth Smith Miller but came to be known as the "Bloomer Costume" or "Bloomers." Amelia Bloomer died at Council Bluffs, IA, Dec 30, 1894.

CARSON, RACHEL (LOUISE): BIRTH ANNIVERSARY. May 27, 1907. American scientist and author, born at Springdale, PA. Author of *Silent Spring* (1962), a book that provoked widespread controversy over the use of pesticides. Died Apr 14, 1964, at Silver Spring, MD.

CELLOPHANE TAPE PATENTED: ANNIVERSARY. May 27, 1930. Richard Gurley Drew received a patent for his adhesive tape, later manufactured by 3M as Scotch tape.

DUNCAN, ISADORA: BIRTH ANNIVERSARY. May 27, 1878. American-born interpretive dancer who revolutionized the entire concept of dance. Bare-footed, freedom-loving, liberated woman and rebel against tradition, she experienced worldwide professional success and profound personal tragedy (her two children drowned, her marriage failed and she met a bizarre death when the long scarf she was wearing caught in a wheel of the open car in which she was riding, strangling her). Born at San Francisco, CA; died at Nice, France, Sept 14, 1927.

FIRST FLIGHT INTO THE STRATOSPHERE: ANNIVERSARY. May 27, 1931. In a balloon launched from Augsburg, Germany, Paul Kipfer and Auguste Piccard became the first to reach the stratosphere. In a pressurized cabin they rose almost 10 miles during their flight.

FIRST RUNNING OF PREAKNESS: ANNIVERSARY. May 27, 1873. The first running of the Preakness Stakes at Pimlico, MD, was won by Survivor with a time of 2:43. The winning jockey was G. Barbee.

GOLDEN GATE BRIDGE OPENED: ANNIVERSARY. May 27, 1937. 200,000 people crossed San Francisco's Golden Gate Bridge on its opening day.

GRUBSTAKE DAYS. May 27–31. Yucca Valley, CA. Includes parade, PRCA rodeo, demolition derby, gold panning demonstration, carnival, dances, food and community booths, arts and crafts booths and breakfasts offered by local service organizations. Est attendance: 20,000. For info: Yucca Valley Chamber of Commerce, 56711 29 Palms Hwy, Yucca Valley, CA 92284. Phone: (760) 365-6323. Fax: (760) 365-0763. E-mail: chamber @yuccavalley.org. Web: www.yuccavalley.org.

HAMMETT, (SAMUEL) DASHIELL: BIRTH ANNIVERSARY. May 27, 1894. The man who brought realism to the genre of mystery writing, Dashiell Hammett was born at St. Mary's County, MD. His first two novels, *Red Harvest* (1929) and *The Dain Curse* (1929), were based on his eight years spent as a Pinkerton detective. Hammett is recognized as the founder of the "hard-boiled" school of detective fiction. Three of his novels have been made into films: *The Maltese Falcon* (1930), considered by many to be his finest work; *The Thin Man* (1932), which provided the basis for a series of five movies starring William Powell and Myrna Loy; and *The Glass Key* (1931). Hammett was called to testify but refused to name members of an alleged sub-

295

May 27 ☆ Chase's 2004 Calendar of Events ☆

versive organization during House Un-American Activities Committee hearings. He died Jan 10, 1961, at New York City.

HERRINFESTA ITALIANA. May 27–31. Herrin Civic Center, Herrin, IL. Authentic Italian food, name Italian and American entertainers, bocce tournament, Midwest Pasta Sauce Contest, road races, grape stomp and more. Est attendance: 55,000. For info: Herrinfesta Italiana, PO Box 2005, Herrin, IL 62948. Phone: (800) ITFESTA. Web: www.herrinfesta.com.

HICKOK, WILD BILL: BIRTH ANNIVERSARY. May 27, 1837. Born at Troy Grove, IL, and died Aug 2, 1876, at Deadwood, SD. American frontiersman, legendary marksman, lawman, army scout and gambler. Hickock's end came when he was shot dead at a poker table by a drunk in the Number Ten saloon.

HUMPHREY, HUBERT HORATIO: BIRTH ANNIVERSARY. May 27, 1911. Born at Wallace, SD. The 38th vice president of the US (1965–1969). Democratic candidate for president in 1968 who lost to Richard Nixon. Died at Waverly, MN, Jan 13, 1978.

IRIS FESTIVAL. May 27–30. Swan Lake, Sumter, SC. In the largest Japanese iris gardens in the world. Annually, the weekend before Memorial Day beginning on Thursday evening. For info: Sumter Tourism, 32 E Calhoun St, Sumter, SC 29150. Phone: (800) 688-4748. Web: www.sumter-sc-tourism.com.

KODIAK CRAB FESTIVAL. May 27–31. Kodiak, AK. A celebration of spring and the Emerald Isle. Featured are parades, carnival booths and midway, running events, a golf tournament, bicycle and survival suit races, a blessing of the fleet ceremony and memorial services. Annually, Memorial Day weekend. Est attendance: 15,000. For info: Kodiak Chamber of Commerce, Box 1485, Kodiak, AK 99615. Phone: (907) 486-5557. Fax: (907) 486-7605. E-mail: chamber@kodiak.org or lisa@kodiak.org. Web: www.kodiak.org.

MARDI GRAS IN MAY. May 27–30. Branson, MO. An authentic Cajun/Zydeco Festival with a Mardi Gras twist. Music, food, arts & crafts from Louisiana. Est attendance: 20,000. For info: Cedric Benoit, Mardi Gras in May, 406 Sherry Ln, Branson, MO 65616. Phone: (417) 335-8842. Fax: (417) 336-2502. E-mail: cedric@cedricbenoit.com. Web: www.mardigrasinmay.com.

MEMORY DAYS. May 27–30. Grayson, KY. Parade, art show and horse show. Est attendance: 10,000. For info: Robert L. Caummisar, Chamber of Commerce, 301 W Main St, Grayson, KY 41143. Phone: (606) 474-9522. Fax: (606) 474-4422.

MOON PHASE: FIRST QUARTER. May 27. Moon enters First Quarter phase at 3:57 AM, EDT.

MUDBUG MADNESS. May 27–30. Riverfront, Shreveport, LA. The state's delectable crustacean, the crawfish, and Cajun heritage are celebrated during this four-day festival. Est attendance: 150,000. For info: DSU, PO Box 235, Shreveport, LA 71162. Phone: (318) 222-7403. E-mail: mbacon@softdisk.com. Web: www.mudbugmadness.com.

NAIA MEN'S AND WOMEN'S OUTDOOR TRACK AND FIELD NATIONAL CHAMPIONSHIPS. May 27–29. Olathe District Activity Center, Olathe, KS. 53rd annual men's and 24th annual women's competition. Est attendance: 2,500. For info: Natl Assn of Intercollegiate Athletics, 23500 W 105th St, PO Box 1325, Olathe, KS 66051-1325. Phone: (913) 791-0044. Fax: (913) 791-9555. E-mail: thasseltine@naia.org. Web: www.naia.org.

★ ★ ★

	S	M	T	W	T	F	S
May 2004							1
	2	3	4	5	6	7	8
	9	10	11	12	13	14	15
	16	17	18	19	20	21	22
	23	24	25	26	27	28	29
	30	31					

NCAA DIVISION I WOMEN'S SOFTBALL CHAMPIONSHIP. May 27–31. University of Oklahoma, Oklahoma City, OK. For info: NCAA, PO Box 6222, Indianapolis, IN 46206-6222. Phone: (317) 917-6222. Fax: (317) 917-6888. Web: www.ncaasports.org.

PRICE, VINCENT: BIRTH ANNIVERSARY. May 27, 1911. Actor, best known for his portrayal of sinister villains in horror films and as host for the TV series "Mystery." Born at St. Louis, MO, and died at Los Angeles, CA, Oct 25, 1993.

RMS *QUEEN MARY*: MAIDEN VOYAGE: ANNIVERSARY. May 27, 1936. Anniversary of the maiden voyage from Southampton, England, to New York Harbor. In 1967 the ship sailed to Long Beach, California, where it is permanently berthed and used as a hotel.

SAINT PETERSBURG FOUNDED: ANNIVERSARY. May 27, 1703. Czar Peter the Great founded the city of St. Petersburg on the banks of the Neva River by laying the first stone of the Peter and Paul Fortress. It became the capital of Russia in 1712. See also: "St. Petersburg Name Restored: Anniversary" (Sept 6).

SNEAD, SAM: BIRTH ANNIVERSARY. May 27, 1912. The winningest US Tour golfer of the 20th century was born at Hot Springs, VA. He turned pro in 1934 and went on to become the only golfer to win tournaments in six different decades. He won 84 US Tour events and 182 tournaments in total. Snead always wore a snappy straw hat and was a favorite on the Tour. He was one of the founders of the US Senior Tour. Snead died at Hot Springs on May 23, 2002.

BIRTHDAYS TODAY

Jeff Bagwell, 36, baseball player, born Boston, MA, May 27, 1968.
John Barth, 74, author (*Last Voyage of Somebody the Sailor, Letters*), born Cambridge, MD, May 27, 1930.
Todd Bridges, 39, actor ("Diff'rent Strokes"), born San Francisco, CA, May 27, 1965.
Pat Cash, 39, former tennis player, born Melbourne, Australia, May 27, 1965.
Christopher J. Dodd, 60, US Senator (D, Connecticut), born Willimantic, CT, May 27, 1944.
Joseph Fiennes, 34, actor (*Shakespeare In Love*), born Salisbury, England, May 27, 1970.
Peri Gilpin, 43, actress ("Frasier"), born Waco, TX, May 27, 1961.
Louis Gossett, Jr, 68, actor (Emmy for "Roots"; Oscar for *An Officer and a Gentleman*), born Brooklyn, NY, May 27, 1936.
Henry Kissinger, 81, former secretary of state, author, born Fuerth, Germany, May 27, 1923.
Christopher Lee, 82, actor (*Dracula, The Mummy*), born London, England, May 27, 1922.
Ramsey Lewis, 69, jazz musician, winner of three Grammy awards, born Chicago, IL, May 27, 1935.
Lee Meriwether, 69, actress, former Miss America ('55), born Los Angeles, CA, May 27, 1935.
Jamie Oliver, 29, chef, television personality ("The Naked Chef"), born Clavering, Essex, England, May 27, 1975.
Richard Schiff, 49, actor ("The West Wing"), born Bethesda, MD, May 27, 1955.
Frank Thomas, 36, baseball player, born Columbus, GA, May 27, 1968.
Bruce Weitz, 61, actor ("Hill Street Blues"), born Norwalk, CT, May 27, 1943.
Herman Wouk, 89, writer (*Marjorie Morningstar, The Winds of War*), born New York, NY, May 27, 1915.

☆ Chase's 2004 Calendar of Events ☆ May 28

MAY 28 — FRIDAY
Day 149 — 217 Remaining

AGASSIZ, LOUIS: BIRTH ANNIVERSARY. May 28, 1807. Professor of zoology and geology at Harvard, born at Motier, Switzerland. He was a major influence in spawning American interest in natural history and helped to establish the Harvard Museum of Comparative Zoology. "The eye of the trilobite," Agassiz wrote in 1870, "tells us that the sun shone on the old beach where he lived; for there is nothing in nature without a purpose, and when so complicated an organ was made to receive the light, there must have been light to enter it." Died at Cambridge, MA, Dec 14, 1873.

AZERBAIJAN: DAY OF THE REPUBLIC. May 28. Public holiday. Commemorates the declaration of the Azerbaijan Democratic Republic in 1918.

BROOKINGS-HARBOR AZALEA FESTIVAL. May 28–31. Brookings, OR. 65th festival. Parade, street fair, art shows, seafood, 10K run, Bonsai exhibit, regional quilt show, crafts fair, Coast Guard demonstration, live music. Annually, Memorial Day weekend. Est attendance: 12,000. For info: Brookings-Harbor Chamber of Commerce, PO Box 940, Brookings, OR 97415. Phone: (800) 535-9469. Fax: (541) 469-4094. E-mail: chamber@brookingsor.com.

DIONNE QUINTUPLETS: 70th BIRTHDAY. May 28, 1934. Five daughters (Marie, Cecile, Yvonne, Emilie and Annette) were born to Oliva and Elzire Dionne, near Callander, ON, Canada. They were the first quints known to have lived for more than a few hours after birth. Emilie died in 1954, Marie in 1970, Yvonne in 2001. The other two sisters are still living.

ETHIOPIA: NATIONAL DAY. May 28. National holiday. Commemorates the downfall of the Dergue, the military government that ruled Ethiopia from 1974 to 1991.

FLEMING, IAN: BIRTH ANNIVERSARY. May 28, 1908. English novelist, creator of the James Bond series. Born at London, died Aug 12, 1964, at Sandwich, England.

GUILLOTIN, JOSEPH IGNACE: BIRTH ANNIVERSARY. May 28, 1738. French physician and member of the Constituent Assembly who urged the use of a machine that was sometimes called the "Maiden" for the execution of death sentences—a less painful, more certain way of dispatching those sentenced to death. The guillotine was first used on Apr 25, 1792, for the execution of a highwayman, Nicolas Jacques Pelletier. Other machines for decapitation had been in use in other countries since the Middle Ages. Guillotin was born at Saintes, France and died at Paris, Mar 26, 1814.

MID-AMERICA NATIONAL STREET ROD ASSOCIATION CAR SHOW. May 28–30. Ozark Empire Fairgrounds, Springfield, MO. More than 2000 pre-1949 street rods on display. More than 80 commercial vendors for shopping. For info: Nancy Bright, Ozark Empire Fair, PO Box 630, Springfield, MO 65801. Phone: (417) 833-2660. Fax: (417) 833-3769. E-mail: nancy@ozarkempirefair.com. Web: www.ozarkempirefair.com.

MORNING RADIO WISE GUY DAY. May 28. To honor all morning radio disc jockeys who get your day started with humor, music and information. For info: Rob and Mark, KISC-FM, 808 E Sprague, Spokane, WA 99202. Phone: (509) 242-2400. Fax: (509) 624-5957. E-mail: wiseguys@clearchannel.com.

NAIA BASEBALL WORLD SERIES. May 28–June 4. Lewiston, ID. 48th annual competition. Est attendance: 20,000. For info: Natl Assn of Intercollegiate Athletics, 23500 W 105th St, PO Box 1325, Olathe, KS 66051-1325. Phone: (913) 791-0044. Fax: (913) 791-9555. E-mail: mchiarucci@naia.org. Web: www.naia.org.

NORTHWEST FOLKLIFE FESTIVAL. May 28–31. Seattle Center, Seattle, WA. Ethnic and traditional arts event celebrating world cultures in the Northwest Region. Includes music, dance, food, crafts, visual arts exhibits, children's programs, demonstrations, films and more. More than 6,000 performers. Annually, Friday–Monday of Memorial Day weekend. Est attendance: 225,000. For info: Northwest Folklife Fest, 305 Harrison St, Seattle, WA 98109-4623. Phone: (206) 684-7300. Fax: (206) 684-7190. E-mail: folklife@nwfolklife.org. Web: www.nwfolklife.org/folklife/.

PENNSYLVANIA ARTS & CRAFTS COUNTRY FESTIVAL. May 28–31. Fayette County Fairgrounds, Uniontown, PA. More than 170 exhibits of handcrafted furniture, gift items, children's toys, dolls, dried floral arrangements, clothing, jewelry and much more. Food and entertainment. Est attendance: 15,000. For info: Debbie or Dave Stoner, Family Festivals Assn, Inc, PO Box 166, Irwin, PA 15642. Phone: (724) 863-4577. Fax: (724) 863-4577. E-mail: familyfestivals@hotmail.com. Web: www.familyfestivals.com.

PITT, WILLIAM: BIRTH ANNIVERSARY. May 28, 1759. British prime minister from 1783 to 1801 and from 1804 to 1806, Pitt was influenced by Adam Smith's economic theories and reduced England's large national debt caused by the American Revolution. Born at Hayes, Kent, England, he died Jan 23, 1806, at Putney. He was the son of William Pitt, first earl of Chatham, for whom the city of Pittsburgh was named.

RIVERFEST. May 28–30. Riverfront Park, Little Rock, and North Shore Riverwalk, North Little Rock, AR. 27th annual outdoor festival of the visual and performing arts with 100 acts on six stages, food vendors, visual artists, kid stuff. Est attendance: 200,000. For info: Riverfest, Exec Director, PO Box 3232, Little Rock, AR 72203. Phone: (501) 255-FEST. Fax: (501) 255-3379. E-mail: director@riverfestarkansas.com. Web: www.riverfestarkansas.com.

ROANOKE FESTIVAL IN THE PARK. May 28–June 6. Roanoke, VA. 35th annual celebration. Three-day juried fine art and crafts show, children's activities, antique car show, land yacht race, children's theatre, parade, USSSA softball tournament, youth art show, garden festival, Senior Citizen Day, 5K and 10K races, concerts, product and service area. Est attendance: 200,000. For info: Stuart Israel, Exec Dir, Roanoke Festival in the Park, PO Box 8276, Roanoke, VA 24014. Phone: (540) 342-2640. E-mail: info@roanokefestival.org. Web: www.roanokefestival.org.

SACRAMENTO JAZZ JUBILEE. May 28–31. Sacramento, CA. More than 100 bands from the US, Canada and foreign countries perform American traditional jazz music in approximately 40 venues around Sacramento at the world's largest traditional jazz festival. Est attendance: 100,000. For info: Roger Krum, Exec Dir, Sacramento Traditional Jazz Society, 2787 Del Monte Blvd, Sacramento, CA 95691. Phone: (916) 372-5277. Fax: (916) 372-3429. E-mail: stjs@earthlink.net. Web: www.sacjazz.com.

SAINT BERNARD OF MONTJOUX: FEAST DAY. May 28. Patron saint of mountain climbers, founder of Alpine hospices of the Great and Little St. Bernard, died at age 85, probably on May 28, 1081.

SIERRA CLUB FOUNDED: ANNIVERSARY. May 28, 1892. Founded by famed naturalist John Muir, the Sierra Club promotes conservation of the natural environment by influencing public policy. It has been especially important in the founding and protection of our national parks. For info: Sierra Club, 85 Second St, 2nd Fl, San Francisco, CA 94105-3441. Phone: (415) 977-5500. Web: www.sierraclub.org.

May 28–29 ☆ Chase's 2004 Calendar of Events ☆

SLUGS RETURN FROM CAPISTRANO DAY. May 28. It's a little known secret that slimy slugs spend their winters in lovely Capistrano and return to our patios and gardens on this date. Bare feet not a good idea now through first frost. [©2003 by WH.] For info: Thomas & Ruth Roy, Wellcat Holidays, 2418 Long Ln, Lebanon, PA 17046. Phone: (717) 279-0184. E-mail: info @wellcat.com. Web: www.wellcat.com.

SPIRIT OF WOVOKA DAYS POWWOW. May 28–29. Yerington, NV. Powwow held in honor of Wovoka, sponsored by the Mason Valley Wind Spirit dancers. For local info: Chamber of Commerce, 227 S Main St, Yerington, NV 89447. Phone: (775) 463-2350. Fax: (775) 463-3369. Web: www.tele-net.net/lyon.

SPOLETO FESTIVAL USA. May 28–June 13. Charleston, SC. Comprehensive arts festival with a mix of more than 120 performances of opera, dance, theater, chamber and symphonic music, jazz and visual arts set in one of America's most beautiful and historic cities. For info: Spoleto Festival USA, PO Box 157, Charleston, SC 29402. Phone: (843) 579-3100. Web: www.spoletousa.org.

THORPE, JAMES FRANCIS (JIM): BIRTH ANNIVERSARY. May 28, 1888. Jim Thorpe, Pro Football Hall of Famer, distinguished Native American athlete, winner of pentathlon and decathlon events at the 1912 Olympic Games, professional baseball and football player. Born near Prague, OK, and died at Lomita, CA, Mar 28, 1953.

WALES: HAY-ON-WYE FESTIVAL OF LITERATURE. May 28–June 6. Hay-on-Wye, Powys. Largest annual festival of literature takes place in the beautiful market town of Hay-on-Wye in the Black Mountains of the Welsh Marches. Est attendance: 30,000. For info: The Hay Festival, Hay-on-Wye, Wales, UK HR3 5AD. Phone: (44) (149) 782-1299. Fax: (44) (149) 782-1066. E-mail: boxoffice@litfest.co.uk. Web: www.hayfestival.co.uk.

WORLD CHAMPIONSHIP OLD-TIME PIANO PLAYING CONTEST. May 28–30. Hotel Père Marquette, Peoria, IL. Competition and festival of ragtime, honky-tonk and old-time music. Annually, Memorial Day weekend. Sponsor: Old-Time Music Preservation Association (OMPA) Inc. Est attendance: 1,000. For info: Judy Leschewski, PO Box 4714, Decatur, IL 62525. Phone: (217) 428-2403. Web: oldtimepiano.com.

"ZOO PARADE" TV PREMIERE: ANNIVERSARY. May 28, 1950. NBC's half-hour program on animals and animal behavior was hosted by Marlin Perkins and Jim Hurlbut. Initially, it was broadcast from Lincoln Park Zoo in Chicago, but after 1955, the show was broadcast from other locales throughout the country. A successor program, "Mutual of Omaha's Wild Kingdom," was shot almost entirely in the wild and ran into the 1980s.

BIRTHDAYS TODAY

Carroll Baker, 73, actress (*Baby Doll, Harlow*), born Johnstown, PA, May 28, 1931.
Barry Commoner, 87, biologist, politician, born Brooklyn, NY, May 28, 1917.
Kirk Harold Gibson, 47, former baseball player, born Pontiac, MI, May 28, 1957.
Armon Louis Gilliam, 40, former basketball player, born Pittsburgh, PA, May 28, 1964.
Rudolph Giuliani, 60, former mayor of New York City, born Brooklyn, NY, May 28, 1944.
Gladys Knight, 60, singer (and the Pips; "Neither One of Us," "If I Were Your Woman"), born Atlanta, GA, May 28, 1944.
Sondra Locke, 57, actress (*The Heart Is a Lonely Hunter, Bronco Billy*), director (*Ratboy*), born Shelbyville, TN, May 28, 1947.

May 2004

S	M	T	W	T	F	S
						1
2	3	4	5	6	7	8
9	10	11	12	13	14	15
16	17	18	19	20	21	22
23	24	25	26	27	28	29
30	31					

Christa Miller, 40, actress ("The Drew Carey Show"), born New York, NY, May 28, 1964.
Glen Rice, 37, basketball player, born Flint, MI, May 28, 1967.
Mark Sanford, 44, Governor of South Carolina (R), born Fort Lauderdale, FL, May 28, 1960.

MAY 29 — SATURDAY
Day 150 — 216 Remaining

ALABAMA JUBILEE HOT AIR BALLOON CLASSIC. May 29–31. Point Mallard, Decatur, AL. Hot air balloon races, arts, crafts, antique cars, water and air shows. Annually, Memorial Day weekend. Est attendance: 100,000. For info: Jacklyn Bailey, Decatur Conv and Visitors Bureau, Box 2349, 719 6th Ave SE, Decatur, AL 35602. Phone: (256) 350-2028 or (800) 524-6181. E-mail: info@decaturcvb.org. Web: www.decaturcvb.org.

ALMA HIGHLAND FESTIVAL AND GAMES. May 29–30. Alma College, Alma, MI. 37th annual festival. Old-world pageantry honoring Scottish traditions—Highland dancing, piping, drumming, athletic competitions, clan tents and grand parade. Annually, Memorial Day weekend. Est attendance: 30,000. For info: Alma Highland Festival, 110 W Superior St, PO Box 516, Alma, MI 48801. Phone: (989) 463-8979. Fax: (989) 463-6588. E-mail: highland@almahighlandfestival.com. Web: www.almahighlandfestival.com.

AMNESTY ISSUED FOR SOUTHERN REBELS: ANNIVERSARY. May 29, 1865. President Andrew Johnson issued a proclamation giving a general amnesty to all who participated in the rebellion against the US. High-ranking members of the Confederate government and military and those who owned more than $20,000 worth of property were excepted and had to apply individually to the President for a pardon. Once an oath of allegiance was taken, all former property rights, except those in slaves, were returned to the former owners.

ASCENSION OF BAHA'U'LLAH: ANNIVERSARY. May 29. Baha'i observance of the anniversary of the death in exile of Baha'u'llah (the prophet-founder of the Baha'i Faith), May 29, 1892. One of the nine days of the year when Baha'is suspend work. For info: Baha'is of the US, Office of Public Information, 1320 Nineteenth St NW, Ste 350, Washington, DC 20036. Phone: (202) 466-9870. Fax: (202) 466-9873. E-mail: opi@usbnc.org. Web: www.us.bahai.org.

CATFISH DERBY. May 29–31. Huntington, OR. Annually, Memorial Day weekend. Est attendance: 400. For info: Baker County Chamber & Visitors Center, 490 Campbell St, Baker City, OR 97814. Phone: (800) 523-1235.

CHARLES II: RESTORATION ANNIVERSARY. May 29, 1660. Restoration of Charles II to English throne. Also his birthday (May 29, 1630). English monarchy restored after Commonwealth period under Oliver Cromwell.

CHESTERTON, GILBERT KEITH: BIRTH ANNIVERSARY. May 29, 1874. English author and critic born at London, England. Died June 14, 1936, at Beaconsfield, Buckinghamshire, England.

CHESTERTOWN TEA PARTY FESTIVAL. May 29–30. Chestertown, MD. Reenactment of 1774 tea dumping, crafts, music, food and games, 10 mile and 5K runs. Est attendance: 15,000. For info: Chestertown Tea Party Festival, Inc, Box 526, Chestertown, MD 21620. Phone: (410) 778-0416. Web: www.kentcounty.com.

★ Chase's 2004 Calendar of Events ★   May 29

CONSTANTINOPLE FALLS TO THE TURKS: ANNIVERSARY. May 29, 1453. The city of Constantinople was captured by the Turks, who later renamed it Istanbul. This conquest marked the end of the Byzantine Empire; the city became the capital of the Ottoman Empire.

DAKOTA COWBOY POETRY GATHERING. May 29–30. Medora Community Center, Medora, ND. 18th annual. This cowboy event hosts some of the most colorful cowboy poets in North Dakota and Montana. There are also singers and songwriters who perform. Annually, Memorial Day Weekend. Est attendance: 700. For info: Dakota Cowboy Poetry Gathering, Dickinson CVB, 72 Museum Dr, Dickinson, ND 58601. Phone: (800) 279-7391 or (701) 872-4746.

1836 ENCAMPMENT. May 29–30. Westville-Lumpkin, GA. Reenactment of an encampment of soldiers who had been dispatched to protect local citizens against Indian attacks. An Indian camp will also be demonstrated. Est attendance: 1,500. For info: Patty Cannington, Westville, PO Box 1850, Lumpkin, GA 31815. Phone: (912) 838-6310 or (888) 733-1850. Web: www.westville.org.

ENGLAND: ENGLISH RIVIERA DANCE FESTIVAL. May 29–June 6. Torquay, Devon. Demonstrations by world champions and participatory events including Modern, Ballroom, Disco and Latin American dance styles. Est attendance: 2,000. For info: Philip Wylie, 73 Hoylake Crescent, Ickenham, Middlesex, England UB10 8JQ. Phone: (44) (1895) 632-143. Fax: (44) (1895) 635-684. Email: holidayanddance@hotmail.com.

FAIRMOUNT ACADEMY 1800s FESTIVAL. May 29. Fairmount, MD. Rain date the following Saturday. Restored school, spelling bees, square dancing, quilt show, folk arts and crafts, music and plenty of good food. Annually, the last Saturday in May. Est attendance: 2,500. For info: Nevette Muir, Fairmount Academy Historical Assn, PO Box 134, Upper Fairmount, MD 21867. Phone: (410) 651-0351 or (410) 651-3945.

FARMINGTON INVITATIONAL BALLOON FESTIVAL. May 29–30. Farmington, NM. Hot air balloons launch off the banks of Farmington Lake. Famous Splash and Dash and Hare and Hound races included in the two-day event. Est attendance: 2,000. For info: Farmington Conv and Visitors Bureau, 3041 E Main St, Farmington, NM 87402. Phone: (800) 448-1240 or (505) 326-7602. Fax: (505) 327-0577. E-mail: fmncvb@cyberport.com. Web: www.farmingtonnm.org.

FREDERICKSBURG MUSIC FESTIVAL. May 29–June 5 (tentative). A series of concerts featuring some of the nation's top musicians with musical styles from Dixieland to symphony and jazz to chamber. Occasionally, dance performances are offered. Annually, the first week of June. Est attendance: 4,500. For info: Fredericksburg Festival of the Arts, Inc, PO Box 7816, Fredericksburg, VA 22404. Phone: (540) 374-5040. Fax: (540) 368-1098. Web: www.fredfest.org.

GREAT MISSISSIPPI RIVER ARTS AND CRAFTS FESTIVAL. May 29–30. Mark Twain Historic District, Hannibal, MO. 17th annual art fair featuring 80 exhibitors in the areas of fine art, fine crafts and traditional arts. Concession stands with fried catfish, BBQ pork-chop sandwiches and lemonade, a variety of entertainment groups and creative learning fun in the children's area. Est attendance: 15,000. For info: Hannibal Arts Council, PO Box 1202, Hannibal, MO 63401. Phone: (573) 221-6545. E-mail: arts@nemonet.com.

HALFWAY PARK DAYS. May 29–30. Martin L. (Marty) Snook Memorial Park, Hagerstown, MD. Family fun in the park with arts and crafts, free entertainment, food and children's rides. Annually, Memorial Day weekend. Est attendance: 9,000. For info: Lions Club of Halfway, 10923 Holly Terrace, Hagerstown, MD 21740-7804. Phone: (301) 739-3219.

HEAD-OF-THE-MON-RIVER HORSESHOE TOURNAMENT. May 29–31. Fairmont, WV. Open to horseshoe pitchers with a current State/National Horseshoe Pitchers Association membership card. Est attendance: 300. For info: Tri-County Horseshoe Club Dir, Beverly Tiano, 1133 Sunset Dr, Fairmont, WV 26554. Phone: (304) 366-3819. E-mail: btiano1133@aol.com.

HENRY, PATRICK: BIRTH ANNIVERSARY. May 29, 1736. American revolutionary leader and orator, born at Studley, VA, and died near Brookneal, VA, June 6, 1799. Especially remembered for his speech (Mar 23, 1775) for arming the Virginia militia, at St. Johns Church, Richmond, VA, when he declared: "I know not what course others may take, but as for me, give me liberty or give me death."

HOPE, BOB: BIRTH ANNIVERSARY. May 29, 1903. The comedic actor was born Leslie Townes Hope at Eltham, England. Hope had a long career in vaudeville, stage, radio, film and TV. His first film appearance was in *The Big Broadcast of 1938* (in which he sang his signature song, "Thanks for the Memory"). Hope went on to appear in more than 75 films—most memorably with crooner Bing Crosby in their series of "Road" movies. He received five honorary Oscars (among them the Jean Hersholt Humanitarian Award) and numerous other honors. Hope tirelessly entertained US troops during every war from WWII to the Gulf War. President Johnson presented him with the Medal of Freedom and he was knighted in 1998. Hope died July 27, 2003, at Toluca Lake, CA.

INTERNATIONAL JAZZ DAY. May 29. Jazz lovers worldwide attend local festivals (or can start their own) to celebrate jazz on the Saturday of the Memorial Day weekend. Originated by the New Jersey Jazz Society and sanctioned by the American Federation of Jazz Societies, the United Nations Jazz Society and the Sacramento Traditional Jazz Society. For info: Web: www.geocities.com/BourbonStreet/4270.

IROQUOIS ARTS SHOWCASE. May 29–30 (also Sept 4–6). Iroquois Indian Museum, Howes Cave, NY. Demonstrations of Iroquois arts and crafts including beadwork, cornhusk dolls, pottery and more. Many items for sale by the artists. Children's activities. Iroquois social dancing and nature walks. Annually, Memorial Day weekend and Labor Day weekend. Est attendance: 3,500. For info: Iroquois Indian Museum, PO Box 7, Caverns Rd, Howes Cave, NY 12092. Phone: (518) 296-8949. Fax: (518) 296-8955. E-mail: info@IroquoisMuseum.org.

KENNEDY, JOHN FITZGERALD: BIRTH ANNIVERSARY. May 29, 1917. 35th president of the US (1961–63), born at Brookline, MA. Assassinated while riding in an open automobile at Dallas, TX, Nov 22, 1963. (Accused assassin Lee Harvey Oswald was killed at the Dallas police station by a gunman, Jack Ruby, two days later.) Kennedy was the youngest man ever elected to the presidency, the first Roman Catholic and the first president to have served in the US Navy. He was the fourth US president to be killed by an assassin, and the second to be buried at Arlington National Cemetery (first was William Howard Taft).

LOBSTERFEST. May 29–31. Mystic Seaport, Mystic, CT. A New England lobster bake on the banks of the Mystic River over the Memorial Day weekend, put on by the Rotary Club of Mystic. Est attendance: 10,000. For info: Mystic Seaport, 75 Greenmanville Ave, PO Box 6000, Mystic, CT 06355-0990. Phone: (860) 572-5315 or (888) 9SEAPORT. Web: www.visitmysticseaport.org.

LONGWOOD GARDENS FESTIVAL OF FOUNTAINS. May 29–Sept 4. Kennett Square, PA. A magical mixture of rainbow-hued fountains, alfresco concerts, fireworks and leisurely evenings in the Conservatory. Est attendance: 275,000. For info: Elizabeth Sullivan, Publicity Director, Longwood Gardens, PO

Box 501, Kennett Square, PA 19348-0501. Phone: (610) 388-1000. Web: www.longwoodgardens.org.

MEMORIAL DAY GETAWAY. May 29–31. Live Oak, FL. Fun for the whole family with a variety of entertainment. For info: Spirit of the Suwannee Music Park, 3076 95th Dr, Live Oak, FL 32060. Phone: (386) 364-1683. Fax: (386) 364-2998. E-mail: spirit@musicliveshere.com. Web: www.musicliveshere.com.

MOSCOW COMMUNIQUE: ANNIVERSARY. May 29, 1972. President Richard Nixon and Soviet Party leader Leonid Brezhnev released a joint communique after Nixon's week-long visit to Moscow. During the visit the two men acknowledged their major differences on the Vietnam War, signed a treaty on antiballistic missile systems as well as an interim agreement on limitation of strategic missiles and an agreement for a joint space flight in 1975. This was the first visit ever to Moscow by a US president (May 22–30, 1972).

MOUNT EVEREST SUMMIT REACHED: ANNIVERSARY. May 29, 1953. New Zealand explorer Sir Edmund Hillary and Tensing Norgay, a Sherpa guide, became the first team to reach the summit of Mount Everest, the world's highest mountain.

RHODE ISLAND: RATIFICATION DAY. May 29. The last of the 13 original states to ratify the Constitution in 1790.

SOCCER TRAGEDY: ANNIVERSARY. May 29, 1985. A riot at Heysel stadium at Brussels, Belgium, killed 39 people. Fans attending the European Cup Final, between Liverpool and Juventus of Turin, clashed before the match started. Some 400 people were injured in the riot. The incident was televised and viewed by millions throughout Europe. More than two years later, Sept 2, 1987, the British government announced that 26 British soccer fans (identified from television tapes) would be extradited to Belgium for trial. Hooliganism at soccer matches became the target of increased security measures for England's professional teams following the 1985 tragedy.

SPENGLER, OSWALD: BIRTH ANNIVERSARY. May 29, 1880. German historian, author of *The Decline of the West*, born at Blankenburg-am-Harz, Germany. Died at Munich, Germany, May 8, 1936.

TASTE OF CINCINNATI. May 29–31. Cincinnati, OH. Greater Cincinnati is famous for its fine food, from elegant five-star dining to five-way chili. This popular eating extravaganza presents a taste of the most delicious culinary delights available. Annually, Memorial Day weekend. Est attendance: 500,000. For info: Raymond Buse, Greater Cincinnati Chamber of Commerce, 441 Vine St, Ste 300, Cincinnati, OH 45202. Phone: (513) 579-3100. Fax: (513) 579-3101. E-mail: chooven@gccc.com. Web: www.tasteofcincinnati.com.

TIVOLI FEST. May 29–30. Elk Horn, IA. Annual Danish celebration with parade, Danish Folk Dancers, Danish foods, unique gift shops, historical tours and much more. Annually, Memorial Day weekend. Sponsors: Better Elk Horn Club. Est attendance: 5,000. For info: Lisa Riggs, Danish Windmill, PO Box 245, Elk Horn, IA 51531. Phone: (712) 764-7472 or (800) 451-7960. Fax: (712) 764-7475. E-mail: info@danishwindmill.com. Web: www.danishwindmill.com.

UTICA OLD-FASHIONED ICE CREAM FESTIVAL. May 29–31. Utica, OH. Saluting "America's favorite dessert," ice cream, with a weekend of fun and entertainment: parade, queen contest, arts and crafts, antique gas engines, sheep herding with border collies and plenty of delicious ice cream. Est attendance: 30,000. For info: Utica Ice Cream Festival, St Rt 13, Utica, OH 43080. Phone: (740) 892-3921. Web: www.velvet-icecream.com.

VIRGINIA PLAN PROPOSED: ANNIVERSARY. May 29, 1787. Just five days after the Constitutional Convention met at Philadelphia, PA, the "Virginia Plan" was proposed. It called for establishment of a new governmental organization consisting of a legislature with two houses, an executive (chosen by the legislature) and a judicial branch.

WAR OF JENKIN'S EAR: LIVING HISTORY. May 29. Wormsloe Historic Site, Savannah, GA. A colonial living history event focusing on the conflict between England and Spain. Features musket demonstrations, military drill, musket ball casting, tomahawk throwing and more. Annually, the Saturday of Memorial Day Weekend. Est attendance: 500. For info: Wormsloe State Historic Site, 7601 Skidaway Rd, Savannah, GA 31406. Phone: (912) 353-3023. E-mail: wormsloe@g-net.net.

WISCONSIN: ADMISSION DAY: ANNIVERSARY. May 29. Became 30th state in 1848.

BIRTHDAYS TODAY

Annette Bening, 46, actress (*The American President, Bugsy, The Grifters*), born Topeka, KS, May 29, 1958.
Kevin Conway, 62, actor (*When You Comin' Back, Red Ryder?, Of Mice and Men, Other People's Money*), born New York, NY, May 29, 1942.
Eric Davis, 42, former baseball player, born Los Angeles, CA, May 29, 1962.
Paul Ehrlich, 72, population biologist, born Philadelphia, PA, May 29, 1932.
Melissa Etheridge, 43, singer, guitarist, born Leavenworth, KS, May 29, 1961.
Rupert Everett, 45, actor (*An Ideal Husband, My Best Friend's Wedding*), born Norfolk, England, May 29, 1959.
Anthony Geary, 56, actor ("General Hospital"), born Coalville, UT, May 29, 1948.
Adrian Paul, 45, actor ("Highlander" series), born London, England, May 29, 1959.
Alfred (Al) Unser, Sr, 65, former auto racer, born Albuquerque, NM, May 29, 1939.
Francis Thomas (Fay) Vincent, Jr, 66, former commissioner of baseball, born Waterbury, CT, May 29, 1938.
Lisa Whelchel, 41, actress ("Facts of Life"), born Fort Worth, TX, May 29, 1963.

MAY 30 — SUNDAY
Day 151 — 215 Remaining

BATTLE OF THE ALEUTIAN ISLANDS: ANNIVERSARY. May 30, 1943. The islands of Kiska and Attu in the Aleutian Islands off the coast of Alaska were retaken by the US 7th Infantry Division. The battle (Operation Landgrab) began when an American force of 11,000 landed on Attu May 12. In three weeks of fighting US casualties numbered 552 killed and 1,140 wounded. Only 28 wounded Japanese were taken prisoner. Their dead amounted to 2,352, of whom 500 committed suicide.

	S	M	T	W	T	F	S
May 2004							1
	2	3	4	5	6	7	8
	9	10	11	12	13	14	15
	16	17	18	19	20	21	22
	23	24	25	26	27	28	29
	30	31					

☆ Chase's 2004 Calendar of Events ☆ May 30

COAL MINER DAYS. May 30–31. Downtown and fairgrounds, Novinger, MO. Turn-of-the-century coal mining boom town celebrates its heritage with old-time contests, music, dancing and displays. Est attendance: 3,000. For info: Glenna Daniels, Novinger Renewal Inc, 15892 State Hwy 6, Novinger, MO 63559. Phone: (660) 488-5280. E-mail: ddaniels@nemr.net.

CROATIA: STATEHOOD DAY. May 30. Public holiday commemorating attainment of statehood in 1990.

CULLEN, COUNTEE: BIRTH ANNIVERSARY. May 30, 1903. One of the leading poets of the Harlem Renaissance (*Color*, 1925). He died at New York City, Jan 9, 1946.

FIRST AMERICAN DAILY NEWSPAPER PUBLISHED: ANNIVERSARY. May 30, 1783. *The Pennsylvania Evening Post* became the first daily newspaper published in the US. The paper was published at Philadelphia, PA, by Benjamin Towne.

INDIANAPOLIS 500: ANNIVERSARY. May 30, 1911. Ray Harroun won the first Indy 500, averaging 74.6 [MPH]. The race was created by Carl Fisher, who in 1909 replaced the stone surface of his 2.5-mile racetrack with a brick one—hence the nickname "The Brickyard."

INDIANAPOLIS 500-MILE RACE. May 30. Indianapolis, IN. Recognized as the world's largest single-day sporting event. First race was in 1911. Annually, the Sunday of Memorial Day weekend. For info: Indianapolis Motor Speedway Corp, 4790 W 16th St, Indianapolis, IN 46222. Phone: (317) 481-8500. Web: www.indy500.com.

ITALY: PALIO DEI BALESTRIERI. May 30. Gubbio. The last Sunday in May is set aside for a medieval crossbow contest between Gubbio and Sansepolcro; medieval costumes, arms.

LINCOLN MEMORIAL DEDICATION: ANNIVERSARY. May 30, 1922. The memorial is made of marble from Colorado and Tennessee and limestone from Indiana. It stands in West Potomac Park at Washington, DC. The Memorial was designed by architect Henry Bacon and its cornerstone was laid in 1915. A skylight lets light into the interiors where the compelling statue "Seated Lincoln," by sculptor Daniel Chester French, is situated.

LOOMIS DAY. May 30. To honor Mahlon Loomis, a Washington, DC, dentist who received a US patent on wireless telegraphy in 1872 (before Marconi was born). Titled "An Improvement in Telegraphing," the patent described how to do without wires; this patent was backed up by experiment on the Massanutten Mountains of Virginia. For info: Robert L. Birch, Puns Corps, Box 2364, Falls Church, VA 22042-0364. Phone: (703) 533-3668.

MAINLY MOZART FESTIVAL. May 30–June 20. San Diego County and Baja California, Mexico. David Atherton conducts world-class artists in a bi-national celebration of Mozart and his contemporaries in San Diego and Escondido, CA, and Tijuana, Rosarito and Tecate, Mexico. Chamber orchestra, chamber music and recitals are presented. Est attendance: 20,000. For info: Public Relations, Mainly Mozart, PO Box 124705, San Diego, CA 92112-4705. Phone: (619) 239-0100. Fax: (619) 233-4292. E-mail: admin@mainlymozart.com. Web: www.mainlymozart.org.

MEMORIAL DAY CEREMONIES. May 30. Andersonville, GA. Ceremonies pay tribute to our country's men and women who paid for our freedom with their lives. Est attendance: 800. For info: Alan Marsh, Park Ranger, Andersonville National Historic Site, 496 Cemetery Rd, Andersonville, GA 31711. Phone: (229) 924-0343.

MEMORIAL DAY (TRADITIONAL). May 30. This day honors the tradition of making memorial tributes to the dead, especially remembering those who have died in battle. Observed as a legal public holiday on the last Monday in May.

ORTHODOX PENTECOST. May 30. Observed by Eastern Orthodox churches.

PENTECOST. May 30. The Christian feast of Pentecost commemorates descent of the Holy Spirit unto the Apostles, 50 days after Easter. Observed on the seventh Sunday after Easter. Recognized since the third century. See also: "Whitsunday" (below).

PETER I: BIRTH ANNIVERSARY. May 30, 1672. Peter I (Peter the Great), Czar and Emperor of all the Russias. His primary aim was to make Russia a major power equal to its size and potential, and the way he saw to do this was through education and technology. He established printing presses and published translations of foreign books, particularly scientific and technical material. The Russian alphabet was simplified, and Arabic numerals were introduced. Peter encouraged trade with foreign countries, mercantilism within Russia and the entrepreneurial skills of resident foreigners; he allowed industrialists to own serfs, a right previously limited to landholders. He completely overhauled the government, the Russian Orthodox Church, the military system and the structure of taxes, ultimately increasing the power of the monarchy at the expense of the nobility and the national church. Upon his death, Jan 28, 1725, he was succeeded by his wife Catherine.

POPE OPPOSES ORDINATION OF WOMEN: 10th ANNIVERSARY. May 30, 1994. Pope John Paul II, in a letter to Roman Catholic bishops, declared the debate on the ordination of women closed. He stated that, based on New Testament practices and tradition, the church could not ordain women to the priesthood. This announcement put the Roman Catholic church at odds with the Anglican Communion, which had ordained a group of women earlier in the year.

SAINT JOAN OF ARC: FEAST DAY. May 30. French heroine and martyr, known as the Maid of Orleans, led the French against the English invading army. Captured, found guilty of heresy and burned at the stake in 1431 (at age 19). Innocence declared in 1456. Canonized in 1920.

SPACE MILESTONE: *MARINER 9* (US). May 30, 1971. Unmanned spacecraft was launched, entering Martian orbit the following Nov 13. The craft relayed temperature and gravitational field information and sent back spectacular photographs of both the surface of Mars and of her two moons. First spacecraft to orbit another planet.

TRINIDAD: INDIAN ARRIVAL DAY. May 30. Port of Spain, West Indies. Public holiday. For info: Info Dept, Tourism Div, Tourism and Industrial Development Co, Trinidad and Tobago Ltd, 10–14 Phillips St, West Indies. Phone: (800) 595-1868.

WHITSUNDAY. May 30. Whitsunday, the seventh Sunday after Easter, is a popular time for baptism. "White Sunday" is named for the white garments formerly worn by the candidates for baptism and occurs at the Christian feast of Pentecost. See also: "Pentecost" (above).

WORLD TRADE CENTER RECOVERY AND CLEANUP ENDS: ANNIVERSARY. May 30, 2002. New York, NY. A solemn and mostly silent ceremony marked the symbolic end of recovery operations at Ground Zero, the former site of the World Trade Center, after the Sept 11, 2001, terrorist attacks. The last standing steel girder was cut down on May 28. An honor guard carried an empty stretcher draped with an American flag to represent those victims who were not recovered from the ruins. Members of the NYFD, NYPD and city, state and federal workers, as well as family members and Ground Zero recovery teams, participated in the ceremony.

May 30–31 ☆ Chase's 2004 Calendar of Events ☆

BIRTHDAYS TODAY

Blake Bashoff, 23, actor (*Bushwhacked, Big Bully*), born Philadelphia, PA, May 30, 1981.

Keir Dullea, 68, actor (*David and Lisa; 2001: A Space Odyssey*), born Cleveland, OH, May 30, 1936.

Bob Evans, 86, restaurant executive, born Sugar Ridge, OH, May 30, 1918.

Wynonna Judd, 40, singer (*Wynonna*, "Tell Me Why"), born Ashland, KY, May 30, 1964.

Ted McGinley, 46, actor ("Married . . . With Children," *Revenge of the Nerds*), born Newport Beach, CA, May 30, 1958.

Colm Meaney, 51, actor ("Star Trek: The Next Generation," *Last of the Mohicans*), born Dublin, Ireland, May 30, 1953.

Trey Parker, 32, director, creator ("South Park"), born Auburn, AL, May 30, 1972.

Michael J. Pollard, 65, actor (*Bonnie and Clyde*, "Leo & Liz in Beverly Hills"), born Passaic, NJ, May 30, 1939.

Manny Ramirez, 32, baseball player, born Santo Domingo, Dominican Republic, May 30, 1972.

Gale Eugene Sayers, 61, Hall of Fame football player, born Wichita, KS, May 30, 1943.

Stephen Tobolowsky, 53, actor (*The Grifters, Groundhog Day*), born Dallas, TX, May 30, 1951.

Clint Walker, 77, actor (*The Dirty Dozen*, "Cheyenne"), born Hartford, IL, May 30, 1927.

MAY 31 — MONDAY
Day 152 — 214 Remaining

AMECHE, DON: BIRTH ANNIVERSARY. May 31, 1908. Film, stage, radio and TV actor. Born Dominic Felix Amici at Kenosha, WI, and died Dec 6, 1993, at Scottsdale, AZ.

BOLDER BOULDER 10K. May 31. Boulder, CO. A 10K race of walkers, joggers and world-class runners through the streets of Boulder. Annually, on Memorial Day. Est attendance: 45,000. For info: Bolder Boulder, 4571 N Broadway, Boulder, CO 80304. Phone: (303) 444-7223. Fax: (303) 444-6411. E-mail: race@bolderboulder.com. Web: www.bolderboulder.com.

COPYRIGHT LAW PASSED: ANNIVERSARY. May 31, 1790. President George Washington signed the first US copyright law. It gave protection for 14 years to books written by US citizens. In 1891 the law was extended to cover books by foreign authors as well.

ENGLAND: DICING FOR BIBLES. May 31. An old Whitmonday ceremony at All Saints Church, St. Ives, Huntingdonshire. A bequest (in 1675) with the intent of providing Bibles for poor children of the parish required winning them at a dice game played in the church. In recent years the dicing has been moved from the altar to a "more suitable" place. Six Bibles are given on Whitmonday each year.

HARRIS, PATRICIA ROBERTS: 80th BIRTH ANNIVERSARY. May 31, 1924. Born at Matoon, IL. The first African American woman to serve in an ambassadorial post, the first African American to hold a cabinet position (Secretary of Housing and Urban Development) and the first woman to serve as dean of a law school. Died Mar 23, 1985.

JOHNSTOWN FLOOD: ANNIVERSARY. May 31, 1889. Heavy rains caused the Connemaugh River Dam to burst. At nearby Johnstown, PA, the resulting flood killed more than 2,300 people and destroyed the homes of thousands more. Nearly 800 unidentified drowning victims were buried in a common grave at Johnstown's Grandview Cemetery. So devastating was the flood and so widespread the sorrow for its victims that "Johnstown Flood" entered the language as a phrase to describe a disastrous event. The valley city of Johnstown, in the Allegheny Mountains, has been damaged repeatedly by floods. Floods in 1936 (25 deaths) and 1977 (85 deaths) were the next most destructive.

MAD CITY MARATHON. May 31. Madison, WI. Running events include marathon, relays, half-marathon, 10K and 5K Run/Walks, kid's race, pasta dinner and a Health & Fitness Fair. Annually, on Memorial Day weekend. For info: Kristi Kent-Bracken, Director, Madison Festivals Inc, PO Box 46427, Madison, WI 53744-6427. Phone: (608) 850-4900. Fax: (608) 850-4929. E-mail: globalcelebrations@tds.net. Web: www.madcitymarathon.com.

MEMORIAL DAY. May 31. Legal public holiday. (PL90–363 sets Memorial Day on last Monday in May. Applicable to federal employees and District of Columbia.) Also known as Decoration Day because of the tradition of decorating the graves of servicemen. An occasion for honoring those who have died in battle. (Observance dates from Civil War years in US: first documented observance at Waterloo, NY, May 5, 1866.) See also: "Confederate Memorial Day" (Apr 26, May 10 and June 3).

MEMORIAL DAY PARADE. May 31. Aurora, IL. Annual parade featuring veterans groups, scouts, bands, floats and more. The parade begins at 12:00 PM. Est attendance: 15,000. For info: City of Aurora, Mayor's Office of Special Events, 43 E Downer Place, Aurora, IL 60507. Phone: (630) 844-3640. Fax: (630) 906-7068.

MEMORIAL DAY PARADE AND CEREMONIES. May 31. Gettysburg National Cemetery, Gettysburg, PA. 2,000 schoolchildren scatter flowers over the unknown graves. Memorial services follow parade. For info: Gettysburg CVB, PO Box 4117, Gettysburg, PA 17325. Phone: (717) 334-6274. Fax: (717) 334-1166. E-mail: gettysburgcvb@dejazzd.com. Web: www.gettysburgcvb.org.

PEALE, NORMAN VINCENT: BIRTH ANNIVERSARY. May 31, 1898. American religious leader Norman Vincent Peale was born at Bowersville, OH. He is best known for his book *The Power of Positive Thinking* (1952), which combines religion and psychiatry. He was a minister at the Marble Collegiate Church at New York, NY. He died Dec 24, 1993, at Pawling, NY.

POPE PIUS XI: BIRTH ANNIVERSARY. May 31, 1857. Ambrogio Damiano Achille Ratti, 259th pope of the Roman Catholic Church, born at Desio, Italy. Elected pope Feb 6, 1922. Died Feb 10, 1939, at Rome, Italy.

★ **PRAYER FOR PEACE, MEMORIAL DAY.** May 31. Presidential Proclamation issued each year since 1948. PL81–512 of May 11, 1950, asks President to proclaim annually this day as a day of prayer for permanent peace. PL90–363 of June 28, 1968, requires that beginning in 1971 it will be observed the last Monday in May. Often titled "Prayer for Peace Memorial Day," and traditionally requests the flying of the flag at half-staff "for the customary forenoon period."

	S	M	T	W	T	F	S
May							1
2004	2	3	4	5	6	7	8
	9	10	11	12	13	14	15
	16	17	18	19	20	21	22
	23	24	25	26	27	28	29
	30	31					

☆ Chase's 2004 Calendar of Events ☆   May 31

"SEINFELD" TV PREMIERE: ANNIVERSARY. May 31, 1990. "Seinfeld"—the show about nothing—premiered on NBC to wide acclaim. The show revolved around the lives and exploits of its four main leads whose storylines were intertwined for some surprising plot twists. Comedian Jerry Seinfeld used his stand-up routines as an introduction to the show; some of the programs concerned relationships, valet parking, annoying dogs and waiting for Chinese food. The cast featured Seinfeld as himself; Julia Louis-Dreyfus as his ex-girlfriend, Elaine Benes; Jason Alexander as his best friend, George Costanza; Wayne Knight as Newman and Michael Richards as his neighbor, Cosmo Kramer. The series ended with the May 14, 1998 episode.

STOCK EXCHANGE HOLIDAY (MEMORIAL DAY). May 31. The holiday schedules for the various exchanges are subject to change if relevant rules, regulations or exchange policies are revised. If you have questions, phone: American Stock Exchange (212) 306-1000; Chicago Board of Trade (312) 435-3500; Chicago Board of Options Exchange (312) 786-5600; New York Stock Exchange (215) 656-2065; Pacific Stock Exchange (415) 393-4000; Philadelphia Stock Exchange (215) 496-5000.

"SURVIVOR" TV PREMIERE: ANNIVERSARY. May 31, 2000. On this immensely popular "reality TV" show, 16 people were sequestered on a deserted island in Malaysia for 39 days. They competed for the right to remain on the island, with the final survivor winning $1,000,000. Hosted by Jeff Probst, the show drew a total audience of 51 million people. On Jan 28, 2001, another group of "Survivor" contestants began their stay in the Australian outback; later that year another group went to Africa.

TOUR OF SOMERVILLE. May 31. Somerville, NJ. 60th running. The oldest continuously run major bicycle race in America. Attracts more than 500 top amateur cyclists for four events. Annually, on Memorial Day. Est attendance: 40,000. For info: Dan Puntillo, 98 Grove St, Somerville, NJ 08876. Phone: (908) 725-7223.

UNITED KINGDOM: SPRING BANK HOLIDAY. May 31. Bank and public holiday in England, Wales, Scotland and Northern Ireland. Annually, the last Monday in May.

UNITED NATIONS: WORLD NO-TOBACCO DAY. May 31.

WHAT YOU THINK UPON GROWS DAY. May 31. A day to remind people of the power of positive thinking. For info: Stephanie West Allen, PO Box 9311, Denver, CO 80209. Phone: (303) 742-4790. E-mail: stephanie@allen-nichols.com. Web: www.allen-nichols.com.

WHITMAN, WALT: BIRTH ANNIVERSARY. May 31, 1819. Poet and journalist, born at West Hills, Long Island, NY. Whitman's best known work, *Leaves of Grass* (1855), is a classic of American poetry. His poems celebrated all of modern life, including subjects that were considered taboo at the time. Died Mar 26, 1892, at Camden, NJ.

WHITMONDAY. May 31. The day after Whitsunday is observed as a public holiday in some countries.

BIRTHDAYS TODAY

Tom Berenger, 54, actor (*Born on the Fourth of July, Major League, Gettysburg*), born Chicago, IL, May 31, 1950.
Clint Eastwood, 74, actor, director (Oscar for *Unforgiven*), former mayor of Carmel, CA, born San Francisco, CA, May 31, 1930.
Chris Elliott, 44, writer ("Late Night with David Letterman"), actor ("Get a Life"), born New York, NY, May 31, 1960.
Colin Farrell, 28, actor (*Minority Report, The Recruit*), born Castleknock, Dublin, Ireland, May 31, 1976.
Sharon Gless, 61, actress (Emmys for "Cagney & Lacey"), born Los Angeles, CA, May 31, 1943.
Gregory Harrison, 54, actor ("Logan's Run," "Trapper John, MD"), born Avalon, Catalina Island, CA, May 31, 1950.
Kenny Lofton, 37, baseball player, born East Chicago, IN, May 31, 1967.
Joseph William (Joe) Namath, 61, Hall of Fame football player, former sportscaster, actor, born Beaver Falls, PA, May 31, 1943.
Kyle Secor, 46, actor ("Homicide: Life on the Streets"), born Tacoma, WA, May 31, 1958.
Brooke Shields, 39, actress (*Pretty Baby, The Blue Lagoon*, "Suddenly Susan"), born New York, NY, May 31, 1965.
Lea Thompson, 43, actress ("Caroline in the City," *Back to the Future, Howard the Duck*), born Rochester, MN, May 31, 1961.
Terry Waite, 65, Church of England special envoy, former hostage in Lebanon (1987–91), born Bollington, Cheshire, England, May 31, 1939.
Peter Yarrow, 66, composer, singer (Peter, Paul and Mary), born New York, NY, May 31, 1938.

June 1 ☆ *Chase's 2004 Calendar of Events* ☆

Iune.

JUNE 1 — TUESDAY
Day 153 — 213 Remaining

ADOPT-A-SHELTER-CAT MONTH. June 1–30. To promote the adoption of cats from local shelters, the ASPCA sponsors this important observance. "Make Pet Adoption Your First Option®" is a message the organization promotes throughout the year in an effort to end the euthanasia of all adoptable animals. For info: ASPCA Media Relations Dept, 424 E 92nd St, New York, NY 10128. Phone: (212) 876-7700 x 4655. E-mail: press@aspca.org. Web: www.aspca.org.

ATLANTIC, CARIBBEAN AND GULF HURRICANE SEASON. June 1–Nov 30. For info: US Dept of Commerce, Natl Oceanic and Atmospheric Admin, Rockville, MD 20852.

BLACK HILLS PASSION PLAY—SOUTH DAKOTA. June 1–Aug 31. Passion Play Amphitheater, Spearfish, SD. Spectacular outdoor drama on a huge stage depicts the last seven days in the life of Christ. It features a professionally led cast of more than 200 and live animals. Annually, Sunday, Tuesday and Thursday evenings. Est attendance: 50,000. For info: Black Hills Passion Play—South Dakota, PO Box 489, Spearfish, SD 57783. Phone: (605) 642-2646 or (800) 457-0160. Fax: (605) 642-7993. E-mail: bhpp@blackhills.com. Web: www.blackhills.com/bhpp.

CANCER FROM THE SUN MONTH. June 1–30. To promote education and awareness of the dangers of skin cancer from too much exposure to the sun. Kit of materials available for $15 from this nonprofit organization. For info: Frederick Mayer, Pres, Pharmacy Council on Dermatology (PCD), 101 Lucas Valley Rd, Ste 210, San Rafael, CA 94903. Phone: (415) 479-8628. Fax: (415) 479-8608. E-mail: ppsi@aol.com. Web: www.ppsinc.org.

CENTRAL PACIFIC HURRICANE SEASON. June 1–Oct 31. Central Pacific is defined as 140 West Longitude to the International Date Line (180 West Longitude). For info: US Dept of Commerce, Natl Oceanic and Atmospheric Admin, Rockville, MD 20852.

CHILD VISION AWARENESS MONTH. June 1–30. To better educate and counsel the public on children's vision problems and detection of eye diseases in infants and children, to increase the number of school-aged children who have an eye exam by an eye doctor and to increase the number of children with learning disabilities having a developmental vision exam to rule out vision problems. There is a $15 charge for kit materials. For info: PPSI, c/o Pharmacy Council on Vision Care, 101 Lucas Valley Rd. Ste 210, San Rafael, CA 94903. Phone: (415) 479-8628. Fax: (415) 479-8608. E-mail: ppsi@aol.com. Web: www.ppsinc.org.

June 2004

S	M	T	W	T	F	S
		1	2	3	4	5
6	7	8	9	10	11	12
13	14	15	16	17	18	19
20	21	22	23	24	25	26
27	28	29	30			

CHILDREN'S AWARENESS MONTH. June 1–30. A month-long celebration of America's children in our everyday lives and communities that lovingly remembers all of America's children that we have lost through violence. These could have been our children or grandchildren. We choose to remember the living during the month of June by celebrating the gift of children. For info: Judith Natale, CEO & Founder, NCAC America–USA, 2091 Del Monte Ave, Monterey, CA 93940. Fax: (831) 655-4547. E-mail: childaware@aol.com.

CHINA: INTERNATIONAL CHILDREN'S DAY. June 1. Shanghai.

CNN DEBUTED: ANNIVERSARY. June 1, 1980. The Cable News Network, TV's first all-news service, went on the air.

EFFECTIVE COMMUNICATIONS MONTH. June 1–30. The most important cog in the wheel of interpersonal relationships is communication. Active listening, verbal language, paralanguage, body language and written communication skills are the essence of how humans relate to each other personally and professionally. This month is dedicated to learning how to, improving upon, and committing to communicating more effectively in our lives. For info: Sylvia Henderson, Springboard Training, 18005 Lafayette Dr, Ste B, Olney, MD 20832. Phone: (301) 646-1668. Fax: (301) 856-8000. E-mail: admin@springboardtraining.com. Web: www.springboardtraining.com.

ENTREPRENEURS "DO IT YOURSELF" MARKETING MONTH. June 1–30. Stand out from your competition and get media attention and more clients, while achieving your goals. Are you looking for better results from your marketing efforts? Remember, your success is a matter of choice, not chance. Discover and apply creative and effective problem-solving marketing ideas that will help you gain the competitive edge. Act now and remove the barriers that are stopping you from achieving your goals. Pamphlet available for $5. For info: Lorrie Walters Marsiglio, Lorimar Communications, PO Box 284-CC, Wasco, IL 60183-0284. Phone: (630) 584-9368.

FIREWORKS EYE SAFETY MONTH. June 1–July 4. Although fireworks are used as a way to celebrate various occasions, they send more than 11,000 people to the emergency room each year. Fireworks Eye Safety Month spreads the message to play it safe this year by letting the professionals handle the fireworks because 18% of those injuries were eye-related and nearly half resulted in legal blindness. For info: American Academy of Ophthalmology, PO Box 7424, San Francisco, CA 94120-7424. Phone: (415) 561-8500. Fax: (415) 561-8533. E-mail: eyemd@aao.org. Web: www.medem.com/eyemd.

FIREWORKS SAFETY MONTHS. June 1–July 31. Activities during these months are designed to warn and educate parents and children about the dangers of playing with fireworks. Prevent Blindness America will offer suggestions for safer ways to celebrate the Fourth of July. For info: Prevent Blindness America®, 500 E Remington Rd, Schaumburg, IL 60173. Phone: (800) 331-2020. Fax: (847) 843-8458. Web: www.preventblindness.org.

GAY AND LESBIAN PRIDE MONTH. June 1–30. Observed this month because on June 28, 1969, the clientele of a gay bar at New York City rioted after the club was raided by the police. President Clinton issued a presidential proclamation for this month in 1999 and 2000, but President Bush has not declared it during his first term. See also: "Stonewall Riot: Anniversary" (June 28).

GERMANY: WALDCHESTAG. June 1. Frankfurt. Since the 19th century Frankfurters have spent the Tuesday after Whitsunday in their forest. See also: "Whitsunday" (May 30).

HEIMLICH MANEUVER INTRODUCED: 30th ANNIVERSARY. June 1, 1974. The June issue of the journal *Emergency Medicine* published an article by Dr. Henry Heimlich outlining a better method for aiding choking victims. Instead of the prevailing method of backslaps (which merely pushed foreign objects further into the airways), Dr. Heimlich advocated "subdiaphragmatic pressure" to force objects out. Three months later, the method was dubbed "the Heimlich Maneuver" by the *Journal of the American Medical Association*.

INTERNATIONAL MEN'S MONTH. June 1–30. This program was initiated in 1996 to increase media and local community awareness of the many unique issues that impact men's lives and that are of concern to the people who love them. In an effort to promote positive changes in male roles and relationships, a different issue is addressed each day of the month during June and information and resources on that issue are provided on the website. This free information can be received automatically by signing up at menstuff-subscribe@topica.com. For info: Gordon Clay, Exec Dir, Natl Men's Resource Center, PO Box 800, San Anselmo, CA 94979-0800. E-mail: menstuff@menstuff.org. Web: www.menstuff.org.

INTERNATIONAL PEOPLE SKILLS MONTH. June 1–30. Get a better job, improve the office atmosphere and increase rapport with your family. How? By refining your people skills and learning how to "de-puzzle" human behavior. More information is available on resolving conflicts, gaining influence and encouraging others. For info: Karla Brandau, Pres, People Skills Intl, 4985 Chartley Circle, Lilburn, GA 30047. Phone: (770) 923-0883. Fax: (770) 931-2530. E-mail: karla@karlaspeaks.com. Web: www.4peopleskills.com.

INTERNATIONAL VOLUNTEERS WEEK. June 1–7. To honor men and women throughout the world who serve as volunteers, rendering valuable service without compensation to the communities in which they live and to honor nonprofit organizations dedicated to making the world a better place in which to live. For complete info, send $5 to cover expense of printing, handling and postage. Annually, the first seven days of June. For info: Dr. Stanley Drake, Pres, Intl Society of Friendship and Good Will, 999 Hood Rd, Ste 127, Marietta, GA 30068. Phone: (770) 565-2322. E-mail: ISFGW@bellsouth.net.

JUNE DAIRY MONTH. June 1–30. Since 1937 the dairy industry has set aside June as a time to pay tribute to the vital role milk and dairy products play in the American diet and the outstanding contribution of America's dairy farmers.

JUNE IS PERENNIAL GARDENING MONTH. June 1–30. June is the perfect month to celebrate the versatility and beauty of perennial garden plants. We'll offer some good gardening tips on how to keep your perennial garden beautiful all season long and highlight many individual perennials that bloom for the month of June. For info: Steven Still, 3383 Schrirtzinger Rd, Hilliard, OH 43026. Phone: (614) 771-8431. E-mail: ppa@perennialplant.org. Web: www.perennialplant.org.

JUNE IS TURKEY LOVERS' MONTH. June 1–30. Month-long campaign to promote awareness and increase turkey consumption at a nonholiday time. Annually, the month of June. For info: Natl Turkey Federation, 1225 New York Ave NW, Ste 400, Washington, DC 20005. Phone: (202) 898-0100. Fax: (202) 898-0203. E-mail: info@turkeyfed.org. Web: www.eatturkey.com.

KENTUCKY: ADMISSION DAY: ANNIVERSARY. June 1. Became 15th state in 1792.

KENYA: MADARAKA DAY: ANNIVERSARY. June 1. Madaraka Day (Self-Rule Day) is observed as a national public holiday. Commemorates attainment of self-government in 1963.

LITTLE, CLEAVON: 65th BIRTH ANNIVERSARY. June 1, 1939. Best known for his role as the black sheriff who cleaned up a town of bumbling redneck toughs in the movie *Blazing Saddles*, Cleavon Little was born at Chickasha, OK. Little was the winner of a Tony award for the 1970 musical *Purlie* and an Emmy in 1989 for a guest appearance on the television series "Dear John." Died Oct 22, 1992, near Sherman Oaks, CA.

MARQUETTE, JACQUES: BIRTH ANNIVERSARY. June 1, 1637. Father Jacques Marquette (Père Marquette), Jesuit missionary-explorer of the Great Lakes region. Born at Laon, France. Died at Ludington, MI, May 18, 1675.

MONROE, MARILYN: BIRTH ANNIVERSARY. June 1, 1926. American actress and sex symbol of the '50s, born at Los Angeles as Norma Jean Mortensen or Baker. She had an unstable childhood in a series of orphanages and foster homes. Her film career came to epitomize Hollywood glamour. In 1954 she wed Yankee legend "Jolting Joe" DiMaggio, but the marriage didn't last. Monroe remained fragile and insecure, tormented by the pressures of Hollywood life. Her death from an overdose Aug 5, 1962, at Los Angeles shocked the world. Among her films: *The Seven Year Itch, Bus Stop, Some Like It Hot, Gentlemen Prefer Blondes* and *The Misfits*.

NATIONAL ACCORDION AWARENESS MONTH. June 1–30. To increase public awareness of this multicultural instrument and its influence and popularity in today's music. For info: Tom Torriglia, All Things Accordion, PO Box 475136, San Francisco, CA 94147-5136. Phone: (415) 440-0800. E-mail: bellows@ladyofspain.com. Web: www.ladyofspain.com.

NATIONAL APHASIA AWARENESS MONTH. June 1–30. More than one million Americans have acquired aphasia. Aphasia is a language-processing disorder that impairs a person's ability to speak or understand speech. The mission of the National Aphasia Association (NAA) is to reduce the social and emotional consequences of aphasia by raising awareness of and giving a voice to people who cannot use their own. Annually, the month of June. For info: Penny Montgomery-West, Response Center Dir, Natl Aphasia Assn, 29 John St #1103, New York, NY 10038. Phone: (800) 922-4622. E-mail: naa@aphasia.org. Web: www.aphasia.org.

NATIONAL CANDY MONTH. June 1–30. Celebrated throughout the confectionary industry. Retailers will host special events in stores, and there will be special promotions and merchandising contests. Get the facts on these fun products: candy is good food and can definitely be enjoyed as a part of a balanced diet. A great month to host a special candy event. Logo available for use. For info: Lisbeth Echeandia, American Consulting Corporation, PO Box 388, Savoy, TX 75479. Phone: (903) 965-9300. Fax: (903) 965-9144. E-mail: lisbeth@texoma.net.

NATIONAL GLBT BOOK MONTH. June 1–30. Created to increase the recognition of lesbian, gay, bisexual and transgender writing. Begun in 1992 by the Publishing Triangle, June was selected in honor of the anniversary of the 1969 Stonewall Riot in New York City. It was this brave resistance to police harassment that kickstarted the gay pride movement in the United States. Libraries, bookstores, publishers and bibliophiles everywhere are invited to form a chorus line and celebrate with the community. Annually, the month of June. For info: GLBT Services Committee, Tucson-Pima Public Library, 101 N Stone Ave, Tucson, AZ 85701. Phone: (520) 791-4393. Fax: (520) 791-2672. E-mail: glbt@ci.tucson.az.us. Web: www.lib.ci.tucson.az.us/glbt/bookmonth.

NATIONAL ICED TEA MONTH. June 1–30. To celebrate one of the most widely consumed beverages in the world and one of nature's most perfect beverages, and to encourage Americans to refresh themselves with this all-natural, low-calorie, refreshing thirst-quencher. For info: Joseph P. Simrany, Pres, The Tea Council of the USA, 420 Lexington Ave, Ste 825, New York, NY 10170. Phone: (212) 986-6998. Fax: (212) 697-8658. E-mail: info@teausa.org. Web: www.teausa.org.

June 1 ☆ *Chase's 2004 Calendar of Events* ☆

NATIONAL RIVERS MONTH. June 1–30. Commemorated by local groups in many states.

NATIONAL ROSE MONTH. June 1–30. To recognize American-grown roses, our national floral emblem. America's favorite flower is grown in all 50 states and more than 1.2 billion fresh-cut roses are sold at retail each year. For info: Web: www.roses inc.org.

NATIONAL SAFETY MONTH. June 1–30. For info: Natl Safety Council, 1121 Spring Lake Dr, Itasca, IL 60143-3201. Phone: (800) 621-7615. Web: www.nsc.org.

NATIONAL SOUL FOOD MONTH. June 1–30. A month to recognize, educate and celebrate the heritage and history of the foods and foodways of African Americans and peoples from the African diaspora. The culinary contributions of this group have had an indelible impact on the menu of the American table and on mainstream American life and culture. For info: Culinary Historians of Chicago, PO Box 805987, Chicago, IL 60680. E-mail: saridgeway0622@yahoo.com. Web: www.culinaryhistorians.org.

NCAA DIVISION I MEN'S GOLF CHAMPIONSHIP. June 1–4. The Homestead, Cascades Golf Course, Hot Springs, VA. For info: NCAA, 700 W Washington Ave, PO Box 6222, Indianapolis, IN 46206-6222. Phone: (317) 917-6222. Fax: (317) 917-6888. Web: www.ncaasports.com.

PHARMACISTS DECLARE WAR ON ALCOHOLISM. June 1–30. To encourage pharmacists, healthcare professionals and consumers to better educate and counsel the public on alcoholism and other substance abuse illnesses. By promoting alcohol abuse awareness and education to healthcare professionals and the general public, PCAA strives to break the stereotype surrounding alcoholism that keeps millions of Americans from receiving proper treatment. There is a $15 charge for kit materials. For info: Pharmacists Planning Service, Inc, Pharmacy Council on Alcohol Abuse, 101 Lucas Valley Rd, #210, San Rafael, CA 94903. Phone: (415) 479-8628. Fax: (415) 479-8608. E-mail: ppsi@aol.com. Web: www.ppsinc.org.

PLYMOUTH PLANTATION EARTHQUAKE: ANNIVERSARY. June 1, 1638. The first earthquake in the US to have been recorded and described in writing occurred at Plymouth, MA, at 2 PM. Governor William Bradford described the event in his *History*: ". . . it was very terrible for ye time; and as ye men were set talking in ye house, some women and others were without ye doors, and ye earth shooke with ye violence as they could not stand without catching hold of ye posts . . . but ye violence lasted not long. And about halfe an hower, or less, came an other noyse & shaking, but neither so loud nor strong as ye former, but quickly passed over, and so it ceased."

POTTY TRAINING AWARENESS MONTH. June 1–30. Potty training can be an exciting yet frustrating time for parents. That's why Kimberly-Clark Pull-Ups® sponsors this month devoted to educating parents about the potty training process and helping make this milestone in a child's life easier. Annually, the month of June. For info: Denise Young, Edelman Public Relations, 200 E Randolph St, 63rd Fl, Chicago, IL 60601. Phone: (312) 240-3000. Fax: (312) 240-1501. E-mail: denise.young@edelman.com. Web: www.pull-ups.com.

"THE PRISONER" TV PREMIERE: ANNIVERSARY. June 1, 1968. "The Prisoner" was one of the most imaginative shows on TV, regarded by some as the finest dramatic series in TV history. Patrick McGoohan, who produced and starred in the series, also wrote and directed some episodes. In the series, McGoohan found himself in a self-contained community known as "the village" where he was referred to, not by name, but as Number 6. Number 6 realized he was a prisoner and spent most of the series trying to escape or to learn the identity of the leader, Number 1.

PROFESSIONAL WELLNESS MONTH. June 1–30. Increase your worth in the marketplace. Add value to your company and your customers. Be accessible, reliable and fair. Update your resume, increase your skills and learn your business completely. Become a source of reference: be visible, attend meetings and company or community socials. For info: Angela Brown, Words of Wellness, PO Box 49266, Charlotte, NC 28277. Phone: (704) 849-2900. Fax: (704) 845-3060. E-mail: Angela@WordsofWellness.com. Web: www.WordsofWellness.com.

REBUILD YOUR LIFE MONTH. June 1–30. This is an opportunity for adults neglected and/or abused as children to celebrate their self-worth and discover inner power. They can learn to heal their lives and emotional pain by helping others. For info send SASE: Donald Etkes, PhD, PMB 148, 112 Harvard Ave, Claremont, CA 91711. Phone: (909) 981-7333.

SAMOA: INDEPENDENCE DAY. June 1. National holiday. Commemorates independence from New Zealand in 1962. The former Western Samoa changed its name in 1997.

SEED TO STALK. June 1–30. Jamestown Settlement, Williamsburg, VA, and Yorktown Victory Center, Yorktown, VA. Explore American agriculture of the 17th and 18th centuries. Compare Powhatan and European planting and cultivation methods and learn which crops were grown for sustenance and which were for profit. Throughout the month, visitors can try their hand at tending and watering gardens and learn about the many practical uses of herbs and plants. For info: Jamestown-Yorktown Foundation, PO Box 1607, Williamsburg, VA 23187. Phone: (757) 253-4838 or toll-free (888) 593-4682. Fax: (757) 253-5299. Web: www.historyisfun.org.

SGT PEPPER'S LONELY HEARTS CLUB BAND RELEASED: ANNIVERSARY. June 1, 1967. After 700 hours of studio work, The Beatles released what many consider one of the greatest rock albums of the twentieth century. No singles were released, but the album included such popular tracks as "Lucy in the Sky with Diamonds," "With a Little Help from My Friends," "When I'm Sixty-Four" and "Day in the Life."

SPORTS AMERICA KIDS MONTH. June 1–30. To encourage the health and well-being of all America's children. Physical fitness and healthy thinking, through the efforts of teamwork with individual self-esteem, can help America's children to appreciate the gift of life and the value of respecting the lives of others. A time for adults and kids to embrace the wonderful outdoors and the benefits of healthy living with physical fitness. For info: Judith Natale, NCAC America–USA, 2091 Del Monte Ave, Monterey, CA 93940. Fax: (831) 655-4547. E-mail: childaware@aol.com.

STEPPARENTS' WEEK. June 1–7. The statistics on family life in the '90s are: 50 percent of all marriages end in divorce and 67 percent of all second marriages end in divorce. This week is in recognition of those courageous souls who flaunt convention and plow forward despite the odds. Annually, the first week in June. [©1996] To alleviate the escalating costs of Eventological® Literature a charge of $7 must be assessed for each request. Checks are to be made payable to: Adrienne Sioux Koopersmith, 1437 W Rosemont, #1W, Chicago, IL 60660-1319. Phone: (773) 743-5341. Fax: (773) 743-5395. E-mail: la_koop@yahoo.com.

STUDENT SAFETY MONTH. June 1–30. Heightening the awareness of safety and making sound decisions following graduations, parties, senior proms and other special events. Encourages young people everywhere not to drink and drive and to use

June 2004	S	M	T	W	T	F	S
			1	2	3	4	5
	6	7	8	9	10	11	12
	13	14	15	16	17	18	19
	20	21	22	23	24	25	26
	27	28	29	30			

good judgment while celebrating throughout the month. For info: Carole Copeland Thomas, 400 W Cummings Pk, Ste 1725-154, Woburn, MA 01801. Phone: (508) 947-5755 or (800) 801-6599. Fax: (508) 947-3903. E-mail: carole@TellCarole.com. Web: www.TellCarole.com.

TENNESSEE: ADMISSION DAY: ANNIVERSARY. June 1. Became 16th state in 1796. Observed as a holiday in Tennessee.

VISION RESEARCH MONTH. June 1–30. While millions of Americans benefit from vision research, many eye diseases have no effective treatments or cures. An overview of vision research successes and the urgent need for future studies will be offered. For info: Prevent Blindness America®, 500 E Remington Rd, Schaumburg, IL 60173. Phone: (800) 331-2020. Fax: (847) 843-8458. Web: www.preventblindness.org.

YOUNG, BRIGHAM: BIRTH ANNIVERSARY. June 1, 1801. Mormon church leader born at Whittingham, VT. Known as "the American Moses," having led thousands of religious followers across 1,000 miles of wilderness to settle more than 300 towns in the West. He died at Salt Lake City, UT, Aug 29, 1877, and was survived by 17 wives and 47 children. Utah observes, as a state holiday, the anniversary of his entrance into the Salt Lake Valley, July 24, 1847.

ZOUK MONTH. June 1–30. To celebrate Zouk music and dancing throughout the US. For info: Huntley Harvey, 141-15 85th Rd, Briarwood, NY 11435. Phone: (718) 974-8887. E-mail: huntley@sitordance.com. Web: www.sitordance.com.

BIRTHDAYS TODAY

Rene Auberjonois, 64, actor (*M*A*S*H*, "Benson"; stage: *Coco* [Tony Award]), born New York, NY, June 1, 1940.
James Hadley Billington, 75, Librarian of Congress, born Bryn Mawr, PA, June 1, 1929.
Lisa Hartman Black, 48, actress ("Tabitha," "Knots Landing"), born Houston, TX, June 1, 1956.
Pat Boone, 70, singer, actor (*State Fair*), author, born Jacksonville, FL, June 1, 1934.
Pat Corley, 74, actor ("Bay City Blues," "Murphy Brown"), born Dallas, TX, June 1, 1930.
Mark Curry, 40, comedian, actor ("Hangin' With Mr Cooper"), born Oakland, CA, June 1, 1964.
Morgan Freeman, 67, stage and film actor (*Driving Miss Daisy*), born Memphis, TN, June 1, 1937.
Andy Griffith, 78, actor ("Matlock," "The Andy Griffith Show"), born Mount Airy, NC, June 1, 1926.
Justine Henin-Hardenne, 22, tennis player, born Liege, Belgium, June 1, 1982.
Alexi Lalas, 34, soccer player, born Detroit, MI, June 1, 1970.
Alanis Morissette, 30, singer, born, Ottawa, ON, Canada, June 1, 1974.
Jonathan Pryce, 57, actor (*The Age of Innocence, Glengarry Glen Ross*; stage: *Miss Saigon*; Tony Awards for *Comedians* and *Hamlet*), born Holywell, North Wales, June 1, 1947.
Frederica von Stade, 59, opera mezzo-soprano, born Somerville, NJ, June 1, 1945.
Ron Wood, 57, musician (guitarist with the Rolling Stones), born London, England, June 1, 1947.
Edward Woodward, 74, actor, singer ("The Equalizer," *Wicker Man, Breaker Morant*), born Croydon, England, June 1, 1930.

JUNE 2 — WEDNESDAY
Day 154 — 212 Remaining

BELGIUM: PROCESSION OF THE GOLDEN CHARIOT. June 2. Mons. Horse-drawn coach carrying a reliquary of St. Waudru circles the town of Mons. Procession commemorates delivery of Mons from the plague in 1349. In the town square, in afternoon, St. George fights the dragon.

BHUTAN: CORONATION DAY. June 2. National holiday. Commemorates the crowning of the fourth king in 1974.

BOOKEXPO AMERICA TRADE EXHIBIT. June 2–6. McCormick Place, Chicago, IL. Publishers display fall titles for booksellers and all interested in reaching the retail bookseller. Book-related items also on display. For info: BookExpo America, 383 Main Ave, Norwalk, CT 06851-1543. Phone: (800) 840-5614. Fax: (203) 855-9101. Web: bookexpo.reedexpo.com.

BULGARIA: HRISTO BOTEV DAY. June 2. Poet and national hero Hristro Botev fell fighting Turks, 1876.

COLORADO SHAKESPEARE FESTIVAL. June 2–Aug 17 (Vail performances Aug 21–23). Boulder, CO. One of the top Shakespeare festivals in the country. Est attendance: 43,000. For info: Richard Devin, Producing Artistic Dir, Colorado Shakespeare Festival Admin Office, University of Colorado, 277 UCB, Boulder, CO 80309-0277. Phone: (303) 492-1527 or box office at (303) 492-0554. Fax: (303) 735-5140. E-mail: shakes@colorado.edu. Web: www.coloradoshakes.org.

ENGLAND: ROYAL BATH AND WEST SHOW. June 2–5. Royal Bath and West Showground, Shepton Mallet, Somerset. One of the largest agricultural shows for the whole family in the country. 227th year. Est attendance: 155,000. For info: Royal Bath and West Society, The Showground, Shepton Mallet, Somerset, England BA4 6QN. Phone: (44) (174) 982-2200. Fax: (44) (174) 982-3169. E-mail: info@bathandwest.co.uk. Web: www.bathandwest.co.uk.

ITALY: REPUBLIC DAY. June 2. National holiday. Commemorates 1946 referendum in which republic status was selected instead of return to monarchy.

MAINE LAW: ANNIVERSARY. June 2, 1851. America's first statewide statute prohibiting the sale of alcoholic beverages was enacted in the state of Maine. The following Independence Day the mayor of Bangor showed his support of the new law by smashing 10 kegs of confiscated booze.

MARQUIS DE SADE: BIRTH ANNIVERSARY. June 2, 1740. Donatien-Alphonse-François, Comte de Sade, was born at Paris, France. French military man, governor-general and author, who spent much of his life in prison because of his acts of cruelty and violence, outrageous behavior and debauchery. The word *sadism* was created from his name to describe gratification in inflicting pain. He died near Paris, at the Charenton lunatic asylum, Dec 2, 1814.

MUSIC IN THE PARK. June 2–Aug 27. Anchorage, AK. An outdoor summer concert series, free to the public. Every Wednesday and Friday from noon to 1 PM. Live, cross-generational bands perform. This is a fun-for-all event, with a tremendous following! For info: Erin Schutte, Anchorage Downtown Partnership, Ltd, 245 W 5th St, Anchorage, AK 99501. Phone: (907) 279-5650. Fax: (907) 279-5651. E-mail: ancdp@alaska.net. Web: www.ancdp.com.

NATIONAL BUBBA DAY. June 2. Comedian and public speaker T. Bubba Bechtol has created a holiday for Bubbas everywhere. Annually, June 2. For info: T. Bubba Bechtol, 339 Panferio Drive, Pensacola Beach, FL 32561. Phone: (850) 932-3162. E-mail: BubbaBechtol@aol.com. Web: www.tbubbabechtol.com.

NATIONAL SPELLING BEE FINALS. June 2–3. Washington, DC. Newspapers and other sponsors across the country send 240–250 youngsters to the finals at Washington, DC. Annually, Wednesday and Thursday of Memorial Day Week. Est attendance: 1,000. For info: Scripps-Howard Natl Spelling Bee, 312 Walnut

St, 28th Fl, Cincinnati, OH 45202. Phone: (513) 977-3040. Fax: (513) 977-3090. E-mail: bee@scripps.com. Web: www.spelling bee.com.

NATIONAL TAILORS DAY. June 2. To honor tailors across the US. Our company, Tom James Clothiers, sells clothing to individuals in their office or home. Without our clothing tailors, we wouldn't be able to perform our jobs! Annually, the first Wednesday in June. For info: Doug Foley, Tom James Clothiers, 9302 N Meridian, Indianapolis, IN 46290. Phone: (317) 571-9191. E-mail: d.foley@tjm068.com. Web: www.tomjamesco.com.

SAINT PIUS X: BIRTH ANNIVERSARY. June 2, 1835. Giuseppe Melchiorre Sarto, 257th pope of the Roman Catholic Church, born at Riese, Italy. Elected pope Aug 4, 1903. Died Aug 20, 1914, at Rome. Canonized May 29, 1954.

SALEM WITCH TRIALS BEGIN: ANNIVERSARY. June 2, 1692. As the village of Salem was gripped by terror of witches, Massachusetts Bay Colony governor Sir William Phips ordered a special court created on May 27, 1692, to expedite judgment of the more than 150 people accused of witchcraft. Unpopular resident Bridget Bishop, first accused in April, was the first of the jailed brought to trial on June 2. At her April examination her accusers—teenaged girls—had collapsed in fits as she appeared, but Bishop adamantly denied the charges: "I am no witch—I know not what a witch is." She was convicted June 2 and hung June 10. See also: "Salem Witch Hysteria Begins: Anniversary" (Mar 1).

UNITED KINGDOM: CORONATION DAY: ANNIVERSARY. June 2. Commemorates the crowning of Queen Elizabeth II in 1953.

WEISSMULLER, JOHNNY: 100th BIRTH ANNIVERSARY. June 2, 1904. Peter John (Johnny) Weissmuller, actor and Olympic gold medal swimmer, born at Windber, PA. Weissmuller won three gold medals at the 1924 Olympics and two more at the 1928 games. He set 24 world records and in 1950 was voted the best swimmer of the first half of the 20th century. After retiring from amateur competition, he appeared as Tarzan in a dozen movies and as "Jungle Jim" in the movies and on television. Died at Acapulco, Mexico, Jan 20, 1984.

YELL "FUDGE" AT THE COBRAS IN NORTH AMERICA DAY. June 2. Anywhere north of the Panama Canal. In order to keep poisonous cobra snakes out of North America, all citizens are asked to go outdoors at noon, local time, and yell "Fudge." Fudge makes cobras gag and the mere mention of it makes them skedaddle. Annually, June 2. [©2003 by WH.] For info: Thomas & Ruth Roy, Wellcat Holidays, 2418 Long Ln, Lebanon, PA 17046. Phone: (717) 279-0184. E-mail: info@wellcat .com. Web: www.wellcat.com.

BIRTHDAYS TODAY

Diana Canova, 51, actress ("Soap," "I'm a Big Girl Now"), born West Palm Beach, FL, June 2, 1953.
Dana Carvey, 49, comedian, actor (*Wayne's World*, "Saturday Night Live"), born Missoula, MT, June 2, 1955.
Gary Grimes, 49, actor (*Summer of '42, Class of '44*), born San Francisco, CA, June 2, 1955.
Charles Haid, 61, actor ("Hill Street Blues," "Delvecchio"), producer, born San Francisco, CA, June 2, 1943.
Marvin Hamlisch, 60, composer (Oscars for *The Sting, The Way We Were*; Tony for *A Chorus Line*), born New York, NY, June 2, 1944.
Dennis Haysbert, 50, actor ("24," *Waiting to Exhale, Major League*), born San Mateo, CA, June 2, 1954.

	S	M	T	W	T	F	S
June			1	2	3	4	5
2004	6	7	8	9	10	11	12
	13	14	15	16	17	18	19
	20	21	22	23	24	25	26
	27	28	29	30			

Stacy Keach, Jr, 63, actor (*Conduct Unbecoming*, "Mickey Spillane's Mike Hammer"), born Savannah, GA, June 2, 1941.
Sally Kellerman, 68, actress (*M*A*S*H, Back to School*), born Long Beach, CA, June 2, 1936.
Jerry Mathers, 56, actor ("Leave It to Beaver"), born Sioux City, IA, June 2, 1948.
Milo O'Shea, 78, actor (*The Purple Rose of Cairo*), born Dublin, Ireland, June 2, 1926.
Charlie Watts, 63, musician (drummer with the Rolling Stones), born Islington, England, June 2, 1941.

JUNE 3 — THURSDAY
Day 155 — 211 Remaining

ALBANY ALIVE AT FIVE. June 3 (also June 10, 17, 24, July 1, 15, 22 and 29). Tricentennial Park on Broadway, Albany, NY. A free eight-week summer concert series on Thursday evenings from 5–8 PM. A different theme of music each week, food and refreshment vendors. Est attendance: 80,000. For info: City of Albany Office of Special Events, Eagle St, City Hall, 4th Fl, Albany, NY 12207. Phone: (518) 434-2032. Fax: (518) 426-0759. Web: www.albanyevents.org.

BATTLE OF COLD HARBOR: ANNIVERSARY. June 3, 1864. Although Confederate Gen Robert E. Lee had placed his troops behind considerable breastworks, Union Gen Ulysses S. Grant launched an all-out attack on the Southern army in Virginia. More than 7,000 Federal troops were killed within one-half hour of battle on the first attack. After a second unsuccessful attack, Grant's orders for a third assault were all but ignored. Battlefield tradition held that the first commander who sought a truce in order to tend to the wounded was the loser. Grant refused to admit defeat by seeking such a truce and the wounded were left on the ground for three days following the battle. As a consequence, all but two of the thousands of wounded men died either from their wounds, hunger, thirst or exposure.

CANADA: SHELBURNE COUNTY LOBSTER FESTIVAL. June 3–6. Shelburne County, NS. Four days of activities in celebration of the lobster-fishing industry. Local community groups and businesses throughout the county host lobster suppers, sporting events, craft shows, yacht, boat and dorey races and much more. "Shelburne County—The Lobster Capital of Canada." Annually, the first full weekend in June. Est attendance: 10,000. For info: Marilyn Johnston, Lobster Fest Secy, PO Box 280, Shelburne, NS, Canada B0T 1W0. Phone: (902) 875-3544. Fax: (902) 875-1278. E-mail: shelburnemunrec@canada.com.

CHIMBORAZO DAY. June 3. To bring the shape of the earth into focus by publicizing the fact that Mount Chimborazo, Ecuador, near the equator, pokes farther out into space than any other mountain on earth, including Mount Everest. (The distance from sea level at the equator to the center of the earth is 13 miles greater than the radius to sea level at the North Pole. This means that New Orleans is about six miles farther from the center of the earth than is Lake Itasca at the headwaters of the Mississippi, so the Mississippi flows uphill.) For info: Robert L. Birch, Puns Corps, Box 2364, Falls Church, VA 22042-0364. Phone: (703) 533-3668.

CONFEDERATE MEMORIAL DAY IN KENTUCKY, LOUISIANA AND TENNESSEE. June 3. Ceremonial holiday on the birthday of Jefferson Davis. Also observed as Jefferson Davis Day in Kentucky and Confederate Decoration Day in Tennessee.

☆ Chase's 2004 Calendar of Events ☆ — June 3

CURWOOD FESTIVAL. June 3–6. Owosso, MI. Homecoming celebration commemorating James Oliver Curwood, Owosso-born author and conservationist (June 12, 1878–Aug 13, 1927). The Curwood castle was built for a studio. Open to the public. 40 events including parades, races and music. Annually, the first full weekend in June. Est attendance: 75,000. For info: Owosso Curwood Festival, Box 461, Owosso, MI 48867. Phone: (989) 723-2161. Fax: (989) 723-8353. E-mail: curwood.festivalinc@verizon.net. Web: www.curwoodfestival.com.

DAVIS, JEFFERSON: BIRTH ANNIVERSARY. June 3, 1808. American statesman, US senator, only president of the Confederate States of America. Imprisoned May 10, 1865–May 13, 1867, but never brought to trial, deprived of rights of citizenship after the Civil War. Davis was born at Todd County, KY, and died at New Orleans, LA, Dec 6, 1889. His citizenship was restored, posthumously, Oct 17, 1978, when President Carter signed an Amnesty Bill. This bill, he said, "officially completes the long process of reconciliation that has reunited our people following the tragic conflict between the states." Davis's birth anniversary is observed in Florida, Kentucky and South Carolina on this day, in Alabama on the first Monday in June and in Mississippi on the last Monday in May. Davis's birth anniversary is observed as Confederate Memorial Day in Tennessee.

DEWHURST, COLLEEN: 80th BIRTH ANNIVERSARY. June 3, 1924. Colleen Dewhurst was born at Quebec, Canada. Her 40-year career as an actress spanned stage, screen and television. After making her Broadway debut in Eugene O'Neill's *Desire Under the Elms* in 1952, she became the actress most associated with O'Neill's works in the later part of this century, also performing in *Long Day's Journey into Night, Mourning Becomes Electra, Ah, Wilderness!* and *A Moon for the Misbegotten*, for which she won her second Tony award. At the time of her death, she was president of Actor's Equity Association, the union for professional actors. She won three Emmy awards. She died Aug 22, 1991, at South Salem, NY.

DREW, CHARLES RICHARD: 100th BIRTH ANNIVERSARY. June 3, 1904. African-American physician who discovered how to store blood plasma and who organized the blood bank system in the US and UK during WWII. Born at Washington, DC, he was killed in an automobile accident near Burlington, NC, Apr 1, 1950.

DUKE OF WINDSOR MARRIAGE: ANNIVERSARY. June 3, 1937. The Duke of Windsor who, as King Edward VIII, had abdicated the British throne on Dec 11, 1936, was married to Mrs Wallis Warfield Simpson of Baltimore, MD, at Monts, France. The couple made their home in France after their marriage and had little contact with the royal family. The Duke died at Paris on May 28, 1972, and was buried near Windsor Castle in England. The Duchess died Apr 24, 1986.

EVERETT SALTY SEA DAYS. June 3–6. Everett, WA. Funtastic Shows Carnival, food booths, music, fireworks, grand parade, classic car show, limited hydro races and Hawaiian Outrigger Boat Races. Sponsors include City of Everett, Port of Everett, Cascade Bank and Dwayne Lane's Family Auto Centers. Est attendance: 150,000. For info: Marion Pope, Exec Dir, Salty Sea Days Assn, 2520 Colby Ave, Ste 101, Everett, WA 98201. Phone: (425) 339-1113. Fax: (425) 259-0131. E-mail: saltysea@aol.com. Web: www.saltyseadays.org.

FIRST WOMAN RABBI IN US: ANNIVERSARY. June 3, 1972. Sally Jan Priesand was ordained the first woman rabbi in the US. She became assistant rabbi at the Stephen Wise Free Synagogue, New York City, Aug 1, 1972.

GINSBERG, ALLEN: BIRTH ANNIVERSARY. June 3, 1926. Poet of the Beat Generation ("Howl"), born Newark, NJ. Died Apr 5, 1997, at New York, NY.

HOBART, GARRET AUGUSTUS: BIRTH ANNIVERSARY. June 3, 1844. 24th vice president of the US (1897–99), born at Long Branch, NJ. Died at Paterson, NJ, Nov 21, 1899.

HONE, WILLIAM: BIRTH ANNIVERSARY. June 3, 1780. English author and bookseller born at Bath, England; died at Tottenham, Nov 6, 1842. Compiler of *The Every-Day Book, or Everlasting Calendar of Popular Amusements* (1826). It was William Hone who said: "A good lather is half the shave."

IRELAND: BANK HOLIDAY. June 3. National holiday in the Republic of Ireland.

JACK JOUETT'S RIDE: ANNIVERSARY. June 3, 1781. Jack Jouett made a heroic 45-mile ride on horseback during the night of June 3–4, 1781, to warn Virginia Governor Thomas Jefferson and the legislature that the British were coming. Jouett rode from a tavern in Louisa County to Charlottesville, VA, in about 6½ hours, arriving at Jefferson's home at dawn on June 4. Lieutenant Colonel Tarleton's British forces raided Charlottesville, but Jouett's warning gave the Americans time to escape. Jouett was born at Albemarle County, VA, Dec 7, 1754, and died at Bath, KY, in 1822 (exact date unknown).

KHOMEINI, AYATOLLAH RUHOLLA: 15th DEATH ANNIVERSARY. June 3, 1989. The Ayatollah Ruholla Khomeini, leader of the Islamic Revolution, lifelong foe of the Shah of Iran, was arrested in 1963 after giving a speech accusing the Shah of seeking to destroy Islam. He was exiled to Turkey in 1964, following which he spent 13 years in Iraq and Paris, where he gained exposure to the world press for his cause. On Jan 16, 1979, the Shah of Iran left the country for a supposed vacation, setting the stage for Khomeini's triumphant return on Jan 31. The monarchy fell on Feb 11, 1979. Khomeini proceeded to reorganize the government based on Islamic principles. On Nov 11, 1979, a group of students loyal to Khomeini occupied the American Embassy in Teheran after the Shah was given admittance to the US for medical treatment, placing the Ayatollah at the center of a diplomatic crisis that consumed the presidency of Jimmy Carter. Khomeini focused attention on the US as the "Great Satan" and blamed many of his country's problems on imperialistic intervention. The anniversary of his death is a national holiday in Iran.

MIGHTY CASEY HAS STRUCK OUT: ANNIVERSARY. June 3, 1888. The famous comic baseball ballad "Casey at the Bat" was printed in the Sunday *San Francisco Examiner*. Appearing anonymously, it was written by Ernest L. Thayer. Recitation of "Casey at the Bat" became part of the repertoire of actor William DeWolf Hopper. The recitation took 5 minutes and 40 seconds. Hopper claimed to have recited it more than 10,000 times, the first being at Wallack's Theater at New York, NY, in 1888. See also: "Thayer, Ernest Lawrence: Birth Anniversary" (Aug 14).

MISSION SAN CARLOS BORROMEO DE CARMELO: FOUNDING ANNIVERSARY. June 3, 1770. California mission to the Indians founded on this date.

MOON PHASE: FULL MOON. June 3. Moon enters Full Moon phase at 12:20 AM, EDT.

PERIGEAN SPRING TIDES. June 3. Spring tides, the highest possible tides, occur when New Moon or Full Moon takes place within 24 hours of the moment the Moon is nearest Earth (perigee) in its monthly orbit. The word *spring* refers not to the season but comes from the German word *springen*, "to rise up."

June 3–4 ☆ Chase's 2004 Calendar of Events ☆

PORTLAND ROSE FESTIVAL. June 3–20. Portland, OR. 97th annual celebration includes more than 50 events featuring three parades, the Portland Arts Festival, dragon boat races, a waterfront village with amusement rides and Navy fleet visits. Est attendance: 2,000,000. For info: Portland Rose Festival Assn, 5603 SW Hood Ave, Portland, OR 97239. Phone: (503) 227-2681. Fax: (503) 227-6603. E-mail: info@rosefestival.org. Web: www.rosefestival.org.

SPACE MILESTONE: *GEMINI 4* (US). June 3, 1965. James McDivitt and Edward White made 66 orbits of Earth. White took the first space walk by an American and maneuvered 20 minutes outside the capsule.

US INTERNATIONAL FILM AND VIDEO FESTIVAL AWARDS PRESENTATIONS. June 3–4. Los Angeles, CA. World's largest awards competition honoring business, television, documentary, informational and industrial productions. Founded in 1968. Est attendance: 300. For info: Lee W. Gluckman, Jr, Chairman, US Intl Film and Video Festival Awards, 713 S Pacific Coast Hwy, Ste A, Redondo Beach, CA 90277-4233. Phone: (310) 540-0959. Fax: (310) 316-8905. E-mail: filmfestinfo@filmfestawards.com. Web: www.filmfestawards.com.

ZOOT SUIT RIOTS: ANNIVERSARY. June 3–8, 1943. In Los Angeles, CA, simmering racial unease exploded as 200 white sailors stormed into East LA and began beating Hispanics in response to an earlier altercation between a few sailors and some street kids. The sailors targeted Zoot Suiters—youths outfitted in the defiant, exaggerated suit of their community (long jackets, wide trousers and ankle-length watch chains). The rioting grew as police either stood by or arrested the victims. The media, antagonistic to the Hispanic community, spurred on the violence with sensational headlines. Finally, military brass declared Los Angeles off limits to its personnel and the LA City Council banned zoot suits. There were no deaths, but the injuries and mayhem were such that a special state committee was convened and First Lady Eleanor Roosevelt fretted in her newspaper column that the riots were symptomatic of a problem with deep roots.

BIRTHDAYS TODAY

Chuck Barris, 75, TV producer ("Dating Game," "Newlywed Game," "Gong Show"), born Philadelphia, PA, June 3, 1929.

Tony Curtis, 79, actor (*Some Like It Hot, The Boston Strangler, The Defiant Ones*), born Bernard Schwartz, New York, NY, June 3, 1925.

Jan-Michael Gambill, 27, tennis player, born Spokane, WA, June 3, 1977.

Charles Hart, 43, lyricist, composer, born London, England, June 3, 1961.

Hale S. Irwin, 59, golfer, born Joplin, MO, June 3, 1945.

Scott Valentine, 46, actor ("Family Ties"), born Saratoga Springs, NY, June 3, 1958.

Deniece Williams, 53, singer ("Free," "It's Gonna Take a Miracle"), born Gary, IN, June 3, 1951.

June 2004	S	M	T	W	T	F	S
			1	2	3	4	5
	6	7	8	9	10	11	12
	13	14	15	16	17	18	19
	20	21	22	23	24	25	26
	27	28	29	30			

JUNE 4 — FRIDAY
Day 156 — 210 Remaining

BAHAMAS: LABOR DAY. June 4. Public holiday. First Friday in June celebrated with parades, displays and picnics.

BATTLE OF MIDWAY: ANNIVERSARY. June 4–6, 1942. A Japanese task force attempted to capture Midway Island in the Central Pacific. American bombers from Midway and from two nearby aircraft carriers sent the Japanese into retreat, having lost four carriers, two large cruisers and three destroyers. Midway was one of the most decisive naval battles of World War II. Japan never regained its margin in carrier strength and the Central Pacific was made safe for American troops.

BUFFALO DAYS CELEBRATION (WITH BUFFALO CHIP THROWING). June 4–6. Luverne, MN. Parade, Arts in the Park, auto shows, free barbecued buffalo burgers (while they last) and unique buffalo chip throwing contest. Annually, the first weekend in June. Est attendance: 12,000. For info: Dave Smith, Exec Dir, Luverne Area Chamber of Commerce, 102 E Main, Luverne, MN 56156. Phone: (507) 283-4061. Fax: (507) 283-4061. E-mail: luvernechamber@dtgnet.com. Web: www.luvernemn.com.

"CAVALCADE OF STARS" TV PREMIERE: 55th ANNIVERSARY. June 4, 1949. Although the Dumont network was not very successful, it was around long enough to launch this popular show. The one-hour variety show was hosted by Jack Carter (1949–50), Jackie Gleason (1950–52) and Larry Storch (in the summer of 1952). It also served as a showcase for the soon-to-be immortal "The Honeymooners" with Gleason and Pert Kelton starring as the Kramdens.

CHICAGO GOSPEL MUSIC FESTIVAL. June 4–6. Grant Park, Chicago, IL. 20th annual. Largest free outdoor gospel music festival in the world. Features local, national and international performers. Est attendance: 150,000. For info: Mayor's Office of Special Events, City Hall, 121 N LaSalle St, #703, Chicago, IL 60602. Phone: (312) 744-3370. Fax: (312) 744-8523. E-mail: moseinquiry@cityofchicago.org. Web: www.cityofchicago.org/specialevents.

CHICKEN AND EGG FESTIVAL. June 4–5. Prescott, AR. Two days of athletic events, shows and entertainment for the entire family. Come and watch our famous Cackling and Crowing contest in Southwest Arkansas's friendliest city. Other activities include: 5K run and walk, tennis tournament, softball, weight lifting, antique car show, Little Miss Hen and Little Mr Rooster Beauty Pageants and much more. Est attendance: 2,000. For info: Mary Godwin, PO Box 307, Prescott, AR 71857. Phone: (870) 887-2101. Fax: (870) 887-5317. E-mail: mgodwin@iocc.com. Web: partnership.pcfa.org/.

CHILDREN'S MIRACLE NETWORK CELEBRATION. June 4–6. The largest televised fund-raiser in history. More than $250 million was raised in 2002. Benefits 170 nonprofit hospitals for children in North America. For info: Children's Miracle Network, 4525 S 2300 E, Salt Lake City, UT 84117. Phone: (801) 278-8900. Web: www.cmn.org.

CHINA: TIANANMEN SQUARE MASSACRE: 15th ANNIVERSARY. June 4, 1989. After almost a month and a half of student demonstrations for democracy, the Chinese government ordered its troops to open fire on the unarmed protestors at Tiananmen Square at Beijing. The demonstrations began Apr 18 as several thousand students marched to mourn the death of Hu Yaobang, a pro-reform leader within the Chinese government. A ban was imposed on such demonstrations; Apr 22, 100,000 gathered in Tiananmen Square in defiance of the ban. On May 13, 2,000 of the students began a hunger strike, and on May 20 the government imposed martial law and began to bring in troops. On June 2 the demonstrators turned back an advance of unarmed troops in the first clash with the People's Army. Under the cover of darkness, early June 4, troops opened fire on the assembled crowds and armored personnel carriers rolled into the square crushing many of the students as they lay sleeping in their tents. Although the government claimed that few died in the attack, estimates range from several hundred to several thousand casualties. In the following months thousands of demonstrators were rounded up and jailed.

DONUT DAY. June 4–5. Chicago, IL. Founded in 1938 by the Salvation Army for fund-raising during the Great Depression, Donut Day is now an annual tradition. Recalling the donuts served to doughboys by the Salvation Army during World War I, symbolic paper "donuts" are given to contributors. Annually, the first Friday and Saturday in June. For info: Richard Grozik, Dir of Communications, The Salvation Army, Metro Div HQ, 5040 N Pulaski, Chicago, IL 60630. Phone: (773) 205-3546. Fax: (773) 725-2822.

FARMINGTON COUNTRY DAYS. June 4–6. Farmington, MO. Three-day event featuring amusement rides, a free "oldies" concert and a Nashville country star concert, talent show and lots more fun for the whole family. Est attendance: 30,000. For info: Farmington Chamber of Commerce, PO Box 191, Farmington, MO 63640. Phone: (573) 756-3615. Fax: (573) 756-1003. E-mail: ursulak@farmingtonmo.org.

FINLAND: FLAG DAY. June 4, 1867. Finland's armed forces honor the birth anniversary of Carl Gustaf Mannerheim.

FIRST FREE FLIGHT BY A WOMAN: ANNIVERSARY. June 4, 1784. Marie Thible, of Lyons, France, accompanied by a pilot (Monsieur Fleurant), became the first woman in history to fly in a free balloon. She drifted across Lyons in a balloon named *Le Gustave* (for King Gustav III of Sweden, who was watching the ascent). The balloon reached a height of 8,500 feet in a flight that lasted about 45 minutes. The event occurred one day short of a year after the first flight in history by a man. See also: "First Balloon Flight: Anniversary" (June 5).

GEORGE III: BIRTH ANNIVERSARY. June 4, 1738. The English king against whom the American Revolution was directed. Born at London, England, died Jan 29, 1820, at Windsor Castle, near London.

GHANA: REVOLUTION DAY. June 4. National holiday.

GREAT WISCONSIN CHEESE FESTIVAL. June 4–6. Little Chute, WI. Festival features cheese breakfast, parade, cheese tasting, cheese-carving demo and cheesecake contest. Est attendance: 10,000. For info: Great Wisconsin Cheese Festival, 1940 Buchanan St, Little Chute, WI 54140-1414. Phone: (920) 788-7390. Fax: (920) 788-7820.

HARVARD MILK DAYS™ FESTIVAL. June 4–6. Harvard, IL. This salute to the dairy farmer includes a parade, evening entertainment, arts and crafts fair, Avenue of Display, milk-drinking contest, farm tours, antique farm tractor display, carnival, fireworks, prince and princess contest, 2-mile milk run/walk and 10K milk run, cattle show, talent show and wee farm. Est attendance: 125,000. For info: Harvard Milk Days, Inc, 201 W Front St, PO Box 325, Harvard, IL 60033. Phone: (815) 943-4614. Fax: (815) 943-7404. E-mail: milkdays@avenew.com. Web: www.milkdays.com.

HUG YOUR CAT DAY. June 4. Cats act like they don't want or need attention—but they do. Apricat, the pampered star of her own book series, has created a special day for humans to hug their cats without fear of scratches or hisses. For info: Marisa D'Vari, 220 Boylston #1206, Boston, MA 02116. Phone: (617) 451-9914. Fax: (617) 351-2030. E-mail: mdvari@deg.com. Web: www.apricat.com.

IDAHO SHAKESPEARE FESTIVAL. June 4–Sept 25. Boise, ID. Idaho's renowned professional repertory theater company presents a full summer season of The Bard, plus other classical and contemporary playwrights, in its outdoor amphitheater along the Boise River. Bring your picnic dinner and enjoy "Shakespeare Under the Stars." Est attendance: 54,000. For info: Idaho Shakespeare Festival, PO Box 9365, Boise, ID 83707. Phone: (208) 429-9908. Box Office: (208) 336-9221 Fax: (208) 429-8798. E-mail: info@idahoshakespeare.org. Web: www.idahoshakespeare.org.

LEWIS AND CLARK DAYS. June 4–6. Washburn, ND. Rediscover the land that Lewis and Clark called home in 1804–05. Fur traders of the 1800s hold a rendezvous at Ft Mandan, while downtown Washburn celebrates with a parade, carnival, street dance, family fishing derby, plus many more fun activities. Est attendance: 4,500. For info: (701) 462-8535 or North Dakota Tourism, Century Center, 1600 E Century Ave, Ste 2, Bismarck, ND 58503. Phone: (701) 328-2525 or (800) 435-5663. Web: www.fortmandan.com.

LILAC FESTIVAL. June 4–13. Mackinac Island, MI. This summer festival provides an excellent chance to see the various lilacs on Mackinac Island. Includes a parade and entertainment. Est attendance: 30,000. For info: Mackinac Island Tourism Bureau, PO Box 451, Mackinac Island, MI 49757. Phone: (906) 847-6418 or (800) 4-LILACS. Fax: (906) 847-3571. Web: www.mackinacisland.org.

MIAMI/BAHAMAS GOOMBAY FESTIVAL. June 4–6. Miami, FL. 28th annual celebration of the black culture and heritage of Bahamian settlers in Miami's Coconut Grove area in the 1800s. Largest black heritage special event in the US. More than 400 vendor booths. Pre-festival events include golf tournament, beauty pageant, sailing regatta. Annually, the first full weekend in June. Est attendance: 600,000. For info: Susan Neuman, Miami/Bahamas Goombay Festival, 555 NE 15th St, #25-K, Miami, FL 33132. Phone: (305) 372-9966. Fax: (305) 372-9967. E-mail: miamipr@bellsouth.net. Web: www.miamigoombay.com.

PULITZER PRIZES FIRST AWARDED: ANNIVERSARY. June 4, 1917. The first Pulitzer Prizes were awarded on this date: for biography, *Julia Ward Howe* by Laura E. Richards and Maude H. Elliott assisted by Florence H. Hall; for history, *With Americans of Past and Present Days* by Jean Jules Jusserand, the French ambassador to the US. Prizes were also awarded for journalistic achievement.

RED EARTH NATIVE AMERICAN CULTURAL FESTIVAL. June 4–6. Oklahoma City, OK. Named to ABA Top 100 Events in North America for 1997. Thousands of Native Americans representing more than 100 tribes from across North America celebrate their proud heritage at one of the largest intertribal gatherings in the world. Dance competitions, art exhibits, lectures, storytelling and parade. Est attendance: 100,000. For info: Jhane Myers, Red Earth, Inc, 2100 NE 52 St, Oklahoma City, OK 73111. Phone: (405) 427-5228. Fax: (405) 427-8079. E-mail: jhanemyers@redearth.org. Web: www.redearth.org.

ROME LIBERATED: 60th ANNIVERSARY. June 4, 1944. The US 9th Army, commanded by General Mark Clark, entered the southern suburbs of Rome as the last of the German rear guard retreated from Mussolini's former capital. Fearful of a last-ditch effort by the Germans to hold the city, the populace remained behind closed doors as Clark's forces entered the Eternal City.

ROUTE 66 SUMMERFEST. June 4–5. Rolla, MO. 10th annual citywide celebration including sporting events, car shows, crafts, entertainment and food. Est attendance: 4,000. For info: Rolla Chamber of Commerce, 1301 Kingshighway, Rolla, MO 65401. Phone: (573) 364-3577. Web: www.rollachamber.org/summerfest.

June 4–5 ☆ Chase's 2004 Calendar of Events ☆

SITKA SUMMER MUSIC FESTIVAL. June 4–25. (Tuesdays, Fridays and Saturdays) Sitka, AK. Sitka hosts a highly acclaimed chamber music festival that attracts performers and spectators from all over the world. Est attendance: 5,000. For info: Sitka Summer Music Festival, PO Box 3333, Sitka, AK 99835. Phone: (907) 747-6774. Fax: (907) 747-6853. E-mail: director@sitkamusicfestival.org. Web: www.sitkamusicfestival.org.

TASTE OF OMAHA. June 4–6. Heartland of America Park, Omaha, NE. Festival of great foods and live entertainment and fun rides for the kids. Est attendance: 40,000. For info: Robert P. Mancuso, Pres, Mid-America Expositions, Inc, 7015 Spring St, Omaha, NE 68106-3518. Phone: (402) 346-8003. Fax: (402) 346-5412. E-mail: showoffice@aol.com. Web: www.showoffice online.com.

TONGA: EMANCIPATION DAY. June 4. National holiday. Commemorates independence from Britain in 1970.

TRIAL TECHNOLOGY DAY. June 4. A day to mark the emerging technologies used for trials. For info: Joyce Mullen, DOAR, 170 Earle Ave, Lynbrook, NY 11563. Phone: (516) 823-3954. Fax: (516) 823-4400. E-mail: joyce@doar.com. Web: www.doar.com.

UNITED NATIONS: INTERNATIONAL DAY OF INNOCENT CHILDREN VICTIMS OF AGGRESSION. June 4. On Aug 19, 1982, the General Assembly decided to commemorate June 4 of each year as a day to call attention to the urgent need to protect the rights of chidren. It reminds people that throughout the world there are many children suffering from different forms of abuse. For info: United Nations, Dept of Public Info, New York, NY 10017. Web: www.un.org.

BIRTHDAYS TODAY

Cecilia Bartoli, 38, mezzo-soprano, born Rome, Italy, June 4, 1966.
Keith David, 50, actor (*Platoon, Bird*), born New York, NY, June 4, 1954.
Eldra DeBarge, 43, singer, musician, lead singer (DeBarge), born Grand Rapids, MI, June 4, 1961.
Bruce Dern, 68, actor (*Coming Home, The Burbs*), born Chicago, IL, June 4, 1936.
Freddy Fender, 67, singer/songwriter ("Before the Next Teardrop Falls," "Wasted Days and Wasted Nights"), born Baldemar Huerta, San Benito, TX, June 4, 1937.
Bettina Gregory, 58, journalist, born New York, NY, June 4, 1946.
Andrea Jaeger, 39, former tennis player, born Chicago, IL, June 4, 1965.
Angelina Jolie, 29, actress (Oscar for *Girl, Interrupted*), daughter of Jon Voight, born Los Angeles, CA, June 4, 1975.
Linda Lingle, 51, Governor of Hawaii (R), born St. Louis, MO, June 4, 1953.
Robert Merrill, 87, singer, born New York, NY, June 4, 1917.
Michelle Phillips, 59, singer (with The Mamas and the Papas; "California Dreamin'"), actress ("Knots Landing"), born Long Beach, CA, June 4, 1945.
Parker Stevenson, 51, actor ("Falcon Crest," "Baywatch," *Lifeguard*), born Philadelphia, PA, June 4, 1953.
Dennis Weaver, 80, actor ("Gunsmoke," "McCloud"), born Joplin, MO, June 4, 1924.
Dr. Ruth Westheimer, 75, TV, radio host for shows on sexual relationships, born Frankfurt, Germany, June 4, 1929.
Scott Wolf, 36, actor ("Party of Five," *The Evening Star*), born Boston, MA, June 4, 1968.
Noah Wyle, 33, actor (*A Few Good Men*, "ER"), born Hollywood, CA, June 4, 1971.

June 2004

S	M	T	W	T	F	S
		1	2	3	4	5
6	7	8	9	10	11	12
13	14	15	16	17	18	19
20	21	22	23	24	25	26
27	28	29	30			

JUNE 5 — SATURDAY
Day 157 — 209 Remaining

AIDS FIRST NOTED: ANNIVERSARY. June 5, 1981. The Centers for Disease Control first described a new illness striking gay men in a newsletter on June 5, 1981. On July 27, 1982, Acquired Immune Deficiency Syndrome was adopted as the official name for the new disease by the CDC. The virus that causes AIDS was identified in 1983 and in May 1985 was named Human Immunodeficiency Virus (HIV) by the International Committee on the Taxonomy of Viruses. The first person killed by this disease in the developed world died in 1959. More than 450,000 Americans have died of AIDS. Worldwide, more than 22 million people have died of AIDS. About 42 million people worldwide are living with HIV/AIDS.

AMERICAN BAHA'I COMMUNITY: ANNIVERSARY. June 5, 1894. The first formal classes on the Baha'i were held at Chicago, IL.

APPLE II COMPUTER RELEASED: ANNIVERSARY. June 5, 1977. The Apple II computer, with 4K of memory, went on sale for $1,298. Its predecessor, the Apple I, was sold largely to electronic hobbyists the previous year. Apple released the Macintosh computer Jan 24, 1984.

BELMONT STAKES. June 5. Belmont Park, NY. 136th annual. Final race of the "Triple Crown" was inaugurated in 1867. Traditionally run on the fifth Saturday after Kentucky Derby (third Saturday after Preakness). Est attendance: 60,000. For info: Press Office, New York Racing Assn, PO Box 90, Jamaica, NY 11417. Phone: (718) 641-4700. Web: www.nyra.com.

BOYD, WILLIAM: BIRTH ANNIVERSARY. June 5, 1895. Born at Hendrysburg, OH, Boyd went to Hollywood in 1919 and got a job as a film extra. In 1935 he got the role of Hopalong Cassidy in a series of popular westerns. He made 66 of these films between 1935 and 1948. Some of them were edited and shown on television; Boyd then made some episodes especially for TV. Died at Hollywood, CA, Sept 12, 1972. See also: "Hopalong Cassidy TV Premiere" (June 24).

CALIFORNIA: FREE-FISHING DAYS IN PUBLIC WATERS. June 5 (also Sept 25). In observance of National Fishing Week these days are free fishing days in all California waters. A fishing license is not required on these days but all other rules and regulations must be followed. For info: Conservation Education, Dept of Fish and Game, 1416 Ninth St, Sacramento, CA 95814. Fax: (916) 653-1856. E-mail: smorris@hq.dfg.ca.gov.

CAPITOL HILL PEOPLE'S FAIR. June 5–6. Civic Center Park, Denver, CO. More than 500 arts and crafts and other exhibit booths; live entertainment featuring local talent on five stages. Est attendance: 300,000. For info: Capitol Hill United Neighborhoods, 1490 Lafayette, #104, Denver, CO 80218. Phone: (303) 830-1651. Fax: (303) 830-1782. E-mail: info@peoplesfair.com. Web: www.peoplesfair.com.

CHEER COACH DAY. June 5. Show appreciation for the hard work and dedication of those who coach our cheerleaders. Annually, the first Saturday in June. For info: Lindy Lundy, 59 County Rd 3474, Cleveland, TX 77327. Phone: (281) 399-8357. Fax: (713) 451-6205. E-mail: linda@unitedcheer.com.

COUNTRYSIDE VILLAGE ART FAIR. June 5–6. Omaha, NE. 34th annual show. Exhibits by 140 artists from 15 states. Juried fine arts show. Est attendance: 10,000. For info: Judy Drawbaugh, Countryside Merchants Assn, 2336 S 138th St, Omaha, NE 68144. Phone: (402) 333-9629.

DENMARK: CONSTITUTION DAY. June 5. National holiday. Commemorates Denmark's becoming a constitutional monarchy in 1849 and the new constitution adopted in 1953.

DO-DAH PARADE. June 5. Kalamazoo, MI. "Salute to Silliness." Since 1981 offbeat entries have included a precision grill team (complete with spatulas) and a herbie curbie brigade. Annually, the first Saturday in June. Est attendance: 60,000. For info: WKMI/WKFR Radio, 4154 Jennings Dr, Kalamazoo, MI 49005-

0911. Phone: (269) 344-0111. Fax: (269) 344-4223. E-mail: sbell@wkfr.com. Web: www.wkfr.com.

ENGLAND: THE DERBY. June 5. Epsom Downs. Horse races. Annually, the Saturday after the first Wednesday in June.

FIESTA BULLWHACKER. June 5–6. Mahaffie Stagecoach Stop and Farm, Olathe, KS. A multicultural celebration of Olathe's Santa Fe Trail heritage with 1800s-period demonstrations, Mexican and American music, children's games and stagecoach rides. The Mahaffie Farmstead on the Santa Fe and Oregon Trails served warm meals for travelers as a stagecoach stop from 1863 to 1869. "Bullwhackers" were the men who drove teams of oxen. Annually, the first weekend in June. Est attendance: 6,000. For info: Fiesta Bullwhacker, 1100 Kansas City Rd, Olathe, KS 66061. Phone: (913) 971-5111. Web: www.mahaffie.com.

FIRST BALLOON FLIGHT: ANNIVERSARY. June 5, 1783. The first public demonstration of a hot-air balloon flight took place at Annonay, France, where brothers Joseph and Jacques Montgolfier succeeded in launching the 33-foot-diameter *globe aerostatique* that they had invented. The unmanned balloon rose an estimated 1,500 feet and traveled, windborne, about 7,500 feet before landing after a 10-minute flight—the first sustained flight of any object achieved by man.

FORT SISSETON HISTORICAL FESTIVAL. June 5–6. Fort Sisseton State Park, Lake City, SD. Fort Sisseton comes alive the first weekend in June every year. See life as it was in 1864 when the fort was established. Cavalry drills, military costume ball, Indian dancing, Dakota Dan's medicine show, wagon train, muzzle-loader shoot, rendezvous, draft-horse pulls, fiddlers, square dancing, melodramas and arts and crafts are popular features of the festival. Est attendance: 40,000. For info: Dave Daberkow, Fort Sisseton State Park, Dept of Game, Fish and Parks, 11545 Northside Dr, Lake City, SD 57247-6142. Phone: (605) 448-5701. Fax: (605) 448-5572. Web: www.state.sd.us/gfp/.

FREDERICK FESTIVAL OF THE ARTS. June 5–6. Carroll Creek Linear Park, Frederick, MD. A juried market of more than 130 exhibitors of fine arts and fine craft. Two food courts, canoe and kayak rentals, children's interactive art center, art demos, literary activities, film festival, paved and tented booth sites and three stages of entertainment. Annually, the first weekend in June. Est attendance: 20,000. For info: Frederick Festival of the Arts, PO Box 3080, Frederick, MD 21705. Phone: (301) 694-9632. Fax: (301) 682-7378. E-mail: festarts@fred.net. Web: frederickarts.org.

GHOST TOURS. June 5–Oct 31. New Hope, PA. (Saturdays, June–November; Fridays in October, plus Halloween.) Tours meet at 8 PM sharp at Main and Perry streets. No reservations required. Rain or shine. $9 per person. No tours July 4th weekend or Labor Day weekend. For info: Ghost Tours, PO Box 3354, Warminster, PA 18974. Phone: (215) 957-9988. E-mail: ghstofpa@aol.com.

HEIRLOOM SEED DAY. June 5. Woodstock, VT. Learn about the importance of heirloom vegetables and the many seed varieties available. Take home a packet of select seeds saved from the museum's 19th-century garden. For info: Billings Farm & Museum, Box 489, Woodstock, VT 05091. Phone: (802) 457-2355. Fax: (802) 457-4663. E-mail: billings.farm@valley.net. Web: www.billingsfarm.org.

HOCKHOCKING FOLK FESTIVAL. June 5. Robbins Crossing, Hocking College Campus, Nelsonville, OH. A celebration of music, culture and heritage set in an authentic pioneer village. Headline entertainment and other musicians. Visitors are encouraged to bring instruments for jam sessions, lawn chairs and blankets. Instrument building, make and take area, storytelling, dancing and food. For info: Ken Bowald, Hocking College, 3301 Hocking Pkwy, Nelsonville, OH 45764. Phone: (740) 753-3591, ext 2875. E-mail: bowald_k@hocking.edu.

HORSERADISH FESTIVAL. June 5–6. Collinsville, IL. Join in the fun at the horseradish capital of the world. Root toss competition, "Root Derby" (build a race car out of a horseradish root and win prizes), races, food, music and more. For info: Collinsville Chamber of Commerce, 221 W Main St, Collinsville, IL 62234. Phone: (618) 344-2884.

IRAN: FIFTEENTH OF KHORDAD. June 5. National holiday. Commemorates the deaths of Islamic clerics in a clash with the shah's forces in 1963.

KENNEDY, ROBERT F.: ASSASSINATION: ANNIVERSARY. June 5, 1968. Senator Kennedy was shot while campaigning for the Democratic presidential nomination at Los Angeles, CA; he died the following day. Sirhan Sirhan was convicted of his murder.

KEYNES, JOHN MAYNARD: BIRTH ANNIVERSARY. June 5, 1883. British economist born at Cambridge, England. Author of *Treatise on Money* and *The General Theory of Employment, Interest and Money* that focused on "expansionist" economic policy. Died at Firle, England, Apr 21, 1946.

LOVELADIES FAIR. June 5–6 (tentative). Loveladies, NJ. 15th annual preseason introduction to Island and mainland merchants. Sponsored by Long Beach Island Foundation of Arts & Sciences. Est attendance: 1,500. For info: Long Beach Island Foundation of Arts & Sciences, 120 Long Beach Blvd, Loveladies, NJ 08008. Phone: (609) 494-1241. Fax: (609) 494-0662.

MALAYSIA: HEAD OF STATE'S OFFICIAL BIRTHDAY. June 5. National holiday. The first Saturday in June.

MISSOURI STATE CHAMPIONSHIP RACKING HORSE SHOW. June 5. Stoddard County Fairgrounds, Dexter, MO. At this 27th annual event elegant showmanship by both horse and rider provides an afternoon and evening of spectator pleasure. Annually, the first Saturday in June. Est attendance: 500. For info: Missouri State Championship Racking Horse Show, PO Box 21, Dexter, MO 63841. Phone: (573) 624-7458 or (800) 332-8857. Fax: (573) 624-7459.

NATIONAL HUNGER AWARENESS DAY. June 5. This day was created to increase awareness of the serious problem of hunger in the US. One in five children in this country lives in poverty and is at risk for hunger. One in ten households isn't sure where the next meal is coming from. We hope to enlist your support. Annually, June 5. For info: Jo Grant, 2802 Dairy Dr, Madison, WI 53716. Phone: (608) 223-9121. Fax: (608) 223-9840. E-mail: jgrant@secondharvest.org. Web: www.secondharvestmadison.org.

NATIONAL TRAILS DAY. June 5. National Trails Day celebrates trails and the volunteers who maintain them. The first Saturday of every June more than 3,000 trail organizations, agencies and businesses across the country host a variety of events including new trail dedications, workshops, educational exhibits, equestrian and mountain bike rides, boat paddling, rollerblading, trail maintenance projects and, as always, hikes on backcountry trails in America's wild lands. For info: American Hiking Society, 1422 Fenwick Ln, Silver Spring, MD 20910. Phone: (301) 565-6704. E-mail: info@americanhiking.org. Web: www.americanhiking.org.

PEDDLER'S VILLAGE FINE ART & CONTEMPORARY CRAFTS SHOW. June 5–6. Juried competition of paintings, prints, photography and more created by fine artists, plus contemporary crafts. Hands-on art activities for children. Shops offer various in-store exhibits and art-related events. Live music, face painting and balloons. Free admission. Est attendance: 12,000. For info: Peddler's Village, Routes 202 & 263, Lahaska, PA 18931. Phone: (215) 794-4000. Fax: (215) 794-4001. Web: www.peddlersvillage.com.

June 5 ☆ Chase's 2004 Calendar of Events ☆

PET PARADE. June 5. LaGrange, IL. Children and their pets parade through the streets of LaGrange in costume, accompanied by clowns, floats, celebrities and marching bands. Trophies awarded to the most original entries in 10 costume categories. Annually, the first Saturday in June. Est attendance: 100,000. For info: West Suburban Chamber of Commerce, PO Box 187, LaGrange, IL 60525. Phone: (708) 352-7079. Fax: (708) 352-0620. E-mail: wscc@megsinet.net. Web: www.westsuburbanchamber.org.

PRINTERS ROW BOOK FAIR. June 5-6. South Dearborn Street between Congress and Polk at Chicago, IL. More than 170 booksellers and publishers from all over the US and Canada fill the streets with new, used, rare and antiquarian books for sale; demonstrations of paper making, paper marbling and book binding; author readings, panel discussions, poetry tent and an elaborate children's program are all part of the free programs. Food, music and much more at the largest book event in the Midwest. Est attendance: 75,000. For info: Printers Row Book Fair, Chicago Tribune, 435 N Michigan, LL2, Chicago, IL 60611. Phone: (312) 222-3986. E-mail: bookfair@tribune.com. Web: www.printersrowbookfair.org.

REOPENING OF THE SCHOHARIE VALLEY RAILROADS MUSEUM. June 5. Depot Lane Complex, Schoharie, NY. Open each weekend, 1-4 PM June through October. Est attendance: 500. For info: Schoharie Colonial Heritage Assn, PO Box 554, Schoharie, NY 12157. Phone: (518) 295-7505. E-mail: scha@midtel.net.

SCARRY, RICHARD McCLURE: 85th BIRTH ANNIVERSARY. June 5, 1919. Author and illustrator of children's books was born at Boston, MA. Two widely known books of the more than 250 Scarry authored are *Richard Scarry's Best Word Book Ever* (1965) and *Richard Scarry's Please & Thank You* (1973). The pages are crowded with small animal characters who live like humans. More than 100 million copies of his books sold worldwide. Died Apr 30, 1994, at Gstaad, Switzerland.

SEASPACE. June 5-6. Reliant Arena, Astrodome, Houston, TX. Scuba diving convention featuring seminars, photo and video courses, workshops, photo contest and exhibit, film festivals, halls of exhibits, special kids talk, environmental awareness area, free intro to scuba and snorkeling and receptions. Sponsor: Houston Underwater Club. For more info send SASE. Est attendance: 10,000. For info: Seaspace, PO Box 3753, Houston, TX 77253-3753. Phone: (713) 467-6675. Web: www.seaspace.org.

SMITH, ADAM: BIRTH ANNIVERSARY. June 5, 1723 (OS). Scottish economist and philosopher, author of *An Enquiry into the Nature and Causes of the Wealth of Nations* (published in 1776), born at Kirkaldy, Fifeshire, Scotland. Died at Edinburgh, Scotland, July 17, 1790. "Consumption," he wrote, "is the sole end and purpose of production; and the interest of the producer ought to be attended to only so far as it may be necessary for promoting that of the consumer."

SOUTH JERSEY CANOE AND KAYAK CLASSIC. June 5. Ocean County Park, Rt 88, Lakewood, NJ. Canoe and kayak vendors from around the country set up on the beach to show the public the thrill of water sports. You may test paddle the boats of your choice, talk with company reps and attend a clinic or demo. Manufacturers, clubs, paddling accessories and more. Concessions. Free ($2 to test paddles). Rain or shine. Annually, the first Saturday in June. Est attendance: 1,500. For info: Michelle Urban, Coord, Wells Mills County Park, 905 Wells Mills Rd, Waretown, NJ 08758. Phone: (609) 971-3085. Fax: (609) 971-9540. Web: www.co.ocean.nj.us/parks/default.htm.

SPACE MILESTONE: *SOYUZ T-2* (USSR). June 5, 1980. Launched on this date, cosmonauts Yuri Malyshev and Vladimir Aksenov docked at *Salyut 6* on June 6 and returned to Earth June 9. First piloted flight of new T (Transport) spacecraft.

STRAWBERRY FESTIVAL. June 5. Vaile Mansion, Independence, MO. Outdoor Victorian-type festival featuring strawberry treats, crafts, antiques, children's activities, carriage rides, flea market and entertainment. Annually, first Saturday in June. Est attendance: 810. For info: Stephanie Roush, Tourism Dir, 111 E Maple, Independence, MO 64050. Phone: (816) 325-7111. Fax: (816) 325-7400. Web: www.visitindependence.com.

SUMMER READING CLUB. June 5-July 24. El Paso, TX. Every summer the El Paso Public Library has a summer reading club program. The program is open to all children from birth through 8th grade. Children are required to read/have been read to, 8 books or 8 hours, during the program to receive a certificate. The 10 libraries plus Bookmobile feature weekly special programs in the libraries for the children. For info: Laurel Indalecio, El Paso Public Library, 501 N Oregon, El Paso, TX 79901. Phone: (915) 543-5470. Fax: (915) 543-5410. E-mail: indalecioL@ci.elpaso.tx.us. Web: www.elpasolibrary.org/kidszone/kidszone_library/.

SWAP MEET AND TRACTOR SHOW. June 5-6. Washington, KS. The celebration includes swap meet, flea market, antique tractor and parts auction, antique tractor show, vehicle parade, car races, entertainment, children's games, historic demonstrators, toy show, buckle show, crafts, etc. Est attendance: 5,000. For info: Washington County Travel and Tourism, Courthouse, 214 C St, Washington, KS 66968. Phone: (785) 325-2116. Fax: (785) 325-2830. E-mail: washcott@washingtonks.net.

TOPPENISH MURAL SOCIETY'S "MURAL-IN-A-DAY." June 5. Railroad Park, Toppenish, WA. 12 professional artists paint a complete, historically authentic mural in eight hours. Starting at 9 AM they work until finished, usually until 4 PM. Accompanied by an arts and crafts show and an ethnic food fair. Annually, the first Saturday in June. Est attendance: 12,000. For info: Toppenish Mural Society, PO Box 1172, Toppenish, WA 98948. Phone: (509) 865-6516. E-mail: murals@wolfenet.com. Web: www.wolfenet.com/~murals/.

UNITED NATIONS: WORLD ENVIRONMENT DAY. June 5. Observed annually June 5, the anniversary of the opening of the UN Conference on the Human Environment held in Stockholm in 1972, which led to establishment of UN Environment Programme, based in Nairobi. The General Assembly has urged marking the day with activities reaffirming concern for the preservation and enhancement of the environment. For info: United Nations, Dept of Public Info, New York, NY 10017. Web: www.un.org.

BIRTHDAYS TODAY

Chad Allen, 30, actor ("Dr. Quinn, Medicine Woman"), cartoon voice (Charlie Brown), born Cerritos, CA, June 5, 1974.
Margaret Drabble, 65, British novelist (*The Gates of Ivory*), born Sheffield, Yorkshire, England, June 5, 1939.
Ken Follett, 55, British novelist (*The Eye of the Needle*), born Wales, UK, June 5, 1949.
Spalding Gray, 63, performance artist, actor, writer (*The Killing Fields, Swimming to Cambodia, Beyond Rangoon*), born Providence, RI, June 5, 1941.
Brian McKnight, 35, singer, born Buffalo, NY, June 5, 1969.
Bill Moyers, 70, journalist ("Bill Moyers' Journal"), born Hugo, OK, June 5, 1934.
Mark Wahlberg, 33, actor (*Boogie Nights*), also known as rapper Marky Mark (Marky Mark and the Funky Bunch, "Good Vibrations"), born Dorchester, MA, June 5, 1971.

	S	M	T	W	T	F	S
June 2004			1	2	3	4	5
	6	7	8	9	10	11	12
	13	14	15	16	17	18	19
	20	21	22	23	24	25	26
	27	28	29	30			

☆ Chase's 2004 Calendar of Events ☆

JUNE 6 — SUNDAY
Day 158 — 208 Remaining

BLACK SINGLE PARENTS' WEEK. June 6–12. This week is to honor all the black single parents who have successfully raised their sons and daughters despite poor schools, crime and drug-infested neighborhoods to be responsible, self-sufficient (and sometimes famous) citizens. For info: Will Barnes, Exec Dir, The Black Single Parents' Network, 7732 S Cottage Grove, #431, Chicago, IL 60619. Phone: (773) 933-1061. Fax: (773) 933-1059. E-mail: wwbarnes@lycos.com.

BONZA BOTTLER DAY™. June 6. To celebrate when the number of the day is the same as the number of the month. Bonza Bottler Day™ is an excuse to have a party at least once a month. For more information, see Jan 1. For info: Gail M. Berger, 14 Fernwood Dr, Taylors, SC 29687. Phone: (864) 609-9874. E-mail: gberger5@aol.com.

CHILDREN'S AWARENESS MEMORIAL DAY. June 6. A day set aside each year to remember all of America's children who have died from violence. A day to bring flowers to the gravesite, have memorial services, spend time with or write a letter to a grieving parent or grandparent. A day to mourn and reach out with healing hands of love to those in need of support. Annually, the first Sunday in June. For info: Judith Natale, NCAC America–USA, 2091 Del Monte Ave, Monterey, CA 93940. Fax: (831) 655-4547. E-mail: childaware@aol.com.

D-DAY: 60th ANNIVERSARY. June 6, 1944. In the early-morning hours Allied forces landed in Normandy on the north coast of France. In an operation that took months of planning, a fleet of 2,727 ships of every description converged from British ports from Wales to the North Sea. Operation *Overlord* involved 2,000,000 tons of war materials, including more than 50,000 tanks, armored cars, jeeps, trucks and half-tracks. The US alone sent 1,700,000 fighting men. The Germans believed the invasion would not take place under the adverse weather conditions of this early June day. But as the sun came up the village of Saint Mère Eglise was liberated by American parachutists, and by nightfall the landing of 155,000 Allies attested to the success of D-Day. The long-awaited second front had at last materialized.

FIRST DRIVE-IN MOVIE OPENS: ANNIVERSARY. June 6, 1933. Richard M. Hollingshead, Jr, opened America's first drive-in movie theater in Camden, NJ, on this date. At the height of their popularity in 1958, there were more than 4,000 drive-ins across America. In the 1990s fewer than 600 remained open.

GERMANFEST. June 6–12. Fort Wayne, IN. A celebration of German heritage with folk music, folk dancing, beer tents, German food, beer and wine tastings, Männerchor (men's choir) singing, Gottesdienste (masses), classical organ music, Family Fest, German films, lectures and demonstrations. Est attendance: 80,000. For info: Germanfest Committee, PO Box 10971, Fort Wayne, IN 46855. Phone: (800) 767-7752. Fax: (260) 436-4064. E-mail: kscheib@mail.fwi.com. Web: www.germanfest.org.

HALE, NATHAN: BIRTH ANNIVERSARY. June 6, 1755. American patriot Nathan Hale was born at Coventry, CT. During the battles for New York in the American Revolution, he volunteered to seek military intelligence behind enemy lines and was captured on the night of Sept 21, 1776. In an audience before General William Howe, Hale admitted he was an American officer and was ordered hanged the following morning. Although some question them, his dying words, "I only regret that I have but one life to lose for my country," have become a symbol of American patriotism. He was hanged Sept 22, 1776, at Manhattan, NY.

INTERNATIONAL CARILLON FESTIVAL. June 6–13. Springfield, IL. A week of recitals by the world's best carillonneurs on Washington Park's carillon of 67 bronze bells. Since it began in 1961, this has become the world's best-known carillon festival. Est attendance: 25,000. For info: Karl Keldermans, Springfield Park District, PO Box 5052, Springfield, IL 62705. Phone: (217) 753-6219. E-mail: KKRees@Carillon-Rees.org.

ITALY: GIOCO DEL PONTE. June 6. Pisa. The first Sunday in June is set aside for the Battle of the Bridge, a medieval parade and a contest for possession of the bridge.

JAPAN: DAY OF THE RICE GOD. June 6. Chiyoda. Annual rice-transplanting festival observed on first Sunday in June. Centuries-old rural folk ritual revived in 1930s and celebrated with colorful costumes, parades, music, dancing and prayers to the Shinto rice god Wbai-sama.

KHACHATURIAN, ARAM (ILICH): BIRTH ANNIVERSARY. June 6, 1903. Armenian musician and composer, noted for compositions based on folk music and legend, born at Tbilisi, Georgia, Russia. Died at Moscow, May 1, 1978.

KOREA: MEMORIAL DAY. June 6. Nation pays tribute to the war dead and memorial services are held at the National Cemetery in Seoul. Legally recognized Korean holiday.

NATIONAL CANCER SURVIVORS DAY. June 6. More than 700 communities nationwide honor survivors who are living with and beyond cancer. The 17th annual celebration of life. Annually, the first Sunday in June. For info: Natl Cancer Survivors Day Foundation, PO Box 682285, Franklin, TN 37068-2285. Phone: (615) 793-3006. Fax: (615) 794-0179. Web: www.ncsdf.org.

NATIONAL HEADACHE AWARENESS WEEK. June 6–12. Educating the public about the reality and severity of headache pain as a legitimate biological disease. Encouraging sufferers to consult with a physician for proper diagnosis and treatment, and to let sufferers know that there are new treatments available. For info: Suzanne E Simons, Exec Dir, National Headache Foundation, 820 N Orleans, Ste 217, Chicago, IL 60610-3132. Phone: (312) 640-5399. Fax: (312) 640-9049.

ORTHODOX FESTIVAL OF ALL SAINTS. June 6. Observed by Eastern Orthodox churches on the Sunday following Orthodox Pentecost (May 30 in 2004). Marks the end of the 18-week Triodion cycle.

PROPOSITION 13: ANNIVERSARY. June 6, 1978. California voters (65 percent of them) supported a primary election ballot initiative to cut property taxes 57 percent. Regarded as a possible omen of things to come across the country—a taxpayers' revolt against high taxes and government spending.

PUSHKIN, ALEXANDER: BIRTH ANNIVERSARY. June 6, 1799. Russian poet (*Eugene Onegin*, a novel in verse), born at Moscow. Died Feb 10, 1837, at St. Petersburg as the result of a duel.

RED CLOUD INDIAN ART SHOW. June 6–Aug 15. Pine Ridge, SD. Encourages Native American artists and gives their artwork exposure to the general public. Juried art show with cash awards. Est attendance: 12,500. For info: Brother C.M. Simon, Red Cloud Indian School, Pine Ridge, SD 57770. Phone: (605) 867-5491. Fax: (605) 867-1291. Web: www.redcloudschool.org.

REOPENING OF THE 1743 PALATINE HOUSE MUSEUM. June 6. Schoharie, NY. Open Thursday through Monday 12–4 PM, June through October. The Palatine House is a living museum and is the oldest existing building in Schoharie County. Est attendance: 900. For info: Angela DeGroff, Program Dir, Schoharie Colonial Heritage Assn, PO Box 554, Schoharie, NY 12157. Phone: (518) 295-7505 or (518) 295-7585. E-mail: scha@midtel.net.

June 6-7 ☆ Chase's 2004 Calendar of Events ☆

SCOTT, ROBERT FALCON: BIRTH ANNIVERSARY. June 6, 1868. British naval officer and polar explorer, born at Devonport, England. Led the ill-starred expedition to the South Pole that arrived on Jan 18, 1912—one month after Norwegian Roald Amundsen's team became the first humans to set foot on the South Pole. Scott and four team members died on the return journey and their bodies were found November 1912. Scott's diary, with a final entry of Mar 29, 1912, had a message to the public: "Had we lived, I should have had a tale to tell of the hardihood, endurance, and courage of my companions which would have stirred the heart of every Englishman. These rough notes and our dead bodies must tell the tale. . . ."

SECURITIES AND EXCHANGE COMMISSION CREATED: 70th ANNIVERSARY. June 6, 1934. President Franklin D. Roosevelt signed the Securities Exchange Act that established the SEC. Wall Street had operated almost unfettered since the end of the eighteenth century. However, the stock market crash of 1929 necessitated regulation of the exchanges. The Securities and Exchange Commission is composed of five members appointed by the president of the US.

"SEX AND THE CITY" TV PREMIERE: ANNIVERSARY. June 6, 1998. HBO's modern comedy of manners focuses on four fashionable women navigating the perilous waters of New York City's dating scene. Stars Sarah Jessica Parker (Carrie Bradshaw), Kristin Davis (Charlotte York), Kim Cattrall (Samantha Jones) and Cynthia Nixon (Miranda Hobbes).

SPACE MILESTONE: SOYUZ 11 (USSR). June 6, 1971. Launched with cosmonauts G.T. Dobrovolsky, V.N. Volkov and V.I. Patsayev, who died during the return landing June 30, 1971, after a 24-day space flight. Soyuz 11 had docked at Salyut orbital space station June 7-29; the cosmonauts entered the space station for the first time and conducted scientific experiments. First humans to die in space.

SUSAN B. ANTHONY FINED FOR VOTING: ANNIVERSARY. June 6, 1872. Seeking to test for women the citizenship and voting rights extended to black males under the 14th and 15th Amendments, Susan B. Anthony led a group of women who registered and voted at a Rochester, NY, election. She was arrested, tried and sentenced to pay a fine. She refused to do so and was allowed to go free by a judge who feared she would appeal to a higher court.

SUYDAM HOMESTEAD AND BARN MUSEUM. June 6–Oct 3 (Sundays). Centerport, NY. This 1730 home, listed in the National Register of Historic Places, has been restored to the way it looked in 1790. The Suydam House has a gallery that contains one of Long Island's largest archeological finds of Huntington Redware, English China and early Creamware, unearthed from under the west wing of the House. The Barn Museum features old farm tools and wagons and an exhibit of local early 19th-century furnishings. For info: Michelle Athanas, Director, Greenlawn Centerport Historical Association, PO Box 354, Greenlawn, NY 11740. Phone: (631) 754-1180. Fax: (631) 757-7216. E-mail: gcha-info@usa.net. Web: gcha.suffolk.lib.ny.us.

SWEDEN: FLAG DAY. June 6. Commemorates the day upon which Gustavus I (Gustavus Vasa) ascended the throne of Sweden in 1523.

TRINITY SUNDAY. June 6. Christian Holy Day on the Sunday after Pentecost commemorates the Holy Trinity, the three divine persons—Father, Son and Holy Spirit—in one God. See also: "Pentecost" (May 30).

★ ★ ★

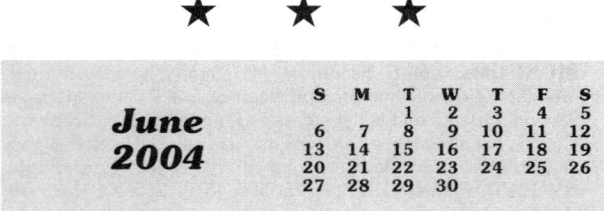

"20/20" TV PREMIERE: ANNIVERSARY. June 6, 1978. An hourly newsmagazine developed by ABC to compete with CBS's "60 Minutes." Its original hosts, Harold Hayes and Robert Hughes, were cut after the first show and replaced by Hugh Downs. Barbara Walters became coanchor in 1984. The show consisted of investigative and background reports. Contributors to the show have included Tom Jarriel, Sylvia Chase, Geraldo Rivera, Thomas Hoving, John Stossel, Lynn Sherr and Stone Phillips.

BIRTHDAYS TODAY

Sandra Bernhard, 49, comedienne, actress ("Roseanne"), born Flint, MI, June 6, 1955.
Gary U.S. Bonds, 65, singer ("Quarter to Three"), songwriter, born Gary Anderson, Jacksonville, FL, June 6, 1939.
Bjorn Rune Borg, 48, former tennis player, born Sodertalje, Sweden, June 6, 1956.
Dalai Lama, 69, Tibet's spiritual leader and Nobel Peace Prize winner, born Taktser, China, June 6, 1935.
Marian Wright Edelman, 65, president of Children's Defense Fund, civil rights activist, born Bennettsville, SC, June 6, 1939.
Harvey Fierstein, 50, playwright (Tony Awards for *Hairspray*, *Torch Song Trilogy*, *Tidy Endings*), born Brooklyn, NY, June 6, 1954.
Kenny G, 48, sax player, born Kenny Gorelick, Seattle, WA, June 6, 1956.
Amanda Pays, 45, actress ("Max Headroom," *Exposure*), born Berkshire, England, June 6, 1959.
Billie Whitelaw, 72, actress (*The Dressmaker*, "Masterpiece Theater"), born Coventry, England, June 6, 1932.

JUNE 7 — MONDAY
Day 159 — 207 Remaining

APGAR, VIRGINIA: 95th BIRTH ANNIVERSARY. June 7, 1909. Dr. Apgar developed the simple assessment method that permits doctors and nurses to evaluate newborns while they are still in the delivery room to identify those in need of immediate medical care. The Apgar score was first published in 1953, and the Perinatal Section of the American Academy of Pediatrics is named for Dr. Apgar. Born at Westfield, NJ, Apgar died Aug 7, 1974, at New York, NY.

BOONE DAY. June 7. Each year on June 7, the Kentucky Historical Society celebrates the anniversary of the day in 1767 when Daniel Boone, America's most famous frontiersman, reportedly first sighted the land that would become Kentucky. The June 7 date is taken from the book *The Discovery, Settlement and Present State of Kentucky*, by John Filson, published in 1784, with an appendix titled "The Adventures of Colonel Daniel Boone." The information in the appendix supposedly originated with Boone, although Filson is the actual author. The work is not considered completely reliable by historians.

BRUMMELL, GEORGE BRYAN "BEAU": BIRTH ANNIVERSARY. June 7, 1778. Born at London, England, Beau Brummell was, early in his life, a popular English men's fashion leader, the "arbiter elegantarium" of taste in dress. His extravagance and lack of tact (it was he who reportedly said—

316

indicating the Prince of Wales, later George IV—"Who's your fat friend?") led him from wealth and popularity to poverty and disrepute. Once imprisoned for debt, he became careless of dress and personal appearance. He died in a charitable asylum at Caen, France, Mar 30, 1840.

GAUGUIN, (EUGENE HENRI) PAUL: BIRTH ANNIVERSARY. June 7, 1848. French painter born at Paris, France. Formerly a stockbroker, he became a painter in his middle age and three years later renounced his life at Paris to move to Tahiti. He is remembered best for his broad, flat tones and bold colors. Gauguin died May 8, 1903, at Atoana on the island of Hiva Oa in the Marquesas.

INTERNATIONAL PIANO COMPETITION FOR OUTSTANDING AMATEURS. June 7–12. Fort Worth, TX. This 4th competition presented by the Van Cliburn Foundation features pianists above the age of 35 whose principal source of income is not derived from piano performance or teaching piano. These amateurs engage in the study of music as a serious pastime rather than as a profession. Held every two years. Sponsored by Steinway & Sons. For info: Van Cliburn Foundation, 2525 Ridgmar Blvd, Ste 307, Fort Worth, TX 76116. Phone: (817) 738-6536. Fax: (817) 738-6534. E-mail: clistaff@cliburn.org. Web: www.cliburn.org.

MALTA: NATIONAL DAY. June 7. National day or (in Maltese) Sette Giugno.

MARTIN, DEAN: BIRTH ANNIVERSARY. June 7, 1917. Actor/singer Dean Martin was born Dino Paul Crocetti, at Steubenville, OH. Martin's career was barely moving in 1946, when he met Jerry Lewis. Together they formed an unforgettable comedy act that carried them to dizzying heights of success. When the team broke up, Martin found continued success as a singer as well as a Hollywood film star. He died Dec 25, 1995, at Beverly Hills, CA.

OLD TIME SCHOOL. June 7–July 9. West Riverside Historic Site, Cambridge, MN. Children attend school in a one-room schoolhouse from 1898. They dress in the style of Laura Ingalls Wilder, carry their lunch in a pail, play games and learn lessons from the year 1900, do art projects, give a program for parents and actually have homework. There are five one-week sessions beginning in mid-June. Students in grades 1–8 may apply. $40 fee. Est attendance: 300. For info: Kathy McCully, Dir, Isanti County Historical Society, PO Box 525, Cambridge, MN 55008. Phone: (763) 689-4229. Fax: (763) 689-4229. E-mail: mccully @usfamily.net.

SHUTTLE CAMP®. June 7–July 30. New Mexico Museum of Space History, Alamogordo, NM. Annual series of week-long residential and day space science camps. Rocket-building classes, field trips and astronomy classes. Est attendance: 750. For info: Shuttle Camp®, New Mexico Museum of Space History, PO Box 5430, Alamogordo, NM 88311-0533. Phone: (877) 333-6589. Fax: (505) 437-7722. E-mail: space-ed@zianet.com. Web: www.spacefame.org/camp.html.

"THE $64,000 QUESTION" TV PREMIERE: ANNIVERSARY. June 7, 1955. This game show was a big hit, and the first of prime time's big money shows. Contestants, each an expert in one area, answered questions; each time a question was answered correctly, contestants doubled their money and the questions became harder. Players, if successful, could come back the following week. For the $64,000 question, a player could bring along an expert, but if neither got the correct answer, the player left with $4,000. The host was Hal March, assisted by Lynn Dollar and later Pat Donovan, and questions were compiled by Dr. Bergen Evans. Some famous contestants were Dr. Joyce Brothers, Barbara Feldon and Jack Benny (as a joke). The show was dropped in 1958 amid the game show scandals.

SUPREME COURT STRIKES DOWN CONNECTICUT LAW BANNING CONTRACEPTION: ANNIVERSARY. June 7, 1965. In *Griswold v Connecticut*, the Supreme Court guaranteed the right to privacy, including the freedom from government intrusion into matters of birth control.

UPPERVILLE COLT AND HORSE SHOW. June 7–13. A week-long "A-rated" horse show involving hundreds of horse and rider combinations from 8- to 10-year-old children in the pony divisions to leading Olympic and World Cup riders and horses in the Hunter, Jumper and Grand Prix divisions. Sunday's highlight is the prestigious $100,000 Budweiser/Upperville Jumper Classic sponsored by Budweiser. Est attendance: 6,000. For info: Tommy L. Jones, Upperville Colt and Horse Show, PO Box 317, The Plains, VA 20198. Phone: (540) 253-5760. Fax: (540) 253-5761. E-mail: uchs@crosslink.net. Web: www.upperville.com.

VCR INTRODUCED: ANNIVERSARY. June 7, 1975. The Sony Corporation released its videocassette recorder, the Betamax, which sold for $995. Eventually, another VCR format, VHS, proved more successful and Sony stopped making the Betamax.

BIRTHDAYS TODAY

Louise Erdrich, 50, author (*Love Medicine*, *The Beet Queen*), born Little Falls, MN, June 7, 1954.
Allen Iverson, 29, basketball player, born Hampton, VA, June 7, 1975.
Jenny Jones, 58, talk-show host, born London, ON, Canada, June 7, 1946.
Tom Jones, 64, singer ("It's Not Unusual"), born Thomas Woodward, Pontypridd, Wales, UK, June 7, 1940.
Anna Kournikova, 23, tennis player, born Moscow, Russia, June 7, 1981.
Bill Kreutzmann, Jr, 58, drummer, singer, cofounder of The Grateful Dead, born Palo Alto, CA, June 7, 1946.
Mike Modano, 34, hockey player, born Livonia, MI, June 7, 1970.
Liam Neeson, 52, actor (*Excalibur*, *Ethan Frome*, *Schindler's List*), born Ballymena, Northern Ireland, June 7, 1952.
Prince, 46, musician, singer, born Prince Rogers Nelson, Minneapolis, MN, June 7, 1958.
John Napier Turner, 75, Canada's 17th prime minister (served June 30, 1984–Sept 17, 1984), born Richmond, Surrey, England, June 7, 1929.

JUNE 8 — TUESDAY
Day 160 — 206 Remaining

AMERICAN HEROINE REWARDED: ANNIVERSARY. June 8, 1697. On Mar 16, 1697, in an attack on Haverhill, MA, Indians captured Hannah Duston and killed her baby, killing or capturing 39 others in addition. After being taken to an Indian camp, she escaped on Apr 29 after killing 10 Indians with a tomahawk and scalping them as proof of her deed. On June 8 her husband was awarded, on her behalf, the sum of 25 pounds for her heroic efforts, the first public award to a woman in America.

ATTACK ON THE USS *LIBERTY*: ANNIVERSARY. June 8, 1967. At 2 PM local time, the unescorted US intelligence ship USS *Liberty*, sailing in international waters off the Egyptian coast, was attacked without warning by Israeli jet planes and three Israeli torpedo boats. She was strafed and hit repeatedly by rockets, cannon, napalm and finally a torpedo. Casualties: out of a crew of 294 Americans, there were 34 dead and 171 wounded. Israel apologized, claiming mistaken identity, but surviving crew members charged deliberate attack by Israel and cover-up by US authorities.

June 8 ☆ Chase's 2004 Calendar of Events ☆

BEEF EMPIRE DAYS. June 8–20. Finney County Fairgrounds, Garden City, KS. 36th annual celebration of the beef industry. Live and carcass show; PRCA rodeo (three nights); parade; beef tasting for the public; cowboy poetry; Professional Western Art Show; feedlot roping and riding; walk/run; golf, softball and tennis tournaments; children's events. Annually, in June. Est attendance: 75,000. For info: Beef Empire Days, PO Box 1197, Garden City, KS 67846-1197. Phone: (620) 275-6807. Web: www.beefempiredays.com.

BILL OF RIGHTS PROPOSAL: ANNIVERSARY. June 8, 1789. The Bill of Rights, which led to the first 10 amendments to the US Constitution, was first proposed by James Madison.

CHUY'S NATIONAL TACO DAY™. June 8. To honor and celebrate the taco, one of our most versatile and convenient foods. The taco is a small meal made by simply rolling up your favorite ingredient in a fresh tortilla. Celebration festivities include cheap tacos and fun giveaways. Annually, the second Tuesday in June. For info: Ashley Mokry, Chuy's, 1623 Toomey Rd, Austin, TX 78704. Phone: (888) HEY-CHUY. Web: www.chuys.com.

COCHISE: DEATH ANNIVERSARY. June 8, 1874. Born around 1810 in the Chiricahua Mountains of Arizona, Cochise became a fierce and courageous leader of the Apache. After his arrest in 1861, he escaped and launched the Apache Wars, which lasted for 25 years. He died 13 years later near his stronghold in southeastern Arizona.

ICELAND: LAKI VOLCANO ERUPTION: ANNIVERSARY. June 8, 1783. One of the most violent and important volcanic eruptions of recorded history began on this date. Laki, or Skafta, volcano in southern Iceland continued erupting for eight months, expelling an estimated 4½ cubic miles of lava, ultimately causing a famine and the deaths of nearly 10,000 persons. Acid rain reached western Europe, and other climatic and atmospheric changes were worldwide. English naturalist Gilbert White described some of the "horrible phenomena" of the summer of 1783, including the "peculiar haze, or smokey fog . . . unlike anything known within the memory of man." The effects of this volcanic eruption and its possible long-term consequences are still being studied by scientists. See also: "White, Gilbert: Birth Anniversary" (July 18).

McKINLEY, IDA SAXTON: BIRTH ANNIVERSARY. June 8, 1847. Wife of William McKinley, 25th president of the US, born at Canton, OH. Died at Canton, OH, May 26, 1907.

SPACE MILESTONE: *VENERA 9* AND *10* (USSR). June 8 and 14, 1975. Launched on this date, unmanned exploration vehicles landed on Venus Oct 22 and 25. Sent first pictures ever transmitted from Venus, atmospheric analysis and other data.

TRANSIT OF VENUS. June 8. Passage of Venus across the face of the sun. Visible in Alaska, Australia, Asia, Africa, Europe, Greenland, South America (except southern part) and North America (except western part). Very rare phenomena that has only happened six times in the last 400 years. Transits of Venus occur in pairs roughly every 125 years–the last times in 1874 and 1882. The next transit of Venus (and the last of the 21st century) occurs June 6, 2012.

UPSY DAISY DAY. June 8. A day to remind people to get up gloriously, gratefully and gleefully each morning. For info: Stephanie West Allen, PO Box 9311, Denver, CO 80209. Phone: (303) 742-4790. E-mail: stephanie@allen-nichols.com. Web: www.allen-nichols.com.

WHITE, BYRON RAYMOND: BIRTH ANNIVERSARY. June 8, 1917. One of the longest serving justices of the Supreme Court of the US, Byron White was born June 8, 1917, at Fort Collins, CO. He was a football star in college (College Football Hall of Fame) and in the National Football League, as well as an academic standout: he was a Rhodes Scholar among other honors. A graduate of Yale Law School, White was a successful lawyer and director of the Justice Department before being nominated by President Kennedy for the highest court on Apr 3, 1962. White took the oath of office Apr 16, 1962, and served 31 years before retiring in 1993. He died on April 15, 2002, at Denver, CO.

WRIGHT, FRANK LLOYD: BIRTH ANNIVERSARY. June 8, 1867. American architect born at Richland Center, WI. In his autobiography Wright wrote: "No house should ever be *on* any hill or on anything. It should be *of* the hill, belonging to it, so hill and house could live together each the happier for the other." Wright died at Phoenix, AZ, Apr 9, 1959.

WYTHE, GEORGE: DEATH ANNIVERSARY. June 8, 1806. Signer of the Declaration of Independence. Born at Elizabeth County, VA, about 1726 (exact date unknown). Died at Richmond, VA.

BIRTHDAYS TODAY

Scott Adams, 47, cartoonist ("Dilbert"), born Windham, NY, June 8, 1957.
Kathy Baker, 54, actress ("Picket Fences," *The Right Stuff*), born Midland, TX, June 8, 1950.
Tim Berners-Lee, 49, inventor of the World Wide Web, born London, England, June 8, 1955.
Barbara Pierce Bush, 79, former First Lady, wife of George H.W. Bush, 41st president of the US, born Rye, NY, June 8, 1925.
Bernie Casey, 65, former football player, actor (*I'm Gonna Git You Sucka, Bill & Ted's Excellent Adventure, Roots: The Next Generations*), born Wyco, WV, June 8, 1939.
Kim Clijsters, 21, tennis player, born Bilzen, Belgium, June 8, 1983.
Francis Crick, 88, discoverer (with James Watson) of the structure of DNA, born Northhampton, England, June 8, 1916.
James Darren, 68, singer ("Goodbye Cruel World"), actor (*Gidget*), born Philadelphia, PA, June 8, 1936.
Lindsay Davenport, 28, tennis player, born Palos Verdes, CA, June 8, 1976.
Griffin Dunne, 49, actor (*Straight Talk*), producer, born New York, NY, June 8, 1955.
Don Grady, 60, actor ("My Three Sons," "Mickey Mouse Club"), born San Diego, CA, June 8, 1944.
Julianna Margulies, 38, actress ("ER"), born Spring Valley, NY, June 8, 1966.
Sara Paretsky, 57, writer (*Killing Orders, Burn Marks*), born Ames, IA, June 8, 1947.
Joan Rivers, 67, comedienne, talk-show host, born New York, NY, June 8, 1937.
Boz Scaggs, 60, singer, musician, songwriter (*Silk Degrees, Middle Man*), born Dallas, TX, June 8, 1944.
Nancy Sinatra, 64, singer ("These Boots Are Made for Walkin'," "Something Stupid"), born Jersey City, NJ, June 8, 1940.
Jerry Stiller, 75, comedian, actor (*Hairspray*, "Seinfeld," "The King of Queens"), born Brooklyn, NY, June 8, 1929.
Keenen Ivory Wayans, 46, actor ("In Living Color"), born New York, NY, June 8, 1958.
Andrew Weil, MD, 62, physician and writer on natural healing, born Philadelphia, PA, June 8, 1942.

	S	M	T	W	T	F	S
June 2004			1	2	3	4	5
	6	7	8	9	10	11	12
	13	14	15	16	17	18	19
	20	21	22	23	24	25	26
	27	28	29	30			

☆ Chase's 2004 Calendar of Events ☆   June 9

JUNE 9 — WEDNESDAY
Day 161 — 205 Remaining

BOCA GRANDE TARPON TOURNAMENT ("WORLD'S RICHEST"). June 9–10. Boca Grande Pass, Boca Grande, FL. Tarpon fishing; field limited to 60 boats; entry fee $5,200 per boat. With 60 entries, first place (largest tarpon) pays off $150,000. Est attendance: 1,000. For info: Boca Grande Chamber of Commerce, PO Box 704, Boca Grande, FL 33921. Phone: (941) 964-0568. Fax: (941) 964-0620. E-mail: chamber@bocagrande.net. Web: www.worldsrichesttarpon.com.

CANADA: THE NATIONAL TOURNAMENT. June 9–13. Spruce Meadows, Calgary, AB. The National Tournament features the Spruce Meadows Show Jumping Championship, including the Direct Energy Grand Prix Cup and the Shell Cup. Enjoy country atmosphere in the Agrium Country Fair on the Spruce Meadows Plaza. Live entertainment and activities daily. First week of June, Wednesday through Sunday. Est attendance: 85,750. For info: Spruce Meadows, RR 9, Calgary, AB, Canada T2J 5G5. Phone: (403) 974-4200. Fax: (403) 974-4270. E-mail: information@sprucemeadows.com. Web: www.sprucemeadows.com.

CUMMINGS, ROBERT: BIRTH ANNIVERSARY. June 9, 1908. American actor Robert Cummings was born Charles Clarence Robert Orville Cummings at Joplin, MO. His best-known role was in the film *Dial M for Murder* (1954). He won an Emmy for his role in the television version of *Twelve Angry Men* (1954) and starred in the popular comedy "The Bob Cummings Show" (1955–59). He died Dec 2, 1990, at Woodland Hills, CA.

DONALD DUCK: BIRTHDAY. June 9, 1934. Donald Duck was "born."

GLENN MILLER BIRTHPLACE SOCIETY FESTIVAL. June 9–13. Clarinda, IA. To commemorate Glenn Miller's contribution to big band music through exhibits, concerts, films, performances by winners of Glenn Miller scholarships and a big band dance. Annually, the second full weekend in June. Est attendance: 5,000. For info: Glenn Miller Birthplace Society, PO Box 61, Clarinda, IA 51632. Phone: (712) 542-2461. Fax: (712) 542-2461. E-mail: gmbs@heartland.net. Web: www.glennmiller.org.

HONG KONG: LEASE SIGNING ANNIVERSARY. June 9, 1898. Hong Kong, consisting of about 400 square miles (islands and mainland) with more than five million persons, was administered as a British Crown Colony after a 99-year lease was signed on June 9, 1898. In 1997 Hong Kong's sovereignty reverted to the People's Republic of China.

JORDAN: ACCESSION DAY. June 9. National holiday. Commemorates the accession to the throne of King Abdullah II in 1999, following the death of his father, King Hussein.

KUTNER, LUIS: BIRTH ANNIVERSARY. June 9, 1908. Human rights attorney Luis Kutner was born at Chicago, IL. Responsible for the release of many unjustly confined prisoners, he came to be known as "The Springman." He helped free Hungarian Cardinal Josef Mindszenty, poet Ezra Pound and former Congo President Moïse Tshombe. He was the author of the living will and founded the World Habeas Corpus. Kutner was nominated nine times for the Nobel Peace Prize. He died Mar 1, 1993, at Chicago, IL.

LOLOMA, CHARLES: BIRTH ANNIVERSARY. June 9, 1921. Charles Loloma was a major influence on modern Native American art and was famous for changing the look of American Indian jewelry. A painter, sculptor and potter, he was best known for his jewelry, which broke tradition with previous Indian styles using materials such as coral, fossilized ivory, pearls and diamonds. Loloma was born at Hotevilla on the Hopi Indian Reservation and died June 9, 1991, at Scottsdale, AZ.

MOON PHASE: LAST QUARTER. June 9. Moon enters Last Quarter phase at 4:02 PM, EDT.

NCAA DIVISION I MEN'S & WOMEN'S OUTDOOR TRACK & FIELD CHAMPIONSHIPS. June 9–12. University of Texas, Austin, TX. Est attendance: 20,000. For info: NCAA, 700 W Washington Ave, PO Box 6222, Indianapolis, IN 46206-6222. Phone: (317) 917-6222. Fax: (317) 917-6825. Web: www.ncaasports.com.

PAYNE, JOHN HOWARD: BIRTH ANNIVERSARY. June 9, 1791. American author, actor, diplomat, born at New York, NY. Died at Tunis, Apr 9, 1852. Author of opera libretto (*Clari, or The Maid of Milan*), that contained the song "Home, Sweet Home."

PORTER, COLE: BIRTH ANNIVERSARY. June 9, 1891. Cole Porter published his first song, "The Bobolink Waltz," at the age of 10. His career as a composer and lyricist for Broadway was launched in 1928 when five of his songs were used in the musical play *Let's Do It*. His prolific contributions to the Broadway stage include *Fifty Million Frenchmen, Wake Up and Dream, The Gay Divorcée, Anything Goes, Leave It to Me, Du Barry Was a Lady, Something for the Boys, Kiss Me Kate, Can Can* and *Silk Stockings*. Porter was born at Peru, IN, and died at Santa Monica, CA, Oct 15, 1964.

RED RIVER RODEO. June 9–12. Wichita Falls, TX. Professional circuit rodeo held at the Wichita County Mounted Patrol Arena, this event features all of the traditional rodeo attractions as well as a dance. Est attendance: 10,000. For info: Wichita Falls Conv & Visitors Bureau, 1000 5th St, Wichita Falls, TX 76301. Phone: (940) 716-5500. Fax: (940) 716-5509. Web: www.wichitafalls.org.

STEPHENSON, GEORGE: BIRTH ANNIVERSARY. June 9, 1781. English inventor, developer of the steam locomotive, born near Newcastle, England. Died near Chesterfield, England, Aug 12, 1848.

THAYER, SYLVANUS: BIRTH ANNIVERSARY. June 9, 1785. A military engineer and educator, born at Braintree, MA. He was appointed superintendent of West Point at 32 and became known as the "Father of the Military Academy." Thayer died at Braintree, MA, Sept 7, 1872.

VIRGINIA PORK FESTIVAL. June 9. Emporia, VA. One of the east coast's largest food festivals promoting the pork industry and featuring 37 different products that are available on an all-you-can-eat basis. Festival also features five stages of live entertainment. Est attendance: 20,000. For info: Kendra Novey, Admit One Festivals, 425-E S Main St, PO Box 1001, Emporia, VA 23847-1001. Phone: (800) 482-7675. Fax: (434) 348-0119. E-mail: knovey@admit1fest.com. Web: www.vaporkfestival.com.

BIRTHDAYS TODAY

George Axelrod, 82, writer (screenplays *Bus Stop, Breakfast at Tiffany's*), born New York, NY, June 9, 1922.

Patricia Cornwell, 48, mystery writer (*All That Remains, Postmortem*), born Miami, FL, June 9, 1956.

Johnny Depp, 41, actor ("21 Jump Street," *Edward Scissorhands, Ed Wood*), born Owensboro, KY, June 9, 1963.

Michael J. Fox, 43, actor ("Family Ties," "Spin City," *Back to the Future* films), born Edmonton, AB, Canada, June 9, 1961.

Marvin Kalb, 74, educator, journalist, born New York, NY, June 9, 1930.

Jackie Mason, 70, comedian ("Chicken Soup," *The World According to Me*), born Yacov Moshe Maza, Sheboygan, WI, June 9, 1934.

Robert S. McNamara, 88, banker, former cabinet member, born San Francisco, CA, June 9, 1916.

David Gene (Dave) Parker, 53, former baseball player, born Calhoun, MS, June 9, 1951.

Les Paul, 89, musician, singer (with the late Mary Ford; "Hummingbird"), born Waukesha, WI, June 9, 1915.

Natalie Portman, 23, actress (*Star Wars* trilogy, *Anywhere But Here*), born Jerusalem, June 9, 1981.

319

June 9–10 ☆ *Chase's 2004 Calendar of Events* ☆

Ashley Postell, 18, gymnast, born Cheverly, MD, June 9, 1986.
Gloria Reuben, 40, actress ("ER"), born Toronto, ON, Canada, June 9, 1964.
Peja Stojakovic, 27, basketball player, born Predrag Stojakovic at Belgrade, Yugoslavia, June 9, 1977.
Dick Vitale, 65, sportscaster, ESPN and ABC analyst, born East Rutherford, NJ, June 9, 1939.

JUNE 10 — THURSDAY
Day 162 — 204 Remaining

ALCOHOLICS ANONYMOUS: FOUNDING ANNIVERSARY. June 10, 1935. On this day at Akron, OH, Dr. Robert Smith completed his first day of permanent sobriety. "Doctor Bob" and William G. Wilson are considered to have founded Alcoholics Anonymous on that day.

BALL-POINT PEN PATENTED: ANNIVERSARY. June 10, 1943. Hungarian Laszlo Biro patented the ball-point pen, which he had been developing since the 1930s. He was living at Argentina, where he had gone to escape the Nazis. In many languages, the word for ball-point pen is "biro."

BATTLE CREEK CEREAL FESTIVAL (WITH WORLD'S LARGEST BREAKFAST TABLE). June 10–13. Battle Creek, MI. Thursday: festival parade, downtown from 6 to 8 PM. Saturday events include arts and crafts, 5K and 10K races, family fun walk, food bank fund-raiser, vendor booths and children's games. The World's Largest Breakfast Table will be on Saturday 8 AM–12 noon. Est attendance: 60,000. For info: Battle Creek Cereal Festival, Greater Battle Creek Visitor and Conv Bureau, 77 E Michigan Ave, Battle Creek, MI 49015. Phone: (269) 962-2240 or (800) 397-2240.

CANADA: WINNIPEG INTERNATIONAL CHILDREN'S FESTIVAL. June 10–13 (tentative). The Forks, Winnipeg, MB. Festival features song, dance, theater, mime, puppetry and music by local, national and international artists. Est attendance: 20,000. For info: Box Office, Winnipeg Intl Children's Fest, 219 Provencher Blvd, 3rd Fl, Winnipeg, MB, Canada R2H 0G4. Phone: (204) 958-4730 or (800) 527-1515. Fax: (204) 231-8017. Web: www.kidsfest.ca.

CHICAGO BLUES FESTIVAL. June 10–13. Grant Park, Chicago, IL. 21st annual. Largest free blues festival in the world. Est attendance: 650,000. For info: Mayor's Office of Special Events, City Hall, 121 N LaSalle St, #703, Chicago, IL 60602. Phone: (312) 744-3370. Fax: (312) 744-8523. E-mail: SpecialEvents@cityofchicago.org. Web: www.ci.chi.il.us/SpecialEvents.

CONGO (BRAZZAVILLE): DAY OF NATIONAL RECONCILIATION. June 10. National holiday. Commemorates official conference in 1991.

CORPUS CHRISTI. June 10. Roman Catholic festival celebrated in honor of the Eucharist. A solemnity observed on the Thursday following Trinity Sunday since 1246. In the US Corpus Christi is celebrated on the Sunday following Trinity Sunday. See also: "Corpus Christi (US Observance)" (June 13).

CZECHOSLOVAKIA: RAPE OF LIDICE: ANNIVERSARY. June 10, 1942. Nazi German troops executed, by shooting, all male inhabitants of the Czechoslovakian village of Lidice (total population about 500 persons), burned every house and deported the women and children to Germany for "re-education." One of the most-remembered atrocities of World War II. June 10, Lidice Memorial Day, is observed in New Jersey.

FESTIVAL OF THE BLUEGRASS. June 10–13. Lexington, KY. Bluegrass music in an outdoor setting. Previous artists have included Valerie Smith and Liberty Pike, Honi Deaton and Dream, Dry Branch Fire Squad, Mountain Heart, Seldom Scene and others. Est attendance: 20,000. For info: James Cornett, Spirit of the Suwannee Music Park, 3076 95th Dr, Live Oak, FL 32060. Phone: (904) 364-1683. Fax: (904) 364-2998. Web: www.festivalofthebluegrass.com.

FIRST MINT IN AMERICA: ANNIVERSARY. June 10, 1652. In defiance of English colonial law, John Hull, a silversmith, established the first mint in America. The first coin issued was the Pine Tree Shilling, designed by Hull.

GARLAND, JUDY: BIRTH ANNIVERSARY. June 10, 1922. American actress and singer born Frances Gumm at Grand Rapids, MN. While Garland played in many films and toured widely as a singer, she is probably most remembered for her portrayal of Dorothy Gale in the now-classic *The Wizard of Oz*. Died June 22, 1969, at London, England.

JORDAN: GREAT ARAB REVOLT AND ARMY DAY. June 10. Commemorates the beginning of the Great Arab Revolt in 1916. National holiday.

McDANIEL, HATTIE: BIRTH ANNIVERSARY. June 10, 1889. Hattie McDaniel was the first African American to win an Academy Award. She won it in 1940 for her role in the 1939 film *Gone With the Wind*. Her career spanned radio and vaudeville in addition to her screen roles in *Judge Priest, The Little Colonel, Showboat* and *Saratoga*, among others. She was born at Wichita, KS, and died Oct 26, 1952, at Los Angeles, CA.

NURSING ASSISTANTS DAY AND WEEK. June 10–17. 27th annual. Recognizes those nursing assistants who provide care to all ill, elderly and long-term residents in nursing homes and other long-term nursing care centers. Begins on Career Nurse Assistants' Day, June 10, 2004. For info: Career Nurse Assistant's Programs Inc, 3577 Easton Rd, Norton, OH 44203. Phone: (330) 825-9342. Fax: (330) 825-9378. E-mail: cnajeni@aol.com. Web: www.cna-network.org.

PORTUGAL: DAY OF PORTUGAL. June 10. National holiday. Anniversary of the death in 1580 of Portugal's national poet, Luis Vas de Camoes (Camoens), born in 1524 (exact date unknown) at either Lisbon or Coimbra. Died at Lisbon, Portugal.

ROCK CREEK PARK NATIONALIZED: ANNIVERSARY. June 10, 1933. Rock Creek Park, authorized Sept 27, 1890, was transferred to the National Park Service. For further park info: Rock Creek Park, 5000 Glover Rd NW, Washington, DC 20015.

SEA MUSIC FESTIVAL. June 10–13. Mystic, CT. World-famous musicians perform aboard Mystic Seaport's tall ships or in concert. Est attendance: 6,000. For info: Mystic Seaport, 75 Greenmanville Ave, Box 6000, Mystic, CT 06355. Phone: (860) 572-5315 or (888) 9-SEAPORT. Web: www.visitmysticseaport.com.

SUPERMAN CELEBRATION. June 10–13. Metropolis, IL. Weekend full of Super activities. See 15-ft Superman Statue, live entertainment, super museum, road race, carnival, tennis tourney, Supertrek bicycle ride, super car show, washer pitch tournament, weight lifting, arm wrestling, children's games and food fair. Est attendance: 30,000. For info: Metropolis Area Chamber of Commerce, Tourism & Economic Development, PO Box 188, Metropolis, IL 62960. Phone: (618) 524-2714 or (800) 949-5740. Fax: (618) 524-4780. E-mail: metrochamber@hcis.net. Web: www.metropolischamber.com.

TEXAS FOLKLIFE FESTIVAL. June 10–13. San Antonio, TX. Provides an entertaining and historic understanding of the crafts, art, food, music, history and heritage of the more than 40 different cultures and ethnic groups that settled and developed the state of Texas. Est attendance: 70,000. For info: Public Relations Office, Institute of Texan Cultures, 801 S Bowie St, San Antonio, TX 78205-3296. Phone: (210) 458-2257. Fax: (210) 458-2380. E-mail: ymoreno@utsa.edu. Web: www.texasfolklifefestival.org.

June 2004	S	M	T	W	T	F	S
			1	2	3	4	5
	6	7	8	9	10	11	12
	13	14	15	16	17	18	19
	20	21	22	23	24	25	26
	27	28	29	30			

☆ Chase's 2004 Calendar of Events ☆   June 10–11

VIVA EL PASO. June 10–Aug 14 (Thursday–Saturday). McKelligon Canyon Amphitheater, El Paso, TX. Outdoor drama celebrating El Paso's cultural history through song, dance, narration and dramatic scenes about early Native American, Spanish, Mexican and Western American settlers. Dinner at 6:00 PM, showtime 8:00 PM. Est attendance: 60,000. For info: El Paso Assn for the Performing Arts, PO Box 31340, El Paso, TX 79931-0340. Phone: (915) 565-6900 or (800) 915-8482. Fax: (915) 565-6999. E-mail: epapa@viva-ep.org. Web: www.viva-ep.org.

BIRTHDAYS TODAY

F. Lee Bailey, 71, lawyer, born Waltham, MA, June 10, 1933.
John Edwards, 51, US Senator (D, North Carolina), born Seneca, SC, June 10, 1953.
Linda Evangelista, 39, model, born St. Catharines, ON, Canada, June 10, 1965.
Jeff Greenfield, 61, author, journalist, born New York, NY, June 10, 1943.
Nat Hentoff, 79, music critic, journalist, born Boston, MA, June 10, 1925.
Elizabeth Hurley, 39, model, actress (*Austin Powers: International Man of Mystery*), born Basingstoke, England, June 10, 1965.
Tara Lipinski, 22, figure skater, born Philadelphia, PA, June 10, 1982.
Doug McKeon, 38, actor (*On Golden Pond*), born Pomptain Plains, NJ, June 10, 1966.
Prince Philip, 83, Duke of Edinburgh, husband of Queen Elizabeth II, born Corfu, Greece, June 10, 1921.
Maurice Sendak, 76, author, illustrator (*Chicken Soup with Rice, Where the Wild Things Are*), born Brooklyn, NY, June 10, 1928.
Leelee Sobieski, 22, actress (*A Soldier's Daughter Never Cries*), born New York, NY, June 10, 1982.
Jeanne Tripplehorn, 41, actress (*The Firm, Waterworld, Mickey Blue Eyes*), born Tulsa, OK, June 10, 1963.

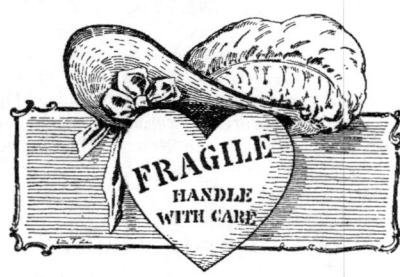

JUNE 11 — FRIDAY
Day 163 — 203 Remaining

"AMERICAN IDOL" TV PREMIERE: ANNIVERSARY. June 11, 2002. FOX's phenomenally successful talent show was based on a British program. Talented singers compete for a major label record deal while being judged by a panel of (at times) highly critical music experts. The audience participates by phoning in votes for favorites.

CARSON CITY RENDEZVOUS. June 11–13. Mills Park, Carson City, NV. A living history event with something for every member of the family. Mountain Men encampment demonstrates black powder shooting and tomahawk and knife throwing. Nevada, Utah and Oregon Civil War volunteers have their own encampments and stage skirmishes on the Rendezvous grounds. Other features include farrier demonstrations, authentic Indian and Hispanic arts and crafts and dance exhibits, live music and food. Annually, the second full weekend in June. Est attendance: 2,500. For info: Carson City Convention & Visitor's Bureau, 1900 S Carson St, Ste 100, Carson City, NV 89701. Phone: (775) 687-7410 or 800-NEVADA-1. Fax: (775) 687-7416. Web: www.carson-city.org.

CONNECTICUT EARLY MUSIC FESTIVAL. June 11–27. New London, CT, and nearby towns. Concert series of pre-19th century music performed on period instruments in historically informed styles. Annually, three weekends in June. Est attendance: 3,000. For info: Connecticut Early Music Festival, PO Box 329, New London, CT 06320. Phone: (860) 444-2419. Web: www.ctearlymusic.org.

CONSTABLE, JOHN: BIRTH ANNIVERSARY. June 11, 1776. English landscape painter. Born at East Bergholt, Suffolk, England, he died at London, Mar 31, 1837.

COUSTEAU, JACQUES: BIRTH ANNIVERSARY. June 11, 1910. French undersea explorer, writer and filmmaker born at St. Andre-de-Cubzac, France. He invented the Aqualung, which allowed him and his colleagues to produce more than 80 documentary films about undersea life, two of which won Oscars. This scientist and explorer was awarded the French Legion of Honor for his work in the Resistance in WWII. He died June 25, 1997, at Paris.

CRAWFORDSVILLE STRAWBERRY FESTIVAL. June 11–13. Crawfordsville, IN. Festival at historic Lane Place includes 3 days of arts and crafts, food, music and children's activities. Great music, classic car show (Sunday), softball and tennis tournaments, bike tour, antique tractor exhibits and 4-mile run. All city museums open. Est attendance: 20,000. For info: Montgomery County Visitors & Conv Bureau, Inc, 218 E Pike St, Crawfordsville, IN 47933. Phone: (800) 866-3973. Fax: (317) 362-5215. E-mail: mcvcb@tctc.com. Web: www.crawfordsville.org.

DOWNTOWN ALIVE!. June 11 (also June 18 & 25, July 9, 16 & 30 and Aug 6, 13 & 20). Downer Place, Aurora, IL. A summer concert series of events on Friday nights, each having a different theme: Jump, Jive and Wail; Motown Memories; Rock on the Fox; Sensational '60s; Blues on the Fox; British Invasion Night; and Friday Night Fever. Free carriage rides, inflatable games and admission to various museums. Specialty food and beverages available. For info: Gina Moga, Events Coord, City of Aurora, 43 E Downer Pl, Aurora, IL 60507. Phone: (630) 844-3640. Hotline: (630) 844-4FUN. Fax: (630) 906-7068. E-mail: gmoga@aurora-il.org.

INTERNATIONAL OLD-TIME FIDDLERS CONTEST. June 11–12. International Peace Garden, Dunseith, ND. The International Old-Time Fiddlers Contest draws young and old fiddlers alike from both Canada and the US. Contestants compete for two days performing a required list of fiddle music in pursuit of cash prizes and trophies. Est attendance: 1,500. For info: Joseph T. Alme, 1725 11th St SW, Minot, ND 58701. Phone: (701) 838-8472. Fax: (701) 838-8472. E-mail: info@internationalmusiccamp.com.

JONSON, BEN: BIRTH ANNIVERSARY. June 11, 1572 (OS). English playwright and poet. "Talking and eloquence," he wrote, "are not the same: to speak and to speak well, are two things." Born at London, England, he died there Aug 6, 1637 (OS). The epitaph written on his tombstone in Westminster Abbey: "O rare Ben Jonson."

KING KAMEHAMEHA I DAY. June 11. Designated state holiday in Hawaii honors memory of Hawaiian monarch (1737–1819). Governor appoints state commission to plan annual celebration.

KUSTOM KEMPS OF AMERICA CAR SHOW. June 11–13. Oakside Community Park, Biglerville, PA. Est attendance: 3,500. For info: Gettysburg CVB, PO Box 4117, Gettysburg, PA 17325. Phone: (717) 637-5229. Fax: (717) 334-1166. E-mail: gettysburgcvb@dejazzd.com. Web: www.gettysburgcvb.org.

LIBYA: EVACUATION DAY. June 11. National day. Commemorates the closing of US base in 1970.

LOMBARDI, VINCE: BIRTH ANNIVERSARY. June 11, 1913. Vincent Thomas (Vince) Lombardi, Pro Football Hall of Fame coach, born at New York, NY. Lombardi played football for Fordham's famed "Seven Blocks of Granite" line in the mid-1930s, became a teacher and began to coach high school football. He became offensive line coach at West Point in 1949 and moved to the New York Giants in 1954. Five years later, he was

June 11 ☆ Chase's 2004 Calendar of Events ☆

named head coach of the Green Bay Packers. His Packers won five NFL titles and two Super Bowls in nine years, and Lombardi was generally regarded as the greatest coach and the finest motivator in pro football history. He retired in 1968, but was lured back to coach the Washington Redskins a year later. Inducted into the Pro Football Hall of Fame in 1971. Died at Washington, DC, Sept 3, 1970.

MINNESOTA INVENTORS CONGRESS. June 11–13. Redwood Falls, MN. 47th Congress. To promote creativity and development of ideas into marketable products, to educate inventors and to bring the inventor to experts in the appropriate field. Highlights include more than 170 inventions from around the world on display, 100 student inventors, the Minnesota Inventors Hall of Fame and the Marketplace with inventions for sale. Also features a Successful Invention Development Workshop on the Thursday preceding the three-day Congress. Annually, the second Friday of June. Est attendance: 10,000. For info: Minnesota Inventors Congress, PO Box 71, Redwood Falls, MN 56283-0071. Phone: (507) 637-2344 or (800) INVENT-1. Fax: (507) 637-8399. E-mail: mic@invent1.org. Web: www.invent1.org.

MOUNT PINATUBO ERUPTS IN PHILIPPINES: ANNIVERSARY. June 11, 1991. Long-dormant volcano Mount Pinatubo erupted with a violent explosion, spewing ash and gases that could be seen for more than 60 miles, into the air. The surrounding areas were covered with ash and mud created by rainstorms. US military bases Clark and Subic Bay were also damaged. On July 6, 1992, Ellsworth Dutton of the National Oceanic and Atmospheric Administration's Climate Monitoring and Diagnostics Laboratory announced that a layer of sulfuric acid droplets released into the Earth's atmosphere by the eruption had cooled the planet's average temperature by about 1 degree Fahrenheit. The greatest difference was noted in the Northern Hemisphere with a drop of 1.5 degrees. Although the temperature drop was temporary, the climate trend made determining the effect of greenhouse warming on the Earth more difficult.

NEBRASKALAND DAYS AND PRCA BUFFALO BILL RODEO. June 11–20 (also June 25–26). North Platte, NE. To relive the Old West. Parades, contests, shoot-outs, art shows, frontier revue, top concert entertainment. Est attendance: 100,000. For info: Claudia Coble, NEBRASKAland DAYS, Box 706, North Platte, NE 69103. Phone: (308) 532-7939. Fax: (308) 532-3789. E-mail: nld@nebraskalanddays.com. Web: www.nebraskalanddays.com.

OK MOZART INTERNATIONAL FESTIVAL. June 11–19. Bartlesville, OK. Festival features world-class artists performing with Solisti New York Orchestra, Ransom Wilson conducting. Est attendance: 40,000. For info: Jeanette Swindell, Public Relations, OK Mozart Intl Festival, Box 2344, Bartlesville, OK 74005. Phone: (918) 336-9900. Fax: (918) 336-9525. Web: www.okmozart.com.

RANKIN, JEANNETTE: BIRTH ANNIVERSARY. June 11, 1880. First woman elected to the US Congress, a reformer, feminist and pacifist, was born at Missoula, MT. She was the only member of Congress to vote against a declaration of war against Japan in December 1941. Died May 18, 1973, at Carmel, CA.

RED ARMY DEPARTS BERLIN: 10th ANNIVERSARY. June 11, 1994. After 49 years, the Russian military occupation of the region once called East Germany ended. At one time there had been 337,800 Soviet troops stationed in Germany. The departure was celebrated with a parade in Wupnsdorf south of Berlin, which was the Soviet Union's military headquarters in the former German Democratic Republic.

June 2004

S	M	T	W	T	F	S
		1	2	3	4	5
6	7	8	9	10	11	12
13	14	15	16	17	18	19
20	21	22	23	24	25	26
27	28	29	30			

RIVERBEND FESTIVAL. June 11–19. Chattanooga, TN. Nine-day festival on the banks of the Tennessee River includes world-class entertainment, sporting events and an evening finale on the final night featuring musically synchronized fireworks. More than 100 artists perform a variety of musical styles before a diverse audience. Est attendance: 650,000. For info: Friends of the Festival, Inc, 1001 Market St, Ste 130, Chattanooga, TN 37402. Phone: (423) 756-2212. E-mail: information@riverbendfestival.com. Web: www.riverbendfestival.com.

SCOTLAND: ROYAL SCOTTISH AUTOMOBILE CLUB INTERNATIONAL SCOTTISH RALLY. June 11–13 (tentative). Throughout Scotland with base at Dumfries. Scotland's top international rally that attracts many of the world's leading drivers. Est attendance: 200,000. For info: Jonathan Lord, Royal Scottish Automobile Club (Motor Sport) Ltd, 11 Blythswood Sq, Glasgow, Scotland G2 4AG. Phone: (44) (141) 204-4999. E-mail: RSAC_motorsport@compuserve.com. Web: www.brcweb.co.uk or www.scottishrally.co.uk.

"SPACE ODDITY" SONG RELEASE: 35th ANNIVERSARY. June 11, 1969. This single recorded by David Bowie was released to coincide with the *Apollo 11*'s trip to the moon, during which Neil Armstrong and Edwin Aldrin, Jr, landed and walked on the surface of the moon.

SPECIAL OLYMPICS CONNECTICUT 2004 SUMMER GAMES. June 11–13. New Haven, Milford and Woodbridge, CT. More than 2,000 athletes, ages 8 to 70, will gather for competition in aquatics, track & field, gymnastics, cycling, soccer and tennis. The Games are free and open to the public. Opening ceremonies will commence Friday evening, June 11, at Southern Connecticut State University in New Haven. Est attendance: 8,000. For info: Special Olympics Connecticut, 2666 State St, Ste 1, Hamden, CT 06517. Phone: (800) 443-6105. Fax: (203) 230-1202. Web: www.soct.org.

STRAUSS, RICHARD GEORG: BIRTH ANNIVERSARY. June 11, 1864. German composer, musician and conductor whose best-remembered works are *Till Eulenspiegel* (1895), *Also Sprach Zarathrustra* (1896) and *Don Quixote* (1898). Born at Munich, he died at Garmisch-Partenkirchen, Germany, after a heart attack Sept 8, 1949, at age 85.

SUMMER FARM TOY SHOW. June 11–13. Beckman HS and National Farm Toy Museum, Dyersville, IA. Features tractor parade, tractor pull, citywide garage sales, live entertainment, antique tractors and farm machinery and indoor/outdoor farm toy show. Annually, the second full weekend in June. Est attendance: 9,000. For info: Dyersville Area Chamber of Commerce, 1100 16th Ave Ct SE, Dyersville, IA 52040. Phone: (563) 875-2311. Fax: (563) 875-8391. E-mail: dyersvillechamber@dyersville.net. Web: www.dyersville.org.

TAKE A KID FISHING WEEKEND. June 11–13. St. Paul, MN. Resident adults may fish without a license on these days when fishing with a child under age 16. For info: Ron Payer, Fisheries Dir, DNR, Box 12, 500 Lafayette Rd, St. Paul, MN 55155-4012. Phone: (651) 296-0792 or (651) 296-3325. Fax: (651) 297-4916. Web: www.dnr.state.mn.us/.

TECUMSEH!: THE EPIC OUTDOOR DRAMA. June 11–Aug 28. Chillicothe, OH. Witness the spectacular reenactment of the life and death of the great Shawnee leader Tecumseh. Held in the large, tiered amphitheater nestled in the hardwood forest of Sugarloaf Mountain. Take a backstage tour, visit the Prehistoric Museum, dine in the open-air Tecumseh Restaurant Terrace. Est attendance: 80,000. For info: Tecumseh!, PO Box 73, Chillicothe, OH 45601-0073. Phone toll-free Mar 1–Aug 28: (866) 775-0700. Fax: (740) 775-4349. E-mail: tecumseh@bright.net. Web: www.tecumsehdrama.com.

WINDSURFING REGATTA/UNVARNISHED MUSIC FESTIVAL. June 11–13. Worthington, MN. Windsurfing on Lake Okabena. Regatta, surfing instruction, swap meet. Traditional music. At sunset, "unvarnished and unamplified" music on the beach. Beach barbecue, food vendors. Tour the largest wind generator farm in the world. Est attendance: 8,000. For info: Worthington Conv & Visitors Bureau, 1121 Third Ave, Worthington, MN 56187. Phone: (800) 279-2919 or (507) 372-2919. Fax: (507) 372-2827. E-mail: wcofc@frontiernet.net.

BIRTHDAYS TODAY

Adrienne Barbeau, 59, actress ("Maude"), born Sacramento, CA, June 11, 1945.
Peter Bergman, 51, actor ("All My Children," "The Young & the Restless"), born Guantanamo Bay, Cuba, June 11, 1953.
Chad Everett, 68, actor ("The Dakotas," "Medical Center"), born Raymond Cramton, South Bend, IN, June 11, 1936.
Joshua Jackson, 26, actor ("Dawson's Creek," *Scream 2*), born Vancouver, BC, Canada, June 11, 1978.
Joseph C. (Joe) Montana, Jr, 48, former sportscaster and Hall of Fame football player, born New Eagle, PA, June 11, 1956.
Jackie Stewart, 65, former auto racer, born Dunbartonshire, Scotland, June 11, 1939.
William Styron, 79, author (*The Confessions of Nat Turner, Sophie's Choice*), born Newport News, VA, June 11, 1925.
Gene Wilder, 65, actor (*The Producers, Willy Wonka & the Chocolate Factory, Blazing Saddles, Young Frankenstein*), director, born Milwaukee, WI, June 11, 1939 (some sources say 1935 or 1933).

JUNE 12 — SATURDAY
Day 164 — 202 Remaining

ANTIQUES ON THE DIAMOND. June 12 (also Aug 28). Ligonier, PA. 70 quality antique dealers from six states set up their products along the Diamond. Est attendance: 10,000. For info: Ligonier Chamber of Commerce, 120 E Main St, Ligonier, PA 15658. Phone: (724) 238-4200. Fax: (724) 238-4610. E-mail: ligonier@ligonier.com. Web: www.ligonier.com.

ART IN THE PARK. June 12 (rain date June 13). Bay Head, NJ. Juried outdoor art show. Est attendance: 300. For info: Anne Neff, Chair, Anchor and Palette Gallery, 45 Mount St, PO Box 96, Bay Head, NJ 08742. Phone: (732) 892-7776 or (800) 4-BAYHED. E-mail: info@anchorandpalette.org. Web: www.bayhead.org.

BASEBALL'S FIRST PERFECT GAME: ANNIVERSARY. June 12, 1880. Lee Richmond of the Worcester Ruby Legs (National League) pitched baseball's first perfect game (not allowing a single opposing player to reach first base), 1-0, against the Cleveland Indians.

BETTY PICNIC. June 12. Tom Pierce Park, Grants Pass, OR. To celebrate the Bettys of this world for their vivacity, impulsiveness and similarities. Annually, the second Saturday in June. Send SASE since this is a nonprofit organization. For info: Betty Wilder and Betty Patterson, c/o Betty Club, 1753 Darrell Circle, Grants Pass, OR 97527. Phone: (541) 476-4104.

BIG BEND NATIONAL PARK ESTABLISHED: 60th ANNIVERSARY. June 12, 1944. Area on the "big bend" of the Rio Grande River in western Texas along the Mexican border, authorized June 20, 1935, was established as a national park. For further park info: Big Bend Natl Park, Big Bend Natl Park, TX 79834.

A BLAST FROM THE PAST. June 12–13. Mount Hope Estate & Winery, Manheim, PA. Relive those happy days with music, dance, record swaps, dance contests, hundreds of classic cars and an end-of-the-day concert by the original performers of some of your favorite rock 'n' roll. Est attendance: 20,000. For info: Thomas Roy, PRF, PO Box 685, Cornwall, PA 17016. Phone: (717) 665-7021. Fax: (717) 664-3466. E-mail: tom@parenfaire.com. Web: www.parenfaire.com.

BUSH, GEORGE HERBERT WALKER: 80th BIRTHDAY. June 12, 1924. 41st president of US (1989–93), 43rd vice president of US (1981–89), born at Milton, MA.

BUZZARD DAY FESTIVAL. June 12. Makoshika State Park, Glendive, MT. Just as the swallows return to Capistrano each year, so do the turkey vultures come back to Makoshika. Festival activities include an 8K run, pancake breakfast, kids fun fest, nature walks, FOLF (frisbee golf) tournament and lots more. For info: Makoshika State Park, Box 1242, Glendive, MT 59330. Phone: (406) 377-6256. Fax: (406) 377-8043. E-mail: makoshikapark@mcn.net.

CENTER OF THE NATION ALL-CAR RALLY. June 12–13. Belle Fourche, SD. This two-day event includes Sunday's big "Show 'n Shine," held all day in Hermann Park, plus food booths, vendors, live '50s and '60s music. Est attendance: 5,000. For info: Belle Fourche Chamber of Commerce, 415 5th Ave, Belle Fourche, SD 57717. Phone: (605) 892-2676. Fax: (605) 892-4633. E-mail: chamber@bellefourche.org.

CHICAGO SOUTHLAND'S FINEST ANTIQUES SHOW. June 12–13. Tinley Park Convention Center, Tinley Park, IL. 120 exhibitors will offer a broad range of art, antiques, and select collectibles—everything from toys to Tiffany. Treasures for first-time buyers to breathtaking investment-quality pieces will be on display. Est attendance: 8,000. For info: Chicago Southland's Finest Shows and Events, 701 Marley Rd, New Lenox, IL 60451. Phone: (815) 485-6666. Fax: (815) 485-1105. E-mail: antiqueshow2004@hotmail.com.

EISENHOWER FIFTIES WEEKEND. June 12–13. Eisenhower National Historic Site, Gettysburg, PA. Revisit the popular culture of the 1950s. See Detroit's finest 1950s cars. Remember rock & roll, the Hula Hoop and more. Ranger programs on the issues of the day. Est attendance: 1,000. For info: Gettysburg CVB, PO Box 4117, Gettysburg, PA 17325. Phone: (717) 334-6274. Fax: (717) 334-1166. E-mail: gettysburgcvb@dejazzd.com. Web: www.gettysburgcvb.org.

ENGLAND: CURTIS CUP. June 12–13. Formby Golf Club, Merseyside, England. Biennial competition between teams of women golfers from the US and the UK. Named after British golfing sisters Harriot and Margaret Curtis. Contested in even-numbered years since 1932 (except during WWII). For info: US Golf Assn, Golf House, Far Hills, NJ 07931. Phone: (908) 234-2300. Fax: (908) 234-9687. E-mail: usga@usga.org. Web: www.usga.org.

ENGLAND: TROOPING THE COLOUR—THE QUEEN'S OFFICIAL BIRTHDAY PARADE. June 12 (tentative). Horse Guards Parade, Whitehall, London. Colorful ceremony with music and pageantry during which Her Majesty The Queen takes the salute from her Household Division. Observance dates from 1805 in the reign of King George III. Starts at 11 AM. When requesting info, send SASE. Trooping the Colour is always the second or third Saturday in June; The Queen's real birthday is Apr 21. Est attendance: 6,500. For info: The Ticket Office, HQ Household Division, Horse Guards, Whitehall, London, England SW1A 2AX. Phone: (44) (020) 7414-2479. Web: www.army.mod.uk/ceremonialandheritage/household/.

June 12 ☆ *Chase's 2004 Calendar of Events* ☆

FIRST MAN-POWERED FLIGHT ACROSS ENGLISH CHANNEL: 25th ANNIVERSARY. June 12, 1979. Bryan Allen, 26-year-old Californian, pedaled the 70-pound *Gossamer Albatross* 22 miles across the English Channel, from Folkestone, England, to Cape Gris-Nez, France, in 2 hours, 49 minutes, winning (with the craft's designer, Paul MacCready of Pasadena, CA) the £100,000 prize offered by British industrialist Henry Kremer for the first man-powered flight across the English Channel.

FOUNDERS' DAY STREET FAIR—THE GOOD LIFE. June 12 (rain date June 13). Toms River, NJ. Street fair for Dover Township nonprofit organizations with a parade, vendor booths, entertainment, prizes, food, literature and games. Crafters welcome. Est attendance: 30,000. For info: Toms River–Ocean County Chamber of Commerce, 1200 Hooper Ave, Toms River, NJ 08753. Phone: (732) 349-0220. Fax: (732) 349-1252. Web: www.oc-chamber.com.

FRANK, ANNE: 75th BIRTH ANNIVERSARY. June 12, 1929. Born at Frankfurt, Germany. Anne Frank's family moved to Amsterdam to escape the Nazis, but after Holland was invaded by Germany, they had to go into hiding. In 1942 Anne began to keep a diary. She died at Bergen-Belsen concentration camp in 1945. After the war, her father published her diary, on which a stage play and movie were later based. See also: "Diary of Anne Frank: Last Entry" (Aug 1).

GREAT AMERICAN BRASS BAND FESTIVAL. June 12–13. Centre College Campus, Danville, KY. Brass bands and ensembles from throughout the country in concert Saturday and Sunday. Free to the public. Est attendance: 55,000. For info: Great American Brass Band Festival, PO Box 429, Danville, KY 40422. Phone: (800) 755-0076. Fax: (859) 236-3197. Web: www.danvillekentucky.com.

HERITAGE DAYS FESTIVAL. June 12–13. Cumberland, MD. 36th annual. Held in historic downtown Cumberland, the festival showcases more than 200 arts and crafts booths. Also music, entertainment, children's activities, carnivals, tours of historic homes and buildings as well as historic reenactments. Annually, the second weekend in June. Est attendance: 25,000. For info: Heritage Days Festival, PO Box 6349, Cumberland, MD 21501. Phone: (301) 777-2787. Web: www.heritagedaysfestival.com.

JUNE JAMBOREE MOTORCYCLE RALLY. June 12. Lovington, NM. Gigantic sales (stores, sidewalk, garage, etc) and special events all day, all over town! For info: Andra Conner, Lovington Chamber of Commerce, 201 S Main St, Lovington, NM 88260. Phone: (505) 396-5311. Fax: (505) 396-2823. E-mail: visit us@leaconet.com. Web: www.lovington.net.

***LOVING v VIRGINIA*: ANNIVERSARY.** June 12, 1967. The US Supreme Court decision in *Loving v Virginia* swept away all 16 remaining state laws prohibiting interracial marriages.

MARBLE MEET AT AMANA. June 12–13 (tentative). Holiday Inn, Amana, IA. Seminar, banquet and exhibits. Collectors buy, sell and trade marbles. Est attendance: 800. For info: Marble Collectors Unltd, Box 206, Northboro, MA 01532. Phone: (319) 642-3891 or (508) 393-2923. E-mail: marblesbev@aol.com or judyhuxford@excite.com.

MELROSE PLANTATION ARTS AND CRAFTS FESTIVAL. June 12–13. Melrose, LA. Held on the grounds of Historic Melrose Plantation, this event features quality handcrafted items from more than 150 juried exhibitors. Food, including the famous meat pies and soft drinks will be available. Annually, the second full weekend in June. Est attendance: 20,000. For info: Calendar of Events, Natchitoches Parish Tourist Commission, 781 Front St, Natchitoches, LA 71457. Phone: (318) 352-8072 or (800) 259-1714. Fax: (318) 352-2415. Web: www.natchitoches.net.

NATIONAL AUTOMOTIVE SERVICE PROFESSIONALS DAY. June 12. Sponsored by the National Institute for Automotive Service Excellence (ASE), which was incorporated on June 12, 1972. ASE was founded to improve the quality of automotive service through voluntary testing and certification of service professionals. Today the nonprofit organization also serves as an information source for professionals and consumers about automotive repair and related topics. For info: Trish Serratore, 101 Blue Seal Dr, Leesburg, VA 20175. Phone: (703) 669-6600. Fax: (703) 669-6127. E-mail: tserratore@asecert.org. Web: www.ase.com.

NATIONAL BASEBALL HALL OF FAME DEDICATED: 65th ANNIVERSARY. June 12, 1939. The National Baseball Hall of Fame and Museum, Inc, was dedicated at Cooperstown, NY. More than 200 individuals have been honored for their contributions to the game of baseball by induction into the Baseball Hall of Fame. The first players chosen for membership (1936) were Ty Cobb, Honus Wagner, Babe Ruth, Christy Mathewson and Walter Johnson. Relics and memorabilia from the history of baseball are housed at this shrine of America's national sport.

PARAGUAY: PEACE WITH BOLIVIA DAY. June 12. Commemorates the end of the Chaco War in 1935.

PHILIPPINES: INDEPENDENCE DAY. June 12. National holiday. Declared independence from Spain in 1898.

POTOMAC CELTIC FESTIVAL. June 12–13. Morven Park Equestrian Center, Leesburg, VA. Featuring Cornwall in 2004, the Festival celebrates all the Celtic nations: Scotland, Wales, Cornwall, the Isle of Man, Ireland, Brittany (France), Galicia & Asturias (Spain) and North America. Nine stages of live music, dance stage, storytelling, drama, poetry, children's entertainment, workshops, crafts, sports and food. Est attendance: 24,000. For info: Barnaby Council for Celtic Studies, PO Box 1106, Vienna, VA 22183. Phone: (800) 752-6118. E-mail: prez@pobox.com. Web: www.PCFest.org.

RENDEZVOUS FESTIVAL. June 12–13 (tentative). Icelandic State Park, Cavalier, ND. A festival of culture and art celebrating the history of North Dakota's Rendezvous Region. Activities include a muzzle-loader's shoot, ethnic singers, dancers and performers, pioneer demonstrations and trades. There will also be a buckskinner's encampment, ceremonies and a Chautauqua. Est attendance: 2,500. For info: (701) 265-4561 or North Dakota Tourism, Century Center, 1600 E Century Ave, Ste 2, Bismarck, ND 58503. Phone: (701) 328-2525 or (800) 435-5663. Web: www.ndparks.com.

RUSSIA: INDEPENDENCE DAY. June 12. National holiday. Commemorates the election in 1991 of the first popularly elected leader (Yeltsin) in the 1,000-year history of the Russian state.

SPACE MILESTONE: *VENERA 4* (USSR). June 12, 1967. Launched on this date, this instrumental capsule landed on Venus by parachute on Oct 18 and reported a temperature of 536°F.

TURTLE RACES. June 12. Knights of Columbus, Danville, IL. More than 100 turtles compete in 40th annual races throughout the day. Concessions available. Food and fun. Proceeds go to help people in the area with disabilities. Annually, the second Saturday in June. Est attendance: 3,000. For info: Nadine Schramm, Turtle Club, 2932 Batestown Rd, Oakwood, IL 61858. Phone: (217) 446-5327 or (800) 383-4386.

★ ★ ★

June 2004

S	M	T	W	T	F	S
		1	2	3	4	5
6	7	8	9	10	11	12
13	14	15	16	17	18	19
20	21	22	23	24	25	26
27	28	29	30			

☆ Chase's 2004 Calendar of Events ☆ June 12–13

BIRTHDAYS TODAY

Spencer Abraham, 52, US Secretary of Energy, former US Senator (R, Michigan), born Lansing, MI, June 12, 1952.
Marv Albert, 61, sportscaster, born Marvin Philip Aufrichtig, New York, NY, June 12, 1943.
Timothy Busfield, 47, actor ("thirtysomething," *Field of Dreams*), born Lansing, MI, June 12, 1957.
George Herbert Walker Bush, 80, 41st president of the US, born Milton, MA, June 12, 1924.
Chick Corea, 63, musician, born Chelsea, MA, June 12, 1941.
Vic Damone, 76, singer ("On the Street Where You Live"), born Vito Farinola, New York, NY, June 12, 1928.
Hideki Matsui, 30, baseball player, born Ishikawa, Japan, June 12, 1974.
Jim Nabors, 72, actor ("The Andy Griffith Show," "Gomer Pyle, U.S.M.C."), born Sylacauga, AL, June 12, 1932.
Frances O'Connor, 35, actress (*The Importance of Being Earnest, Mansfield Park*), born Oxford, England, June 12, 1969.
David Rockefeller, 89, banker, born New York, NY, June 12, 1915.

JUNE 13 — SUNDAY
Day 165 — 201 Remaining

ABUSED WOMEN AND CHILDREN'S AWARENESS DAY. June 13. A day to reflect on how we can help stop the violence in America that is destroying the lives and well-being of women and children. A day to prayerfully put an end to violent behavior in American homes, schools, workplaces and communities. Annually, the second Sunday in June. For info: Judith Natale, CEO & Founder, NCAC America–USA, 2091 Del Monte Ave, Monterey, CA 93940. Fax: (831) 655-4547. E-mail: childaware@aol.com.

BELGIUM: MILITARY MUSIC FESTIVAL. June 13. Tournai. Traditional cultural observance. Annually, the second Sunday in June.

BOLLES, DON: DEATH ANNIVERSARY. June 13, 1976. Don Bolles, investigative reporter for *The Arizona Republic*, died as a result of injuries received when a bomb exploded in his automobile, June 2, 1976, while he was engaged in journalistic investigation of an alleged Mafia story. Bolles was awarded, posthumously, the University of Arizona's John Peter Zenger Award, Dec 9, 1976.

CHILDREN'S DAY IN MASSACHUSETTS. June 13. Annually, the second Sunday in June. The governor proclaims this day each year.

CHILDREN'S SUNDAY. June 13. Traditionally the second Sunday in June is observed as Children's Sunday in many Christian churches.

CORPUS CHRISTI (US OBSERVANCE). June 13. A movable Roman Catholic celebration commemorating the institution of the Holy Eucharist. The solemnity has been observed on the Thursday following Trinity Sunday since 1246, except in the US, where it is observed on the Sunday following Trinity Sunday.

EVERS, MEDGAR ASSASSINATED: ANNIVERSARY. June 13, 1963. Civil rights leader Medgar Wiley Evers was active in seeking integration of schools and voter registration. He was assassinated by Byron de la Beckwith. The public outrage following his death was one of the factors that led President John F. Kennedy to propose a comprehensive civil rights law.

GRANGE, RED: BIRTH ANNIVERSARY. June 13, 1903. Harold Edward ("Red") Grange, Pro Football Hall of Fame halfback and broadcaster, born at Forksville, PA. Perhaps the most famous football player of all time, Grange had a spectacular college career at the University of Illinois, being named an All-American in 1923, 1924 and 1925. When Illinois dedicated its Memorial Stadium on Oct 18, 1924, Grange scored four touchdowns against Michigan in the game's first 12 minutes. Known as the "Galloping Ghost," Grange joined the Chicago Bears in 1925 for what amounted to a barnstorming tour, the start of a professional career dictated by Grange and his manager, Charles C. ("Cash and Carry") Pyle. He retired in 1934 following a knee injury, having put pro football on the sports map. Grange entered business and did announcing work on radio and television. In retirement, he lived quietly and humbly. Inducted into the Hall of Fame as a charter member in 1963. Died at Lake Wales, FL, Jan 28, 1991.

GRANT WOOD ART FESTIVAL. June 13. Stone City–Anamosa, IA. Juried art exhibits, demonstrations, stage entertainment, tours of historic Stone City and more. Annually, the second Sunday in June. Est attendance: 8,000. For info: Grant Wood Art Festival, Inc, 124 E Main St, Anamosa, IA 52205. Phone: (319) 462-4267. E-mail: staff@grantwoodartfestival.org. Web: www.grantwoodartfestival.org.

HOME OWNERS LOAN ACT: ANNIVERSARY. June 13, 1933. The Federal Savings and Loan Association was authorized with the passage of the Home Owners Loan Act. The purpose of the legislation was to provide a convenient place for investment and to lend money on first mortgages. The first association was the First Federal Savings and Loan Association of Miami, FL, which was chartered on Aug 8, 1933.

INTERNATIONAL MUSIC CAMP. June 13–Aug 3. International Peace Garden, Dunseith, ND. In its 49th season, more than 3,000 students from 70 countries enjoy the many different programs of IMC. Music camps include concert band, jazz, choir, vocal jazz, orchestra, piano, guitar, marimba and total percussion. Also visual arts, dance, drama and creative-writing sessions. Est attendance: 3,000. For info: Joseph T. Alme, Dir, Intl Music Camp, 1725 11th St SW, Minot, ND 58701. Phone: (701) 838-8472. Fax: (701) 838-8472. E-mail: info@internationalmusiccamp.com.

MIRANDA DECISION: ANNIVERSARY. June 13, 1966. The US Supreme Court rendered a 5–4 decision in the case of *Miranda v Arizona*, holding that the Fifth Amendment of the Constitution "required warnings before valid statements could be taken by police." The decision has been described as "providing basic legal protections to persons who might otherwise not be aware of their rights." Ernesto Miranda, the 23-year-old whose name became nationally known, was retried after the Miranda Decision, convicted and sent back to prison. Miranda was stabbed to death in a card game dispute at Phoenix, AZ, in 1976. A suspect in the killing was released by police after he had been read his "Miranda rights." Police procedures now routinely require the reading of a prisoner's constitutional rights ("Miranda") before questioning.

MISSION SAN LUIS REY DE FRANCIA: FOUNDING ANNIVERSARY. June 13, 1798. California mission to the Indians founded on this date. Abandoned by 1846; restoration begun in 1892.

MULTICULTURAL AMERICAN CHILD AWARENESS DAY. June 13. Celebrated every second Sunday in June. All children of every culture have been gifted with many talents and uniqueness. As Americans we can all benefit from the sharing of our individual cultural contributions that bring real character and greatness to a nation where all children are precious and deserve our praise. A time to share our many individual talents and treasures. For info: Judith Natale, NCAC America–USA, 2091 Del

325

Monte Ave, Monterey, CA 93940. Fax: (831) 655-4547. E-mail: childaware@aol.com.

★ **NATIONAL FLAG WEEK.** June 13–19. Presidential Proclamation issued each year since 1966 for the week including June 14. (PL89–443 of June 9, 1966.) In addition, the president often calls upon the American people to participate in public ceremonies in which the Pledge of Allegiance is recited.

NATIONAL HERMIT WEEK. June 13–20. This week take an adventure in solitude. Be transformed by the renewing of your mind. Discover truth by going off the grid. Celebrate the contributions of others who found truth through hermiting. Whether you seek inner peace or spiritual release, this 8-day week is for reflection, meditation and prayer. Annually, beginning the 13th of June. For info: Dr. Susan Phelps, The Hermit Project, PO Box 482, Lima, NY 14485.

RACE UNITY DAY. June 13. Baha'i-sponsored observance promoting racial harmony and understanding and the essential unity of humanity. Annually, the second Sunday in June. Established in 1957 by the Baha'is of the US. For info: Baha'is of the US, Office of Public Information, 1320 Nineteenth St NW, Suite 350, Washington, DC 20036. Phone: (202) 466-9870. Fax: (202) 466-9873. E-mail: opi@usbnc.org. Web: www.us.bahai.org.

SAINT ANTHONY OF PADUA: FEAST DAY: DEATH ANNIVERSARY. June 13. Born at Lisbon, Portugal, Aug 15, 1195, St. Anthony is patron of the illiterate and the poor. Died at Padua, June 13, 1231. Public holiday, Lisbon.

SCOTT, WINFIELD: BIRTH ANNIVERSARY. June 13, 1786. American army general, negotiator of peace treaties with Indians and twice nominated for president (1848 and 1852). Leader of brilliant military campaign in Mexico in 1847. Scott was born at Petersburg, VA, and died at West Point, NY, May 29, 1866.

YEATS, WILLIAM BUTLER: BIRTH ANNIVERSARY. June 13, 1865. Nobel prize–winning Irish poet and dramatist, born at Dublin, Ireland. He once wrote: "If a poet interprets a poem of his own he limits its suggestibility." Yeats died at France, Jan 28, 1939. After World War II his body was returned, as he had wished, for reburial in a churchyard at Drumcliff, Ireland.

BIRTHDAYS TODAY

Tim Allen, 51, comedian, actor ("Home Improvement," *Galaxy Quest*), born Denver, CO, June 13, 1953.
Christo, 69, conceptual artist (*Running Fence, Valley Curtain*), born Christo Javacheff, Babrovo, Bulgaria, June 13, 1935.
Malcolm McDowell, 61, actor (*A Clockwork Orange, O Lucky Man*), born Leeds, England, June 13, 1943.
Ashley Olsen, 18, actress ("Full House," "Two of a Kind"), born Los Angeles, CA, June 13, 1986.
Mary-Kate Olsen, 18, actress ("Full House," "Two of a Kind"), born Los Angeles, CA, June 13, 1986.
Ally Sheedy, 42, actress (*St. Elmo's Fire, The Breakfast Club*), born New York, NY, June 13, 1962.
Richard Thomas, 53, actor ("The Waltons," *Roots: The Next Generations*), born New York, NY, June 13, 1951.

	S	M	T	W	T	F	S
June 2004			1	2	3	4	5
	6	7	8	9	10	11	12
	13	14	15	16	17	18	19
	20	21	22	23	24	25	26
	27	28	29	30			

JUNE 14 — MONDAY
Day 166 — 200 Remaining

ALZHEIMER, ALOIS: BIRTH ANNIVERSARY. June 14, 1864. The German psychiatrist and pathologist Alois Alzheimer was born at Markbreit am Mainz, Germany. In 1907 an article by Alzheimer appeared in *Allgemeine Zeitschrift für Psychiatrie*, first describing the disease that was named for him. It was thought of as a kind of pre-senile dementia, usually beginning at age 40–60. Alzheimer died Dec 19, 1915, at Breslau, Germany.

BARTLETT, JOHN: BIRTH ANNIVERSARY. June 14, 1820. American editor and compiler (Bartlett's *Familiar Quotations* [1855]) was born at Plymouth, MA. Though he had little formal education, he created one of the most-used reference works of the English language. No quotation of his own is among the more than 22,000 listed today, but in the preface to the first edition he wrote that the object of this work "originally made without any view of publication" was to show "the obligation our language owes to various authors for numerous phrases and familiar quotations which have become 'household words.' " Bartlett died at Cambridge, MA, Dec 3, 1905.

BOURKE-WHITE, MARGARET: 100th BIRTH ANNIVERSARY. June 14, 1904. Margaret Bourke was born at New York City. One of the original photojournalists, she developed her personal style while photographing the Krupp Iron Works in Germany and the Soviet Union during the first Five-Year Plan. Bourke-White was one of the four original staff photographers for *Life* magazine in 1936. The first woman attached to the US armed forces during World War II, she covered the Italian campaign, the siege of Moscow and American soldiers' crossing of the Rhine into Germany, and she shocked the world with her photographs of the concentration camps. Bourke-White photographed Mahatma Gandhi and covered the migration of millions of people after the Indian subcontinent was divided into Hindu India and Muslim Pakistan. She served as a war correspondent during the Korean War. Among her several books, the most famous was her collaboration with her second husband, novelist Erskine Caldwell, a study of rural poverty in the American South called *You Have Seen Their Faces*. She died Aug 27, 1971, at Stamford, CT.

CHICAGO BULLS WIN THIRD STRAIGHT TITLE FOR THE SECOND TIME: ANNIVERSARY. June 14, 1998. The Chicago Bulls defeated the Utah Jazz to win their third consecutive NBA championship. This was their second "three-peat." They had accomplished this feat the first time with wins in 1991, 1992 and 1993.

FAMILIES IN BUSINESS WEEK. June 14–18. A variety of activities planned to acknowledge and honor families in business. Annually, the week preceding Father's Day. For info: Greg Ast, 121 N Mead, Ste 109, Witchita, KS 67202. Phone: (316) 681-0444. Fax: (316) 681-0589. E-mail: gast@legasusgroup.com. Web: www.legasusgroup.com.

FAMILY HISTORY DAY. June 14. Every summer family reunions are so busy with games and activities that most of us forget the true purpose: to share the folklore, legends and myths that bind us together. Each participant should share at least one good recollection (fact or fiction). Don't forget the hot dogs and lemonade. [©2003 by WH.] For info: Thomas & Ruth Roy, Wellcat Holidays, 2418 Long Ln, Lebanon, PA 17046. Phone: (717) 279-0184. E-mail: info@wellcat.com. Web: www.wellcat.com.

FIRST NONSTOP TRANSATLANTIC FLIGHT: 85th ANNIVERSARY. June 14–15, 1919. Captain John Alcock and Lieutenant Arthur W. Brown flew a Vickers Vimy bomber 1,900 miles nonstop from St. Johns, Newfoundland, to Clifden, County Galway, Ireland. In spite of their crash landing in an Irish peat bog, their flight inspired public interest in aviation. See also: "Lindbergh Flight: Anniversary" (May 20).

FIRST US BREACH OF PROMISE SUIT: ANNIVERSARY. June 14, 1623. The first breach of promise suit in the US was filed in the Virginia Council of State, at Charles City, VA.

326

★ Chase's 2004 Calendar of Events ★   June 14

Reverend Greville Pooley brought suit against Cicely Jordan, who had jilted him in favor of another man.

★**FLAG DAY.** June 14. Presidential Proclamation issued each year for June 14. Proclamation 1335, of May 30, 1916, covers all succeeding years. Has been issued annually since 1941. (PL81–203 of Aug 3, 1949.) Customarily issued as "Flag Day and National Flag Week," as in 1986; the president usually mentions "a time to honor America," Flag Day to Independence Day (89 Stat. 211). See also: "National Flag Day USA: Pause for the Pledge" (below).

FLAG DAY: ANNIVERSARY OF THE STARS AND STRIPES. June 14, 1777. John Adams introduced the following resolution before the Continental Congress, meeting at Philadelphia, PA: "Resolved, That the flag of the thirteen United States shall be thirteen stripes, alternate red and white; that the union be thirteen stars, white on a blue field, representing a new constellation." Legal holiday in Pennsylvania.

"THE GONG SHOW" TV PREMIERE: ANNIVERSARY. June 14, 1976. This popular show featured a panel of three celebrities judging amateur and professional acts, from the ordinary to the unusual. At any time, a judge could bang a gong to end the act; this was often done with gusto. Completed acts were then rated and the winner received a cash prize. Chuck Barris created (along with Chris Bearde) and hosted the show for all seasons and in syndication with the exception of one syndicated season hosted by Gary Owens. Celebrities who frequently appeared were Jaye P. Morgan, Rex Reed, Arte Johnson, Phyllis Diller and Jamie Farr.

IVES, BURL: 95th BIRTH ANNIVERSARY. June 14, 1909. American singer and actor Burl Icle Ivanhoe Ives was born at Hunt, IL. He helped to reintroduce Anglo-American folk music in the '40s and '50s. Ives won an Academy Award for his supporting role in *The Big Country* (1958), and he is well known for his role as Big Daddy in both the film and Broadway productions of *Cat On a Hot Tin Roof*. He died Apr 14, 1995, at Anacortes, WA.

JAPAN: RICE PLANTING FESTIVAL. June 14. Osaka. Ceremonial transplanting of rice seedlings in paddy field at Sumiyashi Shrine, Osaka.

MALAWI: FREEDOM DAY. June 14. National holiday. Commemorates free elections in 1994.

MEET A MATE WEEK. June 14–20. To inspire singles seeking a mate to take advantage of summer by pursuing warm weather meeting opportunities. Options include singles travel, sports activities, New Blood parties and volunteer work. For info: Robin Gorman Newman, 44 Somerset Dr N, Great Neck, NY 11020. Phone: (516) 773-0911. E-mail: robin@lovecoach.com. Web: www.lovecoach.com.

NATIONAL FLAG DAY USA: PAUSE FOR THE PLEDGE. June 14. Held simultaneously across the country at 7 PM, EDT. PL 99–54 recognizes the Pause for the Pledge as part of National Flag Day ceremonies. The concept of the Pause for the Pledge of Allegiance was conceived as a way for all citizens to share a patriotic moment. National ceremony at Fort McHenry National Monument and Historic Shrine.

★**NATIONAL LITTLE LEAGUE BASEBALL WEEK.** June 14–20. Presidential Proclamation 3296, of June 4, 1959, covers all succeeding years. Always the week beginning with the second Monday in June. (H.Con.Res. 17 of June 1, 1959.)

QUEEN'S OFFICIAL BIRTHDAY. June 14. A holiday in Australia (except for Western Australia), Belize, Cayman Islands, Fiji and Papua New Guinea on the second Monday in June. In New Zealand and Tuvalu it is commemorated on the first Monday in June. Celebrating Queen Elizabeth II's "official" birthday, not the day she was actually born (which is Apr 21).

SPACE MILESTONE: *MARINER 5* (US). June 14, 1967. Launched on this date, interplanetary probe of Venus established that 72½–87½ percent of its atmosphere is carbon dioxide on Oct 18 flyby of planet.

STOWE, HARRIET BEECHER: BIRTH ANNIVERSARY. June 14, 1811. American writer Harriet Beecher Stowe, daughter of the Reverend Lyman Beecher and sister of Henry Ward Beecher. Author of *Uncle Tom's Cabin*, an antislavery novel that provoked a storm of protest and resulted in fame for its author. Two characters in the novel attained such importance that their names became part of the English language—the Negro slave, Uncle Tom, and the villainous slaveowner, Simon Legree. The reaction to *Uncle Tom's Cabin* and its profound political impact are without parallel in American literature. It is said that during the Civil War, when Harriet Beecher Stowe was introduced to President Abraham Lincoln, his words to her were, "So you're the little woman who wrote the book that made this great war." Stowe was born at Litchfield, CT, and died at Hartford, CT, July 1, 1896.

UNIVAC COMPUTER: ANNIVERSARY. June 14, 1951. Univac 1, the world's first commercial computer, designed for the US Bureau of the Census, was unveiled, demonstrated and dedicated at Philadelphia, PA. Though this milestone of the computer age was the first commercial electronic computer, it had been preceded by ENIAC (Electronic Numeric Integrator and Computer). It was completed under the supervision of J. Presper Eckert, Jr, and John W. Mauchly at the University of Pennsylvania in 1946.

US ARMY ESTABLISHED BY CONGRESS: ANNIVERSARY. June 14, 1775. Anniversary of Resolution of the Continental Congress establishing the army as the first US military service.

WARREN G. HARDING BECOMES FIRST PRESIDENT TO BROADCAST ON RADIO: ANNIVERSARY. June 14, 1922. Warren G. Harding became the first president to broadcast a message over the radio. The event was the dedication of the Francis Scott Key Memorial at Baltimore, MD. The first official government message was broadcast Dec 6, 1923.

WORLD JUGGLING DAY. June 14. Juggling clubs all over the world hold local festivals to demonstrate, teach and celebrate their art. For info: Intl Jugglers' Assn, PO Box 218, Montague, MA 01351. Phone: (413) 367-2401. Fax: (413) 367-0259. E-mail: IJugglersA@aol.com. Web: www.juggle.org/wjd.

BIRTHDAYS TODAY

Gene Barry, 83, actor (*War of the Worlds*, "Bat Masterson"), born Eugene Klass, New York, NY, June 14, 1921.
Yasmine Bleeth, 36, actress ("Baywatch," "Nash Bridges"), born New York, NY, June 14, 1968.
Boy George, 43, lead singer (Culture Club), born George Alan O'Dowd, London, England, June 14, 1961.
Marla Gibbs, 58, actress ("227," "The Jeffersons"), born Chicago, IL, June 14, 1946 (some sources say 1931 or 1941).
Stephanie Maria (Steffi) Graf, 35, former tennis player, born Brühl, West Germany, June 14, 1969.
Eric Arthur Heiden, 46, Olympic gold medal speed skater, born Madison, WI, June 14, 1958.
Traylor Howard, 38, actress ("Two Guys and a Girl"), born Orlando, FL, June 14, 1966.
Eddie Mekka, 52, actor ("Laverne and Shirley"), born Worcester, MA, June 14, 1952.

Will Patton, 50, actor (*Silkwood, Desperately Seeking Susan*; stage: *Tourists and Refugees #2* [Obie Award]), born Charleston, SC, June 14, 1954.
Samuel Bruce (Sam) Perkins, 43, former basketball player, born New York, NY, June 14, 1961.
Patricia (Pat) Summitt, 52, college basketball coach and former player, born Clarksville, TN, June 14, 1952.
Donald Trump, 58, real estate mogul, born New York, NY, June 14, 1946.

JUNE 15 — TUESDAY
Day 167 — 199 Remaining

ARKANSAS: ADMISSION DAY: ANNIVERSARY. June 15. Became 25th state in 1836.

BURLINGTON STEAMBOAT DAYS/AMERICAN MUSIC FESTIVAL. June 15–20. Mississippi Riverfront at Port of Burlington, IA. 42nd annual. Weeklong event offers community and visitors a chance to enjoy top-name entertainment and a carnival setting. Est attendance: 100,000. For info: Steamboat Days, PO Box 271, Burlington, IA 52601. Phone: (319) 754-4334. Fax: (319) 752-1299. Web: www.steamboatdays.com.

ENGLAND: ROYAL ASCOT. June 15–18. Ascot, Berkshire. Horse races. Annually, the third Tuesday to Friday in June.

FIRST FATAL AVIATION ACCIDENT: ANNIVERSARY. June 15, 1785. Two French aeronauts, Jean François Pilatre de Rozier and P.A. de Romain, attempting to cross the English Channel from France to England in a balloon, were killed when their balloon caught fire and crashed to the ground. Pilatre de Rozier, the first man to fly, thus became a fatality in the first fatal accident in aviation history.

GREAT SMOKY MOUNTAINS NATIONAL PARK ESTABLISHED: 70th ANNIVERSARY. June 15, 1934. Area along southern section of Tennessee–North Carolina boundary was authorized May 22, 1926, established for administration and protection only Feb 6, 1930, and finally established for full development as a national park in 1934. For further park info: Great Smoky Mountains Natl Park, Gatlinburg, TN 37738.

GRIEG, EDVARD: BIRTH ANNIVERSARY. June 15, 1843. Pianist, composer, conductor and teacher, the first Scandinavian to compose nationalistic music. Born at Bergen, Norway, and died there Sept 4, 1907.

"HEE HAW" TV PREMIERE: 35th ANNIVERSARY. June 15, 1969. "Hee Haw" has been described as a country-western version of "Laugh-In," composed of fast-paced sketches, silly jokes and songs. Though critics didn't like it, it had popular appeal and did well as a syndicated show. It was cohosted by Buck Owens and Roy Clark, alternating with guest hosts. Regular performers included Louis M. "Grandpa" Jones, Junior Samples, Jeannine Riley, Lulu Roman, David "Stringbean" Akeman, Sheb Wooley, Marianne Gordon, Minnie Pearl and Gordie Tapp.

JACKSON, RACHEL DONELSON ROBARDS: BIRTH ANNIVERSARY. June 15, 1767. Wife of Andrew Jackson, 7th president of the US, born at Halifax County, NC. Died at Nashville, TN, Dec 22, 1828.

MAGNA CARTA DAY: ANNIVERSARY. June 15. Anniversary of King John's sealing, in 1215, of the Magna Carta "in the meadow called Ronimed between Windsor and Staines on the fifteenth day of June in the seventeenth year of our reign." This document is regarded as the first charter of English liberties and one of the most important documents in the history of political and human freedom. Four original copies of the 1215 charter survive.

"MY LITTLE MARGIE" TV PREMIERE: ANNIVERSARY. June 15, 1952. "My Little Margie" was a half-hour sitcom about a "womanizing widower and his meddlesome daughter." Margie was played by Gale Storm and Charles Farrell played her father, Vern Albright.

NATIVE AMERICAN CITIZENSHIP DAY. June 15. Commemorates the day in 1924 when the US Congress passed legislation recognizing the citizenship of Native Americans.

NORWAY: CELEBRATION OF EDVARD GRIEG'S BIRTH ANNIVERSARY. June 15. Special celebrations at Lofthus on the Hardanger fjord where Grieg's cabin still stands.

PETIT JEAN ANTIQUE AUTO SHOW AND SWAP MEET. June 15–19. Petit Jean Mountain, Morrilton, AR. 46th annual show and meet with more than 100 antique and classic cars competing for awards, from turn-of-the-century to 1979 models. More than 1,500 vendor spaces filled with antique cars, parts and related items. Also, arts and crafts. Est attendance: 85,000. For info: Buddy Hoelzeman, Museum of Automobiles, 8 Jones Lane, Morrilton, AR 72110. Phone: (501) 727-5427. Fax: (501) 727-6482. E-mail: moa@ipa.net. Web: www.museumofautos.com.

QUARTERLY ESTIMATED FEDERAL INCOME TAX PAYERS' DUE DATE. June 15. For those individuals whose fiscal year is the calendar year and who make quarterly estimated federal income tax payments, today is one of the due dates. (Jan 15, Apr 15, June 15 and Sept 15, 2004.)

TWELFTH AMENDMENT TO US CONSTITUTION RATIFIED: 200th ANNIVERSARY. June 15, 1804. The 12th Amendment to the Constitution was ratified. It changed the method of electing the president and vice president after a tie in the electoral college during the election of 1800. Rather than each elector voting for two candidates with the candidate receiving the most votes elected president and the second-place candidate elected vice president, each elector was now required to designate his choice for president and vice president, respectively.

UNIVERSAL FATHER'S WEEK. June 15–21. The purpose of this week, which is celebrated throughout the world the third full week in June, is to stress the importance of fatherhood in family life. For complete info and quotations about the importance of the father, send $5 to cover expense of printing, handling and postage. For info: Dr Stanley Drake, Pres, Intl Society of Friendship and Goodwill, 999 Hood Rd, Ste 127, Marietta, GA 30068. Phone: (770) 565-2322. E-mail: ISFGW@bellsouth.net.

US LANDING ON SAIPAN: 60th ANNIVERSARY. June 15, 1944. In a continued effort to penetrate the Japanese inner defenses, US amphibious forces invaded the Mariana Islands. A huge fleet of 800 ships from Guadalcanal and Hawaii carried the 2nd and 4th Marine Divisions, consisting of 162,000 men. By the end of the day 20,000 of these men had established a 5½-mile-long beachhead on the island of Saipan. Though the American forces suffered heavy losses during an overnight counterattack, on the morning of June 16 the Marines still held the area they had taken the day before.

US WOMEN'S AMATEUR PUBLIC LINKS (GOLF) CHAMPIONSHIP. June 15–20 (tentative). Site TBD. For info: US Golf Assn, Golf House, PO Box 708, Championship Dept, Far Hills, NJ 07931. Phone: (908) 234-2300. Fax: (908) 234-9687. E-mail: usga@usga.org. Web: www.usga.org or www.uswapl.org.

BIRTHDAYS TODAY

Courteney Cox Arquette, 40, actress ("Family Ties," "Friends"), born Birmingham, AL, June 15, 1964.
Jim Belushi, 50, actor ("Saturday Night Live," *Men at Work*), born Chicago, IL, June 15, 1954.

☆ Chase's 2004 Calendar of Events ☆ June 15–16

Wade Anthony Boggs, 46, former baseball player, born Omaha, NE, June 15, 1958.
Simon Callow, 55, actor (*A Room with a View, Mr and Mrs Bridge, Howards End*); author (*Orson Welles*), born London, England, June 15, 1949.
Julie Hagerty, 49, actress (*Airplane!, Lost in America, Reversal of Fortune*; stage: *The House of Blue Leaves* [Theatre World Award]), born Cincinnati, OH, June 15, 1955.
Neil Patrick Harris, 31, actor ("Doogie Howser, MD," "Stark Raving Mad," *Clara's Heart*), born Albuquerque, NM, June 15, 1973.
Mike Holmgren, 56, football coach, born San Francisco, CA, June 15, 1948.
Helen Hunt, 41, actress ("Mad About You," *Twister*, Oscar for *As Good As It Gets*), born Los Angeles, CA, June 15, 1963.
Justin Leonard, 32, golfer, born Dallas, TX, June 15, 1972.
Nicola Pagett, 59, actress ("Upstairs Downstairs," *There's a Girl in My Soup*), born Cairo, Egypt, June 15, 1945.
Leah Remini, 34, actress ("The King of Queens," "Saved By the Bell"), born Brooklyn, NY, June 15, 1970.

JUNE 16 — WEDNESDAY
Day 168 — 198 Remaining

BLOOMSDAY: 100th ANNIVERSARY. June 16, 1904. Anniversary of events in Dublin recorded in James Joyce's *Ulysses*, whose central character is Leopold Bloom.

DICK TRACY DAYS. June 16–20. Woodstock, IL. A hometown 5-day celebration including a band concert, family-oriented block party on Main Street, entertainment, water fights, dance, parade, drum and bugle corps pageant. For info: Woodstock Chamber of Commerce, 136 Cass St, Woodstock, IL 60098. Phone: (815) 338-2436. Fax: (815) 338-2927. E-mail: chamber@woodstockilchamber.com. Web: www.woodstockilchamber.com.

GRIFFIN, JOHN HOWARD: BIRTH ANNIVERSARY. June 16, 1920. American author and photographer deeply concerned about racial problems in US. To better understand blacks in the American South, Griffin blackened his skin by the use of chemicals and ultraviolet light, keeping a journal as he traveled through the South, resulting in his best-known book, *Black Like Me*. Born at Dallas, TX. Died at Fort Worth, TX, Sept 9, 1980.

HOMESTEAD DAYS. June 16–20. Beatrice, NE. This community-wide celebration recognizes the importance of the Homestead Act of 1862 to the settlement of Nebraska. Entertainment, parades and special museum exhibits. Est attendance: 30,000. For info: Homestead Days, Beatrice Chamber of Commerce, 226 S 6th St, Beatrice, NE 68310. Phone: (402) 223-2338 or (800) 755-7745. E-mail: info@beatricechamber.com.

ILLINOIS SHAKESPEARE FESTIVAL. June 16–Aug 14 (start date tentative). Ewing Manor, Bloomington, IL. Productions of three Shakespeare plays (*Hamlet, Two Gentlemen of Verona* and *Troilus and Cressida*) presented under the stars on alternating nights. Est attendance: 15,000. For info: Illinois Shakespeare Festival, Campus Box 5700, Normal, IL 61790-5700. Phone: (309) 438-8110. Web: www.thefestival.org.

LADIES' DAY INITIATED IN BASEBALL: ANNIVERSARY. June 16, 1883. The New York Giants hosted the first Ladies' Day baseball game. Both escorted and unescorted ladies were admitted to the game free.

LAST DUSKY SEASIDE SPARROW: DEATH ANNIVERSARY. June 16, 1987. The last survivor of dusky seaside sparrows, whose habitat was a 10-mile stretch of marshland on Florida's east coast (near Titusville), died at age 12. The last specimen, named "Orange Band," lived its last days in a cage at Walt Disney World. For possible experimental cloning its heart and lungs were frozen and preserved.

LAUREL, STAN: BIRTH ANNIVERSARY. June 16, 1890. Worked with Oliver Hardy as the comedy team of Laurel & Hardy for more than 30 years. Born at Ulverston, England, Laurel died Feb 23, 1965, at Santa Monica, CA.

OUTDOOR SUMMER THEATER. June 16–Aug 7. Farmington, NM. Featuring *Black River Traders*. Performances are held in a natural sandstone amphitheater at the Lion's Wilderness park, with an optional southwest-style dinner served prior to each performance at 6:30 PM. Performances Wednesday through Saturday at 8 PM. Est attendance: 9,000. For info: Farmington Conv and Visitors Bureau, 3041 E Main St, Farmington, NM 87402. Phone: (800) 448-1240 or (505) 326-7602. Fax: (505) 327-0577. E-mail: fmncvb@cyberport.com. Web: www.farmingtonnm.org.

SMACKOVER OIL TOWN FESTIVAL. June 16–19. Smackover, AR. A celebration of the impact the oil industry has had on Smackover and the surrounding area. Included is an oil run, bass fishing tournament, arts and crafts, music, an ice cream social and events for all ages. Est attendance: 8,000. For info: Smackover Chamber of Commerce, PO Box 275, Smackover, AR 71762. Phone: (870) 725-3521. Fax: (870) 725-3521. E-mail: schamber@ipa.net.

SONOMA-MARIN FAIR. June 16–20. Petaluma Fairgrounds, Petaluma, CA. 65th annual country fair with livestock exhibitions, flowers, ugly dog contest, carnival and entertainment. Est attendance: 67,000. For info: Sonoma-Marin Fair, 175 Fairgrounds Dr, Petaluma, CA 94952. Phone: (707) 283-FAIR. Fax: (707) 283-3250. E-mail: info@sonoma-marinfair.org. Web: www.sonoma-marinfair.org.

SOUTH AFRICA: YOUTH DAY. June 16. National holiday. Commemorates a student uprising in Soweto against "Bantu Education" and the enforced teaching of Afrikaans in 1976.

SPACE MILESTONE: *VOSTOK 6* (USSR): FIRST WOMAN IN SPACE: ANNIVERSARY. June 16, 1963. Valentina Tereshkova, 26, former cotton-mill worker, born on collective farm near Yaroslavl, USSR, became the first woman in space when her spacecraft, *Vostok 6*, took off from the Tyuratam launch site. She manually controlled *Vostok 6* during the 70.8-hour flight through 48 orbits of Earth and landed by parachute (separate from her cabin) June 19, 1963. In November 1963 she married cosmonaut Andrian Nikolayev, who had piloted *Vostok 3* through 64 earth orbits, Aug 11–15, 1962. Their child Yelena (1964) was the first born to space-traveler parents.

WHITEWATER WEDNESDAY. June 16. Kernville, CA. One-hour and two-hour raft trips on the "Wild and Scenic" Kern River. BBQ lunch included. Fill out reservation form at www.kernvillechamber.org. Est attendance: 1,000. For info: Kernville Chamber of Commerce, PO Box 397, Kernville, CA 93238. Phone: (760) 376-2629 or toll free (866) KERNVILLE. Fax: (760) 376-4371. E-mail: kernvillechamber@lightspeed.net.

BIRTHDAYS TODAY

Sonia Braga, 54, actress ("American Family," *Kiss of the Spider Woman*), born Maringá, Paraná, Brazil, June 16, 1950.
Billy "Crash" Craddock, 65, singer ("Don't Destroy Me," "Ruby, Baby"), born Greensboro, NC, June 16, 1939.
Roberto Duran, 53, boxer, born Chorillo, Panama, June 16, 1951.
Cobi Jones, 34, soccer player, played in 1994, 1998 and 2002 World Cups, born Westlake Village, CA, June 16, 1970.
Laurie Metcalf, 49, actress (Emmy for "Roseanne"; "The Norm Show"), born Edwardsville, IL, June 16, 1955.

Phil Mickelson, 34, golfer, born San Diego, CA, June 16, 1970.
Joyce Carol Oates, 66, writer (*Triumph of the Spider Monkey, The Time Traveler*), born Lockport, NY, June 16, 1938.
Irving Penn, 87, photographer, born Plainfield, PA, June 16, 1917.
Erich Segal, 67, author (*Acts of Faith, Love Story*), born Brooklyn, NY, June 16, 1937.
Joan Van Ark, 61, actress ("Knots Landing"), born New York, NY, June 16, 1943.
Kerry Wood, 27, baseball player, born Irving, TX, June 16, 1977.

JUNE 17 — THURSDAY
Day 169 — 197 Remaining

BADGER STATE SUMMER GAMES SECTIONALS AND FINALS. June 17–20. Sectional competition in four Wisconsin communities, finals in Madison, WI, June 23–26. 20th annual sports festival for Wisconsin residents of all ages and abilities, featuring 28 sports and opening ceremonies. Major sponsors: American Family Insurance, Wisconsin Milk Marketing Board, Mobil and St. Joseph's Hospital. Est attendance: 20,000. For info: Badger State Games, PO Box 7788, Madison, WI 53707-7788. Phone: (608) 226-4780. Fax: (608) 226-9550. E-mail: info@SportsinWisconsin.com. Web: www.SportsinWisconsin.com.

BELLAMY, RALPH: 100th BIRTH ANNIVERSARY. June 17, 1904. American actor Ralph Rexford Bellamy was born at Chicago, IL. He appeared in more than 100 films and was best known for his stage and film portrayals of President Franklin D. Roosevelt. He was a founder of the Screen Actors' Guild and president of Actors' Equity. Bellamy was awarded an honorary Academy Award in 1987. He died Nov 29, 1991, at Los Angeles, CA.

BOARDWALK ART SHOW & FESTIVAL. June 17–20. Virginia Beach, VA. 49th annual. The works of approximately 300 artists are displayed along the boardwalk in this nationally ranked fine art and crafts show and sale. High quality evening performances. Annually, on Father's Day weekend. Est attendance: 250,000. For info: Contemporary Art Center of Virginia, 2200 Parks Ave, Virginia Beach, VA 23451. Phone: (757) 425-0000. Fax: (757) 425-8186. Web: www.cacv.org.

BUNKER HILL DAY. June 17. Suffolk County, MA. Legal holiday in the county in commemoration of the Battle of Bunker Hill that took place in 1775.

CANADA: SAM STEELE DAYS. June 17–20. Cranbrook, BC. Parade, Sweetheart Pageant, banquet and ball, railway museum tours, bocce tournament, wild west show, black powder shoot, ball tournament, loggers' sports, soccer tournament, live entertainment, climbing wall and children's festival. Est attendance: 19,000. For info: Sam Steele Society, PO Box 115, Cranbrook, BC, Canada V1C 4H6. Phone: (250) 426-4161. Fax: (250) 426-3873. E-mail: cbkchamber@cyberlink.bc.ca.

FAIN, SAMMY: BIRTH ANNIVERSARY. June 17, 1902. American composer Sammy Fain was born Samuel Feinberg at New York, NY. He won an Academy Award for his song "Secret Love" from *Calamity Jane* (1953) and for "Love Is a Many-Splendored Thing" from the film of the same name (1955). He died Dec 6, 1989, at Los Angeles, CA.

FINLAND: KUOPIO DANCE FESTIVAL. June 17–23. Kuopio, Finland. Some 70 events centering on classical ballet, contemporary dance, folklore plus types depending on the theme for the festival. World-renowned dance and music companies; seminars, lectures, exhibits and films; selection of dance courses with internationally known dance teachers. Est attendance: 45,000. For info: Finnish Tourist Board, 655 Third Ave, New York, NY 10017. Phone: (212) 885-9700 or (358) (17) 282-1541. Fax: (358) (17) 261-1990. E-mail: kuopio.dance.festival@travel.fi. Web: www.kuopiodancefestival.fi.

FORT UNION TRADING POST RENDEZVOUS. June 17–20. 25 miles SW of Williston, ND. Re-creation of the fur trade era. Fur trade fair, music, blacksmith and craft demonstrations plus Trader's Row. Sponsor: National Park Service, Fort Union Trading Post National Historic Site. Est attendance: 5,000. For info: Fort Union Trading Post NHS, 15550 Hwy 1804, Williston, ND 58801. Phone: (701) 572-9083. Fax: (701) 572-7321. Web: www.nps.gov/fous.

HERSEY, JOHN: 90th BIRTH ANNIVERSARY. June 17, 1914. American novelist, born at Tientsin, China, who wrote *A Bell for Adano*, which won the Pulitzer Prize in 1945. *The Wall* and *Hiroshima* are both based on fact and set in Poland and Japan respectively in World War II. Died at Key West, FL, Mar 24, 1993.

HOOPER, WILLIAM: BIRTH ANNIVERSARY. June 17, 1742. Signer of the Declaration of Independence, born at Boston, MA. Died Oct 14, 1790, at Hillsboro, NC.

ICELAND: INDEPENDENCE DAY: 60th ANNIVERSARY. June 17. National holiday. Anniversary of founding of republic and independence from Denmark in 1944 is major festival, especially in Reykjavik. Parades, competitions, street dancing.

LOUISIANA PEACH FESTIVAL. June 17–19. Ruston, LA. The 54th annual Louisiana Peach Festival will feature rodeo, parade, concerts, cooking contests, sporting events, arts & crafts and more. Est attendance: 50,000. For info: Becky O'Nan, Ruston/Lincoln Convention & Visitors Bureau, 104 E Mississippi Ave, Ruston, LA 71270. Phone: (800) 392-9032. E-mail: info@rustonlincoln.com. Web: www.rustonlincoln.com.

MISS LOUISIANA PAGEANT. June 17–19. Monroe Civic Center, Monroe, LA. Preliminaries followed by the main event of crowning the new Miss Louisiana. Always culminates on the 3rd Saturday in June. Est attendance: 5,500. For info: Miss Louisiana Organization, PO Box 6003, Monroe, LA 71211. Phone: (318) 387-1658. Fax: (318) 387-6171. E-mail: LKing411@msn.com. Web: www.misslouisiana.com.

MOON PHASE: NEW MOON. June 17. Moon enters New Moon phase at 4:27 PM, EDT.

PARTY IN THE PLAZA. June 17–Aug 26 (Thursdays). Millennium Plaza, Aurora, IL. Weekly music series held every Thursday from 12:00 PM to 1:30 PM. For info: Lisa Garcia, City of Aurora, Mayor's Office of Special Events, 43 E Downer Place, Aurora, IL 60507. Phone: (630) 844-3640. Fax: (630) 906-7068.

PRAIRIE VILLA RENDEZVOUS. June 17–20. Prairie du Chien, WI. Rendezvous with history and learn about life during the fur trading days and experience the fur trader lifestyle firsthand. Many participants come from around the country to display furs, others demonstrate the cumbersome process of loading a rifle with gunpowder and some prepare Indian fry bread and buffalo burgers. Workshops offer information on a variety of subjects including plants and medicines, basket weaving and beadworking. With more than 600 lodges and teepees, this is one of the largest Midwest trading rendezvous. Est attendance: 25,000. For info: Prairie du Chien Area Chamber of Commerce, PO Box 326, Prairie du Chien, WI 53821. Phone: (800) 732-1673.

SOUTH AFRICA REPEALS LAST APARTHEID LAW: ANNIVERSARY. June 17, 1991. The Parliament of South Africa repealed the Population Registration Act, removing the law that was the foundation of apartheid. The law, first enacted in 1950, required the classification by race of all South Africans at birth. It established four compulsory racial categories: white, mixed race, Asian and black. Although this marked the removal of the last of the apartheid laws, blacks in South Africa still could not vote.

STRAVINSKY, IGOR FYODOROVICH: BIRTH ANNIVERSARY. June 17, 1882. Russian composer and author, born

☆ Chase's 2004 Calendar of Events ☆ June 17–18

at Oranienbaum (near Leningrad). Among his best-known music: the ballets *The Firebird*, *Petrushka* and *The Rite of Spring*; the choral work *Symphony of Psalms*; and *Abraham and Isaac, A Sacred Ballet*. Died at New York, NY, Apr 6, 1971.

UNITED NATIONS: WORLD DAY TO COMBAT DESERTIFICATION AND DROUGHT. June 17. Proclaimed by the General Assembly Dec 19, 1994 (Res 49/115). States were invited to promote public awareness of the need for international cooperation to combat desertification and the effects of drought and the implementation of the UN Convention to Combat Desertification. For info: United Nations, Dept of Public Info, New York, NY 10017. Web: www.un.org.

US OPEN (GOLF) CHAMPIONSHIP. June 17–20. Shinnecock Hills Golf Club, Southampton, NY. For info: US Golf Assn, Golf House, PO Box 708, Championship Dept, Far Hills, NJ 07931. Phone: (908) 234-2300. Fax: (908) 234-9687. E-mail: usga@usga.org. Web: www.usga.org.

WATERGATE DAY: ANNIVERSARY. June 17, 1972. Anniversary of arrests at Democratic Party Headquarters (in Watergate complex, Washington, DC) that led to revelations of political espionage, threats of imminent impeachment of the president and, on Aug 9, 1974, the resignation of President Richard M. Nixon.

WESLEY, JOHN: BIRTH ANNIVERSARY. June 17, 1703. Born at Epworth, England. Wesley, along with his younger brother Charles, was the founder of Methodism. John Wesley died Mar 2, 1791.

WEST ALLIS WESTERN DAYS FAMILY JAMBOREE. June 17–20. West Allis, WI. This four-day, fun-filled festival kicks off at 7:00 PM on June 17 with one of the largest non-motorized parades in the world. Live music every day, rodeo, midway, carnival, treats & eats. 40th annual celebration. Est attendance: 150,000. For info: WAND, c/o West Allis Charities, Inc, PO Box 14544, West Allis, WI 53214. Web: www.westerndays.com.

YOUTH COWBOY POETRY GATHERING. June 17–20. Boys Ranch, TX. Boys and girls from around the country gather for this free educational event featuring such well-known poets and musicians as Red Steagall, Don Edwards, Waddie Mitchell, R.W. Hampton and Sons of the San Joaquin. Youths learn about western heritage, cowboy values, creative writing and songwriting. There will be youth poetry and music sessions and a variety of seminars. For info: Cal Farley's Boys Ranch & Affiliates, Attn: Darci Johnson, PO Box 1890, Amarillo, TX 79174. Phone: (806) 372-2341. Fax: (806) 372-6638. E-mail: darcijohnson@calfarley.org. Web: www.calfarley.org.

BIRTHDAYS TODAY

Dermontti Dawson, 39, former football player, born Lexington, KY, June 17, 1965.
Tommy R. Franks, 59, general, US Army, commander-in-chief of US forces during Operation Enduring Freedom in Iraq, born Wynnewood, OK, June 17, 1945.
Elroy Leon ("Crazylegs") Hirsch, 81, Hall of Fame football player, born Wausau, WI, June 17, 1923.
Dan Jansen, 39, former speed skater, sportscaster, born West Allis, WI, June 17, 1965.
Greg Kinnear, 41, actor (*Sabrina*, *As Good As It Gets*), born Logansport, IN, June 17, 1963.

Mark Linn-Baker, 51, actor ("Perfect Strangers," *My Favorite Year*), born St. Louis, MO, June 17, 1953.
Barry Manilow, 58, singer ("Mandy," "I Write the Songs"), songwriter, born Brooklyn, NY, June 17, 1946.
Roderick R. (Rod) Paige, 71, US Secretary of Education, born Monticello, MS, June 17, 1933.
Joe Piscopo, 53, comedian (former "Saturday Night Live" regular), born Passaic, NJ, June 17, 1951.
Venus Williams, 24, tennis player, born Lynwood, CA, June 17, 1980.

JUNE 18 — FRIDAY
Day 170 — 196 Remaining

ANTIQUES BY THE BAY. June 18–19. St. Ignace, MI. 8th annual show for antique and classic original vehicles 25 years or older. Special tours and awards plus auto world celebrities. For info: Nostalgia Productions, Inc, 268 Hillcrest Blvd, St. Ignace, MI 49781. Phone: (906) 643-8087. Fax: (906) 643-9784. E-mail: edreavie@nostalgia-prod.com. Web: www.nostalgia-prod.com or www.auto-shows.com.

BATTLE OF WATERLOO: ANNIVERSARY. June 18, 1815. Date of the decisive defeat of Napoleon by British generals Wellington and Blucher, near Waterloo in central Belgium.

CAHN, SAMMY: BIRTH ANNIVERSARY. June 18, 1913. Tin Pan Alley legend Sammy Cahn was born Samuel Cohen at New York City. He was nominated for 26 Academy Awards and won four times for "Three Coins in the Fountain" (1954), "All the Way" (1957), "High Hopes" (1959) and "Call Me Irresponsible" (1963). In the late 1940s he began working with composer Jimmy Van Heusen, and the two in essence were the personal songwriting team for Frank Sinatra. Cahn wrote the greatest number of Sinatra hits, including "Love and Marriage," "The Second Time Around," "High Hopes" and "The Tender Trap." Sammy Cahn died Jan 15, 1993, at Los Angeles, CA.

CANADA: NOVA SCOTIA MULTICULTURAL FESTIVAL. June 18–20. Dartmouth, NS. 18th annual. Cultural events include five tents housing exhibits, food booths, children's tent, performances, beer tent with live bands and fashion show. Est attendance: 45,000. For info: Barbara Campbell, Exec Dir, Multicultural Assn of Nova Scotia, 1113 Marginal Rd, Halifax, NS, Canada B3H 4P7. Phone: (902) 423-6534. Fax: (902) 422-0881. E-mail: info@multifest.ca. Web: www.multifest.ca.

CZECH DAYS. June 18–19. Tabor, SD. 56th annual. Czechs dressed in their festive costumes gather with people from all parts of the world in this gala celebration. Fine Czech foods, dancing, music and entertainment. Est attendance: 15,000. For info: Tabor Area Chamber of Commerce, Inc, Box 21, Tabor, SD 57063. Phone: (605) 463-2476. E-mail: czechdays@yahoo.com. Web: www.byelectric.com/~tabor.

DELMARVA CHICKEN FESTIVAL. June 18–19 Salisbury, MD. 56th annual. A family event focusing on chicken, the leading agricultural enterprise on the Delmarva Peninsula. Food, entertainment and consumer information are featured. Est attendance: 25,000. For info: Connie Parvis, Delmarva Poultry Industry, Inc, 16686 County Seat Hwy, Georgetown, DE 19947-4881. Phone: (302) 856-9037. E-mail: dpi@dpichicken.com.

DENMARK: VIKING FESTIVAL. June 18–July 4. Frederiksund (about 25 miles northwest of Copenhagen). Famous outdoor plays based on Danish legends. Annually, the next-to-last Friday in June through the first Sunday in July.

DOLLARS AGAINST DIABETES (DAD'S) DAY. June 18–20. DAD's Day is a national fund-raising event conducted in more than 300 cities to help the Diabetes Research Institute find a permanent cure for the disease. Annually, on Father's Day weekend. Sponsor: Building and Construction Trades Dept of the AFL-CIO. Participation 30,000. For info: Building and Construction Trades Dept, 815 16th St NW, Ste 600, Washington, DC 20006. Phone: (888) 883-DADS. E-mail: dadbctd@aol.com. Web: www.dadsday.org.

June 18 ☆ Chase's 2004 Calendar of Events ☆

EGYPT: EVACUATION DAY. June 18. Public holiday celebrating the anniversary of the withdrawal of the British Army from the Suez Canal area of Egypt in 1954.

FIRST AMERICAN WOMAN IN SPACE: ANNIVERSARY. June 18, 1983. Dr. Sally Ride, 32-year-old physicist and pilot, functioned as a "mission specialist" and became the first American woman in space when she began a six-day mission aboard the space shuttle *Challenger*. The "near-perfect" mission was launched from Cape Canaveral, FL, and landed June 24, 1983, at Edwards Air Force Base, CA. See also: "Ride, Sally Kristen: Birthday" (May 26) and "Space Milestone: First Woman in Space" (June 16).

FOLGER, HENRY CLAY, JR: BIRTH ANNIVERSARY. June 18, 1857. American businessman and industrialist who developed one of the finest collections of Shakespeareana in the world and bequeathed it (The Folger Shakespeare Library, Washington, DC) to the American people. Born at New York, NY. Died June 11, 1930, at Brooklyn, NY.

FULTON COUNTY HISTORICAL POWER SHOW. June 18–20. Rochester, IN. Power show will include antique tractors, hit'n'miss engines, equipment and antique trucks. Also: vendors of swap parts, crafts, food and more. Contests held for exhibitors. Admission fee. Annually, third weekend in June. Est attendance: 6,000. For info: Fulton County Historical Power Assn, c/o Fulton County Historical Society, 37 E 375 N, Rochester, IN 46975. Phone: (574) 223-4436. E-mail: melinda@rtcol.com. Web: icss.net/~fchs.

GETTYSBURG BRASS BAND FESTIVAL. June 18–20. Gettysburg, PA. Brass bands, ensembles, drum and bugle corps converge on Gettysburg for many musical events along Gettysburg's "Historical Pathways." Workshops, concerts and performances culminate in one grand finale at the Gettysburg College Stadium on Saturday evening. Est attendance: 8,000. For info: Gettysburg CVB, PO Box 4117, Gettysburg, PA 17325. Phone: (717) 334-6274. Fax: (717) 334-1166. E-mail: gettysburgcvb@dejazzd.com. Web: www.gettysburgcvb.org.

HUCK FINN'S JUBILEE. June 18–20. Mojave Narrows Regional Park, Victorville, CA. A Huck Finn celebration with river raft building, country and bluegrass music, hayrides, old-time tent circus, crafts and food, plus Route 66 car show and the California State Arm Wrestling Championships. Annually, on Father's Day weekend. Est attendance: 16,000. For info: Don or Barbara Tucker, PO Box 56419, Riverside, CA 92517. Phone: (909) 780-8810. E-mail: huckfinn@huckfinn.com. Web: www.huckfinn.com.

KIAMICHI OWA-CHITO FESTIVAL OF THE FOREST. June 18–19. Beavers Bend State Park, Broken Bow, OK. A celebration of American Indian culture and of the forest industry. Compete in ax throwing, cross-buck sawing, pole climbing, pole filling and logging to become the "Bull of the Woods." Also kids' games, food booths, Miss Owa-Chito contest, photography contest, golf tournament, canoe races, archery contest, turkey-calling contest, 5K road race, talent contest and more. Annually, the weekend of the third Friday in June. Est attendance: 30,000. For info: Chamber of Commerce, 113 W Martin Luther King, Broken Bow, OK 74728. Phone: (580) 584-3393. Fax: (580) 584-7698. E-mail: bbchamber@pine-net.com.

KYSER, KAY: BIRTH ANNIVERSARY. June 18, 1906. American bandleader whose band, "Kay Kyser's Kollege of Musical Knowledge," enjoyed immense popularity in the swing era. He was born James King Kern Kyser at Rocky Mount, NC. A shrewd showman and performer, he said he never learned to read music or play an instrument. Among his hit recordings were "Three Little Fishes" and "Praise the Lord and Pass the Ammunition," a World War II favorite. Kyser retired from show business in 1951 and died at Chapel Hill, NC, July 23, 1985.

LONG BEACH BAYOU FESTIVAL. June 18–20. Queen Mary Events Park, Long Beach, CA. Celebrate Cajun/Creole cultures with food, live nonstop music, arts & crafts, activities. Est attendance: 5,000. For info: Phone: (562) 427-3713. Web: www.LongBeachFestival.com.

LUDINGTON HARBOR FESTIVAL. June 18–20. Ludington, MI. Nautical festival celebrating proud past and prosperous future of Ludington's harbor. Featuring kids' activities, arts & crafts show, Coast Guard Open House, Old Time baseball, entertainment. Est attendance: 30,000. For info: Ludington Area Chamber of Commerce, 5300 W US 10, Ludington, MI 49431. Phone: (800) 542-4600. Fax: (231) 845-6857. Web: www.ludingtoncvb.com.

MALLORY, GEORGE LEIGH: BIRTH ANNIVERSARY. June 18, 1886. English explorer and mountain climber born at Mobberley, Cheshire, England. Last seen climbing through the mists toward the summit of the highest mountain in the world, Mount Everest, on the morning of June 8, 1924. Best remembered for his answer when asked why he wanted to climb Mount Everest: "Because it is there." In 1999 Mallory's body was found by an expedition to Mount Everest, 75 years after his death at age 37.

MEDFORD CRUISE. June 18–20. Medford, OR. Fun Run and Grudge Races on Friday, Show'n Shine and Cruise on Saturday, pancake breakfast and Show'n Shine on Sunday. 600 classic pre-1972 cars. Come join the food and fun! Kids' activities provided. For info: Medford Cruise, PO Box 629, Medford, OR 97501. Phone: (541) 779-4847 or (541) 772-5222. E-mail: vcb@medfordchamber.com.

MIDNIGHT SUN BASEBALL GAME. June 18. Fairbanks, AK. To celebrate the summer solstice. Game is played without artificial lights at 10:35 PM. Est attendance: 4,000. For info: Alaska Goldpanners, Box 71154, Fairbanks, AK 99707. Phone: (907) 451-0095. Web: www.goldpanners.com.

NATIONAL SPLURGE DAY. June 18. Today is the day to go out and do something extraordinarily indulgent. Motto: Have fun! [©1994.] Because of the escalating costs of Eventological® Literature, a charge of $7 must be assessed for each request. Checks are to be made payable to: Adrienne Sioux Koopersmith, 1437 W Rosemont, #1W, Chicago, IL 60660-1319. Phone: (773) 743-5341. Fax: (773) 743-5395. E-mail: la_koop@yahoo.com.

NCAA DIVISION I MEN'S BASEBALL CHAMPIONSHIP. June 18–28. Creighton University, Omaha, NE. For info: Natl Collegiate Athletic Assn, 700 W Washington Ave, PO Box 6222, Indianapolis, IN 46206-6222. Phone: (317) 917-6222. Web: www.ncaasports.com.

PENNSYLVANIA RIB, WING AND MUSIC FESTIVAL. June 18–20. Westmoreland Fairgrounds, Greensburg, PA. More than 30 booths of national and local rib, wing and food vendors, fantastic entertainment, crafts, car and motorcycle shows, games, rides and much more. Fun for the whole family! Est attendance: 18,000. For info: Debbie or Dave Stoner, Family Festivals Assn, Inc, PO Box 166, Irwin, PA 15642. Phone/fax: (724) 863-4577. Web: www.familyfestivals.com.

June 2004	S	M	T	W	T	F	S
			1	2	3	4	5
	6	7	8	9	10	11	12
	13	14	15	16	17	18	19
	20	21	22	23	24	25	26
	27	28	29	30			

☆ Chase's 2004 Calendar of Events ☆   June 18–19

PORTER, SYLVIA: BIRTH ANNIVERSARY. June 18, 1913. American financial journalist Sylvia Feldman Porter was born at Patchogue, NY. Her column was syndicated by the *Los Angeles Times*, reaching 450 newspapers worldwide. She also wrote more than 20 books and was noted for her ability to turn complex economic language into readable prose. Porter died June 5, 1991, at Pound Ridge, NY.

RED RIVER VALLEY FAIR. June 18–26. Fargo, ND. One of the largest fairs in the state with 4-H and commercial exhibits, horse shows, car shows, large carnival midway, free entertainment. Big-name country-western and rock entertainers perform everyday. Est attendance: 30,000. For info: (701) 282-2200 or North Dakota Tourism, Century Center, 1600 E Century Ave, Ste 2, Bismarck, ND 58503. Phone: (701) 328-2525 or (800) 435-5663. Web: www.redrivervalleyfair.com.

ROGUE RIVER JET BOAT MARATHON. June 18–20 (tentative). Gold Beach, OR. Watch jet boats ply the twisted, rushing whitewater rapids of the mighty Rogue at speeds faster than your eyes can focus. Festivities start Friday afternoon with a Boat Show at Jot's Resort from 3–6 PM. Saturday and Sunday will be full days of racing from 9 AM–4 PM, starting with the Mail Boat Dock to Lobster Creek. A total of six legs are planned due to the shorter course. The approximate time for the last boat to run the course is 10 minutes. The small high-pitched hydroplanes will also hit the river this weekend for action. Hydroplane races begin at 11:30 AM and run four legs each day, finishing at 2 PM. Est attendance: 4,000. For info: Gold Beach Chamber of Commerce, 29279 Ellensburg Ave, #3, Gold Beach, OR 97444. Phone: (541) 474-0029 or (800) 525-2334. Fax: (541) 247-0188. Web: www.goldbeachchamber.com.

SECRET CITY FESTIVAL. June 18–19. Oak Ridge, TN. A unique event highlighting the genesis of Oak Ridge, TN, as a major site of the Manhattan Project. Oak Ridge was created in 1942 in an almost unknown area in the hills of East Tennessee, specifically for government research. It has grown to be one of this nation's most important technology sites and is a mecca for scientific and technological innovations. Est attendance: 12,000. For info: Oak Ridge CVB, 302 S Tulane Ave, Oak Ridge, TN 37830. Phone: (865) 482-7821. Fax: (865) 481-3543. E-mail: or cvb@visit-or.org. Web: www.visit-or.org.

SEYCHELLES: CONSTITUTION DAY. June 18. National holiday commemorating adoption of constitution in 1993.

SOUTH CAROLINA FESTIVAL OF FLOWERS. June 18–20. Greenwood, SC. Come and see the beautiful flowers of South Carolina. Includes arts and crafts displays, entertainment, sports events and more. Est attendance: 25,000. For info: Greenwood Chamber of Commerce, SC Festival of Flowers, PO Box 980, Greenwood, SC 29648. Phone: (864) 223-8411. Fax: (864) 229-9785. E-mail: frank@greenwoodscchamber.org. Web: www.scfestivalofflowers.org.

SPACE MILESTONE: *CHALLENGER* STS-7 (US): ANNIVERSARY. June 18, 1983. Shuttle *Challenger* launched from Kennedy Space Center, FL, with crew of five, including Sally K. Ride (first American woman in space), Robert Crippen, Norman Thagard, John Fabian and Frederick Houck. Landed at Edwards Air Force Base, CA, on June 24 after near-perfect six-day mission.

SPLINTERFEST. June 18–20. Amana, IA. A craft show with displays, products, demonstrations, equipment, supplies, entertainment, and food. Annually, the third weekend in June. Est attendance: 6,000. For info: Tammy Meyer, Splinterfest/Holzfest, PO Box 215, Dyersville, IA 52040. Phone: (563) 875-7017. Fax: (563) 875-9506. E-mail: dwwi1@msn.com.

STAMP EXPO. June 18–20. Radisson Hotel, Sherman Oaks, CA. Est attendance: 5,000. For info: Intl Stamp Collectors Society, PO Box 854, Van Nuys, CA 91408. Phone: (818) 997-6496. Fax: (818) 988-4337. E-mail: iibick@aol.com. Web: www.bick.net.

WAR OF 1812: DECLARATION ANNIVERSARY. June 18, 1812. After much debate in Congress between "hawks" such as Henry Clay and John Calhoun, and "doves" such as John Randolph, Congress issued a declaration of war on Great Britain. The action was prompted primarily by Britain's violation of America's rights on the high seas and British incitement of Indian warfare on the frontier. War was seen by some as a way to acquire Florida and Canada. The hostilities ended with the signing of the Treaty of Ghent on Dec 24, 1814, at Ghent, Belgium.

WORK@HOME FATHER'S DAY. June 18. One day each year to honor and celebrate those fathers who have elected to work from home—either as home-based entrepreneurs or teleworkers—as a means to improve family interaction and professional satisfaction. Annually, the Friday before Father's Day. For info: Jeff Zbar, PO Box 8263, Coral Springs, FL 33075. Phone: (954) 346-4393. Fax: (954) 346-0251. E-mail: jeff@chiefhomeofficer.com. Web: www.chiefhomeofficer.com.

BIRTHDAYS TODAY

Lou Brock, 65, Hall of Fame baseball player, born El Dorado, AR, June 18, 1939.
Eddie Cibrian, 31, actor ("Third Watch"), born Burbank, CA, June 18, 1973.
Roger Ebert, 62, film critic ("Siskel and Ebert"), born Urbana, IL, June 18, 1942.
Carol Kane, 52, actress (*Hester Street*, *The Princess Bride*, "Taxi"), born Cleveland, OH, June 18, 1952.
Donald Keene, 82, literary critic, translator, educator, born New York, NY, June 18, 1922.
Paul McCartney, 62, singer, songwriter (The Beatles, Wings), born Liverpool, England, June 18, 1942.
John D. Rockefeller IV, 67, US Senator (D, West Virginia), born New York, NY, June 18, 1937.
Isabella Rossellini, 52, model, actress (*Blue Velvet*, *Cousins*), born Rome, Italy, June 18, 1952.
Tom Wicker, 78, journalist, author (*One of Us: Richard Nixon & the American Dream*), born Hamlet, NC, June 18, 1926.

JUNE 19 — SATURDAY
Day 171 — 195 Remaining

BASCOM, EARL W.: BIRTH ANNIVERSARY. June 19, 1906. Rodeo showman and pioneer, Earl W. Bascom was born at Vernal, UT. During his career he developed the first side-delivery rodeo chute (1916), the first hornless bronc saddle (1922) and the first one-handed bareback rigging (1924). He produced the first rodeo in Mississippi and also produced the first rodeo performed at night under electric lights (1935). Bascom died Aug 28, 1995, at Victorville, CA.

BATTLE OF PHILIPPINE SEA: 60th ANNIVERSARY. June 19–20, 1944. Determined to prevent any further advancement by the Allies in Japan's area of inner defense, Vice-Admiral Jisaburo Ozawa ordered the Imperial fleet to the Mariana Islands. Admiral Raymond Spruance, possibly the US's greatest and most successful naval commander, ordered a strike force against the Japanese fleet in the Philippine Sea. A furious battle developed in the skies between US carrier-borne aircraft and Japanese aircraft from their carriers and land bases on the Marianas. The Japanese lost three aircraft carriers (*Shokaku*, *Taiho* and *Hiyo*), two destroyers and one tanker. Three carriers, one battleship, three cruisers, one destroyer and three tankers were seriously damaged. The Japanese lost at least 400 aircraft, the Americans 130.

333

COYOTE CHASE. June 19. Wellington, NV. Annual Beta Sigma Phi 10K and 5K runs and a two-mile walk. Pancake breakfast, art, crafts and more. Annually, the third Saturday in June. For info: Mason Valley Chamber of Commerce, 227 S Main St, Yerington, NV 89447. Phone: (775) 463-2245. Fax: (775) 463-3369. Web: www.tele-net.net/lyon.

EMANCIPATION DAY IN TEXAS. June 19, 1865. In honor of the emancipation of the slaves in Texas. See also: "Juneteenth" (below).

FIRST RUNNING OF THE BELMONT STAKES: ANNIVERSARY. June 19, 1867. The first running of the Belmont Stakes took place at Jerome Park, NY. The team of jockey J. Gilpatrick and his horse Ruthless finished in a time of 3:05. The Belmont Stakes continued at Jerome Park until 1889, then moved to Morris Park, NY, between 1890–1905, and in 1906 settled at Belmont Park, NY, where it has continued to the present day. The Belmont Stakes is the oldest event of horse racing's Triple Crown.

FORTAS, ABE: BIRTH ANNIVERSARY. June 19, 1910. Abe Fortas was born at Memphis, TN. He was appointed to the Supreme Court by President Lyndon Johnson in 1965. Prior to his appointment he was known as a civil libertarian, having argued cases for government employees and other individuals accused by Senator Joe McCarthy of having communist affiliations. He argued the 1963 landmark Supreme Court case of *Gideon v Wainwright*, which established the right of indigent defendants to free legal aid in criminal prosecutions. In 1968 he was nominated by Johnson to succeed Chief Justice Earl Warren, but his nomination was withdrawn after much conservative opposition in the Senate. In 1969 Fortas became the first Supreme Court Justice to be forced to resign after revelations about questionable financial dealings were made public. He died Apr 5, 1982, at Washington, DC.

GARFIELD: BIRTHDAY. June 19, 1978. America's favorite lasagna-loving cat celebrates his birthday. "Garfield," a modern classic comic strip created by Jim Davis, first appeared in 1978, and has brought laughter to millions. For info: Kim Campbell, Paws, Inc, 5440 E Co Rd 450 N, Albany, IN 47320. Web: www.garfield.com.

GEHRIG, LOU: BIRTH ANNIVERSARY. June 19, 1903. Baseball great Henry Louis Gehrig (lifetime batting average of .341), who played in seven World Series, was born at New York, NY, and died there June 2, 1941, from the degenerative muscle disease amyotrophic lateral sclerosis, which has become known as Lou Gehrig's disease.

HERITAGE CRAFT AND OLDE-TIME MUSIC FESTIVAL. June 19–20. Coshocton, OH. Old-time musical entertainment; guitar, fiddle, dulcimer and banjo workshops; games and flat-pick guitar contest. Annually, third weekend in June. Est attendance: 5,000. For info: Roscoe Village Fdtn, 381 Hill St, Coshocton, OH 43812. Phone: (800) 877-1830 or (740) 622-9310. Fax: (740) 623-6555. E-mail: rvmarketing@roscoevillage.com. Web: www.roscoevillage.com.

HOWARD, MOE: BIRTH ANNIVERSARY. June 19, 1897. The head stooge in the Three Stooges, Moe Howard was born Moses Horwitz at Bensonhurst, NY. He died May 4, 1975, at Hollywood, CA. Howard began his show business career at age 12 by running errands at Vitagraph studios. He worked with Ted Healy in various comedy and singing acts, and together they teamed with Shemp Howard and Larry Fine in the mid-1920s for an early Stooges act. In 1930 the Stooges made their film debut in *Soup to Nuts*. Although the members of the Three Stooges changed over the years, Moe Howard was one of the constants. Howard appeared in four feature films without the other Stooges, including *Doctor Death, Seeker of Souls*.

HUBBARD, ELBERT: BIRTH ANNIVERSARY. June 19, 1856. Born at Bloomington, IL, Elbert Green Hubbard, American author and craftsman, founded the Roycroft Press at East Aurora, NY. Best known of his writings were *A Message to Garcia* and a series of essays titled *Little Journeys*. He also became famous for his furniture designs. Hubbard lost his life with the sinking of the *Lusitania*, May 7, 1915.

"I'VE GOT A SECRET" TV PREMIERE: ANNIVERSARY. June 19, 1952. Celebrity panelists tried to guess the guests' secrets on this popular game show; celebrity guests also came on to baffle the panel. Guests whispered their secret to the host and the audience saw it on the screen. Garry Moore hosted the show, followed by Steve Allen and Bill Cullen. Allen Sherman ("My Son the Folk Singer") created the show and most of the celebrity "secrets." Celebrity panelists included Bill Cullen, Betsy Palmer, Henry Morgan, Bess Myerson, Steve Allen and Jayne Meadows.

JUNETEENTH. June 19. Celebrated in Texas to commemorate the day in 1865 when Union General Granger proclaimed the slaves of Texas free. Also proclaimed as Emancipation Day by the Florida legislature. Juneteenth has become an occasion for commemoration by African Americans in many parts of the US.

KCQ COUNTRY MUSIC FEST. June 19. Saginaw, MI. Country music's hottest artists perform on stage on Ojibway Island. Also featuring a classic car show, art fair and great food, this is mid-Michigan's hottest summer attraction. Free admission. Call to receive a free program of this year's performers. Est attendance: 70,000. For info: WKCQ, Box 1776, Saginaw, MI 48605. Phone: (989) 752-8161. Fax: (989) 752-8102. Web: www.98FMKCQ.com.

LAKESTRIDE HALF-MARATHON. June 19. Ludington, MI. Half-marathon race that begins at Lakeshore Drive and Tinkham (by the beach) takes runners along a scenic course through the wooded trails and sand dunes of Lake Michigan at Ludington State Park. Annually, the third Saturday in June. Est attendance: 10,000. For info: Ludington Area CVB, 5300 W US 10, Ludington, MI 49431. Phone: (800) 542-4600. Fax: (231) 845-6857. Web: www.ludingtoncvb.com.

LOCKPORT OLD CANAL DAYS. June 19–20. Lockport, IL. Festival in historic canal community. Crafts, parade. Annually, the third weekend in June. Est attendance: 20,000. For info: Lockport Old Canal Days, PO Box 31, Lockport, IL 60441. Phone: (815) 838-4744.

LONGEST DAM RUN. June 19. Fort Peck, MT. This is a sanctioned 5K and 10K run. There are also 5K walks and a 1-mile run/walk. The run crosses 1.8 miles of Fort Peck Dam. At two miles into the 10K race, the course rises in elevation some 350 feet over a distance of approximately two miles. The 5K is flat. Both distances finish running downhill grade from the top of the dam. Included in the events is a triathlon, 22-mile bike ride and canoeing/kayaking. Annually, the third weekend in June. Est attendance: 550. For info: Glasgow Chamber of Commerce and Agriculture, Box 832, Glasgow, MT 59230. Phone: (406) 228-2222. Fax: (406) 228-2244. E-mail: chamber@nemontel.net.

MARCHAND, NANCY: BIRTH ANNIVERSARY. June 19, 1928. Actress ("Lou Grant," "The Sopranos") born at Buffalo, NY. Died June 18, 2000, at Stratford, CT.

MIDNIGHT SUN FESTIVAL. June 19–20. Nome, AK. A celebration of the summer solstice, which is when Nome experiences the midnight sun with more than 22 hours of direct sunlight. The festival usually includes a parade, raft race and barbecue. Annually, on the Saturday and Sunday closest to the summer solstice. Est attendance: 500. For info: Nome Conv & Visitors Bureau, PO Box 240, Nome, AK 99762. Phone: (907) 443-6624. Fax: (907) 443-5832. Web: www.nomealaska.org.

NEW OXFORD OUTDOOR ANTIQUE SHOW. June 19. New Oxford, PA. Arts, crafts, antiques and flea market. Annually, the third Saturday in June. Est attendance: 30,000. For info: Gettysburg CVB, PO Box 4117, Gettysburg, PA 17325. Phone: (717) 334-6274. Fax: (717) 334-1166. E-mail: gettysburgcvb@dejazzd.com. Web: www.gettysburgcvb.org.

NORSKEDALEN'S MIDSUMMER FEST. June 19–20. Norskedalen Nature and Heritage Center, Coon Valley, WI. Celebrate the summer solstice and Sankt Hans Dag (Saint John's Day) in Scandinavian style. Pioneer crafts and demonstrations; children's activities, entertainment, food and raffle; nature hikes, animal presentations and horse-drawn wagon rides. Woodcarving show and competition, open air museum; artisans demonstrating and selling their works. Est attendance: 1,500. For info: Nature and Heritage Center, Inc, Norskedalen, PO Box 235, Coon Valley, WI 54623. Phone: (608) 452-3424. Fax: (608) 452-3157. E-mail: info@norskedalen.org. Web: www.norskedalen.org.

OIL BOWL FOOTBALL CLASSIC. June 19. Memorial Stadium, Wichita Falls, TX. 65th annual. For more than 60 years, high school all-stars from Texas and Oklahoma tangle in Memorial Stadium, to benefit disadvantaged children. Est attendance: 14,000. For info: Wichita Falls CVB, 1000 5th St, Wichita Falls, TX 76301. Phone: (940) 716-5500. Fax: (940) 716-5509. E-mail: mpec@wf.net. Web: www.wichitafalls.org.

PASCAL, BLAISE: BIRTH ANNIVERSARY. June 19, 1623. French philosopher, physicist and mathematician born at Clermont-Ferrand and died at Paris, Aug 19, 1662. It was Pascal who said, "Had Cleopatra's nose been shorter, the whole history of the world would have been different." And, in his *Provincial Letters*, he wrote, "I have made this letter longer than usual because I lack the time to make it short."

ROCHESTERFEST. June 19–27. Rochester, MN. This community festival includes Midwestern lumberjack championships, cultural diversity, children's and senior events, gigantic street parade, street vendors with exotic foods, country night, rock and roll night, street dance and breakfast on the farm. Est attendance: 150,000. For info: Carole Brown, Exec Dir, Box 007, Rochester, MN 55903. Phone: (507) 285-8769. Fax: (507) 285-8718.

ROSENBERG EXECUTION: ANNIVERSARY. June 19, 1953. Anniversary of the electrocution of the only married couple ever executed together in the US. Julius (35) and Ethel (37) Rosenberg were executed for espionage at Sing Sing Prison, Ossining, NY. Time for the execution was advanced several hours to avoid conflict with the Jewish Sabbath. Their conviction has been a subject of controversy over the years.

SANDPOINT SADDLE CLUB HORSE SHOW. June 19–20. Sandpoint, ID. English, Western, Parade, Spanish Fiesta classes. Annually, the third weekend in June. For info: Denise Mills, PO Box 243, Sandpoint, ID 83864. Phone: (208) 263-4091. E-mail: deniselm@netw.com. Web: www.sandpointsaddleclub.org.

SPACE MILESTONE: *ARIANE* (ESA). June 19, 1981. Launched from Kourou, French Guiana by the European Space Administration, *Ariane* carried two satellites into orbit: *Meteostat 2*, an ESA weather satellite, and *Apple*, a geostationary communications satellite for India, to be stationed over Sumatra.

STONE MOUNTAIN VILLAGE ARTS AND CRAFTS FESTIVAL. June 19–20. Stone Mountain Village, GA. 32nd annual juried arts and crafts show featuring more than 100 of the southeast's finest artists and crafters. With extraordinary entertainment and the best country cooking around. Est attendance: 8,000. For info: Dir, Village Festivals, PO Box 667, Stone Mountain Village, GA 30086. Phone: (770) 498-2097. Web: www.stonemountainvillage.com.

SULLY, THOMAS: BIRTH ANNIVERSARY. June 19, 1783. Artist born at Horncastle, Lincolnshire, England; died at Philadelphia, PA, Nov 5, 1872. He is best known as a painter of nearly 2,000 portraits. Sully studied art first with his brother, a miniaturist, and then with Gilbert Stuart, Benjamin West and others. Among the people Sully painted were Queen Victoria, the Marquis de Lafayette and presidents Thomas Jefferson, James Madison and Andrew Jackson.

URUGUAY: ARTIGAS DAY. June 19. National holiday. Commemorates the birth in 1764 of General José Gervasio Artigas, the father of Uruguayan independence.

"WAR IS HELL": 125th ANNIVERSARY. June 19, 1879. Addressing the graduating class at Michigan Military Academy, General William Tecumseh Sherman uttered his famous words on war—more than a decade after the Civil War had ended. He said, "War is at best barbarism. . . . Its glory is all moonshine. It is only those who have neither fired a shot nor heard the shrieks and groans of the wounded who cry aloud for blood, more vengeance, more desolation. War is hell."

WORLD SAUNTERING DAY. June 19. A day to revive the lost art of Victorian sauntering and to discourage jogging, lollygagging, sashaying, fast walking and trotting. [Originated by the late W.T. Rabe of Saulte Ste. Marie, MI.]

BIRTHDAYS TODAY

Paula Abdul, 42, singer ("Forever Your Girl"), dancer, choreographer, born Los Angeles, CA, June 19, 1962.
Aung San Suu Kyi, 59, Nobel Peace Prize winner, born Rangoon, Burma, June 19, 1945.
Charles Gwathmey, 66, architect, born Charlotte, NC, June 19, 1938.
Andy Lauer, 39, actor ("Caroline in the City," *I'll Be Home for Christmas*), born Santa Monica, CA, June 19, 1965.
Brian McBride, 32, soccer player, born Arlington Heights, IL, June 19, 1972.
Dirk Nowitzki, 26, basketball player, born Würzburg, West Germany, June 19, 1978.
Marisa Pavan, 72, actress (*The Diary of Anne Frank*), born Cagliari, Sardinia, June 19, 1932.
Phylicia Rashad, 56, actress ("The Cosby Show"), born Houston, TX, June 19, 1948.
Gena Rowlands, 68, actress ("Peyton Place," *A Woman Under the Influence*), born Cambria, WI, June 19, 1936 (some sources say 1943 or 1930).
Salman Rushdie, 57, author (*The Jaguar Smile, Satanic Verses, Midnight's Children*), born Bombay, India, June 19, 1947.
Kathleen Turner, 50, actress (*Body Heat, Peggy Sue Got Married, Romancing the Stone*), born Springfield, MO, June 19, 1954.
Ann Wilson, 53, musician, lead singer (Heart), born San Diego, CA, June 19, 1951.

June 20 ☆ *Chase's 2004 Calendar of Events* ☆

JUNE 20 — SUNDAY
Day 172 — 194 Remaining

ARGENTINA: FLAG DAY. June 20. National holiday. Commemorates the death in 1820 of Manuel Belgrano, the designer of the Argentine flag.

CARPENTER ANT AWARENESS WEEK. June 20–26. Wood-destroying organisms cause Americans to spend $3.5 billion annually. This week will focus attention on the identification, biology and habits of carpenter ants, and provide consumers with information on the elimination of these costly pests. Annually, the last full week of June. For info: Jerry Batzner, Pres, Batzner Pest Management, Inc, 16700 W Victor Rd, New Berlin, WI 53151. Phone: (262) 797-4160. Fax: (262) 797-4166. E-mail: JerryB @batzner.com.

CHESNUTT, CHARLES W.: BIRTH ANNIVERSARY. June 20, 1858. Born at Cleveland, OH, Chesnutt was considered by many as the first important black novelist. His collections of short stories included *The Conjure Woman* (1899) and *The Wife of His Youth and Other Stories of the Color Line* (1899). *The Colonel's Dream* (1905) dealt with the struggles of the freed slave. His work has been compared to later writers such as William Faulkner, Richard Wright and James Baldwin. He died Nov 15, 1932, at Cleveland.

"THE ED SULLIVAN SHOW" ("TOAST OF THE TOWN") TV PREMIERE: ANNIVERSARY. June 20, 1948. "The Ed Sullivan Show" was officially titled "Toast of the Town" until 1955. It was the longest-running variety show (through 1971) and the most popular for decades. Ed Sullivan, the host, signed all types of acts, both well-known and new, trying to have something to please everyone. Thousands of performers appeared, many making their television debut, such as Irving Berlin, Victor Borge, Hedy Lamarr, Walt Disney, Fred Astaire and Jane Powell. Two acts attracted the largest audience of the time: Elvis Presley and the Beatles.

EIGHTEENTH-CENTURY WHEAT HARVEST. June 20. The Claude Moore Colonial Farm at Turkey Run, McLean, VA. Help the colonial farm family cut and bind wheat, the farmer's second most important cash crop. Light refreshments and 18th-century games. Annually, the third Sunday in June. Est attendance: 500. For info: Liz Hauris, The Claude Moore Colonial Farm, Turkey Run, 6310 Georgetown Pike, McLean, VA 22101. Phone: (703) 442-7557. Fax: (703) 442-0714. Web: www.1771 .org.

FAMILY AWARENESS DAY. June 20. A day to reflect on the important role of fathers in the American family. "Remembering always that every kid needs a Dad." A day and time to reestablish and reaffirm every man's place in our culture. Annually, third Sunday in June. For info: Judith Natale, CEO & Founder, NCAC America–USA, 2091 Del Monte Ave, Monterey, CA 93940. Fax: (831) 655-4547. E-mail: childaware@aol.com.

★**FATHER'S DAY.** June 20. Presidential Proclamation issued for third Sunday in June in 1966 and annually since 1971. (PL 92–278 of Apr 24, 1972.)

FATHER'S DAY. June 20. Recognition of the third Sunday in June as Father's Day occurred first at the request of Mrs John B. Dodd of Spokane, WA, on June 19, 1910. It was proclaimed for that date by the mayor of Spokane and recognized by the governor of Washington. The idea was publicly supported by President Calvin Coolidge in 1924, but not presidentially proclaimed until 1966. It was assured of annual recognition by PL 92–278 of April 1972. Also celebrated on this day in Britain.

	S	M	T	W	T	F	S
June			1	2	3	4	5
2004	6	7	8	9	10	11	12
	13	14	15	16	17	18	19
	20	21	22	23	24	25	26
	27	28	29	30			

FATHER'S DAY CELEBRATION. June 20. Jenkinson's Aquarium, Point Pleasant Beach, NJ. Calling all kids! Bring your dad for a special day together to learn about the roles of fathers in the marine environment. One father admitted free with each paid child's admission. Est attendance: 800. For info: Jenkinson's Aquarium, 300 Ocean Ave, Point Pleasant Beach, NJ 08742. Phone: (732) 899-1212. Fax: (732) 899-1717. E-mail: aquarium @jenkinsons.com. Web: www.jenkinsons.com.

FIRST BALLOON HONEYMOON: 95th ANNIVERSARY. June 20, 1909. Roger Burnham and Eleanor Waring took the first balloon honeymoon, ascending at 12:40 PM in the balloon *Pittsfield*. They began their trip at Woods Hole, Cape Cod, MA, and landed at 4:30 PM in an orchard at Holbrook, MA.

FIRST DOCTOR OF SCIENCE DEGREE EARNED BY A WOMAN: ANNIVERSARY. June 20, 1895. Caroline Willard Baldwin became the first woman to earn a doctor of science degree at Cornell University, Ithaca, NY.

FORT SEWARD WAGON TRAIL. June 20–26. Jamestown, ND. Relive an important part of western history as you travel in a covered wagon across the great prairies region of North Dakota. This year's ride is called the "Prairie Rose Trail" and follows an historic route. Enjoy fresh air, good campfire cooking and sleeping under the stars in the great North Dakota sky. For info: (701) 252-6844 or North Dakota Tourism, Century Center, 1600 E Century Ave, Ste 2, Bismarck, ND 58503. Phone: (701) 328-2525 or (800) 435-5663.

HUSBAND CAREGIVER DAY. June 20. Coinciding with Father's Day, today we will honor husbands who give health care to their wives or children. For info: Richard Boyd, MD, 1111 W Spruce St, #30, Yakima, WA 98902. Phone: (509) 575-1922. Fax: (509) 248-2501. E-mail: rboyd@cwmed.com.

LEVITT PAVILION PERFORMING ARTS/MUSIC FESTIVAL. June 20–Aug 22. Levitt Pavilion, Westport, CT. 31st annual. Performing Arts/Music Festival conducts more than 50 nights of high-quality entertainment offered free to the general public. In addition, a few concerts are presented with a nominal admission charged to raise money to underwrite the free nights of the festival. Est attendance: 60,000. For info: Freda Welsh, Exec Dir, Levitt Pavilion, 260 S Compo Rd, Westport, CT 06880. Phone: (203) 226-7600. Fax: (203) 226-2330. E-mail: levitt@ci .westport.ct.us. Web: www.levittpavilion.com.

LIZZIE BORDEN VERDICT: ANNIVERSARY. June 20, 1893. Spectators at her trial cheered when the "not guilty" verdict was read by the jury foreman in the murder trial of Lizzy Borden on this date. Elizabeth Borden had been accused of and tried for the hacking deaths of her father and stepmother in their Fall River, MA, home, Aug 4, 1892.

MANCHESTER FATHER'S DAY SALMON BAKE. June 20. Manchester Library, Manchester, WA. Annually on Father's Day. Outdoor grilled salmon and all the fixings, raffles, door prizes and used book sale. Sponsored by the Friends of the Manchester Library, proceeds are used for library maintenance. For info: Manchester Library, 8067 E Main St, PO Box 128, Manchester, WA 98353. Phone: (360) 871-3921. Fax: (360) 871-6152. E-mail: manchester@krl.org.

MIDSUMMER. June 20. One of the "Lesser Sabbats" during the Wiccan year, celebrating the peak of the Sun God in his annual cycle. Annually, on the summer solstice.

MURPHY, AUDIE: 80th BIRTH ANNIVERSARY. June 20, 1924. Born at Kingston, TX, Murphy was the most decorated soldier in World War II and later became an actor in western and war movies. He died May 28, 1971, in a plane crash near Roanoke, VA.

336

☆ Chase's 2004 Calendar of Events ☆ June 20-21

SPANISH-AMERICAN WAR SURRENDER OF GUAM TO US: ANNIVERSARY. June 20, 1898. Having not known that a war was in progress and having no ammunition on the island, the Spanish commander of Guam surrendered to Captain Glass of the USS *Charleston*.

SUMMER. June 20–Sept 22. In the Northern Hemisphere summer begins today with the summer solstice, at 8:57 PM EDT. Note that in the Southern Hemisphere today is the beginning of winter. Anywhere between the Equator and the Arctic Circle, the sun rises and sets farthest north on the horizon for the year and length of daylight is maximum (12 hours, 8 minutes at equator, increasing to 24 hours at the Arctic Circle).

TOAD HOLLOW DAY OF THANK YOU. June 20. A day to say or write a thank-you to the people who have helped us along the way. For info: Ralph Morrison, Toad Hollow, PO Box 45, Vicksburg, MI 49097. Phone: (800) 574-8623.

UNITED NATIONS: WORLD REFUGEE DAY. June 20. A day to bring attention to the situation of refugees—their rights, as well as their suffering. First observed on June 20, 2001, the 50th anniversary of the 1951 Convention on the Status of Refugees. Date chosen to coincide with Africa Refugee Day. For info: United Nations, Dept of Public Info, New York, NY 10017. Web: www.un.org.

VEGAN WORLD DAY. June 20. Vegan World Day, celebrated annually on the first day of summer—the day of most light, and most hope—is designed to recognize the benefits of the vegan (completely vegetarian) lifestyle and its positive impact on human and environmental health, world hunger and animal suffering. People are asked to go vegan on this day and not consume or wear any animal products and avoid entertainment based on animal exploitation. It is a day of celebration of life! Annually, first day of summer. For info: Bob Linden, PO Box 220025, Newhall, CA 91322. Phone: (661) 259-1675. Fax: (661) 259-1675. E-mail: vegan@acninc.net. Web: www.goveganradio.com.

WEST VIRGINIA: ADMISSION DAY: ANNIVERSARY. June 20, 1863. Became 35th state in 1863. Observed as a holiday in West Virginia. The state of West Virginia is a product of the Civil War. Originally part of Virginia, West Virginia became a separate state when Virginia seceded from the Union.

WOMAN RUNS THE HOUSE: ANNIVERSARY. June 20, 1921. Alice Robertson of Oklahoma became the first woman to preside in the US House of Representatives. Robertson presided for half an hour.

BIRTHDAYS TODAY

Danny Aiello, Jr, 71, actor ("Lady Blue," *Do the Right Thing*), born New York, NY, June 20, 1933.
LaVar Arrington, 26, football player, born Pittsburgh, PA, June 20, 1978.
Olympia Dukakis, 73, actress, theatrical director (Oscar for *Moonstruck; Steel Magnolias*), born Lowell, MA, June 20, 1931.
John Goodman, 52, actor ("Roseanne," *The Flintstones*), born Afton, MO, June 20, 1952.
Nicole Kidman, 37, actress (Oscar for *The Hours*), born Honolulu, HI, June 20, 1967.
Martin Landau, 73, actor (*Tucker: The Man and His Dream; Crimes and Misdemeanors*; Oscar for *Ed Wood*), born Brooklyn, NY, June 20, 1931.
Michael Landon, Jr, 40, actor ("Bonanza: The Return," "Bonanza: The Ghosts"), born Encino, CA, June 20, 1964.
Cyndi Lauper, 51, singer ("Girls Just Want to Have Fun"), born Brooklyn, NY, June 20, 1953.
John Mahoney, 64, actor ("Frasier"), born Manchester, England, June 20, 1940.
Anne Murray, 59, singer (*Country*, "Snowbird," "Could I Have This Dance"), born Springhill, NS, Canada, June 20, 1945.
Lionel Richie, 55, singer ("Truly"), songwriter, born Tuskegee, AL, June 20, 1949.
Robert Rodriguez, 36, director/screenwriter (*Spy Kids, Desperado*), born San Antonio, TX, June 20, 1968.

James Tolkan, 73, actor (*Serpico, Back to the Future, Dick Tracy*), born Calumet, MI, June 20, 1931.
Bob Vila, 58, handyman, TV show host, born Miami, FL, June 20, 1946.
Andre Watts, 58, pianist, born Nuremberg, Germany, June 20, 1946.
Brian Wilson, 62, singer (The Beach Boys), songwriter, born Hawthorne, CA, June 20, 1942.

JUNE 21 — MONDAY
Day 173 — 193 Remaining

BABY BOOMERS RECOGNITION DAY. June 21. As baby boomers, we'll never forget the Beatles, Vietnam War and other sixties events. However, many of us accomplished a great deal, becoming successful in business, education, medicine and other fields. This special day commemorates our contributions. Annually, June 21. For info: Dorothy Zjawin, 61 W Colfax Ave, Roselle Park, NJ 07204. Phone: (908) 241-6241.

BATTLE OF OKINAWA ENDS: ANNIVERSARY. June 21, 1945. With American grenades exploding in the background, inside the Japanese command cave at Mabuni the battle for Okinawa was ended when Major General Isamu Cho and Lieutenant General Mitsuru Ushijima killed themselves in the ceremonial rite of hara-kiri. In the long battle that had begun Apr 1, the American death toll reached enormous proportions by Pacific battle standards—7,613 died on land and 4,907 in the air or from kamikaze attacks. A total of 36 US warships were sunk. More than 70,000 Japanese and 80,000 civilian Okinawans died in the course of the battle.

CANADA: NEWFOUNDLAND DISCOVERY DAY. June 21. Commemorates the discovery of Newfoundland by John Cabot, June 24, 1497. Commemorated on the Monday nearest June 24.

CANCER, THE CRAB. June 21–July 22. In the astronomical/astrological zodiac, which divides the sun's apparent orbit into 12 segments, the period June 21–July 22 is identified, traditionally, as the sun sign of Cancer, the Crab. The ruling planet is the moon.

EASTERN MUSIC FESTIVAL. June 21–July 26 (tentative). Guilford College, Greensboro, NC. 43rd annual summer festival of classical concerts and recitals performed by resident professionals and a corps of talented young students from the US and abroad. Est attendance: 63,000. For info: Eastern Music Festival, PO Box 22026, Greensboro, NC 27420. Phone: (336) 333-7450. Fax: (336) 333-7454. E-mail: info@easternmusicfestival.org. Web: www.easternmusicfestival.org.

ENGLAND: CITY OF LONDON FESTIVAL. June 21–July 8. London. Annual multi-arts festival held in some of the city's most historically interesting buildings, including St. Paul's Cathedral and the Tower of London. Est attendance: 30,000. For info: City of London Festival, Bishopsgate Hall, 230 Bishopsgate, London, England EC2M 4HW. Phone: (44) (020) 7377-0540. Fax: (44) (020) 7377-1972. Web: www.colf.org.

ENGLAND: LAWN TENNIS CHAMPIONSHIPS AT WIMBLEDON. June 21–July 4. Wimbledon, London. World famous men's and women's singles and doubles championships for the most coveted titles in tennis. Tickets are allocated via public ballot. Send SASE for details between August and December 2003. For info: All England Lawn Tennis and Croquet Club, PO Box 98,

June 21 ☆ Chase's 2004 Calendar of Events ☆

Wimbledon, London, England SW19 5AE. Phone: (44) (20) 8944-1066. Fax: (44) (20) 8947-8752. Web: www.wimbledon.org.

GREENLAND: NATIONAL DAY. June 21. National holiday.

HIRSCHFELD, AL: BIRTH ANNIVERSARY. June 21, 1903. Caricature artist known for his inimitable sketches of Broadway and Hollywood stars, Al Hirschfeld was born at St. Louis, MO. His first cartoon appeared in 1926 in the now-defunct *New York Herald Tribune*. Later moving to *The New York Times*, his drawings appeared on the drama page for seven decades. He was known for always hiding the name "Nina" (his daughter's name) somewhere in every caricature that he published. His art is found in many museums, including the Metropolitan Museum of Art in New York City. He died Jan 20, 2003, at New York, NY.

HURRICANE AGNES: ANNIVERSARY. June 21–26, 1972. Hurricane Agnes hit the eastern seaboard wreaking havoc across seven Atlantic Coast states. Casualties included 118 lives and 116,000 homes, leaving more than 200,000 homeless after Agnes dumped 28.1 trillion gallons of water over 5,000 square miles.

NATIONAL OLD-TIME FIDDLERS' CONTEST AND FESTIVAL. June 21–26. Weiser, ID. 52nd anniversary. Largest fiddling event in the world to help perpetuate the old-time fiddling of pioneer America. Annually, the third full week in June. Est attendance: 15,000. For info: National Old-Time Fiddlers' Contest, 309 State St, Weiser, ID 83672. Phone: (800) 437-1280. E-mail: notfc@ruralnetwork.net. Web: www.fiddlecontest.com.

NEW HAMPSHIRE RATIFIES CONSTITUTION: ANNIVERSARY. June 21, 1788. By a vote of 57 to 47, New Hampshire became the ninth state to ratify the Constitution. With this ratification, the Constitution became effective for all ratifying states, as the approval of nine states was required for the Constitution to go into effect.

POLAR BEAR SWIM. June 21. Nome, AK. 2 PM on the red sand beaches. Dozens of intrepid swimmers have plunged into the frigid Bering Sea on this day since 1975. The swim may be rescheduled if the ocean ice hasn't sufficiently broken up. For info: Leo B. Rasmussen, Nome Rotary Club, PO Box 275, Nome, AK 99762. Phone: (907) 443-2798. E-mail: leaknome@nook.net.

SARTRE, JEAN-PAUL: BIRTH ANNIVERSARY. June 21, 1905. French philosopher, "father of existentialism," born at Paris, France. In 1964 Sartre rejected the Nobel Prize for Literature when it was awarded to him. He died at Paris, Apr 15, 1980. In *Being and Nothingness*, he wrote: "Man can will nothing unless he has first understood that he must count on no one but himself; that he is alone, abandoned on earth in the midst of his infinite responsibilities, without help, with no other aim than the one he sets for himself, with no other destiny than the one he forges for himself on this earth."

TANNER, HENRY OSSAWA: BIRTH ANNIVERSARY. June 21, 1859. Henry Ossawa Tanner was one of the first black artists to be exhibited in galleries in the US. He was born at Pittsburgh, PA. He died May 25, 1937, at Paris.

TEXAS-OKLAHOMA JUNIOR GOLF TOURNAMENT. June 21–26. Wichita Falls, TX. More than 1,000 golfers 18 years old and under from 33 states and several foreign countries participate each year. Est attendance: 1,600. For info: Wichita Falls Conv & Visitors Bureau, 1000 5th St, Wichita Falls, TX 76301. Phone: (940) 716-5500. Fax: (940) 716-5509. Web: www.wichitafalls.org.

★ ★ ★

TOMPKINS, DANIEL D.: BIRTH ANNIVERSARY. June 21, 1774. 6th vice president of the US (1817–25), born at Fox Meadows, NY. Died at Staten Island, NY, June 11, 1825.

US VIRGIN ISLANDS: ORGANIC ACT DAY. June 21. Commemorates the enactment by the US Congress, July 22, 1954, of the Revised Organic Act, under which the government of the Virgin Islands is organized. Observed annually on the third Monday in June.

WASHINGTON, MARTHA DANDRIDGE CUSTIS: BIRTH ANNIVERSARY. June 21, 1731. Wife of George Washington, first president of the US, born at New Kent County, VA. Died at Mount Vernon, VA, May 22, 1802.

BIRTHDAYS TODAY

Meredith Baxter, 57, actress ("Bridget Loves Bernie," "Family," "Family Ties"), born Los Angeles, CA, June 21, 1947.
Benazir Bhutto, 51, Pakistani political leader, born Karachi, Pakistan, June 21, 1953.
Berke Breathed, 47, cartoonist ("Bloom County"), born Croatia, June 21, 1957.
Thomas Doane (Tom) Chambers, 45, former basketball player, born Ogden, UT, June 21, 1959.
Derrick D. Coleman, 37, basketball player, born Mobile, AL, June 21, 1967.
Sammi Davis-Voss, 40, actress ("Homefront," *Hope and Glory*), born Kidderminster, Worcestershire, England, June 21, 1964.
Jim Douglas, 53, Governor of Vermont (R), born Springfield, MA, June 21, 1951.
Joe Flaherty, 64, writer, actor ("Second City TV," "SCTV Network 90"), born Pittsburgh, PA, June 21, 1940.
Michael Gross, 57, actor ("Family Ties"), born Chicago, IL, June 21, 1947.
Mariette Hartley, 63, actress ("Peyton Place"), born New York, NY, June 21, 1941.
Richard Jefferson, 24, basketball player, born Los Angeles, CA, June 21, 1980.
Bernie Kopell, 71, actor ("Get Smart," "The Love Boat," "When Things Were Rotten"), born New York, NY, June 21, 1933.
Juliette Lewis, 31, actress (*The Other Sister, The Evening Star*), born Los Angeles, CA, June 21, 1973.
Nils Lofgren, 53, musician, singer, songwriter, born Chicago, IL, June 21, 1951.
Monte Markham, 66, actor ("Mr Deeds Goes to Town," "Dallas"), born Manatee, FL, June 21, 1938.
Robert Pastorelli, 50, actor (*Dances with Wolves, Michael*, "Murphy Brown"), born New Brunswick, NJ, June 21, 1954.
Jane Russell, 83, actress (*The Outlaw, Gentlemen Prefer Blondes*), born Bemidji, MN, June 21, 1921.
Maureen Stapleton, 79, actress (Oscar for *Reds*; stage: *The Little Foxes*), born Troy, NY, June 21, 1925.
Rick Sutcliffe, 48, former baseball player, born Independence, MO, June 21, 1956.
Larry Wachowski, 39, filmmaker with brother Andy Wachowski (*The Matrix*), born Chicago, IL, June 21, 1965.
Prince William (William Arthur Philip Louis), 22, son of Prince Charles and Princess Diana, born London, England, June 21, 1982.

JUNE 22 — TUESDAY
Day 174 — 192 Remaining

BLASS, BILL: BIRTH ANNIVERSARY. June 22, 1922. Born at Fort Wayne, IN, William Ralph Blass moved to New York at 17 to study fashion design. After service in World War II, he returned to New York and went to work for Anne Klein. By 1970 he had his own company and put American fashion on the map—favoring a sporty yet classy silhouette. His client list soon included Jacqueline Kennedy, Barbra Streisand and Gloria Vanderbilt, and he became one of the most successful fashion designers in history. He was known as a philanthropist in his later years, and died soon after retirement at New Preston, CT, June 12, 2002.

CHESAPEAKE-LEOPARD AFFAIR: ANNIVERSARY. June 22, 1807. One of the events leading to the War of 1812 occurred about 40 miles east of Chesapeake Bay. The US frigate *Chesapeake* was fired upon and boarded by the crew of the British man-of-war *Leopard*. The *Chesapeake*'s commander, James Barron, was court-martialed and convicted of not being prepared for action. Later Barron killed one of the judges (Stephen Decatur) in a duel fought at Bladensburg, MD, Mar 22, 1820.

CHINA: DRAGON BOAT FESTIVAL. June 22. An important Chinese observance, the Dragon Boat Festival commemorates a hero of ancient China, poet Qu Yuan, who drowned himself in protest against injustice and corruption. It is said that rice dumplings were cast into the water to lure fish away from the body of the martyr, and this is remembered by the eating of zhong zi, glutinous rice dumplings filled with meat and wrapped in bamboo leaves. Dragon boat races are held on rivers. The Dragon Boat Festival is observed in many countries by their Chinese populations (date will differ; in North America the date will be June 21). Also called Fifth Month Festival or Summer Festival. Annually, the fifth day of the fifth lunar month.

CIRCUS TRAIN WRECK: ANNIVERSARY. June 22, 1918. A Michigan Central Railroad troop train, after several days shuttling soldiers to New York from Chicago, was deadheading back to the Midwest when it struck the rear of the Hagenbeck–Wallace Circus train. The circus train had stopped to have its brake box overhauled at Ivanhoe, IN. Fifty-three circus performers were killed. Of the circus animals not killed outright, many that were crippled and maimed had to be destroyed by police officers. The performers, of whom only three could be identified, were buried in a mass grave. The engineer, A.K. Sargent, who was accused of falling asleep at the throttle, was tried and acquitted.

CROATIA: ANTIFASCIST STRUGGLE DAY. June 22. National holiday. Commemorates uprising against fascist invaders in 1941.

DONNA REED PERFORMING ARTS FESTIVAL. June 22–26. Denison, IA. Performing arts festival in Donna Reed's hometown. Focus of the festival is educational workshops in various areas of the performing arts taught by Hollywood and New York professionals. Also included are celebrity golf tournament, auction, beach party, parade, lunch with the stars, 10K run and theatrical performances for the general public. Annually, the third full week in June. Est attendance: 10,000. For info: Gwen Ecklund, Exec Dir, Donna Reed Foundation for the Performing Arts, 1305 Broadway, Denison, IA 51442. Phone: (712) 263-3334. Fax: (712) 263-8026. E-mail: info@donnareed.org. Web: www.donnareed.org.

JOE LOUIS v BRADDOCK/SCHMELING FIGHT ANNIVERSARIES. June 22, 1937. At Chicago's Comiskey Park Joe Louis won the World Heavyweight Championship title by knocking out James J. Braddock (eighth round). Louis retained the title until his retirement in 1949. Exactly one year after the Braddock fight, on June 22, 1938, Louis met Germany's Max Schmeling, at New York City's Yankee Stadium. Louis knocked out Schmeling in the first round.

KOREA: TANO DAY. June 22. Fifth day of fifth lunar month. Summer food offered at the household shrine of the ancestors. Also known as Swing Day, since girls, dressed in their prettiest clothes, often compete in swinging matches. The Tano Festival usually lasts from the third through eighth day of the fifth lunar month.

LINDBERGH, ANNE MORROW: BIRTH ANNIVERSARY. June 22, 1906. American author and aviator, born at Englewood, NJ. Wife of aviator Charles A. Lindbergh, she served as his copilot and navigator when he broke the transatlantic speed record in 1930. A prolific author and poet, in *Gift from the Sea* she wrote: "By and large, mothers and housewives are the only workers who do not have regular time off. They are the great vacationless class." She died Feb 7, 2001, at Passumpsic, VT.

MALTA: MNARJA. June 22–23. Buskett Gardens. A folk-cum-harvest festival. An all-night traditional Maltese "festa" with folk music, dancing and impromptu Maltese folk singing (ghana). This festival originated in the Middle Ages, and the word *Mnarja* is derived from *luminarja* because the countryside and the bastions around Mdina, Malta's ancient capital, used to be illuminated by "Fjakkoli" (torches made of sand mixed with oil and animal fat) on the eve of and on the feast day itself.

MIRTHDAY. June 22. A day on which a person can celebrate their own "self-mirth"—the ability to make choices that are to one's own highest good. A day to appreciate one's uniqueness, sense of humor and outlook on life—as well as your effect on the people around you. One person CAN make a difference—including making differences in himself or herself—every single day. So forget birthdays, celebrate Mirthdays instead! For info: E-mail: stepeast33@cartel.net.

PAPP, JOSEPH: BIRTH ANNIVERSARY. June 22, 1921. Born Yosl Papirofsky at Brooklyn, NY, Joe Papp became one of the leading figures in American theatre. At the helm of the New York Public Theatre, Papp produced a wide range of work from the classical to that of the newest American dramatists, including *Hair, Two Gentlemen of Verona, The Pirates of Penzance, The Mystery of Edwin Drood, That Championship Season* and *A Chorus Line*. He began in 1954 with the Shakespeare Theatre Workshop, taking touring productions around the city on a flatbed truck. When the truck broke down in Central Park, Papp turned his touring company into Shakespeare-in-the-Park. Producing and directing more than 400 productions, Papp garnered three Pulitzer Prizes, six New York Critics Circle Awards and 28 Tonys. He died Oct 31, 1991, at New York, NY.

SOVIET UNION INVADED: ANNIVERSARY. June 22, 1941. German troops invaded the Soviet Union, beginning a conflict that left 27 million Soviet citizens dead. Ceremonies are held this day in Russia, Belarus and Ukraine, the areas of the former Soviet Union which bore the brunt of the initial invasion.

SWEDISH DAYS FESTIVAL. June 22–27. Geneva, IL. Geneva celebrates its Swedish heritage with this midsummer festival. Six days of crafts, rosemailing display, music competitions, entertainment, carnival, Kids' Day activities and parade provide unlimited opportunities. Annually, begins the Tuesday after Father's Day. Est attendance: 250,000. For info: Geneva Chamber of Commerce, 8 S Third St., PO Box 481, Geneva, IL 60134. Phone: (630) 232-2060. Fax: (630) 232-6083. Web: www.genevachamber.com.

SWITZERLAND: MORAT BATTLE ANNIVERSARY. June 22, 1476. The little, walled town of Morat played a decisive part in Swiss history. There, the Confederates were victorious over Charles the Bold of Burgundy, laying the basis for French-speaking areas to become Swiss. Now an annual children's festival.

US DEPARTMENT OF JUSTICE: ANNIVERSARY. June 22. Established by an act of Congress, the Department of Justice is headed by the attorney general. Prior to 1870, the attorney general (whose office had been created Sept 24, 1789) had been a member of the president's cabinet but had not been the head of a department.

VANCOUVER, GEORGE: BIRTH ANNIVERSARY. June 22, 1757. English navigator, explorer and author for whom Vancouver Island and the cities of Vancouver (British Columbia and

Washington) are named was born at Norfolk, England, and joined the navy at the age of 13. He surveyed the coasts of Australia, New Zealand and western North America and sailed with Captain James Cook to the Arctic in 1780. Vancouver died at Petersham, Surrey, England, May 10, 1798, just as he was correcting the final pages of his *Journal*, which was published at London later that year.

V-MAIL DELIVERY: ANNIVERSARY. June 22, 1942. The first V-Mail (V for victory) was dispatched from New York on this date. The system was devised during WWII to conserve cargo space for war materials and supplies. Special paper was used for writing the letters. At post offices, the letters were opened, censored and photographed in reduced proportions. The film was then transported overseas. A complete roll of film contained 1,600 letters.

WILDER, BILLY: BIRTH ANNIVERSARY. June 22, 1906. One of the greatest directors of Hollywood's Golden Age was born Samuel Wilder at Sucha Beskidzka in the Austro-Hungarian Empire. After a short career in Berlin, Wilder fled Germany in 1933 and eventually landed in Hollywood, where he directed and cowrote some of the twentieth century's greatest films. His classics include the film noir works *Double Indemnity* and *Sunset Boulevard*, the searing dramas *Stalag 17* and *The Lost Weekend* and the comic gem *Some Like It Hot*. He received 6 Oscars (out of 21 nominations), and Best Film Oscars went to *The Lost Weekend* and *The Apartment*. Wilder died at Los Angeles, CA, on Mar 27, 2002.

WINDJAMMER DAYS. June 22–23. Boothbay Harbor, ME. Windjammer Days, the premier maritime event along the coast of Maine. Parades, concerts, waterfront food, interactive children's activities, arts showcase, live music, fireworks, visiting military vessels, windjammers sailing into harbor under full sail and much more. Fun for the whole family. Est attendance: 20,000. For info: Boothbay Harbor Region Chamber of Commerce, PO Box 356, Boothbay Harbor, ME 04538. Phone: (207) 633-2353. Fax: (207) 633-7448. E-mail: seamaine@boothbayharbor.com. Web: www.boothbayharbor.com.

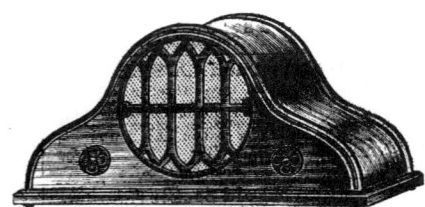

BIRTHDAYS TODAY

Darrell Armstrong, 36, basketball player, born Gastonia, NC, June 22, 1968.
Ed Bradley, 63, broadcast journalist ("60 Minutes"), born Philadelphia, PA, June 22, 1941.
Klaus Maria Brandauer, 60, actor (*Out of Africa*, *White Fang*), born Altausse, Austria, June 22, 1944.
Amy Brenneman, 40, actress ("Judging Amy"), born Glastonbury, CT, June 22, 1964.
Carson Daly, 31, host ("MTV Live," "Last Call with Carson Daly"), born Santa Monica, CA, June 22, 1973.
Clyde Austin Drexler, 42, basketball coach and former player, born Houston, TX, June 22, 1962.
Dianne Feinstein, 71, US Senator (D, California), born San Francisco, CA, June 22, 1933.

	S	M	T	W	T	F	S
June 2004			1	2	3	4	5
	6	7	8	9	10	11	12
	13	14	15	16	17	18	19
	20	21	22	23	24	25	26
	27	28	29	30			

Kris Kristofferson, 68, singer, actor (*Alice Doesn't Live Here Anymore*, *A Star Is Born*), born Brownsville, TX, June 22, 1936.
Michael Lerner, 63, actor (*The Candidate*, *Eight Men Out*, *Barton Fink*), born Brooklyn, NY, June 22, 1941.
Tracy Pollan, 44, actress ("Family Ties," *Bright Lights, Big City*), born New York, NY, June 22, 1960.
Todd Rundgren, 56, singer (*Something/Anything*), producer, born Upper Darby, PA, June 22, 1948.
Meryl Streep, 55, actress (Oscars for *Kramer vs Kramer* and *Sophie's Choice*), born Summit, NJ, June 22, 1949.
Kurt Wagner, 33, football player, born Burlington, IA, June 22, 1971.
Lindsay Wagner, 55, actress ("The Bionic Woman," *The Paper Chase*), born Los Angeles, CA, June 22, 1949.

JUNE 23 — WEDNESDAY
Day 175 — 191 Remaining

"THE BREAKFAST CLUB" RADIO PREMIERE: ANNIVERSARY. June 23, 1933. "The Breakfast Club with Don McNeil," which hit radio airwaves on this date, had a 35-year run. It was carried by 400 affiliates and tickets became as sought-after as those for a taping of "The Tonight Show" are today. The hour-long show included celebrities such as Fran Allison of "Kukla, Fran and Ollie" fame. Its popularity, however, stemmed mainly from regular features such as "Memory Time," when McNeil read poems and letters from listeners. During World War II "Prayer Time" was started. McNeil's "Call to Breakfast," which was announced every 15 minutes, invited listeners to get up and march around the breakfast table. McNeil died in 1996.

DENMARK: MIDSUMMER EVE. June 23. Celebrated all over the country with bonfires and merrymaking.

ESTONIA: VICTORY DAY. June 23. National holiday. Commemorates victory against Germany in 1919.

FIRST TYPEWRITER: ANNIVERSARY. June 23, 1868. First US typewriter was patented by Luther Sholes.

FOSSE, ROBERT LOUIS (BOB): BIRTH ANNIVERSARY. June 23, 1927. Bob Fosse was born at Chicago, IL. The son of a vaudeville singer, he began his show business career at the age of 13. He was the only director in history to win an Oscar, an Emmy and a Tony for his work. As a choreographer he was known for his unique dance style that focused on explosive angularity of the human body in its movement. His body of work included the plays *Pippin*, *Sweet Charity*, *Pajama Game*, *Chicago* and *Damn Yankees*. His films included *Cabaret*, *Lenny* and the autobiographical *All That Jazz*. Fosse died Sept 23, 1987, at Washington, DC.

LAST FORMAL SURRENDER OF CONFEDERATE TROOPS: ANNIVERSARY. June 23, 1865. The last formal surrender of Confederate troops took place in the Oklahoma Territory. Cherokee leader and Confederate Brigadier General Waite surrendered his command of a battalion formed by Indians.

LET IT GO DAY. June 23. Whatever it is that's bugging you, drop it! It's only eating away at you and providing nothing positive. [©2003 by WH.] For info: Thomas & Ruth Roy, Wellcat Holidays, 2418 Long Ln, Lebanon, PA 17046-1708. Phone: (717) 279-0184. E-mail: info@wellcat.com. Web: www.wellcat.com.

LITTLE BIGHORN DAYS. June 23–27. Hardin, MT. To celebrate the history of the Old West. This annual celebration commemorates the anniversary of Custer's Last Stand (June 25). Activities include carnival, Custer's Last Stand reenactment, trial of George Custer, parade, rodeo, shows, Military Ball and dances. Est attendance: 11,000. For info: Promotions, Hardin Area Chamber of Commerce, 10 E Railway St, Hardin, MT 59034. Phone: (406) 665-1672 or (888) 450-3577. E-mail: hardinchamber@cotcomsol.com. Web: www.custerslaststand.org.

LUXEMBOURG: NATIONAL HOLIDAY. June 23. Official birthday of His Royal Highness Grand Duke Jean in 1921. Also, Luxembourg's independence is celebrated June 23.

☆ Chase's 2004 Calendar of Events ☆ June 23-24

MIDSUMMER DAY/EVE CELEBRATIONS. June 23. Celebrates the beginning of summer with maypoles, music, dancing and bonfires. Observed mainly in northern Europe, including Finland, Latvia and Sweden. Day of observance is sometimes St. John's Day (June 24), with celebration on St. John's Eve (June 23) as well, or June 19. Time approximates the summer solstice. See also: "Summer" (June 20).

RUDOLPH, WILMA: BIRTH ANNIVERSARY. June 23, 1940. Olympic gold medal sprinter, born at Bethlehem, TN. She won the 100 meters, the 200 meters and the 400-meter relay at the 1960 Rome games, thus becoming the first woman to win three gold medals at the same Olympics. She overcame polio as a child and went on to Tennessee State University to become an athlete. Rudolph won the Sullivan Award in 1961. Died at Brentwood, TN, Nov 12, 1994.

SWEDEN: MIDSUMMER. June 23–24. Celebrated throughout Sweden. Maypole dancing, games and folk music.

BIRTHDAYS TODAY

Bryan Brown, 57, actor (*A Town Like Alice, Breaker Morant, F/X*), born Sydney, Australia, June 23, 1947.
James Levine, 61, American conductor and pianist, Metropolitan Opera of New York City, born Cincinnati, OH, June 23, 1943.
Frances McDormand, 47, actress (*Fargo, Mississippi Burning, Almost Famous*), born Chicago, IL, June 23, 1957.
Ted Shackelford, 58, actor ("Knots Landing," "Dallas"), born Oklahoma City, OK, June 23, 1946.
Clarence Thomas, 56, Supreme Court Associate Justice, born Pinpoint, GA, June 23, 1948.
LaDanian Tomlinson, 25, football player, born Waco, TX, June 23, 1979.

JUNE 24 — THURSDAY
Day 176 — 190 Remaining

AMERICAN LIBRARY ASSOCIATION ANNUAL CONFERENCE. June 24–30. Orlando, FL. The American Library Association (ALA), the oldest and largest library association in the world, holds its Annual Conference each June. Its attendees include librarians, educators, writers, publishers, Friends of libraries, trustees and special guests. More than 2,000 meetings, discussion groups, tours, special events and awards ceremonies (including the presentation of the Newbery and Caldecott medals) are spread throughout the weeklong conference. Est attendance: 25,000. For info: Public Information Office, American Library Assn, 50 E Huron St, Chicago, IL 60611. Phone: (312) 280-5044. Fax: (312) 944-8520. E-mail: pio@ala.org. Web: www.ala.org.

ASPEN MUSIC FESTIVAL. June 24–Aug 22. Aspen, CO. Nine weeks of concerts performed by highly acclaimed artists. Est attendance: 100,000. For info: Aspen Music Festival, 2 Music School Rd, Aspen, CO 81611. Phone: (970) 925-3254. Fax: (970) 925-3802. E-mail: festival@aspenmusic.org. Web: www.AspenMusicFestival.com.

BEECHER, HENRY WARD: BIRTH ANNIVERSARY. June 24, 1813. Famous American clergyman and orator was born at Litchfield, CT. Died Mar 8, 1887, at Brooklyn, NY. His dying words were "Now comes the mystery."

BERLIN AIRLIFT: ANNIVERSARY. June 24, 1948. In the early days of the Cold War the Soviet Union challenged the West's right of access to Berlin. The Soviets created a blockade, and an airlift to supply some 2,250,000 people resulted. The airlift lasted a total of 321 days and brought into Berlin 1,592,787 tons of supplies. Joseph Stalin finally backed down and the blockade ended May 12, 1949.

CANADA: ST. JEAN-BAPTISTE DAY. June 24. Public holiday in Quebec.

CELEBRATION OF THE SENSES. June 24. Treat yourself to a stimulation of the five senses—taste, touch, scent, sight and sound—and you may experience the elevation known to many mystics as the elusive sixth sense. [©2003 by WH.] For info: Thomas & Ruth Roy, Wellcat Holidays, 2418 Long Ln, Lebanon, PA 17046. Phone: (717) 279-0184. E-mail: info@wellcat.com. Web: www.wellcat.com.

CHINA: MACAU DAY. June 24. Celebrates defeat of the Dutch invasion forces of 1622 and pays homage to patron saint of Macau, Saint John the Baptist. Macau is a former Portuguese colony that is now part of China.

CIARDI, JOHN: BIRTH ANNIVERSARY. June 24, 1916. American poet, critic, translator, teacher, etymologist and author of children's books, born at Boston, MA. John Anthony Ciardi's criticism and other writings were often described as honest and sometimes as harsh. Died at Edison, NJ, Mar 30, 1986.

CLARKSON CZECH FESTIVAL. June 24–27. Main St, Clarkson, NE. Czech food, entertainment, music, polkas, cooking, demonstrations, carnival, rodeo, arts and crafts. Annually, the fourth full weekend in June. Sponsor: Clarkson Commercial Club. Est attendance: 10,000. For info: Robert Brabec, 515 Elm St, Clarkson, NE 68629. Phone: (402) 892-3331 or (402) 892-3561. Fax: (402) 892-3318.

DEMPSEY, JACK: BIRTH ANNIVERSARY. June 24, 1895. William Harrison Dempsey, known as "The Manassa Mauler," was world heavyweight boxing champion from 1919 to 1926. Following his boxing career Dempsey became a successful New York restaurant operator. Born at Manassa, CO, Dempsey died May 31, 1983, at New York, NY.

HELEN KELLER FESTIVAL. June 24–27. Tuscumbia, AL. Commemorates the remarkable life of Helen Keller with stage shows for all ages, arts and crafts fair, free musical entertainment, races, historic tours of Helen Keller's Birthplace and other beautiful homes and much more. *The Miracle Worker* play performed evenings during festival and for five weekends following. Annually, the last weekend in June. Est attendance: 105,000. For info: Debbie Wilson, Dir, Florence/Lauderdale Tourism, One Hightower Pl, Florence, AL 35630. Phone: (256) 740-4141 or (888) FLO-TOUR. Fax: (256) 740-4142. E-mail: dwilson@flo-tour.org. Web: www.flo-tour.org.

"HOPALONG CASSIDY" TV PREMIERE: 55th ANNIVERSARY. June 24, 1949. A Western series starring William Boyd in the title role as a hero who wore black and rode a white horse. The original episodes were segments edited from 66 movie features of Hopalong Cassidy and his sidekick, Red Connors (Edgar Buchanan). The films were so popular that Boyd produced episodes especially for TV.

ITALY: CALCIO FIORENTINO. June 24–28. Florence. Revival of a 16th-century football match in medieval costumes. Fireworks also June 24.

LATVIA: JOHN'S DAY (MIDSUMMER NIGHT DAY). June 24. The festival of Jani, which commemorates the summer solstice and the name day of (Janis) John, is one of Latvia's most ancient as well as joyous rituals. This festival is traditionally celebrated in the countryside, as it emphasizes fertility and the beginning of summer. Festivities begin June 23.

MERAMEC COMMUNITY FAIR. June 24–26. Fairgrounds, Sullivan, MO. 18th annual. Ticket price includes big-name entertainment, huge carnival, truck and tractor pulls, arts and crafts, motocross, kids' games, FFA-4H displays, pageants, Bull Bash and commercial booths. Est attendance: 40,000. For info: Sullivan Chamber of Commerce, PO Box 536, Sullivan, MO 63080. Phone: (573) 468-3314 or (573) 860-2861. E-mail: chamber@sullivanmo.com. Web: www.sullivanmo.com.

MISS VIRGINIA PAGEANT. June 24–26. Roanoke Civic Center Auditorium, Roanoke, VA. Est attendance: 4,000. For info: Stephen Musselwhite, 102 N Mitchell Rd, Vinton, VA 24179. Phone: (540) 989-4531.

ONIZUKA, ELLISON S.: BIRTH ANNIVERSARY. June 24, 1946. Lieutenant Colonel Ellison S. Onizuka, 39-year-old aerospace engineer, was mission specialist aboard the Space Shuttle *Challenger* when it exploded Jan 28, 1986 (killing all aboard). Onizuka was born at Kealakekua, Kona, HI. See also: "Challenger Space Shuttle Explosion Anniversary" (Jan 28).

PERU: COUNTRYMAN'S DAY. June 24. Half-day public holiday.

SAINT IGNACE AUTO SHOW. June 24–26. St. Ignace, MI. 29th anniversary. Parade, cruise night and swap meet. Entries from 25 states and Canada. Est attendance: 107,000. For info: Edward K. Reavie, 268 Hillcrest Blvd, St. Ignace, MI 49781. Phone: (906) 643-8087 or (906) 643-1USA. Fax: (906) 643-9784. E-mail: edreavie@nostalgia-prod.com. Web: www.nostalgia-prod.com or www.auto-shows.com.

SAINT JOHN THE BAPTIST DAY. June 24. Celebrates the birth of the saint.

SCOTLAND: BANNOCKBURN DAY. June 24, 1314. Anniversary of the Battle of Bannockburn when Robert the Bruce won independence for Scotland.

SHAKESPEARE ON THE GREEN. June 24–27 (also June 30–July 3 and July 7–10). Elmwood Park, Univ of Nebraska, Omaha, NE. Nonprofit professional presentations of the works of William Shakespeare in a beautiful outdoor setting for the families of the Great Plains region. One of a handful of "free" festivals across the country. Includes pre-show seminars and workshops. Picnic area and concessions, Elizabethan entertainment featuring music, dancing, singing, juggling and acrobatics. Est attendance: 35,000. For info: Michael Markey, Managing Dir, Nebraska Shakespeare Festival, Dept of Fine Arts, Creighton Univ, Omaha, NE 68178. Phone: (402) 280-2391. E-mail: neshakes@creighton.edu.

SOUTH ST. PAUL KAPOSIA DAYS. June 24–27. South St. Paul, MN. Family-oriented city festival including parades, pageant, children's activities, athletic competitions, craft & flea markets, musical entertainment and fireworks. Annually, the last full weekend in June. For info: South St. Paul Kaposia Days, PO Box 144, South St. Paul, MN 55075. Phone: (651) 451-2266. Fax: (651) 451-0846. E-mail: carol@riverheights.com. Web: www.kaposiadays.com.

SUMMERFEST. June 24–July 4. Milwaukee, WI. Music festival. Est attendance: 1,000,000. For info: Summerfest, 200 N Harbor Dr, Milwaukee, WI 53202. Phone: (800) 273-3378 or (414) 273-2680. Web: www.summerfest.com.

THORNTON, MATTHEW: DEATH ANNIVERSARY. June 24, 1803. Signer of the Declaration of Independence. Born at Ireland about 1714, he died at Newburyport, MA.

VENEZUELA: BATTLE OF CARABOBO DAY. June 24. National holiday. Commemorates a victory in 1821 that assured Venezuelan independence from Spain.

	S	M	T	W	T	F	S
June 2004			1	2	3	4	5
	6	7	8	9	10	11	12
	13	14	15	16	17	18	19
	20	21	22	23	24	25	26
	27	28	29	30			

WATERMELON THUMP (WITH WORLD CHAMPION SEED-SPITTING CONTEST). June 24–27. Luling, TX. Features World Champion Seed-Spitting Contest, street dance each night, giant parade on Saturday, free live entertainment in the Beer Garden, champion melon auction, arts and crafts exhibit and sales, food, games, fun run and rides. Annually, the last weekend in June (Thursday–Sunday). Est attendance: 45,000. For info: Susan H. Ward, Sec, Luling Watermelon Thump Assn, Box 710, Luling, TX 78648. Phone: (830) 875-3214 x 2. Fax: (830) 875-2082. E-mail: susan@watermelonthump.com. Web: www.watermelonthump.com.

BIRTHDAYS TODAY

Nancy Allen, 54, actress (*Carrie, Blow Out, Robocop*), born New York, NY, June 24, 1950.
Claude Chabrol, 74, filmmaker (*La Femme Infidèle, The Cousins*), born Sardent, France, June 24, 1930.
Mick Fleetwood, 62, musician (drummer with Fleetwood Mac, "Dreams," "Don't Stop"), born Cornwall, England, June 24, 1942.
Phyllis George, 55, former sportscaster, former Miss America, born Denton, TX, June 24, 1949.
Juli Inkster, 44, golfer, born Santa Cruz, CA, June 24, 1960.
Michele Lee, 62, actress ("Knots Landing"), born Los Angeles, CA, June 24, 1942.
George Pataki, 59, Governor of New York (R), born Peekskill, NY, June 24, 1945.
Predrag "Preki" Radosavljevic, 41, soccer player, born Belgrade, Yugoslavia, June 24, 1963.
Sherry Stringfield, 37, actress ("NYPD Blue," "ER"), born Colorado Springs, CO, June 24, 1967.
Peter Weller, 57, actor (*Robocop, Naked Lunch*), born Stevens Point, WI, June 24, 1947.

JUNE 25 — FRIDAY
Day 177 — 189 Remaining

AMERICAN NURSES ASSOCIATION CONVENTION. June 25–30. Minneapolis, MN. Informative and useable educational sessions, nurses from around the country and the world, the industry's leading suppliers and employers. The ANA convention occurs every two years and rotates around the country. For info: American Nurses Assn, 600 Maryland Ave SW, Washington, DC 20024. Phone: (202) 651-7203. Web: www.nursingworld.org.

ARNOLD, HENRY H. "HAP": BIRTH ANNIVERSARY. June 25, 1886. US general and commander of the Army Air Force in all theaters throughout WWII, Arnold was born at Gladwyne, PA. Although no funds were made available, as early as 1938 Arnold was persuading the US aviation industry to step up manufacturing of airplanes. Production grew from 6,000 to 262,000 per year from 1940–44. He supervised pilot training and by 1944 Air Force personnel strength had grown to two million from a prewar high of 21,000. Made a full general in 1944, he became the US Air Force's first five-star general when the Air Force was made a separate military branch equal to the Army and Navy. Arnold died Jan 15, 1950, at Sonoma, CA.

BATTLE OF LITTLE BIGHORN: ANNIVERSARY. June 25, 1876. Lieutenant Colonel George Armstrong Custer, leading military forces of more than 200 men, attacked an encampment of Sioux Indians led by Chiefs Sitting Bull and Crazy Horse near Little Bighorn River, MT. Custer and all men in his immediate command were killed in the brief battle (about two hours) of Little Bighorn. One horse, named Comanche, is said to have been the only survivor among Custer's forces.

BHUTAN: NATIONAL DAY. June 25. National holiday observed.

CBS SENDS FIRST COLOR TV BROADCAST OVER THE AIR: ANNIVERSARY. June 25, 1951. Columbia Broadcast System broadcast the first color television program. The four-hour program was carried by stations at New York City,

Baltimore, Philadelphia, Boston and Washington, DC, although no color sets were owned by the public. At the time CBS, itself, owned fewer than 40 color receivers.

CENTRAL CHINA FLOOD: ANNIVERSARY. June 25, 1991. The Huai River flooded its banks and ravaged major portions of the central Chinese province of Anhui. The poor agricultural region was devastated and approximately 3,000 people were killed. The Anhui region sustained enormous damages when the government ordered dikes broken and sluice gates opened in the rural area to prevent flooding of economically important rivers farther downstream.

CIVIL WAR IN YUGOSLAVIA: ANNIVERSARY. June 25, 1991. In an Eastern Europe freed from the iron rule of communism and the USSR, separatist and nationalist tensions suppressed for decades rose to a violent boiling point. The republics of Croatia and Slovenia declared their independence, sparking a fractious and bitter war that spread throughout what was formerly Yugoslavia. Ethnic rivalries between Serbians and Croatians began the military conflicts that spread to Slovenia, and in 1992 fighting began in Bosnia-Herzegovina between Serbians and ethnic Muslims. Although the new republics were recognized by the UN and sanctions passed to stop the fighting, it raged on through 1995 despite the efforts of UN peacekeeping forces.

CLEARWATER CHAMBER OF COMMERCE RODEO. June 25–27. Clearwater, NE. 7:30 PM each day. Annually, the last full weekend of June. Est attendance: 6,000. For info: Clearwater Chamber of Commerce, Box 201, Clearwater, NE 68726.

DALESBURG MIDSUMMER FESTIVAL. June 25 (tentative). Dalesburg Lutheran Church, rural Vermillion, SD. Celebration of Scandinavian and rural heritage. Programs, dances to raise the Midsummer Pole, a smorgasbord, arts and crafts area, band concert and more. Est attendance: 800. For info: Ronald Johnson, Midsummer Committee, Dalesburg Midsummer Festival, 30595 University Rd, Vermillion, SD 57069-6507. Phone: (605) 253-2575. Web: www.angelfire.com/sd/dalesburg99/.

ENGLAND: SHREWSBURY INTERNATIONAL MUSIC FESTIVAL. June 25–July 2. Shrewsbury, Shropshire. 26th annual. Noncompetitive festival that brings together music and dance groups from all over the world. Est attendance: 2,700. For info: Nichola Stokes, Fest Mgr, Festival Office, Victoria Court, Ste 3, Bexton Rd, Knutsford, Cheshire, England WA16 OPF. Phone: (44) (174) 328-1200. E-mail: wsconcerts@aol.com.

GENUINE JAZZ IN BRECKENRIDGE. June 25–27. Breckenridge, CO. Set amid the picturesque Rocky Mountains, this weekend jazz festival features nighttime jams in clubs and restaurants within walking distance, and continuous daytime concerts on two stages: a floating stage on Maggie Pond and the main Street Station stage. Est attendance: 5,000. For info: Kim DiLallo, Genuine Jazz, PO Box 4988, Breckenridge, CO 80424. Phone: (970) 453-4906. E-mail: kdilallo@colorado.net. Web: www.genuinejazz.com.

GETTYSBURG CIVIL WAR HERITAGE DAYS. June 25–July 4. Gettysburg, PA. Commemorates the Battle of Gettysburg. Living history encampment with both Union and Confederate army campsites, concerts, Civil War lecture series, a battle of Gettysburg reenactment, firefighter's festival, encampment church service and Civil War book fair. Est attendance: 350,000. For info: Gettysburg CVB, PO Box 4117, Gettysburg, PA 17325. Phone: (717) 334-6274. Fax: (717) 334-1166. E-mail: gettysburgcvb@dejazzd.com. Web: www.gettysburgcvb.org.

GILLARS, MILDRED "AXIS SALLY" E.: DEATH ANNIVERSARY. June 25, 1988. Mildred E. Gillars received the nickname "Axis Sally" during World War II, when she broadcast Nazi propaganda to US troops in Europe. An American citizen, born about 1900 at Portland, ME, she was arrested after the war, tried and convicted of treason. She was sentenced to 10 to 30 years in prison and fined $10,000. She was released after 12 years and later taught music in a convent school at Columbus, OH. She died June 25, 1988, at Columbus, OH.

GRAND EXCURSION 2004. June 25–July 4. Mississippi River from Quad Cities (Davenport/Bettendorf, IA, and Rock Island/Moline, IL) to Twin Cities (Minneapolis/St. Paul, MN). One dozen steamboats will re-create and commemorate the 150th anniversary of the Grand Excursion. In 1854 dignitaries from across the nation rode by train to Rock Island to celebrate the arrival of the railroad to the Mississippi River, then traveled upriver on steamboats. This was the opening to development of the Upper Midwest. Est attendance: 1,000,000. For info: Clara Littig, 2021 River Dr, Moline, IL 61265. Phone: (309) 764-3678. Fax: (309) 764-9443. E-mail: clittig@grandexcursion.com. Web: www.grandexcursion.com.

GRANTSVILLE DAYS. June 25–27. Grantsville Park, Grantsville, MD. Three-day annual homecoming weekend. Free entertainment Friday 7:15 PM–Sunday 5 PM. Lion's chicken BBQ, local noncommercial food booths, children's games, tennis, horse- and tractor-pulling contests, gospel music, fireworks Friday and Saturday nights. Annually, the last weekend in June. Est attendance: 18,000. For info: Gerry Beachy. Fax: (301) 895-3623. E-mail: gbeachy@qcol.net.

KIM CAMPBELL SWORN IN AS CANADIAN PRIME MINISTER: ANNIVERSARY. June 25, 1993. After winning the June 13 election to the leadership of the ruling Progressive-Conservative Party, Kim Campbell became Canada's 19th prime minister and its first woman prime minister. However, in the general election held Oct 25, 1993, the Liberal Party routed the Progressive-Conservatives in the worst defeat for a governing political party in Canada's 126-year history, reducing the former government's seats in the House of Commons from 154 to 2. Campbell was among those who lost their seats.

KOREAN WAR BEGAN: ANNIVERSARY. June 25, 1950. Forces from northern Korea invaded southern Korea, beginning a civil war. US ground forces entered the conflict June 30. An armistice was signed at Panmunjom July 27, 1953, formally dividing the country into two—North Korea and South Korea.

LONG GROVE STRAWBERRY FESTIVAL. June 25–27. Long Grove, IL. Country village of nearly 100 specialty shops and restaurants celebrates summer with strawberries in every form, outdoor food booths, free music and family entertainment. Admission and parking free. Annually, the weekend after Father's Day. Est attendance: 50,000. For info: Long Grove Merchants Assn, Rtes 53 & 83, Long Grove, IL 60047. Phone: (847) 634-0888. Web: www.longgroveonline.com.

MARBLE WEEKEND. June 25–27. Millville, NJ. Marble artists and collectors conference. Rain or shine, the sale will go on. Est attendance: 1,000. For info: Wheaton Village, 1501 Glasstown Rd, Millville, NJ 08332. Phone: (800) 998-4552 or (856) 825-6800. Fax: (856) 825-2410. E-mail: mail@wheatonvillage.org. Web: www.wheatonvillage.org.

MONTSERRAT: VOLCANO ERUPTS: ANNIVERSARY. June 25, 1997. After lying dormant for 400 years, the Soufrière Hills volcano began to come to life in July 1995. It finally erupted, wiping out the capital city of Plymouth and two-thirds of the rest of this lush Carribean island on June 25, 1997. Two-thirds of the population relocated to other islands or to Great Britain.

MOON PHASE: FIRST QUARTER. June 25. Moon enters First Quarter phase at 3:08 PM, EDT.

MOZAMBIQUE: INDEPENDENCE DAY. June 25. National holiday. Commemorates independence from Portugal in 1975.

O'NEILL, ROSE CECIL: BIRTH ANNIVERSARY. June 25, 1874. Rose O'Neill was born at Wilkes-Barre, PA. Her career included work as an illustrator, author and doll designer, the latter gaining her commercial success with the Kewpie Doll. In 1910 *The Ladies Home Journal* devoted a full page to her Kewpie Doll designs, which were a marketing phenomenon for three decades. Died at Springfield, MO, Apr 6, 1944.

OREGON BACH FESTIVAL. June 25–July 11. Hult Center for the Performing Arts and the University of Oregon, Eugene, OR. Artistic Director and conductor Helmuth Rilling leads an international gathering of musicians in choral-orchestral masterworks, intimate concerts and chamber music, informal free concerts and family events, adult education programs and master classes for conductors and composers. Emphasis is on J.S. Bach and his influence on succeeding generations of composers. Est attendance: 30,000. For info: George Evano, Oregon Bach Fest, 1257 University of Oregon, Eugene, OR 97403. Phone: (800) 457-1486 or (541) 346-5666. Fax: (541) 346-5669. Web: www.oregonbachfestival.com.

ORWELL, GEORGE: BIRTH ANNIVERSARY. June 25, 1903. English satirist, author of *Animal Farm, 1984* and other works, was born at Motihari, Bengal. George Orwell was the pseudonym of Eric Arthur Blair. Died at London, England, Jan 21, 1950.

QUAD CITY AIR SHOW. June 25–27 (tentative). Davenport Municipal Airport, Davenport, IA. 17th annual. Largest family aviation fun-filled weekend in the area featuring the very best of civilian and military aviation. Come and enjoy the "Festival in the Sky!" Friday night twilight show with fireworks starts 6 PM. Sat and Sun: gates open at 8 AM, and flying starts at 9 AM with the WWII Dawn Patrol. Action continues nonstop both in the sky and on the ground. For info: Phone: (563) 285-7469. Web: www.quadcityairshow.com. For info on the Quad Cities: Quad Cities CVB. Phone: (800) 747-7800. Web: www.visitquadcities.com.

REVERE, ANNE: BIRTH ANNIVERSARY. June 25, 1903. American actress Anne Revere was born at New York, NY. She won an Academy Award for her supporting role in *National Velvet* (1944), but was barred from films for 20 years after she refused to testify before the House Committee on Un-American Activities in the 1950s. In 1960 she won a Tony Award for her role in *Toys in the Attic*. Revere died Dec 18, 1990, at Locust Valley, NY.

SAINTE-CROIX 1604–2004. June 25–July 4. Calais, ME and Bayside, NB, Canada. History, culture, cuisine and the performing arts take center stage as the communities around Ste. Croix Island commemorate 400 years of French presence in North America. The official ceremony, with concert and fireworks, takes place June 26. Est attendance: 10,000. For info: Norma Stewart, Ste-Croix 2004, PO Box 805, Calais, ME 04619. Phone: (506) 466-7403. Fax: (506) 466-7438. E-mail: celebrate@stecroix2004.org. Web: www.stecroix2004.org.

SCANDINAVIAN HJEMKOMST FESTIVAL. June 25–27. Moorhead, MN. 27th annual. Named as "One of North America's Top 100 Events" of 2002 by the American Bus Association. Featuring activities for all ages, including authentic ethnic entertainment, music and folk dancing, a marketplace, foods, exhibitions, and demonstrations of arts, fine crafts and ethnic traditions from Denmark, Finland, Iceland, Norway, Sweden and Scandinavian-America. Est attendance: 10,000. For info: Festival Director, Hjemkomst Center, 202 First North Ave, Moorhead, MN 56560. Phone: (218) 299-5452. Web: www.scandinavianhjemkomstfestival.org.

SEVEN DAYS CAMPAIGN: ANNIVERSARY. June 25–July 1, 1862. In an effort to prevent an attack on Richmond, VA, Confederate General Robert E. Lee launched a series of engagements that became known as the Seven Days Campaign. Battles at Oak Grove, Gaine's Mills, Garnett's Farm, Golding's Farm, Savage's Station, White Oak Swamp and finally Malvern Hill left more than 35,000 casualties on both sides. Despite losing the final assault at Malvern Hill, the Confederates succeeded in preventing the Union army from taking Richmond.

SLOVENIA: NATIONAL DAY. June 25. Public holiday. Commemorates independence from the former Yugoslavia in 1991.

STERNWHEELER DAYS. June 25–27. Port Marina Park, Cascade Locks, OR. Home of the 599-passenger sternwheeler *Columbia Gorge*. Salmon Bake, Mountain Men Encampment, bingo, parade, food, crafts, live music, RV parking. Annually, the last weekend in June. Est attendance: 4,000. For info: Columbia Gorge Lions, PO Box 522, Cascade Locks, OR 97014. Phone: (541) 374-8313.

SUPREME COURT ABORTION NOTIFICATION RULING: ANNIVERSARY. June 25, 1990. The Supreme Court ruled, in a 5–4 decision, that it was unconstitutional for a state to require, without providing other options, that a minor notify both her parents before obtaining an abortion.

SUPREME COURT BANS SCHOOL PRAYER: ANNIVERSARY. June 25, 1962. The US Supreme Court ruled that a prayer read aloud in public schools violated the First Amendment's separation of church and state. The court again struck down a law pertaining to the First Amendment when it disallowed an Alabama law that permitted a daily one-minute period of silent meditation or prayer in public schools June 1, 1985. (Vote 6–3.)

SUPREME COURT UPHOLDS RIGHT TO DIE: ANNIVERSARY. June 25, 1990. In the case *Cruzan v Missouri*, the Supreme Court, in a 5–4 ruling, upheld the constitutional right of a person whose wishes are clearly known to refuse life-sustaining medical treatment.

TAKE YOUR DOG TO WORK DAY. June 25. A day to celebrate the great companions dogs make and to encourage adoptions from animal shelters. Annually, the first Friday after Father's Day. For info: Pet Sitters Intl, 201 E King St, King, NC 27021. Phone: (336) 983-9222. Fax: (336) 983-5266. E-mail: tydtwd@petsit.com. Web: www.petsit.com.

TWO YUGOSLAV REPUBLICS DECLARE INDEPENDENCE: ANNIVERSARY. June 25, 1991. The republics of Slovenia and Croatia formally declared independence from Yugoslavia. The two northwestern republics did not, however, secede outright.

VIRGINIA: RATIFICATION DAY. June 25. 10th state to ratify the Constitution in 1788.

WATER SKI DAYS. June 25–27. Lake City, MN. Grand day parade, arts and crafts fair, Venetian boat parade, food, beer tent, live entertainment, carnival and games. Fun for the whole family. Annually, the last full weekend in June. Est attendance: 25,000. For info: Lake City Area Chamber of Commerce, 212 S Washington St, Lake City, MN 55041. Phone: (800) 369-4123. E-mail: lcchamber@earthlink.net.

	S	M	T	W	T	F	S
June 2004			1	2	3	4	5
	6	7	8	9	10	11	12
	13	14	15	16	17	18	19
	20	21	22	23	24	25	26
	27	28	29	30			

☆ Chase's 2004 Calendar of Events ☆ June 25–26

WORLD CHAMPIONSHIP ROTARY TILLER RACE AND PURPLEHULL PEA FESTIVAL. June 25–26. Emerson, AR. 15th annual festival. World Cup purplehull pea-shelling competition, rotary tiller race, domino tournaments, concessions, arts, crafts, entertainment, children's games, Queen's pageant (various ages), 3-on-3 basketball. Est attendance: 10,000. For info: Publicity, Purplehull Pea Fest, PO Box 1, Emerson, AR 71740. Phone: (501) 315-7373. E-mail: purplehull@juno.com. Web: www.purplehull.com.

BIRTHDAYS TODAY

Linda Cardellini, 29, actress (Scooby-Doo, Legally Blonde), born Redmond City, CA, June 25, 1975.
Carlos Delgado, 32, baseball player, born Mayaguez, Puerto Rico, June 25, 1972.
June Lockhart, 79, actress (mom in second "Lassie" series, "Lost in Space"), born New York, NY, June 25, 1925.
Sidney Lumet, 80, director (12 Angry Men, Serpico, Dog Day Afternoon, Network), born Philadelphia, PA, June 25, 1924.
George Michael, 41, singer (Wham!, "Wake Me Up Before You Go-Go," "Faith"), born Radlett, England, June 25, 1963.
Dikembe Mutombo, 38, basketball player, born Kinshasa, Zaire, June 25, 1966.
Willis Reed, Jr, 62, Hall of Fame basketball player, basketball executive and former coach, born Hico, LA, June 25, 1942.
Carly Simon, 59, singer ("You're So Vain," "Nobody Does It Better"), songwriter, born New York, NY, June 25, 1945.
Billy Wagner, 33, baseball player, born Tannersville, VA, June 25, 1971.
Jimmie Walker, 56, actor, comedian ("Good Times," "B.A.D. Cats"), born New York, NY, June 25, 1948.

JUNE 26 — SATURDAY
Day 178 — 188 Remaining

BAR CODE INTRODUCED: 30th ANNIVERSARY. June 26, 1974. A committee formed in 1970 by US grocers and food manufacturers recommended in 1973 a Universal Product Code (i.e., a bar code) for supermarket items that would allow electronic scanning of prices. On this day in 1974 a pack of Wrigley's gum was swiped across the first checkout scanner at a supermarket in Troy, OH. Today bar codes are used to keep track of everything from freight cars to cattle.

BEARTOOTH RUN. June 26. Red Lodge, MT. 8.2-mile or 4.4-mile footrace up scenic Beartooth Pass. Race will start at 7,000 feet and finish at 9,000 feet. Est attendance: 350. For info: Denise Parsons, Beartooth Run, Box 988, Red Lodge, MT 59068. Phone: (406) 446-1718. E-mail: information@redlodge.com. Web: www.redlodge.com.

BEETHOVEN BY THE BEACH. June 26–July 12. Fort Lauderdale, FL. The Florida Philharmonic Orchestra Summer Music Festival. Experience Beethoven's symphonies, chamber pieces and piano concertos plus lectures and more. For info: Greater Fort Lauderdale Conv & Visitors Bureau, 1850 Eller Dr, Ste 303, Fort Lauderdale, FL 33316. Phone: (800) 226-1812. Web: www.sunny.org.

BORDEN, SIR ROBERT LAIRD: 150th BIRTH ANNIVERSARY. June 26, 1854. Canadian statesman and prime minister, born at Grand Pre, Nova Scotia. Died at Ottawa, June 10, 1937.

BUCK, PEARL SYDENSTRICKER: BIRTH ANNIVERSARY. June 26, 1892. American author (The Good Earth), noted authority on China, and humanitarian. Nobel Prize winner. Born at Hillsboro, WV. Died Mar 6, 1973, at Danby, VT.

CELTIC FLING. June 26–27. Mount Hope Estate & Winery, Manheim, PA. 'Tis but a wee journey to the Scottish Highlands or the Emerald Isle when you dance a jig through the gates of the Pennsylvania Renaissance Faire's annual "Celtic Fling." It's an official Highland Dance competition, Highland Games, 35 acres of authentic Celtic arts and crafts, music and dance, concerts by nationally acclaimed Celtic recording artists and, of course, beer and bagpipes. For info: Thomas Roy, PRF, PO Box 685, Cornwall, PA 17016. Phone: (717) 665-7021. Fax: (717) 664-3466. E-mail: tom@parenfaire.com. Web: www.parenfaire.com.

CN TOWER OPENED: ANNIVERSARY. June 26, 1976. Birthday of the world's tallest building and freestanding structure, the CN Tower, 1,815 feet, 5 inches high, at Toronto, Ontario, Canada. For info: CN Tower, 301 Front St W, Toronto, ON, Canada M5V 2T6. Phone: (416) 360-8500. Fax: (416) 601-4713.

DESCENDANTS DAY. June 26–27. The day in each year when all the world's citizens take an accounting of their activities during the preceding year that will impact our descendants and our neighbors across time. Annually, last weekend in June. For info: Charles A. Howell, Trust for the Future, 2704 12th Ave S, Nashville, TN 37204. Phone: (615) 297-7206. Fax: (615) 269-6268. E-mail: cahowell@edge.net.

DOUBLEDAY, ABNER: BIRTH ANNIVERSARY. June 26, 1819. Abner Doubleday served in the US Army during the Mexican War and the Seminole War in Florida prior to his service in the American Civil War. His service found him at the battles of Second Bull Run, Antietam, Fredricksburg and as a major general commanding a division at Gettysburg. A commission set up to investigate the origins of baseball by sporting goods manufacturer Albert Spalding credited Doubleday with inventing the game in the year 1839. Subsequent research has debunked the commission's finding. Abner Doubleday was born at Ballston Spa, NY, and died at Mendham, NJ, Jan 26, 1893.

FEDERAL CREDIT UNION ACT: 70th ANNIVERSARY. June 26, 1934. Commemorates signing by President Franklin Delano Roosevelt of the Federal Credit Union Act, thus enabling the formation of credit unions anywhere in the US.

FISHING HAS NO BOUNDARIES—BEMIDJI. June 26–27. Lake Bemidji, Bemidji, MN. A two-day fishing experience for disabled persons. Any disability, age, sex, race, etc, eligible. Fishing with experienced guides; attended by 75 participants and 130 volunteers. For info: Carol Olson, Bemidji Chamber of Commerce, Fishing Has No Boundaries, 300 Bemidji Ave, PO Box 850, Bemidji, MN 56619-0850. Phone: (800) 458-2223. Fax: (218) 444-4276. Web: www.paulbunyan.net/FHNB.

FLAG AMENDMENT DEFEATED: ANNIVERSARY. June 26, 1990. The Senate rejected a proposed constitutional amendment that would have permitted states to prosecute those who destroyed or desecrated American flags. Similar legislation continues to be introduced in Congress.

GALESBURG RAILROAD DAYS. June 26–27. Galesburg, IL. 27th annual festival celebrating the city's railroad heritage that dates back to 1854. Carnival, street fair, railroad exhibits and displays, 5K run and concerts. Includes more than 40 events. Annually, in June. Est attendance: 55,000. For info: Galesburg Area CVB, PO Box 60, Galesburg, IL 61402-0060. Phone: (309) 343-2485. Fax: (309) 343-2521. E-mail: visitors@visitgalesburg.com. Web: www.visitgalesburg.com.

June 26 ☆ Chase's 2004 Calendar of Events ☆

"GUIDING LIGHT" TV PREMIERE: ANNIVERSARY. June 26, 1952. "Guiding Light," previously on radio, holds the title of longest-lasting daytime show and longest-lasting series. Set in the fictional midwestern town of Springfield, this soap is still on the air.

HAYMARKET PARDON: ANNIVERSARY. June 26, 1893. Illinois Governor John Peter Altgeld pardoned Samuel Fielden, Michael Schwab and Oscar Neebe, three of the anarchists who had been convicted in the violence connected with the Haymarket Riot on May 4, 1886. At a protest meeting at Haymarket Square an unknown individual threw a bomb which caused the death of several policemen. Eight anarchists were tried and convicted of the bombing. Of those, one committed suicide the day before he was to be hanged; three were hanged; and Fielden, Schwab and Neebe were imprisoned. In 1893 the newly elected Altgeld, at the urging of Clarence Darrow, reviewed the transcripts of the trial of these men and concluded that they had been railroaded. The pardon was widely criticized. It was an act of political suicide for Altgeld.

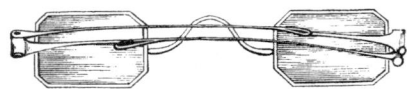

HUMAN GENOME MAPPED: ANNIVERSARY. June 26, 2000. Biologists J. Craig Venter and Francis S. Collins announced that their research groups had mapped the human genome, a strand of DNA with three billion parts that spells out our genetic code.

LADIES OF COUNTRY MUSIC SHOW. June 26. Waretown, NJ. Featuring Albert Music Hall's ladies of country and bluegrass. No alcoholic beverages or smoking allowed. For info: Albert Music Hall, PO Box 657, Waretown, NJ 08758. Phone: (609) 971-1593. Web:www.alberthall.org.

LEWIS & CLARK TRAD'N DAYS. June 26–27. Weston, MO. 3rd annual. This 2-day event commemorates the contributions that the Lewis & Clark Expedition made to the founding of Weston in 1837—some 33 years after camping at the site on the Missouri River on July 2, 1804. Living history presentations, musical entertainment, Native Drum & Dance, demonstrations by Missouri Free Traders, crafts and more at this unique cultural event. Free. For info: Weston Development Co, 502 Main St, Weston, MO 64098-1138. Phone: (888) 635-7457 or (816) 640-2909. E-mail: westonmo@kc.rr.com. Web: ci.weston.mo.us.

MADAGASCAR: INDEPENDENCE DAY. June 26. National holiday. Commemorates independence from France in 1960.

MIDDLETON, ARTHUR: BIRTH ANNIVERSARY. June 26, 1742. American Revolutionary leader and signer of the Declaration of Independence, born near Charleston, SC. Died at Goose Creek, SC, Jan 1, 1787.

NATIONAL CELEBRATE YOUR MARRIAGE DAY. June 26. Time set aside for married couples to refocus on their relationship, and rekindle that romance. Annually, the fourth Saturday in June. For info: James Wilson, Marriagebliss.com, 15759 Wormer, Redford Township, MI 48239. Phone: (248) 790-9994. E-mail: james@marriagebliss2002.com. Web: www.marriagebliss.com.

PIZARRO, FRANCESCO: DEATH ANNIVERSARY. June 26, 1541. Spanish conqueror of Peru, born at Extremadura, Spain, ca 1471. Pizarro died at Lima, Peru.

	S	M	T	W	T	F	S
June 2004			1	2	3	4	5
	6	7	8	9	10	11	12
	13	14	15	16	17	18	19
	20	21	22	23	24	25	26
	27	28	29	30			

PSFCA EAST WEST ALL-STAR GAME. June 26. Mansion Park, Altoona, PA. All-star football game featuring the finest college-bound athletes in Pennsylvania. Come see the "Beasts of the East" take on the "Best of the West" in a must-see, action-packed game. Annually, the last Saturday in June. Est attendance: 10,000. For info: Cheryl Ebersole, Allegheny Mountains CVB, One Convention Center Dr, Altoona, PA 16602. Phone: (814) 943-4183. Fax: (814) 943-8094. E-mail: amcvb@aol.com. Web: visitcentralpa.com.

SAINT LAWRENCE SEAWAY DEDICATION: 45th ANNIVERSARY. June 26, 1959. President Dwight D. Eisenhower and Queen Elizabeth II jointly dedicated the St. Lawrence Seaway in formal ceremonies held at St. Lambert, QC, Canada. A project undertaken jointly by Canada and the US, the waterway (which provides access between the Atlantic Ocean and the Great Lakes) had been opened to traffic Apr 25, 1959.

SNAKE HUNT. June 26–27. Cross Fork, PA. To raise funds for the fire company. Est attendance: 5,000. For info: Barry Gipe, Chmn, Kettle Creek Hose Co #1, 2605 Steward Hill Rd, Cross Fork, PA 17729. Phone: (570) 923-0848.

UNITED NATIONS CHARTER SIGNED: ANNIVERSARY. June 26, 1945. The UN Charter was signed at San Francisco by representatives of 50 nations.

UNITED NATIONS: INTERNATIONAL DAY AGAINST DRUG ABUSE AND ILLICIT TRAFFICKING. June 26. Following a recommendation of the 1987 International Conference on Drug Abuse and Illicit Trafficking, the United Nations General Assembly (Res 42/112) expressed its determination to strengthen action and cooperation for an international society free of drug abuse and proclaimed June 26 as an annual observance to raise public awareness. For info: UN, Dept of Public Info, Public Inquiries Unit, RM GA-57, New York, NY 10017. Phone: (212) 963-4475. E-mail: inquiries@un.org.

UNITED NATIONS: INTERNATIONAL DAY IN SUPPORT OF VICTIMS OF TORTURE. June 26. For info: United Nations, Dept of Public Info, New York, NY 10017. Web: www.un.org.

ZAHARIAS, MILDRED "BABE" DIDRIKSON: 90th BIRTH ANNIVERSARY. June 26, 1914. Born Mildred Ella Didrikson at Port Arthur, TX, the great athlete was nicknamed "Babe" after legendary baseball player Babe Ruth. She was named to the women's All-America basketball team when she was 16. At the 1932 Olympic Games, she won two gold medals and also set world records in the javelin throw and the 80-meter high hurdles; only a technicality prevented her from obtaining the gold in the high jump. Didrikson married professional wrestler George Zaharias in 1938, six years after she began playing golf casually. In 1946 Babe won the US Women's Amateur tournament, and in 1947 she won 17 straight golf championships and became the first American winner of the British Ladies' Amateur Tournament. Turning professional in 1948, she won the US Women's Open in 1950 and 1954, the same year she won the All-American Open. Babe also excelled in softball, baseball, swimming, figure skating, billiards—even football. In a 1950 Associated Press poll she was named the woman athlete of the first half of the 20th century. She died of cancer, Sept 27, 1956, at Galveston, TX.

BIRTHDAYS TODAY

Claudio Abbado, 71, conductor, born Milan, Italy, June 26, 1933.
Paul Thomas Anderson, 34, director/screenwriter (*Punch-Drunk Love, Magnolia, Boogie Nights*), born Studio City, CA, June 26, 1970.
Sean P. Hayes, 34, actor ("Will & Grace"), born Glen Ellyn, IL, June 26, 1970.
Chris Isaak, 48, singer, musician, actor ("The Chris Isaak Show"), born Stockton, CA, June 26, 1956.
Derek Jeter, 30, baseball player, born Pequannock, NJ, June 26, 1974.
Greg LeMond, 43, former cyclist, born Lakewood, CA, June 26, 1961.

☆ Chase's 2004 Calendar of Events ☆ June 26–27

Chris O'Donnell, 34, actor (*Scent of a Woman*), born Winnetka, IL, June 26, 1970.

Eleanor Parker, 82, actress (*The Sound of Music*), born Cedarsville, OH, June 26, 1922.

Jason Schwartzman, 24, actor (*Rushmore*), born Los Angeles, CA, June 26, 1980.

Charlotte Zolotow, 89, author (*The Moon Was the Best, Peter and the Pigeons*), born Norfolk, VA, June 26, 1915.

JUNE 27 — SUNDAY
Day 179 — 187 Remaining

AMERICA'S KIDS DAY. June 27. A day set aside to reach out and teach our children in America the value of life, liberty and the pursuit of happiness. A time to help our kids to learn about the great nation that they live in and to help by demonstrating what it means to be an American. A time to teach them the historical value of their heritage as America's kids. Annually, the fourth Sunday in June. For info: Judith Natale, NCAC America–USA, 2091 Del Monte Ave, Monterey, CA 93940. Fax: (831) 644-4547. E-mail: childaware@aol.com.

"CAPTAIN VIDEO AND HIS VIDEO RANGERS" TV PREMIERE: 55th ANNIVERSARY. June 27, 1949. "Captain Video" was the first of several TV space shows. The show was set in the 22nd century and starred Richard Coogan as Captain Video, a human who led a squad of agents (the Video Rangers) fighting villains from their own and other worlds. Al Hodge later replaced Coogan. Also featured were Ernest Borgnine, Jack Klugman and Tony Randall as guest villains.

"DARK SHADOWS" TV PREMIERE: ANNIVERSARY. June 27, 1966. This soap opera was completely different from all others because it featured vampires as main characters and had a dark, Gothic feel to it. The show focused on the Collins family living at Collinsport, ME, mainly Barnabas Collins (Jonathan Frid), a 200-year-old vampire. Other cast members included David Selby, Kate Jackson, Lara Parker and Jerry Lacy. Action shifted between the 1800s and the 1960s. This show was very popular with teenagers and was remade as a short-lived series in 1991.

DECIDE TO BE MARRIED DAY. June 27. To focus attention on the joy of deciding to get married. Based on my poem *Decide to Be Married*: "It's in the deciding to be united in love, to express your joyful oneness to every person you meet, and in every action you take and together a perfect marriage you'll make." For info: Barbara Gaughen-Muller, Pres, Gaughen Global Public Relations, 7456 Evergreen Dr, Santa Barbara, CA 93117. Phone: (805) 968-8567. Fax: (805) 968-5747. E-mail: Barbara@robertmuller.org.

DJIBOUTI: INDEPENDENCE DAY. June 27. National day. Commemorates independence from France in 1977.

GAY AND LESBIAN PRIDE PARADE. June 27. Chicago, IL. Chicago's 35th annual parade begins at 12 PM. Est attendance: 375,000. For info: Gay and Lesbian Pride Parade, 3712 N Broadway, PMB #544, Chicago, IL 60613. Phone: (773) 348-8243. E-mail: pridechgo@aol.com. Web: www.chicagopridecalendar.org.

HAPPY BIRTHDAY TO "HAPPY BIRTHDAY TO YOU." June 27, 1859. The melody of probably the most often sung song in the world, "Happy Birthday to You," was composed by Mildred J. Hill, a schoolteacher born at Louisville, KY, on this date. Her younger sister, Patty Smith Hill, was the author of the lyrics which were first published in 1893 as "Good Morning to All," a classroom greeting published in the book *Song Stories for the Sunday School*. The lyrics were amended in 1924 to include a stanza beginning "Happy Birthday to You." Now it is sung somewhere in the world every minute of the day. Although the authors are believed to have earned very little from the song, reportedly it later generated about $1 million a year for its copyright owner. The song is expected to enter public domain upon expiration of copyright in 2010. Mildred Hill died at Chicago, IL, June 5, 1916, without knowing that her melody would become the world's most popular song. See also: "Hill, Patty Smith: Birth Anniversary" (Mar 27).

HEARN, LAFCADIO: BIRTH ANNIVERSARY. June 27, 1850. Author, born on the Greek island of Santa Maura. Hearn, who had been a newspaper reporter at Cincinnati, OH, and at New Orleans, LA, went to Japan in 1890 as a magazine writer. Deeply attracted to the country and to the Japanese people, he stayed there as a writer and teacher until his death at Okubo, Japan, Sept 26, 1904. Though his writings are little remembered in America, he remains a popular figure in Japan, where his books are still used, especially in language classes. His home at Matsue is a tourist shrine.

HELEN KELLER DEAF-BLINDNESS AWARENESS WEEK. June 27–July 3. Presidential proclamation since 1984. A week to observe the birth anniversary of Helen Keller who was born June 27, 1880. Annually, the full week that includes Helen Keller's birthday. For info: Library for Deaf Action, 2930 Craiglawn Rd, Silver Spring, MD 20904-1816. Phone: (301) 572-5168 (TTY). Fax: (301) 572-4134. E-mail: alicehagemeyer@aol.com.

HUTCHFEST. June 27–July 4. Hutchinson, KS. Family festival with free entertainment, games, activities, arts and crafts, prairie heritage and name entertainment. Est attendance: 60,000. For info: Dan Popp. Phone: (620) 663-7448. Web: www.hutchchamber.com.

INDEPENDENCE SUNDAY IN IOWA. June 27. Sunday preceding July 4, by proclamation of the governor.

INTERNATIONAL SIT-ON-THE-FRONT-PEW SUNDAY. June 27. An event that can be fun for the whole family, designed to fill churches from the front pew back so that clergy will feel encouraged that their people really do care and do want to see and hear them. Annually, the fourth Sunday in June. For info: Don Hughes, Pres, CEO, KJIL—Great Plains Christian Radio, PO Box 991, Meade, KS 67864. Phone: (620) 873-2991. Fax: (620) 873-2755. E-mail: kjil@kjil.com. Web: www.kjil.com.

KELLER, HELEN: BIRTH ANNIVERSARY. June 27, 1880. Born at Tuscumbia, AL, Helen Keller was left deaf and blind by a disease she contracted at 18 months of age. With the help of her teacher, Anne Sullivan, she graduated from college and had a career as an author and lecturer. She died June 1, 1968, at Westport, CT.

LOG CABIN DAY. June 27. Commemorates log cabins with tours, open houses and special festivities throughout the state of Michigan. Est attendance: 4,000. For info: Virginia Handy, Sec/Treas, Log Cabin Society of Michigan, 3503 Rock Edwards Dr, Sodus, MI 49126. Phone: (269) 925-3836. E-mail: logcabincrafts@qtm.net. Web: www.qtm.net/logcabincrafts.

June 27–28 ☆ Chase's 2004 Calendar of Events ☆

NATIONAL HIV TESTING DAY. June 27. A nationwide campaign encouraging education, voluntary HIV testing and counseling to people at risk for HIV. For info: Natl Assn of People with AIDS, 1413 K St NW, 7th Fl, Washington, DC 20005. Phone: (202) 898-0414. E-mail: cperkins@napwa.org. Web: www.nhtd.org.

NATIONAL PREVENTION OF EYE INJURIES AWARENESS WEEK. June 27–July 5. For info: LoRetta Mann, US Eye Injury Registry, 1201 11th Ave S, Ste 300, Birmingham, AL 35205. Phone: (205) 933-0064. Fax: (205) 933-1341. E-mail: loretta@useironline.org. Web: www.useironline.org.

OPERA FESTIVAL OF NEW JERSEY. June 27–July 17 (tentative). McCarter Theatre Center for the Performing Arts, Princeton, NJ. A professional organization founded in 1984 to present opera productions that are accessible to audiences of all ages and backgrounds. New Jersey's leading producer of professional opera, known for creating artistically focused new productions of opera that feature young American artists of excellence. Est attendance: 17,000. For info: Opera Festival of New Jersey, 29 Emmons Dr, Ste G-50, Princeton, NJ 08540. Phone: (609) 919-1003. Fax: (609) 919-1008. E-mail: info@operafest.org. Web: www.operafest.org.

PARNELL, CHARLES STEWART: BIRTH ANNIVERSARY. June 27, 1846. Irish nationalist leader and home-rule advocate born at Avondale, County Wicklow, Ireland. Politically ruined as a result of an affair with Katherine O'Shea, the estranged wife of a member of Parliament. O'Shea was divorced by her husband (who named Parnell corespondent), and on June 25, 1891, she married Parnell. Less than a month later Parnell was defeated in a by-election. He made his last public speech Sept 27, 1891, and died in the arms of his wife, at Brighton, Oct 6, 1891. Reportedly he was given "a magnificent funeral" by the city of Dublin, where he was buried. The anniversary of Parnell's death is observed by some as Ivy Day when a sprig of ivy is worn on the lapel to remember him. See also: "Ivy Day" (Oct 6).

SINGING ON THE MOUNTAIN. June 27. Grandfather Mountain, Linville, NC. 80th annual sing. Modern and traditional gospel music featuring top groups and nationally known speakers. Annually, the fourth Sunday in June. Free admission. Est attendance: 12,000. For info: Grandfather Mountain, US Highway 221 N, PO Box 129, Linville, NC 28646. Phone: (800) 468-7325. Web: www.grandfather.com.

SMITH, JOSEPH, JR, AND HYRUM: DEATH ANNIVERSARY. June 27, 1844. The founding prophet of The Church of Jesus Christ of Latter-day Saints and his brother Hyrum were shot to death by an armed mob in Carthage, IL. At the time, Joseph Smith was the presidential candidate of the National Reform Party, the first US presidential candidate to be assassinated. Joseph Smith was born at Sharon, VT, Dec 3, 1805; Hyrum Smith was born at Sharon, VT.

SMITHSON, JAMES: 175th DEATH ANNIVERSARY. June 27, 1829. Scientist and founder of the Smithsonian Institution, James Smithson was born at Paris, France in 1765 (exact date unknown). His will, dated Oct 23, 1826, bequeathed his great wealth to a nation he had never visited, to found "at Washington under the name of the Smithsonian Institution, establishment for the increase and diffusion of knowledge among men." In spite of opposition, the Congress approved, on Aug 10, 1846, an act to establish the Smithsonian Institution. Most of Smithson's personal documents, books and collections were destroyed by fire in 1865. Smithson died at Genoa, Italy. His remains were removed from there to Washington, DC, in 1904.

SOCIETY FOR THE PRESERVATION & ENCOURAGEMENT OF BARBER SHOP QUARTET SINGING IN AMERICA (SPEBSQSA) INTERNATIONAL CONVENTION. June 27–July 4. Louisville, KY. More than 10,000 members attend a week of shows, meetings, chorus and quartet contests. Est attendance: 10,000. For info: Reed Sampson, Public Relations Dir, SPEBSQSA, 6315 Third Ave, Kenosha, WI 53143. Phone: (800) 876-SING. E-mail: info@spebsqsa.org. Web: www.spebsqsa.org.

THURGOOD MARSHALL RESIGNS FROM SUPREME COURT: ANNIVERSARY. June 27, 1991. Signaling an end to the era of a liberal Supreme Court, Associate Justice Thurgood Marshall announced his resignation from the United States Supreme Court, effective once his successor was confirmed by the US Senate. Marshall was a pioneering civil rights lawyer who helped lead the fight to end racial segregation and served as US Solicitor General prior to his appointment to the high court by President Lyndon Johnson in 1967 as the first black ever to sit on the Supreme Court. As an attorney for the NAACP, he successfully argued the case of *Brown v Board of Education* before the Supreme Court, ending the doctrine of "separate but equal." Marshall's 24-year tenure on the bench was marked by his strong liberal voice championing the rights of criminal defendants and defending abortion rights, his opposition to the death penalty and his commitment to civil rights. On July 1, 1991, President George Bush selected Clarence Thomas, a conservative black jurist, to succeed Marshall. See also: "Marshall, Thurgood: Birth Anniversary" (July 2).

BIRTHDAYS TODAY

Isabelle Adjani, 49, actress (*The Story of Adele H., Camille Claudel*), born Paris, France, June 27, 1955.
Julia Duffy, 53, actress ("Newhart," "Designing Women"), born St. Paul, MN, June 27, 1951.
Shirley-Anne Field, 66, actress (*Alfie, My Beautiful Laundrette, Getting It Right*), born London, England, June 27, 1938.
Norma Kamali, 59, fashion designer, born New York, NY, June 27, 1945.
Captain Kangaroo (Bob Keeshan), 77, TV personality, born Lynbrook, NY, June 27, 1927.
Tobey Maguire, 29, actor (*Spiderman, Pleasantville, The Cider House Rules*), born Santa Monica, CA, June 27, 1975.
Anna Moffo, 70, opera singer, born Wayne, PA, June 27, 1934.
Jason Patric, 38, actor (*Speed 2, Sleepers*), born Queens, NY, June 27, 1966.
H. Ross Perot, 74, philanthropist, businessman, 1992 and 1996 presidential candidate, born Texarkana, TX, June 27, 1930.
Chuck Connors Person, 40, former basketball player, born Brantley, AL, June 27, 1964.

JUNE 28 — MONDAY
Day 180 — 186 Remaining

"AMOS 'N' ANDY" TV PREMIERE: ANNIVERSARY. June 28, 1951. This show was based on the popular radio show about black characters played by white dialecticians Freeman Gosden and Charles Correll. In fact, it was the first dramatic series with an all-black cast. The cast included Tim Moore, Spencer Williams, Alvin Childress, Ernestine Wade, Amanda Randolph, Johnny Lee, Nick O'Demus and Jester Hairston. The series was widely syndicated until pressure from civil rights groups, who claimed the show was stereotypical and prejudicial, caused CBS to withdraw it from syndication.

	S	M	T	W	T	F	S
June 2004			1	2	3	4	5
	6	7	8	9	10	11	12
	13	14	15	16	17	18	19
	20	21	22	23	24	25	26
	27	28	29	30			

Chase's 2004 Calendar of Events — June 28-29

BISCAYNE NATIONAL PARK ESTABLISHED: ANNIVERSARY. June 28, 1980. Including the coral reefs and waters of Biscayne Bay and the area of the Atlantic Ocean that surrounds the northernmost Florida Keys, Biscayne National Monument was authorized Oct 18, 1968. It became a national park in 1980.

COMECON AND WARSAW PACT DISBAND: ANNIVERSARY. June 28, 1991. The last vestiges of the Cold War-era Soviet bloc, the Council for Mutual Economic Assistance (COMECON) and the Warsaw Pact, formally disbanded on June 28 and July 1, 1991, respectively.

CYPRUS: SAINT PAUL'S FEAST. June 28-29. Kato Paphos, Cyprus. Religious festivities at Kato Paphos at which the archbishop officiates. Procession of the icon of Saint Paul through the streets.

MAASS, CLARA: BIRTH ANNIVERSARY. June 28, 1876. Commemorates the birth in 1876 of Clara Louise Maass, the heroic nurse who gave her life in the yellow fever experiments of 1901. Created by the Clara Maass Foundation. Maass died at Havana, Cuba, Aug 24, 1901.

MAYER, MARIA GOEPPERT: BIRTH ANNIVERSARY. June 28, 1906. German-American physicist Maria Goeppert Mayer was born at Kattowitz, Germany. A participant in the Manhattan Project, she worked on the separation of uranium isotopes for the atomic bomb. Mayer became the first American woman to win the Nobel Prize when she shared the 1963 prize for physics with J. Hans Daniel Jensen and Eugene P. Wigner for their explanation of the atomic nucleus, known as the nuclear shell theory. Mayer died Feb 20, 1972, at San Diego, CA.

MONDAY HOLIDAY LAW: ANNIVERSARY. June 28, 1968. President Lyndon B. Johnson approved PL 90-363, which amended section 6103(a) of title 5, United States Code, establishing Monday observance of Washington's Birthday, Memorial Day, Labor Day, Columbus Day and Veterans Day. The new holiday law took effect Jan 1, 1971. Veterans Day observance subsequently reverted to its former observance date, Nov 11. See individual holidays for further details.

NATIONAL COLUMNIST'S DAY. June 28. Newspaper columnists, who bring you joy all year long, deserve to be celebrated by their readers at least once a year. Now you can send your favorite columnists, local or nationally syndicated, your own wishes for a Happy Columnist's Day and make him or her feel wonderful. Annually, the fourth Tuesday in June. For info: Jim Six, Columnist, *The Gloucester County Times*, 309 S Broad St, Woodbury, NJ 08096. Phone: (856) 845-3300. Fax: (856) 845-5480. E-mail: jimsix@reporters.net.

RADNER, GILDA: BIRTH ANNIVERSARY. June 28, 1946. Actress, comedienne ("Saturday Night Live," *Hanky Panky*), born at Detroit, MI. Died May 20, 1989, at Los Angeles, CA.

ROUSSEAU, JEAN-JACQUES: BIRTH ANNIVERSARY. June 28, 1712. Philosopher, born at Geneva, Switzerland. Died July 2, 1778, at Ermenonville, France. "Man is born free," he wrote in *The Social Contract*, "and everywhere he is in chains."

RUBENS, PETER PAUL: BIRTH ANNIVERSARY. June 28, 1577. Flemish painter and diplomat born at Siegen, Westphalia. Died of gout at Antwerp, Belgium, May 30, 1640.

STONEWALL RIOT: 35th ANNIVERSARY. June 28, 1969. Early in the morning of June 28, 1969, the clientele of a gay bar, the Stonewall Inn at New York City, rioted after the club was raided by police. The riot was followed by several days of demonstrations. Stonewall is now recognized as the start of the gay liberation movement.

TREATY OF VERSAILLES: 85th ANNIVERSARY. June 28, 1919. The signing of the Treaty of Versailles at Versailles, France, formally ended WWI.

BIRTHDAYS TODAY

Kathy Bates, 56, actress (Oscar for *Misery*; *Fried Green Tomatoes*), born Memphis, TN, June 28, 1948.
Donald Edward (Don) Baylor, 55, baseball manager, former player, born Austin, TX, June 28, 1949.
Danielle Brisebois, 35, actress ("All in the Family," "Knots Landing"), born Brooklyn, NY, June 28, 1969.
Mel Brooks, 76, actor, director (*The Producers*, *Blazing Saddles*), born Melvyn Kaminsky, New York, NY, June 28, 1928.
John Cusack, 38, actor (*Say Anything*, *The Grifters*, *Bullets Over Broadway*), born Chicago, IL, June 28, 1966.
Bruce Davison, 58, actor (*Ulzana's Raid*, *Longtime Companion*, *Six Degrees of Separation*), born Philadelphia, PA, June 28, 1946.
John Albert Elway, 44, former football player, born Port Angeles, WA, June 28, 1960.
Mark Grace, 40, baseball player, born Winston-Salem, NC, June 28, 1964.
Alice Krige, 50, actress (*Chariots of Fire*, *Barfly*), born Upington, South Africa, June 28, 1954.
Carl Levin, 70, US Senator (D, Michigan), born Detroit, MI, June 28, 1934.
Mary Stuart Masterson, 38, actress (*Fried Green Tomatoes*, *Benny & Joon*), born New York, NY, June 28, 1966.

JUNE 29 — TUESDAY
Day 181 — 185 Remaining

BOSTON HARBORFEST. June 29-July 5. Boston, MA. Patriotic waterfront festival with reenactments, concerts, chowder competition, Children's Day and much more. Est attendance: 2,500,000. For info: Boston Harborfest, 45 School St, Boston, MA 02108. Phone: (617) 227-1528. Fax: (617) 227-1886. E-mail: festival@bostonharborfest.com. Web: www.bostonharborfest.com.

CANADA: NOVA SCOTIA INTERNATIONAL TATTOO. June 29-July 7. Halifax, NS. The Tattoo combines more than 2,000 international military and civilian performers in bands, singing, dancing, marching, gymnastics and comedy. Annually, June 29-July 7. Est attendance: 60,000. For info: The Nova Scotia Intl Tattoo, 1586 Queen St, Halifax, NS, Canada B3J 2J1. Phone: (902) 420-1114. Fax: (902) 423-6629. E-mail: info@nstattoo.ca. Web: www.nstattoo.ca.

DEATH PENALTY BANNED: ANNIVERSARY. June 29, 1972. In a decision that spared the lives of 600 individuals then sitting on death row, the US Supreme Court, in a 5-4 vote, found capital punishment a violation of the Eighth Amendment, which prohibits "cruel and unusual punishment." Later overruling themselves, the court determined on July 2, 1976, that the death penalty was not cruel and unusual punishment and on Oct 4, 1976, lifted the ban on the death penalty in murder cases. On Jan 15, 1977, Gary Gilmore became the first individual executed in the US in more than 10 years.

ELVIS PRESLEY BOULEVARD NAMED: ANNIVERSARY. June 29, 1971. The City of Memphis, TN, voted to name a road in honor of Elvis—a 12-mile portion of the highway that passes Graceland.

FINLAND: SATA-HAME ACCORDION FESTIVAL. June 29–July 4. Ikaalinen. Est attendance: 40,000. For info: Finnish Tourist Board, 655 Third Ave, New York, NY 10017. Phone: (212) 885-9700 or (358) (3) 440-0224. Fax: (358) (3) 450-1365. E-mail: juhlat@satahamesoi.fi. Web: www.satahamesoi.fi.

FINLAND: TIME OF MUSIC. June 29–July 4. Viitasaari. Festival in a town of 300 lakes focuses on contemporary music with top international and Finnish artists performing more than 100 works from some of the most interesting composers of our time, many being performed for the first time ever. Est attendance: 8,000. For info: Finnish Tourist Board, 655 Third Ave, New York, NY 10017. Phone: (212) 885-9700, or Time of Music, Kestitie 10, Finland 44500 Viitasaari. Phone: (358) (14) 573195. E-mail: info @timeofmusic.org. Web: www.timeofmusic.org.

GOETHALS, GEORGE WASHINGTON: BIRTH ANNIVERSARY. June 29, 1858. American engineer and army officer, chief engineer of the Panama Canal and first civil governor of the Canal Zone, born at Brooklyn, NY. Died at New York, NY, Jan 21, 1928.

GRAND TETON MUSIC FESTIVAL. June 29–Aug 21. Walk Festival Hall, Teton Village, WY. Full symphony orchestra concerts on Friday and Saturday evenings, chamber music Tuesday through Thursday, performed by professional musicians from America's finest symphony orchestras with internationally acclaimed guest soloists and conductors at 8 PM each night. Est attendance: 25,000. For info: Grand Teton Music Festival, 4015 W Lake Creek Dr, #1, Wilson, WY 83014. Phone: (307) 733-1128. Fax: (307) 739-9043. E-mail: gtmf@gtmf.org. Web: www.gtmf.org.

INTERSTATE HIGHWAY SYSTEM BORN: ANNIVERSARY. June 29, 1956. President Dwight Eisenhower signed a bill providing $33.5 billion for highway construction. It was the biggest public works program in history.

LATHROP, JULIA C.: BIRTH ANNIVERSARY. June 29, 1858. A pioneer in the battle to establish child-labor laws, Julia C. Lathrop was the first woman member of the Illinois State Board of Charities and in 1900 was instrumental in establishing the first juvenile court in the US. In 1912 President Taft named Lathrop chief of the newly created Children's Bureau, then part of the US Dept of Commerce and Labor. In 1925 she became a member of the Child Welfare Committee of the League of Nations. Born at Rockford, IL, she died there Apr 15, 1932.

MAYO, WILLIAM JAMES: BIRTH ANNIVERSARY. June 29, 1861. American surgeon, one of the Mayo brothers, establishers of the Mayo Foundation, born at LeSueur, MN. Died July 28, 1939, at Rochester, MN.

MESA VERDE NATIONAL PARK ESTABLISHED: ANNIVERSARY. June 29, 1906. Area of southwest Colorado established as a national park. For further park info: Mesa Verde Natl Park, Mesa Verde Natl Park, CO 81330.

OLYMPIC NATIONAL PARK ESTABLISHED: ANNIVERSARY. June 29, 1938. Washington's Mount Olympus National Monument, proclaimed Mar 2, 1909, was transferred from the US Dept of Agriculture's Forest Service to the National Park Service Aug 10, 1933, then established as Olympic National Park five years later. For further park info: Olympic Natl Park, 600 E Park Ave, Port Angeles, WA 98362.

PETER AND PAUL DAY. June 29. Feast day for Saint Peter and Saint Paul. Commemorates dual martyrdom of Christian apostles Peter (by crucifixion) and Paul (by beheading) during persecution by Roman Emperor Nero. Observed since third century.

PLEASE TAKE MY CHILDREN TO WORK DAY. June 29. To recognize and celebrate the tough job that stay-at-home mothers do every day. Please Take My Children to Work Day lets stay-at-home moms laugh at themselves while getting a much needed pat on the back. Sponsored by www.MommaSaid.net, the stay-at-home mom's coffee break™. For info: Jen Singer, PO Box 117, Butler, NJ 07405. Phone: (973) 492-8780. E-mail: jensinger @MommaSaid.net. Web: www.MommaSaid.net.

SAINT PETER'S DAY. June 29. Antakya, Turkey. Peter first preached Christianity at this place. Ceremonies at Saint Peter's Grotto, early Christian cave near Antakya.

SEYCHELLES: INDEPENDENCE DAY. June 29. National holiday. Gained independence from Great Britain in 1976.

SPACE MILESTONE: *ATLANTIS* (US) AND *MIR* (USSR) DOCK. June 29, 1995. An American space shuttle docked with a Russian space station for the first time, resulting in the biggest craft ever assembled in space. The cooperation involved in this linkup was to serve as a stepping-stone to building the International Space Station.

BIRTHDAYS TODAY

Gary Busey, 60, musician, actor ("The Texas Wheelers," *The Buddy Holly Story*), born Goose Creek, TX, June 29, 1944.
Theo Fleury, 36, hockey player, born Oxbow, SK, Canada, June 29, 1968.
Fred Grandy, 56, former congressman (R, Iowa), former actor ("Love Boat"), born Sioux City, IA, June 29, 1948.
Harmon Clayton Killebrew, 68, Hall of Fame baseball player, born Payette, ID, June 29, 1936.
Sharon Lawrence, 42, actress ("Fired Up," "NYPD Blue"), born Charlotte, NC, June 29, 1962.
Ann Veneman, 55, US Secretary of Agriculture, born Sacramento, CA, June 29, 1949.
Ruth Warrick, 89, actress (*Citizen Kane*, "All My Children"), born St. Louis, MO, June 29, 1915.

JUNE 30 — WEDNESDAY
Day 182 — 184 Remaining

CHARLES BLONDIN'S CONQUEST OF NIAGARA FALLS: ANNIVERSARY. June 30, 1859. Charles Blondin, a French acrobat and aerialist (whose real name was Jean François Gravelet), in view of a crowd estimated at more than 25,000 persons, walked across Niagara Falls on a tightrope. The walk required only about five minutes. On separate occasions he crossed blindfolded, pushing a wheelbarrow, carrying a man on his back and even on stilts. Blondin was born Feb 28, 1824, at St. Omer, France, and died at London, England, Feb 19, 1897.

CONGO (KINSHASA): INDEPENDENCE DAY. June 30. National holiday. The Democratic Republic of Congo was previously known as Zaire. Commemorates independence from Belgium in 1960.

	S	M	T	W	T	F	S
June			1	2	3	4	5
2004	6	7	8	9	10	11	12
	13	14	15	16	17	18	19
	20	21	22	23	24	25	26
	27	28	29	30			

☆ Chase's 2004 Calendar of Events ☆   June 30

ENGLAND: HENLEY ROYAL REGATTA. June 30–July 4. Henley-on-Thames, Oxfordshire. International rowing event that is one of the big social events of the year. Est attendance: 245,000. For info: The Secretary, Henley Royal Regatta, Regatta Headquarters, Henley-on-Thames, Oxfordshire, England RG9 2LY. Phone: (44) (149) 157-2153. Fax: (44) (149) 157-5509. Web: www.hrr.co.uk.

GUATEMALA: ARMED FORCES DAY. June 30. Public holiday.

LAST HURRAH FOR BRITISH HONG KONG: ANNIVERSARY. June 30, 1997. The crested flag of the British Crown Colony was officially lowered at midnight and replaced by a new flag (marked by the bauhinia flower) representing China's sovereignty and the official transfer of power. Though Britain owned Hong Kong in perpetuity, the land areas surrounding the city were leased from China and the lease expired July 1, 1997. Rather than renegotiate a new lease, Britain ceded its claim to Hong Kong.

LEAP SECOND ADJUSTMENT TIME. June 30. June 30 is one of the times that has been favored for the addition or subtraction of a second from our clock time (to coordinate atomic and astronomical time). The determination to adjust is made by the International Earth Rotation Service of the International Bureau of Weights and Measures, at Paris, France. See also: "Note about Leap Seconds" (see Contents).

MANISTEE NATIONAL FOREST FESTIVAL. June 30–July 4. Manistee, MI. Grand Parade, a Venetian boat parade, fireworks over Lake Michigan and children's parade. Tours of historic buildings, the Big Manistee River by canoe, North Country Trail and other local attractions. Juried arts and crafts show, entertainment, flea market, races, Twiggy the Water-Skiing Squirrel, high-action bikes, Aquapalooza and a hand-wood carver. Annually, on a weekend near the Fourth of July. Est attendance: 40,000. For info: Manistee Area Chamber of Commerce, 50 Filer St, Ste 224, Manistee, MI 49660. Phone: (231) 723-2575 or (800) 288-2286. E-mail: chamber@manistee.com. Web: www.manisteecounty.com.

MONROE, ELIZABETH KORTRIGHT: BIRTH ANNIVERSARY. June 30, 1768. Wife of James Monroe, fifth president of the US, born at New York, NY. Died at their Oak Hill estate at Loudon County, VA, Sept 23, 1830.

NOW FOUNDED: ANNIVERSARY. June 30, 1966. The National Organization for Women was founded at Washington, DC, by people attending the Third National Conference on the Commission on the Status of Women. NOW's purpose is to take action to bring women into full partnership in the mainstream of American society, exercising all privileges and responsibilities in equal partnership with men. For info: Natl Organization for Women, 733 15th St NW, 2nd Fl, Washington, DC 20005. Phone: (202) 331-0066. Web: www.now.org.

RIVERFEST. June 30–July 4. Riverside Park, LaCrosse, WI. 22nd annual Riverfest—the city's premier summer event! National stage acts, river activities including air shows, five stages to provide continuous entertainment, a children's area with games, face painting, etc. We also provide a food pavilion featuring 16 different vendors, beverage tent, and an Arts and Crafts area. July 4th features a fireworks display. Est attendance: 40,000. For info: Riverfest, Inc, PO Box 1745, LaCrosse, WI 54602. Phone: (608) 782-6000. Fax: (608) 784-1580. E-mail: riverfest@centurytel.net. Web: www.riverfestlacrosse.com.

SIBERIAN EXPLOSION: ANNIVERSARY. June 30, 1908. Early in the morning, a spectacular explosion occurred over central Siberia. The seismic shock, firestorm, ensuing "black rain" and the illumination that was reportedly visible for hundreds of miles led to speculation that a meteorite was the cause. Said to have been the most powerful explosion in history.

SUDAN: REVOLUTION DAY. June 30. National holiday. Commemorates a bloodless coup in 1989.

TAIWAN: BIRTHDAY OF CHENG HUANG. June 30. Thirteenth day of fifth moon. Celebrated with a procession of actors on stilts doing dragon and lion dances.

WHEELER, WILLIAM ALMON: BIRTH ANNIVERSARY. June 30, 1819. 19th vice president of the US (1877–81), born at Malone, NY. Died there June 4, 1887.

BIRTHDAYS TODAY

Vincent D'Onofrio, 45, actor (*Ed Wood, Men in Black*), born Brooklyn, New York, NY, June 30, 1959.
Nancy Dussault, 68, actress ("Too Close for Comfort," "The Ted Knight Show"), born Pensacola, FL, June 30, 1936.
Rupert Graves, 41, actor (*A Room with a View, Maurice*), born Weston-Super-Mare, England, June 30, 1963.
David Alan Grier, 49, actor (*A Soldier's Story, I'm Gonna Git You Sucka*), born Detroit, MI, June 30, 1955.
Lena Horne, 87, singer, actress (*Stormy Weather, Jamaica, Death of a Gunfighter, The Wiz*), born Brooklyn, NY, June 30, 1917.
Mitchell James (Mitch) Richmond, 39, former basketball player, born Ft Lauderdale, FL, June 30, 1965.
Patricia Schroeder, 64, former member of Congress from Colorado, born Portland, OR, June 30, 1940.
Michael Gerard (Mike) Tyson, 38, former heavyweight champion boxer, born New York, NY, June 30, 1966.

Iulye.

JULY 1 — THURSDAY
Day 183 — 183 Remaining

ANTI-BOREDOM MONTH. July 1–31. 19th annual sponsorship of a "self-awareness" event to encourage people to examine whether they, coworkers, family or friends are experiencing "an extended period of boredom" in their lives. The Boring Institute identifies this as "a warning sign" of problems that include depression, self-destructive behavior and even suicide. Advice is offered on how to avoid and overcome boredom. For info: The Boring Institute, Alan Caruba, Founder, 9 Brookside Rd, Maplewood, NJ 07040. Phone: (973) 763-6392. E-mail: acaruba@aol.com. Web: www.boringinstitute.com.

ARAFAT RETURNS TO PALESTINE: 10th ANNIVERSARY. July 1, 1994. Yasser Arafat, head of the Palestine Liberation Organization (PLO), returned to Palestine for the first time in 33 years. Israel's control of Palestine had prevented his visiting the region because he was a sworn enemy of the State of Israel and was regarded by Israelis as a terrorist. The agreement between Israel and the PLO, signed in September 1993, made possible Arafat's return. He went first to Gaza City in the Gaza Strip, where he was welcomed by a crowd estimated at 200,000. Three days later he flew by helicopter to the city of Jericho. Both areas were granted Palestinian rule by the treaty.

ARTOWN. July 1–31. Reno, NV. More than 200 arts-related events including dance, plays, concerts, fine arts exhibits and demonstrations, hands-on programs for children and film. For info: Artown, PO Box 3058, Reno, NV 89505. Phone: (775) 322-1538 or (800) 227-7909. Fax: (775) 322-8777. Web: www.artown.org.

BATTLE OF GETTYSBURG: ANNIVERSARY. July 1, 1863. After the Southern success at Chancellorsville, VA, Confederate General Robert E. Lee led his forces on an invasion of the North, initially targeting Harrisburg, PA. As Union forces moved to counter the invasion, the battle lines were eventually formed at Gettysburg, PA, in one of the Civil War's most crucial battles. On the climactic third day of the battle (July 3), Lee ordered an attack on the center of the Union line, later to be known as Pickett's Charge. The 15,000 rebels were repulsed, ending the Battle of Gettysburg. After the defeat, Lee's forces retreated back to Virginia, listing more than one-third of the troops as casualties in the failed invasion. Union General George Meade initially failed to pursue the retreating rebels, allowing Lee's army to escape across the rain-swollen Potomac River. With more than 50,000 casualties, this was the worst battle of the Civil War.

July 2004	S	M	T	W	T	F	S
					1	2	3
	4	5	6	7	8	9	10
	11	12	13	14	15	16	17
	18	19	20	21	22	23	24
	25	26	27	28	29	30	31

BELGIUM: OMMEGANG PAGEANT. July 1. Splendid historic festival of medieval pageantry at the illuminated Grand-Palace in Brussels. The annual event (first Thursday in July) re-creates an entertainment given in honor of Charles V and his court.

"BIG TOP" TV PREMIERE: ANNIVERSARY. July 1, 1950. Charles Vanda produced this CBS kiddie circus program that broadcast weekly for seven years from Camden, NJ. Jack Sterling played ringmaster. The show also featured Dan Lurie and Ed McMahon (as a clown, in his first TV appearance).

BIOTERRORISM/DISASTER EDUCATION AND AWARENESS MONTH. July 1–31. To educate consumers, healthcare professionals, nonprofit organizations and healthcare facilities about being prepared for natural disasters, emergency care, bioterrorism and acts of God. For info: Fred Mayer, PPSI, 101 Lucas Valley Rd, Ste 210, San Rafael, CA 94903. Phone: (415) 479-8628. Fax: (415) 479-8608. E-mail: ppsi@aol.com. Web: www.ppsinc.org.

BLERIOT, LOUIS: BIRTH ANNIVERSARY. July 1, 1872. Louis Bleriot, aviation pioneer and first man to fly an airplane across the English Channel (July 25, 1909), was born at Cambrai, France. He died at Paris, Aug 2, 1936.

BOTSWANA: SIR SERETSE KHAMA DAY. July 1. National holiday. Commemorates the birth in 1921 of the first president of Botswana.

BUREAU OF INTERNAL REVENUE ESTABLISHED: ANNIVERSARY. July 1, 1862. The Bureau of Internal Revenue was established by an act of Congress.

BURUNDI: INDEPENDENCE DAY. July 1. National holiday. Anniversary of establishment of independence from Belgian administration in 1962. Had been part of Ruanda-Urundi.

CANADA: CANADA DAY. July 1. National holiday. Canada's national day, formerly known as Dominion Day. Observed on following day when July 1 is a Sunday. Commemorates the confederation of Upper and Lower Canada and some of the Maritime Provinces into the Dominion of Canada in 1867.

CANADA: CANADA DAY CELEBRATION. July 1. Ottawa, ON. Annual event celebrating Canada's anniversary. The heart of the capital comes alive at four main sites with shows, street performers, concerts, games and activities for the whole family. In the evening a spectacular show featuring top Canadian performers is staged on Parliament Hill and culminates with a fireworks display. Est attendance: 350,000. For info: Natl Capital Commission, 40 Elgin St, Ste 202, Ottawa, ON, Canada K1P 1C7. Phone: (800) 465-1867 or (613) 239-5000.

CANADA: CANADA DAY CELEBRATIONS. July 1. Squamish, BC. Celebrate Canada's birthday with cake, games and entertainment. For info: Squamish Chamber of Commerce, PO Box 1009, Squamish, BC, Canada V0N 3G0. Phone: (604) 892-9244. Fax: (604) 892-2034. E-mail: information@squamishchamber.bc.ca. Web: www.squamishchamber.bc.ca.

CANADA: CANADA DAY PARTY IN THE PARK. July 1. Bancroft, ON. Canada Day fireworks. Craft show, kids' games and local musicians. Est attendance: 5,000. For info: Bancroft and Dist Chmbr of Commerce, PO Box 539, Bancroft, ON, Canada K0L 1C0. Phone: (613) 332-1513. Fax: (613) 332-2119. E-mail: chamber@commerce.bancroft.on.ca. Web: www.BancroftDistrict.com.

CANADA: YUKON GOLD PANNING CHAMPIONSHIPS. July 1. Dawson City, YT. Yukon residents compete for the honor of Territorial Champion Gold Panner. Dawson visitors can join in and compete for the Cheechako Award. Annually, July 1, Canada Day. Est attendance: 200. For info: Klondike Visitors Assn, PO Box 389, Dawson City, YT, Canada Y0B 1G0. Phone: (867) 993-5575. Fax: (867) 993-6415. E-mail: kva@dawson.net. Web: www.dawsoncity.ca.

CELL PHONE COURTESY MONTH. July 1–31. There are approximately 137 million cell phone users in the US. This month

☆ Chase's 2004 Calendar of Events ☆ July 1

is dedicated to encouraging the increasingly unmindful corps of cell phone users to be more respectful of their surroundings and those around them. Annually, the month of July. For info: Jacqueline Whitmore, Etiquette Expert, PO Box 3073, Palm Beach, FL 33480. Phone: (561) 586-9026. Fax: (561) 586-6689. E-mail: info@etiquetteexpert.com. Web: www.etiquetteexpert.com.

CHINA: HALF-YEAR DAY. July 1. National holiday in China. Midyear Day in Thailand.

CLEMSON, THOMAS GREEN: BIRTH ANNIVERSARY. July 1, 1807. The man for whom Clemson University was named was born at Philadelphia, PA. The mining engineer and agriculturist married John C. Calhoun's daughter, Anna. Clemson bequeathed the old Calhoun plantation to South Carolina, and Clemson Agricultural College (now Clemson University) was founded there in 1889. Clemson died at Clemson, SC, Apr 6, 1888.

CLEVELAND'S SECRET SURGERY: ANNIVERSARY. July 1, 1893. President Grover Cleveland boarded the yacht *Oneida* for surgery to be performed in secret on a cancerous growth in his mouth. As this was during the 1893 depression, secrecy was thought desirable to avoid further panic by the public. The whole left side of Cleveland's jaw was removed as well as a small portion of his soft palate. A second, less extensive operation was performed July 17. He was later fitted with a prosthesis of vulcanized rubber that he wore until his death June 24, 1908. A single leak of the secret was plugged by Cleveland's Secretary of War, Daniel Lamont, the only member of the administration to know about the surgery. The illness did not become public knowledge until an article appeared Sept 22, 1917, in the *Saturday Evening Post*, written by William W. Keen, who assisted in the surgery.

COURT TV DEBUT: ANNIVERSARY. July 1, 1991. The continuing evolution of entertainment brought on by the advent of cable television added another twist on July 1, 1991, with the debut of Court TV. Trials are broadcast in their entirety, with occasional commentary from the channel's anchor desk and switching between several trials in progress. Trials with immense popular interest, such as the William Kennedy Smith rape trial, the sentencing hearing of Marlon Brando's son and the Jeffrey Dahmer and O.J. Simpson trials, are broadcast along with more low-profile cases.

DIANA, PRINCESS OF WALES: BIRTH ANNIVERSARY. July 1, 1961. Former wife of Charles, Prince of Wales, and mother of Prince William and Prince Harry. Born Lady Diana Spencer at Sandringham, England, she died in an automobile accident at Paris, France, Aug 31, 1997.

DIXON, WILLIE: BIRTH ANNIVERSARY. July 1, 1915. Blues legend Willie Dixon was born at Vicksburg, MI. He moved to Chicago in 1936 and began his career as a musician with the Big Three Trio. With the advent of instrument amplification Dixon migrated away from his acoustic upright bass into producing and songwriting with Chess Studios, where he became one of the primary architects of the classic Chicago sound in the 1950s. His songs were performed by Elvis Presley, the Everly Brothers, the Rolling Stones, Led Zeppelin, the Doors, Cream, the Yardbirds, Aerosmith, Jimi Hendrix and the Allman Brothers, among others. Dixon died Jan 29, 1992, at Burbank, CA.

DORSEY, THOMAS A.: BIRTH ANNIVERSARY. July 1, 1899. Thomas A. Dorsey, the father of gospel music, was born at Villa Rica, GA. Originally a blues composer, Dorsey eventually combined blues and sacred music to develop gospel music. It was Dorsey's composition "Take My Hand, Precious Lord" that Reverend Dr. Martin Luther King, Jr, had asked to have performed just moments before his assassination. Dorsey, who composed more than 1,000 gospel songs and hundreds of blues songs in his lifetime, died Jan 23, 1993, at Chicago, IL.

EASTPORT FOURTH OF JULY AND "OLD HOME WEEK CELEBRATION." July 1–4 (tentative). Eastport, ME. Event features a flea market, craft fair, theater, music, dance, demonstrations and exhibits, fireworks display, public entertainment July 3–4, US naval ship in port and a variety of contests. Eastport, the easternmost city in the US, is bounded by the Atlantic Ocean on the Bay of Fundy and surrounded by Canadian Islands. Canada Day, July 1, is celebrated every year. Est attendance: 10,000. For info: Eastport 4th of July Committee Inc, PO Box 187, Eastport, ME 04631. Phone: (207) 853-2930. Web: www.eastport.net.

EYE INJURY PREVENTION MONTH. July 1–31. Accidental eye injury is a leading cause of visual impairment in the United States. Eye Injury Prevention Month informs the public that prevention is the first and most important step in avoiding serious eye injuries and that with appropriate protective eyewear, 90 percent of eye injuries can be prevented. For info: American Academy of Ophthalmology, PO Box 7424, San Francisco, CA 94120. Phone: (415) 561-8525. Fax: (415) 561-8533. E-mail: eyemd@aao.org. Web: www.medem.com/eyemd.

FIRST PHOTOGRAPHS USED IN A NEWSPAPER REPORT: ANNIVERSARY. July 1, 1848. The first instance of photojournalism occurred during the Paris Riots of 1848, when an enterprising French photographer known only as Thibault scrambled to a rooftop to chronicle the events. Taken on June 25 and 26, the two resulting daguerreotypes show first a deserted street, the rue St. Maur, with barricades, then show the same street with insurgents and the military in combat. Wood engravings were made of the daguerreotypes, and on July 1, 1848, the images appeared in the weekly newspaper *L'Illustration Journal Universel*. More than 3,000 Parisians lost their lives during the June revolt.

FIRST SCHEDULED TELEVISION BROADCAST: ANNIVERSARY. July 1, 1941. The National Broadcasting Company (NBC) began broadcasting from the Empire State Building on this day. The Federal Communications Commission had granted the first commercial TV licenses to ten stations on May 2, 1941.

FIRST US POSTAGE STAMPS ISSUED: ANNIVERSARY. July 1, 1847. The first US postage stamps were issued by the US Postal Service, a 5¢ stamp picturing Benjamin Franklin and a 10¢ stamp honoring George Washington. Stamps had been issued by private postal services in the US prior to this date.

FIRST US ZOO: ANNIVERSARY. July 1, 1874. The Philadelphia Zoological Society, the first US zoo, opened. Three thousand visitors traveled by foot, horse and carriage and steamboat to visit the exhibits. Price of admission was 25¢ for adults and 10¢ for children. There were 1,000 animals in the zoo on opening day.

GHANA: REPUBLIC DAY. July 1. National holiday. Commemorates the inauguration of the Republic in 1960.

HALFWAY POINT OF 2004. July 1. Because 2004 is a leap year, when July 1, 2004, ends at midnight, 183 days will remain before Jan 1, 2005.

HEMOCHROMATOSIS SCREENING AWARENESS MONTH. July 1–31. To promote awareness, encourage routine screening, early diagnosis and treatment of the disorder of iron metabolism characterized by excess iron absorption and gradual increased iron accumulation in vital organs and joints. Early treatment can prevent and even reverse organ damage if not advanced. For info: Hemochromatosis Foundation, PO Box 8569, Albany, NY 12208. Phone: (518) 489-0972.

July 1 ☆ *Chase's 2004 Calendar of Events* ☆

HERBAL/PRESCRIPTION AWARENESS MONTH. July 1–31. To educate health professionals and consumers on dietary supplements, herbs and nutritionals along with mixing those products with prescription drugs. There is a $15 charge for kit materials. For info: PPSI, c/o Pharmacy Council on Dietary Supplements, 101 Lucas Valley Rd, Ste 210, San Rafael, CA 94903. Phone: (415) 479-8628. Fax: (415) 479-8608. E-mail: ppsi @aol.com. Web: www.ppsinc.org.

I FORGOT DAY. July 1. A day to make up for all the birthdays, anniversaries, new births, graduations, etc, that you forgot to acknowledge with a greeting or gift. Annually, the 183rd day of the year—exact center. For info: Gaye Andersen, Davenport University, 8200 Georgia St, Merrillville, IN 46410. Phone: (219) 650-5218. Fax: (219) 756-8911. E-mail: gaye.andersen@davenport.edu.

ICE CREAM DAYS. July 1–4 (tentative). Le Mars, IA. July 4 parade, children's activities, art fair, flea market, food and souvenirs from the "Ice Cream Capital of the World," home of Wells's Blue Bunny. Est attendance: 10,000. For info: Sue Butcher, Operations Mgr, Le Mars Area Chamber of Commerce, 50 Central Ave SE, Le Mars, IA 51031. Phone: (712) 546-8821. Fax: (712) 546-7218. E-mail: lmchmbr@lemarscomm.net. Web: www.lemarsiowa.com.

LEAVENWORTH RIVER FEST. July 1–4. Leavenworth, KS. Joint celebration of the 150th birthday of the founding of Leavenworth and the commemoration of the bicentennial of the Lewis & Clark expedition that came through this area in 1804. Reenactments, keel boats and pirogues, fireworks, arts and crafts, parade, children's carnival, plenty of entertainment, food and several feature attractions. Est attendance: 35,000. For info: Leavenworth Main Street Program, 213 B3 Delaware, Leavenworth, KS 66048. Phone: (913) 682-3924. Fax: (913) 682-3928. E-mail: lvcvb@lvnworth.com.

"THE LIBERACE SHOW" TV PREMIERE: ANNIVERSARY. July 1, 1952. A pianist known for his outrageous style and a candelabra on his piano, Liberace hosted popular shows in the '50s and '60s. The first premiered on KLAC-TV in Los Angeles and went national in 1953. That did so well that he began a half-hour syndicated series which featured his brother George as violinist and orchestra leader. After a brief leave, he returned to TV in 1958 with a half-hour show. Liberace also hosted a British series and a summer series produced in London.

LINCOLN SIGNS INCOME TAX: ANNIVERSARY. July 1, 1862. President Abraham Lincoln signed into law a bill levying a 3 percent income tax on annual incomes of $600–$10,000, and 5 percent on incomes of more than $10,000. The revenues were to help pay for the Civil War. This tax law actually went into effect, unlike an earlier law passed August 5, 1861, making it the first income tax levied by the US. It was rescinded in 1872.

"MAMA" TV PREMIERE: 55th ANNIVERSARY. July 1, 1949. One of TV's first popular sitcoms, "Mama" told the story of a Norwegian family living in San Francisco in 1917. The show aired live through 1956; after it was cancelled, a second, filmed version lasted only 13 weeks. Cast members included Peggy Wood, Judson Laire, Rosemary Rice, Dick Van Patten, Iris Mann, Robin Morgan, Ruth Gates, Malcolm Keen, Carl Frank, Alice Frost, Patty McCormack and Kevin Coughlin. Toni Campbell replaced Robin Morgan in the revival.

MAMMOTH CAVE NATIONAL PARK ESTABLISHED: ANNIVERSARY. July 1, 1941. Area of central Kentucky, originally authorized May 25, 1926, was established as a national park. For more info: Mammoth Cave Natl Park, Mammoth Cave, KY 42259.

MEDICARE: ANNIVERSARY. July 1, 1968. Medicare, the US health insurance program for senior citizens, went into effect. The legislation authorizing the program had been signed by President Lyndon Johnson July 30, 1965. Former President Harry Truman received the first Medicare card.

MERMAIDS ON PARADE. July 1–31. Norfolk, VA. All around the city you'll find delightful mermaids welcoming you to the city. Similar to Chicago's Cows on Parade, our mermaids display the artistic talents of local artists. Rowena's is one of the sponsors—begin your city tour by viewing our mermaid. Annually, the month of July. For info: Rowena's, 758 W 22nd St, Norfolk, VA 23517. Phone: (757) 627-8699. Fax: (757) 627-1505. E-mail: cameron@rowenas.com. Web: www.rowenas.com.

MESCALERO APACHE MAIDEN'S PUBERTY RITES. July 1–4. Mescalero, NM. Mescalero's longest ceremony is four days long and culminates on the Fourth of July in the dramatic, pre-dawn Maiden's Puberty Rite each year. Visitors are welcome to come and share in this cultural tradition of the Mescalero Apache rite of passage experience, which includes clowns and Crown Dancers. This event is open to the public, but all non-Mescalero Apaches must vacate the reservation ceremony by late evening. For info: Mescalero Apache Tribe Resort Information. Phone: (800) 545-9011. Web: www.innofthemountaingods.com. For news requests only: Quill Communications. Email: sonya@quillcommunications.com. Web: www.quillcommunications.com.

MORRILL LAND GRANT ACT PASSED: ANNIVERSARY. July 1, 1862. This federal legislation led to the creation of the Land Grant universities and Agricultural Experiment Stations in each state.

NATIONAL BAKED BEAN MONTH. July 1–31. To pay tribute to one of America's favorite and most healthful and nutritious foods, baked beans, made with dry or canned beans. For info: Therese Schueneman, Bean Education & Awareness Network, 303 E Wacker Dr, Ste 418, Chicago, IL 60601. Phone: (312) 861-5200. Fax: (312) 861-5252. Web: www.americanbean.org.

NATIONAL CULINARY ARTS MONTH. July 1–31. Promotes awareness of professional cooks' and chefs' contributions to new culinary trends and dining excellence. Coincides with the American Culinary Federation's National Convention held in July. The ACF convention attracts the nation's most influential and exciting chefs, culinary educators and food industry representatives. The 2004 ACF convention will be held in Orlando, FL, July 16–20. The American Culinary Foundation, founded in 1929, is the nation's largest and most prestigious organization of culinary professionals with more than 25,000 members. For info: ACF, 10 San Bartola Dr, St. Augustine, FL 32086. Phone: (800) 624-9458. Web: www.acfchefs.org.

NATIONAL "DOGHOUSE REPAIRS" MONTH. July 1–31. Celebrate "Doghouse Repairs" Month by staying out of trouble with those you love and care about by doing something extra special. For info: Heidi Richards, Eden Florist and Gift Baskets, 7100 Pembroke Blvd, Miramar, FL 33023. Phone: (954) 981-5515. E-mail: flowers@edenflorist.com. Web: www.edenflorist.com.

	S	M	T	W	T	F	S
July 2004					1	2	3
	4	5	6	7	8	9	10
	11	12	13	14	15	16	17
	18	19	20	21	22	23	24
	25	26	27	28	29	30	31

Chase's 2004 Calendar of Events — July 1

NATIONAL HOT DOG MONTH. July 1–31. Celebrates one of America's favorite handheld foods with fun facts and new topping ideas. More than 16 billion hot dogs per year are sold in the US. Sponsor: National Hot Dog and Sausage Council. For info: Natl Hot Dog & Sausage Council, 1700 N Moore St, Ste 1600, Arlington, VA 22209. Phone: (703) 841-2400. Web: www.hot-dog.org.

NATIONAL JULY BELONGS TO BLUEBERRIES MONTH. July 1–31. To make the public aware that this is the peak month for fresh blueberries. For info: North American Blueberry Council, 4995 Golden Foothill Parkway, Ste #2, El Dorado Hills, CA 95762. E-mail: mnnabc@compuserve.com. Web: www.blueberry.org.

NATIONAL PURPOSEFUL PARENTING MONTH. July 1–31. Encourages parents to incorporate "purpose" in their parenting. Designed to elevate the level of parental effectiveness by building awareness and providing interested participants with tips for positive, conscientious parenting. For info send SASE to: Teresa Langston, Dir, Parenting Without Pressure (PWOP), 1330 Boyer St, Longwood, FL 32750-6311. Phone: (407) 767-2524. Web: www.parentingwithoutpressure.com.

NATIONAL RECREATION AND PARKS MONTH. July 1–31. To showcase and invite community participation in quality leisure activities for all segments of the population. For info: Natl Recreation and Park Assn, 22377 Belmont Ridge Rd, Ashburn, VA 20148. Phone: (703) 858-2162. Fax: (703) 858-0794. E-mail: programs@nrpa.org. Web: www.nrpa.org.

NATIONAL TOM SAWYER DAYS (WITH FENCE PAINTING CONTEST). July 1–4. Hannibal, MO. Frog jumping, mud volleyball, Tom and Becky Contest, parade, Tomboy Sawyer Contest, 10K run, arts & crafts show and fireworks launched from the banks of the Mississippi River. Highlight is the National Fence Painting Contest. Sponsor: Hannibal Jaycees. Est attendance: 100,000. For info: Hannibal Visitors Bureau, 505 N 3rd St, Hannibal, MO 63401. Phone: (573) 221-2477. Web: www.hannibaljaycees.com.

NATIONAL UNASSISTED HOMEBIRTH WEEK. July 1–7. Conferences and activities to create awareness and encouragement for couples who intentionally seek to give birth without a midwife or doctor. For info: Lynn M. Griesemer, 4103 Plaza Ln, Fairfax, VA 22033. Phone: (703) 263-2468. E-mail: greeze@juno.com. Web: www.unassistedhomebirth.com.

NATIONAL WATER GARDENING MONTH. July 1–31. To celebrate and promote the hobby of water gardening throughout the United States. Numerous events are sponsored in local communities to educate pond keepers about the proper way to install and maintain ornamental garden ponds. Water garden centers host local festivities, pond tours and seminars. For info: Roseanne Conrad, *Pondkeeper Magazine*, 1000 Whitetail Ct, Duncansville, PA 16635. Phone: (888) 356-9895. Fax: (814) 695-1722. E-mail: videorose@aol.com. Web: www.pondkeeper.com.

NICK AT NITE PREMIERE: ANNIVERSARY. July 1, 1985. The first broadcast of Nick at Nite, the creation of the kids' network Nickelodeon, occurred. Owned and operated by MTV Networks, Nick at Nite presents many of the old classic television series.

ROOTS AND BRANCHES MONTH. July 1–31. Created to inspire others to nurture their roots. An annual observance sponsored by Milford-Haven Enterprises, who believe in the synchronistic links between ourselves and everyone we're intended to meet. For info: Mara Purl, Milford-Haven Enterprises, 4411 Cahuenga Blvd, Ste 8, North Hollywood, CA 91602. Phone: (818) 762-2945. Fax: (818) 508-0299. E-mail: milfordhaven@aol.com. Web: www.milfordhaven.com.

RUSSIAN RUBLE BECOMES CONVERTIBLE: ANNIVERSARY. July 1, 1992. The Russian ruble became convertible with other currencies worldwide. Convertibility had long been held to be an important first move toward bringing the Russian economy into the mainstream of the world's economy. The official rate on July 1 was approximately 125 rubles to the dollar, and authorities hoped that it would eventually stabilize at approximately 80 rubles to the dollar. Previously it was illegal to convert rubles, although they traded briskly on the black market.

RWANDA: INDEPENDENCE DAY. July 1. National holiday. Commemorates independence from Belgium in 1962.

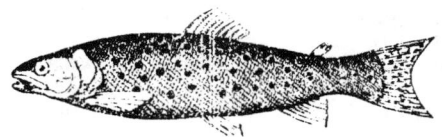

SALMON RIVER DAYS. July 1–4. Salmon, ID. Fourth of July celebration with a parade, boat races, auction, family reunions, rodeo, arts & crafts festival, theater and motorcycle exhibitions. Also, Cowboy Poets & Concert, fireworks, sidewalk sales, quilt show, horse races, kids' fishing derby and demolition derby. Est attendance: 3,000. For info: Salmon Valley Chamber of Commerce, 200 Main, Ste 1, Salmon, ID 83467. Phone: (208) 756-2100 or (800) 727-2540. E-mail: svcc1@salmoninternet.com.

SAND, GEORGE: 200th BIRTH ANNIVERSARY. July 1, 1804. French novelist, author of more than 100 volumes, whose real name was Amandine Aurore Lucile (Dupin) Dudevant, was born at Paris, France. Died at Nohant, France, June 8, 1876. She is better remembered for having been a liberated woman during a romantic epoch than for her literary works.

SOCIAL WELLNESS MONTH. July 1–31. Improve your social and communication skills and learn to act appropriately in prominent situations. Create a positive and lasting first impression. Be distinguished, earn respect, and appear confident under public pressure. For info: Angela Brown, Words of Wellness, PO Box 49266, Charlotte, NC 28277. Phone: (704) 849-2900. Fax: (704) 845-3060. E-mail: Angela@WordsofWellness.com. Web: www.WordsofWellness.com.

SPACE MILESTONE: *KOSMOS 1383* (USSR). July 1, 1982. First search and rescue satellite—equipped to hear distress calls from aircraft and ships—launched in cooperative project with the US and France.

SURINAME: LIBERATION DAY. July 1. National holiday. Commemorates the 1863 abolition of slavery in Dutch territory.

TWENTY-SIXTH AMENDMENT RATIFIED: ANNIVERSARY. July 1, 1971. The 26th Amendment to the Constitution granted the right to vote in all federal, state and local elections to all persons 18 years or older. On the date of ratification the US gained an additional 11 million voters. Up until this time, the minimum voting age was set by the states; in most states it was 21.

US WOMEN'S OPEN CHAMPIONSHIP. July 1–4. The Orchards Golf Club, South Hadley, MA. Est attendance: 40,000. For info: USGA, PO Box 708, Far Hills, NJ 07931-0708. Phone: (908) 234-2300. Fax: (908) 234-9687. E-mail: usga@usga.org. Web: www.usga.org.

WALKMAN DEBUTS: 25th ANNIVERSARY. July 1, 1979. This month Sony introduced the Walkman under the name Soundabout, selling for $200. It had been released in Japan six months earlier. More than 185 million have been sold.

WOMEN'S MOTORCYCLE MONTH. July 1–31. This month is dedicated to honoring women who ride, co-ride, or wish they could ride motorcycles or their derivatives (sidecar rigs, trikes, etc). For info: Sylvia Henderson, Springboard Training, 18005 Lafayette Dr, Ste B, Olney, MD 20832. Phone: (301) 646-1668. Fax: (301) 856-8000. E-mail: admin@v-twinvalues.com. Web: www.v-twinvalues.com.

ZIP CODES INAUGURATED: ANNIVERSARY. July 1, 1963. The US Postal Service introduced the five-digit zip code on this day.

July 1–2 ☆ *Chase's 2004 Calendar of Events* ☆

BIRTHDAYS TODAY

Pamela Anderson, 37, model, actress ("Baywatch," "Home Improvement"), born Ladysmith, BC, Canada, July 1, 1967.

Dan Aykroyd, 52, actor (*The Blues Brothers, Dragnet, Ghostbusters*, "Saturday Night Live"), born Ottawa, ON, Canada, July 1, 1952.

Karen Black, 62, actress (*Five Easy Pieces, Nashville*), born Park Ridge, IL, July 1, 1942.

Andre Braugher, 42, actor ("Homicide," *City of Angels*), born Chicago, IL, July 1, 1962.

Genevieve Bujold, 62, actress (*Choose Me, Trouble in Mind, Dead Ringers*), born Montreal, QC, Canada, July 1, 1942.

Leslie Caron, 73, actress (*Gigi, An American in Paris*), dancer, born Paris, France, July 1, 1931.

Olivia de Havilland, 88, actress (Oscars for *To Each His Own, The Heiress; Gone with the Wind*), born Tokyo, Japan, July 1, 1916.

Jamie Farr, 70, actor ("M*A*S*H," *The Blackboard Jungle*), born Jameel Farah, Toledo, OH, July 1, 1934.

Debbie Harry, 59, lead singer (Blondie, "The Tide Is High"), born Miami, FL, July 1, 1945.

Estée Lauder, 96, cosmetics executive, born New York, NY, July 1, 1908.

Frederick Carlton (Carl) Lewis, 43, Olympic gold medal track athlete, born Birmingham, AL, July 1, 1961.

Jean Marsh, 70, writer, actress (*Upstairs, Downstairs*), born Stoke Newington, England, July 1, 1934.

Sydney Pollack, 70, filmmaker (*Tootsie, The Way We Were, The Fabulous Baker Boys*), born Lafayette, IN, July 1, 1934.

Alan Ruck, 48, actor ("Spin City," *Ferris Bueller's Day Off*), born Cleveland, OH, July 1, 1956.

Twyla Tharp, 63, dancer, choreographer, born Portland, IN, July 1, 1941.

Liv Tyler, 27, actress (*That Thing You Do, Armageddon*), born Portland, ME, July 1, 1977.

JULY 2 — FRIDAY
Day 184 — 182 Remaining

"THE ANDY WILLIAMS SHOW" TV PREMIERE: ANNIVERSARY. July 2, 1957. Singer Andy Williams hosted many variety shows, including "The Andy Williams–June Valli Show," "The Chevy Showroom" and "The Andy Williams Show." His shows featured Dick Van Dyke and the Bob Hamilton Trio, the New Christy Minstrels, the Osmond Brothers, Charlie Callas, Irwin Corey and Janos Prohaska. In 1976 Williams hosted "Andy," a syndicated show.

AUSTIN COMMUNITY FESTIVAL. July 2–4. Austin, MN. 19th annual. Includes Independence Day Parade, stage entertainment, sports events, Street Dance, classic car cruise, concerts, Hambone Blues Jam, games, mini-golf, foods galore, fireworks and more. Est attendance: 20,000. For info: Austin's Festival Office, 329 N Main St, Ste 102, Austin, MN 55912. Phone: (507) 437-3448. E-mail: spamtown@smig.net.

BLACK HILLS ROUNDUP. July 2–4. Roundup Grounds, Belle Fourche, SD. This 85th annual Independence Day celebration includes an exciting PRCA rodeo each day, the Miss Rodeo South Dakota pageant, a big Fourth of July parade downtown at 10 AM and a thrilling carnival and midway. Est attendance: 10,000. For info: Belle Fourche Chamber of Commerce, 415 Fifth Ave, Belle Fourche, SD 57717. Phone: (605) 892-2676. Fax: (605) 892-4633. E-mail: chamber@bellefourche.org.

	S	M	T	W	T	F	S
July					1	2	3
	4	5	6	7	8	9	10
2004	11	12	13	14	15	16	17
	18	19	20	21	22	23	24
	25	26	27	28	29	30	31

CANADA: ABBOTSFORD BERRY FESTIVAL. July 2–3. Abbotsford, BC. July heralds the height of the Raspberry Capital of Canada's berry season. Sample delicious local strawberry, raspberry and blueberry products. Linger to cheer the top musicians, magicians and clowns; play bingo; fish the pond; take the kids on fun rides and browse through local craft and market-style food stands. Est attendance: 40,000. For info: Abbotsford Downtown Business Assn, 33728 Essendene Av, Abbotsford, BC, Canada V2S 2G9. Phone: (604) 850-6547. Fax: (604) 859-6507. E-mail: info@abbotsforddowntownbia.bc.ca. Web: www.abbotsforddowntownbia.bc.ca.

CIVIL RIGHTS ACT OF 1964: 40th ANNIVERSARY. July 2, 1964. President Lyndon Johnson signed the Voting Rights Act of 1964 into law, prohibiting discrimination on the basis of race in public accommodations, in publicly owned or operated facilities, in employment and union membership and in the registration of voters. The bill included Title VI, which allowed for the cutoff of federal funding in areas where discrimination persisted.

CONSTITUTION OF THE US TAKES EFFECT: ANNIVERSARY. July 2, 1788. Cyrus Griffin of Virginia, the president of the Congress, announced that the Constitution had been ratified by the required nine states (the ninth being New Hampshire June 21, 1788), and a committee was appointed to make preparations for the change of government.

CRANMER, THOMAS: BIRTH ANNIVERSARY. July 2, 1489. English clergyman, reformer and martyr, born at Aslacton, Nottinghamshire, England. One of the principal authors of *The English Book of Common Prayer*. Archbishop of Canterbury. Tried for treason and burned at the stake at Oxford, England, Mar 21, 1556.

DECLARATION OF INDEPENDENCE RESOLUTION: ANNIVERSARY. July 2, 1776. Anniversary of adoption by the Continental Congress, Philadelphia, PA, of a resolution introduced June 7, 1776, by Richard Henry Lee of Virginia: "Resolved, That these United Colonies are, and of right ought to be, free and independent States, that they are absolved from all allegiance to the British Crown, and that all political connection between them and the State of Great Britain is, and ought to be, totally dissolved. That it is expedient forthwith to take the most effectual measures for forming foreign Alliances. That a plan of confederation be prepared and transmitted to the respective Colonies for their consideration and approbation." This resolution prepared the way for adoption, July 4, 1776, of the Declaration of Independence. See also: "Declaration of Independence: Anniversary" (July 4).

DENMARK: AALBORG AND REBILD FESTIVAL (AMERICAN INDEPENDENCE DAY CELEBRATION). July 2–4. Aalborg. This celebration of the American Independence Day, at the Rebild National Park, Aalborg, Denmark, is described as "the largest single gathering for this occasion in the world." Guest speakers and Danish and American entertainment. Est attendance: 10,000. For info: 4 July Committee, Aalborg Tourist and Convention Bureau, Oesteragade 8, DK-9100 Aalborg, Denmark. Phone: (45) (98) 12-6022. Fax: (45)

(98) 16-6922. E-mail: info@visitaalborg.com. Web: www.visitaalborg.com.

ENGLAND: CHELTENHAM INTERNATIONAL FESTIVAL OF MUSIC. July 2–18. Cheltenham, Gloucestershire. The best of contemporary British music including symphony and chamber music, opera, late night events and fringe. Est attendance: 30,000. For info: Mr Toby Smith, Festival Administrator, Town Hall, Imperial Square, Cheltenham, Gloucestershire, England GL50 1QA. Phone: (44) (1242) 52-1621. Fax: (44) (1242) 57-3902. E-mail: townhall@cheltenham.gov.uk. Web: www.cheltenhamfestivals.co.uk.

FIRST SOLO ROUND-THE-WORLD BALLOON FLIGHT: ANNIVERSARY. July 2, 2002. In his sixth attempt, Steve Fossett became the first person to circumnavigate the world nonstop and in a nonmotorized craft. In his "Spirit of Freedom" balloon, Fossett traveled 19,400 miles. He began his odyssey on June 18, 2002 from Northam, Australia, and arrived at his starting longitude (117° east) on July 2, 2002. (The first balloon flight around the world was accomplished by a two-man team in 1999. See "First Round-the-World Balloon Flight: Anniversary" [Mar 21].)

FOURTH OF JULY CELEBRATION. July 2–4. Live Oak, FL. Rock-n-Blues BBQ and kids' activities. For info: Spirit of the Suwanee Music Park, 3076 95th Dr, Live Oak, FL 32060. Phone: (386) 364-1683. Fax: (386) 364-2998. E-mail: spirit@musicliveshere.com. Web: www.musicliveshere.com.

FOURTH OF JULY EXTRAVAGANZA. July 2–4. Hettinger, ND. Parade, free noon meal, events happening all week long and dances, food, booths and the largest fireworks display in SW North Dakota. Est attendance: 4,000. For info: Community Promotions Office, Box 1031, Hettinger, ND 58639. Phone: (701) 567-2531. Fax: (701) 567-2690. E-mail: adamschmbr@ndsupernet.com. Web: hettingernd.com.

FREEDOM DAYS. July 2–5. Farmington, NM. Celebration with a variety of special events, including spectacular fireworks, food fair, auction, gem and mineral show, parade, triathlon, BBQ cookoff. Est attendance: 70,000. For info: Farmington Conv and Visitors Bureau, 3041 E Main St, Farmington, NM 87402. Phone: (800) 448-1240 or (505) 326-7602. Fax: (505) 327-0577. E-mail: fmncvb@cyberport.com. Web: www.farmingtonnm.org.

GARFIELD, JAMES ABRAM: ASSASSINATION ANNIVERSARY. July 2, 1881. President James A. Garfield was shot as he entered the railway station at Washington, DC. He died Sept 19, 1881, never having recovered from the wound. The assassin, Charles J. Guiteau, was hanged June 30, 1882.

ITALY: PALIO. July 2 (also Aug 16). Siena. Colorful medieval horse race, competing for the banner (Palio).

LACOSTE, RENE: 100th BIRTH ANNIVERSARY. July 2, 1904. Jean Rene Lacoste, tennis player and clothier born at Paris, France. Lacoste, known as the Crocodile, was one quarter of the great French tennis players in the 1920s known as the Four Musketeers. He won Wimbledon and the US championship twice each, the French Open three times and was ranked No. 1 in the world in 1926–27. He designed the first shirt specifically for tennis, a loose-fitting cotton polo shirt that soon became the standard. He adorned the Lacoste shirt with a small crocodile, the first apparel logo. Died at St. Jean-de-Luz, France, Oct 12, 1996.

"THE LAWRENCE WELK SHOW" TV PREMIERE: ANNIVERSARY. July 2, 1955. This musical series, hosted by accordionist and bandleader Lawrence Welk, lasted for almost three decades. In its early years it was known as "The Dodge Dancing Party." Regulars included the Lennon Sisters, Alice Lon, Norma Zimmer, Tanya Falan, Arthur Duncan, Joe Feeney, Guy Hovis, Jim Roberts, Ralna English, Larry Hooper, Jerry Burke and Bobby Burgess. From 1956–59, this show was on concurrently with either "Lawrence Welk's Top Tunes and New Talent" or "The Plymouth Show Starring Lawrence Welk (Lawrence Welk's Little Band)."

LIVINGSTON ROUNDUP. July 2–4. Park County Fairgrounds, Livingston, MT. Livingston is the trout capital of the world and the Gateway to Yellowstone National Park. Parade on July 2 at 3 PM. Rodeo held nightly followed by a fireworks display. Performances begin at 8 PM each evening. Est attendance: 10,500. For info: Bruce Becker, Pres of Livingston Roundup, PO Box 800, Livingston, MT 59047. Phone: (406) 222-2905. Fax: (406) 222-7725. For tickets: Stacy Sunvison, phone: (406) 222-6787 or (406) 222-3199.

MARSHALL, THURGOOD: BIRTH ANNIVERSARY. July 2, 1908. Thurgood Marshall, the first African American on the US Supreme Court, was born at Baltimore, MD. For more than 20 years, he served as director-counsel of the NAACP Legal Defense and Educational Fund. He experienced his greatest legal victory May 17, 1954, when the Supreme Court decision on *Brown v Board of Education* declared an end to the "separate but equal" system of racial segregation in public schools in 21 states. Marshall argued 32 cases before the Supreme Court, winning 29 of them, before becoming a member of the high court himself. Nominated by President Lyndon Johnson, he began his 24-year career on the high court Oct 2, 1967, becoming a voice of dissent in an increasingly conservative court. Marshall announced his retirement June 27, 1991, and he died Jan 24, 1993, at Washington, DC.

MISSISSIPPI VALLEY BLUES FESTIVAL. July 2–4. LeClaire Park, Davenport, IA. Outstanding in its quality, quantity and variety of blues; enjoy great jams, performances and workshops on the banks of the Mississippi River. Est attendance: 35,000. For info: Mississippi Valley Blues Society, 102 S Harrison St, Ste 300, Davenport, IA 52801. Phone: (563) 32-BLUES. E-mail: mvbs@revealed.net. Web: www.mvbs.org.

MOON PHASE: FULL MOON. July 2. Moon enters Full Moon phase at 7:09 AM, EDT.

NATIONAL EDUCATION ASSOCIATION MEETING. July 2–7. Washington, DC. Representative Assembly. For info: Natl Education Assn, 1201 16th St NW, Washington, DC 20036-3290. Phone: (202) 822-7769. Web: www.nea.org.

OLD-TIME FIDDLERS' JAMBOREE AND CRAFTS FESTIVAL. July 2–3. Smithville, TN. Thirty-one categories of old-time bluegrass including clogging, buck dancing, old-time fiddle band, five-string banjo, dulcimer, dobro, flat-top guitar and fiddle-off to decide the Grand Champion Fiddler. Annually, the weekend nearest July 4. Est attendance: 130,000. For info: Smithville Fiddlers' Jamboree, PO Box 83, Smithville, TN 37166. Phone: (615) 597-8500. Dekalb Chamber of Commerce, phone: (615) 597-4163. Web: www.dekalbtn.com or www.dekalbtn.com/jamboree.

PERIGEAN SPRING TIDES. July 2. Spring tides, the highest possible tides, occur when New Moon or Full Moon falls within 24 hours of the moment the Moon is nearest Earth (perigee) in its monthly orbit. The word *spring* refers not to the season but comes from the German word, *springen*, "to rise up."

RED LODGE HOME OF CHAMPIONS RODEO AND PARADE. July 2–4. Red Lodge, MT. This rodeo is part of the Professional Rodeo Cowboys Association circuit and brings nearly all of the national champions to Red Lodge each year. At noon

July 2-3 ☆ Chase's 2004 Calendar of Events ☆

each day the Home of Champions Parade struts its way through downtown Red Lodge with colorful floats, antique cars, horses, dancing girls, wagons and more. Annually, July 2-4. Sponsor: Red Lodge Rodeo Association. Est attendance: 15,000. For info: Red Lodge Area Chamber of Commerce, Box 988, Red Lodge, MT 59068. Phone: (888) 281-0625. Fax: (406) 446-1718. E-mail: info@redlodge.com.

RED, WHITE & BOOM. July 2. Columbus, OH. Central Ohio's Independence Day celebration features one of the largest fireworks displays in the Midwest. Est attendance: 500,000. For info: Michael L. Collins, Exec Dir, Red, White & Boom, Inc, 929 Harrison Ave, Ste 202, Columbus, OH 43215. Phone: (614) 421-BOOM. Fax: (614) 291-9211. Web: www.redwhiteandboom.org.

SAINT LOUIS RACE RIOTS: ANNIVERSARY. July 2, 1917. Between 20 and 75 blacks were killed in a race riot in St. Louis, MO; hundreds more were injured. To protest this violence against blacks, W.E.B. DuBois and James Weldon Johnson of the NAACP led a silent march down Fifth Avenue at New York City.

SAUK TRAIL HERITAGE DAYS RENDEZVOUS. July 2-4. Johnson's Sauk Trail State Park, Kewanee, IL. Three-day event features artifact display, powwow, Native American crafts, circa 1800 fur traders rendezvous, voyager canoe rides and tours of the Ryan Round Barn, one of the largest in the state of Illinois. Est attendance: 20,000. For info: Mark Mikenas, Exec VP, Kewanee Chamber of Commerce, 113 E 2nd St, Kewanee, IL 61443. Phone: (309) 852-2175. Fax: (309) 852-2176. E-mail: chamber@kewanee-il.com.

STAMP EXPO. July 2-4. Elks Lodge, Pasadena, CA. Est attendance: 4,000. For info: Intl Stamp Collectors Society, Box 854, Van Nuys, CA 91408. Phone: (818) 997-6496. Fax: (818) 988-4337. E-mail: iibick@aol.com. Web: www.bick.net.

VESEY, DENMARK: DEATH ANNIVERSARY. July 2, 1822. Planner of what would have been the biggest slave revolt in US history, Denmark Vesey was executed at Charleston, SC. He was born around 1767, probably in the West Indies, where he was sold at around age 14 to Joseph Vesey, captain of a slave ship. He purchased his freedom in 1800. In 1818 Vesey and others began to plot an uprising; he held secret meetings, collected disguises and firearms and chose a date in June 1822. But authorities were warned, and police and the military were out in full force. Over the next two months 130 blacks were taken into custody; 35, including Vesey, were hanged and 31 were exiled. As a result of the plot Southern legislatures passed more rigorous slave codes.

WESTMORELAND ARTS & HERITAGE FESTIVAL. July 2-5. Twin Lakes Park, Greensburg, PA. Celebrating 30 years of arts and humanities. Multicultural celebration including food booths, children's area, crafts, fine art exhibition, continuous entertainment on five stages. Est attendance: 130,000. For info: WAHF, RR 2, Box 355 A, Latrobe, PA 15650. Phone: (724) 834-7474. E-mail: info@artsandheritage.com. Web: www.artsandheritage.com.

BIRTHDAYS TODAY

José Canseco, Jr, 40, former baseball player, born Havana, Cuba, July 2, 1964.
Sean Casey, 30, baseball player, born Willingsboro, NJ, July 2, 1974.
Vicente Fox Quesada, 62, president of Mexico, born Mexico City, July 2, 1942.

July 2004	S	M	T	W	T	F	S
					1	2	3
	4	5	6	7	8	9	10
	11	12	13	14	15	16	17
	18	19	20	21	22	23	24
	25	26	27	28	29	30	31

Polly Holliday, 67, actress ("Alice," "Home Improvement"), born Jasper, AL, July 2, 1937.
Jimmy McNichol, 43, actor ("The Fitzpatricks," "California Fever"), born Los Angeles, CA, July 2, 1961.
Richard Petty, 67, race car driver, born Level Cross, NC, July 2, 1937.
Ron Silver, 58, actor, director (*Silkwood, Enemies: A Love Story*; stage: *Speed-the-Plow*), born New York, NY, July 2, 1946.

JULY 3 — SATURDAY
Day 185 — 181 Remaining

AIR CONDITIONING APPRECIATION DAYS. July 3-Aug 15. Northern Hemisphere. During Dog Days, the hottest time of the year in the Northern Hemisphere, to acknowledge the contribution of air conditioning to a better way of life. Annually, July 3-Aug 15. For info: Air-Conditioning and Refrig Institute, 4100 N Fairfax Dr, Ste 200, Arlington, VA 22203. Phone: (703) 524-8800. Fax: (703) 528-3816. E-mail: ari@ari.org. Web: www.ari.org.

BELARUS: INDEPENDENCE DAY: 60th ANNIVERSARY. July 3. National holiday. Commemorates liberation of Minsk in 1944.

BENNETT, RICHARD BEDFORD: BIRTH ANNIVERSARY. July 3, 1870. Canadian prime minister, born at Hopewell Hill, NB. Died at Mickelham, England, June 26, 1947.

CANADA: MINERAL COLLECTING FIELD TRIPS. July 3-Aug 31. Bancroft, ON. Geologist-led mineral collecting field trips visit nearby rock dumps, abandoned mines and collecting sites. Participants are educated about mineral identification, collecting techniques and earth sciences. Annually, every Tuesday, Thursday and Saturday in July and August. Est attendance: 2,500. For info: Bancroft and Dist Chamber of Commerce, PO Box 539, Bancroft, ON, Canada K0L 1C0. Phone: (613) 332-1513. Fax: (613) 332-2119. E-mail: chamber@commerce.bancroft.on.ca. Web: www.bancroftdistrict.com.

COMPLIMENT-YOUR-MIRROR DAY. July 3. Participation consists of complimenting your mirror on having such a wonderful owner and keeping track of whether other mirrors you meet during the day smile at you. For info: Bob Birch, Grand Punscorpion, Puns Corps, Box 2364, Falls Church, VA 22042-0364. Phone: (703) 533-3668.

CRAFT DAY BY THE BAY. July 3. Harvey Cedars, NJ. More than 100 crafters and artists displaying and selling their handcrafted goods. Est attendance: 2,000. For info: Harvey Cedars Activity Committee, PO Box 3185, Harvey Cedars, NJ 08008. Phone: (609) 361-7990. Fax: (609) 494-8343. Web: www.harveycedars.org.

THE DAM EXPERIENCE. July 3 (tentative, rain date July 4). Truman Dam, Warsaw, MO. Gigantic fireworks display viewed from land and boat. Est attendance: 10,000. For info: Warsaw Area Chamber of Commerce, PO Box 264, Warsaw, MO 65355. Phone: (800) WARSAW-4. E-mail: warsawcc@iland.net. Web: www.warsawmo.org.

DOG DAYS. July 3-Aug 11. Hottest days of the year in Northern Hemisphere. Usually about 40 days, but variously reckoned at 30-54 days. Popularly believed to be an evil time "when the sea boiled, wine turned sour, dogs grew mad, and all creatures became languid, causing to man burning fevers, hysterics and phrensies" (from Brady's *Clavis Calendarium*, 1813). Originally the days when Sirius, the Dog Star, rose just before or at about the same time as sunrise (no longer true owing to precession of the equinoxes). Ancients sacrificed a brown dog at beginning of Dog Days to appease the rage of Sirius, believing that star was the cause of the hot, sultry weather.

ENNIS RODEO AND PARADE. July 3–4. Ennis, MT. Billed as the fastest two-day rodeo in Montana, this is a nonstop weekend of excitement. Parade with clowns, bucking broncos and everything imaginable. Annually, July 3–4. Est attendance: 4,000. For info: Pat Hamilton, PR, Ennis Rodeo Club, PO Box 236, Ennis, MT 59729. Phone: (406) 682-4700.

FIREFALL. July 3 (tentative). Springfield/Branson Regional Airport, Springfield, MO. The Springfield Symphony provides live music choreographed to fireworks. Also other live entertainment and concert performances. Annually, the Saturday before July 4th. Est attendance: 60,000. For info: Springfield Convention & Visitors Bureau, 3315 E Battlefield Rd, Springfield, MO 65804. Phone: (417) 881-5300 or (800) 678-8767. Web: www.springfieldmo.org.

FIREWORKS CELEBRATION. July 3–4. Demopolis, AL. Each year the Demopolis Area Chamber of Commerce presents a spectacular array of fireworks in celebration of Independence Day. The fireworks celebration is held at the Demopolis City Landing and begins at 9 PM. Two-day event also includes Best Burger on the River competition, duck race and children's day at Bluff Hall. Est attendance: 15,000. For info: Kathy Leverett, Pres, Demopolis Area Chamber of Commerce, Box 667, Demopolis, AL 36732. Phone: (334) 289-0270. Fax: (334) 289-1382. Web: www.demopolischamber.com.

FIREWORKS ON THE FJORD. July 3. Waterfront, Poulsbo, WA. Courtesy 3rd of July. Family event featuring displays, food booths, entertainment and a giant fireworks display on picturesque Liberty Bay. Voted "Best in the West Sound (Puget)"; only fireworks display on July 3rd in the Puget Sound area, it's a great way to celebrate Independence Day early! Est attendance: 25,000. For info: Fireworks on the Fjord, Community Events Productions, PO Box 1976, Poulsbo, WA 98370. Phone: (360) 779-8018.

FOURTH OF JULY. July 3–4. Winston-Salem, NC. Craft demonstrations, reenactments of events in early Salem and other special activities. Reenactment of state's first 4th of July celebration by legislative proclamation (1783). Sponsor: Old Salem Inc. Est attendance: 5,000. For info: Bill Cissna, Box F, Salem Station, Winston-Salem, NC 27108. Phone: (888) OLD-SALEM.

GEORGE WASHINGTON TAKES COMMAND OF THE CONTINENTAL ARMY: ANNIVERSARY. July 3, 1775. George Washington took command of the Continental Army at Cambridge, MA.

HAINES STAMPEDE AND RODEO. July 3–4. Baker City, OR. Fourth of July celebration with rodeo, fireworks, parade, food, entertainment and more. Est attendance: 500. For info: Baker County Chamber & Visitors Center, 490 Campbell St, Baker City, OR 97814. Phone: (800) 523-1235.

HEART OF AMERICA: A JOURNEY FOURTH (LEWIS AND CLARK BICENTENNIAL EVENT). July 3–4. Atchison, Leavenworth and Kansas City, MO. Salutes first independence day celebrated in the American West. On July 4, 1804, the Lewis and Clark Expedition celebrated the 28th birthday of the Declaration of Independence by firing its swivel cannon. Events include air show, July 4 fireworks over the Missouri River and cultural and historical programs. For info: Ms Emilie Jester, 1100 Main St, Ste 2550, Kansas City, MO 64105. Phone: (816) 691-3846. E-mail: ejester@visitkc.com. Web: www.visitkc.com.

HUNTINGTON, SAMUEL: BIRTH ANNIVERSARY. July 3, 1731. President of the Continental Congress, Governor of Connecticut, signer of the Declaration of Independence, born at Windham, CT, died at Norwich, CT, Jan 5, 1796.

IDAHO: ADMISSION DAY: ANNIVERSARY. July 3. Became 43rd state in 1890.

INTERNATIONAL CHERRY PIT SPITTING CONTEST. July 3. Tree-Mendus Fruit Farm, Eau Claire, MI. A nutritious sport—is there a better way to dispose of the pits once you have eaten the cherry? Entrants eat a cherry and then spit the pit as far as possible on a blacktop surface. The entrant who spits the pit the farthest including the roll is the champ. Annually, the first Saturday in July. Est attendance: 1,000. For info: Herb Teichman, Adv and Promo Mgr, Tree-Mendus Fruit Farm, 9351 E Eureka Rd, Eau Claire, MI 49111. Phone: (616) 782-7101. Fax: (616) 461-4187. E-mail: mendus@qtm.net. Web: www.treemendus-fruit.com.

IRAN AIR FLIGHT 655 DISASTER: ANNIVERSARY. July 3, 1988. At 10:54 AM in the Persian Gulf, the US Navy warship *Vincennes* fired two surface-to-air missiles at Iran Air Flight 655 which destroyed the airbus, killing all 290 passengers aboard. The *Vincennes*, boasting the world's most sophisticated radar detection equipment, reportedly misread radio signals of the airbus, mistaking it for a hostile F-14 fighter plane. A self-conducted military inquiry blamed human failure—stress on the tense crew rather than equipment malfunction—for the disaster. In the summer of 1992 the public learned that the ship had been in Iranian waters at the time in the course of an operation aimed at preventing Iranian boats from laying mines.

KILLDEER MOUNTAIN ROUNDUP RODEO DAYS. July 3–4. Killdeer, ND. More than a rodeo, the Western celebration features many events, including parades, contests, dances, musical entertainment, western art show, animal shows, historical reenactments of the Old West, cultural foods, Native American demonstrations, fireworks and two performances of great rodeo action. Est attendance: 6,000. For info: (701) 573-5254, (701) 764-5641 or North Dakota Tourism, Century Center, 1600 E Century Ave Ste 2, Bismarck, ND 58503. Phone: (701) 328-2525 or (800) 435-5663.

"MR PEEPERS" TV PREMIERE: ANNIVERSARY. July 3, 1952. This sitcom was broadcast live and focused on mild-mannered junior high school science teacher, Robinson J. Peepers (Wally Cox). The cast also included Tony Randall, Georgann Johnson, Marion Lorne, Reta Shaw, Jack Warden and Ernest Truex. This half-hour series was a summer replacement, but it earned such positive reviews that it was brought back as a regular series. In 1954 TV Guide wrote that "Mr Peepers . . . comes close to being the perfect TV show."

MOUNT RUSHMORE FOURTH OF JULY CELEBRATION. July 3–4. Mount Rushmore National Memorial, SD. Fireworks July 3 and musical performances both days. Est attendance: 10,000. For info: Mt Rushmore Natl Memorial, 13000 Highway 244, Bldg 31, Ste 1, Keystone, SD 57751. Phone: (605) 574-2523. Fax: (605) 574-2307. Web: www.nps.gov/moru.

OLD GLORY JUBILEE. July 3. Elsberry, MO. Old-time picnic, fireworks, parade, entertainment, games, crafts and lots of food. Est attendance: 1,500. For info: Elsberry City Hall, 201 Broadway, Elsberry, MO 63343. Phone: (573) 898-5588. Fax: (573) 898-2249.

July 3 ☆ Chase's 2004 Calendar of Events ☆

PEPSI 400 NASCAR WINSTON CUP SERIES RACE. July 3. Daytona International Speedway, Daytona Beach, FL. 46th running. Drivers battle for Independence Day glory under the lights. For info: Daytona Intl Speedway, PO Box 28014, Daytona Beach, FL 32120-2801. Phone: (386) 253-7223. Fax: (386) 947-6791. Web: www.daytonainternationalspeedway.com.

RAID ON ENTEBBE: ANNIVERSARY. July 3, 1976. An Israeli commando unit staged a raid on Entebbe airport in Uganda and rescued 103 hostages on a hijacked Air France airliner. Three of the hostages, seven hijackers and 20 Ugandan soldiers were killed in the raid. The plane had been en route from Tel Aviv to Paris when taken over by the pro-Palestinian guerrillas.

ROAD TO INDEPENDENCE. July 3–4. Jamestown Settlement, Williamsburg, VA, and the Yorktown Victory Center, Yorktown, VA. Salute America during the third annual Fourth of July event leading up to 2006, the 225th anniversary of the momentous American victory at Yorktown. The two-day event explores the important personalities of the American Revolution. Visitors can join in military drills and learn about the sacrifices of our nation's founders, including those who signed the Declaration of Independence. For info: Jamestown–Yorktown Foundation, PO Box 1607, Williamsburg, VA 23187. Phone: (757) 253-4838 or (888) 593-4682. Fax: (757) 253-5299. Web: www.historyisfun.org.

ROCK–N–BLUES AND BBQ. July 3. Spirit of the Suwannee Music Park and Campground, Live Oak, FL. Previous artists featured: The Laney Strickland Band, Keith Caton and the Accelerators, Walter Smith's Chicago Nights and more. For info: Spirit of the Suwannee Music Park, Hwy 29, Live Oak, FL 32060. Phone: (386) 364-1683. Web: www.musicliveshere.com.

ROCKPORT ART FESTIVAL. July 3–4. Rockport Festival Grounds, Rockport, TX. The work of top artists from across the US lines the waterfront for two days. Music and plenty of good food. Est attendance: 20,000. For info: Rockport Center for the Arts, 902 Navigation Circle, Rockport, TX 78382. Phone: (361) 729-5519. Fax: (361) 729-3551. E-mail: rockart@2fords.net. Web: www.rockportartcenter.org.

SEAFAIR. July 3–Aug 8 (tentative). Seattle, WA. In 2004 SEAFAIR will celebrate its 55th anniversary as the northwest's largest summer festival. More than 40 events in all highlighted by the Milk Carton Derby, Triathalon Torchlight Run and Torchlight Parade, Unlimited Hydroplane Race and Air Show. Also dozens of community parades and events. Est attendance: 1,000,000. For info: Seafair, 2200 6th Ave, Ste 400, Seattle, WA 98121. Phone: (206) 728-0123. Fax: (206) 728-9506. Web: www.seafair.com.

SPIRIT OF AMERICA (WITH FREEDOM AND AUDIE MURPHY PATRIOTISM AWARDS). July 3–4. Point Mallard, Decatur, AL. Event was started in 1966 to lift patriotic spirits during the tragedy of the Vietnam War. Presentation of Freedom Award and Audie Murphy Patriotism Award. Also includes the crowning of Miss Point Mallard and a booming fireworks display. Est attendance: 2,000. For info: Jacklyn Bailey, Decatur CVB, PO Box 2349, 719 6th Ave SE, Decatur, AL 35602. Phone: (800) 524-6181. E-mail: info@decaturcvb.org. Web: www.decaturcvb.org.

STAY OUT OF THE SUN DAY. July 3. For health's sake, give your skin a break today. [©2003 by WH.] For info: Thomas & Ruth Roy, Wellcat Holidays, 2418 Long Ln, Lebanon, PA 17046. Phone: (717) 279-0184. E-mail: info@wellcat.com. Web: www.wellcat.com.

STERLING RENAISSANCE FESTIVAL. July 3–Aug 15 (Saturdays and Sundays only). Sterling, NY. 28th annual re-creation of an English village set in the time period of Queen Elizabeth I. The festival features authentic jousting, more than 80 stage and street performances, music and dance of the period, beautiful arts and handcrafts, unique and delicious foods and drink and much more. Est attendance: 100,000. For info: Festival Office, Sterling Renaissance Festival, 15385 Farden Rd, Sterling, NY 13156. Phone: (800) 879-4446. Web: sterlingfestival.com.

SUNDOWN SALUTE. July 3–4. Junction City, KS. Free Independence Day celebration includes Coors 10K Freedom Run, parade, Veterans Ceremony, family activities, music, crafts and much more. Sundown Salute is a nonprofit organization made up of citizens in the interest of freedom. The celebration is run completely from corporate, private and individual donations. Est attendance: 35,000. For info: Michelle Avritt, Comm Coord, City of Junction City, PO Box 287, Junction City, KS 66441. Phone: (785) 238-7529. Fax: (785) 210-1930. E-mail: avritt@jcks.com.

TEN THOUSAND CRESTONIANS. July 3–4. Downtown and McKinley Park, Creston, IA. Parade, fireworks, flea market, talent show, historical village, carnival and food. All to celebrate US founding. Est attendance: 10,000. For info: Creston Chamber of Commerce, PO Box 471, Creston, IA 50801. Phone: (641) 641-7021. E-mail: chamber@mddc.com. Web: www.mdcc.com/chamber.

"TONY ORLANDO AND DAWN" TV PREMIERE: 30th ANNIVERSARY. July 3, 1974. Tony Orlando and Dawn (Telma Hopkins and Joyce Vincent Wilson) were a recording trio in the early '70s who hosted a summer replacement for "The Sonny and Cher Show" and then a series. In fall of 1976 the show was renamed "Tony Orlando and Dawn Rainbow Hour" and included George Carlin, Edie McClurg and Susan Lanier.

TOUR DE FRANCE. July 3–25. One of the great sporting events in the world. Cycling's best compete for more than 3,427 kilometers in 20 stages in the country of France. Ten stages are flat terrain races, seven are mountain races and three are time-trails (individual and team). For info: Amaury Sport Organisation, 2 rue Rouget de Iisle, 92 130 Issy-les-Moulineaux, France. Web: www.letour.fr.

UNITED NATIONS: INTERNATIONAL DAY OF COOPERATIVES. July 3. On Dec 16, 1992, the General Assembly proclaimed this observance for the first Saturday of July 1995 (Res 47/60). On Dec 23, 1994, recognizing that cooperatives are becoming an indispensable factor of economic and social development, the Assembly invited governments, international organizations, specialized agencies and national and international cooperative organizations to observe this day annually (Res 49/155). For info: United Nations, Dept of Public Info, New York, NY 10017. Web: www.un.org.

US VIRGIN ISLANDS: DANISH WEST INDIES EMANCIPATION DAY: ANNIVERSARY. July 3, 1848. Commemorates freeing of slaves in the Danish West Indies. Ceremony at Frederiksted, St. Croix, where actual proclamation was first read by Governor-General Peter Von Scholten.

VICKSBURG SURRENDERS: ANNIVERSARY. July 3, 1863. After weeks of immediate siege at the end of a yearlong campaign, Vicksburg, MS, surrendered to General Ulysses S. Grant. Formal surrender was consummated on July 4, and on July 8 the besieged city of Port Hudson also surrendered, giving the Union complete control of the Mississippi River. This cut off the western Confederacy from the rest of the South.

WORLD'S GREATEST LIZARD RACE. July 3. Chaparral Park, Lovington, NM. Participants and observers cheer as their lizards and iguanas race down a 16-ft ramp; winners are awarded trophies. Many other lizard events will be held throughout the day. Entertainment and other games are also featured. For info: Lovington Chamber of Commerce, 201 S Main St, Lovington, NM 88260. Phone: (505) 396-5311. Fax: (505) 396-2823. E-mail: visitus@leaconet.com. Web: visitus.leaco.net.

July 2004

S	M	T	W	T	F	S
				1	2	3
4	5	6	7	8	9	10
11	12	13	14	15	16	17
18	19	20	21	22	23	24
25	26	27	28	29	30	31

☆ Chase's 2004 Calendar of Events ☆   July 3–4

BIRTHDAYS TODAY

Moises Alou, 38, baseball player, born Atlanta, GA, July 3, 1966.
Dave Barry, 57, humorist, author, born Brooklyn, NY, July 3, 1947.
Laura Branigan, 47, singer ("Gloria," "How Am I Supposed to Live Without You"), born Brewster, NY, July 3, 1957.
Betty Buckley, 57, actress (*Cats, Sunset Boulevard*, "Eight Is Enough"), born Fort Worth, TX, July 3, 1947.
Tom Cruise, 42, actor (*Eyes Wide Shut, The Color of Money, Born on the Fourth of July*), born Syracuse, NY, July 3, 1962.
Pete Fountain, 74, jazz musician, born New Orleans, LA, July 3, 1930.
Thomas Gibson, 42, actor ("Dharma & Greg"), born Charleston, SC, July 3, 1962.
Teemu Selanne, 34, hockey player, born Helsinki, Finland, July 3, 1970.
Kurtwood Smith, 62, actor (*Robocop, Dead Poets Society*), born New Lisbon, WI, July 3, 1942.
Tom Stoppard, 67, playwright (*Travesties, On the Razzle, The Real Thing, Arcadia*), born Zlin, Czechoslovakia, July 3, 1937.
Montel Williams, 48, talk-show host ("The Montel Williams Show"), born Baltimore, MD, July 3, 1956.

JULY 4 — SUNDAY
Day 186 — 180 Remaining

ADAMS, JOHN, AND JEFFERSON, THOMAS: DEATH ANNIVERSARY. July 4, 1826. Former US presidents John Adams and Thomas Jefferson died on the same day, July 4, 1826, the 50th anniversary of adoption of the Declaration of Independence. Adams had once written to Jefferson (1813): "You and I ought not to die before we have explained ourselves to each other." They thus began a spirited correspondence until their deaths. Adams's last words: "Thomas Jefferson still survives." Jefferson's last words: "This is the Fourth?"

AMERICA THE BEAUTIFUL PUBLISHED: ANNIVERSARY. July 4, 1895. The poem "America the Beautiful" by Katherine Lee Bates, a Wellesley College professor, was first published in the *Congregationalist*, a church publication.

"AMERICAN TOP 40" RADIO PROGRAM: ANNIVERSARY. July 4. Casey Kasem's hit parade music countdown radio program, "American Top 40," was first broadcast on seven AM stations in the US on July 4, 1970. It is now heard in hundreds of markets around the world. This year marks the program's 34th anniversary. For info: Pete Battistini, 6576 Lake Forest Dr, Avon, IN 46123. Phone: (317) 839-1421. E-mail: at40@aol.com.

ANVIL MOUNTAIN RUN. July 4. Nome, AK. 25th annual running. At 8 AM the 17K run up 1,134-ft Anvil Mountain and return to the city of Nome starts the day's activities. Record time: 1 hr, 11 min, 23 sec. Annually, July 4. Est attendance: 1,500. For info: Rasmussen's Music Mart, PO Box 2, Nome, AK 99762-0002. Phone: (907) 443-2798. Fax: (907) 443-5777.

BE NICE TO NEW JERSEY WEEK. July 4–10. A time to recognize the assets of the state most maligned by American comedians. Annually, the first full week of July. For info: Lauren Barnett, Lone Star Publications of Humor, 8452 Fredericksburg Rd, PMB 103, San Antonio, TX 78229. E-mail: lspubs@aol.com. Web: members.aol.com/lspubs/lsindex.html.

BOOM BOX PARADE. July 4. Main St, Willimantic, CT. Connecticut's unique people's parade. Anyone can march, enter a float or watch; only requirement—bring a radio. No "real" bands allowed. (Marching music broadcast on WILI-AM Radio and played by "boom boxes" along the parade route.) 12 PM. Est attendance: 10,000. For info: Wayne Norman, Prog Dir, WILI-AM, 720 Main St, Willimantic, CT 06226. Phone: (860) 456-1111. Fax: (860) 456-9501. E-mail: wayne@wili.com. Web: www.wili.com/am.

CALITHUMPIAN PARADE. July 4. Biwabik, MN. Funny parade, clowns and bands; Biwabik's population of 1,000 jumps to more than 15,000 for a day. Annually, on the Fourth of July. Est attendance: 15,000. For info: Darlene Jackson, Committee Co-Chair, Biwabik Area Civic Assn, Box 449, Biwabik, MN 55708. Phone: (218) 865-4183 or (218) 865-6033.

CELEBRATION ON THE CANE: AN OLD-FASHIONED FOURTH OF JULY. July 4. Natchitoches, LA. Featuring hot dogs, apple pie, lemonade and a variety of traditional Fourth of July fare. Musical entertainment and fireworks over the scenic Cane River Lake. Est attendance: 10,000. For info: Calendar of Events, Natchitoches Parish Tourist Commission, 781 Front St, Natchitoches, LA 71457. Phone: (318) 352-8072 or (800) 259-1714. Fax: (318) 352-2415.

COOLIDGE, CALVIN: BIRTH ANNIVERSARY. July 4, 1872. The 30th President of the US was born John Calvin Coolidge at Plymouth, VT. He succeeded to the presidency Aug 3, 1923, following the death of Warren G. Harding. Coolidge was elected president once, in 1924, but did "not choose to run for president in 1928." Nicknamed Silent Cal, he is reported to have said, "If you don't say anything, you won't be called on to repeat it." Coolidge died at Northampton, MA, Jan 5, 1933.

DECLARATION OF INDEPENDENCE APPROVAL AND SIGNING: ANNIVERSARY. July 4, 1776. The Declaration was approved by the Continental Congress: "Signed by Order and in Behalf of the Congress, John Hancock, President, Attest, Charles Thomson, Secretary." The official signing occurred Aug 2, 1776. The manuscript journals of the Congress for that date state: "The declaration of independence being engrossed and compared at the table was signed by the members."

DUCKTONA 500. July 4. Riverview Park, Sheboygan Falls, WI. Plastic duck race in the park lagoon, dunk tank, antique car show, craft show, games for children, pancake breakfast, burgers, brats, beverages. Annually, the first Sunday in July. Est attendance: 5,000. For info: Lynn Buehler, Program Assistant, Sheboygan Falls Chamber Main St Office, 504 Broadway, Sheboygan Falls, WI 53085. Phone: (920) 467-6206. Fax: (920) 467-9571.

FAMILY DAY/INDEPENDENCE DAY CELEBRATION. July 4. Historic Square, Dahlonega, GA. Voted as "Top 20 Event" by the Southeast Tourism Society. Craft booths of all kinds, continuous music all day, food booths, kids' fun booths with prizes, clogging and buckdancing. Est attendance: 18,000. For info: Dahlonega-Lumpkin Chamber of Commerce, 13 S Park St, Dahlonega, GA 30533. Phone: (706) 864-3711. Fax: (706) 864-7917. E-mail: dahlonega@alltel.net. Web: www.dahlonega.org.

FARM SANCTUARY'S ANNUAL PIGNIC. July 4. Farm Sanctuary, Watkins Glen, NY. Celebrate July 4th by sampling free vegetarian hot dogs and giving a pig a belly rub at the country's premier farm animal shelter. Meet other rescued farm animals, including cows, goats, sheep, turkeys and more. Free farm tours from 11 AM to 3 PM. Est attendance: 200. For info: Education Coord, Farm Sanctuary, PO Box 150, Watkins Glen, NY 14891. Phone: (607) 583-2225. Fax: (607) 583-2041. Web: www.farmsanctuary.org.

July 4 ☆ *Chase's 2004 Calendar of Events* ☆

FIRESTORM 2004. July 4. Lakemont Park, Altoona, PA. The region's largest Fourth of July celebration with live entertainment on stage all day and a spectacular fireworks show. Free soda! Est attendance: 20,000. For info: Lakemont Park, I-99 Frankstown Rd Exit, Altoona, PA 16602. Phone: (814) 949-7275 or (800) 434-8006. Fax: (814) 949-9207. E-mail: lakemont99@aol.com. Web: www.lakemontparkfun.com.

FOSTER, STEPHEN: BIRTH ANNIVERSARY. July 4, 1826. Stephen Collins Foster, one of America's most famous and best-loved songwriters, was born at Lawrenceville, PA. Among his nearly 200 songs: "Oh! Susanna," "Camptown Races," "Old Folks at Home" ("Swanee River"), "Jeanie with the Light Brown Hair," "Old Black Joe" and "Beautiful Dreamer." Foster died in poverty at Bellevue Hospital at New York, NY, Jan 13, 1864. The anniversary of his death was observed as Stephen Foster Memorial Day by Presidential Proclamation from 1952 to 1997.

FOURTH OF JULY PATRIOTIC CONCERT AND FIREWORKS. July 4. Aurora, IL. Annual patriotic concert and fireworks display. Concert begins at 8 PM and fireworks display begins at dusk. For info: Lisa Garcia, City of Aurora, Mayor's Office of Special Events, 43 E Downer Pl, Aurora, IL 60507. Phone: (630) 844-3640. Fax: (630) 906-7068. E-mail: lgarcia@aurora-il.org.

FREDERICKSBURG HERITAGE FESTIVAL. July 4. Fredericksburg, VA. To create an awareness of Fredericksburg's historic heritage. Parade, raft race, street festival, country music, jazz, rock and roll and fireworks. Est attendance: 15,000. For info: Visitor Center, 706 Caroline St, Fredericksburg, VA 22401. Phone: (800) 678-4748. Fax: (540) 372-6587. E-mail: gboswell@fburg.city.state.va.us.

FREEDOM FEST. July 4 (rain date July 5). Lake of the Woods, Mahomet, IL. Annual celebration of patriotism. Family activities capped off by a spectacular fireworks display. Admission charged. Est attendance: 7,000. For info: Andee Chestnut, PR Director, Champaign Co Forest Preserve District, PO Box 1040, Mahomet, IL 61853. Phone: (217) 586-3360. Fax: (217) 586-5724. E-mail: hq@ccfpd.org. Web: www.ccfpd.org.

FREEDOM FROM FEAR OF SPEAKING DAY. July 4. This day is dedicated to stamping out the fear monster of public speaking. Priscilla Richardson, President of WriteSpeakforSuccess, has had to tame her own fear monster of public speaking to get her own speaking freedom. For info: Priscilla Richardson, Pres, WriteSpeakforSuccess, PO Box 275, Cloverdale, VA 24077-0275. Phone: (540) 992-1279. E-mail: guru@WriteSpeakforSuccess.com. Web: www.WriteSpeakforSuccess.com.

FREEDOM WEEK. July 4–10. To disseminate throughout the world information about freedom and liberty. For complete info and many famous quotations about freedom and liberty, send $5 to cover expense of printing, handling and postage. Annually, July 4–10. For info: Dr. Stanley Drake, Pres, Intl Society of Friendship and Good Will, 999 Hood Rd, Ste 127, Marietta, GA 30068. Phone: (770) 565-2322. E-mail: ISFGW@bellsouth.net.

GOLDBERG, RUBE: BIRTH ANNIVERSARY. July 4, 1883. The cartoonist with an engineering degree who put his education to work inventing elaborate machines with involved steps to accomplish ludicrously simple tasks. He is best remembered for the creative inventions of his cartoon character Lucifer Gorgonzola Butts. Born at San Francisco, Goldberg died Dec 7, 1970, at New York City.

★ ★ ★

	S	M	T	W	T	F	S
July 2004					1	2	3
	4	5	6	7	8	9	10
	11	12	13	14	15	16	17
	18	19	20	21	22	23	24
	25	26	27	28	29	30	31

GREAT CARDBOARD BOAT REGATTA. July 4. Rotary Riverview Park, Sheboygan, WI. The most spectacular and hilarious races of somewhat seaworthy craft ever launched in Wisconsin. Person-powered cardboard boats compete in various classes for prizes. Awards for the most spirited team, the most beautiful boats, boats following a theme and the most spectacular sinking (Titanic Award). Prizes for top finishers in three boat classes: propelled by oars or paddles; propelled by mechanical means such as paddle wheels or propellers; and "Instant Boats" made from "Secret Kits" by spectators-turned-participants. Est attendance: 16,000. For info: John Michael Kohler Arts Center, 608 New York Ave, PO Box 489, Sheboygan, WI 53082-0489. Phone: (920) 458-6144. Fax: (920) 458-4473. Web: www.jmkac.org.

GREAT SEAL OF THE US PROPOSED: ANNIVERSARY. July 4, 1776. The Continental Congress, meeting at Philadelphia, PA, after voting to adopt the Declaration of Independence, went on to approve the following: "Resolved, that Dr. Franklin, Mr J. Adams and Mr Jefferson, be a committee, to bring in a device for a seal for the United States of America," thus beginning the history of the Great Seal of the US on the first day of independence. The seal wasn't designed and used until 1782.

HAWTHORNE, NATHANIEL: 200th BIRTH ANNIVERSARY. July 4, 1804. Novelist and short-story writer, born at Salem, MA. Works included *The Scarlet Letter*, *The House of the Seven Gables* and *The Blithedale Romance*. Hawthorne died at Plymouth, NH, May 19, 1864.

HOMETOWN FAMILY FOURTH. July 4. Hollywood, FL. Family event featuring evening popular music at the Hollywood Beach Theater and a spectacular fireworks display offshore Hollywood Beach. Est attendance: 90,000. For info: Roguey Doyle, City of Hollywood, Dept of Parks, Recreation & Cultural Arts, 1940 Harrison St, Ste 101, Hollywood, FL 33020. Phone: (954) 921-3404.

HOOD RIVER OLD-FASHIONED FOURTH OF JULY. July 4. Hood River, OR. Parade, barbecue, fun run, entertainment and fireworks over the Columbia River. Est attendance: 2,000. For info: Hood River County Chamber of Commerce, 405 Portway Ave Hood River, OR 97031. Phone: (800) 366-3530. Fax: (541) 386-2057. E-mail: hrccc@hoodriver.org. Web: www.hoodriver.org.

ICE CREAM SOCIAL. July 4. Indianapolis, IN. Independence Day celebration. Music, lawn games and living history. Est attendance: 1,000. For info: President Benjamin Harrison Home, PR Dept, 1230 N Delaware St, Indianapolis, IN 46202. Phone: (317) 631-1888. Fax: (317) 632-5488.

INDEPENDENCE DAY (FOURTH OF JULY). July 4, 1776. The US commemorates adoption of the Declaration of Independence by the Continental Congress. The nation's birthday. Legal holiday in all states and territories.

INDEPENDENCE DAY SYMPHONY CONCERT AND FIREWORKS. July 4. Wheeling, WV. Independence Day celebration on the Wheeling waterfront. Est attendance: 30,000. For info: Wheeling Conv and Visitors Bureau, 1401 Main, Wheeling,

362

☆ Chase's 2004 Calendar of Events ☆   July 4

WV 26003. Phone: (800) 828-3097 or (304) 233-7709. Web: www.wheelingcvb.com/calendar.

INDEPENDENCE-FROM-MEAT DAY. July 4. Don't be a slave to tradition. Declare your freedom from flesh foods. Your fiery Fourth will be fantastic with a good-for-you vegetarian barbecue. Why not fix a freedom feast featuring veggie burgers and veggie dogs for your family and friends? It will be fun for you and your animal friends too! For info: Vegetarian Awareness Network, Communications Center, PO Box 321, Knoxville, TN 37901-0321. Phone: (800) USA-VEGE.

JULY 4th FAMILY CELEBRATION. July 4. Fort Lauderdale, FL. Featuring live music, fireworks and food. Annually, July 4. Est attendance: 300,000. For info: City of Fort Lauderdale. Phone: (954) 828-5363. Web: www.sunny.org.

KOKO THE GORILLA: BIRTHDAY. July 4, 1971. Koko, a lowland gorilla (full name: Hanabi-Ko, or "Fireworks Child" in Japanese), was born this day at the San Francisco Zoo. She is probably the most famous gorilla in the world due to her participation in the longest continuous experiment to teach language to animals. She was taught sign language beginning when she was about a year old, and she currently has a vocabulary of 1,000 signs.

LANDERS, ANN: BIRTH ANNIVERSARY. July 4, 1918. Born at Sioux City, IA, the advice columnist Esther Pauline Friedman was beloved worldwide. In 1955 she won a contest to be the new "Ann Landers" columnist for *The Chicago Sun-Times*. For 47 years, with spunky yet compassionate replies that were a refreshing change from prior columnists' styles, she helped everyday people overcome their problems. A trademark admonishment was "40 lashes with a wet noodle." (Her twin sister, Pauline Friedman, followed in her footsteps with a "Dear Abby" column.) By 2002 her column was carried in more than 1,200 newspapers worldwide and had a readership of 30 million. She died June 22, 2002, at Chicago, IL.

LAVALLETTE INDEPENDENCE EXTRAVAGANZA. July 4. Lavallette, NJ. 45-piece orchestra plays patriotic music during an outstanding fireworks display on the bay. Very suitable for boaters to watch from the water. Annually, the first Sunday in July. (Rain date: following Sunday) Est attendance: 30,000. For info: Lavallette Heritage Committee, Inc, Ocean County Public Affairs, PO Box 2191, Toms River, NJ 08754. Phone: (732) 793-3652. Fax: (732) 854-9038. E-mail: tgroskol@juno.com.

MACKINAW CITY'S FOURTH OF JULY FIREWORKS. July 4. State Dock on South Huron Ave, Mackinaw City, MI. Starting at 1:30 PM on the marina lawn, there will be fun and games for all ages. One of the largest fireworks displays in the north will be shot off over the harbor at dusk. For info: Mackinaw City Chamber of Commerce, PO Box 856, Mackinaw City, MI 49701. Phone: (231) 436-5574. Web: www.mackinawchamber.com.

MONETT FOURTH OF JULY CELEBRATION. July 4. Monett South Park, Monett, MO. All-day event includes Li'l Miss & Li'l Mister Liberty Contest; kiddie rides, children's games and contests; gospel, country and other types of music on three stages; hot air balloon rides; patriotic address; food and a fireworks display with a dance following. Annually, the Fourth of July. Est attendance: 5,000. For info: Deborah Schoen, 1304 Hemingway Dr, Monett, MO 65708. Phone: (417) 235-7967.

MOUNT MARATHON RACE. July 4. Seward, AK. 76th running. Grueling footrace begins in downtown Seward, then ascends and descends 3,022-ft Mt Marathon. Race began as a wager between two sourdoughs. Est attendance: 20,000. For info: Seward Chamber of Commerce, PO Box 749, Seward, AK 99664. Phone: (907) 224-8051. Fax: (907) 224-5353. E-mail: events@seward.net. Web: www.sewardak.org.

NATIONAL LAUNDRY WORKERS' WEEK. July 4–10. To promote public awareness of the importance of the laundry worker. For info: Nemaha County Good Samaritan Center, Rt 1, Box 4, Auburn, NE 68305.

OLD-FASHIONED FOURTH OF JULY. July 4. Pioneer Village, Worthington, MN. Open to the general public. Children under 12 are admitted if accompanied by an adult. Events that emphasize the heritage of Southwest Minnesota are on display. Refreshments available and there are performances of a melodrama and shows in the Red Garter Saloon throughout the day. Est attendance: 700. For info: Nobles County Historical Society, 407 12th St, Ste 2, Worthington, MN 56187. Phone: (507) 376-4011 or (507) 376-4431.

OLD VERMONT FOURTH. July 4. Woodstock, VT. A traditional Fourth of July with patriotic speeches and debates, making "1890" flags, a spelling bee for adults, ice cream making, sack race and more. Est attendance: 750. For info: Billings Farm and Museum, PO Box 489, Woodstock, VT 05091. Phone: (802) 457-2355. Fax: (802) 457-4663. E-mail: billings.farm@valley.net. Web: www.billingsfarm.org.

PEACHTREE ROAD RACE. July 4. Atlanta, GA. 10K run. 55,000-runner limit; advance registration only. Send SASE by Mar 1, 2004. 45,000 entrants on first-come basis and 10,000 selected by lottery from other entries postmarked in March 2004. Est attendance: 55,000. For info: Atlanta Track Club, 3097 E Shadowlawn Ave, Atlanta, GA 30305. Phone: (404) 231-9064. E-mail: info@atlantatrackclub.org. Web: www.atlantatrackclub.org.

PHILIPPINES: FIL-AMERICAN FRIENDSHIP DAY. July 4. Formerly National Independence Day, when the Philippines were a colony of the US, now celebrated as Fil-American Friendship Day.

PRAIRIE PIONEER DAYS. July 4. Arapahoe, NE. Parade, games for kids, food booths, free swimming, watermelon bust, quilt show, baseball games, fireworks and more. For info: Tammie Middagh, Secy, Arapahoe Chamber of Commerce, PO Box 624, Arapahoe, NE 68922.

"THE SOUPY SALES SHOW" TV PREMIERE: ANNIVERSARY. July 4, 1955. Soupy Sales hosted a number of national and local children's shows from 1955 to 1979. All of his programs included some of these features: jokes, puns, songs, sketches, puppets, silent films and pies in the face. Sales's humor occasionally went over the edge and got him in trouble; for example, in 1965 his show was suspended for a week because he asked his viewers to send him the green paper in their parents' wallets!

SPACE MILESTONE: *MARS PATHFINDER* (US). July 4, 1997. Unmanned spacecraft landed on Mars after a seven-month flight. Carried *Sojourner*, a roving robotic explorer that sent back photographs of the landscape. One of its missions was to find if life ever existed on Mars. See also: "Space Milestone: *Mars Global Surveyor*" (Sept 11).

SPACE MILESTONE: *NOZOMI* (JAPAN). July 4, 1998. Japan launched this mission to Mars, making it the third country (after the US and Russia) to attempt an interplanetary space mission. *Nozomi*, which means "Hope," is to orbit 84 miles above Mars and beam images back to Earth.

SPECIAL RECREATION FOR DISABLED DAY. July 4. To focus attention on the recreation abilities, aspirations, needs and rights of people with disabilities. See "Special Recreation Week" (July 4–10). For info: John A. Nesbitt, EdD, Pres/CEO, SRDI–Special Recreation for disABLED Intl, 701 Oaknoll Drive, Iowa City, IA 52246. Phone: (319) 466-3192. E-mail: john-nesbitt@uiowa.edu. Also for info: Global Vision for disABLED, web: www.jccniowa.org/~recdsabl or Prevention of Fireworks Disabilities/Deaths, web: www.bailiwick.lib.uiowa.edu/fireworks/.

July 4–5 ☆ Chase's 2004 Calendar of Events ☆

SPECIAL RECREATION WEEK. July 4–10. To focus attention on the recreation rights, needs, aspirations and abilities of people with disabilities—infants, children, youth, young adults, adults and seniors; living in the community, in residential services and in institutions; in 40 types of play, recreation and leisure pursuits. See "Special Recreation for the Disabled Day" (July 4). For info: John A. Nesbitt, Pres/CEO, SRDI–Special Recreation for disABLED Intl, 701 Oaknoll Dr, Iowa City, IA 52246. Phone: (319) 466-3192. E-mail: john-nesbitt@uiowa.edu.

SPIRIT OF FREEDOM CELEBRATION. July 4. Florence, AL. Celebrate America's birthday on the banks of the beautiful Tennessee River at McFarland Park. Enjoy sunning, swimming, bicycling, golf and entertainment. Playground, picnic tables and campground available. Annually, on July 4. Est attendance: 60,000. For info: Florence/Lauderdale Tourism, One Hightower Place, Florence, AL 35630. Phone: (256) 740-4141 or (888) FLO-TOUR. Fax: (256) 740-4142. E-mail: dwilson@flo-tour.org. Web: www.flo-tour.org.

SULLIVAN FREEDOM FESTIVAL. July 4. Sullivan Fairgrounds, Sullivan, MO. Festival open 6 PM–10 PM. Features children's activities, contests, games, entertainment, food and fireworks. Est attendance: 5,000. For info: Sullivan Chamber of Commerce, PO Box 536, Sullivan, MO 63080. Phone: (573) 468-3314. E-mail: chamber@sullivanmo.com. Web: www.sullivanmo.com.

TRADITIONAL SOUSA CONCERT. July 4. The American Club, Kohler, WI. Kohler Village Concert Series presents the Kiel Municipal Band featuring the distinctive swing and vigor that marks the work of the "March King," John Philip Sousa. Entertaining with a selection of marches, show tunes and contemporary favorites, this nationally recognized community concert ensemble has been awarded the Sudler Scroll for musical excellence by the Sousa Foundation. Fireworks and refreshments. Est attendance: 1,000. For info: The American Club, Highland Dr, Kohler, WI 53044. Phone: (800) 344-2838. Fax: (920) 457-6372. Web: www.destinationkohler.com.

TUSKEGEE INSTITUTE OPENING: ANNIVERSARY. July 4, 1881. Booker T. Washington's famed agricultural-industrial institution was built from the ground up by dedicated students seeking academic and vocational training. The institute started in a shanty before Washington purchased an abandoned plantation at Tuskegee, AL. The students built the dormitories, classrooms and chapel from bricks out of their own kiln.

WESTON JAYCEES' ANNUAL JULY 4th CELEBRATION. July 4. Weston, MO. The evening begins with an ice cream social and a presentation by the Missouri Valley Skydivers with fireworks beginning at 9 PM. For info: Steve Whitt, 19550 Shane Ln, Weston, MO 64098. Phone: (816) 640-2211.

WSB-TV SALUTE 2 AMERICA PARADE. July 4. Atlanta, GA. One of the largest 4th of July parades in the US. 44th annual parade steps off at 1 PM. Est attendance: 250,000. For info: WSB-TV Salute 2 America Parade, 1601 W Peachtree St NE, Atlanta, GA 30309. Phone: (404) 897-7385. Fax: (404) 897-6236. E-mail: argonne.parades@wsbtv.com.

ZOOBALEE. July 4. Lee Richardson Zoo, Garden City, KS. Old-fashioned Independence Day celebration featuring dunk tank, food, moon walk, face painting and more. Est attendance: 5,000. For info: Dvmt Dir, Friends of Lee Richardson Zoo, Box 1638, Garden City, KS 67846. Phone: (620) 276-6243. Fax: (620) 276-0910. E-mail: folrz@odsgc.net. Web: www.folrz.com.

July 2004

S	M	T	W	T	F	S
				1	2	3
4	5	6	7	8	9	10
11	12	13	14	15	16	17
18	19	20	21	22	23	24
25	26	27	28	29	30	31

BIRTHDAYS TODAY

Signy Coleman, 44, actress ("The Young and the Restless"), born Bolinas, CA, July 4, 1960.

Allen (Al) Davis, 75, Hall of Fame football player, executive, born Brockton, MA, July 4, 1929.

Harvey Grant, 39, former basketball player, born Augusta, GA, July 4, 1965.

Horace Grant, 39, former basketball player, born Augusta, GA, July 4, 1965.

Leona Helmsley, 84, former hotel executive, born Brooklyn, NY, July 4, 1920.

Gina Lollobrigida, 76, actress (*Belles de Nuit; Bread, Love and Dreams*), born Auviaco, Italy, July 4, 1928.

Geraldo Rivera, 61, journalist, talk-show host ("Geraldo," *Exposing Myself*), born New York, NY, July 4, 1943.

Eva Marie Saint, 80, actress (Oscar for *On the Waterfront*; *North by Northwest*, *Exodus*), born Newark, NJ, July 4, 1924.

Pamela Howard (Pam) Shriver, 42, broadcaster and former tennis player, born Baltimore, MD, July 4, 1962.

Neil Simon, 77, playwright (*The Odd Couple*, *Barefoot in the Park*), born New York, NY, July 4, 1927.

George Michael Steinbrenner III, 74, baseball executive, born Rocky River, OH, July 4, 1930.

Abigail Van Buren, 86, advice columnist, born Pauline Esther Friedman, Sioux City, IA, July 4, 1918.

JULY 5 — MONDAY
Day 187 — 179 Remaining

ALGERIA: INDEPENDENCE DAY. July 5. National holiday. Commemorates the day in 1962 when Algeria gained independence from France.

BARNUM, PHINEAS TAYLOR: BIRTH ANNIVERSARY. July 5, 1810. Promoter of the bizarre and unusual. Barnum's American Museum opened in 1842, promoting unusual acts including the Feejee Mermaid, Chang and Eng (the original Siamese twins) and General Tom Thumb. In 1850 he began his promotion of Jenny Lind, "The Swedish Nightingale," and parlayed her singing talents into a major financial success. Barnum also cultivated a keen interest in politics. A founder of the newspaper *Herald of Freedom*, he wrote outspoken editorials that resulted not only in lawsuits but also in at least one jail sentence. In 1852 he declined the Democratic nomination for governor of Connecticut but did serve two terms in the Connecticut legislature beginning in 1865. He was defeated in a bid for US Congress in 1866 but served as mayor of Bridgeport, CT, from 1875 to 1876. In 1871 "The Greatest Show on Earth" opened at Brooklyn, NY; Barnum merged with his rival J.A. Bailey in 1881 to form the Barnum and Bailey Circus. P.T. Barnum was born at Bethel, CT, and died at Bridgeport, CT, Apr 7, 1891.

BIKINI DEBUTED: ANNIVERSARY. July 5, 1946. The skimpy two-piece bathing suit created by Louis Reard debuted at a fashion show in Paris. It was named after an atoll in the Pacific where the hydrogen bomb was first tested.

BRISTOL CIVIC, MILITARY AND FIREMEN'S PARADE. July 5. Bristol, RI. The nation's oldest 4th of July parade. Features floats, bands, veteran and patriotic organizations and military units. Patriotic exercises, a tradition dating to 1785, are held prior to the parade. Annually, July 4 except when July 4 is a Sunday, then the parade is held Monday, July 5. Est attendance: 175,000. For info: Chamber of Commerce, 654 Metacom Ave, Warren, RI 02885. Phone: (401) 245-0750. Web: www.eastbayritourism.com.

CAPE VERDE: NATIONAL DAY. July 5. Public holiday. Commemorates independence from Portugal in 1975.

CARIBBEAN OR CARICOM DAY. July 5. The anniversary of the treaty establishing the Caribbean Community (also called the Treaty of Chaguaramas), signed by the prime ministers of Barbados, Guyana, Jamaica and Trinidad and Tobago July 4,

☆ Chase's 2004 Calendar of Events ☆   July 5

1973. Observed as a public holiday in Guyana and St. Vincent. Annually, the first Monday in July.

EARTH AT APHELION. July 5. At approximately 7 AM, EDT, planet Earth will reach aphelion, that point in its orbit when it is farthest from the sun (about 94,510,000 miles). The Earth's mean distance from the sun (mean radius of its orbit) is reached early in the months of April and October. Note that Earth is farthest from the sun during Northern Hemisphere summer. See also: "Earth at Perihelion" (Jan 4).

ENGLAND: EXETER FESTIVAL. July 5–19 (tentative). Various venues, Exeter, Devon. A broad ranging eclectic program of classical and contemporary performance in a variety of city venues, featuring the best of British arts and culture. Est attendance: 32,000. For info: David Whitelock, Exeter City Council, Paris Street, Exeter, England EX1 1JJ. Phone: (44) (139) 226-5200. Fax: (44) (139) 226-5366. E-mail: festival@exeter.gov.uk. Web: exeter.gov.uk/festival.

ENGLAND: HAMPTON COURT PALACE FLOWER SHOW CHARITY GALA PREVIEW. July 5. Hampton Court Palace, East Molesey, Surry, England. A charity event that launches the world's largest flower show. For info: Royal Horticulture Society, 80 Vincent Square, London SW1P 2PE, England. Phone: (44) (207) 6305-999. Fax: (44) (207) 6308-178. E-mail: galatickets@rhs.org.uk. Web: www.rhs.org.uk/hamptoncourt.

FARRAGUT, DAVID: BIRTH ANNIVERSARY. July 5, 1801. Born near Knoxville, TN, and died Aug 14, 1870, at Portsmouth, NH. Admiral in the American Civil War who was famous for his naval victories. At Mobile Bay, AL, in a disastrous attack on his entire fleet by the Confederates' Fort Morgan, Farragut proclaimed the famous cry, "Damn the torpedoes, full speed ahead!" They escaped the attack and Mobile Bay surrendered.

ISLE OF MAN: TYNWALD DAY. July 5. Tynwald Hill at St. John's. Traditionally, on July 5, Old Midsummer Day, the island's parliament of Tynwald assembles at the meeting place of the Vikings to promulgate new laws.

NATIONAL LABOR RELATIONS ACT (THE WAGNER ACT): ANNIVERSARY. July 5, 1935. This bill guaranteed workers the right to organize and bargain collectively with their employers. It also prohibited the formation of company unions. An enforcement agency, the National Labor Relations Board, was created by the Act.

NUDE RECREATION WEEK. July 5–11. A week to promote acceptance of the body and understanding of the nude recreation movement with special events at clothes-optional beaches and resorts throughout North America. For info: The Naturist Society, Box 132, Oshkosh, WI 54903. Phone: (920) 426-5009. Fax: (920) 426-5184. E-mail: naturist@naturistsociety.com. Web: www.naturistsociety.com.

OLIVER NORTH ROLE IN IRAN-CONTRA SCANDAL: 15th ANNIVERSARY. July 5, 1989. Retired Marine Lieutenant Colonel Oliver North was sentenced on this date for his role in the Iran-Contra scandal after being convicted in May of falsifying and destroying documents, accepting an illegal gratuity and aiding and abetting in the obstruction of Congress. North became the focal point of an investigation surrounding allegations that the US sold weapons to Iran in order to secure the release of American hostages and funneled the proceeds from the sales to aid the Contras in Nicaragua. As a member of the National Security Council staff, North became a key operator in antiterrorism, hostage rescues and efforts to overthrow the Sandinista government. On July 20, 1990, a federal appeals court overturned his conviction on the destruction-of-documents charge and suspended the other charges. At issue was whether parts of North's Congressional testimony had been used in the trial resulting in his conviction. On May 28, 1991, the Supreme Court let the appeals court ruling stand. On Sept 16, 1991, all charges against North were dropped.

RAFFLES, STAMFORD: BIRTH ANNIVERSARY. July 5, 1781. Sir Stamford Raffles, English colonial official, founder of Singapore, where he is supposed to have landed Jan 29, 1819, was born at sea, off Jamaica. He discovered with Joseph Arnold an East Indian fungus that is named after them, *Rafflesia Arnoldi*. Raffles died near London, England, on his birthday, July 5, 1826.

RHODES, CECIL JOHN: BIRTH ANNIVERSARY. July 5, 1853. English-born, South African millionaire politician. Said to have controlled at one time 90 percent of the world's diamond production. His will founded the Rhodes Scholarships at Oxford University for superior scholastic achievers. Rhodesia (now Zimbabwe) was named for him. Born at Bishop's Stortford, Hertfordshire, Rhodes died Mar 26, 1902, at Cape Town, South Africa.

SLOVAKIA: SAINT CYRIL AND METHODIUS DAY. July 5. This day is dedicated to the Greek priests and scholars from Thessalonniki, who were invited by Prince Rastislav of Great Moravia to introduce Christianity and the first Slavic alphabet to the pagan people of the kingdom in AD 863.

STOCK EXCHANGE HOLIDAY (INDEPENDENCE DAY). July 5 (observed). The holiday schedules for the various exchanges are subject to change if relevant rules, regulations or exchange policies are revised. If you have questions, phone: American Stock Exchange (212) 306-1000; Chicago Board of Trade (312) 435-3500; Chicago Board of Options Exchange (312) 786-5600; New York Stock Exchange (212) 656-2065; Pacific Stock Exchange (415) 393-4000; Philadelphia Stock Exchange (215) 496-5000.

SWITZERLAND: SEMPACH BATTLE COMMEMORATION. July 5. On the morning of the first Monday after July 4, the Lucerne government, military and student delegations and historical groups make their way in solemn procession to the battlefield of 1386. Commemorative address, battle report and solemn service in the chapel. Also an evening procession.

VENEZUELA: INDEPENDENCE DAY. July 5. National holiday. Commemorates Proclamation of Independence from Spain in 1811. Independence was not achieved until 1821.

WOOD PELLET BBQ INTRODUCTION DAY. July 5. Commemorating the introduction of the revolutionary Wood Pellet BBQ Grill, invented by Joseph P. Traeger of Mt Angel, Oregon. The BBQ grill is sold around the world and is now the most revolutionary bio-mass cooking appliance ever invented in America. For info: Bruce Bjorkman, Traeger Industries, PO Box 829, Mt Angel, OR 97362. Phone: (503) 845-9234. E-mail: marketing @traegerindustries.com. Web: www.traegerindustries.com.

ZAMBIA: HEROES DAY. July 5. First Monday in July is Zambian national holiday—memorial day for Zambians who died in the struggle for independence. Political rallies stress solidarity.

ZETKIN, CLARA: BIRTH ANNIVERSARY. July 5, 1857. Women's rights advocate, born at Wiederau, Germany. Zetkin has been credited with being the initiator of International Women's Day, which has been observed on Mar 8 at least since 1910. She died at Arkhangelskoe, Russia, June 20, 1933. See also: "International (Working) Women's Day" (Mar 8).

July 5-6 ☆ Chase's 2004 Calendar of Events ☆

BIRTHDAYS TODAY

Edie Falco, 41, actress ("The Sopranos"), born Brooklyn, NY, July 5, 1963.
Eliot Feld, 62, dancer, born Brooklyn, NY, July 5, 1942.
Richard Michael ("Goose") Gossage, 53, former baseball player, born Colorado Springs, CO, July 5, 1951.
Chris Gratton, 29, hockey player, born Brantford, ON, Canada, July 5, 1975.
Katherine Helmond, 70, actress (stage: *The House of Blue Leaves*; "Soap," "Who's the Boss?"), born Galveston, TX, July 5, 1934.
Shirley Knight, 68, actress (stage: *Kennedy's Children* [Tony Award, 1976]; *The Dark at the Top of the Stairs, Sweet Bird of Youth, Petulia*), born Goessel, KS, July 5, 1936.
Huey Lewis, 54, singer (Huey Lewis and the News), born Hugh Anthony Cregg III, New York, NY, July 5, 1950.
James David Lofton, 48, former football player, born Fort Ord, CA, July 5, 1956.
Robbie Robertson, 60, musician (guitarist with The Band), born Toronto, ON, Canada, July 5, 1944.
Janos Starker, 80, musician, born Budapest, Hungary, July 5, 1924.

JULY 6 — TUESDAY
Day 188 — 178 Remaining

BARN DAY. July 6. Two miles south of Filley, NE. Threshing demonstration, antique farm equipment, entertainment. The barn is on the National Register of Historic Sites and is the largest limestone barn in Nebraska. Est attendance: 300. For info: Lesa Arterburn, Dir, Gage County Historical Society, PO Box 793, Beatrice, NE 68310. Phone: (402) 228-1679. E-mail: gagecountymuseum@beatricene.com. Web: www.beatricene.com/gagecountymuseum.

BUSH, GEORGE W.: BIRTHDAY. July 6, 1946. 43d president of the US (2001–2005). Born at New Haven, CT.

COMOROS: INDEPENDENCE DAY: ANNIVERSARY. July 6. Federal and Islamic Republic of Comoros commemorates declaration of independence from France in 1975.

CZECH REPUBLIC: COMMEMORATION DAY OF BURNING OF JOHN HUS. July 6. National holiday. In honor of Bohemian religious reformer John Hus, who was condemned as a heretic and burned at the stake July 6, 1415.

FAST OF TAMMUZ. July 6. Jewish holiday. Hebrew calendar date: Tammuz 17, 5764. Shiva Asar B'Tammuz begins at first light of day and commemorates the first-century Roman siege that breached the walls of Jerusalem. Begins a three-week time of mourning. Began at sundown July 5.

FINLAND: JYVASKYLA ARTS FESTIVAL. July 6–10. Jyvaskyla. Annual festival begun in 1955 for the purpose of stimulating discussion of contemporary philosophical and social concerns and building a bridge between different national and ethnic traditions. About 50 events including seminars, music, visual arts and film. Est attendance: 10,000. For info: Finnish Tourist Board, 655 Third Ave, New York, NY 10017. Phone: (212) 885-9700 or (358) (14) 624378. Fax: (358) (14) 214808. Web: www.jyvaskla.fi/kesa.

FIRST AIRSHIP CROSSING OF ATLANTIC: 85th ANNIVERSARY. July 6, 1919. The first airship crossing of the Atlantic was completed as a British dirigible landed at New York's Roosevelt Field.

	S	M	T	W	T	F	S
July					1	2	3
2004	4	5	6	7	8	9	10
	11	12	13	14	15	16	17
	18	19	20	21	22	23	24
	25	26	27	28	29	30	31

FIRST BLACK US STATE'S ATTORNEY: ANNIVERSARY. July 6, 1961. Cecil Francis Poole became the first black US state's attorney when he was sworn in as US attorney for the Northern District of California. He served until his retirement on Feb 3, 1970.

FIRST SUCCESSFUL ANTIRABIES INOCULATION: ANNIVERSARY. July 6, 1885. Louis Pasteur gave the first successful antirabies inoculation to a boy who had been bitten by an infected dog.

GREAT CIRCUS PARADE WEEK. July 6–11. Baraboo/Milwaukee, WI. Circus wagons make their annual journey to Milwaukee from Baraboo, home of the world's largest collection of antique circus wagons. Visit the parade showgrounds off the shores of Lake Michigan, July 6–10, for a free viewing of a 40-tent display of circus wagons and performances under the Big Top. The Great Circus Parade, winding its way through the streets of Milwaukee on Sunday, July 11, is the only parade of its kind in the world—an authentic re-creation of a 19th-century parade complete with 50+ restored circus wagons, 750 horses, clowns, animals and marching bands. Est attendance: 500,000. For info: Great Circus Parade, Circus World Museum, 550 Water St, Baraboo, WI 53913. Phone: (608) 356-8341 or (866) 693-1500. E-mail: ringmaster@circusworldmuseum.com. Web: www.circusworldmuseum.com.

JONES, JOHN PAUL: BIRTH ANNIVERSARY. July 6, 1747 (OS). American naval officer born at Kirkbean, Scotland. Remembered for his victory in the battle of his ship, the *Bonhomme Richard*, with the British frigate *Serapis*, Sept 23, 1779. When Jones was queried: "Do you ask for quarter?" he made his famous reply: "I have not yet begun to fight!" Jones was victorious, but the *Bonhomme Richard*, badly damaged, sank two days later. Jones died at Paris, France, July 18, 1792.

KAHLO, FRIDA: BIRTH ANNIVERSARY. July 6, 1907. The great surrealist painter was born Magdalena Carmen Frida Kahlo Calderón at Coyoacán, Mexico. In 1925 she endured severe injuries in a bus accident that would plague her for the rest of her life (and become artistic subject matter). She turned to art at about this time, encouraged by the great muralist Diego Rivera, whom she married in 1929 (and 1941). She is known almost as much for her tumultuous life (she had an affair with Soviet exile Leon Trotsky and was active in leftist politics) as for her vibrant artworks filled with symbols and the flora and fauna of her beloved Mexico. She was one of the first women painters to sell a work to the Louvre. She died at her Casa Azul family home in Coyoacán on July 13, 1954.

LITHUANIA: DAY OF STATEHOOD. July 6. National holiday. Commemorates the 1252 crowning of Mindaugas, who united Lithuania.

LUXEMBOURG: ETTELBRUCK REMEMBRANCE DAY: ANNIVERSARY. July 6. In honor of US General George Patton, Jr, liberator of the Grand-Duchy of Luxembourg in 1945, who is buried at the American Military Cemetery at Hamm, Germany, among 5,100 soldiers of his famous Third Army.

MAJOR LEAGUE BASEBALL HOLDS FIRST ALL-STAR GAME: ANNIVERSARY. July 6, 1933. The first midsummer All-Star Game was held at Comiskey Park, Chicago,

☆ *Chase's 2004 Calendar of Events* ☆   July 6–7

IL. Babe Ruth led the American League with a home run, as they defeated the National League 4–2. Prior to the summer of 1933, All-Star contests consisted of pre- and postseason exhibitions that often found teams made up of a few stars playing beside journeymen and even minor leaguers.

MALAWI: REPUBLIC DAY. July 6. National holiday. Commemorates attainment of independence from Britain in 1965 and Malawi's becoming a republic in 1966. Malawi was formerly known as Nyasaland.

"NAME THAT TUNE" TV PREMIERE: ANNIVERSARY. July 6, 1953. "Name That Tune" was a musical identification show that appeared in different formats in the '50s and the '70s. Red Benson was the host of the NBC series and Bill Cullen (and later George DeWitt) was the CBS host. Two contestants listened while an orchestra played a musical selection, and the first contestant who could identify it raced across the stage to ring a bell. The winner of the round then tried to identify a number of tunes within a specific time period. After 11 years, the show was brought back with Richard Hayes as host. In 1974 new network and syndicated versions appeared.

NATIONAL ASSOCIATION OF THE DEAF CONFERENCE. July 6–10. Kansas City, MO. Held biennially. 47th conference. For info: Natl Assn of the Deaf, 814 Thayer Ave, Silver Spring, MD 20910-4500. TTY: (301) 587-1789. Phone: (301) 587-1788. Fax: (301) 587-1791. E-mail: NADinfo@nad.org. Web: www.nad.org.

OPERATION OVERCAST: ANNIVERSARY. July 6, 1945. As the end of the war approached, the US Army had begun to move German scientists and scientific equipment from the German territory designated for Russian occupation. On this date, the American Joint Chiefs of Staff authorized Operation Overcast, under which 350 German and Austrian scientists were transported to the US in a matter of months.

"THE QUIZ KIDS" TV PREMIERE: 55th ANNIVERSARY. July 6, 1949. This show began on radio and continued on TV with the original host, Joe Kelly, and later with Clifton Fadiman. The format was a panel of five child prodigies who answered questions sent in by viewers. Four were regulars, staying for weeks or months, while the fifth was a "guest child." The ages of the panelists varied from 6 to 16.

REPUBLICAN PARTY FORMED: 150th ANNIVERSARY. July 6, 1854. The Republican Party originated at a convention at Ripon, WI, on Feb 28, 1854. A state convention meeting in Michigan formally adopted the name Republican on July 6.

SPACE MILESTONE: *SOYUZ 21* **(USSR).** July 6, 1976. Launched this date. Two cosmonauts, Colonel B. Volynov and Lieutenant Colonel V. Zholobov, traveled to *Salyut 5* space station (launched June 22, 1976) to study Earth's surface and conduct zoological-botanical experiments. Forty-eight–day stay on space station. Return landing on Aug 24.

TAKE YOUR WEBMASTER TO LUNCH DAY. July 6. Keep the person running your website happy by making sure they're well fed. It makes them feel loved and gives them the energy to fix all the typos that you have on your site. [©2003 by WH.] For info: Thomas & Ruth Roy, Wellcat Holidays, 2418 Long Ln, Lebanon, PA 17046. Phone: (717) 279-0184. E-mail: info@wellcat.com. Web: www.wellcat.com.

WALES: LLANGOLLEN INTERNATIONAL MUSICAL EISTEDDFOD. July 6–11. Eisteddfod Field, Llangollen, Denbighshire, North Wales. 58th annual. Thousands of singers and folk dancers from more than 30 countries take part in this annual international music festival. Friendly rivalry among amateur groups performing amid the Welsh rivers and mountains. Est attendance: 80,000. For info: Caroline Sanger-Davies, Mktg Dir, Llangollen Intl Musical Eisteddfod, Llangollen, North Wales, UK LL20 8SW. Phone: (44) (1978) 862000. Fax: (44) (1978) 862002. E-mail: info@international-eisteddfod.co.uk. Web: www.international-eisteddfod.co.uk.

ZAMBIA: UNITY DAY. July 6. Memorial day for Zambians who died in the struggle for independence. Political rallies stressing solidarity throughout country. Annually, the first Tuesday in July.

BIRTHDAYS TODAY

Allyce Beasley, 50, actress ("Moonlighting"), born Brooklyn, NY, July 6, 1954.
Ned Beatty, 67, actor (*Deliverance*, "Homicide," *Hear My Song*), born Louisville, KY, July 6, 1937.
George W. Bush, 58, 43rd president of the US, former governor of Texas (R), born New Haven, CT, July 6, 1946.
Donal Donnelly, 73, actor (*The Knack, The Dead, The Godfather Part III*), born Bradford, England, July 6, 1931.
Pau Gasol, 24, basketball player, born Barcelona, Spain, July 6, 1980.
Grant Goodeve, 52, actor ("Eight Is Enough," "Dynasty"), born New Haven, CT, July 6, 1952.
Merv Griffin, 79, TV host, business executive, born San Mateo, CA, July 6, 1925.
Janet Leigh, 77, actress (*That Forsyte Woman, Psycho*), born Merced, CA, July 6, 1927.
Nancy Davis Reagan, 83, former First Lady, wife of Ronald Reagan, 40th president of the US, born New York, NY, July 6, 1921.
Della Reese, 72, singer ("Don't You Know," "And That Reminds Me"), actress ("Touched by an Angel"), born Deloreese Patricia Early, Detroit, MI, July 6, 1932.
Geoffrey Rush, 53, actor (*Quills, Shakespeare in Love*, Oscar for *Shine*), born Toowoomba, Queensland, Australia, July 6, 1951.
Sylvester Stallone, 58, actor (*Rocky* and *Rambo* films), director, born New York, NY, July 6, 1946.
Burt Ward, 59, actor ("Batman"), born Los Angeles, CA, July 6, 1945.

JULY 7 — WEDNESDAY
Day 189 — 177 Remaining

BONZA BOTTLER DAY™. July 7. To celebrate when the number of the day is the same as the number of the month. Bonza Bottler Day™ is an excuse to have a party at least once a month. For more information, see Jan 1. For info: Gail M. Berger, 14 Fernwood Dr, Taylors, SC 29687. Phone: (864) 609-9874. E-mail: gberger5@aol.com.

CANADA: THE NORTH AMERICAN TOURNAMENT. July 7–11. Spruce Meadows, Calgary, AB. Show jumping tournament featuring the Spruce Meadows North American Championships. Sun Life Days at Fort Meadows will offer a great variety of entertainment and food kiosks for your enjoyment. Est attendance: 98,000. For info: Spruce Meadows, RR 9, Calgary, AB, Canada T2J 5G5. Phone: (403) 974-4200. Fax: (403) 974-4270. E-mail: information@sprucemeadows.com. Web: www.sprucemeadows.com.

DINOSAUR ROUNDUP RODEO. July 7–10. Vernal, UT. 54th annual presentation of one of the top PRCA rodeos, fun for the entire family. Annually, the second weekend in July. Est attendance: 28,000. For info: Vernal Chamber of Commerce, 134 W Main St, Vernal, UT 84078. Phone: (800) 421-9635 or (435) 789-1352.

FATHER-DAUGHTER TAKE A WALK TOGETHER DAY. July 7. A special time in the summer for fathers and daughters of all ages to spend time together in the beautiful weather. Annually, July 7. For info: Janet Dellaria, 202 N Bennett St, Geneva, IL 60134. Phone: (630) 232-0425.

July 7–8 ★ Chase's 2004 Calendar of Events ★

HAWAII ANNEXED BY US: ANNIVERSARY. July 7, 1898. President William McKinley signed a resolution annexing Hawaii. No change in government took place until 1900, when Congress passed an act making Hawaii an "incorporated" territory of the US. This act remained in effect until Hawaii became a state in 1959.

JAPAN: TANABATA (STAR FESTIVAL). July 7. As an offering to the stars, children set up bamboo branches to which colorful strips of paper bearing poems are tied.

JIMMY AND ROSALYNN CARTER WEDDING: ANNIVERSARY. July 7, 1946. Plains Methodist Church, Plains, GA. James Earl Carter, Jr, was 21 and Eleanor Rosalynn Smith was 18. They have four children: John William "Jack" Carter was born in 1947, James Carl "Chip" Carter, 1950, Donnell Jeffrey Carter, 1952, and Amy Lynn Carter, 1968.

KUNSTLER, WILLIAM: 85th BIRTH ANNIVERSARY. July 7, 1919. Radical attorney, defense lawyer for the Chicago Seven, born at New York, NY. Died Sept 4, 1995, at New York, NY.

LINCOLN ASSASSINATION CONSPIRATORS HANGING: ANNIVERSARY. July 7, 1865. Four persons convicted of complicity with John Wilkes Booth in the assassination of President Abraham Lincoln on Apr 14, 1865, were hanged at Washington, DC. The four: Mary E. Surratt, Lewis Payne, David E. Harold and George A. Atzerodt. Mary Surratt became the first woman executed for a crime in the US. Her conviction was and is a subject of controversy, as the only crime she appeared to have committed was to own the boarding house where John Wilkes Booth planned the assassination.

MOTHER FRANCES XAVIER CABRINI CANONIZED: ANNIVERSARY. July 7, 1946. Pope Pius XII presided over the canonization ceremonies for Mother Frances Xavier Cabrini, as she became the first American to be canonized. She was the founder of the Missionary Sisters of the Sacred Heart of Jesus, and her principal shrine is at Mother Cabrini High School, New York, NY. Cabrini was born at Lombardy, Italy, July 15, 1850, and died at Chicago, IL, Dec 22, 1917. Her feast day is celebrated on Dec 22.

NEPAL: BIRTHDAY OF HIS MAJESTY THE KING. July 7. National holiday of Nepal commemorating the birth of King Gyanendra in 1946.

PAIGE, LEROY ROBERT (SATCHEL): BIRTH ANNIVERSARY. July 7, 1906. Baseball Hall of Fame pitcher born at Mobile, AL. Paige was the greatest attraction in the Negro Leagues and was also, at age 42, the first black pitcher in the American League. Inducted into the Hall of Fame in 1971. Died at Kansas City, MO, June 8, 1982.

"RYAN'S HOPE" TV PREMIERE: ANNIVERSARY. July 7, 1975. This ABC soap ran until 1989 and was set mostly at the fictional Ryan's Tavern or Riverside Hospital at New York City. The show depicted the lives of the ardently Irish Ryan family. The original cast included Faith Catlin, Justin Deas, Bernard Barrow, Helen Gallagher, Michael Hawkins, Ilene Kristen, Malcom Groome and Kate Mulgrew. Marg Helgenberger, Nell Carter, Yasmine Bleeth, Gloria DeHaven, Corbin Bernsen and Grant Show have been among the show's other regulars.

July 2004	S	M	T	W	T	F	S
					1	2	3
	4	5	6	7	8	9	10
	11	12	13	14	15	16	17
	18	19	20	21	22	23	24
	25	26	27	28	29	30	31

SOLOMON ISLANDS: INDEPENDENCE DAY: ANNIVERSARY. July 7. National holiday. Commemorates independence from Britain in 1978.

SPAIN: RUNNING OF THE BULLS. July 7–14. Pamplona, Spain. Event made famous by Hemingway in his novel *The Sun Also Rises*, in which young men run through the streets of Pamplona chased by bulls from the bull ring. Part of the festival of San Fermin.

SPRING SUWANNEE RIVER GOSPEL JUBILEE. July 7–10. Live Oak, FL. Past artists featured have included Dixie Echoes, Florida Boys, Dixie Melody Boys, Perry Sisters and more. Est attendance: 10,000. For info: James Cornett, Spirit of the Suwannee Music Park, 3076 95th Dr, Live Oak, FL 32060. Phone: (386) 364-1683. Fax: (386) 364-2998. E-mail: spirit@musicliveshere.com. Web: www.musicliveshere.com.

TANZANIA: SABA SABA DAY. July 7. Tanzania's mainland ruling party, TANU, was formed on this day in 1954. Saba Saba means "Seven-Seven."

BIRTHDAYS TODAY

Billy Campbell, 45, actor ("Once and Again"), born Charlottesville, VA, July 7, 1959.
Pierre Cardin, 82, fashion designer, born Venice, Italy, July 7, 1922.
Shelley Duvall, 55, actress (*Popeye, Nashville, Roxanne*), born Houston, TX, July 7, 1949.
Jorja Fox, 36, actress ("CSI," "ER"), born New York, NY, July 7, 1968.
Michelle Kwan, 24, figure skater, born Torrance, CA, July 7, 1980.
Lisa Leslie, 32, WNBA player, 1996 Women's Olympic Basketball team player, born Inglewood, CA, July 7, 1972.
Gian Carlo Menotti, 93, composer, born Cadigliano, Italy, July 7, 1911.
Joe Sakic, 35, hockey player, born Burnaby, BC, Canada, July 7, 1969.
Ralph Lee Sampson, 44, former basketball player, born Harrisonburg, VA, July 7, 1960.
Doc Severinsen, 77, composer, conductor, musician (former bandleader on "The Tonight Show"), born Arlington, OR, July 7, 1927.
Ringo Starr, 64, singer, musician (The Beatles), born Richard Starkey, Liverpool, England, July 7, 1940.

JULY 8 — THURSDAY

Day 190 — 176 Remaining

ASPINWALL CROSSES US ON HORSEBACK: ANNIVERSARY. July 8, 1911. Nan Jane Aspinwall rode into New York City carrying a letter to Mayor William Jay Gaynor from San Francisco Mayor Patrick Henry McCarthy, becoming the first woman to cross the US on horseback. She began her trip in San Francisco on Sept 1, 1910, and covered 4,500 miles in 301 days.

DECLARATION OF INDEPENDENCE FIRST PUBLIC READING: ANNIVERSARY. July 8, 1776. Colonel John Nixon read the Declaration of Independence to the assembled residents at Philadelphia's Independence Square.

ECKSTINE, BILLY: 90th BIRTH ANNIVERSARY. July 8, 1914. Bandleader and bass-baritone singer Billy Eckstine was born William Clarence Eckstein at Pittsburgh, PA. After performing with the Earl Hines band for almost 20 years, Eckstine formed his own band in 1944. At one time or another the band's ranks included Charlie Parker, Dizzy Gillespie, Miles Davis, Fats Navarro, Dexter Gordon, Gene Ammons, Art Blakey and vocalist Sarah Vaughan—some of the greatest bebop musicians of all time. Among Eckstine's hits were "Fools Rush In," "Everything I Have Is Yours," "My Foolish Heart," "Blue Moon" and "Body and Soul." Billy Eckstine died Mar 8, 1993, at Pittsburgh, PA.

FINLAND: SAVONLINNA OPERA FESTIVAL. July 8–Aug 7. Savonlinna. Staged in the magnificent 15th-century Olavinlinna Castle in the beautiful lake district of Finland. Music includes Verdi, Wagner and Gounod. Est attendance: 55,000. For info:

368

☆ Chase's 2004 Calendar of Events ☆   July 8

Savonlinna Opera Festival, Olavinkatu 27, Savonlinna, Finland, 57130. Phone: (358) 15-47-67-50. Fax: (358) 15-4767-540. E-mail: info@operafestival.fi. Web: www.operafestival.fi.

HODAG COUNTRY FESTIVAL. July 8–11. Hodag "50" Track, Rhinelander, WI. 27th anniversary country music festival, one of the oldest open-air festivals in the Midwest. Annually, the second full weekend in July. Est attendance: 70,000. For info: Diane Eckert, Hodag Country Fest, PO Box 1184, Rhinelander, WI 54501-1184. Phone: (715) 369-1300. Fax: (715) 362-3919. E-mail: hfc@hodag.com. Web: www.hodag.com.

HOT DOG NIGHT. July 8. Luverne, MN. More than 12,000 hot dogs are served free of charge, free drink is also provided. Various demonstrations. Est attendance: 5,000. For info: Dave Smith, Exec Dir, Luverne Area Chamber of Commerce, 102 E Main, Luverne, MN 56156. Phone: (507) 283-4061. Fax: (507) 283-4061. E-mail: luvernechamber@dtgnet.com. Web: www.luvernemn.com.

KIM IL SUNG: 10th DEATH ANNIVERSARY. July 8, 1994. President Kim Il Sung, the only leader in the history of North Korea, died just a few weeks before an historic summit with the president of South Korea was to take place, at Pyongyang, North Korea. A Stalinist-styled dictator, born at Man'gyandae, Korea, Apr 15, 1912, Kim had created a godlike personality cult surrounding himself and his son and presumed heir apparent Kim Jong Il. His death came at a crucial time in world politics. North Korea and the US had recently cooled rhetoric regarding North Korea's nuclear program and had begun further talks just hours prior to the announcement of Kim's death. The North-South Summit and the US-North Korean talks were postponed.

MARION COUNTY FAIR. July 8–11 (tentative). State Fairgrounds, Salem, OR. Exceptional food and entertainment, carnival, talent show, commercial exhibits, open class exhibits, Longhorns, horse and llama shows and livestock. Est attendance: 28,000. For info: Marion County Fair, PO Box 7166, Salem, OR 97303. Phone: (503) 585-9998. Fax: (503) 588-1659.

MICHIGAN STORYTELLERS FESTIVAL. July 8–10. Flint, MI. Storytelling performances, workshops and swaps come together for family fun and professional support at this 24th annual event. Est attendance: 1,500. For info: Flint Public Library, 1026 E Kearsley, Flint, MI 48502. Phone: (810) 232-7111. Fax: (810) 249-2635. E-mail: cstilley@flint.lib.mi.us.

MONTANA GOVERNOR'S CUP WALLEYE TOURNAMENT. July 8–10. Fort Peck, MT. Two-person team event, limited to 200 teams. First place award of $10,000. There is an 80 percent payback of $300 entry fee. Kids' fishing event also. Annually, the second weekend in July. Est attendance: 2,000. For info: Glasgow Area Chamber of Commerce & Agriculture, Box 832, Glasgow, MT 59230. Phone: (406) 228-2222. Fax: (406) 228-2244. E-mail: chamber@nemontel.net.

MOULIN, JEAN: DEATH ANNIVERSARY. July 8, 1943. Jean Moulin, a Free French representative, born at Beziers, France, June 20, 1899, was parachuted into occupied France on Jan 1, 1942, with the task of uniting the underground resistance. Moulin had with him (in the false bottom of a matchbox) a personal message of admiration for the resistance from General Charles DeGaulle. On May 27, 1943, the underground agreed to the creation of a National Resistance Council with Moulin as president. A month later he was arrested at Lyon by the Gestapo. He was tortured for 11 days but betrayed no one. Moulin died on a train while being transferred by the Nazis to a concentration camp.

NEW JERSEY STATE ROWING CHAMPIONSHIPS. July 8. Brick, NJ. Rowers of all ages will gather at Beaton Boat Yard to experience competition, camaraderie and a wide array of unique craft in the largest lifeguard rowing event in the country. The race covers 7 miles of open water of the Barnegat Bay in Ocean County, NJ. There are many different boat classes, age groups and rowing combinations allowed. A portion of all proceeds will benefit the Toms River Seaport Society and Maritime Museum, a volunteer association that houses, restores and maintains wooden boats as part of American history. For info: Viking Promotions, LLC, 54 Beach Ave, Bayville, NJ 08721-1108. Phone: (732) 237-0576. Fax: (732) 237-9933. E-mail: rich@vikingpromotions.com. Web: www.vikingpromotions.com.

OLIVE BRANCH PETITION: ANNIVERSARY. July 8, 1775. Representatives of New Hampshire, Massachusetts Bay, Rhode Island, Providence, Connecticut, New York, New Jersey, Pennsylvania, Delaware, Maryland, Virginia, North Carolina and South Carolina signed a petition from the Congress to King George III, a final attempt by moderates in the Second Continental Congress to avoid a complete break with England.

OREGON TRAIL DAYS. July 8–11. Gering, NE. Oldest continuing celebration in state of Nebraska commemorating Oregon Trail. Parades, barbecues, street dances, International Food Fair, concert, Nebraska State CASI Chili Cookoff, musical plays and a Western art show highlight the annual celebration. Annually, the second full weekend in July. Est attendance: 30,000. For info: Event Coord, PO Box 222, Gering, NE 69341. Phone/fax: (308) 436-4457. Web: www.oregontraildays.com.

ROCKEFELLER, NELSON ALDRICH: BIRTH ANNIVERSARY. July 8, 1908. Born at Bar Harbor, ME. Governor of New York state (1958–73). Nominated as vice president by President Ford, Aug 20, 1974, under provisions of the 25th Amendment. Sworn in Dec 19, 1974, after confirmation by the Senate and served until Jan 20, 1977. Died at New York, NY, Jan 26, 1979. Rockefeller was the second person to become vice president without having been elected (Gerald R. Ford was the first).

SCUD DAY (SAVOR THE COMIC, UNPLUG THE DRAMA). July 8. A day to remind people of the benefits of spending more time in the Comic Zone and less in the Drama Zone. For info: Stephanie West Allen, PO Box 9311, Denver, CO 80209. Phone: (303) 742-4790. E-mail: stephanie@allen-nichols.com. Web: www.allen-nichols.com.

TURKEY RAMA. July 8–10. McMinnville, OR. This annual event at McMinnville, once known as the Turkey Capital of the world, continues to include Famous Turkey BBQ, Biggest Turkey contest, vendor street sales, 8K fun run, carnival, entertainment. Est attendance: 25,000. For info: McMinnville Area Chamber of Commerce, 417 NW Adams, McMinnville, OR 97128. Phone: (503) 472-6196. Fax: (503) 472-6198. Web: www.mcminnville.org.

BIRTHDAYS TODAY

Kevin Bacon, 46, actor (stage: *Forty Deuce* [Obie Award]; *A Few Good Men*, *Apollo 13*), born Philadelphia, PA, July 8, 1958.

Raffi Cavoukian, 56, children's singer and songwriter, born Cairo, Egypt, July 8, 1948.

Billy Crudup, 36, actor (*Sleepers*, *Almost Famous*), born Manhasset, NY, July 8, 1968.

Kim Darby, 56, actress ("Rich Man, Poor Man," *True Grit*), born Los Angeles, CA, July 8, 1948.

Phil Gramm, 62, former US Senator (R, Texas), born Fort Benning, GA, July 8, 1942.

Cynthia Gregory, 58, ballerina, born Los Angeles, CA, July 8, 1946.

Beck Hansen, 34, rock singer/songwriter, born Bek David Campbell, Los Angeles, CA, July 8, 1970.

Anjelica Huston, 53, actress (Oscar for *Prizzi's Honor*; *The Addams Family*), born Los Angeles, CA, July 8, 1951.

Steve Lawrence, 69, singer ("Party Doll," "Go Away Little Girl"), born Sidney Liebowitz, New York, NY, July 8, 1935.

Jeffrey Tambor, 60, actor ("Hill Street Blues," "The Larry Sanders Show," *City Slickers*), born San Francisco, CA, July 8, 1944.

Alyce Faye Wattleton, 61, former executive director of Planned Parenthood Federation, born St. Louis, MO, July 8, 1943.

JULY 9 — FRIDAY
Day 191 — 175 Remaining

AFRMA FANCY RAT & MOUSE DISPLAY AND SHOW. July 9–Aug 1. Costa Mesa, CA. American Fancy Rat and Mouse Association exhibits rats and mice of "fancy" species that make good pets. For info: AFRMA, PO Box 2589, Winnetka, CA 91396-2589. Phone: (818) 992-5564 or (909) 685-2350. Fax: (818) 592-6590. E-mail: afrma@afrma.org. Web: www.afrma.org.

ALASKA FLAG DAY CELEBRATION. July 9, 1927. This day celebrates the first time Alaska's flag was unfurled over the Jesse Lee Home at Seward, AK. In 1927 Territorial Governor George Parks announced a contest in which children all over Alaska in grades 7–12 were encouraged to design Alaska's flag. The winning flag was designed by John Ben (Benny) Benson, a resident of the Jesse Lee Home, an orphanage. He was the only child in US history to design a state flag. Each year this day is celebrated at Alaska Children's Services (formerly the Jesse Lee Home). Est attendance: 2,000. For info: Alaska Children's Services, 4600 Abbott Rd, Anchorage, AK 99507-4314. Phone: (907) 346-2101. E-mail: akchild@ak.net. Web: www.acs.ak.org.

ARGENTINA: INDEPENDENCE DAY. July 9. Anniversary of establishment of independent republic, with the declaration of independence from Spain in 1816.

BASTILLE DAY CELEBRATION. July 9. Boston, MA. A street celebration with typical Parisian joie de vivre; dining and dancing under the stars. Est attendance: 3,000. For info: The French Library and Cultural Center, 53 Marlborough St, Boston, MA 02116-2099. Phone: (617) 912-0400. Fax: (617) 912-0450. E-mail: info@frenchlib.org. Web: www.frenchlib.org.

BEREA CRAFT FESTIVAL. July 9–11. Berea, KY. Craftspeople from 20 states gather to exhibit, demonstrate and sell their work. Est attendance: 12,000. For info: Sandy Chowning, Berea Craft Enterprises, Box 128, Berea, KY 40403. Phone: (859) 986-2818.

BLISSFEST. July 9–11. Cross Village, MI. Traditional, acoustic and folk music, three stages, four workshop areas, camping, kids' area and activities. Music styles from jazz to bluegrass. Est attendance: 5,000. For info: Blissfest, Box 441, Harbor Springs, MI 49740. Phone: (231) 348-2815. Web: www.blissfest.org.

CANADA: CALGARY STAMPEDE. July 9–18. Calgary, AB. One of the world's largest rodeos, plus an agricultural fair, entertainment, parade and carnival. Est attendance: 1,218,000. For info: Calgary Exhibition and Stampede, PO Box 1060, Station M, Calgary, AB, Canada T2P 2K8. Phone: (403) 261-0101. Web: www.calgarystampede.com.

CANADA: GREAT RENDEZVOUS. July 9–11. Old Fort William, Thunder Bay, ON. Join hundreds of reenactors as they celebrate the arrival of the partners, clerks and voyageurs to the inland headquarters of the North West Company. Take part in Rendezvous games and activities with colorful fur trade characters! Annually, in mid-July. Est attendance: 4,000. For info: Marty Mascarin, Communications Officer, Vickers Heights Post Office, Thunder Bay, ON, Canada P0T 2Z0. Phone: (807) 473-2326 or (807) 577-8461. Fax: (807) 473-2327. E-mail: info@oldfortwilliam.on.ca. Web: www.oldfortwilliam.on.ca.

July 2004	S	M	T	W	T	F	S
					1	2	3
	4	5	6	7	8	9	10
	11	12	13	14	15	16	17
	18	19	20	21	22	23	24
	25	26	27	28	29	30	31

EDWARDS, VINCE: BIRTH ANNIVERSARY. July 9, 1928. As Dr. Ben Casey on the 1961 television show "Ben Casey," Edwards's muscular, brooding charm made him an overnight sex symbol. Medical school enrollment increased while he was on the air. After conquering a gambling addiction, he became a real-life hero. Born at Brooklyn, NY, he died at Los Angeles, CA, Mar 11, 1996.

ENGLAND: WAYS WITH WORDS LITERATURE FESTIVAL. July 9–19. Dartington Hall, Dartington, Devon. Some 200 writers give lectures, seminars, interviews, discussions and readings. Book stalls, workshops and plays are also included. Est attendance: 12,000. For info: Steven Bristow, Dir, Ways With Words Literature Festival, Droridge Farm, Dartington, Totnes, Devon, England TQ9 6JQ. Phone: (44) (180) 386-7373. E-mail: admin@wayswithwords.co.uk.

FIRST OPEN-HEART SURGERY: ANNIVERSARY. July 9, 1893. In Provident Hospital on Chicago's south side, black surgeon Dr. Daniel Hale Williams performed the first successful open-heart surgery.

FOURTEENTH AMENDMENT TO US CONSTITUTION RATIFIED: ANNIVERSARY. July 9, 1868. The 14th Amendment defined US citizenship and provided that no state shall have the right to abridge the rights of any citizen without due process and equal protection under the law. Coming three years after the Civil War, the 14th Amendment also included provisions for barring individuals who assisted in any rebellion or insurrection against the US from holding public office, and releasing federal and state governments from any financial liability incurred in the assistance of rebellion or insurrection against the US.

HERITAGEFEST. July 9–11 (also July 16–18). New Ulm, MN. This unique Old World celebration features European music, New Ulm's own Concord Singers, five stages, air-conditioned Fest Halle, ethnic food and beverages. Est attendance: 40,000. For info: Discover Germany in Minnesota, PO Box 461, New Ulm, MN 56073-0461. Phone: (507) 354-8850. E-mail: hfest@newulmtel.net. Web: www.heritagefest.net.

HIGHEST TSUNAMI IN RECORDED HISTORY: ANNIVERSARY. July 9, 1958. An earthquake registering at 8.3 on the Richter Scale caused a massive landslide at the head of Lituya Bay, AK, which in turn created a tsunami of 1,700 feet—higher than the Sears Tower in Chicago (which is 1,450 feet). A 300-foot wave immediately followed, scouring bare about 4 to 5 square miles of land on both sides of the bay. Of 3 boats anchored at this remote spot, 1 was sunk with the loss of 2 lives; miraculously, the other 2 boats with their passengers survived the powerful waves.

HOWE, ELIAS: BIRTH ANNIVERSARY. July 9, 1819. American inventor of the sewing machine. Born at Spencer, MA, he died Oct 3, 1867, at Brooklyn, NY.

LAURA INGALLS WILDER PAGEANT. July 9–11 (also July 16–18 and 23–25). De Smet, SD. An outdoor pageant on the natural prairie stage depicting scenes historically based on Laura Ingalls Wilder's life and books. Est attendance: 10,000. For info: The Laura Ingalls Wilder Pageant, PO Box 154, De Smet, SD 57231. Phone: (605) 692-2108. Web: www.desmetpageant.org.

☆ Chase's 2004 Calendar of Events ☆ July 9

LITCHFIELD OPEN HOUSE TOUR. July 9–10. Litchfield, CT. Preview tour and cocktail reception on Friday. Open house tour features an assortment of homes as well as additional attractions of historical and architectural significance. Annually, the second weekend in July. Est attendance: 1,500. For info: Connecticut Junior Republic, PO Box 161, Goshen Road, Litchfield, CT 06759. Phone: (860) 567-9423. Fax: (860) 567-8127. E-mail: info@ctjuniorrepublic.org. Web: www.ctjuniorrepublic.org.

MAINE POTATO BLOSSOM FESTIVAL. July 9–18 (tentative). Fort Fairfield, ME. 56th annual. Promotes and observes the importance of Maine's prime agricultural product. Est attendance: 35,000. For info: Fort Fairfield Chamber of Commerce, 128 Main St, Fort Fairfield, ME 04742. Phone: (207) 472-3802. Fax: (207) 472-3886. E-mail: ffcc@mfx.net. Web: www.fortfairfield.org.

MARTYRDOM OF THE BAB. July 9. Baha'i observance of the anniversary of the execution by a firing squad, July 9, 1850, at Tabriz, Persia, of the 30-year-old Siyyid Ali Muhammed, the Bab (prophet-herald of the Baha'i Faith). One of the nine days of the year when Baha'is suspend work. For info: Baha'is of the US, Office of Public Information, 1320 Nineteenth St NW, Ste 350, Washington, DC 20036. Phone: (202) 466-9870. Fax: (202) 466-9873. E-mail: opi@usbnc.org. Web: www.us.bahai.org.

MOON PHASE: LAST QUARTER. July 9. Moon enters Last Quarter phase at 3:33 AM, EDT.

MOROCCO: YOUTH DAY. July 9. National holiday. On the birthday in 1929 of King Hassan II.

NETHERLANDS: NORTH SEA JAZZ FESTIVAL. July 9–11. Nederlands Congresgebouw (Netherlands Congress Centre), The Hague. Live jazz festival with top-name entertainment. Annually, the second full weekend in July. Est attendance: 13,000. For info: North Sea Jazz Fest, PO Box 3325, 2601 DH Delft, Netherlands. Phone: (31) (15) 215-7756 or fax (31) (15) 214-8393. For tickets, phone: (31) (10) 591-9000 or fax: (31) (10) 592-6130. E-mail: info@northseajazz.nl. Web: www.northseajazz.nl.

NEWPORT MUSIC FESTIVAL. July 9–25. Newport, RI. Three, four and even five concerts held daily in Newport's fabled mansions featuring unique chamber music programs, American debuts, world class artists and special events. Est attendance: 25,000. For info: Dr. Mark P. Malkovich III, Gen Dir, The Newport Music Festival, PO Box 3300, Newport, RI 02840-0992. Phone: (401) 846-1133. Box Office Phone: (401) 849-0700. Fax: (401) 849-1857. E-mail: staff@newportmusic.org. Web: www.newportmusic.org.

PROSPECT PARK FISHING CONTEST. July 9–10, 13–17 (tentative). Prospect Park, Brooklyn, NY. A contest for young anglers, 15 and under, with prizes for the largest or most fish. At the Rustic Shelter Lakeside near the Kate Wollman Rink parking lot. Groups must register ahead of time. Est attendance: 3,000. For info: Public Info Mgr, Public Info Office—Litchfield Villa, 95 Prospect Park W, Prospect Park, Brooklyn, NY 11215. Phone: (718) 965-8954. Fax: (718) 965-8972. E-mail: cmark@prospectpark.org. Web: www.prospectpark.org.

RADCLIFFE, ANN WARD: BIRTH ANNIVERSARY. July 9, 1764. English novelist famous for her gothic novels (fiction works especially popular in the late 18th and early 19th centuries). Among her works are *The Romance of the Forest, The Mysteries of Udolpho* and *The Italian*. She was born at London, England, and died there Feb 7, 1823.

RESPIGHI, OTTORINO: 125th BIRTH ANNIVERSARY. July 9, 1879. Italian composer (*The Fountains of Rome*) born at Bologna, Italy. He died at Rome, Apr 18, 1936.

RIVERWALK FESTIVAL. July 9–10. Riverwalk Plaza, Lowell, MI. A fun-filled family festival featuring a pet parade, pontoon rides on the Flat River, arts & crafts, used book sale, children's area, antique tractor show, food booths, live entertainment, health fair and much, much more. The $1,500 Duck Race is held on the Grand River, July 10 from 10 AM to 4 PM. Est attendance: 7,000. For info: Liz Baker, Lowell Area Chamber of Commerce, PO Box 224, Lowell, MI 49331. Phone: (616) 897-9161. Fax: (616) 897-9101. E-mail: info@lowellchamber.org. Web: www.lowellchamber.org.

SLOW PITCH SOFTBALL TOURNAMENT. July 9–11. Elm Park, Williamsport, PA. 31st annual charitable tournament with 40 teams. Sponsor: Yuengling Mid-State Beverage Co. Est attendance: 8,500. For info: Don Phillips, 532 Sylvan Dr, South Williamsport, PA 17702. Phone: (570) 322-3331 or (570) 322-2856.

STATE GAMES OF OREGON. July 9–11. Portland, OR. Oregon's Olympic-style amateur sports festival. Normally, the first weekend after July 4th. Est attendance: 17,500. For info: Dan Duffy, Exec Dir, 4840 SW Western Ave, Ste 900, Beaverton, OR 97005. Phone: (503) 520-1319. Fax: (503) 520-9747.

TRAILS WEST!®. July 9–11. Civic Center Park, St. Joseph, MO. Arts festival celebrating St. Joseph's unique cultural heritage. Fine arts, crafts and folk art, wide variety of taste-tempting food, beer and wine garden, children's activities and four entertainment stages. Est attendance: 80,000. For info: Marketing Manager, Allied Arts Council, 118 S 8th, St. Joseph, MO 64501. Phone: (800) 216-7080 or (816) 233-0231. Fax: (816) 233-6704. E-mail: artstaff@stjoearts.org. Web: www.StJoeArts.org.

WAYNE CHICKEN SHOW. July 9–10. Wayne, NE. To allow humankind to pay tribute to chickenkind (without laying the proverbial egg). Parade, National Cluck-Off, craft show and entertainment. Est attendance: 10,000. For info: Wayne Area Chamber of Commerce, 108 W Third St, Wayne, NE 68787. Phone: (402) 375-2240. E-mail: chamber_btriick@hotmail.com. Web: www.chickenshow.com.

WILD HORSE STAMPEDE. July 9–11. Wolf Point, MT. The "Granddaddy" of all Montana rodeos features a wild-horse race, three rodeos, three parades and Native American culture. This is the oldest PRCA rodeo in Montana. Est attendance: 12,000. For info: Chairman, Wolf Point Chamber of Commerce, 218 3rd Ave S, Ste B, Wolf Point, MT 59201. Phone: (406) 653-2012. E-mail: wpchmber@nemontel.net.

BIRTHDAYS TODAY

Brian Dennehy, 66, actor (Tony for *Long Day's Journey into Night*), born Bridgeport, CT, July 9, 1938.
Margaret Gillis, 51, dancer, choreographer, born Montreal, QC, Canada, July 9, 1953.
Lindsey Graham, 49, US Senator (R, South Carolina), born Pickens County, SC, July 9, 1955.
James Hampton, 68, actor ("F Troop," "Love, American Style"), born Oklahoma City, OK, July 9, 1936.
Tom Hanks, 48, actor (*Big, Sleepless in Seattle, Saving Private Ryan, Cast Away*; Oscars for *Philadelphia, Forrest Gump*), born Concord, CA, July 9, 1956.
David Hockney, 67, artist, born Bradford, England, July 9, 1937.
Mathilde Krim, 78, geneticist, philanthropist, born Como, Italy, July 9, 1926.
Courtney Love, 39, singer ("Live Through This"), actress (*The People vs. Larry Flynt*), born San Francisco, CA, July 9, 1965.
Kelly McGillis, 47, actress (*Witness, Top Gun, The Accused*), born Newport Beach, CA, July 9, 1957.
Donald Rumsfeld, 72, US Secretary of Defense (Ford and George W. Bush administrations), born Evanston, IL, July 9, 1932.
Fred Savage, 28, actor ("The Wonder Years," "Working," *The Princess Bride*), born Highland Park, IL, July 9, 1976.
Orenthal James (O.J.) Simpson, 57, former sportscaster and actor, Hall of Fame football player, born San Francisco, CA, July 9, 1947.
Jimmy Smits, 49, actor (*Glitz*, "LA Law," "NYPD Blue"), born New York, NY, July 9, 1955.
John Tesh, 52, TV host ("Entertainment Tonight"), born Garden City, NY, July 9, 1952.

JULY 10 — SATURDAY
Day 192 — 174 Remaining

ALLIED INVASION OF SICILY: ANNIVERSARY. July 10, 1943. Operation Husky, the Allied infantry attack on Italy, began on the island of Sicily. The British entry into Syracuse was the first Allied success in Europe. General Dwight D. Eisenhower, the Allied Commander-in-Chief, described the invasion as "the first page in the liberation of the European Continent."

ART FAIR ON THE SQUARE. July 10–11. Madison, WI. This is one of the largest and most popular juried art fairs in the Midwest, with nearly 500 artists from around the country selling their works. The fair occupies eight blocks around Madison's state Capitol building and attracts large crowds. There's also entertainment and lots of food. For info: Madison Art Center, 211 State St, Madison, WI 53703-2288. Phone: (608) 257-0158. Web: www.madisonartcenter.org.

ASH LAWN OPERA FESTIVAL. July 10–Aug 15 (tentative). Ash Lawn–Highland, Charlottesville, VA. Established in 1978, Ash Lawn Opera Festival presents opera in English, musical theatre, and concerts at the beautiful Boxwood Gardens of Ash Lawn–Highland, home of President James Monroe. Est attendance: 12,000. For info: Connie Edwards, Ash Lawn Opera Festival, 2000 Holiday Dr, Ste 100, Charlottesville, VA 22901. Phone: (434) 293-4500. Fax: (434) 293-0736. E-mail: info@ashlawnopera.org. Web: www.ashlawnopera.org.

ASHE, ARTHUR: BIRTH ANNIVERSARY. July 10, 1943. Born at Richmond, VA, Arthur Ashe became a legend for his list of firsts as a black tennis player. Ashe was chosen for the US Davis Cup team in 1963 and became captain in 1980. He won the US men's singles championship and US Open in 1968 and in 1975 the men's singles at Wimbledon. Ashe won a total of 33 career titles. In 1985 he was inducted into the International Tennis Hall of Fame. He helped create inner-city tennis programs for youth and wrote the three-volume *A Hard Road to Glory: A History of the African-American Athlete*. Ashe announced Apr 8, 1992, that he probably contracted HIV through a transfusion during bypass surgery in 1983. In September 1992 he began a $5 million fund-raising effort on behalf of the Arthur Ashe Foundation for the Defeat of AIDS and campaigned for public awareness regarding the AIDS epidemic. He died at New York, NY, Feb 6, 1993, from pneumonia.

BAHAMAS: INDEPENDENCE DAY: ANNIVERSARY. July 10. Public holiday. At 12:01 AM in 1973 the Bahamas gained their independence after 250 years as a British Crown Colony.

BETHUNE, MARY McLEOD: BIRTH ANNIVERSARY. July 10, 1875. Mary Jane McLeod Bethune was born at Mayesville, SC, the first in her family to be born free. Bethune became a teacher and in 1904 founded her own school in Florida, the Daytona Normal and Industrial School for Negro Girls. In 1931 the school merged with a local men's college, Cookman Institute, and was renamed Bethune-Cookman College. An adviser on minority affairs under President Franklin D. Roosevelt, she directed the Division of Negro Affairs of the National Youth Administration. She died May 18, 1955, at Daytona Beach, FL.

BON ODORI "FESTIVAL OF THE LANTERNS." July 10. Chicago, IL. One hundred performers, most clad in colorful kimonos, dance in celebration to music of different prefectures of Japan. The beat of the huge *taiko* (drum) helps keep tempo. Dances are performed outdoors, and public participation is encouraged. 8 PM. Est attendance: 750. For info: Office Secy, Midwest Buddhist Temple, 435 W Menomonee St, Chicago, IL 60614. Phone: (312) 943-7801. Fax: (312) 943-8069.

	S	M	T	W	T	F	S
July 2004					1	2	3
	4	5	6	7	8	9	10
	11	12	13	14	15	16	17
	18	19	20	21	22	23	24
	25	26	27	28	29	30	31

BORIS YELTSIN INAUGURATED AS RUSSIAN PRESIDENT: ANNIVERSARY. July 10, 1991. Boris Yeltsin took the oath of office as the first popularly elected president in Russia's 1,000-year history. He defeated the Communist Party candidate resoundingly, establishing himself as a powerful political counterpoint to Mikhail Gorbachev, the president of the Soviet Union, of which Russia was the largest republic. Yeltsin had been dismissed from the Politburo in 1987 and resigned from the Communist Party in 1989. His popularity forced Gorbachev to make concessions to the republics in the new union treaty forming the Confederation of Independent States. Suffering from poor health, Yeltsin resigned as president at the end of 1999.

BRINKLEY, DAVID: BIRTH ANNIVERSARY. July 10, 1920. Born at Wilmington, NC, David Brinkley was one of the most recognizable faces in American broadcast journalism for more than 50 years. He got his start as NBC's first White House correspondent, and his outstanding coverage of the 1956 Democratic and Republican national conventions landed him the anchor job of NBC's nightly TV newscast, paired with Chet Huntley. They remained on the air until Huntley's retirement in 1970. In 1981 Brinkley moved to ABC, creating a Sunday morning interview show called "This Week With David Brinkley." His 1995 memoir was titled *David Brinkley: 11 Presidents, 4 Wars, 22 Political Conventions, 1 Moon Landing, 3 Assassinations, 2000 Weeks of News and Other Stuff on Television, and 18 Years of Growing Up in North Carolina*. He died on June 12, 2003, at Houston, TX.

CALVIN, JOHN: BIRTH ANNIVERSARY. July 10, 1509. Theologian, born at Noyon, France. Reformer and founder of Presbyterianism. Calvin died at Geneva, Switzerland, May 27, 1564.

CANADA: HARRISON FESTIVAL OF THE ARTS. July 10–18. Harrison Hot Springs, BC. A celebration of world music, dance, theatre and visual art including a large outdoor art market. Various venues throughout the village. Variety of activities for the entire family. Est attendance: 12,000. For info: Ed Stenson, Gen Mgr, Harrison Fest, Box 399, Harrison Hot Springs, BC, Canada V0M 1K0. Phone: (604) 796-3664. Fax: (604) 796-3694. E-mail: harrfest@uniserve.com. Web: www.harrisonfestival.com.

CHILDREN'S CELEBRATION. July 10. Island Park, Springfield, OR. Bring your family for a fun-filled day of activity and excitement. Island Park will be transformed into a child's world of life-size characters, creative craft booths, magnificent music, on-stage entertainment and demonstrations and fantastic foods. The dozens of booths and activities range from a petting zoo to exploring the universe. Annually, the second Saturday in July. Est attendance: 5,000. For info: Willamalane Park and Recreation District, 765 A St, Springfield, OR 97477. Phone: (541) 736-4544. Web: www.willamalane.org.

CLERIHEW DAY. July 10. A day recognized in remembrance of Edmund Clerihew Bentley, journalist and author of the celebrated detective thriller *Trent's Last Case* (1912), but perhaps best known for his invention of a popular humorous verse form, the clerihew, consisting of two rhymed couplets of unequal length:/Edmund's middle name was Clerihew/A name possessed by very few,/But verses by Mr Bentley/Succeeded eminently./ Bentley was born at London, July 10, 1875, and died there, Mar 30, 1956.

CORN HILL ARTS FESTIVAL. July 10–11. Corn Hill neighborhood, Rochester, NY. Fine arts and crafts show organized by neighborhood residents for more than 35 years. Food and music from around the world, live entertainment, activities for children. All proceeds are reinvested in neighborhood projects. Annually, the first weekend following the 4th of July. Est attendance: 325,000. For info: Corn Hill Arts Festival, 133 S Fitzhugh St, Rochester, NY 14608. Phone: (585) 262-3142. Fax: (585) 546-4788. E-mail: festival@cornhill.org. Web: www.cornhill.org.

DALLAS, GEORGE MIFFLIN: BIRTH ANNIVERSARY. July 10, 1792. 11th vice president of the US (1845–49), born at Philadelphia, PA. Died there, Dec 31, 1864.

☆ Chase's 2004 Calendar of Events ☆ July 10

DON'T STEP ON A BEE DAY. July 10. Wellcat Holidays reminds kids and grown-ups that now is the time of year when going barefoot can mean getting stung by a bee. If you get stung tell Mom. [©2003 by WH.] For info: Thomas & Ruth Roy, Wellcat Holidays, 2418 Long Ln, Lebanon, PA 17046. Phone: (717) 279-0184. E-mail: info@wellcat.com. Web: www.wellcat.com.

FINLAND: KAUSTINEN FOLK MUSIC FESTIVAL. July 10–18. Kaustinen. The largest annual international festival of folk music and dance in the Nordic countries. Thousands of Finnish and hundreds of foreign artists perform. Every visitor has the opportunity to join in the music, dance and song. First organized in 1968. Est attendance: 110,000. For info: Finnish Tourist Board, 655 Third Ave, New York, NY 10017. Phone: (212) 885-9700 or (358) (6) 860-4111. Fax: (358) (6) 860-4222. E-mail: folk.art@kaustinen.inet.fi. Web: www.kaustinen.net.

GERMANY: LOVE PARADE. July 10. Tiergarten, Berlin. The world's biggest techno music rave takes place annually the second Saturday in July. The street festival features lots of music, style and more than 40 floats. Est attendance: 750,000. For info: Loveparade Berlin GmbH, Alexanderplatz 5, 10178 Berlin, Germany. Phone: (49) (30) 284-62-0. E-mail: infopool@loveparade.net. Web: www.loveparade.de.

GILBERT, JOHN: BIRTH ANNIVERSARY. July 10, 1897. Silent film star John Gilbert was born John Pringle at Logan, UT. In 1916 he had his billed screen debut in *Bullets and Brown Eyes*. In the early 1920s Gilbert had leading roles in several films, such as *The Merry Widow* and *The Big Parade*. Although he was a popular leading man, he was unable to succeed when sound came to movies and MGM released him from his contract in 1934. He died Jan 9, 1936, at Los Angeles, CA.

GWYNNE, FREDERICK HUBBARD: BIRTH ANNIVERSARY. July 10, 1926. Stage, screen and TV actor, best known for the TV roles Herman Munster in "The Munsters" and Officer Muldoon in "Car 54, Where Are You?" Gwynne was born at New York, NY, and died at Taneytown, MD, July 2, 1993.

HOGG, IMA: BIRTH ANNIVERSARY. July 10, 1882. American collector and philanthropist Ima Hogg was born at Mineola, TX. She founded the Houston Symphony and created the Bayou Bend Collection of the Museum of Fine Arts. She was the only daughter of Texas Governor (1891–95) James Stephen Hogg who, some have suggested, deliberately named his daughter "Ima" for political attention. She died at age 93, Aug 19, 1975, following an auto accident at London, England.

PEDDLER'S VILLAGE TEDDY BEAR'S PICNIC. July 10–11. Lahaska, PA. Bring your teddy bear for the festivities: competitions, teddy bear craftspeople from across the country, puppet shows, parades and live entertainment. Est attendance: 14,000. For info: Peddler's Village, Routes 202 & 263, Lahaska, PA 18931. Phone: (215) 794-4000. Fax: (215) 794-4001. Web: www.peddlersvillage.com.

PROUST, MARCEL: BIRTH ANNIVERSARY. July 10, 1871. Famed French author, born at Auteuil, France. He gained an international reputation for his 13-volume masterpiece, *A la Recherche du Temps Perdu* (*Remembrance of Things Past*). "Happiness," he wrote in *The Past Recaptured*, "is beneficial for the body but it is grief that develops the powers of the mind." Proust died Nov 19, 1922, at Paris, France.

***RAINBOW WARRIOR* SINKING: ANNIVERSARY.** July 10, 1985. The 160-ft ship, the *Rainbow Warrior*, operated by Greenpeace, an environmental organization, was sunk and a photographer aboard was killed while the ship was at Auckland, New Zealand. Reportedly a bomb was attached to the underside of the ship by saboteurs. The ship had been scheduled for use in a protest against nuclear tests in the South Pacific Ocean by the French government.

SODBUSTER DAYS. July 10–11. Fort Ransom State Park, Fort Ransom, ND. Remember the way things were done in rural North Dakota during the early 1920s with shelling corn by hand, rope weaving, horse-drawn plowing and haying. Ladies' demonstrations, kids' games, live music. Est attendance: 2,000. For info: Fort Ransom State Park, 5981 Walt Hjelle Parkway, Ft Ransom, ND 58033-9712. Phone: (701) 973-4331. Fax: (701) 973-4271.

SPACE MILESTONE: *TELSTAR* (US). July 10, 1962. First privately owned satellite (American Telephone and Telegraph Company) and first satellite to relay live TV pictures across the Atlantic was launched.

STONE HOUSE DAY. July 10. Hurley, NY. Tour six to nine privately owned, 250-plus-year-old stone houses, six within a 150-yard radius. Annually, the second Saturday in July. Est attendance: 1,000. For info: Stone House Day, Hurley Reformed Church, PO Box 328, Hurley, NY 12443. Phone: (845) 331-4121. E-mail: hrchurch@ulster.net.

TALKEETNA MOOSE-DROPPING FESTIVAL (WITH MOOSE-DROPPING TOSS GAME). July 10–11. Talkeetna, AK. Parade, booths, entertainment, 5K fun run, Mountain Mother contest and the famous moose-dropping toss game. Est attendance: 6,500. For info: Talkeetna Historical Soc, PO Box 76, Talkeetna, AK 99676. Phone: (907) 733-2487. Fax: (907) 733-2484. E-mail: ths@matnet.com.

THREE RIVERS FESTIVAL. July 10–18. Fort Wayne, IN. A citywide extravaganza of more than 200 events including a parade, food, juried art show, concerts, children's events and fireworks. Est attendance: 500,000. For info: Three Rivers Festival, 102 Three Rivers North, Fort Wayne, IN 46802. Phone: (260) 426-5556. Fax: (260) 420-8611. Web: www.threeriversfestival.org.

TIVOLI-VIKING DAYS AT THE NORDIC HERITAGE MUSEUM. July 10–11. Nordic Heritage Museum, Seattle, WA. A two-day outdoor Scandinavian festival featuring crafts, foods, entertainment and children's activities. Swedish pancake breakfast Saturday morning, Sunday barbecued salmon in afternoon, roast pig and café Sunday morning and food booths throughout both days. Viking crafts and demonstrations. Est attendance: 3,500. For info: Marianne Forssblad, Dir, Nordic Heritage Museum, 3014 NW 67th St, Seattle, WA 98117. Phone: (206) 789-5707. Fax: (206) 789-3271.

TUPPER LAKE WOODSMEN'S DAYS (WITH CHAIN-SAW SCULPTURING CONTEST). July 10–11. Tupper Lake, NY. Competitions for woodsmen and lumberjacks—including horse pulls. Includes the annual Northeast Regional Chain-saw Sculpturing Contest. Banquet takes place on July 9. Annually, the second weekend in July. Est attendance: 10,000. For info: Tupper Lake Woodsmen's Assn, PO Box 759, 19 Front St, Tupper Lake, NY 12986. Phone: (518) 359-9444. Fax: (518) 359-8244.

US LIFTS SANCTIONS AGAINST SOUTH AFRICA: ANNIVERSARY. July 10, 1991. President George H.W. Bush lifted US trade and investment sanctions against South Africa. The sanctions had been imposed through the Comprehensive Anti-Apartheid Act of 1986, which Congress had passed to punish South Africa for policies of racial separation.

WHISTLER, JAMES ABBOTT McNEILL: BIRTH ANNIVERSARY. July 10, 1834. American painter (especially known for painting of his mother) born at Lowell, MA. Died at London, England, July 17, 1903. When a woman declared that a landscape reminded her of Whistler's paintings, he reportedly said, "Yes, madam, Nature is creeping up."

July 10–11 ☆ Chase's 2004 Calendar of Events ☆

WINTER PARK JAZZ FESTIVAL. July 10–11 (tentative). Winter Park Resort, Winter Park, CO. A two-day jazz festival located on the slopes of Winter Park Resort. Loyal fans come equipped with lawn chairs, blankets and sunscreen to hear national jazz performers. Est attendance: 2,000. For info: Winter Park Resort, PO Box 36, Winter Park, CO 80482. Phone: (800) 729-5813. Fax: (970) 726-1572. E-mail: wpinfo@mail.skiwinterpark.com. Web: winterparkresort.com.

WORLD FOLKFEST. July 10–17. Springville, UT. 18th annual. Large international folk dance event. Est attendance: 20,000. For info: Springville World Folkfest, PO Box 306, 50 S Main, Springville, UT 84663. Phone: (801) 489-2726 or (801) 489-3657. Fax: (801) 489-4811. Web: www.springville.org.

WYOMING: ADMISSION DAY: ANNIVERSARY. July 10. Became 44th state in 1890.

BIRTHDAYS TODAY

Saul Bellow, 89, author (*Herzog, The Bellarosa Connection*), born Lachine, QC, Canada, July 10, 1915.
Andre Nolan Dawson, 50, former baseball player, born Miami, FL, July 10, 1954.
David Norman Dinkins, 77, former and first black mayor of New York City (D), born Trenton, NJ, July 10, 1927.
Ron Glass, 59, actor ("Barney Miller," voice on "Rugrats"), born Evansville, IN, July 10, 1945.
Arlo Guthrie, 57, singer ("The City of New Orleans," "Alice's Restaurant"), son of Woody Guthrie, born Brooklyn, NY, July 10, 1947.
Brad Henry, 41, Governor of Oklahoma (D), born Shawnee, OK, July 10, 1963.
Jerry Herman, 71, composer, lyricist, born New York, NY, July 10, 1933.
Sue Lyon, 58, actress (*Lolita, The Flim Flam Man*), born Davenport, IA, July 10, 1946.
Lawrence Pressman, 65, actor ("Doogie Howser MD," *The Hanoi Hilton*), born Cynthiana, KY, July 10, 1939.
Eunice Mary Kennedy Shriver, 83, founder of the Special Olympics, born Brookline, MA, July 10, 1921.
Virginia Wade, 59, former tennis player, born Bournemouth, England, July 10, 1945.

	S	M	T	W	T	F	S
July					1	2	3
2004	4	5	6	7	8	9	10
	11	12	13	14	15	16	17
	18	19	20	21	22	23	24
	25	26	27	28	29	30	31

JULY 11 — SUNDAY
Day 193 — 173 Remaining

ADAMS, JOHN QUINCY: BIRTH ANNIVERSARY. July 11, 1767. Sixth president of the US and the son of the second president, John Quincy Adams was born at Braintree, MA. After his single term as president, he served 17 years as a member of Congress from Plymouth, MA. He died Feb 23, 1848, at the House of Representatives (in the same room in which he had taken the presidential Oath of Office Mar 4, 1825). John Quincy Adams was the only president whose father had also been president of the US until George W. Bush became president in January 2001.

BABE RUTH'S DEBUT IN THE MAJORS: 90th ANNIVERSARY. July 11, 1914. Babe Ruth made his debut in major league baseball when he took the mound in Fenway Park for the Boston Red Sox against the Cleveland Indians. Ruth was relieved for the last two innings but was the winning pitcher in a 4–3 game.

BOWDLER'S DAY. July 11. A day to remember the prudish medical doctor, Thomas Bowdler, born near Bath, England, on July 11, 1754. He gave up the practice of medicine and undertook the cleansing of the works of Shakespeare by removing all the words and expressions he considered to be indecent or impious. His *Family Shakespeare*, in 10 volumes, omitted all those words "which cannot with propriety be read aloud in a family." He also "purified" Edward Gibbon's *History of the Decline and Fall of the Roman Empire* and selections from the Old Testament. His name became synonymous with self-righteous expurgation, and the word *bowdlerize* has become part of the English language. Bowdler died at Rhyddings, in South Wales, Feb 24, 1825.

BURR-HAMILTON DUEL: 200th ANNIVERSARY. July 11, 1804. US Vice President Aaron Burr shot and mortally wounded former Secretary of the Treasury (and primary author of *The Federalist Papers*) Alexander Hamilton in a duel at Weehawken, NJ, on this date. Hamilton had insulted Burr and refused to make a public apology. Hamilton died the next day. Although Burr returned to Washington to execute his duties as vice president, the duel ended his political career.

CHURCH AND SYNAGOGUE LIBRARY ASSOCIATION CONFERENCE. July 11–13. Indianapolis, IN. Est attendance: 200. For info: Judith Janzen, Administrator, Church and Synagogue Library Assn, Box 19357, Portland, OR 97280-0357. Phone: (503) 244-6919 or (800) LIB-CSLA. Fax: (503) 977-3734. E-mail: csla@worldaccessnet.com. Web: www.worldaccessnet.com/~csla.

DAY OF THE FIVE BILLION: ANNIVERSARY. July 11, 1987. An eight-pound baby boy, Matej Gaspar, born at 1:35 AM, EST, at Zagreb, Yugoslavia, was proclaimed the five billionth inhabitant of Earth. The United Nations Fund for Population Activities, hoping to draw attention to population growth, proclaimed July 11 as "Day of the Five Billion," noting that 150 babies are born each minute. See also: "World Population Six Billion: Anniversary" (Oct 12).

FAIR IN THE SQUARE CRAFTERS SHOW. July 11. Historic Square, Woodstock, IL. Crafters from all over the Midwest sell their handcrafted wares. Est attendance: 5,000. For info: Woodstock Chamber of Commerce, 136 Cass St, Woodstock, IL 60098. Phone: (815) 338-2436. Fax: (815) 338-2927. E-mail: chamber@woodstockilchamber.com. Web: www.woodstockilchamber.com.

FAMILY, CAREER AND COMMUNITY LEADERS OF AMERICA NATIONAL LEADERSHIP MEETING. July 11–15. Chicago, IL. This meeting is a unique opportunity to gain a national perspective on FCCLA activities and issues, elect officers, receive specialized leadership training and enhance chapter activities. Est attendance: 5,800. For info: Beth Carpenter, Family, Career and Community Leaders of America, Inc, 1910 Association Dr, Reston, VA 20191. Phone: (703) 476-4900. Fax: (703) 860-2713. E-mail: natlhdqtrs@fcclainc. Web: www.fcclainc.org

☆ Chase's 2004 Calendar of Events ☆ July 11–12

MONGOLIA: NAADAM NATIONAL HOLIDAY: ANNIVERSARY. July 11. Public holiday. Commemorates overthrow of the feudal monarch in 1921.

NAPALM USED: ANNIVERSARY. July 11, 1945. The US dropped several thousand pounds of the recently developed weapon napalm on Japanese forces still holed up on Luzon in the Philippines. Napalm, which was later used heavily as a defoliant in Vietnam, was a thickener consisting of a mixture of aluminum soaps used to jell gasoline.

NATIONAL FARRIER'S WEEK. July 11–17. A salute from horse owners to the men and women who keep their horses shod and equine feet and legs in top-notch condition. Annually, the second or third week in July. For info: Frank Lessiter, American Farriers Journal, PO Box 624, Brookfield, WI 53008-0624. Phone: (262) 782-4480. Fax: (262) 782-1252. E-mail: lesspub@aol.com.

NATIONAL THERAPEUTIC RECREATION WEEK. July 11–17. To increase awareness of therapeutic recreation programs and services, and to expand leisure opportunities for individuals with disabilities in their local communities. Annually, the second full week in July. For info: Natl Therapeutic Recreation Society, Ahren's NRPA Institute, 22377 Belmont Ridge Rd, Ashburn, VA 20148. Phone: (703) 858-2153. E-mail: ntrsnrpa@aol.com. Web: www.nrpa.org.

"THE NEWLYWED GAME" TV PREMIERE: ANNIVERSARY. July 11, 1966. Four newly married couples competed for prizes on this game show created by the inimitable Chuck Barris (mastermind of "The Gong Show"). The winners were determined by the couple that could best predict the responses of their respective spouses. Barris, Bob Eubanks and Paul Rodriguez have served as hosts.

OLD MISSION HISTORIC SKILLS FAIR. July 11. Old Mission State Park, Cataldo, ID. An event featuring old-fashioned skills such as spinning, quilting and black powder cannon demonstrations. Annually, the second Sunday of July. Est attendance: 2,000. For info: Bill Scudder, Park Mgr, Old Mission State Park, PO Box 30, Cataldo, ID 83810-0030. Phone: (208) 682-3814. Fax: (208) 682-4032. E-mail: old@idpr.state.id.us.

SMITH, JAMES: DEATH ANNIVERSARY. July 11, 1806. Signer of the Declaration of Independence, born at Ireland about 1719 (exact date unknown). Died at York, PA.

SPACE MILESTONE: *SKYLAB* (US): FALLS TO EARTH: 25th ANNIVERSARY. July 11, 1979. The 82-ton spacecraft launched May 14, 1973, re-entered Earth's atmosphere. Expectation was that 20–25 tons probably would survive to hit Earth, including one piece of about 5,000 pounds. This generated intense international public interest in where it would fall. The chance that some person would be hit by a piece of *Skylab* was calculated at one in 152. Targets were drawn and *Skylab* parties were held but *Skylab* broke up and fell to Earth in a shower of pieces over the Indian Ocean and Australia, with no known casualties.

TAKE CHARGE OF CHANGE WEEK. July 11–17. To increase awareness of the individual's power to control his own destiny, ChangeWorks will sponsor a series of events demonstrating the principles of taking charge of the changes that affect each of us. You can reduce stress and improve the quality of your life when you put yourself in the driver's seat. Learn how to accept the change you cannot control, manage the change you can and make change a positive force in your life. Free articles for publishers and webmasters at IdeaLady.com/content.htm. For info: Cathy Stucker, Special Interests Publishing, 4646 Hwy 6, PMB 123, Sugar Land, TX 77478. Phone: (281) 265-7342. E-mail: cathy@idealady.com. Web: www.idealady.com.

UNITED NATIONS: WORLD POPULATION DAY. July 11. In June 1989 the Governing Council of the United Nations Development Programme recommended that July 11 be observed by the international community as World Population Day. An outgrowth of the Day of Five Billion (July 11, 1987), the Day seeks to focus public attention on the urgency and importance of population issues, particularly in the context of overall development plans and programs and the need to create solutions to these problems. For info: United Nations, Dept of Public Info, Public Inquiries Unit, RM GA-57, New York, NY 10017. Phone: (212) 963-4475. E-mail: inquiries@un.org.

WHITE, E.B.: BIRTH ANNIVERSARY. July 11, 1899. Versatile author of books for adults and children (*Charlotte's Web*) and *New Yorker* editor. Born at Mount Vernon, NY, White died at North Brooklyn, ME, Oct 1, 1985.

BIRTHDAYS TODAY

Giorgio Armani, 68, fashion designer, born Romagna, Italy, July 11, 1936.
Harold Bloom, 74, literary critic, born New York, NY, July 11, 1930.
Mike Foster, Jr, 74, Governor of Louisiana (R), born Shreveport, LA, July 11, 1930.
John Henson, 37, TV talk-show host ("Talk Soup"), born Stamford, CT, July 11, 1967.
Tab Hunter, 73, actor (*Damn Yankees, Judge Roy Bean*, "The Tab Hunter Show"), born Arthur Gelien, New York, NY, July 11, 1931.
Stephen Lang, 52, actor (*Last Exit to Brooklyn, Tombstone*), born Queens, NY, July 11, 1952.
Mark Lester, 46, actor (*Fahrenheit 451, Oliver*), born Oxford, England, July 11, 1958.
Al MacInnis, 41, hockey player, born Inverness, NS, Canada, July 11, 1963.
Theodore Maiman, 77, physicist, developed first working laser, born Los Angeles, CA, July 11, 1927.
Bonnie Pointer, 53, singer (Pointer Sisters, "Steam Heat"), born East Oakland, CA, July 11, 1951.
Michael Rosenbaum, 32, actor ("Smallville," *Sweet November*), born Oceanside, NJ, July 11, 1972.
Richie Sambora, 44, musician (Bon Jovi), born Amboy, NJ, July 11, 1960.
Leon Spinks, 51, former boxer, born St. Louis, MO, July 11, 1953.
Rod Strickland, 38, basketball player, born the Bronx, NY, July 11, 1966.
Beverly Todd, 58, actress, director, producer (*Baby Boom, Clara's Heart*), born Chicago, IL, July 11, 1946.
Suzanne Vega, 45, singer ("Luka"), born Santa Monica, CA, July 11, 1959.
Sela Ward, 48, actress ("Sisters," "Once and Again"), born Meridian, MS, July 11, 1956.

JULY 12 — MONDAY
Day 194 — 172 Remaining

BATTLE OF KURSK: ANNIVERSARY. July 12, 1943. The largest tank battle in history took place outside the small village of Prohorovka, Russia. Nine hundred Russian tanks attacked an equal number of German Panther and Porsche tanks. Though the German equipment was larger, that advantage was lost in a close-range battle where they lacked maneuverability. When Hitler ordered a cease-fire, 300 German tanks remained strewn over the field.

BERLE, MILTON: BIRTH ANNIVERSARY. July 12, 1908. His nickname was "Mr Television," but Milton Berle had a long career as a vaudeville, film, radio and theater comedian as well. He was born Mendel Berlinger at Harlem, NY. He was popular before becoming the host of NBC's "Texaco Star Theater" in 1948, but that variety show made him a huge national star. Dressing in drag, rattling off corny jokes and drawing the day's biggest stars, "Uncle Miltie" made the show a television event until its end in 1953. He was one of the first seven inductees into the Academy of Television Arts and Sciences' TV Hall of Fame. Berle died Mar 27, 2002, at Los Angeles, CA.

375

July 12 ☆ Chase's 2004 Calendar of Events ☆

De RITA, JOE: 95th BIRTH ANNIVERSARY. July 12, 1909. American comedian Curly Joe De Rita was the last surviving member of the Three Stooges comedy team. He joined the team in 1959 after Joe Besser left. He appeared in *Have Rocket, Will Travel* (1959), *Snow White and the Three Stooges* (1961) and *The Outlaw is Coming* (1965). Born at Philadelphia, PA, De Rita died July 3, 1993, at Los Angeles, CA.

"EVENING AT POPS" TV PREMIERE: ANNIVERSARY. July 12, 1970. PBS's popular concert series premiered with conductor Arthur Fiedler heading the Boston Pops Orchestra. Conductor/composer John Williams took over the post upon Fiedler's death in 1979; Keith Lockhart is the current conductor.

"FAMILY FEUD" TV PREMIERE: ANNIVERSARY. July 12, 1976. From the production team of Mark Goodson and Bill Todman, this game show set two families against each other to raise the greater number of points. The contestants had to predict the most common answers to a given survey question. Richard Dawson (TV's famous kissing host), the late Ray Combs, Louie Anderson and Richard Karn have been hosts.

FOLKMOOT USA: THE NORTH CAROLINA INTERNATIONAL FOLK FESTIVAL. July 12–25. Waynesville, NC. A festival of international folk dance featuring groups from 10 countries. Est attendance: 75,000. For info: Folkmoot USA, PO Box 658, Waynesville, NC 28786. Phone: (828) 452-2997 or (877) FOLK-USA. Fax: (828) 452-5762. E-mail: folkmoot@pobox.com. Web: www.folkmoot.com.

FULLER, BUCKMINSTER: BIRTH ANNIVERSARY. July 12, 1895. Architect, inventor, engineer and philosopher, born Richard Buckminster Fuller at Milton, MA. His geodesic dome is one of the most important structural innovations of the 20th century. He died July 1, 1983, at Los Angeles, CA.

GERMANY ENDS MILITARY BAN: 10th ANNIVERSARY. July 12, 1994. Germany's Constitutional Court ended the ban on sending German troops to fight outside the country. The ban had been in effect since shortly after World War II, when Germany was disarmed. (Japan has a similar ban.) The ruling would allow German troops to join in peacekeeping missions of the United Nations or the North Atlantic Treaty Organization (NATO). As if to signal the change in status, German military units marched in the Bastille Day celebration at Paris on July 14, the first time German troops had appeared in France since the German occupation ended in 1945.

INTERNATIONAL TOWN CRIERS DAY. July 12. A day recognizing the ancient and honorable art and tradition of town crying and the significant contribution town criers make to promoting their respective towns and cities. Annually, a Monday in July. For info: David Phillips, Official Town Crier, Box 58, Dutton, ON, Canada N0L IJ0. E-mail: tcrier@hotmail.com.

KIRIBATI: INDEPENDENCE DAY: 25th ANNIVERSARY. July 12. Republic of Kiribati attained independence from Britain in 1979. Formerly known as the Gilbert Islands.

"NORTHERN EXPOSURE" TV PREMIERE: ANNIVERSARY. July 12, 1990. CBS's comedy-drama was essentially a fish-out-of-water (or rather a New Yorker out of Manhattan) series. Dr. Joel Fleischman (Rob Morrow) was forced to practice medicine in remote Cicely, Alaska, to pay off his student loans. He gradually accepted his lot with the help of the town's quirky citizens who needed him because he was the only doctor in town. The show's cast featured Barry Corbin as Maurice Minnefield, a former NASA astronaut and Cicely's most prominent businessman, Janine Turner as bush pilot Maggie O'Connell, Elaine Miles as Joel's assistant Marilyn, Darren E. Burrows as Ed Chigliak, a half-Indian aspiring filmmaker, John Cullum as tavern owner Holling Vincoeur, Cynthia Geary as Holling's girlfriend and waitress Shelley Tambo, Peg Phillips as store proprietor Ruth-Anne and John Corbett as deejay Chris Stevens. The last episode aired in 1995.

NORTHERN IRELAND: ORANGEMEN'S DAY. July 12. National holiday commemorates Battle of Boyne, July 1 (OS), 1690, in which the forces of King William III of England, Prince of Orange, defeated those of James II, at Boyne River in Ireland. Ordinarily observed July 12. If July 12 is a Saturday or a Sunday the holiday observance is on the following Monday.

SAO TOME AND PRINCIPE: INDEPENDENCE DAY: ANNIVERSARY. July 12. National holiday observed. Gained independence from Portugal in 1975.

SPACE MILESTONE: *PHOBOS 2* (USSR). July 12, 1988. Sent back the first close-up photos of Phobos, one of two small moons of Mars. Launched from Soviet space probe in central Asia on July 12, 1988.

THOREAU, HENRY DAVID: BIRTH ANNIVERSARY. July 12, 1817. American author and philosopher, born at Concord, MA. Died there May 6, 1862. In *Walden* he wrote, "I frequently tramped eight or ten miles through the deepest snow to keep an appointment with a beechtree, or a yellow birch, or an old acquaintance among the pines."

TURNER'S FRONTIER ADDRESS: ANNIVERSARY. July 12, 1893. Historian Frederick Jackson Turner delivered his paper, "The Significance of the Frontier in American History," at a meeting of the American Historical Association at Chicago during the Columbian Exposition. Stating that the frontier was a spawning ground for many of the social and intellectual traits that made Americans different from Europeans, Turner saw the end of the frontier as a major break in the psychology of the nation. Turner's formalization of this idea came in part from his reading the *Extra Census Bulletin No. 2: Distribution of Population According to Density: 1890* which said that, "Up to and including 1890 the country had a frontier of settlement, but at present the unsettled area has been so broken into by isolated bodies of settlement that there can hardly be said to be a frontier line."

US AMATEUR PUBLIC LINKS (GOLF) CHAMPIONSHIP. July 12–17. Rush Creek Golf Club, Maple Grove, MN. For info: US Golf Assn, Golf House, PO Box 708, Championship Dept, Far Hills, NJ 07931. Phone: (908) 234-2300. Fax: (908) 234-9687. E-mail: usga@usga.org. Web: www.usga.org.

WEDGWOOD, JOSIAH: BIRTH ANNIVERSARY. July 12, 1730. Famed English pottery designer and manufacturer, born at Burslem, Staffordshire, England. Died at Etruria, Staffordshire, England, Jan 3, 1795.

BIRTHDAYS TODAY

Lisa Nicole Carson, 35, actress ("ER," "Ally McBeal"), born Brooklyn, NY, July 12, 1969.
Van Cliburn, 70, pianist, born Harvey Lavan Cliburn, Jr, Shreveport, LA, July 12, 1934.
Bill Cosby, 66, comedian, actor (Emmys for "I Spy," "The Cosby Show"), born Philadelphia, PA, July 12, 1938.

	S	M	T	W	T	F	S
July 2004					1	2	3
	4	5	6	7	8	9	10
	11	12	13	14	15	16	17
	18	19	20	21	22	23	24
	25	26	27	28	29	30	31

☆ Chase's 2004 Calendar of Events ☆ July 12–13

Paul Guilfoyle, 49, actor ("CSI"), born Boston, MA, July 12, 1955.
Mel Harris, 47, actress ("Something So Right," "thirtysomething"), born Bethlehem, PA, July 12, 1957.
Cheryl Ladd, 52, actress ("Charlie's Angels," "Grace Kelly"), born Huron, SD, July 12, 1952.
Christine McVie, 61, singer, musician (Fleetwood Mac, "Got a Hold On Me"), born Birmingham, England, July 12, 1943.
Denise Nicholas, 59, actress ("Room 222," "In the Heat of the Night," *Let's Do It Again*), born Detroit, MI, July 12, 1945.
Jamey Sheridan, 53, actor ("Shannon's Deal," *The House on Carroll Street*), born Pasadena, CA, July 12, 1951.
Richard Simmons, 56, TV personality, weight loss guru, author, born New Orleans, LA, July 12, 1948.
Erik Per Sullivan, 13, actor ("Malcolm in the Middle," *The Cider House Rules*), born Worcester, MA, July 12, 1991.
Rolonda Watts, 45, talk-show host ("Rolonda"), born Winston-Salem, NC, July 12, 1959.
Kristi Tsuya Yamaguchi, 33, Olympic gold medal figure skater, born Hayward, CA, July 12, 1971.

JULY 13 — TUESDAY
Day 195 — 171 Remaining

ALPENFEST. July 13–17. Gaylord, MI. Swiss-inspired festival that has something for the whole family. Annual traditions include "The World's Largest Coffee Break," Lampion Parade, Burning of the Boogg and a Grand Parade. Free food and entertainment daily, 100 arts & crafts booths, free kids' games, contests and a carnival. Est attendance: 50,000. For info: Pam Duczkowski, Alpenfest, PO Box 513, Gaylord, MI 49734. Phone: (800) 345-8621. Fax: (989) 732-7990. E-mail: events@gaylordmichigan.net. Web: www.gaylordchamber.com.

"BROTHERS" TV PREMIERE: 20th ANNIVERSARY. July 13, 1984. This sitcom was rejected by ABC and NBC before airing on Showtime, partly because one of its characters was openly gay. "Brothers" thus became the first original sitcom made for cable television. Robert Walden starred as Joe Waters, an ex-football player and restaurant owner; Brandon Maggart as eldest brother Lou, a conservative construction worker; and Paul Regina as youngest brother Clifford, who disclosed his orientation in the very first episode. Set in Philadelphia, the series dealt with sensitive topics such as gay-bashing, AIDS and male-to-male intimacy.

EMBRACE YOUR GEEKNESS DAY. July 13. Into dungeon games, comic books and doing vampire dress-up? Spend endless hours going strange places on the Internet? You're a geek, and this is the day to roar! [©2003 by WH.] For info: Thomas & Ruth Roy, Wellcat Holidays, 2418 Long Lane, Lebanon, PA 17046. Phone: (717) 279-0184. E-mail: info@wellcat.com. Web: www.wellcat.com.

FORREST, NATHAN BEDFORD: BIRTH ANNIVERSARY. July 13, 1821. Confederate cavalry commander whose birthday is observed in schools in Tennessee, Forrest was also one of the founders of the short-lived original Ku Klux Klan. Forrest was born at Bedford County, TN, and died Oct 29, 1877, at Memphis, TN.

FRANCE: NIGHT WATCH or LA RETRAITE AUX FLAMBEAUX. July 13. France. Celebrates eve of the Bastille's fall. On the eve of Bastille Day, there are parades and fireworks.

GRUNTLED WORKERS DAY. July 13. There's so much news about disgruntled workers that today's the day for Gruntled Workers to Unite! Drive to a fast-food restaurant and say, "Thanks, your service is fast, have a nice day." [©2003 by WH.] For info: Thomas & Ruth Roy, Wellcat Holidays, 2418 Long Ln, Lebanon, PA 17046. Phone: (717) 279-0184. E-mail: info@wellcat.com. Web: www.wellcat.com.

JAPAN: BON FESTIVAL (FEAST OF LANTERNS). July 13–15. Religious rites throughout Japan in memory of the dead, who, according to Buddhist belief, revisit Earth during this period. Lanterns are lighted for the souls. Spectacular bonfires in the shape of the character *dai* are burned on hillsides on the last day of the Bon or O-Bon Festival, bidding farewell to the spirits of the dead.

"LIVE AID" CONCERTS: ANNIVERSARY. July 13, 1985. Concerts at Philadelphia, PA, and London, England (Kennedy and Wembley stadiums) were seen by 162,000 attendees and an estimated 1.5 billion television viewers. Organized to raise funds for African famine relief; the musicians performed without a fee, and nearly $100 million was pledged toward aid to the hungry.

MAJOR LEAGUE BASEBALL ALL-STAR GAME. July 13. Minute Maid Park, Houston, TX. This marks the 75th anniversary of the all-star game. For info: Major League Baseball. Web: www.mlb.com.

NORTHWEST ORDINANCE: ANNIVERSARY. July 13, 1787. The Northwest Ordinance, providing for government of the territory north of the Ohio River, became law. The ordinance guaranteed freedom of worship and the right to trial by jury, and it prohibited slavery.

WORLD CUP INAUGURATED: ANNIVERSARY. July 13, 1930. The first World Cup soccer competition was held at Montevideo, Uruguay, with 14 countries participating. The host country had the winning team.

BIRTHDAYS TODAY

Cameron Crowe, 47, director, screenwriter (*Fast Times at Ridgemont High, Jerry Maguire*, Oscar for *Almost Famous*), born Palm Springs, CA, July 13, 1957.
Harrison Ford, 62, actor (*Witness, The Fugitive*, the first Star Wars trilogy, the Indiana Jones films), born Chicago, IL, July 13, 1942.
Robert Forster, 63, actor ("Banyon," *Diamond Men, Jackie Brown*), born Rochester, NY, July 13, 1941.
John French (Jack) Kemp, 69, former US Secretary of Housing and Urban Development, former football player, born Los Angeles, CA, July 13, 1935.
Louise Mandrell, 50, country-western singer, born Corpus Christi, TX, July 13, 1954.
Cheech Marin, 58, writer, actor (Cheech and Chong films, "Nash Bridges"), born Los Angeles, CA, July 13, 1946.
Roger McGuinn, 62, musician (The Byrds), born James Joseph McGuinn, Chicago, IL, July 13, 1942.
Erno Rubik, 60, inventor of the Rubik's Cube, born in a hospital air raid shelter, Budapest, Hungary, July 13, 1944.
Wole Soyinka, 70, Nobel Prize–winning author (*The Lion and the Jewel, The Strong Breed*), born Abeokuta, Nigeria, July 13, 1934.
Michael Spinks, 48, former boxer, born St. Louis, MO, July 13, 1956.
Patrick Stewart, 64, actor ("Star Trek: The Next Generation," *Excalibur, LA Story*), born Mirfield, England, July 13, 1940.
David Storey, 71, author, playwright (*The Performance of Small Firms*), born Wakefield, England, July 13, 1933.
Anthony Jerome ("Spud") Webb, 41, former basketball player, born Dallas, TX, July 13, 1963.

377

JULY 14 — WEDNESDAY
Day 196 — 170 Remaining

BASCOM, FLORENCE: BIRTH ANNIVERSARY. July 14, 1862. After receiving her third bachelor's degree from the University of Wisconsin in 1884 and a master's degree in 1887, Florence Bascom entered Johns Hopkins University and received a doctorate in 1893. She taught at Ohio State and became a professor at Bryn Mawr. She also was the first woman appointed a geologist with the US Geological Survey, was associate editor of "American Geologist" (1890–1905) and became the first woman elected a Fellow of the Geological Society of America. Born at Williamstown, MA; died at Northhampton, MA, June 18, 1945.

CANADA: WINNIPEG FRINGE THEATRE FESTIVAL. July 14–25. Winnipeg, MB. A 12-day, noon-to-midnight, nonstop theatrical smorgasbord with more than 120 theatre companies from around the world. The Winnipeg Fringe Festival: Pushing the envelope in theatrical entertainment since 1988. Est attendance: 130,000. For info: The Winnipeg Fringe Festival, 174 Market Ave, Winnipeg, MB, Canada R3B 0P8. Fax: (204) 947-3741. E-mail: fringe@mtc.mb.ca. Web: www.mtc.mb.ca.

CHANCELLOR, JOHN: BIRTH ANNIVERSARY. July 14, 1927. Television broadcast journalist John Chancellor was born at Chicago, IL. He rose through the ranks at the *Chicago Sun-Times*, from copyboy to feature writer. Chancellor spent more than four decades with the NBC network, beginning in 1950. During that time, he took a two-year respite from journalism to serve President Lyndon Johnson as director of the Voice of America. Chancellor retired in 1993, but his distinctive, familiar voice was still heard, for example, when he narrated a PBS documentary in 1996. He died July 12, 1996, at Princeton, NJ.

CHILDREN'S PARTY AT GREEN ANIMALS. July 14. Green Animals Topiary Garden, Portsmouth, RI. Annual party for children and adults at Green Animals, a delightful topiary garden and children's toy museum. Party includes pony rides, games, clowns, refreshments, hot dogs, hamburgers and more. Annually, July 14. Est attendance: 1,500. For info: The Preservation Society of Newport County, 424 Bellevue Ave, Newport, RI 02840. Phone: (401) 847-1000. Web: www.NewportMansions.org.

CHOCTAW INDIAN FAIR. July 14–17. Philadelphia, MS. The fair presents cultural programs demonstrating native arts, crafts, social dancing, stickball, archery, blowgun and rabbit stick competition. Also native foods are prepared and served on the reservation. Annually, the Wednesday through Saturday after July 4. Est attendance: 60,000. For info: Choctaw Fair Desk, 101 Industrial Rd, Choctaw, MS 39350. Phone: (601) 650-1604. Web: www.choctawindianfair.com.

EDWARDS, DOUGLAS: BIRTH ANNIVERSARY. July 14, 1917. American television journalist Douglas Edwards was born at Ada, OK. He began his career in radio, but in 1947 he became the first major announcer to move to television. He was anchor for CBS's first nightly news program, "Douglas Edwards with the News" (1948–62), where he gave memorable on-scene coverage of such events as the sinking of the *Andrea Doria* in 1956. Edwards worked for CBS until his retirement, two years before he died on Oct 13, 1990, at Sarasota, FL.

ENGLAND: BIRMINGHAM RIOT: ANNIVERSARY. July 14, 1791. Following a dinner celebrating the second anniversary of the fall of the Bastille, an angry mob rioted at Birmingham, England. The main target of their wrath was the home of scientist (discoverer of oxygen) Joseph Priestley, who was unpopular because of his religious views and his approval of the American and French revolutionary causes. The mob ruled Birmingham for three days, burning Priestley's home and laboratory as well as the homes of his friends. Priestley, in disguise, and his family narrowly escaped with their lives. They lived for a time at London before moving in 1794 to America. See also: "Priestley, Joseph: Birth Anniversary" (Mar 13).

FORD, GERALD RUDOLPH: BIRTHDAY. July 14, 1913. 38th president of the US (1974–77). Born Leslie King at Omaha, NE, Ford became 41st vice president of the US on Dec 6, 1973, by appointment, following the resignation of Spiro T. Agnew from that office on Oct 10, 1973. Ford became president on Aug 9, 1974, following the resignation from that office on that day of Richard M. Nixon. He was the first nonelected vice president and president of the US.

FRANCE: BASTILLE DAY OR FÊTE NATIONAL. July 14. Public holiday commemorating the fall of the Bastille at the beginning of the French Revolution, July 14, 1789. Also celebrated or observed in many other countries.

GUTHRIE, WOODROW WILSON "WOODY": BIRTH ANNIVERSARY. July 14, 1912. American folksinger, songwriter ("This Land Is Your Land," "Union Maid," "Hard Traveling"), born at Okemah, OK. Traveled the country by freight train, singing and listening. Died Oct 3, 1967, at New York, NY. Father of Arlo Guthrie.

HANNA, WILLIAM: BIRTH ANNIVERSARY. July 14, 1910. Born at Melrose, New Mexico, William Hanna was the co-creator of such popular characters as Tom and Jerry, Yogi Bear, Snagglepuss and Magilla Gorilla. With partner Joe Barbera, he won seven Academy Awards for his Tom and Jerry cartoon shorts, and another eight works were nominated. The Hanna-Barbera team created the first TV animated sitcom for adults, *The Flintstones* (1960), and such favorites as *The Jetsons* and *Scooby-Doo, Where Are You?*. Hanna died at Los Angeles, CA, on Mar 22, 2001.

MISSION SAN ANTONIO DE PADUA: FOUNDING ANNIVERSARY. July 14. California. Mission to the Indians founded July 14, 1771.

MURRAY, KEN: BIRTH ANNIVERSARY. July 14, 1903. American comedian Ken Murray was born at New York, NY. He began in vaudeville, then moved to films and television. He died Oct 12, 1988, at Beverly Hills, CA.

SARTO, ANDREA DEL: BIRTH ANNIVERSARY. July 14, 1486. Celebrated Italian painter was born near Florence, Italy. "Sarto," a nickname referring to his father's trade as a tailor, was the name he chose during his lifetime, though the real surname was probably either Vanucchi or di Francesco. One of the most renowned artists of his time, his paintings hang in the great galleries of the world. He died at Florence, Jan 22, 1531.

SINCLAIR LEWIS DAYS. July 14–18. Sauk Centre, MN. Parade, kids' activities, dance, fireworks, Miss Sauk Centre pageant, flea market, craft sale, Heart of Lakes Bike Tour and softball tournament in Sinclair Lewis's hometown. Est attendance: 10,000. For info: Sauk Centre Chamber of Commerce, PO Box 222, Sauk Centre, MN 56378. Phone: (320) 352-5201. Fax: (320) 352-5202. Web: www.saukcentrechamber.com.

WYANDOTTE STREET ART FAIR. July 14–17. Downtown Wyandotte, MI. More than 350 artists and craftspeople display and sell their wares. Also, music, street entertainers, Children's

July 2004	S	M	T	W	T	F	S
					1	2	3
	4	5	6	7	8	9	10
	11	12	13	14	15	16	17
	18	19	20	21	22	23	24
	25	26	27	28	29	30	31

Emporium and sidewalk sales. Sponsored by Anheuser Busch. Est attendance: 250,000. For info: Leslie Lupo, Dir, 3131 Biddle Ave, Wyandotte, MI 48192. Phone: (734) 324-4506. Fax: (734) 324-4552.

BIRTHDAYS TODAY

Polly Bergen, 74, actress ("To Tell the Truth," *The Winds of War*), singer, born Knoxville, TN, July 14, 1930.

Ingmar Bergman, 86, filmmaker (*The Seventh Seal, Wild Strawberries, Cries and Whispers*), born Uppsala, Sweden, July 14, 1918.

Gerald Rudolph Ford, 91, 38th president of the US, born Leslie King, Omaha, NE, July 14, 1913.

Matthew Fox, 38, actor ("Party of Five"), born Crowheart, WY, July 14, 1966.

Missy Gold, 34, actress ("Benson"), born Great Falls, MT, July 14, 1970.

Roosevelt (Rosey) Grier, 72, actor, former football player, born Cuthbert, GA, July 14, 1932.

Joel Silver, 52, producer (*Lethal Weapon, Die Hard*), born South Orange, NJ, July 14, 1952.

Harry Dean Stanton, 78, actor (*Repo Man; Paris, Texas; Wild at Heart*), born West Irvine, KY, July 14, 1926.

Steven Michael (Steve) Stone, 57, sportscaster, former baseball player, born Euclid, OH, July 14, 1947.

Robin Ventura, 37, baseball player, born Santa Maria, CA, July 14, 1967.

JULY 15 — THURSDAY
Day 197 — 169 Remaining

BATTLE OF THE MARNE: ANNIVERSARY. July 15, 1918. General Erich Ludendorff launched Germany's fifth, and last, offensive to break through the Chateau-Thierry salient. This all-out effort involved three armies branching out from Rheims to cross the Marne River. The Germans were successful in crossing the Marne near Chateau-Thierry before American, British and Italian divisions stopped their progress. On July 18 General Foch, Commander-in-Chief of the Allied troops, launched a massive counteroffensive that resulted in a German retreat that continued for four months until they sued for peace in November.

CANADA: JUST FOR LAUGHS: THE MONTREAL INTERNATIONAL COMEDY FESTIVAL. July 15–25. Montreal, QC. Make the trip to the worldwide capital of comedy! More than 2,500 artists from 16 countries play in more than 2,000 shows and performances at indoor and outdoor venues that blanket the entire city. In the past, the Just for Laughs bilingual comedy marathon has featured some of the world's most impressive talent including Tim Allen, Jerry Seinfeld, Drew Carey, Kelsey Grammer, Rowan "Mr Bean" Atkinson, Jim Carrey and David Hyde Pierce, to name but a few. Est attendance: 1,700,000. For info: Just for Laughs Festival, 2101 St-Laurent Blvd, Montreal, QC, Canada H2X 2T5. Phone: (514) 845-3155 or (888) 244-3155. Fax: (514) 845-4140. E-mail: info@hahaha.com. Web: www.hahaha.com.

CANADA: SAINT SWITHUN'S SOCIETY ANNUAL CELEBRATION. July 15. Toronto, ON. Goals include the promotion of feelings of goodwill, the encouragement of the celebration of St. Swithun's Day and the patterning of members' lives after the example of our patron. Affiliated with the Friends of Winchester Cathedral. Publishes "The Water Spout" newsletter, free upon request. Annually, July 15. Est attendance: 100. For info: Norman A. McMullen, Pres, St. Swithun's Society, 427 Lynett Crescent, Richmond Hill, ON, Canada L4C 2V6. Phone: (905) 883-0984. E-mail: st._swithuns_society@angelfire.com.

COMMERCIAL AIR FLIGHT BETWEEN THE US AND USSR BEGINS: ANNIVERSARY. July 15, 1968. A Soviet Aeroflot jet landed at Kennedy Airport at New York, NY, marking the start of direct commercial air flight between the US and the then USSR.

CRAFT FAIR OF THE SOUTHERN HIGHLANDS. July 15–18 (also Oct 21–24). Asheville Civic Center, Asheville, NC. In 1948 this fair started the crafts revival so evident today. More than a craft fair, this event includes demonstrations and traditional mountain music—all in addition to the 170 craftspeople representing the finest crafts in a nine-state mountain region. Est attendance: 11,000. For info: Lindsay Hearn, Southern Highland Craft Guild, PO Box 9545, Asheville, NC 28815. Phone: (828) 298-7928. Fax: (828) 298-7962. E-mail: lindsay@craftguild.org.

DOWNTOWN ART STREET FAIR. July 15–17. Fargo, ND. Whether your interest is in baskets, pottery, jewelry, paintings, photography or sculpture, you'll find something at this fair with more than 350 exhibiting artists. Three days of unique arts and crafts, incredible food and free entertainment. Est attendance: 4,000. For info: North Dakota Tourism, Century Center, 1600 E Century Ave, Ste 2, Bismarck, ND 58503. Phone: (701) 241-1570 or (800) 435-5663. Web: www.fmdowntown.com.

JAMBOREE IN THE HILLS. July 15–18. St. Clairsville, OH. 28th year. Billed as the "Super Bowl of Country Music," this festival is a four-day outdoor country music show featuring the top names in country music today. Sponsors: Jamboree USA, WWVA Radio and WOVK Radio. Annually, the third weekend in July. Est attendance: 110,000. For info: Terri A. Phillips, Publicity Dir, Jamboree In The Hills, 1015 Main St, Wheeling, WV 26003. Phone: (800) 624-5456. Fax: (304) 234-0067. Web: www.jamboreeinthehills.com.

MOORE, CLEMENT CLARKE: 225th BIRTH ANNIVERSARY. July 15, 1779. American author and teacher, best remembered for his popular verse "A Visit from Saint Nicholas" ("'Twas the Night Before Christmas"), which was first published anonymously and without Moore's knowledge in a newspaper, Dec 23, 1823. Moore was born at New York, NY, and died at Newport, RI, July 10, 1863. (In recent years, Moore's authorship of the poem has been challenged, with Henry Livingston, Jr, offered as the creator.)

"ONE LIFE TO LIVE" TV PREMIERE: ANNIVERSARY. July 15, 1968. Set in a fictional Pennsylvania town, the show was created by Agnes Nixon to depict the class and ethnic struggles of the town's denizens. The initial cast featured many Jewish, Polish and African-American characters. The show departed from inter-ethnic storytelling in the 1980s for more fantastic adventures set in locales such as heaven, the old West and a futuristic mountain silo called Eternia. Since then, the show has returned to its strengths of traditional storytelling by featuring Latino and African-American actors as integral characters. Award-winning actress Erika Slezak heads the cast as the venerable Viki Lord Riley Buchanan Carpenter, the town's matron with five alternate personalities. Among those who have appeared on "OLTL" are Tom Berenger, Judith Light, Robert Desiderio, Tommy Lee Jones, Laurence Fishburne, Jameson Parker, Phylicia Rashad, Christine Ebersole, Richard Grieco, Blair Underwood, Joe Lando, Audrey Landers, Christian Slater and Yasmine Bleeth.

July 15–16 ☆ Chase's 2004 Calendar of Events ☆

REMBRANDT: BIRTH ANNIVERSARY. July 15, 1606. Dutch painter and etcher, born at Leiden, Holland. One of the undisputed giants of Western art. Known for *The Night Watch* and many portraits and self-portraits, died at Amsterdam, Holland, Oct 4, 1669.

SAINT FRANCES XAVIER CABRINI: BIRTH ANNIVERSARY. July 15, 1850. First American saint, founder of schools, orphanages, convents and hospitals, born at Lombardy, Italy. Died of malaria at Chicago, IL, Dec 22, 1917. Canonized July 7, 1946.

SAINT SWITHIN'S DAY. July 15. Swithun (Swithin), Bishop of Winchester (AD 852–862), died July 2, 862. Little is known of his life, but his relics were transferred into Winchester Cathedral July 15, 971, a day on which there was a heavy rainfall. According to old English belief, it will rain for 40 days thereafter when it rains on this day. "St. Swithin's Day, if thou dost rain, for 40 days it will remain; St. Swithin's Day, if thou be fair, for 40 days, will rain nea mair."

THE SCOPES TRIAL. July 15–18. Dayton Courthouse, Dayton, TN. Five performances of an original drama written from the actual transcript of the Scopes trial—"the world's most famous court trial." Also, an arts and crafts fair, an antique car show and much more. Est attendance: 1,500. For info: Cynthia Rodriguez, Dayton Chamber of Commerce, Scopes Festival, 107 Main St, Dayton, TN 37321. Phone: (423) 775-0361. E-mail: chamber@volstate.net. Web: www.bryan.edu.

SCOTLAND: THE OPEN (GOLF) CHAMPIONSHIP. July 15–18. Royal Troon Golf Club, Ayrshire, Troon. Major event on the golfing calendar. Est attendance: 160,000. For info: The Royal and Ancient Golf Club of St. Andrews, St. Andrews, Fife, Scotland KY16 9JD. Phone: (44) (1334) 460-000. Fax: (44) (1334) 460-002. E-mail: championships@randagc.org.

TOPS INTERNATIONAL RECOGNITION DAYS. July 15–17. Pittsburgh, PA. TOPS (Take Off Pounds Sensibly), the leading nonprofit international weight management group, will draw thousands of people throughout the world to celebrate weight-loss support and success. Features include numerous group seminars and workshops, celebration activities and ceremonial events honoring members' weight-loss successes. Est attendance: 3,000. For info: Melissa Baxter, TOPS Club, Inc, 4575 S Fifth St, Milwaukee, WI 53207. Phone: (414) 482-4620. E-mail: mbaxter@tops.org. Web: www.tops.org.

BIRTHDAYS TODAY

Willie Aames, 44, actor ("Eight Is Enough," "Charles in Charge"), born Newport Beach, CA, July 15, 1960.
Kim Alexis, 44, model, born Lockport, NY, July 15, 1960.
Julian Bream, 71, musician (classical guitar, lute), born London, England, July 15, 1933.
Lolita Davidovich, 43, actress (*Indictment, Cobb*), born London, ON, Canada, July 15, 1961.
Brian Austin Green, 31, actor ("Beverly Hills 90210"), singer, born Van Nuys, CA, July 15, 1973.
Irene Jacob, 38, actress (*Red, Othello*), born Paris, France, July 15, 1966.
Alex George Karras, 69, former football player, actor ("Webster," *Babe, Victor/Victoria*), born Gary, IN, July 15, 1935.
Ken Kercheval, 69, actor ("Dallas," "Search for Tomorrow"), born Wolcottville, IN, July 15, 1935.
Linda Ronstadt, 58, singer ("Heart Like a Wheel," "Simple Dreams"), songwriter, born Tucson, AZ, July 15, 1946.

	S	M	T	W	T	F	S
July 2004					1	2	3
	4	5	6	7	8	9	10
	11	12	13	14	15	16	17
	18	19	20	21	22	23	24
	25	26	27	28	29	30	31

Jesse Ventura, 53, former professional wrestler, former Governor of Minnesota (I), born Minneapolis, MN, July 15, 1951.
Jan-Michael Vincent, 60, actor ("The Winds of War," "Airwolf"), born Denver, CO, July 15, 1944.
George V. Voinovich, 68, US Senator (R, Ohio), born Cleveland, OH, July 15, 1936.
Forest Whitaker, 43, actor (*Platoon, Bird, The Crying Game*), director (*Waiting to Exhale*), born Longview, TX, July 15, 1961.

JULY 16 — FRIDAY
Day 198 — 168 Remaining

AMUNDSEN, ROALD: BIRTH ANNIVERSARY. July 16, 1872. Norwegian explorer born near Oslo, Roald Amundsen was the first man to sail from the Atlantic to the Pacific Ocean via the Northwest Passage (1903–05). He discovered the South Pole (Dec 14, 1911) and flew over the North Pole in a dirigible in 1926. He flew, with five companions, from Norway, June 18, 1928, in a daring effort to rescue survivors of an Italian Arctic expedition. No trace of the rescue party or the airplane was ever located. See also: "South Pole: Discovery Anniversary" (Dec 14).

ATOMIC BOMB TESTED: ANNIVERSARY. July 16, 1945. In the New Mexican desert at Alamogordo Air Base, 125 miles southeast of Albuquerque, the experimental atomic bomb was set off at 5:30 AM. Dubbed "Fat Boy" by its creator, the plutonium bomb vaporized the steel scaffolding holding it as the immense fireball rose 8,000 ft in a fraction of a second—ultimately creating a mushroom cloud to a height of 41,000 ft. At ground zero the bomb emitted heat three times the temperature of the interior of the sun. All plant and animal life for a mile around ceased to exist. When informed by President Truman at Potsdam of the successful experiment, Winston Churchill responded, "It's the Second Coming in wrath!"

BIG SKY STATE GAMES. July 16–18. Billings, MT. An Olympic-styled festival for Montana citizens. This statewide multisport program is designed to inspire people of all ages and skill levels to develop their physical and competitive abilities to the height of their potential through participation in fitness activities. Est attendance: 30,000. For info: Big Sky State Games, Box 7136, Billings, MT 59103-7136. Phone: (406) 254-7426. Fax: (406) 254-7439. E-mail: info@bigskygames.org. Web: www.bigskygames.org.

BOLIVIA: LA PAZ DAY. July 16, 1548. Founding of city, now capital of Bolivia, on this day, 1548.

CANADA: COUNTRY GOOD TIMES. July 16–18. Wilberforce, ON. Family fun celebrating music and local musicians featuring amateur contest, flea market, carnival midway, vendors and bingo. Annually, the third weekend in July. Est attendance: 5,000. For info: Bancroft and Dist Chamber of Commerce, PO Box 539, Bancroft, ON, Canada K0L 1C0. Phone: (613) 332-1513. Fax: (613) 332-2119. E-mail: chamber@commerce.bancroft.on.ca. Web: www.bancroftdistrict.com.

CENTRAL MONTANA FAIR. July 16–25. Lewistown, MT. Draft and open-to-all-class horse show, two sessions of rodeo, carnival, 4-H and open exhibits, night shows and AMX & Demolition Derby. Annually, last full week in July. Est attendance: 20,000. For info: Central Montana Fair, PO Box 1098, Lewistown, MT 59457. Phone: (406) 538-8841. Fax: (406) 538-4060. E-mail: cmtfair@tein.net. Web: centralmontanafair.com.

☆ Chase's 2004 Calendar of Events ☆ — July 16

COMET CRASHES INTO JUPITER: 10th ANNIVERSARY. July 16, 1994. The first fragment of the comet Shoemaker-Levy crashed into the planet Jupiter, beginning a series of spectacular collisions, each unleashing more energy than the combined effect of an explosion of all our world's nuclear arsenal. Video imagery from earthbound telescopes as well as the Hubble telescope provided vivid records of the explosions and their aftereffects. In 1993 the comet had shattered into a series of about a dozen large chunks that resembled "pearls on a string" after its orbit brought it within the gravitational effects of our solar system's largest planet.

DECOY AND WILDLIFE ART SHOW. July 16–18. Clayton Recreation Park Arena, Clayton, NY. 36th annual juried show. World championship wildlife carvers, artists, taxidermists, collectors and dealers. Events include hunting decoy contest, gunning rig contest, vintage decoy contest and auction. Displays of handcrafted wildlife from wood, silver, gold and pewter. Annually, the third weekend in July. Est attendance: 5,000. For info: Thousand Islands Museum, PO Box 27, Clayton, NY 13624. Phone: (315) 686-5794. Fax: (315) 686-4867. E-mail: timuseum@gisco.net. Web: www.timuseum.org.

DISTRICT OF COLUMBIA ESTABLISHING LEGISLATION: ANNIVERSARY. July 16, 1790. George Washington signed legislation that selected the District of Columbia as the permanent capital of the US. Boundaries of the district were established in 1792. Plans called for the government to remain housed at Philadelphia, PA, until 1800, when the new national capital would be ready for occupancy.

EARTHQUAKE JOLTS PHILIPPINES: ANNIVERSARY. July 16, 1990. An earthquake measuring 7.7 on the Richter scale struck the Philippines, killing an estimated 1,621 persons and leaving approximately 1,000 missing. The quake struck in an area north of Manila, and heavy damage was reported at Cabanatuan, Baguio and on Luzon island. The quake was the worst in the Philippines in 14 years.

EDDY, MARY BAKER: BIRTH ANNIVERSARY. July 16, 1821. Founder of Christian Science; born near Concord, NH, she died at Chestnut Hill, MA, Dec 3, 1910.

ENGLAND: BBC PROMS (BBC HENRY WOOD PROMENADE CONCERTS). July 16–Sept 11. London. 110th season. "The BBC Proms" consists of more than 73 concerts at the Royal Albert Hall, including symphonic and chamber music, choral music, opera, world music and jazz. For info: BBC Proms, Rm 4096, Broadcasting House, London, England W1A 1AA. Phone: (44) (20) 7765-5575. Fax: (44) (20) 7765 0619. E-mail: proms@bbc.co.uk. Web: www.bbc.co.uk/proms/.

LOGGER DAYS. July 16–18. Libby, MT. Celebration of logging heritage. Est attendance: 5,000. For info: Libby Chamber of Commerce, PO Box 704, Libby, MT 59923. Phone: (406) 293-4167. Fax: (406) 293-2197. E-mail: libbyacc@libby.org. Web: www.libby.org/libbyacc/.

MIDSUMMER NIGHTS' FAIR. July 16–17. Lions Park, Norman, OK. 27th annual. Juried and invited artists and craftspeople display their work for show and sale in booths under the stars. Festival foods, free entertainment and free art activities for the whole family, 6:30 PM–11:30 PM. Est attendance: 8,000. For info: Receptionist, Firehouse Art Center, 444 S Flood, Norman, OK 73069. Phone: (405) 329-4523. E-mail: firehouse@telepath.com.

MINERS JUBILEE. July 16–18. Baker City, OR. Est attendance: 10,000. For info: Baker County Chamber & Visitors Center, 490 Campbell St, Baker City, OR 97814. Phone: (800) 523-1235 or (541) 523-5855.

MISSION SAN DIEGO DE ALCALA: FOUNDING ANNIVERSARY. July 16, 1769. First of 21 California missions to the Indians.

MOZART FESTIVAL. July 16–Aug 1. San Luis Obispo County, CA. Variety of music in unique venues celebrating the spirit of Wolfgang Amadeus Mozart. Est attendance: 15,000. For info: Mozart Festival, PO Box 311, San Luis Obispo, CA 93406. Phone: (805) 781-3008. Fax: (805) 781-3011. E-mail: slo@mozartfestival.com. Web: www.mozartfestival.com.

NATCHITOCHES/NORTHWESTERN STATE UNIVERSITY FOLK FESTIVAL. July 16–17. Prather Coliseum, Northwestern State University, Natchitoches, LA. The festival is a "purist" folk festival in that folk artists who are reviving a traditional Louisiana folk art or still working a Louisiana tradition are invited. Music, food, crafts and storytellers. A four-time winner of the Top Twenty Events in the Southeast, as determined by the Southeast Tourism Society. Annually, the third weekend in July. Est attendance: 10,000. For info: Dr. Lisa Abney, Louisiana Folklife Center, Natchitoches/NSU Folk Fest, NSU PO Box 3663, Natchitoches, LA 71497. Phone: (318) 357-4332 or (800) 259-1714. Fax: (318) 357-4331. E-mail: folklife@nsula.edu. Web: www.liberalarts.nsula.edu/folklife or www.natchitoches.net.

REYNOLDS, JOSHUA: BIRTH ANNIVERSARY. July 16, 1723 (OS). English portrait painter whose paintings of 18th-century English notables are among the best of the time. Born at Plympton, Devon, England, Sir Joshua died at London, Feb 23, 1792, at age 68. "He who resolves never to ransack any mind but his own," Reynolds told students of the Royal Academy in 1774, "will be soon reduced, from mere barrenness, to the poorest of all imitations; he will be obliged to imitate himself, and to repeat what he has before often repeated."

ROGERS, GINGER: BIRTH ANNIVERSARY. July 16, 1911. Ginger Rogers is best remembered as Fred Astaire's dance partner in a series of romantic musicals. She appeared in 70 films during her six-decade career, winning an Oscar for her leading role in the 1940 film *Kitty Foyle*. Rogers was born at Independence, MO, and died Apr 25, 1995, at Rancho Mirage, CA.

SALEM ART FAIR AND FESTIVAL. July 16–18. Bush's Pasture Park, Salem, OR. A celebration of the arts with 200 arts/crafts booths, continuous performing arts, food, children's parade and art activities, historic Bush House Museum and living history performances, special art exhibition, 5K walk and run for the arts. Annually, the third full weekend in July. Est attendance: 120,000. For info: Salem Art Assn, 600 Mission St SE, Salem, OR 97302. Phone: (503) 581-2228. Web: www.salemart.org.

SHERWOOD ROBIN HOOD FESTIVAL. July 16–17. Sherwood, OR. Renaissance group, knighting ceremony, kids and family area, parade, world's only archery contest between Sherwood and Nottingham, England, flower & castle contest, teen dance, music, food and crafts vendors and much more! Annually, the third weekend in July. Est attendance: 18,000. For info: Robin Hood Festival Assn, PO Box 496, Sherwood, OR 97140. Phone: (503) 625-4233.

SHOW ME STATE GAMES. July 16–18 (also July 23–25 and July 30–Aug 1). Columbia, MO. An Olympic-style athletic festival for Missouri citizens. This statewide multisport program is designed to inspire Missourians of every age and skill level to develop their physical and competitive abilities to the height of their potential through participation in fitness activities. Est attendance: 40,000. For info: Ken Ash, Exec Dir, Show Me State Games, 1105 Carrie Francke Dr, Columbia, MO 65211. Phone: (573) 882-2101. Fax: (573) 884-4004. E-mail: ashk@missouri.edu. Web: www.smsg.org.

July 16–17 ☆ Chase's 2004 Calendar of Events ☆

SPACE MILESTONE: *APOLLO 11* (US): MAN SENT TO THE MOON: 35th ANNIVERSARY. July 16, 1969. This launch resulted in man's first moon landing, the first landing on any extraterrestrial body. See also: "Space Milestone: Moon Day" (July 20).

STANWYCK, BARBARA: BIRTH ANNIVERSARY. July 16, 1907. Actress Barbara Stanwyck was born Ruby Stevens at the Flatbush section of Brooklyn, NY. At the age of 18 she won a leading role in the Broadway melodrama *Noose*, appearing for the first time as Barbara Stanwyck. She appeared in 82 films including *Stella Dallas; Double Indemnity; Sorry, Wrong Number; The Lady Eve* and the television series "The Big Valley." In 1944 the government listed her as the nation's highest paid woman, earning $400,000 per year. Stanwyck died at Santa Monica, CA, Jan 21, 1990.

UKRAINIAN FESTIVAL. July 16–18. Dickinson, ND. This three-day festival features Ukranian food, arts and crafts, music and the talented Stepoui Dity dancers. If you are of Ukranian culture, you don't want to miss this. Annually, third weekend in July. Est attendance: 2,000. For info: Agnes Palanuk, Ukranian Cultural Institute. Phone: (701) 483-1486. Fax: (701) 483-4366. E-mail: uci@pop.ctctel.com. Web: www.ukrainiannd.org.

VIRGINIA LAKE FESTIVAL. July 16–18. Clarksville, VA. Fun-filled weekend with Pig Pickin, opening ceremonies on Friday; arts and crafts show, flea market, balloons, five-mile run, fish fry, live entertainment for children and adults and fireworks on Saturday; beach music festival on Sunday. Annually, the third weekend in July (Friday–Sunday). Est attendance: 50,000. For info: Clarksville Lake Country Chamber of Commerce, 105 2nd St, Box 1017, Clarksville, VA 23927. Phone: (804) 374-2436 or (800) 557-5582. E-mail: clarksville@kerrlake.com. Web: www.clarksvilleva.org.

WELLS, IDA B.: BIRTH ANNIVERSARY. July 16, 1862. African-American journalist and anti-lynching crusader Ida B. Wells was born the daughter of slaves at Holly Springs, MS, and grew up as Jim Crow and lynching were becoming prevalent. Wells argued that lynchings occurred not to defend white women but because of whites' fear of economic competition from blacks. She traveled extensively, founding anti-lynching societies and black women's clubs. Wells's *Red Record* (1895) was one of the first accounts of lynchings in the South. She died Mar 25, 1931, at Chicago, IL.

YARMOUTH CLAM FESTIVAL. July 16–18. Yarmouth, ME. 39th annual. Family-oriented festival featuring clams and more. Annually, starts the third Friday in July. Est attendance: 150,000. For info: Yarmouth Chamber of Commerce, Carolyn Schuster, 162 Main St, Yarmouth, ME 04096. Phone: (207) 846-3984. Fax: (207) 846-5419. E-mail: yarmouth@yarmouthmaine.org. Web: www.clamfestival.com.

July 2004

S	M	T	W	T	F	S
				1	2	3
4	5	6	7	8	9	10
11	12	13	14	15	16	17
18	19	20	21	22	23	24
25	26	27	28	29	30	31

ZIPPO/CASE INTERNATIONAL SWAP MEET. July 16–17. Zippo/Case Visitors Center, Bradford, PA. Fans and collectors of Zippo windproof lighters and Case knives come from around the world to admire, sell and swap their prized collectibles. Hosted by Zippo Manufacturing Company and its subsidiary W.R. Case & Sons Cutlery. Est attendance: 2,000. For info: Communications Coord, Zippo Manufacturing Co, 33 Barbour St, Bradford, PA 16701. Phone: (814) 368-2700. Fax: (814) 368-2874. Web: zippo.com or wrcase.com.

BIRTHDAYS TODAY

Ruben Blades, 56, singer (two Grammy Awards), actor (*Crossover Dreams, The Milagro Beanfield War*), born Panama City, Panama, July 16, 1948.
Phoebe Cates, 41, actress (*Fast Times at Ridgemont High, Gremlins*), born New York, NY, July 16, 1963.
Corey Feldman, 33, actor (*Stand By Me, The Lost Boys*), born Reseda, CA, July 16, 1971.
Michael Flatley, 46, dancer (*Lord of the Dance, Feet of Flames*), born Chicago, IL, July 16, 1958.
Alexis Herman, 57, former Secretary of Labor (Clinton administration), born Mobile, AL, July 16, 1947.
Barnard Hughes, 89, actor (*Sisters*, "Doc"), born Bedford Hills, NY, July 16, 1915.
Bess Myerson, 80, former Miss America ('45), former government official, born New York, NY, July 16, 1924.
Barry Sanders, 36, former football player, born Wichita, KS, July 16, 1968.
Pinchas Zukerman, 56, violinist, born Tel Aviv, Israel, July 16, 1948.

JULY 17 — SATURDAY
Day 199 — 167 Remaining

ABBOTT, BERENICE: BIRTH ANNIVERSARY. July 17, 1898. Berenice Abbott was born at Springfield, OH, and went on to become a pioneer of American photography. She is best remembered for her black and white photographs of New York City in the 1930s, many of which appeared in the book *Changing New York*. After publishing this collection she began photographing scientific experiments that illustrated the laws and processes of physics. She died at Monson, ME, Dec 11, 1991.

BANNACK DAYS. July 17–18. Bannack, MT. Montana's first territorial capital, now a living ghost town, comes to life with a celebration of Montana's mining and pioneer history. Stagecoach rides, main street gunfights, old-time dancing, lots of music and fun are provided during this two-day celebration along Grasshopper Creek each year. Bannack State Park allows visitors to explore the old town and imagine what life was like in the mid-1800s. It is open year-round to the public. Admission fee. Est attendance: 4,000. For info: Angela Hurley, Montana Fish, Wildlife and Parks, 4200 Bannack Rd, Dillon, MT 59725. Phone: (406) 834-3413.

CARVER DAY COMMEMORATIVE CELEBRATION. July 17. Diamond, MO. Family-oriented educational programs, gospel singing, storytelling, environmental education and guided historic tours at the George Washington Carver National Monument. Est attendance: 1,300. For info: George Washington Carver Natl Monument, 5646 Carver Rd, Diamond, MO 64840. Phone: (417) 325-4151. Fax: (417) 325-4231.

CHAMBERSFEST. July 17–25. Chambersburg, PA. Annual Civil War festival including gala opening, Old Market Day, Celebrate the Arts, Civil War Seminar, Pet Parade and Almost Anything Goes Games. Est attendance: 10,000. For info: Melissa Knepper, Dir Member Services, Greater Chambersburg Chamber of Commerce, 75 S Second St, Chambersburg, PA 17201. Phone: (717) 264-7101. Fax: (717) 267-0399. E-mail: mknepper@chambersburg.org.

CIRCUS CITY FESTIVAL. July 17–24. Peru, IN. Youth amateur circus performed by children 7 to 21 years of age helping to preserve the circus heritage of Miami County, IN. Circus parade, July 24, 10 AM. Annually, beginning the Saturday before and ending the Saturday after the third Wednesday of July. Est attendance: 75,000. For info: Circus City Festival Inc, 154 N Broadway, Peru, IN 46970. Phone: (765) 472-3918. Fax: (765) 472-2826. Web: www.perucircus.com.

CIVIL WAR REENACTMENT. July 17–18. Coshocton, OH. Features battles, living history scenarios, Civil War artifacts exhibit, period wedding, style show and outdoor church service. Annually, the third weekend in July. Est attendance: 5,000. For info: Roscoe Village Fdtn, 381 Hill St, Coshocton, OH 43812. Phone: (800) 877-1830 or (740) 622-9310. Fax: (740) 623-6555. E-mail: rvmarketing@roscoevillage.com. Web: www.roscoevillage.com.

COLLECTABLES/ANTIQUES/CRAFT/FLEA MARKET SALE. July 17. Sauk Centre, MN. 33rd year for this sale, sponsored by St. Michael's Auxiliary in conjunction with Sinclair Lewis Days. Sale features 75 exhibitors. The Auxiliary offers lunches at their food stand for a fee, also bake sale and raffle. Annually, the third Saturday in July. Est attendance: 1,500. For info: Joyce C. Lyng, St. Michael's Auxiliary, 750 Railroad Ave, Unit 123, Sauk Centre, MN 56378. Phone: (320) 352-2624. E-mail: gramlyng@hotmail.com.

COLTON COUNTRY DAY. July 17. Colton, NY. Annual flea market, live entertainment, museum exhibits. Special programs to be announced. Annually, the third weekend in July. Sponsor: Colton Historical Society. Est attendance: 1,500. For info: Dennis Eickhoff, Town Historian, PO Box 493, South Colton, NY 13687. Phone: (315) 262-2800. E-mail: eickhoff@northnet.org.

COW APPRECIATION DAY. July 17. Woodstock, VT. A "cowledge bowl" competition, dairy education programs, butter and ice cream making and more. Est attendance: 300. For info: Billings Farm & Museum, Box 489, Woodstock, VT 05091. Phone: (802) 457-2355. Fax: (802) 457-4663. E-mail: billings.farm@valley.net. Web: www.billingsfarm.org.

CZAR NICHOLAS II AND FAMILY EXECUTED: ANNIVERSARY. July 17, 1918. Russian Czar Nicholas II; his wife Alexandra; son and heir Alexis; and daughters Anastasia, Tatiana, Olga and Marie were executed by firing squad on this date. The murder of the last of the 300-year-old Romanov dynasty occurred at Yekaterinburg, in the Ural mountains of Siberia where Nicholas had been imprisoned since his abdication in 1917. Local Soviet officials, concerned about advancing pro-monarchist forces, executed the royal family rather than have them serve as a rallying point for the White Russians. In 1992 two of nine skeletons dug up the previous summer from a pit at Yekaterinburg were identified as the remains of the czar and czarina.

DISNEYLAND OPENED: ANNIVERSARY. July 17, 1955. Disneyland, America's first theme park, opened at Anaheim, CA.

EIGHTEENTH-CENTURY SUMMER MARKET FAIR. July 17–18. McLean, VA. Eighteenth-century games, music and crafts. Militia will drill. Est attendance: 5,000. For info: Claude Moore Colonial Farm at Turkey Run, 6310 Georgetown Pike, McLean, VA 22101. Phone: (703) 442-7557. Fax: (703) 442-0714. Web: www.1771.org.

FINLAND: PORI JAZZ FESTIVAL. July 17–25. Pori. 39th international festival presenting the jazz music of today with top-name performances. 13 different venues; some go on all night. Est attendance: 150,000. For info: Finnish Tourist Board, 655 Third Ave, New York, NY 10017. Phone: (212) 885-9700 or (358) (2) 626-2200. Fax: (358) (2) 626-2225. E-mail: festival@porijazz.fi. Web: www.porijazz.com.

GARDNER, ERLE STANLEY: BIRTH ANNIVERSARY. July 17, 1889. American author of detective fiction, born at Malden, MA. Best remembered for his series about lawyer-detective Perry Mason, Gardner also wrote novels under the pen name A.A. Fair. Gardner died at Temecula, CA, Mar 11, 1970.

GERRY, ELBRIDGE: BIRTH ANNIVERSARY. July 17, 1744. Fifth vice president of the US (1813–14), born at Marblehead, MA. Died at Washington, DC, Nov 23, 1814. His name became part of the language (gerrymander) after he signed a redistricting bill favoring his party while governor of Massachusetts in 1812.

HIGHLIGHTS® FOUNDATION WRITER'S WORKSHOP. July 17–24. Chautauqua, NY. This workshop is designed to help authors interested in writing for children. Writer workshops offered at beginner, intermediate and advanced levels. Classes offered include Children's Poetry, Book Promotion, Autobiographical Writing, and more. Workshop is held annually. Scholarships are available for first-time attendees. For info: Highlights Foundation, 814 Court St, Honesdale, PA 18431. Phone: (570) 253-1192. Fax: (570) 253-0179. E-mail: contact@highlightsfoundation.org. Web: www.highlightsfoundation.org.

JOHN MICHAEL KOHLER ARTS CENTER'S OUTDOOR ARTS FESTIVAL. July 17–18. Sheboygan, WI. 34th annual festival. A multiarts extravaganza featuring the works of 145 artists, demonstrations, live entertainment, children's workshops and exhibition tours. Est attendance: 20,000. For info: John Michael Kohler Arts Center, 608 New York Ave, PO Box 489, Sheboygan, WI 53082-0489. Phone: (920) 458-6144. Fax: (920) 458-4473. Web: www.jmkac.org.

KANSAS CITY HOTEL DISASTER: ANNIVERSARY. July 17, 1981. Anniversary of the collapse of aerial walkways at the Hyatt Regency Hotel at Kansas City, MO. About 1,500 people were attending the popular weekly tea dance when, at about 7 PM, two concrete and steel skywalks that were suspended from the ceiling of the hotel's atrium broke loose and fell on guests in the crowded lobby, killing 114 people. In 1986 a state board revoked the licenses of two engineers convicted of gross negligence for their part in designing the hotel.

KBCO WORLD-CLASS ROCKFEST. July 17–18 (tentative). Winter Park Resort, Winter Park, CO. Music lovers have the opportunity to catch major national rock acts as well as up-and-coming regional performers within an ideal concert setting. Concert-goers set up blankets and coolers on Parkway trail for a great view of the stage amid a natural amphitheater. Est attendance: 16,000. For info: Winter Park Resort, PO Box 36, Winter Park, CO 80482. Phone: (800) 729-5813. Fax: (970) 726-1572. E-mail: wpinfo@mail.skiwinterpark.com. Web: winterparkresort.com.

KIDSPREE. July 17–18. Bicentennial Park, Aurora, CO. The Denver metro area's only free outdoor festival for kids, featuring 70 hands-on activities ranging from educational and recreational to the arts, including local and national children's entertainment. Annually, the third weekend in July. Est attendance: 35,000. For info: Special Events Assistant, City of Aurora, Aurora, CO 80012. Phone: (303) 360-0045. Fax: (303) 361-2954. E-mail: maddlema@auroragov.org. Web: www.auroraevents.org.

KOREA: CONSTITUTION DAY. July 17, 1948. Legal national holiday. Commemorates the proclamation of the constitution of the Republic of Korea in 1948. Ceremonies at Seoul's capitol plaza and all major cities.

MINIMUM LEGAL DRINKING AGE AT 21: 20th ANNIVERSARY. July 17, 1984. Mothers Against Drunk Driving (MADD) helped pass the 21 Minimum Legal Drinking Age (MLDA) law because it makes sense and saves lives. President Ronald Reagan signed MLDA federal legislation making it illegal for anyone under 21 to purchase or publicly possess alcohol. Approximately 20,000 young lives have been saved since the law was passed. For info: MADD. Phone: (800) GET-MADD. Web: www.madd.org.

July 17–18 ☆ Chase's 2004 Calendar of Events ☆

MOON PHASE: NEW MOON. July 17. Moon enters New Moon phase at 7:24 AM, EDT.

OREGON COAST MUSIC FESTIVAL. July 17–31. Coos Bay, OR. Musical celebration features regional, national and international artists performing symphonic, choral and chamber music, plus jazz and world music. Est attendance: 15,000. For info: Oregon Coast Music Festival, PO Box 663, Coos Bay, OR 97420. Phone/Fax: (541) 267-0938 or toll-free (877) 897-9350. Web: www.coosnet.com/music.

PUERTO RICO: MUÑOZ-RIVERA DAY. July 17. Public holiday on the anniversary of the birth of Luis Muñoz-Rivera. The Puerto Rican patriot, poet and journalist was born at Barranquitas, Puerto Rico, in 1859. He died at Santurce, a suburb of San Juan, Puerto Rico, Nov 15, 1916.

SHARK AWARENESS DAY. July 17. Jenkinson's Aquarium, Point Pleasant Beach, NJ. 10 AM–10 PM. Are sharks dangerous? Learn all about sharks and what you can do to protect them. A special artifact cart and shark stories for children will be presented throughout the day. You can even touch a live shark in our touch tank. Sharks are fed at 9 PM. Est attendance: 1,200. For info: Jenkinson's Aquarium, 300 Ocean Ave, Point Pleasant Beach, NJ 08742. Phone: (732) 899-1212. Fax: (732) 899-1717. E-mail: aquarium@jenkinsons.com. Web: www.jenkinsons.com.

SPACE MILESTONE: *APOLLO-SOYUZ* TEST PROJECT (US, USSR). July 17, 1975. After three years of planning, negotiation and preparation, the first US–USSR joint space project reached fruition with the linkup in space of *Apollo 18* (crew: T. Stafford, V. Brand, D. Slayton; landed in Pacific Ocean July 24, during 136th orbit) and *Soyuz 19* (crew: A.A. Leonov, V.N. Kubasov; landed July 21, after 96 orbits). *Apollo 18* and *Soyuz 19* were linked for 47 hours (July 17–19) while joint experiments and transfer of personnel and materials back and forth between craft took place. Launch date was July 15, 1975.

SPACE MILESTONE: *SOYUZ T-12* (USSR): 20th ANNIVERSARY. July 17, 1984. Cosmonaut Svetlana Savitskaya became the first woman to walk in space (July 25) and the first woman to make more than one space voyage. Docked at *Salyut 7* July 18 and returned to Earth July 29.

STEALTH BOMBER FLIGHT: 15th ANNIVERSARY. July 17, 1989. The B-2 Stealth bomber airplane was flown successfully over the desert near Palmdale, CA, for almost two hours. A decade of work and $22 billion reportedly were spent on the project prior to the first flight. Designed to penetrate Soviet radar, the B-2 Stealth bomber was said to be capable of delivering up to 25 tons of nuclear or other bombs. Average cost of each of the 132 bombers requested by the Air Force was estimated to be $530 million. On this first test flight the plane flew at speeds of up to 180 knots (200 mph) and was put through several types of turns. Higher speeds and retraction of the landing gear were left for subsequent test flights.

SUMMERSWAP. July 17. Heritage Park, Frankenmuth, MI. A beer can collectors and breweriana trade show. Breweriana is the collection of brewery memorabilia, including steins, cans, bottles, signs, coasters, mirrors, neon signs, etc. The show is attended by collectors from a 10–12-state area and Canada. Annually, the third Saturday in July. Est attendance: 350. For info: Dave Van Hine, Show Chairman, Beer Can Collectors of America, Mid-Michigan Chapter, 357 N Harvest Lane, Frankenmuth, MI 48734. Phone: (989) 652-9818. E-mail: davevanh@aol.com.

★ ★ ★

July 2004	S	M	T	W	T	F	S
					1	2	3
	4	5	6	7	8	9	10
	11	12	13	14	15	16	17
	18	19	20	21	22	23	24
	25	26	27	28	29	30	31

TOSS AWAY THE "COULD HAVES" AND "SHOULD HAVES" DAY. July 17. On this day, everyone will write down their "could haves" and "should haves" on a piece of paper, then throw that list in the trash. Then they will make this resolution: "From this day forward, I choose not to live in the past—the past is history that I can't change. I can do something about the present—I choose to live in the present." Annually, the third Saturday in July. For info: Martha Ross-Rodgers, 2442 Annie Circle, Chesapeake, VA 23323. Phone: (757) 558-4964. Fax: (757) 558-4965. E-mail: MRossrodge@aol.com. Web: www.jirehpublishers.com.

"WRONG WAY" CORRIGAN DAY: ANNIVERSARY. July 17, 1938. Douglas Groce Corrigan, an unemployed airplane mechanic, left Brooklyn, NY's Floyd Bennett Field, ostensibly headed for Los Angeles, CA, in a 1929 Curtiss Robin monoplane. He landed 28 hours, 13 minutes later at Dublin, Ireland's Baldonnell Airport after a 3,150-mile nonstop flight without radio or special navigation equipment and in violation of American and Irish flight regulations. Born at Galveston, TX, Jan 22, 1907, Corrigan received a hero's welcome home; he was nicknamed "Wrong Way" Corrigan because he claimed he accidentally followed the wrong end of his compass needle. Died at New York, NY, Dec 9, 1995.

BIRTHDAYS TODAY

Lucie Arnaz, 53, actress ("Here's Lucy," "The Lucie Arnaz Show," *Lost in Yonkers*), born Los Angeles, CA, July 17, 1951.

Diahann Carroll, 69, singer, actress ("Julia," "Dynasty"), born Carol Diahann Johnson, New York, NY, July 17, 1935.

Phyllis Diller, 87, actress ("The Beautiful Phyllis Diller Show," *Boy, Did I Get a Wrong Number!*), born Phyllis Driver, Lima, OH, July 17, 1917.

David Hasselhoff, 52, actor ("Knight Rider," "Baywatch"), born Baltimore, MD, July 17, 1952.

Jason Jennings, 26, baseball player, born Dallas, TX, July 17, 1978.

Aaron Lansky, 49, founder of National Yiddish Book Center, born New Bedford, MA, July 17, 1955.

Pat McCormick, 70, writer ("The Jack Paar Show," "The Tonight Show"), actor (*Buffalo Bill and the Indians*), born Rocky River, OH, July 17, 1934.

Phoebe Snow, 52, singer ("Poetry Man"), born New York, NY, July 17, 1952.

Donald Sutherland, 69, actor (*M*A*S*H, Klute, Backdraft*), born St. John, NB, Canada, July 17, 1935.

Alex Winter, 39, actor (*Bill & Ted's Excellent Adventure*), born London, England, July 17, 1965.

JULY 18 — SUNDAY
Day 200 — 166 Remaining

ART FESTIVAL. July 18. Harvey Cedars, NJ. More than 75 artists participate in this festival. Est attendance: 1,500. For info: Harvey Cedars Activity Committee, PO Box 3185, Harvey Cedars, NJ 08008. Phone: (609) 361-7990. Web: www.harveycedars.org.

★**CAPTIVE NATIONS WEEK.** July 18–24. Presidential proclamation issued each year since 1959 for the third week of July. (PL86–90 of July 17, 1959.)

CHICAGO GOLF CLUB: ANNIVERSARY. July 18, 1893. The first 18-hole golf course in America, laid out by Charles Blair MacDonald, was incorporated at Wheaton, IL. MacDonald was the architect of many of the early US courses which he attempted to model on the best in Scotland and England. It was his belief that at each tee a golfer should face a hazard at the average distance of his shot.

CONCOURS d'ELEGANCE. July 18 (tentative). Forest Grove, OR. Set among the beauty of the Pacific University Campus, this is one of the premier car shows on the West Coast with 300+ beautifully restored vintage autos. A great family event. Annually, the third Sunday in July. Est attendance: 10,000. For info: Forest Grove Rotary Club, PO Box 387, Forest Grove, OR 97116. Phone: (503) 357-2300. Web: www.forestgroveconcours.org.

DIETARY MANAGERS ASSOCIATION ANNUAL MEETING AND EXPO. July 18–22. Silver Legacy, Reno, NV. 43rd annual meeting. Est attendance: 700. For info: Dennis Leopold, VP, Dietary Mgrs Assn, 406 Surrey Woods Dr, St. Charles, IL 60174-2386. Phone: (630) 587-6336. Fax: (630) 587-6308.

EVANS, CHICK: BIRTH ANNIVERSARY. July 18, 1890. Charles (Chick) Evans, Jr, golfer born at Indianapolis, IN. Evans competed as an amateur against the best professionals in the early 20th century, winning the US Open in 1916. In the 1920s he established the Chick Evans Caddie Foundation, later called the Evans Scholarship Fund, that has helped send more than 4,000 people to college. Died at Chicago, IL, Nov 6, 1979.

FAIRBANKS SUMMER ARTS FESTIVAL. July 18–Aug 1. University of Alaska, Fairbanks, AK. A unique study-performance festival involving workshops and master classes in visual and performing arts with more than 75 prestigious guest artists. Performance opportunities in orchestra, jazz band, jazz, choral groups, dance, opera theatre and ice skating. Est attendance: 12,500. For info: Jo Ryman Scott, Fairbanks Summer Arts Festival, Box 80845, Fairbanks, AK 99708. Phone: (907) 474-8869. Fax: (907) 479-4329. E-mail: festival@ptialaska.net. Web: www.fsaf.org.

FIRST PERFECT SCORE IN OLYMPIC HISTORY: ANNIVERSARY. July 18, 1976. At the Montreal Olympics, Romanian gymnast Nadia Comaneci scored the first "10" in Olympic history with her flawless performance of the compulsory exercise on the uneven bars. The scoreboard displayed a "1.00" because it couldn't go up to "10." Comaneci had seven total perfect scores and won five medals, including the gold for all-around performance. Four months previous to the Olympics, Comaneci had scored the first perfect score in international gymnastic competition history.

FULLER, BOBBY: DEATH ANNIVERSARY. July 18, 1966. Bobby Fuller, leader of the rock group Bobby Fuller Four, was found dead in his car at Los Angeles, CA. No definite cause of death was ever proven. The Bobby Fuller Four is best remembered for their 1966 hit song "I Fought the Law," which was written by Sonny Curtis, a member of Buddy Holly's Crickets. Fuller was born Oct 22, 1942, at Baytown, TX.

GROMYKO, ANDREI ANDREYEVICH: 95th BIRTH ANNIVERSARY. July 18, 1909. Soviet diplomat and statesman, born at Byelorussia, USSR. Gromyko played a leading role in Soviet history from World War II until the early days of Mikhail Gorbachev's reform programs. He entered diplomatic service in 1939 with a post in the Soviet Embassy in Washington, DC, and four years later was promoted to ambassador at the age of 34. He was instrumental in bringing the US, Britain and the USSR together for conferences in Yalta, Potsdam and Tehran. He became deputy foreign minister and permanent representative to the United Nations in 1946. Appointed foreign minister in February 1957, he became the voice of the Soviet Union in international debate. He was given the mostly ceremonial post of state president after Gorbachev's ascension in 1985 and retained that post until his death July 2, 1989, at Moscow.

HAYAKAWA, SAMUEL ICHIYE: BIRTH ANNIVERSARY. July 18, 1906. S.I. Hayakawa was born at Vancouver, BC, and came to the US in 1927. An academic, in 1968 he was appointed acting president of San Francisco State College. During student demonstrations on his first day in office he climbed atop a sound truck and disconnected the wires, silencing the demonstrators. His actions gained him enormous popularity among conservatives and he was promoted to permanent president by Governor Ronald Reagan. As his popularity grew he switched from the Democratic to the Republican party and in 1976 was elected to the US Senate. He led the successful California initiative to declare English the state's official language in 1986. Hayakawa wrote nine textbooks on language and semantics. He died Feb 27, 1992, at Greenbrae, CA.

ITALY: FEAST OF THE REDEEMER. July 18. Venice. Procession of gondolas and other craft commemorating the end of the epidemic of 1575. Annually, the third Sunday in July.

JAPAN'S RULING PARTY SINCE 1955 LOSES PARLIAMENT MAJORITY: ANNIVERSARY. July 18, 1993. Japan's Liberal Democratic Party, the ruling conservative branch of the government, lost the majority in the general elections. They won only 223 seats in the 511-seat lower house, the more powerful of Japan's two houses. The party had held the majority since its inception in 1955. On July 22 Premier Kiichi Miyazawa resigned.

LUXEMBOURG: BEER FESTIVAL. July 18. At Diekirch an annual beer festival is held on the third Sunday in July.

MANDELA, NELSON: BIRTHDAY. July 18, 1918. Former South African President Nelson Rolihlahla Mandela was born the son of a Tembu tribal chieftain at Qunu, near Umtata, in the Transkei territory of South Africa. Giving up his hereditary rights, Mandela chose to become a lawyer and earned his degree at the University of South Africa. He joined the African National Congress (ANC) in 1944, eventually becoming deputy national president in 1952. His activities in the struggle against apartheid resulted in his conviction for sabotage in 1964. During his 28 years in jail, Mandela remained a symbol of hope to South Africa's nonwhite majority, the demand for his release a rallying cry for civil rights activists. That release finally came Feb 11, 1990, as millions watched via satellite television. In 1994 Mandela was elected President of South Africa in the first all-race election there. See also: "Mandela, Nelson: Prison Release Anniversary" (Feb 11).

NATIONAL ICE CREAM DAY. July 18. To promote America's favorite dessert, ice cream, on "Sundae Sunday." Annually, the third Sunday in July.

NATIONAL INDEPENDENT RETAILERS WEEK. July 18–24. The week to celebrate and promote those who own and manage the thousands of independent retail businesses around the world. For info: Tom Shay, Profits Plus Seminars, PO Box 1577, St. Petersburg, FL 33731. Phone: (727) 464-2182. Fax: (727) 898-3179. E-mail: TomShay@profitsplus.org. Web: www.profitsplus.org.

ODETS, CLIFFORD: BIRTH ANNIVERSARY. July 18, 1906. Clifford Odets began his writing career as a poet before turning to acting. He helped found the Group Theatre in 1931. In 1935 he returned to writing with works for the Group Theatre such as *Waiting for Lefty, Awake and Sing!* and *Golden Boy*. His proletarian views helped make him a popular playwright during the Depression years. Odets was born at Philadelphia, PA, and died at Los Angeles, CA, Aug 15, 1963.

PRESIDENTIAL SUCCESSION ACT: ANNIVERSARY. July 18, 1947. President Harry S Truman signed an Executive Order determining the line of succession should the president be temporarily incapacitated or die in office. The speaker of the house and president pro tem of the senate are next in succession after the vice president. This line of succession became the 25th Amendment to the Constitution, which was ratified Feb 10, 1967.

RUTLEDGE, JOHN: DEATH ANNIVERSARY. July 18, 1800. American statesman, associate justice on the Supreme Court, born at Charleston, SC, in September 1739. Nominated second Chief Justice of the Supreme Court to succeed John Jay

July 18-19 ☆ Chase's 2004 Calendar of Events ☆

and served as Acting Chief Justice until his confirmation was denied because of his opposition to the Jay Treaty. He died at Charleston, SC.

SAINT CYRIL'S PARISH FESTIVAL. July 18. Kiwanis Park, Sheboygan, WI. Slovenian foods, music, games, raffle 10:30 AM–7 PM. Polka Mass at 10:30 AM, $3,000 bingo at 1 PM under the Big Top tent. Est attendance: 5,000. For info: St. Cyril & Methodius Parish, 822 New Jersey Ave, Sheboygan, WI 53081. Phone: (414) 457-7110.

SANTA FE CHAMBER MUSIC FESTIVAL. July 18–Aug 23. St. Francis Auditorium, Museum of Fine Arts and the Lensic Performing Arts Center, Santa Fe, NM. Highly acclaimed chamber music festival celebrates its 32nd season. Draws on international talent, featuring works from the baroque, romantic and classical periods, as well as contemporary works, including world premiere performances. Est attendance: 15,000. For info: Santa Fe Chamber Music Festival, PO Box 2227, Santa Fe, NM 87504. Phone: (505) 983-2075. Fax: (505) 986-0251. E-mail: info@sfcmf.org. Web: www.sfcmf.org.

SPACE MILESTONE: *ROHINI 1* (INDIA). July 18, 1980. First successful launch from India, orbited 77-lb satellite.

SPAIN: CIVIL WAR BEGINS: ANNIVERSARY. July 18, 1936. General Francisco Franco led an uprising of army troops based in North Africa against the elected government of the Spanish Republic. Spain was quickly divided into a Nationalist and a Republican zone. Franco's Nationalists drew support from Fascist Italy and Nazi Germany. On Apr 1, 1939, the Nationalists won a complete victory when they entered Madrid. Franco ruled as dictator in Spain until his death in 1975.

THACKERAY, WILLIAM MAKEPEACE: BIRTH ANNIVERSARY. July 18, 1811. English author, best remembered for his novels *Pendennis* and *Vanity Fair*, was born at Calcutta, India, and died at London, England, Dec 23, 1863.

URUGUAY: CONSTITUTION DAY. July 18. National holiday. Commemorates the country's first constitution in 1830.

WHITE, GILBERT: BIRTH ANNIVERSARY. July 18, 1720. Born at Selborne, Hampshire, England, Gilbert White has been called the "father of British naturalists." His book *The Natural History of Selborne*, published in 1788, enjoyed immediate success and is said never to have been out of print. White died near his birthplace, June 26, 1793. His home survives as a museum.

WOODSTOCK FOLK FESTIVAL. July 18. Woodstock, IL. Folk, blues, storytelling and fiddle tunes will ring out at the 18th annual festival and musicians will fill the square with the sounds of guitars and singing, banjo and fiddle. Hammered dulcimer and harmonica. 12:30 PM–6:30 PM. For info: John Wetterholt, Woodstock Folk Festival, 3314 Elaine Dr, Woodstock, IL 60098. Phone: (815) 337-0353. E-mail: johnwbanjo@owc.net. Web: www.woodstockfolkmusic.com.

	S	M	T	W	T	F	S
July					1	2	3
	4	5	6	7	8	9	10
2004	11	12	13	14	15	16	17
	18	19	20	21	22	23	24
	25	26	27	28	29	30	31

BIRTHDAYS TODAY

James Brolin, 63, actor (Emmy for "Marcus Welby, MD"; "Hotel"), born Los Angeles, CA, July 18, 1941.
Richard Totten (Dick) Button, 75, sportscaster, Olympic gold medal figure skater, born Englewood, NJ, July 18, 1929.
Vin Diesel, 37, actor (*XXX, The Fast and the Furious, Pitch Black*), born Mark Vincent, New York, NY, July 18, 1967.
Dion DiMucci, 65, singer (Dion and the Belmonts), born the Bronx, NY, July 18, 1939.
Nick Faldo, 47, golfer, born Welwyn Garden City, England, July 18, 1957.
Steve Forbes, 57, publisher, chairman, Forbes Newspapers, born Morristown, NJ, July 18, 1947.
John Glenn, 83, astronaut, first American to orbit Earth, former US senator (D, Ohio), born Cambridge, OH, July 18, 1921.
Anfernee ("Penny") Hardaway, 32, basketball player, born Memphis, TN, July 18, 1972.
Elizabeth McGovern, 43, actress (*Ordinary People, Racing with the Moon*), born Evanston, IL, July 18, 1961.
Calvin Peete, 61, golfer, born Detroit, MI, July 18, 1943.
Martha Reeves, 63, lead singer (Martha & the Vandellas, "Power of Love"), born Detroit, MI, July 18, 1941.
Ricky Skaggs, 50, musician (bluegrass guitar), singer ("I Don't Care"), born Cordell, KY, July 18, 1954.
Hunter S. Thompson, 65, journalist, author (*Fear and Loathing on the Campaign Trail*), born Louisville, KY, July 18, 1939.
Joe Torre, 64, baseball manager and former player, born New York, NY, July 18, 1940.
Yevgeny Yevtushenko, 71, poet, born Zima, USSR, July 18, 1933.

JULY 19 — MONDAY
Day 201 — 165 Remaining

ATTACK ON FORT WAGNER: ANNIVERSARY. July 19, 1863. In a second attempt to capture Fort Wagner, outside Charleston, SC, Federal troops were repulsed after losing 1,515 men as opposed to Southern losses of only 174. The attack was led by the 54th Massachusetts Colored Infantry, commanded by Colonel Robert Gould Shaw, who was killed in the action. This was the first use of black troops in the war. The film *Glory* was based on the Massachusetts 54th, and this was the attack featured in the film. Fort Wagner was never taken by the Union.

DAYS OF '47 CELEBRATION. July 19–24. Salt Lake City, UT. Commemorates the arrival of pioneers into Great Salt Lake Valley on July 24, 1847 (a state holiday). Celebration includes royalty pageant, pops concert, art show, family fun day (town picnic), essay contest, Pioneers of Progress awards banquet honoring modern pioneers and three great parades—youth parade (all children and mini floats), horse parade and annual 24th of July parade (one of the nation's oldest and largest). PRCA World Champion Rodeo nightly (except Sundays). Sponsor: Days of '47 Committee. Est attendance: 500,000. For info: Days of '47, Inc, PO Box 112287, Salt Lake City, UT 84147-2287. Phone: (801) 250-3890. Web: www.daysof47.com.

DEGAS, EDGAR: BIRTH ANNIVERSARY. July 19, 1834. French Impressionist painter, especially noted for his paintings of dancers in motion, was born at Paris, France, and died there Sept 26, 1917.

ELVIS PRESLEY'S FIRST SINGLE RELEASED: 50th ANNIVERSARY. July 19, 1954. "That's All Right (Mama)" backed by "Blue Moon of Kentucky" was released on this date by Sun Records of Memphis, TN. It was 19-year-old Elvis Presley's first professional record. Presley recorded it with guitarist Scotty Moore and bassist Bill Black. Memphis DJ Dewey Phillips previewed the single on July 7—literally two days after it was recorded—on his radio show and his listeners went crazy, demanding that Phillips play it again and again. See also "Elvis Presley's First Concert Appearance: Anniversary" (July 30).

☆ Chase's 2004 Calendar of Events ☆ July 19–20

FIRST WOMAN VICE-PRESIDENTIAL CANDIDATE: 20th ANNIVERSARY. July 19, 1984. Congresswoman Geraldine Ferraro was nominated to run with presidential candidate Walter Mondale on the Democratic ticket. They were defeated by the Republican ticket headed by Ronald Reagan.

***THE LORD OF THE RINGS*: FIRST PART PUBLISHED: 50th ANNIVERSARY.** July 19, 1954. *The Fellowship of the Ring*, the first part of J.R.R. Tolkien's epic *The Lord of the Rings* was published on this date in London, England by George Allen and Unwin. The publishers chose to publish the book in three parts because it was so long. *The Two Towers* was published on Nov 11, 1954, and *The Return of the King* was published on Oct 20, 1955.

MARILYN MONROE'S FIRST SCREEN TEST: ANNIVERSARY. July 19, 1946. Marilyn Monroe was given her first screen test at Twentieth Century-Fox Studios. Even with no sound, this test was all they needed to sign her first contract. Beginning with *Scudda-Hoo! Scudda-Hay!* in 1948 and ending with *The Misfits* in 1961, Monroe made a total of 29 films during her short career.

MAYO, CHARLES HORACE: BIRTH ANNIVERSARY. July 19, 1865. American surgeon, one of the Mayo brothers, founders of the Mayo Clinic and Mayo Foundation, born at Rochester, MN. Died at Chicago, IL, May 26, 1939.

MERRIAM, EVE: BIRTH ANNIVERSARY. July 19, 1916. A poet, playwright and author of more than 50 books for both adults and children. Merriam's works, which often focused on feminism, include *It Doesn't Always Have to Rhyme*; *After Nora Slammed the Door: The Women's Unfinished Revolution*; *Mommies at Work* and a book of poems attacked by authorities as glamorizing crime, *The Urban Mother Goose*. Her play *Out of Our Father's House*, portraying the lives of American women, was presented on public television's "Great Performances" series. She also wrote the first documentary on women's rights for network TV, *We the Women*. Born at Philadelphia, PA, she died at New York, NY, Apr 11, 1992.

NATIONAL GET OUT OF THE DOGHOUSE DAY. July 19. In trouble with someone you know and care about? This is the day when anyone can "Get out of the doghouse!" Annually, the third Monday in July. For info: Heidi Richards, Eden Florists and Gift Baskets, 7100 Pembroke Rd, Miramar, FL 33023. Phone: (954) 981-5515. E-mail: flowers@edenflorist.com. Web: www.eden florist.com.

NICARAGUA: NATIONAL LIBERATION DAY: 25th ANNIVERSARY. July 19. Following the National Day of Joy (July 17—anniversary of date in 1979 when dictator Anastasio Somoza Debayle fled Nicaragua) is annual July 19 observance of National Liberation Day, anniversary of day the National Liberation Army claimed victory over the Somoza dictatorship.

SAINT VINCENT DE PAUL: OLD FEAST DAY. July 19. A day remembering the founder of the Vincentian Congregation and the Sisters of Charity, born at Pouy, France, Apr 24, 1581. He died Sept 27, 1660, at Paris, France. His Feast Day was formerly observed on July 19 but is now observed on the anniversary of his death, Sept 27.

WOMEN'S RIGHTS CONVENTION AT SENECA FALLS: ANNIVERSARY. July 19, 1848. A convention concerning the rights of women, called by Lucretia Mott and Elizabeth Cady Stanton, was held at Seneca Falls, NY, July 19–20, 1848. The issues discussed included voting, property rights and divorce. The convention drafted a "Declaration of Sentiments" that paraphrased the Declaration of Independence, addressing man instead of King George, and called for women's "immediate admission to all the rights and privileges which belong to them as citizens of the United States." This convention was the beginning of an organized women's rights movement in the US. The most controversial issue was Stanton's demand for women's right to vote.

YALOW, ROSALYN: BIRTHDAY. July 19, 1921. Medical physicist Rosalyn Yalow was born at New York City. Along with Andrew V. Schally and Roger Guillemin, in 1977 Yalow was awarded the Nobel Prize for Physiology or Medicine. Through her research on medical applications of radioactive isotopes, Yalow developed RIA, a sensitive and simple technique used to measure minute concentrations of hormones and other substances in blood or other body fluids. First applied to the study of insulin concentration in the blood of diabetics, RIA was soon used in hundreds of other applications.

BIRTHDAYS TODAY

Vikki Carr, 63, singer ("It Must Be Him," "With Pen in Hand"), born Florencia Bisenta de Casilla, El Paso, TX, July 19, 1941.
Anthony Edwards, 42, actor ("ER," *Fast Times at Ridgemont High*, *Top Gun*), born Santa Barbara, CA, July 19, 1962.
Topher Grace, 26, actor ("That 70s Show," *Traffic*), born Christopher Grace, New York, NY, July 19, 1978.
Clea Lewis, 39, actress ("Ellen," *The Rich Man's Wife*), born Cleveland Heights, OH, July 19, 1965.
George Stanley McGovern, 82, former US senator and '72 Democratic presidential nominee, born Avon, SD, July 19, 1922.
Ilie Nastase, 58, former tennis player, born Bucharest, Romania, July 19, 1946.
Campbell Scott, 42, actor (*The Daytrippers*, *Hi-Life*), born Westchester County, NY, July 19, 1962.

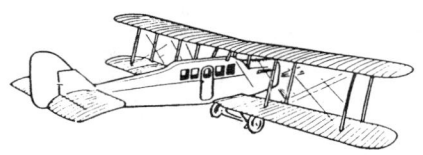

JULY 20 — TUESDAY
Day 202 — 164 Remaining

"ARTHUR MURRAY PARTY" TV PREMIERE: ANNIVERSARY. July 20, 1950. This ballroom dancing show appeared on all four networks (ABC, Dumont, CBS and NBC) and was hosted by Kathryn Murray, wife of famed dance school founder Arthur Murray.

ATTEMPT ON HITLER'S LIFE: 60th ANNIVERSARY. July 20, 1944. During the daily staff meeting at German Headquarters at Rastenburg, an attempt was made to assassinate Adolf Hitler. Count Claus Schenk von Stauffenberg, chosen from a group of German military and civil servants involved in the plot, left a briefcase containing a bomb only six feet from Hitler under the staff table in the briefing room. Four people were killed in the blast, but Hitler's life was saved probably because Colonel Heinz Brandt (who was among those killed) found the briefcase in his way and moved it farther from the German dictator.

BASEBALL DECLARED NON-ESSENTIAL OCCUPATION: ANNIVERSARY. July 20, 1918. Secretary of War Newton D. Baker ruled that baseball was a non-essential occupation. He stated that all players of draft age should seek "employment to aid successful prosecution of the war or shoulder guns and fight." On July 26, Baker allowed baseball to continue until Sept 1. Nearly 250 ballplayers entered the armed services.

COLOMBIA: INDEPENDENCE DAY. July 20. National holiday. Commemorates the beginning of the independence movement with an uprising against Spanish officials in 1810 at Bogotá. Colombia gained independence from Spain in 1819 when Simon Bolívar decisively defeated the Spanish.

GENEVA ACCORDS: 50th ANNIVERSARY. July 20, 1954. An agreement covering cessation of hostilities in Vietnam,

July 20 ☆ Chase's 2004 Calendar of Events ☆

signed at Geneva, Switzerland, on behalf of the commanders-in-chief of French forces at Vietnam and the People's Army of Vietnam. A further declaration of the Geneva Conference was released July 21, 1954. Partition, foreign troop withdrawal and elections for a unified government, within two years, were among provisions.

HILLARY, SIR EDMUND PERCIVAL: 85th BIRTHDAY. July 20, 1919. Explorer, mountaineer born at Auckland, New Zealand. With Tenzing Norgay, a Sherpa guide, became first to ascend summit of highest mountain in the world, Mt Everest (29,028 ft), at 11:30 AM, May 29, 1953. "We climbed because nobody climbed it before," he said.

JAPAN: MARINE DAY. July 20. National holiday.

LOCUST PLAGUE OF 1874: ANNIVERSARY. July 20–30, 1874. The Rocky Mountain locust, long a pest in the American Midwest, became an even bigger threat in the summer of 1874. Beginning in late July, the largest recorded swarm of this insect descended on the Great Plains. It is estimated that 124 billion insects formed a swarm 1,800 miles long and 110 miles wide that ranged from Canada and the Dakotas down to Texas. Contemporary accounts said that the locusts blocked out the sun and devastated farms in mere minutes. The swarms continued in smaller size for the next several years and caused an estimated $200 million in crop destruction.

"POORMAN'S PARADISE" GOLD PANNER CONTEST. July 20. Nome, AK. 104th anniversary. Open to all ages. Contestants pan a coffee can of beach material to free 3 small gold nuggets. All contestants are timed to determine the fastest gold-panner. Trophies for 1st, 2nd and 3rd place overall; 1st, 2nd and 3rd place 12 years and younger; 1st woman. Held on the Red Sand Beaches of the Bering Sea. Est attendance: 500. For info: Rasmussen's Music Mart, PO Box 2, Nome, AK 99762. Phone: (907) 443-2798 or (907) 443-2919. Or, Gold Prospector's Assn of America, 43445 Business Park Dr, Ste 113, Temecula, CA 92590. Phone: (800) 551-9707.

RIOT ACT: ANNIVERSARY. July 20, 1715. To "read the riot act" now usually means telling children to be quiet or less boisterous, but in 18th-century England reading the riot act was a more serious matter. On July 20, 1715, the Riot Act took effect. By law in England, if 12 or more persons were unlawfully assembled to the disturbance of the public peace an authority was required "with a loud voice" to command silence and read the riot act proclamation: "Our sovereign lord the king chargeth and commandeth all persons, being assembled, immediately to disperse themselves, and peaceably to depart to their habitations, or to their lawful business, upon the pains contained in the act made in the first year of King George, for preventing tumults and riotous assemblies. God save the king." Any persons who failed to obey within one hour were to be seized, apprehended and carried before a justice of the peace.

ROCKBRIDGE REGIONAL FAIR. July 20–24. Lexington, VA. Held at the Virginia Horse Center. 4-H Show, rodeo, carnival, exhibits (commercial and crafts), activities of all kinds. For info: Lexington Visitors Bureau, 106 E Washington St, Lexington, VA 24450. Phone: (540) 463-3777. Fax: (540) 463-1105. E-mail: lexington@rockbridge.net.

SAINT ANN'S ITALIAN STREET FESTIVAL. July 20–26. Hoboken, NJ. 94th annual festival features live entertainment nightly with top stars. Also, rides, games of chance, international foods, crafts and much more. Est attendance: 150,000. For info: Church of St. Ann, 704 Jefferson St, Hoboken, NJ 07030-2010. Phone: (201) 659-1114. Fax: (201) 659-1416. E-mail: churchan@bellatlantic.net. Web: www.st-annchurch.com.

SNAKE RIVER STAMPEDE. July 20–24. Nampa, ID. In its 89th year this is one of the top 15 professional rodeo events in the nation featuring the world's top cowboys and cowgirls in action. Events include bareback bronc riding, saddle bronc riding, bull riding, calf roping, team roping, steer wrestling and barrel racing. Est attendance: 40,000. For info: Jimmie Hurley, Snake River Stampede, PO Box 231, Nampa, ID 83653. Phone: (208) 466-8497. Fax: (208) 465-4438. E-mail: sstampede@earthlink.net.

SPACE MILESTONE: MOON DAY: 35th ANNIVERSARY. July 20, 1969. Anniversary of man's first landing on moon. Two US astronauts (Neil Alden Armstrong and Edwin Eugene Aldrin, Jr) landed lunar module *Eagle* at 4:17 PM, EDT and remained on lunar surface 21 hours, 36 minutes and 16 seconds. The landing was made from the Apollo XI's orbiting command and service module, code named *Columbia*, whose pilot, Michael Collins, remained aboard. Armstrong was first to set foot on the moon. Armstrong and Aldrin were outside the spacecraft, walking on the moon's surface, approximately 2¼ hours. The astronauts returned to Earth July 24, bringing photographs and rock samples.

SPECIAL OLYMPICS DAY. July 20. Official anniversary of the first ever International Special Olympics Competition, held in 1968 at Soldier Field, Chicago, IL. Special Olympics is an international year-round program of sports training and competition for individuals with mental retardation. More than one million athletes in over 150 countries train and compete in 26 Olympic-style summer and winter sports. Founded in 1968 by Eunice Kennedy Shriver, Special Olympics provides people with mental retardation continuing opportunities to develop fitness, demonstrate courage and experience joy as they participate in the sharing of gifts and friendship with other athletes, their families and the community. For info: Media Relations Mgr, Special Olympics, Inc, 1325 G St NW, Ste 500, Washington, DC 20005. Phone: (202) 824-0328. Fax: (202) 824-0337. E-mail: jenwezor@specialolympics.org. Web: www.specialolympics.org.

BIRTHDAYS TODAY

Ray Allen, 29, basketball player, born Merced, CA, July 20, 1975.
Kim Carnes, 58, singer ("Bette Davis Eyes"), songwriter (cowrote score *Flashdance*), born Hollywood, CA, July 20, 1946.
Judy Chicago, 65, artist, feminist, born Judy Cohen, Chicago, IL, July 20, 1939.
Larry E. Craig, 59, US Senator (R, Idaho), born Council, ID, July 20, 1945.
John Daley, 19, actor ("Freaks and Geeks"), born New York, NY, July 20, 1985.
Charles Joseph (Chuck) Daly, 74, Hall of Fame basketball coach, sportscaster, born St. Mary's, PA, July 20, 1930.
Donna Dixon, 47, actress ("Bosom Buddies," *Dr. Detroit*), born Alexandria, VA, July 20, 1957.
Peter Forsberg, 31, hockey player, born Ornskoldvik, Sweden, July 20, 1973.
Sir Edmund Hillary, 85, explorer (first to climb Mount Everest), born Auckland, New Zealand, July 20, 1919.
Sally Ann Howes, 74, actress (*Dead of Night, The History of Mr Polly*), singer, born London, England, July 20, 1930.
Michael Ilitch, 75, sports executive, former minor league baseball player, born Detroit, MI, July 20, 1929.
Barbara Ann Mikulski, 68, US Senator (D, Maryland), born Baltimore, MD, July 20, 1936.
Claudio Reyna, 31, soccer player, born Livingston, NJ, July 20, 1973.
Diana Rigg, 66, actress (Tony for *Medea; King Lear, Witness for the Prosecution*, "The Avengers"), born Doncaster, Yorkshire, England, July 20, 1938.
Carlos Santana, 57, musician, born Autlan, Mexico, July 20, 1947.

July 2004	S	M	T	W	T	F	S
					1	2	3
	4	5	6	7	8	9	10
	11	12	13	14	15	16	17
	18	19	20	21	22	23	24
	25	26	27	28	29	30	31

☆ Chase's 2004 Calendar of Events ☆   July 21

JULY 21 — WEDNESDAY
Day 203 — 163 Remaining

ANN ARBOR SUMMER ART FAIR®. July 21–24. Ann Arbor, MI. Juried art fair with more than 464 of the nation's finest artists and contemporary craftspeople. Free family art activity area, performance areas, artist showcase tent and print tent. Est attendance: 500,000. For info: John Yanchula, Art Fair Dir, Michigan Guild of Artists and Artisans, 118 N Fourth Ave, Ann Arbor, MI 48104-1402. Phone: (734) 662-3382. Fax: (734) 662-0339. E-mail: guild@michiganguild.org. Web: www.michiganguild.org.

BATTLE OF BULL RUN: ANNIVERSARY. July 21, 1861. Union Gen Irvin McDowell was defeated by Confederate troops led by Gen Joseph E. Johnston at the first Battle of Bull Run at Manassas, VA. It was the first major engagement of the war. It was during this battle that Confederate Gen T.J. Jackson won the nickname "Stonewall." In the Second Battle of Bull Run, Aug 29–30, 1862, Union Gen John Pope was badly defeated by Gen Robert E. Lee.

BELGIUM: NATIONAL HOLIDAY. July 21. Marks accession of first Belgian king, Leopold I in 1831, after independence from Netherlands.

CLEVELAND, FRANCES FOLSOM: BIRTH ANNIVERSARY. July 21, 1864. Wife of Grover Cleveland, 22nd and 24th president of the US, born at Buffalo, NY. She was the youngest First Lady at age 22, and the first to marry a president in the White House. Died at Princeton, NJ, Oct 29, 1947.

FAIRFEST. July 21–25. Adams County Fairgrounds, Hastings, NE. Annual county fair featuring midway; open-class competitions in culinary arts, needlework, floral culture, woodworking and the visual arts; Adams County 4-H competition, livestock show; strolling acts and live entertainment in the Grand Stand. Est attendance: 85,000. For info: Sandy Himmelberg, Genl Mgr, 947 S Baltimore, Hastings, NE 68901. Phone: (402) 462-3247. Fax: (402) 462-4731. Web: www.adamscountyfairgrounds.com.

FIRST ROBOT HOMICIDE: 20th ANNIVERSARY. July 21, 1984. The first reported killing of a human by a robot occurred at Jackson, MI. A robot turned and caught a 34-year-old worker between it and a safety bar, crushing him. He died of the injuries July 26, 1984. According to the National Institute for Occupational Safety and Health, it was "the first documented case of a robot-related fatality in the US."

GEORGIA MOUNTAIN FAIR. July 21–Aug 1. Georgia Mountain Fairgrounds, Hiawassee, GA. Authentic mountain demonstrations including corn millin', board splittin', soap and hominy makin' and others. Pioneer village with re-created one-room school, log cabin, barn and corncrib. Nashville talent, clogging, midway, arts and crafts and much more. Est attendance: 130,000. For info: Georgia Mountain Fair, PO Box 444, Hiawassee, GA 30546. Phone: (706) 896-4191.

GUAM: LIBERATION DAY: 60th ANNIVERSARY. July 21. National holiday. Commemorates US forces return to Guam in 1944, freeing the island from the Japanese.

HEMINGWAY BIRTHDAY CELEBRATION. July 21. Hemingway Birthplace, Oak Park, IL. Annual celebration of Ernest Hemingway's birth with a lecture and reception. For info: The Ernest Hemingway Foundation of Oak Park, PO Box 2222, Oak Park, IL 60303-2222. Phone: (800) HEMINGWAY. Fax: (708) 386-2952. Web: www.hemingway.org.

HEMINGWAY, ERNEST: BIRTH ANNIVERSARY. July 21, 1899. American short story writer and novelist born at Oak Park, IL. Made his name with such works as *The Sun Also Rises* (1926), *A Farewell to Arms* (1929), *For Whom the Bell Tolls* (1940) and *The Old Man and the Sea* (1952). He was awarded the Nobel Prize in 1954 and wrote little thereafter; he shot himself July 2, 1961, at Ketchum, ID, having been seriously ill for some time.

McLUHAN, MARSHALL: BIRTH ANNIVERSARY. July 21, 1911. (Herbert) Marshall McLuhan, university professor and author, called "the Canadian sage of the electronic age," was born at Edmonton, AB, Canada. *Understanding Media* and *The Medium Is the Massage* (not to be confused with his widely quoted aphorism: "The medium is the message"), among other books, were widely acclaimed for their fresh view of communication. McLuhan is reported to have said: "Most people are alive in an earlier time, but you must be alive in our own time." He died at Toronto, ON, Dec 31, 1980.

NATIONAL WOMEN'S HALL OF FAME: 25th ANNIVERSARY. July 21, 1979. Seneca Falls, NY. Founded to honor American women whose contributions "have been of the greatest value in the development of their country" and located in the community known as the "birthplace of women's rights," where the first Women's Suffrage Movement convention was held in 1848, the Hall of Fame was dedicated with 23 inductees. Earlier National Women's Hall of Fame, honoring "Twenty Outstanding Women of the Twentieth Century," was dedicated at New York World's Fair, on May 27, 1965.

NATIONAL WOODIE WAGON DAY. July 21. The "woodie wagon," made famous in the 1940s and '50s, romanticized the American outing. From Route 66 to the surfer lifestyle, the woodie wagon was there. On July 21 of each year, we will celebrate the dramatic comeback and popularity of woodies in the US. For info: Gregory Raymer, 11827 Brook Road, Golden, CO 80403. Phone: (303) 642-1510. Fax: (303) 642-3087. E-mail: gregoryraymer@yahoo.com.

BIRTHDAYS TODAY

Brandi Chastain, 36, soccer player, born San Jose, CA, July 21, 1968.
Lance Guest, 44, actor ("Lou Grant," *The Last Starfighter*), born Saratoga, CA, July 21, 1960.
Josh Hartnett, 26, actor (*Pearl Harbor, Halloween H2O*), born San Francisco, CA, July 21, 1978.
Edward Herrmann, 61, actor (*The Paper Chase, Eleanor and Franklin*), born Washington, DC, July 21, 1943.
Norman Jewison, 78, producer, director (*Moonstruck, Fiddler on the Roof*), born Toronto, ON, Canada, July 21, 1926.
Don Knotts, 80, actor, comedian ("The Andy Griffith Show," *The Ghost and Mr Chicken*), born Morgantown, WV, July 21, 1924.
Jon Lovitz, 47, actor (*A League of Their Own*, "NewsRadio"), born Tarzana, CA, July 21, 1957.
Matt Mulhern, 44, actor ("Major Dad," *Biloxi Blues*), born Philadelphia, PA, July 21, 1960.
Janet Reno, 66, former US Attorney General (Clinton administration), born Miami, FL, July 21, 1938.
C.C. Sabathia, 24, baseball player, born Vallejo, CA, July 21, 1980.
Cat Stevens, 56, singer, songwriter, born Stephen Demetri Georgiou (chosen Muslim name is Yusuf Islam), London, England, July 21, 1948.
Garry Trudeau, 55, political cartoonist ("Doonesbury"), born New York, NY, July 21, 1949.
Robin Williams, 52, actor ("Mork and Mindy," *Mrs Doubtfire, Dead Poets Society, Good Will Hunting*), born Chicago, IL, July 21, 1952.

JULY 22 — THURSDAY
Day 204 — 162 Remaining

ALLIES TAKE PALERMO: ANNIVERSARY. July 22, 1943. Two weeks after the July 10 Allied invasion of Sicily, the principal northern town of Palermo was captured. Americans had cut off 50,000 Italian troops in the west, but Germans were escaping to the northeastern corner of the island. After 39 days, on Aug 17, 1943, the entire island of Sicily was under the control of Allied forces. The official total of Germans and Italians captured was put at 130,000. The Germans, however, managed to transfer 60,000 of their 90,000 men back to the Italian mainland.

BIX BEIDERBECKE MEMORIAL JAZZ FESTIVAL. July 22–25. Davenport, IA. 33rd annual. Four-day jazz festival honoring the memory of and perpetuating the music of world-renowned cornetist, pianist and composer Bix Beiderbecke. Includes concerts in four venues, several races, arts, crafts, food, etc. Est attendance: 12,000. For info: Bix Beiderbecke Memorial Society, PO Box 3688, Davenport, IA 52808. Phone: (563) 324-7170. Fax: (563) 326-1732. E-mail: info@bixsociety.org. Web: www.bixsociety.org or www.visitquadcities.com.

CANADA: CALGARY FOLK MUSIC FESTIVAL. July 22–25. Calgary, AB. Celebration of local, national and international folk music. Est attendance: 40,000. For info: Kerry Clarke, Assoc Producer, Folk Festival Society of Calgary, PO Box 2897 Station M, Calgary, AB, Canada T2P 3C3. Phone: (403) 233-0904. E-mail: folkfest@canuck.com. Web: www.calgaryfolkfest.com.

DELAWARE STATE FAIR. July 22–31. Harrington, DE. 85th annual fair will feature major concert and motor events, acres of carnival rides, livestock shows, petting zoos, commercial and competitive events, exotic food and free attractions throughout the grounds. Est attendance: 280,000. For info: Delaware State Fair, PO Box 28, Harrington, DE 19952. Phone: (302) 398-3269. Fax: (302) 398-5030. E-mail: fair@delawarestatefair.com. Web: www.delawarestatefair.com.

DILLINGER, JOHN: 70th DEATH ANNIVERSARY. July 22, 1934. Bank robber, murderer, prison escapee and the first person to receive the FBI's appellation "Public Enemy No. 1" (July 1934). After nine years in prison (1924–33), Dillinger traveled through the Midwest, leaving a path of violent crimes. Reportedly betrayed by the "Lady in Red," he was killed by FBI agents as he left Chicago's Biograph movie theater (where he had watched *Manhattan Melodrama*, starring Clark Gable and Myrna Loy), July 22, 1934. He was born at Indianapolis, IN, June 28, 1902.

FALCON RIDGE FOLK FESTIVAL. July 22–25. Hillsdale, NY. A four-day community of folk music and dance at the foot of the Berkshires. Mainstage concerts, all-day and into the night dancing, camping, crafts and workshops. Plenty of activities for everyone in the family to enjoy at Long Hill Farm. For info: Falcon Ridge Folk Festival, 74 Modley Rd, Sharon, CT 06069. Phone: (860) 364-0366. Web: www.falconridgefolk.com.

GOLD DISCOVERY DAYS. July 22–25. Custer, SD. Parade, historic "Pageant of Paha Sapa," park festival, carnival, pancake breakfast, bed races, boat regatta, fun run, volksmarch and hot-air balloon rally. Est attendance: 6,000. For info: Custer Chamber of Commerce, 615 Washington St, Custer, SD 57730. Phone: (605) 673-2244 or (800) 992-9818. E-mail: custerchamber@gwtc.net. Web: www.custersd.com.

MENDEL, GREGOR JOHANN: BIRTH ANNIVERSARY. July 22, 1822. Botanist Gregor Mendel was born of peasant parents at Heinzendorf, Austria. His pioneering work in genetics became the basis for the modern science of genetics and heredity. Around 1856 Mendel began experiments in the small monastery garden, crossing different varieties of the garden pea. The import of Mendel's work was not seen until many years after his death, Jan 6, 1884, at Brünn. In 1900 other European botanists discovered his papers and confirmed and extended his theories, which formed the basis of the study of heredity and genetics.

MENNINGER, KARL: BIRTH ANNIVERSARY. July 22, 1893. American psychiatrist Karl Augustus Menninger was born at Topeka, KS. Along with his father and brother, he founded the Menninger Clinic and Foundation at Topeka in the 1920s. He died July 18, 1990, at Topeka.

PIED PIPER OF HAMELIN: ANNIVERSARY—MAYBE. July 22, 1376. According to legend, the German town of Hamelin, plagued with rats, bargained with a piper who promised to, and did, pipe the rats out of town and into the Weser River. Refused payment for his work, the piper then piped the children out of town and into a hole in a hill, never to be seen again. More recent historians suggest that the event occurred in 1284 when young men of Hamelin left the city on colonizing adventures.

RAT-CATCHERS DAY. July 22. A day to recognize the rat-catchers who labor to exterminate members of the genus *Rattus*, disease-carrying rodents that infest most of the "civilized" world. Observed on anniversary of the legendary feat of the Pied Piper of Hamelin on July 22, 1376 (according to 16th-century chronicler Richard Rowland Verstegen).

RILEY, JAMES WHITCOMB: DEATH ANNIVERSARY. July 22, 1916. American "Hoosier" poet, born at Greenfield, IN, Oct 7, probably in 1853, but possibly several years earlier. Riley died at Indianapolis, IN.

SPACE MILESTONE: *SOYUZ TM-3* (USSR). July 22, 1987. Two Soviet cosmonauts, Aleksandr Viktorenko and Aleksandr Aleksandrov, along with the first Syrian space traveler, Mohammed Faris, were launched on a projected 10-day mission. Launched from the Baikonur base in Central Asia, the spacecraft orbited Earth for two days before linking with Soviet space station *Mir*. The *Soyuz TM* spacecraft was used as a shuttle to *Mir* into the 1990s.

SPAIN: SAN SEBASTIAN JAZZ FESTIVAL. July 22–27. San Sebastian. This 39th annual festival is the oldest surviving jazz festival in Europe. Est attendance: 50,000. For info: Festival de Jazz San Sebastian, 2 Calle Camino, 20004 Donostia-San Sebastian, Spain. Phone: (34) (943) 440-034. Fax: (34) (943) 421-117. E-mail: jazzaldia.donostia@donostia.org. Web: www.jazzaldia.com.

SPOONER'S DAY (WILLIAM SPOONER BIRTH ANNIVERSARY). July 22. A day named for the Reverend William Archibald Spooner (born at London, England, July 22, 1844, warden of New College, Oxford, 1903–24, died at Oxford, England, Aug 29, 1930), whose frequent slips of the tongue led to coinage of the term *spoonerism* to describe them. A day to remember the scholarly man whose accidental transpositions gave us blushing crow (for crushing blow), tons of soil (for sons of toil), queer old dean (for dear old queen), swell foop (for fell swoop) and half-warmed fish (for half-formed wish).

☆ Chase's 2004 Calendar of Events ☆   July 22–23

BIRTHDAYS TODAY

Orson Bean, 76, actor ("To Tell the Truth," "Mary Hartman, Mary Hartman"), born Dallas Frederick Burroughs, Burlington, VT, July 22, 1928.

Irene Bedard, 37, actress ("Grand Avenue," "Crazy Horse," *Squanto: A Warrior's Tale*; voice of Pocahontas in the Disney film), born Anchorage, AK, July 22, 1967.

Albert Brooks, 57, comedian, director, actor (*Broadcast News, Mother*), born Albert Einstein, Los Angeles, CA, July 22, 1947.

Willem Dafoe, 49, actor (*Platoon, Mississippi Burning*), born Appleton, WI, July 22, 1955.

Oscar De La Renta, 72, fashion designer, born Santo Domingo, Dominican Republic, July 22, 1932.

Robert J. Dole, 81, former US senator (R, Kansas), born Russell, KS, July 22, 1923.

Rob Estes, 41, actor ("Melrose Place," "Silk Stalkings"), born Norfolk, VA, July 22, 1963.

Danny Glover, 57, actor ("Chiefs," *Lethal Weapon, The Color Purple*), born San Francisco, CA, July 22, 1947.

Don Henley, 57, musician (The Eagles), songwriter (cowrote "The Boys of Summer"), born Linden, TX, July 22, 1947.

Kay Bailey Hutchison, 61, US Senator (R, Texas), born Galveston, TX, July 22, 1943.

Rhys Ifans, 37, actor (*Notting Hill, Dancing at Lughnasa*), born Ruthin, Wales, July 22, 1967.

Keyshawn Johnson, 32, football player, born Los Angeles, CA, July 22, 1972.

John Leguizamo, 39, actor (*Carlito's Way*; stage: *Mambo Mouth* [also writer; Obie Award], *Spic-O-Rama* [also writer; Theatre World Award]), born Bogotá, Colombia, July 22, 1965.

Alan Menken, 55, film score composer (*Pocahontas, Aladdin*), born New Rochelle, NY, July 22, 1949.

Bobby Sherman, 59, singer, actor, born Santa Monica, CA, July 22, 1945.

David Spade, 39, actor ("Saturday Night Live," "Just Shoot Me," *Black Sheep*), born Birmingham, MI, July 22, 1965.

Terence Stamp, 65, actor (*Superman, Wall Street, Alien Nation*), born London, England, July 22, 1939.

Keith Sweat, 43, R&B singer, born New York, NY, July 22, 1961.

Alex Trebek, 64, game-show host ("Concentration," "Jeopardy"), born Sudbury, ON, Canada, July 22, 1940.

Margaret Whiting, 80, singer ("The Money Tree," "The Wheel of Hurt"), born Detroit, MI, July 22, 1924.

JULY 23 — FRIDAY
Day 205 — 161 Remaining

AEBLESKIVER DAYS. July 23–25. Tyler, MN. A celebration of the city's Danish heritage with Danish food, crafts and folk dancing. Est attendance: 3,000. For info: Tyler Area Chamber of Commerce, Box Q, Tyler, MN 56178. Phone: (507) 247-3905. Fax: (507) 247-5502. E-mail: tribute@tylertribute.com. Web: www.aebleskiverdays.com.

ANNIE OAKLEY DAYS. July 23–25. Greenville, OH. To keep alive the memory of Annie Oakley. Large antique and collectibles market. Est attendance: 60,000. For info: Annie Oakley Days Committee, Inc, PO Box 129, Greenville, OH 45331. Phone: (937) 548-1582. Fax: (937) 548-6711.

ARCADIA DAZE. July 23–25. Arcadia, MI. The scenic village of Arcadia is the setting for this midsummer event. Activities include a parade on Sunday at 1:30 PM on Lake Street. An art fair, steak fry, fishing contest, games for the children, pancake breakfast, 5K running race on Saturday and a street dance on Friday and Saturday. Car Show on Saturday. An old-fashioned good time for the whole family. Annually, the fourth weekend in July. Sponsor: Arcadia Lion's Club. Est attendance: 2,500. For info: Wesley Hull, Arcadia Daze, 3269 Lake St, Arcadia, MI 49613. Phone: (231) 889-5555.

ARTS IN THE PARK. July 23–25. Kalispell, MT. Annual juried arts and crafts show and fair, food and entertainment. Est attendance: 12,000. For info: AIP Coordinator, Hockaday Museum of Art, 302 Second Ave E, Kalispell, MT 59901. Phone: (406) 755-5268. Fax: (406) 755-2023. E-mail: artsinthepark@centurytel.net. Web: www.hockadayartmuseum.org.

BELE CHERE. July 23–25. Asheville, NC. A community celebration featuring three food courts, eight music stages, regional and national artists, children's area and events. The largest free outdoor street festival in the Southeast. Est attendance: 350,000. For info: Paul Clarke, Festival Coord, Asheville Parks & Rec/Festival Division, PO Box 7148, Asheville, NC 28802. Phone: (828) 259-5800. Web: www.belechere.com.

CANADA: ANNUAL NOVA SCOTIA BLUEGRASS AND OLDTIME MUSIC FESTIVAL. July 23–25. Mt Denson, NS. 33rd annual family event featuring acoustic music by groups from the US and Canada's Atlantic area. Annually, the last full weekend in July. Est attendance: 3,000. For info: Marilyn Craft, Promotions Director, Downeast Bluegrass Oldtime Music Society, 1766 Hwy #2, Alton, RR #2, Stewiacke, NS, Canada B0N 2J0. Phone: (902) 673-2597. E-mail: croftmd@ns.sympatico.ca.

CENTRAL NEBRASKA ETHNIC FESTIVAL. July 23–25 (tentative). Downtown Grand Island, NE. The streets come alive with color, music and foods from all ethnic cultures in the Central Nebraska area. Singing, dancing, eating, laughter and enjoyment for the whole family. Annually, the fourth weekend in July. Est attendance: 40,000. For info: Central Nebraska Ethnic Fest, PO Box 1306, Grand Island, NE 68802. Phone: (308) 385-5444. Fax: (308) 385-5423. Web: www.grand-island.com/ethnic.

CHEYENNE FRONTIER DAYS. July 23–Aug 1. Frontier Park, Cheyenne, WY. Held annually since 1897, the world's largest outdoor rodeo is the "Daddy of 'em All" with nine rodeos, nine night shows, three free pancake breakfasts, four parades, chuckwagon racing, carnival midway and exhibitors. Annually, the last full week in July. Est attendance: 210,000. For info: Cheyenne Frontier Days, PO Box 2477, Cheyenne, WY 82003. Phone: (800) 227-6336 or (307) 778-7200. Web: www.cfdrodeo.com.

DRYSDALE, DON: BIRTH ANNIVERSARY. July 23, 1936. Elected to the Baseball Hall of Fame in 1984, Don Drysdale was a pitcher for the Brooklyn and Los Angeles Dodgers from 1956 to 1969, compiling a won-lost record of 209–166 with a career ERA of 2.95. Following his playing career he became a successful and popular broadcast announcer for the Chicago White Sox and then for the Los Angeles Dodgers. He was born at Van Nuys, CA, and died at Montreal, QC, Canada, July 3, 1993.

EGYPT: REVOLUTION DAY. July 23, 1952. National holiday. Anniversary of the Revolution in 1952, which was launched by army officers and changed Egypt from a monarchy to a republic led by Nasser.

FIRST US SWIMMING SCHOOL OPENED: ANNIVERSARY. July 23, 1827. The first swimming school in the US opened at Boston, MA. Its pupils included John Quincy Adams and James Audubon.

"THE GENE AUTRY SHOW" TV PREMIERE: ANNIVERSARY. July 23, 1950. Popular CBS Western ran for six years starring movie actor Gene Autry. Along with sidekick Pat Buttram, Autry helped bring criminals to justice.

391

GILROY GARLIC FESTIVAL. July 23–25. Gilroy, CA. Midsummer harvest celebration in the "Garlic Capital of the World." Great garlic recipe contest/cookoff. Ethnic foods, continuous entertainment on three stages, arts, crafts and children's area. Est attendance: 130,000. For info: Gilroy Garlic Festival Assn, PO Box 2311, Gilroy, CA 95021. Phone: (408) 842-1625. Web: www.gilroygarlicfestival.com.

HARVEST WEEKENDS. July 23–25 (also July 30–Aug 1, Aug 6–8, 13–15 and 20–22). Bryan, TX. Step into the romance of winemaking by joining the Harvest Pickers Club and participate in hand-harvesting. A typical harvest weekend begins with a walk through the vines followed by the leisurely hand-harvesting of grapes. Afterward, you're invited to attend a classic European-style harvest luncheon that is followed by a wine and food pairing seminar. Annually, last two weekends of July and first three weekends of August to coincide with the grape harvest. For info: Steve Wiley, Mktg Dir, Messina Hof Wine Cellars, 4545 Old Reliance Rd, Bryan, TX 77808. Phone: (979) 778-9463. Fax: (979) 778-1729. Web: www.messinahof.com.

HOT ENOUGH FOR YA DAY. July 23. We are permitted today to utter the words that suffice when nothing of intelligence comes to mind. "Is is hot enough for ya?" Annually, July 23. [©2003 by WH.] For info: Thomas & Ruth Roy, Wellcat Holidays, 2418 Long Ln, Lebanon, PA 17046-1708. Phone: (717) 279-0184. E-mail: info@wellcat.com. Web: www.wellcat.com.

IOWA STORYTELLING FESTIVAL. July 23–24. City Park, Clear Lake, IA. This 16th annual storytelling event is held in a scenic lakeside setting. Friday evening "Stories After Dark." Two performances Saturday plus story exchange for novice tellers. Est attendance: 800. For info: Jean Casey, Dir, Clear Lake Public Library, 200 N 4th St, Clear Lake, IA 50428. Phone: (641) 357-6133. Fax: (641) 357-4645.

JAPAN: SOMA NO UMAOI (WILD HORSE CHASING). July 23–25. Hibarigahara, Haramachi, Fukushima Prefecture, Japan. 1,000 horsemen clad in ancient armor compete for possession of three shrine flags shot aloft on Hibarigahara Plain, and men in white costumes attempt to catch wild horses corralled by the horsemen.

LEO, THE LION. July 23–Aug 22. In the astronomical/astrological zodiac, which divides the sun's apparent orbit into 12 segments, the period July 23–Aug 22 is identified, traditionally, as the sun sign of Leo, the Lion. The ruling celestial body is the sun.

MOUNTAIN MAN RENDEZVOUS. July 23–31. Red Lodge, MT. Montana's fur-trapping era is re-created at an authentic mountain men rendezvous camp outside of Red Lodge. The camp residents are from around the country and they offer historical goods and crafts for sale as well as provide an opportunity for visitors to join in their rendezvous celebrations. There is music, dancing, games and food. Est attendance: 8,000. For info: Joan Cline, Red Lodge Chamber of Commerce, PO Box 988, Red Lodge, MT 59068. Phone: (406) 446-1718. Fax: (406) 446-1718. E-mail: information@redlodge.com. Web: www.redlodge.com.

NESHOBA COUNTY FAIR. July 23–30 (tentative). Philadelphia, MS. Billed as "Mississippi's Giant Houseparty," this is one of the nation's last Campground Fairs. At this 114th annual fair, harness racing, state and national political speaking, crafts, music and amusement are the order each day. Est attendance: 175,000. For info: Neshoba County Fair Assoc, 16800 Hwy 21 South, Philadelphia, MS 39350. Phone: (601) 656-8480. Fax: (601) 656-8461. E-mail: ncfa@netalpha.net. Web: www.neshobacountyfair.org.

NORTH DAKOTA STATE FAIR. July 23–31. Minot, ND. For nine days the State Fair features the best in big-name entertainment, farm and home exhibits, displays, the Midway and NPRA rodeo. Est attendance: 250,000. For info: North Dakota State Fair, Box 1796, Minot, ND 58702. Phone: (701) 857-7620. Fax: (701) 857-7622. E-mail: ndsf@minot.com. Web: www.ndstatefair.com.

OREGON BREWERS FESTIVAL. July 23–25. Tom McCall Waterfront Park, Portland, OR. Up to 90 microbreweries from across the country showcase their handcrafted brews to beer lovers. Annually, the last full weekend in July. Est attendance: 80,000. For info: Oregon Brewer's Festival. Phone: (503) 778-5917. Web: www.oregonbrewfest.com.

QUILT SHOW. July 23–25. K of C Hall, Clayton, NY. New and old quilts on display in this 11th annual show. For info: 1000 Islands Museum of Clayton, 312 James St, Clayton, NY 13624. Phone: (315) 686-5794. Fax: (315) 686-4867. E-mail: timuseum@gisco.net. Web: www.timuseum.org.

REESE, HAROLD HENRY ("PEE WEE"): BIRTH ANNIVERSARY. July 23, 1918. Hall of Fame shortstop, born at Ekron, KY. Died Aug 14, 1999, at Louisville, KY.

SAINT APOLLINARIS: FEAST DAY. July 23. First bishop of Ravenna, and a martyr, of unknown date. Observed July 23.

SONG OF HIAWATHA PAGEANT. July 23–25 (also July 30–Aug 1 and Aug 6–8). Pipestone, MN. 56th annual presentation of pageant based on Longfellow's poem, held in a natural outdoor amphitheater. Elaborate lighting, lovely costumes and cast of 200 help make an unforgettable event. Annually, last two weekends in July and first weekend in August. Sponsor: The Hiawatha Club. Est attendance: 12,000. For info: Mick Myers, Exec Dir, Pipestone Chamber of Commerce, PO Box 8 CAE, Pipestone, MN 56164. Phone: (507) 825-3316 or (800) 430-4126. Fax: (507) 825-3317. E-mail: pipecham@pipestoneminnesota.com. Web: www.pipestoneminnesota.com.

SPACE MILESTONE: FIRST FEMALE COMMANDER: *COLUMBIA* (US): 5th ANNIVERSARY. July 23, 1999. Colonel Eileen Collins led a shuttle mission to deploy a $1.5 billion x-ray telescope, the Chandra observatory, into space. It is a sister satellite to the Hubble Space Telescope. The observatory is named after Nobel Prize winner Subrahamyar Chandrasekhar.

SPACE MILESTONE: *SOYUZ 37* (USSR). July 23, 1980. Cosmonauts Viktor Gorbatko and, the first non-Caucasian in space, Lieutenant Colonel Pham Tuan (Vietnam), docked at *Salyut 6* July 24. Returned to Earth July 31.

STATE CRAFT FAIR. July 23–25 (tentative). Franklin & Marshall College, Lancaster, PA. 58th annual fair. High-quality juried craft show featuring the work of more than 250 members of the Pennsylvania Guild of Craftsmen. Demonstrations, seminars, Crafts and Antiques Road Show, food available. Indoors and air conditioned! Est attendance: 18,000. For information about tickets, or how to become a member, contact the PA Guild of Pennsylvania Guild of Craftsmen, 10 Stable Mill Trail, Richboro, PA 18954. Phone: (800) 684-7440. E-mail: pacraft@comcat.com. Web: www.pacrafts.com.

UFO DAYS. July 23–25. Elmwood, WI. Starts Friday evening at 6; ends Sunday. Annually, the last full weekend in July. Est attendance: 3,000. For info: Elmwood Community Club, PO Box 207, Elmwood, WI 54740.

July 2004	S	M	T	W	T	F	S
					1	2	3
	4	5	6	7	8	9	10
	11	12	13	14	15	16	17
	18	19	20	21	22	23	24
	25	26	27	28	29	30	31

☆ Chase's 2004 Calendar of Events ☆ July 23-24

BIRTHDAYS TODAY

Ronny Cox, 66, actor (*Deliverance, Bound for Glory, Total Recall*), born Cloudcroft, NM, July 23, 1938.
Gloria DeHaven, 79, actress (*Two Girls and a Sailor*, "Nakia"), born Los Angeles, CA, July 23, 1925.
Omar Epps, 31, actor (*Love & Basketball*), born Brooklyn, NY, July 23, 1973.
Nicholas Gage, 65, journalist, film producer, writer (*Eleni*), born Lia, Greece, July 23, 1939.
Nomar Garciaparra, 31, baseball player, born Whittier, CA, July 23, 1973.
Woody Harrelson, 43, actor (Emmy for "Cheers"; *White Men Can't Jump, Natural Born Killers*), born Midland, TX, July 23, 1961.
Don Imus, 64, radio talk-show host, media icon and author, born Riverside, CA, July 23, 1940.
Arata Isozaki, 73, architect, born Oita, Japan, July 23, 1931.
Anthony M. Kennedy, 68, Supreme Court Associate Justice, born Sacramento, CA, July 23, 1936.
Eriq La Salle, 42, actor ("ER," *Coming to America*), born Hartford, CT, July 23, 1962.
Edie McClurg, 53, actress ("WKRP in Cincinnati," *Eating Raoul, A River Runs Through It*), born Kansas City, MO, July 23, 1951.
Belinda Montgomery, 54, actress ("The Man From Atlantis," "Doogie Howser, MD"), born Winnipeg, MB, Canada, July 23, 1950.
Gary Dwayne Payton, 36, basketball player, born Oakland, CA, July 23, 1968.
Daniel Radcliffe, 15, actor (the Harry Potter films), born London, England, July 23, 1989 (some sources say July 31).
Marlon Wayans, 32, actor ("In Living Color," *Scary Movie*), born New York, NY, July 23, 1972.

JULY 24 — SATURDAY

Day 206 — 160 Remaining

ANTIQUE AND CLASSIC BOAT RENDEZVOUS. July 24–25. Mystic Seaport, Mystic, CT. Pre-1952 power and sailing yachts on view for Mystic Seaport visitors. Mystic River parade on Sunday. Est attendance: 4,000. For info: Mystic Seaport, 75 Greenmanville Ave, Box 6000, Mystic, CT 06355. Phone: (860) 527-5315 or (888) 9-SEAPORT. Web: www.visitmysticseaport.org.

ANTIQUE POWER EXHIBITION. July 24–25. Burton, OH. More than 100 old-time engines toot whistles and puff smoke as they demonstrate yesterday's feats such as wood sawing and grain threshing. Daily parades, slow races, tractor pulls. Est attendance: 2,600. For info: Century Village Museum, PO Box 153, Burton, OH 44021. Phone: (440) 834-1492. Fax: (440) 834-4012.

BOLÍVAR, SIMON: BIRTH ANNIVERSARY. July 24, 1783. "The Liberator," born at Caracas, Venezuela. Commemorated in Venezuela and other Latin American countries. Died Dec 17, 1830, at Santa Marta, Colombia. Bolivia is named after him.

CANADA: MINERAL CAPITAL ROCK SHOW. July 24. Bancroft, ON. Mineral specimens from central Ontario and Quebec dealers, mineral exhibits, lapidary demonstrations, silent auctions and grand live auction. Est attendance: 1,500. For info: Bancroft and District Chamber of Commerce, PO Box 539, Bancroft, ON, Canada K0L 1C0. Phone: (613) 332-1513. Fax: (613) 332-2119. E-mail: chamber@commerce.bancroft.on.ca. Web: www.BancroftDistrict.com.

COUSINS DAY. July 24. A day to celebrate, honor and appreciate our cousins. For info: Claudia A. Evart, 30 Park Ave, #2P, New York, NY 10016-3833. Phone: (212) 779-2227. E-mail: cevart1@earthlink.net.

DETROIT: ANNIVERSARY. July 24, 1701. Anniversary of the landing at the site of Detroit by Antoine de la Mothe Cadillac in the service of Louis XIV of France. Fort Pontchartrain du Detroit was first settlement on site.

DUMAS, ALEXANDRE: BIRTH ANNIVERSARY. July 24, 1802. French playwright and novelist, born at Villers-Cotterets, France. He is said to have written more than 300 volumes, including *The Count of Monte Cristo* and *The Three Musketeers*. Father of Alexandre Dumas (Dumas fils), also a novelist and playwright (1824–95). Dumas died near Dieppe, France, Dec 5, 1870.

EARHART, AMELIA: BIRTH ANNIVERSARY. July 24, 1897. American aviatrix lost on flight from New Guinea to Howland Island, in the Pacific Ocean, July 2, 1937. First woman to cross the Atlantic solo and fly solo across the Pacific from Hawaii to California. Born at Atchison, KS.

MID-SUMMER ANTIQUES AND COLLECTIBLES SHOW AND SALE. July 24–25. Millville, NJ. Rain or shine. Est attendance: 2,000. For info: Wheaton Village, 1501 Glasstown Rd, Millville, NJ 08332. Phone: (856) 825-6800 or (800) 998-4552. Fax: (856) 825-2410. E-mail: mail@wheatonvillage.org. Web: www.wheatonvillage.org.

MOON PHASE: FIRST QUARTER. July 24. Moon enters First Quarter phase at 11:37 PM, EDT.

NATHAN HALE ANCIENT FIFES AND DRUMS COLONIAL ENCAMPMENT AND MUSTER. July 24–25. Nathan Hale Homestead, Coventry, CT. Colonial battle reenactments, camp-life demonstrations, Colonial fashion show, open-hearth cooking and colonial crafts are highlights on Saturday. On Sunday, in addition to the above there is also a battle of colonial bands when fife and drum corps amass for a muster. Annually, the fourth Saturday and Sunday in July. For info: The Nathan Hale Homestead, 2299 South St, Coventry, CT 06238. Phone: (860) 742-6917.

PIONEER DAY: ANNIVERSARY. July 24, 1847. Utah. State holiday. Commemorates the day when Brigham Young and his followers entered the Salt Lake Valley.

RAF JAMS NAZI RADAR IN OPERATION GOMORRAH: ANNIVERSARY. July 24, 1943. On the first of the Royal Air Force Operation Gomorrah raids on Hamburg, Germany, "windows" (bales of 10½" strips of aluminum foil) were pushed out of the bombers causing the German radar screens to see a snowstorm of false echo "aircraft" on their screens. As a result only 12 of the 791 bombers sent on the mission were shot down.

VIRTUAL LOVE DAY. July 24. A worldwide celebration of online love and romance for all those who have experienced the excitement, joy and sorrow of Internet dating and relationships. For info: Judy Calheiros, PO Box 450236, Sunrise, FL 33345. Phone: (229) 392-0628. Fax: (954) 530-0700. E-mail: info@56days.com. Web: www.56days.com.

BIRTHDAYS TODAY

Barry Bonds, 40, baseball player, born Riverside, CA, July 24, 1964.
Ruth Buzzi, 68, comedienne, actress ("Rowan & Martin's Laugh-In," "Sesame Street"), born Westerly, RI, July 24, 1936.
Lynda Carter, 53, actress ("Wonder Woman," "Partners in Crime"), former Miss World–USA, singer, born Phoenix, AZ, July 24, 1951.
Kristin Chenoweth, 36, singer, actress (Tony for *You're A Good Man, Charlie Brown*; "Kristin"), born Tulsa, OK, July 24, 1968.
Kadeem Hardison, 39, actor ("A Different World," "The Sixth Man"), born New York, NY, July 24, 1965.
Robert Hays, 57, actor (*Airplane!*, "Starman"), born Bethesda, MD, July 24, 1947.
Julie A. Krone, 41, former jockey, first woman in National Racing Hall of Fame, born Benton Harbor, MI, July 24, 1963.

393

July 24–25 ☆ *Chase's 2004 Calendar of Events* ☆

Jennifer Lopez, 34, actress (*Selena, Blood and Wine*), born the Bronx, NY, July 24, 1970.
Karl Malone, 41, basketball player, born Summerfield, LA, July 24, 1963.
Pat Oliphant, 69, cartoonist, born Adelaide, Australia, July 24, 1935.
Anna Paquin, 22, actress (*The Piano, Fly Away Home*), born Winnipeg, MB, Canada, July 24, 1982.
Chris Sarandon, 62, actor (*Dog Day Afternoon, The Princess Bride*), born Beckley, WV, July 24, 1942.
Peter Serkin, 57, musician, born New York, NY, July 24, 1947.
Billy Taylor, 83, jazz musician, born Greenville, NC, July 24, 1921.

JULY 25 — SUNDAY
Day 207 — 159 Remaining

ANDREA DORIA SINKS: ANNIVERSARY. July 25, 1956. The Italian luxury liner collided with the *Stockholm*, a Swedish liner, on its way to New York. Other ships in the area came to the rescue of the *Andrea Doria*. 1,634 people were rescued during the ordeal, including the captain and the crew.

COSTA RICA: GUANACASTE DAY. July 25. National holiday. Commemorates the 1814 transfer of the region of Guanacaste from Nicaragua to Costa Rica by Spain.

DAY-OUT-OF-TIME. July 25. The worldwide festival of human creativity on Earth in tune to a New Time is a synchronized renewal of the Earth occuring each July 25. This planetary holiday has been celebrated for 10+ years by planetary kin following the Thirteen Moon/28-day calendar of natural time. For info: Foundation for the Law of Time, PAN World Headquarters, PO Box 513, Brightwood, OR 97011. Phone: (503) 622-1976. Fax: (503) 622-0198. E-mail: foundation@tortuga.com. Web: www.tortuga.com.

FIRST AIRPLANE CROSSING OF ENGLISH CHANNEL: 95th ANNIVERSARY. July 25, 1909. Louis Bleriot, after asking from the cockpit, "Where is England?" took off from Les Baraques (near Calais), France, and landed on English soil at Northfall Meadow, near Dover, where he was greeted first by English police and customs officers. This, the world's first international overseas airplane flight, was accomplished in a 28-hp monoplane with a wingspan of 23 ft. See also: "Bleriot, Louis: Birth Anniversary" (July 1).

GERMANY: WAGNER FESTSPIELE. July 25–Aug 28. Bayreuth. The works of Richard Wagner are performed daily at the Festival Theatre, which Wagner had built in 1872–76. For info: Bayreuther Festspiele, Pressebüro, Postfach 100262, Bayreuth, Germany D-95402.

GILFORD, JACK: BIRTH ANNIVERSARY. July 25, 1907. American actor Jack Gilford was born Jacob Gellman at New York, NY. Though he was blacklisted for 10 years following refusal to answer questions before the House Un-American Activities Committee in the 1950s, he appeared in many films, stage productions and television programs including an Academy Award–nominated role opposite Jack Lemmon in *Save the Tiger* (1973) and his best-known role as Hysterium in the stage and film versions of *A Funny Thing Happened on the Way to the Forum*. He died June 4, 1990, at New York, NY.

HARRISON, ANNA SYMMES: BIRTH ANNIVERSARY. July 25, 1775. Wife of William Henry Harrison, ninth president of the US, born at Morristown, NJ. Died at North Bend, IN, Feb 25, 1864.

LAVALLETTE HERITAGE ARTS AND CRAFTS SHOW. July 25 (rain date Aug 3). Lavallette, NJ. Juried arts, crafts and antiques show. Only the best of the best welcome to exhibit. One of the best shows on the eastern seaboard. 10 AM to dusk. Ribbon and cash awards given in both categories. Annually, the last Sunday in July. Est attendance: 20,000. For info: Joy Grosko, Heritage Committee of Lavallette, 13 Camden Ave, Lavallette, NJ 08735. Phone: (732) 793-3652. E-mail: tgrosko1@juno.com.

MUSSOLINI OUSTED: ANNIVERSARY. July 25, 1943. Two weeks after the Allied attack on Sicily began, the Fascist Grand Council met for the first time since December of 1939 and took a confidence vote resulting in Mussolini's being removed from office and placed under arrest. Italy's King Victor Emmanuel ordered Marshal Pietro Badoglio to form a new government.

NATIONAL SALAD WEEK. July 25–31. A week to educate consumers of the importance of incorporating more raw vegetables in their diet. Entrée salads are full healthy meals when served with breads. They can be made with or without grilled meats, tossed with tasty homemade dressings and garnished with fruits, nuts or raisins. Annually, the last week in July. For info: Teresa Penkwitz, MBA Marketing Company, c/o The Terrace Restaurant of Lawsonia Golf Courses, State Hwy 23, Green Lake, WI 54941. Phone: (920) 745-2873. E-mail: teresapenkwitz@charter.net.

★ **PARENTS' DAY.** July 25. To pay tribute to the men and women across our country whose devotion as parents strengthens our society and forms the foundation for a bright future for America. Public Law 103-362. Annually, the fourth Sunday in July.

PUERTO RICO: CONSTITUTION DAY. July 25. Also called Commonwealth Day or Occupation Day. Commemorates proclamation of constitution in 1952.

PUERTO RICO: LOIZA ALDEA FIESTA. July 25–28. Best known of Puerto Rico's patron saint festivities. Villagers of Loiza Aldea, 20 miles east of San Juan, don devil masks and colorful costumes for a variety of traditional activities.

REGISTER'S ANNUAL GREAT BICYCLE RIDE ACROSS IOWA. July 25–31. A weeklong bicycle ride across Iowa with 10,000 riders from across the country (and around the world). Annually, the last full week of July. After Nov 1 and before Mar 1 send a business-size SASE (two stamps) to the address below. Sponsor: *Des Moines Register*. Est attendance: 10,000. For info: RAGBRAI, PO Box 622, Des Moines, IA 50303-0622. Phone: (800) 474-3342. Fax: (515) 284-8138. E-mail: info@ragbrai.org. Web: www.ragbrai.org.

SPAIN: SAINT JAMES DAY. July 25. Holy day of the patron saint of Spain. When this day falls on a Sunday it is a holy year and pilgrims make the pilgrimage to Santiago de Compostela, the site of the saint's tomb. 2004 is thus a holy year.

SWITZERLAND: DORNACH BATTLE COMMEMORATION. July 25. The victory at Dornach in 1499 is remembered on the battlefield and in the city of Solothurn on the Sunday nearest to July 22. Dornach observes commemorative festival every five years.

TEST-TUBE BABY: BIRTHDAY. July 25, 1978. Anniversary of the birth of Louise Brown at Oldham, England. First documented birth of a baby conceived outside the body of a woman. Parents: Gilbert John and Lesley Brown, of Bristol, England. Physicians: Patrick Christopher Steptoe and Robert Geoffrey Edwards.

☆ **Chase's 2004 Calendar of Events** ☆   July 25–26

TUNISIA: REPUBLIC DAY. July 25. National holiday. Commemorates the proclamation of the republic in 1957.

W.C. HANDY MUSIC FESTIVAL. July 25–31. Florence, AL. A weeklong street-strutting, toe-tapping and hand-clapping celebration of the musical heritage of Florence native W.C. Handy—"the father of the blues"—culminating in a spectacular Saturday evening concert. Also includes athletic events. Est attendance: 150,000. For info: Nancy Gonce, Exec Dir, Music Preservation Society, PO Box 1827, Florence, AL 35631. Phone: (256) 766-7642. Fax: (256) 766-7549. Web: www.wchandyfest.org.

WSBA/WARM 103 SUMMER CRAFT SHOW. July 25. York Fairgrounds, York, PA. More than 150 crafts, from country to contemporary, Victorian and southwestern, handcrafted furniture, wood carvings, dolls, jewelry, pottery, collectibles, quilts, baskets and much more. Admission fee. Est attendance: 4,000. For info: Joe Alfano, Asst Promo Dir, PO Box 910, York, PA 17402-0910. Phone: (717) 764-1155. Fax: (717) 252-4708. E-mail: jalfano@suscom.com. Web: www.warm103.com.

BIRTHDAYS TODAY

Midge Decter, 77, journalist, born St. Paul, MN, July 25, 1927.
Illeana Douglas, 39, actress (*Message in a Bottle, Grace of My Heart*), born Boston, MA, July 25, 1965.
Estelle Getty, 80, actress ("Golden Girls"), born New York, NY, July 25, 1924.
Iman, 49, model, actress (*Star Trek VI*), born Iman Mohamed Abdulmajid, Mogadishu, Somalia, July 25, 1955.
Matt LeBlanc, 37, actor ("Friends"), born Newton, MA, July 25, 1967.
Evgeni Nabokov, 29, hockey player, born Kamenogorsk, the former USSR, July 25, 1975.
Brad Renfro, 22, actor (*Telling Lies in America, Tom and Huck*), born Knoxville, TN, July 25, 1982.
Nathaniel (Nate) Thurmond, 63, Hall of Fame basketball player, born Akron, OH, July 25, 1941.

JULY 26 — MONDAY
Day 208 — 158 Remaining

AMERICANS WITH DISABILITIES ACT SIGNED: ANNIVERSARY. July 26, 1990. President Bush signed the Americans with Disabilities Act, which went into effect two years later. It required that public facilities be made accessible to the disabled.

ARMED FORCES UNIFIED: ANNIVERSARY. July 26, 1947. President Truman signed legislation unifying the two branches of the armed forces into the Department of Defense. The branches merged were the War Department (Army) and the Navy. The Air Force was separated from the Army at the same time and made an independent force. Truman nominated James Forrestal to be the first Secretary of Defense. The legislation also provided for the National Security Council, the Central Intelligence Agency and the Joint Chiefs of Staff.

ATOMIC BOMB DELIVERED: ANNIVERSARY. July 26, 1945. The US cruiser *Indianapolis* arrived at Tinian Island in the Marianas with a deadly cargo. Aboard were the makings of the atomic bomb. On the island waited scientists prepared to complete the assembly. See also: "*Indianapolis* Sunk: Anniv" (July 29).

CATLIN, GEORGE: BIRTH ANNIVERSARY. July 26, 1796. American artist famous for his paintings of Native American life, born at Wilkes-Barre, PA. In 1832 he toured North and South American tribes, recording their lives in his work. He died Dec 23, 1872, at Jersey City, NJ.

CLINTON, GEORGE: BIRTH ANNIVERSARY. July 26, 1739 (OS). Fourth vice president of the US (1805–12), born at Little Britain, NY. Died at Washington, DC, Apr 20, 1812.

CUBA: NATIONAL DAY: ANNIVERSARY OF REVOLUTION. July 26. Anniversary of the 1953 beginning of Fidel Castro's revolutionary "26th of July Movement." He launched a failed attack on the Moncada army barracks, and most involved were killed or captured. He was captured and given a trial, during which he made his famous speech, "History Will Absolve Me." Sentenced to 15 years, he was pardoned after just two.

CURAÇAO: CURAÇAO DAY. July 26. "Although not officially recognized by the government as a holiday, various social entities commemorate the fact that on this day Alonso de Ojeda, a companion of Christopher Columbus, discovered the Island of Curaçao in 1499, sailing into Santa Ana Bay, the entrance of the harbor of Willemstad." Festivities on this day.

DEMOCRATIC NATIONAL CONVENTION. July 26–29. FleetCenter, Boston, MA. The Democratic Party meets to select its nominees for president and vice president in the 2004 election. Est attendance: 50,000. For info: Democratic National Committee, 430 S Capitol St SE, Washington, DC 20003. Phone: (202) 863-8000. Web: www.democrats.org.

HUXLEY, ALDOUS: BIRTH ANNIVERSARY. July 26, 1894. English author, satirist, mystic and philosopher, Aldous Leonard Huxley was born at Godalming, Surrey, England. Best known of his works are *Brave New World* and *Point Counter Point*. Huxley died at Los Angeles, CA, Nov 22, 1963.

JOHNSON COUNTY 4H AND FFA FAIR. July 26–29. Johnson County Fairgrounds, Iowa City, IA. For info: Gene Mohling, Secy, 4265 Crest Hill Rd SE, 4H Fairgrounds, Iowa City, IA 52246. Phone: (319) 337-6592 or (319) 337-5865. E-mail: plichte@iastate.edu.

KUBRICK, STANLEY: BIRTH ANNIVERSARY. July 26, 1928. American film writer and producer, born at the Bronx, NY. Kubrick started out in photography at the age of 16 with *Look* magazine. His first film, *Day of the Fight*, produced in 1950, was a documentary of his photo series about fighter Walter Cartier. His film credits include *Dr. Strangelove, Full Metal Jacket* and *2001: A Space Odyssey. Eyes Wide Shut*, Kubrick's final film, was released posthumously in the summer of 1999. He died at London, England, Mar 7, 1999.

LIBERIA: INDEPENDENCE DAY. July 26. National holiday. Became republic in 1847, under aegis of the US societies for repatriating former slaves in Africa.

MALDIVES: INDEPENDENCE DAY. July 26. National holiday. Commemorates independence from Britain in 1965.

NEW YORK RATIFICATION DAY. July 26, 1788. 11th state to ratify Constitution in 1788.

POTSDAM DECLARATION: ANNIVERSARY. July 26, 1945. As the Potsdam Conference came to a close in Germany, Churchill, Truman and China's representatives fashioned a communique to Japan offering it an opportunity to end the war. It demanded that Japan completely disarm, allowed them sovereignty to the four main islands and to minor islands to be determined by the Allies, and insisted that all Japanese citizens be given immediate and complete freedom of speech, religion and thought. The Japanese would be allowed to continue enough industry to maintain their economy. The communique concluded with a demand for unconditional surrender. Unaware these demands were backed up by an atomic bomb, on July 28 Japanese Prime Minister Admiral Kantaro Suzuki rejected the Potsdam Declaration.

July 26–27 ☆ Chase's 2004 Calendar of Events ☆

ROBARDS, JASON: BIRTH ANNIVERSARY. July 26, 1922. A staple on the American stage and screen for six decades, Robards was born at Chicago, IL, and was a decorated World War II veteran. He won the Oscar for Best Supporting Actor two years in a row, for 1976's *All the President's Men* and 1977's *Julia*. His most famous stage roles were in the plays of Eugene O'Neill, including *The Iceman Cometh* and *Long Day's Journey into Night*. He won the Tony Award in 1959 for his portrayal of a fictionalized F. Scott Fitzgerald in *The Disenchanted*. He died in Bridgeport, CT, Dec 26, 2000.

SHAW, GEORGE BERNARD: BIRTH ANNIVERSARY. July 26, 1856. Irish playwright, essayist, vegetarian, socialist, antivivisectionist and, he said, ". . . one of the hundred best playwrights in the world." Born at Dublin, Ireland. Died at Ayot St. Lawrence, England, Nov 2, 1950.

SOUTH DAKOTA STATE FAIR. July 26–Aug 1. Huron, SD. Grandstand entertainment nightly, two free stages with multiple shows daily, hundreds of commercial exhibits and thousands of livestock exhibits. One of the largest agricultural fairs in the US. Est attendance: 110,000. For info: South Dakota State Fair, PO Box 1275, Huron, SD 57350-1275. Phone: (605) 353-7340 or (800) 529-0900. Fax: (605) 353-7348. E-mail: statefair@state.sd.us.

SPACE MILESTONE: *APOLLO 15* (US). July 26, 1971. Launched this date. Astronauts David R. Scott and James B. Irwin landed on moon (lunar module *Falcon*) while Alfred M. Worden piloted command module *Endeavor*. *Rover 1*, a four-wheel vehicle, was used for further exploration. Departed moon Aug 2, after nearly three days. Pacific landing Aug 7.

US ARMY FIRST DESEGREGATION: 60th ANNIVERSARY. July 26, 1944. During WWII the US Army ordered desegregation of its training camp facilities. Later the same year black platoons were assigned to white companies in a tentative step toward integration of the battlefield. However, it was not until after the War—July 26, 1948—that President Harry Truman signed an order officially integrating the armed forces.

VIRGIN ISLANDS: HURRICANE SUPPLICATION DAY. July 26. Legal holiday. Population attends churches to pray for protection from hurricanes. Annually, the fourth Monday in July.

BIRTHDAYS TODAY

Kate Beckinsale, 31, actress (*Cold Comfort Farm, Pearl Harbor*), born London, England, July 26, 1973.
Sandra Bullock, 40, actress (*Speed, While You Were Sleeping*), born Arlington, VA, July 26, 1964.
Blake Edwards, 82, producer, writer, director (*Victor/Victoria, The Pink Panther*), born Tulsa, OK, July 26, 1922.
Susan George, 54, actress (*Straw Dogs*), born London, England, July 26, 1950.

	S	M	T	W	T	F	S
July 2004					1	2	3
	4	5	6	7	8	9	10
	11	12	13	14	15	16	17
	18	19	20	21	22	23	24
	25	26	27	28	29	30	31

Mick Jagger, 61, musician, lead singer (Rolling Stones), born Michael Philip Jagger, Dartford, England, July 26, 1943.
Helen Mirren, 58, actress ("Prime Suspect"; *The Cook, The Thief, His Wife and Her Lover*), born London, England, July 26, 1946.
Jeremy Piven, 40, actor ("Ellen," *Grosse Pointe Blank*), born New York, NY, July 26, 1964.
Kevin Spacey, 45, actor (Oscar for *American Beauty*; *The Usual Suspects, Working Girl*; stage: *Lost in Yonkers*), born South Orange, NJ, July 26, 1959.

JULY 27 — TUESDAY
Day 209 — 157 Remaining

ATLANTIC TELEGRAPH CABLE LAID: ANNIVERSARY. July 27, 1866. Cable laying successfully completed.

BARBOSA, JOSÉ CELSO: BIRTH ANNIVERSARY. July 27, 1857. Puerto Rican physician and patriot, born at Bayamon, Puerto Rico. His birthday is a holiday in Puerto Rico. He died at San Juan, Puerto Rico, Sept 21, 1921.

BROOME COUNTY FAIR. July 27–Aug 1. Whitney Point, NY. County agricultural fair. Est attendance: 39,000. For info: Rita Smith, Broome County Fair, PO Box 747, Whitney Point, NY 13862. Phone: (607) 692-4149.

DUMAS, ALEXANDRE (DUMAS FILS): BIRTH ANNIVERSARY. July 27, 1824. French novelist and playwright, as was his father. Author of *La Dame aux Camélias*. Dumas fils was born at Paris, and died at Marly-le-Roi, France, Nov 27, 1895.

DUROCHER, LEO: BIRTH ANNIVERSARY. July 27, 1905. Leo Durocher was born at West Springfield, MA. He began his major league baseball career with the New York Yankees in 1925. He also played for the St. Louis Cardinals' "Gashouse Gang" and the Brooklyn Dodgers, where he first served as player-manager in 1939. It was during that season that he used the phrase "Nice guys finish last," which would become his trademark. As a manager, he guided the New York Giants into two World Series. Following a five-year period away from baseball, he resurfaced as a coach with the Los Angeles Dodgers in 1961. In 1966 he signed with the Chicago Cubs as manager. After leaving the Cubs, he spent one season with the Houston Astros, then retired from baseball in 1973. He died Oct 7, 1991, at Palm Springs, CA.

EAA AIRVENTURE OSHKOSH. July 27–Aug 2. Wittman Regional Airport, Oshkosh, WI. World's largest sport aviation event. More than 10,000 airplanes annually fly in for this Experimental Aircraft Association event. Daily air shows, special programs, more than 500 forums, workshops and seminars. Est attendance: 750,000. For info: Dick Knapinski, Corporate Communications, Experimental Aircraft Assn, PO Box 3086, Oshkosh, WI 54903-3086. Phone: (920) 426-4800. E-mail: communications@eaa.org. Web: www.eaa.org.

HEALTH AND HAPPINESS WITH HYPNOSIS DAY. July 27. Participating members of the International Registry of Professional Hypnotherapists offer free seminars, free introductory hypnotherapy sessions, media appearances to publicize how hypnosis can help people be healthier and happier. Annually, the fourth Tuesday in July. For info: Dr. Bryan Knight, Intl Registry of Professional Hypnotherapists, 7306 Sherbrooke St West, Montreal, QC, Canada H4B 1R7. Phone: (514) 489-6733. Fax: (514) 485-3828. E-mail: drknight@hypnosis.org. Web: www.hypnosis.org.

INSULIN FIRST ISOLATED: ANNIVERSARY. July 27, 1921. Dr. Frederick Banting and his assistant at the University of Toronto Medical School, Charles Best, gave insulin to a dog whose pancreas had been removed. In 1922 insulin was first administered to a diabetic, a 14-year-old boy.

KOREAN WAR ARMISTICE: ANNIVERSARY. July 27, 1953. Armistice agreement ending war that had lasted three years and 32 days was signed at Panmunjom, Korea (July 26, US time)

☆ Chase's 2004 Calendar of Events ☆ July 27–28

by US and North Korean delegates. Both sides claimed victory at conclusion of two years, 17 days of truce negotiations.

★ **NATIONAL KOREAN WAR VETERANS ARMISTICE DAY.** July 27.

NORTH CENTRAL MISSOURI FAIR. July 27–31. North Central Missouri Fairgrounds, Trenton, MO. Carnival rides, professional vendors, parade, livestock, dairy demo. Art exhibits. Nightly events, such as Demolition Derby, bull riding, Mud Run and other entertainment. Est attendance: 2,500. For info: Trenton Area Chamber of Commerce, PO Box 84, Trenton, MO 64683. Phone: (660) 359-4324.

TAKE YOUR HOUSEPLANTS FOR A WALK DAY. July 27. Walking your plants around the neighborhood enables them to know their environment, thereby providing them with a sense of knowing, bringing on wellness. [©2003 by WH.] For info: Thomas & Ruth Roy, Wellcat Holidays, 2418 Long Ln, Lebanon, PA 17046. Phone: (717) 279-0184. E-mail: info@wellcat.com. Web: www.wellcat.com.

TISHA B'AV OR FAST OF AB. July 27. Hebrew calendar date: Ab 9, 5764. Commemorates and mourns the destruction of the first and second Temples in Jerusalem (586 BC and AD 70). Began at sundown July 26.

US DEPARTMENT OF STATE FOUNDED: ANNIVERSARY. July 27, 1789. The first presidential cabinet department, called the Department of Foreign Affairs, was established by the Congress. Later the name was changed to Department of State.

US JUNIOR AMATEUR (GOLF) CHAMPIONSHIP. July 27–31. The Olympic Club, San Francisco, CA. For info: US Golf Assn, Golf House, PO Box 708, Championship Dept, Far Hills, NJ 07931. Phone: (908) 234-2300. Fax: (908) 234-9687. E-mail: usga@usga.org. Web: www.usga.org.

BIRTHDAYS TODAY

Donald Evans, 58, US Secretary of Commerce, born Houston, TX, July 27, 1946.
Peggy Gale Fleming, 56, Olympic gold medal figure skater, sportscaster, born San Jose, CA, July 27, 1948.
Bobbie Gentry, 62, singer, songwriter ("Ode to Billie Joe"), born Roberta Streeter, Chicasaw County, MS, July 27, 1942.
Courtney Kupets, 18, gymnast, born Bedford, TX, July 27, 1986.
Norman Lear, 82, TV scriptwriter, producer ("All in the Family," "Maude"), born New Haven, CT, July 27, 1922.
Maureen McGovern, 55, singer ("The Morning After"), actress, born Youngstown, OH, July 27, 1949.
Alex Rodriguez, 29, baseball player, born New York, NY, July 27, 1975.
Betty Thomas, 56, director, actress ("Hill Street Blues"), born St. Louis, MO, July 27, 1948.
Jerry Van Dyke, 73, actor ("Coach," "Teen Angel"), born Danville, IL, July 27, 1931.
James Victor, 65, actor (*Fuzz, Stand and Deliver*), born Santiago, Dominican Republic, July 27, 1939.

JULY 28 — WEDNESDAY
Day 210 — 156 Remaining

AMERICAN PSYCHOLOGICAL ASSOCIATION ANNUAL MEETING. July 28–Aug 1. Honolulu, HI. For info: Convention Office, American Psychological Assn, 750 First St NE, Washington, DC 20002-4242. Phone: (202) 336-6020. E-mail: convention.office@apa.org. Web: www.apa.org.

BAGELFEST. July 28–31. Peterson Park, Mattoon, IL. 19th annual summer festival celebrating all things bagel. World's biggest bagel breakfast free on Saturday. Bagel parade Friday night. Bagel contests, arts and crafts vendors, food vendors and live free big-name entertainment Friday and Saturday nights (tickets required). Annually, the last full weekend of July. Est attendance: 40,000. For info: Mattoon Welcome Center, PO Box 431, Mattoon, IL 61938. Phone: (800) 500-6286. Fax: (217) 258-6480. Web: www.mattoonillinois.org.

CHINCOTEAGUE PONY PENNING. July 28–29. Chincoteague Island, VA. To round up the 150 wild ponies living on Assateague Island and swim them across the inlet to Chincoteague, where about 80–90 of them are sold. Annually, the last Wednesday and Thursday of July. Est attendance: 50,000. For info: Chincoteague Chamber of Commerce, Box 258, Chincoteague, VA 23336. Phone: (757) 336-6161. Fax: (757) 336-1242. E-mail: pony@intercom.net. Web: www.chincoteaguechamber.com.

FOX, TERRY: BIRTH ANNIVERSARY. July 28, 1958. With cancer requiring amputation of his right leg at age 18, Fox was determined to devote his life to a fight against the disease. His "Marathon of Hope," a planned 5,200-mile run westward across Canada, started Apr 12, 1980, at St. John's, NF, and continued 3,328 miles to Thunder Bay, ON, Sept 1, 1980, when he was forced to stop by spread of the disease. During the run (on an artificial leg) he raised $24 million for cancer research and inspired millions with his courage. Terry Fox was born at Winnipeg, MB, and died at New Westminster (near Vancouver), BC, Canada, June 28, 1981.

GARFIELD COUNTY FAIR. July 28–Aug 1. Burwell, NE. County fair, carnival, rodeo and commercial and craft concessions. Est attendance: 10,000. For info: Peggy Haskell, Garfield County Frontier Fair Assn, Box 747, Burwell, NE 68823. Phone: (308) 346-5210. Web: www.BurwellNebr.com.

HAMBURG FIRESTORM: ANNIVERSARY. July 28, 1943. More than 42,000 civilians were killed when 2,326 tons of bombs, predominantly incendiaries, were dropped on Hamburg, Germany, by the Allies on this date. At the center of the firestorm the winds uprooted trees, and flames burned eight square miles in the eight hours the fire lasted. A firestorm occurs when the fires in a given area become so intense they devour all the oxygen nearby and suck more into themselves creating hurricane-force winds which feed the fires and move them at great speeds.

HEYWARD, THOMAS: BIRTH ANNIVERSARY. July 28, 1746. American Revolutionary soldier, signer of the Declaration of Independence. Died Mar 6, 1809.

HOOD RIVER COUNTY FAIR. July 28–31. Hood River, OR. From 4-H activities to the excitement of the carnival, this annual old-fashioned country fair is bustling with things to do! 9 AM to 11:30 PM, Wed and Thurs; 9 AM to 12:30 PM, Fri and Sat EST. Est attendance: 23,000. For info: Hood River County Fair, Box 385, Odell, OR 97044. Phone: (541) 354-2865. Fax: (541) 354-2875.

NATIONAL DRIVE–THRU DAY. July 28. After WW II, California sunshine and a love affair with automobiles spurred the growth of roadside businesses in the Golden State catering specifically to motorists. As America's first major drive-thru hamburger chain, Jack in the Box® restaurants (founded in 1951) helped pave the way for a delicious new dining experience. Annually, on July 28. For info: Brian Luscomb, Jack in the Box, 9330 Balboa Ave, San Diego, CA 92123. Phone: (858) 571-2121. Web: www.jackinthebox.com.

397

July 28–29 ☆ Chase's 2004 Calendar of Events ☆

ONASSIS, JACQUELINE LEE BOUVIER KENNEDY: 75th BIRTH ANNIVERSARY. July 28, 1929. Editor, widow of John Fitzgerald Kennedy (35th president of the US), born at Southampton, NY. Later married (Oct 20, 1968) Greek shipping magnate Aristotle Socrates Onassis, who died Mar 15, 1975. The widely admired and respected former First Lady died May 19, 1994, at New York City.

PERU: INDEPENDENCE DAY. July 28. San Martin declared independence from Spain on this day in 1821. After the final defeat of Spanish troops by Simon Bolívar in 1824, Spanish rule ended.

POTTER, (HELEN) BEATRIX: BIRTH ANNIVERSARY. July 28, 1866. Author and illustrator of the Peter Rabbit stories for children, born at London, England. Died at Sawrey, Lancashire, Dec 22, 1943.

SINGING TELEGRAM: ANNIVERSARY. July 28, 1933. Anniversary of the first singing telegram, said to have been delivered to singer Rudy Vallee on his 32nd birthday. Early singing telegrams often were delivered in person by uniformed messengers on bicycle. Later they were usually sung over the telephone.

SPACE MILESTONE: SKYLAB 3 (US): ANNIVERSARY. July 28, 1973. Alan L. Bean, Owen K. Garriott and Jack R. Lousma started 59-day mission in the space station to test man's space flight endurance. Pacific splashdown Sept 25.

VALLEE, RUDY: BIRTH ANNIVERSARY. July 28, 1901. American singer, saxophone player and radio idol of millions during the 1930s. Born Hubert Prior Vallee at Island Pond, VT, the crooner used a megaphone to amplify his voice and introduced his performances with the salutation, "Heigh-ho-everybody!" Vallee appeared in a number of movies, including *How to Succeed in Business Without Really Trying*. Among his best-remembered songs are "I'm Just a Vagabond Lover," "Say It Isn't So" and his signature song, "My Time Is Your Time." Vallee died at age 84 at North Hollywood, CA, July 3, 1986.

VETERANS BONUS ARMY EVICTION: ANNIVERSARY. July 28, 1932. Some 15,000 unemployed veterans of World War I marched on Washington, DC, in the summer of 1932, demanding payment of a war bonus. After two months' encampment in Washington's Anacostia Flats, eviction of the bonus marchers by the US Army was ordered by President Herbert Hoover. Under the leadership of General Douglas MacArthur, Major Dwight D. Eisenhower and Major George S. Patton, Jr (among others), cavalry, tanks and infantry attacked. Fixed bayonets, tear gas and the burning of the veterans' tents hastened the end of the confrontation. One death was reported.

July 2004

S	M	T	W	T	F	S
				1	2	3
4	5	6	7	8	9	10
11	12	13	14	15	16	17
18	19	20	21	22	23	24
25	26	27	28	29	30	31

WORLD WAR I BEGINS: 90th ANNIVERSARY. July 28, 1914. Archduke Francis Ferdinand of Austria-Hungary and his wife were assassinated at Sarajevo, Bosnia, by a Serbian nationalist June 28, 1914, touching off the conflict that became WWI. Austria-Hungary declared war on Serbia July 28, the formal beginning of the war. Within weeks, Germany entered the war on the side of Austria-Hungary and Russia, France and Great Britain on the side of Serbia.

BIRTHDAYS TODAY

William Warren (Bill) Bradley, 61, former US senator, Hall of Fame basketball player, born Crystal City, MO, July 28, 1943.
Jim Davis, 59, cartoonist ("Garfield"), born Marion, IN, July 28, 1945.
Darryl Hickman, 73, actor ("The Many Loves of Dobie Gillis," "The Americans"), born Los Angeles, CA, July 28, 1931.
Linda Kelsey, 58, actress ("Lou Grant"), born Minneapolis, MN, July 28, 1946.
Lori Loughlin, 40, actress ("Full House," *Back to the Beach*), born Long Island, NY, July 28, 1964.
Judy Martz, 61, Governor of Montana (R), born Big Timber, MT, July 28, 1943.
Jacques Piccard, 82, inventor, explorer, born Brussels, Belgium, July 28, 1922.
Sally Struthers, 56, actress ("All in the Family"), born Portland, OR, July 28, 1948.
Rick Wright, 59, singer, musician (keyboard player with Pink Floyd), born London, England, July 28, 1945.

JULY 29 — THURSDAY
Day 211 — 155 Remaining

ADAMS COUNTY FAIR/RODEO. July 29–Aug 1. Hettinger, ND. 5th annual fair with booths, exhibits and special events. Est attendance: 2,500. For info: Community Promotions Office, PO Box 1031, Hettinger, ND 58639. Phone: (701) 567-2531. E-mail: adamschmbr@ndsupernet.com. Web: hettingernd.com.

BERNE SWISS DAYS. July 29–31. Berne, IN. Discover Switzerland in Indiana with Swiss food, dancing, yodeling and a parade. See quilt show, art show, "stein-toss" contest, polka bands, old-fashioned horse pull, musical, factory tours and more. Est attendance: 75,000. For info: Berne Chamber of Commerce, PO Box 85, Berne, IN 46711. Phone: (260) 589-8080. Web: www.berneswissdays.com.

CANADA: AGRIFAIR. July 29–Aug 2. Abbotsford, BC. Fun for everyone with attractions like draft horses, dairy, beef, llama and poultry; hands-on milking display; motor sports; my marketplace trade show; antique farm display bursting with antique toys; midway; plus everything from national and international stage entertainment to a pro rodeo and fireworks. Est attendance: 57,000. For info: Harvey Carroll, Abbotsford Agrifair, PO Box 2334, Abbotsford, BC, Canada V2T 4X2. Phone: (604) 852-6674. Fax: (604) 852-6631. E-mail: agrifair@telus.net.

CANADA: BIG VALLEY JAMBOREE. July 29–Aug 1. Camrose, AB. Canada's premier country music festival, featuring top-name entertainers and more than 25 acts. Beer gardens, trade shows, unserviced camping and parking. Est attendance: 70,000. For info: Glen Vinet, 4238-37 St, Camrose, AB, Canada T4V 4L6. Phone: (780) 672-0224 or (888) 404-1234. Fax: (780) 672-9530. E-mail: bvj@bigvalleyjamboree.com. Web: www.bigvalleyjamboree.com.

CANADA: ROCKHOUND GEMBOREE. July 29–Aug 1. Bancroft, ON. Daily expeditions to prime mineral locations; dealers, demonstrations and displays, swapping. Est attendance: 16,000. For info: Bancroft and District Chamber of Commerce, PO Box 539, Bancroft, ON, Canada K0L 1C0. Phone: (613) 332-1513. Fax: (613) 332-2119. E-mail: chamber@commerce.bancroft.on.ca. Web: www.bancroftdistrict.com.

☆ Chase's 2004 Calendar of Events ☆   July 29

GREAT TEXAS MOSQUITO FESTIVAL. July 29–31. Clute, TX. More than 100 booths: arts and crafts, food, entertainment, novelty games and carnival. Meet "Willie Man Chew," a 25-ft inflatable mosquito dressed in cowboy boots and hat. Annually, the last weekend in July. Est attendance: 20,000. For info: City of Clute Pks and Rec Dept, PO Box 997, Clute, TX 77531. Phone: (979) 265-8392 or (800) 371-2971. Fax: (979) 265-8767. E-mail: buzz@mosquitofestival.com. Web: www.mosquitofestival.com.

***INDIANAPOLIS* SUNK: ANNIVERSARY.** July 29, 1945. After delivering the atomic bomb to Tinian Island, the American cruiser *Indianapolis* was headed for Okinawa to train for the invasion of Japan when it was torpedoed by a Japanese submarine. Of 1,196 crew members, more than 350 were immediately killed in the explosion or went down with the ship. There were no rescue ships nearby, and those fortunate enough to survive endured the next 84 hours in ocean waters. By the time they were spotted by air on Aug 2, only 318 sailors remained alive, the others either having drowned or been eaten by sharks. This is the US Navy's worst loss at sea.

MUSSOLINI, BENITO: BIRTH ANNIVERSARY. July 29, 1883. Italian Fascist leader, born at Dovia, Italy. Self-styled "Il Duce" (the leader), Mussolini governed Italy, first as prime minister and later as absolute dictator, 1922–43. Reportedly, under his regime "the trains ran on time." It was Mussolini who said: "War alone . . . puts the stamp of nobility upon the peoples who have the courage to face it." But military defeat of Italy in World War II was Mussolini's downfall. Repudiated and arrested by the Italian government, he was temporarily rescued by German paratroops in 1943. Later, as they attempted to flee in disguise to Switzerland, he and his mistress, Clara Petacci, were killed by Italian partisans near Lake Como, Italy, Apr 28, 1945.

NASA ESTABLISHED: ANNIVERSARY. July 29, 1958. President Eisenhower signed a bill creating the National Aeronautics and Space Administration to direct US space policy.

NEBRASKA'S BIG RODEO. July 29–31. Fairgrounds, Burwell, NE. Professional rodeo. Contestants compete in four exciting performances in historic, outdoor rodeo arena. Added thrills: chuckwagon races, wild horse races, Dinnerbell Derby, bull fighting Burwell-style. Also, quilt and art shows, parade, flea market, beef and longhorn cattle show, country and western music and dancing. Est attendance: 10,000. For info: Peggy Haskell, Garfield County Frontier Fair Assn, Box 747, Burwell, NE 68823. Phone: (308) 346-5210 or (308) 346-5010 July 12–21. Web: www.BurwellNebr.com.

NEWBERRY LIBRARY'S TWENTIETH ANNUAL BOOK FAIR. July 29–Aug 1. Chicago, IL. More than 100,000 books have been sorted into 50 categories for your browsing convenience. With many books priced under a dollar, it's easy to restock your library with titles ranging from classics to pulp fiction. Est attendance: 7,000. For info: Newberry Library, 60 W. Walton, Chicago, IL 60610. Phone: (312) 255-3510. Web: www.newberry.org.

NORWAY: OLSOK EVE. July 29. Commemorates Norway's Viking king St. Olav, who fell in battle at Stiklestad near Trondheim, Norway, July 29, 1030. Bonfires, historical pageants.

QUILT SHOW. July 29–Aug 19. Woodstock, VT. A juried showing of quilts made by Windsor County quilters, displayed with selected 19th-century Vermont quilts. Daily quilting demonstrations and activities. Est attendance: 9,700. For info: Billings Farm and Museum, PO Box 489, Woodstock, VT 05091. Phone: (802) 457-2355. Fax: (802) 457-4663. E-mail: billings.farm@valley.net. Web: www.billingsfarm.org.

RAIN DAY AT WAYNESBURG, PENNSYLVANIA. July 29. Legend has it that rain will fall at Waynesburg, PA, on July 29 as it has most years for the last century, according to local records in this community, which was laid out in 1796 and incorporated in 1816.

ROOSEVELT, ALICE HATHAWAY LEE: BIRTH ANNIVERSARY. July 29, 1861. First wife of Theodore Roosevelt, 26th President of the US, whom she married in 1880. Born at Chestnut Hill, MA, she died at New York, NY, Feb 14, 1884.

TARKINGTON, BOOTH: BIRTH ANNIVERSARY. July 29, 1869. American novelist (*The Magnificent Ambersons*), born at Indianapolis, IN. Died there May 19, 1946.

THAT FAMOUS PRESTON NIGHT RODEO. July 29–31. Preston, ID. The second under-the-lights rodeo in America, this PRCA-approved rodeo has top national cowboys. Est attendance: 20,000. For info: Preston Chamber of Commerce, 49 N State, Ste A, Preston, ID 83263. Phone: (208) 852-2703. E-mail: pacc@dcdi.net.

US SENIOR OPEN (GOLF) CHAMPIONSHIP. July 29–Aug 1. Bellerive Country Club, St. Louis, MO. For info: US Golf Assn, Golf House, PO Box 708, Championship Dept, Far Hills, NJ 07931. Phone: (908) 234-2300. Fax: (908) 234-9687. E-mail: usga@usga.org. Web: www.usga.org.

WAUKESHA RIVERFEST. July 29–Aug 1. Frame Park, Waukesha, WI. 10th annual family festival featuring entertainment, ethnic and traditional food, children's entertainment, arts and crafts marketplace, river activities, carnival midway and more. Est attendance: 60,000. For info: Waukesha Riverfest. Phone: (262) 542-0330. E-mail: patty@rspr.com.

BIRTHDAYS TODAY

Debbie Black, 38, basketball player, born Philadelphia, PA, July 29, 1966.

Ken Burns, 51, documentary filmmaker ("Civil War" series), born New York, NY, July 29, 1953.

Elizabeth Hanford Dole, 68, US Senator (R, North Carolina), former president, American Red Cross, former secretary of transportation and secretary of labor, born Salisbury, NC, July 29, 1936.

Peter Jennings, 66, journalist (anchorman for "ABC Evening News"), born Toronto, ON, Canada, July 29, 1938.

Martina McBride, 38, country singer, born Sharon, KS, July 29, 1966.

Ronnie Musgrove, 48, Governor of Mississippi (D), born David Ronald Musgrove, Panola County, MS, July 29, 1956.

Alexandra Paul, 41, actress ("Baywatch," *Dragnet*), born New York, NY, July 29, 1963.

Patty Scialfa, 48, singer, born Deal, NJ, July 29, 1956.

Paul Taylor, 74, dancer, choreographer, born Allegheny, NY, July 29, 1930.

David Warner, 63, actor ("Holocaust," *Tron*), born Manchester, England, July 29, 1941.

Wil Wheaton, 32, actor ("Star Trek: The Next Generation," *Stand by Me*), born Burbank, CA, July 29, 1972.

JULY 30 — FRIDAY
Day 212 — 154 Remaining

AMERICAN LEGACY. July 30–Aug 1. Fort Abraham Lincoln State Park, Mandan, ND. Frontier Army reenactments of military life and fur trading. Activities, demonstrations, and Mandan Indian Nu-eta Corn Festival. July 30 new events will include noted speakers and authors presenting frontier military and Native American topics followed by a melodrama at 7:50. Est attendance: 5,000. For info: Jeff Hoffer, Park Historian, Fort Abraham Lincoln State Park, 4480 Fort Lincoln Rd, Mandan, ND 58554. Phone: (701) 663-9571. Fax: (701) 663-9234.

BANGOR STATE FAIR. July 30–Aug 8. Auditorium Civic Center State Fairgrounds, Bangor, ME. For info: Bangor State Fair, 100 Dutton St, Bangor, ME 04401. Phone: (207) 947-5555. Fax: (207) 947-5105. E-mail: info@bangorstatefair.com. Web: www.bangorstatefair.com.

BRONTË, EMILY: BIRTH ANNIVERSARY. July 30, 1818. English novelist, one of the Brontë sisters, best known for *Wuthering Heights*. Born at Thornton, Yorkshire, England. Died Dec 19, 1848, at Haworth, Yorkshire, England.

CANADA: CANADA'S NATIONAL UKRAINIAN FESTIVAL. July 30–Aug 1. Dauphin, MB. Experience the richness and flavours of Ukrainian culture. From the colorful, energized dancers to the powerful folk songs of Ukraine, there is something for everyone to enjoy. Est attendance: 10,000. For info: Canada's National Ukrainian Festival, Box 368, 1550 Main St S, Dauphin, MB, Canada R7N 2V2. Phone: (204) 622-4600. Fax: (204) 622-4606. E-mail: CNUF@mb.sympatico.ca. Web: www.cnuf.ca.

CANADA: PIONEER DAYS. July 30–Aug 2. Mennonite Heritage Village, Steinbach, MB. Pioneer demonstrations and related activities in a heritage village setting. Est attendance: 14,500. For info: Sue Barkman, Exec Dir, Box 1136, Steinbach, MB, Canada R0A 2A0. Phone: (204) 326-9661. Fax: (204) 326-5046. E-mail: info@mennoniteheritagevillage.com. Web: www.mennoniteheritagevillage.com.

DODGE CITY DAYS. July 30–Aug 8. Dodge City, KS. Western heritage celebration with concerts, arts and crafts, parades, PRCA rodeo, street dances, cookouts, art show, antique car show. Est attendance: 75,000. For info: Dodge City Conv & Visitors Bureau, Third & W Wyatt Earp, PO Box 1474, Dodge City, KS 67801. Phone: (800) OLD-WEST. Fax: (620) 225-8268. E-mail: cvb@dodgecity.org. Web: www.visitdodgecity.org.

ELVIS PRESLEY'S FIRST CONCERT APPEARANCE: 50th ANNIVERSARY. July 30, 1954. Elvis Presley appeared in concert for the first time at Overton Park Orchestra Shell in Memphis, TN. He was billed third and country crooner Slim Whitman was the headliner. Presley, only 19 years old, nervously began gyrating his leg and a legend was born. See also: "Elvis Presley's First Single Released: Anniversary" (July 19).

FESTIVAL OF NATIONS. July 30–Aug 1. Red Lodge, MT. A nine-day extravaganza. All events are free, following the philosophy of festival founders that the festival should be a fun, educational experience including information on cooking, crafts, customs, dances and languages. Est attendance: 16,000. For info: Joan Cline, Exec Secy, Red Lodge Chamber of Commerce, PO Box 988, Red Lodge, MT 59068. Phone: (888) 281-0625. Fax: (406) 446-1718. E-mail: information@redlodge.com. Web: www.redlodge.com.

	S	M	T	W	T	F	S
July					1	2	3
2004	4	5	6	7	8	9	10
	11	12	13	14	15	16	17
	18	19	20	21	22	23	24
	25	26	27	28	29	30	31

FORD, HENRY: BIRTH ANNIVERSARY. July 30, 1863. Industrialist Henry Ford, whose assembly-line method of automobile production revolutionized the industry, was born at Wayne County, MI, on the family farm. His Model T made up half of the world's output of cars during its years of production. Ford built racing cars until in 1903 he and his partners formed the Ford Motor Company. In 1908 the company presented the Model T, which was produced until 1927, and in 1913 Ford introduced the assembly line and mass production. This innovation reduced the time it took to build each car from 12½ hours to only 1½. This enabled Ford to sell cars for $500, making automobile ownership a possibility for an unprecedented percentage of the population. He is also remembered for introducing a $5-a-day wage for automotive workers and for his statement: "History is bunk." Died Apr 7, 1947, at age 83 at Dearborn, MI, where his manufacturing complex was located.

HOFFA, JAMES: DISAPPEARANCE ANNIVERSARY. July 30, 1975. Former Teamsters Union leader, 62-year-old James Riddle Hoffa was last seen on this date outside a restaurant in Bloomfield Township, near Detroit, MI. His 13-year federal prison sentence had been commuted by former President Richard M. Nixon in 1971. On Dec 8, 1982, seven years and 131 days after his disappearance, an Oakland County judge declared Hoffa officially dead as of July 30, 1982.

INTERNATIONAL FESTIVAL. July 30–Aug 8. Calais, ME, and St. Stephen, NB, Canada. Festival of international cooperation between St. Stephen and Calais with the theme "The Spirit of International Friendship and Goodwill." Celebrating the friendship of two countries joining as one. Est attendance: 14,000. For info: Keith Guttormsen, Exec Chamber Dir, International Fest Committee, PO Box 368, Calais, ME 04619. Phone: (207) 454-2308 or (800) 377-9748. Web: www.calaismaine.com.

LOGGING MUSEUM FESTIVAL DAYS. July 30–31. Rangeley, ME. Bean-hole beans, Logger's Hall of Fame, Miss Woodchip Contest, parade, logging competition. Sponsor: Logging Museum. Est attendance: 1,500. For info: Rangeley Logging Museum, Box 154, Rangeley, ME 04970. Phone: (207) 864-5595.

MOORE, HENRY: BIRTH ANNIVERSARY. July 30, 1898. English sculptor born at Castleford, Yorkshire. Died at Hertfordshire, Aug 31, 1986.

NATIONAL BALLOON CLASSIC. July 30–Aug 7. Indianola, IA. A spectator-oriented balloon extravaganza involving fun events utilizing up to 100 balloons. It is held on the Classic's specially designed balloon field with a natural amphitheater for perfect viewing. Balloons fly morning and evening, weather permitting. The Classic stage features live local & regional entertainment. Est attendance: 75,000. For info: Gerald Knoll, PO Box 346, Indianola, IA 50125. Phone: (800) FLY-IOWA or (515) 961-8415. Fax: (515) 961-8415. E-mail: classicgk@aol.com. Web: www.nationalballoonclassic.com.

OZARK EMPIRE FAIR. July 30–Aug 8. Springfield, MO. Regional fair with carnival, exhibits, livestock and entertainment. Est attendance: 230,000. For info: Ozark Empire Fair, PO Box 630, Springfield, MO 65801. Phone: (417) 833-2660. Fax: (417) 833-3769. Web: www.ozarkempirefair.com.

PAPERBACK BOOKS INTRODUCED: ANNIVERSARY. July 30, 1935. Although books bound in soft covers were first introduced in 1841 at Leipzig, Germany, by Christian Bernhard Tauchnitz, the modern paperback revolution dates to the publication of the first Penguin paperback by Sir Allen Lane at London in 1935. Penguin Number 1 was *Ariel*, a life of Shelley by Andre Maurois.

SNOWBIRD, UTAH JAZZ & BLUES FESTIVAL. July 30–31. Snowbird, UT. Come and join the fun with plenty of jazz and blues music. Festival also includes food booths and much more. Annually, the last weekend in July. Est attendance: 6,000. For info: Snowbird & Ski Summer Resort, PO Box 92900, Snowbird, UT 84092-9000. Phone: (801) 742-2222. Fax: (801) 933-2298. E-mail: www.snowbird.com. Web: info@snowbird.com.

☆ Chase's 2004 Calendar of Events ☆ July 30–31

STENGEL, CHARLES DILLON (CASEY): BIRTH ANNIVERSARY. July 30, 1890. Baseball Hall of Fame outfielder and manager born at Kansas City, MO. His success as manager of the New York Yankees (10 pennants and 7 World Series titles in 12 years) made him one of the game's enduring stars. Inducted into the Hall of Fame in 1966. Died at Glendale, CA, Sept 29, 1975.

TAYLOR HORSEFEST. July 30–31. Taylor, ND. This annual celebration is highlighted by a parade of horses and horse-drawn equipment, ethnic food fest, craft vendors, exhibits, demonstrations, music and cowboy poetry. Horse-drawn taxis provide transportation throughout the town during the day. Est attendance: 3,500. For info: Taylor Horsefest, PO Box 7, Taylor, ND 58656. Phone: (701) 974-4210 or (877) 757-7545. Web: www.taylorhorsefest.com.

VANUATU: INDEPENDENCE DAY: ANNIVERSARY. July 30. Vanuatu became an independent republic in 1980 (from France and the UK) and observes its national holiday.

VEBLEN, THORSTEIN: BIRTH ANNIVERSARY. July 30, 1857. American economist, born at Valders, WI, and died at Menlo Park, CA, Aug 3, 1929. "Conspicuous consumption," he wrote in *The Theory of the Leisure Class*, "of valuable goods is a means of reputability to the gentleman of leisure."

BIRTHDAYS TODAY

Lamar Alexander, 64, US Senator (R, Tennessee), born Maryville, TN, July 30, 1940.
Paul Anka, 63, singer, songwriter ("Diana," "My Way" for Frank Sinatra), born Ottawa, ON, Canada, July 30, 1941.
William Atherton, 57, actor (*The Day of the Locust, Ghostbusters, Die Hard, Die Hard 2*), born New Haven, CT, July 30, 1947.
Peter Bogdanovich, 65, producer, director (*The Last Picture Show, Paper Moon*), born Kingston, NY, July 30, 1939.
Delta Burke, 48, actress ("Designing Women"), former Miss Florida, born Orlando, FL, July 30, 1956.
Kate Bush, 46, singer ("The Man with the Child in His Eyes"), songwriter, born Lewisham, England, July 30, 1958.
Edd Byrnes, 71, actor ("77 Sunset Strip," *Darby's Rangers*), born New York, NY, July 30, 1933.
Laurence Fishburne, 43, actor (*Boyz N the Hood, What's Love Got to Do with It, Higher Learning*; stage: *Two Trains Running* [Tony Award]), born Augusta, GA, July 30, 1961.
Anita Faye Hill, 48, law professor, born on an Oklahoma farm, July 30, 1956.
Lisa Kudrow, 41, actress ("Friends," *Romy and Michele's High School Reunion*), born Encino, CA, July 30, 1963.
Christopher Paul (Chris) Mullin, 41, former basketball player, born New York, NY, July 30, 1963.
Ken Olin, 50, actor ("LA Doctors," "thirtysomething"), born Chicago, IL, July 30, 1954.
David Sanborn, 59, saxophonist, composer, born Tampa, FL, July 30, 1945.
Arnold Schwarzenegger, 57, bodybuilder, actor (*The Terminator, Twins, True Lies*), born Graz, Austria, July 30, 1947.
Allan Huber ("Bud") Selig, 70, Commissioner of Major League Baseball, born Milwaukee, WI, July 30, 1934.
Hilary Swank, 30, actress (Oscar for *Boys Don't Cry*), born Lincoln, NE, July 30, 1974.

JULY 31 — SATURDAY
Day 213 — 153 Remaining

ALL-AMERICAN SOAP BOX DERBY. July 31. Derby Downs, Akron, OH. A weeklong festival culminating in world championship race by regional champs from US, New Zealand, Germany, Japan and the Philippines. 67th annual derby. Est attendance: 20,000. For info: Jeff Iula, Genl Mgr, Intl Soap Box Derby, Inc, PO Box 7225, Derby Downs, Akron, OH 44306. Phone: (330) 733-8723. Fax: (330) 733-1370. E-mail: 2077607@mcimail.com. Web: pages.prodigy.com/soapbox.

ARTS AND CRAFTS FESTIVAL. July 31–Aug 1 (tentative). Loveladies, NJ. 10th annual. Featuring juried arts and crafts displays, entertainment, food and more. For info: Long Beach Island Foundation of the Arts and Sciences, 120 Long Beach Blvd, Loveladies, NJ 08008. Phone: (609) 494-1241. Fax: (609) 494-0662.

BLUE MOON. July 31. When two full moons fall within the same month, the second is called the "Blue Moon."

CANADA: CANMORE FOLK MUSIC FESTIVAL. July 31–Aug 2. Centennial Park, Canmore, AB. 27th annual. Alberta's longest-running folk festival. Featuring food and craft booths, entertainment, workshops and free pancake breakfast on Monday. Est attendance: 13,000. For info: Canmore Folk Music Festival, PO Box 8098, Canmore, AB, Canada T1W 2T8. Phone: (403) 678-2524. Fax: (403) 678-2524. E-mail: info@canmorefolkfestival.com. Web: www.canmorefolkfestival.com.

FEAST OF SAINT IGNATIUS OF LOYOLA. July 31. 1491–1556. Founder of the Society of Jesus (Jesuits). Canonized in 1622.

FIRST INDIAN SAINT: ANNIVERSARY. July 31, 2002. In Mexico City, Mexico, Pope John Paul II canonized the Roman Catholic Church's first Indian saint, Juan Diego. In 1531 Diego claimed to have seen the Virgin of Guadalupe, whose rose-framed image appeared on his cloak. See also: "Day of Our Lady of Guadalupe" (Dec 12).

FIRST US GOVERNMENT BUILDING: ANNIVERSARY. July 31, 1792. The cornerstone of the Philadelphia Mint, the first US government building, was laid on this day.

KENNEDY INTERNATIONAL AIRPORT DEDICATION: ANNIVERSARY. July 31, 1948. New York's International Airport at Idlewild Field was dedicated by President Harry S Truman. It was later renamed John F. Kennedy International Airport.

MONTANA STATE FAIR. July 31–Aug 7. Great Falls, MT. Carnival, petting zoo, discount days, nightly entertainment and plenty of food. Est attendance: 185,000. For info: Michelle Kohut, State Fair, Box 1888, Great Falls, MT 59403. Phone: (406) 727-8900. Fax: (406) 452-8955. E-mail: mkohut@ci.great-falls.mt.us.

MOON PHASE: FULL MOON. July 31. Moon enters Full Moon phase at 2:05 PM, EDT.

MUTT'S DAY. July 31. Dedicated to the mutts of the world. Honor the dogs that aren't just one breed. Annually, on July 31. For info: Terry Runion, 2461 E Hale St, Mesa, AZ 85213. Phone: (480) 671-5202. Fax: (480) 474-9752. E-mail: runion@cybermutz.com. Web: www.cybermutz.com.

NORFOLK PUBLIC LIBRARY LITERATURE FESTIVAL. July 31. Lifelong Learning Center, Norfolk, NE. Presentations by award-winning, nationally known authors, book reviews, book displays and sales and autograph sessions. Est attendance: 300. For info: Karen Drevo, Youth Services Librarian, Norfolk Public Library, 308 Prospect Ave, Norfolk, NE 68701. Phone: (402) 844-2100. Fax: (402) 844-2102. E-mail: kdrevo@ci.norfolk.ne.us.

PRESIDENT'S ENVIRONMENTAL YOUTH AWARD NATIONAL COMPETITION DEADLINE. July 31. Young people in all 50 states are invited to participate in the President's Environmental Youth Awards program, which offers them, individually and collectively, an opportunity to be recognized for environmental efforts in their community. The program encour-

July 31 ☆ *Chase's 2004 Calendar of Events* ☆

ages individuals, school classes, schools, summer camps and youth organizations to promote local environmental awareness and positive community involvement. (The annual deadline is always July 31.) For info: Office of Environmental Education, US Environmental Protection Agency, 1200 Pennsylvania Ave NW (MC 1704A), Washington, DC 20460. Phone: (202) 564-0443. Fax: (202) 564-2754. Web: www.epa.gov/enviroed.

SALVADOR, FRANCIS: DEATH ANNIVERSARY. July 31, 1776. The first Jew to die in the American Revolution, Salvador was also the first Jew elected to office in Colonial America. He was voted a member of the South Carolina Provincial Congress in January 1775.

TIDEWATER ARCHAEOLOGY DIG. July 31–Aug 1. St. Mary's City, MD. Hands-on opportunity to dig at an archaeology site at Maryland's first capital. Special behind-the-scenes tours. Annually, usually the last weekend in July. Est attendance: 1,000. For info: Visitors Services, Historic St. Mary's City, PO Box 39, St. Mary's City, MD 20686. Phone: (240) 895-4990 or (800) SMC-1634. Fax: (240) 895-4968. Web: www.stmaryscity.org.

US PATENT OFFICE OPENS: ANNIVERSARY. July 31, 1790. The first US Patent Office opened its doors and the first US patent was issued to Samuel Hopkins of Vermont for a new method of making pearlash and potash. The patent was signed by George Washington and Thomas Jefferson.

WALES: NATIONAL EISTEDDFOD OF WALES. July 31–Aug 7. Newport, Gwent. In 1880 the National Eisteddfod association was formed and charged with the responsibility of staging an annual festival to be held in North and South Wales alternately, and with the exception of 1914 and 1940, this target has been successfully achieved. The National Eisteddfod of Wales is a cultural event with competitive festivals of music, drama, literature, art and crafts. All events conducted in Welsh with simultaneous translation into English available. Est attendance: 160,000. For info: Natl Eisteddfod of Wales, 40 Parc Ty Glas, Llanishen, Cardiff, Wales, UK CF14 5WU. Phone: (44) (2920) 763777. Fax: (44) (2920) 763737. Web: www.eisteddfod.org.uk.

WORLD FUTURE SOCIETY ANNUAL CONFERENCE. July 31–Aug 2. Grand Hyatt Regency Washington, Washington, DC. For info: World Future Society, 7910 Woodmont Ave, Ste 450, Bethesda, MD 20814. Phone: (800) 989-8274 or (301) 656-8274. Fax: (301) 951-0394. E-mail: sechard@wfs.org. Web: www.wfs.org.

BIRTHDAYS TODAY

Dean Cain, 38, actor ("Lois & Clark: The New Adventures of Superman"), born Mount Clemens, MI, July 31, 1966.
Geraldine Chaplin, 60, actress (*Nashville, Roseland, Chaplin*), born Santa Monica, CA, July 31, 1944.
Susan Flannery, 61, actress ("The Bold & the Beautiful," "Dallas"), born Jersey City, NJ, July 31, 1943.
Milton Friedman, 92, economist, journalist, born Brooklyn, NY, July 31, 1912.
Evonne Goolagong, 53, former tennis player, born Griffith, Australia, July 31, 1951.
Irv Kupcinet, 92, former TV talk-show host, columnist, born Chicago, IL, July 31, 1912.
Sherry Lansing, 60, producer (*Fatal Attraction, The Accused*), born Chicago, IL, July 31, 1944.
Gary Lewis, 58, singer ("This Diamond Ring"), born New York, NY, July 31, 1946.
Don Murray, 75, actor (*Bus Stop*, "Knots Landing"), born Hollywood, CA, July 31, 1929.
France Nuyen, 65, actress ("St. Elsewhere"), born Marseilles, France, July 31, 1939.
Jonathan Ogden, 30, football player, born Washington, DC, July 31, 1974.
J.K. Rowling, 39, author (the Harry Potter series), born Joanne Rowling, Bristol, England, July 31, 1965.
Wesley Snipes, 42, actor (*Blade, US Marshals, Jungle Fever, White Men Can't Jump*), born Orlando, FL, July 31, 1962.

☆ Chase's 2004 Calendar of Events ☆   Aug 1

August.

AUGUST 1 — SUNDAY
Day 214 — 152 Remaining

ADMINISTRATIVE PROFESSIONALS INTERNATIONAL ANNUAL CONVENTION AND EDUCATION FORUM. Aug 1–4. Washington, DC. Est attendance: 2,000. For info: Intl Assn for Administrative Professionals, 10502 NW Ambassador Dr, PO Box 20404, Kansas City, MO 64195-0404. Phone: (816) 891-6600 x 2223. Fax: (816) 891-9118. E-mail: meetings@iaap-hq.org. Web: www.iaap-hq.org.

ADMIT YOU'RE HAPPY MONTH. Aug 1–31. This 5th annual month, sponsored by the Secret Society of Happy People, encourages people to express happiness and discourages parade-raining. Visit our website to find out about activities, or order your Admit You're Happy Month Celebration Kit for $5. For info: Secret Society of Happy People, 1315 Riverchase Dr #2316, Coppell, TX 75019. Phone: (972) 471-1485. E-mail: pjohnson@sohp.com. Web: www.sohp.com.

AMERICAN FAMILY DAY IN ARIZONA. Aug 1. Observed in Arizona on the first Sunday in August. The observance date is designated by statute.

AMERICAN HISTORY ESSAY CONTEST. Aug 1–Dec 15. American History Committee activities are promoted throughout the year with the essay contest conducted in grades 5–8 beginning in August. Essays are submitted for judging by Dec 15, with the winners announced in April at the Daughters of the American Revolution Continental Congress. Events vary, but include programs, displays, spot announcements and recognition of essay writers. Essay topic can be obtained from DAR Headquarters. For info: Natl Society of Daughters of the American Revolution, Office of the Historian-General, Admin Bldg, 1776 D St NW, Washington, DC 20006-5392. Phone: (202) 628-1776. Web: www.dar.org.

BENIN: INDEPENDENCE DAY. Aug 1. Public holiday. Commemorates independence from France in 1960. Benin at that time was known as Dahomey.

BLACK BUSINESS MONTH. Aug 1–31. Six months after Black History Month, the focus on and awareness of black-owned and operated enterprises needs a boost. This month is dedicated to starting, maintaining, growing, buying from and committing to black-owned businesses and entrepreneurs. For info: Sylvia Henderson, Springboard Training, 18005 Lafayette Dr, Ste B, Olney, MD 20832. Phone: (301) 646-1668. Fax: (301) 856-8000. E-mail: admin@springboardtraining.com. Web: www.springboardtraining.com.

BROWN, RONALD H.: BIRTH ANNIVERSARY. Aug 1, 1941. Born at Washington, DC, Brown served as chief council for the Senate Judiciary Committee. He went on to become the first African-American partner at the law firm of Patton Boggs & Blow, the first African-American leader of the Democratic National Committee and later served as the US Secretary of Commerce during the Clinton administration. Brown died in a plane crash at Dubrovnik, Croatia, Apr 3, 1996, while on government business.

BURK, MARTHA (CALAMITY JANE): DEATH ANNIVERSARY. Aug 1, 1903. Known as a frontierswoman and companion to Wild Bill Hickock, Calamity Jane Burk was born Martha Jane Cannary at Princeton, MO, in May 1852. As a young girl living in Montana, she became an excellent markswoman. She went to the Black Hills of South Dakota as a scout for a geological expedition in 1875. Several opposing traditions account for her nickname, one springing from her kindness to the less fortunate, while another attributes it to the harsh warnings she would give men who offended her. She died Aug 1, 1903, at Terry, SD, and was buried at Deadwood, SD, next to Wild Bill Hickock.

CANADA: FOLKLORAMA—CANADA'S CULTURAL CELEBRATION. Aug 1–14. Winnipeg, MB. 35th festival. More than 45 pavilions representing various cultures offer traditionally prepared cuisine, exhilarating entertainment and captivating cultural displays for 14 prairie summer nights. Folklorama is the largest multicultural celebration of its kind in the world and has been named the Internationally Known Super Event by the American Bus Association. Est attendance: 450,000. For info: Judy Murphy, Exec Dir, Folklorama, 183 Kennedy St, 2nd Fl, Winnipeg, MB, Canada R3C 1S6. Phone: (204) 982-6210 or (800) 665-0234. Fax: (204) 943-1956. E-mail: folkarts@folklorama.ca. Web: www.folklorama.ca.

CATARACT AWARENESS MONTH. Aug 1–31. Cataracts are the leading cause of blindness in the world. Cataract Awareness Month informs the public on what cataracts are, when they should be treated and the procedures that can be used to restore good vision. For info: American Academy of Ophthamology, PO Box 7424, San Francisco, CA 94120-7424. Phone: (415) 561-8500. Fax: (415) 561-8533. E-mail: eyemd@aao.org. Web: www.aao.org.

CHILDREN'S EYE HEALTH AND SAFETY MONTH. Aug 1–31. Information will be available about amblyopia, a condition that can affect two to three percent of children and cause permanent vision loss. Also, get tips about preventing eye injuries in children, signs of possible eye problems and general eye health. For info: Prevent Blindness America, 500 E. Remington Rd, Schaumburg, IL 60173. Phone: (800) 331-2020 or (847) 843-2020. Web: www.preventblindness.org.

CLARK, WILLIAM: BIRTH ANNIVERSARY. Aug 1, 1770. The soldier, explorer and public servant was born at Caroline County, VA. He served seven years in the US Army and then gained his lasting fame when Meriwether Lewis asked him to join an expedition exploring the Louisiana Territory (1803–1806). Clark was an able leader, and contributed detailed maps and animal illustrations on the journey. A grateful President Thomas Jefferson made Clark brigadier general of militia for the Louisiana Territory (1807–1813) and superintendent of Indian Affairs (1807–1838). Clark was also governor of the Missouri Territory (1813–1820) and surveyor general for Illinois, Missouri and Arkansas (1824–1825). Clark foresaw the tension between US interests and the native peoples of the western US, and he urged that the US treat western tribes with respect. Clark died at St. Louis, MO, on Sept 1, 1838.

COLORADO: ADMISSION DAY: ANNIVERSARY. Aug 1, 1876. Colorado admitted to the Union as the 38th state. The first Monday in August is celebrated as Colorado Day.

DIARY OF ANNE FRANK: THE LAST ENTRY: 60th ANNIVERSARY. Aug 1, 1944. To escape deportation to concentration camps, the Jewish family of Otto Frank hid for two years in the warehouse of his food products business at Amsterdam. Gentile friends smuggled in food and other supplies during their confinement. Thirteen-year-old Anne Frank, who kept a journal during the time of their hiding, penned her last entry in the diary Aug 1, 1944: "[I] keep on trying to find a way of becoming what I would like to be, and what I could be, if . . . there weren't any other people living in the world." Three days later (Aug 4, 1944) Grüne Polizei raided the "Secret Annex" where the

Aug 1 ☆ Chase's 2004 Calendar of Events ☆

Frank family was hidden. Anne and her sister were sent to Bergen-Belsen concentration camp where Anne died at age 15, two months before the liberation of Holland. Young Anne's diary, later found in the family's hiding place, has been translated into 30 languages and has become a symbol of the indomitable strength of the human spirit. See also: "Frank, Anne: Birth Anniversary" (June 12).

EMANCIPATION OF 500: ANNIVERSARY. Aug 1, 1791. Virginia planter Robert Carter III confounded his family and friends by filing a deed of emancipation for his 500 slaves. One of the wealthiest men in the state, Carter owned 60,000 acres over 18 plantations. The deed included the following words: "I have for some time past been convinced that to retain them in Slavery is contrary to the true principles of Religion and Justice and therefore it is my duty to manumit them." The document established a schedule by which 15 slaves would be freed each Jan 1, over a 21-year period, plus slave children would be freed at age 18 for females and 21 for males. It is believed this was the largest act of emancipation in US history and predated the Emancipation Proclamation by 70 years.

FIRST US CENSUS: ANNIVERSARY. Aug 1, 1790. The first census revealed that there were 3,939,326 citizens in the 16 states and the Ohio Territory. The US has taken a census every 10 years since 1790. The next one will be in 2010.

GARCIA, JERRY: BIRTH ANNIVERSARY. Aug 1, 1942. Jerome John Garcia was born at San Francisco, CA. Country, bluegrass and folk musician, a guitar player of remarkable ability, Garcia was the leading force behind the legendary Grateful Dead, the band that sustained a veritable industry for its legion of followers. He died Aug 9, 1995, at Forest Knolls, CA, ending a musical career that spanned more than three decades.

GIRLFRIEND'S DAY. Aug 1. Celebrate this special day by taking your girlfriend(s) shopping, to a play, to the movies, out to eat, to the spa and/or to the park. A fun slumber party is also recommended. Annually, Aug 1. For info: Thema Martin, Floffee, Inc. Phone: (404) 849-1249. E-mail: girlfriendsday@hotmail.com or floffee@hotmail.com.

HAWAII VOLCANOES NATIONAL PARK ESTABLISHED: ANNIVERSARY. Aug 1, 1916. Area of Hawaii's Hawaii Island, including active volcanoes Kilauea and Mauna Loa, was established as Hawaii National Park in 1916 but its name was changed to Hawaii Volcanoes National Park in 1961. For further park info: Hawaii Volcanoes Natl Park, Hawaii Natl Park, HI 96718.

HOT AUGUST NIGHTS. Aug 1–8. Reno and Sparks, NV. Celebration of the music and cars of the '50s and '60s features show and shine, parade, cruises, proms and concerts by the entertainers of the era. For info: Hot August Nights, 1425 E Greg St, Sparks, NV 89431. Phone: (775) 356-1956. Web: www.hotaugustnights.net.

ITALY: JOUST OF THE QUINTANA. Aug 1. Ascoli/Piceno. The first Sunday in August is set aside for the Torneo della Quintana, an historical pageant with 15th-century costumes.

JAMAICA: ABOLITION OF SLAVERY. Aug 1, 1838. National day. Spanish settlers introduced the slave trade into Jamaica in 1509 and sugar cane in 1640. Slavery continued until Aug 1, 1838, when it was abolished by the British.

KEY, FRANCIS SCOTT: 225th BIRTH ANNIVERSARY. Aug 1, 1779. American attorney, social worker, poet and author of the US national anthem. While on a legal mission, Key was detained on shipboard off Baltimore, during the British bombardment of Fort McHenry on the night of Sept 13–14, 1814. Thrilled to see the American flag still flying over the fort at daybreak, Key wrote the poem "The Star Spangled Banner." Printed in the *Baltimore American* Sept 21, 1814, it was soon popularly sung to the music of an old English tune, "Anacreon in Heaven." It did not become the official US national anthem until 117 years later when, on Mar 3, 1931, President Herbert Hoover signed into law an act for that purpose. Key was born at Frederick County, MD, and died at Baltimore, MD, Jan 11, 1843.

LUGHNASADH. Aug 1. (Also called August Eve, Lammas Eve, Lady Day Eve and Feast of Bread.) One of the "Greater Sabbats" during the Wiccan year, Lughnasadh marks the first harvest. Annually, Aug 1.

MAY YOUR READING BE A HAVEN MONTH. Aug 1–31. Created to encourage readers to choose books and audio books that inspire, inform, transport, edify, expand and enhance awareness—books that are "about something." An annual observance sponsored by Haven Books, which believes in nurturing talent and the creative spirit within. Celebrate this month from the comfort of your favorite reading chair! For info: Reya Patton, Haven Books, 10153½ Riverside Dr, North Hollywood, CA 91602. Phone: (818) 503-2518. Fax: (818) 508-0299. E-mail: reya@havenbooks.net. Web: www.havenbooks.net.

MELVILLE, HERMAN: BIRTH ANNIVERSARY. Aug 1, 1819. American author, best known for his novel *Moby-Dick*, born at New York, NY, and died there Sept 28, 1891.

MITCHELL, MARIA: BIRTH ANNIVERSARY. Aug 1, 1818. An interest in her father's hobby and an ability for mathematics resulted in Maria Mitchell's becoming the first female professional astronomer. In 1847, while assisting her father in a survey of the sky for the US Coast Guard, Mitchell discovered a new comet and determined its orbit. She received many honors because of this, including being elected to the American Academy of Arts and Sciences—its first woman. Mitchell joined the staff at Vassar Female College in 1865—the first US female professor of astronomy—and in 1873 was a cofounder of the Association for the Advancement of Women. Born at Nantucket, MA, Mitchell died June 28, 1889, at Lynn, MA.

MTV PREMIERE: ANNIVERSARY. Aug 1, 1981. The all-music-video channel debuted on this date. VH1, another music channel owned by MTV Networks that is aimed at older pop music fans, premiered in 1985.

NATIONAL IMMUNIZATION AWARENESS MONTH. Aug 1–31. Immunization is critical to maintaining health and preventing life-threatening diseases among people of all ages and cultures throughout the US. Each year in the US, tens of thousands of people die because of vaccine-preventable diseases or their complications, and even more experience pain, suffering and disability. This month calls attention to the importance of infant, child, adolescent and adult immunization, and seeks to reduce disparities in vaccine use while maintaining public trust in their value and safety. A National Immunization Awareness Month promotional kit is available. For info: National Partnership for Immunization, 121 N Washington St, Ste 300, Alexandria, VA 22314. Phone: (703) 836-6110. Fax: (703) 836-3470. E-mail: npi@hmhb.org. Web: www.partnersforimmunization.org.

August 2004	S	M	T	W	T	F	S
	1	2	3	4	5	6	7
	8	9	10	11	12	13	14
	15	16	17	18	19	20	21
	22	23	24	25	26	27	28
	29	30	31				

☆ Chase's 2004 Calendar of Events ☆ Aug 1

NATIONAL INVENTORS' MONTH®. Aug 1–31. To educate the American public about the value of creativity and inventiveness and the importance of inventions and inventors to the quality of our lives. This will be accomplished by specially designed displays for libraries, an interactive website and through the placement of media stories about living inventors in most of the top national, local and trade publications. Sponsored by the United Inventors Association of the USA (UIA-USA), the Academy of Applied Science and *Inventors' Digest*. For info: Joanne Hayes-Rines, Inventors' Digest. Phone: (617) 367-4540. Fax: 617 723-6988. E-mail: joanne@inventorsdigest.com. Web: www.inventorsdigest.com.

NATIONAL KIDSDAY. Aug 1. A day to celebrate and honor children by spending meaningful time with them. Sponsored by KidsPeace® and the Boys and Girls Clubs of America. Annually, the first Sunday in August. For info: National Kidsday Mgmt, c/o Boys & Girls Clubs of America, 1230 W Peachtree St., Atlanta, GA 30309. Phone: (404) 487-5700. Fax: (404) 487-5787. E-mail: kidsday@bgca.org. Web: www.kidsday.net.

NATIONAL WIN WITH CIVILITY MONTH. Aug 1–31. When we are civil to each other we confirm our worth and acknowledge the worth of others. We can move in and out of all levels of society confident that we are always doing the "right thing." We gain recognition for civility and we secure the respect of our fellow human beings. For info: Thomas Danaher, PO Box 85147, Las Vegas, NV 89185. Phone: (702) 386-9115. Web: www.societyforcivility.org.

OAK RIDGE ATOMIC PLANT BEGUN: ANNIVERSARY. Aug 1, 1943. Ground was broken at Oak Ridge, TN, for the first plant built to manufacture the uranium 235 needed to build an atomic bomb. The plant was largely completed by July of 1944 at a final cost of $280 million. By August 1945 the total cost for development of the A-bomb ran to $1 billion.

RESPECT FOR PARENTS DAY. Aug 1. A day set aside to think of positive things parents contribute to society. Annually, August 1. For info: Marilyn Dalrymple, PO Box 1563, Lancaster, CA 93539. Phone: (661) 945-2360. E-mail: marilyn@global.net. Web: members.tripod.com/MarilynDalrymple/index-4.html.

ROUNDS RESOUNDING DAY. Aug 1. To sing rounds, catches and canons in folk contrapuntal tradition. Motto: "As rounds re-sound and resound, all the world's joined in a circle of harmony." Annually, Aug 1. For info: Gloria T. Delamar, Founder, Rounds Resounding Society. E-mail: Rounds.Resounding.Society@juno.com. Web: www.delamar.org/roundsresounding.

"THE RUSH LIMBAUGH SHOW" NATIONAL RADIO PREMIERE: ANNIVERSARY. Aug 1, 1988. Conservative political commentator and radio personality Rush Limbaugh began his nationally syndicated show on this date with 56 stations. It quickly became the nation's top-rated show and rejuvenated the radio talk format. Today, more than 645 stations carry the program to an estimated 20 million listeners.

SIMPLIFY YOUR LIFE WEEK. Aug 1–7. A week to encourage people to simplify their lives and reduce clutter, thereby reducing stress and acquiring a happier and more peaceful lifestyle. For information about this worldwide organization and 100 ways to simplify one's life, send $5 to cover expenses of printing, handling and postage. For info: Dr. Stanley Drake, Pres, Intl Society of Friendship and Good Will, 999 Hood Rd, Ste 127, Marietta, GA 30068. Phone: (770) 565-2322. E-mail: ISFGW@bellsouth.net.

SISTERS' DAY®. Aug 1. Celebrating the spirit of sisterhood—sisters nationwide show appreciation and give recognition to one another for the special relationship they share. Send a card, make a phone call, share memories, photos, flowers, candy, etc. Sisters may include biological sisters, sorority sisters, sisterly friends, etc. Annually, the first Sunday in August. For info: Tricia Eleogram, 5112 Normandy Ave, Memphis, TN 38117. Phone: (901) 681-2145 or (901) 755-0751. Fax: (901) 754-9923. E-mail: sistersday@aol.com.

SPINAL MUSCULAR ATROPHY AWARENESS MONTH. Aug 1–31. To promote awareness of this congenital disease. For info: Families of Spinal Muscular Atrophy, PO Box 196, Libertyville, IL 60048. Phone: (800) 886-1762. E-mail: info@fsma.org. Web: www.curesma.com or www.fsma.org.

SWITZERLAND: CONFEDERATION DAY. Aug 1. National holiday. Anniversary of the founding of the Swiss Confederation. Commemorates a pact made in 1291. Parades, patriotic gatherings, bonfires and fireworks. Young citizens' coming-of-age ceremonies. Observed since 600th anniversary of Swiss Confederation was celebrated in 1891.

TOOLS OF THE TRADE. Aug 1–31. Jamestown Settlement, Williamsburg, VA, and Yorktown Victory Center, Yorktown, VA. Discover tools and technology of the 17th and 18th centuries, from the navigation instruments that led English colonists to the New World to the medical instruments used to treat injured soldiers in the Revolutionary War. For info: Jamestown-Yorktown Foundation, PO Box 1607, Williamsburg, VA 23187. Phone: (757) 253-4838 or toll-free (888) 593-4682. Fax: (757) 253-5299. Web: www.historyisfun.org.

TRINIDAD AND TOBAGO: EMANCIPATION DAY. Aug 1. Public holiday. Slavery was abolished in all British colonies on this day in 1834. Also called Discovery Day.

US CUSTOMS: ANNIVERSARY. Aug 1, 1789. "The first US customs officers began to collect the revenue and enforce the Tariff Act of July 4, 1789, on this date. Since then, the customhouse and the customs officer have stood as symbols of national pride and sovereignty at ports of entry along the land and sea borders of our country." (From Presidential Proclamation 4306.)

VALENTOWN ANTIQUE PEDDLER'S MARKET. Aug 1. Valentown Museum, Victor, New York. More than 100 antique dealers, artisans and craftsmen. Food vendors, entertainment, Valentown Museum tours and Mennonite quilt raffle. Sponsored by the Victor Historical Society. Annually, the first Sunday in August. Est attendance: 3,000. For info: Victor Historical Society, PO Box 456, Fishers, NY 14453. Phone: (716) 924-4170. E-mail: mail@valentown.org. Web: www.valentown.org.

WARSAW UPRISING: 60th ANNIVERSARY. Aug 1, 1944. Having received radio reports from Moscow promising aid from the Red Army, the Polish Home Army rose up against the Nazi oppressors. At 5 PM thousands of windows were thrown open and Polish patriots, 40,000 strong, began shooting at German soldiers in the streets. The Germans responded by throwing eight divisions into the battle. Despite appeals from the London-based Polish government-in-exile, no assistance was forthcoming from the Allies, and after two months of horrific fighting the rebellion was quashed.

WORLD BREASTFEEDING WEEK. Aug 1–7. Commemoration of signing of Innocenti Declaration. Includes a World Walk for Breastfeeding. Breastfeeding advocates, healthcare professionals and social service agencies focus attention on the importance and benefits of breastfeeding. Fairs, picnics, fund-raising and government proclamations highlight the week. Annually, the first seven days of August. For info: La Leche League Intl, 1400 N Meacham, Schaumburg, IL 60168-4079. Phone: (847) 519-7730 or (800) LA LECHE. Fax: (847) 519-0035. E-mail: PRManager@llli.org or PRAssociate@llli.org. Web: www.lalecheleague.org.

Aug 1–2 ☆ Chase's 2004 Calendar of Events ☆

WORLD WIDE WEB: ANNIVERSARY. Aug 1, 1990. The creation of what would become the World Wide Web was suggested this month in 1990 by Tim Berners-Lee and Robert Cailliau at CERN, the European Laboratory for Particle Physics at Switzerland. By October they had designed a prototype Web browser. They also introduced HTML (Hypertext Markup Language) and the URL (Universal Resource Locator). Mosaic, the first graphical Web browser, was designed by Marc Andreessen and released in 1993. By early 1993 there were 50 Web servers worldwide.

ZIMBABWE: INTERNATIONAL BOOK FAIR. Aug 1–9 (tentative). Harare. Celebrate literature and reading, meet publishers, librarians and booksellers. Open to the public on certain dates, see website for more information. Held annually during the first week of August in the beautiful Harare Sculpture Gardens. For info: David Brine, Zimbabwe Intl Book Fair Ltd, PO Box 21303, London, England WC2E 8PH. Phone/fax: 44 (020) 7836-8501. E-mail: international@zibf.org. Web: www.zibf.org.

BIRTHDAYS TODAY

Tempestt Bledsoe, 31, talk-show host, actress ("Tempestt," "The Cosby Show"), born Chicago, IL, Aug 1, 1973.
Robert Cray, 51, singer, guitarist, songwriter, born Columbus, GA, Aug 1, 1953.
Dom DeLuise, 71, comedian, actor (*Cannonball Run*), born Brooklyn, NY, Aug 1, 1933.
Giancarlo Giannini, 62, actor (*Swept Away . . . , Seven Beauties*), born La Spezia, Italy, Aug 1, 1942.
Arthur Hill, 82, actor (*Harper, The Andromeda Strain,* "Owen Marshall"), born Melfort, SK, Canada, Aug 1, 1922.
Yves Saint Laurent, 68, fashion designer, born Oran, Algeria, Aug 1, 1936.
Tom Wilson, 73, cartoonist ("Ziggy"), born Grant Town, WV, Aug 1, 1931.

AUGUST 2 — MONDAY
Day 215 — 151 Remaining

ALBERT EINSTEIN'S ATOMIC BOMB LETTER: 65th ANNIVERSARY. Aug 2, 1939. Albert Einstein, world-famous scientist, a refugee from Nazi Germany, wrote a letter to US President Franklin D. Roosevelt, first mentioning a possible "new phenomenon . . . chain reactions . . . vast amounts of power." "A single bomb of this type," he wrote, "carried by boat and exploded in a port, might very well destroy the whole port together with some of the surrounding territory." Six years and four days later, Aug 6, 1945, the Japanese port of Hiroshima was destroyed by the first atomic bombing of a populated place.

ANTIGUA AND BARBUDA: AUGUST MONDAY. Aug 2–3. The first Monday in August and the day following form the August Monday Public Holiday.

AUSTRALIA: PICNIC DAY. Aug 2. The first Monday in August is a bank holiday in New South Wales and Picnic Day in Northern Territory, Australia.

BAHAMAS: EMANCIPATION DAY. Aug 2. Public holiday in Bahamas. Annually, the first Monday in August. Commemorates the emancipation of slaves by the British in 1834.

BALDWIN, JAMES: 80th BIRTH ANNIVERSARY. Aug 2, 1924. Black American author noted for descriptions of black life in the US. Born at New York, NY. His best-known work, *Go Tell It on the Mountain*, was published in 1953. Died at Saint Paul-de-Vence, France, Nov 30, 1987.

August 2004

S	M	T	W	T	F	S
1	2	3	4	5	6	7
8	9	10	11	12	13	14
15	16	17	18	19	20	21
22	23	24	25	26	27	28
29	30	31				

CANADA: CIVIC HOLIDAY. Aug 2. The first Monday in August is observed as a holiday in seven of Canada's 10 provinces. Civic holiday in Manitoba, New Brunswick, Northwest Territories, Ontario and Saskatchewan, British Columbia Day in British Columbia and Heritage Day in Alberta.

COLORADO DAY. Aug 2. Colorado. Annually, the first Monday in August. Commemorates Admission Day, Aug 1, 1876, when Colorado became the 38th state.

COSTA RICA: FEAST OF OUR LADY OF ANGELS. Aug 2. National holiday.

DECLARATION OF INDEPENDENCE: OFFICIAL SIGNING: ANNIVERSARY. Aug 2, 1776. Contrary to widespread misconceptions, the 56 signers did not sign as a group and did not do so July 4, 1776. John Hancock and Charles Thomson signed only draft copies that day, the official day the Declaration was adopted by Congress. The signing of the official declaration occurred Aug 2, 1776, when 50 men probably took part. Later that year, five more apparently signed separately and one added his name in a subsequent year. (From "Signers of the Declaration . . ." US Dept of the Interior, 1975.) See also: "Declaration of Independence Approval and Signing: Anniversary" (July 4).

GRENADA: EMANCIPATION DAY. Aug 2. Grenada observes public holiday annually on the first Monday in August. Commemorates the emancipation of slaves by the British in 1834.

ICELAND: AUGUST HOLIDAY. Aug 2. National holiday. The first Monday in August. Commemorates Iceland's constitution of 1874.

IRAQ INVADES KUWAIT: ANNIVERSARY. Aug 2, 1990. On President Saddam Hussein's orders, the Iraqi army invaded Kuwait. Hussein claimed that Kuwait presented a serious threat to Iraq's economic existence by overproducing oil and driving prices down on the world market. After conquering the capital, Kuwait City, Hussein installed a military government in Kuwait, prior to annexing it to Iraq on the claim that Kuwait was historically part of Iraq. The US and most other nations immediately condemned the aggression and the UN passed measures calling for broad economic sanctions against Iraq. As Iraqi forces began to mass along the border with Saudi Arabia, the US and other nations sent troops to Saudi Arabia to protect that country from invasion with an operation named Desert Shield. The multinational force included troops from other Arab countries such as Egypt, Syria and Morocco in addition to forces from Western governments with large economic interests in the region. Approximately 21,000 foreign nationals from several countries were detained by Iraq and were transported to various strategic locations to deter possible retaliatory attacks. The US military action was the largest mobilization of forces since the Vietnam War. The following January, Desert Shield became Operation Desert Storm as the Allied forces went to war against Iraq.

JAMAICA: INDEPENDENCE DAY. Aug 2. National holiday observing achievement of Jamaican independence from Britain Aug 6, 1962. Annually, the first Monday in August.

L'ENFANT, PIERRE CHARLES: 250th BIRTH ANNIVERSARY. Aug 2, 1754. The architect, engineer and Revolutionary War officer who designed the plan for the city of Washington, DC, L'Enfant was born at Paris, France. He died at Prince Georges County, MD, June 14, 1825.

☆ Chase's 2004 Calendar of Events ☆   Aug 2–3

LOY, MYRNA (WILLIAMS): BIRTH ANNIVERSARY. Aug 2, 1905. Actress known for her film roles in the *Thin Man* series. Born near Helena, MT, and died at New York, NY, Dec 14, 1993.

MACEDONIA: NATIONAL DAY: ANNIVERSARY. Aug 2. Commemorates the nationalist uprising against the Ottoman Empire in 1903. Called Prophet Elias Day or *Illinden*.

NATIONAL PRETTY IS AS PRETTY DOES DAY. Aug 2. Celebrated by Ms National American Rose Queen Tamar Alexia Fleishman, Esq, as well as by many other "beautiful people," this holiday encourages all pageant winners, beauty queens, models, actresses, cheerleaders, performers and other "beautiful people" to devote a day to helping the community. For info: Tamar A. Fleishman, Esq, 925 St. Paul St, Baltimore, MD 21202. Phone: (410) 685-5553. Fax: (410) 685-3771. E-mail: tfleishman@toad.net.

O'CONNOR, CARROLL: 80th BIRTH ANNIVERSARY. Aug 2, 1924. Television, stage and screen actor born in New York, NY. He was best known for his portrayal of the bigoted, blue-collar Archie Bunker on "All in the Family." He played the role of Bunker from 1971 to 1979, and was nominated for eight Emmy Awards, winning four. He won a fifth Emmy in 1989 for "In the Heat of the Night." He was also inducted into the Television Hall of Fame in 1989. He died in Culver City, CA, on June 21, 2001.

PSYCHIC WEEK. Aug 2–6. To utilize the power of the psyche to bring peace, find lost individuals and concentrate "psychic power" on beneficial causes. Annually, the first week in August (Monday–Friday). [Created by the late Richard R. Falk.]

SAINT ELIAS DAY (ILLINDEN): MACEDONIAN UPRISING: ANNIVERSARY. Aug 2, 1903. Most sacred, honored and celebrated day of the Macedonian people. Anniversary of the uprising of Macedonians against the Ottoman Empire. Turkish reprisals against the insurgents were ruthless, including the destruction of 105 villages and the execution of more than 1,700 noncombatants.

SCOTLAND: SUMMER BANK HOLIDAY. Aug 2. Bank and public holiday in Scotland. The first Monday in August.

US VIRGIN ISLANDS NATIONAL PARK ESTABLISHED: ANNIVERSARY. Aug 2, 1956. The US Virgin Islands, including areas on St. John and St. Thomas, were established as a national park and preserve. On Oct 5, 1962, the Virgin Islands National Park was enlarged to include offshore areas, including coral reefs, shorelines and sea grass beds.

WORLD FOOTBAG CHAMPIONSHIPS. Aug 2–8. San Francisco, CA. 25th annual. Seven-day sports event spotlights competition of footskills—the Super Bowl of footbag (also known as Hacky Sack®)! It attracts the world's top footbag competitors from the US and six other countries. Prize money exceeds $10,000. Sponsors: Sipa Sipa Footbags and The World Footbag Association. Est attendance: 5,000. For info: Bruce Guettich, Dir, World Footbag Assn, PO Box 775208, Steamboat Springs, CO 80477. Phone: (800) 878-8797. Fax: (970) 870-2846. E-mail: wfa@worldfootbag.com. Web: www.worldfootbag.com.

ZAMBIA: YOUTH DAY. Aug 2. National holiday. Youth activities are order of the day. Focal point is Lusaka's Independence Stadium. Annually, the first Monday in August.

BIRTHDAYS TODAY

Joanna Cassidy, 60, actress ("Buffalo Bill," *Under Fire*), born Camden, NJ, Aug 2, 1944.
Wes Craven, 65, writer, director (*The Nightmare on Elm Street*, *Scream*), born Cleveland, OH, Aug 2, 1939.
James Fallows, 55, journalist, former editor (*US News & World Report*), born Philadelphia, PA, Aug 2, 1949.
Edward Furlong, 27, actor (*Before and After*, *Terminator 2*), born Glendale, CA, Aug 2, 1977.
Kathryn Harrold, 54, actress ("I'll Fly Away," "The Larry Sanders Show," *Modern Romance*), born Tazewell, VA, Aug 2, 1950.

Lamar Hunt, 72, Hall of Fame football executive; Hall of Fame soccer executive, born El Dorado, AR, Aug 2, 1932.
Victoria Jackson, 45, actress ("Saturday Night Live," *I Love You to Death*), born Miami, FL, Aug 2, 1959.
Peter O'Toole, 71, actor (*Lawrence of Arabia*, *Becket*), born Connemara, Ireland, Aug 2, 1933.
Mary-Louise Parker, 40, actress (Tony Award for *Proof*, "The West Wing," *Fried Green Tomatoes*), born Fort Jackson, SC, Aug 2, 1964.
John Snow, 65, US Secretary of the Treasury, born Toledo, OH, Aug 2, 1939.
Michael Weiss, 28, figure skater, born Washington, DC, Aug 2, 1976.

AUGUST 3 — TUESDAY
Day 216 — 150 Remaining

COLT LEAGUE WORLD SERIES. Aug 3–10. Lafayette, IN. International amateur baseball World Series for players of league ages 15 and 16. Est attendance: 20,000. For info: PONY Baseball, PO Box 225, Washington, PA 15301. Phone: (724) 225-1060. Fax: (724) 225-9852. E-mail: info@pony.org. Web: www.pony.org.

COLUMBUS SAILS FOR THE NEW WORLD: ANNIVERSARY. Aug 3, 1492. Christopher Columbus, "Admiral of the Ocean Sea," set sail half an hour before sunrise from Palos, Spain, Aug 3, 1492. With three ships, *Niña*, *Pinta* and *Santa Maria*, and a crew of 90, he sailed "for Cathay" but found instead a New World of the Americas, first landing at Guanahani (San Salvador Island in the Bahamas) Oct 12. See also: "Columbus Day" (Oct 12).

EQUATORIAL GUINEA: ARMED FORCES DAY. Aug 3. National holiday.

GUINEA-BISSAU: COLONIZATION MARTYR'S DAY. Aug 3. National holiday. Also called Pidjiguiti Day.

KUHN, MARGARET (MAGGIE): BIRTH ANNIVERSARY. Aug 3, 1905. When she was forced into retirement because she'd reached the age of 65, Maggie Kuhn founded the Gray Panthers organization to fight age discrimination. Subsequently she waged a battle that resulted in mandatory retirement being banned. Born at Buffalo, NY, Kuhn died Apr 22, 1995, at Philadelphia, PA.

NATIONAL NIGHT OUT. Aug 3. Designed to heighten crime prevention awareness and to promote police-community partnerships. Annually, the first Tuesday in August. For info: Matt A. Peskin, Dir, Natl Assn of Town Watch. PO Box 303, Wynnewood, PA 19096. Phone: (610) 649-7055 or (800) 648-3688. Fax: (610) 649-5456. E-mail: info@natw.org. Web: www.natw.org.

NIGER: INDEPENDENCE DAY. Aug 3. Niger gained its independence from France on this day in 1960.

"PRIMETIME LIVE" TV PREMIERE: 15th ANNIVERSARY. Aug 3, 1989. Sam Donaldson and Diane Sawyer were the first hosts of this magazine show that features investigative and consumer reports as well as human interest stories.

Aug 3–4 ☆ Chase's 2004 Calendar of Events ☆

PYLE, ERNEST TAYLOR: BIRTH ANNIVERSARY. Aug 3, 1900. Ernie Pyle was born at Dana, IN, and began his career in journalism in 1923. After serving as managing editor of the Washington *Daily News*, he returned to his first journalistic love of working as a roving reporter in 1935. His column was syndicated by nearly 200 newspapers and often focused on figures behind the news. His reports of the bombing of London in 1940 and subsequent reports from Africa, Sicily, Italy and France earned him a Pulitzer Prize in 1944. He was killed by machine-gun fire at the Pacific island of Ie Shima, Apr 18, 1945.

SANTA CRUZ BEACH BOARDWALK LOOFF CAROUSEL: ANNIVERSARY. Aug 3, 1911. Danish wood-carver Charles I.D. Looff delivered the classic carousel on Aug 3, 1911. A furniture-maker by trade, Looff began carving carousel animals as a hobby after immigrating to America. His first carousel was installed at Coney Island in New York in 1875. The Boardwalk carousel features jeweled horses and a 342-pipe Ruth band organ built in 1894. The carousel and the park's Giant Dipper roller coaster were designated National Historic Landmarks by the US National Park Service in June 1987.

SCOPES, JOHN T.: BIRTH ANNIVERSARY. Aug 3, 1900. Central figure in a cause célèbre (the "Scopes Trial" or the "Monkey Trial"), John Thomas Scopes was born at Paducah, KY. An obscure 24-year-old schoolteacher at the Dayton, TN, high school in 1925, he became the focus of world attention. Scopes never uttered a word at his trial, which was a contest between two of America's best-known lawyers, William Jennings Bryan and Clarence Darrow. The trial, July 10–21, 1925, resulted in Scopes's conviction. He was fined $100 "for teaching evolution" in Tennessee. The verdict was upset on a technicality and the statute he was accused of breaching was repealed in 1967. Scopes died at Shreveport, LA, Oct 21, 1970.

TEXAS COUNTY FAIR/OLD SETTLERS REUNION. Aug 3–7. Fair Grounds, Houston, MO. A fun festival with arts and crafts, carnival midway, gospel music concert, bluegrass and country bands, demolition derby, livestock exhibit and sale. Est attendance: 8,000. For info: Texas County Fair/Old Settlers Reunion, PO Box 374, Houston, MO 65483. Phone: (417) 967-2220. Fax: (417) 967-2178.

URIS, LEON: 80th BIRTH ANNIVERSARY. Aug 3, 1924. American novelist born to a family of Russian Jews at Baltimore, MD. His most successful novels were those that chronicled the Holocaust (1960's *Mila 18*) and the founding of Israel (1958's *Exodus*). His novels sold millions and were made into several feature films. Later titles included *QB VII*, a fictionalized account of his own trial for libel, and *Trinity*, which followed the life of three generations of an Irish family. Uris died June 21, 2003, at Shelter Island, NY.

August 2004

S	M	T	W	T	F	S
1	2	3	4	5	6	7
8	9	10	11	12	13	14
15	16	17	18	19	20	21
22	23	24	25	26	27	28
29	30	31				

BIRTHDAYS TODAY

Tony Bennett, 78, singer ("I Left My Heart in San Francisco"), born Anthony Dominick Benedetto, New York, NY, Aug 3, 1926.
Steven Berkoff, 67, actor, director, writer (*A Clockwork Orange, Beverly Hills Cop*), born London, England, Aug 3, 1937.
Tom Brady, 27, football player, born San Mateo, CA, Aug 3, 1977.
P.D. James, 84, mystery novelist (*Devices and Desires, Innocent Blood*), born Phyllis Dorothy James, Oxford, England, Aug 3, 1920.
John McGinley, 45, actor (*Platoon, Born on the Fourth of July*), born New York, NY, Aug 3, 1959.
Martin Sheen, 64, actor (*Apocalypse Now*, "The West Wing"), born Ramon Estevez, Dayton, OH, Aug 3, 1940.
Martha Stewart, 63, lifestyle consultant, TV personality, writer, born Nutley, NJ, Aug 3, 1941.
Blaine Wilson, 30, gymnast, born Columbus, OH, Aug 3, 1974.

AUGUST 4 — WEDNESDAY
Day 217 — 149 Remaining

ARMSTRONG, LOUIS: BIRTH ANNIVERSARY. Aug 4, 1900 (or 1901). Jazz musician extraordinaire born at New Orleans, LA. Died at New York, NY, July 6, 1971. Armstrong often said he was born on the 4th of July, but documents in the Louis Armstrong Archives of Queens College, Flushing, NY, indicate that he was actually born Aug 4, 1900 or 1901. Asked to define jazz, Armstrong reportedly replied, "Man, if you gotta ask, you'll never know." The trumpet player was also known as Satchmo. He appeared in many films. Popular singles included "What a Wonderful World" and "Hello, Dolly" (with Barbra Streisand).

BURKINA FASO: REVOLUTION DAY: ANNIVERSARY. Aug 4. National holiday. Commemorates 1983 coup.

CANADA: CANADIAN OPEN FIDDLE CHAMPIONSHIP. Aug 4–8. Shelburne, ON. 54th annual competition. Est attendance: 10,000. For info: Shelburne Rotary Club, PO Box 27, Shelburne, ON, Canada L0N 1S0. Phone: (519) 925-3551. E-mail: cindy.sabo@sympatico.ca. Web: www.shelburnefiddlecontest.on.ca.

CANADA: DIGBY SCALLOP DAYS FESTIVAL. Aug 4–8. Digby, NS. A celebration of our seafaring heritage, honoring the fishermen of the world-famous Digby Scallop Fleet. Savor the marvelous mollusks of the deep. Cheer the scallop shuckers in competition. Enjoy five days of events for all ages including local talent, craft sales, coronation of a new Scallop Days queen, the grand street parade, a nighttime sail-past of fishing boats and scallop draggers, the Ceremony of the Flags and fireworks. Est attendance: 12,000. For info: Digby Scallop Days Assn, PO Box 983, 147 First Ave 2nd Fl, Digby, NS, Canada B0V 1A0. Phone: (877) NS-DIGBY. Fax: (902) 245-2121. Web: www.townofdigby.ns.ca.

CIVIL RIGHTS WORKERS FOUND SLAIN: 40th ANNIVERSARY. Aug 4, 1964. After disappearing on June 21, three civil rights workers were found murdered and buried in an earthen dam outside Philadelphia, MS. The three young men were workers on the Mississippi Summer Project organized by the Student Nonviolent Coordinating Committee (SNCC) to increase black voter registration. Prior to their disappearance, James Chaney, Andrew Goodman and Michael Schwerner were detained by Neshoba County police on charges of speeding. When their car was found, burned, on June 23, President Johnson ordered an FBI search for the men.

COAST GUARD DAY. Aug 4. Celebrates anniversary of founding of the Revenue Cutter Service in 1790 which merged with the Life Saving Service in 1915 to become the US Coast Guard.

CUNNINGHAM, GLENN: 95th BIRTH ANNIVERSARY. Aug 4, 1909. Glenn Clarence Cunningham, the "Kansas Ironman," American track athlete and 1934–37 world-record holder for the mile, member of the US Olympic teams in 1932 and 1936, was born at Atlanta, KS. On June 16, 1934, at Princeton, NJ, Cunningham set a world record for the mile (4:06.7 min). Cunningham died at Menifee, AR, Mar 10, 1988.

MAINE LOBSTER FESTIVAL. Aug 4–8. Harbor Park, Public Landing, Rockland, ME. Annual celebration and promotion of the lobster industry featuring lobster dinners, arts, crafts, exhibits, live entertainment, parade, contests and a road race. Est attendance: 100,000. For info: Rockland Thomaston Area Chamber of Commerce, PO Box 508, Harbor Park Public Landing, Rockland, ME 04841. Phone: (207) 596-0376. Fax: (207) 596-6549. E-mail: info@mainelobsterfestival.com. Web: www.mainelobsterfestival.com.

MANDELA, NELSON: ARREST: ANNIVERSARY. Aug 4, 1962. Nelson Rolihlahla Mandela, charismatic black South African leader, was born in 1918, the son of the Tembu tribal chief, at Umtata, Transkei territory of South Africa. A lawyer and political activist, Mandela, who in 1952 established the first black law partnership in South Africa, had been in conflict with the white government there much of his life. Acquitted of a treason charge after a trial that lasted from 1956 to 1961, he was apprehended again by security police Aug 4, 1962. The subsequent trial, widely viewed as an indictment of white domination, resulted in Mandela's being sentenced to five years in prison. In 1963 he was taken from the Pretoria prison to face a new trial—for sabotage, high treason and conspiracy to overthrow the government—and in June 1964 he was sentenced to life in prison. See also: "Mandela, Nelson: Prison Release Anniversary" (Feb 11).

McHENRY COUNTY FAIR. Aug 4–8. Woodstock, IL. Rides, food, entertainment, animal and antique competitions, talent and queen contests, demolition derby, exhibits, livestock judging and more. Est attendance: 125,000. For info: McHenry County Fairgrounds, PO Box 375, Woodstock, IL 60098. Phone: (815) 338-5315. Fax: (815) 338-5310. Web: www.mchenrycountyfair.com.

MISS CRUSTACEAN USA BEAUTY PAGEANT AND OCEAN CITY CREEP. Aug 4. 6th Street Beach, Ocean City, NJ. Participants are hermit tree crabs. To determine most beautiful tree crab and fastest tree crab on earth. Begins at 1 PM, EST. Est attendance: 500. For info: Mark Soifer, PR Dir, City of Ocean City, City Hall, Ocean City, NJ 08226. Phone: (609) 525-9300. Fax: (609) 399-0374. E-mail: MTSoifer@aol.com.

MUSTANG LEAGUE WORLD SERIES. Aug 4–7. Irving, TX. International youth baseball World Series for players of league ages 9 and 10. Est attendance: 6,000. For info: PONY Baseball, Inc, PO Box 225, Washington, PA 15301. Phone: (724) 225-1060. Fax: (724) 225-9852. E-mail: info@pony.org. Web: www.pony.org.

QUEEN ELIZABETH THE QUEEN MOTHER: BIRTH ANNIVERSARY. Aug 4, 1900. One of the most beloved members of the English royal family, the Queen "Mum" saw England through some of its most trying times in the 20th century. She was born Elizabeth Angela Marguerite Bowes-Lyon at London, England, and married the then Duke of York in 1923. When her husband was unexpectedly crowned King George IV in 1936 (after the abdication of Edward VIII), she became his strong and guiding support. She won the undying gratitude of her subjects, moreover, when she refused to remove the royal family to the safety of the countryside during the German bombing of London in World War II. After the King's death in 1952, she took on a different role, that of the Queen Mother, but kept up a busy schedule of public duties almost until her death. She died on March 30, 2002.

RICHARD, MAURICE ("ROCKET"): BIRTH ANNIVERSARY. Aug 4, 1921. Hockey Hall of Fame right wing, born at Montreal, QC, Canada. Died May 27, 2000, at Montreal.

SATCHMO SUMMER FEST. Aug 4–8. New Orleans, LA. The spirit of "Satchmo" lives with this annual birthday celebration of Louis "Satchmo" Armstrong's music, legacy and cultural contributions. The free event, centered around the Louisiana State Museum's Old US Mint (400 Esplanade Ave) will include a jazz-filled music festival, children's activities, edutaining seminars and panels, photo exhibits and cultural displays, a jazz mass and Satchmo-inspired New Orleans cuisine served up in "Red Bean Alley." It's all part of New Orleans' ongoing tribute to the "International Ambassador of Jazz" in the birthplace of jazz. Est attendance: 22,000. For info: French Quarter Festivals, Inc, 400 N Peters St, #205, New Orleans, LA 70130. Phone: (800) 673-5725 or (504) 522-5730. E-mail: feedback@fqfi.org. Web: www.satchmosummerfest.com.

SCALIGER, JOSEPH JUSTUS: BIRTH ANNIVERSARY. Aug 4, 1540 (OS). French scholar who has been called the founder of scientific chronology. Born at Agen, France, the son of classical scholar Julius Caesar Scaliger. In 1582 he suggested a new system for measuring time and numbering years. His "Julian Period" (named for his father), which consisted of 7,980 consecutive years (beginning Jan 1, 4713 BC), is still in use by astronomers. He died at Leiden, Netherlands, Jan 21, 1609 (OS).

SCHUMAN, WILLIAM HOWARD: BIRTH ANNIVERSARY. Aug 4, 1910. American composer who won the first Pulitzer Prize for composition and founded the Juilliard School of Music, born at New York. His compositions include *American Festival Overture, New England Triptych*, the baseball opera *The Mighty Casey* and *On Freedom's Ground*, written for the centennial of the conception of the Statue of Liberty in 1986. He was instrumental in the conception of the Lincoln Center for the Performing Arts and served as its first president. In 1985 he was awarded a special Pulitzer Prize for his contributions. He also received a National Medal of Arts in 1985 and a Kennedy Center Honor in 1989. Schuman died at New York City, Feb 15, 1992.

SCOTLAND: ABERDEEN INTERNATIONAL YOUTH FESTIVAL. Aug 4–14. Aberdeen. Talented young people from all areas of the performing arts come from around the world to participate in this festival. Est attendance: 30,000. For info: Stephen Stenning, Linksfield Community Centre, 520 King St, Aberdeen, Scotland AB24 5SS. Phone: (44) (1224) 484400. Fax: (44) (1224) 484114. E-mail: admin@aiyf.org. Web: www.aiyf.org.

SEASHORE OPEN HOUSE TOUR. Aug 4. Loveladies, NJ. 38th annual. Come and enjoy the fabulous shoreline houses. For info: Long Beach Island Foundation of the Arts and Sciences, 120 Long Beach Blvd, Loveladies, NJ 08008. Phone: (609) 494-1241. Fax: (609) 494-0662.

SHELLEY, PERCY BYSSHE: BIRTH ANNIVERSARY. Aug 4, 1792. Poet Percy Bysshe Shelley, one of the leading English Romantic poets and embodiment of a free spirit, was born at Warnham, Sussex. He lived abroad in Italy until his death at sea off the coast of Viareggio, just a month before his 30th birthday, July 8, 1822. Shelley's important works include "Ozymandias," published in 1818; "Ode to the West Wind," "The Cloud," "To a Skylark" and *Prometheus Unbound* in 1819; and *Adonais* (an elegy for John Keats) in 1821.

Aug 4–5 ☆ *Chase's 2004 Calendar of Events* ☆

BIRTHDAYS TODAY

Yasser Arafat, 75, president of the Palestinian National Authority, chairman of the Executive Committee of the PLO, born Jerusalem, Aug 4, 1929.

Richard Belzer, 60, comedian, actor (*Mad Dog and Glory*, "Homicide: Life on the Street"), born Bridgeport, CT, Aug 4, 1944.

(William) Roger Clemens, 42, baseball player, born Dayton, OH, Aug 4, 1962.

Jeff Gordon, 33, race car driver, born Pittsboro, IN, Aug 4, 1971.

Kristoffer Tabori, 52, actor ("Seventh Avenue," "Chicago Story"), born Los Angeles, CA, Aug 4, 1952.

Helen Thomas, 84, journalist (longtime White House correspondent), born Winchester, KY, Aug 4, 1920.

Billy Bob Thornton, 49, actor (*The Man Who Wasn't There*, *A Simple Plan*), director, screenwriter (Oscar for *Sling Blade*), born Hot Springs, AR, Aug 4, 1955.

AUGUST 5 — THURSDAY
Day 218 — 148 Remaining

AIKEN, CONRAD: BIRTH ANNIVERSARY. Aug 5, 1899. American poet, short-story writer, critic and Pulitzer Prize winner (poetry, 1930). He was born at Savannah, GA, and died there Aug 17, 1973.

"AMERICAN BANDSTAND" TV PREMIERE: ANNIVERSARY. Aug 5, 1957. "American Bandstand" and Dick Clark are synonymous; he hosted the show for more than 30 years. "AB" started out as a local show at Philadelphia in 1952. Clark, then a disk jockey, took over as host at the age of 26. The format was simple: teens dancing, performers doing their latest hits, Clark introducing songs and listing the top 10 songs each week. This hour-long show was not only TV's longest-running musical series, but also the first one devoted exclusively to rock and roll. The show was cancelled six months after Clark turned over the hosting duties to David Hirsch in 1989.

BATTLE OF MOBILE BAY: ANNIVERSARY. Aug 5, 1864. A Union fleet under Admiral David Farragut attempted to run past three Confederate forts into Mobile Bay, AL. After coming under fire, the Union fleet headed into a maze of underwater mines, known at that time as torpedos. The ironclad *Tecumseh* was sunk by a torpedo, after which Farragut is said to have exclaimed, "Damn the torpedoes, full steam ahead." The Union fleet was successful and Mobile Bay was secured.

BEARD, MARY R.: BIRTH ANNIVERSARY. Aug 5, 1876. American historian Mary Ritter Beard was born at Indianapolis, IN. Many of her books were written in collaboration with her husband, Charles A. Beard. She died at Phoenix, AZ, Aug 14, 1958.

BRONCO LEAGUE WORLD SERIES. Aug 5–10. Monterey, CA. International youth baseball World Series for players of league ages 11 and 12. Est attendance: 15,000. For info: PONY Baseball, PO Box 225, Washington, PA 15301. Phone: (724) 225-1060. Fax: (724) 225-9852. E-mail: info@pony.org. Web: www.pony.org.

BURKINA FASO: REPUBLIC DAY. Aug 5. Burkina Faso (formerly Upper Volta) gained autonomy from France in 1960.

	S	M	T	W	T	F	S
August	1	2	3	4	5	6	7
2004	8	9	10	11	12	13	14
	15	16	17	18	19	20	21
	22	23	24	25	26	27	28
	29	30	31				

CANADA: EDMONTON FOLK MUSIC FESTIVAL. Aug 5–8. Gallagher Park, Edmonton, AB. Folk music and fun for the entire family highlighting blues, country, Celtic, traditional folk and bluegrass music, arts and crafts displays and a food fair. Est attendance: 80,000. For info: Edmonton Folk Music Festival Society, PO Box 4130, Edmonton, AB, Canada T6E 4T2. Phone: (780) 429-1899. E-mail: folkfest@edmontonfolkfest.org. Web: www.edmontonfolkfest.org.

CANADA: HALIFAX INTERNATIONAL BUSKER FESTIVAL. Aug 5–15. Halifax, NS. Street performers and artists from around the world, vaudeville nights and entertainment tent. Est attendance: 500,000. For info: Halifax Intl Busker Fest, c/o Pickford & Black, 1869 Upper Water St, 5th Fl, Halifax, NS, Canada B3J 1S9. Phone: (902) 429-3910. Fax: (902) 429-7554. E-mail: buskers@ns.sympatico.ca.

CROATIA: HOMELAND THANKSGIVING DAY. Aug 5. National holiday.

ELIOT, JOHN: 300th BIRTH ANNIVERSARY. Aug 5, 1604 (OS). American "Apostle to the Indians," translator of the Bible into an Indian tongue (the first Bible to be printed in America), was born at Hertfordshire, England. He died at Roxbury, MA, May 21, 1690 (OS).

FESTIVAL AT SANDPOINT. Aug 5–8, 11–15. Sandpoint, ID. Summer music concert series featuring classical, country, jazz, pop, world, blues and folk. Est attendance: 20,000. For info: Dyno Wahl, Exec Dir, Festival at Sandpoint, PO Box 695, Sandpoint, ID 83864. Phone: (888) 265-4554. Fax: (208) 263-0858. E-mail: festival@sandpoint.net. Web: www.festivalatsandpoint.com.

FIRST ENGLISH COLONY IN NORTH AMERICA: ANNIVERSARY. Aug 5, 1583. Sir Humphrey Gilbert, English navigator and explorer, aboard his sailing ship, the *Squirrel*, sighted the Newfoundland coast and took possession of the area around St. John's harbor in the name of the Queen, thus establishing the first English colony in North America. Gilbert was lost at sea, in a storm off the Azores, on his return trip to England.

IRELAND: BANK HOLIDAY. Aug 5. Bank holiday in the Republic of Ireland.

LYNCH, THOMAS: BIRTH ANNIVERSARY. Aug 5, 1749. Signer, Declaration of Independence, born Prince George's Parish, SC. Died 1779 (lost at sea, exact date of death unknown).

MOUNTAIN DANCE AND FOLK FESTIVAL. Aug 5–7. Asheville, NC. 77th annual festival. More than 400 performers in this three-day fest, which celebrates the cultural heritage of the Southern Appalachian Mountains. Includes dance teams, mountain fiddlers, banjo pickers, old-time string bands, storytellers, bluegrass bands and dulcimer sweepers. Oldest of its kind, founded in 1928 by Bascom Lamar Lunsford. Est attendance: 3,500. For info: Asheville Area Chamber of Commerce, Folk Heritage, PO Box 1010, Asheville, NC 28802. Phone: (828) 258-6101 x789.

OMARR, SIDNEY: BIRTH ANNIVERSARY. Aug 5, 1926. Born Sidney Kimmelman at Philadelphia, PA, this world-famous astrologer became fascinated by numerology and astrology, and changed his name to "Sydney Omarr" at the age of 15. He began contributing to astrology magazines, and eventually became well known in Hollywood. He wrote dozens of books, an average of thirteen per year, that sold more than 50 million copies. His newspaper astrology column was syndicated in more than 200 newspapers. He died Jan 16, 2003, at Santa Monica, CA.

QUILT ODYSSEY 2004. Aug 5–8. Gettysburg, PA. Judged quilt competition; antique and special quilt exhibits. Large merchants' mall. Classes and lectures by nationally known professional quilters. Est attendance: 7,000. For info: Quilt Odyssey, 15004 Burnt Mill Rd, Shippensburg, PA 17257. Phone: (717) 423-5148. E-mail: dmolino@cvn.net.

RIBFEST. Aug 5–7. Kalamazoo, MI. Features the smell of sizzling ribs as rib-burners from throughout the US tantalize the taste buds of West Michigan. Festival will feature live entertainment, family-oriented events, food booths and the "Sponsors Choice

410

Award" for best ribs. Annually, the first full weekend in Aug (including Thursday). Est attendance: 24,000. For info: Deborah Droppers, Community Advocates for Persons with Developmental Disabilities, 814 S Westnedge St, Kalamazoo, MI 49008-1162. Phone: (269) 388-2830. E-mail: eventkzoo@ chartermi.net. Web: www.eventkalamazoo.com.

WALLENBERG, RAOUL: BIRTH ANNIVERSARY. Aug 5, 1912. Swedish architect Raoul Gustaf Wallenberg was born at Stockholm, Sweden. He was the second person in history (Winston Churchill was the first) to be voted honorary American citizenship (US House of Representatives 396-2, Sept 22, 1981). He is credited with saving 100,000 Jews from almost certain death at the hands of the Nazis during WWII. Wallenberg was arrested by Soviet troops at Budapest, Hungary, Jan 17, 1945, and, according to the official Soviet press agency Tass, died in prison at Moscow, July 17, 1947.

WISCONSIN STATE FAIR. Aug 5–15. State Fair Park, Milwaukee, WI. Wisconsin celebrates its rural heritage at the state's most popular and most historic annual event. Features more than 150 midway rides; 28 free stages of entertainment; livestock, food and flower judging and top-name entertainment. [Call 24-hour recorded information line at 1-800-884-FAIR for up-to-date information.] Est attendance: 910,000. For info: PR Dept, Wisconsin State Fair Park, PO Box 14990, West Allis, WI 53214-0990. Phone: (414) 266-7000. Fax: (414) 266-7007. E-mail: wsfp@sfp.state.wi.us. Web: www.wistatefair.com.

BIRTHDAYS TODAY

Loni Anderson, 58, actress ("WKRP in Cincinnati," *The Jayne Mansfield Story*), born St. Paul, MN, Aug 5, 1946.
Neil Alden Armstrong, 74, former astronaut (first man to walk on moon), born Wapakoneta, OH, Aug 5, 1930.
Ja'net DuBois, 66, actress ("Good Times," "Beverly Hills 90210"), born Philadelphia, PA, Aug 5, 1938.
Patrick Aloysius Ewing, 42, basketball player, born Kingston, Jamaica, Aug 5, 1962.
Lorrie Fair, 26, soccer player, born Los Altos, CA, Aug 5, 1978.
Eric Hinske, 27, baseball player, born Menasha, WI, Aug 5, 1977.
John Olerud, 36, baseball player, born Seattle, WA, Aug 5, 1968.
John Saxon, 68, actor ("Falcon Crest," *Enter the Dragon, Nightmare on Elm Street*), born Brooklyn, NY, Aug 5, 1936.
Jonathan Silverman, 38, actor ("The Single Guy," *Weekend at Bernie's*), born Los Angeles, CA, Aug 5, 1966.
Erika Slezak, 58, actress ("One Life to Live"), born Los Angeles, CA, Aug 5, 1946.
Sammi Smith, 61, singer ("Help Me Make It Through the Night"), born Orange, CA, Aug 5, 1943.

AUGUST 6 — FRIDAY
Day 219 — 147 Remaining

ATOMIC BOMB DROPPED ON HIROSHIMA: ANNIVERSARY. Aug 6, 1945. At 8:15 AM, local time, an American B-29 bomber, the *Enola Gay*, dropped an atomic bomb named "Little Boy" over the center of the city of Hiroshima, Japan. The bomb exploded about 1,800 ft above the ground, killing more than 105,000 civilians and destroying the city. It is estimated that another 100,000 persons were injured and died subsequently as a direct result of the bomb and the radiation it produced. This was the first time in history that such a devastating weapon had been used by any nation.

BALL, LUCILLE: BIRTH ANNIVERSARY. Aug 6, 1911. Film and television pioneer and comedienne born at Jamestown, NY. In addition to her many film and television credits, Lucille Ball always will be remembered for her role in the 1950's CBS sitcom "I Love Lucy." As Lucy Ricardo, the wife of bandleader Ricky Ricardo (her real-life husband Desi Arnaz), she exhibited a comedic style that became a trademark of early television comedy. She died Apr 26, 1989, at Los Angeles, CA.

BAY HARBOR SUMMER ART FAIR. Aug 6–7. Bay Harbor, MI. 5th annual fine art and fine craft show, located in the Marina District, near Charlevoix and Petosky. Est attendance: 8,700. For info: Audree Levy, 1809 Morning Glory, Carrollton, TX 75007. E-mail: audree@levyartfairs.com. Web: www.levyartfairs.com.

BLUEBERRY FESTIVAL. Aug 6–7. Library Lawn and Village Green, Montrose, PA. 25th annual fund-raiser for the Susquehanna County Library and Historical Society. Two days filled with food, fun and festivity. Raffles, book sale, children's games, silent auction, hand-stitched quilt, commemorative items and more. Annually, the first Friday and Saturday in August. Est attendance: 5,000. For info: Hilary Caws-Elwitt, Susquehanna County Library, 2 Monument Sq, Montrose, PA 18801. Phone: (570) 278-1881. Fax: (570) 278-9336. E-mail: sctylibrary@stny.rr.com. Web: www.susqcolib.org/bf.htm.

BOLIVIA: INDEPENDENCE DAY. Aug 6. National holiday. Gained freedom from Spain in 1825. Named after Simon Bolívar.

BOOM DAYS. Aug 6–8. Leadville, CO. The city's oldest annual celebration features a large parade, street races, mining events, pack burro race and arts and crafts. Fun for the whole family. Est attendance: 35,000. For info: Chamber of Commerce, PO Box 861, Leadville, CO 80461. Phone: (719) 486-3900 or (800) 933-3901. Fax: (719) 486-8478. E-mail: leadville@leadvilleusa.com. Web: www.leadvilleusa.com.

BRAHAM PIE DAY. Aug 6. Freedom Park, Braham, MN. Celebrate Braham's status as "Homemade Pie Capital of Minnesota" during this one-day festival. Visitors will find homemade pies, craft displays, pie-eating contests, a pie auction, a pie race and performing artists in Braham's main street park. Activities also include an exotic pie-eating contest, a pi R squared contest, a pie art show and the "Pie-alluia" chorus. Est attendance: 5,000. For info: Kathy McCully, Isanti County Historical Society, PO Box 525, Cambridge, MN 55008. Phone: (763) 689-4229 or (320) 396-4956. Fax: (763) 689-4229. E-mail: mccully@usfamily.net. Web: www.braham.com. Or Andrea Downing. Phone: (320) 393-4956. E-mail: dandrea@ecenet.com.

CANADA: BOISSEVAIN TURTLE ISLAND FESTIVAL. Aug 6–8. Boissevain, MB. A fun-filled family event, adjacent to the famous International Peace Garden. Ball and volleyball tourneys, golf tournament and children's entertainment. Outdoor Art Gallery with more than 24 murals! Moncur Gallery of Prehistory, bird watching, artisans at work painting and weaving. Ample camping available. For info: Ivan Strain, PO Box 122, Boissevain, MB, Canada R0K 0E0. Phone: (204) 534-6000. Fax: (204) 534-6825. E-mail: istrain@goldenwestradio.com.

Aug 6 ☆ Chase's 2004 Calendar of Events ☆

CRAFTSMEN'S CLASSIC ARTS & CRAFTS FESTIVAL. Aug 6–8. Myrtle Beach Convention Center, Myrtle Beach, SC. 22nd annual. Features work from more than 260 talented artists and craftspeople. All juried exhibitors' work has been handmade by the exhibitors and must be their own original design and creation. See the creative process in action with several exhibitors demonstrating their craft. Something for every style, taste, and budget with items from the most contemporary to the most traditional. Est attendance: 15,000. For info: Gilmore Enterprises, Inc, 1240 Oakland Ave, Greensboro, NC 27403. Phone: (336) 274-5550. E-mail: gilmoreshows@triad.rr.com.

DECATUR CELEBRATION. Aug 6–8. Decatur, IL. The largest free family street festival in Illinois; within 22 city blocks of fun there are 13 entertainment stages, 110 arts and crafts vendors, 46 commercial vendors, and 69 one-of-a-kind food vendors. Est attendance: 300,000. For info: Decatur Celebration, 132 S Water, Ste 418, Decatur, IL 62523. Phone: (217) 423-4222. Fax: (217) 423-4271. Web: decaturcelebration.com.

ELECTROCUTION FIRST USED TO CARRY OUT DEATH PENALTY: ANNIVERSARY. Aug 6, 1890. At Auburn Prison, Auburn, NY, William Kemmler of Buffalo, NY, became the first man to be executed by electrocution. He had been convicted of the hatchet murder of his common-law wife, Matilde Ziegler, on Mar 28, 1889. This first attempt at using electrocution to carry out the death penalty was a botched affair. As reported by George Westinghouse, Jr, "It has been a brutal affair. They could have done better with an axe."

FIRST WOMAN SWIMS THE ENGLISH CHANNEL: ANNIVERSARY. Aug 6, 1926. The first woman to swim the English Channel was 19-year-old Gertrude Ederle of New York, NY. Her swim was completed in 14 hours and 31 minutes.

FLEMING, ALEXANDER: BIRTH ANNIVERSARY. Aug 6, 1881. Sir Alexander Fleming, Scottish bacteriologist, discoverer of penicillin and 1945 Nobel Prize recipient, was born at Lochfield, Scotland. He died at London, England, Mar 11, 1955.

GIFT OF THE WATERS PAGEANT & ART FESTIVAL IN THE PARK. Aug 6–8. Hot Springs State Park, Thermopolis, WY. Indian dance demonstrations and pageant, powwow, parade, arts & crafts festival, craft demonstrations. Est attendance: 6,000. For info: Toddi Darlington, Thermopolis Chamber of Commerce, 700 Broadway, Thermopolis, WY 82443. Phone: (307) 864-3192. E-mail: thercc@trib.com. Web: www.thermopolis.com.

GIGGLEFEET DANCE FESTIVAL. Aug 6 & 8. Ketchikan, AK. Two evening performances celebrating dance in the community, including jazz, tap, ballet, modern, hip-hop, Native Alaskan, break dancing and more. Annually, the first Friday and Sunday in August, part of the Blueberry Arts Festival. Est attendance: 1,000. For info: Ketchikan Area Arts & Humanities Council, 716 Totem Way, Ketchikan, AK 99901. Phone: (907) 225-2211. Fax: (907) 225-4330. E-mail: ketchart@kpunet.net.

GREAT ARKANSAS PIG-OUT. Aug 6–7. Morrilton, AR. 16th annual pig-out. Focus is on food of all kinds: barbecue, chicken-on-a-stick, funnel cakes, hamburgers. Activities include pig chase, hog calling, children's pig-tail, arts, crafts, games, entertainment, Tour de Oink, 5K fun run. Est attendance: 25,000. For info: Chamber of Commerce, 120 N Division, Morrilton, AR 72110. Phone: (501) 354-2393. Fax: (501) 354-8642. E-mail: mcc@mev.net. Web: www.pigout.org.

"GREAT DEBATE": ANNIVERSARY. Aug 6–Sept 10, 1787. The Constitutional Convention engaged in the "Great Debate" over the draft constitution, during which it determined that Congress should have the right to regulate foreign trade and interstate commerce, established a four-year term of office for the president and appointed a five-man committee to prepare a final draft of the Constitution.

HALFWAY POINT OF SUMMER. Aug 6. On this day at 4:43 PM EDT, 46 days, 19 hours and 46 minutes will have elapsed and the equivalent will remain before Sept 22, 2004, the autumnal equinox and the beginning of autumn.

HIROSHIMA DAY: ANNIVERSARY. Aug 6. Memorial observances in many places for victims of the first atomic bombing of a populated place, which occurred at Hiroshima, Japan in 1945, when an American B-29 bomber dropped an atomic bomb over the center of the city. More than 205,000 civilians died either immediately in the explosion or subsequently of radiation.

INDIAN ARTIFACT SHOW. Aug 6–8. Owensboro, KY. To promote the art and culture of prehistoric Indians and to display outstanding collections of relics; buying, selling and trading. Est attendance: 3,000. For info: Kathy Pohl Finley, Box 93, Cannelton, IN 47520-0093. Phone: (812) 547-3255. Fax: (812) 547-2525. E-mail: kpohl@psci.net.

JAPAN: PEACE FESTIVAL. Aug 6. Hiroshima. The festival held annually at Peace Memorial Park is observed in memory of the victims of the Aug 6, 1945, atomic bomb explosion there.

JUDGE CRATER DISAPPEARANCE: ANNIVERSARY. Aug 6, 1930. Anniversary of mysterious disappearance at age 41, on Aug 6, 1930, of Joseph Force Crater, justice of the New York State Supreme Court. Never seen or heard from after disappearance on this date. Declared legally dead in 1939.

MITCHUM, ROBERT: BIRTH ANNIVERSARY. Aug 6, 1917. Film actor (*The Night of the Hunter, The Story of GI Joe*), born at Bridgeport, CT. Died July 1, 1997, at Santa Barbara County, CA.

MODEL BOAT SHOW. Aug 6–8. K of C Hall, Clayton, NY. 7th annual. Static model show with scratch-built and kit-built classic boats. Fri & Sat, 9 AM to 5 PM, Sun 10 AM to 4 PM. Admission is $3 for adults, $1 for students, to benefit The Thousand Islands Museum. Annually, the first weekend in August. For info: Pete Strouse, Chairman, Thousand Islands Museum, PO Box 27, Clayton, NY 13624. Phone: (315) 686-5260 or (315) 686-5794. E-mail: timuseum@gisco.net. Web: www.timuseum.org.

MUSIKFEST. Aug 6–15. Bethlehem, PA. Entertainment, ethnic foods and music—more than 1,000 live performances from Bach to bluegrass to rock. Fourteen indoor and outdoor stages. Est attendance: 1,000,000. For info: ArtsQuest, 25 W Third St, Bethlehem, PA 18015-1238. Phone: (610) 861-0678. Fax: (610) 861-2644. E-mail: info@fest.org. Web: www.musikfest.org.

NATIONAL CZECHOSLOVAKIAN FESTIVAL. Aug 6–8. Wilber, NE. Festival to promote preservation of Czech culture,

August 2004

S	M	T	W	T	F	S
1	2	3	4	5	6	7
8	9	10	11	12	13	14
15	16	17	18	19	20	21
22	23	24	25	26	27	28
29	30	31				

foods, traditions—accordion, polka and Czech band music, parades, national queen contest, museum, art show, Czech dinners, programs, contests, fellowship, reunions. Annually, the first weekend in August. Cosponsored by Nebraska Czechs of Wilber. Est attendance: 40,000. For info: Wilber Chamber of Commerce, PO Box 1164, Wilber, NE 68465. Phone: (888) 4-WILBER.

NATIONAL FRESH BREATH DAY. Aug 6. Offensive breath wafts across all boundaries of age, income and intelligence. It manifests itself at the worst possible times: breaking business deals, stopping love in its tracks and just ruining otherwise fine relationships. National Fresh Breath Day is an educational awareness day designed to bring attention to the importance of fresh breath as an integral part of your overall health and wellness, as well as the impact it has on your personal and professional image. For info: Carol Meyer, Personal Breath Consultants, PO Box 65, Westhampton Beach, NY 11978-0065. Phone: (631) 288-7285. E-mail: Breathlady@hotmail.com.

NATIONAL PAMPER YOURSELF DAY. Aug 6. Indulge yourself today! Take the time to be good to yourself. Take a bubble bath, read a new book, get a massage, buy some fine chocolate. Whatever you choose to do, make an effort to do it—just for you! Annually, Aug 6. For info: Angela Grose, PO Box 1023, Sandia Park, NM 87047. Phone: (505) 286-7754. E-mail: hbbath@yahoo.com.

NEARING, SCOTT: BIRTH ANNIVERSARY. Aug 6, 1883. American sociologist, antiwar crusader, back-to-the-land advocate and author, with his wife Helen, of *Living the Good Life* (1954). He was born at Morris Run, PA, and died a century later at his farm at Harborside, ME, Aug 24, 1983.

NEW JERSEY STATE FAIR. Aug 6–15. Sussex County Fairgrounds, Augusta, NJ. For info: New Jersey State Fair, PO Box 2456, Branchville, NJ 07826. Phone: (973) 948-5500. Fax: (973) 948-0147. E-mail: thefair@njstatefair.com. Web: www.njstatefair.com.

O'CONNELL, DANIEL: BIRTH ANNIVERSARY. Aug 6, 1775. Irish Catholic political leader Daniel O'Connell, known as "the Liberator" for his role in achieving the right of Catholics to sit in Parliament, was born near Cahirciveen, County Kerry. He died at age 81, May 15, 1847, at Genoa, Italy.

OHIO STATE FAIR. Aug 6–22. Columbus, OH. Family fun, amusement rides, games, food booths, parades, entertainment, agriculture exhibits and educational displays. Est attendance: 900,000. For info: Ohio State Fair, 717 E 17th Ave, Columbus, OH 43211. Phone: (614) 644-4000. Fax: (614) 644-4031. Web: www.ohiostatefair.com.

PALOMINO LEAGUE WORLD SERIES. Aug 6–9. Santa Clara, CA. International young adult baseball World Series for players of league ages 17 and 18. Est attendance: 3,000. For info: PONY Baseball, Inc, Box 225, Washington, PA 15301. Phone: (724) 225-1060. Fax: (724) 225-9852. E-mail: info@pony.org. Web: www.pony.org.

ROOSEVELT, EDITH KERMIT CAROW: BIRTH ANNIVERSARY. Aug 6, 1861. Second wife of Theodore Roosevelt, 26th president of the US, whom she married in 1886. Born at Norwich, CT, she died at Long Island, NY, Sept 30, 1948.

SCOTLAND: EDINBURGH MILITARY TATTOO: THE MAIN EVENT. Aug 6–28. Edinburgh Castle, Edinburgh, Lothian. Display of military color and pageantry held at night on the flood-lit esplanade of Edinburgh Castle. A unique blend of music, ceremony, entertainment and theater. Est attendance: 217,000. For info: The Edinburgh Military Tattoo, The Tattoo Office, 32 Market St, Edinburgh, Scotland EH1 1QB. Phone: (44) (131) 225-1188. Fax: (44) (131) 225-8627. E-mail: edintattoo@edintattoo.co.uk. Web: www.edintattoo.co.uk.

SPACE MILESTONE: *VOSTOK 2* (USSR). Aug 6, 1961. Launched on Aug 6, 1961, Gherman Titov orbited Earth 17 times over a period of 25 hours, 18 minutes. Titov broadcast messages in passage over countries, controlled spaceship manually for two hours.

SUSSEX COUNTY FARM AND HORSE SHOW/NEW JERSEY STATE FAIR. Aug 6–15. Augusta, NJ. The state's largest livestock and horse show also includes educational exhibits, amusements, commercial exhibits and entertainment. Located off Rt 206 Plains Rd. Gate opens 1 PM Friday and closes 7 PM Sunday. Est attendance: 220,000. For info: Howard Worts, Mgr, PO Box 2456, Branchville, NJ 07826. Phone: (973) 948-5500. Fax: (973) 948-0147. E-mail: thefair@njstatefair.com. Web: www.newjerseystatefair.org.

TELLURIDE JAZZ CELEBRATION. Aug 6–8. Telluride, CO. Some of jazz's hottest rising stars and most accomplished musicians team up in the town park by day and in intimate nightclubs at night. Annually, the first weekend in August. Est attendance: 1,500. For info: Telluride Mountain Village Visitor Services, PO Box 1009, Telluride, CO 81435. Phone: (800) 525-8455. Fax: (970) 728-6475. E-mail: info@visittelluride.com. Web: www.visittelluride.com.

TENNYSON, ALFRED, LORD: BIRTH ANNIVERSARY. Aug 6, 1808. English poet born at Somersby, Lincolnshire, England. His most celebrated works include the poems "The Lady of Shalott" and "The Lotos-Eaters" and the verse novelettes *Maud, Enoch Arden, In Memoriam, Locksley Hall Sixty Years After* and *The Idylls of the King*. Appointed English poet laureate in 1850 in succession to William Wordsworth and made a peer in 1884. Died at Aldworth, England, Oct 6, 1892.

TWINS DAY FESTIVAL. Aug 6–8. Twinsburg, OH. According to *Guinness Book of World Records*, this is the world's largest gathering of twins. Annually, the first weekend in August. For info: Twins Day Festival Committee, PO Box 29, Twinsburg, OH 44087. Phone: (330) 425-3652. E-mail: info@twinsdays.org. Web: www.twinsdays.org.

VOTING RIGHTS ACT OF 1965 SIGNED: ANNIVERSARY. Aug 6, 1965. Signed into law by President Lyndon Johnson, the Voting Rights Act of 1965 was designed to thwart attempts to discriminate against minorities at the polls. The act suspended literacy and other disqualifying tests, authorized appointment of federal voting examiners and provided for judicial relief on the federal level to bar discriminatory poll taxes. Congress voted to extend the Act in 1975, 1984 and 1991.

WARHOL, ANDY: BIRTH ANNIVERSARY. Aug 6, 1928. The artist, filmmaker and provocateur was born Andrew Warhola to Czech immigrant parents at Forest City, PA. (Some sources cite his birth year as 1927.) A leader of the Pop art movement, Warhol challenged the definitions of art. After a stint as a commercial artist, Warhol gained attention in 1962 with paintings of ordinary commercial products—most famously, Campbell's soup cans—and pop culture figures. He moved on to silk-screen portraits (of subjects like Marilyn Monroe, Elvis Presley and Mao Tse-Tung) and experimental film projects (*Empire* [1964] was a static depiction of the Empire State Building that ran more than eight hours). Warhol was at the center of New York's celebrity scene, and in 1968 it was he who claimed, "In the future everyone will be world-famous for fifteen minutes." Warhol died Feb 22, 1987, at New York, NY.

☆ Chase's 2004 Calendar of Events ☆

Aug 6-7

WHITE RIVER WATER CARNIVAL. Aug 6–7. Batesville, AR. Public receptions, Miss White River pageant, bass classic tournament, four-mile run, four-ball golf tournament, arts, crafts, parade, children's activities, entertainment in the park, ski show, car and bike show. Est attendance: 9,000. For info: Batesville Area Chamber of Commerce, 409 Vine, Batesville, AR 72501. Phone: (870) 793-2378. Fax: (870) 793-3061. E-mail: batesvillechamber@cox-internet.com. Web: watercarnival.com.

WORK LIKE A DOG DAY. Aug 6. A celebration (during the Dog Days of summer) of the professional and personal satisfaction experienced by entrepreneurs and small businesses that work like a dog to be successful. Take this day to lap up and celebrate the rewards of your success. Stop by a spa: just because you work like a dog, it doesn't mean you have to look like one. Annually, the first Friday of August. For info: Aida Rodriquez, Evil Twin Productions, 5201 Fulton Ave, Los Angeles, CA 91401. Phone: (818) 986-8551. E-mail: Aida@eviltwinproductions.com. Web: www.eviltwinproductions.com.

WORLD FREEFALL CONVENTION. Aug 6–15. Rantoul, IL. More than 5,400 skydivers converge in Rantoul and fill the skies with their brilliant-colored parachutes. Spectators can enjoy the sights and take part in helicopter rides and hot-air balloon rides. Those wishing to skydive may purchase a tandem skydive or take lessons and skydive on their own. Est attendance: 100,000. For info: World Freefall Convention, 1659 Hwy 104, Quincy, IL 62301. Phone: (217) 222-5867. Fax: (217) 885-3141. E-mail: wffc@freefall.com. Web: www.freefall.com.

BIRTHDAYS TODAY

Peter Bonerz, 66, actor ("The Bob Newhart Show," "9 to 5"), director, born Portsmouth, NH, Aug 6, 1938.
Soleil Moon Frye, 28, actress ("Punky Brewster"), born Glendora, CA, Aug 6, 1976.
Dorian Harewood, 54, actor (*The Falcon and the Snowman, Full Metal Jacket*), born Dayton, OH, Aug 6, 1950.
Catherine Hicks, 53, actress (*Marilyn, Peggy Sue Got Married*), born Scottsdale, AZ, Aug 6, 1951.
Shirley Ann Jackson, 58, first woman to chair US Nuclear Regulatory Commission, born Washington, DC, Aug 6, 1946.
Freddie Laker, 82, former airline executive, born Kent, England, Aug 6, 1922.
Jim McGreevey, 47, Governor of New Jersey (D), born Jersey City, NJ, Aug 6, 1957.
David Maurice Robinson, 39, basketball player, born Key West, FL, Aug 6, 1965.
Michelle Yeoh, 42, actress (*Crouching Tiger, Hidden Dragon; Tomorrow Never Dies*), born Yang Zi Chong at Ipoh, Perak, Malaysia, Aug 6, 1962.

August 2004

S	M	T	W	T	F	S
1	2	3	4	5	6	7
8	9	10	11	12	13	14
15	16	17	18	19	20	21
22	23	24	25	26	27	28
29	30	31				

AUGUST 7 — SATURDAY
Day 220 — 146 Remaining

AMHERST'S TEDDY BEAR RALLY. Aug 7. Amherst, MA. 21st annual rally features teddy bear parade, used bear lot, coloring event, Teddy Bear Hospital, UMass Oompah Band, Winnie-the-Pooh readings and more than 165 teddy bear dealers and exhibits. Entertainment free; refreshments available. Est attendance: 20,000. For info: Amherst Rotary Club, Teddy Bear Rally Committee, PO Box 542, Amherst, MA 01004. E-mail: baldrich@admin.umass.edu. Web: www.amherst-teddybear-rally.org.

BLUEBERRY ARTS FESTIVAL. Aug 7. State Office Building, Methodist Church and Mainstay Gallery and Theatre, Ketchikan, AK. A street fair featuring arts and crafts, food, games and contests for all ages, performing arts events and poetry and prose reading. Annually, the first Saturday in August. Est attendance: 7,000. For info: Ketchikan Area Arts and Humanities Council, 716 Totem Way, Ketchikan, AK 99901. Phone: (907) 225-2211. Fax: (907) 225-4330. E-mail: ketchart@kpunet.net.

BUNCHE, RALPH JOHNSON: 100th BIRTH ANNIVERSARY. Aug 7, 1904. American statesman, UN official, Nobel Peace Prize recipient (the first black to win the award), born at Detroit, MI. Died Dec 9, 1971, at New York, NY. See also: "Bunche, Ralph: Awarded Nobel Peace Prize: Anniv" (Dec 10).

COLOMBIA: BATTLE OF BOYACÁ. Aug 7. National holiday. Commemorates victory over Spanish forces in 1819.

CÔTE D'IVOIRE: NATIONAL DAY. Aug 7. Commemorates the independence of the Ivory Coast from France in 1960.

DESERT SHIELD: ANNIVERSARY. Aug 7, 1990. Five days after the Iraqi invasion of Kuwait, US President George Bush ordered the military buildup that would become known as Desert Shield to prevent further Iraqi advances.

ELEANOR ROOSEVELT DAY. Aug 7–9. Menlo, WA. Celebration of this great lady's life includes speakers, music, picnic. Sponsored by Willapa Valley Grange #527 and Willapa DAWN. Annually, the long weekend culminating in the second Monday in August. For info: Anne Louise Grimm, 434-6th St #206, Raymond, WA 98577-1804. Phone: (360) 942-4596. E-mail: anne@willapabay.org. Web: www.willapabay.org/grange05.htm.

ELVIS WEEK. Aug 7–16. Memphis, TN. Each year Elvis fans from around the world visit Memphis as Aug 16 marks the anniversary of Elvis Presley's death (Aug 16, 1977) at his beloved home, Graceland Mansion. More than 35 events occur throughout the city with special events sponsored by Graceland. Est attendance: 40,000. For info: Graceland, 3734 Elvis Presley Blvd, Memphis, TN 38116. Phone: (800) 238-2000 or (901) 332-3322. Web: www.elvis.com.

ENGLAND: SKANDIA COWES WEEK. Aug 7–14. Cowes, Isle of Wight. Yachting festival for 35 classes of yacht racing. Est attendance: 14,000. For info: Cowes Combined Clubs Ltd, 18 Bath Rd, Cowes, Isle of Wight, England PO31 7QN. Phone: (44) (198) 329-5744. Fax: (44) (198) 329-5329. E-mail: ccc@cowesweek.co.uk. Web: www.cowesweek.co.uk.

E.P. "TOM" SAWYER STATE PARK/LOUISVILLE LANDSHARKS TRIATHLON XXII. Aug 7. Tom Sawyer State Park, Louisville, KY. Participants swim ½ mile, bicycle 14 miles and run 5K. Est attendance: 500. For info: Gary M. Parsons, Recreation Supervisor, E.P. "Tom" Sawyer Park, 3000 Freys Hill Rd, Louisville, KY 40241-2172. Phone: (502) 426-8950.

FANCY FARM PICNIC. Aug 7. Downtown Fancy Farm, KY. Southern hospitality at its best. The small community volunteers its time to entertain with games, prizes and great fun. Raffle for a brand new car. Bingo with wonderful prizes. Down home country dinners including the famous Fancy Farm Picnic Barbeque. Annually, the first Saturday in August. Est attendance: 20,000. For info: Sharon Hayden, c/o Fancy Farm Picnic, 2759 Carrico Rd, Fancy Farm, KY 42039. Phone: (270) 623-6129.

414

☆ Chase's 2004 Calendar of Events ☆   Aug 7

FIRST PICTURE OF EARTH FROM SPACE: 45th ANNIVERSARY. Aug 7, 1959. US satellite *Explorer VI* transmitted the first picture of Earth from space. For the first time we had a likeness of our planet based on more than projections and conjectures.

GREENE, NATHANIEL: BIRTH ANNIVERSARY. Aug 7, 1742 (OS). Born at Patowomut, RI, American Revolutionary War General Nathaniel Greene was described as the "ablest military officer of the Revolution under Washington." Greene died at Savannah, GA, June 19, 1786.

GULF OF TONKIN RESOLUTION: 40th ANNIVERSARY. Aug 7, 1964. Congress approved the "Gulf of Tonkin Resolution," pertaining to the war in Vietnam, which gave President Lyndon Johnson authority "to take all necessary measures to repel any armed attack against the forces of the United States and to prevent further aggression."

HATFIELD-McCOY FEUD ERUPTS: ANNIVERSARY. Aug 7–9, 1882. The long-simmering tension between two Appalachian families who lived by Tug Fork on the Kentucky-West Virginia border erupted into full-scale violence on Election Day 1882. Brothers Tolbert, Pharmer and Randolph McCoy knifed and shot Ellison Hatfield. The Hatfield family captured the three McCoys. When Ellison Hatfield died on Aug 9, the Hatfields executed the brothers. The feud continued with much loss of life. In 1888, when Kentucky authorities sought to detain feud murder suspects and West Virginia authorities complained, the dispute went all the way to the US Supreme Court, who decided in Kentucky's favor. The feud sputtered out by the end of the century.

HOME OF THE HAMBURGER CELEBRATION. Aug 7. Seymour, WI. Giant parade, live music, kids' games and entertainment, Hamburger Meet, lots of hamburgers to eat. Annually, first Saturday in August. Est attendance: 10,000. For info: Home of the Hamburger, Inc, PO Box 173, Seymour, WI 54165.

INTER-STATE FAIR AND RODEO. Aug 7–15. Coffeyville, KS. "Largest outdoor fair and rodeo event in southeast Kansas and northeast Oklahoma." Includes truck & tractor pull, concerts, demo derby, four nights of PRCA rodeo and livestock shows. Est attendance: 75,000. For info: Montgomery County Fair Assn, Box 457, Coffeyville, KS 67337. Phone: (620) 251-2550. Fax: (620) 251-5448. E-mail: fairandrodeo@coffeyville.com. Web: www.coffeyville.com.

ISING, RUDOLF C.: BIRTH ANNIVERSARY. Aug 7, 1903. Rudolf C. Ising, cocreator with Hugh Harmon of "Looney Tunes" and "Merrie Melodies," was born at Kansas City, MO. Ising and Harmon's initial production, "Bosko the Talk-Ink Kid" (1929), was the first talkie cartoon synchronizing dialogue on the soundtrack with the action on screen. Ising received an Academy Award in 1940 for *Milky Way*, a cartoon about three kittens. During WWII he headed the animation division for the Army Air Corps movie unit developing training films. Rudolf Ising died July 18, 1992, at Newport Beach, CA.

JONATHAN HAGER FRONTIER CRAFT DAYS. Aug 7–8. Jonathan Hager House, City Park, Hagerstown, MD. Featuring dozens of demonstrating craftsmen, great bluegrass music and great food. Annually, the first weekend in August. Est attendance: 10,000. For info: John Nelson, Jonathan Hager House and Museum, 110 Key St, Hagerstown, MD 21740. Phone: (301) 739-8393. E-mail: hagerhouse@hagerstownmd.org.

KNIGHTS OF COLUMBUS FAMILY WEEK. Aug 7–14. Held annually in August as a celebration of the importance of the family. Local councils throughout the countries in which the K of C is present hold family-oriented activities throughout this observance. The birth (Aug 12) and death (Aug 14) anniversaries of Father Michael J. McGivney, founder of the Knights of Columbus, fall during this event. For info: Robert A. Goossens, Director, Fraternal Services, Knights of Columbus, 1 Columbus Plaza, New Haven, CT 06510-3326.

KRXL CAR CRUISE. Aug 7. Kirksville, MO. Motorcycles, cars, antiques, hot rods, classics, originals and street rods. Est attendance: 1,000. For info: Steve Lloyd, General Mgr, KRXL, PO Box 130, Kirksville, MO 63501. Phone: (660) 665-9841.

LEAGUE OF NEW HAMPSHIRE CRAFTSMEN ANNUAL CRAFTSMEN'S FAIR. Aug 7–15. Mount Sunapee Resort, Newbury, NH. "America's oldest crafts fair"—71st annual fair. More than 200 crafts booths, Living with Crafts exhibit, CraftWear exhibit, New Hampshire Art Association exhibit, daily performing arts, children's activities and more. Est attendance: 40,000. For info: League of NH Craftsmen, 205 N Main St, Concord, NH 03301. Phone: (603) 224-3375. Fax: (603) 225-8452. Web: www.nhcrafts.org.

LEITERSBURG PEACH FESTIVAL. Aug 7–8. Leitersburg Ruritan Community Park, Leitersburg, MD. This peach-oriented event features crafts, horse and wagon rides, petting zoo, antique tractor display, oldies and country music and a quilt raffle. Annually, the second weekend in August. Est attendance: 10,000. For info: Leitersburg Ruritan Club, 21378 Leiters Mill Rd, Hagerstown, MD 21742-1633. Phone: (301) 797-6387.

MOON PHASE: LAST QUARTER. Aug 7. Moon enters Last Quarter phase at 6:01 PM, EDT.

NATIONAL MUSTARD DAY. Aug 7. Mustard lovers across the nation pay tribute to the king of condiments by slathering their favorite mustard on hot dogs, pretzels, circus peanuts and all things edible. The Mount Horeb Mustard Museum holds the world's largest collection of prepared mustards and mustard memorabilia. Activities include the mustard games, street music, and lots of great food (with mustard, of course!). Join in the mustard college fight song with the "POUPON U" marching band. Annually, the first Saturday in August. Est attendance: 4,000. For info: Barry M. Levenson, Curator, The Mount Horeb Mustard Museum, 100 W Main St, Mount Horeb, WI 53572. Phone: (608) 437-3986. Fax: (608) 437-4018. E-mail: curator@mustardmuseum.com. Web: www.mustardmuseum.com.

NATIONAL SCRABBLE CHAMPIONSHIP. Aug 7–12. New Orleans, LA. Players compete for the national championship in the popular game invented by unemployed architect Alfred Butts in 1931. For info: John Williams, Natl SCRABBLE Assn, Box 700, Greenport, NY 11944. Phone: (631) 477-0033. Fax: (631) 477-0294. E-mail: info@scrabble-assoc.com. Web: www.scrabble-assoc.com.

PARTICULARLY PREPOSTEROUS PACKAGING DAY. Aug 7. Buy anything lately? Did you succeed in getting the durn thing open? What do older people do when even mainstream society can't open a simple bottle of aspirin, let alone a milk carton? Annually, Aug 7. [©2003 by WH.] For info: Thomas & Ruth Roy, Wellcat Holidays, 2418 Long Ln, Lebanon, PA 17046. Phone: (717) 279-0184. E-mail: info@wellcat.com. Web: www.wellcat.com.

PURPLE HEART: ANNIVERSARY. Aug 7, 1782. At Newburgh, NY, General George Washington ordered the creation of a Badge of Military Merit. The badge consisted of a purple cloth heart with silver braided edge. Only three are known to have been awarded during the Revolutionary War. The award was reinstituted on the bicentennial of Washington's birth, Feb 22, 1932, and recognizes those wounded in action.

SCOTLAND: EDINBURGH INTERNATIONAL BOOK FESTIVAL. Aug 7–23 (tentative). Charlotte Square Gardens, Edinburgh, Lothian. Europe's biggest book event for the public—with more than 500 local and international authors, an extensive program for children, plus thousands of books to buy. Est atten-

Aug 7–8 ☆ Chase's 2004 Calendar of Events ☆

dance: 160,000. For info: Edinburgh Intl Book Festival, Scottish Book Centre, 137 Dundee St, Edinburgh, Scotland EH1 11BG. Phone: (44) (131) 228-5444. E-mail: admin@edbookfest.co.uk. Web: www.edbookfest.co.uk.

SHARON ON THE GREEN ARTS AND CRAFTS FAIR. Aug 7. Sharon, CT. A high-quality, juried art show with 140 regional artists and crafters offering a broad range of unique handmade items of glass, ceramics, pewter, jewelry, quilts, woodcrafts, photos, paintings, art-to-wear and gourmet items. 10:00 AM to 5:00 PM. Est attendance: 1,500. For info: Sharon, Rec/Youth, PO Box 385, Sharon, CT 06069. Phone: (860) 364-1400.

SIZZLIN' SUMMER GARAGE SALE. Aug 7. Live Oak, FL. Gigantic garage sale held throughout the Park, with fun for all ages. With vendors and live music. For info: Spirit of the Suwannee Music Park, 3076 95th Dr, Live Oak, FL 32060. Phone: (386) 364-1683. Fax: (386) 364-2998. E-mail: spirit@musicliveshere.com. Web: www.musicliveshere.com.

TALL TIMBER DAYS FESTIVAL. Aug 7–8. Grand Rapids, MN. Festival features the Sheer Brothers Lumberjack Show, chainsaw carvers, arts and crafts, Applecords Quartet, competitions, YMCA run and bed racing. Families welcome. Annually, the first full weekend in August. Est attendance: 30,000. For info: Tall Timber Days, PO Box 134, Grand Rapids, MN 55744. Phone: (218) 326-5618. E-mail: ecrowe@paulbunyan.net.

US WAR DEPARTMENT ESTABLISHED: ANNIVERSARY. Aug 7, 1789. The second presidential cabinet department, the War Department, was established by Congress.

WHITE OAK RENDEZVOUS. Aug 7–8. Deer River, MN. Voted one of the top 25 festivals by the Minnesota Office of Tourism. One big weekend for reenactment of fur trade history in a setting of 80 acres of pasture and wilderness. 200 tipis and white canvas lodges placed around a North West Company Fur Post from 1798. Blacksmith shop, root cellar, clerk's quarters and store, birchbark canoe–building shed, Ojibwe village. Country, bluegrass and old-time music, dance, puppetry and nature trail with plants labeled to explain their use in 1798 for medicine, shelter or food. 18th-century craft demonstrations and sales. Also, specialty foods from the fur trade period. RV and tent campground available. Est attendance: 4,000. For info: White Oak Society, 33155 State Highway 6, Deer River, MN 56636. Phone: (218) 246-9393. Fax: (218) 246-9393. E-mail: whiteoak@paulbunyan.net. Web: www.whiteoak.org.

BIRTHDAYS TODAY

Lana Cantrell, 61, singer, actress, born Sydney, Australia, Aug 7, 1943.
David Duchovny, 44, actor ("The X-Files"), born New York, NY, Aug 7, 1960.
Stan Freberg, 78, satirist, born Pasadena, CA, Aug 7, 1926.
John Glover, 60, actor (stage: *Great God Brown*; *Julia*, *Melvin and Howard*), born Salisbury, MD, Aug 7, 1944.
Garrison Keillor, 62, humorist, producer (host "The Prairie Home Companion"), writer (*Lake Wobegon Days*), born Anoka, MN, Aug 7, 1942.
DeLane Matthews, 43, actress ("Dave's World"), born Rockledge, FL, Aug 7, 1961.
Alberto Salazar, 47, marathon runner, born Havana, Cuba, Aug 7, 1957.
Charlize Theron, 29, actress (*The Cider House Rules*, *The Legend of Bagger Vance*), born Benoni, South Africa, Aug 7, 1975.
Billy Joe (B.J.) Thomas, 62, singer ("Raindrops Keep Falling on My Head"), born Houston, TX, Aug 7, 1942.

August 2004	S	M	T	W	T	F	S
	1	2	3	4	5	6	7
	8	9	10	11	12	13	14
	15	16	17	18	19	20	21
	22	23	24	25	26	27	28
	29	30	31				

AUGUST 8 — SUNDAY
Day 221 — 145 Remaining

ADMIT YOU'RE HAPPY DAY. Aug 8. This day celebrates the 6th birthday of the Secret Society of Happy People by encouraging the expression of happiness and discouraging parade-raining. Suggested celebration activities are available on our website, or order your Admit You're Happy Day Celebration Kit for $5. For info: Secret Society of Happy People, 1315 Riverchase Dr, #2316, Coppell, TX 75019. Phone: (972) 471-1485. E-mail: pjohnson@sohp.com. Web: www.sohp.com.

BONZA BOTTLER DAY™. Aug 8. To celebrate when the number of the day is the same as the number of the month. Bonza Bottler Day™ is an excuse to have a party at least once a month. For more information, see Jan 1. For info: Gail M. Berger, 14 Fernwood Dr, Taylors, SC 29687. Phone: (864) 609-9874. E-mail: gberger5@aol.com.

BURRO RACE. Aug 8. Leadville, CO. International Pack Burro Race leaves from Main Street up Mosquito Pass and back. Est attendance: 35,000. For info: Chamber of Commerce, Box 861, Leadville, CO 80461. Phone: (719) 486-3900 or (800) 933-3901. Fax: (719) 486-8478. E-mail: leadville@leadvilleusa.com. Web: www.leadvilleusa.com.

THE DATE TO CREATE. Aug 8. A day to increase awareness of individual and organizational potential to solve problems and make things happen. All of us have this potential but may not realize it. Learn your innovative capacity and plan activities that increase it. Rediscover your creative spark. Annually, Aug 8. For info: Diane Decker. Phone: (847) 394-0994. E-mail: dcdecker@msn.com. Web: www.qualitytransitions.com.

HENSON, MATTHEW A.: BIRTH ANNIVERSARY. Aug 8, 1866. American black explorer, born at Charles County, MD. He met Robert E. Peary while working in a Washington, DC, store in 1888 and was hired to be Peary's valet. He accompanied Peary on his seven subsequent Arctic expeditions. During the successful 1908–09 expedition to the North Pole, Henson and two of the four Eskimo guides reached their destination Apr 6, 1909. Peary arrived minutes later and verified the location. Henson's account of the expedition, *A Negro Explorer at the North Pole*, was published in 1912. In addition to the Congressional medal awarded all members of the North Pole expedition, Henson received the Gold Medal of the Geographical Society of Chicago and, at 81, was made an honorary member of the Explorers Club at New York, NY. Died Mar 9, 1955, at New York, NY.

HERBERT HOOVER DAY. Aug 8. Iowa. Annually, the Sunday nearest Aug 10th, the birthday of Herbert Hoover.

ITALY: PALIO DEL GOLFO. Aug 8. La Spezia. A rowing contest over a 2,000-meter course is held on the second Sunday in August.

MARCH, FREDRIC: BIRTH ANNIVERSARY. Aug 8, 1897. Award–winning actor Fredric March was born Frederick McIntyre Bickel at Racine, WI. Over the course of his long and distinguished career, March performed on both the stage and screen. He made more than 65 movies and was nominated for five Academy Awards, winning in 1932 for his role in *Dr. Jekyll and Mr Hyde* and in 1947 for *The Best Years of Our Lives*. In

1956 he appeared on stage in the world premiere of Eugene O'Neill's *Long Day's Journey into Night*. He received the Tony Award for that performance. He died Apr 14, 1975, at Los Angeles, CA.

MARKERT, RUSSELL: BIRTH ANNIVERSARY. Aug 8, 1899. American choreographer Russell Markert was born at Jersey City, NJ. He founded and directed the Radio City Music Hall Rockettes from 1932 to 1971. He died Dec 1, 1990, at Waterbury, CT.

MORRIS, ESTHER HOBART McQUIGG: BIRTH ANNIVERSARY. Aug 8, 1814. Esther Hobart McQuigg Morris was born at Tioga County, NY, but eventually moved to the Wyoming Territory, where she worked in the women's rights movement and had a key role in getting a women's suffrage bill passed. Morris became justice of the peace of South Pass City, WY, in 1870, one of the first times a woman held public office in the US. She represented Wyoming at the national suffrage convention in 1895. She died Apr 2, 1902, at Cheyenne, WY.

NATIONAL RESURRECT ROMANCE WEEK. Aug 8–14. Event focuses on celebrating creative romance. Encourages men and women to find ways to be romantic every day this week by using their hearts. For info: Michael Webb, Romance Expert and Author, PO Box 1567, Cary, NC 27512. Phone: (919) 462-0900. E-mail: chase@theromantic.com. Web: www.TheRomantic.com.

ODIE: BIRTHDAY. Aug 8, 1978. Commemorates the birthday of Odie, Garfield's sidekick, who first appeared in the Garfield comic strip Aug 8, 1978. For info: Kim Campbell, Paws, Inc, 5440 E Co Rd, 450 N, Albany, IN 47320. Web: www.garfield.com.

RAWLINGS, MARJORIE KINNAN: BIRTH ANNIVERSARY. Aug 8, 1896. American short-story writer and novelist (*The Yearling*), born at Washington, DC. Rawlings died at St. Augustine, FL, Dec 14, 1953.

SCOTLAND: EDINBURGH FESTIVAL FRINGE. Aug 8–30. Edinburgh. Three weeks of nonstop entertainment with more than 1,000 different events in 200 venues around the city, including theater, comedy, dance, music and children's shows. Est attendance: 750,000. For info: Edinburgh Festival Fringe Society, 180 High St, Edinburgh, Scotland EH1 1QS. Phone: (44) (131) 226-0026. Fax: (44) (131) 226-0016. E-mail: admin@edfringe.com. Web: www.edfringe.com.

SECOND BATTLE OF AMIENS: ANNIVERSARY. Aug 8, 1918. Two days after the Battle of Marne ended, the British Fourth Army mounted an offensive at Amiens with the objective of freeing the Amiens-Paris railway from bombardment by the German Second and Eighteenth Armies. More than 16,000 German prisoners were taken in two hours of fighting the first day. The German forces were forced back to the Hindenburg line by Sept 3. This battle is considered a turning point by many historians because of its impact on the psyche of Germany. Aug 8 was described by General Erich Ludendorff as a "Black Day" for Germany.

SHILTS, RANDY: BIRTH ANNIVERSARY. Aug 8, 1951. Journalist known for his reporting on the AIDS epidemic. One of the first openly homosexual journalists to work for a mainstream newspaper and the author of *And the Band Played On: Politics, People and the AIDS Epidemic*. Born at Davenport, IA, and died at Guerneville, CA, Feb 17, 1994.

SNEAK SOME ZUCCHINI ONTO YOUR NEIGHBORS' PORCH NIGHT. Aug 8. Due to overzealous planting of zucchini, citizens are asked to drop off baskets of the squash on neighbors' doorsteps. Annually, Aug 8. [©2003 by WH.] For info: Thomas & Ruth Roy, Wellcat Holidays, 2418 Long Ln, Lebanon, PA 17046. Phone: (717) 279-0184. E-mail: info@wellcat.com. Web: www.wellcat.com.

SPACE MILESTONE: *GENESIS* (US). Aug 8, 2001. The robotic explorer *Genesis* was launched on a mission to gather tiny particles of the sun. Its three-year, 20 million-mile round-trip mission is to shed light on the origin of the solar system. It will travel to a spot where the gravitational pulls of the sun and the Earth are equal and will gather atoms from the solar wind hurtling by. In September 2004 the solar samples will return to Earth in a capsule where they will be studied by scientists.

SPACE MILESTONE: *PIONEER VENUS* MULTIPROBE (US): ANNIVERSARY. Aug 8, 1978. Second craft in *Pioneer Venus* program. Split into five and probed Venus atmosphere Dec 9. Launched on Aug 8, 1978.

TANZANIA: FARMERS' DAY. Aug 8. National holiday. Also called "Nane Nane" (8–8).

THANKS FOR ALL THE GIFTS WEEK. Aug 8–14. Designed for procrastinators, this is a time to catch up on all the thank-you notes and cards for birthdays, graduations, weddings, etc, that you forgot to send. Annually, the third week in August. For info: Eva Rosenberg, Giftech Corp, 2961 Industrial Rd, Ste 731, Las Vegas, NV 89109. Phone: (800) 594-9829. Web: www.giftsurf.com.

WYATT EARP BIRTHDAY CELEBRATION. Aug 8. Monmouth, IL. "OK Corral Reenactment" show at 4 PM. Birthplace home, listed on the National Register of Historic Places, open 1 PM to 4 PM. Annually, second Sunday in August. Est attendance: 200. For info: Wyatt Earp Birthplace, Historic House Museum, Office: 1020 E Detroit Ave, Monmouth, IL 61462. Phone: (309) 734-6419 or Chamber of Commerce (309) 734-3181. E-mail:wyattearpbirthp@webtv.net.

BIRTHDAYS TODAY

Keith Carradine, 54, actor (*Nashville, Will Rogers Follies*), singer, born San Mateo, CA, Aug 8, 1950.

Dino De Laurentiis, 85, producer, born Torre Annunziata, Italy, Aug 8, 1919.

The Edge, 43, musician (U2), born David Evans, East London, England, Aug 8, 1961.

Dustin Hoffman, 67, actor (Oscars for *Rain Man* and *Kramer vs. Kramer; The Graduate, Midnight Cowboy, Outbreak*), born Los Angeles, CA, Aug 8, 1937.

Deborah Norville, 46, TV host ("Inside Edition"), born Dalton, GA, Aug 8, 1958.

Roberta Cooper Ramo, 62, first woman president of the American Bar Association, born Denver, CO, Aug 8, 1942.

Connie Stevens, 66, actress ("Hawaiian Eye"), born Brooklyn, NY, Aug 8, 1938.

Mel Tillis, 72, singer, songwriter, born Pahokee, FL, Aug 8, 1932.

Esther Williams, 81, swimmer, actress (*Take Me Out to the Ball Game, Dangerous When Wet*), born Los Angeles, CA, Aug 8, 1923.

AUGUST 9 — MONDAY
Day 222 — 144 Remaining

ATOMIC BOMB DROPPED ON NAGASAKI: ANNIVERSARY. Aug 9, 1945. Three days after the atomic bombing of Hiroshima, an American B-29 bomber named *Bock's Car* left its base on Tinian Island carrying a plutonium bomb nicknamed "Fat Man." Its target was the Japanese city of Kokura, but because of clouds and poor visibility the bomber headed for a secondary target, Nagasaki, where at 11:02 AM, local time, it dropped the bomb, killing an estimated 70,000 persons and destroying about half the city. Memorial services are held annually at Nagasaki and also at Kokura, where those who were spared because of the bad weather also grieve for those at Nagasaki who suffered in their stead.

COCHRAN, JACQUELINE: DEATH ANNIVERSARY. Aug 9, 1980. American pilot Jacqueline Cochran was born at Pensacola, FL, about 1910. She began flying in 1932 and by the time of her death she had set more distance, speed and altitude records than any other pilot, male or female. She was founder and head of the WASPs (Women's Air Force Service Pilots) during WWII; she won the Distinguished Service Medal in 1945 and the US Air Force Distinguished Flying Cross in 1969. She died at Indio, CA.

FINLAND: LAHTI ORGAN FESTIVAL. Aug 9–15. Lahti. Annual festival emphasizing organ music. Also, choirs, orchestras, instrumental groups and solo artists. Plus master classes, seminars and panel discussions. Est attendance: 10,000. For info: Finnish Tourist Board, 655 Third Ave, New York, NY 10017. Phone: (212) 885-9700 or (358) (3) 782-3184. Fax: (358) (3) 783-2190 or Lahti Organ Festival, Kirkkokatu 5, 15110 Lahti, Finland. Fax: 358-3-783 2190. E-mail: lof@pp.phnet.fi. Web: www.lahtiorgan.net.

JAPAN: MOMENT OF SILENCE. Aug 9. Nagasaki. Memorial observance held at Peace Memorial Park for victims of second atomic bomb, which was dropped on Nagasaki by an American bomber Aug 9, 1945.

LASSEN VOLCANIC NATIONAL PARK ESTABLISHED: ANNIVERSARY. Aug 9, 1916. California's Lassen Peak and Cinder Cone National Monument, proclaimed May 6, 1907, and other wilderness land were combined and established as a national park. For further park info: Lassen Volcanic Natl Park, Mineral, CA 96063.

MORTON, WILLIAM THOMAS GREEN: BIRTH ANNIVERSARY. Aug 9, 1819. Dentist, born at Charlton, MA. Morton was the first to use ether as a general anesthetic. Died at New York, NY, July 15, 1868.

NIXON RESIGNS: 30th ANNIVERSARY. Aug 9, 1974. Richard Milhous Nixon's resignation from the presidency of the US, which he had announced in a speech to the American people Thursday evening, Aug 8, became effective at noon. Nixon, under threat of impeachment as a result of the Watergate scandal, became the first person to resign the presidency. He was succeeded by Vice President Gerald Rudolph Ford, the first person to serve as vice president and president without having been elected to either office. Ford granted Nixon "full, free and absolute pardon" Sept 8, 1974. Although Nixon was the first US president to resign, two vice presidents had resigned: John C. Calhoun, Dec 18, 1832, and Spiro T. Agnew, Oct 10, 1973.

★ ★ ★

August 2004

S	M	T	W	T	F	S
1	2	3	4	5	6	7
8	9	10	11	12	13	14
15	16	17	18	19	20	21
22	23	24	25	26	27	28
29	30	31				

OLD FIDDLERS' CONVENTION. Aug 9–14. Galax, VA. 69th annual event features dance, folk songs, old-time and bluegrass music competition. Est attendance: 25,000. For info: Thomas L. Jones Jr, Box 655, Galax, VA 24333. Phone: (276) 236-8541.

PERSEID METEOR SHOWERS. Aug 9–13. Among the best-known and most spectacular meteor showers are the Perseids, peaking about Aug 10–12. As many as 50–100 may be seen in a single night. Wish upon a "falling star"!

PGA CHAMPIONSHIP. Aug 9–15. Whistling Straits, Kohler, WI. The 86th championship conducted by the Professional Golfers' Association of America. Est attendance: 150,000. For info: PGA of America, 100 Avenue of the Champions, Palm Beach Gardens, FL 33418. Phone: (561) 624-8495. Fax: (561) 624-8429. Web: www.pga.com.

SCOTTS BLUFF COUNTY FAIR. Aug 9–15. County Fairgrounds, Mitchell, NE. County fair including stock displays and shows, special events such as large-name country and western concert, largest amateur rodeo in Nebraska, tractor pull, free stage acts, grounds act, rubber-check races, demolition derby. Est attendance: 47,000. For info: Diane Wurdeman, Operations Mgr, Scotts Bluff County Fair, Box 157, Mitchell, NE 69357. Phone: (308) 623-1828. Fax: (308) 623-1328. E-mail: sbcofair@scottsbluff.net. Web: www.scbcountyfair.com.

SINGAPORE: NATIONAL DAY: ANNIVERSARY. Aug 9, 1965. Most festivals in Singapore are Chinese, Indian or Malay, but celebration of national day is shared by all to commemorate the withdrawal of Singapore from Malaysia and its becoming an independent state in 1965. Music, parades, dancing.

SOUTH AFRICA: NATIONAL WOMEN'S DAY. Aug 9. National holiday. Commemorates the march of women in Pretoria to protest the pass laws in 1956.

STURGIS RALLY. Aug 9–15. Sturgis, SD. The granddaddy of all motorcycle rallies and races. For 61 years the small community of Sturgis has welcomed motorcycle enthusiasts from around the world to a week of varied cycle racing, tours of the beautiful Black Hills, trade shows and thousands of bikes on display. Annually, beginning the Monday after the first full weekend in August. Est attendance: 350,000. For info: Sturgis Bike Week Productions, PO Box 999, Sturgis, SD 57785. Phone: (605) 347-0200. Fax: (605) 347-8888. E-mail: jr@sbwproductions.com. Web: www.sturgisrallynews.com.

UNITED NATIONS: INTERNATIONAL DAY OF THE WORLD'S INDIGENOUS PEOPLE. Aug 9. On Dec 23, 1994, the General Assembly decided that the International Day of the World's Indigenous People shall be observed Aug 9 every year during the International Decade of the World's Indigenous People (1994–2004) (Res 49/214). The date marks the anniversary of the first day of the meeting in 1992 of the Working Group on Indigenous Populations of the Subcommission on Prevention of Discrimination and Protection of Minorities. For info: United Nations, Dept of Public Info, Public Inquiries Unit, RM GA-57, New York, NY 10017. Phone: (212) 963-4475. E-mail: inquiries@un.org.

US WOMEN'S AMATEUR (GOLF) CHAMPIONSHIP. Aug 9–14. The Kwahkwa Club, Erie, PA. For info: US Golf Assn, Golf House, PO Box 708, Championship Dept, Far Hills, NJ 07931. Phone: (908) 234-2300. Fax: (908) 234-9687. E-mail: usga@usga.org. Web: www.usga.org.

VEEP DAY. Aug 9. Commemorates the day in 1974 when Richard Nixon's resignation let Gerald Ford succeed to the presidency of the US. This was the first time the new Constitutional provisions for presidential succession took effect. For info: c/o Bob Birch, The Puns Corps, PO Box 2364, Falls Church, VA 22042-0364. Phone: (703) 533-3668.

VICTORY DAY. Aug 9. Rhode Island. State holiday commemorating President Truman's announcement of the surrender of the Japanese to the Allies on Aug 14, 1945. Annually, the second Monday in August.

☆ Chase's 2004 Calendar of Events ☆   Aug 9–10

WALTON, IZAAK: BIRTH ANNIVERSARY. Aug 9, 1593 (OS). English author of classic treatise on fishing, *The Compleat Angler*, published in 1653, was born at Stafford, England. Died at Winchester, England, Dec 15, 1683 (OS). "Angling," Walton wrote, "may be said to be so like the mathematics, that it can never be fully learnt."

WEBSTER-ASHBURTON TREATY SIGNED: ANNIVERSARY. Aug 9, 1842. The treaty delimiting the eastern section of the Canadian-American border was negotiated by the US Secretary of State, Daniel Webster, and Alexander Baring, president of the British Board of Trade. The treaty established the boundaries between the St. Croix and Connecticut rivers, between Lake Superior and the Lake of the Woods and between Lakes Huron and Superior. The treaty was signed at Washington, DC.

BIRTHDAYS TODAY

Gillian Anderson, 36, actress ("The X-Files," *The House of Mirth*), born Chicago, IL, Aug 9, 1968.
Amanda Bearse, 46, actress ("Married . . . With Children"), born Winter Park, FL, Aug 9, 1958.
Robert Joseph (Bob) Cousy, 76, Hall of Fame basketball player, former coach, born New York, NY, Aug 9, 1928.
Sam Elliott, 60, actor ("Mission Impossible," *Gettysburg*), born Sacramento, CA, Aug 9, 1944.
Melanie Griffith, 47, actress (*Working Girl, Something Wild, Milk Money*), born New York, NY, Aug 9, 1957.
Chamique Holdsclaw, 27, former basketball player, born Astoria, NY, Aug 9, 1977.
Whitney Houston, 41, singer ("And I Will Always Love You"), actress (*Waiting to Exhale*), born Newark, NJ, Aug 9, 1963.
Brett Hull, 40, hockey player, born Belleville, ON, Canada, Aug 9, 1964.
Rodney George (Rod) Laver, 66, former tennis player, born Rockhampton, Australia, Aug 9, 1938.
Kenneth Howard (Ken) Norton, Sr, 59, former boxer, born Jacksonville, IL, Aug 9, 1945.
Deion Sanders, 37, former football player, former baseball player, born Fort Myers, FL, Aug 9, 1967.
David Steinberg, 62, comedian ("The David Steinberg Show"), born Winnipeg, MB, Canada, Aug 9, 1942.

AUGUST 10 — TUESDAY
Day 223 — 143 Remaining

BAHAMAS: FOX HILL DAY. Aug 10. Nassau. Annually, the second Tuesday in August.

"CANDID CAMERA" TV PREMIERE: ANNIVERSARY. Aug 10, 1948. This show—which appeared at various times on the big three networks and in syndication—was created and hosted by Allen Funt. The show was initially an Armed Forces Radio program based on Funt's success in recording and broadcasting soldiers' gripes. The show's modus operandi was to catch people unawares on camera—either as part of a practical joke or just being themselves. It spawned numerous imitators such as "Totally Hidden Video," "People Do the Craziest Things" and "America's Funniest Home Videos."

ECUADOR: INDEPENDENCE DAY. Aug 10. National holiday. Celebrates declaration of independence in 1809. Freedom from Spain was attained May 24, 1822.

HOOVER, HERBERT CLARK: BIRTH ANNIVERSARY. Aug 10, 1874. The 31st president of the US (1929–33) was born at West Branch, IA. Hoover was the first president born west of the Mississippi River and the first to have a telephone on his desk (installed Mar 27, 1929). "Older men declare war. But it is youth that must fight and die," he said at Chicago, IL, at the Republican National Convention, June 27, 1944. Hoover died at New York, NY, Oct 20, 1964. The Sunday nearest Aug 10th is observed in Iowa as Herbert Hoover Day.

JAPAN'S UNCONDITIONAL SURRENDER: ANNIVERSARY. Aug 10, 1945. A gathering to discuss surrender terms took place in Emperor Hirohito's bomb shelter; the participants were stalemated. Hirohito settled the question, believing continuation of the war would only result in further loss of Japanese lives. A message was transmitted to Japanese ambassadors in Switzerland and Sweden to accept the terms issued at Potsdam July 26, 1945, except that the Japanese emperor's sovereignty must be maintained. The Allies devised a plan under which the emperor and the Japanese government would administer under the rule of the Supreme Commander of the Allied Powers and the Japanese surrendered.

MISSOURI: ADMISSION DAY: ANNIVERSARY. Aug 10. Became 24th state in 1821.

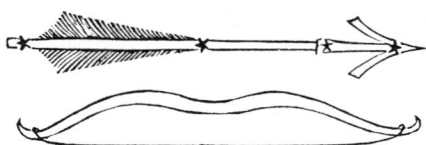

NATIONAL DURAN DURAN APPRECIATION DAY. Aug 10. This is a day for everyone to enjoy the underrated beauty of '80s rock icons, Duran Duran. For info: Matt Kennedy, 2025 US 41 W, Marquette, MI 49855. Phone: (906) 227-7777. E-mail: matt@greatlakesradio.org.

SIOUX EMPIRE FAIR. Aug 10–15. W.H. Lyon Fairgrounds, Sioux Falls, SD. Grandstand concerts, free entertainment, livestock exhibits, 4-H activities, flower and vegetable displays and craft exhibits. Est attendance: 250,000. For info: Sioux Empire Fair, W.H. Lyon Fairgrounds, 4000 W 12th St, Sioux Falls, SD 57107. Phone: (605) 367-7178. Fax: (605) 367-7886. Web: www.siouxempirefair.com.

SMITHSONIAN INSTITUTION FOUNDED: ANNIVERSARY. Aug 10, 1846. Founding of the Smithsonian Institution at Washington, DC. For info: Smithsonian Institution, 900 Jefferson Dr SW, Washington, DC 20560. Phone: (202) 357-2700.

BIRTHDAYS TODAY

Ian Anderson, 57, musician, lead singer (Jethro Tull, "Bungle in the Jungle"), born Blackpool, England, Aug 10, 1947.
Rosanna Arquette, 45, actress (*Desperately Seeking Susan, New York Stories*), born New York, NY, Aug 10, 1959.
Antonio Banderas, 44, actor (*Spy Kids, The Mask of Zorro, Desperado*), born Malaga, Spain, Aug 10, 1960.
Riddick Bowe, 37, boxer, born Brooklyn, NY, Aug 10, 1967.
Jimmy Dean, 76, singer ("Big Bad John," "P.T. 109"), born Seth Ward, Plainview, TX, Aug 10, 1928.
Eddie Fisher, 76, singer ("Heart," "Cindy, Oh Cindy"), born Philadelphia, PA, Aug 10, 1928.
Rhonda Fleming, 81, actress ("Stage Door," *The Best of Broadway*), born Marilyn Lewis, Los Angeles, CA, Aug 10, 1923.
Angie Harmon, 32, actress ("Law & Order," "Baywatch Nights"), born Dallas, TX, Aug 10, 1972.
Betsy Johnson, 62, fashion designer, born Wethersfield, CT, Aug 10, 1942.

AUGUST 11 — WEDNESDAY
Day 224 — 142 Remaining

ATCHISON, DAVID R.: BIRTH ANNIVERSARY. Aug 11, 1807. Missouri legislator who was president of the US for one day. Born at Frogtown, KY, Atchison's strong pro-slavery opinions made his name prominent in legislative debates. He served as president pro tempore of the Senate a number of times, and he became president of the US for one day—Sunday, Mar 4, 1849—pending the swearing in of President-elect Zachary Taylor on Monday, Mar 5, 1849. The city of Atchison, KS, and the county of Atchison, MO, are named for him. He died at Gower, MO, Jan 26, 1886.

BEATLES' NATIONAL APPLE WEEK: ANNIVERSARY. Aug 11–18. The Beatles proclaimed this week to be "National Apple Week" in 1968, when they launched their Apple recording label. Presentation boxes of "Our First Four" releases were sent to Queen Elizabeth II, the Queen Mother and Princess Margaret.

BOND, CARRIE JACOBS: BIRTH ANNIVERSARY. Aug 11, 1862. American composer of well-known songs, including "I Love You Truly" and "A Perfect Day," and of scores for motion pictures, Carrie Jacobs Bond was born at Janesville, WI. She died at Hollywood, CA, at age 84, Dec 28, 1946.

CHAD: INDEPENDENCE DAY. Aug 11. National holiday. Commemorates independence from France in 1960.

FIRST FOREIGN-BORN OFFICER APPOINTED CHAIR OF JOINT CHIEFS: ANNIVERSARY. Aug 11, 1993. President Bill Clinton appointed Army General John Shalikashvili to succeed Colin Powell as Chairman of the Joint Chiefs of Staff. Shalikashvili was born at Poland, but his family fled to Germany in 1944 to escape advancing Soviet troops. After moving to the US, his family lived at Peoria, IL. "General Shali" has a distinguished military record and is a Vietnam war veteran.

FREDERICK DOUGLASS SPEAKS: ANNIVERSARY. Aug 11, 1841. Having escaped from slavery only three years earlier, Frederick Douglass was legally a fugitive when he first spoke before an audience. At an antislavery convention on Nantucket Island, Douglass spoke simply but eloquently about his life as a slave. His words were so moving that he was asked to become a full-time lecturer for the Massachusetts Anti-Slavery Society. Douglass became a brilliant orator, writer and abolitionist who championed the rights of blacks as well as the rights of all humankind.

HALEY, ALEX PALMER: BIRTH ANNIVERSARY. Aug 11, 1921. Born at Ithaca, NY, Alex Palmer Haley was raised by his grandmother at Henning, TN. In 1939 he entered the US Coast Guard and served as a cook, but eventually he became a writer and college professor. His interview with Malcolm X for *Playboy* led to his first book, *The Autobiography of Malcolm X*, which sold six million copies and was translated into eight languages. *Roots*, his Pulitzer Prize–winning novel published in 1976, sold millions, was translated into 37 languages and was made into an eight-part TV miniseries in 1977. The story generated an enormous interest in family ancestry. Haley died at Seattle, WA, Feb 13, 1992.

INDIANA STATE FAIR. Aug 11–22. Indiana State Fairgrounds, Indianapolis, IN. Top-rated livestock exhibition, world-class harness racing, top music and entertainment, giant midway and Pioneer Village. Est attendance: 750,000. For info: Andy Klotz, Public Relations Dir, Indiana State Fair, 1202 E 38th St, Indianapolis, IN 46205-2869. Phone: (317) 927-7524. Fax: (317) 927-7578. Web: www.indianastatefair.com.

August 2004	S	M	T	W	T	F	S
	1	2	3	4	5	6	7
	8	9	10	11	12	13	14
	15	16	17	18	19	20	21
	22	23	24	25	26	27	28
	29	30	31				

PRESIDENTIAL JOKE DAY: 20th ANNIVERSARY. Aug 11, 1984. Anniversary of President Ronald Reagan's voice-test joke. In preparation for a radio broadcast, during a thought-to-be-off-the-record voice level test, instead of counting "one, two, three . . ." the president said: "My fellow Americans, I am pleased to tell you I just signed legislation which outlaws Russia forever. The bombing begins in five minutes." The statement was picked up by live television cameras and was heard by millions worldwide. The incident provoked national and international reactions, including a news network proposal of new ground rules concerning the use of "off-the-record" remarks.

SAINT CLARE OF ASSISI: FEAST DAY. Aug 11, 1253. Chiara Favorone di Offreduccio, a religious leader inspired by St. Francis of Assisi, was the first woman to write her own religious order rule. Born at Assisi, Italy, July 16, 1194, she died there Aug 11, 1253. A "Privilege of Poverty" freed her order from any constraint to accept material security, making the "Poor Clares" totally dependent on God.

SPACE MILESTONE: *VOSTOK 3* (USSR). Aug 11, 1962. Launched on this date, Andrian Nikolayev orbited Earth 64 times over a period of 94 hours, 25 minutes, covering a distance of 1,242,500 miles. Achieved radio communication with *Vostok 4* and telecast from spacecraft.

SWEDEN: CRAYFISH PREMIERE. Aug 11. Crayfish may be sold and served in restaurants the following day after the season opens. Annually, the second Wednesday in August.

WATTS RIOT: ANNIVERSARY. Aug 11, 1965. A minor clash between the California Highway Patrol and two young blacks set off six days of riots in the Watts area of Los Angeles. Thirty-four deaths were reported and more than 3,000 people were arrested. Damage to property was listed at $40 million. The less-immediate cause of the disturbance and the others that followed was racial tension between whites and blacks in American society.

ZIMBABWE: HEROES' DAY. Aug 11. National holiday. Followed by Defense Forces Day on August 12.

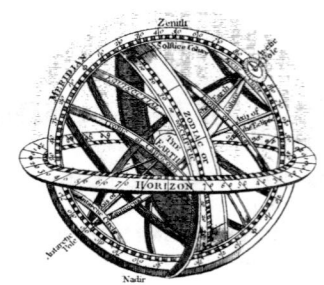

BIRTHDAYS TODAY

Joanna Coles, 60, children's author, born Newark, NJ, Aug 11, 1944.
Arlene Dahl, 76, actress ("One Life to Live," "Fantasy Island"), born Minneapolis, MN, Aug 11, 1928.
Mike Douglas, 79, TV host, singer, born Michael Delaney Dowd, Jr, Chicago, IL, Aug 11, 1925.
Jerry Falwell, 71, clergyman (head of Moral Majority PAC), born Lynchburg, VA, Aug 11, 1933.
Will Friedle, 28, actor ("Boy Meets World"), born Hartford, CT, Aug 11, 1976.
Hulk Hogan, 51, wrestler, actor, born Terry Gene Bollea, Augusta, GA, Aug 11, 1953.
Joe Jackson, 49, musician, songwriter, born Burton-on-Trent, England, Aug 11, 1955.
Anna Massey, 67, actress (*Bunny Lake Is Missing*, *A Doll's House*), born Thankeham, England, Aug 11, 1937.
Marilyn vos Savant, 58, columnist ("Ask Marilyn"), claims world's highest IQ, born St. Louis, MO, Aug 11, 1946.
Stephen Wozniak, 54, Apple computer cofounder, born Sunnyvale, CA, Aug 11, 1950.

AUGUST 12 — THURSDAY
Day 225 — 141 Remaining

AMISH ACRES ARTS & CRAFTS FESTIVAL. Aug 12–15. Nappanee, IN. Displays of traditional arts and crafts including furniture and other objects. Also features a variety of entertainment. Est attendance: 60,000. For info: Amish Acres Arts & Crafts Festival, 1600 W Market St, Nappanee, IN 46550. Phone: (574) 773-4188 x 215. Fax: (574) 773-4180. E-mail: Jenni Wysong@AmishAcres.com. Web: www.amishacres.com.

BEWICK, THOMAS: BIRTH ANNIVERSARY. Aug 12, 1753. English artist, wood engraver and author, remembered especially for his book illustrations in *General History of Quadrupeds*, *A History of British Birds* and *Aesop's Fables*. Born at Cherryburn, Northumberland, and died at Gateshead, Durham, England, Nov 8, 1828.

CANADA: FRINGE THEATRE FESTIVAL. Aug 12–22 (tentative). Edmonton, AB. A ten-day extravaganza of new plays, old plays, dance, music, mime and street entertainment. More than 800 performances of 150 productions in 18 theatres, in the parks and on the streets. Performers from around the world. Regarded as the largest and most exciting festival of alternative theatre in North America. Est attendance: 470,000. For info: Fringe Festival Adventures, #300, 10330-84 Av, Edmonton, AB, Canada T6E 2G9. Phone: (780) 448-9000. Web: www.fringetheatreadventures.ca.

CANADA: YUKON RIVER BATHTUB RACE. Aug 12–16. Beginning in Whitehorse, YT. 13th annual 462-mile bathtub race from Whitehorse to Dawson. Est attendance: 1,500. For info: Yukon Sourdough Rendezvous Society, Box 31721, Whitehorse, YT, Canada Y1A 6L3. Phone: (867) 667-2148. Fax: (867) 668-6755. E-mail: ysr@yukon.net. Web: www.tubrace.com.

CANTINFLAS: BIRTH ANNIVERSARY. Aug 12, 1911. Mexico's most famous comic actor, Cantinflas, was born at Mexico City as Mario Moreno Reyes. Particularly popular with the poor of Mexico because he most often portrayed the underdog, Cantinflas got his start in Mexico City *carpas*, the equivalent of vaudeville. He became internationally known for his role in *Around the World in 80 Days*. The name Cantinflas was invented by the comic to prevent his parents from learning he was in show business, which they considered a shameful endeavor. Died Apr 20, 1993, at Mexico City.

COLUMBUS DAYS. Aug 12–15. Columbus, NE. Citywide. Concerts, prayer breakfast, coronation ball, baby show, arts and crafts, horseshoes, lip-sync, talent show, quilt show, book sale, pet show, fly-in breakfast, parades, senior activities, tractor pull, historic tours, biathlon, children's carnival and big-wheel races. Est attendance: 20,000. For info: Columbus Area Chamber of Commerce, PO Box 515, Columbus, NE 68602-0515. Phone: (402) 564-2769. Fax: (402) 564-2026. E-mail: chamber@megavision.com. Web: www.ci.columbus.ne.us/columbusdays.htm.

De MILLE, CECIL B.: BIRTH ANNIVERSARY. Aug 12, 1881. Film pioneer, born at Ashfield, MA. Cecil Blount De Mille was a film showman extraordinaire known for lavish screen spectacles. He produced more than 70 major films which were noted more for their large scale than for their subtle artistry. He produced one of the earliest four-reel films, *The Squaw Man*, in 1913, which boasted the first use of indoor lighting on an actor and was the first film to publicize the names of its stars. His other innovations included the sneak preview and the idea of producing different versions of a popular film. His films include *The Crusades*, *The Sign of the Cross*, *King of Kings*, *Cleopatra*, *The Plainsman*, *The Buccaneer*, *Reap the Wild Wind* and *The Ten Commandments*, which was made in 1923 and then in a new version in 1956. De Mille was awarded an Oscar for *The Greatest Show on Earth* in 1953. He died Jan 21, 1959, at Hollywood, CA.

ENGLAND: JERSEY BATTLE OF FLOWERS. Aug 12–13. St. Helier, Jersey Channel Islands. Colorful parade of floats decorated with hundreds of flowers. First held in 1902 to mark the coronation of Edward VII and Queen Alexandra. Annually, the second Thursday in August. Est attendance: 27,500. For info: The Jersey Battle of Flowers Assn, Meadow Bank, St. Lawrence, Jersey, Channel Islands, England JE3 1EE. Phone: (44) (153) 639-000. E-mail: battle@battleofflowers.com. Web: www.battleofflowers.com.

FLOOD VICTIMS RECEIVE $6.2 BILLION: ANNIVERSARY. Aug 12, 1993. President Bill Clinton signed a bill Aug 12, 1993, providing $6.2 billion in federal relief to victims of floods in July and August for nine states from North Dakota to Missouri. Due to the record rains in the spring of up to 200 percent above average, the Midwest suffered 50 deaths, 70,000 left homeless and an estimated $12 billion in damage as of Aug 9, 1993.

HOME SEWING MACHINE INVENTED: ANNIVERSARY. Aug 12, 1851. Isaac Singer developed the sewing machine for use in homes.

HOPE WATERMELON FESTIVAL. Aug 12–15. Hope, AR. An event in which the entire family can participate while promoting the city of Hope and having fun. Hope is the birthplace of 42nd president of the US, Bill Clinton. Annually, in August. Est attendance: 40,000. For info: Mktg Dept, Hope–Hempstead County Chamber of Commerce, 108 W 3rd, PO Box 250, Hope, AR 71802-0250. Phone: (870) 777-3640. Fax: (870) 722-6154. E-mail: hopeark@arkansas.net. Web: www.hopemelonfest.com.

IBM PERSONAL COMPUTER INTRODUCED: ANNIVERSARY. Aug 12, 1981. IBM's first personal computer was released. The computer cost the equivalent of $3,000 in today's currency. Although IBM was one of the pioneers in making mainframe and other large computers, this was the company's first foray into the desktop computer market. Eventually, more IBM-compatible computers were manufactured by IBM's competitors than by IBM itself.

IOWA STATE FAIR. Aug 12–22. Iowa State Fairgrounds, Des Moines, IA. One of America's oldest and largest state fairs proudly celebrates its sesquecentennial! After 150 years, the Iowa State Fair is "still the one" for showcasing Iowa pride, talent and tradition. The Fair boasts one of the world's largest livestock shows. Ten-acre carnival, superstar grandstand stage shows, track events, spectacular free entertainment. 160-acre campgrounds. Est attendance: 1,008,000. For info: Kathie Swift, Mktg Dir, Iowa State Fair, PO Box 57130, Des Moines, IA 50317-0003. Phone: (515) 262-3111. Fax: (515) 262-6906. E-mail: info@iowastatefair.org. Web: www.iowastatefair.org.

KING PHILIP ASSASSINATION: ANNIVERSARY. Aug 12, 1676. Native American, Philip, son of Massasoit, chief of the Wampanog tribe, was killed near Mt Hope, RI, by a renegade Indian of his own tribe, bringing to an end the first and bloodiest war between American Indians and white settlers of New England, a war that had raged for nearly two years and was known as King Philip's War.

"LIL" MARGARET'S BLUEGRASS AND OLD-TIME MUSIC FESTIVAL. Aug 12–15. Leonardtown, MD. Bluegrass music, crafts, old-time cars and tractors, plenty of home-cooked meals and lots of fun. Annually, the second weekend in August. Est attendance: 1,000. For info: Joseph H. Goddard, Lil Margaret's Bluegrass, 20529 White Point Rd, Leonardtown, MD 20650. Phone: (301) 475-8191. Web: www.gotech.com/.

MATHEWSON, CHRISTY: BIRTH ANNIVERSARY. Aug 12, 1880. Famed American baseball player Christopher (Christy) Mathewson, one of the first players named to Baseball's Hall of Fame, was born at Factoryville, PA. Died at Saranac Lake, NY, Oct 7, 1925. He pitched three complete games during the 1905 World Series without allowing opponents to score a run. In 17 years he won 372 games while losing 188 and striking out 2,499 players.

MISSOURI STATE FAIR. Aug 12–22. Sedalia, MO. Livestock shows, commercial and competitive exhibits, horse show, car races, tractor pulls, carnival and headline musical entertainment. Economical family entertainment. Est attendance: 360,000. For info: Kimberly Allen, PR Dir, Missouri State Fair, 2503 W 16th, Sedalia, MO 65301. Phone: (660) 530-5600. Fax: (660) 530-5609. Web: www.mostatefair.com.

MOUNT OGURA PLANE CRASH: ANNIVERSARY. Aug 12, 1985. A Japan Airlines plane crashed into the side of Mount Ogura, Japan, claiming 520 lives. The worst air disaster involving a single plane. See also: "Canary Islands Plane Disaster: Anniv" (Mar 27).

NATIONAL BLUEBERRY FESTIVAL. Aug 12–15. South Haven, MI. At the World's Highbush Blueberry Capital, enjoy events such as a sand-sculpting contest and beach volleyball on the shores of Lake Michigan. Est attendance: 50,000. For info: South Haven Chamber of Commerce, 606 Philips, South Haven, MI 49090. Phone: (269) 637-5171. E-mail: cofc@southhavenmi.com.

SKOWHEGAN STATE FAIR. Aug 12–21. Fairgrounds, Skowhegan, ME. 186th annual. Huge fair with horse pulling, tractor pulls, harness racing, carnival midway, exhibits, flower show, grandstand shows, coliseum events, truck pulls, demolition derby and much more. Annually, beginning three weeks before Labor Day. Est attendance: 100,000. For info: Skowhegan State Fair Assn, PO Box 39, Skowhegan, ME 04976. Phone: (207) 474-2947.

SPACE MILESTONE: *ECHO I* (US). Aug 12, 1960. First successful communications satellite in Earth's orbit to relay voice and TV signals from one ground station to another was launched.

SPACE MILESTONE: *ENTERPRISE* (US). Aug 12, 1977. Reusable orbiting vehicle (space shuttle) makes first successful flight on its own within Earth's atmosphere. Launched from Boeing 747 on Aug 12, 1977.

THAILAND: BIRTHDAY OF THE QUEEN. Aug 12. The entire kingdom of Thailand celebrates the birthday of Queen Sirikit.

UNITED NATIONS: INTERNATIONAL YOUTH DAY. Aug 12. Day to increase public awareness of the World Programme of Action for Youth to the Year 2000 and Beyond, which calls for action in 10 priority areas: education, employment, hunger and poverty, health, environment, drug abuse, juvenile delinquency, leisure-time activities, girls and young women, and full and effective participation of youth (15 to 24 years old) in the life of society and in decision making. For info: United Nations, Dept of Public Info, New York, NY 10017. Web: www.un.org.

	S	M	T	W	T	F	S
August	1	2	3	4	5	6	7
2004	8	9	10	11	12	13	14
	15	16	17	18	19	20	21
	22	23	24	25	26	27	28
	29	30	31				

VINYL RECORD DAY. Aug 12. We all need a reminder sometimes that life is good, regardless of national news and daily challenges. Favorite songs can bring back fond memories, and Vinyl Record Day encourages celebrating these music memories with family and friends. Our nonprofit organization also seeks to recognize and preserve the tremendous cultural influence that vinyl records and album covers have had for more than 60 years. Annually, on Aug 12—the day Thomas Edison invented the phonograph in 1877. For info: Gary Freiberg, 734 Pacific, San Luis Obispo, CA 93401. Phone: (805) 541-6674. Fax: (805) 546-0783. E-mail: gary@VinylRecordDay.com. Web: www.VinylRecordDay.com.

BIRTHDAYS TODAY

William Goldman, 73, writer (*The Princess Bride, Marathon Man*), born Chicago, IL, Aug 12, 1931.
George Hamilton, 65, actor (*Love at First Bite, Act One,* "The Survivors"), born Memphis, TN, Aug 12, 1939.
Sam J. Jones, 50, actor (*Flash Gordon, 10*), born Chicago, IL, Aug 12, 1954.
Michael Kidd, 85, choreographer, born Milton Greenwald, Brooklyn, NY, Aug 12, 1919.
Peter Krause, 39, actor ("Six Feet Under," "Sports Night"), born Minneapolis, MN, Aug 12, 1965.
Ann Martin, 49, author (The Baby-Sitter's Club series), born Princeton, NJ, Aug 12, 1955.
Pat Metheny, 50, jazz guitarist ("Song X," "Letter from Home"), born Lee's Summit, MO, Aug 12, 1954.
Alvis Edgar ("Buck") Owens, 75, singer ("Hee Haw," "Act Naturally"), songwriter, born Sherman, TX, Aug 12, 1929.
Pete Sampras, 33, tennis player, born Washington, DC, Aug 12, 1971.
George Soros, 74, billionaire, financier, philanthropist in Eastern Europe and the US, born Budapest, Hungary, Aug 12, 1930.
Porter Wagoner, 74, singer ("The Carroll County Accident"), born West Plains, MO, Aug 12, 1930.
Antoine Walker, 28, basketball player, born Chicago, IL, Aug 12, 1976.
Jane Wyatt, 91, actress (Emmies for "Father Knows Best," *Lost Horizon*), born New York, NY, Aug 12, 1913.

AUGUST 13 — FRIDAY
Day 226 — 140 Remaining

BERLIN WALL ERECTED: ANNIVERSARY. Aug 13, 1961. Early in the morning, the East German government closed the border between east and west sectors of Berlin with barbed wire fence to discourage further population movement to the west. Telephone and postal services were interrupted, and, later in the week, a concrete wall was built to strengthen the barrier between official crossing points. The dismantling of the wall began Nov 9, 1989. See also: "Berlin Wall: Dismantling Anniversary" (Nov 9).

BLUEGRASS FESTIVAL. Aug 13–15. Grand Targhee Ski and Summer Resort, Alta, WY. 17th annual. Set in a beautiful outdoor venue on a pristine mountainside on the gorgeous western slopes of the Grand Teton Mountains, this festival is three days of incredible bluegrass music featuring national, regional and local talent such as Alison Krauss, Del McCoury Band, Peter Rowan and David Grisman. Also, arts and crafts, food and beverages. Est attendance: 7,000. For info: Grand Targhee Ski & Summer Resort, PO Box SKI, Alta, WY 83414. Phone: (800) TAR-GHEE. Fax: (307) 353-8148. E-mail: info@targhee.com. Web: www.grandtarghee.com.

CANADA: ABBOTSFORD INTERNATIONAL AIRSHOW. Aug 13–15. Abbotsford Airport, Abbotsford, BC. "Canada's National Airshow," 42nd annual. Leading air show in North America attracts the world's top aeronautical performers. Thrill to the grace of the Canadian Snowbirds, the raw power of the international air demonstration squadrons, dramatic teams of daring performers and soloists. Static displays and food booths. Open daily 8–6; aerial show 10–5. Airshow camping facilities. Est

☆ Chase's 2004 Calendar of Events ☆ Aug 13

attendance: 250,000. For info: Abbotsford Intl Airshow, Unit 4-1276 Tower St, Abbotsford, BC, Canada V2T 6H5. E-mail: info@abbotsfordairshow.com. Web: www.abbotsfordairshow.com.

CAXTON, WILLIAM: BIRTH ANNIVERSARY. Aug 13, 1422. First English printer, born at Kent, England. Died at London, England, 1491. Caxton produced his first book printed in English (while he was still at Bruges), the *Recuyell of the Histories of Troy*, in 1476, and in the autumn of 1476 set up a print shop at Westminster, becoming the first printer in England.

CENTRAL AFRICAN REPUBLIC: INDEPENDENCE DAY. Aug 13. Commemorates Proclamation of Independence from France in 1960.

FINLAND: TURKU MUSIC FESTIVAL. Aug 13–22. Turku. One of Finland's oldest music festivals in its oldest city. Music ranges from the medieval era to present day, performed by world-famous artists and groups in halls with fine acoustics, churches and even museums. Est attendance: 17,000. For info: Finnish Tourist Board, 655 Third Ave, New York, NY 10017. Phone: (212) 885-9700. Or Turku Music Festival, Uudenmaankatu 1, 20500 Turku, Finland. Phone: (358) (2) 251-1162. Fax: (358) (2) 231-3316. E-mail: info@turkumusicfestival.fi. Web: www.turkumusicfestival.fi.

GAMES OF THE XXVIII OLYMPIAD. Aug 13–29. Athens, Greece. More than 10,500 athletes and 3,000 officials will attend the 2004 summer Olympics, featuring more than 300 events in 38 different venues. For info: United States Olympic Committee, One Olympic Plaza, Colorado Springs, CO 80909. Phone: (719) 866-4500. E-mail: media@usoc.org. Web: www.athens2004.com.

GREAT RIVER TUG FEST. Aug 13–14. Port Byron, IL, and LeClaire, IA. The Tug is the only tug-of-war across the mighty Mississippi River or any other moving body of water in the world. For two hours barge traffic, pleasure boats, gambling and paddle boats yield the right of way to a 400-ft, 680-lb rope that stretches between Illinois and Iowa. At 1 PM Saturday, the first team of 20 tuggers grip the rope, the crowd counts down and dirt starts flying! Festivals on both sides of the river Friday and Saturday. Fireworks Friday evening. For info: Phone: (563) 289-3946 or (309) 523-3734. Web: www.tugfest.org or www.qconline.com/tugfest. For info on the Quad Cities: Quad Cities CVB. Phone: (800) 747-7800. Web: www.visitquadcities.com.

HITCHCOCK, ALFRED (JOSEPH): BIRTH ANNIVERSARY. Aug 13, 1899. English film director and master of suspense born at London. Hitchcock's career as a filmmaker dates back to the silent film era when he made *The Lodger* in 1926, based on the tale of Jack the Ripper. American audiences were introduced to the Hitchcock style in 1935 with *The Thirty-Nine Steps* and *The Lady Vanishes* in 1938, after which he went to Hollywood. There he produced a string of classics including *Rebecca, Suspicion, Notorious, Rear Window, To Catch a Thief, The Birds, Psycho* and *Frenzy*, in addition to his TV series "Alfred Hitchcock Presents." He died Apr 29, 1980, at Beverly Hills, CA.

HOGAN, BEN: BIRTH ANNIVERSARY. Aug 13, 1912. Golfer born at Dublin, TX. Hogan was one of only four players to win all four major professional championships, and his 63 career victories rank him third after Sam Snead and Jack Nicklaus. Died at Ft Worth, TX, July 25, 1997.

ILLINOIS STATE FAIR. Aug 13–22. Springfield, IL. Amusement rides, food booths, parade, various types of entertainment, and tractor pulls. Est attendance: 1,100,000. For info: Illinois State Fair, PO Box 19427, Springfield, IL 62794. Phone: (217) 782-6661. Fax: (217) 782-9115. Web: www.illinoisstatefair.com.

JOHN DEERE TRACTOR & MEMORABILIA AUCTION. Aug 13–14. John Deere Collectors Center, Moline, IL. 5th annual. This is a premier event for enthusiasts of John Deere tractors, equipment and parts, and for collectors of John Deere memorabilia. For info: Sarah Johnson, John Deere Collectors Center, 320 16th St, Moline, IL 61265. Phone: (800) 240-5265. Fax: (309) 748-7946. E-mail: JohnsonSarah@johndeere.com. Web: www.johndeerecollectorsctr.com.

KOOL-AID DAYS. Aug 13–15. Hastings, NE. Family festival in the town where Kool-Aid was invented. Large inflatable games, live entertainment, festival foods, commemoratives, games for kids. Purchase a mug and receive free Kool-Aid all day from the world's largest Kool-Aid stand where we pour more than a gallon a minute of 22 flavors. Annually, the second weekend in August. Est attendance: 8,000. For info: Kool-Aid Days, PO Box 541, Hastings, NE 68902-0541. E-mail: koolaiddays@alltel.net. Web: www.kool-aiddays.com.

KRUPP, ALFRIED von BOHLEN und HALBACH: BIRTH ANNIVERSARY. Aug 13, 1907. As sole owner of the massive Krupp industries, Alfried Krupp took over the factories of German-occupied countries and used them for the Nazi war machine. Sometimes he had complete facilities dismantled and reassembled inside Germany. He used prisoners of war, civilians from occupied countries and inmates of concentration camps as forced labor in his factories. Found guilty as a war criminal by the Military Court at Nuremberg in 1948, he regained his property after serving three years of a twelve-year sentence. He was named Alfried von Bohlen und Halbach at birth but the family was authorized by Emperor Wilhelm II to add the mother's maiden name of Krupp to their own. Born at Essen, Germany, he died there July 30, 1967.

MONTGOMERY COUNTY AGRICULTURAL FAIR. Aug 13–21. Gaithersburg, MD. Maryland's largest county fair, family-oriented entertainment, farm animals, arts and crafts exhibits of all types, many contests, carnival rides, grandstand entertainment to include demolition derby, horse events, musical performances, tractor pulls. Est attendance: 250,000. For info: Montgomery County Agricultural Fair, 16 Chestnut St, Gaithersburg, MD 20877. Phone: (301) 926-3100. Fax: (301) 926-1532. Web: www.mcagfair.com.

OAKLEY, ANNIE: BIRTH ANNIVERSARY. Aug 13, 1860. Annie Oakley was born at Darke County, OH. She developed an eye as a markswoman early as a child, becoming so proficient that she was able to pay off the mortgage on her family farm by selling the game she killed. A few years after defeating vaudeville marksman Frank Butler in a shooting match, she married him and they toured as a team until joining Buffalo Bill's Wild West Show in 1885. She was one of the star attractions for 17 years. She died Nov 3, 1926, at Greenville, OH.

SAINT JOHNS MINT FESTIVAL. Aug 13–15. St. Johns, MI. Arts & crafts, flea market, collectibles, sports events, parade, mint tours and a three-night rodeo. Est attendance: 70,000. For info: St. Johns Area Chamber of Commerce, Box 61, St. Johns, MI 48879. Phone: (989) 224-7248. Fax: (989) 224-7667. E-mail: stjohnschamber@power-net.net.

SHANTY DAYS: CELEBRATION OF THE LAKE. Aug 13–15. Legion Park, Algoma, WI. Three-day festival to celebrate lakeshore heritage. Entertainment, ethnic food, arts and crafts, street fair, 5K walk/run, fishing contest, kids' area, book sale, community parade, photo contest and fireworks finale. Est attendance: 23,000. For info: Pam Ritchie, Algoma Area Chamber of Commerce, 1226 Lake St, Algoma, WI 54201. Phone: (920) 487-2041 or (800) 498-4888. Fax: (920) 487-5519. E-mail: chamber@itol.com. Web: www.algoma.org.

Aug 13–14 ☆ *Chase's 2004 Calendar of Events* ☆

SPACE MILESTONE: *HELIOS* SOLAR WING. Aug 13, 2001. The solar-powered plane *Helios* broke the altitude records for propeller-driven aircraft and non-rocket planes on this date, soaring higher than 96,500 feet. The plane has a wingspan longer than a Boeing 747 and uses solar-powered motors to power 14 propellers, flying at speeds as high as 170 (mph). NASA plans to develop similar craft for unmanned flights on Mars.

STONE, LUCY: BIRTH ANNIVERSARY. Aug 13, 1818. American women's rights pioneer, born near West Brookfield, MA, Lucy Stone dedicated her life to the abolition of slavery and the emancipation of women. Although she graduated from Oberlin College, she had to finance her education by teaching for nine years because her father did not favor college education for women. An eloquent speaker for her causes, she headed the list of 89 men and women who signed the call to the first national Woman's Rights Convention, held at Worcester, MA, October 1850. On May 1, 1855, she married Henry Blackwell. She and her husband aided in the founding of the American Suffrage Association, taking part in numerous referendum campaigns to win suffrage amendments to state constitutions. She died Oct 18, 1893, at Dorchester, MA.

SWITZERLAND: LUCERNE FESTIVAL, SOMMER. Aug 13–Sept 18. Lucerne. Directed by Michael Haefliger since 1999, the summer festival has been restructured and now intensively focuses on specific festival topics, concert cycles and programs such as "moderne," "debut," and "Children's Corner." Important artistic accents are set by each year's Artiste étoile, Composers-in-residence and Orchestras-in-residence. Annually, in August and September. For info: Sheila Huber, Lucerne Festival, PO Box CH-6002, Lucerne, Switzerland. Phone: (41) (0) 41-226-44-00. Fax: (41) (0) 41-226-4460. E-mail: info@lucernefestival.ch. Web: www.lucernefestival.ch.

TETONKAHA RENDEZVOUS. Aug 13–15. Hole in the Mountain County Park, Lake Benton, MN. Presents the fur-trading atmosphere of the 1840s. Muzzle-loader contest, tomahawk and knife throw, log sawing, canoe races, kids' games. Est attendance: 300. For info: Dave Huebner, Brookings Renegade Muzzle Loaders, 47826 Main St, Bushnell, SD 57276. Phone: (605) 693-4589.

TUNISIA: WOMEN'S DAY. Aug 13. General holiday. Celebration of independence of women.

WEST VIRGINIA STATE FAIR. Aug 13–22. Lewisburg, WV. For info: The State Fair of West Virginia, PO Drawer 986, Lewisburg, WV 24901. Phone: (301) 645-1090. E-mail: wvstatefair@wvstatefair.com. Web: www.wvstatefair.com.

BIRTHDAYS TODAY

Kathleen Battle, 56, opera soprano, born Portsmouth, OH, Aug 13, 1948.
Danny Bonaduce, 45, radio personality, actor ("The Partridge Family"), born Broomall, PA, Aug 13, 1959.
Fidel Castro, 77, President of Cuba, former amateur baseball player, born Mayari, Oriente Province, Cuba, Aug 13, 1927.
Quinn Cummings, 37, actress (*The Goodbye Girl*, "Family"), born Los Angeles, CA, Aug 13, 1967.
Dan Fogelberg, 53, composer, singer ("Same Old Lang Syne," "Leader of the Band"), born Peoria, IL, Aug 13, 1951.
Pat Harrington, Jr, 75, actor, comedian ("The Jack Paar Show," "One Day at a Time"), born New York, NY, Aug 13, 1929.
Don Ho, 74, singer ("Tiny Bubbles"), born Oahu, HI, Aug 13, 1930.
Kevin Tighe, 60, actor ("Emergency," *The Graduate, What's Eating Gilbert Grape?*), born Los Angeles, CA, Aug 13, 1944.

August 2004

S	M	T	W	T	F	S
1	2	3	4	5	6	7
8	9	10	11	12	13	14
15	16	17	18	19	20	21
22	23	24	25	26	27	28
29	30	31				

AUGUST 14 — SATURDAY
Day 227 — 139 Remaining

ALBANY RIVERFEST. Aug 14. Riverfront Park, Albany, NY. A daylong summer family festival featuring music, food, entertainment on water and land, a lighted boat parade and fireworks. For info: Albany Special Events, City Hall, 4th Fl, Eagle St, Albany, NY 12207. Phone: (518) 434-2032. Fax: (518) 426-0759. E-mail: info@albanyevents.org. Web: www.albanyevents.org.

AMERICAN SOCIETY OF ASSOCIATION EXECUTIVES ANNUAL MEETING AND EXPOSITION. Aug 14–17. Minneapolis, MN. Major meeting for ASAE members, nonmembers and suppliers including education sessions, trade show, speakers and networking events. Est attendance: 5,000. For info: American Society of Assn Executives, 1575 I St NW, Washington, DC 20005. Phone: (202) 626-2723. Fax: (202) 371-8825. E-mail: pr@asaenet.org. Web: www.asaenet.org.

ANTIQUE SHOW. Aug 14. Somerset, PA. 34th annual. More than 100 vendors dealing in quality antiques and collectibles. Est attendance: 5,000. For info: Sandy Berkebile, Somerset County Chamber of Commerce, 601 N Center Ave, Somerset, PA 15501. Phone: (814) 445-6431. E-mail: info@somersetcountychamber.com.

ATLANTIC CHARTER SIGNING: ANNIVERSARY. Aug 14, 1941. The eight-point agreement was signed by US President Franklin D. Roosevelt and British Prime Minister Winston S. Churchill. The charter grew out of a three-day conference aboard ship in the Atlantic Ocean, off the Newfoundland coast, and stated policies and hopes for the future agreed to by the two nations.

BLUE CLAW CRAB CRAFT SHOW & CRAB RACE. Aug 14. Harvey Cedars, NJ. Crafters displaying their goods at Sunset Park. Crab race determines fastest crab on Long Beach Island. For info: Harvey Cedars Activity Committee, PO Box 3185, Harvey Cedars, NJ 08008. Phone: (609) 361-7990. Fax: (609) 494-8343. Web: www.harveycedars.org.

BUD BILLIKEN PARADE. Aug 14. Chicago, IL. A parade especially for children begun in 1929 by Robert S. Abbott. The second largest parade in the US, it features bands, floats, drill teams and celebrities. Annually, the second Saturday in August. For info: Michael Brown, PR Dir, Chicago Defender Charities, 2400 S Michigan, Chicago, IL 60616. Phone: (312) 225-2400. Fax: (312) 255-9231.

CANADA: OJIBWA KEESHIGUN. Aug 14–15. Old Fort William, Thunder Bay, ON. A celebration of Old Fort William's native culture. Taste historic foods, enjoy unique demonstrations and join in crafts and games. Experience the atmosphere with traditional singing and dancing. Annually, late August. Est attendance: 3,000. For info: Marty Mascarin, Communications Officer, Vickers Heights PO, Thunder Bay, ON, Canada P0T 2Z0. Phone: (807) 473-2326 or (807) 577-8461. Fax: (807) 473-2327. E-mail: info@oldfortwilliam.on.ca. Web: www.oldfortwilliam.on.ca.

CHENEY, LYNNE: BIRTHDAY. Aug 14, 1941. Wife of Vice President Richard (Dick) Cheney, born at Casper, WY. Former chairman of the National Endowment for the Humanities (1986–1993).

424

☆ Chase's 2004 Calendar of Events ☆   Aug 14

COLOGNE CATHEDRAL: COMPLETION ANNIVERSARY. Aug 14, 1880. The largest Gothic church in northern Europe, the Cologne Cathedral at Cologne, Germany, was completed Aug 14, 1880, just 632 years after rebuilding began on Aug 14, 1248. In fact, there had been a church on its site since 873, but a fire in 1248 made rebuilding necessary. The cathedral was again damaged, by bombing, during World War II.

CRATER LAKE RIM RUNS AND MARATHON. Aug 14. Crater Lake National Park, OR. One of the toughest and most spectacular races you'll ever run! Race routes are around Crater Lake, the deepest lake in the US. Included are a 6.7-mile walk and 6.7-mile run, a 13-mile and a full marathon. Est attendance: 500. For info: Crater Lake Rim Runs, 5830 Mack Ave, Klamath Falls, OR 97603. Phone: (541) 884-6939. E-mail: rimruns@aol.com.

ELVIS PRESLEY REMEMBERED. Aug 14. St. Louis, MO. Singer Elvis Presley, his entire family and Colonel Tom Parker are impersonated in a live display titled "From Tupelo to Graceland" to mark the anniversary week of his death. Later a two-hour live music show featuring Steve Davis and the TCB Band will be held in the Duck Room at Blueberry Hill. Est attendance: 400. For info: Blueberry Hill, 6504 Delmar, St. Louis, MO 63130. Phone: (314) 727-0880. Web: www.blueberryhill.com.

GREATER PITTSBURGH RENAISSANCE FESTIVAL. Aug 14–15 (also Aug 21–22, Aug 28–29, Sept 4–6, Sept 11–12 and Sept 18–19). West Newton, PA. A re-creation of a 16th-century marketplace where the king and queen come on holiday. Featured are more than 100 craft shops, six themed stages, games, food and armoured contact jousting. Est attendance: 60,000. For info: Lori Hughes, Greater Pittsburgh Renaissance Festival, PO Box 1670, Greensburg, PA 15601-7670. Phone: (724) 872-1670.

INTERNATIONAL NAGGING DAY. Aug 14. A day to celebrate and remember the gift of positive nagging—particularly parental and cultural sayings handed down from one generation to the next. Annually, Aug 14. For info: Sharon Hague, PO Box 591, Avalon Beach, NSW 2107, Australia. E-mail: naggingday@naggingqueen.com. Web: www.naggingqueen.com/naggingday.

JOURS DE FÊTE (DAYS OF CELEBRATION). Aug 14–15. Ste. Genevieve, MO. Celebration of town's French heritage. Tours of historic homes dating to the 1700s that exemplify some of the finest French Creole architecture. Also more than 600 arts and crafts booths and colonial crafts demonstrations by authentically costumed crafters. Annually, the second full weekend of August. Est attendance: 40,000. For info: Ste. Genevieve Tourist Info Center, 66 S Main, Ste. Genevieve, MO 63670. Phone: (573) 883-7097 or (800) 373-7007.

JUST, ERNEST E.: BIRTH ANNIVERSARY. Aug 14, 1883. American marine biologist Ernest E. Just was born at Charleston, SC. He was the first recipient of the NAACP's Spingarn Medal and was a professor at Howard University from 1907 to 1941, where he was head of physiology at the medical school (1912–20) and head of zoology (1912–41). He died Oct 27, 1941, at Washington, DC.

LEADVILLE TRAIL 100 BIKE RACE. Aug 14. Leadville, CO. Some 600 cyclists compete in this 100-mile off-road bike race over Colorado's high peaks—out 50 miles to a peak above Twin Lakes and back to Leadville. Sponsor: Leadville Trail 100, Inc. Est attendance: 5,000. For info: Leadville Chamber of Commerce, PO Box 861, Leadville, CO 80461. Phone: (719) 486-3900 or (800) 933-3901. Fax: (719) 486-8478. E-mail: leadville@leadvilleusa.com. Web: www.leadvilleusa.com.

MINNESOTA RENAISSANCE FESTIVAL. Aug 14–Sept 26 (weekends and Labor Day only). Shakopee, MN. A celebration of 16th-century Renaissance Europe with entertainment on 12 lively stages, food, arts and crafts, games and live jousting. Est attendance: 300,000. For info: Minnesota Renaissance Festival, 1244 S Canterbury Rd, Ste 306, Shakopee, MN 55379. Phone: (800) 966-8215 or (952) 445-7361. Fax: (952) 445-7380. Web: www.renaissancefest.com.

MISSOURI RIVER FESTIVAL OF THE ARTS. Aug 14, 27–28 (tentative). Thespian Hall, Boonville, MO. Performing arts festival with major symphony, jazz, children's program, Broadway music, dance and contemporary music. Est attendance: 5,000. For info: Maryellen H. McVicker, Admin, Friends of Historic Boonville, PO Box 1776, Boonville, MO 65233. Phone: (660) 882-7977. Fax: (660) 882-9194. E-mail: friendsart@mid-mo.net.

NATIONAL GARAGE SALE DAY. Aug 14. A day to turn the nation into a giant shopping mall! Annually, the second Saturday in August. For info: C. Daniel Rhodes, 1900 Crossvine Rd, Hoover, AL 35244. Phone: (205) 987-2986. E-mail: drhodes2986@charter.net.

O-BON FESTIVAL. Aug 14. Morikami Museum, Delray Beach, FL. Traditional Japanese summer festival welcomes the ancestral spirits back to Earth with folk dancing, music, games and amusements, culminating with the floating of paper lanterns on Morikami pond at dusk and a fireworks display. Est attendance: 10,000. For info: The Morikami Museum, 4000 Morikami Park Rd, Delray Beach, FL 33446. Phone: (561) 495-0233. Fax: (561) 499-2557. Web: www.morikami.org.

PAKISTAN: INDEPENDENCE DAY. Aug 14, 1947. Gained independence from Britain in 1947.

PONY LEAGUE WORLD SERIES. Aug 14–21. Washington, PA. International youth baseball World Series for teams of players ages 13 and 14. Est attendance: 14,000. For info: PONY Baseball, PO Box 225, Washington, PA 15301. Phone: (724) 225-1060. Fax: (724) 225-9852. E-mail: info@pony.org. Web: www.pony.org.

RIVER REGALIA. Aug 14. Hot Springs State Park, Thermopolis, WY. River-floating parade. Decorate any legal flotation device, including inner tube, raft and canoe, and join the floating fun. Est attendance: 800. For info: Toddi Darlington, Thermopolis Chamber of Commerce, 700 Broadway, Thermopolis, WY 82443. Phone: (307) 864-3192. E-mail: thercc@trib.com. Web: www.thermopolis.com.

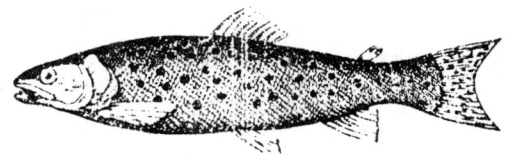

SEWARD SILVER SALMON DERBY. Aug 14–22. Seward, AK. Alaska's largest salmon derby. Fishermen vie for cash prizes, including tagged fish, daily top fish awards and sweepstakes drawing. 49th annual. Est attendance: 10,000. For info: Seward Chamber of Commerce, PO Box 749, Seward, AK 99664. Phone: (907) 224-8051. Fax: (907) 224-5353. E-mail: chamber@seward.net. Web: www.sewardak.org.

SILVER VALLEY CLASSIC HORSESHOE TOURNAMENT. Aug 14–15. Kellogg, ID. Annually, the second weekend of August. Saturday, sanctioned National Horseshoe Association singles tournament. Sunday, sanctioned singles half or half not. Est attendance: 120. For info: Vicki McEnany, PO Box 770, Pinehurst, ID 83850-0770.

SOCIAL SECURITY ACT: ANNIVERSARY. Aug 14, 1935. President Franklin D. Roosevelt signed the Social Security Act, which contained provisions for the establishment of a Social Security Board to administer federal old-age and survivors' insurance in the US. By signing the bill into law, Roosevelt was fulfilling a 1932 campaign promise.

STREETSCENE. Aug 14. Covington, VA. Car Show, open to all types of vehicles! 10–4. Entertainment throughout the day. Annually, the second Saturday in August. Est attendance: 8,000. For info: Kars Unlimited, Inc, PO Box 851, Covington, VA 24426. Phone: (540) 962-3642.

Aug 14–15 ☆ Chase's 2004 Calendar of Events ☆

THAYER, ERNEST LAWRENCE: BIRTH ANNIVERSARY. Aug 14, 1863. The man who wrote the famous comic baseball ballad "Casey at the Bat" was born at Lawrence, MA. He wrote a series of comic poems for the *San Francisco Examiner*, of which "Casey at the Bat" was the last. It was published Sunday, June 3, 1888, and Thayer received $5 in payment for it. Thayer, who regarded the poem's fame as a nuisance and whose other writings are largely forgotten, died at Santa Barbara, CA, Aug 21, 1940.

365-INNING SOFTBALL GAME: ANNIVERSARY. Aug 14–15, 1976. The Gager's Diner softball team played the Bend'n Elbow Tavern in a 365-inning softball game. Starting at 10 AM Aug 14, the game was called because of rain and fog at 4 PM, Aug 15. The 70 players, including 20 women, raised $4,000 for construction of a new softball field and for the Monticello, NY, Community General Hospital. The Gagers beat the Elbows 491–467. To date, this remains the longest softball game on record.

TRADITIONAL GYROSCOPE AND TOP SPINNING CONTEST. Aug 14. Burlington, WI. Friendly contest for the longest spinning gyroscope and trick division, followed by the universal peg top and throw top contests of accuracy, and tricks. Basic top spinning classes given earlier in the afternoon. The contest is followed by a tour and show at the Spinning Top Museum. 9 AM classes, 4 PM contest, 6 PM Museum Show at the world's only Spinning Top Museum. For info: Spinning Top Museum, 533 Milwaukee Ave (Hwy 36), Burlington, WI 53105. Phone: (262) 763-3946.

V-J DAY: ANNIVERSARY. Aug 14, 1945. Anniversary of President Truman's announcement that Japan had surrendered to the Allies, setting off celebrations across the nation. Official ratification of surrender occurred aboard the USS *Missouri* at Tokyo Bay, Sept 2 (Far Eastern time).

WATERMELON FESTIVAL. Aug 14. Rush Springs, OK. Beginning with watermelon judging and ending with the crowning of the festival queen, the highlight of the celebration is the serving of 50,000 pounds of free watermelon at Jeff Davis Park. Est attendance: 20,000. For info: Rush Springs Lions Club, Box 298, Rush Springs, OK 73082. Phone: (580) 476-3277 or (580) 476-3255.

WYOMING STATE FAIR AND RODEO. Aug 14–21. Douglas, WY. Recognizing the products, achievements and cultural heritage of the people of Wyoming. Bringing together rural and urban citizens for an inexpensive, entertaining and educational experience. Features Livestock show for beef, goats, swine, sheep and horses, Junior Livestock show for beef, swine, sheep, horses, goats, dogs and rabbits, competitions and displays for culinary arts, needlework, visual arts, and floriculture, 4-H and FFA County/Chapters State qualification competitions; Youth Talent Show, Demo Derby, live entertainment, midway, PRCA Rodeo, Ranch Rodeo and an All Women Rodeo (rough stock). Est attendance: 48,000. For info: Wyoming State Fair, PO Drawer 10, Douglas, WY 82633. Phone: (307) 358-2398. Fax: (307) 358-6030. E-mail: wystfair@coffey.com. Web: www.wystatefair.com.

BIRTHDAYS TODAY

Russell Baker, 79, journalist, author, TV host ("Masterpiece Theatre"), born Loudoun County, VA, Aug 14, 1925.
Catherine Bell, 36, actress ("JAG"), born London, England, Aug 14, 1968.
Halle Berry, 36, actress (*Die Another Day, X-Men*, Oscar for *Monster's Ball*), born Cleveland, OH, Aug 14, 1968.
Lynne Cheney, 63, wife of Dick Cheney, 46th vice president of the US, born Casper, WY, Aug 14, 1941.
David Crosby, 63, singer (Crosby, Stills & Nash), songwriter, born Los Angeles, CA, Aug 14, 1941.
Antonio Fargas, 58, actor (*Shaft, I'm Gonna Git You Sucka!, Car Wash*), born the Bronx, NY, Aug 14, 1946.
Alice Ghostley, 78, actress ("Designing Women," "Bewitched"), born Eve, MO, Aug 14, 1926.
Buddy Greco, 78, singer ("Mr Lonely"), composer, musician, born Philadelphia, PA, Aug 14, 1926.
Marcia Gay Harden, 45, actress (Oscar for *Pollock; Space Cowboys*), born La Jolla, CA, Aug 14, 1959.
Terin Humphrey, 18, gymnast, born St. Louis, MO, Aug 14, 1986.
Earvin ("Magic") Johnson, Jr, 45, former basketball player, born Lansing, MI, Aug 14, 1959.
Mila Kunis, 21, actress ("That 70s Show," "Family Guy"), born Kiev, Ukraine, Aug 14, 1983.
Arthur Betz Laffer, 64, economist (The Laffer Curve), born Youngstown, OH, Aug 14, 1940.
Gary Larson, 54, cartoonist ("The Far Side"), born Tacoma, WA, Aug 14, 1950.
Steve Martin, 59, comedian, actor ("Saturday Night Live," *LA Story, Roxanne, Parenthood*), born Waco, TX, Aug 14, 1945.
Susan Saint James, 58, actress ("MacMillan and Wife," "Kate and Allie"), born Long Beach, CA, Aug 14, 1946.
Danielle Steel, 57, author (*Vanished, Wanderlust*), born New York, NY, Aug 14, 1947.
Rusty Wallace, 48, auto racer, born St. Louis, MO, Aug 14, 1956.

AUGUST 15 — SUNDAY
Day 228 — 138 Remaining

ALLIED LANDINGS IN SOUTH OF FRANCE: 60th ANNIVERSARY. Aug 15, 1944. After several postponements, Allied forces began Operation Dragoon, the landing on the south coast of France. More than 2,000 transports and landing craft transported 94,000 men to an area between Toulon and Cannes, with only 183 Allied losses. They encountered minimal opposition, and by the end of August the French coast from the mouth of the Rhone to Nice was in Allied hands.

ASSUMPTION OF THE VIRGIN MARY. Aug 15. Greek and Roman Catholic churches celebrate Mary's ascent to Heaven. In Orthodox Churches called the Dormition of the Theotokos and commemorated on Aug 15 or 28. A holiday in many Christian countries.

BARRYMORE, ETHEL: 125th BIRTH ANNIVERSARY. Aug 15, 1879. Celebrated award-winning actress of stage, screen and television, born Ethel Blythe at Philadelphia, PA. Sister of John and Lionel Barrymore. Died at Beverly Hills, CA, June 18, 1959.

BONAPARTE, NAPOLEON: BIRTH ANNIVERSARY. Aug 15, 1769. Anniversary of birth of French emperor Napoleon Bonaparte on the island of Corsica. He died in exile at 5:49 PM, May 5, 1821, on the island of St. Helena. Public holiday at Corsica, France.

☆ Chase's 2004 Calendar of Events ☆   Aug 15

CHAUVIN DAY. Aug 15. A day named for Nicholas Chauvin, French soldier from Rochefort, France, who idolized Napoleon and who eventually became a subject of ridicule because of his blind loyalty and dedication to anything French. Originally referring to bellicose patriotism, chauvinism has come to mean blind or absurdly intense attachment to any cause. Observed on Napoleon's birth anniversary because Chauvin's birth date is unknown.

COEUR D'ALENE TRIBAL PILGRIMAGE. Aug 15. Old Mission State Park, Cataldo, ID. The annual Feast of the Assumption pilgrimage by the Coeur d'Alene Indians. Annually, Aug 15. Est attendance: 1,800. For info: Bill Scudder, Park Mgr, Old Mission State Park, PO Box 30, Cataldo, ID 83810-0030. Phone: (208) 682-3814. Fax: (208) 682-4032. E-mail: old@idpr.state.id.us.

CONGO (BRAZZAVILLE): NATIONAL DAY. Aug 15. National day of the People's Republic of the Congo. Commemorates independence from France in 1960.

DORMITION OF THEOTOKOS. Aug 15. Orthodox observance. According to New Calendar (Gregorian), the Dormition Fast is observed Aug 1–14, followed by Dormition of Theotokos Aug 15.

EQUATORIAL GUINEA: CONSTITUTION DAY. Aug 15. National holiday. Commemorates the 1982 revision of the original constitution of 1968.

FERBER, EDNA: BIRTH ANNIVERSARY. Aug 15, 1887. Edna Ferber was born at Kalamazoo, MI. She wrote her first novel, *Dawn O'Hara*, in 1911 and became a prolific writer, producing many popular magazine stories. Her novel *So Big* brought her commercial success in 1924 as well as a Pulitzer Prize. Her other novels include *Show Boat, Cimarron, Saratoga Trunk, Giant* and *Ice Palace*, all of which were made into successful films. Ferber collaborated with George Kaufman in writing for the stage on *The Royal Family, Dinner at Eight, Stage Door* and *Bravo*. Ferber died at New York, NY, Apr 16, 1968.

HARDING, FLORENCE KLING DeWOLFE: BIRTH ANNIVERSARY. Aug 15, 1860. Wife of Warren Gamaliel Harding, 29th president of the US, born at Marion, OH. Died at Marion, OH, Nov 21, 1924.

HOLLYWOOD BEACH LATIN FESTIVAL. Aug 15. Hollywood, FL. 11th annual. Weekend festival features Latin entertainment, arts and crafts, food and health court. Est attendance: 40,000. For info: Roguey Doyle, City of Hollywood, Dept of Parks, Recreation & Cultural Arts, 1940 Harrison St, Ste 101, Hollywood, FL 33020. Phone: (954) 921-3404.

INDIA: INDEPENDENCE DAY. Aug 15. National holiday. Anniversary of Indian independence from Britain in 1947.

KOREA: INDEPENDENCE DAY. Aug 15. National holiday commemorates acceptance by Japan of Allied terms of surrender in 1945, thereby freeing Korea from 36 years of Japanese domination. Also marks formal proclamation of the Republic of Korea in 1948. Military parades and ceremonies throughout country.

LIECHTENSTEIN: NATIONAL DAY. Aug 15. Public holiday on Assumption Day.

MOON PHASE: NEW MOON. Aug 15. Moon enters New Moon phase at 9:24 PM, EDT.

★**NATIONAL HEALTH CENTER WEEK.** Aug 15–21. A month to celebrate the importance of health centers to our communities. Participants are encouraged to take part in health fairs and screenings, blood drives, immunizations and open house events.

NATIONAL RELAXATION DAY. Aug 15. An excuse for every overworked and underpaid individual to do what they would rather be doing. Annually, Aug 15. For info: Sean M. Moeller, 11723 Sundrop Circle, Allendale, MI 49401. E-mail: relax15@yahoo.com.

PANAMA CANAL OPENS: 90th ANNIVERSARY. Aug 15, 1914. A waterway connecting the Atlantic and the Pacific oceans was a focus of explorers and countries seeking quicker trade routes as early as the 16th century. Congress authorized President Theodore Roosevelt to acquire the rights and property of the New Panama Canal Zone from the French, providing that Colombia, of which the Isthmus of Panama was a province, agreed to grant perpetual control of the required land. On Jan 22, 1903, a treaty was signed leasing the US a 10-mile wide zone for 100 years. Colombia delayed ratification of the treaty, and the citizens of Panama revolted, encouraged by the presence of a US warship offshore. Panama declared its independence Nov 3, 1903, and Nov 18 Panama signed the Hay-Buana-Varilla Treaty, giving the US the right to build a canal in return for a payment of $10 million. The treaty gave the US all rights, in perpetuity, to the 10- by 50-mile strip of land. Construction began in 1904, and Jan 7, 1914, a self-propelled crane boat made the first passage through the canal. The first ocean steamer, the SS *Ancon*, passed through Aug 3, 1914, and the canal officially opened Aug 15, 1914. In 1977, a treaty was signed that transfered control of the canal to Panama at the end of 1999.

PANAMA: PANAMA CITY FOUNDATION DAY. Aug 15. Traditional annual cultural observance recognizes foundation of Panama City.

REDUCE THE CLUTTER WEEK. Aug 15–21. By reducing the clutter in your environment, you'll reduce the clutter in your mind and live a more fulfilled life. Take this week to tackle one cluttered area in your home or office. Choose a highly visible space that will give you immediate gratification. You'll simply feel better! Annually, the third full week in Aug. For info: Clutter MD. Phone: (260) 403-2226. Web: www.cluttermd.com.

SCOTLAND: EDINBURGH INTERNATIONAL FESTIVAL. Aug 15–Sept 4. Edinburgh, Lothian. Now in its 58th year, this is one of the world's largest arts festivals, attracting many international stars. The festival includes symphonic music, opera, theater and dance. Est attendance: 420,000. For info: Edinburgh Festival Society, The Hub, Castlehill, The Royal Mile, Edinburgh, Scotland EH1 2NE. Phone: (44) (131) 473-2099. Fax: (44) (131) 473-2002. E-mail: eif@eif.co.uk. Web: www.eif.co.uk.

SCOTT, SIR WALTER: BIRTH ANNIVERSARY. Aug 15, 1771. Born at Edinburgh, Scotland. Famed poet and novelist. "But no one shall find me rowing against the stream," he wrote in the introduction to *The Fortunes of Nigel*; "I care not who knows it—I write for the general amusement." Died at Abbotsford, Scotland, Sept 21, 1832.

TRANSCONTINENTAL US RAILWAY COMPLETION: ANNIVERSARY. Aug 15, 1870. The Golden Spike ceremony at Promontory Point, UT, May 10, 1869, was long regarded as the final link in a transcontinental railroad track reaching from an Atlantic port to a Pacific port. In fact, that link occurred unceremoniously on another date in another state. Diaries of engineers working at the site establish "the completion of a transcontinental track at a point 928 feet east of today's milepost 602, or 3,812 feet east of the present Union Pacific depot building at Strasburg (formerly Comanche)," CO. The final link was made at 2:53 PM, Aug 15, 1870. Annual celebration at Strasburg, CO, on a weekend in August. See also: "Golden Spike Driving: Anniversary" (May 10).

Aug 15–16 ☆ Chase's 2004 Calendar of Events ☆

WEIRD CONTEST WEEK. Aug 15–20. Music Pier, Ocean City, NJ. One contest daily. Contests include artistic pie eating (chewing something meaningful out of a TastyKake Pie), saltwater taffy sculpting, french fry sculpting, wet T-shirt throwing, animal and celebrity impersonation, Little Miss and Little Mister Chaos and Miss Miscellaneous Contest. 11 AM. Annually, the third week in August. Sponsors: The City of Ocean City, TastyKake Baking Company, Shriver's Saltwater Taffy, The Promenade. Est attendance: 4,500. For info: Mark Soifer, PR Dir, City of Ocean City, City Hall, 9th Asbury Ave, Ocean City, NJ 08226. Phone: (609) 525-9300. Fax: (609) 399-0374. E-mail: MTSoifer@aol.com.

WOODSTOCK: 35th ANNIVERSARY. Aug 15, 1969. The Woodstock Music and Art Fair opened on this day on an alfalfa field on or near Yasgur's Farm at Bethel, NY. The three-day rock concert featured 24 bands and drew a crowd of more than 400,000 people.

WORLD DAY OF REIKI. Aug 15. A day to unite all Reiki practitioners in commemoration of the birthday of Dr. Mikao Usui (Aug 15, 1865) and his legacy of Reiki. Practitioners are encouraged to sponsor local, national and international events. For info: Rinda-Mary Payne, RMT, The-Reiki-Works, 30 Gardner Rd #4H, Brookline, MA 02445. Phone: (617) 734-1219. E-mail: TheReikiWorks1@aol.com.

BIRTHDAYS TODAY

Ben Affleck, 32, actor (*Good Will Hunting, Forces of Nature*), born Berkeley, CA, Aug 15, 1972.
Princess Anne, 54, Princess Royal of the UK, horsewoman, born London, England, Aug 15, 1950.
Stephen G. Breyer, 66, US Supreme Court justice, born San Francisco, CA, Aug 15, 1938.
Julia Child, 92, food authority, author (*The French Chef*), born Pasadena, CA, Aug 15, 1912.
Mike Connors, 79, actor ("Mannix"), born Krekor Ohanian, Fresno, CA, Aug 15, 1925.
Linda Ellerbee, 60, journalist, born Bryan, TX, Aug 15, 1944.
Zeljko Ivanek, 47, actor ("24," *Donnie Brasco*), born Ljubljana, Slovenia, Aug 15, 1957.
Vernon Jordan, Jr, 69, civil rights leader, born Atlanta, GA, Aug 15, 1935.
Debra Messing, 36, actress ("Ned and Stacey," "Will & Grace"), born Brooklyn, NY, Aug 15, 1968.
Phyllis Stewart Schlafly, 80, antifeminist, author, born St. Louis, MO, Aug 15, 1924.
Eugene (Gene) Upshaw, 59, Hall of Fame football player, union executive, born Robstown, TX, Aug 15, 1945.
Kathryn Whitmire, 58, first woman mayor of Houston, Texas, born Houston, TX, Aug 15, 1946.

August 2004	S	M	T	W	T	F	S
	1	2	3	4	5	6	7
	8	9	10	11	12	13	14
	15	16	17	18	19	20	21
	22	23	24	25	26	27	28
	29	30	31				

AUGUST 16 — MONDAY
Day 229 — 137 Remaining

BABE RUTH: DEATH ANNIVERSARY. Aug 16, 1948. Baseball fans of all ages and all walks of life mourned when the great Bambino died of cancer at New York City at the age of 53. Born Feb 6, 1895, at Baltimore, MD, the left-handed pitcher and "Sultan of Swat" hit 714 home runs in 22 major league seasons of play and played in 10 World Series. His body lay in state at the main entrance of Yankee Stadium where people waited in line for hours to march past the coffin. On Aug 19, countless people surrounded St. Patrick's Cathedral for the funeral mass and lined the streets along the route to the cemetery as America bade farewell to one of baseball's greatest legends.

BATTLE OF CAMDEN: ANNIVERSARY. Aug 16, 1780. Revolutionary War battle fought near Camden, SC. American troops led by General Horatio Gates suffered disastrous losses. Nearly 1,000 Americans killed and another 1,000 captured by the British. British losses about 325. One of America's worst defeats in the war.

BEGIN, MENACHEM: BIRTH ANNIVERSARY. Aug 16, 1913. Born at Brest-Litovsk, Poland. A militant Zionist and anticommunist, he fled to Russia in 1939 ahead of the advancing Nazis; he was soon arrested and sent to Siberia. Freed in 1941, he went to Palestine and became a leader in the Jewish underground, fighting for Israel's independence; by 1943 he headed the national military organization. Elected Prime Minister of Israel in 1977, he signed the historic peace treaty between Israel and Egypt with President Anwar el Sadat of Egypt and US president Jimmy Carter at Camp David in 1979. He died Mar 9, 1992, at Tel Aviv, Israel.

BENNINGTON BATTLE DAY: ANNIVERSARY. Aug 16, 1777. Anniversary of battle is legal holiday in Vermont.

CANADA: YUKON DISCOVERY DAY. Aug 16. In the Klondike region of the Yukon, at Bonanza Creek (formerly known as Rabbit Creek), George Washington Carmack discovered gold Aug 16 or 17, 1896. During the following year more than 30,000 people joined the gold rush to the area. Anniversary is celebrated as a holiday (Discovery Day) in the Yukon, on nearest Monday.

DOMINICAN REPUBLIC: RESTORATION OF THE REPUBLIC. Aug 16. The anniversary of the Restoration of the Republic in 1863 is celebrated as an official public holiday.

HARMONIC CONVERGENCE: ANNIVERSARY. Aug 16, 1987. At about 20 designated "sacred sites" around the world (including Lake Titicaca, Bolivia; Boulder, CO; Niagara Falls and the Grand Canyon in the US) believers gathered to meditate about peace and to ward off any impending doom. The harmonic convergence, projected from ancient Mayan and Aztec calendars to begin on this date, was said to signal the beginning of a period of cleansing that would last until 1992, in preparation for alien intelligence to be confronted in the next century.

JOE MILLER'S JOKE DAY. Aug 16. A day to tell a joke in honor of the English comic actor Joseph (or Josias) Miller, who was born in 1684 (exact date unknown). Miller acted at the Drury Lane Theatre at London and was a popular favorite. He died at London, Aug 16, 1738. A book with which Miller had no direct connection, *Joe Miller's Jests*, was compiled by John Mottley and first published in 1739. It contained 247 jokes. Revised and expanded hundreds of times, it contained more than 1,500 jokes in the ensuing two centuries. From *Joe Miller's Jests*, London, 1739: "A melting Sermon being preached in a country Church, all fell a weeping but one Man, who being asked, why he did not weep with the rest? O! said he, I belong to another Parish."

KLONDIKE GOLD DISCOVERY: ANNIVERSARY. Aug 16, 1896. According to the oral tradition of the Tagish First Nations People, Skookum Jim, Dawson Charlie and George Carmack found gold in Rabbit Creek, a tributary of the Klondike River, lying "thick between the flaky slabs like cheese sandwiches." This event that led to the great Klondike Gold Rush is celebrated

☆ Chase's 2004 Calendar of Events ☆   Aug 16–17

in the Yukon each year with a public holiday, Discovery Day, observed on the nearest Monday.

LAWRENCE (OF ARABIA), T.E.: BIRTH ANNIVERSARY. Aug 16, 1888. British soldier, archaeologist and writer, born at Tremadoc, North Wales. During WWI, led the Arab revolt against the Turks and served as a spy for the British. His book, *Seven Pillars of Wisdom*, is a personal account of the Arab revolt. He was killed in a motorcycle accident at Dorset, England, May 19, 1935.

MacFADDEN, BERNARR: BIRTH ANNIVERSARY. Aug 16, 1868. Physical culture enthusiast and publisher, born at Mill Springs, MO. He was publisher of *Physical Culture Magazine, True Story Magazine, True Romances, True Detective Mysteries Magazine* and many others. MacFadden made parachute jumps on his 81st, 83rd and 84th birthdays. He died at Jersey City, NJ, of jaundice, following a three-day fast, Oct 12, 1955.

MEANY, GEORGE: BIRTH ANNIVERSARY. Aug 16, 1894. American labor leader George Meany was born at New York, NY. A plumber by trade, he became president of the AFL (American Federation of Labor) in 1952, and when he merged the AFL with the CIO (Congress of Industrial Organizations) he became the leading labor spokesperson in the US. In 1957 he expelled Jimmy Hoffa's Teamsters Union from the AFL-CIO and lost the United Auto Workers in 1967. His tenure as president lasted until 1979. He died Jan 10, 1980, at Washington, DC.

★**NATIONAL AIRBORNE DAY.** Aug 16. Commemorating the first official Army parachute jump on Aug 16, 1940. Honors all soldiers, past and present, who have served in an Airborne capacity.

NATIONAL AVIATION WEEK. Aug 16–22. A celebration of flight designed to increase public awareness, knowledge and appreciation of aviation. Annually, the week of Orville Wright's birthday, Aug 19. For info: Lafayette Natural History Museum and Planetarium, 433 Jefferson St, Lafayette, LA 70501. Phone: (337) 291-5547. Fax: (337) 291-5464.

NEWSPAPERS TAKEN TO COURT FOR PRO-CONFEDERATE SYMPATHIES: ANNIVERSARY. Aug 16, 1861. Beginning on Aug 16, several newspapers in Union states were brought to court for alleged pro-Confederate sympathies, including the Brooklyn *Eagle*, the New York *Journal of Commerce* and the New York *Daily News*. On Aug 19, an editor for the *Essex County Democrat*, at Haverhill, MA, was tarred and feathered for his Southern leanings expressed in the newspaper.

PRESLEY, ELVIS: DEATH ANNIVERSARY. Aug 16, 1977. One of America's most popular singers, Elvis Presley was pronounced dead at the Memphis Baptist Hospital at 3:30 PM, Aug 16, 1977, at age 42. The anniversary of his death is an occasion for pilgrimages by admirers to Graceland, his home and gravesite at Memphis, TN. See also: "Presley, Elvis: Birth Anniversary" (Jan 8).

STAGG, AMOS ALONZO: BIRTH ANNIVERSARY. Aug 16, 1862. Amos Alonzo Stagg, football player and coach born at West Orange, NJ. Stagg played baseball and football at Yale and then forsook the ministry for physical education. He built the football program at the University of Chicago as an integral part of William Rainey Harper's plan to build a great university. Over 40 years at Chicago, he became the game's greatest innovator and master strategist. When Chicago de-emphasized football, he moved to the College of the Pacific, finishing his career with a record of 314-181-15. In 1959 he was inducted into the Basketball Hall of Fame as a contributor. Died at Stockton, CA, Mar 17, 1965.

STAY HOME WITH YOUR KIDS DAY. Aug 16. To encourage and support those parents who have chosen to be at home with their children. The day is sponsored by WAHM.com—the online magazine for work-at-home moms and is a day for celebration for all parents who are happy with their at-home decision. Annually, the third Monday in August. For info: Cheryl Demas, PO Box 366, Folsom, CA 95630. Phone: (916) 985-2078. Fax: (916) 985-3932. E-mail: cheryl@wahm.com. Web: www.wahm.com.

US AMATEUR (GOLF) CHAMPIONSHIP. Aug 16–22. Winged Foot Golf Club, Mamaroneck, NY. For info: US Golf Assn, Golf House, PO Box 708, Championship Dept, Far Hills, NJ 07931. Phone: (908) 234-2300. Fax: (908) 234-9687. E-mail: usga@usga.org. Web: www.usga.org.

BIRTHDAYS TODAY

Angela Bassett, 46, actress (*Malcolm X, What's Love Got to Do with It, Waiting to Exhale*), born New York, NY, Aug 16, 1958.
James Cameron, 50, director (Oscar for *Titanic; True Lies*), born Kapuskasing, ON, Canada, Aug 16, 1954.
Robert Culp, 74, actor ("I Spy," *Bob and Carol and Ted and Alice*), born Berkeley, CA, Aug 16, 1930.
Frank Newton Gifford, 74, sportscaster, Hall of Fame football player, born Santa Monica, CA, Aug 16, 1930.
Kathie Lee Gifford, 51, TV personality, singer, born Paris, France, Aug 16, 1953.
Eydie Gorme, 72, singer ("Blame It on the Bossa Nova"), born Edith Gormezano, New York, NY, Aug 16, 1932.
Timothy Hutton, 44, actor (*Taps, Made in Heaven*), born Malibu, CA, Aug 16, 1960.
Laura Innes, 44, actress ("ER," "Wings"), born Pontiac, MI, Aug 16, 1960.
Madonna, 46, singer ("Material Girl"), actress (*Desperately Seeking Susan, A League of Their Own, Evita*), born Madonna Louise Veronica Ciccone, Bay City, MI, Aug 16, 1958.
Julie Newmar, 69, actress (Cat Woman on TV's "Batman," *Li'l Abner*), born Hollywood, CA, Aug 16, 1935.
Fess Parker, 77, actor ("Daniel Boone," *Davy Crockett*), born Fort Worth, TX, Aug 16, 1927.
Jeff Perry, 49, actor ("Nash Bridges"), founder of Chicago's Steppenwolf Theater, born Highland Park, IL, Aug 16, 1955.
Seth Peterson, 34, actor ("Providence"), born the Bronx, NY, Aug 16, 1970.
Reginald VelJohnson, 52, actor (*Ghostbusters, Die Hard, Die Hard 2*), born Queens, NY, Aug 16, 1952.
Lesley Ann Warren, 58, actress (*Victor/Victoria, Choose Me*, "Cinderella"), born New York, NY, Aug 16, 1946.

AUGUST 17 — TUESDAY

Day 230 — 136 Remaining

ARGENTINA: DEATH ANNIVERSARY OF SAN MARTÍN. Aug 17. National holiday. Commemorates the death in 1850 of the hero of the struggle for independence.

BALLOON CROSSING OF ATLANTIC OCEAN: ANNIVERSARY. Aug 17, 1978. Three Americans—Maxie Anderson, 44, Ben Abruzzo, 48, and Larry Newman, 31—all of Albuquerque, NM, became first to complete transatlantic trip in a balloon. Starting from Presque Isle, ME, Aug 11, they traveled some 3,200 miles in 137 hours, 18 minutes, landing at Miserey, France (about 60 miles west of Paris), in their craft, named the *Double Eagle II*.

CHASE, HARRISON V.: BIRTH ANNIVERSARY. Aug 17, 1913. Cofounder and coeditor of *Chase's Annual Events*, professor at Florida State University, born at Big Rapids, MI. Died Feb 6, 2000, at Tallahassee, FL.

CROCKETT, DAVID "DAVY": BIRTH ANNIVERSARY. Aug 17, 1786. American frontiersman, adventurer and soldier, born at Hawkins County, TN. Died during final heroic defense of the Alamo, Mar 6, 1836, at San Antonio, TX. In his *Autobiography* (1834), Crockett wrote, "I leave this rule for others when I'm dead, Be always sure you're right—then go ahead."

429

Aug 17–18 ☆ Chase's 2004 Calendar of Events ☆

FORT SUMTER SHELLED BY NORTHERN FORCES: ANNIVERSARY. Aug 17, 1863. In what would become a long siege, Union forces began shelling Fort Sumter at Charleston, SC. The site of the first shots fired during the Civil War on Apr 12, 1861, Sumter endured the siege for a year and a half before being returned to Union hands.

FULTON SAILS STEAMBOAT: ANNIVERSARY. Aug 17, 1807. Robert Fulton began the first American steamboat trip between Albany and New York, NY, on a boat later called the *Clermont*. After years of promoting submarine warfare, Fulton engaged in a partnership with Robert R. Livingston, the US minister to France, allowing Fulton to design and construct a steamboat. His first success came in August 1803 when he launched a steam-powered vessel on the Seine. That same year the US Congress granted Livingston and Fulton exclusive rights to operate steamboats on New York waters during the next 20 years. The first Albany–to–New York trip took 32 hours to travel the 150-mile course. Although his efforts were labeled "Fulton's Folly" by his detractors, his success allowed the partnership to begin commercial service the next year, Sept 4, 1808.

GABON: NATIONAL DAY. Aug 17. National holiday. Commemorates independence from France in 1960.

GOLDWYN, SAMUEL: BIRTH ANNIVERSARY. Aug 17, 1882. Motion picture producer and industry pioneer, born Samuel Goldfish, at Warsaw, Poland. Goldwyn died at Los Angeles, CA, Jan 31, 1974. Attributed to Goldwyn is the observation: "Anybody who goes to see a psychiatrist ought to have his head examined."

INDONESIA: INDEPENDENCE DAY: 55th ANNIVERSARY. Aug 17. National holiday. Republic proclaimed in 1945. It was only after several years of fighting, however, that Indonesia was formally granted its independence by the Netherlands, Dec 27, 1949.

PENN STATE'S AGRI PROGRESS DAYS. Aug 17–19. The Larson Agricultural Research Center, Rock Springs, PA. To provide the public with the latest information on agricultural industries and developments Penn State has made in the field of agriculture. More than 350 commercial exhibitors. Est attendance: 50,000. For info: Robert Oberheim, Penn State Univ, 420 Agricultural Admin Bldg, University Park, PA 16802. Phone: (814) 865-2081. Fax: (814) 865-1677. Web: apd.cas.psu.edu.

POWERS, FRANCIS GARY: 75th BIRTH ANNIVERSARY. Aug 17, 1929. One of America's most famous aviators, Francis Gary Powers was born at Jenkins, KY. The CIA agent, pilot of a U-2 overflight across the Soviet Union, was shot down May 1, 1960, near Sverdlovsk, USSR. He was tried, convicted and sentenced to 10 years' imprisonment, at Moscow, USSR, in August 1960. Returned to the US in 1962, in exchange for an imprisoned Soviet spy (Colonel Rudolf Abel), he found an unwelcoming homeland. Powers died in a helicopter crash near Los Angeles, CA, Aug 2, 1977.

SANDCASTLE DAY. Aug 17. Making sandcastles at the beach is a time-honored family tradition. Today is a day to recognize this tradition and celebrate it at beaches everywhere! For info: David Benson, 13116 Frog Hollow Ct, Oak Hill, VA 20171. Phone: (703) 471-5784. E-mail: David.C.Benson@saic.com.

TURKISH EARTHQUAKE: 5th ANNIVERSARY. Aug 17, 1999. A quake with a magnitude of 7.4 struck northwest Turkey where 45 percent of the population lives. More than 17,000 died and thousands more remained missing. Many of the deaths were due to the shoddy construction of apartment houses. Aftershocks in the region through September 1999 resulted in more deaths. On Nov 12, 1999, a magnitude 7.2 earthquake struck Turkey, killing more than 800 people. Also in 1999 there were earthquakes in Greece (139 dead) and Taiwan (2,200 dead and many missing).

BIRTHDAYS TODAY

Belinda Carlisle, 46, singer, (The Go-Go's, "Mad About You"), born Hollywood, CA, Aug 17, 1958.
Norm Coleman, 55, US Senator (R, Minnesota), born Brooklyn, NY, Aug 17, 1949.
Robert De Niro, 61, actor (Oscars for *Raging Bull*, *The Godfather Part II*; *Taxi Driver*), born New York, NY, Aug 17, 1943.
Robert Joy, 53, actor (*Atlantic City*, *Desperately Seeking Susan*, *Longtime Companion*), born Montreal, QC, Canada, Aug 17, 1951.
Christian Laettner, 35, NBA forward, member of the Dream Team in the 1992 Olympics, born Angola, NY, Aug 17, 1969.
Maureen O'Hara, 84, actress (*Miracle on 34th Street*, *The Hunchback of Notre Dame*), born Dublin, Ireland, Aug 17, 1920.
Sean Penn, 44, actor (*Fast Times at Ridgemont High*, *Dead Man Walking*), born Santa Monica, CA, Aug 17, 1960.
Nelson Piquet, 52, former auto racer, born Brasilia, Brazil, Aug 17, 1952.
Guillermo Vilas, 52, former tennis player, born Mar del Plata, Argentina, Aug 17, 1952.
Donnie Wahlberg, 35, singer (New Kids on the Block), actor ("Band of Brothers," *Ransom*), born Boston, MA, Aug 17, 1969.

AUGUST 18 — WEDNESDAY
Day 231 — 135 Remaining

AMERICAN NEUTRALITY APPEAL: 90th ANNIVERSARY. Aug 18, 1914. President Woodrow Wilson followed his Aug 4th Proclamation of Neutrality with an appeal to the American people to remain impartial in thought and deed with respect to the war that was raging in Europe (World War I).

AMERICAN QUILTER'S SOCIETY QUILT EXPOSITION. Aug 18–21. Nashville, TN. Contest quilts and special quilt exhibits. Workshops, lectures. Est attendance: 25,000. For info: American Quilter's Society, PO Box 3290, Paducah, KY 42002. Phone: (270) 898-7903. Web: www.AQSquilt.com.

ARTISTS IN THE PARK. Aug 18. Cate Park, Wolfeboro, NH. 25th annual juried exhibit and sale including 41 artists and craftspeople, demonstrations throughout the day and family entertainment. Held rain or shine, 10 AM–5 PM. Sponsor: Governor Wentworth Arts Council. Est attendance: 4,000. For info: Deborah Hopkins, Chair, PO Box 1379, Wolfeboro, NH 03894. Phone: (603) 569-4994.

BAD POETRY DAY. Aug 18. After all the "good" poetry you were forced to study in school, here's a chance for a payback. Invite some friends over, compose some really rotten verse and send it to your old high school English teacher. (©2003 by WH.) For info: Thomas & Ruth Roy, Wellcat Holidays, 2418 Long Ln, Lebanon, PA 17046. Phone: (717) 279-0184. E-mail: info@wellcat.com. Web: www.wellcat.com.

BIRTH CONTROL PILLS SOLD: ANNIVERSARY. Aug 18, 1960. The first commercially produced oral contraceptives were marketed by the G.D. Searle Company of Illinois. The pill, developed by Gregory Pincus, had been undergoing clinical trials since 1954.

August 2004	S	M	T	W	T	F	S
	1	2	3	4	5	6	7
	8	9	10	11	12	13	14
	15	16	17	18	19	20	21
	22	23	24	25	26	27	28
	29	30	31				

☆ Chase's 2004 Calendar of Events ☆ Aug 18–19

CLEMENTE, ROBERTO: 70th BIRTH ANNIVERSARY. Aug 18, 1934. National League baseball player, born at Carolina, Puerto Rico. Drafted by the Pittsburgh Pirates in 1954, he played his entire major league career with them. Clemente died in a plane crash Dec 31, 1972, while on a mission of mercy to Nicaragua to deliver supplies he had collected for survivors of an earthquake. He was elected to the Baseball Hall of Fame in 1973.

DARE, VIRGINIA: BIRTH ANNIVERSARY. Aug 18, 1587 (OS). Virginia Dare, the first child of English parents to be born in the New World, was born to Ellinor and Ananias Dare, at Roanoke Island, NC, Aug 18, 1587. When a ship arrived to replenish their supplies in 1591, the settlers (including Virginia Dare) had vanished, without leaving a trace of the settlement.

LEWIS, MERIWETHER: BIRTH ANNIVERSARY. Aug 18, 1774. American explorer (of Lewis and Clark expedition), born at Albemarle County, VA. Died Oct 11, 1809, near Nashville, TN.

MAIL-ORDER CATALOG: ANNIVERSARY. Aug 18, 1872. The first mail-order catalog was published by Montgomery Ward. It was only a single sheet of paper. By 1904 the Montgomery Ward catalog weighed four pounds. In 1985 Montgomery Ward closed its catalog operation; in 2000 it announced the closing of its retail stores.

MICHIGAN FIBER FESTIVAL. Aug 18–22. Allegan County Fairgrounds, Allegan, MI. A unique opportunity to see and learn about natural fibers and the animals and plants that produce them. Includes classes and displays of fiber animals and processes of fiber into garments or décor. Est attendance: 8,000. For info: Michigan Fiber Festival, PO Box 744, Hastings, MI 49058. Phone: (269) 948-2497. E-mail: mff@Iserv.net. Web: www.michiganfiberfestival.org.

NINETEENTH AMENDMENT TO US CONSTITUTION RATIFIED: ANNIVERSARY. Aug 18, 1920. The 19th Amendment extended the right to vote to women.

TENNESSEE WALKING HORSE NATIONAL CELEBRATION. Aug 18–28. Celebration Grounds, Shelbyville, TN. More than 3,800 entries compete for more than $650,000 in prizes and awards—and the World Grand Championship titles. An 11-day festival for the whole family, plus trade show. Est attendance: 250,000. For info: Chip Walters, Dir Public & Media Relations, Tennessee Walking Horse Natl Celebration, Calhoun and Evans, PO Box 1010, Shelbyville, TN 37162. Phone: (931) 684-5915. Fax: (931) 684-5949. E-mail: twhnc@twhnc.com. Web: www.twhnc.com.

BIRTHDAYS TODAY

Elayne Boosler, 52, comedienne, born Brooklyn, NY, Aug 18, 1952.
Rosalynn (Eleanor) Smith Carter, 77, former First Lady, wife of Jimmy Carter, 38th president of the US, born Plains, GA, Aug 18, 1927.
Bobby Higginson, 34, baseball player, born Philadelphia, PA, Aug 18, 1970.
Mike Johanns, 54, Governor of Nebraska (R), born Osage, IA, Aug 18, 1950.
Luc Montagnier, 72, virologist, discovered the AIDS virus in 1983, born Chabris, France, Aug 18, 1932.
Martin Mull, 61, actor, comedian ("Sabrina, the Teenage Witch," "Roseanne"), born Chicago, IL, Aug 18, 1943.
Edward Norton, 35, actor (*Primal Fear, American History X*), born Boston, MA, Aug 18, 1969.
Roman Polanski, 71, filmmaker (Oscar for *The Pianist*; *Rosemary's Baby, Chinatown*), born Paris, France, Aug 18, 1933.
Robert Redford, 67, actor (*Butch Cassidy and the Sundance Kid, The Sting, The Natural*), director (*A River Runs Through It*, Oscar for *Ordinary People*), born Santa Monica, CA, Aug 18, 1937.
Christian Slater, 35, actor (*Heathers, Broken Arrow, Pump Up the Volume*), born New York, NY, Aug 18, 1969.

Madeleine Stowe, 46, actress (*The Last of the Mohicans, Short Cuts*), born Los Angeles, CA, Aug 18, 1958.
Patrick Swayze, 50, dancer, actor ("North and South," *Dirty Dancing*), born Houston, TX, Aug 18, 1954.
Malcolm-Jamal Warner, 34, actor ("The Cosby Show"), born Jersey City, NJ, Aug 18, 1970.
Shelley Winters, 82, actress (Oscars for *A Patch of Blue, The Diary of Anne Frank*), born Shelly Schrift, St. Louis, MO, Aug 18, 1922.

AUGUST 19 — THURSDAY
Day 232 — 134 Remaining

AFGHANISTAN: INDEPENDENCE DAY: 85th ANNIVERSARY. Aug 19. National day. Gained independence from British control, Treaty of Rawalpindi in 1919.

"BLACK COW" ROOT BEER FLOAT CREATED: ANNIVERSARY. Aug 19, 1893. Frank J. Wisner, owner of Cripple Creek Brewing, served the first "Black Cow" root beer float in Cripple Creek, CO. Inspired by the moon-lit view of the snow-capped Cow Mountain, which reminded him of vanilla ice cream floating on top of the pitch-black mountain, he added a scoop of ice cream to his Myers Avenue Red root beer and began serving it as the "Black Cow Mountain." Kids loved it and shortened the name to "Black Cow." Cripple Creek Brewing, now located in Naperville, IL, celebrating its 111th anniversary, still sells beverages based on the original formulas. For info: Michael Lynn, Cripple Creek Brewing, 23244 Rebecca Ct, Naperville, IL 60564. Phone: (630) 393-0540. E-mail: lbartl6415@aol.com. Web: www.cripplecreekbrewing.com.

CHANEL, COCO: BIRTH ANNIVERSARY. Aug 19, 1883. The most important fashion designer of the twentieth century was born Gabrielle Chanel in rural Saumur, France. After starting out in a millinery shop, she began a fashion revolution when moving on to couture fashion in the late teens: using men's clothing (pants) for women's wear; creating simple, comfortable clothing that was nonetheless elegant; making dramatic use of costume jewelry (especially ropes of pearls) and popularizing the "little black dress" and sportswear. She was the first couturier to put her name on a signature perfume: Chanel No. 5 (created in 1921, it was an immediate sensation and today sells every 30 seconds around the world). After closing her shop with the outbreak of World War II, Chanel reopened it in 1954 and introduced her signature suit of collarless, bias-trimmed jacket with skirt. "Elegance does not consist in putting on a new dress," she once stated. The fashion icon died on Jan 10, 1971, at Paris, France.

CLINTON, WILLIAM JEFFERSON (BILL): BIRTHDAY. Aug 19, 1946. The 42nd US President (1993–2001), born at Hope, AR.

FORBES, MALCOLM: 85th BIRTH ANNIVERSARY. Aug 19, 1919. Publisher, born at New York, NY. Malcolm Forbes was an unabashed proponent of capitalism, and his beliefs led to his colorful and successful climb to the top of the magazine-publishing industry. Known as much for his lavish lifestyle as his publishing acumen, Forbes was also an avid motorcyclist and hot-air balloonist. He died Feb 24, 1990, at Far Hills, NJ.

GERMAN PLEBISCITE: 70th ANNIVERSARY. Aug 19, 1934. In a plebiscite, 89.9 percent of German voters approved giving Chancellor Adolf Hitler the additional office of president, placing the Führer in uncontestable supreme command of that country's destiny.

431

Aug 19 ☆ Chase's 2004 Calendar of Events ☆

KENTUCKY STATE FAIR (WITH WORLD CHAMPIONSHIP HORSE SHOW). Aug 19–29. Kentucky Fair and Expo Center, Louisville, KY. Midway, concerts by nationally known artists and the World's Championship Horse Show. In 2004 we celebrate the 100th anniversary of the Fair. Est attendance: 700,000. For info: Marketing Dept, KY Fair and Expo Ctr, Box 37130, Louisville, KY 40233. Phone: (502) 367-5000 or (502) 367-5291. Web: www.kyfairexpo.org or www.kystatefair.org.

LARDNER, RING, JR: BIRTH ANNIVERSARY. Aug 19, 1915. Born Chicago, IL, Aug 19, 1915, son of fabled baseball writer and humorist Ring Lardner. Lardner Jr was an Academy Award–winning screenwriter (Oscar for *Woman of the Year*; *M*A*S*H*), and he also wrote for television. He was a member of the Hollywood Ten, a group of film industry executives sent to federal prison in 1950 for their refusal to tell the House Un-American Activities Committee if they were members of the Communist Party. He served nine months, and was blacklisted for many years. Died at New York, NY, Oct 31, 2000.

MILWAUKEE IRISH FEST. Aug 19–22. Milwaukee, WI. World's largest and most comprehensive Irish music and cultural event, featuring 15 stages of Irish and Irish American music, dance and theater. Activities include sports, contests, parades, displays, food, marketplace, dance and children's activities. Weeklong summer school precedes the festival with lectures and demonstrations in Irish music, dance and culture. Annually, the third weekend in August. Est attendance: 130,000. For info: Milwaukee Irish Fest, 1532 Wauwatosa Ave, Milwaukee, WI 53213. Phone: (414) 476-3378. Fax: (414) 476-7712. E-mail: ifest@execpc.com. Web: www.irishfest.com.

NASH, OGDEN: BIRTH ANNIVERSARY. Aug 19, 1902. American writer, best remembered for his humorous verse. Born at Rye, NY; died May 19, 1971, at Baltimore, MD. "Undeniably brash/Was young Ogden Nash/Whose notable verse/Was admirably terse/And written with panache."

★**NATIONAL AVIATION DAY.** Aug 19. Presidential Proclamation 2343, of July 25, 1939, covers all succeeding years. Always Aug 19 of each year since 1939. Observed annually on anniversary of birth of Orville Wright, who piloted "first self-powered flight in history," Dec 17, 1903. First proclaimed by President Franklin D. Roosevelt.

RIVERFRONT RIBFEST. Aug 19–22. Harris Riverfront Park, Huntington, WV. World-class ribs cooked by rib vendors from around the country, competing for prizes. Continuous entertainment for all ages. Annually, the third weekend in August. Est attendance: 15,000. For info: Heath Brown, Big Sandy Superstore Arena, One Civic Center Plaza, Huntington, WV 25701. Phone: (304) 696-5990. Fax: (304) 696-4463. E-mail: brown@bigsandyarena.com. Web: www.bigsandyarena.com.

RODDENBERRY, GENE: BIRTH ANNIVERSARY. Aug 19, 1921. The creator of the popular TV series "Star Trek," Gene Roddenberry was born at El Paso, TX. Turning from his first career as an airline pilot to writing, he created one of the most successful TV science fiction series ever. The original series, which ended its run in 1969, lives on in reruns, and led to other popular spin-off series. Ten films also have been spawned from the original concept. Roddenberry died Oct 24, 1991, at Santa Monica, CA.

SOLDIERS' REUNION CELEBRATION. Aug 19. Newton, NC. Parade climaxes the 115th annual soldiers' reunion celebration—"oldest patriotic event of its kind in the US, honoring all veterans." Annually, the third Thursday in August. Concerts, arts, crafts, food and games. Est attendance: 29,000. For info: Soldiers' Reunion Committee, Box 267, Newton, NC 28658. Phone: (828) 464-2383.

SPACE MILESTONE: *SOYUZ T-7* (USSR). Aug 19, 1982. Launched from Tyuratam, USSR, with second woman in space (test pilot Svetlana Savitskaya) and two other cosmonauts. Docked at *Salyut 7* and visited the cosmonauts who had been in residence there for the three previous months before returning to Earth on Aug 27 in the *Soyuz T-5* vehicle that had been docked there. The *Soyuz T-7* returned to Earth Dec 10 with the remaining two cosmonauts.

SPACE MILESTONE: *SPUTNIK 5* (USSR). Aug 19, 1960. Space menagerie satellite with dogs Belka and Strelka, mice, rats, houseflies and plants launched. These passengers became first living organisms recovered from orbit when the satellite returned safely to Earth the next day.

SUN PRAIRIE'S SWEET CORN FESTIVAL. Aug 19–22. Sun Prairie, WI. Family-oriented fun. Carnival, midget auto races, parade, beer, brats, food, exhibits, entertainment, craft fair and tons of hot, buttered sweet corn. Est attendance: 100,000. For info: Chamber of Commerce, 109 E Main, Sun Prairie, WI 53590. Phone: (608) 837-4547. Fax: (608) 837-8765. E-mail: sprairie@merr.com. Web: www.sunprairiechamber.com.

SWEDEN: SOUR HERRING PREMIERE. Aug 19. By ordinance, the year's supply of sour herring may begin to be sold on the third Thursday in August.

WRIGHT, ORVILLE: BIRTH ANNIVERSARY. Aug 19, 1871. Aviation pioneer born at Dayton, OH, and died there Jan 30, 1948. See also: "Wright Brothers First Powered Flight" (Dec 17).

BIRTHDAYS TODAY

Adam Arkin, 48, actor ("Chicago Hope," "Northern Exposure"), born Brooklyn, NY, Aug 19, 1956.
William Jefferson Clinton, 58, 42nd president of the US, born Hope, AK, Aug 19, 1946.
Kevin Dillon, 39, actor (*Platoon, The Doors*), born Mamaroneck, NY, Aug 19, 1965.
Peter Gallagher, 49, actor (*sex, lies and videotape, Short Cuts, The Hudsucker Proxy*), born New York, NY, Aug 19, 1955.
Tipper Gore, 56, wife of Al Gore, 45th vice president of the US, advocate for the homeless, mental health and children's causes, born Mary Elizabeth Aitcheson, Washington, DC, Aug 19, 1948.
Gerald McRaney, 56, actor ("Simon & Simon," "Major Dad"), born Collins, MS, Aug 19, 1948.
Diana Muldaur, 66, actress ("Star Trek: The Next Generation," "LA Law," *The Swimmer*), born New York, NY, Aug 19, 1938.
(Franklin) Storey Musgrave, 69, former astronaut, born Boston, MA, Aug 19, 1935.
Cindy Nelson, 49, former alpine skier, born Lutsen, MN, Aug 19, 1955.
Matthew Perry, 35, actor ("Friends," *Fools Rush In*), born Williamstown, MA, Aug 19, 1969.
Jill St. John, 64, actress (*Diamonds Are Forever*), born Jill Oppenheim, Los Angeles, CA, Aug 19, 1940.
Kyra Sedgwick, 39, actress (*Born on the Fourth of July*), born New York, NY, Aug 19, 1965.
William Lee (Willie) Shoemaker, 73, former jockey, born Fabens, TX, Aug 19, 1931.
John Stamos, 41, actor ("General Hospital," "Full House"), born Los Angeles, CA, Aug 19, 1963.
Fred Thompson, 62, former US Senator (R, Tennessee), actor ("Law & Order," *In the Line of Fire*), born Sheffield, AL, Aug 19, 1942.

August 2004

S	M	T	W	T	F	S
1	2	3	4	5	6	7
8	9	10	11	12	13	14
15	16	17	18	19	20	21
22	23	24	25	26	27	28
29	30	31				

☆ Chase's 2004 Calendar of Events ☆ Aug 20

AUGUST 20 — FRIDAY
Day 233 — 133 Remaining

CALIFORNIA STATE FAIR. Aug 20–Sept 6. Sacramento, CA. Top-name entertainment, fireworks, California counties exhibits, livestock nursery, culinary delights, carnival rides and award-winning wines and microbrews. For info: California State Fair, PO Box 15649, Sacramento, CA 95852. Phone: (916) 263-FAIR. Web: www.bigfun.org.

CANADA: COE HILL AGRICULTURAL FAIR. Aug 20–21. Coe Hill, ON. Competitions for best vegetables and animals, along with kids' games, auto thrill show and music. Est attendance: 5,000. For info: Bancroft and District Chamber of Commerce, PO Box 539, Bancroft, ON, Canada K0L 1C0. Phone: (613) 332-1513. Fax: (613) 332-2119. E-mail: chamber@commerce.bancroft.on.ca. Web: www.bancroftdistrict.com.

CANADA: NOVA SCOTIA'S GEM AND MINERAL SHOW. Aug 20–22. Parrsboro, NS. Geological tours by foot, rock collectors' workshops and demonstrations, lectures about Nova Scotia. Est attendance: 2,000. For info: Marilyn Smith, Box 640, 162 Two Island Rd, Parrsboro, NS, Canada B0M 1S0. Phone: (902) 254-3814. Fax: (902) 254-3666. E-mail: smithmf@gov.ns.ca. Web: museum.gov.ns.ca.

COBBLESTONE FESTIVAL. Aug 20–22. Falls City, NE. Includes games, sporting events, contests, draft horse pull, bull riding, carnival rides, flea market, food concessions, fishing contest, parade, craft demos and more. Est attendance: 5,000. For info: Chamber of Commerce, 107 E 17th, PO Box 146, Falls City, NE 68355. Phone: (402) 245-4228. Fax: (402) 245-4228. E-mail: fcchamber@sentco.net.

ELWOOD GLASS FESTIVAL. Aug 20–22. Elwood, IN. Glass factory tours, parade, craft market, flea market, quilt show, entertainment, carnival, kids' activities and more. Est attendance: 20,000. For info: Chamber of Commerce, 108 S Anderson St, Elwood, IN 46036. Phone: (765) 552-0180. E-mail: elwoodchamber@earthlink.net.

FESTIVAL OF THE LITTLE HILLS. Aug 20–22. Frontier Park and Historic Main, St. Charles, MO. The largest festival of the year; activities include demonstrations by craftspeople and artisans. Annually, the third weekend in August. Est attendance: 300,000. For info: St. Charles Conv and Visitors Bureau, 230 S Main, St. Charles, MO 63301. Phone: (800) 366-2427 or (636) 946-7776. Web: www.festivalofthelittlehills.com.

GINZA HOLIDAY: JAPANESE CULTURAL FESTIVAL. Aug 20–22. Midwest Buddhist Temple, Chicago, IL. Experience the Waza (National Treasures tradition) by viewing 300 years of Edo craft tradition and seeing it come alive as master craftsmen from Tokyo demonstrate their arts. Japanese folk and classical dancing, martial arts, taiko (drums), flower arrangements and cultural displays. Chicken teriyaki, sushi, udon, shaved ice, corn on the cob and refreshments. Annually, the third weekend in August. Est attendance: 15,000. For info: Office Secretary, Midwest Buddhist Temple, 435 W Menomonee St, Chicago, IL 60614. Phone: (312) 943-7801. Fax: (312) 943-8069.

GUEST, EDGAR ALBERT: BIRTH ANNIVERSARY. Aug 20, 1881. Newspaperman and author of folksy, homespun verse that enjoyed great popularity and was syndicated in more than 100 newspapers. Born at Birmingham, England; died at Detroit, MI, Aug 5, 1959. "Eddie Guest Day" usually proclaimed on birth anniversary in Detroit.

HARRISON, BENJAMIN: BIRTH ANNIVERSARY. Aug 20, 1833. The 23rd president of the US, born at North Bend, OH. He was the grandson of William Henry Harrison, 9th president of the US. His term of office, Mar 4, 1889–Mar 3, 1893, was preceded and followed by the presidential terms of Grover Cleveland (who thus became the 22nd and 24th president of the US). Harrison died at Indianapolis, IN, Mar 13, 1901.

HAWAII ADMISSION DAY HOLIDAY. Aug 20. The third Friday in August is observed as a state holiday each year, recognizing the anniversary of Hawaii's statehood. Hawaii became the 50th state Aug 21, 1959.

HOLZFEST. Aug 20–22. Amana, IA. A woodcraft show with displays, products, demonstrations, equipment, supplies, entertainment and food. Annually, the third weekend in August. Est attendance: 10,000. For info: Tammy Meyer, Splinterfest/Holzfest, PO Box 215, Dyersville, IA 52040. Phone: (563) 875-7017. Fax: (563) 875-9506. E-mail: dww1@msn.com.

HUNGARY: ST. STEPHEN'S DAY. Aug 20. National holiday. Commemorates the canonization of St. Stephen, king and founder of the state, in 1083. Under the Communists, commemorated as Constitution Day.

ITALY: STRESA MUSIC WEEKS. Aug 20–Sept 14 (tentative). Stresa. 44th annual festival. International festival includes concerts by symphonic orchestras, chamber music, recitals and a series by young winners of international musical contests. For info: Settimane Musicali di Stresa del Lago Maggiore, Via Carducci, 38, 28838 Stresa (VB), Italy. Phone: (39) (0323) 31095. Fax: (39) (0323) 33006. E-mail: info@settimanemusicali.net. Web: www.settimanemusicali.net.

KRUISIN' WEEKEND. Aug 20–22. Lakemont Park, Altoona, PA. 15th annual. More than 400 custom street rods and classic cars will be on display throughout the park all weekend, plus terrific live oldies music. For info: Lakemont Park, I-99 Frankstown Rd Exit, Altoona, PA 16602. Phone: (814) 949-7275 or (800) 434-8006. Fax: (814) 949-9207. E-mail: Lakemont99@aol.com. Web: www.lakemontparkfun.com.

LITTLE LEAGUE BASEBALL WORLD SERIES. Aug 20–29. Williamsport, PA. Sixteen teams from the US and foreign countries compete for the World Championship. Est attendance: 315,000. For info: Little League Baseball HQ, Box 3485, Williamsport, PA 17701. Phone: (570) 326-1921. Web: www.littleleague.org.

LOVECRAFT, H.P.: BIRTH ANNIVERSARY. Aug 20, 1890. Howard Phillips Lovecraft, American author of horror tales of the supernatural, a pioneering science fiction writer and a notable epistolarian, was born at Providence, RI and died there Mar 15, 1937.

MACHIAS WILD BLUEBERRY FESTIVAL. Aug 20–22. Machias, ME. Harvest festival includes crafts sale, lobster boil, five-mile race, entertainment, children's parade, blueberry foods and a wild blueberry pie-eating contest. Annually, the third weekend in August. Est attendance: 22,000. For info: Machias Wild Blueberry Festival, PO Box 265, Machias, ME 04654. Phone: (207) 255-6665. Web: www.machiasblueberry.com.

MICHIGAN STATE FAIR. Aug 20–Sept 6 (tentative). State Fairgrounds, Detroit, MI. Est attendance: 450,000. For info: State Fairgrounds, Eight Mile Road and Woodward Ave, Detroit, MI 48203. Phone: (313) 369-8250. Fax: (313) 369-8410. Web: www.michiganstatefair.com.

MOROCCO: REVOLUTION OF THE KING AND THE PEOPLE: ANNIVERSARY. Aug 20. National holiday. Commemorates the response of the people to Sultan (later King) Sidi Muhammed being sent into exile in 1953 by the French.

MOUNTAIN MAN RENDEZVOUS. Aug 20–22. Old Mission State Park, Cataldo, ID. 1800s fur trappers and traders, in period clothing. Est attendance: 2,500. For info: Roger Howard, Old Mission State Park, PO Box 30, Cataldo, ID 83810-0030. Phone: (208) 682-3814. Fax: (208) 682-4032. E-mail: old@idpr.state.id.us.

MUDDY FROGWATER COUNTRY CLASSIC FESTIVAL. Aug 20–22. Yantis Park, Milton-Freewater, OR. Arts, crafts, food, karaoke, country music, frog jumping contest, book sale, square dancing, firefighters' water fight, 3-on-3 basketball tournament, corn roast, watermelon feed and softball tournament. Annually, the third weekend in August. Est attendance: 5,000. For info: Milton-Freewater Area Chamber of Commerce, 505 Ward St, Milton-Freewater, OR 97862. Phone: (541) 938-5563. Fax: (541) 938-5564. E-mail: mfmdfrog@oregontrail.net. Web: www.mfchamber.com.

Aug 20 ☆ Chase's 2004 Calendar of Events ☆

NORTHEASTERN WISCONSIN ANTIQUE POWER AND MACHINERY SHOW THRESHEREE. Aug 20–22. Sturgeon Bay, WI. Continuous display of operating antique machinery, antique tractor pull, barefoot horse pull, crafts, games for kids, food and refreshments. Annually, the third weekend in August. Est attendance: 3,000. For info: Josephine Bochek, Northeastern Wisconsin Antique Power Assn, 5005 Country View Rd, Sturgeon Bay, WI 54235. Phone: (920) 743-5251 or Bernie Geisel (920) 743-4859. E-mail: coldcomfortfarms@hotmail.com.

NORTHERN PLAINS HERITAGE FESTIVAL. Aug 20–22. Dickinson, ND. Celebrate the Russian, German and Scandinavian heritage of our local homesteaders at this annual event. Ethnic foods, dress, music, demonstrations and displays round it out. Est attendance: 1,000. For info: Northern Plains Heritage Festival, 72 Museum Dr, Dickinson, ND 58601. Phone: (800) 279-7391 or (701) 483-4988. Fax: (701) 483-9261. Web: www.dickinsoncvb.com.

O'HIGGINS, BERNARDO: BIRTH ANNIVERSARY. Aug 20, 1778. First ruler of Chile after its declaration of independence. Called the "Liberator of Chile." Born at Chillan, Chile. Died at Lima, Peru, Oct 24, 1842.

PLUTONIUM FIRST WEIGHED: ANNIVERSARY. Aug 20, 1942. University of Chicago scientist Glen Seaborg and his colleagues first weighed plutonium, the first man-made element.

PRESIDENT BENJAMIN HARRISON'S BIRTHDAY CELEBRATION. Aug 20. Indianapolis, IN, Harrison's hometown. Also free tours of the Victorian mansion. Est attendance: 500. For info: PR Dept, President Benjamin Harrison Home, 1230 N Delaware St, Indianapolis, IN 46202. Phone: (317) 631-1888. Fax: (317) 632-5488.

REEVES, JIM: 80th BIRTH ANNIVERSARY. Aug 20, 1924. Country music star Jim Reeves was born at Galloway, Panola County, TX, and died at Nashville, TN, July 31, 1964, when the single-engine plane in which he was traveling crashed in a dense fog. Reeves's biggest hit was "He'll Have to Go" (1959), and he was inducted into the Country Music Hall of Fame in 1967.

RE/MAX BALLUNAR LIFTOFF FESTIVAL. Aug 20–22. NASA/Johnson Space Center, Clear Lake Area, Houston, TX. Featuring more than 100 hot-air balloons, sky diving competitions, arts and crafts, midway game area, food, music and other entertainment. Sponsored by NASA/Johnson Space Center, Clear Lake Area Chamber of Commerce, ReMax and Space Center Houston. For info: Clear Lake Area Chamber of Commerce, 1201 NASA Rd One, Houston, TX 77058. Phone: (281) 488-7676. Fax: (281) 488-8981.

SAARINEN, (GOTTLIEB) ELIEL: BIRTH ANNIVERSARY. Aug 20, 1873 (OS). Famed architect. Born at Helsinki, Finland. Died at Bloomfield Hills, MI, July 1, 1950.

SACAJAWEA HERITAGE DAYS. Aug 20–21. Sacajawea Center, Salmon, ID. Grand opening of the Sacajawea Interpretive Center with tribal ceremonies, performances, tours of the facilities, rendezvous, exhibits, period crafts and demonstrations. Also featuring a concert, arts & crafts, BBQs, dutch-oven "gathering," Lewis & Clark Reenactment Troupe and much more. Est attendance: 4,000. For info: Salmon Valley Chamber of Commerce, 200 Main St, Ste 1, Salmon, ID 83467. Phone: (208) 756-2100 or (800) 727-2540. E-mail: svcc1@salmoninternet.com.

SPACE MILESTONE: VIKING 1 AND 2 (US). Aug 20 and Sept 9, 1975. Sister ships launched toward Mars from Cape Canaveral, FL, on Aug 20 and Sept 9, 1975. Viking 1's lander touched down on Mars July 20, 1976, and Viking 2's lander on Sept 3, 1976. Sent back to Earth high-quality photographs, analysis of atmosphere, weather information and results of sophisticated experiments intended to determine whether life may be present on Mars.

SPACE MILESTONE: VOYAGER 2 (US). Aug 20, 1977. This unmanned spacecraft journeyed past Jupiter in 1979, Saturn in 1981, Uranus in 1986 and Neptune in 1989, sending photographs and data back to scientists on Earth.

TEXAS RANCH ROUNDUP. Aug 20–22. MPEC Exhibit Hall & Kay Yeager Coliseum, Wichita Falls, TX. Cowboys from prestigious ranches in Texas compete in the events that make up their daily work. Cattle roping and penning and other rodeo-type events plus ranch cooking contests, ranch talent contests. Est attendance: 18,000. For info: Wichita Falls Conv and Visitors Bureau, 1000 5th St, Wichita Falls, TX 76301. Phone: (800) 799-6732 or (940) 716-5500. Fax: (940) 716-5509. Web: www.wichitafalls.org.

WESTERN IDAHO FAIR. Aug 20–28. Boise, ID. 107th annual. Largest fair in the state, including four stages of entertainment on the grounds with local and regional talent, seven nights of grandstand concerts, two days of Idaho Cowboy Association Rodeo finals, carnival midway, 70 food booths and a power equipment display. Est attendance: 254,000. For info: Bob Batista, Mgr, Western Idaho Fair, 5610 Glenwood, Boise, ID 83714. Phone: (208) 287-5650. Fax: (208) 375-9972.

WILD WEST WEEKEND AND COUNTRY MUSIC FESTIVAL. Aug 20–22. Clifton, KS. Cowboys, mountainmen, bank robbers, gunfighters, lawmen, drovers, blacksmiths, hide tanners, dance hall girls. Music competition in 12 country music categories with more than $3,000 in prize monies plus trophies. Also car show, citywide garage sale, and flea market. For info: Washington County Travel and Tourism, Courthouse, 214 C St, Washington, KS 66968. Phone: (785) 325-2116. Fax: (785) 325-2830. E-mail: washcott@washingtonks.net.

XEROX 914 DONATED TO SMITHSONIAN: ANNIVERSARY. Aug 20, 1985. The original Xerox 914 copying machine (which had been introduced to the public 25 years earlier—in March 1960) was formally presented to the Smithsonian Institution's National Museum of American History at Washington, DC. Invented by Chester Carlson, a patent lawyer, the quick and easy copying of documents by machine revolutionized the world's offices.

BIRTHDAYS TODAY

Joan Allen, 48, actress (Searching for Bobby Fischer, Nixon, The Contender), born Rochelle, IL, Aug 20, 1956.
Andy Benes, 37, former baseball player, born Evansville, IN, Aug 20, 1967.
Connie Chung, 58, journalist, born Constance Yu-Hwa, Washington, DC, Aug 20, 1946.
Tara Dakides, 29, snowboarder, born Mission Viejo, CA, Aug 20, 1975.
Isaac Hayes, 62, musician, singer, songwriter, born Covington, TN, Aug 20, 1942.
Todd Helton, 31, baseball player, born Knoxville, TN, Aug 20, 1973.
Donald (Don) King, 73, boxing promoter, born Cleveland, OH, Aug 20, 1931.
Mark Edward Langston, 44, former baseball player, born San Diego, CA, Aug 20, 1960.
Alfonso Raymond (Al) Lopez, 96, Hall of Fame baseball player and manager, born Tampa, FL, Aug 20, 1908.
Robert Plant, 56, singer, born Bromwich, England, Aug 20, 1948.
Al Roker, 50, meteorologist ("Today Show"), born Brooklyn, NY, Aug 20, 1954.
Theresa Saldana, 49, actress ("The Commish"), born Brooklyn, NY, Aug 20, 1955.

AUGUST 21 — SATURDAY
Day 234 — 132 Remaining

AMERICAN BAR ASSOCIATION FOUNDING: ANNIVERSARY. Aug 21, 1878. Organized at Saratoga, NY.

AQUINO, BENIGNO: ASSASSINATION ANNIVERSARY. Aug 21, 1983. Filipino opposition leader Benigno S. Aquino, Jr, was shot and killed at the Manila airport on his return to the Philippines on Aug 21, 1983. The killing precipitated greater anti-Marcos feeling and figured significantly in the Feb 7, 1986, election that brought about the collapse of the government administration of Ferdinand E. Marcos and the inauguration of Corazon C. Aquino, widow of the slain man, as president.

ARGENTINA: INTERNATIONAL FEDERATION OF LIBRARY ASSOCIATIONS ANNUAL CONFERENCE. Aug 21–28. Buenos Aires, Argentina. The theme for the 70th annual conference is "Libraries: Tools for Education and Development." For info: Intl Federation of Library Assns Conf, Asociación de Bibliotecarios, Graduados de la República Argentina, Tucumán 1424, 8 piso Of. D, C1050AAB, Buenos Aires, Argentina. Phone: (54) (11) 4371-5269. Email: ifla2004secr@el-libro.com.ar. Web: www.ifla.org.

BATTLE OF BLUE LICKS CELEBRATION. Aug 21–22. Blue Licks Battlefield State Park, Mount Olivet, KY. Commemorates the anniversary of Revolutionary War Battle of Blue Licks (which involved Daniel Boone). Living-history demonstrations, arts, crafts, games, competitions and battle reenactment. Annually, the third weekend in August. Est attendance: 3,000. For info: Doug Price, Park Mgr, Blue Licks Battlefield State Resort Pk, PO Box 66, Mt Olivet, KY 41064-0066. Phone: (859) 289-5507. Fax: (859) 289-5409. Web: www.state.ky.us/agencies/parks/bluelick.htm.

BEARDSLEY, AUBREY VINCENT: BIRTH ANNIVERSARY. Aug 21, 1872. English artist and illustrator born at Brighton. Died at Menton, France, Mar 16, 1898.

BIKE VAN BUREN. Aug 21–22. Van Buren County, IA. A laid-back bicycle tour of the villages, landmarks and landscape of this rural Iowa county. The "red carpet of hospitality" is rolled out for the bikers as they pass through. Annually, the third weekend in August. Est attendance: 500. For info: Villages of Van Buren, Inc, PO Box 9, Keosauqua, IA 52565. Phone: (800) TOU-RVBC. Fax: (319) 293-7116. Web: www.800-tourvbc.com.

CHAMBERLAIN, WILT: BIRTH ANNIVERSARY. Aug 21, 1936. Basketball Hall of Fame center, born at Philadelphia, PA. Died Oct 12, 1999, at Los Angeles, CA.

CHILDREN'S DAY. Aug 21. Woodstock, VT. Traditional farm activities from corn shelling to sawing firewood—19th-century games, traditional spelling bee, ice cream and butter making, wagon rides. For info: Billings Farm Museum, PO Box 489, Woodstock, VT 05091. Phone: (802) 457-2355. Fax: (802) 457-4663. E-mail: billings.farm@valley.net. Web: www.billingsfarm.org.

COLORADO STATE FAIR. Aug 21–Sept 4. State Fairgrounds, Pueblo, CO. One of the nation's oldest western fairs, it is also Colorado's largest single event. Family fun, top-name entertainment, lots of food and festivities. Est attendance: 650,000. For info: Colorado State Fair, 1001 Beulah Ave, Pueblo, CO 81004. Phone: (719) 561-8484. Web: www.coloradostatefair.com.

COSHOCTON CANAL FESTIVAL. Aug 21–22. Coshocton, OH. Celebrates the arrival of first canal boat at Port Roscoe. Crafts, demonstrations and live entertainment. Annually, the third weekend in August. Est attendance: 14,000. For info: Roscoe Village Fdtn, 381 Hill St, Coshocton, OH 43812. Phone: (800) 877-1830 or (740) 622-9310. Fax: (740) 623-6555. E-mail: rvmarketing@roscoevillage.com. Web: www.roscoevillage.com.

A DAY ON THE FARM. Aug 21. Dorris Ranch, Springfield, OR. Hayrides, pony rides, entertainment, kids' crafts, petting zoo. Take an interpretive walking tour of the Dorris Ranch living history filbert farm. Costumed trappers, farmers and Kalapuya Indians guide the tours. Or you can browse the displays in the historic barn and watch old-time farming demonstrations. Refreshments will be available, or you are welcome to bring a picnic lunch. For info: Willamalane Park and Recreation District, 200 S Mill St, Springfield, OR 97477. Phone: (541) 736-4544. Web: www.willamalane.org.

HAWAII: ADMISSION DAY: 45th ANNIVERSARY. Aug 21, 1959. President Dwight Eisenhower signed a proclamation admitting Hawaii to the Union. The statehood bill had passed the previous March with a stipulation that statehood should be approved by a vote of Hawaiian residents. The referendum passed by a huge margin in June and Eisenhower proclaimed Hawaii the 50th state on Aug 21.

HOMETOWN DAYS. Aug 21–22. Strasburg, CO. To remind people of the first continuous chain of rails from an Atlantic to a Pacific port. The rails were joined Aug 15, 1870, at Comanche, which was later renamed Strasburg. Annually, the third weekend in August. Est attendance: 1,000. For info: Sandy Miller, Curator-Comanche Crossing Museum, 7433 S Rd 157, Strasburg, CO 80136. Phone: (303) 622-4690.

LEADVILLE TRAIL 100 ULTRAMARATHON. Aug 21–22. Leadville, CO. One of the toughest 100-mile foot races in the country, the course goes through the Rocky Mountains 50 miles to the ghost town of Winfield and back. Runners begin at 4 AM and must complete the race in 30 hours. All race applications mailed by Jan 2. Sponsor: Leadville Trail 100, Inc. Est attendance: 5,000. For info: Leadville Chamber of Commerce, PO Box 861, Leadville, CO 80461. Phone: (719) 486-3900 or (800) 933-3901. Fax: (719) 486-8478. E-mail: leadville@leadvilleusa.com. Web: www.leadvilleusa.com.

MAINE HIGHLAND GAMES. Aug 21. Thomas Point Beach, Brunswick, ME. 26th annual. Presented by the Saint Andrew's Society of Maine. Bagpipe bands, Highland and Scottish dancing, Scottish arts and crafts fair, folksingers, Scottish fiddling, children's games, adult athletics including tossing of the caber, wheat sheaf toss and putting of the stone, Border collie herding demonstrations, Highland cattle and individual piping contests. American and Scottish foods galore. The only Scottish event of its kind held in Maine! Scots and non-Scots will enjoy the color, pageantry and friendly atmosphere. Est attendance: 8,000. For info: Thomas Point Beach, 29 Meadow Rd, Brunswick, ME 04011. Phone: (207) 725-6009. Web: www.thomaspointbeach.com.

MARCIE'S PLACE: A CAMP FOR GRIEVING CHILDREN. Aug 21–22 (tentative). Ingleside, IL. A special camp for children ages 5–16 who have had someone that they love die. Grief-directed as well as traditional camp activities. Nondenominational, no cost to the campers, completely funded through private donations. Annually, the third weekend in August. For info: Marcie's Place, PO Box 457, Grayslake, IL 60030. Phone: (847) 223-9889. E-mail: marciesplacecamp@yahoo.com.

NATIONAL HOMELESS ANIMALS DAY AND CANDLELIGHT VIGILS. Aug 21. A day to call attention to the fact that millions of healthy dogs and cats are killed each year in the US in animal shelters because of overpopulation—a problem that has a solution: Spay/Neuter! It stops the killing! The vigils memorialize the animals killed in the preceding year and sympathize with the caring shelter personnel who must take the lives of the animals. Vigils will be held throughout the US and beyond. For info: Intl Society for Animal Rights, Inc, Susan Dapsis, Pres,

Aug 21–22 ☆ Chase's 2004 Calendar of Events ☆

965 Griffin Pond Rd, Clarks Summit, PA 18411-9214. Phone: (570) 586-2200. Fax: (570) 586-9580. E-mail: contact@ISARonline.org.

PENNSYLVANIA RENAISSANCE FAIRE. Aug 21–Oct 31 (Saturdays, Sundays, Labor Day). Manheim, PA. Re-creation of 16th-century Elizabethan village. Lords and ladies, mongers, merchants, jousting, human chess match, medieval foods and crafts. Est attendance: 150,000. For info: Thomas Roy, Mount Hope Estate and Winery, PO Box 685, Cornwall, PA 17016. Phone: (717) 665-7021. Fax: (717) 664-3466. E-mail: Tom@parenfaire.com. Web: www.parenfaire.com.

POCONO STATE CRAFT FAIR. Aug 21–22 (tentative). Sun Mountain Recreation Club, Shawnee-on-the-Delaware, PA. High-quality juried craft show featuring the work of 80 members of the Pennsylvania Guild of Craftsmen. Enjoy a day in this lakeside setting with festival food, craft demonstrations, children's activities, and strolling musical entertainment. For information about tickets, or how to become a member of the PA Guild, contact PGC at the address below. Est attendance: 5,000. PGC, 10 Stable Mill Trail, Richboro, PA 18954. Phone: (800) 684-7440. E-mail: pacraft@comcat.com. Web: www.pacrafts.com.

POET'S DAY. Aug 21. A day for all poets to celebrate their special talents and the vision that makes them so wonderful and dear. Poet's Day is a time to share special thoughts about poets and poetry. (©2001 C. Daniel Rhodes) For info: C. Daniel Rhodes or Natalie Danielle Rhodes, 1900 Crossvine Rd, Hoover, AL 35244. Phone: (205) 908-6781. Fax: (205) 987-2986. E-mail: drhodes2986@charter.net.

QUANTRILL'S RAID ON LAWRENCE, KANSAS: ANNIVERSARY. Aug 21, 1863. Confederate raider William Clarke Quantrill launched a predawn terrorist raid on Lawrence, KS, leaving 150 civilians dead and much of the town ruined. Quantrill had been denied a commission in the Southern army for his barbaric approach to war.

ROCKBRIDGE COMMUNITY FESTIVAL. Aug 21. Lexington, VA. Fun for all ages—crafts, exhibits, live music, food and games. For info: Lexington Visitors Bureau, 106 E Washington St, Lexington, VA 24450. Phone: (540) 463-3777. Fax: (540) 463-1105. E-mail: lexington@rockbridge.net.

SANDCASTLE & SCULPTURE DAY. Aug 21. Jetties Beach, Nantucket, MA. Islanders and visitors create masterpiece sandcastles and sand sculptures on the beach. This 30th annual contest will last all afternoon and ribbons will be awarded in various categories. For info: Nantucket Chamber of Commerce, 48 Main St, Nantucket, MA 02554. Phone: (508) 228-1700. E-mail: info@nantucketchamber.org. Web: www.nantucketchamber.org.

SEMINOLE TRIBE OF FLORIDA LEGALLY ESTABLISHED: ANNIVERSARY. Aug 21, 1957. In 1953 Congress adopted a proposal to terminate assistance to nonrecognized Indian tribes. Seminole leaders and tribal members began to fight the proposal by drafting a constitution and charter for the Seminole Tribe. These were later approved by the Secretary of the Interior. On this date, a majority of tribal members voted to establish the Seminole Tribe of Florida. Today, 2,200 Seminoles live on five reservations in Florida.

SOUTHERN HEMISPHERE HOODIE-HOO DAY. Aug 21. Long awaited by our Southern-half friends, this is the day to go outdoors at high noon and yell "Hoodie-Hoo" to chase winter and make ready for spring. [©2003 by WH.] For info: Thomas & Ruth Roy, Wellcat Holidays, 2418 Long Ln, Lebanon, PA 17046. Phone: (717) 279-0184. E-mail: info@wellcat.com. Web: www.wellcat.com.

August 2004	S	M	T	W	T	F	S
	1	2	3	4	5	6	7
	8	9	10	11	12	13	14
	15	16	17	18	19	20	21
	22	23	24	25	26	27	28
	29	30	31				

SPACE MILESTONE: GEMINI 5 (US). Aug 21, 1965. Launched on this date, this craft carrying astronauts Lieutenant Colonel Cooper and Lieutenant Commander Conrad orbited Earth 128 times for new international record of eight days.

VINEGAR DAY. Aug 21. A day set aside to celebrate the virtues of vinegar. All over the world people will conduct vinegar tasting contests and host events connected with vinegar. There will be an International Vinegar Festival in Roslyn, SD, to commemorate. For info: Lawrence Diggs, Vinegar Connoisseurs Intl, PO Box 41, Roslyn, SD 57261. Phone: (605) 486-4536. E-mail: vinegarday@vinegarman.com. Web: www.vinegarman.com.

BIRTHDAYS TODAY

Steve Case, 46, founder of America Online, born Oahu, HI, Aug 21, 1958.
Kim Cattrall, 48, actress ("Sex and the City," *Mannequin*), born Liverpool, England, Aug 21, 1956.
Jackie DeShannon, 60, singer, songwriter ("Put a Little Love in Your Heart"), born Hazel, KY, Aug 21, 1944.
James Robert (Jim) McMahon, 45, former football player, born Jersey City, NJ, Aug 21, 1959.
Kenny Rogers, 66, singer ("Lucille," "Lady"), born Houston, TX, Aug 21, 1938.
Melvin Van Peebles, 72, playwright (*Ain't Supposed to Die a Natural Death*), born Chicago, IL, Aug 21, 1932.
Peter Weir, 60, director (*Dead Poets Society, Gallipoli, The Truman Show*), born Sydney, Australia, Aug 21, 1944.
Clarence Williams III, 65, actor ("The Mod Squad," *Purple Rain*), born New York, NY, Aug 21, 1939.
Alicia Witt, 29, actress ("Cybill"), born Worcester, MA, Aug 21, 1975.

AUGUST 22 — SUNDAY
Day 235 — 131 Remaining

BATTLE OF STALINGRAD BEGINS: ANNIVERSARY. Aug 22, 1942. Having captured Sevastopol on the Crimea on July 2, after an eight-month seige, the Germans began an offensive to capture Stalingrad. During this five-month-long battle the city of 500,000 people dwindled to a population of 1,515. In the fighting Russia lost 750,000 troops, the Germans 400,000, the Romanians nearly 200,000 and the Italians 130,000—a total of 1,480,000. The last German strongholds at Stalingrad surrendered to the Russian Army on Feb 2, 1943.

BE AN ANGEL DAY. Aug 22. A day to do "one small act of service for someone. Be a blessing in someone's life." Annually, Aug 22. For info: Angel Heights Healing Center, Rev Jayne M. Howard-Feldman, PO Box 95, Upperco, MD 21155. Phone: (410) 833-6912. E-mail: earthangel4peace@aol.com. Web: earthangel4peace.com.

BELGIUM: WEDDING OF THE GIANTS. Aug 22. Traditional cultural observance. Annually, the fourth Sunday in August.

CAMEROON: VOLCANIC ERUPTION: ANNIVERSARY. Aug 22, 1986. Deadly fumes from a presumed volcanic eruption under Lake Nios at Cameroon killed more than 1,500 persons. A similar occurrence two years earlier had killed 37 persons.

DEBUSSY, CLAUDE: BIRTH ANNIVERSARY. Aug 22, 1862. (Achille) Claude Debussy, French musician and composer, especially remembered for his impressionistic "tone poems," was born at St. Germain-en-Laye, France. He died at Paris, France, Mar 25, 1918.

HERRIMAN, GEORGE: BIRTH ANNIVERSARY. Aug 22, 1880. In 1910 when George Herriman introduced a cat and mouse as subplot characters to his comic strip "The Dingbat Family," their non-sequitur dialogue gained enough attention to result in a spin-off strip of their own. The superbly drafted "Krazy Kat and Ignatz" had as its central theme unrequited love. Kat loved Ignatz, but the malevolent mouse took every opportunity to throw bricks at the devoted cat. "Krazy Kat" was popular with a mass audience as well as artists and intellectuals, and it remained enormously popular after Herriman's death. Born at New Orleans, LA, he died at Hollywood, CA, Apr 25, 1944.

INTERNATIONAL YACHT RACE: ANNIVERSARY. Aug 22, 1851. A silver trophy (then known as the "Hundred Guinea Cup," and offered by the Royal Yacht Squadron) was won in a race around the Isle of Wight by the US yacht *America*. The trophy, later turned over to the New York Yacht Club, became known as the America's Cup.

KGB FOUNDER STATUE DISMANTLED: ANNIVERSARY. Aug 22, 1991. In the wake of the popular revolt that smashed the right-wing Soviet coup, a crowd of 10,000 Muscovites watched as cranes dismantled a 14-ton statue of Felix Dzerzhinsky, a Polish intellectual tapped by Vladimir Lenin to organize the fledgling Soviet Union's secret police. After trucks had hauled away the massive likeness of Dzerzhinsky, Moscow residents adorned the statue's pedestal and the nearby KGB headquarters with graffiti.

LANGLEY, SAMUEL PIERPONT: BIRTH ANNIVERSARY. Aug 22, 1834. American astronomer, physicist and aviation pioneer for whom Langley Air Force Base, VA, is named. Born at Roxbury, MA, Langley died at Aiken, SC, Feb 27, 1906.

LUXEMBOURG: SCHUEBERMESS SHEPHERD'S FAIR. Aug 22–Sept 4. Fair dates from 1340. (Two weeks beginning on the next to last Sunday of August.)

MORMON CHOIR FIRST PERFORMANCE: ANNIVERSARY. Aug 22, 1847. What would later become the world-famous Mormon Tabernacle Choir gave its first public performance at Salt Lake City, UT, for an outdoor meeting of The Church of Jesus Christ of Latter-day Saints. Widely known for its concert tours, recordings and weekly radio and television broadcasts from Temple Square, the choir's radio program "Music and the Spoken Word" is the longest continuously running radio program in network history, dating back to 1929.

NATIONAL PUNCTUATION DAY. Aug 22. A celebration of the lowly comma, the correctly used quote and other proper uses of periods, semi-colons and the ever mysterious ellipsis. For info: Jeff Rubin, Put It in Writing Publishers, 1517 Buckeye Court, Pinole, CA 94564. Phone: (877) 588-1212 (toll-free) or (510) 724-9507. Fax: (510) 741-8698. E-mail: jeff@put-it-in-writing.com. Web: www.put-it-in-writing.com.

NATIONAL SAVE YOUR SMILE WEEK. Aug 22–29. A week dedicated to the prevention of adult tooth loss. Seeing the mouth as part of the whole body, correct selection of dental professionals and most important reversing gum disease naturally. For info: S. Senzon, RDH, 32 Bridies Path, Southampton, NY 11968. Phone: (516) 287-6671. Fax: (516) 287-9737. E-mail: S.Senzon961@aol.com. Web: www.tooth.qpg.com.

NATIONAL TRUCK DRIVER APPRECIATION WEEK. Aug 22–28 (tentative). Sponsored by the American Truck Driving Association to thank the men and women of the American trucking industry for their tireless efforts during the year. Annually. For info: American Trucking Assn, 2200 Mill Road, Alexandria, VA 22314-4677. Phone: (703) 838-1700. Web: www.truckline.com.

TOBACCO HARVEST. Aug 22. McLean, VA. Help cut and hang tobacco to dry. Enjoy 18th-century games and light refreshment afterward. Est attendance: 400. For info: Claude Moore Colonial Farm at Turkey Run, 6310 Georgetown Pike, McLean, VA 22101. Phone: (703) 442-7557. Fax: (703) 442-0714. Web: www.1771.org.

VIETNAM CONFLICT BEGINS: ANNIVERSARY. Aug 22, 1945. Less than a week after the Japanese surrender ended WWII, a team of Free French parachuted into southern Indochina in response to a successful coup by a Communist guerrilla named Ho Chi Minh in the French colony.

WILLARD, ARCHIBALD M.: BIRTH ANNIVERSARY. Aug 22, 1836. American artist, best known for his painting *The Spirit of '76*, was born at Bedford, OH. Willard died at Cleveland, OH, Oct 11, 1918.

BIRTHDAYS TODAY

Tori Amos, 41, musician, singer, songwriter, born Newton, NC, Aug 22, 1963.

Ray Bradbury, 84, author (*The Toynbee Convector, Fahrenheit 451*), born Waukegan, IL, Aug 22, 1920.

Gerald Paul Carr, 72, former astronaut, born Denver, CO, Aug 22, 1932.

Henri Cartier-Bresson, 96, photographer, born Chanteloup, France, Aug 22, 1908.

Valerie Harper, 63, actress ("The Mary Tyler Moore Show," "Rhoda"), born Suffern, NY, Aug 22, 1941.

Steve Kroft, 59, coeditor, correspondent ("60 Minutes"), born Kokomo, IN, Aug 22, 1945.

Paul Leo Molitor, 48, former baseball player, born St. Paul, MN, Aug 22, 1956.

Duane Charles (Bill) Parcells, 63, football coach, born Englewood, NJ, Aug 22, 1941.

Leni Riefenstahl, 102, actress (*The Blue Light*), director (*Triumph of the Will, Olympia*), born Berta Helene Amalie Riefenstahl at Berlin, Germany, Aug 22, 1902.

Norman H. Schwarzkopf, 70, retired army general, born Trenton, NJ, Aug 22, 1934.

Cindy Williams, 56, actress (*American Graffiti*, "Laverne & Shirley"), born Van Nuys, CA, Aug 22, 1948.

Carl Michael Yastrzemski, 65, Hall of Fame baseball player, born Southampton, NY, Aug 22, 1939.

AUGUST 23 — MONDAY
Day 236 — 130 Remaining

FIRST MAN-POWERED FLIGHT: ANNIVERSARY. Aug 23, 1977. At Schafter, CA, Bryan Allen pedaled the 70-lb *Gossamer Condor* for a mile at a "minimal altitude of two pylons" in a flight certified by the Royal Aeronautical Society of Britain, winning a £50,000 prize offered by British industrialist Henry Kremer. See also: "First Man-Powered Flight Across English Channel: Anniversary" (June 12).

KELLY, GENE: BIRTH ANNIVERSARY. Aug 23, 1912. Actor, dancer, director, choreographer born at Pittsburgh, PA. His movies included the musicals *Singin' in the Rain* and *An American in Paris*. Kelly died at Beverly Hills, CA, Feb 2, 1996.

MASTERS, EDGAR LEE: BIRTH ANNIVERSARY. Aug 23, 1869. American poet, author of the *Spoon River Anthology*, was born at Garnett, KS. He died at Melrose Park, PA, Mar 5, 1950.

MOON PHASE: FIRST QUARTER. Aug 23. Moon enters First Quarter phase at 6:12 AM, EDT.

PERRY, OLIVER HAZARD: BIRTH ANNIVERSARY. Aug 23, 1785. American naval hero, born at South Kingston, RI. Died Aug 23, 1819, at sea. Best remembered is his announcement of victory at the Battle of Lake Erie, Sept 10, 1813: "We have met the enemy, and they are ours."

ROMANIA SURRENDERS TO USSR: 60th ANNIVERSARY. Aug 23, 1944. Romanian King Michael I removed pro-German Premier Jon Antonescue from his position, dismissed his entire government and broadcast to the people of Romania that all hostilities had ceased and that he had accepted all peace terms demanded by the Allies. Most important, the Ploesti oil fields would be secured by the Allies.

SACCO-VANZETTI MEMORIAL DAY: ANNIVERSARY. Aug 23, 1927. Nicola Sacco and Bartolomeo Vanzetti were electrocuted at the Charlestown, MA, prison on this date. Convicted of a shoe factory payroll robbery during which a guard had been killed, Sacco and Vanzetti maintained their innocence to the end. Six years of appeals marked this American cause célèbre during which substantial evidence was presented to show that both men were elsewhere at the time of the crime. On the 50th anniversary of their execution, Massachusetts governor Michael S. Dukakis proclaimed Aug 23, 1977, a memorial day, noting that the 1921 trial had been "permeated by prejudice."

SPACE MILESTONE: *INTELSAT-4 F-7* (US): ANNIVERSARY. Aug 23, 1973. International Communications Satellite Consortium's *Intelsat* launched Aug 23, 1973, to relay communications from North and South America to Europe and Africa.

"STOCKHOLM SYNDROME" BANK ROBBERY: ANNIVERSARY. Aug 23–28, 1973. In a botched bank robbery at Stockholm, Sweden, Jan Erik Olsson took four hostages and barricaded himself with them and a friend, Clark Olofsson, in the vault. After a six-day siege, the police piped in gas and the hostages were freed. Afterwards, it emerged that the hostages were more afraid of the police than of their captors, and Swedish professor Nils Bejerot coined the term "Stockholm Syndrome" to explain the phenomena of hostages identifying and sympathizing with their captors.

August 2004

S	M	T	W	T	F	S
1	2	3	4	5	6	7
8	9	10	11	12	13	14
15	16	17	18	19	20	21
22	23	24	25	26	27	28
29	30	31				

SWEDISH LANGUAGE AND CULTURE DAY CAMP. Aug 23–27. West Riverside Historic Site, Cambridge, MN. Children learn to speak Swedish and understand Swedish culture through songs, games, language classes and craft classes. Families can see what the children have learned through a program at the end of the week. For info: Kathy McCully, Dir, Isanti County Historical Society, PO Box 525, Cambridge, MN 55008. Phone: (763) 689-4229. Fax: (763) 689-4229. E-mail: mccully@usfamily.net.

UNITED NATIONS: INTERNATIONAL DAY FOR THE REMEMBRANCE OF THE SLAVE TRADE AND ITS ABOLITION. Aug 23. For info: United Nations, Dept of Public Info, New York, NY 10017. Web: www.un.org.

VALENTINO MEMORIAL SERVICE. Aug 23. Hollywood Cathedral Mausoleum, Hollywood Forever Cemetery, Los Angeles, CA. Since 1927 annual memorial service celebrating the life of the silent screen's biggest male star, Rudolph Valentino. Held each year on the anniversary of his 1926 death, at 12:10 PM—the time he died. Attendees include the "Lady in Black." For info: Hollywood Forever Cemetery, 6000 Santa Monica Blvd, Los Angeles, CA, 90038.

VIRGO, THE VIRGIN. Aug 23–Sept 22. In the astronomical/astrological zodiac, which divides the sun's apparent orbit into 12 segments, the period Aug 23–Sept 22 is identified, traditionally, as the sun sign of Virgo, the Virgin. The ruling planet is Mercury.

BIRTHDAYS TODAY

Tony Bill, 64, actor (*You're a Big Boy Now*), director (*My Bodyguard*), born San Diego, CA, Aug 23, 1940.
Kobe Bryant, 26, basketball player, born Philadelphia, PA, Aug 23, 1978.
Barbara Eden, 70, actress ("I Dream of Jeannie," *The Wonderful World of the Brothers Grimm*), born Barbara Huffman, Tucson, AZ, Aug 23, 1934.
Sonny Jurgensen, 70, Hall of Fame football player, born Wilmington, NC, Aug 23, 1934.
Cortez Kennedy, 36, former football player, born Osceola, AR, Aug 23, 1968.
Shelley Long, 55, actress ("Cheers," *Irreconcilable Differences*), born Fort Wayne, IN, Aug 23, 1949.
Patricia McBride, 62, dancer, born Teaneck, NJ, Aug 23, 1942.
Vera Miles, 74, actress (*The Wrong Man, Psycho*), born Boise City, OK, Aug 23, 1930.
Jay Mohr, 34, actor ("Saturday Night Live," *Jerry Maguire*), born Verona, NJ, Aug 23, 1970.
Antonia Novello, 60, first woman and first Hispanic US Surgeon General (1990–93), born Fajardo, Puerto Rico, Aug 23, 1944.
Mark Russell, 72, political comedian ("Real People"), born Mark Ruslander, Buffalo, NY, Aug 23, 1932.
Richard Sanders, 64, actor ("WKRP in Cincinnati," "Berrengers"), born Harrisburg, PA, Aug 23, 1940.
Rik Smits, 38, former basketball player, born Eindhoven, Netherlands, Aug 23, 1966.
Rick Springfield, 55, singer, actor, born Sydney, Australia, Aug 23, 1949.

☆ Chase's 2004 Calendar of Events ☆   Aug 24–25

AUGUST 24 — TUESDAY
Day 237 — 129 Remaining

"THE FACTS OF LIFE" TV PREMIERE: 25th ANNIVERSARY. Aug 24, 1979. This NBC sitcom was spun off from "Diff'rent Strokes" with Drummond family housekeeper Edna Garrett (Charlotte Rae) moving to Peekskill, NY, to take over as housemother at Eastland, a boarding school for girls. During the first season, the cast included John Lawlor as Headmaster Steven Bradley, Jenny O'Hara as Miss Mahoney, Lisa Whelchel as Blair Warner, Mindy Cohn as Natalie Green, Kim Fields as Dorothy "Tootie" Ramsey, Felice Schachter as Nancy Olson, Julie Piekarski as Sue Ann Weaver, Julie Anne Haddock as Cindy Webster and Molly Ringwald as Molly Parker. The last episode aired in 1986.

JARVIS, GREGORY B.: 60th BIRTH ANNIVERSARY. Aug 24, 1944. Gregory B. Jarvis, a civilian engineer with Hughes Aircraft Co, was born at Detroit, MI. He was the 41-year-old payload specialist who perished with other crew members and Christa McAuliffe in the Space Shuttle *Challenger* explosion on Jan 28, 1986. See also: "*Challenger* Space Shuttle Explosion: Anniversary" (Jan 28).

KAHANAMOKU, DUKE: BIRTH ANNIVERSARY. Aug 24, 1890. Duke Paoa Kahanamoku, Olympic gold medal swimmer and "Father of International Surfing," born at Honolulu, HI. Kahanamoku won gold medals in the 100-meter freestyle at the 1912 Olympics and at the 1920 Olympics. In total, he won five medals in four Olympics. Credited with inventing the flutter kick, he enjoyed a long career, not retiring from competition until age 42. Kahanamoku was also Hawaii's ambassador of surfing, popularizing the sport around the world. In 1917, on a 16-foot, 114-pound board, he rode a wave off Waikiki for 1.75 miles. The "Duke" acted in movies and served as sheriff of Honolulu, running alternately on the Republican and Democratic tickets. Died at Honolulu, Jan 22, 1968. Hawaii has honored him with a statue on Waikiki Beach, on which fans place leis.

LIBERIA: FLAG DAY. Aug 24. National holiday.

SAINT BARTHÉLEMY: PATRON SAINT DAY. Aug 24. The festival of St. Barthélemy is celebrated for several days, beginning on Aug 24. The "look and feeling of a French country fair."

SAINT BARTHOLOMEW'S DAY MASSACRE: ANNIVERSARY. Aug 24, 1572. Anniversary of the massacre in Paris and throughout France of thousands of Protestant Huguenots. The massacre began when the church bells tolled at dawn on St. Bartholomew's Day, Aug 24, 1572, and continued for several days. Pope Gregory XIII ordered a medal struck to commemorate the event, but Protestant countries abhorred the killings, estimated at 2,000 to 70,000.

SOUTHERN CYCLONE: ANNIVERSARY. Aug 24, 1893. A hurricane hit Savannah, GA, and Charleston, SC, killing between 1,000 and 2,000 people.

SPACE MILESTONE: *VOYAGER 2* (US) REACHES NEPTUNE: 15th ANNIVERSARY. Aug 24, 1989. Launched in 1977, *Voyager 2* had its first close encounter with Neptune.

UKRAINE: INDEPENDENCE DAY. Aug 24. National day. Commemorates independence from the former Soviet Union in 1991.

VESUVIUS DAY: 1,925th ANNIVERSARY. Aug 24, AD 79. Anniversary of the eruption of Vesuvius, an active volcano in southern Italy, which destroyed the cities of Pompeii, Stabiae and Herculaneum. Pliny the Younger, who escaped the disaster, wrote of it to the historian Tacitus: "[B]lack and horrible clouds, broken by sinuous shapes of flaming winds, were opening with long tongues of fire . . ."

WARNER WEATHER QUOTATION: ANNIVERSARY. Aug 24, 1897. Charles Dudley Warner, American newspaper editor for the *Hartford Courant*, published this now-famous and oft-quoted sentence, "Everybody talks about the weather, but nobody does anything about it." The quotation is often mistakenly attributed to his friend and colleague Mark Twain. Warner and Twain were part of the most notable American literary circle during the late 19th century. Warner was a journalist, essayist, novelist, biographer and author who collaborated with Mark Twain in writing *The Gilded Age* in 1873.

WASHINGTON, DC: INVASION ANNIVERSARY. Aug 24–25, 1814. British forces briefly invaded and raided Washington, DC, burning the Capitol, the president's house and most other public buildings. President James Madison and other high US government officials fled to safety until British troops (not knowing the strength of their position) departed the city two days later.

BIRTHDAYS TODAY

Gerry Cooney, 48, former boxer, born New York, NY, Aug 24, 1956.
Stephen Fry, 47, actor (*Gosford Park, Wilde*, "Jeeves and Wooster"), novelist, born Hampstead, London, England, Aug 24, 1957.
Rafael Furcal, 26, baseball player, born Loma de Cabrera, Dominican Republic, Aug 24, 1978.
Rupert Grint, 16, actor (*Harry Potter and the Sorcerer's Stone*), born Hertfordshire, England, Aug 24, 1988.
Kenny Guinn, 68, Governor of Nevada (R), born Garland, AR, Aug 24, 1936.
Steve Guttenberg, 46, actor ("Billy," *Three Men and a Baby*), born Brooklyn, NY, Aug 24, 1958.
Bob Holden, 55, Governor of Missouri (D), born Kansas City, MO, Aug 24, 1949.
Mike Huckabee, 49, Governor of Arkansas (R), born Hope, AR, Aug 24, 1955.
Craig Kilborn, 42, TV host ("The Late Late Show"), born Hastings, MN, Aug 24, 1962.
Marlee Matlin, 39, actress (Oscar for *Children of a Lesser God*), born Morton Grove, IL, Aug 24, 1965.
Reginald Wayne (Reggie) Miller, 39, basketball player, born Riverside, CA, Aug 24, 1965.
Michael Richards, 54, actor ("Seinfeld," *Trial and Error*), born Culver City, CA, Aug 24, 1950.
Calvin Edward (Cal) Ripken, Jr, 44, former baseball player, born Havre de Grace, MD, Aug 24, 1960.
Louis Teicher, 80, pianist (Ferrante and Teicher), composer, born Wilkes-Barre, PA, Aug 24, 1924.
Mason Williams, 66, composer, born Abilene, TX, Aug 24, 1938.

AUGUST 25 — WEDNESDAY
Day 238 — 128 Remaining

BE KIND TO HUMANKIND WEEK. Aug 25–31. 16th annual observance. All the negative news that you read and hear about in the media is disheartening—but the truth is the positive stories outweigh the negative stories by a long shot! We just don't hear about them as often. Take heart—most people are caring individuals! Show you care by being kind. Daily affirmations: Motorist Consideration Monday. Touch-a-Heart Tuesday. Willing to Lend a Hand Wednesday. Thoughtful Thursday. Forgive Your Foe Friday. Speak Kind Words Saturday. Sacrifice Our Wants for Others' Needs Sunday. For info: Lorraine Jara, PO Box 586, Island Heights, NJ 08732-0586. Phone: (732) 255-0553. E-mail: Lsays BeKind@comcast.net.

BERNSTEIN, LEONARD: BIRTH ANNIVERSARY. Aug 25, 1918. American conductor and composer Leonard Bernstein was born at Lawrence, MA. One of the greatest conductors in American music history, he first conducted the New York Philharmonic Orchestra at age 25 and was its director from 1959 to 1969. His musicals include *West Side Story* and *On the Town*, and his operas and operettas include *Candide*. He died five days after his retirement, Oct 14, 1990, at New York, NY.

EAST COAST SURFING CHAMPIONSHIPS AND SPORTS FESTIVAL. Aug 25–29. Virginia Beach, VA. 42nd annual championship. Pro and amateur surfing and extreme sports, volleyball, 5K run, skimboarding, bands, food. Est attendance: 150,000. For info: Virginia Beach Jaycees, PO Box 62041, Virginia Beach, VA 23466. Phone: (800) 861-7873 or (757) 499-8822. Web: www.surfecsc.com.

HARTE, BRET: BIRTH ANNIVERSARY. Aug 25, 1836. Francis Bret(t) Harte, journalist, poet, printer, teacher and novelist, especially remembered for his early stories of California ("The Luck of Roaring Camp," "The Outcasts of Poker Flat" and "How Santa Claus Came to Simpson's Bar"), was born at Albany, NY. He died at London, England, May 5, 1902.

KELLY, WALT: BIRTH ANNIVERSARY. Aug 25, 1913. American cartoonist and creator of the comic strip "Pogo" was born at Philadelphia, PA. It was Kelly's character Pogo who paraphrased Oliver Hazard Perry to say, "We has met the enemy, and it is us." Kelly died at Hollywood, CA, Oct 18, 1973. See also: "Perry, Oliver Hazard: Birth Anniversary" (Aug 23).

KISS-AND-MAKE-UP-DAY. Aug 25. A day to make amends and for relationships that need mending! For info: Jacqueline V. Milgate, Media Dept, Jay Inc, 500 Linden Oaks Dr, Rochester, NY 14625.

NEVADA STATE FAIR. Aug 25–29. Reno Livestock Events Center, Reno, NV. State entertainment and carnival, with creative living, agriculture and commercial exhibits. Est attendance: 60,000. For info: Nevada State Fair, 1350-A N Wells Ave, Reno, NV 89512. Phone: (775) 688-5767. Fax: (775) 688-5763. E-mail: nvstatefair@inetworld.com. Web: www.nevadastatefair.org.

PARIS LIBERATED: 60th ANNIVERSARY. Aug 25, 1944. As dawn broke, the men of the 2nd French Armored Division entered Paris, ending the long German occupation of the City of Light. That afternoon General Charles de Gaulle led a parade down the Champs Elysées. Though Hitler had ordered the destruction of Paris, German occupying-officer General Dietrich von Choltitz refused that order and instead surrendered to French Major General Jacques Le Clerc.

PINKERTON, ALLAN: BIRTH ANNIVERSARY. Aug 25, 1819. Scottish-born American detective, founder of detective agency at Chicago, IL, in 1850, first chief of US Army's secret service, remembered now because of his strike-breaking and his lack of sympathy for working people. Pinkerton was born at Glasgow, Scotland, and died at Chicago, IL, July 1, 1884.

SPAIN: LA TOMATINA. Aug 25. Buñol (near Valencia). The world's biggest food fight takes place today as 35,000 revelers hurl 120 tons of tomatoes at each other (and the town) for 2 hours. La Tomatina ("Tomato Festival") occurs annually the last Wednesday of August. Festivities kick off with a competition to see who can reach a ham at the top of a greased pole. With the ham secured, the trucks arrive with tomatoes.

URUGUAY: INDEPENDENCE DAY. Aug 25. National holiday. Declared independence from Brazil in 1825. Independence granted in 1828.

THE WIZARD OF OZ RELEASED: 65th ANNIVERSARY. Aug 25, 1939. This motion-picture classic directed by Victor Fleming was a musical adaptation of the L. Frank Baum children's book with both black-and-white and color sequences. It starred Judy Garland as Dorothy as well as Frank Morgan as the Wizard (and four other characters), Ray Bolger as the Scarecrow, Bert Lahr as the Lion, Jack Haley as the Tin Man and Margaret Hamilton as the Wicked Witch of the West. Nominated for six Academy Awards, it won two for best original music score and best song, "Over the Rainbow" (Harold Arlen music and E.Y. Harburg lyrics).

BIRTHDAYS TODAY

Martin Amis, 55, author (*The Information, London Fields*), critic, born Oxford, England, Aug 25, 1949.
Anne Archer, 57, actress ("Falcon Crest"; stage: *A Couple of White Chicks Sitting Around Talking*), born Los Angeles, CA, Aug 25, 1947.
Albert Jojuan Belle, 38, baseball player, born Shreveport, LA, Aug 25, 1966.
Cornelius O'Landa Bennett, 38, former football player, born Birmingham, AL, Aug 25, 1966.
Tim Burton, 46, director (*Edward Scissorhands, The Nightmare Before Christmas*), born Burbank, CA, Aug 25, 1958.
Sean Connery, 74, actor (James Bond movies; *The Man Who Would Be King*), born Edinburgh, Scotland, Aug 25, 1930.
Elvis Costello, 50, musician, songwriter ("Oliver's Army"), born London, England, Aug 25, 1954.
Billy Ray Cyrus, 43, country singer ("Achy Breaky Heart"), born Flatwoods, KY, Aug 25, 1961.
Mel Ferrer, 87, actor (*Scaramouche, The Sun Also Rises*), born Elberon, NJ, Aug 25, 1917.
Frederick Forsyth, 66, author (*The Day of the Jackal*), born Ashford, Kent, England, Aug 25, 1938.
Althea Gibson, 77, former tennis player, born Silver, SC, Aug 25, 1927.
Monty Hall, 81, former TV host ("Let's Make a Deal"), born Winnipeg, MB, Canada, Aug 25, 1923.
Anthony Heald, 60, actor (*The Silence of the Lambs, Searching for Bobby Fischer*), born New Rochelle, NY, Aug 25, 1944.
Regis Philbin, 71, TV show host ("Live with Regis & Kelly," "Who Wants to Be a Millionaire?"), born New York, NY, Aug 25, 1933.
John Savage, 55, actor (*The Deer Hunter, Hair*), born Long Island, NY, Aug 25, 1949.
Claudia Schiffer, 34, model, born Rheinberg, Germany, Aug 25, 1970.
Wayne Shorter, 71, jazz musician ("High Life"), born Newark, NJ, Aug 25, 1933.
Gene Simmons, 55, cofounder of KISS, actor, born Chaim Witz, Haifa, Israel, Aug 25, 1949.
Tom Skerritt, 71, actor ("Picket Fences," *Steel Magnolias*), born Detroit, MI, Aug 25, 1933.
Blair Underwood, 40, actor ("One Life to Live," "LA Law"), born Tacoma, WA, Aug 25, 1964.
Ally Walker, 43, actress ("The Profiler"), born Tullahoma, TN, Aug 25, 1961.
Joanne Whalley, 40, actress ("The Singing Detective"; stage: *What the Butler Saw*), born Manchester, England, Aug 25, 1964.

AUGUST 26 — THURSDAY
Day 239 — 127 Remaining

ACTON FAIR. Aug 26–29. Acton, ME. A country fair featuring horse and ox pulls, antique tractor pull, firemen's muster, 4-H projects, flowers, arts and crafts, stage shows and handicraft. Vendors call Douglas Roberts at (207) 324-1250. Est attendance: 15,000. For info: Lista C. Staples, Secy, 178 Nason Rd, Shapleigh, ME 04076. Phone: (207) 636-2026.

ALASKA STATE FAIR. Aug 26–Sept 6. Palmer, AK. Cows and critters, music and dancing, rides, excitement and family fun at the state's largest summer extravaganza. See 100-lb cabbages, native art, more than 500 events including demonstrations, high-caliber entertainment, rodeos, horse shows, crafts and agricultural exhibits. Est attendance: 300,000. For info: Alaska State Fair, Inc, 2075 Glenn Hwy, Palmer, AK 99645. Phone: (907) 745-4827 or (800) 850-FAIR. Fax: (907) 746-2699. Web: www.alaskastatefair.org.

De FOREST, LEE: BIRTH ANNIVERSARY. Aug 26, 1873. American inventor of the electron tube, radio knife for surgery and the photoelectric cell and a pioneer in the creation of talking pictures and television. Born at Council Bluffs, IA, De Forest was holder of hundreds of patents but perhaps best remembered by the moniker he gave himself in the title of his autobiography, *Father of Radio*, published in 1950. So unbelievable was the idea of wireless radio broadcasting that De Forest was accused of fraud and arrested for selling stock to underwrite the invention that later was to become an essential part of daily life. De Forest died at Hollywood, CA, June 30, 1961.

FIRST BASEBALL GAMES TELEVISED: 65th ANNIVERSARY. Aug 26, 1939. WXBS television, at New York City, broadcast the first major league baseball games—a doubleheader between the Cincinnati Reds and the Brooklyn Dodgers at Ebbets Field. Announcer Red Barber interviewed Leo Durocher, manager of the Dodgers, and William McKechnie, manager of the Reds, between games.

GETTYSBURG FALL BLUEGRASS FESTIVAL. Aug 26–29. Gettysburg, PA. Granite Hill Campground on Rt 116. Features some of the country's best stars of bluegrass music. Est attendance: 5,000. For info: Gettysburg CVB, PO Box 4117, Gettysburg, PA 17325. Phone: (717) 334-6274. Fax: (717) 332-1166. E-mail: gettysburgcvb@dejazzd.com. Web: www.gettysburgcvb.org.

HOTTER 'N HELL HUNDRED BIKE RACE/FESTIVAL. Aug 26–29. Wichita Falls, TX. Cyclists of all ages participate in the largest sanctioned century ride in the US. Treks of 100, 50 or 25 miles. Est attendance: 10,000. For info: Wichita Falls CVB, 1000 5th St, Wichita Falls, TX 76301. Phone: (940) 716-5500 or (940) 322-3223. Fax: (940) 716-5509. E-mail: hh100@wf.net. Web: www.hh100.org.

ISHERWOOD, CHRISTOPHER: 100th BIRTH ANNIVERSARY. Aug 26, 1904. Author of short stories, plays and novels, Christopher William Isherwood was born at High Lane, Cheshire, England. The play and motion picture *I Am a Camera* and the musical *Cabaret* were based on the short story "Sally Bowles" in his collection from the 1930s titled *Goodbye to Berlin*, which contained the line "I am a camera with its shutter open, quite passive, recording, not thinking." Isherwood died at Santa Monica, CA, Jan 4, 1986.

KRAKATOA ERUPTION: ANNIVERSARY. Aug 26, 1883. Anniversary of the biggest explosion in historic times. The eruption of the Indonesian volcanic island, Krakatoa (Krakatau) was heard 3,000 miles away, created tidal waves 120 ft high (killing 36,000 persons), hurled five cubic miles of earth fragments into the air (some to a height of 50 miles) and affected the oceans and the atmosphere for years.

MINNESOTA STATE FAIR. Aug 26–Sept 6. St. Paul, MN. Twelve days of fun ending on Labor Day. Major entertainers, agricultural displays, arts, crafts, food, carnival rides, animal judging and performances. Est attendance: 1,700,000. For info: Minnesota State Fair, 1265 Snelling Ave N, St. Paul, MN 55108-3099. Phone: (651) 642-2200. E-mail: fairinfo@mnstatefair.org. Web: www.mnstatefair.org.

MONTGOLFIER, JOSEPH MICHEL: BIRTH ANNIVERSARY. Aug 26, 1740. French merchant and inventor, born at Vidalonlez-Annonay, France, who, with his brother Jacques Etienne in November 1782, conducted experiments with paper and fabric bags filled with smoke and hot air, which led to invention of the hot-air balloon and man's first flight. Died at Balaruc-les-Bains, France, June 26, 1810. See also: "Montgolfier, Jacques Etienne: Birth Anniversary" (Jan 7), "First Balloon Flight: Anniversary" (June 5) and "Aviation History Month" (Nov 1).

NAMIBIA: HEROES' DAY. Aug 26. National holiday. Commemorates beginning of struggle for independence in 1966.

NEW YORK STATE FAIR. Aug 26–Sept 6. Syracuse, NY. Agricultural and livestock competitions, top-name entertainment, the International Horse Show, business and industrial exhibits, the midway and ethnic presentations. Est attendance: 1,000,000. For info: Joseph LaGuardia, Dir of Mktg, NY State Fair, 581 State Fair Blvd, Syracuse, NY 13209. Phone: (315) 487-7711. Fax: (315) 487-9260.

OREGON STATE FAIR. Aug 26–Sept 6. Salem, OR. Exhibits, products and displays illustrate Oregon's role as one of the nation's major agricultural and recreational states. Floral gardens, carnival, big-name entertainment, horse show and food. Annually, 12 days ending on Labor Day. Est attendance: 400,000. For info: Oregon State Fair, 2330 17th St NE, Salem, OR 97303-3201. Phone: (503) 947-3247.

SABIN, ALBERT BRUCE: BIRTH ANNIVERSARY. Aug 26, 1906. American medical researcher Albert Bruce Sabin was born at Bialystok, Poland. He is most noted for his oral vaccine for polio, which replaced Jonas Salk's injected vaccine because Sabin's provided lifetime protection. He was awarded the US National Medal of Science in 1971. Sabin died Mar 3, 1993, at Washington, DC.

SPACE MILESTONE: *SOYUZ 31* **(USSR): ANNIVERSARY.** Aug 26, 1978. Launched on Aug 26, Valery Bykovsky and Sigmund Jaehn docked at *Salyut 6* on Aug 27, stayed for a week, then returned to Earth in *Soyuz 29* vehicle, leaving their *Soyuz 31* docked at space station. Earth landing on Sept 3.

TELLURIDE MUSHROOM FESTIVAL. Aug 26–29. Telluride, CO. To educate people about the types of wild mushrooms—edible, poisonous, psychoactive—and their cultivation. Est attendance: 250. For info: Fungophile, Inc, Box 480503, Denver, CO 80248-0503. Phone: (303) 296-9359. Fax: (303) 296-9359. E-mail: lodomyco@earthlink.net. Web: www.telluridemm.com.

★**WOMEN'S EQUALITY DAY.** Aug 26. Presidential Proclamation issued in 1973 and 1974 at request and since 1975 without request.

WOMEN'S EQUALITY DAY. Aug 26. Anniversary of certification as part of US Constitution, in 1920, of the 19th Amendment, prohibiting discrimination on the basis of sex with regard to voting. Congresswoman Bella Abzug's bill to designate Aug 26 of each year as "Women's Equality Day" in August 1974 became Public Law 93-382.

Aug 26–27 ☆ Chase's 2004 Calendar of Events ☆

BIRTHDAYS TODAY

Benjamin Crowninshield Bradlee, 83, journalist, editor, born Boston, MA, Aug 26, 1921.
Christopher Burke, 39, actor ("Life Goes On"), born New York, NY, Aug 26, 1965.
Macaulay Culkin, 24, actor (*Home Alone, My Girl*), born New York, NY, Aug 26, 1980.
Geraldine Ferraro, 69, first woman vice-presidential candidate, born Newburgh, NY, Aug 26, 1935.
Irving R. Levine, 82, broadcast journalist, born Pawtucket, RI, Aug 26, 1922.
Branford Marsalis, 44, musician, born Beaux Bridge, LA, Aug 26, 1960.
Thomas J. Ridge, 59, US Secretary of Homeland Security; former Governor of Pennsylvania (R), born Munhall, PA, Aug 26, 1945.
Robert G. Torricelli, 53, former US Senator (D, New Jersey), born Paterson, NJ, Aug 26, 1951.

AUGUST 27 — FRIDAY
Day 240 — 126 Remaining

CANADA: CLASSIC BOAT FESTIVAL. Aug 27–29. Victoria, BC. Classic sail and power vessels from all over the west coast of the US, Canada and beyond gather in Victoria's Inner Harbour. View these lovingly restored and maintained boats with their polished brass fittings and rich teak and oak decks and hulls. Schooner races, sail-past, steamboat parade. Sponsored by Victoria Real Estate Board and Monday Publications. For info: Classic Boat Festival, 3035 Nanaimo St, Victoria, BC, Canada V8T 4W2. Phone: (604) 385-7766. Fax: (604) 385-8773. E-mail: msampson@vreb.org.

CANADA: MORDEN CORN AND APPLE FESTIVAL. Aug 27–29. Morden, MB. It's fun and it's free! Est attendance: 50,000. For info: Morden Chamber of Commerce, 102-195 Stephen St, Morden, MB, Canada R6M 1V3. Phone: (204) 822-5630. Fax: (204) 822-2041. E-mail: chamber@mordenmb.com.

CORVETTE SHOW. Aug 27–28. State Dock, Mackinaw City, MI. Show and visitor viewing, awards and Sunset Dessert Boat Cruise on Saturday. Est attendance: 4,000. For info: Corvette Show, 216 E Central Av, Mackinaw City, MI 49701. Phone: (231) 436-5574 or (888) 455-8100. Web: www.mackinawchamber.com.

DAWES, CHARLES GATES: BIRTH ANNIVERSARY. Aug 27, 1865. Thirtieth vice president of the US (1925–1929), born at Marietta, OH. Won the Nobel Peace Prize in 1925 for the Dawes Plan for German reparations. Died at Evanston, IL, Apr 23, 1951.

DREISER, THEODORE: BIRTH ANNIVERSARY. Aug 27, 1871. American novelist Theodore Dreiser was born at Terre Haute, IN. As part of the Chicago group he was an exponent of American naturalism in literature. His first novel, *Sister Carrie* (1900), was suppressed by his publisher on moral grounds. Dreiser's finest achievement is widely considered to be his novel *An American Tragedy* (1925). He died Dec 28, 1945, at Hollywood, CA.

"THE DUCHESS" WHO WASN'T DAY. Aug 27. At least once on Aug 27 repeat the following now-famous quotation from the novel *Molly Bawn*: "Beauty is in the eye of the beholder." Margaret Wolfe Hungerford often wrote under the pseudonym "The Duchess," which was the title of her most popular novel—hence the name of this event. A popular romance novelist with about 40 books published, Hungerford was born at Rosscarbery, County Cork, Ireland, on Aug 27, 1850; she died at Bandon, County Cork, in 1897. For info: Peggy Shirley, 3800 Treyburn Dr, #4402, Williamsburg, VA 23185. Phone: (757) 220-6870.

FIRST COMMERCIAL OIL WELL: ANNIVERSARY. Aug 27, 1859. W.A. "Uncle Billy" Smith discovered oil in a shaft being sunk by Colonel E.L. Drake at Titusville, in western Pennsylvania. Drilling had reached 69 ft, 6 inches when Smith saw a dark film floating on the water below the derrick floor. Soon 20 barrels of crude were being pumped each day. The first oil was refined to make kerosene for lighting, replacing whale oil. Later it was refined to make gasoline for cars. The first gas station opened in 1907.

FIRST PLAY PRESENTED IN NORTH AMERICAN COLONIES: ANNIVERSARY. Aug 27, 1655. Acomac, VA, was the site of the first play presented in the North American colonies. The play was *Ye Bare and Ye Cubb*, by Phillip Alexander Bruce. Three local residents were arrested and fined for acting in the play. At the time, most colonies had laws prohibiting public performances; Virginia, however, had no such ordinance.

"GOOD SEX! WITH DR. RUTH WESTHEIMER" TV PREMIERE: 20th ANNIVERSARY. Aug 27, 1984. This program premiered on the Lifetime Cable Channel with sex therapist Ruth Westheimer counseling actors appearing as her patients. The show's format later also changed to include celebrity and physician interviews and call-ins.

HAMLIN, HANNIBAL: BIRTH ANNIVERSARY. Aug 27, 1809. Fifteenth vice president of the US (1861–1865) born at Paris, ME. Died at Bangor, ME, July 4, 1891.

JOHNSON, LYNDON BAINES: BIRTH ANNIVERSARY. Aug 27, 1908. The 36th president of the US succeeded to the presidency following the assassination of John F. Kennedy. Johnson's term of office: Nov 22, 1963–Jan 20, 1969. In 1964, he said: "The challenge of the next half-century is whether we have the wisdom to use [our] wealth to enrich and elevate our national life—and to advance the quality of American civilization." Johnson was born near Stonewall, TX, and died at San Antonio, TX, Jan 22, 1973. His birthday is observed as a holiday in Texas.

MAKAH DAYS. Aug 27–29. Neah Bay, WA. Makah Day originated Aug 26, 1913, with the presentation of the American Flag to the Makah Tribe. Flag-raising honors were shared by three tribal members whose present-day descendants still carry on this Makah's Day tradition. Makahs proud to be American citizens celebrate with traditional dance and song, canoe races, salmon bake, parade, fireworks, and Sla-Hal, or "Bone Games," an Indian form of gambling. Makah Day has expanded to Makah Days, and the Makah are proud of their rich heritage that we are able to share with the rest of the world. Annually, on the weekend closest to Aug 26. For info: Leonard A. Denney, Jr, PO Box 115, Neah Bay, WA 98357. Phone: (360) 645-3281. Fax: (360) 645-2033. E-mail: mtcbic@olypen.com. Web: www.makah.com.

MARYLAND STATE FAIR. Aug 27–Sept 6. Timonium, MD. Home arts, agricultural and livestock presentations, midway rides, live entertainment and thoroughbred horse racing. Est attendance: 500,000. For info: Maryland State Fair, Publicity Dept, State Fairgrounds, PO Box 188, Timonium, MD 21094. Phone: (410) 252-0200. E-mail: msfair@msn.com. Web: www.marylandstatefair.com.

	S	M	T	W	T	F	S
August 2004	1	2	3	4	5	6	7
	8	9	10	11	12	13	14
	15	16	17	18	19	20	21
	22	23	24	25	26	27	28
	29	30	31				

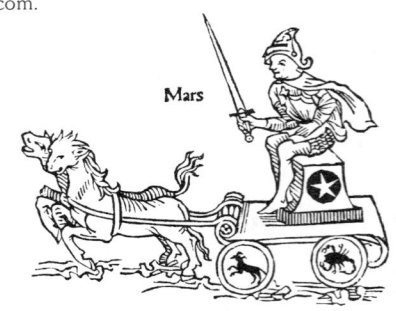
Mars

442

★ Chase's 2004 Calendar of Events ★ Aug 27–28

MEXICAN FIESTA INTERNACIONAL. Aug 27–29. Milwaukee, WI. Mexican Fiesta brings the sound and taste of Mexico to Milwaukee's lakefront. Three days of fun, food, Mariachi and fiesta for everyone. Plus the traditional jalapeño-eating contest, national and international entertainment and the best Mexican cuisine. Est attendance: 70,000. For info: Mexican Fiesta, 1220 W Windlake Ave, Milwaukee, WI 53215. Phone: (414) 383-7066. Fax: (414) 383-6677. E-mail: mexicanf@aol.com. Web: www.mexicanfiesta.org.

MOLDOVA: INDEPENDENCE DAY. Aug 27. Republic of Moldova. Moldova declared its independence from the Soviet Union in 1991.

MOTHER TERESA: BIRTH ANNIVERSARY. Aug 27, 1910. Albanian Roman Catholic nun born Agnes Gonxha Bojaxhiu at Skopje, Macedonia. She founded the Order of the Missionaries of Charity, which cared for the destitute of Calcutta, India. She won the Nobel Peace Prize in 1979. She died at Calcutta, Sept 5, 1997.

MOUNTBATTEN, LOUIS: 25th ASSASSINATION ANNIVERSARY. Aug 27, 1979. Lord Mountbatten (Louis Francis Albert Victor Nicholas Mountbatten), celebrated British war hero, cousin of Queen Elizabeth II, last viceroy of India, was killed by bomb, along with his 14-year-old grandson and two others, while on his yacht in Donegal Bay off the coast of Ireland, on Aug 27, 1979. Provisional Irish Republican Army claimed responsibility for the explosion and for the killing of 18 British soldiers later the same day, deepening the crisis and conflict between Protestants and Catholics and between England and Ireland. Lord Mountbatten was born at Windsor, England, June 25, 1900.

OZARK ANTIQUE AUTO CLUB SWAP MEET. Aug 27–29. Ozark Empire Fairgrounds, Springfield, MO. Hundreds of booths fill the fairgrounds with antique auto parts to buy, sell and swap. For info: Nancy Bright, Ozark Empire Fair, PO Box 630, Springfield, MO 65801. Phone: (417) 833-2660. Fax: (417) 833-3769. E-mail: nancy@ozarkempirefair.com. Web: www.ozarkempirefair.com.

PRAIRIE VILLAGE JAMBOREE. Aug 27–29. Prairie Village, Madison, SD. Come and join the fun with 40 restored buildings, parades, tractor pulls, threshing, plowing, wagon trains, flea market, train and carousel rides, entertainment and much more. Est attendance: 15,000. For info: Prairie Village Jamboree, PO Box 256, Madison, SD 57042. Phone: (800) 693-3644. E-mail: prairiev@rapidnet.com. Web: www.prairievillage.org.

RAYE, MARTHA: BIRTH ANNIVERSARY. Aug 27, 1916. Born at Butte, MT, Martha Raye began singing when she was three. Raye performed for American servicemen during three wars and received the Jean Hersholt Humanitarian Award from the Academy of Motion Picture Arts and Sciences (1969) for that service. She appeared in her first film, *Rhythm on the Range*, in 1936. She had several TV shows, including "The Martha Raye Show" (1955–56). In 1993 Raye was awarded the Presidential Medal of Freedom. Martha Raye died Oct 19, 1994, at Los Angeles, CA.

RIVER ROCKIN' RIBFEST. Aug 27–29. LeClaire Park, Mississippi Riverfront, downtown Davenport, IA. Three days of national and local BBQ rib vendors, variety of live music and children's activities. Bring the whole family! Admission $3. Free for children 8 and under. Presented by DavenportOne-Downtown Partnership. For info: Phone: (563) 322-1706. Web: www.downtowndavenport.com. For info on the Quad Cities: Quad Cities CVB. Phone: (800) 747-7800. Web: www.visitquadcities.com.

ROCKY MOUNTAIN BALLOON FESTIVAL. Aug 27–29. Chatfield State Park, Denver, CO. Hot air balloon festival and outdoor celebration. Fun, free, family event with dawn balloon ascensions and Saturday sunset "Lites in the Nite" mass balloon illumination. Annually, the weekend before Labor Day weekend. Est attendance: 60,000. For info: Rocky Mountain Balloon Festival, 9871 S Deer Creek Rd, Littleton, CO 80127. Phone: (303) 697-1039. E-mail: info@rockymountainballoonfestival.com. Web: www.rockymountainballoonfestival.com.

TOTAH FESTIVAL. Aug 27–29. Farmington, NM. Native American arts and crafts show and marketplace—highlighted by an Indian rug auction. Est attendance: 10,000. For info: Farmington Conv and Visitors Bureau, 3041 E Main St, Farmington, NM 87402. Phone: (800) 448-1240 or (505) 326-7602. Fax: (505) 327-0577. E-mail: fmncvb@cyberport.com. Web: farmingtonnm.org.

WISCONSIN STATE COW-CHIP THROW. Aug 27–28. Prairie du Sac, WI. Cow-Chip Throw, 5K and 10K runs, arts and crafts fair, live music and parade. Annually, the Friday night and Saturday of Labor Day weekend. Est attendance: 50,000. For info: Wisconsin State Cow-Chip Throw, PO Box 3, Prairie du Sac, WI 53578. Phone: (608) 643-4317. Fax: (608) 643-5421. E-mail: marietta@merr.com.

BIRTHDAYS TODAY

Sarah Chalke, 28, actress ("Roseanne"), born Ottawa, ON, Canada, Aug 27, 1976.
Daryl Dragon, 62, musician (Captain and Tennille), songwriter, born Studio City, CA, Aug 27, 1942.
Carlos Moya, 28, tennis player, born Palma, Majorca, Spain, Aug 27, 1976.
Paul Rubens (Pee-wee Herman), 52, actor, writer ("Pee-wee's Playhouse," *Pee-wee's Big Adventure*), born Peekskill, NY, Aug 27, 1952.
Tommy Sands, 67, singer ("Teen-Age Crush," "Goin' Steady"), born Chicago, IL, Aug 27, 1937.
Jim Thome, 34, baseball player, born Peoria, IL, Aug 27, 1970.
Tuesday Weld, 61, actress ("The Many Loves of Dobie Gillis," *Looking for Mr Goodbar*), born Susan Kerr, New York, NY, Aug 27, 1943.

AUGUST 28 — SATURDAY
Day 241 — 125 Remaining

BOYER, CHARLES: BIRTH ANNIVERSARY. Aug 28, 1889. Film star (*Mayerling, Gaslight*), born at Figeac, France. Died at Scottsdale, AZ, Aug 26, 1978.

CELTIC HIGHLAND GAMES OF THE QUAD CITIES. Aug 28. Mississippi Valley Fair, Davenport, IA. One-day festival celebrating the sports, music, dance, and cultures of the seven Celtic nations of Scotland, Ireland, Wales, Cornwall, Brittany, Galicia, and the Isle of Man. Activities include athletic competitions, dancing and piping, children's games, workshops, genealogy and heritage displays, and an evening Ceilidh. Annually, the fourth Saturday in August. For info: Phone: (309) 764-9886. E-mail: infocelt@celtichighlandgames.org. Web: www.celtichighlandgames.org. For info on the Quad Cities: Quad Cities CVB. Phone: (800) 747-7800. Web: www.visitquadcities.com.

CHAMPLAIN VALLEY FAIR. Aug 28–Sept 6. Essex Junction, VT. Vermont's largest fair. Agricultural exhibits and competitions, variety of entertainment, arts and crafts, midway rides, commercial exhibits, great food and much more. Est attendance: 300,000. For info: George Rousseau, Dir of Sales and Mktg, PO Box 209, Essex Junction, VT 05453. Phone: (802) 878-5545. Fax: (802) 879-5404. E-mail: info@cvfair.com. Web: www.cvfair.com.

Aug 28 ☆ Chase's 2004 Calendar of Events ☆

COUNTRY FEST AND AUCTION. Aug 28. Garrett County Fairgrounds, Deep Creek Lake, McHenry, MD. Family-oriented activities, demonstrations, crafts, baked goods, horse-and-buggy and pony rides, farm animal petting zoo, gospel music, chicken BBQ and an auction featuring handcrafted wood items, locally made hand-quilted quilts and much more. Event sponsored by the Dry Run Mennonite Church. Annually, the fourth Saturday in August. Est attendance: 2,500. For info: Country Fest & Auction, 1705 Foy Rd, Accident, MD 21520. Phone: (301) 245-4564 or (301) 245-4326. E-mail: countryfest@juno.com. Web: www.countryfest.org.

DANKFEST. Aug 28–29. Harmony Museum, Harmony, PA. Pioneer crafts, historic-district tours, food and entertainment. Est attendance: 2,500. For info: Kathy Luek, Administrator, Historic Harmony, 218 Mercer St, PO Box 524, Harmony, PA 16037. Phone: (724) 452-7341. Web: www.harmonymuseum.org.

DENMARK: HO SHEEP MARKET. Aug 28. The village of Ho, near Esbjerg, holds its annual sheep market on the last Saturday in August, when some 50,000 people visit the fair.

FEAST OF SAINT AUGUSTINE. Aug 28. Bishop of Hippo, author of *Confessions* and *The City of God*, born Nov 13, 354, at Tagaste, in what is now Algeria. Died Aug 28, 430, at Hippo, also in North Africa.

GOETHE, JOHANN WOLFGANG von: BIRTH ANNIVERSARY. Aug 28, 1749. German author, poet, dramatist and philosopher, born at Frankfurt. Died Mar 22, 1832, at Weimar, Germany. Best known for the novels *The Sorrows of Young Werther* and *Wilhelm Meister* and the play *Faust*.

HAYES, LUCY WARE WEBB: BIRTH ANNIVERSARY. Aug 28, 1831. Wife of Rutherford Birchard Hayes, nineteenth president of the US, born at Chillicothe, OH. Died at Fremont, OH, June 25, 1889. She was nicknamed "Lemonade Lucy" because she and the president, both abstainers, served no alcoholic beverages at White House receptions.

ITALY: VENICE FILM FESTIVAL. Aug 28–Sept 7 (approximate dates). Palazzo del Cinema on the Lido, Venice, Italy. The 61st festival of the first international film event. Juried competition awarding Golden and Silver Lions to films from around the world. For info: Mostra Internazionale d'Arte Cinematografica, San Marco, 1364, Ca Giustinian, 30124, Venice, Italy. Phone: (39) (041) 5218878. E-mail: cinema@labiennale.com. Web: www.labiennaledivenezia.net.

LABOR DAY PICNIC. Aug 28–31. Live Oak, FL. For info: Spirit of the Suwannee Music Park, 3076 95th Dr, Live Oak, FL 32060. Phone: (386) 364-1683. Fax: (386) 364-2998. E-mail: spirit@musicliveshere.com. Web: www.musicliveshere.com.

MARCH ON WASHINGTON: ANNIVERSARY. Aug 28, 1963. More than 250,000 people attended this Civil Rights rally at Washington, DC, at which the Reverend Dr. Martin Luther King, Jr, made his famous "I have a dream" speech.

MARYLAND RENAISSANCE FESTIVAL. Aug 28–Oct 24 (Saturdays, Sundays and Labor Day). Annapolis, MD. A 16th-century English festival with Henry VIII, sword swallowers, magicians, authentic jousting, juggling, music, theater, games, food and crafts. Est attendance: 298,000. For info: Jules Smith, Maryland Renaissance Festival, PO Box 315, Crownsville, MD 21032. Phone: (410) 266-7304. Fax: (410) 573-1508. E-mail: rennfest@erols.com. Web: www.rennfest.com.

NEBRASKA STATE FAIR. Aug 28–Sept 6 (tentative). Lincoln, NE. Food booths, variety of entertainment, amusement rides, concerts, livestock shows and tractor pulls. Est attendance: 350,000. For info: Nebraska State Fair, PO Box 81223, Lincoln, NE 68501. Phone: (402) 474-5371. Fax: (402) 473-4114. E-mail: nestatefair@statefair.org.

PETERSON, ROGER TORY: BIRTH ANNIVERSARY. Aug 28, 1908. Naturalist, author of *A Field Guide to Birds*, born at Jamestown, NY. Peterson died at Old Lyme, CT, July 28, 1996.

PORT ROYAL HURRICANE: ANNIVERSARY. Aug 28, 1722. The hapless Jamaican town of Port Royal was devastated twice within a 30-year span by two natural disasters—an earthquake in 1692 and a hurricane in 1722. The hurricane killed 400 townspeople and sank 26 merchant ships.

RACE YOUR MOUSE AROUND THE ICONS DAY. Aug 28. While you're waiting for any number of endless items to finally come up on your screen, don't just sit there. Race your mouse in and around the icons! You'll feel peppy for doing it. [©2003 by WH.] For info: Thomas & Ruth Roy, Wellcat Holidays, 2418 Long Ln, Lebanon, PA 17046. Phone: (717) 279-0184. E-mail: info@wellcat.com. Web: www.wellcat.com.

RADIO COMMERCIALS: ANNIVERSARY. Aug 28, 1922. Broadcasters realized radio could earn profits from the sale of advertising time. WEAF in New York ran a commercial "spot," which was sponsored by the Queensboro Realty Corporation of Jackson Heights to promote Hawthorne Court, a group of apartment buildings at Queens. The commercial rate was $100 for 10 minutes.

TASTE OF MADISON. Aug 28–29. Capitol Square, Madison, WI. Food and entertainment festival, including booths from more than 60 restaurants, five stages, waiters' race and Kiddie Korner. Est attendance: 175,000. For info: Kristi Kent-Bracken, Dir, Madison Festivals, Inc, PO Box 46427, Madison, WI 53744-6427. Phone: (608) 850-4900. Fax: (608) 850-4929. E-mail: globalcelebrations@tds.net. Web: www.madfest.org.

VIVA! CHICAGO LATIN MUSIC FESTIVAL. Aug 28–29. Grant Park, Chicago, IL. 16th annual. The spectrum of Latin music: cumbias, tropical, merengue, salsa, norteñas, ranchero and mariachi. Est attendance: 160,000. For info: Mayor's Office of Special Events, City Hall, 121 N LaSalle St, #703, Chicago, IL 60602. Phone: (312) 744-3370 (hotline). Fax: (312) 744-8523. Web: www.cityofchicago.org/specialevents.

BIRTHDAYS TODAY

Mamadou Diallo, 33, soccer player, born Dakar, Senegal, Aug 28, 1971.
Ben Gazzara, 74, actor (*Anatomy of a Murder*, "Run for Your Life"), born New York, NY, Aug 28, 1930.
Ronald Ames (Ron) Guidry, 54, former baseball player, born Lafayette, LA, Aug 28, 1950.
Scott Hamilton, 46, Olympic gold medal figure skater, born Toledo, OH, Aug 28, 1958.
Noriyuki ("Pat") Morita, 72, actor ("Sanford and Son," "Happy Days," *The Karate Kid*), born Isleton, CA, Aug 28, 1932.
Donald O'Connor, 79, actor, dancer ("Donald O'Connor Texaco Show," *Singin' in the Rain*), born Houston, TX, Aug 28, 1925.
Lou Piniella, 61, baseball manager and former player, born Tampa, FL, Aug 28, 1943.
Jason Priestley, 35, actor ("Beverly Hills 90210," *Tombstone*), born Vancouver, BC, Canada, Aug 28, 1969.
LeAnn Rimes, 22, country and western singer, born Jackson, MS, Aug 28, 1982.
Rick Rossovich, 47, actor (*The Terminator*, *Roxanne*), born Palo Alto, CA, Aug 28, 1957.
Emma Samms, 44, actress ("General Hospital," "Dynasty"), born Emma Samuelson, London, England, Aug 28, 1960.
David Soul, 58, actor ("Starsky and Hutch," *Salem's Lot*), born Chicago, IL, Aug 28, 1946.
Daniel Stern, 47, actor (*City Slickers*, *Home Alone*), born Bethesda, MD, Aug 28, 1957.
Shania Twain, 39, country singer, born Eileen Twain, Windsor, ON, Canada, Aug 28, 1965.

August 2004	S	M	T	W	T	F	S
	1	2	3	4	5	6	7
	8	9	10	11	12	13	14
	15	16	17	18	19	20	21
	22	23	24	25	26	27	28
	29	30	31				

☆ Chase's 2004 Calendar of Events ☆ Aug 29

AUGUST 29 — SUNDAY
Day 242 — 124 Remaining

"ACCORDING TO HOYLE" DAY (EDMOND HOYLE DEATH ANNIVERSARY). Aug 29, 1769. A day to remember Edmond Hoyle and a day for fun and games *according to the rules*. He is believed to have studied law. For many years he lived at London, England, and gave instructions in the playing of games. His "Short Treatise" on the game of whist (published in 1742) became a model guide to the rules of the game. Hoyle's name became synonymous with the idea of correct play according to the rules, and the phrase "according to Hoyle" became a part of the English language. Hoyle was born at London about 1672 and died there.

***AMISTAD* SEIZED: ANNIVERSARY.** Aug 29, 1839. In January 1839, 53 Africans were seized near modern-day Sierra Leone, taken to Cuba and sold as slaves. While being transferred to another part of the island on the ship *Amistad*, led by the African, Cinque, they seized control of the ship, telling the crew to take them back to Africa. However, the crew secretly changed course and the ship landed at Long Island, NY, where it and its "cargo" were seized as salvage. The *Amistad* was towed to New Haven, CT, where the Africans were imprisoned and a lengthy legal battle began to determine if they were property to be returned to Cuba or free men. John Quincy Adams took their case all the way to the Supreme Court, where on Mar 9, 1841, it was determined that they were free and could return to Africa.

BARNEGAT BAY CRAB RACE AND FESTIVAL. Aug 29. Seaside Heights, NJ. Crab race, festival and craft fair. Est attendance: 5,000. For info: Lucy Greene, Pres, Barbara Morgan, Admin Asst, Toms River–Ocean Co Chmbr of Com, 1200 Hooper Ave, Toms River, NJ 08753. Phone: (732) 349-0220. Fax: (732) 349-1252. Web: www.oc-chamber.com.

BERGMAN, INGRID: BIRTH ANNIVERSARY. Aug 29, 1915. One of cinema's greatest actresses. Bergman was born at Stockholm, Sweden, and died at London, England, on her 67th birthday, Aug 29, 1982. Three-time Academy Award winner for *Gaslight, Anastasia, Murder on the Orient Express*. Controversy over her personal life made her and her films unpopular to American audiences during an interval of several years between periods of awards and adulation.

ENGLAND: NOTTING HILL CARNIVAL. Aug 29–30. London. The biggest street carnival in Europe: annual multicultural celebration on the streets of Notting Hill and Ladbroke Grove. Three-mile route for spectacular costume bands, steel bands, calypsonians and soca-on-the-move. 45 static sound systems, live stages featuring top national and international musicians, 240 street-trading stalls selling food from all over the world, and arts and crafts. Free event. Late August summer bank holiday weekend. Est attendance: 2,000,000. For info: Notting Hill Carnival Trust, Grand Union Centre, 332 Ladbroke Grove, London, England W10 5AH. Phone: (44) (0208) 964-0544. Fax: (44) (0208) 964-0545.

FAMILY DAY IN TENNESSEE. Aug 29. Observed annually on the last Sunday in August.

HOLMES, OLIVER WENDELL: BIRTH ANNIVERSARY. Aug 29, 1809. Physician and author, father of Supreme Court justice Oliver Wendell Holmes, born at Cambridge, MA. Died at Boston, MA, Oct 7, 1894. "A moment's insight," he wrote, "is sometimes worth a life's experience."

LOCKE, JOHN: BIRTH ANNIVERSARY. Aug 29, 1632 (OS). English philosopher, founder of philosophical liberalism, born at Wrington, England. His ideas influenced the American colonists and were enshrined in the Constitution. Locke died at Essex, England, Oct 28, 1704 (OS).

MOON PHASE: FULL MOON. Aug 29. Moon enters Full Moon phase at 10:22 PM, EDT.

MORE HERBS, LESS SALT DAY. Aug 29. It's healthier, zestier and lustier! [©2003 by WH.] For info: Thomas & Ruth Roy, Wellcat Holidays, 2418 Long Ln, Lebanon, PA 17046. Phone: (717) 279-0184. E-mail: info@wellcat.com. Web: www.wellcat.com.

NATIONAL OLD-TIME COUNTRY MUSIC CONTEST, FESTIVAL & EXPO. Aug 29–Sept 5. Harrison County Fairgrounds, Missouri Valley, IA. Country music fans come from all around to hear their favorites. Also many arts and crafts displays, other musical entertainment and food booths. Est attendance: 50,000. For info: Natl Old-Time Country Music Contest, Fest & Expo, PO Box 492, Anita, IA 50020. Phone: (712) 762-4363. E-mail: bobeverhart@yahoo.com. Web: www.oldtimemusic.bigstep.com.

PARKER, CHARLIE: BIRTH ANNIVERSARY. Aug 29, 1920. Jazz saxophonist Charlie Parker was born at Kansas City, KS. He earned the nickname "Yardbird" (later "Bird") from his habit of sitting in the backyard of speakeasies, fingering his saxophone. His career as a jazz saxophonist took him from jam sessions in Kansas City to New York, where he met Dizzy Gillespie and others who were creating a style of music that would become known as bop or bebop. Although his musical genius was unquestioned, Parker's addiction to heroin haunted his life. He died at Rochester, NY, Mar 12, 1955, at the age of 34.

PHILIPPINES: NATIONAL HEROES' DAY. Aug 29. National holiday. The last Sunday in August. Commemorates the Aug 26, 1896, beginning of the Philippine fight for independence from Spain.

PONY EXPRESS FESTIVAL. Aug 29. Hollenberg Pony Express Station, State Historic Site, Hanover, KS. Reenactment of Pony Express ride with mochila exchange, pioneer living-history demonstrations, 1860s historic dress group, circuit-rider church service and a noon meal on the grounds. Annually, the last Sunday in August. Sponsor: Kansas State Historical Society, Friends of Hollenberg Station. Est attendance: 2,000. For info: Duane Durst, Curator, Hollenberg Pony Express Station, State Historic Site, RR1, 2889 23rd Rd, Hanover, KS 66945. Phone: (785) 337-2635. Fax: (785) 337-2309. E-mail: hollenberg@kshs.org.

***ROYAL GEORGE* SINKS: ANNIVERSARY.** Aug 29, 1792. Prized British battleship *Royal George* sank due to fatal human error in one of the worst maritime disasters in history. While the ship was being repaired at Spithead, the port side was tilted too close to the waterline. A gust of wind lowered the ship even further, allowing tons of water to flood into its open gunports. The ship sank within minutes before many of the 1,300 on board realized what was happening and more than 900 people drowned.

Aug 29-30 ☆ Chase's 2004 Calendar of Events ☆

SHAYS REBELLION: ANNIVERSARY. Aug 29, 1786. Daniel Shays, veteran of the battles of Lexington, Bunker Hill, Ticonderoga and Saratoga, was one of the leaders of more than 1,000 rebels who sought redress of grievances during the depression days of 1786–87. They prevented general court sessions and on Sept 26 they prevented Supreme Court sessions at Springfield, MA. On Jan 25, 1787, they attacked the federal arsenal at Springfield; Feb 2, Shays's troops were routed and fled. Shays was sentenced to death but pardoned June 13, 1788. Later he received a small pension for services in the American Revolution.

SLOVAKIA: NATIONAL UPRISING DAY. Aug 29. National holiday. Commemorates resistance to Nazi occupation in 1944.

SOVIET COMMUNIST PARTY SUSPENDED: ANNIVERSARY. Aug 29, 1991. The Supreme Soviet, the parliament of the USSR, suspended all activities of the Communist Party, seizing its property and bringing to an end the institution that ruled the Soviet Union for nearly 75 years. The action followed an unsuccessful coup Aug 19–21 that sought to overthrow the government of Soviet President Mikhail Gorbachev but instead prompted a sweeping wave of democratic change. Gorbachev quit as party leader Aug 24.

BIRTHDAYS TODAY

Sir Richard Attenborough, 81, filmmaker (*In Which We Serve, The Great Escape*), born Cambridge, England, Aug 29, 1923.
Rebecca De Mornay, 42, actress (*Risky Business, The Hand That Rocks the Cradle*), born Santa Rosa, CA, Aug 29, 1962.
William Friedkin, 65, filmmaker (Oscar for *The French Connection; The Exorcist*), born Chicago, IL, Aug 29, 1939.
Richard Gere, 55, actor (*An Officer and a Gentleman, Pretty Woman*), born Philadelphia, PA, Aug 29, 1949.
Elliott Gould, 66, actor (*M*A*S*H, The Long Goodbye*), born Elliott Goldstein, Brooklyn, NY, Aug 29, 1938.
Michael Jackson, 46, singer, songwriter ("We Are the World," *Bad, Thriller, Beat It*), born Gary, IN, Aug 29, 1958.
Robin Leach, 63, TV host ("Lifestyles of the Rich and Famous"), born London, England, Aug 29, 1941.
Pablo Mastrioeni, 28, soccer player, born Mendoza, Argentina, Aug 29, 1976.
John Sidney McCain III, 68, US Senator (R, Arizona), born Panama Canal Zone, Aug 29, 1936.
Mark Morris, 48, choreographer, dancer, born Seattle, WA, Aug 29, 1956.
Roy Oswalt, 27, baseball player, born Kosciusko, MS, Aug 29, 1977.
William Edward (Will) Perdue III, 39, former basketball player, born Melbourne, FL, Aug 29, 1965.
Pierre Turgeon, 35, hockey player, born Rouyn, QC, Canada, Aug 29, 1969.

August 2004

S	M	T	W	T	F	S
1	2	3	4	5	6	7
8	9	10	11	12	13	14
15	16	17	18	19	20	21
22	23	24	25	26	27	28
29	30	31				

AUGUST 30 — MONDAY
Day 243 — 123 Remaining

ARTHUR, ELLEN LEWIS HERNDON: BIRTH ANNIVERSARY. Aug 30, 1837. Wife of Chester Alan Arthur, 21st president of the US, born at Fredericksburg, VA. Died at New York, Jan 12, 1880.

BOOTH, SHIRLEY: BIRTH ANNIVERSARY. Aug 30, 1898. American actress Shirley Booth was born Thelma Booth Ford at New York, NY. She won a Tony Award and an Oscar for her roles in the stage (1950) and film (1952) productions of *Come Back, Little Sheba*, but she is best known for her title role in the television program "Hazel" (1961–66). She died at Chatham, MS, Oct 16, 1992.

BURNING MAN 2004. Aug 30–Sept 6. Black Rock Desert, NV. A temporary art community in the desert. On the Saturday of this annual experiment in radical self-expression, a 50′ statue will be burned. Participants must bring all necessities for survival, including food, water and shelter. Est attendance: 29,000. For info: Burning Man 2004, PO Box 884688, San Francisco, CA 94188-4688. Phone: (415) TO-FLAME. E-mail: questions@burningman.com. Web: www.burningman.com.

CHINA: FESTIVAL OF HUNGRY GHOSTS. Aug 30. Important Chinese festival, also known as the Chung Yuan Festival. According to Chinese legend, during the seventh lunar month the souls of the dead are released from purgatory to roam the Earth. Joss sticks are burned in homes; prayers, food and "ghost money" are offered to appease the ghosts. Market stallholders combine to hold celebrations to ensure that their businesses will prosper in the coming year. Wayang (Chinese street opera) and puppet shows are performed, and fruit and Chinese delicacies are offered to the spirits of the dead. Chung Yuan is observed on the 15th day of the 7th lunar month. Date in other countries will differ from China's.

FIRST WHITE HOUSE PRESIDENTIAL BABY: BIRTH ANNIVERSARY. Aug 30, 1893. Frances Folsom Cleveland (Mrs Grover Cleveland) was the first presidential wife to have a baby at the White House when she gave birth to a baby girl (Esther). The first child ever born in the White House was a granddaughter to Thomas Jefferson in 1806.

HONG KONG: LIBERATION DAY. Aug 30. Public holiday to celebrate liberation from the Japanese in 1945. Annually, the last Monday in August.

HUEY P. LONG DAY. Aug 30. A legal holiday in Louisiana.

MacMURRAY, FRED: BIRTH ANNIVERSARY. Aug 30, 1908. Fred MacMurray was born at Kankakee, IL. His film and television career included a wide variety of roles, ranging from comedy (*The Absent-Minded Professor, Son of Flubber, The Shaggy Dog, The Happiest Millionaire*) to serious drama (*The Caine Mutiny, Fair Wind to Java, Double Indemnity*). During 1960–72 he portrayed the father on "My Three Sons," which was second only to "Ozzie and Harriet" as network TV's longest running family sitcom. He died Nov 5, 1991, at Santa Monica, CA.

PERU: SAINT ROSE OF LIMA DAY. Aug 30. Saint Rose of Lima was the first saint of the Western Hemisphere. She lived at the time of the colonization by Spain in the 16th century. Patron saint of the Americas and the Philippines. Public holiday in Peru.

REPUBLICAN NATIONAL CONVENTION. Aug 30–Sept 2. Madison Square Garden, New York, NY. The Republican Party meets to select its nominees for president and vice president in the 2004 election. For info: Republican National Committee, 310 First St SE, Washington, DC 20003. Phone: (202) 863-8500. Fax: (202) 863-8820. E-mail: info@rnc.org. Web: www.rnc.org.

RUTHERFORD, ERNEST: BIRTH ANNIVERSARY. Aug 30, 1871. Physicist, born at Nelson, New Zealand. He established the nuclear nature of the atom, the electrical structure of matter and achieved the transmutation of elements, research which later resulted in the atomic bomb. Rutherford died at Cambridge, England, Oct 19, 1937.

☆ Chase's 2004 Calendar of Events ☆   Aug 30–31

SHELLEY, MARY WOLLSTONECRAFT: BIRTH ANNIVERSARY. Aug 30, 1797. English novelist Mary Shelley, daughter of the philosopher William Godwin and the feminist Mary Wollstonecraft and wife of the poet Percy Bysshe Shelley, was born at London and died there Feb 1, 1851. In addition to being the author of the famous novel *Frankenstein*, Shelley is important in literary history for her work in the editing and publishing of her husband's unpublished work after his early death.

SPACE MILESTONE: *CHALLENGER* STS-8 (US): ANNIVERSARY. Aug 30, 1983. Shuttle *Challenger* with five astronauts (Richard Truly, Daniel Brandenstein, Guion Bluford, Jr, Dale Garner and William Thornton) was launched from Kennedy Space Center, FL, on this date. Return landing six days later on Sept 5 at Edwards Air Force Base, CA.

SPACE MILESTONE: *DISCOVERY* (US): 20th ANNIVERSARY. Aug 30, 1984. Space shuttle *Discovery* was launched from Kennedy Space Center, FL, for its maiden flight with six-member crew. During the flight the crew deployed three satellites and used a robot arm before landing at Edwards Air Force Base, CA, Sept 5.

STRAITH, CLAIRE, MD: BIRTH ANNIVERSARY. Aug 30, 1891. Innovator in plastic and cosmetic surgery, born at Southfield, MI. After attending an international meeting at Paris, France, at the end of World War I to share information regarding reconstructive surgical techniques used on the battlefield, Dr. Claire Straith dedicated his career to the new field of plastic surgery. He developed many of the techniques used in plastic and cosmetic surgery, designed new surgical instruments and led a campaign that convinced automakers, in 1930, to use safety glass and remove dangerous projections from the interior of cars. Dr. Straith died July 13, 1958.

TURKEY: VICTORY DAY. Aug 30. Commemorates victory in War of Independence in 1922. Military parades, performing of the Mehtar band (the world's oldest military band), fireworks.

UNITED KINGDOM: SUMMER BANK HOLIDAY. Aug 30. Bank and public holiday in England, Wales and Northern Ireland. (Scotland not included.) Annually, the last Monday in August.

WILKINS, ROY: BIRTH ANNIVERSARY. Aug 30, 1901. Roy Wilkins, grandson of a Mississippi slave, civil rights leader, active in the National Association for the Advancement of Colored People (NAACP), retired as its executive director in 1977. Born at St. Louis, MO. Died at New York, NY, Sept 8, 1981.

WILLIAMS, TED: BIRTH ANNIVERSARY. Aug 30, 1918. Born Theodore Samuel Williams at San Diego, CA, Ted Williams played his first major league baseball game for the Boston Red Sox on Apr 22, 1939. In the years that followed, he became known as perhaps the best hitter ever to play the game. His career batting average was .344, and his record average of .406 set during the 1941 season stands unsurpassed. He played 19 seasons for the Red Sox, but during the prime of his career, missed three full seasons while serving as a Navy pilot in WWII, and most of two seasons serving as a Marine pilot in the Korean War. He was elected to the Baseball Hall of Fame in 1966. He died July 5, 2002, at Inverness, FL.

BIRTHDAYS TODAY

Elizabeth Ashley, 63, actress (*Agnes of God, Cat on a Hot Tin Roof*, "Evening Shade"), born Elizabeth Ann Cole, Ocala, FL, Aug 30, 1941.
Timothy Bottoms, 53, actor (*The Last Picture Show, The Paper Chase*), born Santa Barbara, CA, Aug 30, 1951.
Michael Chiklis, 41, actor ("The Shield"), born Lowell, MA, Aug 30, 1963.
Cameron Diaz, 32, actress (*My Best Friend's Wedding, There's Something about Mary*), born San Diego, CA, Aug 30, 1972.
Jean-Claude Killy, 61, Olympic gold medal alpine skier, born Saint Cloud, France, Aug 30, 1943.
Peggy Lipton, 57, actress (Golden Globe Award for "The Mod Squad"; "Twin Peaks"), born New York, NY, Aug 30, 1947.

Michael Michele, 38, actress ("Homicide: Life on the Street," "ER"), born Evansville, IN, Aug 30, 1966.
Robert Lee Parish, 51, former basketball player, born Shreveport, LA, Aug 30, 1953.
David Paymer, 50, actor (*City Slickers, Mr Saturday Night*), born Long Island, NY, Aug 30, 1954.
Andy Roddick, 22, tennis player, born Omaha, NE, Aug 30, 1982.
Kitty Wells, 85, singer ("Jealousy"), born Muriel Deason, Nashville, TN, Aug 30, 1919.

AUGUST 31 — TUESDAY
Day 244 — 122 Remaining

"ALICE" TV PREMIERE: ANNIVERSARY. Aug 31, 1976. Linda Lavin played the title role in this CBS comedy that was based on the 1975 film *Alice Doesn't Live Here Anymore*. Alice Hyatt was the new girl in town—a widow raising her son while trying to make ends meet by waitressing at a diner. She had dreams of making it big as a singer. Nine years later, Alice was able to leave her "temp" job for a gig. Lavin's co-stars were: Vic Tayback as diner owner Mel Sharples, Philip McKeon as Alice's son Tommy, Beth Howland as waitress Vera Gorman, Polly Holliday as sassy waitress Flo Castleberry, Diane Ladd as Flo's replacement Belle Dupree, Celia Weston as waitress Jolene Hunnicutt, Martha Raye as Mel's mother Carrie and Marvin Kaplan as customer Henry Beesmyer. The last telecast aired on July 2, 1985.

CHARLESTON EARTHQUAKE: ANNIVERSARY. Aug 31, 1886. Charleston, SC. The first major earthquake in the recorded history of the eastern US occurred on this date. It is believed that about 100 persons perished in the quake, centered near Charleston but felt up to 800 miles away. Though a number of smaller eastern US quakes had been described and recorded since 1638, this affected persons living in an area of some 2 million square miles.

COBURN, JAMES: BIRTH ANNIVERSARY. Aug 31, 1928. Academy Award–winning actor born at Laurel, NE. He rose to fame as the knife thrower in *The Magnificent Seven* and became known for his tough-guy roles in films such as *The Great Escape* and *Our Man Flint*. He received an Oscar for his supporting role in 1999's *Affliction*. He died at Los Angeles, CA, Nov 18, 2002.

"CRANKSHAFT": ANNIVERSARY. Aug 31. Celebrating the anniversary of the nationally syndicated comic strip that premiered Aug 31, 1987. For info: Tom Batiuk, 2750 Substation Rd, Medina, OH 44256. Phone: (330) 722-8755.

447

Aug 31 ☆ Chase's 2004 Calendar of Events ☆

KAZAKHSTAN: CONSTITUTION DAY. Aug 31. National holiday. Commemorates the constitution of 1995.

KLONDIKE ELDORADO GOLD DISCOVERY: ANNIVERSARY. Aug 31, 1896. Two weeks after the Rabbit/Bonanza Creek claim was filed, gold was discovered on Eldorado Creek, a tributary of Bonanza. More than $30 million worth of gold (worth some $600–$700 million in today's dollars) was mined from the Eldorado Claim in 1896.

KYRGYZSTAN: INDEPENDENCE DAY. Aug 31. National holiday. Commemorates independence from the former Soviet Union in 1991.

LOVE LITIGATING LAWYERS DAY. Aug 31. Lawyer jokes abound, but when push comes to shove, these are the folks who can end up saving the day. [©2003 by WH.] For info: Thomas & Ruth Roy, Wellcat Holidays, 2418 Long Ln, Lebanon, PA 17046. Phone: (717) 279-0184. E-mail: info@wellcat.com. Web: www.wellcat.com.

MALAYSIA: FREEDOM DAY. Aug 31. National holiday. Commemorates independence from Britain in 1957.

MOLDOVA: NATIONAL LANGUAGE DAY. Aug 31. National holiday. Also called Mother Tongue Day. Commemorates the replacement of the Cyrillic alphabet with the Latin alphabet in 1991.

MONTESSORI, MARIA: BIRTH ANNIVERSARY. Aug 31, 1870. Italian physician and educator, born at Chiaraville, Italy. Founder of the Montessori method of teaching children. Montessori died at Noordwijk, Holland, May 6, 1952.

POLAND: SOLIDARITY FOUNDED: ANNIVERSARY. Aug 31, 1980. The Polish trade union Solidarity was formed at the Baltic Sea port of Gdansk, Poland. Outlawed by the government, many of its leaders were arrested. Led by Lech Walesa, Solidarity persisted in its opposition to the Communist-controlled government, and on Aug 19, 1989, Polish president Wojciech Jaruzelski astonished the world by nominating for the post of prime minister Tadeusz Mazowiecki, a deputy in the Polish Assembly, 1961–72, and editor-in-chief of Solidarity's weekly newspaper, bringing to an end 42 years of Communist Party domination.

SAROYAN, WILLIAM: BIRTH ANNIVERSARY. Aug 31, 1908. American writer of Armenian descent, author of *The Human Comedy* and of the Pulitzer Prize–winning play *The Time of Your Life*, was born at Fresno, CA, and died there May 18, 1981. In April 1981 he gave reporters a final statement for publication after his death: "Everybody has got to die, but I have always believed an exception would be made in my case. Now what?"

SHAWN, WILLIAM: BIRTH ANNIVERSARY. Aug 31, 1907. William Shawn, editor of *The New Yorker* for 35 years, was born at Chicago, IL. He was virtual dictator of editorial policy for the magazine, which in turn had an impact on the literary and reportorial styles of writers throughout the country. Nonfiction pieces in *The New Yorker* contributed to public opinion on important issues during Shawn's tenure. Shawn died Dec 8, 1992, at New York, NY.

TRINIDAD AND TOBAGO: INDEPENDENCE DAY. Aug 31. National holiday. Became an independent nation within the British Commonwealth on this day in 1962. Trinidad became a republic, Sept 24, 1976.

WHITECHAPEL MURDERS BEGIN: ANNIVERSARY. Aug 31, 1888. At 3:40 AM, the body of Mary Ann Nichols was found in the impoverished Whitechapel district of London, England. This was (debatably) the first in a series of brutal murders that autumn that claimed the lives of at least five women, perhaps more, by a serial killer who has come to be known as "Jack the Ripper" because of the mutilations he inflicted on his victims. The ferocity of the Whitechapel killings created an "Autumn of Terror" in which the entire populace of London was terrified and where mobs frequently tried to mete out justice to suspects they picked. Mary Kelly, found Nov 9, is considered the last victim. No suspect was ever tried for the murders. See also: "'Jack the Ripper' Letter: Anniversary" (Sept 27).

BIRTHDAYS TODAY

Jennifer Azzi, 36, basketball player, born Oak Ridge, TN, Aug 31, 1968.
Debbie Gibson, 34, singer ("Only in My Dreams," "Foolish Beat"), born Brooklyn, NY, Aug 31, 1970.
Van Morrison, 59, singer, songwriter ("Brown Eyed Girl," "Domino"), born Belfast, Northern Ireland, Aug 31, 1945.
Edwin Corley Moses, 49, Olympic gold medal track athlete, born Dayton, OH, Aug 31, 1955.
Hideo Nomo, 36, baseball player, born Osaka, Japan, Aug 31, 1968.
Itzhak Perlman, 59, violinist, born Tel Aviv, Israel, Aug 31, 1945.
Frank Robinson, 69, Hall of Fame baseball player, former baseball executive and manager, born Beaumont, TX, Aug 31, 1935.
Daniel Schorr, 88, journalist, born New York, NY, Aug 31, 1916.
G.D. Spradlin, 84, actor (*The Godfather Part II, North Dallas Forty, The War of the Roses*), born Garvin County, OK, Aug 31, 1920.
Jack Thompson, 64, actor (*The Chant of Jimmie Blacksmith, Breaker Morant*), born Sydney, Australia, Aug 31, 1940.
Glenn Tilbrook, 47, singer, musician, born London, England, Aug 31, 1957.
Chris Tucker, 32, actor (*Rush Hour, The Fifth Element*), born Decatur, GA, Aug 31, 1972.
Noble Willingham, 73, actor (*Ace Ventura: Pet Detective, Up Close and Personal*), born Mineola, TX, Aug 31, 1931.

☆ Chase's 2004 Calendar of Events ☆   Sept 1

September.

SEPTEMBER 1 — WEDNESDAY
Day 245 — 121 Remaining

"ART LINKLETTER'S HOUSE PARTY" TV PREMIERE: ANNIVERSARY. Sept 1, 1952. Television's longest-running daytime variety show was hosted by Art Linkletter. This blend of talk and audience participation started on radio. In 1968 the show was renamed "The Linkletter Show" and moved from the afternoon to a morning slot. The series was well known for its daily interview with four schoolchildren.

ATTENTION DEFICIT HYPERACTIVITY DISORDER MONTH. Sept 1–30. To educate healthcare groups, children and family organizations, teachers, parents and others interested in childhood health issues by providing information on effective treatments for ADHD. Some treatments have been scientifically validated, tested and proven to reduce the severity of ADHD symptoms and thereby reduce adverse consequences in the child's current and future life. There is a $15 charge for kit materials. For info: PPSI, c/o Pharmacy Council on Children's Health, 101 Lucas Valley Rd, Ste 210, San Rafael, CA 94903. Phone: (415) 479-8628. Fax: (415) 479-8608. E-mail: ppsi@aol.com. Web: www.ppsinc.org.

BACKPACK SAFETY AMERICA MONTH. Sept 1–30. Thousands of school-age children are straining in pain under backpacks that are too heavy for their growing bodies. This month is set aside to remind students, parents and teachers about the safe and proper ways to choose, pack, lift and carry a backpack. Annually, the month of September. For info: John Carroll, PO Box 2430, Mt Pleasant, SC 29465. Phone: (800) 672-4277. Fax: (843) 881-6746. E-mail: info@backpacksafe.com. Web: www.backpacksafe.com.

BE KIND TO EDITORS AND WRITERS MONTH. Sept 1–30. A time for editors and writers to show uncommon courtesy toward each other. For info: Lauren Barnett, Lone Star Publications of Humor, 8452 Fredericksburg Rd, PMB 103, San Antonio, TX 78229. E-mail: lspubs@aol.com. Web: members.aol.com/lspubs/lsindex.html.

BRAZIL: INDEPENDENCE WEEK. Sept 1–7. The independence of Brazil from Portugal in 1822 is commemorated with civic and cultural ceremonies promoted by federal, state and municipal authorities. On Sept 7, a grand military parade takes place and the National Defense League organizes the Running Race in Honor of the Symbolic Torch of the Brazilian Nation.

BURROUGHS, EDGAR RICE: BIRTH ANNIVERSARY. Sept 1, 1875. US novelist (*Tarzan of the Apes*), born at Chicago, IL. Correspondent for the *Los Angeles Times*, died at Encino, CA, Mar 19, 1950.

CANADA: GREAT KLONDIKE INTERNATIONAL OUTHOUSE RACE AND BATHROOM WALL LIMERICK CONTEST. Sept 1. Dawson City, YT. 27th annual. Crazy race of outhouses on wheels over a 1.5-mile course through the streets of downtown Dawson City. Awards presentation at Diamond Tooth Gertie's gambling hall following the race. Est attendance: 500. For info: Klondike Visitors Assn, PO Box 389V, Dawson City, YT, Canada Y0B 1G0. Phone: (867) 993-5575. Fax: (867) 993-6415. E-mail: kva@dawson.net. Web: www.dawsoncity.ca.

CARTIER, JACQUES: DEATH ANNIVERSARY. Sept 1, 1557. French navigator and explorer who sailed from St. Malo, France, Apr 20, 1534, in search of a northwest passage to the Orient. Instead, he discovered the St. Lawrence River, explored Canada's coastal regions and took possession of the country for France. Cartier was born at St. Malo, about 1491 (exact date unknown) and died there.

CHICKEN BOY'S BIRTHDAY. Sept 1. Chicken Boy is a 22-ft statue of a boy with a chicken's head, holding a bucket of chicken. Formerly the signage for the restaurant for which he is named, he was rescued from destruction when the restaurant went out of business by Future Studio of Los Angeles, a graphic design studio. Chicken Boy has since become a pop culture icon. (Some call him the Statue of Liberty of Los Angeles.) For info: Amy Inouye, Future Studio, PO Box 292000, Los Angeles, CA 90029. Phone: (323) 660-0620. Fax: (323) 660-2571. E-mail: futurestu@attbi.com. Web: www.chickenboy.com.

CHILDREN'S GOOD MANNERS MONTH ™. Sept 1–30. Starts the school year with a national program of teachers and parents encouraging good manners in children. The yearlong program includes monthly objectives that work in conjunction with a reinforcing home program. For info: "Dr. Manners," Fleming Allaire, PhD, 35 Eastfield St, Manchester, CT 06040. Phone: (860) 643-0051. E-mail: dr.manners@cox.net. Web: www.goodmannersclub.com and askdrmanners.com.

CHILE: NATIONAL MONTH. Sept 1–30. A month of special significance in Chile: arrival of spring, a Day of Unity on the first Monday in September, Independence of Chile anniversary (proclaimed Sept 18, 1810) and celebration of the 1980 Constitution and Army Day, Sept 19.

CHRISTMAS SEAL CAMPAIGN®. Sept 1–Dec 31. An American tradition dating back to 1907 when the first Christmas Seals® were made available in the US, the annual campaign is a major support of American Lung Association programs dedicated to fighting lung diseases such as asthma, emphysema, tuberculosis and lung cancer, as well as their causes. For info: American Lung Assn, 61 Broadway, 6th Fl, New York, NY 10006. Phone: (800) LUNG-USA. Web: www.lungusa.org.

COLUMBIA RIVER CROSS CHANNEL SWIM. Sept 1. Hood River, OR. The annual swim across the mighty Columbia River draws 550 contestants each year to swim the approximately one-mile distance for fun. Est attendance: 1,000. For info: Columbia River Cross Channel Swim, Hood River County Chamber of Commerce, 405 Portway Ave, Hood River, OR 97031. Phone: (800) 366-3530. E-mail: hrccc@hoodriver.org. Web: www.hoodriver.org.

CORN PALACE FESTIVAL. Sept 1–6. Mitchell, SD. Celebration of the harvest and the annual redecoration of the world's only Corn Palace (with ears of corn). Midway and carnival rides, games, specialty vendors, food and top-name entertainment on the stage of the Corn Palace. Est attendance: 30,000. For info: Corn Palace, Box 250, Mitchell, SD 57301. Phone: (605) 995-8427. Fax: (605) 995-8410. E-mail: mschilling.cityofmitchell@midconetwork.com. Web: www.cornpalacefestival.com.

EMMA M. NUTT DAY. Sept 1. A day to honor the first woman telephone operator, Emma M. Nutt, who reportedly began her professional career at Boston, MA, Sept 1, 1878, and continued working as a telephone operator for some 33 years.

449

Sept 1 ☆ *Chase's 2004 Calendar of Events* ☆

FALL HAT MONTH. Sept 1–30. A month of celebration during which the straw hat is put aside in favor of the felt or fabric hat by both men and women. Local businesses and the media are encouraged to plan hat-related activities. For info: Casey Bush, Exec Dir, Headwear Info Bureau, 302 W 12 St, PH-C, New York, NY 10014. Phone: (212) 627-8333. E-mail: milicase@aol.com. Web: www.hatsny.com/hib.

FALL IN LOVE WITH FOND DU LAC!. Sept 1–Oct 31. Fond du Lac, WI. Hike, bike or bird-watch in the Horicon National Wildlife Refuge, home to more than 260 species of birds, including the world's largest flock of migrating Canada geese. Horicon Marsh viewing area is located 12 miles south of Fond du Lac on Hwy 49. Also explore colorful Kettle Moraine State Forest. Enjoy harvest dinners, orchard hayrides, art galleries, farm markets, country roads tours and more. Annually, September and October. Est attendance: 4,500. For info: Fond du Lac Area Conv and Visitors Bureau, 171 S Pioneer Rd, Fond du Lac, WI 54935. Phone: (800) 937-9123 x92. Fax: (920) 929-6846. E-mail: market@fdl.com. Web: www.fdl.com.

GERMANY: CAPITAL RETURNS TO BERLIN: 5th ANNIVERSARY. Sept 1, 1999. In July the monthlong process of moving the German government from Bonn to Berlin began, eight years after Parliament had voted to return to its prewar seat. Berlin officially became the capital of Germany on Sept 1, 1999, and Parliament reconvened at the newly restored Reichstag on Sept 7, 1999.

GO WILD DURING CALIFORNIA WILD RICE MONTH. Sept 1–30. To promote greater appreciation and use of cultivated wild rice. California wild rice growers want America to know that wild rice is no longer simply hiding inside a holiday turkey. This versatile grain can add a gourmet touch to meals year-round. Stuff it inside pork chop pockets and chicken breasts or toss it into soups, salads, stir-frys and even pancake and muffin batters. Let your imagination run wild! Annually, the month of September. For info: The Thacker Group, 4550 Post Oak Pl, Ste 307, Houston, TX 77027. Phone: (877) 748-9693. Fax: (713) 355-1952. E-mail: julie@thackergroup.com. Web: www.cawildrice.com.

GREAT AMERICAN LOW-CHOLESTEROL, LOW-FAT PIZZA BAKE. Sept 1–30. Pizza parlors, restaurants and volunteer agencies nationwide create healthy pizza recipes to increase the public's awareness of the benefits of controlling high cholesterol levels through diet. For info: Frederick S. Mayer, Pres, Cholesterol Council of America, c/o PPSI, 101 Lucas Valley Rd, #210, San Rafael, CA 94903. Phone: (415) 479-8628. Fax: (415) 479-8608. E-mail: ppsi@aol.com. Web: www.ppsinc.org.

HOME AND SPORTS EYE HEALTH AND SAFETY MONTH. Sept 1–30. There are thousands of eye injuries each year related to common household products and sports. Tips on how to protect yourself and your children from such eye injuries will be discussed. For info: Prevent Blindness America®, 500 E Remington Rd, Schaumburg, IL 60173. Phone: (800) 331-2020. Fax: (847) 843-8458. Web: www.preventblindness.org.

HUG A TEXAS CHEF MONTH. Sept 1–30. Everybody knows when Texans set out to do something, they do it in a BIG way. This month show a Texas-size thanks to chefs across the Lone Star State for all the hard work and dedication that go into each dining experience. Send a note out to the kitchen and let them know you appreciate 'em. For info: Texas Chefs Assn, 320 Kitty Hawk Rd, Ste 103, Universal City, TX 78148. Phone: (210) 566-5003. E-mail: TCA@texchef.org. Web: www.texchef.org.

	S	M	T	W	T	F	S
September				1	2	3	4
2004	5	6	7	8	9	10	11
	12	13	14	15	16	17	18
	19	20	21	22	23	24	25
	26	27	28	29	30		

INTERNATIONAL ENTHUSIASM WEEK. Sept 1–7. Display genuine enthusiasm to every person, every project, every possibility that comes your way. It will change your week, your month, your year, your life. For info: Carolyn Stein, 1901 S Oak Haven Circle, Miami, FL 33179. Phone: (305) 931-3237. Fax: (305) 682-1416. E-mail: carolyn@carolynstein.com. Web: www.carolynstein.com.

INTERNATIONAL GAY SQUARE DANCE MONTH. Sept 1–30. Emphasis on square dancing as a healthy, fun, recreational activity. For info: Intl Assn of Gay Square Dance Clubs (IAGSDC), PO Box 87507, San Diego, CA 92138-7507. Phone: (800) 835-6462. E-mail: information@iagsdc.org. Web: www.iagsdc.org.

INTERNATIONAL SELF-AWARENESS MONTH. Sept 1–30. Cathcart Institute Inc of Lake Sherwood, CA, hosts this month each year to draw attention to the value of knowing oneself. Taking Socrates's advice "Know Thyself," this effort is targeted to identify, highlight and explore all the various means and models people use for improved understanding. Jim Cathcart, founder, is the author of *The Acorn Principle (Know Yourself–Grow Yourself)* and one of the premier professional speakers on self-awareness. For info: Jim Cathcart, Cathcart Institute Inc, 1650 Oakcottage Court, Lake Sherwood, CA 91361. Phone: (800) 222-4883. Fax: (805) 777-7013. E-mail: info@cathcart.com. Web: www.cathcart.com.

INTERNATIONAL STRATEGIC THINKING MONTH. Sept 1–30. A monthlong effort to bring awareness of the universal need to improve thinking skills. The International Center for Strategic Planning hosts this month each year to draw attention to the value of proactively seeking to expand individual views of the world and to remove thought barriers that prevent professional achievement, personal fulfillment, cultural awareness and tolerance. For info: Sherrin Ross Ingram, Intl Center for Strategic Planning, 104 W Chestnut St, #101, Hinsdale, IL 60521. Phone: (800) 962-4750. Fax: (800) 962-0177. E-mail: info@icfsp.com. Web: www.icfsp.com.

JAPAN: KANTO EARTHQUAKE MEMORIAL DAY: ANNIVERSARY. Sept 1, 1923. A day to remember the 57,000 people who died during Japan's greatest earthquake.

KOREAN AIR LINES FLIGHT 007 DISASTER: ANNIVERSARY. Sept 1, 1983. Korean Air Lines Flight 007, en route from New York, NY, to Seoul, Korea, reportedly strayed more than 100 miles off course, flying over secret Soviet military installations on the Kamchatka Peninsula and Sakhalin Island. Two and one half hours after it was said to have entered Soviet airspace, a Soviet interceptor plane destroyed the Boeing 747 with 269 persons on board which then crashed in the Sea of Japan. There were no survivors. President Reagan, in Proclamation 5093, named Sunday, Sept 11, 1983, as a National Day of Mourning as "homage to the memory of those who died."

LIBRARY CARD SIGN-UP MONTH. Sept 1–30. This observance was launched in 1987 to meet the challenge of then Secretary of Education William J. Bennett who said, "Let's have a national compaign. . . . every child should obtain a library card—and use it." Since then, thousands of public and school libraries join each fall in a national effort to ensure every child does just that. Annually, the month of September. For info: American Library Assn, Public Information Office, 50 E Huron St, Chicago, IL 60611. Phone: (312) 280-5043 or (312) 280-5042. E-mail: pio@ala.org. Web: www.ala.org.

LIBYA: REVOLUTION DAY: 35th ANNIVERSARY. Sept 1. Commemorates the revolution in 1969 when King Idris I was overthrown by Colonel Qaddafi. National holiday.

MARCIANO, ROCKY: BIRTH ANNIVERSARY. Sept 1, 1923. Rocky Marciano, boxer born Rocco Francis Marchegiano at Brockton, MA. Marciano used superb conditioning to fashion an impressive record that propelled him to fight against Jersey Joe Walcott for the heavyweight title on Sept 23, 1952. Marciano knocked Walcott out and in 1956 he retired as the only undefeated heavyweight champion. Died in a plane crash at Newton, IA, Aug 31, 1969. The film *Somebody Up There Likes Me* recounts his life story.

MENOPAUSE AWARENESS MONTH. Sept 1–30. More than 1,500 American women reach menopause every day. This is the month to make an appointment with your healthcare provider and take charge of your health during and after menopause. For info: American Menopause Foundation, 350 Fifth Ave, Ste 2822, New York, NY 10118. Phone: (212) 714-2398. E-mail: menopause@earthlink.net. Web: www.americanmenopause.org.

METAPHYSICAL AWARENESS MONTH. Sept 1–30. A time to review our holistic lifestyle and reconnect to the Source of all living and nonliving things, which we are and are not aware of, which contantly keep us healthy and safe. A newsletter is available. For info: Margaret Allbritten, Light Paths, 211 Cherry St, Roseville, CA 95678. Phone: (916) 446-4961. E-mail: goldenfire@mail.com.

MEXICO: PRESIDENT'S STATE OF THE UNION ADDRESS. Sept 1. National holiday.

MILLION MINUTE FAMILY CHALLENGE™. Sept 1–Dec 31. Fourth annual. A national effort to bring family, friends and neighbors together through board games. Goal is for 1,000 families or groups from each state to play a board game together for at least 20 minutes. Add your minutes to the running total at www.millionminute.com. Special teacher material and media information available, including press kits, interviews, etc. Annually, September through December. For info: Frank Beres, Million Minute Family Challenge, PO Box 268, Beloit, WI 53512-0268. Phone: (800) 524-4263. Fax: (608) 362-8178. E-mail: millionminute@patchproducts.com. Web: www.millionminute.com.

MISSION SAN LUIS OBISPO DE TOLOSA: FOUNDING ANNIVERSARY. Sept 1, 1772. California mission to the Indians.

NATIONAL BISCUIT MONTH. Sept 1–30. To promote usage of biscuits in restaurants and other foodservice outlets. Biscuits are a classic American food, good at any time of day—morning, noon or night. They're great alone and make a perfect partner to all sorts of dishes. For info: Tom O'Brien, Bakery Chef, Inc. Phone: (312) 372-6142.

NATIONAL CHICKEN MONTH. Sept 1–30. Focuses food shoppers' and restaurant customers' attention on chicken as the most healthy, convenient, economical and versatile food available; in short, "America's favorite." For info: Bill Roenigk, Sr VP, Natl Chicken Council, 1015 15th St NW, Ste 930, Washington, DC 20005. Phone: (202) 296-2622. Fax: (202) 293-4005. E-mail: WRoenigk@chickenUSA.org. Web: www.eatchicken.com.

NATIONAL CHILDHOOD INJURY PREVENTION WEEK. Sept 1–7. Injuries continue to be the #1 killer of American children. This month promotes prevention and intervention of unintentional injuries to children and emphasizes community involvement. Although money cannot buy social change, no significant change can happen without it. We invite you to join our mission. "Because the worst kind of childhood injury is the one that could have been prevented."® For info on our strategic partnership and sponsorship opportunities to help us mobilize the necessary human and financial resources to accomplish our objectives, contact the As Safe As Possible Campaign, PO Box 715, Richboro, PA 18954. E-mail: nobooboos@AsSafeAsPossible.org. Web: www.AsSafeAsPossible.org.

NATIONAL COUPON MONTH. Sept 1–30. Sponsored by the Coupon Council of the Promotional Marketing Association and celebrates the nearly four billion dollar savings American consumers receive each year by redeeming coupons for their favorite brands. Contests and fun activities are planned on a national level to raise the awareness of coupons and their redemption value. For info: Stacie McAnuff, Valassis, 19775 Victor Parkway, Livonia, MI 47152. Phone: (734) 591-7375. Fax: (734) 591-4503. E-mail: mcanuffs@valassis.com. Web: www.couponmonth.com.

NATIONAL 5-A-DAY MONTH. Sept 1–30. To encourage all Americans to increase the amount of fruits and vegetables they eat to five or more servings per day, to better their health and reduce their risk of cancer and other chronic diseases. For info: Produce for Better Health Foundation, 5301 Limestone Rd, Ste 101, Wilmington, DE 19808. Web: www.5aday.com.

NATIONAL FOOD ALLERGY AWARENESS MONTH. Sept 1–30. A month for all to learn about the seriousness of food allergies. For info: Robyn Rogers, 41 Massachusetts Av, Norfolk, MA 02056. Phone: (508) 553-3858. E-mail: rrhearts@attbi.com. Web: www.seafoodallergy.com.

NATIONAL HOMESCHOOL MONTH. Sept 1–30. Every year thousands of parents choose not to send their children to school but to educate them at home instead. This month is a chance to take your child's education in your hands. Follow in the footsteps of many famous people who were homeschooled: Thomas Edison, Alexander Graham Bell, Abraham Lincoln, the Wright Brothers, Mark Twain and more. Sponsored by Patchwork Primers Homeschool Unit Studies author Sharon Wilharm. For info: Sharon Wilharm, Patchwork Primers, 34 E Main St, DeFuniak Springs, FL 32435. Phone: (850) 951-0399. E-mail: sharon@patchworkprimers.com. Web: www.patchworkprimers.com.

NATIONAL HONEY MONTH. Sept 1–30. To honor the US's 211,600 beekeepers and 2.63 million colonies of honeybees, which produce more than 220 million pounds of honey each year. For info: Natl Honey Bd, 390 Lashley St, Longmont, CO 80501-6045. Phone: (303) 776-2337. Web: www.honey.com.

NATIONAL MUSHROOM MONTH. Sept 1–30. To promote the greater appreciation and use of fresh mushrooms. For info: Ruth Lowenberg, Lewis & Neale, Inc, 49 E 21st St, New York, NY 10010. Phone: (212) 420-8808. Fax: (212) 254-2452. E-mail: ruth@lewis-neale.com. Web: www.mushroominfo.com.

NATIONAL ORGANIC HARVEST MONTH. Sept 1–30. National celebration to educate all ages about organic agriculture and products sponsored by Organic Trade Association. Local and regional events organized by retailers, manufacturers, distributors and consumer groups include food fairs, tastings, farm tours, cooking demonstrations and meet-the-farmer days. Annually, the month of September. For info: Holly Givens, Organic Trade Assn, PO Box 547, Greenfield, MA 01302. Phone: (413) 774-7511. Fax: (413) 774-6432. E-mail: info@ota.com.

★**NATIONAL OVARIAN CANCER AWARENESS MONTH.** Sept 1–30.

NATIONAL PEDICULOSIS PREVENTION MONTH. Sept 1–30. To promote awareness of how to prevent pediculosis and protect against unnecessary and potentially harmful pesticide treatments for head lice. For info: Natl Pediculosis Assn, 50 Kearney Rd, Newton, MA 02494. Phone: (781) 449-NITS. Fax: (781) 449-8129. Web: www.headlice.org or www.licemeister.org.

Sept 1 ☆ Chase's 2004 Calendar of Events ☆

NATIONAL PIANO MONTH. Sept 1–30. Recognizes America's most popular instrument and its more than 20 million players; also encourages piano study by people of all ages. For info: Donald W. Dillon, Exec Dir, Natl Piano Foundation, 13140 Coit Rd, Ste 320, LB 120, Dallas, TX 75240-5737. Phone: (972) 233-9107. Fax: (972) 490-4219. E-mail: don@dondillon.com. Web: www.pianonet.com.

NATIONAL POTATO MONTH. Sept 1–30. To celebrate the taste, variety and nutrition of potatoes. This month is dedicated to the celebration of one of America's most popular foods—the potato. For info: Cape Cod Potato Chips, 100 Breed's Hill Rd, Hyannis, MA 02601. Phone: (508) 775-3358. Web: www.capecodchips.com.

NATIONAL RICE MONTH. Sept 1–30. To focus attention on the importance of rice to the American diet and to salute the US rice industry. For info: Molly Johnson, Mgr Retail Trade Development, USA Rice Federation, 9800 Richmond, Ste 235, Houston, TX 77042. Phone: (713) 270-6699. Web: www.usarice.com or www.nationalricemonth.com.

NATIONAL SCHOOL SUCCESS MONTH. Sept 1–30. Today's young people have many distractions from school and are sometimes overwhelmed when it comes to academics. Parents are often unskilled at effectively redirecting the attention of their children, especially their teenagers. This observance is to recognize parents who want to support and encourage their children to succeed in school and to explore ways to do that. Annually, the month of September. For info send SASE to: Teresa Langston, Dir, Parenting Without Pressure, 1330 Boyer St, Longwood, FL 32750-6311. Phone: (407) 767-2524. Web: www.parentingwithoutpressure.com.

NATIONAL SEWING MONTH. Sept 1–30. Celebrates the art, craft and hobby of sewing. Sponsored by the Home Sewing Association, the nonprofit trade association representing the home sewing industry. Recognized by HSA member and nonmember retailers, suppliers and manufacturers, the monthlong celebration includes special sales, promotions and education programs directed at increased awareness for sewing. For info: Home Sewing Assn, 494 Eighth Ave, Ste 802, New York, NY 10001-1806. Phone: (212) 714-1633. Fax: (212) 714-1655. E-mail: info@sewing.org. Web: www.sewing.org.

NATIONAL SKIN CARE AWARENESS MONTH. Sept 1–30. This special month focuses on providing education on caring for your skin. Topics include protecting your skin from the dangers of the sun, how diet and lifestyle affect your skin, developing a proper skin care routine and myths and facts about skin care products. All important knowledge for great-looking skin. For info: Renée Rouleau Skin Care, 19009 Preston Rd, Ste 206, Dallas, TX 75252. Phone: (972) 248-6131. Web: www.reneerouleau.com.

NATIONAL SPINAL CORD INJURY AWARENESS MONTH. Sept 1–30. National campaign to create awareness about the prevention and treatment of spinal cord injuries. Activities include visits to schools teaching students, parents and teachers about the many causes and effects of spinal cord injuries. An annual art contest is held to design the current year's logo. Annually, the month of September. For info: Patty Lance, c/o Regional Spinal Cord Injury Center of Delaware Valley, 132 S 10th St, Philadelphia, PA 19107. Phone: (877) 452-6231. Fax: (215) 955-8652. E-mail: pattylance5@aol.com. Web: www.geofflance.com.

NATIONAL VERY IMPORTANT PARENTS (VIP) MONTH™. Sept 1–30. Family Information Services (FIS) is an organization serving professionals who provide information and support about parenting, child guidance and family relationships in their communities. VIP Month celebrates the crucial role parents play in the growth and development of their children, and focuses on a different important area of parenting each year. Free ready-to-copy master page for promoting VIP Month is available. Annually, in September. For info, send SASE to: Family Information Services, 12565 Jefferson St NE, Ste 102, Minneapolis, MN 55434-2102. Phone: (800) 852-8112 or (763) 755-6233. Fax: (763) 755-7355. E-mail: staff@familyinfoserv.com. Web: www.familyinfoserv.com.

OVARIAN CANCER AWARENESS MONTH. Sept 1–30. For info: Natl Ovarian Cancer Coalition, 500 NE Spanish River Blvd, Ste 14, Boca Raton, FL 33431. Phone: (888) OVA-RIAN. E-mail: nocc@ovarian.org. Web: www.ovarian.org.

PEDIATRIC CANCER AWARENESS MONTH. Sept 1–30. Cancer is the chief cause of death by disease in children. More than 2,300 children in the US die of cancer every year, more than die of AIDS. For info: Bear Necessities Pediatric Cancer Foundation, 85 W Algonquin Rd, Ste 165, Arlington Heights, IL 60005. Phone: (847) 952-9164. Web: www.bearnecessities.org.

PICATINNY PEAK FALL HAWKWATCH. Sept 1–Dec 1. Picatinny Arsenal, Dover, NJ. Fall hawkwatch to count migrating raptors. Between 9,000 and 12,000 raptors per year are counted. Member site of Hawk Migration Association of North America (HMANA). Annually, Sept 1 through Dec 1. For info: John J. Reed, 31 Croft Rd, Lake Hopatcong, NJ 07849-1023. Phone: (201) 724-2703. E-mail: eagle76@bellatlantic.net.

PLEASURE YOUR MATE MONTH. Sept 1–30. To promote love and show appreciation to your mate. Look for new ways to create happiness together. Use this event to establish a lifelong habit of sharing pleasure. Annually, the month of September. For info: Donald Etkes, PhD, PMB 148, 112 Harvard Ave, Claremont, CA 91711. Phone: (909) 981-7333.

REUTHER, WALTER PHILIP: BIRTH ANNIVERSARY. Sept 1, 1907. American labor leader who began work in a steel factory at age 16 and later became president of the United Automobile Workers (UAW) and the Congress of Industrial Organizations (CIO). Born at Wheeling, WV, Reuther worked for two years in a Russian automobile factory. Often at the center of controversy, he was the target of an assassin in 1948. Reuther and his wife died in an airplane crash May 9, 1970, at Black Lake, MI. The UAW Family Education Center, a project which he had cherished, was later named for Walter and May Reuther.

SEA CADET MONTH. Sept 1–30. Nationwide year-round youth program for boys and girls 11–17 teaches leadership and self-discipline with emphasis on nautically oriented training without military obligation. Est attendance: 10,000. For info: US Naval Sea Cadet Corps, 2300 Wilson Blvd, Arlington, VA 22201. Phone: (703) 243-6910. Fax: (703) 243-3985. E-mail: mford@NAVYLEAGUE.org. Web: www.seacadets.org.

SELF-IMPROVEMENT MONTH. Sept 1–30. To disseminate information about the importance of lifelong learning and self-improvement. For complete information and lists of books, materials and cassettes, send $5 to cover expense of printing, handling and postage. Annually, the month of September. For info: Dr. Stanley Drake, Pres, Intl Society of Friendship and Good Will, 999 Hood Rd, Ste 127, Marietta, GA 30068. Phone: (770) 565-2322. E-mail: ISFGW@bellsouth.net.

SELF-UNIVERSITY WEEK. Sept 1–7. Reminds adults (in or out of school) that each of us has a responsibility to help shape the future by pursuing lifelong learning. Committed to self-education as the lifeblood of democracy and the key to living life to its fullest. Dedicated to furthering education not as something you get but as something you take. We assert that America's greatest treasures are found not in our shopping malls but in our libraries. Annually, the first seven days of September. For info: Charles Hayes, Publisher, Autodidactic Press, PO Box 872749,

☆ Chase's 2004 Calendar of Events ☆   Sept 1

Wasilla, AK 99687. Phone: (907) 376-2932. Fax: (907) 376-2932. E-mail: autpress@alaska.net. Web: www.autodidactic.com.

SEPTEMBER IS CHILDHOOD CANCER MONTH. Sept 1–30. Public awareness of infants, children and teens with cancer and the need to make research into a higher national priority are stressed each year in September. For info: National Childhood Cancer Foundation, 440 E Huntington Dr, Ste 402, Arcadia, CA 91006. Phone: (800) 458-6223. Fax: (626) 447-6359. Web: www.nccf.org or www.childhoodcancermonth.org.

SEPTEMBER IS HEALTHY AGING® MONTH. Sept 1–30. Healthy Aging® Month is an annual health observance designed to focus national attention on the positive aspects of growing older. The month is part of the Healthy Aging® Campaign, a national, ongoing health promotion designed to broaden awareness of the positive aspects of aging and to provide inspiration for adults, ages 50+, to improve their physical, mental, social and financial health. The Campaign is developed and produced by Educational Television Network, Inc. (ETNET), a nonprofit corporation based in Pennsylvania. For info: Carolyn Worthington, The Healthy Aging® Campaign, PO Box 442, Unionville, PA 19375. Phone: (610) 793-0979. E-mail: info@healthyaging.net. Web: www.healthyaging.net.

SHAMELESS PROMOTION MONTH. Sept 1–30. This is the month for you to go out and promote yourself, your business, your book or your product shamelessly. For outrageous tips, visit our website. For info: Marisa D'Vari, 220 Boylstown St, #1206, Boston, MA 02116. Phone: (617) 451-9914. Fax: (617) 351-2030. E-mail: mdvari@deg.com. Web: www.GetBookedNow.com.

SIGOURNEY, LYDIA: BIRTH ANNIVERSARY. Sept 1, 1791. Prolific American author, Lydia Howard Huntley Sigourney was born at Norwich, CT. Her writings, mainly moral and religious works, included such titles as *How to Be Happy, Letters to Young Ladies* and *Pleasant Memories of Pleasant Lands*. She wrote more than 65 books before her death June 10, 1865, at Hartford, CT.

SLOVAKIA: CONSTITUTION DAY. Sept 1. Anniversary of the adoption of the Constitution of the Slovak Republic in 1992.

SOUTHERN GOSPEL MUSIC MONTH. Sept 1–30. To promote the growth, enjoyment and awareness nationwide of Southern Gospel music, a cherished American art form, by promoting radio airplay, concert attendance and retail awareness. For info: Southern Gospel Music Guild, PO Box 150264, Nashville, TN 37215. E-mail: info@sgmg.org. Web: www.sgmg.org.

SUBLIMINAL COMMUNICATIONS MONTH. Sept 1–30. Not getting the results you want? Make a change for the positive and learn how to maximize your effectiveness. Learn how to put to use your entrepreneurial thinking to achieve your goals and increase your visibility socially or in the corporate world. Recognize and apply prosperity-building opportunities for increasing your networking, marketing and publicity goals through the use of color, scents and language. Finish the last quarter of the year successfully by using the powerful resources you already possess. It's your choice! For info send large SASE to: Lorrie Walters Marsiglio, Lorimar Comunications, PO Box 284-CC, Wasco, IL 60183-0284. Phone: (630) 584-9368.

TITANIC DISCOVERED: ANNIVERSARY. Sept 1, 1985. Almost 75 years after the *Titanic* sank in the North Atlantic after striking an iceberg, a joint American-French expedition force led by marine geologist Dr. Robert Ballard located the wreck. The luxury liner was resting on the ocean floor 12,500 feet down—about 350 miles southeast from Newfoundland, Canada. In July 1986 Ballard returned in an expedition aboard the *Atlantis II* to explore the ship with underwater robots. Two memorial bronze plaques were left on the deck. See also: "Sinking of the *Titanic*: Anniversary" (Apr 15).

TOY TIPS EXECUTIVE TOY TEST. Sept 1. New York, NY. Annual event where senior executives of various companies test toys and learn how to use creativity in the workplace. For info: Toy Tips, Inc. Phone: (414) 421-9668. Web: www.toytips.com.

TWITTY, CONWAY: BIRTH ANNIVERSARY. Sept 1, 1933. Country and western music star who began his career as a rock and roll performer in the style of Elvis Presley, born at Friars Point, MS. Died June 5, 1993, at Springfield, MO.

UNITED PLANET MONTH. Sept 1–30. Sponsored by United Planet, a Boston-based nonprofit public charity. A monthlong holiday dedicated to the promotion of cross-cultural understanding, friendship, world unity and peace. During the month of September, United Planet sponsors a diverse and creative range of events and initiatives to celebrate these ideals. Come join the fun in the celebration of a global community beyond borders! Annually, every September. For info: David Santulli, United Planet, 41 Appleton St, Ste 303, Boston, MA 02116. Phone: (617) 292-0711. Fax: (617) 292-0712. E-mail: info@unitedplanet.org. Web: www.unitedplanet.org.

UPDATE YOUR RESUME MONTH. Sept 1–30. The Professional Resume Writing and Research Association is an international group of resume writing and career coaching professionals who are "Setting the Standard for Resume Excellence" by encouraging the updating and maintenance of resumes for every employed individual. For info: Laurie Roy, Professional Resume Writing and Research Assn, 1106 Coolidge Blvd, Lafayette, LA 70503. Phone: (800) 225-8688. Fax: (337) 233-1871. E-mail: laurie@prwra.com. Web: www.prwra.com.

UZBEKISTAN: INDEPENDENCE DAY. Sept 1. National holiday. Commemorates independence upon the dissolution of the Soviet Union in 1991.

WORLD WAR II BEGINS: GERMANY INVADES POLAND: 65th ANNIVERSARY. Sept 1, 1939. After securing a nonaggression pact with the USSR (which secretly allowed for the partition of Poland by the Soviet Union and Germany) on Aug 23, Germany invaded Poland without a declaration of war at 4:45 AM. Two days later, Britain and France declared war, with Canada, Australia, New Zealand and South Africa soon following with their own declarations. Poland, overwhelmed by German air and land power, was in German and Soviet hands before the month concluded.

BIRTHDAYS TODAY

Yvonne De Carlo, 82, actress ("The Munsters," *Salome*), born Peggy Yvonne Middleton, Vancouver, BC, Canada, Sept 1, 1922.

Alan Dershowitz, 66, attorney, author, born Brooklyn, NY, Sept 1, 1938.

Gloria Estefan, 47, singer (Miami Sound Machine, "Don't Want to Lose You"), born Havana, Cuba, Sept 1, 1957.

Barry Gibb, 58, singer (with the Bee Gees, "Staying Alive"), songwriter, born Manchester, England, Sept 1, 1946.

Timothy Duane (Tim) Hardaway, 38, former basketball player, born Chicago, IL, Sept 1, 1966.

Ron O'Neal, 67, actor (*Super Fly, Red Dawn*; stage: *No Place to Be Somebody* [Obie Award]), born Utica, NY, Sept 1, 1937.

Seiji Ozawa, 69, conductor, born Hoten, Japan, Sept 1, 1935.

Don Stroud, 67, actor ("Mike Hammer," *The Buddy Holly Story, License to Kill*), born Honolulu, HI, Sept 1, 1937.

Lily Tomlin, 65, actress ("Laugh-In," *The Search for Signs of Intelligent Life in the Universe*), comedienne, born Detroit, MI, Sept 1, 1939.

SEPTEMBER 2 — THURSDAY
Day 246 — 120 Remaining

BISON-TEN-YELL DAY. Sept 2. Honoring the "bicentennial" of the birth of Bison-Ten-Yell, imaginary inventor of a set of ten battle yells as signals, based on the traditional memory aid system eventually adopted by football players. For info: Bob Birch, Grand Punscorpion, Puns Corps, Box 2364, Falls Church, VA 22042-0364. Phone: (703) 533-3668.

BLUE HILL FAIR. Sept 2–6. Blue Hill, ME. A "down-to-earth" country fair. Annually, Labor Day weekend. Est attendance: 35,000. For info: Blue Hill Fair, PO Box 390, Blue Hill, ME 04614. Phone: (207) 374-3701. Fax: (207) 374-3702.

CALENDAR ADJUSTMENT DAY: ANNIVERSARY. Sept 2. Pursuant to the British Calendar Act of 1751, Britain (and the American colonies) made the "Gregorian Correction" in 1752. The Act proclaimed that the day following Wednesday, Sept 2, should become Thursday, Sept 14, 1752. There was rioting in the streets by those who felt cheated and who demanded the eleven days back. The Act also provided that New Year's Day (and the change of year number) should fall Jan 1 (instead of Mar 25) in 1752 and every year thereafter. As a result, 1751 only had 282 days. See also: "Gregorian Calendar Adjustment: Anniversary" (Feb 24, Oct 4).

CHICAGO JAZZ FESTIVAL. Sept 2–5. Grant Park, Chicago, IL. 26th annual. International line-ups on three stages. Free. Est attendance: 315,000. For info: Mayor's Office of Special Events, City Hall, 121 N LaSalle St #703, Chicago, IL 60602. Phone: (312) 744-3370. Fax: (312) 744-8523. E-mail: moseinquiry@cityofchicago.org. Web: www.cityofchicago.org/specialevents.

COLUMBIA COUNTY FAIR. Sept 2–6. Chatham, NY. Midway and agricultural exhibits for the family to enjoy. For info: Columbia County Tourism Dept, 401 State St, Hudson, NY 12534. Phone: (800) 724-1846. Web: www.columbiacountyny.org or www.columbiafair.com.

FORTEN, JAMES: BIRTH ANNIVERSARY. Sept 2, 1766. James Forten was born of free black parents at Philadelphia, PA. As a powder boy on an American Revolutionary warship, he escaped being sold as a slave when his ship was captured due to the intervention of the son of the British commander. While in England he became involved with abolitionists. On his return to Philadelphia, he became an apprentice to a sailmaker and eventually purchased the company for which he worked. He was active in the abolition movement, and in 1816 his support was sought by the American Colonization Society for the plan to settle American blacks at Liberia. He rejected their ideas and their plans to make him the ruler of the colony. From the large profits of his successful sailmaking company, he contributed heavily to the abolitionist movement and was a supporter of William Lloyd Garrison's antislavery journal, *The Liberator*. Died at Philadelphia, PA, Mar 4, 1842.

GREAT FIRE OF LONDON: ANNIVERSARY. Sept 2–5, 1666 (OS). The fire generally credited with bringing about our system of fire insurance started Sept 2, 1666 (OS), in the wooden house of a baker named Farryner, at London's Pudding Lane, near the Tower. During the ensuing three days more than 13,000 houses were destroyed, though it is believed that only six lives were lost in the fire.

HISTORIC MARATHON RUNS: ANNIVERSARY. Sept 2–9, 490 BC. Anniversary of the event during the Persian Wars from which the marathon race is derived. Phidippides, "an Athenian and by profession and practice a trained runner," according to Herodotus, was dispatched from Marathon to Sparta (26 miles) Sept 2 to seek help in repelling the invading Persian army. Help being unavailable by religious law until after the next full moon, Phidippides ran the 26 miles back to Marathon Sept 4. Without Spartan aid, the Athenians defeated the Persians at the Battle of Marathon Sept 9. According to legend Phidippides carried the news of the battle to Athens and died as he spoke the words, "Rejoice, we are victorious." The marathon race was revived at the 1896 Olympic Games at Athens. Course distance, since 1924, is 26 miles, 385 yards. See also: "Battle of Marathon: Anniversary" (Sept 9).

HOPKINTON STATE FAIR. Sept 2–6. Contoocook, NH. 89th fair. "A Labor Day Weekend Tradition." For info: Hopkinton State Fair, PO Box 700, Contoocook, NH 03229-0700. Phone: (603) 746-4191. Fax: (603) 746-3037. E-mail: info@hsfair.org. Web: www.hsfair.org.

LITTLE BALKANS DAYS/PAACA FOLKLIFE FESTIVAL. Sept 2–6. Pittsburg, KS. This event, featuring more than 100 arts and crafts booths, is spread all over Pittsburg from the mall on the south to the Historical Museum on the north and in the parks in between. Contests, tournaments, food, live entertainment, street dances, quilt show and much more. Annually, Labor Day weekend. Est attendance: 25,000. For info: Little Balkans Festival Assn, PO Box 1933, Pittsburg, KS 66762. Phone: (620) 231-1000 or (800) 879-1212. Fax: (620) 231-3178. E-mail: cvb@pittsburgkschamber.com.

LOUISIANA SHRIMP AND PETROLEUM FESTIVAL AND FAIR. Sept 2–6. Morgan City, LA. Free admission to this event that recognizes and celebrates the importance of the shrimp and oil industry to the area. Arts, crafts, water and street parades, Cajun culinary classic, shrimp cook-off, music in the park, unique children's village (a magical adventureland), gospel tent, coronation pageant and ball, carnival, blessing of the fleet. Chosen as the American Bus Association's "Festival of the Year" for the past four years. Est attendance: 175,000. For info: Louisiana Shrimp and Petroleum Festival and Fair Assn, Box 103, Morgan City, LA 70381. Phone: (504) 385-0703. Fax: (504) 384-4628. E-mail: info@shrimp-petrofest.org.

MARION POPCORN FESTIVAL. Sept 2–4. Marion, OH. Performances by nationally known entertainers every evening; parade, athletic competition, arts and crafts. 11 AM to midnight daily. Est attendance: 350,000. For info: Marion Popcorn Festival, PO Box 1101, Marion, OH 43301-1101. Phone: (740) 387-3378.

McAULIFFE, CHRISTA: BIRTH ANNIVERSARY. Sept 2, 1948. Christa McAuliffe, a 37-year-old Concord, NH, high school teacher, was to have been the first "ordinary citizen" in space. Born Sharon Christa Corrigan at Boston, MA, she perished with six crew members in the Space Shuttle *Challenger* explosion Jan 28, 1986. See also: "Challenger Space Shuttle Explosion: Anniversary" (Jan 28).

NATIONAL SWEETCORN FESTIVAL. Sept 2–6. McFerron Park, Hoopeston, IL. Annual festival includes 29 tons of free corn on the cob, nationally sanctioned beauty pageant, carnival, flea market, horse show, demolition derby, bands and talent shows. Est attendance: 50,000. For info: Jeanie Cooke, Exec Dir, Danville Area Conv/Visitors Bureau, PO Box 992, Danville, IL 61834. Phone: (217) 442-2096.

☆ Chase's 2004 Calendar of Events ☆ Sept 2–3

NUGGET BEST IN THE WEST RIB COOK-OFF. Sept 2–6. Victorian Square, Sparks, NV. Rib cookers from across the country compete for the title of Nugget Best in the West Rib Cooker. Competing cookers sell ribs to the crowd over the Labor Day weekend. Free concerts nightly feature groups like BTO, War and Terri Clark. Other music groups presented throughout the day—all free. Hundreds of craft booths and activities for the whole family. Est attendance: 300,000. For info: John Ascuaga's Nugget, 1100 Nugget Ave, Sparks, NV 89431. Phone: (800) 648-1177. Web: www.janugget.com.

OLD THRESHERS REUNION. Sept 2–6. McMillan Park, Mount Pleasant, IA. The reunion began in 1950. Old Threshers is a celebration of our rich agricultural heritage. Attractions range from displays of steam engines and agricultural exhibits to turn-of-the-century living and antique cars, tractors and gas engines. There are also steam trains, trolleys, crafts, museums, music and camping. Annually, five days ending on Labor Day. Est attendance: 100,000. For info: Midwest Old Threshers, 405 E Threshers Rd, Mt Pleasant, IA 52641. Phone: (319) 385-8937. Fax: (319) 385-0563. Web: www.oldthreshers.org.

ON THE WATERFRONT. Sept 2–5. Rockford, IL. Illinois's largest music festival. Eight music stages, more than 150 performers, more than 50 specialty foods and dozens of special events. Est attendance: 350,000. For info: On the Waterfront, Inc, 308 W State St, Ste 115, Rockford, IL 61101. Phone: (815) 964-4388 or (815) 963-4FUN. E-mail: 4fun@onthewaterfront.com. Web: www.onthewaterfront.com.

SHERMAN ENTERS ATLANTA: ANNIVERSARY. Sept 2, 1864. After a four-week siege, Union General William Tecumseh Sherman entered Atlanta, GA. The city had been evacuated on the previous day by Confederate troops under General John B. Hood. Hood had mistakenly assumed Sherman was ending the siege Aug 27, when actually Sherman was beginning the final stages of his attack. Hood then sent troops to attack the Union forces at Jonesboro. Hood's troops were defeated, opening the way for the capture of Atlanta.

THOMAS POINT BEACH BLUEGRASS FESTIVAL. Sept 2–5. Brunswick, ME. Featuring world-class bluegrass musicians on the southern coast of Maine. Swimming, playground, picnic area, snack bar, free camping, Sunday morning worship service on the beach. Fun for the whole family! 27th annual festival. Enjoy an end-of-summer family outing and terrific bluegrass music. Est attendance: 4,000. For tickets and info: Thomas Point Beach, 29 Meadow Rd, Brunswick, ME 04011. Phone: (207) 725-6009 or (877) TPB-4321. Web: www.thomaspointbeach.com.

UNITED TRIBES POWWOW. Sept 2–5. United Tribes Technical College, Bismarck, ND. Enjoy one of the largest international powwows in the nation. This colorful pageant includes Native Americans from across the country singing and dancing in friendly competition. Indian foods, artifacts and jewelry are sold on the premises. Est attendance: 20,000. For info: (701) 255-3285 or North Dakota Tourism, Century Center, 1600 E Century Ave, Ste 2, Bismarck, ND 58503. Phone: (701) 328-2525 or (800) 435-5663. Web: www.unitedtribespowwow.com.

US TREASURY DEPARTMENT: ANNIVERSARY. Sept 2, 1789. The third presidential cabinet department, the Treasury Department, was established by Congress.

VIETNAM: INDEPENDENCE DAY. Sept 2. Ho Chi Minh formally proclaimed the independence of Vietnam from France and the establishment of the Democratic Republic of Vietnam on this day in 1945. National holiday.

V-J DAY: ANNIVERSARY. Sept 2, 1945. Official ratification of Japanese surrender to the Allies occurred aboard the USS *Missouri* at Tokyo Bay Sept 2 (Far Eastern time) in 1945, thus prompting President Truman's declaration of this day as Victory-over-Japan Day. Japan's initial, informal agreement of surrender was announced by Truman and celebrated in the US Aug 14.

BIRTHDAYS TODAY

Nathaniel ("Tiny") Archibald, 56, Hall of Fame basketball player, born New York, NY, Sept 2, 1948.
Terry Paxton Bradshaw, 56, sportscaster, Hall of Fame football player, born Shreveport, LA, Sept 2, 1948.
Marge Champion, 81, dancer, actress ("Marge and Gower Champion Show," *Show Boat*), born Los Angeles, CA, Sept 2, 1923.
Jimmy Connors, 52, former tennis player, born East St. Louis, IL, Sept 2, 1952.
Eric Demetric Dickerson, 44, Hall of Fame football player, born Sealy, TX, Sept 2, 1960.
Mark Harmon, 53, actor ("St. Elsewhere," "Chicago Hope"), born Burbank, CA, Sept 2, 1951.
Salma Hayek, 38, actress (*Fools Rush In, Frida*), born Veracruz, Mexico, Sept 2, 1966.
Linda Purl, 49, actress ("Happy Days," "Matlock"), born Greenwich, CT, Sept 2, 1955.
Keanu Reeves, 40, actor (*Bill and Ted's Excellent Adventure, My Own Private Idaho, Speed*), born Beirut, Lebanon, Sept 2, 1964.
John Thompson, 63, college basketball coach, former player, born Washington, DC, Sept 2, 1941.
Peter Victor Ueberroth, 67, former commissioner of baseball and Olympic organizer, born Evanston, IL, Sept 2, 1937.
Carlos Valderrama, 43, soccer player, born Santa Marta, Colombia, Sept 2, 1961.

SEPTEMBER 3 — FRIDAY
Day 247 — 119 Remaining

BEGINNING OF THE PENNY PRESS: ANNIVERSARY. Sept 3, 1833. Benjamin H. Day launched the *New York Sun* on this date, the first truly successful penny newspaper in the US. The *Sun* was sold on sidewalks by newspaper boys. By 1836 the paper was the largest seller in the country with a circulation of 30,000. It was possibly Day's concentration on human interest stories and sensationalism that made his publication a success while efforts at penny papers at Philadelphia and Boston had failed.

BENTON NEIGHBOR DAY. Sept 3–4. Benton, MO. Large festival that includes exhibits, greased pole climb, amusement park, Little Mr and Miss contest, greased pig chase, live bands, antique car show, horseshoe tournament, sky divers, queen contest, kid tractor pull, parade and talent show. Antique Tractor Pull, outdoor games for kids and adults. Annually, the Friday and Saturday before Labor Day. Est attendance: 3,000. For info: Benton Chamber of Commerce, PO Box 477, Benton, MO 63736. Phone: (573) 545-3125.

BRITAIN DECLARES WAR ON GERMANY: 65th ANNIVERSARY. Sept 3, 1939. British ultimatum to Germany, demanding halt to invasion of Poland (which had started at dawn on Sept 1), expired at 11 AM, GMT, Sept 3, 1939. At 11:15 AM, in a radio broadcast, Prime Minister Neville Chamberlain announced the declaration of war against Germany. France, Canada, Australia, New Zealand and South Africa quickly issued separate declarations of war. Winston Churchill was named First Lord of the Admiralty. See also: "World War II Begins: Germany Invades Poland" (Sept 1).

455

Sept 3 ☆ *Chase's 2004 Calendar of Events* ☆

BRITT DRAFT HORSE SHOW. Sept 3–5. Hancock County Fairgrounds, Britt, IA. One of the largest draft horse hitch shows in North America, featuring 18 six-horse hitches from the US and Canada representing the very best of the Belgian, Percheron and Clydesdale performance horses. Annually, Labor Day weekend. Est attendance: 10,000. For info: Randel or Melodie Hiscocks, Britt Draft Horse Assn, PO Box 312, Britt, IA 50423. Phone: (641) 843-4181.

BUMBERSHOOT: THE SEATTLE ARTS FESTIVAL. Sept 3–6. Seattle Center, Seattle, WA. Celebrates the arts in every genre; includes kids' activities. Annually, Labor Day weekend. Est attendance: 250,000. For info: One Reel, PO Box 9750, Seattle, WA 98109. Phone: (206) 281-8111. E-mail: info@onereel.org. Web: www.bumbershoot.org.

CRANDALL, PRUDENCE: BIRTH ANNIVERSARY. Sept 3, 1803. Born to a Quaker family at Hopkinton, RI, this American schoolteacher sparked controversy in the 1830s with her efforts to educate black girls. When her private academy for girls was boycotted because she admitted a black girl, she started a school for "young ladies and misses of colour." Died Jan 28, 1890, at Elk Falls, KS.

DANIEL BOONE PIONEER FESTIVAL. Sept 3–5 (tentative). Winchester, KY. Take yourself back to the days of Daniel Boone and the pioneers. Features entertainment, arts and crafts displays and food booths. Est attendance: 35,000. For info: Daniel Boone Pioneer Fest, 2 S Maple St, Ste A, Winchester, KY 40391. Phone: (859) 744-0556. Fax: (859) 744-9229.

DOUGLASS'S ESCAPE TO FREEDOM: ANNIVERSARY. Sept 3, 1838. Dressed as a sailor and carrying identification papers borrowed from a retired merchant seaman, Frederick Douglass boarded a train in Baltimore, MD, a slave state, and rode to Wilmington, DE, where he caught a steamboat to the free city of Philadelphia. He then transferred to a train headed for New York City where he entered the protection of the Underground Railway network. Douglass later became a great orator and one of the leaders of the antislavery struggle.

ENGLAND: BLACKPOOL ILLUMINATIONS. Sept 3–Nov 7. The Promenade, Blackpool, Lancashire. "A five-mile spectacle of lighting." Est attendance: 8,000,000. For info: Tourism and Services Dept, 1 Clifton St, Blackpool, Lancashire, England FY1 1LY. Phone: (44) 1253 478203. Fax: (44) 1253 478210. E-mail: tourism@blackpool.gov.uk. Web: www.blackpooltourism.com.

EVERLY BROTHERS/CENTRAL CITY ROCK 'N ROLL CRUISE-IN & CONCERT. Sept 3-4. Central City, KY. Cruise the "famous Central City Strip" in your street rod or muscle car. Enjoy the concert on Sept 4. Lots of concessions, booths and fun. Est attendance: 10,000. For info: Central City Music Festival, 203 N Second St, Central City, KY 42330. Phone: (270) 754-2360. Fax: (270) 754-2365. Web: www.centralcityky.com.

FESTIVAL OF MOUNTAIN AND PLAIN . . . A TASTE OF COLORADO. Sept 3–4. Denver, CO. The Rocky Mountain region's largest free outdoor festival, this four-day food and entertainment extravaganza over Labor Day weekend features 50 of Colorado's best restaurants. Musical entertainment on six outdoor stages, gourmet cooking demonstrations, 280 arts and crafts vendors and children's music and activities. Friday, Saturday and Sunday 11 AM–10:30 PM. Monday 11 AM–8:30 PM. Est attendance: 500,000. For info: John Kerns, Event Mgr, Downtown Denver Partnership, Inc, 511 16th St, Ste 200, Denver, CO 80202. Phone: (303) 534-6161 or (303) 478-7878 (Hotline). Fax: (303) 534-2803. E-mail: jkerns@downtowndenver.com. Web: www.atasteofcolorado.com.

September 2004

S	M	T	W	T	F	S
			1	2	3	4
5	6	7	8	9	10	11
12	13	14	15	16	17	18
19	20	21	22	23	24	25
26	27	28	29	30		

FILENE, EDWARD ALBERT: BIRTH ANNIVERSARY. Sept 3, 1860. American merchant and philanthropist, born at Salem, MA, who established the US credit union movement in 1921. Died at Paris, France, Sept 26, 1937.

FIRST SECRET SERVICE AGENT TO DIE IN THE LINE OF DUTY: ANNIVERSARY. Sept 3, 1902. While on duty protecting President Theodore Roosevelt, William Craig was killed when a streetcar collided with the carriage carrying the president (who suffered some cuts). The United States Secret Service was founded in 1865 as a branch of the Treasury Department entrusted with foiling counterfeiting, but was given the additional role of protecting the US president upon the assassination of William McKinley. Craig, born in Glasgow, Scotland, in 1855, was also a bodyguard for Queen Victoria before moving to Chicago. Roosevelt affectionately called Craig his "shadow."

FORT BRIDGER RENDEZVOUS. Sept 3–6. Fort Bridger, WY. Come and join in the family fun with entertainment, food booths, merchandise exhibits and much more. Est attendance: 30,000. For info: Traci Hardy, Fort Bridger Rendezvous Assn, PO Box 9, Woodruff, UT 84086. Phone: (435) 793-4570. E-mail: fbrainc@hotmail.com. Web: www.fortbridgerrendezvous.net.

HOG CAPITAL OF THE WORLD FESTIVAL. Sept 3–6. Kewanee, IL. World's largest pork chop BBQ. Also features professional entertainment, carnival, flea market, Model T races, parade, four-mile run (Hog Stampede) and the Hogatta Regatta. Annually, Labor Day weekend. Est attendance: 60,000. For info: Mark Mikenas, Exec VP, Kewanee Chamber of Commerce, 113 E 2nd St, Kewanee, IL 61443. Phone: (309) 852-2175. Fax: (309) 852-2176. E-mail: chamber@kewanee-il.com. Web: www.kewanee-il.com.

HOISINGTON CELEBRATION. Sept 3–6. Bicentennial Park, Hoisington, KS. Annual event includes dances, demolition derby, parade, car show, carnival, kiddie events, baby contest, float contest. Annually, Labor Day weekend. Est attendance: 30,000. For info: Hoisington Labor Day Committee, 123 N Main, Hoisington, KS 67544. Phone: (620) 653-4311.

ITALY SURRENDERS: ANNIVERSARY. Sept 3, 1943. General Giuseppe Castellano signed three copies of the "short armistice," effectively surrendering "unconditionally" for the Italian government. That same day the British Eighth Army, commanded by General Bernard Montgomery, invaded the Italian mainland.

JOHNSON CITY FIELD DAYS. Sept 3–6. Northside Park, Johnson City, NY. Amusement rides, game booths, live entertainment, food concessions, area's largest fireworks display. The annual celebration benefits many nonprofit organizations in Johnson City. Annually, Labor Day weekend. For info: Johnson City Celebration Committee, 243 Main St, Johnson City, NY 13790. Phone: (607) 798-7861. Fax: (607) 798-7865. E-mail: jcmayor@stny.rr.com.

JOHNSTOWN FOLKFEST. Sept 3–5. Johnstown, PA. A three-day heritage festival held over Labor Day weekend. Includes five performance stages, nationally known music performers from a variety of genres, more than 50 food vendors and free admission. Est attendance: 150,000. For info: Juli Gardill, Johnstown Area Heritage Assn, PO Box 1889, Johnstown, PA 15907-1889. Phone: (814) 539-1889. Web: www.jaha.org.

☆ Chase's 2004 Calendar of Events ☆   Sept 3

MARSHALL COUNTY BLUEBERRY FESTIVAL. Sept 3–6. Plymouth, IN. More than 600 craft and commercial booths, parade, circus, fireworks, 15K run, antique car show, horse pull and luscious blueberry treats. Est attendance: 500,000. For info: Marshall County Blueberry Festival, 220 N Center St, PO Box 639, Plymouth, IN 46563-0639. Phone: (574) 936-5020 or (888) 936-5020. Fax: (574) 936-9845. E-mail: blueberry@blueberryfestival.org. Web: www.blueberryfestival.org.

NATIONAL CHAMPIONSHIP CHUCKWAGON RACES. Sept 3–5. Clinton, AR. 19th annual. Five divisions of chuckwagon races, bronc fanning, Snowy River race, live entertainment, trail rides, barn dance, Western show, Western art, saddles, tack-clothing vendors. Annually, Labor Day weekend. Est attendance: 20,000. For info: Dan Eoff, 2848 Shake Rag Rd, Clinton, AR 72031. Phone: (501) 745-8407. Fax: (501) 745-4416. E-mail: chuckwag@artelco.com. Web: www.chuckwagonraces.com.

NEW MEXICO STATE FAIR. Sept 3–20. Albuquerque, NM. Nationally known recording artists perform at Tingley Coliseum. PRCA rodeo competitions. Thoroughbred and Quarterhorse racing. Villa Hispana and Native American villages. Free entertainment. Est attendance: 622,000. For info: New Mexico State Fair, Attn: Events Dept, PO Box 8546, Albuquerque, NM 87198. Phone: (505) 265-1791. Fax: (505) 268-6753. Web: www.nmstatefair.com.

NORTH CAROLINA APPLE FESTIVAL. Sept 3–6. Hendersonville, NC. Festival includes arts and crafts displays, entertainment, food booths, sports events and much more. Est attendance: 200,000. For info: North Carolina Apple Festival, PO Box 886, Hendersonville, NC 28793. Phone: (828) 697-4557.

OATMEAL FESTIVAL. Sept 3–4. Bertram/Oatmeal, TX. Annual festival to honor Oatmeal, the community and the cereal, and to have a weekend of family fun, good food and a whole lot of foolishness. Annually, Friday and Saturday before Labor Day. Est attendance: 7,000. For info: Oatmeal Fest, PO Box 70, Bertram/Oatmeal, TX 78605. Phone: (512) 355-2197. Fax: (512) 355-3182.

ODYSSEY—A GREEK FESTIVAL. Sept 3–6. Orange, CT. An indoor/outdoor festival celebrating Greek culture, featuring authentic Greek cuisine, live music and marketplace. Est attendance: 15,000. For info: St. Barbara Greek Orthodox Church, 480 Racebrook Rd, Orange, CT 06477. Phone: (203) 795-1347. Web: www.saintbarbara.org. Or: Greater New Haven Conv & Visitors Bureau, One Long Wharf Dr, New Haven, CT, 06511. Phone: (203) 777-8550 or (800) 332-STAY. Fax: (203) 782-7755.

OREGON TRAIL RODEO. Sept 3–5. Hastings, NE. PRCA-sponsored rodeo. Annually, Friday–Sunday of Labor Day weekend. Est attendance: 7,600. For info: Sandy Himmelberg, Genl Mgr, Oregon Trail Rodeo, 947 S Baltimore, Hastings, NE 68901. Phone: (402) 462-3247. Fax: (402) 462-4731. Web: www.adamscountyfairgrounds.com.

PAYSON GOLDEN ONION DAYS. Sept 3–6. Payson, UT. This unique festival includes amusement rides, fireworks, a parade, arts and crafts displays, entertainment, food booths, a demolition derby and much more. Annually, Labor Day weekend. Est attendance: 13,000. For info: Payson Community Services Dir, 439 W Utah Ave, Payson, UT 84651. Phone: (801) 465-5226. Fax: (801) 465-5208.

PENNSYLVANIA ARTS & CRAFTS COLONIAL FESTIVAL. Sept 3–6. Westmoreland Fairgrounds, Greensburg, PA. Step back to Colonial times with more than 200 exhibits of handcrafted furniture, floral arrangements, ceramics, tole, decorative paintings and wrought iron. Civil War encampment, fife and drum music and food booths. Est attendance: 30,000. For info: Debbie & Dave Stoner, Family Festivals Assn, Inc, PO Box 166, Irwin, PA 15642. Phone: (724) 863-4577. Fax: (724) 863-4577. E-mail: familyfestivals@hotmail.com. Web: www.familyfestivals.com.

QATAR: INDEPENDENCE DAY. Sept 3. National holiday. Commemorates the severing in 1971 of treaty with Britain which had handled Qatar's foreign relations.

SAN MARINO: NATIONAL DAY. Sept 3. Public holiday. Honors St. Marinus, the traditional founder of San Marino.

SANTA-CALI-GON DAYS FESTIVAL. Sept 3–6. Historic Square, Independence, MO. Regional celebration for the three trails—Santa Fe, California, Oregon—which all started in Independence. Huge arts and crafts show, live Nashville performers, large carnival midway and free admission. Largest Labor Day weekend event in Kansas City metropolitan area. Est attendance: 225,000. For info: Santa-Cali-Gon Days, 210 W Truman Rd, Independence, MO 64051. Phone: (816) 252-4745. Web: www.santacaligon.com.

"SEARCH FOR TOMORROW" TV PREMIERE: ANNIVERSARY. Sept 3, 1951. This soap lasted for 35 years. It began as a 15-minute program and expanded to 30 minutes in 1968, when performances began to be videotaped instead of airing live. "Search" was set in the town of Henderson, and its central character was Joanne Gardner Barron Tate Vincente Tourneur (played by Mary Stuart). Other notable cast members have included: Don Knotts, Robert Mandan, Ken Kercheval, Jill Clayburgh, Natalie Schafer, Susan Sarandon, Robert Loggia, Hal Linden, Morgan Fairchild, Joe Morton, Robby Benson, Kevin Kline, Cynthia Gibb and Olympia Dukakis.

SHAKESPEARE-ON-THE-ROCKS. Sept 3–26 (Fridays–Sundays). McKelligon Canyon Amphitheater, El Paso, TX. Festival presents three Shakespeare plays in repertory. Renaissance dinner served at 6 PM, showtime 8 PM. Nightly backstage tours, green show. Est attendance: 16,000. For info: El Paso Assn for the Performing Arts, PO Box 31340, El Paso, TX 79931-0340. Phone: (915) 565-6900 or (800) 915-8482. Fax: (915) 565-6999. E-mail: epapa@viva-ep.org. Web: www.viva-ep.org.

SONOMA VALLEY HARVEST WINE AUCTION. Sept 3–6. Sonoma Mission Inn & Spa, Sonoma, CA. Wine tasting, winery dinners, a vintner & grower picnic, golf tournament, live and silent auctions and the main event charity auction which has raised more than $2.8 million during the first ten years. For info or tickets: Sonoma Valley Vintners & Growers Assn. Phone: (707) 935-0803. Web: www.sonomavalleywine.com.

TELLURIDE FILM FESTIVAL. Sept 3–6. Telluride, CO. 31st film festival attracts film lovers, artists and scholars from all over the globe. National and international premieres, world archive treasures, filmmaker discussions, innovative or experimental filmmaking and retrospectives. 8 venues. Annually, Labor Day weekend. Est attendance: 5,000. For info: Telluride Film Festival, The Natl Film Preserve, 379 State St, Portsmouth, NH 03801. Phone: (603) 433-9202. Fax: (603) 433-9206. Web: www.telluridefilmfestival.org.

TREATY OF PARIS ENDS AMERICAN REVOLUTION: ANNIVERSARY. Sept 3, 1783. Treaty between Britain and the US, ending the Revolutionary War, signed at Paris, France. American signatories: John Adams, Benjamin Franklin and John Jay.

VERMONT STATE FAIR. Sept 3–12. Fairgrounds, Rutland, VT. Est attendance: 100,000. For info: Vermont State Fair, 175 S Main St, Rutland, VT 05701. Phone: (802) 775-5200. Web: www.vermontstatefair.net.

WEST VIRGINIA ITALIAN HERITAGE FESTIVAL. Sept 3–5. Clarksburg, WV. Includes Pasta Cook-off—participants cook a pasta dish to compete for prizes. Est attendance: 150,000. For info: West Virgina Italian Heritage Festival Office, Box 1632, Clarksburg, WV 26302. Phone: (304) 622-7314. Fax: (304) 622-5727. E-mail: benvenuto79@aol.com. Web: www.wvihf.com.

WESTERN MINNESOTA STEAM THRESHER'S REUNION. Sept 3–6. Rollag, MN. 51st annual. Visit the living museum of early machines, farm equipment, crafts and pioneer days covering more than 230 open acres and 2½ acres of building space. Features machinery and life from days gone by with operating, rare and unusual equipment, demonstrations of pioneer crafts and farming, a full-size operating railroad locomotive, five passenger cars, boxcar and caboose, authentic log cabins, entertainment and food. For info: Ilene Osten, Secy, Western Steam Thresher's Reunion, 3305 15th Ave S, #E, Fargo, MN 58103. Phone: (218) 789-7792. E-mail: iosten@fargocity.com. Web: www.rollag.com.

WOODSTOCK FAIR. Sept 3–6. Woodstock, CT. Annually, Labor Day weekend. Est attendance: 250,000. For info: Woodstock Fair, PO Box 1, South Woodstock, CT 06267. Phone: (860) 928-3246.

BIRTHDAYS TODAY

Eileen Brennan, 67, actress (*The Last Picture Show, Private Benjamin*), born Los Angeles, CA, Sept 3, 1937.
Kitty Carlisle, 89, actress (*A Night at the Opera*, "To Tell the Truth"), singer, born New Orleans, LA, Sept 3, 1915.
Pauline Collins, 64, actress ("Upstairs, Downstairs"; stage: *Shirley Valentine* [won Olivier Award and Tony Award]), born Exmouth, England, Sept 3, 1940.
Anne Jackson, 78, actress (*Lovers and Other Strangers*), born Allegheny, PA, Sept 3, 1926.
Valerie Perrine, 61, actress (*Lenny, W.C. Fields and Me*), born Galveston, TX, Sept 3, 1943.
Charlie Sheen, 39, actor (*Platoon, Hot Shots!*), born Carlos Irwin Estevez, New York, NY, Sept 3, 1965.
Damon Stoudamire, 31, basketball player, born Portland, OR, Sept 3, 1973.
Mort Walker, 81, cartoonist ("Beetle Bailey"), born Mortimer Walker Addison, El Dorado, KS, Sept 3, 1923.

SEPTEMBER 4 — SATURDAY
Day 248 — 118 Remaining

BRUCKNER, ANTON: BIRTH ANNIVERSARY. Sept 4, 1824. Austrian composer born at Ansfelden, Austria. Died at Vienna, Austria, Oct 11, 1896.

BURNHAM, DANIEL: BIRTH ANNIVERSARY. Sept 4, 1846. American architect and city planner born at Henderson, NY. Daniel Hudson Burnham was an advocate of tall, fireproof buildings, probably the first to be called "sky-scrapers." In 1909 he proposed a long-range city plan for Chicago, IL, that was a key factor in the "forever open, clear and free" policy which resulted in Chicago having the most beautiful lakefront of any major city in the US. Died June 1, 1912, at Heidelberg, Germany.

	S	M	T	W	T	F	S
September				1	2	3	4
	5	6	7	8	9	10	11
2004	12	13	14	15	16	17	18
	19	20	21	22	23	24	25
	26	27	28	29	30		

CAL FARLEY'S BOYS RANCH RODEO. Sept 4–5. Boys Ranch, TX. From young stick-horse riders to more experienced bareback bronc riders, the two-day event provides recognition and rewards for children living at Boys Ranch, Girlstown, USA and Cal Farley's Family Program. Winners in each event are presented with rodeo belt buckles. Special awards are given to the All-Around Cowboy, the All-Around Cowgirl and the Junior All-Around Cowboy. Annually, Labor Day weekend. Est attendance: 10,000. For info: Darci Johnson, PO Box 1890, Amarillo, TX 79174. Phone: (806) 372-2341. Fax: (806) 372-6638. Web: www.calfarley.org.

CANADA: MAYNOOTH MADNESS AND LOGGERS GAMES. Sept 4–5. Maynooth, ON. An exciting, fun-filled weekend for the whole family, with loggers' games and parade, children's activities, petting zoo, pony rides and a craft show featuring original arts and crafts. Est attendance: 7,000. For info: Bancroft and District Chamber of Commerce, PO Box 539, Bancroft, ON, Canada K0L 1C0. Phone: (613) 332-1513. Fax: (613) 332-2119. E-mail: chamber@commerce.bancroft.on.ca. Web: www.bancroftdistrict.com.

"CAPTAIN MIDNIGHT" TV PREMIERE: 50th ANNIVERSARY. Sept 4, 1954. A children's show starring Richard Webb as Captain Midnight, a World War I flying ace who battled crime as part of the Secret Squadron. Webb was joined by Sid Melton as Ichabod (Ikky) Mudd, his assistant, and Olan Soule as Tut, an eccentric scientist. "Captain Midnight" moved to TV from radio, where it was sponsored by Ovaltine. In reruns the name was changed to "Jet Jackson, Flying Commando" because Ovaltine owned the rights to the Captain Midnight name.

CHATEAUBRIAND, FRANCOIS RENE DE: BIRTH ANNIVERSARY. Sept 4, 1768. French poet, novelist, historian, explorer and statesman, witness to the French Revolution. Born at St. Malo, France, he died at Paris, France, July 4, 1848.

CLEVELAND NATIONAL AIR SHOW. Sept 4–6. Burke Lakefront Airport, Cleveland, OH. Country's oldest air show, featuring extensive military and foreign aircraft participation. Est attendance: 80,000. For info: Cleveland Natl Air Show, Burke Lakefront Airport, Cleveland, OH 44114. Phone: (216) 781-0747. Fax: (216) 781-7810. E-mail: cknacle@aol.com. Web: www.clevelandairshow.com.

CLOTHESLINE FAIR. Sept 4–6. Prairie Grove Battlefield State Park, Prairie Grove, AR. 52nd annual fair with more than 200 arts and crafts exhibitors; parade; folk, bluegrass, gospel and country music; square-dancing exhibitions and competitions; living history programs and tours. Annually, Labor Day weekend. Est attendance: 45,000. For info: Rhonda Escobedo, Prairie Grove Battlefield State Park, PO Box 306, Prairie Grove, AR 72753. Phone: (479) 846-2990. Fax: (479) 846-4035.

COMMONWHEEL LABOR DAY WEEKEND ARTS AND CRAFTS FESTIVAL. Sept 4–6. Memorial Park, Manitou Springs, CO. 30th annual juried arts and crafts festival, featuring 120 fine artists and craftsmen and a variety of foods with continuous live entertainment ranging from Celtic harp music to jazz to mime. Est attendance: 30,000. For info: Commonwheel Artists Fair, PO Box 42, Manitou Springs, CO 80829. Phone: (719) 577-7700.

CURAÇAO: ANIMALS' DAY. Sept 4. In Curaçao the Association for the Protection of Animals organizes an animal show for this day and the best-kept animals are awarded prizes.

DENMARK: AARHUS FESTIVAL WEEK. Sept 4–12. Observed from the first Saturday in September and for nine days after since 1965, with theater, ballet, opera, sports, exhibitions and special programs for children. For info: www.aarhusfestuge.dk.

EASTERN IDAHO STATE FAIR. Sept 4–11. Blackfoot, ID. Family fun, amusement rides, food booths, entertainment, tractor pulls and more. Est attendance: 212,000. For info: Manager, Eastern Idaho State Fair, PO Box 250, Blackfoot, ID 83221.

☆ Chase's 2004 Calendar of Events ☆   Sept 4

Phone: (208) 785-2480. Fax: (208) 785-2483. E-mail: theFair@idaho-state-fair.com. Web: www.idaho-state-fair.com.

FIRST ELECTRIC LIGHTING: ANNIVERSARY. Sept 4, 1882. Four hundred electric lights came on in offices on Spruce, Wall, Nassau and Pearl streets in lower Manhattan as Thomas Edison hooked up light bulbs to an underground cable carrying direct current electrical power. Edison had demonstrated his first incandescent light bulb in 1879. See also: "Incandescent Lamp Demonstrated: Anniversary" (Oct 21).

FRANKFORT FALL FESTIVAL. Sept 4–6. Frankfort, IL. One of the largest arts and crafts festivals in the Midwest, featuring 300 crafters, carnival, entertainment tent, community parade and civic food booths. Annually, on Labor Day weekend. Est attendance: 200,000. For info: Lynne Doogan, Exec Dir, Frankfort Chamber of Commerce, 123 Kansas St, Frankfort, IL 60423. Phone: (877) 469-3356. Fax: (815) 469-4352. E-mail: Lynne@frankfortchamber.com. Web: www.frankfortchamber.com.

IROQUOIS INDIAN FESTIVAL. Sept 4–6. Iroquois Indian Museum, Howes Cave, NY. 22nd annual celebration of Iroquois arts. Performing artists, craft demonstrations, speakers, storytellers, native foods, children's activities, Nature Park walks and fine-quality Iroquois art market. Est attendance: 2,000. For info: Iroquois Indian Museum, PO Box 7, Howes Cave, NY 12092. Phone: (518) 296-8949. Fax: (518) 296-8955. E-mail: info@iroquoismuseum.org.

JUBILEE DAYS FESTIVAL. Sept 4–6. Zion, IL. 56th annual communitywide festival featuring arts and crafts, Queen's Pageant, Illinois's largest Labor Day parade and fireworks. Annually, Labor Day weekend. Est attendance: 10,000. For info: Richard Walker, Exec Dir, Jubilee Days Fest, Inc, PO Box 23, Zion, IL 60099. Phone: (847) 746-5500.

KANSAS CITY RENAISSANCE FESTIVAL. Sept 4–Oct 17 (weekends, Labor Day and Columbus Day). Bonner Springs, KS. Re-creation of a 16th-century harvest fair featuring more than 160 artisans selling handcrafted wares and continuous entertainment on 12 stages. Food, special events and the Children's Realm are highlights. Est attendance: 200,000. For info: Director of PR, The Kansas City Renaissance Festival, 207 Westport Rd, Ste 206, Kansas City, MO 64111. Phone: (800) 373-0357. Fax: (816) 561-6493. E-mail: renfest@kcrenfest.com. Web: www.kcrenfest.com.

LITTLE ROCK NINE: ANNIVERSARY. Sept 4, 1957. Governor Oval Faubus called out the Arkansas National Guard to turn away nine black students who had been trying to attend Central High School in Little Rock. President Eisenhower sent in troops to enforce the law allowing the students to integrate the school.

LOS ANGELES, CALIFORNIA, FOUNDED: ANNIVERSARY. Sept 4, 1781. Los Angeles founded by decree and called "El Pueblo de Nuestra Senora La Reina de Los Angeles de Porciuncula."

NEWSPAPER CARRIER DAY. Sept 4. Anniversary of the hiring of the first "newsboy" in the US, 10-year-old Barney Flaherty, who is said to have answered the following classified advertisement which appeared in The New York Sun in 1833: "To the Unemployed—a number of steady men can find employment by vending this paper. A liberal discount is allowed to those who buy to sell again."

OLDE-TIME ANTIQUES AND COLLECTIBLES FAIRE. Sept 4. Toms River, NJ. More than 100 dealers, appraisals, displays and demonstrations and museum exhibits. Free admission. 20th annual. Annually, Saturday of Labor Day weekend. Est attendance: 5,000. For info: Ocean County Historical Society, PO Box 2191, 26 Hadley Ave, Toms River, NJ 08754-2191. Phone: (732) 341-1880. Fax: (732) 341-4372. Web: www.oceancountyhistory.org.

POLK, SARAH CHILDRESS: BIRTH ANNIVERSARY. Sept 4, 1803. Wife of James Knox Polk, 11th president of the US. Born at Murfreesboro, TN, and died at Nashville, TN, Aug 14, 1891.

POWERS' CROSSROADS COUNTRY FAIR AND ART FESTIVAL. Sept 4–6. Newnan, GA. 300 top US artists and craftsmen. Old plantation skills revived including gristmill, blacksmithing; entertainment, continuous music and down-home cooking. Est attendance: 45,000. For info: Coweta Festivals, Inc, 4766 W Hwy 34, Newnan, GA 30263. Phone: (770) 253-2011. Fax: (770) 253-8180. E-mail: cowetafestivals@charter.net.

SCOTLAND: BRAEMAR ROYAL HIGHLAND GATHERING. Sept 4. Princess Royal and Duke of Fife Memorial Park, Braemar, Grampian. Kilted clansmen from all over the world gather. Traditional activities including tossing cabers, dancing and playing bagpipes. Est attendance: 18,000. For info: Mr W.A. Meston, Secretary, Coilacriech, Ballater, Aberdeenshire, Scotland AB35 5UH. Phone/fax: (44) (133) 975-5377. E-mail: info@braemargathering.org.

SEPTEMBER SKIRMISH. Sept 4–5. Point Mallard, Decatur, AL. Staged in honor of local Confederate generals John Hunt Morgan and Joe Wheeler. More than 200 authentically clad Yankee and Rebel soldiers meet in daily battles. Visitors may join a young recruit and follow his life as a soldier during the Candlelight Camp Tour on Saturday night or join the Civil War roundtable discussion. Est attendance: 1,000. For info: Jacklyn Bailey, Decatur CVB, 719 6th Ave SE, PO Box 2349, Decatur, AL 35602. Phone: (800) 524-6181. E-mail: info@decaturcvb.org. Web: www.decaturcvb.org.

SNOWBIRD OKTOBERFEST. Sept 4–6. (Also Sept 11, 13, 18–19, 25–26, Oct 2–3, 9–10). Snowbird, UT. Festival includes traditional European music, shopping, dancing and food. For info: Snowbird & Ski Summer Resort, PO Box 929000, Snowbird, UT 84092-9000. Phone: (801) 742-2222. Fax: (801) 933-2298. E-mail: info@snowbird.com. Web: www.snowbird.com.

STA-BIL NATIONALS CHAMPIONSHIP LAWN MOWER RACE. Sept 4–5. Mansfield, OH. Five classes of races for winners of regional races held across the US. Mowers will travel at speeds ranging from 10 mph to more than 50 mph. Est attendance: 2,000. For info: US Lawn Mower Racing Assn, 1812 Glenview Rd, Glenview, IL 60025. Phone: (847) 729-7363. E-mail: letsmow@aol.com. Web: www.letsmow.com/.

TOOLS AND SKILLS THAT BUILT THE COLONY. Sept 4. Wormsloe Historic Site, Savannah, GA. Living history demonstrations relating to the tools and skills that were used to build the colony. These will include woodworking, blacksmithing, spinning, candlemaking and more. Museum, film and trails. 11 AM to 4 PM. Annually, the Saturday before Labor Day. Est attendance: 500. For info: Wormsloe State Historic Site, 7601 Skidaway Rd, Savannah, GA 31406. Phone: (912) 353-3023. E-mail: wormsloe@g-net.net.

WESTFEST. Sept 4–5. West, TX. West celebrates its Czech heritage with folk dances, Czech pastries, sausage, polka music, arts and crafts, children's area, 5K run, parade. Est attendance: 35,000. For info: Westfest, Box 65, West, TX 76691. Phone: (254) 826-5058. Web: www.westfest.com.

WORLD CHAMPIONSHIP BARBECUE GOAT COOK-OFF AND ARTS AND CRAFTS FAIR. Sept 4. Richards Park, Brady, TX. 31st annual cook-off to promote Brady/McCulloch County and the sheep and goat industry. Arts and crafts fair featuring local and statewide artists. Est attendance: 17,000. For info: Brady/McCulloch County Chamber of Commerce, 101 E First St, Brady, TX 76825. Phone: (915) 597-3491. Fax: (915) 792-9181. E-mail: dpcofc@hotmail.com. Web: www.bradytx.com.

WRIGHT, RICHARD: BIRTH ANNIVERSARY. Sept 4, 1908. Novelist and short story writer whose works included *Native Son, Uncle Tom's Children* and *Black Boy*, born at Natchez, MS. Wright died at Paris, France, Nov 28, 1960.

BIRTHDAYS TODAY

Mitzi Gaynor, 73, singer, dancer, actress (*South Pacific*), born Franchesca Mitzi Marlene de Charney von Gerber, Chicago, IL, Sept 4, 1931.

Paul Harvey, 86, broadcaster, commentator ("The Rest of the Story"), born Tulsa, OK, Sept 4, 1918.

Judith Ivey, 53, actress (*Compromising Positions, Brighton Beach Memoirs*; stage: *Steaming*), born El Paso, TX, Sept 4, 1951.

Michael Joseph (Mike) Piazza, 36, baseball player, born Norristown, PA, Sept 4, 1968.

Carlos Romero Barcelo, 72, US Resident Commissioner (D, Commonwealth of Puerto Rico), born San Juan, Puerto Rico, Sept 4, 1932.

Jennifer Salt, 60, actress ("Soap"), born Los Angeles, CA, Sept 4, 1944.

Ione Skye, 34, actress (*Say Anything . . .; Gas, Food, Lodging*), born Hertfordshire, England, Sept 4, 1970.

Thomas Sturges (Tom) Watson, 55, golfer, born Kansas City, MO, Sept 4, 1949.

Damon Wayans, 44, actor, comedian ("In Living Color"), born New York, NY, Sept 4, 1960.

SEPTEMBER 5 — SUNDAY
Day 249 — 117 Remaining

BABE RUTH'S FIRST PRO HOMER: 90th ANNIVERSARY. Sept 5, 1914. Babe Ruth hit his first home run as a professional while playing for Providence in the International League, a type of minor league affiliate of the Boston Red Sox. He pitched a one-hit shutout against Toronto.

BE LATE FOR SOMETHING DAY. Sept 5. To create a release from the stresses and strains resulting from a consistent need to be on time. For info: Les Waas, Pres, Procrastinators' Club of America, Inc, Box 712, Bryn Athyn, PA 19009. Phone: (215) 947-9020. Fax: (215) 947-7210. E-mail: procrastinators_club_of_america@yahoo.com.

BELGIUM: HISTORICAL PROCESSION. Sept 5. Tournai. Traditional cultural observance. Annually, the Sunday closest to Sept 8.

CAGE, JOHN: BIRTH ANNIVERSARY. Sept 5, 1912. Avant-garde American composer John Cage was born at Los Angeles, CA. He pioneered the experimental music and performance art schools. He used non-traditional instruments such as flower pots and cowbells in innovative situations, such as performances governed by chance, in which the *I Ching* was consulted to determine the direction of the performance. In 1978 he was elected to the American Academy of Arts and Sciences, and in 1982 was awarded France's highest honor for cultural contributions, Commandeur de l'Ordre des Arts et des Lettres. He died Aug 12, 1992, at New York, NY.

CARNOVSKY, MORRIS: BIRTH ANNIVERSARY. Sept 5, 1897. American actor Morris Carnovsky was born at St. Louis, MO. In 1931 with actor Lee Strasberg and others he founded the Group Theater at New York, NY. He was blacklisted in the 1950s by the House Un-American Activities Committee, but was still asked by John Houseman to perform in the American Shakespeare Festival in 1956 and began a successful Shakespearean career. He was elected to the Theater Hall of Fame in 1979. Carnovsky died Sept 1, 1992, at Easton, CT.

FIRST CONTINENTAL CONGRESS ASSEMBLY: ANNIVERSARY. Sept 5, 1774. The first assembly of this forerunner of the US Congress took place at Philadelphia, PA. Peyton Randolph, delegate from Virginia, was elected president.

GERALD FORD: ASSASSINATION ATTEMPTS: ANNIVERSARY. Sept 5, 1975. Lynette A. "Squeaky" Fromme, a follower of convicted murderer Charles Manson, attempted to shoot President Gerald Ford. On Sept 22 of the same year, another attempt on Ford's life occurred when Sara Jane Moore shot at him.

HARVEST WINE CELEBRATION. Sept 5–6. Livermore, CA. The Harvest Wine Celebration is an open-house event offering the public an opportunity to visit 26 wineries, sample wines, learn more about this historic wine region, enjoy entertainment and shop for arts and crafts. Shuttle bus service is available between the wineries. Annually, Labor Day weekend. Est attendance: 10,000. For info: Livermore Valley Winegrowers Assn, 1984 Railroad Ave, Ste A, Livermore, CA 94550. Phone: (925) 447-9463. Fax: (925) 447-0433. E-mail: lvwa@livermorewine.com.

ISRAELI OLYMPIAD MASSACRE: ANNIVERSARY. Sept 5–6, 1972. Eleven members of the Israeli Olympic Team were killed in an attack on the Olympic Village at Munich and attempted kidnapping of team members. Four of seven guerrillas, members of the Black September faction of the Palestinian Liberation Army, were also killed. In retaliation, Israeli jets bombed Palestinian positions at Lebanon and Syria on Sept 8, 1972.

ITALY: HISTORICAL REGATTA. Sept 5. Venice. Traditional competition among two-oar racing gondolas, preceded by a procession of Venetian ceremonial boats of the epoch of the Venetian Republic. Annually, the first Sunday in September.

ITALY: JOUST OF THE SARACEN. Sept 5. Arezzo. The first Sunday in September is set aside for the Giostra del Saracino, a tilting contest of the 13th century, with knights in armor.

JAMES, JESSE: BIRTH ANNIVERSARY. Sept 5, 1847. Western legend and bandit Jesse Woodson James was born at Centerville (now Kearney), MO. His criminal exploits were glorified and romanticized by writers for Eastern readers looking for stories of Western adventure and heroism. After the Civil War, James and his brother, Frank, formed a group of eight outlaws who robbed banks, stagecoaches and stores. In 1873 the James gang began holding up trains. The original James gang was put out of business Sept 7, 1876, while attempting to rob a bank at Northfield, MN. Every member of the gang except for the James brothers was killed or captured. The brothers formed a new gang and resumed their criminal careers in 1879. Two years later, the governor of Missouri offered a $10,000 reward for their capture, dead or alive. On Apr 3, 1882, at St. Joseph, MO, Robert Ford, a member of the gang, shot 34-year-old Jesse in the back of the head and claimed the reward.

JERRY LEWIS MUSCULAR DYSTROPHY ASSOCIATION TELETHON. Sept 5–6. The annual Labor Day TV broadcast to raise money for 40 neuromuscular diseases. For info: Muscular Dystrophy Assn, 3300 E Sunrise Dr, Tucson, AZ 85718. Phone: (800) 572-1717. Web: www.mdausa.org.

September 2004

S	M	T	W	T	F	S
			1	2	3	4
5	6	7	8	9	10	11
12	13	14	15	16	17	18
19	20	21	22	23	24	25
26	27	28	29	30		

KOESTLER, ARTHUR: BIRTH ANNIVERSARY. Sept 5, 1905. Born at Budapest, Hungary, Koestler is best known for his novel about his disillusionment with Communism, *Darkness at Noon*, and for *The God That Failed*. Died at London, England, Mar 3, 1983.

"THE MacNEIL–LEHRER NEWSHOUR" TV PREMIERE: ANNIVERSARY. Sept 5, 1983. Originally, this PBS news show was called "The MacNeil-Lehrer Report" and was on every weeknight for a half hour starting in 1976. Robert MacNeil and Jim Lehrer were joined by Charlayne Hunter-Gault and Judy Woodruff. In 1983 the show was expanded to an hour and became TV's first regularly scheduled daily hour news show. The show has been praised for its depth and objectivity. In 1995 Robert MacNeil retired and the show was retitled "The Newshour with Jim Lehrer."

MICHIGAN'S GREAT FIRE OF 1881: ANNIVERSARY. Sept 5, 1881. According to Michigan Historical Commission, "Small fires were burning in the forests of the 'Thumb area of Michigan,' tinder-dry after a long, hot summer, when a gale swept in from the southwest on Sept 5, 1881. Fanned into an inferno, the fire raged for three days. A million acres were devastated in Sanilac and Huron counties alone. At least 125 persons died, and thousands more were left destitute. The new American Red Cross won support for its prompt aid to the fire victims. This was the first disaster relief furnished by this great organization."

NATIONAL EMERGENCY PREPAREDNESS WEEK. Sept 5–12. To inspire employers and their employees to learn about and prepare an emergency and/or disaster preparedness plan for their families. Also to provide educational programs in the workplace and community designed to help families reduce stress, anxiety and impact on job performance, and to ultimately minimize serious consequences to people, property and business continuity. For info: Sara Shepard, 1450 S New Wilke Rd, #102, Arlington Heights, IL 60005. Phone: (877) 670-7444. Fax: (847) 670-7466. E-mail: sara@getprepared.org. Web: www.getprepared.org.

NATIONAL WAFFLE WEEK. Sept 5–11. A celebration of the wonderful, crispy breakfast orb and its contributions to American society. Annually, the first week of September. For info: Pat Warner, PO Box 6450, Norcross, GA 30091. Phone: (770) 729-5842. Fax: (770) 729-5999. E-mail: patwarner@wafflehouse.com. Web: www.waffleweek.com.

NIELSEN, ARTHUR CHARLES: BIRTH ANNIVERSARY. Sept 5, 1897. Marketing research engineer, founder of AC Nielsen Company, in 1923, known for radio and TV audience surveys, was born at Chicago, IL, and died there June 1, 1980.

SCANDINAVIAN FEST. Sept 5. Waterloo Village, Stanhope, NJ. Celebrate and sample the cultures, traditions and contemporary life of the Nordic countries: Denmark, Estonia, Finland, Iceland, Norway and Sweden through food, entertainment, music, dancing, handicrafts and lectures. Annually, the Sunday before Labor Day. Est attendance: 6,000. For info: Carl Anderson, PO Box 5103, Bethlehem, PA 18015. Phone: (610) 868-7525. E-mail: info@ScanFest.org. Web: www.ScanFest.org.

SPACE MILESTONE: *VOYAGER 1* (US). Sept 5, 1977. Twin of *Voyager 2* which was launched Aug 20. On Feb 18, 1998, *Voyager 1* set a new distance record when after more than 20 years in space it reached 6.5 billion miles from Earth.

SWITZERLAND: SAINT GOTTHARD AUTOMOBILE TUNNEL OPENING: ANNIVERSARY. Sept 5, 1980. The longest underground motorway in the world, the St. Gotthard Auto Tunnel in Switzerland, was opened to traffic. More than 10 miles long, requiring $417,000,000 and 10 years for construction, it became the most direct route from Switzerland to the southern regions of the continent. The St. Gotthard Pass, the main passage since the Middle Ages, was closed much of every year by massive snow drifts.

ZANUCK, DARRYL F.: BIRTH ANNIVERSARY. Sept 5, 1902. Born at Wahoo, NE, Darryl F. Zanuck became a celebrated—and controversial—movie producer. He was also a cofounder of Twentieth Century Studios, which later merged with Fox. His film credits include *The Jazz Singer* (the first sound picture), *Forever Amber*, *The Snake Pit* and *The Grapes of Wrath*. He died Dec 21, 1979, at Palm Springs, CA.

BIRTHDAYS TODAY

Kristian Alfonso, 40, actress ("Days of Our Lives," "Melrose Place"), born Brockton, MA, Sept 5, 1964.
William Devane, 65, actor ("From Here to Eternity," "Knots Landing"), born Albany, NY, Sept 5, 1939.
Dennis Dugan, 58, actor (*The Howling, Parenthood, Problem Child*), born Wheaton, IL, Sept 5, 1946.
Cathy Lee Guisewite, 54, cartoonist (*Cathy*), born Dayton, OH, Sept 5, 1950.
Carol Lawrence, 69, singer, actress (*West Side Story*), born Carol Maria Laraia, Melrose Park, IL, Sept 5, 1935.
Rose McGowan, 31, actress (*Jawbreaker*, "Charmed"), born Florence, Italy, Sept 5, 1973.
Bob Newhart, 75, comedian ("The Bob Newhart Show," "Newhart"), born Chicago, IL, Sept 5, 1929.
Raquel Welch, 62, actress (*The Three Musketeers, Woman of the Year*), model, born Chicago, IL, Sept 5, 1942.
Dweezil Zappa, 35, singer, actor ("Normal Life"), born Hollywood, CA, Sept 5, 1969.

SEPTEMBER 6 — MONDAY
Day 250 — 116 Remaining

ADDAMS, JANE: BIRTH ANNIVERSARY. Sept 6, 1860. American worker for peace, social welfare, rights of women, founder of Hull House (Chicago), cowinner of Nobel Prize, 1931. Born at Cedarville, IL, she died May 21, 1935, at Chicago, IL.

BALTIC STATES' INDEPENDENCE RECOGNIZED: ANNIVERSARY. Sept 6, 1991. The Soviet government recognized the independence of the Baltic states—Latvia, Estonia and Lithuania. The action came 51 years after the Baltic states were annexed by the Soviet Union. All three Baltic states had earlier declared their independence, and many nations had already recognized them diplomatically, including the US, Sept 2, 1991.

BEECHER, CATHARINE ESTHER: BIRTH ANNIVERSARY. Sept 6, 1800. Catharine Esther Beecher was born at East Hampton, NY. In addition to teaching herself mathematics, philosophy and Latin, Beecher had been formally educated in art and music. An early advocate for equal education for women, she founded the Hartford Female Seminary, which was widely recognized for its advanced curriculum. She was also instrumental in the founding of women's colleges in Iowa, Illinois and Wisconsin. Beecher died May 12, 1878, at Elmira, NY.

461

☆ Chase's 2004 Calendar of Events ☆

Sept 6

BUHL DAY. Sept 6. Buhl Farm, Sharon, PA. To honor the laboring man. Observed annually on Labor Day. Est attendance: 25,000. For info: Karen Campman-Emmett, 36 Dogwood Ln, West Middlesex, PA 16159. Phone: (724) 528-1071. E-mail: kpemmett@worldnet.att.net.

BULGARIA: UNIFICATION DAY. Sept 6. National holiday. Commemorates the anniversary of the reunification of the southern part of Bulgaria with the rest of the country in 1885.

CANADA: LABOR DAY. Sept 6. Annually, the first Monday in September.

DALTON, JOHN: BIRTH ANNIVERSARY. Sept 6, 1766. English chemist, physicist, teacher and developer of atomic theory, was born at Eaglesfield, near Cockermouth, England. Dalton died at Manchester, England, July 27, 1844.

FIRST RADIO BROADCAST OF A PRIZEFIGHT: ANNIVERSARY. Sept 6, 1920. In the first boxing match broadcast on radio, Jack Dempsey knocked out Billy Miske in the third round of a scheduled 10-round fight.

GREAT BATHTUB RACE. Sept 6. Nome, AK. 27th annual. Bathtubs mounted on wheels are raced down Front Street. Each team has five members, one in the tub, with bubbles apparent in the bath water. Tub must be full of water at beginning and have at least 10 gallons at the finish line. The other four team members must wear large-brim hats and suspenders and carry either a bar of soap, washcloth, towel or bath mat for the entire race. Winning team claims trophy: a statue of Miss Piggy and Kermit taking a bath, which is handed down from year to year. Annually, at noon on Labor Day. Est attendance: 1,500. For info: Rasmussen's Music Mart, PO Box 2, Nome, AK 99762-0002. Phone: (907) 443-2798 or (907) 443-2919. Fax: (907) 443-5777.

LABOR DAY. Sept 6. Legal public holiday. Public Law 90–363 sets Labor Day on the first Monday in September. Observed in all states. First observance believed to have been a parade on Tuesday, Sept 5, 1882, at New York, NY, probably organized by Peter J. McGuire, a Carpenters and Joiners Union secretary. In 1883 a union resolution declared "the first Monday in September of each year a Labor Day." By 1893 more than half of the states were observing Labor Day on one or another day and a bill to establish Labor Day as a federal holiday was introduced in Congress. On June 28, 1894, President Grover Cleveland signed into law an act making the first Monday in September a legal holiday for federal employees and the District of Columbia. Canada also celebrates Labor Day on the first Monday in September. In most other countries, Labor Day is observed May 1.

September 2004	S	M	T	W	T	F	S
				1	2	3	4
	5	6	7	8	9	10	11
	12	13	14	15	16	17	18
	19	20	21	22	23	24	25
	26	27	28	29	30		

LAFAYETTE, MARQUIS DE: BIRTH ANNIVERSARY. Sept 6, 1757. French general and aristocrat, Marquis de Lafayette, whose full name was Marie-Joseph-Paul-Yves-Roch-Gilbert du Motier, came to America to assist in the revolutionary cause and volunteered to serve without compensation. He was awarded a major-generalship and began a long friendship with the American commander-in-chief, George Washington. After an alliance was signed with France, he returned to his native country and persuaded Louis XVI to send a 6,000-man force to assist the Americans. On his return, he was given command of an army at Virginia and was instrumental in forcing the surrender of Lord Cornwallis at Yorktown, leading to the end of the war and American independence. He was called "The Hero of Two Worlds" and was appointed a brigadier general on his return to France in 1782. He became a leader of the liberal aristocrats during the early days of the French revolution. As the commander of the newly formed national guard of Paris, he rescued Louis XVI and Marie-Antoinette from a crowd that stormed Versailles Oct 6, 1789. His popularity waned after his guards opened fire on angry demonstrators demanding abdication of the king in 1791. He fled to Austria with the overthrow of the monarchy in 1792, returning when Napoleon Bonaparte came to power. Born at Chavaniac, he died at Paris, May 20, 1834.

MACKINAC BRIDGE WALK. Sept 6. St. Ignace, MI. 47th annual event. Labor Day is the only day of the year pedestrians are permitted to walk across the five-mile-long span, one of the world's longest suspension bridges, connecting Michigan's two peninsulas. Walk is from St. Ignace to Mackinaw City. Est attendance: 55,000. For info: Mackinac Bridge Authority, 333 Interstate 75, St. Ignace, MI 49781. Phone: (906) 643-7600. Fax: (906) 643-7668. Web: www.mackinacbridge.org.

MOON PHASE: LAST QUARTER. Sept 6. Moon enters Last Quarter phase at 11:10 AM, EDT.

NATIONAL PAYROLL WEEK. Sept 6–10. Founded in 1995 by the American Payroll Association to recognize the important partnership of America's workers and the payroll professionals who pay them on time and accurately. Provides an annual opportunity to proudly proclaim "America Works Because We're Working for America!" For info: Lori Martin, American Payroll Assn, 660 N Main Ave, Ste 100, San Antonio, TX 78205. Phone: (210) 226-4600. Fax: (210) 224-2028. E-mail: lmartin@americanpayroll.org. Web: www.nationalpayrollweek.com.

PAKISTAN: DEFENSE OF PAKISTAN DAY. Sept 6. National holiday. Commemorates the Indo-Pakistan War of 1965.

PROTECTING YOUR HOME FURNISHINGS WEEK. Sept 6–11. Week dedicated to taking care of the valuable furnishings in your home—furniture, window treatments, paintings, objects of art, decorative accessories, etc. A Home Furnishings laminated maintenance chart is now available: "How to Care for Your Valuable Furnishings"—weekly, monthly and annually with special prevention and repair tips ($5). Annually, the second week in September before holiday preparations begin. For info: Darvas Interiors, 1835 F Tanglewood Dr, Glenview, IL 60025. Phone: (847) 832-1414. Fax: (847) 832-1417. E-mail: DarvasInteriors@msn.com.

ROSE, BILLY: BIRTH ANNIVERSARY. Sept 6, 1899. Billy Rose (William S. Rosenberg), American theatrical producer, author, songwriter and husband of Fanny Brice, was born at New York, NY. His songs include: "That Old Gang of Mine," "Me and My Shadow," "Without a Song," "It's Only a Paper Moon" and hundreds of others. Rose died at Montego Bay, Jamaica, Feb 10, 1966.

SAINT PETERSBURG NAME RESTORED: ANNIVERSARY. Sept 6, 1991. Russian legislators voted to restore the name Saint Petersburg to the nation's second largest city. The city had been known as Leningrad for 67 years in honor of the Soviet Union's founder, Vladimir I. Lenin. The city, founded in 1703 by Peter the Great, has had three names in the 20th century with Russian leaders changing its German-sounding name to Petrograd at the beginning of WWI in 1914 and Soviet Communist

☆ Chase's 2004 Calendar of Events ☆   Sept 6–7

leaders changing its name to Leningrad in 1924 following their leader's death.

SNAKE RIVER DUCK RACE. Sept 6. Nome, AK. 15th annual race. Since 1992 thousands of plastic ducks have negotiated the historic Snake River to Nome's power plant. 2 PM. For info: Leo B. Rasmussen, Nome Rotary Club, PO Box 275, Nome, AK 99762. Phone: (907) 443-2798. E-mail: leaknome@nook.net.

STEARMAN FLY-IN DAYS. Sept 6–12. Galesburg, IL. The largest gathering of Stearman airplanes—the biplane trainers that gave wings to more military pilots than any other series of aircraft in the world. Est attendance: 7,500. For info: Galesburg Area CVB, PO Box 60, Galesburg, IL 61402-0060. Phone: (309) 343-2485. Fax: (309) 343-2521. E-mail: visitors@visitgalesburg.com. Web: www.visitgalesburg.com.

STOCK EXCHANGE HOLIDAY (LABOR DAY). Sept 6. The holiday schedules for the various exchanges are subject to change if relevant rules, regulations or exchange policies are revised. If you have questions, phone: American Stock Exchange (212) 306-1000; Chicago Board of Trade (312) 435-3500; Chicago Board of Options Exchange (312) 786-5600; New York Stock Exchange (212) 656-2065; Pacific Stock Exchange (415) 393-4000; Philadelphia Stock Exchange (215) 496-5000.

SWAZILAND: INDEPENDENCE DAY: ANNIVERSARY. Sept 6. National holiday. Commemorates attainment of independence from Britain in 1968. Also called Somhlolo Day in honor of the great 19th-century Swazi leader.

UNITED NATIONS: MILLENNIUM SUMMIT: ANNIVERSARY. Sept 6–8, 2000. More than 150 world leaders met at the United Nations in New York City, the largest gathering of such leaders in history. Among the kings, prime ministers, presidents and generals attending were US President Bill Clinton, Fidel Castro and Yasser Arafat. These leaders adopted a declaration which committed them to promote democracy, strengthen respect for human rights, reverse the spread of AIDS, cut poverty, protect our planet and improve the ability of the UN to keep the peace.

WAIKIKI ROUGHWATER SWIM. Sept 6. Waikiki Beach, Honolulu, HI. The 35th annual swim is 2.4 miles from Sans Souci Beach to Duke Kahanamoku Beach. "The World's Most Prestigious Open Water Swimming Event." Preregistration is required. Annually, Labor Day. Est attendance: 1,000. For info: Jim Anderson, One Keahole Place #1607, Honolulu, HI 96825-3414. Phone: (808) 396-8866. Fax: (808) 396-8868. E-mail: waikikijim@aol.com. Web: www.WaikikiRoughwaterSwim.com.

"WYATT EARP" TV PREMIERE: ANNIVERSARY. Sept 6, 1955. Officially titled "The Life and Legend of Wyatt Earp," this half-hour series marked the beginning of the trend toward "adult Westerns." It was loosely based on fact, with Hugh O'Brian as Earp, marshall of Dodge City, KS, and later of Tombstone, AZ.

BIRTHDAYS TODAY

Jane Curtin, 57, actress ("Saturday Night Live," "3rd Rock from the Sun"), comedienne, born Cambridge, MA, Sept 6, 1947.
Jeff Foxworthy, 46, comedian (You Know You're a Redneck), actor ("The Jeff Foxworthy Show"), author (No Shirt, No Shoes . . . No Problem), born Atlanta, GA, Sept 6, 1958.
Tim Henman, 30, tennis player, born Oxford, Great Britian, Sept 6, 1974.
Swoosie Kurtz, 60, actress ("Sisters," The World According to Garp; Tony for The House of Blue Leaves), born Omaha, NE, Sept 6, 1944.
Rosie Perez, 40, actress (King of the Jungle, White Men Can't Jump), born Brooklyn, NY, Sept 6, 1964.
Justin Whalin, 30, actor ("Charles in Charge," "Lois & Clark"), born San Francisco, CA, Sept 6, 1974.
Jo Anne Worley, 67, comedienne, actress ("Rowan & Martin's Laugh-In"), born Lowell, IA, Sept 6, 1937.

TEA PLANT.   SUGAR CANE.   COFFEE PLANT.

SEPTEMBER 7 — TUESDAY
Day 251 — 115 Remaining

ANOTHER LOOK UNLIMITED DAY. Sept 7. Your house, garage, barn, shed, attic or yard. Encourages everyone to look over their possessions and give surplus to charity or reuse in other projects. Lessen the flow to landfills. Annually, the day after Labor Day. For info: ENVIRA MYNYTL, PO Box 220, Holts Summit, MO 65043. E-mail: envira-myntyl@cal-a-co.com.

BRAZIL: INDEPENDENCE DAY. Sept 7. Declared independence from Portugal in 1822. National holiday.

CORBETT-SULLIVAN PRIZE FIGHT: ANNIVERSARY. Sept 7, 1892. John L. Sullivan was knocked out by James J. Corbett in the 21st round of a prize fight at New Orleans, LA. It was the first major fight under the Marquess of Queensberry Rules.

DO IT! DAY (aka FIGHT PROCRASTINATION DAY). Sept 7. Feeling overwhelmed? Too many things left undone? Hard to focus? Today is your day to turn your Do Its into Did Its! Annually, the first Wednesday after Labor Day. For info: Productivity Coach Ethel Cook, 4 Hilda Rd, Bedford, MA 01730. Phone: (781) 275-2326. Fax: (781) 275-7136. E-mail: coachethel@ethelcook.com.

"THE FLYING NUN" TV PREMIERE: ANNIVERSARY. Sept 7, 1967. This sitcom about a nun at a convent in Puerto Rico who discovers that she can fly starred Sally Field as Elsie Ethrington (Sister Bertrille) and featured Madeleine Sherwood, Marge Redmond, Shelley Morrison, Alejandro Rey and Vito Scotti.

GRANDMA MOSES DAY. Sept 7. Anna Mary (Robertson) Moses, modern primitive American painter born at Greenwich, NY, Sept 7, 1860. Started painting at the age of 78. Her 100th birthday was proclaimed Grandma Moses Day in New York state. Died at Hoosick Falls, NY, Dec 13, 1961.

HOLLY, BUDDY: BIRTH ANNIVERSARY. Sept 7, 1936. American popular music performer, composer and bandleader. Called one of the most innovative and influential musicians of his time, he was a pioneer of rock 'n' roll. His hits included "That'll Be the Day" and "Peggy Sue." Born Charles Harden Holley, at Lubbock, TX, he died at age 22 in an airplane crash near Mason City, IA, Feb 3, 1959.

LAWRENCE, JACOB: BIRTH ANNIVERSARY. Sept 7, 1917. African-American painter, born at Atlantic City, NJ. Lawrence was best known for his series of historical paintings on John Brown and on the migration of African Americans out of the South. A recipient of the NAACP's Spingarn Medal, he won many other awards during his lifetime. Lawrence died June 9, 2000, in Seattle, WA.

"NEITHER SNOW NOR RAIN" DAY: 90th ANNIVERSARY. Sept 7, 1914. Anniversary of the opening to the public on Labor Day 1914 of the New York Post Office Building at Eighth Avenue between 31st and 33rd Streets. On the front of this building was an inscription supplied by William M. Kendall of the architectural firm that planned the building. The inscription, a free translation from Herodotus, reads: "Neither snow nor rain nor heat nor gloom of night stays these couriers from the swift completion of their appointed rounds." This has long been believed to be the motto of the US Post Office and Postal Service. They have, in fact, no motto . . . but the legend remains. [Info from: New York Post Office, Public Info Office and US Postal Service.]

463

Sept 7–8 ☆ Chase's 2004 Calendar of Events ☆

PLAY DAYS. Sept 7–11. In a world filled with downsizing, rightsizing and shaftsizing, we need humor to reaffirm our humanity and sanity. In the week after Labor Day, the HUMOR Project will playfully spread the word on 1,001 ways to add humor to your life and work. Jest for success—humor works—the funny line and bottom line intersect! Annually, the Tuesday through Saturday after Labor Day. For a free information packet on the positive power of humor, send a $1.06 SASE. For info: The HUMOR Project, 480 Broadway, Ste 210-C, Sarasota Springs, NY 12866-2288. Phone: (518) 587-8770. Fax: (518) 587-8771. E-mail: chase @HumorProject.com. Web: www.HumorProject.com.

QUEEN ELIZABETH I: BIRTH ANNIVERSARY. Sept 7, 1533. Queen of England, daughter of Henry VIII and Anne Boleyn, after whom the Elizabethan era was named, was born at Greenwich Palace. She ascended the throne in 1558 at the age of 25. During her reign, the British defeated the Spanish Armada in July 1588, the Anglican Church was essentially established and England became a world power. She died at Richmond, England, Mar 24, 1603.

"TRUTH OR CONSEQUENCES" TV PREMIERE: ANNIVERSARY. Sept 7, 1950. This game show lasted for many years on both radio and TV. The half-hour show was based on a parlor game: contestants who failed to answer a question before the buzzer (nicknamed Beulah) went off had to perform stunts (i.e. pay the consequences). Ralph Edwards created and hosted the show until 1954, then it became a prime-time show hosted by Jack Bailey. Bob Barker succeeded him in 1966 and hosted it through its syndicated run. In 1977 the show was revived as "The New Truth or Consequences" with Bob Hilton as host.

BIRTHDAYS TODAY

Corbin Bernsen, 50, actor ("LA Law," "Ryan's Hope," *Major League*), born North Hollywood, CA, Sept 7, 1954.
Susan Blakely, 54, actress (*The Way We Were, The Lords of Flatbush, Shampoo*), born Frankfurt, Germany, Sept 7, 1950.
Michael DeBakey, 96, distinguished heart surgeon, born Lake Charles, LA, Sept 7, 1908.
Michael Feinstein, 48, singer, pianist, born Columbus, OH, Sept 7, 1956.
Arthur Ferrante, 83, pianist (Ferrante and Teicher), composer, born New York, NY, Sept 7, 1921.
Chrissie Hynde, 53, lead singer (Pretenders), songwriter, born Akron, OH, Sept 7, 1951.
Daniel Ken Inouye, 80, US Senator (D, Hawaii), born Honolulu, HI, Sept 7, 1924.
Julie Kavner, 53, actress (*Radio Days*, "Rhoda," Marge Simpson's voice on "The Simpsons"), born Los Angeles, CA, Sept 7, 1951.

	S	M	T	W	T	F	S
September				1	2	3	4
2004	5	6	7	8	9	10	11
	12	13	14	15	16	17	18
	19	20	21	22	23	24	25
	26	27	28	29	30		

Elia Kazan, 95, filmmaker (*On the Waterfront, East of Eden*), born Elia Kazanjoglou, Constantinople, Turkey, Sept 7, 1909.
John Philip Law, 67, actor (*The Russians Are Coming, the Russians Are Coming; Barbarella*), born Hollywood, CA, Sept 7, 1937.
Richard Roundtree, 62, actor (*Shaft, Q, Once upon a Time When We Were Colored*), born New Rochelle, NY, Sept 7, 1942 (some sources say 1939).
Devon Sawa, 26, actor (*Wild America, The Boy's Club*), born Vancouver, BC, Canada, Sept 7, 1978.
Briana Scurry, 33, soccer player, born Minneapolis, MN, Sept 7, 1971.

SEPTEMBER 8 — WEDNESDAY
Day 252 — 114 Remaining

ANDORRA: NATIONAL HOLIDAY. Sept 8. Honors our Lady of Meritxell.

CANADA: THE MASTERS. Sept 8–12. Spruce Meadows, Calgary, AB. International show jumping competition, along with Equi-Fair, TELUS Battle of the Breeds and the BP Amoco Festival of Nations. Featured events are the EnCana Cup, the ATCO Electric Circuit "Six-Bar," the BMO Financial Group Nations' Cup and the CN International. Est attendance: 175,000. For info: Spruce Meadows, RR 9, Calgary, AB, Canada T2J 5G5. Phone: (403) 974-4200. Fax: (403) 974-4270. E-mail: information @sprucemeadows.com. Web: www.sprucemeadows.com.

CLINE, PATSY: BIRTH ANNIVERSARY. Sept 8, 1932. Country and western singer, born Virginia Patterson Hensley at Winchester, VA. Patsy Cline got her big break in 1957 when she won an Arthur Godfrey Talent Scout show, singing "Walking After Midnight." Her career took off and she became a featured singer at the Grand Ole Opry, attaining the rank of top female country singer. She died in a plane crash Mar 5, 1963, at Camden, TN, along with singers Hawkshaw Hawkins and Cowboy Copas.

FARMERS AND THRESHERMENS JUBILEE. Sept 8–12. New Centerville, PA. Many steam engines, threshing demonstrations using manpower, horses and steam, quilt show, crafts, truck and tractor pulls. Live entertainment, good food. Est attendance: 25,000. For info: Farmers & Threshermens Jubilee, 1428 Casselman Rd, Rockwood, PA 15557. Phone: (814) 926-3142.

GALVESTON HURRICANE: ANNIVERSARY. Sept 8, 1900. The worst national disaster in US history in terms of lives lost. More than 6,000 people were killed when a hurricane struck Galveston, TX, with winds of more than 120 mph, followed by a huge tidal wave. More than 2,500 buildings were destroyed.

MACEDONIA: INDEPENDENCE DAY. Sept 8. National holiday. Commemorates independence from the Yugoslav Union in 1991.

MALTA: SIEGE BROKEN: ANNIVERSARY. Sept 8. "Two Sieges and Regatta Day" festivities now commemorate victory over the Turks, Sept 8, 1565, when the siege that began in May 1565 was broken by the Maltese and the Knights of St. John after a loss of nearly 10,000 lives. Also commemorated is survival of the 1943 siege by the Axis Powers. Parades, fireworks, boat races, etc, especially at the capital, Valleta, and the Grand Harbour.

McGWIRE BREAKS HOME RUN RECORD: ANNIVERSARY. Sept 8, 1998. Mark McGwire of the St. Louis Cardinals hit his 62nd home run, breaking Roger Maris's 1961 record for the most home runs in a single season. McGwire hit his homer at Busch Stadium at St. Louis against pitcher Steve Trachsel of the Chicago Cubs as the Cardinals won, 6–3. McGwire finished the season with 70 home runs. On Oct 5, 2001, Barry Bonds hit his 71st home run, breaking McGwire's record. Bonds finished the season with 73 homers.

MISS AMERICA FIRST CROWNED: ANNIVERSARY. Sept 8, 1921. Margaret Gorman of Washington, DC, was crowned the first Miss America at the end of a two-day pageant at Atlantic City, NJ.

464

☆ Chase's 2004 Calendar of Events ☆ Sept 8–9

MISSION SAN GABRIEL ARCHANGEL: FOUNDING ANNIVERSARY. Sept 8, 1771. California mission to the Indians founded on this date.

NIXON PARDONED: 30th ANNIVERSARY. Sept 8, 1974. Anniversary of the "full, free, and absolute pardon unto Richard Nixon, for all offenses against the United States which he, Richard Nixon, has committed or may have committed or taken part in during the period from January 20, 1969, through August 9, 1974." (Presidential Proclamation 4311, Sept 8, 1974, by Gerald R. Ford.)

NORTHERN PACIFIC RAILROAD COMPLETED: ANNIVERSARY. Sept 8, 1883. After 19 years of construction, the Northern Pacific Railroad became the second railroad to link the two coasts. The Union Pacific and Central Pacific lines met at Utah in 1869.

"THE OPRAH WINFREY SHOW" TV PREMIERE: ANNIVERSARY. Sept 8, 1986. This daytime talk show was the top-rated talk show for years and also has the distinction of being the first talk show hosted by a black woman, Oprah Winfrey. Her show is taped in front of a studio audience who are solicited for their questions and feedback. In the mid-1990s, fed up with the plethora of trashy talk shows that had sprung up everywhere, Winfrey decided to upgrade the quality of topics that her show presented. Her "book club" feature has been a popular element of her show, and chosen books usually become bestsellers.

PEPPER, CLAUDE DENSON: BIRTH ANNIVERSARY. Sept 8, 1900. US Representative and Senator, born near Dudleyville, AL. Pepper's career in politics spanned 53 years and 10 presidents, and he became the champion for America's senior citizens. He was elected to the US Senate in 1936, where he was a principal architect of many of the nation's "safety net" social programs including Social Security, the minimum wage and medical assistance for the elderly and for handicapped children. After a 14-year career in the Senate, he returned to Congress in the House of Representatives where he served 14 terms. He served as chairman of the House Select Committee on Aging, drafted legislation banning forced retirement and fought against cutting Social Security benefits. Pepper died at Washington, DC, May 30, 1989.

SELLERS, PETER: BIRTH ANNIVERSARY. Sept 8, 1925. Award-winning British comedian and film star, born Richard Henry Sellers at Southsea, Hampshire, England. Sellers is remembered for his multiple roles in *Dr. Strangelove*, his Oscar-nominated role as Chance the Gardener in *Being There* and for his role as the bumbling Inspector Clouseau in the *Pink Panther* films. Died at London, England, July 24, 1980.

"STAR TREK" TV PREMIERE: ANNIVERSARY. Sept 8, 1966. The first of 79 episodes of the TV series "Star Trek" was aired on the NBC network. Although the science fiction show set in the future only lasted a few seasons, it has remained enormously popular through syndication reruns. It has been given new life through ten motion pictures, a cartoon TV series and popular spin-off TV series such as "Star Trek: The Next Generation," "Star Trek: Enterprise" and others. It has consistently ranked among the biggest titles in the motion picture, television, home video and licensing divisions of Paramount Pictures.

"TARZAN" TV PREMIERE: ANNIVERSARY. Sept 8, 1966. This hour adventure series was based on Edgar Rice Burroughs's character, who appeared for the first time on TV. Tarzan, an English lord who preferred the jungle, was played by Ron Ely. Manuel Padilla, Jr was Jai, a jungle orphan, Alan Caillou was Jason Flood, Jai's tutor, and Rockne Tarkington was Rao, a veterinarian. There was no Jane.

"THAT GIRL" TV PREMIERE: ANNIVERSARY. Sept 8, 1966. "That Girl" was a half-hour sitcom starring Marlo Thomas as Ann Marie, an independent aspiring actress in New York City. Ted Bessell also starred as her boyfriend Don Hollinger. They were finally engaged in 1970. Also featured were Lew Parker, Rosemary De Camp and Bonnie Scott. Well-known performers who appeared on the show include Dabney Coleman, George Carlin and Bernie Kopell.

UNITED NATIONS: INTERNATIONAL LITERACY DAY. Sept 8. An international day observed by the organizations of the United Nations system. For info: United Nations, Dept of Public Info, New York, NY 10017. Web: www.un.org.

BIRTHDAYS TODAY

David Arquette, 33, actor (*Scream, Muppets from Space*), born Winchester, VA, Sept 8, 1971.
Sid Caesar, 82, comedian, actor ("Your Show of Shows"), born Yonkers, NY, Sept 8, 1922.
Alan Feinstein, 63, actor ("Edge of Night," "Love of Life," "Search for Tomorrow"), born New York, NY, Sept 8, 1941.
Marilyn (Williamson) Mims, 50, opera singer, born Collins, MS, Sept 8, 1954.
Latrell Sprewell, 34, basketball player, born Milwaukee, WI, Sept 8, 1970.
Heather Thomas, 47, actress ("The Fall Guy"), born Greenwich, CT, Sept 8, 1957.
Henry Thomas, 33, actor (*E.T. The Extra-Terrestrial, Legends of the Fall*), born San Antonio, TX, Sept 8, 1971.
Jonathan Taylor Thomas, 23, actor ("Home Improvement"), born Bethlehem, PA, Sept 8, 1981.
Rogatien (Rogie) Vachon, 59, former hockey executive and player, born Palmarolle, QC, Canada, Sept 8, 1945.

SEPTEMBER 9 — THURSDAY
Day 253 — 113 Remaining

BATTLE OF MARATHON: ANNIVERSARY. Sept 9. On the day of the ninth month's full moon in the year 490 BC, the numerically superior invading army of Persia was met and defeated on the Plain of Marathon by the Athenian army, led by Miltiades. More than 6,000 men died in the day's battle, which drove the Persians to the sea. The mound of earth covering the dead is still visible at the site. This date is in dispute. See also: "Historic Marathon Runs: Anniversary" (Sept 2) for the legendary running of Phidippides and the origin of the marathon race.

BATTLE OF SALERNO: ANNIVERSARY. Sept 9–16, 1943. US General Mark Clark's Fifth Army made an amphibious assault on Salerno, Italy (Operation Avalanche), at 3:30 AM. The British 1st Airborne Division seized the southern Italian port of Taranto (Operation Slapstick) without opposition. Initial gains along the western coast of Italy were checked by strong German forces by Sept 12. In some places the Allied forces were pushed back to within two miles of the coast. On Sept 15 US 82nd Airborne and British 7th Armoured counterattacked and on Sept 16 units of the American 5th Army and the British 8th Army joined up near Vallo di Lucania.

BONZA BOTTLER DAY™. Sept 9. To celebrate when the number of the day is the same as the number of the month. Bonza Bottler Day™ is an excuse to have a party at least once a month. For more information, see Jan 1. For info: Gail M. Berger, 14 Fernwood Dr, Taylors, SC 29687. Phone: (864) 609-9874. E-mail: gberger5@aol.com.

465

Sept 9 ☆ *Chase's 2004 Calendar of Events* ☆

CALIFORNIA: ADMISSION DAY: ANNIVERSARY. Sept 9. Became 31st state in 1850.

CANADA: TORONTO INTERNATIONAL FILM FESTIVAL. Sept 9–18. Toronto, ON. 29th annual. A 10-day festival of contemporary Canadian and international cinema at various downtown theatres. Call or write for info or to be put on mailing list. Est attendance: 250,000. For info: Toronto Intl Film Festival, 2 Carlton St, Ste 1600, Toronto, ON, Canada M5B 1J3. Phone: (416) 968-FILM. Fax: (416) 967-9477. E-mail: tiffg@torfilmfest.ca. Web: www.bell.ca/filmfest

DEFEAT OF JESSE JAMES DAYS. Sept 9–12. Northfield, MN. Bank raid reenactment, 5K and 15K runs, arts, crafts, bike race, parade and professional rodeo. Est attendance: 150,000. For info: Northfield Chamber of Commerce, PO Box 198, Northfield, MN 55057. Phone: (507) 645-5604. Fax: (507) 663-7782.

"FAT ALBERT AND THE COSBY KIDS" TV PREMIERE: ANNIVERSARY. Sept 9, 1972. This cartoon series was hosted by Bill Cosby, with characters based on his childhood friends at Philadelphia. Its central characters—Fat Albert, Weird Harold, Mush Mouth and Donald—were weird-looking but very human. The show sent messages of tolerance and harmony. In 1979 the show was renamed "The New Fat Albert Show."

THE 59 MINUTE 37 SECOND ANVIL MOUNTAIN CHALLENGE. Sept 9. Nome, AK. A running event that starts at the base of Anvil Mountain, where runners must run 834 ft up the face of the mountain and return in less than 59 minutes and 37 seconds or be disqualified from the competition. Trophies awarded for first–third finishers, first woman finisher and first finisher 16 years of age and under. Record time is 25 minutes 37 seconds. Annually, the second Thursday in September. Est attendance: 1,000. For info: Rasmussen's Music Mart, PO Box 2, Nome, AK 99762-0002. Phone: (907) 443-2798 or (907) 443-2919. Fax: (907) 443-5777.

GREAT PEANUT TOUR. Sept 9–12. Skippers, VA. Assorted bicycle rides from 13 to 125 miles. Special peanut tour ride to examine peanuts growing, method of harvesting and a sampling of more than 40 peanut goodies. Unique water stops, nature walks, music, campfires with marshmallow roast. Annually, the weekend following Labor Day. Est attendance: 1,500. For info: Robert C. Wrenn, Emporia Bicycle Club, PO Box 631, Emporia, VA 23847. Phone: (804) 348-4215. Fax: (804) 348-4020. E-mail: gpt@3rddoor.com. Web: www.greatpeanuttour.com.

JAPAN: CHRYSANTHEMUM DAY. Sept 9. Traditional chrysanthemum festival.

KOREA, DEMOCRATIC PEOPLE'S REPUBLIC OF: NATIONAL DAY. Sept 9. National holiday in the Democratic People's Republic of [North] Korea.

LONGS PEAK SCOTTISH/IRISH HIGHLAND FESTIVAL. Sept 9–12. Estes Park, CO. This 28th annual Scottish-Irish celebration festival with pipe bands, Highland and Irish dancing, jousting and gathering of the clans. Featuring professional Scottish and Irish entertainers, "Dogs of the British Isles" dog competition, professional Scottish athletes and vendors with imported and handcrafted merchandise. Annually, the first weekend after Labor Day. Est attendance: 60,000. For info: Longs Peak Scottish/Irish Highland Festival, Inc, Box 1820, Estes Park, CO 80517. Phone: (800) 903-7837. Fax: (970) 586-5328. E-mail: staff@scotfest.com. Web: www.scotfest.com.

LUXEMBOURG: LIBERATION CEREMONY: 60th ANNIVERSARY. Sept 9. Petange. Commemoration of liberation of Grand-Duchy by the Allied forces in 1944. Ceremony at monument of the American soldier.

September 2004

S	M	T	W	T	F	S
			1	2	3	4
5	6	7	8	9	10	11
12	13	14	15	16	17	18
19	20	21	22	23	24	25
26	27	28	29	30		

MAO TSE-TUNG: DEATH ANNIVERSARY. Sept 9, 1976. People's Republic of China pays tribute to memory of the Chinese revolutionary leader, who died at Beijing. Memorial Hall, where his flag-draped body lies encased in crystal, was opened at Tiananmen Square at Beijing on the first anniversary of his death. Mao was born Dec 26, 1893, at Hunan Province, China.

"RHODA" TV PREMIERE: 30th ANNIVERSARY. Sept 9, 1974. This spin-off from "The Mary Tyler Moore Show" starred Valerie Harper as Rhoda Morgenstern, who returns to New York, finds a job and gets married (she also gets separated and divorced). Other characters included her husband Joe Gerard (David Groh), her sister Brenda (Julie Kavner), her mother Ida (Nancy Walker), her father Martin (Harold Gould) and Carlton, the heard-but-not-seen doorman (Lorenzo Music). Other regulars included Richard Masur, Ron Silver, Anne Meara and Kenneth McMillan. The last episode aired in 1978.

SANDERS, COLONEL HARLAND DAVID: BIRTH ANNIVERSARY. Sept 9, 1890. Founder of Kentucky Fried Chicken, born near Henryville, IN. Died Dec 16, 1980, at Shelbyville, KY.

TAJIKISTAN: INDEPENDENCE DAY. Sept 9. National holiday commemorating independence from the Soviet Union in 1991.

TOLSTOY, LEO: BIRTH ANNIVERSARY. Sept 9, 1828. Russian novelist and moral philosopher, born at Tula Province, Russia. Best known for his novels (*War and Peace, Anna Karenina*), Tolstoy also wrote short stories, plays and essays. A member of the nobility, in his moral and religious writings he condemned private property and championed nonviolent protest. Died Nov 20, 1910, at Astapovo, Russia.

UTAH STATE FAIR. Sept 9–19. Utah State Fairpark, Salt Lake City, UT. PRCA Rodeo Sept 4–7. Exhibits, livestock, family contests, cook-offs, concerts and entertainment. Annually, beginning the first Thursday after Labor Day. Est attendance: 275,000. For info: Utah State Fair Park, 155 N 1000 W, Salt Lake City, UT 84116. Phone: (801) 538-8440. Fax: (801) 538-8455. E-mail: donna@fiber.net.

"WELCOME BACK, KOTTER" TV PREMIERE: ANNIVERSARY. Sept 9, 1975. In this half-hour sitcom, Gabe Kotter (Gabe Kaplan) returned to James Buchanan High School, his alma mater, to teach the "sweathogs," a group of hopeless underachievers. Other cast members included Marcia Strassman, John Travolta, Robert Hegyes, Ron Palillo, Lawrence Hilton-Jacobs and John Sylvester White. Later in the series, two new sweathogs were added, played by Melonie Haller and Stephen Shortridge. The theme song, "Welcome Back," was sung by John Sebastian. The last telecast was Aug 10, 1979.

WILLIAM, THE CONQUEROR: DEATH ANNIVERSARY. Sept 9, 1087. William I, The Conqueror, King of England and Duke of Normandy, whose image is portrayed in the Bayeux Tapestry, was born about 1028 at Falaise, Normandy. Victorious over Harold at the Battle of Hastings (the Norman Conquest) in 1066, William was crowned King of England at Westminster Abbey on Christmas Day of that year. Later, while waging war in France, William met his death at Rouen, Sept 9, 1087.

☆ Chase's 2004 Calendar of Events ☆ Sept 9–10

WILLIAMSBURG OLD-FASHIONED TRADING DAYS. Sept 9–11. Courthouse Square, Williamsburg, KY. Arts and crafts, bluegrass and gospel singing, antique car show and more. Annually, the first Thursday, Friday and Saturday after Labor Day. Est attendance: 25,000. For info: Theresa Estes, Coord, 522 Main St, Williamsburg, KY 40769. Phone: (606) 549-2285. Fax: (606) 549-5565.

WONDERFUL WEIRDOS DAY. Sept 9. All of us are blessed with one or two wonderful weirdos in our lives. These are the folks who remind us to think outside the box, to be a little more true to ourselves. Today's the day to thank them. So give them a hug, and say "I love you, you weirdo!" [©2003 by WH.] For info: Thomas & Ruth Roy, Wellcat Holidays, 2418 Long Lane, Lebanon, PA 17046. Phone: (717) 279-0184. E-mail: info@wellcat.com. Web: www.wellcat.com.

YELLOW DAISY FESTIVAL. Sept 9–12. Stone Mountain Park, Stone Mountain, GA. Arts and crafts festival with more than 450 exhibitors. Continuous entertainment and foods. Annually, the weekend after Labor Day. Est attendance: 225,000. For info: Special Events Office, Stone Mountain Park, PO Box 778, Stone Mountain, GA 30086. Phone: (770) 498-5633. Fax: (770) 413-5059. E-mail: jbattle@stonemountainpark.com. Web: www.stonemountainpark.com.

BIRTHDAYS TODAY

Benjamin Roy ("BJ") Armstrong, 37, former basketball player, born Detroit, MI, Sept 9, 1967.
Shane Battier, 26, basketball player, born Birmingham, MI, Sept 9, 1978.
Angela Cartwright, 52, actress ("Lost in Space," *The Sound of Music*), born Cheshire, England, Sept 9, 1952.
Hugh Grant, 44, actor (*Impromptu, Sense and Sensibility, Four Weddings and a Funeral*), born London, England, Sept 9, 1960.
Mike Hampton, 32, baseball player, born Brooksville, FL, Sept 9, 1972.
Rachel Hunter, 35, model, born New Zealand, Sept 9, 1969.
Kazuhiro Ishii, 31, baseball player, born Chiba, Japan, Sept 9, 1973.
Michael Keaton, 53, actor ("Report to Murphy," *Batman, The Dream Team*), born Michael Douglas, Pittsburgh, PA, Sept 9, 1951.
Daniel Lewis (Dan) Majerle, 39, basketball player, born Traverse City, MI, Sept 9, 1965.
Sylvia Miles, 70, actress (*Midnight Cowboy; Farewell, My Lovely*), born New York, NY, Sept 9, 1934.
Billy Preston, 58, musician, songwriter, singer ("Nothing from Nothing"), born Houston, TX, Sept 9, 1946.
Cliff Robertson, 79, actor ("Falcon Crest," *Brainstorm, Charly, PT-109*), born La Jolla, CA, Sept 9, 1925.
Adam Sandler, 38, actor, comedian ("Saturday Night Live," *The Wedding Singer*), born Brooklyn, NY, Sept 9, 1966.
Joseph Robert (Joe) Theisman, 55, sportscaster, Hall of Fame football player, born New Brunswick, NJ, Sept 9, 1949.
Goran Visnjic, 32, actor ("ER," *The Deep End*), born Sibenik, Croatia, Sept 9, 1972.
Tom Wopat, 53, actor ("The Dukes of Hazzard," "Cybill," *Annie Get Your Gun*), born Lodi, WI, Sept 9, 1951.

SEPTEMBER 10 — FRIDAY
Day 254 — 112 Remaining

ALOHA FESTIVALS OPENING CEREMONY AND ROYAL PA'INA. Sept 10. Hilton Hawaiian Village, Honolulu, HI. Hawaii's Aloha Festivals are a six-week, six-island annual celebration. They're kicked off with the Opening Ceremony with traditional chant and hula. The O'ahu Royal Court, dressed in royal garments, will gather on the steps of the only royal palace on US soil—the 'Iolani Palace—at 5:30 PM. Immediately following will be the Royal Pa'ina, a dinner held on the grounds of 'Iolani Palace. The Aloha Festivals Floral Parade takes place on Sept 18. For info: Aloha Festivals. Phone: (808) 589-1771. Fax: (808) 589-1770. E-mail: info@alohafestivals.com. Web: www.alohafestivals.com.

ARCOLA BROOM CORN FESTIVAL. Sept 10–12. Arcola, IL. The whole town celebrates. Free entertainment, arts and crafts, flea markets, food. Est attendance: 60,000. For info: Arcola Chamber of Commerce, PO Box 274, Arcola, IL 61910. Phone: (800) 336-5456. Web: www.arcola-il.org.

BALD IS BEAUTIFUL CONVENTION. Sept 10–12. Morehead City, NC. To cultivate a sense of pride for all bald-headed men (folks) everywhere and eliminate the vanity associated with the loss of one's hair. As seen on national television; Bald is Beautiful Contests, family events. Annually, the second weekend in September. Est attendance: 250. For info: John T. Capps III, Founder, Bald Headed Men of America, 102 Bald Dr, Morehead City, NC 28557. Phone: (252) 726-1855. Fax: (252) 726-6061. E-mail: jcapps4102@aol.com. Web: members.aol.com/BaldUSA.

BELIZE: SAINT GEORGE'S CAYE DAY. Sept 10. Public holiday celebrated in honor of the battle between the European Baymen Settlers and the Spaniards for the territory of Belize.

BRAXTON, CARTER: BIRTH ANNIVERSARY. Sept 10, 1736. American revolutionary statesman and signer of the Declaration of Independence. Born at Newington, VA, he died Oct 10, 1797, at Richmond, VA.

DOODLE SOUP DAYS. Sept 10–11. Bradford, TN. This weeklong event celebrates the town of Bradford, famous for its Doodle Soup. Includes car show, BBQ cook-off, quilt show, flea market, art show, street dance, Doodle Soup beauty pageant and a Doodle Soup supper. For info: Bradford City Hall. Phone: (731) 742-3465.

FESTIVAL OF THE VINE. Sept 10–12. Geneva, IL. Flavors of fall are celebrated with music, wine tasting, antique carriage rides, arts and crafts, entertainment and specialties of Geneva's fine restaurants. For info: Geneva Chamber of Commerce, 8 S Third St., PO Box 481, Geneva, IL 60134. Phone: (630) 232-6060. Fax: (630) 232-6083. E-mail: chamberinfo@genevachamber.com. Web: www.genevachamber.com.

"GENTLE BEN" TV PREMIERE: ANNIVERSARY. Sept 10, 1967. This show was about the adventures of a boy, Mark Wedloe (Clint Howard) and his pet bear, Ben. Also featured were Dennis Weaver as his father Tom, a game warden, Beth Brickell as his mother Ellen, Jack Worley as Tom's friend Spencer and Angelo Rutherford as his friend Willie. It was filmed on location in Florida.

GOAT DAYS. Sept 10–12. USA Stadium, Millington, TN. Goat contests with large cash prizes and trophies, children's area, camping, fishing, goat races, dancing, music, food, rodeo, crafts, Cabrito Challenge Cook-Off, Dutch-oven cook-offs, ice cream making and National Anvil Shoot. Huge display of antique engines and tractors and national stock dog trials. Est attendance: 20,000. For info: Goat Days Intl, 4880 Navy Rd, Millington, TN 38053. Phone: (901) 872-4559. Fax: (901) 872-7700. E-mail: goatdays@bigriver.net.

GOULD, STEPHEN JAY: BIRTH ANNIVERSARY. Sept 10, 1941. Evolutionary biologist and influential writer for academic and lay audiences. With colleague Niles Eldredge, he proposed the theory of punctuated equilibrium to explain sudden

467

changes (and lack of) in fossil records. He died in his birthplace city, New York, NY, on May 20, 2002.

"GUNSMOKE" TV PREMIERE: ANNIVERSARY. Sept 10, 1955. "Gunsmoke" was TV's longest-running Western, moving from radio to TV. John Wayne turned down the role of Marshall Matt Dillon but recommended James Arness, who got the role. Other regulars included Amanda Blake as Kitty Russell, saloon-owner; Dennis Weaver as Chester B. Goode, Dillon's deputy and Milburn Stone as Doc Adams. In 1962 a fifth character was added—the "rugged male." Burt Reynolds played Quint Asper, followed by Roger Ewing as Thad Greenwood, and Buck Taylor as Newly O'Brien. In 1964 Ken Curtis was added as funnyman Festus Haggen, the new deputy. "Gunsmoke" was the number-one rated series for four seasons, and a top ten hit for six seasons. The last telecast was Sept 1, 1975.

HISTORIC NORWICHTOWN DAYS. Sept 10–12. Norwich, CT. Experience and explore living history on one of the country's most pristine 18th-century town greens. Colonial and Native American craft, trade and military demonstrations; lectures and colonial music. Also, Patriot Parade with famous figures from history. Est attendance: 25,000. For info: Bob Whatley, Chair, Historic Norwichtown Days, PO Box 108, Yantic, CT 06389. Phone: (860) 887-7845. E-mail: chilibob@webtv.net.

INDIAN SUMMER FESTIVAL. Sept 10–12. Maier Festival Park, Milwaukee, WI. Festival dedicated to promoting the unique culture of the American Indian. Cultural events and exhibits, authentic villages, competition powwow, juried fine arts show, marketplace with traditional and contemporary entertainment and traditional food. Est attendance: 70,000. For info: Indian Summer Festivals, Inc, 10809 W Lincoln Ave, West Allis, WI 53227. Phone: (414) 604-1000. Fax: (414) 774-6810. Web: www.indiansummer.org.

INTREPID MEDIA ANNIVERSARY EVENT. Sept 10–12. Contributors worldwide determine the new location each year for an event honoring creative people. Intrepid Media is an online magazine and ideal-driven organization launched in an effort to provide a forum and a podium for those creative people. Whether you're a writer, a musician, a graphic artist, a publisher, a producer, an editor, this site and event promotes and encourages you to come together with others to increase your skills and levels of opportunity. For info: Joe Procopio, Intrepid Media. Phone: (919) 740-9009. E-mail: joe@intrepidmedia.com. Web: www.intrepidmedia.com.

KANSAS STATE FAIR. Sept 10–19. Hutchinson, KS. Commercial and competitive exhibits, entertainment, carnival, car racing and other special attractions. Annually, beginning the first Friday after Labor Day. Est attendance: 400,000. For info: Denny Stocklein, Gen Mgr, Kansas State Fair, 2000 N Poplar, Hutchinson, KS 67502. Phone: (316) 669-3600. E-mail: info@kansasstatefair.com. Web: www.kansasstatefair.com.

KEYSTONE COUNTRY FAIR. Sept 10–12. Lakemont Park, Altoona, PA. More than 300 arts and crafts vendors display their wares throughout the weekend. Attractions include an ethnic food village and entertainment. Admission to fair includes amusement rides and waterpark. For info: Allegheny Mountains Convention and Visitors Bureau, One Convention Center Dr, Altoona, PA 16602. Phone: (814) 943-4183. Fax: (814) 943-8094. E-mail: amcvb@aol.com. Web: www.alleghenymountains.com.

KURALT, CHARLES: 70th BIRTH ANNIVERSARY. Sept 10, 1934. TV journalist ("On the Road with Charles Kuralt") born at Wilmington, NC. Died at New York, NY, July 4, 1997.

September 2004

S	M	T	W	T	F	S
			1	2	3	4
5	6	7	8	9	10	11
12	13	14	15	16	17	18
19	20	21	22	23	24	25
26	27	28	29	30		

LIGONIER HIGHLAND GAMES. Sept 10–11. Ligonier, PA. Scottish bagpipe bands on parade, Highland dancers and athletes in daylong performances. Clan gatherings, dog show. Offers imported woolens, china, jewelry, records and foods. Mail SASE for schedule of events. Est attendance: 10,000. For info: David L. Peet, Ligonier Highland Games, PO Box 884, Bethel Park, PA 15102-0884. Phone: (412) 851-9900. E-mail: ligdir@icubed.com. Web: www.ligoniergames.org.

MARIGOLD FESTIVAL. Sept 10–12. Pekin, IL. Parade, flower judging, arts, crafts, golf, carnival, Festive Foods and other family-oriented activities. Est attendance: 100,000. For info: Chamber of Commerce, PO Box 636, Pekin, IL 61555-0636. Phone: (309) 346-2106. Fax: (309) 346-2104.

MARIS, ROGER: 70th BIRTH ANNIVERSARY. Sept 10, 1934. Roger Eugene Maris, baseball player born Roger Eugene Maras at Hibbing, MN. In 1961 Maris surpassed the mark set by Babe Ruth in 1927, hitting 61 home runs, a record which wasn't broken until 1998. He won the American League MVP award in 1960 and 1961 and finished his career with the St. Louis Cardinals. Died at Houston, TX, Dec 14, 1985.

MOUNTAIN CRAFT DAYS. Sept 10–12. Somerset, PA. Southwestern Pennsylvania's premier traditional craft festival along the Somerset Historical Center's trails. Entertainment, food, trades and crafts. Est attendance: 15,000. For info: Mark Ware, Mountain Craft Days, 10649 Somerset Pike, Somerset, PA 15501. Phone: (814) 445-6077.

NATIONAL CHAMPIONSHIP INDIAN POWWOW. Sept 10–12. Traders Village, Grand Prairie, TX. Hundreds of Indians gather for colorful traditional dance contests, Indian arts and crafts shows, homemade tepee competition and Indian food. Est attendance: 80,000. For info: Dallas–Fort Worth Inter-Tribal Assn, Traders Village, 2602 Mayfield Rd, Grand Prairie, TX 75052-7246. Phone: (972) 647-2331. E-mail: tvgp@flash.net. Web: www.tradersvillage.com.

NORDICFEST. Sept 10–12. Libby, MT. Scandinavian festival with food booths, dinners, cultural exhibits, craft shows, quilt show, art show, folk dance performances, big name performances and the international Fjord horse show. Parade showcases a contingent of Norwegian fjord horses plus a variety of floats. Est attendance: 10,000. For info: Libby Nordicfest, Inc, Box 791, Libby, MT 59923. Phone: (800) 785-6541. E-mail: smokesignal@libby.org. Web: www.libbynordicfest.org.

NORWALK SEAPORT OYSTER FESTIVAL. Sept 10–12. Norwalk, CT. Huge festival with vintage ships on display, 225 juried crafters, main stage entertainment, oyster shucking and slurping contests and Kids Cove (children's entertainment). Annually, the weekend following Labor Day. Est attendance: 82,000. For info: Norwalk Seaport Assn, 132 Water St, Norwalk, CT 06854. Phone: (203) 838-9444. Fax: (203) 855-1017.

OHIO RIVER STERNWHEEL FESTIVAL. Sept 10–12. Ohio River Levee, Marietta, OH. A three-day riverfront extravaganza. More than two dozen sternwheelers line the Ohio River shore in Marietta, OH. Continuous musical entertainment for all ages, food concessions, queen coronation, sternwheel races, fireworks. Annually, the weekend following Labor Day. Est attendance: 85,000. For info: Ohio River Sternwheel Festival Committee, 316 Third St, Marietta, OH 45750. Phone: (740) 373-5178 or (740) 374-4913. Fax: (740) 374-4959. E-mail: mtourist@ee.net. Web: www.rivertowns.org.

OKTOBERFEST. Sept 10–12. MainStrasse Village, Covington, KY. Celebration of the German "storybook wedding reception" kicks off with a beer-tapping ceremony. Features include German and American food, live Bavarian music and dancing, arts and crafts, children's rides and much more. Est attendance: 175,000. For info: Donna Kremer, Administrative Coord, MainStrasse Village, 605 Philadelphia St, Covington, KY 41011. Phone: (859) 491-0458. Fax: (859) 655-7932. Web: www.mainstrasse.org.

ON THE WATERFRONT SWAP MEET AND CAR SHOW. Sept 10–12. Downtown St. Ignace, MI. 14th anniversary. Car show, toy show, truck display and swap meet. Est attendance: 10,000. For info: Ed Reavie, President, Nostalgia Prod, Inc, 268 Hillcrest Blvd, St. Ignace, MI 49781. Phone: (906) 643-8087 or (906) 643-1USA. Fax: (906) 643-9784. E-mail: edreavie@nostalgia-prod.com. Web: www.nostalgia-prod.com or www.auto-shows.com.

PUYALLUP FAIR. Sept 10–26. Puyallup, WA. Entertainment, animals, rides, displays and food. The 104th fair. Est attendance: 1,300,000. For info: Western Washington Fair, PO Box 430, Puyallup, WA 98371-0162. Phone: (253) 841-5045. E-mail: info@thefair.com. Web: www.thefair.com.

RICHARD CRANE MEMORIAL TRUCK SHOW. Sept 10–12. St. Ignace, MI. 9th annual show featuring 18-wheeler competition. $2,000 cash Best of Show. Parade of Lights across the Mackinac Bridge. Est attendance: 10,000. For info: Nostalgia Productions, Inc, 268 Hillcrest Blvd, St. Ignace, MI 49781. Phone: (906) 643-8087 or (906) 643-1USA. Fax: (906) 643-9784. E-mail: edreavie@nostalgia-prod.com. Web: www.nostalgia-prod.com or www.auto-shows.com.

ROCHESTER FAIR. Sept 10–19 (tentative). Rochester, NH. Agricultural Fair. Est attendance: 150,000. For info: Rochester Fair Assn, 72 Lafayette St, Rochester, NH 03867. Phone: (603) 332-6585. Fax: (603) 332-1896. Web: rochesterfair.com.

SEW BE IT! DAY. Sept 10. Celebrating the anniversary of the patent on the sewing machine on Sept 10, 1846. Recognizing that when a hem loosens or a button pops off, Sew Be It! [©1995] Because of the escalating costs of Eventological® Literature, a charge of $7 must be assessed for each request. Checks are to be made payable to: Adrienne Sioux Koopersmith, 1437 W Rosemont, #1W, Chicago, IL 60660-1319. Phone: (773) 743-5341. Fax: (773) 743-5395. E-mail: la_koop@yahoo.com.

STAMP EXPO. Sept 10–12. Radisson Hotel, Anaheim, CA. Est attendance: 4,000. For info: Intl Stamp Collectors Society, PO Box 854, Van Nuys, CA 91408. Phone: (818) 997-6496. Fax: (818) 988-4337. E-mail: iibick@aol.com. Web: www.bick.net.

SUGARLOAF CRAFTS FESTIVAL. Sept 10–12. Prince William County Fairgrounds, Manassas, VA. This show, now in its 24th year, features 300 nationally recognized craft designers and fine artists displaying and selling their original creations. Craft demonstrations, children's entertainment, live music, food, hourly gift certificate drawings and more. Est attendance: 20,500. For info: Sugarloaf Mountain Works, 200 Orchard Ridge Dr, #215, Gaithersburg, MD 20878. Phone: (800) 210-9900. Fax: (301) 253-9620. Web: www.sugarloafcrafts.com.

SWAP IDEAS DAY. Sept 10. To encourage people to explore ways in which their ideas can be put to work for the benefit of humanity, and to encourage development of incentives that will encourage use of creative imagination. For info: Robert L. Birch, Publicity Chair, Puns Corps, Box 2364, Falls Church, VA 22042-0364. Phone: (703) 533-3668.

TENNESSEE STATE FAIR. Sept 10–19. Nashville, TN. A huge variety of exhibits, carnival midway, animal and variety shows, live stage presentations, livestock, agricultural and craft competitions and food and game booths. Annually, beginning the first Friday after Labor Day. Est attendance: 200,000. For info: Tennessee Fair Office, PO Box 40208, Melrose Station, Nashville, TN 37204. Phone: (615) 862-8980. Fax: (615) 862-8992. Web: www.tennesseestatefair.org.

WERFEL, FRANZ: BIRTH ANNIVERSARY. Sept 10, 1890. Austrian author (*The Song of Bernadette*, *The Forty Days of Musa Dagh*), born at Prague, Czechoslovakia. Died at Hollywood, CA, Aug 26, 1945.

WINFIELD GOOD OLD DAYS. Sept 10–12. Winfield, IL. 37th annual festival involving current Miss Illinois USA and entire Winfield community, including live music, carnival, ladies shoe-kicking contest, bed races, underhand free-throw tournaments, pony rides, petting zoo, duck race, dunk tank, expo tent, food concession, beer garden and parade. Annually, the three-day weekend following Labor Day. Est attendance: 10,000. For info: Winfield Chamber of Commerce, 0S125 Church St, Winfield, IL 60190. Phone: (630) 682-3712. Fax: (630) 682-3726. E-mail: bysina@winfield-chamber.com. Web: www.winfield-chamber.com.

WOLLSTONECRAFT, MARY: DEATH ANNIVERSARY. Sept 10, 1797. Writer and advocate of equality for women, Mary Wollstonecraft died at London 11 days after giving birth to her second daughter (Mary Wollstonecraft Shelley, the author of *Frankenstein*). Wollstonecraft was born Apr 27, 1759, at London. Rebelling against her father, she left home at age 18 and served as a lady's companion, opened a school and worked as a governess. Beginning with *Thoughts on the Education of Daughters* in 1787, Wollstonecraft attracted notice as a writer in favor of women's rights. Her *A Vindication of the Rights of Woman* (1792) argued that women should be given an education that would allow them to gain economic independence.

WYANDOTTE HERITAGE DAYS. Sept 10–12. Bishop Park Area, Wyandotte, MI. Outdoor craft show, living history encampments, Teddy Bear picnic, costume show, Historic Home and Church Tours and Colonial dinners. Est attendance: 50,000. For info: Marc Partin, Museum Dir, 2610 Biddle Ave, Wyandotte, MI 48192. Phone: (734) 324-7297. Fax: (734) 324-7283.

"THE X-FILES" TV PREMIERE: ANNIVERSARY. Sept 10, 1993. "The Truth Is Out There" was the mantra of FOX's scary and brainy sci-fi drama. Special FBI agents Fox Mulder (David Duchovny) and Dana Scully (Gillian Anderson) solved the cases too weird for the Bureau and also uncovered a vast conspiracy involving aliens and human-alien hybrids. *TV Guide* named "The X-Files" one of the greatest TV shows of all time. A feature-length film was created as well. The series ended in 2002.

ZIEGLER KETTLE MORAINE JAZZ FESTIVAL. Sept 10–11. Riverside Park, West Bend, WI. Features nationally recognized jazz musicians and vocalists. Past performers have included David Sanborn, Dave Koz and Rick Braun. Est attendance: 5,000. For info: Dave Amoroso, Ron Sonntag Public Relations, 9406 N 107th St, Milwaukee, WI 53224. Phone: (877) 271-6903. Fax: (414) 354-5317. E-mail: dave@rspr.com. Web: www.kmjazz.com.

Sept 10–11 ☆ Chase's 2004 Calendar of Events ☆

BIRTHDAYS TODAY

José Feliciano, 59, singer, musician ("Light My Fire," "Hi-Heel Sneakers"), born Lares, Puerto Rico, Sept 10, 1945.
Colin Firth, 44, actor (*Shakespeare in Love, Valmont*, "Pride and Prejudice"), born Grayshott, Hampshire, England, Sept 10, 1960.
Judy Geeson, 56, actress (*To Sir with Love, The Eagle Has Landed*), born Arundel, Sussex, England, Sept 10, 1948.
Matt Geiger, 35, former basketball player, born Salem, MA, Sept 10, 1969.
Amy Irving, 51, actress (*Carrie, Honeysuckle Rose*; singing voice of Jessica Rabbit), born Palo Alto, CA, Sept 10, 1953.
Clark Johnson, 40, actor ("Homicide"), born Philadelphia, PA, Sept 10, 1964.
Randy Johnson, 41, baseball player, born Walnut Creek, CA, Sept 10, 1963.
Karl Lagerfeld, 66, fashion designer, born Hamburg, Germany, Sept 10, 1938.
Joe Nieuwendyk, 38, hockey player, born Oshawa, ON, Canada, Sept 10, 1966.
Arnold Palmer, 75, golfer, born Latrobe, PA, Sept 10, 1929.
Yma Sumac, 76, singer, born Ichocan, Peru, Sept 10, 1928.
John Sununu, 40, US Senator (R, New Hampshire), born Boston, MA, Sept 10, 1964.
Robert Wise, 90, filmmaker (*The Curse of the Cat People, The Sound of Music*), born Winchester, IN, Sept 10, 1914.

SEPTEMBER 11 — SATURDAY

Day 255 — 111 Remaining

AEROSPACE WALK OF HONOR. Sept 11. Lancaster, CA. In the tradition of the aerospace industry of the Antelope Valley, the City of Lancaster Aerospace Walk of Honor attracts visitors to Lancaster Boulevard to the unveiling of granite monuments honoring Edwards Air Force Base test pilots whose aviation careers are marked by significant achievements. Honorees such as Neil Armstrong, Chuck Yeager and William "Pete" Knight are selected because they have soared above the rest. Est attendance: 5,000. For info: Anne Aldrich, Public Information Officer, City of Lancaster, 44933 Fern Ave, Lancaster, CA 93534. Phone: (661) 723-6053. Fax: (661) 723-6141. Web: city.cityoflancasterca.org.

ALBANY RIVERFRONT JAZZ FESTIVAL. Sept 11. Riverfront Ampitheater, Albany, NY. A daylong celebration of traditional and smooth jazz music. Great food and beverages, as well as children's activities, make for a great free festival. Est attendance: 15,000. For info: Albany Special Events, City Hall, 4th Fl, Eagle St, Albany, NY 12207. Phone: (518) 434-2032. Fax: (518) 426-0759. E-mail: info@albanyevents.org. Web: www.albanyevents.org.

ARTIST RECEPTION & ART IN THE GARDEN. Sept 11–12. Washington, PA. Est attendance: 1,200. For info: Joyce Mullen, Washington County Historical Society, 49 E Maiden St, Washington, PA 15317. Phone: (724) 225-6740. Fax: (724) 225-8495. E-mail: info@wchspa.org. Web: www.wchspa.org.

ATTACK ON AMERICA: ANNIVERSARY. Sept 11, 2001. Terrorists hijacked four planes, piloting two of them into the World Trade Center's twin towers in New York City and one into the Pentagon in Washington, DC. Passengers on the fourth plane appear to have attempted to overcome the hijackers, causing the plane to crash in western Pennsylvania instead of reaching its target in Washington. The twin towers at the WTC collapsed about an hour after being hit. More than 3,000 people died as a result of the attacks. The hijackers were agents of the Al Qaeda terrorist group led by Islamic extremist Osama bin Laden, who was headquartered in Afghanistan. In response, the US began unprecedented internal security measures and launched a war on terrorism with the support of many nations. See also: "The Fall of Kabul: Anniversary" (Nov 13) and "World Trade Center Recovery and Cleanup Ends: Anniversary" (May 30).

BATTLE OF BRANDYWINE: ANNIVERSARY. Sept 11, 1777. The largest engagement of the American Revolution, between the Continental Army led by General George Washington and British troops led by General William Howe. General Howe was marching to take Philadelphia when Washington chose to try and stop the British advance at the Brandywine River near Chadds Ford, PA. The American forces were defeated and the British went on to take Philadelphia Sept 26. They spent the winter in the city while Washington's troops suffered at their encampment at Valley Forge, PA.

BOONESBOROUGH DAYS. Sept 11–12. Shafer Memorial Park, Boonsboro, MD. Crafts, antiques, living history, demonstrations, food. Boonesborough was the original spelling of the town's name. Est attendance: 10,000. For info: Boonsboro Historical Society, PO Box 213, Boonsboro, MD 21713. Phone: (301) 432-5889.

"THE CAROL BURNETT SHOW" TV PREMIERE: ANNIVERSARY. Sept 11, 1967. This popular comedy/variety show starred comedienne Carol Burnett, who started the show by taking questions from the audience and ended with an ear tug. Sketches and spoofs included recurring characters like "The Family" (later to be spun off as "Mama's Family") and "As the Stomach Turns." Regular cast members included Harvey Korman, Lyle Waggoner and Vicki Lawrence. Later, Tim Conway joined the cast. Dick Van Dyke briefly joined after Korman left in 1977.

CARRY NATION FESTIVAL. Sept 11. Downtown Holly, MI. 31st annual festival re-creates the historical visit of Carry Nation, the Kansas City saloon smasher. Includes pageant, parade, entertainment tent, carnival, street dance and craft show. Annually, the Saturday after Labor Day. Est attendance: 25,000. For info: Holly Chamber of Commerce, PO Box 214, Holly, MI 48442. Phone: (248) 634-1900. Fax: (248) 634-1049.

CHADDS FORD DAYS. Sept 11–12. Chadds Ford, PA. Open-air Colonial fair with 18th-century craft demonstrations, Brandywine Valley art, live old-time music, country rides and games, colonial and contemporary crafts for sale, good food. Est attendance: 8,000. For info: Chadds Ford Historical Society, Box 27, Chadds Ford, PA 19317. Phone: (610) 388-7376. Web: www.chaddsfordhistory.org.

CHESTER COUNTY OLD FIDDLERS' PICNIC. Sept 11 (rain date Sept 12). Hibernia County Park, Coatesville, PA. Old-time musicians gather to make their traditional music. Est attendance: 4,200. For info: Chester County Parks and Recreation Dept, PO Box 2747, 601 Westtown Rd, Ste 160, West Chester, PA 19380-0990. Phone: (610) 344-6415 or (610) 383-3812. Web: www.chesco.org/ccparks.

CIVIL WAR DAYS. Sept 11–12. Chesapeake Central Library, Chesapeake, VA. 12th annual reenactment and living history event. Skirmish both days, encampment drills, demonstrations,

	S	M	T	W	T	F	S
September				1	2	3	4
2004	5	6	7	8	9	10	11
	12	13	14	15	16	17	18
	19	20	21	22	23	24	25
	26	27	28	29	30		

☆ Chase's 2004 Calendar of Events ☆   Sept 11

speakers, displays, children's activities and much more. Music groups and food vendors on site. Est attendance: 15,000. For info: Rhonda Riddick, Chesapeake Central Library, 298 Cedar Rd, Chesapeake, VA 23322. Phone: (757) 382-8571. Fax: (757) 382-8400. E-mail: rriddick@chesapeake.lib.va.us. Web: www.chesapeake.lib.va.us.

ETHIOPIA: NEW YEAR'S DAY. Sept 11. In the year 2004, this day will start the year 1998 on the Ethiopian Orthodox calendar. On the Coptic Orthodox calendar, it begins the year 1721.

FINE ART FAIR. Sept 11–12. Historic Woodstock Square, Woodstock, IL. A juried show featuring paintings, ceramics, photography, sculpture, fiber arts, jewelry and other fine work. Est attendance: 5,000. For info: Woodstock Chamber of Commerce, 136 Cass St, Woodstock, IL 60098. Phone: (815) 338-2436. Fax: (815) 338-2927. E-mail: chamber@woodstockilchamber.com. Web: www.woodstockilchamber.com.

FLAX SCUTCHING FESTIVAL. Sept 11–12. Stahlstown, PA. PA Turnpike Exit 9; four miles north on Rte 711. Demonstrations of the art of making linen from the flax plant. Second oldest continuous complete flax demonstration festival in the world. Annually, the second full weekend in September. Est attendance: 15,000. For info: Frank Newell, Flax Scutching Festival, RR 1, Rt 130W, Box 216, Stahlstown, PA 15687. Phone: (724) 593-2119 or (724) 238-9244.

FOOD STAMPS AUTHORIZED: 45th ANNIVERSARY. Sept 11, 1959. Congress passed a bill authorizing food stamps for low-income Americans.

GARDENFEST AT LONGWOOD GARDENS. Sept 11–Oct 10. Kennett Square, PA. Longwood celebrates September beauty and bounty with harvest displays, flower shows, gardening demonstrations, family entertainment, and a miniature garden railway. Est attendance: 50,000. For info: Elizabeth Sullivan, Pub Dir, Longwood Gardens, PO Box 501, Kennett Square, PA 19348-0501. Phone: (610) 388-1000. Web: www.longwoodgardens.org.

HANG AROUND VICTOR DAY. Sept 11. Victor, NY. Festival with artists, craftsmen, antique dealers, civic and social organizations, family entertainment, pet parade and pet contest, cloggers, magicians, clowns and food vendors. Annually, the first Saturday after Labor Day. Est attendance: 25,000. For info: Susan Stehling, Victor Chamber of Commerce, 31 E Main St, Victor, NY 14564. Phone: (585) 924-7260 or (585) 742-1476. Fax: (585) 924-0523.

HERITAGE DAY FESTIVAL. Sept 11 (rain date Sept 12). Lavallette, NJ. Clowns, antique cars, four live bands, games, food, children's games, train rides and finale with Ocean County String Band performing. 10 AM–dusk. Annually, the first Saturday after Labor Day. Est attendance: 30,000. For info: Joy Grosko, Dir, Heritage Committee Inc, 13 Camden Ave, Lavallette, NJ 08735. Phone: (732) 793-3652. Fax: (732) 854-9038. E-mail: tgrosko1@juno.com.

HILLTOP FESTIVAL. Sept 11–12. Huntington Museum of Art, Huntington, WV. Book fair, arts and crafts and demonstrations, children's activities and food booths. HMA is fully accessible. Annually, first weekend after Labor Day. Est attendance: 3,000. For info: Huntington Museum of Art, 2033 McCoy Rd, Huntington, WV 25701. Phone: (304) 529-2701. Fax: (304) 529-7447. Web: www.hmoa.org.

ISRA AL MI'RAJ: ASCENT OF THE PROPHET MUHAMMAD. Sept 11. Islamic calendar date: Rajab 27, 1425. Commemorates the journey of the Prophet Muhammad from Mecca to Jerusalem, his ascension into the Seven Heavens and his return on the same night. Muslims believe that on that night Muhammad prayed together with Abraham, Moses and Jesus in the area of the Al-Aqsa Mosque in Jerusalem. The rock from which he is believed to have ascended to heaven to speak with God is the one inside The Dome of the Rock. Different methods for "anticipating" the visibility of the new moon crescent at Mecca are used by different Muslim groups. US date may vary. Began at sunset the preceding day.

JACKSON HILL CIDER DAY. Sept 11. Jackson House, Portsmouth, NH. Noon–5 PM. A harvest celebration for families and children in the orchards of the oldest house in New Hampshire. Children can wield picking poles and assist in pressing cider and cranking the paring machines. Fiddle music, beekeeping, samples of traditional sauce and pie and free tours of the house are included in the celebration. Annually, second Saturday in September. Est attendance: 120. For info: Society for Preservation of New England Antiquities, 143 Pleasant St, Portsmouth, NH 03801. Phone: (603) 436-3205. Fax: (603) 436-4651.

KANABEC FALL FEST. Sept 11. Kanabec History Center, Mora, MN. A beautiful setting for this 15th annual festival that showcases a diverse blend of demonstrating and performing folk artists. Arts activities and fun for all ages. Est attendance: 2,500. For info: Kanabec History Center, 805 W Forest Ave, PO Box 113, Mora, MN 55051. Phone: (320) 679-1665. Fax: (320) 679-1673. E-mail: center@kanabechistory.org. Web: www.kanabechistory.org.

LAWRENCE, DAVID HERBERT: BIRTH ANNIVERSARY. Sept 11, 1885. English novelist, author of *Lady Chatterley's Lover*. Born at Eastwood, Nottinghamshire, England, D.H. Lawrence died Mar 2, 1930, at Vence, France.

LIND, JENNY: US PREMIERE: ANNIVERSARY. Sept 11, 1850. Jenny Lind, the "Swedish Nightingale," gave her first American performance in the Castle Garden Theatre, New York, NY, on this day.

LITTLE FALLS ARTS AND CRAFTS FAIR. Sept 11–12. Little Falls, MN. 950 artists, craftspeople and hobbyists displaying and selling their items. Est attendance: 100,000. For info: Chamber of Commerce, 200 NW First St, Little Falls, MN 56345. Phone: (320) 632-5155. Fax: (320) 632-2122. E-mail: assistance@littlefallsmnchamber.com. Web: www.littlefallsmnchamber.com.

"LITTLE HOUSE ON THE PRAIRIE" TV PREMIERE: 30th ANNIVERSARY. Sept 11, 1974. This hour-long family drama was based on books by Laura Ingalls Wilder. It focused on the Ingalls family and their neighbors living at Walnut Grove, MN: Michael Landon as Charles (Pa), Karen Grassle as Caroline (Ma), Melissa Sue Anderson as daughter Mary, Melissa Gilbert as daughter Laura, from whose point of view the stories were told, Lindsay and Sidney Greenbush as daughters Carrie and Wendi and Brenda Turnbaugh as daughter Grace. In its last season (1982), the show's name was changed to "Little House: A New Beginning." Landon appeared less often and the show centered around Laura and her husband.

LOUISIANA FOLKLIFE FESTIVAL. Sept 11–12. Monroe, LA. A festival of Louisiana's culture, heritage and music, featuring five entertainment stages, craft demonstrations and food. For info: Mike Luster. Phone: (318) 324-1665. Web: www.louisianafolklifefest.org.

MARCOS, FERDINAND EDRALIN: BIRTH ANNIVERSARY. Sept 11, 1917. Former ruler of the Philippines, born at Sarrat, Philippines. Ferdinand Marcos served as head of state from 1966 until his ouster in 1986. His authoritarian regime was marred by widespread corruption and suppression of democratic processes. After the assassination of Benigno Aquino, Jr in 1983, antigovernment protests increased and Marcos called for an election in 1986, hoping to reassert his mandate. Although he defeated Corazon Aquino in the election, it was widely asserted he did so through massive vote fraud, leading to a decline in support, and Corazon Aquino became the new president of the Philippines. Marcos died in exile Sept 28, 1989, at Honolulu, HI.

MUSHROOM FESTIVAL. Sept 11–12. Downtown Kennett Square, PA. Weekend of fun, food and fungi at the mushroom capital of the world! Help taste and judge the soup cook-off, attend cooking or growing demos. Also mushroom judging, art show, car show, BrewFest, WineFest, Street Festival with entertainment and mushroom farm tours. Est attendance: 80,000. For info: The Mushroom Festival, PO Box 1000, Kennett Square, PA 19348. Phone: (888) 440-9920. E-mail: info@mushroomfest.com. Web: www.mushroomfestival.org.

NANTICOKE INDIAN POWWOW. Sept 11–12. Millsboro, DE. Annual gathering of Native Americans during which Native American dances, music and storytelling are presented and Native American foods and arts and crafts are sold. 40 different tribes participate. Dance sessions: Saturday, noon–5 PM, Sunday, 2–5 PM. Sunday worship service, 10:30 AM–noon. Annually, the weekend after Labor Day. Est attendance: 40,000. For info: Nanticoke Indian Assn, Rte 13, Box 107A, Millsboro, DE 19966. Phone: (302) 945-3400. E-mail: nanticok@bellatlantic.net.

O. HENRY (WILLIAM S. PORTER): BIRTH ANNIVERSARY. Sept 11, 1862. William Sydney Porter, American author, who wrote under the pen name O. Henry. Best known for his short stories, including "Gift of the Magi." Born at Greensboro, NC, he died at New York, NY, June 5, 1910.

PAKISTAN: FOUNDER'S DEATH ANNIVERSARY. Sept 11. Pakistan observes the death anniversary in 1948 of Qaid-e-Azam Mohammed Ali Jinnah (founder of Pakistan) as a national holiday. His birth date of Dec 25 is also a national holiday.

PATRIOT DAY. Sept 11. On Dec 18, 2001, a joint resolution of Congress amended Title 36, Chapter 1, Sec. 144 of the US Code to permit the President to declare Sept 11 of each year as Patriot Day, in commemoration of the terrorist attacks on the United States on Sept 11, 2001. The resolution requests that all state and local governments observe this day "with appropriate programs and activities," that the flag be displayed at half-staff from sunrise till sundown and that a moment of silence be observed in honor of those who lost their lives in the attacks.

POTATO DAY FESTIVAL. Sept 11. Centennial Village Museum, Greeley, CO. Living history demonstrations, musical entertainment, square dancing, cloggers, children's activities spread over five-acre site. Free baked potato and trimmings. Ages 12 and over $5. Children free. Est attendance: 3,000. For info: Greeley Museums, 919 7th St, Greeley, CO 80631. Phone: (970) 350-9220. Fax: (970) 350-9700. Web: www.greeleymuseums.com.

PRAIRIE DAY. Sept 11. Diamond, MO. A celebration of life on the Missouri prairie. Prairie walks, wagon rides, basket weaving, candle making, Dutch oven cooking and numerous other activities. For info: George Washington Carver National Monument, 5646 Carver Rd, Diamond, MO 64840. Phone: (417) 325-4151. Fax: (417) 325-4231. E-mail: superintendent@nps.gov. Web: www.nps.gov/gwca.

QUADRANGLE FESTIVAL. Sept 11–12. Downtown Texarkana, TX and AR. 23rd annual festival features 5K BiState Race on the Texas-Arkansas state line. Also, three stages of entertainment, more than 150 artists and craftsmen, antique autos, pet shows; country/rock, traditional and contemporary music; street dancing and food vendors. Est attendance: 35,000. For info: Dir of Mktg, Texarkana Museums System, PO Box 2343, Texarkana, TX 75504. Phone: (903) 793-4831. Fax: (903) 793-7108. Web: www.texarkanamuseums.com.

SCOTT COUNTY "UGLY WOMAN" CONTEST. Sept 11. Downtown Courthouse, Scottsburg, IN. Part of the 24th annual CourtFest, a fund-raising activity where the biggest men in the area compete for the title and crown. Money raised goes to the winner's favorite charity. "Ugly Women" compete in various categories, including costume and stage presence, trivia and fund-raising success. Also arts & crafts and a free concert featuring a national entertainer. Always the first weekend after Labor Day. For info: Exec Dir, Scott County Visitors Commission, 5809 W Oak Hill Road, Scottsburg, IN 47170. Phone: (812) 752-9211. Fax: (812) 752-0151. E-mail: tourscott@aol.com. Web: www.greatscottindiana.org.

1786 ANNAPOLIS CONVENTION: ANNIVERSARY. Sept 11–14, 1786. Twelve delegates from New York, New Jersey, Delaware, Pennsylvania and Virginia met at Annapolis, MD, to discuss commercial matters of mutual interest. The delegates voted, on Sept 14, to adopt a resolution prepared by Alexander Hamilton asking all states to send representatives to a convention at Philadelphia, PA, in May 1787 "to render the constitution of the Federal Government adequate to the exigencies of the Union."

SIDEWALK ARTS FESTIVAL. Sept 11. Sioux Falls, SD. Live entertainment, music, great food, cultural activities and more than 400 booths featuring the area's best art and folk displays. Est attendance: 60,000. For info: Visual Arts Center at the Washington Pavilion, 301 S Main Ave, Sioux Falls, SD 57104. Phone: (605) 367-7397 x 2353. Fax: (605) 731-2402. E-mail: vac@washingtonpavilion.org. Web: www.washingtonpavilion.org.

SODBUSTER DAYS—THE HARVEST. Sept 11–12. Sunne Farm, Fort Ransom State Park, Fort Ransom, ND. Demonstrations of life on a small family farm of the 1920s during the fall harvest. Activities include threshing, fall field work, gathering prairie hay, ladies' demonstrations, kids' games, food, music. Most farm machinery is horse drawn. Annually, the weekend after Labor Day. Est attendance: 2,000. For info: Fort Ransom State Park, 5981 Walt Hjelle Pkwy, Fort Ransom, ND 58033-9712. Phone: (701) 973-4331. Fax: (701) 973-4271.

SOUTHEAST MISSOURI DISTRICT FAIR. Sept 11–18. Arena Park Fairgrounds, Cape Girardeau, MO. Oldest outdoor fair in the state. Celebrating its 149th year with beauty pageants, livestock exhibition, horse show, entertainment, carnival, food and 4-H and FFA displays. Annually, starts the Saturday after Labor Day and continues to the next Saturday. Est attendance: 100,000. For info: SEMO District Fair Assn, PO Box 234, Cape Girardeau, MO 63702-0234. Phone: (800) 455-FAIR or (573) 334-9250. Web: www.semofair.com.

SPACE MILESTONE: *MARS GLOBAL SURVEYOR* (US). Sept 11, 1997. Launched Nov 7, 1996, this unmanned vehicle was put into orbit around Mars. It was designed to compile global maps of Mars by taking high-resolution photos. This mission inaugurated a new series of Mars expeditions in which NASA launched pairs of orbiters and landers to Mars. *Mars Global Surveyor* was paired with the lander *Mars Pathfinder*. See also: "Space Milestone: *Mars Pathfinder*" (July 4).

TYLER'S CABINET RESIGNS: ANNIVERSARY. Sept 11, 1841. In protest of President John Tyler's veto of the Banking Bill all of his cabinet except Secretary of State Daniel Webster resigned on this day.

VALPARAISO POPCORN FESTIVAL. Sept 11. Valparaiso, IN. Celebration of popcorn with a parade, the Popcorn Panic and Little Kernel Puff running races, arts, crafts, food booths, music and entertainment, kiddie carnival and a hot-air balloon show. Annually, the first Saturday after Labor Day. Est attendance: 65,000. For info: Glennas Kueck, Exec Dir, 204 E Lincolnway, PO Box 189, Valparaiso, IN 46384. Phone: (219) 464-8332. Fax: (219) 464-2343. E-mail: popcorn@netnitco.net. Web: www.popcornfest.org.

WILLOW TREE FESTIVAL. Sept 11–12. Gordon, NE. This festival is a cornucopia of arts and crafts, three quality performing stages including a children's stage, children's activities, fun and

September 2004

S	M	T	W	T	F	S
			1	2	3	4
5	6	7	8	9	10	11
12	13	14	15	16	17	18
19	20	21	22	23	24	25
26	27	28	29	30		

☆ Chase's 2004 Calendar of Events ☆   Sept 11–12

food. Annually, the second weekend in September. Est attendance: 4,600. For info: Willow Tree Festival, PO Box 303, Gordon, NE 69343-0303. Phone: (308) 282-2464. E-mail: barth@gpcom.net.

WOODLAND INDIAN DISCOVERY DAY. Sept 11. St. Mary's City, MD. Explore the lifeways of the Yaocomaco Indian people at the Woodland Indian Hamlet. Hands-on demonstrations, storytelling and more. Est attendance: 800. For info: Visitors Services, Historic St. Mary's City, PO Box 39, St. Mary's City, MD 20686. Phone: (240) 895-4990 or (800) SMC-1634. Fax: (240) 895-4968. Web: www.stmaryscity.org.

BIRTHDAYS TODAY

Daniel K. Akaka, 80, US Senator (D, Hawaii), born Honolulu, HI, Sept 11, 1924.
Harry Connick, Jr, 37, singer (Grammy for *We Are in Love*), actor (*When Harry Met Sally...*), born New Orleans, LA, Sept 11, 1967.
Brian De Palma, 64, filmmaker (*The Untouchables, Bonfire of the Vanities, Carrie*), born Newark, NJ, Sept 11, 1940.
Lola Falana, 61, actress ("The New Bill Cosby Show," "Ben Vereen—Comin' at Ya"), born Camden, NJ, Sept 11, 1943.
William Xavier Kienzle, 76, author (*Body Count, The Rosary Murders*), former priest, born Detroit, MI, Sept 11, 1928.
Donna Lopiano, 58, women's sports executive and former softball player, born Stamford, CT, Sept 11, 1946.
Amy Madigan, 53, actress (*Places in the Heart, Field of Dreams, Uncle Buck*), born Chicago, IL, Sept 11, 1951.
Virginia Madsen, 41, actress (*Dune, The Hot Spot, Candyman*), born Winnetka, IL, Sept 11, 1963.
Kristy McNichol, 42, actress (Emmys for "Family"; "Empty Nest"; *Little Darlings, Two Moon Junction*), born Los Angeles, CA, Sept 11, 1962.
Moby, 39, rock singer/songwriter, born Richard Melville Hall, New York, NY, Sept 11, 1965.

SEPTEMBER 12 — SUNDAY

Day 256 — 110 Remaining

BATTLE OF SAINT-MIHIEL: ANNIVERSARY. Sept 12, 1918. Under the command of General John J. Pershing, the 1st US Army attacked the Germans at the Saint-Mihiel salient. This was the first major US offensive of the war. Sixteen army divisions, coupled with French II Colonial Corps tanks and artillery support, forced back the Germans after 36 hours of heavy fighting and reclaimed 200 square miles of French territory that had been in the hands of the Germans since 1914. The 1st US Army lost about 7,000 soldiers in the Battle of Saint-Mihiel.

CATONSVILLE ARTS & CRAFTS FESTIVAL. Sept 12. Catonsville, MD. Fall festival featuring handmade items by 200 artisans and crafters in the revitalized village of Catonsville. Continuous music, children's entertainment and local food vendors. Annually, the Sunday after Labor Day. Est attendance: 30,000. For info: Greater Catonsville Chamber of Commerce, PO Box 21100, Catonsville, MD 21228. Phone: (410) 719-9609.

CHARLES LEROUX'S LAST JUMP: ANNIVERSARY. Sept 12, 1889. American aeronaut of French extraction, born in New York, NY, about 1857, achieved world fame as a parachutist. After his first public performance (Philadelphia, PA, 1887) he toured European cities where his parachute jumps attracted wide attention. Credited with 238 successful jumps. On Sept 12, 1889, he jumped from a balloon over Tallinn, Estonia, and perished in the Bay of Reval.

CZECH REPUBLIC: PRAGUE AUTUMN INTERNATIONAL MUSIC FESTIVAL. Sept 12–Oct 1. Symphonic and chamber orchestras, instrumental concerts and recitals. For info: Prague Autumn International Music Festival, 130 00 - CZ, Prague 3, Pribenicka 20, Czech Republic. Phone: (42 2) 22 540 484. Fax: (42 2) 22 540 415. E-mail: festival@pragueautumn.cz. Web: pragueautumn.cz.

DEFENDERS DAY. Sept 12. Maryland. Public holiday. Annual reenactment of bombardment of Fort McHenry in 1814 that inspired Francis Scott Key to write the "Star-Spangled Banner."

FESTIVAL-IN-THE-PARK. Sept 12 (rain date Sept 26). Memorial Park, Nutley, NJ. 31st annual festival, a craft and collectibles show to benefit the Nutley Historical Society and the Historic Restoration Trust. Annually, the first Sunday after Labor Day. Est attendance: 16,000. For info: Douglas J. Eisenfelder, Festival-in-the-Park, 51 Enclosure, Nutley, NJ 07110. Phone: (973) 667-3013.

"FRAGGLE ROCK" TV PREMIERE: ANNIVERSARY. Sept 12, 1987. This children's show was a cartoon version of the live Jim Henson puppet production on HBO. It was set in the rock underneath a scientist's house and featured characters such as the Fraggles, the Doozers and the Gorgs.

GRANDPARENT'S DAY CELEBRATION. Sept 12. Jenkinson's Aquarium, Point Pleasant Beach, NJ. Calling all kids! Join your grandparents for a special day together at the aquarium. We will focus on families in the animal kingdom. Stories about animal families will be read throughout the day. One grandparent is admitted free with each paid child's admission (child is 3–12 years). Est attendance: 800. For info: Jenkinson's Aquarium, 300 Ocean Ave, Point Pleasant Beach, NJ 08742. Phone: (732) 899-1212. Fax: (732) 899-1717. E-mail: aquarium@jenkinsons.com. Web: www.jenkinsons.com.

GUINEA-BISSAU: NATIONAL HOLIDAY. Sept 12. Amilcar Cabral's birthday, Sept 12, is observed as a national holiday.

HOMESTEADER HARVEST FESTIVAL. Sept 12. Beaver Creek Nature Area, Brandon, SD. This is a re-creation of the harvest and celebration that went with it back in the pioneer days. Annually, the Sunday after Labor Day. Est attendance: 1,200. For info: Palisades State Park, 25495 485th Ave, Garretson, SD 57030-6117. Phone: (605) 594-3824.

ITALY: GIOSTRA DELLA QUINTANA. Sept 12. Foligno. A revival of a 17th-century joust of the Quintana, featuring 600 knights in full costume. Annually, the second Sunday in September.

"LASSIE" TV PREMIERE: 50th ANNIVERSARY. Sept 12, 1954. This long-running series was originally about a boy and his courageous and intelligent dog, Lassie (played by more than six different dogs, all male). For the first few seasons, Lassie lived on the Miller farm. The family included Jeff (Tommy Rettig), his widowed mother Ellen (Jan Clayton) and George Cleveland as Gramps. Throughout the years there were many format and cast changes, as Lassie was exchanged from one family to another in order to have a variety of new perils and escapades. Other featured performers included Cloris Leachman, June Lockhart and Larry Wilcox.

Sept 12 ☆ Chase's 2004 Calendar of Events ☆

LISCO OLD-TIMERS DAY. Sept 12. Lisco, NE. Local talent puts on program and skits about an honored old-timer or couple. Parade, barbecue (free-will offering), horseshoe tournament and more. Annually, Sunday after Labor Day. Sponsor: Lisco Old-timers Day Committee. Est attendance: 2,000. For info: Lisco State Bank, Lisco Old-Timers Day Committee, Lisco, NE 69148.

"MAUDE" TV PREMIERE: ANNIVERSARY. Sept 12, 1972. Bea Arthur's character, Maude Findlay, was first introduced as Edith Bunker's cousin on "All in the Family." She was a loud, opinionated liberal, living with her fourth husband Walter (Bill Macy). Other characters on the show were her divorced daughter by a previous marriage, Carol Trainer (Adrienne Barbeau), Conrad Bain as Dr. Arthur Harmon, Rue McClanahan as Arthur's wife Vivian, Esther Rolle as Florida Evans, Maude's maid and John Amos as her husband, Henry. This was one of the first shows to tackle the controversial issue of abortion.

MENCKEN, HENRY LOUIS: BIRTH ANNIVERSARY. Sept 12, 1880. American newspaperman, lexicographer and critic, "the Sage of Baltimore" was born at Baltimore, MD, and died there Jan 29, 1956. "If, after I depart this vale," he wrote in 1921 (Epitaph, *Smart Set*), "you ever remember me and have thought to please my ghost, forgive some sinner and wink your eye at some homely girl."

MERCEDES-BENZ FASHION WEEK SPRING 05. Sept 12–18 (tentative). New York, NY. Fashion designers present their Spring 2005 lines. For info: 7th on Sixth, 420 W 45th St, 6th Fl, New York, NY 10036. Phone: (212) 253-2692. E-mail: info@7thonsixth.com. Web: www.7thonsixth.com.

"THE MONKEES" TV PREMIERE: ANNIVERSARY. Sept 12, 1966. Featuring a rock group that was supposed to be an American version of the Beatles, this half-hour show featured a blend of comedy and music. Four young actors were chosen from more than 400 to play the group members: Micky Dolenz, Davy Jones, Mike Nesmith and Peter Tork. Dolenz and Jones had previous acting experience and Tork and Nesmith had previous musical experience. The music that they performed on the show proved to be immensely popular; at first they sang with a studio band but later insisted on writing and performing their own music. They released several albums and toured several times. In 1986, the Monkees, except for Nesmith, were reunited for a 20th Anniversary tour and the show was broadcast in reruns on MTV. The Monkees sans Nesmith also toured in 1996 for the 30th reunion celebration.

NATIONAL ASSISTED LIVING WEEK. Sept 12–18. A weeklong observance designed to raise awareness of the role assisted living plays in serving the nation's elderly. Annually, Grandparents' Day through the following Saturday. For info: Natl Center for Assisted Living, 1201 L St NW, Washington, DC 20005. Phone: (202) 842-4444. Fax: (202) 842-3860.

NATIONAL GRANDPARENTS' DAY. Sept 12. To honor grandparents, to give grandparents an opportunity to show love for their children's children and to help children become aware of the strength, information and guidance older people can offer. Annually, the first Sunday after Labor Day.

NATIONAL GRANDPARENT'S DAY AT THE TOP MUSEUM. Sept 12. Burlington, WI. Grandparents and great-grandparents are honored with a special program. Enjoy the traditional, universal toys of tops, yo-yos and gyroscopes with your grandchildren. See the amazing exhibit of more than 2,000 items, play with 35 different games and tops, view videos and enjoy a show by a top collector. Grandparents admitted free with a paying grandchild. For info: Top Museum, 533 Milwaukee Ave (Hwy 36), Burlington, WI 53105. Phone: (262) 763-3946.

September 2004	S	M	T	W	T	F	S
				1	2	3	4
	5	6	7	8	9	10	11
	12	13	14	15	16	17	18
	19	20	21	22	23	24	25
	26	27	28	29	30		

NORTHEAST MISSOURI TRIATHLON CHAMPIONSHIP. Sept 12. Thousand Hills State Park, Kirksville, MO. Swim 3/4 mile, bike 18 miles, run 5 miles. USA Triathlon sanctioned. Qualifier for International Course Nationals. Annually, the Sunday after Labor Day. Est attendance: 350. For info: KCOM-TCC, 210 S Osteopathy, Kirksville, MO 63501. Phone: (660) 626-2213. Fax: (660) 626-2071. E-mail: lcrossgrove@kcom.edu. Web: www.nemotriathlon.org.

OCEAN COUNTY BLUEGRASS FESTIVAL. Sept 12. Waretown, NJ. An indoor bluegrass festival. No alcoholic beverages or smoking allowed. Est attendance: 400. For info: Albert Music Hall, PO Box 657, Waretown, NJ 08758. Phone: (609) 971-1593. Web: www.alberthall.org.

OWENS, JESSE: BIRTH ANNIVERSARY. Sept 12, 1913. James Cleveland (Jesse) Owens, American athlete, winner of four gold medals at the 1936 Olympic Games at Berlin, Germany, was born at Oakville, AL. Owens set 11 world records in track and field. During one track meet, at Ann Arbor, MI, May 23, 1935, Owens, representing Ohio State University, broke three world records and tied a fourth in the space of 70 minutes. Died at Tucson, AZ, Mar 31, 1980.

PROSTATE CANCER AWARENESS WEEK. Sept 12–18. Free or low-cost prostate cancer screenings for all men 40–75 and men in high-risk groups such as African-American men and Hispanics over age 35. Annually, the third week in September. For info: Prostate Cancer Education Council, 5299 DTC Blvd, Ste 345, Greenwood Village, CO 80111. Phone: (303) 316-4685. Web: www.pcaw.com.

SPACE MILESTONE: *LUNA 2* (USSR): 45th ANNIVERSARY. Sept 12, 1959. First spacecraft to land on moon was launched.

UNITED KINGDOM: BATTLE OF BRITAIN WEEK. Sept 12–18. Annually, the week of September containing Battle of Britain Day (Sept 15).

VIDEO GAMES DAY. Sept 12. A day for kids who love video games to celebrate the fun they have playing them and to thank their parents for all the cartridges and quarters they have provided to indulge this enthusiasm.

WARNER, CHARLES DUDLEY: 175th BIRTH ANNIVERSARY. Sept 12, 1829. American newspaperman, born at Plainfield, MA, authored many works, but is perhaps best remembered for a single sentence (in an editorial, *Hartford Courant*, Aug 24, 1897): "Everybody talks about the weather, but nobody does anything about it." The quotation is often mistakenly attributed to his friend, Mark Twain. Died at Hartford, CT, Oct 20, 1900.

BIRTHDAYS TODAY

Sam Brownback, 48, US Senator (R, Kansas), born Garnett, KS, Sept 12, 1956.
Irene Dailey, 84, actress ("Another World"), born New York, NY, Sept 12, 1920.
Linda Gray, 63, actress ("Dallas," "Melrose Place"), born Santa Monica, CA, Sept 12, 1941.
Ian Holm, 73, actor (*Alien*, Academy Award for *Chariots of Fire*), born Goodmayes, England, Sept 12, 1931.
George Jones, 73, singer ("White Lightning," "Race Is On," "He Stopped Loving Her Today"), born Saratoga, TX, Sept 12, 1931.

☆ Chase's 2004 Calendar of Events ☆ Sept 12–13

Yao Ming, 24, basketball player, born Shanghai, China, Sept 12, 1980.
Maria Muldaur, 61, singer ("Midnight at the Oasis," "I'm a Woman"), born New York, NY, Sept 12, 1943.
Joe Pantoliano, 50, actor (*Risky Business, The Fugitive*; stage: *Orphans*), born Jersey City, NJ, Sept 12, 1954.
Peter Scolari, 50, actor ("Bosom Buddies," "Newhart"), born New Rochelle, NY, Sept 12, 1954.
Rachel Ward, 47, actress ("The Thorn Birds," *Against All Odds*), born London, England, Sept 12, 1957.
Amy Yasbeck, 41, actress (*The Mask*, "Wings"), born Cincinnati, OH, Sept 12, 1963.

SEPTEMBER 13 — MONDAY
Day 257 — 109 Remaining

ANDERSON, SHERWOOD: BIRTH ANNIVERSARY. Sept 13, 1876. American author and newspaper publisher, born at Camden, OH. His best remembered book is *Winesburg, Ohio*. Anderson died at Colon, Panama, Mar 8, 1941.

BARRY, JOHN: DEATH ANNIVERSARY. Sept 13, 1803. Revolutionary War hero John Barry, first American to hold the rank of commodore, died at Philadelphia, PA. He was born at Tacumshane, County Wexford, Ireland, in 1745. He has been called the "Father of the American Navy."

"BENSON" TV PREMIERE: 25th ANNIVERSARY. Sept 13, 1979. This half-hour sitcom was a spin-off from the popular series "Soap." Benson, played by Robert Guillaume, went to work for Jessica's Tate's widowed cousin Governor James Gatling, played by James Noble. The series centered around Benson trying to keep the household intact while the governor performed his duties for the state. The last telecast aired Aug 30, 1986. Other cast members included Missy Gold, Rene Auberjonois, Ethan Phillips, Didi Conn, Caroline McWilliams, Inga Swenson and Lewis J. Stadlen.

"CHICO AND THE MAN" TV PREMIERE: 30th ANNIVERSARY. Sept 13, 1974. This sitcom starred Jack Albertson as Ed Brown, a cranky garage owner, and Freddie Prinze as Chico Rodriguez, his Mexican-American employee. It was set in the barrio of East Los Angeles. However, the show was widely criticized for its use of the term "Chico," which was derogatory to many Chicanos, and for the lack of Mexican Americans in the cast or crew. To remedy this, the cast was expanded to include Issac Ruiz as Chico's friend Ramon and Rodolfo Hoyos as Ed's friend Rudy. Also added were Scatman Crothers as Louie Wilson, the garbage collector; Bonnie Boland as Mabel, the letter carrier; Ronny Graham as Reverend Bemis and Della Reese as Della Rogers, Ed's landlady. Prinze committed suicide in 1977 but the series continued with Gabriel Melgar as Raul Garcia, a Mexican kid adopted by Ed. Charo also joined the show as Aunt Charo.

COLBERT, CLAUDETTE: BIRTH ANNIVERSARY. Sept 13, 1903. Actress and comedienne Colbert, born Lily Claudette Chauchoin at Paris, France, was a beloved movie star of the '30s. She was best known for her films *Midnight, Cleopatra* and *It Happened One Night*, for which she won an Oscar in 1934. In addition to more than 60 movies, she appeared in Broadway shows and won a Golden Globe award for her role in the 1986 miniseries "The Two Mrs Grenvilles." She also received a Life Achievement Award from the Kennedy Center for Performing Arts in 1989. She died July 30, 1996, at Bridgetown, Barbados.

DAHL, ROALD: BIRTH ANNIVERSARY. Sept 13, 1916. Author (*Charlie and the Chocolate Factory, James and the Giant Peach*), born at Llandaff, South Wales, Great Britain. Died Nov 23, 1990, at Oxford, England.

FORTUNE COOKIE DAY. Sept 13. San Francisco, CA. San Francisco—birthplace of the fortune cookie—is the Fortune Cookie Capital of the World. Celebrate good fortune and family fun today! For info: Margaret Speaker Yuan, 17 Mt Darwin Ct, San Rafael, CA 94903. Phone: (415) 492-1074. E-mail: books4women@yahoo.com. Web: www.fortunecookieday.com.

HABITAT FOR HUMANITY'S INTERNATIONAL BUILDING ON FAITH WEEK. Sept 13–19. An opportunity to celebrate Habitat for Humanity's partnerships with denominations around the world building houses as a global witness to faith in action. Uniting people of diverse faiths in the common cause of eliminating poverty housing and rebuilding communities, Habitat for Humanity affiliates around the country are reaching out to families in need by holding multi-faith builds. For info: Habitat for Humanity, 121 Habitat St, Americus, GA 31709-3498. Phone: (800) HABITAT or (229) 924-6935. E-mail: publicinfo@hfhi.org. Web: www.habitat.org.

"LAW & ORDER" TV PREMIERE: ANNIVERSARY. Sept 13, 1990. This hour-long series, filmed on location at New York City, shows the interaction between the police and the district attorney's office in dealing with a crime. Almost the entire cast has changed over the life of this program; Steven Hill (District Attorney Adam Schiff) was the only constant until 2000 when he was replaced by Dianne Wiest, followed by Fred Dalton Thompson in 2002. Michael Moriarty (Assistant District Attorney Benjamin Stone) was followed by Sam Waterston (ADA Jack McCoy). The police have been represented by George Dzundza (Detective Max Greevey), followed by Paul Sorvino (Detective Phil Cerreta), followed by Jerry Orbach (Detective Lennie Briscoe). Christopher Noth (Detective Mike Logan) was replaced by Benjamin Bratt (Detective Reynaldo Curtis) followed by Jesse L. Martin (Detective Edward Green). Dann Florek (Captain Donald Cragen) was followed by S. Epatha Merkerson (Lieutenant Anita Van Buren). Other stars have included Richard Brooks, Jill Hennessy, Carey Lowell, Angie Harmon and Elisabeth Rohm.

LOVE A MENSCH WEEK. Sept 13–19. Mensches are decent, responsible men or women. During this week singles look to meet a mensch as well as take time to appreciate how mensches enhance our lives. For info: Robin Gorman Newman, 44 Somerset Dr N, Great Neck, NY 11020. Phone: (516) 773-0911. E-mail: robin@lovecoach.com. Web: www.lovecoach.com.

LUNCH PROWL WEEK. Sept 13–19. A week dedicated to teaching women how to use their lunch hour to find single men. This event introduces women to a new method of mate-searching that is based on the compatability of a man's profession with hers. Women will learn how to follow simple techniques to maximize their mate-searching efforts. For info: Nancy Fagan, MS. Phone: (408) 499-9010. E-mail: AskDrRomance@aol.com. Web: www.ExpertDatingAdvice.com.

"THE MUPPET SHOW" TV PREMIERE: ANNIVERSARY. Sept 13, 1976. This comedy-variety show was hosted by Kermit the Frog of "Sesame Street." The new Jim Henson puppet characters included Miss Piggy, Fozzie Bear and The Great Gonzo. Many celebrities appeared as guests on the show, which was broadcast in more than 100 countries. The show ran until 1981. "Muppet Babies" was a Saturday morning cartoon that ran from 1984 until 1992. *The Muppet Movie* (1979) was the first of five films based on "The Muppet Show." In 1996 a new show, *Muppets Tonight!*, was created.

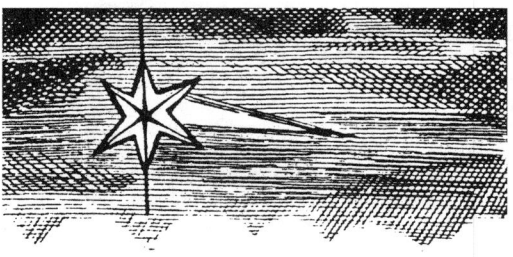

Sept 13–14 ☆ Chase's 2004 Calendar of Events ☆

NATIONAL BOSS/EMPLOYEE EXCHANGE DAY. Sept 13. To help bosses and employees appreciate each other by sharing each other's point of view for a day. Annually, the first Monday after Labor Day. For info: A.C. Moeller, Box 71, Clio, MI 48420-1042.

PEDDLER'S VILLAGE SCARECROW CONTEST AND OUTDOOR DISPLAY. Sept 13–Oct 31. Peddler's Village, Lahaska, PA. Contestants compete for $4,900 in cash prizes. Categories include: "A Scarecrow Whirligig"—a scarecrow that makes noise and moves with the wind; "An Extraordinary Contemporary Scarecrow"—an imaginative piece created to give a good scare in the garden; "A Traditional Scarecrow"—an outstanding example of the American Scarecrow; and "The Amateur Scarecrow"—for those who haven't won previously. Free admission. Est attendance: 650,000. For info: Peddler's Village, Routes 202 and 263, Lahaska, PA 18931. Phone: (215) 794-4000. Fax: (215) 794-4001. Web: www.peddlersvillage.com.

PERSHING, JOHN J.: BIRTH ANNIVERSARY. Sept 13, 1860. US Army general who commanded the American Expeditionary Force (AEF) during World War I, Pershing was born at Laclede, MO. The AEF, as part of the inter-Allied offensive, successfully assaulted the Saint-Mihiel salient in September 1918 and later that month quickly regrouped for the Meuse-Argonne operation that led to the Armistice of Nov 11, 1918. Pershing died July 15, 1948, at Washington, DC.

REED, WALTER: BIRTH ANNIVERSARY. Sept 13, 1851. American army physician (especially known for his Yellow Fever research). Born at Gloucester County, VA, he served as an army surgeon for more than 20 years and as a professor at the Army Medical College. He died at Washington, DC, Nov 22, 1902. The US Army's general hospital at Washington, DC, is named in his honor.

"SCOOBY-DOO, WHERE ARE YOU?" TV PREMIERE: ANNIVERSARY. Sept 13, 1969. A tremendously popular Saturday morning cartoon, Hanna-Barbera's show featured four wacky kids and lovable Great Dane Scooby-Doo solving spooky (and often hilarious) mysteries. Fred, Daphne and Velma usually do the work, while Shaggy (originally voiced by radio personality Casey Kasem) and Scooby-Doo look for something to eat. A live-action feature film was released in 2002 starring Freddie Prinze, Jr, Sarah Michelle Gellar, Matthew Lillard, Linda Cardellini and a digital Scooby.

"SOAP" TV PREMIERE: ANNIVERSARY. Sept 13, 1977. "Soap" was a prime-time comedy that parodied soap operas. It had plots that were funny (e.g., Corinne's baby is possessed by the devil), controversial (e.g., Billy joins a cult) and downright bizarre (e.g., Burt is abducted by aliens). The show focused on two families, the wealthy Tates and the middle-class Campbells. It starred Katherine Helmond, Robert Mandan, Jennifer Salt, Diana Canova, Jimmy Baio, Robert Guillaume, Cathryn Damon, Richard Mulligan, Ted Wass, Billy Crystal, Richard Libertini, Kathryn Reynolds, Robert Urich, Arthur Peterson, Roscoe Lee Browne and Jay Johnson. Rod Roddy was the announcer who recapped what had happened on the previous episode.

"STAR-SPANGLED BANNER" INSPIRED: ANNIVERSARY. Sept 13–14, 1814. On the night of Sept 13, Francis Scott Key was aboard a ship that was delayed in Baltimore harbor by the British attack there on Fort McHenry. Key had no choice but to anxiously watch the battle. That experience and seeing the American flag still flying over the fort the next morning inspired him to pen the verses that, coupled with the tune of a popular drinking song, became our official national anthem in 1931, 117 years after the words were written.

	S	M	T	W	T	F	S
September 2004				1	2	3	4
	5	6	7	8	9	10	11
	12	13	14	15	16	17	18
	19	20	21	22	23	24	25
	26	27	28	29	30		

SUBSTITUTE TEACHER APPRECIATION WEEK. Sept 13–17. Although substitute teachers get no sick days or respect, they teach when the regular teacher cannot and continually adjust to different classroom situations. Annually, the second week of September. For info: Dorothy Zjawin, Dir, 61 W Colfax Ave, Roselle Park, NJ 07204. Phone: (908) 241-6241.

US CAPITAL ESTABLISHED AT NEW YORK CITY: ANNIVERSARY. Sept 13, 1788. Congress picked New York, NY, as the location of the new US government in place of Philadelphia, which had served as the capital up until this time. In 1790 the capital moved back to Philadelphia for ten years, before moving permanently to Washington, DC.

BIRTHDAYS TODAY

Fiona Apple, 27, singer, born New York, NY, Sept 13, 1977.
Jacqueline Bisset, 60, actress (*Rich & Famous, The Deep*), born Weybridge, England, Sept 13, 1944.
Peter Cetera, 60, singer (former lead singer of Chicago; solo hit "Glory of Love"), songwriter, born Chicago, IL, Sept 13, 1944.
Robert Indiana, 76, artist (*As I Opened Fire*), born New Castle, IA, Sept 13, 1928.
Michael Johnson, 37, track athlete, born Dallas, TX, Sept 13, 1967.
Richard Kiel, 65, actor (*The Longest Yard, Silver Streak, The Spy Who Loved Me*), born Detroit, MI, Sept 13, 1939.
Judith Martin, 66, author, journalist ("Miss Manners"), born Washington, DC, Sept 13, 1938.
Stella McCartney, 33, fashion designer, born London, England, Sept 13, 1971.
Ben Savage, 24, actor ("Boy Meets World"), born Chicago, IL, Sept 13, 1980.
Fred Silverman, 67, TV producer, born New York, NY, Sept 13, 1937.
Jean Smart, 45, actress ("Designing Women"), born Seattle, WA, Sept 13, 1959.
Bernabe ("Bernie") Williams, 36, baseball player, born San Juan, Puerto Rico, Sept 13, 1968.

SEPTEMBER 14 — TUESDAY
Day 258 — 108 Remaining

DANTE ALIGHIERI: DEATH ANNIVERSARY. Sept 14, 1321. Italian poet, author of the *Divine Comedy*, died at Ravenna, Italy. He was born in May 1265 (exact date unknown) at Florence, Italy.

"THE GOLDEN GIRLS" TV PREMIERE: ANNIVERSARY. Sept 14, 1985. This comedy starred Bea Arthur, Betty White, Rue McClanahan and Estelle Getty as four divorced/widowed women sharing a house in Florida during their golden years. It was unique in that all four main characters were women. The last episode aired Sept 14, 1992, but the show remains popular in syndication.

"HAVE GUN WILL TRAVEL" TV PREMIERE: ANNIVERSARY. Sept 14, 1957. "Have Gun, Will Travel..." so read the business card of Paladin (Richard Boone), a loner whose professional services were available for a price. This half-hour Western also featured Kam Tong as his servant, Hey Boy. The show was extremely popular and ranked in the top five for most of its run.

☆ Chase's 2004 Calendar of Events ☆   Sept 14

HUSKER HARVEST DAYS. Sept 14–16. Grand Island, NE. The largest irrigated working agricultural show on a permanent site in the United States. 80 acres of exhibits, 700 acres of field demonstrations and more. Annually, the Tuesday–Thursday of the second full week of September. Est attendance: 50,000. For info: Renee Seifert, Grand Island/Hall County CVB, 309 West Second St, Grand Island, NE 68801. Phone: (308) 382-4400. Fax: (308) 382-1154. E-mail: info@visitgrandisland.com. Web: www.visitgrandisland.com.

"IRONSIDE" TV PREMIERE: ANNIVERSARY. Sept 14, 1967. This crime series starred Raymond Burr as Robert T. Ironside, Chief of Detectives for the San Francisco Police Department (he was in a wheelchair, paralyzed from an assassination attempt). Also featured were Don Galloway as his assistant, Detective Sergeant Ed Brown, Barbara Anderson as Officer Eve Whitfield, Don Mitchell as Mark Sanger, Ironside's personal assistant, Gene Lyons as Commissioner Dennis Randall, Elizabeth Baur as Officer Fran Belding and Joan Pringle as Diana, Mark's wife.

McKINLEY, WILLIAM: DEATH ANNIVERSARY. Sept 14, 1901. President William McKinley was shot at Buffalo, NY, Sept 6, 1901. He died eight days later. Assassin Leon Czolgosz was executed Oct 29, 1901.

MOON PHASE: NEW MOON. Sept 14. Moon enters New Moon phase at 10:29 AM, EDT.

MOTLEY, CONSTANCE BAKER: BIRTHDAY. Sept 14, 1921. New York's first black woman state senator and federal judge, and the first woman elected borough president of Manhattan, Constance Baker Motley became interested in law and civil rights when she was barred from a public beach at age 15. She went on to become one of the top civil rights lawyers of the '50s and '60s. She presented arguments before the US Supreme Court for seven cases and won them all. Motley was born at New Haven, CT.

NICARAGUA: BATTLE OF SAN JACINTO DAY. Sept 14. National holiday. Commemorates the 1856 defeat of US invader William Walker.

RYDER CUP MATCHES. Sept 14–19. Oakland Hills Country Club, Bloomfield Hills, MI. Held every two years, this match pits American golfers against a European team. First held in 1927, this is the 35th match. For info: Professional Golfers' Association of America, 100 Ave of the Champions, Palm Beach Gardens, FL 33418. Phone: (561) 630-1737. Fax: (561) 624-8448. Web: www.pga.com.

SANGER, MARGARET (HIGGINS): 125th BIRTH ANNIVERSARY. Sept 14, 1879. Feminist, nurse and founder of the birth control movement in the US. Born at Corning, NY. (Note: birth year not entirely certain because, apparently, Sanger often used a later date when obliged to divulge her birthday. Best evidence now points to Sept 14, 1879, rather than the frequently used 1883 date.) She died at Tucson, AZ, Sept 6, 1966.

SETON, ELIZABETH ANN: CANONIZATION ANNIVERSARY. Sept 14, 1975. Elizabeth Ann Seton became the first native-born American to be canonized. She was declared a saint in 1974 by Pope Paul VI.

SOLO TRANSATLANTIC BALLOON CROSSING: 20th ANNIVERSARY. Sept 14–18, 1984. Joe W. Kittinger, 56-year-old balloonist, left Caribou, ME, in a 10-story-tall helium-filled balloon named *Rosie O'Grady's Balloon of Peace* Sept 14, 1984, crossed the Atlantic Ocean and reached the French coast, above the town of Capbreton, in bad weather Sept 17 at 4:29 PM, EDT. He crash-landed amid wind and rain near Savone, Italy, at 8:08 AM, EDT, Sept 18. Kittinger suffered a broken ankle when he was thrown from the balloon's gondola during the landing. His nearly 84-hour flight, covering about 3,535 miles, was the first solo balloon crossing of the Atlantic Ocean and a record distance for a solo balloon flight.

TEXAS-OKLAHOMA FAIR. Sept 14–19. Multi-Purpose Events Center, Wichita Falls, TX. Largest fair in the North Texas area. Exhibits, carnival, food, arts and crafts, animal barn, special entertainment. Est attendance: 80,000. For info: Wichita Falls Conv & Visitors Bureau, 1000 5th St, Wichita Falls, TX 76301. Phone: (940) 716-5500. Fax: (940) 716-5509. Web: www.wichitafalls.org.

"THE WALTONS" TV PREMIERE: ANNIVERSARY. Sept 14, 1972. This epitome of the family drama spawned nearly a dozen knock-offs during its nine-year run on CBS. The drama was based on creator/writer Earl Hamner Jr's experiences growing up during the Depression in rural Virginia. It began as the TV movie "The Homecoming," which was turned into a weekly series covering the years 1933–43. The cast went through numerous changes through the years; the principals were: Michael Learned as Olivia Walton, mother of the clan; Ralph Waite as John Walton, father; Richard Thomas as John-Boy, eldest son; Jon Walmsley as son Jason; Judy Norton-Taylor as daughter Mary Ellen; Eric Scott as son Ben; Mary Beth McDonough as daughter Erin; David W. Harper as son Jim-Bob and Kami Cotler as daughter Elizabeth. The Walton grandparents were played by Ellen Corby and Will Geer. The last telecast aired Aug 20, 1981.

WILSON, JAMES: BIRTH ANNIVERSARY. Sept 14, 1742. Signer of the Declaration of Independence and one of the first associate justices of the US Supreme Court. Born at Fifeshire, Scotland, he died Aug 21, 1798, at Edenton, NC.

BIRTHDAYS TODAY

Zoe Caldwell, 71, actress (*Medea, The Prime of Miss Jean Brodie*), born Melbourne, Australia, Sept 14, 1933.
Dan Cortese, 37, actor ("Veronica's Closet," *Public Enemies*), born Sewickley, PA, Sept 14, 1967.
Mary Crosby, 45, actress ("Dallas," *Tapeheads*), born Los Angeles, CA, Sept 14, 1959.
Faith Ford, 40, actress ("Murphy Brown"), born Alexandria, LA, Sept 14, 1964.
Joey Heatherton, 60, actress (*Cry Baby, Bluebeard*, "Dean Martin and the Golddiggers"), born Rockville Centre, NY, Sept 14, 1944.
Walter Koenig, 68, actor, writer, director, producer ("Star Trek" and *Star Trek* movies), born Chicago, IL, Sept 14, 1936.
Kate Millett, 70, feminist, writer (*Sexual Politics, Flying*), born St. Paul, MN, Sept 14, 1934.
Sam Neill, 57, actor (*My Brilliant Career, Jurassic Park, The Piano*), born Northern Ireland, Sept 14, 1947.
Nicol Williamson, 66, actor (*Robin and Marian, Excalibur*), born Hamilton, Scotland, Sept 14, 1938.

477

SEPTEMBER 15 — WEDNESDAY
Day 259 — 107 Remaining

ACUFF, ROY: BIRTH ANNIVERSARY. Sept 15, 1903. Grand Ole Opry "King of Country Music" Roy Acuff was born at Maynardville, TN. Singer and fiddler Acuff (who was cofounder of Acuff-Rose Publishing Company, the leading publisher of country music) was a regular host on weekly Grand Ole Opry broadcasts. He frequently appeared at the Opry with his group, the Smoky Mountain Boys. In December of 1991 Acuff became the first living member elected to the Country Music Hall of Fame. Some of his more famous songs were "The Wabash Cannonball" (his theme song), "Pins and Needles (In My Heart)" and "Night Train to Memphis." Roy Acuff died Nov 23, 1992, at Nashville, TN.

"BACHELOR FATHER" TV PREMIERE: ANNIVERSARY. Sept 15, 1957. John Forsythe (Bentley Gregg) and Noreen Corcoran (Kelly Gregg) starred in this sitcom about a bachelor attorney's life turning upside-down after his orphaned niece moves in with him. The last episode aired Sept 25, 1962. Supporting players included: Sammee Tong as Peter Tong, the butler, and Jimmy Boyd as Kelly's boyfriend, Howard Meechim.

"CHiPs" TV PREMIERE: ANNIVERSARY. Sept 15, 1977. A popular action-packed NBC police series depicting cases and chases of the motorcycle-riding California Highway Patrol. The show starred Erik Estrada as Francis "Ponch" Poncherello and Larry Wilcox as Jon Baker, two quick-witted cops. Wilcox left the show, and Estrada's new partner, Bobby "Hot Dog" Nelson, was played by Tom Reilly. The last telecast aired July 17, 1983.

CHRISTIE, AGATHA: BIRTH ANNIVERSARY. Sept 15, 1890. English author of nearly a hundred books (mysteries, drama, poetry and nonfiction), born at Torquay, England. Died at Wallingford, England, Jan 12, 1976. "Every murderer," she wrote, in *The Mysterious Affair at Styles,* "is probably somebody's old friend."

"COLUMBO" TV PREMIERE: ANNIVERSARY. Sept 15, 1971. "Columbo," based on a 1968 made-for-TV movie, entered the lineup of NBC's "Mystery Movie" series on this date. Peter Falk starred as one of TV's great characters, Lieutenant Columbo, the crime-solving policeman dressed in rumpled raincoat and bearing a chewed up cigar. The first episode, "Murder by the Book," was directed by Steven Spielberg. In almost every episode, Columbo latches himself onto the main suspect, usually a polished sophisticate in comparison to Columbo's seeming simpleness, and nags him or her to death with questions and comments such as: "Just another thing . . ." or "What did you pay for those shoes?" or "But one thing bothers me, Sir." The series ended in 1978, but reemerged in the form of periodic movies beginning in 1989.

COOPER, JAMES FENIMORE: BIRTH ANNIVERSARY. Sept 15, 1789. American novelist, historian and social critic, born at Burlington, NJ, James Fenimore Cooper was one of the earliest American writers to develop a native American literary tradition. His most popular works are the five novels comprising *The Leatherstocking Tales,* featuring the exploits of one of the truly unique American fictional characters, Natty Bumppo. These novels, *The Deerslayer, The Last of the Mohicans, The Pathfinder, The Pioneers* and *The Prairie,* chronicle Natty Bumppo's continuing flight away from the rapid settlement of America. Other works, including *The Monikins* and *Satanstoe,* reveal him as an astute critic of American life. He died Sept 14, 1851, at Cooperstown, NY, the town founded by his father.

COSTA RICA: INDEPENDENCE DAY. Sept 15. National holiday. Gained independence from Spain in 1821.

EL SALVADOR: INDEPENDENCE DAY. Sept 15. National holiday. Gained independence from Spain in 1821.

FIRST NATIONAL CONVENTION FOR BLACKS: ANNIVERSARY. Sept 15, 1830. The first national convention for blacks was held at Bethel Church, Philadelphia, PA. The convention was called to find ways to better the condition of black people and was attended by delegates from seven states. Bishop Richard Allen was elected as the first convention president.

GOLDEN ASPEN MOTORCYCLE RALLY. Sept 15–19. Ruidoso, NM. Trade show, bike shows, riding tours, skill events, parade, awards banquet, stunt shows and thousands in prizes. Est attendance: 35,000. For info: Golden Aspen Rally Assn, PO Box 1467, Ruidoso, NM 88355. Phone: (800) 452-8045. E-mail: gara@zianet.com. Web: www.motorcyclerally.com.

GREENPEACE FOUNDED: ANNIVERSARY. Sept 15, 1971. The environmental organization Greenpeace, committed to a green and peaceful world, was founded by 12 members of the Don't Make a Wave committee of Vancouver, BC, Canada, when the boat *Phyllis Cormack* sailed to Amchitka, AK, to protest US nuclear testing. Greenpeace's basic principle is "that determined individuals can alter the actions and purposes of even the overwhelmingly powerful by 'bearing witness'—drawing attention to an environmental abuse through their mere unwavering presence, whatever the risk."

GUATEMALA: INDEPENDENCE DAY. Sept 15. National holiday. Gained independence from Spain in 1821.

HONDURAS: INDEPENDENCE DAY. Sept 15. National holiday. Gained independence from Spain in 1821.

"I SPY" TV PREMIERE: ANNIVERSARY. Sept 15, 1965. Bill Cosby made television history as the first African-American actor starring in a major dramatic role in this spy series. Cosby played Alexander "Scotty" Scott, an intellectual spy with a cover as a tennis trainer. Robert Culp played Kelly Robinson, the "tennis pro" and Scotty's partner in espionage. The series was notable for filming worldwide.

JAPAN: RESPECT FOR THE AGED DAY. Sept 15. National holiday to honor Japan's senior citizens—especially those who are centenarians.

KENTUCKY BOURBON FESTIVAL. Sept 15–19. Bardstown, KY. Visit the "Bourbon Capital of the World" and celebrate the history and making of Kentucky's finest product, Kentucky bourbon. Enjoy tours, displays, music, food, competitions and much more. For info: Kentucky Bourbon Festival, 107 E Stephen Foster Ave, Bardstown, KY 40004. Phone: (502) 348-3623. Fax: (502) 349-0804. E-mail: info@kybourbonfestival.com. Web: www.kybourbonfestival.com.

"THE LONE RANGER" TV PREMIERE: 55th ANNIVERSARY. Sept 15, 1949. This character was created for a radio serial in 1933 by George W. Trendle. The famous masked man was the alter ego of John Reid, a Texas Ranger who was the only survivor of an ambush. He was nursed back to health by his Native American friend, Tonto. Both men traveled around the West on their trusty steeds, Silver and Scout, fighting injustice. Clayton Moore played the Lone Ranger/John Reid and Jay Silverheels costarred as Tonto. The theme music was Rossini's "William Tell Overture." The last episode aired Sept 12, 1957.

MORTON PUMPKIN FESTIVAL. Sept 15–18. Morton, IL. Carnival, parade, entertainment and fantastic food to celebrate the pumpkin in the "Pumpkin Capital of the World." Est attendance: 70,000. For info: Morton Chamber of Commerce, 415 W Jefferson St, Morton, IL 61550. Phone: (309) 263-2491. Fax: (309) 263-2401. E-mail: chamber@mtco.com. Web: www.pumpkincapital.com.

★**NATIONAL HISPANIC HERITAGE MONTH.** Sept 15–Oct 15. Presidential Proclamation. Beginning in 1989, always issued for Sept 15–Oct 15 of each year (PL100-402 of Aug 17, 1988). Previously issued each year for the week including Sept 15 and 16 since 1968 at request (PL90-498 of Sept 17, 1968).

NICARAGUA: INDEPENDENCE DAY. Sept 15. National holiday. Gained independence from Spain in 1821.

PETIT JEAN FALL ANTIQUE AUTO SWAP MEET. Sept 15–18. Petit Jean Mountain, Morrilton, AR. 7th annual antique auto swap meet, car corral, flea market and arts and crafts. Military vehicle show Friday and Saturday. More than 1,400 vendor spaces. Est attendance: 30,000. For info: Buddy Hoelzeman, Museum of Automobiles, 8 Jones Ln, Morrilton, AR 72110. Phone: (501) 727-5427. Fax: (501) 727-6482. E-mail: moa@ipa.net. Web: museumofautos.com.

QUARTERLY ESTIMATED FEDERAL INCOME TAX PAYERS' DUE DATE. Sept 15. For those individuals whose fiscal year is the calendar year and who make quarterly estimated federal income tax payments, today is one of the due dates. (Jan 15, Apr 15, June 15 and Sept 15, 2004.)

ROSH HASHANAH BEGINS AT SUNDOWN. Sept 15. Jewish New Year. See also: "Rosh Hashanah" (Sept 16).

16th STREET BAPTIST CHURCH BOMBING: ANNIVERSARY. Sept 15, 1963. In a horrific episode of the civil rights struggle, a bomb blast in the basement of the 16th Street Baptist Church in Birmingham, AL, killed four girls preparing for church: Denise McNair, Carole Robertson, Cynthia Wesley and Addie Mae Collins. Previously, the church had been the center for marches led by Dr. Martin Luther King, Jr. Three suspects were brought to trial in 1977, 2001 and 2002 and found guilty.

SOMEDAY. Sept 15. You know all those things you're going to do "someday"—lose weight, start a business, learn another language, skydive, whatever. Well, someday is here! This is the day to tackle new challenges and experience the joy of accomplishment. Free articles available for publishers and webmasters at IdeaLady.com/content.htm. For info: Cathy Stucker, Special Interests Publishing, 4646 Hwy 6, PMB 123, Sugar Land, TX 77478. Phone: (281) 265-7342. E-mail: cathy@idealady.com. Web: www.idealady.com.

SPACE MILESTONE: *ARIANE-3* (ESA). Sept 15, 1987. European Space Agency rocket carrying two (Australian and European) communications satellites into Earth's orbit marked the reentry of western nations into commercial space projects. Launched this date from Kourou, French Guiana, with Arianespace, a private company operating the rocket for the 13-nation European Space Agency.

TAFT, WILLIAM HOWARD: BIRTH ANNIVERSARY. Sept 15, 1857. The 27th president of the US was born at Cincinnati, OH. His term of office was Mar 4, 1909–Mar 3, 1913. Following his presidency he became a law professor at Yale University until his appointment as Chief Justice of the US Supreme Court in 1921. Died at Washington, DC, Mar 8, 1930, and was buried at Arlington National Cemetery.

UNITED KINGDOM: BATTLE OF BRITAIN DAY. Sept 15. Commemorates end of biggest daylight bombing raid of Britain by German Luftwaffe, in 1940. Said to have been the turning point against Hitler's siege of Britain in WWII.

US TROOPS ENTER GERMANY: 60th ANNIVERSARY. Sept 15, 1944. US troops of the VII and V Corps reached the southwestern frontier of Germany. The war had finally moved into the Third Reich's backyard.

***USA TODAY* FIRST PUBLISHED: ANNIVERSARY.** Sept 15, 1982. Media corporation Gannett published a new kind of daily—the "Nation's Newspaper"—that featured general interest articles for a national audience on this date.

BIRTHDAYS TODAY

Jackie Cooper, 82, actor (*Our Gang* shorts, "The People's Choice"), producer, born Los Angeles, CA, Sept 15, 1922.
Norm Crosby, 77, comedian, host ("The Comedy Shop"), born Boston, MA, Sept 15, 1927.
Sherman Douglas, 38, former basketball player, born Washington, DC, Sept 15, 1966.
Prince Harry (Henry Charles Albert David), 20, second son of Prince Charles and Princess Diana, born London, England, Sept 15, 1984.
Tommy Lee Jones, 58, actor (Oscar for *The Fugitive*; *Coal Miner's Daughter*), born San Saba, TX, Sept 15, 1946.
Daniel Constantine (Dan) Marino, Jr, 43, former football player, born Pittsburgh, PA, Sept 15, 1961.
Carmen Maura, 59, actress (*Women on the Verge of a Nervous Breakdown*), born Madrid, Spain, Sept 15, 1945.
Jessye Norman, 59, soprano, opera singer, born Augusta, GA, Sept 15, 1945.
Merlin Jay Olsen, 64, Hall of Fame football player, sportscaster, actor ("Little House on the Prairie"), born Logan, UT, Sept 15, 1940.
Gaylord Jackson Perry, 66, Hall of Fame baseball player, born Williamston, NC, Sept 15, 1938.
Bobby Short, 78, singer, pianist, cafe song stylist, born Robert Waltrip, Danville, IL, Sept 15, 1926.
Oliver Stone, 58, director (*Platoon*, *JFK*, *Wall Street*), screenwriter, born New York, NY, Sept 15, 1946.

SEPTEMBER 16 — THURSDAY
Day 260 — 106 Remaining

ANNE BRADSTREET DAY. Sept 16. An official date proclaimed by the governor of the Commonwealth of Massachusetts to honor Anne Bradstreet, America's first poet who is also recognized as the first published woman poet in the English language. Anne Bradstreet was born in 1612 in England and came to America in 1630. Unbeknownst to Anne, her brother-in-law took some of her poetry back to England where it was published in 1630 as *The Tenth Muse Lately Sprung Up in America*. Subsequent editions were also published in Boston. She died at Old Andover, MA, Sept 16, 1672. For info: Sue Ellen Holmes, Dir, Stevens Memorial Library, PO Box 8, North Andover, MA 01845. Phone: (978) 688-9505. Fax: (978) 688-9507. E-mail: SHolmes@mailserv.mvlc.lib.ma.us.

CHEROKEE STRIP DAY: ANNIVERSARY. Sept 16, 1893. Optional school holiday, Oklahoma. Greatest "run" for Oklahoma land in 1893.

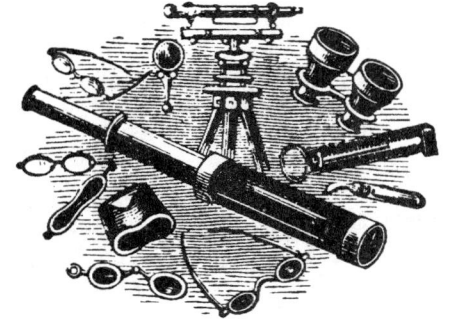

Sept 16 ☆ *Chase's 2004 Calendar of Events* ☆

CORN ISLAND STORYTELLING FESTIVAL. Sept 16–18. Louisville, KY. Festival locations are Waterfront Park, the *Belle of Louisville* (featuring a storytelling cruise on the old paddlewheeler) and the Kentucky Theater. Est attendance: 10,000. For info: Corn Island Storytelling, 651 S Fourth St, Louisville, KY 40202. Phone: (502) 245-0643. E-mail: cornislandstorytelling@msn.com.

"FRASIER" TV PREMIERE: ANNIVERSARY. Sept 16, 1993. In this spin-off of "Cheers," psychiatrist Dr. Frasier Crane (Kelsey Grammer) has moved to Seattle where he dispenses advice on the radio. He lives with his ex-cop father Martin (John Mahoney) and Martin's physical therapist Daphne Moon (Jane Leeves). His brother, Dr. Niles Crane (David Hyde Pierce), frequently asks for Frasier's advice about his love life. Roz Doyle, the producer of Frasier's show, is played by Peri Gilpin.

FRIENDS OF LAKE FOREST LIBRARY ANNUAL BOOK SALE. Sept 16–19. Lake Forest, IL. A three-day sale of used books in excellent condition set up in 20 categories. Sept 16 is a presale for members and volunteers only. Est attendance: 5,000. For info: Kaye Grabbe, Lake Forest Library, 360 E Deerpath, Lake Forest, IL 60045. Phone: (847) 234-0636. Fax: (847) 234-1453. E-mail: kgrabbe@lfl.alibrary.com. Web: lfkhome.northstarnet.org/FriendsofLFL.html.

GENERAL MOTORS: FOUNDING ANNIVERSARY. Sept 16, 1908. The giant automobile manufacturing company was founded by William Crapo "Billy" Durant, a Flint, MI, entrepreneur.

GREAT SEAL OF THE US: FIRST USE ANNIVERSARY. Sept 16, 1782. On this date the Great Seal of the United States was, for the first time, impressed upon an official document. That document authorized George Washington to negotiate a prisoner of war agreement with the British. See also: "Great Seal of the United States: Anniversary" (Jan 28 and July 4).

HUMMER/BIRD CELEBRATION. Sept 16–19. Rockport and Fulton, TX. To celebrate the spectacular fall migration of the ruby-throated hummingbird and other birds from their summer nesting grounds in the north along the eastern Gulf Coast on the way to their winter grounds in Mexico and Central America, and its 500-mile journey across the Gulf. There are programs, workshops, booths, concessions, bus and boat tours. Est attendance: 5,000. For info: Rockport Fulton Area Chamber of Commerce, Hummer/Bird Celebration, 404 Broadway, Rockport, TX 78382. Phone: (800) 242-0071 or (361) 729-6445. Fax: (361) 729-7681. E-mail: visitor@1rockport.org. Web: www.rockport-fulton.org.

"MANNIX" TV PREMIERE: ANNIVERSARY. Sept 16, 1967. Mike Connors starred as Joe Mannix, a Los Angeles private investigator working for the computer organization Intertect, in this long-running CBS crime series. Joseph Campanella played his boss, Lou Wickersham, during the first season. The show then changed format with Mannix setting up his own agency. The new cast members were Gail Fisher as Peggy Fair, his secretary, Robert Reed as Lieutenant Adam Tobias and Ward Wood as Lieutenant Art Malcolm.

MAYFLOWER DAY: ANNIVERSARY. Sept 16, 1620. Anniversary of the departure of the *Mayflower* from Plymouth, England with 102 passengers and a small crew. Vicious storms were encountered en route which caused serious doubt about the wisdom of continuing, but she reached Provincetown, MA, Nov 21, and discharged the Pilgrims at Plymouth, MA, Dec 26, 1620.

MEXICO: INDEPENDENCE DAY. Sept 16. National Day. The official celebration begins at 11 PM, Sept 15, and continues through Sept 16. On the night of the 15th, the President of Mexico steps onto the balcony of the National Palace at Mexico City and voices the same "El Grito" (Cry for Freedom) that Father Hidalgo gave on the night of Sept 15, 1810, that began Mexico's rebellion from Spain.

MIDDLEMARK, MARVIN: 85th BIRTH ANNIVERSARY. Sept 16, 1919. Marvin Middlemark was born at Long Island, NY. His passion for inventing and tinkering led to many inventions, most of which enjoyed little commercial success, like the water-driven automatic potato peeler. But it was as the inventor of a device to improve TV reception, known as "rabbit ears," that he became successful. He died Sept 14, 1989, at Old Westbury, NY.

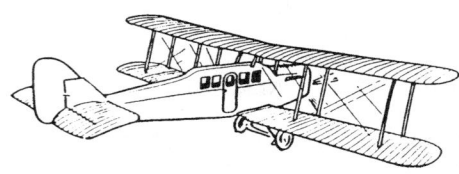

NATIONAL CHAMPIONSHIP AIR RACES. Sept 16–19. Reno, NV. Six classes of races—Unlimited, Sport, Jet, Formula One, T-6 and Biplane—compete. The event includes thrilling aerobatics and displays of military, vintage and contemporary aircraft. Est attendance: 223,000. For info: National Championship Air Races, PO Box 1429, Reno, NV 89505. Phone: (775) 972-6663. Web: www.airrace.org.

NATIONAL GUITAR FLAT-PICKING CHAMPIONSHIPS AND WALNUT VALLEY FESTIVAL. Sept 16–19. Cowley County Fairgrounds, Winfield, KS. The Walnut River is the site of this 33rd annual family event featuring four stages with 8 contests, at least 14 workshops and many first-class concerts. The Walnut Valley Arts and Crafts Festival features handmade instruments and a large variety of arts and crafts items, both ornamental and functional. All-weather facilities. Est attendance: 45,000. For info: Walnut Valley Assn, Bob Redford, PO Box 245, Winfield, KS 67156. Phone: (620) 221-3250. Fax: (620) 221-3109. E-mail: hq@wvfest.com. Web: www.wvfest.com.

NEWPORT INTERNATIONAL BOAT SHOW. Sept 16–19. Newport, RI. More than 300 new sail and power boats in the water and displays of accessories, equipment and services. New product information, free sail/power boat rides in Newport harbor. Est attendance: 30,000. For info: Newport Exhibition Group, PO Box 698, 366 Thames St, Newport, RI 02840. Phone: (401) 846-1115. Web: www.newportboatshow.com.

PALESTINIAN MASSACRE: ANNIVERSARY. Sept 16, 1982. Christian militiamen (the Phalangists) entered Sabra and Shatila, two Palestinian refugee camps in West Beirut. They began open shooting and by Sept 18 hundreds of Palestinians, including elderly men, women and children, were dead. Phalangists had demanded blood of Palestinians since the assassination of their president, Bashir Gemayel, on Sept 14. Survivors of the massacre said they had not seen Israeli forces inside the camp; however, they claimed Israelis sealed off boundaries to the camps and allowed Christian militiamen to enter.

PANIZZI, ANTHONY: BIRTH ANNIVERSARY. Sept 16, 1797. Sir Anthony Panizzi, the only librarian ever hanged in effigy, was born Antonio Genesio Maria Panizzi at Brescello, Italy. As a young man he joined a forbidden Italian patriotic society that advocated the overthrow of the oppressive Austrians who then controlled most of northern Italy. Tried in absentia by an Austrian court in 1820, he was sentenced to death and all his property was confiscated. He fled to England in 1823, learned the language and by 1831 was employed in the British Museum where, in 1856, he was named principal librarian. Later described as the "prince of librarians," Panizzi died at London, England, Apr 8, 1879.

September 2004	S	M	T	W	T	F	S
				1	2	3	4
	5	6	7	8	9	10	11
	12	13	14	15	16	17	18
	19	20	21	22	23	24	25
	26	27	28	29	30		

☆ Chase's 2004 Calendar of Events ☆ Sept 16–17

PAPUA NEW GUINEA: INDEPENDENCE DAY. Sept 16. National holiday. Commemorates independence from Australian administration in 1975.

PARKMAN, FRANCIS: BIRTH ANNIVERSARY. Sept 16, 1823. American historian, author of *The Oregon Trail*, was born at Boston, MA, and died there Nov 8, 1893.

PAUSE THE WORLD DAY. Sept 16. New York, NY, and other cities. Annual worldwide concert and media event to celebrate the wonderful world we live in and to pause, calm down, be nice and plant a seed. Not-for-profit. Annually, Sept 16—on United Nations' International Day of Peace. For info: Paul Sladkus, 126 Fifth Ave, Ste 3D, New York, NY 10011. Phone: (212) 647-1212. Fax: (212) 647-1216. E-mail: pause@pausetheworld.org. Web: www.pausetheworld.org.

POWERED PARACHUTE FLY-IN. Sept 16–19. Columbus, KS. Largest powered parachute fly-in in the United States. More than 20 machines participating. Annually, begins the third Thursday in Sept. Est attendance: 5,000. For info: Dawn Bonet, 800 Powrachute Way, Columbus, KS 66725. Phone: (620) 429-1397. Fax: (620) 429-3827. Web: www.powrachute.com.

ROSH HASHANAH or JEWISH NEW YEAR. Sept 16–17. Jewish holy day observed on 2 consecutive days. Hebrew calendar date: Tishri 1–2, 5765. Rosh Hashanah (literally "Head of the Year") is the beginning of 10 days of repentance and spiritual renewal. (Began at sundown Sept 15.)

"SKY KING" TV PREMIERE: ANNIVERSARY. Sept 16, 1951. This half-hour children's adventure series began on radio in 1947. Kirby Grant starred as Schuyler J. (Sky) King, owner of the Flying Crown Ranch, who used his plane, *The Songbird*, to help victims and capture criminals. To help him was a cast that included Gloria Winters as his niece, Penny, Ron Hagerthy as his nephew, Clipper, Ewing Mitchell as the sheriff, Mitch, Norman Ollstead as Bob Carey and Gary Hunley as Mickey.

TORQUEMADA, TOMAS DE: DEATH ANNIVERSARY. Sept 16, 1498. One of history's most malevolent persons, feared and hated by millions. As Inquisitor-General of Spain, he ordered burning at the stake for more than 10,000 persons and burning in effigy for another 7,000 (according to 18th-century estimates). Torquemada persuaded Ferdinand and Isabella to rid Spain of the Jews. More than a million families were driven from the country and Spain suffered a commercial decline from which it never recovered. Torquemada was born at Valladolid, Spain, in 1420 (exact date unknown) and died at Avila, Spain.

UNITED NATIONS: INTERNATIONAL DAY FOR THE PRESERVATION OF THE OZONE LAYER. Sept 16. On Dec 19, 1994, the General Assembly proclaimed this day to commemorate the date in 1987 on which Montreal Protocol on Substances that Deplete the Ozone Layer was signed (Res 49/114). States are invited to devote the Day to promote, at the national level, activities in accordance with the objectives of the Protocol. The ozone layer filters sunlight and prevents the adverse effects of ultraviolet radiation from reaching the Earth's surface, thereby preserving life on the planet. For info: United Nations, Dept of Public Info, Public Inquiries Unit, Rm GA-57, New York, NY 10017. Phone: (212) 963-4475. E-mail: inquiries@un.org. Web: www.un.org.

BIRTHDAYS TODAY

Marc Anthony, 35, singer, actor (*Bringing Out the Dead*), born New York, NY, Sept 16, 1969.

Lauren Bacall, 80, actress (*Applause, Woman of the Year, Key Largo*), born Betty Joan Perske, New York, NY, Sept 16, 1924.

Elgin Gay Baylor, 70, Hall of Fame basketball player, former coach, born Washington, DC, Sept 16, 1934.

Ed Begley, Jr, 55, actor ("St. Elsewhere"), born Los Angeles, CA, Sept 16, 1949.

Alexis Bledel, 22, actress ("Gilmore Girls"), born Houston, TX, Sept 16, 1982.

David Copperfield (Kotkin), 48, illusionist, born Metuchen, NJ, Sept 16, 1956.

Peter Falk, 77, actor (*The Great Race*, "Columbo"), born New York, NY, Sept 16, 1927.

Anne Francis, 72, actress (*Bad Day at Black Rock, Blackboard Jungle, Forbidden Planet*), born Ossining, NY, Sept 16, 1932.

Henry Louis Gates, Jr, 54, professor of African-American studies at Harvard, editor of the *Norton Anthology of African American Literature*, born Keyser, WV, Sept 16, 1950.

Orel Leonard Hershiser IV, 46, former baseball player, born Buffalo, NY, Sept 16, 1958.

B.B. King, 79, singer ("Rock Me Baby," "The Thrill Is Gone"), born Itta Bena, MS, Sept 16, 1925.

Richard Marx, 41, singer, born Chicago, IL, Sept 16, 1963.

Mark McEwen, 50, weatherman, music editor, born San Antonio, TX, Sept 16, 1954.

Janis Paige, 81, singer, actress (stage: *The Pajama Game, Silk Stockings*), born Tacoma, WA, Sept 16, 1923.

Tim Raines, 45, former baseball player, born Sanford, FL, Sept 16, 1959.

Mickey Rourke, 48, actor (*9½ Weeks, Bar Fly*), born Schenectady, NY, Sept 16, 1956.

Susan Ruttan, 54, actress ("LA Law"), born Oregon City, OR, Sept 16, 1950.

Molly Shannon, 40, actress ("Saturday Night Live"), born Shaker Heights, OH, Sept 16, 1964.

Jennifer Tilly, 43, actress (*Johnny Be Good, Made in America*), born Los Angeles, CA, Sept 16, 1961.

Robin R. Yount, 49, Hall of Fame baseball player, born Danville, IL, Sept 16, 1955.

SEPTEMBER 17 — FRIDAY
Day 261 — 105 Remaining

ALOHA FESTIVALS DOWNTOWN HO'OLAULE'A. Sept 17. Downtown Honolulu, HI. One of the best attended and most enjoyed events in Honolulu. An estimated 150,000 residents and visitors stroll through downtown Honolulu enjoying the various lei and food booths and the exciting dancing and entertainment on nine stages featuring music to suit every taste. (Also the Waikiki Ho'olaule'a on Kalakaua Avenue, Honolulu, HI, Sept 11.) Est attendance: 150,000. For info: Aloha Festivals. Phone: (808) 589-1771. Fax: (808) 589-1770. E-mail: info@alohafestivals.com. Web: www.alohafestivals.com.

ANGOLA: DAY OF THE NATIONAL HERO. Sept 17. National holiday.

ANTIQUE AND CLASSIC CAR SHOW. Sept 17–19. Willow Park, Bennington, VT. Classic cars, Woodies. A flea market with auto-related parts and memorabilia entices collectors seeking that elusive fender or gas running lamp. A display and demonstration of antique motorcycles, tractor and farm machinery are also featured. Annually, the second weekend after Labor Day. Est attendance: 10,000. For info: Bennington Area Chamber of Commerce, 100 Veterans Memorial Dr, Bennington, VT 05201. Phone: (802) 447-3311. Fax: (802) 447-1163. E-mail: chamber@bennington.com. Web: www.bennington.com.

Sept 17 ☆ *Chase's 2004 Calendar of Events* ☆

BATTLE OF ANTIETAM: ANNIVERSARY. Sept 17, 1862. This date has been called America's bloodiest day in recognition of the high casualties suffered in the Civil War battle between General Robert E. Lee's Confederate forces and General George McClellan's Union army. Estimates vary, but more than 25,000 Union and Confederate soldiers were killed or wounded in this battle on the banks of the Potomac River at Maryland.

"BEWITCHED" TV PREMIERE: 40th ANNIVERSARY. Sept 17, 1964. This sitcom centered around blonde-haired witch Samantha Stephens (Elizabeth Montgomery). Although she promises not to use her witchcraft in her daily life, Samantha finds herself twitching her nose in many situations. Her husband, Darrin Stephens, was played by Dick York and Dick Sargent, and her daughter, Tabitha Stephens, was played by Erin and Diane Murphy. The last episode aired July 1, 1972. Other cast members included Agnes Moorehead, David White, Alice Ghostley, Bernard Fox and Paul Lynde.

THE BIG E. Sept 17–Oct 3. West Springfield, MA. New England's autumn tradition and one of the nation's largest fairs. Each September, The Big E features all free entertainment including top-name talent, a big-top circus and horse show. Also children's attractions, daily parade with custom-built Mardi Gras floats, historic village, Avenue of States, Better Living Center and much more. Annually, beginning the second Friday after Labor Day. Est attendance: 1,000,000. For info: Eastern States Exposition, 1305 Memorial Ave, West Springfield, MA 01089. Phone: (413) 737-2443. Fax: (413) 787-0127. E-mail: info@thebige.com. Web: www.thebige.com.

BURGER, WARREN E.: BIRTH ANNIVERSARY. Sept 17, 1907. Former Chief Justice of the US Supreme Court, Warren E. Burger was born at St. Paul, MN. A conservative on criminal matters, but a progressive on social issues, he had the longest tenure (1969–86) of any chief justice in this century. Appointed by President Nixon, he voted in the majority on *Roe v Wade* (1973), which upheld a woman's right to an abortion, and on *US v Nixon* (1974), which forced Nixon to surrender audiotapes to the Watergate special prosecutor. He died June 25, 1995, at Washington, DC.

★**CITIZENSHIP DAY.** Sept 17. Presidential Proclamation always issued for Sept 17 at request (PL82-261 of Feb 29, 1952). Customarily issued as "Citizenship Day and Constitution Week." Replaces Constitution Day.

CONNOLLY, MAUREEN: 70th BIRTH ANNIVERSARY. Sept 17, 1934. Maureen ("Little Mo") Catherine Connolly Brinker, tennis player born at San Diego, CA. Connolly became the second-youngest woman to win the US National championship at Forest Hills, NY, when she captured that title in 1951. She repeated in 1952 and won Wimbledon as well. In 1953 she became the first woman to win the Grand Slam, taking the US, French, Australian and Wimbledon championships. After winning a second straight French title and a third straight Wimbledon, she suffered a crushed leg in a horseback riding accident and never competed again. Died at Dallas, TX, June 21, 1969.

CONSTITUTION COMMEMORATION DAY IN ARIZONA. Sept 17. Arizona. This state holiday commemorates the signing of the US Constitution on Sept 17, 1787.

CONSTITUTION OF THE US: ANNIVERSARY. Sept 17, 1787. Delegations from 12 states (Rhode Island did not send a delegate) at the Constitutional Convention at Philadelphia, PA, voted unanimously to approve the proposed document. Thirty-nine of the 42 delegates present signed it and the Convention adjourned, after drafting a letter of transmittal to the Congress. The proposed constitution stipulated that it would take effect when ratified by nine states. This day is a legal holiday in Florida.

★**CONSTITUTION WEEK.** Sept 17–23. Presidential Proclamation always issued for the period of Sept 17–23 each year since 1955 (PL84-915 of Aug 2, 1956).

CRESTON/SOUTHWEST IOWA BALLOON DAYS. Sept 17–19. Creston, IA. Hare and hound races held at sunrise and sunset; parade and marching band contest and much more. Annually, the third weekend in September. Est attendance: 7,000. For info: Creston Chamber of Commerce, Box 471, Creston, IA 50801. Phone: (641) 641-7021. E-mail: chamber@mddc.com. Web: www.mddc.com/chamber.

ENGLAND: HARROGATE AUTUMN FLOWER SHOW. Sept 17–19. Great Yorkshire Showground, Harrogate, N Yorkshire. See Britain's finest blooms, talk to the experts and witness the giants in the National Onion Championship. Est attendance: 35,000. For info: Roger Brownbridge, North of England Horticultural Society, 4A South Park Rd, Harrogate, North Yorkshire, England HG1 5QU. Phone: (44) (1423) 561049. Fax: (44) (1423) 536880. E-mail: info@flowershow.org.uk. Web: www.flowershow.org.uk.

FLORIDA MUSIC HARVEST. Sept 17–19. Spirit of Suwannee Music Park and Campground, Live Oak, FL. Three days of music. Previous artists who have performed include James Brown, Train, The Roots, Sister Hazel, The Wailers and many more. Ethnic and handmade instruments sold by vendors. Food, beverages, arts, crafts and jewelry booths. Est attendance: 8,000. For info: Spirit of the Suwannee Music Park, 3076 95th Dr, Live Oak, FL 32060. Phone: (386) 364-1683. Web: www.musicliveshere.com.

FOSTER, ANDREW (RUBE): 125th BIRTH ANNIVERSARY. Sept 17, 1879. Rube Foster's efforts in baseball earned him the title of "The Father of Negro Baseball." He was a manager and star pitcher, pitching 51 victories in one year. In 1919, he called a meeting of black baseball owners and organized the first black baseball league, the Negro National League. He served as its president until his death in 1930. Foster was born at Calvert, TX, the son of a minister. He died Dec 9, 1930, at Kankakee, IL.

"THE FUGITIVE" TV PREMIERE: ANNIVERSARY. Sept 17, 1963. A nail-biting adventure series on ABC. Dr. Richard Kimble (David Janssen) was wrongly convicted and sentenced to death for his wife's murder, but escaped from his captors in a train wreck. This popular program aired for four years detailing Kimble's search for the one-armed man (Bill Raisch) who had killed his wife, Helen (Diane Brewster). In the meantime Kimble himself was being pursued by Lieutenant Philip Gerard (Barry Morse). The final episode aired Aug 29, 1967, and featured Kimble extracting a confession from the one-armed man as they struggled from the heights of a water tower in a deserted amusement park. That single episode was the highest-rated show ever broadcast until 1976. The TV series generated a hit movie in 1993 with Harrison Ford as Kimble and Oscar-winner Tommy Lee Jones as Gerard.

	S	M	T	W	T	F	S
September 2004				1	2	3	4
	5	6	7	8	9	10	11
	12	13	14	15	16	17	18
	19	20	21	22	23	24	25
	26	27	28	29	30		

HANKFEST. Sept 17. Chicago, IL. Celebrating the music and birthday of perhaps the greatest American songwriter who ever lived, Hiram "Hank" Williams, Sr. This 3rd annual event features live bands, "Twang-a-Long" audience participation, guest performances by various musicians, plus homemade jambalaya (in honor of one of Hank's best songs). For info: Marty Larkin, Hankfest, 1924 W Montrose, Ste 117, Chicago, IL 60613. E-mail: info@hankfest.com. Web: www.hankfest.com.

HENDRICKS, THOMAS ANDREWS: BIRTH ANNIVERSARY. Sept 17, 1819. Twenty-first vice president of the US (1885) born at Muskingum County, OH. Died at Indianapolis, IN, Nov 25, 1885.

HERZOG, CHAIM: BIRTH ANNIVERSARY. Sept 17, 1918. President of Israel, an ex-general and chief delegate to the UN, author, lawyer, born at Belfast, Northern Ireland. He was a British army officer in World War II. Died at Tel Aviv, Israel, Apr 17, 1997.

"HOME IMPROVEMENT" TV PREMIERE: ANNIVERSARY. Sept 17, 1991. This comedy was a TV program about a TV program. Tim Taylor, played by Tim Allen, was host of the popular fix-it show "Tool Time." His wife Jill, played by Patricia Richardson, was a housewife going back to school to get a degree in psychology. The couple's three sons were played by Zachery Ty Bryan, Jonathan Taylor Thomas and Taran Noah Smith. Other cast members included Richard Karn as Tim's TV assistant, and Earl Hindman, Debbe Dunning and Pamela Anderson. The last episode aired May 25, 1999.

MacNELLY, JEFF: BIRTH ANNIVERSARY. Sept 17, 1947. Pulitzer prize–winning editorial cartoonist, comic strip cartoonist ("Shoe"), born at New York, NY. Died June 9, 2000, at Baltimore, MD.

"M*A*S*H" TV PREMIERE: ANNIVERSARY. Sept 17, 1972. This popular CBS series was based on the 1970 Robert Altman movie and a book by Richard Hooker. Set during the Korean War, the show aired for 11 years (lasting longer than the war). It followed the lives of doctors and nurses on the war front with both humor and pathos. The cast included: Alan Alda as Captain Benjamin Franklin "Hawkeye" Pierce, Wayne Rogers as Captain John "Trapper John" McIntyre, McLean Stevenson as Lieutenant Colonel Henry Blake, Loretta Swit as Major Margaret "Hot Lips" Houlihan, Larry Linville as Major Frank Burns, Gary Burghoff as Corporal Walter "Radar" O'Reilly, William Christopher as Father Francis Mulcahy, Jamie Farr as Corporal Max Klinger, Harry Morgan as Colonel Sherman Potter, Mike Farrell as Captain B.J. Hunnicut and David Ogden Stiers as Major Charles Emerson Winchester III. The show won numerous awards during its run. Its final episode, "Goodbye, Farewell and Amen" was the highest-rated program of all time, topping the "Who Shot J.R.?" revelation on "Dallas." See also: "M*A*S*H: The Final Episode: Anniversary" (Feb 28). The show generated two spin-offs: "Trapper John, MD" and "After M*A*S*H."

"MISSION: IMPOSSIBLE" TV PREMIERE: ANNIVERSARY. Sept 17, 1966. This action-adventure espionage series was produced by Bruce Geller, appearing on CBS for seven years. The premise of the show was simple: each week the IMF (Impossible Missions Force) leader would receive instructions on a super-secret mission to be carried out by the crew. Steven Hill played the first IMF leader, Dan Briggs. He was replaced by Peter Graves who played Jim Phelps. The crew included: Martin Landau as Rollin Hand, master of disguise; Barbara Bain, real-life wife of Landau, as Cinnamon Carter; Greg Morris as Barney Collier, technical expert; Peter Lupus as Willy Armitage, tough guy; Leonard Nimoy as Hand's replacement, Paris; Lesley Ann Warren as Dana Lambert; Sam Elliott as Doug; Lynda Day George as Lisa Casey and Barbara Anderson as Mimi Davis. The show was remade for ABC in 1988; it lasted two seasons.

MONTEREY JAZZ FESTIVAL. Sept 17–19. Monterey, CA. Celebrating its 47th year, the country's oldest continuous jazz festival features sounds of some of the world's finest jazz musicians. Est attendance: 40,000. For info: Monterey Jazz Festival, PO Box Jazz, Monterey, CA 93942. Phone: (925) 275-9259 (tickets and info) or (831) 373-3366 (corporate offices). Web: www.montereyjazzfestival.org.

NATIONAL CONSTITUTION CENTER CONSTITUTION WEEK. Sept 17–23. To celebrate and commemorate the signing of the US Constitution Sept 17, 1787. The National Constitution Center sponsors special events and activities. Annually, Sept 17–23. Est attendance: 150,000. For info: Natl Constitution Center, 525 Arch St, Independence Mall, Philadelphia, PA 19106. Phone: (215) 923-0004. Fax: (215) 923-1749. Web: www.constitutioncenter.org.

NATIONAL FOOTBALL LEAGUE FORMED: ANNIVERSARY. Sept 17, 1920. The National Football League was formed at Canton, OH.

★**NATIONAL POW/MIA RECOGNITION DAY.** Sept 17. Annually, the third Friday of September.

NATIONAL SCHOOL CELEBRATION. Sept 17. "Pledge Across America": every school is invited to join a synchronized recitation of the Pledge of Allegiance and the preamble to the Constitution coast to coast, 8 AM Hawaiian time to 2 PM Eastern time. Supported by the US Department of Education, this event enables our nation's youth to unite for a patriotic observance. Teleconference lines (check website for number) will allow schools to hear President Bush and/or Secretary Rod Paige start off the event. The national recitation will be followed by a roll call of the 50 states in the order they joined the union. The original 1892 National School Celebration, declared by President Benjamin Harrison, was the event for which the Pledge of Allegiance was written. Free resources available from Farmers Insurance and Celebration USA, including a CD with musical renditions of the Pledge and other selections, as well as teacher's resources. For info: Paula Burton, Pres, Celebration USA, 17853 Santiago Blvd, Ste 107, Villa Park, CA 92861. Phone: (714) 283-1892. Web: www.americanpromise.com or www.celebrationusa.org.

NORTH PARK'S COLONIAL ARTS AND CRAFTS FESTIVAL. Sept 17–19. North Park, Pittsburgh, PA. More than 250 colonial artists & craftsmen, period reenactments and entertainment, fantastic food in big, beautiful North Park! Est attendance: 14,000. For info: Debbie and Dave Stoner, Family Festivals Association, Inc, PO Box 166, Irwin, PA 15642. Phone: (724) 863-4577. Web: www.familyfestivals.com.

OKLAHOMA STATE FAIR. Sept 17–Oct 3 (ending date tentative). State Fair Park, Oklahoma City, Oklahoma. One of the top ten state fairs in North America includes six buildings of commercial exhibits, ten barns for livestock and horse competitions, Disney on Ice, the State Fair Circus, PRCA championship rodeo, live entertainment and motor sports events. Annually, begins the second Friday after Labor Day. Est attendance: 1,000,000. For info: Oklahoma State Fair, PO Box 74943, Oklahoma City, OK 73147. Phone: (405) 948-6700. Fax: (405) 948-6828. E-mail: mail@oklahomastatefair.com. Web: www.oklahomastatefair.com.

Sept 17 ☆ Chase's 2004 Calendar of Events ☆

OSAGE RIVER MOUNTAIN MAN FESTIVAL AND BLACK POWDER SHOOT. Sept 17–19. Lake Ozark, MO. 17th annual. Mountain men, Indians, musicians, storytellers in authentic attire gather to reenact a pre-1840s wilderness rendezvous. Annually, the third full weekend in September. Est attendance: 6,000. For info: Lake Area Chamber of Commerce, PO Box 1570, Lake Ozark, MO 65049. Phone: (800) 451-4117 or (573) 964-1008. Fax: (573) 964-1010. E-mail: mtman@lakeareachamber.com. Web: lakeareachamber.com.

PARALYMPIC GAMES 2004. Sept 17–28. Athens, Greece. Two weeks following the conclusion of the summer Olympics, disabled athletes will have their chance to compete in the same venues at similar events. Highlights include wheelchair basketball, track and field, archery, judo and wheelchair rugby. Some 4,000 athletes from around the world are expected to compete. For info: International Paralympic Committee, Adenauerallee 212-214, 53113 Bonn, Germany. Phone: (49) (228) 209-7200. Fax: (49) (228) 209-7209. E-mail: info@paralympic.org. Web: www.paralympic.org or www.athens2004.com.

RACKING WORLD CELEBRATION. Sept 17–25. Decatur, AL. Weeklong event featuring racking horses from across the nation. The highlight of the 75-class event is the crowning of the World Grand Racking Horse Champion on the last night. Annually, the last full week in September. Est attendance: 10,000. For info: Jacklyn Bailey, Decatur/Morgan County CVB, 719 6th Ave SE, PO Box 2349, Decatur, AL 35602. Phone: (256) 350-2028 or (800) 524-6181. E-mail: info@decaturcvb.org. Web: www.decaturcvb.org.

RIVER CITY ROUNDUP. Sept 17–26. Omaha, NE. Take a moment to reflect on the Midwest's proud past. A celebration of Omaha's agricultural and Western heritage; PRCA rodeo, barbecue contest, trail rides, western/wildlife art show, dances, the world's largest 4-H Livestock Expo and a downtown parade. Est attendance: 300,000. For info: Christy Aegerter, Dir of PR, River City Roundup and Rodeo, 302 S 36th, Ste 800, Omaha, NE 68114. E-mail: knights@aksarben.org. Web: www.aksarben.org.

SELFRIDGE, THOMAS E.: DEATH ANNIVERSARY. Sept 17, 1908. Lieutenant Thomas E. Selfridge, 26-year-old passenger in 740-lb biplane piloted by Orville Wright, was killed when, after four minutes in the air, the plane fell from a height of 75 feet. Nearly 2,000 spectators witnessed the crash at Fort Myer, VA. The plane was being tested for possible military use by the Army Signal Corps. Orville Wright was seriously injured in the crash. Selfridge Air Force Base, MI, was named after the young lieutenant, a West Point graduate, who was the first fatality of powered airplane travel.

SEVEN SWEETS AND SEVEN SOURS FESTIVAL. Sept 17–18. Intercourse, PA. The biggest time of the year is when we put up our fruits and vegetables for the long winter. The whole Village is invaded with wonderful end-of-the-garden creations. Est attendance: 30,000. For info: Lisa Horn, Kitchen Kettle Village, Box 380, Intercourse, PA 17534. Phone: (800) 732-3538 or (717) 768-8261. Web: www.kitchenkettle.com.

SOUTHSIDE FALL FESTIVAL. Sept 17–19. St. Joseph, MO. The highlight of this event is a professional rodeo the United Rodeo Association named "Rodeo of the Year." Also featured are a parade, arts and crafts, street dances, food and much more. Annually, the third weekend in September. Est attendance: 40,000. For info: Beth Bush, 11330 SW State Route JJ, St. Joseph, MO, 64504. Phone: (816) 238-3515. Fax: (816) 238-2218. Web: www.stjomo.com.

	S	M	T	W	T	F	S
September 2004				1	2	3	4
	5	6	7	8	9	10	11
	12	13	14	15	16	17	18
	19	20	21	22	23	24	25
	26	27	28	29	30		

SPACE MILESTONE: *PEGASUS 1* (US). Sept 17, 1978. 23,000-pound research satellite broke up over Africa and fell to Earth. Major pieces are believed to have fallen into Atlantic Ocean off the coast of Angola. The satellite had been orbiting Earth for more than 13 years since being launched Feb 16, 1965.

STREET MACHINE FALL NATIONALS. Sept 17–19. Ozark Empire Fairgrounds, Springfield, MO. Car & truck show with Family Fun Zone and Performance Market Place. For info: Nancy Bright, Ozark Empire Fair, PO Box 630, Springfield, MO 65801. Phone: (417) 833-2660. Fax: (417) 833-3769. E-mail: nancy@ozarkempirefair.com. Web: www.ozarkempirefair.com.

VFW LADIES AUXILIARY ORGANIZED: 90th ANNIVERSARY. Sept 17, 1914. This organization is loyal to the issues and actions affecting America's heroes. Its members offer assistance in addition to supporting veterans' issues in Congress. Part of the organization's mission, according to its charter, is "to assist the Posts and members thereof . . . to foster true patriotism; and to preserve and defend the United States from all her enemies, whomsoever." For info: Veterans of Foreign Wars of the US, Women's Auxiliary, 406 W 34th St, Kansas City, MO 64111. Phone: (816) 561-8655. Fax: (816) 931-4753. Web: www.ladiesauxvfw.com.

VON STEUBEN, BARON FRIEDRICH: BIRTH ANNIVERSARY. Sept 17, 1730. Prussian-born general who volunteered to serve in the American Revolution. He died at Remsen, NY, Nov 28, 1794. Von Steuben Day is commemorated on this day, on the following Saturday or on the 4th Sunday in September.

WILLIAMS, HANK, SR: BIRTH ANNIVERSARY. Sept 17, 1923. Hiram King Williams, country and western singer, born at Georgia, AL. He achieved his first hit with "Lovesick Blues," which brought him a contract with the Grand Ole Opry. His string of hits included "Cold, Cold Heart," "Honky Tonk Blues," "Jambalaya," "Your Cheatin' Heart," "Take These Chains from My Heart" and "I'll Never Get Out of This World Alive," which was released prior to his death Jan 1, 1953, at Oak Hill, VA.

WIZARD OF OZ FESTIVAL. Sept 17–19. Chesterton, IN. 23rd annual festival. Parade, costumed Oz characters, original Munchkins, arts and crafts, food. Est attendance: 80,000. For info: Chesterton/Duneland Chamber of Commerce, 220 W Broadway, Chesterton, IN 46304. Phone: (219) 926-5513. Fax: (219) 926-7593. E-mail: info@chestertonchamber.org. Web: www.chestertonchamber.org.

WO-ZHA-WA DAYS FALL FESTIVAL. Sept 17–19. Wisconsin Dells, WI. Celebrates the beginning of the fall season. Arts, crafts, 100-unit parade, Maxwell Street Days, Wo-Zha-Wa Run and antique flea market. Est attendance: 100,000. For info: Wisconsin Dells Visitors Bureau, PO Box 390, Wisconsin Dells, WI 53965. Phone: (800) 223-3557. E-mail: info@wisdells.com. Web: www.wisdells.com.

BIRTHDAYS TODAY

Anne Bancroft, 73, actress (Tony and Oscar for *The Miracle Worker*; *The Graduate*, *The Turning Point*), born Anna Maria Italiano, New York, NY, Sept 17, 1931.

Paul Benedict, 66, actor ("The Jeffersons," many stage roles), born Silver City, NM, Sept 17, 1938.

☆ Chase's 2004 Calendar of Events ☆ Sept 17–18

George Blanda, 77, Hall of Fame football player, born Youngwood, PA, Sept 17, 1927.
Mark Brunell, 34, football player, born Los Angeles, CA, Sept 17, 1970.
Kyle Chandler, 39, actor ("Early Edition," "Homefront"), born Buffalo, NY, Sept 17, 1965.
Charles Grassley, 71, US Senator (R, Iowa), born New Hartford, IA, Sept 17, 1933.
Philip D. (Phil) Jackson, 59, basketball coach, former player, born Deer Lodge, MT, Sept 17, 1945.
Dorothy Loudon, 71, actress, singer ("The Garry Moore Show"), born Boston, MA, Sept 17, 1933.
Cassandra Peterson, 53, actress (movie hostess Elvira), born Manhattan, KS, Sept 17, 1951.
John Ritter, 56, actor (Emmy for "Three's Company"; *Problem Child*), born Burbank, CA, Sept 17, 1948.
Rita Rudner, 48, comedienne, actress (*Peter's Friends*), born Miami, FL, Sept 17, 1956.
David H. Souter, 65, Associate Justice of the US Supreme Court, born Melrose, MA, Sept 17, 1939.
Rasheed Wallace, 30, basketball player, born Philadelphia, PA, Sept 17, 1974.

SEPTEMBER 18 — SATURDAY
Day 262 — 104 Remaining

"THE ADDAMS FAMILY" TV PREMIERE: 40th ANNIVERSARY. Sept 18, 1964. Charles Addams's quirky *New Yorker* cartoon creations were brought to life in this ABC sitcom about a family full of oddballs. John Astin played lawyer Gomez Addams, with Carolyn Jones as his morbid wife Morticia, Ken Weatherwax as son Pugsley, Lisa Loring as daughter Wednesday, Jackie Coogan as Uncle Fester, Ted Cassidy as both Lurch, the butler, and Thing, a disembodied hand, Blossom Rock as Grandmama and Felix Silla as Cousin Itt. The last episode aired Sept 2, 1966. In 1991, *The Addams Family* movie was released, followed by a sequel. Both starred Anjelica Huston as Morticia, Raul Julia as Gomez, Christopher Lloyd as Uncle Fester, Jimmy Workman as Pugsley and Christina Ricci as Wednesday.

ALABAMA COASTAL CLEANUP. Sept 18. Mobile, Baldwin and Escambia counties, AL. 17th annual. Volunteers convene to "get the trash out of the splash" by cleaning up Alabama's beaches and waterways. This event provides participants with a firsthand experience that improves the ecosystem. Annually, the third Saturday in September. Est attendance: 3,000. For info: Alabama Dept of Conservation & Natural Resources, State Lands Division Coastal Section, Stonebrook Executive Complex, Ste B-1, 23210 Highway 98, Fairhope, AL 36532. Phone: (251) 929-0900. Fax: (251) 990-9293. Web: www.alabamacoastalcleanup.com.

ALOHA FESTIVALS FLORAL PARADE. Sept 18. Hobron Lane to Waikiki's Kalakaua Ave, Honolulu, HI. The Floral Parade has become synonymous with Aloha Festivals. The colorful display is a celebration of the history and spirit of the islands, set amidst the fragrant blossoms of Hawaii. For info: Aloha Festivals. Phone: (808) 589-1771. Fax: (808) 589-1770. E-mail: info@alohafestivals.com. Web: www.alohafestivals.com.

AL'S MEMORIAL RUN AND WALK FOR CHILDREN'S HOSPITAL. Sept 18. Milwaukee, WI. Presented by Briggs & Stratton. Choose from an 8K run, 5-mile walk or 3-mile walk along the lake and through the streets. Benefit fund-raiser for Children's Hospital of Wisconsin. Finish line party on Summerfest grounds with free entertainment and fitness expo. Est attendance: 16,000. For info: Children's Hospital Foundation, PO Box 1997 MS#3050, Milwaukee, WI 53201. Phone: (414) 266-6320. Fax: (414) 266-6139. Web: www.alsmemorialrun.com.

AMERICAN HERITAGE BLUEGRASS FESTIVAL. Sept 18. Stolberg-Jackson Community Bldg, Arrow Rock, MO. Workshops on traditional folk instruments and afternoon and evening concerts. 2nd annual. Est attendance: 300. For info: Linda Moore, H.A.R.C., PO Box 121, Arrow Rock, MO 65320. Phone: (660) 837-3306.

APPLEJACK FESTIVAL. Sept 18–19. Nebraska City, NE. To promote local orchards and their abundant apple harvest. Est attendance: 40,000. For info: Nebraska City Tourism & Events, 806 First Ave, Nebraska City, NE 68410. Phone: (402) 873-3000. Fax: (402) 873-6701. E-mail: tourism@nebraskacity.com. Web: www.nebraskacity.com.

BANNED BOOKS WEEK—CELEBRATING THE FREEDOM TO READ. Sept 18–25. Brings to the attention of the general public the importance of the freedom to read and the harm censorship causes to our society. Sponsors: American Library Association, American Booksellers Association, American Booksellers Association for Free Expression, American Society of Journalists and Authors, Association of American Publishers, National Association of College Stores. For info: Judith F. Krug, American Library Assn, Office for Intellectual Freedom, 50 E Huron St, Chicago, IL 60611. Phone: (312) 280-4223. Fax: (312) 280-4227. E-mail: oif@ala.org. Web: www.ala.org/bbooks.

BELLE MEADE PLANTATION FALL FEST. Sept 18–19. Belle Meade Plantation, Nashville, TN. Annual fund-raiser, crafts, antiques, art, food, market, fine jewelry, garage treasures and children's fest. Annually, the third weekend of September. Est attendance: 10,000. For info: Belle Meade Plantation, 5025 Harding Rd, Nashville, TN 37205. Phone: (615) 356-0501 or (800) 270-3991. Fax: (615) 356-2336. Web: www.bellemeadeplantation.com.

BIG WHOPPER LIAR'S CONTEST. Sept 18. Murphy Auditorium, New Harmony, IN. Thirty "storytellers" compete to see who can tell the BIGGEST Whopper. Annually, the third Saturday in September. Est attendance: 425. For info: Jeff Fleming, PO Box 598, Olney, IL 62450. Phone: (618) 395-8491. Fax: (618) 392-3174.

BRAZZI, ROSSANO: BIRTH ANNIVERSARY. Sept 18, 1916. Hollywood actor Rossano Brazzi was born at Bologna, Italy. A leading romantic figure in the 1950s and 1960s, he appeared in more than 200 films (*South Pacific, Summertime*). He died Dec 24, 1994, at Rome, Italy.

CAPE MAY FOOD & WINE FESTIVAL. Sept 18–22. Cape May, NJ. Come see why *The New York Times* calls Cape May "the restaurant capital of New Jersey." Take classes and seminars taught by Cape May chefs. Attend workshops and tours that invite visitors into the kitchens of Cape May's critically acclaimed restaurants. Enjoy special dinner and lunch meal packages and visit the Gourmet Marketplace, featuring the People's Choice Chowder Contest. For info: Jenn Heinold, Mid-Atlantic Center for the Arts, 1048 Washington St, Cape May, NJ 08204. Phone: (800) 275-4278. Fax: (609) 884-0574. E-mail: mac4arts@capemaymac.org. Web: www.capemaymac.org.

CHAUTAUQUA OF THE ARTS. Sept 18–19. Columbus, IN. Fine artists and craftsmen gather to demonstrate and sell their works. Annually, the third weekend in September. Est attendance: 20,000. For info: Chautauqua of the Arts, 1119 W Main St, Madison, IN 47250-3047. Phone: (812) 265-5080. E-mail: jim@chautauquaofthearts.com. Web: www.chautauquaofthearts.com.

CHEROKEE STRIP CELEBRATION. Sept 18. Perry, OK. To commemorate the opening of the Cherokee Strip to settlement on Sept 16, 1893. Annually, the Saturday or weekend nearest Sept 16. Est attendance: 10,000. For info: Carolyn Briegge, Chamber of Commerce, Box 426, Perry, OK 73077. Phone: (580) 336-4684. Fax: (580) 336-3522. E-mail: information@parrychamber.org.

Sept 18 ☆ Chase's 2004 Calendar of Events ☆

CHILE: INDEPENDENCE DAY. Sept 18. National holiday. Declared independence from Spain in 1810. Sept 19 is commemorated as Armed Forces Day in Chile.

COLUMBUS'S LAST VOYAGE TO THE NEW WORLD: ANNIVERSARY. Sept 18, 1502. Columbus landed at Costa Rica on his fourth and last voyage to the New World. He returned to Spain in 1504 and died there in 1506.

COVERED BRIDGE FESTIVAL. Sept 18–19. Washington and Greene County, PA. Arts and crafts, entertainment and lots of homestyle food at each of ten covered bridges. Annually, the third weekend in September. Est attendance: 110,000. For info: Washington Co Tourism, 273 S Main St, Washington, PA 15301. Phone: (800) 531-4114 or (724) 228-5520. E-mail: info@washpatourism.org. Web: www.washpatourism.org.

DeMILLE, AGNES: BIRTH ANNIVERSARY. Sept 18, 1905. Dancer, choreographer for ballet and Broadway shows such as *Oklahoma*, born at New York, NY. DeMille died at New York, NY, Oct 7, 1993.

DIEFENBAKER, JOHN: BIRTH ANNIVERSARY. Sept 18, 1895. Canadian lawyer, statesman and Conservative prime minister (1957–63). Born at Normandy Township, ON, Canada, he died at Ottawa, ON, Aug 16, 1979. Diefenbaker was a member of the Canadian Parliament from 1940 until his death.

EISENHOWER WORLD WAR II WEEKEND. Sept 18–19. Eisenhower National Historic Site, Gettysburg, PA. A living history encampment featuring Allied soldiers, German prisoners of war, tanks and military vehicles of that time. Annually, the third weekend in September. Est attendance: 2,500. For info: Gettysburg CVB, PO Box 4117, Gettysburg, PA 17325. Phone: (717) 334-6274. Fax: (717) 334-1166. E-mail: gettysburgcvb@dejazzd.com. Web: www.gettysburgcvb.org.

FESTIVAL OF ADVENTURES. Sept 18–19. Aitkin, MN. This annual festival celebrates the area's fur-trading history. Rendezvous at the City Park with trappers, traders, ethnic dancers, music and food. Est attendance: 5,000. For info: Aitkin Area Chamber of Commerce, PO Box 127, Aitkin, MN 56431. Phone: (218) 927-2316 or (800) 526-8342. Fax: (218) 927-4494. E-mail: upnorth@aitkin.com. Web: www.aitkin.com.

FESTIVAL OF THE SEA. Sept 18 (rain date Sept 19). Point Pleasant Beach, NJ. Come join the fun with arts, crafts, food, games for the kids, pony rides, antiques, nonprofit and commercial exhibits. Free admission. Est attendance: 55,000. For info: Point Pleasant Beach Chamber of Commerce, 517A Arnold Ave, Point Pleasant Beach, NJ 08742. Phone: (732) 899-2424. Fax: (732) 899-0103. E-mail: info@pointpleasantbeachnj.com. Web: www.pointpleasantbeachnj.com.

FESTIVAL 2004: FESTIVAL OF FINE ARTS AND FINE CRAFTS. Sept 18–19. Downtown, Dalton, GA. 41st annual. Fine arts and fine crafts festival includes outdoor artist booths, food vendors, children's arts festival, entertainment for adults and children, cash awards. Est attendance: 7,000. For info: Creative Arts Guild, Box 1485, Dalton, GA 30722-1485. Phone: (706) 278-0168. Fax: (706) 278-6996. E-mail: cagarts@creativeartsguild.org.

GARBO, GRETA: BIRTH ANNIVERSARY. Sept 18, 1905. International film actress Greta Garbo was born Greta Lovisa Gustafsson at Stockholm, Sweden. A famous recluse, she retired temporarily, then permanently, from films after 19 years and 27 films, which spanned the late-silent era and beginning of sound movies. Her on-screen roles were characterized by an image of a seductress involved in tragic love affairs. She died Apr 15, 1990, at New York, NY.

September 2004	S	M	T	W	T	F	S
				1	2	3	4
	5	6	7	8	9	10	11
	12	13	14	15	16	17	18
	19	20	21	22	23	24	25
	26	27	28	29	30		

"GET SMART" TV PREMIERE: ANNIVERSARY. Sept 18, 1965. A spy-thriller spoof appearing on both NBC (1965–69) and CBS (1969–70). Don Adams starred as bumbling CONTROL Agent 86, Maxwell Smart. His mission was to thwart the evildoings of the KAOS organization. Agent Smart was usually successful with the help of his friends: Barbara Feldon as Agent 99 (whom Smart eventually married), Edward Platt as The Chief, Robert Karvelas as Agent Larrabee, Dick Gautier as Hymie the Robot and David Ketchum as Agent 13.

HERITAGE DAY. Sept 18. Houston, MO. Arts & crafts, demonstrations of old-time crafts. For info: Houston Area Chamber of Commerce, PO Box 374, Houston, MO 65483. Phone: (417) 967-2220. Fax: (417) 967-2178.

HULL HOUSE OPENS: ANNIVERSARY. Sept 18, 1889. This settlement house was founded in Chicago by Jane Addams and Ellen Gates Starr. It soon became the heart of one of the country's most influential social reform movements, offering a mix of cultural and education programs to new immigrants. See also: "Addams, Jane: Birth Anniversary" (Sept 6).

INTERNATIONAL COASTAL CLEANUP. Sept 18. A million volunteers remove and tabulate 12 million pieces of trash on 21,000 miles of beaches as well as below the water in 100 countries. Annually, the third Saturday in Sept. For info: The Ocean Concervancy, 1725 DeSales St NW, Washington, DC 20036. Phone: (202) 429-5609. Fax: (202) 872-0619. E-mail: cleanup@oceanconcervancyva.org. Web: www.oceanconcervancy.org.

IRON HORSE OUTRACED BY HORSE: ANNIVERSARY. Sept 18, 1830. In a widely celebrated race, the first locomotive built in America, the Tom Thumb, lost to a horse. Mechanical difficulties plagued the steam engine over the nine-mile course between Riley's Tavern and Baltimore, MD, and a boiler leak prevented the locomotive from finishing the race. In the early days of trains, engines were nicknamed "Iron Horses."

JOHNNY APPLESEED FESTIVAL. Sept 18–19. Fort Wayne, IN. A return to the pioneer spirit of the early 1800s, at the gravesite of John Chapman, known as "Johnny Appleseed," who planted hundreds of apple orchards along the early Indiana frontier. Crafts, music, food and demonstrators. Annually, the third full weekend in September. Est attendance: 350,000. For info: Johnny Appleseed Festival, Inc, 1502 Harry Baals Dr, Fort Wayne, IN 46805. Phone: (260) 427-6003. Fax: (260) 427-6020. Web: johnnyappleseedfest.com.

JOHNSON, SAMUEL: BIRTH ANNIVERSARY. Sept 18, 1709 (OS). English lexicographer and literary lion, creator of the first great dictionary of the English language (1755) and author of poems, novels and essays. Johnson was born at Lichfield, Staffordshire, England, and died at London, England, Dec 13, 1784. Johnson, master of the quip, stated, "Patriotism is the last refuge of a scoundrel."

KING TURKEY DAYS (WITH TURKEY RACE). Sept 18. Worthington, MN. Community celebration which includes live turkey race between Paycheck, Worthington, MN and Ruby Begonia, Cuero, TX. Also included are a grand parade, live entertainment, free pancake breakfast and family activities. Est attendance: 15,000. For info: King Turkey Days, Inc, 1121 Third Ave, Worthington, MN 56187. Phone: (800) 279-2919 or (507) 372-2919. Fax: (507) 372-2827. E-mail: wcofc@frontiernet.net.

"LOVE IS A MANY SPLENDORED THING" TV PREMIERE: ANNIVERSARY. Sept 18, 1967. A soap opera created by veteran writer Irna Phillips, airing on CBS for five years. It was based on the 1955 film starring William Holden and Jennifer Jones. Irna Phillips left the show after the network nixed interracial romance in favor of political storylines. David Birney, Bibi Besch and Donna Mills appeared on the show.

MITCHELL PERSIMMON FESTIVAL. Sept 18–25. Main Street, Mitchell, IN. 58th annual. Persimmon pudding and novelty contests, parade, carnival, arts and crafts, fine arts and photography shows, antique autos and machinery, pioneer village candlelight tour, free entertainment nightly. Annually, the last full week in September. Est attendance: 90,000. For info: Greater Mitchell Chamber of Commerce, PO Box 216, Mitchell, IN 47446. Phone: (800) 580-1985. E-mail: mitchell@kiva.net. Web: www.persimmonfestival.org.

NATIONAL STORYTELLER OF THE YEAR CONTEST. Sept 18. Columbus, OH. Official Storyteller of the Year named at this event. Sponsored by the Creative Arts Institute Inc and the Columbus Storytellers Guild. Annually, the third Saturday in September. Est attendance: 2,000. For info: Donna Foster, Creative Arts, 8021 Kennedy Rd, Blacklick, OH 43004. Phone: (614) 759-9407. Fax: (614) 759-8480. E-mail: curtcain@ohiohills.com.

***THE NEW YORK TIMES* FIRST PUBLISHED: ANNIVERSARY.** Sept 18, 1851. The *Times* debuted as *The New-York Daily Times*. The name was changed to the current one in 1857.

NORSKEDALEN'S THRESHING BEE. Sept 18. Norskedalen Nature and Heritage Center, Coon Valley, WI. Antique engines and pioneer demonstrations, such as winnowing, threshing, corn shredding, shelling and grinding; cream separating and butter-making; horse-drawn wagon rides, rope braiding, sawmill, quilt show and farm tool displays. Threshers' meal served, reservations required. Est attendance: 500. For info: Nature and Heritage Center, Inc, Norskedalen, PO Box 235, Coon Valley, WI 54623. Phone: (608) 452-3424. Fax: (608) 452-3157.

PEDDLER'S VILLAGE SCARECROW FESTIVAL. Sept 18–19. Peddler's Village, Lahaska, PA. Weekend festival includes scarecrow making, pumpkin-painting workshops, musical entertainment and scarecrow competition display. Free admission and free live entertainment, charge for workshops. Est attendance: 16,000. For info: Peddler's Village, Routes 202 & 263, Lahaska, PA 18931. Phone: (215) 794-4000. Fax: (215) 794-4001. Web: www.peddlersvillage.com.

READ, GEORGE: BIRTH ANNIVERSARY. Sept 18, 1733. Lawyer and signer of the Declaration of Independence, born at Cecil County, MD. Died Sept 21, 1798, at New Castle, DE.

RELIGIOUS FREEDOM WEEK. Sept 18–26. This date commemorates the anniversary of the Bill of Rights and the right to believe and practice the religion of one's own choice as laid out in the First Amendment. Annually, the week including the anniversary date, Sept 25. For info: Rev Susan Taylor, Religious Freedom Week Committee, c/o Church of Scientology, 1701 20th St NW, Washington, DC 20009. Phone: (202) 667-6404. Fax: (202) 667-6314. E-mail: suetaylor1@juno.com.

ROAD CHURCH COUNTRY FAIR. Sept 18. Road Congregational Church, Pequot Trail, Stonington, CT. White elephants, bake table, harvest table, crafts and children's midway. Famous Barnes's Chowder Luncheon at noon (served in Civil War kettles). Auction at 2 PM. 10 AM–3 PM. Est attendance: 300. For info: Libby Kennedy, 21 Roosevelt Ave, Mystic, CT 06355. Phone: (860) 536-1514. E-mail: roadchurch@juno.com. Web: www.roadchurch.org.

SAM RAYBURN CHILI COOK-OFF. Sept 18. Sam Rayburn House Museum, Bonham, TX. 5th annual. Sponsored by the Friends of Sam Rayburn, this event will again feature live music, family fun-and-games horseshoe tournament, face painting, tours and more! Most importantly there will be lots of great chili to sample and winners to select. Annually, third Saturday in September. For info: Bridget Jones, Sam Rayburn House Museum, PO Box 308, Bonham, TX 75418. Phone: (903) 583-5558. Fax: (903) 640-0800. E-mail: srhmdir@texoma.net.

"SHIRLEY TEMPLE THEATRE" TV PREMIERE: ANNIVERSARY. Sept 18, 1960. An NBC children's anthology of specials appearing on Sundays, hosted by Shirley Temple. Reruns were broadcast on ABC on the following Mondays. "Beauty and the Beast," "Rumplestiltskin," "Rapunzel," "Mother Goose," "The Land of Oz" and "Babes in Toyland" were among the stories presented.

SPACE MILESTONE: *SOYUZ 38* (USSR). Sept 18, 1980. Launched on this date with Cosmonauts Arnaldo Tamayo Mendes (Cuba) and Yuri Romanenko aboard and docked at *Salyut 6* for weeklong mission, returning to Earth Sept 26.

STORY, JOSEPH: 225th BIRTH ANNIVERSARY. Sept 18, 1779. Associate justice of the US Supreme Court (1811–45) was born at Marblehead, MA. "It is astonishing," he wrote a few months before his death, "how easily men satisfy themselves that the Constitution is exactly what they wish it to be." Story died Sept 10, 1845, at Cambridge, MA, having served 33 years on the Supreme Court bench.

TASTE OF HISTORY. Sept 18. Frontier Culture Museum, Staunton, VA. Progressive dinner at historic farm sites. Modern adaptions of historic recipes representing Germany, Ulster, England and early America. Meet at the Museum Visitor Center and stroll from farm to farm with a guide to a tasty progressive meal. For info: Debbie Cole, Frontier Museum, 1290 Richmond Rd, PO Box 810, Staunton, VA 24401. Phone: (540) 332-7850. Fax: (540) 332-9989. E-mail: dcole@frontiermuseum.state.va.us. Web: www.frontiermuseum.org.

TRAIL OF COURAGE LIVING-HISTORY FESTIVAL. Sept 18–19. Rochester, IN. Portrayal of life in frontier Indiana when it was Indian territory. Historic skits, music, dancing, wigwam and tepee villages, historic encampments for Revolutionary War, French and Indian War, Voyageurs, Western Fur Trade and Plains Indians; re-created 1832 Chippeway Village, also Woodland Indian village, pioneer foods and crafts, muzzle-loading and tomahawk contests, canoe rides. Museum, round barn and Living History Village on grounds. Special honored Potawatomi family from Indiana's history each year. Est attendance: 18,000. For info: Fulton County Historical Society, 37 E 375N, Rochester, IN 46975. Phone: (574) 223-4436. E-mail: fchs@rtcol.com. Web: www.icss.net/~fchs.

TRAIL OF TEARS COMMEMORATION AND MOTORCYCLE RIDE. Sept 18. Waterloo, AL. A day to gather and remember the tragic Trail of Tears when Native Americans were removed from their homes in the 1830s and forced to walk a trail to the West. Arts and crafts, museum exhibits and great entertainment. An organized motorcycle ride begins at Chattanooga the same morning and arrives in Waterloo for afternoon activities. Est attendance: 10,000. For info: Debbie Wilson, Florence/Lauderdale Tourism, One Hightower Place, Florence, AL 35630. Phone: (256) 740-4141 or (888) FLO-TOUR. Fax: (256) 740-4142. E-mail: dwilson@flo-tour.org. Web: www.flo-tour.org.

US AIR FORCE ESTABLISHED: ANNIVERSARY. Sept 18, 1947. Although its heritage dates back to 1907 when the Army first established military aviation, the US Air Force became a separate military service on this date. Responsible for providing an Air Force that is capable, in conjunction with the other armed forces, of preserving the peace and security of the US, the department is separately organized under the Secretary of the Air Force and operates under the authority, direction and control of the Secretary of Defense.

US CAPITOL CORNERSTONE LAID: ANNIVERSARY. Sept 18, 1793. President George Washington laid the Capitol cornerstone at Washington, DC, in a Masonic ceremony. That event was the first and last recorded occasion at which the stone with its engraved silver plate was seen. In 1958, during the extension of the east front of the Capitol, an unsuccessful effort was made to find it.

US TAKES OUT ITS FIRST LOAN: ANNIVERSARY. Sept 18, 1789. The first loan taken out by the US was negotiated and secured by Alexander Hamilton on Feb 17, 1790. After beginning negotiations with the Bank of New York and the Bank of North America on Sept 18, 1789, Hamilton obtained the sum of $191,608.81 from the two banks in what became known as the Temporary Loan of 1789. The loan was obtained without authority of law and was used to pay the salaries of the president, senators, representatives and officers of the first Congress. Repayment was completed on June 8, 1790.

"WAGON TRAIN" TV PREMIERE: ANNIVERSARY. Sept 18, 1957. "Wagon Train" was a popular western on NBC and ABC, airing for eight years with its last telecast Sept 5, 1965. Each week travelers on a journey along the wagon trail from Missouri to California encountered new surroundings and interacted with different guest stars. Ward Bond played wagonmaster Major Seth Adams until his death in 1960. He was replaced by John McIntire as Chris Hale. Other regulars were: Robert Horton as scout Flint McCullough, Frank McGrath as cook Charlie Wooster, Terry Wilson as Bill Hawks, Denny (Scott) Miller as scout Duke Shannon, Michael Burns as Barnaby West, a teen passenger, and Robert Fuller as scout Cooper.

WHITE WOMAN MADE AMERICAN INDIAN CHIEF: ANNIVERSARY. Sept 18, 1891. Harriet Maxwell Converse was made a chief of the Six Nations Tribe at the Tonawanda Reservation, NY. She was given the name Ga-is-wa-noh, which means "The Watcher." She had been adopted as a member of the Seneca tribe in 1884 in appreciation of her efforts on behalf of the tribe.

WIFE APPRECIATION DAY. Sept 18. Husbands, show your wives how much you love and appreciate them. Communicate the difference your wife makes in your life. Annually, the third Saturday in September. For info: Brooke Espinoza, PO Box 1054, Arcadia, CA 91007. Phone: (626) 574-7571. E-mail: brookeespinoza@equipyourmarriage.com. Web: www.equipyourmarriage.com.

WINGS 'N' WATER FESTIVAL. Sept 18–19. Wetlands Institute, Stone Harbor, NJ. Coastal arts celebration of the environment throughout seaside towns of Stone Harbor and Avalon. 22nd annual award-winning festival features Wildlife, Duck Stamp, Maritime & Landscape art. Plus bird and fish carvings, decoys, photography, crafts, quilts, music, retriever demos, boat cruises, kayaking, seafood and more. Est attendance: 5,000. For info: Nancy Morrow, Wetlands Institute, 1075 Stone Harbor Blvd, Stone Harbor, NJ 08247-1424. Phone: (609) 368-1211. Fax: (609) 368-3871. Web: www.wetlandsinstitute.org.

BIRTHDAYS TODAY

Lance Armstrong, 33, cyclist, national and world champion, two-time Olympian, five-time winner of the Tour de France, born Plano, TX, Sept 18, 1971.
Frankie Avalon, 65, singer ("Venus"), actor (teen flicks with Annette Funicello), born Philadelphia, PA, Sept 18, 1939.
Robert F. Bennett, 71, US Senator (R, Utah), born Salt Lake City, UT, Sept 18, 1933.
Robert Blake, 66, actor ("Baretta," *In Cold Blood, Little Rascals*), born Michael Gubitosi, Nutley, NJ, Sept 18, 1938.
Scotty Bowman, 71, Hall of Fame hockey coach, born Montreal, QC, Canada, Sept 18, 1933.
James Gandolfini, 43, actor ("The Sopranos"), born Westwood, NJ, Sept 18, 1961.
Jada Pinkett Smith, 33, actress (*The Nutty Professor, Menace II Society*), born Baltimore, MD, Sept 18, 1971.
Ryne Dee Sandberg, 45, former baseball player, born Spokane, WA, Sept 18, 1959.
Jack Warden, 84, actor ("NYPD Blue," "Bad News Bears," "Crazy Like a Fox"), born Newark, NJ, Sept 18, 1920.

SEPTEMBER 19 — SUNDAY

Day 263 — 103 Remaining

ARTS/QUINCY RIVERFEST. Sept 19. Quincy, IL. Celebration of the arts and the Mississippi River in the riverfront parks. Fine arts and crafts and a children's area featuring hands-on activities and performances. Annually, the third Sunday in September. Est attendance: 5,000. For info: Quincy Society of Fine Arts, 300 Civic Center Plaza, Ste 244, Quincy, IL 62301-4162. Phone: (217) 222-3432. Fax: (217) 228-2787. E-mail: art@artsqcy.org. Web: www.artsqcy.org.

BALANCE AWARENESS WEEK. Sept 19–25. To develop public awareness of balance and disorders of balance system (vestibular disorders); to unite professionals, educators, support groups, medical facilities in a weeklong effort to focus attention of the public and the media. Annually, the third full week in Sept. For info: Vestibular Disorders Assn, PO Box 4467, Portland, OR 97208-4467. Phone: (800) 837-8428. Fax: (503) 229-8064. E-mail: veda@vestibular.org. Web: www.vestibular.org.

BALTIMORE HIGHLANDS ARTS & CRAFTS FESTIVAL. Sept 19. Baltimore, MD. Homemade crafts, food, children's activities, entertainment and much more. Annually, the third Sunday in September. For info: Greater Baltimore Highlands Community Assn, PO Box 18213, Halethorpe, MD 21227. Phone: (410) 789-4334.

BROUGHAM, HENRY PETER: BIRTH ANNIVERSARY. Sept 19, 1778. Scottish jurist and orator born at Edinburgh, Scotland. Died at Cannes, France, May 7, 1868. The Brougham carriage was named after him. "Education," he said, "makes a people easy to lead, but difficult to drive; easy to govern, but impossible to enslave."

BUILD A BETTER IMAGE WEEK. Sept 19–25. In order to be a success, you need to look like one. This week is set aside for people to evaluate their professional image and take the steps necessary to improve on it. For "10 Steps to a Better Image" tip sheet, send #10 SASE. Annually, the third full week of September. For info: Marlys K. Arnold, ImageSpecialist, 7885 NW Roanridge Rd, Ste A, Kansas City, MO 64151. Phone: (816) 746-7888.

September 2004	S	M	T	W	T	F	S
				1	2	3	4
	5	6	7	8	9	10	11
	12	13	14	15	16	17	18
	19	20	21	22	23	24	25
	26	27	28	29	30		

E-mail: marnold@imagespecialist.com. Web: www.imagespecialist.com.

CARROLL, CHARLES: BIRTH ANNIVERSARY. Sept 19, 1737 (OS). American Revolutionary leader and signer of the Declaration of Independence, born at Annapolis, MD. The last surviving signer of the Declaration, he died Nov 14, 1832, at Baltimore, MD.

DEAF AWARENESS WEEK. Sept 19–25. Nationwide celebration to promote deaf culture, American Sign Language and deaf heritage. Activities might include library displays, interpreted story hours, Open Houses in residential schools and mainstream programs, exhibit booths in shopping malls with "Five Minute Sign Language Lessons," material distribution. Annually, the last full week of September. For info: Natl Assn of the Deaf, 814 Thayer Ave, Silver Spring, MD 20910-4500. Fax: (301) 587-1791. E-mail: nadinfo@nad.org. Web: www.nad.org.

"ER" TV PREMIERE: 10th ANNIVERSARY. Sept 19, 1994. This medical drama takes place in the emergency room of the fictional County General Hospital in Chicago. Doctors and nurses care for life-and-death cases while experiencing their personal traumas as well. Cast has included Anthony Edwards, George Clooney, Sherry Stringfield, Noah Wylie, Laura Innes, Gloria Reuben, Eriq La Salle, Maura Tierney, Goran Visnjic and Alex Kingston. On May 8, 2003, the 200th episode aired.

FAST OF GEDALYA. Sept 19. Jewish holiday. Hebrew calendar date: Tishri 3, 5765. Tzom Gedalya begins at first light of day and commemorates the 6th-century BC assassination of Gedalya Ben Achikam. Began at sundown Sept 18.

"FLIPPER" TV PREMIERE: 40th ANNIVERSARY. Sept 19, 1964. An adventure series starring Flipper, the intelligent, communicative and helpful dolphin. The human cast members included Brian Kelly as Chief Ranger Porter Ricks, Luke Halpin as his son Sandy, Tommy Norden as his son Bud and Ulla Strömstedt as biochemist Ulla Norstrand. The last telecast of this series was Sept 1, 1968. The series was briefly re-created under the same title in the '90s.

FOUNDER'S DAY CORN ROAST. Sept 19. Pacific University, Forest Grove, OR. 1–5 PM. Mountain men, interactive pioneer displays, Native and other entertainment, buffalo burgers, family activities and lots of CORN!!! Est attendance: 2,000. For info: Founder's Day Corn Roast, 2417 Pacific Ave, Forest Grove, OR 97116. Phone: (503) 357-3006. Fax: (503) 357-2367. E-mail: fgchamber@groveweb.net. Web: www.fgchamber.com.

GOLDING, SIR WILLIAM: BIRTH ANNIVERSARY. Sept 19, 1911. Born at Columb Minor at Cornwall, England, this celebrated author was recognized for his contributions to literature with a Nobel Prize in 1983. His first and most popular novel was *Lord of the Flies*. He died June 19, 1993, near Truro, Cornwall.

HEY RUBE GET A TUBE OCEAN INNER TUBE RACE. Sept 19. Jenkinsons Beach, Point Pleasant, NJ. Contestants paddle thru a 300-yard course in the ocean. All monies benefit the Point Pleasant Lions Club charities. For info: Philip Crincoli, PO Box 444, Point Pleasant, NJ 08742. Phone: (732) 714-9749. Fax: (732) 714-9750. E-mail: crincolip@netscape.net. Web: community.nj.com/cc/pt.pleasantlionsclub.

"ICEMAN" MUMMY DISCOVERED: ANNIVERSARY. Sept 19, 1991. At 10,531 feet in the Austrian-Italian Alps, two hikers discovered a 5,300-year-old frozen mummy from late Neolithic times. The man carried rough bow and arrows as well as a copper axe, and wore a grass cloak for warmth. His shoes were made from bearskin, deer hide and tree bark. He now rests as a frozen exhibit at the South Tyrol Museum of Archaeology at Bolzano, Italy. The "Iceman" was gently thawed in September 2000 in order for scientists to conduct valuable DNA analysis and determine his last meal.

INTERNATIONAL DAY OF PRAYER AND ACTION FOR HUMAN HABITAT. Sept 19. This day is set aside to encourage churches to pray for those in need of shelter and guidance in what God would have them do to help eliminate poverty housing. Annually, the third Sunday in September, as the end of Building on Faith Week. For info: Habitat for Humanity, 121 Habitat St, Americus, GA 31709-3498. Phone: (800) HABITAT or (229) 924-6935. E-mail: publicinfo@hfhi.org. Web: www.habitat.org.

JAMESTOWN BURNED BY BACON'S REBELLION: ANNIVERSARY. Sept 19, 1676. In the Virginia colony every adult male could vote. When Charles II was restored to the English throne, he sought to exploit the colony to the fullest. Virginia Governor Sir William Berkeley, supporting the king, adopted new laws to facilitate these efforts including measures allowing only property holders to vote, raising taxes and raising the cost of shipping while lowering the price for tobacco. The resulting discontent exploded when the frontier of the colony was attacked by Indians and the governor refused to defend the settlers. Nathaniel Bacon, a colonist on the governor's council, was made leader by the frontier farmers, and his troops successfully defeated the Indians. Denounced by Berkeley as rebels, Bacon and his men occupied Jamestown, forcing the governor to call an election, the first in 15 years. The Berkeley laws were repealed and election and tax reforms were instituted. While Bacon and his troops were gone on a raiding party against the Indians, Berkeley again denounced them. They returned and attacked Berkeley's forces, defeating them and burning Jamestown on Sept 19, 1676. Berkeley fled and Bacon became ruler of Virginia. When he died suddenly a short time later, the rebellion collapsed. Berkeley returned to power and Bacon's followers were hunted down, some executed and their property confiscated. Berkeley was replaced the next year and peace was restored.

"THE MARY TYLER MOORE SHOW": TV PREMIERE: ANNIVERSARY. Sept 19, 1970. This show—one of the most popular sitcoms of the '70s—combined good writing, an effective supporting cast and contemporary attitudes. The show centered around the two most important places in Mary Richards's (Mary Tyler Moore) life—the WJM-TV newsroom and her apartment at Minneapolis. At home she shared the ups and downs of life with her friend Rhoda Morgenstern (Valerie Harper) and the manager of her apartment building, Phyllis Lindstrom (Cloris Leachman). At work, as the associate producer (later producer) of "The Six O'Clock News," Mary struggled to function in a man's world. Figuring in her professional life were her irascible boss Lou Grant (Ed Asner), levelheaded and softhearted news writer Murray Slaughter (Gavin MacLeod) and narcissistic anchorman Ted Baxter (Ted Knight). In the last of 168 episodes (Mar 19, 1977), the unthinkable happened: everyone in the WJM newsroom except the inept Ted was fired.

MEXICO CITY EARTHQUAKE: ANNIVERSARY. Sept 19–20, 1985. Nearly 10,000 persons perished in the earthquakes (8.1 and 7.5 respectively, on the Richter scale) that devastated Mexico City. Damage to buildings was estimated at more than $1 billion, and 100,000 homes were destroyed or severely damaged.

NATIONAL ADULT DAY SERVICES WEEK. Sept 19–25. To promote day care services for older adults. For info: Natl Adult Day Services Assn, 8201 Greensboro Dr, Ste 300, McLean, VA 22102. Phone: (703) 610-9035. E-mail: info@nadsa.org. Web: www.nadsa.org.

Sept 19 ☆ *Chase's 2004 Calendar of Events* ☆

NATIONAL DOG WEEK. Sept 19–25. To promote the relationship of dogs to mankind and emphasize the need for the proper care and treatment of dogs. Annually, the last full week in September. For info: Morris Raskin, Secy, Dogs on Stamps Study Unit (DOSSU), 202 A Newport Rd, Monroe Township, NJ 08831. Phone: (609) 655-7411. E-mail: mraskin@nerc.com.

★**NATIONAL FARM AND RANCH SAFETY AND HEALTH WEEK.** Sept 19–25. Presidential Proclamation issued since 1982 for the third week in September. Previously, from 1944, for one of the last two weeks in July.

NATIONAL FARM ANIMALS AWARENESS WEEK. Sept 19–25. A week to promote awareness of farm animals and their natural behaviors. The week is dedicated to learning about farm animals and appreciating their many interesting and unique qualities. Annually, the third full week in September. For info: Karen Graham, The Humane Society of the US, Farm Animal Section, 2100 L St NW, Washington, DC 20037. Phone: (301) 258-3110. E-mail: kgraham@hsus.org. Web: www.hsus.org.

★**NATIONAL HISTORICALLY BLACK COLLEGES AND UNIVERSITIES WEEK.** Sept 19–25 (tentative).

NATIONAL PERSONAL CHEF DAYS. Sept 19–21. A national day for clients to honor the hardworking, creative personal chefs who provide them with delicious, affordable, custom-designed meals from fresh ingredients on a regular basis that may be enjoyed in the comfort of the client's own home. Our clients don't have to be celebrities to eat like celebrities! For info: Candy Wallace, 4572 Delaware St, San Diego, CA 92116. Phone: (800) 644-8389. Fax: (619) 294-2823. E-mail: chefcandy@personalchef.com. Web: www.personalchef.com.

NATIONAL REHABILITATION AWARENESS CELEBRATION. Sept 19–25. The observance salutes the determination of the more than 50 million Americans with disabilities. It is a time to applaud the efforts of rehab professionals, provide a forum for education and offer an occasion to call upon our citizens to find new ways to fulfill needs that still exist. Annually, the third full week in Sept. For info: Natl Rehabilitation Awareness Foundation, PO Box 71, Scranton, PA 18501. Phone: (570) 341-4637 or (800) 943-6723. Fax: (570) 341-4331. Web: www.nraf-rehabnet.org.

NATIONAL SINGLES WEEK. Sept 19–25. To celebrate single life and to recognize singles and their contributions to society. For info: Singles Press Assn, Box 6243, Scottsdale, AZ 85261-6243. Phone: (480) 945-6746. E-mail: singles@primenet.com.

OLD-FASHIONED HARVESTFEST AND FIDDLERS CONTEST. Sept 19. Woodstock, IL. A daylong celebration, Harvestfest features farmers' markets, old-time craftspeople including weavers, spinners and quilters, vintage farm equipment, blacksmithing, woodworking, wagon rides and a fiddlers contest for youth and adults. Hours: 10 AM–5 PM. Est attendance: 3,000. For info: Woodstock Chamber of Commerce, 136 Cass St, Woodstock, IL 60098. Phone: (815) 338-2436. Fax: (815) 338-2927. E-mail: chamber@woodstockilchamber.com. Web: www.woodstockilchamber.com.

"PEOPLE ARE FUNNY" TV PREMIERE: 50th ANNIVERSARY. Sept 19, 1954. This half-hour show combined audience participation and stunts. One feature was a Univac computer that played matchmaker for eligible men and women. Art Linkletter hosted the show until 1958; reruns were shown for the next few seasons. The show was revived for a short time in 1984; Flip Wilson was the host.

September 2004

S	M	T	W	T	F	S
			1	2	3	4
5	6	7	8	9	10	11
12	13	14	15	16	17	18
19	20	21	22	23	24	25
26	27	28	29	30		

POWELL, LEWIS F., JR: BIRTH ANNIVERSARY. Sept 19, 1907. Former associate justice of the Supreme Court of the US, nominated by President Nixon Oct 21, 1971. (Took office Jan 7, 1972.) Justice Powell was born at Suffolk, VA. In 1987, he announced his retirement from the Court. He died Aug 25, 1998, at Richmond, VA.

ROYKO, MIKE: BIRTH ANNIVERSARY. Sept 19, 1932. Syndicated columnist to more than 600 newspapers nationwide, Pulitzer Prize–winner and author (*Boss, Slats Grobnick*). Born at Chicago, IL, he died there Apr 29, 1997.

SAINT CHRISTOPHER (SAINT KITTS) AND NEVIS: INDEPENDENCE DAY: ANNIVERSARY. Sept 19. National holiday. Commemorates independence from Britain in 1983.

SAINT JANUARIUS (GENNARO): FEAST DAY. Sept 19. Fourth-century bishop of Benevento, martyred near Naples, Italy, whose relics in the Naples Cathedral are particularly famous because on his feast days the blood in a glass vial is said to liquefy in response to prayers of the faithful. In September 1979, the Associated Press reported that some 5,000 persons gathered at the cathedral at dawn, and that "the blood liquefied after 63 minutes of prayers." This phenomenon is said to occur also on the first Saturday in May.

TALK LIKE A PIRATE DAY. Sept 19. A day when people everywhere add a touch of larceny to their dialogue by talking like pirates: for example, "Arr, matey, it be a fine day." While it's inherently a guy thing, women have been known to enjoy the day, because they have to be addressed as "me beauty." Arr! Annually, Sept 19. For info: John Baur. Phone: (541) 928-3513. Also: Mark Summers. Email: slappy@talklikeapirate.com.

TITAN II MISSILE EXPLOSION: ANNIVERSARY. Sept 19, 1980. The third major accident involving America's most powerful single weapon occurred near Damascus, AR. The explosion, at 3 AM, came nearly 11 hours after a fire had started in the missile silo. The multimegaton nuclear warhead (a hydrogen bomb) reportedly was briefly airborne, but came to rest a few hundred feet away. One dead, 21 injured in accident. Previous major Titan Missile accidents: Aug 9, 1965, near Searcy, AR (53 dead); and Aug 24, 1978, near Rock, KS (2 dead, 29 injured).

TOLKIEN WEEK. Sept 19–25. To promote appreciation and enjoyment of the works of J.R.R. Tolkien. Annually, the week that includes Hobbit Day (Sept 22). For info: Phil Helms, American Tolkien Society, PO Box 7871, Flint, MI 48507-0871. Phone/fax: (727) 585-0985.

"THE VIRGINIAN" TV PREMIERE: ANNIVERSARY. Sept 19, 1962. TV's first 90-minute Western starred James Drury as the Virginian, a foreman trying to come to terms with the westward expansion of civilization. It was set on the Shiloh Ranch, in Wyoming. Key players included Doug McClure (with Drury, the only cast member to stay for the entire run), Lee J. Cobb, Roberta

☆ Chase's 2004 Calendar of Events ☆ Sept 19–20

Shore, Pippa Scott, Gary Clarke, David Hartman and Tim Matheson. In the last season, the title was changed to "The Men From Shiloh," and Stewart Granger and Lee Majors joined the cast.

WOMEN'S FRIENDSHIP DAY. Sept 19. Every woman has special friends she can't live without; those women to whom she tells everything, friends who will always listen and who know just what to say. Women's Friendship Day provides the perfect opportunity for women to acknowledge the special people in their lives. Annually, the third Sunday in September. For info: Kappa Delta Sorority, 3205 Players Ln, Memphis, TN 38125. Phone: (901) 748-1897. Fax: (901) 748-0949. E-mail: commspec@kappadelta.org.

WOOL DAY: SHEEP TO SHAWL AND BORDER COLLIES. Sept 19. Billings Farm and Museum, Woodstock, VT. This daylong event focuses on the many aspects of wool production, including a "sheep to shawl" demonstration and sheep herding, as well as many hands-on activities for all ages to enjoy. These activities include carding wool, drop spindle spinning, weaving, knitting and rug hooking. Border collie demonstrations will show how these natural shepherds efficiently round up sheep, drive them from one area to another and corral them. Est attendance: 1,000. For info: Billings Farm & Museum, PO Box 489, Woodstock, VT 05091. Phone: (802) 457-2355. Fax: (802) 457-4663. E-mail: billings.farm@valley.net. Web: www.billingsfarm.org.

WORLD PRIEST DAY. Sept 19. World Priest Day is a celebration and affirmation of the men who commit their lives to the Lord and the Church via the Sacrament of Holy Orders. It is an opportunity for Catholic parishoners to thank, affirm and share their love and support for our priests. Sponsored by WorldWide Marriage Encounter since 2000. Annually, third Sunday in September. For info: Gary & Marcia Daigle, WorldWide Marriage Encounter, 2210 E Highland Ave, #106, San Bernardino, CA 92404. Phone: (985) 649-0999. Fax: (909) 863-9986. E-mail: gemgd@worldnet.att.net. Web: wpd.wwme.org.

BIRTHDAYS TODAY

James Anthony (Jim) Abbott, 37, former baseball player, born Flint, MI, Sept 19, 1967.
Kevin Hooks, 46, actor, director ("The White Shadow," *Sounder*), born Philadelphia, PA, Sept 19, 1958.
Jeremy Irons, 56, actor (Oscar for *Reversal of Fortune; Lolita, Dead Ringers*), born Cowes, Isle of Wight, England, Sept 19, 1948.
Nick Johnson, 26, baseball player, born Sacramento, CA, Sept 19, 1978.
Joan Lunden, 53, broadcast journalist (former cohost of "Good Morning America"), born Sacramento, CA, Sept 19, 1951.
Randolph Mantooth, 59, actor ("Emergency"), born Sacramento, CA, Sept 19, 1945.
David McCallum, 71, actor ("The Man from U.N.C.L.E.," *The Great Escape*), born Glasgow, Scotland, Sept 19, 1933.
Joe Morgan, 61, broadcaster, Hall of Fame baseball player, born Bonham, TX, Sept 19, 1943.
Twiggy, 55, actress (*The Boy Friend, The Blues Brothers*), model, born Leslie Hornby, London, England, Sept 19, 1949.
Adam West, 76, actor ("Batman," "The Last Precinct"), born Walla Walla, WA, Sept 19, 1928 (some sources say 1929 or 1930).
Paul Williams, 64, singer, composer ("Love Boat" theme song), born Omaha, NE, Sept 19, 1940.
Trisha Yearwood, 40, singer, born Monticello, GA, Sept 19, 1964.

SEPTEMBER 20 — MONDAY
Day 264 — 102 Remaining

BILLIE JEAN KING WINS THE "BATTLE OF THE SEXES": ANNIVERSARY. Sept 20, 1973. Billie Jean King defeated Bobby Riggs in the nationally televised "Battle of the Sexes" tennis match in three straight sets.

"THE COSBY SHOW" TV PREMIERE: 20th ANNIVERSARY. Sept 20, 1984. This Emmy Award–winning comedy set in New York City revolved around the members of the Huxtable family. Father Dr. Heathcliff Huxtable was played by Bill Cosby; his wife Clair, an attorney, was played by Phylicia Rashad. Their four daughters were played by Sabrina Le Beauf (Sondra), Lisa Bonet (Denise), Tempestt Bledsoe (Vanessa) and Keshia Knight Pulliam (Rudy); Malcolm-Jamal Warner played son Theo. By the end of the series in 1992, the two oldest daughters had finished college and were married. "A Different World" was a spin-off set at historically black Hillman College where Denise was a student.

EQUAL RIGHTS PARTY FOUNDING: ANNIVERSARY. Sept 20, 1884. The Equal Rights Party was formed at San Francisco, CA. Its candidate for president, nominated in convention, was Mrs Belva Lockwood. The vice presidential candidate was Marietta Stow.

FAMILY DAY—A DAY TO EAT DINNER WITH YOUR CHILDREN. Sept 20. A national event meant to remind Americans of the value of parental engagement and to encourage them to make family dinners a regular feature of their lives. Research by the National Center on Addiction and Substance Abuse (CASA) at Columbia University has shown that the more often children eat dinner with their parents, the less likely they are to smoke, use illegal drugs or abuse alcohol. Materials available on how to eat dinner with your children and address tough issues. For info: Family Day Coord, CASA, 633 Third Ave, 19th Fl, New York, NY 10017. Phone: (212) 841-5200. Fax: (212) 956-8020. Web: www.casacolumbia.org.

FINANCIAL PANIC OF 1873: ANNIVERSARY. Sept 20, 1873. For the first time in its history, the New York Stock Exchange was forced to close because of a banking crisis. Although the worst of the panic and crisis was over within a week, the psychological effect on businessmen, investors and the nation at large was more lasting.

HOLLYWOOD MAGIC DAY. Sept 20. Spirituality meets Hollywood in "Hollywood Magic" Day. It's a time for screenwriters to forget the formulaic approach to Hollywood films and focus on the stories within. For info: Marisa D'Vari, 220 Boylston St, #1206, Boston, MA 02116. Phone: (617) 451-9914. Fax: (617) 351-2279. E-mail: mdvari@deg.com. Web: www.deg.com.

"THE LORETTA YOUNG SHOW" TV PREMIERE: ANNIVERSARY. Sept 20, 1953. NBC half-hour dramatic anthology series (initially titled "Letter to Loretta") hosted by and frequently starring Oscar-winning actress Loretta Young. At the beginning of each episode Young would swirl through a door in a spectacular gown. Young garnered two Emmys during the show's eight-year run. In 1972 it was reported that Young had been awarded $559,000 in a suit against NBC for syndicating reruns of the show without her permission. Young did not want them shown because her clothes and hairstyles in the shows were long out of date by the '70s.

"LOU GRANT" TV PREMIERE: ANNIVERSARY. Sept 20, 1977. This hour-long dramatic series was a spin-off of "The Mary Tyler Moore Show." Ed Asner reprised his role as newspaper editor Lou Grant, now a city editor for the *Los Angeles Tribune*. The show tackled many serious issues, including child abuse, gun control and the plight of Vietnamese refugees. The cast included Mason Adams, Nancy Marchand, Jack Bannon, Robert Walden, Daryl Anderson, Rebecca Balding, Linda Kelsey, Allen Williams and Emilio Delgado. This series was an unusual spin-off because it was the first time a character left a sitcom to headline a drama.

Sept 20-21 ☆ Chase's 2004 Calendar of Events ☆

MORTON, FERDINAND "JELLY ROLL": BIRTH ANNIVERSARY. Sept 20, 1885. American jazz pianist, composer and orchestra leader, was born at New Orleans, LA (some scholars believe in 1890). Morton, subject of a biography titled *Mr Jelly Roll* by Alan Lomax, died July 10, 1941, at Los Angeles, CA.

NATIONAL INVISIBLE CHRONIC ILLNESS AWARENESS WEEK. Sept 20–26. San Diego, CA. Activities include online events and outreach to communities and churches, encouraging them to participate in calling attention to reaching out to those with chronic illness. Annually, last full week of September. For info: Lisa Copen, PO Box 502928, San Diego, CA 92150. Phone: (888) 751-7378. Fax: (800) 933-1078. E-mail: rest@restministries.org. Web: www.mychronicillness.com.

NATIONAL LOVE YOUR FILES WEEK. Sept 20–24. A good filing system can be a powerful asset. Filing gets a bad rap because people do it the hard way. If a filing system is set up correctly, it's easy to maintain and a pleasure to use. Annually, the third full week in September. For info: Jan Jasper. Phone: (212) 465-7472. Fax: (509) 356-2803. E-mail: jan@janjasper.com. Web: www.janjasper.com.

NATIONAL RESEARCH COUNCIL: FIRST MEETING: ANNIVERSARY. Sept 20, 1916. Anniversary of first meeting of National Research Council, at New York, NY. Formed at request of President Woodrow Wilson for ". . . encouraging the investigation of natural phenomena . . ." for American business and national security.

"THE PHIL SILVERS SHOW" TV PREMIERE: ANNIVERSARY. Sept 20, 1955. This popular half-hour sitcom starred Phil Silvers as Sergeant Ernie Bilko, a scheming but good-natured con man whose schemes rarely worked out. Guest stars included Fred Gwynne, Margaret Hamilton, Dick Van Dyke and Alan Alda in his first major TV role.

ROCK OF CHICKAMAUGA: ANNIVERSARY. Sept 20, 1863. After disastrous moves by Union General William Starke Rosecrans, Confederate forces appeared to be carrying the day at the Battle of Chickamauga in Tennessee. With Rosecrans in flight to Chattanooga, Union General Henry Thomas and his men maintained their position and repeatedly turned back Southern attacks until they were reinforced. Thomas's actions saved the Union forces from a complete rout and earned him the nickname, "Rock of Chickamauga." Rosecrans was relieved of his command.

SINCLAIR, UPTON (BEALL): BIRTH ANNIVERSARY. Sept 20, 1878. American novelist and politician born at Baltimore, MD. He worked for political and social reforms, and his best-known novel, *The Jungle*, prompted one of the nation's first pure food laws. Died at Bound Brook, NJ, Nov 25, 1968.

BIRTHDAYS TODAY

Arnold Jacob ("Red") Auerbach, 87, Hall of Fame basketball coach, born Brooklyn, NY, Sept 20, 1917.
Joyce Brothers, 76, psychologist, author, born New York, NY, Sept 20, 1928.
Donald A. Hall, 76, poet, author (*Lucy's Christmas, Ox Cart Man*), born New Haven, CT, Sept 20, 1928.
Kristen Johnston, 37, actress ("3rd Rock from the Sun"), born Washington, DC, Sept 20, 1967.
Guy Damien LaFleur, 53, Hall of Fame hockey player, born Thurso, QC, Canada, Sept 20, 1951.
Sophia Loren, 70, actress (Oscar for *Two Women*; *Black Orchid*, *Marriage Italian Style*, "Brief Encounter"), born Sofia Scicoloni, Rome, Italy, Sept 20, 1934.
Anne Meara, 75, actress ("Fame"), comedienne (Stiller and Meara), born New York, NY, Sept 20, 1929.

	S	M	T	W	T	F	S
September 2004				1	2	3	4
	5	6	7	8	9	10	11
	12	13	14	15	16	17	18
	19	20	21	22	23	24	25
	26	27	28	29	30		

SEPTEMBER 21 — TUESDAY
Day 265 — 101 Remaining

ARMENIA: INDEPENDENCE DAY. Sept 21. Public holiday. Commemorates independence from Soviet Union in 1991.

BELIZE: INDEPENDENCE DAY. Sept 21. National holiday. Commemorates independence of the former British Honduras from Britain in 1981.

HOPKINSON, FRANCIS: BIRTH ANNIVERSARY. Sept 21, 1737. Signer of the Declaration of Independence. Born at Philadelphia, PA, he died there May 9, 1791.

HURRICANE HUGO HITS AMERICAN COAST: 15th ANNIVERSARY. Sept 21, 1989. After ravaging the Virgin Islands, Hurricane Hugo hit the American coast at Charleston, SC. In its wake, Hugo left destruction totaling at least eight billion dollars.

JACKSON COUNTY APPLE FESTIVAL. Sept 21–25. Jackson County, OH. Mountains of apples and barrels of cider. Homemade apple butter, apple pies and candy apples. Est attendance: 225,000. For info: Jackson County Apple Festival, Inc, PO Box 8, Jackson, OH 45640-0008. Phone: (740) 286-1339. Web: www.jacksonapplefestival.com.

JONES, CHUCK: BIRTH ANNIVERSARY. Sept 21, 1912. Born at Spokane, WA, Chuck Jones worked as a child extra in Hollywood in the 1920s. After attending art school, he landed a job washing animation cels for famed Disney animator Ub Iwerks. He learned the craft, and by 1962 he headed his own unit at Warner Bros. Animation. He created the characters Road Runner and Wile E. Coyote, Marvin the Martian and Pepe le Pew. He worked on the development of Bugs Bunny, Elmer Fudd, Daffy Duck and Porky Pig, and also produced, directed and wrote the screenplay for the animated 1966 television classic "Dr. Seuss' How the Grinch Stole Christmas." He won several Academy Awards for his work and his cartoon "What's Opera, Doc?" is in the National Film Registry. He died on Feb 22, 2002, at Corona del Mar, CA.

JOSEPH, CHIEF: 100th DEATH ANNIVERSARY. Sept 21, 1904. Admirable Nez Percé chief, whose Indian name was In-mut-yoo-yah-lat-lat, was born about 1840 at Wallowa Valley, Oregon Territory, and died on the Colville Reservation at Washington. Faced with war or resettlement to a reservation, Chief Joseph led a dramatic attempt to escape to Canada. After three months and more than 1,000 miles, he and his people were surrounded 40 miles from Canada and sent to a reservation at Oklahoma. Though the few survivors were later allowed to relocate to another reservation at Washington, they never regained their ancestral lands.

MALTA: INDEPENDENCE DAY: 40th ANNIVERSARY. Sept 21. National Day. Commemorates independence from Britain in 1964.

MOON PHASE: FIRST QUARTER. Sept 21. Moon enters First Quarter phase at 11:53 AM, EDT.

NETHERLANDS: PRINSJESDAG. Sept 21. Official opening of parliament at The Hague. The queen of the Netherlands, by tradition, rides in a golden coach to the hall of knights for the annual opening of parliament. Annually, on the third Tuesday in September.

"NYPD BLUE" TV PREMIERE: ANNIVERSARY. Sept 21, 1993. This gritty New York City police drama has had a large and changing cast. The central characters were partners Detective Bobby Simone (who later died), played by Jimmy Smits, and Detective Andy Sipowicz, played by Dennis Franz. Other cast members have included Kim Delaney as Detective Diane Russell,

James McDaniel as Lieutenant Arthur Fancy, Gordon Clapp as Detective Gregory Medavoy, Rick Schroder as Detective Danny Sorenson, Nicholas Turturro as Detective James Martinez, Mark-Paul Gosselaar as Detective John Clark and Esai Morales as Lieutenant Tony Rodriguez.

"PERRY MASON" TV PREMIERE: ANNIVERSARY. Sept 21, 1957. Raymond Burr will forever be associated with the character of Perry Mason, a criminal lawyer who won the great majority of his cases. Episodes followed a similar format: the action took place in the first half, with the killer's identity unknown, and the courtroom drama took place in the latter half. Mason was particularly adept at eliciting confessions from the guilty parties. Regulars and semi-regulars included Barbara Hale, William Hopper, William Talman and Ray Collins. Following the series' end, with the last telecast on Jan 27, 1974, a number of successful "Perry Mason" TV movies aired and the show remains popular in reruns.

TAYLOR, MARGARET SMITH: BIRTH ANNIVERSARY. Sept 21, 1788. Wife of Zachary Taylor, 12th president of the US, born at Calvert County, MD. Died Aug 18, 1852.

"THE TEXACO STAR THEATER" TV PREMIERE: ANNIVERSARY. Sept 21, 1948. Also known as "The Milton Berle Show" and sponsored by Texaco until 1953, this popular variety show was a good sign for the fledgling TV industry. Milton Berle became a superstar. The show featured singing and comedy, especially sight gags and outrageous costumes, and guest stars. Changes were made in the fourth season: Berle cut back his appearances, new writers and a new director were added and the format was changed to a show-within-a-show. Ruth Gilbert, Fred Clark and Arnold Stang were featured, along with the new pitchman, ventriloquist Jimmy Nelson and his dummy Danny O'Day.

UNITED NATIONS: INTERNATIONAL DAY OF PEACE/OPENING DAY OF GENERAL ASSEMBLY. Sept 21. The United Nations General Assembly, Nov 30, 1981, declared "that the third Tuesday of September, the opening day of the regular sessions of the General Assembly, shall be officially proclaimed and observed as International Day of Peace and shall be devoted to commemorating and strengthening the ideals of peace both within and among all nations and peoples." For info: United Nations, Dept of Public Info, New York, NY 10017. Web: www.un.org.

WELLS, HERBERT GEORGE: BIRTH ANNIVERSARY. Sept 21, 1866. English novelist and historian, born at Bromley, Kent, England. Among his books: *The Time Machine, The Invisible Man, The War of the Worlds* and *The Outline of History*. H.G. Wells died at London, Aug 13, 1946. "Human history," he wrote, "becomes more and more a race between education and catastrophe."

BIRTHDAYS TODAY

Ethan Coen, 47, writer, producer (*Fargo*), born Minneapolis, MN, Sept 21, 1957.
Leonard Cohen, 70, singer, songwriter, born Montreal, QC, Canada, Sept 21, 1934.
David James Elliott, 44, actor ("JAG"), born Toronto, ON, Canada, Sept 21, 1960.
Cecil Grant Fielder, 41, former baseball player, born Los Angeles, CA, Sept 21, 1963.
Fannie Flagg, 60, actress, writer (*Fried Green Tomatoes*), born Birmingham, AL, Sept 21, 1944.
Henry Gibson, 69, comedian ("Rowan and Martin's Laugh-In"), actor (*Nashville*), born Germantown, PA, Sept 21, 1935.
Artis Gilmore, 55, former basketball player, born Chipley, FL, Sept 21, 1949.
Larry Hagman, 73, actor ("I Dream of Jeannie," "Dallas"), born Fort Worth, TX, Sept 21, 1931.
Faith Hill, 37, country singer, born Jackson, MS, Sept 21, 1967.
Stephen King, 57, author (*Christine, Pet Sematary, The Shining, Misery, The Stand*), born Portland, ME, Sept 21, 1947.
Bill Kurtis, 64, TV journalist ("Investigative Reports"), born Pensacola, FL, Sept 21, 1940.
Ricki Lake, 36, talk-show host, actress (*Hairspray, Serial Mom*), born New York, NY, Sept 21, 1968.
Rob Morrow, 42, actor ("Northern Exposure," *Quiz Show*), born New Rochelle, NY, Sept 21, 1962.
Bill Murray, 54, comedian ("Saturday Night Live"), actor (*Ghostbusters, Groundhog Day, Caddyshack*), born Evanston, IL, Sept 21, 1950.
Nancy Travis, 43, actress ("Almost Perfect," *Married to the Mob, Chaplin*), born New York, NY, Sept 21, 1961.
Luke Wilson, 33, actor (*The Royal Tenenbaums, Legally Blonde*), born Dallas, TX, Sept 21, 1971.

SEPTEMBER 22 — WEDNESDAY
Day 266 — 100 Remaining

AMERICAN BUSINESS WOMEN'S DAY. Sept 22. A day set forth by Congress on which all Americans can recognize the important contributions more than 57 million American working women have made and are continuing to make to this nation. Annually, Sept 22. For info: Carolyn Elman, American Business Women's Assn, 9100 Ward Pkwy, Kansas City, MO 64114. Phone: (816) 361-6621. Fax: (816) 361-4991. E-mail: cbelman@abwa.org. Web: www.abwa.org.

AUTUMN. Sept 22–Dec 21. In the Northern Hemisphere, autumn begins today with the autumnal equinox, at 12:30 PM, EDT. Note that in the Southern Hemisphere today is the beginning of spring. Everywhere on Earth (except near the poles) the sun rises due east and sets due west and daylight length is nearly identical—about 12 hours, 8 minutes.

BLACK WALNUT FESTIVAL. Sept 22–25. Stockton, MO. 44th annual. Tours of the largest, in fact the only, black walnut processing plant in the world. Also included are a parade, craft demonstrations, queen contest, carnival and musical entertainment. Est attendance: 20,000. For info: Stockton Area Chamber of Commerce, PO Box 410, Stockton, MO 65785. Phone: (417) 276-5213.

"CHARLIE'S ANGELS" TV PREMIERE: ANNIVERSARY. Sept 22, 1976. This extremely popular show of the '70s featured three attractive women solving crimes. Sabrina Duncan (Kate Jackson), Jill Munroe (Farrah Fawcett-Majors) and Kelly Garrett (Jaclyn Smith) signed on with detective agency Charles Townsend Associates. Their boss was never seen, only heard (the voice of John Forsythe); messages were communicated to the women by his associate John Bosley (David Doyle). During the course of the series, Cheryl Ladd replaced Fawcett, Shelley Hack and Tanya Roberts succeeded Kate Jackson. The show went off the air in 1981 but feature films were made in 2000 and 2003.

DEAR DIARY DAY. Sept 22. Put it on paper. You'll feel better. No need to be a professional writer. [©2003 by WH.] For info: Thomas & Ruth Roy, Wellcat Holidays, 2418 Long Ln, Lebanon, PA 17046. Phone: (717) 279-0184. E-mail: info@wellcat.com. Web: www.wellcat.com.

ELEPHANT APPRECIATION DAY. Sept 22. Celebrate the earth's largest, most interesting and most noble endangered land animal. Free info kit from: Wayne Hepburn, Mission Media, Inc, PO Box 50095, Sarasota, FL 34232. Phone: (941) 355-4552. Fax: (941) 355-6592. E-mail: elefunt@gte.net. Web: www.himandus.net/elephanteria.

Sept 22 ☆ *Chase's 2004 Calendar of Events* ☆

EMANCIPATION PROCLAMATION: ANNIVERSARY. Sept 22, 1862. One of the most important presidential proclamations of American history is that of Sept 22, 1862, in which Abraham Lincoln, by executive proclamation, freed the slaves in the rebelling states. "That on . . . [Jan 1, 1863] . . . all persons held as slaves within any state or designated part of a state, the people whereof shall then be in rebellion against the United States, shall be then, thenceforward, and forever, free. . . ." See also: "13th Amendment Anniversary" (Dec 18) for abolition of slavery in all states.

FAMILY FARM DAY. Sept 22. The family farm is a part of Americana that has been celebrated in lierature, song and tradition for centuries. For info: Ron Kaisen, 84 Irish Meetinghouse Rd, Perkasie, PA 18944. Phone: (215) 249-3870.

"FAMILY TIES" TV PREMIERE: ANNIVERSARY. Sept 22, 1982. This popular '80s sitcom was set at Columbus, OH, and focused on the Keaton family: Ex-hippies Elyse (Meredith Baxter-Birney), an architect, and Steven (Michael Gross), a station manager of the local public TV station, Alex (Michael J. Fox), their smart, conservative and financially driven son, Mallory (Justine Bateman), their materialistic, ditzy daughter and Jennifer (Tina Yothers), their tomboy youngest daughter. Later in the series Elyse gave birth to Andrew (Brian Bonsall). Marc Price played Irwin "Skippy" Handleman, the nerdy next-door neighbor who adored the Keatons, and Mallory in particular. The last episode aired Sept 17, 1989.

FARADAY, MICHAEL: BIRTH ANNIVERSARY. Sept 22, 1791. English scientist and early experimenter with electricity, born at Newington, Surrey, England. Died at Hampton Court, Aug 25, 1867.

FIRST ALL-WOMAN JURY EMPANELED IN COLONIES. Sept 22, 1656. The General Provincial Court at Patuxent, MD, empaneled the first all-woman jury in the colonies to hear the case of Judith Catchpole, accused of murdering her child. The defendant claimed she had never even been pregnant, and after all the evidence was heard, the jury acquitted her.

"FRIENDS" TV PREMIERE: 10th ANNIVERSARY. Sept 22, 1994. This NBC comedy brings together six single friends and the issues in their personal lives, ranging from their jobs to their love lives. Cast includes Courteney Cox Arquette, Lisa Kudrow, Jennifer Aniston, Matthew Perry, David Schwimmer and Matt Le Blanc.

HOBBIT DAY. Sept 22. To commemorate the birthdays of Frodo and Bilbo Baggins and their creator J.R.R. Tolkien. For info: American Tolkien Society, PO Box 7871, Flint, MI 48507-0871. Phone/fax: (727) 585-0985.

HOUSEMAN, JOHN: BIRTH ANNIVERSARY. Sept 22, 1902. American actor and producer John Houseman was born Jacques Haussmann at Bucharest. He is best known for his collaboration with Orson Welles on the 1938 radio production of *War of the Worlds* and for his role as Professor Kingsfield in the film and television version of *The Paper Chase*. He won an Oscar for that film role in 1974 and helped establish the Juilliard drama school and the Acting Company repertory group. He died Oct 30, 1988, at Malibu, CA.

ICE CREAM CONE: ANNIVERSARY. Sept 22, 1903. Italo Marchiony emigrated from Italy in the late 1800s and soon thereafter went into business at New York, NY, with a pushcart dispensing lemon ice. Success soon led to a small fleet of pushcarts, and the inventive Marchiony was inspired to develop a cone, first made of paper, later of pastry, to hold the tasty delicacy. On Sept 22, 1903, his application for a patent for his new mold was filed, and US Patent No 746971 was issued to him Dec 15, 1903.

JAPAN: AUTUMNAL EQUINOX DAY. Sept 22. National holiday in Japan.

LONG COUNT DAY: ANNIVERSARY. Sept 22, 1927. Anniversary of world championship boxing match between Jack Dempsey and Gene Tunney, at Soldier Field, Chicago, IL. It was the largest fight purse ($990,446) in the history of boxing to that time. Nearly half the population of the US is believed to have listened to the radio broadcast of this fight. In the seventh round of the 10-round fight, Tunney was knocked down. Following the rules, Referee Dave Barry interrupted the count when Dempsey failed to go to the farthest corner. The count was resumed and Tunney got to his feet at the count of nine. Stopwatch records of those present claimed the total elapsed time from the beginning of the count until Tunney got to his feet at 12–15 seconds. Tunney, awarded seven of the 10 rounds, won the fight and claimed the world championship. Dempsey's appeal was denied and he never fought again. Tunney retired the following year after one more (successful) fight.

MABON. Sept 22. (Also called Alban Elfed.) One of the "Lesser Sabbats" during the Wiccan year, Mabon marks the second harvest as Nature prepares for the coming of winter. Annually, on the autumnal equinox.

MALI: INDEPENDENCE DAY. Sept 22. National holiday commemorating independence from France in 1960. Mali, in West Africa, was known as the French Sudan while a colony.

"MAVERICK" TV PREMIERE: ANNIVERSARY. Sept 22, 1957. This popular Western starred James Garner as Bret Maverick, a clever man who preferred card playing to fighting. A second Maverick was introduced when production was behind schedule—Jack Kelly played his brother Bart. Garner and Kelly played most episodes separately, and when Garner left in 1961, Kelly was in almost all the episodes. Other performers included Roger Moore, Robert Colbert and Diane Brewster. This Western distinguished itself by its light touch and parody of other Westerns.

MID-SOUTH FAIR. Sept 22–Oct 3. Fairgrounds, Memphis, TN. Regional fair featuring concerts, free entertainment, midway, rodeo, livestock, exhibits and special events. Est attendance: 500,000. For info: Sandra Ireland, Mid-South Fair, 940 Early Maxwell Blvd, Memphis, TN 38104. Phone: (901) 274-8800. Fax: (901) 274-8804. E-mail: sireland@midsouthfair.com. Web: www.midsouthfair.com.

NATIONAL CENTENARIANS DAY. Sept 22. A day to recognize and honor elderly individuals who have lived a century or longer. A day not only to recognize these individuals, but to listen to them discuss the memories—filled with historical information—that they have of their rich lives. Take time today to listen to a centenarian. Special celebration held annually at Williamsport Retirement Village. For info: Amy Olack, Comm Rel Dir, Williamsport Retirement Village, Founders, A Division of Brooke Grove Fdtn, 154 N Artizan St, Williamsport, MD 21795. Phone: (301) 223-7971. Fax: (301) 223-6031. Web: www.wrv-bgf.org.

STANHOPE, PHILIP DORMER: BIRTH ANNIVERSARY. Sept 22, 1694 (OS). Philip Dormer Stanhope, the 4th Earl of Chesterfield, was born at London, England. He was a brilliant politician and orator. On Feb 20, 1751, he brought a bill into the House of Lords that caused the "New Style" Gregorian calendar to replace the "Old Style" Julian calendar in 1752. His influential political career was eclipsed by the fame of the letters he wrote to his son Philip, giving shrewd counsel on manners, morals and the ways of the world. Published less than a year after his own death at London, Mar 24, 1773, the *Letters* became

	S	M	T	W	T	F	S
September 2004				1	2	3	4
	5	6	7	8	9	10	11
	12	13	14	15	16	17	18
	19	20	21	22	23	24	25
	26	27	28	29	30		

494

immensely popular, were translated and republished in many editions. The Chesterfield, a kind of sofa, is said to be named for him.

US POSTMASTER GENERAL ESTABLISHED: ANNIVERSARY. Sept 22, 1789. Congress established office of Postmaster General, following the Departments of State, War and Treasury.

BIRTHDAYS TODAY

Scott Baio, 43, actor ("Happy Days," "Diagnosis Murder," "Charles in Charge"), born Brooklyn, NY, Sept 22, 1961.
Shari Belafonte-Harper, 50, model, actress, born New York, NY, Sept 22, 1954.
Debbie Boone, 48, singer ("You Light Up My Life," "Baby, I'm Yours"), born Hackensack, NJ, Sept 22, 1956.
Bonnie Hunt, 40, actress (*Jerry Maguire, Jumanji*), born Chicago, IL, Sept 22, 1964.
Joan Jett, 44, singer ("I Love Rock 'n' Roll," "Crimson and Clover"), musician, born Philadelphia, PA, Sept 22, 1960.
Thomas Charles (Tommy) Lasorda, 77, Hall of Fame baseball manager and former player, born Norristown, PA, Sept 22, 1927.
Paul Le Mat, 59, actor (*American Graffiti, Melvin and Howard, Strange Invaders*), born Rahway, NY, Sept 22, 1945.
Catherine Oxenberg, 43, actress ("Dynasty"), born New York, NY, Sept 22, 1961.
Mike Richter, 38, hockey player, born Philadelphia, PA, Sept 22, 1966.
Eugene Roche, 76, actor ("Soap," "Webster"), born Boston, MA, Sept 22, 1928.
Ronaldo, 28, Brazilian soccer player, born Ronaldo Luiz Nazario de Lima, Rio de Janeiro, Brazil, Sept 22, 1976.
Arthur O. Sulzberger, 53, publisher (*The New York Times*), born Mount Kisco, NY, Sept 22, 1951.
Junko Tabei, 65, mountaineer (first woman to climb Mount Everest), born Fukushima Prefecture, Japan, Sept 22, 1939.

SEPTEMBER 23 — THURSDAY
Day 267 — 99 Remaining

BARNESVILLE PUMPKIN FESTIVAL. Sept 23–26. Downtown Barnesville, OH. This 41st annual festival features King Pumpkin contest, Queen Pageant, Giant Pumpkin Parade, classic car show, banjo & fiddle contest and more. Annually, the last full weekend of September. Est attendance: 100,000. For info: Tom Michelli, President, Barnesville Pumpkin Festival, Inc, PO Box 5, Barnesville, OH 43713. Phone: (740) 425-2593. Fax: (740) 425-1755. E-mail: bacc@1st.net.

BASEBALL'S GREATEST DISPUTE: ANNIVERSARY. Sept 23, 1908. In the decisive game between the Chicago Cubs and the New York Giants, the National League pennant race erupted in controversy during the bottom of the ninth with the score tied 1–1, at the Polo Grounds, New York, NY. New York was at bat with two men on. The batter hit safely to center field, scoring the winning run. Chicago claimed that the runner on first, Fred Merkle, seeing the winning run scored, headed toward the dugout without advancing to second base, thus invalidating the play. The Chicago second baseman, Johnny Evers, attempted to get the ball and tag Merkle out, but was prevented by the fans streaming onto the field. Days later Harry C. Pulliam, head of the National Commission of Organized Baseball, decided to call the game a tie. The teams were forced to play a postseason play-off game, which the Cubs won 4–2. Fans invented the terms "boner" and "bonehead" in reference to the play and it has gone down in baseball history as "Merkle's Boner."

CHECKERS DAY: ANNIVERSARY. Sept 23. Anniversary of the nationally televised "Checkers Speech" by then vice presidential candidate Richard M. Nixon, on Sept 23, 1952. Nixon was found "clean as a hound's tooth" in connection with a private fund for political expenses, and he declared he would never give back the cocker spaniel dog, Checkers, which had been a gift to his daughters. Other dogs prominent in American politics: Abraham Lincoln's dog, Fido; Franklin D. Roosevelt's much-traveled terrier, Fala; Harry S. Truman's dogs, Mike and Feller; Dwight D. Eisenhower's dog, Heidi; Lyndon Johnson's beagles, Him and Her; Ronald Reagan's dogs, Lucky and Rex; and George H.W. Bush's dog, Millie.

FALL BLUEGRASS FESTIVAL. Sept 23–25. Spirit of the Suwannee Music Park, Live Oak, FL. Weekend filled with bluegrass music and other great activities. Previously featured artists include Goldwing Express, Tater Hill, Southern Gentlemen, Liberty Bluegrass, The Adairs and Lonesome Whistle. Est attendance: 7,000. For info: James Cornett, Spirit of Suwannee Music Park, 3076 95th Dr, Live Oak, FL 32060. Phone: (386) 364-1683. Fax: (386) 364-2998. E-mail: spirit@musicliveshere.com. Web: www.musicliveshere.com.

INNERGIZE DAY. Sept 23. A day set aside for anyone who has said "I don't have time to do the personal things I want to do for myself." Today is the day to set time aside for yourself to do anything you want to do. Annually, the day after autumn. For info: Michelle Porchia, inner dimensions, 4 Daniels Farm Rd, Ste 137, Trumbull, CT 06611. Phone: (203) 924-1012. Fax: (203) 924-1012. E-mail: michelle@porchia.net. Web: www.porchia.net.

"THE JETSONS" TV PREMIERE: ANNIVERSARY. Sept 23, 1962. "Meet George Jetson. His boy Elroy. Daughter Judy. Jane, his wife. . . . " These words introduced us to the Jetsons, a cartoon family living in the twenty-first century, the Flintstones of the Space Age. We followed the exploits of George and his family, as well as his work relationship with his greedy, ruthless boss Cosmo Spacely. Voices were provided by George O'Hanlon as George, Penny Singleton as Jane, Janet Waldo as Judy, Daws Butler as Elroy, Don Messick as Astro, the family dog, and Mel Blanc as Spacely. New episodes were created in 1985 which also introduced a new pet, Orbity.

LEWIS & CLARK EXPEDITION RETURNS: ANNIVERSARY. Sept 23, 1806. After more than two years in the American West, the Corps of Discovery returned to St. Louis amid much fanfare. They had traveled—with the assistance of guides Toussaint Charbonneau and his wife Sacagawea (a member of the Shoshone tribe)—to what is now North Dakota and Montana, over the Continental Divide and to the Columbia River, which took them to the Pacific (Nov 1805). They lost only one man from the 33-member group. Their valuable findings on western tribes, geography, plants and animals dispelled many longstanding myths about the region. (See also Jan 18 and May 14.)

LIBRA, THE BALANCE. Sept 23–Oct 22. In the astronomical/astrological zodiac that divides the sun's apparent orbit into 12 segments, the period Sept 23–Oct 22 is identified traditionally as the sun sign of Libra, the Balance. The ruling planet is Venus.

LIPPMANN, WALTER: BIRTH ANNIVERSARY. Sept 23, 1889. American journalist, political philosopher and author. Born at New York, NY, he died there Dec 14, 1974. As a syndicated newspaper columnist he was the foremost and perhaps the most influential commentator in the nation. "Without criticism," he said in an address to the International Press Institute in 1965, "and reliable and intelligent reporting, the government cannot govern."

Sept 23-24 ☆ Chase's 2004 Calendar of Events ☆

McGUFFEY, WILLIAM HOLMES: BIRTH ANNIVERSARY. Sept 23, 1800. American educator and author of the famous *McGuffey Readers*, born at Washington County, PA. Died at Charlottesville, VA, May 4, 1873.

PAULUS, FRIEDRICH: BIRTH ANNIVERSARY. Sept 23, 1890. The German commander of the Sixth Army who led the advance on Stalingrad in 1942, Friedrich von Paulus was born at Breitenau, Germany. Paulus's troops succeeded in taking most of Stalingrad in November 1942, but eventually became trapped within the city they had captured. Paulus surrendered to the Russians Jan 31, 1943, the same day that Hitler promoted him to field marshal. He appeared as a key witness for the Soviet prosecution at the Nuremberg trials. Paulus died Feb 1, 1957, at Dresden, East Germany.

PIDGEON, WALTER: BIRTH ANNIVERSARY. Sept 23, 1897. Actor Walter Pidgeon was born at East St. John, NB, Canada. He died at age 87, Sept 25, 1984, at Santa Monica, CA. He made his film debut in 1925 in *Mannequin*. Among his films are *Saratoga* and *Mrs Miniver*.

PLANET NEPTUNE DISCOVERY: ANNIVERSARY. Sept 23, 1846. Neptune is 2,796,700,000 miles from the sun (about 30 times as far from the sun as Earth). Eighth planet from the sun, Neptune takes 164.8 years to revolve around the sun. Diameter is about 31,000 miles compared to Earth at 7,927 miles. Discovered by German astronomer Johann Galle.

SAUDI ARABIA: KINGDOM UNIFICATION. Sept 23. National holiday. Commemorates unification in 1932.

STATE FAIR OF VIRGINIA. Sept 23–Oct 3. Richmond Raceway Complex, Richmond, VA. The pride of Virginia's industry of agriculture can be seen in more than 3,000 exhibitions, competitions and shows. Virginia's greatest annual educational and entertainment event. Est attendance: 600,000. For info: Glen Sink, Fair Mgr, PO Box 26805, Richmond, VA 23261-6805. Phone: (804) 569-3200. Fax: (804) 569-3252. Web: www.statefair.com.

WOODHULL, VICTORIA CHAFLIN: BIRTH ANNIVERSARY. Sept 23, 1838. American feminist, reformer and first female candidate for the presidency of the US. Born at Homer, OH, she died at Norton Park, Bremmons, Worcestershire, England, June 10, 1927.

WORLD BEEF EXPO. Sept 23–26. Milwaukee, WI. World-class cattle shows and sales representing 15 beef cattle breeds. Trade show featuring agribusinesses catering to the beef industry. Also includes activities for children and adults, such as Taste of Beef, Pfizer Supreme Champions, microbrewery sampling, scarecrow making and Kids Corral. Est attendance: 50,000. For info: Wisconsin State Fair Park, World Beef Expo, 8100 W Greenfield Ave, PO Box 14990, West Allis, WI 53214-0990. Phone: (800) 884-FAIR or (414) 266-7000. Web: www.worldbeefexpo.com.

BIRTHDAYS TODAY

Jason Alexander, 45, actor ("Seinfeld," *Pretty Woman; Bye, Bye, Birdy;* stage: *Jerome Robbins' Broadway*), born Newark, NJ, Sept 23, 1959.
Ray Charles (Robinson), 74, singer ("Georgia on My Mind," "What'd I Say"), composer, born Albany, GA, Sept 23, 1930.
Ani DiFranco, 34, folk-punk singer and songwriter, born Buffalo, NY, Sept 23, 1970.
Julio Iglesias, 61, singer ("To All the Girls I've Loved Before" with Willie Nelson), songwriter, born Madrid, Spain, Sept 23, 1943.
Tony Joseph Mandarich, 38, former football player, born Oakville, ON, Canada, Sept 23, 1966.

Larry Hogan Mize, 46, golfer, born Augusta, GA, Sept 23, 1958.
Elizabeth Peña, 43, actress (*Rush Hour, Lone Star, Jacob's Ladder*), born Elizabeth, NJ, Sept 23, 1961.
Paul Petersen, 59, actor ("The Donna Reed Show," *Houseboat*), born Glendale, CA, Sept 23, 1945.
Mary Kay Place, 57, writer, actress ("Mary Hartman, Mary Hartman," *The Big Chill*), born Tulsa, OK, Sept 23, 1947.
Mickey Rooney, 84, actor (*Andy Hardy* movies, *The Black Stallion*), born Joe Yule, Jr, Brooklyn, NY, Sept 23, 1920.
Bruce Springsteen, 55, singer, songwriter ("Born in the USA"), born Freehold, NJ, Sept 23, 1949.

SEPTEMBER 24 — FRIDAY
Day 268 — 98 Remaining

BAYFEST. Sept 24–26. Corpus Christi, TX. Plenty of fun at this waterfront festival. Includes amusement rides, games, fireworks, arts and crafts displays, various musical entertainment, food booths, merchandise exhibitors and much more. Est attendance: 165,000. For info: Bayfest, PO Box 1858, Corpus Christi, TX 78403. Phone: (361) 887-0868. Fax: (361) 887-9773. E-mail: lidia bayfest@interconnect.net. Web: www.bayfesttexas.com.

CAMBODIA: CONSTITUTIONAL DECLARATION DAY: ANNIVERSARY. Sept 24. National holiday. Commemorates the new constitution of 1993.

CELTIC CLASSIC HIGHLAND GAMES & FESTIVAL. Sept 24–26. Bethlehem, PA. America's largest highland games and festival, celebrating Celtic culture with three free days of Celtic music, Irish dance, world-class highland athletic competitions, Border Collie exhibitions, bagpipe and drum major competitions, art and history workshops, foods, crafts, entertainment and much more. For info: Helen Foraste, Celtic Classic, 561 Main St, Ste 260, Bethlehem, PA 18018. Phone: (610) 868-9599. Fax: (610) 868-9730. E-mail: info@celticfest.org. Web: www.celticfest.org.

CHASE'S 2005 CALENDAR OF EVENTS PUBLISHED. Sept 24. The 2005 *Chase's* is now available. Order a copy on our website at www.chases.com or call (800) 722-4726.

COMMON GROUND COUNTRY FAIR. Sept 24–26. MOFGA's Common Ground, Unity, ME. Old-time country fair celebrating rural life with the revival of forgotten skills and demonstrations of technology appropriate for the future. Features Maine-produced food, crafts, entertainment, farming demonstrations and talks, a very special children's area with daily and ongoing participatory activities. Annually, the third weekend after Labor Day. Sponsor: Maine Organic Farmers and Gardeners Assn. Est attendance: 60,000. For info: Babara Luce, Fair Dir, Common Ground Country Fair, PO Box 170, Unity, ME 04988. Phone: (207) 568-4142. Fax: (207) 568-4141. E-mail: cgcf@mofga.org. Web: www.mofga.org.

September 2004

S	M	T	W	T	F	S
			1	2	3	4
5	6	7	8	9	10	11
12	13	14	15	16	17	18
19	20	21	22	23	24	25
26	27	28	29	30		

☆ Chase's 2004 Calendar of Events ☆ Sept 24

"DANIEL BOONE" TV PREMIERE: 40th ANNIVERSARY. Sept 24, 1964. A successful show based loosely on the life of pioneer Daniel Boone, who helped settle Kentucky in the 1770s. Fess Parker starred as the American hero. Ed Ames played Mingo, Boone's friend, an educated Cherokee, and Pat Blair played his wife, Rebecca. Also featured were Albert Salmi, Jimmy Dean, Roosevelt Grier, Darby Hinton, Veronica Cartwright and Dallas McKennon.

"A DIFFERENT WORLD" TV PREMIERE: ANNIVERSARY. Sept 24, 1987. In this spin-off from "The Cosby Show," Denise Huxtable (Lisa Bonet) went off to Hillman College. The first season's cast included Marisa Tomei, Dawnn Lewis, Jasmine Guy, Loretta Devine, Amir Williams, Kadeem Hardison, Darryl Bell, Marie-Alise Recasner, Mary Alice and Sinbad. Bonet left the series and returned to "The Cosby Show." Joining the show were Charnele Brown, Cree Summer and Glynn Turman. Aretha Franklin (Turman's wife) sang the show's theme song. The last telecast was in 1993.

FABULOUS 1890s WEEKEND. Sept 24–25. Mansfield, PA. Night football in America began in 1892 with a game between Mansfield University and Wyoming Seminary. Annually, Mansfield celebrates a "Fabulous 1890s Weekend" to commemorate the event. Motorless parade, period exhibits, crafts and other events, including the re-creation of the first night football game. Sponsors: Mansfield University of Pennsylvania and Greater Area Mansfield Chamber of Commerce. Est attendance: 10,000. For info: Dennis Miller, Dir PR, Mansfield University, Beecher House, Mansfield, PA 16933. Phone: (570) 662-4293. Fax: (570) 662-4965. E-mail: dmiller@mansfield.edu. Web: www.mansfield.edu.

FAIRMOUNT MUSEUM DAYS/REMEMBERING JAMES DEAN FESTIVAL. Sept 24–26. Fairmount, IN. The town where James Dean grew up honors Dean and other celebrated former citizens such as Jim Davis, creator of Garfield, journalist Phil Jones and Robert Sheets, retired director of the National Hurricane Center. The Fairmount Museum boasts "the Authentic James Dean Exhibit" of memorabilia and personal items of Dean's and it sponsors the festival that also includes a parade, James Dean Look-Alike Contest, custom car show featuring the James Dean Run for pre-1970 autos, Garfield Cat Photo and Art Contest, Garfield Great Run, carnival, booths, live '50s entertainment and more. Annually, the last full weekend in September. Est attendance: 40,000. For info: Fairmount Historical Museum, Inc, 203 E Washington St, PO Box 92, Fairmount, IN 46928. Phone: (765) 948-4555. Web: www.jamesdeanartifacts.com.

FALL FESTIVAL OF THE ARTS AND CRAFTS. Sept 24–26. Washington, MO. Juried festival featuring the creative talents of two- and three-dimensional artists and crafters. Free children's area, beer and wine garden, specialty foods, music and live entertainment. For info: Downtown Washington, Inc, PO Box 144, Washington, MO 63090. Phone: (636) 239-1743. Fax: (636) 239-4832. E-mail: dwinc@yhti.net. Web: downtownwashmo.org.

FANEUIL HALL OPENED TO THE PUBLIC: ANNIVERSARY. Sept 24, 1742. On this date Faneuil Hall at Boston, MA, opened to the public. Designed by painter John Smibiert, it was enlarged in 1805 according to plans by Charles Bulfinch. Today it is on the Freedom Trail, as part of the Boston Historical Park administered by the National Park Service.

FITZGERALD, F. SCOTT: BIRTH ANNIVERSARY. Sept 24, 1896. American short story writer and novelist; author of *This Side of Paradise, The Great Gatsby* and *Tender Is the Night*. Born Francis Scott Key Fitzgerald, at St. Paul, MN, he died at Hollywood, CA, Dec 21, 1940.

GUINEA-BISSAU: INDEPENDENCE DAY: ANNIVERSARY. Sept 24. National holiday. Commemorates declaration of independence from Portugal in 1973.

HENSON, JIM: BIRTH ANNIVERSARY. Sept 24, 1936. Puppeteer, born at Greenville, MS. Jim Henson created a unique family of puppets known as the Muppets. Kermit the Frog, Big Bird, Rowlf, Bert and Ernie, Gonzo, Animal, Miss Piggy and Oscar the Grouch are a few of the puppets that captured the hearts of children and adults alike in television and film productions including "Sesame Street," "The Jimmy Dean Show," "The Muppet Show," *The Muppet Movie, The Muppets Take Manhattan, The Great Muppet Caper* and *The Dark Crystal*. Henson began his career in 1954 as producer of the TV show "Sam and Friends" at Washington, DC. He introduced the Muppets in 1956. His creativity was rewarded with 18 Emmy Awards, seven Grammy Awards, four Peabody Awards and five ACE Awards from the National Cable Television Association. Henson died unexpectedly May 16, 1990, at New York, NY.

LAVITSEF. Sept 24–26. Norfolk, NE. Concerts, pet show, quilt show, pancake feed, craft fair, ice cream social, museum events, adult spelling bee, car show, BBQ, German dinner, boiled fish dinner, kids fun events. Parade at 10 AM on Saturday. Est attendance: 15,000. For info: LaVitsef, Inc, PO Box 1512, Norfolk, NE 68702-1512. Web: www.lavitsef.com.

LIBERTY FALL FESTIVAL. Sept 24–26. Liberty, MO. Arts and crafts booth, food booths, children's activities, a carnival, a parade, car show, entertainment provided throughout the three-day festival. Annually, the fourth weekend in September. Est attendance: 30,000. For info: Liberty Area Chamber of Commerce, 9 S Leonard St, Liberty, MO 64068. Phone: (816) 781-5200. Fax: (816) 781-4901. E-mail: info@libertychamber.com. Web: www.libertychamber.com.

"THE LOVE BOAT" TV PREMIERE: ANNIVERSARY. Sept 24, 1977. This one-hour comedy-drama featured guest stars aboard a cruise ship, the Pacific Princess. All stories had to do with finding or losing love. The ship's crew were the only regulars (though there were occasional recurring roles, such as Charo as April): Gavin MacLeod as Captain Merrill Stubing, Bernie Kopell as Doctor Adam Bricker, Fred Grandy as assistant purser Burl "Gopher" Smith, Ted Lange as bartender Isaac Washington and Lauren Tewes as cruise director Julie McCoy. Also featured were Jill Whelan as Vicki, Stubing's daughter, Pat Klous as Julie, who replaced Tewes and Ted McGinley as photographer Ashley Covington "Ace" Evans. The series ended with the last telecast on Sept 5, 1986, but three two-hour specials were broadcast the next year. MacLeod, Lange, Kopell and Whelan were reunited in a Love Boat special in 1990.

"LOVE OF LIFE" TV PREMIERE: ANNIVERSARY. Sept 24, 1951. This serial, which began as a 15-minute show, ran for 28 years. The story lines shifted from a focus on two sisters to a larger number of characters. The diverse cast included such notables as Christopher Reeve, Karen Grassle, Roy Scheider, Dana Delaney, John Aniston, Marsha Mason, Bert Convy, Warren Beatty and Barnard Hughes.

MARSHALL, JOHN: BIRTH ANNIVERSARY. Sept 24, 1755. Fourth Chief Justice of Supreme Court, born at Germantown, VA. Served in House of Representatives and as Secretary of State under John Adams. Appointed by President Adams to the position of chief justice in January 1801, he became known as "The Great Chief Justice." Marshall's court was largely responsible for defining the role of the Supreme Court and basic organizing principles of government in the early years after adoption of the Constitution in such cases as *Marbury v Madison, McCulloch v Maryland, Cohens v Virginia* and *Gibbons v Ogden*. He died at Philadelphia, PA, July 6, 1835.

MOUNT PLEASANT GLASS & ETHNIC FESTIVAL. Sept 24–26. Mount Pleasant, PA. Large outdoor street festival featuring glass blowing demos, arts and crafts, two parades, national and regional entertainment and ethnic foods. Free entertainment on three stages, a carnival and unique activities. Est attendance: 45,000. For info: Jeff Landy, Mount Pleasant Glass and Ethnic Festival, Municipal Bldg, 1 Etze Ave, Mt Pleasant, PA

15666. Phone: (724) 547-7738. Fax: (724) 547-0115. Web: www.mtpleasantglassandethnicfestival.com.

MOZAMBIQUE: ARMED FORCES DAY. Sept 24. National holiday. Commemorates the beginning of the war for independence in 1964.

"THE MUNSTERS" TV PREMIERE: 40th ANNIVERSARY. Sept 24, 1964. "The Munsters" was a half-hour sitcom about an unusual family who thought they were ordinary. Each family member resembled a different type of monster: Herman Munster (Fred Gwynne) was Frankenstein's monster; Lily, his wife (Yvonne DeCarlo), and Grandpa, her father (Al Lewis), were vampires and his son Eddie (Butch Patrick) was a werewolf. Only their niece, Marilyn (Beverly Owen and Pat Priest), looked normal, and they considered her the unattractive family member. Most of the show's laughs came from the family's interactions with outsiders. The last telecast was on Sept 1, 1966.

NEPTUNE FESTIVAL BOARDWALK WEEKEND. Sept 24–26. Virginia Beach, VA. A major mid-Atlantic regional festival. Events include sand sculpture contests, a parade, wine-tasting, sport events and more. Est attendance: 750,000. For info: Neptune Festival Boardwalk Weekend, 265 Kings Grant Rd, #102, Virginia Beach, VA 23452. Phone: (757) 498-0215. Web: www.neptunefestival.com.

NEW HAMPSHIRE HIGHLAND GAMES. Sept 24–26. Hopkinton Fair Grounds, Contoocook, NH. From the tossing of the caber to the lilting melodies of the clarsach plus massed pipe bands on parade, there's something for everyone at New Hampshire's Highland Games: a three-day Scottish festival crammed with music, dance, crafts, athletic events, Scottish food and more. For those of Scottish heritage, there's also a chance to look up one's clan connection, as more than 60 Scottish clans and societies have tents with displays. Admission charged. Est attendance: 42,000. For info: New Hampshire Highland Games, PO Box 4197, Concord, NH 03302-4197. Phone: (603) 229-1975. Fax: (603) 223-6678. E-mail: info@nhscot.org. Web: www.nhscot.org.

OKTOBERFEST. Sept 24–Oct 2 (tentative). LaCrosse, WI. German fall festival featuring family events, live entertainment, lots of food, Torchlight Parade on Thursday night and Maple Leaf Parade on Saturday. Fun for the whole family. For info: Michelle Hoch-Tourism & Mktg Coordinator, LaCrosse Area Conv & Visitors Bureau, 410 Veterans Memorial Dr, LaCrosse, WI 54601. Phone: (800) 658-9424. E-mail: info@explorelacrosse.com. Web: www.explorelacrosse.com.

SCHWENKFELDER THANKSGIVING. Sept 24. On this day in 1734 members of the Schwenkfelder Society gave thanks for their deliverance from Old World persecution as they prepared to take up new lives in the Pennsylvania-Dutch counties of Pennsylvania. Still celebrated.

"60 MINUTES" TV PREMIERE: ANNIVERSARY. Sept 24, 1968. TV's longest-running prime-time program was originally hosted by Harry Reasoner and Mike Wallace. Dan Rather and Diane Sawyer were also reporters on TV's first news magazine. Today the show's correspondents include Ed Bradley, Steve Kroft, Lesley Stahl, Morley Safer, Andy Rooney and Mike Wallace.

SOUTH AFRICA: HERITAGE DAY. Sept 24. A celebration of South African nationhood, commemorating the multicultural heritage of this rainbow nation.

STATE FAIR OF TEXAS. Sept 24–Oct 17. Fair Park, Dallas, TX. Features a Broadway musical, college football games, new car show, concerts, livestock shows and traditional events and entertainment including exhibits, creative arts and parades. Est attendance: 3,000,000. For info: Public Relations, State Fair of Texas, PO Box 150009, Dallas, TX 75315. Phone: (214) 421-8716. Fax: (214) 421-8710. E-mail: pr@greatstatefair.com. Web: www.bigtex.com.

TACA FALL CRAFTS FAIR. Sept 24–26. Centennial Park, Nashville, TN. 26th annual fair. Festival of fine crafts featuring 180 selected American craft artists. Annually, the last weekend in September. Est attendance: 35,000. For info: Alice C. Merritt, Exec Dir, Tennessee Assn of Craft Artists, PO Box 120066, Nashville, TN 37212. Phone: (615) 385-1904. Web: www.tennesseecrafts.org.

VIRGINIA PEANUT FESTIVAL. Sept 24–25. Emporia, VA. Annual celebration promoting peanuts and harvesting. Features musical concerts, arts and crafts, parade, corporate village, luncheon/fashion show, carnival, car show and fireworks. Sponsored by Emporia-Greensville Chamber of Commerce. Est attendance: 20,000. For info: Virginia Peanut Festival, Attn: Lisa Council, PO Box 956, Emporia, VA 23847. Phone: (434) 634-5405.

YOM KIPPUR BEGINS AT SUNDOWN. Sept 24. Jewish Day of Atonement. See "Yom Kippur" (Sept 25).

BIRTHDAYS TODAY

Gordon Clapp, 56, actor ("NYPD Blue"), born North Conway, NH, Sept 24, 1948.
Morgan Hamm, 22, gymnast, born Ashland, WI, Sept 24, 1982.
Paul Hamm, 22, gymnast, born Ashland, WI, Sept 24, 1982.
Sheila MacRae, 81, singer, actress, born London, England, Sept 24, 1923.
James Kenneth (Jim) McKay, 83, sportscaster, born James Kenneth McManus, Philadelphia, PA, Sept 24, 1921.
Rafael Corrales Palmeiro, 40, baseball player, born Havana, Cuba, Sept 24, 1964.
Kevin Sorbo, 46, actor ("Hercules"), born Mound, MN, Sept 24, 1958.
Nia Vardalos, 42, screenwriter, actress (*My Big Fat Greek Wedding*), born Winnipeg, MB, Canada, Sept 24, 1962.

SEPTEMBER 25 — SATURDAY
Day 269 — 97 Remaining

APPLE FESTIVAL. Sept 25 (rain date Sept 26). Forked River, NJ. 9th annual. Pie-baking contest, music, clowns, apple crafts, artist exhibition. Apples, candied apples, apple pies and much more on sale. Sponsored by the Lacey Township Historical Society. Est attendance: 900. For info: Lacey Township Historical Society, PO Box 412, Forked River, NJ 08731.

"BEAUTY AND THE BEAST" TV PREMIERE: ANNIVERSARY. Sept 25, 1987. This updated version of the fairy tale was a romantic hit and acquired a cult following. It followed the experiences of Catherine Chandler (Linda Hamilton), a Manhattan lawyer who is beaten and abandoned and subsequently found and cared for by Vincent (Ron Perlman), a man-beast living under the city. Other cast members included Roy Dotrice, Jay Acovone, Ren Woods, Cory Danziger and David Greenlee. Hamilton left the series at the beginning of the third season; the series ended shortly thereafter.

DESOTO CAVERNS PARK INDIAN DANCE FESTIVAL. Sept 25–26 (tentative). DeSoto Caverns Park, Childersburg, AL. 29th annual event, featuring Native American dancing, singing and lifeways demonstrations. Arts and crafts and great food. Est attendance: 8,000. For info: DeSoto Caverns Park, 5181 DeSoto Caverns Pkwy, Childersburg, AL 35044. Phone: (205) 378-7252 or (800) 933-2283. E-mail: fun@desotocavernspark.com. Web: www.DeSotoCavernsPark.com.

	S	M	T	W	T	F	S
September				1	2	3	4
2004	5	6	7	8	9	10	11
	12	13	14	15	16	17	18
	19	20	21	22	23	24	25
	26	27	28	29	30		

☆ Chase's 2004 Calendar of Events ☆ — Sept 25

DuPONT RIVERFEST. Sept 25. Wilmington, DE. Everyone is invited to enjoy a variety of amusements including Wilmington Trust's children's entertainment, Fleet Credit Card's kids corner, river taxi rides, live music on the Bank One Stage of Harmony and refreshments at the Acme Market Café Court. Also featuring the Delaware Transportation Festival. Proceeds benefit the Boys & Girls Clubs of Delaware. Annually, the last Saturday in September. Est attendance: 12,000. For info: Danae Banning, DuPont RiverFest, 669 S Union St, Wilmington, DE 19805. Phone: (302) 658-1870. Fax: (302) 658-3907. E-mail: dbanning@bgclubs.org. Web: www.dupontriverfest.com.

DYERSVILLE FESTIVAL OF THE ARTS. Sept 25–26. Beckman High School, Dyersville, IA. The "Farm Toy Capital of the World," near the film site of the movie *Field of Dreams*. Features the Dyersville Quilt & Craft Show, with hundreds of quilts and hundreds of crafts, all handmade. Entertainment and food. Annually, the last full weekend in September. Est attendance: 4,000. For info: Dyersville Area Chamber of Commerce, 1100 16th Ave Ct SE, Dyersville, IA 52040. Phone: (563) 875-2311 or (866) DYERSVILLE. Fax: (563) 875-8391. E-mail: dyersvillechamber@dyersville.org. Web: www.dyersville.org.

EVERYBODY'S DAY FESTIVAL. Sept 25. Thomasville, NC. A downtown street festival for "everybody." Crafts, food vendors and live entertainment. Annually, the last Saturday in September. Est attendance: 80,000. For info: Thomasville Area Chamber of Commerce, Box 1400, Thomasville, NC 27361. Phone: (336) 475-6134. Fax: (336) 475-4802. E-mail: tvillecoc@northstate.net. Web: www.everybodysday.com.

FALL FIESTA. Sept 25–26. Andrews Airport Grounds, Andrews, TX. 4th annual event featuring arts & crafts, classic cars, motorcycle display, antique farm equipment, airplanes, carnival, concessions and live entertainment. For info: Andrews Chamber of Commerce, 700 W Broadway, Andrews, TX 79714. Phone: (432) 523-2695. E-mail: achamber@andrewstx.com. Web: www.andrewstx.com.

FALLASBURG FALL FESTIVAL. Sept 25–26. Fallasburg Park, Lowell, MI. Unique event with 80 artists displaying and selling their work. Historical setting, arts, entertainment, kids' activities and food. Annually, the last full weekend in September. For info: Michelle Ellison, Lowell Area Arts Council, 149 S Hudson, Lowell, MI 49331. Phone: (616) 897-8545. Fax: (616) 897-3061. E-mail: info@lowellartscouncil.org.

FAMILY HEALTH AND FITNESS DAY—USA. Sept 25. 8th annual national event promoting family health and fitness. Families across the country will be involved in locally organized health promotion activities at hundreds of locations all on the same day. Always held the last Saturday in September. Est attendance: 25,000. For info: Pat Henze, Exec Dir, Health Info Resource Center, 1850 Winchester Rd, Ste 213, Libertyville, IL 60048. Phone: (800) 828-8225. Fax: (847) 816-8662. E-mail: fitnessday@aol.com. Web: www.fitnessday.com.

FAULKNER, WILLIAM CUTHBERT: BIRTH ANNIVERSARY. Sept 25, 1897. American novelist and short story writer William Faulkner (born Falkner) was born at New Albany, MS. A Nobel Prize–winner who changed the style and structure of the American novel, he died at Byhalia, MS, on July 6, 1962. Faulkner's first novel, *Soldiers' Pay*, was published in 1926. His best-known book, *The Sound and the Fury*, appeared in 1929. Shunning literary circles, Faulkner moved to a pre-Civil War house on the outskirts of Oxford, MS, in 1930. From 1930 until the onset of World War II he published an incredible body of work. In June 1962 Faulkner published his last novel, *The Reivers*.

FIRST AMERICAN NEWSPAPER PUBLISHED: ANNIVERSARY. Sept 25, 1690. The first (and only) edition of *Publick Occurrences Both Foreign and Domestick* was published by Benjamin Harris, at the London-Coffee-House, Boston, MA. Authorities considered this first newspaper published in the US offensive and ordered immediate suppression.

FIRST WOMAN SUPREME COURT JUSTICE: ANNIVERSARY. Sept 25, 1981. Sandra Day O'Connor was sworn in as the first woman associate justice on the US Supreme Court on this date. She had been nominated by President Ronald Reagan in July 1981.

GENEVA AREA GRAPE JAMBOREE. Sept 25–26. Geneva, OH. Grape harvest and products. 41st annual Jamboree. Annually, the last full weekend in September. Est attendance: 250,000. For info: Geneva Grape Jamboree, Box 92, Geneva, OH 44041. Phone: (440) 466-5262. Web: www.grapejamboree.com.

GETTYSBURG OUTDOOR ANTIQUE SHOW. Sept 25. Gettysburg, PA. More than 150 dealers displaying their wares on the sidewalk. Annually, the fourth Saturday in September. Est attendance: 25,000. For info: Gettysburg Conv & Visitors Bureau, PO Box 4117, Gettysburg, PA 17325. Phone: (717) 334-6274. Fax: (717) 334-1166. E-mail: gettysburgcvb@dejazzd.com. Web: www.gettysburgcvb.org.

GREENWICH MEAN TIME BEGINS: ANNIVERSARY. Sept 25, 1676 (OS). Two very accurate clocks were set in motion at the Royal Observatory at Greenwich, England. Greenwich Mean Time (now known as Universal Time) became the standard for England; in 1884 it became the standard for the world.

"THE KATE SMITH HOUR" TV PREMIERE: ANNIVERSARY. Sept 25, 1950. Singer Kate Smith hosted radio before beginning a successful but short TV career. This late afternoon show was the most successful (she also had two prime-time shows, "The Kate Smith Evening Hour" (1951–52) and "The Kate Smith Show" (1960) that were less well received). It included interviews, musical numbers and comedy or drama sketches. The sketches spun off many series, including "The World of Mr Sweeney" and "Ethel and Albert."

KECHI FALL "OUTDOOR" ANTIQUE SWAP MEET AND FLEA MARKET. Sept 25–26. Kechi, KS. This is Kechi's fall event: all antique dealers are invited to town to set up their booths in between local antique & specialty shops. Hours 8 AM to 5 PM. Free admission. Kechi is the official "Antique Capital of Kansas." Est attendance: 1,200. For info: Rick Eberhard, Kechi Area Chamber of Commerce, 205 Heritage Ct, Kechi, KS 67067-8710. Phone: (316) 744-1337. For vendor booths call (316) 744-8710. E-mail: kechichamber@kechikscoc.com. Web: www.kechikscoc.com.

KIWANIS KIDS' DAY. Sept 25. To honor and assist youth—our greatest resource. Annually, the fourth Saturday in September. For info: Kiwanis Intl, Member Services, 3636 Woodview Trace, Indianapolis, IN 46268. E-mail: kiwanismail@kiwanis.org. Web: www.kiwanis.org.

MAJOR LEAGUE BASEBALL'S FIRST DOUBLEHEADER: ANNIVERSARY. Sept 25, 1882. The first major league baseball doubleheader was played between the Providence and Worcester teams.

MARION COUNTY COUNTRY HAM DAYS. Sept 25–26. Lebanon, KY. Country ham breakfast served under a tent in downtown Lebanon. Pokey pig 5K run, PIGasus parade, more than 125 arts and crafts booths and free entertainment. Est attendance: 50,000. For info: Kathy Browning, Lebanon-Marion County Chamber of Commerce, 21 Court Sq, Lebanon, KY 40033. Phone: (270) 692-9594. Fax: (270) 692-2661. E-mail: chamber@hamdays.com. Web: www.hamdays.com.

Sept 25 ☆ Chase's 2004 Calendar of Events ☆

NATIONAL ONE-HIT WONDER DAY. Sept 25. Honors the one-hit wonders of rock 'n' roll. Anyone who ever had a hit single deserves eternal remembrance. For info: Steven Rosen, 1944 S Glendon Ave, #105, Los Angeles, CA 90025. Phone: (310) 441-5102. E-mail: srosenone@aol.com.

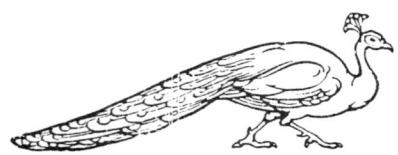

NORTHEAST MONTANA THRESHING BEE AND ANTIQUE SHOW. Sept 25–26. Culbertson, MT. See how grandma and grandpa worked and lived. At the threshing grounds one mile southeast of town. Annually, the fourth full weekend in September. Est attendance: 2,000. For info: Rodney Iverson or David Krogedal, Northeast Montana Threshing Bee/Antique Show, Culbertson, MT 59218. Phone: (406) 787-5265. E-mail: elk1@nemontel.net.

OCEAN COUNTY DECOY AND GUNNING SHOW. Sept 25–26. Pinelands High and Middle Schools, Tip Seaman County Park and Tuckerton Seaport, Tuckerton, NJ. 22nd annual. Gathering to celebrate the local waterfowling heritage. Emphasizes traditional skills such as decoy carving, working decoy rigs, sneakbox building, gunning, retrieving and goose-calling contests. Wildlife art, outdoor clothing and gear, hunting and fishing supplies. More than 500 vendors. Free. Rain or shine. Est attendance: 35,000. For info: Wells Mills Co Park. Phone: (609) 971-3085. Web: www.co.ocean.nj.us/parks/default.htm.

OCTOBERFEST. Sept 25. Lawrence University, Appleton, WI. Come enjoy a family event with ethnic foods, arts & crafts, fun and entertainment. Annually, the last Saturday in September. Est attendance: 150,000. For info: Campus Activities, Lawrence University, PO Box 599, Appleton, WI 54912.

PACIFIC OCEAN DISCOVERED: ANNIVERSARY. Sept 25, 1513. Vasco Núñez de Balboa, a Spanish conquistador, stood high atop a peak in the Darien, in present-day Panama, becoming the first European to look upon the Pacific Ocean, claiming it as the South Sea in the name of the King of Spain.

PALATINE MUSEUM FALL EVENT. Sept 25. Palatine House Museum, Schoharie, NY. Fall harvest festival. This event is fun for the whole family. Est attendance: 1,700. For info: Angela DeGroff, Program Dir, Schoharie Colonial Heritage Assn, Box 554, Schoharie, NY 12157. Phone: (518) 295-7505 or (518) 295-7585. E-mail: scha@midtel.net.

PROWSE, JULIET: BIRTH ANNIVERSARY. Sept 25, 1936. Dancer, actress, born Bombay, India. Died Sept 14, 1996.

RAMEAU, JEAN PHILLIPPE: BIRTH ANNIVERSARY. Sept 25, 1683. French composer Jean Phillippe Rameau was baptised at Dijon, France, Sept 25, 1683. Called by some the greatest French composer and musical theorist of the 18th century, Rameau died at Paris, France, Sept 12, 1764.

RWANDA: REPUBLIC DAY. Sept 25. National holiday. Marks the 1961 abolition of the monarchy.

SEQUOIA AND KINGS CANYON NATIONAL PARK ESTABLISHED: ANNIVERSARY. Sept 25, 1890. Area in central California established as a national park. For further park info: Sequoia Natl Park, Three Rivers, CA 93271.

September 2004

S	M	T	W	T	F	S
			1	2	3	4
5	6	7	8	9	10	11
12	13	14	15	16	17	18
19	20	21	22	23	24	25
26	27	28	29	30		

SHEYENNE VALLEY ARTS & CRAFTS FESTIVAL. Sept 25–26. Fort Ransom, ND. This 37th annual festival is one of the oldest and best in the area. Artists and crafters from several states join local people in offering 200 displays, church bazaar and dinner, turkey barbecue, cavalry performance—all in a rustic historic atmosphere. Annually, the last full weekend in September. Sponsor: Sheyenne Valley Arts and Crafts Assn, Inc, a nonprofit organization. Est attendance: 10,000. For info: SVACA, PO Box 21, Fort Ransom, ND 58033. Phone: (701) 973-4461. E-mail: svaca1@juno.com.

SHOSTAKOVICH, DMITRI: BIRTH ANNIVERSARY. Sept 25, 1906. Russian composer born at St. Petersburg, Russia. Died at Moscow, USSR, Aug 9, 1975.

"SILVER SPOONS" TV PREMIERE: ANNIVERSARY. Sept 25, 1982. This half-hour sitcom was about a wealthy, immature toy company owner and his sensible son. Joel Higgins was Edward Stratton III, Rick Schroder played his son Ricky, who left military school to be with his divorced father. Erin Gray was Kate Summers, Edward's secretary and later, his wife. Leonard Lightfoot was his lawyer, Leonard Rollins, and Franklyn Seales played his business manager, Dexter Stuffins. Alfonso Ribeiro was Ricky's friend and Dexter's nephew, Alfonso Spears; Jason Bateman played Derek Taylor, Ricky's sneaky friend; and Corky Pigeon played geeky Freddie Lippincottleman. Ray Walston appeared as Kate's uncle, and John Houseman had a recurring role as Edward's stuffy father.

SINGLE PARENT FAMILY DAY. Sept 25. Columbus, OH. A celebration for single parent families. Annually, the fourth Saturday in September. For info: Sheryl Fenderson, A Cup of Joy Single Parent Family Resource Center, PO Box 29711, Columbus, OH 43229. E-mail: singleparents@acupofjoy.org.

SMITH, WALTER WESLEY "RED": BIRTH ANNIVERSARY. Sept 25, 1905. Pulitzer Prize–winning sports columnist and newspaperman for 54 years, Walter Wesley (Red) Smith was born at Green Bay, WI. Called the "nation's most respected sportswriter," Smith's columns appeared in some 500 newspapers. He died at Stamford, CT, Jan 15, 1982.

TASTE OF MORGAN HILL. Sept 25–26. Downtown Morgan Hill, CA. 15th annual family festival featuring fine arts and quality crafts, entertainment, wine and beer garden, local restaurants and food booths, custom and classic car show, and kids' zone. Annually, the last full weekend in September. Est attendance: 50,000. For info: Sunday Minnich, Morgan Hill Chamber of Commerce, PO Box 786, Morgan Hill, CA 95038. Phone: (408) 779-9444. Fax: (408) 779-5405. E-mail: mhcc@morganhill.org. Web: www.morganhill.org.

TRI-STATE BAND FESTIVAL. Sept 25. Luverne, MN. 54th annual festival with more than 2,500 high school students from Minnesota, South Dakota and Iowa; trophies awarded in four classes. Annually, the last Saturday in September. Est attendance: 10,000. For info: Dave Smith, Exec Dir, Luverne Area Chamber of Commerce, 102 E Main, Luverne, MN 56156. Phone: (507) 283-4061. Fax: (507) 283-4061. E-mail: luvernechamber@dtgnet.com. Web: www.luvernemn.com.

YOM KIPPUR or DAY OF ATONEMENT. Sept 25. Holiest Jewish observance. A day for fasting, repentance and seeking forgiveness. Hebrew calendar date: Tishri 10, 5765. Began at sundown on Sept 24.

BIRTHDAYS TODAY

Tate Donovan, 41, actor ("Friends," "Partners"), born New York, NY, Sept 25, 1963.
Michael Douglas, 60, actor ("The Streets of San Francisco," *Fatal Attraction, Basic Instinct*), director, born New York, NY, Sept 25, 1944.
Mark Hamill, 53, actor ("General Hospital," *Star Wars*), born Oakland, CA, Sept 25, 1951.
Heather Locklear, 43, actress ("T.J. Hooker," "Dynasty," "Melrose Place"), born Los Angeles, CA, Sept 25, 1961.

Michael Madsen, 45, actor (*Species II, Donnie Brasco*), born Chicago, IL, Sept 25, 1959.
Scottie Pippen, 39, basketball player, born Hamburg, AR, Sept 25, 1965.
Christopher Reeve, 52, actor (*Superman*), born New York, NY, Sept 25, 1952.
Philip Francis (Phil) Rizzuto, 87, Hall of Fame baseball player, born New York, NY, Sept 25, 1917.
Will Smith, 36, actor (*Independence Day*, "The Fresh Prince of Bel-Air"), singer, born Philadelphia, PA, Sept 25, 1968.
Robert Walden, 61, actor ("Lou Grant," *All the King's Men*), born New York, NY, Sept 25, 1943.
Barbara Walters, 73, journalist, interviewer, TV host ("20/20"), born Boston, MA, Sept 25, 1931.
Catherine Zeta-Jones, 35, actress (*The Mask of Zorro, Chicago*), born Swansea, Glamorgan, Wales, Sept 25, 1969.

SEPTEMBER 26 — SUNDAY
Day 270 — 96 Remaining

ALL ABOUT APPLES. Sept 26. Billings Farm and Museum, Woodstock, VT. Learn more about this most basic American fruit that boasts hundreds of varieties. Activities include cider pressing, making apple butter in the farmhouse kitchen, apples-on-a-string, harvest dolls and horse-drawn wagon rides. For info: Billings Farm and Museum, PO Box 489, Woodstock, VT 05091. Phone: (802) 457-2355. Fax: (802) 457-4663. E-mail: billings.farm@valley.net. Web: www.billingsfarm.org.

APPLESEED, JOHNNY: BIRTH ANNIVERSARY. Sept 26, 1774. John Chapman, better known as Johnny Appleseed, believed to have been born at Leominster, MA. Died at Allen County, IN, Mar 11, 1845. Planter of orchards and friend of wild animals, he was regarded as a great medicine man by the Indians.

BATTLE OF MEUSE–ARGONNE FOREST: ANNIVERSARY. Sept 26, 1918. As part of four major efforts to break the Hindenburg line, a Franco-American offensive began on this date, with the US First Army striking between the Meuse River and the Argonne Forest and the French Fourth Army to their west. After four taxing weeks of attack, the Germans were gradually pushed back. By Oct 31, the Americans had advanced 10 miles, the French had reached the Aisne River 20 miles away and the Argonne Forest was rid of the Central Power forces. This was the final great battle of World War I.

"THE BEVERLY HILLBILLIES" TV PREMIERE: ANNIVERSARY. Sept 26, 1962. This half-hour comedy was one of the most successful "rural" comedies on TV; in addition, according to Nielsen, the eight most-watched half-hour shows are episodes of this series. "The Beverly Hillbillies" was about an Appalachian man, Jed Clampett (Buddy Ebsen) who found oil on his property, so he moved his family to a better life in Beverly Hills, CA. Most of its jokes were based on its fish-out-of-water premise. Also in the cast were Irene Ryan as Granny, Jed's mother-in-law; Donna Douglas as his daughter Elly May; Max Baer, Jr, as his nephew Jethro Bodine; Raymond Bailey as neurotic Milburn Drysdale, Jed's neighbor; Nancy Kulp as Jane Hathaway, Drysdale's secretary; and Harriet MacGibbon as Margaret Drysdale, Milburn's wife.

"THE BRADY BUNCH" TV PREMIERE: 35th ANNIVERSARY. Sept 26, 1969. This popular sitcom starred Robert Reed as widower Mike Brady who has three sons and is married to Carol (played by Florence Henderson), who has three daughters. Housekeeper Alice was played by Ann B. Davis. Sons Greg (Barry Williams), Peter (Christopher Knight) and Bobby (Mike Lookinland) and daughters Marcia (Maureen McCormick), Jan (Eve Plumb) and Cindy (Susan Olsen) experienced the typical crises of youth. The program steered clear of social issues and portrayed childhood as a time of innocence. The last episode was telecast on Aug 30, 1974. The program continues to be popular in reruns in the after-school time slot. There were also many spin-offs: "The Brady Kids" (1972–74), a Saturday morning cartoon; "The Brady Bunch Hour" (1976–77), a variety series; "The Brady Brides" (1981), a sitcom about the two older daughters adjusting to marriage and "The Bradys" (1990), a short-lived dramatic series. *A Very Brady Christmas* (1988) was CBS's highest rated special for the season. In 1995 *The Brady Bunch Movie* appealed to fans who had watched the program 25 years before.

CABRILLO FESTIVAL. Sept 26–Oct 3. San Diego, CA. Colorful pageant reenacts the historic landing of explorer Juan Rodríguez Cabrillo who sailed into San Diego Bay on Sept 28, 1542. Kumeyaay basket-weaving, acorn grinding and flint knapping demonstrations. Knot tying exhibition. Reenactment of Spanish encampment. Portuguese, Spanish, Native American and Mexican dances and food. Pageant, annually the last Sunday in September. Est attendance: 9,500. For info: Cabrillo Natl Monument, 1800 Cabrillo Memorial Dr, San Diego, CA 92106. Phone: (619) 557-5450. TTY: (619) 222-8211. Fax: (619) 557-5469. Web: www.nps.gov/cabr/.

CHRISTIAN LEADERSHIP WEEK INTERNATIONAL. Sept 26–Oct 2. Nowhere is exemplary leadership expected more than in Christian organizations, whether the church or parachurch. This event is dedicated to developing Christian leaders in all areas of life and to establishing an example of great and morally good leadership for both secular and faith-based organizations. For info: DiFrances & Assoc, LLC, 208 E Oak Crest Dr, Ste 200, Wales, WI 53183-9700. Phone: (262) 968-9850. Fax: (262) 968-9854. E-mail: christianleadership@difrances.com. Web: www.difrances.com/christianleadershipweek.

DONIZETTI'S "LUCIA DI LAMMERMOOR" PREMIERE: ANNIVERSARY. Sept 26, 1835. *Lucia di Lammermoor*, one of opera's greatest tragic love stories, premiered in Naples, Italy. The opera was composed by Gaetano Donizetti with a libretto by Salvatore Cammarano. The plot was based on Sir Walter Scott's *The Bride of Lammermoor* and takes place in 17th-century Scotland. Lucia, thwarted by a blood feud from marrying the man she loves, kills her husband and then herself.

ELIOT, T.S.: BIRTH ANNIVERSARY. Sept 26, 1888. Thomas Stearns Eliot, Nobel Prize winner, poet, playwright and critic, was born at St. Louis, MO. "There never was a time," he believed, "when those that read at all, read so many more books by living authors than books by dead authors; there never was a time so completely parochial, so shut off from the past." Eliot died at London, England, Jan 4, 1965.

FESTIFALL. Sept 26. Friendship Hill National Historic Site, Point Marion, PA. To celebrate the 19th-century arts, crafts and music of the Allegheny Plateau. Historic foods are available for purchase. Annually, the last Sunday in September. Est attendance: 3,000. For info: Friendship Hill Natl Historic Site, 223 New Geneva Rd, Point Marion, PA 15474. Phone: (724) 725-9190. Fax: (724) 725-1999. Web: www.nps.gov/frhi/.

FIRST TELEVISED PRESIDENTIAL DEBATE: ANNIVERSARY. Sept 26, 1960. The debate between presidential candidates John F. Kennedy and Richard Nixon was televised from WBBM-TV, a Chicago TV studio.

Sept 26–27 ☆ Chase's 2004 Calendar of Events ☆

GERSHWIN, GEORGE: BIRTH ANNIVERSARY. Sept 26, 1898. American composer remembered for his many enduring songs and melodies, including: "The Man I Love," "Strike Up the Band," "Funny Face," "I Got Rhythm" and the opera *Porgy and Bess*. Many of his works were in collaboration with his brother, Ira. Born at Brooklyn, NY, he died of a brain tumor at Beverly Hills, CA, July 11, 1937. See also: "Gershwin, Ira: Birth Anniversary" (Dec 6).

"GILLIGAN'S ISLAND" TV PREMIERE: 40th ANNIVERSARY. Sept 26, 1964. Seven people set sail aboard the *Minnow* for a three-hour tour and became stranded on an island. They used the resources on the island for food, shelter and entertainment. The cast included Bob Denver as Gilligan, Alan Hale, Jr, as the Skipper, Jim Backus as Thurston Howell III, Natalie Schafer as Mrs "Lovey" Howell, Russell Johnson as the Professor, Dawn Wells as Mary Ann and Tina Louise as Ginger Grant, the movie star. The last telecast aired on Sept 4, 1967.

★ **GOLD STAR MOTHER'S DAY.** Sept 26. Presidential Proclamation always for last Sunday of each September since 1936. Proclamation 2424 of Sept 14, 1940, covers all succeeding years.

"KNIGHT RIDER" TV PREMIERE: ANNIVERSARY. Sept 26, 1982. David Hasselhoff starred in this one-hour adventure series about a cop who was nearly killed, then brought back to life with a new identity (Michael Knight) by a mysterious millionaire. Together with a car that talked, a Pontiac Trans Am called KITT (Knight Industries Two Thousand), Knight had various adventures. Other cast members included: Edward Mulhare as Devon Miles, aide to the deceased millionaire, Patricia McPherson as mechanic Bonnie Barstow, Rebecca Holden as April Curtis, William Daniels as the voice of KITT and Peter Parros as Reginald Cornelius III, truck driver/chauffeur for KITT.

★ **MINORITY ENTERPRISE DEVELOPMENT WEEK.** Sept 26–Oct 2. Presidential Proclamation issued without request since 1983.

NATIONAL CHIMNEY SAFETY WEEK. Sept 26–Oct 2. Each year CSIA Certified Chimney Sweeps work to raise awareness of chimney safety. For a list of Certified Chimney Sweeps in your state, call CSIA at (800) 536-0118. Annually, the week prior to National Fire Prevention Week. For info: CSIA, 2155 Commercial Dr, Plainfield, IN 46168. Phone: (317) 837-5362. Fax: (317) 837-5365. E-mail: office@csia.org. Web: www.csia.org.

NATIONAL GOOD NEIGHBOR DAY. Sept 26. To build a nation and world that cares by increasing appreciation and understanding of our fellow man. Annually, the fourth Sunday in September. For info: Natl Good Neighbor Day Fdtn, Box 379, Lakeside, MT 59922. Phone: (406) 844-3000. Web: www.natgoodneighborday.com.

POPE PAUL VI: BIRTH ANNIVERSARY. Sept 26, 1897. Giovanni Battista Montini, 262nd pope of the Roman Catholic Church, born at Concesio, Italy. Elected pope June 21, 1963. Died at Castel Gandolfo, near Rome, Italy, Aug 6, 1978.

SHAMU'S BIRTHDAY: ANNIVERSARY. Sept 26, 1985. Shamu was born at Sea World at Orlando, FL, and is the first killer whale born in captivity to survive. Shamu is now living at Sea World's Texas park.

BIRTHDAYS TODAY

Lynn Anderson, 57, singer ("Rose Garden"), born Grand Forks, ND, Sept 26, 1947.
Melissa Sue Anderson, 42, actress ("Little House on the Prairie"), born Berkeley, CA, Sept 26, 1962.

	S	M	T	W	T	F	S
September				1	2	3	4
	5	6	7	8	9	10	11
2004	12	13	14	15	16	17	18
	19	20	21	22	23	24	25
	26	27	28	29	30		

Bryan Ferry, 59, lead singer (Roxy Music, "Heart on My Sleeve"), songwriter, born Durham, England, Sept 26, 1945.
Linda Hamilton, 47, actress (*Terminator, Terminator 2*), born Salisbury, MD, Sept 26, 1957.
Mary Beth Hurt, 56, actress (*The World According to Garp, Six Degrees of Separation*), born Marshalltown, IA, Sept 26, 1948.
Olivia Newton-John, 56, singer ("Physical"), actress (*Grease*), born Cambridge, England, Sept 26, 1948.
Christine T. Whitman, 58, former administrator of the Environmental Protection Agency, former Governor of New Jersey (R), born New York, NY, Sept 26, 1946.
Serena Williams, 23, tennis player, born Saginaw, MI, Sept 26, 1981.

SEPTEMBER 27 — MONDAY
Day 271 — 95 Remaining

ADAMS, SAMUEL: BIRTH ANNIVERSARY. Sept 27, 1722. Revolutionary leader and Massachusetts state politician Samuel Adams, cousin to President John Adams (1797–1801), was born at Boston. He died there Oct 2, 1803. As a delegate to the First and Second Continental Congresses Adams urged a vigorous stand against England. He signed the Declaration of Independence and the Articles of Confederation and supported the war for independence. Adams served as lieutenant governor of Massachusetts under John Hancock from 1789 to 1793 and then as governor until 1797.

ANCESTOR APPRECIATION DAY. Sept 27. A day to learn about and appreciate one's forebears. For info: A.A.D. Assn, PO Box 3, Montague, MI 49437-0003.

BATTLE OF CAMBRAI–SAINT QUENTIN: ANNIVERSARY. Sept 27, 1918. British General Sir Douglas Haig moved his armies toward Cambrai and St. Quentin as part of four major efforts to break the Hindenburg line in the German salient that extended from Verdun to the sea. To the south the New Zealand and Canadian divisions smashed through the Hindenburg line on Oct 6. German General Erich Ludendorff resigned Oct 16, and the line was taken between Oct 18 and 20.

CONRAD, WILLIAM: BIRTH ANNIVERSARY. Sept 27, 1920. Actor, best known for his roles in the TV series "Cannon" and "Jake and the Fat Man." Born at Louisville, KY, and died at North Hollywood, CA, Feb 11, 1994.

CRUIKSHANK, GEORGE: BIRTH ANNIVERSARY. Sept 27, 1792. English illustrator, especially known for caricatures and for illustrations of Charles Dickens's books. Born at London, England, and died there Feb 1, 1878.

ETHIOPIA: TRUE CROSS DAY. Sept 27. National holiday. Commemorates the finding of the true cross (*Maskal*). Also a holiday in Eritrea.

FALL FOLIAGE FESTIVAL. Sept 27–Oct 3. Walden, Cabot, Plainfield, Peacham, Barnet, Groton and St. Johnsbury, VT. Seven towns welcome visitors during Vermont's famous fall foliage season. Est attendance: 2,500. For info: Northeast Chamber of Commerce, Fall Festival, 357 Western Ave, Ste 2, St. Johnsbury, VT 05819. Phone: (802) 563-2472. Web: www.vermontnekchamber.org.

502

★ Chase's 2004 Calendar of Events ★ Sept 27–28

"JACK THE RIPPER" LETTER: ANNIVERSARY. Sept 27, 1888. In the midst of the "Autumn of Terror" in which London, England, was convulsed over the crimes of a brutal serial killer, the city's Central News Agency received a letter written in red ink purporting to be written by the killer. He dubbed himself "Jack the Ripper" and threatened more killings. Police at the time and most historians today believe(d) the letter to be a hoax by an irresponsible journalist, but the name took hold in the public imagination and is forever associated with the Whitechapel murders of 1888. See also: "Whitechapel Murders Begin: Anniversary" (Aug 31).

NAST, THOMAS: BIRTH ANNIVERSARY. Sept 27, 1840. American political cartoonist born at Landau, Germany, best known for his cartoons attacking New York's Tweed ring. Died Dec 7, 1902, at Guayaquil, Ecuador.

SAINT VINCENT DE PAUL: FEAST DAY. Sept 27. French priest, patron of charitable organizations, and cofounder of the Sisters of Charity. Canonized 1737 (lived 1581?–1660).

SEMMES, RAPHAEL: BIRTH ANNIVERSARY. Sept 27, 1809. Born at St. Charles County, MD, and died Aug 30, 1877, at Mobile, AL. Daring Confederate naval officer, best known for his incredible raids on Union merchant ships during the middle two years of the Civil War. As commander of the *Alabama*, he captured, sank or burned 82 Union ships valued at more than $6,000,000.

SPACE MILESTONE: *SOYUZ 12* (USSR): ANNIVERSARY. Sept 27, 1973. Because of the death of the crew of *Soyuz 11* upon reentry, it was decided that cosmonauts must wear pressurized space suits on takeoff and landing. Thus there was no longer room for three cosmonauts on a flight. Two Soviet cosmonauts (V.G. Lazarev and O.G. Makarov) made the two-day flight launched on this date.

"THE TONIGHT SHOW" TV PREMIERE: 50th ANNIVERSARY. Sept 27, 1954. "The Tonight Show" has gone through numerous changes over the years, yet it has remained a top-rated show that set the standards for all variety/talk shows to come. Steve Allen served as host from 1954–57. He introduced the format of the show with an opening monologue, games or segments for the studio audience, and then the interview on a simple desk and couch set. Jack Paar hosted from 1957–62 and Johnny Carson reigned as the king of comedy from 1962–92. Comedian Jay Leno serves as its current host.

WARREN COMMISSION REPORT: 40th ANNIVERSARY. Sept 27, 1964. On this day, the Warren Commission issued a report stating that Lee Harvey Oswald acted alone in the assassination of President John F. Kennedy on Nov 22, 1963. Congress reopened the investigation and in 1979 the House Select Committee on Assassinations issued a report stating a conspiracy was most likely involved. See also: "Committee on Assassinations Report: Anniversary" (Mar 29).

WORLD TOURISM DAY. Sept 27. Observed on the anniversary of the adoption of the World Tourism Organization Statutes in 1970. For info: World Tourism Organization, Calle Capitan Haya 42, 28020 Madrid, Spain. Phone: (34) (91) 5678100. Fax: (34) (91) 571373. Web: www.world-tourism.org.

BIRTHDAYS TODAY

Wilford Brimley, 70, actor (*Cocoon*, "Our House"), born Salt Lake City, UT, Sept 27, 1934.
Shaun Cassidy, 45, singer ("Da Doo Ron Ron"), actor ("The Hardy Boys," "General Hospital"), born Los Angeles, CA, Sept 27, 1959.
Claude Jarman, Jr, 70, actor (*The Yearling*, *Rio Grande*), born Nashville, TN, Sept 27, 1934.
Stephan Jenkins, 39, musician (Third Eye Blind), born Southern CA, Sept 27, 1965.
Steve Kerr, 39, basketball player, born Beirut, Lebanon, Sept 27, 1965.
Jayne Meadows, 80, actress ("I've Got a Secret," "The Steve Allen Show," *Lady in the Lake*), born Chang, China, Sept 27, 1924.
Meat Loaf, 57, singer, musician (*The Rocky Horror Picture Show*), born Marvin Lee Aday, Dallas, TX, Sept 27, 1947.
Arthur Heller Penn, 82, filmmaker (*Bonnie and Clyde*, *The Miracle Worker*), born Philadelphia, PA, Sept 27, 1922.
Michael Jack (Mike) Schmidt, 55, Hall of Fame baseball player, born Dayton, OH, Sept 27, 1949.
Delores Taylor, 65, actress, writer, producer (*Billy Jack*, *The Trial of Billy Jack*), born Winner, SD, Sept 27, 1939.
Sada Thompson, 75, actress (*Twigs*, "Family"), born Des Moines, IA, Sept 27, 1929.

SEPTEMBER 28 — TUESDAY
Day 272 — 94 Remaining

CABRILLO DAY: ANNIVERSARY OF DISCOVERY OF CALIFORNIA. Sept 28, 1542. California. Commemorates discovery of California by Portuguese navigator Juan Rodriguez Cabrillo who reached San Diego Bay. Cabrillo died at San Miguel Island, CA, Jan 3, 1543. His birth date is unknown. The Cabrillo National Monument marks his landfall and Cabrillo Day is still observed in California (in some areas on the Saturday nearest Sept 28).

CAPP, AL: 95th BIRTH ANNIVERSARY. Sept 28, 1909. The creator of the fictitious village of Dogpatch, KY, Al Capp was born Alfred Gerald Caplin at New Haven, CT. The comic strip "Li'l Abner" appeared in daily newspapers from 1934 until its final episode was published Nov 13, 1977. Along with the misadventures of Abner Yokum, Capp lampooned famous public figures. The minor American institution of "Sadie Hawkins Day" made its debut in "Li'l Abner." Al Capp died Nov 5, 1979, at Cambridge, MA.

CHINA: MOON FESTIVAL (OR MID-AUTUMN FESTIVAL). Sept 28. According to folk legend this day is the birthday of the earth god T'u-ti Kung. The festival indicates the year's hard work in the fields will soon end with the harvest. People express gratitude to heaven as represented by the moon and to earth as symbolized by the earth god for all good things from the preceding year. Special harvest foods are eaten, especially "moon cakes." Observed on the 15th day of the eighth month of the Chinese lunar calendar, this festival is called by different names in different places, but is widely recognized throughout the Far East, including Taiwan, Korea, Singapore and Hong Kong. Date here is for China, date in other countries will differ.

FIRST NIGHT FOOTBALL GAME: ANNIVERSARY. Sept 28, 1892. The first night football game in America was played between Mansfield State Normal School (now Mansfield University) and Wyoming Seminary.

HARVEST MOON. Sept 28. So called because the full moon nearest the autumnal equinox extends the hours of light into the evening and helps the harvester with his long day's work. Moon enters Full Moon phase at 9:09 AM, EDT.

Sept 28–29 ☆ Chase's 2004 Calendar of Events ☆

"HAZEL" TV PREMIERE: ANNIVERSARY. Sept 28, 1961. "Hazel" was based on a comic strip of the same name about a maid working for the Baxter family who gets into everyone's business. Hazel was played by Shirley Booth, and the Baxters were played by Don DeFore, Whitney Blake and Bobby Buntrock. "Hazel" moved from NBC to CBS after the third season and Hazel switched families from George to younger brother, Steve Baxter. These Baxters were played by Ray Fulmer, Lynn Borden and Julia Benjamin. This successful series also featured Mala Powers and Ann Jillian.

KOREA: CHUSOK. Sept 28. Gala celebration by Koreans everywhere. Autumn harvest thanksgiving moon festival. Observed on 15th day of eighth lunar month (eighth full moon of lunar calendar) each year. Koreans pay homage to ancestors and express gratitude to guarding spirits for another year of rich crops. A time to visit tombs, leave food and prepare for the coming winter season. Traditional food is the "moon cake," made on the eve of Chusok, with rice, chestnuts and jujube fruits. Games, dancing and gift exchanges. Observed since Silla Dynasty (beginning of First Millennium).

MASTROIANNI, MARCELLO: 80th BIRTH ANNIVERSARY. Sept 28, 1924. One of the great international stars of cinema, born at Fontana Liri, Italy. Mastroianni worked with the master directors of the mid-twentieth century, among them Federico Fellini and Luchino Visconti. Two of his most famous roles were the world-weary journalist of *La Dolce Vita* (1960) and the in-crisis movie director of *8½* (1963)—both films directed by Fellini. He was nominated for Oscars three times and twice won the Best Actor Award at the Cannes Film Festival. Died at Paris, France, Dec 19, 1996.

MOON PHASE: FULL MOON. Sept 28. Moon enters Full Moon phase at 9:09 AM, EDT.

SULLIVAN, ED: BIRTH ANNIVERSARY. Sept 28, 1901. Known as the "King of TV Variety," born at New York, NY. Sullivan started his media career in 1932 as a sportswriter for the *Daily News* in New York. His popular variety show, "The Ed Sullivan Show" ("Toast of the Town"), ran from 1948 until 1971. It included such sensational acts as Elvis Presley and the Beatles. He died at New York, NY, Oct 13, 1974.

TAIWAN: CONFUCIUS'S BIRTHDAY AND TEACHERS' DAY. Sept 28. National holiday, designated as Teachers' Day. Confucius is the Latinized name of Kung-futzu, born at Shantung province on the 27th day of the tenth moon (lunar calendar) in the 22nd year of Kuke Hsiang of Lu (551 BC). He died at age 72, having spent some 40 years as a teacher. Teachers' Day is observed annually on Sept 28.

WIGGIN, KATE DOUGLAS: BIRTH ANNIVERSARY. Sept 28, 1856. Kate Wiggin was born Kate Douglas Smith at Philadelphia, PA. She helped organize the first free kindergarten on the West Coast in 1878 at San Francisco and in 1880 she and her sister established the California Kindergarten Training School. After moving back east she devoted herself to writing, producing a number of children's books including *The Birds' Christmas Carol, Polly Oliver's Problem* and *Rebecca of Sunnybrook Farm*. She died at Harrow, England, Aug 24, 1923.

September 2004

S	M	T	W	T	F	S
			1	2	3	4
5	6	7	8	9	10	11
12	13	14	15	16	17	18
19	20	21	22	23	24	25
26	27	28	29	30		

WILLARD, FRANCES ELIZABETH CAROLINE: BIRTH ANNIVERSARY. Sept 28, 1839. American educator and reformer, president of the Women's Christian Temperance Union, 1879–98, and women's suffrage leader, born at Churchville, NY. Died at New York, NY, Feb 18, 1898.

BIRTHDAYS TODAY

Brigitte Bardot, 70, actress (*And God Created Woman, Viva Maria*), animal rights activist, born Camille Javal, Paris, France, Sept 28, 1934.
Jerry Clower, 78, comedian ("Nashville on the Road"), born Liberty, MS, Sept 28, 1926.
Janeane Garofalo, 40, actress (*Reality Bites, The Truth About Cats and Dogs*), born Newton, NJ, Sept 28, 1964.
Jeffrey Jones, 57, actor (*Beetlejuice, Stay Tuned*), born Buffalo, NY, Sept 28, 1947.
Ben E. King, 66, singer, musician ("There Goes My Baby"), born Henderson, NC, Sept 28, 1938.
Steve M. Largent, 50, Hall of Fame football player, born Tulsa, OK, Sept 28, 1954.
Se Ri Pak, 27, golfer, born Daejeon, South Korea, Sept 28, 1977.
Gwyneth Paltrow, 31, actress (*Emma, Shakespeare in Love*), born Los Angeles, CA, Sept 28, 1973.
Brian Rafalski, 31, hockey player, born Dearborn, MI, Sept 28, 1973.
William Windom, 81, actor (Emmy for "My World and Welcome to It," "Murder, She Wrote"), born New York, NY, Sept 28, 1923.

SEPTEMBER 29 — WEDNESDAY
Day 273 — 93 Remaining

DAVIDSON FELLOWS AWARD RECEPTION. Sept 29. Library of Congress, Washington, DC. Each year, the Davidson Institute for Talent Development honors our nation's brightest young minds, students under the age of 18, who have completed prodigious works in science, mathematics, technology, music, literature and/or philosophy. These students are recognized as Davidson Fellows Award recipients and receive up to a $50,000 scholarship to attend an accredited institute of learning. The Davidson Institute is a national nonprofit foundation dedicated to supporting America's most intelligent young people. Annually, the last Wednesday in September. For info: Julie Dudley, Davidson Institute, 9665 Gateway Dr, Ste B, Reno, NV 89521. Phone: (775) 852-3483, ext 424. Fax: (775) 852-2184. E-mail: davidsonfellows@ditd.org. Web: www.davidsonfellows.org.

FERMI, ENRICO: BIRTH ANNIVERSARY. Sept 29, 1901. Nuclear physicist, born at Rome, Italy. Played a prominent role in the splitting of the atom and the construction of the first American nuclear reactor. Died at Chicago, IL, Nov 28, 1954.

HOWARD, TREVOR: BIRTH ANNIVERSARY. Sept 29, 1916. British actor Trevor Howard was born at Cliftonville, England. He appeared in more than 70 films including *The Third Man* (1950) and *Mutiny on the Bounty* (1962). He died Jan 7, 1988, at Bushey, England.

"MAKE ROOM FOR DADDY" TV PREMIERE: ANNIVERSARY. Sept 29, 1953. Danny Thomas starred as Danny Williams, a nightclub singer and comedian, in this family sitcom. The series was renamed "The Danny Thomas Show" in 1956 after Jean Hagen (who played his wife, Margaret) left the show. Thomas's costars were: Sherry Jackson and Penney Parker as Danny's daughter Terry; Rusty Hamer as son Rusty; Amanda Randolph as housekeeper Louise; Horace McMahon as Danny's agent, Phil Arnold; Jesse White as agent Jesse Leeds; Sid Melton as Charlie Halper, owner of the Copa Club; Ben Lessy as Danny's pianist, Ben; Mary Wickes as his publicist, Liz O'Neal; Hans Conried as Uncle Tonoose; Nan Bryant as Danny's mother-in-law and Marjorie Lord as his new wife Kathy. Many cast members returned for the show's sequel, "Make Room for Granddaddy," in 1970.

☆ Chase's 2003 Calendar of Events ☆ Sept 29–30

MICHAELMAS. Sept 29. The feast of St. Michael and All Angels in the Greek and Roman Catholic Churches.

NATIONAL ATTEND YOUR GRANDCHILD'S BIRTH DAY. Sept 29. Bonding with your grandchild should begin at birth. This day is set aside to encourage grandparents to participate in their grandchild's birth as well as his/her life. Annually, on Sept 29. For info: Carolynn Zorn, PO Box 744, Agoura, CA 91376. Phone: (818) 889-8377. E-mail: carolynn@attendingthebirth.com. Web: www.attendingthebirth.com.

NATIONAL WOMEN'S HEALTH AND FITNESS DAY. Sept 29. 3rd annual event to promote the value of health and fitness for women of all ages. More than 700 local women's health events will be held across the country on the same day. Call the toll-free number for further info and a list of local events. Annually, the last Wednesday in September. Est attendance: 70,000. For info: Pat Henze, Exec Dir, Health Information Resource Center, 1850 W Winchester Rd #213, Libertyville, IL 60048. Phone: (800) 828-8225. Fax: (847) 816-8662. E-mail: fitnessday@aol.com. Web: www.fitnessday.com.

NELSON, HORATIO: BIRTH ANNIVERSARY. Sept 29, 1758. English naval hero of the Battle of Trafalgar, born at Burnham Thorpe, Norfolk, England. Died during a battle at sea off Cape Trafalgar, Spain, Oct 21, 1805.

PARAGUAY: BOQUERÓN DAY. Sept 29. National holiday. Commemorates a battle during the 1932 Chaco War.

SCOTLAND YARD FIRST APPEARANCE: 175th ANNIVERSARY. Sept 29, 1829. The first public appearance of Greater London's Metropolitan Police occurred amid jeering and abuse from disapproving political opponents. Public sentiment turned to confidence and respect in the ensuing years. The Metropolitan Police had been established by an act of Parliament in June 1829, at the request of Home Secretary Sir Robert Peel, after whom the London police officers became more affectionately known as "bobbies." Scotland Yard, the site of their first headquarters near Charing Cross, soon became the official name of the force.

SPACE MILESTONE: *DISCOVERY* (US): ANNIVERSARY. Sept 29, 1988. Space Shuttle *Discovery*, after numerous reschedulings, launched from Kennedy Space Center, FL, with a five-member crew on board, and landed Oct 3 at Edwards Air Force Base, CA. It marked the first American manned flight since the Challenger tragedy in 1986. See also: "Challenger, Space Shuttle Explosion: Anniversary" (Jan 28).

SPACE MILESTONE: *SALYUT 6* (USSR). Sept 29, 1977. Soviet space station launched this date. *Salyut* stayed in space for four years, during which 31 spacecraft docked with the space station. Burned up when it reentered Earth's atmosphere after nearly five years on July 29, 1982.

SUKKOT BEGINS AT SUNDOWN. Sept 29. Jewish Feast of Tabernacles. See "Sukkot" (Sept 30).

"THIRTYSOMETHING" TV PREMIERE: ANNIVERSARY. Sept 29, 1987. This ABC drama series about a group of seven baby boomers was created by Ed Zwick and Marshall Herskovitz. Viewers were able to identify with the struggles of the show's characters—such as the death of a parent, illness, single-hood, marriage, divorce, career setbacks and the birth of a child. The cast featured Ken Olin as Michael Steadman; Mel Harris as his wife, Hope; Timothy Busfield as Michael's business partner, Elliot Weston; Patricia Wettig (Olin's real-life wife) as Elliot's wife, Nancy; Polly Draper as Hope's friend Ellyn Warren; Melanie Mayron as Michael's cousin, Melissa Steadman, and Peter Horton as family friend Gary Shepherd. The last telecast was Sept 3, 1991.

VETERANS OF FOREIGN WARS ESTABLISHED: ANNIVERSARY. Sept 29, 1899. This organization is loyal to the issues and actions affecting America's heroes. Its members offer assistance in addition to supporting veterans issues in Congress. Part of the organization's mission, according to its charter, is "to preserve and strengthen comradeship among its members; to foster true patriotism; and to preserve and defend the United States from all her enemies, whomsoever." For info: Veterans of Foreign Wars of the United States, 406 W 34th St, Kansas City, MO 64111. Phone: (816) 756-3390. Fax: (816) 968-1129. Web: www.vfw.org.

BIRTHDAYS TODAY

Michelangelo Antonioni, 92, filmmaker (*Blow-Up, Zabriskie Point*), born Ferrara, Italy, Sept 29, 1912.

Anita Ekberg, 73, actress (*La Dolce Vita*), born Malmo, Sweden, Sept 29, 1931.

Bryant Gumbel, 56, TV host ("Today," "The Public Eye," "CBS This Morning"), sportscaster, born New Orleans, LA, Sept 29, 1948.

Hersey R. Hawkins, Jr, 38, former basketball player, born Chicago, IL, Sept 29, 1966.

Patricia Hodge, 58, actress ("Rumpole of the Bailey," *The Elephant Man, Betrayal*), born Cleethorpes, Lincolnshire, England, Sept 29, 1946.

Jerry Lee Lewis, 69, singer, musician ("Whole Lot of Shakin' Goin' On," "Great Balls of Fire"), born Ferriday, LA, Sept 29, 1935.

Emily Lloyd, 34, actress (*Wish You Were Here, In Country, A River Runs Through It*), born North London, England, Sept 29, 1970.

Ian McShane, 62, actor ("Lovejoy," *The Last of Sheila*), born Blackburn, England, Sept 29, 1942.

Bill Nelson, 62, US Senator (D, Florida), born Miami, FL, Sept 29, 1942.

John MacBeth Paxson, 44, former basketball player, born Dayton, OH, Sept 29, 1960.

Lech Walesa, 61, Polish labor leader, Solidarity founder, born Popowo, Poland, Sept 29, 1943.

Dave Wilcox, 62, Hall of Fame football player, born Ontario, OR, Sept 29, 1942.

SEPTEMBER 30 — THURSDAY
Day 274 — 92 Remaining

AMERICAN DENTAL ASSOCIATION ANNUAL SESSION. Sept 30–Oct 3. Philadelphia, PA. Est attendance: 38,000. For info: Vicki Guinta, American Dental Assn, 211 E Chicago Ave, Ste 200, Chicago, IL 60611. Fax: (312) 440-2707. E-mail: annualsession@ada.org. Web: www.ada.org/goto/session.

BABE RUTH SETS HOME RUN RECORD: ANNIVERSARY. Sept 30, 1927. George Herman "Babe" Ruth hit his 60th home run of the season off Tom Zachary, of the Washington Senators. Ruth's record for the most homers in a single season stood for 34 years—until Roger Maris hit 61 in 1961. Maris's record was broken in 1998 by Mark McGwire with 62 home runs. Barry Bonds broke McGwire's record on Oct 5, 2001.

BABE RUTH'S LAST GAME AS YANKEE: 70th ANNIVERSARY. Sept 30, 1934. On this date Babe Ruth played his last game for the New York Yankees. Soon after, while watching the fifth game of the World Series (between the St. Louis Cardinals and Detroit Tigers) and angry that he was not to be named Yankees manager, Ruth told Joe Williams, sports editor of the Scripp-Howard newspapers, that after 15 seasons he would no longer be playing for the Yankees.

Sept 30 ☆ *Chase's 2003 Calendar of Events* ☆

BOTSWANA: INDEPENDENCE DAY. Sept 30. National holiday. The former Bechuanaland Protectorate (British Colony) became the independent Republic of Botswana in 1966.

CAPOTE, TRUMAN: 80th BIRTH ANNIVERSARY. Sept 30, 1924. American novelist and literary celebrity, was born Truman Streckfus Persons at New Orleans, LA. He later took the name of his stepfather to become Truman Capote. Among his best-remembered books: *Other Voices, Other Rooms; Breakfast at Tiffany's* and *In Cold Blood*. He was working on a new novel, *Answered Prayers*, at the time of his death at Los Angeles, CA, Aug 25, 1984.

"CHEERS" TV PREMIERE: ANNIVERSARY. Sept 30, 1982. NBC sitcom revolving around the owner, employees and patrons of a Beacon Street bar at Boston. Original cast: Ted Danson as owner Sam Malone, Shelley Long and Rhea Perlman as waitresses Diane Chambers and Carla Tortelli, Nicholas Colasanto as bartender Ernie "Coach" Pantusso, John Ratzenberger as mailman Cliff Clavin and George Wendt as accountant Norm Peterson. Later cast members: Woody Harrelson as bartender Woody Boyd, Kelsey Grammer as Dr. Frasier Crane, Kirstie Alley as Rebecca Howe and Bebe Neuwirth as Dr. Lilith Sternin Crane. The theme song "Where Everybody Knows Your Name," was sung by Gary Portnoy. The last episode aired Aug 19, 1993.

COWBOY HALL OF FAME CEREMONY AND BANQUET. Sept 30. Willcox Community Center, Willcox, AZ. The Cowboy Hall of Fame events lead into the Rex Allen Days celebration. Open house 6 PM, dinner 7 PM. Includes "Cowboy Hall of Fame" induction ceremony, favorite son/daughter award. Sponsored by the Willcox Chamber of Commerce & Agriculture. Est attendance: 340. For info: (520) 384-2272 or (800) 200-2272. Web: www.willcoxchamber.com.

DODGE POETRY FESTIVAL. Sept 30–Oct 3. Location to be announced. Twelfth biennial Geraldine R. Dodge Poetry Festival will include the participation of more than 100 poets and will offer dozens of simultaneous poetry readings and discussions. Est attendance: 15,000. For info: Geraldine R. Dodge Foundation, 163 Madison Ave, PO Box 1239, Morristown, NJ 07962-1239. Phone: (973) 540-8443 x 5. E-mail: festival@grdodge.org. Web: grdodge.org/poetry/.

FALL SUWANNEE RIVER GOSPEL JUBILEE. Sept 30–Oct 2. Live Oak, FL. Featuring well-known musical groups for a weekend of music in this beautiful park. Previous artists featured include Naomi and the Segos, Bibletones, Jody Brown Indian Family and more. Est attendance: 5,000. For info: James Cornett, Spirit of the Suwannee Music Park, 3076 95th Dr, Live Oak, FL 32060. Phone: (386) 364-1683. E-mail: spirit@musicliveshere.com. Web: www.musicliveshere.com.

September 2004

S	M	T	W	T	F	S
			1	2	3	4
5	6	7	8	9	10	11
12	13	14	15	16	17	18
19	20	21	22	23	24	25
26	27	28	29	30		

FEAST OF SAINT JEROME. Sept 30. Patron saint of scholars and librarians.

FIRST ANNUAL FAIR IN AMERICA: ANNIVERSARY. Sept 30, 1641. According to the Laws and Ordinances of New Netherlands (now New York and New Jersey), on Sept 30, 1641, authorities declared that "henceforth there shall be held annually at Fort Amsterdam" a Cattle Fair (Oct 15) and a Hog Fair (Nov 1), and that "whosoever hath any things to sell or buy can regulate himself accordingly."

FIRST CRIMINAL EXECUTION IN AMERICAN COLONIES: ANNIVERSARY. Sept 30, 1630. John Billington, one of the first Pilgrims to land in America, was hanged for murder, becoming the first criminal to be executed in the American colonies.

"THE FLINTSTONES" TV PREMIERE: ANNIVERSARY. Sept 30, 1960. This Hanna Barbera cartoon comedy was set in prehistoric times. Characters included two Stone Age families, Fred and Wilma Flintstone, and neighbors Barney and Betty Rubble. In 1994 *The Flintstones* movie was released, starring John Goodman, Rick Moranis and Rosie O'Donnell.

GUADALUPE MOUNTAINS NATIONAL PARK ESTABLISHED: ANNIVERSARY. Sept 30, 1972. Area in western Texas along Texas–New Mexico border, originally authorized Oct 15, 1966, was established as a national park. For further park info: Guadalupe Mountains Natl Park, HC 60, Box 400, Salt Flat, TX 79847-9400.

GUTENBERG BIBLE PUBLISHED: ANNIVERSARY. Sept 30, 1452. The first section of the Gutenberg Bible, the first book printed from movable type, was published at Mainz, Germany. Johann Gutenberg was the printer. The book was completed by 1456.

HALEAKALA NATIONAL PARK ESTABLISHED: ANNIVERSARY. Sept 30, 1960. Summit of a volcano on Maui in the Hawaiian Islands was authorized as a part of Hawaii National Park on Aug 1, 1916. In 1960 Haleakala was established as a separate national park. The park was expanded in 1969 to include the Kipahulu Valley. For further park info: Haleakala Natl Park, PO Box 369, Makawao, HI 96768.

MEREDITH ENROLLS AT OLE MISS: ANNIVERSARY. Sept 30, 1962. Rioting broke out when James Meredith became the first black to enroll in the all-white University of Mississippi. President Kennedy sent US troops to the area to force compliance with the law. Three people died in the fighting and 50 were injured. On June 6, 1966, Meredith was shot while participating in a civil rights march at Mississippi. On June 25 Meredith, barely recovered, rejoined the marchers near Jackson, MS.

"MURDER, SHE WROTE" TV PREMIERE: 20th ANNIVERSARY. Sept 30, 1984. Angela Lansbury starred as crime novelist Jessica Fletcher from Cabot Cove, Maine, who traveled the country solving murders. This top-rated detective show also featured Tom Bosley as Sheriff Amos Tupper and William Windom as Dr. Seth Hazlett. The program aired for 12 years and is still in syndication.

OKLAHOMA INTERNATIONAL BLUEGRASS FESTIVAL. Sept 30–Oct 2. Guthrie, OK. Festival featuring top international bluegrass bands and musicians, children's activities, music workshops, RV camping, antique shopping, food booths and a Celebrity Golf Tournament on Sunday. Est attendance: 45,000. For info: Oklahoma Intl Bluegrass Festival, PO Box 1585, Guthrie, OK 73044. Phone: (800) 299-1889 or (405) 282-4446. Fax: (405) 282-0061.

☆ Chase's 2003 Calendar of Events ☆   Sept 30

ORPHAN TRAIN HERITAGE SOCIETY OF AMERICA: ANNUAL REUNION. Sept 30–Oct 2. Concordia, KS. Between 1854 and 1929, more than 150,000 homeless children and poor families were transported out of New York City, Boston and Chicago aboard trains accompanied by "agents" for the New York Children's Aid Society who arranged for midwestern families to take the children under a contract agreement. Infants placed by the New York Foundling Hospital were indentured. Annual reunion, plus regional reunions in Oklahoma, Missouri, Kansas, Texas, Iowa, Illinois, Indiana, California, Louisiana, Nebraska and Minnesota bring together survivors of the Orphan Trains era, their descendants and interested persons. All gatherings are open to the public, with a small registration fee charged at each. Books containing stories of the Orphan Train Riders are available at each reunion. Est attendance: 250. For info: OTHSA, Inc. E-mail: othsa@msn.com. Web: www.orphantrainriders.com.

PRESTON COUNTY BUCKWHEAT FESTIVAL. Sept 30–Oct 3. Kingwood, WV. Celebrating the fall harvest, with coronations, parades, exhibits, arts and crafts, antique cars, livestock, carnival, country music and Buckwheat Cake Dinners. Annually, beginning the last Thursday in September. Est attendance: 100,000. For info: Lucille H. Crogan, Fest Secy, Kingwood Volunteer Fire Dept, PO Box 74, Kingwood, WV 26537. Phone: (304) 329-0021. Fax: (304) 329-0021. Web: www.buckwheatfest.com.

"THE RED SKELTON SHOW" TV PREMIERE: ANNIVERSARY. Sept 30, 1951. Vaudevillian and radio performer Red Skelton hosted several popular variety shows on NBC and CBS in a career that spanned 20 years. He was a gifted comedian, famous for his loony characters, sight gags, pantomimes and ad-libs. His show was also notable for introducing Johnny Carson and the Rolling Stones to a national audience.

SUKKOT, SUCCOTH or FEAST OF TABERNACLES, FIRST DAY. Sept 30. Hebrew calendar date: Tishri 15, 5765 begins nine-day festival in commemoration of Jewish people's 40 years of wandering in the desert and thanksgiving for the fall harvest. This high holiday season closes with Shemini Atzeret (see entry on Oct 7) and Simchat Torah (see entry on Oct 8). Began at sundown Sept 29.

BIRTHDAYS TODAY

Deborah Allen, 51, singer ("Baby I Lied"), songwriter ("Don't Worry 'Bout Me"), born Memphis, TN, Sept 30, 1953.
Crystal Bernard, 40, actress ("Wings"), born Garland, TX, Sept 30, 1964.
Angie Dickinson, 73, actress (Emmy for "Police Woman"; *Dressed to Kill*), born Angeline Brown, Kulm, ND, Sept 30, 1931.
Fran Drescher, 47, actress ("The Nanny," *Jack*), born Flushing, NY, Sept 30, 1957.
Jenna Elfman, 33, actress ("Dharma & Greg," "Townies"), born Los Angeles, CA, Sept 30, 1971.
Martina Hingis, 24, tennis player, born Kosice, Slovakia, Sept 30, 1980.
Deborah Kerr, 83, actress (*From Here to Eternity, The King and I*), born Helensburgh, Scotland, Sept 30, 1921.
Blanche Lambert Lincoln, 44, US Senator (D, Arkansas), born Helena, MT, Sept 30, 1960.
Johnny Mathis, 69, singer ("It's Not for Me to Say," "Chances Are"), born Gilmer, TX, Sept 30, 1935.
Marilyn McCoo, 61, singer (Fifth Dimension, "Up, Up and Away"), actress, born Jersey City, NJ, Sept 30, 1943.
Dominique Moceanu, 23, gymnast, born Hollywood, CA, Sept 30, 1981.
Eric Stoltz, 43, actor (*Fast Times at Ridgemont High, Pulp Fiction*), born Los Angeles, CA, Sept 30, 1961.
Victoria Tennant, 51, actress ("Winds of War," *All of Me, LA Story*), born London, England, Sept 30, 1953.
Elie Wiesel, 76, author, human rights activist, Nobel Peace Prize recipient, founder of the Elie Wiesel Foundation for Humanity, born Sighet, Romania, Sept 30, 1928.

Oct 1   ☆ *Chase's 2004 Calendar of Events* ☆

October.

OCTOBER 1 — FRIDAY
Day 275 — 91 Remaining

ADOPT-A-SHELTER-DOG MONTH. Oct 1–31. To promote the adoption of dogs from local shelters, the ASPCA sponsors this important observance. "Make pet adoption your first option®" is a message the organization promotes throughout the year in an effort to end the euthanasia of all adoptable animals. For info: ASPCA Media Relations Dept, 424 E 92nd St, New York, NY 10128. Phone: (212) 876-7700 x 4655. E-mail: press @aspca.org. Web: www.aspca.org.

ANIMALSALOUD! MONTH. Oct 1–31. Teachers of students at the K–3 reading level are encouraged to spend at least 20 minutes during every school day in October reading aloud an animal-friendly book to their class. Each teacher who does this and verifies their participation by sending in a contest entry form is eligible to win free books with humane themes for their students. For info: Doris Day Animal Foundation, AnimalsAloud!, 227 Massachusetts Ave NE, Ste 100, Washington, DC 20002. Phone: (202) 546-1761. Fax: (202) 546-2193. E-mail: info@ddaf.org. Web: www.ddaf.org/aloud.html.

BABE RUTH CALLS HIS SHOT?: ANNIVERSARY. Oct 1, 1932. In the fifth inning of game three of the World Series, with a count of two balls and two strikes and with hostile Cubs fans shouting epithets at him, Babe Ruth pointed to the center field bleachers in Chicago's Wrigley Field and followed up by hitting a soaring home run high above the very spot to which he had just gestured. With that homer Ruth squashed the Chicago Cubs' hopes of winning the game, and the Yankees went on to sweep the Series with four straight victories. For more than half a century the question has remained: Did Ruth actually call his shot that day? Even eyewitnesses disagree. Joe Williams of *The New York Times* wrote, "In no mistaken motions, the Babe notified the crowd that the nature of his retaliation would be a wallop right out of the confines of the park." But Cubs pitcher Charlie Root said, "Ruth did *not* point at the fence before he swung. If he'd made a gesture like that, I'd have put one in his ear and knocked him on his ass." Ruth's daughter has said that he denied it. But the Babe himself also claimed he had. Fact or folklore? Either way, legend!

	S	M	T	W	T	F	S
October						1	2
	3	4	5	6	7	8	9
	10	11	12	13	14	15	16
2004	17	18	19	20	21	22	23
	24	25	26	27	28	29	30
	31						

BILLIARD AWARENESS MONTH. Oct 1–31. Sponsored by the Billiard Congress of America, a national nonprofit organization, Billiard Awareness Month celebrates the historic, recreational and educational aspects of cue sports. Cue sports are recognized as part of amateur and professional competitive sports, but more importantly promote camaraderie among participants of all ages and abilities. Throughout this month, BCA will highlight the skills learned at billiards: hand-eye coordination, physics, sportsmanship, strategy, discipline, concentration and goal-setting. For info: Amy Long, Billiard Congress of America, 4345 Beverly St, Colorado Springs, CO 80918. Phone: (719) 264-8300. Fax: (719) 264-0900. E-mail: amy-long@bca-pool.com. Web: www.bca-pool.com.

BLOODY BREWERY IN 3-D. Oct 1–3 (also Oct 7–10, 14–17, 21–24 and 28–31). Columbus, OH. A 3-D haunted house in Columbus's historic brewery district. Artwork and actors literally "pop out" as visitors tour the region's largest 3-D indoor haunted house with special glasses. Completely wheelchair accessible. All proceeds go to Easter Seals of Central and Southeastern Ohio. For info: Bloody Brewery, 477 S Front St, Columbus, OH 43213. Phone: (614) 235-5555. Fax: (614) 236-3236. E-mail: info@bloody brewery.com. Web: www.bloodybrewery.com.

BRAZIL: FESTIVAL OF PENHA. Oct 1–31. Rio de Janeiro. Pilgrimages, especially on Saturdays during October, to the Church of Our Lady of Penha, which is built on top of a rock, requiring a climb of 365 steps (representing the days of the year), or ride in car on inclined plane (for children, invalids and aged), for those troubled and sick who seek hope or cure.

CANADA: HERITAGE DAYS—"THE FAIRE AT THE FORKS." Oct 1–3. Chatham, ON. A family-oriented, historical "faire" and reenactment of the Battle of the Thames where the great native leader Tecumseh was killed during the War of 1812. Est attendance: 10,000. For info: Jim Gilbert, Chair of the Faire, 508 King St W, Chatham, ON, Canada N7M 1G9. Phone: (519) 351-2058. Fax: (519) 351-5059. E-mail: jgilbert@ciaccess.com.

CARTER, JIMMY: 80th BIRTHDAY. Oct 1, 1924. 39th president of US (1977–81), Nobel Peace Prize recipient, born James Earl Carter, Jr, at Plains, GA.

CD PLAYER DEBUTS: ANNIVERSARY. Oct 1, 1982. The first compact disc player, developed jointly by Sony, Philips and Polygram, went on sale. It cost $625.

CELEBRATE SUN DRIED TOMATOES MONTH. Oct 1–31. Celebrate all that's great about sun dried tomatoes—it's more than taste! Before modern canning methods were available, Italians dried tomatoes on their tile roofs for use in winter when fresh tomatoes were not available. These nutrient-dense tomatoes contain lycopene, a phytochemical and antioxidant that fights free radicals in the body and can help reduce the risk factors for many types of cancer and heart disease. To obtain recipes and health info: Mooney Farms, 1220 Fortress St, Chico, CA 95973. Phone: (530) 899-2661. Fax: (530) 899-7746. Web: www.mooney farms.com.

CELIAC SPRUE AWARENESS MONTH. Oct 1–31. For info: Celiac Sprue Assn/USA, PO Box 31700, Omaha, NE 68131-0700. Phone: (402) 558-0600 or toll-free (877) CSA-4CSA. Fax: (402) 558-1347. E-mail: celiacs@csaceliacs.org. Web: www.csa celiacs.org.

CHESAPEAKE WILDFOWL EXPO. Oct 1–3. Ward Museum of Wildfowl Art, Salisbury, MD. Annual Chesapeake Challenge Shootin' Stool competition. Frank & Frank Decoy Aviation. Buy/sell/trade, exhibit opening and reception, plus the finest collection of contemporary and antique wildfowl sculpture in the world. Est attendance: 1,000. For info: Kevan Wroten, Ward Museum of Wildfowl Art, 909 S Schumaker Dr, Salisbury, MD 21804. Phone: (410) 742-4988 x 106. Fax: (410) 742-3107. E-mail: ward@ward museum.org. Web: www.wardmuseum.org.

CHILDREN'S MAGAZINE MONTH. Oct 1–31. Nationwide literacy initiative to raise awareness and create interest in chil-

508

☆ Chase's 2004 Calendar of Events ☆   Oct 1

dren's magazines. For info: Assn of Educational Publishers, 510 Heron Dr, Ste 309, Logan Township, NJ 08085. Web: www.childmagmonth.org.

CHINA, PEOPLE'S REPUBLIC OF: NATIONAL DAY: 55th ANNIVERSARY. Oct 1. Commemorates the founding of the People's Republic of China in 1949.

COHOCTON FALL FOLIAGE FESTIVAL. Oct 1–3. Cohocton, NY. 37th annual. World-famous tree-sitting contest. Parade, more than 100 food, antiques, arts and crafts booths. Est attendance: 50,000. For info: Bill Berry, 6950 Lain Rd, Hornell, NY 14843-9419.

COMPUTER LEARNING MONTH. Oct 1–31. A monthlong focus of events and activities for learning new uses of computers and software, sharing ideas and helping others gain the benefits of computers and software. Numerous national contests are held to recognize students, educators and parents for their innovative ideas; computers and software are awarded to winning entries. Annually, the month of October. For info: Computer Learning Foundation, Dept CHS, 440 Hawkcrest Circle, Sacramento, CA 95385. Phone: (408) 720-8898. Fax: (408) 730-1191. E-mail: clf@computerlearning.org. Web: www.computerlearning.org.

CO-OP AWARENESS MONTH. Oct 1–31. Co-op Awareness Month was created to remind retailers of their co-op advertising funds in time for them to research and spend these remaining funds by the end of the calendar year. For info: Christine Hunt, Sales Development Services, Inc, 445 Hutchinson Ave, Ste 800, Columbus, OH 43235. Phone: (800) 4-ADMALL. Fax: (740) 548-0397. E-mail: info@admall.com. Web: www.admall.com.

CRAFTSMEN'S CLASSIC ARTS & CRAFTS FESTIVAL. Oct 1–3 (tentative). Roanoke Civic Center, Roanoke, VA. Features work from more than 250 talented artists and craftspeople. All juried exhibitors work has been handmade by the exhibitors and must be their own original design and creation. See the creative process in action with several exhibitors demonstrating their craft. Something for every style, taste and budget with items from the most contemporary to the most traditional. Est attendance: 20,000. For info: Gilmore Enterprises, 1240 Oakland Ave, Greensboro, NC 27403. Phone: (336) 274-5550. Web: gilmoreshows@triad.rr.com.

CYPRUS: INDEPENDENCE DAY. Oct 1. National holiday. Commemorates independence from Britain in 1960.

DALTON DEFENDERS DAY. Oct 1–2. Coffeyville, KS. Event to honor citizens killed during Dalton Gang's robbery of two banks on Oct 5, 1892. Est attendance: 5,000. For info: Coffeyville Area Chamber of Commerce, PO Box 457, Coffeyville, KS 67337. Phone: (620) 251-2550 or (800) 626-3357. Fax: (620) 251-5448. E-mail: chamber@coffeyville.com.

DISNEY WORLD OPENED: ANNIVERSARY. Oct 1, 1971. Disney's second theme park opened at Orlando, FL. See also "Disneyland Opened: Anniversary" (July 17).

DIVERSITY AWARENESS MONTH. Oct 1–31. Celebrating, promoting and appreciating the diversity of our society. Also, a month to foster and further our understanding of the inherent value of all races, genders, nationalities, age groups, religions, sexual orientations, classes and physical disabilities. Annually, in October. For info: Carole Copeland Thomas, C. Thomas & Assoc, 400 W Cummings Park, Ste 1725-154, Woburn, MA 01801. Phone: (800) 801-6599 or (508) 947-5755. Fax: (508) 947-3903. E-mail: Carole@TellCarole.com. Web: www.TellCarole.com.

EAT BETTER, EAT TOGETHER MONTH. Oct 1–31. Time to encourage families to eat together. Research indicates that children who eat with their families not only have better nutrition, but they do better in school and have fewer behavior problems. A tool kit has been created to show how family meals can be simple, easy and nutritious. Call for the top ten ways to eat better, eat together. For info: Sue Butkus, Nutrition Education Network of Washington State, Cooperative Extension, Washington State University, 7612 Pioneer Way E, Puyallup, WA 98317-4989. Phone: (253) 445-4553. Web: www.nutrition.wsu.edu.

EMOTIONAL WELLNESS MONTH. Oct 1–31. Get more out of every day with laughter and enjoyment. This is a time to reduce stress and seek moderation in mood swings. Balance your activities to support your emotional state, and keep your positive attitude in check. Take an anger management course to learn how to control explosive tempers. Seek the help of a therapist. Distance yourself from drama and chaos. Create a humor file with clipped columns and cartoons, and watch comedy on TV and film. Lighten up and learn to laugh at yourself. For info: Angela Brown, Words of Wellness, PO Box 49266, Charlotte, NC 28277. Phone: (704) 849-2900. Fax: (661) 215-9683. E-mail: angela@wordsofwellness.com. Web: www.wordsofwellness.com.

ENERGY MANAGEMENT IS A FAMILY AFFAIR—IMPROVE YOUR HOME. Oct 1–Mar 31, 2005. Replace energy-consuming units with new efficient home conveniences and remodel to prevent heating and cooling loss. Editorial package includes approximately 100 camera-ready stories and photos free to editors. Also available on disk. For info: James A. Stewart, Jr, Home Improvement Time Inc, PO Box 247, Oakdale, PA 15071-0247. Phone: (412) 787-2881. Fax: (412) 787-3233. E-mail: hitdirect@aol.com. Web: homeimprovementtime.com.

FALL ON NANTUCKET. Oct 1–Nov 30. Nantucket Island, MA. Includes the Nantucket Arts Festival, Chowder Contest, Octoberfest, Harvest Fair and more. Est attendance: 2,000. For info: Nantucket Island Chamber of Commerce, 48 Main St, Nantucket, MA 02554-3595. Phone: (508) 228-1700. Web: www.nantucketchamber.org.

FIREPUP'S® BIRTHDAY. Oct 1. Firepup spends his time teaching fire and burn prevention and life safety awareness to children and their parents in a fun-filled and nonthreatening manner. Materials are available through local fire departments. For info: Natl Fire Safety Council, Inc, PO Box 378, Michigan Center, MI 49254-0378. Phone: (517) 764-2811.

GAY AND LESBIAN HISTORY MONTH. Oct 1–31. October was selected to commemorate the first two lesbian and gay marches on Washington in October 1979 and 1987.

GERMAN-AMERICAN HERITAGE MONTH. Oct 1–31. A month celebrating America's German heritage. Numerous historical programs, museum and library exhibits, cultural events, genealogical workshops and more planned. For info: Dr. Don Heinrich Tolzmann, Dir, German-American Studies Program, 806 Blegen Library, Univ of Cincinnati, PO Box 210113, Cincinnati, OH 45221-0113. Phone: (513) 556-1955. Fax: (513) 556-2113. E-mail: don.tolzmann@uc.edu.

GO HOG WILD—EAT COUNTRY HAM MONTH. Oct 1–31. Suuu-eee! It's not just a word, it is a state of mind. For more than 200 years, Americans have been curing and eating country ham. The custom of curing that began in the state of Virginia during the mid-1700s continues today from Georgia to Missouri and points in between. Discover the difference between "city ham" and "country ham" and get some great recipes to boot during Eat Country Ham Month. For info: Natl Country Ham Assn, PO Box 948, Conover, NC 28613. Phone: (800) 820-4HAM. E-mail: eatham@countryham.org. Web: www.countryham.org.

GO NUTS OVER TEXAS PEANUTS MONTH. Oct 1–31. Everything's big in Texas, including the pride in its peanut industry! Texas is the nation's second largest peanut-producing state

Oct 1 — Chase's 2004 Calendar of Events

and is one of only two states that grow all four US peanut varieties: Runner, Spanish, Virginia and Valencia. "Go Nuts Over Texas Peanuts Month" celebrates America's favorite nut. For info: Julie Scott, Texas Peanut Producers Board. Phone: (877) 748-9693. Web: www.texaspeanutboard.com.

HALLOWEEN SAFETY MONTH. Oct 1–31. There are steps you can take to make it a safe Halloween for children and teens. Information about the dangers of cosmetic contact lenses will be included, as the use of these lenses increases at this time of the year. For info: Prevent Blindness America®, 500 E Remington Rd, Schaumburg, IL 60173. Phone: (800) 331-2020. Fax: (847) 843-8458. Web: www.prevent-blindness.org.

HARRIS, RICHARD: BIRTH ANNIVERSARY. Oct 1, 1930. Born at Limerick, Ireland, Richard Harris became known as a stage actor on the London theater scene in the 1950s. Although his first love was the stage, it was in films that he earned his highest degree of success. He was unforgettable as King Arthur in the film version of *Camelot* (1967) and was twice nominated for best actor Oscars: for 1963's *This Sporting Life* and 1991's *The Field*. He portrayed headmaster Albus Dumbledore in the first two Harry Potter films in 2001 and 2002. He died Oct 25, 2002, at London, England.

HARRISON, CAROLINE LAVINIA SCOTT: BIRTH ANNIVERSARY. Oct 1, 1832. First wife of Benjamin Harrison, 23rd president of the US, born at Oxford, OH. Died at Washington, DC, Oct 25, 1892. She was the second First Lady to die in the White House.

HEALTH LITERACY MONTH. Oct 1–31. Promoting understandable health information around the world. For info: Health Literacy Consulting, 31 Highland St, Ste 201, Natick, MA 01760. Phone: (508) 653-1199. Fax: (508) 650-9492. E-mail: Helen @healthliteracy.com. Web: www.healthliteracymonth.com.

HISPANIC HERITAGE FESTIVAL. Oct 1–31. Dade County, Miami, FL. A series of special, cultural, educational and sporting events to celebrate and enhance Hispanic culture and traditions. Est attendance: 350,000. For info: Eduardo Mendoza, Hispanic Heritage Council, Inc, 5040 NW 7 St, Ste 690, Miami, FL 33126. Phone: (305) 461-1014. Fax: (305) 461-1015. Web: www.hispanic festival.com.

HISTORY ALIVE! Oct 1–3 (tentative). Norfolk Botanical Garden, Norfolk, VA. Features historical groups from various periods, with reenactors participating in field maneuvers and constructing encampments and featuring display areas with equipment, clothing, food and bedding authentic to the era they represent. Interpreters at each site explain the life and times of the characters, providing an accurate and exciting chronicle of our past. Est attendance: 2,000. For info: Norfolk Botanical Garden, 6700 Azalea Garden Rd, Norfolk, VA 23518. Phone: (757) 441-5838. Fax: (757) 853-8294. Web: www.norfolkbotanicalgarden.org.

HOROWITZ, VLADIMIR: 100th BIRTH ANNIVERSARY. Oct 1, 1904. Virtuoso pianist, born at Berdichev, Russia. Horowitz was widely hailed as one of the world's greatest pianists, renowned for his masterful technique. His debut was at Kiev in 1920, and at the age of 20 he played a series of 23 recitals at Leningrad, performing a total of more than 200 works with no duplications. He made his US debut in 1928 with the New York Philharmonic. He settled in the US in 1940 and became a citizen in 1944. His career swung full circle Apr 20, 1986, when he performed his first concert in his native Russia after a self-imposed absence of 60 years. He died Nov 5, 1989, at New York, NY.

October 2004	S	M	T	W	T	F	S
						1	2
	3	4	5	6	7	8	9
	10	11	12	13	14	15	16
	17	18	19	20	21	22	23
	24	25	26	27	28	29	30
	31						

INTERNATIONAL STARMAN MONTH. Oct 1–31. Celebrates the TV series "Starman," which first aired in 1986 and inspired many people around the world to change their lives in positive ways. Spotlight Starman International is a group of people who appreciate the quality, consciousness and themes of the show and continue to gather annually to celebrate that spirit while raising funds for environmental, social and/or educational causes. (The organization is open to all without membership dues.) See also "Starman Family-Con 2004" (Apr 23). For info: Vicki Werkley, Spotlight Starman Intl, 16563 Ellen Springs Dr, Lower Lake, CA 95457-9477. Phone: (707) 995-1228. E-mail: spotlight_starman@bigfoot.com. Web: www.starmanet.com.

INTERNATIONAL STRATEGIC PLANNING MONTH. Oct 1–31. The start of the final quarter of the year provides a great opportunity for businesses and individuals to review the results of their efforts to date, make adjustments to meet this year's goals and begin thinking about next year's goals. Strategic planning is a systematic and continuous process of evaluation, decision, implementation and measuring. For info: Sherrin Ross Ingram, Intl Center for Strategic Planning, 104 W Chestnut St, #101, Hinsdale, IL 60521. Phone: (800) 962-4750. Fax: (800) 962-0177. E-mail: info@icfsp.com. Web: www.icfsp.com.

JAPAN: NEWSPAPER WEEK. Oct 1–7. During this week newspapers make an extensive effort to acquaint the public with their functions and attempt to carry out the role of a newspaper in a free society. Annually, the first week in October.

KENTUCKY APPLE FESTIVAL. Oct 1–2. Paintsville, KY. Apple blossom beauty pageants, country music show, arts and crafts, flea market, antique car show, Corvette show, Apple Bowl, Terrapin Trot, amusement rides, food booths, clogging and square dancing. Annually, the first Friday and Saturday in October. Est attendance: 75,000. For info: Kentucky Apple Festival, Inc, Ray Tosti, Chmn, PO Box 1245, Paintsville, KY 41240-5245. Phone: (606) 789-4355 or (800) 542-5790.

"KUNG FU" TV PREMIERE: ANNIVERSARY. Oct 1, 1972. David Carradine starred in this unusual ABC western as Kwai Chang Caine, a half-Chinese martial arts master drifter who was exiled from China. Appearing in flashback were: Keye Luke as Master Po, Philip Ahn as Master Kan and Radames Pera as the younger Caine. The show ran for three years. "Kung Fu" returned as a 1986 TV movie introducing the late Brandon Lee as Caine's son. A sequel series currently appears in syndication starring a much older Carradine.

LAWRENCE, JAMES: BIRTH ANNIVERSARY. Oct 1, 1781. Brilliant American naval officer, whose last battle was a defeat, but whose dying words became a most honored naval motto. Lawrence, born at Burlington, NJ, was captain of the *Chesapeake* when she engaged in a naval duel with HMS *Shannon* off Boston, June 1, 1813. The *Chesapeake* was captured and towed to Halifax as a British prize. Lawrence was mortally wounded by a musket ball during the engagement and uttered his famous last words, "Don't give up the ship," as he was being carried off the ship's deck.

☆ Chase's 2004 Calendar of Events ☆   Oct 1

LISTEN TO YOUR INNER CRITIC MONTH. Oct 1–31. Turn that nagging voice into your personal success coach. This month is set aside to explore and learn ways to overcome the negativity of self-criticism. Self-criticism affects everything—from your feelings of confidence as a parent, to your sense of competence as an employee or boss to your feelings about yourself as a lover. But when the negativity of your "self-critical voice" is neutralized, your inner critic can become a strong, responsive resource that supports personal and professional development. For a free "how-to" handout, send a SASE. For info: TransformationWorks Center, 5909 W Loop South, Ste 620, Bellaire, TX 77401. Phone: (713) 667-6047. Fax: (713) 667-1745. E-mail: Transworks@aol.com. Web: www.TransformationWorks.com.

LITERALLY, A HAUNTED HOUSE. Oct 1–2 (also Oct 8–9, 15–16, 22–23, 29–30). New Albany, IN. Friends of Culbertson Mansion fund-raiser. Est attendance: 7,500. For info: Culbertson Mansion, 914 E Main, New Albany, IN 47150. Phone: (812) 944-9600. Web: www.indianamuseum.org.

LONG GROVE APPLE FEST. Oct 1–3. Long Grove, IL. Bushels of fun and apple-inspired treats everywhere await visitors to this country village of nearly 100 specialty shops. Outdoor food booths, free music and entertainment and special events. Admission and parking free. 10 AM–6 PM. Est attendance: 45,000. For info: Long Grove Merchants Assoc, Rtes 53 & 83, Long Grove, IL 60047. Phone: (847) 634-0888. Web: www.longgroveonline.com.

LUPUS AWARENESS CAMPAIGN. Oct 1–Nov 15. To promote public awareness of lupus symptoms to aid in early diagnosis and treatment of this disease. For info: Duane Peters, VP of Communications & Advocacy, Lupus Foundation of America, 2000 L St NW, Ste 710, Washington, DC 20036. Phone: (202) 349-1145. Fax: (202) 349-1156. E-mail: peters@lupus.org. Web: www.lupus.org.

MARIS BREAKS HOME RUN RECORD: ANNIVERSARY. Oct 1, 1961. Roger Maris of the New York Yankees hit his 61st home run, breaking Babe Ruth's record for the most home runs in a season. Maris hit his homer against pitcher Tracy Stallard of the Boston Red Sox as the Yankees won, 1–0. Controversy over the record arose because the American League had adopted a 162-game schedule in 1961, and Maris played in 161 games. In 1927, when Ruth set his record, the schedule called for 154 games, and Ruth played in 151. On Sept 8, 1998, Mark McGwire of the St. Louis Cardinals hit his 62nd home run, breaking Maris's record. On Oct 5, 2001, Barry Bonds of the San Francisco Giants broke McGwire's record

MATTHAU, WALTER: BIRTH ANNIVERSARY. Oct 1, 1920. Actor (*The Odd Couple, Grumpy Old Men*), born at New York, NY. Died July 1, 2000, at Santa Monica, CA.

"THE MERV GRIFFIN SHOW" TV PREMIERE: ANNIVERSARY. Oct 1, 1962. Singer and game show king Merv Griffin's first effort as an afternoon talk-show host premiered on NBC but was later dropped for syndication. The afternoon show continued until 1969 when Griffin was tapped to host a late-night program on CBS to compete with "The Tonight Show with Johnny Carson."

MODEL T INTRODUCED: ANNIVERSARY. Oct 1, 1908. Ford introduced the Model T at a price of $850 but by 1924 the basic model sold for as little as $260. Between 1908 and 1927 Ford sold 15,007,033 Model Ts in the US. Although the first Model Ts were not built on an assembly line, the demand for the cars was so high that Ford developed a system where workers remained at their stations and cars came to them. This enabled Ford to turn out a Model T every 10 seconds.

NATIONAL ANIMAL SAFETY AND PROTECTION MONTH. Oct 1–31. Observance to promote the appropriate ways to protect and care for domestic and wild animals and help people strengthen skills for staying safe around animals. For info: PALS Foundation, PO Box 1271, San Luis Obispo, CA 93406. Phone: (805) 544-0984. Web: www.PALS.mailme.org.

NATIONAL BREAST CANCER AWARENESS MONTH. Oct 1–31. Entering its second decade of public and professional education and awareness. This month is promoted by 19 major national nonprofit cancer organizations to ensure that the media and communities everywhere focus a spotlight on the problem of breast cancer. For info: call the Natl Breast Cancer Awareness Month Program toll-free at (877) 88-NBCAM. Web: www.nbcam.org.

★**NATIONAL BREAST CANCER AWARENESS MONTH.** Oct 1–31.

NATIONAL CHILI MONTH. Oct 1–31. National observance and celebration of chili, one of the most historical and traditional American dishes. For info: Williams Foods, Inc, 13301 W 99th St, Lenexa, KS 66215. Phone: (913) 888-4343. Fax: (913) 888-0727.

NATIONAL COMMUNICATE WITH YOUR KID MONTH. Oct 1–31. The generation gap—parents and teens are often on different wavelengths and complain that they cannot talk to each other. The purpose of this observance is to open the doors to better communication between parents and teens and to build positive teen/parent relationships. Annually, the month of October. For info send SASE to: Teresa Langston, Dir, Parenting Without Pressure, 1330 Boyer St, Longwood, FL 32750-6311. Phone: (407) 767-2524. Web: www.parentingwithoutpressure.com.

NATIONAL CONSTRUCTION TOY MONTH. Oct 1–31. A monthlong celebration of the creativity and educational value children gain from building with construction toys. For info: Knex Industries, Inc, 2990 Bergey Rd, Hatfield, PA 19440. Phone: (215) 997-7722. Fax: (215) 996-4222. E-mail: email@knex.com. Web: www.knex.com.

NATIONAL COOKIE MONTH. Oct 1–31. Remember the aroma and tradition of fresh-baked cookies? Remember how the delicious scent filled the house? Celebrate the All-American favorite treat, the cookie, during National Cookie Month. Make, bake or buy a batch of fresh homemade cookies in any of your favorite flavors this month. Share a little love today—share a fresh-baked cookie! For info: Cookies For You, 117 S Main, Minot, ND 58701. Phone: (701) 839-4975 or (800) 814-5334. Web: www.cookiesforyou.com.

NATIONAL CRIME PREVENTION MONTH. Oct 1–31. During Crime Prevention Month, individuals can commit to working on at least one of three levels—family, neighborhood or community—to drive violence and drugs from our world. It is also a time to honor individuals who have accepted personal responsibility for their neighborhoods and groups who work for the community's common good. Annually, every October. For info: Natl Crime Prevention Council. 1000 Connecticut Ave NW, 13th Fl, Washington, DC 20036. Phone: (202) 466-6272. Fax: (202) 296-1356. Web: www.weprevent.org or www.ncpc.org.

NATIONAL DENTAL HYGIENE MONTH. Oct 1–31. To increase public awareness of the importance of preventive oral health care and the dental hygienist's role as the preventive professional. Annually, during the month of October. For info: Public Relations, American Dental Hygienists' Assn, 444 N Michigan Ave, Ste 3400, Chicago, IL 60611. Phone: (312) 440-8900. Web: www.adha.org.

Oct 1 ☆ Chase's 2004 Calendar of Events ☆

NATIONAL DEPRESSION EDUCATION AND AWARENESS MONTH. Oct 1–31. A nonprofit campaign to educate patients, the elderly and professionals about depression disorders. Kit of materials available for $15. Annually, the month of October. For info: PPSI, c/o Pharmacy Council on Depression Education, 101 Lucas Valley Rd, #210, San Rafael, CA 94903. Phone: (415) 479-8628. Fax: (415) 479-8608. E-mail: ppsi@aol.com. Web: www.ppsinc.org.

★**NATIONAL DISABILITY EMPLOYMENT AWARENESS MONTH.** Oct 1–31. Presidential Proclamation issued for the month of October (PL100–630, Title III, Sec 301a of Nov 7, 1988). Previously issued as "National Employ the Handicapped Week" for a week beginning during the first week in October since 1945.

NATIONAL DISABILITY EMPLOYMENT AWARENESS MONTH. Oct 1–31. To foster the full integration of people with disabilities into the workforce. For info: US Dept of Labor, Office of Disability Employment Policy, 200 Constitution Ave NW, Rm S1303, Washington, DC 20210-0002. Phone: (202) 693-7880. Fax: (202) 693-7888. E-mail: infoODEP@dol.gov. Web: www.dol.gov/odep.

NATIONAL DIVORCED PARENTS FOR CHILDREN WEEK. Oct 1–7. All divorced parents with children show a gesture of honor and respect to the other parent for the benefit and sake of the children. For info: Barbara Rose, 13401-9 Summerlin Rd, #191, Fort Myers, FL 33919. Phone: (239) 357-5092. E-mail: barbara@borntoinspire.com. Web: www.borntoinspire.com.

★**NATIONAL DOMESTIC VIOLENCE AWARENESS MONTH.** Oct 1–31.

NATIONAL DOWN SYNDROME MONTH. Oct 1–31. To promote better understanding of Down Syndrome. For info: Natl Down Syndrome Congress, 1370 Center Dr, Ste 102, Atlanta, GA 30338. Phone: (800) 232-NDSC. E-mail: info@ndsccenter.org. Web: www.ndsccenter.org.

NATIONAL FAMILY SEXUALITY EDUCATION MONTH. Oct 1–31. A national coalition effort to support parents as the first and primary sexuality educators of their children by providing information for parents and young people. For info: Planned Parenthood Federation of America, Education Dept, 434 W 33 St, New York, NY 10001. Phone: (212) 261-4628. Fax: (212) 247-6269. E-mail: education@ppfa.org. Web: www.plannedparenthood.org.

NATIONAL "GAIN THE INSIDE ADVANTAGE" MONTH. Oct 1–31. Gaining "The Inside Advantage" is how ordinary people accomplish extraordinary things. It refers to taking control of your life from the inside out. It means learning how to live deeply, joyfully and successfully. For info: Cathy W. Lauro. Phone: (800) 215-3644. E-mail: mind@CWLauro.com. Web: www.CWLauro.com.

NATIONAL GO ON A FIELD TRIP MONTH. Oct 1–31. A month to highlight the importance of the field trip as a way to help children learn. Studies show that children learn 40–60% more outside the classroom, and the field trip is a great way to teach valuable life skills and career education. For info: Field Trip Factory, 1735 N Paulina, #413, Chicago, IL 60622. Phone: (773) 342-9510. Web: www.fieldtripfactory.com.

NATIONAL HOME INSPECTION MONTH. Oct 1–31. Raise awareness of the need for, and benefits of, a professional home inspection. For info: Brad Meyer, LandSafe Home Inspection Services, 6400 Legacy Drive, PTX-83, Plano, TX 75024.

	S	M	T	W	T	F	S
October 2004						1	2
	3	4	5	6	7	8	9
	10	11	12	13	14	15	16
	17	18	19	20	21	22	23
	24	25	26	27	28	29	30
	31						

Phone: (800) 577-6967. Fax: (972) 608-2177. E-mail: landsafe_public_relations@landsafe.com. Web: www.landsafe.com.

NATIONAL LIVER AWARENESS MONTH. Oct 1–31. To increase understanding of the importance of liver functions, to promote healthful practices and to encourage research into the causes and cures of liver disease. Annually, the month of October. For info: Public Relations Dept, American Liver Fdtn, 75 Maiden Lane, Ste 603, New York, NY 10038. Phone: (800) GO LIVER. Fax: (212) 483-8179. E-mail: info@liverfoundation.org. Web: www.liverfoundation.org.

NATIONAL LONG TERM CARE PLANNING WEEK. Oct 1–7. As lifespans increase and family structures change, this week promotes awareness and discussion of how to meet the challenge of providing compassionate long term care. Raising awareness of the importance of long term care planning in everyone's retirement plan. Annually, the first week in October. For info: Marilee Driscoll, Long Term Care Learning Institute, PO Box 956, Plymouth, MA 02362. Phone: (508) 830-9975. Fax: (508) 830-9976. E-mail: mdriscoll@longtermcarelearning.com. Web: www.LongTermCareLearning.com.

NATIONAL MEDICAL LIBRARIANS MONTH. Oct 1–31. Recognizes and celebrates the importance and the achievements of health sciences information professionals. Medical librarians offer efficient access to quality print and online medical and health-related information within a wide variety of health-care settings. Librarians representing 23 specialty groups and 14 regional chapters of the Medical Library Association (MLA) sponsor several events and educational opportunities throughout the month of October. For info: Medical Library Assn, 65 E Wacker Place, Ste 1900, Chicago, IL 60601. Phone: (312) 419-9094. Fax: (312) 419-8950. E-mail: info@mlahg.org. Web: www.mlanet.org.

NATIONAL ORTHODONTIC HEALTH MONTH. Oct 1–31. A beautiful, healthy smile is only the most obvious benefit of orthodontic treatment. Orthodontic care plays an important role in dental health, overall physical health and emotional well-being. National Orthodontic Health Month is sponsored by the American Association of Orthodontists (AAO), the oldest and largest dental specialty organization in the world, established in 1900. The AAO supports research and education leading to quality patient care, as well as increased public awareness of the need for and benefits of orthodontic treatment. For info: Pam Paladin, American Assn of Orthodontists, 401 N Lindbergh St. Louis, MO 63141-7816. Phone: (314) 993-1700. E-mail: ppaladin@aaortho.org. Web: www.braces.org.

NATIONAL PHYSICAL THERAPY MONTH. Oct 1–31. To increase awareness of the role of physical therapy in health care, thousands of physical therapists nationwide celebrate by hosting special activities such as fitness clinics, open houses, hotlines, athletic events, health seminars and exhibits. Annually, the month of October. For info: The American Physical Therapy Assn, 1111 N Fairfax St, Alexandria, VA 22314. Phone: (800) 999-2782 or (703) 706-3248. Web: www.apta.org.

NATIONAL POPCORN POPPIN' MONTH. Oct 1–31. To celebrate the wholesome, economical, natural food value of popcorn, America's native snack. For info: The Popcorn Board, 401 N Michigan Ave, Chicago, IL 60611-4267. Phone: (312) 644-6610. Web: www.popcorn.org.

NATIONAL PORK MONTH. Oct 1–31. The National Pork Board, in cooperation with state pork producers associations, celebrates October as National Pork Month. While pork promotions

☆ Chase's 2004 Calendar of Events ☆   Oct 1

are conducted throughout the year, special emphasis is placed on Pork: The Other White Meat® during October. For info: National Pork Board, PO Box 9114, Des Moines, IA 50306. Phone: (515) 223-2600. Fax: (515) 223-2646. E-mail: porkboard@porkboard.org. Web: www.porkboard.org.

NATIONAL READING GROUP MONTH. Oct 1–31. Reading group members celebrate the joy of a book shared and inspire individuals who do not belong to a reading group to join one or start their own. Organizations, bookstores and libraries are encouraged to sponsor reading group events during this month. For info: Alice Dillon, 14511 Pfeifer Way, Lake Oswego, OR 97035. Phone: (503) 636-1242. Fax: (503) 635-5119. E-mail: NotesintheMargin@aol.com or Martha Burns, 41 Park Ln, Essex Fells, NJ 07021. E-mail: mlbwrite@aol.com.

NATIONAL ROLLER SKATING MONTH. Oct 1–31. A monthlong celebration recognizing the health benefits and recreational enjoyment of this long-loved pastime. Also includes in-line skating and an emphasis on safe skating. For info: Roller Skating Assn, 6905 Corporate Dr, Indianapolis, IN 46278. Phone: (317) 347-2626. Fax: (317) 347-2636. E-mail: rsa@rollerskating.com. Web: www.rollerskating.com.

NATIONAL RSV AWARENESS MONTH. Oct 1–31. Most babies get Respiratory Syncytial Virus (RSV) before they turn 2, and it generally has symptoms much like a common cold. However, other children who get RSV, especially those born early or with ongoing lung problems, may develop serious complications associated with it such as pneumonia or bronchiolitis. Each year, 125,000 babies are hospitalized because of complications with RSV and some of these babies die. There are things we can do to help protect our babies. A free booklet on RSV is available. For info: Preemie Care, c/o MOST (Mothers of Supertwins), PO Box 951, Brentwood, NY 11717-6027. Phone: (631) 859-1110. Web: www.MOSTonline.org.

NATIONAL SARCASTICS AWARENESS MONTH. Oct 1–31. To help people everywhere understand the positive and negative aspects of sarcasm. For info: Dr. Virginia Tooper, Dir of Barbs, Sarcastics Anonymous, 100 Bay Pl, #2112, Oakland, CA 94610. Phone: (510) 891-8479. E-mail: vtooper@ix.netcom.com.

NATIONAL SEAFOOD MONTH. Oct 1–31. To promote the taste, variety and nutrition of fish and shellfish. For info and recipes: Linda Candler, Natl Fisheries Institute, 1901 N Ft Myer Dr, Ste 700, Arlington, VA 22209. Phone: (703) 524-8881. E-mail: lcandler@nfi.org. Web: www.nfi.org.

NATIONAL SPINA BIFIDA AWARENESS MONTH. Oct 1–31. Promoting public awareness of current scientific, medical and educational issues related to spina bifida—the most frequently occurring, permanently disabling birth defect. For info: Natl Resource Center, Natl Spina Bifida Assn of America, 4590 McArthur Blvd NW, Ste 250, Washington, DC 20007-4226. Phone: (202) 944-3285 or (800) 621-3141. Fax: (202) 944-3295. E-mail: sbaa@sbaa.org. Web: www.sbaa.org.

NATIONAL SPINAL HEALTH MONTH. Oct 1–31. For info: American Chiropractic Assn, 1701 Clarendon Blvd, Arlington, VA 22209. Phone: (800) 986-4636. E-mail: memberinfo@amerchiro.org. Web: www.acatoday.com.

NATIONAL STAMP COLLECTING MONTH. Oct 1–31. An annual promotion during the entire month of October sponsored by the US Postal Service. For info: Stamp Services, US Postal Service, 475 L'Enfant Plaza SW, Rm 5670, Washington, DC 20260-2437. Web: www.usps.gov.

NATIONAL STORYTELLING FESTIVAL. Oct 1–3. Jonesborough, TN. Tennessee's oldest town plays host to the most dynamic storytelling event dedicated to the oral tradition. This three-day celebration showcases storytellers, stories and traditions from across America and around the world. Annually, the first full weekend in October. Est attendance: 10,000. For info: Intl Storytelling Center, 116 W Main, Jonesborough, TN 37659. Phone: (800) 952-8392. Fax: (423) 913-8219. E-mail: info@storytellingcenter.net. Web: www.storytellingfestival.org.

NATIONAL SUDDEN INFANT DEATH SYNDROME AWARENESS MONTH. Oct 1–31. Monthlong focus on sudden infant death syndrome (also called crib death), the nation's major cause of death for infants beyond one month of age. The BACK TO SLEEP CAMPAIGN hopes to increase public awareness and funds available for medical research and family services. For info: First Candle/SIDS Alliance, 1314 Bedford Ave, Ste 210, Baltimore, MD 21208. Phone: (800) 221-7437. Fax: (410) 653-8709. E-mail: info@firstcandle.org. Web: www.firstcandle.org.

NATIONAL TOILET TANK REPAIR MONTH. Oct 1–31. Monthlong observance dedicated to the value and benefits of a properly tuned toilet with special emphasis on do-it-yourself repairs and water conservation. For info: Greg Wisner, Mktg Mgr, Fluidmaster Inc, 30800 Rancho Viejo Rd, San Juan Capistrano, CA 92675. Phone: (949) 728-2000. Fax: (949) 728-2805.

NEW YORK FILM FESTIVAL. Oct 1–17. Lincoln Center, New York City. The 42nd annual film festival presented by the Film Society of Lincoln Center. 17-day showcase of the newest and most important films from around the world. All features are US premieres, and more than 20 nations are represented. The festival closes with the Grand Marnier Film Fellowship Awards given to graduate students for excellence in filmmaking, videomaking and film criticism. For info: New York Film Festival, The Film Society of Lincoln Center, 70 Lincoln Center Plaza, New York, NY 10023-6595. E-mail: webmaster@filmlinc.com. Web: www.filmlinc.com.

NIGERIA: INDEPENDENCE DAY. Oct 1. National holiday. Became independent of Great Britain in 1960 and a republic in 1963.

NO SALT WEEK. Oct 1–5. Give no-salt cooking and food preparation a try! This celebration will help with recipes and combinations. Annually, the first week in October. For ideas send a large, self-addressed stamped envelope. For info: Make It Tasty Spice Co, Box 416, Denver, CO 80201. Phone: (303) 575-5676. E-mail: mail@foodservicecookbooks.com.

NORWAY: PAGEANTRY IN OSLO. Oct 1. The Storting (Norway's Parliament) convenes on first weekday in October, when it decides date for the ceremonial opening of the Storting—usually the following weekday—and the parliamentary session is then opened by King Harald V in the presence of Corps Diplomatique, preceded and followed by a military procession between the Royal Palace and the Storting.

OCTOBER FROZEN FOOD FESTIVAL. Oct 1–31. Promotes a national awareness of the economical and nutritional benefits of frozen foods. Annually, the month of October. For info: Julie Henderson, VP Communications, Natl Frozen & Refrigerated Foods Assn, 4755 Linglestown Rd, Ste 300, Harrisburg, PA 17112. Phone: (717) 657-8601. Fax: (717) 657-9862. E-mail: info@nfraweb.org. Web: www.nfraweb.org.

513

Oct 1 ☆ Chase's 2004 Calendar of Events ☆

OCTOBER IS DISCOVER AMERICA MONTH. Oct 1–31. Celebrate the anniversary of Columbus's discovery of America by visiting a place in the United States, Canada, Mexico or South America between July 1 and October 31. Take a snapshot, write a 50-word description of the scene and submit the image and words to the Second Annual "Discover America Through Postcards" contest. Winning images will be made into e-postcards and featured on the website www.postcardsfrom.com. For info: Kristine Krom, Postcards From, PO Box 25, N Billerica, MA 01862. Phone: (978) 663-8832. Fax: (978) 663-4828. E-mail: travel@post cardsfrom.com. Web: www.postcardsfrom.com.

OHIO SWISS FESTIVAL. Oct 1–2. Sugarcreek, OH. Swiss music, games, costumes, parades. Continuous entertainment and tons of Swiss cheese. Annually, the fourth Friday and Saturday following Labor Day. Est attendance: 50,000. For info: Patricia Kaser, Info Coord, Ohio Swiss Festival, PO Box 158, Sugarcreek, OH 44681. Phone: (330) 852-4113 or (888) 609-7592.

OKTOBERFEST. Oct 1–2 (also Oct 8–9). New Ulm, MN. Celebrating Minnesota's German heritage, with musical entertainment, food, craft shows and dancing. Est attendance: 5,000. For info: New Ulm Chamber of Commerce, Box 384, New Ulm, MN 56073. Phone: (507) 233-4300 or (888) 4NEW-ULM. E-mail: nuchamber@newulmtel.net. Web: www.newulm.com.

OZARK FALL FARMFEST. Oct 1–3. Ozark Empire Fairgrounds, Springfield, MO. The largest agricultural trade show in the Ozarks. Exhibits fill the grounds and all buildings. Free admission and free parking. For info: Nancy Bright, Ozark Empire Fair, PO Box 630, Springfield, MO 65801. Phone: (417) 833-2660. Fax: (417) 833-3769. E-mail: nancy@ozarkempirefair.com. Web: www.ozarkempirefair.com.

PAUL BUNYAN SHOW. Oct 1–3. Hocking College Campus, Nelsonville, OH. Live demonstrations of forestry equipment, lumberjack contests, professional timber harvester competitions, forest industry trade show, chainsaw sculptors, Robbins Crossing interpretive history program, activities and steam show exhibits. Est attendance: 60,000. For info: Judy Sinnott, Public Info Dir, Hocking College, 3301 Hocking Pkwy, Nelsonville, OH 45764. Phone: (740) 753-3591 x 2102. Fax: (740) 753-9018. E-mail: sinnott_j@hocking.edu.

POLISH AMERICAN HERITAGE MONTH. Oct 1–31. A national celebration of Polish history, culture and pride, in cooperation with the Polish American Congress and Polonia Across America. For info: Michael Blichasz, Chair, Polish American Cultural Center, Natl HQ, 308 Walnut St, Philadelphia, PA 19106. Phone: (215) 922-1700. Fax: (215) 922-1518. E-mail: mail@polishamericancenter.org. Web: www.polishamericancenter.org.

POSITIVE ATTITUDE MONTH. Oct 1–31. Sometimes it just comes down to attitude! Zig Ziglar says that attitude, more than aptitude, affects altitude. Keith Harrell says attitude is everything. I say atta-tude is a self-reflection of who you think you are. This month is dedicated to establishing, boosting, or forcing ourselves to adopt positive attitudes and discovering and/or creating positive self-images. For info: Sylvia Henderson, Springboard Training, 18005 Lafayette Dr, Ste B, Olney, MD 20832. Phone: (301) 646-1668. Fax: (301) 856-8000. E-mail: admin@springboard-training.com. Web: www.springboardtraining.com.

October 2004

S	M	T	W	T	F	S
					1	2
3	4	5	6	7	8	9
10	11	12	13	14	15	16
17	18	19	20	21	22	23
24	25	26	27	28	29	30
31						

PROFESSIONAL UNDERWRITER'S WEEK. Oct 1–7. A time to recognize the work of the commercial insurance underwriters. For info: Barbara Reardon, 403 Walnut St, Batavia, IL 60510. Phone: (630) 406-9540. Fax: (630) 406-9539. E-mail: reardon@educatingunderwriters.com.

"REMINGTON STEELE" TV PREMIERE: ANNIVERSARY. Oct 1, 1982. Laura Holt (played by Stephanie Zimbalist, daughter of Efrem Zimbalist, Jr), an imaginative private detective, could not get a case of her own—until she made up a partner, Remington Steele, who was conveniently out of the office when clients came calling. Then she met the suave stranger (Pierce Brosnan) with a foreign accent who called himself Remington Steele. They began a working partnership . . . which ended in marriage. The show aired on NBC, with the last telecast on Mar 9, 1987, and costarred James Read, Janet DeMay and Doris Roberts.

RETT SYNDROME AWARENESS MONTH. Oct 1–31. To promote awareness of this neurological disease. For info: Intl Rett Syndrome Assn, 9121 Piscataway Rd, Ste 2B, Clinton, MD 20735. Phone: (301) 856-3334 or (800) 818-RETT. E-mail: irsa@rettsyndrome.org. Web: www.rettsyndrome.org.

REX ALLEN DAYS. Oct 1–3. Willcox, AZ. Annual celebration honors hometown boy the late Rex Allen, who gained fame as a singer, cowboy movie star and narrator for Walt Disney Productions. Celebration also honors Rex Allen, Jr, famed singer, who appeared on TNN's Yesteryears and Statler Brothers' Show. Activities include golf tournament, parade, country fair, rodeo, General Willcox Turtle Race, arts and crafts, country-western concert, carnival, softball tournament, cowboy dances. Est attendance: 20,000. For info: Willcox Chamber of Commerce, 1500 N Circle I Rd, Willcox, AZ 85643. Phone: (520) 384-2272 or (800) 200-2272. Fax: (520) 384-0293. Web: www.rexallendays.com or www.willcoxchamber.com.

RIGHT-BRAINERS RULE MONTH. Oct 1–31. Right-brainers are often ridiculed and reprimanded for their unorthodox and creative ways of doing things. The month of October is a chance to show how the right-brained person can survive and thrive in a very left-brained world. For info: Lee Silber, Creative Lee Speaking, 822 Redondo Ct, San Diego, CA 92109. Phone: (858) 792-5312. Web: www.creativelee.com.

SCARE A FRIEND DAY. Oct 1. Begin October with innocent fun by scaring friends and family. Watch a horror movie, visit a haunted house attraction, play a harmless prank or do anything that gets the old blood pumping. Have a screaming good time starting with Scare a Friend Day on Oct 1 and ending on Halloween. For info: Christopher Cook, Fearmakers Studios, 108 Maple St, McArthur, OH 45651. Phone: (614) 262-9573. E-mail: ccook@fearmakers.com. Web: www.fearmakers.com.

SELF-PROMOTION MONTH. Oct 1–31. Learn how to toot your own horn and promote your business to another level of success. Unique marketing strategies with a twist are shared by some of the most successful marketing gurus in the nation. Discover some of these insightful and shameless marketing strategies for yourself! Sign up for Debbie Allen's marketing expertise newsletter free. For info: Debbie Allen, Allen & Assoc Consulting, Inc, PO Box 27946, Scottsdale, AZ 85255-0149. Phone: (800) 359-4544. Web: www.academyofmarketing.net.

SOUTH KOREA: ARMED FORCES DAY. Oct 1. Marked by many colorful military parades, aerial acrobatics and honor guard ceremonies, held around the reviewing plaza at Yoido, an island in the Han River.

SPINACH LOVERS MONTH. Oct 1–31. Spinach has finally become "the darling of vegetables": from its delectable taste to the breaking news on its lutein content for the prevention of macular degeneration. "Spinach—it's not just for breakfast anymore!" For info: Burgundy L. Olivier, "The Spinach Lady", PO Box 61952, Dept C, Lafayette, LA 70596. E-mail: email@ilovespinach.com. Web: www.ilovespinach.com.

☆ Chase's 2004 Calendar of Events ☆ Oct 1

SPRINGS FOLK FESTIVAL. Oct 1–2. Springs, PA. 47th annual festival during the peak of fall foliage in Amish country. 135 craftsmen, Dutch food and continuous live music. Est attendance: 15,000. For info: Springs Folk Festival, PO Box 293, Springs, PA 15562. Phone: (814) 662-4158.

STAMP EXPO. Oct 1–3. Radisson Hotel, Anaheim, CA. Est attendance: 4,000. For info: Intl Stamp Collectors Society, PO Box 854, Van Nuys, CA 91408. Phone: (818) 997-6496. Fax: (818) 988-4337. E-mail: iibick@aol.com. Web: www.bick.net.

STOCKTON, RICHARD: BIRTH ANNIVERSARY. Oct 1, 1730. Lawyer and signer of the Declaration of Independence, born at Princeton, NJ. Died there, Feb 8, 1781.

SUGARLOAF CRAFTS FESTIVAL. Oct 1–3. Maryland State Fairgrounds, Timonium, MD. This show, now in its 28th year, features more than 350 nationally recognized fine artists and craft designers displaying and selling their original creations. Includes craft demonstrations, live music, specialty food, hourly gift certificate drawings and more. Est attendance: 26,500. For info: Sugarloaf Mountain Works, 200 Orchard Ridge Dr, #215, Gaithersburg, MD 20878. Phone: (800) 210-9900. Fax: (301) 253-9620. Web: www.sugarloafcrafts.com.

SWAPPIN' MEETIN'. Oct 1–2. Southeast Community College, Cumberland, KY. A celebration of the rich heritage of the mountain people. Handmade goods such as quilts and woodwork are displayed; demonstrations include lye soap making, sorghum molasses making and folk singing. Est attendance: 10,000. For info: Michael Corriston, Facility Dir, Appalachian Cntr, 700 College Rd, Cumberland, KY 40823. Phone: (606) 589-2145 x 2102. Fax: (606) 589-2275. E-mail: michael.corriston@kctcs.net. Web: www.state.ky.us.

TALK ABOUT PRESCRIPTIONS MONTH. Oct 1–31. For info: Natl Council on Patient Information and Education, 4915 Saint Elmo Ave, Ste 505, Bethesda, MD 20814-6082. Phone: (301) 656-8565. Fax: (301) 656-4464. E-mail: ncpie@ncpie.info. Web: www.talkaboutrx.org or www.bemedwise.org.

TEXAS ON THE PLATE MONTH. Oct 1–31. Fredericksburg, TX. A celebration of all that's great about Texas cuisine and the salsas, rubs, jellies and sauces that make Texas food haute cuisine with a down-home flair. Texas on the Plate Month calls attention to the combination of trend-setting flavors and diverse ethnic cooking styles to create exciting examples of the new Texas Cuisine. For info: Fischer & Wieser Specialty Foods, Inc. Phone: (800) 369-9257. Web: www.jelly.com or www.texasontheplate.com.

"THIS IS YOUR LIFE" TV PREMIERE: ANNIVERSARY. Oct 1, 1952. Ralph Edwards hosted this program that lured unsuspecting guests on the show and surprised them by detailing their lives and achievements with their family and friends. It began as a radio show in 1948.

"TOM CORBETT, SPACE CADET" TV PREMIERE: ANNIVERSARY. Oct 1, 1950. This space show was set in the 2350s at the Space Academy and starred Frankie Thomas in the title role as an eager cadet. "Tom Corbett" was one of the few shows to be aired on all four major networks, including running on two different networks (NBC and ABC) at the same time.

TUVALU: NATIONAL HOLIDAY: ANNIVERSARY. Oct 1. Gained independence from Britain on this day in 1978.

UNITED NATIONS: INTERNATIONAL DAY OF OLDER PERSONS. Oct 1. Designated by the General Assembly on Dec 14, 1990 (originally "International Day for the Elderly," the name was changed later on Dec 21, 1995). A day to encourage all societies to better integrate aging issues into the larger context of development. States are encouraged to do everything in their power to enable all men and women to age with security and dignity. For info: United Nations, Dept of Public Info, Public Inquiries Unit, Rm GA-57, New York, NY 10017. Phone: (212) 963-4475. E-mail: inquiries@un.org. Web: www.un.org.

UNIVERSAL CHILDREN'S WEEK. Oct 1–7. To disseminate throughout the world info on the needs of children and to distribute copies of the Declaration of the Rights of the Child. For complete info, send $5 to cover expense of printing, handling and postage. Annually, the first seven days of October. For info: Dr. Stanley Drake, Pres, Intl Society of Friendship and Good Will, 999 Hood Rd, Ste 127, Marietta, GA 30068. Phone: (770) 565-2322. E-mail: ISFGW@bellsouth.net.

UNIVERSITY OF CHICAGO FIRST DAY OF CLASSES: ANNIVERSARY. Oct 1, 1892. The University of Chicago opened with an enrollment of 594 and a faculty of 103, including eight former college presidents.

US OPEN STOCK DOG TRIALS & FARM FESTIVAL. Oct 1–3. Hubert Bailey Farm, Dawsonville, GA. In the foothills of the Appalachian mountains, handlers from across the country will work both sheep and cattle. Also a petting zoo for children. Est attendance: 10,000. For info: Dawson County Chamber of Commerce, PO Box 299, Dawsonville, GA 30534. Phone: (706) 265-6278. Fax: (706) 265-6279. E-mail: info@dawson.org. Web: www.dawson.org.

US 2005 FEDERAL FISCAL YEAR BEGINS. Oct 1, 2004–Sept 30, 2005.

VEGETARIAN MONTH. Oct 1–31. This educational event advances awareness of the many surprising ethical, environmental, economic, health, humanitarian and other benefits of the increasingly popular vegetarian lifestyle. For info: Vegetarian Awareness Network, Communications Center, PO Box 321, Knoxville, TN 37901-0321. Phone: (800) USA-VEGE.

WOMEN'S SMALL BUSINESS MONTH. Oct 1–31. National events celebrate women's small businesses. Seminars, award ceremonies and prize giveaways annually every October. For info: Linda Hollander, 4214 Glencoe Ave, Marina Del Rey, CA 90292. Phone: (310) 337-1430. Fax: (310) 641-5823. E-mail: linda@wealthybaglady.com. Web: www.wealthybaglady.com.

WORLD BLINDNESS AWARENESS MONTH. Oct 1–31. Every five seconds, one person in our world goes blind, with a child going blind nearly every minute. World Blindness Awareness Month educates the public about the nearly 180 million people throughout the world who suffer from some degree of visual impairment, and how needless blindness can be eliminated if people worldwide have access to sight-saving medical and surgical techniques. For info: American Academy of Ophthalmology, PO Box 7424, San Francisco, CA 94120-7424. Phone: (415) 561-8525. Fax: (415) 561-8533. E-mail: eyemd@aao.org. Web: www.medem.com/eyemd.

WORLD SMILE DAY. Oct 1. A day dedicated to good works and good cheer throughout the world. The official theme for the day is "Do an act of kindness. Help one person smile." The symbol for the day is the world-famous "smiley face" icon, created in 1963 by Harvey Ball of Worcester, MA. This icon is now the international symbol of happiness and goodwill. Annually, the first Friday in October. For info: Charles P. Ball, President, World Smile Corp, 22 Front St, PO Box 171, Worcester, MA 01614. Web: www.worldsmileday.com.

Oct 1–2 ☆ Chase's 2004 Calendar of Events ☆

WORLD VEGETARIAN DAY. Oct 1. Celebration of vegetarianism's benefits to humans, animals and our planet. In addition to individuals, participants include libraries, schools, colleges, restaurants, food services, health-care centers, health food stores, workplaces and many more. For info: North American Vegetarian Society, Box 72, Dolgeville, NY 13329. Phone: (518) 568-7970. Fax: (518) 568-7979. E-mail: navs@telenet.net. Web: www.navs-online.org.

YOSEMITE NATIONAL PARK ESTABLISHED: ANNIVERSARY. Oct 1, 1890. Yosemite Valley and Mariposa Big Tree Grove, granted to the State of California June 30, 1864, were combined and established as a national park. For further park info: Yosemite Natl Park, PO Box 577, Yosemite Natl Park, CA 95389.

BIRTHDAYS TODAY

Julie Andrews, 69, actress, singer (Emmy for "The Julie Andrews Hour"; Oscar for *Mary Poppins*), born Julia Wells, Walton-on-Thames, England, Oct 1, 1935.
Tom Bosley, 77, actor ("Happy Days," "Father Dowling Mysteries"), born Chicago, IL, Oct 1, 1927.
Rodney Cline (Rod) Carew, 59, Hall of Fame baseball player, born Gatun, Panama Canal zone, Oct 1, 1945.
Jimmy Carter, 80, 39th president of the US, born James Earl Carter, Jr, Plains, GA, Oct 1, 1924.
Stephen Collins, 57, actor ("7th Heaven," *All the President's Men*), born Des Moines, IA, Oct 1, 1947.
Mark McGwire, 41, former baseball player, born Pomona, CA, Oct 1, 1963.
Esai Morales, 42, actor ("American Family," "NYPD Blue"), born Brooklyn, NY, Oct 1, 1962.
Philippe Noiret, 74, actor (*The Day of the Jackal, Coup de Torchon, Il Postino*), born Lille, France, Oct 1, 1930.
Randy Quaid, 54, actor (*The Last Picture Show, Dead Solid Perfect*), born Houston, TX, Oct 1, 1950.
William Hubbs Rehnquist, 80, Chief Justice of the US Supreme Court, born Milwaukee, WI, Oct 1, 1924.
Stella Stevens, 68, actress ("Ben Casey," "Flamingo Road"), born Hot Coffee, MS, Oct 1, 1936.
Grete Waitz, 51, marathoner, born Oslo, Norway, Oct 1, 1953.

OCTOBER 2 — SATURDAY
Day 276 — 90 Remaining

ALBUQUERQUE INTERNATIONAL BALLOON FIESTA. Oct 2–10. Balloon Fiesta Park, Albuquerque, NM. Held since 1972, the largest hot air balloon gathering in the world features more than 750 hot air and gas balloons, mass ascensions, balloon glows and specially shaped balloons. The ten-day event includes entries from more than 28 countries. Annually, the first through second weekends in October. For info: Albuquerque Intl Balloon Fiesta, Inc, 4401 Alameda NE, Albuquerque, NM 87113. Phone: (505) 821-1000 or (888) 422-7277. Fax: (505) 828-2887. E-mail: balloons@balloonfiesta.com. Web: www.balloonfiesta.com.

"ALFRED HITCHCOCK PRESENTS" TV PREMIERE: ANNIVERSARY. Oct 2, 1955. Alfred Hitchcock was already an acclaimed director when he began hosting this mystery anthology series that aired on CBS and NBC for 10 years. Each episode began with an introduction by Hitchcock, the man with the world's most recognized profile. Hitchcock directed about 22 episodes of the series; Robert Altman also directed. Among the many stars who appeared on the show are: Barbara Bel Geddes, Brian Keith, Gena Rowlands, Dick York, Cloris Leachman, Joanne Woodward, Steve McQueen, Peter Lorre, Dick Van Dyke, Robert Redford and Katherine Ross.

AMERICAN DIETETIC ASSOCIATION FOOD & NUTRITION CONFERENCE & EXPO. Oct 2–5. Anaheim, CA. Est attendance: 10,000. For info: Public Relations, American Dietetic Assn, 120 S Riverside Plaza, Ste 2000, Chicago, IL 60606-6995. Phone: (312) 899-0040. Fax: (312) 899-0008. E-mail: mtgsinfo@eatright.org. Web: www.eatright.org.

APPLE HARVEST FESTIVAL. Oct 2–3 (also Oct 9–10). South Mountain Fairgrounds, Gettysburg, PA. 40th annual celebration includes tours of orchards, apple-butter boiling and antique cider press. Est attendance: 100,000. For info: Gettysburg CVB, PO Box 4117, Gettysburg, PA 17325. Phone: (717) 334-6274. Fax: (717) 334-1166. E-mail: gettysburgcvb@dejazzd.com. Web: www.gettysburgcvb.org.

APPLEFEST. Oct 2–3. Downtown Weston, MO. Pressing apple cider, cooking apple butter, music, parade and Lost Arts demonstrations on Main Street. Est attendance: 8,500. For info: Weston Development Co, 502 Main, Weston, MO 64098. Phone: (816) 640-2909 or (888) 635-7457. E-mail: westonmo@kc.rr.com. Web: ci.weston.mo.us.

ARTS & CRAFTS FESTIVAL. Oct 2. Rolla, MO. Approximately 150 crafters plus food vendors. Annually, the first Saturday in October. Est attendance: 3,000. For info: Rolla Chamber of Commerce, 1301 Kingshighway, Rolla, MO 65401. Phone: (573) 364-3577.

BATTLE OF GERMANTOWN REENACTMENT. Oct 2. Philadelphia, PA. Annual reenactment of the Oct 4, 1777, Battle of Germantown. Featured are more than 400 authentically costumed troops re-creating the original battle at noon and at 3 PM. Shuttles run throughout the day between battle site and six other participating historical sites. Annually, the first Saturday in October. Est attendance: 4,000. For info: Public Relations, Cliveden of the National Trust, 6401 Germantown Ave, Philadelphia, PA 19144. Phone: (215) 848-1777. Fax: (215) 438-2892. Web: www.cliveden.org.

BIG ISLAND RENDEZVOUS. Oct 2–3. Bancroft Bay City Park, Albert Lea, MN. Minnesota's largest early American reenactment with 1,000 costumed participants—including New Ulm Battery Civil War group. With old-time bluegrass and country music, black powder shoot, tipi village, Colonial crafts for sale, workshops, traditional and ethnic foods. Est attendance: 13,000. For info: Big Island Rendezvous and Festival, Inc, 143 W Clark St, Albert Lea, MN 56007-2547. Phone: (800) 658-2526. Fax: (507) 373-0344. E-mail: bigisland@albertlea.org.

	S	M	T	W	T	F	S
October 2004						1	2
	3	4	5	6	7	8	9
	10	11	12	13	14	15	16
	17	18	19	20	21	22	23
	24	25	26	27	28	29	30
	31						

BUFFALO ROUNDUP ARTS FESTIVAL. Oct 2–4. Custer, SD. South Dakota artists and craftsmen display and sell their arts and crafts. Also Western and Native American entertainment, pancake feeds, chili cook-off and much more. 11th annual. Est attendance: 15,000. For info: Craig Pugsley, Visitor Services Coord, Custer State Park, HC 83, Box 70, Custer, SD 57730. Phone: (605) 255-4515. Fax: (605) 255-4460. E-mail: craig.pugsley@state.sd.us. Web: www.custerstatepark.info.

CARSON CITY LIBRARY FOUNDATION OKTOBERFEST. Oct 2. Pony Express Pavillion, Mills Park, Carson City, NV. Live oompah music, polka dancing, beer-grilled sausages, craft faire, book sale and fun for the entire family amidst the colorful autumn season. This annual fund-raiser, benefitting the Carson City Library, is held the first Saturday in October. Est attendance: 2,000. For info: Andrea Moore, Carson City Library, 900 N Roop St, Carson City, NV 89701. Phone: (775) 887-2244. Fax: (775) 887-2273. E-mail: awmoore@clan.lib.nv.us.

CELEBRATION OF FINE CRAFTS. Oct 2–3. Coolidge Park, Chattanooga, TN. 9th annual fair. Marketing the creative work of the hand by 100 select American craft artists. Annually, the first weekend in October. Est attendance: 10,000. For info: Alice C. Merritt, Exec Director, Tennessee Assn of Craft Artists, PO Box 120066, Nashville, TN 37212. Phone: (615) 385-1904. Web: www.tennesseecrafts.org.

COME AND TAKE IT FESTIVAL. Oct 2–3. Gonzales, TX. This celebration commemorating the first shot fired for Texas independence in 1835 is named for the defiant battle cry of the colonists when the Mexican military demanded the return of a cannon. Est attendance: 30,000. For info: Chamber of Commerce, Box 134, Gonzales, TX 78629. Phone: (830) 672-6532. Fax: (830) 672-6533. E-mail: info@gonzalestexas.com. Web: www.gonzalestexas.com.

FALL CITYWIDE GARAGE SALE. Oct 2. Electra, TX. Sales throughout the Electra area. Chamber of Commerce will provide free coffee and maps at 7 AM. The Chamber of Commerce office will close at 8 AM so that we too may enjoy all of the bargains. Est attendance: 500. For info: Sherry Strange, Electra Chamber of Commerce, 112 W Cleveland, Electra, TX 76360. Phone: (940) 495-3577. E-mail: ElectraCoC@aol.com. Web: www.electratexas.org.

FEAST OF THE HUNTERS' MOON. Oct 2–3. Fort Ouiatenon Historic Park, Lafayette, IN. Re-creation of French and Native American life at mid-1700s fur-trading outpost. 8,000 participants. Est attendance: 65,000. For info: Gina Settle, Tippecanoe County Historical Assn, 909 South St, Lafayette, IN 47901. Phone: (765) 476-8402. Fax: (765) 476-8414. E-mail: feastinfo@tcha.mus.in.us. Web: www.tcha.mus.in.us.

FELL'S POINT FUN FESTIVAL. Oct 2–3. Fell's Point National Historic District, Baltimore, MD. 38th annual popular outdoor street festival held in Baltimore's original seaport. 400+ arts and crafts vendors, antique market, carnival rides, Hispanic area, five stages featuring rock and roll, bluegrass, jazz, blues, folk, gospel, dancing, etc, family and children's area, three beer gardens, international bazaar retail area, 40+ food vendors in three food courts and much more. Annually, the first full weekend in October. Sponsor: The Preservation Society. Est attendance: 700,000. For info: Fell's Point Fun Festival, 812 S Ann St, Baltimore, MD 21231. Phone: (410) 675-6756. Fax: (410) 675-6769. Web: www.preservationsociety.com.

FESTIVAL OF FINE CRAFT. Oct 2–3. Millville, NJ. Snow, rain or shine, the show will go on. Est attendance: 10,000. For info: Wheaton Village, 1501 Glasstown Rd, Millville, NJ 08332. Phone: (856) 825-6800 x 2739 or (800) 998-4552. Fax: (856) 825-2410. E-mail: mail@wheatonvillage.org. Web: www.wheatonvillage.org.

FINE ARTS AND CRAFTS FESTIVAL. Oct 2. Barrett House, New Ipswich, NH. 3rd annual festival features 80 juried artists and craftsmen, food, entertainment. Rain or shine. Admission is $5 per person with proceeds to benefit museum. Annually, first Saturday in October. For info: Roseland Cottage, PO Box 186, Woodstock, CT 06281. Phone: (860) 928-4074. Fax: (860) 963-2208. E-mail: prusso@spnea.org. Web: spnea.org.

GANDHI, MOHANDAS KARAMCHAND (MAHATMA): BIRTH ANNIVERSARY. Oct 2, 1869. Indian political and spiritual leader who achieved world honor and fame for his advocacy of nonviolent resistance as a weapon against tyranny was born at Porbandar, India. He was assassinated in the garden of his home at New Delhi, Jan 30, 1948. On the anniversary of Gandhi's birth (Gandhi Jayanti) thousands gather at the park on the Jumna River at Delhi where Gandhi's body was cremated. Hymns are sung, verses from the Gita, the Koran and the Bible are recited and cotton thread is spun on small spinning wheels (one of Gandhi's favorite activities). Other observances held at his birthplace and throughout India on this public holiday.

"THE GEORGE GOBEL SHOW" TV PREMIERE: 50th ANNIVERSARY. Oct 2, 1954. George Gobel hosted this comedy-variety show for five years on NBC. Chanteuse Peggy King and Jeff Donnell were also on the show, with Eddie Fisher as "permanent guest star." In 1959 Gobel switched networks to CBS and appeared for a year with Joe Flynn, Anita Bryant and Harry von Zell.

GREENE, GRAHAM: 100th BIRTH ANNIVERSARY. Oct 2, 1904. British author Graham Greene was born at Berkhamsted, Hertfordshire, England. He centered his works around characters facing salvation and damnation in a world of chaos, often with complex Catholic settings. His works include *The Power and The Glory* (1940) and *The Third Man* (1950). He died Apr 3, 1991, at Vevey, Switzerland.

GUINEA: INDEPENDENCE DAY: ANNIVERSARY. Oct 2. National Day. Guinea gained independence from France in 1958.

GUNN, MOSES: 75th BIRTH ANNIVERSARY. Oct 2, 1929. The 1981 winner of the NAACP Image Award for his performance as Booker T. Washington in the film *Ragtime* was born at St. Louis, MO. His appearances on stage ranged from the title role in *Othello* to Jean Genet's *The Blacks*. He received an Emmy nomination for his role in *Roots* and was awarded several Obies for off-Broadway performances. On film he appeared in *Shaft* and *The Great White Hope*. He died Dec 17, 1993, at Guilford, CT.

HULL, CORDELL: BIRTH ANNIVERSARY. Oct 2, 1871. American statesman who served in both houses of the Congress and as secretary of state was born at Pickett County, TN. Noted for his contributions to the "Good Neighbor" policies of the US with regard to countries of the Americas and to the establishment of the United Nations. Hull died at Bethesda, MD, July 23, 1955.

INTERNATIONAL FRUGAL FUN DAY. Oct 2. A day to celebrate that having fun doesn't have to be costly. Do at least one fun thing for yourself and/or your family that is free of cost or under $5 a person: a concert or play, a hike, a meal out, a picnic, an art gallery or museum tour, a day trip, a boat ride. Annually, the first Saturday in October. For info: Shel Horowitz, PO Box 1164, Northampton, MA 01061-1164. Phone: (413) 586-2388. Fax: (617) 249-0153. E-mail: shel@frugalfun.com. Web: www.frugalfun.com/frugalfundayideas.html.

Oct 2 ☆ *Chase's 2004 Calendar of Events* ☆

ISSAQUAH SALMON DAYS FESTIVAL. Oct 2–3. Issaquah, WA. To celebrate the return of the spawning salmon to the hatchery. Annually, the first weekend in October. Est attendance: 150,000. For info: Issaquah Salmon Days Festival, 155 NW Gilman Blvd, Issaquah, WA 98027. Phone: (425) 270-2532. Fax: (425) 392-8101. E-mail: info@salmondays.org. Web: www.salmondays.org.

"THE JIMMY DURANTE SHOW" TV PREMIERE: 50th ANNIVERSARY. Oct 2, 1954. Affectionately known as "The Schnozz," Durante hosted a Saturday night variety show with his former vaudeville partner, Eddie Jackson. It alternated with "The Donald O'Connor Show" on NBC and aired for two years.

JOHNNY APPLESEED DAYS. Oct 2–3. Lake City, MN. Apple pie, apple pancake breakfast, arts and crafts fair, silent auction, games. Annually, the first full weekend in October. Est attendance: 6,500. For info: Lake City Area Chamber of Commerce, 212 S Washington St, Lake City, MN 55041. Phone: (800) 369-4123. E-mail: lcchambr@earthlink.net.

KNOX COUNTY SCENIC DRIVE. Oct 2–3 (also Oct 9–10). Knox County, IL. A self-conducted 100-mile driving tour through rural Spoon River Valley resplendent with fall colors. Different attractions at every stop feature food, crafts, art, antiques, fresh produce, old skills demonstrations, flea markets or games. Annually, the first two full weekends in October. Est attendance: 75,000. For info: Galesburg Area CVB, PO Box 60, Galesburg, IL 61402-0060. Phone: (309) 343-2485. Fax: (309) 343-2521. E-mail: visitors@visitgalesburg.com. Web: www.visitgalesburg.com.

LONG BEACH ISLAND CHOWDER COOK-OFF. Oct 2–3. Bayfront Park, Beach Haven, NJ. Weekend-long festival featuring unlimited tasting of up to 30 different red/white clam chowders prepared by area restaurants. Entertainment; other food/beverages available. Annually, the weekend before Columbus Day weekend. Est attendance: 24,000. For info: Southern Ocean County Chamber of Commerce, 265 W 9th St, Ship Bottom, NJ 08008. Phone: (800) 292-6372 or (609) 494-7171. Fax: (609) 494-5807. E-mail: sochamber@aol.com. Web: www.chowderfest.com.

MAKOTI THRESHING BEE SHOW. Oct 2–3. Makoti, ND. To acquire, rebuild and maintain antique farm machinery and motor vehicles. Threshing and other demonstrations. Annually, the first weekend in October. Est attendance: 8,000. For info: Loren Quandt, Makoti Threshers, Inc, PO Box 124, Makoti, ND 58756. Phone: (701) 726-5649.

MAPLE LEAF RAG PREMIERE: ANNIVERSARY. Oct 2, 1990. The last work choreographed by Martha Graham premiered at City Center at New York City. One of the 181 works created by Graham, *The Maple Leaf Rag* appeared on stage for the first time just six months before the dancer and choreographer died at the age of 96.

MARSHALL, THURGOOD, SWORN IN TO SUPREME COURT: ANNIVERSARY. Oct 2, 1967. Thurgood Marshall was sworn in as the first black associate justice to the US Supreme Court. On June 27, 1991, he announced his resignation, effective upon the confirmation of his successor. See also: "Marshall, Thurgood: Birth Anniversary" (July 2).

MARX, GROUCHO: BIRTH ANNIVERSARY. Oct 2, 1890. Born Julius Henry Marx at New York, NY. Comedian who along with his brothers constituted the famous Marx Brothers. The Marx Brothers began as a singing group and then acted in such movies as *Duck Soup* and *Animal Crackers*. During the '40s and '50s, Groucho was the host of the television and radio show "You Bet Your Life." Died at Los Angeles, CA, Aug 19, 1977.

	S	M	T	W	T	F	S
October						1	2
2004	3	4	5	6	7	8	9
	10	11	12	13	14	15	16
	17	18	19	20	21	22	23
	24	25	26	27	28	29	30
	31						

McFARLAND, GEORGE (SPANKY): BIRTH ANNIVERSARY. Oct 2, 1928. Chubby child star of the "Our Gang" comedy film shorts. Born at Dallas, TX, and died at Grapevine, TX, June 30, 1993.

MORRO BAY HARBOR FESTIVAL. Oct 2–3. Morro Bay, CA. Celebrates a working waterfront at play! Showcases seafood, fishing industry and diversity of marine life and coastal lifestyles. Features California Seafood Faire, wine and premium beer tasting, and a flotilla of family-oriented attractions. Annually, the first full weekend in October. Phone in California: (800) 366-6043. Est attendance: 30,000. For info: Exhibits Coord, Morro Bay Harbor Festival, Inc, PO Box 1869, Morro Bay, CA 93443. Phone: (805) 772-1155. Fax: (805) 772-2107. E-mail: info@mbharborfest.com. Web: www.mbharborfest.com.

NATIONAL CUSTODIAL WORKERS DAY. Oct 2. A day to honor all custodial workers—those who clean up after us. For info: Bette Tadajewski, Saint John the Baptist Church, 2425 Frederick, Alpena, MI 49707. Phone: (517) 354-3019.

NORTH CASCADES NATIONAL PARK ESTABLISHED: ANNIVERSARY. Oct 2, 1968. Located in Washington state.

OKTOBERFEST. Oct 2–3. St. Charles, MO. A citywide celebration of French and German heritage. Activities include a parade, German bands, foods and costumes. Annually, the first full weekend in October. Est attendance: 40,000. For info: Convention and Visitors Bureau, 230 S Main St, St. Charles, MO 63301. Phone: (800) 366-2427 or (636) 946-7776. Web: www.historicstcharles.com.

"PEANUTS" DEBUTS: ANNIVERSARY. Oct 2, 1950. This comic strip by Charles Schulz featured Charlie Brown, Lucy, Linus, Sally, Peppermint Patty and Charlie's dog Snoopy. The last new *Peanuts* strip was published Feb 13, 2000.

PHILEAS FOGG'S WAGER DAY: ANNIVERSARY. Oct 2, 1872. Anniversary, from Jules Verne's *Around the World in Eighty Days*, of the famous wager upon which the book is based: "I will bet twenty thousand pounds against any one who wishes, that I will make the tour of the world in eighty days or less." Then, consulting a pocket almanac, Phileas Fogg said: "As today is Wednesday, the second of October, I shall be due in London, in this very room of the Reform Club, on Saturday, the twenty-first of December, at a quarter before nine PM; or else the twenty thousand pounds . . . will belong to you." See also: "Phileas Fogg Wins a Wager Day" (Dec 21).

PUMPKIN DAY. Oct 2. Woodstock, VT. Learn about the many uses and varieties of pumpkin through activities and programs and take home a miniature pumpkin. Also harvest activities and wagon rides. For info: Billings Farm & Museum, Box 489, Woodstock, VT 05091. Phone: (802) 457-2355. Fax: (802) 457-4663. E-mail: billings.farm@valley.net. Web: www.billingsfarm.org.

REDWOOD NATIONAL PARK ESTABLISHED: ANNIVERSARY. Oct 2, 1968. California's Redwood National Park was established. For further park info: Redwood Natl Park, 1111 Second St, Crescent City, CA 95531.

☆ Chase's 2004 Calendar of Events ☆   Oct 2–3

SPOON RIVER VALLEY SCENIC DRIVE. Oct 2–3 (also Oct 9–10). Fulton County, IL. Fall festival with fall foliage, arts and crafts, antiques and collectibles, demonstrations, exhibits, food and the beauty of the 100-mile-long Spoon River Valley. *Spoon River Anthology* in Lewistown. Annually, the first two weekends in October. Est attendance: 100,000. For info: Spoon River Valley Scenic Drive Assn, PO Box 525, Canton, IL 61520. Phone: (309) 647-8980.

STREETER, RUTH CHENEY: BIRTH ANNIVERSARY. Oct 2, 1895. Born at Brookline, MA, Ruth Cheney Streeter was the first director of the US Marine Corps Women's Reserve. She was active in unemployment relief, public health, welfare and old-age assistance in New Jersey during the 1930s. A student of aeronautics, she learned to fly while serving as an adjutant of a flight group in the Civil Air Patrol during the early years of World War II. She died Sept 30, 1990, at Morristown, NJ.

TOMS RIVER CANOE RACE. Oct 2. Old Toms River Bus Terminal, Toms River, NJ. 8½-mile race, 13 categories, every skill level. Prizes awarded. Preregistration is a must for entering the contest or come and observe. Est attendance: 500. For info: Mickey Coen, Coord, Wells Mills County Park, 905 Wells Mills Rd, Waretown, NJ 08758. Phone: (609) 971-3085. Fax: (609) 971-9540. Web: www.co.ocean.nj.us/parks/default.htm.

"THE TWILIGHT ZONE" TV PREMIERE: 45th ANNIVERSARY. Oct 2, 1959. "The Twilight Zone" went on the air with these now-familiar words: "There is a fifth dimension, beyond that which is known to man. It is a dimension as vast as space and as timeless as infinity. It is the middle ground between light and shadow, between science and superstition, and it lies between the pit of man's fear and the summit of his knowledge. This is the dimension of imagination. It is an area which we call The Twilight Zone." The anthology program ran five seasons for 154 installments, with a one-year hiatus between the third and fourth seasons. Created and hosted by Rod Serling, it is now considered to have been one of the best dramas to appear on television. The last episode was telecast on Sept 31, 1965.

WINFIELD ART-IN-THE-PARK FESTIVAL. Oct 2. Scenic Island Park, Winfield, KS. More than 100 artists and craftspersons display and sell their wares. Entertainment; food services available. $2 admission for those over 12 years of age. Annually, the first Saturday in October. Est attendance: 8,000. For info: Madeline Norland, Program Coord, Winfield Arts and Humanities Council, 700 Gary, Stes A & B, Winfield, KS 67156-3731. Phone: (620) 221-2161. Fax: (620) 221-0587. E-mail: wahc@iwinfield.net.

WOLLERSHEIM WINERY GRAPE STOMP FESTIVAL. Oct 2–3. Wollersheim Winery, Prairie du Sac, WI. Festive event of grape-stomping contests, cork-toss, grilled food and wine tasting. Fun for the whole family. Annually, the first weekend in October. Est attendance: 2,500. For info: Wollersheim Winery, PO Box 87, 7876 State Rd 188, Prairie du Sac, WI 53578. Phone: (800) VIP-WINE. Web: www.wollersheim.com.

WORLD FARM ANIMALS DAY. Oct 2. Celebrated on Gandhi's birthday. To expose and memorialize the needless suffering and death of billions of innocent, sentient animals in factories, farms and slaughterhouses. Local actions include memorial services, vigils, street theater, picketing, leafletting and information tables. For info: Farm Animal Reform Movement, Box 30654, Bethesda, MD 20824. Phone: (301) 530-1737. Fax: (301) 530-5747. E-mail: info@wfad.org. Web: www.wfad.org.

BIRTHDAYS TODAY

Lorraine Bracco, 49, actress (*Goodfellas, Medicine Man*), born Brooklyn, NY, Oct 2, 1955.
Clay S. Felker, 76, publisher, born St. Louis, MO, Oct 2, 1928.
Donna Karan, 56, fashion designer, born Forest Hills, NY, Oct 2, 1948.
Don McLean, 59, singer ("Crying"), songwriter ("American Pie," "Vincent"), born New Rochelle, NY, Oct 2, 1945.
Rex Reed, 65, movie critic, born Fort Worth, TX, Oct 2, 1939.

Kelly Ripa, 34, actress ("All My Children"), TV host ("Live with Regis & Kelly"), born Stratford, NJ, Oct 2, 1970.
Sting, 53, musician, lead singer (Police), songwriter ("Every Breath You Take"), actor (*Dune*), born Gordon Sumner, London, England, Oct 2, 1951.

OCTOBER 3 — SUNDAY
Day 277 — 89 Remaining

"THE ANDY GRIFFITH SHOW" TV PREMIERE: ANNIVERSARY. Oct 3, 1960. Marks the airing of the first of 249 episodes. Set in rural Mayberry, NC, the show starred Griffith as Sheriff Andy Taylor, Ron Howard as his son Opie, Frances Bavier as Aunt Bee Taylor and Don Knotts as Deputy Barney Fife. Although the last telecast aired Sept 16, 1968, more than 12,000 members of "The Andy Griffith Show" Rerun Watchers Club and others celebrate this day with festivities every year.

APPLE FESTIVAL. Oct 3. Historic Ward-Meade Park, Topeka, KS. Celebration of harvest and heritage of Kansas located in 5½-acre historical park. Ethnic foods, live entertainment, special shows, turn-of-the-century town square activities, nearly 100 craft booths. Annually, the first Sunday in October. Est attendance: 10,000. For info: Sara Leeth, Historic Ward-Meade Park, 124 NW Fillmore, Topeka, KS 66606. Phone: (785) 368-3888. Fax: (785) 368-3890.

BANCROFT, GEORGE: BIRTH ANNIVERSARY. Oct 3, 1800. American historian, known as "The Father of American History," born at Worcester, MA. Died at Washington, DC, Jan 27, 1891.

BLESSING OF THE FISHING FLEET. Oct 3. Church of Saints Peter and Paul and Fisherman's Wharf, San Francisco, CA. Annually, the first Sunday in October.

BUFFALO WALLOW CHILI COOKOFF. Oct 3. Custer State Park, Custer, SD. Musical entertainment, art fair and lots of chili cooking and tasting. Est attendance: 4,000. For info: Custer Area Chamber of Commerce, 615 Washington St, Custer, SD 57730. Phone: (800) 992-9818. Fax: (605) 673-3726.

"CAPTAIN KANGAROO" TV PREMIERE: ANNIVERSARY. Oct 3, 1955. On the air until 1985, this was the longest-running children's TV show until it was surpassed by "Sesame Street." Starring Bob Keeshan as Captain Kangaroo, it was broadcast on CBS and PBS. Other characters included Mr Green Jeans, Grandfather Clock, Bunny Rabbit, Mr Moose and Dancing Bear. Keeshan was an advocate for excellence in children's programming and even supervised which commercials would appear on the program. In 1997 "The All New Captain Kangaroo" debuted, starring John McDonough.

CATTUS ISLAND NATURE FESTIVAL. Oct 3. Cattus Island County Park, Toms River, NJ. Environmental organizations fair with natural history programs throughout the day. Annually, the first Sunday in October. Est attendance: 1,200. For info: Christopher Claus, Cattus Island Park, 1170 Cattus Island Blvd, Toms River, NJ 08753. Phone: (732) 270-6960.

Oct 3 ☆ Chase's 2004 Calendar of Events ☆

COUNCIL OF LOGISTICS MANAGEMENT ANNUAL CONFERENCE. Oct 3–6. Chicago, IL. Professional development and dialogue. Est attendance: 4,000. For info: Council of Logistics Management, 2805 Butterfield Rd, Ste 200, Oak Brook, IL 60523. Phone: (630) 574-0985. Fax: (630) 574-0989. E-mail: membership@clm1.org. Web: www.clm1.org.

"THE DICK VAN DYKE SHOW" TV PREMIERE: ANNIVERSARY. Oct 3, 1961. This Carl Reiner–created sitcom wasn't an immediate success but soon became a hit. It starred Dick Van Dyke as Rob Petrie, a TV show writer, and Mary Tyler Moore as his wife Laura, a former dancer. This was one of the first shows revolving around the goings-on at a TV series. Other cast members included: Morey Amsterdam, Rose Marie, Richard Deacon, Carl Reiner, Jerry Paris, Ann Morgan Guilbert and Larry Matthews. The last episode aired Sept 7, 1966, but the show remains popular in reruns.

★**FIRE PREVENTION WEEK.** Oct 3–9. Presidential Proclamation issued annually for the first or second week in October since 1925. For many years prior to 1925, National Fire Prevention Day was observed in October. Sponsored by the National Fire Protection Association. Annually, the Sunday-through-Saturday period during which the Oct 9 anniversary date falls.

FIRE PREVENTION WEEK. Oct 3–9. To increase awareness of the dangers of fire and to educate the public on how to stay safe from fire. For info: Natl Fire Protection Assn, One Batterymarch Park, Quincy, MA 02269. Phone: (617) 770-3000. E-mail: public_affairs@nfpa.org. Web: www.nfpa.org, www.sparky.org or www.firepreventionweek.org.

FRYEBURG FAIR. Oct 3–10. Rte 5, Fryeburg, ME. Agricultural exposition, draft horse competitions, oxen and horse pulling, midway, country shows each evening, harness racing, Woodsmen's Day (always Monday), tractor pulling, baking contests, Forestry Resource Center, Fireman's Muster, sheepdog trials and juried crafts show. Annually, the week that includes the first Wednesday in October. Est attendance: 325,000. For info: June Hammond, Secy, PO Box 78, Fryeburg, ME 04037. Phone: (207) 935-3268. Fax: (207) 935-3662. E-mail: info@fryeburgfair.com.

GERMAN REUNIFICATION: ANNIVERSARY. Oct 3, 1990. After 45 years of division, East and West Germany reunited just four days short of East Germany's 41st founding anniversary (Oct 7, 1949). The new united Germany took the name the Federal Republic of Germany, the formal name of the former West Germany and adopted the constitution of the former West Germany. Today is a national holiday in Germany, Tag der Deutschen Einheit (Day of German Unity).

GERMANY: ERNTEDANKFEST. Oct 3. A harvest thanksgiving festival, or potato harvest festival, Erntedankfest (or Erntedanktag) is generally observed on the first Sunday in October.

GET ORGANIZED WEEK. Oct 3–9. This is an opportunity to streamline your life, create more time, lower your stress and increase your profit. Simplify your situation and make it more manageable by taking advantage of this time to get organized. Annually, the first full week in October. For info: National Assn of Professional Organizers, 35 Technology Parkway S, Ste 150, Norcross, GA 30092. Phone: (770) 325-3440. Web: www.napo.net.

GORGAS, WILLIAM CRAWFORD: 150th BIRTH ANNIVERSARY. Oct 3, 1854. Physician and sanitary engineer, born at Toulminville, AL. He eradicated yellow fever from Havana and the Panama Canal, allowing the completion of the canal. Gorgas died at London, England, July 4, 1920.

October 2004

S	M	T	W	T	F	S
					1	2
3	4	5	6	7	8	9
10	11	12	13	14	15	16
17	18	19	20	21	22	23
24	25	26	27	28	29	30
31						

HERRIOT, JAMES: BIRTH ANNIVERSARY. Oct 3, 1916. Author and veterinarian born James Alfred Wight at Glasgow, Scotland. Under the pen name Herriot he wrote more than 12 books chronicling his life as a veterinarian in northern England. His *All Creatures Great and Small* (1974) was made into a TV series that was an international hit. He was made a member of the Order of the British Empire in 1979. Herriot died Feb 23, 1995, at Yorkshire, England.

HOME COMFORT AWARENESS WEEK. Oct 3–9. This week, consider the quality of home comfort for all seasons. Put to use money-saving ideas to reduce energy, improve heating and cooling, make indoor air cleaner and keep equipment running efficiently with a trusted contractor partnership. Receive money-saving tips and information for each day of this week. (Send SASE to address listed below.) Annually, first full week in October. For info: Comfort Awareness Office, ServiceMark, PO Box 2167, West Chester, PA 19380. E-mail: info@servicemark.ws. Web: www.servicemark.ws.

HONDURAS: FRANCISCO MORAZÁN HOLIDAY. Oct 3. Public holiday in honor of Francisco Morazán, national hero, who was born in 1799.

INTERGENERATION DAY. Oct 3. Connecting generations through communication, celebration and education. Annually, the first Sunday in October. For info: Intergeneration Foundation, 430 N Tejon St, Ste 300, Colorado Springs, CO 80903. Phone: (719) 471-3691. Fax: (719) 471-3696. E-mail: information@intergenerationday.org. Web: www.intergenerationday.org.

KOREA: NATIONAL FOUNDATION DAY. Oct 3. National holiday also called Tangun Day, as it commemorates day when legendary founder of the Korean nation, Tangun, established his kingdom of Chosun in 2333 BC.

KURTZMAN, HARVEY: BIRTH ANNIVERSARY. Oct 3, 1902. Cartoonist and founder of *Mad* magazine, Harvey Kurtzman was born at Brooklyn, NY. At the age of 14 he had his first cartoon published, and he began his career in comic books in 1943. His career led him to EC (Educational Comics), and with the support of William Gaines, he created *Mad* magazine, which first appeared in 1952. He died Feb 21, 1993, at Mount Vernon, NY.

"LA LAW" TV PREMIERE: ANNIVERSARY. Oct 3, 1986. Set in the Los Angeles law firm of McKenzie, Brackman, Chaney and Kuzak, this drama had a large cast. Divorce lawyer Arnie Becker was played by Corbin Bernsen, public defender Victor Sifuentes by Jimmy Smits and managing partner Douglas Brackman by Alan Rachins. Other cast members included Harry Hamlin as Michael Kuzak, Richard Dysart as Leland McKenzie, Susan Dey as Grace Van Owen, Jill Eikenberry as Ann Kelsey, Michael Tucker as Stuart Markowitz and Susan Ruttan as Roxanne Melman. The last telecast was May 19, 1994.

LITTLE RED SCHOOL HOUSE ANNUAL ART FAIR. Oct 3. Willow Springs, IL. Est attendance: 12,000. For info: Little Red School House Nature Center, Forest Preserve Dist of Cook County, 9800 S 104th Ave, Willow Springs, IL 60480. Phone: (708) 839-6897.

THE MAGIC OF DIFFERENCES™ WEEK. Oct 3–9. All wars, divorces and child abuse are rooted in feeling threatened by differences. Yet, each individual and each culture or nationality has been created to be different from all others. The Magic of Differences™ Week is devoted to affirming the wondrous discovery and adventure, learning and expansion that are only possible through experiencing the value of our differences. School and church programs, public workshops, premarital seminars and media events will celebrate the power of differences to transform society for the better. Annually, the first full week of October. For info: Judith Sherven and James Sniechowski, PO Box 975, Windham, NY 12496. Phone: (518) 734-3657. E-mail: shervsniec@aol.com. Web: www.themagicofdifferences.com.

MANSON, PATRICK: BIRTH ANNIVERSARY. Oct 3, 1844. British parasitologist and surgeon sometimes called the "father of tropical medicine." Sir Patrick's research into insects as carriers of parasites was instrumental in later understanding of mosquitoes as transmitters of malaria. Born at Aberdeen, Scotland, Manson died Apr 9, 1922, at London, England.

MENTAL ILLNESS AWARENESS WEEK. Oct 3–9. To increase public awareness of the causes of, symptoms of and treatments for mental illnesses. Annually, the first full week in October. For info: Div of Public Affairs, American Psychiatric Assn, 1000 Wilson Blvd, Ste 1825, Arlington, VA 22209-3901. Phone: (703) 907-7300. E-mail: apa@psych.org. Web: www.psych.org.

"MICKEY MOUSE CLUB" TV PREMIERE: ANNIVERSARY. Oct 3, 1955. This afternoon show for children was on ABC. Among its young cast members were Mouseketeers Annette Funicello and Shelley Fabares. A later version, "The New Mickey Mouse Club," starred Keri Russell, Christina Aguilera and Britney Spears.

MYSTERY SERIES WEEK. Oct 3–9. A celebration of continuing characters in mystery fiction. Two-thirds of all new mysteries each year feature a series detective. The series tradition has been alive and well for more than 100 years. Series readers today can choose from more than 12,500 adult mysteries featuring more than 2,500 continuing characters from living writers. Mystery Series Week will celebrate fictional cops, private eyes and amateur sleuths from all walks of life—solving crimes from 55 BC to the 22nd century. Annually, the first full week in October. For info: Purple Moon Press, 3319 Greenfield Rd, #317, Dearborn, MI 48120-1212. Phone: (313) 593-1033. Fax: (313) 593-4087. E-mail: info@purplemoonpress.com. Web: www.mysteryseriesweek.com.

NATIONAL CARRY A TUNE WEEK. Oct 3–9. This week celebrates favorite tunes from the past by performing them in a concert, at school, at church or at home. The purpose is to remember tunes from America's past and keep them alive. Annually, the week nearest the birthday of William Billings (born Oct 7, 1746), America's first important tune composer ("Chester"). Sponsor: Tune Lovers Society. For info: Pine Tree Productions, 235 Prospect St, Stoughton, MA 02072. Phone: (781) 344-6954. E-mail: tunes1342@aol.com.

NATIONAL NEWSPAPER WEEK. Oct 3–9. To emphasize the importance of newspapers to the public. Annually, the first full week in October. For info: Newspaper Assn Managers, Inc, 70 Washington St, Salem, MA 01970. Phone: (978) 744-8940. Fax: (978) 744-0333. E-mail: mlp@nenews.org.

NATIONAL WORK FROM HOME WEEK. Oct 3–9. A week to celebrate the trends, technology and tactics that allow millions of Americans to work from home as entrepreneurs and corporate teleworkers. For info: Jeff Zbar, PO Box 8263, Coral Springs, FL 33075-8263. Phone: (954) 346-4393. Fax: (954) 346-0251. E-mail: jeff@chiefhomeofficer.com. Web: www.chiefhomeofficer.com.

NETHERLANDS: RELIEF OF LEIDEN DAY. Oct 3. Celebration of the liberation of Leiden in 1574.

NUCLEAR MEDICINE WEEK. Oct 3–9. In recognition of the diagnostic revolution nuclear medicine has provided to the medical profession. Special events are scheduled in thousands of nuclear medicine departments and imaging centers across the US. For info: Society of Nuclear Medicine, 1850 Samuel Morse Dr, Reston, VA 20190. Phone: (703) 708-9000. Fax: (703) 708-9015. Web: www.snm.org.

"OUR MISS BROOKS" TV PREMIERE: ANNIVERSARY. Oct 3, 1952. This half-hour sitcom began on the radio, and unlike many radio programs that moved to TV, most of the original radio cast was retained. It was about a favorite high school English teacher named Connie Brooks (played by Eve Arden). Also featured were Gale Gordon, Richard Crenna, Gloria McMillan and Jane Morgan.

"OZZIE AND HARRIET" TV PREMIERE: ANNIVERSARY. Oct 3, 1952. "Ozzie and Harriet" was TV's longest-running sitcom. The successful radio-turned-TV show about the Nelson family starred the real-life Nelsons—Ozzie, his wife Harriet and their sons David and Ricky. Officially titled "The Adventures of Ozzie and Harriet," this show was set in the family's home. The boys were one reason the show was successful, and Ricky used the advantage to become a pop star. David and Rick's real-life wives—June Blair and Kris Nelson—also joined the cast. The show was cancelled at the end of the 1965–66 season after 435 episodes, 409 of which were in black and white and 26 in color. The last episode aired Sept 3, 1966.

"THE PAT BOONE SHOW" TV PREMIERE: ANNIVERSARY. Oct 3, 1957. Clean-cut singer Pat Boone hosted three shows between 1957 and 1969. The first was a prime-time variety series with the McGuire Sisters and the Mort Lindsey Orchestra as regulars. The second show featured the Paul Smith Orchestra and was a daytime variety and talk show. "Pat Boone in Hollywood" was the title of the third, a 90-minute talk show.

PICKLE FESTIVAL. Oct 3. Greenlawn, NY. Commemorating the history of the pickle industry in Greenlawn. Pickle lovers will be able to taste and buy such homemade favorites as bread & butter pickles, sweet pickles, corn relish, red pepper relish, assorted jams and jellies, as well as some of the most delicious cakes and baked goods found anywhere. There will be displays telling all about the pickle industry in Greenlawn from the 1880s until the 1920s. For info: Michelle Athanas, Dir, Greenlawn Centerport Historical Assn, PO Box 354, Greenlawn, NY 11740. Phone: (631) 754-1180. Fax: (631) 757-7216. E-mail: gcha-info@usa.net. Web: gcha.suffolk.library.ny.us.

PULASKI DAY PARADE. Oct 3. Philadelphia, PA. Parade honoring the Polish patriot known as the "Father of the American Cavalry." Begins at 20th and Benjamin Franklin Pkwy and ends at 19th and Benjamin Franklin Pkwy. For info: Polish American Congress, Eastern Pennsylvania District, 308 Walnut St, Philadelphia, PA 19106. Phone: (215) 739-3408. Fax: (215) 922-1518. Web: www.polishamericancongress.com.

"QUINCY" TV PREMIERE: ANNIVERSARY. Oct 3, 1976. This medically-oriented crime show starred Jack Klugman as Dr. Raymond Quincy, a medical examiner for the L.A. coroner's office. Quincy's curiosity about his cases led to investigative work which often solved them. Later in the series, the show focused on social issues that were unrelated to forensic medicine. In the final season, Quincy married Dr. W. Emily Hanover (Anita Gillette). The last telecast aired on Sept 5, 1983.

"THE REAL McCOYS" TV PREMIERE: ANNIVERSARY. Oct 3, 1957. This first successful rural comedy program was one of the most popular, predating similar shows such as "The Beverly Hillbillies" by many seasons. It was set in rural California and featured the McCoys, played by Walter Brennan, Richard Crenna, Kathleen Nolan, Michael Winkelman and Lydia Reed.

Oct 3-4 ☆ Chase's 2004 Calendar of Events ☆

ROBINSON NAMED BASEBALL'S FIRST BLACK MAJOR LEAGUE MANAGER: 30th ANNIVERSARY. Oct 3, 1974. The only major league player selected most valuable player in both the American and National Leagues, Frank Robinson was hired by the Cleveland Indians as baseball's first black major league manager. During his playing career Robinson represented the American League in four World Series playing for the Baltimore Orioles, led the Cincinnati Reds to a National League pennant and hit 586 home runs in 21 years of play.

"SCARECROW AND MRS KING" TV PREMIERE: ANNIVERSARY. Oct 3, 1983. A one-hour adventure series starring Bruce Boxleitner as Lee Stetson (code name "Scarecrow"), a government agent working with Mrs Amanda King (Kate Jackson), a housewife-turned-agent. Mr King, played by Sam Melville, appeared once, but he was out of the picture when Mrs King and Scarecrow were married in the final season.

SQUIRREL AWARENESS WEEK (SAW). Oct 3-9. Set aside to honor one of our friendliest forms of wildlife, squirrels. "I SAW a squirrel today." Annually, the first Sunday in October through the following Saturday. For info: Gregg Bassett, The Squirrel Lover's Club, 318 W Fremont Ave, Elmhurst, IL 60126. Phone: (630) 833-1117. Fax: (630) 833-1449. E-mail: sqrlman@thesquirreloversclub.com. Web: www.thesquirreloversclub.com.

WORLD COMMUNION SUNDAY. Oct 3. Communion is celebrated by Christians all over the world. Annually, the first Sunday in October.

BIRTHDAYS TODAY

Jeff Bingaman, 61, US Senator (D, New Mexico), born El Paso, TX, Oct 3, 1943.
Lindsey Buckingham, 57, singer, songwriter (with Fleetwood Mac, "Go Your Own Way"), born Palo Alto, CA, Oct 3, 1947.
Neve Campbell, 31, actress ("Party of Five," Scream), born Guelph, ON, Canada, Oct 3, 1973.
Chubby Checker, 63, musician, singer ("The Twist"), born Ernest Evans, Philadelphia, PA, Oct 3, 1941.
Fred Couples, 45, golfer, born Seattle, WA, Oct 3, 1959.
Dennis Lee Eckersley, 50, former baseball player, born Oakland, CA, Oct 3, 1954.
Janel Maloney, 35, actress ("From the Earth to the Moon," "The West Wing"), born Woodland Hills, CA, Oct 3, 1969.
Madlyn Rhue, 70, actress (It's a Mad Mad Mad Mad World, "Executive Suite"), born Washington, DC, Oct 3, 1934.
Bob Riley, 60, Governor of Alabama (R), born Ashland, AL, Oct 3, 1944.
Gore Vidal, 79, author (Burr, Myra Breckinridge), born West Point, NY, Oct 3, 1925.
Jack P. Wagner, 45, actor ("Melrose Place," "General Hospital"), born Washington, MO, Oct 3, 1959.
David Mark (Dave) Winfield, 53, Hall of Fame baseball player, born St. Paul, MN, Oct 3, 1951.

October 2004

S	M	T	W	T	F	S
					1	2
3	4	5	6	7	8	9
10	11	12	13	14	15	16
17	18	19	20	21	22	23
24	25	26	27	28	29	30
31						

OCTOBER 4 — MONDAY
Day 278 — 88 Remaining

"THE ALVIN SHOW" TV PREMIERE: ANNIVERSARY. Oct 4, 1961. This prime-time cartoon was based on Ross Bagdasarian's novelty group The Chipmunks, which began as recordings with speeded-up vocals. In the series, the three chipmunks, Alvin, Simon and Theodore, sang and had adventures along with their songwriter-manager David Seville. Bagdasarian supplied the voices. "Alvin" was more successful as a Saturday morning cartoon. It returned in reruns in 1979 and also prompted a sequel, "Alvin and the Chipmunks," in 1983.

BUFFALO ROUND-UP. Oct 4. Custer, SD. To round up, brand and separate 1,500 buffalo before auction in November. 39th annual. Est attendance: 7,500. For info: Craig Pugsley, Custer State Park, HC 83, Box 70, Custer, SD 57730. Phone: (605) 255-4515. Fax: (605) 255-4460. E-mail: craig.pugsley@state.sd.us. Web: www.custerstatepark.info.

CALIFORNIA RIDESHARE WEEK. Oct 4-8. Reduce pollution and traffic! Form a carpool to take to work, or try public transportation. Annually, the first full business week in October. For info: Donna Blanchard, LA County MTA, One Gateway Pl, Los Angeles, CA 90012. Phone: (213) 922-5614. Fax: (213) 236-1803. E-mail: blanchardd@mta.net. Web: www.mta.net.

★**CHILD HEALTH DAY.** Oct 4. Presidential Proclamation always issued for the first Monday of October. Proclamation has been issued since 1928. In 1959 Congress changed celebration day from May 1 to the present observance (Pub Res No. 46 of May 18, 1928, and PL86-352 of Sept 22, 1959).

CORSICA LIBERATED: ANNIVERSARY. Oct 4, 1943. The Island of Corsica became the first French territory in Europe freed from Nazi control when Free French troops entered the city of Bastia, the culmination of a French uprising that had begun on the island on Sept 19.

"DECEMBER BRIDE" TV PREMIERE: 50th ANNIVERSARY. Oct 4, 1954. This sitcom was filmed before a live audience at Desilu Studios and took place mainly in a living room. It starred Spring Byington as widow Lily Ruskin, Frances Rafferty as her daughter Ruth Henshaw, Dean Miller as Ruth's husband, Matt, Harry Morgan as wisecracking next-door neighbor, Pete Porter (his wife Gladys was talked about but never seen), Verna Felton as Lily's friend Hilda Crocker and Arnold Stang as Private Marvin Fisher, Pete's brother-in-law. This series spun off "Pete and Gladys" in 1960.

GREGORIAN CALENDAR ADJUSTMENT: ANNIVERSARY. Oct 4, 1582. Pope Gregory XIII issued a bulletin that decreed that the day following Thursday, Oct 4, 1582, should be Friday, Oct 15, 1582, thus correcting the Julian Calendar, then 10 days out of date relative to the seasons. This reform was effective in most Catholic countries; the Julian Calendar continued in use in Britain and the American colonies until 1752, in Russia until 1918 and in Greece until 1923. See also: "Gregorian Calendar Adjustment: Anniversary" (Feb 24) and "Calendar Adjustment Day: Anniversary" (Sept 2).

HAYES, RUTHERFORD BIRCHARD: BIRTH ANNIVERSARY. Oct 4, 1822. Rutherford Birchard Hayes, 19th president of the US (Mar 4, 1877-Mar 3, 1881), was born at Delaware, OH. In his inaugural address, Hayes said: "He serves his party best who serves the country best." He died at Fremont, OH, Jan 17, 1893.

IMPROVE YOUR HOME OFFICE WEEK. Oct 4-8. Spend the week improving the way you work from home—find the best place to work, equip your office with the right technology, make your home office fit your work style. Annually, the second week in October. For info: Lisa Kanarek, HomeOfficeLife.com, 660 Preston Forest Center, #120, Dallas, TX 75230. Phone: (214) 361-0556. E-mail: lisa@homeofficelife.com. Web: www.homeofficelife.com.

☆ Chase's 2004 Calendar of Events ☆   Oct 4

INTERNATIONAL TOOT YOUR FLUTE DAY. Oct 4. A day dedicated to selling yourself on the idea of selling yourself—and telling others how good you are. This is your day to celebrate you, to remind yourself that you're too good to be your own best secret, to accept credit where credit is due and to reject the idea that self-promotion is "bragging." For info: Fred Berns, Power Promotion, 394 Rendezvous Dr, Lafayette, CO 80026. Phone: (303) 665-6688. Fax: (303) 665-5599. E-mail: FredTalks@aol.com. Web: www.fredberns.com.

JOHNSON, ELIZA McCARDLE: BIRTH ANNIVERSARY. Oct 4, 1810. Wife of Andrew Johnson, 17th president of the US, born at Leesburg, TN. Died at Greeneville, TN, Jan 15, 1876.

KEATON, BUSTER: BIRTH ANNIVERSARY. Oct 4, 1895. Born Joseph Francis Keaton at Piqua, KS, Buster Keaton (supposedly nicknamed by Harry Houdini) would become one of America's greatest filmmakers. He became a star on the vaudeville stage by age 6 in a family show with his parents, but moved on to films at age 21, costarring in several comic shorts with Roscoe "Fatty" Arbuckle, then starring, writing, directing and producing his own shorts—which featured improbable stunts and physical gags along with Keaton's deadpan expression. His full-length silent films are regarded as masterpieces of American comedy, especially *Sherlock, Jr* (1924) and the Civil War epic *The General* (1927)—both of which are on the Library of Congress's National Film Registry. Alcoholism and troubled relations with the MGM studio sidelined his career in the 1930s and 40s, but he later began a quieter career writing gags, making comic cameos in such films as *Around the World in Eighty Days*, appearing on TV's "Candid Camera" and even performing as a clown in Paris's Cirque Medrano. Keaton died on Feb 1, 1966, at Los Angeles, CA.

"LEAVE IT TO BEAVER" TV PREMIERE: ANNIVERSARY. Oct 4, 1957. This family sitcom was a stereotypical portrayal of American family life. It focused on Theodore "Beaver" Cleaver (Jerry Mathers) and his family: his patient, understanding and all-knowing father, Ward (Hugh Beaumont), impeccably dressed housewife and mother June (Barbara Billingsley) and Wally (Tony Dow), Beaver's good-natured, all-American brother. The "perfectness" of the Cleaver family was balanced by other, less-than-perfect characters played by Ken Osmond, Frank Bank, Richard Deacon, Diane Brewster, Sue Randall, Rusty Stevens and Madge Blake. The last episode aired Sept 12, 1963. "Leave It to Beaver" remained popular in reruns.

LESOTHO: INDEPENDENCE DAY. Oct 4. National holiday. Commemorates independence from Britain in 1966. Formerly Basutoland.

REMINGTON, FREDERIC S.: BIRTH ANNIVERSARY. Oct 4, 1861. Born at Canton, NY. Artist and writer Frederic Remington was devoted to the outdoors of New York's North Country and the rugged characters and landscapes of the Old West. He began as an illustrator for popular magazines and worked to become a fine artist and sculptor, capturing images of Native Americans, Buffalo Soldiers, cowboys, horses and Western adventure. Died Dec 26, 1909, at age 48, at Ridgefield, CT, following an appendectomy. Illustrations, watercolors, oil paintings, sketches, bronzes on display at the Frederic Remington Art Museum. For museum info: Frederic Remington Art Museum, 303 Washington St, Ogdensburg, NY 13669. Phone: (315) 393-2425. E-mail: info@fredericremington.org. Web: www.fredericremington.org.

RUNYAN, DAMON: BIRTH ANNIVERSARY. Oct 4, 1884. American newspaperman and author, born at Manhattan, KS, and died at New York, NY, Dec 10, 1946. The musical *Guys and Dolls* was based on one of his short stories. ". . . always try to rub up against money," he wrote, "for if you rub up against money long enough, some of it may rub off on you."

SAINT FRANCIS OF ASSISI: FEAST DAY. Oct 4. Giovanni Francesco Bernardone, religious leader, founder of the Friars Minor (Franciscan Order), born at Assisi, Umbria, Italy, in 1181. Died at Porziuncula, Oct 3, 1226. One of the best-loved saints of all time.

SPACE MILESTONE: *LUNA 3* **(USSR): 45th ANNIVERSARY.** Oct 4, 1959. First satellite to photograph moon's distant side was launched on this date.

SPACE MILESTONE: *SPUTNIK* **(USSR).** Oct 4, 1957. Anniversary of launching of first successful man-made earth satellite. *Sputnik I* ("satellite") weighing 184 lbs was fired into orbit from the USSR's Tyuratam launch site. Transmitted radio signal for 21 days, decayed Jan 4, 1958. Beginning of Space Age and man's exploration beyond Earth. This first-in-space triumph by the Soviets resulted in a stepped-up emphasis on the teaching of science in American classrooms.

SPINNING AND WEAVING WEEK. Oct 4–10. To celebrate the timeless craft of weaving and spinning and to honor craftsmen and women past and present who perpetuate a legacy of fine handmade textiles. Annually, the first full week in October, Monday–Sunday. For info: Handweavers Guild of America, Inc, 1255 Buford Hwy, Ste 211, Suwanee, GA 30024. Phone: (678) 730-0010. E-mail: weavespindye@compuserve.com. Web: www.weavespindye.org.

STRATEMEYER, EDWARD L.: BIRTH ANNIVERSARY. Oct 4, 1862. American author of children's books, Stratemeyer was born at Elizabeth, NJ. He created numerous series of popular children's books including The Bobbsey Twins, The Hardy Boys, Nancy Drew and Tom Swift. He and his Stratemeyer Syndicate, using 60 or more pen names, produced more than 800 books. More than four million copies were in print in 1987. Stratemeyer died at Newark, NJ, May 10, 1930.

SUPREME COURT 2004–2005 TERM BEGINS. Oct 4. Traditionally, the Supreme Court's annual term begins on the first Monday in October and continues with seven two-week sessions of oral arguments. Between the sessions are six recesses during which the opinions are written by the Justices. Ordinarily, all cases are decided by the following June or July.

TEN-FOUR DAY. Oct 4. The fourth day of the tenth month is a day of recognition for radio operators, whose code words, "Ten-Four," signal an affirmative reply.

UNITED NATIONS: WORLD HABITAT DAY. Oct 4. The United Nations General Assembly, by a resolution of Dec 17, 1985, has designated the first Monday of October each year as World Habitat Day—a day to reflect on the living conditions of human beings and for actions to be taken to address the shortcomings of those conditions. The first observance of this day, Oct 5, 1986, marked the 10th anniversary of the first international conference on the subject. For info: United Nations, Dept of Public Info, Public Inquiries Unit, Rm GA-57, New York, NY 10017. Phone: (212) 963-4475. E-mail: inquiries@un.org. Web: www.un.org.

UNITED NATIONS: WORLD SPACE WEEK. Oct 4–10. To celebrate the contributions of space science and technology to the betterment of the human condition. The dates recall the launch, on Oct 4, 1957, of the first artificial satellite, *Sputnik*, and the entry into force, on Oct 10, 1967, of the Treaty on Principles Governing the Activities of States in the Exploration and Use of Outer Space. For info: United Nations, Dept of Public Info, New York, NY 10017. Web: www.un.org.

WOMEN'S NEWS DAY. Oct 4. A day for businesswomen to submit their press releases, events and articles to the media. Businesswomen who need help writing their press releases and articles can request assistance from the Women's News Bureau. Annually, the first Monday in October. For info: Jerrilynn B. Thomas. Phone: (770) 603-6521. E-mail: pr@jerrilynnbthomas.com. Web: www.womensnewsbureau.com.

WOOFSTOCK. Oct 4. Wichita, KS. An annual celebration of peace, love and pets, Woofstock invites canines and their owners to participate in activities catered exclusively for them, including a one-mile mutt strut, two-mile fun run, pet trick and costume contests and much more. Silent auction, more than 40 pet-friendly vendors, demonstrations of dog agility, canine search and rescue and sheepherding. All proceeds benefit the Kansas Humane Society and the 12,000 animals it receives each year. For info: Jennifer Campbell, Kansas Humane Society, 4218 Southeast Blvd, Wichita, KS 67210. Phone: (316) 524-1590. Fax: (316) 554-0356. E-mail: jcampbell@kshumane.org. Web: www.kshumane.org.

BIRTHDAYS TODAY

Michael David (Mike) Adamle, 55, sportscaster, former football player, born Kent, OH, Oct 4, 1949.
Armand Assante, 55, actor (*Belizaire the Cajun, The Mambo Kings, Fatal Instinct*), born New York, NY, Oct 4, 1949.
Jackie Collins, 63, author (*Lucky*), born London, England, Oct 4, 1941.
Rachael Leigh Cook, 25, actress (*She's All That*, "The Baby-Sitter's Club"), born Minneapolis, MN, Oct 4, 1979.
Clifton Davis, 59, singer, actor ("That's My Mama," "Amen"), composer, born Chicago, IL, Oct 4, 1945.
Anita L. DeFrantz, 52, Olympics executive and former rower, born Philadelphia, PA, Oct 4, 1952.
Charles (Chuck) Hagel, 58, US Senator (R, Nebraska), born North Platte, NE, Oct 4, 1946.
Charlton Heston, 82, actor (*The Ten Commandments, Ben-Hur, Planet of the Apes*), born Evanston, IL, Oct 4, 1922.
Tony La Russa, Jr, 60, baseball manager and former player, born Tampa, FL, Oct 4, 1944.
Jan Murray, 87, comedian (emcee of "Dollar a Second," "Treasure Hunt"), born Murry Janofsky, New York, NY, Oct 4, 1917.
Anne Rice, 63, novelist (*Interview with the Vampire*), born New Orleans, LA, Oct 4, 1941.
Susan Sarandon, 58, actress (Oscar for *Dead Man Walking; Atlantic City, Thelma and Louise, Lorenzo's Oil*), born Susan Tomaling, New York, NY, Oct 4, 1946.
Alicia Silverstone, 28, actress (*Clueless, Batman & Robin*), born San Francisco, CA, Oct 4, 1976.
Alvin Toffler, 76, author (*Future Shock, Power Shift*), born New York, NY, Oct 4, 1928.
Jimy Williams, 61, baseball manager and former player, born Santa Maria, CA, Oct 4, 1943.

OCTOBER 5 — TUESDAY
Day 279 — 87 Remaining

ARTHUR, CHESTER ALAN: 175th BIRTH ANNIVERSARY. Oct 5, 1829. The 21st president of the US, Chester Alan Arthur, was born at Fairfield, VT, and succeeded to the presidency following the death of James A. Garfield. Term of office: Sept 20, 1881–Mar 3, 1885. Arthur was not successful in obtaining the Republican party's nomination for the following term. He died at New York, NY, Nov 18, 1886.

BONDS BREAKS HOME RUN RECORD: ANNIVERSARY. Oct 5, 2001. Barry Bonds of the San Francisco Giants broke Mark McGwire's 1998 home run record when he hit his 71st homer of the season in a game against the Los Angeles Dodgers at Pacific Bell Park. Later in the game he hit another homer. The Dodgers beat the Giants, 11–10, eliminating them from the playoffs. On Oct 7 Bonds hit one more homer to finish the season with 73. He also broke Babe Ruth's slugging record of .847 with .863.

CHIEF JOSEPH SURRENDER: ANNIVERSARY. Oct 5, 1877. After a 1,700-mile retreat, Chief Joseph and the Nez Percé Indians surrendered to US Cavalry troops at Bear's Paw near Chinook, MT, Oct 5, 1877. Chief Joseph made his famous speech of surrender, "From where the sun now stands, I will fight no more forever."

CIVIL WAR "SUBMARINE" ATTACK: ANNIVERSARY. Oct 5, 1863. In an attempt to disrupt the Union blockade of Charleston Harbor, the Confederate semi-submersible *David* rammed the Federal ironclad *New Ironsides* with a spar torpedo. This was the first successful Southern attack using a submersible craft. Although both sides experimented with submarine warfare during the Civil War, the results were far from encouraging, as the submarines caused more fatalities to their own crews than to the opposing side.

EDWARDS, JONATHAN: BIRTH ANNIVERSARY. Oct 5, 1703 (OS). The great theologian and leader of the "Great Awakening," the religious revival in the Colonies, was born at East Windsor, CT. His "Sinners in the Hands of an Angry God" is the most famous sermon in American history. He later became president of Princeton College (then the College of New Jersey). Edwards died at Princeton, NJ, Mar 22, 1758, when he contracted smallpox from an inoculation.

ENRICO FERMI ATOMIC POWER PLANT ACCIDENT: ANNIVERSARY. Oct 5, 1966. A radiation alarm and Class I alert at 3:09 PM, EST, signaled a problem at the Enrico Fermi Atomic Power Plant, Lagoona Beach, near Monroe, MI. The accident was contained, but nearly a decade was required to complete the decommissioning and disassembly of the plant.

GODDARD, ROBERT HUTCHINGS: BIRTH ANNIVERSARY. Oct 5, 1882. The "father of the Space Age," born at Worcester, MA. Largely ignored or ridiculed during his lifetime because of his dreams of rocket travel, including travel to other planets. Launched a liquid-fuel-powered rocket Mar 16, 1926, at Auburn, MA. Died Aug 10, 1945, at Baltimore, MD. See also: "Goddard Day" (Mar 16).

LUMIÈRE, LOUIS: BIRTH ANNIVERSARY. Oct 5, 1864. Born at Besançon, France, Louis Lumière with brother Auguste were film pioneers who created the first movie, "Workers Leaving the Lumière Factory" (1895). He died at Bandol, France, on June 6, 1948.

"MONTY PYTHON'S FLYING CIRCUS" TV PREMIERE: 35th ANNIVERSARY. Oct 5, 1969. This wacky comedy series debuted on BBC-1 in Great Britain and aired until 1974. The cast was made up of Graham Chapman, John Cleese, Eric Idle, Terry Jones, Michael Palin and American Terry Gilliam. John Phillip Sousa's "Liberty Bell March" got the show started, and viewers were treated to surreal animation and such skits as "The Spanish Inquisition" and "The Ministry of Silly Walks." On October 6, 1974, "Monty Python's Flying Circus" began airing in the US. The cast members also made four films together.

☆ Chase's 2004 Calendar of Events ☆   Oct 5

NOBEL CONFERENCE XXXX. Oct 5-6. Gustavus Adolphus College, St. Peter, MN. Annual two-day scientific symposium (40th year), and the only one sanctioned by the Nobel Foundation, Stockholm. Annually, the first Tuesday and Wednesday in October. Est attendance: 6,000. For info: Dean Wahlund, Dir of Special Events, Gustavus Adolphus College, 800 W College Avenue, St. Peter, MN 56082-1498. Phone: (507) 933-7520.

NORSK HOSTFEST. Oct 5-9. State Fairgrounds, Minot, ND. The Northern Plains' biggest ethnic festival draws thousands of people to Minot for Scandinavian and American entertainment, Scandinavian delicacies, arts and crafts exhibits and dignitaries representing Sweden, Norway, Denmark, Iceland and Finland with big-name entertainment nightly. Est attendance: 60,000. For info: (701) 852-2368 or North Dakota Tourism, Century Center, 1600 E Century Ave, Ste 2, Bismarck, ND 58503. Phone: (701) 328-2525 or (800) 435-5663. Web: www.hostfest.com.

PORTUGAL: REPUBLIC DAY. Oct 5. National holiday. Commemorates establishment of the republic in 1910.

SPACE MILESTONE: *CHALLENGER* STS 41-G: 20th ANNIVERSARY. Oct 5, 1984. Space shuttle *Challenger*'s sixth mission with crew of seven, including two women. Launched from Kennedy Space Center, FL, on this date and landed there on Oct 13, 1984. Kathryn D. Sullivan became the first American woman to walk in space.

STONE, THOMAS: DEATH ANNIVERSARY. Oct 5, 1787. Signer of the Declaration of Independence, born 1743 (exact date unknown) at Charles County, MD. Died at Alexandria, VA.

TECUMSEH: DEATH ANNIVERSARY. Oct 5, 1813. Shawnee Indian chief and orator, born at Old Piqua near Springfield, OH, in March 1768. Tecumseh was one of the greatest of Native American leaders. He came to prominence between the years 1799 and 1804 as a powerful orator, defending his people against whites. He denounced as invalid all treaties by which Indians ceded their lands and condemned the chieftains who had entered into such agreements. With his brother Tenskwatawa, the Prophet, he established a town on the Tippecanoe River near Lafayette, IN, and then embarked on a mission to organize an Indian confederation to stop white encroachment. Although he advocated peaceful methods and negotiation, he did not rule out war as a last resort as he visited tribes throughout the country. While he was away, William Henry Harrison defeated the Prophet at the Battle of Tippecanoe Nov 7, 1811, and burned the town. Tecumseh organized a large force of Indian warriors and assisted the British in the War of 1812. Tecumseh was defeated and killed at the Battle of the Thames, Oct 5, 1813.

UNITED NATIONS: WORLD TEACHERS' DAY. Oct 5. A day to honor teachers and their contributions to learning. For info: United Nations, Dept of Public Info, New York, NY 10017. Web: www.un.org.

"YOU BET YOUR LIFE" TV PREMIERE: ANNIVERSARY. Oct 5, 1950. This funny game show began on radio in 1947 and moved to TV with Groucho Marx as host and George Fenneman as announcer and scorekeeper. Players tried to answer questions in the category of their choice, but Groucho's improvised interviews stole the show. Many guests appeared, including Phyllis Diller and Candice Bergen, who would later become famous. Players could also win money by uttering the secret word, an everyday word suspended above the stage on a duck that dropped when the word was spoken. This was one of the few shows to be filmed, because the interviews needed to be edited. Two short-lived revivals of the series aired, with Buddy Hackett as host in 1980, and with Bill Cosby in 1992.

"ZANE GREY THEATER" TV PREMIERE: ANNIVERSARY. Oct 5, 1956. Officially titled "Dick Powell's Zane Grey Theater," this western anthology series was hosted by Powell and featured both stories by Grey and original telecasts. Powell occasionally starred in an episode. Guest stars included Hedy Lamarr (in her only dramatic TV role), Ginger Rogers, Claudette Colbert and Esther Williams.

BIRTHDAYS TODAY

Karen Allen, 53, actress (*The Wanderers, Raiders of the Lost Ark, Starman*), born Carrollton, IL, Oct 5, 1951.
Michael Andretti, 42, race car driver, son of Mario Andretti, born Bethlehem, PA, Oct 5, 1962.
Raymond Lester ("Trace") Armstrong, 39, football player, born Bethesda, MD, Oct 5, 1965.
Josie Bissett, 34, actress ("Melrose Place"), born Seattle, WA, Oct 5, 1970.
Jeff Conaway, 54, actor ("Taxi," *Grease*), born New York, NY, Oct 5, 1950.
Bill Dana, 80, actor, comedian ("The Steve Allen Show," "The Bill Dana Show"), born Quincy, MA, Oct 5, 1924.
Laura Davies, 41, golfer, 1994 LPGA Championship winner, born Coventry, England, Oct 5, 1963.
Bob Geldof, 53, singer, lead singer (Boomtown Rats), born Dublin, Ireland, Oct 5, 1951.
Vaclav Havel, 68, dramatist, President of the Czech Republic, born Prague, Czechoslovakia, Oct 5, 1936.
Grant Hill, 32, basketball player, born Dallas, TX, Oct 5, 1972.
Glynis Johns, 81, actress (*Mary Poppins, The Ref, A Little Night Music*), born Pretoria, South Africa, Oct 5, 1923.
Bil Keane, 82, cartoonist ("Family Circus"), born Philadelphia, PA, Oct 5, 1922.
Mario Lemieux, 39, Hall of Fame hockey player, hockey executive, born Montreal, QC, Canada, Oct 5, 1965.
Bernie Mac, 46, actor ("The Bernie Mac Show," *The Original Kings of Comedy*), born Chicago, IL, Oct 5, 1958.
Steve Miller, 61, musician, singer (Steve Miller Band, "The Joker," "Abracadabra"), born Dallas, TX, Oct 5, 1943.
Patrick Roy, 39, former hockey player, born Quebec City, QC, Canada, Oct 5, 1965.
Kate Winslet, 29, actress (*Titanic*), born Reading, England, Oct 5, 1975.

OCTOBER 6 — WEDNESDAY
Day 280 — 86 Remaining

AMERICAN LIBRARY ASSOCIATION FOUNDING: ANNIVERSARY. Oct 6, 1876. Founded at Philadelphia, PA, by 103 librarians attending the Centennial Exposition.

AMERICAN MASSAGE THERAPY ASSOCIATION® NATIONAL CONVENTION. Oct 6–10. Nashville Convention Center, Nashville, TN. Annual meeting and convention of the American Massage Therapy Association (established 1943), the largest association of professional massage therapists and massage schools, representing more than 46,000 members from throughout the US. Includes continuing education classes, association governance and current massage research. Exhibit area of products and services pertinent to the profession. Est attendance: 800. For info: American Massage Therapy Assn, 820 Davis St, Ste 100, Evanston, IL 60201-4444. Phone: (847) 864-0123. Fax: (847) 864-1178. E-mail: media@amtamassage.org. Web: www.amtamassage.org.

"CSI: CRIME SCENE INVESTIGATION" TV PREMIERE: ANNIVERARY. Oct 6, 2000. CBS's consistently top-rated mystery drama focuses on the Las Vegas Police forensics team led by preternaturally calm Gil Grissom (William Petersen). "CSI" brings science to the foreground, with close-up looks at technology and lab techniques. The show has spawned an equally successful spin-off: "CSI: Miami."

EGYPT: ARMED FORCES DAY: ANNIVERSARY. Oct 6. The Egyptian Army celebrates crossing into Sinai in 1973.

EL-SADAT, ANWAR: ASSASSINATION ANNIVERSARY. Oct 6, 1981. Egyptian president and Nobel Peace Prize recipient Anwar el-Sadat was killed by assassins at Cairo while he was reviewing a military parade commemorating the 1973 Egyptian-Israeli War. At least eight other persons were reported killed in the attack on Sadat. Anwar el-Sadat was born Dec 25, 1918, at Mit Abu Al-Kom, a village near the Nile River delta.

ENGLAND: NOTTINGHAM GOOSE FAIR. Oct 6–9. Forest Recreation Ground, Nottingham. Held annually since 1284 (except during the Great Plague in 1665 and the two World Wars), the fair formerly lasted three weeks and boasted as many as 20,000 geese on display. Now lasting four days, the Nottingham Goose Fair always operates in early October. A traditional fair with modern amusements. For info: Markets Division, Victoria Market Offices, Glasshouse St, Nottingham, England NG1 3LP. Phone: (44) (115) 915-6970 or (44) (115) 915-6973. E-mail: markets.fairs@nottinghamcity.gov.uk. Web: www.nottinghamgoosefair.co.uk.

GERMANY: FRANKFURT BOOK FAIR. Oct 6–11. Fairgrounds, Frankfurt. World's largest international book fair; also important event for electronic media. Best place for international rights and licenses. Open to trade for four days and to the public for two. Est attendance: 265,000. For info: Frankfurt Book Fair, Reineckstr. 3, D-60313 Frankfurt am Main, Germany. Phone: (49) 69 2102-0. Fax: (49) 69 2102-227. E-mail: info@book-fair.com. Web: www.frankfurt-book-fair.com.

HEYERDAHL, THOR: 90th BIRTH ANNIVERSARY. Oct 6, 1914. The anthropologist and explorer was born at Larvik, Norway. Seeking to prove the plausibility of South American peoples having settled Polynesia, he embarked on an epic raft ride with 5 companions in 1947. The "Kon-Tiki" made the 4,300-mile voyage from Peru to Raroia in 101 days. Heyerdahl's book chronicling the adventure became an international best-seller. He continued his travels (including a solo 1970 trip in a reed boat from North Africa to Barbados) and writing until his death. He died at Italy on Apr 18, 2002.

IRELAND: IVY DAY. Oct 6. The anniversary of the death of Irish nationalist leader and Home Rule advocate Charles Stewart Parnell is observed, especially in Ireland, as Ivy Day. A sprig of ivy is worn on the lapel to remember Parnell. James Joyce's short story "Ivy Day in the Committee Room," published in the collection titled *Dubliners*, addresses this event. See also: "Parnell, Charles Stewart: Birth Anniversary" (June 27).

JACKIE MAYER REHAB DAY. Oct 6. Sandusky, OH. Known as Sandusky's "favorite daughter," Jacquelyn Jeanne Mayer, Miss America 1963 and stroke survivor since 1970, is honored on Oct 6, the anniversary of the 1997 renaming of Providence Hospital's rehab and nursing facility as the Jackie Mayer Rehab Center. After her stroke in 1970, it took Jackie Mayer seven years of self-directed rehab to regain her speech and mobility. Since then, she has been a motivational speaker and tireless advocate on behalf of stroke survivors across the US and Canada. She was national spokesperson about stroke for the American Heart Association and the National Stroke Association (NSA). She has received NSA's "Award of Hope and Courage," is a 1997 inductee in the Ohio Women's Hall of Fame and holds an Honorary Doctorate from Lourdes College, Sylvania, OH. For info: Dr. Nancy Linenkugel, OSF, Chatfield College, 20918 State Route 251, St. Martin, OH 45118-9705. Phone: (513) 875-3344. Fax: (513) 875-3912. Web: www.jackiemayer.com. To contact Ms Mayer, phone (419) 433-6163.

LIND, JENNY: BIRTH ANNIVERSARY. Oct 6, 1820. Opera singer known as the "Swedish Nightingale," born at Stockholm, Sweden. She died at Malvern, England, Nov 2, 1887.

MISSISSIPPI STATE FAIR. Oct 6–17. Jackson, MS. Features nightly professional entertainment, livestock show, midway carnival, domestic art exhibits. Est attendance: 620,000. For info: Mississippi Fair Commission, PO Box 892, Jackson, MS 39205. Phone: (601) 961-4000. Fax: (601) 354-6545.

MOON PHASE: LAST QUARTER. Oct 6. Moon enters Last Quarter phase at 6:12 AM, EDT.

★NATIONAL GERMAN-AMERICAN DAY. Oct 6. Celebration of German heritage and contributions German Americans have made to the building of the nation. A Presidential Proclamation has been issued each year since 1987. Annually, Oct 6.

PHYSICIAN ASSISTANT (PA) DAY. Oct 6. To acknowledge the unique contribution of Physician Assistants in providing access to medical care on the anniversary of the graduation of the first class of PAs from Duke University. For info: Nancy Hughes, VP, American Academy of Physician Assistants, 950 N Washington St, Alexandria, VA 22314-1534. Phone: (703) 836-2272. Fax: (703) 684-1924. E-mail: aapa@aapa.org. Web: www.aapa.org.

SEIBERT, FLORENCE: BIRTH ANNIVERSARY. Oct 6, 1897. American physician Florence B. Seibert was born at Easton, PA. She developed the test for tuberculosis that was adopted by the US and used worldwide by the World Health Organization. She died Aug 23, 1991, at St. Petersburg, FL.

WESTINGHOUSE, GEORGE: BIRTH ANNIVERSARY. Oct 6, 1846. Engineer and inventor of the air brake for trains, born at Central Bridge, NY. He was the first employer to give his employees paid vacations. Westinghouse died at New York, NY, Mar 12, 1914.

YOM KIPPUR WAR: ANNIVERSARY. Oct 6–25, 1973. A surprise attack by Egypt and Syria pushed Israeli forces several miles behind the 1967 cease-fire lines. Israel was caught off guard, partly because the attack came on the holiest Jewish religious day. After 18 days of fighting, hostilities were halted by the UN Oct 25. Israel partially recovered from the initial setback but failed to regain all the land lost in the fighting.

October 2004	S	M	T	W	T	F	S
						1	2
	3	4	5	6	7	8	9
	10	11	12	13	14	15	16
	17	18	19	20	21	22	23
	24	25	26	27	28	29	30
	31						

☆ Chase's 2004 Calendar of Events ☆   Oct 6–7

BIRTHDAYS TODAY

Shana Alexander, 79, journalist (formerly of "60 Minutes" Point-Counterpoint segment), author, born Boston, MA, Oct 6, 1925.
Britt Ekland, 62, actress (*The Night They Raided Minsky's*), born Stockholm, Sweden, Oct 6, 1942.
James Gilmore III, 55, former Governor of Virginia (R), born Richmond, VA, Oct 6, 1949.
Rebecca Lobo, 31, basketball player, born Southwick, MA, Oct 6, 1973.
Elisabeth Shue, 41, actress (*Adventures in Babysitting, Leaving Las Vegas*), born Wilmington, DE, Oct 6, 1963.
Fred Travalena, 62, actor ("Keep On Truckin'," "ABC Comedy Hour"), born New York, NY, Oct 6, 1942.
Stephanie Zimbalist, 48, actress ("Remington Steele"), born Encino, CA, Oct 6, 1956.
David Zucker, 57, writer, producer, with his brother Jerry, (*Naked Gun* movies, *Airplane!*), born Milwaukee, WI, Oct 6, 1947.

OCTOBER 7 — THURSDAY
Day 281 — 85 Remaining

ARIZONA STATE FAIR. Oct 7–24. Phoenix, AZ. Festival, concerts, flea markets, entertainment and food. For info: Arizona State Fair, 1826 W McDowell Rd, Phoenix, AZ 85007. Phone: (602) 252-6771. Fax: (602) 495-1302. E-mail: info@azstatefair.com. Web: www.azstatefair.com.

CATS PREMIERES: ANNIVERSARY. Oct 7, 1982. The longest-running production in Broadway history opened this day. *Cats* was based on a book of poetry by T.S. Eliot and had a score by Andrew Lloyd Webber. More than 10 million theatergoers saw the New York City production, which closed Sept 10, 2000, after 7,485 performances. *Cats* was also produced in 30 other countries.

CHICAGO INTERNATIONAL FILM FESTIVAL. Oct 7–21. Chicago, IL. North America's oldest competitive film festival. Some of cinema's greatest filmmakers have been introduced at this festival. Gold and Silver Hugos awarded at its conclusion. For info: Chicago Intl Film Fest, 32 W Randolph St, Ste 600, Chicago, IL 60601. Phone: (312) 425-9400. Fax: (312) 425-0944. E-mail: info@chicagofilmfestival.com or entries@chicagofilmfestival.com. Web: www.chicagofilmfestival.com.

DOW-JONES INDUSTRIAL AVERAGE: ANNIVERSARY. Oct 7, 1896. Dow Jones began reporting an average of the prices of 12 industrial stocks in the *Wall Street Journal* on this day. In the early years these were largely railroad stocks. In 1928 Mr Dow expanded the number of stocks to 30, where it remains today. Today, the large, frequently traded stocks in the DJIA represent about a fifth of the market value of all US stocks.

EAST TEXAS POULTRY FESTIVAL. Oct 7–9. Shelby County Courthouse Square, Center, TX. County fair–style festival featuring carnival rides, food booths run by local charities, art and craft exhibits, live entertainment, chicken clucking contest, street dance, 4-H broiler show and auction. Annually, the first Thursday, Friday and Saturday of October. Est attendance: 15,000. For info: Shelby County Chamber of Commerce, 100 Courthouse Square, Center, TX 75935. Phone: (936) 598-3682. Web: www.shelbycountychamber.com.

IG® NOBEL PRIZE CEREMONY. Oct 7 (scheduled). Sanders Theatre, Harvard University, Cambridge, MA. The "Fourteenth 1st Annual." Honors scientific achievements that cannot or should not be reproduced, with prizes awarded by Nobel laureates. Sponsored by the science humor magazine *Annals of Improbable Research*. Annually, first Thursday in October, pending theatre availability. For info: Marc Abrahams, Annals of Improbable Research, PO Box 380853, Cambridge, MA 02238. Phone: (617) 491-4437. E-mail: marca@chem2.harvard.edu. Web: www.improbable.com.

NATIONAL DEPRESSION SCREENING DAY. Oct 7. Offers free, anonymous education and screening for depression, bipolar disorder, generalized anxiety disorder and post-traumatic stress disorder. The screenings connect people in need with treatment and provide support and resources for friends and family members. For info: Screening for Mental Health, One Washington St, Ste 304, Wellesley Hills, MA 02481-1706. Phone: (781) 239-0071. Fax: (781) 431-7447. Web: www.mentalhealthscreening.org.

RODNEY, CAESAR: BIRTH ANNIVERSARY. Oct 7, 1728 (OS). Signer of the Declaration of Independence who cast a tie-breaking vote. Born near Dover, DE, he died June 26, 1784. Rodney is on the Delaware quarter issued by the US Mint in 1999, the first in a series of quarters that will commemorate each of the 50 states.

SHEMINI ATZERET. Oct 7. Hebrew calendar date: Tishri 22, 5765. The eighth day of Solemn Assembly, part of the Sukkot Festival (see entry on Sept 30), with memorial services and cycle of Biblical readings in the synagogue. Began at sundown on Oct 6.

SOUTH CAROLINA STATE FAIR. Oct 7–17. Columbia, SC. Conklin Shows, rides, musical entertainment, food booths and children's activities. Est attendance: 576,000. For info: South Carolina State Fair, PO Box 393, Columbia, SC 29202. Phone: (803) 799-3387. Fax: (803) 799-1760. E-mail: geninfo@scstatefair.org.

TENNESSEE FALL HOMECOMING. Oct 7–10. Museum of Appalachia, Norris, TN. A celebration of the culture and heritage of Appalachian, pioneer, mountain and rural life. Four stages provide continuous musical performances by more than 260 old-time musicians and legendary greats. Scores of traditional mountain activities such as molasses making, sheepherding, rail splitting, soap making and sawmilling are demonstrated to help preserve the old ways in an interesting and educational manner. For info: John Rice Irwin or Elaine Irwin Meyer, Museum of Appalachia, PO Box 1189, Norris, TN 37828. Phone: (865) 494-0514 or (865) 494-7680. Web: www.museumofappalachia.com.

WALLACE, HENRY AGARD: BIRTH ANNIVERSARY. Oct 7, 1888. Thirty-third vice president of the US (1941–45) born at Adair County, IA. Died at Danbury, CT, Nov 18, 1965.

WISE, THOMAS J.: BIRTH ANNIVERSARY. Oct 7, 1859. English bibliophile and literary forger, born at Gravesend, England. One of England's most distinguished bibliographic experts, he was revealed, in 1934, to have forged dozens of "first editions" and "unique" publications over a period of more than 20 years. Many of them had been sold at high prices to collectors and libraries. The forgeries in some cases purported to pre-date the real first editions. Wise died at Hampstead, England, May 13, 1937.

"YOUR HIT PARADE" TV PREMIERE: ANNIVERSARY. Oct 7, 1950. "Your Hit Parade" began as a radio show in 1935. When it finally made it to TV, the format was simple: the show's cast performed the week's top musical hits. To sustain interest, since many of the same songs appeared weekly, eye-catching production sequences were created. "YHP" was the starting point for many famous choreographers and dancers, including Peter Gennaro and Bob Fosse. Regulars included Dorothy Collins, Eileen Wilson, Snooky Lanson and Sue Bennett. The show was overhauled many times and switched networks before leaving the air in 1959. A summer revival in 1974 was short-lived. See also: "'Your Hit Parade' Radio Premiere: Anniversary" (Apr 12).

Oct 7–8 ☆ Chase's 2004 Calendar of Events ☆

BIRTHDAYS TODAY

June Allyson, 87, actress (*Little Women, The Shrike*, "The June Allyson Show"), born Ella Geisman, Lucerne, NY, Oct 7, 1917.

Imamu Amiri Baraka, 70, poet, dramatist, born Leroi Jones, Newark, NJ, Oct 7, 1934.

Toni Braxton, 37, singer, born Severn, MD, Oct 7, 1967.

Charles Dutoit, 68, Swiss conductor, born Lausanne, Switzerland, Oct 7, 1936.

Thomas Keneally, 69, novelist (*Schindler's List*), born New South Wales, Australia, Oct 7, 1935.

Yo-Yo Ma, 49, cellist, born Paris, France, Oct 7, 1955.

Al Martino, 77, actor, singer (*Hello Dolly, Phantom of the Opera*), born Alfred Cini, Philadelphia, PA, Oct 7, 1927.

John Mellencamp, 53, singer (*American Fool, Uh-Huh*), born Seymour, IN, Oct 7, 1951.

Oliver Laurence North, 61, US Marine Corps Lieutenant Colonel, center of Iran-Contra controversy, born San Antonio, TX, Oct 7, 1943.

Vladimir Putin, 52, Russian president, born St. Petersburg, Russia, Oct 7, 1952.

Desmond Tutu, 73, South African archbishop, Nobel Peace Prize winner, born Klerksdorp, South Africa, Oct 7, 1931.

OCTOBER 8 — FRIDAY
Day 282 — 84 Remaining

ALABAMA NATIONAL FAIR. Oct 8–17. Garrett Coliseum/Fairgrounds, Montgomery, AL. A midway filled with exciting rides and games, arts and crafts, exhibits, livestock shows, racing pigs, a circus, a petting zoo, food and entertainment. Est attendance: 225,000. For info: Hazel Ashmore, PO Box 3304, Montgomery, AL 36109-0304. Phone: (334) 272-6831. Fax: (334) 272-6835. Web: www.alnationalfair.org.

ALGONQUIN MILL FALL FESTIVAL. Oct 8–10. Four miles south of Carrollton, OH. Presented by the Carroll County Historical Society. An 1800s pioneer festival featuring steam-powered grist and sawmill in operation. Also featured are antique tools and farm machinery and quilting, spinning and weaving demonstrations. Log buildings include a bookstore, print shop, souvenir shop and a two-story home. A one-room school and a railroad station are on exhibit. More than 70 quality craftsmen will be demonstrating and selling their products. Est attendance: 35,000. For info: Jeanie Stevens, 3007 Mayham Rd NE, Carrollton, OH 44615. Phone: (330) 627-2946 or (330) 627-5910. Web: www.carrollcountyohio.com.

ALVIN C. YORK DAY. Oct 8, 1918. Sergeant Alvin C. York (while in the Argonne Forest, France, and separated from his patrol) killed 20 enemy soldiers and captured a hill, 132 enemy soldiers and 35 machine guns. He was awarded the US Medal of Honor and French Croix de Guerre. Ironically, York had petitioned for exemption from the draft as a conscientious objector, but was turned down by his local draft board.

APPLE BUTTER MAKIN' DAYS. Oct 8–10. Mt Vernon, MO. A huge festival highlighting the making of apple butter in large copper kettles on the courthouse lawn. Also, 375 crafters displaying and selling handmade goods, free entertainment all three days, apple pie eating contest, hairy legs contest, log sawing contest, bubblegum blowing contest, nail driving contest, pet parade, terrapin race and fiddlers. Annually, the second full weekend in October. Est attendance: 60,000. For info: Chamber of Commerce, PO Box 373, Mt Vernon, MO 65712. Phone: (417) 466-7654.

ARKANSAS STATE FAIR AND LIVESTOCK SHOW. Oct 8–17. Barton Coliseum and State Fairground, Little Rock, AR. Est attendance: 400,000. For info: Arkansas State Fair, 2600 Howard St, Little Rock, AR 72206. Phone: (501) 372-8341. Fax: (501) 372-4197. Web: www.arkfairgrounds.com.

BUTTERFIELD OVERLAND STAGE DAYS. Oct 8–9. Benson, AZ. Commemorates when Benson was a stop for the Overland Stage and the Southern Pacific Railroad came through to make Benson a "Hub City" for three major rail lines. Parade, blues concert, rodeo, food booths and arts and crafts. Est attendance: 7,000. For info: Benson-San Pedro Valley C of C, PO Box 2255, Benson, AZ 85602. Phone: (520) 586-2842. Fax: (520) 586-1972.

CANADA: OKTOBERFEST. Oct 8–16. Kitchener and Waterloo, ON. "The second largest Oktoberfest in the world." More than 70 events and Festhalls including one of the premier parades in Canada on Canadian Thanksgiving morning. Est attendance: 700,000. For info: Kitchener-Waterloo Oktoberfest Inc, PO Box 1053, Kitchener, ON, Canada N2G 4G1. Phone: (519) 570-4267 or (888) 294-HANS. E-mail: info@oktoberfest.ca. Web: www.oktoberfest.ca.

COLUMBUS DAY FESTIVAL AND HOT AIR BALLOON REGATTA. Oct 8–10. Downtown square and Industrial Park, Columbus, KS. Hot Air Balloon Regatta starts with Balloon Glow Friday evening; prizes are awarded for both Saturday and Sunday races. Also, car show, arts and crafts fair, entertainment, children's festival and more. Est attendance: 10,000. For info: Jean Pritchett, Mgr, Columbus Chamber of Commerce, 320 E Maple, Columbus, KS 66725. Phone: (620) 429-1492. Fax: (620) 429-1674. E-mail: columbuschamber@columbus-ks.com. Web: www.columbus-ks.com.

FALL HOME & GARDEN EXPO. Oct 8–10. Omaha Convention Center, Omaha, NE. A consumer show for indoor and outdoor living with seminars and feature areas throughout the show. Est attendance: 25,000. For info: Robert P. Mancuso, Pres, Mid-America Expositions, Inc, 7015 Spring St., Omaha, NE 68106-3518. Phone: (402) 346-8003. Fax: (402) 346-5412. E-mail: showoffice@aol.com. Web: www.showofficeonline.com.

FIREANT FESTIVAL. Oct 8–10. Marshall, TX. Arts and crafts, chili cook-off, Tour de FireAnt bike ride, 5K run, fireant calling contest, fireant roundup, rubber chicken chunking, gurning contest (ugly face), Diaper Derby Contest (crawling), parade, men's crazy leg contest and street dance. Est attendance: 50,000. For info: Marshall Chamber of Commerce, PO Box 520, Marshall, TX 75671. Phone: (903) 935-7868. Fax: (903) 935-9982. E-mail: marshallcvd@hotmail.com. Web: www.marshalltxchamber.com.

FORT LIGONIER DAYS. Oct 8–10. Ligonier, PA. Commemorates the Battle of Ligonier. Reenactments, parade, outdoor entertainment, craft booths and food booths. For info: Rachel Roehrig, Ligonier Chamber of Commerce, 120 E Main St, Ligonier, PA 15658. Phone: (724) 238-4200. Fax: (724) 238-4610. E-mail: ligonier@ligonier.com.

GEORGIA NATIONAL FAIR. Oct 8–17. Georgia National Fairgrounds, Perry, GA. Traditional state agricultural fair features thousands of entries in horse, livestock, horticultural, youth, home and fine arts categories. Family entertainment, education and fun. Sponsored by the State of Georgia. Annually, beginning the fifth Friday after Labor Day. Est attendance: 366,000. For info: John P. Webb, Jr, CFE, Georgia Natl Fair, PO Box 1367, Perry, GA 31069. Phone: (478) 987-3247. E-mail: webb1@alltel.net. Web: www.gnfa.com.

	S	M	T	W	T	F	S
October 2004						1	2
	3	4	5	6	7	8	9
	10	11	12	13	14	15	16
	17	18	19	20	21	22	23
	24	25	26	27	28	29	30
	31						

☆ Chase's 2004 Calendar of Events ☆ Oct 8

GREAT CHICAGO FIRE: ANNIVERSARY. Oct 8, 1871. Great fire of Chicago began, according to legend, when Mrs O'Leary's cow kicked over the lantern in her barn on DeKoven Street. The fire leveled 3½ sq miles, destroying 17,450 buildings and leaving 98,500 people homeless and about 250 people dead. Financially, the loss was $200 million. On the same day a fire destroyed the entire town of Peshtigo, WI, killing more than 1,100 people.

GUMBO FESTIVAL. Oct 8–10. Bridge City, LA. To promote Cajun-French culture and provide the opportunity for people from everywhere to enjoy continuous Cajun entertainment on an outdoor stage and cuisine. Gumbo cooking contests and 5K Bridge Run. Annually, the second weekend in October. Est attendance: 150,000. For info: Rev Msgr J. Anthony Luminais, Pastor, Holy Guardian Angels Church, Box 9069, Bridge City, LA 70096. Phone: (504) 436-4712. Fax: (504) 436-4070. E-mail: gumbofestival@cox.net.

LEE NATIONAL DENIM DAY. Oct 8 (tentative). Lee Jeans invites companies nationwide to participate by allowing employees to wear denim to work in exchange for a contribution of $5 to the Susan G. Komen Breast Cancer Foundation. Since 1996 this program has raised more than $36 million—and the foundation receives 100% of these donations. Sponsored by Lee Jeans. For info: Lee Jeans, One Lee Dr, Merriam, KS 66202. Phone: (800) 521-5533. Fax: (888) 254-4794. E-mail: denimday@vfc.com. Web: www.denimday.com.

MEDFORD JAZZ JUBILEE. Oct 8–10. Medford, OR. 15 nationally known bands will play in downtown Medford locations. More than 100 performances along with fun, food and music for all ages. Est attendance: 6,000. For info: Medford Jazz Jubilee, PMB 201, 221 N Central, Medford, OR 97501. Phone: (541) 770-6972 or (800) 599-0039. E-mail: info@medfordjazz.org. Web: www.medfordjazz.org.

MISSISSINEWA 1812. Oct 8–10. Marion, IN. Largest War of 1812 living history event in US includes reenactment of battle. Military, trappers and woodland Indians living as they did 190 years ago. Est attendance: 32,000. For info: Mississinewa Battlefield Society, PO Box 1812, Marion, IN 46952. Phone: (800) 822-1812. Fax: (765) 662-1809. E-mail: war1812@aol.com.

NATCHEZ FALL PILGRIMAGE. Oct 8–25. Natchez, MS. Tours of 18 antebellum mansions furnished with fine antiques and surrounded by lovely gardens. Carriage and bus sightseeing tours, evening entertainment. Est attendance: 10,000. For info: Natchez Pilgrimage Tours, PO Box 347, Corner of Canal and State Streets, Natchez, MS 39121. Phone: (800) 647-6742 or (601) 446-6631. Fax: (601) 446-8687. E-mail: tours@natchezpilgrimage.com. Web: www.natchezpilgrimage.com.

NATCHITOCHES HISTORIC PILGRIMAGE. Oct 8–10. Natchitoches, LA. Tour of homes in the National Historic Landmark District and plantation homes in Cane River Country. Est attendance: 5,000. For info: Natchitoches Parish Tourist Commission, 781 Front St., Natchitoches, LA 71457. Phone: (318) 352-8072 or (800) 259-1714. Fax: (318) 352-2415. Web: www.natchitoches.net.

NORMAN ROCKWELL'S SELF-PORTRAIT: ANNIVERSARY. Oct 8, 1938. For the *Saturday Evening Post* cover for this date Norman Rockwell chose to portray himself in a quandary he frequently had to grapple with—trying to come up with a cover for the *Post* on deadline.

OKTOBERFEST!. Oct 8–9. Frontier Culture Museum, Staunton, VA. A traditional Oktoberfest celebration with music, dancing, brews, beverages and German foods. Special children's activities during the day on Saturday. For info: Debbie Cole, Frontier Culture Museum, 1290 Richmond Rd, PO Box 810, Staunton, VA 24401. Phone: (540) 332-7850. Fax: (540) 332-9989. E-mail: dcole@frontiermuseum.state.va.us. Web: www.frontiermuseum.org.

"OZZIE AND HARRIET SHOW" RADIO DEBUT: 60th ANNIVERSARY. Oct 8, 1944. Ozzie and Harriet Nelson made their CBS Radio debut in "The Adventures of Ozzie and Harriet." Although their sons David and Ricky were referred to frequently on air and eventually played by others, it was not until Feb 20, 1949, that David (age 12) and Rick (age 8) first appeared playing themselves on the show. "The Adventures of Ozzie and Harriet" hit television airwaves Oct 3, 1952, on ABC.

PARKE COUNTY COVERED BRIDGE FESTIVAL. Oct 8–17. Rockville, IN. Covered bridge capital of the world, 32 historic covered bridges. Headquarters: Courthouse Lawn, Rockville. Guided bus tours on covered bridge routes. Hundreds of booths of arts, crafts, demonstrations, old-fashioned homemade foods and a farmers' market. Annually, beginning on the second Friday in October. Est attendance: 2,000,000. For info: Anne Lynk, Exec Secy, Covered Bridge Capital, PO Box 165, Rockville, IN 47872-0165. Phone: (765) 569-5226. Fax: (765) 569-3900. E-mail: pci@ticz.com. Web: www.coverbridges.com.

PESHTIGO FOREST FIRE: ANNIVERSARY. Oct 8, 1871. One of the most disastrous forest fires in history began at Peshtigo, WI, the same day the Great Chicago Fire began. The Wisconsin fire burned across six counties, killing more than 1,100 people.

RHINELANDER'S OKTOBERFEST. Oct 8–9. Rhinelander, WI. The entire weekend enjoy German music, dancers and food. Est attendance: 9,000. For info: Rhinelander Area Chamber of Commerce, PO Box 795, Rhinelander, WI 54501. Phone: (800) 236-4386. Fax: (715) 365-7467. Web: www.rhinelanderchamber.com.

RICKENBACKER, EDWARD V.: BIRTH ANNIVERSARY. Oct 8, 1890. American aviator, auto racer, war hero, born at Columbus, OH. Died July 23, 1973, at Zurich, Switzerland.

ROCKPORT SEAFAIR. Oct 8–10. Ski Basin area, Rockport, TX. Features fresh-from-the-bay seafood, gumbo cook-off, ongoing live musical entertainment, crab races, arts and crafts booths and land parade on Saturday. Annually, Columbus Day weekend. Est attendance: 20,000. For info: Rockport Seafair, 404 Broadway, Rockport, TX 78381. Phone: (800) 242-0071 or (361) 729-6445. E-mail: leadership@1rockport.org. Web: www.rockport-fulton.org.

Oct 8–9 ☆ ***Chase's 2004 Calendar of Events*** ☆

SAINT CHARLES SCARECROW FESTIVAL. Oct 8–10. St. Charles, IL. More than 100 handcrafted scarecrows invade St. Charles along with live musical entertainment, carnival, children's activities, great food, huge craft show and much more. Est attendance: 100,000. For info: St. Charles Conv & Visitors Bureau, 311 N Second St, Ste 100, St. Charles, IL 60174. Phone: (630) 377-6161 or (800) 777-4373. Web: www.scarecrowfest.com.

SCHÜTZ, HEINRICH: BIRTH ANNIVERSARY. Oct 8, 1585. German musician and composer sometimes called the father of German music. Born at Kostritz, Saxony, Schütz died at Dresden, Germany, Nov 6, 1672. His works enjoyed renewed attention on the occasions of the bicentennial (1885) and tricentennial (1985) of two of his most devoted followers: George Frederick Handel and Johann Sebastian Bach.

SIMCHAT TORAH. Oct 8. Hebrew calendar date: Tishri 23, 5765. Rejoicing in the Torah concludes the nine-day Sukkot Festival (see entry on Sept 30). Public reading of the Pentateuch is completed and begun again, symbolizing the need for ever-continuing study. Began at sundown on Oct 7.

SOUTHERN FESTIVAL OF BOOKS: A CELEBRATION OF THE WRITTEN WORD. Oct 8–10. War Memorial Plaza, Nashville, TN. To promote reading, writing, the literary arts and a broader understanding of the language and culture of the South, this annual festival will feature readings, talks and panel discussions by more than 200 authors, exhibit booths of publishing companies and bookstores, autographing sessions, a comprehensive children's program and a Cafe Stage, which is a performance corner for authors, storytellers and musicians. Annually, the second weekend in October. Est attendance: 30,000. For info: Serenity Gerbman, Dir, Southern Festival of Books, Tennessee Humanities Council, 1003 18th Ave S, Nashville, TN 37212. Phone: (615) 320-7001 x 12. Fax: (615) 321-4586. E-mail: serenity@tn-humanities.org. Web: www.tn-humanities.org.

SUGARLOAF CRAFTS FESTIVAL. Oct 8–10. Montgomery County Fairgrounds, Gaithersburg, MD. This show, now in its 4th year, features more than 475 nationally recognized craft designers and fine artists displaying and selling their original creations. Includes craft demonstrations, live music, specialty food, hourly gift certificate drawings and more. Est attendance: 22,000. For info: Sugarloaf Mountain Works, 200 Orchard Ridge Dr, #215, Gaithersburg, MD 20878. Phone: (800) 210-9900. Fax: (310) 253-9620. Web: www.sugarloafcrafts.com.

VICTORIAN WEEK. Oct 8–17. Cape May, NJ. Hailed as "A Top 100 Event in North America," the 32nd annual Victorian Week is a 10-day celebration of Cape May's Victorian heritage, with self-guided tours of Victorian homes, antiques and crafts shows, brass band concerts, murder mystery dinners, authentic Victorian feasts, Victorian fashion shows, workshops, tours and lectures. Annually, 10 days beginning the Friday before Columbus Day. Est attendance: 20,000. For info: Mid-Atlantic Center for the Arts, 1048 Washington St, Cape May, NJ 08204. Phone: (800) 275-4278. Fax: (609) 884-0574. E-mail: mac4arts@capemaymac.org. Web: www.capemaymac.org.

WINCHELL'S DONUT HOUSE ESTABLISHED: ANNIVERSARY. Oct 8, 1948. Since the grand opening of its first donut house in Temple City, CA, Winchell's has offered warm and fresh donuts from its own speciality mixes featuring the finest ingredients. Winchell's even invented the apple fritter in 1964! For more than 50 years, Winchell's donuts have been an American institution. Winchell's Donut House, 2223 Wellington Ave, Ste 300, Santa Ana, CA 92701. Phone: (714) 565-1800. Fax: (714) 565-1801. Web: winchells.com.

October 2004

S	M	T	W	T	F	S
					1	2
3	4	5	6	7	8	9
10	11	12	13	14	15	16
17	18	19	20	21	22	23
24	25	26	27	28	29	30
31						

WORLD EGG DAY. Oct 8. Dedicated to the global appeal of the billions of nutritious eggs produced worldwide. Annually, the second Friday of October. For info: Linda Braun, Consumer Services Dir, American Egg Bd, 1460 Renaissance Dr, Park Ridge, IL 60068. Web: www.aeb.org.

BIRTHDAYS TODAY

Rona Barrett, 68, gossip columnist, born New York, NY, Oct 8, 1936.
Craig Benson, 50, Governor of New Hampshire (R), born New York, NY, Oct 8, 1954.
Chevy Chase, 61, comedian, actor ("Saturday Night Live," *Caddyshack*), born Cornelius Crane, New York, NY, Oct 8, 1943.
Clodagh, 67, designer, born Clodagh Aubry, Galway, Ireland, Oct 8, 1937.
Matt Damon, 34, actor (*Good Will Hunting, The Rainmaker*), born Cambridge, MA, Oct 8, 1970.
Bill Elliott, 49, race car driver, born Dawsonville, GA, Oct 8, 1955.
Paul Hogan, 65, actor, writer (*Crocodile Dundee, Crocodile Dundee II*), born Lightning Ridge, Australia, Oct 8, 1939.
Jesse Jackson, 63, clergyman, civil rights leader ("I am somebody," "Keep hope alive"), born Greenville, NC, Oct 8, 1941.
Sarah Purcell, 56, TV personality ("Real People"), born Richmond, IN, Oct 8, 1948.
Faith Ringgold, 74, artist, writer (*Tar Beach, My Dream of Martin Luther King*), born New York, NY, Oct 8, 1930.
Rashaan Salaam, 30, former football player, born San Diego, CA, Oct 8, 1974.
R.L. Stine, 61, author (Goosebumps series), born Columbus, OH, Oct 8, 1943.
Sigourney (Susan) Weaver, 55, actress (*Ghostbusters, Gorillas in the Mist, Aliens*), born New York, NY, Oct 8, 1949.

OCTOBER 9 — SATURDAY
Day 283 — 83 Remaining

APPLE BUTTER FESTIVAL. Oct 9–10. Berkeley Springs, WV. Fall festival with spicy apple butter simmering in copper kettles in the town square. A parade, two days of mountain music and old-fashioned contests. Fine crafts, farmers' market, down-home cooking and fall foliage. Annually, Columbus Day weekend. Est attendance: 40,000. For info: Apple Butter Festival, 127 Fairfax St, Berkeley Springs, WV 25411. Phone: (304) 258-3738. Web: www.berkeleysprings.com.

ARROW ROCK HERITAGE CRAFT FESTIVAL. Oct 9–10. Arrow Rock, MO. 1850s crafters demonstrate and sell crafts of daily living: bobbin lace making, rope braiding, basketmaking, candle dipping, soapmaking, silhouettes, blacksmithing and more. Historic buildings open to tour, entrance fee is $1 per person, 5 & under are free. Annually, the second full weekend in October. Est attendance: 6,500. For info: Historic Arrow Rock Council, PO Box 121, Arrow Rock, MO 65320. Phone: (660) 837-3306. E-mail: garlin@mid-mo.net.

☆ Chase's 2004 Calendar of Events ☆   Oct 9

CATOCTIN COLORFEST ARTS AND CRAFTS SHOW. Oct 9–10. Thurmont, MD. Live music, food. 350 arts and crafts booths featuring artists from Maryland, Virginia, West Virginia and Pennsylvania. Annually, the second weekend in October. Est attendance: 100,000. For info send a SASE to: Catoctin ColorFest, Inc, Box 33, Thurmont, MD 21788. Phone: (301) 271-4432. Web: www.colorfest.org.

CHOWDERFEST. Oct 9–11. Mystic Seaport, Mystic, CT. Columbus Day weekend. A riverfront festival of New England chowders. Est attendance: 9,000. For info: Mystic Seaport, 75 Greenmanville Ave, PO Box 6000, Mystic, CT 06355-0990. Phone: (860) 572-5315 or (888) 9SEAPORT. Web: www.visitmysticseaport.org.

CHRYSLER CLASSIC SPEED FESTIVAL. Oct 9–10. Naval Air Station, North Island, Coronado, San Diego, CA. This San Diego bayside vintage auto racing event is a presentation of the Holiday Bowl, a production of General Racing, Ltd. Est attendance: 30,000. For info: Mark Neville, Holiday Bowl, PO Box 601400, San Diego, CA 92160-1400. Phone: (619) 283-5808. Fax: (619) 281-7947. Web: www.pacificlifeholidaybowl.com.

COAST DAY NJ. Oct 9–10. Long Beach Island, NJ, on Oct 9 and Cape May, NJ, on Oct 10. Celebrating New Jersey's marine and coastal environment and all that it provides. Enjoy music, dock and ship tours, eco-tours and lots of hands-on family fun designed to help you learn more about our 127-mile coastline. Meet scientists, researchers, educators, commercial fishers and government agencies all on hand to tell you about their work and programs. Annually, Columbus Day weekend. For info: New Jersey Marine Sciences Consortium, Sandy Hook Field Station, Building 22, Fort Hancock, NJ 07732. Phone: (732) 872-1300. Fax: (732) 872-9573. E-mail: cvalkos@njmsc.org. Web: www.njmsc.org.

ELDON TURKEY FESTIVAL. Oct 9. Eldon, MO. A celebration of Miller County's state and national ranking as a top producer of wild and domestic turkeys. Event includes more than 200 crafters and exhibitors, turkey events, food, quilt show and old-time machinery show. Annually, the second Saturday in October. Est attendance: 10,000. For info: Eldon Chamber of Commerce, PO Box 209, Eldon, MO 65026. Phone: (573) 392-3752. Fax: (573) 392-0634. Web: www.eldonchamber.com.

FAIRE ON THE SQUARE ART & CRAFT FAIR. Oct 9. Sauk County Courthouse Square Park, Downtown Baraboo, WI. Annual outdoor event. Features all handmade work of 150 artists and crafters, local cuisine food stands, farmers' market, live entertainment, carnival, kids' activities and Creation Station craft workshops for kids. Held during peak fall color time for travelers in this area of scenic Wisconsin. Visit local orchards and browse the unique specialty shops in historic downtown Baraboo. Annually, the second Saturday in October. Est attendance: 8,000. For info: Cindy Doescher, Fan Faire Promotions, LLC, 1801 Jefferson St, Baraboo, WI 53913. Phone: (608) 356-7995. E-mail: info@downtownbaraboo.com. Web: www.downtownbaraboo.com.

FOREST CRAFT/SCENIC DRIVE FESTIVAL. Oct 9–10. Van Buren County, IA. Scenic landscapes, historic architecture, wood carvers, buckskinners camp, flea market, arts festival, crafts and more. Annually, the second full weekend in October. Est attendance: 18,000. For info: Villages of Van Buren, Inc, PO Box 9, Keosauqua, IA 52565. Phone: (800) TOU-RVBC. Fax: (319) 293-7116. Web: www.800-tourvbc.com.

HARVEST WEEKEND. Oct 9–10. Woodstock, VT. Traditional celebration of the harvest featuring a husking bee and the arrival of the giant pumpkins. Also, farm harvest activities including food preservation, traditional toy making and cider pressing. Est attendance: 1,600. For info: Billings Farm and Museum, PO Box 489, Woodstock, VT 05091. Phone: (802) 457-2355. Fax: (802) 457-4663. E-mail: billings.farm@valley.net. Web: www.billingsfarm.org.

ICELAND: LEIF ERIKSON DAY. Oct 9. Celebrates discovery of North America in the year 1000 by Norse explorer.

INDIAN SUMMER DAYS AT AUDUBON ACRES. Oct 9. Audubon Acres, Chattanooga, TN. Enjoy the games of Native Americans and pioneers, participate in Native American dance, listen to stories and talk to and watch Native American craftspersons and demonstrations of pioneer skills. Sponsor: Chattanooga Audubon Society. Est attendance: 1,500. For info: Lynda Logan, Audubon Acres, 900 N Sanctuary Rd, Chattanooga, TN 37421. Phone: (423) 892-1499. Fax: (423) 892-6376. E-mail: caudubons@aol.com. Web: www.audubonchattanooga.org.

JAY PEAK ANNUAL ARTS AND CRAFTS FAIR. Oct 9–10. Jay Peak Ski Resort, Jay, VT. This annual event features primarily Vermont artists and artisans. The show is juried, providing many crafters the opportunity to display their wares such as jewelry, woodworking, painting, slate, maple syrup and other food products, clothing, quilting, candle making, toys, dolls, pottery, glass, just to name a few. Fall foliage tramway rides, hiking, brunch both Sat & Sun, buffets. Annually, the Saturday and Sunday before Columbus Day. Est attendance: 6,000. For info: Jay Peak Resort, Rte 242, Jay, VT 05859. Phone: (802) 988-2611, x 8215 or 8205. Fax: (802) 988-2049. E-mail: bkeet@jaypeakresort.com. Web: www.jaypeakresort.com.

KOREA: ALPHABET DAY (HANGUL): ANNIVERSARY. Oct 9. Celebrates anniversary of promulgation of Hangul (24-letter phonetic alphabet) by King Sejong of the Yi Dynasty in 1446.

★**LEIF ERIKSON DAY.** Oct 9. Presidential Proclamation always issued for Oct 9 since 1964 (PL88–566 of Sept 2, 1964) at request.

LENNON, JOHN: BIRTH ANNIVERSARY. Oct 9, 1940. John Winston Lennon, English composer, musician and member of The Beatles, the sensationally popular group of musical performers who captivated audiences first in England and Germany, and later throughout the world. A fervent activist for peace. Born at Liverpool, England, Lennon was murdered at New York City, Dec 8, 1980.

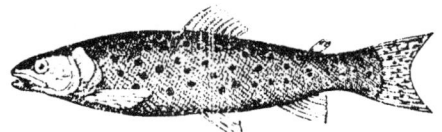

LONG BEACH ISLAND SURF FISHING TOURNAMENT. Oct 9–Nov 21. Long Beach Island, NJ. 50th annual LBI Surf Fishing Tournament. Thousands of dollars in daily, weekly, and grand prizes for bluefish and striped bass. Always starts the Saturday of Columbus Day weekend. For info: Southern Ocean County Chamber of Commerce, 265 W 9th St, Ship Bottom, NJ 08008. Phone: (800) 292-6372. Fax: (609) 494-5807. E-mail: sochamber@aol.com. Web: www.discoversouthernocean.org.

LONGWOOD GARDENS AUTUMN'S COLORS. Oct 9–22. Kennett Square, PA. Outdoor display features a harvest rainbow of brilliant foliage on 1,050 acres. Est attendance: 50,000. For info: Elizabeth Sullivan, PR Dir, Longwood Gardens, PO Box 501, Kennett Square, PA 19348-0501. Phone: (610) 388-1000. Web: www.longwoodgardens.org.

MAPLE LEAF FESTIVAL. Oct 9–16. Carthage, MO. Brilliant fall foliage gives this Victorian city the perfect backdrop. A 150+ unit parade, four-state marching band competition, nationwide car show (more than 500 entries), arts and crafts show, plus entertainment and much more. Est attendance: 60,000. For info: Chamber of Commerce, 107 E 3rd St, Carthage, MO 64836. Phone: (417) 358-2373. Fax: (417) 358-7479. E-mail: info@carthagechamber.com.

MISSION DELORES FOUNDING: ANNIVERSARY. Oct 9, 1776. The oldest building at San Francisco, CA. Formerly known as Mission San Francisco de Asis, the mission survived the great earthquake and fire of 1906.

531

Oct 9 ☆ Chase's 2004 Calendar of Events ☆

MOUNTAIN GLORY FESTIVAL. Oct 9. Marion, NC. A celebration of mountain heritage in western North Carolina. Arts, crafts, children's area and continuous entertainment. Also, "Mountain Glory Metric Century" bicycle ride. Annually, the second Saturday in October. Est attendance: 20,000. For info: Robert Parker, PO Drawer 700, Marion, NC 28752. Phone: (828) 652-3551. Fax: (828) 652-1983. E-mail: mtglory@wnclink.com. Web: www.mtgloryfestival.com.

NORTHEAST MARBLE MEET. Oct 9–10. Radisson Inn, Marlborough, MA. Auction, exhibits; dealers and collectors buy, sell and trade marbles. Est attendance: 1,000. For info: Bert Cohen, 169 Marlborough St, Boston, MA 02116. Phone: (617) 247-4754. Fax: (617) 247-9093. E-mail: marblebert@aol.com. Web: www.marblebert.com.

OYSTER FESTIVAL. Oct 9. Chincoteague Island, VA. Oysters fixed every way possible—all you can eat. Annually, Saturday of Columbus Day weekend. Tickets can be obtained in advance by contacting Chincoteague Chamber of Commerce. Est attendance: 2,700. For info: Chincoteague Chamber of Commerce, 6733 Maddox Blvd, Chincoteague Island, VA 23336. Phone: (757) 336-6161. Fax: (757) 336-1242. E-mail: pony@intercom.net. Web: www.chincoteaguechamber.com.

PERU: DAY OF NATIONAL HONOR: ANNIVERSARY. Oct 9. Public holiday. Commemorates nationalization of the oil fields in 1968.

PINE BARRENS JAMBOREE. Oct 9. Wells Mills County Park, Waretown, NJ. Celebrate the culture and natural history of the New Jersey Pinelands. Folk and country music, crafts, wood carvers, nature walks, canoeing, children's games, food and more. Free rain or shine. Est attendance: 1,500. For info: Michelle Urban, Wells Mills County Park, 905 Wells Mills Rd, Waretown, NJ 08758. Phone: (609) 971-3085. Fax: (609) 971-9540. Web: www.co.ocean.nj.us/Parks.

PRATER'S MILL COUNTRY FAIR. Oct 9–10. Dalton, GA. A Southern festival of artists, craftsmen, music and food. Est attendance: 15,000. For info: Judy Alderman, Prater's Mill Fdtn, Inc, 500 Prater's Mill Rd, GA Hwy 2, Dalton, GA 30721. Phone: (706) 694-MILL or (800) 331-3258. Fax: (706) 694-8413. E-mail: pratersmill@daton.net. Web: PratersMill.org.

SEDONA ARTS FESTIVAL. Oct 9–10. Sedona, AZ. Annual celebration of visual, performing and culinary arts. Creative artisans present a unique collection of fine arts, crafts, foods, music and entertainment, surrounded by the scenic grandeur of towering red rocks. Application deadline: April 15. Admission $7; children 12 and under free with paid adult. Proceeds will benefit the cultural arts of Sedona. Rated best arts festival in Northern Arizona. Est attendance: 5,000. For info: Sedona Arts Festival, PO Box 2729, Sedona, AZ 86339-2729. Phone: (928) 204-9456. Fax: (928) 204-9456.

"TOPPER" TV PREMIERE: ANNIVERSARY. Oct 9, 1953. In this sitcom a man moves into a new home with his wife, only to discover that it's haunted by ghosts only he can see. Leo G. Carroll starred as Cosmo Topper and Anne Jeffreys and Robert Sterling starred as Marion and George Kerby, who had been killed in a skiing accident and returned to their former home as ghosts. The show was based on Thorne Smith's novel and used trick photography for some of the ghost scenes.

UGANDA: INDEPENDENCE DAY. Oct 9. National holiday commemorating achievement of autonomy from Britain in 1962.

UNITED NATIONS: WORLD POST DAY. Oct 9. An annual special observance of Postal Administrations of the Universal Postal Union (UPU). For info: United Nations, Dept of Public Info, Public Inquiries Unit, Rm GA-57, New York, NY 10017. Phone: (212) 963-4475. E-mail: inquiries@un.org. Web: www.un.org.

USGA SENIOR AMATEUR (GOLF) CHAMPIONSHIP. Oct 9–14. Bel-Air Country Club, Los Angeles, CA. For info: US Golf Assn, Golf House, PO Box 708, Championship Dept, Far Hills, NJ 07931. Phone: (908) 234-2300. Fax: (908) 234-9687. E-mail: usga@usga.org. Web: www.usga.org.

VERMONT APPLE FESTIVAL. Oct 9–10. Riverside Middle School, Springfield, VT. Craft fair, apples, games and other family entertainment. Annually, Columbus Day weekend. Est attendance: 6,000. For info: Springfield Chamber of Commerce, 14 Clinton St, Springfield, VT 05156. Phone: (802) 885-2779. E-mail: spfldcoc@vermontel.com.

VIVA ITALIA!. Oct 9–10. Hollywood, FL. A celebration of Italian culture complete with traditional entertainment, dancing, food and crafts highlighted by Italian sauce tasting contest. Children's activities. Est attendance: 10,000. For info: Roguey Doyle, City of Hollywood, Dept of Parks, Recreation & Cultural Arts, 1940 Harrison St, Hollywood, FL 33020. Phone: (954) 921-3404.

WORLD WRISTWRESTLING CHAMPIONSHIPS. Oct 9. Petaluma, CA. Nationally recognized event with more than 500 entrants vying for the title of World Wristwrestling Champion. Est attendance: 1,000. For info: Bill Soberanes, c/o *Argus Courier*, 423 E Washington St, Petaluma, CA 94952. Phone: (707) 778-1430. Web: www.armwrestling.com.

BIRTHDAYS TODAY

Scott Bakula, 49, actor ("Enterprise," "Quantum Leap"), born St. Louis, MO, Oct 9, 1955.

Jackson Browne, 54, singer, songwriter ("Running on Empty," "Lawyers in Love"), born Heidelberg, Germany, Oct 9, 1950.

Zachery Ty Bryan, 23, actor ("Home Improvement"), born Aurora, CO, Oct 9, 1981.

Trent Lott, 63, US Senator (R, Mississippi), born Duck Hill, MS, Oct 9, 1941.

Russell Myers, 66, cartoonist ("Broom Hilda"), born Pittsburg, KS, Oct 9, 1938.

Michael Pare, 45, actor (*Streets of Fire, The Philadelphia Experiment*), born Brooklyn, NY, Oct 9, 1959.

Joseph Anthony (Joe) Pepitone, 64, former baseball player, born New York, NY, Oct 9, 1940.

Tony Shalhoub, 51, actor ("Wings," "Stark Raving Mad"), born Green Bay, WI, Oct 9, 1953.

Donald Sinden, 81, actor (*The Day of the Jackal*), born Plymouth, England, Oct 9, 1923.

Michael (Mike) Singletary, 46, Hall of Fame football player, born Houston, TX, Oct 9, 1958.

Annika Sorenstam, 34, golfer, born Stockholm, Sweden, Oct 9, 1970.

Robert Wuhl, 53, writer, actor (*Bull Durham, Cobb*), born Union, NJ, Oct 9, 1951.

October 2004

S	M	T	W	T	F	S
					1	2
3	4	5	6	7	8	9
10	11	12	13	14	15	16
17	18	19	20	21	22	23
24	25	26	27	28	29	30
31						

OCTOBER 10 — SUNDAY
Day 284 — 82 Remaining

AGNEW RESIGNATION: ANNIVERSARY. Oct 10, 1973. Spiro Theodore Agnew became the second person to resign the office of vice president of the United States. Agnew entered a plea of no contest to a charge of income tax evasion (on contract kickbacks received while he was governor of Maryland and after he became vice president). He was sentenced to pay a $10,000 fine and serve three years probation. Agnew was elected vice president twice, serving under President Richard M. Nixon. See also "Agnew, Spiro: Birth Anniversary" (Nov 9).

ASSOCIATION FOR DRESSINGS AND SAUCES ANNUAL MEETING. Oct 10–12. Ritz-Carlton, Amelia Island, FL. For info: Jacque Knight, Assn for Dressings and Sauces, 5775 Peachtree-Dunwoody Rd, Bldg G, Ste 500, Atlanta, GA 30342. Phone: (404) 252-3663. Fax: (404) 252-0774. E-mail: ads@kellencompany.com. Web: www.dressings-sauces.org.

"THE BOB NEWHART SHOW" TV PREMIERE: ANNIVERSARY. Oct 10, 1962. This half-hour variety series was hosted by Bob Newhart, a successful stand-up comedian famous for his trademark "telephone conversation" monologues. The show was critically acclaimed, winning both an Emmy and a Peabody in its short time on the air. Newhart later starred in situation comedies. In "The Bob Newhart Show," which aired 1972–78, he played a psychologist. See also: "Newhart TV Premiere: Anniversary" (Oct 25).

BONZA BOTTLER DAY™. Oct 10. To celebrate when the number of the day is the same as the number of the month. Bonza Bottler Day™ is an excuse to have a party at least once a month. For more information, see Jan 1. For info: Gail M. Berger, 14 Fernwood Dr, Taylors, SC 29687. Phone: (864) 609-9874. E-mail: gberger5@aol.com.

BRAZIL: CIRIO DE NAZARE. Oct 10–23. Greatest festival of northern Brazil, the Feast of Cirio starts on second Sunday of October in city of Belem (St. Mary of Bethlehem), capital of the state of Para. Festival lasts two weeks.

BUILD YOUR BUSINESS WITH BUSINESS CARDS WEEK. Oct 10–16. Celebrate the power of the world's most portable, affordable and versatile marketing tool—the business card. An excellent reason to contact previous customers and cultivate new relationships. Event ideas and materials available. Annually, the week beginning with the second Sunday in October. For info: Diana Ratliff. E-mail: diana@businesscarddesign.com. Web: www.businesscardweek.com.

CHINA: BIRTHDAY OF CONFUCIUS. Oct 10. Observed on 27th day of 8th lunar month.

CUBA: BEGINNING OF INDEPENDENCE WARS DAY. Oct 10. National holiday. Commemorates the beginning of struggle against Spain in 1868.

DOUBLE TENTH DAY: ANNIVERSARY. Oct 10, 1911. Tenth day of 10th month, Double Tenth Day, is observed by many Chinese as the anniversary of the outbreak of the revolution against the imperial Manchu dynasty, Oct 10, 1911. Sun Yat-sen and Huan Hsing were among the revolutionary leaders. This is a holiday in Taiwan.

EMERGENCY NURSES WEEK. Oct 10–16. Sponsored by the Emergency Nurses Association (ENA) since 1989, this is a weeklong celebration recognizing emergency nurses for their dedication, service and commitment to their patients and communities. Special focus is given on Wednesday, which is Emergency Nurses Day (Oct 13), to honor nursing professionals who provide care to those whose lives have been touched by life's tragedies. For info: Debra Bethard-Caplick, ENA, 915 Lee St, Des Plaines, IL 60016. Phone: (847) 460-4049. Fax: (847) 460-4002. E-mail: dcaplick@ena.org. Web: www.ena.org.

FIJI: INDEPENDENCE DAY: ANNIVERSARY. Oct 10. National holiday. Commemorates independence from Britain in 1970.

GETTING THE WORLD TO BEAT A PATH TO YOUR DOOR WEEK. Oct 10–16. To focus attention on improving "public relationships" in order to create success for companies, products and individuals. Free self-evaluation available. Annually, the third week in October. For info: Barbara Gaughen, Pres, Gaughen Global Public Relations, 7456 Evergreen Dr, Santa Barbara, CA 93117. Phone: (805) 968-8567. Fax: (805) 968-5747. E-mail: bgaughenmu@aol.com.

GRANDMOTHER'S DAY IN FLORIDA. Oct 10. A ceremonial day on the second Sunday in October.

HAYES, HELEN: BIRTH ANNIVERSARY. Oct 10, 1900. Actress Helen Hayes, often called the First Lady of the American Theater, was born at Washington, DC. Hayes's greatest stage triumph was her role as the long-lived British monarch Queen Victoria in the play *Victoria Regina*. Her first great success was in *Coquette* (1927). She won an Academy Award for best actress for her first major film role in *The Sin of Madelon Claudet* (1931) and won best supporting actress for her role in *Airport* (1971). Helen Hayes died Mar 17, 1993, at Nyack, NY.

HOME-BASED BUSINESS WEEK. Oct 10–16. To celebrate, recognize and promote the home-based entrepreneur. Annually, the week including the second Tuesday of October. For info: Beverley Williams, The Home Business Advocate. E-mail: bevspeaks@earthlink.net. Web: www.aahbb.org.

THE LASALLE BANK CHICAGO MARATHON. Oct 10. Grant Park, Chicago, IL. The world's fastest 26.2-mile marathon attracts an international field of top athletes. Est attendance: 40,000. For info: The LaSalle Bank Chicago Marathon, 11 E Adams, Lower Level II, Chicago, IL 60604. Phone: (312) 904-9800. Fax: (312) 904-9820. Web: www.chicagomarathon.com.

NATIONAL ADULT IMMUNIZATION AWARENESS WEEK. Oct 10–16. Thousands of deaths occur each year—deaths which could be easily prevented by today's available vaccines. NAIAW emphasizes the importance of appropriately vaccinating adults against measles, mumps, rubella, hepatitis A, hepatitis B, tetanus, diphtheria, influenza, pneumococcal disease and varicella. A campaign kit of materials is available. For info: Natl Coalition for Adult Immunization, 4733 Bethesda Ave, Ste 750, Bethesda, MD 20814-5278. Phone: (301) 656-0003. Fax: (301) 907-0878. E-mail: ncai@nfid.org. Web: www.NFID.org/NCAI.

NATIONAL FOOD BANK WEEK. Oct 10–16. Educates and recognizes efforts of food banks, their donors and volunteers to alleviate hunger in the US. Annually, the week encompassing World Food Day (Oct 16). For info: Jo Grant, 2802 Dairy Dr, Madison, WI 53718. Phone: (608) 223-9121. Fax: (608) 223-9840. E-mail: jgrant@secondharvest.org. Web: www.secondharvestmadison.org.

NATIONAL METRIC WEEK. Oct 10–16. To maintain an awareness of the importance of the metric system as the primary system of measurement for the US. Annually, the week of the tenth month containing the tenth day of the month. For info: US Metric Assn, 10245 Andasol Ave, Northridge, CA 91325-1504. Phone: (818) 363-5606. Web: www.metric.org.

NATIONAL SCHOOL LUNCH WEEK. Oct 10–16. To celebrate good nutrition and healthy, safe school lunches. Annually, the second full week in October. For info: Service Center, American School Food Service Assn, 700 S Washington St, Ste 300, Alexandria, VA 22314-4287. Phone: (703) 739-3900. Web: www.asfsa.org.

★**NATIONAL SCHOOL LUNCH WEEK.** Oct 10–16. Presidential Proclamation issued for the week beginning with the second Sunday in October since 1962 (PL87–780 of Oct 9, 1962). Note: Not issued in 1981.

OKLAHOMA HISTORICAL DAY. Oct 10. Oklahoma.

PEARL, DANIEL: BIRTH ANNIVERSARY. Oct 10, 1963. Born at Princeton, NJ, Daniel Pearl was a foreign correspondent for the *Wall Street Journal* when he was assassinated by a terrorist group in Pakistan. His body was found in Karachi, Pakistan, where he had been researching terrorist threats against America. British-born Islamic militant Ahmed Omar Sheikh, a leader of the National Movement for the Restoration of Pakistani Sovereignty, was convicted of Pearl's kidnapping and murder. Pearl was 38 at the time he was kidnapped, on Jan 23, 2002.

SAMOA AND AMERICAN SAMOA: WHITE SUNDAY. Oct 10. The second Sunday in October. For the children of Samoa and American Samoa, this is the biggest day of the year. Traditional roles are reversed, as children lead church services, are served special foods and receive gifts of new church clothes and other special items. All the children dress in white. The following Monday is an official holiday.

TAIWAN: DOUBLE TENTH DAY. Oct 10. Commemorates the proclamation of the Chinese Republic in 1911.

TUXEDO CREATED: ANNIVERSARY. Oct 10, 1886. Griswold Lorillard of Tuxedo Park, NY, fashioned the first tuxedo for men by cutting the tails off a tailcoat.

UNITED NATIONS: WORLD MENTAL HEALTH DAY. Oct 10. For info: United Nations, Dept of Public Info, New York, NY 10017. Web: www.un.org.

"UPSTAIRS, DOWNSTAIRS" TV PREMIERE: ANNIVERSARY. Oct 10, 1971. The 52 episodes of this Masterpiece Theatre series covered the years 1903 to 1930 in the life of a wealthy London family ("Upstairs") and their many servants ("Downstairs"). Produced by London Weekend Television, cast members included Angela Baddeley, Pauline Collins, Gordon Jackson and Jean Marsh. Won a Golden Globe for Best Drama TV Show in 1975 and an Emmy for Outstanding Limited Series in 1976. The last episode aired May 1, 1977, though the series has been rerun several times on PBS.

US NAVAL ACADEMY FOUNDED: ANNIVERSARY. Oct 10, 1845. A college to train officers for the navy was established at Annapolis, MD. Women were admitted in 1976. The Academy's motto is "Honor, Courage, Commitment." For more info: www.usna.edu.

VERDI, GIUSEPPI: BIRTH ANNIVERSARY. Oct 10, 1813. Italian composer, born at Le Roncole, Italy. His 26 operas include *Rigoletto*, *Il Trovatore*, *La Traviata* and *Aida*, and are among the most popular of all operatic music today. Died at Milan, Italy, Jan 27, 1901.

	S	M	T	W	T	F	S
October 2004						1	2
	3	4	5	6	7	8	9
	10	11	12	13	14	15	16
	17	18	19	20	21	22	23
	24	25	26	27	28	29	30
	31						

BIRTHDAYS TODAY

Bob Burnquist, 28, skateboarder, born Rio de Janeiro, Brazil, Oct 10, 1976.
Charles Dance, 58, actor (*The Jewel in the Crown, White Mischief*), born Worcestershire, England, Oct 10, 1946.
Dale Earnhardt, Jr, 30, race car driver, born Concord, NC, Oct 10, 1974.
Brett Favre, 35, football player, born Gulfport, MS, Oct 10, 1969.
Jessica Harper, 55, actress (*Stardust Memories, Pennies from Heaven, My Favorite Year*), born Chicago, IL, Oct 10, 1949.
Mario Lopez, 31, actor ("Saved by the Bell," "Pacific Blue"), born San Diego, CA, Oct 10, 1973.
Harold Pinter, 74, director (*Butley*), playwright (*Betrayal, The Birthday Party*), born London, England, Oct 10, 1930.
Chris Pronger, 30, hockey player, born Dryden, ON, Canada, Oct 10, 1974.
David Lee Roth, 49, singer, musician (Van Halen, "Jump," *Eat 'Em and Smile*), born Bloomington, IN, Oct 10, 1955.
Tanya Tucker, 46, singer ("Delta Dawn," "Lizzie and the Rain Man"), born Seminole, TX, Oct 10, 1958.
Ben Vereen, 58, actor, singer, dancer (Tony for *Pippin; Roots, All That Jazz*, "Webster"), born Miami, FL, Oct 10, 1946.

OCTOBER 11 — MONDAY
Day 285 — 81 Remaining

AMERICAN INDIAN HERITAGE DAY (ALABAMA). Oct 11. First declared in 2000, this state holiday will also be observed as Columbus Day in Alabama. Annually, the second Monday in October.

BILL AND HILLARY CLINTON WEDDING: ANNIVERSARY. Oct 11, 1975. William Jefferson (Blythe) Clinton was 29 and Hillary Rodham was 27. They have one child, Chelsea Victoria Clinton, born in 1980.

BLAKEY, ART: 85th BIRTH ANNIVERSARY. Oct 11, 1919. Born at Pittsburgh, PA, jazz musician Blakey recorded many albums with his group, The Jazz Messengers. Died at New York, NY, Oct 16, 1990.

CANADA: THANKSGIVING DAY. Oct 11. Observed on second Monday in October each year.

★**COLUMBUS DAY.** Oct 11. Presidential Proclamation always the second Monday in October. Observed on Oct 12 from 1934 to 1970 (Pub Res No 21 of Apr 30, 1934). PL90–363 of June 28, 1968, required that beginning in 1971 it would be observed on the second Monday in October.

COLUMBUS DAY OBSERVANCE. Oct 11. Public Law 90–363 sets observance of Columbus Day on the second Monday in October. Applicable to federal employees and to the District of Columbia, but observed also in most states. Commemorates the landfall of Columbus in the New World, Oct 12, 1492. See also: "Columbus Day (Traditional)" (Oct 12).

★ Chase's 2004 Calendar of Events ★   Oct 11

"DAVID BRINKLEY'S JOURNAL" TV PREMIERE: ANNIVERSARY. Oct 11, 1961. Newscaster David Brinkley anchored this NBC public affairs show which covered a range of issues, both serious and light. There were also filmed features. "Journal" won both an Emmy and a Peabody in 1962 and was widely respected by the critics.

DISCOVERERS' DAY IN HAWAII. Oct 11. Honors all discoverers, including Pacific and Polynesian navigators. Second Monday in October.

★ **GENERAL PULASKI MEMORIAL DAY.** Oct 11. Presidential Proclamation always issued for Oct 11 since 1929. Requested by Congressional Resolution each year from 1929–1946. (Since 1947 has been issued by custom.) Note: Proclamation 4869, of Oct 5, 1981, covers all succeeding years.

JAPAN: HEALTH-SPORTS DAY ANNIVERSARY. Oct 11. National holiday to encourage physical activity for building sound body and mind. Created in 1966 to commemorate the day of the opening of the 18th Olympic Games at Tokyo, Oct 10, 1964. Annually, the second Monday in October.

NATIONAL COMING OUT DAY. Oct 11. A project of the Human Rights Campaign. An international day of visibility for the lesbian, gay, bisexual and transgender community since 1988. Local community groups sponsor activities and events which in the past have included "coming out" dances, rallies and demonstrations, educational films, fairs and workshops, literature drops, fund-raisers, and religious blessings of lesbian and gay couples and families. Annually, Oct 11. For info: Candace Gingrich, Mgr, Natl Coming Out Project, 1640 Rhode Island Ave NW, Washington, DC 20036. Phone: (800) 866-6263. Fax: (202) 347-5323. E-mail: ncop@hrc.org. Web: www.hrc.org.

NATIONAL KICK-BUTT DAY. Oct 11. On this day we commit to kicking ourselves in the butts to take action on goals we've set and not achieved, actions we've committed to and not taken, promises we've made and not kept, excuses we've created that have us stalled and difficulties we've faced and not overcome. This is the day we get our butts in gear and move forward in our lives. No butts about it! Annually, the second Monday of October. For info: Sylvia Henderson, Springboard Training, 18005 Lafayette Dr, Ste B, Olney, MD 20832. Phone: (301) 646-1668. Fax: (301) 856-8000. E-mail: admin@springboardtraining.com. Web: www.springboardtraining.com.

NATIONAL NETWORKING WEEK. Oct 11–17. Whether the goal is to grow a business or enrich your personal life, networking is invaluable. One can never meet enough new people, exchange business cards and share one's goals and desires with others who may offer leads. Cameraderie is another benefit that can result from successfully connecting with others through a concerted, consistent effort. For info: Robin Gorman Newman, Independent Business Women's Circle, 44 Somerset Dr N, Great Neck, NY 10020. Phone: (516) 773-0911. E-mail: robin@love coach.com. Web: www.ibwc.org.

NATIONAL PET PEEVE WEEK. Oct 11–15. A chance for people to make others aware of all the little things in life they find so annoying, in the hope of changing some of them. Annually, the second full week of October. When requesting info, please send SASE. For info: Ad-America, Pine Tree Center Indust Park, 2215 29th St SE, Ste B-7, Grand Rapids, MI 49508. Phone: (616) 247-3797. Fax: (616) 247-3798. E-mail: adamerica@aol.com.

NATIVE AMERICANS' DAY (SOUTH DAKOTA). Oct 11. Observed in the state of South Dakota as a legal holiday, dedicated to the remembrance of the great Native American leaders who contributed so much to the history of South Dakota. Annually, the second Monday in October.

PATENT ISSUED FOR FIRST ADDING MACHINE: ANNIVERSARY. Oct 11, 1887. A patent was granted to Dorr Eugene Felt for the Comptometer, which was the first adding machine known to be absolutely accurate at all times.

ROBBINS, JEROME: BIRTH ANNIVERSARY. Oct 11, 1918. Choreographer and ballet dancer, born at New York, NY. Robbins choreographed several Broadway musicals including *Fiddler On the Roof*, *The King and I* and *On the Town*. He died at New York, NY, July 29, 1998.

ROBINSON, ROSCOE, JR: BIRTH ANNIVERSARY. Oct 11, 1928. The first black American to achieve the Army rank of four-star general. Born at St. Louis, MO, and died at Washington, DC, July 22, 1993.

ROOSEVELT, (ANNA) ELEANOR: BIRTH ANNIVERSARY. Oct 11, 1884. Wife of Franklin Delano Roosevelt, 32nd president of the US, was born at New York, NY. She led an active and independent life and was the first wife of a president to give her own news conference in the White House (1933). Widely known throughout the world, she was affectionately called "the first lady of the world." She served as US delegate to the United Nations General Assembly for a number of years before her death at New York, NY, Nov 7, 1962. A prolific writer, she wrote in *This Is My Story*, "No one can make you feel inferior without your consent."

"SATURDAY NIGHT LIVE" TV PREMIERE: ANNIVERSARY. Oct 11, 1975. Through the years this show has been through numerous cast, writing, producing and musical staff changes, but its format has remained the same: skits, commercial parodies and news parodies, with a different guest host and musical guest performing every week—live. It used to be known for its outrageous comedy topics and parodies that almost bordered on slander, and for having the best in alternative musical groups. Its title was originally "NBC's Saturday Night," with its first host being comedian George Carlin. Notable cast members have included: Chevy Chase, Dan Aykroyd, John Belushi, Jane Curtin, Garrett Morris, Laraine Newman, Gilda Radner, Bill Murray, Joe Piscopo, Eddie Murphy, Billy Crystal, Martin Short, Christopher Guest, Harry Shearer, Joan Cusack, Robert Downey, Jr, Nora Dunn, Jon Lovitz, Dana Carvey, Phil Hartman, Jan Hooks, Dennis Miller, Chris Farley, Mike Myers, Adam Sandler, Will Ferrell and Molly Shannon.

SPACE MILESTONE: *DISCOVERY STS-92*: **100th SHUTTLE FLIGHT.** Oct 11, 2000. *Discovery* was launched on its 28th flight. This marked the shuttle program's 100th mission. On this flight, *Discovery* headed to the International Space Station, where it docked on Oct 13. On earlier flights, the shuttles *Columbia, Challenger, Endeavour, Atlantis* and *Discovery* had launched the Hubble Space Telescope and Chandra X-Ray Observatory, docked with the *Mir* space station, and supported scientific research. The first shuttle flight took place in 1981. Since the first mission, space shuttles have carried 261 individuals and nearly 3 million pounds of payload, logging an estimated 350 million miles. See: "Space Milestone: *Columbia STS-1*" (Apr 12).

STONE, HARLAN FISKE: BIRTH ANNIVERSARY. Oct 11, 1872. Former associate justice and later chief justice of the US Supreme Court who wrote more than 600 opinions and dissents for that court, Stone was born at Chesterfield, NH. He served on the Supreme Court from 1925 until his death, at Washington, DC, Apr 22, 1946.

VATICAN COUNCIL II: ANNIVERSARY. Oct 11, 1962. The 21st ecumenical council of the Roman Catholic Church was convened by Pope John XXIII. It met in four annual sessions, concluding Dec 8, 1965. It dealt with the renewal of the Church and introduced sweeping changes, such as the use of the vernacular rather than Latin in the Mass.

VIRGIN ISLANDS–PUERTO RICO FRIENDSHIP DAY. Oct 11. Columbus Day (second Monday in October) also celebrates historical friendship between peoples of Virgin Islands and Puerto Rico.

WEEMS, PARSON (MASON LOCKE): BIRTH ANNIVERSARY. Oct 11, 1759. Mason Locke Weems was born at Anne Arundel County, MD. An Episcopal clergyman and traveling bookseller, Weems is remembered for the fictitious stories he presented as historical fact. Best known of his "fables" is the story describing George Washington cutting down his father's cherry tree with a hatchet. Weems's fictionalized histories, however, delighted many readers who accepted them as true. They became immensely popular and were bestsellers for many years. Weems died May 23, 1825, at Beaufort, SC.

WEST, DOTTIE: BIRTH ANNIVERSARY. Oct 11, 1932. American singer Dottie West was born at McMinnville, TN. In 1964 she won the first Grammy ever by a country vocalist for "Here Comes My Baby." She died Sept 4, 1991, at Nashville, TN.

YORKTOWN VICTORY DAY. Oct 11. Observed as a holiday in Virginia. Annually, the second Monday in October. Commemorates the Revolutionary War battle fought in 1781.

BIRTHDAYS TODAY

Joan Cusack, 42, actress (*Working Girl, In & Out*), born Evanston, IL, Oct 11, 1962.
Robert Gale, 59, physician, cofounder of the International Bone Marrow Registry, born Brooklyn Heights, NY, Oct 11, 1945.
Daryl Hall, 56, singer, musician (Hall and Oates), born Pottstown, PA, Oct 11, 1948.
Orlando Hernandez, 35, baseball player, known as "El Duque," born Villa Clara, Cuba, Oct 11, 1969.
Ron Leibman, 67, actor (*Norma Rae*; stage: *We Bombed in New Haven*, *Angels in America* [Tony Award]), born New York, NY, Oct 11, 1937.
Elmore Leonard, 79, writer (*Glitz, Get Shorty*), born New Orleans, LA, Oct 11, 1925.
David Morse, 51, actor ("St. Elsewhere," *The Indian Runner*), born Beverly, MA, Oct 11, 1953.
Patty Murray, 54, US Senator (D, Washington), born Seattle, WA, Oct 11, 1950.
Luke Perry, 38, actor ("Beverly Hills 90210," *Buffy the Vampire Slayer*), born Fredricktown, MO, Oct 11, 1966.
Steve Young, 43, former football player, born Salt Lake City, UT, Oct 11, 1961.

October 2004

S	M	T	W	T	F	S
					1	2
3	4	5	6	7	8	9
10	11	12	13	14	15	16
17	18	19	20	21	22	23
24	25	26	27	28	29	30
31						

OCTOBER 12 — TUESDAY
Day 286 — 80 Remaining

BAHAMAS: DISCOVERY DAY. Oct 12. Commemorates the landing of Columbus in the Bahamas in 1492.

BALI TERRORIST BOMBING: ANNIVERSARY. Oct 12, 2002. Two bombs detonated in Kuta on the Indonesian island of Bali killed more than 200 people and injured hundreds. The bombs were placed at bars where vacationing tourists were known to gather. Although the terrorist group Al Qaeda claimed responsibility, suspects who later confessed to the crime stated that they were working independently.

BELIZE: COLUMBUS DAY. Oct 12. Public holiday.

"THE BOB HOPE SHOW" TV PREMIERE: ANNIVERSARY. Oct 12, 1953. Premiere funnyman, well-known and loved Bob Hope made monthly appearances on TV in the 1950s. During the first season he hosted "The Colgate Comedy Hour," and during the later seasons his show was seen replacing and then alternating with Milton Berle (and in 1955–56 with Martha Raye and Dinah Shore). Leo Robin and Ralph Rainger wrote Hope's trademark show-closing song, "Thanks for the Memory."

BOER WAR: ANNIVERSARY. Oct 12, 1899. The Boers of the Transvaal and Orange Free State in southern Africa declared war on the British. The Boer states were annexed by Britain in 1900 but guerrilla warfare on the part of the Boers caused the war to drag on. It was finally ended May 31, 1902, by the Treaty of Vereeniging.

"THE BURNS AND ALLEN SHOW" TV PREMIERE: ANNIVERSARY. Oct 12, 1950. The comedic husband and wife duo of George Burns and Gracie Allen starred as themselves in this comedy series in which Burns was the straight man and Allen was known for her ditziness. The show employed the technique of speaking directly to the camera ("breaking the fourth wall"); Burns often commented on the plot, told jokes or tried to make sense of Allen's actions and statements. Also on the show were their real-life son, Ronnie Burns, Bea Benaderet, Hal March, John Brown (until blacklisted by McCarthyites in the "red scare"), Fred Clark, Larry Keating, Bill Goodwin and Harry von Zell. The show was done live for the first two seasons and included vaudeville scenes at the end of each episode.

COLUMBUS DAY (TRADITIONAL). Oct 12. Public holiday in most countries in the Americas and in most Spanish-speaking countries. Observed under different names (Dia de la Raza or Day of the Race) and on different dates (most often, as in US, on the second Monday in October). Anniversary of Christopher Columbus's arrival, Oct 12, 1492, after a dangerous voyage across "shoreless Seas," at the Bahamas (probably the island of Guanahani), which he renamed El Salvador and claimed in the name of the Spanish crown. In his *Journal*, he wrote: "As I saw that they (the natives) were friendly to us, and perceived that they could be much more easily converted to our holy faith by gentle means than by force, I presented them with some red caps, and strings of beads to wear upon the neck, and many other trifles of small value, wherewith they were much delighted, and becamed wonderfully attached to us." See also: "Columbus Day Observance" (Oct 11).

DAY OF THE SIX BILLION: 5th ANNIVERSARY. Oct 12, 1999. According to the United Nations, the population of the world reached six billion on this date. More than one-third of the world's people live in China and India. It wasn't until 1804 that the world's population reached one billion; now a billion people are added to the population about every 12 years. See also: "Day of the Five Billion" (July 11).

EQUATORIAL GUINEA: INDEPENDENCE DAY: ANNIVERSARY. Oct 12. National holiday. Gained independence from Spain in 1968.

536

☆ Chase's 2004 Calendar of Events ☆   Oct 12–13

GORDONE, CHARLES: BIRTH ANNIVERSARY. Oct 12, 1925. First black playwright to win the Pulitzer Prize for drama, for his play *No Place to Be Somebody*. Born at Cleveland, OH. Died Nov 17, 1995, at College Station, TX.

INTERNATIONAL MOMENT OF FRUSTRATION SCREAM DAY. Oct 12. To share any or all of our frustrations, all citizens of the world will go outdoors at twelve hundred hours Greenwich time and scream for 30 seconds. We will all feel better or Earth will go off its orbit. Annually, Oct 12. [©2003 by WH.] For info: Thomas & Ruth Roy, Wellcat Holidays, 2418 Long Ln, Lebanon, PA 17046. Phone: (717) 279-0184. E-mail: info@wellcat.com. Web: www.wellcat.com.

MacDONALD, ANNE THOMPSON: DEATH ANNIVERSARY. Oct 12, 1993. Born in 1896, MacDonald founded a nonprofit organization, Recording for the Blind, that produces audio tapes of books to benefit blind and learning disabled people. MacDonald founded the organization in 1948; its library currently contains more than 80,000 titles. She died at Huntington, NY.

McNAIR, RONALD E.: BIRTH ANNIVERSARY. Oct 12, 1950. Ronald E. McNair, a 35-year-old physicist, was the second black American astronaut in space (Feb 1984). He was born at Lake City, SC. As mission specialist for the crew, he perished in the space shuttle *Challenger* explosion Jan 28, 1986. See also: "Challenger Space Shuttle Explosion: Anniversary" (Jan 28).

MEXICO: DIA DE LA RAZA. Oct 12. Columbus Day is observed as the "Day of the Race," a fiesta time to commemorate the discovery of America as well as the common interests and cultural heritage of the Spanish and Indian peoples and the Hispanic nations.

"SNEAK PREVIEWS" TV PREMIERE: ANNIVERSARY. Oct 12, 1978. This show with film critics Gene Siskel and Roger Ebert got its start on public television in Chicago in 1975. In 1978 it went national on PBS. In 1981 the program moved to network TV and the name was changed to "At the Movies." After Siskel's death in 1999, a rotating panel of critics joined Ebert and in 2000 journalist Richard Roeper was named the permanent cohost. The title was changed to "Ebert & Roeper and the Movies."

SPAIN: NATIONAL HOLIDAY. Oct 12. Called Hispanity Day or Day of Spanish Consciousness. Honors Christopher Columbus and the Spanish conquerors of Latin America.

TRUMBULL, JONATHAN: BIRTH ANNIVERSARY. Oct 12, 1710. American patriot, counselor and friend of George Washington, governor of Connecticut Colony, born at Lebanon, CT. Died there, Aug 17, 1785.

VAUGHAN WILLIAMS, RALPH: BIRTH ANNIVERSARY. Oct 12, 1872. English composer and conductor Ralph Vaughan Williams was born at Down Ampney, Gloucestershire. He is considered England's first great truly national composer, having rooted "modern" composition techniques in traditional English folk and Tudor music and themes to create a uniquely English style. Among his many works are nine symphonies, church and choral music, film and stage music and several operas. His major compositions include the *Mass in G Minor* and the opera *The Pilgrim's Progress*. He died Aug 26, 1958, at London.

WORLD HERBAL HEALTH DAY. Oct 12. Celebrates and recognizes the use and importance of naturally grown herbal and botanical therapies to advance human health and wellness. Annually, the second Tuesday in October. For info: Thom Reece, PO Box 6074, Ocean View, HI 96737. Phone: (808) 929-7377. Fax: (808) 929-9991. E-mail: kaubiz@hialoha.net. Web: st4.yahoo.net/kaubusiness/naturalhealth.html.

BIRTHDAYS TODAY

Susan Anton, 54, singer ("Killin' Time" with Fred Knoblock), actress (*Goldengirl*), born Yucaipa, CA, Oct 12, 1950.
Kirk Cameron, 34, actor ("Growing Pains," "Kirk"), born Panorama City, CA, Oct 12, 1970.
Chris Chandler, 39, football player, born Everett, WA, Oct 12, 1965.
Dave Freudenthal, 54, Governor of Wyoming (D), born Thermopolis, WY, Oct 12, 1950.
Dick Gregory, 72, comedian, author, activist, born St. Louis, MO, Oct 12, 1932.
Marion Jones, 29, track runner, born Los Angeles, CA, Oct 12, 1975.
Anthony Christopher (Tony) Kubek, 68, sportscaster, former baseball player, born Milwaukee, WI, Oct 12, 1936.
Jean Nidetch, 81, founder of Weight Watchers, born Brooklyn, NY, Oct 12, 1923.
Luciano Pavarotti, 69, opera singer, one of the "Three Tenors," born Modena, Italy, Oct 12, 1935.
Adam Rich, 36, actor ("Eight Is Enough"), born Brooklyn, NY, Oct 12, 1968.
Chris Wallace, 57, broadcaster ("Dateline"), White House correspondent, born Chicago, IL, Oct 12, 1947.

OCTOBER 13 — WEDNESDAY
Day 287 — 79 Remaining

AMERICAN BUSINESS WOMEN'S ASSOCIATION NATIONAL CONVENTION. Oct 13–17. Richmond, VA. Businesswomen gather to learn, network and elect ABWA's national board of directors for the coming year. Seminars, speakers and the announcement of the Top Ten Business Women of ABWA and the American Business Woman of ABWA are featured. Est attendance: 3,000. For info: Carolyn Elman, American Business Women's Assn, 9100 Ward Parkway, PO Box 8728, Kansas City, MO 64114-0728. Phone: (816) 361-6621. Fax: (816) 361-4991. E-mail: abwa@abwa.org. Web: www.abwa.org.

AMERICAN ROSE SOCIETY FALL NATIONAL CONVENTION. Oct 13–18. Tulsa, OK. Amateur rose growers from all over the US display thousands of their roses in this major competition. Hobbyists from all over the country come together to talk shop, attend seminars and show their roses. Est attendance: 800. For info: American Rose Society, PO Box 30000, Shreveport, LA 71130. Phone: (800) 637-6534. E-mail: ars@ars-hq.org. Web: www.ars.org. Alternate contact: Norma Hedrick. Phone: (918) 825-1646. E-mail: hedrick@sbcglobal.net.

BROWN, JESSE LEROY: BIRTH ANNIVERSARY. Oct 13, 1926. Jesse Leroy Brown was the first black American naval aviator and also the first black naval officer to lose his life in combat when he was shot down over Korea, Dec 4, 1950. On Mar 18, 1972, USS *Jesse L. Brown* was launched as the first ship to be named in honor of a black naval officer. Brown was born at Hattiesburg, MS.

BURUNDI: ASSASSINATION OF THE HERO OF THE NATION DAY. Oct 13. National holiday. Commemorates the assassination of Prince Louis Rwagasore in 1961.

EMERGENCY NURSES DAY. Oct 13. Sponsored by the Emergency Nurses Association (ENA) since 1989, this day serves to recognize emergency nurses for their dedication, service and commitment to their patients and communities. It honors nursing professionals who provide care to those whose lives have been touched by life's tragedies. For info: Debra Bethard-Caplick, ENA, 915 Lee St, Des Plaines, IL 60016. Phone: (847) 460-4049. Fax: (847) 460-4002. E-mail: dcaplick@ena.org. Web: www.ena.org.

Oct 13 ☆ *Chase's 2004 Calendar of Events* ☆

FRANTIC WOMEN EXTRAVAGANZA. Oct 13. Pittsburgh, PA. The annual event will kick off with a "live" workshop at the beginning of the most stress-filled season for women. The celebration includes sharing information and concrete tips for those women in need of a less stressful life. Refreshments include the Frantic Woman Cocktail, the Frantic Woman Revitalizer (nonalcoholic beverage) and Frantic Woman Power Bar. (Location and time to be announced.) The Internet Celebration will commence with a newsletter to all Frantic Women and the FranticWomen.com website will offer a ten-step plan for jump-starting the chaotic season ahead. Est attendance: 100. For info: Mary Jo Rulnick, Frantic Woman Co-Director, PO Box 14282, Pittsburgh, PA 15239. Phone: (724) 325-4964. Fax: (724) 387-1438. E-mail: mjrwrites@aol.com. Web: www.franticwoman.com.

MONTAND, YVES: BIRTH ANNIVERSARY. Oct 13, 1921. French actor Yves Montand was born Ivo Livi at Monsummano Alto, Italy. His career was successful in both France and America, including more than 50 films. He died Nov 9, 1991, at Senlis, France.

MOON PHASE: NEW MOON. Oct 13. Moon enters New Moon phase at 10:48 PM, EDT.

NATIONAL BRING YOUR TEDDY BEAR TO WORK AND SCHOOL DAY. Oct 13. A celebration and observation of the help, stress relief and joy that teddy bears bring into the lives of people of all ages and stages! Annually, the second Wednesday in October. For info: Susan E. Schwartz, Teddies Are the Answer, 454 26th Ave, San Mateo, CA 94403. Phone: (650) 349-3184. Fax: (650) 345-4944. E-mail: suwho2@rcn.com.

NAVY BIRTHDAY. Oct 13. Since 1972 a Navywide celebration (for members of the active forces, as well as retirees and dependents) recognizing the authorization of the Continental Navy on this date in 1775. The celebration is meant "to enhance a greater appreciation of [the] Navy heritage and to provide a positive influence toward pride and professionalism in the naval service." See also: "US Navy: Authorization Anniversary" below. For info: www.history.navy.mil.

PITCHER, MOLLY: 250th BIRTH ANNIVERSARY. Oct 13, 1754. "Molly Pitcher," heroine of the American Revolution, was a water carrier at the Battle of Monmouth (Sunday, June 28, 1778) where she distinguished herself by loading and firing a cannon after her husband, William Hays, was wounded. Affectionately known as "Sergeant Molly" after General Washington issued her a warrant as a noncommissioned officer. Her real name was Mary Hays McCauley (née Ludwig). Born near Trenton, NJ, she died at Carlisle, PA, Jan 22, 1832.

SAINT EDWARD, THE CONFESSOR: FEAST DAY. Oct 13. King of England, 1042–66, Edward was the son of King Ethelred the Unready. Born at Islip, England, in 1003, he died Jan 5, 1066, at London, England. On Oct 13, 1163, his remains were transported in a ceremony that was of national interest. Since then Oct 13 has been observed as his principal feast day.

SOLAR ECLIPSE. Oct 13–14. Partial eclipse of the sun. Eclipse begins at 8:54 PM, EDT on Oct 13, reaches greatest eclipse at 10:59 PM and ends Oct 14 at 1:04 AM. Visible in northeast Asia, Japan, the western Pacific Ocean, Hawaiian Islands and western Alaska.

UNITED NATIONS: INTERNATIONAL DAY FOR NATURAL DISASTER REDUCTION. Oct 13. The General Assembly made this designation for the second Wednesday of October each year as part of its efforts to foster international cooperation in reducing the loss of life, property damage and social and economic disruption caused by natural disasters. For info: United Nations, Dept of Public Info, New York, NY 10017. Web: www.un.org.

US NATIONAL COMMISSION ON SPACE: 20th ANNIVERSARY. Oct 13, 1984. President Reagan signed executive order creating a National Commission on Space to prepare 20-year agenda for civilian space program.

US NAVY: AUTHORIZATION ANNIVERSARY. Oct 13, 1775. Commemorates legislation passed by Second Continental Congress authorizing the acquisition of ships and establishment of a navy.

VIRCHOW, RUDOLF: BIRTH ANNIVERSARY. Oct 13, 1821. German political leader, scientist, teacher and author. Called "the founder of cellular pathology." Born at Schivelbein, Prussia, died at Berlin, Sept 5, 1902.

WHITE HOUSE CORNERSTONE LAID: ANNIVERSARY. Oct 13, 1792. The presidential residence at 1600 Pennsylvania Ave NW, Washington, DC, designed by James Hoban (q.v.), observes its birthday Oct 13. The cornerstone was laid; the first presidential family to occupy it was that of John Adams, in November 1800. With three stories and more than 100 rooms, the White House is the oldest building at Washington. First described as the "presidential palace," it acquired the name "White House" about 10 years after construction was completed. Burned by British troops in 1814, it was reconstructed, refurbished and reoccupied by 1817.

WORLDWIDE CELEBRATION: TOP SPINNING AT NOON. Oct 13. The world is a large top, spinning on its axis. To celebrate this big and important top, students and grown-ups everywhere spin any kind of top at noon (their local time) for one minute. Sponsored by the Spinning Top Museum—where there will be free top spinning activities at noon. For info: Spinning Top Museum, 533 Milwaukee Ave (Hwy 36), Burlington, WI 53105. Phone: (262) 763-3946.

BIRTHDAYS TODAY

Maria Cantwell, 46, US Senator (D, Washington), born Indianapolis, IN, Oct 13, 1958.
Chris Carter, 47, creator of "The X-Files," born Bellflower, CA, Oct 13, 1957.
Melinda Dillon, 65, actress (*Close Encounters of the Third Kind, Absence of Malice, A Christmas Story*), born Hope, AR, Oct 13, 1939.
Sammy Hagar, 55, singer, musician ("Your Love Is Driving Me Crazy"), born Monterrey, CA, Oct 13, 1949.
Nancy Kerrigan, 35, figure skater, born Woburn, MA, Oct 13, 1969.
Jermaine O'Neal, 26, basketball player, born Columbia, SC, Oct 13, 1978.
Marie Osmond, 45, actress, singer ("Donny and Marie"), born Ogden, UT, Oct 13, 1959.
Paul Pierce, 27, basketball player, born Oakland, CA, Oct 13, 1977.
Kelly Preston, 42, actress (*Christine, Twins*), born Honolulu, HI, Oct 13, 1962.
Jerry Lee Rice, 42, football player, born Starkville, MS, Oct 13, 1962.

	S	M	T	W	T	F	S
October 2004						1	2
	3	4	5	6	7	8	9
	10	11	12	13	14	15	16
	17	18	19	20	21	22	23
	24	25	26	27	28	29	30
	31						

Glenn Anton ("Doc") Rivers, 43, basketball coach and former player, born Maywood, IL, Oct 13, 1961.
Nipsey Russell, 80, comedian, actor, born Atlanta, GA, Oct 13, 1924.
Paul Simon, 63, singer, songwriter (with Art Garfunkel: "The Sounds of Silence," "Mrs Robinson"; solo album: *Graceland*), born Newark, NJ, Oct 13, 1941.
Margaret Hilda Roberts Thatcher, 79, former Prime Minister of England, born Grantham, England, Oct 13, 1925.
Pamela Tiffin, 62, actress (*Harper*; stage: *Dinner at Eight* [Theatre World Award]), born Oklahoma City, OK, Oct 13, 1942.

OCTOBER 14 — THURSDAY
Day 288 — 78 Remaining

"THE ADVENTURES OF ELLERY QUEEN" TV PREMIERE: ANNIVERSARY. Oct 14, 1950. The first of many series to portray fictional detective Ellery Queen, it began on the Dumont network and later moved to ABC. Queen was played by Richard Hart. In the next four series, he would also be played by Lee Bowman, Hugh Marlowe, George Nadar, Lee Philips, Peter Lawford and Jim Hutton. In each series Queen talked to the home audience at the show's climax to see if they were able to identify the killer. Future series were titled "Ellery Queen" and "The Further Adventures of Ellery Queen." The last telecast aired on Sept 5, 1976.

BE BALD AND BE FREE DAY. Oct 14. For those who are bald and who either do wear or do not wear a wig or toupee, this is the day to go "shiny" and be proud. Annually, Oct 14. [©2003 by WH.] For info: Thomas & Ruth Roy, Wellcat Holidays, 2418 Long Ln, Lebanon, PA 17046. Phone: (717) 279-0184. E-mail: info@wellcat.com. Web: www.wellcat.com.

CANADA: TORONTO SKI, SNOWBOARD AND TRAVEL SHOW. Oct 14–17. Exhibition Place, Toronto, ON. Ski manufacturers (equipment, fashions, accessories), retailers, ski resorts, hotels, travel agencies, tourist bureaus, ski clinics and demonstrations, ski clubs, associations, movies and live entertainment. Catering to all ski disciplines—alpine, cross country and snowboarding. Est attendance: 35,000. For info: Canadian Natl Sportsmen's Shows, 703 Evans Ave, Ste 202, Toronto, ON, Canada M9C 5E9. Phone: (416) 695-0311. Fax: (416) 695-0381. Web: www.torontoskishow.com or www.snowboardshow.ca.

EISENHOWER, DWIGHT DAVID: BIRTH ANNIVERSARY. Oct 14, 1890. The 34th president of the US, Dwight David Eisenhower, was born at Denison, TX. Serving two terms as president, Jan 20, 1953–Jan 20, 1961, Eisenhower was the first president to be baptized after taking office (Sunday, Feb 1, 1953). Nicknamed "Ike," he held the rank of five-star general of the army (resigned in 1952, and restored by act of Congress in 1961). He served as supreme commander of the Allied forces in western Europe during WWII. In his Farewell Address (Jan 17, 1961), speaking about the "conjunction of an immense military establishment and a large arms industry," he warned: "In the councils of government, we must guard against the acquisition of unwarranted influence, whether sought or unsought, by the military-industrial complex. The potential of the disastrous rise of misplaced power exists and will persist." An American hero, Eisenhower died at Washington, DC, Mar 28, 1969.

FODOR, EUGENE: BIRTH ANNIVERSARY. Oct 14, 1905. Travel writer Eugene Fodor was born at Leva, Hungary. His first travel book was published in 1936, after which he published more than 140, bringing to them a human element previously lacking in travel books. He died Feb 18, 1991, at Torrington, CT.

GISH, LILLIAN: BIRTH ANNIVERSARY. Oct 14, 1893. American actress Lillian Diana Gish was born at Springfield, OH. Her film and stage career spanned more than 85 years, 100 films, the silent and sound eras of film and numerous stage productions. She was awarded an honorary Oscar in 1970 and made her last film appearance in *The Whales of August* (1987). She died Feb 27, 1993, at New York, NY.

JAPAN: MEGA KENKA MATSURI or ROUGHHOUSE FESTIVAL. Oct 14–15. Himeji. Palanquin bearers jostle one another to demonstrate their skill and balance in handling their burdens.

KING AWARDED NOBEL PEACE PRIZE: 40th ANNIVERSARY. Oct 14, 1964. Martin Luther King, Jr, became the youngest recipient of the Nobel Peace Prize when awarded the honor. Dr. King donated the entire $54,000 prize money to furthering the causes of the civil rights movement.

LEE, FRANCIS LIGHTFOOT: BIRTH ANNIVERSARY. Oct 14, 1734. Signer of the Declaration of Independence. Born at Westmoreland County, VA, he died Jan 11, 1797, at Richmond County, VA.

MAGNOLIA FEST. Oct 14–17. Live Oak, FL. Music festival. Previous artists have included David Grisman Quintet, Dickey Betts and Great Southern, Peter Rowan, Tony Rice, Vassar Clements, Laura Love Band and many more. Also available are workshops, vendors and activities for children. Est attendance: 8,000. For info: Spirit of the Suwannee Music Park, 3076 95th Dr, Live Oak, FL 32060. Phone: (386) 364-1683. Fax: (386) 364-2998. E-mail: spirit@musicliveshere.com. Web: www.musicliveshere.com.

PEACE CORPS PROPOSED: ANNIVERSARY. Oct 14, 1960. At the improbable hour of 2 AM, on Oct 14, 1960, then presidential candidate John F. Kennedy spoke impromptu to several thousand students from the steps of the University of Michigan Union building. He asked: "How many of you who are going to be doctors are willing to spend your days in Ghana? How many of you (technicians and engineers) are willing to work in the Foreign Service?" The response was favorable, and 19 days later in San Francisco, Kennedy formally proposed the Peace Corps, which was created by Executive Order Mar 1, 1961.

PENN, WILLIAM: BIRTH ANNIVERSARY. Oct 14, 1644. Founder of Pennsylvania, born at London, England. Penn died July 30, 1718, at Buckinghamshire, England. Presidential Proclamation 5284 of Nov 28, 1984, conferred honorary citizenship of the USA upon William Penn and his second wife, Hannah Callowhill Penn. They were the third and fourth persons to receive honorary US citizenship (following Winston Churchill and Raoul Wallenberg).

SOUND BARRIER BROKEN: ANNIVERSARY. Oct 14, 1947. Flying a Bell X-1 at Muroc Dry Lake Bed, CA, Air Force pilot Chuck Yeager broke the sound barrier, ushering in the era of supersonic flight.

TEA PLANT.   SUGAR CANE.   COFFEE PLANT.

BIRTHDAYS TODAY

Harry Anderson, 52, actor ("Night Court," "Dave's World"), born Newport, RI, Oct 14, 1952.
Beth Daniel, 48, Hall of Fame golfer, born Charleston, SC, Oct 14, 1956.
John Dean, 66, lawyer (White House counsel during Watergate), born Akron, OH, Oct 14, 1938.
Greg Evigan, 51, actor ("B.J. and the Bear," "Masquerade"), born South Amboy, NJ, Oct 14, 1953.
Gary Graffman, 76, pianist, director of the Curtis Institute of Music (Philadelphia), born New York, NY, Oct 14, 1928.
Charles Everett Koop, 88, former US Surgeon General, born Brooklyn, NY, Oct 14, 1916.
Ralph Lauren, 65, designer, born the Bronx, NY, Oct 14, 1939.
Roger Moore, 76, actor (James Bond movies, "The Saint"), born London, England, Oct 14, 1928.

OCTOBER 15 — FRIDAY
Day 289 — 77 Remaining

APPLE BUTTER STIRRIN'. Oct 15–17. Coshocton, OH. Kettles of apple butter simmer over open fires; demonstrations, craft show, contests in Roscoe Village, a restored canal town. Also, live musical entertainment. Annually, the third weekend of October. Est attendance: 35,000. For info: Roscoe Village Fdtn, 381 Hill St, Coshocton, OH 43812. Phone: (800) 877-1830 or (740) 622-9310. Fax: (740) 623-6555. E-mail: rvmarketing@roscoevillage.com. Web: www.roscoevillage.com.

CHINA: CANTON AUTUMN TRADE FAIR. Oct 15–Nov 15. The Guangzhou (Canton) Autumn Trade Fair is held during the same dates each year.

CRAFTSMEN'S CLASSIC ARTS & CRAFTS FESTIVAL. Oct 15–17. Dulles Expo and Convention Center, Chantilly, VA. 9th annual. Features work from more than 400 talented artists and craftspeople. All juried exhibitors' work has been handmade by the exhibitors and must be their own original design and creation. See the creative process in action with several exhibitors demonstrating their craft. Something for every style, taste, and budget with items from the most contemporary to the most traditional. Est attendance: 30,000. For info: Gilmore Enterprises, Inc, 1240 Oakland Ave, Greensboro, NC 27403. Phone: (336) 274-5550. E-mail: gilmoreshows@triad.rr.com.

CREOLE HERITAGE DAY. Oct 15–17. Natchitoches, LA. This festival celebrates the Creole culture with music, crafts and Creole cuisine. Held on the grounds of the historic St. Augustine Catholic Church. Admission. Annually, the third weekend in October. Est attendance: 10,000. For info: Natchitoches Parish Tourist Commission. Phone: (800) 259-1714. Web: www.caneriver.net.

CROW RESERVATION OPENED FOR SETTLEMENT: ANNIVERSARY. Oct 15, 1892. By Presidential Proclamation 1.8 million acres of Crow Indian reservation were opened to settlers. The government had induced the Crow to give up a portion of their land in the mountainous western area in the state of Montana, for which they received 50 cents per acre.

FALL FESTIVAL OF LEAVES. Oct 15–17. Bainbridge, Ross County, OH. Celebrating the beauty of the season and region. Folk arts, crafts, music, antique car show, log sawing contest, flea markets and parades. To obtain a map of self-guided scenic tours send SASE to sponsor. For info: Fall Festival of Leaves, Box 571, Bainbridge, Ross County, OH 45612. Phone: (740) 634-2085 or (740) 634-3173.

FALL MARYLAND HOME & GARDEN SHOW/MARYLAND HOLIDAY CRAFT SHOW. Oct 15–17. Timonium Fairgrounds, Baltimore, MD. A variety of home products and services to get your home ready for winter. Also educational exhibits, a plant market area and beautiful landscaped gardens. The Maryland Holiday Craft Show is in the same building with more than 150 artists and craftspeople selling something for everyone to fill their Christmas lists. Also a festive Christmas tree decorating contest and wonderful holiday entertainment. For info: S & L Productions, Inc, 1916 Crain Highway, Ste 16, Glen Burnie, MD 21061. Phone: (410) 863-1180. Fax: (410) 863-1187.

FALL STATE CRAFT FESTIVAL. Oct 15–17 (tentative). Tyler State Park, Richboro, PA. High quality juried craft show featuring the work of 200 members of the Pennsylvania Guild of Craftsmen. Demonstrations, seminars, Crafts and Antiques Road Show, festival food, children's activities, musical entertainment. Est attendance: 15,000. For information about tickets, or how to become a member of the PA Guild, contact: Pennsylvania Guild of Craftsmen, 10 Stable Mill Trail, Richboro, PA 18954. Phone: (800) 684-7440. E-mail: pacraft@comcat.com. Web: www.pacrafts.com.

FIRST MANNED FLIGHT: ANNIVERSARY. Oct 15, 1783. Jean Francois Pilatre de Rozier and Francois Laurent, Marquis d'Arlandes became the first people to fly when they ascended in a Montgolfier hot-air balloon at Paris, France, less than three months after the first public balloon flight demonstration (June 5, 1783), and only a year after the first experiments with small paper and fabric balloons by the Montgolfier brothers, Joseph and Jacques, in November 1782. The first manned free flight lasted about 4 minutes and carried the passengers at a height of about 84 feet. On Nov 21, 1783, they soared 3,000 feet over Paris for 25 minutes.

FOOTHILLS ART FESTIVAL. Oct 15–17. Jackson, OH. Visual arts exhibits with more than 600 works by 150 artists from the tri-state area. Also live music and arts activities for the entire family. Est attendance: 4,000. For info: Barbara Summers, Southern Hills Arts Council, PO Box 149, Jackson, OH 45640. Phone/fax: (740) 286-6355. E-mail: shac@zoomnet.net.

HOOD RIVER VALLEY HARVEST FEST. Oct 15–17. Hood River, OR. The valley welcomes visitors for three days of continuous entertainment, crafts, fresh locally grown produce and fruits. Est attendance: 30,000. For info: Hood River County Chamber of Commerce, 405 Portway Ave, Hood River, OR 97031. Phone: (800) 366-3530. Fax: (541) 386-2057. E-mail: hrccc@hoodriver.org. Web: www.hoodriver.org.

"I LOVE LUCY" TV PREMIERE: ANNIVERSARY. Oct 15, 1951. This enormously popular sitcom, TV's first smash hit, starred the real-life husband and wife team of Cuban actor/bandleader Desi Arnaz and talented redheaded actress/comedienne Lucille Ball. They played Ricky and Lucy Ricardo, a New York bandleader and his aspiring actress/homemaker wife who was always scheming to get on stage. Costarring were William Frawley and Vivian Vance as Fred and Ethel Mertz, the Ricardos' landlords and good friends who participated in the escapades and dealt with the consequences of Lucy's often well-intentioned plans. Famous actors guest-starred on the show, including Harpo Marx, Rock Hudson, William Holden, Hedda Hopper and John Wayne. This was the first sitcom to be filmed live before a studio audience, and it did extremely well in the ratings both the first time around and in reruns. The last telecast ran Sept 24, 1961.

LEE COUNTY COTTON FESTIVAL. Oct 15–16. Bishopville, SC. Join the festivities with amusement rides, parade, entertainment, sports events, food booths and much more. Annually, the third weekend in October. Est attendance: 20,000. For info: Lee County Chamber of Commerce, Lee County Cotton Fest, PO Box 187, Bishopville, SC 29010. Phone: (803) 484-5145. Fax: (803) 484-4270.

MANN, MARTY: 100th BIRTH ANNIVERSARY. Oct 15, 1904. American social activist and author was born at Chicago, IL. She was founder in 1944 of the National Committee for Education on Alcoholism and author of *A New Primer on Alcoholism*. She died at Bridgeport, CT, July 22, 1980.

MATA HARI: EXECUTION ANNIVERSARY. Oct 15, 1917. Possibly history's most famous spy, Mata Hari refused a blindfold and threw a kiss to the firing squad at her execution. Early estimates claimed her espionage for Germany in World War I was responsible for 50,000 Allied deaths. More recent studies suggest that she was a double agent (secret code name: "H-21") and that her "intelligence" was of little value to either side. She was born Margaret Gertrude Zelle, at Leewarden, Netherlands. Her life as a courtesan, blackmailer and spy—and her liaisons with high officials in the British, French and German governments—fascinated millions of readers.

MISSOURI DAY FESTIVAL. Oct 15–17. North Central Missouri Fairgrounds, Trenton, MO. Annual festival in conjunction with high school marching band competitions. Features a parade, car show, baby show, quilt show, craft booths, a talent show, flea

October 2004

S	M	T	W	T	F	S
					1	2
3	4	5	6	7	8	9
10	11	12	13	14	15	16
17	18	19	20	21	22	23
24	25	26	27	28	29	30
31						

market, food vendors and entertainment of all kinds. Est attendance: 20,000. For info: Missouri Day Festival, PO Box 84, Trenton, MO 64683. Phone: (660) 359-4324. Fax: (660) 359-4325.

NATIONAL GROUCH DAY. Oct 15. Honor a grouch; all grouches deserve a day to be recognized. Annually, Oct 15. For info: Alan R. Miller, Carter Middle School, 300 Upland Dr, Room 207, Clio, MI 48420. Phone: (810) 591-0503.

NATIONAL MAMMOGRAPHY DAY. Oct 15. On this day, or throughout the month of October, radiologists provide discounted or free screening mammograms. Annually, the third Friday of October. For info: Web: www.nbcam.org.

NIETZSCHE, FRIEDRICH WILHELM: BIRTH ANNIVERSARY. Oct 15, 1844. Influential German philosopher born at Rocken. Especially remembered among his philosophical beliefs are contempt for the weak and expected ultimate triumph of a superman. Nietzsche died at Weimar, Aug 25, 1900, a decade after suffering a mental breakdown.

NORTH CAROLINA STATE FAIR. Oct 15–24. State Fairgrounds, Raleigh, NC. Agricultural fair with livestock, arts and crafts, home arts, entertainment and carnival. Est attendance: 750,000. For info: Wesley Wyatt, Mgr, North Carolina State Fair, 1025 Blue Ridge Blvd, Raleigh, NC 27607. Phone: (919) 821-7400. Fax: (919) 733-5079. Web: www.ncstatefair.org.

PENNSYLVANIA ARTS & CRAFTS CHRISTMAS FESTIVAL. Oct 15–17 (also Oct 23–24). Washington County Fairgrounds, Washington, PA. More than 165 exhibits of handcrafted furniture, gift items, children's toys, dolls, dried floral arrangements and clothing. Holiday food and entertainment. Est attendance: 22,000. For info: Debbie & Dave Stoner, Family Festivals Assn, Inc, PO Box 166, Irwin, PA 15642. Phone: (724) 863-4577. Fax: (724) 863-4577. E-mail: familyfestivals@hotmail.com. Web: www.familyfestivals.com.

PREGNANCY AND INFANT LOSS AWARENESS DAY. Oct 15. Babylifeline is dedicated to raising awareness of pregnancy and infant loss in order to reduce maternal and infant mortality. Many of these deaths are preventable! For info: Jackie Wicks, RN, Babylifeline, 1615 Akridge Dr, Tallahassee, FL 32308. Phone: (850) 656-1165. E-mail: babylifeline@email.com. Web: www.babylifeline.org.

SENATE CONFIRMS THOMAS TO SUPREME COURT: ANNIVERSARY. Oct 15, 1991. After three days of Senate Judiciary Committee hearings on charges of sexual harassment made against Judge Clarence Thomas by a former aide, Anita F. Hill, the Senate confirmed Thomas as the 106th US Supreme Court Justice with a 52–48 vote on Oct 15, 1991. The vote was the closest for a 20th-century justice and made Thomas, who would replace retired Justice Thurgood Marshall, the second African American to sit on the Supreme Court.

SPACE MILESTONE: *CASSINI* (US). Oct 15, 1997. The plutonium-powered spacecraft was launched to arrive at Saturn in July 2004. It will orbit the planet, take pictures of its 18 known moons and dispatch a probe to Titan, the largest of these moons.

SUGARLOAF CRAFTS FESTIVAL. Oct 15–17. Fort Washington Expo Center, Fort Washington, PA. This show, now in its 10th year, features more than 350 nationally recognized craft designers and fine artists displaying and selling their original creations. Includes craft demonstrations, live music, specialty foods, hourly gift certificate drawings and more. Est attendance: 25,500. For info: Sugarloaf Mountain Works, 200 Orchard Ridge Dr, #215, Gaithersburg, MD 20878. Phone: (800) 210-9900. Fax: (301) 253-9620. Web: www.sugarloafcrafts.com.

★ **WHITE CANE SAFETY DAY.** Oct 15. Presidential Proclamation always issued for Oct 15 since 1964 (PL88–628 of Oct 6, 1964).

WILSON, EDITH BOLLING GALT: BIRTH ANNIVERSARY. Oct 15, 1872. Second wife of Woodrow Wilson, 28th president of the US, born at Wytheville, VA. Died at Washington, DC, Dec 28, 1961.

WODEHOUSE, PELHAM GRENVILLE: BIRTH ANNIVERSARY. Oct 15, 1881. English author, lyricist ("Bill"), humorist, creator of Bertie Wooster and Jeeves. Born at Guildford, Surrey, England, P.G. Wodehouse died at Southampton, Long Island, NY, Feb 14, 1975.

BIRTHDAYS TODAY

Victor Banerjee, 58, actor (*A Passage to India, The Home and the World*), born Calcutta, India, Oct 15, 1946.
John Kenneth Galbraith, 96, economist, diplomat, author, born Iona Station, ON, Canada, Oct 15, 1908.
Lee Iacocca, 80, former automobile executive (Ford and Chrysler), born Allentown, PA, Oct 15, 1924.
Tito Jackson, 51, singer, musician (Jackson 5), born Toriano Adaryll Jackson, Gary, IN, Oct 15, 1953.
Linda Lavin, 65, actress (Tony for *Broadway Bound*; "Alice"), born Portland, ME, Oct 15, 1939.
Penny Marshall, 62, director (*Big, A League of Their Own*), actress ("Laverne & Shirley"), born New York, NY, Oct 15, 1942.
James Alvin (Jim) Palmer, 59, Hall of Fame baseball player, sportscaster, born New York, NY, Oct 15, 1945.
Sarah (Ferguson), 45, Duchess of York (former wife of Prince Andrew), born London, England, Oct 15, 1959.
Arthur Meier Schlesinger, Jr, 87, historian, author, born Columbus, OH, Oct 15, 1917.

OCTOBER 16 — SATURDAY
Day 290 — 76 Remaining

ADAI CADDO INDIAN NATION POW WOW. Oct 16. Marthaville, LA. Held on the grounds of historic St. Anne Catholic Church. Celebrate the Adai Caddo Indian heritage through music, dance, arts and crafts, and food. Admission. Est attendance: 2,500. For info: Natchitoches Parish Tourist Commision. Phone: (800) 259-1714. Web: www.natchitoches.net.

AMERICA'S FIRST DEPARTMENT STORE: ANNIVERSARY. Oct 16, 1868. Salt Lake City, UT. America's first department store, "ZCMI" (Zion's Co-Operative Mercantile Institution), is still operating at Salt Lake City. It was founded under the direction of Brigham Young. For info: Museum of Church History and Art, 45 North West Temple, Salt Lake City, UT 84150. Phone: (801) 240-4604.

AUTUMN HISTORIC FOLKLIFE FESTIVAL. Oct 16–17. Downtown Historic District, Hannibal, MO. The Hannibal Arts Council sponsors its 28th annual festival celebrating heritage and tradition of the 1800s. Artisans demonstrate the folk arts of the mid-1800s, vendors prepare food and drink over wood fires and street performers play traditional tunes. Also living history and children's areas with many activities. Est attendance: 25,000. For info: Hannibal Arts Council, PO Box 1202, Hannibal, MO 63401. Phone: (573) 221-6545. E-mail: arts@nemonet.com.

BEN-GURION, DAVID: BIRTH ANNIVERSARY. Oct 16, 1886. First prime minister of the state of Israel. Born at Plonsk, Poland, died at Tel Aviv, Israel, Dec 1, 1973.

Oct 16 ☆ Chase's 2004 Calendar of Events ☆

BIRTH CONTROL CLINIC OPENED: ANNIVERSARY. Oct 16, 1916. Margaret Sanger, Fania Mindell and Ethel Burne opened the first birth control clinic in the US at 46 Amboy St, Brooklyn, NY. Sanger believed that the poor should be able to control the size of their families.

BRIDGE DAY 2004. Oct 16. New River Gorge Bridge, Fayetteville, WV. World's biggest extreme sports event and West Virginia's largest festival. Up to 500 BASE jumpers leap off North America's longest single span bridge at a height of 876 feet. Annually, the third Saturday in October. Est attendance: 250,000. For info: Fayette County Chamber of Commerce, 310 Oyler Av, Oak Hill, WV 25901. Phone: (800) 927-0263 or (304) 465-5617. Web: www.newrivercvb.com or www.officialbridgeday.com.

COUNTRY AFFAIR. Oct 16–17. Ben Franklin School, Menomonee Falls, WI. Community League's 22nd annual fair features antiques, folk art and country collectibles. More than 90 exhibitors; a Country Luncheon of homemade food and desserts; a Quilt Raffle; and a "Country Pantry" and silent auction. Admission charged. Est attendance: 6,000. For info: Jeanne Verbsky, Community League, Inc, Publicity—ACA, PO Box 101, Menomonee Falls, WI 53052. Phone: (414) 297-9446.

CRIMEAN WAR: ANNIVERSARY. Oct 16, 1853. The Ottoman Empire declared war on Russia on this day to stem Russian expansionist policies in the Empire. Britain, France and parts of Italy allied themselves with the Turks against Russia. A battle in this war was immortalized in Tennyson's poem, "The Charge of the Light Brigade." Health conditions for soldiers were scandalous, leading Florence Nightingale to work in the British hospital at Istanbul. This was the first war to be observed firsthand by newspaper reporters and photographers.

DEUTSCH COUNTRY DAYS. Oct 16–17. Luxenhaus Farm, Marthasville, MO. 23rd annual. An authentic re-creation of early German life in Missouri as 80 costumed artisans present log hewing, kloppolei, bee keeping, broom making, wood turning, quilting and more. Period music, meals, a sorghum press driven by Missouri mules and a steam-powered sawmill add to the festivities. Est attendance: 9,000. For info: Lois Mueller, Deutsch Country Days, Historic Luxenhaus Farm, 5437 Highway O, Marthasville, MO 63357. Phone: (636) 433-5669. E-mail: luxenhaus@yhti.net. Web: www.deutschcountrydays.org.

DICTIONARY DAY. Oct 16. The birthday of Noah Webster, American teacher and lexicographer, is occasion to encourage every person to acquire at least one dictionary—and to use it regularly.

DOUGLAS, WILLIAM ORVILLE: BIRTH ANNIVERSARY. Oct 16, 1898. American jurist, world traveler, conservationist, outdoorsman and author. Born at Maine, MN, he served as justice of the US Supreme Court longer than any other (36 years). Died at Washington, DC, Jan 19, 1980.

EIGHTEENTH-CENTURY AUTUMN MARKET FAIR. Oct 16–17. McLean, VA. Crafts, games, music and dancing. Period food and wares. Est attendance: 5,500. For info: Liz Hauris, Claude Moore Colonial Farm at Turkey Run, 6310 Georgetown Pike, McLean, VA 22101. Phone: (703) 442-7557. Fax: (703) 442-0714. Web: www.1771.org.

FINE ARTS AND CRAFTS FESTIVAL. Oct 16–17. Roseland Cottage, Bowen House, Woodstock, CT. 22nd annual festival features 175 juried artists and craftsmen, food court and entertainment for children and adults. Rain or shine. Admission is $5 per person with proceeds to benefit museum. Annually, the weekend after Columbus Day. Est attendance: 10,000. For info: Roseland Cottage, Bowen House, PO Box 186, Woodstock, CT 06281. Phone: (860) 928-4074. Fax: (860) 963-2208. E-mail: prusso@spnea.org. Web: www.spnea.org.

GRAND MILITIA MUSTER. Oct 16. St. Mary's City, MD. The largest gathering of 17th-century military reenactment groups in the US. Tacticals, contests of skill and camp life demonstrations. Est attendance: 1,000. For info: Visitors Services, Historic St. Mary's City, PO Box 39, St. Mary's City, MD 20686. Phone: (240) 895-4990 or (800) SMC-1634. Fax: (240) 895-4968. Web: www.stmaryscity.org.

GRANT PUT IN CHARGE OF THE MISSISSIPPI REGION: ANNIVERSARY. Oct 16, 1863. After his impressive success taking Vicksburg, MS, Ulysses S. Grant, a brigadier general of the militia, was appointed a general in the regular army and, with the subsequent reorganization of the departments of war in Ohio, Cumberland and Tennessee, was placed in charge of the newly formed Military Division of the Mississippi. Grant's first priority was to save the besieged and starving Union troops at Chattanooga, TN.

HARTVILLE ANNUAL FALL FESTIVAL. Oct 16. Hartville, MO. Annual festival includes local entertainment, parade, games, rides for the kids and craft booths. A day of fun for all—young and old. Est attendance: 2,500. For info: Hartville Area Chamber of Commerce, PO Box 307, Hartville, MO 65667. Phone: (417) 741-7777. Fax: (417) 741-7741.

HORSE EXPO. Oct 16–17. Multi-Purpose Events Center, Wichita Falls, TX. Area horse show. Awards, show horses. For info: Wichita Falls CVB, 1000 5th St, Wichita Falls, TX 76301. Phone: (940) 716-5500. Fax: (940) 716-5509. E-mail: mpec@wf.net. Web: www.wichitafalls.org or www.mpecwf.com.

INTERNATIONAL GOLD CUP. Oct 16. Great Meadow, The Plains, VA. A day of steeplechasing in the heart of Virginia's hunt country, to promote steeplechase racing and to encourage open space land use. Gates open at 10 AM for special events and activities. Corporate and chalet entertainment packages available. Est attendance: 40,000. For info: Virginia Gold Cup Assn, PO Box 840, Warrenton, VA 20188. Phone: (540) 347-2612. Fax: (540) 349-1829. Web: www.vagoldcup.com.

JOHN BROWN'S RAID: ANNIVERSARY. Oct 16, 1859. White abolitionist John Brown, with a band of about 20 men, seized the US Arsenal at Harpers Ferry, WV. Brown was captured and the insurrection put down by Oct 19. Brown was hanged at Charles Town, WV, Dec 2, 1859.

MARIE ANTOINETTE: EXECUTION ANNIVERSARY. Oct 16, 1793. Queen Marie Antoinette, whose extravagance and "let them eat cake" attitude toward the starving French underclass made her a target of the French Revolution, was beheaded on this date.

MILLION MAN MARCH: ANNIVERSARY. Oct 16, 1995. Hundreds of thousands of black men met at Washington, DC, for a "holy day of atonement and reconciliation" organized by Louis Farrakhan, leader of the Nation of Islam. Marchers pledged to take responsibility for themselves, their families and their communities.

MONSTER MYTHS BY MOONLIGHT. Oct 16. Milford State Park, Milford, KS. Learn the truth about spiders, snakes, bats, vultures, owls and other Halloween "monsters." Meet the real creatures as you walk our nature trail and learn the truth about them from witches, snake charmers and Little Red Riding Hood. Wear costumes. Cookies and cider served by Mother Nature. Sponsored by Friends of Milford Nature Center and State Park. Est attendance: 650. For info: Milford Nature Center, 3115 Hatchery Dr, Junction City, KS 66441. Phone: (785) 238-5323. Fax: (785) 238-5775.

NATIONAL BOSS DAY. Oct 16. For all employees to honor their bosses. Annually, Oct 16. Mrs Patricia Bays Haroski originated this event. For info: Edward A. Haroski, 1315 Forestwood Dr, Lewisville, NC 27023.

NATIONAL CUT UP YOUR CREDIT CARD DAY. Oct 16. National Cut Up Your Credit Card Day is an organized effort by Stowers Innovations, Inc, a Kansas City–based publisher that helps people discover the good life by sharing the philosophies, beliefs and practices of self-made billionaire James E. Stowers, to expose the country's growing dependence on credit. For 24 hours, people are encouraged to put away their credit cards and pay cash only. For info: Stowers Innovations, Inc, 4500 Main, 14th Fl, Kansas City, MO 64111. Phone: (816) 340-7615. Fax: (816) 753-7787. E-mail: sam_goller@americancentury.com. Web: www.stowers-innovations.com.

O'NEILL, EUGENE GLADSTONE: BIRTH ANNIVERSARY. Oct 16, 1888. American playwright (*Long Day's Journey into Night, Ah, Wilderness*), recipient of Pulitzer and Nobel Prize. Born at New York, NY, he died at Boston, MA, Nov 27, 1953.

QUINCY PRESERVES FALL ARCHITECTURAL TOUR. Oct 16. Quincy, IL. 10 AM–5 PM. Tour historic homes decked out in their finest. Homes range in size from Quincy's grandest mansions to quaint cottages. Inside each home, ticket holders are awed by the architectural splendors. Annually, the third Saturday in October. Est attendance: 1,500. For info: Fran Cook, Quincy Preserves, 310 S 16th St, Quincy, IL 62301. Phone: (217) 224-2587.

RAMADAN: THE ISLAMIC MONTH OF FASTING. Oct 16–Nov 13. Begins on Islamic lunar calendar date Ramadan 1, 1425. Ramadan, the ninth month of the Islamic calendar, is holy because it was during this month that the Holy Qur'an [Koran] was revealed. All adults of sound body and mind fast from dawn (before sunrise) until sunset to achieve spiritual and physical purification and self-discipline, abstaining from food, drink and intimate relations. It is a time for feeling a common bond with the poor and needy, a time of piety and prayer. Different methods for "anticipating" the visibility of the new moon crescent at Mecca are used by different Muslim groups. US date may vary. Began at sunset the preceding day.

REPTILE AWARENESS DAY. Oct 16. Jenkinson's Aquarium, Point Pleasant Beach, NJ. Learn how alligators, snakes and turtles are related. Meet our live reptiles up close! A special artifact cart and reptile stories for children will be presented throughout the day. Alligators are fed at 1:30 PM. Crafts 1–4 PM. Face Painting 10 AM–1 PM. Est attendance: 700. For info: Jenkinson's Aquarium, 300 Ocean Ave, Point Pleasant Beach, NJ 08742. Phone: (732) 899-1212. Fax: (732) 899-1717. E-mail: aquarium@jenkinsons.com. Web: www.jenkinsons.com.

ROMP IN THE SWAMP FUN WALK. Oct 16. Gordon Bubolz Nature Preserve, Appleton, WI. Choose to hike ¼-, 1½-, 2½- or 4-mile distances on the Preserve's beautiful trail system. Food and activities at rest stops along the way. Est attendance: 1,000. For info: Joann Engel, Naturalist, 4815 N Lynndale Dr, Appleton, WI 54913. Phone: (920) 731-6041. Fax: (920) 731-9593. E-mail: bubolz@dataex.com.

SAINT MARY'S COUNTY MD OYSTER FESTIVAL. Oct 16–17. Fairgrounds, Leonardtown, MD. Oysters served every style, national oyster shucking contest and national oyster cookoff. Est attendance: 20,000. For info: David L. Taylor, Admin, Oyster Fest Office, Box 766, California, MD 20619-0766. Phone: (301) 863-5015. Fax: (301) 363-7789. Web: www.usoysterfest.com.

SPECIAL CHEFS™ BLUE RIBBON RECIPE AND COOKING CONTEST. Oct 16. Chicago, IL. Special Chefs™ encourages people with developmental disabilities to comfortably and enthusiastically embrace the vital independent living skill of food preparation so their lives will be healthier and richer. Special Chefs™ sponsors national recipe and cooking competitions to celebrate the culinary capabilities of these inspired chefs. Finalists from across the country will compete in a cook-off in Chicago, IL. All expenses paid by Special Chefs™. For info: Special Chefs Inc, 456 Frontage Rd, Ste 9, Northfield, IL 60093. Phone: (847) 501-5060. Fax: (847) 501-5074. E-mail: blueribbon@specialchefs.org. Web: www.specialchefs.org.

SWEETEST DAY. Oct 16. About 65 years ago, a candy company employee named Herbert Birch Kingston decided that it would be a wonderful thing to distribute candy to the sick, shut-ins and orphans of Cleveland, OH. Thus, Sweetest Day was born. Do something nice for someone today, something that will make them say, "Oh, that's so sweet!" Annually, the third Saturday in October.

TAMARACK TIME!. Oct 16. Bigfork, MT. Old-fashioned village celebration of harvest and autumn. Local chefs prepare their specialties for a taste treat. Est attendance: 600. For info: Elna Darrow, Box 400, Bigfork, MT 59911-0400. Phone: (406) 837-4400. E-mail: crossbow@cyberport.net.

UNITED NATIONS: WORLD FOOD DAY. Oct 16. Annual observance to heighten public awareness of the world food problem and to strengthen solidarity in the struggle against hunger, malnutrition and poverty. Date of observance is anniversary of founding of Food and Agriculture Organization (FAO), Oct 16, 1945, at Quebec, Canada. For info: United Nations, Dept of Public Info, New York, NY 10017. Web: www.un.org.

WEBSTER, NOAH: BIRTH ANNIVERSARY. Oct 16, 1758. American teacher and journalist whose name became synonymous with the word "dictionary" after his compilations of the earliest American dictionaries of the English language. Born at West Hartford, CT, he died at New Haven, CT, May 28, 1843.

WILDE, OSCAR: 150th BIRTH ANNIVERSARY. Oct 16, 1854. Irish wit, poet and playwright Oscar (Fingal O'Flahertie Wills) Wilde was born at Dublin, Ireland. At the height of his career he was imprisoned for two years on a morals offense, during which time he wrote "A Ballad of Reading Gaol." Best known of his plays is *The Importance of Being Earnest*. "We are all in the gutter," he wrote in *Lady Windermere's Fan*, "but some of us are looking at the stars." Wilde died at Paris, France, Nov 30, 1900.

WOOLLY WORM FESTIVAL. Oct 16–17. Banner Elk, NC. Annual woolly worm races, mountain entertainment, crafts and food. Third full weekend in October. Est attendance: 25,000. For info: Chamber of Commerce, PO Box 335, Banner Elk, NC 28604. Phone: (828) 898-5605. Fax: (828) 898-8287. E-mail: chamber@averycounty.com. Web: www.averycounty.com.

Oct 16–17 ☆ Chase's 2004 Calendar of Events ☆

WORLD FOOD DAY. Oct 16. To increase awareness, understanding and informed action on hunger. Annually, on the founding date of the UN Food and Agriculture Organization. For info: Patricia Young, US Natl Committee for World Food Day, 2175 K St NW, Washington, DC 20437. Phone: (202) 653-2404. Web: www.worldfooddayusa.org.

YALE UNIVERSITY FOUNDED: ANNIVERSARY. Oct 16, 1701 (OS). The Collegiate School was founded at Branford, CT, by Congregationalists dissatisfied with the growing liberalism at Harvard. In 1716, the school was moved to New Haven, CT, where it became Yale College, named after Elihu Yale, a governor of the East India Company. The first degrees were awarded in 1716. Yale became a university in 1887. Founded as a school for men, Yale began admitting women undergraduates in 1969.

YORKTOWN VICTORY CELEBRATION. Oct 16–17. Yorktown Victory Center, Yorktown, VA. Military life and artillery demonstrators mark the 223rd anniversary of America's climactic victory at Yorktown. To experience Continental Army life firsthand, visitors may enroll in "A School for the Soldier," where they can try on uniforms, march to the beat of a Revolutionary drum and join in other hands-on military activities. Special programs are also held at Yorktown Battlefield, administered by the Colonial National Historical Park. For info: Jamestown-Yorktown Foundation, PO Box 1607, Williamsburg, VA 23187. Phone: (757) 253-4838 or toll-free (888) 593-4682. Fax: (757) 253-5299. Web: www.historyisfun.org.

BIRTHDAYS TODAY

Melissa Louise Belote, 48, Olympic gold medal swimmer, born Washington, DC, Oct 16, 1956.
Manute Bol, 42, former basketball player, born Gogrial, Sudan, Oct 16, 1962.
Barry Corbin, 64, actor ("Northern Exposure," *Stir Crazy, Any Which Way You Can*), born Dawson County, TX, Oct 16, 1940.
Juan Gonzalez, 35, baseball player, born Vaga Baja, Puerto Rico, Oct 16, 1969.
Günter Grass, 77, author (*The Tin Drum, Dog Years*), born Danzig, Germany, Oct 16, 1927.
Paul Kariya, 30, hockey player, born Vancouver, BC, Canada, Oct 16, 1974.
Angela Lansbury, 79, actress ("Murder, She Wrote," *National Velvet*; Tony for *Sweeney Todd*), born London, England, Oct 16, 1925.
Kellie Martin, 29, actress ("Life Goes On," "ER"), born Riverside, CA, Oct 16, 1975.
Tim Robbins, 46, actor (*Top Gun, Shawshank Redemption*), born West Covina, CA, Oct 16, 1958.
Suzanne Somers, 58, actress ("Three's Company," "Step by Step," *American Graffiti*), born San Bruno, CA, Oct 16, 1946.
Kordell Stewart, 32, football player, born New Orleans, LA, Oct 16, 1972.
Bob Weir, 57, cofounder (The Grateful Dead), born San Francisco, CA, Oct 16, 1947.

October 2004

S	M	T	W	T	F	S
					1	2
3	4	5	6	7	8	9
10	11	12	13	14	15	16
17	18	19	20	21	22	23
24	25	26	27	28	29	30
31						

OCTOBER 17 — SUNDAY
Day 291 — 75 Remaining

ARTHUR, JEAN: BIRTH ANNIVERSARY. Oct 17, 1900. American actress Jean Arthur was born Gladys Georgianna Greene at Plattsburg, NY. Her films included *Mr Deeds Goes to Town* (1936), *Mr Smith Goes to Washington* (1939) and *Shane* (1953). She died June 19, 1991, at Carmel, CA.

BLACK POETRY DAY. Oct 17. To recognize the contribution of black poets to American life and culture and to honor Jupiter Hammon, first black in America to publish his own verse. Jupiter Hammon of Huntington, Long Island, NY, was born Oct 17, 1711. The celebration includes a poetry reading by an important black poet. Est attendance: 200. For info: Black Poetry Day Committee, EOP Office, Algonquin Hall, SUNY-Plattsburgh, Plattsburgh, NY 12901-2681. Phone: (518) 564-2263. E-mail: fieldsme@plattsburgh.edu.

HAMMON, JUPITER: BIRTH ANNIVERSARY. Oct 17, 1711. America's first published black poet, whose birth anniversary is celebrated annually as Black Poetry Day, was born into slavery, probably at Long Island, NY. He was taught to read, however, and as a trusted servant was allowed to use his master's library. "With the publication on Christmas Day, 1760, of the 88-line broadside poem 'An Evening Thought,' Jupiter Hammon, then 49, became the first black in America to publish poetry." Hammon died in 1790. The exact date and place of his death are unknown.

"THE HOLLYWOOD SQUARES" TV PREMIERE: ANNIVERSARY. Oct 17, 1966. On this game show, nine celebrities sat in a giant grid. Two contestants played tic-tac-toe by determining if an answer given by a celebrity was correct. Peter Marshall hosted the show for many years with panelists Paul Lynde, Rose Marie, Cliff Arquette, Wally Cox, John Davidson and George Gobel among others. John Davidson took over as host in 1986 for a new version of the game show with Joan Rivers and, later, Shadoe Stevens at center square. In 1998 "Hollywood Squares" appeared again with Tom Bergeron as host and Whoopi Goldberg as the center square.

JOHNSON, RICHARD MENTOR: BIRTH ANNIVERSARY. Oct 17, 1780. Ninth vice president of the US (1837–41). Born at Floyd's Station, KY. Died at Frankfort, KY, Nov 19, 1850.

★**NATIONAL CHARACTER COUNTS WEEK.** Oct 17–23. One of the greatest building blocks of character is citizen service. The future belongs to those who have the strength of character to live a life of service to others.

NATIONAL CHEMISTRY WEEK. Oct 17–23. To celebrate the contributions of chemistry to modern life and to help the public understand that chemistry affects every part of our lives. Activities include an array of outreach programs such as open houses, contests, workshops, exhibits and classroom visits. 10 million participants nationwide. For info: Office of Community Activities, American Chemical Society, 1155 16th St NW, Washington, DC 20036. Phone: (202) 872-6078. Fax: (202) 872-4353. E-mail: ncw@acs.org. Web: www.chemistry.org/ncw.

★**NATIONAL FOREST PRODUCTS WEEK.** Oct 17–23. Presidential Proclamation always issued for the week beginning with the third Sunday in October since 1960 (PL86–753 of Sept 13, 1960).

NATIONAL SCHOOL BUS SAFETY WEEK. Oct 17–23. This week is set aside to focus attention on school bus safety—from the standpoint of the bus drivers, students and the motoring public. The theme for 2004 is "Shhh—Railroad Crossing!" Annually, the third full week of October, starting on Sunday. For info: Natl Assn for Pupil Transportation, 1840 Western Ave, Albany, NY 12203. Phone: (800) 989-6278. E-mail: sbsw@napt.org. Web: www.napt.org.

POPE JOHN PAUL I: BIRTH ANNIVERSARY. Oct 17, 1912. Albino Luciani, 263rd pope of the Roman Catholic Church. Born at Forno di Canale, Italy, he was elected pope Aug 26, 1978.

☆ Chase's 2004 Calendar of Events ☆   Oct 17–18

Died at Rome, 34 days after his election, Sept 28, 1978. Shortest papacy since Pope Leo XI (Apr 1–27, 1605).

SAN FRANCISCO 1989 EARTHQUAKE: 15th ANNIVERSARY. Oct 17, 1989. The San Francisco Bay area was rocked by an earthquake registering 7.1 on the Richter scale at 5:04 PM, EDT, just as the nation's baseball fans settled in to watch the 1989 World Series. A large audience was tuned in to the pregame coverage when the quake hit and knocked the broadcast off the air. The quake caused damage estimated at $10 billion and killed 67 people, many of whom were caught in the collapse of the double-decked Interstate 80, at Oakland, CA.

SUNDAY SCHOOL TEACHER APPRECIATION DAY. Oct 17. Established in 1993, this is a day set aside for churches to honor the 15 million men and women who faithfully serve as Sunday School teachers—one of the largest volunteer forces in America. For info: Sunday School Teacher Appreciation Day, Gospel Light, 2300 Knoll Dr, Ventura, CA 93003. Phone: (800) 354-4224. Fax: (805) 677-6818. E-mail: marlenebaer@gospellight.com. Web: www.mysundayschoolteacher.com.

TEEN READ WEEK. Oct 17–24. The teen years are a time when many kids reject reading as being just another dreary assignment. The goal of Teen Read Week is to encourage young adults to read for the fun of it. Also to remind parents, teachers, booksellers and others that reading for fun is important for teens as well as young children and to increase awareness of the resources available at libraries. More than 1,400 school and public libraries are registered to participate. For info: Young Adult Library Services Assn, American Library Assn, 50 E Huron St, Chicago, IL 60611. Phone: (800) 545-2433 x 4390. E-mail: yalsa@ala.org. Web: www.ala.org/teenread.

UNITED NATIONS: INTERNATIONAL DAY FOR THE ERADICATION OF POVERTY. Oct 17. The General Assembly proclaimed this observance (Res 47/196) to promote public awareness of the need to eradicate poverty and destitution in all countries, particularly the developing nations. For info: United Nations, Dept of Public Info, New York, NY 10017. Web: www.un.org.

WSBA/WARM 103 HOLIDAY CRAFT SHOW. Oct 17. York Fairgrounds, York, PA. More than 250 craft displays, from country to contemporary, Victorian and southwestern, handcrafted furniture, wood carvings, dolls, jewelry, pottery, collectibles, quilts, baskets, fine arts and much more. Admission fee. Est attendance: 4,000. For info: Joe Alfano, Asst Promo Dir, PO Box 910, York, PA 17402-0910. Phone: (717) 764-1155. Fax: (717) 252-4807. E-mail: jalfano@suscom.com. Web: www.warm103.com.

BIRTHDAYS TODAY

Ernie Els, 35, golfer, born Johannesburg, South Africa, Oct 17, 1969.
Eminem, 32, musician, rapper (*The Slim Shady LP, The Marshall Mathers LP*), born Marshall Bruce Mathers III, Kansas City, MO, Oct 17, 1972.
Beverly Garland, 78, actress ("My Three Sons," "Scarecrow and Mrs King"), born Santa Cruz, CA, Oct 17, 1926.
Mae Jemison, 48, scientist, astronaut, host ("Susan B. Anthony Slept Here"), born Decatur, AL, Oct 17, 1956.
Margot Kidder, 56, actress (Lois Lane in *Superman* movies), born Yellowknife, NT, Canada, Oct 17, 1948.
Robert Craig ("Evel") Knievel, 66, motorcycle stunt performer, born Butte, MT, Oct 17, 1938.
Norm Macdonald, 41, comedian, actor ("Saturday Night Live," "Norm"), born Quebec City, QC, Canada, Oct 17, 1963.
Michael McKean, 57, actor ("Laverne & Shirley," *This Is Spinal Tap*), born New York, NY, Oct 17, 1947.
Arthur Miller, 89, dramatist (*Death of a Salesman, A View from the Bridge, All My Sons*), born New York, NY, Oct 17, 1915.
Tom Poston, 77, actor ("Grace Under Fire," Emmy for "The Steve Allen Show," *Soldier in the Rain*), born Columbus, OH, Oct 17, 1927.

Richard Roeper, 45, newspaper columnist, film reviewer ("At the Movies" with Roger Ebert), born Chicago, IL, Oct 17, 1959.
George Wendt, 56, actor ("Cheers," "The Naked Truth"), born Chicago, IL, Oct 17, 1948.

OCTOBER 18 — MONDAY
Day 292 — 74 Remaining

ALASKA DAY. Oct 18. Alaska. Anniversary of transfer of Alaska on Oct 18, 1867, from Russia to the US. The transfer became official on Sitka's Castle Hill. This is a holiday in Alaska; when it falls on a weekend, it is observed on the following Monday.

ANDREE, SALOMON AUGUSTE: 150th BIRTH ANNIVERSARY. Oct 18, 1854. Swedish explorer and balloonist born at Grenna, Sweden. His North Pole expedition of 1897 attracted world attention but ended tragically. With two companions, Andree left Spitzbergen, July 11, 1897, in a balloon, hoping to place the Swedish flag at the North Pole. The last message from Andree, borne by carrier pigeons, was dated noon, July 13, 1897. The frozen bodies of the explorers were found 33 years later by another polar expedition in the summer of 1930. Diaries, maps and exposed photographic negatives also were found. The photos were developed successfully, providing a pictorial record of the ill-fated expedition.

AZERBAIJAN: INDEPENDENCE DAY. Oct 18. National holiday. Commemorates declaration of independence from the Soviet Union in 1991.

BERGSON, HENRI: BIRTH ANNIVERSARY. Oct 18, 1859. French philosopher, Nobel Prize winner and author of *Creative Evolution*, born at Paris, France. Died there Jan 4, 1941.

BROOKS, JAMES DAVID: BIRTH ANNIVERSARY. Oct 18, 1906. Born at St. Louis, MO, during the Depression Brooks worked as a muralist in the Federal Art Project of the Works Progress Administration. His best-known work of that period was "Flight," a mural on the rotunda of the Marine Air Terminal at La Guardia National Airport in New York. It was painted over during the 1950s but restored in 1980. Brooks served with the US Army from 1942 to 1945. When he returned to New York, his interest shifted to abstract expressionism. His paintings were exhibited in the historic "Ninth Street Exhibition" as a part of the Museum of Modern Art's exhibits "Twelve Americans" and "New American Painting," among others. He died Mar 8, 1992, at Brookhaven, NY.

CANADA: PERSONS DAY. Oct 18. A day to commemorate the anniversary of the 1929 ruling that declared women to be persons in Canada. Prior to this ruling English common law prevailed ("Women are persons in matters of pains and penalties, but are not persons in matters of rights and privileges"). The celebrated cause, popularly known as the "Persons Case," was brought by five women of Alberta, Canada; leader of the courageous "Famous Five" was Emily Murphy (1868–1933). This ruling by the Judicial Committee of England's Privy Council, Oct 18, 1929, overturned a 1928 decision of the Supreme Court of Canada. Fifty years after the Persons Case decision, in 1979, the Governor General's Awards in Commemoration of the Persons Case were established to recognize deserving persons who have made outstanding contributions to the quality of life of women in Canada.

545

CANALETTO, GIOVANNI ANTONIO: BIRTH ANNIVERSARY. Oct 18, 1697. Italian painter Giovanni Antonio Canaletto (born Canale), who is best known for his detailed landscapes of Venice and London, was born at Venice and died there at age 70, Apr 20, 1768. He was known for his accurate use of perspective, shadow and light. He went to England in 1746 and expanded his range of subjects to include English landscapes and country homes.

FACILITY SERVICE WORKERS DAY. Oct 18. This day is dedicated to recognizing the invisible workforce that insures our safety and security by maintaining our workplaces, restaurants, healthcare facilities and other places where we take personal well-being for granted. Annually, the third Monday in October. For info: Kurt Zachhuber, 19 Harvey Road, #15, Bedford, NH 03110. Phone: (603) 624-8899. Fax: (603) 624-6002. E-mail: info@cleanvalue.com. Web: www.cleanvalue.com.

FIRST NEWSPAPER COMIC STRIP: ANNIVERSARY. Oct 18, 1896. Although cartoons had appeared in newspapers for many years, the comic strip—a narrative told in cartoons over several panels—took its main form with the appearance of "The Yellow Kid Takes a Hand at Golf" in the *New York Journal*'s weekly supplement *American Humorist*. The creator was Richard Fenton Outcault. In March 1897 the *Yellow Kid Magazine* gathered the strips and became the first published collection of a comic strip—setting the stage for the first comic books in the late 1920s. See also: "Outcault, Richard Fenton: Birth Anniversary" (Jan 14).

INTERNATIONAL CREDIT UNION WEEK. Oct 18–22. Worldwide observance to recognize the contribution of credit unions to the development and practice of democracy. For info: Public Relations, Credit Union Natl Assn, PO Box 431, Madison, WI 53701-0431. Phone: (800) 356-9655. Fax: (608) 231-4858.

INTERNATIONAL INFECTION CONTROL WEEK. Oct 18–24. To promote awareness of prevention and treatment of infection. Annually, the third week in October. For info: Assn for Professionals in Infection Control and Epidemiology, 1275 K St NW, Ste 1000, Washington, DC 20005-4006. Phone: (202) 789-1890. Fax: (202) 789-1899. E-mail: APICinfo@apic.org. Web: www.apic.org.

JAMAICA: NATIONAL HEROES DAY. Oct 18. National holiday established in 1969. Always observed on third Monday of October.

	S	M	T	W	T	F	S
October						1	2
	3	4	5	6	7	8	9
2004	10	11	12	13	14	15	16
	17	18	19	20	21	22	23
	24	25	26	27	28	29	30
	31						

LATINO BOOK & FAMILY FESTIVAL—HOUSTON. Oct 18–19. Houston, TX. Produced along with actor Edward James Olmos, this festival is a celebration of books, careers, culture, education, health, recreation, travel and more. It is the largest Latino consumer trade show in the US. Attendees will enjoy hundreds of booths and activities including book signings, storytelling, poetry readings, food, entertainment and workshops. For info: Latino Book & Family Festivals, 3980 Cazador St, Los Angeles, CA 90065. E-mail: kathy@latinobookfestival.com. Web: www.latinobookfestival.com.

LIEBLING, A.J.: 100th BIRTH ANNIVERSARY. Oct 18, 1904. American journalist and author who said "Freedom of the press belongs to those who own one." Abbott Joseph Liebling was born at New York, NY, and died there Dec 28, 1963.

MERCOURI, MELINA: BIRTH ANNIVERSARY. Oct 18, 1922. Greek actress and politician Melina Mercouri was born Maria Amalia Mercouri at Athens, Greece, Oct 18, 1922 or 1925 (both reported). Of her more than 70 films and plays she is most known for her role in *Never on Sunday* (1960). In 1977 she was elected to Greece's parliament and became the first woman in Greece's senior cabinet when appointed by Premier Andreas Papandreou to the position of minister of culture in 1981. She died Mar 6, 1994, at New York, NY.

NATIONAL BUSINESS WOMEN'S WEEK. Oct 18–22. Celebrates the contributions of working women to American society, the economy and the family. It is commemorated nationwide by special activities. Annually, starting the third Monday in October. For info: Business and Professional Women/USA, 1900 M St NW, #310, Washington, DC 20036. Phone: (202) 293-1100. Web: www.bpwusa.org.

NATIONAL HEALTH EDUCATION WEEK. Oct 18–24. Annually, the third week in October. For info: Elaine Sheehan, National Center for Health Education, 375 Hudson St, New York, NY 10014. Phone: (212) 463-4053.

"ROSEANNE" TV PREMIERE: ANNIVERSARY. Oct 18, 1988. This comedy showed the blue-collar Conner family trying to make ends meet. Rosanne played wise-cracking Roseanne Conner, John Goodman played her husband Dan and Laurie Metcalf played her sister Jackie. The Conner children were played by Sara Gilbert (Darlene), Alicia Goranson and Sarah Chalke (Becky) and Michael Fishman (D.J). The last episode aired Nov 14, 1997, but it remains popular in reruns.

SAINT LUKE: FEAST DAY. Oct 18. Patron saint of doctors and artists, himself a physician and painter, authorship of the third Gospel and Acts of the Apostles is attributed to him. Died about AD 68. Legend says that he painted portraits of Mary and Jesus.

SILVERSTEIN, SHEL: BIRTH ANNIVERSARY. Oct 18, 1932. Cartoonist and children's author, best remembered for his poetry that included *A Light in the Attic* and *The Giving Tree*. Silverstein won the Michigan Young Reader's Award for *Where the Sidewalk Ends*. Also a songwriter, he wrote "The Unicorn Song" and "A Boy Named Sue" for Johnny Cash. Born at Chicago, IL, he died at Key West, FL, May 9, 1999.

TRUDEAU, PIERRE ELLIOTT: 85th BIRTH ANNIVERSARY. Oct 18, 1919. Prime Minister of Canada 1968–79, 1980–84, Born at Montreal, QC, Canada on Oct 18, 1919, he died there Sept 28, 2000.

VIRGIN ISLANDS: HURRICANE THANKSGIVING DAY. Oct 18. Third Monday of October is a legal holiday celebrating the end of hurricane season.

WATER POLLUTION CONTROL ACT: ANNIVERSARY. Oct 18, 1972. Overriding President Nixon's veto, Congress passed a $25 billion Water Pollution Control Act.

WORLD MENOPAUSE DAY. Oct 18. The World Menopause Day challenge calls on every nation to make menopausal health a principal issue in their research and public health agendas in order to help women prevent unpleasant symptoms that can affect productivity and quality of life, as well as reduce rates of osteo-

☆ Chase's 2004 Calendar of Events ☆   Oct 18–20

porosis, heart disease, colon cancer and other aging- and hormone-related diseases. For info: Intl Menopause Society, Chez Maitre M Steyaert, Av des Cattleyas, 3, box 1, 1150 Brussels, Belgium. Phone: (32 2) 772-2183. E-mail: imsociety@Filink.net. Web: www.imsociety.org.

WORLD RAINFOREST WEEK. Oct 18–25 (tentative). Rainforest activists worldwide will sponsor events to increase public awareness of rainforest destruction and motivate people to protect the Earth's rainforest and support the rights of their inhabitants. The global rate of destruction of rainforests is 2.4 acres per second—equivalent to two US football fields. For info: Grassroots Coord, Rainforest Action Network, 221 Pine St, 5th Fl, San Francisco, CA 94104. Phone: (415) 398-4404. E-mail: grassroots@ran.org. Web: www.ran.org.

BIRTHDAYS TODAY

Chuck Berry, 78, singer, songwriter ("Johnny B. Goode," "Roll Over Beethoven"), musician, born Charles Edward Anderson, St. Louis, MO, Oct 18, 1926.
Peter Boyle, 71, actor (*Medium Cool, The Dream Team,* "Everybody Loves Raymond"), born Philadelphia, PA, Oct 18, 1933.
Pam Dawber, 53, actress ("Mork & Mindy," "My Sister Sam"), born Farmington, MI, Oct 18, 1951.
Mike Ditka, 65, Hall of Fame football player, former coach, sportscaster, born Carnegie, PA, Oct 18, 1939.
Jesse Helms, 83, retired five-term US Senator (R, North Carolina), born Monroe, NC, Oct 18, 1921.
Wynton Marsalis, 43, jazz musician, born New Orleans, LA, Oct 18, 1961.
Erin Moran, 43, actress ("Happy Days," "Joanie Loves Chachi"), born Burbank, CA, Oct 18, 1961.
Joe Morton, 57, actor (*The Brother from Another Planet, Trouble in Mind, City of Hope*), born New York, NY, Oct 18, 1947.
Martina Navratilova, 48, former tennis player, born Martina Subertova, Prague, Czechoslovakia, Oct 18, 1956.
Ntozake Shange, 56, dramatist, poet, born Paulette L. Williams, Trenton, NJ, Oct 18, 1948.
Vincent Spano, 42, actor (*Baby, It's You; Rumblefish*), born New York, NY, Oct 18, 1962.
Jim Talent, 48, US Senator (R, Missouri), born Des Peres, MO, Oct 18, 1956.
Jean-Claude Van Damme, 44, actor (*Kickboxer*), born Brussels, Belgium, Oct 18, 1960.
Wendy Wasserstein, 54, playwright (*The Heidi Chronicles, The Sisters Rosenzweig*), born Brooklyn, NY, Oct 18, 1950.

OCTOBER 19 — TUESDAY
Day 293 — 73 Remaining

BROWNE, THOMAS: BIRTH ANNIVERSARY. Oct 19, 1605 (OS). Physician, scholar and author, Thomas Browne was born at London, England. At age 55 he wrote: "The long habit of living indisposeth us for dying." His most famous work, *Religio Medici*, was published in 1642. Browne died at Norwich, England, Oct 19, 1682 (OS).

DOW-JONES BIGGEST DROP: ANNIVERSARY. Oct 19, 1987. The Dow-Jones Industrial Average plunged 508 points, or 22.6 percent, after frenzied selling, the largest percentage drop in history.

EVALUATE YOUR LIFE DAY. Oct 19. To encourage everyone to check and see if they're really headed where they want to be. [©2003 by WH.] For info: Thomas & Ruth Roy, Wellcat Holidays, 2418 Long Ln, Lebanon, PA 17042-0774. Phone: (717) 279-0184. E-mail: info@wellcat.com. Web: www.wellcat.com.

JEFFERSON, MARTHA WAYLES SKELTON: BIRTH ANNIVERSARY. Oct 19, 1748. Wife of Thomas Jefferson, third president of the US. Born at Charles City County, VA, she died at Monticello, VA, Sept 6, 1782.

LUMIÈRE, AUGUSTE: BIRTH ANNIVERSARY. Oct 19, 1862. Born at Besançon, France, Auguste Lumière with brother Louis were film pioneers who created the first movie, "Workers Leaving the Lumière Factory" (1895). He died at Lyon, France, on Apr 10, 1954.

PECK, ANNIE S.: BIRTH ANNIVERSARY. Oct 19, 1850. World-renowned mountain climber Annie S. Peck won an international following in 1895 when she climbed the Matterhorn in the Swiss Alps. Peck climbed the Peruvian peak Huascaran (21,812 ft), giving her the record for the highest peak climbed in the Western Hemisphere by an American man or woman, and at age 61 she climbed Mt Coropuna in Peru (21,250 ft) and placed a "Votes for Women" banner at its pinnacle. Annie Peck died July 18, 1935, at New York City.

YORKTOWN DAY: ANNIVERSARY. Oct 19, 1781. More than 7,000 English and Hessian troops, led by British General Lord Cornwallis, surrendered to General George Washington at Yorktown, VA, effectively ending the war between Britain and her American colonies. There were no more major battles, but the provisional treaty of peace was not signed until Nov 30, 1782, and the final Treaty of Paris, Sept 3, 1783.

BIRTHDAYS TODAY

Jack Anderson, 82, journalist, columnist, author (*Japan Conspiracy, Stormin' Norman*), born Long Beach, CA, Oct 19, 1922.
Michael Gambon, 64, actor ("The Singing Detective," *The Cook, The Thief, His Wife & Her Lover*), born Dublin, Ireland, Oct 19, 1940.
Evander Holyfield, 42, boxer, born Atlanta, GA, Oct 19, 1962.
Patricia Ireland, 59, feminist, social activist, former president of National Organization for Women, born Oak Park, IL, Oct 19, 1945.
John LeCarre, 73, author (*The Russia House*), born David John Moore Cornwell, Poole, England, Oct 19, 1931.
John Lithgow, 59, actor (*Don Quixote, Harry & the Hendersons,* "3rd Rock from the Sun"), born Rochester, NY, Oct 19, 1945.
Peter Max, 67, artist, designer, born Berlin, Germany, Oct 19, 1937.
Simon Ward, 63, actor (*The Three Musketeers, The Four Musketeers*), born London, England, Oct 19, 1941.

OCTOBER 20 — WEDNESDAY
Day 294 — 72 Remaining

BIRTH OF THE BAB: ANNIVERSARY. Oct 20, 1819. Baha'i observance of anniversary of the birth in Shiraz, Persia, of Siyyid Ali Muhammad, who later took the title "the Bab"; the Bab was the prophet-herald of the Baha'i Faith. One of the nine days of the year when Baha'is suspend work. For info: Baha'is of the US, Office of Public Information, 1320 Nineteenth St NW, Ste 350, Washington, DC 20036. Phone: (202) 466-9870. Fax: (202) 466-9873. E-mail: opi@usbnc.org. Web: www.us.bahai.org.

CIRCLEVILLE PUMPKIN SHOW. Oct 20–23. Circleville, OH. More than 100,000 pounds of pumpkins, squash and gourds. Est attendance: 300,000. For info: Hugh Dresbach, Secy, Pumpkin Show Inc, 159 E Franklin St, Circleville, OH 43113. Phone: (740) 474-7000. Fax: (740) 474-6611. Web: www.pumpkinshow.com.

547

Oct 20 ☆ Chase's 2004 Calendar of Events ☆

DEWEY, JOHN: BIRTH ANNIVERSARY. Oct 20, 1859. American psychologist, philosopher and educational reformer born at Burlington, VT. His philosophical views of education have been termed pragmatism, instrumentalism and experimentalism. Died at New York, NY, June 1, 1952.

EAST TEXAS YAMBOREE. Oct 20–23. Gilmer, TX. Est attendance: 100,000. For info: Joan Small, Exec Dir, Gilmer Area Chamber of Commerce, Box 854, Gilmer, TX 75644. Phone: (903) 843-2413 or (903) 843-3981. Fax: (903) 843-3759. E-mail: upchamber@aol.com. Web: www.yamboree.com.

GUATEMALA: REVOLUTION DAY: 60th ANNIVERSARY. Oct 20. Public holiday. Commemorates the overthrow of dictator Jorge Ubico Castañada in 1944.

KENYA: KENYATTA DAY. Oct 20. Public holiday.

LUGOSI, BELA: BIRTH ANNIVERSARY. Oct 20, 1882. Born Bela Ferenc Denzso Blasko at Lugos, Hungary. Known best for his role as Count Dracula in *Dracula*. Lugosi died of a heart attack at Los Angeles, CA, Aug 16, 1956.

MacARTHUR RETURNS: US LANDINGS ON LEYTE, PHILIPPINES: 60th ANNIVERSARY. Oct 20, 1944. In mid-September of 1944 American military leaders made the decision to begin the invasion of the Philippines on Leyte, a small island north of the Surigao Strait. With General Douglas MacArthur in overall command, US aircraft dropped hundreds of tons of bombs in the area of Dulag. Four divisions were landed on the east coast, and after a few hours General MacArthur set foot on Philippine soil for the first time since he was ordered to Australia Mar 11, 1942, thus fulfilling his promise, "I shall return."

MANN, JAMES ROBERT: BIRTH ANNIVERSARY. Oct 20, 1856. American lawyer and legislator, born near Bloomington, IL. Republican member of Congress from Illinois from 1896 until his death, Nov 30, 1922, at Washington, DC. Mann was the author and sponsor of the "White Slave Traffic Act," also known as the "Mann Act," passed by Congress on June 25, 1910. The act prohibited, under heavy penalties, the interstate transportation of women for immoral purposes.

MANTLE, MICKEY: BIRTH ANNIVERSARY. Oct 20, 1931. Baseball Hall of Famer, born at Spavinaw, OK. Died Aug 13, 1995, at Dallas, TX.

MISS AMERICAN ROSE DAY. Oct 20. Miss American Rose is a pageant devoted to high achievement and community service for girls and women of all ages. On this day, treat the women in your life like beautiful American roses. For info: Lynanne White, Miss American Rose Pageants, 19689 7th Av, PMB 323, Poulsbo, WA 98370. E-mail: miss@americanrose.com. Web: www.americanrose.com.

MISSOURI DAY. Oct 20. Observed by teachers and pupils of schools with appropriate exercises throughout state of Missouri. Annually, the third Wednesday of October.

MOON PHASE: FIRST QUARTER. Oct 20. Moon enters First Quarter phase at 5:59 PM, EDT.

MOSCOW SOCCER TRAGEDY: ANNIVERSARY. Oct 20, 1982. The world's worst soccer disaster occurred at Moscow when 340 sports fans were killed during a game between Soviet and Dutch players. Details of the event, blaming police for the tragedy in which spectators were crushed to death in an open staircase, were not published until nearly seven years later (July 1989) in *Sovietsky Sport*. In 1985, three soccer game disasters in England and Belgium took 93 lives and injured nearly 800 persons. In April 1989, 95 persons perished in a crush at a soccer match in Sheffield, England.

	S	M	T	W	T	F	S
October 2004						1	2
	3	4	5	6	7	8	9
	10	11	12	13	14	15	16
	17	18	19	20	21	22	23
	24	25	26	27	28	29	30
	31						

NORTHERN INTERNATIONAL LIVESTOCK EXPOSITION. Oct 20–23. MetraPark, Billings, MT. PRCA rodeo, trade show exhibits, cattle, sheep, swine and horse sales. Est attendance: 30,000. For info: Joyce Laughery, Genl Mgr, NILE Office, PO Box 1981, Billings, MT 59103. Phone: (406) 256-2495. Fax: (406) 256-2494. Web: www.thenile.org.

OMAHA PRODUCTS SHOW. Oct 20–21. Omaha Convention Center, Omaha, NE. A marketing center for buyers and sellers with products, services and supplies for business and industry. Est attendance: 12,500. For info: Robert P. Mancuso, Pres, Mid-America Expositions, Inc, 7015 Spring St, Omaha, NE 68106-3518. Phone: (402) 346-8003. Fax: (402) 346-5412. Web: www.showofficeonline.com.

PIONEER DAYS. Oct 20–21. Washington, MS. Through talks and demonstrations, youngsters learn how children lived 200 years ago. Annually, in October. Est attendance: 1,500. For info: Anne L. Gray, Historian, Historic Jefferson College, PO Box 700, Washington, MS 39190. Phone: (601) 442-2901. E-mail: hjc@bkbank.com. Web: www.mdah.state.ms.us.

SATURDAY NIGHT MASSACRE: ANNIVERSARY. Oct 20, 1973. Anniversary of dramatic turning point in the Watergate affair. On Oct 20, 1973, the White House announced at 8:24 PM, EDT, that President Richard M. Nixon had discharged Archibald Cox (Special Watergate Prosecutor) and William B. Ruckelshaus (Deputy Attorney General), and that the Attorney General, Elliot L. Richardson, had resigned. Immediate and widespread demands for impeachment of the president ensued and were not stilled until President Nixon resigned, Aug 9, 1974.

"THE SIX MILLION DOLLAR MAN" TV PREMIERE: ANNIVERSARY. Oct 20, 1973. This action-adventure series based on the novel "Cyborg" was a monthly feature on "The ABC Suspense Movie" before becoming a regular series in 1974. Lee Majors starred as astronaut Steve Austin, who, after an accident, was "rebuilt" with bionic legs, arms and an eye. He worked for the Office of Strategic Information (OSI) carrying out sensitive missions. Also in the cast were Richard Anderson, Alan Oppenheimer and Martin E. Brooks. "The Bionic Woman," starring Lindsay Wagner, was a spin-off from this show, and the two main characters were paired for several made-for-TV sequels.

TACOMA HOLIDAY FOOD AND GIFT FESTIVAL. Oct 20–24. Tacoma Dome, Tacoma, WA. Gifts, crafts, gourmet foods and more amidst this glittering extravaganza which transforms the Tacoma Dome into a fairyland of twinkling lights, trees and Christmas cheer. Est attendance: 50,000. For info: Showcase Northwest, Inc, PO Box 2815, Kirkland, WA 98083. Phone: (425) 889-9494 or (800) 521-7469. Fax: (425) 889-8165. E-mail: tacoma@showcaseproductionsnw.com. Web: www.showcaseproductionsnw.com.

WREN, CHRISTOPHER: BIRTH ANNIVERSARY. Oct 20, 1632 (OS). Sir Christopher Wren, English architect, astronomer and mathematician, was born at East Knoyle, Wiltshire, England. Died Feb 25, 1723 (OS), at London, England. His epitaph, written by his son, is inscribed over the interior of the north door at St. Paul's Cathedral, London: "Si monumentum requiris, circumspice." (If you would see his monument, look about you.)

☆ Chase's 2004 Calendar of Events ☆   Oct 20–21

BIRTHDAYS TODAY

Art Buchwald, 79, columnist, author (*While Reagan Slept*), born Mount Vernon, NY, Oct 20, 1925.
William Christopher, 72, actor ("M*A*S*H," *With Six You Get Eggroll*), born Evanston, IL, Oct 20, 1932.
Peter Fitzgerald, 44, US Senator (R, Illinois), born Elgin, IL, Oct 20, 1960.
Keith Hernandez, 51, former baseball player, born San Francisco, CA, Oct 20, 1953.
Eddie Jones, 33, basketball player, born Pompano Beach, FL, Oct 20, 1971.
Melanie Mayron, 52, actress (Emmy for "thirtysomething"; *Car Wash, My Blue Heaven*), born Philadelphia, PA, Oct 20, 1952.
Viggo Mortensen, 46, actor (*The Lord of the Rings* trilogy), born New York, NY, Oct 20, 1958.
Jerry Orbach, 69, actor ("Law & Order," *Crimes and Misdemeanors, Dirty Dancing*; stage: *The Fantasticks*; Tony for *Promises Promises*), born the Bronx, NY, Oct 20, 1935.
Tom Petty, 51, musician, singer ("Stop Draggin' My Heart Around"), born Gainesville, FL, Oct 20, 1953.

OCTOBER 21 — THURSDAY
Day 295 — 71 Remaining

BATTLE OF TRAFALGAR: ANNIVERSARY. Oct 21, 1805. This famous naval action between the British Royal Navy and the combined French and Spanish fleets removed the threat of Napoleon's invasion of England. The British victory, off Trafalgar on the coast of Spain, guaranteed the fame of Viscount Horatio Nelson who died in the battle.

BIKETOBERFEST. Oct 21–24. Daytona Beach, FL. Bikers return to Daytona Beach for that last chance to ride before winter. Parades, concerts and expos highlight the weekend. Est attendance: 100,000. For info: Daytona Beach Area CVB, 126 E Orange, Daytona Beach, FL 32114. Phone: (866) 296-8970. Fax: (386) 255-5478. E-mail: info@daytonabeach.com. Web: www.biketoberfest.org.

CARLETON, WILL: BIRTH ANNIVERSARY. Oct 21, 1845. Anniversary of the birth of poet Will Carleton, observed (by 1919 statute) in Michigan schools where poems of Carleton must be read on this day. Best known of his poems: "Over the Hill to the Poorhouse." Carleton died in 1912.

CARVEL, TOM: DEATH ANNIVERSARY. Oct 21, 1990. American inventor and businessman Tom Carvel was born Thomas Andreas Carvelas at Greece in 1906. He invented the machine that makes soft-serve ice cream (or frozen custard). His chain of ice cream stores began with a $15 loan and grew into the third-largest ice cream chain in America. He died at Pine Plains, NY.

COLERIDGE, SAMUEL TAYLOR: BIRTH ANNIVERSARY. Oct 21, 1772. English poet ("The Rime of the Ancient Mariner") and essayist born at Ottery St. Mary, Devonshire, England. Died at Highgate, England, July 25, 1834. In *Table Talk*, he wrote: "I wish our clever young poets would remember my homely definitions of prose and poetry; that is, prose = words in their best order; poetry = the *best* words in the best order."

CRUZ, CELIA: BIRTH ANNIVERSARY. Oct 21, 1924. The Grammy Award-winning singer was dubbed the "Queen of Salsa" by her adoring fans. Born as Celia de la Caridad Cruz Alonso at Havana, Cuba (some sources cite her birth year as 1925 or 1929), Cruz had a career spanning six decades and recorded some 70 albums. Her energetic performances were punctuated by her call of "Azucar!" ("Sugar!") and flamboyant costumes. President Bill Clinton awarded her the National Medal of Arts in 1994. Cruz died at New York, NY, on July 16, 2003.

DAY OF NATIONAL CONCERN ABOUT YOUNG PEOPLE AND GUN VIOLENCE. Oct 21 (tentative). Students across America are asked to voluntarily sign a "Student Pledge Against Gun Violence," a solemn promise never to bring a gun to school, never to use a gun to settle a dispute and to discourage their friends from using a gun. Formerly issued as a presidential proclamation. For info: Student Pledge Against Gun Violence, 112 Nevada St, Northfield, MN 55057. Phone: (507) 645-5378. Web: www.pledge.org.

FALL CYCLE SCENE MOTORCYCLE RACES. Oct 21–24. Daytona International Speedway, Daytona Beach, FL. For info: Daytona International Speedway, PO Box 2801, Daytona Beach, FL 32120-2801. Phone: (386) 253-7223. Fax: (386) 947-6791. Web: www.daytonainternationalspeedway.com.

FILLMORE, CAROLINE CARMICHAEL McINTOSH: BIRTH ANNIVERSARY. Oct 21, 1813. Second wife of Millard Fillmore, 13th president of the US, born at Morristown, NJ. Died at New York, Aug 11, 1881.

GILLESPIE, JOHN BIRKS "DIZZY": BIRTH ANNIVERSARY. Oct 21, 1917. Dizzy Gillespie, trumpet player, composer, bandleader and one of the founding fathers of modern jazz, was born at Cheraw, SC. In the early 1940s Gillespie and alto saxophonist Charlie (Yardbird) Parker created be-bop. In the late '40s he created a second music revolution by incorporating Afro-Cuban music into jazz. In 1953 someone fell on Gillespie's trumpet and bent it. Finding he could hear the sound better, he kept it that way; his puffed cheeks and bent trumpet became his trademarks. He won a Grammy in 1975 for *Oscar Peterson and Dizzy Gillespie* and again in 1991 for *Live at the Royal Festival Hall*. He died Jan 6, 1993, at Englewood, NJ.

GREAT PUMPKIN CARVE. Oct 21–23. Chadds Ford, PA. Local artists carve huge pumpkins on the grounds of the Chadds Ford Historical Society, 5–9 PM. Attractions include hayrides, live music and food. Est attendance: 10,000. For info: Chadds Ford Historical Society, Box 27, Chadds Ford, PA 19317. Phone: (610) 388-7376. Fax: (610) 388-7480. Web: www.chaddsfordhistory.org.

INCANDESCENT LAMP DEMONSTRATED: 125th ANNIVERSARY. Oct 21, 1879. Thomas A. Edison demonstrated the first incandescent lamp that could be used economically for domestic purposes. This prototype, developed at his Menlo Park, NJ, laboratory, could burn for 13½ hours.

INTERNATIONAL CREDIT UNION DAY. Oct 21. A celebration of the credit union movement's significant points in history. On Jan 17, 1927, the Credit Union League of Massachusetts celebrated the first official holiday for credit union members and staff on the birthday of Benjamin Franklin, America's apostle of thrift. In 1948, the 100th anniversary of the credit union movement, Credit Union National Association (CUNA) set aside the third Thursday in October as the day of observance. More than 39,000 credit unions, representing 97 million people in 84 countries, celebrate the credit union difference on this day and during International Credit Union Week (Oct 18–22). For info: Joe Day, CUNA and Affiliates, PO Box 431, Madison, WI 53701. Phone: (608) 231-4370. Fax: (608) 231-5791.

NOBEL, ALFRED BERNHARD: BIRTH ANNIVERSARY. Oct 21, 1833. Swedish chemist and engineer who invented dynamite was born at Stockholm, Sweden, and died at San Remo, Italy, Dec 10, 1896. His will established the Nobel Prize.

Oct 21–22 ☆ *Chase's 2004 Calendar of Events* ☆

OKTOBERFEST. Oct 21–24. Tulsa, OK. This colorful ethnic festival reflects an authentic German flavor in food, music and entertainment with biergartens located at River West Festival Park. Attractions include German Bands, dancing, sing-alongs, contests, visual arts and crafts and German collectibles and children's entertainment. Est attendance: 175,000. For info: Kathy Baker, Oktoberfest Inc, 2121 S Columbia, #LL8, Tulsa, OK 74114. Phone: (918) 744-9700. Fax: (918) 744-9702. E-mail: admin@tulsaoktoberfest.org. Web: www.tulsaoktoberfest.org.

SHAWN, TED: BIRTH ANNIVERSARY. Oct 21, 1891. Named Edwin Myers Shawn at birth, Ted Shawn was born at Kansas City, MO. Partially paralyzed by diphtheria, Shawn was introduced to ballet for therapeutic purposes and became a professional dancer by the age of 21. The Denishawn School of Dancing was established with the help of his wife, Ruth St. Denis, and became the epicenter of much innovation in 20th-century dance and choreography. Among his many achievements is Jacob's Pillow Dance Festival, which he inaugurated and directed for the remainder of his years, and such modern ballets as *Osage-Pawnee*, *Labor Symphony* and *John Brown*. He died Jan 9, 1972.

SOLTI, GEORG: BIRTH ANNIVERSARY. Oct 21, 1912. Conductor born at Budapest, Hungary. Sir Georg conducted orchestras at London (for which he was knighted), Paris and Chicago. He died at Antibes, France, Sept 5, 1997.

SOMALIA DEMOCRATIC REPUBLIC: NATIONAL DAY. Oct 21. National holiday. Anniversary of the revolution.

TAIWAN: OVERSEAS CHINESE DAY. Oct 21. Thousands of overseas Chinese come to Taiwan for this and other occasions that make October a particularly memorable month.

VIETNAM WAR PROTESTORS STORM PENTAGON: ANNIVERSARY. Oct 21, 1967. Some 250 protestors were arrested when thousands of the 50,000 participants in a rally against the Vietnam War at Washington, DC, crossed the Potomac River and stormed the Pentagon. No shots were fired, but many demonstrators were struck with nightsticks and rifle butts.

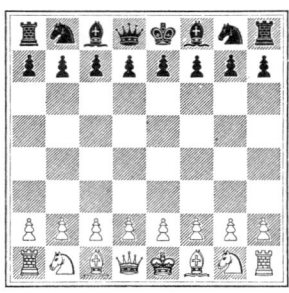

BIRTHDAYS TODAY

Sir Malcolm Arnold, 83, composer, born Northampton, England, Oct 21, 1921.
Elvin Bishop, 62, musician, born Glendale, CA, Oct 21, 1942.
Carrie Fisher, 48, actress (*Star Wars, Shampoo*), novelist (*Postcards from the Edge*), born Beverly Hills, CA, Oct 21, 1956.
Frances Fitzgerald, 64, journalist, author (*The Fire in the Lake*), born New York, NY, Oct 21, 1940.
Edward Charles ("Whitey") Ford, 76, Hall of Fame baseball player, born New York, NY, Oct 21, 1928.
Ursula K. LeGuin, 75, author (*The Wind's Twelve Quarters, A Wizard of Earthsea*), born Berkeley, CA, Oct 21, 1929.

	S	M	T	W	T	F	S
October 2004						1	2
	3	4	5	6	7	8	9
	10	11	12	13	14	15	16
	17	18	19	20	21	22	23
	24	25	26	27	28	29	30
	31						

OCTOBER 22 — FRIDAY
Day 296 — 70 Remaining

BEADLE, GEORGE: BIRTH ANNIVERSARY. Oct 22, 1903. Born on a farm near Wahoo, NE, Beadle began his professional career as a professor of genetics at Harvard, eventually becoming president of the University of Chicago. Dr. Beadle won many international prizes, including the Nobel Prize for Medicine in 1958 for his work in genetic research, as well as the National Award of the American Cancer Society in 1959 and the Kimber Genetica Award of the National Academy of Science in 1960. Beadle demonstrated how the genes control the basic chemistry of the living cell. Because of his work, he has been termed "the man who did most to put modern genetics on its chemical basis." Beadle died June 9, 1989, at Pomona, CA.

BOO AT THE ZOO. Oct 22–24 (also Oct 29–31). Cleveland Metroparks Zoo, Cleveland, OH. Six nights of spooky but not too scary Halloween fun at Cleveland Metroparks Zoo. Safe family fun takes place after-hours at the zoo, with seasonal entertainment for all ages to enjoy. Many of your favorite zoo animals will be on exhibit. Est attendance: 30,000. For info: Attn: Marketing, Cleveland Metroparks Zoo, 3900 Wildlife Way, Cleveland, OH 44109. Phone: (216) 661-6500 or TDD (216) 661-1090. Fax: (216) 661-3312. E-mail: zooinfo@clevelandmetroparks.com. Web: www.clemetzoo.com.

"BREAK THE BANK" TV PREMIERE: ANNIVERSARY. Oct 22, 1948. As with many shows of the late '40s and '50s, this game show began on radio. Contestants had to answer up to eight questions in their area of expertise in order to answer a ninth question in order to "break the bank." Winners were paid on the spot. Bert Parks was the first host, followed by Bud Collyer. Parks returned as host to a revised show renamed "Break the $250,000 Bank." After 20 years, "BTB" resurfaced with a panel of celebrities who gave different answers to the same question, while the contestants had to choose which answer was correct. Tom Kennedy hosted the network version, and Jack Barry, the syndicated version.

CHINA: CHUNG YEUNG FESTIVAL (OR DOUBLE 9 FESTIVAL). Oct 22. This festival relates to the old story of the Han Dynasty, when a soothsayer advised a man to take his family to a high place on the ninth day of the ninth moon for 24 hours in order to avoid disaster. The man obeyed and found, on returning home, that all living things had died a sudden death in his absence. Part of the celebration is climbing to high places. Date in other countries will differ from China's.

CUBAN MISSILE CRISIS: ANNIVERSARY. Oct 22, 1962. President John F. Kennedy, in a nationwide television address Oct 22, 1962, demanded the removal from Cuba of Soviet missiles, launched equipment and bombers, and imposed a naval "quarantine" to prevent further weaponry from reaching Cuba. On Oct 28, the USSR announced it would remove the weapons in question. In return, the US removed missiles from Turkey that were aimed at the USSR.

FANTASY FEST. Oct 22–31. Key West, FL. Ten-day adult costume festival with street parties, masked balls and nighttime grand parade. Est attendance: 75,000. For info: Fantasy Fest, Linda O'Brien, Box 230, Key West, FL 33041. Phone: (305) 296-1817. Fax: (305) 294-3335. Web: www.fantasyfest.net.

HOLY SEE: NATIONAL HOLIDAY. Oct 22. The state of Vatican City and the Holy See observe Oct 22 as a national holiday.

HUMORESILIENCE: TICKLING STRESS BEFORE IT TICKLES YOU. Oct 22–24. Lake George, NY. This 27th annual workshop, which draws participants from around the world, is designed to help you move from "grim and bear it" to "grin and share it." Led by Margie Ingram and Joel Goodman, this program is fun but not for fun. Attendees laugh while learning practical ideas and skills they can use both personally as well as on the job. For workshop information and a free Humor Sourcebook, send SASE ($1.06). For info: The HUMOR Project, Inc, 480 Broadway, Ste 210-C, Saratoga Springs, NY 12866-

550

☆ Chase's 2004 Calendar of Events ☆ Oct 22–23

2288. Phone: (518) 587-8770. Fax: (518) 587-8771. E-mail: Chase@HumorProject.com. Web: www.HumorProject.com.

INTERNATIONAL STUTTERING AWARENESS DAY. Oct 22. For info: National Stuttering Assn, 4071 E La Palma, Ste A, Anaheim, CA 92807. Phone: (800) 364-1677. Fax: (714) 630-7707. Web: www.nsastutter.org or www.stutteringhomepage.com.

LEARY, TIMOTHY: BIRTH ANNIVERSARY. Oct 22, 1920. Timothy Francis Leary was born at Springfield, MA. Prominent psychologist and professor at Harvard, Leary became an icon of the countercultural movement in the 1960s. He lost his professorship after giving a hallucinogenic drug, psilocybin, to students. Leary was arrested numerous times, and on one occasion, while being held at a California prison, he was forced to submit to a personality test that he had designed himself several years earlier. He continued to advocate the use of LSD in the pursuit of spiritual and political freedom and simply for the fun of it, until his death, of prostate cancer, May 31, 1996, at Beverly Hills, CA.

LISZT, FRANZ: BIRTH ANNIVERSARY. Oct 22, 1811. Hungarian pianist and composer (*Hungarian Rhapsodies*). Born at Raiding, Hungary. Died July 31, 1886, at Bayreuth, Germany.

METROPOLITAN OPERA HOUSE: OPENING ANNIVERSARY. Oct 22, 1883. Grand opening of the original New York Metropolitan Opera House was celebrated with a performance of Gounod's *Faust*.

NATIONAL COLOR DAY. Oct 22. Making people aware of how color affects them and how their names are color coded. Fashion show will show how this color philosophy works. Est attendance: 250. For info: D.G. Rolliet, PO Box 21, Crockett, CA 94525. E-mail: dgrolliet@aol.com. Web: www.namecolorology.com.

RANDOLPH, PEYTON: DEATH ANNIVERSARY. Oct 22, 1775. First president of the Continental Congress, died at Philadelphia, PA. Born about 1721 (exact date unknown), at Williamsburg, VA.

SAINT LOUISE DE MARILLAC LOUISIANA BAR-B-Q FESTIVAL. Oct 22–24. St. Louise de Marillac Church, Arabi, LA. Festival includes live entertainment, booths, rides, raffle and home-cooked foods. Foods featured include Bar-B-Q chicken, ribs and sausage topped with our own homemade Bar-B-Q sauce, Crawfish Pizza, Muffulattas, Pasta Louise, Jambalaya, Shish kabobs and more. Est attendance: 7,000. For info: St. Louise de Marillac Church, 6800 Patricia St, Arabi, LA 70032.

STATE FAIR OF LOUISIANA. Oct 22–Nov 7. Fairgrounds, Shreveport, LA. Educational, agricultural, commercial exhibits, entertainment. Est attendance: 250,000. For info: Sam Giordano, Pres/Genl Mgr, Louisiana State Fairgrounds, 3701 Hudson St, Shreveport, LA 71109. Phone: (318) 635-1361. Fax: (318) 631-4909.

SUGARLOAF ART FAIR. Oct 22–24. Novi Expo Center, Novi, MI. This show, now in its 10th year, features more than 325 nationally recognized craft designers and fine artists displaying and selling their original creations. Includes craft demonstrations, live music, specialty foods, hourly gift certificate drawings and more. Est attendance: 20,000. For info: Sugarloaf Mountain Works, 200 Orchard Ridge Dr, #215, Gaithersburg, MD 20878. Phone: (800) 210-9900. Fax: (310) 253-9620. Web: www.sugarloafcrafts.com.

WORLD'S END DAY: ANNIVERSARY. Oct 22, 1844. Anniversary of the day set as the one on which the world would end by followers of William Miller, religious leader and creator of a movement known as Millerism. Stories about followers disposing of all earthly possessions and climbing to high places on that date are believed to be apocryphal. (Miller was born at Pittsfield, MA, Feb 15, 1782. Died at Low Hampton, NY, Dec 20, 1849.)

BIRTHDAYS TODAY

Brian Anthony Boitano, 41, Olympic gold medal figure skater, born Mountain View, CA, Oct 22, 1963.
Jan De Bont, 61, director (*Speed, Twister*), born Amsterdam, the Netherlands, Oct 22, 1943.
Catherine Deneuve (Dorleac), 61, actress (*Repulsion, Indochine*), born Paris, France, Oct 22, 1943.
Annette Funicello, 62, singer, actress ("Mickey Mouse Club," Beach Party movies), born Utica, NY, Oct 22, 1942.
Jeff Goldblum, 52, actor (*The Big Chill, The Fly, Jurassic Park*), born Pittsburgh, PA, Oct 22, 1952.
Valeria Golino, 38, actress (*Big Top Pee-wee, Hot Shots!, Hot Shots! Part Deux*), born Naples, Italy, Oct 22, 1966.
Derek Jacobi, 66, actor ("I Claudius," *The Day of the Jackal*), born London, England, Oct 22, 1938.
Christopher Lloyd, 66, actor ("Taxi," *Back to the Future, Who Framed Roger Rabbit?*), born Stamford, CT, Oct 22, 1938.
Bill Owens, 54, Governor of Colorado (R), born Fort Worth, TX, Oct 22, 1950.
Robert Rauschenberg, 79, artist (*Monogram*), born Port Arthur, TX, Oct 22, 1925.
Tony Roberts, 65, actor (*Victor/Victoria, Annie Hall*), born New York, NY, Oct 22, 1939.
Ichiro Suzuki, 31, baseball player, born Kasugai, Japan, Oct 22, 1973.

OCTOBER 23 — SATURDAY
Day 297 — 69 Remaining

ALABAMA RENAISSANCE FAIRE. Oct 23–24. Florence, AL. Celebration in grand 16th-century style with music, arts and crafts, costumes, theater and dance. Listen to minstrels, dulcimers and autoharps, watch as knights in shining armor transform Wilson Park into "Fountain-on-the-Green," the scene of a 16th-century faire. Annually, the fourth weekend in October. Est attendance: 30,000. For info: Debbie Wilson, Dir, Florence/Lauderdale Tourism, One Hightower Pl, Florence, AL 35630. Phone: (256) 740-4141 or (800) 888-FLO-TOUR. Fax: (256) 740-4142. E-mail: dwilson@flo-tour.org. Web: www.flo-tour.org.

APPERT, NICOLAS: BIRTH ANNIVERSARY. Oct 23, 1752. Also known as "Canning Day," this is the anniversary of the birth of French chef, chemist, confectioner, inventor and author Nicolas Appert, at Chalons-Sur-Marne. Appert, who also invented the bouillon tablet, is best remembered for devising a system of heating foods and sealing them in airtight containers. Known as the "father of canning," Appert won a prize of 12,000 francs from the French government in 1809, and the title "Benefactor of Humanity" in 1812, for his inventions which revolutionized our previously seasonal diet. Appert died at Massy, France, June 3, 1841.

BATTLE OF LEYTE GULF: 60th ANNIVERSARY. Oct 23–26, 1944. In response to the Allied invasion of the Philippines at Leyte, the Japanese initiated "Sho-Go" (*Operation Victory*), an attempt to counter the Allies' next invasion by heavy air attacks. Four carriers were sent south from Japanese waters to lure the US aircraft carriers away from Leyte Gulf. At the same time Japanese naval forces from Singapore were sent to Brunei Bay, split up into two groups and converged on Leyte Gulf from the north and southwest. The group in the north, under Vice Admiral Kurita Takeo, was to enter the Pacific through the San Bernardino Strait between the Philippine islands of Samar and

Oct 23 ☆ *Chase's 2004 Calendar of Events* ☆

Luzon. On Oct 23 Kurita lost two of his heavy cruisers to US submarine attack, and one of Japan's greatest battleships, the *Musashi*, was sunk in an aerial attack the next day, but Kurita made his way unopposed through the San Bernardino Strait on Oct 25. The southern group commanded by Vice Admiral Nishimura Teiji was detected on its way to the Surigao Strait and was practically annihilated by the US 7th Fleet as it entered the Leyte Gulf on Oct 25. Kurita, as a result, was forced to turn back from his planned rendezvous with Nishimura. Japan's "Sho-Go," rather than inflicting damage on the Americans, resulted in serious losses for the Japanese.

BEIRUT TERRORIST ATTACK: ANNIVERSARY. Oct 23, 1983. A suicidal terrorist attack on American forces at Beirut, Lebanon, killed 240 US personnel when a truck loaded with TNT was driven into and exploded at US Headquarters there. A similar attack on French forces killed scores more.

BLUE RIDGE FOLKLIFE FESTIVAL. Oct 23. Ferrum College/Blue Ridge Institute and Museum, Ferrum, VA. The largest celebration of authentic folkways in Virginia featuring food, crafts, music and exhibits. Annually, the fourth Saturday in October. Est attendance: 20,000. For info: Roddy Moore, BRI Dir, Ferrum College/BRI, PO Box 1000, Rte 40 West, Ferrum, VA 24088. Phone: (540) 365-4416. Fax: (540) 365-4419. E-mail: bri@ferrum.edu. Web: www.blueridgeinstitute.org.

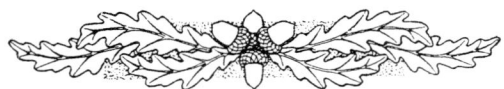

CAMBODIA: PEACE TREATY DAY. Oct 23. National holiday. Commemorates peace treaty of 1991.

EDERLE, GERTRUDE: BIRTH ANNIVERSARY. Oct 23, 1906. American swimming champion, born at New York City, Gertrude Caroline Ederle was the first woman to swim the English Channel (from Cape Gris-nez, France, to Dover, England). At age 19 she broke the previous world record by swimming the 35-mile distance in 14 hours, 31 minutes, on Aug 6, 1926. During her swimming career she broke many other records and was a gold medal winner at the 1924 summer Olympic Games.

HOGEYE FESTIVAL. Oct 23. Elgin, TX. The main feature of this festival is Cow Patty Bingo. Buy a square painted on Depot Street and hope the cow plops on your space to win you $1,500. Day's events also include pork and bean cook-off, crowning of King Hog or Queen Sowpreme, arts & crafts, kids' activities and Elgin's famous hot sausage and live music. Annually, the fourth Saturday in October. Est attendance: 20,000. For info: Amy Miller, PO Box 591, Elgin, TX 78621. Phone: (512) 285-5721. Fax: (512) 285-5962. E-mail: economic@totalaccess.net. Web: www.elgintx.com.

HUNGARY: ANNIVERSARY OF 1956 REVOLUTION. Oct 23. National holiday. Also called Uprising Day of Remembrance. Commemorates revolt against Soviet domination which was crushed on Nov 4, 1956.

HUNGARY DECLARES INDEPENDENCE: 15th ANNIVERSARY. Oct 23, 1989. Hungary declared itself an independent republic, 33 years after Russian troops crushed a popular revolt against Soviet rule. The announcement followed a weeklong purge by Parliament of the Stalinist elements from Hungary's 1949 constitution, which defined the country as a socialist people's republic. Acting head of state Matyas Szuros made the declaration in front of tens of thousands of Hungarians at Parliament Square, speaking from the same balcony from which Imre Nagy addressed rebels 33 years earlier. Nagy was hanged for treason after Soviet intervention. Free elections held in March 1990 removed the Communist party to the ranks of the opposition for the first time in four decades.

LONGWOOD GARDENS CHRYSANTHEMUM FESTIVAL. Oct 23–Nov 21. Kennett Square, PA. 15,000 chrysanthemums and amazing topiaries are featured in indoor displays accompanied by performances and activities throughout this late autumn festival. Est attendance: 50,000. For info: Elizabeth Sullivan, PR Dir, Longwood Gardens, PO Box 501, Kennett Square, PA 19348-0501. Phone: (610) 388-1000. Web: www.longwoodgardens.org.

MAKE A DIFFERENCE DAY. Oct 23. This national day of community service is sponsored by *USA Weekend* Magazine. Volunteer projects that take place that day are judged by well-known celebrities. Selected projects receive $10,000 charitable awards to further their good work. Key projects are honored in April during National Volunteer Week. More than two million people nationwide participate. For info: Make A Difference Day, USA Weekend Magazine, 7950 Jones Branch Dr, McLean, VA 22107. Phone: (800) 416-3824. Web: www.makeadifferenceday.com.

NATIONAL MOLE DAY. Oct 23. Celebrated on Oct 23 each year from 6:02 AM to 6:02 PM in observance of the "mole." The "mole" is a way of counting the Avogadro number, 6.02×10 to the 23rd power of anything (just like a "dozen" is a way of counting 12 of anything). Mole Day owes its existence to an early-19th-century Italian physics professor named Amedeo Avogadro. He discovered that the number of molecules in a mole is the same for all substances. Because of this, chemists are able to precisely measure quantities of chemicals in the laboratory. Mole Day is celebrated to help all persons, especially chemistry students, become enthused about chemistry, which is the central science. Individual teachers develop their own ways of observing Mole Day. For 2004 the Mole Day theme is "Pi a la Mole." For info: Maurice Oehler, Exec Dir, National Mole Day Fdtn, 1220 S 5th St, Prairie du Chien, WI 53821. Fax: (608) 326-6036. E-mail: mole@mhtc.net. Web: moleday.org.

OKTOBERFEST. Oct 23 (tentative). Monett, MO. Street festival in historic downtown featuring live entertainment, including line dancing, cloggers, storytelling, and pancake breakfast, pork steak barbeque, last car show of the season with antique and classic vehicles from four states, food and craft booths, full carnival, children's rides, climbing wall, carriage rides, ARTExpo display, Karaoke, Little Miss & Mr Oktoberfest, best downtown window display contest and more. Annually, on the fourth Saturday of October. For info: Monett Chamber of Commerce, 705 E Broadway, Monett, MO 65708. Phone: (417) 235-7919.

PIONEER AND INDIAN FESTIVAL. Oct 23–24. Mississippi Crafts Center, Natchez Trace Parkway, Ridgeland, MS. Pioneer-era crafts (basket weaving, blacksmithing, pottery, spinning), Indian stickball dance, mules, blowguns, tomahawk throw, music and food. Annually, the fourth Saturday and Sunday in October. Sponsor: Craftsmen's Guild of Mississippi, Inc. Est attendance: 4,000. For info: Mississippi Crafts Center, PO Box 69, Ridgeland, MS 39158. Phone: (601) 856-7546. Fax: (601) 856-7546. E-mail: mscraftsmen@aol.com.

RICHMOND HIGHLAND GAMES AND CELTIC FESTIVAL. Oct 23–24. Richmond, VA. Celebration of Scottish and Celtic heritage featuring athletic competition, clan tents, two entertainment stages, pipe bands, dogs, livestock and horses of the British Isles, fiddle, harp and Highland and Irish dance competitions, food, pubs and whisky tasting and more. Est attendance: 20,000. For info: Richmond Highland Games & Celtic Fest, Richmond Raceway Complex, PO Box 26805, Richmond, VA 23261. Phone: (804) 569-3200. Fax: (804) 569-3252.

SAINT JOHN OF CAPISTRANO: DEATH ANNIVERSARY. Oct 23, 1456. Giovanni da Capistrano, Franciscan lawyer, educator and preacher, was born at Capistrano, Italy, in 1386, and died of plague on Oct 23, 1456. Feast Day is Mar 28.

October 2004

S	M	T	W	T	F	S
					1	2
3	4	5	6	7	8	9
10	11	12	13	14	15	16
17	18	19	20	21	22	23
24	25	26	27	28	29	30
31						

SCORPIO, THE SCORPION. Oct 23–Nov 22. In the astronomical/astrological zodiac that divides the sun's apparent orbit into 12 segments, the period Oct 23–Nov 22 is identified, traditionally, as the sun sign of Scorpio, the Scorpion. The ruling planet is Pluto or Mars.

SORGHUM DAY FESTIVAL. Oct 23. Wewoka, OK. The autumn air fills with the sweet-smelling aroma of sorghum during this old-time festival and fall tradition. Visitors can witness sorghum-making, a quilt show, antique car show and pioneer demonstrations and visit more than 100 craft booths. Annually, the fourth Saturday in October. Est attendance: 40,000. For info: Wewoka Chamber of Commerce, PO Box 719, Wewoka, OK 74884. Phone: (405) 257-5485. Fax: (405) 257-7020.

STEVENSON, ADLAI EWING: BIRTH ANNIVERSARY. Oct 23, 1835. Twenty-third vice president of the US (1893–97) born at Christian County, KY. Died at Chicago, IL, June 14, 1914. He was grandfather of Adlai E. Stevenson, the Democratic candidate for president in 1952 and 1956. See also: "Stevenson, Adlai Ewing: Birth Anniversary" (Feb 5).

SWALLOWS DEPART FROM SAN JUAN CAPISTRANO. Oct 23. Traditional date for swallows to depart for the winter from old mission of San Juan Capistrano, CA. See also: "Swallows Return to San Juan Capistrano" (Mar 19).

THAILAND: CHULALONGKORN DAY. Oct 23. Annual commemoration of the death of King Chulalongkorn the Great, who died Oct 23, 1910, after a 42-year reign. King Chulalongkorn abolished slavery at Thailand. Special ceremonies with floral tributes and incense at the foot of his equestrian statue in front of Bangkok's National Assembly Hall.

TV TALK-SHOW HOST DAY. Oct 23. To celebrate the many TV talk-show hosts whose personalities and intellects enable them to bring out the best in their guests. For info: Glenn Rothenberger, Blue Collar Show, 541 Clinton St, Ste 2B, Brooklyn, NY 11231. Phone: (718) 802-1689. E-mail: gnlroth@aol.com.

WISCONSIN DELLS AUTUMN HARVEST FEST. Oct 23–24. Wisconsin Dells, WI. Celebration of the autumn harvest season. A variety of events for the entire family including fall color tours, Dells on Tap, craft fair, live entertainment, straw dig, scarecrow stuffing, pumpkin decorating contests, Kid's Kookie Corner, petting zoo, hayrides, pony rides, caricatures, face painting and clowns for the kids. Est attendance: 25,000. For info: Wisconsin Dells Visitor & Convention Bureau, PO Box 390, Wisconsin Dells, WI 53965. Phone: (800) 223-3557. E-mail: info@wisdells.com. Web: www.wisdells.com.

BIRTHDAYS TODAY

Jim Bunning, 73, US Senator (R, Kentucky), born Southgate, KY, Oct 23, 1931.
Johnny Carson, 79, former TV talk-show host ("The Tonight Show"), born Corning, IA, Oct 23, 1925.
Michael Crichton, 62, writer (*Jurassic Park, Rising Sun*), born Chicago, IL, Oct 23, 1942.
Douglas Richard (Doug) Flutie, 42, football player, born Manchester, MD, Oct 23, 1962.
Ang Lee, 50, director (Oscar for *Crouching Tiger, Hidden Dragon*; *Sense and Sensibility*, *The Ice Storm*), born Taiwan, Oct 23, 1954.
Melquiades (Mel) R. Martinez, 58, US Secretary of Housing and Urban Development, born Sagua la Grande, Cuba, Oct 23, 1946.
Tiffeny Milbrett, 32, soccer player, born Portland, OR, Oct 23, 1972.
Pelé, 64, former soccer player, born Edson Arantes do Nascimento, Tres Coracoes, Brazil, Oct 23, 1940.
Juan ("Chi-Chi") Rodriguez, 70, golfer, born Rio Piedras, Puerto Rico, Oct 23, 1934.
Michael John (Mike) Tomczak, 42, former football player, born Calumet City, IL, Oct 23, 1962.
Keith Van Horn, 29, basketball player, born Fullerton, CA, Oct 23, 1975.
Alfred Matthew ("Weird Al") Yankovic, 45, singer, satirist, born Lynwood, CA, Oct 23, 1959.
Dwight Yoakam, 48, country singer, actor (*Sling Blade*), born Pikeville, KY, Oct 23, 1956.

OCTOBER 24 — SUNDAY
Day 298 — 68 Remaining

BATTLE OF VITTORIO VENETO: ANNIVERSARY. Oct 24–Nov 3, 1918. Italian forces, commanded by General Armando Diaz, began the last offensive against Austrian troops in upper Italy on this date. The battle began north of the Piave River, and on Oct 30 the Austrian headquarters at Vittorio Veneto was taken. By Nov 1 Austrian troops were breaking up into deserting mobs. A truce was signed at Villa Giusti on Nov 3, which provided for fighting to end the next day. This Allied victory led to the collapse of the Austro-Hungarian Empire.

A FAMILY HALLOWEEN. Oct 24. Billings Farm and Museum, Woodstock, VT. Mystery stories, doughnuts on a string, pumpkin carving, costume parades, plus wagon rides. Children in costume accompanied by an adult admitted free. For info: Billings Farm and Museum, PO Box 489, Woodstock, VT 05091. Phone: (802) 457-2355. Fax: (802) 457-4663. E-mail: billings.farm@valley.net. Web: www.billingsfarm.org.

LOCKWOOD, BELVA A. BENNETT: BIRTH ANNIVERSARY. Oct 24, 1830. Belva Lockwood, an educator, lawyer and advocate for women's rights, was born at Royalton, NY. In 1879 she was admitted to practice before the US Supreme Court—the first woman to do so. While practicing law at Washington, DC, she secured equal property rights for women. By adding amendments to statehood bills, Lockwood helped to provide voting rights for women in Oklahoma, New Mexico and Arizona. In 1884 she was the first woman formally nominated for the US presidency. Died May 19, 1917, at Washington, DC.

MOTHER-IN-LAW DAY. Oct 24. Traditionally, the fourth Sunday in October is occasion to honor mothers-in-law for their contribution to the success of families and for their good humor in enduring bad jokes.

NATIONAL MASSAGE THERAPY AWARENESS WEEK®. Oct 24–30. Sponsored by the American Massage Therapy Association® (AMTA) to increase public awareness of the value of massage therapy in health and wellness. Results of an annual national survey of consumer usage of and attitudes about massage are released. Special attention is given to research confirming the efficacy of massage and of massage for relief of stress. AMTA provides information about how to locate and choose a qualified massage therapist and AMTA chapters emphasize the importance of legislation in states that do not yet regulate the profession. Annually, the last full week of October. For info: American Massage Therapy Assn (AMTA), 820 Davis St, Ste 100, Evanston, IL 60201. Phone: (847) 864-0123. Fax: (847) 864-1178. E-mail: media@amtamassage.org. Web: www.amtamassage.org.

NATIONAL SAVE YOUR BACK WEEK. Oct 24–30. To educate the population on proper back care. For info: Daniel S. Romm, MD, c/o VAMC (117), Rehab Medicine Dept, 400 Veteran's Ave, Biloxi, MS 39531. Phone: (228) 523-4557. Fax: (228) 523-4517. E-mail: Daniel.Romm@med.va.gov.

NISSAN XTERRA WORLD CHAMPIONSHIP. Oct 24. Wailea, Maui, HI. Heralded as the hot, new king of multisport, the Nissan XTERRA World Championship is the culmination of more than 50 events held across the globe. Includes 1.5K roughwater swim, 30K mountain bike race and 11K cross-country run. $105,000 pro purse. CBS one-hour television feature. Est attendance: 8,000. For info: TEAM Unlimited, 500 Ala Moana Blvd, 2-Waterfront Plaza, #302, Honolulu, HI 96813. Phone: (808) 521-4322. Fax: (808) 538-0314. E-mail: info@xterraplanet.com. Web: www.xterraplanet.com.

PASTORAL CARE WEEK. Oct 24–30. Honors clergy of all faiths who provide pastoral care in congregations and in such specialized settings as hospitals, correctional facilities, mental health systems, the military and counseling centers. For info: Pastoral Care Week. Web: www.pastoralcareweek.org.

SHERMAN, JAMES SCHOOLCRAFT: BIRTH ANNIVERSARY. Oct 24, 1855. Twenty-seventh vice president of the US (1909–12), born at Utica, NY. Died there Oct 30, 1912.

STOCK MARKET PANIC: 75th ANNIVERSARY. Oct 24, 1929. After several weeks of a downward trend in stock prices, investors began panic selling on Black Thursday, Oct 24, 1929. More than 13 million shares were dumped. Desperate attempts to support the market brought a brief rally. See also: "Stock Market Crash: Anniversary" (Oct 29).

★**UNITED NATIONS DAY.** Oct 24. Presidential Proclamation. Always issued for Oct 24 since 1948. (By unanimous request of the UN General Assembly.)

UNITED NATIONS DAY: ANNIVERSARY OF FOUNDING. Oct 24, 1945. Official United Nations holiday commemorates founding of the United Nations and effective date of the United Nations Charter. In 1971 the General Assembly recommended this day be observed as a public holiday by UN Member States (Res 2782/xxvi). For info: United Nations, Dept of Public Info, Public Inquiries Unit, Rm GA-57, New York, NY 10017. Phone: (212) 963-4475. Fax: (212) 963-0071. E-mail: inquiries @un.org. Web: www.un.org.

UNITED NATIONS: DISARMAMENT WEEK. Oct 24–30. In 1978 the General Assembly called on member states to highlight the danger of the arms race, propogate the need for its cessation and increase public understanding of the urgent task of disarmament. Observed annually, beginning on the anniversary of the founding of the UN. For info: United Nations, Dept of Public Info, New York, NY 10017. Web: www.un.org.

UNITED NATIONS: WORLD DEVELOPMENT INFORMATION DAY. Oct 24. Anniversary of 1970 adoption by United Nations General Assembly of the International Development Strategy for the Second United Nations Development Decade. Object is to "draw the attention of the world public opinion each year to development problems and the necessity of strengthening international cooperation to solve them." For info: United Nations, Dept of Public Info, New York, NY 10017. Web: www.un.org.

BIRTHDAYS TODAY

F. Murray Abraham, 64, actor (Oscar for *Amadeus*), born El Paso, TX, Oct 24, 1940.
Kevin Kline, 57, actor (Oscar for *A Fish Called Wanda; Silverado*), born St. Louis, MO, Oct 24, 1947.

★ ★ ★

October 2004	S	M	T	W	T	F	S
						1	2
	3	4	5	6	7	8	9
	10	11	12	13	14	15	16
	17	18	19	20	21	22	23
	24	25	26	27	28	29	30
	31						

Kweisi Mfume, 56, NAACP president, born Baltimore, MD, Oct 24, 1948.
Monica, 24, singer, born Monica Arnold, Atlanta, GA, Oct 24, 1980.
David Nelson, 68, actor ("The Adventures of Ozzie and Harriet"), born New York, NY, Oct 24, 1936.
Mike Rounds, 50, Governor of South Dakota (R), born Huron, SD, Oct 24, 1954.
Yelberton Abraham (Y.A.) Tittle, Jr, 78, Hall of Fame football player, born Marshall, TX, Oct 24, 1926.
Bill Wyman, 68, musician (Rolling Stones), born William Perks, London, England, Oct 24, 1936.

OCTOBER 25 — MONDAY
Day 299 — 67 Remaining

CARTOONISTS AGAINST CRIME DAY™. Oct 25. A day in honor of all those cartoonists, graphic designers and illustrators who join together to promote the prevention of crime through the art and medium of cartooning. Motto: "Cartoonists Against Crime: We Draw Cartoons—Not Guns!" CAC's slogan is to "Toon Out Crime" by employing comic art as an educational tool for implanting seeds of safety prevention into the minds of viewers/readers. To alleviate the escalating costs of Eventological® Literature, a charge of $7 must be assessed for each request. Checks are to be made payable to: Adrienne Sioux Koopersmith, Cartoonists Against Crime, 1437 W Rosemont, #1W, Chicago, IL 60660-1319. Phone: (773) 743-5341. Fax: (773) 743-5395. E-mail: la_koop@yahoo.com.

CHAUCER, GEOFFREY: DEATH ANNIVERSARY. Oct 25, 1400. English poet and the best-known English writer of the Middle Ages, was born at London, England, probably about 1340. His greatest work, *Canterbury Tales*, consists of some 17,000 poetic lines. Unfinished at his death, it tells the stories of 23 pilgrims. Among his lesser-known prose writings was a treatise on the Astrolabe titled *Brede and Milke for Children* (1387), written for "little Lewis, my son." Chaucer died at London and is buried at Westminster Abbey.

FIRST FEMALE FBI AGENTS: ANNIVERSARY. Oct 25, 1972. The first women to become FBI agents completed training at Quantico, VA. The new agents, Susan Lynn Roley and Joanne E. Pierce, graduated from the 14-week course with a group of 45 men.

GRENADA INVADED BY US: ANNIVERSARY. Oct 25, 1983. Some 2,000 US Marines and Army Rangers invaded the Caribbean island of Grenada, taking control after a political coup the previous week had made the island a "Soviet-Cuban colony," according to President Reagan. Commemorated as Thanksgiving Day in Grenada, a public holiday.

INDIA: DIWALI (DEEPAVALI). Oct 25. Diwali, the five-day festival of lights, is the prettiest of all Indian festivals. It celebrates the return of Lord Rama to Ayodhya after a 14-year exile. Thousands of flickering lights illuminate houses and transform urban landscapes while fireworks add color and noise. The goddess of wealth, Lakshmi, is worshipped in Hindu homes on Diwali. Houses are white-washed and cleaned and elaborate designs drawn on thresholds with colored powder to welcome the fastidious goddess. Because there is no one universally accepted Hindu calendar, this holiday may be celebrated on a different date in some parts of India but it always falls in the months of October or November.

KAZAKHSTAN: INDEPENDENCE DAY. Oct 25. National Day. Commemorates independence from the Soviet Union in 1991.

MACAULAY, THOMAS BABINGTON: BIRTH ANNIVERSARY. Oct 25, 1800. English essayist and historian, born at Rothley Temple, Leicestershire, England. Died at Campden Hill, London, England, Dec 28, 1859. "Nothing," he wrote, "is so useless as a general maxim."

NEW ZEALAND: LABOR DAY. Oct 25. National holiday on the 4th Monday in October.

★ Chase's 2004 Calendar of Events ★   Oct 25–26

"NEWHART" TV PREMIERE: ANNIVERSARY. Oct 25, 1982. Bob Newhart starred in this sitcom as Dick Loudon, an author of "how-to" books who moved with his wife, Joanna (Mary Frann), to Vermont to take over the Stratford Inn. Regulars included Tom Poston as George Utley, caretaker of the inn, Steven Kampmann as Kirk Devane, the owner of the Minute Man Café, Jennifer Holmes as the maid, Leslie Vanderkellen and Julia Duffy as "princess" Stephanie Vanderkellen, who, through bad luck, had to take on the maid's job. Changes in the third season introduced the characters of Michael Harris (Peter Scolari), producer of Dick's talk show and Stephanie's squeeze, and the new owners of the cafe, Larry (William Sanderson) and his silent brothers, both named Darryl (Tony Papenfuss and John Volstad). The last telecast was Sept 8, 1990.

PEACE, FRIENDSHIP AND GOOD WILL WEEK. Oct 25–31. To encourage and foster international understanding, good human relations, friendship, good will and peace throughout the world. For complete info, send $5 to cover expense of printing, handling and postage. Annually, the last seven days in October. For info: Dr. Stanley Drake, Pres, Intl Society of Friendship and Good Will, 999 Hood Rd, Ste 127, Marietta, GA 30068. Phone: (770) 565-2322. E-mail: ISFGW@bellsouth.net.

PEARL, MINNIE: BIRTH ANNIVERSARY. Oct 25, 1912. Comedian, Grand Ole Opry star born at Centerville, TN. Pearl died at Nashville, TN, Mar 4, 1996.

PICASSO, PABLO RUIZ: BIRTH ANNIVERSARY. Oct 25, 1881. Called by many the greatest artist of the 20th century, Pablo Picasso excelled as a painter, sculptor and engraver. He is said to have commented once: "I am only a public entertainer who has understood his time." Born at Málaga, Spain, he died Apr 8, 1973, at Mougins, France.

SAINT CRISPIN'S DAY. Oct 25. Martyr in the reign of Diocletian. Saint Crispin's Day is famous as the day in 1415 when King Henry V defeated the superior forces of France at the Battle of Agincourt. A passage in Shakespeare's *Henry V* notes this.

SOUREST DAY. Oct 25. To emphasize the balance of things in nature. A day for sour (Sauer) people. For info: Richard Ankli, The Fifth Wheel Tavern, 639 Fifth St, Ann Arbor, MI 48103.

SOUTHERN CALIFORNIA FIRESTORMS: ANNIVERSARY. Oct 25, 1993. The Southern California fire season began viciously when fires swept from the celebrity-studded beachfront homes of Malibu to the Mexican border. Blown out of the desert by the fierce Santa Anna winds, the fires destroyed suburban enclaves south of LA at Laguna Beach and northeast of LA at Altadena. As winds died down, firefighters appeared to gain control as the flames reached the Santa Monica Mountains, but the winds roared again, spreading the fire into Malibu—often jumping the Pacific Coast Highway to destroy the beachfront homes of the wealthy celebrities who lived there. Damage from the fires was estimated at more than $1 billion.

TAIWAN EXPELLED FROM UN: ANNIVERSARY. Oct 25, 1971. The United Nations General Assembly voted to admit mainland China and expel Taiwan. This was after many years of debate about which government was the "official" government of China. In 1979 the US accorded diplomatic recognition to mainland China.

TAIWAN: RETROCESSION DAY. Oct 25. Commemorates restoration of Taiwan to Chinese rule in 1945, after half a century of Japanese occupation.

ZAMBIA: INDEPENDENCE DAY. Oct 25. Zambia. National holiday commemorates the independence of what was then Northern Rhodesia from Britain in 1964. Celebrations in all cities, but main parades of military, labor and youth organizations are at capital, Lusaka. The fourth Monday in October.

BIRTHDAYS TODAY

Anthony Franciosa, 76, actor ("The Name of the Game," "Wheels"), born Anthony Papaleo, New York, NY, Oct 25, 1928.
Brian Kerwin, 55, actor ("Lobo," "The Blue and the Gray"), born Chicago, IL, Oct 25, 1949.
Robert Montgomery (Bobby) Knight, 64, college basketball coach and former player, born Orrville, OH, Oct 25, 1940.
Pedro Martinez, 33, baseball player, born Manoguyabo, Dominican Republic, Oct 25, 1971.
Midori, 33, violinist, born Osaka, Japan, Oct 25, 1971.
Helen Reddy, 62, singer, songwriter ("I Am Woman"), born Melbourne, Australia, Oct 25, 1942.
Marion Ross, 68, actress ("Happy Days," *The Evening Star*), born Albert Lea, MN, Oct 25, 1936.
Anne Tyler, 63, author (*The Accidental Tourist, Breathing Lessons*), born Minneapolis, MN, Oct 25, 1941.

OCTOBER 26 — TUESDAY
Day 300 — 66 Remaining

AUSTRIA: NATIONAL DAY. Oct 26. National holiday. Commemorates the withdrawal of Soviet troops in 1955.

ERIE CANAL: ANNIVERSARY. Oct 26, 1825. The Erie Canal, first US major man-made waterway, was opened, providing a water route from Lake Erie to the Hudson River. Construction started July 4, 1817, and the canal cost $7,602,000. Cannons fired and celebrations were held all along the route for the opening.

HANSOM, JOSEPH: BIRTH ANNIVERSARY. Oct 26, 1803. English architect and inventor Joseph Aloysius Hansom registered his "Patent Safety Cab" in 1834. The two-wheeled, one-horse, enclosed cab, with driver seated above and behind the passengers, quickly became a familiar and favorite vehicle for public transportation. Hansom was born at York, England, and died at London, June 29, 1882.

JACKSON, MAHALIA: BIRTH ANNIVERSARY. Oct 26, 1911. Born at New Orleans, LA, Jackson was the most famous gospel singer of her time. After moving to Chicago in 1928, Jackson sang with the Johnson Gospel Singers. Thomas A. Dorsey, the father of gospel music, was her advisor and accompanist from 1937 to 1946. By the 1950s, Jackson could be heard in concert halls around the world. She sang at the inauguration of President John F. Kennedy and at the 1963 March on Washington rally. Dr. Martin Luther King, Jr, described her voice as "one heard once in a millennium." She died at Chicago, IL, on Jan 27, 1972, and was buried in New Orleans, where her funeral procession was thronged with mourners.

MERCEDES-BENZ SHOWS LA. Oct 26–29 (tentative). Los Angeles, CA. Fashion designers present their spring 2005 lines. For info: 7th on Sixth, 420 W 45th St, 6th Fl, New York, NY 10036. Phone: (212) 253-2692. E-mail: info@7thonsixth.com. Web: www.7thonsixth.com.

MULE DAY. Oct 26. Anniversary of the first importation of Spanish jacks to the US, a gift from King Charles III of Spain. Mules are said to have been bred first in this country by George Washington from a pair delivered at Boston, Oct 26, 1785.

Oct 26–27 ☆ *Chase's 2004 Calendar of Events* ☆

ROCKEFELLER, ABBY GREENE ALDRICH: BIRTH ANNIVERSARY. Oct 26, 1874. A philanthropist and art patron, Abby Rockefeller was one of the three founders of the New York Museum of Modern Art in 1929. Born at Providence, RI, she died Apr 5, 1948, at New York City.

"ST. ELSEWHERE" TV PREMIERE: ANNIVERSARY. Oct 26, 1982. A popular one-hour medical drama set in St. Eligius Hospital at Boston. Among its large and changing cast were Ed Flanders, William Daniels, Ed Begley, Jr, David Morse, Howie Mandel, Christina Pickles, Denzel Washington, Norman Lloyd, David Birney, G.W. Bailey, Kavi Raz, Stephen Furst, Mark Harmon and Alfre Woodard. The last episode of the series, aired on Aug 10, 1988, cast doubt on the reality of the whole series, suggesting that a child's imagination had dreamed it up.

SCARLATTI, DOMENICO: BIRTH ANNIVERSARY. Oct 26, 1685. Italian keyboard composer, born at Naples, Italy. Died July 23, 1757, at Madrid, Spain.

SPACE MILESTONE: *SOYUZ 3* (USSR): ANNIVERSARY. Oct 26, 1968. After the crash of *Soyuz 1* and the death of its cosmonaut, *Soyuz 3* was launched this date with Colonel Georgi Beregovoy. It orbited Earth 64 times, rendezvousing but not docking with unmanned *Soyuz 2*, which had been launched the day before. Both vehicles returned to Earth under ground control. *Soyuz* means "union."

BIRTHDAYS TODAY

Tom Cavanagh, 36, actor ("Ed"), born Ottawa, ON, Canada, Oct 26, 1968.
Hillary Rodham Clinton, 57, US Senator (D, New York), former First Lady, wife of Bill Clinton, 42nd president of the US, born Park Ridge, IL, Oct 26, 1947.
Sasha Cohen, 20, figure skater, born Westwood, CA, Oct 26, 1984.
Nick Collison, 24, basketball player, born Orange City, IA, Oct 26, 1980.
Pat Conroy, 59, writer (*The Prince of Tides, The Lords of Discipline*), born Atlanta, GA, Oct 26, 1945.
Cary Elwes, 42, actor (*The Princess Bride, Glory, Bram Stoker's Dracula*), born London, England, Oct 26, 1962.
Bob Hoskins, 62, actor (*Mona Lisa, Who Framed Roger Rabbit?*), born Bury St. Edmonds, Suffolk, England, Oct 26, 1942.
Dylan McDermott, 42, actor ("The Practice"), born Waterbury, CT, Oct 26, 1962.
Natalie Merchant, 41, singer, born Jamestown, NY, Oct 26, 1963.
Jeff Probst, 42, TV host ("Survivor," "Rock and Roll Jeopardy"), born Wichita, KS, Oct 26, 1962.
Ivan Reitman, 58, filmmaker (*Ghostbusters* movies), born Komarno, Czechoslovakia, Oct 26, 1946.
Pat Sajak, 58, TV personality ("Wheel of Fortune"), born Chicago, IL, Oct 26, 1946.
Jaclyn Smith, 57, actress ("Charlie's Angels"), former Breck Girl, born Houston, TX, Oct 26, 1947.

October 2004	S	M	T	W	T	F	S
						1	2
	3	4	5	6	7	8	9
	10	11	12	13	14	15	16
	17	18	19	20	21	22	23
	24	25	26	27	28	29	30
	31						

OCTOBER 27 — WEDNESDAY
Day 301 — 65 Remaining

ARKALALAH FESTIVAL. Oct 27–30. Arkansas City, KS. Ark City's largest celebration features three parades (lighted evening, children's and giant Arkalalah Parade), crowning of Queen Alalah, high school band contest, street events, food concessions, crafts show, dances and reunions. Est attendance: 40,000. For info: Bonnie Givens, Arkalalah, 106 S Summit, Arkansas City, KS 67005. Phone: (620) 442-6077. Fax: (620) 442-5790. E-mail: elite advertising@cox.net.

COOK, JAMES: BIRTH ANNIVERSARY. Oct 27, 1728 (OS). English sea captain of the ship *Endeavour* and explorer who brought Australia and New Zealand into the British Empire. Born at Marton-in-Cleveland, Yorkshire, England, he was killed Feb 14, 1779, at the Hawaiian Islands, which he discovered.

CRANKY CO-WORKERS DAY. Oct 27. Because all of us have bad days (some more than others), here's a day when crankiness at work is actually encouraged. [©2003 by WH.] For info: Thomas & Ruth Roy, Wellcat Holidays, 2418 Long Ln, Lebanon, PA 17046. Phone: (717) 279-0184. E-mail: info@wellcat.com. Web: www.wellcat.com.

FEDERALIST PAPERS: ANNIVERSARY. Oct 27, 1787. The first of the 85 "Federalist" papers appeared in print in a New York City newspaper, Oct 27, 1787. These essays, written by Alexander Hamilton, James Madison and John Jay, argued in favor of adoption of the new Constitution and the new form of federal government. The last of the essays was completed Apr 4, 1788.

HUNTER'S MOON. Oct 27. The full moon following Harvest Moon. So called because the moon's light in evening extends day's length for hunters. Moon enters Full Moon phase at 11:07 PM, EDT.

HURRICANE MITCH: ANNIVERSARY. Oct 27, 1998. More than 7,000 people were killed at Honduras by flooding caused by Hurricane Mitch. Thousands more were killed in other Central American countries, especially Nicaragua.

LICHTENSTEIN, ROY: BIRTH ANNIVERSARY. Oct 27, 1923. Pop artist who used comic strips and other elements of pop culture in his paintings. Born at New York City, he died there Sept 29, 1997.

LOUISIANA YAMBILEE. Oct 27–31. Opelousas, LA. Sweet potato, corn, rice and soybean shows, cooked foods contest, yam auction, "yum-yum contest," carnival, grand parade and the crowning of King Will Yam and Queen Marigold and the 2004 Louisiana Yambilee Queen. Est attendance: 50,000. For info: Sheryl Badeaux, Louisiana Yambilee, Inc, 1939 W Landry St, #103, Opelousas, LA 70570-2010. Phone: (800) 210-5298. Fax: (337) 948-4331. E-mail: yambilee1@aol.com.

LUNAR ECLIPSE. Oct 27–28. Total eclipse of the moon. Moon enters penumbra at 8:05 PM, EDT on Oct 27, reaches middle of eclipse at 11:04 PM and leaves penumbra Oct 28 at 2:02 AM. Visible in the Arctic region, North America, Central America, South America, parts of Antarctica, Greenland, Africa, western Madagascar, Arabia, western Russia, Europe and the eastern Pacific Ocean.

MOON PHASE: FULL MOON. Oct 27. Moon enters Full Moon phase at 11:07 PM, EDT.

NAVY DAY. Oct 27. Established in 1922 to honor the "past and present services" of the US Navy to the nation. Also honored Theodore Roosevelt, whose birth date is Oct 27 (and who had been Assistant Secretary of the Navy early in his public career). Not a national holiday, it was last observed in 1949.

NEW YORK CITY SUBWAY: 100th ANNIVERSARY. Oct 27, 1904. Running from City Hall to West 145th Street, the New York City subway began operation. It was privately operated by the Interborough Rapid Transit Company and later became part of the system operated by the New York City Transit Authority.

PAGANINI, NICOLO: BIRTH ANNIVERSARY. Oct 27, 1782. Hailed as the greatest violin virtuoso of all time, Paganini was born at Genoa, Italy. Unusually long arms contributed to his legendary Mephistophelian appearance—and probably to his unique skills as a performer. His immensely popular concerts brought him great wealth, but his compulsive gambling repeatedly humbled the genius. Paganini died at Nice, France, May 27, 1840.

ROOSEVELT, THEODORE: BIRTH ANNIVERSARY. Oct 27, 1858. Twenty-sixth president of the US, succeeded to the presidency on the death of William McKinley. His term of office: Sept 14, 1901–Mar 3, 1909. Roosevelt was the first president to ride in an automobile (1902), to submerge in a submarine (1905) and to fly in an airplane (1910). Although his best-remembered quote was perhaps, "Speak softly and carry a big stick," he also said: "The first requisite of a good citizen in this Republic of ours is that he shall be able and willing to pull his weight." Born at New York, NY, Roosevelt died at Oyster Bay, NY, Jan 6, 1919. His last words: "Put out the light."

SAINT VINCENT AND THE GRENADINES: INDEPENDENCE DAY: 25th ANNIVERSARY. Oct 27. National Day commemorating independence from Britain in 1979.

SEPARATION OF CHURCH & STATE DAY. Oct 27. 6th annual recognition of this day, now proclaimed jointly by two separate national groups, American Atheists, Inc, and the Freedom from Religion Foundation. The purpose of the day is to honor James Madison's "Remonstrance Against Taxes for Religious Uses," Thomas Jefferson's "Virginia Statute for Religious Freedom" and the Establishment Clause of the First Amendment of the Constitution of the United States. For info: John Simpson, American Atheist Publications, PO Box 4338, Ann Arbor, MI 48106-4338. Phone: (734) 944-1381. E-mail: js@Atheism.org.

THOMAS, DYLAN MARLAIS: 90th BIRTH ANNIVERSARY. Oct 27, 1914. Welsh poet and playwright, born at Swansea, Wales. Died at New York, NY, Nov 9, 1953.

TURKMENISTAN: INDEPENDENCE DAY. Oct 27. National holiday. Commemorates independence from the Soviet Union in 1991.

"WALT DISNEY" TV PREMIERE: 50th ANNIVERSARY. Oct 27, 1954. This highly successful and long-running show appeared on different networks under different names but was essentially the same show. It was the first ABC series to break the Nielsen's Top Twenty and the first prime-time anthology series for kids. "Walt Disney" was originally titled "Disneyland" to promote the park and upcoming Disney releases. When it switched networks, it was called "Walt Disney's Wonderful World of Color" to highlight its being broadcast in color. Presentations included edited versions of previously released Disney films and original productions (including natural history documentaries, behind-the-scenes at Disney shows and dramatic shows, including the popular Davy Crockett segments that were the first TV miniseries). The show went off the air in December 1980 after 25 years, making it the longest-running series in prime-time TV history. In 1997 ABC revived the series as "Wonderful World of Disney."

BIRTHDAYS TODAY

Roberto Benigni, 52, actor, director (Oscar for *Life Is Beautiful*), born Arezzo, Italy, Oct 27, 1952.
John Cleese, 65, actor, writer ("Monty Python's Flying Circus," *A Fish Called Wanda*), born Weston-Super-Mare, England, Oct 27, 1939.
Ruby Dee, 80, actress ("Ossie and Ruby," *Zora Is My Name, Do the Right Thing*), born Cleveland, OH, Oct 27, 1924.
Nanette Fabray, 84, actress (Emmy for "Caesar's Hour"; "One Day at a Time," *Our Gang* comedies), born San Diego, CA, Oct 27, 1920.
Simon LeBon, 46, singer (Duran Duran), born Bushey, England, Oct 27, 1958.

Fran Lebowitz, 54, magazine columnist famous for essays on urban life (*Social Studies*), born Morristown, NJ, Oct 27, 1950.
Marla Maples, 41, model, actress, born Dalton, GA, Oct 27, 1963.
Carrie Snodgress, 58, actress (*Diary of a Mad Housewife*), born Chicago, IL, Oct 27, 1946.

OCTOBER 28 — THURSDAY
Day 302 — 64 Remaining

CZECH REPUBLIC: INDEPENDENCE DAY. Oct 28. National Day, anniversary of the bloodless revolution at Prague in 1918 resulting in independence from the Austro-Hungarian Empire, after which the Czechs and Slovaks united to form Czechoslovakia (a union they dissolved without bloodshed in 1993).

DONNER PARTY FAMINE: ANNIVERSARY. Oct 28, 1846–Apr 21, 1847. The pioneering Donner Party, a group of 90 people consisting of immigrants, families and businessmen led by George and Jacob Donner and James F. Reed, headed toward California in 1846 from Springfield, IL, in hopes of beginning a new life. They experienced the normal travails of caravan travel until their trip took several sensational twists. Indian attacks and winter weather which forced them to interrupt their journey led to famine and outright cannibalism which took their toll on members of the party whose numbers dwindled to 48 by journey's end.

ERASMUS, DESIDERIUS: BIRTH ANNIVERSARY. Oct 28, 1467. Dutch author and scholar Desiderius Erasmus was born at Rotterdam, probably Oct 28, 1467. Best known of his writings is *Encomium Moriae* (In Praise of Folly). Erasmus died at Basel, Switzerland, July 12, 1536.

ESCOFFIER, GEORGES AUGUSTE: BIRTH ANNIVERSARY. Oct 28, 1846. Celebrated French chef and author, inventor of the peche Melba (honoring the operatic singer Dame Nellie Melba), Escoffier became known as the "king of chefs and the chef of kings." Born at Villeneuve-Loubet, France. He was awarded the Legion d'Honneur in recognition of his contribution to the international reputation of French cuisine and his service at the Savoy and Carlton hotels at London, England, brought him world fame. He died at Monte Carlo, Monaco, Feb 12, 1935.

FIRST WOMAN US AMBASSADOR APPOINTED: 55th ANNIVERSARY. Oct 28, 1949. Helen Eugenie Moore Anderson became the first woman to hold the post of US ambassador when she was sworn in by President Harry S. Truman on this date. She served as Ambassador to Denmark.

FORT LAUDERDALE INTERNATIONAL BOAT SHOW. Oct 28–Nov 1. Fort Lauderdale, FL. Everything from small boats to mega-yachts to boating equipment. Visitors attend from all over the world. For info: Greater Ft Lauderdale Conv/Visitors Bureau, 1850 Eller Dr, Ste 303, Ft Lauderdale, FL 33316. Phone: (954) 765-4466 or (954) 764-7642. Web: www.sunny.org.

Oct 28–29 ☆ *Chase's 2004 Calendar of Events* ☆

GERMAN REVOLUTION OF 1918: ANNIVERSARY. Oct 28, 1918. On this date in the final days of World War I, crews of six German battleships protested a series of planned cruiser raids. A mutiny broke out in the fleet at Kiel. All but one of the ships remaining in port ran up the red flag of revolution, 600 sailors were arrested and imprisoned on shore. The uprising spread to Hamburg, Bremen and Lubeck. On Nov 9 a general strike at Berlin brought the administration to a halt. The abdication of Kaiser Wilhelm began to be seen as the only way to avoid a full-scale revolution.

GREECE: "OCHI DAY": ANNIVERSARY. Oct 28. National holiday commemorating Greek resistance and refusal to open her borders when Mussolini's Italian troops attacked Greece, Oct 28, 1940. "Ochi" means no! Celebrated with military parades, especially at Athens and Thessaloniki.

HANSON, HOWARD: BIRTH ANNIVERSARY. Oct 28, 1896. Born at Wahoo, NE, Howard Hanson in 1921 became the first American to win the Prix de Rome. In 1924 he became head of the Eastman School of Music at the University of Rochester, NY, where he served for 40 years. Best known for the music he composed, Hanson was awarded the Pulitzer Prize as outstanding contemporary composer in 1944 for his composition *Symphony No. 4*, the George Foster Peabody Award in 1946, the Laurel Leaf of the American Composers Alliance in 1957 and the Huntington Hartford Foundation Award in 1959. He died at Rochester, Feb 26, 1981.

HARVARD UNIVERSITY FOUNDED: ANNIVERSARY. Oct 28, 1636 (OS). Harvard University founded at Cambridge, MA, when the Massachusetts General Court voted to provide £400 for a "schoale or colledge."

IRELAND: BANK HOLIDAY. Oct 28. Bank holiday in the Republic of Ireland.

"THE JACK BENNY PROGRAM" TV PREMIERE: ANNIVERSARY. Oct 28, 1950. One of radio's favorite comedians, Jack Benny made the transition to favorite TV personality with this situation comedy–variety show in 1950. Regulars included Eddie Anderson, Don Wilson, Dennis Day, Mel Blanc, Mary Livingstone (Benny's real-life wife) and Frank Nelson. Benny also had guest stars, including Ken Murray, Frank Sinatra, Claudette Colbert, Basil Rathbone and TV newcomers Johnny Carson, Marilyn Monroe and Humphrey Bogart. Famous for his cheapness, Benny had a guard for his vaults which created many laughs.

SAINT JUDE'S DAY. Oct 28. St. Jude, the saint of hopeless causes, was martyred along with St. Simon at Persia, and their feast is celebrated jointly. St. Jude was supposedly the brother of Jesus, and, like his brother, a carpenter by trade. He is most popular with those who attempt the impossible and with students, who often ask for his help on exams.

SALK, JONAS: 90th BIRTH ANNIVERSARY. Oct 28, 1914. Dr. Jonas Salk, developer of the Salk polio vaccine, was born at New York, NY. Salk announced his development of a successful vaccine in 1953, the year after a polio epidemic claimed some 3,300 lives in the US. Polio deaths were reduced by 95 percent after the introduction of the vaccine. Salk spent the last 10 years of his life doing AIDS research. He died June 23, 1995, at La Jolla, CA.

SPACE MILESTONE: INTERNATIONAL SPACE RESCUE AGREEMENT. Oct 28, 1970. US and USSR officials agreed upon space rescue cooperation.

STATUE OF LIBERTY: DEDICATION ANNIVERSARY. Oct 28, 1886. Frederic Auguste Bartholdi's famous sculpture, the statue of *Liberty Enlightening the World*, on Bedloe's Island in New York Harbor, was dedicated. Ground breaking for the structure was in April 1883. A sonnet by Emma Lazarus, inside the pedestal of the statue, contains the words: "Give me your tired, your poor, your huddled masses yearning to breathe free, the wretched refuse of your teeming shore. Send these, the homeless, tempest-tost to me, I lift my lamp beside the golden door!"

WILSON'S VOLSTEAD PROHIBITION ACT VETO OVERRIDDEN: 85th ANNIVERSARY. Oct 28, 1919. Woodrow Wilson's veto of the Volstead Prohibition Act was overridden by Congress.

BIRTHDAYS TODAY

Jane Alexander, 65, actress (*The Great White Hope, Kramer v Kramer*), former chair of the National Endowment for the Arts, born Jane Quigley, Boston, MA, Oct 28, 1939.

Charlie Daniels, 68, musician, singer, songwriter ("Devil Went Down to Georgia"), born Wilmington, NC, Oct 28, 1936.

Jeremy Davies, 35, actor (*Saving Private Ryan*), born Rockford, IA, Oct 28, 1969.

Terrell Davis, 32, football player, born San Diego, CA, Oct 28, 1972.

Dennis Franz, 60, actor ("Hill Street Blues," "NYPD Blue"), born Maywood, IL, Oct 28, 1944.

Bill Gates, 49, computer software executive (Microsoft), born Seattle, WA, Oct 28, 1955.

Jami Gertz, 39, actress ("ER," *Twister*), born Chicago, IL, Oct 28, 1965.

Lauren Holly, 41, actress (*Dumb & Dumber, Sabrina*), born Geneva, NY, Oct 28, 1963.

Telma Hopkins, 56, singer, actress ("Family Matters"), born Louisville, KY, Oct 28, 1948.

William Bruce Jenner, 55, sportscaster, Olympic gold medal decathlete, born Mount Kisco, NY, Oct 28, 1949.

Bowie Kent Kuhn, 78, former commissioner of baseball, born Tacoma Park, MD, Oct 28, 1926.

Annie Potts, 52, actress ("Designing Women," *Ghostbusters, Pretty in Pink*), born Nashville, TN, Oct 28, 1952.

Andy Richter, 38, former cohost ("Late Night with Conan O'Brien"), born Grand Rapids, MI, Oct 28, 1966.

Julia Roberts, 37, actress (Oscar for *Erin Brockovich; My Best Friend's Wedding*), born Smyrna, GA, Oct 28, 1967.

OCTOBER 29 — FRIDAY
Day 303 — 63 Remaining

BOSWELL, JAMES: BIRTH ANNIVERSARY. Oct 29, 1740 (OS). Scottish biographer, born at Edinburgh, Scotland. Died at London, England, May 19, 1795. "I think," he wrote in his monumental biography, the *Life of Samuel Johnson*, "no innocent species of wit or pleasantry should be suppressed: and that a good pun may be admitted among the smaller excellencies of lively conversation."

BRING YOUR JACK-O-LANTERN TO WORK DAY. Oct 29. Pumpkins, patterns and tools—what is more exciting than carving pumpkins for Halloween? We invite you to carve pumpkins and bring your favorite to work. Share this fun and exciting tradition with everyone in your workplace. For info: Pumpkin Masters, PO Box 44068, Denver, CO 80201. Phone: (303) 860-8006. E-mail: pumpkin@pumpkinmasters.com. Web: www.pumpkinmasters.com.

	S	M	T	W	T	F	S
October 2004						1	2
	3	4	5	6	7	8	9
	10	11	12	13	14	15	16
	17	18	19	20	21	22	23
	24	25	26	27	28	29	30
	31						

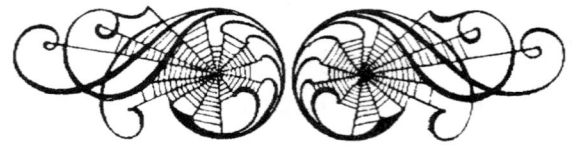

☆ Chase's 2004 Calendar of Events ☆ Oct 29

CREEPY TALES: HAUNTED HISTORY. Oct 29–31. Frontier Culture Museum, Staunton, VA. Folktales or traditional ghost stories from America's past enhanced by the ambiance of night and authentic surroundings on a lantern-lit tour to the historic farms for a session of creepy tales. For info: Debbie Cole, Frontier Museum, 1290 Richmond Rd, PO Box 810, Staunton, VA 24401. Phone: (540) 332-7850. Fax: (540) 332-9989. E-mail: dcole@frontiermuseum.state.va.us. Web: www.frontiermuseum.org.

EDGAR ALLAN POE EVERMORE. Oct 29–Nov 14. Mount Hope Estate, Manheim, PA. Friday, Saturday and Sunday evenings. Nights of suspense featuring the spine-chilling short stories of Edgar Allan Poe. Professionals from the Pennsylvania Renaissance Faire Actors Conservatory perform, wine served. Est attendance: 10,000. For info: Thomas Roy, Mount Hope Estate and Winery, PO Box 685, Cornwall, PA 17016. Phone: (717) 665-7021. Fax: (717) 664-3466. E-mail: Tom@parenfaire.com. Web: www.parenfaire.com/.

EMMETT, DANIEL DECATUR: BIRTH ANNIVERSARY. Oct 29, 1815. Creator of words and music for the song "Dixie's Land" ("Dixie"), which became a fighting song for Confederate troops and unofficial anthem of the South. Emmett was born at Mount Vernon, OH, and died there June 28, 1904.

FRANKENSTEIN FRIDAY. Oct 29. This holiday has been designed to honor and celebrate the "mother" and "father" of Frankenstein, Mary Shelley and Boris Karloff. Every year a different venue will be used to celebrate this occasion. In years past it has included a torch lighting ceremony, film festival and awarding of the Franky. Annually, the last Friday in October. For info: Ron MacCloskey, 219 Loring Ave, Edison, NJ 08817. E-mail: ronmac55@aol.com.

FRIENDLY FOREST HALLOWEEN HIKE. Oct 29–30. Savannah, GA. A safe, not-so-scary, fun-filled alternative suited for young children. Guided hike will take your child "Trick or Treating" to visit some lovable, huggable critters that will surprise and delight them. Children are encouraged to wear their costumes and comfortable walking shoes. Treat bags will be provided at the admissions counter. Children must be accompanied by an adult. Est attendance: 600. For info: Oatland Island Education Center, 711 Sandtown Rd, Savannah, GA 31410. Phone: (912) 898-3980. Web: www.oatlandisland.org.

GHOST TALES AROUND THE CAMPFIRE. Oct 29. Jefferson College, Washington, MS. Storytellers weave their spells of mystery, surprise and suspense as they tell tales around a bonfire. Annually, the Friday before Halloween. Est attendance: 300. For info: Anne L. Gray, Historian, Jefferson College, PO Box 700, Washington, MS 39190. Phone: (601) 442-2901.

GOEBBELS, PAUL JOSEF: BIRTH ANNIVERSARY. Oct 29, 1897. German Nazi leader, born at Rheydt, Germany, who became Hitler's minister of propaganda, had earlier been rejected by the military because of a limp caused by infantile paralysis. Killed himself, his wife and children May 1, 1945, in Hitler's bunker in Berlin as Russian forces advanced into the city.

INTERNET CREATED: 35th ANNIVERSARY. Oct 29, 1969. The first connection on what would become the Internet was made on this day when bits of data flowed between computers at UCLA and the Stanford Research Institute. This was the beginning of ARPANET, the precurser to the Internet developed by the Department of Defense. By the end of 1969 four sites were connected: UCLA, the Stanford Research Institute, the University of California, Santa Barbara and the University of Utah. By the next year there were 10 sites and soon there were applications like e-mail and file transfer utilities. The @ symbol was adopted in 1972 and a year later 75 percent of ARPANET traffic was e-mail. ARPANET was decommissioned in 1990 and the National Science Foundation's NSFnet took over the role of backbone of the Internet.

NATIONAL TRAIL RIDE GATHERING. Oct 29–Nov 2. Live Oak, FL. Dust off your boots and be prepared for a grand time including daily trail rides, auctions, dances and much more! For info: Spirit of the Suwannee Music Park, 3076 95th Dr, Live Oak, FL 32060. Phone: (386) 364-1683. Fax: (386) 364-2998. E-mail: spirit@musicliveshere.com. Web: www.musicliveshere.com.

SEA WITCH HALLOWEEN & FIDDLERS FESTIVAL. Oct 29–31. Rehoboth Beach/Dewey Beach, DE. Sea Witch Hunt, broom tossing contest on beach, best costumed pet contest, scarecrow making, haunted house, costume parade, spook show, horse-drawn hayrides and entertainment. Annually, the last full weekend in October. Est attendance: 100,000. For info: Patty Burkentine, Festival Dir, PO Box 216, Rehoboth Beach, DE 19971. Phone: (800) 441-1329. Fax: (302) 227-8351. E-mail: rehoboth@beach-fun.com. Web: www.beach-fun.com.

SPACE MILESTONE: OLDEST MAN IN SPACE: *DISCOVERY* (US): ANNIVERSARY. Oct 29, 1998. Former astronaut and senator John Glenn became the oldest man in space when he traveled on the space shuttle *Discovery* at the age of 77. In 1962 on *Friendship 7* Glenn had been the first American to orbit Earth. See "Space Milestone: Friendship 7" (Feb 20).

STOCK MARKET CRASH: 75th ANNIVERSARY. Oct 29, 1929. Prices on the New York Stock Exchange plummeted and virtually collapsed four days after President Herbert Hoover had declared "The fundamental business of the country . . . is on a sound and prosperous basis." More than 16 million shares were dumped and billions of dollars were lost. The boom was over and the nation faced nearly a decade of depression. Some analysts had warned that the buying spree, with prices 15 to 150 times above earnings, had to stop at some point. Frightened investors ordered their brokers to sell at whatever price. The resulting Great Depression, which lasted until about 1939, involved North America, Europe and other industrialized countries. In 1932 one out of four US workers was unemployed.

SUGARLOAF CRAFTS FESTIVAL. Oct 29–31. Garden State Exhibit Center, Somerset, NJ. This show, now in its 11th year, features more than 250 nationally recognized craft designers and fine artists displaying and selling their original creations. Includes craft demonstrations, live music, specialty foods, hourly gift certificate drawings and more. Est attendance: 17,500. For info: Sugarloaf Mountain Works, 200 Orchard Ridge Dr, #215, Gaithersburg, MD 20878. Phone: (800) 210-9900. Fax: (301) 253-9620. Web: www.sugarloafcrafts.com.

TAKE BACK YOUR TIME DAY. Oct 29. A nationwide initiative to challenge the epidemic of overwork by encouraging workers to take all or part of their work day off. Held annually nine weeks before the end of the year—because Americans now work nine weeks more than Western Europeans do. For info: The Simplicity Forum, PO Box 9955, Glendale, CA 91226. Phone: (877) 867-8833. E-mail: contact@timeday.org. Web: www.timeday.org or www.simplicityforum.org.

TURKEY: REPUBLIC DAY: ANNIVERSARY. Oct 29. Anniversary of the founding of the republic in 1923.

UGLY PICKUP PARADE AND CONTEST. Oct 29. Chadron, NE. Honors beat-up old pickups, US manufacturing prowess and ingenuity and selects the ugliest pickup in all the

559

land. Ugly pickup queen contest held prior to the parade. Annually, the Friday before Halloween. Est attendance: 2,500. For info: *Chadron Record*, PO Box 1141, Chadron, NE 69337. Phone: (308) 432-5511. Fax: (308) 432-2385. E-mail: cdrrecord@bbc.net.

WMAS 94.7 FM ANNUAL HALLOWEEN BALL. Oct 29. Springfield, MA. Our annual listener appreciation ball, where listeners come dressed in their wildest and most creative costumes. Lots of prize categories in which people can win trips, VCRs, TVs, jewelry and more. Est attendance: 3,500. For info: Dina McMahon, PO Box 9500, Springfield, MA 01102. Phone: (413) 737-1414. Fax: (413) 737-1488.

WURSTFEST. Oct 29–Nov 7. Landa Park, New Braunfels, TX. To honor and celebrate German heritage. Music, dancing, food, arts and crafts, historical exhibits, sporting events and special demonstrations. For accommodation info: (800) 572-2626. Est attendance: 100,000. For info: Wurstfest Assn, PO Box 310309, New Braunfels, TX 78131. Phone: (830) 625-9167 or (800) 221-4369. Fax: (830) 620-1318. E-mail: info@wurstfest.com. Web: www.wurstfest.com.

BIRTHDAYS TODAY

Richard Dreyfuss, 57, actor (*American Graffiti, Jaws*; Oscar for *The Goodbye Girl*), born Brooklyn, NY, Oct 29, 1947.
Joely Fisher, 39, actress ("Ellen"), born Los Angeles, CA, Oct 29, 1965.
Finola Hughes, 44, actress ("Blossom," "Pacific Palisades"), born London, England, Oct 29, 1960.
Kate Jackson, 56, actress ("Charlie's Angels," "Scarecrow and Mrs King"), born Birmingham, AL, Oct 29, 1948.
Randy Jackson, 43, singer (Jackson 5), born Steven Randall Jackson, Gary, IN, Oct 29, 1961.
Dirk Kempthorne, 53, Governor of Idaho (R), born San Diego, CA, Oct 29, 1951.
Melba Moore, 59, singer ("You Stepped into My Life"), actress ("Melba"), born New York, NY, Oct 29, 1945.
Winona Ryder, 33, actress (*Beetlejuice, Edward Scissorhands, Little Women*), born Winona, MN, Oct 29, 1971.

OCTOBER 30 — SATURDAY
Day 304 — 62 Remaining

ADAMS, JOHN: BIRTH ANNIVERSARY. Oct 30, 1735. Second president of the US (term of office: Mar 4, 1797–Mar 3, 1801), had been George Washington's vice president, and was the father of John Quincy Adams (6th president of the US). Born at Braintree, MA, he once wrote in a letter to his wife Abigail: "I must study politics and war that my sons may have liberty to study mathematics and philosophy." Adams and Thomas Jefferson died on the same day, July 4, 1826. Adams died at Quincy, MA. See also: "Adams, John, and Jefferson, Thomas: Death Anniversary" (July 4).

ATLAS, CHARLES: BIRTH ANNIVERSARY. Oct 30, 1893. Charles Atlas (ex-97-lb weakling), whose original name was Angelo Siciliano, was born at Acri, Calabria, Italy. A bodybuilder and physical culturist, he created a popular mail-order bodybuilding course. The legendary sand-kicking episode used later in advertising for his course occurred at Coney Island when a lifeguard kicked sand in Atlas's face and stole his girlfriend. Three generations of comic book fans read his advertisements. He died Dec 24, 1972, at Long Beach, NY.

CLOSING OF COLUMBIAN EXPOSITION: ANNIVERSARY. Oct 30, 1893. After a rousing success, the Columbian Exposition held "American Cities Day" Oct 28, and Chicago Mayor Carter Harrison gave a speech before the visiting mayors. After he arrived home, Harrison's doorbell rang. When the mayor answered the door he was shot by Patrick Eugene Pendergast, who had been disappointed when his request for a position with the city as corporation counsel was turned down. Instead of the elaborate ceremony that had been planned to close the exposition on Oct 30, a single speech was given and the flags lowered to half-mast.

CREATE A GREAT FUNERAL DAY. Oct 30. A day to remind people of all the benefits of creating their own unique funerals or memorial services, regardless of age or state of health. For info: Stephanie West Allen, PO Box 9311, Denver, CO 80209. Phone: (303) 742-4790. Fax: (303) 935-8842. E-mail: stephanie@allen-nichols.com. Web: www.allen-nichols.com.

DEVIL'S NIGHT. Oct 30. Formerly a "Mischief Night" on the evening before Halloween and an occasion for harmless pranks, chiefly observed by children. However, in some areas of the US, the destruction of property and endangering of lives has led to the imposition of dusk-to-dawn curfews during the last two or three days of October. Not to be confused with "Trick or Treat," or "Beggar's Night," usually observed on Halloween. See also: "Hallowe'en" (Oct 31).

EMMA CRAWFORD FESTIVAL AND MEMORIAL COFFIN RACE. Oct 30. Manitou Springs, CO. Ghost tours, 5K, coffin races and parade. Annually, the Saturday before Halloween. Est attendance: 3,000. For info: Manitou Springs Chamber of Commerce, 354 Manitou, Manitou Springs, CO 80829. Phone: (800) 642-2567. Fax: (719) 685-0355. Web: www.manitousprings.org.

HALLOWEEN HAUNTED WALK AND CARNIVAL. Oct 30. Prospect Park, Brooklyn, NY. Carnival games, musicians, storytellers and a haunted walk through Lookout Hill with many scary surprises. Hours 12–3 PM; free. "Scary Stories from the Past" on Oct 30–31 at Lefferts Homestead Children's Historic House. Est attendance: 4,500. For info: Public Info Office, Prospect Park, 95 Prospect Park W, Brooklyn, NY 11215. Phone: (718) 965-8954. Fax: (718) 965-8972. E-mail: cmark@prospectpark.org. Web: www.prospectpark.org.

HALLOWEEN PARADE. Oct 30. Toms River, NJ. Reported as the second largest Halloween parade in the nation with 8,000 participants, 118 prizes and 100,000 spectators. Parade covers a one-mile route. Est attendance: 100,000. For info: Carl Weingroff, c/o Toms River Fire Co. 1, PO Box 1035, Toms River, NJ 08754. Phone: (723) 349-0144. Fax: (732) 349-5024.

THE HALLOWEEN TRAIL. Oct 30. Pioneer Village, Worthington, MN. Open to all children, third grade and under, accompanied by their parents or a responsible adult. Treats are provided at stations located in various parts of Pioneer Village. Refreshments are available for all in the Fire Hall at the end of the trail. For info: Nobles County Historical Society, 407 12th St, Ste 2, Worthington, MN 56187. Phone: (507) 376-4011 or (507) 376-4431.

HALSEY, WILLIAM "BULL" FREDERICK: BIRTH ANNIVERSARY. Oct 30, 1882. American admiral and fleet

	S	M	T	W	T	F	S
October 2004						1	2
	3	4	5	6	7	8	9
	10	11	12	13	14	15	16
	17	18	19	20	21	22	23
	24	25	26	27	28	29	30
	31						

commander who played a leading role in the defeat of the Japanese in the Pacific naval battles of WWII, William Halsey was born at Elizabeth, NJ. In April 1942, aircraft carriers under his command ferried Jimmy Doolittle's B-25s to within several hundred miles of Japan's coast. From that location the aircraft were launched from the decks of the carriers for a raid on Tokyo. In October 1942, as commander of all the South Pacific area, Halsey led naval forces in the defeat of Japan at Guadalcanal, and in November 1943, he directed the capture of Bougainville. He supported the landings in the Philippines in June 1944. In the great naval battle of Leyte (Oct 23–25, 1944) he assisted in an overwhelming defeat of the Japanese. On Sept 2, 1945, Japan's final instrument of surrender was signed in Tokyo Bay aboard Halsey's flagship, the USS *Missouri*. Halsey died at Fishers Island, NY, Aug 16, 1959.

HAUNTED REFRIGERATOR NIGHT. Oct 30. Who knows what evil lurks in the refrigerators of men and women. It's time to be afraid, very afraid. Gather friends, open the refrigerator door and venture unto the realm of the lower shelf, rear. That "thing" inside that container is much more horrifying than any haunted hayride. Annually, Oct 30. [©2003 by WH.] For info: Thomas & Ruth Roy, Wellcat Holidays, 2418 Long Ln, Lebanon, PA 17046. Phone: (717) 279-0184. E-mail: info@wellcat.com. Web: www.wellcat.com.

MALLE, LOUIS: BIRTH ANNIVERSARY. Oct 30, 1932. Born at Thumeries, France, film director Louis Malle was known for his experimental approach to filmmaking and his investigation of controversial topics. *Le Souffle Au Coeur* (1971), *Lancombe, Lucien* (1974) and *Pretty Baby* (1978), for instance, dealt with the issues of incest, the collaboration of France with its Nazi occupiers and child prostitution, respectively. Of all his films, Malle wished most to be remembered for *Au Revoir Les Enfants* (1987). Died Nov 23, 1995, at Beverly Hills, CA.

POST, EMILY: BIRTH ANNIVERSARY. Oct 30, 1872. Emily Post was born at Baltimore, MD. Published in 1922, her book *Etiquette: The Blue Book of Social Usage* instantly became the American bible of manners and social behavior and established Post as the household name in matters of etiquette. It was in its 10th edition at the time of her death Sept 25, 1960, at New York, NY. *Etiquette* inspired a great many letters asking Post for advice on manners in specific situations. She used these letters as the basis for her radio show and her syndicated newspaper column, which eventually appeared in more than 200 papers.

POUND, EZRA LOOMIS: BIRTH ANNIVERSARY. Oct 30, 1885. Modernist poet, editor and critic, born at Hailey, ID. His success as a poet began in 1909 with the publication of *Personae*. In 1912 Pound initiated the Imagist movement, edited its first anthology in 1914, and collaborated with James Joyce and T.S. Eliot. He moved to Italy in 1924. As a result of his pro-Fascist radio broadcasts from Italy Pound was indicted for treason July 26, 1943, and arrested near Genoa, by the US Army. Confined to St. Elizabeth's Hospital, Washington, DC, from 1946 to 1958 as being mentally unable to stand trial, he was never tried for treason. Died at Venice, Italy, Nov 1, 1972.

SHERIDAN, RICHARD BRINSLEY: BIRTH ANNIVERSARY. Oct 30, 1751. Dramatist, born at Dublin, Ireland. Died at London, England, July 7, 1816. Sheridan is said to have extended the following invitation to a young lady: "Won't you come into the garden? I would like my roses to see you."

SISLEY, ALFRED: BIRTH ANNIVERSARY. Oct 30, 1839. French impressionist painter, born at Paris, France. One of the most influential artists of his time, he died near Fontainebleau, Jan 29, 1899.

"WAR OF THE WORLDS": BROADCAST ANNIVERSARY. Oct 30, 1938. As part of a series of radio dramas based on famous novels, Orson Welles with the Mercury Players produced H.G. Wells's *War of the Worlds*. Near panic resulted when listeners believed the simulated news bulletins, which described a Martian invasion of New Jersey, to be real.

BIRTHDAYS TODAY

Dick Gautier, 67, actor (*Bye Bye Birdie*, "Here We Go Again"), born Los Angeles, CA, Oct 30, 1937.
Harry Hamlin, 53, actor ("LA Law," "Studs Lonigan"), born Pasadena, CA, Oct 30, 1951.
Ed Lauter, 64, actor (*The Longest Yard, Fat Man and Little Boy*), born Long Beach, NY, Oct 30, 1940.
Diego Armando Maradona, 44, former soccer player, born Lanus, Argentina, Oct 30, 1960.
Andrea Mitchell, 58, news correspondent, born New York, NY, Oct 30, 1946.
Kevin Pollak, 46, actor (*A Few Good Men, Grumpy Old Men*), born San Francisco, CA, Oct 30, 1958.
Grace Slick, 65, singer (Jefferson Airplane, "White Rabbit"), born Chicago, IL, Oct 30, 1939.
Charles Martin Smith, 51, actor (*American Graffiti, The Buddy Holly Story, The Untouchables*), director, born Los Angeles, CA, Oct 30, 1953.
Dick Vermeil, 68, football coach, born Calistoga, CA, Oct 30, 1936.
Henry Winkler, 59, actor ("Happy Days," "An American Christmas Carol"), coproducer ("MacGyver"), born New York, NY, Oct 30, 1945.

OCTOBER 31 — SUNDAY
Day 305 — 61 Remaining

BIG TEN MEN'S AND WOMEN'S CROSS COUNTRY CHAMPIONSHIP. Oct 31. University of Iowa, Iowa City, IA. For info: Sue Lister, Big Ten Conference, 1500 W Higgins Rd, Park Ridge, IL 60068-6300. Phone: (847) 696-1010. Fax: (847) 696-1110. Web: www.bigten.org.

CANDY, JOHN: BIRTH ANNIVERSARY. Oct 31, 1950. Comedic actor who got his start in Second City improvisation at Toronto and graduated to film stardom (*Uncle Buck, Home Alone*). Born at Toronto, Ontario, Canada, and died Mar 4, 1994, while on location for a film at Chupederos, Mexico.

"CAR TALK" NATIONAL RADIO PREMIERE: ANNIVERSARY. Oct 31, 1987. "Car Talk," the irreverent talk show that diagnoses auto ills, premiered nationally on National Public Radio on this date. Hosted by brothers Ray and Tom Magliozzi (also known as "Click and Clack, the Tappet Brothers"), "Car Talk" originally debuted in Boston in 1977. Today, almost 4 million listeners tune in to the Peabody Award–winning show on 550 NPR stations.

CHIANG KAI-SHEK: BIRTH ANNIVERSARY. Oct 31, 1887. Chinese soldier and statesman, born at Chekiang, China. Educated at the Wampoa Military Academy, Chiang led the KMT (nationalist) forces in the struggle against the Communist army led by Mao Tse-Tung and eventually had to flee mainland China. He died at Taipei, Taiwan, Apr 5, 1975.

DAYLIGHT SAVING TIME ENDS; STANDARD TIME RESUMES. Oct 31–Apr 3, 2005. Standard Time resumes at 2 AM on the last Sunday in October in each time zone, as provided by the Uniform Time Act of 1966 (as amended in 1986 by Public Law 99–359). Many use the popular rule: "spring forward, fall back" to remember which way to turn their clocks. See also: "Daylight Saving Time" (Apr 4).

FIRST BLACK PLAYS IN NBA GAME: ANNIVERSARY. Oct 31, 1950. Earl Lloyd became the first black ever to play in an NBA game when he took the floor for the Washington Capitols at Rochester, NY. Lloyd was actually one of three blacks to become an NBA player in the 1950 season, the others being Nat "Sweetwater" Clifton, who was signed by the New York Knicks, and Chuck Cooper, who was drafted by the Boston Celtics (and debuted the night after Lloyd).

HALLOWEEN IN ARAPAHOE. Oct 31. Arapahoe, NE. Merchants and business personnel dress in Halloween costume, children's parade and prizes. Est attendance: 200. For info: Secretary, Chamber of Commerce, PO Box 624, Arapahoe, NE 68922.

HALLOWE'EN or ALL HALLOW'S EVE. Oct 31. An ancient celebration combining Druid autumn festival and Christian customs. Hallowe'en (All Hallow's Eve) is the beginning of Hallowtide, a season that embraces the Feast of All Saints (Nov 1) and the Feast of All Souls (Nov 2). The observance, dating from the sixth or seventh century, has long been associated with thoughts of the dead, spirits, witches, ghosts and devils. In fact, the ancient Celtic Feast of Samhain, the festival that marked the beginning of winter and of the New Year, was observed Nov 1. See also: "Trick or Treat or Beggar's Night" (Oct 31).

HAUTE DOG CHARITY HOWL'OWEEN PARADE. Oct 31. Belmont Shore, Long Beach, CA. Just about every breed from boxer to poodle—even a potbellied pig—will take over Belmont Shore for the annual Haute Dog Howl'oween Parade. The event has raised thousands of dollars for animal shelters and rescue organizations. About 400 pooches—some colorfully costumed for Halloween—are expected to pack Livingston Park for a Yappy Hour before beginning their parade down Second Street. Prizes awarded for the best canine costumes. Annually, the Sunday before Halloween. Est attendance: 3,000. For info: Justin Rudd. Phone: (562) 439-3316. E-mail: justinrudd@aol.com. Web: www.hautedogs.org.

HOUDINI, HARRY: DEATH ANNIVERSARY. Oct 31, 1926. Harry Houdini (whose real name was Ehrich Weisz), magician, illusionist and escape artist, died at 10:30 PM at Grace Hospital, Detroit, MI, of peritonitis following a blow to the abdomen. Houdini's death anniversary, on Halloween, is occasion for meetings of magicians. See also: "Houdini, Harry: Birth Anniversary" (Mar 24).

KEATS, JOHN: BIRTH ANNIVERSARY. Oct 31, 1795. One of England's greatest poets, born at London, England. Keats wrote to Fanny Brawne (in 1820): "If I should die . . . I have left no immortal work behind me—nothing to make my friends proud of my memory—but I have loved the principle of beauty in all things, and if I had had time I would have made myself remembered." Died at the age of 25 at Rome, Italy, Feb 23, 1821.

October 2004	S	M	T	W	T	F	S
						1	2
	3	4	5	6	7	8	9
	10	11	12	13	14	15	16
	17	18	19	20	21	22	23
	24	25	26	27	28	29	30
	31						

LANDON, MICHAEL: BIRTH ANNIVERSARY. Oct 31, 1936. American actor, born Eugene Maurice Orowitz, at Forest Hills, NY. He is best known for his roles in the television series "Bonanza" (1959–73), "Little House on the Prairie" (1974–83) and "Highway to Heaven" (1984–89). He died July 1, 1991, at Malibu, CA.

LOW, JULIET GORDON: BIRTH ANNIVERSARY. Oct 31, 1860. Founded Girl Scouts of the USA Mar 12, 1912, at Savannah, GA. Born at Savannah, Low died there Jan 17, 1927.

MOUNT RUSHMORE COMPLETION: ANNIVERSARY. Oct 31, 1941. The Mount Rushmore National Memorial was completed after 14 years of work. First suggested by Jonah Robinson of the South Dakota State Historical Society, the memorial was dedicated in 1925, and work began in 1927. The memorial contains sculptures of the heads of Presidents George Washington, Thomas Jefferson, Abraham Lincoln and Theodore Roosevelt. The 60-foot-tall sculptures represent, respectively, the nation's founding, political philosophy, preservation, expansion and conservation.

NATIONAL KNOCK-KNOCK DAY. Oct 31. Celebrated in tandem with Halloween, National Knock-Knock Day answers the age-old question "who's there?" A day for kids of all ages to try out their best knock-knock jokes (ie Knock Knock/Who's there?/Weirdo/Weirdo who?/Weirdo you keep all your Halloween candy? I'm starving!). For a list of Halloween Knock-Knock Jokes, contact children's joke book authors Matt Rissinger and Philip Yates. Annually, on October 31. For info: Matt Rissinger/Philip Yates, Phone: (610) 650-9136. E-mail: mrissinger@aol.com.

NATIONAL MAGIC DAY. Oct 31. Traditionally observed on the anniversary of the death of Harry Houdini in 1926.

NATIONAL PARK OF AMERICAN SAMOA AUTHORIZED: ANNIVERSARY. Oct 31, 1988. An area of American Samoa was authorized to be developed as a national park. For further park info: Natl Park of American Samoa, c/o Pacific Area Office, PO Box 50165, Honolulu, HI 96850.

★**NATIONAL UNICEF DAY.** Oct 31. Presidential Proclamation 3817, of Oct 27, 1967, covers all succeeding years. Annually, Oct 31.

NEVADA: ADMISSION DAY: ANNIVERSARY. Oct 31, 1864. Became 36th state in 1864. Observed as a holiday in Nevada.

NORTHERN IRELAND: BELFAST FESTIVAL AT QUEEN'S. Oct 31–Nov 16. Queen's University, Belfast, County Antrim. International festival of the arts that includes theatre, dance, opera and all types of music from folk to rock and pop to classical. Est attendance: 70,000. For info: Ms S Hall, Festival House, 25 College Gardens, Belfast, Northern Ireland BT9 6BS. Phone: (44) (2890) 667687. Fax: (44) (2890) 663733. E-mail: festival@qub.ac.uk. Web: www.qub.ac.uk/festival.

PACA, WILLIAM: BIRTH ANNIVERSARY. Oct 31, 1740. Signer of the Declaration of Independence and governor of Maryland. Born near Abingdon, MD, he died Oct 13, 1799, at Talbot County, MD.

REFORMATION DAY: ANNIVERSARY. Oct 31, 1517. Anniversary on which Martin Luther nailed his 95 theses to the door of Wittenberg's Palace church, denouncing the selling of papal indulgences—the beginning of the Reformation in Germany. Observed by many Protestant churches on Reformation Sunday, on this day if it is a Sunday or on the Sunday before Oct 31.

REFORMATION SUNDAY. Oct 31. Many Protestant churches commemorate Reformation Day (Oct 31—anniversary of the day on which Martin Luther nailed his 95 theses to the door of Wittenberg's Palace church, protesting the sale of papal indulgences, in 1517), on the Sunday preceding Oct 31, each year or on the 31st, if a Sunday.

SAMHAIN. Oct 31. (Also called November Eve, Hallowmas, Hallowe'en, All Hallow's Eve, Feast of Souls, Feast of the Dead, Feast of Apples and Calan Gaeaf.) One of the "Greater Sabbats" dur-

★ Chase's 2004 Calendar of Events ★   Oct 31

ing the Wiccan year, Samhain or "Summer's end" marks the death of the Sun-God, who then awaits his rebirth from the Mother Goddess at Yule (Dec 21 in 2004). In the Celtic tradition, the feast of Samhain was also celebrated as New Year's Eve, as their new year began on Nov 1. Annually, Oct 31.

SLEIDANUS, JOHANNES: DEATH ANNIVERSARY. Oct 31, 1556. German historian, born at Schleiden in 1506. His *Famous Chronicle of Oure Time*, called *Sleidanes Comentaires*, was first translated into English in 1560. The translator spoke thus to the book: "Go forth my painful Boke, Thou art no longer mine. Eche man may on thee loke, The Shame or praise is thine." He died at Strasbourg, Oct 31, 1556.

TAIWAN: CHIANG KAI-SHEK DAY: ANNIVERSARY. Oct 31. National holiday to honor the memory of Generalissimo Chiang Kai-Shek, the first constitutional president of the Republic of China, born Oct 31, 1887.

TRICK OR TREAT or BEGGAR'S NIGHT. Oct 31. A popular custom on Hallowe'en, in which children wearing costumes visit neighbors' homes, calling out "Trick or Treat" and "begging" for candies or gifts to place in their beggars' bags. In recent years there has been increased participation by adults, often parading in elaborate or outrageous costumes and also requesting candy.

WATERS, ETHEL: BIRTH ANNIVERSARY. Oct 31, 1896. Married when she was 13, Ethel Waters began her singing career at the urging of friends. At age 17 she was singing at Baltimore, billing herself as Sweet Mama Stringbean. Her career took her to New York, where she divided her work between the stage, nightclubs and films. She made her Broadway debut in 1927 in the revue *Africana*, and her other stage credits included *Black-birds* and *Thousands Cheer*. Her memorable stage roles in *Cabin in the Sky* and *A Member of the Wedding* (for which she won the Drama Critics' Award) were re-created for film. Born at Chester, PA, she died Sept 9, 1977, at Chatsworth, GA.

BIRTHDAYS TODAY

Michael Collins, 73, former astronaut, born Rome, Italy, Oct 31, 1931.

Deidre Hall, 56, actress ("Our House," "Days of Our Lives"), born Lake Worth, FL, Oct 31, 1948.

Peter Jackson, 43, director (*Lord of the Rings* trilogy), born Pukerua Bay, North Island, New Zealand, Oct 31, 1961.

Frederick Stanley (Fred) McGriff, 41, baseball player, born Tampa, FL, Oct 31, 1963.

Larry Mullen, 43, musician (drummer with U2; Grammy for *The Joshua Tree*), born Dublin, Ireland, Oct 31, 1961.

Dermot Mulroney, 41, actor (*Young Guns, Longtime Companion*), born Alexandria, VA, Oct 31, 1963.

Jane Pauley, 54, TV personality, born Indianapolis, IN, Oct 31, 1950.

Dan Rather, 73, journalist (coanchor "CBS Evening News"), born Wharton, TX, Oct 31, 1931.

Stephen Rea, 61, actor (*The Crying Game, Michael Collins*), born Belfast, Northern Ireland, Oct 31, 1943.

Rob Schneider, 41, actor ("Saturday Night Live," "Men Behaving Badly"), born San Francisco, CA, Oct 31, 1963.

David Ogden Stiers, 62, actor ("M*A*S*H," *North and South*), born Peoria, IL, Oct 31, 1942.

Vanilla Ice, 37, rapper, actor (*Teenage Mutant Ninja Turtles, Cool As Ice*), born Robert Van Winkle, Miami, FL, Oct 31, 1967.

Nov 1 ☆ *Chase's 2004 Calendar of Events* ☆

November.

NOVEMBER 1 — MONDAY
Day 306 — 60 Remaining

ALGERIA: REVOLUTION DAY. Nov 1. National holiday. Commemorates beginning of revolt against France in 1954.

ALL HALLOWS or ALL SAINTS' DAY. Nov 1. Roman Catholic Holy Day of Obligation. Commemorates the blessed, especially those who have no special feast days. Observed on Nov 1 since Pope Gregory IV set the date of recognition in 835. All Saints' Day is a legal holiday in Louisiana. Halloween is the evening before All Hallows Day.

AMERICAN DIABETES MONTH. Nov 1–30. American Diabetes Month is designed to communicate the seriousness of diabetes and the importance of proper diabetes control and treatment to those diagnosed with the disease and their families. Throughout the month, the American Diabetes Association holds special events and programs on a variety of topics related to diabetes care and treatment. For info contact: American Diabetes Assn at (800) DIABETES or www.diabetes.org.

ANTIGUA AND BARBUDA: INDEPENDENCE DAY. Nov 1. National holiday. Commemorates independence from Britain in 1981.

AUSTRALIA: RECREATION DAY. Nov 1. The first Monday in November is observed as Recreation Day at Northern Tasmania, Australia.

AVIATION HISTORY MONTH. Nov 1–30. Anniversary of aeronautical experiments in November 1782 (exact dates unknown) by Joseph Michel Montgolfier and Jacques Etienne Montgolfier, brothers living at Annonay, France. Inspired by Joseph Priestley's book *Experiments Relating to the Different Kinds of Air*, the brothers experimented with filling paper and fabric bags with smoke and hot air, leading to the invention of the hot air balloon, man's first flight and the entire science of aviation and flight.

COZY CUDDLES FOR KIDS. Nov 1–Dec 20. Communities are encouraged to provide basics such as new blankets, coats, hats, mittens and boots for foster and needy children. Event includes Kids Helping Kids, scout participation and Crafting for Kids events. Donations will go to Grant-A-Wish, Inc. Sponsors and donors needed. For info or to host an event: Kathleen Quinn, ProQuest/2020, PO Box 2373, Glenview, IL 60025-6373. Phone: (847) 998-9950. Fax: (847) 998-9945. E-mail: shfk2000@aol.com.

November 2004	S	M	T	W	T	F	S
		1	2	3	4	5	6
	7	8	9	10	11	12	13
	14	15	16	17	18	19	20
	21	22	23	24	25	26	27
	28	29	30				

CRANE, STEPHEN: BIRTH ANNIVERSARY. Nov 1, 1871. American author (*The Red Badge of Courage*), born at Newark, NJ. Died June 5, 1900, at Badenweiler, Germany.

DIABETIC EYE DISEASE MONTH. Nov 1–30. Can people with diabetes prevent the onset of diabetic eye disease? During this observance Prevent Blindness America® tells how early detection and treatment of diabetes can help save sight. For info: Prevent Blindness America®, 500 Remington Rd, Schaumburg, IL 60173. Phone: (800) 331-2020. Fax: (847) 843-8458. Web: www.preventblindness.org or www.diabetes-sight.org.

EPILEPSY AWARENESS MONTH. Nov 1–30. To increase public awareness that despite dramatic gains in treatment, epilepsy is a serious and chronic health condition for which there is no cure. Annually, the month of November. For info: PR Dept, Epilepsy Foundation, 4351 Garden City Dr, Landover, MD 20785. Phone: (301) 459-3700 or (800) 332-1000. Fax: (301) 459-0412. E-mail: pvanhaverbeke@efa.org. Web: www.epilepsyfoundation.org.

EUROPEAN UNION ESTABLISHED: ANNIVERSARY. Nov 1, 1993. The Maastricht Treaty went into effect this day, formally establishing the European Union. The treaty was drafted in 1991. By 1993, 12 nations had ratified it. In 1995 three more nations ratified the treaty. The European Union grew out of the European Economic Community (also known as the Common Market) which was established in 1958.

FAMILY STORIES MONTH. Nov 1–30. November starts out with crisper weather and ends with the gathering of family and friends around the table, which makes it the perfect month to start telling and saving family stories. For info: EFG, Inc, 2207 S 39th St, St Louis, MO 63110. Phone: (314) 762-9762. Fax: (314) 762-0811. E-mail: quicknews@aol.com. Web: www.scrapbookstorytelling.com.

GUATEMALA: KITE FESTIVAL OF SANTIAGO SACATEPEQUEZ. Nov 1. Long ago, when evil spirits disturbed the good spirits in the local cemetery, a magician told the townspeople a secret way to get rid of the evil spirits—by flying kites (because the evil spirits were frightened by the noise of wind against paper). Since then, the kite festival has been held at the cemetery each year on Nov 1 or Nov 2, and it is said that "to this day no one knows of bad spirits roaming the streets or the cemetery of Santiago Sacatepequez," a village about 20 miles from Guatemala City. Nowadays, the youth of the village work for many weeks to make the elaborate and giant kites to fly on All Saints' Day (Nov 1) or All Souls' Day (Nov 2).

HOCKEY MASK INVENTED: 45th ANNIVERSARY. Nov 1, 1959. Tired of stopping hockey pucks with his face, Montreal Canadiens goalie Jacques Plante, having received another wound, reemerged from the locker room with seven new stitches—and a plastic face mask he had made from fiberglass and resin. Although Cliff Benedict had tried a leather mask back in the '20s, the idea didn't catch on, but after Plante wore his, goalies throughout the NHL began wearing protective plastic face shields.

I AM SO THANKFUL MONTH. Nov 1–30. This month is dedicated to giving thanks and counting your blessings daily. Share with others the things you are thankful for! For info: Nancy J. Lewis, MS, PHR, PO Box 342, Fayetteville, GA 30214. Phone: (404) 559-7614. Fax: (404) 767-2988. E-mail: nanjlewis@aol.com. Web: www.nancyjlewis.com.

☆ Chase's 2004 Calendar of Events ☆   Nov 1

JOURNEY'S END NATIONAL ART EXHIBITION. Nov 1–30. Astoria, OR. Juried show intended primarily to interpret the exploration and history of the Northwest. In honor of the bicentennial of the Lewis and Clark Expedition, our show will focus on the epic journey of Jefferson's "Corps of Discovery." Cash awards to be determined. For info: Journey's End Natl Art Exhibition, PO Box 2005, Astoria, OR 97103. E-mail: journey's@pacifier.com. Web: www.jsend.org.

KIDS' GOAL SETTING WEEK. Nov 1–5. Encourages parents, teachers and coaches to foster goal-setting habits in children's lives so that the children can make their dreams come true. For info: Gary Ryan Blair, The GoalsGuy, 36181 E Lake Rd, Ste 139, Palm Harbor, FL 34685. Phone: (877) GOALSGUY. Fax: (800) 731-GOAL. E-mail: info@goalsguy.com. Web: www.goalsguy.com.

LUNG CANCER AWARENESS MONTH. Nov 1–30. A month created to increase awareness of the need for screening, early detection, more research and compassion for lung cancer survivors. ALCASE is the only organization in the world solely dedicated to helping people at risk for and living with lung cancer. Support and education resources are available free of charge by phone, mail or Internet. For info: Alliance for Lung Cancer Advocacy, Support and Education, 500 W 8th St, #240, Vancouver, WA 98660. Phone: (800) 298-2436. Fax: (360) 735-1305. E-mail: info@alcase.org. Web: www.alcase.org.

MEDICAL SCHOOL FOR WOMEN OPENED AT BOSTON: ANNIVERSARY. Nov 1, 1848. Founded by Samuel Gregory, a pioneer in medical education for women, the Boston Female Medical School opened as the first medical school exclusively for women. The original enrollment was 12 students. In 1874 the school merged with the Boston University School of Medicine and formed one of the first coed medical schools in the world.

MEXICO: DAY OF THE DEAD. Nov 1–2. Observance begins during last days of October when "Dead Men's Bread" is sold in bakeries—round loaves, decorated with sugar skulls. Departed souls are remembered not with mourning but with a spirit of friendliness and good humor. Cemeteries are visited and graves are decorated.

MISSION SAN JUAN CAPISTRANO: FOUNDING ANNIVERSARY. Nov 1, 1776. California mission founded on this date, collapsed during the 1812 earthquake. The swallows of Capistrano nest in the ruins of the old mission church, departing each year on Oct 23, and returning the following year on or near St. Joseph's Day (Mar 19).

★**NATIONAL ADOPTION MONTH.** Nov 1–30.

NATIONAL AIDS AWARENESS MONTH. Nov 1–30. To educate consumers, patients, students and professionals on the prevention of AIDS and sexually transmitted diseases. Kit of materials available for $15. For info: Frederick Mayer, Pres, Pharmacists Planning Service, Inc, 101 Lucas Valley Rd, #210, San Rafael, CA 94903. Phone: (415) 479-8628. Fax: (415) 479-8608. E-mail: ppsi@aol.com. Web: www.ppsinc.org.

NATIONAL ALZHEIMER'S DISEASE MONTH. Nov 1–30. To increase awareness of Alzheimer's disease and what the Alzheimer's Association is doing to advance research and help patients, their families and their caregivers. For info: Alzheimer's Assn, 225 N Michigan, 17th Fl, Chicago, IL 60601. Phone: (312) 335-8700. Fax: (312) 335-1110. E-mail: info@alz.org. Web: www.alz.org.

★**NATIONAL AMERICAN INDIAN HERITAGE MONTH.** Nov 1–30.

NATIONAL AUTHORS' DAY. Nov 1. This observance was adopted by the General Federation of Women's Clubs in 1929 and in 1949 was given a place on the list of special days, weeks and months prepared by the US Dept of Commerce. The resolution states: "by celebrating an Authors' Day as a nation, we would not only show patriotism, loyalty, and appreciation of the men and women who have made American literature possible, but would also encourage and inspire others to give of themselves in making a better America. . . ." It was also resolved "that we commemorate an Authors' Day to be observed on November First each year."

NATIONAL COPD AWARENESS MONTH. Nov 1–30. Established by EFFORTS (Emphysema Foundation for Our Right to Survive) to raise public awareness about the prevalence of chronic obstructive pulmonary disease and the serious problems associated with the disease. Annually, the month of November. For info: Gary Bain, EFFORTS, Claycomo Plaza, 411 NE US Highway 69, Claycomo, MO 64119. Phone: (816) 452-3132. Fax: (816) 413-0176. E-mail: 1efforts@emphysema.net. Web: www.emphysema.net.

NATIONAL FAMILY CAREGIVERS MONTH. Nov 1–30. A nationwide month of recognition for the millions of family caregivers. For info: Suzanne Geffen Mintz, Pres, Natl Family Caregivers Assn, 10400 Connecticut Ave, Ste 500, Kensington, MD 20895-3944. Phone: (800) 896-3650. Fax: (301) 942-2302. E-mail: info@nfcacares.org. Web: www.nfcacares.org.

★**NATIONAL FAMILY CAREGIVERS MONTH.** Nov 1–30. To honor family members who care for aging relatives or those with disabilities.

NATIONAL FAMILY LITERACY DAY®. Nov 1. Celebrated all over the country with special activities and events that showcase the importance of family literacy programs. Family literacy programs bring parents and children together in the classroom to learn and support each other in efforts to further their education and improve their life skills. Sponsored by the National Center for Family Literacy and Toyota. Annually, Nov 1. For info: Natl Center for Family Literacy, 325 W Main St, Ste 300, Louisville, KY 40202. Phone: (502) 584-1133 or (877) FAMLIT 1. Fax: (502) 584-0172. E-mail: ncfl@famlit.org. Web: www.famlit.org.

NATIONAL FIG WEEK. Nov 1–7. To celebrate the completion of the California fig harvest and encourage consumers to use California figs as part of their diet for the taste, high fiber and nutritional value. For info: California Fig Advisory Board, PO Box 709, Fresno, CA 93712. Phone: (800) 588-2344. Fax: (559) 224-3449. E-mail: info@californiafigs.com. Web: www.californiafigs.com.

NATIONAL FUN WITH FONDUE MONTH. Nov 1–30. Fondue—pronounced (fahn-doo)—originated in Switzerland as a way of using up hardened cheese. It was melted with wine in a communal pot and became a dip for leftover pieces of bread. Today, from cheese to chocolate, fondue is back! It's a vehicle for easy, intimate entertaining and a way to involve guests in the cooking and serving. And don't forget the kids—they think fondue's fun too! For info: Chantal Corp. Phone: (800) 365-4354, ext 624. Web: www.chantal.com.

NATIONAL GEORGIA PECAN MONTH. Nov 1–30. To herald the Georgia pecan harvest and recognize Georgia's status as the nation's top pecan-producing state, providing 50 percent of the nation's supply. For info: Marcia Crowley, Georgia Agricultural Commodity Commission for Pecans (GACCP), Commodities Promotion Div, GA Dept of Agriculture, 328 Agriculture Bldg, Capitol Square, Atlanta, GA 30334. Phone: (404) 656-3678. Fax: (404) 656-9380.

Nov 1-2 ☆ Chase's 2004 Calendar of Events ☆

NATIONAL HOMELESS WEEK. Nov 1–7. To recognize the homeless as a part of our society and to put forth effort to treat them with respect, dignity and as human beings regardless of how or why they are homeless. For info: Steve Dawson, PO Box 5278, Englewood, CO 80155. Phone: (303) 221-5364. E-mail: sjdaws @yahoo.com.

NATIONAL HOSPICE MONTH. Nov 1–30. To promote greater awareness of hospice care and the advantages it offers; to educate physicians and other health care professionals about the concept of hospice; to honor patients and family members, as well as the thousands of dedicated professionals and volunteers who devote their time, love and support to the terminally ill and their families; and to educate public officials to ensure hospice care remains a key component in the health care delivery system. For info: Public Relations, Hospice Assn of America, 228 Seventh St SE, Washington, DC 20003. Phone: (202) 546-4759. Fax: (202) 547-3540. Web: www.nahc.org/.

NATIONAL LIFEWRITING MONTH. Nov 1–30. An opportunity to celebrate and share ourselves by putting our lifestories in writing. Celebration by preserving our autobiographies in writing allows us to share our stories with future generations. For info: Soleil Lifestory Network, 95-33 Gould Rd, Lisbon Falls, ME 04252.

NATIONAL MARROW AWARENESS MONTH. Nov 1–30. More than 30,000 Americans are diagnosed each year with leukemia or another life-threatening blood disease for which a bone marrow or blood stem cell transplant offers hope for survival. The National Marrow Donor Program maintains a computerized registry of nearly 4,000,000 volunteer donors. For info: Natl Marrow Donor Program, 3001 Broadway St NE, Ste 500, Minneapolis, MN 55413-2197. Phone: (800) MAR-ROW2. Web: www.marrow.org.

OZARK MOUNTAIN CHRISTMAS/BRANSON AREA FESTIVAL OF LIGHTS. Nov 1–Dec 31. Branson, MO. A tradition for more than 1.4 million visitors, who relish the opportunity to celebrate a traditional Christmas ambiance with a dash of dazzle as only Branson can offer. The area is illuminated in twinkling lights, special holiday events and shows galore. For info: Branson Area CVB, PO Box 1897, Branson, MO 65615. Phone: (800) 296-0529. Fax: (417) 334-4139. E-mail: info@bransoncvb .com. Web: www.explorebranson.com.

PEANUT BUTTER LOVERS' MONTH. Nov 1–30. Celebration of America's favorite food and #1 sandwich. For info: Peanut Advisory Board, 1025 Sugar Pike Way, Canton, GA 30115. Web: www.peanutbutterlovers.com.

PRESIDENT OCCUPIES THE WHITE HOUSE: ANNIVERSARY. Nov 1, 1800. Philadelphia had served as the nation's capital from 1790 to 1800. On Nov 1, 1800, President John Adams and his family moved into the newly completed White House, as Washington, DC, became the new capital.

PRIME MERIDIAN SET: ANNIVERSARY. Nov 1, 1884. Delegates from 25 nations met in October at Washington, DC, at the International Meridian Conference to set up time zones for the world. On this day the treaty adopted by the Conference took effect, making Greenwich, England, the Prime Meridian (i.e., zero° longitude) and setting the International Date Line at 180° longitude in the Pacific. Every 15° of longitude equals one hour and there are 24 meridians. While some countries do not strictly observe this system (for example, while China stretches over five time zones, it is the same time everywhere in China) this system has brought predictability and logic to time throughout the world.

★ ★ ★

November 2004

S	M	T	W	T	F	S
	1	2	3	4	5	6
7	8	9	10	11	12	13
14	15	16	17	18	19	20
21	22	23	24	25	26	27
28	29	30				

US VIRGIN ISLANDS: LIBERTY DAY. Nov 1. Officially "D. Hamilton Jackson Memorial Day," commemorating establishment of the first press in the Virgin Islands in 1915.

VEGAN MONTH. Nov 1–30. This outreach event encourages everyone to GO VEGAN! Vegans choose to neither eat nor use any animal products (e.g., meat, poultry, seafood, dairy products, eggs, gelatin, leather, fur, etc). A growing number of caring, compassionate people are adopting this conscientious lifestyle. Primarily ethical reasons, but also health and environmental concerns, motivate them to GO VEGAN. For info: VEGANET, PO Box 3545, Washington, DC 20027-0045. Phone: (888) GO-VEGAN.

WORLD COMMUNICATION WEEK. Nov 1–7. To stress the importance of communication among the more than six billion human beings in the world who speak more than 3,000 languages and to promote communication by means of the international language, Esperanto. For complete info, send $5 to cover expense of printing, handling and postage. Annually, the first seven days of November. For info: Dr. Stanley Drake, Pres, Intl Society of Friendship and Goodwill, 999 Hood Rd, Ste 127, Marietta, GA 30068. Phone: (770) 565-2322. E-mail: ISFGW@bellsouth.net.

BIRTHDAYS TODAY

Toni Collette, 32, actress (*The Sixth Sense, About a Boy, Muriel's Wedding*), born Sidney, New South Wales, Australia, Nov 1, 1972.
Larry Claxton Flynt, 62, publisher, born Magoffin County, KY, Nov 1, 1942.
James Jackson Kilpatrick, 84, journalist (conservative side of "60 Minutes" Point-Counterpoint segment), born Oklahoma City, OK, Nov 1, 1920.
Lyle Lovett, 47, country and western singer ("Cowboy Man"), born Klein, TX, Nov 1, 1957.
Jenny McCarthy, 32, model, actress ("Jenny"), born Chicago, IL, Nov 1, 1972.
Betsy Palmer, 78, actress ("I've Got a Secret," "Knots Landing," "Today"), born Patricia Bromek, East Chicago, IN, Nov 1, 1926.
Tim Pawlenty, 44, Governor of Minnesota (R), born St. Paul, MN, Nov 1, 1960.
Gary Jim Player, 69, golfer, born Johannesburg, South Africa, Nov 1, 1935.
Rachel Ticotin, 46, actress (*Total Recall, Natural Born Killers*), born the Bronx, NY, Nov 1, 1958.
Fernando Anguamea Valenzuela, 44, former baseball player, born Navojoa, Sonora, Mexico, Nov 1, 1960.

NOVEMBER 2 — TUESDAY
Day 307 — 59 Remaining

ALL SOULS' DAY. Nov 2. Commemorates the faithful departed. Catholic observance.

BOONE, DANIEL: BIRTH ANNIVERSARY. Nov 2, 1734 (NS). American frontiersman, explorer and militia officer, born at Berks County, near Reading, PA. In February 1778, he was captured at Blue Licks, KY, by Shawnee Indians, under Chief Blackfish, who adopted Boone when he was inducted into the tribe as "Big Turtle." Boone escaped after five months, and in 1781 was captured briefly by the British. He experienced a series of personal and financial disasters during his life, but continued a rugged existence, hunting until his 80s. Boone died at St. Charles County, MO, Sept 26, 1820. The bodies of Daniel Boone and his wife, Rebecca, were moved to Frankfort, KY, in 1845.

★ Chase's 2004 Calendar of Events ★ Nov 2–3

FIRST SCHEDULED RADIO BROADCAST: ANNIVERSARY. Nov 2, 1920. Station KDKA at Pittsburgh, PA, broadcasted the results of the presidential election. The station got its license to broadcast Nov 7, 1921. By 1922 there were about 400 licensed radio stations in the US.

GENERAL ELECTION DAY. Nov 2. Annually, the first Tuesday after the first Monday in November. Many state and local government elections are held on this day, as well as presidential and congressional elections in the appropriate years. All US Congressional seats and one-third of US Senatorial seats are up for election in even-numbered years. Presidential elections are held in even-numbered years that can be divided equally by four. This day is a state holiday in 12 states.

HARDING, WARREN GAMALIEL: BIRTH ANNIVERSARY. Nov 2, 1865. Twenty-ninth president of the US was born at Corsica, OH. His term of office: Mar 4, 1921–Aug 2, 1923 (died in office). His undistinguished administration was tainted by the Teapot Dome scandal, and his sudden death in San Francisco, CA, while on a western speaking tour prompted many rumors.

LANCASTER, BURT: BIRTH ANNIVERSARY. Nov 2, 1913. Distinguished American actor, born Burton Stephen Lancaster, who began his career in show business as a circus acrobat. In a career spanning 45 years, he appeared in nearly 80 films. Some of his more memorable roles are in *From Here to Eternity* (1953), *The Bird Man of Alcatraz* (1962) and *The Leopard* (1963); he received an Academy Award for his performance in the title role of *Elmer Gantry* (1961). Some of his later popular movies include *Atlantic City* (1981), *Local Hero* (1983) and *Field of Dreams* (1989). Born at New York City, he died Oct 20, 1994, at Los Angeles.

NEW YORK SUBWAY ACCIDENT: ANNIVERSARY. Nov 2, 1918. The Brighton Beach Express, exceeding its speed limit five times over (going 30 mph) while approaching the station near Malbone Street tunnel at Brooklyn, jumped the tracks, killing 97 people and injuring 100. The supervisor-engineer, taking the place of a striking motorman of the Brotherhood of Locomotive Engineers, was tried and acquitted of charges of negligence.

NORTH DAKOTA: ADMISSION DAY: ANNIVERSARY. Nov 2. Became 39th state in 1889.

PLAN YOUR EPITAPH DAY. Nov 2. Dedicated to the proposition that a forgettable gravestone is a fate worse than death, and that everyone can be in the same league with William Shakespeare and W.C. Fields. Annually, coincides with the Day of the Dead. For info: Lance Hardie, Dead or Alive, PO Box 4595, Arcata, CA 95518. Phone: (707) 822-6924. E-mail: sunrise@hardiehouse.org. Web: www.hardiehouse.org/epitaph.

POLK, JAMES KNOX: BIRTH ANNIVERSARY. Nov 2, 1795. The 11th president of the US was born at Mecklenburg County, NC. His term of office: Mar 4, 1845–Mar 3, 1849. A compromise candidate at the 1844 Democratic Party convention, Polk was awarded the nomination on the ninth ballot. He declined to be a candidate for a second term and declared himself to be "exceedingly relieved" at the completion of his presidency. He died shortly thereafter at Nashville, TN, June 15, 1849.

SENECA FALLS CONVENTION SURVIVOR VOTES: ANNIVERSARY. Nov 2, 1920. The only woman who attended the historic Seneca Falls Women's Rights Convention in 1848 who lived long enough to exercise her right to vote under the 19th Amendment, Charlotte Woodward voted at Philadelphia in the general election Nov 2, 1920.

SOUTH DAKOTA: ADMISSION DAY: ANNIVERSARY. Nov 2. Became 40th state in 1889.

SPACE MILESTONE: INTERNATIONAL SPACE STATION INHABITED. Nov 2, 2000. On Oct 31, 2000, a *Soyuz* shuttle left with the first crew to live in the International Space Station, consisting of American commander Bill Shepherd and two Russians cosmonauts. The flight left from the same site in Central Asia where *Sputnik* was launched in 1957, beginning the Space Age. The astronauts stayed on board the International Space Station (ISS) until March, 2001, when they were replaced by a crew that arrived on the shuttle *Discovery*. Sixteen nations are participating in the ISS project. The construction of the station will be complete in 2006.

SPRUCE GOOSE FLIGHT: ANNIVERSARY. Nov 2, 1947. The mammoth flying boat *Hercules*, then the world's largest airplane, was designed, built and flown (once) by Howard Hughes. Its first and only flight was about one mile and at an altitude of 70 feet over Long Beach Harbor, CA. The $25 million, 200-ton plywood craft was nicknamed the "Spruce Goose." It is now housed at the Evergreen Aviation Museum in McMinnville, OR.

BIRTHDAYS TODAY

Patrick Buchanan, 66, political columnist, born Washington, DC, Nov 2, 1938.
Shere Hite, 62, author (*The Hite Report, Women and Love*), born St. Joseph, MO, Nov 2, 1942.
k.d. lang, 43, singer, born Kathryn Dawn Lang, Consort, AB, Canada, Nov 2, 1961.
Stefanie Powers, 62, actress ("Hart to Hart"), born Hollywood, CA, Nov 2, 1942.
David Knapp (Dave) Stockton, 63, golfer, born San Bernardino, CA, Nov 2, 1941.

NOVEMBER 3 — WEDNESDAY
Day 308 — 58 Remaining

AUSTIN, STEPHEN FULLER: BIRTH ANNIVERSARY. Nov 3, 1793. A principal founder of Texas, for whom its capital city was named, Austin was born at Wythe County, VA. He first visited Texas in 1821 and established a settlement there the following year, continuing a colonization project started by his father, Moses Austin. Thrown in prison when he advocated formation of a separate state (Texas still belonged to Mexico), he was freed in 1835, lost a campaign for the presidency (of the Republic of Texas) to Sam Houston (q.v.) in 1836, and died (while serving as Texas secretary of state) at Austin, TX, Dec 27, 1836.

BRYANT, WILLIAM CULLEN: BIRTH ANNIVERSARY. Nov 3, 1794. American poet (*Thanatopsis*), born at Cummington, MA. Died at New York, NY, June 12, 1878.

CANADA: BANFF MOUNTAIN BOOK FESTIVAL. Nov 3–5. Banff, AB. An international mountain book competition that features guest speakers, readings, seminars, book signings, book launches and a book fair. Est attendance: 3,000. For info: Banff Mountain Book Festival, Banff Centre, Box 1020, Banff, AB, Canada T1L 1H5. Phone: (403) 762-6369. Fax: (403) 762-6277. E-mail: banffmountainbooks@banffcentre.ca. Web: www.banffmountainfestivals.ca.

CANADA: NEW INUIT TERRITORY APPROVED: ANNIVERSARY. Nov 3, 1992. Canada's Inuit people voted to accept a federal land-claim package granting them control over a new territory, Nunavut, to be carved out of the existing Northwest Territories by 1999. The voting on Nov 3–5, 1992, indicated that 69 percent of the 9,648 eligible Inuit voters accepted the settlement. In exchange for the new territory, approximately 135,000 square miles, the Inuits gave up their rights to a territory of 775,000 square miles. See also: "Canada: Nunavut Independence" (Apr 1).

567

☆ Chase's 2004 Calendar of Events ☆

Nov 3–4

CLICHÉ DAY. Nov 3. Use clichés as much as possible today. Hey, why not? Give it a shot! Win some, lose some. You'll never know 'til you try it. Annually, Nov 3. [©2003 by WH.] For info: Thomas & Ruth Roy, Wellcat Holidays, 2418 Long Ln, Lebanon, PA 17046-1708. Phone: (717) 279-0184. E-mail: info@wellcat.com. Web: www.wellcat.com.

"DEWEY DEFEATS TRUMAN" HEADLINE: ANNIVERSARY. Nov 3, 1948. This headline in the *Chicago Tribune* notwithstanding, Harry Truman defeated Republican candidate Thomas E. Dewey for the US presidency.

DOMINICA: NATIONAL DAY: ANNIVERSARY. Nov 3. National holiday. Commemorates independence from Britain in 1978.

JAPAN: CULTURE DAY. Nov 3. National holiday.

MICRONESIA, FEDERATED STATES OF: INDEPENDENCE DAY. Nov 3. National holiday commemorating independence from US in 1980.

NAGURSKI, BRONKO: BIRTH ANNIVERSARY. Nov 3, 1908. Bronislau ("Bronko") Nagurski, College Football Hall of Fame and charter member of the Pro Football Hall of Fame. Born at Rainy River, Ontario, Canada, he played football at the University of Minnesota, earning All-American honors at both tackle and fullback, and for the Chicago Bears. After retiring from football, Nagurski wrestled professionally. He died at International Falls, MN, Jan 7, 1990.

NATIONAL ASSOCIATION FOR GIFTED CHILDREN CONVENTION. Nov 3–7. Salt Lake City, UT. Educational sessions for administrators, counselors, coordinators, teachers and parents. Est attendance: 4,000. For info: Natl Assn for Gifted Children, 1707 L St NW, Ste 550, Washington, DC 20036. Phone: (202) 785-4268.

PANAMA: INDEPENDENCE DAY: ANNIVERSARY. Nov 3. Independence Day. Panama declared itself independent of Colombia in 1903.

PUBLIC TELEVISION DEBUTS: 35th ANNIVERSARY. Nov 3, 1969. A string of local educational TV channels united on this day under the Public Broadcasting System banner. Today there are more than 350 PBS stations.

SANDWICH DAY: BIRTH ANNIVERSARY OF JOHN MONTAGUE. Nov 3, 1718. A day to recognize the inventor of the sandwich, John Montague, Fourth Earl of Sandwich, born at London, England. England's first lord of the admiralty, secretary of state for the northern department, postmaster general and the man after whom Captain Cook named the Sandwich Islands in 1778. A rake and a gambler, he is said to have invented the sandwich as a time-saving nourishment while engaged in a 24-hour-long gambling session in 1762. He died at London, England, Apr 30, 1792.

SPACE MILESTONE: *SPUTNIK 2* (USSR). Nov 3, 1957. A dog named Laika became the first animal sent into space. Total weight of craft and dog was 1,121 lbs. The satellite was not capable of returning the dog to Earth and she died when her air supply was gone. Nicknamed "Muttnik" by the American press.

WHITE, EDWARD DOUGLASS: BIRTH ANNIVERSARY. Nov 3, 1845. Ninth Chief Justice of the Supreme Court, born at La Fourche Parish, LA. During the Civil War, he served in the Confederate Army after which he returned to New Orleans to practice law. Elected to the US Senate in 1891, he was appointed to the Supreme Court by Grover Cleveland in 1894. He became Chief Justice under President William Taft in 1910 and served until 1921. He died at Washington, DC, May 19, 1921.

November 2004	S	M	T	W	T	F	S
		1	2	3	4	5	6
	7	8	9	10	11	12	13
	14	15	16	17	18	19	20
	21	22	23	24	25	26	27
	28	29	30				

BIRTHDAYS TODAY

Adam Ant, 50, singer ("Goody Two Shoes"), born Stewart Goddard, London, England, Nov 3, 1954.
Ken Berry, 71, actor ("F Troop," "Mayberry RFD," "Mama's Family"), singer, dancer, born Moline, IL, Nov 3, 1933.
Charles Bronson, 82, actor (*The Dirty Dozen, Death Wish*), born Charles Buchinsky, Ehrenfeld, PA, Nov 3, 1922.
Kate Capshaw, 51, actress ("Duke of Groove," *How to Make an American Quilt*), born Fort Worth, TX, Nov 3, 1953.
Michael S. Dukakis, 71, former Governor of Massachusetts (D), 1988 presidential candidate, born Brookline, MA, Nov 3, 1933.
Robert William Andrew (Bob) Feller, 86, Hall of Fame baseball player, born Van Meter, IA, Nov 3, 1918.
Kathy Kinney, 50, actress ("The Drew Carey Show"), born Stevens Point, WI, Nov 3, 1954.
Steve Landesberg, 59, actor ("Barney Miller," "Friends and Lovers"), born the Bronx, NY, Nov 3, 1945.
Dolph Lundgren, 45, actor (*A View to a Kill, Rocky IV*), born Stockholm, Sweden, Nov 3, 1959.
Dennis Miller, 51, comedian, actor ("Saturday Night Live," "The Dennis Miller Show"), born Pittsburgh, PA, Nov 3, 1953.
Evgeny Plushenko, 22, figure skater, born Vologograd, Russia, Nov 3, 1982.
Roseanne, 51, comedienne, actress ("Roseanne," *She-Devil*), born Roseanne Barr, Salt Lake City, UT, Nov 3, 1953.
Philip (Phil) Simms, 48, sportscaster, former football player, born Lebanon, KY, Nov 3, 1956.
Monica Vitti, 71, actress (*The Red Desert*), born Monica Luisa Ceciarelli, Rome, Italy, Nov 3, 1933.

NOVEMBER 4 — THURSDAY
Day 309 — 57 Remaining

BALSAM, MARTIN: 85th BIRTH ANNIVERSARY. Nov 4, 1919. Actor ("Archie Bunker's Place," *Twelve Angry Men*), born at New York, NY. Died at Rome, Italy, Feb 13, 1996.

BIG TEN WOMEN'S SOCCER TOURNAMENT. Nov 4–7. Ohio State University, Columbus, OH. Est attendance: 1,000. For info: Sue Lister, Big Ten Conference, 1500 W Higgins Rd, Park Ridge, IL 60068-6300. Phone: (847) 696-1010. Fax: (847) 696-1110. Web: www.bigten.org.

BUSH, LAURA: BIRTHDAY. Nov 4, 1946. First Lady, wife of President George W. Bush, born Laura Welch at Midland, TX.

INTERNATIONAL GIFT FESTIVAL. Nov 4–6. Fairfield, PA. Traditional handcrafts from more than 30 countries. Est attendance: 4,500. For info: Gettysburg CVB, PO Box 4117, Gettysburg, PA 17325. Phone: (717) 334-6274. Fax: (717) 334-1166. E-mail: gettysburgcvb@dejazzd.com. Web: www.gettysburgcvb.org.

ITALY: VICTORY DAY. Nov 4. Commemorates the signing of a WWI treaty by Austria in 1918, which resulted in the transfer of Trentino and Trieste from Austria to Italy.

KING TUT TOMB DISCOVERY: ANNIVERSARY. Nov 4, 1922. In 1922, one of the most important archaeological discoveries of modern times occurred at Luxor, Egypt. It was the tomb of Egypt's child-king, Tutankhamen, who became pharaoh at the age of nine and died, probably in the year 1352 BC, when he was 19. Perhaps the only ancient Egyptian royal tomb to have escaped plundering by grave robbers, it was discovered more than 3,000 years after Tutankhamen's death by English archaeologist Howard Carter, leader of an expedition financed by Lord Carnarvon. The priceless relics yielded by King Tut's tomb were placed in Egypt's National Museum at Cairo.

☆ Chase's 2004 Calendar of Events ☆ Nov 4–5

MAPPLETHORPE, ROBERT: BIRTH ANNIVERSARY. Nov 4, 1946. Born at Floral Park, NY, Mapplethorpe was one of photography's most controversial artists, known initially for his photographs of sadomasochistic rituals and later for his still lifes, nudes and portraits. Mapplethorpe died at Boston, Mar 9, 1989. Exhibits of his work sparked controversy in 1989 and 1990, leading to intense political debate about the funding practices of the National Endowment for the Arts when its charter was up for renewal by Congress. An exhibition of his work in Cincinnati led to the arrest of the museum's curator, causing an additional uproar over First Amendment freedoms and obscenity issues.

MISCHIEF NIGHT. Nov 4. Observed in England, Australia and New Zealand. Nov 4, the eve of Guy Fawkes Day, is occasion for bonfires and firecrackers to commemorate failure of the plot to blow up the Houses of Parliament Nov 5, 1605. See also: "England: Guy Fawkes Day" (Nov 5).

NATIONAL CHICKEN LADY DAY. Nov 4. Miami Shores, FL. The Chicken Lady has helped thousands to learn the art of public speaking through her nonprofit organization The Professional Speakers Network, Inc. Each year as a thank-you, people come out and have a celebration to show their appreciation for what she has done to help them. Forty-three of them, thanks to the Chicken Lady, have published their own books. For info: Dr. Marthenia "Tina" Dupree, The Chicken Lady, PO Box 540821, Ofa Locka, FL 33054. Phone: (305) 759-7655. Fax: (305) 759-7656. E-mail: chickenlady@prodigy.net. Web: www.thechickenlady.com.

NATIONAL MEN MAKE DINNER DAY. Nov 4. One day set aside for "Non-Cooking Men Only" in the kitchen. Give wives a break and let the men whip up some culinary delight with no help from family members. In the true spirit of Men Make Dinner Day, barbecues are not allowed! For info: Sandy Sharkey, KOOL FM Radio, 87 George St, Ottawa, ON, Canada K1N 9H7. Phone: (613) 738-2372. Fax: (613) 739-4040. E-mail: ssharkey@planetkool.com. Web: www.menmakedinnerday.com.

PANAMA: FLAG DAY. Nov 4. Public holiday.

PHILLPOTTS, EDEN: BIRTH ANNIVERSARY. Nov 4, 1862. English novelist, poet and playwright, born at Mount Abu, Rajasthan, India. A friend of Arnold Bennett, Phillpotts wrote more than a hundred novels. He died near Exeter, England, Dec 29, 1960.

RETURN DAY. Nov 4. Georgetown, DE. The day when officially tabulated election returns are read from the balcony of Georgetown's red brick, Greek Revival courthouse to the throngs of voters assembled below. Always the second day after a general election. An official "half-holiday" in Sussex County. Reportedly Return Day has become so popular "that it is for all intents and purposes a state holiday as well."

ROGERS, WILL: 125th BIRTH ANNIVERSARY. Nov 4, 1879. William Penn Adair Rogers, American writer, actor, humorist and grassroots philosopher, born at Oologah, Indian Territory (now Oklahoma). With aviator Wiley Post, he was killed in an airplane crash near Point Barrow, AK, Aug 15, 1935. "My forefathers," he said, "didn't come over on the *Mayflower*, but they met the boat."

SEIZURE OF US EMBASSY IN TEHERAN: 25th ANNIVERSARY. Nov 4, 1979. About 500 Iranians seized the US Embassy in Teheran, taking some 90 hostages, of whom about 60 were Americans. They vowed to hold the hostages until the former Shah, Mohammed Reza Pahlavi (in the US for medical treatments), was returned to Iran for trial. The Shah died July 27, 1980, in an Egyptian military hospital near Cairo. The remaining 52 American hostages were released and left Teheran on Jan 20, 1981, after 444 days of captivity. The release occurred on America's Presidential Inauguration Day, during the hour in which the American presidency was transferred from Jimmy Carter to Ronald Reagan.

UNESCO: ANNIVERSARY. Nov 4, 1946. The United Nations Educational, Scientific and Cultural Organization was formed.

VIRGINIA CHRISTMAS SHOW. Nov 4–7. Showplace Exhibition Center, Richmond, VA 19th annual show featuring 450 artisans and crafters, Christmas gourmet food shops and Christmas Holiday Theatre, entertainment, legendary "Sgt Santa." Est attendance: 40,000. For info: Virginia Show Productions, PO Box 305, Chase City, VA 23924. Phone: (434) 372-3996. Fax: (434) 372-3410. E-mail: vashowsinc@aol.com.

WILL ROGERS DAY. Nov 4. Oklahoma.

BIRTHDAYS TODAY

Laura Bush, 58, First Lady, wife of George W. Bush, 43rd president of the US, born Midland, TX, Nov 4, 1946.
Art Carney, 86, actor (Oscar for *Harry and Tonto*; six Emmys for "The Honeymooners"), born Mount Vernon, NY, Nov 4, 1918.
Sean ("Puffy") Combs, 34, rapper known as Puff Daddy, born New York, NY, Nov 4, 1970.
Walter Leland Cronkite, Jr, 88, journalist (former anchor for "CBS Evening News"), born St. Joseph, MO, Nov 4, 1916.
Kathy Griffin, 38, comedienne, actress ("Suddenly Susan"), born Chicago, IL, Nov 4, 1966.
Ralph Macchio, 42, actor ("Eight Is Enough," *The Karate Kid*), born Huntington, NY, Nov 4, 1962.
Andrea McArdle, 41, singer, actress (Broadway's *Annie*), born Philadelphia, PA, Nov 4, 1963.
Matthew McConaughey, 35, actor (*Dazed and Confused, A Time to Kill*), born Uvalde, TX, Nov 4, 1969.
Orlando Pace, 29, football player, born Sandusky, OH, Nov 4, 1975.
Markie Post, 54, actress ("Night Court," "Hearts Afire"), born Palo Alto, CA, Nov 4, 1950.
Doris Roberts, 74, actress ("Everybody Loves Raymond," "Remington Steele"), born St. Louis, MO, Nov 4, 1930.
Loretta Swit, 67, actress ("M*A*S*H"), born Passaic, NJ, Nov 4, 1937.

NOVEMBER 5 — FRIDAY
Day 310 — 56 Remaining

BIG TEN FIELD HOCKEY TOURNAMENT. Nov 5–7. Michigan State University, East Lansing, MI. Est attendance: 1,000. For info: Sue Lister, Big Ten Conference, 1500 W Higgins Rd, Park Ridge, IL 60068-6300. Phone: (847) 696-1010. Fax: (847) 696-1110. Web: www.bigten.org.

BRANSON VETERANS HOMECOMING 2004. Nov 5–11. Branson, MO. An areawide celebration honoring America's veterans. Annually, the first seven days in November ending with the 11th. Est attendance: 50,000. For info: Bill Groninger, Branson Veterans Task Force, PO Box 1726, Branson, MO 65615. Phone: (417) 593-1072. E-mail: bvtf@sofnet.com. Web: www.bransonveterans.com.

BRUMOS CONTINENTAL HISTORICS/GRAND AMERICAN FINALE. Nov 5–7. Daytona International Speedway, Daytona Beach, FL. For info: Daytona Intl Speedway, PO Box 2801, Daytona Beach, FL 32120-2801. Phone: (386) 253-7223. Fax: (386) 947-6791. Web: www.daytonainternationalspeedway.com.

569

CANADA: BANFF MOUNTAIN FILM FESTIVAL. Nov 5–7. Banff, AB. The 29th annual festival brings the best films and videos on mountain subjects to the town of Banff. The weekend's activities, which take place at The Banff Centre, include continuous film screenings, guest speakers, public forums on mountain issues, a climbing wall, adventure fair, trade fair and a mountain art and craft sale. Presented by Eagle Creek and National Geographic. Est attendance: 8,000. For info: Deb Smythe, Fest Mgr, Mountain Film Festival, PO Box 1020, Station 38, Banff, AB, Canada T1L 1H5. Phone: (403) 762-6125. Fax: (403) 762-6277. E-mail: mountainculture@banffcentre.ca. Web: www.banffmountainfestivals.ca.

CHRISTMAS MAGIC. Nov 5–7. Multi-Purpose Events Center, Wichita Falls, TX. "A Christmas marketplace," with vendors from Texas and other states. Food, gift items, arts and crafts, entertainment. Est attendance: 10,000. For info: Wichita Falls CVB, 1000 5th St, Wichita Falls, TX 76301. Phone: (940) 716-5500 or (800) 799-6732. Fax: (940) 716-5509. E-mail: MPEC@wf.net. Web: www.wichitafalls.org.

CRAFTSMEN'S CHRISTMAS CLASSIC ARTS & CRAFTS FESTIVAL. Nov 5–7. Richmond Raceway Complex, Richmond, VA. Features work from more than 500 talented artists and craftspeople. All juried exhibitors' work has been handmade by the exhibitors and must be their own original design and creation. See the creative process in action with several exhibitors demonstrating their craft. Visit Christmas Tree Village to view the uniquely decorated Christmas Trees by some of our exhibitors. Something for every style, taste and budget with items from the most contemporary to the most traditional. Est attendance: 35,000. For info: Gilmore Enterprises Inc, 1240 Oakland Ave, Greensboro, NC 27403. Phone: (336) 274-5550. E-mail: gilmoreshows@triad.rr.com.

DEAR SANTA LETTER WEEK. Nov 5–9. Consumer advocate Bob O'Brien answers "Dear Santa" letters for the holiday season. For info: Bob O'Brien, Consumer Advocate, 1061 Koelle Blvd, Secaucus, NJ 07094. Phone: (201) 860-1595. Fax: (201) 865-4775. E-mail: bobthebestthebest@yahoo.com.

DEBS, EUGENE VICTOR: BIRTH ANNIVERSARY. Nov 5, 1855. American politician, first president of the American Railway Union, founder of the Social Democratic Party of America, and Socialist Party candidate for president of the US in 1904, 1908, 1912 and 1920, sentenced to 10-year prison term in 1918 (for sedition) and pardoned by President Harding in 1921. Debs was born at Terre Haute, IN, and died at Elmhurst, IL, Oct 20, 1926.

DURANT, WILL: BIRTH ANNIVERSARY. Nov 5, 1885. American author and popularizer of history and philosophy. Among his books: *The Story of Philosophy* and *The Story of Civilization* (a 10-volume series of which the last four were coauthored by his wife, Ariel). Born at North Adams, MA, and died Nov 7, 1981, at Los Angeles, CA.

EL SALVADOR: DAY OF THE FIRST SHOUT FOR INDEPENDENCE. Nov 5. National holiday. Commemorates the first Central American battle for independence in 1811.

ENGLAND: GUY FAWKES DAY. Nov 5. United Kingdom. Anniversary of the "Gunpowder Plot." Conspirators planned to blow up the Houses of Parliament and King James I, Nov 5, 1605 (OS). Twenty barrels of gunpowder, which they had secreted in a cellar under Parliament, were discovered on the night of Nov 4, the very eve of the intended explosion, and the conspirators were arrested. They were tried and convicted, and Jan 31, 1606, eight (including Guy Fawkes) were beheaded and their heads displayed on pikes at London Bridge. Though there were at least 11 conspirators, Guy Fawkes is most remembered. In 1606, the Parliament, which was to have been annihilated, enacted a law establishing Nov 5 as a day of public thanksgiving. It is still observed, and on the night of Nov 5, "the whole country lights up with bonfires and celebration." "Guys" are burned in effigy and the old verses repeated: "Remember, remember the fifth of November,/ Gunpowder treason and plot;/I see no reason why Gunpowder Treason/Should ever be forgot."

GEORGE W. AND LAURA BUSH WEDDING: ANNIVERSARY. Nov 5, 1977. George W. Bush and Laura Welch were married at Midland, TX. They have twin daughters, Barbara Pierce Bush and Jenna Welch Bush, born in 1981.

GREAT AMERICAN WARM-UP. Nov 5–7. Just as the weather outside begins to change, this weekend is set aside to clean out those closets and take your warm, wearable coats, jackets, scarves, hats and mittens that you no longer use and donate them to a homeless shelter or agency for distribution. Do it now, before it gets even colder outside. Annually, the second full weekend in November. [© 1995] To alleviate the escalating costs of Eventological® Literature, a charge of $7 must be assessed for each request. Checks are to be made payable to: Adrienne Sioux Koopersmith, 1437 W Rosemont, #1W, Chicago, IL 60660-1319. Phone: (773) 743-5341. Fax: (773) 743-5395. E-mail: la_koop@yahoo.com.

GREAT NY STATE SNOW & TRAVEL EXPO. Nov 5–7. Empire State Plaza, Albany, NY. Top-of-the-line equipment, apparel and destinations for the outdoor winter sports enthusiast. Annually, the first full weekend in November. Sponsor: Alpine Haus. Est attendance: 20,000. For info: Candace Stazio, Ed Lewi Assoc, 6 Chelsea Pl, Clifton Park, NY 12065. Phone: (518) 383-6183. Fax: (518) 383-6755. Web: www.edlewi.com.

GREATER PITTSBURGH ARTS & CRAFTS HOLIDAY SPECTACULAR. Nov 5–7. Expo Center at Greengate Mall, Greensburg, PA. Approximately 200 booths including pottery, jewelry, quilts, furniture, tole and decorative painting, leather, toys and much more. Find that perfect gift for the holidays. Est attendance: 21,000. For info: Debbie & Dave Stoner, PO Box 166, Irwin, PA 15642. Phone: (724) 863-4577. Fax: (724) 863-4577. E-mail: familyfestivals@hotmail.com. Web: www.familyfestivals.com.

HOLIDAY MARKET. Nov 5–7. Greensboro Coliseum Complex Special Events Center, Greensboro, NC. 14th annual commercial holiday gift show. Celebrate the season at Holiday Market, a true feast for all the senses. Of course there is shopping with a capital SHOP! Enjoy the singing of the Victorian-costumed strolling carolers and let the children visit with Santa. You'll come away with ideas, recipes, samples, beauty makeovers and lots of holiday gifts and ideas. Est attendance: 25,000. For info: Gilmore Enterprises, Inc, 1240 Oakland Ave, Greensboro, NC 27403. Phone: (336) 274-5550. E-mail: gilmoreshows@triad.rr.com.

LAILAT UL QADR: THE NIGHT OF POWER. Nov 5 (also Nov 7, 9, 11 or 13). "The Night of Power" falls on one of the last

	S	M	T	W	T	F	S
November 2004		1	2	3	4	5	6
	7	8	9	10	11	12	13
	14	15	16	17	18	19	20
	21	22	23	24	25	26	27
	28	29	30				

10 days of Ramadan on an odd-numbered night (Islamic calendar dates: Ramadan 21, 23, 25, 27 or 29, 1425). It commemorates the night of the first revelation of the Holy Qur'an to Muhammad by the angel Gabriel. The Holy Qur'an states that praying on this night is better than praying 1,000 months. Since it is not known which day it is, Muslims feel it is best to pray on each of the possible nights. Different methods for "anticipating" the visibility of the new moon crescent at Mecca are used by different Muslim sects or groups. US date may vary.

LOEWY, RAYMOND: BIRTH ANNIVERSARY. Nov 5, 1893. Raymond Fernand Loewy, the "father of streamlining," an inventor, engineer and industrial designer whose ideas changed the look of 20th-century life, was born at Paris, France. His designs are evident in almost every area of modern life—the US Postal Service logo, the president's airplane, *Air Force One*, in streamlined automobiles, trains, refrigerators and pens. "Between two products equal in price, function and quality," he said, "the better looking will outsell the other." Loewy died at Monte Carlo, July 14, 1986.

MAXWELL, ROBERT: DEATH ANNIVERSARY. Nov 5, 1991. Media mogul Robert Maxwell's mysterious death added more controversy to his already controversial and intriguing larger-than-life story. Born Jan Ludwig Hoch to a poor farm family in the Carpathian mountains of Czechoslovakia, he ended his life a billionaire with a media empire that included TV stations in France, Macmillan Publishing Company in the US, newspapers in Hungary and the former East Germany, MTV Europe, the only official English language newspaper in China and two of the biggest tabloids in the English-speaking world: New York's *Daily News* and London's *Daily Mirror*. He earned his first million publishing scientific books. After a brief career as a member of Parliament, he began his rise as a media baron. Maxwell died after falling overboard from his yacht near the Canary Islands. After his death, his empire was found to be in significant financial disrepair.

McCREA, JOEL: BIRTH ANNIVERSARY. Nov 5, 1905. American actor Joel McCrea was born at South Pasadena, CA. His more than 80 films include *Wells Fargo* (1937), *Union Pacific* (1939), *Sullivan's Travels* (1941) and *Foreign Correspondent* (1940). He died Oct 20, 1990, at Los Angeles, CA.

MOON PHASE: LAST QUARTER. Nov 5. Moon enters Last Quarter phase at 12:53 AM, EST.

"THE NAT KING COLE SHOW" TV PREMIERE: ANNIVERSARY. Nov 5, 1956. Popular African-American pianist and singer Cole hosted his own variety show for NBC. The Nelson Riddle Orchestra and the Randy Van Horne Singers also appeared as regulars on the show. It began as a 15-minute show which was expanded to half an hour. The show was dropped as a result of lack of sponsorship and because many affiliates declined to carry it.

NATIONAL FARM TOY SHOW. Nov 5–7. Beckman HS and National Farm Toy Museum, The Commercial Club Park, Dyersville, IA. This "granddaddy" of farm toy shows features tours of farm toy manufacturers, auction, craft bazaar, pedal pull and more than 200 vendors dealing in farm toys and implements. Annually, the first full weekend in November. For info: Dyersville Area Chamber of Commerce, 1100 16th Ave Ct SE, Dyersville, IA 52040. Phone: (563) 875-2311. Fax: (563) 875-8391. E-mail: dyersvillechamber@dyersville.org. Web: www.dyersville.org.

NEW YORK WEEKLY JOURNAL: FIRST ISSUE ANNIVERSARY. Nov 5, 1733. John Peter Zenger, colonial American printer and journalist, published the first issue of the *New York Weekly Journal* newspaper. He was arrested and imprisoned on Nov 17, 1734, for libel. The trial remains an important landmark in the history of the struggle for freedom of the press. See also: "Zenger, John Peter: Arrest Anniversary" (Nov 17).

PACIFIC DANCESPORT CHAMPIONSHIPS. Nov 5–7. Los Angeles, CA. Launched in 1990, the Pacific DanceSport Championships, which is a part of the DanceSport Super Bowl Series, captures the best that ballroom has to offer. It is now considered one of the most prestigious and largest ballroom dance events west of the Mississippi. Competitiors arrive from around the world to vie for a $75,000 purse. For info: A. Marashi, Pacific DanceSport Championships, 924 Bellevue Way NE, Ste 200, Bellevue, WA 98004. Phone: (425) 688-1010 or (877) 553-5735. Fax: (425) 688-7484. E-mail: info@pacificdancesport.com. Web: www.pacificdancesport.com.

ROGERS, ROY: BIRTH ANNIVERSARY. Nov 5, 1912. Known as the "King of the Cowboys," Rogers was born Leonard Slye at Cincinnati, OH. His many songs included "Don't Fence Me In" and "Happy Trails to You." He made his acting debut in *Under Western Stars* in 1935 and later hosted his own show, "The Roy Rogers Show," in 1951. Rogers died at Apple Valley, CA, July 6, 1998. See also: "'The Roy Rogers Show' TV Premiere: Anniversary" (Dec 30).

SAMOA: ARBOR DAY. Nov 5. The first Friday in November is observed as Arbor Day in Samoa (formerly Western Samoa).

TARBELL, IDA M.: BIRTH ANNIVERSARY. Nov 5, 1857. American writer born at Erie County, PA. She edited the muckraking journal *McClure's Magazine*, which exposed the political and industrial corruption of the day and emphasized the need for reform. Died at Bethel, CT, Jan 6, 1944.

WALSH INVITATIONAL RIFLE TOURNAMENT. Nov 5–7 (also Nov 12–14 and 19–21, tentative). Xavier University, Cincinnati, OH. To promote marksmanship and sportsmanship in the competitive spirit of collegiate athletics. International smallbore rifle and air rifle match open to all competitors. Recognized as "the largest indoor rifle match in the nation." Sponsor: Xavier University Athletic Department. Est attendance: 300. For info: Pete Holterman, Office of Sports Info, Dept of Athletics, Xavier Univ, 3800 Victory Pkwy, Cincinnati, OH 45207-7530. Fax: (513) 745-2825.

BIRTHDAYS TODAY

Bryan Adams, 45, singer ("Heaven," "Summer of '69"), songwriter ("Everything I Do"), born Vancouver, BC, Canada, Nov 5, 1959.
Arthur (Art) Garfunkel, 63, singer (Simon and Garfunkel), actor (*Carnal Knowledge*), born Forest Hills, NY, Nov 5, 1941.
Ted Kulongoski, 64, Governor of Oregon (D), born in rural Missouri, Nov 5, 1940.
Javy Lopez, 34, baseball player, born Ponce, Puerto Rico, Nov 5, 1970.
Corin Nemec, 33, actor ("Parker Lewis Can't Lose," *Tucker: The Man and His Dream*), born Little Rock, AR, Nov 5, 1971.
Tatum O'Neal, 41, actress (Oscar for *Paper Moon*; *Bad News Bears*), born Los Angeles, CA, Nov 5, 1963.
Sam Shepard, 61, dramatist, actor (*Buried Child*, *The Right Stuff*), born Samuel Shepard Rogers, Ft Sheridan, IL, Nov 5, 1943.
Elke Sommer, 63, actress (*A Shot in the Dark*, *The Prize*), born Elke Schletze, Berlin, Germany, Nov 5, 1941.
Jerry Stackhouse, 30, basketball player, born Kinston, NC, Nov 5, 1974.
Ike Turner, 73, singer (Ike and Tina Turner Revue), born Clarksdale, MS, Nov 5, 1931.
Bill Walton, 52, broadcaster, Hall of Fame basketball player, born Mesa, CA, Nov 5, 1952.
Geoffrey Wolff, 67, author (*The Duke of Deception*, *The Age of Consent*), born Los Angeles, CA, Nov 5, 1937.

NOVEMBER 6 — SATURDAY
Day 311 — 55 Remaining

DOWNTOWN FESTIVAL AND ART SHOW. Nov 6–7. Downtown Gainesville, FL. 23rd annual. 240 fine artists display one-of-a-kind art for purchase. Two full days of live music on three stages, children's activity area, food vendors, hands-on art opportunities. Est attendance: 100,000. For info: Linda Piper, City of Gainesville, Dept of Cultural Affairs, PO Box 490, Gainesville, FL 32602. Phone: (352) 334-5064. Fax: (352) 334-2249. E-mail: piperLr@ci.gainesville.fl.us. Web: www.gvlculturalaffairs.org.

FALL COUNTRY JAMBOREE. Nov 6–7. Pioneer Settlement for the Creative Arts, Barberville, FL. A celebration of pioneer life and food. More than 100 demonstrating craftsmen and tradesmen, three continuous musical stages featuring more than 75 noted artists. Historical displays include Indian and Cracker camps, antique autos, turpentine stills, flywheelers and model railroaders. For info: Pioneer Settlement for the Creative Arts, PO Box 6, Barberville, FL 32105. Phone: (386) 749-2959.

"GOOD MORNING AMERICA" TV PREMIERE: ANNIVERSARY. Nov 6, 1975. This ABC morning program, set in a living room, is a mixture of news reports, features and interviews with newsmakers and people of interest. It was the first program to compete with NBC's "Today" show and initially aired as "A.M. America." Hosts have included David Hartman, Nancy Dussault, Sandy Hill, Charles Gibson, Joan Lunden, Lisa McRee, Kevin Newman and Diane Sawyer.

HALFWAY POINT OF AUTUMN. Nov 6. On this day at 9:06 AM EST, 44 days, 21 hours and 36 minutes of autumn will have elapsed and the equivalent will remain before Dec 21, 2004, which is the winter solstice and the beginning of winter.

INTERNATIONAL END GOSSIP DAY. Nov 6. A day in which everyone is asked to not gossip (engage in any negative or hurtful communications) for at least this one day. For info: Bob Burg, PO Box 7002, Jupiter, FL 33468-7002. Phone: (561) 575-2114. Fax: (561) 575-2304. E-mail: bob@burg.com. Web: www.EndGossip.com.

INTERNATIONAL TONGUE TWISTER CONTEST. Nov 6. Burlington, WI. Classic and modern phrases plus poems will twist the tongues of everyone. The question is "how long can you go?" Prizes and smiles from the rest of us, to the winners. For info: Hall of Logic Puzzles Museum, 533 Milwaukee Ave (Hwy 36), Burlington, WI 53105. Phone: (262) 763-3946.

LOVINGTON FALL ARTS AND CRAFTS FESTIVAL. Nov 6–7. Lea County Fairgrounds, Lovington, NM. Displays from more than 100 local and regional crafters. No commercially manufactured items allowed. 27th annual festival. Annually, the first weekend in November. Est attendance: 10,000. For info: Lovington Chamber of Commerce, 201 S Main St, Lovington, NM 88260. Phone: (505) 396-5311. Fax: (505) 396-2823. E-mail: visitus@leaconet.com. Web: visitus.leaco.net.

"MEET THE PRESS" TV PREMIERE: ANNIVERSARY. Nov 6, 1947. "Meet the Press" holds the distinction of being the oldest program on TV. It originally debuted on radio in 1945. The show has changed its format little since it began: a well-known guest (usually a politician) is questioned on current, relevant issues by a panel of journalists. The moderators throughout the years have included Martha Rountree, Lawrence E. Spivak, Ned Brooks, Bill Monroe, Marvin Kalb, Chris Wallace and Garrick Utley with the current host being Tim Russert.

MOROCCO: ANNIVERSARY OF THE GREEN MARCH. Nov 6. National holiday. Commemorates the march into the Spanish Sahara in 1975 to claim the land for Morocco.

NAISMITH, JAMES: BIRTH ANNIVERSARY. Nov 6, 1861. Inventor of the game of basketball was born at Almonte, Ontario, Canada. Died at Lawrence, KS, Nov 28, 1939. Inducted into the Basketball Hall of Fame in 1959. Basketball became an Olympic sport in 1936.

NORTHERN ILLINOIS GATHERINGS POWWOW. Nov 6. Student Recreation Center, Dekalb, IL. Gathering of Native American drummers, dancers and vendors. A traditional powwow—admission is free and everyone is welcome. Annually, the first Saturday in November. Est attendance: 4,800. For info: Rita Reynolds, Northern Illinois Univ, Dekalb, IL 60115. Phone: (815) 753-0722. E-mail: rreynolds@niu.edu.

PADEREWSKI, IGNACE JAN: BIRTH ANNIVERSARY. Nov 6, 1860. Polish composer, pianist, patriot born at Kurylowka, Podolia, Poland. He died at New York, NY, June 29, 1941. When Poland fell into the hands of the Soviets after WWII, his family decided he would remain buried in Arlington National Cemetery. In May 1963, President John F. Kennedy dedicated a plaque to Paderewski's memory and declared that the pianist would rest in Arlington until Poland was free. Paderewski's remains were returned to his native country on June 29, 1992, the 51st anniversary of his death, after Poland held its first parliamentary election following its independence from the Soviet Union.

"THE PHIL DONAHUE SHOW" TV PREMIERE: ANNIVERSARY. Nov 6, 1967. The forerunner of Oprah, Jerry, Montel, etc, this first talk show with audience participation went on the air on this date at Dayton, OH. The first guest interviewed by host Phil Donahue was atheist Madalyn Murray O'Hair. In 1970 the program went national; it moved to Chicago in 1974 and to New York in 1985. In later years the program was titled "Donahue." After winning 19 Emmy Awards, the show left daytime TV in 1996. Phil Donahue briefly aired a show on the MSNBC cable network, but it was cancelled after six months Feb 25, 2003.

SADIE HAWKINS DAY. Nov 6. Widely observed in US, usually on the first Saturday in November. Tradition established in "Li'l Abner" comic strip in 1930s by cartoonist Al Capp. A popular occasion when women and girls are encouraged to take the initiative in inviting the man or boy of their choice for a date. A similar tradition is associated with Feb 29 in leap years.

SAXOPHONE DAY (ADOLPHE SAX BIRTH ANNIVERSARY). Nov 6. A day to recognize the birth anniversary of Adolphe Sax, Belgian musician and inventor of the saxophone and the saxotromba. Born at Dinant, Belgium, in 1814, Antoine Joseph Sax, later known as Adolphe, was the eldest of 11 children of a musical instrument builder. Sax contributed an entire family of brass wind instruments for band and orchestra use. He was accorded fame and great wealth, but business misfortunes led to bankruptcy. Sax died in poverty at Paris, Feb 7, 1894.

SOUSA, JOHN PHILIP: 150th BIRTH ANNIVERSARY. Nov 6, 1854. American composer and band conductor, remembered for stirring marches such as "The Stars and Stripes Forever," "Semper Fidelis," "El Capitan," born at Washington, DC. Died at Reading, PA, Mar 6, 1932. See also: "The Stars and Stripes Forever Day: Anniversary" (May 14).

November 2004	S	M	T	W	T	F	S
		1	2	3	4	5	6
	7	8	9	10	11	12	13
	14	15	16	17	18	19	20
	21	22	23	24	25	26	27
	28	29	30				

STEEPLECHASE AT CALLAWAY GARDENS. Nov 6. Pine Mountain, GA. A six-race steeplechase "meet" where riders match their horses for speed and split-second timing over brush jumps. Box seating and infield tailgating spaces available. Est attendance: 10,000. For info: The Steeplechase at Callaway Gardens, PO Box 2311, Columbus, GA 31902. Phone: (706) 324-6252. Fax: (706) 324-3651.

SWEDEN: ALL SAINTS' DAY. Nov 6. Honors the memory of deceased friends and relatives. Annually, the Saturday following Oct 30.

SWEDEN: GUSTAVUS ADOLPHUS DAY. Nov 6. Honors Sweden's King and military leader killed in 1632.

UNITED NATIONS: INTERNATIONAL DAY FOR PREVENTING THE EXPLOITATION OF THE ENVIRONMENT IN WAR AND ARMED CONFLICT. Nov 6. A day calling attention to the irreparable damage to ecosystems and natural resources caused by armed conflict. For info: United Nations, Dept of Public Info, New York, NY 10017. Web: www.un.org.

BIRTHDAYS TODAY

Sally Field, 58, actress (Oscars for *Norma Rae, Places in the Heart*; Emmy for *Sybil*), born Pasadena, CA, Nov 6, 1946.
Glenn Frey, 56, musician, songwriter, singer ("The Heat Is On"), born Detroit, MI, Nov 6, 1948.
Nigel Havers, 55, actor (*Chariots of Fire, Empire of the Sun*), born London, England, Nov 6, 1949.
Ethan Hawke, 34, actor (*Training Day, Dead Poets Society*), novelist, born Austin, TX, Nov 6, 1970.
Lance Kerwin, 44, actor ("James at 15," "The Family Holvak"), born Newport Beach, CA, Nov 6, 1960.
Thandie Newton, 32, actress (*Beloved, Mission Impossible II*), born in Zambia, Nov 6, 1972.
Mike Nichols, 73, comedian, actor, theater producer, director, filmmaker (Oscar for *The Graduate; Working Girl*), born Michael Igor Peschkowsky, Berlin, Germany, Nov 6, 1931.
Rebecca Romijn-Stamos, 32, model, host (MTV's "House of Style"), actress (*X-Men*), born Berkeley, CA, Nov 6, 1972.
Maria Owings Shriver, 49, broadcast journalist ("Today"), born Chicago, IL, Nov 6, 1955.

NOVEMBER 7 — SUNDAY
Day 312 — 54 Remaining

BANGLADESH: SOLIDARITY DAY. Nov 7. National holiday. Commemorates a coup in 1975.

CAMUS, ALBERT: BIRTH ANNIVERSARY. Nov 7, 1913. French writer and philosopher, winner of the Nobel Prize for Literature in 1957, was born at Mondavi, Algeria. "The struggle to reach the top is itself enough to fulfill the heart of man. One must believe that Sisyphus is happy," he wrote, in *Le Mythe de Sisyphe*. Camus was killed in an automobile accident in France, Jan 4, 1960.

CANADIAN PACIFIC RAILWAY: TRANSCONTINENTAL COMPLETION ANNIVERSARY. Nov 7, 1885. At 9:30 AM the last spike was driven at Craigellachie, British Columbia, completing the Canadian Pacific Railway's 2,980-mile transcontinental railroad track between Montreal, Quebec, in the east and Port Moody, British Columbia, in the west.

CONTINENT-SIZED WINDSTORMS DISCOVERED: ANNIVERSARY. Nov 7, 1991. A satellite that had been launched from the space shuttle *Discovery* on Sept 15, 1991, discovered large windstorms in Earth's upper atmosphere. The satellite's 10 instruments became functional on Nov 7 and detected the continent-sized windstorms, which measured up to 200 mile-per-hour velocities in areas that are 600 to 6,000 miles wide in the mesosphere. The largest storm was discovered in the Southern hemisphere and reached from western Australia eastward to points halfway across the Atlantic Ocean.

CURIE, MARIE SKLODOWSKA: BIRTH ANNIVERSARY. Nov 7, 1867. Polish chemist and physicist, born at Warsaw, Poland. In 1903 she was awarded, with her husband, the Nobel Prize for physics for their discovery of the element radium. Died near Sallanches, France, July 4, 1934.

ENGLAND: LONDON TO BRIGHTON VETERAN CAR RUN. Nov 7. London. A 57-mile run for approximately 450 veteran cars, along the A23 road from Serpentine Road, Hyde Park, London, to Madiera Drive, Brighton. Only cars built before Dec 31, 1904, are eligible to participate. Celebrates emancipation—the abolition in 1896 of English law requiring that a man walk in front of motor vehicles carrying a red flag. Annually, the first Sunday in November. For info: Intl Motor Sports Ltd, Motor Sports House, Riverside Park, Colnbrook, SL3 OHG, England. Phone: (44) (1753) 765100. Fax: (44) (1753) 765106. E-mail: vcr @msaevents.co.uk. Web: www.msauk.org.

"FACE THE NATION" TV PREMIERE: 50th ANNIVERSARY. Nov 7, 1954. The CBS counterpart to NBC's "Meet the Press," this show employed a similar format: panelists interviewed a well-known guest. In 1983 the panel was changed to include experts in addition to journalists. Though usually produced at Washington, DC, the show occasionally interviewed people elsewhere (such as Khrushchev in Moscow in 1957).

FIRST BLACK GOVERNOR ELECTED: 15th ANNIVERSARY. Nov 7, 1989. L. Douglas Wilder was elected governor of Virginia, becoming the first elected black governor in US history. Wilder had previously served as lieutenant governor of Virginia.

GREAT OCTOBER SOCIALIST REVOLUTION: ANNIVERSARY. Nov 7, 1917. This holiday in the old Soviet Union was observed for two days with parades, military displays and appearances by Soviet leaders. In the mid-1990s, President Yeltsin issued a decree renaming the holiday the "Day of National Reconciliation and Agreement." According to the old Russian calendar, the revolution took place Oct 25, 1917. Soviet calendar reform causes observance to fall Nov 7 (Gregorian). The Bolshevik Revolution began at Petrograd, Russia, on the evening of Nov 6 (Gregorian), 1917. A new government headed by Nikolai Lenin took office the following day under the name Council of People's Commissars. Leon Trotsky was commissar for foreign affairs and Josef Stalin became commissar of national minorities.

JAGGER, DEAN: BIRTH ANNIVERSARY. Nov 7, 1903. American actor Dean Jagger was born at Columbus Grove, OH. Predominantly a character actor, he appeared in more than 120 films, including *Twelve O'Clock High* (1950), for which he won an Oscar for best supporting actor. He died Feb 5, 1991, at Santa Monica, CA.

NEW YORK CITY MARATHON. Nov 7. New York, NY. 30,000 runners from all over the world gather to compete with more than 2.5 million spectators watching from the sidelines. For info: Phone: (212) 423-2249. Web: www.nycmarathon.org.

NIXON'S "LAST" PRESS CONFERENCE: ANNIVERSARY. Nov 7, 1962. Richard M. Nixon, having been narrowly defeated in his bid for the presidency by John F. Kennedy in the 1960 election, returned to politics two years later as a candidate for governor of California in the election of Nov 6, 1962. Defeated again (this time by incumbent governor Edmund G. Brown), Nixon held his "last" press conference with assembled reporters in Los Angeles at mid-morning the next day at which he said: ". . . just think how much you're going to be missing. You won't have Nixon to kick around any more, because, gentlemen, this is my last press conference."

Nov 7–8 ☆ *Chase's 2004 Calendar of Events* ☆

OLD STOUGHTON MUSICAL SOCIETY: ANNIVERSARY. Nov 7, 1786. Founded at Stoughton, MA, the Stoughton Musical Society is the oldest choral society in the US. Originally consisting of 25 men, it now includes both men and women. The society performed at the Chicago World's Columbian Exposition in 1893.

REPUBLICAN SYMBOL: ANNIVERSARY. Nov 7, 1874. Thomas Nast used an elephant to represent the Republican Party in a satirical cartoon in *Harper's Weekly*. Today the elephant is still a well-recognized symbol for the Republican Party in political cartoons.

ROOSEVELT ELECTED TO FOURTH TERM: 60th ANNIVERSARY. Nov 7, 1944. Defeating Thomas Dewey, Franklin D. Roosevelt became the first, and only, person elected to four terms as President of the US. Roosevelt was inaugurated the following Jan 20 but died in office Apr 12, 1945, serving only 53 days of the fourth term.

RUSSIA: OCTOBER REVOLUTION. Nov 7. National holiday in Russia and Ukraine. Commemorates the Great Socialist Revolution which occurred in October 1917 under the Old Style calendar. In 1997, the holiday was renamed the "Day of National Reconciliation and Agreement."

SYNERGY WEEK INTERNATIONAL. Nov 7–13. Synergy enables organizations to consistently achieve exponential outcomes through the optimal integration of all of their resources. Conference themes will promote awareness of methods for achieving synergy within organizations. For info: DiFrances & Assoc, LLC, 208 E Oak Crest Dr, Ste 200, Wales, WI 53183-9700. Phone: (262) 968-9850. Fax: (262) 968-9854. E-mail: synergy@difrances.com. Web: www.difrances.com/synergyweek.

BIRTHDAYS TODAY

Billy Graham, 86, evangelist, born William Franklin Graham, Charlotte, NC, Nov 7, 1918.
Jeremy London, 32, actor ("I'll Fly Away," "Party of Five"), born San Diego, CA, Nov 7, 1972.
Joni Mitchell, 61, singer, songwriter ("Both Sides Now," "Big Yellow Taxi," "Woodstock"), born Roberta Joan Anderson, McLeod, AB, Canada, Nov 7, 1943.
Barry Newman, 66, actor ("Petrocelli," *Vanishing Point*), born Boston, MA, Nov 7, 1938.
Johnny Rivers, 62, singer ("Poor Side of Town," "Secret Agent Man"), born John Ramistella, New York, NY, Nov 7, 1942.
Joan Sutherland, 78, opera singer, born Sydney, Australia, Nov 7, 1926.
Mary Travers, 67, composer, singer (Peter, Paul and Mary, "Blowin' in the Wind"), born Louisville, KY, Nov 7, 1937.

November 2004

S	M	T	W	T	F	S
	1	2	3	4	5	6
7	8	9	10	11	12	13
14	15	16	17	18	19	20
21	22	23	24	25	26	27
28	29	30				

NOVEMBER 8 — MONDAY
Day 313 — 53 Remaining

ABET AND AID PUNSTERS DAY. Nov 8. Laugh instead of groan at incredibly dreadful puns. All-time greatest triple pun: "Though he's not very humble, there's no police like Holmes," from the register of worst puns of Punsters Unlimited. (Originated by Earl Harris, retired, and the late William Rabe.)

COOK SOMETHING BOLD AND PUNGENT DAY. Nov 8. Especially for those of us who have tightly closed up the house against chill weather for the next six months. Now is the time to create the heavenly, homey odor of pungently bold cooking. Don't forget the sauerkraut and garlic! [©2003 by WH.] For info: Thomas & Ruth Roy, Wellcat Holidays, 2418 Long Ln, Lebanon, PA 17046. Phone: (717) 279-0184. E-mail: info@wellcat.com. Web: www.wellcat.com.

CORTÉS CONQUERS MEXICO: ANNIVERSARY. Nov 8, 1519. After landing on the Yucatan peninsula in April, Spaniard Hernan Cortés and his troops marched into the interior of Mexico to the Aztec capital and took the Aztec emperor Montezuma hostage.

"DAYS OF OUR LIVES" TV PREMIERE: ANNIVERSARY. Nov 8, 1965. This popular daytime serial, like many others, has gone through many changes throughout its run. It expanded from 30 minutes to an hour; it went to number one in the ratings and slipped to nine out of 12 in the 1980s; and it dropped or deemphasized older characters, which angered its audience. The soap is set in Salem and centers around the Horton and Brady families. Notable cast members included Mary Frann, Joan Van Ark, Susan Oliver, Mike Farrell, Kristian Alfonso, Garry Marshall, John Aniston, Josh Taylor, Wayne Northrop, John DeLancie, Andrea Barber, Deidre Hall, Thaao Penghlis, Jason Bernard, Marilyn McCoo, Charles Shaughnessy, Peter Reckell, Francis Reid, Patsy Pease and Genie Francis.

HALLEY, EDMUND: BIRTH ANNIVERSARY. Nov 8, 1656 (OS). Astronomer and mathematician born at London, England. Astronomer Royal, 1721–42. Died at Greenwich, England, Jan 14, 1742 (OS). He observed the great comet of 1682 (now named for him), first conceived its periodicity and wrote in his *Synopsis of Comet Astronomy*: ". . . I may venture to foretell that this Comet will return again in the year 1758." It did, and Edmund Halley's memory is kept alive by the once-every-generation appearance of Halley's Comet. There have been 28 recorded appearances of this comet since 240 BC. Average time between appearances is 76 years. Halley's Comet is next expected to be visible in 2061.

MERCHANT SAILING SHIP PRESERVATION DAY: ANNIVERSARY. Nov 8, 1941. The whaler *Charles W. Morgan* arrived at Mystic, CT, to be restored. This was the beginning of the modern era of preservation of merchant sailing ships.

MITCHELL, MARGARET: BIRTH ANNIVERSARY. Nov 8, 1900. American novelist who won a Pulitzer Prize (1937) for her only book, *Gone with the Wind*, a romantic novel about the Civil War and Reconstruction. *Gone with the Wind* sold about 10,000,000 copies and was translated into 30 languages. Born at Atlanta, GA, Mitchell died there after being struck by an automobile Aug 16, 1949.

MONTANA: ADMISSION DAY: ANNIVERSARY. Nov 8. Became 41st state in 1889.

MOUNT HOLYOKE COLLEGE FOUNDED: ANNIVERSARY. Nov 8, 1837. The first college for women in the United States was founded as Mt Holyoke Seminary in 1837 at South Hadley, MA. While many colleges for women became coeducational institutions in the 1970s and 1980s, Mt Holyoke remains a women's college.

NATIONAL AMPLE TIME DAY. Nov 8. One day set aside each year to recognize the importance of time management—of making ample time in one's life for priorities. Make the most of each day and live a completely fulfilling life! Annually, Nov 8. For

☆ Chase's 2004 Calendar of Events ☆ Nov 8–9

info: Lorie Hicks, Author, Ample Time, 5222 E 78th Pl, Tulsa, OK 74136. Phone: (918) 499-8777. Web: www.LorieHicks.com.

NATIONAL PARENTS AS TEACHERS DAY. Nov 8. To pay tribute to the more than 3,000 Parents as Teachers programs located in 50 states and other countries. These programs give all parents, regardless of social or economic circumstance, the support and guidance necessary to be their children's best first teacher in the critical early years. National PAT Day is celebrated on November 8, the birthday of Mildred Winter, PAT Founding Director. For info: Parents as Teachers Natl Center, 2228 Ball Dr, St. Louis, MO 63146. Phone: (314) 432-4330. Fax: (314) 432-8963. E-mail: info@patnc.org. Web: www.patnc.org

PURSUIT OF HAPPINESS WEEK. Nov 8–14. The purpose of this week is to remind everyone, as stated in the Declaration of Independence, that all men and women are "endowed by their Creator with certain unalienable rights, that among them are life, liberty and the pursuit of happiness." For complete info and quotations about happiness by famous people, send $5 to cover expense of printing, handling and postage. For info: Dr. Stanley Drake, Pres, Intl Society of Friendship and Goodwill, 999 Hood Rd, Ste 127, Marietta, GA 30068. Phone: (770) 565-2322. E-mail: ISFGW@bellsouth.net.

TEXAS BOOK FESTIVAL. Nov 8–9. State Capitol and Capitol Extension, Austin, TX. 8th annual fair benefiting the public libraries of Texas. More than 150 authors will give readings, participate in panel discussions and sign books. Outdoor book fair with displays by publishers and booksellers. Free. For info: Texas Book Festival, PO Box 13143, Austin, TX 78711. Phone: (512) 477-4055. Fax: (512) 322-0722. Web: www.texasbookfestival.org.

X-RAY DISCOVERY DAY: ANNIVERSARY. Nov 8, 1895. Physicist Wilhelm Conrad Roentgen (q.v.) discovered X-rays, beginning a new era in physics and medicine. Although X-rays had been observed previously, it was Roentgen, a professor at the University of Würzburg (Germany), who successfully repeated X-ray experimentation and who is credited with the discovery.

BIRTHDAYS TODAY

Edgardo Alfonzo, 31, baseball player, born St. Teresa, Venezuela, Nov 8, 1973.
Mary Hart, 53, TV host, born Madison, SD, Nov 8, 1951.
June Havoc, 88, actress (*Brewster's Millions*, "Willy"), born Vancouver, BC, Canada, Nov 8, 1916.
Christie Hefner, 52, business executive (*Playboy*), daughter of Hugh Hefner, born Chicago, IL, Nov 8, 1952.
Ricki Lee Jones, 50, singer, musician ("Chuck E.'s In Love"), born Chicago, IL, Nov 8, 1954.
Virna Lisi, 67, actress (*How to Murder Your Wife, The Secret of Santa Vittoria*), born Ancona, Italy, Nov 8, 1937.
Patti Page, 77, singer ("The Doggie in the Window," "Allegheny Moon"), born Clara Ann Fowler, Clarence, OK, Nov 8, 1927.
Parker Posey, 36, actress (*The House of Yes*), born Baltimore, MD, Nov 8, 1968.
Bonnie Raitt, 55, singer ("Sweet Forgiveness"), actress, daughter of John Raitt, born Los Angeles, CA, Nov 8, 1949.
Morley Safer, 73, journalist ("60 Minutes"), born Toronto, ON, Canada, Nov 8, 1931.
Courtney Thorne-Smith, 37, actress ("Melrose Place," "Ally McBeal"), born San Francisco, CA, Nov 8, 1967.
Alfre Woodard, 51, actress (*Cross Creek, Miss Evers' Boys, How to Make an American Quilt*), born Tulsa, OK, Nov 8, 1953.

NOVEMBER 9 — TUESDAY
Day 314 — 52 Remaining

AGNEW, SPIRO THEODORE: BIRTH ANNIVERSARY. Nov 9, 1918. 39th vice president of the US, born at Baltimore, MD. Twice elected vice president (1968 and 1972), Agnew became the second person to resign that office Oct 10, 1973. Agnew entered a plea of no contest to a charge of income tax evasion (on contract kickbacks received while he was governor of Maryland and after he became vice president). He died Sept 17, 1996, at Berlin, MD. See also: "Vice Presidential Resignation: Anniversary" (Dec 28) and "Calhoun, John Caldwell: Birth Anniversary" (Mar 18).

BANNEKER, BENJAMIN: BIRTH ANNIVERSARY. Nov 9, 1731. American astronomer, mathematician, clockmaker, surveyor and almanac author, called "first black man of science." Took part in original survey of city of Washington. Banneker's *Almanac* was published 1792–97. Born at Elliott's Mills, MD, he died at Baltimore, MD, Oct 9, 1806. A fire that started during his funeral destroyed his home, library, notebooks, almanac calculations, clocks and virtually all belongings and documents related to his life.

BERLIN WALL OPENED: 15th ANNIVERSARY. Nov 9, 1989. After 28 years as a symbol of the Cold War, the Berlin Wall was opened on this evening, and citizens of both sides walked freely through the barrier as others danced atop the structure to celebrate the end of an historic era. Coming amidst the celebration of East Germany's 40-year anniversary, pro-democracy demonstrations led to the resignation of Erich Honecker, East Germany's head of state and party chief. It was Honecker who had supervised the construction of the 27.9-mile wall across the city during the night of Aug 13, 1961, because US President John Kennedy had ordered a troop build-up in response to the blockade of West Berlin by the Soviets.

BOSTON FIRE: ANNIVERSARY. Nov 9, 1872. Though Boston had experienced several damaging fires, the worst one started on this Saturday evening in a dry-goods warehouse. Spreading rapidly in windy weather, it devastated several blocks of the business district, destroying nearly 800 buildings. Damage was estimated at more than $75 million. It was said that the fire caused a bright red glare in the sky that could be seen from nearly 100 miles away. The Boston fire came one year, one month and one day after the Great Chicago Fire of Oct 8, 1871.

CAMBODIA: INDEPENDENCE DAY: 55th ANNIVERSARY. Nov 9. National Day. Declared independence from France in 1949.

DANDRIDGE, DOROTHY: BIRTH ANNIVERSARY. Nov 9, 1923. Actress and singer Dandridge was a child star, born at Cleveland, OH, who toured with her sisters, Vivian and Etta Jones, as The Dandridge Sisters. They played at the Cotton Club, sharing the stage with artists such as Cab Calloway and W.C. Handy. Dandridge went solo in 1941 to perform in Hollywood movies and on stage with the Desi Arnaz Band. Her big break came with the lead role in Otto Preminger's musical, *Carmen Jones*. Dandridge received an Oscar nomination for her performance. Unfortunately, she could not overcome Hollywood's racism and tendency to typecast and her career foundered. She died at West Hollywood, CA, Sept 8, 1965.

EAST COAST BLACKOUT: ANNIVERSARY. Nov 9, 1965. Massive electric power failure starting in western New York state at 5:16 PM, cut electric power to much of northeastern US and Ontario and Quebec in Canada. More than 30 million people in an area of 80,000 square miles were affected. The experience provoked studies of the vulnerability of 20th-century technology.

FULBRIGHT, J. WILLIAM: BIRTH ANNIVERSARY. Nov 9, 1905. US Senator, born at Sumner, MO. He sponsored the legislation that created the Fulbright scholarships for international study for graduate students, faculty and researchers. Died Feb 9, 1995.

Nov 9–10 ☆ *Chase's 2004 Calendar of Events* ☆

KRISTALLNACHT (CRYSTAL NIGHT): ANNIVERSARY. Nov 9–10, 1938. During the evening of Nov 9 and into the morning of Nov 10, 1938, mobs in Germany destroyed thousands of shops and homes carrying out a pogrom against Jews. Synagogues were burned down or demolished. There were bonfires in every Jewish neighborhood, fueled by Jewish prayer books, Torah scrolls and volumes of philosophy, history and poetry. More than 30,000 Jews were arrested and 91 killed. The night got its name from the smashing of glass store windows.

THE LINKS, INC: ANNIVERSARY. Nov 9, 1946. Thousands of African Americans fought in WWII, but after the war the same old injustices and hatred prevailed. In Philadelphia Margaret Roselle Hawkins and Sarah Strickland Scott founded a nonpartisan, volunteer organization called The Links, "linking" their friendship and resources in an effort to better the lives of disadvantaged African Americans. From the first group of nine, The Links has grown to an incorporated organization of 8,000 women in 240 local chapters in 40 states plus the District of Columbia and two foreign countries. The Links promotes educational, cultural and community activities through a variety of projects here and in Africa. In May of 1985 The Links became an official Non-Governmental Organization of the UN.

LOVEJOY, ELIJAH P.: BIRTH ANNIVERSARY. Nov 9, 1802. American newspaper publisher and abolitionist born at Albion, ME. Died Nov 7, 1837, at Alton, IL, in a fire started by a mob angry about his anti-slavery views.

NATIONAL CHILD SAFETY COUNCIL: FOUNDING ANNIVERSARY. Nov 9, 1955. National Child Safety Council (NCSC) at Jackson, MI, is the oldest and largest nonprofit organization in the US dedicated solely to child safety. Distributes comprehensive safety education materials to children and adults through local law enforcement, and the Council's mascot, Safetypup®. For info: Barbara Handley Huggett, Dir, R & D, NCSC, Box 1368, Jackson, MI 49204-1368. Phone: (517) 764-6070. E-mail: bhugget@nfcd.org.

NATIONAL YOUNG READER'S DAY. Nov 9. Pizza Hut and the Center for the Book in the Library of Congress established National Young Reader's Day to remind Americans of the joys and importance of reading for young people. Schools, libraries, families and communities nationwide use this day to celebrate youth reading in a variety of creative and educational ways. Ideas on ways you can celebrate this special day available. For info: Shelley Morehead, The BOOK IT! Program, PO Box 2999, Wichita, KS 67201. Phone: (800) 426-6548. Fax: (316) 685-0977. E-mail: bookit@pizzahut.com.

"OMNIBUS" TV PREMIERE: ANNIVERSARY. Nov 9, 1952. This eclectic series deserved its name, offering a variety of presentations, including dramas, documentaries and musicals for more than 10 years. Alistair Cooke hosted the program, which was the first major TV project to be underwritten by the Ford Foundation. Notable presentations included: James Agee's "Mr Lincoln"; "Die Fledermaus," with Eugene Ormandy conducting the Metropolitan Opera Orchestra; Agnes DeMille's ballet "Three Virgins and the Devil" (presented as "Three Maidens and the Devil"); and documentaries from underwater explorer Jacques Cousteau.

SAGAN, CARL: 70th BIRTH ANNIVERSARY. Nov 9, 1934. Astronomer, biologist, author (*Broca's Brain, Cosmos*), born at New York, NY. Died at Seattle, WA, Dec 20, 1996.

TRIPLE CROWN OF SURFING. Nov 9–Dec 20. Oahu, HI. The 22nd annual Triple Crown includes three professional big wave surf meets on Oahu's North Shore that mark the conclusion of the yearlong Association of Surfing Professionals (ASP) world tour. Following the Triple Crown the ASP Men's and Women's Champions are crowned. Est attendance: 20,000. For info: Randy Rarick, 59-063-A Hoalua St, Haleiwa, HI 96712. Phone: (808) 638-7266. Fax: (808) 638-7764. E-mail: surfpro@hawaii.rr.com.

VIETNAM VETERANS MEMORIAL STATUE UNVEILING: 20th ANNIVERSARY. Nov 9, 1984. The Vietnam Veterans Memorial was completed by the addition of a statue, "Three Servicemen" (sculpted by Frederick Hart), which was unveiled on this date. The statue faces the black granite wall on which are inscribed the names of more than 58,000 Americans who were killed or missing in action in the Vietnam War.

WHITE, STANFORD: BIRTH ANNIVERSARY. Nov 9, 1853. American architect who designed the old Madison Square Garden, the Washington Square Arch, and the Players, Century and Metropolitan Clubs at New York City. Stanford White was born at New York City and was shot to death on the roof of the Madison Square Garden by Harry Thaw, June 25, 1906.

WILHELM II ABDICATES: ANNIVERSARY. Nov 9, 1918. As World War I was coming to a close and it became clear their cause was lost, a revolt broke out in Germany. The Kaiser was advised by his military staff that the loyalty of the army could not be guaranteed. On Nov 9, 1918, it was announced in Berlin that Kaiser Wilhelm II had abdicated his throne. The former leader then fled to Holland. Philip Scheidemann, a Socialist leader, proclaimed a German Republic and became its first Chancellor.

BIRTHDAYS TODAY

Adam Dunn, 25, baseball player, born Houston, TX, Nov 9, 1979.
David Duval, 33, golfer, born Jacksonville, FL, Nov 9, 1971.
Lou Ferrigno, 53, actor (*Pumping Iron*, "The Incredible Hulk"), former bodybuilder, born Brooklyn, NY, Nov 9, 1951.
Robert (Bob) Gibson, 69, Hall of Fame baseball player, born Omaha, NE, Nov 9, 1935.
Robert Graham, 68, US Senator (D, Florida), born Dade County, FL, Nov 9, 1936.
Thomas Daniel (Tom) Weiskopf, 62, broadcaster, former golfer, born Massillon, OH, Nov 9, 1942.

NOVEMBER 10 — WEDNESDAY
Day 315 — 51 Remaining

AREA CODES INTRODUCED: ANNIVERSARY. Nov 10, 1951. The 10-digit North American Numbering Plan which provides area codes for Canada, the US, and many Caribbean nations was devised in 1947 by AT&T and Bell Labs. Eighty-four area codes were assigned. However, all long-distance calls at that time were operator-assisted. On this date in 1951, the mayor of Englewood, NJ (area code 201) direct-dialed the mayor of Alameda, CA. By 1960 all telephone customers could dial long-distance calls. Because of the proliferation of faxes, modems and cell phones, the US could run out of area codes as early as 2007. The system is administered by the North American Numbering Plan Administration. For more info: www.nanpa.com

BADLANDS NATIONAL PARK ESTABLISHED: ANNIVERSARY. Nov 10, 1978. South Dakota's Badlands National Monument, authorized Mar 4, 1929, was established as a national park and preserve.

	S	M	T	W	T	F	S
November		1	2	3	4	5	6
2004	7	8	9	10	11	12	13
	14	15	16	17	18	19	20
	21	22	23	24	25	26	27
	28	29	30				

576

☆ Chase's 2004 Calendar of Events ☆ — Nov 10

BURTON, RICHARD: BIRTH ANNIVERSARY. Nov 10, 1925. Welsh-born stage and film actor. Richard Burton was never knighted and never an Oscar winner, but he was generally regarded as one of the great acting talents of his time. Born Richard Jenkins at Pontrhydyfen, South Wales, the son of a coal miner, he later took the name of his guardian, schoolmaster Philip Burton. His films include *Cleopatra, Becket, Who's Afraid of Virginia Woolf?, Anne of the Thousand Days* and *Equus*. An intense and tempestuous personal life and career suggested a self-destructive bent. Burton died at Geneva, Switzerland, Aug 5, 1984.

CHRISTMAS GIFT AND HOBBY SHOW. Nov 10–14. West Pavilion, Indiana State Fairgrounds, Indianapolis, IN. 55th annual event. Selling show of arts, crafts, collectibles and other gift items. Est attendance: 60,000. For info: Donell Heberer Walton, Show Mgr, HSI Show Productions, Box 502797, Indianapolis, IN 46250. Phone: (317) 576-9933. Fax: (317) 576-9955. Web: www.hsishows.com.

EDMUND FITZGERALD MEMORIAL BEACON LIGHTING. Nov 10. Noon–6 PM, Split Rock Lighthouse, Two Harbors, MN. Includes information on *Edmund Fitzgerald* and other shipwrecks on Lake Superior; beacon lighting at dusk in memory of the 29 men lost on the *Edmund Fitzgerald* on Nov 10, 1975, and of all those who lost their lives in other Great Lakes shipwrecks. Lighthouse open. Est attendance: 1,000. For info: Lee Radzak, 3713 Split Rock Lighthouse Rd, Two Harbors, MN 55616. Phone: (218) 226-6372.

EDMUND FITZGERALD SINKING: ANNIVERSARY. Nov 10, 1975. The ore carrier *Edmund Fitzgerald* broke in two during a heavy storm in Lake Superior (near Whitefish Point). There were no survivors of this, the worst Great Lakes ship disaster of the decade, which took the lives of 29 crew members.

GATEWAY FARM EXPO. Nov 10–11. Buffalo County Fairgrounds, Kearney, NE. Est attendance: 6,000. For info: Kearney Area Chamber of Commerce, PO Box 607, Kearney, NE 68848. Phone: (877) 720-4885. Web: www.gatewayfarmexpo.org.

GOLDSMITH, OLIVER: BIRTH ANNIVERSARY. Nov 10, 1728. Irish writer, author of the play *She Stoops to Conquer*. Born at Pallas, County Longford, Ireland, he died Apr 4, 1774, at London. "A book may be amusing with numerous errors," he wrote (Advertisement to *The Vicar of Wakefield*), "or it may be very dull without a single absurdity."

HOGARTH, WILLIAM: BIRTH ANNIVERSARY. Nov 10, 1697. English painter and engraver, famed for his satiric series of engravings (*A Harlot's Progress, A Rake's Progress, Four Stages of Cruelty*, etc). Born at London, England, he died there, Oct 26, 1764.

KIRTLAND, JARED: BIRTH ANNIVERSARY. Nov 10, 1793. American-born physician and naturalist, Dr. Jared Potter Kirtland (for whom Kirtland's Warbler is named) was born at Wallingford, CT. The first of the now rare Kirtland's Warblers to be identified and studied was found on his farm near Cleveland, OH, in 1851. Dr. Kirtland died at Rockport, near Cleveland, Dec 10, 1877.

LUTHER, MARTIN: BIRTH ANNIVERSARY. Nov 10, 1483. Augustinian monk who was a founder and leader of the Protestant Reformation was born at Eisleben, Saxony. Luther tacked his 95 Theses "On the Power of Indulgences" on the door of Wittenberg's castle church, on Oct 31, 1517, the eve of All Saints' Day. Luther asserted that the Bible was the sole authority of the church, called for reformation of abuses by the Roman Catholic Church and denied the supremacy of the Pope. Tried for heresy by the Roman Church, threatened with excommunication and finally banned by a papal bull (Jan 2, 1521), he responded by burning the bull. In 1525 he married Katherine von Bora, one of nine nuns who had left the convent due to his teaching. Luther died near his birthplace, at Eisleben, Feb 18, 1546.

MARINE CORPS BIRTHDAY: ANNIVERSARY. Nov 10, 1775. Commemorates the Marine Corps' establishment in 1775. Originally part of the navy, it became a separate unit July 11, 1789.

MICROSOFT RELEASES WINDOWS: ANNIVERSARY. Nov 10, 1983. In 1980 Microsoft signed a contract with IBM to design an operating system, MS-DOS, for a personal computer that IBM was developing. On Nov 10, 1983, Microsoft released Windows, an extension of MS-DOS with a graphical user interface. Windows 3.1 was released Apr 6, 1992.

PANAMA: FIRST SHOUT OF INDEPENDENCE. Nov 10. National holiday. Commemorates Panama's first battle for independence from Spain in 1821.

"SESAME STREET" TV PREMIERE: 35th ANNIVERSARY. Nov 10, 1969. An important, successful long-running children's show, "Sesame Street" educates children while they have fun. It takes place along a city street, featuring a diverse cast of humans and puppets. Through singing, puppetry, film clips and skits, kids are taught letters, numbers, concepts and other lessons. Shows are "sponsored" by letters and numbers. Human cast members have included: Loretta Long, Matt Robinson, Roscoe Orman, Bob McGrath, Linda Bove, Buffy Sainte-Marie, Ruth Buzzi, Will Lee, Northern J. Calloway, Emilio Delgado and Sonia Manzano. Favorite Jim Henson Muppets include Ernie, Bert, Grover, Oscar the Grouch, Kermit the Frog, the Cookie Monster, life-sized Big Bird and Mr Snuffleupagus.

SOUTHERN CHRISTMAS SHOW. Nov 10–21. Charlotte, NC. Show filled with exquisite art and crafts from nationally known artisans. Ideas for decorating trees, mantels, doors and wreaths; festive foods for holiday celebrations from fresh hot strudel to plum pudding. Gifts for everyone on your holiday list. Plus cooking demonstrations, Christmas Tree Lane, Santa Claus, Olde Towne Craft demonstrations and musical performances. Est attendance: 130,000. For info: Christine Cipriano, Asst Show Mgr, Southern Shows, Inc, PO Box 36859, Charlotte, NC 28236. Phone: (704) 376-6594. Fax: (704) 376-6345. E-mail: ccipriano@southernshows.com. Web: www.southernchristmasshow.com.

SPACE MILESTONE: *LUNA 17* (USSR). Nov 10, 1970. Launched in 1970, this unmanned spacecraft landed and released *Lunakhod 1* (8-wheel, radio-controlled vehicle) on Moon's Sea of Rains Nov 17, which explored lunar surface, sending data back to Earth.

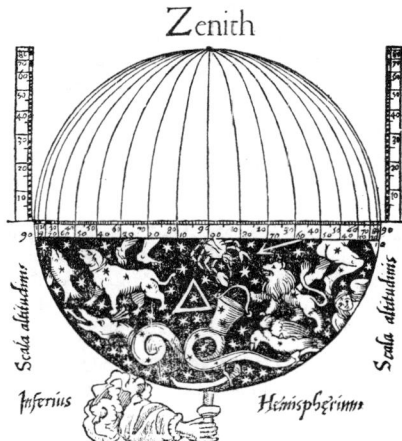

STANLEY FINDS LIVINGSTONE: ANNIVERSARY. Nov 10, 1871. Having begun his search the previous March for the then two-years-missing explorer-missionary David Livingstone, explorer Henry M. Stanley found him on this day at Ujiji (Africa) and uttered those now immortal words, "Dr. Livingstone, I presume?"

Nov 10–11   ☆ *Chase's 2004 Calendar of Events* ☆

BIRTHDAYS TODAY

Vanessa Angel, 41, actress (*Spies Like Us, Kingpin*), born London, England, Nov 10, 1963.
Isaac Bruce, 32, football player, born Ft Lauderdale, FL, Nov 10, 1972.
Saxby Chambliss, 61, US Senator (R, Georgia), born Warrenton, NC, Nov 10, 1943.
Roland Emmerich, 49, director, producer (*Independence Day, Eye of the Storm*), born Stuttgart, Germany, Nov 10, 1955.
Donna Fargo, 55, singer ("Funny Face"), songwriter, born Yvonne Vaughan, Mount Airy, NC, Nov 10, 1949.
Russell Charles Means, 64, Native American rights activist, born Pine Ridge, SD, Nov 10, 1940.
Mackenzie Phillips, 45, actress ("One Day at a Time," *American Graffiti*), daughter of John Phillips of the Mamas and Papas, born Alexandria, VA, Nov 10, 1959.
Ann Reinking, 55, dancer, actress (*Pippin*), born Seattle, WA, Nov 10, 1949.
Tim Rice, 60, lyricist (*Evita*), born Amersham, England, Nov 10, 1944.
Roy Scheider, 69, actor (*Jaws, All That Jazz*, "Seaquest DSV"), born Orange, NJ, Nov 10, 1935.
Sinbad, 48, actor (*Unnecessary Roughness*, "A Different World"), born David Adkins, Benton Harbor, MI, Nov 10, 1956.

NOVEMBER 11 — THURSDAY
Day 316 — 50 Remaining

ANGOLA: INDEPENDENCE DAY. Nov 11. National holiday. Angola gained its independence from Portugal in 1975.

BIG TEN MEN'S SOCCER CHAMPIONSHIP. Nov 11–14. University of Michigan, Ann Arbor, MI. For info: Sue Lister, Big Ten Conference, 1500 W Higgins Rd, Park Ridge, IL 60068-6300. Phone: (847) 696-1010. Fax: (847) 696-1110. Web: www.bigten.org.

BONZA BOTTLER DAY™. Nov 11. To celebrate when the number of the day is the same as the number of the month. Bonza Bottler Day™ is an excuse to have a party at least once a month. For more information, see Jan 1. For info: Gail M. Berger, 14 Fernwood Dr, Taylors, SC 29687. Phone: (864) 609-9874. E-mail: gberger5@aol.com.

CANADA: REMEMBRANCE DAY. Nov 11. Public holiday in Alberta.

CHRISTKINDL MARKT. Nov 11–13. Cultural Center, Canton, OH. Fine arts and crafts show and sale with a Christmas flair. Est attendance: 8,000. For info: Canton Museum of Art, 1001 Market Ave N, Canton, OH 44702. Phone: (330) 453-7666. Fax: (330) 453-1034. Web: www.cantonart.org/events.html.

COLOMBIA: CARTAGENA INDEPENDENCE DAY. Nov 11. National holiday. Commemorates declaration of independence from Spain of the city of Cartagena in 1811.

November 2004	S	M	T	W	T	F	S
		1	2	3	4	5	6
	7	8	9	10	11	12	13
	14	15	16	17	18	19	20
	21	22	23	24	25	26	27
	28	29	30				

DEATH/DUTY DAY. Nov 11. Honoring soldiers on both sides who died on Nov 11, 1918, the armistice or Waffenstillstand day that ended the fighting in the First World War of 1914–18. The order was to stop fighting at 11 AM, rather than on receipt of the order. For info: Bob Birch, Punscorpion, The Puns Corps, PO Box 2364, Falls Church, VA 22042-0364. Phone: (703) 533-3668.

DOSTOYEVSKY, FYODOR MIKHAILOVICH: BIRTH ANNIVERSARY. Nov 11, 1821. Russian novelist, author of *The Brothers Karamazov*, *Crime and Punishment* and *The Idiot*, was born at Moscow, and died at St. Petersburg, Feb 9, 1881. A political revolutionary, he was arrested, tried, convicted and sentenced to death, but instead of execution he served a sentence in a Siberian prison and later served in the army there.

"GOD BLESS AMERICA" FIRST PERFORMED: ANNIVERSARY. Nov 11, 1938. Irving Berlin wrote this song especially for Kate Smith. She first sang it during her regular radio broadcast. It quickly became a great patriotic favorite of the nation and one of Smith's most requested songs.

LONGHORN CHAMPIONSHIP FINALS RODEO. Nov 11–13. Murfreesboro, TN. 39th annual. Best 72 of 1,200+ qualifiers compete each performance in 6 contests for the 2004 Championships. Awards include gold and silver diamond-studded trophy belt buckles and hand-tooled trophy saddles. Large Western Trade Show will include retail vendor booths, Indian dancers and Texas-style cowboy meals served off a genuine ranch chuckwagon. Free beginners horsemanship clinic 40 minutes before each performance. Contests include Big, Bad BONUS bull riding! Est attendance: 20,000. For info: W. Bruce Lehrke, Longhorn World Chmpshp Rodeo, Inc, PO Box 70159, Nashville, TN 37207. Phone: (615) 876-1016. Fax: (615) 876-4685. E-mail: info@longhornrodeo.com. Web: www.longhornrodeo.com.

MALDIVES: REPUBLIC DAY: ANNIVERSARY. Nov 11. National holiday. Commemorates the abolition of the sultanate in 1968.

MARTINMAS. Nov 11. The Feast Day of St. Martin of Tours, who lived about AD 316–397. A bishop, he became one of the most popular saints of the Middle Ages. The period of warm weather often occurring about the time of his feast day is sometimes called St. Martin's Summer (especially in England).

PATTON, GEORGE S., JR: BIRTH ANNIVERSARY. Nov 11, 1885. American military officer, graduate of West Point (1909), George Smith Patton, Jr, was born at San Gabriel, CA. Ambitious and flamboyant, he lived for combat. He served in the punitive expedition into Mexico (1916), in Europe in World War I and in North Africa and Europe in World War II. He received world attention and official censure in 1943 for slapping a hospitalized shell-shocked soldier. While a full general, owing to his critical public statements, he was relieved of his command in 1945. He died at Heidelberg, Germany, Dec 21, 1945, of injuries received in an automobile accident.

POLAND: INDEPENDENCE DAY. Nov 11. Poland regained independence in 1918, after having been partitioned among Austria, Prussia and Russia for more than 120 years.

SPACE MILESTONE: *COLUMBIA* STS-5 (US). Nov 11, 1982. Shuttle *Columbia* launched from Kennedy Space Center, FL, with four astronauts: Vance Brand, Robert Overmyer, William Lenoir and Joseph Allen. "First operational mission" delivered two satellites into orbit for commercial customers. *Columbia* landed at Edwards Air Force Base, CA, Nov 16, 1982.

SPACE MILESTONE: *GEMINI 12* (US). Nov 11, 1966. Last Project Gemini manned Earth orbit launched. Buzz Aldrin spent five hours on a space walk, setting a new record.

SWEDEN: SAINT MARTIN'S DAY. Nov 11. Originally in memory of St. Martin of Tours; also associated with Martin Luther, who is celebrated the day before. Marks the end of the autumn's work and the beginning of winter activities.

SWITZERLAND: MARTINMAS GOOSE (MARTINIGIANS). Nov 11. Sursee, Canton Lucerne. At 3 PM on Martinmas (the day on which interest is due), the "Gansabhauet" is staged in front of Town Hall. Blindfolded participants try to bring down, with a single sword stroke, a dead goose suspended on a wire.

★**VETERANS DAY.** Nov 11. Presidential Proclamation. Formerly called "Armistice Day" and proclaimed each year since 1926 for Nov 11. PL 83-380 of June 1, 1954, changed the name to "Veterans Day." PL 90-363 of June 28, 1968, required that beginning in 1971 it would be observed the fourth Monday in October. PL 94-97 of Sept 18, 1975, required that effective Jan 1, 1978, the observance would revert to Nov 11.

VETERANS DAY. Nov 11. Veterans Day was observed on Nov 11 from 1919 through 1970. Public Law 90-363, the "Monday Holiday Law," provided that, beginning in 1971, Veterans Day would be observed on "the fourth Monday in October." This movable observance date, which separated Veterans Day from the Nov 11 anniversary of World War I Armistice, proved unpopular. State after state moved its observance back to the traditional Nov 11 date, and finally Public Law 94-97 of Sept 18, 1975, required that, effective Jan 1, 1978, the observance of Veterans Day revert to Nov 11. As Armistice Day this is a holiday in Belgium, France and other European countries. "At the eleventh hour of the eleventh day of the eleventh month" fighting ceased in World War I.

VETERANS DAY CELEBRATION. Nov 11. Mamou, LA. Memorial services, a patriotic parade and speeches, Cajun dance. Annually, on Veterans Day. Sponsor: American Legion Post 123. Est attendance: 1,000. For info: Frank Gurvis Bihm, Jr, PO Box 123, Mamou, LA 70554. Phone: (337) 468-5059. E-mail: fbihm @yahoo.com.

VICTOR EMMANUEL III: BIRTH ANNIVERSARY. Nov 11, 1869. Last king of Italy Victor Emmanuel III was born at Naples, Italy, and became king upon the assassination of his father in July 1900. For the first 20 years of his reign, Victor Emmanuel followed Italy's constitutional custom of selecting a prime minister based on the parliamentary majority, but with parliament in disarray after World War I, he named Benito Mussolini to form a cabinet and then failed to prevent Mussolini and the Fascists from seizing power. The king became little more than a figurehead. In 1946 Victor Emmanuel abdicated the throne, and he and the Crown Prince went into exile. He died at Alexandria, Egypt, Dec 28, 1947.

VIETNAM WOMEN'S MEMORIAL DEDICATION: ANNIVERSARY. Nov 11, 1993. In recognition of the 11,500 women who served in the Vietnam War, the bronze sculpture erected at Washington, DC, was dedicated this day.

VOX POPULI DAY. Nov 11. Vox Populi is the Latin term for "People's Voice." Today is the day to make your voice count. Speak up and out for social change on impending cultural issues in international, national, regional and local news via the mediums of print, radio, TV, the internet and open assemblies. [©1994] To alleviate the escalating costs of Eventological® Literature, a charge of $7 must be assessed for each request. Checks are to be made payable to: Adrienne Sioux Koopersmith, 1437 W Rosemont, #1W, Chicago, IL 60660-1319. Phone: (773) 743-5341. Fax: (773) 743-5395. E-mail: la_koop@yahoo.com.

WASHINGTON: ADMISSION DAY: ANNIVERSARY. Nov 11. Became 42nd state in 1889.

WORLD WAR I ARMISTICE: ANNIVERSARY. Nov 11, 1918. Anniversary of armistice between Allied and Central Powers ending WWI, signed at 5 AM, Nov 11, 1918, in Marshal Foch's railway car in the Forest of Compiegne, France. Hostilities ceased at 11 AM. Recognized in many countries as Armistice Day, Remembrance Day, Veterans Day, Victory Day or World War I Memorial Day. Many places observe silent memorial at the 11th hour of the 11th day of the 11th month each year. See also: "Veterans Day" (Nov 11).

BIRTHDAYS TODAY

Bibi Andersson, 69, actress (*Story of a Woman*), born Birgitta Anderson, Stockholm, Sweden, Nov 11, 1935.
Barbara Boxer, 64, US Senator (D, California), born Brooklyn, NY, Nov 11, 1940.
Leonardo DiCaprio, 29, actor (*What's Eating Gilbert Grape, Titanic*), born Ridgewood, NJ, Nov 11, 1975.
Calista Flockhart, 40, actress ("Ally McBeal"), born Freeport, IL, Nov 11, 1964.
Philip McKeon, 40, actor ("Alice"), born Westbury, NY, Nov 11, 1964.
Demi Moore, 42, actress ("General Hospital," *Ghost, GI Jane*), born Roswell, NM, Nov 11, 1962.
Reynaldo Ordonez, 32, baseball player, born Havana, Cuba, Nov 11, 1972.
Kurt Vonnegut, Jr, 82, novelist (*Slaughterhouse Five, Cat's Cradle*), born Indianapolis, IN, Nov 11, 1922.
Jonathan Winters, 79, comedian, actor ("The Jonathan Winters Show," "Mork & Mindy"), born Dayton, OH, Nov 11, 1925.
Frank Urban ("Fuzzy") Zoeller, 53, golfer, born New Albany, IN, Nov 11, 1951.

NOVEMBER 12 — FRIDAY
Day 317 — 49 Remaining

ARCHES NATIONAL PARK ESTABLISHED: ANNIVERSARY. Nov 12, 1971. Area of natural wind-eroded formations in eastern Utah, originally proclaimed a national monument Apr 12, 1929, was established as a national park. For further park info: Arches Natl Park, PO Box 907, Moab, UT 84532.

BIRTH OF BAHA'U'LLAH. Nov 12, 1817. Baha'i observance of anniversary of the birth of Baha'u'llah (born Mirza Husayn Ali) at Nur, Persia. Baha'u'llah was prophet-founder of the Baha'i Faith. One of the nine days of the year when Baha'is suspend work. For info: Baha'is of the US, Office of Public Information, 1320 Nineteenth St NW, Ste 350, Washington, DC 20036. Phone: (202) 466-9870. Fax: (202) 466-9873. E-mail: opi@usbnc.org. Web: www.us.bahai.org.

BLACKMUN, HARRY A.: BIRTH ANNIVERSARY. Nov 12, 1908. Former associate justice of the Supreme Court of the US, nominated by President Nixon Apr 14, 1970. He retired from the Court Aug 3, 1994. Justice Blackmun was born at Nashville, IL, and died at Arlington, VA, Mar 4, 1999.

AN 1890S CHRISTMAS AT BELLE MEADE. Nov 12–Jan 2, 2005. Belle Meade Plantation, Nashville, TN. See magnificent period holiday decorations inside the 1853 Greek Revival Mansion. Tour guides in 1890s dress for the holidays. For info: Belle Meade Plantation, 5025 Harding Rd, Nashville, TN 37205. Phone: (615) 356-0501 or (800) 270-3991. Fax: (615) 356-2336. Web: www.bellemeadeplantation.com.

FOUR CORNER STATES BLUEGRASS FESTIVAL. Nov 12–14. Wickenburg, AZ. 26th annual old-time fiddle, banjo, mandolin, flat-pick guitar championships. Includes gospel music. Special entertainment by nationally known bands as well as 13 competitive events. Annually, the second weekend in November.

Est attendance: 5,000. For info: J Brooks, Exec Dir, Chamber of Commerce, 216 N Frontier Street, Wickenburg, AZ 85390. Phone: (928) 684-5479 or (928) 684-0977. Fax: (928) 684-5470. E-mail: info@wickenburgchamber.com. Web: www.wickenburgchamber.com.

KELLY, GRACE PATRICIA: 75th BIRTH ANNIVERSARY. Nov 12, 1929. American award-winning actress (*Rear Window, To Catch a Thief*) who became Princess Grace of Monaco when she married that country's ruler, Prince Rainier III, in 1956. Born at Philadelphia, PA, she died of injuries sustained in an automobile accident, Sept 14, 1982, at Monte Carlo, Monaco.

MEXICO: POSTMAN'S DAY. Nov 12. Every year on "Día del cartero," Mexicans show their appreciation for their postal carriers by leaving a little something in their mail boxes.

MOON PHASE: NEW MOON. Nov 12. Moon enters New Moon phase at 9:27 AM, EST.

NATIONAL DONOR SABBATH. Nov 12–14. To increase awareness about the dire need for organs and tissues for transplantation and to dispel fears that religion and tissue and organ donation are incompatible. Annually, two weekends before Thanksgiving. For info: Health Resources and Services Admin, US Dept of Health and Human Services. Phone: (301) 443-7577. Web: www.organdonor.gov.

RODIN, AUGUSTE: BIRTH ANNIVERSARY. Nov 12, 1840. French sculptor (*The Kiss, The Thinker*), born at Paris, France. Died Nov 17, 1917, near Paris.

SALT LAKE'S FAMILY CHRISTMAS GIFT SHOW. Nov 12–14. Salt Lake City, UT. A delightful holiday experience. Shoppers will find gifts and decorations from vendors across the nation. A festive shopping atmosphere with music, entertainment, Santa Claus and a Specialty Food area for all to enjoy. Est attendance: 21,000. For info: Showcase Northwest, Inc, PO Box 2815, Kirkland, WA 98083. Phone: (800) 521-SHOW. E-mail: saltlake@showcaseproductionsnw.com. Web: www.showcaseproductions.com.

SPACE MILESTONE: *COLUMBIA* STS-2 (US). Nov 12, 1981. Shuttle *Columbia*, launched from Kennedy Space Center, FL, with Joe Engle and Richard Truly on board, became first spacecraft launched from Earth for a second orbiting mission. Landed at Edwards Air Force Base, CA, Nov 14, 1981.

STAMP EXPO: AMERICA. Nov 12–14. Radisson Hotel, Anaheim, CA. Est attendance: 4,000. For info: Intl Stamp Collectors Society, PO Box 854, Van Nuys, CA 91408. Phone: (818) 997-6496. Fax: (818) 988-4337. E-mail: iibick@aol.com. Web: www.bick.net.

STANTON, ELIZABETH CADY: BIRTH ANNIVERSARY. Nov 12, 1815. American woman suffragist and reformer, Elizabeth Cady Stanton was born at Johnstown, NY. "We hold these truths to be self-evident," she said at the first Women's Rights Convention, in 1848, "that all men and women are created equal." She died at New York, NY, Oct 26, 1902.

SUN YAT-SEN: BIRTH ANNIVERSARY (TRADITIONAL). Nov 12. Although his actual birth date in 1866 is not known, Dr. Sun Yat-Sen's traditional birthday commemoration is held Nov 12. Heroic leader of China's 1911 revolution, he died at Peking, Mar 12, 1925. A holiday in Taiwan. His death anniversary is also widely observed. See also: "Sun Yat-Sen: Death Anniversary" (Mar 12).

★ ★ ★

November 2004

S	M	T	W	T	F	S
	1	2	3	4	5	6
7	8	9	10	11	12	13
14	15	16	17	18	19	20
21	22	23	24	25	26	27
28	29	30				

TYLER, LETITIA CHRISTIAN: BIRTH ANNIVERSARY. Nov 12, 1790. First wife of John Tyler, tenth president of the US, born at New Kent County, VA. Died at Washington, DC, Sept 10, 1842.

WATERFOWL FESTIVAL. Nov 12–14. Easton, MD. A family wildlife art adventure, featuring paintings, carvings, sculpture, decoys, photography and crafts in gallery and shop venues throughout town. Lots of food, music and kids activities. Also, retriever, shooting and fly fishing demonstrations, World Championship Goose and Mason-Dixon Duck Calling contests, Antique Decoy Auction. Annually, the second full weekend in November. Proceeds contributed to wildlife conservation. Est attendance: 19,000. For info: Waterfowl Festival, PO Box 929, Easton, MD 21601. Phone: (410) 822-4567. Fax: (410) 820-9286. E-mail: facts@waterfowlfestival.org. Web: www.waterfowlfestival.org.

WISCONSIN HOLIDAY MARKET. Nov 12–14. The American Club, Kohler, WI. More than 100 artists and craftspeople display their specialties in a glittering holiday market setting. Christmas shoppers can browse for crafts and collectibles to find the perfect holiday gift. Held in The American Club's Grand Hall of the Great Lakes. Est attendance: 6,000. For info: The American Club, Highland Dr, Kohler, WI 53044. Phone: (800) 344-2838. Fax: (920) 457-4441. Web: www.destinationkohler.com.

BIRTHDAYS TODAY

Nadia Comaneci, 43, Olympic gold medal gymnast, born Onesti, Romania, Nov 12, 1961.

Tonya Harding, 34, figure skater, born Portland, OR, Nov 12, 1970.

Norman Mineta, 73, US Secretary of Transportation, born San Jose, CA, Nov 12, 1931.

Megan Mullally, 46, actress ("Will & Grace," *How to Succeed in Business Without Really Trying*), born Los Angeles, CA, Nov 12, 1958.

Jack Reed, 55, US Senator (D, Rhode Island), born Providence, RI, Nov 12, 1949.

David Schwimmer, 38, actor ("Friends"), born Queens, NY, Nov 12, 1966.

Sammy Sosa, 36, baseball player, born San Pedro de Macoris, Dominican Republic, Nov 12, 1968.

Neil Young, 59, singer (Buffalo Springfield and Crosby, Stills, Nash & Young), songwriter, born Toronto, ON, Canada, Nov 12, 1945.

NOVEMBER 13 — SATURDAY
Day 318 — 48 Remaining

BOOTH, EDWIN (THOMAS): BIRTH ANNIVERSARY. Nov 13, 1833. Famed American actor and founder of the Players Club, born near Bel Air, MD. His brother, John Wilkes Booth, assassinated President Lincoln. Died at New York, NY, June 7, 1893.

BRANDEIS, LOUIS DEMBITZ: BIRTH ANNIVERSARY. Nov 13, 1856. American jurist, associate justice of US Supreme Court (1916–39), born at Louisville, KY. Died at Washington, DC, Oct 5, 1941.

580

CANE GRINDING AND CRAFTS FESTIVAL. Nov 13. Oatland Island Education Center, Savannah, GA. This festive fall celebration is centered around Oatland's Heritage Homesite where area farmers grind sugar cane and make syrup as it was done 150 years ago. The sites and sounds of music and dancing fill the forest and flavor the air with traditional rhythms. Regional artisans and crafters will be selling and demonstrating their work. Hayrides, pony rides and children's activities are planned and Oatland's Native Animal Nature Trail will be open. Est attendance: 4,000. For info: Oatland Island Education Center, 711 Sandtown Rd, Savannah, GA 31410. Phone: (912) 898-3980. Web: www.oatlandisland.org.

ENGLAND: LORD MAYOR'S SHOW. Nov 13. The City of London. The 677th show. Each year a colorful parade steps off at 11 AM from the Guildhall to the Royal Courts of Justice to mark the inauguration of the new Lord Mayor, who pledges allegiance to the Crown. Annually, the second Saturday in November. Est attendance: 500,000. For info: Pageantmaster, The Lord Mayor's Show, 1 Queens Rd, Hertford, Herts, England SG14 1EN. Phone: (44) (1992) 505-306. E-mail: webmaster@lordmayorsshow.org. Web: www.lordmayorsshow.org.

FALL OF KABUL: ANNIVERSARY. Nov 13, 2001. Northern Alliance troops opposing the Islamic extremist regime of the Taliban moved into the capital of Afghanistan on this date—the first major victory in the war on terrorism prompted by the Sept 11, 2001, attacks on America. After fleeing Kabul (which they had controlled since 1996), the Taliban regime quickly collapsed. The US had demanded that the Taliban regime give up Al Qaeda terrorists and their leader, Osama Bin Laden, or face reprisals. Upon the Taliban's prevarication, the US led a multinational force in support of the Northern Alliance that began with a bombardment and then ground warfare in Afghanistan. The Fall of Kabul was the major first step to destroying Al Qaeda's Afghanistan stronghold. See also "Attack on America: Anniversary" (Sept 11).

HOLLAND TUNNEL: ANNIVERSARY. Nov 13, 1927. The Holland Tunnel, running under the Hudson River between New York, NY, and Jersey City, NJ, was opened to traffic. The tunnel was built and operated by the New York–New Jersey Bridge and Tunnel Commission. Comprised of two tubes, each large enough for two lanes of traffic, the Holland was the first underwater tunnel built in the US.

MAXWELL, JAMES CLERK: BIRTH ANNIVERSARY. Nov 13, 1831. British physicist noted for his work in the field of electricity and magnetism. Born at Edinburgh, Scotland, he died of cancer Nov 5, 1879, at Cambridge, England.

MESSINA HOF'S WINE PREMIERE. Nov 13 (tentative). Bryan, TX. Traditional celebration of the new vintages. Wine aficionados' palates are treated to the premiere of all the new wines, and also the prize-winning wine label from our Texas Artist Competition earlier in the year. There are several wine-related activities like the Winemaker's Blending Lab and wine and food pairing seminars. In the evening a new vintage reception will be followed by an elegant gourmet wine premiere dinner. Est attendance: 2,500. For info: Messina Hof Wine Cellars, 4545 Old Reliance Rd, Bryan, TX 77808. Phone: (979) 778-9463. Fax: (979) 778-1729.

STEVENSON, ROBERT LOUIS: BIRTH ANNIVERSARY. Nov 13, 1850. Scottish author, born at Edinburgh, Scotland, known for his *Child's Garden of Verses* and novels such as *Treasure Island* and *Kidnapped*. Died at Samoa, Dec 3, 1894.

STOKES BECOMES FIRST BLACK MAYOR IN US: ANNIVERSARY. Nov 13, 1967. Carl Burton Stokes became the first black in the US elected mayor when he won the Cleveland, OH, mayoral election Nov 13, 1967. Died Apr 3, 1996.

TRELAWNEY, EDWARD JOHN: BIRTH ANNIVERSARY. Nov 13, 1792. English traveler and author, friend of Shelley and Byron, born at London. He died at Sompting, Sussex, Aug 13, 1881, and was buried at Rome, next to Shelley.

WORLD KINDNESS DAY. Nov 13. The Kindness Movement has gone global! The World Kindness Movement grew out of a series of Kindness Conferences convened by the Japanese Small Kindness Movement in 1996. The Random Acts of Kindness Foundation, USA has been a part of these conferences along with representatives from Japan, Singapore, Australia, Canada, Thailand and England. This day represents the pledge of each of these countries to join together to build a kinder and more compassionate world. For info: Random Acts of Kindness Foundation. Phone: (800) 660-2811. Web: www.actsofkindness.org.

BIRTHDAYS TODAY

Sheila E. Frazier, 56, actress (*Super Fly, I'm Gonna Git You Sucka*), born the Bronx, NY, Nov 13, 1948.
Whoopi Goldberg, 55, comedienne, actress (*Ghost, Sister Act, The Color Purple*), born New York, NY, Nov 13, 1949.
Jimmy Kimmel, 37, late night talk-show host, comedian ("The Man Show," "Jimmy Kimmel Live"), born Brooklyn, NY, Nov 13, 1967.
Joe Mantegna, 57, actor (stage: Tony for *Glengarry Glen Ross*; *House of Games, Things Change*), born Chicago, IL, Nov 13, 1947.
Garry Marshall, 70, producer, director (*Beaches, Pretty Woman*), actor ("Murphy Brown"), born New York, NY, Nov 13, 1934.
Chris Noth, 47, actor ("Sex and the City," "Law & Order," *Burnzy's Last Call*), born Madison, WI, Nov 13, 1957.
Tracy Scoggins, 45, actress ("The Colbys," *Some Kind of Hero*), born Galveston, TX, Nov 13, 1959.
Madeline Sherwood, 82, actress ("The Flying Nun"), born Montreal, QC, Canada, Nov 13, 1922.
Vincent Frank (Vinny) Testaverde, 41, football player, born New York, NY, Nov 13, 1963.

NOVEMBER 14 — SUNDAY
Day 319 — 47 Remaining

★**AMERICAN EDUCATION WEEK.** Nov 14–20. Presidential Proclamation 5403, of Oct 30, 1985, covers all succeeding years. Always the first full week preceding the fourth Thursday in November. Issued from 1921–25 and in 1936, sometimes for a week in December and sometimes as National Education Week. After an absence of a number of years, this proclamation was issued each year from 1955–82 (issued in 1955 as a prelude to the White House Conference on Education). Previously, Proclamation 4967, of Sept 13, 1982, covered all succeeding years as the second week in November.

AMERICAN EDUCATION WEEK. Nov 14–20. Focuses attention on the importance of education and all that it stands for. Annually, the week preceding the week of Thanksgiving. For info: Natl Education Assn (NEA), 1201 16th St NW, Washington, DC 20036. Phone: (202) 833-4000. Web: www.nea.org.

Nov 14 ☆ *Chase's 2004 Calendar of Events* ☆

AROUND THE WORLD IN 72 DAYS: ANNIVERSARY. Nov 14, 1889. Newspaper reporter Nellie Bly (pen name used by Elizabeth Cochrane Seaman) set off Nov 14, 1889, to attempt to break Jules Verne's imaginary hero Phileas Fogg's record of voyaging around the world in 80 days. She did beat Fogg's record, taking 72 days, 6 hours, 11 minutes and 14 seconds to make the trip.

BLOOD TRANSFUSION: ANNIVERSARY. Nov 14, 1666. Samuel Pepys, diarist and Fellow of the Royal Society, wrote in his diary for Nov 14, 1666: "Dr. Croone told me . . . there was a pretty experiment of the blood of one dog let out, till he died, into the body of another on one side, while all his own run out on the other side. The first died upon the place, and the other very well and likely to do well. This did give occasion to many pretty wishes, as of the blood of a Quaker to be let into an Archbishop, and such like; but, as Dr. Croone says, may, if it takes, be of mighty use to man's health, for the amending of bad blood by borrowing from a better body."

COPLAND, AARON: BIRTH ANNIVERSARY. Nov 14, 1900. American composer Aaron Copland was born at Brooklyn, NY. Incorporating American folk music and, later, the 12-tone system, he strove to create an American music style that was both popular and artistic. He composed ballets, film scores and orchestral works including *Fanfare for the Common Man* (1942), *Appalachian Spring* (1944) (for which he won the Pulitzer Prize) and the score for *The Heiress* (1948) (for which he won an Oscar). He died Dec 2, 1990, at North Tarrytown, NY.

DOW-JONES TOPS 1,000: ANNIVERSARY. Nov 14, 1972. The Dow-Jones Index of 30 major industrial stocks topped the 1,000 mark for the first time.

EID-AL-FITR: CELEBRATING THE FAST. Nov 14. Islamic calendar date: Shawwal 1, 1425. This feast/festival celebrates the completion of the Ramadan fasting and usually lasts for several days. Everyone wears new clothes; children receive gifts from parents and relatives; children are allowed to stay up late and participate in games, folktales, plays, puppet shows, trips to amusement parks. This holiday is known as Seker Bayram in Turkey and Hari Raya Puasa in South East Asia. Different methods for "anticipating" the visibility of the new moon crescent at Mecca are used by different Muslim groups. US date may vary. Began at sunset the preceding day.

EISENHOWER, MAMIE DOUD: BIRTH ANNIVERSARY. Nov 14, 1896. Wife of Dwight David Eisenhower, 34th president of the US, born at Boone, IA. Died Nov 1, 1979, at Gettysburg, PA.

ENGLAND: REMEMBRANCE DAY SERVICE AND PARADE. Nov 14. Cenotaph, Whitehall, London. Wreath-laying ceremony to commemorate the dead of both World Wars by Her Majesty The Queen, members of the Royal Family, government and service organizations. Annually, the Sunday closest to Nov 11. For info: Public Info Office, HQ London District Military, Horse Guards, Whitehall, London, England SW1A 2AX. Phone: (44) (171) 414-2353. Fax: (44) (171) 414-2352.

FULTON, ROBERT: BIRTH ANNIVERSARY. Nov 14, 1765. Inventor of the steamboat, born at Little Britain, PA. Died Feb 24, 1815, at New York, NY.

GERMANY: VOLKSTRAUERTAG. Nov 14. Memorial Day and national day of mourning in all German states for victims of National Socialism and the dead of both world wars. Observed on the Sunday before Totensonntag. See also: "Germany: Totensonntag" (Nov 21).

GUINEA-BISSAU: RE-ADJUSTMENT MOVEMENT'S DAY. Nov 14. National holiday.

INDIA: CHILDREN'S DAY. Nov 14. Holiday observed throughout India.

JORDAN: KING HUSSEIN: BIRTH ANNIVERSARY. Nov 14. H.M. King Hussein's birthday is honored each year on the anniversary of his birth in 1935. He died in Jordan Feb 7, 1999.

LOOSEN UP, LIGHTEN UP DAY. Nov 14. A day to remind people of all the benefits of joy and laughter. For info: Stephanie West Allen, PO Box 9311, Denver, CO 80209. Phone: (303) 742-4790. Fax: (303) 935-8842. E-mail: stephanie@allen-nichols.com. Web: www.allen-nichols.com.

MONET, CLAUDE: BIRTH ANNIVERSARY. Nov 14, 1840. French Impressionist painter (*Water Lillies*), born at Paris. Died at Giverny, France, Dec 5, 1926.

"MURPHY BROWN" TV PREMIERE: ANNIVERSARY. Nov 14, 1988. This intelligent, often acerbic sitcom set in Washington, DC, starred Candice Bergen as an egotistical, seasoned journalist working for the fictitious TV news show "FYI." Featured were Grant Shaud, as the show's high-strung producer, Miles Silverberg (later replaced by Lily Tomlin); Faith Ford as the former Miss America-turned-anchor, Corky Sherwood; Joe Regalbuto as neurotic reporter Frank Fontana; Charles Kimbrough as uptight anchorman, Jim Dial; Pat Corley as Phil, owner of the local watering hole and Robert Pastorelli as Eldin Bernecky, perfectionist housepainter and aspiring artist. The show often blurred the line between reality and fiction by dealing with topical issues and including real-life journalists as guest stars playing themselves. The series ended with the May 31, 1998 episode.

NATIONAL AMERICAN TEDDY BEAR DAY. Nov 14. The Vermont Teddy Bear Company® annually celebrates the birth of America's most beloved companion, the Teddy Bear. The legend goes that President Theodore Roosevelt spared the life of a bear cub while on a big game hunt in Mississippi in 1902. Clifford Berryman, a political cartoonist, recorded the incident. President Theodore Roosevelt was most often depicted alongside a Teddy Bear and thus America's love affair with the Teddy Bear began. For info: The Vermont Teddy Bear Company®, 6655 Shelburne Rd, Shelburne, VT 05482. Phone: 1-800-829-BEAR. Web: www.VermontTeddyBear.com.

NEHRU, JAWAHARLAL: BIRTH ANNIVERSARY. Nov 14, 1889. Indian leader and first prime minister after independence. Born at Allahabad, India, he died May 27, 1964, at New Delhi.

PERIOPERATIVE (OR) NURSE WEEK. Nov 14–20. To inform health care consumers that the nurse in the operating room cares for patients before, during and after surgery. Annually, the week including Nov 14. For info: PR Mgr, AORN, 2170 S Parker Rd, Ste 300, Denver, CO 80231-5711. Phone: (303) 755-6300. Fax: (303) 338-4838. E-mail: jpaulson@aorn.org. Web: www.aorn.org.

SALISBURY, HARRISON: BIRTH ANNIVERSARY. Nov 14, 1908. American journalist Harrison Evans Salisbury was born at Minneapolis, MN. *New York Times* Moscow correspondent

November 2004	S	M	T	W	T	F	S
		1	2	3	4	5	6
	7	8	9	10	11	12	13
	14	15	16	17	18	19	20
	21	22	23	24	25	26	27
	28	29	30				

from 1949 to 1954. Salisbury won the Pulitzer Prize in 1955 for a series of articles on the Soviet Union. He died July 5, 1993, at Providence, RI.

SPACE MILESTONE: *APOLLO 12* (US): 35th ANNIVERSARY. Nov 14, 1969. Launched this date. This was the second manned lunar landing—in Ocean of Storms. First pinpoint landing. Astronauts Conrad, Bean and Gordon visited *Surveyor 3* and took samples. Earth splashdown Nov 24.

TUNISIA: TREE FESTIVAL. Nov 14. National agricultural festival. Annually, the second Sunday in November.

BIRTHDAYS TODAY

Boutros Boutros-Ghali, 82, former Secretary-General of the UN, born Cairo, Egypt, Nov 14, 1922.
Prince Charles, 56, Prince of Wales, heir to the British throne, born London, England, Nov 14, 1948.
Condoleezza Rice, 50, US National Security Adviser, born Birmingham, AL, Nov 14, 1954.
Laura San Giacomo, 42, actress (*sex, lies and videotape*, "Just Shoot Me"), born Hoboken, NJ, Nov 14, 1962.
Curt Schilling, 38, baseball player, born Anchorage, AK, Nov 14, 1966.
Joseph ("Run") Simmons, 40, rapper (*Run-DMC*), born Queens, NY, Nov 14, 1964.
Don Stewart, 69, singer, actor ("Guiding Light"), born Staten Island, NY, Nov 14, 1935.
D.B. Sweeney, 43, actor (*Spawn*, *The Cutting Edge*), born Shoreham, Long Island, NY, Nov 14, 1961.
Yanni, 50, New Age composer, born Yanni Chrysomalis, Kalamata, Greece, Nov 14, 1954.

NOVEMBER 15 — MONDAY

Day 320 — 46 Remaining

AMERICA RECYCLES DAY. Nov 15. To promote recycling and recycled products. More than 40 states will participate. Annually, every Nov 15. For info: Natl Program Mgr, America Recycles Day, 1325 G St NW, Ste 1025, Washington, DC 20005. Phone: (202) 347-0450. Web: www.americarecyclesday.org.

BELGIUM: DYNASTY DAY. Nov 15. National holiday in honor of Belgian monarchy.

BRAZIL: REPUBLIC DAY. Nov 15. Commemorates the Proclamation of the Republic in 1889. Celebrated on the Monday nearest Nov 15.

CHILDREN'S BOOK WEEK. Nov 15–21. An annual event, sponsored by The Children's Book Council, to encourage the enjoyment of reading for young people. For info: The Children's Book Council, Inc, 12 W 37th St, 2nd Fl, New York, NY 10018. Phone: (800) 999-2160. Fax: (888) 807-9355. E-mail: paula.quint @cbcbooks.org. Web: www.cbcbooks.org/html/book_week.html.

FIRST BLACK PROFESSIONAL HOCKEY PLAYER: ANNIVERSARY. Nov 15, 1950. When Arthur Dorrington signed a contract to play hockey with the Atlantic City Seagulls of the Eastern Amateur League, he became the first black man to play organized hockey in the US. He played for the Seagulls during the 1950 and 1951 seasons.

GEORGE SPELVIN DAY. Nov 15. Believed to be the anniversary of George Spelvin's theatrical birth—in Charles A. Gardiner's play *Karl the Peddler* on Nov 15, 1886, in a production at New York, NY. The name (or equivalent Georgina, Georgetta, etc) is used in play programs to conceal the fact that an actor is performing in more than one role. The fictitious Spelvin is said to have appeared in more than 10,000 Broadway performances. See also: "England: Walter Plinge Day" (Dec 2) for British equivalent.

GYPSY CONDEMNATION ORDER: ANNIVERSARY. Nov 15, 1943. An order was issued by Heinrich Himmler for nomadic Gypsies and part-Gypsies to be placed in concentration camps. In cases of doubt, it was up to local heads of police to determine who was a Gypsy. Some estimates put the number of Gypsies killed in the Holocaust as high as half a million.

JAPAN: SHICHI-GO-SAN. Nov 15. Annual children's festival. The *Shichi-Go-San* (Seven-Five-Three) rite is "the most picturesque event in the autumn season." Parents take their three-year-old children of either sex, five-year-old boys and seven-year-old girls to the parish shrines dressed in their best clothes. There the guardian spirits are thanked for the healthy growth of the children and prayers are offered for their further development.

O'KEEFFE, GEORGIA: BIRTH ANNIVERSARY. Nov 15, 1887. Described as one of the greatest American artists of the 20th century, Georgia O'Keeffe was born at Sun Prairie, WI. In 1924, she married the famous photographer Alfred Stieglitz. His more than 500 photographs of her have been called "the greatest love poem in the history of photography." She painted desert landscapes and flower studies. She died at Santa Fe, NM, Mar 6, 1986.

ROMMEL, ERWIN: BIRTH ANNIVERSARY. Nov 15, 1891. Field marshal and commander of the German Afrika Korps in WWII, Erwin Rommel was born at Heidenheim, in Wurttemberg, Germany. Rommel commanded the Seventh Panzer Division in the Battle of France. Considered an excellent commander, Rommel's early success in Africa made him a legend as the "Desert Fox," but in early 1943 he was outmaneuvered by Field Marshal Bernard Montgomery and Germany surrendered Tunis in May of that year. Implicated in July 1944 in an attempted assassination of Hitler, he was given the choice of suicide or a trial and chose the former. Rommel died by his own hand at age 52, Oct 14, 1944, near Ulm, Germany.

SPACE MILESTONE: *BURAN* (USSR): ANNIVERSARY. Nov 15, 1988. The Soviet Union's first reusable space plane, *Buran*, landed on this date, completing a smooth, unmanned mission at approximately 1:25 AM, EST, after orbiting the Earth twice in 3 hours, 25 minutes. Launched at Baikonur, Soviet central Asia, the importance of this mission was in its computer-controlled liftoff and return.

BIRTHDAYS TODAY

Ed Asner, 75, actor ("The Mary Tyler Moore Show," "Lou Grant," *Roots*), born Kansas City, MO, Nov 15, 1929.
Daniel Barenboim, 62, musician, conductor, born Buenos Aires, Argentina, Nov 15, 1942.
Joanna Barnes, 70, actress ("The Trials of O'Brien"), born Boston, MA, Nov 15, 1934.
Petula Clark, 72, singer ("Downtown," "I Know a Place," "This Is My Song"), actress, born Ewell, Surrey, England, Nov 15, 1932.
Beverly D'Angelo, 50, actress (*Hair*, *Coal Miner's Daughter*), born Columbus, OH, Nov 15, 1954.
Kevin Eubanks, 47, "The Tonight Show" bandleader, born Philadelphia, PA, Nov 15, 1957.
Yaphet Kotto, 67, actor ("Homicide," *Nothing But a Man*, *Blue Collar*, *Midnight Run*), born New York, NY, Nov 15, 1937.
Jonny Lee Miller, 32, actor (*Dracula 2000*, *Behind the Lines*, *Mansfield Park*), born Kingston, England, Nov 15, 1972.
Bill Richardson, 57, Governor of New Mexico (D), former Secretary of Energy (Clinton Administration), born Pasadena, CA, Nov 15, 1947.
Joseph Wapner, 85, TV personality ("People's Court"), retired judge, born Los Angeles, CA, Nov 15, 1919.
Sam Waterston, 64, actor (*The Killing Fields*, *The Great Gatsby*, "I'll Fly Away," "Law & Order"), born Cambridge, MA, Nov 15, 1940.

Nov 16–17 ☆ *Chase's 2004 Calendar of Events* ☆

★ ★ ★

NOVEMBER 16 — TUESDAY
Day 321 — 45 Remaining

ESTONIA: DAY OF NATIONAL REBIRTH: ANNIVERSARY. Nov 16. National holiday. Commemorates the 1988 Declaration of Sovereignty. Became independent from the Soviet Union in 1991.

HANDY, WILLIAM CHRISTOPHER: BIRTH ANNIVERSARY. Nov 16, 1873. American composer, bandleader, "Father of the Blues," W.C. Handy was born at Florence, AL. He died at New York, NY, Mar 28, 1958.

HINDEMITH, PAUL: BIRTH ANNIVERSARY. Nov 16, 1895. Prolific composer and teacher, born at Hanau, Germany. Became a resident and citizen of the US during World War II. Died at Frankfurt, Germany, Dec 28, 1963.

MEREDITH, BURGESS: BIRTH ANNIVERSARY. Nov 16, 1907. Actor (*Of Mice and Men, Rocky*) born at Cleveland, OH. Some sources give his year of birth as 1908 or 1909. Died at Malibu, CA, Sept 9, 1997.

OKLAHOMA: ADMISSION DAY: ANNIVERSARY. Nov 16. Became 46th state in 1907.

RIEL, LOUIS: HANGING ANNIVERSARY. Nov 16, 1885. Born at St. Boniface, Manitoba, Canada, Oct 23, 1844, Louis Riel, leader of the Metis (French/Indian mixed ancestry), was elected to Canada's House of Commons in 1873 and 1874, but never seated. Confined to asylums for madness (feigned or falsely charged, some said), Riel became a US citizen in 1883. In 1885 he returned to western Canada to lead the North West Rebellion. Defeated, he surrendered and was tried for treason, convicted and hanged, at Regina, Northwest Territory, Canada. Seen as a patriot and protector of French culture in Canada, Riel's life and death became a legend and a symbol of the problems between French and English Canadians.

ROMAN CATHOLICS ISSUE NEW CATECHISM: ANNIVERSARY. Nov 16, 1992. For the first time since 1563, the Roman Catholic Church issued a new universal catechism, which addressed modern-day issues.

SAINT EUSTATIUS, WEST INDIES: STATIA AND AMERICA DAY. Nov 16, 1776. St. Eustatius, Leeward Islands. To commemorate the first salute to an American flag by a foreign government, from Fort Oranje in 1776. Festivities include sports events and dancing. During the American Revolution St. Eustatius was an important trading center and a supply base for the colonies.

SPACE MILESTONE: SKYLAB 4 (US): ANNIVERSARY. Nov 16, 1973. 30th manned US space flight launched with three astronauts, G.P. Carr, W.R. Page and E.G. Gibson who spent 84 days on the space station. Space walks totalled 22 hours. Returned to Earth on Feb 8, 1974.

SPACE MILESTONE: VENERA 3 (USSR). Nov 16, 1965. Launched this date, this unmanned space probe crashed into Venus, Mar 1, 1966. First man-made object on another planet.

UNITED NATIONS: INTERNATIONAL DAY FOR TOLERANCE. Nov 16. On Dec 12, 1996, the General Assembly established the International Day for Tolerance, to commemorate the adoption by UNESCO member states of the Declaration of Principles on Tolerance in 1995. For info: United Nations, Dept of Public Info, New York, NY 10017. Web: www.un.org.

November 2004

S	M	T	W	T	F	S
	1	2	3	4	5	6
7	8	9	10	11	12	13
14	15	16	17	18	19	20
21	22	23	24	25	26	27
28	29	30				

BIRTHDAYS TODAY
Oksana Baiul, 27, Olympic gold medal figure skater, born Dniepropetrovsk, Ukraine, Nov 16, 1977.
Lisa Bonet, 37, actress ("The Cosby Show," "A Different World," *Angel Heart*), born San Francisco, CA, Nov 16, 1967.
Elizabeth Drew, 69, journalist, born Cincinnati, OH, Nov 16, 1935.
Dwight Eugene Gooden, 40, former baseball player, born Tampa, FL, Nov 16, 1964.
Marg Helgenberger, 46, actress ("CSI," "China Beach"), born Fremont, NE, Nov 16, 1958.
Martha Plimpton, 34, actress ("The Defenders"), born New York, NY, Nov 16, 1970.

NOVEMBER 17 — WEDNESDAY
Day 322 — 44 Remaining

GERMANY: BUSS UND BETTAG. Nov 17. Buss und Bettag (Repentance Day) is observed on the Wednesday before the last Sunday of the church year. A legal public holiday in all German states except Bavaria (where it is observed only in communities with predominantly Protestant populations).

HOMEMADE BREAD DAY. Nov 17. A day for the family to remember and enjoy the making, baking and eating of nutritious homemade bread. For info: Homemade Bread Day Committee, PO Box 3, Montague, MI 49437-0003.

MOBIUS, AUGUST: BIRTH ANNIVERSARY. Nov 17, 1790. German astronomer, mathematician, teacher and author, August Ferdinand Mobius was born at Schulpforte, Germany. Mobius was a pioneer in the field of topology, and first described the Mobius net and the Mobius strip. He died at Leipzig, Sept 26, 1868.

MONTGOMERY, BERNARD LAW: BIRTH ANNIVERSARY. Nov 17, 1887. Bernard Law Montgomery, who commanded the British Eighth Army to victory at El Alamein in north Africa in 1943, was born at St. Mark's Vicarage, Kennington Oval, London, England. He also led the Eighth Army in the Sicilian and Italian campaigns and commanded all ground forces in the 1944 Normandy landing. Montgomery died Mar 24, 1976, at Alton, Hampshire, England.

NATIONAL EDUCATIONAL SUPPORT PERSONNEL DAY. Nov 17. A mandate of the delegates to the 1987 National Education Association Representative Assembly called for a special day during American Education Week to honor the contributions of school support employees. Local associations and school districts salute support staff on this 17th annual observance, the Wednesday of American Education Week. For info: Communications, Natl Education Assn (NEA), 1201 16th St NW, Washington, DC 20036. Phone: (202) 822-7200. Fax: (202) 822-7292. Web: www.nea.org.

QUEEN ELIZABETH I: ACCESSION ANNIVERSARY. Nov 17, 1558. Anniversary of accession of Elizabeth I to English throne; celebrated as a holiday in England for more than a century after her death in 1603.

SUEZ CANAL: ANNIVERSARY. Nov 17, 1869. Formal opening of the Suez Canal. It had taken 1.5 million men a decade to dig the 100-mile canal. It shortened the sea route from Europe to India by 6,000 miles. An Anglo-French commission ran the canal until 1956, when Egypt's President Gamal Abdel Nasser seized it.

ZENGER, JOHN PETER: ARREST ANNIVERSARY. Nov 17, 1734. Colonial printer and journalist who established the *New York Weekly Journal* (first issue, Nov 5, 1733). Zenger was arrested Nov 17, 1734, for libel against the colonial governor, but continued to edit his newspaper from jail. Trial was held during August 1735. Zenger's acquittal was an important early step toward freedom of the press in America. Zenger was born at Germany in 1697, came to the US in 1710 and died July 28, 1746, at New York, NY.

584

☆ Chase's 2004 Calendar of Events ☆ Nov 17–18

BIRTHDAYS TODAY

Justin Cooper, 16, actor ("Brother's Keeper," *Liar, Liar*), born Southern California, Nov 17, 1988.
Howard Dean, 56, former Governor of Vermont (D), born East Hampton, NY, Nov 17, 1948.
Danny DeVito, 60, actor ("Taxi," *Twins*), director (*Throw Mama from the Train*), born Neptune, NJ, Nov 17, 1944.
Shelby Foote, 88, writer, historian (*Civil War*), born Greenville, MS, Nov 17, 1916.
Daisy Fuentes, 38, MTV veejay, host ("America's Funniest Home Videos"), born Havana, Cuba, Nov 17, 1966.
Isaac Hanson, 24, singer (Hanson), born Tulsa, OK, Nov 17, 1980.
Lauren Hutton, 60, model, actress (*American Gigolo*), born Charleston, SC, Nov 17, 1944.
James M. Inhofe, 70, US Senator (R, Oklahoma), born Des Moines, IA, Nov 17, 1934.
Gordon Lightfoot, 66, singer ("Sundown"), songwriter ("Early Morning Rain"), born Orilla, ON, Canada, Nov 17, 1938.
Keith Lockhart, 45, Boston Pops conductor, born Poughkeepsie, NY, Nov 17, 1959.
Sophie Marceau, 38, actress (*Braveheart*), born Paris, France, Nov 17, 1966.
Mary Elizabeth Mastrantonio, 46, actress (*The Color of Money, Thieves*), born Oak Park, IL, Nov 17, 1958.
Robert Bruce (Bob) Mathias, 74, former congressman, Olympic gold medal decathlete, born Tulare, CA, Nov 17, 1930.
Lorne Michaels, 60, producer ("Saturday Night Live"), born Toronto, ON, Canada, Nov 17, 1944.
RuPaul, 44, model, actor ("The RuPaul Show"), born RuPaul Andre Charles, San Diego, CA, Nov 17, 1960.
Martin Scorsese, 62, director (*Mean Streets, The Color of Money, Raging Bull, Goodfellas*), born Flushing, NY, Nov 17, 1942.
George Thomas (Tom) Seaver, 60, Hall of Fame baseball player, broadcaster, born Fresno, CA, Nov 17, 1944.

NOVEMBER 18 — THURSDAY

Day 323 — 43 Remaining

AMERICAN SPEECH-LANGUAGE-HEARING ASSOCIATION CONVENTION. Nov 18–20. Philadelphia, PA. Scientific sessions held on language, speech disorders, hearing science and hearing disorders and matters of professional interest to speech-language pathologists and audiologists. Est attendance: 10,000. For info: American Speech-Language-Hearing Assn, 10801 Rockville Pike, Rockville, MD 20852-3279. Phone: (301) 897-5700. Web: www.professional.asha.org.

DAGUERRE, LOUIS JACQUES MANDE: BIRTH ANNIVERSARY. Nov 18, 1789. French tax collector, theater scene-painter, physicist and inventor, was born at Cormeilles-en-Parisis, France. He is remembered for his invention of the daguerreotype photographic process—one of the earliest to permit a photographic image to be chemically fixed to provide a permanent picture. The process was presented to the French Academy of Science Jan 7, 1839. Daguerre died near Paris, France, July 10, 1851.

GILBERT, SIR WILLIAM SCHWENCK: BIRTH ANNIVERSARY. Nov 18, 1836. English author of librettos for the famed Gilbert and Sullivan comic operas, born at London, England. Died May 29, 1911, at Harrow Weald, Middlesex, England, as a result of a heart attack experienced while saving a woman from drowning.

GRAY, ASA: BIRTH ANNIVERSARY. Nov 18, 1810. Botanist and natural history professor at Harvard, born at Paris, NY. Gray was known as a pioneer in the field of plant geography and a chief advocate of Darwin. Died at Cambridge, MA, Jan 30, 1888.

GREAT AMERICAN SMOKEOUT. Nov 18. A day observed annually to celebrate smoke-free environments. Annually, the third Thursday in November. For info: American Cancer Society, 1599 Clifton Rd NE, Atlanta, GA 30329. Phone: (800) 227-2345. Web: www.cancer.org.

HAITI: ARMY DAY: ANNIVERSARY. Nov 18, 1803. Commemorates the Battle of Vertiéres, Nov 18, 1803, in which Haitians defeated the French.

"HOWARD STERN SHOW" RADIO PREMIERE: ANNIVERSARY. Nov 18, 1985. Radio's pioneering shock jock, Howard Stern, began broadcasting with sidekick Robin Quivers on New York radio station WXRK-FM. With outrageous humor and a gleeful disregard for taste, Stern quickly became popular nationally, but many remain outraged at his show elements. The FCC has frequently fined his broadcasting company. Radio listeners today number around 25 million.

JONESTOWN MASSACRE: ANNIVERSARY. Nov 18, 1978. On this date, Indiana-born, 47-year-old Reverend Jim Jones, leader of the "People's Temple," was reported to have directed the suicides of more than 900 persons at Jonestown, Guyana. US Representative Leo J. Ryan, of California, and four members of his party were killed in ambush at Port Kaituma airstrip on Nov 18, 1978, when they attempted to leave after an investigative visit to the remote jungle location of the religious cult. On the following day, Jones and his mistress killed themselves after watching the administration of Kool-Aid laced with the deadly poison cyanide to members of the cult. At least 912 persons died in the biggest murder-suicide in history.

LATVIA: INDEPENDENCE DAY. Nov 18. National holiday. Commemorates the declaration of an independent Latvia from Germany and Russia in 1918.

LOMBROSO, CESARE: BIRTH ANNIVERSARY. Nov 18, 1836. Italian founder of criminology, born at Verona, Italy. A professor of psychiatry, Lombroso believed that criminality could be identified with certain physical types of people. He died at Turin, Oct 19, 1909.

MARRIED TO A SCORPIO SUPPORT DAY. Nov 18. A worldwide day of remembrance to honor all those married to Scorpios and who suffer greatly. Assert yourself today! Hide their household flow charts. Annually, Nov 18. [©2003 by WH.] For info: Thomas & Ruth Roy, Wellcat Holidays, 2418 Long Ln, Lebanon, PA 17046. Phone: (717) 279-0184. E-mail: info@wellcat .com. Web: www.wellcat.com.

MERCER, JOHN HERNDON (JOHNNY): 95th BIRTH ANNIVERSARY. Nov 18, 1909. American songwriter, singer, radio performer and actor, born at Savannah, GA. Johnny Mercer wrote lyrics (and often the music) for some of the great American popular music from the 1930s through the 1960s, including "Autumn Leaves," "One for My Baby," "Satin Doll," "On the Achison, Topeka, and the Santa Fe," "You Must Have Been a Beautiful Baby," "Come Rain or Come Shine," "Hooray for Hollywood," "Jeepers Creepers" and countless more. Mercer died June 25, 1976, at Bel Air, CA.

MICKEY MOUSE'S BIRTHDAY. Nov 18. The comical activities of squeaky-voiced Mickey Mouse first appeared in 1928, on the screen of the Colony Theatre at New York City. The film, Walt Disney's "Steamboat Willie," was the first animated cartoon talking picture.

Nov 18 ☆ Chase's 2004 Calendar of Events ☆

MOROCCO: INDEPENDENCE DAY. Nov 18. National holiday. Commemorates the return from exile in 1955 of Sultan (later King) Sidi Muhammed to form a constitutional government.

★**NATIONAL GREAT AMERICAN SMOKEOUT DAY.** Nov 18.

OMAN: NATIONAL HOLIDAY. Nov 18. Sultanate of Oman celebrates its national day, the birthday in 1942 of Sultan Qaboos bin Said.

PINCHBECK, CHRISTOPHER: DEATH ANNIVERSARY. Nov 18, 1732. English inventor, jeweler and clockmaker. Inventor of the copper and zinc alloy which looked like gold but became synonymous with cheapness. Noted manufacturer of automated musical clocks and instruments. Born at Clerkenwell, London, England, about 1670 (exact date unknown). Died at London, England, Nov 18, 1732.

PREMATURITY AWARENESS DAY. Nov 18. Sponsored by the March of Dimes to alert Americans to the common, serious and costly problem of premature birth (before 37 weeks). One in eight babies is born prematurely in this country, many without warning and with no known cause. Prematurity is the leading cause of newborn death (before the first month in life) and babies who do survive often face chronic health and developmental disabilities for the rest of their lives. For info: Beth Rowan, March of Dimes, 1275 Mamaroneck Ave, White Plains, NY 10605. Phone: (914) 997-4533. Fax: (914) 997-4585. E-mail: browan@marchofdimes.com. Web: www.marchofdimes.com.

PUSH-BUTTON PHONE DEBUTS: ANNIVERSARY. Nov 18, 1963. Push-button telephones went into service as an alternative to rotary-dial phones. Touch-tone service was available as an option at an extra charge. This option was only available in two Pennsylvania cities.

QUAD CITY ARTS FESTIVAL OF TREES. Nov 18–28. RiverCenter, Davenport, IA. 19th annual. This brilliant 10-day festival with activities for children and adults of all ages features designer trees, room vignettes, hearth and home arrangements, door designs, miniatures, handcrafted stockings and ornaments, gingerbread creations, 14 special events and a "Holiday Parade" with giant helium balloons. (Chosen by the American Bus Assn as one of the top 100 events for 2001.) For info: Phone: (563) 324-FEST or (309) 793-1213. Web: www.quadcityarts.com/festoftrees. For info on the Quad Cities: Quad Cities CVB. Phone: (800) 747-7800. Web: www.visitquadcities.com.

"SEE IT NOW" TV PREMIERE: ANNIVERSARY. Nov 18, 1951. "See It Now" was a high quality and significant public affairs show of the 1950s. Known for using its own film footage, unrehearsed interviews and no dubbing, "See It Now" covered many relevant and newsworthy stories of its time, including desegregation, lung cancer and anti-Communist fervor. One of the most notable shows focused on Senator Joseph McCarthy, leading to McCarthy's appearance on the show which damaged his credibility. The show was hosted by Edward R. Murrow, who also produced it jointly with Fred W. Friendly. Its premiere was the first live commercial coast-to-coast broadcast. The show had premiered on radio the year before as "Hear It Now."

SHEPARD, ALAN: BIRTH ANNIVERSARY. Nov 18, 1923. Former astronaut and the first American in space (in 1961), Shepard was born at East Derry, NH. He was one of only 12 Americans who have walked on the moon and was America's only lunar golfer, practicing his drive in space with a six iron. He was awarded the Medal of Honor in 1979. Shepard died near Monterey, CA, July 21, 1998.

SOUTH AFRICA ADOPTS NEW CONSTITUTION: ANNIVERSARY. Nov 18, 1993. After more than 300 years of white majority rule, basic civil rights were finally granted to blacks in South Africa. The constitution providing such rights was approved by representatives of the ruling party, as well as members of 20 other political parties.

SUGARLOAF CRAFTS FESTIVAL. Nov 18–21. Montgomery County Fairgrounds, Gaithersburg, MD. This show, now in its 29th year, features more than 550 nationally recognized craft designers and fine artists displaying and selling their original creations. Includes craft demonstrations, live music, specialty foods, hourly gift certificate drawings and more. Est attendance: 37,500. For info: Sugarloaf Mountain Works, 200 Orchard Ridge Dr, #215, Gaithersburg, MD 20878. Phone: (800) 210-9900. Fax: (301) 253-9620. Web: www.sugarloafcrafts.com.

US UNIFORM TIME ZONE PLAN: ANNIVERSARY. Nov 18, 1883. Charles Ferdinand Dowd, a college professor and one of the early advocates of uniform time, proposed a time zone plan of the US (four zones of 15 degrees), which he and others persuaded the railroads to adopt and place in operation on this date. Because it didn't involve the enactment of any law, some localities didn't change their clocks. A year later an international conference applied the same procedure to create time zones for the entire world. US time zones weren't nationally legalized until 1918, with the passage of the Standard Time Act. See also: "Prime Meridian Set: Anniversary" (Nov 1) and "US Standard Time Act: Anniversary" (Mar 19).

WEBER, CARL MARIA VON: BIRTH ANNIVERSARY. Nov 18, 1786. Composer, "founder of German romantic school," was born at Eutin, Germany. Member of a musical family, he is remembered mainly for his operas, especially the immensely popular *Der Freischutz* (1821). He died at London, England, June 5, 1826, at age 39.

BIRTHDAYS TODAY

Margaret Eleanor Atwood, 65, author (*Cat's Eye*, *The Handmaid's Tale*), born Ottawa, ON, Canada, Nov 18, 1939.

Dante Bichette, 41, former baseball player, born West Palm Beach, FL, Nov 18, 1963.

Linda Evans, 62, actress ("Dynasty," "Bachelor Father"), born Hartford, CT, Nov 18, 1942.

Wilma Mankiller, 59, Chief of the Cherokee Nation 1985–95, born Tahlequah, OK, Nov 18, 1945.

Andrea Marcovicci, 56, actress ("Trapper John, MD"), singer, born New York, NY, Nov 18, 1948.

Harold Warren Moon, 48, former football player, born Los Angeles, CA, Nov 18, 1956.

Kevin Nealon, 51, comedic actor ("Champs," "Saturday Night Live"), born St. Louis, MO, Nov 18, 1953.

Jameson Parker, 57, actor ("Simon and Simon," *A Small Circle of Friends*), born Baltimore, MD, Nov 18, 1947.

Elizabeth Perkins, 44, actress (*About Last Night . . .*, *Big*, *The Flintstones*), born Queens, NY, Nov 18, 1960.

November 2004

S	M	T	W	T	F	S
	1	2	3	4	5	6
7	8	9	10	11	12	13
14	15	16	17	18	19	20
21	22	23	24	25	26	27
28	29	30				

★ Chase's 2004 Calendar of Events ★   Nov 18–19

Katey Sagal, 48, actress ("Married . . . With Children," "8 Simple Rules for Dating My Teenage Daughter"), born Los Angeles, CA, Nov 18, 1956.
Gary Sheffield, 36, baseball player, born Tampa, FL, Nov 18, 1968.
Ted Stevens, 81, US Senator (R, Alaska), born Indianapolis, IN, Nov 18, 1923.
Susan Sullivan, 60, actress ("Falcon Crest," "Dharma & Greg"), born New York, NY, Nov 18, 1944.
Brenda Vaccaro, 65, actress (*Cactus Flower, How Now Dow Jones, The Goodbye People*), born Brooklyn, NY, Nov 18, 1939.
Owen Wilson, 36, actor (*The Royal Tenenbaums, Behind Enemy Lines, Bottle Rocket*), screenwriter, born Dallas, TX, Nov 18, 1968.

NOVEMBER 19 — FRIDAY
Day 324 — 42 Remaining

BELIZE: GARIFUNA DAY. Nov 19. Public holiday celebrating the first arrival of Black Caribs from St. Vincent and Rotan to southern Belize in 1823.

CAMPANELLA, ROY: BIRTH ANNIVERSARY. Nov 19, 1921. Roy Campanella, one of the first black major leaguers and a star of one of baseball's greatest teams, the Brooklyn Dodgers' "Boys of Summer," was born at Philadelphia, PA. He was named the National League MVP three times in his 10 years of play, in 1951, 1953 and 1955. Campanella had his highest batting average in 1951 (.325), and in 1953 he established three single-season records for a catcher—most putouts (807), most home runs (41) and most runs batted in (142)—as well as having a batting average of .312. His career was cut short on Jan 28, 1958, when an automobile accident left him paralyzed. Campanella gained even more fame after his accident as an inspiration and spokesman for the handicapped. He was named to the Baseball Hall of Fame in 1969. Roy Campanella died June 26, 1993, at Woodland Hills, CA.

CHRISTMAS IN ROSELAND. Nov 19–Dec 30. American Rose Center, Shreveport, LA. A fantasyland featuring millions of twinkling lights, live entertainment, fascinating railroad and model train display and unique gift shop. Est attendance: 25,000. For info: American Rose Center, 8877 Jefferson-Paige Rd, Shreveport, LA 71119. Phone: (318) 938-5402. Fax: (318) 938-5405. E-mail: ars@ars-hq.org. Web: www.ars.org.

CHRISTMAS IN SEATTLE HOLIDAY GIFT SHOW. Nov 19–21. Washington State Convention Center, Seattle, WA. A holiday shopper's paradise! Unique gifts and specialty foods to sample and buy. Seattle's largest holiday gift show. Crafters from across the nation and Canada await the shoppers. Santa Claus, holiday music and complimentary child care (2-hour limit). For info: Susie O'Brien Borer, Showcase Northwest, Inc, PO Box 2815, Kirkland, WA 98083. Phone: (800) 521-SHOW. E-mail: seattle@showcaseproductionsnw.com.

CLARK, GEORGE ROGERS: BIRTH ANNIVERSARY. Nov 19, 1752. American soldier and frontiersman, born at Albemarle County, VA. Died at Louisville, KY, Feb 13, 1818.

COLD WAR FORMALLY ENDED: ANNIVERSARY. Nov 19–21, 1990. A summit was held at Paris with the leaders of the Conference on Security and Cooperation in Europe (CSCE). The highlight of the summit was the signing of a treaty to dramatically reduce conventional weapons in Europe, thereby ending the Cold War.

COLORADO RIVER CROSSING BALLOON FESTIVAL. Nov 19–21. Cibola High School, Yuma, AZ. 14th annual. 55 balloons. Sunrise balloon liftoffs on Saturday and Sunday at Cibola High School. Sunset balloon glow and fireworks on Saturday evening at Ray Kroc Complex/Desert Sun Stadium. Entertainment, food, vendors. Free admission. Est attendance: 17,000. For info: Caballeros de Yuma, Inc, PO Box 5987, Yuma, AZ 85366. Phone: (928) 343-1715. Fax: (928) 783-1609. Web: www.caballeros.org.

FANTASY OF LIGHT PARADE. Nov 19. Wheeling, WV. Night parade with more than 100 lighted floats and musical units. Est attendance: 80,000. For info: Wheeling Conv and Visitors Bureau, 1401 Main St, Wheeling, WV 26003. Phone: (800) 828-3097 or (304) 233-7709. Fax: (304) 233-1470. Web: www.wheelingcvb.com/calendar.

FIRST AUTOMATIC TOLL COLLECTION MACHINE: 50th ANNIVERSARY. Nov 19, 1954. At the Union Toll Plaza on New Jersey's Garden State Parkway motorists dropped 25¢ into a wire mesh hopper and a green light would flash. The first modern toll road was the Pennsylvania Turnpike which opened in 1940.

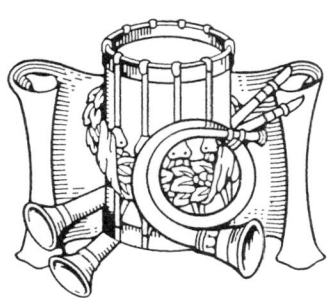

FIRST PRESIDENTIAL LIBRARY: 65th ANNIVERSARY. Nov 19, 1939. President Franklin D. Roosevelt laid the cornerstone for his presidential library at Hyde Park, NY. He donated the land, but public donations provided funds for the building which was dedicated on June 30, 1941.

GARFIELD, JAMES ABRAM: BIRTH ANNIVERSARY. Nov 19, 1831. Twentieth president of the US (and the first left-handed president) was born at Orange, OH. Term of office: Mar 4–Sept 19, 1881. While walking into the Washington, DC, railway station on the morning of July 2, 1881, Garfield was shot by disappointed office seeker Charles J. Guiteau. He survived, in very weak condition, until Sept 19, 1881, when he succumbed to blood poisoning at Elberon, NJ (where he had been taken for recuperation). Guiteau was tried, convicted and hanged at the jail at Washington, June 30, 1882.

GETTYSBURG ADDRESS MEMORIAL CEREMONY. Nov 19. Gettysburg, PA. 141st anniversary of Lincoln's Gettysburg Address is celebrated with brief memorial services at the Soldiers' National Monument in Gettysburg National Cemetery. Est attendance: 2,000. For info: Gettysburg CVB, PO Box 4117, Gettysburg, PA 17325. Phone: (717) 334-6274. Fax: (717) 334-1166. E-mail: gettysburgcvb@dejazzd.com. Web: www.gettysburgcvb.org.

GRAND ILLUMINATION. Nov 19. Lahaska, PA. At dusk the Village's brilliant outdoor holiday lights display debuts. Free cider and toasted marshmallows. Preview of new gift ideas in shops. Free admission. Est attendance: 5,000. For info: Peddler's Village, Routes 202 & 263, Lahaska, PA 18931. Phone: (215) 794-4000. Fax: (215) 794-4001. Web: www.peddlersvillage.com.

HAVE A BAD DAY DAY. Nov 19. For those who are filled with revulsion at being told endlessly to "have a nice day," this day is a brief respite. Store and business owners are to ask workers to tell customers to "have a bad day." Annually, Nov 19. [©2003 by WH.] For info: Thomas & Ruth Roy, Wellcat Holidays, 2418 Long Ln, Lebanon, PA 17046. Phone: (717) 279-0184. E-mail: info@wellcat.com. Web: www.wellcat.com.

HOLIDAY FOLK FAIR INTERNATIONAL. Nov 19–21. Wisconsin State Fair Park, Milwaukee, WI. International festival featuring costumes, dancing, entertainment, exhibits, workshops, folk wares and cuisine from 65 cultures. Also children's activities. Annually, the weekend before Thanksgiving. Est attendance: 65,000. For info: Holiday Folk Fair Intl, Intl Institute of Wisconsin, 1110 N Old World Third St, Ste 420, Milwaukee, WI 53203. Phone: (414) 225-6220. Fax: (414) 225-6235. E-mail: iiw@execpc.com.

Nov 19 ☆ *Chase's 2004 Calendar of Events* ☆

LINCOLN'S GETTYSBURG ADDRESS: ANNIVERSARY. Nov 19, 1863. In 1863, 17 acres of the battlefield at Gettysburg, PA, were dedicated as a national cemetery. Noted orator Edward Everett spoke for two hours; the address that Lincoln delivered in less than two minutes was later recognized as one of the most eloquent of the English language. Five manuscript copies in Lincoln's hand survive, including the rough draft begun in ink at the executive Mansion at Washington and concluded in pencil at Gettysburg on the morning of the dedication (kept at the Library of Congress).

MEXICO CITY EXPLOSION: 20th ANNIVERSARY. Nov 19, 1984. More than 300 people were killed when a gas truck explosion set off a series of explosions at a butane and liquefied gas storage facility in the Mexico City suburb Tlalnepantla. An area of approximately 60 acres was razed by the blasts and resulting fires. The four storage tanks involved held more than three million gallons of liquified gas.

MONACO: NATIONAL HOLIDAY. Nov 19.

MOON PHASE: FIRST QUARTER. Nov 19. Moon enters First Quarter phase at 12:50 AM, EST.

NAIA MEN'S & WOMEN'S SOCCER NATIONAL CHAMPIONSHIP. Nov 19–25. 12-team field competes for national championship. 46th annual for men takes place in Olathe, KS; 21st annual for women takes place in Santa Barbara, CA. For info: Natl Assn of Intercollegiate Athletics, 23500 W 105th St, PO Box 1325, Olathe, KS 66051-1325. Phone: (913) 791-0044. Fax: (913) 791-9555. Web: www.naia.org.

★**NATIONAL FARM-CITY WEEK.** Nov 19–25. Presidential Proclamation issued for a week in November since 1956, customarily for the week ending with Thanksgiving Day. Requested by congressional resolutions from 1956–1958; since 1959 issued annually without request.

PEDDLER'S VILLAGE GINGERBREAD HOUSE COMPETITION & DISPLAY. Nov 19–Jan 6, 2005. Lahaska, PA. More than 100 gingerbread house entries from throughout the US compete for more than $4,800 in cash prizes in such categories as: Traditional, Authentic Reproduction of a Significant Building, Amateur, Incredibly Unusual 3-Dimensional and Childrens (12 and under; 13–18). The creative masterpieces are displayed throughout the holiday season in the Village Gazebo. Free admission. Est attendance: 850,000. For info: Peddler's Village, Routes 202 & 263, Lahaska, PA 18931. Phone: (215) 794-4000. Fax: (215) 794-4001. Web: www.peddlersvillage.com.

PUERTO RICO: DISCOVERY DAY. Nov 19. Public holiday. Columbus discovered Puerto Rico in 1493 on his second voyage to the New World.

"ROCKY AND HIS FRIENDS" TV PREMIERE: 45th ANNIVERSARY. Nov 19, 1959. This popular cartoon featured the adventures of a talking squirrel, Rocky (Rocket J. Squirrel), and his friend Bullwinkle, a flaky moose. The tongue-in-cheek dialogue contrasted with the simple plots in which Rocky and Bullwinkle tangled with Russian bad guys Boris Badenov and Natasha (who worked for Mr Big). Other popular segments on the show included "Fractured Fairy Tales," "Bullwinkle's Corner" and the adventures of Sherman and Mr Peabody (an intelligent talking dog). In 1961 the show was renamed "The Bullwinkle Show," but the cast of characters remained the same.

SILVER BELLS IN THE CITY. Nov 19 (weather permitting). Lansing, MI. Michigan's capital city sparkles with hospitality on the streets of downtown Lansing's business district for this celebration of lights, music and holiday cheer including an electric light parade, lighting of the State of Michigan Holiday Tree and a fireworks display over the State Capital dome. Annually, the Friday before Thanksgiving. Coordinated by Arts Council of Greater Lansing, Inc. Est attendance: 50,000. For info: Arts Council of Greater Lansing, Inc, Center for the Arts, 425 S Grand Ave, Lansing, MI 48933. Phone: (517) 372-4636 x 6. Fax: (517) 484-2564. Web: www.lansingarts.org.

SOUTH TEXAS WILDLIFE AND BIRDING FESTIVAL. Nov 19–21. Kingsville, TX. Birding and wildlife field trips, speakers, demonstrations and a nature marketplace. Est attendance: 3,000. For info: Kingsville Conv & Visitors Bureau, 1501 N Hwy 77, Kingsville, TX 78363. Phone: (800) 333-5032. Fax: (361) 592-3227. E-mail: visitors@kingsvilletexas.com. Web: www.kingsvilletexas.com.

STAMP EXPO: CALIFORNIA. Nov 19–21. Pasadena Convention Center, Pasadena, CA. Est attendance: 4,000. For info: Intl Stamp Collectors Society, PO Box 854, Van Nuys, CA 91408. Phone: (818) 997-6496. Fax: (818) 988-4337. E-mail: iibick@aol.com. Web: www.bick.net.

SUFFRAGISTS' VOTING ATTEMPT: ANNIVERSARY. Nov 19, 1868. Testing the wording of the 14th Amendment that says "no State shall make or enforce any law which shall abridge the privileges or immunities of citizens of the United States," 172 New Jersey suffragists, including four black women, attempted to vote in the presidential election. Denied, they cast their votes instead into a women's ballot box overseen by 84-year-old Quaker Margaret Pryer.

TELLABRATION! A WEEKEND OF STORYTELLING FOR GROWN-UPS. Nov 19–21. Many sites throughout Connecticut. Simultaneous storytelling concerts for adults. Annually, the weekend before Thanksgiving. Est attendance: 1,000. For info: Ann Shapiro, Adm, Connecticut Storytelling Center, Connecticut College, Box 5295, 270 Mohegan Ave, New London, CT 06320. Phone: (860) 439-2764. Fax: (860) 439-5431. E-mail: csc@conncoll.edu. Web: www.connstorycenter.com.

WOMEN'S CHRISTIAN TEMPERANCE UNION ORGANIZED: ANNIVERSARY. Nov 19, 1874. Developed out of the Women's Temperance Crusade of 1873, the Women's Christian Temperance Union was organized at Cleveland, OH. The Crusade had swept through 23 states with women going into saloons to sing hymns, pray and ask saloonkeepers to stop selling liquor. Today the temperance group, headquartered at Evanston, IL, includes more than a million members with chapters in 72 countries and continues to be concerned with educating people on the potential dangers of the use of alcohol, narcotics and tobacco.

YORK INTERNATIONAL POSTCARD FAIR. Nov 19–20. York Fairgrounds, York, PA. Est attendance: 1,000. For info: Mary Martin Ltd, 4899 Pulaski Hwy, Rt 40, Perryville, MD 21903. Phone: (410) 642-3581. Fax: (410) 642-2053.

ZION NATIONAL PARK ESTABLISHED: 85th ANNIVERSARY. Nov 19, 1919. Utah's Mukuntuweap National Monument, proclaimed July 31, 1909, and later incorporated in Zion National Monument by proclamation Mar 18, 1918, was established as Zion National Park in 1919.

BIRTHDAYS TODAY

Dick Cavett, 68, entertainer ("The Dick Cavett Show"), born Gibbon, NE, Nov 19, 1936.
Eileen Collins, 48, first female shuttle commander, Lieutenant Colonel USAF, born Elmira, NY, Nov 19, 1956.
Gail Devers, 38, Olympic gold medal sprinter, born Seattle, WA, Nov 19, 1966.
Terry Farrell, 41, actress ("Star Trek: Deep Space Nine," "Becker"), born Cedar Rapids, IA, Nov 19, 1963.

November 2004

S	M	T	W	T	F	S
	1	2	3	4	5	6
7	8	9	10	11	12	13
14	15	16	17	18	19	20
21	22	23	24	25	26	27
28	29	30				

Jodie Foster, 42, actress (Oscars for *The Accused, The Silence of the Lambs; Taxi Driver*), director (*Home for the Holidays*), born Los Angeles, CA, Nov 19, 1962.

Savion Glover, 31, dancer, choreographer (*Bring in 'Da Noise, Bring in 'Da Funk*), born Newark, NJ, Nov 19, 1973.

Thomas R. Harkin, 65, US Senator (D, Iowa), born Cumming, IA, Nov 19, 1939.

Scott Jacoby, 48, actor (*The Little Girl Who Lives Down the Lane, Return to Horror High*), born Chicago, IL, Nov 19, 1956.

Allison Janney, 44, actress (*American Beauty*, "The West Wing"), born Dayton, OH, Nov 19, 1960.

Larry King, 71, talk-show host ("Larry King Live"), born Brooklyn, NY, Nov 19, 1933.

Calvin Klein, 62, fashion designer, born New York, NY, Nov 19, 1942.

Glynnis O'Connor, 49, actress (*Ode to Billy Joe, Johnny Dangerously*), born New York, NY, Nov 19, 1955.

Kathleen Quinlan, 50, actress (*Twilight Zone: The Movie; The Doors*), born Pasadena, CA, Nov 19, 1954.

Ahmad Rashad, 55, sportscaster, former football player, born Bobby Moore, Portland, OR, Nov 19, 1949.

Meg Ryan, 43, actress (*When Harry Met Sally . . ., Sleepless in Seattle*), born Fairfield, CT, Nov 19, 1961.

Kerri Strug, 27, Olympic gymnast, born Tucson, AZ, Nov 19, 1977.

Tommy G. Thompson, 63, US Secretary of Health and Human Services, former Governor of Wisconsin (R), born Elroy, WI, Nov 19, 1941.

Ted Turner, 66, baseball, basketball and cable TV executive, born Cincinnati, OH, Nov 19, 1938.

Garrick Utley, 65, journalist, born Chicago, IL, Nov 19, 1939.

NOVEMBER 20 — SATURDAY
Day 325 — 41 Remaining

ANN ARBOR WINTER ART FAIR. Nov 20–21. Ann Arbor, MI. 31st annual. Fine art and selected craft show. Some of the best artists and craftspersons in the country. Est attendance: 10,000. For info: Audree Levy, 1809 Morning Glory, Carrollton, TX 75007. Phone: (972) 394-5236. Fax: (972) 394-6236. E-mail: audree@levyartfairs.com. Web: www.levyartfairs.com.

BATTLE OF TARAWA-MAKIN: ANNIVERSARY. Nov 20, 1943. The US began its offensive against Japan in the Central Pacific (Operation Galvanic) by attacking the Gilbert Islands, particularly the islets of Betio and Makin. The Japanese had heavily fortified the Tarawa chain of atolls, especially Tarawa, with pillboxes, blockhouses and ferroconcrete bombproofs. In the eight days it took the 5th Amphibious Corps, 2nd Marine Division and the 27th Infantry Division to take the Tarawa and Makin Islands, 1,000 US soldiers were killed and 2,311 wounded. The Japanese loss was tallied at 4,700 men killed, 17 wounded captured and 129 Koreans surrendered. The US public, who through censorship previously had been kept in the dark about the human cost of the war, was appalled by casualty figures and photographs from this battle.

BILL OF RIGHTS: ANNIVERSARY OF FIRST STATE RATIFICATION. Nov 20, 1789. New Jersey became the first state to ratify 10 of the 12 amendments to the US Constitution proposed by Congress Sept 25. These 10 amendments came to be known as the Bill of Rights.

CALICO CRAFTS BAZAAR. Nov 20. Event Center on the Beach, Gold Beach, OR. 10 AM–5 PM. Est attendance: 500. For info: Mary Ann Gray, Calico Country Bazaar, PO Box 964, Gold Beach, OR 97444. Phone: (800) 525-2334 or (541) 247-5064. Fax: (541) 247-0188. E-mail: maryann@g.b.wave.net. Web: www.goldbeachchamber.com.

CANADA: RALLY OF THE TALL PINES. Nov 20. Bancroft, ON, Canada. Combining winter road surfaces with the scenic, winding backroads of the Canadian Shield makes this event of the Canadian Rally Car Race Circuit one of the most popular. For info: Chris Fouts, Bancroft & District Chamber of Commerce, Box 539, Bancroft, ON, K0L 1C0, Canada. Phone: (613) 332-1513. Fax: (613) 332-2119. E-mail: chamber@commerce.bancroft.on.ca. Web: www.BancroftDistrict.com.

CHATTERTON, THOMAS: BIRTH ANNIVERSARY. Nov 20, 1752. English poet Thomas Chatterton was born at Bristol, England, and killed himself at age 17 by taking arsenic at his London garret, Aug 24, 1770. A gifted but lonely child, before he reached his teens Chatterton had created a fantasy poet-priest, Thomas Rowley, who lived in the 16th century. With his own pen, Chatterton created enough verses "by" Rowley to fill more than 600 printed pages. Chatterton's fantasy-forgery poems attracted little attention during his short life, but they were later admired by Wordsworth, Coleridge, Shelley, Keats and Byron. In addition, he became the subject of at least one play, an opera and a novel.

CUSTER STATE PARK BUFFALO AUCTION. Nov 20. Custer, SD. A live sale at 10 AM, (MST), of 300–400 surplus buffalo (calves, yearlings, mature cows and two-year-old bulls). Est attendance: 600. For info: Ron Walker, Custer State Park, HC 83, Box 70, Custer, SD 57730. Phone: (605) 255-4515. Fax: (605) 255-4460. E-mail: ron.walker@state.sd.us.

DELAND FALL FESTIVAL OF THE ARTS. Nov 20–21. DeLand, FL. Showcasing the works of more than 200 artists, the festival features more than $20,000 in prize money awarded during this two-day juried and judged event. Artist demonstrations, a youth art exhibition, children's workshops, specialty foods and live entertainment enhance the show. Categories featuring the traditional mediums of oil, acrylic, watercolor, pottery, sculpture and jewelry are enhanced by original video, computer and performance arts categories. Annually, the weekend before Thanksgiving. Est attendance: 40,000. For info: DeLand Area Chamber of Commerce. Phone: (386) 734-4331.

GINGERBREAD ON PARADE. Nov 20–Dec 20. Mormon Trail Center at Historic Winter Quarters Visitors Center, Omaha, NE. View more than 225 gingerbread houses of every shape and size delightfully decorated for the holidays. Gingerbread houses given to charities before Christmas. Est attendance: 22,000. For info: Director, Mormon Trail Center, 3215 State St, Omaha, NE 68112. Phone: (402) 453-9372.

GOULD, CHESTER: BIRTH ANNIVERSARY. Nov 20, 1900. In 1931, Chester Gould created comic strip character Dick Tracy, the clean-cut, square-jawed, plainclothed detective who represented the code that "crime doesn't pay." The strip first appeared Oct 4, 1931, in the *Detroit Daily Mirror* and later was syndicated in nearly 1,000 newspapers worldwide. *Dick Tracy* (originally called *Plainclothes Tracy*) featured Tess Trueheart (later Mrs Tracy) and a host of bad guys with ugly names and faces to match their ugly ways—Mole, Pruneface, Flat Top, B-B Eyes, Mumbles and others. Closely following actual police methods of crime prevention, it included a "Crimestopper Notebook" with tips on self-protection. More violent than most comic strips, *Dick Tracy* was a combination of realism and science fiction. Chester Gould was born at Pawnee, OK, and died May 11, 1985, at Woodstock, IL.

Nov 20 ☆ Chase's 2004 Calendar of Events ☆

HANDEL'S *MESSIAH*. Nov 20. Community of Christ Auditorium, Independence, MO. 88th annual performance of Handel's *Messiah* by the Independence Messiah Choir, Messiah Festival Orchestra and renowned soloists. Est attendance: 5,000. For info: Public Relations, Community of Christ Headquarters, 1001 W Walnut St, Independence, MO 64050-3562. Phone: (816) 521-3041. Fax: (816) 521-3043. E-mail: kfriend@CofChrist.org. Web: www.CofChrist.org/messiah.

HOLIDAY CRAFT SHOW. Nov 20–22. Depot Lane, Schoharie, NY. Handcrafted items offered, bake sale, country kitchen. Est attendance: 1,000. For info: Paul Piela, Show Mgr, Schoharie Colonial Heritage Assn, PO Box 554, Schoharie, NY 12157. Phone: (518) 295-7505. E-mail: scha@midtel.net.

HOLIDAY LIGHTS ON THE LAKE. Nov 20–Jan 2, 2005. Lakemont Park, Altoona, PA. Drive-through displays of more than 51 acres of animated holiday lights, plus a holiday gift shop, food, model train displays and visits from Santa Claus. Est attendance: 75,000. For info: Lakemont Park, 1-99 Frankstown Exit, Altoona, PA 16602. Phone: (814) 949-7275 or (800) 434-8006. Fax: (814) 949-9207. E-mail: Lakemont99@aol.com. Web: www.lakemontparkfun.com.

HOLIDAYS IN THE CITY GRAND ILLUMINATION PARADE. Nov 20. Norfolk, VA. All of Norfolk's downtown skyscrapers and many of its smaller buildings outline their profiles in lights for Holidays in the City. On the first evening of the illumination a downtown lighted street parade kicks off the celebration of the season. All of the floats, bands and entries in this nighttime parade are lighted. Annually, the Saturday before Thanksgiving. Est attendance: 100,000. For info: Parade Mgr, Downtown Norfolk Council, 201 Granby St, Ste 101, Norfolk, VA 23510. Phone: (757) 623-1757. Fax: (757) 623-1756. E-mail: dnc@downtownnorfolk.org. Web: www.downtownnorfolk.org.

HOMEPLACE FESTIVAL. Nov 20. Waretown, NJ. Featuring families playing country, bluegrass and traditional music. No alcoholic beverages or smoking allowed. For info: Albert Music Hall, PO Box 657, Waretown, NJ 08758. Phone: (609) 971-1593. Web: www.alberthall.org.

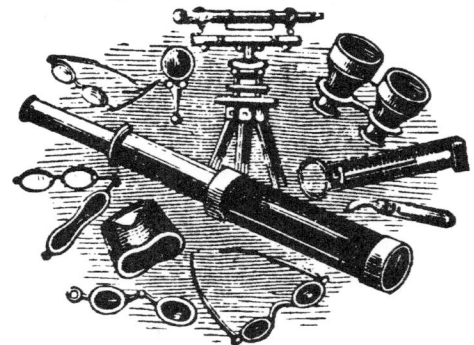

HUBBLE, EDWIN POWELL: BIRTH ANNIVERSARY. Nov 20, 1889. American astronomer Edwin Hubble was born at Marshfield, MO. His discovery and development of the concept of an expanding universe has been described as the "most spectacular astronomical discovery" of the 20th century. As a tribute, the Hubble Space Telescope, deployed Apr 25, 1990, from US Space Shuttle *Discovery*, was named for him. The Hubble Space Telescope, with a 240-centimeter mirror, was to allow astronomers to see farther into space than they had ever seen from telescopes on Earth. Hubble died at San Marino, CA, Sept 28, 1953.

November 2004	S	M	T	W	T	F	S
		1	2	3	4	5	6
	7	8	9	10	11	12	13
	14	15	16	17	18	19	20
	21	22	23	24	25	26	27
	28	29	30				

KECHI'S "ANTIQUE COUNTRY CHRISTMAS." Nov 20. Kechi, KS. Spend the day in "The Antique Capital of Kansas" strolling through our small quaint community of 12 antique and speciality shops. Plan to tour the Karg Art Glass & Gallery for free glass-blowing demonstrations and the Turkey Creek Weaving Studio. Hours 10 AM to 5 PM. Free admission. Motel accommodations and bed & breakfast all located within two miles. Est attendance: 800. For info: Rick Eberhard, Exec Dir, Kechi KS Chamber of Commerce, 205 Heritage Ct, Kechi, KS 67067-8710. Phone: (316) 744-1337. Fax: (316) 744-1337. E-mail: kechichamber@kechikscoc.com. Web: www.kechikscoc.com.

KENNEDY, ROBERT FRANCIS: BIRTH ANNIVERSARY. Nov 20, 1925. US Senator and younger brother of John F. Kennedy (thirty-fifth president) was born at Brookline, MA. An assassin shot him at Los Angeles, CA, June 5, 1968, while he was campaigning for the presidential nomination. He died the next day. Sirhan Sirhan was convicted of his murder.

LAGERLOF, SELMA: BIRTH ANNIVERSARY. Nov 20, 1858. Swedish author, member of the Swedish Academy and the first woman to receive the Nobel Prize for literature (1909) was born at Sweden's Varmland Province. She died there Mar 16, 1940.

LAND OF MARK TWAIN BLUEGRASS MUSIC FESTIVAL. Nov 20–21. Hannibal Inn, Hannibal, MO. Annually, the third weekend in November. Est attendance: 1,500. For info: Tri-State Bluegrass Assn, RR 1, Box 71, Kahoka, MO 63445. Phone: (573) 853-4344. E-mail: edspray@marktwain.net.

LANDIS, KENESAW MOUNTAIN: BIRTH ANNIVERSARY. Nov 20, 1866. Baseball Hall of Fame executive born at Millville, OH. Landis, a federal judge, was named the first Commissioner of Baseball in 1920. He ruled with an absolutely firm hand and imposed his view of how baseball should operate upon owners and players alike. Inducted into the Hall of Fame in 1944. Died at Chicago, IL, Nov 25, 1944.

LAURIER, SIR WILFRED: BIRTH ANNIVERSARY. Nov 20, 1841. Canadian statesman (premier, 1896–1911), born at St. Lin, Quebec. Died Feb 17, 1919, at Ottawa, Ontario.

MARRIAGE OF ELIZABETH AND PHILIP: ANNIVERSARY. Nov 20, 1947. The Princess Elizabeth Alexandra Mary was wed to Philip Mountbatten on Nov 20, 1947. Elizabeth was the first child of King George VI and Queen Elizabeth. Philip, the former Prince Philip of Greece, had become a British subject nine months earlier and the title Duke of Edinburgh was bestowed on him. The bride later became Elizabeth II, Queen of the United Kingdom of Great Britain and Northern Ireland and Head of the Commonwealth, upon the death of her father on Feb 6, 1952, her coronation taking place at Westminster Abbey on June 2, 1953.

MEXICO: REVOLUTION DAY. Nov 20. Anniversary of the social revolution launched by Francisco I. Madero in 1910. National holiday.

NAIA MEN'S AND WOMEN'S CROSS COUNTRY NATIONAL CHAMPIONSHIPS. Nov 20. Location TBD. Men compete on an 8K course and women compete on a 5K course with the top 25 individual finishers in each championship receiving All-America honors. 49th men's championship; 25th women's. For info: Kelly Noonan, Natl Assn of Intercollegiate Athletics, 23500 W 105th St, PO Box 1325, Olathe, KS 66051-1325. Phone: (913) 791-0044. Fax: (913) 791-9555. E-mail: knoonan@naia.org. Web: www.naia.org.

NAME YOUR PC DAY. Nov 20. Hey, why not? People name their boats! There are a lot more PCs than boats these days. "Binky" is already taken. Annually, Nov 20. [©2003 by WH.] For info: Thomas & Ruth Roy, Wellcat Holidays, 2418 Long Ln, Lebanon, PA 17046. Phone: (717) 279-0184. E-mail: info@wellcat.com. Web: www.wellcat.com.

NORDIC YULEFEST. Nov 20–21. Seattle, WA. A Scandinavian holiday extravaganza with typical Nordic Christmas foods, music and dance. Crafts throughout the museum, kid's room for decoration making, one-of-a-kind gifts. Est attendance: 5,000. For info: Marianne Forssblad, Dir, Nordic Heritage Museum, 3014 NW 67th St, Seattle, WA 98117. Phone: (206) 789-5707. Fax: (206) 789-3271.

NUREMBERG WAR CRIMES TRIAL: ANNIVERSARY. Nov 20, 1945. The first session of the German war crimes trials started at Berlin with indictments against 24 former Nazi leaders. Later sessions were held at Nuremberg, starting Nov 20, 1945. One defendant committed suicide during the trial, and another was excused because of his physical and mental condition. The trial lasted more than 10 months, and delivery of the judgment was completed on Oct 1, 1946. Twelve were sentenced to death by hanging, three to life imprisonment, four to lesser prison terms and three were acquitted.

RANCH HAND BREAKFAST. Nov 20 (tentative). King Ranch, Kingsville, TX. A breakfast cooked and served outdoors at the world-famous King Ranch. See longhorn cattle and real cowboys on horseback. Annually, the Saturday before Thanksgiving. Est attendance: 7,000. For info: Kingsville Convention & Visitors Bureau, 1501 N Hwy 77, Kingsville, TX 78364-1562. Phone: (800) 333-5032. Fax: (361) 592-3227. E-mail: visitors@kingsvilletexas.com. Web: www.kingsvilletexas.com.

REMEMBRANCE DAY. Nov 20. Gettysburg, PA. An annual event held in conjunction with the Lincoln Observance, with a parade of Civil War troops to the High Water Mark and then to the Albert Woolson Monument for a wreath-laying ceremony. Civil War Ball held in the evening at Eisenhower Inn & Conference Center. Sponsored by the Sons of Union Veterans. Est attendance: 5,000. For info: Gettysburg CVB, PO Box 4117, Gettysburg, PA 17325. Phone: (717) 334-6274. Fax: (717) 334-1166. E-mail: gettysburgcvb@dejazzd.com. Web: www.gettysburgcvb.org.

THAILAND: ELEPHANT ROUND-UP AT SURIN. Nov 20. Elephant demonstrations in morning, elephant races and tug-of-war between 100 men and one elephant. Observed since 1961 on third Saturday in November. Special trains from Bangkok on previous day.

TIERNEY, GENE: BIRTH ANNIVERSARY. Nov 20, 1920. Known best for the title role in the film *Laura*, actress Gene Tierney was born at Brooklyn, NY. Her other films include *Heaven Can Wait, A Bell for Adano, Advise and Consent* and her last film, *The Pleasure Seekers*. She died Nov 6, 1991, at Houston, TX.

UNITED NATIONS: AFRICA INDUSTRIALIZATION DAY. Nov 20. The General Assembly proclaimed this day for the purpose of mobilizing the commitment of the international community to the industrialization of the continent (Res 44/237, Dec 22, 1989). For info: United Nations, Dept of Public Info, New York, NY 10017. Web: www.un.org.

UNITED NATIONS: UNIVERSAL CHILDREN'S DAY. Nov 20. Designated by the United Nations General Assembly as Universal Children's Day. First observance was in 1953. A time to honor children with special ceremonies and festivals and to make children's needs known to governments. Observed on different days and in different ways in more than 120 nations. For info: United Nations, Dept of Public Info, New York, NY 10017. Web: www.un.org.

WARM SPRINGS THANKSGIVING. Nov 20. Little White House, Warm Springs, GA. Dr. Tom Wentland portrays Pres Franklin D. Roosevelt in this presentation of what it was like when FDR spent the holiday here. Antique cars, harvest decor. Annually, the Saturday before Thanksgiving. Est attendance: 800. For info: Frankie Mewborn, Mgr, FDR's Little White House, 401 Little White House Rd, Warm Springs, GA 31830. Phone: (706) 655-5870. Fax: (706) 655-5870.

WOLCOTT, OLIVER: BIRTH ANNIVERSARY. Nov 20, 1726. Signer of the Declaration of Independence, Governor of Connecticut, born at Windsor, CT. Died Dec 1, 1797, at Litchfield, CT.

BIRTHDAYS TODAY

Joseph (Joe) Robinette Biden, Jr, 62, US Senator (D, Delaware), born Scranton, PA, Nov 20, 1942.
Robert C. Byrd, 87, US Senator (D, West Virginia), born North Wilkesboro, NC, Nov 20, 1917.
Steve Dahl, 50, Chicago radio personality, born La Canada, CA, Nov 20, 1954.
Richard Dawson, 72, actor, TV game-show host ("Hogan's Heroes"; Emmy for "Family Feud"), born Gosport, England, Nov 20, 1932.
Bo Derek, 48, actress (*10, Bolero, Tarzan, A Change of Seasons*), born Cathleen Collins, Long Beach, CA, Nov 20, 1956.
Nadine Gordimer, 81, writer (*July's People, Lifetimes Under Apartheid*), born Springs, South Africa, Nov 20, 1923.
Veronica Hamel, 61, actress ("Hill Street Blues"), born Philadelphia, PA, Nov 20, 1943.
Ruth Laredo, 67, concert pianist, born Detroit, MI, Nov 20, 1937.
Sabrina Lloyd, 34, actress (*Sliders*), born Mount Dora, FL, Nov 20, 1970.
Richard Masur, 56, actor ("One Day at a Time," *Who'll Stop the Rain, Under Fire, Heartburn*), born New York, NY, Nov 20, 1948.
Ricardo Montalban, 84, actor ("Fantasy Island," *Star Trek II: The Wrath of Kahn*), born Mexico City, Mexico, Nov 20, 1920.
Estelle Parsons, 77, actress ("Roseanne," *Bonnie and Clyde, Dick Tracy*; stage: *Next Time I'll Sing to You* [Obie], *In the Summer House* [Obie]), born Marblehead, MA, Nov 20, 1927.
Dick Smothers, 65, comedian, folksinger (with brother Tom, "The Smothers Brothers Comedy Hour"), born New York, NY, Nov 20, 1939.
Ming-Na Wen, 37, actress ("ER," *One Night Stand*), born Macau, China, Nov 20, 1967.
Judy Woodruff, 58, journalist, author, born Tulsa, OK, Nov 20, 1946.
Sean Young, 45, actress (*Blade Runner, No Way Out*), born Louisville, KY, Nov 20, 1959.

NOVEMBER 21 — SUNDAY
Day 326 — 40 Remaining

ALASCATTALO DAY. Nov 21. Anchorage, AK. To honor humor in general and Alaskan humor in particular. Event is named after "alascattalo," said to be the genetic cross between a moose and a walrus. For info: Steven C. Levi, Parsnackle Press, PO Box 241467, Anchorage, AK 99524. Phone/fax: (907) 337-2021. E-mail: afscl@alaska.net.

BARTLETT, JOSIAH: 275th BIRTH ANNIVERSARY. Nov 21, 1729. Signer of the Declaration of Independence. Born at Amesbury, MA, he died at Kingston, NH, May 19, 1795.

BEAUMONT, WILLIAM: BIRTH ANNIVERSARY. Nov 21, 1785. US Army surgeon whose contribution to classic medical literature and world fame resulted from another man's shotgun wound. When Canadian fur trapper Alexis St. Martin received a wound June 6, 1822—a nearly point-blank blast to the abdomen—Dr. Beaumont began observing his stomach and digestive processes through an opening in his abdominal wall. His findings were published in 1833 in *Experiments and Observations on the Gastric Juice and the Physiology of Digestion*. St. Martin returned to Canada in 1834 and resisted Beaumont's efforts to

Nov 21 ☆ ***Chase's 2004 Calendar of Events*** ☆

have him return for further study. He outlived his doctor by 20 years and was buried at a depth of eight feet to discourage any attempt at posthumous examination. Beaumont, born at Lebanon, CT, died Apr 25, 1853, at St. Louis, MO.

CONGRESS FIRST MEETS AT WASHINGTON: ANNIVERSARY. Nov 21, 1800. Congress met at Philadelphia from 1790 to 1800, when the north wing of the new Capitol at Washington, DC, was completed. The House and the Senate had been scheduled to meet in the new building Nov 17, 1800, but a quorum wasn't achieved until Nov 21, 1800.

DOW-JONES TOPS 5,000: ANNIVERSARY. Nov 21, 1995. The Dow-Jones Index of 30 major industrial stocks topped the 5,000 mark for the first time.

DRC-FM CARAVAN OF CARRIAGES. Nov 21. Windsor, CT. 10th annual. "DRC-FM Drive for Foodshare" consists of listeners soliciting monetary donations, purchasing a shopping cart full of food and walking a five-mile route in the "Caravan of Carriages" from a local grocery store to Foodshare in Windsor, which collects food for 200 shelters and kitchens across Connecticut. Annually, the last Sunday before Thanksgiving. Est attendance: 1,000. For info: WDRC-FM, 869 Blue Hills Ave, Bloomfield, CT 06002. Phone: (860) 243-1115. Fax: (860) 286-8257. Web: www.drcfm.com.

EIGHTEENTH-CENTURY THRESHING DAY. Nov 21. McLean, VA. Help the farm family thresh wheat, make yeast cakes and celebrate the end of the season with light refreshment. Annually, the third Sunday in November. Est attendance: 500. For info: Pat Dubbin, Claude Moore Colonial Farm at Turkey Run, 6310 Georgetown Pike, McLean, VA 22101. Phone: (703) 442-7557. Fax: (703) 442-0714. Web: www.1771.org.

FRENCHMAN ROWS ACROSS PACIFIC: ANNIVERSARY. Nov 21, 1991. Gerard d'Aboville completed a four-month solo journey across the Pacific Ocean on this date. D'Aboville began rowing across the Pacific on July 11 when he left Choshi, Japan. His journey ended at Ilwaco, WA.

GERMANY: TOTENSONNTAG. Nov 21. In Germany, Totensonntag is the Protestant population's day for remembrance of the dead. It is celebrated on the last Sunday of the church year (the Sunday before Advent).

GREEN, HETTY: BIRTH ANNIVERSARY. Nov 21, 1835. Henrietta Howland Robinson Green, better known as Hetty Green, reported to have been the richest woman in America, was born at New Bedford, MA. She was an able financier who managed her own wealth, which was estimated to have been in excess of $100 million. Died at New York, NY, July 3, 1916.

LA POSADA de KINGSVILLE: A CELEBRATION OF LIGHTS. Nov 21–Dec 12 (tentative). Kingsville, TX. While a celebration of lights recaptures the joy and spirit of Christmas as businesses and neighborhoods twinkle with lights from the weekend before Thanksgiving, many holiday events with a South Texas flavor are scheduled: special activities for children, nighttime parade with lighted floats and holiday music and much more. Call for dates of specific events. Est attendance: 50,000. For info: Kingsville Conv and Visitors Bureau, 1501 N Hwy 77, Kingsville, TX 78364-1562. Phone: (800) 333-5032. Fax: (361) 592-3227. Web: www.kingsvilletexas.com.

MARX, HARPO: BIRTH ANNIVERSARY. Nov 21, 1893. Harpo (Adolph Arthur) Marx was born at New York, NY. He was the second born of the famed Marx brothers who were a popular comedy team of stage, screen and radio for 30 years. Harpo wore a blond curly wig and pretended to be a mute who communicated by honking a horn. He was an expert player of the harp. He died Sept 28, 1964, at Hollywood, CA. Other family members who participated in the comedy team were Groucho (Julius), Chico (Leonard) and, briefly, Zeppo (Herbert) and Gummo (Milton).

MOTHER GOOSE PARADE. Nov 21. El Cajon, CA. "A celebration of children." Floats depict Mother Goose rhymes and fairy tales and/or annual theme. Bands, equestrians and clowns. Traditionally, the Sunday before Thanksgiving. Est attendance: 450,000. For info: Mother Goose Parade Assn, 480 N Magnolia Ave, Ste 106, El Cajon, CA 92020. Phone: (619) 444-8712. Fax: (619) 444-3971. E-mail: mothergooseparade@att.net. Web: www.mothergooseparade.com.

NATIONAL ADOPTION WEEK. Nov 21–27. To commemorate the success of three kinds of adoption—infant, special needs and intercountry—through a variety of special events. Annually, the week of Thanksgiving. For info: Natl Council for Adoption, 225 N Washington St, Alexandria, VA 22314-2520. Phone: (703) 299-6633. Fax: (703) 299-6004. Web: www.adoptioncouncil.org.

NATIONAL BIBLE WEEK. Nov 21–28. An interfaith campaign to promote reading of the Bible. Resource packets available. Governors and mayors across the country proclaim National Bible Week observance to their constituencies. Annually, from the Sunday preceding Thanksgiving to the following Sunday. For info: Thomas R. May, Pres, Natl Bible Assn, 1865 Broadway, New York, NY 10023. Phone: (212) 408-1390. E-mail: tmay@nationalbible.org. Web: www.nationalbible.org.

★**NATIONAL FAMILY WEEK.** Nov 21–27.

NATIONAL GAME AND PUZZLE WEEK™. Nov 21–27. 10th annual event to increase appreciation of board games and puzzles while preserving the tradition of investing time with family and friends. Part of The Million Minute Family Challenge™, conducted Sept 1–Dec 31. Special teacher material and media information available, including press kits, interviews, etc. Annually, the Sunday through Saturday of Thanksgiving week. For info: Frank Beres, National Game & Puzzle Week, PO Box 268, Beloit, WI 53512-0268. Phone: (800) 524-4263. Fax: (608) 362-8178. E-mail: patch@patchproducts.com. Web: www.millionminute.com.

NORTH CAROLINA: RATIFICATION DAY. Nov 21. 12th state to ratify Constitution in 1789.

PASADENA DOO DAH PARADE. Nov 21. Pasadena, CA. No theme, no judging, no prizes, no order of march, no motorized vehicles and no animals. Annually, the Sunday before Thanksgiving Day. Light Bringer Project, 64 N Raymond Ave, Pasadena, CA 91103. Phone: (626) 440-7379. E-mail: pasadenadoodahparade@yahoo.com. Web: www.pasadenadoodahparade.com.

POPE BENEDICT XV: 150th BIRTH ANNIVERSARY. Nov 21, 1854. Giacomo dela Chiesa, 258th pope of the Roman

	S	M	T	W	T	F	S
November		1	2	3	4	5	6
	7	8	9	10	11	12	13
2004	14	15	16	17	18	19	20
	21	22	23	24	25	26	27
	28	29	30				

Catholic Church, born at Pegli, Italy, and elected pope Sept 3, 1914. Died at Rome, Italy, Jan 22, 1922.

PUMPKIN PIE DAY. Nov 21. Making pumpkin pies is a family tradition that goes back generations. People associate the sweet smell of pumpkin pie with the late fall. For info: Cindy Benson, 13116 Frog Hollow Ct, Oak Hill, VA 20171. Phone: (703) 471-5784. E-mail: benson1984@aol.com.

PURCELL, HENRY: DEATH ANNIVERSARY. Nov 21, 1695 (OS). English composer of the early Baroque period was born at London circa 1659. Purcell's work includes more than 100 songs, the opera *Dido and Aeneas* and *The Fairy Queen*, incidental music for a version of Shakespeare's *A Midsummer Night's Dream*. Purcell died at London.

UNITED NATIONS: WORLD TELEVISION DAY. Nov 21. On Dec 17, 1996, the General Assembly proclaimed this day as World Television Day, commemorating the date in 1996 on which the first World Television Forum was held at the UN. For info: United Nations, Dept of Public Info, New York, NY 10017. Web: www.un.org.

VOLTAIRE, JEAN FRANÇOIS MARIE: BIRTH ANNIVERSARY. Nov 21, 1694. French author and philosopher to whom is attributed (perhaps erroneously) the statement: "I disapprove of what you say, but I will defend to the death your right to say it." His most famous work is the novel *Candide*. Born at Paris, he died there May 30, 1778.

WORLD HELLO DAY. Nov 21. 32nd annual observance. Everyone who participates greets 10 people. People in 180 countries have participated in this annual activity for advancing peace through personal communication. Heads of state of 114 countries have expressed approval of the event. For info: Michael McCormack, The McCormack Brothers, PO Box 15592, Beverly Hills, CA 90209. Web: www.worldhelloday.org.

BIRTHDAYS TODAY

Troy Aikman, 38, former football player, born West Covina, CA, Nov 21, 1966.
Phil Bredesen, 61, Governor of Tennessee (D), born Shortsville, NY, Nov 21, 1943.
Marcy Carsey, 60, TV producer, born South Weymouth, MA, Nov 21, 1944.
James (Anderson) DePreist, 68, conductor (Oregon Symphony), born Philadelphia, PA, Nov 21, 1936.
Richard J. Durbin, 60, US Senator (D, Illinois), born East St. Louis, IL, Nov 21, 1944.
George Kenneth (Ken) Griffey, Jr, 35, baseball player, born Donora, PA, Nov 21, 1969.
Goldie Hawn, 59, actress ("Rowan & Martin's Laugh-In," *Private Benjamin*; Oscar for *Cactus Flower*), born Washington, DC, Nov 21, 1945.
David Hemmings, 63, actor (*Blow-Up, The Charge of the Light Brigade*), born Guildford, England, Nov 21, 1941.
Laurence Luckinbill, 70, actor ("The Delphi Bureau," *The Boys in the Band, Star Trek V*), born Fort Smith, AR, Nov 21, 1934.
Lorna Luft, 52, actress ("Trapper John, MD"), daughter of Judy Garland, born Los Angeles, CA, Nov 21, 1952.
Juliet Mills, 63, actress ("Nanny and the Professor," "Passions," *So Well Remembered, Carry on Jack*), daughter of actor John Mills, sister of actress Hayley Mills, born London, England, Nov 21, 1941.
Stanley Frank ("Stan the Man") Musial, 84, Hall of Fame baseball player, born Donora, PA, Nov 21, 1920.
Harold Ramis, 60, actor, director, writer, producer (*Ghostbusters, Back to School*), born Chicago, IL, Nov 21, 1944.
Cynthia Rhodes, 48, actress, dancer (*Flashdance, Dirty Dancing*), born Nashville, TN, Nov 21, 1956.
Tasha Schwikert, 20, gymnast, born Las Vegas, NV, Nov 21, 1984.
Nicollette Sheridan, 41, actress ("Knots Landing," *The Sure Thing*), born Worthing, Sussex, England, Nov 21, 1963.
Marlo Thomas, 66, actress ("That Girl"), author (*Free to Be . . . You and Me*), born Detroit, MI, Nov 21, 1938.

NOVEMBER 22 — MONDAY
Day 327 — 39 Remaining

ADAMS, ABIGAIL SMITH: BIRTH ANNIVERSARY. Nov 22, 1744. Wife of John Adams, second president of the US, born at Weymouth, MA. Died Oct 28, 1818, at Quincy, MA.

BETTER CONVERSATION WEEK. Nov 22–28. In order to have better, more satisfying conversations, you must follow some simple guidelines. This week focuses on making better conversation with friends and relatives. For "10 Ways to Better Conversation" tip sheet, send #10 SASE or check RESOURCES at website below. For info: Dr Loren Ekroth, Working Knowledge, 9030 W Sahara Ave, #430, Las Vegas, NV 89117. Phone: (702) 214-6782. E-mail: loren@conversation-matters.com. Web: www.conversation-matters.com.

BRITTEN, (EDWARD) BENJAMIN: BIRTH ANNIVERSARY. Nov 22, 1913. English composer born at Lowestoft, Suffolk, England. Lord Britten, Baron Britten of Aldeburgh, died at Aldeburgh, Dec 4, 1976.

CANADA: CANADIAN WESTERN AGRIBITION. Nov 22–27. Regina, SK. Canada's premiere international livestock show and marketplace featuring North America's finest livestock genetics. More than 4,000 cattle, sheep, goats, llamas and horses are on display to the public at this trade show featuring more than 400 exhibitors. Major attractions include Saskatchewan's largest indoor pro rodeo, Grain and Forage showcase, Prairie Cuisine, draft horse events, light horse competitions, our award-winning Agri-ed program for youth, and the Agribition grandstand, featuring cowboy poetry, musical performers and fashion shows. Est attendance: 145,000. For info: Western Agribition, Box 3535, Regina, SK, Canada S4P 3J8. Phone: (306) 565-0565. E-mail: agribition@sk.sympatico.ca. Web: www.agribition.com.

CARMICHAEL, HOAGIE: BIRTH ANNIVERSARY. Nov 22, 1899. Hoagland Howard Carmichael, attorney who gave up the practice of law to become an actor and songwriter, was born at Bloomington, IN. Among his many popular songs: "Stardust," "Lazybones," "Two Sleepy People" and "Skylark." Carmichael died at Rancho Mirage, CA, Dec 27, 1981.

CHINA CLIPPER: ANNIVERSARY. Nov 22, 1935. A Pan American Martin 130 "flying boat" called the *China Clipper* began regular trans-Pacific mail service on Nov 22, 1935. The plane, powered by four Pratt and Whitney Twin Wasp engines, took off from San Francisco. It reached Manila, Philippines, 59 hours and 48 minutes later. About 20,000 persons watched the historic takeoff. Commercial passenger service was established the following year (Oct 21, 1936).

CHRISTMAS AT THE BENJAMIN HARRISON HOME. Nov 22–Dec 31. Indianapolis, IN. (Closed Thanksgiving, Christmas Eve and Christmas Day.) Daily guided tours of the 23rd President's home decorated in seasonal, Victorian style. For info: PR Dept, President Benjamin Harrison Home, 1230 N Delaware St, Indianapolis, IN 46202-2598. Phone: (317) 631-1888. Fax: (317) 632-5488.

Nov 22 ☆ *Chase's 2004 Calendar of Events* ☆

De GAULLE, CHARLES ANDRE MARIE: BIRTH ANNIVERSARY. Nov 22, 1890. President of France from December 1958 until his resignation in April 1969, Charles de Gaulle was born at Lille, France. A military leader, he wrote *The Army of the Future* (1934) in which he predicted just the type of armored warfare that was used against his country by Nazi Germany in WWII. After France's defeat at the hands of the Germans, he declared the existence of "Free France" and made himself head of that organization. When the French Vichy government began to collaborate openly with the Germans, the French citizenry looked to de Gaulle for leadership. His greatest moment of triumph was when he entered liberated Paris on Aug 26, 1944. De Gaulle died at Colombey-les-Deux-Eglises, France, Nov 19, 1970.

ELIOT, GEORGE: BIRTH ANNIVERSARY. Nov 22, 1819. English novelist George Eliot, whose real name was Mary Ann Evans, was born at Chilvers Coton, Warwickshire, England. Her works include *Silas Marner* and *Middlemarch*. She died at Chelsea, Dec 22, 1880.

GARNER, JOHN NANCE: BIRTH ANNIVERSARY. Nov 22, 1868. Thirty-second vice president of US (1933–41) born at Red River County, TX. Died at Uvalde, TX, Nov 7, 1967.

KENNEDY, JOHN F.: ASSASSINATION: ANNIVERSARY. Nov 22, 1963. President John F. Kennedy was slain by a sniper while riding in an open automobile at Dallas, TX. Accused assassin Lee Harvey Oswald was killed by Jack Ruby while in police custody awaiting trial.

LATINO BOOK & FAMILY FESTIVAL—CHICAGO. Nov 22–23. McCormick Place, Chicago, IL. Produced along with actor Edward James Olmos, this festival is a celebration of books, careers, culture, education, health, recreation, travel and more. It is the largest Latino consumer trade show in the US. Attendees will enjoy hundreds of booths and activities including book signings, storytelling, poetry readings, food, entertainment and workshops. For info: Latino Book & Family Festivals, 3980 Cazador St, Los Angeles, CA 90065. E-mail: kathy@latinobookfestival.com. Web: www.latinobookfestival.com.

LEBANON: INDEPENDENCE DAY: ANNIVERSARY. Nov 22. National Day. Gained independence from France in 1943.

***ON THE ORIGIN OF SPECIES* PUBLISHED: ANNIVERSARY.** Nov 22, 1859. Charles Darwin's monumental work, *On the Origin of Species by Means of Natural Selection, or the Preservation of Favoured Races in the Struggle for Life*, was published on this date by London publisher John Murray. The print run of 1,250 (priced at 15 shillings) sold out the same day. A second print run of 3,000 in December also sold quickly. The book immediately generated a firestorm of public and private discussion. The word "evolution" did not appear until the 1872 (last) edition of *Origin*.

POST, WILEY: BIRTH ANNIVERSARY. Nov 22, 1898. Barnstorming aviator, stunt parachutist and adventurer, Wiley Post was born at Grand Plain, TX. Post, who taught himself to fly, and his plane, the *Winnie Mae*, were the center of world attention in the 1930s. He was co-author (with his navigator, Harold Gatty) of *Around the World in Eight Days*. In 1935, Post and friend Will Rogers started on a flight to Asia. Their plane crashed near Point Barrow, AK, Aug 15, 1935; both were killed.

November 2004

S	M	T	W	T	F	S
	1	2	3	4	5	6
7	8	9	10	11	12	13
14	15	16	17	18	19	20
21	22	23	24	25	26	27
28	29	30				

PRIME MINISTER THATCHER RESIGNS: ANNIVERSARY. Nov 22, 1990. Margaret Thatcher announced that she would resign from her position as England's prime minister. She was named prime minister in May 1979 and served until Nov 22, 1990. No other prime minister in the UK in the 20th century has served the post as long as she.

SAGITTARIUS, THE ARCHER. Nov 22–Dec 21. In the astronomical/astrological zodiac that divides the sun's apparent orbit into 12 segments, the period Nov 22–Dec 21 is identified, traditionally, as the sun sign of Sagittarius, the Archer. The ruling planet is Jupiter.

SAINT CECILIA: FEAST DAY. Nov 22. Roman virgin, Christian martyr and patron of music and musicians lived during third century. Survived sentences of burning and beheading. Subject of poetry and musical compositions and her feast day is still an occasion for musical events.

SWITZERLAND: ONION MARKET (ZIBELEMARIT). Nov 22. Berne. Best known and most popular of Switzerland's many autumn markets. Great heaps of onions in front of Federal Palace. Fourth Monday in November commemorates granting of market right to people after great fire of Berne in 1405.

BIRTHDAYS TODAY

Boris Becker, 37, former tennis player, born Leimen, Germany, Nov 22, 1967.

Guion S. Bluford, Jr, 62, first black astronaut in space, born West Philadelphia, PA, Nov 22, 1942.

Tom Conti, 63, actor (*Reuben, Reuben*), born Paisley, Scotland, Nov 22, 1941.

Jamie Lee Curtis, 46, actress (*True Lies, Halloween, A Fish Called Wanda*), born Los Angeles, CA, Nov 22, 1958.

Rodney Dangerfield, 83, comedian, actor (*Easy Money, Caddyshack*, "The Dean Martin Show"), born Jacob Cohen, Babylon, NY, Nov 22, 1921.

Harry Edwards, 62, sports sociologist, born St. Louis, MO, Nov 22, 1942.

Allen Garfield, 65, actor (*Bananas, The Conversation, Dick Tracy*), born Newark, NJ, Nov 22, 1939.

Stephen Geoffreys, 45, actor (*Heaven Help Us, 976-EVIL*), born Cincinnati, OH, Nov 22, 1959.

Terry Gilliam, 64, actor, writer ("Monty Python's Flying Circus," *Life of Brian*), director (*Brazil*), born Minneapolis, MN, Nov 22, 1940.

Mariel Hemingway, 43, actress (*Manhattan, Personal Best, Superman IV*), born Ketchum, ID, Nov 22, 1961.

Richard Kind, 47, actor ("Spin City," "Mad About You"), born Trenton, NJ, Nov 22, 1957.

Billie Jean King, 61, former tennis player, born Long Beach, CA, Nov 22, 1943.

Robert Vaughn, 72, actor ("The Man From U.N.C.L.E.," *The Magnificent Seven*), born New York, NY, Nov 22, 1932.

NOVEMBER 23 — TUESDAY
Day 328 — 38 Remaining

ASHFORD, EMMETT LITTLETON: 90th BIRTH ANNIVERSARY. Nov 23, 1914. Emmett Littleton Ashford, born at Los Angeles, CA, was the first black to officiate at a major league baseball game. Ashford began his pro career calling games in the minors in 1951 and went to the majors in 1966. He was noted for his flamboyant style when calling strikes and outs as well as for his dapper dress which included cufflinks with his uniform. He died Mar 1, 1980, at Marina del Rey, CA.

BILLY THE KID: BIRTH ANNIVERSARY. Nov 23, 1859. Legendary outlaw of western US. Probably named Henry McCarty at birth (New York, NY), he was better known as William H. Bonney. Ruthless killer, a failure at everything legal, he escaped from jail at age 21 while under sentence of hanging. Recaptured at Stinking Springs, NM, and returned to jail, he again escaped, only to be shot through the heart by pursuing Lincoln County Sheriff Pat Garrett at Fort Sumner, NM, during the night of July 14, 1881. His last words, answered by two shots, reportedly were "Who is there?"

CARRS/SAFEWAY GREAT ALASKA SHOOTOUT. Nov 23–27. Sullivan Arena, Anchorage, AK. Top NCAA basketball action as eight men's and four women's Division I teams from around the country compete. Est attendance: 48,000. For info: Univ of Alaska–Anchorage, Athletic Dept, 3211 Providence Dr, Anchorage, AK 99508. Phone: (907) 786-1230. Fax: (907) 563-4565. E-mail: antlm@uaa.alaska.edu. Web: www.goseawolves.com.

"DR. WHO" TV PREMIERE: ANNIVERSARY. Nov 23, 1963. First episode of "Dr. Who" premiered on British TV with William Hartnell as the first doctor. Traveling through time and space in the TARDIS (an acronym for Time and Relative Dimensions in Space), the doctor and his companions found themselves in mortal combat with creatures such as the Daleks. "Dr. Who" didn't air in the US until Sept 29, 1975.

FIRST PLAY-BY-PLAY FOOTBALL GAME BROADCAST: 85th ANNIVERSARY. Nov 23, 1919. The first play-by-play football game radio broadcast in the US took place on this day. Texas A&M blanked the University of Texas 7–0.

GILBERT ISLANDS TAKEN: ANNIVERSARY. Nov 23, 1943. The US Second Marine Division took control of the Gilbert Islands after fierce fighting on the heavily fortified Tarawa Atoll. In the 76-hour battle the Marines beat back a "death charge" in which the Japanese ran directly at the American guns. American troops sustained 3,500 killed and wounded. The Japanese suffered 5,000 killed and 17 wounded and captured. (The Gilbert Islands are the westernmost of the Polynesians, midway between Australia and Hawaii and today are part of the nation of Kiribati.)

JAPAN: LABOR THANKSGIVING DAY. Nov 23. National holiday.

KARLOFF, BORIS: BIRTH ANNIVERSARY. Nov 23, 1887. Born William Henry Pratt at London, England. An actor known for his portrayal of ghoulish figures, his movies included *Frankenstein*, *The Body Snatcher* and *The Bride of Frankenstein*. Karloff died Feb 2, 1969, at Sussex, England.

***LIFE* MAGAZINE DEBUTED: ANNIVERSARY.** Nov 23, 1936. The illustrated magazine *Life* debuted on this day. The first cover depicted a doctor slapping a baby with the caption "Life begins."

NATCHITOCHES FESTIVAL OF LIGHTS. Nov 23–Jan 6, 2005. Natchitoches, LA. A fairyland of multi-colored lights, created by 170,000 Christmas bulbs strung along city streets and incorporated into 72 unique set pieces along Cane River Lake. Est attendance: 500,000. For info: Natchitoches Parish Tourist Commission, Calendar of Events, 781 Front St, Natchitoches, LA 71457. Phone: (318) 352-8072 or (800) 259-1714. Fax: (318) 352-2415. Web: www.natchitoches.net.

PIERCE, FRANKLIN: 200th BIRTH ANNIVERSARY. Nov 23, 1804. The fourteenth president of the US was born at Hillsboro, NH. Term of office: Mar 4, 1853–Mar 3, 1857. Not nominated until the 49th ballot at the Democratic party convention in 1852, he was refused his party's nomination in 1856 for a second term. Pierce died at Concord, NH, Oct 8, 1869.

RUTLEDGE, EDWARD: BIRTH ANNIVERSARY. Nov 23, 1749. Signer of the Declaration of Independence, governor of South Carolina, born at Charleston, SC. Died there Jan 23, 1800.

SWITZERLAND: LUCERNE FESTIVAL, PIANO. Nov 23–28. Concert Hall of the Culture and Convention Centre, Lucerne. This piano festival presents recitals with first-class classical and jazz pianists at the Concert Hall. In addition, exhibitions, workshops, and films on the topic of keyboard instruments complement the events offered to the public. For info: Sheila Huber, Lucerne Festival, PO Box CH-6002, Lucerne, Switzerland. Phone: (41) (0) 41-226-44-00. Fax: (41) (0) 41-226-44-60. E-mail: info@lucernefestival.ch. Web: www.lucernefestival.ch.

BIRTHDAYS TODAY

Susan Anspach, 59, actress (*Five Easy Pieces, Play It Again Sam, Montenegro*), born New York, NY, Nov 23, 1945.
Vin Baker, 33, basketball player, born Lake Wales, FL, Nov 23, 1971.
Jerry Bock, 76, composer ("Fiddler on the Roof," "Fiorello"), born New Haven, CT, Nov 23, 1928.
Jim Doyle, 59, Governor of Wisconsin (D), born Madison, WI, Nov 23, 1945.
Steve Harvey, 48, comedian, actor (*The Original Kings of Comedy*, "The Steve Harvey Show"), born Welch, WV, Nov 23, 1956.
Mary L. Landrieu, 49, US Senator (D, Louisiana), born Arlington, VA, Nov 23, 1955.
Krzysztof Penderecki, 71, composer, born Debica, Poland, Nov 23, 1933.
Charles E. Schumer, 54, US Senator (D, New York), born Brooklyn, NY, Nov 23, 1950.

NOVEMBER 24 — WEDNESDAY
Day 329 — 37 Remaining

BARKLEY, ALBEN WILLIAM: BIRTH ANNIVERSARY. Nov 24, 1877. Thirty-fifth vice president of the US (1949–53), born at Graves County, KY. Died at Lexington, VA, Apr 30, 1956.

BATTLE OF CHATTANOOGA: ANNIVERSARY. Nov 24, 1863. After reinforcing the besieged Union army at Chattanooga, TN, General Ulysses S. Grant launched the Battle of Chattanooga on this date. Falsely secure in the knowledge that his troops were in an impregnable position on Lookout Mountain, Confederate General Braxton Bragg and his army were overrun by the Union forces, Bragg himself barely escaping capture. The battle is famous for the Union Army's spectacular advance up a heavily fortified slope into the teeth of the enemy guns.

CARNEGIE, DALE: BIRTH ANNIVERSARY. Nov 24, 1888. American inspirational lecturer and author, Dale Carnegie was born at Maryville, MO. His best known book, *How to Win Friends and Influence People*, published in 1936, sold nearly five million copies and was translated into 29 languages. Carnegie died at New York, NY, Nov 1, 1955.

Nov 24–25 ☆ Chase's 2004 Calendar of Events ☆

"D.B. COOPER" HIJACKING: ANNIVERSARY. Nov 24–25, 1971. A middle-aged man whose plane ticket was made out to "D.B. Cooper" parachuted from a Northwest Airlines 727 jetliner on Nov 25, 1971, carrying $200,000 which he had collected from the airline as ransom for the plane and passengers as a result of threats made during his Nov 24 flight from Portland, OR, to Seattle, WA. He jumped from the plane over an area of wilderness south of Seattle and was never apprehended. Several thousand dollars of the marked ransom money turned up in February 1980, along the Columbia River, near Vancouver, WA.

DUFF, HOWARD: BIRTH ANNIVERSARY. Nov 24, 1913. American actor Howard Duff was born at Bremerton, WA. He played detective Sam Spade on radio in the 1940s and then went on to films and television ("Knots Landing"). He died July 8, 1990, at Santa Barbara, CA.

JOPLIN, SCOTT: BIRTH ANNIVERSARY. Nov 24, 1868. American musician and composer famed for his piano rags, born at Texarkana, TX. Died at New York, NY, Apr 1, 1917.

MANSTEIN, ERICH von: BIRTH ANNIVERSARY. Nov 24, 1887. Considered by many to be the greatest strategist of World War II, Erich von Manstein was born at Berlin, Germany. His plan for the invasion of France in 1940 was a complete success. He was dismissed by Hitler in March 1944. Manstein died at Irschenhausen, Germany, June 10, 1973.

SPINOZA, BARUCH: BIRTH ANNIVERSARY. Nov 24, 1632 (OS). Dutch philosopher, born at Amsterdam. Died at The Hague, Feb 21, 1677 (OS). "Peace is not an absence of war," wrote Spinoza, in 1670, "it is a virtue, a state of mind, a disposition for benevolence, confidence, justice."

STERNE, LAURENCE: BIRTH ANNIVERSARY. Nov 24, 1713. Novelist, born at Clonmel, Ireland. Died at London, England, Mar 18, 1768. In his dedication to *Tristram Shandy*, Sterne wrote: "I live in a constant endeavour to fence against the infirmities of ill health, and other evils of life, by mirth; being firmly persuaded that every time a man smiles—but much more so, when he laughs, that it adds something to this Fragment of Life."

TAYLOR, ZACHARY: BIRTH ANNIVERSARY. Nov 24, 1784. The soldier who became twelfth president of the US was born at Orange County, VA. Term of office: Mar 4, 1849–July 9, 1850. He was nominated at the Whig party convention in 1848, but, the story goes, he did not accept the letter notifying him of his nomination because it had postage due. He cast his first vote in 1846, when he was 62 years old. Becoming ill July 4, 1850, he died at the White House, July 9. His last words: "I am sorry that I am about to leave my friends."

TOULOUSE-LAUTREC, HENRI DE: BIRTH ANNIVERSARY. Nov 24, 1864. French painter and designer of posters. Born at Albi, France, he died Sept 9, 1901, at Bordeaux, France.

US MILITARY LEAVES PHILIPPINES: ANNIVERSARY. Nov 24, 1992. The Philippines became a US colony at the turn of the century when it was taken over from Spain after the Spanish-American War. Though President Franklin D. Roosevelt signed a bill Mar 24, 1934, granting the Philippines independence to be effective July 4, 1946, before that date Manila and Washington signed a treaty allowing the US to lease military bases on the island. In 1991 the Philippine Senate voted to reject a renewal of that lease, and Nov 24, 1992, after almost 100 years of military presence on the island, the last contingent of US marines left Subic Base.

November 2004

S	M	T	W	T	F	S
	1	2	3	4	5	6
7	8	9	10	11	12	13
14	15	16	17	18	19	20
21	22	23	24	25	26	27
28	29	30				

WHAT DO YOU LOVE ABOUT AMERICA DAY. Nov 24. One day to talk about what's great about our country and its people. In the midst of cynicism, let's talk to each other about what we love. Annually, the day before Thanksgiving. For info: Chuck Sutherland, 6906 Waggoner Pl, Dallas, TX 75230. Phone: (214) 696-9214. Fax: (214) 722-1266. E-mail: sutherla@swbell.net.

WONDERLAND OF LIGHTS. Nov 24–Dec 30. Marshall, TX. More than ten million tiny white lights cover the city. Features the living Christmas tree, JC's lighted Christmas parade, candlelight home tours. Outdoor ice skating on the square and live entertainment on the square Tuesdays, Thursdays, Fridays and Saturdays. Second Saturday (Dec 4), Cowboy Christmas Celebration with breakfast, entertainment, stick-horse races, mule rides, carriage rides, bus tours and Santa Claus. Est attendance: 750,000. For info: Patsy Dreesen, Dir of Conv & Visitors Dvmt, Greater Marshall Chamber of Commerce, PO Box 520, Marshall, TX 75671. Phone: (903) 935-7868. Fax: (903) 935-9982. E-mail: marshallcvd@hotmail.com. Web: www.marshalltxchamber.com.

BIRTHDAYS TODAY

William Frank Buckley, Jr, 79, editor (*The National Review*), author (*God and Man at Yale*), born New York, NY, Nov 24, 1925.

Stanley Livingston, 54, actor ("My Three Sons"), born Los Angeles, CA, Nov 24, 1950.

Keith Primeau, 33, hockey player, born Toronto, ON, Canada, Nov 24, 1971.

Oscar Palmer Robertson, 66, Hall of Fame basketball player, born Charlotte, TN, Nov 24, 1938.

Dwight Schultz, 57, actor ("Star Trek: The Next Generation," *Fat Man and Little Boy*), born Baltimore, MD, Nov 24, 1947.

Brad Sherwood, 40, comedian, actor ("Whose Line Is It Anyway?"), born Chicago, IL, Nov 24, 1964.

Rudolph (Rudy) Tomjanovich, 56, basketball coach and former player, born Hamtramck, MI, Nov 24, 1948.

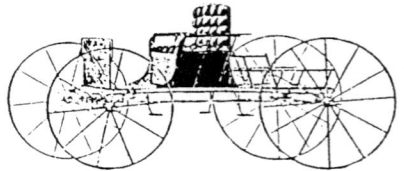

NOVEMBER 25 — THURSDAY
Day 330 — 36 Remaining

ATLANTA MARATHON AND ATLANTA HALF MARATHON. Nov 25. Atlanta, GA. 26.2-mile and 13.1-mile races (USATF certified). Advance registration only; entry forms available in July, please send SASE. Est attendance: 8,000. For info: Atlanta Track Club, 3097 E Shadowlawn Ave, Atlanta, GA 30305. Phone: (404) 231-9064. Fax: (404) 364-0708. E-mail: info@atlantatrackclub.org. Web: www.atlantatrackclub.org.

AUTOMOBILE SPEED REDUCTION: ANNIVERSARY. Nov 25, 1973. Anniversary of the presidential order requiring a cutback from the 70 mile-per-hour speed limit. The 55 mile-per-hour National Maximum Speed Limit (NMSL) was established by Congress in January 1974 (PL 93–643). The National Highway Traffic Administration reported that "analysis of available data shows that the 55 mph NMSL forestalled 48,310 fatalities through 1980. There were also reductions in crash-related injuries and property damage." Motor fuel savings were estimated at 2.4 billion gallons per year. Notwithstanding, in 1987 Congress permitted states to increase speed limits on rural interstate highways to 65 miles per hour.

BOSNIA AND HERZEGOVINA: NATIONAL DAY. Nov 25. National holiday. Commemorates the declaration of statehood within the federation of Yugoslavia in 1943.

CARNEGIE, ANDREW: BIRTH ANNIVERSARY. Nov 25, 1835. American financier, philanthropist and benefactor of more than 2,500 libraries, was born at Dunfermline, Scotland. Carnegie Hall, Carnegie Foundation and the Carnegie Endowment for International Peace are among his gifts. Carnegie wrote in 1889, "Surplus wealth is a sacred trust which its possessor is bound to administer in his lifetime for the good of the community. . . . The man who dies . . . rich dies disgraced." Carnegie died at his summer estate, "Shadowbrook," MA, Aug 11, 1919.

DAYTONA TURKEY RUN. Nov 25-28. Daytona International Speedway, Daytona Beach, FL. 31st annual car show of all makes of 1980 and older collector vehicles. Show includes display of classics, street rods, muscle cars, race cars, customs and special trucks on the speedway infield with a large swap meet of auto parts and accessories and car sales corral. Also a craft sale. Annually, Thanksgiving weekend. Est attendance: 150,000. For info: Ron Baynton, Mgr of Show Operations, Daytona Beach Racing and Recreational Facilities District, PO Box 1958, Daytona Beach, FL 32115-1958. Phone: (386) 255-7355. Fax: (386) 255-5755. Web: www.turkeyrun.com.

DiMAGGIO, JOSEPH PAUL (JOE): 90th BIRTH ANNIVERSARY. Nov 25, 1914. Baseball Hall of Fame outfielder, born at Martinez, CA. In 1941 he was on "the streak," getting a hit in 56 consecutive games. He was the American League MVP for three years, was the batting champion in 1939 and led the league in RBIs in both 1941 and 1948. DiMaggio was married to actress Marilyn Monroe in 1954, but they later divorced. He died at Harbour Island, FL, Mar 8, 1999.

FOODS & FEASTS OF COLONIAL VIRGINIA. Nov 25–27. Jamestown Settlement, Williamsburg, VA, and Yorktown Victory Center, Yorktown, VA. Explore the 17th- and 18th-century culinary practices of Virginia at this three-day event starting on Thanksgiving day. At Jamestown Settlement learn how food was gathered, preserved and prepared on land and at sea by Virginia's English colonists and Powhatan Indians. At Yorktown Victory Center, learn about typical soldiers' fare during the American Revolution and trace the bounty of a 1780s farm from field to kitchen. For info: Jamestown-Yorktown Foundation, PO Box 1607, Williamsburg, VA 23187. Phone: (757) 253-4838 or toll-free (888) 593-4682. Fax: (757) 253-5299. Web: www.historyisfun.org.

GARDEN OF LIGHTS. Nov 25–Jan 1, 2005. Honor Heights Park, Muskogee, OK. Park sparkles and shimmers with more than one million lights. Three graceful doves with 12-ft wingspans; four lighted nature exhibits; lighted waterfall with sound effects is 200 ft long with a family of deer resting nearby. Lights all over! Est attendance: 280,000. For info: Ervalene Jenkins, Muskogee Convention & Tourism, 425 Boston, Muskogee, OK 74402-0797. Phone: (918) 684-6363. Fax: (918) 684-6364.

GERMANY: FRANKFURT CHRISTMAS MARKET. Nov 25–Dec 23. "Weinachtsmarkt auf dem Romerberg," the Christmas market in Frankfurt, is one of Germany's best. Bells are rung simultaneously from nine downtown churches. Glockenspiels are sounded by hand and trumpets blown from the old St. Nicolas Church.

KENNEDY, JOHN F., JR: BIRTH ANNIVERSARY. Nov 25, 1960. Lawyer, editor (*George* magazine), born at Washington, DC. Son of John F. Kennedy (35th president of the US) and Jacqueline Bouvier Kennedy. He died along with his wife, Carolyn, and his sister-in-law, Lauren Bessette, when the plane he was piloting crashed off of Cape Cod, MA, July 16, 1999.

LONGWOOD GARDENS CHRISTMAS DISPLAY. Nov 25–Jan 2, 2005. Kennett Square, PA. Indoor Conservatory display of thousands of poinsettias and decorated trees. Outdoors, more than 400,000 lights and holiday fountain displays. Est attendance: 200,000. For info: Elizabeth Sullivan, PR Dir, Longwood Gardens, PO Box 501, Kennett Square, PA 19348-0501. Phone: (610) 388-1000. Web: www.longwoodgardens.org.

MACY'S THANKSGIVING DAY PARADE. Nov 25. New York, NY. 78th annual parade. Starts at 9 AM, EST, in Central Park West. A part of everyone's Thanksgiving, the parade grows bigger and better each year. Featuring floats, giant balloons, marching bands and famous stars, the parade is televised for the whole country. For info: New York Conv/Visitors Bureau, 810 7th Ave, 3rd Fl, New York, NY 10019. Phone: (212) 484-1222. Web: www.nycvisit.com.

NATION, CARRY AMELIA MOORE: BIRTH ANNIVERSARY. Nov 25, 1846. American temperance leader, famed as hatchet-wielding smasher of saloons, born at Garrard County, KY. Died at Leavenworth, KS, June 9, 1911.

OLD TYME FARM DAYS. Nov 25–28. Live Oak, FL. You will experience the past in the present, from cane syrup making and mule-pulled wagon rides to a living old tyme village and an old tyme gospel sing. There will be vendors selling all kinds of old tyme wares. Est attendance: 5,000. For info: Spirit of the Suwannee Music Park, 3076 95th Dr, Live Oak, FL 32060. Phone: (386) 364-1683. Fax: (386) 364-2998. E-mail: spirit@musicliveshere.com. Web: www.musicliveshere.com.

PLAZA LIGHTS. Nov 25–mid-January, 2005. Country Club Plaza, Kansas City, MO. Annual lighting ceremony heralds the beginning of the holiday season. More than 200,000 jewel-colored lights, spanning 80 miles, illuminate the outline of every tower, balcony and courtyard of a 14-square block area. Christmas shopping against a backdrop of the Plaza Lights is a Kansas City tradition that began with a single strand of lights over a store entrance in 1925. Est attendance: 250,000. For info: Highwoods Properties, 310 Ward Pkwy, Kansas City, MO 64112. Phone: (816) 753-0100. Fax: (816) 753-4625. Web: www.countryclubplaza.com.

POPE JOHN XXIII: BIRTH ANNIVERSARY. Nov 25, 1881. Angelo Roncalli, 261st pope of the Roman Catholic Church, born at Sotte il Monte, Italy. Elected pope, Oct 28, 1958. Died June 3, 1963, at Rome, Italy.

SAINT CATHERINE'S DAY. Nov 25. Patron saint of maidens, mechanics and philosophers, as well as of all who work with wheels.

SCOTLAND: SCOTTISH INTERNATIONAL BADMINTON CHAMPIONSHIP. Nov 25–28. Kelvin Hall International Sports Arena, Glasgow. A European Badminton Union Grand Prix Tournament. Est attendance: 7,000. For info: Badminton Scotland, Cockburn Centre, 40 Bogmoor Pl, Glasgow, Scotland G51 4TQ. Phone: (44) (141) 445-1218. Fax: (44) (141) 425-1218. E-mail: enquiries@badmintonscotland.org.uk.

SHOPPING REMINDER DAY. Nov 25. One month before Christmas, a reminder to shoppers that after today there are only 28 more shopping days (excluding Thanksgiving and Christmas Eve) until Christmas.

Nov 25–26 ☆ *Chase's 2004 Calendar of Events* ☆

STOCK EXCHANGE HOLIDAY (THANKSGIVING DAY). Nov 25. The holiday schedules for the various exchanges are subject to change if relevant rules, regulations or exchange policies are revised. If you have questions, phone: American Stock Exchange (212) 306-1000; Chicago Board of Trade (312) 435-3500; Chicago Board of Options Exchange (312) 786-5600; New York Stock Exchange (212) 656-2065; Pacific Stock Exchange (415) 393-4000; Philadelphia Stock Exchange (215) 496-5000.

SURINAME: INDEPENDENCE DAY. Nov 25. Holiday. Gained independence from the Netherlands in 1975.

★**THANKSGIVING DAY.** Nov 25. Presidential Proclamation. Always issued for the fourth Thursday in November. See also: "First US Holiday by Presidential Proclamation: Anniversary" (Nov 26).

THANKSGIVING DAY. Nov 25. Legal public holiday. (Public Law 90–363 sets Thanksgiving Day on the fourth Thursday in November.) Observed in all states. In most states, the Friday after Thanksgiving is also a holiday; in Nevada it is called Family Day.

TURKEY-FREE THANKSGIVING. Nov 25. This is a time for you to take turkey off your table, forgoing flesh foods "cold turkey" and having a harvest of health. Why not carve a compassionate celebration centerpiece—a tasty mock turkey made from tofu, tempeh or seitan? The turkeys will thank you for having a humane holiday! For info: Vegetarian Awareness Network, Communications Center, PO Box 321, Knoxville, TN 37901-0321. Phone: (800) USA-VEGE.

TURKEY TROT. Nov 25. Parkersburg City Park Pavilion, Parkersburg, WV. Three-mile fun run/walk on Thanksgiving morning. Drawings held for frozen turkeys and first 500 participants receive a long-sleeved T-shirt. Est attendance: 800. For info: The Rehab Center, 1900 Garfield Ave, Parkersburg, WV 26101. Phone: (304) 424-3678. Fax: (304) 424-4430.

UNITED NATIONS: INTERNATIONAL DAY FOR THE ELIMINATION OF VIOLENCE AGAINST WOMEN. Nov 25. Women's activists have marked Nov 25 as a day against violence since 1981. On that date in 1961 the three Mirabel sisters, political activists in the Dominican Republic, were assassinated on orders of ruler Rafael Trujillo. For info: United Nations, Dept of Public Info, New York, NY 10017. Web: www.un.org.

BIRTHDAYS TODAY

Christina Applegate, 33, actress ("Married . . . With Children," "Jesse"), born Hollywood, CA, Nov 25, 1971.
Cris Carter, 39, former football player, born Troy, OH, Nov 25, 1965.
Russell Earl ("Bucky") Dent, 53, former baseball player and manager, born Russell Earl O'Dey, Savannah, GA, Nov 25, 1951.
Robert Ehrlich, Jr, 47, Governor of Maryland (R), born Baltimore, MD, Nov 25, 1957.
Joe Jackson Gibbs, 64, Hall of Fame football coach, sportscaster, born Mocksville, NC, Nov 25, 1940.
Amy Grant, 44, singer ("Baby, Baby"), born Augusta, GA, Nov 25, 1960.

	S	M	T	W	T	F	S
November 2004		1	2	3	4	5	6
	7	8	9	10	11	12	13
	14	15	16	17	18	19	20
	21	22	23	24	25	26	27
	28	29	30				

Jill Hennessy, 35, actress ("Law & Order," "Crossing Jordan"), born Edmonton, AB, Canada, Nov 25, 1969.
Bernie Joseph Kosar, Jr, 41, former football player, born Boardman, OH, Nov 25, 1963.
John Larroquette, 57, actor (Emmies for "Night Court"; "Payne," "The John Larroquette Show"), born New Orleans, LA, Nov 25, 1947.
Lenny Moore, 71, Hall of Fame football player, born Reading, PA, Nov 25, 1933.
Ben Stein, 60, actor, game show host ("Win Ben Stein's Money"), born Washington, DC, Nov 25, 1944.

NOVEMBER 26 — FRIDAY
Day 331 — 35 Remaining

BELSNICKEL CRAFT SHOW. Nov 26–27. Boyertown, PA. Sale of juried crafts with folk art emphasis. Annually, the first Friday and Saturday after Thanksgiving. Est attendance: 5,000. For info: Lindsay Dieroff, Collection Dir, Boyertown Area Historical Society, 43 S Chestnut St, Boyertown, PA 19512. Phone: (610) 367-5255. E-mail: boyertownhistory@juno.com.

BLACK FRIDAY. Nov 26. The traditional beginning of the Christmas shopping season on the Friday after Thanksgiving.

BUY NOTHING DAY. Nov 26. A 24-hour moratorium on consumer spending. A celebration of simplicity, about getting our runaway consumer culture back onto a sustainable path. Annually, on the first shopping day after Thanksgiving. For info: The Media Foundation, 1243 W 7th Ave, Vancouver, BC, Canada V6H 1B7. Phone: (800) 663-1243 or (604) 736-9401. Fax: (604) 737-6021. E-mail: buynothingday@adbusters.org. Web: www.adbusters.org/campaigns.

CASABLANCA **PREMIERE: ANNIVERSARY.** Nov 26, 1942. Due to the landing of the Allies in North Africa on Nov 8, the premiere and release of the film were moved up from June 1943 to Nov 26, 1942, when it premiered at New York City on Thanksgiving Day. The general nationwide release followed on Jan 23, 1943, during the Roosevelt-Churchill conferences in Casablanca.

CHRISTMAS CANDLELIGHT TOUR. Nov 26–28 (also Dec 3–5 and 10–12). My Old Kentucky Home State Park, Bardstown, KY. Christmas in the style and flavor of the 1800s. Annually, the first three weekends after Thanksgiving. Est attendance: 10,000. For info: My Old Kentucky Home State Pk, PO Box 323, Hwy 150, Bardstown, KY 40004. Phone: (800) 323-7803 or (502) 348-3502. Fax: (502) 349-0054. Web: www.kystateparks.com.

CHRISTMAS TRADITIONS. Nov 26–Dec 22. St. Charles, MO. Holiday festivities include yule-log burning, caroling, chestnut roasting and authentically costumed Santas. Enjoy evening shopping on Wednesdays and Fridays. Annually, after Thanksgiving until Christmas. Est attendance: 50,000. For info: St. Charles CVB, 230 S Main St, St. Charles, MO 63301. Phone: (800) 366-2427. Web: www.stcharleschristmas.com.

CRAFTSMEN'S CHRISTMAS CLASSIC ARTS & CRAFTS FESTIVAL. Nov 26–28. Greensboro Coliseum Complex Special Events Center, Greesboro, NC. Features work from more than 500 talented artists and craftspeople. All juried exhibitors' work has been handmade by the exhibitors and must be their own original design and creation. See the creative process in action as many exhibitors demonstrate their craft. Visit Christmas Tree Village to view the uniquely decorated Christmas Trees by some of our exhibitors. Something for every style, taste, and budget with items from the most contemporary to the most traditional. Est attendance: 35,000. For info: Gilmore Enterprises, 1240 Oakland Ave, Greensboro, NC 27403. Phone: (336) 274-5550. E-mail: gilmoreshows@triad.rr.com.

CUSTER BATTLEFIELD BECOMES LITTLE BIGHORN BATTLEFIELD: ANNIVERSARY. Nov 26, 1991. The US Congress approved a bill renaming Custer Battlefield National Monument as Little Bighorn Battlefield National Monument. The bill also authorized the construction of a memorial to the Native

★ Chase's 2004 Calendar of Events ★   Nov 26

Americans who fought and died at the battle known as Custer's Last Stand. Introduced by then Representative Ben Nighthorse Campbell, the only Native American in Congress, the bill was signed into law by President George H.W. Bush.

CUT YOUR OWN CHRISTMAS TREE. Nov 26–Dec 24. Charlottesville, VA. Est attendance: 100. For info: Ash Lawn–Highland, James Monroe Parkway, Charlottesville, VA 22902. Phone: (434) 293-9539. Fax: (434) 293-8000. E-mail: info@ashlawnhighland.org. Web: www.ashlawnhighland.org.

DICKENS OLDE-FASHIONED CHRISTMAS FESTIVAL. Nov 26–28 (also Dec 4–5, 11–12, 18–19). Holly, MI. Circa 1850 comes to life in downtown Holly. Bah humbug with Scrooge, encourage Tiny Tim, sing with the carolers, banter with the street vendors. Enjoy delicacies such as roasted chestnuts, open-flame baked potatoes and plum pudding. Entertainment on the hour. Est attendance: 55,000. For info: Holly Area Chamber of Commerce, PO Box 214, Holly, MI 48442. Phone: (248) 634-1900. Fax: (248) 634-1049. Web: www.hollymi.com.

DICKENS VILLAGE FESTIVAL. Nov 26–27 (also Dec 3–4 and Dec 10–11). Garrison, ND. Walk the streets of downtown and eat delicious hot baked potatoes and sausages on a stick, warm up with a cup of English tea, shop the Fezziwig's Warehouse, an English Market for Victorian treasures and English gifts. In the evening be outside for a parade of lights led by Christmas carolers and then attend the nightly performance of Dickens *A Christmas Carol*. Est attendance: 4,000. For info: North Dakota Tourism, Century Center, 1600 E Century Ave, Ste 2, Bismarck, ND 58503. Phone: (800) 799-4242 or (800) 435-5663. Web: www.dickensfestival.com.

FAMILY DAY IN NEVADA. Nov 26. Observed annually on the Friday following the fourth Thursday in November.

FIRST US HOLIDAY BY PRESIDENTIAL PROCLAMATION: ANNIVERSARY. Nov 26, 1789. President George Washington proclaimed Nov 26, 1789, to be Thanksgiving Day. Both Houses of Congress, by their joint committee, had requested him to recommend "a day of public thanksgiving and prayer, to be observed by acknowledging with grateful hearts the many and signal favors of Almighty God, especially by affording them an opportunity to peaceably establish a form of government for their safety and happiness." Proclamation issued Oct 3, 1789. Next proclaimed by President Lincoln in 1863 for the last Thursday in November. In 1939 President Roosevelt moved Thanksgiving to the fourth Thursday in November.

FISH HOUSE PARADE. Nov 26. Aitkin, MN. 14th annual special parade of uniquely and humorously decorated fish houses used for ice fishing during the winter. Annually, the Friday after Thanksgiving. Est attendance: 6,000. For info: Carroll Kukowski, Exec Dir, Aitkin Area Chamber of Commerce, PO Box 127, Aitkin, MN 56431. Phone: (800) 526-8342. Fax: (218) 927-4494. E-mail: upnorth@aitkin.com. Web: www.aitkin.com.

GETTYSBURG YULETIDE FESTIVAL. Nov 26–28. (Also Dec 3–5, 10–12, 17–19, 24–26, 31) Gettysburg, PA. Tours of decorated historic homes, live nativity scene, caroling and handbell choirs, Christmas parade, community concerts, holiday dessert tasting, candlelight walking tour and Adams County New Years Eve Bash. Annually, the last weekend in November, weekends in December and New Year's Eve. Est attendance: 10,000. For info: Gettysburg CVB, PO Box 4117, Gettysburg, PA 17325. Phone: (717) 334-6274. Fax: (717) 334-1166. E-mail: gettysburgcvb@dejazzd.com. Web: www.gettysburgcvb.org.

GIVING THANKS: HEARTH AND HOME IN EARLY MARYLAND. Nov 26–27. St. Mary's City, MD. From everyday meals to feasts, join us as we examine the colonial table. Demonstrations of food preservation and hearth cooking. 10 AM–5 PM. Est attendance: 1,000. For info: Visitors Services, Historic St. Mary's City, PO Box 39, St. Mary's City, MD 20686. Phone: (240) 895-4990 or (800) SMC-1634. Fax: (240) 895-4968. Web: www.stmaryscity.org.

GRIMKE, SARAH MOORE: BIRTH ANNIVERSARY. Nov 26, 1792. American antislavery and women's rights advocate along with her sister Angelina. Born at Charleston, SC, and died Dec 23, 1873, at Hyde Park, MA.

HOLIDAY MAGIC. Nov 26. Galena Blvd in downtown Aurora, IL. Annual celebration as Santa Claus arrives in our Parade of Lights, followed by the annual lighting of the City Christmas tree and fireworks. For info: Tess Wackerlin, City of Aurora, Mayor's Office of Special Events, 43 E Downer Pl, Aurora, IL 60507. Phone: (630) 844-3640. Fax: (630) 906-7068.

IDAHO FESTIVAL OF LIGHTS. Nov 26–27. Preston, ID. Annual festival featuring a lighted parade, fireworks in the evenings, kids' parade and international bed race. Annually, the Friday and Saturday after Thanksgiving. Est attendance: 18,000. For info: Preston Chamber of Commerce, 49 N State, Ste A, Preston, ID 83263. Phone: (208) 852-2703. E-mail: pacc@dcdi.net.

JAPAN AGREES TO END USE OF DRIFT NETS: ANNIVERSARY. Nov 26, 1991. Japan agreed to comply with a 1989 United Nations moratorium on the use of huge fishing nets in the Northern Pacific Ocean. The large nets extend up to 40 miles and have been criticized as "walls of death," causing widespread destruction of marine life, including whales, turtles, birds and many varieties of fish. Japan agreed to end half of its driftnet fishing by the June 30, 1992, deadline, and the remainder by the end of 1992.

JOHN HARVARD DAY: BIRTH ANNIVERSARY. Nov 26, 1607. English clergyman and scholar, founder of Harvard College. Born in England, he died Sept 24, 1638, at the Massachusetts Bay colony.

JULE FEST. Nov 26–28. Elk Horn, IA. Danish Christmas festival. Est attendance: 3,000. For info: Lisa Riggs, Danish Windmill, PO Box 245, Elk Horn, IA 51531. Phone: (712) 764-7472 or (800) 451-7960. Fax: (712) 764-7475. E-mail: info@danishwindmill.com. Web: www.danishwindmill.com.

LIGHTING OF THE SQUARE. Nov 26. Woodstock, IL. Kick off the Christmas season by visiting the merchants throughout Woodstock who will be open all day and evening. There will be holiday decorations and special discounts. At 7PM, Christmas will offically come alive in Woodstock with a flip of the switch that will light the buildings and trees on the square. There will be caroling before and after. Est attendance: 1,000. For info: Woodstock Chamber of Commerce, 136 Cass St, Woodstock, IL 60098. Phone: (815) 338-2436. Fax: (815) 338-2927. E-mail: chamber@woodstockilchamber.com. Web: www.woodstockilchamber.com.

LONG GROVE COUNTRYSIDE CHRISTMAS. Nov 26–Dec 24. Long Grove, IL. Discover an old-fashioned country Christmas in historic village of nearly 100 specialty shops. Covered bridge, carriage rides, Victorian buildings outlined in lights.

Breakfast and lunch with Santa, Nutcracker Teas, weekend carolers. Fee for selected events. Free parking. 10 AM–5 PM; Sundays 11 AM–5 PM. For info: Long Grove Merchants Assn, Rtes 53 & 83, Long Grove, IL 60047. Phone: (847) 634-0888. Web: www.longgroveonline.com.

MAYOR'S CHRISTMAS TREE. Nov 26. Crown Center Square, Kansas City, MO. The lighting of the nation's tallest Christmas tree celebrates Kansas City's 97-year-old tradition of holiday giving. Local celebrities, musical entertainment, costume characters and outdoor ice skating are all part of the evening's festivities. The Mayor's Christmas Tree stands 100 ft tall and shines with thousands of white lights and colorful ornaments. Each evening throughout the holiday season, more than 55,000 lights illuminate Crown Center Square, creating a holiday atmosphere beyond compare. Est attendance: 15,000. For info: Crown Center, 2405 Grand Blvd, Ste 200, Kansas City, MO 64108-2519. Phone: (816) 274-8444 or (800) 721-STAY. Fax: (816) 274-4567. Web: www.crowncenter.com.

MONGOLIA: REPUBLIC DAY. Nov 26. National holiday. Commemorates the declaration of the republic in 1924.

MOON PHASE: FULL MOON. Nov 26. Moon enters Full Moon phase at 3:07 PM, EST.

MYSTIC SEAPORT FIELD DAYS. Nov 26–27. Mystic Seaport, Mystic, CT. Families enjoy special Thanksgiving weekend activities including wagon rides, food, entertainment and outdoor games on the green. Est attendance: 3,000. For info: Mystic Seaport Museum, 75 Greenmanville Ave, PO Box 6000, Mystic, CT 06355-0990. Phone: (860) 572-5315 or (888) 9SEAPORT. Web: www.mysticseaport.org.

"THE PRICE IS RIGHT" TV PREMIERE: ANNIVERSARY. Nov 26, 1956. This popular show is also TV's longest-running daily game show, surviving changes in format, networks, time slots and hosts. It began in 1956 with Bill Cullen as host, Don Pardo as announcer; four contestants had to bid on an item and the one who bid closest to the manufacturer's suggested price without going over won the item. In 1972, after a seven-year hiatus, "The Price Is Right" came back in two versions. Bob Barker was the host of the network version, which expanded to an hour and which he hosts to this day. Johnny Olsen was the announcer until his death in 1985; Rod Roddy took his place. Also on the show are attractive women who model the prizes to be won and help set up the price-guessing games. "Price" contestants are drawn from the studio audience.

QUEEN ELIZABETH II AGREES TO PAY TAXES: ANNIVERSARY. Nov 26, 1992. Prime Minister John Major announced that Britain's monarch, Queen Elizabeth, had decided to begin paying taxes on her personal income.

SCHULZ, CHARLES: BIRTH ANNIVERSARY. Nov 26, 1922. Cartoonist, born at Minneapolis, MN. Created the "Peanuts" comic strip that debuted on Oct 2, 1950. The strip included Charlie Brown, his sister Sally, his dog Snoopy, friends Linus and Lucy and a variety of other characters. Schulz's last daily strip was published Jan 3, 2000, and his last Sunday strip was published Feb 13, 2000. The strip ran in more than 2,500 newspapers in many different countries. Schulz won the Reuben Award in both 1955 and 1964 and was named International Cartoonist of the Year in 1978. Several TV specials were spin-offs of the strip including "It's the Great Pumpkin Charlie Brown" and "You're a Good Man Charlie Brown." Schulz died at Santa Rosa, CA Feb 12, 2000. See also "Peanuts Debuts: Anniversary" (Oct 2).

SEVAREID, ERIC: BIRTH ANNIVERSARY. Nov 26, 1912. American journalist Eric (Arnold) Sevareid was born at Velva, ND. He worked for CBS News as a radio reporter during World War II, appeared regularly on "The CBS News with Walter Cronkite" from 1964 to 1977, won the Peabody Award for news interpretations (1950, 1964 and 1967) and earned two Emmys in 1973. He died July 9, 1992, at Washington, DC.

SINKIE DAY. Nov 26. "Sinkies" (people who occasionally dine over the kitchen sink) are encouraged to celebrate this time-honored, casual-yet-tasteful cuisine culture. This is a particularly appropriate day to become acquainted with the sinkie style of dining. Christmas shopping and Thanksgiving leftovers provide the perfect reasons to enjoy a quick meal. Also the day the annual list of "Six Prominent Suspected Closet-Sinkies" is announced. Annually, the day after Thanksgiving. If it has anything to do with having a quick bite, it has everything to do with being a sinkie. For info: Norm Hankoff, Founder, Intl Assn of People Who Dine Over the Kitchen Sink, PO Box 221413, Sacramento, CA 95822. E-mail: normh@sinkie.com. Web: www.sinkie.com.

TRUTH, SOJOURNER: DEATH ANNIVERSARY. Nov 26, 1883. A former slave who had been sold four different times, Sojourner Truth became an evangelist who argued for abolition and women's rights. After a troubled early life, she began her evangelical career in 1843, traveling through New England until she discovered the utopian colony called the Northampton Association of Education and Industry. It was there she was exposed to, and became an advocate for, the cause of abolition, working with Frederick Douglass, Wendell Phillips, William Lloyd Garrison and others. In 1850 she befriended Lucretia Mott, Elizabeth Cady Stanton and other feminist leaders and actively began supporting calls for women's rights. In 1870 she attempted to petition Congress to create a "Negro State" on public lands in the west. Born at Ulster County, NY, about 1790, with the name Isabella Van Wagener, she died Nov 26, 1883, at Battle Creek, MI.

"TWENTY QUESTIONS" TV PREMIERE: 55th ANNIVERSARY. Nov 26, 1949. This game show was based on the old guessing game. A celebrity panel had to guess the identity of an object (at the start they were told only if it was animal, vegetable or mineral) by asking up to 20 questions. Bill Slater hosted two network versions of the show on NBC and Dumont. Jay Jackson took over when it switched from NBC to ABC. "Twenty Questions" first began on radio. Regular panelists included Fred Van Deventer, Florence Rinard, Herb Polesie and Johnny McPhee.

A VICTORIAN CHRISTMAS AT MOUNT HOPE MANSION. Nov 26–Dec 19 (Fridays, Saturdays, Sundays). Mount Hope Estate and Winery, Manheim, PA. An open house in colorfully decorated Mount Hope Mansion, wine sampling in the billiards room, actors portraying such Dickens favorites as Tiny Tim, Oliver Twist and Ebenezer Scrooge. Est attendance: 10,000. For info: Thomas Roy, Mgr, Mount Hope Estate and Winery, PO Box 685, Cornwall, PA 17016. Phone: (717) 665-7021, ext 127. Fax: (717) 664-3466. E-mail: tom@parenfaire.com. Web: www.parenfaire.com.

	S	M	T	W	T	F	S
November 2004		1	2	3	4	5	6
	7	8	9	10	11	12	13
	14	15	16	17	18	19	20
	21	22	23	24	25	26	27
	28	29	30				

★ Chase's 2004 Calendar of Events ★ Nov 26–27

VICTORIAN CHRISTMAS CELEBRATION. Nov 26–Dec 31. Gordon-Roberts House, Cumberland, MD. Victorian Christmas tea and candlelight tours with musical entertainment. Various workshops and children's programs. Theme decorating in an 1867 Victorian mansion museum. Est attendance: 1,500. For info: Sharon Nealis, Admin, Gordon-Roberts House, 218 Washington St, Cumberland, MD 21502. Phone: (301) 777-8678. Web: www.historyhouse.allconet.org.

WALKER, MARY EDWARDS: BIRTH ANNIVERSARY. Nov 26, 1832. American physician and women's rights leader, born at Oswego, NY. First female surgeon in US Army (Civil War). Spent four months in Confederate prison. First and only woman ever to receive Medal of Honor (Nov 11, 1865). Two years before her death, on June 3, 1916, a government review board asked that her award be revoked. She continued to wear it, in spite of official revocation, until her death, Feb 21, 1919, at Oswego. On June 11, 1977, the secretary of the army posthumously restored the Medal of Honor to Dr. Walker.

WORLD'S CHAMPIONSHIP DUCK-CALLING CONTEST AND WINGS OVER THE PRAIRIE FESTIVAL. Nov 26–27. Stuttgart, AR. Annually, Thanksgiving weekend. Duck-calling contests, duck gumbo cookoff, carnival, 10K race, arts and crafts, beauty pageant, concessions, sporting collectibles, Sportsman's Dinner and Dance, commercial exhibitors, fun shoot. Est attendance: 65,000. For info: Stuttgart Chamber of Commerce, 507 S Main, Stuttgart, AR 72160. Phone: (870) 673-1602. Fax: (870) 673-1604. Web: www.stuttgartarkansas.com.

YOU'RE WELCOMEGIVING DAY. Nov 26. The day after Thanksgiving, to create a four-day weekend. For info: Richard Ankli, The Fifth Wheel Tavern, 639 Fifth St, Ann Arbor, MI 48103-4840.

BIRTHDAYS TODAY

Shannon Dunn, 32, Olympic snowboarder, born Arlington Heights, IL, Nov 26, 1972.
Robert Goulet, 71, entertainer, actor (*Camelot, Naked Gun 2½*), born Lawrence, MA, Nov 26, 1933.
Dale Jarrett, 48, race car driver, born Conover, NC, Nov 26, 1956.
Shawn Kemp, 35, basketball player, member of Dream Team II, born Elkhart, IN, Nov 26, 1969.
Richard (Rich) Caruthers Little, 66, impressionist, born Ottawa, ON, Canada, Nov 26, 1938.
Tina Turner, 66, singer (with Ike: "A Fool in Love"; solo: "What's Love Got to Do With It"), born Nutbush, TN, Nov 26, 1938.

NOVEMBER 27 — SATURDAY
Day 332 — 34 Remaining

AGEE, JAMES: 95th BIRTH ANNIVERSARY. Nov 27, 1909. Poet, novelist (*Let Us Now Praise Famous Men*), scriptwriter (*A Death in the Family*), born at Knoxville, TN. Died at New York, NY, May 16, 1955.

BANK BAILOUT BILL: ANNIVERSARY. Nov 27, 1991. Both houses of Congress approved legislation authorizing $70 billion in additional borrowing authority for the Federal Deposit Insurance Corporation (FDIC) because of the record number of savings and loan failures.

BEARD, CHARLES A.: BIRTH ANNIVERSARY. Nov 27, 1874. American historian Charles Austin Beard who wrote many books in collaboration with his wife, Mary R. Beard, was born near Knightstown, IN. He died at New Haven, CT, Sept 1, 1948.

CHICAGO SOUTHLAND'S FINEST ANTIQUES SHOW. Nov 27–28. Tinley Park Convention Center, Tinley Park, IL. 120 exhibitors will offer a broad range of art, antiques, and select collectibles—everything from toys to Tiffany. Treasures for first-time buyers to breathtaking investment-quality pieces will be on display. Est attendance: 8,000. For info: T. Ruane, Chicago Southland's Finest Shows and Events, 701 Marley Rd, New Lenox, IL 60451. Phone: (815) 485-6666. Fax: (815) 485-1105. E-mail: antiqueshow2004@hotmail.com.

CHRISTMAS AT UNION STATION. Nov 27–Dec 31. Omaha, NE. Celebration of the Christmas holiday around a giant 45-ft Christmas tree in the splendor of Omaha's old Union Station. Est attendance: 45,000. For info: Durham Western Heritage Museum, 801 S 10th St, Omaha, NE 68108-3299. Phone: (402) 444-5701. Fax: (402) 444-5397. Web: www.dwhm.org.

"THE DINAH SHORE SHOW" TV PREMIERE: ANNIVERSARY. Nov 27, 1951. Dinah Shore hosted a successful 15-minute musical show until 1957 and then an hour variety show from 1957 to 1962, one of the few females to have done so. The music show was sponsored by Chevrolet (and was officially known as "The Dinah Shore Chevy Show") and featured a backup group called the Skylarks. Shore also starred in specials and hosted a variety series with a guest host filling in for her every fourth week. She later moved on to hosting a talk show.

DUBCEK, ALEXANDER: BIRTH ANNIVERSARY. Nov 27, 1921. The man who attempted to give his country "socialism with a human face," Alexander Dubcek was born at Uhrocev, a village in western Slovakia. As first secretary of the Czechoslovak Communist Party during the "Prague Spring" of 1968, he moved to achieve the "widest possible democratization" and to loosen the dominant influence of the Soviet Union. As a result, Czechoslovakia was invaded by armed forces of the Warsaw Pact on Aug 21, 1968. Dubcek died Nov 7, 1992, at Prague.

GARDEN OF LIGHTS. Nov 27–Dec 31. Norfolk Botanical Garden, Norfolk, VA. This holiday festival includes more than 500,000 twinkling lights along a 2.5-mile route through the Garden. Proceeds to benefit the Norfolk Botanical Garden Society, a nonprofit organization. Est attendance: 95,000. For info: Norfolk Botanical Garden, 6700 Azalea Garden Rd, Norfolk, VA 23518. Phone: (757) 441-5830. Fax: (757) 853-8294. Web: www.norfolkbotanicalgarden.org.

HANGING OF THE GREENS. Nov 27. Main Street, Arrow Rock, MO. The village puts on its winter greenery as the historic boardwalk is decorated with traditional living greenery. Event includes a visit from Santa and Mrs Claus via fire truck and a merchants open house. Est attendance: 200. For info: HARC, PO Box 121, Arrow Rock, MO 65320. Phone: (660) 837-3398. E-mail: garlin@mid-mo.net.

HENDRIX, JIMI: BIRTH ANNIVERSARY. Nov 27, 1942. American musician and songwriter Jimi Hendrix was born at Seattle, WA. One of the greatest rock guitarists in history, he revolutionized the guitar sound with heavy use of feedback and incredible fretwork. His success first came in England, then in the US after his appearance at the Monterey Pop Festival (1967). His albums included *Are You Experienced?*, *Electric Ladyland* and *Band of Gypsys*. He died Sept 18, 1970, at London, England.

Nov 27–28 ☆ Chase's 2004 Calendar of Events ☆

HOLIDAY CRAFT FAIR. Nov 27–28 (tentative). Franklin and Marshall College, Lancaster, PA. High-quality juried craft show featuring the work of more than 175 members of the Pennsylvania Guild of Craftsmen. Don't miss our annual gallery showcasing the Best of the Best in a variety of media! For information about tickets or how to become a member contact the Guild. Est attendance: 10,000. For info: PGC, 10 Stable Mill Trail, Richboro, PA 18954. Phone: (800) 684-7440. E-mail: pacraft@comcat.com. Web: www.pacrafts.com.

HOLIDAYS AT WHEATON VILLAGE. Nov 27–Jan 2, 2005. Millville, NJ. Snow, rain or shine, the sale will go on. Est attendance: 6,000. For info: Wheaton Village, 1501 Glasstown Rd, Millville, NJ 08332. Phone: (856) 825-6800 x 2739. Fax: (856) 825-2410. E-mail: janet@wheatonvillage.org. Web: www.wheatonvillage.org.

INTERNATIONAL AURA AWARENESS DAY. Nov 27. A day to increase awareness of the human energy body, or aura. Annually, the fourth Saturday in Nov. For info: Cynthia Larson, PO Box 7393, Berkeley, CA 94707. Phone: (510) 528-2044. E-mail: cynthia@realityshifters.com. Web: realityshifters.com/pages/auradon.html.

KEMBLE, FANNY: BIRTH ANNIVERSARY. Nov 27, 1809. Frances Anne Kemble, English actress, born at London, England, and died there Jan 15, 1893.

LEE, BRUCE: BIRTH ANNIVERSARY. Nov 27, 1940. The actor and martial artist was born at San Francisco, CA, but raised in Hong Kong. In 1959, he returned to the US to teach martial arts, opening schools in Seattle, WA, and Oakland, CA. Spotted at a competition by a TV producer, Lee was cast as Kato in TV's *The Green Hornet* in 1966. He moved on to film, where he displayed an intense charisma that would make him a star. Before he could enjoy this new success, Lee died of a cerebral edema on July 20, 1973, in Hong Kong. His films included *Fists of Fury* (1972) and *Enter the Dragon* (1973).

"THE LIGHT OF THE WORLD" CHRISTMAS PAGEANT. Nov 27 (also Dec 5 and 12). Courthouse square, Minden, NE. Pageant presented on three sides of the courthouse square with around 115 local citizens performing in beautiful costumes. At the climax some 12,000 Christmas lights are turned on the courthouse. 7 PM; free admission. Annually, the first Saturday after Thanksgiving and the first two Sundays in December. Est attendance: 10,000. For info: Dena Beck, Mgr, Minden Chamber of Commerce, PO Box 375, Minden, NE 68959. Phone: (308) 832-1811. E-mail: mindenchamber@gtmc.net. Web: www.mindenne.org.

LIVINGSTON, ROBERT R.: BIRTH ANNIVERSARY. Nov 27, 1746 (OS). Member of the Continental Congress, farmer, diplomat and jurist, was born at New York, NY. It was Livingston who administered the oath of office to President George Washington in 1789. He died at Clermont, NY, Feb 26, 1813.

MASTERSON, BAT: BIRTH ANNIVERSARY. Nov 27, 1853. Old American West gambler, saloonkeeper, lawman and news writer/editor. Born at Henryville, Quebec, Canada; died Oct 25, 1921, at New York, NY.

MEXICO: GUADALAJARA INTERNATIONAL BOOK FAIR. Nov 27–Dec 5. Mexico's largest book fair with exhibitors from all over the Spanish-speaking world. Est attendance: 325,000. For info: David Unger, Guadalajara Book Fair–US Office, Div of Hum, NAC 5225, City College, New York, NY 10031. Phone: (212) 650-7925. Fax: (212) 650-7912. E-mail: filny@aol.com.

November 2004

S	M	T	W	T	F	S
	1	2	3	4	5	6
7	8	9	10	11	12	13
14	15	16	17	18	19	20
21	22	23	24	25	26	27
28	29	30				

SPACE MILESTONE: SOYUZ T-3 (USSR). Nov 27, 1980. Launched this date with three cosmonauts, O. Makarov, L. Kizim and G. Strekalov, docked at *Salyut 6* space station on Nov 28. Returned to Earth, Dec 10, 1980. This was the first Soviet crew of three since 1971.

TERRITORIAL CHRISTMAS CELEBRATION. Nov 27–Dec 24. Guthrie, OK. Take a step back in time and celebrate Christmas in grand Victorian style. Enjoy the Pollard's production of "A Territorial Christmas Carol," the Victorian Walk, Bed & Breakfast Home Tour, Lion's Club Christmas Parade, Christmas light tour on the trolley, street carolers, peanut vendors, Christmas Tree Auction and Reception and Election of the Territorial Governor. Est attendance: 13,000. For info: Guthrie Conv & Visitors Bureau, PO Box 995, Guthrie, OK 73044-0995. Phone: (800) 299-1889 or (405) 282-1947. Fax: (405) 282-0061. E-mail: gchamber@theshop.net. Web: www.guthrieok.com.

WEIZMANN, CHAIM: BIRTH ANNIVERSARY. Nov 27, 1874. Israeli statesman born near Pinsk, Byelorussia. He played an important role in bringing about the British government's Balfour Declaration, calling for the establishment of a national home for Jews at Palestine. He died at Tel Aviv, Israel, Nov 9, 1952.

BIRTHDAYS TODAY

Robin Givens, 40, actress ("Head of the Class," *A Rage in Harlem*), born New York, NY, Nov 27, 1964.
Jimmy Rollins, 26, baseball player, born Oakland, CA, Nov 27, 1978.
Gail Henion Sheehy, 67, author, journalist (*The Silent Passage: Menopause; Pathfinders*), born Mamaroneck, NY, Nov 27, 1937.
Fisher Stevens, 41, actor (*The Brother from Another Planet, Bob Roberts*), born Chicago, IL, Nov 27, 1963.
Nick Van Exel, 33, basketball player, born Kenosha, WI, Nov 27, 1971.
Jaleel White, 28, actor ("Family Matters"), born Los Angeles, CA, Nov 27, 1976.

NOVEMBER 28 — SUNDAY
Day 333 — 33 Remaining

ADVENT, FIRST SUNDAY. Nov 28. Advent includes the four Sundays before Christmas, Nov 28, Dec 5, Dec 12 and Dec 19 in 2004.

ALBANIA: INDEPENDENCE DAY. Nov 28. Commemorates independence from the Ottoman Empire in 1912.

ALSTON, CHARLES H.: BIRTH ANNIVERSARY. Nov 28, 1907. African-American painter and sculptor born at Charlotte, NC, and died at New York, NY, Apr 27, 1977. Throughout his career, Alston experimented with styles ranging from realism to abstraction. His realistic WPA murals at Harlem Hospital depict a narrative in the style of Diego Rivera. The Cubist painting of *The Family* (1955), is an excellent example of Alston's early work, influenced by Italian artist Amedeo Modigliani. *Black Man, Black Woman USA* has a decidedly Egyptian style of portraiture. *Walking* (1958), which depicts a silent crowd, almost prophesies the turmoil and social agitation of the Civil Rights Movement.

BLAKE, WILLIAM: BIRTH ANNIVERSARY. Nov 28, 1757. English poet (*Songs of Innocence*), artist and philosopher, born at London, England. Died there Aug 12, 1827.

BUNYAN, JOHN: BIRTH ANNIVERSARY. Nov 28, 1628 (OS). English cleric and author of *A Pilgrim's Progress*, born at Elstow, Bedfordshire. Died at London, Aug 31, 1688 (OS).

602

☆ Chase's 2004 Calendar of Events ☆   Nov 28–29

CHAD: REPUBLIC DAY: ANNIVERSARY. Nov 28. National holiday. Commemorates proclamation of the republic in 1958.

CHRISTMAS ON THE RIVER. Nov 28–Dec 4. Demopolis, AL. Fun with arts and crafts, children's parade, Alabama State BBQ Cook-off and a river boat parade. Annually, the week concluding with the first Saturday of December. Est attendance: 40,000. For info: Kathy Leverett, Pres, Demopolis Area Chamber of Commerce, Box 667, Demopolis, AL 36732. Phone: (334) 289-0270. Fax: (334) 289-1382. Web: www.demopolischamber.com.

CHRISTMAS PARADE. Nov 28. Woodstock, IL. Santa will officially arrive in a parade around the square at 2 PM. Est attendance: 1,000. For info: Woodstock Chamber of Commerce, 136 Cass St, Woodstock, IL 60098. Phone: (815) 338-2436. Fax: (815) 338-2927. E-mail: chamber@woodstockilchamber.com. Web: www.woodstockilchamber.com.

D & G BARREL RACE. Nov 28–30. Multi-Purpose Events Center, Wichita Falls, TX. Barrel riders from Texas, Oklahoma, New Mexico, Kansas and other areas compete in this national Barrel Racing Show. For info: Wichita Falls CVB, 1000 5th St, Wichita Falls, TX 76301. Phone: (940) 716-5500. Fax: (940) 716-5509. E-mail: mpec@wf.net. Web: www.wichitafalls.com or www.mpecwf.com.

DESERT STORM: UN DEADLINE RESOLUTION: ANNIVERSARY. Nov 28, 1990. The United Nations passed the twelfth in a series of resolutions concerning the Iraqi invasion of Kuwait. Resolution 678 authorized states "to use all necessary means" against Iraq unless it withdrew its forces from Kuwait by Jan 15, 1991. Iraq did not comply, and the Allied Forces began their attack with the code-name Operation Desert Storm within hours of the expiration of the deadline.

LULLY, JEAN BAPTISTE: BIRTH ANNIVERSARY. Nov 28, 1632. Versatile musician and composer, born at Florence, Italy, who chose France for his homeland. Noted for his quick temper, it is said that he struck his own foot with a baton while in a rage. The resulting wound led to blood poisoning, from which he died, at Paris, France, Mar 22, 1687.

MAURITANIA: INDEPENDENCE DAY. Nov 28. National holiday. Attained sovereignty from France in 1960.

NETHERLANDS: MIDWINTER HORN BLOWING. Nov 28–Jan 6, 2005. Twente and several other areas in the Netherlands. Midwinter horn blowing, folklore custom of announcing the birth of Christ, begins with Advent and continues until Epiphany (Jan 6) of the following year.

PANAMA: INDEPENDENCE FROM SPAIN. Nov 28. Public holiday. Commemorates the independence of Panama (which at the time was part of Colombia) from Spain in 1821.

RADIOLOGICAL SOCIETY OF NORTH AMERICA SCIENTIFIC ASSEMBLY AND ANNUAL MEETING. Nov 28–Dec 3. McCormick Place, Chicago, IL. 90th annual. Est attendance: 61,000. For info: Radiological Society of North America, 820 Jorie Blvd, Oak Brook, IL 60523-2251. Phone: (630) 571-2670. Fax: (630) 571-7837.

SPACE MILESTONE: *COLUMBIA STS-9* (US): ANNIVERSARY. Nov 28, 1983. Shuttle *Columbia* launched from Kennedy Space Center, FL, with five astronauts (John Young, Brewster Shaw, Jr, Owen Garriot, Robert Parker, Byron Lichtenberg) and German physicist Ulf Merbold. Landed Edwards Air Force Base, CA, on Dec 8.

SPACE MILESTONE: *MARINER 4* (US): 40th ANNIVERSARY. Nov 28, 1964. The first successful mission to Mars. Approached within 6,118 miles of Mars on July 14, 1965. Took photographs and instrument readings.

TEHERAN CONFERENCE: ANNIVERSARY. Nov 28–Dec 1, 1943. President Franklin D. Roosevelt, British Prime Minister Winston Churchill and Soviet Premier Joseph Stalin met at Teheran, Iran, to formulate a plan for an Allied assault, a second front, in western Europe. The resulting plan was "Operation Overlord," which commenced with the landing on Normandy's beaches on June 6, 1944 ("D-Day").

TRAVELERS WITH DISABILITIES AWARENESS WEEK. Nov 28–Dec 5. To promote the economic well-being of Americans with disabilities who travel and to create an environment free of obstacles throughout the tourism and travel industry for Americans with disabilities. Annually, the week following Thanksgiving. For info: Society for Accessible Travel and Hospitality, 347 Fifth Ave, Ste 610, New York, NY 10016. Phone: (212) 447-7284. E-mail: SATHTRAVEL@aol.com. Web: www.sath.org.

BIRTHDAYS TODAY

Berry Gordy, Jr, 75, record and motion picture executive (cofounder of Motown), born Detroit, MI, Nov 28, 1929.
Ed Harris, 54, actor (*Pollock, The Right Stuff*), born Englewood, NJ, Nov 28, 1950.
Gary Hart, 66, former senator, former presidential candidate, born Gary Hartpence, Ottawa, KS, Nov 28, 1938.
Hope Lange, 71, actress ("The Ghost and Mrs Muir," *Bus Stop*), born Reading Ridge, CT, Nov 28, 1933.
S. Epatha Merkerson, 52, actress ("Law & Order"), born Detroit, MI, Nov 28, 1952.
Judd Nelson, 45, actor (*The Breakfast Club, St. Elmo's Fire*, "Suddenly Susan"), born Portland, ME, Nov 28, 1959.
Randy Newman, 61, singer, songwriter ("Short People"), composer (film scores *Ragtime, The Natural*), born New Orleans, LA, Nov 28, 1943.
Paul Shaffer, 55, bandleader ("Late Night with David Letterman"), comedian, born Thunder Bay, ON, Canada, Nov 28, 1949.
Jon Stewart, 42, comedian, host ("The Daily Show with Jon Stewart"), born Trenton, NJ, Nov 28, 1962.
Matt Williams, 39, baseball player, born Bishop, CA, Nov 28, 1965.

NOVEMBER 29 — MONDAY
Day 334 — 32 Remaining

ALCOTT, LOUISA MAY: BIRTH ANNIVERSARY. Nov 29, 1832. American author, born at Philadelphia, PA. Died at Boston, MA, Mar 6, 1888. Her most famous novel was *Little Women*, the classic story of Meg, Jo, Beth and Amy.

BERKELEY, BUSBY: BIRTH ANNIVERSARY. Nov 29, 1895. William Berkeley Enos was born at Los Angeles, CA. After serving in World War I as an entertainment officer, he changed his name to Busby Berkeley and began a career as an actor. He turned to directing in 1921, and his lavish Broadway and Hollywood creations include *Forty-Second Street, Gold Diggers of 1933, Footlight Parade, Stage Struck, Babes in Arms, Strike Up the Band, Girl Crazy* and *Take Me Out to the Ball Game*. He retired in 1962 and returned to Broadway in 1970 to supervise a revival of *No, No, Nanette*. He died Mar 14, 1976, at Palm Springs, CA.

CZECHOSLOVAKIA ENDS COMMUNIST RULE: 15th ANNIVERSARY. Nov 29, 1989. Czechoslovakia ended 41 years of one-party communist rule when the Czechoslovak parliament voted unanimously to repeal the constitutional clauses giving the Communist Party a guaranteed leading role in the country and promoting Marxism-Leninism as the state ideology. The vote came at the end of a 12-day revolution sparked by the beating of protestors Nov 17. Although the Communist party remained in power, the tide of reform led to its ouster by the Civic Forum, headed by playwright Vaclav Havel. The Civic Forum demanded free elections with equal rights for all parties, a mixed economy and support for foreign investment. In the first free elections in Czechoslovakia since WWII, Vaclav Havel was elected president.

Nov 29–30 ☆ Chase's 2004 Calendar of Events ☆

ELECTRONIC GREETINGS DAY. Nov 29. Save a letter carrier, save a tree, save a stamp! Today's the day to send your greetings the free, electronic way, via the Internet! [©2003 by WH.] For info: Thomas & Ruth Roy, Wellcat Holidays, 2418 Long Ln, Lebanon, PA 17046. Phone: (717) 279-0184. E-mail: info@wellcat.com. Web: www.wellcat.com.

"KUKLA, FRAN AND OLLIE" TV PREMIERE: ANNIVERSARY. Nov 29, 1948. This popular children's show featured puppets created and handled by Burr Tillstrom and was equally popular with adults. Fran Allison was the only human on the show. Tillstrom's lively and eclectic cast of characters, called the "Kuklapolitans," included the bald, high-voiced Kukla, the big-toothed Oliver J. Dragon (Ollie), Fletcher Rabbit, Cecil Bill, Beulah the Witch, Colonel Crackie, Madame Ooglepuss and Dolores Dragon. Most shows were performed without scripts.

LEWIS, C.S. (CLIVE STAPLES): BIRTH ANNIVERSARY. Nov 29, 1898. British scholar, novelist and author (*The Screwtape Letters, Chronicles of Narnia*), born at Belfast, Ireland, died at Oxford, England, Nov 22, 1963.

ROSS, NELLIE TAYLOE: BIRTH ANNIVERSARY. Nov 29, 1876. Nellie Tayloe Ross became the first female governor in the US when she was chosen to serve out the last month and two days of her husband's term as governor of Wyoming after he died in office. She was elected in her own right in the Nov 4, 1924, election but lost the 1927 race. Ross was appointed vice chairman of the Democratic National Committee in 1926 and named director of the US Mint by President Franklin D. Roosevelt in 1933. She served in that capacity for 20 years. Born at St. Joseph, MO, she died Dec 20, 1977, at Washington, DC.

THOMSON, CHARLES: 275th BIRTH ANNIVERSARY. Nov 29, 1729. America's first official record keeper. Chosen secretary of the First Continental Congress Sept 5, 1774, Thomson recorded proceedings for 15 years and delivered his journals together with tens of thousands of records to the federal government in 1789. Born in Ireland, he died Aug 16, 1824. It was Thomson who notified George Washington of his election as president.

UNITED NATIONS: INTERNATIONAL DAY OF SOLIDARITY WITH THE PALESTINIAN PEOPLE. Nov 29. Annual observance proclaimed by UN General Assembly in 1977. At request of Assembly, observance is organized by secretary-general in consultation with Committee on the Exercise of the Inalienable Rights of the Palestinian People. Recommendations include a plan for return of the Palestinians to their homes and the establishment of an "independent Palestinian entity." For info: United Nations, Dept of Public Info, New York, NY 10017. Web: www.un.org.

WAITE, MORRISON R.: BIRTH ANNIVERSARY. Nov 29, 1816. Seventh Chief Justice of the Supreme Court, born at Lyme, CT. Appointed Chief Justice by President Ulysses S. Grant Jan 19, 1874. The Waite Court is remembered for its controversial rulings that did much to rehabilitate the idea of states' rights after the Civil War and early Reconstruction years. Waite died at Washington, DC, Mar 23, 1888zz.

BIRTHDAYS TODAY

Jacques Rene Chirac, 72, President of France, born Paris, France, Nov 29, 1932.
Joel Coen, 50, producer, screenwriter (*Fargo*), born Minneapolis, MN, Nov 29, 1954.
Kim Delaney, 43, actress ("NYPD Blue"), born Philadelphia, PA, Nov 29, 1961.

	S	M	T	W	T	F	S
November 2004		1	2	3	4	5	6
	7	8	9	10	11	12	13
	14	15	16	17	18	19	20
	21	22	23	24	25	26	27
	28	29	30				

Diane Ladd, 72, actress (*Alice Doesn't Live Here Anymore, Ramblin' Rose, The Cemetery Club*), born Rose Diane Ladner, Meridian, MS, Nov 29, 1932.
Madeleine L'Engle, 86, writer (*A Wrinkle in Time, Summer of the Great-Grandmother*), born New York, NY, Nov 29, 1918.
Howie Mandel, 49, comedic actor ("Howie Mandel's Sunny Skies," "Bobby's World"), born Toronto, ON, Canada, Nov 29, 1955.
Chuck Mangione, 64, musician, composer (Grammy for "Bellavia"), born Rochester, NY, Nov 29, 1940.
John Mayall, 71, musician, bandleader (The Bluesbreakers), born Manchester, England, Nov 29, 1933.
Andrew McCarthy, 42, actor (*Pretty in Pink, Weekend at Bernie's*), born Westfield, NJ, Nov 29, 1962.
Cathy Moriarty, 44, actress (*Raging Bull, The Mambo Kings*), born The Bronx, NY, Nov 29, 1960.
Janet Napolitano, 47, Governor of Arizona (D), born Pittsburgh, PA, Nov 29, 1957.
Mariano Rivera, 35, baseball player, born Panama City, Panama, Nov 29, 1969.
Vincent Edward (Vin) Scully, 77, sportscaster, Ford Frick award winner, born New York, NY, Nov 29, 1927.
Garry Shandling, 55, comedian ("The Larry Sanders Show"), born Chicago, IL, Nov 29, 1949.

NOVEMBER 30 — TUESDAY
Day 335 — 31 Remaining

ARTICLES OF PEACE BETWEEN GREAT BRITAIN AND THE US: ANNIVERSARY. Nov 30, 1782. These provisional articles of peace, which were to end America's War of Independence, were signed at Paris, France. The refined and definitive treaty of peace between Great Britain and the US was signed at Paris, on Sept 3, 1783. In it "His Britannic Majesty acknowledges the said United States. . .to be free, sovereign and independent states; that he treats them as such; and for himself, his heirs and successors, relinquishes all claims to the government, propriety and territorial rights of the same, and every part thereof. . . ."

BARBADOS: INDEPENDENCE DAY. Nov 30. National holiday. Gained independence from Great Britain in 1966.

CHURCHILL, WINSTON: BIRTH ANNIVERSARY. Nov 30, 1874. Winston Leonard Spencer Churchill, British statesman and the first man to be made an honorary citizen of the US (by an act of Congress, Apr 9, 1963), born at Blenheim Palace, Oxfordshire, England. Died Jan 24, 1965, at London, England. Dedicated to Britain and total victory over Germany, Churchill as minister of defense and prime minister was a strong leader during WWII.

CLEMENS, SAMUEL LANGHORNE (MARK TWAIN): BIRTH ANNIVERSARY. Nov 30, 1835. Celebrated American author, whose books include: *The Adventures of Tom Sawyer, The Adventures of Huckleberry Finn* and *The Prince and the Pau-*

per. Born at Florida, MO, Twain is quoted as saying, "I came in with Halley's Comet in 1835. It is coming again next year, and I expect to go out with it." He did. Twain died at Redding, CT, Apr 21, 1910 (just one day after Halley's Comet's perihelion).

COMPUTER SECURITY DAY. Nov 30. The use of computers and the concern for security increases daily. This annual observance reminds people to protect their computers, programs and data at home and at work. More than 1,500 companies participate worldwide. For info: Assn for Computer Security Day, PO Box 39110, Washington, DC 20016. E-mail: computer_security_day@acm.org. Web: www.computersecurityday.com or www.geocities.com/a4csd.

EL SALVADOR ADOPTS US DOLLAR: ANNIVERSARY. Nov 30, 2000. El Salvador became the third Latin American country to adopt the US dollar as its official currency. Ecuador and Panama also use the US dollar and Bermuda, a British colony, uses it as well.

HOFFMAN, ABBOT (ABBIE): BIRTH ANNIVERSARY. Nov 30, 1936. Political activist, born at Worcester, MA, Abbie Hoffman rose to prominence during the 1968 Democratic National Convention at Chicago and at his subsequent trial as a member of the Chicago Seven, a group of radicals accused of conspiring to disrupt the convention. Combining politics and street theater was a Hoffman trait. During the 1967 march on the Pentagon, he sought a permit to allow 1,200 demonstrators to encircle and levitate the military headquarters in an attempt to end the war in Vietnam. He, Jerry Rubin and Paul Krassner conceived the Yippie movement as a youth festival of life to run concurrently with the Convention. Hoffman fled underground in 1974 to avoid trial on cocaine-possession charges and remained a fugitive for nearly seven years. Surrendering to authorities in 1980, he served his sentence in a work-release program. Hoffman died Apr 12, 1989, at New Hope, PA.

PHILIPPINES: BONIFACIO DAY. Nov 30. Also known as National Heroes' Day. Commemorates birth of Andres Bonifacio, leader of the 1896 revolt against Spain. Bonifacio was born in 1863.

SAINT ANDREW'S DAY. Nov 30. Feast day of the apostle and martyr, Andrew, who died about AD 60. Patron saint of Scotland.

SIDNEY, PHILIP: 450th BIRTH ANNIVERSARY. Nov 30, 1554. English poet, statesman and soldier was born at Penshurst, Kent, England. Best known of his poems is *Arcadia* (1580). Mortally wounded as he led an English detachment aiding the Dutch near Zutphen, Sept 22, 1586, Sidney gave his water bottle to another dying soldier with the words "Thy necessity is yet greater than mine." He died at Arnheim, Oct 17, 1586, and all England mourned his death.

STATUE OF RAMSES II UNEARTHED: ANNIVERSARY. Nov 30, 1991. Egyptian construction workers in the ancient provincial town of Akhimim, 300 miles south of Cairo, unearthed a statue of Ramses II. Akhimim was an important provincial district that included the city of Ipu, a mecca for worshippers of the fertility god Min. The statue was uncovered during an excavation to prepare a foundation for a post office. An additional statue was uncovered 33 feet away, but the identity of its subject was unknown.

STAY HOME BECAUSE YOU'RE WELL DAY. Nov 30. So we can call in "well," instead of faking illness and stay home from work. [©2003 by WH.] For info: Thomas & Ruth Roy, Wellcat Holidays, 2418 Long Ln, Lebanon, PA 17046. Phone: (717) 279-0184. E-mail: info@wellcat.com. Web: www.wellcat.com.

SWIFT, JONATHAN: BIRTH ANNIVERSARY. Nov 30, 1667 (OS). Clergyman and satirist born at Dublin, Ireland. Died there Oct 19, 1745 (OS). Author of *Gulliver's Travels*. "I never saw, heard, nor read," Swift wrote in *Thoughts on Religion*, "that the clergy were beloved in any nation where Christianity was the religion of the country. Nothing can render them popular but some degree of persecution."

UKRAINIAN FAMINE FILM BROADCAST: ANNIVERSARY. Nov 30, 1991. In the rapidly changing former Soviet Union, the film *Famine 33* produced by Oles Yanchuk, was broadcast on republic-wide TV. The film chronicled the forced collectivization of the agriculture industry in 1933 and the resulting famine which led to the death of more than seven million Ukrainians. The famine was not officially recognized until 1990, when the Central Committee of the Ukrainian Communist Party first acknowledged that the millions of deaths were caused by the seizure of crops. The airing of the film heralded a significant departure from prior Soviet handling of history.

BIRTHDAYS TODAY

Shirley Chisholm, 80, author, former congresswoman, born Brooklyn, NY, Nov 30, 1924.
Dick Clark, 75, long-time host of "American Bandstand," entertainer, producer, born Mount Vernon, NY, Nov 30, 1929.
Joan Ganz Cooney, 75, founder of the Children's Television Workshop and creator of "Sesame Street," born Phoenix, AZ, Nov 30, 1929.
Elisha Cuthbert, 22, actress ("24," "Are You Afraid of the Dark?"), born Calgary, AB, Canada, Nov 30, 1982.
Des'ree, 34, singer (*I Ain't Movin'*), born London, England, Nov 30, 1970.
Robert Guillaume, 77, actor ("Soap," "Benson"), born St. Louis, MO, Nov 30, 1927.
Billy Idol, 49, singer ("Mony Mony," "Eyes Without a Face"), songwriter, born Surrey, England, Nov 30, 1955.
Vincent Edward ("Bo") Jackson, 42, former baseball player, former football player, born Bessemer, AL, Nov 30, 1962.
G. Gordon Liddy, 74, convicted Watergate co-conspirator, radio talk-show host, born New York, NY, Nov 30, 1930.
David Mamet, 57, dramatist, director (*American Buffalo, Oleanna, Things Change*), born Chicago, IL, Nov 30, 1947.
Virginia Mayo, 82, actress (*The Best Years of Our Lives*), born St. Louis, MO, Nov 30, 1922.
Colin Mochrie, 47, comedian, actor ("Whose Line Is It Anyway?"), born Ayrshire, Scotland, Nov 30, 1957.
Gordon Parks, 92, photographer, author, born Fort Scott, KS, Nov 30, 1912.
Mandy Patinkin, 52, actor (Tony for *Evita*; *Sunday in the Park with George*, "Chicago Hope"), born Chicago, IL, Nov 30, 1952.
Ivan ("Pudge") Rodriguez, 33, baseball player, born Vega Baja, Puerto Rico, Nov 30, 1971.
Ridley Scott, 67, director (*Alien, Blade Runner, Gladiator*), born Northumberland, England, Nov 30, 1937.
Ben Stiller, 39, actor, director (*Reality Bites, The Cable Guy*), born New York, NY, Nov 30, 1965.
Noel Paul Stookey, 67, singer, songwriter (Peter, Paul and Mary), born Baltimore, MD, Nov 30, 1937.
Lawrence Summers, 50, president, Harvard University, former US Secretary of the Treasury (Clinton administration), born New Haven, CT, Nov 30, 1954.
Efrem Zimbalist, Jr, 81, actor ("The F.B.I.," *Airport*), born New York, NY, Nov 30, 1923.

Dec 1 ☆ *Chase's 2004 Calendar of Events* ☆

December.

DECEMBER 1 — WEDNESDAY
Day 336 — 30 Remaining

BASKETBALL CREATED: ANNIVERSARY. Dec 1, 1891. James Naismith was a teacher of physical education at the International YMCA Training School at Springfield, MA. To create an indoor sport that could be played during the winter months, he nailed up peach baskets at opposite ends of the gym and gave students soccer balls to toss into them. Thus was born the game of basketball.

BIFOCALS AT THE MONITOR LIBERATION DAY. Dec 1. Our hearts fill with compassion today for co-workers stuck wearing bifocals at the PC. Shed a tear as their heads bob up and down, in and out, trying to read the monitor, trying to decide which set of lenses to use. Annually, Dec 1. [©2003 by WH.] For info: Thomas & Ruth Roy, Wellcat Holidays, 2418 Long Ln, Lebanon, PA 17046. Phone: (717) 279-0184. E-mail: info@wellcat.com. Web: www.wellcat.com.

BINGO'S BIRTHDAY MONTH. Dec 1–31. To celebrate the innovation and manufacture of the game of Bingo in 1929 by Edwin S. Lowe. Bingo has grown into a five-billion-dollar-a-year charitable fundraiser. For info: Tara Snowden, Pres, Bingo Bugle, Inc, Box 527, Vashon, WA 98070. Phone: (800) 327-6437 or (206) 463-5656. E-mail: tara@bingobugle.com.

CANADA: YUKON ORDER OF PIONEERS: ANNIVERSARY. Dec 1, 1894. The Yukon Order of Pioneers held its founding meeting on this date at Fortymile, Yukon. It began as a vigilante police force to deter claim jumping and later inaugurated Discovery Day (Aug 17), a statutory Yukon holiday commemorating the discovery of gold on Bonanza Creek in 1896.

CHRISTMAS—NEW ORLEANS STYLE. Dec 1–31. New Orleans, LA. Cathedral Christmas concerts, caroling in Jackson Square, holiday parades with Papa Noel, cooking demonstrations, Celebration in the Oaks, Christmas Day Concert, tours of 19th-century houses in holiday dress, Reveillon dinners, Papa Noel hotel rates. For info: French Quarters Festivals, Inc, 400 N Peters St, #205, New Orleans, LA 70130. Phone: (800) 673-5725 or (504) 522-5730. E-mail: feedback@fqfi.org. Web: www.christmasneworleans.com.

CIVIL AIR PATROL FOUNDED: ANNIVERSARY. Dec 1, 1941. The Director of Civilian Defense, former New York Mayor Fiorello H. LaGuardia, signed a formal order creating the Civil Air Patrol, a US Air Force Auxiliary. The CAP has a three-part mission: to provide an aerospace education program, a CAP cadet program and an emergency services program. For info: Civil Air Patrol, 105 S Hansell St, Maxwell AFB, AL 36112-6332. Phone: (205) 953-5463.

COLORECTAL CANCER EDUCATION AND AWARENESS MONTH. Dec 1–31. To educate consumers, patients and professionals regarding the need for early diagnosis and treatment of colorectal cancer. For info: PPSI, c/o Pharmacy Council on Colorectal Cancer Education, 101 Lucas Valley Rd, #210, San Rafael, CA 94903. Phone: (415) 479-8628. Fax: (415) 479-8608. E-mail: ppsi@aol.com. Web: www.ppsinc.org.

COOKIE CUTTER WEEK. Dec 1–7. The international cookie cutter collectors club celebrates a special time of baking cookies and collecting cutters. And what better time than the first week of December—baking season? For info: Paula W. Mullins, 207 Ash, Box 8, Lawrenceburg, KY 40342. Phone: (502) 839-4929.

DAY WITH(OUT) ART. Dec 1. An annual observance about the impact of AIDS on the visual arts. Events to increase public awareness through the visual arts, direct services to artists living with HIV/AIDS. For info: Visual AIDS, 526 W 26th St, #510, New York, NY 10001. Phone: (212) 627-9855. Fax: (212) 627-9815. E-mail: info@visualaids.org. Web: www.visualaids.org.

HOLIDAYS AT THE NATIONALITY CLASSROOMS. Dec 1–31. Univ of Pittsburgh, Oakland, PA. Twenty-six rooms depict the city's diverse ethnic culture through authentic examples of architecture and decor from Eastern and Western Europe, Scandinavia, the Middle East, Asia and Africa. For info: Greater Pittsburgh Conv & Visitors Bureau, Regional Enterprise Tower, 30th Fl, 425 6th Ave, Pittsburgh, PA 15219. Phone: (412) 624-6000 or (800) 359-0758. Fax: (412) 644-5512.

HYPNOTIZE YOURSELF OUT OF PAIN NOW DAY. Dec 1. This holiday celebrates and commemorates every person's right to be totally free of physical and mental pain and anguish at least some of the time. It celebrates every human being's ability to change the way he or she thinks about things, un-upset one's self and stop suffering. Physical pain may be mandatory but suffering is optional. Annually, December 1. For info: Bruce Eimer, Alternative Behavior Assoc, PO Box 52538, Philadelphia, PA 19115. Phone: (215) 947-7867. Fax: (215) 947-7860. E-mail: dreimer@comcast.net. Web: www.hypnosisgroup.com.

ICELAND: UNIVERSITY STUDENTS' CELEBRATION: ANNIVERSARY. Dec 1, 1918. Marks the day in 1918 when Iceland became an independent state from Denmark (but still remained under the king of Denmark).

MADD'S TIE ONE ON FOR SAFETY HOLIDAY RIBBON CAMPAIGN. Dec 1–Jan 1, 2005. TOOFS is a drunk driving awareness campaign created by Mothers Against Drunk Driving that encourages the public to tie a MADD red ribbon to their vehicle as a pledge to drive safe and sober and buckle-up seat belts throughout the holidays and year-round. For info: MADD. Phone: (800) GET-MADD. Web: www.madd.org.

MARTIN, MARY: BIRTH ANNIVERSARY. Dec 1, 1913. American stage star was born Mary Virginia Martin at Weatherford, TX. She is best known for her title role in the Broadway and television productions of *Peter Pan*. She won Tony awards for her starring roles in *South Pacific* and *Peter Pan*. She died Nov 3, 1990, at Rancho Mirage, CA.

MOORE, JULIA A. DAVIS: BIRTH ANNIVERSARY. Dec 1, 1847. Julia Moore, known as the "Sweet Singer of Michigan," was born in a log cabin at Plainfield, MI. A writer of homely verse and ballads, Moore enjoyed remarkable popularity and gave many public readings before realizing that her public appearances were occasions for laughter and ridicule. Her poems were said to be "so bad, her subjects so morbid and her naivete so genuine" that they were actually gems of humorous genius. At her final public appearance she told her audience: "You people paid 50 cents to see a fool, but I got $50 to look at a house full of fools." Moore died June 17, 1920, near Manton, MI.

★ ★ ★

December 2004	S	M	T	W	T	F	S
				1	2	3	4
	5	6	7	8	9	10	11
	12	13	14	15	16	17	18
	19	20	21	22	23	24	25
	26	27	28	29	30	31	

☆ Chase's 2004 Calendar of Events ☆   Dec 1

NATIONAL APLASTIC ANEMIA AWARENESS WEEK. Dec 1–7. Annually, Dec 1–7. For info: Marilyn Baker, Aplastic Anemia & MDS Intl Foundation, Inc, PO Box 613, Annapolis, MD 21404-0613. Phone: (800) 747-2820. E-mail: help@aamds.org. Web: www.aamds.org.

★**NATIONAL DRUNK AND DRUGGED DRIVING PREVENTION MONTH.** Dec 1–31.

NATIONAL SIGN UP FOR SUMMER CAMP MONTH. Dec 1–31. Every year more than ten million children continue a national tradition by attending day or resident camps. Building self-confidence, learning new skills and making memories that last a lifetime are just a few examples of what makes camp special and why camp does children a world of good. To find the right program, parents begin looking at summer camps during this month—and sign their children up while there are still vacancies. For a guide to accredited camps, call (800) 428-CAMPS. For info: Public Relations, American Camping Assn, 5000 State Rd 67N, Martinsville, IN 46151. Phone: (765) 342-8456. E-mail: pr@acacamps.org. Web: www.ACAcamps.org.

NATIONAL STRESS-FREE FAMILY HOLIDAYS MONTH. Dec 1–31. The holidays are so fraught with busy schedules that families often miss out on quality time together because outside demands have left them virtually drained. This observance is a reminder for parents to strive for more stress-free holidays for their families. Annually, the month of December. For info send SASE to: Teresa Langston, Dir, Parenting Without Pressure, 1330 Boyer St, Longwood, FL 32750-6311. Phone: (407) 767-2524. Web: www.parentingwithoutpressure.com.

NATIONAL TIE MONTH. Dec 1–31. Annually in December. 20% of all ties sold are bought as Christmas gifts. Celebrate the tie and promote its proper use this month. For info: Sir Nemo Turner, The Protocol Institute, CP 157, Place du Parc, Montreal, QC, H2X 4A4 , Canada. Phone: (514) 849-0888. E-mail: magician@total.net.

***PLAYBOY* FIRST PUBLISHED: ANNIVERSARY.** Dec 1, 1953. *Playboy* magazine was launched at Chicago by publisher Hugh Hefner.

PORTUGAL: INDEPENDENCE DAY. Dec 1. Public holiday. Became independent of Spain in 1640.

RECIPE GREETINGS FOR THE HOLIDAYS. Dec 1–8. A week in which to send recipes as great greetings. Create your own or send a large SASE for ideas. Annually, the second week in December. For info: Recipe Greetings Update, PO Box 416, Denver, CO 80201. Phone: (303) 575-5676. E-mail: mail@contentprovidermedia.com.

ROCKEFELLER CENTER CHRISTMAS TREE: ANNUAL LIGHTING. Dec 1 (tentative). New York, NY. Lighting of the huge Christmas Tree in Rockefeller Center signals the opening of the holiday season at New York City. More than 30,000 lights are strung on 5 miles of electric wire. In 1933 the first formal tree lighting ceremony took place with 700 lights. Date is usually the Wednesday after Thanksgiving.

ROMANIA: NATIONAL DAY. Dec 1. National holiday. Marks unification of Romania and Transylvania in 1918 and the overthrow of the communist regime in 1989.

ROSA PARKS DAY: ANNIVERSARY OF ARREST. Dec 1, 1955. Anniversary of the arrest of Rosa Parks, at Montgomery, AL, for refusing to give up her seat and move to the back of a municipal bus. Her arrest triggered a yearlong boycott of the city bus system and led to legal actions which ended racial segregation on municipal buses throughout the southern US. The event has been called the birth of the modern civil rights movement. Rosa McCauley Parks was born at Tuskegee, AL, Feb 4, 1913.

SAFE TOYS AND GIFTS MONTH. Dec 1–31. What toys are dangerous to children's eyesight? Tips on how to choose age-appropriate toys will be distributed. For info: Prevent Blindness America®, 500 E Remington Rd, Schaumburg, IL 60173. Phone: (800) 331-2020. Fax: (847) 843-8458. Web: www.preventblindness.org.

SUWANNEE LIGHTS. Dec 1–31. Spirit of the Suwannee Music Park and Campground, Live Oak, FL. Monthlong light display, scenes and animation of the wonder of Christmas. Share your childhood memories with your family. Visit Santa and craft villages. For info: Spirit of the Suwannee Music Park, 3076 95th Dr, Live Oak, FL 32060. Phone: (386) 364-1683. Web: www.musicliveshere.com.

TOLERANCE WEEK. Dec 1–7. The purpose of this week is to promote the importance of tolerance among human beings as a means of reducing bigotry and prejudice toward those of a different religion, race or creed. For a copy of quotations about tolerance by famous people, as well as a frameable copy of the Golden Rule of ten religions, send $5 to cover printing, handling and postage. For info: Dr. Stanley Drake, Pres, Intl Society of Friendship and Good Will, 999 Hood Rd, Ste 127, Marietta, GA 30068. Phone: (770) 565-2322. E-mail: ISFGW@bellsouth.net.

UNITED NATIONS: WORLD AIDS DAY. Dec 1. In 1988 the World Health Organization of the United Nations declared Dec 1 as World AIDS Day, an international day of awareness and education about AIDS. The WHO is the leader in global direction and coordination of AIDS prevention, control, research and education. A program called UN-AIDS was created to bring together the skills and expertise of the World Bank, UNDP, UNESCO, UNICEF, UNFPA and the WHO to strengthen and expand national capacities to respond to the pandemic. For info: United Nations, Dept of Public Info, New York, NY 10017. Web: www.un.org.

UNIVERSAL HUMAN RIGHTS MONTH. Dec 1–31. To disseminate throughout the world information about human rights and distribute copies of the Universal Declaration of Human Rights in English and other languages. Please send $5 to cover expense of printing, handling and postage. Annually, the month of December. For info: Dr. Stanley Drake, Pres, Intl Society of Friendship & Good Will, 999 Hood Rd, Ste 127, Marietta, GA 30068. Phone: (770) 565-2322. E-mail: ISFGW@bellsouth.net.

US CONGRESS PASSES GATT TREATY: 10th ANNIVERSARY. Dec 1, 1994. Following the lead of the House of Representatives, the US Senate voted 76–24 to approve the Uruguay Round provisions of the General Agreement on Tariffs and Trade (GATT). The worldwide trade pact is intended to reduce tariffs by a third, eliminate trade quotas and protect intellectual property. The GATT agreement is expected to add $300–500 billion to the global economy through the year 2005. In Jan, 1995, the World Trade Organization (WTO) became the successor to GATT.

★**WORLD AIDS DAY.** Dec 1.

BIRTHDAYS TODAY

Woody Allen, 69, actor, writer, director (Oscar for *Annie Hall; Sleeper, Manhattan, Bullets over Broadway*), born Allen Stewart Konigsberg, Brooklyn, NY, Dec 1, 1935.
Carol Alt, 44, model, born New York, NY, Dec 1, 1960.
Nestor Carbonell, 37, actor ("Suddenly Susan"), born New York, NY, Dec 1, 1967.

Dec 1–2   ☆ *Chase's 2004 Calendar of Events* ☆

Bette Midler, 59, singer ("You Are the Wind Beneath My Wings"), actress (*Beaches, For the Boys, Down and Out in Beverly Hills*), born Paterson, NJ, Dec 1, 1945.
Richard Pryor, 64, actor, comedian (*Blue Collar, Stir Crazy*, "The Richard Pryor Show"), born Peoria, IL, Dec 1, 1940.
Lou Rawls, 69, blues singer ("A Natural Man," "You've Made Me So Very Happy"), actor, born Chicago, IL, Dec 1, 1935.
Reggie Sanders, 37, baseball player, born Florence, SC, Dec 1, 1967.
Lee Buck Trevino, 65, golfer, born Dallas, TX, Dec 1, 1939.
Larry Walker, 38, baseball player, born Maple Ridge, BC, Canada, Dec 1, 1966.
Treat Williams, 52, actor (*Hair, Smooth Talk*), born Rowayton, CT, Dec 1, 1952.

DECEMBER 2 — THURSDAY
Day 337 — 29 Remaining

ARTIFICIAL HEART TRANSPLANT: ANNIVERSARY. Dec 2, 1982. Barney C. Clark, 61, became the first recipient of a permanent artificial heart. The operation was performed at the University of Utah Medical Center at Salt Lake City. Near death at the time of the operation, Clark survived almost 112 days after the implantation. He died Mar 23, 1983.

BELGIUM: LOVER'S FAIR. Dec 2. Arlon, Belgium. Traditional cultural observance. Annually, the first Thursday in December.

BROWN, JOHN: EXECUTION ANNIVERSARY. Dec 2, 1859. Abolitionist leader who is remembered for his raid on the US Arsenal at Harper's Ferry was hanged for treason at Charles Town, WV.

CALLAS, MARIA: BIRTH ANNIVERSARY. Dec 2, 1923. American opera singer born at New York, NY. Died at Paris, Sept 16, 1977.

CHRISTMAS AT PIONEER VILLAGE. Dec 2–3. Worthington, MN. Many different activities are held including Christmas carolers, sleigh rides, Santa and Mrs Claus, their elves, refreshments and the beautiful decorations. Free admission. Est attendance: 1,400. For info: Nobles County Historical Society, 407 12th St, Ste 2, Worthington, MN 56187. Phone: (507) 376-4011 or (507) 376-4431.

ENGLAND: WALTER PLINGE DAY. Dec 2. A day to recognize Walter Plinge, said to have been a London pub landlord in 1900. His generosity to actors led to the use of his name as an actor in play programs to conceal the fact that an actor was playing more than one role. See also: "George Spelvin Day" (Nov 15) for US equivalent.

December 2004

S	M	T	W	T	F	S
			1	2	3	4
5	6	7	8	9	10	11
12	13	14	15	16	17	18
19	20	21	22	23	24	25
26	27	28	29	30	31	

ENRON FILES FOR BANKRUPTCY: ANNIVERSARY. Dec 2, 2001. The once high-flying Houston, TX, energy services company filed for bankruptcy on this date. Subsequent investigations revealed questionable accounting practices and unethical dealings, to the extent that "Enron" became the buzzword for corporate malfeasance of the late 1990s and into the 21st century. Many other corporations were found to have questionable financial statements after the Enron scandal (in which thousands of employees lost their jobs and retirement savings), and investor confidence in the US stock market was shaken. Federal Reserve chairman Alan Greenspan, in a July 16, 2002, report to the Senate Banking Committee, indicted such corporate misbehavior: "An infectious greed seemed to grip much of our business community [in the 1990s]."

FIRST SELF-SUSTAINING NUCLEAR CHAIN REACTION: ANNIVERSARY. Dec 2, 1942. Physicist Enrico Fermi led a team of scientists at the University of Chicago in producing the first controlled, self-sustaining nuclear chain reaction. Their first simple nuclear reactor was built under the stands of the University's football stadium.

HOLLY JOLLY WEEKEND. Dec 2–5. James Roberts Center, Andrews, TX. Events include Light-Up the County contest, 4-H Trim-a-Tree contest, 10th annual Chow-Down, Lakeside Christmas tree lighting and caroling, Christmas Time Festival of Homes and the 28th annual Christmas Bazaar. For info: Andrews Chamber of Commerce, 700 W Broadway, Andrews, TX 79714. Phone: (432) 523-2695. E-mail: achamber@andrewstx.com. Web: www.andrewstx.com.

LANTERN LIGHT TOURS. Dec 2–19 (Thursday–Sunday evenings). Mystic, CT. Step into Christmas past. You may find yourself riding in a horse-drawn omnibus, kicking up your heels with revelers in the tavern or spying on silver-haired St. Nick. Purchase tickets for these nighttime traveling dramas by calling (888) 9SEAPORT. Est attendance: 7,000. For info: Mystic Seaport, 75 Greenmanville Ave, Box 6000, Mystic, CT 06355. Phone: (860) 572-5315 or (888) 9SEAPORT. Web: www.visitmysticseaport.org.

LAOS: NATIONAL DAY. Dec 2. National holiday commemorating declaration of the republic in 1975.

LIBERACE MUSEUM CHRISTMAS TREE LIGHTING CEREMONY. Dec 2. The Liberace Museum, Las Vegas, NV. Santa wearing Liberace's gold lamé Santa suit will pull the switch to light the tree with music of the season provided by Liberace scholars. Free admission to all who donate a new toy or nonperishable food item, which will be given to the Salvation Army for distribution to the needy. Annually, the first Thursday in December. Est attendance: 1,000. For info: Jamie G. James, The James Agency, 3630 Coldwater Canyon Ave, Studio City, CA 91604. Phone: (818) 508-4902. Fax: (818) 508-0562. E-mail: JJames@Liberace.org.

McCARTHY SILENCED BY SENATE: 50th ANNIVERSARY. Dec 2, 1954. On Feb 9, 1950, Joseph McCarthy, a relatively obscure senator from Wisconsin, announced during a speech in Wheeling, WV, that he had a list of Communists in the State Department. Over the next two years he made increasingly sensational charges and in 1953 McCarthyism reached its height as he held Senate hearings in which he bullied defendants. In 1954 McCarthy's tyranny was exposed in televised hearings during which he took on the Army and on Dec 2, 1954, the Senate voted to censure him. McCarthy died May 2, 1957.

MONROE DOCTRINE: ANNIVERSARY. Dec 2, 1823. President James Monroe, in his annual message to Congress, enunciated the doctrine that bears his name and that was long hailed as a statement of US policy. ". . . In the wars of the European powers in matters relating to themselves we have never taken any part . . . we should consider any attempt on their part to extend their system to any portion of this hemi-sphere as dangerous to our peace and safety. . . ."

NATIONAL PARKS ESTABLISHED IN ALASKA: ANNIVERSARY. Dec 2, 1980. Eight national parks were established in Alaska on this date. Mount McKinley National Park, which was

608

established Feb 26, 1917, and Denali National Monument, which was proclaimed Dec 1, 1978, were combined as Denali National Park and Preserve. Gates of the Arctic National Monument, proclaimed Dec 1, 1978; Glacier Bay National Monument, proclaimed Feb 25, 1925; and Katmai National Monument, proclaimed Sept 24, 1918, were established as national parks and preserves. Kenai Fjords National Monument, proclaimed Dec 1, 1978, and Kobuk Valley National Monument, proclaimed Dec 1, 1978, were established as national parks. Lake Clark National Monument, proclaimed Dec 1, 1978, and Wrangell–St. Elias National Monument, proclaimed Dec 1, 1978, were established as national parks and preserves. For info: www.nps.gov.

SAFETY RAZOR PATENTED: ANNIVERSARY. Dec 2, 1901. American King Camp Gillette designed the first razor with disposable blades. Up until this time, men shaved with a straight edge razor that they sharpened on a leather strap.

SAINT OLAF CHRISTMAS FESTIVAL. Dec 2–5. St. Olaf College, Northfield, MN. Annually since 1912. This celebration of the Christmas season brings together 600 student musicians (a 90-piece symphony orchestra and 500 singers) to perform sacred and folk songs from around the world. Annually, the weekend after Thanksgiving, Thurs–Sun. Est attendance: 12,000. For info: Bob Johnson, St. Olaf College, 1520 St. Olaf Ave, Northfield, MN 55057-1098. Phone: (507) 646-3179. Web: www.stolaf.edu.

SEURAT, GEORGES PIERRE: BIRTH ANNIVERSARY. Dec 2, 1859. French Neo-impressionist painter born at Paris, France. Died there Mar 29, 1891. Seurat is known for his style of painting with small spots of color, called "pointillism," as in *Sunday Afternoon on the Island of Grand Jatte*.

UNITED ARAB EMIRATES: NATIONAL DAY. Dec 2. Anniversary of the day in 1971 when a federation of seven sheikdoms known as the Trucial States declared independence from the UK and became known as the United Arab Emirates.

UNITED NATIONS: INTERNATIONAL DAY FOR THE ABOLITION OF SLAVERY. Dec 2. Recalls the date of adoption by the General Assembly in 1949 of the Convention for the Suppression of the Traffic in Persons and the Exploitation of Others. For info: United Nations, Dept of Public Info, New York, NY 10017. Web: www.un.org.

VICTORIAN SLEIGHBELL PARADE & OLD CHRISTMAS WEEKEND. Dec 2–5. Manistee, MI. Re-creation of Manistee history. No motorized vehicles, no amplification. Horse-drawn entries, walking entries, singers, animals and St. Nick in historic garb. Parade on Dec 4. Est attendance: 10,000. For info: Manistee Area Chamber of Commerce, 11 Cypress St, Manistee, MI 49660. Phone: (231) 723-2575 or (800) 288-2286. E-mail: chamber@manistee.com. Web: www.manisteecountychamber.com.

WORLD'S LARGEST OUTLET SALE. Dec 2–12. Pigeon Forge, TN. Pre-holiday savings on famous brands provided by six outlet malls with almost 200 sites. For info: Office of Special Events, Pigeon Forge Dept of Tourism, 3107 Parkway, PO Box 1390, Pigeon Forge, TN 37868. Phone: (800) 251-9100 or (865) 453-8574. Fax: (865) 429-7392. Web: www.mypigeonforge.com.

BIRTHDAYS TODAY

Wayne Allard, 61, US Senator (R, Colorado), born Fort Collins, CO, Dec 2, 1943.
Dan Butler, 50, actor ("Frasier"), born Huntington, IN, Dec 2, 1954.
Dennis Christopher, 49, actor (*Sweet Dreams, Breaking Away*), born Philadelphia, PA, Dec 2, 1955.
Cathy Lee Crosby, 56, actress ("That's Incredible," *Coach*), born Los Angeles, CA, Dec 2, 1948.
Randy Gardner, 46, figure skater, born Marina del Rey, CA, Dec 2, 1958.
Julie Harris, 79, actress (winner of six Tonys), born Grosse Pointe, MI, Dec 2, 1925.

Lucy Liu, 37, actress ("Ally McBeal," *Charlie's Angels*), born Queens, NY, Dec 2, 1967.
Garry Meier, 55, Chicago radio personality, born Chicago, IL, Dec 2, 1949.
Stone Phillips, 50, anchor ("Dateline," "20/20"), born Texas City, TX, Dec 2, 1954.
Harry Reid, 65, US Senator (D, Nevada), born Searchlight, NV, Dec 2, 1939.
Monica Seles, 31, tennis player, born Novi Sad, Yugoslavia, Dec 2, 1973.
Britney Spears, 23, singer, born Kentwood, LA, Dec 2, 1981.
William Wegman, 61, artist, photographer (of dogs), born Holyoke, MA, Dec 2, 1943.

DECEMBER 3 — FRIDAY
Day 338 — 28 Remaining

BHOPAL POISON GAS DISASTER: 20th ANNIVERSARY. Dec 3, 1984. At Bhopal, India, a leak of deadly gas (methyl isocyanate) at a Union Carbide Corp plant killed more than 4,000 persons and injured more than 200,000 in the world's worst industrial accident.

CHRISTMAS CRAFT SHOW. Dec 3–4. H.O. Weeks Recreation Center, Aiken, SC. This show consists of more than 150 Christmas exhibits and other items from the Southeast's top craftsmen. The displays range from woodwork to fine porcelain sculpture. 33rd annual show. Est attendance: 14,000. For info: City of Aiken Park & Rec Dept, PO Box 1177, Aiken, SC 29802. Phone: (803) 642-7631. Fax: (803) 642-7639. E-mail: howeeks@aiken.com.

CHRISTMAS FESTIVAL OF LIGHTS. Dec 3–4. Natchitoches, LA. 78th annual. Featuring a parade, fireworks, food, entertainment, a fun run/walk and Christmas lighting. Listed as one of the "Top 100 Events in North America" by the American Bus Association. Est attendance: 150,000. For info: Natchitoches Parish Tourist Commission, 781 Front St, Natchitoches, LA 71457. Phone: (318) 352-8072 or (800) 259-1714. Fax: (318) 352-2415. Web: www.natchitoches.net or www.christmasfestival.com.

CHRISTMAS GREENS SHOW. Dec 3–5. Jackman-Long Building, State Fairgrounds, Salem, OR. Half the building houses decorated trees, large Christmas displays, hundreds of floral arrangements, wreaths and wall hangings. The other half houses 106 handcrafters and their wares, also fresh greens and wreaths. Food available. Proceeds benefit community projects. Annually, the second Friday, Saturday and Sunday after Thanksgiving. Est attendance: 15,000. For info: Linda Nelson, Willamette Christmas Assn, 543 Lakefair Pl, N, Keizer, OR 97303. Phone: (503) 393-4439. For application write to: Willamette Christmas Assn, PO Box 20817, Keizer, OR 97307.

Dec 3 ☆ Chase's 2004 Calendar of Events ☆

CHRISTMAS STROLL WEEKEND. Dec 3–5. Nantucket Island, MA. Christmas trees, costumed carolers, theatrical performances. Santa arrives via Coast Guard boat and is driven up Main Street in a horse-drawn carriage. Est attendance: 10,000. For info: Nantucket Island Chamber of Commerce, 48 Main St, Nantucket, MA 02554-3595. Phone: (508) 228-1700. Web: www.nantucketchamber.org.

CONRAD, JOSEPH: BIRTH ANNIVERSARY. Dec 3, 1857. English novelist, born Jozef Korzeniowski to Polish parents at Berdichev in the Ukraine. He learned English as a sailor on British ships. Author of *Lord Jim* and *Heart of Darkness*, among others. Died Aug 3, 1924 at Bishopsbourne, Kent, England.

DICKENS' CHRISTMAS EXTRAVAGANZA. Dec 3–5. Cape May, NJ. This three-day celebration features the sights and sounds, tastes and scents of the Dickens era, with lectures, performances, tours and feasts in various locations. For info: Mid-Atlantic Center for the Arts, 1048 Washington St, Cape May, NJ 08204. Phone: (800) 275-4278. Fax: (609) 884-0574. E-mail: mac4arts@capemaymac.org. Web: www.capemaymac.org.

FANTASY OF LIGHTS. Dec 3–Jan 1, 2005. Wichita Falls, TX. A spectacular light and toyland display on the Midwestern State University campus. A Wichita Falls Christmas tradition! Est attendance: 250,000. For info: Wichita Falls Conv & Visitors Bureau, 1000 Fifth St, Wichita Falls, TX 76301. Phone: (940) 716-5500. Fax: (940) 716-5509. E-mail: MPEC@wf.net. Web: www.wichitafalls.org.

FIRST HEART TRANSPLANT: ANNIVERSARY. Dec 3, 1967. Dr. Christiaan Barnard, a South African surgeon, performed the world's first successful heart transplantation at Cape Town, South Africa. See also: "Barnard, Christiaan Neethling: Birthday" (Nov 8).

GENEVA'S CHRISTMAS WALK. Dec 3–4. Geneva, IL. Spend the day touring charming homes aglow with holiday decorations. In the evening, Santa Lucia, the Swedish symbol of the season, arrives and Santa Claus opens his house for children's visits. Merchants graciously serve traditional holiday refreshments, including roasted chestnuts, as carolers fill the air with the sounds of the season. Annually, the first Friday and Saturday in December. Est attendance: 20,000. For info: Mary K. Brown, Geneva Chamber of Commerce, 8 S Third St, PO Box 481, Geneva, IL 60134. Phone: (630) 232-6060 or (866) 4-GENEVA. Fax: (630) 232-6083. E-mail: chamberinfo@genevachamber.com. Web: www.genevachamber.com.

ILLINOIS: ADMISSION DAY: ANNIVERSARY. Dec 3. Became 21st state in 1818.

LEMOYNE HOUSE CANDLELIGHT CHRISTMAS TOURS. Dec 3–5 (also Dec 11–12). Washington, PA. Evening candlelight tours of the beautifully decorated LeMoyne House. Volunteers dressed in period costume guide visitors through this historic home. Est attendance: 500. For info: Joyce Mullen, Washington County Historical Society, 49 E Maiden St, Washington, PA 15317. Phone: (724) 225-6740. Fax: (724) 225-8495. E-mail: info@wchspa.org. Web: www.wchspa.org.

MONTOYA, CARLOS: BIRTH ANNIVERSARY. Dec 3, 1903. Guitarist and composer renowned for popularizing flamenco guitar music. His solo performances of the Spanish folk form lifted flamenco from its traditional accompaniment role. Montoya never learned to read music and relied on the traditional improvisational nature of flamenco rooted in the Andalusian Gypsy form of music that stressed rhythms and harmonic patterns. He was born at Madrid, Spain, and died Mar 3, 1993, at Wainscott, NY.

December 2004

	S	M	T	W	T	F	S
				1	2	3	4
	5	6	7	8	9	10	11
	12	13	14	15	16	17	18
	19	20	21	22	23	24	25
	26	27	28	29	30	31	

NAIA WOMEN'S NATIONAL VOLLEYBALL CHAMPIONSHIP. Dec 3–6. Point Loma Nazarene University, San Diego, CA. 20 teams compete in a pool play tournament to determine the national champion. 25th annual championship, co-hosted by Point Loma Nazarene University with the San Diego International Sports Council. Est attendance: 3,000. For info: Natl Assn of Intercollegiate Athletics, 23500 W 105th St, PO Box 1325, Olathe, KS 66051-1325. Phone: (913) 791-0044. Fax: (913) 791-9555. E-mail: lthomas@naia.org. Web: www.naia.org.

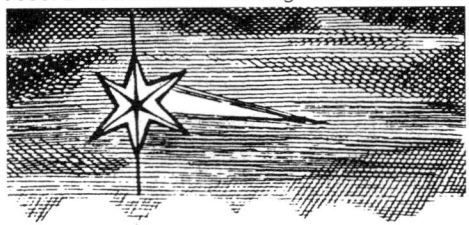

NORTH STAR CLASSIC. Dec 3–5. Valley City, ND. 3-day livestock show and sale featuring 11 breeds of cattle shows and 5 breed sales, plus shows for swine and sheep and a junior livestock show. Also a commercial exhibit area that features only items and equipment related to livestock production. Est attendance: 15,000. For info: Tom Langemo, Mgr, North Star Classic, PO Box 846, Valley City, ND 58072. Phone: (701) 845-1401 or (800) 437-0218. Fax: (701) 845-3914. E-mail: ndws@valleycity.net. Web: www.ndws.org.

OCEAN DANCE. Dec 3–5 (tentative). Hollywood, FL. A two-day celebration of dance featuring a critically acclaimed dance company with performances on the beach as well as indoor educational programs for school children and families. Est attendance: 50,000. For info: Art & Culture Center of Hollywood, 1650 Harrison St, Hollywood, FL 33020. Phone: (954) 921-3274. Web: www.artandculturecenter.org.

PEGGY V. HELMERICH DISTINGUISHED AUTHOR AWARD PRESENTATION. Dec 3–4. Central Library, Tulsa, OK. The award is given annually by the Tulsa Library Trust to a nationally acclaimed author who has written a distinguished body of work and made a major contribution to the field of literature and letters. The award consists of a $25,000 cash prize and an engraved crystal book. The winning author will be the keynote speaker at this black-tie dinner in his or her honor. Past recipients include Neil Simon (1996), David McCullough (1995), Ray Bradbury (1994), Peter Matthiessen (1993), Norman Mailer (1992), Eudora Welty (1991) and John le Carre (1990). Est attendance: 1,000. For info: Larry Bartley, Trust and Development Mgr, Tulsa Public Library, 400 Civic Center, Tulsa, OK 74103. Phone: (918) 596-7985. Fax: (918) 596-7990.

STUART, GILBERT CHARLES: BIRTH ANNIVERSARY. Dec 3, 1755. American portrait painter whose most famous painting is that of George Washington. He also painted portraits of Madison, Monroe, Jefferson and other important Americans. Stuart was born near Narragansett, RI, and died July 9, 1828, at Boston, MA.

UNITED NATIONS: INTERNATIONAL DAY OF DISABLED PERSONS. Dec 3. On Oct 14, 1992 (Res 47/3), at the end of the Decade of Disabled Persons, the General Assembly proclaimed Dec 3 to be an annual observance to promote the continuation of integrating the disabled into general society. For info: United Nations, Dept of Public Info, New York, NY 10017. Web: www.un.org.

WINTERFEST. Dec 3–5. Luverne, MN. Christmas Light Parade, Parade of Homes, craft show, historical tours, dinner theater. For

★ Chase's 2004 Calendar of Events ★ Dec 3–4

info: Dave Smith, Exec Dir, Luverne Area Chamber of Commerce, 102 E Main, Luverne, MN 56156. Phone: (507) 283-4061. Fax: (507) 283-4061. E-mail: luvernechamber@dtgnet.com. Web: www.luvernemn.com.

XCEL ENERGY'S PARADE OF LIGHTS. Dec 3–4. Denver, CO. This 30th annual evening holiday parade features dazzling theme floats, giant helium-filled holiday balloons, magical costumed characters, the area's best marching bands, high-stepping equestrian units and much more. Friday at 8 PM, Saturday at 6 PM. Est attendance: 375,000. For info: John L. Kerns, Event Mgr, Downtown Denver Partnership, Inc, 511 16th St, Ste 200, Denver, CO 80202-4250. Phone: (303) 534-6161. Fax: (303) 534-2803. E-mail: jkerns@downtowndenver.com. Web: www.downtowndenver.com.

BIRTHDAYS TODAY

Brian Bonsall, 23, actor ("Family Ties," *Blank Check*), born Torrance, CA, Dec 3, 1981.
Bruno Campos, 30, actor ("Jesse"), born Rio de Janeiro, Brazil, Dec 3, 1974.
Holly Marie Combs, 31, actress ("Picket Fences," "Charmed"), born San Diego, CA, Dec 3, 1973.
Brendan Fraser, 36, actor (*Mummy, The Quiet American*), born Indianapolis, IN, Dec 3, 1968.
Jean Luc Godard, 74, filmmaker (*Breathless, Weekend*), born Paris, France, Dec 3, 1930.
Daryl Hannah, 43, actress (*Splash, Grumpy Old Men*), born Chicago, IL, Dec 3, 1961.
Ferlin Husky, 77, singer ("Gone," "On the Wings of a Dove"), born Flat River, MO, Dec 3, 1927.
Bucky Lasek, 32, skateboarder, born Baltimore, MD, Dec 3, 1972.
Rick Ravon Mears, 53, former auto racer, born Wichita, KS, Dec 3, 1951.
Julianne Moore, 43, actress (*Far From Heaven*), born Fort Bragg, Fayetteville, NC, Dec 3, 1961.
Jaye P. Morgan, 72, singer ("That's All I Want from You," "The Longest Walk"), born Mancos, CO, Dec 3, 1932.
Sven Vilhem Nykvist, 82, cinematographer (*The Unbearable Lightness of Being*), born Moheda, Sweden, Dec 3, 1922.
Ozzy Osbourne, 56, singer, songwriter (originally lead singer for Black Sabbath), born Birmingham, England, Dec 3, 1948.
Andy Williams, 74, singer (platinum album *Love Story*, 13 gold albums), born Wall Lake, IA, Dec 3, 1930.
Katarina Witt, 39, Olympic figure skater, born Karl-Marx-Stadt, East Germany, Dec 3, 1965.

DECEMBER 4 — SATURDAY
Day 339 — 27 Remaining

ADELPHIAN CLUB CHRISTMAS BAZAAR. Dec 4. American Legion Building, Kennett, MO. Huge sale of arts and crafts with more than 100 exhibitors, plus a bake sale. Free admission. Annually, the first Saturday in December. For info: Adelphian Civic Club, 301 S Everett, Kennett, MO 63857. Phone: (573) 888-9472.

APPALACHIAN POTTERS MARKET. Dec 4. McDowell High School, Marion, NC. One-day display and sale of clay work only by 60 potters. Annually, the first Saturday in December. Sponsor: McDowell Arts and Crafts Association. Est attendance: 1,600. For info: Appalachian Potters Market, c/o MACA, PO Box 1387, Marion, NC 28752. Phone: (828) 652-8610.

BUTLER, SAMUEL: BIRTH ANNIVERSARY. Dec 4, 1835. English author (*Erewhon, The Way of All Flesh*), born at Bingham, Nottinghamshire, England. Died at London, June 18, 1902.

CANDLELIGHT TOURS. Dec 4. The Atheneum, New Harmony, IN. Tours of private and historic homes decorated for the holidays. This event coincides with the local business associates' Christmas in New Harmony festival. Annually, the first weekend in December. Est attendance: 250. For info: Historic New Harmony, PO Box 579, New Harmony, IN 47631. Phone: (812) 682-4488. Fax: (812) 682-4313. E-mail: klinderm@usi.edu.

CARLYLE, THOMAS: BIRTH ANNIVERSARY. Dec 4, 1795. Scottish essayist and historian, born at Ecclefechan, Scotland. Died at London, Feb 4, 1881. "A well-written Life is almost as rare as a well-spent one," Carlyle wrote in his *Critical and Miscellaneous Essays*.

CHASE'S CALENDAR OF EVENTS: BIRTHDAY. Dec 4, 1957. Forty-seven years ago today the first copies of the first edition of *Chase's Calendar of Annual Events* (for the year 1958) were delivered by the printer at Flint, MI. Two thousand copies, consisting of 32 pages and listing 364 events, were printed. Now annual editions are more than 700 pages long and list more than 12,000 events. It has several offspring, including *The Teacher's Calendar*, which debuted in 1999.

CHESTER GREENWOOD DAY PARADE. Dec 4. Farmington, ME. Celebration of Farmington's famous inventor of the earmuff. An earmuff-themed parade with flag raising. Annually, the first Saturday in December. Est attendance: 1,500. For info: Farmington-Wilton Chamber of Commerce, 575 Wilton Rd, Farmington, ME 04938. Phone: (207) 778-4215.

CHIMNEYVILLE CRAFTS FESTIVAL. Dec 4–5. Jackson, MS. The finest crafts for sale by more than 150 craftsmen: woodcarving, blown glass, weaving, leather, baskets, stained glass, pottery. Est attendance: 6,500. For info: Kit Davis Barksdale, Exec Dir, Craftsmen's Guild of Mississippi, Inc, 1150 Lakeland Dr, Jackson, MS 39216. Phone: (601) 981-0019. Fax: (601) 981-0488. E-mail: mscraftsmen@aol.com. Web: www.mscraftsmensguild.org.

CHRISTMAS IN THE VILLAGES. Dec 4–5. Van Buren County, IA. Event features tour of homes, English High Tea, cookie walk, Festival of Trees, horse-drawn carriage rides, bake sales, lighting contests and displays, soup suppers and the natural beauty of the season that is found throughout the county. Est attendance: 5,000. For info: Villages of Van Buren, Inc, PO Box 9, Keosauqua, IA 52565. Phone: (800) 868-7822. Fax: (319) 293-7116. Web: www.800-tourvbc.com.

CHRISTMAS IN WESTON CANDLELIGHT HOMES TOUR. Dec 4–5. Weston, MO. Enjoy a walking tour featuring homes decorated for Christmas, museum, shops, buggy rides and Father Christmas. Limited tickets. For info: Weston Development Co, 502 Main, Weston, MO 64098. Phone: (816) 640-2909. E-mail: westonmo@kc.rr.com. Web: ci.weston.mo.us.

CHRISTMAS ON THE PRAIRIE. Dec 4–5. Saunders County Museum, Wahoo, NE. Old-fashioned Christmas featuring entertainment by local groups, lots of period costumes, special postal cancellation, children's activities common to the 1800s and demonstrations in the historical village decorated in the 1800s style. Annually, the first weekend of December. Sponsor: Christmas on the Prairie Steering Committee. Est attendance: 3,000. For info: Curator, Saunders County Museum, 240 N Walnut, Wahoo, NE 68066-1858. Phone: (402) 443-3090. Web: www.visitsaunderscounty.org.

611

Dec 4 ☆ Chase's 2004 Calendar of Events ☆

CHRISTMAS PAST AT AUDUBON ACRES. Dec 4. Audubon Acres, Chattanooga, TN. Visit Spring Frog Cabin decorated for the season with pioneer cheer; join in with Tom Morgan and Lynn Haas as they play traditional folk and holiday music. Enjoy the sights, tastes, smells and excitement of Christmas long ago; see demonstrations of early skills; enjoy a stroll to the swinging bridge to observe signs of nature in the winter. Sponsor: Chattanooga Audubon Society. Est attendance: 1,500. For info: Lynda Logan, Audubon Acres, 900 N Sanctuary Rd, Chattanooga, TN 37421. Phone: (423) 892-1499. Fax: (423) 892-6376. E-mail: caudubons@aol.com. Web: www.AudubonChattanooga.org.

COMMUNITY CHRISTMAS BAZAAR. Dec 4. Event Center on the Beach, Gold Beach, OR. Local nonprofit organizations sell their wares with all the cheer of the Christmas season. Santa visits at 1 PM. Est attendance: 400. For info: Gold Beach Chamber of Commerce, 29279 Ellensburg Ave, #3, Gold Beach, OR 97444. Phone: (800) 525-2334. Fax: (541) 247-0188. E-mail: gbchamber@wave.net. Web: goldbeachchamber.com.

COUNTRY CHRISTMAS. Dec 4 (also Dec 11 and 18). Roscoe Village, Coshocton, OH. 19th-century holiday atmosphere, 51-room country inn, hot mulled cider in Village. Candlelighting ceremony on the first three Saturdays in December. Special weekend activities including Christmas carriage rides, strolling carolers, visits with Mr & Mrs Santa Claus. Annually, the first three Saturdays of December. Est attendance: 6,500. For info: Roscoe Village Foundation, 381 Hill St, Coshocton, OH 43812. Phone: (740) 622-9310 or (800) 877-1830. Fax: (740) 623-6555. E-mail: rvmarketing@roscoevillage.com. Web: www.roscoevillage.com.

DICKENS ON THE STRAND. Dec 4–5. Galveston, TX. Victorian Christmas celebration focuses on the 19th-century architecture of Galveston's Strand and ties to Charles Dickens's 19th-century London. Annually, the first Saturday–Sunday in December. Est attendance: 50,000. For info: Galveston Historical Foundation, 502 20th St, Galveston, TX 77550. Phone: (409) 765-7834. Fax: (409) 765-7851. E-mail: foundation@galvestonhistory.org. Web: www.dickensonthestrand.org or www.galvestonhistory.org.

EXTRAORDINARY WORK TEAM RECOGNITION DAY. Dec 4. To recognize business teams that work extraordinarily well together, producing significant results/accomplishments for their company or organization. Team leaders and management "champions" are encouraged to recognize exceptional team performance and submit their stories for a chance to win an extraordinary prize for their team! Annually, on Dec 4. For info: Kristin J. Arnold, Quality Process Consultants, Inc, 11304 Megan Dr, Fairfax, VA 22030. Phone: (703) 278-0892. Fax: (703) 278-0891. E-mail: karnold@qpcteam.com. Web: www.qpcteam.com.

"FALCON CREST" TV PREMIERE: ANNIVERSARY. Dec 4, 1981. This nighttime serial was set in California wine country and originally focused on Angela Channing's determined efforts to gain control of the Falcon Crest vineyard and winery; later in the nine-year run the emphasis turned to crime. Famous actors who were a part of the cast at one time or another include: Jane Wyman, Lorenzo Lamas, Billy R. Moses, Cliff Robertson, Lana Turner, Gina Lollobrigida, Parker Stevenson, Anne Archer, Apollonia, Cesar Romero, Morgan Fairchild, Ken Olin and Mary Ann Mobley. In the season finale, Angela received Falcon Crest and everyone was happy.

GINGERBREAD VILLAGE AND BAZAAR. Dec 4–11. St. George's Church, Middlebury, CT. Fairy land of newly baked gingerbread houses—all edible and all for sale. Bazaar, food, handicrafts and gingerbread cookie men. Groups by reservation. Handicapped access available. Est attendance: 3,000. For info: Marilyn, St. George's Church, Gingerbread Village and Bazaar, Tuckerhill Rd at Rte 188, Middlebury, CT 06762. Phone: (203) 758-2165. Group reservations Phone: (203) 723-4143.

HERITAGE CHRISTMAS. Dec 4 (also Dec 11). Old Mill Museum Complex, Lindsborg, KS. A celebration of Christmas past with the music, drama and costumes of a traditional pioneer Christmas on the Kansas prairie. Annually, the first two Saturday evenings in December. Est attendance: 1,200. For info: McPherson County Old Mill Museum, PO Box 94, Lindsborg, KS 67456. Phone: (785) 227-3595. E-mail: oldmillmuseum@hotmail.com. Web: www.oldmillmuseum.org.

HOLIDAY HAPPINESS. Dec 4. Upper Arlington Public Library, Upper Arlington, OH. Holiday crafts, music and activities, including a visit from Santa Claus, for the whole family to enjoy. Annually, the first Saturday of December. For info: Upper Arlington Public Library, 2800 Tremont Rd, Upper Arlington, OH 43221. Phone: (614) 486-9621. Fax: (614) 486-4530. Web: www.ualibrary.org.

LAST AMERICAN HOSTAGE RELEASED IN LEBANON: ANNIVERSARY. Dec 4, 1991. A sad chapter of US history came to a close when Terry Anderson, an Associated Press correspondent, became the final American hostage held in Lebanon to be freed. Anderson had been held since Mar 16, 1985, one of 15 Americans who were held hostage for from two months to as long as six years and eight months. Three of the hostages, William Buckley, Peter Kilburn and Lieutenant Colonel William Higgins, were killed during their captivity. The other hostages, released previously one or two at a time, were Jeremy Levin, Benjamin Weir, the Reverend Lawrence Martin Jenco, David Jacobsen, Thomas Sutherland, Frank Herbert Reed, Joseph Cicippio, Edward Austin Tracy, Alan Steen, Jesse Turner and Robert Polhill.

MADRIGAL DINNER AND CONCERT. Dec 4–5. Mount Mary College, Milwaukee, WI. Saturday dinner concert and Sunday dessert concert. Est attendance: 400. For info: Mary Cain, PR Office, Mount Mary College, 2900 N Menomonee River Pkwy, Milwaukee, WI 53222-4597. Phone: (414) 256-1210. Fax: (414) 256-1239. E-mail: mktg@mtmary.edu. Web: www.mtmary.edu.

MISSION SANTA BARBARA: FOUNDING ANNIVERSARY. Dec 4, 1786. Franciscan Mission to the Indians founded at Santa Barbara, CA. Present structure is the fourth to stand on same site. Last one destroyed by 1812 earthquake.

MOON PHASE: LAST QUARTER. Dec 4. Moon enters Last Quarter phase at 7:53 PM, EST.

NATIONAL DICE DAY. Dec 4. A day for everyone to enjoy playing the game of dice. The goal of the game is to get to 10,000 points. Each player rolls 5 dice. If you roll a 5, it counts for 500 points. If you roll a 1, it counts for 100 points. If you roll neither, you lose your turn. If you roll 3-of-a-kind, it will count for the number x 100. If you roll 4-of-a-kind, double the number; 5-of-a-kind, double the number. If you roll a straight 12345 or 23456, you earn 1,500 points. Once someone reaches 10,000 points, they have to make every die count; once they do that everyone else has a chance to beat their score. For info: Julia Chase, 2681 Balmoral Ct, Ann Arbor, MI 48103. E-mail: FlamingCheese01@hotmail.com.

NATIONAL GRANGE FOUNDING: ANNIVERSARY. Dec 4, 1786. The anniversary of the National Grange, the first organized agricultural movement in the US.

December 2004	S	M	T	W	T	F	S
				1	2	3	4
	5	6	7	8	9	10	11
	12	13	14	15	16	17	18
	19	20	21	22	23	24	25
	26	27	28	29	30	31	

☆ Chase's 2004 Calendar of Events ☆ Dec 4

NORSKEDALEN'S OLD-FASHIONED CHRISTMAS. Dec 4–5. Coon Valley, WI. Celebrate an old-fashioned Christmas with decorated pioneer log homes to view, entertainment, a la carte ethnic foods, raffle, horse-drawn wagon/sleigh rides and outdoor activities. Fun for all ages. 10 AM–4 PM. Est attendance: 500. For info: Norskedalen Nature and Heritage Center, Inc, PO Box 235, Coon Valley, WI 54623. Phone: (608) 452-3424. Fax: (608) 452-3157. E-mail: info@norskedalen.org. Web: www.norskedalen.org.

NORWEGIAN CHRISTMAS. Dec 4–5. Brooklyn Park, MN. Old-fashioned farm Christmas with turn-of-the-century decorations, carolers, making of traditional gifts, lefse and other Norwegian delicacies, a visit by St. Nicholas and sled & hayrides. Est attendance: 1,500. For info: Kay Grotenhuis, Site Mgr, Brooklyn Park Historical Farm, 4345 101st Ave N, Brooklyn Park, MN 55443. Phone: (763) 493-4604 or (763) 493-8368. Web: www.brooklynpark.org.

OLD-FASHIONED CHRISTMAS CELEBRATION. Dec 4–24. Historic Square, Dahlonega, GA. Festival begins with Illumination of the Square and Christmas Parade the first Saturday in December. Events continue during the month of December and include sleighbell tour of b&bs, festival of trees and wreaths and more. Est attendance: 800. For info: Dahlonega-Lumpkin Chamber of Commerce, 13 S Park St, Dahlonega, GA 30533. Phone: (706) 864-3711. Fax: (706) 864-7917. E-mail: dahlonega@alltel.net. Web: www.dahlonega.org/festivals.

PALM HARBOR ART, CRAFT AND MUSIC FESTIVAL. Dec 4–5. Palm Harbor, FL. 30th annual juried arts and crafts show with some 200 exhibitors from all over the US. Artists' cash awards: $16,550. Annually, the first weekend in December. Est attendance: 30,000. For info: Connie Davis, Exec Dir, Palm Harbor Chamber of Commerce, 1151 Nebraska Ave, Palm Harbor, FL 34683. Phone: (727) 784-4287. Fax: (727) 786-2336. E-mail: phchamber@palmharborcc.org. Web: www.palmharborcc.org.

PARADE OF LIGHTS. Dec 4. Kingsville, TX. Breakfast with Santa kicks off a fun-filled day of holiday activities for children ending with an illuminated night-time parade for children of all ages in historic downtown Kingsville. Est attendance: 3,000. For info: Kingsville CVB, 1501 N Hwy 77, Kingsville, TX 78363. Phone: (800) 333-5032. Fax: (361) 592-3227. E-mail: visitors@kingsvilletexas.com. Web: www.kingsvilletexas.com.

RUSSELL, LILLIAN: BIRTH ANNIVERSARY. Dec 4, 1861. American singer and actress who in 1881 gained fame in the comic opera *The Great Mogul*. Born Helen Louise Leonard at Clinton, IA, she died June 6, 1922, at Pittsburgh, PA.

SAINT BARBARA'S DAY. Dec 4. On this day, traditionally the feast day of St. Barbara, a young girl places a twig from a cherry tree in a glass of water. If it blooms by Christmas Eve, she is certain to marry the following year. Because the narratives of her life and martyrdom are legendary, St. Barbara was dropped from the Roman Catholic Calendar of Saints in 1970.

SANTA BY STAGECOACH PARADE. Dec 4. El Centro, CA. Annually, the first Saturday in December. Est attendance: 25,000. For info: El Centro Chamber of Commerce, Box 3006, El Centro, CA 92244. Phone: (760) 352-3681. Fax: (760) 352-3246. Web: www.elcentrochamber.com.

SPACE MILESTONE: INTERNATIONAL SPACE STATION LAUNCH (US): ANNIVERSARY. Dec 4, 1998. The shuttle *Endeavour* took a US component of the space station named *Unity* into orbit 220 miles from Earth where spacewalking astronauts fastened it to a component launched by the Russians Nov 20, 1998. On July 25, 2000, the Russian service module *Zvezda* docked with the station. It will take a total of 45 Russian and US launches over the next five years before the space station is complete. When finished, it will be 356' across and 290' long and will support a crew of up to seven. On Oct 31, 2000, NASA launched the first expedition with a three-man crew to stay aloft for four months.

TAMALE FIESTA. Dec 4. Town Square, El Centro, CA. Tamale contest plus various arts & crafts and entertainment. Annually, the first Saturday in December. Est attendance: 4,000. For info: El Centro Chamber of Commerce, PO Box 3006, El Centro, CA 92244. Phone: (760) 352-3681. Fax: (760) 352-3246. Web: www.elcentrochamber.com.

TWELVE VILLAGES OF CHRISTMAS. Dec 4–25. Each of 12 cities in Washington County, KS, organizes events including special lighting of entire county, craft festivals, drawings, special musical programs, retail open houses. Some towns have a Christmas tree in every yard. Annually, the three weekends before Christmas. Est attendance: 7,000. For info: Washington County Travel and Tourism, Courthouse, 214 C St, Washington, KS 66968. Phone: (785) 325-2116. Fax: (785) 325-2830. E-mail: washcott@washingtonks.net.

VICTORIAN CHRISTMAS HOME TOUR AND MINER'S BALL. Dec 4. Leadville, CO. Highlight of the holiday season—annual showing off of Leadville's historic homes and buildings bedecked in Christmas trimmings. Locals and guests alike dress in period fashions. Est attendance: 350. For info: Chamber of Commerce, Box 861, Leadville, CO 80461. Phone: (719) 486-3900 or (800) 933-3901. Fax: (719) 486-8478. E-mail: leadville@leadvilleusa.com. Web: www.leadvilleusa.com.

BIRTHDAYS TODAY

Max Baer, Jr, 67, actor ("The Beverly Hillbillies"), producer (*Ode to Billy Joe*), born Oakland, CA, Dec 4, 1937.
Tyra Banks, 31, model, actress ("Soul Train Lady of Soul Awards"), born Los Angeles, CA, Dec 4, 1973.
Jeff Bridges, 55, actor (*The Fisher King*), born Los Angeles, CA, Dec 4, 1949.
Helen M. Chase, 80, retired chronicler of contemporary civilization as coeditor of *Chase's Annual Events*, born Whitehall, MI, Dec 4, 1924.
Deanna Durbin, 83, actress (*It Started with Eve, Can't Help Singing*), born Winnipeg, MB, Canada, Dec 4, 1921.
Chris Hillman, 62, musician (the Byrds, the Desert Rose Band), born Los Angeles, CA, Dec 4, 1942.
Stewart Rawlings Mott, 67, philanthropist, born Flint, MI, Dec 4, 1937.
Marisa Tomei, 40, actress (*The Flamingo Kid, My Cousin Vinny*), born Brooklyn, NY, Dec 4, 1964.
Patricia Wettig, 53, actress ("St. Elsewhere," *City Slickers*; Emmys for "thirtysomething"), born Cincinnati, OH, Dec 4, 1951.
Cassandra Wilson, 49, jazz singer, born Jackson, MS, Dec 4, 1955.

DECEMBER 5 — SUNDAY
Day 340 — 26 Remaining

"THE ABBOTT AND COSTELLO SHOW" TV PREMIERE: ANNIVERSARY. Dec 5, 1952. Bud Abbott and Lou Costello made 52 half-hour films for television incorporating many of their best burlesque routines. The show ran for two seasons, until 1954. Costello was born at Paterson, NJ, Mar 6, 1906, and died at East Los Angeles, CA, Mar 3, 1959. In 1966 Hanna-Barbera Productions produced an animated cartoon based on the characters of Abbott and Costello. Abbott supplied his own voice while Stan Irwin imitated Costello. Bud Abbott was born at Asbury Park, NJ, Oct 2, 1895, and died at Woodland Hills, CA, Apr 24, 1974.

ADORATION PARADE. Dec 5. Branson, MO. The 56th annual Adoration Parade will present a celebration of Christmas—the traditional values of faith, family and friendliness. For info: Branson Area CVB, PO Box 1897, Branson, MO 65615. Phone: (800) 296-0529. Fax: (417) 334-4139. E-mail: info@bransoncvb.com. Web: www.explorebranson.com.

AFL-CIO FOUNDED: ANNIVERSARY. Dec 5, 1955. The American Federation of Labor and the Congress of Industrial Organizations joined together in 1955, following 20 years of rivalry, to become the nation's leading advocate for trade unions.

BATHTUB PARTY DAY. Dec 5. Almost everyone nowadays takes showers, so here's a day to recall some of the warm water luxury of days gone by. Invite a few friends. [©2003 by WH.] For info: Thomas & Ruth Roy, Wellcat Holidays, 2418 Long Ln, Lebanon, PA 17046. Phone: (717) 279-0184. E-mail: info@wellcat.com. Web: www.wellcat.com.

BCHS CHRISTMAS OPEN HOUSE AND GINGERBREAD CONTEST. Dec 5. Ainsworth, NE. Displays, gingerbread houses, refreshments, sing-along at 2 PM. Annually, the first Sunday in December. Est attendance: 100. For info: Carol Larson, Brown County Historical Society, HC 65 Box 158, Ainsworth, NE 69210. E-mail: Carolarson10@hotmail.com.

CHRISTMAS TO REMEMBER. Dec 5. Laurel, MT. To officially open the Christmas season in Laurel, this daylong celebration includes the arrival of Santa, a community bazaar, children's craft activities, musical entertainment, lighting ceremony, parade of lights and fireworks. Annually, the first Sunday of December. Est attendance: 5,000. For info: Christmas to Remember Committee, Jean Carroll Thompson, PO Box 463, Laurel, MT 59044. Phone: (406) 248-8557.

CLERC-GALLAUDET WEEK. Dec 5–11. Week in which to celebrate the birth anniversaries of Laurent Clerc (Dec 26, 1785) and Thomas Hopkins Gallaudet (Dec 10, 1787). Clerc and Gallaudet pioneered education for the deaf in the US. Library activities will include a lecture on Clerc and Gallaudet and their contemporaries, storytelling for all ages and a display of books, videotapes, magazines, newspapers and posters. For info: Library for Deaf Action, 2930 Craiglawn Rd, Silver Spring, MD 20904-1816. Phone: (301) 572-5168 (TTY). Fax: (301) 572-4134. E-mail: alicehagemeyer@aol.com.

DISNEY, WALT: BIRTH ANNIVERSARY. Dec 5, 1901. Animator, filmmaker, theme park developer, born at Chicago, IL. Disney died at Los Angeles, CA, Dec 15, 1966.

GRANT'S SPEECH OF APOLOGY: ANNIVERSARY. Dec 5, 1876. President Ulysses S. Grant delivered his speech of apology to Congress claiming mistakes he made while he was president were due to his inexperience. His errors, he said, were "errors of judgment, not intent." While Grant's personal integrity was never formally questioned, he was closely associated with many government scandals which became public during his presidency. He unwittingly aided Jay Gould in an attempt to corner the gold market during his first term. During the second, the Credit Mobilier affair involving many of the president's friends aired, while significant fraud was discovered in the Treasury Department and Indian Service.

HAITI: DISCOVERY DAY: ANNIVERSARY. Dec 5. Commemorates the discovery of Haiti by Christopher Columbus in 1492. Public holiday.

HISTORIC HOMES PARLOR TOUR. Dec 5. Baker City, OR. Est attendance: 300. For info: Baker County Chamber & Visitors Center, 490 Campbell St, Baker City, OR 97814. Phone: (800) 523-1235.

"IRRATIONAL EXUBERANCE" ENTERS LEXICON: ANNIVERSARY. Dec 5, 1996. In a speech to the Washington, D.C.–based American Enterprise Institute for Policy Research, Federal Reserve Chairman Alan Greenspan uttered a new catch phrase that the media quickly saw as a warning about the high-flying 1990s stock market. He asked, "How do we know when irrational exuberance has unduly escalated asset values. . . And how do we factor that assessment into monetary policy?" Those two words, buried in an academic speech, nonetheless sparked panic in markets fearing the Fed would raise interest rates. The Tokyo, Hong Kong, Frankfurt, London and US markets dropped 2–4 percent after his speech. Most economists thought Greenspan was simply suggesting that markets needed to slow down a bit. But "irrational exuberance" lives on as Greenspan's most famous quote.

JINGLEBELL JOURNEY. Dec 5. Mount Wolf, PA. Enjoy a special holiday tour of seven creatively decorated homes and a historical landmark. They are all decked out in their holiday finery and say WELCOME to all. Enjoy more holiday atmosphere as the Northeastern Senior Community Center opens its doors and provides visitors with musical entertainment, a seniors art show, handmade crafts, homemade tea breads, cookies and wassail. Proceeds from the tour provide funding to the Senior Center to supply and improve services offered to the area's senior citizens. Annually, the third Sunday before Christmas. For info: Northeastern Senior Community Center, 131 Center St, PO Box 386, Mt Wolf, PA 17347. Phone: (717) 266-1400.

MONTGOMERY BUS BOYCOTT BEGINS: ANNIVERSARY. Dec 5, 1955. Rosa Parks was arrested at Montgomery, AL, for refusing to give up her seat on a bus to a white man. In support of Parks, and to protest the arrest, the black community of Montgomery organized a boycott of the bus system. The boycott lasted from Dec 5, 1955, to Dec 20, 1956, when a US Supreme Court ruling was implemented at Montgomery, integrating the public transportation system.

NATIONAL COMMUNICATE WITH YOUR KIDS DAY. Dec 5. A day that promotes open and ongoing communication between parents and children with a special emphasis on early childhood communication. Annually, Dec 5. For info: Diane Ryan, 147 Carolwood Blvd, Fern Park, FL 32730. Phone: (407) 767-2966. E-mail: kindersigns@msn.com. Web: www.kindersigns.com.

December 2004	S	M	T	W	T	F	S
				1	2	3	4
	5	6	7	8	9	10	11
	12	13	14	15	16	17	18
	19	20	21	22	23	24	25
	26	27	28	29	30	31	

PICKETT, BILL: BIRTH ANNIVERSARY. Dec 5, 1870. American rodeo cowboy, born at Williamson County, TX; died Apr 21, 1932, at Tulsa, OK. Inventor of bulldogging, the modern rodeo event that involves wrestling a running steer to the ground.

THAILAND: KING'S BIRTHDAY AND NATIONAL DAY. Dec 5. Celebrated throughout the kingdom with colorful pageantry. Stores and houses decorated with spectacular illuminations at night. Public holiday.

THURMOND, STROM: BIRTH ANNIVERSARY. Dec 5, 1902. The longest serving senator in American history, James Strom Thurmond was born at Edgefield, SC. The only senator ever elected by a write-in vote, he joined the US Senate in 1954. He was elected as both a Democrat and a Republican, and is remembered for his record-breaking filibuster protesting pending civil rights legislation. He did not yield the floor for 24 hours, 18 minutes over Aug 28–29, 1957, although the legislation did pass less than 2 hours later. He served in the Senate until Nov 19, 2002, just a few weeks shy of his 100th birthday. He died at Edgefield on June 26, 2003.

TWENTY-FIRST AMENDMENT TO THE US CONSTITUTION RATIFIED: ANNIVERSARY. Dec 5, 1933. Prohibition ended with the repeal of the Eighteenth Amendment, as the Twenty-First Amendment was ratified. Congress proposed repeal of Amendment XVIII (". . . the manufacture, sale, or transportation of intoxicating liquors, within, the importation thereof into, or the exportation thereof from the United States and all territory subject to the jurisdiction thereof, for beverage purposes is hereby prohibited. . . .") Feb 20, 1933. By Dec 5, 1933, the repeal amendment had been ratified by the required 36 states and went into effect immediately as Amendment XXI to the US Constitution.

UNITED NATIONS: INTERNATIONAL VOLUNTEER DAY FOR ECONOMIC AND SOCIAL DEVELOPMENT. Dec 5. In a resolution of Dec 17, 1985, the United Nations General Assembly recognized the desirability of encouraging the work of all volunteers. It invited governments to observe annually on Dec 5 the "International Volunteer Day for Economic and Social Development, urging them to take measures to heighten awareness of the important contribution of volunteer service." A day commemorating the establishment in December 1970 of the UN Volunteers program and inviting world recognition of volunteerism in the international development movement. For info: United Nations, Dept of Public Info, Public Inquiries Unit, Rm GA-57, New York, NY 10017. Phone: (212) 963-4475. E-mail: inquiries@un.org. Web: www.un.org.

VAN BUREN, MARTIN: BIRTH ANNIVERSARY. Dec 5, 1782. The eighth president of the US (term of office: Mar 4, 1837–Mar 3, 1841) was the first to have been born a citizen of the US. He was a widower for nearly two decades before he entered the White House. His daughter-in-law, Angelica, served as White House hostess during an administration troubled by bank and business failures, depression and unemployment. Van Buren was born at Kinderhook, NY, and died there July 24, 1862.

WHEATLEY, PHILLIS: DEATH ANNIVERSARY. Dec 5, 1784. Born at Senegal, West Africa about 1753 or 1754, Phillis Wheatley was brought to the US in 1761 and purchased as a slave by a Boston tailor named John Wheatley. She was allotted unusual privileges for a slave, including being allowed to learn to read and write. She wrote her first poetry at age 14, and her first work was published in 1770. Wheatley's fame as a poet spread throughout Europe as well as the US after her *Poems on Various Subjects, Religious and Moral* was published at England in 1773. She was invited to visit George Washington's army headquarters after she read a poem she had written about him in 1776. Phillis Wheatley died at about age 30, at Boston, MA.

WOLF POINT'S ANNUAL CHRISTMAS PARADE. Dec 5. Wolf Point, MT. The city comes alive with the Christmas spirit in this magical and enchanting evening which features a parade in which all the floats are illuminated with lights, Santa is the master of ceremonies and awards for floats are given in three categories. This event will make you remember what Christmas looks like through the eyes of a child. Est attendance: 1,000. For info: Wolf Point Chamber of Commerce, 218 3rd Ave S, Ste B, Wolf Point, MT 59201. Phone: (406) 653-2012. E-mail: wpchmber@nemontel.net.

WSBA/WARM 103 CHRISTMAS CRAFT SHOW. Dec 5. York Fairgrounds, York, PA. More than 250 craft displays, from country to contemporary, Victorian and southwestern, hand-crafted furniture, wood carvings, dolls, jewelry, pottery, collectibles, quilts, baskets, fine arts and much more. Admission fee. Est attendance: 4,000. For info: Joe Alfano, Asst Promo Dir, PO Box 910, York, PA 17402-0910. Phone: (717) 764-1155. Fax: (717) 252-4807. E-mail: jalfano@suscom.com. Web: www.warm103.com.

BIRTHDAYS TODAY

Morgan Brittany, 54, actress ("Dallas," "Glitter"), born Suzanne Cupito, Hollywood, CA, Dec 5, 1950.
José Carreras, 58, opera singer, one of the "Three Tenors," born Barcelona, Spain, Dec 5, 1946.
Margaret Cho, 36, actress ("All-American Girl"), comedienne, born San Francisco, CA, Dec 5, 1968.
Joan Didion, 70, author, journalist (*After Henry, Run River, The White Album*), born Sacramento, CA, Dec 5, 1934.
Jeroen Krabbe, 60, actor (*A World Apart, King of the Hill, The Fugitive*), born Amsterdam, the Netherlands, Dec 5, 1944.
Little Richard, 69, singer ("Tutti Frutti," "Long Tall Sally"), songwriter, born Richard Penniman, Macon, GA, Dec 5, 1935.
Jim Messina, 57, singer ("Your Mama Don't Dance"), songwriter, born Maywood, CA, Dec 5, 1947.
Chad Mitchell, 68, lead singer (Chad Mitchell trio, "Lizzie Borden"), born Spokane, WA, Dec 5, 1936.
Art Monk, 47, former football player, born White Plains, NY, Dec 5, 1957.
Frankie Muniz, 19, actor ("Malcolm in the Middle," *My Dog Skip*), born Ridgewood, NJ, Dec 5, 1985.
Calvin Trillin, 69, author (*American Stories, Remembering Denny*), born Kansas City, MO, Dec 5, 1935.

DECEMBER 6 — MONDAY
Day 341 — 25 Remaining

ALTAMONT CONCERT: 35th ANNIVERSARY. Dec 6, 1969. A free concert featuring performances by the Rolling Stones, Jefferson Airplane, Santana, Crosby, Stills, Nash and Young and the Flying Burrito Brothers turned into tragedy. The "thank-you" concert for 300,000 fans was marred by overcrowding, drug overdoses and the fatal stabbing of a spectator by a member of the Hell's Angels motorcycle gang, who had been hired as security guards for the event. The concert was held at the Altamont Speedway, Livermore, CA.

CENTRAL AFRICAN REPUBLIC: NATIONAL DAY OBSERVED. Dec 6. Commemorates Proclamation of the Republic Dec 1, 1958. Usually observed on the first Monday in December.

Dec 6   ☆ *Chase's 2004 Calendar of Events* ☆

ECUADOR: DAY OF QUITO. Dec 6. Commemorates founding of city of Quito by Spaniards in 1534.

EISENSTAEDT, ALFRED: BIRTH ANNIVERSARY. Dec 6, 1898. American photojournalist Alfred Eisenstaedt was born at Dirschau, Prussia. One of the greatest photojournalists in US history, he is best known for his 86 photos that were used on covers of *Life* magazine, including the iconic image of a sailor kissing a nurse in New York's Times Square at the end of World War II. He died Aug 23, 1995, at Martha's Vineyard, MA.

ELECTRIC LIGHT PARADE. Dec 6. Downtown Lovington, NM. Christmas shines in Lovington with more than 60 entries including floats, motorhomes, cars and motorcycles decorated with Christmas lights. Annually, early December. Est attendance: 7,000. For info: Lovington Chamber of Commerce, 201 S Main St, Lovington, NM 88260. Phone: (505) 396-5311. E-mail: visitus@leaconet.com. Web: visitus.leaco.net.

EVERGLADES NATIONAL PARK ESTABLISHED: ANNIVERSARY. Dec 6, 1947. Part of vast marshland area on southern Florida peninsula, originally authorized May 30, 1934, was established as a national park.

FINLAND: INDEPENDENCE DAY. Dec 6. National holiday. Declaration of independence from Russia in 1917.

GERALD FORD SWEARING-IN AS VICE PRESIDENT: ANNIVERSARY. Dec 6, 1973. Gerald Ford was sworn in as vice president under Richard Nixon, following the resignation of Spiro Agnew who pled no contest to a charge of income tax evasion. See also "Agnew, Spiro Theodore: Birth Anniversary" (Nov 9) and "Ford, Gerald Rudolph: Birthday" (July 14).

GERSHWIN, IRA: BIRTH ANNIVERSARY. Dec 6, 1896. Pulitzer Prize–winning American lyricist and author who collaborated with his brother, George, and with many other composers. Among his Broadway successes: *Lady Be Good, Funny Face, Strike Up the Band* and such songs as "The Man I Love," "Someone to Watch Over Me," "I Got Rhythm" and hundreds of others. Born at New York, NY, he died at Beverly Hills, CA, Aug 17, 1983.

HALIFAX, NOVA SCOTIA, DESTROYED: ANNIVERSARY. Dec 6, 1917. More than 1,650 people were killed at Halifax when the Norwegian ship *Imo* plowed into the French munitions ship *Mont Blanc*. *Mont Blanc* was loaded with 4,000 tons of TNT, 2,300 tons of picric acid, 61 tons of other explosives and a deck of highly flammable benzene, which ignited and touched off an explosion. In addition to those killed, 1,028 were injured. A tidal wave caused by the explosion washed much of the city out to sea.

KILMER, JOYCE (ALFRED): BIRTH ANNIVERSARY. Dec 6, 1886. American poet most famous for his poem "Trees," which was published in 1913, was born at New Brunswick, NJ. Kilmer was killed in action near Ourcy, France, in World War I, July 30, 1918. Camp Kilmer was named for him.

LEVINE, CHARLES A.: DEATH ANNIVERSARY. Dec 6, 1991. Charles A. Levine, whose efforts to beat Charles Lindbergh across the Atlantic by plane were stymied by a lawsuit, nevertheless became the first air passenger to cross the Atlantic Ocean. Levine's 225-horsepower plane, *The Columbia*, was grounded when one of his copilots filed a suit hours after Lindbergh took off from Roosevelt Field. Not to be overshadowed by Lindbergh's success, Levine announced that his flight, leaving June 4, 1927, would fly beyond Paris to Berlin, with himself as a passenger. Piloted by Clarence Chamberlin, the plane exhausted its fuel and landed at Eisleben, Germany, June 6, 100 miles short of his goal. The flight set a new record of 3,911 miles in 43 hours of nonstop flight, besting Lindbergh by approximately 300 miles. Levine was born at North Adams, MA, in 1897, and died at Washington, DC.

MISSOURI EARTHQUAKES: ANNIVERSARY. Dec 6, 1811. New Madrid, MO. Most prolonged series of earthquakes in US history occured not in California, but in the Midwest. Lasted until Feb 12, 1812. There were few deaths because of the sparse population. These were the most severe earthquakes in the contiguous US; those higher on the Richter scale have all occurred in Alaska.

MOST BORING CELEBRITIES OF THE YEAR. Dec 6. 21st annual list of celebrities chosen because of "massive media over-exposure" during the year. The list is posted prior to the event on our website to facilitate media coverage. For info: The Boring Institute, Alan Caruba, Founder, 9 Brookside Rd, Maplewood, NJ 07040. Phone: (973) 763-6392. E-mail: acaruba@aol.com. Web: www.boringinstitute.com.

NATIONAL PAWNBROKERS DAY. Dec 6. Celebrated on St. Nicholas Day, the patron saint of pawnbroking. Designed to acknowledge the valuable lending and retail services the pawnbroker provides his or her clientele. For info: Michael Goldstein, Empire Loan, 1130 Washington St, Boston, MA 02118. Phone: (617) 423-9366.

OPERATION SANTA PAWS. Dec 6–20. During the holiday season extra help is needed for abused and abandoned animals in the care of local animal shelters. One local grassroots organization, "Operation Santa Paws," is helping by spearheading a canine/feline toy/treat drive to benefit less-fortunate pets this season. Justin Rudd, organizer of this holiday effort, is encouraging animal lovers to purchase a new dog or cat toy, treat or supply that will be delivered in time for Christmas to local shelters and rescue organizations. For info: Justin Rudd. Phone: (562) 439-3316. E-mail: justinrudd@aol.com. Web: www.hautedogs.org.

SAINT NICHOLAS DAY. Dec 6. One of the most venerated saints of both Eastern and Western Christian churches, of whose life little is known, except that he was Bishop of Myra (in what is today's Turkey) in the fourth century, and that from early times he has been especially noted for his charity. Santa Claus and the presentation of gifts is said to derive from Saint Nicholas.

SPAIN: CONSTITUTION DAY. Dec 6. National holiday. Commemorates the voters' approval of a new constitution in 1978.

"TALENT SCOUTS" TV PREMIERE: ANNIVERSARY. Dec 6, 1948. Officially titled "Arthur Godfrey's Talent Scouts," this TV show was created when host Arthur Godfrey took his radio show to TV in 1948. On this talent show, celebrity guests introduced amateur and young professional acts. It was a weekly show until 1958. For several years beginning in 1960 it was a summer replacement series called "Celebrity Talent Scouts" and "Hollywood Talent Scouts." Hosts included Sam Levenson, Jim Backus, Merv Griffin and Art Linkletter. Pat Boone, Shari Lewis and the McGuire Sisters got their start here.

THIRTEENTH AMENDMENT TO THE US CONSTITUTION RATIFIED: ANNIVERSARY. Dec 6, 1865. The Thirteenth Amendment to the Constitution was ratified, abolishing slavery in the US. "Neither slavery nor involuntary servitude, save as a punishment for crime whereof the party shall have been duly convicted, shall exist within the United States, or any place subject to their jurisdiction." This amendment was proclaimed Dec 18, 1865. The Thirteenth, Fourteenth and Fifteenth amendments are considered the Civil War Amendments. See also: "Emancipation Proclamation: Anniversary" (Jan 1) for Lincoln's proclamation freeing slaves in the rebelling states.

December 2004	S	M	T	W	T	F	S
				1	2	3	4
	5	6	7	8	9	10	11
	12	13	14	15	16	17	18
	19	20	21	22	23	24	25
	26	27	28	29	30	31	

☆ Chase's 2004 Calendar of Events ☆   Dec 6–7

BIRTHDAYS TODAY

Dave Brubeck, 84, jazz musician, born Concord, CA, Dec 6, 1920.
Otto Graham, 83, Hall of Fame football player, former coach, born Waukegan, IL, Dec 6, 1921.
Macy Gray, 35, singer, born Canton, OH, Dec 6, 1969.
Thomas Hulce, 51, actor (*Amadeus, Parenthood*), born Plymouth, MI, Dec 6, 1953.
James Naughton, 59, actor (*The Paper Chase, The Good Mother*; stage: *Long Day's Journey into Night*), born Middletown, CT, Dec 6, 1945.
Don Nickles, 56, US Senator (R, Oklahoma), born Ponca City, OK, Dec 6, 1948.
Janine Turner, 42, actress ("Northern Exposure," *Cliffhanger*), born Lincoln, NE, Dec 6, 1962.
JoBeth Williams, 51, actress (*The Big Chill*, "Payne"), born Houston, TX, Dec 6, 1953.
Steven Wright, 49, comedian, born New York, NY, Dec 6, 1955.

DECEMBER 7 — TUESDAY
Day 342 — 24 Remaining

ARMENIAN EARTHQUAKE OF 1988: ANNIVERSARY. Dec 7, 1988. An earthquake measuring 6.9 on the Richter scale rocked the Soviet province of Armenia killing upward of 60,000 people. Many of the deaths were blamed on poor construction practices as many homes had been made of adobe, mud, stones, had unreinforced masonry or were prefabricated structures made of loosely connected concrete slabs. In the quake's aftermath, Soviet President Mikhail Gorbachev cut short his trip to the US to fly home and head the massive worldwide relief efforts.

CATHER, WILLA SIBERT: BIRTH ANNIVERSARY. Dec 7, 1873. American author born at Winchester, VA. Died at New York, NY, Apr 24, 1947. Best known for her novels about the development of early 20th-century American life, such as *O Pioneers!* and *My Antonia*. She won a Pulitzer Prize in 1922 for her book *One of Ours*.

CHAPIN, HARRY: BIRTH ANNIVERSARY. Dec 7, 1942. Folk singer/songwriter Harry Chapin was one of only five songwriters to receive the Special Congressional Gold Medal for his devotion to the issue of hunger throughout the world. Born at New York, NY, he was killed in a car accident July 16, 1981, at Long Island, NY.

CLUTE'S CHRISTMAS IN THE PARK. Dec 7–10. Clute Municipal Park, Clute, TX. A Christmas event with nightly entertainment, Santa's Land, a beautifully decorated Christmas tree forest and a marshmallow roasting pit. Great family fun for all ages. Food and crafts. Annually, in December. Est attendance: 4,500. For info: Clute Parks and Recreation, PO Box 997, Clute, TX 77531. Phone: (800) 371-2971 or (979) 265-8392. Fax: (979) 265-8767.

CÔTE D'IVOIRE: COMMEMORATION DAY. Dec 7. National holiday. Commemorates the death of the first president, Félix Houphouët-Boigny, in 1993.

DELAWARE RATIFIES CONSTITUTION: ANNIVERSARY. Dec 7, 1787. Delaware became the first state to ratify the proposed Constitution. It did so by unanimous vote.

NATIONAL FIRE SAFETY COUNCIL: 25th FOUNDING ANNIVERSARY. Dec 7, 1979. Founded to promote fire and burn prevention and life safety awareness. Council distributes comprehensive material to children and adults through local fire departments and the Council's mascot, Safetypup®. For info: Natl Fire Safety Council Inc, PO Box 378, Michigan Center, MI 49254-0378. Phone: (517) 764-2811.

★**NATIONAL PEARL HARBOR REMEMBRANCE DAY.** Dec 7.

PEARL HARBOR DAY: ANNIVERSARY. Dec 7, 1941. At 7:55 AM (local time) Dec 7, 1941, "a date that will live in infamy," nearly 200 Japanese aircraft attacked Pearl Harbor, Hawaii, long considered the US "Gibraltar of the Pacific." The raid, which lasted little more than one hour, left nearly 3,000 dead. Nearly the entire US Pacific Fleet was at anchor there and few ships escaped damage. Several were sunk or disabled, while 200 US aircraft on the ground were destroyed. The attack on Pearl Harbor brought about immediate US entry into WWII, a Declaration of War being requested by President Franklin D. Roosevelt and approved by the Congress Dec 8, 1941.

SPACE MILESTONE: *APOLLO 17* (US). Dec 7, 1972. Launched this date with three-man crew: Eugene A. Cernan, Harrison H. Schmidt, Ronald E. Evans, who explored the moon, Dec 11–14. Lunar landing module named *Challenger*. Pacific splashdown, Dec 19. This was the last manned mission to the moon.

SPACE MILESTONE: *GALILEO* (US). Dec 7, 1995. Launched Oct 18, 1989, by the space shuttle *Atlantis*, the spacecraft *Galileo* entered the orbit of Jupiter after a six-year journey. It has been orbiting Jupiter ever since, sending out probes to study three of its moons. Organic compounds, the ingredients of life, were found on them. On May 25, 2001, it passed within 86 miles of Callisto, one of Jupiter's moons.

TUSSAUD, MARIE GROSHOLTZ: BIRTH ANNIVERSARY. Dec 7, 1761. Creator of Madame Tussaud's waxwork museum, born at Strasbourg, France. Some of the wax figures she created are still on view at Madame Tussaud's at London. She died at London, Apr 15, 1850.

UNITED NATIONS: INTERNATIONAL CIVIL AVIATION DAY. Dec 7. On Dec 6, 1996, the General Assembly proclaimed Dec 7 as International Civil Aviation Day. On Dec 7, 1944, the convention on International Civil Aviation, which established the International Civil Aviation Organization, was signed. For info: United Nations, Dept of Public Info, New York, NY 10017. Web: www.un.org.

BIRTHDAYS TODAY

Johnny Lee Bench, 57, Hall of Fame baseball player, born Oklahoma City, OK, Dec 7, 1947.
Larry Joe Bird, 48, Hall of Fame basketball player, former coach, born West Baden, IN, Dec 7, 1956.
Ellen Burstyn, 72, actress (*Alice Doesn't Live Here Anymore; The Exorcist; Same Time, Next Year*), born Edna Rae Gilhooley, Detroit, MI, Dec 7, 1932.
Thad Cochran, 67, US Senator (R, Mississippi), born Pontotoc, MS, Dec 7, 1937.
Susan M. Collins, 52, US Senator (R, Maine), born Caribou, ME, Dec 7, 1952.
Edd Hall, 46, announcer ("The Tonight Show with Jay Leno"), born Boston, MA, Dec 7, 1958.
C. Thomas Howell, 38, actor ("Two Marriages," *Soul Man, Tank*), born Los Angeles, CA, Dec 7, 1966.
Tino Martinez, 37, baseball player, born Tampa, FL, Dec 7, 1967.
Tom Waits, 55, singer, songwriter ("I Never Talk to Strangers"), actor (*Down by Law, Short Cuts*), born Pomona, CA, Dec 7, 1949.
Eli Wallach, 89, actor (*The Tiger Makes Out*; Emmy for "The Poppy Is Also a Flower"), born New York, NY, Dec 7, 1915.

DECEMBER 8 — WEDNESDAY
Day 343 — 23 Remaining

AMERICA ENTERS WORLD WAR II: ANNIVERSARY. Dec 8, 1941. One day after the surprise Japanese attack on Pearl Harbor, Congress declared war against Japan and the US entered World War II.

AMERICAN FEDERATION OF LABOR (AFL) FOUNDED: ANNIVERSARY. Dec 8, 1886. Originally founded at Pittsburgh, PA, as the Federation of Organized Trades and Labor Unions of the United States and Canada in 1881, the union was reorganized in 1886 under the name American Federation of Labor (AFL). The AFL was dissolved as a separate entity in 1955 when it merged with the Congress of Industrial Organizations to form the AFL-CIO. See also: "AFL-CIO Founded: Anniversary (Dec 5)."

CHANUKAH. Dec 8–15. Feast of Lights or Feast of Dedication. Festival lasting eight days commemorates victory of Maccabees over Syrians (165 BC) and rededication of Temple of Jerusalem. Begins on Hebrew calendar date Kislev 25, 5765. Began at sundown on Dec 7.

CHINESE NATIONALISTS MOVE TO FORMOSA: 55th ANNIVERSARY. Dec 8, 1949. The government of Chiang Kai-Shek moved to Formosa (Taiwan) after being driven out of Mainland China by the Communists led by Mao Tse-Tung.

DAVIS, SAMMY, JR: BIRTH ANNIVERSARY. Dec 8, 1925. Born at New York, NY, Sammy Davis, Jr, was the son of vaudevillians and first appeared on the stage at the age of four. He made his first film appearance in *Rufus Jones for President* in 1931. He joined the Will Mastin Trio, a song-and-dance team popular on the night club circuit; as Davis matured, his singing, dancing and impersonations became the center of the act. Davis began performing on his own in the 1950s, headlining club engagements, appearing on television variety shows and making numerous records. His Broadway debut came in 1956 in the hit musical *Mr Wonderful*, and in the late '50s and early '60s he starred in a number of films, including a series with Frank Sinatra and the Rat Pack. Davis died at Los Angeles, CA, May 16, 1990.

DURANT, WILLIAM CRAPO: BIRTH ANNIVERSARY. Dec 8, 1861. "Billy" Durant, a leading producer of carriages at Flint, MI; promoter of the Buick car; cofounder of Chevrolet and founder, in 1908, of General Motors. He lost, regained and again lost control of GM, after which he founded Durant Motors, went bankrupt in the Depression and operated a Flint bowling alley in his last working years. Durant was born at Boston, MA, and died at New York, NY, Mar 18, 1947.

FEAST OF THE IMMACULATE CONCEPTION. Dec 8. Roman Catholic Holy Day of Obligation. A public holiday in Nicaragua.

FIRST STEP TOWARD A NUCLEAR-FREE WORLD: ANNIVERSARY. Dec 8, 1987. The former Soviet Union and the US signed a treaty at Washington eliminating medium-range and shorter-range missiles. This was the first treaty completely doing away with two entire classes of nuclear arms. These missiles, with a range of 500 to 5,500 kilometers, were to be scrapped under strict supervision within three years of the signing.

December 2004	S	M	T	W	T	F	S
				1	2	3	4
	5	6	7	8	9	10	11
	12	13	14	15	16	17	18
	19	20	21	22	23	24	25
	26	27	28	29	30	31	

GUAM: LADY OF CAMARIN DAY. Dec 8. Declared a legal holiday by Guam legislature, Mar 2, 1971.

HOBAN, JAMES: DEATH ANNIVERSARY. Dec 8, 1831. Irish-born architect who designed the US President's Executive Mansion, later known as The White House. He was born at Callan, County Kilkenny, Ireland, in 1762 (exact date unknown) and died at Washington, DC. The cornerstone for the White House, Washington's oldest public building, was laid in 1792.

HOLIDAY TOUR OF HOMES. Dec 8, 10–11, 15, 17–18. Natchitoches, LA. Come join us for the magic and the beauty of Christmas in historic Natchitoches. Christmas will be brought to life this holiday season during the "Christmas by Candlelight" tour. Each tour day will have three homes on tour. Come join us for this wonderful experience. Admission. Est attendance: 1,500. For info: Natchitoches Parish Tourist Commission. Phone: (800) 259-1714. Web: www.natchitoches.net.

MORRISON, JIM: BIRTH ANNIVERSARY. Dec 8, 1943. Singer, songwriter, known as "The Lizard King," lead singer of The Doors, Jim Morrison is considered to be one of the fathers of contemporary rock. Born at Melbourne, FL, and died at Paris, France, July 3, 1971.

NAFTA SIGNED: ANNIVERSARY. Dec 8, 1993. President Clinton signed the North American Free Trade Agreement, which cut tariffs and eliminated other trade barriers between the US, Canada and Mexico. The Agreement went into effect Jan 1, 1994.

RIVERA, DIEGO: BIRTH ANNIVERSARY. Dec 8, 1886. Mexican painter whose murals became center of political controversy, born at Guanajuato, Mexico. Died in his studio at San Angel, near Mexico City, Nov 25, 1957.

SEGAR, ELZIE CRISLER: BIRTH ANNIVERSARY. Dec 8, 1894. Popeye creator Elzie Crisler Segar was born at Chester, IL. Originally called *Thimble Theater*, the comic strip that came to be known as *Popeye* had the unusual format of a one-act play in cartoon form. Centered on the Oyl family, especially daughter Olive, the strip introduced a new central character in 1929. A one-eyed sailor with bulging muscles, Popeye became the strip's star attraction almost immediately. Popeye made it to the silver screen in animated form and in 1980 became a movie with Robin Williams playing the lead. Segar died Oct 13, 1938, at Santa Monica, CA.

SOVIET UNION DISSOLVED: ANNIVERSARY. Dec 8, 1991. The Union of Soviet Socialist Republics ceased to exist, as the republics of Russia, Byelorussia and Ukraine signed an agreement at Minsk, Byelorussia, creating the Commonwealth of Independent States. The remaining republics, with the exception of Georgia, joined in the new Commonwealth as it began the slow and arduous process of removing the yoke of Communism and dealing with strong separatist and nationalistic movements within the various republics.

THURBER, JAMES: BIRTH ANNIVERSARY. Dec 8, 1894. James Grover Thurber, American humorist and artist, long-time contributor to the *New Yorker*, born at Columbus, OH. Died at New York, NY, Nov 2, 1961.

UZBEKISTAN: CONSTITUTION DAY. Dec 8. National holiday. Commemorates the constitution of 1991.

WHITNEY, ELI: BIRTH ANNIVERSARY. Dec 8, 1765. Inventor of the cotton gin, born at Westboro, MA. Died at New Haven, CT, Jan 8, 1825.

BIRTHDAYS TODAY

Gregg Allman, 57, singer ("Ramblin' Man"), actor (*Rush*), born Nashville, TN, Dec 8, 1947.
Kim Basinger, 51, actress (*The Natural, The Getaway, My Stepmother Is an Alien*), born Athens, GA, Dec 8, 1953.
Gordon Arthur ("Red") Berenson, 63, former hockey player and coach, born Regina, SK, Canada, Dec 8, 1941.
David Carradine, 64, actor (*Boxcar Bertha*, "Kung-Fu" series), born Hollywood, CA, Dec 8, 1940.
James Galway, 65, flutist, born Belfast, Northern Ireland, Dec 8, 1939.
Jeff George, 37, former football player, born Indianapolis, IN, Dec 8, 1967.
Teri Hatcher, 40, actress ("Lois & Clark"), born Sunnyvale, CA, Dec 8, 1964.
James MacArthur, 67, actor ("Hawaii Five-O"), born Los Angeles, CA, Dec 8, 1937.
Mike Mussina, 36, baseball player, born Williamsport, PA, Dec 8, 1968.
Sinead O'Connor, 38, singer, songwriter, born Dublin, Ireland, Dec 8, 1966.
Maximilian Schell, 74, actor (*Judgment at Nuremberg, The Odessa File*), producer, born Vienna, Austria, Dec 8, 1930.
Mary Woronov, 58, actress (*Rock 'n' Roll High School, Eating Raoul*), born Brooklyn, NY, Dec 8, 1946.

DECEMBER 9 — THURSDAY
Day 344 — 22 Remaining

AMERICA'S FIRST FORMAL CREMATION: ANNIVERSARY. Dec 9, 1792. The first formal cremation of a human body in America took place near Charleston, SC. Henry Laurens, Colonial statesman and signer of the Treaty of Paris, ending the Revolutionary War, in his will provided: "I do solemnly enjoin it on my son, as an indispensable duty, that as soon as he conveniently can, after my decease, he cause my body to be wrapped in twelve yards of tow cloth and burned until it be entirely consumed, and then, collecting my bones, deposit them wherever he may think proper." Laurens died Dec 8, 1792, at his plantation, and was cremated there.

BIRDSEYE, CLARENCE: BIRTH ANNIVERSARY. Dec 9, 1886. American industrialist who developed a way of deep-freezing foods. He was marketing frozen fish by 1925 and was one of the founders of General Foods Corporation. Born at Brooklyn, NY, he died at New York City, Oct 7, 1956.

FOXX, REDD: BIRTH ANNIVERSARY. Dec 9, 1922. Born John Elroy Sanford at St. Louis, MO, Redd Foxx plied his comedic trade on vaudeville stages, in nightclubs, on television, in films and on record albums. His talents reached a national audience with the TV sitcom "Sanford and Son." He died after collapsing during a rehearsal for a new TV sitcom, "The Royal Family," at Los Angeles, CA, Oct 11, 1991.

GENOCIDE CONVENTION: ANNIVERSARY. Dec 9, 1948. The United Nations General Assembly unanimously approved the Convention on Prevention and Punishment of the Crime of Genocide on Dec 9, 1948. It took effect Jan 12, 1951, when ratification by 20 nations had been completed. President Truman sent it to the US Senate for approval on June 16, 1949; it was supported by Presidents Kennedy, Johnson, Nixon, Ford, Carter and Reagan. Thirty-seven years after its submission, and after approval by more than 90 nations, the Senate approved it, Feb 19, 1986, by a vote of 83–11.

HARRIS, JOEL CHANDLER: BIRTH ANNIVERSARY. Dec 9, 1848. American author, creator of the "Uncle Remus" stories, born at Eatonton, GA. Died July 3, 1908, at Atlanta, GA.

HOPPER, GRACE: BIRTH ANNIVERSARY. Dec 9, 1906. Born at New York, NY. When she retired from the US Navy at the age of 79, she was the oldest naval officer ever on active duty. She attained the rank of Rear Admiral and was a leader in the computer revolution, having developed the computer language COBOL. Grace Hopper died Jan 1, 1992, at Arlington, WV.

KELLY, EMMETT: BIRTH ANNIVERSARY. Dec 9, 1898. American circus clown and entertainer, born at Sedan, KS. Kelly was best known for "Weary Willie," a clown dressed in tattered clothes, with a beard and large nose. Died at Sarasota, FL, Mar 28, 1979.

MILTON, JOHN: BIRTH ANNIVERSARY. Dec 9, 1608. English poet and defender of freedom of the press born at Bread Street, Cheapside, London. Died from gout, Nov 8, 1674, at London, England. "No man who knows aught," he wrote, "can be so stupid to deny that all men naturally were born free."

PETRIFIED FOREST NATIONAL PARK ESTABLISHED: ANNIVERSARY. Dec 9, 1962. Arizona's Petrified Forest National Monument, proclaimed Dec 8, 1906, was established as a national park. For further park info: Petrified Forest Natl Park, Petrified Forest Natl Park, AZ 86028.

SANDYS, EDWIN: BIRTH ANNIVERSARY. Dec 9, 1561. Sir Edwin Sandys, English statesman and one of the founders of the Virginia Colony (treasurer, the Virginia Company, 1619–20), born at Worcestershire, England. Died at Kent, England, in October 1629 (exact date unknown).

TANZANIA: INDEPENDENCE AND REPUBLIC DAY. Dec 9. Tanganyika became independent of Britain in 1961. The republics of Tanganyika and Zanzibar joined to become one state (Apr 27, 1964), renamed (Oct 29, 1964) the United Republic of Tanzania.

THOMASVILLE'S VICTORIAN CHRISTMAS. Dec 9–10 (tentative). Thomasville, GA. Downtown Thomasville relives Christmas past as it celebrates the Victorian era of the late 1800s. Costumed strollers and carolers, horse-drawn carriages, bell-ringers and colorful characters from the past fill the streets of downtown. Victorian-clad merchants welcome shoppers with hot cider and confections and street vendors offer Christmas delicacies. Free—wonderful family event. Est attendance: 30,000. For info: Sharlene Celaya, Thomasville Victorian Christmas, Thomasville Main Street, PO Box 1540, Thomasville, GA 31799. Phone: (229) 227-7020. E-mail: mainstrt@rose.net. Web: www.downtownthomasville.com.

BIRTHDAYS TODAY

Joan Armatrading, 54, singer, songwriter (*Me, Myself, I*), born Saint Kitts, West Indies, Dec 9, 1950.
Beau Bridges, 63, actor ("James Brady Story," *The Fabulous Baker Boys*), born Los Angeles, CA, Dec 9, 1941.
Richard Marvin (Dick) Butkus, 62, Hall of Fame football player, sportscaster, actor, born Chicago, IL, Dec 9, 1942.
Thomas Daschle, 57, US Senator (D, South Dakota), born Aberdeen, SD, Dec 9, 1947.
Judi Dench, 70, actress (*Mrs Brown, Iris*), born York, England, Dec 9, 1934.

Dec 9–10 ☆ *Chase's 2004 Calendar of Events* ☆

Kirk Douglas, 88, actor (*Champion, Lust for Life*), author, born Issur Danielovitch Demsky, Amsterdam, NY, Dec 9, 1916.
David Anthony Higgins, 43, actor ("Ellen," "Malcolm in the Middle"), born Des Moines, IA, Dec 9, 1961.
Thomas O. (Tom) Kite, Jr, 55, golfer, born Austin, TX, Dec 9, 1949.
Joe Lando, 43, actor ("Dr. Quinn, Medicine Woman"), born Chicago, IL, Dec 9, 1961.
John Malkovich, 51, actor (*The Killing Fields, The Sheltering Sky*), filmmaker, born Christopher, IL, Dec 9, 1953.
Dina Merrill, 79, actress (*Desk Set, Operation Petticoat*), born New York, NY, Dec 9, 1925.
Michael Nouri, 59, actor ("Search for Tomorrow," "Love and War," *Goodbye Columbus, Flashdance*), born Washington, DC, Dec 9, 1945.
Donny Osmond, 47, actor, singer ("Donny and Marie," stage: *Joseph and the Amazing Technicolor Dreamcoat*), born Ogden, UT, Dec 9, 1957.
Dick Van Patten, 76, actor ("Eight Is Enough," "Mama"), born Richmond Hill, NY, Dec 9, 1928.

DECEMBER 10 — FRIDAY
Day 345 — 21 Remaining

DEWEY, MELVIL: BIRTH ANNIVERSARY. Dec 10, 1851. American librarian and inventor of the Dewey decimal book classification system was born at Adams Center, NY. Born Melville Louis Kossuth Dewey, he was an advocate of spelling reform, urged use of the metric system and was interested in many other education reforms. Dewey died at Highlands County, FL, Dec 26, 1931.

DICKINSON, EMILY: BIRTH ANNIVERSARY. Dec 10, 1830. One of America's greatest poets, Emily Dickinson was born at Amherst, MA. She was reclusive, mysterious and frail in health. Seven of her poems were published during her life, but after her death her sister, Lavinia, discovered almost 2,000 more poems written on the backs of envelopes and other scraps of paper locked in her bureau. They were published gradually, over 50 years, beginning in 1890. She died May 15, 1886, at Amherst, MA. The little-known Emily Dickinson who was born, lived and died at Amherst now is recognized as one of the most original poets of the English-speaking world.

FIRST GRAND OLE OPRY BROADCAST: ANNIVERSARY. Dec 10, 1927. Grand Ole Opry made its first radio broadcast from Nashville, TN.

FIRST US HEAVYWEIGHT CHAMP DEFEATED IN ENGLAND: ANNIVERSARY. Dec 10, 1810. Tom Molineaux, the first unofficial heavyweight champion of the US, was a freed slave from Virginia. He was beaten in the 40th round by Tom Cribb, the English champion, in a boxing match at Copthall Common at London.

FIRST US SCIENTIST RECEIVES NOBEL PRIZE: ANNIVERSARY. Dec 10, 1907. University of Chicago professor Albert Michelson, eminent physicist known for his research on the speed of light and optics became the first US scientist to receive the Nobel Prize.

GALLAUDET, THOMAS HOPKINS: BIRTH ANNIVERSARY. Dec 10, 1787. A hearing educator who, with Laurent Clerc, founded the first public school for deaf people, Connecticut Asylum for the Education and Instruction of Deaf and Dumb Persons (now the American School for the Deaf), at Hartford, CT, Apr 15, 1817. Gallaudet was born at Philadelphia, PA, and died Sept 9, 1851, at Hartford, CT.

HOLIDAY LANTERN TOURS. Dec 10–12 (also Dec 16–23, 26). Frontier Culture Museum, Staunton, VA. Evening guided lantern-light tours of four historic farms to see family vignettes about the holiday heritage of Christmas in 1720s Germany, 1730s Northern Ireland, 1690s England and 1850s Shenandoah Valley. Light refreshments in the Visitor Center after the tours. For info: Debbie Cole, Frontier Museum, 1290 Richmond Rd, PO Box 810, Staunton, VA 24401. Phone: (540) 332-7850. Fax: (540) 332-9989. E-mail: dcole@frontiermuseum.state.va.us. Web: www.frontiermuseum.org.

★**HUMAN RIGHTS DAY.** Dec 10. Presidential Proclamation 2866, of Dec 6, 1949, covers all succeeding years. Customarily issued as "Bill of Rights Day, Human Rights Day and Week."

★**HUMAN RIGHTS WEEK.** Dec 10–16. Presidential Proclamation issued since 1958 for the week of Dec 10–16, except in 1986. See also: "Human Rights Day" (Dec 10) and "Bill of Rights Day" (Dec 15).

LAMOUR, DOROTHY: 90th BIRTH ANNIVERSARY. Dec 10, 1914. Singer, actress (*The Hurricane, Road to Singapore*), born New Orleans, LA. Died Sept 22, 1996, at Los Angeles, CA.

"THE MIGHTY MOUSE PLAYHOUSE" TV PREMIERE: ANNIVERSARY. Dec 10, 1955. An all-time favorite of the Saturday-morning crowd (including adults). CBS had a hit with their pint-sized cartoon character Mighty Mouse, who was a tongue-in-cheek version of Superman. The show had other feature cartoons such as "The Adventures of Gandy Goose."

MISSISSIPPI: ADMISSION DAY: ANNIVERSARY. Dec 10. Became 20th state in 1817.

NOBEL PRIZE AWARDS CEREMONIES. Dec 10. Oslo, Norway and Stockholm, Sweden. Alfred Nobel, Swedish chemist and inventor of dynamite who died in 1896, provided in his will that income from his $9 million estate should be used for annual prizes—to be awarded to people who are judged to have made the most valuable contributions to the good of humanity. The Nobel Peace Prize is awarded by a committee of the Norwegian parliament and the presentation is made at the Oslo City Hall. Five other prizes, for physics, chemistry, medicine, literature and economics, are presented in a ceremony at Stockholm, Sweden. Both ceremonies traditionally are held on the anniversary of the death of Alfred Nobel. First awarded in 1901, the current value of each prize is about $1,000,000. To date, more than 250 Americans have won Nobel prizes. See also "Nobel, Alfred Bernhard: Birth Anniversary" (Oct 21).

NORTON, MARY: BIRTH ANNIVERSARY. Dec 10, 1903. British author Mary Norton was born at London, England. An author of children's books, she is best known for *Bedknob and Broomstick* (1957). She died Aug 29, 1992, at Hartland, England.

RALPH BUNCHE AWARDED NOBEL PEACE PRIZE: ANNIVERSARY. Dec 10, 1950. Dr. Ralph Johnson Bunche became the first black man awarded the Nobel Peace Prize. Bunche was awarded the prize for his efforts in mediation between Israel and neighboring Arab states in 1949.

	S	M	T	W	T	F	S
December				1	2	3	4
2004	5	6	7	8	9	10	11
	12	13	14	15	16	17	18
	19	20	21	22	23	24	25
	26	27	28	29	30	31	

☆ Chase's 2004 Calendar of Events ☆ Dec 10–11

RED CLOUD: 95th DEATH ANNIVERSARY. Dec 10, 1909. Sioux Indian chief Red Cloud was born in 1822 (exact date unknown), near North Platte, NE. A courageous leader and defender of Indian rights, Red Cloud was the son of Lone Man and Walks as She Thinks. His unrelenting determination caused US abandonment of the Bozeman trail and of three forts that interfered with Indian hunting grounds. Red Cloud died at Pine Ridge, SD.

SPACE MILESTONE: *SOYUZ 26* (USSR). Dec 10, 1977. Launched this date with Cosmonauts Yuri Romanenko and Georgi Grechko who linked it with *Salyut 6* space station on Dec 11, after the unsuccessful attempt by *Soyuz 25* earlier that year. Returned to Earth in *Soyuz 27*, Mar 16, 1978, after record-setting 96 days in space.

SUGARLOAF CRAFTS FESTIVAL. Dec 10–12. Montgomery County Fairgrounds, Gaithersburg, MD. This show, now in its 27th year, features more than 300 nationally recognized craft designers and fine artists displaying and selling their original creations. Includes craft demonstrations, live music, specialty foods, hourly gift certificate drawings, and more. Est attendance: 12,500. For info: Sugarloaf Mountain Works, 200 Orchard Ridge Dr, #215, Gaithersburg, MD 20878. Phone: (800) 210-9900. Fax: (301) 253-9620. Web: www.sugarloafcrafts.com.

THAILAND: CONSTITUTION DAY. Dec 10. National holiday. Commemorates the constitution of 1932, the nation's first.

TREATY OF PARIS ENDS SPANISH-AMERICAN WAR: ANNIVERSARY. Dec 10, 1898. Following the conclusion of the Spanish-American War in 1898, American and Spanish ambassadors met at Paris, France, to negotiate a treaty. Under the terms of this treaty, Spain granted the US the Philippine Islands and the islands of Guam and Puerto Rico, and agreed to withdraw from Cuba. Senatorial debate over the treaty centered on the US's move toward imperialism by acquiring the Philippines. A vote was taken Feb 6, 1899, and the treaty passed by a one-vote margin. President William McKinley signed the treaty Feb 10, 1899.

UNITED NATIONS: HUMAN RIGHTS DAY: ANNIVERSARY. Dec 10. Official United Nations observance day. Date is the anniversary of adoption of the "Universal Declaration of Human Rights" in 1948. The Declaration sets forth basic rights and fundamental freedoms to which all men and women everywhere in the world are entitled. For info: United Nations, Dept of Public Info, New York, NY 10017. E-mail: inquiries@un.org. Web: www.un.org.

WASSAIL CELEBRATION. Dec 10–12. Woodstock, VT. Activities include a horse rider and carriage parade, Santa comes to town, Wassail Dance, concert by The Ten Men's Vocal Choir, caroling and burning the yule log on the Village Green. Est attendance: 5,000. For info: David Murison, Exec Dir, Woodstock Area Chamber of Commerce, 18 Central St, PO Box 486, Woodstock, VT 05091. Phone: (802) 457-3555 or (888) 496-6378. E-mail: dave@woodstockvt.com. Web: www.woodstockvt.com.

BIRTHDAYS TODAY

Rod Blagojevich, 48, Governor of Illinois (D), born Chicago, IL, Dec 10, 1956.
Kenneth Branagh, 44, actor, director (*High Season, Henry V*), born Belfast, Northern Ireland, Dec 10, 1960.
Susan Dey, 52, model, actress ("The Partridge Family," "LA Law,"), born Pekin, IL, Dec 10, 1952.
Harold Gould, 81, actor ("Rhoda," "Under One Roof"), born Schenectady, NY, Dec 10, 1923.
Gloria Loring, 58, singer, actress ("Days of Our Lives"), born New York, NY, Dec 10, 1946.

DECEMBER 11 — SATURDAY
Day 346 — 20 Remaining

BUELL, MARJORIE H.: 100th BIRTH ANNIVERSARY. Dec 11, 1904. Cartoonist, creator of comic strip character Little Lulu, Marjorie Buell was considered a pioneer for creating a female character that outsmarted the neighborhood boys. She was born at Philadelphia, PA, and died May 30, 1993, at Elyria, OH.

BURKINA FASO: NATIONAL DAY: ANNIVERSARY. Dec 11. Gained independence within the French community, 1958.

CANNON, ANNIE JUMP: BIRTH ANNIVERSARY. Dec 11, 1863. American astronomer and discoverer of five stars, was born at Dover, DE. Author and winner of the National Academy of Science Draper Medal, she died at Cambridge, MA, Apr 13, 1941.

CHRISTMAS CANDLELIGHT TOUR. Dec 11–12. Fredericksburg, VA. To instill the spirit of Christmases past by opening historic homes to the public. Eighteenth-century music, street dancers, carriage rides throughout the tour. Est attendance: 10,000. For info: Visitor Center, 706 Caroline St, Fredericksburg, VA 22401. Phone: (800) 678-4748. Fax: (540) 372-6587. E-mail: gboswell@fburg.city.state.va.us.

DAY OF THE HORSE. Dec 11. The horse is a living link to the heritage and history of our nation, and represents a common bond among all peoples who led the way in building our country. Today, the horse industry contributes more than $112 billion annually to the American economy. Therefore, the California State Legislature has declared the second Saturday of December to be the Day of the Horse in honor of these magnificent creatures. For info: Reis Ranch, 411 Highland Ave, Penngrove, CA 94951. Phone: (800) 732-8220. E-mail: dreis@reisranch.com. Web: www.reisranch.com.

DICKENS OF A CHRISTMAS. Dec 11–12. Downtown Franklin, TN. 18th annual festival features living characters from *A Christmas Carol* as well as other Victorian characters including Father and Mother Christmas. Street vendors sell roasted chestnuts, plum pudding and hot chocolate. Horse-drawn carriage rides, musical, dramatic performances and town sing. Local artists and crafters create "living windows" by demonstrating their skills in shop windows and on the historic square. Est attendance: 50,000. For info: Shelly Spragins, Downtown Franklin Assn, PO Box 807, Franklin, TN 37065. Phone: (615) 595-1239. Fax: (615) 591-8502. E-mail: sspragins@historicfranklin.com. Web: www.historicfranklin.com.

EDWARD VIII ABDICATION: ANNIVERSARY. Dec 11, 1936. Christened Edward Albert Christian George Andrew Patrick David, King Edward VIII was born at Richmond Park, England, on June 12, 1894, and became Prince of Wales in July 1911. He ascended to the English throne upon the death of his father, George V, on Jan 20, 1936, but coronation never took place. He abdicated on Dec 11, 1936, in order to marry "the woman I love," twice-divorced American Wallis Warfield Simpson. They were married in France, June 3, 1937. Edward was named Duke of Windsor by his brother-successor, George VI. The Duke died at Paris, May 28, 1972, but was buried in England, near Windsor Castle.

HOLIDAY HOUSE TOURS. Dec 11–31. Ash Lawn–Highland, Home of James Monroe, Charlottesville, VA. House decorated inside and out with fresh greens, fruits and woodland seed pods. 10 AM–5 PM. Evening candlelight openings. Est attendance: 1,000.

621

For info: Ash Lawn–Highland, 1000 James Monroe Pkwy, Charlottesville, VA 22902. Phone: (434) 293-9539. Fax: (434) 293-8000. E-mail: info@ashlawnhighland.org. Web: www.ashlawnhighland.org.

HOLLYWOOD BEACH CANDY CANE PARADE. Dec 11. Hollywood, FL. More than 200 floats and marching units line the Hollywood Beach Boardwalk during this popular evening event. Est attendance: 30,000. For info: Roguey Doyle, City of Hollywood, Dept of Parks, Recreation & Cultural Arts, 1940 Harrison St, Ste 101, Hollywood, FL 33020. Phone: (954) 921-3404.

HOMESTEADERS HOLIDAY. Dec 11. Centennial Village Museum, Greeley, CO. Pioneer holiday family festival with candledipping, cowboy Santa, live reindeer, telegrams to North Pole, living history demos, musical entertainment, decorated homes, craft activities and food. Est attendance: 1,500. For info: Greeley Museums, 919 7th St, Greeley, CO 80631. Phone: (970) 350-9220. Fax: (970) 350-9700. Web: www.greeleymuseums.com.

INDIANA: ADMISSION DAY: ANNIVERSARY. Dec 11. Became 19th state in 1816.

INTERNATIONAL SHAREWARE DAY. Dec 11. A day to take the time to reward the efforts of thousands of computer programmers who trust that if we try their programs and like them, we will pay for them. Unfortunately, very few payments are received, thus stifling the programmers' efforts. This observance is meant to prompt each of us to inventory our PCs and Macs, see if we are using any shareware, and then take the time in the holiday spirit to write payment checks to the authors. Hopefully this will keep shareware coming. Annually, the second Saturday in December. For info: David Lawrence, Online Tonight, Net Music Countdown, 145 S Glenoaks Blvd, Ste 336, Burbank, CA 91501. Phone: (818) 563-3123. E-mail: david@onlinetonight.net. Web: onlinetonight.net.

LA GUARDIA, FIORELLO HENRY: BIRTH ANNIVERSARY. Dec 11, 1882. Popularly known as the "Little Flower," Fiorello H. La Guardia was not too busy as mayor of New York City to read the "funnies" to radio listeners during the New York newspaper strike. He said of himself: "When I make a mistake it's a beaut!" La Guardia was born at New York, NY, and died there Sept 20, 1947.

"MAGNUM, PI" TV PREMIERE: ANNIVERSARY. Dec 11, 1980. Premiered on CBS television network, starring Tom Selleck, John Hillerman, Roger E. Mosley and Larry Manetti. Each year on this anniversary, "Magnum" fans turn to the international fan organization "Magnum Memorabilia by David Romas" as the center of observances worldwide. For info: David Romas, Magnum Memorabilia, 1581 Moorhouse, Ferndale, MI 48220-1154. E-mail: ac2942@wayne.edu.

MOON PHASE: NEW MOON. Dec 11. Moon enters New Moon phase at 8:29 PM, EST.

OLD-FASHIONED DANISH CHRISTMAS. Dec 11. Dannebrog, NE. Days filled with Christmas Tree Fantasy, living nativity scene, crafters/working artists expo, music medley, Danish buffet luncheon, Danish pastry, Danish tree ornament cutouts demonstration and spectacular displays of holiday lights. Annually, the second Saturday in December. Est attendance: 1,200. For info: Shirley Johnson, Festival Coord, Dannebrog Area Booster Club, 522 E Roger Welsch Ave, Dannebrog, NE 68831. Phone: (308) 226-2237.

★ ★ ★

December 2004	S	M	T	W	T	F	S
				1	2	3	4
	5	6	7	8	9	10	11
	12	13	14	15	16	17	18
	19	20	21	22	23	24	25
	26	27	28	29	30	31	

PERIGEAN SPRING TIDES. Dec 11. Spring tides, the highest possible tides, which occur when New Moon or Full Moon takes place within 24 hours of the moment the Moon is nearest Earth (perigee) in its monthly orbit. These tides are not named for the season of spring but for the German *springen*, "to leap up."

34th STREET EXPRESS. Dec 11. Chartered Amtrak train leaves from Boston, MA. Christmas shopping special to New York City also takes in the Radio City Christmas Spectacular. Annually, the second Saturday in December. Est attendance: 500. For info: Mystic Valley Railway Society, Inc, PO Box 365486, Hyde Park, MA 02136-0009. Phone: (617) 361-4445. Fax: (617) 361-4445*51 (dial all as one number). Web: www.mysticvalleyrs.org.

UNITED NATIONS: UNICEF ANNIVERSARY. Dec 11, 1946. Anniversary of the establishment by the United Nations General Assembly of the United Nations International Children's Emergency Fund (UNICEF). For info: United Nations, Dept of Public Info, New York, NY 10017. Web: www.unicef.org.

VICTORIAN CHRISTMAS TOURS AT FRANK LLOYD WRIGHT HOME. Dec 11 (also Dec 18). Oak Park, IL. A wonderful Christmas tradition, the Frank Lloyd Wright Preservation Trust presents free Victorian Christmas tours of Wright's home in Oak Park. These tours feature stories of how the Wright family celebrated the holidays at the turn of the 20th century and are led by Junior Interpreters: specially trained middle and high school students who bring a new perspective to the tour experience. Free, but tickets required. Annually, the second and third Saturdays of Dec. For info: Frank Lloyd Wright Preservation Trust, 931 Chicago Ave, Oak Park, IL 60302. Phone: (708) 848-1976. Web: www.wrightplus.org.

A VICTORIAN YULETIDE. Dec 11–13. Clinton, MD. Candlelight tours with holiday greenery, antique toys, cards, ornaments, music and Father Christmas. Est attendance: 800. For info: Surratt House Museum, PO Box 427, Clinton, MD 20735. Phone: (301) 868-1121. Fax: (301) 868-8177. Web: www.surratt.org.

BIRTHDAYS TODAY

Max Baucus, 63, US Senator (D, Montana), born Helena, MT, Dec 11, 1941.

Jay Bell, 39, baseball player, born Pensacola, FL, Dec 11, 1965.

Gary Dourdan, 38, actor ("CSI"), born Philadelphia, PA, Dec 11, 1966.

Teri Garr, 55, actress (*Young Frankenstein, Tootsie, The Black Stallion*), born Lakewood, OH, Dec 11, 1949.

David Gates, 64, singer, songwriter, born Tulsa, OK, Dec 11, 1940.

Tom Hayden, 64, journalist, activist, politician, born Royal Oak, MI, Dec 11, 1940.

Jermaine Jackson, 50, singer, musician (Jackson 5), born Gary, IN, Dec 11, 1954.

John F. Kerry, 61, US Senator (D, Massachusetts), born Denver, CO, Dec 11, 1943.

Brenda Lee, 60, singer ("I'm Sorry," "All Alone Am I"), born Brenda Mae Tarpley, Atlanta, GA, Dec 11, 1944.

Donna Mills, 61, actress ("Knots Landing," "Melrose Place"), born Chicago, IL, Dec 11, 1943.

Rita Moreno, 73, singer, actress (Oscar for *West Side Story*; Tony for *The Ritz*), born Hunacao, Puerto Rico, Dec 11, 1931.

Carlo Ponti, 91, producer, born Milan, Italy, Dec 11, 1913.

Susan Seidelman, 52, filmmaker (*Desperately Seeking Susan, Making Mr Right*), born Philadelphia, PA, Dec 11, 1952.

☆ Chase's 2004 Calendar of Events ☆   Dec 11-12

Aleksandr Isayevich Solzhenitsyn, 86, author (*Cancer Ward, One Day in the Life of Ivan Denisovich, The Gulag Archipelago*), born Kislovodsk, USSR, Dec 11, 1918.

Rider Strong, 25, actor ("Boy Meets World"), born San Francisco, CA, Dec 11, 1979.

Ken Wahl, 51, actor ("Wiseguy," *The Wanderers, Fort Apache: The Bronx*), born Chicago, IL, Dec 11, 1953.

Curtis Williams, 42, musician, singer (Penguins, "Earth Angel"), born Buffalo, NY, Dec 11, 1962.

DECEMBER 12 — SUNDAY
Day 347 — 19 Remaining

BONZA BOTTLER DAY™. Dec 12. To celebrate when the number of the day is the same as the number of the month. Bonza Bottler Day™ is an excuse to have a party at least once a month. For more information, see Jan 1. For info: Gail M. Berger, 14 Fernwood Dr, Taylors, SC 29687. Phone: (864) 609-9874. E-mail: gberger5@aol.com.

DAY OF OUR LADY OF GUADALUPE. Dec 12. The legend of Guadalupe tells how in December 1531, an Indian, Juan Diego, saw the Virgin Mother on a hill near Mexico City, who instructed him to go to the bishop and have him build a shrine to her on the site of the vision. After his request was initially rebuffed, the Virgin Mother appeared to Juan Diego three days later. She instructed him to pick roses growing on a stony and barren hillside nearby and take them to the bishop as proof. Although flowers do not normally bloom in December, Juan Diego found the roses and took them to the bishop. As he opened his mantle to drop the roses on the floor, an image of the Virgin Mary appeared among them. The bishop built the sanctuary as instructed. Our Lady of Guadalupe became the patroness of Mexico City and by 1746 was the patron saint of all New Spain and by 1910 of all Latin America.

EIGHTEENTH-CENTURY CHRISTMAS WASSAIL. Dec 12. McLean, VA. Greet the winter solstice and Christmas season with a toast to the apple trees. Caroling and warm refreshments. Bring pots or other noisemakers to frighten off evil spirits threatening next year's apple crop. Est attendance: 800. For info: Pat Dubbin, Claude Moore Colonial Farm at Turkey Run, 6310 Georgetown Pike, McLean, VA 22101. Phone: (703) 442-7557. Fax: (703) 442-0714. Web: www.1771.org.

FIRST BLACK SERVES IN US HOUSE OF REPRESENTATIVES: ANNIVERSARY. Dec 12, 1870. Joseph Hayne Rainey of Georgetown, SC, was sworn in as the first black to serve in the US House of Representatives. Rainey filled the seat of Benjamin Franklin Whittemore, which had been declared vacant by the House. He served until Mar 3, 1879.

FLAUBERT, GUSTAVE: BIRTH ANNIVERSARY. Dec 12, 1821. French author whose works include one of the greatest French novels, *Madame Bovary*, was born at Rouen. Flaubert died at Croisset, France, May 8, 1880.

GINGERBREAD HOUSE DAY. Dec 12. One of the best activities of the Christmas season is the making of gingerbread houses. It's pure fun for all involved. Spend time with your family and create one today! For info: Allison Benson, 13116 Frog Hollow Ct, Oak Hill, VA 20171. Phone: (703) 471-5784. E-mail: Firebird121212@aol.com.

JAY, JOHN: BIRTH ANNIVERSARY. Dec 12, 1745 (OS). American statesman, diplomat and first chief justice of the US Supreme Court (1789–95), coauthor (with Alexander Hamilton and James Madison) of the influential *Federalist* papers, was born at New York, NY. Jay died at Bedford, NY, May 17, 1829.

KENYA: JAMHURI DAY: ANNIVERSARY. Dec 12. Jamhuri Day (Independence Day) is Kenya's official National Day, commemorating proclamation of the republic and independence from Britain in 1963.

MEXICO: GUADALUPE DAY. Dec 12. One of Mexico's major celebrations. Honors the "Dark Virgin of Guadalupe," the republic's patron saint. Parties and pilgrimages, with special ceremonies at the Shrine of Our Lady of Guadalupe at Mexico City.

NATIONAL CHILDREN'S MEMORIAL DAY. Dec 12. A day to remember the more than 79,000 children who die in the US every year. Annually, the second Sunday in December. For info: The Compassionate Friends, PO Box 3696, Oak Brook, IL 60522-3696. Phone: (877) 969-0010. E-mail: nationaloffice@compassionatefriends.org. Web: www.compassionatefriends.org.

PENNSYLVANIA RATIFIES CONSTITUTION: ANNIVERSARY. Dec 12, 1787. Pennsylvania became the second state to ratify the US Constitution, by a vote of 46 to 23, in 1787.

POINSETTIA DAY (JOEL ROBERTS POINSETT: DEATH ANNIVERSARY). Dec 12. A day to enjoy poinsettias and to honor Dr. Joel Roberts Poinsett, the American diplomat who introduced the Central American plant which is named for him into the US. Poinsett was born at Charleston, SC, Mar 2, 1799. He also served as a member of Congress and as secretary of war. He died near Statesburg, SC, Dec 12, 1851. The poinsettia has become a favorite Christmas season plant.

POLISH CHRISTMAS OPEN HOUSE. Dec 12. Polish American Cultural Center Museum, Philadelphia, PA. Sw. Mikolaj (Polish St. Nicholas) will greet everyone with gifts for the children. Polish Christmas Tree and entertainment. Free admission. For info: Polish American Cultural Center Museum, 308 Walnut St, Philadelphia, PA 19106. Phone: (215) 922-1700. Fax: (215) 922-1518. E-mail: mail@polishamericancenter.org. Web: www.polishamericancenter.org.

PUERTO RICO: LAS MAÑANITAS. Dec 12. Ponce, Puerto Rico. Procession at 5 AM honoring our patron saint, Virgen de la Guadalupe. Mass with music from a mariachi band; free breakfast afterwards. Anually, on Dec 12. For info: Elma Santiago, Tourism Dir, Municipality of Ponce, PO Box 331709, Ponce, PR 00733. Phone: (787) 841-8044. Fax: (787) 259-1316. E-mail: munponce@coqui.net. Web: ponceweb.org.

QUINCY PRESERVES CHRISTMAS CANDLELIGHT TOUR. Dec 12. Quincy, IL. Tour historic homes decked out in their Christmas finest. Each year this walking tour features a different neighborhood. Homes range in size from grand mansions to quaint cottages. Annually, the second Sunday in December. Est attendance: 1,000. For info: Fran Cook, Quincy Preserves, 310 S 16th St, Quincy, IL 62301. Phone: (217) 224-2587.

RUSSIA: CONSTITUTION DAY: ANNIVERSARY. Dec 12. National holiday commemorating the adoption of a new constitution in 1993.

SINATRA, FRANK: BIRTH ANNIVERSARY. Dec 12, 1915. Born at Hoboken, NJ, Frank Sinatra matured from a teen idol to the premier singer of American popular music. Known as the "Chairman of the Board" to his fans, he made more than 200 albums. His signature songs included "All the Way," "New York, New York" and "My Way." His film career included musicals (*On the Town* and *Pal Joey*) and two gritty films: *From Here to Eternity* (Oscar for Best Actor) and *The Man With the Golden Arm* (Oscar nomination). Died May 14, 1998, at Los Angeles, CA.

Dec 12–13 ☆ *Chase's 2004 Calendar of Events* ☆

SUPREME COURT RULES FOR BUSH: ANNIVERSARY. Dec 12, 2000. The Supreme Court ruled by a vote of 5 to 4 that there could be no further counting of Florida's disputed presidential votes, ending deliberations over the 2000 presidential election. After five weeks of conflict over this pivotal vote count in Florida, Democratic candidate Al Gore conceded the election to George W. Bush. While Bush won the electoral vote to become the nation's 43rd president, Gore won the popular vote. Bush was only the fourth president in American history to be elected without winning the popular vote.

TELL SOMEONE THEY'RE DOING A GOOD JOB WEEK. Dec 12–18. Every day this week tell someone "you're doing a good job." For info: Joe Hoppel, Radio Station WCMS, 5589 Greenwich Rd, Virginia Beach, VA 23462. Phone: (757) 671-1000. E-mail: wcmsradio@hotmail.com. Web: www.wcms.com.

TURKMENISTAN: NEUTRALITY DAY. Dec 12. National holiday. Commemorates the UN's recognition of Turkmenistan's neutrality in 1995.

WATIE, STAND: BIRTH ANNIVERSARY. Dec 12, 1806. Born at Rome, GA, and died there Sept 9, 1871. Cherokee chief who, by signing the treaty of New Echota, surrendered his people's land in Georgia, forcing relocation to Oklahoma. Though the three other signers were murdered, Watie escaped and went on to initiate the first volunteer Cherokee regiment for the Confederates in the Civil War. Promoted to brigadier general, he was active in destroying the property of other Native Americans who supported the Union.

BIRTHDAYS TODAY

Tracy Ann Austin, 42, former tennis player, born Rolling Hills Estates, CA, Dec 12, 1962.
Bob Barker, 81, TV personality, game-show host (Emmy for "The Price Is Right"), born Darrington, WA, Dec 12, 1923.
Mayim Bialik, 29, actress ("Blossom"), born San Diego, CA, Dec 12, 1975.
Jennifer Connelly, 34, actress (*Hulk,* Oscar for *A Beautiful Mind*), born Catskill Mountains, NY, Dec 12, 1970.
Sheila E, 45, singer, musician ("The Glamorous Life"), born Sheila Escoveda, San Francisco, CA, Dec 12, 1959.
Connie Francis, 66, singer ("Where the Boys Are"), born Constance Franconero, Newark, NJ, Dec 12, 1938.
Edward Irwin Koch, 80, former mayor of New York City, born New York, NY, Dec 12, 1924.
Robert Lindsay, 55, actor (*Me and My Girl* [Olivier, Tony, Theatre World and Drama Desk Awards]), born Derbyshire, England, Dec 12, 1949.
Robert Lee (Bob) Pettit, Jr, 72, Hall of Fame basketball player, born Baton Rouge, LA, Dec 12, 1932.
Cathy Rigby, 52, former Olympic gymnast, born Long Beach, CA, Dec 12, 1952.
Dionne Warwick, 63, singer ("I Say a Little Prayer for You," "This Girl's in Love With You"), born East Orange, NJ, Dec 12, 1941.
Tom Wilkinson, 56, actor (*In the Bedroom, The Full Monty*), born Leeds, West Yorkshire, England, Dec 12, 1948.

	S	M	T	W	T	F	S
December				1	2	3	4
2004	5	6	7	8	9	10	11
	12	13	14	15	16	17	18
	19	20	21	22	23	24	25
	26	27	28	29	30	31	

DECEMBER 13 — MONDAY
Day 348 — 18 Remaining

BROOKS, PHILLIPS: BIRTH ANNIVERSARY. Dec 13, 1835. American clergyman and composer born at Boston, MA. Best remembered for his lyrics for the Christmas carol "O Little Town of Bethlehem." Brooks died at Boston, Jan 23, 1893.

HEINE, HEINRICH: BIRTH ANNIVERSARY. Dec 13, 1797. German poet and critic, born at Dusseldorf. Died at Paris, France, Feb 17, 1856.

LINCOLN, MARY TODD: BIRTH ANNIVERSARY. Dec 13, 1818. Wife of Abraham Lincoln, sixteenth president of the US, born at Lexington, KY. Died at Springfield, IL, July 16, 1882.

MALTA: REPUBLIC DAY. Dec 13. National holiday. Malta became a republic in 1974.

MEETING OF THE ELECTORS. Dec 13. On the Monday following the second Wednesday in December in presidential election years, the Electors formally cast their ballots for president and vice president of the US, meeting in their respective state capitals. The Electors' ballots will be transmitted "to the Seat of Government of the United States, directed to the President of the Senate," who "in the presence of the Senate and House of Representatives," at 1 PM on Jan 6 following the election, officially counts the electoral votes and announces the result, legally completing the election process if any candidate has received a majority of the electoral votes.

MOORE, ARCHIE: BIRTH ANNIVERSARY. Dec 13, 1913. Born Archibald Lee Wright at Benoit, MS. One of the most colorful fighters ever, Moore boxed from the mid-1930s to 1963, holding the light-heavyweight title for a record nine years. For much of his career, he fought an average of once a month. Moore let an aura of celebrity surround him: he lied about his age, ate an unusual diet, married five times and spoke out on a variety of political and social issues. Died at San Diego, CA, Dec 9, 1998.

NEW ZEALAND FIRST SIGHTED BY EUROPEANS: ANNIVERSARY. Dec 13, 1642. Captain Abel Tasman of the Dutch East India Company first sighted New Zealand but was kept from landing by Maori warriors. In 1769 Captain James Cook landed and claimed formal possession for Great Britain.

NORTH AND SOUTH KOREA END WAR: ANNIVERSARY. Dec 13, 1991. North and South Korea signed a treaty of reconciliation and nonaggression, formally ending the Korean War—38 years after fighting ceased in 1953. This agreement was not hailed as a peace treaty, and the armistice that was signed July 27, 1953, between the UN and North Korea, was to remain in effect until it could be transformed into a formal peace.

SWEDEN: SANTA LUCIA DAY. Dec 13. Nationwide celebration of festival of light, honoring St. Lucia. Many hotels have their own Lucia, a young girl attired in a long, flowing white gown, who serves guests coffee and lussekatter (saffron buns) in the early morning.

BIRTHDAYS TODAY

Steve Buscemi, 46, actor (*Ghost World, Fargo, Reservoir Dogs*), born Brooklyn, NY, Dec 13, 1958.
John Davidson, 63, singer, actor (*Edward Scissorhands,* "Hollywood Squares"), born Pittsburgh, PA, Dec 13, 1941.
Sergei Fedorov, 35, hockey player, born Pskov, Russia, Dec 13, 1969.
Jamie Foxx, 37, actor (*The Truth About Cats and Dogs,* "The Jamie Foxx Show"), born Dallas, TX, Dec 13, 1967.
Wendie Malick, 54, actress ("Just Shoot Me"), born Buffalo, NY, Dec 13, 1950.
Ted Nugent, 55, singer (with Amboy Dukes: "Journey to the Center of the Mind"; solo: "Cat Scratch Fever"), born Detroit, MI, Dec 13, 1949.
Christopher Plummer, 75, actor (Emmy for "The Moneychangers;" *The Sound of Music, Dolores Claiborne*), born Toronto, ON, Canada, Dec 13, 1929.

Robert Prosky, 74, actor ("Hill Street Blues," "Veronica's Closet"), born Philadelphia, PA, Dec 13, 1930.
Dick Van Dyke, 79, comedian, actor (*Mary Poppins*, "The Dick Van Dyke Show," "Diagnosis Murder"), born West Plains, MO, Dec 13, 1925.
Tom Vilsack, 54, Governor of Iowa (D), born Pittsburgh, PA, Dec 13, 1950.

DECEMBER 14 — TUESDAY
Day 349 — 17 Remaining

ALABAMA: ADMISSION DAY: ANNIVERSARY. Dec 14. Became 22nd state in 1819.

DOOLITTLE, JAMES HAROLD: BIRTH ANNIVERSARY. Dec 14, 1896. American aviator and World War II hero General James Doolittle was born at Alameda, CA. A Lieutenant General in the US Army Air Force, he was the first person to fly across North America in less than a day. On Apr 18, 1942, Doolittle led a squadron of 16 B-25 bombers, launched from aircraft carriers, on the first US aerial raid on Japan of WWII. He was awarded the Congressional Medal of Honor for this accomplishment. Doolittle also headed the Eighth Air Force during the Normandy invasion. He died Sept 27, 1993, at Pebble Beach, CA.

EGYPT: MARITIME DISASTER: ANNIVERSARY. Dec 14, 1991. The ferry *Salem Express* sank off the port city of Safaga, Egypt, claiming the lives of 462 passengers and crew members. 180 people survived the disaster, the worst in modern Egypt's maritime history.

HALCYON DAYS. Dec 14–28. Traditionally, the seven days before and the seven days after the winter solstice. To the ancients a time when fabled bird (called the halcyon—pronounced hal-cee-on) calmed the wind and waves—a time of calm and tranquility.

NOSTRADAMUS: BIRTH ANNIVERSARY. Dec 14, 1503. French physician, best remembered for his astrological predictions (written in rhymed quatrains), was born Michel de Notredame, at St. Rémy, Provence, France. Many believed that his book of prophecies actually foretold the future. Nostradamus died at Salon, France, July 2, 1566.

REMICK, LEE: BIRTH ANNIVERSARY. Dec 14, 1935. American actress Lee Remick was born at Quincy, MA. Her films include *A Face in the Crowd* (1957), *Anatomy of a Murder* (1959) and *Days of Wine and Roses* (1963). She died July 2, 1991, at Los Angeles, CA.

SMITH, MARGARET CHASE: BIRTH ANNIVERSARY. Dec 14, 1897. American politician Margaret Madeline Chase Smith was born at Skowhegan, ME. As the first woman to be elected to both houses of Congress (1941 to the House and 1949 to the Senate), she was also one of seven Republican senators to issue a "declaration of conscience" to denounce Senator Joseph R. McCarthy's communist witch-hunt. She died May 29, 1995, at Skowhegan, ME.

SOUTH POLE DISCOVERY: ANNIVERSARY. Dec 14, 1911. The elusive object of many expeditions dating from the seventh century, the South Pole was located and visited by Roald Amundsen with four companions and 52 sled dogs. All five men and 12 of the dogs returned to base camp safely. Next to visit the South Pole, Jan 17, 1912, was a party of five led by Captain Robert F. Scott, all of whom perished during the return trip. A search party found their frozen bodies 11 months later. See also: "Amundsen, Roald: Birth Anniversary" (July 16).

BIRTHDAYS TODAY

Craig Biggio, 39, baseball player, born Smithtown, NY, Dec 14, 1965.
Jane Birkin, 58, actress (*Blow-Up, Death on the Nile, Evil Under the Sun*), born London, England, Dec 14, 1946.
Leonardo Boff, 66, Catholic theologian, born Concordia, Brazil, Dec 14, 1938.
William Joseph (Bill) Buckner, 55, former baseball player, born Vallejo, CA, Dec 14, 1949.
Patty Duke, 58, actress (Oscar for *The Miracle Worker*; Emmy for *My Sweet Charlie*), born New York, NY, Dec 14, 1946.
Don Hewitt, 82, TV news producer, born New York, NY, Dec 14, 1922.
Michael Owen, 25, soccer player (youngest player ever to represent England in World Cup in 20th century), born Chester, England, Dec 14, 1979.
Dee Wallace Stone, 56, actress (*10, E.T. The Extra-Terrestrial*), born Kansas City, MO, Dec 14, 1948.

DECEMBER 15 — WEDNESDAY
Day 350 — 16 Remaining

BATTLE OF SAN PIETRO: 60th ANNIVERSARY. Dec 15, 1943. A German panzer battalion inflicted heavy casualties on American forces trying to take the 700-year-old Italian village of San Pietro, before withdrawing from the town. San Pietro was reduced almost entirely to rubble. The American movie director John Huston, serving as an Army lieutenant, filmed the battle for the military. So graphic was the film that it was described as antiwar by the military brass at the War Department. The film was cut from five to three reels before censors allowed it to be released in 1944. It was later re-edited for the television series "The Big Picture."

BILL OF RIGHTS: ANNIVERSARY. Dec 15, 1791. The first 10 amendments to the US Constitution, known as the Bill of Rights, became effective following ratification by Virginia. The anniversary of ratification and of effect is observed as Bill of Rights Day.

★**BILL OF RIGHTS DAY.** Dec 15. Presidential Proclamation. Has been proclaimed each year since 1962, but was omitted in 1967 and 1968. (Issued in 1941 and 1946 at Congressional request and in 1947 without request.) Since 1968 has been included in Human Rights Day and Week Proclamation.

CURACAO: KINGDOM DAY AND ANTILLEAN FLAG DAY. Dec 15. This day commemorates the Charter of Kingdom, signed in 1954 at the Knight's Hall at The Hague, granting the Netherlands Antilles complete autonomy. The Antillean flag was hoisted for the first time on this day in 1959.

"DAVY CROCKETT" TV PREMIERE: 50th ANNIVERSARY. Dec 15, 1954. This show, a series of five segments, can be considered TV's first miniseries. Shown on Walt Disney's "Disneyland" show, it starred Fess Parker as American western hero Davy Crockett and was immensely popular. The show spawned Crockett paraphernalia, including the famous coonskin cap (even after we found out that Crockett never wore a coonskin cap).

EIFFEL, ALEXANDRE GUSTAVE: BIRTH ANNIVERSARY. Dec 15, 1832. Eiffel, the French engineer who designed the 1,000 ft-high, million-dollar, open-lattice wrought iron Eiffel Tower, and who participated in designing the Statue of Liberty, was born at Dijon, France. The Eiffel Tower, weighing more than 7,000 tons, was built for the Paris International Exposition of 1889. Eiffel died at Paris, France, Dec 23, 1923.

GAL, UZI: BIRTH ANNIVERSARY. Dec 15, 1923. Inventor of the 9-millimeter submachine gun that bears his name, Uziel Gal was born in Germany but spent most of his life in Israel. A mechanical engineer, he fought in the 1948 Arab-Israeli war, to which he brought a homemade submachine gun. He went on to design the Uzi, and by 1956 it was being manufactured by Israeli Military Industries, whose management named it for him against his own wishes. The gun itself revolutionized automatic weaponry, and is currently found in the arsenals of armies, secret-service organizations, bodyguards, etc, worldwide. Gal died at Philadelphia, PA, on Sept 2, 2002.

GONE WITH THE WIND FILM PREMIERE: 65th ANNIVERSARY. Dec 15, 1939. One of the twentieth-century's biggest film blockbusters premiered on this date in Atlanta, GA. Based on Margaret Mitchell's bestselling and Pulitzer-Prize–winning novel of Civil War passions, the film starred Vivian Leigh and Clark Gable and was produced by the dynamic David O. Selznick. It won an unprecedented eight Academy Awards, including Best Picture. Hattie McDaniel won a Best Supporting Actress Oscar—the first time an African-American actor had won or been nominated. No film would touch its Oscar achievement or monetary grosses for decades. At the chilly Atlanta premiere, more than 300,000 people lined the streets to catch sight of the film's stars arriving at the Loew's Grand Theater. See also: "*Gone with the Wind* Published: Anniversary" (May 19).

INTERNATIONAL LANGUAGE WEEK. Dec 15–21. To disseminate information about mankind's quest for an international language to solve the communication problem of humans, and to supply information about the international language, Esperanto. Esperanto was created in 1887 by Dr. L.L. Zamenhof as a solution to the world's language problem. For complete info, send $5 to cover expense of printing, handling and postage. Annually, Dec 15–21. For info: Dr. Stanley Drake, Pres, Intl Society of Friendship and Good Will, 999 Hood Rd, Ste 127, Marietta, GA 30068. Phone: (770) 565-2322. E-mail: ISFGW@bellsouth.net.

MILITARY DICTATORSHIP ENDED IN CHILE: 15th ANNIVERSARY. Dec 15, 1989. In an election on this date, Patricio Aylwin defeated General Augusto Pinochet's former finance minister, Hernan Buchi, bringing the military dictatorship of Pinochet to an end. Fourteen months previously, Pinochet suffered defeat in a national plebiscite on eight more years of his rule. This defeat prompted democratic elections and crippled the Pinochet regime. Pinochet came to power when the military overthrew a democratically elected government and killed Marxist president Salvador Allende in a 1973 coup. Patricio Aylwin avoided a two-candidate runoff by achieving 55.2 percent of the vote. He was inaugurated on Mar 11, 1990.

PUERTO RICO: NAVIDADES. Dec 15–Jan 6. Traditional Christmas season begins mid-December and ends on Three Kings Day. Elaborate nativity scenes, carolers, special Christmas foods and trees from Canada and US. Gifts on Christmas Day and on Three Kings Day.

SITTING BULL: DEATH ANNIVERSARY. Dec 15, 1890. Famous Sioux Indian leader, medicine man and warrior of the Hunkpapa Teton band. Known also by his native name, Tatankayatanka, Sitting Bull was born on the Grand River, SD. He first accompanied his father on the warpath at the age of 14 against the Crow and thereafter rapidly gained influence within his tribe. In 1886 he led a raid on Fort Buford. His steadfast refusal to go to a reservation led General Phillip Sheridan to initiate a campaign against him which led to the massacre of Lieutenant Colonel George Custer's men at the Little Bighorn, after which Sitting Bull fled to Canada, remaining there until 1881. Although many in his tribe surrendered on their return, Sitting Bull remained hostile until his death in a skirmish with the US soldiers along the Grand River.

	S	M	T	W	T	F	S
December				1	2	3	4
	5	6	7	8	9	10	11
2004	12	13	14	15	16	17	18
	19	20	21	22	23	24	25
	26	27	28	29	30	31	

SPACE MILESTONE: *VEGA 1* (USSR): 20th ANNIVERSARY. Dec 15, 1984. Craft launched this date to rendezvous with Halley's Comet in March 1986. *Vega 2*, launched Dec 21, 1984, was part of same mission which, in cooperation with the US, carried US-built "comet-dust" detection equipment.

US FORCES LAND IN MINDORO, PHILIPPINES: 60th ANNIVERSARY. Dec 15, 1944. After the usual barrage from naval guns, the US 24th Division landed on Mindoro, the largest of the islands immediately south of Luzon (the most important island of the Philippines). American soldiers easily advanced eight miles inland, took the perimeter of their beachhead and started construction of an airfield. Japanese kamikaze counterattacks, however, sank two motor torpedo boats and damaged the escort carrier *Marcus Island*, two destroyers and a third motor torpedo boat, making Mindoro a more costly conquest than the island of Leyte had been.

BIRTHDAYS TODAY

Nicholas (Nick) Buoniconti, 64, former football player, born Springfield, MA, Dec 15, 1940.
Dave Clark, 62, musician (leader of the Dave Clark Five, "I Like It Like That"), born London, England, Dec 15, 1942.
Tim Conway, 71, actor, comedian ("McHale's Navy," "The Carol Burnett Show"), born Willoughby, OH, Dec 15, 1933.
Don Johnson, 55, actor ("Miami Vice," "Nash Bridges"), born Flatt Creek, MO, Dec 15, 1949.
Edna O'Brien, 73, author (*Country Girls Trilogy*, *Time and Tide*), born Tuamgraney, Ireland, Dec 15, 1931.
Helen Slater, 41, actress (*City Slickers*, *The Secret of My Success*), born Long Island, NY, Dec 15, 1963.
Alexandra Stevenson, 24, tennis player, born San Diego, CA, Dec 15, 1980.
Garrett Wang, 36, actor ("Star Trek: Voyager"), born Riverside, CA, Dec 15, 1968.
Mark Warner, 50, Governor of Virginia (D), born Indianapolis, IN, Dec 15, 1954.

DECEMBER 16 — THURSDAY

Day 351 — 15 Remaining

AUSTEN, JANE: BIRTH ANNIVERSARY. Dec 16, 1775. English novelist (*Pride and Prejudice*, *Sense and Sensibility*), born at Steventon, Hampshire, England. Died July 18, 1817, at Winchester, England.

BAHRAIN: INDEPENDENCE DAY. Dec 16. National holiday. Commemorates independence from British protection in 1971.

BANGLADESH: VICTORY DAY. Dec 16. National holiday. Commemorates victory over Pakistan in 1971. The former East Pakistan became Bangladesh.

BARBIE AND BARNEY BACKLASH DAY. Dec 16. If we have to explain this to you, you don't have kids. It's one day each year when Mom and Dad can tell the kids that Barbie and Barney don't exist. [©2003 by WH.] For info: Thomas & Ruth Roy, Wellcat Holidays, 2418 Long Ln, Lebanon, PA 17046. Phone: (717) 279-0184. E-mail: info@wellcat.com. Web: www.wellcat.com.

BATTLE OF NASHVILLE: ANNIVERSARY. Dec 16, 1864. On the second day of battle at Nashville, Union troops defeated Confederate forces under General John B. Hood, essentially knocking the Confederate Army of Tennessee out of the war.

BATTLE OF THE BULGE: 60th ANNIVERSARY. Dec 16, 1944. A German offensive was launched in the Belgian Ardennes Forest, where Hitler had managed to concentrate 250,000 men. The Nazi commanders, hoping to minimize any aerial counterattack by the Allies, chose a time when foggy, rainy weather prevailed and the initial attack by eight armored divisions along a 75-mile front took the Allies by surprise, the 5th Panzer Army penetrating to within 20 miles of crossings on the Meuse River. US troops were able to hold fast at bottlenecks in the Ardennes, but by the end of December the German push had penetrated 65 miles into the Allied lines (though their line had narrowed from the initial 75 miles to 20 miles). By that time the Allies began to respond and the Germans were stopped by Montgomery on the Meuse and by Patton at Bastogne. The weather then cleared and Allied aircraft began to bomb the German forces and supply lines by Dec 26. The Allies restablished their original line by Jan 21, 1945.

BEETHOVEN, LUDWIG VAN: BIRTH ANNIVERSARY. Dec 16, 1770. Regarded by many as the greatest orchestral composer of all time, Ludwig van Beethoven was born at Bonn, Germany. Impairment of his hearing began before he was 30, but even total deafness did not halt his composing and conducting. His last appearance on the concert stage was to conduct the premiere of his *Ninth Symphony*, at Vienna, May 7, 1824. He was unable to hear either the orchestra or the applause. Often in love, he never married. Of a stormy temperament, he is said to have died during a violent thunderstorm Mar 26, 1827, at Vienna.

BOSTON TEA PARTY: ANNIVERSARY. Dec 16, 1773. Anniversary of Boston patriots' boarding of British vessel at anchor at Boston Harbor. Contents of nearly 350 chests of tea were dumped into the harbor.

CALABRIA EARTHQUAKE: ANNIVERSARY. Dec 16, 1857. Calabria—an especially quake-prone region near Naples, Italy—experienced a devastating earthquake of great magnitude that left more than 10,000 people dead and entire villages destroyed. Between 1783 (the last big quake) and 1857, about 111,000 people lost their lives in the unstable region.

COWARD, NOËL: BIRTH ANNIVERSARY. Dec 16, 1899. English playwright, actor and wit known for his sophisticated comedies: *Private Lives* (1930), *Design for Living* (1933), *Blithe Spirit* (1941) and others—many of which were later filmed. He is also known for such songs as "Mad Dogs and Englishmen." He advised actors: "Learn the lines and don't bump into the furniture." Born at Teddington, England, Coward died at St. Mary, Jamaica, on Mar 26, 1973.

"DRAGNET" TV PREMIERE: ANNIVERSARY. Dec 16, 1951. This famous crime show stressed authenticity, and episodes were supposedly based on real cases. It starred Jack Webb as stoic and determined Sergeant Joe Friday, a man whose life was his investigative police work and who was recognized by his recurring line, "Just the facts, ma'am." Friday had many partners: Barton Yarborough played Sergeant Ben Romero for three episodes; for the rest of the season Barney Phillips played Sergeant Ed Jacobs and Ben Alexander played his comedic sidekick, Officer Frank Smith. A new version appeared in 1967 with Webb and his new partner, Officer Bill Gannon (Harry Morgan). "Dragnet" is also known for its theme music and its narrative epilogue describing the fate of the bad guys.

MEAD, MARGARET: BIRTH ANNIVERSARY. Dec 16, 1901. American anthropologist and author, especially known for her studies of peoples of the southwest Pacific area, and for her forthright manner in speaking and writing. Born at Philadelphia, PA, Mead died at New York, NY, Nov 15, 1978.

MEXICO: POSADAS. Dec 16–24. A nine-day annual celebration throughout Mexico. Processions of "pilgrims" knock at doors asking for posada (shelter), commemorating the search by Joseph and Mary for a shelter in which the infant Jesus might be born. Pilgrims are invited inside, and fun and merrymaking ensue with blindfolded guests trying to break a "piñata" (papier mache decorated earthenware utensil filled with gifts and goodies) suspended from the ceiling. Once the piñata is broken, the gifts are distributed and celebration continues.

NEW WORLD SYMPHONY PREMIERE: ANNIVERSARY. Dec 16, 1893. Anton Dvorak's *New World Symphony* premiered at the newly erected Carnegie Hall with the New York Philharmonic playing. The composer attended and enjoyed enthusiastic applause from the audience. The symphony contains snatches from black spirituals and American folk music. Dvorak, a Bohemian, had been in the US only a year when he composed it as a greeting to his friends in Europe.

"ONE DAY AT A TIME" TV PREMIERE: ANNIVERSARY. Dec 16, 1975. This sitcom about a divorced mother raising two girls in Indianapolis starred Bonnie Franklin as Ann Romano, Mackenzie Phillips and Valerie Bertinelli as daughters Julie and Barbara Cooper. Other regulars included: Pat Harrington, Jr, as tool-belt-wearing maintenance man Dwayne Schneider, Richard Masur as David Kane, Ann's boyfriend, and Nanette Fabray as Ann's mother. All three female leads got married and Ann opened her own ad agency before the series ended in 1984.

PHILIPPINES: PHILIPPINE CHRISTMAS OBSERVANCE. Dec 16–Jan 6. Philippine Islands. Said to be world's longest Christmas celebration.

PHILIPPINES: SIMBANG GABI. Dec 16–25. Nationwide. A nine-day novena of predawn masses, also called "Misa de Gallo." One of the traditional Filipino celebrations of the holiday season.

SANTAYANA, GEORGE: BIRTH ANNIVERSARY. Dec 16, 1863. Philosopher and author born at Madrid, Spain. At the age of nine he emigrated to the US where he attended and later taught at Harvard University. In 1912 he returned to Europe and traveled extensively. It was Santayana who said, "Those who cannot remember the past are condemned to repeat it." He died at Rome, Italy, Sept 26, 1952.

SOUTH AFRICA: RECONCILIATION DAY. Dec 16. National holiday. Celebrates the spirit of reconciliation, national unity and peace amongst all citizens.

UNITED NATIONS REVOKES RESOLUTION ON ZIONISM: ANNIVERSARY. Dec 16, 1991. The United Nations voted 111 to 25 to revoke Resolution 3379, which equated Zionism with racism. Resolution 3379 was approved Nov 10, 1975, with 72 countries voting in favor, 35 against and 32 abstentions. The largest block of changed votes came from the former Soviet Union and Eastern Europe.

BIRTHDAYS TODAY

Bruce N. Ames, 76, biochemist, cancer researcher, born New York, NY, Dec 16, 1928.
Steven Bochco, 61, TV writer, producer ("Hill Street Blues," "NYPD Blue"), born New York, NY, Dec 16, 1943.
Benjamin Bratt, 41, actor ("Law & Order"), born San Francisco, CA, Dec 16, 1963.
Donald Carcieri, 62, Governor of Rhode Island (R), born East Greenwich, RI, Dec 16, 1942.
Arthur Charles Clarke, 87, author (*2001: A Space Odyssey, Islands in the Sky*), born Minehead, England, Dec 16, 1917.
Alison La Placa, 45, actress ("The John Laroquette Show"), born Lincolnshire, IL, Dec 16, 1959.
William ("The Refrigerator") Perry, 42, former football player, born Aiken, SC, Dec 16, 1962.
Clifford (Cliff) Ralph Robinson, 38, basketball player, born Buffalo, NY, Dec 16, 1966.
Lesley Stahl, 63, journalist ("60 Minutes," former White House correspondent), born Lynn, MA, Dec 16, 1941.
Jon Tenney, 43, actor ("Brooklyn South"), born Princeton, NJ, Dec 16, 1961.
Liv Johanne Ullmann, 65, actress (*The Immigrants, Scenes from a Marriage*), born Tokyo, Japan, Dec 16, 1939.

DECEMBER 17 — FRIDAY
Day 352 — 14 Remaining

AZTEC CALENDAR STONE DISCOVERY: ANNIVERSARY. Dec 17, 1790. One of the wonders of the western hemisphere—the Aztec Calendar or Solar Stone—was found beneath the ground by workmen repairing Mexico City's Central Plaza. The centuries-old, intricately carved stone, 11 ft, 8 inches in diameter and weighing nearly 25 tons, proved to be a highly developed calendar monument to the sun. Believed to have been carved in the year 1479, this extraordinary time-counting basalt tablet originally stood in the Great Temple of the Aztecs. Buried along with other Aztec idols, soon after the Spanish conquest in 1521, it remained hidden until 1790. Its 52-year cycle had regulated many Aztec ceremonies, including grisly human sacrifices to save the world from destruction by the gods.

CLEAN AIR ACT PASSED BY CONGRESS: ANNIVERSARY. Dec 17, 1967. A sweeping set of laws passed to protect the nation from air pollution. This was the first legislation to place pollution controls on the automobile industry.

FIRST FLIGHT ANNIVERSARY CELEBRATION. Dec 17. Kill Devil Hills, NC. Each year since 1928, on the anniversary of the Wright Brothers' first successful heavier-than-air flight at Kitty Hawk, NC, Dec 17, 1903, a celebration has been held at the Wright Brothers National Memorial, with wreaths, flyover and other observances—regardless of weather.

FLOYD, WILLIAM: BIRTH ANNIVERSARY. Dec 17, 1734. Signer of the Declaration of Independence, member of Congress, born at Brookhaven, Long Island. Died at Westernville, NY, Aug 4, 1821.

HENRY, JOSEPH: BIRTH ANNIVERSARY. Dec 17, 1797. Scientist Joseph Henry was born at Albany, NY. One of his great discoveries was the principle of self-induction; the unit used in the measure of electrical inductance was named "the henry" in his honor. In 1831 Henry constructed the first model of an electric telegraph with an audible signal. This formed the basis of nearly all later work on commercial wire telegraphy. In 1832 Henry was named professor of natural philosophy at the College of New Jersey, now Princeton University. Henry was involved in the planning of the Smithsonian Institution and became its first secretary in 1846. President Lincoln named Henry as one of the original 50 scientists to make up the National Academy of Sciences in 1863. He served as that organization's president from 1868 until his death May 13, 1878, at Washington, DC.

KING, W.L. MACKENZIE: BIRTH ANNIVERSARY. Dec 17, 1874. Former Canadian prime minister, born at Berlin, Ontario. Served 21 years, the longest term of any prime minister in the English-speaking world. Died at Kingsmere, July 22, 1950.

LIBBY, WILLARD FRANK: BIRTH ANNIVERSARY. Dec 17, 1908. American educator, chemist, atomic scientist and Nobel Prize winner was born at Grand Valley, CO. He was the inventor of the carbon-14 "atomic clock" method for dating ancient and prehistoric plant and animal remains and minerals. Died at Los Angeles, CA, Sept 8, 1980.

SAMPSON, DEBORAH: BIRTH ANNIVERSARY. Dec 17, 1760. Born at Plympton, MA, Deborah Sampson spent her childhood as an indentured servant. In 1782, wishing to participate in the Revolutionary War, she disguised herself as a man and enlisted in the Continental Army's 4th Massachusetts Regiment under the name Robert Shurtleff. Her identity was unmasked and she was dismissed from the army in 1783. In 1802 Sampson became perhaps the first woman to lecture professionally in the US when she began giving public speeches on her experiences. Deborah Sampson died Apr 29, 1827, at Sharon, MA. Full military pension was provided for her heirs by an act of Congress in 1838.

SATURNALIA. Dec 17–23. Ancient Roman festival honoring Saturnus, the god of agriculture. It was a time of merriment at the end of harvesting and wine-making. Presents were exchanged, sacrifices offered, and masters served their slaves. Approximates the winter solstice. Some say that the date for the observance of the nativity of Jesus was selected by the early Christian church leaders to fall on Dec 25 partly to counteract the popular but disapproved of pre-Christian Roman festival of Saturnalia.

"THE SIMPSONS" TV PREMIERE: 15th ANNIVERSARY. Dec 17, 1989. TV's hottest animated family, "The Simpsons," premiered as a half-hour weekly sitcom. The originator of Homer, Marge, Bart, Lisa and Maggie is cartoonist Matt Groening. The show's 300th episode, "Barting Over," aired Feb 16, 2003.

TINY TIM WEDS MISS VICKI ON "THE TONIGHT SHOW": 35th ANNIVERSARY. Dec 17, 1969. In the highest-rated show in "The Tonight Show" history, 45 million viewers saw ukulele-playing eccentric Tiny Tim marry Miss Vicki (née Budinger), his 17-year-old girlfriend. The live ceremony was accented by thousands of tulips, since Tiny Tim's claim to fame was his falsetto revival of the song "Tiptoe through the Tulips."

UNDERDOG DAY. Dec 17. To salute, before the year's end, all of the underdogs and unsung heroes—the Number Two people who contribute so much to the Number One people we read about. (Sherlock Holmes's Dr. Watson and Robinson Crusoe's Friday are examples.) Observed annually on the third Friday in December since its founding in 1976 by the late Peter Moeller, THE Chief Underdog. For info: A. Moeller, Underdogs Intl, Box 71, Clio, MI 48420-1042.

WHITTIER, JOHN GREENLEAF: BIRTH ANNIVERSARY. Dec 17, 1807. Poet and abolitionist, born at Haverhill, Essex County, MA. Whittier's books of poetry include *Legends of New England* and *Snowbound*. Died at Hampton Falls, NH, Sept 7, 1892.

★**WRIGHT BROTHERS DAY.** Dec 17. Presidential Proclamation always issued for Dec 17 since 1963 (PL88–209 of Dec 17, 1963). Issued twice earlier at Congressional request in 1959 and 1961.

WRIGHT BROTHERS FIRST POWERED FLIGHT: ANNIVERSARY. Dec 17, 1903. Orville and Wilbur Wright, brothers, bicycle shop operators, inventors and aviation pioneers, after three years of experimentation with kites and gliders, achieved the first documented successful powered and controlled flights of an airplane. The flights, near Kitty Hawk, NC, piloted first by Orville then by Wilbur Wright, were sustained for less than one minute but represented man's first powered airplane flight and the beginning of a new form of transportation. Orville Wright was born at Dayton, OH, Aug 19, 1871, and died there Jan 30, 1948. Wilbur Wright was born at Millville, IN, Apr 16, 1867, and died at Dayton, OH, May 30, 1912.

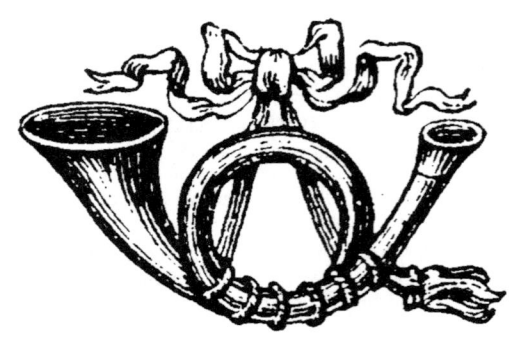

December 2004	S	M	T	W	T	F	S
				1	2	3	4
	5	6	7	8	9	10	11
	12	13	14	15	16	17	18
	19	20	21	22	23	24	25
	26	27	28	29	30	31	

☆ Chase's 2004 Calendar of Events ☆   Dec 17-18

BIRTHDAYS TODAY

Christopher Cazenove, 59, actor (*Zulu Dawn, Eye of the Needle*), born Winchester, England, Dec 17, 1945.
Bob Guccione, 74, publisher, born Brooklyn, NY, Dec 17, 1930.
Bernard Hill, 60, actor (*Gandhi, Shirley Valentine*), born Manchester, England, Dec 17, 1944.
Ernie Hudson, 59, actor (*Ghostbusters, Ghostbusters II, The Hand That Rocks the Cradle*), born Benton Harbor, MI, Dec 17, 1945.
Eugene Levy, 58, comedian, writer ("Second City TV," "SCTV Network 90"), born Hamilton, ON, Canada, Dec 17, 1946.
Bill Pullman, 50, actor (*Independence Day, While You Were Sleeping*), born Delphi, NY, Dec 17, 1954.
William Safire, 75, author, journalist (*Coming to Terms, Words of Wisdom*), born New York, NY, Dec 17, 1929.
Tommy Steele, 68, actor (*The Happiest Millionaire, Half a Sixpence*), born London, England, Dec 17, 1936.
Sean Patrick Thomas, 34, actor (*Save the Last Dance*, "The District"), born Wilmington, DE, Dec 17, 1970.

DECEMBER 18 — SATURDAY
Day 353 — 13 Remaining

AFRICAN AMERICAN HOLIDAY EXPO. Dec 18–19. Washington, DC. The oldest, East Coast marketplace that celebrates Christmas and the cultural holiday, Kwanzaa. The Expo offers food, fun, inner-attainment, workshops and more than 160 merchants in an African Marketplace atmosphere, and supports youth entrepreneurs. Est attendance: 12,000. For info: African American Holiday Assn, PO Box 43255, Washington, DC 20010. E-mail: aaha@aaha-info.org. Web: www.aaha-info.org.

BRANDT, WILLY: BIRTH ANNIVERSARY. Dec 18, 1913. Former West German chancellor Willy Brandt was born Herbert Ernst Karl Frahm at Lubeck, Germany. An anti-Nazi exile during World War II, he won the Nobel Peace Prize in 1971 for seeking better East-West relations. He died Oct 8, 1992, at Unkel, Germany.

CAPITOL REEF NATIONAL PARK ESTABLISHED: ANNIVERSARY. Dec 18, 1971. Area of outstanding geological features, colorful canyons, prehistoric Fremont petroglyphs and Mormon historic fruit orchards and buildings in south central Utah, originally proclaimed a national monument Aug 2, 1937, was established as a national park. For further park info: Capitol Reef Natl Park, Box 15, Torrey, UT 84775. E-mail: care-interpretation@nps.gov. Web: www.nps.gov/care.

CINGULAR WINTERFEST BOAT PARADE PRESENTED BY NOKIA. Dec 18. More than 100 decorated yachts sail up Fort Lauderdale's Intracoastal Waterway starting at Port Everglades. Winterfest Black Tie Ball is Dec 11, Intracoastal Decorating is Dec 15 and Grand Marshal Reception is Dec 17. Est attendance: 850,000. For info: Winterfest, 512 NE 3rd Ave, Fort Lauderdale, FL 33301. Phone: (954) 767-0686. Fax: (954) 767-0665. E-mail: boats@winterfestparade.com. Web: www.winterfestparade.com.

COBB, TYRUS RAYMOND "TY": BIRTH ANNIVERSARY. Dec 18, 1886. Famed American baseball player born at Narrows, GA. Died at Atlanta, GA, July 17, 1961. Lifetime batting average of .367 compiled over 24 years during which he played in more than 3,000 games. Cobb was among the first five players inducted into the National Baseball Hall of Fame in 1936.

A COLONIAL CHRISTMAS. Dec 18–31. Jamestown Settlement, Williamsburg, VA, and Yorktown Victory Center, Yorktown, VA. Experience 17th- and 18th-century holiday traditions. At Jamestown Settlement, a film and special guided tours compare and contrast English Christmas customs of the period with how the season may have been observed in the difficult early years of the Jamestown colony. At the Yorktown Victory Center, hear accounts of Christmas and winter in military encampments during the American Revolution, and glimpse holiday preparations on a 1780s Virginia farm. For info: Jamestown-Yorktown Foundation, PO Box 1607, Williamsburg, VA 23187. Phone: (757) 253-4838 or toll-free (888) 593-4682. Fax: (757) 253-5299. Web: www.historyisfun.org.

DAVIS, BENJAMIN O., JR: BIRTH ANNIVERSARY. Dec 18, 1912. The World War II hero was born at Washington, DC, to the Army's first black general. Davis had a distinguished career serving the US: he was the first African American to graduate from West Point in the 20th century; he led the first all-black air unit, the 99th Pursuit Squadron (the Tuskegee Airmen), in WWII; he helped plan the integration of the US Air Force in 1948–9 and he was the Air Force's first black general (1954). He died at Washington, DC, on July 4, 2002. See also: "Tuskegee Airmen Activated: Anniversary" (Mar 22).

GRIMALDI, JOSEPH: BIRTH ANNIVERSARY. Dec 18, 1778. Known as the "greatest clown in history" and the "king of pantomime," Joseph Grimaldi began his stage career at age two. He was an accomplished singer, dancer and acrobat. Born at London, England, he is best remembered as the original "Joey the Clown" and for the innovative humor he brought to the clown's role in theater. Illness forced his early retirement in 1823, and he died at London, May 31, 1837.

MEXICO: FEAST OF OUR LADY OF SOLITUDE. Dec 18. Oaxaca. Pilgrims venerate the patron of the lonely.

MOON PHASE: FIRST QUARTER. Dec 18. Moon enters First Quarter phase at 11:39 AM, EST.

NEW JERSEY RATIFICATION DAY: ANNIVERSARY. Dec 18, 1787. New Jersey became the third state to ratify the Constitution (following Delaware and Pennsylvania). It did so unanimously.

NIGER: REPUBLIC DAY: ANNIVERSARY. Dec 18. National holiday. Gained autonomy within the French community in 1958.

STRADIVARI, ANTONIO: DEATH ANNIVERSARY. Dec 18, 1737. Celebrated Italian violin maker was born probably in the year 1644, and died at Cremona, at about age 93.

"TO TELL THE TRUTH" TV PREMIERE: ANNIVERSARY. Dec 18, 1956. This long-running popular game show was a production of the Mark Goodson-Bill Todman team. A celebrity panel (and the home audience) tried to guess which of three guests claiming to be the same person was telling the truth. Panelists took turns questioning the guests, and, at the conclusion, the identity of the person was revealed. Hosts have included Bud Collyer, Garry Moore, Joe Garagiola, Robin Ward, Gordon Elliott and Alex Trebek. Celebrity panelists included Dick Van Dyke, Tom Poston, Peggy Cass, Kitty Carlisle and Bill Cullen.

UNITED NATIONS: INTERNATIONAL MIGRANTS DAY. Dec 18. Recognizes the contributions that millions of migrant workers make to the global economy and seeks to draw attention to the precarious state of their rights. For info: United Nations, Dept of Public Info, New York, NY 10017. Web: www.un.org.

BIRTHDAYS TODAY

Christina Aguilera, 24, singer, born Staten Island, NY, Dec 18, 1980.
Ossie Davis, 87, actor (*A Raisin in the Sun, Grumpy Old Men*, "Evening Shade"), born Cogdell, GA, Dec 18, 1917.

Dec 18–20 ☆ *Chase's 2004 Calendar of Events* ☆

Katie Holmes, 26, actress ("Dawson's Creek"), born Toledo, OH, Dec 18, 1978.
Ray Liotta, 49, actor (*Unforgettable, Goodfellas, Field of Dreams, Something Wild*), born Newark, NJ, Dec 18, 1955.
Leonard Maltin, 54, movie critic, author (*Maltin's Guide*), born New York, NY, Dec 18, 1950.
Charles Oakley, 41, basketball player, born Cleveland, OH, Dec 18, 1963.
Brad Pitt, 40, actor (*Ocean's Eleven, Interview with the Vampire, A River Runs Through It*), born Shawnee, OK, Dec 18, 1964.
Keith Richards, 61, musician, singer (Rolling Stones), born Dartford, England, Dec 18, 1943.
Steven Spielberg, 57, producer, director (*E.T. The Extra-Terrestrial*, Indiana Jones movies, *Close Encounters of the Third Kind, Jurassic Park, The Color Purple*; Oscars for *Schindler's List, Saving Private Ryan*), born Cincinnati, OH, Dec 18, 1947.
Kiefer Sutherland, 38, actor ("24," *Flatliners, A Few Good Men*), born Los Angeles, CA, Dec 18, 1966.

DECEMBER 19 — SUNDAY
Day 354 — 12 Remaining

CHRISTMAS GREETINGS FROM SPACE: ANNIVERSARY. Dec 19, 1958. At 3:15 PM, EST, the US Earth satellite *Atlas* transmitted the first radio voice broadcast from space, a 58-word recorded Christmas greeting from President Dwight D. Eisenhower: "to all mankind America's wish for peace on earth and good will toward men everywhere." The satellite had been launched from Cape Canaveral Dec 18.

COMMUNITY CAROL SINGING. Dec 19. Mystic, CT. Lift up your voice in song to celebrate the season. Museum admission is free when you bring a canned good to be donated to charity. A brass quartet and the Mystic Seaport carolers lead an afternoon of joyous musical cheer. Est attendance: 1,000. For info: Mystic Seaport, 75 Greenmanville Ave, Box 6000, Mystic, CT 06355. Phone: (860) 572-5315 or (888) 9SEAPORT. Web: www.visitmysticseaport.org.

FISKE, MINNIE MADDERN: BIRTH ANNIVERSARY. Dec 19, 1865. American theater actress with a long, distinguished career. First stage appearance at the age of three as "Little Minnie Maddern." Born at New Orleans, LA, she died Feb 15, 1932, at Hollis, NY.

LIVERMORE, MARY ASHTON: BIRTH ANNIVERSARY. Dec 19, 1821. American reformer and women's suffrage leader, born at Boston, MA. Died May 23, 1905, at Melrose, MA.

PARRY, WILLIAM: BIRTH ANNIVERSARY. Dec 19, 1790. British explorer Sir William Edward Parry was born at Bath, England. Remembered for his Arctic expeditions and for his search for a Northwest Passage, Parry died at Ems, Germany, July 8, 1855.

December 2004

S	M	T	W	T	F	S
			1	2	3	4
5	6	7	8	9	10	11
12	13	14	15	16	17	18
19	20	21	22	23	24	25
26	27	28	29	30	31	

SPACE MILESTONE: *INTELSAT 4 F-3* (US). Dec 19, 1971. Communications satellite launched by NASA on contract with COMSAT. Mission involved intercontinental relay phone and TV communications.

SUSSKIND, DAVID: BIRTH ANNIVERSARY. Dec 19, 1920. American television producer David (Howard) Susskind was born at New York, NY. In 1952 he started his own television production company and soon was producing more live programs than the three networks combined. He began to host talk shows in 1958 and was widely respected for focusing on serious matters. He died Feb 22, 1987, at New York, NY.

***TITANIC* RELEASED: ANNIVERSARY.** Dec 19, 1997. The most expensive film made (up to that time) at $200 million was released in theaters on this date. *Titanic*, written and directed by James Cameron, featured the drama of star-crossed lovers (Leonardo DiCaprio and Kate Winslet) paired with the amazing special effects recreation of the doomed 1912 ocean liner's first and last voyage. The film won 11 Academy Awards, including Best Picture, which tied it with 1959's *Ben-Hur*. It is widely considered one of the most successful films ever made.

WOODSON, CARTER GODWIN: BIRTH ANNIVERSARY. Dec 19, 1875. Historian who introduced black studies to colleges and universities, born at New Canton, VA. His scholarly works included *The Negro in Our History, The Education of the Negro Prior to 1861*. Known as the father of Black history, he inaugurated Negro History Week. Woodson was working on a six-volume *Encyclopaedia Africana* when he died at Washington, DC, Apr 3, 1950.

BIRTHDAYS TODAY

Jennifer Beals, 41, actress (*Flashdance, The Bride, Into the Soup*), born Chicago, IL, Dec 19, 1963.
Janie Fricke, 52, country singer ("It Ain't Easy"), born Whitney, IN, Dec 19, 1952.
Tom Gugliotta, 35, basketball player, born Huntington Station, NY, Dec 19, 1969.
Richard E. Leakey, 60, anthropologist, born Nairobi, Kenya, Dec 19, 1944.
Kevin Edward McHale, 47, Hall of Fame basketball player, born Hibbing, MN, Dec 19, 1957.
Alyssa Milano, 32, actress ("Charmed," "Melrose Place"), born Brooklyn, NY, Dec 19, 1972.
Tim Reid, 60, actor ("Frank's Place," "WKRP in Cincinnati"), born Norfolk, VA, Dec 19, 1944.
Kristy Swanson, 35, actress (*Buffy the Vampire Slayer*), born Mission Viejo, CA, Dec 19, 1969.
Cicely Tyson, 65, actress (Emmy for *The Autobiography of Miss Jane Pittman; Sounder*), born New York, NY, Dec 19, 1939.
Reggie White, 43, former football player, born Chattanooga, TN, Dec 19, 1961.

DECEMBER 20 — MONDAY
Day 355 — 11 Remaining

AMERICAN POET LAUREATE ESTABLISHMENT: ANNIVERSARY. Dec 20, 1985. A bill empowering the Librarian of Congress to name, annually, a Poet Laureate/Consultant in Poetry was signed into law by President Ronald Reagan. In return for a stipend as Poet Laureate and a salary as the Consultant in Poetry, the person named will present at least one major work of poetry and will appear at selected national ceremonies. The first Poet Laureate of the US was Robert Penn Warren, appointed to that position by the Librarian of Congress Feb 26, 1986. See also: "Warren, Robert Penn: Birth Anniversary" (Apr 24).

BELGIUM: NUTS FAIR. Dec 20. Bastogne. Traditional cultural observance. Annually, the third Monday in December.

CATHODE-RAY TUBE PATENTED: ANNIVERSARY. Dec 20, 1938. The kinescope, today known as the cathode-ray

630

tube, was patented by Russian immigrant Vladimir Zworykin. It is still used today in computer monitors and television sets.

CLINTON IMPEACHMENT PROCEEDINGS: ANNIVERSARY. Dec 20, 1998. President Bill Clinton was impeached by a House of Representatives that was divided along party lines. He was convicted of perjury and obstruction of justice stemming from a sexual relationship with a White House intern. He was then tried by the Senate in January 1999. On Feb 12, 1999, the Senate acquitted him on both charges. Clinton was only the second US president to undergo impeachment proceedings. Andrew Johnson was impeached by the House in 1868 but the Senate voted against impeachment and he finished his term of office. See also: "Johnson Impeachment Proceedings" (Feb 24).

"THE DATING GAME" TV PREMIERE: ANNIVERSARY. Dec 20, 1965. Another game show developed by Chuck Barris, it typically featured a "bachelorette" who questioned three men who were hidden from her view and decided, based on their answers, which guy appealed to her the most. The couple was then sent on a date, courtesy of the show. Occasionally, a bachelor would question three women. Jim Lange was the host of the network series and two syndicated ones. Elaine Joyce and Jeff MacGregor hosted one season each on the retitled "The New Dating Game."

FIRESTONE, HARVEY S.: BIRTH ANNIVERSARY. Dec 20, 1868. American industrialist, businessman and founder of the Firestone Tire and Rubber Company, Harvey Samuel Firestone was born at Columbiana County, OH. A close friend of Henry Ford, Thomas Edison and John Burroughs, Firestone died at Miami Beach, FL, Feb 7, 1938.

LANGER, SUSANNE K.: BIRTH ANNIVERSARY. Dec 20, 1895. Susanne Langer, a leading American philosopher, author of *Philosophy in a New Key: A Study in the Symbolism of Reason, Rite, and Art*, was born at New York, NY. Her studies of esthetics and art exerted a profound influence on thinking in the fields of psychology, philosophy and the social sciences. She died at Old Lyme, CT, July 17, 1985.

MACAU REVERTS TO CHINESE CONTROL: 5th ANNIVERSARY. Dec 20, 1999. Macau, a tiny province on the southeast coast of China, reverted to Chinese rule. It had been a Portuguese colony since 1557.

MENZIES, ROBERT GORDON: BIRTH ANNIVERSARY. Dec 20, 1894. Australian statesman and conservative leader, born at Jeparit, Victoria, Australia, Sir Robert died at Melbourne, Australia, May 14, 1978, at age 83.

MONTGOMERY BUS BOYCOTT ENDS: ANNIVERSARY. Dec 20, 1956. The US Supreme Court ruling of Nov 13, 1956, calling for integration of the Montgomery, AL, public bus system was implemented. Since Dec 5, 1955, the black community of Montgomery had refused to ride on the segregated buses. The boycott was in reaction to the Dec 1, 1955, arrest of Rosa Parks for refusing to relinquish her seat on a Montgomery bus to a white man.

MUDD DAY. Dec 20, 1833. A day to remember Dr. Samuel A. Mudd (born near Bryantown, MD, Dec 20, 1833), sentenced to life imprisonment for giving medical aid to disguised John Wilkes Booth, fleeing assassin of Abraham Lincoln. Imprisoned four years before being pardoned by President Andrew Johnson. Died on Jan 10, 1883.

NAIA FOOTBALL NATIONAL CHAMPIONSHIP GAME. Dec 20. Hardin County, TN. 16-team field competes, ending with the final two teams vying for the national championship. 49th annual game. For info: Natl Assn of Intercollegiate Athletics, 23500 W 105th St, PO Box 1325, Olathe, KS 66051-1325. Phone: (913) 791-0044. Fax: (913) 791-9555. E-mail: thasseltine@naia.org. Web: www.naia.org.

RICKEY, BRANCH: BIRTH ANNIVERSARY. Dec 20, 1881. Wesley Branch Rickey, Baseball Hall of Fame player, manager and executive born at Lucasville, OH. Rickey was baseball's most innovative general manager. He invented the farm system, instituted unique training and teaching methods and, most prominently, signed Jackie Robinson to play major league baseball with the Brooklyn Dodgers. Inducted into the Hall of Fame in 1967. Died at Columbia, MO, Dec 9, 1965.

SACAGAWEA: DEATH ANNIVERSARY. Dec 20, 1812. As a young Shoshone Indian woman, Sacagawea in 1805 (with her two-month-old son strapped to her back) traveled with the Lewis and Clark Expedition, serving as an interpreter. It is said that the expedition could not have succeeded without her aid. She was born about 1787 and died at Fort Manuel on the Missouri River, Dec 20, 1812. Few other women have been so often honored. There are statues, fountains and memorials of her, and her name has been given to a mountain peak. In 2000 the US Mint issued a $1 coin honoring her.

SOUTH CAROLINA: SECESSION ANNIVERSARY. Dec 20, 1860. South Carolina's legislature voted to secede from the US, the first state to do so. Within six weeks, five more states seceded. On Feb 4, 1861, representatives from the six states met at Montgomery, AL to establish a government and on Feb 9 Jefferson Davis was elected president of the Confederate States of America. By June 1861, 11 states had seceded.

US INVASION OF PANAMA: 15th ANNIVERSARY. Dec 20, 1989. The US launched operation "Just Cause," invading Panama in an attempt to seize Manuel Noriega and bring him to justice for narcotics trafficking. Seven months after Noriega had ruled unfavorable election results null and void, the US toppled the Noriega government and oversaw the installation of Guillermo Endara as president. Although the initial military action was declared a success, Noriega eluded capture. He surrendered to US troops on Jan 4, 1990, and was tried, convicted and imprisoned in the US.

VIRGINIA COMPANY EXPEDITION TO AMERICA: ANNIVERSARY. Dec 20, 1606. Three small ships, the *Susan Constant*, the *Godspeed* and the *Discovery*, commanded by Captain Christopher Newport, departed London, England bound for America, where the royally chartered Virginia Company's approximately 120 persons established the first permanent English settlement in what is now the United States at Jamestown, VA, May 14, 1607.

BIRTHDAYS TODAY

Jenny Agutter, 52, actress (Emmy for "The Snow Goose"), born London, England, Dec 20, 1952.
Uri Geller, 58, psychic, clairvoyant, born Tel Aviv, Israel, Dec 20, 1946.
John Hillerman, 72, actor ("The Betty White Show," "Magnum, PI"), born Denison, TX, Dec 20, 1932.
David Levine, 78, artist, caricaturist (*New York Review of Books*), born Brooklyn, NY, Dec 20, 1926.
Sonny Perdue, 58, Governor of Georgia (R), born Perry, GA, Dec 20, 1946.
John Spencer, 58, actor ("The West Wing," "LA Law"), born New York, NY, Dec 20, 1946.
William Julius Wilson, 69, sociologist, educator, writer (*When Work Disappears*), born Derry Township, PA, Dec 20, 1935.

DECEMBER 21 — TUESDAY
Day 356 — 10 Remaining

BOLL, HEINRICH: BIRTH ANNIVERSARY. Dec 21, 1917. German novelist, winner of the 1972 Nobel Prize for Literature, author of some 20 books including *Billiards at Half-Past Nine, The Clown* and *Group Portrait with Lady*, was born at Cologne, Germany. He died near Bonn, Germany, July 16, 1985.

DISRAELI, BENJAMIN: 200th BIRTH ANNIVERSARY. Dec 21, 1804. British novelist and statesman, born at London and died there Apr 19, 1881. "No government," he wrote, "can be long secure without a formidable opposition."

FIRST CROSSWORD PUZZLE: ANNIVERSARY. Dec 21, 1913. The first crossword puzzle was compiled by Arthur Wynne and published in a supplement to the *New York World*.

FOREFATHERS' DAY. Dec 21. Observed mainly in New England in commemoration of landing at Plymouth Rock on this day in 1620.

HUMBUG DAY. Dec 21. Allows all those preparing for Christmas to vent their frustrations. 12 "humbugs" allowed. [©2003 by WH.] For info: Thomas & Ruth Roy, Wellcat Holidays, 2418 Long Ln, Lebanon, PA 17046. Phone: (717) 279-0184. E-mail: info@wellcat.com. Web: www.wellcat.com.

PAN AMERICAN FLIGHT 103 EXPLOSION: ANNIVERSARY. Dec 21, 1988. Pan Am World Airways Flight 103 exploded in midair and crashed into the heart of Lockerbie, Scotland, the result of a terrorist bombing. The 259 passengers and crew members and 11 persons on the ground were killed in the disaster. The tragedy raised questions about security and the notification of passengers in the event of threatened flights. In the resultant investigation it was revealed that government agencies and the airline had known that the flight was possibly the target of a terrorist attack.

PARKINSON, JAMES: DEATH ANNIVERSARY. Dec 21, 1824. The remarkable English physician and paleontologist who first described the "shaking palsy" later had it named for him—Parkinson's disease. He was the author of numerous books and articles on a variety of subjects. His *Organic Remains of a Former World* is called the first attempt to give a scientific account of fossils. Under oath, Parkinson declared that he was a member of the group that hatched the "Pop-gun Plot" to assassinate King George III in a theater, using a poisoned dart for the deed. Parkinson was born at London about 1755, and died there, Dec 21, 1824.

PHILEAS FOGG WINS A WAGER DAY. Dec 21. Anniversary, from Jules Verne's *Around the World in Eighty Days*, of the winning of Phileas Fogg's wager, on Dec 21, 1872, when Fogg walked into the saloon of the Reform Club at London, announcing "Here I am, gentlemen!" exactly 79 days, 23 hours, 59 minutes and 59 seconds after starting his trip "around the world in 80 days," to win his £20,000 wager. See also: "Phileas Fogg's Wager Day" (Oct 2).

PILGRIM LANDING: ANNIVERSARY. Dec 21, 1620. According to Governor William Bradford's *History of Plymouth Plantation*, "On Munday," [Dec 21, 1620, New Style] the Pilgrims, aboard the *Mayflower*, reached Plymouth, MA, "sounded ye harbor, and founde it fitt for shipping; and marched into ye land, & founde diverse cornfields, and ye best they could find, and ye season & their presente necessitie made them glad to accepte of it.... And after wards tooke better view of ye place, and resolved wher to pitch their dwelling; and them and their goods." Plymouth Rock, the legendary place of landing since it first was "identified" in 1769, nearly 150 years after the landing, has been a historic shrine since. The landing anniversary is observed in much of New England as Forefathers' Day. See also: "Forefathers' Day" (Dec 21).

SHERMAN TAKES SAVANNAH: ANNIVERSARY. Dec 21, 1864. Despite efforts by Confederate General William Hardee to defend the city of Savannah, GA, Southern troops were forced to pull out of the city, and on this date Union forces under William Tecumseh Sherman captured the town. By marching from Atlanta to the coast at Savannah, Sherman had cut the lower South off from the center.

SNOW WHITE AND THE SEVEN DWARFS FILM PREMIERE: ANNIVERSARY. Dec 21, 1937. America's first full-length animated feature film (and also the first Technicolor feature) premiered on this date at the Carthay Circle Theater, Hollywood, CA. The labor of love from Walt Disney—who for years wanted to create a feature-length cartoon—involved more than 750 artists and 1,500 colors in four years of development. The film features the classic songs "Some Day My Prince Will Come" and "Whistle While You Work." Walt Disney received a special Oscar for *Snow White*—along with seven miniature Oscars.

SPACE MILESTONE: *APOLLO 8* **(US): ANNIVERSARY.** Dec 21, 1968. First moon voyage launched, manned by Colonel Frank Borman, Captain James A. Lovell, Jr and Major William A. Anders. Orbited moon Dec 24, returned to Earth Dec 27. First men to orbit the moon and see the side of the moon away from Earth.

STALIN, JOSEPH: 125th BIRTH ANNIVERSARY. Dec 21, 1879. Russian dictator whose family name was Dzhugashvili, was born at Gori, Georgia. One of the most powerful and most feared men of the 20th century, Stalin died (of a stroke) at the Kremlin, at Moscow, Mar 5, 1953.

SZOLD, HENRIETTA: BIRTH ANNIVERSARY. Dec 21, 1860. Teacher, writer, social worker, organizer and pioneer Zionist, Henrietta Szold is best remembered as founder and first president of Hadassah, the Women's Zionist Organization of America. Born at Baltimore, MD, she was influenced by her father Rabbi Benjamin Szold, an active and vocal abolitionist. She established the first "Night School" at Baltimore, focused on teaching English and job skills to immigrants. Her trip to Palestine in 1910 sparked the genesis of Hadassah. While there, Szold was alarmed by the lack of social, medical and educational services and returned with the idea that a national women's Zionist organization must be formed to carry out practical projects. The "Mother of Social Service in Palestine," Szold died at Jerusalem, Feb 13, 1945. See also: "Hadassah: Anniversary" (Feb 24).

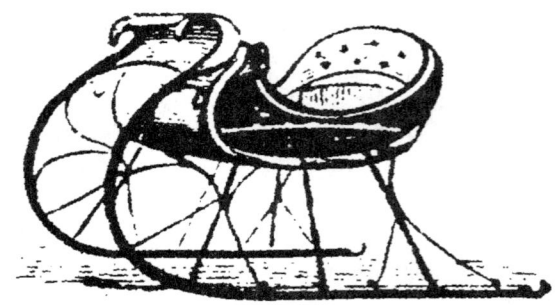

WINTER. Dec 21–Mar 20, 2005. In the Northern Hemisphere winter begins today with the winter solstice, at 7:42 AM, EST. Note that in the Southern Hemisphere today is the beginning of summer. Between Equator and Arctic Circle the sunrise and sunset points on the horizon are farthest south for the year and daylight length is minimum (ranging from 12 hours, 8 minutes, at the equator to zero at the Arctic Circle).

WORLD PEACE DAY/WINTER SOLSTICE. Dec 21. A day on which bells throughout the world will be rung along with prayers for world peace. The Middle East and Iraq will be the main focal point this year. Choose peace now. Annually, on the winter solstice. For info: Donald L. Orne, PO Box 225, Marblehead, MA 01945. Phone: (781) 631-0786. E-mail: don@yingcom.com. Web: www.yingcom.com.

YALDA. Dec 21. Yalda, the longest night of the year, is celebrated by Iranians. The ceremony has an Indo-Iranian origin, where Light and Good were considered to struggle against Darkness and Evil. With fires burning and lights lit, family and friends gather to stay up through the night helping the sun in its battle against darkness. They recite poetry, tell stories and eat special fruits and nuts until the sun, triumphant, reappears in the morning.

YULE. Dec 21. (Also called Alban Arthan.) One of the "Lesser Sabbats" during the Wiccan year, Yule marks the death of the Sun-God and his rebirth from the Earth Goddess. Annually, on the winter solstice.

ZAPPA, FRANK: BIRTH ANNIVERSARY. Dec 21, 1940. Rock musician and composer, Zappa was noted for his satire and as a leading advocate against censorship of contemporary music. He formed the group Mothers of Invention. Born at Baltimore, MD, he died Dec 4, 1993, at Los Angeles, CA, at age 52.

BIRTHDAYS TODAY

Tina Brown, 51, former *New Yorker* editor, born London, England, Dec 21, 1953.
Andy Dick, 39, actor ("NewsRadio"), born Charleston, SC, Dec 21, 1965.
Phil Donahue, 69, former TV talk-show host ("Donahue"), born Cleveland, OH, Dec 21, 1935.
Christine Marie (Chris) Evert, 50, sportscaster, former tennis player, born Ft Lauderdale, FL, Dec 21, 1954.
Jane Fonda, 67, actress (Oscars for *Klute, Coming Home; Julia, On Golden Pond*), born New York, NY, Dec 21, 1937.
Samuel L. Jackson, 56, actor (*Pulp Fiction, Jurassic Park*), born Washington, DC, Dec 21, 1948.
Jane Kaczmarek, 49, actress ("Malcolm in the Middle"), born Milwaukee, WI, Dec 21, 1955.
Joe Paterno, 78, college football coach, born Brooklyn, NY, Dec 21, 1926.
Ray Romano, 47, comedian, actor ("Everybody Loves Raymond"), born Queens, NY, Dec 21, 1957.
Michael Tilson Thomas, 60, conductor, pianist, organist, born Hollywood, CA, Dec 21, 1944.
Andrew James (Andy) Van Slyke, 44, former baseball player, born Utica, NY, Dec 21, 1960.
Karrie Webb, 30, golfer, born Ayr, Queensland, Australia, Dec 21, 1974.
Paul Winchell, 82, ventriloquist, actor, born New York, NY, Dec 21, 1922.

DECEMBER 22 — WEDNESDAY
Day 357 — 9 Remaining

ABILITIES DAY. Dec 22. Celebrates all people with disabilities and their caregivers. To celebrate this day wear a white ribbon. For info: Paul Cannaday, 4971 Wixson Rd, Croswell, MI 48422. Phone: (810) 679-0236. E-mail: paulc@greatlakes.net. Web: www.disabilitygrapevine.com.

ASARAH B'TEVET. Dec 22. Hebrew calendar date: Tevet 10, 5765. The Fast of the 10th of Tevet begins at first morning light and commemorates the beginning of the Babylonian siege of Jerusalem in the 6th century BC. Began at sundown on Dec 21.

ASHCROFT, PEGGY: BIRTH ANNIVERSARY. Dec 22, 1907. British actress Dame Edith Margaret Emily Ashcroft was born at Croyden, England. In addition to her many accolades on the British stage she won an Oscar for her supporting role in *Passage to India* (1985) and a special British Olivier Award for lifetime achievement in 1991. She died June 14, 1991, at London, England.

CAPRICORN, THE GOAT. Dec 22–Jan 19. In the astronomical and astrological zodiac that divides the sun's apparent orbit into 12 segments, the period Dec 22–Jan 19 is identified, traditionally, as the sun-sign of Capricorn, the Goat. The ruling planet is Saturn.

"DING DONG SCHOOL" TV PREMIERE: ANNIVERSARY. Dec 22, 1952. Named by a three-year-old after watching a test broadcast of the opening sequence (a hand ringing a bell), "Ding Dong School" was one of the first children's educational series. Miss Frances (Dr. Frances Horwich, head of Roosevelt College's education department at Chicago) was the host of this weekday show.

ELLERY, WILLIAM: BIRTH ANNIVERSARY. Dec 22, 1727. Signer of the Declaration of Independence, born at Newport, RI, and died there Feb 15, 1820.

FIRST GORILLA BORN IN CAPTIVITY: BIRTH ANNIVERSARY. Dec 22, 1956. "Colo" was born at the Columbus, OH, zoo, weighing in at 3¼ pounds, the first gorilla born in captivity.

OGLETHORPE, JAMES EDWARD: BIRTH ANNIVERSARY. Dec 22, 1696. English general, author and colonizer of Georgia. Founder of the city of Savannah. Oglethorpe was born at London. He died June 30, 1785, at Cranham Hall, Essex, England.

PUCCINI, GIACOMO: BIRTH ANNIVERSARY. Dec 22, 1858. Italian composer of such operas as *La Boheme* and *Madame Butterfly*. Born at Lucca, Tuscany, Italy, he died Nov 29, 1924, at Brussels, Belgium.

ROBINSON, EDWIN ARLINGTON: BIRTH ANNIVERSARY. Dec 22, 1869. Three-time Pulitzer Prize winner best known for his short dramatic poems, including "Richard Cory" and "Miniver Cheevy." Born at Head Tide, ME, and died at Los Angeles, CA, Apr 6, 1935.

BIRTHDAYS TODAY

Barbara Billingsley, 82, actress ("Leave It to Beaver," *Airplane!*), born Los Angeles, CA, Dec 22, 1922.
Steven Norman (Steve) Carlton, 60, Hall of Fame baseball player, born Miami, FL, Dec 22, 1944.
Hector Elizondo, 68, actor (*Pretty Woman, Frankie and Johnny*, "Chicago Hope"), born New York, NY, Dec 22, 1936.
Ralph Fiennes, 42, actor (*Schindler's List, The English Patient*), born Suffolk, England, Dec 22, 1962.
Steve Garvey, 56, former baseball player, born Tampa, FL, Dec 22, 1948.
Robin Gibb, 55, singer, musician (The Bee Gees), born Manchester, England, Dec 22, 1949.
Claudia Alta (Lady Bird) Johnson, 92, former First Lady, widow of Lyndon B. Johnson, 36th president of the US, born Karnack, TX, Dec 22, 1912.
Diane K. Sawyer, 58, journalist ("60 Minutes," "Prime Time Live"), born Glasgow, KY, Dec 22, 1946.
Jan Stephenson, 53, golfer, born Sydney, Australia, Dec 22, 1951.

Dec 23–24   ☆ *Chase's 2004 Calendar of Events* ☆

DECEMBER 23 — THURSDAY
Day 358 — 8 Remaining

FEDERAL RESERVE SYSTEM: ANNIVERSARY. Dec 23, 1913. Established pursuant to authority contained in the Federal Reserve Act of Dec 23, 1913, the system serves as the nation's central bank, with the responsibility for execution of monetary policy. It is called on to contribute to the strength and vitality of the US economy, in part by influencing the lending and investing activities of commercial banks and the cost and availability of money and credit.

FIRST NONSTOP FLIGHT AROUND THE WORLD WITHOUT REFUELING: ANNIVERSARY. Dec 23, 1987. Dick Rutan and Jeana Yeager set a new world record of 216 hours of continuous flight, breaking their own record of 111 hours set July 15, 1986. The aircraft *Voyager* departed from Edwards Air Force Base in California, Dec 14, 1987 and landed Dec 23, 1987. The journey covered 24,986 miles at an official speed of 115 miles per hour.

"IMMACULATE RECEPTION": ANNIVERSARY. Dec 23, 1972. In an AFC first-round play-off game between the Pittsburgh Steelers and the Oakland Raiders, the Raiders were ahead, 7–6, with 22 seconds to play. Pittsburgh had the ball on its own 40-yard line. Steelers quarterback Terry Bradshaw threw a desperation pass intended for Johnny Fuqua. The ball deflected off an Oakland defender into the waiting arms of Franco Harris, who ran into the end zone for the winning touchdown. The Steelers defeated the Raiders, 13–7, and the play has since been known as the "Immaculate Reception."

JAPAN: BIRTHDAY OF THE EMPEROR. Dec 23. National Day. Holiday honoring Emperor Akihito, born in 1933.

METRIC CONVERSION ACT: ANNIVERSARY. Dec 23, 1975. The Congress of the US passed Public Law 94–168, known as the Metric Conversion Act of 1975. This act declares that the SI (International System of Units) will be this country's basic system of measurement and establishes the United States Metric Board which is responsible for the planning, coordination and implementation of the nation's voluntary conversion to SI. (Congress had authorized the metric system as a legal system of measurement in the US by an act passed July 28, 1866. In 1875, the US became one of the original signers of the Treaty of the Metre, which established an international metric system.)

MEXICO: FEAST OF THE RADISHES. Dec 23. Oaxaca. Figurines of people and animals cleverly carved out of radishes are sold during festivities.

MONROE, HARRIET: BIRTH ANNIVERSARY. Dec 23, 1860. American poet, editor and founder of *Poetry* magazine. Born at Chicago, IL. Died Sept 26, 1936, at Arequipa, Peru.

SMILES, SAMUEL: BIRTH ANNIVERSARY. Dec 23, 1812. Scottish writer, born at Haddington, Berwickshire, Scotland. Died at London, England, Apr 17, 1904. "A place for everything," he wrote in *Thrift*, "and everything in its place."

TOJO HIDEKI EXECUTION: ANNIVERSARY. Dec 23, 1948. Tojo Hideki, prime minister of Japan from Oct 16, 1941, until his resignation July 19, 1944. After Japan's surrender in August 1945, Tojo was arrested as a war criminal, tried by a military tribunal and sentenced to death Nov 12, 1948. Born at Tokyo, Japan, Dec 30, 1884, Tojo was hanged (with six other Japanese wartime military leaders) at Sugamo Prison, Tokyo, Dec 23, 1948, the sentence being carried out by the US 8th Army.

	S	M	T	W	T	F	S
December 2004				1	2	3	4
	5	6	7	8	9	10	11
	12	13	14	15	16	17	18
	19	20	21	22	23	24	25
	26	27	28	29	30	31	

TRANSISTOR INVENTED: ANNIVERSARY. Dec 23, 1947. John Bardeen, Walter Brattain and William Shockley of Bell Laboratories shared the 1956 Nobel Prize for their invention of the transistor, which led to a revolution in communications and electronics. It was smaller, lighter, more durable, more reliable and generated less heat than the vacuum tube that had been used up to this time.

BIRTHDAYS TODAY

Akihito, 71, Emperor of Japan, born Tokyo, Japan, Dec 23, 1933.
Robert Bly, 78, author (*Iron John: A Book About Men; What Have I Ever Lost by Dying?*), born Madison, MN, Dec 23, 1926.
Scott Gomez, 25, hockey player, born Anchorage, AK, Dec 23, 1979.
Jose Greco, 86, dancer, born Abruzzi, Italy, Dec 23, 1918.
Corey Haim, 33, actor (*Murphy's Romance, The Lost Boys*), born Toronto, ON, Canada, Dec 23, 1971.
James Joseph (Jim) Harbaugh, 41, former football player, born Toledo, OH, Dec 23, 1963.
Susan Lucci, 55, actress ("All My Children," *Mafia Princess*), born Westchester, NY, Dec 23, 1949.
Gerald O'Loughlin, 83, actor ("The Rookies," "Our House"), born New York, NY, Dec 23, 1921.

DECEMBER 24 — FRIDAY
Day 359 — 7 Remaining

AIDA PREMIERE: ANNIVERSARY. Dec 24, 1871. Giuseppe Verdi's opera *Aida* premiered at Cairo. It was commissioned by the Khedive of Egypt to celebrate the opening of the Suez Canal.

ARNOLD, MATTHEW: BIRTH ANNIVERSARY. Dec 24, 1822. English poet and essayist, born at Laleham, England. Died Apr 15, 1888, at Liverpool, England. "One has often wondered," he wrote in *Culture and Anarchy*, "whether upon the whole earth there is anything so unintelligent, so unapt to perceive how the world is really going, as an ordinary young Englishman of our upper class."

AUSTRIA: "SILENT NIGHT, HOLY NIGHT" CELEBRATIONS. Dec 24. Oberndorf, Hallein and Wagrain, Salzburg, Austria. Commemorating the creation of the Christmas carol here in 1818.

CARSON, CHRISTOPHER "KIT": BIRTH ANNIVERSARY. Dec 24, 1809. American frontiersman, soldier, trapper, guide and Indian agent best known as Kit Carson. Born at Madison County, KY, he died at Fort Lyon, CO, May 23, 1868.

CHRISTMAS BELLS RING AGAIN IN ST. BASIL'S: ANNIVERSARY. Dec 24, 1990. For the first time since the death of Lenin in 1924, the bells of St. Basil's Cathedral, on Red Square in Moscow, rang to celebrate Christmas.

CHRISTMAS EVE. Dec 24. Family gift-giving occasion in many Christian countries.

CHRISTMAS EVE TORCHLIGHT PARADE. Dec 24. Winter Park Resort, Winter Park, CO. One of Winter Park Resort's

☆ Chase's 2004 Calendar of Events ☆ Dec 24–25

most beloved traditions, highlighted by Santa Claus leading a procession of torch-bearing skiers down Lower Hughes trail under a spectacular fireworks display. Est attendance: 1,500. For info: Winter Park Resort, PO Box 36, Winter Park, CO 80482. Phone: (970) 726-1564. Fax: (970) 726-1572. E-mail: wpinfo@mail.ski winterpark.com. Web: winterparkresort.com.

FIRST SURFACE-TO-SURFACE GUIDED MISSILE: ANNIVERSARY. Dec 24, 1942. German rocket engineer Wernher von Braun launched the first surface-to-surface guided missile. Buzz bombs, a form of guided missile, were used by Germany against Great Britain starting Sept 8, 1944. On Feb 24, 1949, the first rocket to reach outer space (an altitude of 25 miles) was fired. The two-stage rocket, a Wac Corporal set in the nose of a German V-2, was launched from the White Sands Proving Grounds, NM, by a team of scientists headed by von Braun.

GARDNER, AVA: BIRTH ANNIVERSARY. Dec 24, 1922. Actress and leading sex symbol of the 1940s and '50s, Ava Lavinnia Gardner was born at Smithfield, NC. Among Gardner's numerous movies are *The Barefoot Contessa, Bhowani Junction, The Sun Also Rises* and *The Life and Times of Judge Roy Bean*. Gardner was married to Mickey Rooney (1942–43), Artie Shaw (1945–46) and Frank Sinatra (1951–57). Died at London, England, Jan 25, 1990.

HUGHES, HOWARD ROBARD: BIRTH ANNIVERSARY. Dec 24, 1905. Wealthy American industrialist, aviator and movie producer who spent his latter years as a recluse. Born at Houston, TX, he died in airplane en route from Acapulco, Mexico, to Houston, Apr 5, 1976.

JOULE, JAMES PRESCOTT: BIRTH ANNIVERSARY. Dec 24, 1818. English physicist and inventor after whom Joule's Law (the first law of thermodynamics) was named was born at Salford, Lancashire, England. The unit of measurement of the mechnical equivalent of heat is known as the Joule. He died at Cheshire, England, Oct 11, 1889.

LIBYA: INDEPENDENCE DAY. Dec 24. Libya gained its independence from Italy in 1951.

"THE PERRY COMO SHOW" TV PREMIERE: ANNIVERSARY. Dec 24, 1948. Singer Perry Como hosted "The Chesterfield Supper Club" when it came to TV from radio. Also featured were the Mitchell Ayres Orchestra and the Fontane Sisters. The show was retitled "The Perry Como Show" during 1955–59 and then "The Kraft Music Hall" during 1959–63. The Ray Charles Singers and the Louis DaPron Dancers were featured. Como's theme song was "Dream Along with Me."

STOCK EXCHANGE HOLIDAY (CHRISTMAS DAY). Dec 24 (observed). The holiday schedules for the various exchanges are subject to change if relevant rules, regulations or exchange policies are revised. If you have questions, phone: American Stock Exchange (212) 306-1000; Chicago Board of Options Exchange (312) 786-5600; Chicago Board of Trade (312) 435-3500; New York Stock Exchange (212) 656-2065; Pacific Stock Exchange (415) 393-4000; Philadelphia Stock Exchange (215) 496-5000.

BIRTHDAYS TODAY

Diedrich Bader, 38, actor ("The Drew Carey Show"), born Alexandria, VA, Dec 24, 1966.
Mary Higgins Clark, 73, author (*Where Are the Children?, Silent Night*), born New York, NY, Dec 24, 1931.
Ricky Martin, 33, singer, actor ("General Hospital"), born Enrique José Martín, San Juan, Puerto Rico, Dec 24, 1971.
Jeff Sessions, 58, US Senator (R, Alabama), born Hybart, AL, Dec 24, 1946.

DECEMBER 25 — SATURDAY
Day 360 — 6 Remaining

A'PHABET DAY. Dec 25. Also known as "No-L" Day, this celebration is for people who do not want to send Christmas cards but who want to greet their friends; so they send out cards listing the letters of the alphabet in order, but with a gap where L would be. For info: Bob Birch, The Puns Corps, PO Box 2364, Falls Church, VA 22042-0364. Phone: (703) 533-3668.

BARTON, CLARA: BIRTH ANNIVERSARY. Dec 25, 1821. Clarissa Harlowe Barton, American nurse and philanthropist, founder of the American Red Cross, was born at Oxford, MA. In 1881, she became first president of the American Red Cross (founded May 21, 1881). She died at Glen Echo, MD, Apr 12, 1912.

BLUE-GRAY ALL STAR FOOTBALL CLASSIC. Dec 25. Cramton Bowl, Montgomery, AL. College seniors from northern schools compete against their southern counterparts. Annually, on Christmas Day. Est attendance: 22,000. For info: Montgomery Lion's Club, 771 S Lawrence St, Ste 106, PO Box 94, Montgomery, AL 36101-0094. Phone: (334) 265-1266. Fax: (334) 265-5944. E-mail: info@bluegrayfootball.com. Web: www.blue grayfootball.com.

BOGART, HUMPHREY: BIRTH ANNIVERSARY. Dec 25, 1899. American stage and screen actor, Humphrey DeForest Bogart was born at New York, NY. Among his best remembered films are: *The African Queen, The Maltese Falcon, Casablanca* and *To Have and Have Not*. Bogart died Jan 14, 1957, at Hollywood, CA.

BOOTH, EVANGELINE CORY: BIRTH ANNIVERSARY. Dec 25, 1865. Salvation Army general, active in England, Canada and the US. Author and composer of songs, Booth was born at London, England. She died at Hartsdale, NY, July 17, 1950.

CALLOWAY, CAB: BIRTH ANNIVERSARY. Dec 25, 1907. American singer and bandleader Cabell Calloway was born at Rochester, NY. George Gershwin modeled the part of Sportin' Life in *Porgy and Bess* (1953) after this jazz singer who also played the role across the US until 1956. He is best known for his song "Minnie the Moocher" (1931). He died Nov 18, 1994, at Hockessin, DE.

CEAUSESCU, NICOLAE: 15th DEATH ANNIVERSARY. Dec 25, 1989. On Christmas evening a broadcast of a Christmas symphony on state-run television was interrupted with

Dec 25 ☆ Chase's 2004 Calendar of Events ☆

the report that Romanian president Nicolae Ceausescu and his wife had been executed, bringing to an end the last hard-line regime in the Soviet bloc. Ceausescu's downfall began when he ordered members of his black-shirted state police, the Securitate, to use force to quell a disturbance in the town of Timisorara. The brutal crackdown led to estimates of as many as 4,500 killed. Ceausescu's rule was marked by corruption, deprivation and terror.

CHRISTMAS. Dec 25. Christian festival commemorating the birth of Jesus of Nazareth. Most popular of Christian observances, Christmas as a Feast of the Nativity dates from the 4th century. Although Jesus's birth date is not known, the Western church selected Dec 25 for the feast, possibly to counteract the non-Christian festivals of that approximate date. Many customs from non-Christian festivals (Roman Saturnalia, Mithraic sun's birthday, Teutonic yule, Druidic and other winter solstice rites) have been adopted as part of the Christmas celebration (lights, mistletoe, holly and ivy, holiday tree, wassailing and gift-giving, for example). Some Orthodox Churches celebrate Christmas Jan 7 based on the "old calendar" (Julian). Theophany (recognition of the divinity of Jesus) is observed on this date and also on Jan 6, especially by the Eastern Orthodox Church.

CHRISTMAS FIRESIDE CHAT WARNING: ANNIVERSARY. Dec 25, 1943. In his Christmas message to the American people, Franklin D. Roosevelt warned, "The war is now reaching the stage when we shall have to look forward to large casualty lists—dead, wounded and missing. War entails just that. There is no easy road to victory. And the end is not yet in sight."

CUBA: CHRISTMAS RETURNS: ANNIVERSARY. Dec 25, 1998. Christmas was celebrated in Cuba after Fidel Castro's government announced that it was again a regular holiday in the Cuban calendar. In 1997 the government had granted a Christmas holiday in deference to Pope John Paul II who was visiting the island the next month. Christmas had been abolished as a holiday in Cuba in 1969.

FARLEY, CAL: BIRTH ANNIVERSARY. Dec 25, 1895. Cal Farley, known as "America's Greatest Foster Father," started Cal Farley's Boys Ranch in 1939 with nine boys. The Ranch has grown into a modern community of 441 boys (and girls since 1992), which has housed and educated more than 4,000 boys and girls over the years. Cal Farley was born at Saxton, IA; he died Feb 19, 1967, at Boys Ranch, TX.

IT'S ABOUT TIME WEEK!. Dec 25–31. Innovative week dedicated to time-to-give, time-to-live and time-to-remember. Encourages creativity applied to problems and honors pioneers and partnerships in research, ideas and services for "ABetterWay; ABetterWorld." Awards to pioneers and partnerships. Send nominations by October. For info: For Goodness Sake! Center, 427 E 7th St, Michigan City, IN 46360. E-mail: ForGood@adsnet.com.

JINNAH, MOHAMMED ALI (QAID-E-AZAM): BIRTH ANNIVERSARY. Dec 25, 1876. The founder of the Islamic Republic of Pakistan, Mohammed Ali Jinnah was born at Karachi, then part of India. When Pakistan became an independent political entity (Aug 15, 1947), Jinnah became its first governor general. He was given the title Qaid-e-Azam (Great Leader) in 1947. He died at Karachi, Sept 11, 1948. This day is a holiday in Pakistan.

December 2004	S	M	T	W	T	F	S
				1	2	3	4
	5	6	7	8	9	10	11
	12	13	14	15	16	17	18
	19	20	21	22	23	24	25
	26	27	28	29	30	31	

"METROPOLITAN OPERA RADIO BROADCASTS" PREMIERE: ANNIVERSARY. Dec 25, 1931. On Christmas Day 1931, the Metropolitan Opera of New York City broadcast an entire opera, *Hansel and Gretel*, on the NBC radio network—the first time this had ever been done. This broadcast was the first of an ongoing radio series of Saturday matinees. On Dec 7, 1940, Texaco (now ChevronTexaco) became a sponsor and began the longest continuous sponsorship in broadcast history. For decades, the Metropolitan Opera radio broadcasts have introduced opera to new fans far from New York. Today, the broadcasts are heard internationally in 42 countries.

"THE STEVE ALLEN SHOW" TV PREMIERE: ANNIVERSARY. Dec 25, 1950. Talented actor, comedian, singer and musician, Steve Allen hosted a number of variety shows from 1950 to 1969 (with a few breaks in between to host specials and "The Tonight Show"). For two years, his television show was similar to his radio show and featured singer Peggy Lee, announcer Bern Bennett and Llemuel the llama. His next show competed with Ed Sullivan's show, though Allen's stressed comedy. Some of his "funny men" were Don Knotts, Tom Poston, Louis Nye, Gabe Dell, Pat Harrington, Jr, Dayton Allen and Bill Dana. His other shows included a talk show, a game show, a comedy show, an educational music show and a flashback-comedy show.

TAIWAN: CONSTITUTION DAY. Dec 25. National holiday. Commemorates the adoption of the 1946 constitution.

UNITED KINGDOM: CHRISTMAS HOLIDAY. Dec 25. Bank and public holiday in England, Wales, Scotland and Northern Ireland.

WEST, REBECCA: BIRTH ANNIVERSARY. Dec 25, 1892. English author, literary critic, prize-winning journalist and noted feminist, Dame Rebecca West was born Cicely Isabel Fairfield at London, England. She died there Mar 15, 1983.

BIRTHDAYS TODAY

Jimmy Buffett, 58, singer ("Margaritaville"), songwriter, born Pascagoula, MS, Dec 25, 1946.
Lawrence Richard (Larry) Csonka, 58, Hall of Fame football player, born Stow, OH, Dec 25, 1946.
Rickey Henley Henderson, 46, baseball player, born Chicago, IL, Dec 25, 1958.
Annie Lennox, 50, singer (Eurythmics, "Sweet Dreams Are Made of This"), born Aberdeen, Scotland, Dec 25, 1954.
Barbara Mandrell, 56, singer ("I Was Country When Country Wasn't Cool"), born Houston, TX, Dec 25, 1948.
Gary Sandy, 59, actor ("All That Glitters," "WKRP in Cincinnati"), born Dayton, OH, Dec 25, 1945.
Hanna Schygulla, 61, actress (*The Marriage of Maria Braun, Berlin Alexanderplatz*), born Kattowitz, Germany, Dec 25, 1943.
Mary Elizabeth (Sissy) Spacek, 55, actress (Oscar for *Coal Miner's Daughter; Missing*), born Quitman, TX, Dec 25, 1949.

DECEMBER 26 — SUNDAY
Day 361 — 5 Remaining

ALLEN, STEVE: BIRTH ANNIVERSARY. Dec 26, 1921. American entertainer and TV pioneer, Steve Allen created the original "Tonight" show for NBC in 1953. Also known as a composer and the author of more than 40 books, he was born at New York, NY, Dec 26, 1921. He died at Encino, CA, Oct 30, 2000.

BABBAGE, CHARLES: BIRTH ANNIVERSARY. Dec 26, 1792. English mathematician, born at Teignmouth, England. He developed the principles on which modern computers are designed. Babbage died at London, England, Oct 18, 1871.

BAHAMAS: JUNKANOO. Dec 26. Kaleidoscope of sound and spectacle combining a bit of Mardi Gras, mummers' parade and ancient African tribal rituals. Revelers in colorful costumes parade through the streets to sounds of cowbells, goat skin drums and many other homemade instruments. Always on Boxing Day.

BOXING DAY. Dec 26. Ordinarily observed on the first day after Christmas. A legal holiday in Canada, the United Kingdom and many other countries. Formerly (according to Robert Chambers) a day when Christmas gift boxes were "regularly expected by a postman, the lamplighter, the dustman and generally by all those functionaries who render services to the public at large, without receiving payment therefore from any individual." When Boxing Day falls on a Saturday or Sunday, the Monday or Tuesday immediately following may be proclaimed or observed as a bank or public holiday.

BOXING DAY AT THE HEMINGWAY BIRTHPLACE. Dec 26. Hemingway Birthplace, Oak Park, IL. The Hemingway family celebrated Boxing Day with extended family, eating special foods, listening to Gilbert and Sullivan, and sharing literary works and poetry. The Ernest Hemingway Foundation of Oak Park will recreate this holiday celebration. Specialty teas, sherry tastings and dramatic readings of Christmas tales will be featured. The Hemingway birthplace will be decorated in Victorian fashion and hosts and hostesses will be in Victorian dress. For info: The Ernest Hemingway Foundation, PO Box 2222, Oak Park, IL 60303-2222. Phone: (877) HEMINGWAY. Fax: (708) 386-8506. Web: www.hemingway.org.

CLERC, LAURENT: BIRTH ANNIVERSARY. Dec 26, 1785. The first deaf teacher in America, Laurent Clerc assisted Thomas Hopkins Gallaudet in establishing the first public school for the deaf, Connecticut Asylum for the Education and Instruction of Deaf and Dumb Persons (now the American School for the Deaf), at Hartford, CT, in 1817. For 41 years Clerc trained new teachers in the use of sign language and in methods of teaching the deaf. Clerc was born at LaBalme, France, and died July 18, 1869.

IRELAND: DAY OF THE WREN. Dec 26. Dingle Peninsula. Masked revelers and musicians go from door to door asking for money. Traditional day and night of public merrymaking.

KIDS AFTER CHRISTMAS. Dec 26–Jan 1, 2005. Mystic, CT. Everyone pays reduced admission and enjoys a full day of crafts, entertainment and the lore of the sea. Est attendance: 3,000. For info: Mystic Seaport, 75 Greenmanville Ave, Box 6000, Mystic, CT 06355. Phone: (860) 572-5315 or (888) 9SEAPORT. Web: www.visitmysticseaport.org.

KWANZAA. Dec 26–Jan 1, 2005. American black family observance created in 1966 by Dr. Maulana Karenga in recognition of traditional African harvest festivals. This seven-day festival stresses unity of the black family, with a harvest feast (karamu) on the first day and a day of meditation on the final one. Kwanzaa means "first fruit" in Swahili.

LOVERA, JUAN: BIRTH ANNIVERSARY. Dec 26, 1778. Venezuelan "Artist of Independence," whose best-known canvases commemorate the independence dates of Apr 19, 1810, and July 5, 1811. Known as the founder of historical painting in Venezuela. Died in 1841 (exact date unknown).

LUXEMBOURG: BLESSING OF THE WINE. Dec 26. Greiveldange, Luxembourg. Winemakers parade to the church, where a barrel of wine is blessed.

MAO TSE-TUNG: BIRTH ANNIVERSARY. Dec 26, 1893. Chinese librarian, teacher, communist revolutionist and "founding father" of the People's Republic of China, born at Hunan Province, China. Died at Beijing, Sept 9, 1976.

MILLER, HENRY (VALENTINE): BIRTH ANNIVERSARY. Dec 26, 1891. Controversial American novelist (*Tropic of Cancer*), born at New York, NY. Died at Pacific Palisades, CA, June 7, 1980.

MOON PHASE: FULL MOON. Dec 26. Moon enters Full Moon phase at 10:06 AM, EST.

NATIONAL WHINER'S DAY™. Dec 26. A day dedicated to whiners, especially those who return Christmas gifts and need lots of attention. People are encouraged to be happy about what they do have, rather than unhappy about what they don't have. The most famous whiner(s) of the year will be announced. Nominations accepted through Dec 15. For more info, please send SASE to: Kevin C. Zaborney, 2023 Vickory Rd, Caro, MI 48723. Phone: (989) 673-6696. E-mail: revkev@avci.net. Web: www.geocities.com/hugging_whining.

NELSON, THOMAS: BIRTH ANNIVERSARY. Dec 26, 1738. Merchant and signer of the Declaration of Independence, born at Yorktown, VA. Died at Hanover County, VA, Jan 4, 1789.

NEW YEAR'S EVE TRAIL RIDE AND PARTY. Dec 26–31. Spirit of the Suwannee Music Park and Campground, Live Oak, FL. Enjoy trail riding in the cool and mild warm weather, good food, music, dancing and fun. For info: Spirit of the Suwannee Music Park and Campground, Hwy 129, Live Oak, FL 32060. Phone: (386) 364-1683. Web: www.musicliveshere.com.

RADIUM DISCOVERED: ANNIVERSARY. Dec 26, 1898. French scientists Pierre and Marie Curie discovered the element radium, for which they later won the Nobel Prize for Physics.

SAINT STEPHEN'S DAY. Dec 26. One of the seven deacons named by the apostles to distribute alms. Died during 1st century. Feast Day is Dec 26 and is observed as a public holiday in Austria and the Republic of Ireland.

SECOND DAY OF CHRISTMAS. Dec 26. Observed as holiday in many countries.

SHENANDOAH NATIONAL PARK ESTABLISHED: ANNIVERSARY. Dec 26, 1935. Area of Blue Ridge Mountains of Virginia, originally authorized May 22, 1926, was established as a national park. For further park info: Shenandoah Natl Park, Rte 4, Box 348, Luray, VA 22835.

SLOVENIA: INDEPENDENCE DAY. Dec 26. National holiday. Commemorates 1990 announcement of separation from the Yugoslav Union.

SOUNDS OF THE SEASON: A HOLIDAY CONCERT. Dec 26–27. Ash Lawn–Highland, Charlottesville, VA. Seasonal music, candlelight house tour and cider. Est attendance: 150. For info: Ash Lawn–Highland, James Monroe Parkway, Charlottesville, VA 22902. Phone: (434) 293-9539. Fax: (434) 293-8000. E-mail: info@ashlawnhighland.org. Web: www.ashlawnhighland.org.

SOUTH AFRICA: DAY OF GOODWILL. Dec 26. National holiday. Replaces Boxing Day.

UNITED KINGDOM: BOXING DAY BANK HOLIDAY. Dec 26. Bank and public holiday in England, Wales, Scotland and Northern Ireland.

Dec 26–28 ☆ Chase's 2004 Calendar of Events ☆

WORLD KARTING ASSOCIATION RACES. Dec 26–30 (tentative). Daytona International Speedway, Daytona Beach, FL. For info: Daytona Intl Speedway, PO Box 2801, Daytona Beach, FL 32120-2801. Phone: (386) 253-7223. Fax: (386) 947-6791. Web: www.daytonainternationalspeedway.com.

BIRTHDAYS TODAY

Evan Bayh, 49, US Senator (D, Indiana), born Shirkleville, IN, Dec 26, 1955.
Susan Butcher, 50, sled dog racer, born Cambridge, MA, Dec 26, 1954.
Gray Davis, 62, Governor of California (D), born The Bronx, NY, Dec 26, 1942.
Carlton Ernest Fisk, 57, Hall of Fame baseball player, born Bellows Falls, VT, Dec 26, 1947.
Alan King, 77, comedian, author ("Seventh Avenue," *Help! I'm a Prisoner in a Chinese Bakery*), born Irwin Kniberg, New York, NY, Dec 26, 1927.
Marcelo Rios, 29, tennis player, born Santiago, Chile, Dec 26, 1975.
Osborne Earl (Ozzie) Smith, 50, Hall of Fame baseball player, born Mobile, AL, Dec 26, 1954.
Phil Spector, 64, music producer, born New York, NY, Dec 26, 1940.
Richard Widmark, 90, actor (*Kiss of Death, Madigan*), born Sunrise, MN, Dec 26, 1914.

DECEMBER 27 — MONDAY
Day 362 — 4 Remaining

CAYLEY, GEORGE: BIRTH ANNIVERSARY. Dec 27, 1773. Aviation pioneer Sir George Cayley, English scientist and inventor, was a theoretician who designed airplanes, helicopters and gliders. He is credited as the father of aerodynamics and he was the pilot of the world's first manned glider flight. Born at Scarborough, Yorkshire, England, he died at Brompton Hall, Yorkshire, Dec 15, 1857.

CHRISTMAS AT THE TOP MUSEUM. Dec 27 & 29. Spinning Top Museum, Burlington, WI. Enjoy the traditional, universal toys of tops and top games, well-loved Christmas gifts around the world in the 2-hour museum program: 35 hands-on games and experiments, two videos, view the exhibit of 2,000 items, plus a live show by top collector. Reservations required. For info: Spinning Top Museum, 533 Milwaukee Ave (Hwy 36), Burlington, WI 53105. Phone: (262) 763-3946.

DIETRICH, MARLENE: BIRTH ANNIVERSARY. Dec 27, 1901. Born at Berlin, Germany, Dietrich enrolled in Max Reinhardt's drama school. Her first big break was in 1930 when Josef Von Sternberg cast her in *The Blue Angel*, the first talkie made in Germany. A year later, she and Sternberg moved to Hollywood and began a string of six films together with *Morocco*, the only film for which she received an Academy Award nomination. Some of her other films were *Destry Rides Again, Around the World in 80 Days, Touch of Evil, Judgment at Nuremberg* and *Witness for the Prosecution*. During the 1950s she was a cabaret singer in a stage revue that toured the globe. Dietrich died May 6, 1992, at Paris, France.

"HOWDY DOODY" TV PREMIERE: ANNIVERSARY. Dec 27, 1947. The first popular children's show was brought to TV by Bob Smith and was one of the first regular NBC shows to be shown in color. It was set in the circus town of Doodyville. Children sat in the bleachers' "Peanut Gallery" and participated in activities such as songs and stories. Human characters were Buffalo Bob (Bob Smith), the silent clown Clarabell (Bob Keeshan, Bobby Nicholson and Lew Anderson), storekeeper Cornelius Cobb (Nicholson), Chief Thunderthud (Bill LeCornec), Princess Summerfall Winterspring (Judy Tyler and Linda Marsh), Bison Bill (Ted Brown) and wrestler Ugly Sam (Dayton Allen). Puppet costars included Howdy Doody, Phineas T. Bluster, Dilly Dally, Flub-a-Dub, Captain Scuttlebutt, Double Doody and Heidi Doody. The filmed adventures of Gumby were also featured. In the final episode, Clarabell broke his long silence to say, "Goodbye, kids."

KEPLER, JOHANNES: BIRTH ANNIVERSARY. Dec 27, 1571. One of the world's greatest astronomers, called "the father of modern astronomy," German mathematician Johannes Kepler was born at Wurttemberg, Germany; he died at Regensburg, Germany, Nov 15, 1630.

PASTEUR, LOUIS: BIRTH ANNIVERSARY. Dec 27, 1822. French chemist-bacteriologist born at Dole, Jura, France. Died at Villeneuve l'Etang, France, Sept 28, 1895. Discoverer of prophylactic inoculation against rabies. Pasteurization process named for him.

RADIO CITY MUSIC HALL: ANNIVERSARY. Dec 27, 1932. Radio City Music Hall, at New York City, opened on this date.

SAINT JOHN, APOSTLE-EVANGELIST: FEAST DAY. Dec 27. Son of Zebedee, Galilean fisherman, and Salome. Died about AD 100. Roman Rite Feast Day is Dec 27. (Observed May 8 by Byzantine Rite.)

SALK, LEE: BIRTH ANNIVERSARY. Dec 27, 1926. American child psychologist Lee Salk was born at New York, NY. He became well known for proving the calming effect of a mother's heartbeat on a newborn infant. Salk's warning during the 1970s that women should not abandon full-time childrearing was met with wide opposition, especially from working mothers. He died May 2, 1992, at New York, NY.

BIRTHDAYS TODAY

Gerard Depardieu, 56, actor (*The Return of Martin Guerre, Cyrano de Bergerac*), born Chateauroux, France, Dec 27, 1948.
Tovah Feldshuh, 52, actress (*Holocaust*), born New York, NY, Dec 27, 1952.
Bernard Lanvin, 69, fashion designer, born Neuilly, France, Dec 27, 1935.
Cokie Roberts, 61, news correspondent, born New Orleans, LA, Dec 27, 1943.
Anna Russell, 93, comedienne, born London, England, Dec 27, 1911.

DECEMBER 28 — TUESDAY
Day 363 — 3 Remaining

AUSTRALIA: PROCLAMATION DAY. Dec 28. Observed in South Australia.

ENDANGERED SPECIES ACT: ANNIVERSARY. Dec 28, 1973. President Richard Nixon signed the Endangered Species Act into law.

HOLY INNOCENTS DAY (CHILDERMAS). Dec 28. Commemoration of the massacre of children at Bethlehem, ordered by King Herod who wanted to destroy, among them, the infant Savior. Early and medieval accounts claimed as many as 144,000 victims, but more recent writers, noting that Bethlehem was a very small town, have revised the estimates of the number of children killed to between six and 20.

	S	M	T	W	T	F	S
December 2004				1	2	3	4
	5	6	7	8	9	10	11
	12	13	14	15	16	17	18
	19	20	21	22	23	24	25
	26	27	28	29	30	31	

☆ Chase's 2004 Calendar of Events ☆   Dec 28-29

IOWA: ADMISSION DAY: ANNIVERSARY. Dec 28. Became 29th state in 1846.

MESSINA EARTHQUAKE: ANNIVERSARY. Dec 28, 1908. Messina, Sicily. The ancient town of Messina was struck by an earthquake. Nearly 80,000 persons died in the disaster, and half of the town's buildings were destroyed.

MOLSON, JOHN: BIRTH ANNIVERSARY. Dec 28, 1763. John Molson, an orphan, left his home at Lincolnshire, England, to settle in Montreal in 1782. He soon acquired a brewery and became patriarch of the Molson brewery family. Born at Lincolnshire, he died at Montreal, Quebec, Canada, Jan 11, 1836.

PLEDGE OF ALLEGIANCE RECOGNIZED: ANNIVERSARY. Dec 28, 1945. The US Congress officially recognized the Pledge of Allegiance and urged its frequent recitation in America's schools. The pledge was composed in 1892 by Francis Bellamy, a Baptist minister. At the time, Bellamy was chairman of a committee of state school superintendents of education, and several public schools adopted his pledge as part of the Columbus Day quadricentennial celebration that year. In 1954 the Knights of Columbus persuaded Congress to add the words "under God" to the pledge. In 2002 a federal appeals court found the pledge unconstitutional for use in public schools due to the "under God" phrase.

POOR RICHARD'S ALMANACK : ANNIVERSARY. Dec 28, 1732. The *Pennsylvania Gazette* carried the first known advertisement for the first issue of *Poor Richard's Almanack* by Richard Saunders (Benjamin Franklin) for the year 1733. The advertisement promised "many pleasant and witty verses, jests and sayings . . . new fashions, games for kisses . . . men and melons . . . breakfast in bed, &c." America's most famous almanac, *Poor Richard's* was published through the year 1758 and has been imitated many times since.

VICE PRESIDENTIAL RESIGNATION: ANNIVERSARY. Dec 28, 1832. John C. Calhoun, who had served as vice president of the US under two presidents (John Quincy Adams and Andrew Jackson), Mar 4, 1825–Dec 28, 1832, finding himself in growing disagreement with President Jackson, resigned the office of vice president, the first to do so. He spent most of his subsequent political life as a US senator from South Carolina.

WILSON, WOODROW: BIRTH ANNIVERSARY. Dec 28, 1856. The 28th president of the US was born Thomas Woodrow Wilson at Staunton, VA. Twice elected president (1912 and 1916), it was Wilson who said, "The world must be made safe for democracy," as he asked the Congress to declare war on Germany, Apr 2, 1917. His first wife, Ellen, died Aug 6, 1914, and he married Edith Bolling Galt, Dec 18, 1915. He suffered a paralytic stroke, Sept 16, 1919, never regaining his health. There were many speculations about who (possibly Mrs Wilson?) was running the government during his illness. His second term of office ended Mar 3, 1921, and he died at Washington, DC, Feb 3, 1924.

BIRTHDAYS TODAY

Ray Bourque, 44, former hockey player, born Montreal, QC, Canada, Dec 28, 1960.
Malcolm Gets, 40, actor ("Caroline in the City"), born near Gainesville, FL, Dec 28, 1964.
Hubert Myatt (Hubie) Green III, 58, golfer, born Birmingham, AL, Dec 28, 1946.
Lou Jacobi, 91, actor (*Irma La Douce*), born Toronto, ON, Canada, Dec 28, 1913.
Tim Johnson, 58, US Senator (D, South Dakota), born Canton, SD, Dec 28, 1946.
Patrick Rafter, 32, tennis player, born Mount Isa, Queensland, Australia, Dec 28, 1972.
Todd Richards, 35, Olympic snowboarder, born Worcester, MA, Dec 28, 1969.
Maggie Smith, 70, actress (Oscar for *The Prime of Miss Jean Brodie*; Tony for *Lettice & Lovage*), born Ilford, England, Dec 28, 1934.

Denzel Washington, 50, actor (*The Hurricane, Malcolm X*; Oscars for *Training Day* and *Glory*), born Mount Vernon, NY, Dec 28, 1954.
Edgar Winter, 58, singer, musician (*Edgar Winter's White Trash, They Only Come Out at Night*), born Beaumont, TX, Dec 28, 1946.

Season's Greetings

DECEMBER 29 — WEDNESDAY
Day 364 — 2 Remaining

CASALS, PABLO: BIRTH ANNIVERSARY. Dec 29, 1876. Famed cellist Pablo Carlos Salvador Defillio de Casals was born at Venrell, Spain, and died at Rio Pedros, Puerto Rico, Oct 22, 1973.

GLADSTONE, WILLIAM EWART: BIRTH ANNIVERSARY. Dec 29, 1809. English statesman and author for whom the Gladstone (luggage) bag was named. Inspiring orator, eccentric individual, intensely loved or hated by all who knew him (cheered from the streets and jeered from the balconies), Gladstone is said to have left more writings (letters, diaries, journals, books) than any other major English politician. However, his preoccupation with the charitable rehabilitation of prostitutes was perhaps easily misunderstood. Born at Liverpool, England, he was four times Britain's prime minister. Gladstone died at Hawarden, Wales, May 19, 1898.

JOHNSON, ANDREW: BIRTH ANNIVERSARY. Dec 29, 1808. Seventeenth president of the US, Andrew Johnson, proprietor of a tailor shop at Laurens, SC, before he entered politics, was born at Raleigh, NC. Upon Abraham Lincoln's assassination Johnson became president. He was the first president to be impeached by the House and was acquitted Mar 26, 1868, by the Senate. After his term of office as president (Apr 15, 1865–Mar 3, 1869) he made several unsuccessful attempts to win public office. Finally he was elected to the US Senate from Tennessee and served in the Senate from Mar 4, 1875, until his death at Carter's Station, TN, July 31, 1875.

RASPUTIN, GRIGORI EFIMOVICH: ASSASSINATION ANNIVERSARY. Dec 29, 1916. Russian monk and mystic, born Grigori Efimovich Novjkh, about 1871, at Siberia. Rasputin gained great influence with Russian emperor Nicholas II and the empress Alexandra, urging severe measures in dealing with the peasant masses, virtually dictating government policy. Notoriously dissolute and corrupt, Rasputin was said to have possessed hypnotic powers. He claimed divine inspiration and the ability to perform miracles. His name became synonymous with corruption and evil, and he was called the "plague pot" of Russia. In fact, Rasputin was a nickname from the Russian word *rasputny*, meaning debauched, profligate, licentious. When an attempt to poison him failed, he was shot to death and his body dropped through a hole in the ice into the Neva River. It was recovered three days later and buried in a silver casket at Tsarkoe Selo. The imperial government was crushed by the 1917 Revolution within a year of his death.

SAINT THOMAS OF CANTERBURY: FEAST DAY. Dec 29. Thomas, Archbishop of Canterbury, was born at London in 1118 and was murdered at the Canterbury Cathedral on this date in 1170.

TEXAS: ADMISSION DAY: ANNIVERSARY. Dec 29. Became 28th state in 1845.

TICK TOCK DAY. Dec 29. Time runs out! All those dreams you've had, all those fantasies? It's time, friend. Do it! Annually, Dec 29. [©2003 by WH.] For info: Thomas & Ruth Roy, Wellcat Holidays, 2418 Long Ln, Lebanon, PA 17046. Phone: (717) 279-0184. E-mail: info@wellcat.com. Web: www.wellcat.com.

Dec 29–30 ☆ *Chase's 2004 Calendar of Events* ☆

WOUNDED KNEE MASSACRE: ANNIVERSARY. Dec 29, 1890. Anniversary of the massacre of more than 200 Native American men, women and children by the US 7th Cavalry at Wounded Knee Creek, SD. Government efforts to suppress a ceremonial religious practice, the Ghost Dance (which called for a messiah who would restore the bison to the plains, make the white men disappear and bring back the old Native American way of life), had resulted in the death of Sitting Bull, Dec 15, 1890, which further inflamed the disgruntled Native Americans and culminated in the slaughter at Wounded Knee, Dec 29.

YMCA ORGANIZED: ANNIVERSARY. Dec 29, 1851. The first US branch of the Young Men's Christian Association was organized at Boston. It was modeled on an organization begun at London in 1844.

BIRTHDAYS TODAY

Ted Danson, 57, actor ("Cheers," "Becker," *Three Men and a Baby*), born San Diego, CA, Dec 29, 1947.

Marianne Faithfull, 58, singer ("As Tears Go By," "Summer Nights"), actress, born London, England, Dec 29, 1946.

Thomas Edwin Jarriel, 70, broadcast journalist, born LaGrange, GA, Dec 29, 1934.

Jason Kreis, 32, soccer player, born Omaha, NE, Dec 29, 1972.

Jude Law, 32, actor (*The Talented Mr Ripley*), born London, England, Dec 29, 1972.

Mary Tyler Moore, 68, actress (two Emmys for "The Dick Van Dyke Show"; three Emmys for "The Mary Tyler Moore Show"; *Ordinary People*), born Brooklyn, NY, Dec 29, 1936.

Jon Polito, 54, actor ("Homicide"), born Philadelphia, PA, Dec 29, 1950.

Paula Poundstone, 45, comedienne, born Sudbury, MA, Dec 29, 1959.

Jon Voight, 66, actor (*Midnight Cowboy, Deliverance*), born Yonkers, NY, Dec 29, 1938.

Andy Wachowski, 37, filmmaker with brother Larry Wachowski (*The Matrix*), born Chicago, IL, Dec 29, 1967.

DECEMBER 30 — THURSDAY
Day 365 — 1 Remaining

FALLING NEEDLES FAMILY FEST. Dec 30. Now that the Yuletide tree's been up for weeks and hasn't been watered since a couple of days before Christmas, gather the gang around and watch the needles gently fall one by one. Live it up! Dance barefoot! (©2003 by WH.) For info: Thomas & Ruth Roy, Wellcat Holidays, 2418 Long Ln, Lebanon, PA 17046. Phone: (717) 279-0184. E-mail: info@wellcat.com. Web: www.wellcat.com.

GUGGENHEIM, SIMON: BIRTH ANNIVERSARY. Dec 30, 1867. American capitalist and philanthropist, born at Philadelphia, PA. He established, in memory of his son, the John Simon Guggenheim Memorial Foundation, in 1925. Died Nov 2, 1941, at New York, NY.

KIPLING, RUDYARD: BIRTH ANNIVERSARY. Dec 30, 1865. English poet, novelist and short story writer, Nobel prize laureate, Kipling was born at Bombay, India. After working as a journalist at India, he traveled around the world. He married an American and lived in Vermont for several years. Kipling is best known for his children's stories, such as the *Jungle Book* and *Just So Stories* and poems such as "The Ballad of East and West" and "If." He died at London, England, Jan 18, 1936.

LEACOCK, STEPHEN: BIRTH ANNIVERSARY. Dec 30, 1869. Canadian economist and humorist, born at Swanmore, Hampshire, England. Died Mar 28, 1944, at Toronto, Canada. "Lord Ronald. . .," he wrote in *Nonsense Novels*, "flung himself upon his horse and rode madly off in all directions."

"LET'S MAKE A DEAL" TV PREMIERE: ANNIVERSARY. Dec 30, 1963. Monty Hall hosted this outrageous and no-skill-required game show. Audience members, many of whom wore costumes, were selected to sit in the trading area, and some were picked to "make a deal" with Hall by trading something of their own for something they were offered. Sometimes prizes were worthless ("zonks"). At the end of the show, the two people who had won the most were given the option to trade their winnings for a chance at the "Big Deal," hidden behind one of three doors. The most recent revival (1990–91) was hosted by Bob Hilton.

***MONITOR* SINKS: ANNIVERSARY.** Dec 30, 1862. The Union ironclad ship USS *Monitor* (which achieved fame after her battle with the *Merrimac*) sank off Cape Hatteras during a storm. Sixteen of her crew were lost. See also: "Battle of the *Monitor* and the *Merrimac*: Anniversary" (Mar 9).

NO INTERRUPTIONS DAY. Dec 30. On this day there shall be no interruptions! At work we will minimize or eliminate interruptions to our thought processes or tasks we are performing. At home we will silence and shut down all devices that interrupt us so we can devote ourselves to our families or to ourselves. This is a day for quiet and/or focus. It is a day to renew our energies to prepare ourselves for the new calendar year ahead. For info: Sylvia Henderson, Springboard Training, 18005 Lafayette Dr, Ste B, Olney, MD 20832. Phone: (301) 646-1668. Fax: (301) 856-8000. E-mail: admin@springboardtraining.com. Web: www.springboardtraining.com.

PACIFIC LIFE HOLIDAY BOWL PARADE AND GAME. Dec 30. Parade along Harbor Drive; game at Qualcomm Stadium, San Diego, CA. The televised parade, the morning of the Pacific Life Holiday Bowl football game (teams picked from Pac 10 and Big 12), features floats, marching bands, giant balloons and unique specialty units. Parade at 10 AM, kickoff for game is 5 PM. Est attendance: 100,000. For info: Mark Neville, Holiday Bowl, PO Box 601400, San Diego, CA 92160-1400. Phone: (619) 283-5808. Fax: (619) 281-7947. Web: www.pacificlifeholidaybowl.com.

PARKS, BERT: 90th BIRTH ANNIVERSARY. Dec 30, 1914. Bert Parks was born at Atlanta, GA. An actor whose career spanned radio, film, television and Broadway, his name became synonymous with the Miss America pageant which he emceed for 25 years. He was fired from the Miss America post in 1980 when pageant officials wanted to acquire a younger look. Parks made a special return appearance for the 1990 pageant, once again singing his signature song "There She Is." He got his big break in show business in 1945 as the emcee for the radio quiz show "Break the Bank" and later as the host of "Stop the Music." When both shows moved to television they did so with Parks at the microphone, launching a television career that included hosting a variety of quiz shows and guest appearances on dramatic series. He died Feb 2, 1992, at La Jolla, CA.

PHILIPPINES: RIZAL DAY. Dec 30. National holiday. Commemorates martyrdom of Dr. Jose Rizal in 1896.

"THE ROY ROGERS SHOW" TV PREMIERE: ANNIVERSARY. Dec 30, 1951. This very popular TV western starred Roy Rogers and his wife, Dale Evans, as themselves. It also featured Pat Brady as Rogers's sidekick who rode a jeep named Nellybelle, the singing group Sons of the Pioneers, Rogers's horse Trigger, Evans's horse Buttermilk and a German shepherd named Bullet. This half-hour show was especially popular with young viewers.

USSR ESTABLISHED: ANNIVERSARY. Dec 30, 1922. After the Russian revolution of 1917 and the subsequent three-year civil war, the Union of Soviet Socialist Republics (or Soviet Union) was founded, a confederation of Russia, Byelorussia, the Ukraine and the Transcaucasian Federation. It was the first state in the world to be based on Marxist communism. The Soviet

December 2004

S	M	T	W	T	F	S
			1	2	3	4
5	6	7	8	9	10	11
12	13	14	15	16	17	18
19	20	21	22	23	24	25
26	27	28	29	30	31	

Union was dissolved Dec 8, 1991. See also: "Soviet Union Dissolved" (Dec 8).

VAN FLEET, JO: BIRTH ANNIVERSARY. Dec 30, 1922. Actress (Oscar for *East of Eden*; "Cinderella"), born at Oakland, CA. Died June 10, 1996.

BIRTHDAYS TODAY

Joseph Bologna, 66, actor, writer (*The Big Bus, My Favorite Year, Blame It on Rio*), born Brooklyn, NY, Dec 30, 1938.
James Burrows, 64, director ("Cheers," "Taxi"), born Los Angeles, CA, Dec 30, 1940.
Skeeter Davis, 73, singer, born Dry Ridge, KY, Dec 30, 1931.
Bo Diddley, 76, singer, songwriter ("Who Do You Love," "I'm a Man"), musician, born McCombs, MS, Dec 30, 1928.
Eliza Dushku, 24, actress ("Buffy the Vampire Slayer," "Angel"), born Boston, MA, Dec 30, 1980.
Davy Jones, 58, actor, singer (The Monkees, "Daydream Believer"), born Manchester, England, Dec 30, 1946.
Sanford (Sandy) Koufax, 69, Hall of Fame baseball player, former sportscaster, born Brooklyn, NY, Dec 30, 1935.
Kristin Kreuk, 22, actress ("Smallville"), born Vancouver, BC, Canada, Dec 30, 1982.
Matt Lauer, 47, news anchor ("Today"), born New York, NY, Dec 30, 1957.
Kenyon Martin, 27, basketball player, born Saginaw, MI, Dec 30, 1977.
Michael Nesmith, 62, singer, songwriter (The Monkees), director, born Houston, TX, Dec 30, 1942.
Patti Smith, 58, singer ("Because the Night"), born Chicago, IL, Dec 30, 1946.
Russ Tamblyn, 69, actor ("Twin Peaks," *Peyton Place, West Side Story*), born Los Angeles, CA, Dec 30, 1935.
Concetta Tomei, 59, actress ("Providence," "China Beach"), born Kenosha, WI, Dec 30, 1945.
Tracey Ullman, 45, actress, singer ("The Tracey Ullman Show," *I Love You to Death*), born Buckinghamshire, England, Dec 30, 1959.
Meredith Vieira, 51, TV host ("The View"), born Providence, RI, Dec 30, 1953.
Eldrick (Tiger) Woods, 29, golfer, born Cypress, CA, Dec 30, 1975.

DECEMBER 31 — FRIDAY
Day 366 — 0 Remaining

CANADA: FIRST NIGHTS. Dec 31. These Canadian cities have First Night celebrations: Banff, Drayton Valley, Edmonton and Red Deer, Alberta; Kamloops and Whistler, British Columbia; Yellowknife, Northwest Territories; and Chatham-Kent, Hamilton, Kingston, Peterborough and Toronto, Ontario. For info: First Night Intl, 200 Lincoln St, Ste 301, Boston, MA 02111-2418. Phone: (617) 357-0065. Web: www.firstnightintl.org.

DENVER, JOHN: BIRTH ANNIVERSARY. Dec 31, 1943. Born Henry John Deutschendorf at Roswell, NM, this singer-songwriter ("Rocky Mountain High," "Sunshine on My Shoulder") died in a plane crash off the coast of California, Oct 12, 1997.

FIRST BANK OPENS IN US: ANNIVERSARY. Dec 31, 1781. The first modern bank in the US, the Bank of North America, was organized by Robert Morris and received its charter from the Confederation Congress. It began operations Jan 7, 1782, at Philadelphia.

FIRST NIGHT ALBANY. Dec 31. Downtown Albany, NY. A New Year's eve celebration of the arts in multiple locations downtown with music, dancing, children's events, fireworks, food and beverages. Annually, on New Year's Eve. Est attendance: 10,000. For info: City of Albany Office of Special Events, City Hall, 4th Fl, Eagle St, Albany, NY 12207. Web: www.albanyevents.org.

FIRST NIGHT ASHEVILLE. Dec 31. Asheville, NC. This alcohol-free celebration of art, music and entertainment includes approximately 15 indoor venues featuring magic, drama and dance, as well as interactive games and children's activities. The grand finale includes live music and a countdown to midnight that culminates with a spectacular fireworks show. Est attendance: 10,000. For info: Paul Clarke, Festival Coord, Asheville Parks & Rec/First Night, PO Box 7148, Asheville, NC 28802-7148. Phone: (828) 259-5800. Fax: (828) 259-5606.

FIRST NIGHT BOSTON. Dec 31. Boston, MA. The largest New Year's arts festival in North America, First Night Boston has grown to be a highly anticipated tradition. The festival features more than 1,000 artists in 250 performances and exhibitions in 50 venues throughout downtown Boston, a Mardi Gras-style Grand Procession, large-scale ice sculptures, music, dance, theater, family entertainment, fireworks at midnight and much more! Boston was the site of the first First Night in 1976. Est attendance: 1,000,000. For info: First Night, Inc, 20 Park Plaza, Ste 1000, Boston, MA 02116. Phone: (617) 542-1399. Web: www.firstnight.org.

FIRST NIGHTS. Dec 31. The following US cities have First Night celebrations: Mobile, AL; Fayetteville, AR; Bakersfield, Escondido, Fullerton, Martinez, Monterey, San Diego, San Luis Obispo, Santa Barbara, Santa Cruz, Santa Fe Springs, Santa Rosa, Stockton and Whittier, CA; Fort Collins and Pikes Peak, CO; Cheshire, Danbury, Hartford, Torrington and Westport/Weston, CT; Dover and Wilmington, DE; Delray Beach, Dunedin, Fort Walton Beach, Miami Beach and St. Petersburg, FL; Athens, Gainesville, Golden Isles, Macon and Savannah, GA; Boise and Idaho Falls, ID; Aurora, Bloomington/Normal, Centralia, Evanston, Pontiac, River Bend, Rockford and Springfield, IL; Evansville, IN; Owensboro, KY; Annapolis, Frederick, Montgomery County and Talbot, MD; Beverly, Boston, Chatham, Fall River, Martha's Vineyard, New Bedford, Northampton, Pittsfield, Quincy, Sharon, Sturbridge, Twin Cities and Worcester, MA; Jackson, MS; Cadillac and Birmingham, MI; St. Paul, MN; Columbia and Springfield, MO; Flathead and Missoula, MT; Portsmouth and Wolfeboro, NH; Bridgewater/Raritan/Somerville, Flemington, Haddonfield, Manasquan, Maplewood/South Orange, Montclair, Moorestown, Morris County, Mount Holly, Newark, Ocean City, Ocean County, Red Bank, Ridgewood, Summit, Teaneck and Westfield, NJ; Albany, Binghamton, Buffalo, Gloversville/Johnstown, Greenport, Middletown, New York City, Nyack, Oneonta, Saratoga, Sayville, Staten Island, Syracuse and Watertown, NY; Asheville and Raleigh, NC; Grand Forks, ND; Akron, Canfield, Columbus, Toledo and Youngstown, OH; Eugene and Salem, OR; Bethlehem, Bloomsburg, Bradford, Bristol, Carlisle, Doylestown, Erie, Hanover, Newtown, Norwin, Oil City, Philipsburg, Pittsburgh, Scranton, State College, Warren and York, PA; Providence and Westerly, RI; Charleston and Varnville, SC; Yankton, SD; Kingsport, TN; The Woodlands, TX; Ogden, Provo, Salt Lake City and St. George, UT; Bennington, Burlington, Montpelier, Rutland and St. Johnsbury, VT; Augusta, Blacksburg, Charlottesville, Fredericksburg, Harrisonburg, Leesburg, Warrenton, Williamsburg and Winchester, VA; Tacoma and Tri-Cities, WA; and Morgantown, WV. For info: First Night Intl, 200 Lincoln St, Ste 301, Boston, MA 02111-2418. Phone: (617) 357-0065. Fax: (617) 357-0066. E-mail: mainoffice@firstnightintl.org. Web: www.firstnightintl.org.

Dec 31 ☆ *Chase's 2004 Calendar of Events* ☆

JAPAN: NAMAHAGE. Dec 31. In evening, groups of "Namahage" men disguised as devils make door-to-door visits, growling, "Any good-for-nothing fellow hereabout?" The object of this annual event is to give sluggards an opportunity to change their minds and become diligent. Otherwise, according to legend, they will be punished by devils. Oga Peninsula, Akita Prefecture, Japan.

LEAP SECOND ADJUSTMENT TIME. Dec 31. One of the times that have been favored for the addition or subtraction of a second from clock time (to coordinate atomic and astronomical time). The determination to adjust is made by the International Earth Rotation Service of the International Bureau of Weights and Measures, at Paris, France. See also: "Leap Seconds" (see Contents).

MADD'S NEW YEAR'S DESIGNATE A DRIVER CAMPAIGN. Dec 31. Mothers Against Drunk Driving (MADD) asks motorists to designate a non-drinking driver before the celebrations begin on New Year's Eve (and for any celebration year-round). As part of its Designate a Driver Campaign, MADD offers a free Safe Party Guide in English and Spanish. For info: Mothers Against Drunk Driving (MADD). Phone: (800) GET-MADD. Web: www.madd.org.

MAINSTAY INDEPENDENCE BOWL. Dec 31 (tentative). Shreveport, LA. Annual football game featuring competitors from the Big 12 and SEC conferences. For info: MainStay Independence Bowl, 401 Market St, Ste 120, Shreveport, LA 71101. Phone: (888) 414-BOWL or (318) 221-0712. Fax: (318) 221-7366. Web: www.independencebowl.org.

MAKE UP YOUR MIND DAY. Dec 31. A day for all those people who have a hard time making up their minds. Make a decision today and follow through with it! Annually, Dec 31. For info: A.C. Moeller and M.A. Dufour, Box 71, Clio, MI 48420-1042.

MARSHALL, GEORGE CATLETT: BIRTH ANNIVERSARY. Dec 31, 1880. Chairman of the newly formed Joint Chiefs of Staff Committee throughout the US's involvement in WWII, General George Marshall was born at Uniontown, PA. He accompanied Roosevelt or represented the US at most Allied war conferences. He served as secretary of state and was designer of the Marshall Plan after the war. Died Oct 16, 1959, at Washington, DC.

MATISSE, HENRI: BIRTH ANNIVERSARY. Dec 31, 1869. Painter born at Le Cateau, France. Matisse also designed textiles and stained glass windows. Died at Nice, France, Nov 3, 1954.

NEW YEAR'S EVE. Dec 31. The last evening of the Gregorian calendar year, traditionally a night for merrymaking to welcome in the new year.

NEW YEAR'S FEST. Dec 31. Kalamazoo, MI. Kalamazoo comes alive as families, teens and seniors come downtown to welcome the New Year. Featuring more than 25 different artists, performances are hosted in 11 different indoor sites throughout downtown Kalamazoo. The cultural celebration offers music, theatre, puppetry, dance, mime and storytelling. Artists come from throughout the Midwest to join in this non-alcoholic celebration. Est attendance: 5,500. For info: Deborah Droppers, New Year's Fest, Inc, 346 W Michigan Ave, Kalamazoo, MI 49007. Phone: (616) 388-2830. E-mail: EventKzoo@chartermi.net. Web: www.eventkalamazoo.com.

NIXON, JOHN: DEATH ANNIVERSARY. Dec 31, 1808. Revolutionary patriot and businessman, Commander of the Philadelphia City Guard, born 1733 (exact date unknown). Appointed to conduct the first public reading of the Declaration of Independence, July 8, 1776. Died at Philadelphia, PA.

ORANGE BOWL PARADE. Dec 31. Miami, FL. Annual New Year's Eve parade for the past 64 years. Nationally televised, parade moves 2.2 miles along downtown Miami's Biscayne Boulevard by the bay. Est attendance: 500,000. For info: Orange Bowl Committee, 703 Waterford Way, Ste 590, Miami, FL 33126. Phone: (305) 371-4700. E-mail: obie@orangebowl.org. Web: www.orangebowl.org/events/parade.asp.

PANAMA: ASSUMES CONTROL OF CANAL: 5th ANNIVERSARY. Dec 31, 1999. With the expiration of the Panama Canal Treaty of 1979 at noon, the Republic of Panama assumed full responsibility for the canal and the US Panama Canal Commission ceased to exist.

SAINT SYLVESTER'S DAY. Dec 31. Observed in Belgium, Germany, France, Switzerland. Commemorates death of Pope Sylvester I in 335. Feasting, particularly upon "St. Sylvester's Carp."

SAMOA: SAMOAN FIRE DANCE. Dec 31. New Year's Eve is occasion for Samoan bamboo fireworks, singing and traditional performances such as the Samoan Fire Dance.

SUN BOWL. Dec 31. Sun Bowl Stadium, El Paso, TX. 71st annual. For info: Sun Bowl Assn, 4100 Rio Bravo, Ste 303, El Paso, TX 79902. Phone: (800) 915-BOWL. Web: www.sunbowl.org.

WORLD PEACE MEDITATION. Dec 31. An opportunity for people around the world to focus their thoughts and energy on peace. The event is observed internationally, beginning at noon Greenwich Mean Time (GMT) and lasting one hour (7 AM–8 AM, EST). For info: Quartus Foundation, PO Box 1768, Boerne, TX 78006. Phone: (830) 249-3985. Fax: (830) 249-3318. E-mail: quartus@texas.net. Web: www.quartus.org.

BIRTHDAYS TODAY

Sir Anthony Hopkins, 67, actor (*The Silence of the Lambs, Legends of the Fall*), born Port Talbot, South Wales, UK, Dec 31, 1937.
Val Kilmer, 45, actor (*Batman Forever, Top Secret, The Doors, Heat*), born Los Angeles, CA, Dec 31, 1959.
Ben Kingsley, 61, actor (Oscar for *Gandhi; Sexy Beast, Schindler's List*), born Krishna Bhanji, Yorkshire, England, Dec 31, 1943.
Tim Matheson, 56, actor (*Animal House*, "The Virginian," "Bonanza"), born Los Angeles, CA, Dec 31, 1948.
Sarah Miles, 63, actress (*The Servant, Blow-Up, Hope and Glory*), born Ingatestone, England, Dec 31, 1941.
Bebe Neuwirth, 46, actress ("Cheers," "Frasier"; stage: *Chicago*), born Newark, NJ, Dec 31, 1958.
Odetta, 74, folksinger, musician, born Odetta Homes Felious Gordon, Birmingham, AL, Dec 31, 1930.
James Remar, 51, actor (*48 Hrs, Drugstore Cowboy*), born Boston, MA, Dec 31, 1953.
Donna Summer, 56, singer ("Bad Girls"), born LaDonna Andrea Gaines, Boston, MA, Dec 31, 1948.
Diane Halfin von Furstenberg, 59, fashion designer, author, born Brussels, Belgium, Dec 31, 1945.

See ya next year!

	S	M	T	W	T	F	S
December 2004				1	2	3	4
	5	6	7	8	9	10	11
	12	13	14	15	16	17	18
	19	20	21	22	23	24	25
	26	27	28	29	30	31	

☆ Chase's 2004 Calendar of Events ☆
CALENDAR INFORMATION FOR THE YEAR 2004

Time shown is Eastern Standard Time. All dates are given in terms of the Gregorian calendar.
(Based in part on information prepared by the Nautical Almanac Office, US Naval Observatory.)

ERAS	YEAR	BEGINS
Byzantine	7513	Sept 14
Jewish*	5765	Sept 15
Chinese (Year of the Monkey)	4702	Jan 22
Roman (AUC)	2757	Jan 14
Nabonassar	2753	Apr 23
Japanese (Heisei)	16	Jan 1
Grecian (Seleucidae)	2316	Sept 14 (or Oct 14)
Indian (Saka)	1926	Mar 21
Diocletian	1721	Sept 12
Islamic (Hegira)**	1425	Feb 21

*Year begins at sunset. **Year begins at moon crescent.

RELIGIOUS CALENDARS
Epiphany . . . . Jan 6
Shrove Tuesday . . . . Feb 24
Ash Wednesday . . . . Feb 25
Lent . . . . Feb 25–Apr 10
Palm Sunday . . . . Apr 4
Good Friday . . . . Apr 9
Easter . . . . Apr 11
Ascension Day . . . . May 20
Whit Sunday (Pentecost) . . . . May 30
Trinity Sunday . . . . June 6
First Sunday in Advent . . . . Nov 28
Christmas Day . . . . Dec 25

Eastern Orthodox Church Observances
Great Lent begins . . . . Feb 23
Pascha (Easter) . . . . Apr 11
Ascension . . . . May 20
Pentecost . . . . May 30

Jewish Holy Days*
Purim . . . . Mar 7
Passover (1st day) . . . . Apr 6
Shavuot . . . . May 26–27
Tisha B'av . . . . July 27
Rosh Hashanah (New Year) . . . . Sept 16–17
Yom Kippur . . . . Sept 25
Succoth . . . . Sept 30–Oct 8
Chanukah . . . . Dec 8–15

*All Jewish holy days begin the previous day at sundown.

Islamic Holy Days**
Islamic New Year (1425) . . . . Feb 21
First Day of Ramadan (1425) . . . . Oct 15
Eid-Al-Fitr (1425) . . . . Nov 13

**All Islamic holy days begin at moon crescent.

CIVIL CALENDAR—USA—2004
New Year's Day . . . . Jan 1
Martin Luther King's Birthday (obsvd) . . . . Jan 19
Lincoln's Birthday . . . . Feb 12
Washington's Birthday (obsvd)/Presidents' Day . . . . Feb 16
Memorial Day (obsvd) . . . . May 31
Independence Day . . . . July 4
Labor Day . . . . Sept 6
Columbus Day (obsvd) . . . . Oct 11
General Election Day . . . . Nov 2
Veterans Day . . . . Nov 11
Thanksgiving Day . . . . Nov 25

Other Days Widely Observed in US—2004
Groundhog Day (Candlemas) . . . . Feb 2
St. Valentine's Day . . . . Feb 14
St. Patrick's Day . . . . Mar 17
Mother's Day . . . . May 9
Flag Day . . . . June 14
Father's Day . . . . June 20
National Grandparents Day . . . . Sept 12
Hallowe'en . . . . Oct 31

CIVIL CALENDAR—CANADA—2004
Victoria Day . . . . May 24
Canada Day . . . . July 1
Labor Day . . . . Sept 6
Thanksgiving Day . . . . Oct 11
Remembrance Day . . . . Nov 11
Boxing Day . . . . Dec 26

CIVIL CALENDAR—MEXICO—2004
New Year's Day . . . . Jan 1
Constitution Day . . . . Feb 5
Benito Juarez Birthday . . . . Mar 21
Labor Day . . . . May 1
Battle of Puebla Day (Cinco de Mayo) . . . . May 5
Independence Day* . . . . Sept 16
Dia de La Raza . . . . Oct 12
Mexican Revolution Day . . . . Nov 20
Guadalupe Day . . . . Dec 12

*Celebration begins Sept 15 at 11:00 p.m.

CIVIL CALENDAR—UNITED KINGDOM—2004
Accession of Queen Elizabeth II . . . . Feb 6
St. David (Wales) . . . . Mar 1
Commonwealth Day . . . . Mar 8
St. Patrick (Ireland) . . . . Mar 17
Birthday of Queen Elizabeth II . . . . Apr 21
St. George (England) . . . . Apr 23
Coronation Day . . . . June 2
The Queen's Official Birthday (tentative) . . . . June 12
Birthday of Prince Philip, Duke of Edinburgh . . . . June 10
Remembrance Sunday . . . . Nov 14
Birthday of the Prince of Wales . . . . Nov 14
St. Andrew (Scotland) . . . . Nov 30

BANK AND PUBLIC HOLIDAYS—UNITED KINGDOM—2004
(Observed during 2004 in England and Wales, Scotland
and Northern Ireland unless otherwise indicated)
New Year . . . . Jan 1
Bank Holiday (Scotland) . . . . Jan 2
St. Patrick's Day (Northern Ireland) . . . . Mar 17
Good Friday . . . . Apr 9
Easter Monday (except Scotland) . . . . Apr 12
May Day Bank Holiday . . . . May 3
Spring Bank Holiday . . . . May 31
Orangeman's Day (Battle of the Boyne) (Northern Ireland) . July 12
Bank Holiday (Scotland) . . . . Aug 2
Summer Bank Holiday (except Scotland) . . . . Aug 30
Christmas Day Holiday . . . . Dec 25
Boxing Day Holiday . . . . Dec 27

SEASONS
Spring (Vernal Equinox) . . . . Mar 20, 1:49 am, EST
Summer (Summer Solstice) . . . . June 20, 8:57 pm, EDT
Autumn (Autumnal Equinox) . . . . Sept 22, 12:30 pm, EDT
Winter (Winter Solstice) . . . . Dec 21, 7:42 am, EST

DAYLIGHT SAVING TIME SCHEDULE—2004
Sunday, Apr 4, 2:00 am–Sunday, Oct 31, 2:00 am—in all time zones.

CHRONOLOGICAL CYCLES
Dominical Letter . . . . DC
Epact 8
Golden Number (Lunar Cycle) X
Julian Period (year of) 6717
Roman Indiction 12
Solar Cycle 25

☆ Chase's 2004 Calendar of Events ☆
CALENDAR INFORMATION FOR THE YEAR 2005

Time shown is Eastern Standard Time. All dates are given in terms of the Gregorian calendar.
(Based in part on information prepared by the Nautical Almanac Office, US Naval Observatory.)

ERAS	YEAR	BEGINS
Byzantine	7514	Sept 14
Jewish*	5766	Oct 3
Chinese (Year of the Horse)	4703	Feb 9
Roman (AUC)	2758	Jan 14
Nabonassar	2754	Apr 23
Japanese (Heisei)	17	Jan 1
Grecian (Seleucidae)	2317	Sept 14 (or Oct 14)
Indian (Saka)	1927	Mar 22
Diocletian	1722	Sept 11
Islamic (Hegira)**	1426	Feb 9

*Year begins at sunset.   **Year begins at moon crescent.

RELIGIOUS CALENDARS
- Epiphany .... Jan 6
- Shrove Tuesday .... Feb 8
- Ash Wednesday .... Feb 9
- Lent .... Feb 9–Mar 26
- Palm Sunday .... Mar 20
- Good Friday .... Mar 25
- Easter .... Mar 27
- Ascension Day .... May 5
- Whit Sunday (Pentecost) .... May 15
- Trinity Sunday .... May 22
- First Sunday in Advent .... Nov 27
- Christmas Day .... Dec 25

Eastern Orthodox Church Observances
- Great Lent begins .... Mar 14
- Pascha (Easter) .... May 1
- Ascension .... June 9
- Pentecost .... June 19

Jewish Holy Days*
- Purim .... Mar 25
- Passover (1st day) .... Apr 24
- Shavuot .... June 13–14
- Tisha B'av .... Aug 14
- Rosh Hashanah (New Year) .... Oct 4–5
- Yom Kippur .... Oct 13
- Succoth .... Oct 18–23
- Chanukah .... Dec 26–Jan 2

*All Jewish holy days begin the previous day at sundown.

Islamic Holy Days**
- Islamic New Year (1426) .... Feb 9
- First Day of Ramadan (1426) .... Oct 3
- Eid-Al-Fitr (1426) .... Nov 2

**All Islamic holy days begin at moon crescent.

CIVIL CALENDAR—USA—2005
- New Year's Day .... Jan 1
- Martin Luther King's Birthday (obsvd) .... Jan 17
- Lincoln's Birthday .... Feb 12
- Washington's Birthday (obsvd)/Presidents' Day .... Feb 21
- Memorial Day (obsvd) .... May 30
- Independence Day .... July 4
- Labor Day .... Sept 5
- Columbus Day (obsvd) .... Oct 10
- General Election Day .... Nov 8
- Veterans Day .... Nov 11
- Thanksgiving Day .... Nov 24

Other Days Widely Observed in US—2005
- Groundhog Day (Candlemas) .... Feb 2
- St. Valentine's Day .... Feb 14
- St. Patrick's Day .... Mar 17
- Mother's Day .... May 8
- Flag Day .... June 14
- Father's Day .... June 19
- National Grandparents Day .... Sept 11
- Hallowe'en .... Oct 31

CIVIL CALENDAR—CANADA—2005
- Victoria Day .... May 23
- Canada Day .... July 1
- Labor Day .... Sept 5
- Thanksgiving Day .... Oct 10
- Remembrance Day .... Nov 11
- Boxing Day .... Dec 26

CIVIL CALENDAR—MEXICO—2005
- New Year's Day .... Jan 1
- Constitution Day .... Feb 5
- Benito Juarez Birthday .... Mar 21
- Labor Day .... May 1
- Battle of Puebla Day (Cinco de Mayo) .... May 5
- Independence Day* .... Sept 16
- Dia de La Raza .... Oct 12
- Mexican Revolution Day .... Nov 20
- Guadalupe Day .... Dec 12

*Celebration begins Sept 15 at 11:00 P.M.

CIVIL CALENDAR—UNITED KINGDOM—2005
- Accession of Queen Elizabeth II .... Feb 6
- St. David (Wales) .... Mar 1
- Commonwealth Day .... Mar 14
- St. Patrick (Ireland) .... Mar 17
- Birthday of Queen Elizabeth II .... Apr 21
- St. George (England) .... Apr 23
- Coronation Day .... June 2
- The Queen's Official Birthday (tentative) .... June 11
- Birthday of Prince Philip, Duke of Edinburgh .... June 10
- Remembrance Sunday .... Nov 13
- Birthday of the Prince of Wales .... Nov 14
- St. Andrew (Scotland) .... Nov 30

BANK AND PUBLIC HOLIDAYS—UNITED KINGDOM—2005
(Observed during 2005 in England and Wales, Scotland and Northern Ireland unless otherwise indicated)

- New Year .... Jan 1
- Bank Holiday (Scotland) .... Jan 2
- St. Patrick's Day (Northern Ireland) .... Mar 17
- Good Friday .... Mar 25
- Easter Monday (except Scotland) .... Mar 28
- May Day Bank Holiday .... May 2
- Bank Holiday .... May 30
- Orangeman's Day (Battle of the Boyne) (Northern Ireland) .... July 12
- Bank Holiday (Scotland) .... Aug 1
- Summer Bank Holiday (except Scotland) .... Aug 29
- Christmas Day Holiday .... Dec 25
- Boxing Day Holiday .... Dec 26

SEASONS
- Spring (Vernal Equinox) .... Mar 20, 7:34 AM, EST
- Summer (Summer Solstice) .... June 21, 2:46 AM, EDT
- Autumn (Autumnal Equinox) .... Sept 22, 6:23 PM, EDT
- Winter (Winter Solstice) .... Dec 21, 1:35 PM, EST

DAYLIGHT SAVING TIME SCHEDULE—2005
Sunday, Apr 3, 2:00 AM–Sunday, Oct 30, 2:00 AM—in all time zones.

CHRONOLOGICAL CYCLES
- Dominical Letter .... B
- Epact 19
- Golden Number (Lunar Cycle) XI
- Julian Period (year of) 6718
- Roman Indiction 13
- Solar Cycle 26

☆ Chase's 2004 Calendar of Events ☆
CALENDAR INFORMATION FOR THE YEAR 2006

Time shown is Eastern Standard Time. All dates are given in terms of the Gregorian calendar.
(Based in part on information prepared by the Nautical Almanac Office, US Naval Observatory.)

ERAS	YEAR	BEGINS
Byzantine	7515	Sept 14
Jewish*	5767	Sept 22
Chinese (Year of the Dog)	4704	Jan 29
Roman (AUC)	2759	Jan 14
Nabonassar	2755	Apr 23
Japanese (Heisei)	18	Jan 1
Grecian (Seleucidae)	2318	Sept 14 (or Oct 14)
Indian (Saka)	1928	Mar 22
Diocletian	1723	Sept 11
Islamic (Hegira)**	1427	Jan 30

*Year begins at sunset.   **Year begins at moon crescent.

RELIGIOUS CALENDARS
- Epiphany . . . Jan 6
- Shrove Tuesday . . . Feb 28
- Ash Wednesday . . . Mar 1
- Lent . . . Mar 1–Apr 15
- Palm Sunday . . . Apr 9
- Good Friday . . . Apr 14
- Easter . . . Apr 16
- Ascension Day . . . May 25
- Whit Sunday (Pentecost) . . . June 4
- Trinity Sunday . . . June 11
- First Sunday in Advent . . . Dec 3
- Christmas Day . . . Dec 25

Eastern Orthodox Church Observances
- Great Lent begins . . . Mar 6
- Pascha (Easter) . . . Apr 23
- Ascension . . . June 1
- Pentecost . . . June 11

Jewish Holy Days*
- Purim . . . Mar 14
- Passover (1st day) . . . Apr 13
- Shavuot . . . June 2–3
- Tisha B'av . . . Aug 3
- Rosh Hashanah (New Year) . . . Sept 23–24
- Yom Kippur . . . Oct 2
- Succoth . . . Oct 7–12
- Chanukah . . . Dec 16–Dec 23

*All Jewish holy days begin the previous day at sundown.

Islamic Holy Days**
- Islamic New Year (1427) . . . Jan 30
- First Day of Ramadan (1427) . . . Sept 23
- Eid-Al-Fitr (1427) . . . Oct 23

**All Islamic holy days begin at moon crescent.

CIVIL CALENDAR—USA—2006
- New Year's Day . . . Jan 1
- Martin Luther King's Birthday (obsvd) . . . Jan 16
- Lincoln's Birthday . . . Feb 12
- Washington's Birthday (obsvd)/Presidents' Day . . . Feb 20
- Memorial Day (obsvd) . . . May 29
- Independence Day . . . July 4
- Labor Day . . . Sept 4
- Columbus Day (obsvd) . . . Oct 9
- General Election Day . . . Nov 7
- Veterans Day . . . Nov 11
- Thanksgiving Day . . . Nov 23

Other Days Widely Observed in US—2006
- Groundhog Day (Candlemas) . . . Feb 2
- St. Valentine's Day . . . Feb 14
- St. Patrick's Day . . . Mar 17
- Mother's Day . . . May 14
- Flag Day . . . June 14
- Father's Day . . . June 18
- National Grandparents Day . . . Sept 10
- Hallowe'en . . . Oct 31

CIVIL CALENDAR—CANADA—2006
- Victoria Day . . . May 22
- Canada Day . . . July 1
- Labor Day . . . Sept 4
- Thanksgiving Day . . . Oct 9
- Remembrance Day . . . Nov 11
- Boxing Day . . . Dec 26

CIVIL CALENDAR—MEXICO—2006
- New Year's Day . . . Jan 1
- Constitution Day . . . Feb 5
- Benito Juarez Birthday . . . Mar 21
- Labor Day . . . May 1
- Battle of Puebla Day (Cinco de Mayo) . . . May 5
- Independence Day* . . . Sept 16
- Dia de La Raza . . . Oct 12
- Mexican Revolution Day . . . Nov 20
- Guadalupe Day . . . Dec 12

*Celebration begins Sept 15 at 11:00 P.M.

CIVIL CALENDAR—UNITED KINGDOM—2006
- Accession of Queen Elizabeth II . . . Feb 6
- St. David (Wales) . . . Mar 1
- Commonwealth Day . . . Mar 13
- St. Patrick (Ireland) . . . Mar 17
- Birthday of Queen Elizabeth II . . . Apr 21
- St. George (England) . . . Apr 23
- Coronation Day . . . June 2
- The Queen's Official Birthday (tentative) . . . June 10
- Birthday of Prince Philip, Duke of Edinburgh . . . June 10
- Remembrance Sunday . . . Nov 12
- Birthday of the Prince of Wales . . . Nov 14
- St. Andrew (Scotland) . . . Nov 30

BANK AND PUBLIC HOLIDAYS—UNITED KINGDOM—2006
(Observed during 2006 in England and Wales, Scotland and Northern Ireland unless otherwise indicated)
- New Year . . . Jan 1
- Bank Holiday (Scotland) . . . Jan 2
- St. Patrick's Day (Northern Ireland) . . . Mar 17
- Good Friday . . . Apr 14
- Easter Monday (except Scotland) . . . Apr 17
- May Day Bank Holiday . . . May 1
- Spring Bank Holiday . . . May 29
- Orangeman's Day (Battle of the Boyne) (Northern Ireland) . . . July 12
- Bank Holiday (Scotland) . . . Aug 7
- Summer Bank Holiday (except Scotland) . . . Aug 28
- Christmas Day Holiday . . . Dec 25
- Boxing Day Holiday . . . Dec 26

SEASONS
- Spring (Vernal Equinox) . . . Mar 20, 1:26 PM, EST
- Summer (Summer Solstice) . . . June 21, 8:26 AM, EDT
- Autumn (Autumnal Equinox) . . . Sept 23, 12:03 AM, EDT
- Winter (Winter Solstice) . . . Dec 21, 7:22 PM, EST

DAYLIGHT SAVING TIME SCHEDULE—2006
Sunday, Apr 2, 2:00 AM–Sunday, Oct 29, 2:00 AM—in all time zones.

CHRONOLOGICAL CYCLES
- Dominical Letter . . . A
- Epact . . . *
- Golden Number (Lunar Cycle) . . . XII
- Julian Period (year of) . . . 6719
- Roman Indiction . . . 14
- Solar Cycle . . . 27

Perpetual Calendar, 1753–2100

A perpetual calendar lets you find the day of the week for any date in any year. Since January 1 may fall on any of the seven days of the week, and may be a leap or non-leap year, 14 different calendars are possible. The number next to each year corresponds to one of the 14 calendars. Calendar 4 will be used in 2003; calendar 12 will be used in 2004.

Year	No.	Year	No.	Year	No.	Year	No.	Year	No.	Year	No.	Year	No.	Year	No.	Year	No.
1753	2	1792	8	1831	7	1870	7	1909	6	1948	12	1987	5	2026	5	2065	5
1754	3	1793	3	1832	8	1871	1	1910	7	1949	7	1988	13	2027	6	2066	6
1755	4	1794	4	1833	3	1872	9	1911	1	1950	1	1989	1	2028	14	2067	7
1756	12	1795	5	1834	4	1873	4	1912	9	1951	2	1990	2	2029	2	2068	8
1757	7	1796	13	1835	5	1874	5	1913	4	1952	10	1991	3	2030	3	2069	3
1758	1	1797	1	1836	13	1875	6	1914	5	1953	5	1992	11	2031	4	2070	4
1759	2	1798	2	1837	1	1876	14	1915	6	1954	6	1993	6	2032	12	2071	5
1760	10	1799	3	1838	2	1877	2	1916	14	1955	7	1994	7	2033	7	2072	13
1761	5	1800	4	1839	3	1878	3	1917	2	1956	8	1995	1	2034	1	2073	1
1762	6	1801	5	1840	11	1879	4	1918	3	1957	3	1996	9	2035	2	2074	2
1763	7	1802	6	1841	6	1880	12	1919	4	1958	4	1997	4	2036	10	2075	3
1764	8	1803	7	1842	7	1881	7	1920	12	1959	5	1998	5	2037	5	2076	11
1765	3	1804	8	1843	1	1882	1	1921	7	1960	13	1999	6	2038	6	2077	6
1766	4	1805	3	1844	9	1883	2	1922	1	1961	1	2000	14	2039	7	2078	7
1767	5	1806	4	1845	4	1884	10	1923	2	1962	2	2001	2	2040	8	2079	1
1768	13	1807	5	1846	5	1885	5	1924	10	1963	3	2002	3	2041	3	2080	9
1769	1	1808	13	1847	6	1886	6	1925	5	1964	11	2003	4	2042	4	2081	4
1770	2	1809	1	1848	14	1887	7	1926	6	1965	6	2004	12	2043	5	2082	5
1771	3	1810	2	1849	2	1888	8	1927	7	1966	7	2005	7	2044	13	2083	6
1772	11	1811	3	1850	3	1889	3	1928	8	1967	1	2006	1	2045	1	2084	14
1773	6	1812	11	1851	4	1890	4	1929	3	1968	9	2007	2	2046	2	2085	2
1774	7	1813	6	1852	12	1891	5	1930	4	1969	4	2008	10	2047	3	2086	3
1775	1	1814	7	1853	7	1892	13	1931	5	1970	5	2009	5	2048	11	2087	4
1776	9	1815	1	1854	1	1893	1	1932	13	1971	6	2010	6	2049	6	2088	12
1777	4	1816	9	1855	2	1894	2	1933	1	1972	14	2011	7	2050	7	2089	7
1778	5	1817	4	1856	10	1895	3	1934	2	1973	2	2012	8	2051	1	2090	1
1779	6	1818	5	1857	5	1896	11	1935	3	1974	3	2013	3	2052	9	2091	2
1780	14	1819	6	1858	6	1897	6	1936	11	1975	4	2014	4	2053	4	2092	10
1781	2	1820	14	1859	7	1898	7	1937	6	1976	12	2015	5	2054	5	2093	5
1782	3	1821	2	1860	8	1899	1	1938	7	1977	7	2016	13	2055	6	2094	6
1783	4	1822	3	1861	3	1900	2	1939	1	1978	1	2017	1	2056	14	2095	7
1784	12	1823	4	1862	4	1901	3	1940	9	1979	2	2018	2	2057	2	2096	8
1785	7	1824	12	1863	5	1902	4	1941	4	1980	10	2019	3	2058	3	2097	3
1786	1	1825	7	1864	13	1903	5	1942	5	1981	5	2020	11	2059	4	2098	4
1787	2	1826	1	1865	1	1904	13	1943	6	1982	6	2021	6	2060	12	2099	5
1788	10	1827	2	1866	2	1905	1	1944	14	1983	7	2022	7	2061	7	2100	6
1789	5	1828	10	1867	3	1906	2	1945	2	1984	8	2023	1	2062	1		
1790	6	1829	5	1868	11	1907	3	1946	3	1985	3	2024	9	2063	2		
1791	7	1830	6	1869	6	1908	11	1947	4	1986	4	2025	4	2064	10		

Calendar 1

JAN
S	M	T	W	T	F	S
1	2	3	4	5	6	7
8	9	10	11	12	13	14
15	16	17	18	19	20	21
22	23	24	25	26	27	28
29	30	31				

FEB
S	M	T	W	T	F	S
			1	2	3	4
5	6	7	8	9	10	11
12	13	14	15	16	17	18
19	20	21	22	23	24	25
26	27	28				

MAR
S	M	T	W	T	F	S
			1	2	3	4
5	6	7	8	9	10	11
12	13	14	15	16	17	18
19	20	21	22	23	24	25
26	27	28	29	30	31	

APR
S	M	T	W	T	F	S
						1
2	3	4	5	6	7	8
9	10	11	12	13	14	15
16	17	18	19	20	21	22
23	24	25	26	27	28	29
30						

MAY
S	M	T	W	T	F	S
	1	2	3	4	5	6
7	8	9	10	11	12	13
14	15	16	17	18	19	20
21	22	23	24	25	26	27
28	29	30	31			

JUNE
S	M	T	W	T	F	S
				1	2	3
4	5	6	7	8	9	10
11	12	13	14	15	16	17
18	19	20	21	22	23	24
25	26	27	28	29	30	

JULY
S	M	T	W	T	F	S
						1
2	3	4	5	6	7	8
9	10	11	12	13	14	15
16	17	18	19	20	21	22
23	24	25	26	27	28	29
30	31					

AUG
S	M	T	W	T	F	S
		1	2	3	4	5
6	7	8	9	10	11	12
13	14	15	16	17	18	19
20	21	22	23	24	25	26
27	28	29	30	31		

SEPT
S	M	T	W	T	F	S
					1	2
3	4	5	6	7	8	9
10	11	12	13	14	15	16
17	18	19	20	21	22	23
24	25	26	27	28	29	30

OCT
S	M	T	W	T	F	S
1	2	3	4	5	6	7
8	9	10	11	12	13	14
15	16	17	18	19	20	21
22	23	24	25	26	27	28
29	30	31				

NOV
S	M	T	W	T	F	S
			1	2	3	4
5	6	7	8	9	10	11
12	13	14	15	16	17	18
19	20	21	22	23	24	25
26	27	28	29	30		

DEC
S	M	T	W	T	F	S
					1	2
3	4	5	6	7	8	9
10	11	12	13	14	15	16
17	18	19	20	21	22	23
24	25	26	27	28	29	30
31						

(2006)

Calendar 2

JAN
S	M	T	W	T	F	S
	1	2	3	4	5	6
7	8	9	10	11	12	13
14	15	16	17	18	19	20
21	22	23	24	25	26	27
28	29	30	31			

FEB
S	M	T	W	T	F	S
				1	2	3
4	5	6	7	8	9	10
11	12	13	14	15	16	17
18	19	20	21	22	23	24
25	26	27	28			

MAR
S	M	T	W	T	F	S
				1	2	3
4	5	6	7	8	9	10
11	12	13	14	15	16	17
18	19	20	21	22	23	24
25	26	27	28	29	30	31

APR
S	M	T	W	T	F	S
1	2	3	4	5	6	7
8	9	10	11	12	13	14
15	16	17	18	19	20	21
22	23	24	25	26	27	28
29	30					

MAY
S	M	T	W	T	F	S
		1	2	3	4	5
6	7	8	9	10	11	12
13	14	15	16	17	18	19
20	21	22	23	24	25	26
27	28	29	30	31		

JUNE
S	M	T	W	T	F	S
					1	2
3	4	5	6	7	8	9
10	11	12	13	14	15	16
17	18	19	20	21	22	23
24	25	26	27	28	29	30

JULY
S	M	T	W	T	F	S
1	2	3	4	5	6	7
8	9	10	11	12	13	14
15	16	17	18	19	20	21
22	23	24	25	26	27	28
29	30	31				

AUG
S	M	T	W	T	F	S
			1	2	3	4
5	6	7	8	9	10	11
12	13	14	15	16	17	18
19	20	21	22	23	24	25
26	27	28	29	30	31	

SEPT
S	M	T	W	T	F	S
						1
2	3	4	5	6	7	8
9	10	11	12	13	14	15
16	17	18	19	20	21	22
23	24	25	26	27	28	29
30						

OCT
S	M	T	W	T	F	S
	1	2	3	4	5	6
7	8	9	10	11	12	13
14	15	16	17	18	19	20
21	22	23	24	25	26	27
28	29	30	31			

NOV
S	M	T	W	T	F	S
				1	2	3
4	5	6	7	8	9	10
11	12	13	14	15	16	17
18	19	20	21	22	23	24
25	26	27	28	29	30	

DEC
S	M	T	W	T	F	S
						1
2	3	4	5	6	7	8
9	10	11	12	13	14	15
16	17	18	19	20	21	22
23	24	25	26	27	28	29
30	31					

3

JAN
S	M	T	W	T	F	S
		1	2	3	4	5
6	7	8	9	10	11	12
13	14	15	16	17	18	19
20	21	22	23	24	25	26
27	28	29	30	31		

APR
S	M	T	W	T	F	S
	1	2	3	4	5	6
7	8	9	10	11	12	13
14	15	16	17	18	19	20
21	22	23	24	25	26	27
28	29	30				

JULY
S	M	T	W	T	F	S
	1	2	3	4	5	6
7	8	9	10	11	12	13
14	15	16	17	18	19	20
21	22	23	24	25	26	27
28	29	30	31			

OCT
S	M	T	W	T	F	S
		1	2	3	4	5
6	7	8	9	10	11	12
13	14	15	16	17	18	19
20	21	22	23	24	25	26
27	28	29	30	31		

FEB
S	M	T	W	T	F	S
					1	2
3	4	5	6	7	8	9
10	11	12	13	14	15	16
17	18	19	20	21	22	23
24	25	26	27	28		

MAY
S	M	T	W	T	F	S
			1	2	3	4
5	6	7	8	9	10	11
12	13	14	15	16	17	18
19	20	21	22	23	24	25
26	27	28	29	30	31	

AUG
S	M	T	W	T	F	S
				1	2	3
4	5	6	7	8	9	10
11	12	13	14	15	16	17
18	19	20	21	22	23	24
25	26	27	28	29	30	31

NOV
S	M	T	W	T	F	S
					1	2
3	4	5	6	7	8	9
10	11	12	13	14	15	16
17	18	19	20	21	22	23
24	25	26	27	28	29	30

MAR
S	M	T	W	T	F	S
					1	2
3	4	5	6	7	8	9
10	11	12	13	14	15	16
17	18	19	20	21	22	23
24	25	26	27	28	29	30
31						

JUNE
S	M	T	W	T	F	S
						1
2	3	4	5	6	7	8
9	10	11	12	13	14	15
16	17	18	19	20	21	22
23	24	25	26	27	28	29
30						

SEPT
S	M	T	W	T	F	S
1	2	3	4	5	6	7
8	9	10	11	12	13	14
15	16	17	18	19	20	21
22	23	24	25	26	27	28
29	30					

DEC
S	M	T	W	T	F	S
1	2	3	4	5	6	7
8	9	10	11	12	13	14
15	16	17	18	19	20	21
22	23	24	25	26	27	28
29	30	31				

4

JAN
S	M	T	W	T	F	S
			1	2	3	4
5	6	7	8	9	10	11
12	13	14	15	16	17	18
19	20	21	22	23	24	25
26	27	28	29	30	31	

APR
S	M	T	W	T	F	S
		1	2	3	4	5
6	7	8	9	10	11	12
13	14	15	16	17	18	19
20	21	22	23	24	25	26
27	28	29	30			

JULY
S	M	T	W	T	F	S
		1	2	3	4	5
6	7	8	9	10	11	12
13	14	15	16	17	18	19
20	21	22	23	24	25	26
27	28	29	30	31		

OCT
S	M	T	W	T	F	S
			1	2	3	4
5	6	7	8	9	10	11
12	13	14	15	16	17	18
19	20	21	22	23	24	25
26	27	28	29	30	31	

FEB
S	M	T	W	T	F	S
						1
2	3	4	5	6	7	8
9	10	11	12	13	14	15
16	17	18	19	20	21	22
23	24	25	26	27	28	

MAY
S	M	T	W	T	F	S
				1	2	3
4	5	6	7	8	9	10
11	12	13	14	15	16	17
18	19	20	21	22	23	24
25	26	27	28	29	30	31

AUG
S	M	T	W	T	F	S
					1	2
3	4	5	6	7	8	9
10	11	12	13	14	15	16
17	18	19	20	21	22	23
24	25	26	27	28	29	30
31						

NOV
S	M	T	W	T	F	S
						1
2	3	4	5	6	7	8
9	10	11	12	13	14	15
16	17	18	19	20	21	22
23	24	25	26	27	28	29
30						

MAR
S	M	T	W	T	F	S
						1
2	3	4	5	6	7	8
9	10	11	12	13	14	15
16	17	18	19	20	21	22
23	24	25	26	27	28	29
30	31					

JUNE
S	M	T	W	T	F	S
1	2	3	4	5	6	7
8	9	10	11	12	13	14
15	16	17	18	19	20	21
22	23	24	25	26	27	28
29	30					

SEPT
S	M	T	W	T	F	S
	1	2	3	4	5	6
7	8	9	10	11	12	13
14	15	16	17	18	19	20
21	22	23	24	25	26	27
28	29	30				

DEC
S	M	T	W	T	F	S
	1	2	3	4	5	6
7	8	9	10	11	12	13
14	15	16	17	18	19	20
21	22	23	24	25	26	27
28	29	30	31			

5

JAN
S	M	T	W	T	F	S
				1	2	3
4	5	6	7	8	9	10
11	12	13	14	15	16	17
18	19	20	21	22	23	24
25	26	27	28	29	30	31

APR
S	M	T	W	T	F	S
			1	2	3	4
5	6	7	8	9	10	11
12	13	14	15	16	17	18
19	20	21	22	23	24	25
26	27	28	29	30		

JULY
S	M	T	W	T	F	S
			1	2	3	4
5	6	7	8	9	10	11
12	13	14	15	16	17	18
19	20	21	22	23	24	25
26	27	28	29	30	31	

OCT
S	M	T	W	T	F	S
				1	2	3
4	5	6	7	8	9	10
11	12	13	14	15	16	17
18	19	20	21	22	23	24
25	26	27	28	29	30	31

FEB
S	M	T	W	T	F	S
1	2	3	4	5	6	7
8	9	10	11	12	13	14
15	16	17	18	19	20	21
22	23	24	25	26	27	28

MAY
S	M	T	W	T	F	S
					1	2
3	4	5	6	7	8	9
10	11	12	13	14	15	16
17	18	19	20	21	22	23
24	25	26	27	28	29	30
31						

AUG
S	M	T	W	T	F	S
						1
2	3	4	5	6	7	8
9	10	11	12	13	14	15
16	17	18	19	20	21	22
23	24	25	26	27	28	29
30	31					

NOV
S	M	T	W	T	F	S
1	2	3	4	5	6	7
8	9	10	11	12	13	14
15	16	17	18	19	20	21
22	23	24	25	26	27	28
29	30					

MAR
S	M	T	W	T	F	S
1	2	3	4	5	6	7
8	9	10	11	12	13	14
15	16	17	18	19	20	21
22	23	24	25	26	27	28
29	30	31				

JUNE
S	M	T	W	T	F	S
	1	2	3	4	5	6
7	8	9	10	11	12	13
14	15	16	17	18	19	20
21	22	23	24	25	26	27
28	29	30				

SEPT
S	M	T	W	T	F	S
		1	2	3	4	5
6	7	8	9	10	11	12
13	14	15	16	17	18	19
20	21	22	23	24	25	26
27	28	29	30			

DEC
S	M	T	W	T	F	S
		1	2	3	4	5
6	7	8	9	10	11	12
13	14	15	16	17	18	19
20	21	22	23	24	25	26
27	28	29	30	31		

6

JAN
S	M	T	W	T	F	S
					1	2
3	4	5	6	7	8	9
10	11	12	13	14	15	16
17	18	19	20	21	22	23
24	25	26	27	28	29	30
31						

APR
S	M	T	W	T	F	S
				1	2	3
4	5	6	7	8	9	10
11	12	13	14	15	16	17
18	19	20	21	22	23	24
25	26	27	28	29	30	

JULY
S	M	T	W	T	F	S
				1	2	3
4	5	6	7	8	9	10
11	12	13	14	15	16	17
18	19	20	21	22	23	24
25	26	27	28	29	30	31

OCT
S	M	T	W	T	F	S
					1	2
3	4	5	6	7	8	9
10	11	12	13	14	15	16
17	18	19	20	21	22	23
24	25	26	27	28	29	30
31						

FEB
S	M	T	W	T	F	S
	1	2	3	4	5	6
7	8	9	10	11	12	13
14	15	16	17	18	19	20
21	22	23	24	25	26	27
28						

MAY
S	M	T	W	T	F	S
						1
2	3	4	5	6	7	8
9	10	11	12	13	14	15
16	17	18	19	20	21	22
23	24	25	26	27	28	29
30	31					

AUG
S	M	T	W	T	F	S
1	2	3	4	5	6	7
8	9	10	11	12	13	14
15	16	17	18	19	20	21
22	23	24	25	26	27	28
29	30	31				

NOV
S	M	T	W	T	F	S
	1	2	3	4	5	6
7	8	9	10	11	12	13
14	15	16	17	18	19	20
21	22	23	24	25	26	27
28	29	30				

MAR
S	M	T	W	T	F	S
	1	2	3	4	5	6
7	8	9	10	11	12	13
14	15	16	17	18	19	20
21	22	23	24	25	26	27
28	29	30	31			

JUNE
S	M	T	W	T	F	S
		1	2	3	4	5
6	7	8	9	10	11	12
13	14	15	16	17	18	19
20	21	22	23	24	25	26
27	28	29	30			

SEPT
S	M	T	W	T	F	S
			1	2	3	4
5	6	7	8	9	10	11
12	13	14	15	16	17	18
19	20	21	22	23	24	25
26	27	28	29	30		

DEC
S	M	T	W	T	F	S
			1	2	3	4
5	6	7	8	9	10	11
12	13	14	15	16	17	18
19	20	21	22	23	24	25
26	27	28	29	30	31	

2005

JAN
S	M	T	W	T	F	S
						1
2	3	4	5	6	7	8
9	10	11	12	13	14	15
16	17	18	19	20	21	22
23	24	25	26	27	28	29
30	31					

FEB
S	M	T	W	T	F	S
		1	2	3	4	5
6	7	8	9	10	11	12
13	14	15	16	17	18	19
20	21	22	23	24	25	26
27	28					

MAR
S	M	T	W	T	F	S
		1	2	3	4	5
6	7	8	9	10	11	12
13	14	15	16	17	18	19
20	21	22	23	24	25	26
27	28	29	30	31		

APR
S	M	T	W	T	F	S
					1	2
3	4	5	6	7	8	9
10	11	12	13	14	15	16
17	18	19	20	21	22	23
24	25	26	27	28	29	30

MAY
S	M	T	W	T	F	S
1	2	3	4	5	6	7
8	9	10	11	12	13	14
15	16	17	18	19	20	21
22	23	24	25	26	27	28
29	30	31				

JUNE
S	M	T	W	T	F	S
			1	2	3	4
5	6	7	8	9	10	11
12	13	14	15	16	17	18
19	20	21	22	23	24	25
26	27	28	29	30		

JULY
S	M	T	W	T	F	S
					1	2
3	4	5	6	7	8	9
10	11	12	13	14	15	16
17	18	19	20	21	22	23
24	25	26	27	28	29	30
31						

AUG
S	M	T	W	T	F	S
	1	2	3	4	5	6
7	8	9	10	11	12	13
14	15	16	17	18	19	20
21	22	23	24	25	26	27
28	29	30	31			

SEPT
S	M	T	W	T	F	S
				1	2	3
4	5	6	7	8	9	10
11	12	13	14	15	16	17
18	19	20	21	22	23	24
25	26	27	28	29	30	

OCT
S	M	T	W	T	F	S
						1
2	3	4	5	6	7	8
9	10	11	12	13	14	15
16	17	18	19	20	21	22
23	24	25	26	27	28	29
30	31					

NOV
S	M	T	W	T	F	S
		1	2	3	4	5
6	7	8	9	10	11	12
13	14	15	16	17	18	19
20	21	22	23	24	25	26
27	28	29	30			

DEC
S	M	T	W	T	F	S
				1	2	3
4	5	6	7	8	9	10
11	12	13	14	15	16	17
18	19	20	21	22	23	24
25	26	27	28	29	30	31

2008

JAN
S	M	T	W	T	F	S
		1	2	3	4	5
6	7	8	9	10	11	12
13	14	15	16	17	18	19
20	21	22	23	24	25	26
27	28	29	30	31		

FEB
S	M	T	W	T	F	S
					1	2
3	4	5	6	7	8	9
10	11	12	13	14	15	16
17	18	19	20	21	22	23
24	25	26	27	28	29	

MAR
S	M	T	W	T	F	S
						1
2	3	4	5	6	7	8
9	10	11	12	13	14	15
16	17	18	19	20	21	22
23	24	25	26	27	28	29
30	31					

APR
S	M	T	W	T	F	S
		1	2	3	4	5
6	7	8	9	10	11	12
13	14	15	16	17	18	19
20	21	22	23	24	25	26
27	28	29	30			

MAY
S	M	T	W	T	F	S
				1	2	3
4	5	6	7	8	9	10
11	12	13	14	15	16	17
18	19	20	21	22	23	24
25	26	27	28	29	30	31

JUNE
S	M	T	W	T	F	S
1	2	3	4	5	6	7
8	9	10	11	12	13	14
15	16	17	18	19	20	21
22	23	24	25	26	27	28
29	30					

JULY
S	M	T	W	T	F	S
		1	2	3	4	5
6	7	8	9	10	11	12
13	14	15	16	17	18	19
20	21	22	23	24	25	26
27	28	29	30	31		

AUG
S	M	T	W	T	F	S
					1	2
3	4	5	6	7	8	9
10	11	12	13	14	15	16
17	18	19	20	21	22	23
24	25	26	27	28	29	30
31						

SEPT
S	M	T	W	T	F	S
	1	2	3	4	5	6
7	8	9	10	11	12	13
14	15	16	17	18	19	20
21	22	23	24	25	26	27
28	29	30				

OCT
S	M	T	W	T	F	S
			1	2	3	4
5	6	7	8	9	10	11
12	13	14	15	16	17	18
19	20	21	22	23	24	25
26	27	28	29	30	31	

NOV
S	M	T	W	T	F	S
						1
2	3	4	5	6	7	8
9	10	11	12	13	14	15
16	17	18	19	20	21	22
23	24	25	26	27	28	29
30						

DEC
S	M	T	W	T	F	S
	1	2	3	4	5	6
7	8	9	10	11	12	13
14	15	16	17	18	19	20
21	22	23	24	25	26	27
28	29	30	31			

2009

JAN
S	M	T	W	T	F	S
				1	2	3
4	5	6	7	8	9	10
11	12	13	14	15	16	17
18	19	20	21	22	23	24
25	26	27	28	29	30	31

FEB
S	M	T	W	T	F	S
1	2	3	4	5	6	7
8	9	10	11	12	13	14
15	16	17	18	19	20	21
22	23	24	25	26	27	28

MAR
S	M	T	W	T	F	S
1	2	3	4	5	6	7
8	9	10	11	12	13	14
15	16	17	18	19	20	21
22	23	24	25	26	27	28
29	30	31				

APR
S	M	T	W	T	F	S
			1	2	3	4
5	6	7	8	9	10	11
12	13	14	15	16	17	18
19	20	21	22	23	24	25
26	27	28	29	30		

MAY
S	M	T	W	T	F	S
					1	2
3	4	5	6	7	8	9
10	11	12	13	14	15	16
17	18	19	20	21	22	23
24	25	26	27	28	29	30
31						

JUNE
S	M	T	W	T	F	S
	1	2	3	4	5	6
7	8	9	10	11	12	13
14	15	16	17	18	19	20
21	22	23	24	25	26	27
28	29	30				

JULY
S	M	T	W	T	F	S
			1	2	3	4
5	6	7	8	9	10	11
12	13	14	15	16	17	18
19	20	21	22	23	24	25
26	27	28	29	30	31	

AUG
S	M	T	W	T	F	S
						1
2	3	4	5	6	7	8
9	10	11	12	13	14	15
16	17	18	19	20	21	22
23	24	25	26	27	28	29
30	31					

SEPT
S	M	T	W	T	F	S
		1	2	3	4	5
6	7	8	9	10	11	12
13	14	15	16	17	18	19
20	21	22	23	24	25	26
27	28	29	30			

OCT
S	M	T	W	T	F	S
				1	2	3
4	5	6	7	8	9	10
11	12	13	14	15	16	17
18	19	20	21	22	23	24
25	26	27	28	29	30	31

NOV
S	M	T	W	T	F	S
1	2	3	4	5	6	7
8	9	10	11	12	13	14
15	16	17	18	19	20	21
22	23	24	25	26	27	28
29	30					

DEC
S	M	T	W	T	F	S
		1	2	3	4	5
6	7	8	9	10	11	12
13	14	15	16	17	18	19
20	21	22	23	24	25	26
27	28	29	30	31		

2010

JAN
S	M	T	W	T	F	S
					1	2
3	4	5	6	7	8	9
10	11	12	13	14	15	16
17	18	19	20	21	22	23
24	25	26	27	28	29	30
31						

FEB
S	M	T	W	T	F	S
	1	2	3	4	5	6
7	8	9	10	11	12	13
14	15	16	17	18	19	20
21	22	23	24	25	26	27
28						

MAR
S	M	T	W	T	F	S
	1	2	3	4	5	6
7	8	9	10	11	12	13
14	15	16	17	18	19	20
21	22	23	24	25	26	27
28	29	30	31			

APR
S	M	T	W	T	F	S
				1	2	3
4	5	6	7	8	9	10
11	12	13	14	15	16	17
18	19	20	21	22	23	24
25	26	27	28	29	30	

MAY
S	M	T	W	T	F	S
						1
2	3	4	5	6	7	8
9	10	11	12	13	14	15
16	17	18	19	20	21	22
23	24	25	26	27	28	29
30	31					

JUNE
S	M	T	W	T	F	S
		1	2	3	4	5
6	7	8	9	10	11	12
13	14	15	16	17	18	19
20	21	22	23	24	25	26
27	28	29	30			

JULY
S	M	T	W	T	F	S
				1	2	3
4	5	6	7	8	9	10
11	12	13	14	15	16	17
18	19	20	21	22	23	24
25	26	27	28	29	30	31

AUG
S	M	T	W	T	F	S
1	2	3	4	5	6	7
8	9	10	11	12	13	14
15	16	17	18	19	20	21
22	23	24	25	26	27	28
29	30	31				

SEPT
S	M	T	W	T	F	S
			1	2	3	4
5	6	7	8	9	10	11
12	13	14	15	16	17	18
19	20	21	22	23	24	25
26	27	28	29	30		

OCT
S	M	T	W	T	F	S
					1	2
3	4	5	6	7	8	9
10	11	12	13	14	15	16
17	18	19	20	21	22	23
24	25	26	27	28	29	30
31						

NOV
S	M	T	W	T	F	S
	1	2	3	4	5	6
7	8	9	10	11	12	13
14	15	16	17	18	19	20
21	22	23	24	25	26	27
28	29	30				

DEC
S	M	T	W	T	F	S
			1	2	3	4
5	6	7	8	9	10	11
12	13	14	15	16	17	18
19	20	21	22	23	24	25
26	27	28	29	30	31	

11

JAN
S	M	T	W	T	F	S
				1	2	3	4
5	6	7	8	9	10	11
12	13	14	15	16	17	18
19	20	21	22	23	24	25
26	27	28	29	30	31

FEB
S	M	T	W	T	F	S
						1
2	3	4	5	6	7	8
9	10	11	12	13	14	15
16	17	18	19	20	21	22
23	24	25	26	27	28	29

MAR
S	M	T	W	T	F	S
1	2	3	4	5	6	7
8	9	10	11	12	13	14
15	16	17	18	19	20	21
22	23	24	25	26	27	28
29	30	31

APR
S	M	T	W	T	F	S
			1	2	3	4
5	6	7	8	9	10	11
12	13	14	15	16	17	18
19	20	21	22	23	24	25
26	27	28	29	30

MAY
S	M	T	W	T	F	S
					1	2
3	4	5	6	7	8	9
10	11	12	13	14	15	16
17	18	19	20	21	22	23
24	25	26	27	28	29	30
31

JUNE
S	M	T	W	T	F	S
	1	2	3	4	5	6
7	8	9	10	11	12	13
14	15	16	17	18	19	20
21	22	23	24	25	26	27
28	29	30

JULY
S	M	T	W	T	F	S
			1	2	3	4
5	6	7	8	9	10	11
12	13	14	15	16	17	18
19	20	21	22	23	24	25
26	27	28	29	30	31

AUG
S	M	T	W	T	F	S
						1
2	3	4	5	6	7	8
9	10	11	12	13	14	15
16	17	18	19	20	21	22
23	24	25	26	27	28	29
30	31

SEPT
S	M	T	W	T	F	S
		1	2	3	4	5
6	7	8	9	10	11	12
13	14	15	16	17	18	19
20	21	22	23	24	25	26
27	28	29	30

OCT
S	M	T	W	T	F	S
				1	2	3
4	5	6	7	8	9	10
11	12	13	14	15	16	17
18	19	20	21	22	23	24
25	26	27	28	29	30	31

NOV
S	M	T	W	T	F	S
1	2	3	4	5	6	7
8	9	10	11	12	13	14
15	16	17	18	19	20	21
22	23	24	25	26	27	28
29	30

DEC
S	M	T	W	T	F	S
		1	2	3	4	5
6	7	8	9	10	11	12
13	14	15	16	17	18	19
20	21	22	23	24	25	26
27	28	29	30	31

12 — 2004

JAN
S	M	T	W	T	F	S
				1	2	3
4	5	6	7	8	9	10
11	12	13	14	15	16	17
18	19	20	21	22	23	24
25	26	27	28	29	30	31

FEB
S	M	T	W	T	F	S
1	2	3	4	5	6	7
8	9	10	11	12	13	14
15	16	17	18	19	20	21
22	23	24	25	26	27	28
29

MAR
S	M	T	W	T	F	S
	1	2	3	4	5	6
7	8	9	10	11	12	13
14	15	16	17	18	19	20
21	22	23	24	25	26	27
28	29	30	31

APR
S	M	T	W	T	F	S
				1	2	3
4	5	6	7	8	9	10
11	12	13	14	15	16	17
18	19	20	21	22	23	24
25	26	27	28	29	30

MAY
S	M	T	W	T	F	S
						1
2	3	4	5	6	7	8
9	10	11	12	13	14	15
16	17	18	19	20	21	22
23	24	25	26	27	28	29
30	31

JUNE
S	M	T	W	T	F	S
		1	2	3	4	5
6	7	8	9	10	11	12
13	14	15	16	17	18	19
20	21	22	23	24	25	26
27	28	29	30

JULY
S	M	T	W	T	F	S
				1	2	3
4	5	6	7	8	9	10
11	12	13	14	15	16	17
18	19	20	21	22	23	24
25	26	27	28	29	30	31

AUG
S	M	T	W	T	F	S
1	2	3	4	5	6	7
8	9	10	11	12	13	14
15	16	17	18	19	20	21
22	23	24	25	26	27	28
29	30	31

SEPT
S	M	T	W	T	F	S
			1	2	3	4
5	6	7	8	9	10	11
12	13	14	15	16	17	18
19	20	21	22	23	24	25
26	27	28	29	30

OCT
S	M	T	W	T	F	S
					1	2
3	4	5	6	7	8	9
10	11	12	13	14	15	16
17	18	19	20	21	22	23
24	25	26	27	28	29	30
31

NOV
S	M	T	W	T	F	S
	1	2	3	4	5	6
7	8	9	10	11	12	13
14	15	16	17	18	19	20
21	22	23	24	25	26	27
28	29	30

DEC
S	M	T	W	T	F	S
			1	2	3	4
5	6	7	8	9	10	11
12	13	14	15	16	17	18
19	20	21	22	23	24	25
26	27	28	29	30	31

13

JAN
S	M	T	W	T	F	S
					1	2
3	4	5	6	7	8	9
10	11	12	13	14	15	16
17	18	19	20	21	22	23
24	25	26	27	28	29	30
31

FEB
S	M	T	W	T	F	S
	1	2	3	4	5	6
7	8	9	10	11	12	13
14	15	16	17	18	19	20
21	22	23	24	25	26	27
28	29

MAR
S	M	T	W	T	F	S
		1	2	3	4	5
6	7	8	9	10	11	12
13	14	15	16	17	18	19
20	21	22	23	24	25	26
27	28	29	30	31

APR
S	M	T	W	T	F	S
					1	2
3	4	5	6	7	8	9
10	11	12	13	14	15	16
17	18	19	20	21	22	23
24	25	26	27	28	29	30

MAY
S	M	T	W	T	F	S
1	2	3	4	5	6	7
8	9	10	11	12	13	14
15	16	17	18	19	20	21
22	23	24	25	26	27	28
29	30	31

JUNE
S	M	T	W	T	F	S
			1	2	3	4
5	6	7	8	9	10	11
12	13	14	15	16	17	18
19	20	21	22	23	24	25
26	27	28	29	30

JULY
S	M	T	W	T	F	S
					1	2
3	4	5	6	7	8	9
10	11	12	13	14	15	16
17	18	19	20	21	22	23
24	25	26	27	28	29	30
31

AUG
S	M	T	W	T	F	S
	1	2	3	4	5	6
7	8	9	10	11	12	13
14	15	16	17	18	19	20
21	22	23	24	25	26	27
28	29	30	31

SEPT
S	M	T	W	T	F	S
				1	2	3
4	5	6	7	8	9	10
11	12	13	14	15	16	17
18	19	20	21	22	23	24
25	26	27	28	29	30

OCT
S	M	T	W	T	F	S
						1
2	3	4	5	6	7	8
9	10	11	12	13	14	15
16	17	18	19	20	21	22
23	24	25	26	27	28	29
30	31

NOV
S	M	T	W	T	F	S
		1	2	3	4	5
6	7	8	9	10	11	12
13	14	15	16	17	18	19
20	21	22	23	24	25	26
27	28	29	30

DEC
S	M	T	W	T	F	S
				1	2	3
4	5	6	7	8	9	10
11	12	13	14	15	16	17
18	19	20	21	22	23	24
25	26	27	28	29	30	31

14

JAN
S	M	T	W	T	F	S
						1
2	3	4	5	6	7	8
9	10	11	12	13	14	15
16	17	18	19	20	21	22
23	24	25	26	27	28	29
30	31

FEB
S	M	T	W	T	F	S
		1	2	3	4	5
6	7	8	9	10	11	12
13	14	15	16	17	18	19
20	21	22	23	24	25	26
27	28	29

MAR
S	M	T	W	T	F	S
			1	2	3	4
5	6	7	8	9	10	11
12	13	14	15	16	17	18
19	20	21	22	23	24	25
26	27	28	29	30	31

APR
S	M	T	W	T	F	S
						1
2	3	4	5	6	7	8
9	10	11	12	13	14	15
16	17	18	19	20	21	22
23	24	25	26	27	28	29
30

MAY
S	M	T	W	T	F	S
	1	2	3	4	5	6
7	8	9	10	11	12	13
14	15	16	17	18	19	20
21	22	23	24	25	26	27
28	29	30	31

JUNE
S	M	T	W	T	F	S
				1	2	3
4	5	6	7	8	9	10
11	12	13	14	15	16	17
18	19	20	21	22	23	24
25	26	27	28	29	30

JULY
S	M	T	W	T	F	S
						1
2	3	4	5	6	7	8
9	10	11	12	13	14	15
16	17	18	19	20	21	22
23	24	25	26	27	28	29
30	31

AUG
S	M	T	W	T	F	S
		1	2	3	4	5
6	7	8	9	10	11	12
13	14	15	16	17	18	19
20	21	22	23	24	25	26
27	28	29	30	31

SEPT
S	M	T	W	T	F	S
					1	2
3	4	5	6	7	8	9
10	11	12	13	14	15	16
17	18	19	20	21	22	23
24	25	26	27	28	29	30

OCT
S	M	T	W	T	F	S
1	2	3	4	5	6	7
8	9	10	11	12	13	14
15	16	17	18	19	20	21
22	23	24	25	26	27	28
29	30	31

NOV
S	M	T	W	T	F	S
			1	2	3	4
5	6	7	8	9	10	11
12	13	14	15	16	17	18
19	20	21	22	23	24	25
26	27	28	29	30

DEC
S	M	T	W	T	F	S
					1	2
3	4	5	6	7	8	9
10	11	12	13	14	15	16
17	18	19	20	21	22	23
24	25	26	27	28	29	30
31

☆ Chase's 2004 Calendar of Events ☆
NATIONAL DAYS OF THE WORLD FOR 2004

(Compiled from publications of the U.S. Department of State, the United Nations and from information received from the countries listed.)

Most nations set aside one or more days each year as national public holidays, often recognizing the anniversary of the attainment of independence, or the birthday of the country's ruler. Below, the national days are listed alphabetically. It should be noted that in some countries the Gregorian Calendar date of observance varies from year to year. See the Index and the main chronology for further details of observance, and for numerous holidays in addition to the national days listed here.

Afghanistan	Aug 19
Albania	Nov 28
Algeria	Nov 1
Andorra	Sept 8
Angola	Nov 11
Antigua and Barbuda	Nov 1
Argentina	May 25
Armenia	Sept 21
Australia	Jan 26
Austria	Oct 26
Azerbaijan	May 28
Bahamas	July 10
Bahrain	Dec 16
Bangladesh	Mar 26
Barbados	Nov 30
Belarus	July 3
Belgium	July 21
Belize	Sept 21
Benin	Aug 1
Bhutan	Dec 17
Bolivia	Aug 6
Bosnia and Herzegovina	Mar 1
Botswana	Sept 30
Brazil	Sept 7
Brunei Darussalam	Feb 23
Bulgaria	Mar 3
Burkina Faso	Dec 11
Burundi	July 1
Cambodia	Nov 9
Cameroon	May 20
Canada	July 1
Cape Verde	July 5
Central African Republic	Dec 1
Chad	Aug 11
Chile	Sept 18
China	Oct 1
Colombia	July 20
Comoros	July 6
Congo	Aug 15
Congo, Democratic Republic of	June 30
Costa Rica	Sept 15
Cote D'Ivoire	Aug 7
Croatia	May 30
Cuba	Jan 1
Cyprus	Oct 1
Czech Republic	Oct 28
Denmark	Apr 16
Djibouti	June 27
Dominica	Nov 3
Dominican Republic	Feb 27
Ecuador	Aug 10
Egypt	July 23
El Salvador	Sept 15
Equatorial Guinea	Oct 12
Eritrea	May 24
Estonia	Feb 24
Ethiopia	May 28
Fiji	Oct 10
Finland	Dec 6
France	July 14
Gabon	Aug 17
Gambia	Feb 18
Georgia	May 26
Germany	Oct 3
Ghana	Mar 6
Greece	Mar 25
Grenada	Feb 7
Guatemala	Sept 15
Guinea	Oct 2
Guinea-Bissau	Sept 24
Guyana	Feb 23
Haiti	Jan 1
Holy See	Oct 22
Honduras	Sept 15
Hungary	Aug 20
Iceland	June 17
India	Jan 26
Indonesia	Aug 17
Iran	Feb 11
Iraq	July 17
Ireland	Mar 17
Israel	Apr 26
Italy	June 2
Jamaica	Aug 6
Japan	Dec 23
Jordan	May 25
Kazakhstan	Oct 25
Kenya	Dec 12
Kiribati	July 12
Korea, Democratic People's Republic of	Sept 9
Korea, Republic of	Aug 15
Kuwait	Feb 25
Kyrgyzstan	Aug 31
Lao People's Democratic Republic	Dec 2
Latvia	Nov 18
Lebanon	Nov 22
Lesotho	Oct 4
Liberia	July 26
Libyan Arab Jamahiriya	Sept 1
Liechtenstein	Aug 15
Lithuania	Feb 16
Luxembourg	June 23
Macedonia, Former Yugoslav Republic of	Aug 2
Madagascar	June 26
Malawi	July 6
Malaysia	Aug 31
Maldives	July 26
Mali	Sept 22
Malta	Sept 21
Marshall Islands	May 1
Mauritania	Nov 28
Mauritius	Mar 12
Mexico	Sept 16
Micronesia (Federated States of)	Nov 3
Moldova, Republic of	Aug 27
Monaco	Nov 19
Mongolia	July 11
Morocco	Mar 3
Mozambique	June 25
Myanmar	Jan 4
Namibia, Republic of	Mar 21
Nauru	Jan 31
Nepal	Dec 28
Netherlands	Apr 30
New Zealand	Feb 6
Nicaragua	Sept 15
Niger	Dec 18
Nigeria	Oct 1
Norway	May 17
Oman	Nov 18
Pakistan	Mar 23
Panama	Nov 3
Papua New Guinea	Sept 16
Paraguay	May 15
Peru	July 28
Philippines	June 12
Poland	May 3
Portugal	June 10
Qatar	Sept 3
Romania	Dec 1
Russian Federation	June 12
Rwanda	July 1
Saint Christopher (St Kitts) and Nevis	Sept 19
Saint Lucia	Feb 22
Saint Vincent and the Grenadines	Oct 27
Samoa	June 1
San Marino	Sept 3
Sao Tome and Principe	July 12
Saudi Arabia	Sept 23
Senegal	Apr 4
Seychelles	June 18
Sierra Leone	Apr 27
Singapore	Aug 9
Slovakia	Sept 1
Slovenia	June 25
Solomon Islands	July 7
Somalia	Oct 21
South Africa	Apr 27
Spain	Oct 12
Sri Lanka	Feb 4
Sudan	Jan 1
Suriname	Nov 25
Swaziland	Sept 6
Sweden	June 6
Switzerland	Aug 1
Syrian Arab Republic	Apr 17
Tajikistan	Sept 9
Tanzania, United Republic of	Apr 26
Thailand	Dec 5
Togo	Apr 27
Tonga	June 4
Trinidad and Tobago	Aug 31
Tunisia	Mar 20
Turkey	Oct 29
Turkmenistan	Oct 27
Tuvalu	Oct 1
Uganda	Oct 9
Ukraine	Aug 24
United Arab Emirates	Dec 2
United Kingdom*	June 2
United Republic of Tanzania	Apr 26
United States of America	July 4
Uruguay	Aug 25
Uzbekistan	Sept 1
Vanuatu	July 30
Venezuela	July 5
Vietnam	Sept 2
Yemen	May 22
Yugoslavia	Apr 27
Zambia	Oct 24
Zimbabwe	Apr 18

*Trooping the Colour—Queen's official birthday.

☆ Chase's 2004 Calendar of Events ☆

SELECTED SPECIAL YEARS: 1972-2005

As sponsored by the United Nations

Intl Book Year: 1972
World Population Year: 1974
Intl Women's Year: 1975
Intl Year of the Child: 1979
Intl Year for Disabled Persons: 1981
World Communications Year: 1983
Intl Youth Year: 1985
Intl Year of Peace: 1986
Intl Year of Shelter for the Homeless: 1987
Year of the Reader: 1987
Year of the Young Reader: 1989
Intl Literacy Year: 1990
US Decade of the Brain: 1990-99
Intl Space Year: 1992
Intl Year for World's Indigenous Peoples: 1993
Intl Year of the Family: 1994
Year for Tolerance: 1995
Intl Year for Eradication of Poverty: 1996
Intl Year of the Ocean: 1998
Intl Year of Older Persons: 1999
Intl Year for the Culture of Peace: 2000
Intl Year of Thanksgiving: 2000
Intl Year of Volunteers: 2001
Year of Dialogue Among Civilizations: 2001
Intl Decade for a Culture of Peace: 2001-10
Intl Year of Mobilization Against Racism: 2001
Intl Year of Mountains: 2002
Intl Year of Ecotourism: 2002
Literacy Decade: Education for All: 2003-2012
Intl Year of Freshwater: 2003
Intl Year of Rice: 2004
Intl Year to Commemorate the Struggle Against Slavery and Its Abolition: 2004
Intl Year of Microcredit: 2005

CHINESE CALENDAR

The Chinese lunar year is divided into 12 months of 29 or 30 days. The calendar is adjusted to the length of the solar year by the addition of extra months at regular intervals. The years are arranged in major cycles of 60 years. Each successive year is named after one of 12 animals. These 12-year cycles are continuously repeated.

1998 . . . . Tiger
1999 . . . . Hare
2000 . . . . Dragon
2001 . . . . Snake
2002 . . . . Horse
2003 . . . . Sheep (Goat)
2004 . . . . Monkey
2005 . . . . Rooster
2006 . . . . Dog
2007 . . . . Pig
2008 . . . . Rat
2009 . . . . Ox

WEDDING ANNIVERSARY GIFTS

1st . . . . paper, plastics, clocks
2nd . . . . cotton, china, calico
3rd . . . . leather, crystal, glass
4th . . . . . . books, electrical appliances, silk, fruit, flowers
5th . . . . wood, silverware
6th . . . . sugar, candy, wood, iron
7th . . . . wool, copper, desk sets
8th . . . . bronze, pottery, linens, laces, electrical appliances
9th . . . . pottery, willow, leather
10th . . . . tin, aluminum, diamond jewelry
11th . . . . steel, fashion jewelry, accessories
12th . . . . silk, linen, pearls, colored gems
13th . . . . lace, textiles, furs
14th . . . . ivory, gold jewelry
15th . . . . crystal, watches, glass
16th . . . . silver hollowware
17th . . . . furniture
18th . . . . porcelain
19th . . . . bronze
20th . . . . china, platinum
21st . . . . brass, nickel
22nd . . . . copper
23rd . . . . silver plate
24th . . . . musical instruments
25th . . . . silver
26th . . . . original pictures
27th . . . . sculpture
28th . . . . orchids
29th . . . . new furniture
30th . . . . pearl, diamond
31st . . . . time pieces
32nd . . . . conveyances (including automobiles)
33rd . . . . amethyst
34th . . . . opal
35th . . . . coral, jade
36th . . . . bone china
37th . . . . alabaster
38th . . . . beryl, tourmaline
39th . . . . lace
40th . . . . ruby
41st . . . . land
42nd . . . . improved real estate
43rd . . . . trips
44th . . . . groceries
45th . . . . sapphire
46th . . . . original poetry tributes
47th . . . . books
48th . . . . optical (spectacles, microscopes, telescopes)
49th . . . . luxuries of any kind
50th . . . . gold
55th . . . . emerald
60th . . . . diamond
75th . . . . diamond

☆ *Chase's 2004 Calendar of Events* ☆
WORLD MAP OF TIME ZONES

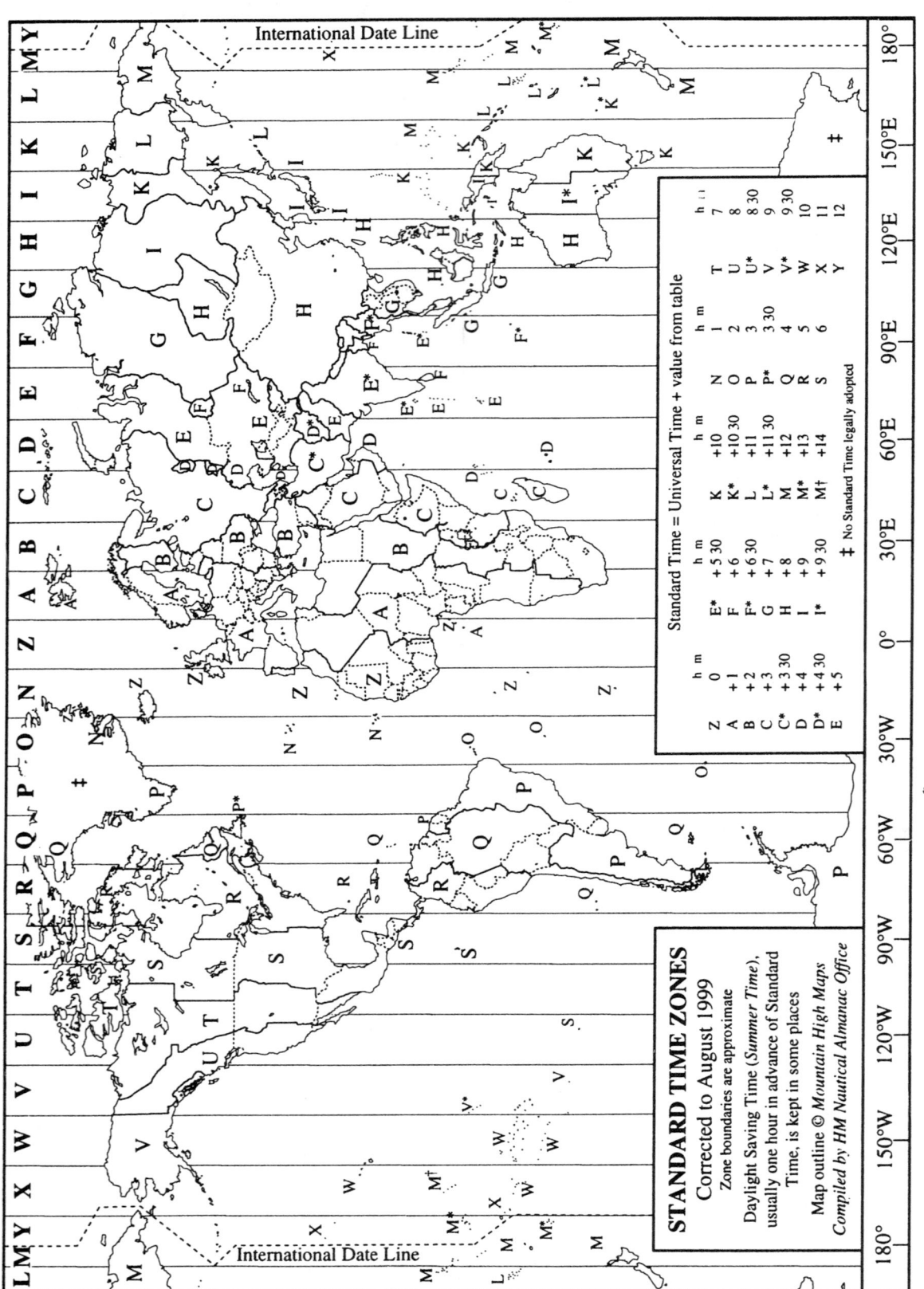

652

☆ *Chase's 2004 Calendar of Events* ☆
UNIVERSAL, STANDARD AND DAYLIGHT TIMES

Universal Time (UT) is also known as Greenwich Mean Time (GMT) and is the standard time of the Greenwich meridian (0° of longitude). A time given in UT may be converted to local mean time by the addition of east longitude (or the subtraction of west longitude), where the longitude of the place is expressed in time-measure at the rate of one hour for every 15°. Local clock times may differ from standard times, especially in summer when clocks are often advanced by one hour ("daylight saving" or "summer" time).

The time used in this book is Eastern Standard Time. The following table provides conversion between Universal Time and all Time Zones in the United States. An asterisk denotes that the time is on the preceding day.

Universal Time	Eastern Daylight Time	Eastern Standard Time and Central Daylight Time	Central Standard Time and Mountain Daylight Time	Mountain Standard Time and Pacific Daylight Time	Pacific Standard Time
0h	* 8 P.M.	* 7 P.M.	* 6 P.M.	* 5 P.M.	* 4 P.M.
1	* 9	* 8	* 7	* 6	* 5
2	*10	* 9	* 8	* 7	* 6
3	*11 P.M.	*10	* 9	* 8	* 7
4	0 Midnight	*11 P.M.	*10	* 9	* 8
5	1 A.M.	0 Midnight	*11 P.M.	*10	* 9
6	2	1 A.M.	0 Midnight	*11 P.M.	*10
7	3	2	1 A.M.	0 Midnight	*11 P.M.
8	4	3	2	1 A.M.	0 Midnight
9	5	4	3	2	1 A.M.
10	6	5	4	3	2
11	7	6	5	4	3
12	8	7	6	5	4
13	9	8	7	6	5
14	10	9	8	7	6
15	11 A.M.	10	9	8	7
16	12 Noon	11 A.M.	10	9	8
17	1 P.M.	12 Noon	11 A.M.	10	9
18	2	1 P.M.	12 Noon	11 A.M.	10
19	3	2	1 P.M.	12 Noon	11 A.M.
20	4	3	2	1 P.M.	12 Noon
21	5	4	3	2	1 P.M.
22	6	5	4	3	2
23	7 P.M.	6 P.M.	5 P.M.	4 P.M.	3 P.M.

The longitudes of the standard meridians for the standard time zones are:

Eastern . . . . . 75° West   Central . . . . . 90° West   Mountain . . . . . 105° West   Pacific . . . . . 120° West

LEAP SECONDS

The information below is developed by the editors from data supplied by the US Naval Observatory.

Because of Earth's slightly erratic rotation and the need for greater precision in time measurement it has become necessary to add a "leap second" from time to time to man's clocks to coordinate them with astronomical time. Rotation of the Earth has been slowing since 1900, making an astronomical second longer than an atomic second. Since 1972, by international agreement, adjustments have been made to keep astronomical and atomic clocks within 0.9 second of each other. The determination to add (or subtract) seconds is made by the Central Bureau of the International Earth Rotation Service, in Paris. Preferred times for adjustment have been June 30 and December 31, but any time may be designated by the International Earth Rotation Service. The first such adjustment was made in 1972, and as of June 30, 2001, a total of 22 leap seconds had been added. The additions have been made at 23:59:60 UTC (Coordinated Universal Time) = 6:59:60 EST (Eastern Standard Time). Leap seconds have been inserted into the UTC time scale on the following dates:

June 30, 1972	Dec 31, 1977	June 30, 1985	June 30, 1994
Dec 31, 1972	Dec 31, 1978	Dec 31, 1987	Dec 31, 1995
Dec 31, 1973	Dec 31, 1979	Dec 31, 1989	June 30, 1997
Dec 31, 1974	June 30, 1981	Dec 31, 1990	Dec 31, 1998
Dec 31, 1975	June 30, 1982	June 30, 1992	
Dec 31, 1976	June 30, 1983	June 30, 1993	

☆ Chase's 2004 Calendar of Events ☆

ASTRONOMICAL PHENOMENA FOR THE YEARS 2004–2006

All dates are given in terms of Eastern Standard or Daylight Time and the Gregorian calendar.
(Based in part on information prepared by the Nautical Almanac Office, US Naval Observatory.)

2004
PRINCIPAL PHENOMENA
EARTH

Perihelion	Jan 4
Aphelion	July 5
Equinoxes	Mar 20, Sept 22
Solstices	June 20, Dec 21

PHASES OF THE MOON

New Moon	First Quarter	Full Moon	Last Quarter
		Jan 7	Jan 14
Jan 21	Jan 29	Feb 6	Feb 13
Feb 20	Feb 27	Mar 6	Mar 13
Mar 20	Mar 28	Apr 5	Apr 11
Apr 19	Apr 27	May 4	May 11
May 19	May 27	June 3	June 9
June 17	June 25	July 2	July 9
July 17	July 24	July 31	Aug 7
Aug 15	Aug 23	Aug 29	Sept 6
Sept 14	Sept 21	Sept 28	Oct 6
Oct 13	Oct 20	Oct 27	Nov 5
Nov 12	Nov 19	Nov 26	Dec 4
Dec 11	Dec 18	Dec 26	

ECLIPSES

Partial eclipse of the Sun	Apr 19
Total eclipse of the Moon	May 4
Partial eclipse of the Sun	Oct 13
Total eclipse of the Moon	Oct 27

TRANSITS

Transit of Venus	June 8

VISIBILITY OF PLANETS
IN MORNING AND EVENING TWILIGHT

	Morning	Evening
Venus	June 15–Dec 31	Jan 1–June 2
Mars	Oct 30–Dec 31	Jan 1–July 31
Jupiter	Jan 4–Mar 4, Oct 5–Dec 31	Mar 4–Sept 8
Saturn	July 27–Dec 31	Jan 1–June 20

2005
PRINCIPAL PHENOMENA
EARTH

Perihelion	Jan 1
Aphelion	July 5
Equinoxes	Mar 20, Sept 22
Solstices	June 21, Dec 21

PHASES OF THE MOON

New Moon	First Quarter	Full Moon	Last Quarter
			Jan 3
Jan 10	Jan 17	Jan 25	Feb 2
Feb 8	Feb 15	Feb 23	Mar 3
Mar 10	Mar 17	Mar 25	Apr 1
Apr 8	Apr 16	Apr 24	May 1
May 8	May 16	May 23	May 30
June 6	June 14	June 22	June 28
July 6	July 14	July 21	July 27
Aug 4	Aug 12	Aug 19	Aug 26
Sept 3	Sept 11	Sept 17	Sept 25
Oct 3	Oct 10	Oct 17	Oct 24
Nov 1	Nov 8	Nov 15	Nov 23
Dec 1	Dec 8	Dec 15	Dec 23
Dec 30			

ECLIPSES

Annular eclipse of the Sun	Apr 8
Penumbral eclipse of the Moon	Apr 24
Annular eclipse of the Sun	Oct 3
Partial eclipse of the Moon	Oct 17

2006
PRINCIPAL PHENOMENA
EARTH

Perihelion	Jan 4
Aphelion	July 2
Equinoxes	Mar 20, Sept 23
Solstices	June 21, Dec 21

PHASES OF THE MOON

New Moon	First Quarter	Full Moon	Last Quarter
	Jan 6	Jan 14	Jan 22
Jan 29	Feb 5	Feb 12	Feb 21
Feb 27	Mar 6	Mar 14	Mar 22
Mar 29	Apr 5	Apr 13	Apr 20
Apr 27	May 5	May 13	May 20
May 27	June 3	June 11	June 18
June 25	July 3	July 10	July 17
July 25	Aug 2	Aug 9	Aug 15
Aug 23	Aug 31	Sept 7	Sept 14
Sept 22	Sept 30	Oct 6	Oct 13
Oct 22	Oct 29	Nov 5	Nov 12
Nov 20	Nov 28	Dec 4	Dec 12
Dec 20	Dec 27		

ECLIPSES

Penumbral eclipse of the Moon	Mar 14–15
Total eclipse of the Sun	Mar 29
Partial eclipse of the Moon	Sept 7
Annular eclipse of the Sun	Sept 22

★ Chase's 2004 Calendar of Events ★
THE NAMING OF HURRICANES

(Compiled from information issued by the US Department of Commerce, National Oceanic and Atmospheric Administration.)

Why are hurricanes named? Experience shows that the use of short, distinctive names greatly reduces confusion when two or more tropical storms occur at the same time. The use of easily remembered names in written and spoken communication is quicker and less subject to error than the older, more cumbersome latitude-longitude identification methods, advantages which are especially important in exchanging detailed storm information between hundreds of widely scattered stations, airports, coastal bases and ships at sea.

The practice of naming hurricanes began hundreds of years ago, but only relatively recently did they begin to be named solely for women. During World War II forecasters and meteorologists began using female names for storms in weather map discussions, and in 1953 the US weather services adopted the practice, creating a new international phonetic alphabet of women's names from A–W to name hurricanes. In 1978 men's names were also introduced into the storm lists.

Because hurricanes affect other nations and are tracked by their weather services, the lists have an international flavor. Names are agreed upon during international meetings of the World Meteorological Organization by the nations involved, and can be retired and replaced with new names in the event of particularly severe storms.

The National Hurricane Center near Miami, FL, keeps a constant watch on oceanic storm-breeding areas for tropical disturbances that may herald the formation of a hurricane. If a disturbance intensifies into a tropical storm—with rotary circulation and wind speeds above 39 miles per hour—the Center will give the storm a name from one of six lists. The Atlantic and Eastern Pacific lists are rotated year by year so that the 2004 set, for example, will be used again to name storms in 2010.

The lists of names for Central Pacific and Western Pacific hurricanes (tropical cyclones) are not rotated on a yearly basis. Meteorologists follow each list until all those names have been used, then go on to the next list. The name of a particularly severe storm is retired and replaced. For example, Iniki—the name of the hurricane that devastated Hawaii—has been replaced with Iolana on List 2.

ATLANTIC HURRICANE NAMES

2004	2005	2006
Alex	Arlene	Alberto
Bonnie	Bret	Beryl
Charley	Cindy	Chris
Danielle	Dennis	Debby
Earl	Emily	Ernesto
Frances	Franklin	Florence
Gaston	Gert	Gordon
Hermine	Harvey	Helene
Ivan	Irene	Isaac
Jeanne	Jose	Joyce
Karl	Katrina	Kirk
Lisa	Lee	Leslie
Matthew	Maria	Michael
Nicole	Nate	Nadine
Otto	Ophelia	Oscar
Paula	Philippe	Patty
Richard	Rita	Rafael
Shary	Stan	Sandy
Tomas	Tammy	Tony
Virginie	Vince	Valerie
Walter	Wilma	William

EASTERN PACIFIC HURRICANE NAMES

2004	2005	2006
Agatha	Adrian	Aletta
Blas	Beatriz	Bud
Celia	Calvin	Carlotta
Darby	Dora	Daniel
Estelle	Eugene	Emilia
Frank	Fernanda	Fabio
Georgette	Greg	Gilma
Howard	Hilary	Hector
Isis	Irwin	Ileana
Javier	Jova	John
Kay	Kenneth	Kristy
Lester	Lidia	Lane
Madeline	Max	Miriam
Newton	Norma	Norman
Orlene	Otis	Olivia
Paine	Pilar	Paul
Roslyn	Ramon	Rosa
Seymour	Selma	Sergio
Tina	Todd	Tara
Virgil	Veronica	Vicente
Winifred	Wiley	Willa
Xavier	Xina	Xavier
Yolanda	York	Yolanda
Zeke	Zelda	Zeke

If more than 24 tropical cyclones occur in a year, then the Greek alphabet will be used following Zelda or Zeke.

CENTRAL PACIFIC TROPICAL CYCLONE NAMES

LIST 1
Akoni (ah-KOH-nee)
Ema (EH-ma)
Hana (HAH-nah)
IO (EE-oo)
Keli (KEH-lee)
Lala (LAH-lah)
Moke (MOH-keh)
Nele (NEH-leh)
Oka (OH-kah)
Peke (PEH-keh)
Uleki (oo-LEH-kee)
Wila (VEE-lah)

LIST 2
Aka (AH-kah)
Ekeka (eh-KEH-kah)
Hali (HAH-lee)
Iolana (ee-OH-lah-nah)
Keoni (keh-OH-nee)
Li (LEE)
Mele (MEH-leh)
Nona (NOH-nah)
Oliwa (oh-LEE-vah)
Paka (PAH-hak)
Upana (oo-PAH-nah)
Wene (WEH-neh)

LIST 3
Alika (ah-LEE-kah)
Ele (EH-leh)
Huko (HOO-koh)
Ioke (ee-OH-keh)
Kika (KEE-kah)
Lana (LAH-nah)
Maka (MAH-kah)
Neki (NEH-kee)
Oleka (oh-LEH-kah)
Peni (PEH-nee)
Ulia (oo-LEE-ah)
Wali (WAH-lee)

LIST 4
Ana (AH-nah)
Ela (EH-lah)
Halola (hah-LOH-lah)
Iune (ee-OO-neh)
Kimo (KEE-moh)
Loke (LOH-keh)
Malia (mah-LEE-ah)
Niala (nee-AH-lah)
Oko (OH-koh)
Pali (PAH-lee)
Ulika (oo-LEE-kah)
Walaka (wah-LAH-kah)

In Hawaiian, all letters are pronounced, including double or triple vowels.

WESTERN PACIFIC TROPICAL CYCLONE NAMES

LIST 1	LIST 2	LIST 3	LIST 4	LIST 5
Damrey	Kong-rey	Nakri	Krovanh	Sarika
Longwang	Yutu	Fengshen	Dujuan	Haima
Kirogi	Toraji	Kalmaegi	Maemi	Meari
Kai-Tak	Man-yi	Fung-wong	Choi-wan	Ma-on
Tenbin	Usagi	Kanmuri	Koppu	Tokage
Bolaven	Pabuk	Phanfone	Ketsana	Nock-ten
Chanchu	Wutip	Vongfong	Parma	Muifa
Jelawat	Sepat	Rusa	Melor	Merbok
Ewinlar	Fitow	Sinlaku	Nepartak	Nanmadol
Bilis	Danas	Hagupit	Lupit	Talas
Gaemi	Nari	Changmi	Sudal	Noru
Prapiroon	Vipa	Megkhla	Nida	Kularb
Maria	Francisco	Higos	Omais	Roke
Saomai	Lekima	Bavi	Conson	Sonca
Bopha	Krosa	Maysak	Chanthu	Nesat
Wukong	Haiyan	Haishen	Dianmu	Haitang
Sonamu	Podul	Pongsona	Mindule	Nalgae
Shanshan	Lingling	Yanyan	Tingting	Banyan
Yagi	Kaziki	Kuzira	Kompasu	Washi
Xangsane	Faxai	Chan-hom	Namtheun	Matsa
Bebinca	Vamei	Linfa	Malou	Sanvu
Rumbia	Tapah	Nangka	Meranti	Mawar
Soulik	Mitag	Soudelor	Rananin	Guchol
Cimaron	Hagibis	Imbudo	Malakas	Talim
Chebi	Noguri	Koni	Megi	Nabi
Durian	Ramasoon	Hanuman	Chaba	Khanun
Utor	Chataan	Etau	Kodo	Vicete
Trami	Halong	Vamco	Songda	Saola

655

☆ *Chase's 2004 Calendar of Events* ☆
SOME FACTS ABOUT THE PRESIDENTS

	Name	Birthdate, Place	Party	Tenure	Died	First Lady	Vice President
1.	George Washington	2/22/1732, Westmoreland Cnty, VA	Federalist	1789–1797	12/14/1799	Martha Dandridge Custis	John Adams
2.	John Adams	10/30/1735, Braintree (Quincy), MA	Federalist	1797–1801	7/4/1826	Abigail Smith	Thomas Jefferson
3.	Thomas Jefferson	4/13/1743, Shadwell, VA	Democratic-Republican	1801–1809	7/4/1826	Martha Wayles Skelton	Aaron Burr, 1801–05 George Clinton, 1805–09
4.	James Madison	3/16/1751, Port Conway, VA	Democratic-Republican	1809–1817	6/28/1836	Dolley Payne Todd	George Clinton, 1809–12 Elbridge Gerry, 1813–14(?)
5.	James Monroe	4/28/1758, Westmoreland Cnty, VA	Democratic-Republican	1817–1825	7/4/1831	Elizabeth Kortright	Daniel D. Tompkins
6.	John Q. Adams	7/11/1767, Braintree (Quincy), MA	Democratic-Republican	1825–1829	2/23/1848	Louisa Catherine Johnson	John C. Calhoun
7.	Andrew Jackson	3/15/1767, Waxhaw Settlement, SC	Democrat	1829–1837	6/8/1845	Mrs. Rachel Donelson Robards	John C. Calhoun, 1829–32 Martin Van Buren, 1833–37
8.	Martin Van Buren	12/5/1782, Kinderhook, NY	Democrat	1837–1841	7/24/1862	Hannah Hoes	Richard M. Johnson
9.	William H. Harrison	2/9/1773, Charles City Cnty, VA	Whig	1841	4/4/1841†	Anna Symmes	John Tyler
10.	John Tyler	3/29/1790, Charles City Cnty, VA	Whig	1841–1845	1/18/1862	Letitia Christian Julia Gardiner	
11.	James K. Polk	11/2/1795, near Pineville, NC	Democrat	1845–1849	6/15/1849	Sarah Childress	George M. Dallas
12.	Zachary Taylor	11/24/1784, Barboursville, VA	Whig	1849–1850	7/9/1850†	Margaret Mackall Smith	Millard Fillmore
13.	Millard Fillmore	1/7/1800, Locke, NY	Whig	1850–1853	3/8/1874	Abigail Powers Mrs. Caroline Carmichael McIntosh	
14.	Franklin Pierce	11/23/1804, Hillsboro, NH	Democrat	1853–1857	10/8/1869	Jane Means Appleton	William R. D. King
15.	James Buchanan	4/23/1791, near Mercersburg, PA	Democrat	1857–1861	6/1/1868		John C. Breckinridge
16.	Abraham Lincoln	2/12/1809, near Hodgenville, KY	Republican	1861–1865	4/15/1865*	Mary Todd	Hannibal Hamlin, 1861–65 Andrew Johnson, 1865
17.	Andrew Johnson	12/29/1808, Raleigh, NC	Democrat	1865–1869	7/31/1875	Eliza McCardle	
18.	Ulysses S. Grant	4/27/1822, Point Pleasant, OH	Republican	1869–1877	7/23/1885	Julia Boggs Dent	Schuyler Colfax, 1869–73 Henry Wilson, 1873–75
19.	Rutherford B. Hayes	10/4/1822, Delaware, OH	Republican	1877–1881	1/17/1893	Lucy Ware Webb	William A. Wheeler
20.	James A. Garfield	11/19/1831, Orange, OH	Republican	1881	9/19/1881*	Lucretia Rudolph	Chester A. Arthur
21.	Chester A. Arthur	10/5/1829, Fairfield, VT	Republican	1881–1885	11/18/1886	Ellen Lewis Herndon	
22.	Grover Cleveland	3/18/1837, Caldwell, NJ	Democrat	1885–1889	6/24/1908	Frances Folsom	Thomas A. Hendricks, 1885
23.	Benjamin Harrison	8/20/1833, North Bend, OH	Republican	1889–1893	3/13/1901	Caroline Lavinia Scott Mrs. Mary Dimmick	Levi P. Morton
24.	Grover Cleveland	3/18/1837, Caldwell, NJ	Democrat	1893–1897	6/24/1908	Frances Folsom	Adlai Stevenson, 1893–97

☆ Chase's 2004 Calendar of Events ☆

Name	Birthdate, Place	Party	Tenure	Died	First Lady	Vice President
25. William McKinley	1/29/1843, Niles, OH	Republican	1897–1901	9/14/1901*	Ida Saxton	Garret A. Hobart, 1897–99 Theodore Roosevelt, 1901
26. Theodore Roosevelt	10/27/1858, New York, NY	Republican	1901–1909	1/6/1919	Alice Hathaway Lee Edith Kermit Carow	Charles W. Fairbanks
27. William H. Taft	9/15/1857, Cincinnati, OH	Republican	1909–1913	3/8/1930	Helen Herron	James S. Sherman
28. Woodrow Wilson	12/28/1856, Staunton, VA	Democrat	1913–1921	2/3/1924	Ellen Louise Axson Edith Bolling Galt	Thomas R. Marshall
29. Warren G. Harding	11/2/1865, near Corsica, OH	Republican	1921–1923	8/2/1923†	Florence Kling DeWolfe	Calvin Coolidge
30. Calvin Coolidge	7/4/1872, Plymouth Notch, VT	Republican	1923–1929	1/5/1933	Grace Anna Goodhue	Charles G. Dawes
31. Herbert C. Hoover	8/10/1874, West Branch, IA	Republican	1929–1933	10/20/1964	Lou Henry	Charles Curtis
32. Franklin D. Roosevelt	1/30/1882, Hyde Park, NY	Democrat	1933–1945	4/12/1945†	Eleanor Roosevelt	John N. Garner, 1933–41 Henry A. Wallace, 1941–45 Harry S. Truman, 1945
33. Harry S. Truman	5/8/1884, Lamar, MO	Democrat	1945–1953	12/26/1972	Elizabeth Virginia (Bess) Wallace	Alben W. Barkley
34. Dwight D. Eisenhower	10/14/1890, Denison, TX	Republican	1953–1961	3/28/1969	Mamie Geneva Doud	Richard M. Nixon
35. John F. Kennedy	5/29/1917, Brookline, MA	Democrat	1961–1963	11/22/1963*	Jacqueline Lee Bouvier	Lyndon B. Johnson
36. Lyndon B. Johnson	8/27/1908, near Stonewall, TX	Democrat	1963–1969	1/22/1973	Claudia Alta (Lady Bird) Taylor	Hubert H. Humphrey
37. Richard M. Nixon	1/9/1913, Yorba Linda, CA	Republican	1969–1974**	4/22/1994	Thelma Catherine (Pat) Ryan	Spiro T. Agnew, 1969–73 Gerald R. Ford, 1973–74
38. Gerald R. Ford	7/14/1913, Omaha, NE	Republican	1974–1977		Elizabeth (Betty) Bloomer	Nelson A. Rockefeller
39. James E. Carter, Jr	10/1/1924, Plains, GA	Democrat	1977–1981		Rosalynn Smith	Walter F. Mondale
40. Ronald W. Reagan	2/6/1911, Tampico, IL	Republican	1981–1989		Nancy Davis	George H. W. Bush
41. George H. W. Bush	6/12/1924, Milton, MA	Republican	1989–1993		Barbara Pierce	J. Danforth Quayle
42. William J. Clinton	8/19/1946, Hope, AR	Democrat	1993–2001		Hillary Rodham	Albert Gore, Jr.
43. George W. Bush	7/6/1946, New Haven, CT	Republican	2001–		Laura Welch	Richard Cheney

*assassinated while in office
** resigned Aug 9, 1974
† died while in office—nonviolently

Sources: *World Book*, 1991 Edition; *Encyclopedia Americana*, 1990 Edition; *Collier's Encyclopedia*, 1994 Edition

☆ Chase's 2004 Calendar of Events ☆
PRESIDENTIAL PROCLAMATIONS ISSUED, MARCH 5, 2002–JUNE 30, 2003

No. Title, Observance Dates, (Date of signing).

2002

7529 To Facilitate Positive Adjustment to Competition From Imports of Certain Steel Products (Mar 5, 2002)
7530 Women's History Month, 2002: March (Mar 6, 2002)
7531 Bicentennial Day of the United States Military Academy at West Point: Mar 16, 2002 (Mar 11, 2002)
7532 National Poison Prevention Week, 2002: Mar 17–23, 2002 (Mar 14, 2002)
7533 National Bone and Joint Decade, 2002–2011: Years 2002–2011 (Mar 21, 2002)
7534 Education and Sharing Day, 2002: Mar 24, 2002 (Mar 21, 2002)
7535 Greek Independence Day: A National Day of Celebration of Greek and American Democracy, 2002: Mar 25, 2002 (Mar 25, 2002)
7536 Cancer Control Month, 2002: April (Apr 1, 2002)
7537 National Child Abuse Prevention Month, 2002: April (Apr 1, 2002)
7538 National Former Prisoner of War Recognition Day, 2002: Apr 9, 2002 (Apr 4, 2002)
7539 National D.A.R.E. (Drug Abuse Resistance Education) Day, 2002: Apr 11, 2002 (Apr 10, 2002)
7540 Pan American Day and Pan American Week, 2002: Apr 14, 2002 and Apr 14–20, 2002 (Apr 12, 2002)
7541 Jewish Heritage Week, 2002: Apr 14–21, 2002 (Apr 12, 2002)
7542 Death of Byron R. White (Apr 17, 2002)
7543 National Crime Victim's Rights Week, 2002: Apr 21–27, 2002 (Apr 18, 2002)
7544 National Organ and Tissue Donor Awareness Week, 2002: Apr 21–27, 2002 (Apr 19, 2002)
7545 National Volunteer Week, 2002: Apr 21–27, 2002 (Apr 19, 2002)
7546 National Park Week, 2002: Apr 22–28, 2002 (Apr 23, 2002)
7547 National Day of Prayer, 2002: May 2, 2002 (Apr 26, 2002)
7548 Law Day, USA, 2002: May 1, 2002 (Apr 30, 2002)
7549 Loyalty Day, 2002: May 1, 2002 (Apr 30, 2002)
7550 Asian/Pacific American Heritage Month, 2002: May (May 1, 2002)
7551 National Older Americans Month, 2002: May (May 1, 2002)
7552 National Charter Schools Week, 2002: Apr 28–May 4, 2002 (May 2, 2002)
7553 To Restore Non-discriminatory Trade Treatment (Normal Trade Relations Treatment) to the Products of Afghanistan (May 3, 2002)
7554 To Extend Duty-Free Treatment for Certain Agricultural Products of Israel (May 3, 2002)
7555 Small Business Week, 2002: May 5–11, 2002 (May 3, 2002)
7556 National Tourism Week, 2002: May 5–11, 2002 (May 6, 2002)
7557 Mother's Day, 2002: May 12, 2002 (May 9, 2002)
7558 Peace Officers Memorial Day and Police Week, 2002: May 15, 2002 and May 12–18, 2002 (May 10, 2002)
7559 National Defense Transportation Day and National Transportation Week, 2002: May 17, 2002 and May 12–18, 2002 (May 10, 2002)
7560 National Hurricane Awareness Week, 2002: May 19–25, 2002 (May 13, 2002)
7561 To Designate the Republic of Côte d'Ivoire as a Beneficiary Sub-Saharan African Country (May 16, 2002)
7562 Armed Forces Day, 2002: May 18, 2002 (May 16, 2002)
7563 National Safe Boating Week, 2002: May 18–24, 2002 (May 17, 2002)
7564 World Trade Week, 2002: May 19–25, 2002 (May 17, 2002)

No. Title, Observance Dates, (Date of signing).

7565 National Maritime Day, 2002: May 22, 2002 (May 21, 2002)
7566 National Missing Children's Day, 2002: May 25, 2002 (May 21, 2002)
7567 Prayer for Peace, Memorial Day, 2002: May 27, 2002 (May 21, 2002)
7568 Black Music Month, 2002: June (May 31, 2002)
7569 National Fishing and Boating Week, 2002: June 2–8, 2002 (May 31, 2002)
7570 National Homeownership Month, 2002: June (June 4, 2002)
7571 National Child's Day, 2002: June 9, 2002 (June 5, 2002)
7572 Great Outdoors Week, 2002: June 9–15, 2002 (June 7, 2002)
7573 Flag Day and National Flag Week, 2002: June 14, 2002 and June 9–15, 2002 (June 7, 2002)
7574 Father's Day, 2002: June 16, 2002 (June 14, 2002)
7575 Lewis and Clark Bicentennial: 2003–2006 (June 28, 2002)
7576 To Provide for the Efficient and Fair Administration of Safeguard Measures on Imports of Certain Steel Products (July 3, 2002)
7577 Captive Nations Week, 2002: July 21–27, 2002 (July 17, 2002)
7578 National Korean War Veteran's Armistice Day, 2002: July 27, 2002 (July 26, 2002)
7579 Anniversary of the Americans with Disabilities Act, 2002: July 26, 2002 (July 26, 2002)
7580 Parent's Day, 2002: July 28, 2002 (July 26, 2002)
7581 The Bicentennial of the United States Patent and Trademark Office, 2002 (July 29, 2002)
7582 National Airborne Day, 2002: Aug 16, 2002 (Aug 14, 2002)
7583 National Health Center Week, 2002: Aug 18–24, 2002 (Aug 16, 2002)
7584 Women's Equality Day, 2002: Aug 26, 2002 (Aug 23, 2002)
7585 To Implement an Agreement Regarding Imports of Line Pipe Under Section 203 of the Trade Act of 1974 (Aug 28, 2002)
7586 To Modify Duty-Free Treatment Under the Generalized System of Preferences for Argentina (Aug 28, 2002)
7587 National Ovarian Cancer Awareness Month, 2002: September (Aug 30, 2002)
7588 National Days of Prayer and Remembrance, 2002: Sept 6–8, 2002 (Aug 31, 2002)
7589 National Alcohol and Drug Addiction Recovery Month, 2002: September (Sept 4, 2002)
7590 Patriot Day, 2002: Sept 11, 2002 (Sept 4, 2002)
7591 National Hispanic Heritage Month, 2002: Sept 15–Oct 15, 2002 (Sept 13, 2002)
7592 National Farm Safety and Health Week, 2002: Sept 15–21, 2002 (Sept 13, 2002)
7593 National Historically Black Colleges and Universities Week, 2002: Sept 15–21, 2002 (Sept 13, 2002)
7594 Citizenship Day and Constitution Week, 2002: Sept 17, 2002 and Sept 17–23, 2002 (Sept 16, 2002)
7595 National POW/MIA Recognition Day, 2002: Sept 20, 2002 (Sept 19, 2002)
7596 Minority Enterprise Development Week, 2002: Sept 22–28, 2002 (Sept 20, 2002)
7597 Family Day, 2002: Sept 23, 2002 (Sept 20, 2002)
7598 Gold Star Mother's Day, 2002: Sept 29, 2002 (Sept 27, 2002)
7599 National Breast Cancer Awareness Month, 2002: October (Oct 1, 2002)
7600 National Disability Employment Awareness Month, 2002: October (Oct 1, 2002)
7601 National Domestic Violence Awareness Month, 2002: October (Oct 1, 2002)
7602 Fire Prevention Week, 2002: Oct 6–12, 2002 (Oct 4, 2002)

☆ Chase's 2004 Calendar of Events ☆

No. Title, Observance Dates, (Date of signing).

7603 Child Health Day, 2002: Oct 7, 2002 (Oct 4, 2002)
7604 German-American Day, 2002: Oct 6, 2002 (Oct 4, 2002)
7605 Leif Erikson Day, 2002: Oct 9, 2002 (Oct 8, 2002)
7606 Columbus Day, 2002: Oct 14, 2002 (Oct 9, 2002)
7607 General Pulaski Memorial Day, 2002: Oct 11, 2002 (Oct 10, 2002)
7608 National Cystic Fibrosis Awareness Week, 2002: Oct 13-19, 2002 (Oct 11, 2002)
7609 National School Lunch Week, 2002: Oct 13-19, 2002 (Oct 11, 2002)
7610 White Cane Safety Day, 2002: Oct 15, 2002 (Oct 11, 2002)
7611 Year of Clean Water, 2002-2003: Oct 18, 2002-Oct 17, 2003 (Oct 17, 2002)
7612 National Character Counts Week, 2002: Oct 20-26, 2002 (Oct 18, 2002)
7613 National Forest Products Week, 2002: Oct 20-26, 2002 (Oct 18, 2002)
7614 United Nations Day, 2002: Oct 24, 2002 (Oct 23, 2002)
7615 National Family Caregivers Month, 2002: November (Oct 29, 2002)
7616 To Implement the Andean Trade Promotion and Drug Eradication Act (Oct 31, 2002)
7617 National Alzheimer's Disease Awareness Month, 2002: November (Oct 31, 2002)
7618 National Diabetes Month, 2002: November (Oct 31, 2002)
7619 National Adoption Month, 2002: November (Nov 1, 2002)
7620 National American Indian Heritage Month, 2002: November (Nov 1, 2002)
7621 National Hospice Month, 2002: November (Nov 1, 2002)
7622 In Celebration of the Centennial of the West Wing of the White House, 2002: West Wing Centennial Day: Nov 6, 2002 (Nov 5, 2002)
7623 Veteran's Day and National Veteran's Awareness Week, 2002: Nov 11 and Nov 10-16, 2002 (Nov 6, 2002)
7624 National Employer Support of the Guard and Reserve Week, 2002: Nov 10-16, 2002 (Nov 8, 2002)
7625 World Freedom Day, 2002: Nov 9, 2002 (Nov 8, 2002)
7626 To Implement Modifications to the Caribbean Basin Economic Recovery Act and the African Growth and Opportunity Act (Nov 13, 2002)
7627 America Recycles Day, 2002: Nov 15, 2002 (Nov 14, 2002)
7628 Thanksgiving Day, 2002: Nov 28, 2002 (Nov 21, 2002)
7629 National Farm-City Week, 2002: Nov 22-28, 2002 (Nov 22, 2002)
7630 National Family Week, 2002: Nov 24-30, 2002 (Nov 22, 2002)
7631 World AIDS Day, 2002: Dec 1, 2002 (Nov 27, 2002)
7632 National Drunk and Drugged Driving Prevention Month, 2002: December (Dec 3, 2002)
7633 National Pearl Harbor Remembrance Day, 2002: Dec 7, 2002 (Dec 6, 2002)
7634 Human Rights Day, Bill of Rights Day and Human Rights Week, 2002: Dec 10, 2002, Dec 15, 2002, and Dec 10-17, 2002 (Dec 9, 2002)
7635 Wright Brothers Day, 2002: Dec 17, 2002 (Dec 16, 2002)

2003

7636 National Mentoring Month, 2003: January (Jan 2, 2003)
7637 To Modify Duty-Free Treatment under the Generalized System of Preferences (Jan 10, 2003)
7638 The Centennial of Korean Immigration to the United States: Jan 13, 2003 (Jan 13, 2003)
7639 National Sanctity of Human Life Day, 2003: Jan 19, 2003 (Jan 14, 2003)
7640 Religious Freedom Day, 2003: Jan 16, 2003 (Jan 15, 2003)
7641 To Modify Rules of Origin under the North American Free Trade Agreement (Jan 17, 2003)
7642 Martin Luther King, Jr. Federal Holiday, 2003: Jan 20, 2003 (Jan 17, 2003)
7643 National Consumer Protection Awareness Week, 2003: Feb 2-8, 2003 (Jan 27, 2003)
7644 American Heart Month, 2003: February (Jan 30, 2003)
7645 National African American History Month, 2003: February (Jan 31, 2003)

No. Title, Observance Dates, (Date of signing).

7646 Honoring the Memory of the Astronauts aboard Space Shuttle *Columbia* (Feb 1, 2003)
7647 Establishment of Governor's Island National Monument (Feb 7, 2003)
7648 American Red Cross Month, 2003: March (Feb 28, 2003)
7649 Irish American Heritage Month, 2003: March (Feb 28, 2003)
7650 National Colorectal Cancer Awareness Month, 2003: March (Feb 28, 2003)
7651 Women's History Month, 2003: March (Feb 28, 2003)
7652 Save Your Vision Week, 2003: Mar 2-8, 2003 (Feb 28, 2003)
7653 National Poison Prevention Week, 2003: Mar 16-22, 2003 (Mar 14, 2003)
7654 Greek Independence Day: A National Day of Celebration of Greek and American Democracy, 2003: Mar 25, 2003 (Mar 18, 2003)
7655 Cancer Control Month, 2003: April (Mar 24, 2003)
7656 National Child Abuse Prevention Month, 2003: April (Mar 26, 2003)
7657 To Take Certain Actions under the African Growth and Opportunities Act with Respect to the Republic of Gambia and the Democratic Republic of Congo (Mar 28, 2003)
7658 National Donate Life Month, 2003: April (Apr 1, 2003)
7659 National Crime Victim's Rights Week, 2003: Apr 6-12, 2003 (Apr 4, 2003)
7660 National Former Prisoner of War Recognition Day, 2003: Apr 9, 2003 (Apr 8, 2003)
7661 National D.A.R.E. (Drug Abuse Resistance Education) Day, 2003: Apr 10, 2003 (Apr 9, 2003)
7662 Education and Sharing Day, 2003: Apr 13, 2003 (Apr 10, 2003)
7663 Pan American Day and Pan American Week, 2003: Apr 14, 2003 and Apr 13-19, 2003 (Apr 11, 2003)
7664 National Fair Housing Month, 2003: April (Apr 15, 2003)
7665 National Park Week, 2003: Apr 21-27, 2003 (Apr 18, 2003)
7666 National Charter Schools Week, 2003: Apr 27-May 3, 2003 (Apr 25, 2003)
7667 National Volunteer Week, 2003: Apr 27-May 3, 2003 (Apr 25, 2003)
7668 Asian/Pacific American Heritage Month, 2003: May (Apr 30, 2003)
7669 Older Americans Month, 2003: May (Apr 30, 2003)
7670 Law Day, USA, 2003: May 1, 2003 (Apr 30, 2003)
7671 Loyalty Day, 2003: May 1, 2003 (Apr 30, 2003)
7672 National Day of Prayer, 2003: May 1, 2003 (Apr 30, 2003)
7673 Jewish Heritage Week, 2003: May 4-11, 2003 (May 2, 2003)
7674 Mother's Day, 2003: May 11, 2003 (May 7, 2003)
7675 Peace Officers Memorial Day and Police Week, 2003: May 15, 2003 and May 11-17, 2003 (May 9, 2003)
7676 National Defense Transportation Day and National Transportation Week, 2003: May 16, 2003 and May 11-17, 2003 (May 9, 2003)
7677 National Safe Boating Week, 2003: May 17-23, 2003 (May 9, 2003)
7678 National Hurricane Awareness Week, 2003: May 18-24, 2003 (May 15, 2003)
7679 World Trade Week, 2003: May 18-24, 2003 (May 16, 2003)
7680 National Maritime Day, 2003: May 22, 2003 (May 21, 2003)
7681 Prayer for Peace, Memorial Day, 2003: May 26, 2003 (May 22, 2003)
7682 National Missing Children's Day, 2003: May 25, 2003 (May 23, 2003)
7683 National Child's Day, 2003: June 1, 2003 (May 30, 2003)
7684 Flag Day and National Flag Week, 2003: June 14, 2003 and June 8-14, 2003 (June 6, 2003)
7685 Father's Day, 2003: June 15, 2003 (June 13, 2003)
7686 National Homeownership Month, 2003: June (June 13, 2003)
7687 Black Music Month, 2003: June (June 24, 2003)
7688 Death of James Strom Thurmond (June 30, 2003)

☆ Chase's 2004 Calendar of Events ☆
SOME FACTS ABOUT THE UNITED STATES

State	Capital	Popular name	Area (sq. mi.)	State bird	State flower	State tree	Admitted to the Union	Order of Admission
Alabama	Montgomery	Cotton or Yellowhammer State; or Heart of Dixie	51,609	Yellowhammer	Camellia	Southern pine (Longleaf pine)	1819	22
Alaska	Juneau	Last Frontier	591,004	Willow ptarmigan	Forget-me-not	Sitka spruce	1959	49
Arizona	Phoenix	Grand Canyon State	114,000	Cactus wren	Saguaro (giant cactus)	Palo Verde	1912	48
Arkansas	Little Rock	The Natural State	53,187	Mockingbird	Apple blossom	Pine	1836	25
California	Sacramento	Golden State	158,706	California valley quail	Golden poppy	California redwood	1850	31
Colorado	Denver	Centennial State	104,091	Lark bunting	Rocky Mountain columbine	Blue spruce	1876	38
Connecticut	Hartford	Constitution State	5,018	Robin	Mountain laurel	White oak	1788	5
Delaware	Dover	First State	2,044	Blue hen chicken	Peach blossom	American holly	1787	1
Florida	Tallahassee	Sunshine State	58,664	Mockingbird	Orange blossom	Cabbage (sabal) palm	1845	27
Georgia	Atlanta	Empire State of the South	58,910	Brown thrasher	Cherokee rose	Live oak	1788	4
Hawaii	Honolulu	Aloha State	6,471	Nene (Hawaiian goose)	Hibiscus	Kukui	1959	50
Idaho	Boise	Gem State	83,564	Mountain bluebird	Syringa (mock orange)	Western white pine	1890	43
Illinois	Springfield	Prairie State	56,345	Cardinal	Native violet	White oak	1818	21
Indiana	Indianapolis	Hoosier State	36,185	Cardinal	Peony	Tulip tree or yellow poplar	1816	19
Iowa	Des Moines	Hawkeye State	56,275	Eastern goldfinch	Wild rose	Oak	1846	29
Kansas	Topeka	Sunflower State	82,277	Western meadowlark	Sunflower	Cottonwood	1861	34
Kentucky	Frankfort	Bluegrass State	40,409	Kentucky cardinal	Goldenrod	Kentucky coffeetree	1792	15
Louisiana	Baton Rouge	Pelican State	47,752	Pelican	Magnolia	Bald cypress	1812	18
Maine	Augusta	Pine Tree State	33,265	Chickadee	White pine cone and tassel	White pine	1820	23
Maryland	Annapolis	Old Line State	10,577	Baltimore oriole	Black-eyed Susan	White oak	1788	7
Massachusetts	Boston	Bay State	8,284	Chickadee	Mayflower	American elm	1788	6
Michigan	Lansing	Wolverine State	58,527	Robin	Apple blossom	White pine	1837	26
Minnesota	St. Paul	North Star State	84,402	Common loon	Pink and white lady's-slipper	Norway, or red, pine	1858	32
Mississippi	Jackson	Magnolia State	47,689	Mockingbird	Magnolia	Magnolia	1817	20
Missouri	Jefferson City	Show Me State	69,697	Bluebird	Hawthorn	Flowering dogwood	1821	24
Montana	Helena	Treasure State	147,046	Western meadowlark	Bitterroot	Ponderosa pine	1889	41
Nebraska	Lincoln	Cornhusker State	77,355	Western meadowlark	Goldenrod	Cottonwood	1867	37
Nevada	Carson City	Silver State	110,540	Mountain bluebird	Sagebrush	Single-leaf piñon	1864	36
New Hampshire	Concord	Granite State	9,304	Purple finch	Purple lilac	White birch	1788	9
New Jersey	Trenton	Garden State	7,787	Eastern goldfinch	Purple violet	Red oak	1787	3
New Mexico	Santa Fe	Land of Enchantment	121,593	Roadrunner	Yucca flower	Piñon, or nut pine	1912	47

☆ Chase's 2004 Calendar of Events ☆

State	Capital	Popular name	Area (sq. mi.)	State bird	State flower	State tree	Admitted to the Union	Order of Admission
New York	Albany	Empire State	49,108	Bluebird	Rose	Sugar maple	1788	11
North Carolina	Raleigh	Tar Heel State or Old North State	52,669	Cardinal	Dogwood	Pine	1789	12
North Dakota	Bismarck	Peace Garden State	70,702	Western meadowlark	Wild prairie rose	American elm	1889	39
Ohio	Columbus	Buckeye State	41,330	Cardinal	Scarlet carnation	Buckeye	1803	17
Oklahoma	Oklahoma City	Sooner State	69,956	Scissortail flycatcher	Mistletoe	Redbud	1907	46
Oregon	Salem	Beaver State	97,073	Western meadowlark	Oregon grape	Douglas fir	1859	33
Pennsylvania	Harrisburg	Keystone State	45,308	Ruffed grouse	Mountain laurel	Hemlock	1787	2
Rhode Island	Providence	Ocean State	1,212	Rhode Island Red	Violet	Red maple	1790	13
South Carolina	Columbia	Palmetto State	31,113	Carolina wren	Carolina jessamine	Palmetto	1788	8
South Dakota	Pierre	Sunshine State	77,116	Ring-necked pheasant	American pasqueflower	Black Hills spruce	1889	40
Tennessee	Nashville	Volunteer State	42,114	Mockingbird	Iris	Tulip poplar	1796	16
Texas	Austin	Lone Star State	266,807	Mockingbird	Bluebonnet	Pecan	1845	28
Utah	Salt Lake City	Beehive State	84,899	Sea Gull	Sego lily	Blue spruce	1896	45
Vermont	Montpelier	Green Mountain State	9,614	Hermit thrush	Red clover	Sugar maple	1791	14
Virginia	Richmond	Old Dominion	40,767	Cardinal	Dogwood	Dogwood	1788	10
Washington	Olympia	Evergreen State	68,139	Willow goldfinch	Coast rhododendron	Western hemlock	1889	42
West Virginia	Charleston	Mountain State	24,231	Cardinal	Rhododendron	Sugar maple	1863	35
Wisconsin	Madison	Badger State	56,153	Robin	Wood violet	Sugar maple	1848	30
Wyoming	Cheyenne	Equality State	97,809	Meadowlark	Indian paintbrush	Cottonwood	1890	44

STATE & TERRITORY ABBREVIATIONS: UNITED STATES

Alabama . . . . AL	Kentucky . . . . KY	Oklahoma . . . . OK
Alaska . . . . AK	Louisiana . . . . LA	Oregon . . . . OR
Arizona . . . . AZ	Maine . . . . ME	Pennsylvania . . . . PA
Arkansas . . . . AR	Maryland . . . . MD	Puerto Rico . . . . PR
American Samoa . . . . AS	Massachusetts . . . . MA	Rhode Island . . . . RI
California . . . . CA	Michigan . . . . MI	South Carolina . . . . SC
Colorado . . . . CO	Minnesota . . . . MN	South Dakota . . . . SD
Connecticut . . . . CT	Mississippi . . . . MS	Tennessee . . . . TN
Delaware . . . . DE	Missouri . . . . MO	Texas . . . . TX
District of Columbia . . . . DC	Montana . . . . MT	Utah . . . . UT
Florida . . . . FL	Nebraska . . . . NE	Vermont . . . . VT
Georgia . . . . GA	Nevada . . . . NV	Virginia . . . . VA
Guam . . . . GU	New Hampshire . . . . NH	Virgin Islands VI
Hawaii . . . . HI	New Jersey . . . . NJ	Washington . . . . WA
Idaho . . . . ID	New Mexico . . . . NM	West Virginia . . . . WV
Illinois IL	New York . . . . NY	Wisconsin . . . . WI
Indiana . . . . IN	North Carolina . . . . NC	Wyoming . . . . WY
Iowa . . . . IA	North Dakota . . . . ND	
Kansas . . . . KS	Ohio . . . . OH	

☆ Chase's 2004 Calendar of Events ☆

STATE GOVERNORS/US SENATORS/US SUPREME COURT

GOVERNORS*
Name (Party, State)

Bob Riley (R, AL)
Frank Murkowski (R, AK)
Janet Napolitano (D, AZ)
Mike Huckabee (R, AR)
Gray Davis (D, CA)
Bill Owens (R, CO)
John Rowland (R, CT)
Ruth Ann Minner (D, DE)
Jeb Bush (R, FL)
Sonny Perdue (R, GA)
Linda Lingle (R, HI)
Dirk Kempthorne (R, ID)
Rod Blagojevich (D, IL)
Frank O'Bannon (D, IN)
Tom Vilsack (D, IA)
Kathleen Sibelius (D, KS)
Paul E. Patton (D, KY)
Mike Foster (R, LA)
John Baldacci (D, ME)
Robert Ehrlich, Jr (R, MD)
Mitt Romney (R, MA)
Jennifer Granholm (D, MI)
Tim Pawlenty (R, MN)
Ronnie Musgrove (D, MS)
Bob Holden (D, MO)
Judy Martz (R, MT)
Mike Johanns (R, NE)
Kenny Guinn (R, NV)
Craig Benson (R, NH)
James McGreevey (R, NJ)
Bill Richardson (D, NM)
George Pataki (R, NY)
Mike Easley (D, NC)
John Hoeven (R, ND)
Bob Taft (R, OH)
Brad Henry (D, OK)
Ted Kulongoski (D, OR)
Ed Rendell (D, PA)
Donald Carcieri (R, RI)
Mark Sanford (R, SC)
Mike Rounds (R, SD)
Phil Bredesen (D, TN)
Rick Perry (R, TX)
Mike Leavitt (R, UT)
Jim Douglas (R, VT)
Mark Warner (R, VA)
Gary Locke (D, WA)
Bob Wise (D, WV)
Jim Doyle (D, WI)
Dave Freudenthal (D, WY)

Office holders were current as of July 2003.

SENATORS*
Name (Party, State)

Jeff Sessions (R, AL)
Richard C. Shelby (R, AL)
Ted Stevens (R, AK)
Lisa Murkowski (R, AK)
Jon Kyl (R, AZ)
John McCain (R, AZ)
Blanche Lambert Lincoln (D, AR)
Mark Pryor (D, AR)
Dianne Feinstein (D, CA)
Barbara Boxer (D, CA)
Wayne Allard (R, CO)
Ben Nighthorse Campbell (R, CO)
Christopher J. Dodd (D, CT)
Joseph I. Lieberman (D, CT)
Thomas Carper (D, DE)
Joseph R. Biden, Jr (D, DE)
Robert Graham (D, FL)
Bill Nelson (D, FL)
Saxby Chambliss (R, GA)
Zell Miller (D, GA)
Daniel K. Inouye (D, HI)
Daniel K. Akaka (D, HI)
Larry E. Craig (R, ID)
Michael Crapo (R, ID)
Richard J. Durbin (D, IL)
Peter Fitzgerald (R, IL)
Richard G. Lugar (R, IN)
Evan Bayh (D, IN)
Charles E. Grassley (R, IA)
Tom Harkin (D, IA)
Sam Brownback (R, KS)
Pat Roberts (R, KS)
Jim Bunning (R, KY)
Mitch McConnell (R, KY)
Mary L. Landrieu (D, LA)
John B. Breaux (D, LA)
Susan M. Collins (R, ME)
Olympia J. Snowe (R, ME)
Paul S. Sarbanes (D, MD)
Barbara A. Mikulski (D, MD)
Edward M. Kennedy (D, MA)
John F. Kerry (D, MA)
Debbie Stabenow (D, MI)
Carl Levin (D, MI)
Mark Dayton (D, MN)
Norm Coleman (R, MN)
Thad Cochran (R, MS)
Trent Lott (R, MS)
Jim Talent (R, MO)
Christopher S. Bond (R, MO)
Max S. Baucus (D, MT)
Conrad Burns (R, MT)
Chuck Hagel (R, NE)
Ben Nelson (D, NE)
Harry M. Reid (D, NV)
John Ensign (R, NV)
John Sununu (R, NH)
Judd Gregg (R, NH)

Frank Lautenberg (D, NJ)
Jon Corzine (D, NJ)
Pete V. Domenici (R, NM)
Jeff Bingaman (D, NM)
Hillary Rodham Clinton (D, NY)
Charles E. Schumer (D, NY)
Elizabeth Dole (R, NC)
John Edwards (D, NC)
Kent Conrad (D, ND)
Byron L. Dorgan (D, ND)
George Voinovich (R, OH)
Mike DeWine (R, OH)
James M. Inhofe (R, OK)
Don Nickles (R, OK)
Gordon Smith (R, OR)
Ron Wyden (D, OR)
Arlen Specter (R, PA)
Rick Santorum (R, PA)
Jack Reed (D, RI)
Lincoln Chafee (R, RI)
Lindsey Graham (R, SC)
Ernest F. Hollings (D, SC)
Tim Johnson (D, SD)
Thomas A. Daschle (D, SD)
William Frist (R, TN)
Lamar Alexander (R, TN)
John Cornyn (R, TX)
Kay Bailey Hutchison (R, TX)
Orrin G. Hatch (R, UT)
Robert F. Bennett (R, UT)
Patrick J. Leahy (D, VT)
James M. Jeffords (I, VT)
John W. Warner (R, VA)
George Allen (R, VA)
Maria Cantwell (D, WA)
Patty Murray (D, WA)
Robert C. Byrd (D, WV)
John D. Rockefeller IV (D, WV)
Herbert H. Kohl (D, WI)
Russell D. Feingold (D, WI)
Michael B. Enzi (R, WY)
Craig Thomas (R, WY)

SUPREME COURT JUSTICES*
Name (Appointed by, Year)

William H. Rehnquist, Chief Justice (Reagan, 1986)
John P. Stevens (Ford, 1975)
Sandra Day O'Connor (Reagan, 1981)
Antonin Scalia (Reagan, 1986)
Anthony M. Kennedy (Reagan, 1988)
David H. Souter (G.H.W. Bush, 1990)
Clarence Thomas (G.H.W. Bush, 1991)
Ruth Bader Ginsburg (Clinton, 1993)
Stephen G. Breyer (Clinton, 1994)

☆ *Chase's 2004 Calendar of Events* ☆

SOME FACTS ABOUT CANADA

Province/Territory	Capital	Population*	Flower	Land/Fresh Water (sq. mi.)	Total Area
Alberta	Edmonton	2,974,807	Wild Rose	248,000/7,541	255,541
British Columbia	Victoria	3,907,738	Pacific dogwood	357,216/7,548	364,764
Manitoba	Winnipeg	1,119,583	Prairie crocus	213,729/36,387	250,116
New Brunswick	Fredericton	729,498	Purple violet	27,587/563	28,150
Newfoundland & Labrador	St. John's	513,930	Pitcher plant	144,343/12,100	156,543
Northwest Territories	Yellowknife	37,360	Mountain avens	456,791/62,943	519,734
Nova Scotia	Halifax	908,007	Mayflower	20,593/752	21,345
Nunavut	Iqaluit	26,745	Purple saxifrage	747,537/60,648	808,185
Ontario	Toronto	11,410,046	White trillium	354,341/61,256	415,599
Prince Edward Island	Charlottetown	135,294	Lady's-slipper	2,185/0	2,185
Quebec	Quebec City	7,237,479	White garden lily	527,079/68.313	595,391
Saskatchewan	Regina	978,933	Western red lily	228.445/22,921	251,366
Yukon Territory	Whitehorse	28,674	Fireweed	183,163/3,109	186,272

*Based on the 2001 Canadian Census

PROVINCE & TERRITORY ABBREVIATIONS: CANADA

Alberta .... AB	Northwest Territories .... NT	Prince Edward Island .... PE
British Columbia .... BC	Nova Scotia .... NS	Quebec .... QC
Manitoba .... MB	Nunavut .... NU	Saskatchewan .... SK
New Brunswick .... NB	Ontario .... ON	Yukon Territory .... YT
Newfoundland & Labrador .... NF		

SOME FACTS ABOUT MEXICO

State	Abbreviation	Capital	Population*	Area (sq. mi.)
Aguascalientes	Ags.	Aguascalientes	944,285	2,156
Baja California	B.C.	Mexicali	2,487,367	27,655
Baja California Sur	B.C.S.	La Paz	424,041	27,979
Campeche	Camp.	Campeche	690,689	19,672
Chiapas	Chis.	Tuxtla Gutiérrez	3,920,892	28,732
Chihuahua	Chih.	Chihuahua	3,052,907	94,831
Coahuila	Coah.	Saltillo	2,298,070	58,067
Colima	Col.	Colima	542,627	2010
Distrito Federal	D.F.	Mexico City	8,605,239	573
Durango	Dgo.	Durango	1,448,661	47,691
Guanajuato	Gto.	Guanajuato	4,663,032	11,805
Guerrero	Gro.	Chilpancingo	3,079,649	24,887
Hidalgo	Hgo.	Pachuca	2,235,591	8058
Jalisco	Jal.	Guadalajara	6,322,002	31,152
México	Mex.	Toluca	13,096,686	8,268
Michoacán	Mich.	Morelia	3,985,667	23,202
Morelos	Mor.	Cuernavaca	1,555,296	1,917
Nayarit	Nay.	Tepic	920,185	10,547
Nuevo León	N.L.	Monterrey	3,834,141	25,136
Oaxaca	Oax.	Oaxaca	3,438,765	36,375
Puebla	Pue.	Puebla	5,076,686	13,126
Querétaro	Qro.	Querétaro	1,404,306	4,432
Quintana Roo	Q.R.	Chetumal	874,963	19,630
San Luis Potosí	S.L.P.	San Luis Potosí	2,229,360	24,417
Sinaloa	Sin.	Culiacán	2,536,844	22,582
Sonora	Son.	Hermosillo	2,216,969	70,484
Tabasco	Tab.	Villahermosa	1,891,829	9,783
Tamaulipas	Tamps.	Ciudad Victoria	2,753,222	30,734
Tlaxcala	Tlax.	Tlaxcala	962,646	1,555
Veracruz	Ver.	Jalapa	6,908,975	27,759
Yucatán	Yuc.	Mérida	1,658,210	14,868
Zacatecas	Zac.	Zacatecas	1,353,610	28,125

*Based on the 2000 Mexican Census

☆ Chase's 2004 Calendar of Events ☆
BROADCASTING HALL OF FAME

The National Association of Broadcasters Broadcasting Hall of Fame, established in 1977, recognizes radio and television personalities or programs that have earned a place in broadcasting history due to outstanding programming and success.

1977
William S. Paley, entrepreneur
Jack Benny, comedian
Fred Allen, comedian
Lowell Thomas, news reporter and commentator
Edward R. Murrow, news reporter and commentator
Milton Cross, music commentator
David Sarnoff, entrepreneur
Ted Husing, sportscaster
Edwin H. Armstrong, inventor
Herbert Hoover, president of the United States
Gene Autry, singer, entertainer
Freeman F. Gosden (Amos) and Charles J. Correll (Andy), comedians
Bob Hope, comedian
Gordon McNamee, announcer

1978
Jim Jordan and Marian Jordan (Fibber McGee and Molly), comedians
Walter Winchell, commentator
Guglielmo Marconi, inventor
Arthur Godfrey, personality
Orson Welles, producer, actor, director of radio, motion pictures and theatre

1979
Paul Harvey, commentator

1980
George Burns, comedian
Bing Crosby, singer/entertainer

1981
Ronald Reagan (Dutch Reagan), president of the United States
Kate Smith, singer, entertainer

1982
Don McNeill, entertainer
Edgar Bergen, comedian

1983
Charles Lauk (Lum) and Norris Goff (Abner), comedians
Benny Goodman, entertainer

1984
Red Skelton, comedian
Bob Elliot and Ray Goulding, entertainers

1985
Fred Palmer, broadcaster, consultant
Casey Kasem, personality, announcer

1986
Mel Allen, sportscaster
Earl Nightingale, commentator

1987
Robert Trout, political journalist
Gordon B. McLendon, innovator
Robert Todd Storz, industry leader

1988
William B. Williams, personality
Roy Acuff, singer
Milton Berle, comedian
Lucille Ball, comedienne

1989
Ernie Kovacs, comedian
Sid Caesar, comedian
Red Barber, sportscaster
Nathan Safir, Spanish broadcasting pioneer

1990
Hal Jackson, entrepreneur
Charles Osgood, correspondent
"The Honeymooners" and Its Original Cast (Art Carney, Audrey Meadows, Joyce Randolph, Jackie Gleason), entertainers
Sylvester L. (Pat) Weaver, TV programming pioneer

1991
Jerry Lewis, comedian
Douglas Edwards, radio correspondent

1992
Larry King, radio personality
"Star Trek," TV series

1993
"Grand Ole Opry," radio program
"60 Minutes," TV program

1994
Harry Caray, radio personality
Roone Arledge, network news president

1995
Gary Owens, radio personality
Carol Burnett, TV entertainer

1996
Don Imus, radio personality
"M*A*S*H," cast of TV series

1997
Wally Phillips, radio personality
"Today," cast of TV's "Today" show

1998
Rush Limbaugh, radio personality
Bob Keeshan, TV entertainer

1999
Wolfman Jack, radio personality
"All in the Family," TV series

2000
Tom Joyner, radio personality
"Saturday Night Live," TV program

2001
Bruce "Cousin Brucie" Morrow, radio personality
Ted Koppel, TV anchor

2002
Dick Orkin, radio personality and producer
"Rowan & Martin's Laugh-In," TV series

2003
Scott Shannon, radio personality
Disney Television Anthology Series, TV series ("The Wonderful World of Disney," "Disneyland," etc.)

☆ *Chase's 2004 Calendar of Events* ☆

THE ACADEMY OF TELEVISION ARTS AND SCIENCES (ATAS) TELEVISION HALL OF FAME

The Academy of Television Arts & Sciences Television Academy Hall of Fame was established in 1984 to recognize the lifelong accomplishments of television's greatest contributors, including, in addition to those who appear before the camera, those who contribute to the industry as writers, executives and producers.

Bronze sculptures and bas reliefs of some of the Hall of Fame's inductees have been erected in the Hall of Fame Plaza. Located in the forecourt of the Television Academy's North Hollywood international headquarters, the plaza's centerpiece is a 27-foot Emmy statue, a replica of the internationally famous Emmy statuette, symbol of television excellence.

1984
Lucille Ball
Milton Berle
Paddy Chayefsky
Norman Lear
Edward R. Murrow
William S. Paley
David Sarnoff

1985
Carol Burnett
Sid Caesar
Walter Cronkite
Joyce C. Hall
Rod Serling
Ed Sullivan
Sylvester "Pat" Weaver

1986
Steve Allen
Fred Coe
Walt Disney
Jackie Gleason
Mary Tyler Moore
Frank Stanton
Burr Tillstrom

1987
Johnny Carson
Jacques-Yves Cousteau
Leonard Goldenson
Jim Henson
Bob Hope
Ernie Kovacs
Eric Sevareid

1988
Jack Benny
George Burns and
  Gracie Allen
Chet Huntley and
  David Brinkley
Red Skelton
David Susskind
David L. Wolper

1989
Roone Arledge
Fred Astaire
Perry Como
Joan Ganz Cooney
Don Hewitt
Carroll O'Connor
Barbara Walters

1990
Desi Arnaz
Leonard Bernstein
James Garner
"I Love Lucy"
Danny Thomas
Mike Wallace

1991
Bill Cosby
Andy Griffith
Ted Koppel
Sheldon Leonard
Dinah Shore
Ted Turner

1992
John Chancellor
Dick Clark
Phil Donahue
Mark Goodson
Bob Newhart
Agnes Nixon
Jack Webb

1993
Alan Alda
Howard Cosell
Barry Diller
Fred W. Friendly
William Hanna and
  Joseph Barbera
Oprah Winfrey

1994
Michael Landon
Richard Levinson and
  William Link
Jim McKay
Bill Moyers
Dick Van Dyke
Betty White

1995
Edward Asner
Steven Bochco
Marcy Carsey and
  Tom Werner
Charles Kuralt
Angela Lansbury
Aaron Spelling
Lew R. Wasserman

1996
James L. Brooks
Garry Marshall
Quinn Martin
Diane Sawyer
Grant Tinker

1997
No inductees

1998
No inductees

1999
Herbert Brodkin
Robert MacNeil and
  Jim Lehrer
Lorne Michaels
Carl Reiner
Fred Rogers
Fred Silverman
Ethel Winant

2000
No inductees

2001
No inductees

2002
Tim Conway
Harvey Korman
John Frankenheimer
Bob Mackie
Jean Stapleton
Bud Yorkin

☆ Chase's 2004 Calendar of Events ☆

THE NATIONAL FILM REGISTRY
2002 Additions

Under the terms of the National Film Preservation Act, each year the Librarian of Congress names 25 "culturally, historically or aesthetically" significant motion pictures to the Registry. The list is designed to reflect the full breadth and diversity of America's film heritage, thus increasing public awareness of the richness of American cinema and the need for its preservation. A film must be at least ten years old to be considered. These are the 2002 additions to the archive; the full list can be found at www.loc.gov/film/titles.html.

Alien (1979)
All My Babies (1953)
The Bad and the Beautiful (1952)
Beauty and the Beast (1991)
The Black Stallion (1979)
Boyz N the Hood (1991)
Theodore Case Sound Test: Gus Visser and his Singing Duck (1925)
The Endless Summer (1966)
From Here to Eternity (1953)
From Stump to Ship (1930)
Fuji (1974)
In the Heat of the Night (1967)
Lady Windermere's Fan (1925)
Melody Ranch (1940)
The Pearl (1948)
Punch Drunks (1934)
Sabrina (1954)
Star Theatre (1901)
Stranger Than Paradise (1984)
This is Cinerama (1952)
This is Spinal Tap (1984)
Through Navajo Eyes (series) (1966)
Why Man Creates (1968)
Wild and Wooly (1917)
Wild River (1960)

THE NATIONAL RECORDING REGISTRY

Founded in 2002 by the National Recording Preservation Board at the Library of Congress, the National Recording Registry maintains and preserves sound recordings and collections of sound recordings that are culturally, historically or aesthetically significant. New recordings will be added to the collection yearly. More information can be found at www.loc.gov/rr/record/nrpb.

Edison Exhibition Recordings (group of three cylinders): "Around the World on the Phonograph," "The Pattison Waltz," "Fifth Regiment March" (1888–1889)
The Jesse Walter Fewkes field recordings of the Passamaquoddy Indians (1890)
"Stars and Stripes Forever," Military Band, Berliner Gramophone disc recording (1897)
Lionel Mapleson cylinder recordings of the Metropolitan Opera (1900–1903)
Scott Joplin ragtime compositions on piano rolls, Scott Joplin on piano (1900s)
Booker T. Washington's 1895 Atlanta Exposition Speech (1906 re-creation)
"Vesti la giubba" from *Pagliacci*, performed by Enrico Caruso (1907)
"Swing Low, Sweet Chariot," performed by Fisk Jubilee Singers (1909)
Lovey's Trinidad String Band recordings for Columbia Records (1912)
"Casey at the Bat," DeWolf Hopper reciting (1915)
"Tiger Rag," performed by Original Dixieland Jazz Band (1918)
"Arkansas Traveler" and "Sallie Gooden," Eck Robertson on fiddle (1922)
"Down-Hearted Blues," performed by Bessie Smith (1923)
Rhapsody in Blue, with George Gershwin on piano; Paul Whiteman Orchestra (1924)
Louis Armstrong's Hot Five and Hot Seven recordings (1925–1928)
Victor Talking Machine Company sessions in Bristol, TN: Carter Family, Jimmie Rodgers, Ernest Stoneman and others (1927)
Harvard Vocarium record series: T.S. Eliot, W.H. Auden and others, reciting (1930–1940s)
Highlander Center Field Recording Collection: Rosa Parks, Esau Jenkins and others (1930s–1980s)
Bell Laboratories experimental stereo recordings of the Philadelphia Orchestra; Leopold Stokowski, conductor (1931–1932)
President Franklin D. Roosevelt's radio "Fireside Chats" (1933–1944)
New Music Recordings series; Henry Cowell, producer (1934–1949)
Description of the crash of the Hindenburg; Herbert Morrison, reporting (1937)
"Who's on First," Abbott and Costello's first radio broadcast version (1938)
"War of the Worlds," Orson Welles and the Mercury Theater (1938)
"God Bless America," Kate Smith, radio broadcast premiere (1938)
The Cradle Will Rock, Marc Blitzstein and the original Broadway cast (1938)
The John and Ruby Lomax Southern States Recording Trip (1939)
Grand Ole Opry, first network radio broadcast: Uncle Dave Macon, Roy Acuff and others (1939)
"Strange Fruit," performed by Billie Holiday (1939)
Duke Ellington Orchestra "Blanton-Webster Era" recordings (1940–1942)
Bela Bartok, piano, and Joseph Szigeti, violin, in concert at the Library of Congress (1940)
Rite of Spring, Igor Stravinsky conducting the New York Philharmonic (1940)
"White Christmas," performed by Bing Crosby (1942)
"This Land Is Your Land," performed by Woody Guthrie (1944)
General Dwight D. Eisenhower's D-Day radio address to the Allied Nations (1944)
"Koko," performed by Charlie Parker, Miles Davis, Dizzy Gillespie and others (1945)
"Blue Moon of Kentucky," performed by Bill Monroe and the Blue Grass Boys (1947)
"How High the Moon," performed by Les Paul and Mary Ford (1951)
Elvis Presley's Sun Records sessions (1954–1955)
Songs for Young Lovers, performed by Frank Sinatra (1954)
Dance Mania, performed by Tito Puente (1958)
Kind of Blue, Miles Davis, John Coltrane, Cannonball Adderley, Bill Evans and others (1959)
"What'd I Say," parts 1 and 2, performed by Ray Charles (1959)
"I Have a Dream," speech by Dr. Martin Luther King, Jr (1963)
Freewheelin', performed by Bob Dylan (1963)
"Respect!" performed by Aretha Franklin (1967)
Philomei: for soprano, recorded soprano, and synthesized sound, Bethany Beardslee, soprano (1971)
Precious Lord: New Recordings of the Great Gospel Songs of Thomas A. Dorsey, Thomas Dorsey, Marion Williams and others (1973)
Crescent City Living Legends Collection (New Orleans Jazz and Heritage Foundation Archive/WWOZ Radio, New Orleans) (1973–1990)
"The Message," performed by Grandmaster Flash and the Furious Five (1982)

☆ Chase's 2004 Calendar of Events ☆
MAJOR AWARDS

TONY AWARDS
57th Annual, for 2002–2003 Achievement

Play: *Take Me Out*
Musical: *Hairspray*
Book of a Musical: Thomas Meehan and Mark O'Donnell, *Hairspray*
Original Musical Score: Scott Whittman and Marc Shaiman *Hairspray*
Revival of a Play: *Long Day's Journey Into Night*
Revival of a Musical: *Nine*
Director of a Play: Joe Mantello, *Take Me Out*
Director of a Musical: Jack O'Brien, *Hairspray*
Leading Actor in a Play: Brian Dennehy, *Long Day's Journey Into Night*
Leading Actress in a Play: Vanessa Redgrave, *Long Day's Journey Into Night*
Leading Actor in a Musical: Harvey Fierstein, *Hairspray*
Leading Actress in a Musical: Marissa Jaret Winokur, *Hairspray*
Featured Actor in a Play: Denis O'Hare, *Take Me Out*
Featured Actress in a Play: Michele Pawk, *Hollywood Arms*
Featured Actor in a Musical: Dick Latessa, *Hairspray*
Featured Actress in a Musical: Jane Krakowski, *Nine*
Scenic Design: Catherine Martin, *La Bohème*
Costume Design: William Ivey Long, *Hairspray*
Lighting Design: Nigel Levings, *La Bohème*
Choreography: Twyla Tharp, *Movin' Out*
Orchestration: Billy Joel & Stuart Malina, *Movin' Out*
Special Theatrical Event: *Russell Simmons' Def Poetry Jam on Broadway*
Special Award for Lifetime Achievement: Cy Feuer
Special Award for Regional Theater: The Children's Theater Company, Minneapolis, MN
Tony Honors for Excellence in Theater: Principal Ensemble of *La Bohème*

2002 ACADEMY AWARDS
75th Annual, for 2002 Achievement

Picture: *Chicago*
Actor: Adrien Brody, *The Pianist*
Actress: Nicole Kidman, *The Hours*
Director: Roman Polanski, *The Pianist*
Supporting Actor: Chris Cooper, *Adaptation*
Supporting Actress: Catherine Zeta-Jones, *Chicago*
Original Screenplay: Pedro Almodóvar, *Talk To Her*
Adapted Screenplay: Ronald Harwood, *The Pianist*
Foreign Language Film: *Nowhere in Africa* (Germany)
Animated Feature: *Spirited Away*
Animated Short Film: *The Chubbchubbs!*
Live Action Short Film: *This Charming Man*
Documentary Feature: *Bowling for Columbine*
Documentary Short Subject: *Twin Towers*
Film Editing: Martin Walsh, *Chicago*
Costume Design: Colleen Atwood, *Chicago*
Cinematography: Conrad L. Hall, *Road to Perdition*
Art Direction: John Myhre (Art Direction) and Gordon Sim (Set Decoration), *Chicago*
Visual Effects: Jim Rygiel, Joe Letteri, Randall William Cook and Alex Funke, *The Lord of the Rings: The Two Towers*
Makeup: John Jackson and Beatrice De Alba, *Frida*
Sound Design: Michael Minkler, Dominick Tavella and David Lee, *Chicago*
Sound Editing: Ethan Van der Ryn and Michael Hopkins, *The Lord of the Rings: The Two Towers*
Original Score: Elliot Goldenthal, *Frida*
Original Song: Eminem, "Lose Yourself" from *8 Mile*
Honorary Award: Peter O'Toole

2003 SUNDANCE FILM FESTIVAL AWARDS
22nd Annual

Dramatic Grand Jury Prize: *American Splendor*
Documentary Grand Jury Prize: *Capturing the Friedmans*
Dramatic Audience Award: *The Station Agent*
Documentary Audience Award: *My Flesh and Blood*
World Cinema Audience Award: *Whale Rider*
Directing Award, Dramatic: Catherine Hardwicke, *Thirteen*
Directing Award, Documentary: Jonathan Karsh, *My Flesh and Blood*
Excellence in Cinemetography Award, Dramatic: Derek Cianfrance, *Quattro Noza*

✯ Chase's 2004 Calendar of Events ✯

Excellence in Cinemetography Award, Documentary: Dana Kupper, Gordon Quinn and Peter Gilbert, *Stevie*
Freedom of Expression Award: *What I Want My Words to Do to You*
Waldo Salt Screenwriting Award: Tom McCarthy, *The Station Agent*
Special Jury Prizes, Documentary: *The Murder of Emmett Till; A Certain Kind of Death*
Special Jury Prize for Outstanding Dramatic Performance: Patricia Clarkson for *The Station Agent, Pieces of April* and *All the Real Girls*
Special Jury Prize for Outstanding Dramatic Performance: Charles Busch for *Die Mommie Die*
Special Jury Prizes for Emotional Truth: *All The Real Girls* and *What Alice Found*
Jury Prize in Short Filmmaking: *Terminal Bar*
Alfred P. Sloan Prize: *Dopamine*

CANNES FILM FESTIVAL
56th Annual

Palme d'Or (Golden Palm): *Elephant*
Grand Prix: *Uzak*
Jury Prize: *At Five in the Afternoon*
Best Short Film: *Cracker Bag*
Jury Prize for Short Film: *The Man Without a Head*
Best Actress: Marie-Josee Croze, *The Barbarian Invasions*
Best Actor: TIE: Muzaffer Ozdemir, *Uzak* and Mehmet Emin Toprak, *Uzak*
Best Director: Gus Van Zant, *Elephant*
Best Screenplay: Denys Arcand, *The Barbarian Invasions*
Golden Camera: Christoffer Boe, *Reconstruction*

2003 GOLDEN GLOBE AWARDS
60th Annual, For 2002 Achievement

MOVIES

Drama: *The Hours*
Musical or Comedy: *Chicago*
Director: Martin Scorsese, *Gangs of New York*
Actor, Drama: Jack Nicholson, *About Schmidt*
Actress, Drama: Nicole Kidman, *The Hours*
Actor, Musical or Comedy: Richard Gere, *Chicago*
Actress, Musical or Comedy: Renée Zellweger, *Chicago*
Supporting Actor: Chris Cooper, *Adaptation*
Supporting Actress: Meryl Streep, *Adaptation*
Screenplay: Alexander Payne and Jim Taylor, *About Schmidt*
Foreign Language Film: Spain, *Talk to Her*
Original Score: Elliot Goldenthal, *Frida*
Original Song: U2, "The Hands That Built America," *Gangs of New York*

TELEVISION

Series, Drama: "The Shield"
Series, Musical or Comedy: "Curb Your Enthusiasm"
Miniseries or TV Movie: *The Gathering Storm*
Actor, Series, Drama: Michael Chiklis, "The Shield"
Actress, Series, Drama: Edie Falco, "The Sopranos"
Actor, Series, Musical or Comedy: Tony Shalhoub, "Monk"
Actress, Series, Musical or Comedy: Jennifer Aniston, "Friends"
Actor, Miniseries or TV Movie: Albert Finney, *The Gathering Storm*
Actress, Miniseries or TV Movie: Uma Thurman, *Hysterical Blindness*
Actor, Supporting Role: Donald Sutherland, *Path to War*
Actress, Supporting Role: Kim Cattrall, "Sex and the City"

2002 PRIME TIME EMMY AWARDS
(Major Categories)
54th Annual

Drama: "The West Wing," NBC
Comedy: "Friends," NBC
Miniseries: *Band of Brothers*, HBO
Made-for-Television Movie: *The Gathering Storm*, HBO
Variety, Music or Comedy Series: "Late Show with David Letterman," CBS
Variety, Music or Comedy Special: "America: A Tribute to Heroes," multiple networks
Children's Program: "Nick News Special Edition: Faces of Hope: The Kids of Afghanistan," Nickelodeon
Animated Program (Less Than One Hour): "Futurama," Fox
Animated Program (One Hour or More): "Walking With Prehistoric Beasts," Discovery Channel
Non-Fiction Program (Reality): "The Osbournes," MTV
Non-fiction Program (Special Class): "The West Wing: Documentary Special," NBC
Lead Actress in a Drama Series: Allison Janney, "The West Wing," NBC
Lead Actor in a Drama Series: Michael Chiklis, "The Shield," FX
Lead Actress in a Comedy Series: Jennifer Aniston, "Friends," NBC
Lead Actor in a Comedy Series: Ray Romano, "Everybody Loves Raymond," CBS
Lead Actress in a Miniseries or TV Movie: Laura Linney, *Wild Iris*, Showtime
Lead Actor in a Miniseries or TV Movie: Albert Finney, *The Gathering Storm*, HBO
Supporting Actress in a Drama Series: Stockard Channing, "The West Wing," NBC
Supporting Actor in a Drama Series: John Spencer, "The West Wing," NBC
Supporting Actress in a Comedy Series: Doris Roberts, "Everybody Loves Raymond," CBS
Supporting Actor in a Comedy Series: Brad Garrett, "Everybody Loves Raymond," CBS
Supporting Actress in a Miniseries or TV Movie: Stockard Channing, *The Matthew Shepard Story*, NBC
Supporting Actor in a Miniseries or TV Movie: Michael Moriarty, *James Dean*, TNT
Performance in a Variety, Music or Comedy Program: Sting, "A&E in Concert: Sting in Tuscany... All This Time," A&E
Drama Series Directing: Alan Ball, "Six Feet Under," HBO
Comedy Series Directing: Michael Patrick King, "Sex and the City," HBO
Variety, Music or Comedy Program Directing: Ron de Moraes, Kenny Ortega and Bucky Gants, "Opening Ceremony, Salt Lake 2002 Olympic Winter Games," NBC

☆ Chase's 2004 Calendar of Events ☆

Miniseries or TV Movie Directing: David Frankel, Tom Hanks, et al, *Band of Brothers,* HBO
Drama Series Writing: Joel Surnow, "24," Fox
Comedy Series Writing: Larry Wilmore, "The Bernie Mac Show," Fox
Variety, Music or Comedy Program Writing: Tina Fey, Dennis McNicholas, et al, "Saturday Night Live," NBC
Miniseries or TV Movie Writing: Larry Ramin and Hugh Whitemore, *The Gathering Storm,* HBO

2003 DAYTIME EMMY AWARDS
30th Annual

Drama: "As the World Turns," CBS
Lead Actress in a Drama Series: Susan Flannery, "The Bold and the Beautiful," CBS
Lead Actor in a Drama Series: Maurice Benard, "General Hospital," ABC
Supporting Actress in a Drama Series: Vanessa Marcil, "General Hospital," ABC
Supporting Actor in a Drama Series: Benjamin Hendrickson, "As the World Turns," CBS
Younger Actress in a Drama Series: Jennifer Finnigan, "The Bold and the Beautiful," CBS
Younger Actor in a Drama Series: Jordi Vilasuso, "The Guiding Light," CBS
Drama Series Writing Team: "General Hospital," ABC
Drama Series Directing Team: "All My Children," ABC
Preschool Children's Series: "Sesame Street," PBS
Children's Series: "Reading Rainbow," PBS
Performer in a Children's Series: Shia LaBeouf, "Even Stevens," The Disney Channel
Children's Series Writing Team: "Sesame Street," PBS
Children's Series Directing Team: "Bear in the Big Blue House," The Disney Channel
Children's Animated Program: "Rugrats," Nickelodeon
Performer in an Animated Program: Gregory Hines, "Little Bill," Nickelodeon
Children's Special: "Bang Bang You're Dead," SHO
Performer in a Children's Special: Ben Foster, "Bang Bang You're Dead," SHO
Children's Special Writing: William Mastrosimone, "Bang Bang You're Dead," SHO
Children's Special Directing: Guy Ferland, "Bang Bang You're Dead," SHO
Special Class Animated Program: "Disney's Teacher's Pet," ABC
Special Class Series: "A Baby Story," TLC
Special Class Special: "Hollywood Rocks the Movies: The 1970's with David Bowie," AMC
Special Class Writing Team: "Jeopardy!," syndicated
Special Class Directing: "Opening Ceremony, Salt Lake 2002 Paralympic Winter Games," NBC
Talk Show: TIE: "The Wayne Brady Show," syndicated, and "The View," ABC
Talk Show Host: Wayne Brady, "The Wayne Brady Show," syndicated
Talk Show Directing: TIE: Brian Chapman, "Live with Regis and Kelly," syndicated, and Liz Plonka, "The Wayne Brady Show," syndicated
Game Show: "Jeopardy!," syndicated
Game Show Host: Alex Trebek, "Jeopardy!," syndicated
Game Show Directing: Bart Eskander, "The Price Is Right," CBS
Service Show: "Martha Stewart Living," syndicated
Service Show Host: Martha Stewart, "Martha Stewart Living," syndicated
Service Show Directing: Gordon Recht and Charlie Ryan, "Wolfgang Puck," Food Network

2002 AMERICAN MUSIC AWARDS
30th Annual Awards, Awarded Jan 14, 2003

Pop/Rock
Male Artist: Eminem
Female Artist: Sheryl Crow
Band, Duo or Group: Creed
Album: *The Eminem Show,* Eminem
New Artist: Ashanti
Hip-Hop/Rhythm & Blues
Male Vocalist: Eminem
Female Vocalist: Mary J. Blige
Band, Duo or Group: OutKast
Album: *The Eminem Show,* Eminem
New Artist: Ashanti
Country
Male Vocalist: Tim McGraw
Female Vocalist: Martina McBride
Band, Duo or Group: Dixie Chicks
Album: *Home,* Dixie Chicks
New Artist: Carolyn Dawn Johnson
Latin
Artist: Enrique Iglesias
Adult Contemporary Inspirational
Artist: Avalon
Adult Contemporary
Artist: Celine Dion
Alternative
Artist: Creed
Soundtrack
Spider-Man
Fans Choice Award
Nelly
Coca-Cola New Music Award
Moe Loughran
Award of Merit
Alabama

2003 GRAMMY AWARDS

Record of the Year: "Don't Know Why," Norah Jones
Album of the Year: *Come Away With Me,* Norah Jones
Song of the Year: "Don't Know Why," Jesse Harris (Norah Jones)
Best New Artist: Norah Jones

☆ Chase's 2004 Calendar of Events ☆

Best Female Pop Vocal Performance: "Don't Know Why," Norah Jones
Best Male Pop Vocal Performance: "Your Body Is a Wonderland," John Mayer
Best Pop Performance by a Duo or Group with Vocal: "Hey Baby," No Doubt
Best Pop Collaboration with Vocals: "The Game of Love," Santana and Michelle Branch
Best Pop Instrumental Performance: "Auld Lang Syne," B.B. King
Best Pop Instrumental Album: *Just Chillin'*, Norman Brown
Best Pop Vocal Album: *Come Away With Me*, Norah Jones
Best Dance Recording: "Days Go By," Dirty Vegas
Best Traditional Pop Vocal Album: *Playin' With My Friends: Bennett Sings the Blues*, Tony Bennett

Best Female Rock Vocal Performance: "Steve McQueen," Sheryl Crow
Best Male Rock Vocal Performance: "The Rising," Bruce Springsteen
Best Rock Performance by a Duo or Group with Vocal: "In My Place," Coldplay
Best Hard Rock Performance: "All My Life," Foo Fighters
Best Metal Performance: "Here To Stay," Korn
Best Rock Instrumental Performance: "Approaching Pavonis Mons By Balloon (Utopia Planitia)," The Flaming Lips
Best Rock Song: "The Rising," Bruce Springsteen (Bruce Springsteen)
Best Rock Album: *The Rising*, Bruce Springsteen
Best Alternative Music Album: *A Rush of Blood to the Head*, Coldplay
Best Female R&B Vocal Performance: "He Think I Don't Know," Mary J. Blige
Best Male R&B Vocal Performance: "U Don't Have to Call," Usher
Best R&B Performance by a Duo or Group with Vocal: "Love's In Need Of Love Today," Stevie Wonder and Take 6
Best Traditional R&B Vocal Performance: "What's Going On," Chaka Khan and The Funk Brothers
Best Urban/Alternative Performance: "Little Things," India.Arie
Best R&B Song: "Love of My Life (An Ode to Hip Hop)," Erykah Badu, Madukwu Chinwah, Rashid Lonnie Lynn, Robert Ozuna, James Poyser, Raphael Saadiq and Glen Standridge (Erykah Badu featuring Common)
Best R&B Album: *Voyage to India*, India.Arie
Best Contemporary R&B Album: *Ashanti*, Ashanti
Best Female Rap Solo Performance: "Scream a.k.a. Itchin'," Missy Elliott
Best Male Rap Solo Performance: "Hot in Herre," Nelly
Best Rap Performance by a Duo or Group: "The Whole World," Outkast featuring Killer Mike
Best Rap/Sung Collaboration: "Dilemma," Nelly featuring Kelly Rowland
Best Rap Album: *The Eminem Show*, Eminem
Best Female Country Vocal Performance: "Cry," Faith Hill

Best Male Country Vocal Performance: "Give My Love to Rose," Johnny Cash
Best Country Performance by a Duo or Group with Vocal: "Long Time Gone," Dixie Chicks
Best Country Collaboration with Vocals: "Mendocino County Line," Willie Nelson with Lee Ann Womack
Best Country Instrumental Performance: "Lil' Jack Slade," Dixie Chicks
Best Country Song: "Where Were You (When the World Stopped Turning)," Alan Jackson (Alan Jackson)
Best Country Album: *Home*, Dixie Chicks
Best Bluegrass Album: *Lost in the Lonesome Pines*, Jim Lauderdale, Ralph Stanley and The Clinch Mountain Boys
Best New Age Album: *Acoustic Garden*, Eric Tingstad and Nancy Rumbel
Best Contemporary Jazz Album: *Speaking of Now*, Pat Metheny Group
Best Jazz Vocal Album: *Live in Paris*, Diana Krall
Best Jazz Instrumental Solo: "My Ship," Herbie Hancock, soloist
Best Jazz Instrumental Album, Individual or Group: *Directions in Music*, Herbie Hancock, Michael Brecker and Roy Hargrove
Best Large Jazz Ensemble Album: *What Goes Around*, Dave Holland Big Band
Best Latin Jazz Album: *The Gathering*, Caribbean Jazz Project
Best Rock Gospel Album: *Come Together*, Third Day
Best Pop/Contemporary Gospel Album: *The Eleventh Hour*, Jars of Clay
Best Southern, Country or Bluegrass Gospel Album: *We Called Him Mr. Gospel Music: The James Blackwood Tribute Album*, The Jordanaires, Larry Ford and The Light Crust Doughboys
Best Traditional Soul Gospel Album: *Higher Ground*, The Blind Boys of Alabama
Best Contemporary Soul Gospel Album: *Sidebars*, Eartha
Best Gospel Album by a Choir or Chorus: *Be Glad*, Carol Cymbala, choir director; The Brooklyn Tabernacle Choir
Best Latin Pop Album: *Caraluna*, Bacilos
Best Latin Rock/Alternative Album: *Revolución de Amor*, Maná
Best Traditional Tropical Latin Album: *El Arte del Sabor*, Bebo Valdés Trio with Israel López "Cachao" & Carlos "Patato" Valdés
Best Salsa Album: *La Negra Tiene Tumbao*, Celia Cruz
Best Merengue Album: *Latino*, Grupo Mania

670

☆ Chase's 2004 Calendar of Events ☆

Best Mexican/Mexican-American Album: *Lo Dijo El Corazón*, Joan Sebastian
Best Tejano Album: *Acuérdate*, Emilio Navaira
Best Traditional Blues Album: *A Christmas Celebration of Hope*, B.B. King
Best Contemporary Blues Album: *Don't Give Up On Me*, Solomon Burke
Best Traditional Folk Album: *Legacy*, Doc Watson and David Holt
Best Contemporary Folk Album: *This Side*, Nickel Creek
Best Native American Music Album: *Beneath the Raven Moon*, Mary Youngblood
Best Reggae Album: *Jamaican E.T.*, Lee "Scratch" Perry
Best World Music Album: *Mundo*, Rubén Blades
Best Polka Album: *Top of the World*, Jimmy Sturr
Best Musical Album for Children: *Monsters, Inc.—Scream Factory Favorites*, Riders In The Sky
Best Spoken Word Album for Children: *There Was An Old Lady Who Swallowed A Fly*, Tom Chapin
Best Spoken Word Album: *A Song Flung Up to Heaven* (Maya Angelou), Maya Angelou
Best Spoken Comedy Album: *Robin Williams—Live 2002*, Robin Williams
Best Musical Show Album: *Hairspray*
Best Compilation Soundtrack Album for a Motion Picture, Television or Other Visual Media: *Standing In the Shadows of Motown*, The Funk Brothers and Various Artists
Best Score Soundtrack Album for a Motion Picture, Television Or Other Visual Media: *The Lord of the Rings—The Fellowship of the Ring*, Howard Shore
Best Song Written for a Motion Picture, Television or Other Visual Media: "If I Didn't Have You" (from *Monsters, Inc*), Randy Newman (Randy Newman)
Best Instrumental Composition: "Six Feet Under Title Theme," Thomas Newman (Thomas Newman)
Best Instrumental Arrangement: "Six Feet Under Title Theme," Thomas Newman (Thomas Newman)
Best Instrumental Arrangement with Accompanying Vocal(s): "Mean Old Man," Dave Grusin, arranger (James Taylor)
Best Recording Package: *Home*, Kevin Reagan, art director (Dixie Chicks)
Best Boxed Recording Package: *Screamin' and Hollerin' the Blues: The World of Charley Patton*, Susan Archie, art director (Charley Patton)
Best Album Notes: *Screamin' and Hollerin' the Blues: The World of Charley Patton*, David Evans, album notes writer (Charley Patton)
Best Historical Album: *Screamin' and Hollerin' the Blues: The World of Charley Patton* (Charley Patton)
Best Engineered Album, Non-Classical: *Come Away With Me*, S. Husky Höskulds & Jay Newland, engineers (Norah Jones)
Producer of the Year, Non-Classical: Arif Mardin, *Come Away With Me*, (Norah Jones)
Best Remixed Recording, Non-Classical: *Hella Good (Roger Sanchez Remix Main)*, Roger Sanchez, remixer (No Doubt)
Best Engineered Album, Classical: *Vaughan Williams: A Sea Symphony (Sym. No. 1)*, Michael Bishop, engineer (Robert Spano & Norman Mackenzie)
Classical Producer of the Year: Robert Woods
Best Classical Album: *Vaughan Williams: A Sea Symphony (Sym. No. 1)*, Robert Spano, conductor. Atlanta Symphony Orchestra; Atlanta Symphony Orchestra Choir
Best Orchestral Performance: *Mahler: Symphony No. 6*, Michael Tilson Thomas, conductor, San Francisco Symphony
Best Opera Recording: *Wagner: Tannhäuser*, Daniel Barenboim, conductor, and other award recipients
Best Choral Performance: *Vaughan Williams: A Sea Symphony (Sym. No. 1)*, Robert Spano, conductor; Norman Mackenzie, chorus director; Atlanta Symphony Orchestra
Best Instrumental Soloist(s) Performance (With Orchestra): *Brahms/Stravinsky: Violin Concertos*, Sir Neville Marriner, conductor; Hilary Hahn, violin
Best Instrumental Soloist Performance (Without Orchestra): *Chopin: Études, Op. 10 & Op. 25*, Murray Perahia, piano
Best Chamber Music Performance: *Beethoven: String Quartets ("Razumovsky" Op. 59, 1–3; "Harp" Op. 74)*, Takács Quartet
Best Small Ensemble Album Performance: *Tavener: Lamentations and Praises*, Joseph Jennings, conductor; Chanticleer
Best Classical Vocal Performance: *Bel Canto (Bellini, Donizetti, Rossini, Etc.)*, Renée Fleming, soprano
Best Classical Contemporary Composition: *Tavener: Lamentations and Praises*, Sir John Tavener
Best Classical Crossover Album: *Previn Conducts Korngold (Sea Hawk; Captain Blood, Etc.)*, André Previn, conductor; London Symphony Orchestra
Best Music Video, Short Form: *Without Me*, Eminem; Joseph Kahn, video director; Greg Tharp, video producer
Best Music Video, Long Form: *Westway To the World*, The Clash, Don Letts, video director

2002 COUNTRY MUSIC AWARDS
36th Annual Awards

Entertainer of the Year: Alan Jackson
Male Vocalist of the Year: Alan Jackson
Female Vocalist of the Year: Martina McBride
Horizon Award: Rascal Flatts
Vocal Group of the Year: Dixie Chicks
Vocal Duo of the Year: Brooks & Dunn
Single of the Year: "Where Were You (When the World Stopped Turning)," Alan Jackson; Keith Stegall, producer

★ Chase's 2004 Calendar of Events ★

Album of the Year: *Drive,* Alan Jackson
Song of the Year: "Where Were You (When the World Stopped Turning)," Alan Jackson
Vocal Event of the Year: Willie Nelson with Lee Ann Womack: "Mendocino County Line"
Musician of the Year: Jerry Douglas—dobro
Music Video of the Year: "I'm Gonna Miss Her (The Fishin' Song)," Brad Paisley; Peter Zavadil, director

2003 DOVE AWARDS
34th Annual Awards, Presented by the Gospel Music Association

Song of the Year: "Holy," Nichole Nordeman and Mark Hammond
Songwriter of the Year: Nichole Nordeman
Male Vocalist of the Year: Michael W. Smith
Female Vocalist of the Year: Nichole Nordeman
Group of the Year: Third Day
Artist of the Year: Michael W. Smith
New Artist of the Year: Paul Colman Trio
Producer of the Year: Brown Bannister
Alternative/Modern Rock Recorded Song: "Breathe Your Name," Sixpence None the Richer
Alternative/Modern Rock Album: *The Eleventh Hour,* Jars of Clay
Rock Recorded Song: "40 Days," Third Day
Rock Album: *Lift,* Audio Adrenaline
Hard Music Recorded Song: "Boom," POD
Hard Music Album: *Fireproof,* Pillar
Rap/Hip Hop/Dance Recorded Song: "All Around the World," Souljahz
Rap/Hip Hop/Dance Album: *The Art of Translation,* GRITS
Pop/Contemporary Recorded Song: "Holy," Nichole Nordeman
Pop/Contemporary Album: *Woven & Spun,* Nichole Nordeman
Inspirational Recorded Song: "Here I Am to Worship," Tim Hughes
Inspirational Album: *Legacy...Hymns & Faith,* Amy Grant
Southern Gospel Recorded Song: "Don't You Wanna Go?," The Crabb Family
Southern Gospel Album: *A Crabb Collection,* The Crabb Family
Bluegrass Recorded Song: "Walkin' and Talkin'," The Lewis Family
Bluegrass Album: *50th Anniversary Celebration,* The Lewis Family
Traditional Gospel Recorded Song: "Holding On," Mississippi Mass Choir
Traditional Gospel Album: *Higher Ground,* Blind Boys of Alabama
Contemporary Gospel Recorded Song: "In the Morning," Mary Mary
Contemporary Gospel Album: *The Rebirth of Kirk Franklin,* Kirk Franklin
Country Recorded Song: "The River's Gonna Keep On Rolling," Amy Grant
Country Album: *Rise and Shine,* Randy Travis
Urban Recorded Song: "Meditate," Out of Eden
Urban Album: TIE: *Fault Is History,* Souljahz; *This is Your Life,* Out of Eden
Special Event Album: *City on a Hill—Sing Alleluia* various artists
Instrumental Album: *Hymnsongs,* Phil Keaggy
Praise and Worship Album: *Worship Again,* Michael W. Smith
Children's Music Album: *Jonah, a Veggie Tales Movie Original Soundtrack,* various artists
Spanish Language Album: *Navidad,* Jaci Velasquez
Musical: *The Christmas Shoes,* Donna VanLiere, Eddie Carswell and J. Daniel Smith
Youth/Children's Musical: *Meet Me at the Manger,* Celeste Clydesdale
Choral Collection: *More Songs For Praise & Worship 2,* Ken Barker and Keith Christopher
Recorded Music Packaging: *Welcome to the Rock 'N' Roll Worship Circus,* The Rock 'N' Roll Worship
Short Form Music Video: "Irene," TobyMac
Long Form Music Video: *Worship,* Michael W. Smith

NOBEL PRIZES
2002 Recipients

The Nobel Prizes are highly prestigious international awards given yearly since 1901, named for founder Alfred E. Nobel. The prize, awarded in October, consists of a medal, a personal diploma, and a prize amount. Details can be found at www.nobel.se.

Peace: Jimmy Carter
Physics: Raymond Davis, Jr, Masatoshi Koshiba, Riccardo Giacconi
Chemistry: John B. Fenn, Koichi Tanaka, Kurt Wüthrich
Physiology or Medicine: Sydney Brenner, H. Robert Horvitz, John E. Sulston
Literature: Imre Kertész
Economics: Daniel Kahneman, Vernon L. Smith

2002/2003 NATIONAL ENDOWMENT AWARDS
Awarded Mar 6, 2003

2002 National Medal of Arts:
Florence Knoll Bassett, designer and architect
Trisha Brown, dancer and choreographer
Uta Hagen, actor and educator
Lawrence Halprin, landscape architect and environmental planner
Al Hirshfeld, artist and caricaturist
George Jones, country singer
Ming Cho Lee, painter and stage designer
Philippe de Montebello, museum designer
William "Smokey" Robinson, Jr, singer and songwriter

2002 National Medal of Humanities:
Frankie Hewitt, theater artistic director
Iowa Writers' Workshop
Donald Kagan, professor and author
Brian Lamb, television executive
Art Linkletter, television entertainer and author
Patricia MacLachlan, author
The Mount Vernon Ladies' Association, preservation society
Thomas Sowell, professor and author

☆ Chase's 2004 Calendar of Events ☆

2003 Jefferson Lecturer in the Humanities:
(This award is the highest honor bestowed by the federal government for distinguished intellectual achievement in the humanities.)

David McCullough, National Book Award and Pulitzer Prize–winning author and historian, who has "made history come alive for millions of Americans."

THE NATIONAL BOOK AWARDS 2002

Given annually by the National Book Foundation.

Fiction: *Three Junes,* Julia Glass
Nonfiction: *Master of the Senate: The Years of Lyndon Johnson,* Robert Caro
Poetry: *In the Next Galaxy,* Ruth Stone
Young People's Literature: *The House of the Scorpion,* Nancy Farmer

THE NATIONAL BOOK CRITICS CIRCLE AWARDS 2002

Fiction: *Atonement,* Ian McEwan
General Nonfiction: *"A Problem From Hell": America and the Age of Genocide,* Samantha Power
Biography/Autobiography: *Charles Darwin: The Power of Place, Vol. II,* Janet Browne
Poetry: *Early Occult Memory Systems of the Lower Midwest,* B.H. Fairchild
Criticism: *Tests of Time,* William H. Gass

PEN/FAULKNER AWARD FOR FICTION 2003

An award given by an organization of writers to honor their peers.

Winner
Sabina Murray, *The Caprices*
Finalists
Peter Cameron, *The City of Your Final Destination*
William Kennedy, *Roscoe*
Victor LaValle, *The Ecstatic*
Gilbert Sorrentino, *Little Casino*

THE BOOK SENSE BOOK OF THE YEAR 2002

Formerly known as the ABBY (American Bookseller's Book of the Year), this award is given annually by the American Bookseller's Association.

Adult Fiction: *The Lovely Bones,* Alice Sebold
Adult Nonfiction: *Don't Let's Go to the Dogs Tonight,* Alexandra Fuller
Paperback: *Bel Canto,* Ann Patchett
Children's Illustrated: *Dear Mrs. LaRue,* Mark Teague
Children's Literature: *The Thief Lord,* Cornelia Funke
Rediscovery Award: *The Children of Green Knowe,* L.M. Boston

2003 AMERICAN LIBRARY ASSOCIATION AWARDS FOR CHILDREN'S BOOKS

NEWBERY MEDAL For most distinguished contribution to American literature for children published in 2002:
Avi, author, *Crispin: The Cross of Lead*
Honor Books
Nancy Farmer, author, *The House of the Scorpion*
Carl Hiaasen, author, *Hoot*
Patricia Reilly Giff, author, *Pictures of Hollis Woods*
Ann M. Martin, author, *A Corner of the Universe*
Stephanie S. Tolan, author, *Surviving the Applewhites*

CALDECOTT MEDAL For most distinguished American picture book for children published in 2002:
Eric Rohmann, illustrator and author, *My Friend Rabbit*
Honor Books
Tony DiTerlizzi, illustrator, *The Spider and the Fly,* based on the poem by Mary Howitt
Peter McCarty, author and illustrator, *Hondo & Fabian*
Jerry Pinkney, illustrator and author, *Noah's Ark*

CORETTA SCOTT KING AWARD For outstanding books by African American authors and illustrators:
Nikki Grimes, author, *Bronx Masquerade*
E.B. Lewis, illustrator, *Talkin' About Bessie: The Story of Aviator Elizabeth Coleman,* written by Nikki Grimes
Honor Books—Authors
Brenda Woods, *The Red Rose Box*
Nikki Grimes, *Talkin' About Bessie: The Story of Aviator Elizabeth Coleman*
Honor Books—Illustrators
Leo & Diane Dillon, authors and illustrators, *Rap a Tap Tap: Here's Bojangles, Think of That*
Bryan Collier, illustrator, *Visiting Langston,* written by Willie Perdomo

☆ Chase's 2004 Calendar of Events ☆

John Steptoe New Talent Award
For narrative: Janet McDonald, *Chill Wind*
For illustration: Randy DuBurke, author and illustrator, *The Moon Ring*

MICHAEL L. PRINTZ AWARD For excellence in writing literature for young adults:
Aidan Chambers, author, *Postcards from No Man's Land*

Honor Books
Jack Gantos, author, *Hole in My Life*
Nancy Farmer, author, *House of the Scorpion*
Garret Freymann-Wehr, author, *My Heartbeat*

ROBERT F. SIBERT AWARD For most distinguished informational book for children published in 2002:
James Cross Giblin, author, *The Life and Death of Adolf Hitler*

Honor Books
Karen Blumenthal, author, *Six Days in October: The Stock Market Crash of 1929*
Jack Gantos, author, *Hole in My Life*
Jan Greenberg & Sandra Jordan, authors, *Action Jackson*, illustrated by Robert Andrew Parker
Pam Muñoz Ryan, author, *When Marian Sang*, illustrated by Brian Selznick

MARGARET A. EDWARDS AWARD For lifetime achievement in writing books for young adults:
Nancy Garden, recipient

LAURA INGALLS WILDER MEDAL For an author or illustrator whose books, published in the United States, have made, over a period of years, a substantial and lasting contribution to literature for children:
Eric Carle, recipient

MILDRED L. BATCHELDER AWARD For the best children's book in English translation (first published in a foreign country) published in the US:
The Chicken House/Scholastic, publisher, *The Thief Lord*, written by Cornelia Funke, translated from German by Oliver Latsch

Honor Book
David R. Godine, publisher, *Henrietta and the Golden Eggs*, written by Hanna Johansen, illustrated by Käthi Bhen, translated from German by John Barrett

ANDREW CARNEGIE MEDAL FOR EXCELLENCE IN CHILDREN'S VIDEO
Paul R. Gagne and Melissa Reilly, producers, *So You Want to Be President?*, based on the book written by Judith St. George and illustrated by David Small

MAY HILL ARBUTHNOT LECTURE AWARD
Ursula K. LeGuin, recipient

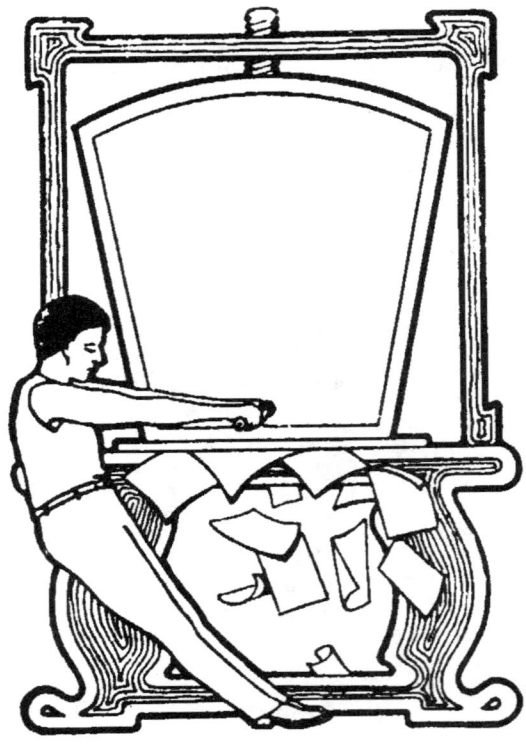

THE MAN BOOKER PRIZE 2002

Sponsored by Booker Prize Foundation and the Man Group in the United Kingdom, this award is given annually to the best full-length novel written in English by a citizen of the U.K., the Commonwealth, Eire, Pakistan, or South Africa.

Life of Pi, Yann Martel
Shortlisted titles
Family Matters, Rohinton Mistry
Unless, Carol Shields
The Story of Lucy Gault, William Trevor
Fingersmith, Sarah Waters
Dirt Music, Tim Winton

2003 ORANGE PRIZE FOR FICTION

Celebrating the excellence of women's writing.

Property, by Valerie Martin

WHITBREAD BOOK AWARDS 2003

An award given to celebrate the most enjoyable British writing of the year.

Novel: *Spies*, Michael Frayn
First Novel: *The Song of Names*, Norman Lebrecht
Poetry: *The Ice Age*, Paul Farley
Biography: *Samuel Pepys: The Unequalled Self*, Claire Tomalin
Children's Book: *Saffy's Angel*, Hilary McKay
Book of the Year: *Samuel Pepys: The Unequalled Self*, Claire Tomalin

☆ Chase's 2004 Calendar of Events ☆

THE KORET JEWISH BOOK AWARDS 2003

Given annually to the most outstanding books on aspects of Jewish life.

Fiction: *Drohobycz, Drohobycz and Other Stories: True Tales from the Holocaust and Life After*, Henryk Grynberg
History: *Beyond the Pale: The Jewish Encounter with Late Imperial Russia*, Benjamin Nathans
Biography, Autobiography and Literary Studies: *Reading the Women of the Bible: A New Interpretation of Their Stories*, Tikva Frymer-Kensky
Philosophy & Thought: *Absorbing Perfections: Kabbalah and Interpretation*, Moshe Idel

THE LAMBDA LITERARY AWARDS

15th annual awards given by the Lambda Literary Foundation to recognize excellence in lesbian/gay/bisexual/transgender (LGBT) literature, for works published in 2002.

Gay Men's Fiction: *At Swim Two Boys*, Jamie O'Neill
Lesbian Fiction: *Fingersmith*, Sarah Waters
Gay Men's Poetry: *Hazmat*, J.D. McClatchy
Lesbian Poetry: *Mules of Love*, Ellen Bass
Gay Men's Mystery: *The Snow Garden*, Christopher Rice
Lesbian Mystery: TIE: *Good Bad Woman*, Elizabeth Woodcraft; and *Immaculate Midnight*, Ellen Hart
Biography: *Ridiculous!*, David Kaufman
Memoir/Autobiography: *Surviving Madness*, Betty Berzon
Anthology (Fiction): *Black Like Us*, edited by Devon Carbado, Dwight McBride and Don Weise
Anthology (Non-fiction): *The Man I Might Become*, edited by Bruce Shenitz
Humor: *Skipping Towards Gomorrah*, Dan Savage
Science Fiction/Fantasy/Horror: *Queer Fear II*, edited by Michael Rowe
Religion/Spirituality: *Courage to Love*, Geoffrey Duncan
Photography/Visual Arts: *A Hidden Love*, Dominique Fernandez
Children/Young Adult: *Letters in the Attic*, Bonnie Shimko
LGBT Independent Press: Kings Crossing Publishing, Robin G. White and Sha Mendon
Erotica: *Best Lesbian Erotica 2003*, edited by Tristan Taormino
Bisexuality/Transgender: *Dress Codes*, Noelle Howey
Romance: *The Winter of Our Discothèque*, Andrew W.M. Beierle
LGBT Studies: *Sex-Crime Panic*, Neil Miller
Editors' Choice Award: *The World Turned*, John D'Emilio
Lambda Literary Foundation Pioneer Awards: Judy Shepard, The Matthew Shepard Foundation; Barbara Greer, Naiad Press
Lambda Literary Foundation Bridgebuilders Award: Betty DeGeneres, author of *Love, Ellen* and *Just a Mom*.

THE EDGAR AWARDS 2003

The Mystery Writers of America honor the best in mystery fiction and nonfiction produced in the previous year. Named in honor of Edgar Allan Poe.

Best Novel: *Winter and Night*, S.J. Rozan
Best First Novel by an American Author: *The Blue Edge of Midnight*, Jonathon King
Best Paperback Original: *Out of Sight*, T.J. MacGregor
Best Fact Crime: *Fire Lover*, Joseph Wambaugh
Best Critical/Biographical Work: *The Mammoth Encyclopedia of Modern Crime Fiction*, Mike Ashley, editor
Best Short Story: "Mexican Gatsby," Raymond Steiber
Best Young Adult: *The Wessex Papers, Vols. 1–3*, Daniel Parker
Best Juvenile: *Harriet Spies Again*, Helen Ericson
Best Television Episode Teleplay: "Law & Order: Special Victims Unit: Waste," Dawn DeNoon and Lisa Marie Petersen
Best Motion Picture Screenplay: *Chicago*, Bill Condon
Best Play: *Easy*, Philip DePoy
Grand Master: Ira Levin
Ellery Queen Award: Ed Gorman
Robert L. Fish Award: "War Can Be Murder," Mike Doogan
Raven Award: Otto Penzler, owner of Mysterious Bookshop, New York, NY; Poe Museum, Richmond, VA; Ed & Pat Thomas, owners of Book Carnival Bookstore, Orange, CA
Simon & Schuster–Mary Higgins Clark Award: *Absolute Certainty*, Rose Connors
Special Award: Dick Wolf, creator of "Law & Order"

THE NEBULA AWARDS 2002

38th annual awards given by Science Fiction and Fantasy Writers of America, Inc.

Novel: *American Gods*, Neil Gaiman
Novella: "Bronte's Egg," Richard Chwedyk
Novelette: "Hell Is the Absence of God," Ted Chiang
Script: *Lord of the Rings: The Fellowship of the Ring*, Frances Walsh, Philippa Boyens and Peter Jackson
Short Story: "Creature," Carol Emshwiller

THE HUGO AWARDS 2002

Also known as the Science Fiction Achievement Award, given annually by the World Science Fiction Society. 50th annual awards.

Best Novel: *American Gods*, Neil Gaiman
Best Novella: "Fast Times at Fairmont High," Vernor Vinge
Best Novelette: "Hell Is the Absence of God," Ted Chiang
Best Related Book: *The Art of Chesley Bonestell*, Ron Miller and Frederick C. Durant III with Melvin H. Schuetz
Best Short Story: "The Dog Said Bow-Wow," Michael Swanwick
John W. Campbell Award for Best New Writer of 2000 or 2001: Jo Walton

☆ Chase's 2004 Calendar of Events ☆

THE JAMES BEARD FOUNDATION/KITCHENAID BOOK AWARDS 2003

Given annually by the James Beard Foundation to the best original, English-language books on culinary topics published in the previous year.

Americana: *Foods of the Southwest Indian Nations,* Lois Ellen Frank
Baking & Desserts: *Baking in America,* Greg Patent
General/Cooking for Everyday: *Local Flavors,* Deborah Madison
General/Cooking from a Professional Point of View: *Zuni Café Cookbook,* Judy Rodgers
International: *Thai Food,* David Thompson
KitchenAid Cookbook Hall of Fame: various titles, Edna Lewis
KitchenAid Cookbook of the Year: *Zuni Café Cookbook,* Judy Rodgers
Literary: *Food Politics: How the Food Industry Influences Nutrition and Health,* Marion Nestle
Mediterranean: *Glorious French Food,* James Peterson
Photography: TIE: *The Anatomy of a Dish,* Victor Schrager, photographer; Diane Forley with Catherine Young, authors; *Belinda Jeffery's Tried and True Recipes,* Rodney Weidland, photographer; Belinda Jeffery, author
Reference: *I'm Just Here for the Food,* Alton Brown
Single Subject: *The Flavors of Olive Oil,* Deborah Krasner
Tools & Technique: *Process This!,* Jean Anderson
Vegetarian/Healthy Focus: *Passionate Vegetarian,* Crescent Dragonwagon
Wines & Spirits: *Michael Broadbent's Vintage Wine,* Michael Broadbent

2003 PULITZER PRIZES

THE ARTS
Fiction: *Middlesex,* Jeffrey Eugenides
Drama: *Anna in the Tropics,* Nilo Cruz
History: *An Army at Dawn: The War in North Africa, 1942–1943,* Rick Atkinson
Biography: *Master of the Senate,* Robert A. Caro
Poetry: *Moy Sand and Gravel,* Paul Muldoon
General Nonfiction: *"A Problem From Hell": America and the Age of Genocide,* Samantha Power
Music: *On the Transmigration of Souls,* John Adams

JOURNALISM
Public Service: *The Boston Globe*
Breaking News Reporting: Staff, *The Eagle-Tribune,* Lawrence, MA
Investigative Reporting: Clifford J. Levy, *The New York Times*
Explanatory Reporting: Staff, *The Wall Street Journal*
Beat Reporting: Diana K. Sugg, *The Baltimore Sun*
National Reporting: Alan Miller and Kevin Sack, *Los Angeles Times*
International Reporting: Kevin Sullivan and Mary Jordan, *The Washington Post*
Feature Writing: Sonia Nazario, *Los Angeles Times*
Commentary: Colbert I. King, *The Washington Post*
Criticism: Stephen Hunter, *The Washington Post*
Editorial Writing: Cornelia Grumman, *Chicago Tribune*
Editorial Cartooning: David Horsey, *Seattle Post-Intelligencer*
Breaking News Photography: Staff, *The Rocky Mountain News*
Feature Photography: Don Bartletti, *Los Angeles Times*

2002 GEORGE POLK AWARDS

Awarded for special achievement in journalism.

Career Award: Morley Safer
International Reporting: Sonia Nazario and Don Bartletti, *Los Angeles Times*
Foreign Reporting: Anthony Shadid, *The Boston Globe*
National Reporting: a team of reporters for "Crisis in the Catholic Church," *The Boston Globe*
Regional Reporting: Clifford J. Levy, *The New York Times*
Healthcare Reporting: Walt Bogdanich, Barry Meier and Mary Williams Walsh, *The New York Times*
Environmental Reporting: Debbie Salamone with Ramsey Campbell and Robert Sargent, *The Orlando Sentinal*
Criminal Justice Reporting: Michael Luo, Associated Press
Financial Reporting: Ellen E. Schultz and Theo Francis, *The Wall Street Journal*
Medical Reporting: Stephen Kiernan and Cadence Mertz, *The Burlington Free Press*
Magazine Reporting: Arnold S. Relman and Marcia Angell, *The New Republic*
Local Reporting: Jason Riley and R.G. Dunlop, *The Courier Journal*
Television Reporting: Phil Williams and Bryan Staples, WTVF, Nashville, TN
Cultural Criticism: Susan Sontag, "Looking at War," *The New Yorker*

☆ Chase's 2004 Calendar of Events ☆

2002 PEABODY AWARDS
62nd Annual Awards

"Terror on Tape," CNN Productions, Atlanta, GA
"Bringing Down a Dictator," York Zimmerman, Inc, presented on PBS
"48 Hours: 9/11," CBS, New York, NY
"The Sonic Memorial Project," Lost and Found Sound from the Kitchen Sisters Productions, presented on NPR and SonicMemorial.org
"Nightline: The Survivors," ABC News, New York, NY
"Frontline: Shattered Dreams of Peace: The Road from Oslo," SET Productions, C-Films Productions for WGBH, in association with FRANCE 2, ABU DHABI Television and Tel Ad Israel
"File on 4: Export Controls," BBC Radio 4
"The Hepatitis C Epidemic: A 15-Year Government Cover-Up," Fuji Television Network, Inc, Japan
"Sounding the Alarm," WISN-TV, Milwaukee, WI
"Fake Drugs, Real Lives," WFAA-TV, Dallas, TX
"DNA Protects Men of Dishonor," KPRC-TV, Houston, TX
"Nightline: Heart of Darkness," ABC News, New York, NY
"How High Is the Mountain," Public Television Service Foundation, Taiwan
"The Yiddish Radio Project," NPR and Sound Portrait Productions
"Stories of Home," WBEZ/Chicago Public Radio, Chicago, IL
"EGG the Arts Show," Thirteen/WNET, New York, NY
"The Complete Angler," ESPN and Lake Champlain Productions
"Monkey Trial," Nebraska ETV and The American Experience, WGBH, Boston, MA
"The Rise and Fall of Jim Crow," Thirteen/WNET, New York, NY
Bang Bang You're Dead, Showtime from Viacom Productions and A Jersey Guys Production, Inc
"Almost Strangers," BBC America with Talkback Productions, presented on BBC
"Stage on Screen: Beckett on Film," Thirteen/WNET, New York, NY
"Russell Simmons Presents Def Poetry Jam," HBO and Simmons/Lathan TV
"The Interrogation of Michael Crowe," Court TV from JB Media and Hearst Entertainment
"Boomtown," NBC/NBC Studios Inc, in association with DreamWorks Television
"ExxonMobil Masterpiece Theatre: Othello," WGBH and London Weekend Television
"ExxonMobil Masterpiece Theatre's American Collection: Almost a Woman," WGBH and ALT Films
The Gathering Storm, HBO and Scott Free Productions
"Boston Public/Chapter 37," FOX from David E. Kelley Productions and 20th Century Fox Television
"Six Feet Under," HBO from Janollari Studios and Actual Size, Inc
"Door to Door," TNT from Rosemont Productions International in association with Angel/Brown Productions

2002 WEBBY AWARDS
6th Annual

Activism: tolerance.org—www.tolerance.org
Best Practices: Google—www.google.com
Broadband: GUGGENHEIM.COM—www.guggenheim.com
Commerce: Amazon.com—www.amazon.com
Community: Idealist.org—www.idealist.org
Education: Exploratorium—www.exploratorium.edu
Fashion: ZOOZOOM.com Magazine—www.zoozoom.com
Film: Donnie Darko—www.donniedarko.com
Finance: Yahoo! Finance—finance.yahoo.com
Games: Netbaby—www.netbabyworld.com
Government & Law: Library of Congress—lcweb.loc.gov
Health: teenwire.com—www.teenwire.com
Humor: The Onion—www.theonion.com
Kids: OLogy—www.ology.amnh.org
Living: epicurious—www.epicurious.com
Music: LOOPLABS—www.looplabs.com
Net Art: 360degrees—www.360degrees.org
News: BBC News—www.bbc.co.uk/news
Personal: The Committee to Free Lori Berenson—www.freelori.org
Politics: Center for Responsive Politics—www.opensecrets.org
Print & Zines: Salon.com—www.salon.com
Radio: BBC Radio 4 website—www.www.bbc.co.uk/radio4
Science: Becoming Human—www.becominghuman.org
Services: evite—www.evite.com
Spirituality: Beliefnet—www.beliefnet.com
Sports: ESPN.com—www.espn.com
Technical Achievement: David Rumsey Historical Map Collection—www.davidrumsey.com
Travel: Lonely Planet Online—www.lonelyplanet.com
TV: The Osbournes—www.mtv.com/onair/osbournes
Weird: Devices of Wonder—www.getty.edu/art/exhibitions/devices

Glossary

Dominical Letter

The basis of a perpetual calendar used in the Christian church to determine the date on which Sundays fall in a particular year. Knowing the Dominical Letter (A to G) of a year gives the entire order of days in that year.

Epact

The number of days in the age of the Moon on Jan 1 of any year. Each year has an epact number that allows the dates of all full moons for the year to be calculated. It is used to determine the date of Easter. The epact is supposed to be an improvement over the Golden number (below) for this purpose.

Eras

Counting years from a particular date as year one. The era of Nabonassar, named after King Nabonassar of Babylon, dated time from the eighth century BC. The ancient Greeks counted years from the Olympics. A period of four years was called an Olympiad, so an event would be described as having occurred in the second year of the 92nd Olympiad. The Seleucid era used in the Asian part of the Roman Empire was named after a Roman general, Seleucus.

Year one was 312 BC, the year he captured Babylon. The Romans counted years from the reign of an emperor or the founding of Rome. The Diocletian era, for example, was counted from AD 284. The Roman Era (AUC) had year one as 753 BC, the traditional founding date of Rome. The Byzantines dated their era back to what they thought was the creation in 5508 BC. The Roman Indiction, an era introduced by the Emperor Constantine, dated time in 15-year intervals (indictions) from AD 313. The Jewish calendar counts from the year established as the date of the creation (3760 BC) and the Muslim calendar from the flight into exile of Muhammad (AD 622). The Japanese count years from the beginning of an emperor's reign, the Chinese calendar dates time from 2637 BC and the Indian Saka era dates time from AD 78.

The Gregorian calendar counts years from the birth of Christ. In the sixth century a monk named Dionysius Exiguus realized that it was the 525th year since the birth of Christ. (We now know that he was slightly off in this calculation; Christ is thought to have been born in 4 BC.) He saw an opportunity to replace the system of calculating years from pagan emperors, who often had been great persecuters of Christians, and instituted a system whereby time is calculated from the birth of Christ. Years are designated as AD (from Latin for "in the year of our Lord"). This system was not widely adopted, however, until the eighth century when it was popularized by the Venerable Bede. Since the system of Roman numerals available to Dionysius and Bede lacked a zero, time was divided at 1 BC and 1 AD; there was no year zero.

Golden Number

The position of any year in the 19-year Metonic cycle, a lunisolar cycle discovered by the Greek astronomer Meton. In modern times it has been used to determine the date of Easter.

Gregorian Calendar

This solar calendar, used in most countries of the world today, was designed on the order of Pope Gregory to improve on the Julian calendar, which over time had grown to exceed the seasons by ten days. In 1582, ten days were deleted from the year as a correction and the Gregorian calendar was adopted in Catholic Europe. To reflect the fact that the solar year has 365.24219 days, not 365.25 days as used in the Julian calendar, the cycle of leap years was changed so that century years must be evenly divisible by 400 to be leap years. Hence, 1600 and 2000 were leap years, 1900 was not. The Gregorian calendar is still 25 seconds longer than the true solar year but will not gain a full day for some 3,400 years.

This calendar, often called New Style as opposed to Old Style (Julian), was adopted in Roman Catholic countries in 1582, but Great Britain and its colonies (including North America) did not switch until 1752. (Great Britain also changed the beginning of the year to January at this time; it had been Annunciation Day, Mar 25.) The Gregorian calendar was not adopted in Russia and Greece until the twentieth century.

Islamic Calendar

This lunar calendar has 354 days and thus is shorter than the solar year. As a result, the fixed holidays in the Islamic calendar move

Glossary

"backward" about 11 days each year in relation to the seasons. In roughly 32 years, Ramadan, the Islamic month of fasting, moves back through the entire solar year. If Ramadan occurs in January one year, about 16 years later it will occur in June. Many Islamic countries use the Gregorian calendar for civil purposes and the Islamic calendar determines the days of religious holidays. The Islamic era began with year one on July 16, 622, the date of the flight into exile of the Prophet Muhammad.

Jewish Calendar

This lunisolar calendar is regulated by both the moon and the sun. The average year is a lunar year with 354 days; adjustments are made by adding a leap month about every three years so that major Jewish holidays fall into their proper season. From year to year, Jewish dates vary from their Gregorian equivalents. For example, the state of Israel was founded on Iyar 5, 5708. In 1948, when this event occurred, the Gregorian date was May 14th. However, in 2002 the Gregorian equivalent is Apr 17th. But the addition of the extra month periodically means that this holiday will always occur in the spring. The Jewish calendar dates year one from 3761 BC, the assumed date of creation.

Julian Calendar

This solar calendar was commissioned by Julius Caesar in 46 BC. Up until that time, the Romans had used a lunar calendar. It had increasingly grown out of sync with the seasons, so the year 46 BC was lengthened to 445 days to make the adjustment. From then on, the year was 365 days long, with a leap year every fourth year. Julian dates are now usually identified as Old Style.

The numbering of years varied, usually dating time from the reign of a Roman emperor. The Julian calendar was used for more than 1,600 years and is still used by Orthodox Christian churches to determine some religious holidays. See Gregorian Calendar for the successor to the Julian calendar.

Julian Period and Julian Day

This system of calculating time, which is used by astronomers, is not related to the Julian Calendar. A Frenchman, Joseph Justus Scaliger, conceived these measures in 1582 and named them after his father, Julius Scaliger. The Julian Period is composed of 7,980 years. Scaliger selected Jan 1, 4713 BC as day one of the period, which will be complete in 3267. Individual Julian days are counted from the beginning of the Julian Period and each day has its own number. Currently, more than 2,451,000 Julian days have elapsed. Astronomical reference books have tables to facilitate converting any date into its Julian-day number for calculations involving large time intervals.

Roman Calendars

Prior to the adoption of the Julian calendar in 46 BC, the Romans used various lunar calendars. The Romans, like many other civilizations, started the year in March; hence the names of the months September, October, November and December have their roots in seven (sept), eight (oct), nine (nov) and ten (dec), when they are our ninth, tenth, eleventh and twelfth months.

About 451 BC the calendar was rearranged to have the year begin in January

Solar Cycle

A cycle designed to show the relation between the day of the week and the day of the month. Because the 365 days in the year are not evenly divisible by the seven days in a week (there is one day left over), if one year begins on a Sunday, the next year must begin on a Monday. During a leap year, with its added day, the calendar leaps ahead from, for example, Sunday to Tuesday. Thus, a perpetual calendar has 14 possible arrangements for days of the year, seven for leap years and seven for nonleap years.

It took 28 years (a solar cycle) for these 14 calendars to occur in the same order in the Julian calendar. In the Gregorian calendar it takes 400 years.

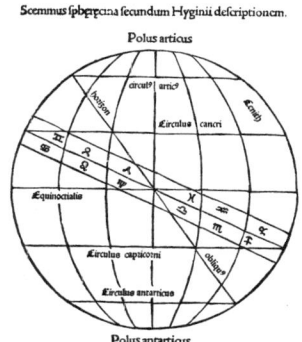

☆ Chase's 2004 Calendar of Events ☆
INDEX

Aames, Willie: Birth, Jul 15
Aaron, Hank: Birth, Feb 5
Aaron, Hank: Home Run Record: Anniv, Apr 8
Abbado, Claudio: Birth, Jun 26
Abbott and Costello Show TV Premiere: Anniv, Dec 5
Abbott, Berenice: Birth Anniv, Jul 17
Abbott, Jim: Birth, Sep 19
Abdul, Paula: Birth, Jun 19
Abdul-Jabbar, Kareem: Birth, Apr 16
Abet and Aid Punsters Day, Nov 8
Abilities Day, Dec 22
Abolition Soc Founded, First American: Anniv, Apr 14
Abortion Counseling, Supreme Court Upholds Ban: Anniv, May 23
Abortion First Legalized: Anniv, Apr 25
Abortion: Roe v Wade Supreme Court Decision: Anniv, Jan 22
Abraham, F. Murray: Birth, Oct 24
Abraham, Spencer: Birth, Jun 12
Abused Women and Children's Awareness Day, Jun 13
Academy Awards Presentation, Feb 1
Academy Awards, First: Anniv, May 16
Acadia Natl Park Established: Anniv, Jan 1
According to Hoyle Day, Aug 29
Accordion Awareness Month, Natl, Jun 1
Accordion Fest, Sata-Hame (Ikaalinen, Finland), Jun 29
Accounting: Internal Audit Awareness Month, Intl, May 1
Ace, Goodman: Birth Anniv, Jan 15
Achelis, Elisabeth: Birth Anniv, Jan 24
Ackland, Joss: Birth, Feb 29
Act Happy Day, Mar 15
Acuff, Roy: Birth Anniv, Sep 15
Adamle, Mike: Birth, Oct 4
Adams County Fair/Rodeo (Hettinger, ND), Jul 29
Adams, Abigail: Birth Anniv, Nov 22
Adams, Ansel: Birth Anniv, Feb 20
Adams, Brooke: Birth, Feb 8
Adams, Bryan: Birth, Nov 5
Adams, Don: Birth, Apr 19
Adams, Edie: Birth, Apr 16
Adams, Joey Lauren: Birth, Jan 6
Adams, John Quincy: Birth Anniv, Jul 11
Adams, John Quincy: Returns to Congress, Mar 4
Adams, John, and Jefferson, Thomas: Death Anniv, Jul 4
Adams, John: Birth Anniv, Oct 30
Adams, Louisa Catherine Johnson: Birth Anniv, Feb 12
Adams, Mason: Birth, Feb 26
Adams, Maud: Birth, Feb 12
Adams, Samuel: Birth Anniv, Sep 27
Adams, Scott: Birth, Jun 8
Addams Family TV Premiere: Anniv, Sep 18
Addams, Charles: Birth Anniv, Jan 7
Addams, Jane: Birth Anniv, Sep 6
Adding Machine, Patent Issued for First: Anniv, Oct 11
Addison, Joseph: Birth Anniv, May 1
Adjani, Isabelle: Birth, Jun 27
Administrative Professionals Day, Apr 21
Administrative Professionals Intl Conv (Washington, DC), Aug 1
Administrative Professionals Week, Apr 18
Admission Day Holiday (HI), Aug 20
Admit You're Happy Day, Aug 8
Admit You're Happy Month, Aug 1
Adolfo: Birth, Feb 15
Adopt-A-Shelter-Cat Month, Jun 1
Adoption Month, Natl, Nov 1
Adoption Week, Natl, Nov 21
Adult Day Services Assn Conference, Natl (New Orleans, LA), Jan 30
Adult Day Services Week, Natl, Sep 19
Adult Immunization Awareness Week, Natl, Oct 10
Advent, First Sunday of, Nov 28
Adventures of Ellery Queen TV Premiere: Anniv, Oct 14
Advertising: Co-op Awareness Month, Oct 1
Advertising: Mobius Awards (Los Angeles, CA), Feb 20
Aebleskiver Days (Tyler, MN), Jul 23
Affleck, Ben: Birth, Aug 15
Afghanistan,
  Fall of Kabul: Anniv, Nov 13
  Independence Day, Aug 19
  Soviet Troop Withdrawal Deadline, Feb 15
AFL Founded: Anniv, Dec 8
AFL-CIO Founded: Anniv, Dec 5
Africa Industrialization Day (UN), Nov 20
African American,
  African American History Month, Natl, Feb 1
  African American Holiday Expo (Washington, DC), Dec 18
  African Methodist Episcopal Church Organized: Anniv, Apr 9

Alpha Kappa Alpha Sorority Founded: Anniv, Jan 15
Amistad Seized: Anniv, Aug 29
Anderson, Marian: Birth Anniv, Feb 27
Anderson, Marian: Easter Concert: Anniv, Apr 9
Ashford, Emmett: Birth Anniv, Nov 23
Attack on Fort Wagner: Anniv, Jul 19
Black Business Month, Aug 1
Black History Month, Feb 1
Black Love Day, Feb 13
Black Page Appointed US House: Anniv, Apr 9
Black Poetry Day, Oct 17
Black Press Day: Anniv of First Black Newspaper in US, Mar 16
Black Senate Page Appointed: Anniv, Apr 8
Black Single Parents' Week, Jun 6
Blacks Ruled Eligible to Vote: Anniv, Apr 3
Bolin, Jane M.: Birth, Apr 11
Brown, Jesse Leroy: Birth Anniv, Oct 13
Bud Billiken Parade (Chicago, IL), Aug 14
Civil Rights Act of 1964: Anniv, Jul 2
Civil Rights Bill of 1866: Anniv, Apr 9
Civil Rights Workers Found Slain: Anniv, Aug 4
Cole, Nat "King": Birth Anniv, Mar 17
Coleman, Bessie: Birth Anniv, Jan 26
Cullen, Countee: Birth Anniv, May 30
Davis, Benjamin O., Jr: Birth Anniv, Dec 18
Desegregation, US Army First: Anniv, Jul 26
Dred Scott Decision: Anniv, Mar 6
Drew, Charles: Birth Anniv, Jun 3
Emancipation of 500: Anniv, Aug 1
Escape to Freedom (F. Douglass): Anniv, Sep 3
First American Abolition Soc Founded: Anniv, Apr 14
First Black Governor Elected: Anniv, Nov 7
First Black Plays in NBA Game: Anniv, Oct 31
First Black Pro Hockey Player: Anniv, Nov 15
First Black Receives Congressional Medal: Anniv, May 23
First Black Serves in US House Reps: Anniv, Dec 12
First Black Senator Sworn in Lt Gov: Anniv, Jan 11
First Black US Cabinet Member: Anniv, Jan 18
First Black US State's Attorney: Anniv, Jul 6
First Natl Convention for Blacks: Anniv, Sep 15
Forten, James: Birth Anniv, Sep 2
Foster, Andrew: Birth Anniv, Sep 17
Frederick Douglass Speaks: Anniv, Aug 11
Freedom Riders: Anniv, May 4
Gibbs, Mifflin Wister: Birth Anniv, Apr 28
Greensboro Sit-in: Anniv, Feb 1
Harlem Globetrotters Play First Game: Anniv, Jan 7
Harris, Patricia Roberts: Birth Anniv, May 31
Historically Black Colleges and Universities Week, Natl (Pres Proc), Sep 19
Hughes, Langston: Birth Anniv, Feb 1
Jackie Robinson Breaks Baseball Color Line: Anniv, Apr 15
Joplin, Scott: Birth Anniv, Nov 24
Juneteenth, Jun 19
King Awarded Nobel Peace Prize: Anniv, Oct 14
King, Martin Luther, Jr: Birth Anniv, Jan 15
Kwanzaa Fest, Dec 26
Links, Inc: Anniv, Nov 9
Little Rock Nine: Anniv, Sep 4
Malcolm X: Assassination Anniv, Feb 21
Malcolm X: Birth Anniv, May 19
Marshall, Thurgood, Resigns from Supreme Court: Anniv, Jun 27
Marshall, Thurgood: Birth Anniv, Jul 2
Marshall, Thurgood: Sworn in to Supreme Court: Anniv, Oct 2
McDaniel, Hattie: Birth Anniv, Jun 10
Medgar Evers Assassinated: Anniv, Jun 13
Meredith (James) Enrolls at Ole Miss: Anniv, Sep 30
Miami/Bahamas Goombay Fest (Miami, FL), Jun 4
Million Man March: Anniv, Oct 16
Minority Enterprise Development Week (Pres Proc), Sep 26
Minority Scientists Showcase (St. Louis, MO), Jan 17
Montgomery Boycott Arrests: Anniv, Feb 22
Montgomery Bus Boycott Begins: Anniv, Dec 5
Montgomery Bus Boycott Ends: Anniv, Dec 20
Motley, Constance Baker: Birth, Sep 14
NAACP Founded: Anniv, Feb 12
New York Slave Revolt: Anniv, Apr 7
Ralph Bunche Awarded Nobel Peace Prize: Anniv, Dec 10
Robinson Named First Black Manager: Anniv, Oct 3
Robinson, Roscoe, Jr: Birth Anniv, Oct 11
Rosa Parks Day, Dec 1
Saint Louis Race Riots: Anniv, Jul 2
Scottsboro Trial: Anniv, Apr 6
16th Street Baptist Church Bombing: Anniv, Sep 15
Soul Food Month, Natl, Jun 1
Spelman College Established: Anniv, Apr 11
Stokes Becomes First Black Mayor in US: Anniv, Nov 13
Tanner, Henry Ossawa: Birth Anniv, Jun 21
Truth, Sojourner: Death Anniv, Nov 26
Tubman, Harriet: Death Anniv, Mar 10
Tuskegee Airmen Activated: Anniv, Mar 22
Tuskegee Institute Opening: Anniv, Jul 4

Unity in Diversity Day, May 1
Wheatley, Phillis: Death Anniv, Dec 5
Willie Covan Loved to Dance Week, Feb 1
Zora Neale Hurston Fest (Eatonville, FL), Jan 28
African American Coaches Day, Feb 4
African American History Month, Natl, Feb 1
African Methodist Episcopal Church Organized: Anniv, Apr 9
African Natl Congress Ban Lifted, Feb 2
Agassi, Andre: Birth, Apr 29
Agassiz, Louis: Birth Anniv, May 28
Agee, James: Birth Anniv, Nov 27
Aggie Muster, Apr 21
Agnew Resignation: Anniv, Oct 10
Agnew, Spiro: Birth Anniv, Nov 9
Agriculture (including state and county fairs),
  Acton Fair (Acton, ME), Aug 26
  Agriculture Day, Natl, Mar 20
  Agriculture Week, Natl, Mar 14
  Agrifair (Abbotsford, BC, Canada), Jul 29
  Alabama Natl Fair (Montgomery, AL), Oct 8
  Alaska State Fair (Palmer, AK), Aug 26
  Arizona State Fair (Phoenix, AZ), Oct 7
  Arkansas State Fair (Little Rock, AR), Oct 8
  Bangor State Fair (Bangor, ME), Jul 30
  Barn Day (Filley, NE), Jul 6
  Big E (West Springfield, MA), Sep 17
  Black Hills Stock Show and Rodeo (Rapid City, SD), Jan 30
  Blue Hill Fair (Blue Hill, ME), Sep 2
  Broome County Fair (Whitney Point, NY), Jul 27
  Calgary Stampede (Calgary, AB, Canada), Jul 9
  California State Fair (Sacramento, CA), Aug 20
  Canadian Western Agribition (Regina, SK, Canada), Nov 22
  Champlain Valley Fair (Essex Junction, VT), Aug 28
  Coe Hill Agricultural Fair (Coe Hill, ON, Canada), Aug 20
  Colorado State Fair (Pueblo, CO), Aug 21
  Columbia County Fair (Chatham, NY), Sep 2
  Common Ground Country Fair (Unity, ME), Sep 24
  Corn Palace Fest (Mitchell, SD), Sep 1
  Day on the Farm (Springfield, OR), Aug 21
  Delaware State Fair (Harrington, DE), Jul 22
  Delmarva Chicken Fest (Salisbury, MD), Jun 18
  Eastern Idaho State Fair (Blackfoot, ID), Sep 4
  Eighteenth-Century Threshing Day (McLean, VA), Nov 21
  Fairfest (Hastings, NE), Jul 21
  Family Farm Day, Sep 22
  Farm Animals Awareness Week, Natl, Sep 19
  Farm Safety Week, Natl (Pres Proc), Sep 19
  Farm Toy Show & Auction (Sauk Centre, MN), Feb 14
  Farm-City Week, Natl (Pres Proc), Nov 19
  Farmers Market (Woodstock, IL), May 6
  FFA Week, Natl, Feb 21
  Florida Citrus Fest (Winter Haven, FL), Jan 15
  Florida State Fair (Tampa, FL), Feb 5
  Fryeburg Fair (Fryeburg, ME), Oct 3
  Garfield County Fair (Burwell, NE), Jul 28
  Gateway Farm Expo (Kearney, NE), Nov 10
  Georgia National Fair (Perry, GA), Oct 8
  Grange Month, Apr 1
  Harvard Milk Days Fest (Harvard, IL), Jun 4
  Hood River County Fair (Hood River, OR), Jul 28
  Hopkinton State Fair (Contoocook, NH), Sep 2
  Husker Harvest Days (Grand Island, NE), Sep 14
  Illinois State Fair (Springfield, IL), Aug 13
  Indiana State Fair (Indianapolis, IN), Aug 11
  Iowa State Fair (Des Moines, IA), Aug 12
  Johnson County 4H and FFA Fair (Iowa City, IA), Jul 26
  Kansas State Fair (Hutchinson, KS), Sep 10
  Kentucky State Fair (Louisville, KY), Aug 19
  Livestock Show, Rio Grande Valley (Mercedes, TX), Mar 20
  Louisiana, State Fair of (Shreveport, LA), Oct 22
  Makoti Threshing Bee Show (Makoti, ND), Oct 2
  Marion County Fair (Salem, OR), Jul 8
  Maryland State Fair (Timonium, MD), Aug 27
  McHenry County Fair (Woodstock, IL), Aug 4
  Michigan State Fair (Detroit, MI), Aug 20
  Mid-South Fair (Memphis, TN), Sep 22
  Minnesota State Fair (St. Paul, MN), Aug 26
  Mississippi State Fair (Jackson, MS), Oct 6
  Missouri State Fair (Sedalia, MO), Aug 12
  Montana State Fair (Great Falls, MT), Jul 31
  Montgomery County Agricultural Fair (Gaithersburg, MD), Aug 13
  Morrill Land Grant Act Passed: Anniv, Jul 2
  Nebraska State Fair (Lincoln, NE), Aug 28
  Nevada State Fair (Reno, NV), Aug 25
  New Jersey State Fair (Augusta, NJ), Aug 6
  New Mexico State Fair (Albuquerque, NM), Sep 3
  New York State Fair (Syracuse, NY), Aug 26
  North Carolina State Fair (Raleigh, NC), Oct 15
  North Central Missouri Fair (Trenton, MO), Jul 27
  North Dakota State Fair (Minot, ND), Jul 23
  Northeast Montana Threshing Bee/Antique Show (Culbertson, MT), Sep 25

680

☆ Chase's 2004 Calendar of Events ☆ Index

Agriculture (cont'd)—Amos

Northeastern Wisconsin Antique Power and Machinery Show Thresheree (Sturgeon Bay, WI), **Aug 20**
Northern Intl Livestock Expo (Billings, MT), **Oct 20**
No-Tillage Conference, Natl (Des Moines, IA), **Jan 7**
Ohio State Fair (Columbus, OH), **Aug 6**
Oklahoma State Fair (Oklahoma City, OK), **Sep 17**
Old Tyme Farm Days (Live Oak, FL), **Nov 25**
Oregon State Fair (Salem, OR), **Aug 26**
Organic Harvest Month, Natl, **Sep 1**
Ozark Empire Fair (Springfield, MO), **Jul 30**
Ozark Fall Farmfest (Springfield, MO), **Oct 1**
Penn State's Agri Progress Days (Rock Springs, PA), **Aug 17**
Pennsylvania Farm Show, **Jan 10**
Red River Valley Fair (Fargo, ND), **Jun 18**
Rice Month, Natl, **Sep 1**
Rochester Fair (Rochester, NH), **Sep 10**
Rockbridge Regional Fair (Lexington, VA), **Jul 20**
Rotary Tiller Race, World Chmpshp/Purplehull Pea Fest (Emerson, AR), **Jun 25**
Royal Bath and West Show (Shepton Mallet, Somerset, England), **Jun 2**
Royal Ulster Agri Soc Balmoral Show (Belfast, N Ireland), **May 12**
Ruffin, Edmund: Birth Anniv, **Jan 5**
Rural Life Sunday, **May 16**
Saint Johns Mint Fest (St. Johns, MI), **Aug 13**
Scotts Bluff County Fair (Mitchell, NE), **Aug 9**
Seed to Stalk (Williamsburg, VA), **Jun 1**
Sheep to Shawl Festival (Savannah, GA), **Mar 20**
Sioux Empire Fair (Sioux Falls, SD), **Aug 10**
Sioux Empire Farm Show (Sioux Falls, SD), **Jan 27**
Sodbuster Days—Harvest (Fort Ransom, ND), **Sep 11**
Sonoma-Marin Fair (Petaluma, CA), **Jun 16**
Sorghum Day Fest (Wewoka, OK), **Oct 23**
South Carolina State Fair (Columbia, SC), **Oct 7**
South Dakota State Fair (Huron, SD), **Jul 26**
Southeast Missouri District Fair (Cape Girardeau, MO), **Sep 11**
Southwestern Expo Livestock Show/Rodeo (Fort Worth, TX), **Jan 17**
State Fair of Texas (Dallas, TX), **Sep 24**
Sussex Farm and Horse Show/New Jersey State Fair (Augusta, NJ), **Aug 6**
Swap Meet and Tractor Show (Washington, KS), **Jun 5**
Tennessee State Fair (Nashville, TN), **Sep 10**
Texas-Oklahoma Fair (Wichita Falls, TX), **Sep 14**
Texoma Farm and Ranch Show (Wichita Falls, TX), **Feb 10**
Traditional Plowing Match (Woodstock, VT), **May 2**
Triumph of Ag Expo (Omaha, NE), **Mar 3**
Utah State Fair (Salt Lake City, UT), **Sep 9**
Vermont State Fair (Rutland, VT), **Sep 3**
Virginia, State Fair of (Richmond, VA), **Sep 23**
West Virginia State Fair (Lewisburg, WV), **Aug 13**
Western Minnesota Steam Thresher's Reunion (Rollag, MN), **Sep 3**
Western Washington Fair (Puyallup, WA), **Sep 10**
Wheat Harvest, 18th-Century (McLean, VA), **Jun 20**
Winter Show (Valley City, ND), **Mar 5**
Wisconsin State Fair (Milwaukee, WI), **Aug 5**
World Ag Expo (Tulare, CA), **Feb 10**
World Beef Expo (Milwaukee, WI), **Sep 23**
Wyoming State Fair & Rodeo (Douglas, WY), **Aug 14**
Aguilera, Christina: Birth, Dec 18
Agutter, Jenny: Birth, Dec 20
Aida Premieres: Anniv, Dec 24
AIDS,
Awareness Month, Natl, **Nov 1**
Condom Week, Natl, **Feb 14**
First Noted: Anniv, **Jun 5**
White, Ryan: Death Anniv, **Apr 8**
World AIDS Day (Pres Proc), **Dec 1**
World AIDS Day (UN), **Dec 1**
Aiello, Danny, Jr: Birth, Jun 20
Aiken, Conrad: Birth Anniv, Aug 5
Aikman, Troy: Birth, Nov 21
Ailey, Alvin: Birth Anniv, Jan 5
Aimee, Anouk: Birth, Apr 27
Ainge, Danny: Birth, Mar 17
Air Conditioning Appreciation Days, Jul 3
Air Force Academy, US, Established: Anniv, Apr 1
Airborne Day, Natl (Pres Proc), Aug 16
Ajaye, Franklyn: Birth, May 13
Akaka, Daniel K.: Birth, Sep 11
Akers, Michelle: Birth, Feb 1
Akihito: Birth, Dec 23
Al Qaeda: Fall of Kabul: Anniv, Nov 13
Alabama,
Admission Day, **Dec 14**
Alabama Coastal Cleanup (Mobile), **Sep 18**
Alabama Jubilee (Decatur), **May 29**
Alabama Renaissance Faire (Florence), **Oct 23**
American Indian Heritage Day, **Oct 11**
Battle of Mobile Bay: Anniv, **Aug 5**
Blue-Gray Classic (Montgomery), **Dec 25**
Christmas on the River (Demopolis), **Nov 28**
Confederate Memorial Day, **Apr 26**
DeSoto Caverns Park Fall Indian Dance Fest (Childersburg), **Sep 25**
DeSoto Caverns Park Spring Indian Dance Fest (Childersburg), **Apr 3**
Do Dah Day (Birmingham), **May 8**
Fireworks Celebration (Demopolis), **Jul 3**
Helen Keller Fest (Tuscumbia), **Jun 24**
Joe Cain Procession (Mobile), **Feb 22**
Longhorn World Chmpshp Rodeo (Huntsville), **Mar 12**
NAIA Softball Chmpshp (Decatur), **May 21**
Natl Fair (Montgomery), **Oct 8**
NCAA Div I Women's Golf Chmpshps (Auburn), **May 18**
Panoply (Huntsville), **Apr 23**
Racking World Celebration (Decatur), **Sep 17**
Riley, Bob: Birth, **Oct 3**
Senior Bowl Football Game (Mobile), **Jan 25**
September Skirmish (Decatur), **Sep 4**
Sessions, Jeff: Birth, **Dec 24**
Shelby, Richard C.: Birth, **May 6**
Southern Appalachian Dulcimer Fest (McCalla), **May 1**
Spirit of America (Decatur), **Jul 3**
Spirit of Freedom Fest (Florence), **Jul 4**
Trail of Tears Commemoration (Waterloo), **Sep 18**
W.C. Handy Fest (Florence), **Jul 25**
Alamo: Anniv of the Fall, Mar 6
Alaska,
Admission Day, **Jan 3**
Alascattalo Day (Anchorage), **Nov 21**
Alaska Day, **Oct 18**
Alaska Flag Day Celebration, **Jul 9**
Anvil Mountain Run (Nome), **Jul 4**
Blueberry Arts Fest (Ketchikan), **Aug 7**
Carrs/Safeway Great Alaska Shootout (Anchorage), **Nov 23**
Earthquake Strikes Alaska: Anniv, **Mar 27**
Fairbanks Summer Arts Fest (Fairbanks), **Jul 18**
Fest of the North (Ketchikan), **Feb 1**
59 Min 37 Sec Anvil Mountain Challenge (Nome), **Sep 9**
Gigglefeet Dance Festival (Ketchikan), **Aug 6**
Great Bathtub Race (Nome), **Sep 6**
Iditarod Trail Sled Dog Race (Anchorage), **Mar 6**
Kodiak Crab Fest (Kodiak), **May 27**
Midnight Sun Baseball Game (Fairbanks), **Jun 18**
Midnight Sun Fest (Nome), **Jun 19**
Mount Marathon Race (Seward), **Jul 4**
Murkowski, Frank: Birth, **Mar 28**
Murkowski, Lisa: Birth, **May 22**
Music in the Park (Anchorage), **Jun 2**
National Parks Established: Anniv, **Dec 2**
Nenana Tripod Raising Fest (Nenana), **Mar 6**
Polar Bear Swim (Nome), **Jun 21**
Poorman's Paradise Gold Panner Contest (Nome), **Jul 20**
Seward Silver Salmon Derby (Seward), **Aug 14**
Seward's Day, **Mar 29**
Sled Dogs Save Nome: Anniv, **Feb 2**
Snake River Duck Race (Nome), **Sep 6**
State Fair (Palmer), **Aug 26**
Stevens, Ted: Birth, **Nov 18**
Summer Music Fest (Sitka), **Jun 4**
Talkeetna Moose-Dropping Fest (Talkeetna), **Jul 10**
Tsunami, Highest Recorded in History: Anniv, **Jul 9**
Alba, Jessica: Birth, Apr 28
Albania: Independence Day, Nov 28
Albany Riverfest (Albany, NY), Aug 14
Albany Riverfront Jazz Festival (Albany, NY), Sep 11
Albee, Edward: Birth, Mar 12
Alberghetti, Anna Maria: Birth, May 15
Albert, Eddie: Birth, Apr 22
Albert, Edward: Birth, Feb 20
Albert, Marv: Birth, Jun 12
Albright, Madeleine: Birth, May 15
Albuquerque Intl Balloon Fiesta (Albuquerque, NM), Oct 2
Alcohol, Alcoholism,
Alcohol and Other Drug-Related Birth Defects Week, Natl, **May 9**
Alcohol-Free Weekend, **Apr 2**
Alcoholics Anonymous: Founding Anniv, **Jun 10**
Awareness Month, **Apr 1**
Pharmacists Declare War on Alcoholism, **Jun 1**
Screening Day, Natl, **Apr 8**
Women's Christian Temperance Union: Anniv, **Nov 19**
Alcott, Amy Strum: Birth, Feb 22
Alcott, Louisa May: Birth Anniv, Nov 29
Alda, Alan: Birth, Jan 28
Aldrin, Edwin "Buzz": Birth, Jan 20
Aleichem, Sholem: Birth Anniv, Feb 18
Alexander, Jane: Birth, Oct 28
Alexander, Jason: Birth, Sep 23
Alexander, Lamar: Birth, Jul 30
Alexander, Shana: Birth, Oct 6
Alexis, Kim: Birth, Jul 15
Alfonso, Kristian: Birth, Sep 5
Alfonzo, Edgardo: Birth, Nov 8
Alfred Hitchcock Presents TV Premiere: Anniv, Oct 2
Alger, Horatio, Jr: Birth Anniv, Jan 13
Algeria,
Independence Day, **Jul 5**
Revolution Day, **Nov 1**
Algonquin Mill Fall Festival (Carrollton, OH), Oct 8
Ali, Muhammad: Birth, Jan 17
Ali, Muhammad: Clay Becomes Heavyweight Champ: Anniv, Feb 25
Ali, Muhammad: Stripped of Title: Anniv, Apr 30
Alice TV Premiere: Anniv, Aug 31
All Fools' Day, Apr 1
All Hallows, Nov 1
All Hallows Eve, Oct 31
All in the Family TV Premiere: Anniv, Jan 12
All My Children TV Premiere: Anniv, Jan 5
All Saints' Day, Nov 1
All Souls' Day, Nov 2
All the News That's Fit to Print: Anniv, Feb 10
Allanson, Susie: Birth, Mar 17
Allard, Wayne: Birth, Dec 2
Allen, Byron: Birth, Apr 22
Allen, Chad: Birth, Jun 5
Allen, Debbie: Birth, Jan 16
Allen, Deborah: Birth, Sep 30
Allen, Ethan: Birth Anniv, Jan 21
Allen, George: Birth, Mar 8
Allen, Joan: Birth, Aug 20
Allen, Karen: Birth, Oct 5
Allen, Marcus: Birth, Mar 26
Allen, Nancy: Birth, Jun 24
Allen, Ray: Birth, Jul 20
Allen, Rex, Days (Willcox, AZ), Oct 1
Allen, Steve: Birth Anniv, Dec 26
Allen, Tim: Birth, Jun 13
Allen, Woody: Birth, Dec 1
Allergy/Asthma Awareness Month, Natl, May 1
Alley, Kirstie: Birth, Jan 12
Allilueva, Svetlana: Birth, Feb 28
Allman, Gregg: Birth, Dec 8
All-Northwest Barbershop Ballad Contest (Forest Grove, OR), Mar 5
All-Star Game, First Major League Baseball, Jul 6
All-Star Game, Major League Baseball, Jul 13
Allyson, June: Birth, Oct 7
Almanack, Poor Richard's: Anniv, Dec 28
Aloha Fest Opening Ceremony & Royal Pa'ina (Honolulu, HI), Sep 10
Alomar, Roberto: Birth, Feb 5
Alou, Moises: Birth, Jul 3
Alpert, Herb: Birth, Mar 31
Alpha Kappa Alpha Sorority Founded: Anniv, Jan 15
Alphabet Day (Korea), Oct 9
Alston, Charles H.: Birth Anniv, Nov 28
Alt, Carol: Birth, Dec 1
Altamont Concert: Anniv, Dec 6
Altman, Robert: Birth, Feb 20
Alvin Show TV Premiere: Anniv, Oct 4
Alzheimer, Alois: Birth Anniv, Jun 14
Alzheimer's Disease Month, Natl, Nov 1
AMA Founded: Anniv, May 5
AMD/Low Vision Awareness Month, Feb 1
Ameche, Don: Birth Anniv, May 31
America Recycles Day, Nov 15
America the Beautiful Published, Jul 4
America, God Bless, 1st Performed: Anniv, Nov 11
America, Spirit of (Decatur, IL), Jul 3
American Assn for the Advancement of Science Annual Meeting (Denver, CO), Feb 13
American Bandstand TV Premiere: Anniv, Aug 5
American Bandstand: Dick Clark Retires: Anniv, Mar 23
American Council on Education Annual Mtg (Miami Beach, FL), Feb 28
American Crossword Puzzle Tournament (Stamford, CT), Mar 12
American Dental Assn: Annual Session (Philadelphia, PA), Sep 30
American Dietetic Assn Food & Nutrition Conf & Expo (Anaheim, CA), Oct 2
American Education Week, Nov 14
American Federation of Labor Founded: Anniv, Dec 8
American Flight Crashes at O'Hare: Anniv, May 25
American Heritage Bluegrass Fest (Arrow Rock, MO), Sep 18
American Historical Assn Annual Meeting (Washington, DC), Jan 8
American History Essay Contest, Aug 1
American Idol TV Premiere: Anniv, Jun 11
American Indian Heritage Day (AL), Oct 11
American Indian Heritage Month, Natl, Nov 1
American Library Assn Annual Conference (Orlando, FL), Jun 24
American Library Assn Founded: Anniv, Oct 6
American Massage Therapy Assn, Natl Conv (Nashville, TN), Oct 6
American Psychological Assn Annual Meeting (Honolulu, HI), Jul 28
American Red Cross: Founding Anniv, May 21
American Samoa,
Park of American Samoa Authorized, Natl: Anniv, **Oct 31**
White Sunday, **Oct 10**
American Top 40 Radio Program: Anniv, Jul 4
Americans with Disabilities Act: Anniv, Jul 26
America's Cup: Intl Yacht Race, Aug 22
America's First Department Store (Salt Lake City, UT), Oct 16
America's Kids Day, Jun 27
America's Subway Day: Anniv, Mar 29
Ames, Bruce N.: Birth, Dec 16
Amis, Kingsley: Birth Anniv, Apr 16
Amis, Martin: Birth, Aug 25
Amis, Suzy: Birth, Jan 5
Amish Acres Arts & Crafts Fest (Nappanee, IN), Aug 12
Amistad Seized: Anniv, Aug 29
Amnesty for Polygamists: Anniv, Jan 4
Amos 'n' Andy TV Premiere: Anniv, Jun 28
Amos, Tori: Birth, Aug 22

Index ☆ Chase's 2004 Calendar of Events ☆

Ampere—Arizona

Ampere, Andre: Birth Anniv, Jan 22
Amtrak: Anniv, May 1
Amundsen, Roald: Birth Anniv, Jul 16
Ancestor Appreciation Day, Sep 27
Ancestor Honor Day, May 24
Andersen, Hans Christian: Birth Anniv, Apr 2
Anderson, Dame Judith: Birth Anniv, Feb 10
Anderson, George Lee (Sparky): Birth, Feb 22
Anderson, Gillian: Birth, Aug 9
Anderson, Harry: Birth, Oct 14
Anderson, Helen E.M.: First Woman US Ambassador: Anniv, Oct 28
Anderson, Ian: Birth, Aug 10
Anderson, Jack: Birth, Oct 19
Anderson, Kevin: Birth, Jan 13
Anderson, Loni: Birth, Aug 5
Anderson, Louie: Birth, Mar 23
Anderson, Lynn: Birth, Sep 26
Anderson, Marian: Birth Anniv, Feb 27
Anderson, Marian: Easter Concert: Anniv, Apr 9
Anderson, Melissa Sue: Birth, Sep 26
Anderson, Pamela: Birth, Jul 1
Anderson, Paul Thomas: Birth, Jun 26
Anderson, Richard Dean: Birth, Jan 23
Anderson, Sherwood: Birth Anniv, Sep 13
Anderson, Wes: Birth, May 1
Andersson, Bibi: Birth, Nov 11
Andorra: National Holiday, Sep 8
Andrea Doria Sinks: Anniv, Jul 25
Andree, Salomon A.: Birth Anniv, Oct 18
Andress, Ursula: Birth, Mar 19
Andretti, Mario: Birth, Feb 28
Andretti, Michael: Birth, Oct 5
Andrew, Prince: Birth, Feb 19
Andrews, Julie: Birth, Oct 1
Andy Griffith Show TV Premiere: Anniv, Oct 3
Andy Williams Show TV Premiere: Anniv, Jul 2
Anesthetic First Used in Surgery: Anniv, Mar 30
Angel Day, Be an, Aug 22
Angel, Vanessa: Birth, Nov 10
Angelou, Maya: Birth, Apr 4
Anglund, Joan Walsh: Birth, Jan 3
Angola,
- Armed Struggle Day, **Feb 4**
- Day of the National Hero, **Sep 17**
- Independence Day, **Nov 11**

Animal Poison Prevention Week, Natl, Mar 14
Animals Aloud Month, Oct 1
Animals. See also Birds; Dogs; Horses; Sled Dogs,
- Adopt-A-Shelter-Cat Month, **Jun 1**
- Adopt-A-Shelter-Dog Month, **Oct 1**
- AFRMA Display & Show (Costa Mesa, CA), **Jul 9**
- AFRMA Display at America's Family Pet Expo (Costa Mesa, CA), **Apr 2**
- AFRMA Fancy Rat & Mouse Display (Newhall, CA), **May 16**
- Animal Poison Prevention Week, Natl, **Mar 14**
- Animal Safety and Protection Month, Natl, **Oct 1**
- Answer Your Cat's Question Day, **Jan 22**
- Bark in the Park (Chicago, IL), **May 1**
- Barnegat Bay Crab Race and Fest (Seaside Heights, NJ), **Aug 29**
- Be Kind to Animals Week, **May 2**
- Blessing of Animals at the Cathedral (Mexico), **Jan 17**
- Boo at the Zoo (Cleveland, OH), **Oct 22**
- Buffalo Auction (Custer, SD), **Nov 20**
- Buffalo Roundup (Custer, SD), **Oct 4**
- Burro Race (Leadville, CO), **Aug 8**
- Buzzard Day Fest (Glendive, MT), **Jun 12**
- Cat Fest (Belgium), **Feb 26**
- Cloning of an Adult Animal, First: Anniv, **Feb 23**
- Cow Appreciation Day (Woodstock, VT), **Jul 17**
- Cow Milked While Flying: Anniv, **Feb 18**
- Crufts Dog Show (Birmingham, England), **Mar 4**
- Day of the Seal Celeb, Intl (Point Pleasant Beach, NJ), **Mar 20**
- Dog Bite Prevention Week, Natl, **May 16**
- Dog Week, Natl, **Sep 19**
- Elephant Appreciation Day, **Sep 22**
- Elephant Round-Up at Surin (Thailand), **Nov 20**
- Faith City Kennel Club Dog Show (Wichita Falls, TX), **Feb 27**
- Fancy Rat and Mouse Annual Show (Riverside, CA), **Jan 17**
- Farm Animals Awareness Week, Natl, **Sep 19**
- Farm Sanctuary's Annual Pignic (Watkins Glen, NY), **Jul 4**
- Field Trial Chmpshp, Natl (Bird Dogs) (Grand Junction, TN), **Feb 9**
- First US Zoo: Anniv (Philadelphia, PA), **Jul 1**
- Goat Days (Millington, TN), **Sep 10**
- Gorilla Born in Captivity, First: Anniv, **Dec 22**
- Grand American Coon Hunt (Orangeburg, SC), **Jan 2**
- Hairball Awareness Day, Natl, **Apr 30**
- Happy Mew Year for Cats Day, **Jan 2**
- Haute Dog Charity Easter Parade (Long Beach, CA), **Apr 11**
- Haute Dog Charity Howl'oween Parade (Long Beach, CA), **Oct 31**
- Ho Sheep Market (Denmark), **Aug 28**
- Homeless Animals Day, Natl/Candlelight Vigils, **Aug 21**
- Hug Your Cat Day, **Jun 4**
- Humanatee/St. Marks Fest (St. Marks, FL), **May 15**
- Jumping Frog Jubilee/Calaveras Fair (Angel Camp, CA), **May 13**
- Koko the Gorilla: Birth, **Jul 4**
- Lizard Race, World's Greatest (Lovington, NM), **Jul 3**
- Miss Crustacean/Ocean City Creep (Ocean City, NJ), **Aug 4**
- Moth-er Day, **Mar 14**
- Mule Day, **Oct 26**
- Mule Day (Columbia, TN), **Apr 1**
- Mutt's Day, **Jul 31**
- North Star Classic (Valley City, ND), **Dec 3**
- Operation Santa Paws, **Dec 6**
- Orange City Blue Spring Manatee Fest (Orange City, FL), **Jan 24**
- Penguin Awareness Day (Point Pleasant Beach, NJ), **Jan 17**
- Pet First Aid Awareness Month, Natl, **Apr 1**
- Pet Owners Independence Day, **Apr 18**
- Pet Parade (LaGrange, IL), **Jun 5**
- Pet Week, Natl, **May 2**
- Pig Day, Natl, **Mar 1**
- Prevention of Animal Cruelty Month, **Apr 1**
- Prof Pet Sitters Week, Natl, **Mar 7**
- Rattlesnake Derby (Mangum, OK), **Apr 23**
- Reptile Awareness Day (Point Pleasant Beach, NJ), **Oct 16**
- Riverfest (Columbus, GA), **Apr 23**
- Save the Rhino Day, **May 1**
- Sea Monkey Day, Natl, **May 16**
- Seal, Intl Day of the, **Mar 22**
- Seeing Eye Established: Anniv, **Jan 29**
- Shamu's Birthday, **Sep 26**
- Snake Hunt (Cross Fork, PA), **Jun 26**
- Spay Day USA, **Feb 24**
- Squirrel Appreciation Day, **Jan 21**
- Squirrel Awareness Week, **Oct 3**
- Stock Dog Trials & Farm Fest, US Open (Dawsonville, GA), **Oct 1**
- Take Your Dog to Work Day, **Jun 25**
- Taylor Horsefest (Taylor, ND), **Jul 30**
- Toad Suck Daze (Conway, AR), **Apr 30**
- Turkey Vultures Return to the Living Sign (Canisteo, NY), **Mar 11**
- Turtle Races (Danville, IL), **Jun 12**
- Walk Your Pet Month, **Jan 1**
- Wayne Chicken Show (Wayne, NE), **Jul 9**
- Westminster Kennel Club Dog Show (New York, NY), **Feb 9**
- What If Cats and Dogs Had Opposable Thumbs Day, **Mar 3**
- Wild Horse Chasing (Japan), **Jul 23**
- Wilderness Wildlife Week of Nature (Pigeon Forge, TN), **Jan 10**
- Wool Day: Sheep to Shawl/Border Collies (Woodstock, VT), **Sep 19**
- Woolly Worm Fest (Banner Elk, NC), **Oct 16**
- World Farm Animals Day, **Oct 2**
- World Habitat Awareness Month, **Apr 1**
- World Turtle Day, **May 23**

Aniston, Jennifer: Birth, Feb 11
Anka, Paul: Birth, Jul 30
Annan, Kofi: Birth, Apr 8
Annapolis Convention: Anniv, Sep 11
Anne, Princess: Birth, Aug 15
Annenberg, Walter: Birth Anniv, Mar 13
Annie Oakley Days (Greenville, OH), Jul 23
Ann-Margret: Birth, Apr 28
Annunciation, Feast of, Mar 25
Anonymous Giving Week, Mar 20
Another Look Unlimited Day, Sep 7
Another World TV Premiere: Anniv, May 4
Anson, Cap: Birth Anniv, Apr 17
Anspach, Susan: Birth, Nov 23
Answer Your Cat's Question Day, Jan 22
Ant, Adam: Birth, Nov 3
Antarctica: Shackleton, Ernest: Birth Anniv, Feb 15
Anthem Day, Natl, Mar 3
Anthony, Marc: Birth, Sep 16
Anthony, Susan B.: Day, Feb 15
Anthony, Susan B.: Fined for Voting: Anniv, Jun 6
Anti-Boredom Month, Natl, Jul 1
Antietam, Battle of: Anniv, Sep 17
Antigua and Barbuda,
- August Monday, **Aug 2**
- Independence Day, **Nov 1**

Antique Power Exhib (Burton, OH), Jul 24
Antiques,
- Antique Show & Sale (Weston, MO), **Mar 6**
- Antique Show (Somerset, PA), **Aug 14**
- Antique Valentine Exhibit (Clinton, MD), **Jan 22**
- Antiques & Collectibles Show & Sale, Mid-Summer (Millville, NJ), **Jul 24**
- Antiques in Schoharie (Schoharie, NY), **Mar 6**
- Antiques on the Diamond (Ligonier, PA), **Jun 12**
- Art & Antiques at the American Club (Kohler, WI), **Mar 13**
- Chelsea Antiques Fair (London, England), **Mar 17**
- Chester Antiques and Fine Art Show (Cheshire, England), **Feb 12**
- Chicago Southland's Finest Antiques Show (Tinley Park, IL), **Nov 27**
- Chicago Southland's Finest Antiques Show (Tinley Park, IL), **Jun 12**
- Collectables-Antiques-Craft-Flea Market Sale (Sauk Centre, MN), **Jul 17**
- Cotton Pickin' Fair (Gay, GA), **May 1**
- Gettysburg Outdoor Antique Show (Gettysburg, PA), **May 22**
- Gettysburg Outdoor Antique Show (Gettysburg, PA), **Sep 25**
- Greenlawn Antiques Show (Greenlawn, NY), **Mar 13**
- Kechi Fall Outdoor Antique Swap Meet (Kechi, KS), **Sep 25**
- Kechi Spring Outdoor Antique Swap Meet & Flea Market (Kechi, KS), **May 1**
- Kechi's Antique Country Christmas (Kechi, KS), **Nov 20**
- Landon Azalea Garden Fest/Antique Show (Bethesda, MD), **Apr 30**
- Mid-Winter Antiques Show (Millville, NJ), **Feb 7**
- New Oxford Outdoor Antique Show (Gettysburg, PA), **Jun 19**
- Olde-Time Antiques and Collectibles Faire (Toms River, NJ), **Sep 4**
- Orange Historical Society Antique Show (Orange, CT), **Feb 28**
- Pec Thing (Pecatonica, IL), **May 15**
- Petersfield Antiques Fair (Petersfield, England), **Feb 6**
- Seven Days in May (Chapel Hill, NC), **May 21**
- Suydam Homestead and Barn Museum (Centerport, NY), **Jun 6**
- Valentown Antique Peddler's Market (Victor, NY), **Aug 1**
- Vegaspex (Las Vegas, NV), **May 21**
- West London Antiques & Fine Art Fair (London, England), **Jan 15**

Anti-Saloon League Founded: Anniv, May 24
Anton, Susan: Birth, Oct 12
Antonioni, Michelangelo: Birth, Sep 29
Anwar, Gabrielle: Birth, Feb 4
Anxiety Disorders Screening Day, Natl, May 5
ANZAC Day, Apr 25
Apache Wars Began: Anniv, Feb 4
Apartheid Law, South Africa Repeals Last: Anniv, Jun 17
Apgar, Virginia: Birth Anniv, Jun 7
A'phabet Day, Dec 25
Aphasia Awareness Month, Natl, Jun 1
Aphelion, Earth at, Jul 5
Aplastic Anemia Awareness Week, Natl, Dec 1
Apollo I: Spacecraft Fire: Anniv, Jan 27
Appert, Nicolas: Birth Anniv, Oct 23
Apple Blossom Fest (Annapolis Valley, NS, Canada), May 26
Apple Blossom Fest (Gettysburg, PA), May 1
Apple Blossom Fest, Washington State (Wenatchee, WA), Apr 29
Apple Butter Makin' Days (Mt Vernon, MO), Oct 8
Apple Butter Stirrin' (Coshocton, OH), Oct 15
Apple Fest (Topeka, KS), Oct 3
Apple Fest, Jackson County (Jackson, OH), Sep 21
Apple Fest, Kentucky (Paintsville, KY), Oct 1
Apple Fest, Vermont (Springfield, VT), Oct 9
Apple Harvest Fest (Gettysburg, PA), Oct 2
Apple II Computer Released: Anniv, Jun 5
Apple Week, Beatles' Natl: Anniv, Aug 11
Apple, Fiona: Birth, Sep 13
Applegate, Christina: Birth, Nov 25
Applejack Fest (Nebraska City, NE), Sep 18
Appleseed Days, Johnny (Lake City, MN), Oct 2
Appleseed, Johnny: Birth Anniv, Sep 26
Appleseed: Johnny Appleseed Day, Mar 11
April Fools' Day, Apr 1
Aquarius Begins, Jan 20
Aquino, Benigno: Assassination Anniv, Aug 21
Aquino, Corazon: Birth, Jan 25
Arab Oil Embargo Lifted: Anniv, Mar 13
Arab-Israeli War (Yom Kippur War), Oct 6
Arafat Returns to Palestine: Anniv, Jul 1
Arafat, Yasser: Birth, Aug 4
Arbor Day (Arizona), Apr 30
Arbor Day (Florida), Jan 16
Arbor Day Fest (Nebraska City, NE), Apr 30
Arbor Day, Natl, Apr 30
Arcadia Daze (Arcadia, MI), Jul 23
Archeology: Iceman Mummy Discovered: Anniv, Sep 19
Archer, Anne: Birth, Aug 25
Arches Natl Park Established: Anniv, Nov 12
Archibald, Nate: Birth, Sep 2
Architecture: First Skyscraper: Anniv, May 1
Area Codes Introduced: Anniv, Nov 10
Argentina,
- Death Anniversary of San Martin, **Aug 17**
- Falkland Islands War: Anniv, **Apr 2**
- Federation of Library Assns Annual Conference, Intl (Buenos Aires), **Aug 21**
- Flag Day, **Jun 20**
- Independence Day, **Jul 9**
- Revolution Day, **May 25**

Aries Begins, Mar 21
Arizona,
- Admission Day: Anniv, **Feb 14**
- All States Picnic (Yuma), **Jan 7**
- American Family Day, **Aug 1**
- Apache Wars Began: Anniv, **Feb 4**
- Arbor Day, **Apr 30**
- Arizona Renaissance Fest (Apache Junction), **Feb 7**
- Arizona State Fair (Phoenix), **Oct 7**
- Butterfield Overland Stage Days (Benson), **Oct 8**
- Colorado River Crossing Balloon Festival (Yuma), **Nov 19**
- Constitution Commemoration Day, **Sep 17**
- Cowboy Hall of Fame Ceremony (Willcox), **Sep 30**

☆ Chase's 2004 Calendar of Events ☆ Index

Arizona (cont'd.)—Arts

Desert Foothills Music Fest (Carefree), **Feb 6**
Fest of the West, Natl (Scottsdale), **Mar 18**
Fiesta De Los Vaqueros (Tucson), **Feb 25**
Four Corner States Bluegrass Fest (Wickenburg), **Nov 12**
Gold Rush Days (Wickenburg), **Feb 13**
Grand Canyon Natl Park Established: Anniv, **Feb 26**
Kyl, Jon: Birth, **Apr 25**
Lost Dutchman Days (Apache Junction), **Feb 27**
McCain, John Sidney, III: Birth, **Aug 29**
Midnight at the Oasis (Yuma), **Mar 5**
Napolitano, Janet: Birth, **Nov 29**
Petrified Forest Natl Park Established: Anniv, **Dec 9**
Rex Allen Days (Willcox), **Oct 1**
RV Workers and Workampers Day (Yuma), **Jan 9**
Scottsdale Culinary Fest (Scottsdale), **Apr 14**
Sedona Arts Fest (West Sedona), **Oct 9**
Sedona Chamber Music Festival (Sedona), **May 12**
Sonora Showcase (Yuma), **Jan 20**
Southwest Senior Chmpshp (Yuma), **Jan 20**
Tempe Spring Fest of Arts (Tempe), **Mar 26**
Tostitos Fiesta Bowl (Tempe), **Jan 2**
Wings Over Willcox—Sandhill Crane Celebration (Willcox), **Jan 16**
Winterfest (Flagstaff), **Feb 1**
Arkansas,
Admission Day: Anniv, **Jun 15**
Bluegrass Fest (Hope), **May 7**
Chicken and Egg Fest (Prescott), **Jun 4**
Chuckwagon Races, Natl Chmpshp (Clinton), **Sep 3**
Clothesline Fair (Prairie Grove), **Sep 4**
Dermott's Annual Crawfish Fest (Dermott), **May 14**
Duck-Calling Contest/Wings Over Prairie Fest (Stuttgart), **Nov 26**
Eagles Et Cetera (Bismarck), **Jan 23**
Fordyce on the Cotton Belt Fest (Fordyce), **Apr 19**
Great Arkansas Pig-Out (Morrilton), **Aug 6**
Hope Watermelon Fest (Hope), **Aug 12**
Hot Springs Natl Park Established: Anniv, **Mar 4**
Huckabee, Mike: Birth, **Aug 24**
Lincoln, Blanche Lambert: Birth, **Sep 30**
Magnolia Blossom Fest (Magnolia), **May 13**
NCAA Indoor Track/Field Chmpshps (Fayetteville), **Mar 12**
Ozark UFO Conf (Eureka Springs), **Apr 9**
Petit Jean Antique Auto Show/Swap Meet (Morrilton), **Jun 15**
Petit Jean Fall Antique Auto Swap Meet (Morrilton), **Sep 15**
Picklefest (Atkins), **May 21**
Pryor, Mark: Birth, **Jan 10**
Quadrangle Fest (Texarkana), **Sep 11**
Riverfest (Little Rock), **May 28**
Rotary Tiller Race, World Chmpshp/Purplehull Pea Fest (Emerson), **Jun 25**
Smackover Oil Town Fest (Smackover), **Jun 16**
State Fair and Livestock Show (Little Rock), **Oct 8**
Steak Cook-off World Chmpshp (Magnolia), **May 15**
Toad Suck Daze (Conway), **Apr 30**
White River Water Carnival (Batesville), **Aug 6**
Arkin, Adam: Birth, Aug 19
Arkin, Alan: Birth, Mar 26
Arlen, Harold: Birth Anniv, Feb 15
Armani, Giorgio: Birth, Jul 11
Armatrading, Joan: Birth, Dec 9
Armed Forces Day (Egypt), Oct 6
Armed Forces Day (Pres Proc), May 15
Armed Forces Unified: Anniv, Jul 26
Armenia,
Armenian Martyrs Day, **Apr 24**
Earthquake of 1988: Anniv, **Dec 7**
Independence Day, **Sep 21**
Armenian Christmas, Jan 6
Armistice Day, Nov 11
Armistice Day: See Veterans Day, Nov 11
Armstrong, BJ: Birth, Sep 9
Armstrong, Darrell: Birth, Jun 22
Armstrong, Lance: Birth, Sep 18
Armstrong, Louis: Birth Anniv, Aug 4
Armstrong, Neil: Birth, Aug 5
Armstrong, Trace: Birth, Oct 5
Armstrong-Jones, Anthony: Birth, Mar 7
Army Established: Anniv, Jun 14
Army, US: First Desegregation: Anniv, Jul 26
Arnaz, Desi, Jr: Birth, Jan 19
Arnaz, Desi: Birth Anniv, Mar 2
Arnaz, Lucie: Birth, Jul 17
Arness, James: Birth, May 26
Arnold, Benedict: Birth Anniv, Jan 14
Arnold, Eddy: Birth, May 15
Arnold, Henry "Hap": Birth Anniv, Jun 25
Arnold, Matthew: Birth Anniv, Dec 24
Arnold, Sir Malcolm: Birth, Oct 21
Arnold, Tom: Birth, Mar 6
Arquette, Courteney Cox: Birth, Jun 15
Arquette, David: Birth, Sep 8
Arquette, Patricia: Birth, Apr 8
Arquette, Rosanna: Birth, Aug 10
Arrington, LaVar: Birth, Jun 20
Arrow Rock Heritage Craft Fest (Arrow Rock, MO), Oct 9
Arsenio Hall Show TV Premiere: Anniv, Jan 3
Art Deco Weekend Fest (Miami Beach, FL), Jan 16
Art Linkletter's House Party TV Premiere: Anniv, Sep 1
Arthritis Month, Natl, May 1
Arthur Murray Party TV Premiere: Anniv, Jul 20
Arthur, Beatrice: Birth, May 13
Arthur, Chester A.: Birth Anniv, Oct 5
Arthur, Ellen: Birth Anniv, Aug 30
Arthur, Jean: Birth Anniv, Oct 17
Articles of Confederation: Ratification Anniv, Mar 1
Articles of Peace: Anniv, Nov 30
Arts and Crafts. See also Quilt,
Adelphian Club Christmas Bazaar (Kennett, MO), **Dec 4**
Alpenfest (Gaylord, MI), **Jul 13**
American Club Teddy Bear and Doll Classic (Kohler, WI), **Feb 21**
Amish Acres Arts & Crafts Fest (Nappanee, IN), **Aug 12**
Appalachian Potters Market (Marion, NC), **Dec 4**
Arrow Rock Heritage Craft Fest (Arrow Rock, MO), **Oct 9**
Artists in the Park (Wolfeboro, NH), **Aug 18**
Arts & Crafts Fest (Loveladies, NJ), **Jul 31**
Arts & Crafts Fest (Rolla, MO), **Oct 2**
Baltimore Highlands Arts & Crafts Fest (Baltimore, MD), **Sep 19**
Belsnickel Craft Show (Boyertown, PA), **Nov 26**
Berea Craft Fest (Berea, KY), **Jul 9**
Blue Claw Crab Craft Show & Crab Race (Harvey Cedars, NJ), **Aug 14**
Blue Ridge Folklife Fest (Ferrum, VA), **Oct 23**
Boardwalk Art Show & Fest (Virginia Beach, VA), **Jun 17**
Calico Crafts Bazaar (Gold Beach, OR), **Nov 20**
Cane Grinding and Crafts Fest (Savannah, GA), **Nov 13**
Capitol Hill People's Fair (Denver, CO), **Jun 5**
Carson City Rendezvous (Carson City, NV), **Jun 11**
Catoctin ColorFest Arts/Crafts (Thurmont, MD), **Oct 9**
Catonsville Arts & Crafts Fest (Catonsville, MD), **Sep 12**
Celebration of Fine Crafts (Chattanooga, TN), **Oct 2**
Children's Craft Day, Natl, **Mar 14**
Chimneyville Crafts Fest (Jackson, MS), **Dec 4**
Christkindl Market (Canton, OH), **Nov 11**
Christmas Craft Show (Aiken, SC), **Dec 3**
Christmas Craft Show (York, PA), **Dec 5**
Clothesline Fair (Prairie Grove, AR), **Sep 4**
Commonwheel Arts and Crafts Fest (Manitou Springs, CO), **Sep 4**
Community Christmas Bazaar (Gold Beach, OR), **Dec 4**
Corn Hill Arts Fest (Rochester, NY), **Jul 10**
Country Affair (Menomonee Falls, WI), **Oct 16**
Country Fest and Auction (Deep Creek Lake, MD), **Aug 28**
Craft Day by the Bay (Harvey Cedars, NJ), **Jul 3**
Craft Fair of the Southern Highlands (Asheville, NC), **Jul 15**
Craft Month, Natl, **Mar 1**
Craftsmen's Christmas Classic Arts & Crafts Fest (Greensboro, NC), **Nov 26**
Craftsmen's Christmas Classic Arts & Crafts Fest (Richmond, VA), **Nov 5**
Craftsmen's Classic Arts & Crafts Fest (Richmond, VA), **Mar 12**
Craftsmen's Classic Arts & Crafts Fest (Chantilly, VA), **Oct 15**
Craftsmen's Classic Arts & Crafts Fest (Chantilly, VA), **Mar 26**
Craftsmen's Classic Arts & Crafts Fest (Columbia, SC), **Mar 5**
Craftsmen's Classic Arts & Crafts Fest (Greensboro, NC), **Apr 2**
Craftsmen's Classic Arts & Crafts Fest (Myrtle Beach, SC), **Aug 6**
Craftsmen's Classic Arts & Crafts Fest (Roanoke, VA), **Oct 1**
Dankfest (Harmony, PA), **Aug 28**
Downtown Art Street Fair (Fargo, ND), **Jul 15**
Dyersville Fest of the Arts (Dyersville, IA), **Sep 25**
Easter Craft Show (York, PA), **Feb 8**
Fair in the Square Crafters Show (Woodstock, IL), **Jul 11**
Faire on the Square Art & Craft Fair (Baraboo, WI), **Oct 9**
Fall Country Jamboree (Barberville, FL), **Nov 6**
Fall Fest of Arts and Crafts (Washington, MO), **Sep 24**
Fall State Craft Fest (Richboro, PA), **Oct 15**
Fallasburg Fall Fest (Lowell, MI), **Sep 25**
Fest of Fine Craft (Millville, NJ), **Oct 2**
Fest of the Little Hills (St. Charles, MO), **Aug 20**
Fest-in-the-Park (Nutley, NJ), **Sep 12**
Festival 2004: Fest of Fine Arts and Fine Crafts (Dalton, GA), **Sep 18**
Fine Arts & Crafts Fest (Woodstock, CT), **Oct 16**
Fine Arts and Crafts Fest (New Ipswich, NH), **Oct 2**
Frankfort Fall Fest (Frankfort, IL), **Sep 4**
Frederick Fest of the Arts (Frederick, MD), **Jun 5**
Gift Fest, Intl (Fairfield, PA), **Nov 4**
Gift of the Waters Pageant & Art Fest in the Park (Thermopolis, WY), **Aug 6**
Great Mississippi River Arts/Crafts Fest (Hannibal, MO), **May 29**
Greater Pittsburgh Arts & Crafts Holiday Spectacular (Greensburg, PA), **Nov 5**
Helen Keller Fest (Tuscumbia, AL), **Jun 24**
Heritage Days Fest (Cumberland, MD), **Jun 12**
Holiday Craft Fair (Lancaster, PA), **Nov 27**
Holiday Craft Show (Schoharie, NY), **Nov 20**
Holiday Craft Show (York, PA), **Oct 17**
Holzfest (Amana, IA), **Aug 20**
Into the Wood Show (Millville, NJ), **Apr 3**
Iroquois Indian Fest (Howes Cave, NY), **Sep 4**
Jay Peak Annual Arts & Crafts Fair (Jay, VT), **Oct 9**
Jonathan Hager Frontier Craft Days (Hagerstown, MD), **Aug 7**
Jours de Fete (Ste. Genevieve, MO), **Aug 14**
Jubilee (Bennettsville, SC), **May 8**
Keystone Country Fair (Altoona, PA), **Sep 10**
Lavallette Heritage Arts & Crafts Show (Lavallette, NJ), **Jul 25**
League of NH Craftsmen Annual Craftsmen's Fair (Newbury, NH), **Aug 7**
Liberty Spring on the Square Festival (Liberty, MO), **May 15**
Little Balkans Days/Folklife Fest (Pittsburg, KS), **Sep 2**
Little Falls Arts/Crafts (Little Falls, MN), **Sep 11**
Lovington Fall Arts/Crafts Fest (Lovington, NM), **Nov 6**
Main Street Fest (Franklin, TN), **Apr 24**
Meet the Artists & Artisans Show (Milford Green, CT), **May 15**
Melrose Plantation Arts/Crafts Fest (Melrose, LA), **Jun 12**
Midsummer Nights' Fair (Norman, OK), **Jul 16**
Mifflin-Juniata Arts Fest (Lewistown, PA), **May 22**
Missouri Day Fest (Trenton, MO), **Oct 15**
Mossy Creek Barnyard Fest (Warner Robins, GA), **Apr 17**
Mount Pleasant Glass & Ethnic Fest (Mt Pleasant, PA), **Sep 24**
Mountain Craft Days (Somerset, PA), **Sep 10**
New Beginning Fest (Coffeyville, KS), **Apr 23**
North Park's Colonial Arts & Crafts Fest (Pittsburgh, PA), **Sep 17**
North Texas Arts & Crafts Show (Wichita Falls, TX), **Mar 27**
Ocean County Wildfowl Art & Decoy Show (Brick, NJ), **Feb 14**
Original Raggedy Ann & Andy Fest (Arcola, IL), **May 22**
Palm Harbor Arts/Crafts/Music Fest (Palm Harbor, FL), **Dec 4**
Peddler's Village Scarecrow Contest and Outdoor Display (Lahaska, PA), **Sep 13**
Pennsylvania Arts & Crafts Christmas Fest (Washington, PA), **Oct 15**
Pennsylvania Arts & Crafts Colonial Fest (Greensburg, PA), **Sep 3**
Pennsylvania Arts & Crafts Country Fest (Uniontown, PA), **May 28**
Pinchot Lake Festival and Craft Show (Wellsville, PA), **May 15**
Pittsburgh Arts & Crafts Spring Fever Fest (PA), **Mar 26**
Pocono State Craft Fair (Shawnee-on-the-Delaware, PA), **Aug 21**
Powers' Crossroads Country Fair/Art Fest (Newnan, GA), **Sep 4**
Quilt Odyssey (Gettysburg, PA), **Aug 5**
Quilting Day, Natl, **Mar 20**
Rappahannock River Waterfowl Show (White Stone, VA), **Mar 20**
Sacajawea Heritage Days (Salmon, ID), **Aug 20**
Salem Art Fair and Fest (Salem, OR), **Jul 16**
Sedona Arts Fest (West Sedona, AZ), **Oct 9**
Sewing Month, Natl, **Sep 1**
Sharon on the Green Arts and Crafts Fair (Sharon,CT), **Aug 7**
Sheep to Shawl Festival (Savannah, GA), **Mar 20**
Sheyenne Valley Arts/Crafts (Fort Ransom, ND), **Sep 25**
Sidewalk Arts Fest (Sioux Falls, SD), **Sep 11**
Southeastern Wildlife Expo (Charleston, SC), **Feb 13**
Spinning and Weaving Week, **Oct 4**
Splinterfest (Amana, IA), **Jun 18**
Spring Arts Fest (Gainesville, FL), **Apr 17**
Spring Craft Celeb (Richboro, PA), **May 15**
Spring Craft Show (York, PA), **Apr 18**
Springs Folk Fest (Springs, PA), **Oct 1**
State Craft Fair (Lancaster, PA), **Jul 23**
Sugarloaf Art Fair (Novi, MI), **Apr 16**
Sugarloaf Art Fair (Novi, MI), **Oct 22**
Sugarloaf Crafts Fest (Chantilly, VA), **Jan 30**
Sugarloaf Crafts Fest (Chantilly, VA), **Apr 30**
Sugarloaf Crafts Fest (Fort Washington, PA), **Mar 19**
Sugarloaf Crafts Fest (Fort Washington, PA), **Oct 15**
Sugarloaf Crafts Fest (Gaithersburg, MD), **Apr 2**
Sugarloaf Crafts Fest (Gaithersburg, MD), **Oct 8**
Sugarloaf Crafts Fest (Gaithersburg, MD), **Nov 18**
Sugarloaf Crafts Fest (Gaithersburg, MD), **Dec 10**
Sugarloaf Crafts Fest (Manassas, VA), **Sep 10**
Sugarloaf Crafts Fest (Somerset, NJ), **Mar 12**
Sugarloaf Crafts Fest (Somerset, NJ), **Oct 29**
Sugarloaf Crafts Fest (Timonium, MD), **Apr 23**
Sugarloaf Crafts Fest (Timonium, MD), **Oct 1**
Summer Craft Show (York, PA), **Jul 25**
Swappin' Meetin' (Cumberland, KY), **Oct 1**
Taca Fall Crafts Fair (Nashville, TN), **Sep 24**
Tarpon Springs Arts & Crafts Fest (Tarpon Springs, FL), **Apr 3**
Tempe Spring Fest of Arts (Tempe, AZ), **Mar 26**

Index ☆ Chase's 2004 Calendar of Events ☆
Arts (cont'd)—Avedon

Totah Fest (Farmington, NM), Aug 27
Virginia Spring Show (Richmond, VA), Mar 11
Ward World Championship Waterfowl Carving Competition (Ocean City, MD), Apr 23
Waterfowl Fest (Easton, MD), Nov 12
Wichita West Spring Arts/Crafts Show (Wichita Falls, TX), Apr 10
Winfield Art-in-the-Park Fest (Winfield, KS), Oct 2
Wisconsin Holiday Market (Kohler, WI), Nov 12
Wyandotte Heritage Days (Wyandotte, MI), Sep 10
Wyandotte Street Art Fair (Wyandotte, MI), Jul 14
Yukon Sourdough Rendezvous (Whitehorse, YT, Canada), Feb 26
Arts, Fine and Performing; Art Shows,
Affaire in Gardens, Beverly Hills (Beverly Hills, CA), May 15
Alabama Jubilee (Decatur, AL), May 29
Ann Arbor Spring Art Fair (Ann Arbor, MI), Mar 27
Ann Arbor Summer Art Fair (Ann Arbor, MI), Jul 21
Ann Arbor Winter Art Fair (Ann Arbor, MI), Nov 20
Art Deco Weekend Fest (Miami Beach, FL), Jan 16
Art Fair & Winefest (Washington, MO), May 21
Art Fair on the Square (Madison, WI), Jul 10
Art Festival (Harvey Cedars, NJ), Jul 18
Art in the Garden (Washington, PA), Sep 11
Art in the Park (Bay Head, NJ), Jun 12
Art in the Park Plus (Oakland Park, FL), Apr 24
Artown (Reno, NV), Jul 1
Arts & Crafts Fest (Stone Mtn Village, GA), Jun 19
Arts in the Park (Kalispell, MT), Jul 23
Arts/Quincy Riverfest (Quincy, IL), Sep 19
Ballet Introduced to the US: Anniv, Feb 7
Bay Harbor Summer Art Fair (Bay Harbor, MI), Aug 6
Belfast Fest at Queen's (Belfast, N Ireland), Oct 31
Buffalo Roundup Arts Fest (Custer, SD), Oct 2
Bumbershoot: The Seattle Arts Fest (Seattle, WA), Sep 3
C.M. Russell Auction Orig Western Art (Great Falls, MT), Mar 17
Cartoonists Against Crime Day, Oct 25
Cartoonists Day, May 5
Chautauqua of the Arts (Columbus, IN), Sep 18
Chowder Fest, Flower and Art Show (Gold Beach, OR), May 1
City of London Fest (London, England), Jun 21
Countryside Village Art Fair (Omaha, NE), Jun 5
Day With(out) Art, Dec 1
Decoy and Wildlife Art Show (Clayton, NY), Jul 16
DeLand Fall Festival of Arts (DeLand, FL), Nov 20
DeLand Outdoor Art Fest (DeLand, FL), Mar 27
Dogwood Arts Fest (Knoxville, TN), Apr 8
Dogwood Fest (Lewiston, ID), Apr 2
Downtown Fest/Art Show (Gainesville, FL), Nov 6
European Fine Art Fair (Maastricht, Netherlands), Mar 5
Fairbanks Summer Arts Fest (Fairbanks, AK), Jul 18
Fest of the North (Ketchikan, AK), Feb 1
Festival 2004: Fest of Fine Arts and Fine Crafts (Dalton, GA), Sep 18
Fine Art & Crafts Show (Lahaska, PA), Jun 5
Fine Art Fair (Woodstock, IL), Sep 11
Foothills Art Fest (Jackson, OH), Oct 15
Grant Wood Art Fest (Stone City–Anamosa, IA), Jun 13
Gum Tree Fest (Tupelo, MS), May 8
Inspire Your Heart With Art Day, Jan 31
Iroquois Arts Showcase (Howes Cave, NY), May 29
Journey's End National Art Exhibition (Astoria, OR), Nov 1
Kennedy Center Imagination Celeb (Colorado Springs, CO), Mar 4
Kohler Arts Center's Outdoor Arts Fest (Sheboygan, WI), Jul 17
Levitt Pavilion Performing Arts/Music Fest (Westport, CT), Jun 20
Little Red School House Annual Art Fair (Willow Springs, IL), Oct 3
Meet the Artists & Artisans Show (Milford Green, CT), May 15
Mural-in-a-Day (Toppenish, WA), Jun 5
Native American Arts Fest (Grants Pass, OR), May 8
Northwest Folklife Fest (Seattle, WA), May 28
Panoply (Huntsville, AL), Apr 23
Red Cloud Indian Art Show (Pine Ridge, SD), Jun 6
Riverfest (Little Rock, AR), May 28
Roanoke Fest in the Park (Roanoke, VA), May 28
Rockport Art Fest (Rockport, TX), Jul 3
Russell, Charles M.: Birth Anniv, Mar 19
Spring Fling (Wichita Falls, TX), Apr 24
Spring Gala (Lovington, NM), May 1
The Present Looks at the Past: Modern Views of the American Revolution (Yorktown, VA), Jan 1
Three Rivers Fest (Fort Wayne, IN), Jul 10
Westmoreland Arts & Heritage Fest (Greensburg, PA), Jul 2
Wildflower Fest of the Arts (Dahlonega, GA), May 15
Wildlife and Western Art Expo (Lakeland, FL), Jan 30
Wine and Garden Fest (Bryan, TX), Apr 17
Youth Art Month, Mar 1
Aruba: Flag Day, Mar 18
As The World Turns TV Premiere: Anniv, Apr 2
As Young as You Feel Day, Mar 22
Asarah B'Tevet, Dec 22
Asarah B'Tevet, Jan 4
Ascension Day, May 20
Ascension of Baha'u'llah, May 29
Ash Wednesday, Feb 25
Ashcroft, John D.: Birth, May 9
Ashcroft, Peggy: Birth Anniv, Dec 22
Ashe, Arthur: Birth Anniv, Jul 10
Asher, Jane: Birth, Apr 5
Ashford, Emmett: Birth Anniv, Nov 23
Ashford, Evelyn: Birth, Apr 15
Ashford, Nickolas: Birth, May 4
Ashley, Elizabeth: Birth, Aug 30
Ashura: Tenth Day (Islamic), Mar 2
Asian Pacific American Heritage Month (Pres Proc), May 1
Asimov, Isaac: Birth Anniv, Jan 2
Asner, Ed: Birth, Nov 15
Aspen Music Fest (Aspen, CO), Jun 24
AspenCash Motorcycle Rally (Ruidoso, NM), May 20
Aspinwall Crosses US on Horseback: Anniv, Jul 8
Assante, Armand: Birth, Oct 4
Assassination Attempt: Pope John Paul II: Anniv, May 13
Assassinations Report, Committee on: Anniv, Mar 29
Assisted Living Week, Natl, Sep 12
Assumption of the Virgin Mary, Aug 15
Astaire, Fred: Birth Anniv, May 10
Astin, John: Birth, Mar 30
Astin, MacKenzie: Birth, May 12
Astin, Sean: Birth, Feb 25
Astor Place Riot: Anniv, May 10
Astor, Brooke: Birth, Mar 30
Astrology,
Aquarius, Jan 20
Aries, Mar 21
Cancer, Jun 21
Capricorn, Dec 22
Gemini, May 21
Leo, Jul 23
Libra, Sep 23
Pisces, Feb 20
Sagittarius, Nov 22
Scorpio, Oct 23
Taurus, Apr 20
Virgo, Aug 23
Astronomers Find New Solar System: Anniv, Apr 15
Astronomy Day, Apr 24
Astronomy Week, Apr 19
AT&T Divestiture: Anniv, Jan 8
Ataturk, Mustafa Kemal: Birth Anniv, Mar 12
Atchison, David R.: Birth Anniv, Aug 11
Atherton, William: Birth, Jul 30
Athletic Training Month, Natl, Mar 1
Atkins, Christopher: Birth, Feb 21
Atkinson, Rowan: Birth, Jan 6
Atlantic Charter Signing: Anniv, Aug 14
Atlantic Telegraph Cable Laid: Anniv, Jul 27
Atlas, Charles: Birth Anniv, Oct 30
Atler, Vanessa: Birth, Feb 17
Atomic Bomb Delivered: Anniv, Jul 26
Atomic Bomb Dropped on Hiroshima: Anniv, Aug 6
Atomic Bomb Dropped on Nagasaki: Anniv, Aug 9
Atomic Bomb Tested: Anniv, Jul 16
Atomic Plant Begun, Oak Ridge: Anniv, Aug 1
Atomic Power Plant Accident, Fermi: Anniv, Oct 5
Attack on America: Anniv, Sep 11
Attack on America: Fall of Kabul: Anniv, Nov 13
Attenborough, David: Birth, May 8
Attenborough, Sir Richard: Birth, Aug 29
Attend Your Grandchild's Birth Day, Natl, Sep 29
Attention Deficit Hyperactivity Disorder Month, Sep 1
Attlee, Clement Richard: Birth Anniv, Jan 3
Attucks, Crispus: Day, Mar 5
Atwood, Margaret: Birth, Nov 18
Auberjonois, Rene: Birth, Jun 1
Auctioneers Day, Natl, Apr 17
Auden, W.H.: Birth Anniv, Feb 2
Audubon, John J.: Birth Anniv, Apr 26
Auerbach, Arnold "Red": Birth, Sep 20
Augusta Futurity (Augusta, GA), Jan 22
Aung San Suu Kyi: Birth, Jun 19
Aura Awareness Day, Intl, Nov 27
Austen, Jane: Birth Anniv, Dec 16
Austin, Stephen F.: Birth Anniv, Nov 3
Austin, Tracy: Birth, Dec 12
Australia,
ANZAC Day, Apr 25
Australia Day, Jan 26
Canberra Day, Mar 15
Commonwealth Formed: Anniv, Jan 1
Eight Hour Day (Labor Day), Mar 1
Picnic Day, Aug 2
Proclamation Day, Dec 28
Recreation Day, Nov 1
Sorry Day, May 26
Austria,
Fasching, Feb 23
Fasching Sunday, Feb 22
Invaded By Nazi Germany: Anniv, Mar 12
National Day, Oct 26
Saint Stephen's Day, Dec 26
Silent Night, Holy Night Celebrations, Dec 24
Authors' Day, Natl, Nov 1
Autism Awareness Month, Natl, Apr 1
Autism: COSAC Annual Conference, May 7
Automatic Toll Collection Machine, First: Anniv, Nov 19
Automobile Speed Reduction: Anniv, Nov 25
Automobiles (including shows, races, etc),
AMA Grand National Kickoff (Daytona Beach, FL), Mar 6
AMA Natl Hot Shoe Kickoff Dirt Track Race (Daytona Beach, FL), Mar 5
Antique and Classic Car Show (Bennington, VT), Sep 17
Antiques by the Bay (St. Ignace, MI), Jun 18
Armed Forces Day Military Vehicle Rally (Hawthorne, NV), May 19
Automotion (Wisconsin Dells, WI), May 22
Automotive Service Professionals Day, Natl, Jun 12
Brumos Continental Historics/Grand American Finale (Daytona Beach, FL), Nov 5
Bud Pole Day for the Daytona 500 (Daytona Beach, FL), Feb 8
Budweiser Shootout at Daytona Winston Cup Series Race (Daytona Beach, FL), Feb 7
Car Care Month, Natl, Apr 1
Center of Nation All-Car Rally (Belle Fourche, SD), Jun 12
Chrysler Classic Speed Fest (San Diego, CA), Oct 9
Collision Awareness Month, Natl, Mar 1
Concours d'Elegance (Forest Grove, OR), Jul 18
Corvette and High Performance Meet (Puyallup, WA), Feb 7
Corvette Show (Mackinaw City, MI), Aug 27
Daytona 200 by Arai Qualifying Day (Daytona Beach, FL), Mar 4
Daytona 500 (Daytona Beach, FL), Feb 15
Daytona Beach Spring Car Show & Swap Meet (Daytona Beach, FL), Mar 19
Daytona Turkey Run (Daytona Beach, FL), Nov 25
55 mph Speed Limit: Anniv, Jan 2
First Car Insurance: Anniv, Feb 1
Florida Dodge Dealers 250 NASCAR Craftsman Truck Series Race (Daytona Beach, FL), Feb 13
4-Wheel Drive Jamboree (Springfield, MO), May 8
Gasoline Rationing: Anniv, May 15
Gatorade 125-Mile Qualifying Races (Daytona Beach, FL), Feb 12
Good Car-Keeping Month, Natl, May 1
Hot August Nights (Reno and Sparks, NV), Aug 1
Indianapolis 500: Anniv, May 30
Indy 500-Mile Race (Indianapolis, IN), May 30
Interstate Highway System Born: Anniv, Jun 29
Intl Ford Mustang Day, Apr 17
Intl Race of Champions (Daytona Beach, FL), Feb 13
Koolerz 300 NASCAR Busch Series Race (Daytona Beach, FL), Feb 14
Kruisin' Weekend (Altoona, PA), Aug 20
KRXL Car Cruise (Kirksville, MO), Aug 7
Kustom Kemps Car Show (Biglerville, PA), Jun 11
London/Brighton Veteran Car Run (London, England), Nov 7
Lost in the '50s (Sandpoint, ID), May 14
MADD's Tie One On for Safety, Dec 1
Magic Dragon Street Meet Nationals Car Show (Lake Ozark, MO), Apr 30
Medford Cruise (Medford, OR), Jun 18
Michigan Camper, Travel & RV Show (Pontiac, MI), Jan 21
Mid-America Natl Street Rod Assn Car Show (Springfield, MO), May 28
Midnight at the Oasis (Yuma, AZ), Mar 5
Model T Introduced: Anniv, Oct 1
Monster Trucks Winter Nationals (Wichita Falls, TX), Jan 10
Mustang 40th Anniv Celebration (Nashville, TN), Apr 15
NC RV and Camping Show (Charlotte, NC), Jan 30
NC RV and Camping Show (Greensboro, NC), Jan 9
NC RV and Camping Show (Raleigh, NC), Feb 13
On the Waterfront Swap Meet/Car Show (St. Ignace, MI), Sep 10
Ozark Antique Auto Club Swap Meet (Springfield, MO), Aug 27
Pepsi 400 (Daytona, FL), Jul 3
Petit Jean Antique Auto Show/Swap Meet (Morrilton, AR), Jun 15
Petit Jean Fall Antique Auto Swap Meet (Morrilton, AR), Sep 15
Rally of the Tall Pines (Bancroft, ON, Canada), Nov 20
Recreational Vehicle Show (Timonium, MD), Feb 20
Richard Crane Memorial Truck Show (St. Ignace, MI), Sep 10
Rolex 24 at Daytona (Daytona, FL), Jan 31
Royal Scottish Auto Club Rally (Scotland), Jun 11
Show of Wheels (Lovington, NM), Feb 7
St. Ignace Auto Show (St. Ignace, MI), Jun 24
Street Machine Fall Nationals (Springfield, MO), Sep 17
Streetscene (Covington, VA), Aug 14
Woodie Wagon Day, Natl, Jul 21
World Karting Assn Races (Daytona Beach, FL), Dec 26
World of Wheels (Wichita Falls, TX), Jan 30
Autumn Begins, Sep 22
Autumn Market Fair, Eighteenth-Century (McLean, VA), Oct 16
Autumn, Halfway Point of, Nov 6
Avalon, Frankie: Birth, Sep 18
Avedon, Richard: Birth, May 15

★ Chase's 2004 Calendar of Events ★ Index

Aviation; Aviation History; Air Shows; Airplane Fly-ins,
Abbotsford Intl Airshow (Abbotsford, BC, Canada), **Aug 13**
Airborne Day, Natl (Pres Proc), **Aug 16**
Amelia Earhart Atlantic Crossing: Anniv, **May 20**
American Flight Crashes at O'Hare: Anniv, **May 25**
Aviation Day, Natl (Pres Proc), **Aug 19**
Aviation History Month, **Nov 1**
Aviation in America: Anniv, **Jan 9**
Aviation Week, Natl, **Aug 16**
Balloon Crossing of Atlantic: Anniv, **Aug 17**
Berlin Airlift: Anniv, **Jun 24**
Campbell Becomes 1st American Air ACE: Anniv, **Apr 14**
Canary Islands Plane Disaster: Anniv, **Mar 27**
Cayley, George: Birth Anniv, **Dec 27**
China Clipper: Anniv, **Nov 22**
Chmpshp Air Races, Natl (Reno, NV), **Sep 16**
Civil Air Patrol Founded: Anniv, **Dec 1**
Civil Aviation Day, Intl (UN), **Dec 7**
Cleveland Natl Air Show (Cleveland, OH), **Sep 4**
Coleman, Bessie: Birth Anniv, **Jan 26**
Commercial Air Flight Between the US and USSR Begins, **Jul 15**
EAA Airventure Oshkosh (Oshkosh, WI), **Jul 27**
First Airplane Crossing English Channel: Anniv, **Jul 25**
First Airship Crossing of Atlantic: Anniv, **Jul 6**
First Balloon Flight Across English Channel: Anniv, **Jan 7**
First Balloon Flight: Anniv, **Jun 5**
First Concorde Flight: Anniv, **Jan 21**
First Fatal Aviation Accident: Anniv, **Jun 15**
First Flight Anniv Celeb (Kill Devil Hills, NC), **Dec 17**
First Flight Attendant: Anniv, **May 15**
First Flight into the Stratosphere: Anniv, **May 27**
First Free Flight by a Woman: Anniv, **Jun 4**
First Manned Balloon Flight: Anniv, **Oct 15**
First Man-Powered Flight Across English Channel: Anniv, **Jun 12**
First Man-Powered Flight: Anniv, **Aug 23**
First Nonstop Flight of World/No Refueling: Anniv, **Dec 23**
First Nonstop Transatlantic Flight: Anniv, **Jun 14**
First Round-the-World Balloon Flight: Anniv, **Mar 21**
First Solo Round-the-World Balloon Flight: Anniv, **Jul 2**
Frequent Flyer Program Debuts: Anniv, **May 1**
Hindenburg Disaster: Anniv, **May 6**
Iran Air Flight 655 Disaster: Anniv, **Jul 3**
Johnson, Amy: Flight Anniv, **May 5**
Kennedy Intl Airport Dedication: Anniv, **Jul 31**
Lady Be Good Lost: Anniv, **Apr 4**
Levine, Charles A.: Death Anniv, **Dec 6**
Lindbergh Flight: Anniv, **May 20**
Lindbergh, Charles A.: Birth Anniv, **Feb 4**
Mint Julep Scale Meet (Falls of Rough, KY), **May 15**
Montgolfier, Jacques: Birth Anniv, **Jan 7**
Pan Am Circles Earth: Anniv, **Jan 6**
Pan Am Flight 103 Explosion: Anniv, **Dec 21**
Post, Wiley: Birth Anniv, **Nov 22**
Quad City Air Show (Davenport, IA), **Jun 25**
Sikorsky, Igor: Birth Anniv, **May 25**
Solo Transatlantic Balloon Crossing: Anniv, **Sep 14**
Sound Barrier Broken: Anniv, **Oct 14**
Spruce Goose Flight: Anniv, **Nov 2**
Stearman Fly-In Days (Galesburg, IL), **Sep 6**
Streeter, Ruth Cheney: Birth Anniv, **Oct 2**
US Air Force Academy Established: Anniv, **Apr 1**
US Air Force Established: Birth, **Sep 18**
Wright Brothers Day (Pres Proc), **Dec 17**
Wright Brothers First Powered Flight: Anniv, **Dec 17**
Wrong Way Corrigan Day, **Jul 17**
Awkward Moments Day, **Mar 18**
Axelrod, George: Birth, **Jun 9**
Aykroyd, Dan: Birth, **Jul 1**
Aylwin, Patricio: Military Dictatorship Ended, **Dec 15**
Azalea Fest (Muskogee, OK), **Apr 1**
Azalea Fest, Brookings-Harbor (Brookings, OR), **May 28**
Azaria, Hank: Birth, **Apr 25**
Azerbaijan,
Day of the Republic, **May 28**
Martyrs' Day, **Jan 20**
Independence Day, **Oct 18**
Aznavour, Charles: Birth, **May 22**
Aztec Calendar Stone Discovery: Anniv, **Dec 17**
Azzi, Jennifer: Birth, **Aug 31**
Bab, Birth of the (Baha'i): Anniv, **Oct 20**
Babbage, Charles: Birth Anniv, **Dec 26**
Babenco, Hector: Birth, **Feb 7**
Baby Boomer Born, First, **Jan 1**
Baby Boomers Recognition Day, **Jun 21**
Baby Food Fest, Natl (Fremont, MI), **Jul 13**
Babysitter Safety Day, **Mar 6**
Babysitters Day, Natl, **May 8**
Bacall, Lauren: Birth, **Sep 16**
Bach, Catherine: Birth, **Mar 1**
Bach, Johann Sebastian: Birth Anniv, **Mar 21**
Bacharach, Burt: Birth, **May 12**
Bachelor Father TV Premiere: Anniv, **Sep 15**
Bachelors Day, **Feb 1**
Back Week, Natl Save Your, **Oct 24**
Backpack Safety America Month, **Sep 1**
Backus, Jim: Birth Anniv, **Feb 25**
Backyard Games Week, Natl, **May 24**

Bacon, Francis: Birth Anniv, **Jan 22**
Bacon, Kevin: Birth, **Jul 8**
Bacon's Rebellion, Jamestown Burned By: Anniv, **Sep 19**
Bad Day Day, Have a, **Nov 19**
Bad Poetry Day, **Aug 18**
Baden-Powell, Robert: Birth Anniv, **Feb 22**
Bader, Diedrich: Birth, **Dec 24**
Badlands Natl Park Established: Anniv, **Nov 10**
Badminton Horse Trials (Badminton, England), **Apr 29**
Badminton: Scottish Intl Chmpshp (Edinburgh, Scotland), **Nov 25**
Badu, Erykah: Birth, **Feb 26**
Baer, Max, Jr: Birth, **Dec 4**
Baez, Joan: Birth, **Jan 9**
Bagelfest (Mattoon, IL), **Jul 28**
Bagwell, Jeff: Birth, **May 27**
Baha'i,
American Baha'i Community: Anniv, **Jun 5**
Ascension of Baha'u'llah, **May 29**
Baha'i New Year's Day: Naw-Ruz, **Mar 21**
Birth of Baha'u'llah, **Nov 12**
Birth of the Bab, **Oct 20**
Declaration of the Bab, **May 23**
Fest of Ridvan, **Apr 21**
Martyrdom of the Bab, **Jul 9**
Race Unity Day, **Jun 13**
Bahamas,
Discovery Day, **Oct 12**
Emancipation Day, **Aug 2**
Fox Hill Day (Nassau), **Aug 10**
Independence Day, **Jul 10**
Junkanoo, **Dec 26**
Labor Day, **Jun 4**
Miami/Bahamas Goombay Fest, **Jun 4**
Bahrain: Independence Day, **Dec 16**
Bailey, F. Lee: Birth, **Jun 10**
Bailey, Pearl Mae: Birth Anniv, **Mar 29**
Baines, Harold: Birth, **Mar 15**
Baio, Scott: Birth, **Sep 22**
Baiul, Oksana: Birth, **Nov 16**
Baisakhi (India), **Apr 13**
Bake for Family Fun Month, **Feb 1**
Baked Bean Month, Natl, **Jul 1**
Baker, Anita: Birth, **Jan 26**
Baker, Carroll: Birth, **May 28**
Baker, Diane: Birth, **Feb 25**
Baker, Joe Don: Birth, **Feb 12**
Baker, Kathy: Birth, **Jun 8**
Baker, Russell: Birth, **Aug 14**
Baker, Vin: Birth, **Nov 23**
Bakker, Jim: Birth, **Jan 2**
Bakula, Scott: Birth, **Oct 9**
Balance Awareness Week, **Sep 19**
Balanchine, George: Birth Anniv, **Jan 22**
Balanchine-Graham Collaboration: Anniv, **May 14**
Balboa: Pacific Ocean Discovered: Anniv, **Sep 25**
Bald and Be Free Day, Be, **Oct 14**
Bald Eagle Appreciation Days (Keokuk, IA), **Jan 16**
Bald Is Beautiful Convention (Morehead City, NC), **Sep 10**
Baldacci, John: Birth, **Jan 30**
Baldwin, Adam: Birth, **Feb 27**
Baldwin, Alec: Birth, **Apr 3**
Baldwin, Caroline: First Woman Dr. Science: Anniv, **Jun 20**
Baldwin, James: Birth Anniv, **Aug 2**
Baldwin, Roger Nash: Birth Anniv, **Jan 21**
Baldwin, Stephen: Birth, **May 12**
Baldwin, William: Birth, **Feb 21**
Bale, Christian: Birth, **Jan 30**
Balfour, Eric: Birth, **Apr 24**
Bali Terrorist Bombing: Anniversary, **Oct 12**
Ball, Lucille: Birth Anniv, **Aug 6**
Ballesteros, Seve: Birth, **Apr 9**
Ballet Introduced to the US: Anniv, **Feb 7**
Balloons, Hot-Air,
Albuquerque Intl Balloon Fiesta (Albuquerque, NM), **Oct 2**
Aviation in America: Anniv, **Jan 9**
Balloon Classic, Natl (Indianola, IA), **Jul 30**
Balloon Crossing of Atlantic: Anniv, **Aug 17**
Colorado River Crossing Balloon Festival (Yuma, AZ), **Nov 19**
Columbus Fest/Hot Air Balloon Regatta (Columbus, KS), **Oct 8**
Creston/Southwest Iowa Balloon Days (Creston, IA), **Sep 17**
Farmington Invitational Balloon Fest (Farmington, NM), **May 29**
First Balloon Flight Across English Channel: Anniv, **Jan 7**
First Balloon Flight: Anniv, **Jun 5**
First Balloon Honeymoon: Anniv, **Jun 20**
First Flight into the Stratosphere: Anniv, **May 27**
First Manned Flight: Anniv, **Oct 15**
First Round-the-World Balloon Flight: Anniv, **Mar 21**
First Solo Round-the-World Balloon Flight: Anniv, **Jul 2**
Macon, GA's Cherry Blossom Fest, 2004 Intl (Macon, GA), **Mar 19**
Re/Max Ballunar Liftoff Festival (Houston, TX), **Aug 20**
Rocky Mountain Balloon Fest (Denver, CO), **Aug 27**
Solo Transatlantic Balloon Crossing: Anniv, **Sep 14**

Ball-Point Pen Patented: Anniv, **Jun 10**
Balsam, Martin: Birth Anniv, **Nov 4**
Balzac, Honore De: Birth Anniv, **May 20**
Bancroft, Anne: Birth, **Sep 17**
Bancroft, George: Birth Anniv, **Oct 3**
Band Fest, Great American Brass (Danville, KY), **Jun 12**
Banderas, Antonio: Birth, **Aug 10**
Banerjee, Victor: Birth, **Oct 15**
Banff Mountain Book Fest (Banff, AB, Canada), **Nov 3**
Banff Mountain Film Fest (Banff, AB, Canada), **Nov 5**
Bangladesh,
Independence Day, **Mar 26**
Martyrs Day, **Feb 21**
Solidarity Day, **Nov 7**
Victory Day, **Dec 16**
Banjo: Guthrie Jazz Banjo Fest (Guthrie, OK), **May 21**
Bank Holiday, Spring (United Kingdom), **May 31**
Bank Holiday, Summer (Scotland), **Aug 2**
Bank Holiday, Summer (United Kingdom), **Aug 30**
Bank Holiday: Anniv, **Mar 5**
Bank Opens in US, First: Anniv, **Dec 31**
Banks, Ernie: Birth, **Jan 31**
Banks, Tyra: Birth, **Dec 4**
Banned Books Week, **Sep 18**
Banneker, Benjamin: Birth Anniv, **Nov 9**
Bannister Breaks Four-Minute Mile: Anniv, **May 6**
Bannister, Dr. Roger: Birth, **Mar 23**
Bar Assn, American Founding: Anniv, **Aug 21**
Bar Code Introduced: Anniv, **Jun 26**
Barak, Ehud: Birth, **Feb 12**
Baraka, Imamu Amiri: Birth, **Oct 7**
Baranski, Christine: Birth, **May 2**
Barbados: Independence Day, **Nov 30**
Barbeau, Adrienne: Birth, **Jun 11**
Barbecue Month, Natl, **May 1**
Barbed Wire Swap/Sell (LaCrosse, KS), **Apr 29**
Barber, Frances: Birth, **May 13**
Barber, Red: Birth Anniv, **Feb 17**
Barber, Red: First Baseball Games Televised: Anniv, **Aug 26**
Barbershop Quartet Day, **Apr 11**
Barbershop Quartet Singing Intl Conv (Louisville, KY), **Jun 27**
Barbershop: SPEBSQSA Convention (Biloxi, MS), **Jan 25**
Barbie and Barney Backlash Day, **Dec 16**
Barbie Debuts: Anniv, **Mar 9**
Barbosa, Jose Celso: Birth Anniv, **Jul 27**
Bardot, Brigitte: Birth, **Sep 28**
Barenboim, Daniel: Birth, **Nov 15**
Baretta TV Premiere: Anniv, **Jan 17**
Barker, Bob: Birth, **Dec 12**
Barkin, Ellen: Birth, **Apr 16**
Barkley, Alben: Birth Anniv, **Nov 24**
Barkley, Charles: Birth, **Feb 20**
Barnaby Jones TV Premiere: Anniv, **Jan 28**
Barnard, Christiaan: First Heart Transplant: Anniv, **Dec 3**
Barnes, Clive: Birth, **May 13**
Barnes, Joanna: Birth, **Nov 15**
Barnesville Pumpkin Fest (Barnesville, OH), **Sep 23**
Barney & Friends TV Premiere: Anniv, **Apr 6**
Barney Miller TV Premiere: Anniv, **Jan 23**
Barnum, Phineas Taylor: Birth Anniv, **Jul 5**
Baron Bliss Day (Belize), **Mar 9**
Barrel Race, Josey's World Champion Jr (Marshall, TX), **Apr 30**
Barrett, Rona: Birth, **Oct 8**
Barrie, Barbara: Birth, **May 23**
Barris, Chuck: Birth, **Jun 3**
Barry, Dave: Birth, **Jul 3**
Barry, Gene: Birth, **Jun 14**
Barry, John: Death Anniv, **Sep 13**
Barrymore, Drew: Birth, **Feb 22**
Barrymore, Ethel: Birth Anniv, **Aug 15**
Barrymore, John: Birth Anniv, **Feb 15**
Barrymore, Lionel: Birth Anniv, **Apr 28**
Barth, John: Birth, **May 27**
Bartholdi, Frederic A.: Birth Anniv, **Apr 2**
Bartholomew, Freddie: Birth Anniv, **Mar 28**
Bartlett, John: Birth Anniv, **Jun 14**
Bartlett, Josiah: Birth Anniv, **Nov 21**
Bartok, Bela: Birth Anniv, **Mar 25**
Bartoli, Cecilia: Birth, **Jun 4**
Barton, Clara: American Red Cross Founding Anniv, **May 21**
Barton, Clara: Birth Anniv, **Dec 25**
Baryshnikov, Mikhail: Birth, **Jan 27**
Bascom, Earl W.: Birth Anniv, **Jun 19**
Bascom, Florence: Birth Anniv, **Jul 14**
Bascom, George N.: Birth Anniv, **Apr 24**
Bascom, Texas Rose: Birth Anniv, **Feb 25**
Baseball. See also Softball,
American League's First Perfect Game: Anniv, **May 5**
Ashford, Emmett: Birth Anniv, **Nov 23**
Babe Ruth Calls His Shot?: Anniv, **Oct 1**
Babe Ruth's First Major League Home Run: Anniv, **May 6**
Babe Ruth's First Pro Homer: Anniv, **Sep 5**
Baseball Declared Non-Essential: Anniv, **Jul 20**
Baseball First Played Under Lights: Anniv, **May 24**
Baseball Hall of Fame Dedicated, Natl: Anniv, **Jun 12**

685

Index ☆ Chase's 2004 Calendar of Events ☆

Baseball (cont'd)—Bicycle

Baseball's Greatest Dispute: Anniv, **Sep 23**
Bell, James: Birth Anniv, **May 17**
Big Ten Baseball Tournament, **May 26**
Bonds Breaks Home Run Record, **Oct 5**
Bronco League World Series (Monterey, CA), **Aug 5**
Caray, Harry: Birth Anniv, **Mar 14**
Cobb, Ty: Birth Anniv, **Dec 18**
Colt League World Series (Lafayette, IN), **Aug 3**
Designated Hitter Rule Adopted: Anniv, **Jan 11**
Doubleday, Abner: Birth Anniv, **Jun 26**
First Baseball Games Televised: Anniv, **Aug 26**
First Baseball Strike Ends: Anniv, **Apr 13**
First Perfect Game: Anniv, **Jun 12**
Gehrig, Lou: Birth Anniv, **Jun 19**
Greenberg, Hank: Birth Anniv, **Jan 1**
Hall of Fame's Charter Members: Anniv, **Feb 2**
Home Run Record: Anniv, **Apr 8**
Jackie Robinson Breaks Baseball Color Line: Anniv, **Apr 15**
Ladies' Day Initiated in Baseball: Anniv, **Jun 16**
Little League Baseball Week, Natl, **Jun 14**
Little League World Series (Williamsport, PA), **Aug 20**
Major League Baseball First All-Star Game: Anniv, **Jul 6**
Major League's First Double Header, **Sep 25**
Maris Breaks Home Run Record: Anniv, **Oct 1**
Martin, Billy: Birth Anniv, **May 16**
McGwire Breaks Home Run Record: Anniv, **Sep 8**
Midnight Sun Baseball Game (Fairbanks, AK), **Jun 18**
Mighty Casey Has Struck Out: Anniv, **Jun 3**
MLB All-Star Game, **Jul 13**
Mustang League World Series (Irving, TX), **Aug 4**
NAIA Baseball World Series (Lewiston, ID), **May 28**
NCAA Div I Men's Baseball Chmpshp (Omaha, NE), **Jun 18**
Palomino League World Series (Santa Clara, CA), **Aug 6**
Pony League World Series (Washington, PA), **Aug 14**
President Taft Opens Baseball Season: Anniv, **Apr 14**
Robinson Named First Black Manager: Anniv, **Oct 3**
Young, Cy: Birth Anniv, **Mar 29**
Bashoff, Blake: Birth, May 30
Basinger, Kim: Birth, Dec 8
Basketball,
Basketball Created: Anniv, **Dec 1**
Big 12 Men's Basketball Chmpshp (Dallas, TX), **Mar 11**
Big 12 Women's Basketball Tourn (Dallas, TX), **Mar 9**
Big Ten Men's Basketball Tournament (Indianapolis, IN), **Mar 11**
Big Ten Women's Basketball Tournament (Indianapolis, IN), **Mar 4**
Carrs/Safeway Great Alaska Shootout (Anchorage, AK), **Nov 23**
Chicago Bulls Third Straight Title for the Second Time, **Jun 14**
First Black Plays in NBA Game: Anniv, **Oct 31**
First Women's Collegiate Basketball Game: Anniv, **Mar 22**
Harlem Globetrotters Play First Game: Anniv, **Jan 7**
NAIA Men's Div I Basketball Chmpshp, **Mar 24**
NAIA Men's Div II Basketball Chmpshp, **Mar 10**
NAIA Wom Div II Basketball Chmpshp Tourn (Sioux City, IA), **Mar 10**
NAIA Women's Div I Basketball Chmpshp (Jackson, TN), **Mar 17**
NBA All-Star Weekend (Los Angeles, CA), **Feb 13**
NCAA Div I Men's Basketball Chmpshp (San Antonio, TX), **Apr 3**
NJCAA Div I Men's Natl Basketball Finals (Danville, IL), **Mar 17**
Bassett, Angela: Birth, Aug 16
Bassey, Shirley: Birth, Jan 8
Bastille Day (France), Jul 14
Bastille Day Celebration (Boston, MA), Jul 9
Bataan Death March: Anniv, Apr 10
Bateman, Jason: Birth, Jan 14
Bateman, Justine: Birth, Feb 19
Bates, Alan: Birth, Feb 17
Bates, Kathy: Birth, Jun 28
Bathtub Party Day, Dec 5
Bathtub Race, Great (Nome, AK), Sep 6
Batman TV Premiere: Anniv, Jan 12
Battier, Shane: Birth, Sep 9
Battle of Blue Licks Celebration (Mount Olivet, KY), Aug 21
Battle of Brandywine: Anniv, Sep 11
Battle of Britain Day (United Kingdom), Sep 15
Battle of Britain Week (United Kingdom), Sep 12
Battle of Germantown Reenactment (Philadelphia, PA), Oct 2
Battle of Kursk: Anniv, Jul 12
Battle of Lexington and Concord: Anniv, Apr 19
Battle of Little Bighorn: Anniv, Jun 25
Battle of Midway: Anniv, Jun 4
Battle, Kathleen: Birth, Aug 13
Baucus, Max: Birth, Dec 11
Baum, L. Frank: Birth Anniv, May 15
Baxter, Meredith: Birth, Jun 21
Bay Harbor Summer Art Fair (Bay Harbor, MI), Aug 6
Bay of Pigs Invasion Launched: Anniv, Apr 17
Bay to Breakers Race (San Francisco, CA), May 14
Bayfest (Corpus Christi, TX), Sep 24
Bayh, Evan: Birth, Dec 26
Baylor, Don: Birth, Jun 28

Baylor, Elgin Gay: Birth, Sep 16
Baywatch TV Premiere: Anniv, Apr 23
BBC Proms (London, England), Jul 16
BCS National Championship Game: Nokia Sugar Bowl, Jan 1
Be an Angel Day, Aug 22
Be Bald and Be Free Day, Oct 14
Be Electrific Day, Feb 11
Be Kind to Animals Week, May 2
Be Kind to Humankind Week, Aug 25
Be Late for Something Day, Sep 5
Be Nice to New Jersey Week, Jul 4
Beach Party (Deadwood, SD), Mar 13
Beadle, George: Birth Anniv, Oct 22
Beals, Jennifer: Birth, Dec 19
Bean Throwing Fest (Japan), Feb 3
Bean, Alan: Birth, Mar 15
Bean, Andy: Birth, Mar 13
Bean, Orson: Birth, Jul 22
Bean, Sean: Birth, Apr 17
Beard, Charles: Birth Anniv, Nov 27
Beard, James: Awards Ceremony (New York, NY), May 10
Beard, James: Birth Anniv, May 5
Beard, Mary R.: Birth Anniv, Aug 5
Beardsley, Aubrey V.: Birth Anniv, Aug 21
Bearse, Amanda: Birth, Aug 9
Beasley, Allyce: Birth, Jul 6
Beasley, DaMarcus: Birth, May 24
Beat the Clock TV Premiere: Anniv, Mar 23
Beatles, The,
Appear on The Ed Sullivan Show: Anniv, **Feb 9**
Bed-in for Peace: Anniv, **Mar 25**
Harrison, George: Birth Anniv, **Feb 25**
Last Concert: Anniv, **Jan 30**
Lennon, John: Birth Anniv, **Oct 9**
McCartney, Paul: Birth, **Jun 18**
Natl Apple Week: Anniv, **Aug 11**
Sgt Pepper's Lonely Hearts Club Band Released: Anniv, **Jun 1**
Starr, Ringo: Birth, **Jul 7**
Take Over Music Charts: Anniv, **Apr 4**
Beatrix, Queen: Birth, Jan 31
Beatty, Ned: Birth, Jul 6
Beatty, Warren: Birth, Mar 30
Beaufort Scale Day, May 7
Beaumont, William: Birth Anniv, Nov 21
Beauregard, Genl: Battle of Shiloh: Anniv, Apr 6
Beauty and the Beast TV Premiere: Anniv, Sep 25
Beauty Contests, Pageants,
Doodle Soup Days (Bradford, TN), **Sep 10**
First Miss America: Anniv, **Sep 8**
Miss American Rose Day, **Jun 17**
Miss Crustacean USA (Ocean City, NJ), **Aug 4**
Miss Louisiana Pageant (Monroe, LA), **Jun 17**
Miss Virginia Pageant (Roanoke, VA), **Jun 24**
Our Town America Fest (Coral Springs, FL), **Feb 27**
Parks, Bert: Birth Anniv, **Dec 30**
Pretty Is as Pretty Does Day, Natl, **Aug 2**
Beavers, Louise: Birth Anniv, Mar 8
Beck, John: Birth, Jan 28
Becker, Boris: Birth, Nov 22
Beckett, Samuel: Birth Anniv, Apr 13
Beckham, David: Birth, May 2
Beckham, Victoria Adams: Birth, Apr 17
Beckinsale, Kate: Birth, Jul 26
Become a YardNerd Month, Apr 1
Bedard, Irene: Birth, Jul 22
Bedelia, Bonnie: Birth, Mar 25
Bed-in for Peace: Anniv, Mar 25
Bednarik, Chuck: Birth, May 1
Beecher, Catharine Esther: Birth Anniv, Sep 6
Beecher, Henry W.: Birth Anniv, Jun 24
Beef Empire Days (Garden City, KS), Jun 8
Beer Cans: Winterfest (Burton, MI), Jan 17
Beer Day (Iceland), Mar 1
Beer Fest (Luxembourg), Jul 18
Beethoven, Ludwig van: Birth Anniv, Dec 16
Beethoven's Ninth Symphony Premiere: Anniv, May 7
Beggar's Night, Oct 31
Begin, Menachem: Birth Anniv, Aug 16
Begley, Ed, Jr: Birth, Sep 16
Behan, Brendan: Birth Anniv, Feb 9
Beirut Terrorist Attack: Anniv, Oct 23
Belafonte, Harry: Birth, Mar 1
Belafonte-Harper, Shari: Birth, Sep 22
Belarus,
Constitution Day, **Mar 15**
Independence Day, **Jul 3**
Bele Chere (Asheville, NC), Jul 23
Belfour, Ed: Birth, Apr 21
Belgium,
Cat Fest, **Feb 26**
Dynasty Day, **Nov 15**
Historical Procession (Tournai), **Sep 5**
Lover's Fair, **Dec 2**
Military Music Fest, **Jun 13**
National Holiday, **Jul 21**
Nuts Fair (Bastogne), **Dec 20**
Ommegang Pageant, **Jul 1**
Play of St. Evermaar, **May 1**
Procession of Golden Chariot (Mons), **Jun 2**
Procession of the Holy Blood, **May 20**
Wedding of the Giants, **Aug 22**
Believe It or Not TV Premiere: Anniv, Mar 1

Belize,
Baron Bliss Day, **Mar 9**
Columbus Day, **Oct 12**
Commonwealth Day, **May 24**
Garifuna Day, **Nov 19**
Independence Day, **Sep 21**
Saint George's Caye Day, **Sep 10**
Bell Telephone Hour TV Premiere: Anniv, Jan 12
Bell, Alexander Graham: Birth Anniv, Mar 3
Bell, Catherine: Birth, Aug 14
Bell, James: Birth Anniv, May 17
Bell, Jay: Birth, Dec 11
Bellamy, Ralph: Birth Anniv, Jun 17
Belle, Albert: Birth, Aug 25
Bellow, Saul: Birth, Jul 10
Belmondo, Jean-Paul: Birth, Apr 9
Belmont Stakes (Belmont Park, NY), Jun 5
Belote, Melissa: Birth, Oct 16
Beltane, Apr 30
Belushi, Jim: Birth, Jun 15
Belushi, John: Birth Anniv, Jan 24
Belzer, Richard: Birth, Aug 4
Benatar, Pat: Birth, Jan 10
Bench, Johnny: Birth, Dec 7
Benchley, Peter: Birth, May 8
Benedict, Paul: Birth, Sep 17
Benes, Andy: Birth, Aug 20
Benet, William Rose: Birth Anniv, Feb 2
Ben-Gurion, David: Birth Anniv, Oct 16
Benigni, Roberto: Birth, Oct 27
Benin: Independence Day, Aug 1
Bening, Annette: Birth, May 29
Benjamin, Richard: Birth, May 22
Bennett, Arnold: Birth Anniv, May 27
Bennett, Cornelius: Birth, Aug 25
Bennett, Joan: Birth Anniv, Feb 27
Bennett, Richard Bedford: Birth Anniv, Jul 3
Bennett, Robert F.: Birth, Sep 18
Bennett, Tony: Birth, Aug 3
Bennington Battle Day, Aug 16
Benny, Jack: Birth Anniv, Feb 14
Benson TV Premiere: Anniv, Sep 13
Benson, Craig: Birth, Oct 8
Benson, George: Birth, Mar 22
Benson, Robby: Birth, Jan 21
Bentley, Edmund Clerihew: Clerihew Day, Jul 10
Benton Neighbor Day (Benton, MO), Sep 3
Benton, Thomas Hart: Birth Anniv, Apr 15
Berenger, Tom: Birth, May 31
Berenson, Marisa: Birth, Feb 15
Berenson, Red: Birth, Dec 8
Bergen, Candice: Birth, May 9
Bergen, Edgar: Birth Anniv, Feb 16
Bergen, Polly: Birth, Jul 14
Bergeron, Tom: Birth, May 6
Bergin, Michael: Birth, Mar 19
Bergman, Ingmar: Birth, Jul 14
Bergman, Ingrid: Birth & Death Anniv, Aug 29
Bergman, Peter: Birth, Jun 11
Bergson, Henri: Birth Anniv, Oct 18
Berkeley, Busby: Birth Anniv, Nov 29
Berkoff, Steven: Birth, Aug 3
Berle, Milton: Birth Anniv, Jul 12
Berlin Airlift: Anniv, Jun 24
Berlin International Film Fest (Berlin, Germany), Feb 5
Berlin Wall Erected: Anniv, Aug 13
Berlin Wall Opened: Anniv, Nov 9
Berlin, Irving: Birth Anniv, May 11
Berman, Shelley: Birth, Feb 3
Bermuda Colonized by English: Anniv, Mar 12
Bermuda: Peppercorn Ceremony, Apr 23
Bernard, Crystal: Birth, Sep 30
Berne Swiss Days (Berne, IN), Jul 29
Berners-Lee, Tim: Birth, Jun 8
Bernhard, Sandra: Birth, Jun 6
Bernsen, Corbin: Birth, Sep 7
Bernstein, Carl: Birth, Feb 14
Bernstein, Elmer: Birth, Apr 4
Bernstein, Leonard: Birth Anniv, Aug 25
Berra, Yogi: Birth, May 12
Berridge, Elizabeth: Birth, May 2
Berry, Chuck: Birth, Oct 18
Berry, Halle: Birth, Aug 14
Berry, Ken: Birth, Nov 3
Bertinelli, Valerie: Birth, Apr 23
Bertolucci, Bernardo: Birth, Mar 16
Bethune, Mary McLeod: Birth Anniv, Jul 10
Bethune, Norman: Birth Anniv, Mar 3
Better Conversation Week, Nov 22
Bettis, Jerome: Birth, Feb 16
Beverly Hillbillies TV Premiere: Anniv, Sep 26
Bewick, Thomas: Birth Anniv, Aug 12
Bewitched TV Premiere: Anniv, Sep 17
Bezos, Jeff: Birth, Jan 12
Bhopal Poison Gas Disaster: Anniv, Dec 3
Bhutan,
Coronation Day, **Jun 2**
Natl Day, **Jun 25**
Bhutto, Benazir: Birth, Jun 21
Bialik, Mayim: Birth, Dec 12
Bibby, Mike: Birth, May 13
Bible Week, Natl, Nov 21
Bichette, Dante: Birth, Nov 18
Bicycle,
Bike Month, Natl, **May 1**

686

☆ Chase's 2004 Calendar of Events ☆ Index

Bicycle (cont'd)—Boll

Bike to Work Day, Natl, **May 21**
Bike Van Buren (Van Buren County, IA), **Aug 21**
Borneo Rhino Challenge (Malaysia), **May 1**
Great Peanut Tour (Skippers, VA), **Sep 9**
Hotter 'n Hell Hundred Bike Race/Fest (Wichita Falls, TX), **Aug 26**
Leadville Trail 100 Bike Race (Leadville, CO), **Aug 14**
Perry's "BRR" (Bike Ride to Rippey) (Perry, IA), **Feb 7**
Register's Bicycle Ride Across Iowa (Des Moines, IA), **Jul 25**
Tour de Cure (Diabetes), **Apr 1**
Tour de France, **Jul 3**
Tour of Somerville (Somerville, NJ), **May 31**
Biddle, Nicholas: Birth Anniv, Jan 8
Biden, Joe: Birth, Nov 20
Biel, Jessica: Birth, Mar 3
Bifocals at the Monitor Liberation Day, Dec 1
Big Bend Natl Park Established: Anniv, Jun 12
Big Bertha Paris Gun: Anniv, Mar 23
Big E, The (West Springfield, MA), Sep 17
Big Island Rendezvous (Albert Lea, MN), Oct 2
Big Top TV Premiere: Anniv, Jul 1
Big Valley Jamboree (Camrose, AB, Canada), Jul 29
Big Whopper Liar's Contest (New Harmony, IN), Sep 18
Big Wind: Anniv, Apr 12
Biggio, Craig: Birth, Dec 14
Biggs, E. Power: Birth Anniv, Mar 29
Biggs, Jason: Birth, May 12
Bike to Work Day, Natl, May 21
Bikel, Theodore: Birth, May 2
Bikini Debuted: Anniv, Jul 5
Bill of Rights: Anniv, Dec 15
Bill of Rights: Anniv of First State Ratification, Nov 20
Bill of Rights: Day (Pres Proc), Dec 15
Bill of Rights: Proposal: Anniv, Jun 8
Bill of Rights: Religious Freedom Week, Sep 18
Bill, Tony: Birth, Aug 23
Billiard Awareness Month, Oct 1
Billings, John S.: Birth Anniv, Apr 12
Billingsley, Barbara: Birth, Dec 22
Billington, James Hadley: Birth, Jun 1
Billionaire Bachelor [Gates]: Wedding Anniv, Jan 1
Billy the Kid: Birth Anniv, Nov 23
Bingaman, Jeff: Birth, Oct 3
Bingo's Birthday Month, Dec 1
Binoche, Juliette: Birth, Mar 9
Biodiesel Day, Natl (Rudolph Diesel Birth Anniv), Mar 18
Biographers Day, May 16
Biological Clock Gene Discovered: Anniv, Apr 28
Biological Diversity, Intl Day for (UN), May 22
Bioterrorism/Disaster Education and Awareness Month, Jul 1
Bird, Larry: Birth, Dec 7
Birds,
Bald Eagle Appreciation Days (Keokuk, IA), **Jan 16**
Bird Feeding Month, Natl, **Feb 1**
Birds & Blossoms Spring Nature Festival (Norfolk, VA), **May 6**
Crane Watch (Kearney, NE), **Mar 1**
Curlew Day, **Mar 16**
Duck-Calling Contest/Wings Over Prairie (Stuttgart, AR), **Nov 26**
Eagle Days (Junction City, KS), **Jan 17**
Eagle Days in Springfield (Springfield, MO), **Jan 17**
Eagles Et Cetera (Bismarck, AR), **Jan 23**
Fall in Love with Fond du Lac (Fond du Lac, WI), **Sep 1**
Great Backyard Bird Count, **Feb 13**
Hummer/Bird Celebration (Rockport, Fulton, TX), **Sep 16**
Kirtland, Jared: Birth Anniv, **Nov 10**
Migratory Bird Celebration, Intl (Chincoteague, VA), **May 8**
Migratory Bird Day, Intl, **May 8**
Migratory Bird Day, Intl (Savannah, GA), **May 8**
Picatinny Peak Fall Hawkwatch (Dover, NJ), **Sep 1**
South Texas Wildlife and Birding Festival (Kingsville, TX), **Nov 19**
Sparrow, Last Dusky Seaside: Death Anniv, **Jun 16**
Swallows Depart San Juan Capistrano (CA), **Oct 23**
Swallows Return to San Juan Capistrano (CA), **Mar 19**
Waterfowl Fest (Easton, MD), **Nov 12**
Wings Over the Platte Spring Migration Season: Sandhill Cranes (Grand Island, NE), **Feb 15**
Wings Over Willcox—Sandhill Crane Celebration (Willcox, AZ), **Jan 16**
Birdseye, Clarence: Birth Anniv, Dec 9
Birkebeiner, American (Cable to Hayward, WI), Feb 19
Birkin, Jane: Birth, Dec 14
Birmingham (AL) Resistance: Anniv, Apr 3
Birmingham Riot: Anniv (England), Jul 14
Birney, David: Birth, Apr 23
Birth Control Clinic Opened, First: Anniv, Oct 16
Birth Control Pills Sold: Anniv, Aug 18
Birthday of Mother's Whistler, May 18
Biscayne Natl Park Established: Anniv, Jun 28
Biscuit Month, Natl, Sep 1
Bishop, Elvin: Birth, Oct 21
Bishop, Joey: Birth, Feb 3
Bison-Ten-Yell Day, Sep 2
Bisset, Jacqueline: Birth, Sep 13
Bissett, Josie: Birth, Oct 5
Black Awareness 365, Mar 25
Black Cow Created: Anniv, Aug 19
Black Friday, Nov 26
Black Love Day, Feb 13
Black Nazarene Fiesta (Philippines), Jan 1
Black Nazarene, Feast of the (Philippines), Jan 9
Black Poetry Day, Oct 17
Black Press Day: Anniv of the First Black Newspaper, Mar 16
Black Single Parents' Week, Jun 6
Black Walnut Fest (Stockton, MO), Sep 22
Black, Clint: Birth, Feb 4
Black, Debbie: Birth, Jul 29
Black, Karen: Birth, Jul 1
Black, Shirley Temple: Birth, Apr 23
Blackmun, Harry A.: Birth Anniv, Nov 12
Blackout, East Coast: Anniv, Nov 9
Blackout, Seattle: Anniv, May 11
Blackpowder Historical Fair (Albert Lea, MN), Feb 14
Blackstone, William: Birth Anniv, Mar 5
Blackwell, Elizabeth, Awarded MD: Anniv, Jan 23
Blackwell, Elizabeth: Birth Anniv, Feb 3
Blades, Ruben: Birth, Jul 16
Blagojevich, Rod: Birth, Dec 10
Blah Blah Blah Day, Apr 17
Blaine, David: Birth, Apr 4
Blair, Bonnie: Birth, Mar 18
Blair, Linda: Birth, Jan 22
Blair, Tony: Birth, May 6
Blake, Eubie: Birth Anniv, Feb 7
Blake, Robert: Birth, Sep 18
Blake, William: Birth Anniv, Nov 28
Blakely, Susan: Birth, Sep 7
Blakey, Art: Birth Anniv, Oct 11
Blame Someone Else Day, Feb 13
Blanchett, Cate: Birth, May 14
Blanda, George: Birth, Sep 17
Blass, Bill: Birth Anniv, Jun 22
Blatty, William: Birth, Jan 7
Bledel, Alexis: Birth, Sep 16
Bledsoe, Drew: Birth, Feb 14
Bledsoe, Tempestt: Birth, Aug 1
Bleeth, Yasmine: Birth, Jun 14
Bleriot, Louis: Birth Anniv, Jul 1
Blessing of Animals at the Cathedral (Mexico), Jan 17
Blethyn, Brenda: Birth, Feb 20
Blige, Mary J.: Birth, Jan 11
Blindness Awareness Month, World, Oct 1
Bliss, Lizzie: Birth Anniv, Apr 11
Blizzard, Great of '88: Anniv, Mar 12
Blondin, Charles: Birth Anniv, Feb 28
Blondin, Charles: Conquest of Niagara Falls: Anniv, Jun 30
Blood Transfusion: Anniv, Nov 14
Bloodworth-Thomason, Linda: Birth, Apr 15
Bloody Brewery in 3-D (Columbus, OH), Oct 1
Bloody Sunday (Northern Ireland): Anniv, Jan 30
Bloom, Claire: Birth, Feb 15
Bloom, Harold: Birth, Jul 11
Bloom, Orlando: Birth, Jan 13
Bloomberg, Michael: Birth, Feb 14
Bloomer, Amelia Jenks: Birth Anniv, May 27
Bloomsday: Anniv, Jun 16
Blue Claw Crab Craft Show & Crab Race (Harvey Cedars, NJ), Aug 14
Blue Hill Fair (Blue Hill, ME), Sep 2
Blue Moon, Jul 31
Blue Ribbon Week, Natl (Child Abuse), Apr 4
Blue Ridge Folklife Fest (Ferrum, VA), Oct 23
Blueberry Arts Fest (Ketchikan, AK), Aug 7
Blueberry Fest (Montrose, PA), Aug 6
Blueberry Fest, Natl (South Haven, MI), Aug 12
Bluegrass. See also Fiddlers,
Blissfest (Cross Village, MI), **Jul 9**
Bluegrass Fest (Alta, WY), **Aug 13**
Bluegrass Fest (Hope, AR), **May 7**
Bluegrass Fest, Ocean County (Waretown, NJ), **Sep 12**
Fall Bluegrass Fest (Live Oak, FL), **Sep 23**
Fest of the Bluegrass (Lexington, KY), **Jun 10**
Four Corner States Bluegrass Fest (Wickenburg, AZ), **Nov 12**
Gettysburg Bluegrass Fest (Gettysburg, PA), **May 13**
Gettysburg Fall Bluegrass Fest (Gettysburg, PA), **Aug 26**
Homeplace Festival (Waretown, NJ), **Nov 20**
Ladies of Country Music Show (Waretown, NJ), **Jun 26**
Land of Mark Twain Bluegrass Music Fest (Hannibal, MO), **Nov 20**
Lil Margaret's Bluegrass and Old-Time Music Fest (Leonardtown, MD), **Aug 12**
Nova Scotia Oldtime Music Fest (Mt Denson, NS), **Jul 23**
Ocean County Bluegrass Fest (Waretown, NJ), **Feb 1**
Oklahoma Intl Bluegrass Fest (Guthrie, OK), **Sep 30**
Old Fiddlers' Conv (Galax, VA), **Aug 9**
Old-Time Fiddlers' Jamboree (Smithville, TN), **Jul 2**
Polk County Ramp Tramp Fest (Benton, TN), **Apr 24**
Spring Bluegrass Fest (Live Oak, FL), **Apr 8**
Thomas Point Beach Bluegrass Fest (Brunswick, ME), **Sep 2**
Blue-Gray Classic (Montgomery, AL), Dec 25
Blues Fest, Chicago (Chicago, IL), Jun 10
Bluford, Guion S., Jr: Birth, Nov 22
Blume, Judy: Birth, Feb 12
Bly, Nellie: Around the World in 72 Days: Anniv, Nov 14
Bly, Nellie: Birth Anniv, May 5
Bly, Robert: Birth, Dec 23
Boats, Ships, Things That Float. See also Rowing,
Antique/Classic Boat Rendezvous (Mystic, CT), **Jul 24**
Big Ten Women's Rowing (Iowa City, IA), **May 1**
Burlington Steamboat Days/Music Fest (Burlington, IA), **Jun 15**
Calgary Boat/Sportsmen's Show (Calgary, AB, Canada), **Feb 12**
Cardboard Boat Regatta, Great (Sheboygan, WI), **Jul 4**
Cingular Winterfest Boat Parade (Fort Lauderdale, FL), **Dec 18**
Civil War Submarine Attack: Anniv, **Oct 5**
Classic Boat Fest (Victoria, BC, Canada), **Aug 27**
Coshocton Canal Fest (Coshocton, OH), **Aug 21**
Devizes/Westminster Intl Canoe Race (Devizes, England), **Apr 9**
Edmund Fitzgerald Sinking: Anniv, **Nov 10**
Egyptian Maritime Disaster: Anniv, **Dec 14**
Everett Salty Sea Days (Everett, WA), **Jun 3**
First American to Circumnavigate Earth: Anniv, **Apr 10**
Fleet Week New York (New York, NY), **May 19**
Fort Lauderdale Intl Boat Show (Fort Lauderdale, FL), **Oct 28**
Frenchman Rows Across Pacific: Anniv, **Nov 21**
Fulton Sails Steamboat: Anniv, **Aug 17**
Grand Excursion 2004 (IA, IL, MN), **Jun 25**
Grand Rapids Boat Show (Grand Rapids, MI), **Feb 17**
Halifax, Nova Scotia, Destroyed: Anniv, **Dec 6**
Head of the River Race (London, England), **Mar 20**
Henley Royal Regatta (Henley-on-Thames, England), **Jun 30**
Historical Regatta (Venice, Italy), **Sep 5**
Lousiana Sportsmen's Show (New Orleans, LA), **Mar 3**
Loyalty Days and Seafair Fest (Newport, OR), **Apr 29**
Merchant Sailing Ship Preservation Day, **Nov 8**
Merrimac Destroyed: Anniv, **May 11**
Miami Intl Boat/Sailboat Show (Miami Beach, FL), **Feb 12**
Michigan Boat, Sport & Fishing Show (Detroit, MI), **Mar 3**
Milwaukee Boat Show & Wisconsin Sportfishing Expo (Milwaukee, WI), **Feb 11**
Monitor Sinking: Anniv, **Dec 30**
New Jersey State Rowing Chmpshps (Brick, NJ), **Jul 8**
New Orleans Boat Show (New Orleans, LA), **Feb 4**
Newport Intl Boat Show (Newport, RI), **Sep 16**
Ohio River Sternwheel Fest (Marietta, OH), **Sep 10**
Ottawa Boat/Sportsmen's Show (Ottawa, ON, Canada), **Feb 26**
Palio del Golfo (La Spezia, Italy), **Aug 8**
Queen Mary, RMS: Anniv, **May 27**
Remember the Maine Day, **Feb 15**
Rogue River Jet Boat Marathon (Gold Beach, OR), **Jun 18**
Royal George Sinks: Anniv, **Aug 29**
Safe Boating Week, Natl, **May 22**
Safe Boating Week, Natl (Pres Proc), **May 22**
San Diego Boat Show (San Diego, CA), **Jan 8**
Schrocers London Intl Boat Show (London, England), **Jan 8**
Sea Music Fest (Mystic, CT), **Jun 10**
Seattle Boat Show (Seattle, WA), **Jan 16**
Skandia Cowes Week (Isle of Wight), **Aug 7**
South Jersey Canoe/Kayak Classic (Lakewood, NJ), **Jun 5**
Spanish War/Maine Memorial Day, **Feb 15**
Sternwheeler Days (Cascade Locks, OR), **Jun 25**
Washington Boat Show (Washington, DC), **Feb 18**
White River Water Carnival (Batesville, AR), **Aug 6**
Whitewater Wednesday (Kernville, CA), **Jun 16**
Windjammer Days (Boothbay Harbor, ME), **Jun 22**
Yacht Race, Intl: Anniv, **Aug 22**
Bob Hope Show TV Premiere: Anniv, Oct 12
Bob Newhart Show TV Premiere: Anniv, Oct 10
Bob Wills Day (Turkey, TX), Apr 24
Bochco, Steven: Birth, Dec 16
Bock, Jerry: Birth, Nov 23
Bocuse, Paul: Birth, Feb 11
Boer War: Anniv, Oct 12
Boff, Leonardo: Birth, Dec 14
Bogart, Humphrey: Birth Anniv, Dec 25
Bogdanovich, Peter: Birth, Jul 30
Boggs, Wade: Birth, Jun 15
Bogosian, Eric: Birth, Apr 24
Bogues, Muggsy: Birth, Jan 9
Boissevain-Morton Summer Festival (Boissevain, MB, Canada), Aug 6
Boitano, Brian: Birth, Oct 22
Bol, Manute: Birth, Oct 16
Bold and the Beautiful TV Premiere: Anniv, Mar 23
Bolin, Jane M.: Birth, Apr 11
Bolivar, Simon: Birth Anniv, Jul 24
Bolivia,
Alacitis Fair, **Jan 24**
Independence Day, **Aug 6**
La Paz Day, **Jul 16**
Boll, Heinrich: Birth Anniv, Dec 21

Bolles, Don: Death Anniv, Jun 13
Bollingen Prize Award: Anniv, Feb 19
Bologna, Joseph: Birth, Dec 30
Bolton, Michael: Birth, Feb 27
Bombeck, Erma: Birth Anniv, Feb 21
Bombing, Oklahoma City: Anniv, Apr 19
Bombing, World Trade Center: Anniv, Feb 26
Bon Fest (Feast of Lanterns) (Japan), Jul 13
Bon Jovi, Jon: Birth, Mar 2
Bonaduce, Danny: Birth, Aug 13
Bonaparte, Napoleon: Birth Anniv, Aug 15
Bond, Carrie Jacobs: Birth Anniv, Aug 11
Bond, Christopher S.: Birth, Mar 6
Bond, Julian: Birth, Jan 14
Bonds Breaks Home Run Record: Anniv, Oct 5
Bonds, Barry: Birth, Jul 24
Bonds, Gary U.S.: Birth, Jun 6
Bonerz, Peter: Birth, Aug 6
Bonet, Lisa: Birth, Nov 16
Bonham Carter, Helena: Birth, May 26
Bonheur, Rosa: Birth Anniv, Mar 16
Bonilla, Bobby: Birth, Feb 23
Bonnie Blue Natl Horse Show (Lexington, VA), May 5
Bono: Birth, May 10
Bonsall, Brian: Birth, Dec 3
Bonza Bottler Day, Jan 1
Bonza Bottler Day, Feb 2
Bonza Bottler Day, Mar 3
Bonza Bottler Day, Apr 4
Bonza Bottler Day, May 5
Bonza Bottler Day, Jun 6
Bonza Bottler Day, Jul 7
Bonza Bottler Day, Aug 8
Bonza Bottler Day, Sep 9
Bonza Bottler Day, Oct 10
Bonza Bottler Day, Nov 11
Bonza Bottler Day, Dec 12
Book and Copyright Day, World (UN), Apr 23
Book Month, Natl, May 1
Books. See also Library/Librarians,
 Authors' Day, Natl, Nov 1
 Banff Mountain Book Fest (Banff, AB, Canada), Nov 3
 Banned Books Week, Sep 18
 Bible Week, Natl, Nov 21
 Biographers Day, May 16
 Book Blitz Month, Jan 1
 Book Day (Spain), Apr 23
 Book Month, Natl, May 1
 BookExpo America (Chicago, IL), Jun 2
 Canada Book Week, Apr 18
 Children's Authors & Illustrators Week, Feb 1
 Children's Book Day, Intl, Apr 2
 Children's Book Week, Natl, Nov 15
 Copyright Law Passed: Anniv, May 31
 Copyright Revision Law: Anniv, Jan 1
 Dia de los Ninos/Dia de los Libros (El Paso, TX), Apr 24
 Dictionary Day, Oct 16
 Edinburgh Intl Book Fest (Edinburgh, Scotland), Aug 7
 First Dictionary of American English Published: Anniv, Apr 14
 Frankfurt Book Fair (Frankfurt, Germany), Oct 6
 Get Caught Reading Month, May 1
 Ghostwriters Month, Natl, Mar 1
 GLBT Book Month, Natl, Jun 1
 Grapes of Wrath Published: Anniv, Apr 14
 Guadalajara Intl Book Fair, Nov 27
 Gutenberg Bible Published: Anniv, Sep 30
 Highlights Foundation Writer's Workshop (Chautauqua, NY), Jul 17
 King James Bible Published: Anniv, May 2
 Latino Book & Family Fest (Chicago, IL), Nov 22
 Linda Dominique Grosvenor Natl Read For Leisure Week, May 1
 Literature Fest (Norfolk, NE), Jul 31
 London (England) Book Fair, Mar 14
 Lord of the Rings, First Part Published: Anniv, Jul 19
 Manchester Father's Day Salmon Bake (Manchester, WA), Jun 20
 May Your Reading Be a Haven Month, Aug 1
 Newberry Library's Twentieth Annual Book Fair (Chicago, IL), Jul 29
 On the Origin of Species Published: Anniv, Nov 22
 Paperback Books Introduced: Anniv, Jul 30
 Printers Row Book Fair (Chicago, IL), Jun 5
 Read an E-Book Week, Mar 7
 Reading Group Month, Natl, Oct 1
 Reading Is Fun Week, May 2
 Return the Borrowed Books Week, Mar 1
 Southern Fest of Books (Nashville, TN), Oct 8
 Teen Read Week, Oct 17
 Young Reader's Day, Natl, Nov 9
 Zimbabwe Intl Book Fair, Aug 1
Boom Box Parade (Willimantic, CT), Jul 4
Boom Days (Leadville, CO), Aug 6
Boomer Bonus Day, Apr 1
Boone, Bret: Birth, Apr 6
Boone, Daniel: Battle of Blue Licks Celeb (Mount Olivet, KY), Aug 21
Boone, Daniel: Birth Anniv, Nov 2
Boone, Daniel: Boone Day, Jun 7
Boone, Debbie: Birth, Sep 22
Boone, Pat: Birth, Jun 1
Boonesborough Days (Boonsboro, MD), Sep 11
Boorman, John: Birth, Jan 18

Boosler, Elayne: Birth, Aug 18
Booth, Edwin: Birth Anniv, Nov 13
Booth, Evangeline: Birth Anniv, Dec 25
Booth, John Wilkes, Escape Route Tour (Clinton, MD), Apr 17
Booth, Shirley: Birth Anniv, Aug 30
Booth, William: Birth Anniv, Apr 10
Borden, Lizzie, Verdict: Anniv, Jun 20
Borden, Sir Robert Laird: Birth Anniv, Jun 26
Boreanaz, David: Birth, May 16
Borg, Bjorn: Birth, Jun 6
Borglum, Gutzon: Birth Anniv, Mar 25
Borgnine, Ernest: Birth, Jan 24
Boring Celebrities of the Year, Most, Dec 6
Borman, Frank: Birth, Mar 14
Borneo Rhino Challenge (Malaysia), May 1
Bosley, Tom: Birth, Oct 1
Bosnia and Herzegovina,
 Independence Day, Mar 1
 National Day, Nov 25
Boss Day, Natl, Oct 16
Boss/Employee Exchange Day, Natl, Sep 13
Boston Fire: Anniv, Nov 9
Boston Harborfest (Boston, MA), Jun 29
Boston Marathon (Boston, MA), Apr 19
Boston Massacre: Anniv, Mar 5
Boston Public Library: Anniv, Apr 3
Boston Tea Party: Anniv, Dec 16
Bostwick, Barry: Birth, Feb 24
Boswell, James: Birth Anniv, Oct 29
Botswana,
 Independence Day, Sep 30
 Sir Seretse Khama Day, Jul 1
Bottoms, Timothy: Birth, Aug 30
Boucher, Brian: Birth, Jan 2
Boulez, Pierre: Birth, Mar 26
Bounty, Mutiny on the: Anniv, Apr 28
Bourke-White, Margaret: Birth Anniv, Jun 14
Bourque, Ray: Birth, Dec 28
Boutros-Ghali, Boutros: Birth, Nov 14
Bowditch, Nathaniel: Birth Anniv, Mar 26
Bowdler's Day, Jul 11
Bowe, Riddick: Birth, Aug 10
Bowen, Julie: Birth, Mar 3
Bowie, David: Birth, Jan 8
Bowling,
 ABC Chmpshp Tourn (Reno, NV), Feb 14
 ABC Convention (Reno, NV), Mar 14
Bowman, Scotty: Birth, Sep 18
Boxer, Barbara: Birth, Nov 11
Boxing,
 Clay Becomes Heavyweight Champ: Anniv, Feb 25
 Corbett-Fitzsimmons Title Fight: Anniv, Mar 17
 Corbett-Sullivan Prize Fight: Anniv, Sep 7
 First US Heavyweight Champ Defeated: Anniv, Dec 10
 Johnson, John (Jack) Arthur: Birth Anniv, Mar 31
 Long Count Day, Sep 22
 Louis v Braddock/Schmeling Fight Anniv, Jun 22
 Louis, Joe: Birth Anniv, May 13
 Muhammad Ali Stripped of Title: Anniv, Apr 30
Boxing Day (United Kingdom), Dec 26
Boxing Day Bank Holiday (United Kingdom), Dec 26
Boxleitner, Bruce: Birth, May 12
Boy George: Birth, Jun 14
Boy Scouts of America Founded: Anniv, Feb 8
Boy Scouts: Baden-Powell, Robert: Birth Anniv, Feb 22
Boycott, Charles C.: Birth Anniv, Mar 12
Boyd, Belle: Birth Anniv, May 9
Boyd, William: Birth Anniv, Jun 5
Boyer, Charles: Birth Anniv, Aug 28
Boyle, Lara Flynn: Birth, Mar 24
Boyle, Peter: Birth, Oct 18
Boyle, Robert: Birth Anniv, Jan 25
Boys' Clubs Founded: Anniv, May 19
Bracco, Lorraine: Birth, Oct 2
Brackett Day, Joseph, May 6
Bradbury, Ray: Birth, Aug 22
Bradford, William: Birth Anniv, Mar 19
Bradlee, Benjamin: Birth, Aug 26
Bradley, Bill: Birth, Jul 28
Bradley, Ed: Birth, Jun 22
Bradshaw, Terry: Birth, Sep 2
Bradstreet: Anne Bradstreet Day, Sep 16
Brady Bunch TV Premiere: Anniv, Sep 26
Brady, Mathew: First Presidential Photograph: Anniv, Feb 14
Brady, Sarah: Birth, Feb 6
Brady, Tom: Birth, Aug 3
Braga, Sonia: Birth, Jun 16
Brahms Requiem Premiere: Anniv, Apr 10
Braille, Louis: Birth Anniv, Jan 4
Brain Awareness Week, Intl, Mar 15
Brain Bee, Intl, Mar 20
Branagh, Kenneth: Birth, Dec 10
Branch Davidian Fire at Waco: Anniv, Apr 19
Brand, Elton: Birth, Mar 11
Brand, Oscar: Birth, Feb 7
Brandauer, Klaus Maria: Birth, Jun 22
Brandeis, Louis D.: Birth Anniv, Nov 13
Brando, Marlon: Birth, Apr 3
Brandt, Willy: Birth Anniv, Dec 18
Brandy: Birth, Feb 11
Branigan, Laura: Birth, Jul 3
Branson Fest (Branson, MO), Apr 6

Branson Veterans Homecoming, Nov 5
Bratt, Benjamin: Birth, Dec 16
Braugher, Andre: Birth, Jul 1
Brawl in US House of Representatives, First: Anniv, Jan 30
Braxton, Carter: Birth Anniv, Sep 10
Braxton, Toni: Birth, Oct 7
Brazil,
 Carnival, Feb 21
 Cirio de Nazare, Oct 10
 Discovery of Brazil Day, Apr 22
 Fest of Penha (Rio de Janeiro), Oct 1
 Independence Day, Sep 7
 Independence Week, Sep 1
 Nosso Senhor Do Bonfim Fest, Jan 20
 Republic Day, Nov 15
 San Sebastian's Day, Jan 20
 Tiradentes Day, Apr 21
Brazleton, T. Berry: Birth, May 10
Brazzi, Rossano: Birth Anniv, Sep 18
Breach of Promise Suit, First US: Anniv, Jun 14
Bread Day, Homemade, Nov 17
Bread Machine Baking Month, Jan 1
Bread Pudding Recipe Exchange, May 1
Break the Bank TV Premiere: Anniv, Oct 22
Breakfast Club Radio Premiere: Anniv, Jun 23
Bream, Julian: Birth, Jul 15
Breast Cancer Awareness Month, Natl, Oct 1
Breast Cancer Awareness Month, Natl (Pres Proc), Oct 1
Breathed, Berke: Birth, Jun 21
Breaux, John B.: Birth, Mar 1
Brecht, Bertolt: Birth Anniv, Feb 10
Breckinridge, John Cabell: Birth Anniv, Jan 21
Bredesen, Phil: Birth, Nov 21
Brennan, Eileen: Birth, Sep 3
Brenneman, Amy: Birth, Jun 22
Brenner, David: Birth, Feb 4
Brent, Margaret: Demands a Political Voice: Anniv, Jan 21
Brett, George: Birth, May 15
Brewer, Theresa: Birth, May 7
Breweriana: Summerswap (Frankenmuth, MI), Jul 17
Brewers Fest, Oregon (Portland, OR), Jul 23
Breyer, Stephen G.: Birth, Aug 15
Brickell, Edie: Birth, Mar 10
Brickhouse, Jack: Birth Anniv, Jan 24
Bridal Expo (Santa Cruz, CA), Feb 1
Bridge Day (Fayetteville, WV), Oct 16
Bridge Fest, Covered (Washington County, PA), Sep 18
Bridge Fest, Parke County Covered (Rockville, IN), Oct 8
Bridge over the Neponset: Anniv, Apr 1
Bridger, Jim: Birth Anniv, Mar 17
Bridges, Beau: Birth, Dec 9
Bridges, Jeff: Birth, Dec 4
Bridges, Todd: Birth, May 27
Brimley, Wilford: Birth, Sep 27
Brinkley, Christie: Birth, Feb 2
Brinkley, David: Birth, Jul 10
Brisebois, Danielle: Birth, Jun 28
Britain Declares War on Germany: Anniv, Sep 3
British Museum: Anniv, Jan 15
British North America Act: Anniv, Mar 29
British Open (Open Golf Chmpshp) (Scotland), Jul 15
Brittany, Morgan: Birth, Dec 5
Britten, (Edward) Benjamin: Birth Anniv, Nov 22
Broadbent, Jim: Birth, May 24
Brock, Lou: Birth, Jun 18
Broderick, Matthew: Birth, Mar 21
Brodeur, Martin: Birth, May 6
Brody, Adrien: Birth, Apr 14
Brokaw, Tom: Birth, Feb 6
Brolin, James: Birth, Jul 18
Brolin, Josh: Birth, Feb 12
Bronco League World Series (Monterey, CA), Aug 5
Bronson, Charles: Birth, Nov 3
Bronte, Charlotte: Birth Anniv, Apr 21
Bronte, Emily: Birth Anniv, Jul 30
Brook, Peter: Birth, Mar 21
Brooklyn Bridge Opened: Anniv, May 24
Brooks, Albert: Birth, Jul 22
Brooks, Garth: Birth, Feb 7
Brooks, James David: Birth Anniv, Oct 18
Brooks, James L.: Birth, May 9
Brooks, Jason: Birth, May 10
Brooks, Mel: Birth, Jun 28
Brooks, Phillips: Birth Anniv, Dec 13
Brosnan, Pierce: Birth, May 16
Brother's Day, May 24
Brothers TV Premiere: Anniv, Jul 13
Brothers, Joyce: Birth, Sep 20
Brougham, Henry P.: Birth Anniv, Sep 19
Brown v Board of Education: Anniv, May 17
Brown, Bobby: Birth, Feb 5
Brown, Bryan: Birth, Jun 23
Brown, Curtis, Jr: Birth, Mar 11
Brown, Helen Gurley: Birth, Feb 18
Brown, James: Birth, May 3
Brown, Jesse Leroy: Birth Anniv, Oct 13
Brown, Jim: Birth, Feb 17
Brown, John: Birth Anniv, May 9
Brown, John: Execution Anniv, Dec 2
Brown, John: Raid Anniv, Oct 16

★ Chase's 2004 Calendar of Events ★ Index

Brown, Louise: First Test-Tube Baby: Birth, Jul 25
Brown, Ronald H.: Birth Anniv, Aug 1
Brown, Tina: Birth, Dec 21
Brown, Tony: Birth, Apr 11
Brownback, Sam: Birth, Sep 12
Browne, Jackson: Birth, Oct 9
Browne, Thomas: Birth Anniv, Oct 19
Browning, Elizabeth Barrett: Birth Anniv, Mar 6
Browning, John Moses: Birth Anniv, Jan 21
Browning, Robert: Birth Anniv, May 7
Brownmiller, Susan: Birth, Feb 15
Broz, Josip "Tito": Birth Anniv, May 25
Brubeck, Dave: Birth, Dec 6
Bruce, Isaac: Birth, Nov 10
Bruckner, Anton: Birth Anniv, Sep 4
Brummell, Beau: Birth Anniv, Jun 7
Brunei: National Day, Feb 23
Brunell, Mark: Birth, Sep 17
Brutus Day, Mar 15
Bryan, William Jennings: Birth Anniv, Mar 19
Bryan, Zachery Ty: Birth, Oct 9
Bryant, Anita: Birth, Mar 25
Bryant, Kobe: Birth, Aug 23
Bryant, William C.: Birth Anniv, Nov 3
Bryce Canyon Natl Park Established: Anniv, Jan 1
Bryson, Peabo: Birth, Apr 13
Bubba Day, Natl, Jun 2
Bubble Wrap Appreciation Day, Jan 26
Buchanan, James: Birth Anniv, Apr 23
Buchanan, Patrick: Birth, Nov 2
Buchwald, Art: Birth, Oct 20
Buck Rogers TV Premiere: Anniv, Apr 15
Buck, Pearl S.: Birth Anniv, Jun 26
Buckingham, Lindsey: Birth, Oct 3
Buckley, Betty: Birth, Jul 3
Buckley, William F., Jr: Birth, Nov 24
Buckner, Bill: Birth, Dec 14
Buckwheat Fest, Preston County (Kingwood, WV), Sep 30
Buddha: Birth Anniv, Apr 8
Buddha: Birthday (China), May 26
Buell, Marjorie H.: Birth Anniv, Dec 11
Buffalo Auction (Custer, SD), Nov 20
Buffalo Bill (William F. Cody): Birth Anniv, Feb 26
Buffalo Days Celebration (Luverne, MN), Jun 4
Buffalo Roundup (Custer, SD), Oct 4
Buffalo Roundup Arts Fest (Custer, SD), Oct 2
Buffett, Jimmy: Birth, Dec 25
Buffy the Vampire Slayer TV Premiere: Anniv, Mar 10
Buhl Day (Sharon, PA), Sep 6
Build a Better Image Week, Sep 19
Building on Faith Week, Habitat for Humanity's, Sep 13
Bujold, Genevieve: Birth, Jul 1
Bulgaria,
    Babin Den (Day of the Midwives), Jan 23
    Culture Day, May 24
    Hristo Botev Day, Jun 2
    Liberation Day, Mar 3
    Saint Lasarus's Day, Apr 1
    Unification Day, Sep 6
    Viticulturists' Day, Feb 14
Bullfinch Exchange Fest (Japan), Jan 7
Bullnanza (Guthrie, OK), Feb 6
Bullock, Sandra: Birth, Jul 26
Bullwinkle Show: Rocky and His Friends TV Premiere: Anniv, Nov 19
Bumbershoot: The Seattle Arts Fest (Seattle, WA), Sep 3
Bun Day (Iceland), Feb 23
Bunche, Ralph: Awarded Nobel Peace Prize: Anniv, Dec 10
Bunche, Ralph: Birth Anniv, Aug 7
Bunker Hill Day (Suffolk County, MA), Jun 17
Bunning, Jim: Birth, Oct 23
Bunsen Burner Day, Mar 31
Bunsen, Robert: Birth, Mar 31
Bunyan, John: Birth Anniv, Nov 28
Buonarroti, Michelangelo: Birth Anniv, Mar 6
Buoniconti, Nick: Birth, Dec 15
Burbank, Luther: Birth Anniv, Mar 7
Burdon, Eric: Birth, Apr 5
Bure, Candace Cameron: Birth, Apr 6
Bure, Pavel: Birth, Mar 31
Bureau of Indian Affairs Established, Mar 11
Bureau of Internal Revenue Established: Anniv, Jul 1
Burger, Warren E.: Birth Anniv, Sep 17
Burgess, Anthony: Birth Anniv, Feb 25
Burghoff, Gary: Birth, May 24
Burk, Martha (Calamity Jane): Death Anniv, Aug 1
Burke, Christopher: Birth, Aug 26
Burke, Delta: Birth, Jul 30
Burke, Edmund: Birth Anniv, Jan 12
Burkina Faso,
    National Day, Dec 11
    Republic Day, Aug 5
    Revolution Day, Aug 4
Burnett, Carol: Birth, Apr 26
Burnham, Daniel: Birth Anniv, Sep 4
Burning Man (Black Rock Desert, NV), Aug 30
Burnquist, Bob: Birth, Oct 10
Burns and Allen Show TV Premiere: Anniv, Oct 12
Burns, Conrad: Birth, Jan 25
Burns, George: Birth Anniv, Jan 20
Burns, Ken: Birth, Jul 29

Burns, Robert: Birth Anniv, Jan 25
Burr, Aaron: Birth Anniv, Feb 6
Burr, Aaron: Duel with Alexander Hamilton: Anniv, Jul 11
Burr, Raymond: Birth Anniv, May 21
Burro Race (Leadville, CO), Aug 8
Burroughs, Edgar Rice: Birth Anniv, Sep 1
Burroughs, John: Birth Anniv, Apr 3
Burrows, James: Birth, Dec 30
Bursting Day (Iceland), Feb 24
Burstyn, Ellen: Birth, Dec 7
Burton, LeVar: Birth, Feb 16
Burton, Richard: Birth Anniv, Nov 10
Burton, Tim: Birth, Aug 25
Burundi,
    Assassination of the Hero of the Nation Day, Oct 13
    Independence Day, Jul 1
Buscemi, Steve: Birth, Dec 13
Busey, Gary: Birth, Jun 29
Busfield, Timothy: Birth, Jun 12
Bush, Barbara Pierce: Birth, Jun 8
Bush, George H.W. and Barbara, Wedding: Anniv, Jan 6
Bush, George Herbert Walker: Birthday, Jun 12
Bush, George W. and Laura, Wedding: Anniv, Nov 5
Bush, George W.: Birthday, Jul 6
Bush, George W.: Supreme Court Rules for Bush: Anniv, Dec 12
Bush, Jeb: Birth, Feb 11
Bush, Kate: Birth, Jul 30
Bush, Laura: Birthday, Nov 4
Business (including history, skills, workplace life, types of). See also Careers,
    American Business Women's Day, Sep 22
    AT&T Divestiture: Anniv, Jan 8
    Better Business Communication Day, Jan 26
    Black Business Month, Aug 1
    Boss/Employee Exchange Day, Natl, Sep 13
    Bring Your Teddy Bear to Work and School Day, Natl, Oct 13
    Build a Better Trade Show Image Week, Feb 15
    Build Your Business with Business Cards Week, Oct 10
    Business Image Improvement Month, Intl, May 1
    Business of America Quotation: Anniv, Jan 17
    Business Success Resolutions Month, Intl, Jan 1
    Business Women's Assn, Amer, Natl Conv of (Richmond, VA), Oct 13
    Business Women's Week, Natl, Oct 18
    Clean-Off-Your-Desk Day, Natl, Jan 12
    Companies That Care Day, Mar 18
    Computer Security Day, Nov 30
    Co-op Awareness Month, Oct 1
    Credit Union Week, Intl, Oct 18
    Customer Loyalty Month, Intl, Apr 1
    Customer Service Day, Jan 15
    Emergency Preparedness Week, Natl, Sep 5
    Enron Files for Bankruptcy: Anniv, Dec 2
    Fair Trade Day, World, May 8
    Families in Business Week, Jun 14
    Federal Govt Seizure of Steel Mills: Anniv, Apr 8
    Five-Dollar-a-Day Minimum Wage: Anniv, Jan 5
    Fun at Work Day, Jan 30
    Fun at Work Day, Natl, Apr 1
    Get To Know Your Customer Day, Jan 15
    Getting World to Beat a Path to Your Door Week, Oct 10
    Home-Based Business Week, Oct 10
    Independent Retailers Week, Natl, Jul 18
    Irrational Exuberance Enters Lexicon: Anniv, Dec 5
    Laugh and Get Rich Day, Feb 8
    Laugh at Work Week, Apr 1
    Leadership Success Day, Feb 10
    Ludlow Mine Incident: Anniv, Apr 20
    Mail-Order Catalog: Anniv, Aug 18
    Mom and Pop Business Owners Day, Natl, Mar 29
    Montgomery Ward Seized: Anniv, Apr 26
    Networking Week, Natl, Oct 11
    New York Stock Exchange: Anniv, May 17
    On-Hold Month, Natl, Mar 1
    Printing Week, Intl, Jan 11
    Professional Wellness Month, Jun 1
    Revise Your Work Schedule Month, May 1
    Scrapbooking Industry Day, Intl, Mar 4
    Shameless Promotion Month, Sep 1
    Small Business Day, Natl, May 10
    Small Business Week, May 12
    Smith, Adam: Birth Anniv, Jun 5
    Stay Home Because You're Well Day, Nov 30
    Stop the Bad Service Day, Mar 3
    Subliminal Communications Month, Sep 1
    Take Back Your Time Day, Oct 29
    Take Our Daughters and Sons to Work Day, Apr 22
    Tell Someone They're Doing a Good Job Week, Dec 12
    Thank-Your-Customers Week, Natl, Jan 5
    Tourism Week, Natl, May 8
    Triangle Shirtwaist Fire: Anniv, Mar 25
    Women's Small Business Month, Oct 1
    Work from Home Week, Natl, Oct 3
    Work Life Enrichment Month, Intl, Apr 1
    Work Like a Dog Day, Aug 6
    Workplace Napping Day, Natl, Apr 5
Butcher, Susan: Birth, Dec 26
Butkus, Dick: Birth, Dec 9

Butler, Benjamin: Butler Issues "Woman Order": Anniv, May 16
Butler, Benjamin: Farragut Captures New Orleans: Anniv, Apr 25
Butler, Brett: Birth, Jan 30
Butler, Dan: Birth, Dec 2
Butler, Samuel: Birth Anniv, Dec 4
Button, Dick: Birth, Jul 18
Buttons, Red: Birth, Feb 5
Butts, Alfred M.: Birth Anniv, Apr 13
Buy Nothing Day, Nov 26
Buzzi, Ruth: Birth, Jul 24
Byrd, Robert C.: Birth, Nov 20
Byrne, David: Birth, May 14
Byrne, Gabriel: Birth, May 12
Byrnes, Edd: Birth, Jul 30
Byron, George Gordon: Birth Anniv, Jan 22
Caan, James: Birth, Mar 26
Cabinet, US: Perkins, Frances (1st Woman Appointed), Mar 4
Cable Car Patent: Anniv, Jan 17
Cabrillo Day (CA), Sep 28
Cabrillo Fest (San Diego, CA), Sep 26
Cabrini, Mother Frances Xavier: Anniv, Jul 7
Caesar, Sid: Birth, Sep 8
Caesarean Section, First: Anniv, Jan 14
Caffeine Awareness Month, Natl, Mar 1
Cage, John: Birth Anniv, Sep 5
Cage, Nicolas: Birth, Jan 7
Cagney & Lacey TV Premiere: Anniv, Mar 25
Cahn, Sammy: Birth Anniv, Jun 18
Cain, Dean: Birth, Jul 31
Caine, Michael: Birth, Mar 14
Calabro, Thomas: Birth, Feb 3
Calamity Jane (Martha Burk): Death Anniv, Aug 1
Caldwell, Sarah: Birth, Mar 6
Caldwell, Zoe: Birth, Sep 14
Calendar Adjustment Day: Anniv, Sep 2
Calendar Day, Gregorian, Feb 24
Calendar Stone, Aztec, Discovery: Anniv, Dec 17
Calhoun, John C.: Birth Anniv, Mar 18
Calhoun, John C.: VP Resignation: Anniv, Dec 28
California,
    Admission Day, Sep 9
    Aerospace Walk of Honor (Lancaster), Sep 11
    AFRMA Display & Show (Costa Mesa), Jul 9
    AFRMA Display at America's Family Pet Expo (Costa Mesa), Apr 2
    AFRMA Fancy Rat & Mouse Display (Newhall), May 16
    American Dietetic Assn Food & Nutrition Conf & Expo (Anaheim), Oct 2
    American Rose Society Spring Natl Convention (San Diego), May 5
    Bay to Breakers Race (San Francisco), May 14
    Beverly Hills Affaire in Gardens (Beverly Hills), May 15
    Blessing of the Fishing Fleet (San Francisco), Oct 3
    Bob Hope Chrysler Golf Classic (La Quinta), Jan 19
    Boxer, Barbara: Birth, Nov 11
    Bridal Expo (Santa Cruz), Jan 1
    Bronco League World Series (Monterey), Aug 5
    Cabrillo Day, Sep 28
    Cabrillo Fest (San Diego), Sep 26
    Calaveras Fair/Jumping Frog Jubilee (Angel Camp), May 13
    California Artichoke Festival (Castroville), May 17
    California Free-Fishing Days, Jun 5
    California Gold Discovery: Anniv, Jan 24
    California Poppy Fest (Lancaster), Apr 17
    California State Fair (Sacramento), Aug 20
    Cesar Chavez Day, Mar 31
    Channel Islands Natl Park Established: Anniv, Mar 5
    Chinese New Year Fest (San Francisco), Jan 17
    Chinese New Year Golden Dragon Parade (Los Angeles), Jan 24
    Chrysler Classic Speed Fest (San Diego), Oct 9
    Clam Chowder Cookoff (Santa Cruz), Feb 21
    Date Fest, Natl (Indio), Feb 13
    Davis, Gray: Birth, Dec 26
    Day of the Horse, Dec 11
    Disneyland Opened: Anniv, Jul 17
    EarthFair (San Diego), Apr 25
    Earthquake Preparedness Month, Apr 1
    Farmers Market (El Centro), Jan 24
    Feinstein, Dianne: Birth, Jun 22
    Footbag Chmpshps, World (San Francisco), Aug 2
    Fortune Cookie Day (San Francisco), Sep 13
    Gilroy Garlic Fest (Gilroy), Jul 23
    Go Wild During California Wild Rice Month, Sep 1
    Golden Gate Bridge Opened: Anniv, May 27
    Grubstake Days (Yucca Valley), May 27
    Harvest Wine Celeb (Livermore), Sep 5
    Haute Dog Charity Easter Parade (Long Beach), Apr 11
    Haute Dog Charity Howl'oween Parade (Long Beach), Oct 31
    Hobby Industry Assn Conv & Trade Show (Anaheim), Feb 5
    Huck Finn's Jubilee (Victorville), Jun 18
    Invisible Chronic Illness Awareness Week, Natl (San Diego), Sep 20
    Jimmy Stewart Relay Marathon (Los Angeles), Apr 18
    Lassen Volcanic Natl Park Established: Anniv, Aug 9
    Laura Ingalls Wilder Gingerbread Sociable (Pomona), Feb 7

Index ☆ Chase's 2004 Calendar of Events ☆
California (cont'd)—Careers

Long Beach Bayou Fest (Long Beach), **Jun 18**
Los Angeles Founded: Anniv, **Sep 4**
Los Angeles Riots: Anniv, **Apr 29**
Mainly Mozart Fest (San Diego), **May 30**
Mercedes-Benz Shows LA (Fall Lines) (Los Angeles), **Mar 30**
Mercedes-Benz Shows LA (Spring Lines) (Los Angeles), **Oct 26**
Mission San Carlos Borromeo de Carmelo: Founding Anniv, **Jun 3**
Mobius Awards (Los Angeles), **Feb 20**
Monterey Jazz Fest (Monterey), **Sep 17**
Morro Bay Harbor Fest (Morro Bay), **Oct 2**
Mother Goose Parade (El Cajon), **Nov 21**
Mozart Fest (San Luis Obispo), **Jul 16**
MS Walk (San Jose), **Apr 17**
Nabisco Championship (Rancho Mirage), **Mar 22**
NBA All-Star Weekend (Los Angeles), **Feb 13**
NCAA Div I Women's Gymnastics (Los Angeles), **Apr 15**
NCAA Skiing Chmpshps (Norden and Soda Springs), **Mar 10**
Nixon Birthday Holiday (Yorba Linda), **Jan 9**
Pacific DanceSport Chmpnshps (Los Angeles), **Nov 5**
Pacific Life Holiday Bowl Parade/Game (San Diego), **Dec 30**
Palomino League World Series (Santa Clara), **Aug 6**
Pasadena Doo Dah Parade (Pasadena), **Nov 21**
Proposition 13: Anniv, **Jun 6**
Rat and Mouse Annual Show, Fancy (Riverside), **Jan 17**
Redwood Natl Park Established: Anniv, **Oct 2**
Rideshare Week, **Oct 4**
Rose Bowl Game (Pasadena), **Jan 1**
Sacramento Jazz Jubilee (Sacramento), **May 28**
San Diego Boat Show (San Diego), **Jan 8**
San Diego Marathon (Carlsbad), **Jan 18**
Santa by Stage Coach Parade (El Centro), **Dec 4**
Sequoia and Kings Canyon Natl Park Established: Anniv, **Sep 25**
Snowbirds Pancake Breakfast (El Centro), **Jan 10**
Sonoma Valley Harvest Wine Auction (Sonoma), **Sep 3**
Sonoma-Marin Fair (Petaluma), **Jun 16**
Southern California Firestorms: Anniv, **Oct 25**
Stamp Expo (Anaheim), **Sep 10**
Stamp Expo (Anaheim), **May 14**
Stamp Expo (Los Angeles), **Apr 2**
Stamp Expo (Pasadena), **Feb 20**
Stamp Expo (Pasadena), **May 21**
Stamp Expo (Pasadena), **Jul 2**
Stamp Expo (Sherman Oaks), **Jun 18**
Stamp Expo America (Anaheim), **Nov 12**
Stamp Expo USA (Anaheim), **Feb 13**
Stamp Expo: Anaheim (Anaheim), **Oct 1**
Stamp Expo: California (Pasadena), **Nov 19**
Stamp Expo: South (Anaheim), **Apr 16**
Starman Family-Con 2004 (Hollywood), **Apr 23**
Swallows Depart from San Juan Capistrano, **Oct 23**
Swallows Return to San Juan Capistrano, **Mar 19**
Tamale Fiesta (El Centro), **Dec 4**
Taste of Morgan Hill (Morgan Hill), **Sep 25**
Tournament of Roses Parade (Pasadena), **Jan 1**
US Industrial Film/Video Awards (Los Angeles), **Jun 3**
US Junior Amateur (Golf) Chmpship (San Francisco), **Jul 27**
USGA Senior Amateur (Golf) Chmpshp (Los Angeles), **Oct 9**
Viva El Mariachi Fest (Fresno), **Mar 20**
Whiskey Flat Days (Kernville), **Feb 13**
Whitewater Wednesday (Kernville), **Jun 16**
World Ag Expo (Tulare), **Feb 10**
World Wristwrestling Chmpshp (Petaluma), **Oct 9**
Yosemite Natl Park Established: Anniv, **Oct 1**
Callas, Maria: Birth Anniv, Dec 2
Callow, Simon: Birth, Jun 15
Calloway, Cab: Birth Anniv, Dec 25
Calvin, John: Birth Anniv, Jul 10
Cambodia,
Constitutional Declaration Day, **Sep 24**
Falls to the Khmer Rouge: Anniv, **Apr 17**
Independence Day, **Nov 9**
Invaded by US: Anniv, **Apr 30**
Peace Treaty Day, **Oct 23**
Pol Pot Overthrown: Anniv, **Jan 7**
Cambodia Invaded by US: Anniv, Apr 30
Camden, Battle of: Anniv, Aug 16
Cameron, James: Birth, Aug 16
Cameron, James: Titanic Released: Anniv, Dec 19
Cameron, Kirk: Birth, Oct 12
Cameroon,
National Holiday: Anniv, **May 20**
Volcanic Eruption: Anniv, **Aug 22**
Youth Day, **Feb 11**
CAMEX (San Antonio, TX), Feb 27
Camp David Accord Signed: Anniv, Mar 26
Camp Fire Birthday Week, Mar 15
Camp Fire Founders Day, Mar 17
Camp Month, Natl Sign Up for Summer, Dec 1
Camp, Walter: Birth Anniv, Apr 7
Campanella, Roy: Birth Anniv, Nov 19
Campbell, Ben Nighthorse: Birth, Apr 13
Campbell, Billy: Birth, Jul 7
Campbell, Christian: Birth, May 12
Campbell, Douglas: Becomes 1st American Air ACE: Anniv, Apr 14
Campbell, Earl: Birth, Mar 29
Campbell, Glen: Birth, Apr 22
Campbell, Kim: Birth, Mar 10
Campbell, Malcolm: Birth Anniv, Mar 11
Campbell, Naomi: Birth, May 22
Campbell, Neve: Birth, Oct 3
Campion, Jane: Birth, Apr 30
Campos, Bruno: Birth, Dec 3
Camus, Albert: Birth Anniv, Nov 7
Canada,
Abbotsford Berry Fest (Abbotsford, BC), **Jul 2**
Abbotsford Intl Airshow (Abbotsford, BC), **Aug 13**
Agrifair (Abbotsford, BC), **Jul 29**
Apple Blossom Fest (Annapolis Valley, NS), **May 26**
Bancroft Frosty Frolics (Bancroft, ON), **Feb 14**
Banff Mountain Book Fest (Banff, AB), **Nov 3**
Banff Mountain Film Fest (Banff, AB), **Nov 5**
Big Valley Jamboree (Camrose, AB), **Jul 29**
Boissevain-Morton Summer Festival (Boissevain, MB), **Aug 6**
British North America Act: Anniv, **Mar 29**
Calgary Boat/Sportsmen's Show (Calgary, AB), **Feb 12**
Calgary Folk Fest (Calgary, AB), **Jul 22**
Calgary Stampede (Calgary, AB), **Jul 9**
Campbell, Kim, 19th Prime Minister: Anniv, **Jun 25**
Canada Book Week, **Apr 18**
Canada Day, **Jul 1**
Canada Day Celebration (Ottawa, ON), **Jul 1**
Canada Day Celebrations (Squamish, BC), **Jul 1**
Canada Day Party in the Park (Bancroft, ON), **Jul 1**
Canada's Natl Ukrainian Fest (Dauphin, MB), **Jul 30**
Canadian Open Fiddle Chmpnshp (Shelburne, ON), **Aug 4**
Canadian Tulip Fest (Ottawa, ON), **May 6**
Canadian Western Agribition (Regina, SK), **Nov 22**
Canmore Folk Music Fest (Canmore, AB), **Jul 31**
Civic Holiday, **Aug 2**
Classic Boat Fest (Victoria, BC), **Aug 27**
CN Tower: Anniv, **Jun 26**
Coe Hill Agricultural Fair (Coe Hill, ON), **Aug 20**
Constitution Act: Anniv, **Apr 18**
Country Good Times (Wilberforce, ON), **Jul 16**
Daylight Saving Time Begins, **Apr 4**
Daylight Saving Time Ends, **Oct 31**
Digby Scallop Days Fest (Digby, NS), **Aug 4**
Edmonton Folk Music Fest (Edmonton, AB), **Aug 5**
Elmira Maple Syrup Fest (Elmira, ON), **Apr 3**
Family Day in Alberta, **Feb 16**
First Nights, **Dec 31**
Folklorama—Canada's Cultural Celeb (Winnipeg, MB), **Aug 1**
Fringe Theatre Fest (Edmonton, AB), **Aug 12**
Great Klondike Outhouse Race (Dawson City, YT), **Sep 1**
Great Rendezvous (Thunder Bay, ON), **Jul 9**
Guelph Spring Fest (Guelph, ON), **Apr 30**
Halifax Intl Busker Fest (Halifax, NS), **Aug 5**
Halifax, Nova Scotia, Destroyed: Anniv, **Dec 6**
Harrison Fest of Arts (Harrison Hot Springs, BC), **Jul 10**
Heritage Days (Chatham, ON), **Oct 1**
Immigrants' Day, **May 22**
International Fest (St. Stephen, NB/Calais, ME), **Jul 30**
Inuit Territory Approved: Anniv, **Nov 3**
Just for Laughs Fest (Montreal, QC), **Jul 15**
Klondike Eldorado Gold Discovery: Anniv, **Aug 31**
Klondike Gold Discovery: Anniv, **Aug 16**
Labor Day, **Sep 6**
Maple Fest of Nova Scotia (Northern Nova Scotia), **Mar 20**
Maple Leaf Flag Adopted: Anniv, **Feb 15**
Masters (Calgary, AB), **Sep 8**
Maynooth Madness (Maynooth, ON), **Sep 4**
Mineral Capital Rock Show (Bancroft, ON), **Jul 24**
Mineral Collecting Field Trips (Bancroft, ON), **Jul 3**
Montreal Sportsmen's Show (Montreal, QC), **Feb 26**
Morden Corn/Apple Fest (Morden, MB), **Aug 27**
Mourning, Natl Day of, **Apr 28**
Multicultural Fest (Dartmouth, NS), **Jun 18**
Natl Tournament (Calgary, AB), **Jun 9**
Newfoundland Discovery Day, **Jun 21**
Newfoundland: Saint George's Day, **Apr 26**
North American Tournament (Calgary, AB), **Jul 7**
North America's Coldest Recorded Temperature: Anniv, **Feb 3**
Nova Scotia Bluegrass/Oldtime Music Fest (Mt Denson, NS), **Jul 23**
Nova Scotia Intl Tattoo (Halifax, NS), **Jun 29**
Nova Scotia's Gem and Mineral Show (Parrsboro, NS), **Aug 20**
Nunavut Independence: Anniv, **Apr 1**
Ojibwa Keeshigun (Thunder Bay, ON), **Aug 14**
Oktoberfest (Kitchener/Waterloo, ON), **Oct 8**
Ontario Winter Carnival Bon Soo (Sault Ste. Marie, ON), **Jan 30**
Ottawa Boat/Sportsmen's Show (Ottawa, ON), **Feb 26**
Persons Day, **Oct 18**
Pioneer Days (Steinbach, MB), **Jul 30**
Quebec City Sportsmen's Show (Quebec City, QC), **Mar 11**
Quebec Winter Carnival (Quebec City, QC), **Jan 30**
Rally of the Tall Pines (Bancroft, ON), **Nov 20**
Remembrance Day, **Nov 11**
Robbie Burns Dinner (Bracebridge, ON), **Jan 24**
Rockhound Gemboree (Bancroft, ON), **Jul 29**
Saint Jean-Baptiste Day (Quebec, QC), **Jun 24**
Saint Swithun's Celeb (Richmond Hill, ON), **Jul 15**
Sam Steele Days (Cranbrook, BC), **Jun 17**
Shelburne County Lobster Fest (Shelburne Co, NS), **Jun 3**
Thanksgiving Day, **Oct 11**
Thunder Bay Chamber of Commerce Trade Show, **May 13**
Toronto Intl Film Fest (Toronto, ON), **Sep 9**
Toronto Ski, Snowboard and Travel Show (Toronto, ON), **Oct 14**
Toronto Sportsmen's Show (Toronto, ON), **Mar 17**
Vancouver Intl Boat Show (Vancouver, BC), **Feb 4**
Victoria Day, **May 24**
Winnipeg Fringe Theatre Fest (Winnipeg, MB), **Jul 14**
Winnipeg Intl Children's Fest (Winnipeg, MB), **Jun 10**
Winterlude (Ottawa, ON), **Feb 6**
Yukon Discovery Day, **Aug 16**
Yukon Gold Panning (Dawson City, YT), **Jul 1**
Yukon Order of Pioneers: Anniv, **Dec 1**
Yukon Quest Intl 1,000-Mile Sled Dog Race (Whitehorse, YT), **Feb 14**
Yukon River Bathtub Race (Whitehorse, YT), **Aug 12**
Yukon Sourdough Rendezvous (Whitehorse, YT), **Feb 26**
Canadian Pacific RR: Transcontinental Completion Anniv, Nov 7
Canal Fest, Coshocton (Coshocton, OH), Aug 21
Canaletto, Giovanni Antonio: Birth Anniv, Oct 18
Canary Islands Plane Disaster: Anniv, Mar 27
Cancer (Zodiac) Begins, Jun 21
Cancer Control Month (Pres Proc), Apr 1
Cancer from the Sun Month, Jun 1
Cancer Prevention Month, Natl, Jan 1
Cancer Survivors Day, Natl, Jun 6
Candid Camera TV Premiere: Anniv, Aug 10
Candlemas Day (Presentation of the Lord), Feb 2
Candy Month, Natl, Jun 1
Candy, John: Birth Anniv, Oct 31
Caniff, Milton: Birth Anniv, Feb 28
Canned Beer, First: Anniv, Jan 24
Cannes Film Fest (Cannes, France), May 12
Canning: Appert, Nicholas: Birth Anniv, Oct 23
Cannon, Annie Jump: Birth Anniv, Dec 11
Cannon, Dyan: Birth, Jan 4
Canova, Diana: Birth, Jun 2
Canseco, Jose, Jr: Birth, Jul 2
Cantinflas: Birth Anniv, Aug 12
Cantrell, Lana: Birth, Aug 7
Cantwell, Maria: Birth, Oct 13
Cape Verde: National Day, Jul 5
Capital One Florida Citrus Bowl (Orlando, FL), Jan 1
Capitol Cornerstone Laid, US: Anniv, Sep 18
Capitol Reef Natl Park Established: Anniv, Dec 18
Capone, Al: Death Anniv, Jan 25
Capote, Truman: Birth Anniv, Sep 30
Capp, Al: Birth Anniv, Sep 28
Capra, Frank: Birth Anniv, May 18
Capriati, Jennifer: Birth, Mar 29
Capricorn Begins, Dec 22
Capshaw, Kate: Birth, Nov 3
Captain Kangaroo TV Premiere: Anniv, Oct 3
Captain Kangaroo: Birth, Jun 27
Captain Midnight TV Premiere: Anniv, Sep 4
Captain Video and His Video Rangers TV Premiere: Anniv, Jun 27
Captive Nations Week (Pres Proc), Jul 18
Car Care Month, Natl, Apr 1
Car Talk Natl Radio Premiere: Anniv, Oct 31
Cara, Irene: Birth, Mar 18
Carabao Fest (Philippines), May 14
Caraway, Hattie Wyatt: Birth Anniv, Feb 1
Caraway, Hattie: First Elected Woman Senator: Anniv, Jan 12
Caray, Harry: Birth Anniv, Mar 14
Carbon-14 Dating Inventor (Libby): Birth Anniv, Dec 17
Carbonell, Nestor: Birth, Dec 1
Carcieri, Donald: Birth, Dec 16
Cardellini, Linda: Birth, Jun 25
Cardiac Rehabilitation Week, Feb 8
Cardin, Pierre: Birth, Jul 7
Cardinale, Claudia: Birth, Apr 15
Care Sunday (England), Mar 28
Careers (including employment, employees, occupations, professions). See also Business, Labor,
Administrative Professionals Day, **Apr 21**
Administrative Professionals Intl Conv (Washington, DC), **Aug 1**
Administrative Professionals Week, **Apr 18**
American Soc of Assn Executives Mtg/Expo (Minneapolis, MN), **Aug 14**
Automotive Service Professionals Day, Natl, **Jun 12**
Be Kind to Editors and Writers Month, **Sep 1**
Boss Day, Natl, **Oct 16**
Columnist's Day, Natl, **Jun 28**
Companies That Care Day, **Mar 18**
Cranky Co-Workers Day, **Oct 27**
Custodial Workers Day, Natl, **Oct 2**
Disability Employment Awareness Month, Natl, **Oct 1**
Emergency Nurses Day, **Oct 13**
Emergency Nurses Week, **Oct 10**

☆ Chase's 2004 Calendar of Events ☆   Index

Empowered Women Entrepreneurs Day, **Apr 1**
Engineers Week, Natl, **Feb 22**
Explore Your Career Options Week, **Apr 12**
Extraordinary Work Team Recognition Day, **Dec 4**
Facility Service Workers Day, **Oct 18**
Family, Career and Community Leaders of America Natl Leadership Mtg (Chicago, IL), **Jul 11**
Family, Career and Community Leaders Week, Natl, **Feb 8**
First Flight Attendant: Anniv, **May 15**
Flexible Work Arrangements Week, **May 2**
Freelance Writers Appreciation Week, **Feb 9**
Get Paid to Shop Week, **Feb 1**
Goodwill Industries Week, **May 2**
Groundhog Job Shadow Day, **Feb 2**
Gruntled Workers Day, **Jul 13**
Hairstylist Day, **Apr 30**
Labor Day, **Sep 6**
Labor Day, **May 3**
Laundry Workers' Week, Natl, **Jul 4**
Legal Assistants Day, **Mar 26**
Meeting Planners Appreciation Day, Natl, **May 3**
Mom and Pop Business Owners Day, Natl, **Mar 29**
Nurse Anesthetists Week, Natl, **Jan 25**
Nurses Day and Week, Natl, **May 6**
Nursing Assistants Day and Week, **Jun 10**
Nursing Conf on Pediatric Primary Care (Dallas, TX), **Mar 23**
Occupational Therapy Month, Natl, **Apr 1**
Pastoral Care Week, **Oct 24**
Pawnbrokers Day, Natl, **Dec 6**
Payroll Week, Natl, **Sep 6**
Peace Officer Memorial Day, Natl, **May 15**
Perioperative (OR) Nurse Week, **Nov 14**
Physician Assistant Day, **Oct 6**
Police Week, Natl, **May 9**
Prof Pet Sitters Week, Natl, **Mar 7**
Receptionists Day, Natl, **May 14**
Salesperson's Day, Natl, **Mar 5**
Social Work Month, Natl Pro, **Mar 1**
Solo-Preneuring Week, **Jan 25**
Sporting Goods Assn Mgmt Conf, Natl (Hilton Head Island, SC), **May 16**
Substitute Teacher Appreciation Week, **Sep 13**
Tailors Day, Natl, **Jun 2**
Take Back Your Time Day, **Oct 29**
Take Our Daughters and Sons to Work Day, **Apr 22**
Tell Someone They're Doing a Good Job Week, **Dec 12**
Thank You, School Librarian Day, **Apr 21**
Third Shift Workers Day, Natl, **May 12**
TV Talk-Show Host Day, **Oct 23**
Update Your References Week, **May 3**
Update Your Resume Month, **Sep 1**
Waitstaff Day, Natl, **May 21**
Weatherman's Day, **Feb 5**
Wordsmith Day, **May 3**
Workers Memorial Day, **Apr 28**
Working Women's Day, Intl, **Mar 8**
Carew, Rod: Birth, **Oct 1**
Carey, Drew: Birth, **May 23**
Carey, Mariah: Birth, **Mar 27**
Caribbean or Caricom Day, **Jul 5**
Caricom or Caribbean Day, **Jul 5**
Carillon Fest, Intl (Springfield, IL), **Jun 6**
Car-Keeping Month, Natl Good, **May 1**
Carleton, Will: Birth Anniv, **Oct 21**
Carlin, George: Birth, **May 12**
Carlisle, Belinda: Birth, **Aug 17**
Carlisle, Kitty: Birth, **Sep 3**
Carlsbad Caverns Natl Park Established: Anniv, **May 14**
Carlton, Steve: Birth, **Dec 22**
Carlyle, Robert: Birth, **Apr 14**
Carlyle, Thomas: Birth Anniv, **Dec 4**
Carmichael, Hoagie: Birth Anniv, **Nov 22**
Carnaval Miami (Miami, FL), **Mar 5**
Carnegie, Andrew: Birth Anniv, **Nov 25**
Carnegie, Dale: Birth Anniv, **Nov 24**
Carnes, Kim: Birth, **Jul 20**
Carney, Art: Birth, **Nov 4**
Carney, Wm, First Black Receives Congressional Medal: Anniv, **May 23**
Carnival, **Feb 23**
Carnival (Malta), **Feb 21**
Carnival (Port of Spain, Trinidad and Tobago), **Feb 23**
Carnival de Ponce (Ponce, PR), **Feb 18**
Carnival Season, **Jan 6**
Carnival Week (Milan, Italy), **Feb 22**
Carnovsky, Morris: Birth Anniv, **Sep 5**
Carol Burnett Show TV Premiere: Anniv, **Sep 11**
Caroline, Princess: Birth, **Jan 23**
Caron, Leslie: Birth, **Jul 1**
Carousel: Santa Cruz Beach Looff Carousel: Anniv, **Aug 3**
Carpenter Ant Awareness Week, **Jun 20**
Carpenter, John: Birth, **Jan 16**
Carpenter, Mary Chapin: Birth, **Feb 21**
Carper, Tom: Birth, **Jan 23**
Carr, Gerald Paul: Birth, **Aug 22**
Carr, Vikki: Birth, **Jul 19**
Carradine, David: Birth, **Dec 8**
Carradine, John: Birth Anniv, **Feb 5**
Carradine, Keith: Birth, **Aug 8**
Carreras, Jose: Birth, **Dec 5**

Carrere, Tia: Birth, **Jan 2**
Carrey, Jim: Birth, **Jan 17**
Carroll, Charles: Birth Anniv, **Sep 19**
Carroll, Diahann: Birth, **Jul 17**
Carroll, Lewis: Birth Anniv. See Dodgson, Charles, **Jan 27**
Carroll, Pat: Birth, **May 5**
Carry a Tune Wk, Natl, **Oct 3**
Carsey, Marcy: Birth, **Nov 21**
Carson, Johnny: Birth, **Oct 23**
Carson, Johnny: Final Show, **May 22**
Carson, Kit: Birth Anniv, **Dec 24**
Carson, Lisa Nicole: Birth, **Jul 12**
Carson, Rachel: Birth Anniv, **May 27**
Carson, Rachel: Silent Spring Publication: Anniv, **Apr 13**
Carter Reinstates Selective Service: Anniv, **Jan 23**
Carter, Chris: Birth, **Oct 13**
Carter, Cris: Birth, **Nov 25**
Carter, Dixie: Birth, **May 25**
Carter, Gary: Birth, **Apr 8**
Carter, Hodding, III: Birth, **Apr 7**
Carter, Jimmy and Rosalynn, Wedding Anniv, **Jul 7**
Carter, Jimmy: Birthday, **Oct 1**
Carter, Lynda: Birth, **Jul 24**
Carter, Robert III: Emancipation of 500: Anniv, **Aug 1**
Carter, Rosalynn: Birth, **Aug 18**
Carter, Vince: Birth, **Jan 25**
Cartier, Jacques: Death Anniv, **Sep 1**
Cartier-Bresson, Henri: Birth, **Aug 22**
Cartoonists Against Crime Day, **Oct 25**
Cartoonists Day, **May 5**
Cartwright, Angela: Birth, **Sep 9**
Cartwright, Edmund: Birth Anniv, **Apr 24**
Caruso, David: Birth, **Jan 7**
Caruso, Enrico: Birth Anniv, **Feb 25**
Carvel, Tom: Death Anniv, **Oct 21**
Carver Day Commemorative Celebration (Diamond, MO), **Jul 17**
Carver, George Washington: Death Anniv, **Jan 5**
Carver, Raymond: Birth Anniv, **May 25**
Carvey, Dana: Birth, **Jun 2**
Casablanca Premiere: Anniv, **Nov 26**
Casady, Jack: Birth, **Apr 13**
Casals, Pablo: Birth Anniv, **Dec 29**
Casanova, Giovanni: Birth Anniv, **Apr 2**
Case, Steve: Birth, **Aug 21**
Casey, Bernie: Birth, **Jun 8**
Casey, Sean: Birth, **Jul 2**
Cash, Johnny: Birth, **Feb 26**
Cash, Pat: Birth, **May 27**
Cassatt, Mary: Birth Anniv, **May 22**
Cassel, Seymour: Birth, **Jan 22**
Cassidy, Butch (Robert Leroy Parker): Birth Anniv, **Apr 13**
Cassidy, David: Birth, **Apr 12**
Cassidy, Joanna: Birth, **Aug 2**
Cassidy, Patrick: Birth, **Jan 4**
Cassidy, Shaun: Birth, **Sep 27**
Cassini, Oleg: Birth, **Apr 11**
Castro, Fidel: Birth, **Aug 13**
Cat Fest (Belgium), **Feb 26**
Cataract Awareness Month, **Aug 1**
Cates, Phoebe: Birth, **Jul 16**
Cather, Willa: Birth Anniv, **Dec 7**
Cathode-Ray Tube Patented: Anniv, **Dec 20**
Catholic Educational Assn Conv/Expo, Natl (Boston, MA), **Apr 13**
Catholic Hour TV Premiere: Anniv, **Jan 4**
Catholic Schools Week, **Jan 25**
Catlin, George: Birth Anniv, **Jul 26**
Cats Premieres: Anniv, **Oct 7**
Catt, Carrie Lane Chapman: Birth Anniv, **Jan 9**
Cattrall, Kim: Birth, **Aug 21**
Cauthen, Steve: Birth, **May 1**
Cavalcade of Stars TV Premiere: Anniv, **Jun 4**
Cavanagh, Tom: Birth, **Oct 26**
Cavett, Dick: Birth, **Nov 19**
Cavoukian, Raffi: Birth, **Jul 8**
Caxton, William: Birth Anniv, **Aug 13**
Caxton's "Mirror of the World" Translation: Anniv, **Mar 8**
Cayley, George: Birth Anniv, **Dec 27**
Cazenove, Christopher: Birth, **Dec 17**
CBS Evening News TV Premiere: Anniv, **May 3**
CD Player Debuts: Anniv, **Oct 1**
Ceausescu, Nicolae: Death Anniv, **Dec 25**
Ceccato, Aldo: Birth, **Feb 18**
Celebrate Your Marriage Day, Natl, **Jun 26**
Celebrate Your Name Week, **Mar 7**
Celebration of Life Day, **Jan 22**
Celebration of Life Month, **Jan 1**
Celebration of Life Week, **Jan 1**
Celebration of Love Week, **Feb 9**
Celebration of the Senses, **Jun 24**
Celebrities, Most Boring of the Year, **Dec 6**
Celiac Sprue Awareness Month, **Oct 1**
Cell Phone Courtesy Month, **Jul 1**
Cellophane Tape Patented: Anniv, **May 27**
Cellucci, A. Paul: Birth, **Apr 24**
Celtic Fest, Southern Maryland (St. Leonard, MD), **Apr 24**
Census, First US: Anniv, **Aug 1**
Centenarians Day, Natl, **Sep 22**

Central African Republic,
   Boganda Day, **Mar 29**
   Independence Day, **Aug 13**
   National Day, **Dec 1**
Cermak, Anton J.: Assassination Anniv, **Feb 15**
Cervantes Saavedra, Miguel de: Death Anniv, **Apr 23**
Cetera, Peter: Birth, **Sep 13**
Cezanne, Paul: Birth Anniv, **Jan 19**
Chabrol, Claude: Birth, **Jun 24**
Chad,
   African Freedom Day, **May 25**
   Independence Day, **Aug 11**
   Republic Day, **Nov 28**
Chadds Ford Days (Chadds Ford, PA), **Sep 11**
Chafee, Lincoln: Birth, **Mar 26**
Chalke, Sarah: Birth, **Aug 27**
Challenger Space Shuttle Explosion: Anniv, **Jan 28**
Chalo Nitka (Big Bass) (Moore Haven, FL), **Mar 5**
Chamberlain, Richard: Birth, **Mar 31**
Chamberlain, Wilt: Birth Anniv, **Aug 21**
Chambers, Tom: Birth, **Jun 21**
Chambersfest (Chambersburg, PA), **Jul 17**
Chambliss, Saxby: Birth, **Nov 10**
Champion of the Month, **Jan 15**
Champion, Marge: Birth, **Sep 2**
Chan, Jackie: Birth, **Apr 7**
Chancellor, John: Birth Anniv, **Jul 14**
Chandler, Chris: Birth, **Oct 12**
Chandler, Kyle: Birth, **Sep 17**
Chanel, Coco: Birth Anniv, **Aug 19**
Chaney, Goodman, Schwerner: Civil Rights Workers Slain, **Aug 4**
Chang, Michael: Birth, **Feb 22**
Channel Islands Natl Park Established: Anniv, **Mar 5**
Channing, Carol: Birth, **Jan 31**
Channing, Stockard: Birth, **Feb 13**
Channing, William Ellery: Birth, **Apr 7**
Chanukah, **Dec 8**
Chao, Elaine: Birth, **Mar 26**
Chapin, Harry: Birth Anniv, **Dec 7**
Chaplin, Charles: Birth Anniv, **Apr 16**
Chaplin, Charlie: Tramp Debuts: Anniv, **Feb 7**
Chaplin, Geraldine: Birth, **Jul 31**
Chapman, John (Johnny Appleseed): Birth Anniv, **Sep 26**
Chapman, John: Death Anniv: Johnny Appleseed Day, **Mar 11**
Chapman, John: Johnny Appleseed Fest (Fort Wayne, IN), **Sep 18**
Chapman, Tracy: Birth, **Mar 30**
Character Counts Week, Natl (Pres Proc), **Oct 17**
Charisse, Cyd: Birth, **Mar 8**
Charles I Execution: Anniv, **Jan 30**
Charles II: Restoration and Birth Anniv, **May 29**
Charles, Prince: Birth, **Nov 14**
Charles, Ray: Birth, **Sep 23**
Charleston Earthquake: Anniv, **Aug 31**
Charlie the Tuna: Sorry Charlie Day, **Apr 1**
Charlie's Angels TV Premiere: Anniv, **Sep 22**
Charo: Birth, **Mar 13**
Charro Days (Brownsville, TX), **Feb 26**
Charvet, David: Birth, **May 15**
Chase, Chevy: Birth, **Oct 8**
Chase, Harrison, V: Birth Anniv, **Aug 17**
Chase, Helen M.: Birth, **Dec 4**
Chase, Salmon Portland: Birth Anniv, **Jan 13**
Chase, Samuel: Birth Anniv, **Apr 17**
Chase, Sylvia: Birth, **Feb 23**
Chase, William D.: Birth, **Apr 8**
Chase's 2005 Calendar of Events Published, **Sep 24**
Chase's Calendar Deadline Approaching, **Mar 8**
Chase's Calendar of Events: Birthday, **Dec 4**
Chastain, Brandi: Birth, **Jul 21**
Chateaubriand, Francois Rene de: Birth Anniv, **Sep 4**
Chatterton, Thomas: Birth Anniv, **Nov 20**
Chaucer, Geoffrey: Death Anniv, **Oct 25**
Chauvin Day, **Aug 15**
Chavez, Cesar Estrada: Birth Anniv, **Mar 31**
Check Your Batteries Day, **Apr 4**
Checker, Chubby: Birth, **Oct 3**
Checkers Day, **Sep 23**
Cheer Coach Day, **Jun 5**
Cheerleading Week, Natl, **Mar 1**
Cheers TV Premiere: Anniv, **Sep 30**
Cheese Fest, Great Wisconsin (Little Chute, WI), **Jun 4**
Chekhov, Anton Pavlovich: Birth Anniv, **Jan 29**
Chelios, Chris: Birth, **Jan 25**
Chelsea Antiques Fair (London, England), **Mar 17**
Chemistry Week, Natl, **Oct 17**
Chen, Joan: Birth, **Apr 26**
Cheney, Dick: Birth, **Jan 30**
Cheney, Lynne: Birth, **Aug 14**
Cheney, Richard (Dick): Birthday, **Jan 30**
Cheng Huang: Birth Anniv Celebration (Taiwan), **Jun 30**
Chenoweth, Kristin: Birth, **Jul 24**
Cher: Birth, **May 20**
Chernobyl Nuclear Reactor Disaster: Anniv, **Apr 26**
Cherokee Rose Fest (Gilmer, TX), **May 15**
Cherokee Strip Celebration (Perry, OK), **Sep 18**
Cherokee Strip Day (OK), **Sep 16**
Cherry Blossom Fest (Washington, DC), **Mar 27**
Cherry Blossom Fest, Macon, GA's 2004 Intl, **Mar 19**
Cherry Month, Natl, **Feb 1**

Careers (cont'd)—Cherry

691

★ Chase's 2004 Calendar of Events ★

Index

Cherry Pit Spitting Contest, Intl (Eau Claire, MI), Jul 3
Chesapeake-Leopard Affair: Anniv, Jun 22
Chesnut, Mary Boykin Miller: Birth Anniv, Mar 31
Chesnutt, Charles W.: Birth Anniv, Jun 20
Chess: First Computer Chess Victory: Anniv, Feb 10
Chesterton, Gilbert: Birth Anniv, May 29
Chiang Kai-Shek Day (Taiwan), Oct 31
Chiang Kai-Shek: Birth Anniv, Oct 31
Chicago Bulls Third Straight Title for the Second Time, Jun 14
Chicago Fire, Great: Anniv, Oct 8
Chicago Flag Exhibit Controversy: Anniv, Feb 17
Chicago Flood, Great: Anniv, Apr 13
Chicago Gospel Music Festival (Chicago, IL), Jun 4
Chicago Jazz Fest (Chicago, IL), Sep 2
Chicago Marathon, The LaSalle Bank (Chicago, IL), Oct 10
Chicago, Judy: Birth, Jul 20
Chicago, Univ of, First Day Classes: Anniv, Oct 1
Chicken and Egg Fest (Prescott, AR), Jun 4
Chicken Boy's Birthday, Sep 1
Chicken Lady Day, Natl, Nov 4
Chicken Month, Natl, Sep 1
Chicken Show, Wayne (Wayne, NE), Jul 9
Chick-fil-A Peach Bowl (Atlanta, GA), Jan 2
Chico and the Man TV Premiere: Anniv, Sep 13
Chief Joseph Surrender: Anniv, Oct 5
Chiklis, Michael: Birth, Aug 30
Child Abuse Prevention Month, Apr 1
Child Abuse Prevention Month, Natl, Apr 1
Child, Julia: Birth, Aug 15
Child, Lydia Maria: Birth Anniv, Feb 11
Childermas, Dec 28
Children,
  Absolutely Incredible Kid Day, Mar 18
  Abused Women and Children's Awareness Day, Jun 13
  Adoption Month, Natl, Nov 1
  Alcohol and Other Drug-Related Birth Defects Week, Natl, May 9
  All-American Soap Box Derby (Akron, OH), Jul 31
  America's Kids Day, Jun 27
  Andersen, Hans Christian: Birth Anniv, Apr 2
  Animals Aloud Month, Oct 1
  Attention Deficit Hyperactivity Disorder Month, Sep 1
  Australia: Sorry Day, May 26
  Babysitters Day, Natl, May 8
  Backpack Safety America Month, Sep 1
  Baraboo Circus Heritage (Baraboo, WI), May 14
  Blue Ribbon Week, Natl (Child Abuse), Apr 4
  Boy Scouts of America Founded: Anniv, Feb 8
  Bud Billiken Parade (Chicago, IL), Aug 14
  Camp Fire Birthday Week, Mar 15
  Camp Fire Founders Day, Mar 17
  Child Abuse Prevention Month, Apr 1
  Child Abuse Prevention Month, Natl, Apr 1
  Child Abuse Prevention Month, Natl (Pres Proc), Apr 1
  Child Health Day (Pres Proc), Oct 4
  Child Safety Council, Natl: Founding Anniv, Nov 9
  Child Vision Awareness Month, Jun 1
  Childhood Depression Awareness Day, May 4
  Childhood Injury Prevention Week, Natl, Sep 1
  Children and Police Day, Natl, May 14
  Children's Awareness Memorial Day, Jun 6
  Children's Awareness Month, Jun 1
  Children's Book Day, Intl, Apr 2
  Children's Book Week, Natl, Nov 15
  Children's Celebration (Springfield, OR), Jul 10
  Children's Day (FL), Apr 13
  Children's Day (Japan), May 5
  Children's Day (MA), Jun 13
  Children's Day (South Korea), May 5
  Children's Day (Woodstock, VT), Aug 21
  Children's Day, Intl (China), Jun 1
  Children's Day/Natl Sovereignty (Turkey), Apr 23
  Children's Dental Health Month, Natl, Feb 1
  Children's Eye Health and Safety Month, Aug 1
  Children's Good Manners Month, Sep 1
  Children's Magazine Month, Oct 1
  Children's Miracle Network Celebration, Jun 4
  Children's Party at Green Animals (Newport, RI), Jul 14
  Children's Sunday, Jun 13
  Circus City Fest (Peru, IN), Jul 17
  Communicate with Your Kid Month, Natl, Oct 1
  Contruction Toy Month, Natl, Oct 1
  Cozy Cuddles for Kids, Nov 1
  Davidson Fellows Award Reception (Washington, DC), Sep 29
  Divorced Parents for Children Week, Natl, Oct 1
  Dr. Seuss (Theodor Geisel): Birth Anniv, Mar 2
  Family Day—A Day to Eat Dinner with Your Children, Sep 20
  Family Month, Natl, May 9
  Family Support Month, May 1
  Firepup's Birthday, Oct 1
  Gifted Children Conv, Natl Assn (Salt Lake City, UT), Nov 3
  Girl Scout Sabbath, Mar 13
  Girl Scout Sunday, Mar 7
  Girl Scout Week, Mar 7
  Girl Scouts Founding: Anniv, Mar 12
  Innocent Children Victims of Aggression, Intl Day of, Jun 4
  Johnson County 4H and FFA Fair (Iowa City, IA), Jul 26
  Kids' Goal Setting Week, Nov 1
  KidsDay, Natl, Aug 1
  KidSpree (Aurora, CO), Jul 17
  Kiwanis Kids' Day, Natl, Sep 25
  Library Card Sign-up Month, Sep 1
  Little League Baseball Week, Natl, Jun 14
  Little League Baseball World Series (Williamsport, PA), Aug 20
  Marcie's Place: A Camp for Grieving Children (Ingleside, IL), Aug 21
  Missing Children's Day, Natl, May 25
  Mother Goose Day, May 1
  Multicultural American Child Awareness Day, Jun 13
  Music in Our Schools Month, Mar 1
  National Children's Memorial Day, Dec 12
  Natl Communicate with Your Kids Day, Dec 5
  New England Conference on Storytelling for Children (Keene, NH), Apr 17
  No Homework Day, May 6
  Peddler's Village Teddy Bear's Picnic (Lahaska, PA), Jul 10
  Pediatric Cancer Awareness Month, Sep 1
  Pediatric Nurse Practitioner Week, Mar 21
  Playground Safety Week, Natl, Apr 26
  Potty Training Awareness Month, Jun 1
  Prematurity Awareness Day, Nov 18
  President's Environmental Youth Award Natl Competition, Jul 31
  Read Across America Day, Mar 2
  Read Me Week (TN), Mar 1
  RSV Awareness Month, Natl, Oct 1
  Safe Kids Week, Natl, May 1
  Safe Place Week, Natl, Mar 14
  Safe Toys and Gifts Month, Dec 1
  Saint Louis Variety Club Telethon (St. Louis, MO), Apr 17
  School Breakfast Week, Natl, Mar 8
  School Lunch Week, Natl, Oct 10
  Sea Cadet Month, Sep 1
  Send a Kid to Kamp Radiothon (Lexington, KY), May 1
  September Is Childhood Cancer Month, Sep 1
  Shoes for Orphans Month, Natl, May 1
  Sign Up for Summer Camp Month, Natl, Dec 1
  Smart Sitter Week, Feb 6
  Spank Out Day USA, Apr 30
  Spelling Bee Finals, Natl, Jun 2
  Spina Bifida Awareness Month, Natl, Oct 1
  Sports America Kids Month, Jun 1
  Stepparents' Week, Jun 1
  Stories Day, Apr 21
  Student Safety Month, Jun 1
  Sudden Infant Death Syndrome Awareness Month, Natl, Oct 1
  Summer Reading Club (El Paso, TX), Jun 5
  Super Scout Sunday (Springfield, MO), May 15
  Swedish Language and Culture Day Camp (Cambridge, MN), Aug 23
  Take a Kid Fishing Weekend (St. Paul, MN), Jun 11
  Talk With Your Teen About Sex Month, Natl, Mar 1
  Teach Children to Save Day, Natl, Apr 22
  Texas Love the Children Day, Mar 29
  Truancy Law: Anniv, Apr 12
  UN: Culture of Peace and Non-Violence for the Children of the World, Intl Decade for a, Jan 1
  Universal Children's Day (UN), Nov 20
  Universal Children's Week, Oct 1
  Vegetarian Resource Group's Essay Contest for Kids, May 1
  Very Important Parents Month, Natl, Sep 1
  Video Games Day, Sep 12
  White Sunday (Samoa, American Samoa), Oct 10
  Window Safety Week, Natl, Apr 18
  Winnipeg Intl Children's Fest (Winnipeg, MB, Canada), Jun 10
  World Breastfeeding Week, Aug 1
  Young Achievers Month, May 1
  Young Child, Month of the (MI), Apr 1
  Young Child, Week of the, Apr 18
  Young People's Poetry Week, Apr 12
  Young Reader's Day, Natl, Nov 9
  Youth Art Month, Mar 1
  Youth Cowboy Poetry Gathering (Boys Ranch, TX), Jun 1
  Youth Day (Cameroon), Feb 11
  Youth Day (Taiwan), Mar 29
  Youth Day (Zambia), Aug 2
  Youth Leadership Month, Feb 1
  Youth Service Day, Natl, Apr 16
  Yo-Yo Conv (Burlington, WI), Apr 3
Children's Authors & Illustrators Week, Feb 1
Children's Craft Day, Natl, Mar 14
Children's Memorial Day, Natl, Dec 12
Chile,
  Battle of Iquique, May 21
  Independence Day, Sep 18
  Military Dictatorship Ended: Anniv, Dec 15
  National Month, Sep 1
  Worst Earthquake of the 20th Century: Anniv, May 22
Chili Cook-off, State Chmpshp (Roanoke, VA), May 8
Chili Month, Natl, Oct 1
Chimborazo Day, Jun 3
Chimney Safety Wk, Natl, Sep 26
China Beach TV Premiere: Anniv, Apr 26
China Clipper: Anniv, Nov 22
China, People's Republic of,
  Birthday of Confucius (Observance), Oct 10
  Birthday of Lord Buddha, May 26
  Canton Autumn Trade Fair, Oct 15
  Canton Spring Trade Fair, Apr 15
  Central China Flood: Anniv, Jun 25
  Chung Yeung Fest (or Double 9 Fest), Oct 22
  Double 10th Day, Oct 10
  Dragon Boat Fest, Jun 22
  Fest of Hungry Ghosts, Aug 30
  Half-Year Day, Jul 1
  International Children's Day, Jun 1
  Lantern Fest, Feb 5
  Macau Day, Jun 24
  Macau Reverts to Chinese Control: Anniv, Dec 20
  Moon Fest (Mid-Autumn Fest), Sep 28
  National Day, Oct 1
  Qing Ming Fest or Tomb Sweeping Day, Apr 4
  Shanghai Communique: Anniv, Feb 27
  Sun Yat-Sen Birth Anniv, Nov 12
  Tiananmen Square Massacre: Anniv, Jun 4
  Youth Day, May 4
China: Taiwan Expelled from UN: Anniv, Oct 25
Chinese Lunar New Year Fest (Baltimore, MD), Jan 25
Chinese Nationalists Move to Formosa: Anniv, Dec 8
Chinese New Year, Jan 22
Chinese New Year Golden Dragon Parade (Los Angeles, CA), Jan 24
Chipotle Day, Totally, May 5
CHiPs TV Premiere: Anniv, Sep 15
Chirac, Jacques: Birth, Nov 29
Chisholm, Shirley: Birth, Nov 30
Cho, Margaret: Birth, Dec 5
Chocolate Fest (Galesburg, IL), Feb 7
Chocolate Fest (Norman, OK), Feb 7
Choctaw Indian Fair (Philadelphia, MS), Jul 14
Chokachi, David: Birth, Jan 16
Chong, Tommy: Birth, May 24
Chou En-Lai: Death Anniv, Jan 8
Chow Yun-Fat: Birth, May 18
Chowder Fest, Flower and Art Show (Gold Beach, OR), May 1
Chowderfest (Mystic, CT), Oct 9
Chretien, Jean: Birth, Jan 11
Christ, Circumcision of, Jan 1
Christensen, Hayden: Birth, Apr 19
Christian Leadership Week Intl, Sep 26
Christian Unity, Week of, Jan 18
Christianity Week, Consider, Mar 28
Christie, Agatha: Birth Anniv, Sep 15
Christie, Julie: Birth, Apr 14
Christie, Lou: Birth, Feb 19
Christmas,
  Adelphian Club Christmas Bazaar (Kennett, MO), Dec 4
  Adoration Parade (Branson, MO), Dec 5
  African American Holiday Expo (Washington, DC), Dec 18
  Armenian Christmas, Jan 6
  BCHS Christmas Open House (Ainsworth, NE), Dec 5
  Black Friday, Nov 26
  Boxing Day at the Hemingway Birthplace (Oak Park, IL), Dec 26
  Candlelight Tours (New Harmony, IN), Dec 4
  Christkindl Market (Canton, OH), Nov 11
  Christmas, Dec 25
  Christmas at Benjamin Harrison Home (Indianapolis, IN), Nov 22
  Christmas at Pioneer Village (Worthington, MN), Dec 2
  Christmas at the Top Museum (Burlington, WI), Dec 27
  Christmas at Union Station (Omaha, NE), Nov 27
  Christmas Bells Ring Again (CIS): Anniv, Dec 24
  Christmas Candlelight Tour (Bardstown, KY), Nov 26
  Christmas Candlelight Tour (Fredricksburg, VA), Dec 11
  Christmas Craft Show (Aiken, SC), Dec 3
  Christmas Craft Show (York, PA), Dec 5
  Christmas Epiphany Celebration (Isanti, MN), Jan 4
  Christmas Eve, Dec 24
  Christmas Eve Torchlight Parade (Winter Park, CO), Dec 24
  Christmas Fest of Lights (Natchitoches, LA), Dec 3
  Christmas Gift and Hobby Show (Indianapolis, IN), Nov 10
  Christmas Greens Show (Salem, OR), Dec 3
  Christmas Greetings from Space: Anniv, Dec 19
  Christmas in Roseland (Shreveport, LA), Nov 19
  Christmas in Seattle Holiday Gift Show (Seattle, WA), Nov 19
  Christmas in the Villages (Van Buren County, IA), Dec 4
  Christmas in Weston Candlelight Homes Tour (Weston, MO), Dec 4
  Christmas Magic (Wichita Falls, TX), Nov 5
  Christmas on the Prairie (Wahoo, NE), Dec 4
  Christmas on the River (Demopolis, AL), Nov 28
  Christmas Parade (Woodstock, IL), Nov 28
  Christmas Past at Audubon Acres (Chattanooga, TN), Dec 4
  Christmas Seal Campaign, Sep 1

692

☆ Chase's 2004 Calendar of Events ☆ Index

Christmas (cont'd)—Clark

Christmas Stroll Weekend (Nantucket Island, MA), **Dec 3**
Christmas to Remember (Laurel, MT), **Dec 5**
Christmas Traditions (St. Charles, MO), **Nov 26**
Christmas-New Orleans Style (New Orleans, LA), **Dec 1**
Clute's Christmas in the Park (Clute, TX), **Dec 7**
Colonial Christmas (Williamsburg, VA), **Dec 18**
Community Carol Singing (Mystic, CT), **Dec 19**
Community Christmas Bazaar (Gold Beach, OR), **Dec 4**
Country Christmas (Coshocton, OH), **Dec 4**
Countryside Christmas (Long Grove, IL), **Nov 26**
Craftsmen's Christmas Classic Arts & Crafts Fest (Greensboro, NC), **Nov 26**
Craftsmen's Christmas Classic Arts & Crafts Fest (Richmond, VA), **Nov 5**
Cuba: Christmas Returns: Anniv, **Dec 25**
Cut Your Own Christmas Tree (Charlottesville, VA), **Nov 26**
Dear Santa Letter Week, **Nov 5**
Dickens' Christmas Extravaganza (Cape May, NJ), **Dec 3**
Dickens of a Christmas (Franklin, TN), **Dec 11**
Dickens Olde-Fashioned Christmas (Holly, MI), **Nov 26**
Dickens Village Fest (Garrison, ND), **Nov 26**
1890s Christmas at Belle Meade (Nashville, TN), **Nov 12**
Eighteenth-Century Christmas Wassail (McLean, VA), **Dec 12**
Electric Light Parade (Lovington, NM), **Dec 6**
Fall Maryland Home & Garden Show/Holiday Craft Show (Baltimore, MD), **Oct 15**
Falling Needles Family Fest, **Dec 30**
Fantasy of Lights (Wichita Falls, TX), **Dec 3**
Frankfurt Christmas Market (Frankfurt, Germany), **Nov 25**
Garden of Lights (Muskogee, OK), **Nov 25**
Garden of Lights (Norfolk, VA), **Nov 27**
Geneva's Christmas Walk (Geneva, IL), **Dec 3**
Gettysburg Yuletide Fest (Gettysburg, PA), **Nov 26**
Gingerbread House Day, **Dec 12**
Gingerbread on Parade (Omaha, NE), **Nov 20**
Hanging of the Greens (Arrow Rock, MO), **Nov 27**
Heritage Christmas (Lindsborg, KS), **Dec 4**
Holiday Happiness (Upper Arlington, OH), **Dec 4**
Holiday House Tours (Charlottesville, VA), **Dec 11**
Holiday Lantern Tours (Staunton, VA), **Dec 10**
Holiday Lights on the Lake (Altoona, PA), **Nov 20**
Holiday Magic (Aurora, IL), **Nov 26**
Holiday Market (Greensboro, NC), **Nov 5**
Holiday Tour of Homes (Natchitoches, LA), **Dec 8**
Holidays at the Nationality Classrooms (Oakland, PA), **Dec 1**
Holidays in the City Grand Illumination Parade (Norfolk, VA), **Nov 20**
Holly Jolly Weekend (Andrews, TX), **Dec 2**
Hollywood Beach Candy Cane Parade (Hollywood, FL), **Dec 11**
Homesteaders Holiday (Greeley, CO), **Dec 11**
Humbug Day, **Dec 21**
Jinglebell Journey (Mt Wolf, PA), **Dec 5**
Jule Fest (Elk Horn, IA), **Nov 26**
La Posada de Kingsville/Celeb of Lights (Kingsville, TX), **Nov 21**
Lantern Light Tours (Mystic, CT), **Dec 2**
LeMoyne House Candlelight Christmas Tours (Washington, PA), **Dec 3**
Liberace Museum Christmas Tree Lighting (Las Vegas, NV), **Dec 2**
Light of the World Christmas Pageant (Minden, NE), **Nov 27**
Lighting of the Square (Woodstock, IL), **Nov 26**
Longwood Gardens Christmas Display (Kennett Square, PA), **Nov 25**
Mayor's Christmas Tree (Kansas City, MO), **Nov 26**
Natchitoches Fest of Lights (Natchitoches, LA), **Nov 23**
Navidades (Puerto Rico), **Dec 15**
Nordic Yulefest (Seattle, WA), **Nov 20**
Norskedalen's Old-Fashioned Christmas (Coon Valley, WI), **Dec 4**
Norwegian Christmas (Brooklyn Park, MN), **Dec 4**
Old-Fashioned Christmas Celebration (Dahlonega, GA), **Dec 4**
Old-Fashioned Danish Christmas (Dannebrog, NE), **Dec 11**
Operation Santa Paws, **Dec 6**
Ozark Mountain Christmas/Branson Fest of Lights (Branson, MO), **Nov 1**
Parade of Lights (Kingsville, TX), **Dec 4**
Peddler's Village Gingerbread House Competition & Display (Lahaska, PA), **Nov 19**
Pennsylvania Arts & Crafts Christmas Fest (Washington, PA), **Oct 15**
Philippines: Christmas Observance, **Dec 16**
Plaza Lights (Kansas City, MO), **Nov 25**
Polish Christmas Open House (Philadelphia, PA), **Dec 12**
Quad City Arts Festival of Trees (Davenport, IA), **Nov 18**
Quincy Preserves Christmas Candlelight Tour (Quincy, IL), **Dec 12**
Recipe Greetings for the Holidays, **Dec 1**
Rockefeller Center Christmas Tree Lighting (New York, NY), **Dec 1**
Russia: Christmas Day, **Jan 7**
Saint Nicholas Day, **Dec 6**
Saint Olaf Christmas Fest (Northfield, MN), **Dec 2**
Salt Lake's Family Christmas Gift Show (Salt Lake City, UT), **Nov 12**
Santa by Stage Coach Parade (El Centro, CA), **Dec 4**
Shopping Reminder Day, **Nov 25**
Silent Night, Holy Night Celebrations (Austria), **Dec 24**
Sounds of Season: Holiday Concert (Charlottesville, VA), **Dec 26**
Southern Christmas Show (Greensboro, NC), **Nov 10**
Suwannee Lights (Live Oak, FL), **Dec 1**
Territorial Christmas Celebration (Guthrie, OK), **Nov 27**
34th St Express (Boston, MA), **Dec 11**
Thomasville's Victorian Christmas (Thomasville, GA), **Dec 9**
Three Kings Day, **Jan 6**
Tie Month, Natl, **Dec 1**
Twelve Villages of Christmas (Washington County, KS), **Dec 4**
Victorian Christmas at Mount Hope Mansion (Manheim, PA), **Nov 26**
Victorian Christmas Celebration (Cumberland, MD), **Nov 26**
Victorian Christmas Home Tour (Leadville, CO), **Dec 4**
Victorian Christmas Sleighbell Parade (Manistee, MI), **Dec 2**
Victorian Christmas Tours at Frank Lloyd Wright Home (Oak Park, IL), **Dec 11**
Victorian Yuletide (Clinton, MD), **Dec 11**
Virginia Christmas Show (Richmond, VA), **Nov 4**
Wassail Celebration (Woodstock, VT), **Dec 10**
Whiner's Day, Natl, **Dec 26**
Winterfest (Luverne, MN), **Dec 3**
Wisconsin Holiday Market (Kohler, WI), **Nov 12**
Wolf Point's Annual Christmas Parade (Wolf Point, MT), **Dec 5**
Wonderland of Lights (Marshall, TX), **Nov 24**
Xcel Energy's Parade of Lights (Denver, CO), **Dec 3**
Christo: Birth, Jun 13
Christopher, Dennis: Birth, Dec 2
Christopher, William: Birth, Oct 20
Chronic Fatigue Syndrome Awareness Month, Natl, Mar 1
Chuckwagon Races, Natl Chmpshp (Clinton, AR), Sep 3
Chung Yeung Fest (China), Oct 22
Chung Yuan Fest (China), Aug 30
Chung, Connie: Birth, Aug 20
Church and Synagogue Library Assn Conf (Indianapolis, IN), Jul 11
Church of England Ordains Women Priests: Anniv, Mar 12
Church of Jesus Christ of Latter-day Saints: Anniv, Apr 6
Church, Charlotte: Birth, Feb 21
Church, Thomas Haden: Birth, Mar 31
Church: Intl Sit-on-the-Front-Pew Sunday, Jun 27
Church: No Excuse Sunday, Apr 25
Churchill, Randolph Henry Spencer: Birth Anniv, Feb 13
Churchill, Winston: Birth Anniv, Nov 30
Churchill, Winston: Day, Apr 9
CIA Agent Arrested as Spy: Anniv, Feb 21
Ciardi, John: Birth Anniv, Jun 24
Cibrian, Eddie: Birth, Jun 18
Cigarette Advertising Banned: Anniv, Apr 1
Cigarettes Reported Hazardous: Anniv, Jan 11
Cinco de Mayo (Mexico), May 5
Cinco de Mayo Fest (Portland, OR), May 5
Circumcision of Christ, Jan 1
Circus,
Baraboo Circus Heritage (Baraboo, WI), **May 14**
Circus City Fest (Peru, IN), **Jul 17**
Circus Festival of Monte Carlo, Intl (Monaco), **Jan 15**
Circus Train Wreck: Anniv, **Jun 22**
Emmett Kelly Clown Fest (Houston, MO), **Apr 29**
Great Circus Parade Week (Milwaukee, WI), **Jul 6**
Greatest Show on Earth: Anniv, **Mar 28**
Kelly, Emmett: Birth Anniv, **Dec 9**
Citizen Kane Premiere: Anniv, May 1
Citizenship Day (Pres Proc), Sep 17
Citrus Bowl, Capital One Florida (Orlando, FL), Jan 1
Citrus Fest, Florida (Winter Haven, FL), Jan 15
Civil Air Patrol Founded: Anniv, Dec 1
Civil Aviation Day, Intl (UN), Dec 7
Civil Rights,
Anderson, Marian: Easter Concert: Anniv, **Apr 9**
Birmingham Resistance: Anniv, **Apr 3**
Blacks Ruled Eligible to Vote: Anniv, **Apr 3**
Brown v Board of Education: Anniv, **May 17**
Civil Rights Act of 1964: Anniv, **Jul 2**
Civil Rights Act of 1968: Anniv, **Apr 11**
Civil Rights Bill of 1866: Anniv, **Apr 9**
Civil Rights Workers Found Slain: Anniv, **Aug 4**
Dred Scott Decision: Anniv, **Mar 6**
Freedom Riders: Anniv, **May 4**
Greensboro Sit-in: Anniv, **Feb 1**
Little Rock Nine: Anniv, **Sep 4**
March on Washington: Anniv, **Aug 28**
Meredith (James) Enrolls at Ole Miss: Anniv, **Sep 30**
Montgomery Bus Boycott Ends: Anniv, **Dec 20**
Montgomery Bus Boycott: Anniv, **Dec 5**
Poll Tax Outlawed: Anniv, **Apr 8**
Rosa Parks Day, **Dec 1**
Saint Louis Race Riots: Anniv, **Jul 2**
Selma Civil Rights March: Anniv, **Mar 21**
16th Street Baptist Church Bombing: Anniv, **Sep 15**
24th Amendment (Eliminated Poll Taxes), **Jan 23**
Civil Rights Act of 1968: Anniv, Apr 11
Civil Service Created: Anniv, Jan 16
Civil War, American,
Amnesty Issued for Southern Rebels: Anniv, **May 29**
Attack on Fort Sumter: Anniv, **Apr 12**
Attack on Fort Wagner: Anniv, **Jul 19**
Battle of Antietam: Anniv, **Sep 17**
Battle of Bull Run: Anniv, **Jul 21**
Battle of Chattanooga: Anniv, **Nov 24**
Battle of Cold Harbor: Anniv, **Jun 3**
Battle of Gettysburg: Anniv, **Jul 1**
Battle of La Glorietta Pass: Anniv, **Mar 28**
Battle of Mobile Bay: Anniv, **Aug 5**
Battle of Nashville: Anniv, **Dec 16**
Battle of Shiloh: Anniv, **Apr 6**
Battle of Spotsylvania: Anniv, **May 12**
Battle of the Wilderness: Anniv, **May 5**
Bread Riot at Richmond: Anniv, **Apr 2**
Butler Issues "Woman Order": Anniv, **May 16**
Carson City Rendezvous (Carson City, NV), **Jun 11**
Civil War Days (Chesapeake, VA), **Sep 11**
Civil War Ending: Anniv, **Apr 9**
Civil War Peace Talks: Anniv, **Feb 3**
Civil War Reenactment (Coshocton, OH), **Jul 17**
Civil War Reenactment (Keokuk, IA), **Apr 23**
Civil War Submarine Attack: Anniv, **Oct 5**
Davis, Jefferson: Inauguration: Anniv, **Feb 18**
Defeat at Five Forks: Anniv, **Apr 1**
Doubleday, Abner: Birth Anniv, **Jun 26**
Fall of Richmond: Anniv, **Apr 3**
Farragut Captures New Orleans: Anniv, **Apr 25**
First Black Receives Congressional Medal: Anniv, **May 23**
Fort Sumter Returned to Union Control: Anniv, **Feb 17**
Fort Sumter Shelled by North: Anniv, **Aug 17**
Fredericksburg Heritage Fest (Fredericksburg, VA), **Jul 4**
Gettysburg Address Memorial Ceremony (Gettysburg, PA), **Nov 19**
Gettysburg Civil War Heritage Days (Gettysburg, PA), **Jun 25**
Grant Commissioned Commander: Anniv, **Mar 9**
Grant Put in Charge of Mississippi: Anniv, **Oct 16**
Hunter Frees the Slaves: Anniv, **May 9**
John Wilkes Booth Escape Route Tour (Clinton, MD), **Apr 17**
Johnson Impeachment Proceedings: Anniv, **Feb 24**
Last Formal Surrender of Confederate Troops: Anniv, **Jun 23**
Lincoln Approves 13th Amendment (Freedom Day), **Feb 1**
Lincoln Assassination Anniv, **Apr 14**
Lincoln Assassination Conspirators Hanging, **Jul 7**
Lincoln Signs Income Tax: Anniv, **Jul 1**
Lincoln's Gettysburg Address: Anniv, **Nov 19**
Massacre at Fort Pillow: Anniv, **Apr 12**
Memorial Day Ceremonies (Andersonville, GA), **May 30**
Memorial Day Parade and Ceremonies (Gettysburg, PA), **May 31**
Merrimac Destroyed: Anniv, **May 11**
Monitor Sinking: Anniv, **Dec 30**
Murder at Ford's Theater: 5th Annual Conf (Clinton, MD), **Mar 19**
Natural Bridge Battle (Tallahassee, FL), **Mar 6**
Newspapers Taken to Court: Anniv, **Aug 16**
Peninsula Campaign Intensified: Anniv, **May 9**
Quantrill's Raid on Lawrence, KS: Anniv, **Aug 21**
Raid on Richmond: Anniv, **Mar 1**
Remembrance Day (Gettysburg, PA), **Nov 20**
Rock of Chickamauga: Anniv, **Sep 20**
Ruffin, Edmund: Birth Anniv, **Jan 5**
September Skirmish (Decatur, AL), **Sep 4**
Seven Days Campaign: Anniv, **Jun 25**
Sherman Enters Atlanta: Anniv, **Sep 2**
Sherman Takes Savannah: Anniv, **Dec 21**
South Carolina: Secession Anniv, **Dec 20**
Sultana Explosion: Anniv, **Apr 27**
Surrender at Durham Station: Anniv, **Apr 18**
Surrender of Fort Donelson: Anniv, **Feb 16**
Union Officers Escape Libby Prison: Anniv, **Feb 9**
Vicksburg Surrenders: Anniv, **Jul 3**
Wade-Davis Reconstruction Bill: Anniv, **May 4**
Civility Month, Natl Win with, Aug 1
Claiborne, Liz: Birth, Mar 31
Clam Chowder Cookoff (Santa Cruz, CA), Feb 21
Clancy, Tom: Birth, Apr 12
Clapp, Gordon: Birth, Sep 24
Clapton, Eric: Birth, Mar 30
Clark, Abraham: Birth Anniv, Feb 15
Clark, Barney: Artificial Heart Transplant: Anniv, Dec 2
Clark, Barney: Death Anniv, Mar 23
Clark, Dave: Birth, Dec 15
Clark, Dick: Birth, Nov 30
Clark, Dick: Retires from American Bandstand: Anniv, Mar 23
Clark, George R: Birth Anniv, Nov 19
Clark, Mark: Birth Anniv, May 1

Index — Chase's 2004 Calendar of Events

Clark, Mary Higgins: Birth, Dec 24
Clark, Petula: Birth, Nov 15
Clark, Roy: Birth, Apr 15
Clark, Susan: Birth, Mar 8
Clark, William: Birth Anniv, Aug 1
Clarke, Arthur C.: Birth, Dec 16
Clay (Muhammad Ali) Becomes Heavyweight Champ: Anniv, Feb 25
Clay, Cassius, Jr (Muhammad Ali): Birth, Jan 17
Clay, Henry: Birth Anniv, Apr 12
Clayburgh, Jill: Birth, Apr 30
Clayton, Adam: Birth, Mar 13
Clean Air Act Passed by Congress: Anniv, Dec 17
Clean Air Month, May 1
Clean Up Your Computer Month, Natl, Jan 1
Cleaning Week, Natl, Mar 28
Clean-Off-Your-Desk Day, Natl, Jan 12
Clear Lake Crawfish Fest (Seabrook, TX), Apr 3
Cleary, Beverly: Birth, Apr 12
Cleese, John: Birth, Oct 27
Clemens, Roger: Birth, Aug 4
Clemens, Samuel (Mark Twain): Birth Anniv, Nov 30
Clemente, Roberto: Birth Anniv, Aug 18
Clements, George Harold: Birth, Jan 26
Clemons, Clarence: Birth, Jan 11
Clemson, Thomas: Birth Anniv, Jul 1
Clerc, Laurent: Birth Anniv, Dec 26
Clerc-Gallaudet Week, Dec 5
Clergy: Pastoral Care Week, Oct 24
Clerihew Day (Edmund Bentley Clerihew Birth Anniv), Jul 10
Cleveland Natl Air Show (Cleveland, OH), Sep 4
Cleveland, Esther: First White House Presidential Baby, Aug 30
Cleveland, Frances: Birth Anniv, Jul 21
Cleveland, Grover: Birth Anniv, Mar 18
Cleveland, Grover: Cleveland's Secret Surgery: Anniv, Jul 1
Cleveland, Grover: Second Inauguration: Anniv, Mar 4
Cliburn, Van: Birth, Jul 12
Cliche Day, Nov 3
Clijsters, Kim: Birth, Jun 8
Cline, Patsy: Birth Anniv, Sep 8
Clinton, George: Birth Anniv, Jul 26
Clinton, Hillary Rodham: Birth, Oct 26
Clinton, William Jefferson,
  Birthday, Aug 19
  Impeachment Proceedings: Anniv, Dec 20
  Senate Acquits: Anniv, Feb 12
  Wedding to Hillary Rodham: Anniv, Oct 11
Clodagh: Birth, Oct 8
Cloning of an Adult Animal, First: Anniv, Feb 23
Clooney, George: Birth, May 6
Clooney, Rosemary: Birth Anniv, May 23
Close, Glenn: Birth, Mar 19
Clothesline Fair (Prairie Grove, AR), Sep 4
Clower, Jerry: Birth, Sep 28
Clowns: Grimaldi, Joseph: Birth Anniv, Dec 18
Clowns: Kelly, Emmett: Birth Anniv, Dec 9
Clute's Christmas in the Park (Clute, TX), Dec 7
Clutter Month, Tackle Your, Apr 1
Clutter Wk, Reduce the, Aug 15
Clymer, George: Birth Anniv, Mar 16
CN Tower: Anniv, Jun 26
CNN Debuted: Anniv, Jun 1
Coaching Week, Intl, Feb 1
Coal Miner Days (Novinger, MO), May 30
Coast Day NJ (Long Beach Island & Cape May, NJ), Oct 9
Coast Guard Day, Aug 4
Coast Guard, US: Fleet Week New York (New York, NY), May 19
Coastal Cleanup, Intl, Sep 18
Cobb, Tyrus "Ty": Birth Anniv, Dec 18
Cobblestone Fest (Falls City, NE), Aug 20
Coburn, James: Birth Anniv, Aug 31
Cochise: Death Anniv, Jun 8
Cochran, Jacqueline: Death Anniv, Aug 9
Cochran, Thad: Birth, Dec 7
Cocker, Joe: Birth, May 20
Cody, William F. "Buffalo Bill": Birth Anniv, Feb 26
Coen, Ethan: Birth, Sep 21
Coen, Joel: Birth, Nov 29
Coffee Gourmet Intl Month, Jan 1
Cohen, Leonard: Birth, Sep 21
Cohen, Rob: Birth, Mar 12
Cohen, Sasha: Birth, Oct 26
Cohocton Fall Foliage Fest (Cohocton, NY), Oct 1
Coin Week, Natl, Apr 18
Coins Stamped "In God We Trust": Anniv, Apr 22
Colantoni, Enrico: Birth, Feb 14
Colbert, Claudette: Birth Anniv, Sep 13
Cold War: Treaty Signed to Mark End: Anniv, Nov 19
Cole, Nat "King": Birth Anniv, Mar 17
Cole, Natalie: Birth, Feb 6
Coleman, Bessie: Birth Anniv, Jan 26
Coleman, Dabney: Birth, Jan 3
Coleman, Derrick: Birth, Jun 21
Coleman, Gary: Birth, Feb 8
Coleman, Norm: Birth, Aug 17
Coleman, Ornette: Birth, Mar 19
Coleman, Signy: Birth, Jul 4
Coleridge, Samuel: Birth Anniv, Oct 21
Coles, Joanna: Birth, Aug 11
Colfax, Schuyler: Birth Anniv, Mar 23

Collectables-Antiques-Craft-Flea Market Sale (Sauk Centre, MN), Jul 17
Collette, Toni: Birth, Nov 1
Collins, Eileen: Birth, Nov 19
Collins, Gary: Birth, Apr 30
Collins, Jackie: Birth, Oct 4
Collins, Joan: Birth, May 23
Collins, Judy: Birth, May 1
Collins, Michael: Birth, Oct 31
Collins, Pauline: Birth, Sep 3
Collins, Phil: Birth, Jan 30
Collins, Stephen: Birth, Oct 1
Collins, Susan M.: Birth, Dec 7
Collins, Wilkie: Birth Anniv, Jan 8
Collinsworth, Cris: Birth, Jan 27
Collision Awareness Month, Natl, Mar 1
Collison, Nick: Birth, Oct 26
Cologne Cathedral Completion: Anniv, Aug 14
Colombia,
  Battle of Boyaca Day, Aug 7
  Cartagena Independence Day, Nov 11
  Independence Day, Jul 20
Colonial Christmas (Williamsburg, VA), Dec 18
Colonialism, Second Intl Decade for Eradication of (UN), Jan 1
Color Day, Natl, Oct 22
Color TV Broadcast, First: Anniv, Jun 25
Colorado,
  Abortion First Legalized: Anniv, Apr 25
  Admission Day, Aug 1
  Allard, Wayne: Birth, Dec 2
  American Assn for the Advancement of Science Meeting (Denver), Feb 13
  Aspen Music Fest (Aspen), Jun 24
  Bolder Boulder 10K (Boulder), May 31
  Boom Days (Leadville), Aug 6
  Burro Race (Leadville), Aug 8
  Campbell, Ben Nighthorse: Birth, Apr 13
  Capitol Hill People's Fair (Denver), Jun 5
  Christmas Eve Torchlight Parade (Winter Park), Dec 24
  Colorado Day, Aug 2
  Colorado Shakespeare Fest (Boulder), Jun 2
  Commonwheel Arts and Crafts Fest (Manitou Springs), Sep 4
  Dole Spring Splash (Winter Park), Apr 11
  Emma Crawford Fest and Memorial Coffin Race (Manitou Springs), Oct 30
  Fest of Mountain and Plain/A Taste of Colorado (Denver), Sep 3
  Genuine Jazz in Breckenridge (Breckenridge), Jun 25
  Great Fruitcake Toss (Manitou Springs), Jan 3
  Homesteaders Holiday (Greeley), Dec 11
  Hometown Days (Strasburg), Aug 21
  KBCO World-Class Rockfest (Winter Park), Jul 17
  Kennedy Center Imagination Celeb (Colorado Springs), Mar 4
  KidSpree (Aurora), Jul 17
  Leadville Trail 100 Bike Race (Leadville), Aug 14
  Leadville Trail 100 Ultramarathon (Leadville), Aug 21
  Longs Peak Scottish/Irish Highland Fest (Estes Park), Sep 9
  Mesa Verde Natl Park Established: Anniv, Jun 29
  Owens, Bill: Birth, Oct 22
  Potato Day Fest (Greeley), Sep 11
  Rocky Mountain Balloon Fest (Denver), Aug 27
  Rocky Mountain Natl Park Established: Anniv, Jan 26
  State Fair (Pueblo), Aug 21
  Telluride Film Fest (Telluride), Sep 3
  Telluride Jazz Celebration (Telluride), Aug 6
  Telluride Mushroom Fest (Telluride), Aug 26
  Victorian Christmas Home Tour (Leadville), Dec 4
  Wells Fargo Bank Cup (Winter Park), Feb 6
  Wells Fargo Golden Bunny Egg Hunt and Race (Winter Park), Apr 10
  Western Stock Show and Rodeo, Natl (Denver), Jan 10
  Winter Park Jazz Fest (Winter Park), Jul 10
  Xcel Energy's Parade of Lights (Denver), Dec 3
Colorado River Crossing Balloon Festival (Yuma, AZ), Nov 19
Colorectal Cancer Awareness Month, Natl, Mar 1
Colorectal Cancer Awareness Month, Natl (Pres Proc), Mar 1
Colorectal Cancer Education/Awareness Month, Dec 1
Colt League World Series (Lafayette, IN), Aug 3
Colter, Jessi: Birth, May 25
Coltrane, Robbie: Birth, Mar 30
Columbia Space Shuttle Disaster: Anniv, Feb 1
Columbian Exposition Opening: Anniv, May 1
Columbian Exposition, Closing: Anniv, Oct 30
Columbine High School Killings: Anniv, Apr 20
Columbo TV Premiere: Anniv, Sep 15
Columbus Days (Columbus, NE), Aug 12
Columbus, Christopher,
  Columbus Day (Observed), Oct 11
  Columbus Day (Traditional), Oct 12
  Columbus Day, Natl (Pres Proc), Oct 11
  Columbus Sails for New World: Anniv, Aug 3
  Columbus's Last Voyage to New World: Anniv, Sep 18
  Discovery of Jamaica by: Anniv, May 4
Columnist's Day, Natl, Jun 28
Comaneci, Nadia: Birth, Nov 12
Comaneci, Nadia: First Perfect Score in Olympic History: Anniv, Jul 18

Combs, Holly Marie: Birth, Dec 3
Combs, Sean "Puffy": Birth, Nov 4
Come and Take It Festival (Gonzales, TX), Oct 2
COMECON and Warsaw Pact Disband: Anniv, Jun 28
Comet, Closest Approach to Earth: Anniv, Feb 20
Comics (including newspaper strips, books, creators and characters),
  Caniff, Milton: Birth Anniv, Feb 28
  Crankshaft: Anniv, Aug 31
  First Newspaper Comic Strip: Anniv, Oct 18
  Funky Winkerbean: Anniv, Mar 27
  Gaines, William M.: Birth Anniv, Mar 1
  Garfield Birthday, Jun 19
  Gould, Chester: Birth Anniv, Nov 20
  Herriman, George: Birth Anniv, Aug 22
  Kelly, Walt: Birth Anniv, Aug 25
  King, Frank: Birth Anniv, Apr 9
  Odie's Birthday, Aug 8
  Outcault, Richard Felton: Birth Anniv, Jan 14
  Peanuts Debuts: Anniv, Oct 2
  Popeye Debuts: Anniv, Jan 17
  Wallet, Skeezix: Birth, Feb 14
  Young, Chic: Birth Anniv, Jan 9
Coming Out Day, Natl, Oct 11
Commercial Air Flight Between the US and USSR Begins, Jul 15
Commercial Bank, First US: Anniv, Jan 7
Commodore Perry Day, Apr 10
Common Courtesy Day, Natl, Mar 17
Common Prayer Day (Denmark), May 7
Common Sense Published: Anniv, Jan 10
Commoner, Barry: Birth, May 28
Commonwealth Day (United Kingdom), Mar 8
Commonwealth Day, Belize, May 24
Communicate with Your Kids Day, Natl, Dec 5
Communication Day, Better Business, Jan 26
Communication Week, World, Nov 1
Communications Month, Effective, Jun 1
Communist Manifesto Published: Anniv, Feb 26
Communist Party Suspended, Soviet: Anniv, Aug 29
Community Spirit Days, Apr 1
Comoros: Independence Day, Jul 6
Companies That Care Day, Mar 18
Compliment Day, Natl, Jan 28
Compliment-Your-Mirror Day, Jul 3
Computer,
  Apple II Computer Released: Anniv, Jun 5
  Babbage, Charles: Birth Anniv, Dec 26
  Bifocals at the Monitor Liberation Day, Dec 1
  Cathode-Ray Tube Patented: Anniv, Dec 20
  Clean Up Your Computer Month, Natl, Jan 1
  Computer Learning Month, Oct 1
  Computer Security Day, Nov 30
  Eckert, J. Presper, Jr: Birth Anniv, Apr 9
  ENIAC Introduced: Anniv, Feb 14
  First Computer Chess Victory: Anniv, Feb 10
  High Tech Month, Natl, Jan 1
  IBM PC Introduced: Anniv, Aug 12
  Internet Created: Anniv, Oct 29
  Lotus 1-2-3 Released: Anniv, Jan 26
  Macintosh Debuts: Anniv, Jan 25
  Microsoft Releases Windows: Anniv, Nov 10
  Name Your PC Day, Nov 20
  Race Your Mouse Around the Icons Day, Aug 28
  Shareware Day, Intl, Dec 11
  Take Your Webmaster to Lunch Day, Jul 6
  Virtual Love Day, Jul 24
  World Wide Web: Anniv, Aug 1
Conaway, Jeff: Birth, Oct 5
Concorde Flight, First: Anniv, Jan 21
Concours d'Elegance (Forest Grove, OR), Jul 18
Condom Week, Natl, Feb 14
Cone, David: Birth, Jan 2
Confederate Decoration Day (TN), Jun 3
Confederate Heroes Day (TX), Jan 19
Confederate Memorial Day (AL), Apr 26
Confederate Memorial Day (FL, GA), Apr 26
Confederate Memorial Day (KY, LA, TN), Jun 3
Confederate Memorial Day (MS), May 24
Confederate Memorial Day (NC, SC), May 10
Confederation, Articles of: Ratification Anniv, Mar 1
Confucius: Birthday and Teacher's Day (Taiwan), Sep 28
Confucius: Birthday Observance (China), Oct 10
Congenital Heart Defect Awareness Day, Feb 14
Congo (Brazzaville),
  Day of Natl Reconciliation, Jun 10
  National Holiday, Aug 15
Congo (Dem Rep of the),
  Independence Day, Jun 30
Congress, US,
  Assembles, Jan 5
  First Meets at Washington: Anniv, Nov 17
  First Meeting Anniv, Mar 4
  First Quorum (House of Reps): Anniv, Apr 1
  Woman Runs the House: Anniv, Jun 20
  First Female Congressional Page: Anniv, Jan 3
Connecticut,
  American Crossword Puzzle Tournament (Stamford), Mar 12
  Antique/Classic Boat Rendezvous (Mystic), Jul 24
  Boom Box Parade (Willimantic), Jul 4
  Chowderfest (Mystic), Oct 9
  Community Carol Singing (Mystic), Dec 19
  Connecticut Early Music Fest (New London), Jun 11
  Connecticut Storytelling Fest (New London), Apr 23

694

☆ Chase's 2004 Calendar of Events ☆ Index

Constitution Ratification: Anniv, **Jan 9**
Dodd, Christopher J.: Birth, **May 27**
DRC-FM Caravan of Carriages (Windsor), **Nov 21**
Fine Arts & Crafts Fest (Woodstock), **Oct 16**
Gingerbread Village and Bazaar (Middlebury), **Dec 4**
Historic Norwichtown Days (Norwich), **Sep 10**
Kids After Christmas (Mystic), **Dec 26**
Lantern Light Tours (Mystic), **Dec 2**
Levitt Pavilion Performing Arts/Music Fest (Westport), **Jun 20**
Lieberman, Joseph: Birth, **Feb 24**
Litchfield Open House Tour (Litchfield), **Jul 9**
Lobsterfest (Mystic), **May 29**
Meet the Artists & Artisans Show (Milford Green), **May 15**
Mystic Seaport Field Days (Mystic), **Nov 26**
Nathan Hale Fife and Drum Muster (Coventry), **Jul 24**
Norwalk Seaport Oyster Fest (Norwalk), **Sep 10**
Odyssey—A Greek Fest (Orange), **Sep 3**
Orange Historical Society Antique Show (Orange), **Feb 28**
Road Church Country Fair (Stonington), **Sep 18**
Road Church Missionary Fair (Stonington), **May 15**
Rowland, John: Birth, **May 24**
Sea Music Fest (Mystic), **Jun 11**
Sharon on the Green Arts and Crafts Fair (Sharon), **Aug 7**
Special Olympics Connecticut 2004 Summer Games (New Haven), **Jun 11**
Supreme Court Strikes Down Law Banning Contraception: Anniv, **Jun 7**
Teen Day, **May 1**
Tellabration! An Evening of Storytelling for Grown-Ups, **Nov 19**
Woodstock Fair (Woodstock), **Sep 3**
Connelly, Jennifer: Birth, Dec 12
Connery, Sean: Birth, Aug 25
Connick, Harry, Jr: Birth, Sep 11
Connolly, Maureen: Birth Anniv, Sep 17
Connors, Chuck: Birth Anniv, Apr 10
Connors, Jimmy: Birth, Sep 2
Connors, Mike: Birth, Aug 15
Conrad, Joseph: Birth Anniv, Dec 3
Conrad, Kent: Birth, Mar 12
Conrad, Robert: Birth, Mar 1
Conrad, William: Birth Anniv, Sep 27
Conroy, Pat: Birth, Oct 26
Consider Christianity Week, Mar 28
Constable, John: Birth Anniv, Jun 11
Constantinople Falls to the Turks: Anniv, May 29
Constitution, US,
  11th Amendment Ratified (States' Sov), **Feb 7**
  12th Amendment Ratified (Electoral College Modified), **Jun 15**
  13th Amendment Ratified (Abolished Slavery), **Dec 6**
  14th Amendment Ratified (Citizenship), **Jul 9**
  15th Amendment Ratified (Voting Rights), **Feb 3**
  16th Amendment Ratified (Income Tax), **Feb 3**
  17th Amendment Ratified, **Apr 8**
  18th Amendment (Prohibition): Anniv, **Jan 16**
  19th Amendment Ratified, **Aug 18**
  20th Amendment Ratified (Inaugural, Congress opening dates), **Jan 23**
  21st Amendment Ratified (Prohibition Repealed), **Dec 5**
  22nd Amendment Ratified (Two-Term Limit), **Feb 27**
  23rd Amendment Ratified (DC Residents Right to Vote), **Mar 29**
  24th Amendment Ratified (Eliminated Poll Taxes), **Jan 23**
  25th Amendment Ratified (Pres Succession, Disability), **Feb 10**
  26th Amendment Ratified (Voting Age to 18), **Jul 1**
  27th Amendment Ratified (No Midterm Congressional Pay Raises), **May 7**
  Bill of Rights: Anniv of First State Ratification, **Nov 20**
  Constitution of the US: Anniv, **Sep 17**
  Constitution Week (Pres Proc), **Sep 17**
  Constitution Week, Natl, **Sep 17**
  Constitutional Convention: Anniv, **May 25**
  Equal Rights Amendment Sent to States for Ratification, **Mar 22**
  Federalist Papers: Anniv, **Oct 27**
  Great Debate (Constitutional Convention): Anniv, **Aug 6**
  Presidential Succession Act: Anniv, **Jul 18**
  Religious Freedom Day, **Jan 16**
  Takes Effect: Anniv, **Jul 2**
  Veep Day, **Aug 9**
  Women's Suffrage Amendment Introduced: Anniv, **Jan 10**
Consumer Awareness Week, Apr 16
Consumer Protection Week, Natl (Pres Proc), Feb 1
Conti, Bill: Birth, Apr 13
Conti, Tom: Birth, Nov 22
Continental Congress Assembly, First: Anniv, Sep 5
Contraband Days (Lake Charles, LA), Apr 27
Contruction Toy Month, Natl, Oct 1
Conversation Week, Better, Nov 22
Converse, Frank: Birth, May 22
Converse, Harriet: White Woman Made Indian Chief: Anniv, Sep 18
Conway, Gary: Birth, Feb 4
Conway, Kevin: Birth, May 29
Conway, Tim: Birth, Dec 15
Coogan, Keith: Birth, Jan 13

Cook Something Bold and Pungent Day, **Nov 8**
Cook, James: Birth Anniv, **Oct 27**
Cook, Rachael Leigh: Birth, **Oct 4**
Cookie Cutter Week, **Dec 1**
Cookie Month, Natl, **Oct 1**
Coolidge, Calvin: Birth Anniv, **Jul 4**
Coolidge, Calvin: Business of America Quotation: Anniv, **Jan 17**
Coolidge, Grace: Birth Anniv, **Jan 3**
Coolidge, Rita: Birth, **May 1**
Coon Hunt, Grand American (Orangeburg, SC), **Jan 2**
Cooney, Gerry: Birth, **Aug 24**
Cooney, Joan Ganz: Birth, **Nov 30**
Co-op Awareness Month, **Oct 1**
Cooper, Alice: Birth, **Feb 4**
Cooper, Bradley: Birth, **Jan 5**
Cooper, Cynthia: Birth, **Apr 14**
Cooper, D.B. Hijacking: Anniv, **Nov 24**
Cooper, Gary: Birth Anniv, **May 7**
Cooper, Jackie: Birth, **Sep 15**
Cooper, James Fenimore: Birth Anniv, **Sep 15**
Cooper, Justin: Birth, **Nov 17**
Cooper, L. Gordon: Birth, **Mar 6**
Cooperatives, Intl Day of (UN), **Jul 3**
COPD Awareness Month, Natl, **Nov 1**
Copernicus, Nicolaus: Birth Anniv, **Feb 19**
Copland, Aaron: Birth Anniv, **Nov 14**
Copperfield, David: Birth, **Sep 16**
Coppola, Francis Ford: Birth, **Apr 7**
Copyright Law Passed: Anniv, **May 31**
Copyright Revision Law: Anniv, **Jan 1**
Coral Sea, Battle of: Anniv, **May 8**
Coray, Melissa Burton: Birth Anniv, **Mar 2**
Corbett-Fitzsimmons Title Fight: Anniv, **Mar 17**
Corbett-Sullivan Prize Fight: Anniv, **Sep 7**
Corbin, Barry: Birth, **Oct 16**
Corea, Chick: Birth, **Jun 12**
Corelli, Arcangelo: Birth Anniv, **Feb 17**
Corley, Pat: Birth, **Jun 1**
Corman, Roger: Birth, **Apr 5**
Corn Fest, Sun Prairie's Sweet (Sun Prairie, WI), **Aug 19**
Corn Palace Fest (Mitchell, SD), **Sep 1**
Cornwall: Saint Piran's Day, **Mar 5**
Cornwell, Patricia: Birth, **Jun 9**
Cornyn, John: Birth, **Feb 2**
Corps of Discovery Departure: Camp River Dubois—Lewis and Clark Bicentennial Event (Hartford and Wood River, IL), **May 13**
Corpus Christi, **Jun 10**
Corpus Christi (US): Observance, **Jun 13**
Corrigan, Mairead: Birth, **Jan 27**
Corrigan, Wrong Way Day, **Jul 17**
Cort, Bud: Birth, **Mar 29**
Cortes Conquers Mexico: Anniv, **Nov 8**
Cortese, Dan: Birth, **Sep 14**
Cortese, Valentina: Birth, **Jan 1**
Corvette and High Performance Meet (Puyallup, WA), **Feb 7**
Corvette Show (Mackinaw City, MI), **Aug 27**
Corzine, Jon: Birth, **Jan 1**
Cosby Show TV Premiere: Anniv, **Sep 20**
Cosby, Bill: Birth, **Jul 12**
Cosell, Howard: Birth Anniv, **Mar 25**
Costa Rica,
  Feast of Our Lady of Angels, **Aug 2**
  Guanacaste Day, **Jul 25**
  Independence Day, **Sep 15**
  Juan Santamaria Day, **Apr 11**
Costas, Bob: Birth, **Mar 22**
Costello, Elvis: Birth, **Aug 25**
Costner, Kevin: Birth, **Jan 18**
Cote D'Ivoire,
  Commemoration Day, **Dec 7**
  Natl Day, **Aug 7**
Cotten, Joseph: Birth Anniv, **May 15**
Cotton Bowl Classic (Dallas, TX), **Jan 1**
Cotton Pickin' Fair (Gay, GA), **May 1**
Council of Nicaea I: Anniv, **May 20**
Counseling Week, Natl School, **Feb 2**
Country Day, Colton (Colton, NY), **Jul 17**
Country Good Times (Wilberforce, ON), **Jul 16**
Country Ham Days, Marion County (Lebanon, KY), **Sep 25**
Country Ham: Go Hog Wild—Eat Country Ham Month, **Oct 1**
Country & Western,
  Acuff, Roy: Birth Anniv, **Sep 15**
  Twitty, Conway: Birth Anniv, **Sep 1**
  Wild West Weekend and Country Music Fest (Clifton, KS), **Aug 20**
  Williams, Hank, Sr: Birth Anniv, **Sep 17**
  Wills, Bob: Birth Anniv, **Mar 6**
Couple Appreciation Month, **Apr 1**
Couples, Fred: Birth, **Oct 3**
Coupon Month, Natl, **Sep 1**
Courageous Follower Day, **Mar 4**
Couric, Katie: Birth, **Jan 7**
Court TV Debut: Anniv, **Jul 1**
Courtenay, Tom: Birth, **Feb 25**
Cousins Day, **Jul 24**
Cousteau, Jacques: Birth Anniv, **Jun 11**
Cousy, Bob: Birth, **Aug 9**
Covan (Willie) Loved to Dance Week, **Feb 1**

Covered Bridge Fest (Washington County, PA), **Sep 18**
Cow Chip-Throwing Chmpshp, World (Beaver, OK), **Apr 17**
Coward, Noel: Birth Anniv, **Dec 16**
Cowboys, Frontier, Old West,
  American Legacy (Mancan, ND), **Jul 30**
  Annie Oakley Days (Greenville, OH), **Jul 23**
  Bannack Days (Bannack, MT), **Jul 17**
  Bascom, Texas Rose: Birth Anniv, **Feb 25**
  Butterfield Overland Stage Days (Benson, AZ), **Oct 8**
  Calamity Jane (Martha Burk): Death Anniv, **Aug 1**
  Cherokee Strip Celebration (Perry, OK), **Sep 18**
  Come and Take It Fest (Gonzales, TX), **Oct 2**
  Cowboy Hall of Fame Ceremony (Willcox, AZ), **Sep 30**
  Cowboy Poetry Gathering, Dakota (Medora, ND), **May 29**
  Cowboy Poetry Gathering, Natl (Elko, NV), **Jan 24**
  Cowboy Poetry Gathering, Texas (Alpine, TX), **Mar 5**
  Defeat of Jesse James Days (Northfield, MN), **Sep 9**
  Dodge City Days (Dodge City, KS), **Jul 30**
  Fest of the West, Natl (Scottsdale, AZ), **Mar 18**
  Fiesta Bullwhacker (Olathe, KS), **Jun 5**
  Fort Seward Wagon Trail (Jamestown, ND), **Jun 20**
  Gold Rush Days (Wickenburg, AZ), **Feb 13**
  Mountain Man Rendezvous (Red Lodge, MT), **Jul 23**
  Nebraskaland Days/Buffalo Bill Rodeo (North Platte, NE), **Jun 11**
  Oakley, Annie: Birth Anniv, **Aug 13**
  Oregon Trail Days (Gering, NE), **Jul 8**
  Pony Express Fest (Hanover, KS), **Aug 29**
  Reenactment of Cowtown's Last Gunfight (Fort Worth, TX), **Feb 8**
  Rex Allen Days (Willcox, AZ), **Oct 1**
  River City Roundup (Omaha, NE), **Sep 17**
  Russell, Charles M.: Birth Anniv, **Mar 19**
  Santa-Cali-Gon Days Fest (Independence, MO), **Sep 3**
  Stagecoach Days (Marshall, TX), **May 15**
  Texas Ranch Roundup (Wichita Falls, TX), **Aug 20**
  Trails West! (St. Joseph, MO), **Jul 8**
  Wild West Weekend and Country Music Fest (Clifton, KS), **Aug 20**
  Wyatt Earp Birthday Celebration (Monmouth, IL), **Aug 8**
Cow-Chip Throw, Wisconsin (Prairie du Sac, WI), **Aug 27**
Cowher, Bill: Birth, **May 8**
Cox, Bobby: Birth, **May 21**
Cox, Ronny: Birth, **Jul 23**
Coyote Chase (Wellington, NV), **Jun 19**
Cozy Cuddles for Kids, **Nov 1**
Craddock, Billy "Crash": Birth, **Jun 16**
Crafts, **Jan 19**
Craig, Larry E: Birth, **Jul 20**
Crandall, Prudence: Birth Anniv, **Sep 3**
Crane, Stephen: Birth Anniv, **Nov 1**
Crankshaft: Anniv, **Aug 31**
Cranky Co-Workers Day, **Oct 27**
Cranmer, Thomas: Birth Anniv, **Jul 2**
Cranston, Bryan: Birth, **Mar 7**
Crapo, Michael: Birth, **May 20**
Crapper, Thomas: Day, **Jan 27**
Crater Lake Natl Park Established: Anniv, **May 22**
Crater Lake Rim Runs and Marathon (Klamath Falls, OR), **Aug 14**
Crater, Judge Joseph F.: Disappearance Anniv, **Aug 6**
Craven, Wes: Birth, **Aug 2**
Crawfish Fest, Dermott's Annual (Dermott, AR), **May 14**
Crawford, Cindy: Birth, **Feb 20**
Crawford, Joan: Birth Anniv, **Mar 23**
Crawford, Michael: Birth, **Jan 19**
Crawford, Wahoo Sam: Birth Anniv, **Apr 18**
Crawfordsville Strawberry Fest (Crawfordsville, IN), **Jun 11**
Cray, Robert: Birth, **Aug 1**
Crayfish Premier (Sweden), **Aug 11**
Create a Great Funeral Day, **Oct 30**
Creative Beginnings Month, **May 1**
Creative Frugality Week, Natl, **Jan 25**
Creativity Month, Intl, **Jan 1**
Credit Education Week, Natl, **Apr 19**
Credit Union Act: Anniv, **Jun 26**
Credit Union Day, Intl, **Oct 21**
Credit Union Law, First US: Anniv, **Apr 6**
Credit Union Week, Intl, **Oct 18**
Creeley, Robert: Birth, **May 21**
Cremation, America's First: Anniv, **Dec 9**
Crenshaw, Ben: Birth, **Jan 11**
Creole Heritage Day (Natchitoches, LA), **Oct 15**
Cribb, Tom: First US Heavyweight Defeated: Anniv, **Dec 10**
Crichton, Michael: Birth, **Oct 23**
Crick, Francis: Birth, **Jun 8**
Crime,
  Billy the Kid: Birth Anniv, **Nov 23**
  Borden, Lizzie, Verdict: Anniv, **Jun 20**
  Capone, Al: Death Anniv, **Jan 25**
  Columbine High School Killings: Anniv, **Apr 20**
  Crime Prevention Month, Natl, **Oct 1**
  Crime Victims' Rights Week, Natl (Pres Proc), **Apr 18**
  D.B. Cooper Hijacking: Anniv, **Nov 24**
  Dillinger, John: Death Anniv, **Jul 22**

695

Index ☆ Chase's 2004 Calendar of Events ☆

Crime (cont'd)—Declaration

Electrocution for Death Penalty, First: Anniv, **Aug 6**
Jack the Ripper Letter: Anniv, **Sep 27**
Miranda Decision: Anniv, **Jun 13**
Stockholm Syndrome Bank Robbery: Anniv, **Aug 23**
Ten Most Wanted List Debuts: Anniv, **Mar 14**
Valentine's Day Massacre: Anniv, **Feb 14**
Whitechapel Murders Begin: Anniv, **Aug 31**
Crimean War Began: Anniv, Oct 16
Crispus Attucks Day, Mar 5
Crist, Judith: Birth, May 22
Croatia,
Antifascist Struggle Day, **Jun 22**
Homeland Thanksgiving Day, **Aug 5**
Statehood Day, **May 30**
Crockett, David: Birth Anniv, Aug 17
Cromwell, James: Birth, Jan 27
Cronenberg, David: Birth, May 15
Cronkite, Walter: Birth, Nov 4
Crosby, Cathy Lee: Birth, Dec 2
Crosby, David: Birth, Aug 14
Crosby, Harry L. "Bing": Birth Anniv, May 3
Crosby, Mary: Birth, Sep 14
Crosby, Norm: Birth, Sep 15
Crossword Puzzle, First: Anniv, Dec 21
Crouse, Lindsay: Birth, May 12
Crow, Sheryl: Birth, Feb 11
Crowe, Cameron: Birth, Jul 13
Crowe, Russell: Birth, Apr 7
Crudup, Billy: Birth, Jul 8
Crufts Dog Show (Birmingham, England), Mar 4
Cruikshank, George: Birth Anniv, Sep 27
Cruise, Tom: Birth, Jul 3
Cruz, Celia: Birth Anniv, Oct 21
Cruz, Penelope: Birth, Apr 28
Cryer, Jon: Birth, Apr 16
Crystal, Billy: Birth, Mar 14
CSI: Crime Scene Investigation TV Premiere: Anniv, Oct 6
CSICOP Annual Superstition Bash, Feb 13
Csonka, Larry: Birth, Dec 25
Cuba,
Anniv of the Revolution, **Jan 1**
Bay of Pigs Invasion Launched: Anniv, **Apr 17**
Beginning of Independence Wars Day, **Oct 10**
Christmas Returns: Anniv, **Dec 25**
Cuban Missile Crisis: Anniv, **Oct 22**
Liberation Day, **Jan 1**
National Day, **Jul 26**
Cuckoo Dancing Week, Jan 11
Culinary Arts Month, Natl, Jul 1
Culkin, Macaulay: Birth, Aug 26
Cullen, Countee: Birth Anniv, May 30
Culligan, Emmett J.: Birth Anniv, Mar 5
Cullum, John: Birth, Mar 2
Culp, Robert: Birth, Aug 16
Cumming, Alan: Birth, Jan 27
Cummings, Quinn: Birth, Aug 13
Cummings, Robert: Birth Anniv, Jun 9
Cummings, Terry: Birth, Mar 15
Cunningham, Glenn: Birth Anniv, Aug 4
Cunningham, Merce: Birth, Apr 16
Cunningham, Randall: Birth, Mar 27
Curacao,
Animals' Day, **Sep 4**
Curacao Day, **Jul 26**
Kingdom Day and Antillean Flag Day, **Dec 15**
Memorial Day, **May 4**
Curie, Marie: Birth Anniv, Nov 7
Curlew Day, Mar 16
Curling is Cool Day, Feb 23
Curry, Mark: Birth, Jun 1
Curry, Tim: Birth, Apr 19
Curtin, Jane: Birth, Sep 6
Curtis Cup (Merseyside, England), Jun 12
Curtis, Charles: Birth Anniv, Jan 25
Curtis, Jamie Lee: Birth, Nov 22
Curtis, Tony: Birth, Jun 3
Curtiss, Glenn: Birth Anniv, May 21
Curwood Festival (Owosso, MI), Jun 3
Cusack, Joan: Birth, Oct 11
Cusack, John: Birth, Jun 28
Custer Battlefield Becomes Little Bighorn Battlefield: Anniv, Nov 26
Custer, George: Battle of Little Bighorn: Anniv, Jun 25
Custer: Little Bighorn Days (Hardin, MT), Jun 23
Custodial Workers Day, Natl, Oct 2
Customer Day, Get To Know Your, Jan 15
Customer Loyalty Month, Intl, Apr 1
Customer Service Day, Jan 15
Customer Service: Stop the Bad Service Day, Mar 3
Customers Week, Natl Thank-Your-, Jan 5
Cut Up Your Credit Card Day, Natl, Oct 16
Cuthbert, Elisha: Birth, Nov 30
Cyprus,
Green Monday, **Feb 23**
Independence Day, **Oct 1**
Procession of Icon of St. Lazarus, **Apr 3**
Saint Paul's Feast, **Jun 28**
Cyrus, Billy Ray: Birth, Aug 25
Czar Nicholas II and Family Executed: Anniv, Jul 17
Czech Republic,
Commemoration Day, **Jul 6**
Foundation of the Republic, **Oct 28**
Liberation Day, **May 8**

Prague Autumn Intl Music Festival, **Sep 12**
Teachers' Day, **Mar 28**
Czechoslovakia,
Clarkson Czech Fest (Clarkson, NE), **Jun 24**
Czech Days (Tabor, SD), **Jun 18**
Czechoslovakia Ends Communist Rule: Anniv, **Nov 29**
Czechoslovakian Fest, Natl (Wilber, NE), **Aug 6**
Czech-Slovak Divorce: Anniv, **Jan 1**
Rape of Lidice: Anniv, **Jun 10**
Westfest (West, TX), **Sep 4**
D.A.R.E. Day, Natl (Pres Proc), Apr 10
D'Abo, Olivia: Birth, Jan 22
Daffodil Fest Weekend (Nantucket Island, MA), Apr 23
Dafoe, Willem: Birth, Jul 22
Daguerre, Louis: Birth Anniv, Nov 18
Dahl, Arlene: Birth, Aug 11
Dahl, Roald: Birth Anniv, Sep 13
Dahl, Steve: Birth, Nov 20
Dailey, Irene: Birth, Sep 12
Dailey, Janet: Birth, May 21
Dairy Month, June, Jun 1
Dakides, Tara: Birth, Aug 20
Dalai Lama Flees Tibet: Anniv, Mar 31
Dalai Lama: Birth, Jun 6
Daley, John: Birth, Jul 20
Daley, Richard M.: Birth, Apr 24
Dali, Salvador: Birth Anniv, May 11
Dallas Cup (Dallas, TX), Apr 4
Dallas TV Premiere: Anniv, Apr 2
Dallas, George: Birth Anniv, Jul 10
Dalton Defenders Day (Coffeyville, KS), Oct 1
Dalton, John: Birth Anniv, Sep 6
Dalton, Timothy: Birth, Mar 21
Daltrey, Roger: Birth, Mar 1
Daly, Carson: Birth, Jun 22
Daly, Chuck: Birth, Jul 20
Daly, John: Birth, Apr 28
Daly, Timothy: Birth, Mar 1
Daly, Tyne: Birth, Feb 21
Damian, Michael: Birth, Apr 26
Damon, Matt: Birth, Oct 8
Damone, Vic: Birth, Jun 12
Dana, Bill: Birth, Oct 5
Dance,
Ailey, Alvin: Birth Anniv, **Jan 5**
Balanchine, George: Birth Anniv, **Jan 22**
Balanchine-Graham Collaboration: Anniv, **May 14**
Ballet Introduced to US: Anniv, **Feb 7**
Dance Day, Natl, **Mar 21**
Duncan, Isadora: Birth Anniv, **May 27**
English Riviera Dance Fest (Torquay, England), **May 29**
Folkmoot USA (Waynesville, NC), **Jul 12**
Fonteyn, Margot: Birth Anniv, **May 18**
Fosse, Bob: Birth Anniv, **Jun 23**
Gay Square Dance Month, Intl, **Sep 1**
Gigglefeet Dance Festival (Ketchikan, AK), **Aug 6**
Graham, Martha: Birth Anniv, **May 11**
Kuopio Dance Fest (Kuopio, Finland), **Jun 17**
Maple Leaf Rag Premiere: Anniv, **Oct 2**
Merrie Monarch Fest & Hula Competition (Hilo, HI), **Apr 11**
Ocean Dance (Hollywood, FL), **Dec 3**
Pacific DanceSport Chmpnshps (Los Angeles, CA), **Nov 5**
Robinson, Bill "Bojangles": Birth Anniv, **May 25**
Shrewsbury Intl Music Fest (Shropshire, England), **Jun 25**
Tap Dance Day, Natl, **May 25**
Willie Covan Loved to Dance Week, **Feb 1**
World Folkfest (Springville, UT), **Jul 10**
Dance, Charles: Birth, Oct 10
Dandridge, Dorothy: Birth Anniv, Nov 9
Danes, Claire: Birth, Apr 12
D'Angelo, Beverly: Birth, Nov 15
Dangerfield, Rodney: Birth, Nov 22
Daniel Boone Pioneer Festival (Winchester, KY), Sep 3
Daniel Boone TV Premiere: Anniv, Sep 24
Daniel, Beth: Birth, Oct 14
Daniels, Charlie: Birth, Oct 28
Daniels, Jeff: Birth, Feb 19
Daniels, William: Birth, Mar 31
Danish,
Aebleskiver Days (Tyler, MN), **Jul 23**
Tivoli Fest (Elk Horn, IA), **May 29**
Dankfest (Harmony, PA), Aug 28
Danner, Blythe: Birth, Feb 3
Danson, Ted: Birth, Dec 29
Dante Alighieri: Death Anniv, Sep 14
Danza, Tony: Birth, Apr 21
Darby, Kim: Birth, Jul 8
Dare, Virginia: Birth Anniv, Aug 18
Dark Day in New England: Anniv, May 19
Dark Shadows TV Premiere: Anniv, Jun 27
Darren, James: Birth, Jun 8
Darrow, Clarence, Death Commemoration (Chicago, IL), Mar 13
Darrow, Clarence: Birth Anniv, Apr 18
Darwin, Charles: Birth Anniv, Feb 12
Darwin, Charles: On the Origin of Species Published: Anniv, Nov 22
Daschle, Thomas: Birth, Dec 9
Date Fest, Natl (Indio, CA), Feb 13

Date to Create, The, **Aug 8**
Dating Game TV Premiere: Anniv, **Dec 20**
Daumier, Honore: Birth Anniv, **Feb 26**
DAV Day, Natl, **Feb 9**
Davenport, Lindsay: Birth, **Jun 8**
David Brinkley's Journal TV Premiere: Anniv, **Oct 11**
David, Keith: Birth, **Jun 4**
Davidovich, Lolita: Birth, **Jul 15**
Davidson, John: Birth, **Dec 13**
Davies, Jeremy: Birth, **Oct 28**
Davies, Laura: Birth, **Oct 5**
Davies, Marion: Birth Anniv, **Jan 3**
Davis, Al: Birth, **Jul 4**
Davis, Angela: Birth, **Jan 26**
Davis, Bette: Birth Anniv, **Apr 5**
Davis, Clifton: Birth, **Oct 4**
Davis, Eric: Birth, **May 29**
Davis, Geena: Birth, **Jan 21**
Davis, Gray: Birth, **Dec 26**
Davis, Jefferson: Birth Anniv, **Jun 3**
Davis, Jefferson: Bread Riot Richmond: Anniv, **Apr 2**
Davis, Jefferson: Inauguration: Anniv, **Feb 18**
Davis, Jim: Birth, **Jul 28**
Davis, Jr, Benjamin O.: Birth Anniv, **Dec 18**
Davis, Judy: Birth, **Apr 23**
Davis, Mac: Birth, **Jan 21**
Davis, Miles: Birth Anniv, **May 25**
Davis, Ossie: Birth, **Dec 18**
Davis, Sammy, Jr: Birth Anniv, **Dec 8**
Davis, Skeeter: Birth, **Dec 30**
Davis, Terrell: Birth, **Oct 28**
Davis-Voss, Sammi: Birth, **Jun 21**
Davison, Bruce: Birth, **Jun 28**
Davy Crockett TV Premiere: Anniv, **Dec 15**
Dawber, Pam: Birth, **Oct 18**
Dawes, Charles: Birth Anniv, **Aug 27**
Dawson, Andre: Birth, **Jul 10**
Dawson, Dermontti: Birth, **Jun 17**
Dawson, Richard: Birth, **Nov 20**
Day of Meditation, **Jan 1**
Day of Natl Concern about Young People and Gun Violence, **Oct 21**
Day of Prayer and Action for Human Habitat, Intl, **Sep 19**
Day of Reason, Natl, **May 6**
Day of the Five Billion: Anniv, **Jul 11**
Day of the Race: See Columbus Day, **Oct 12**
Day of the Six Billion: Anniv, **Oct 12**
Day on the Farm (Springfield, OR), **Aug 21**
Day With(out) Art, **Dec 1**
Day, Doris: Birth, **Apr 3**
Day-Lewis, Daniel: Birth, **Apr 29**
Dayne, Taylor: Birth, **Mar 7**
Day-Out-of-Time, **Jul 25**
Days of Our Lives TV Premiere: Anniv, **Nov 8**
Dayton, Mark: Birth, **Jan 26**
D-Day: Anniv, **Jun 6**
De Bont, Jan: Birth, **Oct 22**
De Carlo, Yvonne: Birth, **Sep 1**
De Forest, Lee: Birth Anniv, **Aug 26**
De Gaulle, Charles: Birth Anniv, **Nov 22**
de Havilland, Olivia: Birth, **Jul 1**
De Klerk, Frederick: Birth, **Mar 18**
de la Hoya, Oscar: Birth, **Feb 4**
De La Renta, Oscar: Birth, **Jul 22**
De Laurentiis, Dino: Birth, **Aug 8**
De Mille, Cecil B.: Birth Anniv, **Aug 12**
De Mornay, Rebecca: Birth, **Aug 29**
De Niro, Robert: Birth, **Aug 17**
De Palma, Brian: Birth, **Sep 11**
De Rita, Joe: Birth Anniv, **Jul 12**
De Sade, Donatien: Birth Anniv, **Jun 2**
De Young, Cliff: Birth, **Feb 12**
Deaf Awareness Week, **Sep 19**
Deaf Conference, Natl Assn of the (Kansas City, MO), **Jul 6**
Deaf Day, Mother, Father, **Apr 25**
Deaf History Month, **Mar 13**
Deaf, First School for: Anniv, **Apr 15**
Dean, Dizzy: Birth Anniv, **Jan 16**
Dean, Howard: Birth, **Nov 17**
Dean, James, Birthday Celebration (Fairmont, IN), **Feb 7**
Dean, James: Birth Anniv, **Feb 8**
Dean, James: Fairmount Fest/Remembering (Fairmount, IN), **Sep 24**
Dean, Jimmy: Birth, **Aug 10**
Dean, John: Birth, **Oct 14**
Dear Diary Day, **Sep 22**
Dear Santa Letter Week, **Nov 5**
Death Penalty Banned: Anniv, **Jun 29**
Death/Duty Day, **Nov 11**
DeBakey, Michael: Birth, **Sep 7**
DeBarge, Eldra: Birth, **Jun 4**
Debate, Great (over Constitution): Anniv, **Aug 6**
Debs, Eugene V: Birth Anniv, **Nov 5**
Debussy, Claude: Birth Anniv, **Aug 22**
Decatur, Stephen: Birth Anniv, **Jan 5**
December Bride TV Premiere: Anniv, **Oct 4**
Decency, Rally for: Anniv, **Mar 23**
Decide to Be Married Day, **Jun 27**
Decisions: Make Up Your Mind Day, **Dec 31**
Declaration of Independence,
Approval and Signing: Anniv, **Jul 4**
First Public Reading: Anniv, **Jul 8**

696

★ Chase's 2004 Calendar of Events ★   Index

Official Signing: Anniv, **Aug 2**
Resolution: Anniv, **Jul 2**
Declaration of the Bab, May 23
Decoration Day (Memorial Day), May 31
Decoy and Wildlife Art Show (Clayton, NY), Jul 16
Decter, Midge: Birth, Jul 25
Dee, Ruby: Birth, Oct 27
Dee, Sandra: Birth, Apr 23
Deepavali (India), Oct 25
Deere, John: Birthday Celeb (Moline, IL), Feb 7
Deere, John: Memorabilia Conf (Moline, IL), Mar 9
Deere, John: Tractor & Memorabilia Auction (Moline, IL), **Aug 13**
Deerfield Massacre: Anniv (Feb 29), Feb 1
Dees, Rick: Birth, Mar 14
Defenders Day, Sep 12
Defense Transportation Day, Natl (Pres Proc), May 21
DeFrantz, Anita L.: Birth, Oct 4
Degas, Edgar: Birth Anniv, Jul 19
DeGeneres, Ellen: Birth, Jan 26
DeHaven, Gloria: Birth, Jul 23
Del Toro, Benicio: Birth, Feb 19
Delaney, Kim: Birth, Nov 29
Delano, Jane: Birth Anniv, Mar 26
Delany, Dana: Birth, Mar 13
Delaware,
   Biden, Joe: Birth, **Nov 20**
   Carper, Tom: Birth, **Jan 23**
   Delaware State Fair (Harrington), **Jul 22**
   DuPont RiverFest (Wilmington), **Sep 25**
   Minner, Ruth Ann: Birth, **Jan 17**
   Nanticoke Indian Powwow (Millsboro), **Sep 11**
   Point-to-Point (Wilmington), **May 2**
   Ratification Day, **Dec 7**
   Return Day (Georgetown), **Nov 4**
   Sea Witch Halloween Fest (Rehoboth Beach/Dewey Beach), **Oct 29**
Delgado, Carlos: Birth, Jun 25
Delmonico, Lorenzo: Birth Anniv, Mar 13
DeLuise, Dom: Birth, Aug 1
DeMille, Agnes: Birth Anniv, Sep 18
Demme, Jonathan: Birth, Feb 22
Democratic National Convention (Boston, MA), Jul 26
Dempsey, Jack: Birth Anniv, Jun 24
Dempsey, Jack: Long Count Day, Sep 22
Dempsey, Patrick: Birth, Jan 13
DeMunn, Jeffrey: Birth, Apr 25
Denali Natl Park: Anniv, Dec 2
Dench, Judi: Birth, Dec 9
Deneuve, Catherine: Birth, Oct 22
Denim Day, Lee Natl, Oct 8
Denmark,
   Aalborg and Rebild Fest (Aalborg and Rebild), **Jul 2**
   Aarhus Fest Week, **Sep 4**
   Common Prayer Day, **May 7**
   Constitution Day, **Jun 5**
   Ho Sheep Market, **Aug 28**
   Midsummer Eve, **Jun 23**
   Queen Margrethe's Birthday, **Apr 16**
   Street Urchins' Carnival, **Feb 23**
   Tivoli Gardens Season (Copenhagen), **May 1**
   Viking Fest, **Jun 18**
Dennehy, Brian: Birth, Jul 9
Dennis, Sandy: Birth Anniv, Apr 27
Dent, Bucky: Birth, Nov 25
Dental Awareness Month, Intl, May 1
Dental Drill Patent: Anniv, Jan 26
Dental Health Month, Natl Children's, Feb 1
Dental Hygiene Month, Natl, Oct 1
Dental School, First Woman to Graduate: Anniv, Feb 21
Denver, Bob: Birth, Jan 9
Denver, John: Birth Anniv, Dec 31
Depardieu, Gerard: Birth, Dec 27
Depp, Johnny: Birth, Jun 9
DePreist, James (Anderson): Birth, Nov 21
Depression Education and Awareness Month, Natl, Oct 1
Depression Screening Day, Natl, Oct 7
Derek, Bo: Birth, Nov 20
Dern, Bruce: Birth, Jun 4
Dern, Laura: Birth, Feb 10
Dershowitz, Alan: Birth, Sep 1
Descartes, Rene: Birth, Mar 31
Descendants Day, Jun 26
Desegregation, US Army First: Anniv, Jul 26
Desert Shield: Anniv, Aug 7
Desert Storm: Ground War Begins: Anniv, Feb 23
Desert Storm: Kuwait Liberated: Anniv, Feb 27
Desert Storm: Persian Gulf War Begins: Anniv, Jan 16
Desert Storm: UN Deadline Resolution: Anniv, Nov 28
DeShannon, Jackie: Birth, Aug 21
Designated Hitter Rule Adopted: Anniv, Jan 11
DeSoto Caverns Park Fall Indian Dance Fest (Childersburg, AL), Sep 25
DeSoto Caverns Park Spring Indian Dance Fest (Childersburg, AL), Apr 3
DeSoto's Winter Encampment (Tallahassee, FL), Jan 17
Des'ree: Birth, Nov 30
Detroit (MI): Anniv, Jul 24
Devane, William: Birth, Sep 5

Development Information Day, World (UN) Oct 24
Devers, Gail: Birth, Nov 19
Devil's Night, Oct 30
DeVito, Danny: Birth, Nov 17
Devlin, Bernadette: Birth, Apr 23
DeVoe, Ronald: Birth, Feb 17
Dewey Defeats Truman Headline: Anniv, Nov 3
Dewey, John: Birth Anniv, Oct 20
Dewey, Melvil: Birth Anniv, Dec 10
Dewhurst, Colleen: Birth Anniv, Jun 3
DeWine, Mike: Birth, Jan 5
Dewitt, Joyce: Birth, Apr 23
Dey, Susan: Birth, Dec 10
Dia de la Raza (Mexico), Oct 12
Dia de la Raza: See Columbus Day, Oct 12
Diabetes Assn Alert Day, American, Mar 23
Diabetes Month, American, Nov 1
Diabetes, Dollars Against (DAD's) Day, Jun 18
Diabetic Eye Disease Month, Nov 1
Diallo, Mamadou: Birth, Aug 28
Diamond, Dustin: Birth, Jan 7
Diamond, Neil: Birth, Jan 24
Diana, Princess of Wales: Birth Anniv, Jul 1
Diary Day, Dear, Sep 22
Diaz, Cameron: Birth, Aug 30
DiCaprio, Leonardo: Birth, Nov 11
Dice Day, Natl, Dec 4
Dicing for Bibles (Huntingdonshire, England), May 31
Dick Cavett Show TV Premiere: Anniv, Mar 4
Dick Van Dyke Show TV Premiere: Anniv, Oct 3
Dick, Andy: Birth, Dec 21
Dickens' Christmas Extravaganza (Cape May, NJ), Dec 3
Dickens of a Christmas (Franklin, TN), Dec 11
Dickens on the Strand (Galveston, TX), Dec 4
Dickens, Charles: Birth Anniv, Feb 7
Dickerson, Eric: Birth, Sep 2
Dickinson, Angie: Birth, Sep 30
Dickinson, Emily: Birth Anniv, Dec 10
Dictionary Day, Oct 16
Dictionary of American English Published, First: Anniv, Apr 14
Diddley, Bo: Birth, Dec 30
Didion, Joan: Birth, Dec 5
Didrikson, Babe: See under Zaharias, Jun 26
Diefenbaker, John: Birth Anniv, Sep 18
Diego, Jose de: Birth Anniv, Apr 16
Dien Bien Phu Falls: Anniv, May 7
Diesel Engine Patented: Anniv, Feb 23
Diesel, Rudolph: Natl Biodiesel Day, Mar 18
Diesel, Vin: Birth, Jul 18
Dietrich, Marlene: Birth Anniv, Dec 27
Diets, Dieting (including weight loss and weight issues). See also Health,
   Diet Resolution Week, **Jan 1**
   Dietary Managers Assn Mtg/Expo (Reno, NV), **Jul 18**
   Family Fit Lifestyle Month, **Jan 1**
   Healthy Weight Week, **Jan 18**
   Lose Weight/Feel Great Week, Natl, **Jan 1**
   No Diet Day, **May 6**
   Rid the World of Fad Diets/Gimmicks Day, **Jan 20**
   TOPS Club, Inc: Anniv, **Jan 21**
   Women's Healthy Weight Day, **Jan 22**
Different World TV Premiere: Anniv, Sep 24
DiFranco, Ani: Birth, Sep 23
Diggs, Taye: Birth, Jan 2
Diller, Phyllis: Birth, Jul 17
Dillinger, John: Death Anniv, Jul 22
Dillman, Bradford: Birth, Apr 14
Dillon, Kevin: Birth, Aug 19
Dillon, Matt: Birth, Feb 18
Dillon, Melinda: Birth, Oct 13
DiMaggio, Joe: Birth Anniv, Nov 25
Dimpled Chad Day, Jan 4
DiMucci, Dion: Birth, Jul 18
Dinah Shore Show TV Premiere: Anniv, Nov 27
Ding Dong School TV Premiere: Anniv, Dec 22
Ding Ling: Death Anniv, Mar 4
Dinkins, David: Birth, Jul 10
Dion, Celine: Birth, Mar 30
Dionne Quintuplets: Birth, May 28
Disabled,
   Abilities Day, **Dec 22**
   Americans with Disabilities Act: Anniv, **Jul 26**
   Bell, Alexander Graham: Birth Anniv, **Mar 3**
   Clerc-Gallaudet Week, **Dec 5**
   Deaf Awareness Week, **Sep 19**
   Deaf History Month, **Mar 13**
   Deep Creek Dunk (McHenry, MD), **Feb 21**
   Disability Employment Awareness Month, Natl, **Oct 1**
   Disability Employment Awareness Month, Natl (Pres Proc), **Oct 1**
   Disabled Persons, Intl Day of (UN), **Dec 3**
   First School for Deaf: Anniv, **Apr 15**
   Fishing Has No Boundaries (Bemidji, MN), **Jun 26**
   Fishing Has No Boundaries (Hayward, WI), **May 14**
   Fishing Has No Boundaries (Monticello, IN), **May 15**
   Goodwill Industries Week, **May 2**
   Helen Keller Deaf-Blindness Awareness Week, **Jun 27**
   Mother, Father Deaf Day, **Apr 25**
   National Association of the Deaf Conference (Kansas City, MO), **Jul 6**
   Rehabilitation Awareness Celebration, Natl, **Sep 19**
   Seeing Eye Established: Anniv, **Jan 29**

Special Chefs Blue Ribbon Recipe and Cooking Contest (Chicago, IL), **Oct 16**
   Special Olympics Day, **Jul 20**
   Special Olympics Winter Games (McHenry, MD), **Feb 22**
   Special Recreation Day, **Jul 4**
   Special Recreation Week, **Jul 4**
   Therapeutic Recreation Week, Natl, **Jul 11**
   Travelers with Disabilities Awareness Week, **Nov 28**
   Wells Fargo Bank Cup (Winter Park, CO), **Feb 6**
Disarmament Week (UN), Oct 24
Discoverers' Day (Hawaii), Oct 11
Discovery Launches Satellite: Anniv, Nov 7
Discovery Walk Festival (Vancouver, WA), Apr 23
Dishonor List, New Year's, Jan 1
Disney World Opened: Anniv, Oct 1
Disney, Walt: Birth Anniv, Dec 5
Disneyland Opened: Anniv, Jul 17
Disraeli, Benjamin: Birth Anniv, Dec 21
Distinguished Service Medal: Anniv, Mar 7
Ditka, Mike: Birth, Oct 18
Divac, Vlade: Birth, Feb 3
Diversity Awareness Month, Oct 1
Divorced Parents for Children Week, Natl, Oct 1
Diwali (India), Oct 25
Dix, Dorothea L.: Birth Anniv, Apr 4
Dixie, Holiday in (Shreveport and Bossier City, LA), Apr 16
Dixon, Donna: Birth, Jul 20
Dixon, Willie: Birth Anniv, Jul 1
Djibouti: Independence Day, Jun 27
Do Dah Day (Birmingham, AL), May 8
Do It Day (aka Fight Procrastination Day), Sep 7
Dobson, Kevin: Birth, Mar 18
Doctorow, E.L.: Birth, Jan 6
Doctor-Patient Trust Day, Mar 17
Doctors' Day, Mar 30
Doctors TV Premiere: Anniv, Apr 1
Dodd, Christopher J.: Birth, May 27
Dodge Poetry Fest (NJ), Sep 16
Dodgson, Charles Lutwidge: Birth Anniv, Jan 27
Dog Days, Jul 3
Doghouse Repairs Month, Natl, Jun 1
Dogs. See also Sled Dogs,
   Adopt-A-Shelter-Dog Month, **Oct 1**
   Bark in the Park (Chicago, IL), **May 1**
   Crufts Dog Show (Birmingham, England), **Mar 4**
   Dog Bite Prevention Week, Natl, **May 16**
   Dog Week, Natl, **Sep 19**
   Faith City Kennel Club Dog Show (Wichita Falls, TX), **Feb 27**
   Field Trial Chmpshp, Natl (Bird Dogs) (Grand Junction, TN), **Feb 9**
   Haute Dog Charity Easter Parade (Long Beach, CA), **Apr 11**
   Haute Dog Charity Howl'oween Parade (Long Beach, CA), **Oct 31**
   Sled Dogs Save Nome: Anniv, **Feb 2**
   Stock Dog Trials & Farm Fest, US Open (Dawsonville, GA), **Oct 1**
   Take Your Dog to Work Day, **Jun 25**
   Westminster Kennel Club Dog Show (New York, NY), **Feb 9**
   What if Cats and Dogs Had Opposable Thumbs Day, **Mar 3**
   Woofstock (Wichita, KS), **Oct 4**
Dogwood Arts Fest (Knoxville, TN), Apr 8
Doherty, Shannen: Birth, Apr 12
Dolby, Ray: Birth, Jan 18
Dole, Elizabeth: Birth, Jul 29
Dole, Robert J.: Birth, Jul 22
Dolenz, Micky: Birth, Mar 8
Doll Classic, American Club's Teddy Bear and (Kohler, WI), Feb 21
Doll Day (Japan), Mar 3
Doll, Kewpie: Rose C. O'Neill: Birth Anniv, Jun 25
Dollars Against Diabetes (DAD's) Day, Jun 18
Domenici, Pete V.: Birth, May 7
Domestic Violence Awareness Month, Natl, Oct 1
Domingo, Placido: Birth, Jan 21
Dominica: National Day, Nov 3
Dominican Republic,
   Independence Day, **Feb 27**
   National Holiday, **Jan 26**
   Restoration of the Republic, **Aug 16**
Domino, Fats: Birth, Feb 26
Donahue, Elinor: Birth, Apr 19
Donahue, Phil: Birth, Dec 21
Donald Duck: Birth, Jun 9
Donaldson, Sam: Birth, Mar 11
Donate a Day's Wages to Charity Day, May 12
Donate Life Month, Natl, Apr 1
Donizetti's "Lucia Di Lammermoor" Premiere: Anniv, Sep 26
Donna Reed Performing Arts Fest (Denison, IA), Jun 22
Donnelly, Donal: Birth, Jul 6
Donner Party Famine: Anniv, Oct 28
Donny and Marie TV Premiere: Anniv, Jan 16
D'Onofrio, Vincent: Birth, Jun 30
Donor Sabbath, Natl, Nov 12
Donovan, Landon: Birth, Mar 4
Donovan, Tate: Birth, Sep 25
Donovan: Birth, Feb 10
Don't Step on a Bee Day, Jul 10
Donut Day (Chicago, IL), Jun 4

Declaration (cont'd)—Donut

697

Index ☆ *Chase's 2004 Calendar of Events* ☆

Dooley, Paul: Birth, Feb 22
Doolittle, Eliza: Day, May 20
Doolittle, James Harold: Birth Anniv, Dec 14
Dorgan, Byron L.: Birth, May 14
Dormition of Theotokos, Aug 15
Dornach Battle Commemoration (Switzerland), Jul 25
Dorrington, Arthur: First Black Pro Hockey Player: Anniv, Nov 15
Dorsett, Tony: Birth, Apr 7
Dorsey, Thomas A.: Birth Anniv, Jul 1
Dostoyevsky, Fyodor M: Birth Anniv, Nov 11
Double 9 Fest (China), Oct 22
Double 10th Day (China), Oct 10
Doubleday, Abner: Birth Anniv, Jun 26
Douglas, Illeana: Birth, Jul 25
Douglas, Jim: Birth, Jun 21
Douglas, Kirk: Birth, Dec 9
Douglas, Michael: Birth, Sep 25
Douglas, Mike: Birth, Aug 11
Douglas, Sherman: Birth, Sep 15
Douglas, Virginia O'Hanlon: Death Anniv, May 13
Douglas, William O.: Birth Anniv, Oct 16
Douglass, Frederick,
   Death Anniv, **Feb 20**
   Escape to Freedom: Anniv, **Sep 3**
   Frederick Douglass Speaks: Anniv, **Aug 11**
Dourdan, Gary: Birth, Dec 11
Dourif, Brad: Birth, Mar 18
Dow, Tony: Birth, Apr 13
Dowie, John: Birth Anniv, May 25
Dow-Jones Biggest Drop: Anniv, Oct 19
Dow-Jones Industrial Average: Anniv, Oct 7
Dow-Jones Tops 1,000: Anniv, Nov 14
Dow-Jones Tops 5,000: Anniv, Nov 21
Dow-Jones Tops 10,000: Anniv, Mar 29
Dow-Jones Tops 11,000: Anniv, May 3
Down Syndrome Month, Natl, Oct 1
Down, Lesley-Anne: Birth, Mar 17
Downey, Robert, Jr: Birth, Apr 4
Downey, Roma: Birth, May 6
Downs, Hugh: Birth, Feb 14
Doyle, Jim: Birth, Nov 23
Doyle, Sir Arthur Conan: Birth Anniv, May 22
Dr. Who TV Premiere: Anniv, Nov 23
Drabble, Margaret: Birth, Jun 5
Dragnet TV Premiere: Anniv, Dec 16
Dragon Boat Fest (China), Jun 22
Dragon, Daryl: Birth, Aug 27
DRC-FM Caravan of Carriages (Windsor, CT), Nov 21
Dream 2004 Day, Mar 11
Dream Hotline, Natl, Apr 23
Dred Scott Decision: Anniv, Mar 6
Dreiser, Theodore: Birth Anniv, Aug 27
Drescher, Fran: Birth, Sep 30
Dresden Firebombing, Feb 13
Drew, Charles: Birth Anniv, Jun 3
Drew, Elizabeth: Birth, Nov 16
Drexler, Clyde Austin: Birth, Jun 22
Dreyfuss, Richard: Birth, Oct 29
Drinking Age: Minimum Legal at 21: Anniv, Jul 17
Drinking Straw Patented: Anniv, Jan 3
Drive-In Movie Opens, First: Anniv, Jun 6
Driver, Minnie: Birth, Jan 31
Drive-Thru Day, Natl, Jul 28
Drug Abuse/Illicit Trafficking, Intl Day Against (UN), Jun 26
Drugs: Just Pray No: Worldwide Weekend Prayer, Apr 17
Drunk and Drugged Driving Prevention Month, Natl (Pres Proc), Dec 1
Drysdale, Don: Birth Anniv, Jul 23
Du Bois, W.E.B.: Birth Anniv, Feb 23
Dubcek, Alexander: Birth Anniv, Nov 27
DuBois, Ja'net: Birth, Aug 5
Duchovny, David: Birth, Aug 7
Duck-Calling Contest, World Chmpshp (Stuttgart, AR), Nov 26
Duff, Howard: Birth Anniv, Nov 24
Duffy, Julia: Birth, Jun 27
Duffy, Patrick: Birth, Mar 17
Dugan, Dennis: Birth, Sep 5
Dukakis, Michael: Birth, Nov 3
Dukakis, Olympia: Birth, Jun 20
Duke, Patty: Birth, Dec 14
Dukes of Hazzard TV Premiere: Anniv, Jan 26
Dulcimer Days (Coshocton, OH), May 14
Dulcimer Fest, Southern Appalachian (McCalla, AL), May 1
Dullea, Keir: Birth, May 30
Dumars, Joe: Birth, May 24
Dumas, Alexandre (Fils): Birth Anniv, Jul 27
Dumas, Alexandre: Birth Anniv, Jul 24
Dumb Week (Greece), Apr 5
Dump Your "Significant Jerk" Day, Feb 3
Dunant, Jean Henri: Birth Anniv, May 8
Dunaway, Faye: Birth, Jan 14
Duncan, Isadora: Birth Anniv, May 27
Duncan, Sandy: Birth, Feb 20
Duncan, Tim: Birth, Apr 25
Dunkirk Evacuated: Anniv, May 26
Dunn, Adam: Birth, Nov 9
Dunn, Nora: Birth, Apr 29
Dunn, Shannon: Birth, Nov 26
Dunn, Warrick: Birth, Jan 5
Dunne, Griffin: Birth, Jun 8

Dunne, Philip: Birth Anniv, Feb 11
Dunst, Kirsten: Birth, Apr 30
Duran Duran Appreciation Day, Natl, Aug 10
Duran, Roberto: Birth, Jun 16
Durang, Christopher: Birth, Jan 2
Durant, Will: Birth Anniv, Nov 5
Durant, William: Birth Anniv, Dec 8
Durante, Jimmy: Birth Anniv, Feb 10
Durbin, Deanna: Birth, Dec 4
Durbin, Richard J.: Birth, Nov 21
Durer, Albrecht: Birth Anniv, May 21
Durning, Charles: Birth, Feb 28
Durocher, Leo: Birth Anniv, Jul 27
Dushku, Eliza: Birth, Dec 30
Dussault, Nancy: Birth, Jun 30
Duston, Hannah: American Heroine Rewarded: Anniv, Jun 8
Dutoit, Charles: Birth, Oct 7
Dutton, Charles S.: Birth, Jan 30
Duval, David: Birth, Nov 9
Duvall, Robert: Birth, Jan 5
Duvall, Shelley: Birth, Jul 7
Dvorak, Anton: New World Symphony Premiere: Anniv, Dec 16
Dykstra, Lenny: Birth, Feb 10
Dylan, Bob: Birth, May 24
Dynasty TV Premiere: Anniv, Jan 12
Dysart, Richard: Birth, Mar 30
E, Sheila: Birth, Dec 12
Eads, George: Birth, Mar 1
Eagle Days in Springfield (Springfield, MO), Jan 17
Eagles Et Cetera (Bismarck, AR), Jan 23
Earhart, Amelia, Atlantic Crossing: Anniv, May 20
Earhart, Amelia: Birth Anniv, Jul 24
Earmuffs Patented: Anniv, Mar 13
Earnhardt, Dale, Jr: Birth, Oct 10
Earnhardt, Dale: Birth Anniv, Apr 29
Earp, Wyatt: Birth Anniv, Mar 19
Earp, Wyatt: Birthday Celebration (Monmouth, IL), Aug 8
Earth at Aphelion, Jul 5
Earth at Perihelion, Jan 4
Earth Day (Environment), Apr 25
Earth, First Picture of, From Space: Anniv, Aug 7
Earthquake,
   Calabria (Italy) Earthquake: Anniv, Dec 16
   California Earthquake Preparedness Month, **Apr 1**
   Earthquake Jolts Philippines: Anniv, **Jul 16**
   Earthquake of 1988, Armenian: Anniv, **Dec 7**
   Earthquake Strikes Alaska: Anniv, **Mar 27**
   Indian Earthquake, **Jan 26**
   Japan Suffers Major Quake: Anniv, **Jan 17**
   Mexico City Earthquake: Anniv, **Sep 19**
   Missouri Earthquakes: Anniv, **Dec 6**
   Plymouth Plantation: Anniv, **Jun 1**
   Richter Scale Day, **Apr 26**
   San Francisco 1906 Earthquake: Anniv, **Apr 18**
   San Francisco 1989 Earthquake: Anniv, **Oct 17**
   Southern California: Anniv, **Jan 17**
   Turkish Earthquake: Anniv, **Aug 17**
   Worst Earthquake of the 20th Century: Anniv, **May 22**
Earth's Rotation Proved: Anniv, Jan 8
Easley, Mike: Birth, Mar 23
East Coast Blackout: Anniv, Nov 9
East Texas Poultry Fest (Center, TX), Oct 7
East Timor: Independence Day: Anniv, May 20
Easter,
   Chincoteague Easter Decoy Show (Chincoteague Island, VA), **Apr 9**
   Consider Christianity Week, **Mar 28**
   Curtis Easter Pageant (Curtis, NE), **Apr 4**
   Easter Bunny Bop and Hop (Aiken, SC), **Apr 10**
   Easter Egg Hunt (Rockford, OH), **Apr 10**
   Easter Even, **Apr 10**
   Easter Monday, **Apr 12**
   Easter Monday Bank Holiday (United Kingdom), **Apr 12**
   Easter Sunday, **Apr 11**
   Easter Sundays Through the Year 2007, **Apr 11**
   Easter Sunrise Service (Chimney Rock, NC), **Apr 11**
   Great Egg Caper at Audubon Acres (Chattanooga, TN), **Apr 10**
   Haute Dog Charity Easter Parade (Long Beach, CA), **Apr 11**
   Holy Humor Month, **Apr 1**
   Holy Week, **Apr 4**
   Longwood Gardens Easter Display (Kennett Square, PA), **Apr 3**
   Lucerne Fest, Ostern (Lucerne, Switzerland), **Mar 27**
   Megga Hunt (Springfield, OR), **Apr 10**
   Moravian Easter Resurrection Service (Winston-Salem, NC), **Apr 11**
   Orthodox Easter Sunday, **Apr 11**
   Passion Week, **Mar 28**
   Passiontide, **Mar 28**
   Wells Fargo Golden Bunny Egg Hunt and Race (Winter Park, CO), **Apr 10**
   White House Easter Egg Roll (Washington, DC), **Apr 12**
   White House Easter Egg Roll: Anniv, **Apr 2**
   World's Largest Easter Egg Hunt (Homer, GA), **Apr 6**
Easter Rising (Ireland), Apr 24
Eastern Idaho State Fair (Blackfoot, ID), Sep 4
Easton, Sheena: Birth, Apr 27
Eastwood, Clint: Birth, May 31
Eat Better, Eat Together Month, Oct 1

Eat Dessert First Month, May 1
Eat What You Want Day, May 11
Eating Disorders Awareness Week, Natl, Feb 22
Ebersole, Christine: Birth, Feb 21
Ebert, Roger: Birth, Jun 18
Ebsen, Buddy: Birth Anniv, Apr 2
Eckersley, Dennis: Birth, Oct 3
Eckert, J. Presper, Jr: Birth Anniv, Apr 9
Eckstine, Billy: Birth Anniv, Jul 8
Eclipses,
   Partial Solar Eclipse, **Apr 19**
   Partial Solar Eclipse, **Oct 13**
   Total Lunar Eclipse, **May 4**
   Total Lunar Eclipse, **Oct 27**
Eco, Umberto: Birth, Jan 5
Ecuador,
   Battle of Pichincha, **May 24**
   Chimborazo Day, **Jun 3**
   Day of Quito, **Dec 6**
   Independence Day, **Aug 10**
Ed Sullivan Show TV Premiere: Anniv, Jun 20
Ed Sullivan Show: The Beatles Appear: Anniv, Feb 9
Eddy, Duane: Birth, Apr 26
Eddy, Mary Baker: Birth Anniv, Jul 16
Edelman, Marian Wright: Birth, Jun 6
Eden, Barbara: Birth, Aug 23
Ederle, Gertrude: Birth Anniv, Oct 23
Ederle, Gertrude: Swims English Channel: Anniv, Aug 6
Edgar Allan Poe Evermore (Manheim, PA), Oct 29
Edge of Night TV Premiere: Anniv, Apr 2
Edge, The: Birth, Aug 8
Edinburgh Festival Fringe (Scotland), Aug 8
Edison, Thomas Alva,
   Birth Anniv, **Feb 11**
   Black Maria Studio: Anniv, **Feb 1**
   First Electric Lighting: Anniv, **Sep 4**
   Incandescent Lamp Demonstrated: Anniv, **Oct 21**
   Record of a Sneeze: Anniv, **Feb 2**
Editors and Writers Month, Be Kind to, Sep 1
Edmonds, Kenneth (Babyface): Birth, Apr 10
Edmund Fitzgerald Beacon Lighting (Two Harbors, MN), Nov 10
Edmund Fitzgerald Sinking: Anniv, Nov 10
Education and Sharing Day (Pres Proc), Mar 27
Education, Learning, Schools,
   American Council on Education Annual Mtg (Miami Beach, FL), **Feb 28**
   American Education Week, **Nov 14**
   American Education Week (Pres Proc), **Nov 14**
   Banned Books Week, **Sep 18**
   CAMEX (San Antonio, TX), **Feb 28**
   Catholic Educational Assn Conv/Expo, Natl (Boston, MA), **Apr 13**
   Catholic Schools Week, **Jan 25**
   Chemistry Week, Natl, **Oct 17**
   Children's Book Day, Intl, **Apr 2**
   Computer Learning Month, **Oct 1**
   Education Assn Meeting, Natl (Washington, DC), **Jul 2**
   Educational Support Personnel Day, Natl, **Nov 17**
   Eliza Doolittle Day, **May 20**
   Family Literacy Day, Natl, **Nov 1**
   Fashion Show (Milwaukee, WI), **May 14**
   FFA Week, Natl, **Feb 21**
   Froebel, Friedrich: Birth Anniv, **Apr 21**
   Geographic Bee Finals, Natl (Washington, DC), **May 25**
   Geographic Bee, School Level, Natl, **Jan 2**
   Geographic Bee, State Level, Natl, **Apr 2**
   Gifted Children Conv, Natl Assn (Salt Lake City, UT), **Nov 3**
   Go On a Field Trip Month, Natl, **Oct 1**
   Graduate and Professional Student Appreciation Week, **Apr 5**
   Harvard Univ Founded: Anniv, **Oct 28**
   Historically Black Colleges and Universities Week, Natl (Pres Proc), **Sep 19**
   Homeschool Month, Natl, **Sep 1**
   Honor Society Awareness Month, **Mar 1**
   Hug a Prom Sponsor Day, **Apr 23**
   Introduce a Girl to Engineering Day, **Feb 26**
   Kindergarten Day, **Apr 21**
   Learning Disabilities Assn Intl Conf (Atlanta, GA), **Mar 17**
   Library Week, Natl, **Apr 18**
   Literacy Day, Intl (UN), **Sep 8**
   Literacy Decade (UN), **Jan 1**
   March to College Day, Natl, **Mar 1**
   Mentoring Month, Natl, **Jan 1**
   Metric Week, Natl, **Oct 10**
   MiAEYC Early Childhood Conference (Grand Rapids, MI), **Mar 25**
   Mole Day, Natl, **Oct 23**
   Morrill Land Grant Act Passed: Anniv, **Jul 1**
   Mount Holyoke College Founded, **Nov 8**
   Museum Day, Intl, **May 18**
   Music in Our Schools Month, **Mar 1**
   Newspaper in Education Week, **Mar 1**
   Paraprofessional Appreciation Day, **Apr 7**
   Parents as Teachers Day, Natl, **Nov 8**
   Peabody, Elizabeth Palmer: Birth Anniv, **May 16**
   Pioneer Days (Washington, DC), **Oct 20**
   PTA Founders' Day, Natl, **Feb 17**
   PTA Teacher Appreciation Week, Natl, **May 3**
   Public School, First in America: Anniv, **Apr 23**

☆ Chase's 2004 Calendar of Events ☆ Index

Education (cont'd)—Epilepsy

Read Across America Day, **Mar 2**
Read Me Week (TN), **Mar 1**
Reading Is Fun Week, **May 2**
Scholarship Month, Natl, **May 1**
School Bus Safety Week, Natl, **Oct 17**
School Celebration, Natl, **Sep 17**
School Counseling Week, Natl, **Feb 2**
School for Deaf Founded, First: Anniv, **Apr 15**
School Library Media Month, **Apr 1**
School Lunch Week, Natl, **Oct 10**
School Principals' Day, **May 1**
School Spirit Season, Intl, **Apr 30**
School Success Month, Natl, **Sep 1**
Self-Improvement Month, **Sep 1**
Self-University Week, **Sep 1**
Spelling Bee Finals, Natl, **Jun 2**
Spelman College Established: Anniv, **Apr 11**
Student Government Day (MA), **Apr 2**
Substitute Teacher Appreciation Week, **Sep 13**
Sullivan, Anne: Birth Anniv, **Apr 14**
Teach Children to Save Day, Natl, **Apr 22**
Teacher Appreciation Week, **May 2**
Teacher Day, Natl, **May 4**
Teachers' Day (Czech Republic), **Mar 28**
Thank You, School Librarian Day, **Apr 21**
Truancy Law: Anniv, **Apr 12**
Tuskegee Institute Opening: Anniv, **Jul 4**
Tutor Appreciation Day, **Apr 5**
Univ of Chicago First Day of Classes, **Oct 1**
World Teachers' Day (UN), **Oct 5**
World's Largest Concert, **Mar 11**
Yale Univ Founded: Anniv, **Oct 16**
Young Child, Week of the, **Apr 18**
Young Reader's Day, Natl, **Nov 9**
Edward VIII: Abdication Anniv, Dec 11
Edward, Jonathan: Birth Anniv, Oct 5
Edward, Prince: Birth, Mar 10
Edwards, Anthony: Birth, Jul 19
Edwards, Blake: Birth, Jul 26
Edwards, Douglas: Birth Anniv, Jul 14
Edwards, Harry: Birth, Nov 22
Edwards, John: Birth, Jun 10
Edwards, Vince: Birth Anniv, Jul 9
Effectiveness Week, Natl, May 17
Egg Month, Natl, May 1
Egg Races (Switzerland), Apr 12
Egg Roll, White House Easter Egg Roll: Anniv, Apr 2
Egg Salad Week, Apr 12
Eggar, Samantha: Birth, Mar 5
Eggert, Nicole: Birth, Jan 13
Eggsibit (Phillipsburg, NJ), Mar 27
Egypt,
Armed Forces Day, **Oct 6**
Camp David Accord Signed: Anniv, **Mar 26**
Egyptian Maritime Disaster: Anniv, **Dec 14**
Evacuation Day, **Jun 18**
Revolution Day, **Jul 23**
Sham El-Nessim, **Apr 12**
Sinai Day, **Apr 25**
Statue of Ramses II Unearthed: Anniv, **Nov 30**
Suez Canal Formal Opening: Anniv, **Nov 17**
Suez Canal Opens: Anniv, **Mar 7**
Ehrlich, Paul: Birth, May 29
Ehrlich, Robert, Jr: Birth, Nov 25
Eichhorn, Lisa: Birth, Feb 4
Eid-al-Adha: Feast of the Sacrifice (Muslim), Feb 1
Eid-al-Fitr: Celebrating the Fast (Muslim), Nov 14
Eiffel Tower: Anniv (Paris, France), Mar 31
Eiffel, Alexandre Gustave: Birth Anniv, Dec 15
Eight Is Enough TV Premiere: Anniv, Mar 15
Eikenberry, Jill: Birth, Jan 21
Einstein on Wine (Tampa, FL), Jan 31
Einstein, Albert: Atomic Bomb Letter Anniv, Aug 2
Einstein, Albert: Birth Anniv, Mar 14
Eisenhower Assumes Command: Anniv, Jan 16
Eisenhower, David: Birth, Apr 1
Eisenhower, Dwight: Birth Anniv, Oct 14
Eisenhower, Dwight: Ike's Farewell (military-industrial warning): Anniv, Jan 17
Eisenhower, Mamie Doud: Birth Anniv, Nov 14
Eisenhower: Interstate Highway System Born: Anniv, Jun 29
Eisenstaedt, Alfred: Birth Anniv, Dec 6
Eisner, Michael: Birth, Mar 7
Ekberg, Anita: Birth, Sep 29
Ekland, Britt: Birth, Oct 6
El Salvador,
Adopts US Dollar: Anniv, **Nov 30**
Day of the First Shout for Independence, **Nov 5**
Day of the Soldier, **May 7**
Independence Day, **Sep 15**
Natl Day of Peace, **Jan 16**
Eldard, Ron: Birth, Feb 20
Eldon Turkey Fest (Eldon, MO), Oct 9
Eleanor Roosevelt Day (Willapa, WA), Aug 7
Election Day, General (US), Nov 2
Election Officials Day, Apr 6
Elections, Caucuses, Political Conventions,
Democratic National Convention (Boston, MA), **Jul 26**
Dimpled Chad Day, **Jan 4**
Election Officials Day, **Apr 6**
Electors, Meeting of Presidential, **Dec 13**
Republican National Convention (New York, NY), **Aug 30**
Return Day (Georgetown, DE), **Nov 4**
Supreme Court Rules for Bush: Anniv, **Dec 12**
Vote Lawyers Out of Office Day, **Apr 8**
Electra, Carmen: Birth, Apr 20
Electric Lighting, First: Anniv, Sep 4
Electricity: Incandescent Lamp Demonstrated: Anniv, Oct 21
Electrocution for Death Penalty, First: Anniv, Aug 6
Electronic Communications Week, Apr 12
Electronic Greetings Day, Nov 29
Elephant Appreciation Day, Sep 22
Elephant Round-Up at Surin (Thailand), Nov 20
Elfman, Jenna: Birth, Sep 30
Eliot, George: Birth Anniv, Nov 22
Eliot, John: Birth Anniv, Aug 5
Eliot, T.S.: Birth Anniv, Sep 26
Elizabeth I, Queen: Accession Anniv, Nov 17
Elizabeth I, Queen: Birth Anniv, Sep 7
Elizabeth II, Queen: Accession Anniv, Feb 6
Elizabeth II, Queen: Agrees to Pay Taxes, Nov 26
Elizabeth II, Queen: Birth, Apr 21
Elizabeth II: Marriage of Elizabeth and Philip: Anniv, Nov 20
Elizabeth, the Queen Mother: Birth Anniv, Aug 4
Elizondo, Hector: Birth, Dec 22
Elkin, Stanley: Birth Anniv, May 11
Ellerbee, Linda: Birth, Aug 15
Ellery, William: Birth Anniv, Dec 22
Ellington, Duke: Birth Anniv, Apr 29
Elliott, Bill: Birth, Oct 8
Elliott, Chris: Birth, May 31
Elliott, David James: Birth, Sep 21
Elliott, Sam: Birth, Aug 9
Elliott, Sean: Birth, Feb 2
Ellis Island Family History Day (New York, NY), Apr 17
Ellis Island Opened: Anniv, Jan 1
Ellison, Ralph Waldo: Birth Anniv, Mar 1
Ellsberg, Daniel: Birth, Apr 7
Ellsworth, Oliver: Birth Anniv, Apr 29
Els, Ernie: Birth, Oct 17
Elvis Presley Remembered (St. Louis, MO), Aug 14
Elvis Week (Memphis, TN), Aug 7
Elway, John: Birth, Jun 28
Elwes, Cary: Birth, Oct 26
Emaishen (Luxembourg), Apr 12
Emancipation Day (Texas), Jun 19
Emancipation of 500: Anniv, Aug 1
Emancipation Proclamation Takes Effect: Anniv, Jan 1
Emancipation Proclamation: Anniv, Sep 22
Embassy Seizure, US, in Teheran: Anniv, Nov 4
Embrace Your Geekness Day, Jul 13
Emergency Medical Services Week, Natl, May 16
Emergency Nurses Day, Oct 13
Emergency Nurses Week, Oct 10
Emergency Preparedness Week, Natl, Sep 5
Emergency TV Premiere: Anniv, Jan 22
Emerson, Ralph Waldo: Birth Anniv, May 25
Eminem: Birth, Oct 17
Emmerich, Roland: Birth, Nov 10
Emmett Kelly Clown Fest (Houston, MO), Apr 29
Emmett, Daniel D.: Birth Anniv, Oct 29
Emotional Wellness Month, Oct 1
Empowerment Week, Women's Self-, Jan 5
Enberg, Dick: Birth, Jan 9
Endangered Species Act: Anniv, Dec 28
Energy Management Is a Family Affair, Oct 1
Engineers Week, Natl, Feb 22
England,
Badminton Horse Trials (Badminton), **Apr 29**
BBC Proms (London), **Jul 16**
Birmingham Riot: Anniv, **Jul 14**
Blackpool Illuminations (Blackpool, Lancashire), **Sep 3**
British Air Raid on Berlin: Anniv, **Jan 16**
British Museum: Anniv, **Jan 15**
Care Sunday, **Mar 28**
Charles II: Restoration and Birth Anniv, **May 29**
Chelsea Antiques Fair (London), **Mar 17**
Chelsea Flower Show (London), **May 25**
Cheltenham Hunt Fest (Prestbury), **Mar 16**
Cheltenham Intl Fest of Music (Cheltenham), **Jul 2**
Chester Antiques and Fine Art Show (Cheshire), **Feb 12**
Christmas Holiday, **Dec 25**
City of London Fest (London), **Jun 21**
Crufts Dog Show (Birmingham), **Mar 4**
Curtis Cup (Merseyside), **Jun 12**
Derby, The, **Jun 5**
Devizes/Westminster Intl Canoe Race (Devizes), **Apr 9**
Dicing for Bibles, **May 31**
English Riviera Dance Fest (Torquay), **May 29**
Exeter Fest (Exeter), **Jul 5**
George VI's Coronation: Anniv, **May 12**
Great Britain Formed: Anniv, **May 1**
Great Fire of London: Anniv, **Sep 2**
Guy Fawkes Day, **Nov 5**
Hallaton Bottle Kicking (Hallaton), **Apr 12**
Hampton Court Palace Flower Show Charity Gala Preview (East Molesey, Surrey), **Jul 5**
Harrogate Autumn Flower Show (Harrogate, N Yorkshire), **Sep 17**
Harrogate Spring Flower Show (Harrogate), **Apr 22**
Head of the River Race (London), **Mar 20**
Helston Furry Dance, **May 8**
Henley Royal Regatta (Henley-on-Thames), **Jun 30**
Jersey Battle of Flowers (St. Lawrence, Channel Is), **Aug 12**
Last Hurrah for British Hong Kong, **Jun 30**
Lawn Tennis Chmpshps at Wimbledon (London), **Jun 21**
London Book Fair (London), **Mar 14**
London/Brighton Veteran Car Run (London), **Nov 7**
Lord Mayor's Show (London), **Nov 13**
Marriage of Elizabeth and Philip: Anniv, **Nov 20**
Mothering Sunday, **Mar 21**
New Year's Day Parade (London), **Jan 1**
Notting Hill Carnival (London), **Aug 29**
Nottingham Goose Fair (Nottingham), **Oct 6**
Petersfield Antiques Fair (Petersfield), **Feb 6**
Plough Monday, **Jan 12**
Queen Elizabeth I: Birth Anniv, **Sep 7**
RAF Bombs Hitler Celebration: Anniv, **Jan 30**
Remembrance Day Service/Parade (London), **Nov 14**
Royal Ascot, **Jun 15**
Royal Bath and West Show (Shepton Mallet, Somerset), **Jun 2**
Royal George Sinks: Anniv, **Aug 29**
Royal Windsor Horse Show (Windsor), **May 12**
Saint George: Feast Day, **Apr 23**
Schroders London Intl Boat Show (London), **Jan 8**
Scotland Yard First Appearance Anniv, **Sep 29**
Shrewsbury Intl Music Fest (Shropshire), **Jun 25**
Shrovetide Pancake Race (Olney, Buckinghamshire), **Feb 24**
Skandia Cowes Week (Isle of Wight), **Aug 7**
Slave Trade Abolished: Anniv, **Mar 25**
Trooping Colours/Queen's Official Birthday, **Jun 12**
Tynwald Day, **Jul 5**
Walter Plinge Day, **Dec 2**
Ways With Words Literature Fest (Dartington), **Jul 9**
West London Antiques & Fine Art Fair (London), **Jan 15**
Words by the Water: A Cumbrian Literature Fest (Lake District), **Mar 9**
English Channel, First Airplane Crossing: Anniv, Jul 25
English Channel, First Man-Powered Flight Across: Anniv, Jun 12
English Colony in North America, First: Anniv, Aug 5
ENIAC Computer Introduced: Anniv, Feb 14
Enigma Machine, British Capture of: Anniv, May 9
Eno, Brian: Birth, May 15
Enron Files for Bankruptcy: Anniv, Dec 2
Ensign, John: Birth, Mar 25
Entebbe, Raid on: Anniv, Jul 3
Enthusiasm Week, Intl, Sep 1
Entrepreneurs Day, Empowered Women, Apr 1
Entrepreneurs 'Do It Yourself' Marketing Month, Jun 1
Environment Day, World (UN), Jun 5
Environmental,
Alabama Coastal Cleanup (Mobile, AL), **Sep 18**
America Recycles Day, **Nov 15**
Arbor Day, Natl, **Apr 30**
Bike to Work Day, Natl, **May 21**
Biodiesel Day, Natl (Rudolph Diesel Birth Anniv), **Mar 18**
Biological Diversity, Intl Day for (UN), **May 22**
Cattus Island Nature Fest (Toms River, NJ), **Oct 3**
Celebrate Earth Day Weekend (Point Pleasant Beach, NJ), **Apr 17**
Chernobyl Reactor Disaster: Anniv, **Apr 26**
Clean Air Act Passed by Congress: Anniv, **Dec 17**
Clean Air Month, **May 1**
Coastal Cleanup, Intl, **Sep 18**
Day for Preventing the Exploitation of the Environment in War and Armed Conflict, Intl (UN), **Nov 6**
Earth Day, **Apr 25**
Earth Day Community Fest (St. Louis, MO), **Apr 25**
EarthFair (San Diego, CA), **Apr 25**
Endangered Species Act: Anniv, **Dec 28**
Environmental Policy Act, Natl, **Jan 1**
Exxon Valdez Oil Spill: Anniv, **Mar 24**
Greenpeace Founded: Anniv, **Sep 15**
Intl Day for Preservation of the Ozone Layer (UN), **Sep 16**
Japan Agrees to End Use of Drift Nets: Anniv, **Nov 26**
Mother Ocean Day, **May 8**
Natural Disaster Reduction, Intl Day For (UN), **Oct 13**
President's Environmental Youth Award Natl Competition, **Jul 31**
Rainbow Warrior Sinking: Anniv, **Jul 10**
Rainforest Week, Natl, **Oct 18**
Recreation and Parks Month, Natl, **Jul 1**
Rivers Month, Natl, **Jun 1**
Rural Life Sunday, **May 16**
Sierra Club Founded: Anniv, **May 28**
Silent Spring Publication: Anniv, **Apr 13**
Sparrow, Last Dusky Seaside: Death Anniv, **Jun 16**
Water Pollution Control Act: Anniv, **Oct 18**
Water, World Day for (UN), **Mar 22**
Week of Ocean Fest Sea-Son, Natl (Fort Lauderdale, FL), **Mar 6**
Week of the Ocean, Natl, **Apr 4**
World Day to Combat Desertification and Drought (UN), **Jun 17**
World Environment Day (UN), **Jun 5**
Enzi, Michael B.: Birth, Feb 1
Ephron, Nora: Birth, May 19
Epilepsy Awareness Month, Nov 1

Index ☆ Chase's 2004 Calendar of Events ☆

Epiphany—Family

Epiphany (Twelfth Day), Jan 6
Episcopal Bishop, First Woman: Anniv, Feb 11
Epps, Omar: Birth, Jul 23
Equal Rights Party Founding: Anniv, Sep 20
Equatorial Guinea,
Armed Forces Day, **Aug 3**
Constitution Day, **Aug 15**
Independence Day, **Oct 12**
Equinox, Autumn, Sep 22
Equinox, Spring, Mar 20
ER TV Premiere: Anniv, Sep 19
Eradication of Poverty, Intl Day for (UN), Oct 17
Erasmus, Desiderius: Birth Anniv, Oct 28
Erdrich, Louise: Birth, Jun 7
Erie Canal: Anniv, Oct 26
Erikson, Leif: Day (Iceland), Oct 9
Erikson, Leif: Day (Pres Proc), Oct 9
Eritrea: Independence Day, May 24
Eritrea: Timket (Epiphany), Jan 19
Ermey, R. Lee: Birth, Mar 24
Ernie Kovacs TV Premiere: Anniv, May 14
Erving, Julius: Birth, Feb 22
Escoffier, Georges: Birth Anniv, Oct 28
Esiason, Boomer: Birth, Apr 17
Esposito, Giancarlo: Birth, Apr 26
Esposito, Phil: Birth, Feb 20
Estefan, Emilio: Birth, Mar 4
Estefan, Gloria: Birth, Sep 1
Estes, Rob: Birth, Jul 22
Estevez, Emilio: Birth, May 12
Estonia,
Independence Day, **Feb 24**
Baltic States' Independence Recognized: Anniv, **Sep 6**
Day of National Rebirth, **Nov 16**
Victory Day, **Jun 23**
Estrada, Erik: Birth, Mar 16
Etheridge, Melissa: Birth, May 29
Ethiopia,
Adwa Day, **Mar 2**
National Day, **May 28**
New Year's Day, **Sep 11**
Patriots Victory Day, **May 5**
Timket (Epiphany), **Jan 19**
True Cross Day, **Sep 27**
Ethnic Awareness Program (Macon, GA), Apr 28
Ethnic Observances. See also nationality names,
Aebleskiver Days (Tyler, MN), **Jul 23**
Asian Pacific American Heritage Month (Pres Proc), **May 1**
Berne Swiss Days (Berne, IN), **Jul 29**
Cabrillo Fest (San Diego, CA), **Sep 26**
Canada's Natl Ukrainian Fest (Dauphin, MB, Canada), **Jul 30**
Central Nebraska Ethnic Fest (Grand Island, NE), **Jul 23**
Chinese New Year Fest (San Francisco, CA), **Jan 17**
Cinco de Mayo Fest (Portland, OR), **May 5**
Clarkson Czech Fest (Clarkson, NE), **Jun 24**
Czech Days (Tabor, SD), **Jun 18**
Czechoslovakian Fest, Natl (Wilber, NE), **Aug 6**
Dalesburg Midsummer Fest (Vermillion, SD), **Jun 25**
Fest of Nations (Red Lodge, MT), **Jul 30**
Festival of Nations (St. Paul, MN), **Apr 29**
German-American Day, Natl, **Oct 6**
German-American Heritage Month, **Oct 1**
Haitian Heritage Month, **May 1**
Heritagefest (New Ulm, MN), **Jul 9**
Herrinfesta Italiana (Herrin, IL), **May 27**
Hispanic Heritage Month, **Sep 15**
Holiday Folk Fair Intl (Milwaukee, WI), **Nov 19**
Hollywood Beach Latin Fest (Hollywood, FL), **Aug 15**
Irish-American Heritage Month, **Mar 1**
Jours de Fete (Ste. Genevieve, MO), **Aug 14**
Midsummer Day/Eve Celebrations, **Jun 23**
Norskedalen's Midsummer Fest (Coon Valley, WI), **Jun 19**
Northern Plains Heritage Fest (Dickinson, ND), **Aug 20**
Odyssey—A Greek Fest (Orange, CT), **Sep 3**
Oktoberfest (LaCrosse, WI), **Sep 24**
Old-Fashioned Danish Christmas (Dannebrog, NE), **Dec 11**
Polish American Heritage Month, **Oct 1**
Polish Christmas Open House (Philadelphia, PA), **Dec 12**
Polish-American in the House (Mikulski): Anniv, **Jan 4**
Pulaski Day Parade (Philadelphia, PA), **Oct 3**
Saint Ann's Italian Street Fest (Hoboken, NJ), **Jul 20**
Saint Paul's Feast, **Jun 28**
Saint Piran's Day (Cornish) Celeb (Kansas City, MO), **Mar 6**
Scandinavian Fest (Stanhope, NJ), **Sep 5**
Scandinavian Hjemkomst Fest (Moorhead, MN), **Jun 25**
St. Patrick's Day Parade & Fest (Hollywood, FL), **Mar 7**
Swedish Days Fest (Geneva, IL), **Jun 22**
Swedish Language and Culture Day Camp (Cambridge, MN), **Aug 23**
Tivoli Fest (Elk Horn, IA), **May 29**
Tivoli-Viking Days at the Nordic Heritage Museum (Seattle, WA), **Jul 10**
Ukrainian Fest (Dickinson, ND), **Jul 16**
Viking Fest (Poulsbo, WA), **May 14**
West Virginia Italian Heritage Fest (Clarksburg, WV), **Sep 3**
Westfest (Czech) (West, TX), **Sep 4**
Etiquette,
Cell Phone Courtesy Month, **Jul 1**
Children's Good Manners Month, **Sep 1**
Civility Month, Natl Win with, **Aug 1**
Electronic Communications Week, **Apr 12**
Etiquette Week, Natl, **May 16**
I Forgot Day, **Jul 2**
Table Manners Wk, Intl, **Feb 8**
Tell Someone They're Doing a Good Job Week, **Dec 12**
Thank You Days, Intl, **Jan 11**
Thanks for All the Gifts Week, **Aug 8**
Thank-Your-Customers Week, Natl, **Jan 5**
Eubanks, Bob: Birth, Jan 8
Eubanks, Kevin: Birth, Nov 15
Euro Introduced: Anniv, Jan 1
Europe: Summer Daylight-Saving Time, Mar 28
European Union Established: Anniv, Nov 1
European Union: Schuman Plan Anniv, May 9
Evacuation Day (Boston, MA), Mar 17
Evacuation Day (Egypt), Jun 18
Evaluate Your Life Day, Oct 19
Evangelista, Linda: Birth, Jun 10
Evans, Bob: Birth, May 30
Evans, Chick: Birth Anniv, Jul 18
Evans, Donald: Birth, Jul 27
Evans, Heloise Cruse: Birth, Apr 15
Evans, Linda: Birth, Nov 18
Evening at Pops TV Premiere: Anniv, Jul 12
Everest: First Woman To Climb: Anniv, May 16
Everett Salty Sea Days (Everett, WA), Jun 3
Everett Summit Reached: Anniv, May 29
Everett, Chad: Birth, Jun 11
Everett, Rupert: Birth, May 29
Everglades Natl Park Established: Anniv, Dec 6
Everly, Don: Birth, Feb 1
Everly, Phil: Birth, Jan 19
Evers, Medgar, Assassinated: Anniv, Jun 13
Evert, Chris: Birth, Dec 21
Everybody's Day Fest (Thomasville, NC), Sep 25
Evigan, Greg: Birth, Oct 14
Ewell, Tom: Birth Anniv, Apr 29
Ewing, Patrick: Birth, Aug 5
Exchange Club Birthday, Natl, Mar 27
Exchange Club: Freedom Shrine Month, May 1
Execution: First Criminal in American Colonies: Anniv, Sep 30
Executives, American Soc of Assn: Mtg/Expo (Minneapolis, MN), Aug 14
Expect Success Month, Intl, Feb 1
Explore Your Career Options Week, Apr 12
Explosion of the Cart (Florence, Italy), Apr 11
Explosion: Halifax, Nova Scotia, Destroyed: Anniv, Dec 6
Explosion: Mexico City: Anniv, Nov 19
Extraordinary Work Team Recognition Day, Dec 4
Extraterrestrial Culture Day (New Mexico), Feb 12
Extreme Sports (Parachuting, etc.),
Bridge Day (Fayetteville, WV), **Oct 16**
Freefall Conv, World (Rantoul, IL), **Aug 6**
Nissan Xterra World Championship (Maui, HI), **Oct 24**
Powered Parachute Fly-in (Columbus, KS), **Sep 16**
Exxon Valdez Oil Spill: Anniv, Mar 24
Eye Donor Month, Natl, Mar 1
Eye Health and Safety Month, Children's, Aug 1
Eye Health and Safety Month, Women's, Apr 1
Eye Injury Prevention Month, Jul 1
Fabares, Shelley: Birth, Jan 19
Fabian: Birth, Feb 6
Fabio: Birth, Mar 15
Fabray, Nanette: Birth, Oct 27
Face the Nation TV Premiere: Anniv, Nov 7
Facility Service Workers Day, Oct 18
Facts of Life TV Premiere: Anniv, Aug 24
Fahrenheit, Gabriel D.: Birth Anniv, May 14
Fain, Sammy: Birth Anniv, Jun 17
Fair Trade Day, World, May 8
Fair, First Annual, in America: Anniv, Sep 30
Fair, Lorrie: Birth, Aug 5
Fairbanks, Charles W.: Birth Anniv, May 11
Fairbanks, Douglas: Birth Anniv, May 23
Fairchild, David G.: Birth Anniv, Apr 7
Fairchild, Morgan: Birth, Feb 3
Faithfull, Marianne: Birth, Dec 29
Fake Howard Hughes Biography: Anniv, Jan 9
Falana, Lola: Birth, Sep 11
Falco, Edie: Birth, Jul 5
Falcon Crest TV Premiere: Anniv, Dec 4
Faldo, Nick: Birth, Jul 18
Falk, Peter: Birth, Sep 16
Falkland Islands War: Anniv, Apr 2
Fall Bluegrass Fest (Live Oak, FL), Sep 23
Fall Fest of Arts and Crafts (Washington, MO), Sep 24
Fall Fest of Leaves (Ross County, OH), Oct 15
Fall Fest, Belle Meade Plantation (Nashville, TN), Sep 18
Fall Fest, Wo-Zha-Wa (Wisconsin Dells, WI), Sep 17
Fall Fiesta (Andrews, TX), Sep 25
Fall Hat Month, Sep 1
Fall in Love with Fond du Lac (Fond du Lac, WI), Sep 1
Fall of Kabul: Anniv, Nov 13
Fall of the Alamo: Anniv, Mar 6
Fall on Nantucket (Nantucket Island, MA), Oct 1
Falling Needles Family Fest, Dec 30
Fallows, James: Birth, Aug 2
Falwell, Jerry: Birth, Aug 11
Family Day—A Day to Eat Dinner with Your Children, Sep 20
Family Feud TV Premiere: Anniv, Jul 12
Family Ties TV Premiere: Anniv, Sep 22
Family,
Absolutely Incredible Kid Day, **Mar 18**
Adoption Week, Natl, **Nov 21**
American Family Day, **Aug 1**
American Mothers, Inc, Natl Conv (San Juan, Puerto Rico), **Apr 27**
Ancestor Appreciation Day, **Sep 27**
Attend Your Grandchild's Birth Day, Natl, **Sep 29**
Bake for Family Fun Month, **Feb 1**
Black Single Parents' Week, **Jun 6**
Brother's Day, **May 24**
Canada: Family Day in Alberta, **Feb 16**
Celebrate Your Marriage Day, Natl, **Jun 26**
Child Abuse Prevention Month, **Apr 1**
Communicate with Your Kid Month, Natl, **Oct 1**
Cousins Day, **Jul 24**
Descendants Day, **Jun 26**
Eat Better, Eat Together Month, **Oct 1**
Ellis Island Family History Day (New York, NY), **Apr 17**
Energy Management Is a Family Affair, **Oct 1**
Families in Business Week, **Jun 14**
Families, Intl Day of (UN), **May 15**
Family Awareness Day, **Jun 20**
Family Caregivers Month, Natl, **Nov 1**
Family Caregivers Month, Natl (Pres Proc), **Nov 1**
Family Day (TN), **Aug 29**
Family Day in Nevada, **Nov 26**
Family Farm Fay, **Sep 22**
Family Fit Lifestyle Month, **Jan 1**
Family Health and Fitness Days—USA, **Sep 25**
Family History Day, **Jun 14**
Family Literacy Day, Natl, **Nov 1**
Family Month, Natl, **May 9**
Family Sexuality Education Month, Natl, **Oct 1**
Family Stories Month, **Nov 1**
Family Support Month, **May 1**
Family Week, Natl, **May 2**
Family Week, Natl (Pres Proc), **Nov 21**
Family Wellness Month, **May 1**
Family, Career and Community Leaders of America Natl Leadership Mtg (Chicago, IL), **Jul 11**
Family, Career and Community Leaders of America Week, Natl, **Feb 8**
Family-Leave Bill: Anniv, **Feb 5**
Father-Daughter Take a Walk Together Day, **Jul 7**
Father's Day, **Jun 20**
Father's Day (Pres Proc), **Jun 20**
Forgive Mom & Dad Day, **Mar 18**
Game and Puzzle Week, Natl, **Nov 21**
Genealogy Day, **Mar 13**
Grandparent's Day at the Top Museum, Natl (Burlington, WI), **Sep 12**
Grandparent's Day Celebration (Point Pleasant Beach, NJ), **Sep 12**
Grandparents' Day, Natl, **Sep 12**
Healthy Vision Month, **May 1**
Hugging Day, Natl, **Jan 21**
Husband Appreciation Day, **Apr 17**
Husband Caregiver Day, **Jun 20**
Immunization Awareness Month, Natl, **Aug 1**
Intergeneration Day, **Oct 3**
KidsDay, Natl, **Aug 1**
Knights of Columbus Family Week, **Aug 7**
Legacy Month, Intl, **Apr 1**
Lifewriting Month, Natl, **Nov 1**
Married to a Scorpio Support Day, **Nov 18**
Michigans Grandparents and Grandchildren Day, **Mar 18**
Million Minute Family Challenge™, **Sep 1**
Mother-in-Law Day, **Oct 24**
Mother's Day, **May 9**
Moving Month, Natl, **May 1**
Parent Leadership Month, Natl, **Feb 1**
Parents as Teachers Day, Natl, **Nov 8**
Parents' Day (Pres Proc), **Jul 25**
Please Take My Children to Work Day, **Jun 29**
Preparing Tomorrow's Parents Month, **May 9**
Purposeful Parenting Month, Natl, **Jul 1**
Respect for Parents Day, **Aug 1**
Second Honeymoon Weekend, **Feb 20**
Sibling Appreciation Day, **May 2**
Siblings Day, Natl, **Apr 10**
Single Parent Family Day, **Sep 25**
Sisters' Day, **Aug 1**
Stay Home With Your Kids Day, **Aug 16**
Stepparents' Week, **Jun 1**
Stress-Free Family Holidays Month, Natl, **Dec 1**
Take Our Daughters and Sons to Work Day, **Apr 22**
Talk With Your Teen About Sex Month, Natl, **Mar 1**
Teen Day, **May 1**
Unassisted Homebirth Week, Natl, **Jul 1**
Universal Children's Week, **Oct 1**
Universal Family Week, **May 11**
Universal Father's Week, **Jun 15**
Very Important Parents Month, Natl, **Sep 1**
Visit Your Relatives Day, **May 18**

☆ Chase's 2004 Calendar of Events ☆ Index

Family (cont'd)—Flag

Weddings Month, Natl, Feb 1
Work@Home Father's Day, Jun 18
World Marriage Day, Feb 8
Yours, Mine and Ours Month, Natl, Jan 1
Famous Preston Night Rodeo (Preston, ID), Jul 29
Faneuil Hall Opened to the Public: Anniv, Sep 24
Fantasy Fest (Key West, FL), Oct 22
Fantasy Island TV Premiere: Anniv, Jan 28
Faraday, Michael: Birth Anniv, Sep 22
Farentino, James: Birth, Feb 24
Fargas, Antonio: Birth, Aug 14
Fargo, Donna: Birth, Nov 10
Farina, Dennis: Birth, Feb 29
Farley, Cal: Birth Anniv, Dec 25
Farm Safety Week, Natl (Pres Proc), Sep 19
Farm Toy Show, Natl (Dyersville, IA), Nov 5
Farm-City Week, Natl (Pres Proc), Nov 19
Farmer, James: Birth Anniv, Jan 12
Farmer, Philip Jose: Birth, Jan 26
Farmers & Threshermens Jubilee (New Centerville, PA), Sep 8
Farmington Country Days (Farmington, MO), Jun 4
Farr, Jamie: Birth, Jul 1
Farragut, David: Battle of Mobile Bay: Anniv, Aug 5
Farragut, David: Birth Anniv, Jul 5
Farragut, David: Farragut Captures New Orleans: Anniv, Apr 25
Farrakhan, Louis: Birth, May 11
Farrell, Colin: Birth, May 31
Farrell, James T.: Birth Anniv, Feb 27
Farrell, Mike: Birth, Feb 6
Farrell, Terry: Birth, Nov 19
Farrier's Week, Natl, Jul 11
Farrow, Mia: Birth, Feb 9
Fasching (Germany, Austria), Feb 23
Fasching Sunday (Germany, Austria), Feb 22
Fashion (including shows, designers),
Blass, Bill: Birth Anniv, Jun 22
Chanel, Coco: Birth Anniv, Aug 19
Fashion Show (Milwaukee, WI), May 14
Mercedes-Benz Fashion Week Fall '04 (New York, NY), Feb 6
Mercedes-Benz Fashion Week Spring '05 (New York, NY), Sep 12
Mercedes-Benz Shows LA (Fall Lines) (Los Angeles, CA), Mar 30
Mercedes-Benz Shows LA (Spring Lines) (Los Angeles, CA), Oct 26
Fast of Esther: Ta'anit Esther, Mar 4
Fast of Gedalya, Sep 19
Fat Albert and the Cosby Kids TV Premiere: Anniv, Sep 9
Father-Daughter Take a Walk Together Day, Jul 7
Father's Day, Jun 20
Father's Day (Pres Proc), Jun 20
Fatima, Pilgrimage to (Portugal), May 12
Faulk, Marshall: Birth, Feb 26
Faulkner, William: Birth Anniv, Sep 25
Fauset, Jessie Redmon: Birth Anniv, Apr 26
Faustino, David: Birth, Mar 3
Favre, Brett: Birth, Oct 10
Fawcett, Farrah: Birth, Feb 2
Fawkes, Guy: Day (England), Nov 5
FBI: First Female FBI Agents: Anniv, Oct 25
Feast of Lanterns (Bon Fest) (Japan), Jul 13
Feast of St. Paul's Shipwreck (Valletta, Malta), Feb 10
Feast of the Immaculate Conception, Dec 8
Feast of the Incappucciati (Gradoli, Italy), Feb 19
Feast of the Redeemer (Venice, Italy), Jul 18
February Is Fabulous Florida Strawberry Month, Feb 1
Federal Communications Commission Created: Anniv, Feb 26
Federal Credit Union Act: Anniv, Jun 26
Federal Reserve System: Anniv, Dec 23
Federalist Papers: Anniv, Oct 27
FedEx Orange Bowl (Miami, FL), Jan 1
Fedorov, Sergei: Birth, Dec 13
Feiffer, Jules: Birth, Jan 26
Feingold, Russell D.: Birth, Mar 2
Feinstein, Alan: Birth, Sep 8
Feinstein, Dianne: Birth, Jun 22
Feinstein, Michael: Birth, Sep 7
Feld, Eliot: Birth, Jul 5
Feldman, Corey: Birth, Jul 16
Feldon, Barbara: Birth, Mar 12
Feldshuh, Tovah: Birth, Dec 27
Feliciano, Jose: Birth, Sep 10
Felker, Clay S.: Birth, Oct 2
Feller, Bob: Birth, Nov 3
Fellini, Federico: Birth Anniv, Jan 20
Fell's Point Fun Fest (Baltimore, MD), Oct 2
Feltsman, Vladimir: Birth, Jan 8
Feminine Mystique Published: Anniv, Feb 19
Fender, Freddy: Birth, Jun 4
Feng Shui Awareness Day, Intl, Apr 8
Fenn, Sherilyn: Birth, Feb 1
Fenwick, Millicent: Birth Anniv, Feb 25
Ferber, Edna: Birth Anniv, Aug 15
Ferguson, Maynard: Birth, May 4
Ferlinghetti, Lawrence: Birth, Mar 24
Fermi Atomic Power Plant: Accident Anniv, Oct 5
Fermi, Enrico: Birth Anniv, Sep 29
Fernandez, Giselle: Birth, May 15
Ferrante, Arthur: Birth, Sep 7
Ferraro, Geraldine: Birth, Aug 26
Ferrell, Conchata: Birth, Mar 28
Ferrer, Jose: Birth Anniv, Jan 8
Ferrer, Mel: Birth, Aug 25
Ferrer, Miguel: Birth, Feb 7
Ferrigno, Lou: Birth, Nov 9
Ferris Wheel Day, Feb 14
Ferry, Bryan: Birth, Sep 26
Fest of the Sea (Point Pleasant Beach, NJ), Sep 18
Fest of the West, Natl (Scottsdale, AZ), Mar 18
Festifall (Point Marion, PA), Sep 26
FFA Week, Natl, Feb 21
Fibromyalgia Education & Awareness Month, May 1
Fiddlers. See also Bluegrass,
Canadian Open Fiddle Chmpnshp (Shelburne, ON, Canada), Aug 4
Chester Old Fiddlers' Picnic (Coatesville, PA), Sep 11
Fiddler's Frolics (Hallettsville, TX), Apr 23
Old Fiddlers' Conv (Galax, VA), Aug 9
Old-Fashioned Harvestfest and Fiddlers Contest (Woodstock, IL), Sep 19
Old-Time Fiddlers' Contest and Fest, Natl (Weiser, ID), Jun 21
Old-Time Fiddlers' Contest, Intl (Dunseith, ND), Jun 11
Spring Fest and Louisiana Fiddler's Chmpnshp (Marthaville, LA), Apr 23
Field Trial Chmpshp (Bird Dogs), Natl (Grand Junction, TN), Feb 9
Field, Sally: Birth, Nov 6
Field, Shirley-Anne: Birth, Jun 27
Fielder, Cecil: Birth, Sep 21
Fields, Kim: Birth, May 12
Fields, W.C.: Birth Anniv, Jan 29
Fiennes, Joseph: Birth, May 27
Fiennes, Ralph: Birth, Dec 22
Fierstein, Harvey: Birth, Jun 6
Fiesta Bowl (Tempe, AZ), Jan 2
Fig Week, Natl, Nov 1
Fiji: Independence Day, Oct 10
Filene, Edward Albert: Birth Anniv, Sep 3
Files Week, Natl Love Your, Sep 20
Fillmore, Abigail P.: Birth Anniv, Mar 13
Fillmore, Caroline: Birth Anniv, Oct 21
Fillmore, Millard: Birth Anniv, Jan 7
Film,
Academy Awards Presentation, Feb 1
Academy Awards, First: Anniv, May 16
Ann Arbor Film Fest (Ann Arbor, MI), Mar 16
Banff Mountain Film Fest (Banff, AB, Canada), Nov 5
Berlin International Film Fest (Berlin, Germany), Feb 5
Black Maria Studio: Anniv, Feb 1
Cannes Film Fest (Cannes, France), May 12
Casablanca Premiere: Anniv, Nov 26
Chaplin's Tramp Debuts: Anniv, Feb 7
Chicago Intl Film Fest (Chicago, IL), Oct 7
Citizen Kane Premiere: Anniv, May 1
First Drive-In Movie Opens: Anniv, Jun 6
First Movie Theater Opens: Anniv, Apr 23
Golden Globe Awards, Jan 25
Gone with the Wind Premiere: Anniv, Dec 15
Hollywood Magic Day, Sep 20
KidFilm® Fest (Dallas, TX), Jan 5
Lumiere, Auguste: Birth Anniv, Oct 19
Lumiere, Louis: Birth Anniv, Oct 5
Marilyn Monroe's First Screen Test: Anniv, Jul 19
New York Film Fest, Oct 1
Pre-Will Hayes Movie Day, Feb 14
Record of a Sneeze: Anniv, Feb 2
Roger Ebert's Overlooked Film Fest (Champaign, IL), Apr 21
Slamdance 2004 (Park City, UT), Jan 17
Snow White and the Seven Dwarfs Film Premiere: Anniv, Dec 21
Star Wars Released: Anniv, May 25
Sundance Film Fest (Park City, UT), Jan 15
Telluride Film Fest (Telluride, CO), Sep 3
Titanic Released: Anniv, Dec 19
Toronto Intl Film Fest (Toronto, ON, Canada), Sep 9
2001: A Space Odyssey Premiere: Anniv, Apr 3
US Industrial Film/Video Awards (Los Angeles, CA), Jun 3
USA Film Fest (Dallas, TX), Apr 22
Valentino (Rudolph) Memorial Service, Aug 23
Venice Film Fest (Venice, Italy), Aug 28
Wildlife Film Fest, Intl (Missoula, MT), May 1
Wizard of Oz Fest (Chesterton, IN), Sep 17
Wizard of Oz Released: Anniv, Aug 25
Financial Panic of 1873: Anniv, Sep 20
Financial Wellness Month, Jan 1
Finland,
Flag Day, Jun 4
Independence Day: Anniv, Dec 6
Jazz Fest, Intl (Pori), Jul 17
Jyvaskyla Arts Fest (Jyvaskyla), Jul 6
Kaustinen Folk Music Fest (Kaustinen), Jul 10
Kuopio Dance Fest (Kuopio), Jun 17
Lahti Organ Fest (Lahti), Aug 9
Sata-Hame Accordion Fest (Ikaalinen), Jun 29
Savonlinna Opera Fest (Savonlinna), Jul 8
Time of Music (Viitasaari), Jun 29
Turku Music Fest (Turku), Aug 13
Finney, Albert: Birth, May 9
Fiorentino, Linda: Birth, Mar 9
Fire,
Apollo Spacecraft Fire: Anniv, Jan 27
Fire Prevention Week, Oct 3
Fire Prevention Week (Pres Proc), Oct 3
Great Chicago Fire: Anniv, Oct 8
Great Fire of London: Anniv, Sep 2
Great Michigan Fire of 1881: Anniv, Sep 5
Peshtigo (WI) Forest Fire: Anniv, Oct 8
Southern California Firestorms: Anniv, Oct 25
Triangle Shirtwaist Fire: Anniv, Mar 25
Fire Safety Council, Natl: Anniv, Dec 7
Fireant Fest (Marshall, TX), Oct 8
Firefall (Springfield, MO), Jul 3
Firepup's Birthday, Oct 1
Fireside Chat, FDR's First: Anniv, Mar 12
Fireside Theatre TV Premiere: Anniv, Apr 5
Firestone, Harvey: Birth Anniv, Dec 20
Fireworks Eye Safety Month, Jun 1
Fireworks on the Fjord (Poulsbo, WA), Jul 3
Fireworks Safety Months, Jun 1
Fireworks: Red, White and Boom (Columbus, OH), Jul 2
First American to Orbit Earth: Anniv, Feb 20
First Baby Boomer Born: Anniv, Jan 1
First Baseball Strike Ends: Anniv, Apr 13
First Black Southern Lt Gov: Anniv, Jan 11
First Car Insurance: Anniv, Feb 1
First Elected Woman Senator: Anniv, Jan 12
First Nights, Dec 31
First Perfect Game: Anniv, Jun 12
First Perfect Score in Olympic History: Anniv, Jul 18
First Round-the-World Balloon Flight: Anniv, Mar 21
First Salem Witches Arrested: Anniv, Feb 1
First Scheduled Radio Broadcast: Anniv, Nov 2
First Scheduled Television Broadcast: Anniv, Jul 1
First Secret Service Agent to Die in the Line of Duty: Anniv, Sep 3
First Session of the Supreme Court: Anniv, Feb 1
First Solo Round-the-World Balloon Flight: Anniv, Jul 2
First Tuxedo Created, Oct 10
First UN General Assembly: Anniv, Jan 10
First US Chamber of Commerce Founded: Anniv, Apr 5
First Winter Olympics: Anniv, Jan 25
First Woman British Prime Minister: Anniv, May 4
First Woman To Climb Mount Everest: Anniv, May 16
First Women's Collegiate Basketball Game: Anniv, Mar 22
Firth, Colin: Birth, Sep 10
Fiscal Year, US Federal, Oct 1
Fischer, Bobby: Birth, Mar 9
Fiscus, Kathy: Death Anniv, Apr 8
Fishburne, Laurence: Birth, Jul 30
Fisher, Carrie: Birth, Oct 21
Fisher, Eddie: Birth, Aug 10
Fisher, Joely: Birth, Oct 29
Fishing,
Blessing of the Fishing Fleet (San Francisco, CA), Oct 3
Boca Grande Tarpon Tourn (Boca Grande, FL), Jun 9
California Free-Fishing Days, Jun 5
Catfish Derby (Huntington, OR), May 29
Chalo Nitka (Big Bass) (Moore Haven, FL), Mar 5
D.C. Booth Day (Spearfish, SD), May 16
Fish House Parade (Aitkin, MN), Nov 26
Fishing Contest (Lakewood, NJ), May 1
Fishing Has No Boundaries (Bemidji, MN), Jun 26
Fishing Has No Boundaries (Hayward, WI), May 14
Fishing Has No Boundaries (Monticello, IN), May 15
Grand Rapids Sport, Fishing & Travel Show (Grand Rapids, MI), Mar 18
Long Beach Island Surf Fishing Tournament (Long Beach Island, NJ), Oct 9
Michigan Boat, Sport & Fishing Show (Detroit, MI), Mar 3
Montana Governor's Cup Walleye Tourn (Fort Peck, MT), Jul 8
Montreal Sportsmen's Show (Montreal, QB, Canada), Feb 26
Morro Bay Harbor Fest (Morro Bay, CA), Oct 2
Ottawa Boat/Sportsmen's Show (Ottawa, ON, Canada), Feb 26
Palmetto Sportsmen's Classic (Columbia, SC), Mar 26
Prospect Park Fishing Contest (Brooklyn, NY), Jul 9
Seward Silver Salmon Derby (Seward, AK), Aug 14
Take a Kid Fishing Weekend (St. Paul, MN), Jun 11
Walton, Izaak: Birth Anniv, Aug 9
Fisk, Carlton: Birth, Dec 26
Fiske, Minnie M.: Birth Anniv, Dec 19
Fitness, Physical, and Sports Month, Natl, May 1
Fitzgerald, Edward: Birth Anniv, Mar 31
Fitzgerald, Ella: Birth Anniv, Apr 25
Fitzgerald, F. Scott: Birth Anniv, Sep 24
Fitzgerald, Frances: Birth, Oct 21
Fitzgerald, Peter: Birth, Oct 20
5-A-Day Month, Natl, Sep 1
Five Billion, Day of the: Anniv, Jul 11
Flack, Roberta: Birth, Feb 10
Flag Act of 1818: Anniv, Apr 4
Flag Amendment Defeated: Anniv, Jun 26
Flag Day (Pres Proc), Jun 14
Flag Day USA, Pause for Pledge, Natl, Jun 14
Flag Day: Anniv of the Stars and Stripes, Jun 14
Flag Exhibit Controversy, Chicago: Anniv, Feb 17
Flag Week, Natl (Pres Proc), Jun 13

Chase's 2004 Calendar of Events

Index — Flagg—Food

Flagg, Fannie: Birth, Sep 21
Flaherty, Joe: Birth, Jun 21
Flaherty, Robert J.: Birth Anniv, Feb 16
Flannery, Susan: Birth, Jul 31
Flatley, Michael: Birth, Jul 16
Flaubert, Gustave: Birth Anniv, Dec 12
Flax Scutching Fest (Stahlstown, PA), Sep 11
Fleet Week New York (New York, NY), May 19
Fleetwood, Mick: Birth, Jun 24
Fleming, Alexander: Birth Anniv, Aug 6
Fleming, Ian: Birth Anniv, May 28
Fleming, Peggy: Birth, Jul 27
Fleming, Rhonda: Birth, Aug 10
Fleury, Theo: Birth, Jun 29
Flexible Work Arrangements Week, May 2
Flight Attendant, First: Anniv, May 15
Flintstones TV Premiere: Anniv, Sep 30
Flipper TV Premiere: Anniv, Sep 19
Flirting Week, Intl, Feb 9
Flockhart, Calista: Birth, Nov 11
Flood of 1889 Commemorative Weekend, Great (Johnstown, PA), May 24
Flood Victims Relief: Anniv, Aug 12
Flood, Curt: Birth Anniv, Jan 18
Flood, Great Chicago: Anniv, Apr 13
Flood, Johnstown: Anniv, May 31
Floral Design Day, Feb 28
Florida,
 Acquired by US: Anniv, Feb 22
 Admission Day, Mar 3
 AHRMA Vintage Motorcycle Races (Daytona Beach), Mar 1
 AMA Grand National Kickoff (Daytona Beach), Mar 6
 AMA Natl Hot Shoe Kickoff Dirt Track Race (Daytona Beach), Mar 5
 American Council on Education Annual Mtg (Miami Beach), Feb 28
 American Library Assn Conference (Orlando), Jun 24
 Arbor Day, Jan 16
 Art Deco Weekend Fest (Miami Beach), Jan 16
 Art in the Park Plus (Oakland Park), Apr 24
 Assn for Dressings and Sauces Annual Meeting (Amelia Island), Oct 10
 Beethoven by the Beach (Fort Lauderdale), Jun 26
 Biketoberfest (Daytona Beach), Oct 21
 Biscayne Natl Park Established: Anniv, Jun 28
 Boca Grande Tarpon Tourn (Boca Grande), Jun 9
 Brumos Continental Historics/Grand American Finale (Daytona Beach), Nov 5
 Bud Pole Day for the Daytona 500 (Daytona Beach), Feb 8
 Budweiser Shootout at Daytona Winston Cup Series Race (Daytona Beach), Feb 7
 Bush, Jeb: Birth Feb 11
 Canadafest (Hollywood), Jan 31
 Carnaval Miami (Miami), Mar 5
 Chalo Nitka (Big Bass) (Moore Haven), Mar 5
 Children's Day, Apr 13
 Cingular Winterfest Boat Parade (Fort Lauderdale), Dec 18
 Citrus Bowl, Capital One Florida (Orlando), Jan 1
 Confederate Memorial Day, Apr 26
 Daytona 200 by Arai Qualifying Day (Daytona Beach), Mar 4
 Daytona 200 by Arai Superbike Classic (Daytona Beach), Mar 6
 Daytona 500 (Daytona Beach), Feb 15
 Daytona Beach Spring Car Show & Swap Meet (Daytona Beach), Mar 19
 Daytona Supercross by Honda (Daytona Beach), Mar 6
 Daytona Turkey Run (Daytona Beach), Nov 25
 DeLand Fall Festival of Arts (DeLand), Nov 20
 DeLand Outdoor Art Fest (DeLand), Mar 27
 DeSoto's Winter Encampment (Tallahassee), Jan 17
 Disney World Opened: Anniv, Oct 1
 Downtown Fest/Art Show (Gainesville), Nov 6
 Dr. Martin Luther King Jr Celebration (Hollywood), Jan 16
 Easter Beach Run (Daytona Beach), Apr 10
 Einstein on Wine (Tampa), Jan 31
 Everglades Natl Park Established: Anniv, Dec 6
 Fall Bluegrass Fest (Live Oak), Sep 23
 Fall Country Jamboree (Barberville), Nov 6
 Fall Cycle Scene Motorcycle Races (Daytona Beach), Oct 21
 Fall Suwannee River Gospel Jubilee (Live Oak), Sep 30
 Fantasy Fest (Key West), Oct 22
 February Is Fabulous Florida Strawberry Month, Feb 1
 FedEx Orange Bowl (Miami), Jan 1
 Florida Citrus Fest (Winter Haven), Jan 15
 Florida Dodge Dealers 250 NASCAR Craftsman Truck Series Race (Daytona Beach), Feb 13
 Florida Folk Fest (White Springs), May 22
 Florida Music Harvest (Live Oak), Sep 17
 Ford Championship at Doral (Miami), Mar 1
 Fort Lauderdale Intl Boat Show (Fort Lauderdale), Oct 28
 Fourth of July Celebration (Live Oak), Jul 2
 Fun-in-the-Sun Postcard Sale (Orlando), Jan 17
 Gasparilla Invasion and Parade (Tampa), Feb 7
 Gatorade 125-Mile Qualifying Races (Daytona Beach), Feb 12
 Graham, Robert: Birth, Nov 9
 Grandmother's Day, Oct 10
 Grant Seafood Fest (Grant), Feb 28
 Hatsume Fair (Delray Beach), Feb 28
 Hispanic Heritage Fest (Miami), Oct 1
 Hoggetowne Medieval Faire (Gainesville), Feb 7
 Hollywood Beach Candy Cane Parade (Hollywood), Dec 11
 Hollywood Beach Latin Fest (Hollywood), Aug 15
 Hometown Family Fourth (Hollywood), Jul 4
 Humanatee/St. Marks Fest (St. Marks), May 15
 Intl Race of Champions (Daytona Beach), Feb 13
 Isle of Eight Flags Shrimp Fest (Fernandina Beach), Apr 30
 July 4th Family Celebration (Fort Lauderdale), Jul 4
 Kissimmee Slough Shootout and Rendezvous (Big Cypress Reservation), Feb 7
 Koolerz 300 NASCAR Busch Series Race (Daytona Beach), Feb 14
 Kuumba Fest (Hollywood), Apr 24
 Labor Day Picnic (Live Oak), Aug 28
 Law Enforcement Appreciation Month, May 1
 Magnolia Fest (Live Oak), Oct 14
 Memorial Day Getaway (Live Oak), May 29
 Miami Intl Boat/Sailboat Show (Miami Beach), Feb 12
 Miami/Bahamas Goombay Fest (Miami), Jun 4
 Natural Bridge Battle (Tallahassee), Mar 6
 Nelson, Bill: Birth, Sep 29
 New Year's Eve Trail Ride and Party (Live Oak), Dec 26
 O-Bon Fest (Delray Beach), Aug 14
 Ocean Dance (Hollywood), Dec 3
 Old Tyme Farm Days (Live Oak), Nov 25
 Orange Bowl Parade (Miami), Dec 31
 Orange City Blue Spring Manatee Fest (Orange City), Jan 24
 Our Town America Fest (Coral Springs), Feb 27
 Outback Bowl (Tampa), Jan 1
 Palm Harbor Arts/Crafts/Music Fest (Palm Harbor), Dec 4
 Pan-American Day, Apr 14
 Pascua Florida Day, Apr 2
 Patriot's Day, Apr 19
 Pepsi 400 (Daytona), Jul 3
 Poetry Day, May 25
 Pompano Beach Seafood Fest (Pompano Beach), Apr 23
 Ponce de Leon Discovers Florida: Anniv, Apr 2
 Renaissance Fest (Live Oak), Mar 19
 Rock-n-Blues and BBQ (Live Oak), Jul 3
 Rolex 24 at Daytona (Daytona Beach), Jan 31
 Saint Petersburg Fest of States (St. Petersburg), Apr 2
 Save the Florida Panther Day, Mar 20
 Seminole Tribe Festival, Powwow and Rodeo (Hollywood), Feb 12
 Seminole Tribe of Florida Legally Established: Anniv, Aug 21
 Sizzlin' Summer Garage Sale (Live Oak), Aug 7
 South Florida Senior Games (Hollywood), Jan 21
 Southeast Florida Scottish Fest & Games (Pembroke Pines), Mar 6
 Spring Arts Fest (Gainesville), Apr 17
 Spring Bluegrass Fest (Live Oak), Apr 8
 Spring Suwannee River Jubilee (Live Oak), Jul 7
 St. Patrick's Day Parade & Fest (Hollywood), Mar 7
 State Fair (Tampa), Feb 5
 Strawberry Fest/Hillsborough County Fair (Plant City), Feb 26
 SunFest (West Palm Beach), Apr 28
 Suwannee Lights (Live Oak), Dec 1
 Suwannee Spring Fest (Live Oak), Mar 18
 Tarpon Springs Arts & Crafts Fest (Tarpon Springs), Apr 3
 Teacher's Day, May 21
 Trail Ride Gathering, Natl (Live Oak), Oct 29
 Viva Italia! (Hollywood), Oct 9
 Week of Ocean Fest Sea-Son, Natl (Fort Lauderdale), Mar 6
 Wildlife and Western Art Expo (Lakeland), Jan 30
 World Karting Assn Races (Daytona Beach), Dec 26
 Zora Neale Hurston Fest (Eatonville), Jan 28
Flowers, Flower Shows,
 Albany Tulip Fest (Albany, NY), May 7
 American Rose Society Fall Natl Convention (Tulsa, OK), Oct 13
 American Rose Society Spring Natl Convention (San Diego, CA), May 5
 Azalea Fest (Muskogee, OK), Apr 1
 California Poppy Fest (Lancaster, CA), Apr 17
 Camellia Fest (Fort Valley, GA), Feb 1
 Canadian Tulip Fest (Ottawa, ON, Canada), May 6
 Chelsea Flower Show (London, England), May 25
 Cherry Blossom Fest (Washington, DC), Mar 27
 Chowder Fest, Flower and Art Show (Gold Beach, OR), May 1
 Daffodil Fest Weekend (Nantucket Island, MA), Apr 23
 Dandelion May Fest (Dover, OH), May 7
 Floral Design Day, Feb 28
 Flower Fest (Japan), Apr 8
 Hampton Court Palace Flower Show Charity Gala Preview (East Molesey, Surrey, England), Jul 5
 Harrogate Autumn Flower Show (Harrogate, England), Sep 17
 Harrogate Spring Flower Show (Harrogate, England), Apr 22
 Holland Tulip Time Fest (Holland, MI), May 1
 Hood River Valley Blossom Fest (Hood River, OR), Apr 17
 Indiana Flower and Patio Show (Indianapolis, IN), Mar 13
 Iris Fest (Sumter, SC), May 27
 Jersey Battle of Flowers (St. Lawrence, Channel Is), Aug 12
 Landon Azalea Garden Fest/Antiques (Bethesda, MD), Apr 30
 Lei Day (Hawaii), May 1
 Lilac Fest (Mackinac Island, MI), Jun 4
 Lilac Fest (Rochester, NY), May 14
 Longwood Gardens Acres of Spring (Kennett Square, PA), Apr 17
 Longwood Gardens Christmas Display (Kennett Square, PA), Nov 25
 Longwood Gardens Chrysanthemum Fest (Kennett Square, PA), Oct 23
 Longwood Gardens Welcome Spring (Kennett Square, PA), Jan 17
 Macon, GA's Cherry Blossom Fest, 2004 Intl (Macon, GA), Mar 19
 Magnolia Blossom Fest (Magnolia, AR), May 13
 Marigold Fest (Pekin, IL), Sep 10
 Maryland Home and Garden Show (Baltimore, MD), Mar 5
 Maymont Flower & Garden Show (Richmond, VA), Feb 19
 Midwest Regional Lawn, Garden and Flower Show (Davenport, IA), Mar 5
 Mother's Day Annual Rhododendron Show (Portland, OR), May 8
 Orchid Show (St. Louis, MO), Jan 31
 Pella Tulip Time Fest (Pella, IA), May 6
 Philadelphia Flower Show (Philadelphia, PA), Mar 7
 Poinsettia Day, Dec 12
 Portland Rose Fest (Portland, OR), Jun 3
 Redbud and Garden Show (Kechi, KS), Apr 24
 Repot Your Plant Day, Natl, Apr 4
 Rhododendron Fest (Florence, OR), May 21
 Rose Month, Natl, Jun 1
 Skagit Valley Tulip Fest (Burlington, WA), Apr 1
 South Carolina Fest of Roses (Orangeburg, SC), Apr 23
 South Carolina Festival of Flowers (Greenwood, SC), Jun 18
 Tournament of Roses Parade (Pasadena, CA), Jan 1
 Washington Home & Garden Show (Washington, DC), Mar 25
 Wildflower Week, Natl, May 2
 Yellow Daisy Fest (Stone Mountain, GA), Sep 9
Floyd, William: Birth Anniv, Dec 17
Flutie, Doug: Birth, Oct 23
Flying Nun TV Premiere: Anniv, Sep 7
Flynt, Larry: Birth, Nov 1
Foch, Nina: Birth, Apr 20
Fodor, Eugene: Birth Anniv, Oct 14
Fogelberg, Dan: Birth, Aug 13
Fogg, Phileas: Wager Day, Oct 2
Fogg, Phileas: Wins a Wager Day, Dec 21
Foley, Dave: Birth, Jan 4
Folger, Henry C.: Birth Anniv, Jun 18
Foliage Fest, Fall (Walden, VT), Sep 27
Folk Fair Intl, Holiday (Milwaukee, WI), Nov 19
Folk Fest, Florida (White Springs, FL), May 22
Folkfest, World (Springville, UT), Jul 10
Folklife Fest (Monroe, LA), Sep 11
Folklife Fest, Autumn Historic (Hannibal, MO), Oct 16
Folklife Fest, Texas (San Antonio, TX), Jun 10
Folklorama—Canada's Cultural Celeb (Winnipeg, MB), Aug 1
Folkmoot USA: The NC Intl Folk Fest (Waynesville, NC), Jul 12
Follett, Ken: Birth, Jun 5
Fonda, Bridget: Birth, Jan 27
Fonda, Henry: Birth Anniv, May 16
Fonda, Jane: Birth, Dec 21
Fonda, Peter: Birth, Feb 23
Fondue Month, National Fun with, Nov 1
Fonteyn, Margot: Birth Anniv, May 18
Food Allergy Awareness Month, Sep 1
Food and Beverage-Related Events and Observances,
 Abbotsford Berry Fest (Abbotsford, BC, Canada), Jul 2
 All About Apples (Woodstock, VT), Sep 26
 American Dietetic Assn Food & Nutrition Conf & Expo (Anaheim, CA), Oct 2
 Anti-Saloon League Founded: Anniv, May 24
 Appert, Nicholas: Birth Anniv, Oct 23
 Apple Butter Fest (Berkeley Springs, WV), Oct 9
 Apple Butter Makin' Days (Mt Vernon, MO), Oct 8
 Apple Butter Stirrin' (Coshocton, OH), Oct 15
 Apple Fest (Long Grove, IL), Oct 1
 Apple Fest (Topeka, KS), Oct 3
 Apple Fest, Kentucky (Paintsville, KY), Oct 1
 Apple Fest, Vermont (Springfield, VT), Oct 9
 Apple Festival (Forked River, NJ), Sep 25
 Apple Harvest Fest (Gettysburg, PA), Oct 2
 Applefest (Weston, MO), Oct 2
 Applejack Fest (Nebraska City, NE), Sep 18
 Art Fair & Winefest (Washington, MO), May 21
 Assn for Dressings and Sauces Annual Meeting (Amelia Island, FL), Oct 10

702

☆ Chase's 2004 Calendar of Events ☆ Index

Food (cont'd)—Football

Baby Food Fest, Natl (Fremont, MI), **Jul 13**
Bagelfest (Mattoon, IL), **Jul 28**
Bake for Family Fun Month, **Feb 1**
Baked Bean Month, Natl, **Jul 1**
Barbecue Month, Natl, **May 1**
Beef Empire Days (Garden City, KS), **Jun 8**
Biscuit Month, Natl, **Sep 1**
Black Cow Created: Anniv, **Aug 19**
Black Walnut Fest (Stockton, MO), **Sep 22**
Blueberry Arts Fest (Ketchikan, AK), **Aug 7**
Blueberry Fest (Montrose, PA), **Aug 6**
Blueberry Fest, Natl (South Haven, MI), **Aug 12**
Braham Pie Day (Braham, MN), **Aug 6**
Bread Machine Baking Month, **Jan 1**
Bread Pudding Recipe Exchange, **May 1**
Brewers Fest, Oregon (Portland, OR), **Jul 23**
Buffalo Wallow Chili Cookoff (Custer, SD), **Oct 3**
Bun Day (Iceland), **Feb 23**
Caffeine Awareness Month, Natl, **Mar 1**
California Artichoke Festival (Castroville, CA), **May 17**
Canadafest (Hollywood, FL), **Jan 31**
Candy Month, Natl, **Jun 1**
Cape May Food & Wine Fest (Cape May, NJ), **Sep 18**
Celebrate Sun Dried Tomatoes Month, **Oct 1**
Cheese Fest, Great Wisconsin (Little Chute, WI), **Jun 4**
Cherry Month, Natl, **Feb 1**
Cherry Pit Spitting Contest, Intl (Eau Claire, MI), **Jul 3**
Chicken Fest, Delmarva (Salisbury, MD), **Jun 18**
Chicken Month, Natl, **Sep 1**
Chili Cook-off, State Chmpshp (Roanoke, VA), **May 8**
Chili Month, Natl, **Oct 1**
Chocolate Fest (Galesburg, IL), **Feb 7**
Chocolate Fest (Long Grove, IL), **Apr 30**
Chocolate Fest (Norman, OK), **Feb 7**
Chowder Fest, Flower and Art Show (Gold Beach, OR), **May 1**
Chowderfest (Mystic, CT), **Oct 9**
Citrus Fest, Florida (Winter Haven, FL), **Jan 15**
Clam Chowder Cookoff (Santa Cruz, CA), **Feb 21**
Clam Fest, Yarmouth (Yarmouth, ME), **Jul 16**
Clear Lake Crawfish Fest (Seabrook, TX), **Apr 3**
Coffee Gourmet Intl Month, **Jan 1**
Cook Something Bold and Pungent Day, **Nov 8**
Cookie Cutter Week, **Dec 1**
Cookie Month, Natl, **Oct 1**
Country Ham Days, Marion County (Lebanon, KY), **Sep 25**
Crawfish Fest, Dermott's Annual (Dermott, AR), **May 14**
Crawfordsville Strawberry Fest (Crawfordsville, IN), **Jun 11**
Crayfish Premiere (Sweden), **Aug 11**
Culinary Arts Month, Natl, **Jul 1**
Dairy Month, June, **Jun 1**
Date Fest, Natl (Indio, CA), **Feb 13**
Diet Resolution Week, **Jan 1**
Digby Scallop Days Fest (Digby, NS), **Aug 4**
DRC-FM Caravan of Carriages (Windsor, CT), **Nov 21**
Drive-Thru Day, Natl, **Jul 28**
Eat Dessert First Month, **May 1**
Eat What You Want Day, **May 11**
Egg Month, Natl, **May 1**
Egg Salad Week, **Apr 12**
Einstein on Wine (Tampa, FL), **Jan 31**
Eldon Turkey Fest (Eldon, MO), **Oct 9**
Electra Goat BBQ Cook-Off (Electra, TX), **May 7**
Elmira Maple Syrup Fest (Elmira, ON, Canada), **Apr 3**
Escoffier, Georges: Birth Anniv, **Oct 28**
Fall on Nantucket (Nantucket Island, MA), **Oct 1**
Feast of the Ramson (Richwood, WV), **Apr 17**
February Is Fabulous Florida Strawberry Month, **Feb 1**
Fest of Mountain and Plain/A Taste of Colorado (Denver, CO), **Sep 3**
Fig Week, Natl, **Nov 1**
First McDonald's Opens: Anniv, **Apr 15**
5-A-Day Month, Natl, **Sep 1**
Florida Strawberry Fest (Plant City, FL), **Feb 26**
Food Bank Week, Natl, **Oct 10**
Foods/Feasts of Colonial Virginia (Williamsburg, VA), **Nov 25**
Fortune Cookie Day, **Sep 13**
Fresh Squeezed Juice Week, Natl, **Jan 15**
Frozen Food Month, Natl, **Mar 1**
Fulton Oysterfest (Fulton, TX), **Mar 4**
Fun with Fondue Month, Natl, **Nov 1**
Georgia Pecan Month, Natl, **Nov 1**
Gilroy Garlic Fest (Gilroy, CA), **Jul 23**
Gingerbread House Day, **Dec 12**
Gingerbread Village and Bazaar (Middlebury, CT), **Dec 4**
Giving Thanks: Hearth and Home in Early Maryland (St. Mary's City, MD), **Nov 26**
Go Hog Wild—Eat Country Ham Month, **Oct 1**
Go Nuts Over Peanuts Month, **Oct 1**
Go Wild During California Wild Rice Month, **Sep 1**
Grant Seafood Fest (Grant, FL), **Feb 28**
Grape Jamboree, Geneva Area (Geneva, OH), **Sep 25**
Great American Low-Cholesterol, Low-Fat Pizza Bake, **Sep 1**
Great American Meatout, **Mar 20**
Great Arkansas Pig-Out (Morrilton, AR), **Aug 6**
Great Peanut Tour (Skippers, VA), **Sep 9**
Gumbo Fest (Bridge City, LA), **Oct 8**
Hamburger Month, Natl, **May 1**
Harvest Weekends (Bryan, TX), **Jul 23**
Harvest Wine Celeb (Livermore, CA), **Sep 5**
Herb Fest (Mattoon, IL), **Apr 24**
Herrinfesta Italiana (Herrin, IL), **May 27**
Highland County Maple Fest (Highland County, VA), **Mar 13**
Hog Capital of the World Fest (Kewanee, IL), **Sep 3**
Home of the Hamburger Celeb (Seymour, WI), **Aug 7**
Homemade Bread Day, **Nov 17**
Honey Month, Natl, **Sep 1**
Hope Watermelon Fest (Hope, AR), **Aug 12**
Horseradish Fest (Collinsville, IL), **Jun 5**
Hot Breakfast Month, Natl, **Feb 1**
Hot Dog Month, Natl, **Jul 1**
Hot Dog Night (Luverne, MN), **Jul 8**
Hot Tea Month, Natl, **Jan 1**
Hug a Texas Chef Month, **Sep 1**
I Want Butterscotch Day, Natl, **Feb 15**
Ice Cream Cone: Anniv, **Sep 22**
Ice Cream Day, Natl, **Jul 18**
Ice Cream Days (Le Mars, IA), **Jul 1**
Ice Cream Fest, Old-Fashioned (Utica, OH), **May 29**
Ice Cream Social (Indianapolis, IN), **Jul 4**
Iced Tea Month, Natl, **Jun 1**
Jackson County Apple Fest (Jackson, OH), **Sep 21**
Jackson Hill Cider Day (Portsmouth, NH), **Sep 11**
James Beard Awards Ceremony (New York, NY), **May 10**
Jell-O Week in Utah, **Feb 8**
July Belongs to Blueberries Month, Natl, **Jul 1**
June Is Turkey Lovers' Month, **Jun 1**
Kentucky Bourbon Fest (Bardstown, KY), **Sep 15**
Kodiak Crab Fest (Kodiak, AK), **May 27**
Kool-Aid Days (Hastings, NE), **Aug 13**
La Tomatina (Spain), **Aug 25**
Leitersburg Peach Fest (Leitersburg, MD), **Aug 7**
Lobster Fest, Maine (Rockland, ME), **Aug 4**
Lobsterfest (Mystic, CT), **May 29**
Long Beach Island Chowder Cook-Off (Beach Haven, NJ), **Oct 2**
Louisiana Peach Fest (Ruston, LA), **Jun 17**
Machias Wild Blueberry Fest (Machias, ME), **Aug 20**
Maple Fair, Parke County (Rockville, IN), **Feb 28**
Maple Fest of Nova Scotia (Northern Nova Scotia, Canada), **Mar 20**
Maple Syrup Fest (Beaver, PA), **Apr 3**
Maple Syrup Saturday (Appleton, WI), **Mar 20**
Marion Popcorn Fest (Marion, OH), **Sep 2**
Marriage of the Port Ceremony (Bryan, TX), **Feb 21**
Marshall County Blueberry Fest (Plymouth, IN), **Sep 3**
Men Make Dinner Day, Natl, **Nov 4**
Messina Hof's Wine Premiere (Bryan, TX), **Nov 13**
Mint Fest, Saint Johns (St. Johns, MI), **Aug 13**
Mitchell Persimmon Fest (Mitchell, IN), **Sep 18**
Morden Corn/Apple Fest (Morden, MB, Canada), **Aug 27**
More Herbs, Less Salt Day, **Aug 29**
Morel Mushroom Fest (Muscoda, WI), **May 14**
Morton Pumpkin Fest (Morton, IL), **Sep 15**
Mudbug Madness (Shreveport, LA), **May 27**
Muffin Wk, Natl, **May 3**
Mushroom Fest (Kennett Square, PA), **Sep 11**
Mushroom Fest, Telluride (Telluride, CO), **Aug 26**
Mushroom Month, Natl, **Sep 1**
Mustard Day, Natl, **Aug 7**
Newport Seafood and Wine Fest (Newport, OR), **Feb 27**
No Salt Week, **Oct 1**
North Carolina Apple Fest (Hendersonville, NC), **Sep 3**
North Carolina SweetPotato Month, **Feb 1**
Norwalk Seaport Oyster Fest (Norwalk, CT), **Sep 10**
Nugget Best in the West Rib Cook-Off (Sparks, NV), **Sep 2**
Nuts Fair (Bastogne, Belgium), **Dec 20**
Oatmeal Month, **Jan 1**
October Frozen Food Fest, **Oct 1**
Onion Market (Zibelemarit, Switzerland), **Nov 22**
Organic Harvest Month, Natl, **Sep 1**
Oyster Fest (Chincoteague Island, VA), **Oct 9**
Oyster Fest, St. Mary's County MD (Leonardtown, MD), **Oct 16**
Paczki Day, **Feb 24**
Pancake Day, Intl (Liberal, KS), **Feb 24**
Pancake Week, Natl, **Feb 22**
Payson Golden Onion Days (Payson, UT), **Sep 3**
Peanut Butter Lover's Month, **Nov 1**
Pecan Day, **Mar 25**
Pecan Month, Natl, **Apr 1**
Pennsylvania Rib, Wing and Music Fest (Greensburg, PA), **Jun 18**
Personal Chef Days, Natl, **Sep 19**
Pickle Festival (Greenlawn, NY), **Oct 3**
Pickle Week, Intl, **May 21**
Picklefest (Atkins, AR), **May 21**
Polk County Ramp Tramp Fest (Benton, TN), **Apr 24**
Popcorn Fest (Valparaiso, IN), **Sep 11**
Popcorn Poppin' Month, Natl, **Oct 1**
Pork Month, Natl, **Oct 1**
Potato Blossom Fest, Maine (Fort Fairfield, ME), **Jul 9**
Potato Day Fest (Greeley, CO), **Sep 11**
Potato Month, Natl, **Sep 1**
Poteet Strawberry Fest (Poteet, TX), **Apr 2**
Prairie Dog Chili Cookoff (Grand Prairie, TX), **Apr 3**
Pumpkin Pie Day, **Nov 21**
Pumpkin Show, Circleville (Circleville, OH), **Oct 20**
Ranch Hand Breakfast (Kingsville, TX), **Nov 20**
Recipe Greetings for the Holidays, **Dec 1**
Return Shopping Carts to the Supermarket Month, **Feb 1**
Rhubarb Fest (Intercourse, PA), **May 21**
Ribfest (Kalamazoo, MI), **Aug 5**
Rice God, Day of the (Chiyoda, Japan), **Jun 6**
Rice Month, Natl, **Sep 1**
Rice Planting Fest (Osaka, Japan), **Jun 14**
Rice, Intl Year of, **Jan 1**
River Rockin' Ribfest (Davenport, IA), **Aug 27**
Riverfest (Columbus, GA), **Apr 23**
Riverfront Ribfest (Huntington, WV), **Aug 19**
Rochesterfest (Rochester, MN), **Jun 19**
Rockport Seafair (Rockport, TX), **Oct 8**
Saint Louise de Marillac Louisiana Bar-B-Q Fest (Arabi, LA), **Oct 22**
Salad Week, Natl, **Jul 25**
Salsa, Month, Natl, **May 1**
Sam Rayburn Chili Cook-off (Bonham, TX), **Sep 18**
Sandwich Day, **Nov 3**
Schmeckfest (Freeman, SD), **Apr 1**
School Breakfast Week, Natl, **Mar 8**
Scottsdale Culinary Fest (Scottsdale, AZ), **Apr 14**
Seafood Fest, Pompano Beach (Pompano Beach, FL), **Apr 23**
Seafood Month, Natl, **Oct 1**
Seven Sweets/Seven Sours Fest (Intercourse, PA), **Sep 17**
Shrimp and Petroleum Fest, Louisiana (Morgan City, LA), **Sep 2**
Shrimp Fest, Low Country (McClellanville, SC), **May 1**
Sinkie Day, **Nov 26**
Sneak Some Zucchini onto Your Neighbors' Porch Night, **Aug 8**
Soft Pretzel Month, Natl, **Apr 1**
Sonoma Valley Harvest Wine Auction (Sonoma, CA), **Sep 3**
Soul Food Month, Natl, **Jun 1**
Sour Herring Premiere (Sweden), **Aug 19**
Soyfoods Month, **Apr 1**
Special Chefs Blue Ribbon Recipe and Cooking Contest (Chicago, IL), **Oct 16**
Spinach Lovers Month, **Oct 1**
Steak Cook-off, World Chmpshp (Magnolia, AR), **May 15**
Strawberry Fest (Lahaska, PA), **May 1**
Strawberry Fest (Long Grove, IL), **Jun 25**
Sun Prairie's Sweet Corn Fest (Sun Prairie, WI), **Aug 19**
Sweetcorn Fest, Natl (Hoopeston, IL), **Sep 2**
Taco Day, Chuy's Natl, **Jun 8**
Tacoma Holiday Food and Gift Fest (Tacoma, WA), **Oct 20**
Taste of Cincinnati (Cincinnati, OH), **May 29**
Taste of History (Staunton, VA), **Sep 18**
Taste of Madison (Madison, WI), **Aug 28**
Taste of Morgan Hill (Morgan Hill, CA), **Sep 25**
Taste of the Town (Wichita Falls, TX), **Mar 2**
Texas on the Plate Month, **Oct 1**
3-A-Day Week, **Mar 3**
Tomato Month, Fresh Florida, **Apr 1**
Totally Chipotle Day, **May 5**
Turkey Rama (McMinnville, OR), **Jul 8**
Turkey-Free Thanksgiving, **Nov 25**
University Kiwanis Pancake Fest (Wichita Falls, TX), **Jan 31**
Vegan Month, **Nov 1**
Vegan World Day, **Jun 20**
Vegetarian Day, World, **Oct 1**
Vegetarian Month, **Oct 1**
Vermont Maple Fest (St. Albans, VT), **Apr 23**
Vinegar Day, **Aug 21**
Virginia Peanut Fest (Emporia,VA), **Sep 24**
Virginia Pork Fest (Emporia, VA), **Jun 9**
Virginia Wine Fest (Charlottesville, VA), **May 15**
Waffle Week, Natl, **Sep 5**
Washington State Apple Blossom Fest (Wenatchee, WA), **Apr 29**
Watermelon Fest (Rush Springs, OK), **Aug 14**
Watermelon Thump (Luling, TX), **Jun 24**
Winchell's Donut House Established: Anniv, **Oct 8**
Wine and Garden Fest (Bryan, TX), **Apr 17**
Wollersheim Winery Grape Stomp Fest (Prairie du Sac, WI), **Oct 2**
World Beef Expo (Milwaukee, WI), **Sep 23**
World Chmpshp BBQ Goat Cook-off (Brady, TX), **Sep 4**
World Egg Day, **Oct 8**
World Food Day, **Oct 16**
World Food Day (UN), **Oct 16**
World's Biggest Fish Fry (Paris, TN), **Apr 18**
World's Largest Breakfast Table (Battle Creek, MI), **Jun 10**
Yambilee, Louisiana (Opelousas, LA), **Oct 27**

Food Bank Week, Natl, Oct 10
Food Fight, World's Largest: La Tomatina (Spain), Aug 25
Food Stamps Authorized: Anniv, Sep 11
Footbag Chmpshps, World (San Francisco, CA), Aug 2
Football,
Blue-Gray Classic (Montgomery, AL), **Dec 25**
Chick-fil-A Peach Bowl (Atlanta, GA), **Jan 2**
Citrus Bowl, Capital One Florida (Orlando, FL), **Jan 1**

Index ☆ Chase's 2004 Calendar of Events ☆

Football (cont'd)—Garden

Fabulous 1890s Weekend (Mansfield, PA), **Sep 24**
FedEx Orange Bowl (Miami, FL), **Jan 1**
First Night Football Game (Mansfield, PA), **Sep 28**
First Play-by-Play Football Game Broadcast, **Nov 23**
First Super Bowl: Anniv, **Jan 15**
Football League, Natl, Formed: Anniv, **Sep 17**
Hula Bowl Maui All Star Classic (Maui, HI), **Jan 17**
Immaculate Reception: Anniv, **Dec 31**
MainStay Independence Bowl (Shreveport, LA), **Dec 31**
NAIA Div II Football Chmpshp Game, **Dec 20**
Nokia Sugar Bowl (New Orleans, LA), **Jan 1**
Oil Bowl Football Classic (Wichita Falls, TX), **Jun 19**
Outback Bowl (Tampa, FL), **Jan 1**
Pacific Life Holiday Bowl Parade/Game (San Diego, CA), **Dec 30**
PSFCA East West All-Star Game (Altoona, PA), **Jun 26**
Rose Bowl Game (Pasadena, CA), **Jan 1**
SBC Cotton Bowl Classic (Dallas, TX), **Jan 1**
Senior Bowl Football Game (Mobile, AL), **Jan 25**
Sun Bowl (El Paso, TX), **Dec 31**
Super Bowl (Houston, TX), **Feb 1**
Tostitos Fiesta Bowl (Tempe, AZ), **Jan 2**
Unitas, Johnny: Birth, **May 7**
Foote, Shelby: Birth, **Nov 17**
Foothills Art Fest (Jackson, OH), **Oct 15**
For Pete's Sake Day, **Feb 26**
Forbes, Malcolm: Birth Anniv, **Aug 19**
Forbes, Michelle: Birth, **Feb 17**
Forbes, Steve: Birth, **Jul 18**
Ford, Eileen: Birth, **Mar 25**
Ford, Elizabeth (Betty): Birth, **Apr 8**
Ford, Faith: Birth, **Sep 14**
Ford, Gerald,
    Assassination Attempts On: Anniv, **Sep 5**
    Birth, **Jul 14**
    Veep Day, **Aug 9**
    Vice Presidential Swearing In: Anniv, **Dec 6**
Ford, Glenn: Birth, **May 1**
Ford, Harrison: Birth, **Jul 13**
Ford, Henry: Birth Anniv, **Jul 30**
Ford, John: Birth Anniv, **Feb 1**
Ford, Whitey: Birth, **Oct 21**
Forefathers' Day, **Dec 21**
Foreman, George: Birth, **Jan 10**
Forest Craft/Scenic Drive Fest (Van Buren Cnty, IA), **Oct 9**
Forest Products Week, Natl (Pres Proc), **Oct 17**
Forgive Mom & Dad Day, **Mar 18**
Forman, Milos: Birth, **Feb 18**
Former Prisoner of War Recognition Day, Natl (Pres Proc), **Apr 9**
Forrest, Nathan Bedford: Birth Anniv, **Jul 13**
Forsberg, Peter: Birth, **Jul 20**
Forster, E.M.: Birth Anniv, **Jan 1**
Forster, Robert: Birth, **Jul 13**
Forsyth, Frederick: Birth, **Aug 25**
Forsythe, John: Birth, **Jan 29**
Fort Ligonier Days (Ligonier, PA), **Oct 8**
Fort Moore Established: Anniv, **Apr 24**
Fort Sumter Shelled by North: Anniv, **Aug 17**
Fort Union Trading Post Rendezvous (Williston, ND), **Jun 17**
Fortas, Abe: Birth Anniv, **Jun 19**
Forten, James: Birth Anniv, **Sep 2**
Fortune Cookie Day, **Sep 13**
48 Hours TV Premiere: Anniv, **Jan 19**
Fosse, Bob: Birth Anniv, **Jun 23**
Foster, Andrew "Rube": Birth Anniv, **Sep 17**
Foster, Jodie: Birth, **Nov 19**
Foster, Meg: Birth, **May 14**
Foster, Mike: Birth, **Jul 11**
Foster, Stephen: Birth Anniv, **Jul 4**
Foucault, Jean: Earth's Rotation Proved: Anniv, **Jan 8**
Foudy, Julie: Birth, **Jan 27**
Foundation Day, Natl (Japan), **Feb 11**
Founders' Day (Toms River, NJ), **Jun 12**
Founder's Day Corn Roast (Forest Grove, OR), **Sep 19**
Fountain, Pete: Birth, **Jul 3**
Fountains, Longwood Gardens Fest of (Kennett Square, PA), **May 29**
Four Chaplains Memorial Day, **Feb 3**
Fox, Bernard: Birth, **May 11**
Fox, Edward: Birth, **Apr 13**
Fox, James: Birth, **May 19**
Fox, Jorja: Birth, **Jul 7**
Fox, Matthew: Birth, **Jul 14**
Fox, Michael J.: Birth, **Jun 9**
Fox, Terry: Birth Anniv, **Jul 28**
Fox, Vicente: Birth, **Jul 2**
Foxfield Races (Charlottesville, VA), **Apr 24**
Foxworthy, Jeff: Birth, **Sep 6**
Foxx, Jamie: Birth, **Dec 13**
Foxx, Redd: Birth Anniv, **Dec 9**
Foyt, A.J.: Birth, **Jan 16**
Fraggle Rock TV Premiere: Anniv, **Sep 12**
Frampton, Peter: Birth, **Apr 22**
France,
    Bastille Day, **Jul 14**
    Cannes Film Fest (Cannes), **May 12**
    Celebrate France Parade (Paris), **Jan 1**
    Eiffel Tower: Anniv (Paris), **Mar 31**
    Nice Carnival, **Feb 13**
    Night Watch, **Jul 13**
    Tour de France, **Jul 3**
    Victory Day, **May 8**
Franciosa, Anthony: Birth, **Oct 25**
Francis, Anne: Birth, **Sep 16**
Francis, Connie: Birth, **Dec 12**
Francis, Genie: Birth, **May 26**
Francis, Ron: Birth, **Mar 1**
Franco, James: Birth, **Apr 19**
Frank, Anne, Diary: Last Entry: Anniv, **Aug 1**
Frank, Anne: Birth Anniv, **Jun 12**
Frankel, Max: Birth, **Apr 3**
Franken, Al: Birth, **May 21**
Frankenstein Friday, **Oct 29**
Frankfurt Book Fair (Frankfurt, Germany), **Oct 6**
Franklin Day, Joe, **Mar 9**
Franklin Prefers Turkey: Anniv, **Jan 26**
Franklin, Aretha: Birth, **Mar 25**
Franklin, Benjamin: Birth Anniv, **Jan 17**
Franklin, Benjamin: Poor Richard's Almanack: Anniv, **Dec 28**
Franklin, Bonnie: Birth, **Jan 6**
Franklin, Pamela: Birth, **Feb 4**
Franks, Tommy: Birth, **Jun 17**
Franz, Arthur: Birth, **Feb 29**
Franz, Dennis: Birth, **Oct 28**
Fraser, Brendan: Birth, **Dec 3**
Frasier TV Premiere: Anniv, **Sep 16**
Frazier, Joe: Birth, **Jan 12**
Frazier, Sheila E.: Birth, **Nov 13**
Freberg, Stan: Birth, **Aug 7**
Fred Waring Show TV Premiere: Anniv, **Apr 17**
Frederick Fest of the Arts (Frederick, MD), **Jun 5**
Freedom Day: Anniv, **Feb 1**
Freedom from Fear of Speaking Day, **Jul 4**
Freedom of Information Day, **Mar 16**
Freedom Riders: Anniv, **May 4**
Freedom Shrine Month, **May 1**
Freedom Week, **Jul 4**
Freedom Week, Religious, **Sep 18**
Freefall Conv, World (Rantoul, IL), **Aug 6**
Freelance Writers Appreciation Week, **Feb 9**
Freeman, Al, Jr: Birth, **Mar 21**
Freeman, Morgan: Birth, **Jun 1**
Freer, Charles L.: Birth Anniv, **Feb 25**
Freethinker's Day, **Jan 29**
Frelich, Phyllis: Birth, **Feb 29**
French and Indian War, Treaty of Paris Ends: Anniv, **Feb 10**
French Quarter Fest (New Orleans, LA), **Apr 16**
French West Indies,
    Carnival (Martinique), **Feb 21**
French, Daniel C.: Birth Anniv, **Apr 20**
Frenchmen Rows Across Pacific: Anniv, **Nov 21**
Frequent Flyer Program Debuts: Anniv, **May 1**
Fresh Breath Day, Natl, **Aug 6**
Fresh Squeezed Juice Week, Natl, **Jan 15**
Freud, Sigmund: Birth Anniv, **May 6**
Freudenthal, Dave: Birth, **Oct 12**
Frey, Glenn: Birth, **Nov 6**
Fricke, Janie: Birth, **Dec 19**
Fricker, Brenda: Birth, **Feb 17**
Friday the Thirteenth, **Feb 13**
Friedan, Betty: Birth, **Feb 4**
Friedel, Brad: Birth, **May 18**
Friedkin, William: Birth, **Aug 29**
Friedle, Will: Birth, **Aug 11**
Friedman, Milton: Birth, **Jul 31**
Friends TV Premiere: Anniv, **Sep 22**
Friends: New Friends, Old Friends Week, Natl, **May 16**
Friendship Week, Intl, **Feb 22**
Friendship: Girlfriend's Day, **Aug 1**
Fringe Theatre Fest (Edmonton, AB, Canada), **Aug 12**
Frisch, Max: Birth Anniv, **May 15**
Frist, William: Birth, **Feb 22**
Froebel, Friedrich: Birth Anniv, **Apr 21**
Frog Jumping Jubilee/Calaveras Fair (Angel Camp, CA), **May 13**
Frontier Address, Turner's: Anniv, **Jul 12**
Frontline TV Premiere: Anniv, **Jan 17**
Frost, David: Birth, **Apr 7**
Frost, Robert: Birth Anniv, **Mar 26**
Frozen Food Month, Natl, **Mar 1**
Frugal Fun Day, Intl, **Oct 2**
Fry, Elizabeth: Birth Anniv, **May 21**
Fry, Stephen: Birth, **Aug 24**
Frye, Soleil Moon: Birth, **Aug 6**
Fuentes, Daisy: Birth, **Nov 17**
Fugitive TV Premiere: Anniv, **Sep 17**
Fulbright, J. William: Birth Anniv, **Nov 9**
Fuller, Alfred Carl: Birth Anniv, **Jan 13**
Fuller, Bobby: Death Anniv, **Jul 18**
Fuller, Buckminster: Birth Anniv, **Jul 12**
Fuller, Margaret: Birth Anniv, **May 23**
Fuller, Melville Weston: Birth Anniv, **Feb 11**
Fulton, Robert: Birth Anniv, **Nov 14**
Fulton, Robert: Sails Steamboat: Anniv, **Aug 17**
Fun at Work Day, **Jan 30**
Fun at Work Day, Natl, **Apr 1**
Fun Facts About Names Day, **Mar 8**
Funeral Day, Create a Great, **Oct 30**
Funeral for Ol' Man Winter, Wayne State Univ (Detroit, MI), **Apr 7**
Funicello, Annette: Birth, **Oct 22**
Funky Winkerbean: Anniv, **Mar 27**
Fur Trade, Voyageurs,
    Big Island Rendezvous (Albert Lea, MN), **Oct 2**
    Fest of Adventures (Aitkin, MN), **Sep 18**
    Fort Union Trading Post Rendezvous (Williston, ND), **Jun 17**
    Great Rendezvous (Thunder Bay, ON, Canada), **Jul 9**
    Mountain Man Rendezvous (Cataldo, ID), **Aug 20**
    Prairie Villa Rendezvous (Prairie du Chien, WI), **Jun 17**
    Tetonkaha Rendezvous (Lake Benton, MN), **Aug 13**
    White Oak Rendezvous (Deer River, MN), **Aug 7**
Furcal, Rafael: Birth, **Aug 24**
Furlong, Edward: Birth, **Aug 2**
Furnishings Market, Intl Home (High Point, NC), **Apr 22**
G.I. Joe Introduced: Anniv, **Feb 1**
Gable, Clark: Birth Anniv, **Feb 1**
Gable, Clark: Gone with the Wind Film Premiere: Anniv, **Dec 15**
Gabon: National Day, **Aug 17**
Gabor, Zsa Zsa: Birth, **Feb 6**
Gabriel, Peter: Birth, **Feb 13**
Gagarin, Yuri A.: Birth Anniv, **Mar 9**
Gage, Nicholas: Birth, **Jul 23**
Gagne, Eric: Birth, **Jan 7**
Gagne, Simon: Birth, **Feb 29**
Gail, Max: Birth, **Apr 5**
Gain the Inside Advantage Month, Natl, **Oct 1**
Gaines, William M.: Birth Anniv, **Mar 1**
Gainsborough, Thomas: Birth Anniv, **May 14**
Gal, Uzi: Birth Anniv, **Dec 15**
Galbraith, John Kenneth: Birth, **Oct 15**
Gale, Robert: Birth, **Oct 11**
Galecki, Johnny: Birth, **Apr 30**
Galilei, Galileo: Birth Anniv, **Feb 15**
Gallagher, Peter: Birth, **Aug 19**
Gallaudet, Thomas Hopkins: Birth Anniv, **Dec 10**
Galligan, Zach: Birth, **Feb 14**
Gallo, Frank: Birth, **Jan 13**
Gallo, Julio: Anniv, **Mar 21**
Galveston Historic Homes Tour (Galveston Island, TX), **May 1**
Galveston, TX Hurricane: Anniv, **Sep 8**
Galway, James: Birth, **Dec 8**
Gambia: Independence Day, **Feb 18**
Gambill, Jan-Michael: Birth, **Jun 3**
Gambon, Michael: Birth, **Oct 19**
Game and Puzzle Week, Natl, **Nov 21**
Games, Multisport Competitions,
    Badger State Summer Games Sectionals and Finals (WI), **Jun 17**
    Badger State Winter Games (Wausau, WI), **Feb 6**
    Big Sky State Games (Billings, MT), **Jul 16**
    Cowboy State Sports Fest (Casper, WY), **Feb 7**
    Dice Day, Natl, **Dec 4**
    Games of the XXVIII Olympiad (Athens, Greece), **Aug 13**
    Maine Highland Games (Brunswick, ME), **Aug 21**
    Paralympic Games 2004 (Athens, Greece), **Sep 17**
    Scrabble Chmpshp, Natl (New Orleans, LA), **Aug 7**
    Show Me State Games (Columbia, MO), **Jul 16**
    Simplot Games (Pocatello, ID), **Feb 19**
    State Games of Oregon (Portland, OR), **Jul 9**
    Wells Fargo Winter Games of Idaho (ID), **Feb 1**
Gandhi, Mohandas, Assassinated: Anniv, **Jan 30**
Gandhi, Mohandas: Birth Anniv, **Oct 2**
Gandhi, Rajiv, Assassinated: Anniv, **May 21**
Gandolfini, James: Birth, **Sep 18**
Ganz, Bruno: Birth, **Mar 22**
Garage Sale Day, Natl, **Aug 14**
Garage Sale Month, Natl, **May 1**
Garagiola, Joe: Birth, **Feb 12**
Garbo, Greta: Birth Anniv, **Sep 18**
Garcia, Andy: Birth, **Apr 12**
Garcia, Jeff: Birth, **Feb 24**
Garcia, Jerry: Birth Anniv, **Aug 1**
Garcia, Sergio: Birth, **Jan 9**
Garcia-Marquez, Gabriel: Birth, **Mar 6**
Garciaparra, Nomar: Birth, **Jul 23**
Garden,
    Become a YardNerd Month, **Apr 1**
    Fall Home & Garden Expo (Omaha, NE), **Oct 8**
    Garden Week, Natl, **Apr 11**
    Gardenfest at Longwood Gardens (Kennett Square, PA), **Sep 11**
    Heirloom Seed Day (Woodstock, VT), **Jun 5**
    Historic Garden Week (Virginia), **Apr 17**
    Home and Garden Fest (Wichita Falls, TX), **Feb 28**
    June Is Perennial Gardening Month, **Jun 1**
    Landscape Architecture Month, Natl, **Apr 1**
    Lawn and Garden Month, Natl, **Apr 1**
    Lawnmower Tune-Up Month, Natl, **Apr 1**
    Longwood Gardens Autumn's Colors (Kennett Square, PA), **Oct 9**
    Mailorder Gardening Month, Natl, **Jan 1**
    Maymont's Herbs Galore (Richmond, VA), **Apr 24**
    Michigan Home & Garden Show (Pontiac, MI), **Mar 4**
    Midwest Regional Lawn, Garden and Flower Show (Davenport, IA), **Mar 5**
    Natl City Cleveland Home and Garden Show (Cleveland, OH), **Feb 7**
    Savannah Tour of Homes and Gardens (Savannah, GA), **Mar 25**
    Spring Gardener's Market and Plant Sale (Norfolk, VA), **May 8**

# ☆ Chase's 2004 Calendar of Events ☆ Index

Washington Home & Garden Show (Washington, DC), **Mar 25**
Water Gardening Month Natl, **Jul 1**
Wisconsin Spring Garden Market (Kohler, WI), **Apr 17**
Gardenia, Vincent: Birth Anniv, Jan 7
Gardner, Ava: Birth Anniv, Dec 24
Gardner, Erle Stanley: Birth Anniv, Jul 17
Gardner, Randy: Birth, Dec 2
Garfield, Allen: Birth, Nov 22
Garfield, James A.: Birth Anniv, Nov 19
Garfield, James: Assassination Anniv, Jul 2
Garfield, Lucretia R.: Birth Anniv, Apr 19
Garfield: Birthday, Jun 19
Garfunkel, Art: Birth, Nov 5
Garland, Beverly: Birth, Oct 17
Garland, Judy: Birth Anniv, Jun 10
Garland, Judy: Wizard of Oz Released: Anniv, **Aug 25**
Garner, James: Birth, Apr 7
Garner, Jennifer: Birth, Apr 17
Garner, John Nance: Birth Anniv, Nov 22
Garnett, Kevin: Birth, May 19
Garofalo, Janeane: Birth, Sep 28
Garr, Teri: Birth, Dec 11
Garrett, Brad: Birth, Apr 14
Garrick, David: Birth Anniv, Feb 19
Garth, Jennie: Birth, Apr 3
Garvey, Steve: Birth, Dec 22
Gasol, Pau: Birth, Jul 6
Gasoline Alley Creator: King, Frank: Birth Anniv, **Apr 9**
Gates of the Arctic Natl Park: Anniv, Dec 2
Gates, Bill: Billionaire Wedding Anniv, Jan 1
Gates, Bill: Birth, Oct 28
Gates, David: Birth, Dec 11
Gates, Henry Louis, Jr: Birth, Sep 16
Gatlin, Larry: Birth, May 2
GATT Treaty, US Congress Passes: Anniv, Dec 1
Gauguin, Paul: Birth Anniv, Jun 7
Gautier, Dick: Birth, Oct 30
Gay & Lesbian,
  Coming Out Day, Natl, **Oct 11**
  Gay and Lesbian History Month, **Oct 1**
  Gay and Lesbian Pride Month, **Jun 1**
  Gay and Lesbian Pride Parade (Chicago, IL), **Jun 27**
  Gay Square Dance Month, Intl, **Sep 1**
  GLBT Book Month, Natl, **Jun 1**
  Stonewall Riot: Anniv, **Jun 28**
Gayle, Crystal: Birth, Jan 9
Gaynor, Mitzi: Birth, Sep 4
Gazzara, Ben: Birth, Aug 28
Geary, Anthony: Birth, May 29
Gedalya, Fast of, Sep 19
Geeson, Judy: Birth, Sep 10
Geffen, David: Birth, Feb 21
Gehrig, Lou: Birth Anniv, Jun 19
Gehry, Frank: Birth, Feb 28
Geiger, Matt: Birth, Sep 10
Geisel, Theodor "Dr. Seuss": Birth Anniv, Mar 2
Gelbart, Larry: Birth, Feb 25
Geldof, Bob: Birth, Oct 5
Gellar, Sarah Michelle: Birth, Apr 14
Geller, Uri: Birth, Dec 20
Gemini Begins, May 21
Gene Autry Show TV Premiere: Anniv, Jul 23
Genealogy Day, Mar 13
General Election Day (US), **Nov 2**
General Electric Theater TV Premiere: Anniv, Feb 1
General Hospital TV Premiere: Anniv, Apr 1
General Motors: Founding Anniv, Sep 16
Geneva Accords: Anniv, Jul 20
Genocide Convention: Anniv, Dec 9
Gentle Ben TV Premiere: Anniv, Sep 10
Gentry, Bobbie: Birth, Jul 27
Geoffreys, Stephen: Birth, Nov 22
Geographers Annual Meeting, Assn American (Philadelphia, PA), **Mar 14**
Geographic Bee Finals, Natl (Washington, DC), **May 25**
Geographic Bee, School Level, Natl, **Jan 2**
Geographic Bee, State Level, Natl, **Apr 2**
George Gobel Show TV Premiere: Anniv, Oct 2
George III: Birth Anniv, Jun 4
George Spelvin Day, Nov 15
George VI's Coronation: Anniv, May 12
George, Jeff: Birth, Dec 8
George, Phyllis: Birth, Jun 24
George, Susan: Birth, Jul 26
Georgia,
  Arts & Crafts Fest (Stone Mtn Village), **Jun 19**
  Atlanta Marathon and Half Marathon (Atlanta), **Nov 25**
  Augusta Futurity (Augusta), **Jan 22**
  Braveheart Scottish Weekend (Moultrie), **Feb 13**
  Camellia Fest (Fort Valley), **Feb 1**
  Cane Grinding and Crafts Fest (Savannah), **Nov 13**
  Chambliss, Saxby: Birth, Nov 10
  Chick-fil-A Peach Bowl (Atlanta), **Jan 2**
  Confederate Memorial Day, **Apr 26**
  Cotton Pickin' Fair (Gay), **May 1**
  1836 Encampment (Lumpkin), **May 29**
  Ethnic Awareness Program (Macon), **Apr 28**
  Family Day Celebration (Dahlonega), **Jul 4**
  FDR Commemorative Ceremony (Warm Springs), **Apr 12**
  Festival 2004: Fest of Fine Arts and Fine Crafts (Dalton), **Sep 18**

Friendly Forest Halloween Hike (Savannah), **Oct 29**
Georgia National Fair (Perry), **Oct 8**
Georgia Pecan Month, Natl, **Nov 1**
Georgia Renaissance Spring Fest (Atlanta), **Apr 17**
Macon, GA's Cherry Blossom Fest, 2004 Intl (Macon), **Mar 19**
May Day (Lumpkin), **May 7**
Memorial Day Ceremonies (Andersonville), **May 30**
Migratory Bird Day, Intl (Savannah), **May 8**
Miller, Zell: Birth, Feb 24
Mossy Creek Barnyard Fest (Warner Robins), **Apr 17**
Mountain Fair (Hiawassee), **Jul 21**
Native American Heritage Day (Jonesboro), **Apr 24**
NCAA Div I Women's Tennis Chmpshps (Athen), **May 20**
Old-Fashioned Christmas Celebration (Dahlonega), **Dec 4**
Peachtree Road Race (Atlanta), **Jul 4**
Perdue, Sonny: Birth, Dec 20
Powers' Crossroads Country Fair/Art Fest (Newnan), **Sep 4**
Prater's Mill Country Fair (Dalton), **Oct 9**
Pro-Am Snipe Excursion and Hunt (Moultrie), **Apr 1**
Ratification Day, **Jan 2**
Rhododendron Fest (Hiawassee), **May 7**
Riverfest (Columbus), **Apr 23**
Savannah Tour of Homes and Gardens (Savannah), **Mar 25**
Sheep to Shawl Festival (Savannah), **Mar 20**
Sherman Enters Atlanta: Anniv, **Sep 2**
Sherman Takes Savannah: Anniv, **Dec 21**
Southern Cyclone: Anniv, **Aug 24**
Steeplechase at Callaway Gardens (Pine Mountain), **Nov 6**
Thomasville's Victorian Christmas (Thomasville), **Dec 9**
Tools and Skills That Built the Colony (Savannah), **Sep 4**
US Open Stock Dog Trials & Farm Fest (Dawsonville), **Oct 1**
War of Jenkin's Ear: Living History (Savannah), **May 29**
Warm Springs Thanksgiving (Warm Springs), **Nov 20**
Wildflower Fest of the Arts (Dahlonega), **May 15**
World Chmpshp Gold Panning Competition (Dahlonega), **May 8**
World's Largest Easter Egg Hunt (Homer), **Apr 6**
WSB-TV Salute 2 America Parade (Atlanta), **Jul 4**
Yellow Daisy Fest (Stone Mountain), **Sep 9**
Georgia (Europe),
  Independence Restoration Day, **May 26**
  Votes Independence, **Mar 31**
Gerard, Gil: Birth, Jan 23
Gere, Richard: Birth, Aug 29
German. See also Octoberfest; Oktoberfest,
  Deutsch Country Days (Marthaville, MO), **Oct 16**
  German-American Day, Natl, **Oct 6**
  German-American Heritage Month, **Oct 1**
  Germanfest (Fort Wayne, IN), **Jun 6**
  Oktoberfest (New Ulm, MN), **Oct 1**
  Oktoberfest (Tulsa, OK), **Oct 11**
  Schmeckfest (Freeman, SD), **Apr 1**
  Wurstfest (New Braunfels, TX), **Oct 29**
Germany,
  Berlin Airlift: Anniv, **Jun 24**
  Berlin International Film Fest (Berlin), **Feb 5**
  Berlin Wall Opened: Anniv, **Nov 9**
  Buss und Bettag, **Nov 17**
  Capital Returns to Berlin: Anniv, **Sep 1**
  Day of Remembrance for Victims of Nazism, **Jan 27**
  Dresden Firebombing, **Feb 13**
  Erntedankfest, **Oct 3**
  Fasching, **Feb 23**
  Fasching Sunday, **Feb 22**
  Frankfurt Book Fair (Frankfurt), **Oct 6**
  Frankfurt Christmas Market (Frankfurt), **Nov 25**
  German Plebiscite: Anniv, **Aug 19**
  German Surrender at Stalingrad: Anniv, **Feb 2**
  Germany Ends Military Ban: Anniv, **Jul 12**
  Hamburg Harbor Birthday, **May 7**
  Kristallnacht: Anniv, **Nov 9**
  Love Parade (Berlin), **Jul 10**
  Munich Fasching Carnival, **Jan 7**
  Nuremberg War Crimes Trial: Anniv, **Nov 20**
  Red Army Departs Berlin: Anniv, **Jun 11**
  Reunification: Anniv, **Oct 3**
  Totensonntag, **Nov 21**
  Volkstrauertag, **Nov 14**
  Wagner Festspiele (Bayreuth), **Jul 25**
  Waldchestag (Frankfurt), **Jun 1**
  Wilhelm II Abdicates: Anniv, **Nov 9**
Germany Invades Poland: Anniv, **Sep 1**
Geronimo: Death Anniv, Feb 17
Gerry, Elbridge: Birth Anniv, Jul 17
Gershwin, George: Birth Anniv, Sep 26
Gershwin, Ira: Birth Anniv, Dec 6
Gertz, Jami: Birth, Oct 28
Get a Different Name Day, Feb 13
Get Organized Week, Oct 3
Get Out of the Doghouse Day, Natl, Jul 19
Get Paid to Shop Week, Feb 1
Get Smart TV Premiere: Anniv, Sep 18
Get to Know an Independent Real Estate Broker Month, Natl, Jan 1
Gets, Malcolm: Birth, Dec 28
Getty, Balthazar: Birth, Jan 22

Getty, Estelle: Birth, Jul 25
Gettysburg Address Memorial Ceremony (Gettysburg, PA), **Nov 19**
Gettysburg Address, Lincoln's: Anniv, Nov 19
Gettysburg Bluegrass Fest (Gettysburg, PA), **May 13**
Gettysburg Outdoor Antique Show (Gettysburg, PA), **May 22**
Getz, Stan: Birth Anniv, Feb 2
Ghana,
  Independence Day, **Mar 6**
  Republic Day, **Jul 1**
  Revolution Day, **Jun 4**
Ghost Tours (New Hope, PA), **Jun 5**
Ghostley, Alice: Birth, Aug 14
Ghosts, Fest of Hungry (China), **Aug 30**
Ghostwriters Month, Natl, **Mar 1**
GI Day, Hug a, Mar 4
Giamatti, Bartlett: Birth Anniv, Apr 4
Giambi, Jason: Birth, Jan 8
Giannini, Giancarlo: Birth, Aug 1
Giant Dipper, Santa Cruz Beach: Anniv, May 17
Gibb, Barry: Birth, Sep 1
Gibb, Robin: Birth, Dec 22
Gibbon, Edward: Birth Anniv, Apr 27
Gibbons, Leeza: Birth, Mar 26
Gibbs, Joe Jackson: Birth, Nov 25
Gibbs, Marla: Birth, Jun 14
Gibbs, Mifflin Wister: Birth Anniv, Apr 28
Gibran, Kahlil: Birth Anniv, Jan 6
Gibson, Althea: Birth, Aug 25
Gibson, Bob: Birth, Nov 9
Gibson, Debbie: Birth, Aug 31
Gibson, Henry: Birth, Sep 21
Gibson, Kirk: Birth, May 28
Gibson, Mel: Birth, Jan 3
Gibson, Thomas: Birth, Jul 3
Gielgud, Sir John: Birth Anniv, Apr 14
Gifford, Frank: Birth, Aug 16
Gifford, Kathie Lee: Birth, Aug 16
Gift Fest, Intl (Fairfield, PA), **Nov 4**
Giguere, Jean-Sebastien: Birth, May 16
Gilbert, John: Birth Anniv, Jul 10
Gilbert, Melissa: Birth, May 8
Gilbert, Sara: Birth, Jan 29
Gilbert, Sir William: Birth Anniv, Nov 18
Gilford, Jack: Birth Anniv, Jul 25
Gillars, Mildred E.: Death Anniv, Jun 25
Gillespie, Dizzy: Birth Anniv, Oct 21
Gilley, Mickey: Birth, Mar 9
Gilliam, Armon: Birth, May 28
Gilliam, Terry: Birth, Nov 22
Gilligan's Island TV Premiere: Anniv, Sep 26
Gillis, Margaret: Birth, Jul 9
Gilmore, Artis: Birth, Sep 21
Gilmour, Dave: Birth, Mar 6
Gilpin, Peri: Birth, May 27
Gilroy Garlic Fest (Gilroy, CA), **Jul 23**
Gingerbread House Day, Dec 12
Gingerbread on Parade (Omaha, NE), **Nov 20**
Gingerbread Village and Bazaar (Middlebury, CT), **Dec 4**
Ginsberg, Allen: Birth Anniv, Jun 3
Ginsburg, Ruth Bader: Birth, Mar 15
Ginza Holiday: Japanese Cultural Fest (Chicago, IL), **Aug 20**
Girl Scout Sabbath, Mar 13
Girl Scout Sunday, Mar 7
Girl Scout Week, Mar 7
Girl Scouts Founding: Anniv, Mar 12
Girlfriend's Day, Aug 1
Girls and Women in Sports Day, Natl, Feb 4
Gish, Lillian: Birth Anniv, Oct 14
Giuliani, Rudolph: Birth, May 28
Givenchy, Hubert de: Birth, Feb 21
Givens, Robin: Birth, Nov 27
Glacier Bay Natl Park: Anniv, Dec 2
Glacier Natl Park: Anniv, May 11
Gladstone, William: Birth Anniv, Dec 29
Glaser, Paul Michael: Birth, Mar 25
Glass Fest, Elwood (Elwood, IN), **Aug 20**
Glass, Ira: Birth, Mar 3
Glass, Philip: Birth, Jan 31
Glass, Ron: Birth, Jul 10
Glaucoma Awareness Month, Natl, **Jan 1**
Glavine, Tom: Birth, Mar 25
GLBT Book Month, Natl, **Jun 1**
Gleason, Jackie: Birth Anniv, Feb 26
Glenn, John: Birth, Jul 18
Glenn, Scott: Birth, Jan 26
Gless, Sharon: Birth, May 31
Glover, Crispin: Birth, Apr 20
Glover, Danny: Birth, Jul 22
Glover, John: Birth, Aug 7
Glover, Savion: Birth, Nov 28
Go Hog Wild—Eat Country Ham Month, Oct 1
Go Nuts Over Peanuts Month, Oct 1
Go On a Field Trip Month, Natl, Oct 1
Goals, Goal Setting (personal and professional growth),
  Be On-Purpose Month, Natl, **Jan 1**
  Business Success Resolutions Month, Intl, **Jan 1**
  Effectiveness Week, Natl, **May 17**
  Evaluate Your Life Day, Oct 19
  Kick-Butt Day, Natl, **Oct 11**
  Kids' Goal Setting Week, **Nov 1**
  New Year's Resolutions Week, **Jan 1**

705

Index — Chase's 2004 Calendar of Events

Take a New Year's Resolution to Stop Smoking, **Jan 1**
Toss Away the Could Haves and Should Haves Day, **Jul 17**
Goat Cook-off, World Chmpshp BBQ/Crafts Fair (Brady, TX), **Sep 4**
God Bless America First Performed: Anniv, **Nov 11**
Godard, Jean Luc: Birth, **Dec 3**
Goddard Day: Anniv, **Mar 16**
Goddard, Robert H.: Birth Anniv, **Oct 5**
Godwin, Mary Wollstonecraft: Birth Anniv, **Apr 27**
Goebbels, Paul Josef: Birth Anniv, **Oct 29**
Goethals, George W.: Birth Anniv, **Jun 29**
Goethe, Johann W.: Birth Anniv, **Aug 28**
Gogol, Nikolai: Birth Anniv, **Mar 31**
Gold Discovery Days (Custer, SD), **Jul 22**
Gold Discovery, California: Anniv, **Jan 24**
Gold Discovery, Klondike Eldorado: Anniv, **Aug 31**
Gold Discovery, Klondike: Anniv, **Aug 16**
Gold Panning Competition, World Chmpshp (Dahlonega, GA), **Apr 17**
Gold Rush Days (Wickenburg, AZ), **Feb 13**
Gold Rush: Whiskey Flat Days (Kernville, CA), **Feb 13**
Gold Star Mother's Day (Pres Proc), **Sep 26**
Gold, Missy: Birth, **Jul 14**
Gold, Tracey: Birth, **May 16**
Goldberg, Rube: Birth Anniv, **Jul 4**
Goldberg, Whoopi: Birth, **Nov 13**
Goldbergs TV Premiere: Anniv, **Jan 17**
Goldblum, Jeff: Birth, **Oct 22**
Golden Aspen Motorcycle Rally (Ruidoso, NM), **Sep 15**
Golden Gate Bridge Opened: Anniv, **May 27**
Golden Girls TV Premiere: Anniv, **Sep 14**
Golden Globe Awards, **Jan 25**
Golden Rule Week, **Apr 1**
Golden Spike Driving: Anniv, **May 10**
Golding, Sir William: Birth Anniv, **Sep 19**
Goldman, William: Birth, **Aug 12**
Goldsmith, Oliver: Birth Anniv, **Nov 10**
Goldwyn, Samuel: Birth Anniv, **Aug 17**
Goldwyn, Tony: Birth, **May 20**
Golf,
  Big 12 Men's Chmpshp (Hutchinson, KS), **Apr 26**
  Big 12 Women's Golf Chmpshp (College Station, TX), **Apr 23**
  Big Ten Men's Golf Chmpshp (Ann Arbor, MI), **May 7**
  Big Ten Women's Chmpshp (Columbus, OH), **Apr 23**
  Bob Hope Chrysler Classic (La Quinta, CA), **Jan 19**
  Chicago Golf Club: Anniv, **Jul 18**
  Curtis Cup (Merseyside, England), **Jun 12**
  First PGA Championship: Anniv, **Apr 10**
  Ford Championship at Doral (Miami, FL), **Mar 1**
  Hogan, Ben: Birth Anniv, **Aug 13**
  Jones, Bobby: Birth Anniv, **Mar 17**
  Nabisco Championship (Rancho Mirage, CA), **Mar 22**
  NAIA Men's Golf Chmpshps, **May 26**
  NAIA Women's Natl Chmpshps, **May 26**
  NCAA Div I Men's Golf Chmpshp (Hot Springs, VA), **Jun 1**
  NCAA Div I Women's Golf Chmpshps (Auburn, AL), **May 18**
  Open Golf Chmpshp (British Open) (Scotland), **Jul 15**
  Ouimet, Francis DeSales: Birth Anniv, **May 8**
  PGA Chmpshp (Kohler, WI), **Aug 9**
  PGA Founded: Anniv, **Jan 17**
  PGA Seniors' Chmpshp (Louisville, KY), **May 24**
  Ryder Cup Matches (Bloomfield Hills, MI), **Sep 14**
  Sarazen, Gene: Birth Anniv, **Feb 27**
  Snead, Sam: Birth Anniv, **May 27**
  Southwest Senior Chmpshp (Yuma, AZ), **Jan 20**
  Texas-Oklahoma Junior Golf Tournament (Wichita Falls, TX), **Jun 21**
  US Amateur Chmpshp (Mamaroneck, NY), **Aug 16**
  US Amateur Public Links Chmpshp (Maple Grove, MN), **Jul 12**
  US Junior Amateur Chmpship (San Francisco, CA), **Jul 27**
  US Open Chmpshp (Southampton, NY), **Jun 17**
  US Senior Open (Golf) Championship (St. Louis, MO), **Jul 29**
  US Women's Amateur Chmpshp (Erie, PA), **Aug 9**
  US Women's Amateur Public Links Chmpshp, **Jun 15**
  US Women's Open Chmpshp (South Hadley, MA), **Jul 1**
  USGA Senior Amateur Chmpshp (Los Angeles, CA), **Oct 9**
  Zaharias, Mildred Babe Didrikson: Birth Anniv, **Jun 26**
Golino, Valeria: Birth, **Oct 22**
Gomez, Scott: Birth, **Dec 23**
Gompers, Samuel: Birth Anniv, **Jan 27**
Gone with the Wind Film Premiere: Anniv, **Dec 15**
Gone with the Wind Published: Anniv, **May 19**
Gong Show TV Premiere: Anniv, **Jun 14**
Gonzales, Pancho: Birth Anniv, **May 9**
Gonzalez, Juan: Birth, **Oct 16**
Good Friday, **Apr 9**
Good Friday Bank Holiday (United Kingdom), **Apr 9**
Good Friday Peace Agreement in Northern Ireland: Anniv, **Apr 10**
Good Morning America TV Premiere: Anniv, **Nov 6**
Good Samaritan Involvement Day, **Mar 13**
Good Sex! with Dr. Ruth Westheimer TV Premiere: Anniv, **Aug 27**
Good Times TV Premiere: Anniv, **Feb 1**
Goodall, Jane: Birth, **Apr 3**

Gooden, Dwight: Birth, **Nov 16**
Goodeve, Grant: Birth, **Jul 6**
Gooding, Cuba, Jr: Birth, **Jan 2**
Goodman, Ellen: Birth, **Apr 11**
Goodman, John: Birth, **Jun 20**
Goodson, Mark: Birth Anniv, **Jan 24**
Goodwill Industries Week, **May 2**
Goodwill: Helms, Edgar J.: Birth Anniv, **Jan 19**
Goof-Off Day, Intl, **Mar 22**
Goolagong, Evonne: Birth, **Jul 31**
Goombay Fest, Miami/Bahamas, **Jun 4**
Goorjian, Michael: Birth, **Feb 4**
Gorbachev, Mikhail: Birth, **Mar 2**
Gordimer, Nadine: Birth, **Nov 20**
Gordon, Jeff: Birth, **Aug 4**
Gordon, Keith: Birth, **Feb 3**
Gordone, Charles: Birth Anniv, **Oct 12**
Gordon-Levitt, Joseph: Birth, **Feb 17**
Gordy, Berry, Jr: Birth, **Nov 28**
Gore, Al: Birth, **Mar 31**
Gore, Lesley: Birth, **May 2**
Gore, Tipper: Birth, **Aug 19**
Gorgas, William Crawford: Birth Anniv, **Oct 3**
Gorilla Born in Captivity, First: Anniv, **Dec 22**
Gorillas: Koko: Birth, **Jul 4**
Gorme, Eydie: Birth, **Aug 16**
Gortner, Marjoe: Birth, **Jan 14**
Gospel. See also Music,
  Chicago Gospel Music Festival (Chicago, IL), **Jun 4**
  Gospel Sing (Arrow Rock, MO), **Apr 25**
  Singing on the Mountain (Linville, NC), **Jun 27**
  Southern Gospel Music Month, **Sep 1**
Gossage, Goose: Birth, **Jul 5**
Gosselaar, Mark-Paul: Birth, **Mar 1**
Gossett, Louis, Jr: Birth, **May 27**
Gossip Day, Intl End, **Nov 6**
Gottlieb, Robert: Birth, **Apr 29**
Gottschalk, Louis Moreau: Birth Anniv, **May 8**
Gould, Chester: Birth Anniv, **Nov 20**
Gould, Elliott: Birth, **Aug 29**
Gould, Harold: Birth, **Dec 10**
Gould, Stephen Jay: Birth Anniv, **Sep 10**
Goulet, Robert: Birth, **Nov 26**
Goya, Francisco Jose de: Birth Anniv, **Mar 30**
Grace, Mark: Birth, **Jun 28**
Grace, Topher: Birth, **Jul 19**
Graduate and Professional Student Appreciation Week, **Apr 5**
Grady, Don: Birth, **Jun 8**
Graf, Steffi: Birth, **Jun 14**
Graffman, Gary: Birth, **Oct 14**
Grafton, Sue: Birth, **Apr 24**
Graham, Billy: Birth, **Nov 7**
Graham, Calvin ("Baby Vet"): Birth Anniv, **Apr 3**
Graham, Heather: Birth, **Jan 29**
Graham, Lauren: Birth, **Mar 16**
Graham, Lindsey: Birth, **Jul 9**
Graham, Martha: Balanchine-Graham Collaboration: Anniv, **May 14**
Graham, Martha: Birth Anniv, **May 11**
Graham, Martha: Maple Leaf Rag Premiere: Anniv, **Oct 2**
Graham, Otto: Birth, **Dec 6**
Graham, Robert: Birth, **Nov 9**
Grahame, Kenneth: Birth Anniv, **Mar 8**
Gramm, Phil: Birth, **Jul 8**
Grammer, Kelsey: Birth, **Feb 21**
Grammy Awards, **Feb 8**
Granato, Cammi: Birth, **Mar 25**
Grand Canyon Natl Park Established: Anniv, **Feb 26**
Grand Excursion 2004 (IA, IL, MN), **Jun 25**
Grand Illumination (Lahaska, PA), **Nov 19**
Grand Militia Muster (St. Mary's City, MD), **Oct 16**
Grand Ole Opry Broadcast, First: Anniv, **Dec 10**
Grand Rapids Sport, Fishing & Travel Show (Grand Rapids, MI), **Mar 18**
Grand Teton Music Fest (Teton Village, WY), **Jun 29**
Grand Teton Natl Park Established: Anniv, **Feb 1**
Grandmother's Day in Florida, **Oct 10**
Grandparents' Day, Natl, **Sep 12**
Grandy, Fred: Birth, **Jun 29**
Grange Founding, Natl: Anniv, **Dec 4**
Grange Month, **Apr 1**
Grange, Red: Birth Anniv, **Jun 13**
Granholm, Jennifer: Birth, **Feb 5**
Grant, Amy: Birth, **Nov 25**
Grant, Cary: Birth Anniv, **Jan 18**
Grant, Harvey: Birth, **Jul 4**
Grant, Horace: Birth, **Jul 4**
Grant, Hugh: Birth, **Sep 9**
Grant, Jennifer: Birth, **Feb 26**
Grant, Julia Dent: Birth Anniv, **Jan 26**
Grant, Richard E.: Birth, **May 5**
Grant, Ulysses S.,
  Battle of Chattanooga: Anniv, **Nov 24**
  Battle of Cold Harbor: Anniv, **Jun 3**
  Battle of Shiloh: Anniv, **Apr 6**
  Battle of the Wilderness: Anniv, **May 5**
  Birth Anniv, **Apr 27**
  Commissioned Commander: Anniv, **Mar 9**
  Put in Charge of Mississippi: Anniv, **Oct 16**
  Speech of Apology: Anniv, **Dec 5**
  Surrender of Fort Donelson: Anniv, **Feb 16**
  Vicksburg Surrenders: Anniv, **Jul 3**
  Battle of Spotsylvania: Anniv, **May 12**

Grantsville Days (Grantsville, MD), **Jun 25**
Grape Jamboree, Geneva Area (Geneva, OH), **Sep 25**
Grapes of Wrath Published: Anniv, **Apr 14**
Grass, Gunter: Birth, **Oct 16**
Grassle, Karen: Birth, **Feb 25**
Grassley, Charles: Birth, **Sep 17**
Gratton, Chris: Birth, **Jul 5**
Graves' Disease Awareness Week, **Jan 12**
Graves, Peter: Birth, **Mar 18**
Graves, Rupert: Birth, **Jun 30**
Gray, Asa: Birth Anniv, **Nov 18**
Gray, Erin: Birth, **Jan 7**
Gray, Harold Lincoln: Birth Anniv, **Jan 20**
Gray, Linda: Birth, **Sep 12**
Gray, Macy: Birth, **Dec 6**
Gray, Robert, Circumnavigates the Earth: Anniv, **Apr 10**
Gray, Spalding: Birth, **Jun 5**
Grayson, Kathryn: Birth, **Feb 9**
Great (Holy) Week, **Apr 4**
Great American Meatout, **Mar 20**
Great American Smokeout, **Nov 18**
Great American Smokeout Day, Natl (Pres Proc), **Nov 18**
Great American Warm-Up, **Nov 5**
Great Backyard Bird Count, **Feb 13**
Great Britain Formed: Anniv, **May 1**
Great NY State Snow & Track Expo (Albany, NY), **Nov 5**
Great Outdoors Show, Northeast (Albany, NY), **Mar 19**
Great Smoky Mountains Natl Park Established: Anniv, **Jun 15**
Greatest Show on Earth Formed: Anniv, **Mar 28**
Greco, Buddy: Birth, **Aug 14**
Greco, Jose: Birth, **Dec 23**
Greece,
  Dumb Week, **Mar 28**
  Games of the XXVIII Olympiad (Athens), **Aug 13**
  Independence Day, **Mar 25**
  Midwife's Day or Women's Day, **Jan 8**
  Ochi Day, **Oct 28**
  Paralympic Games 2004 (Athens), **Sep 17**
Greek Independence Day (Pres Proc), **Mar 25**
Greeley, Father Andrew: Birth, **Feb 5**
Greeley, Horace: Birth Anniv, **Feb 3**
Green Monday (Cyprus), **Feb 23**
Green, Al: Birth, **Apr 13**
Green, Brian: Birth, **Jul 15**
Green, Hetty: Birth Anniv, **Nov 21**
Green, Hubie: Birth, **Dec 28**
Green, Seth: Birth, **Feb 8**
Greenberg, Hank: Birth Anniv, **Jan 1**
Greene, Bob: Birth, **Mar 10**
Greene, Graham: Birth Anniv, **Oct 2**
Greene, Nathaniel: Birth Anniv, **Aug 7**
Greene, Shecky: Birth, **Apr 8**
Greenfield, Jeff: Birth, **Jun 10**
Greenland: National Day, **Jun 21**
Greenpeace Founded: Anniv, **Sep 15**
Greenpeace: Rainbow Warrior Sinking: Anniv, **Jul 10**
Greensboro Sit-in: Anniv, **Feb 1**
Greenspan, Alan: Birth, **Mar 6**
Greenspan, Alan: Irrational Exuberance Enters Lexicon: Anniv, **Dec 5**
Greenwich Mean Time Begins: Anniv, **Sep 25**
Greenwood, Joan: Birth Anniv, **Mar 4**
Greer, Germaine: Birth, **Jan 29**
Gregg, Judd: Birth, **Feb 14**
Gregorian Calendar Adjustment: Anniv, **Oct 4**
Gregorian Calendar Day, **Feb 24**
Gregory, Bettina: Birth, **Jun 4**
Gregory, Cynthia: Birth, **Jul 8**
Gregory, Dick: Birth, **Oct 12**
Greist, Kim: Birth, **May 12**
Grenada,
  Emancipation Day, **Aug 2**
  Independence Day, **Feb 7**
  Invasion by US: Anniv, **Oct 25**
Grenadines and Saint Vincent: Independence Day, **Oct 27**
Gretzky, Wayne: Birth, **Jan 26**
Grey, Jennifer: Birth, **Mar 26**
Grey, Joel: Birth, **Apr 11**
Grey, Zane: Birth Anniv, **Jan 31**
Grieco, Richard: Birth, **Mar 23**
Grieg, Edvard: Birth Anniv, **Jun 15**
Grieg, Edvard: Birth Anniv Celebration (Norway), **Jun 15**
Grier, David Alan: Birth, **Jun 30**
Grier, Pam: Birth, **May 26**
Grier, Roosevelt (Rosey): Birth, **Jul 14**
Griese, Bob: Birth, **Feb 3**
Grieve, Ben: Birth, **May 4**
Griffey, Ken: Birth, **Nov 21**
Griffin, John H.: Birth Anniv, **Jun 16**
Griffin, Kathy: Birth, **Nov 4**
Griffin, Merv: Birth, **Jul 6**
Griffith, Andy, Show TV Premiere: Anniv, **Oct 3**
Griffith, Andy: Birth, **Jun 1**
Griffith, D.W.: Birth Anniv, **Jan 22**
Griffith, Melanie: Birth, **Aug 9**
Griffith, Yolanda: Birth, **Mar 1**
Griffiths, Martha: Speech Against Sex Discrimination, **Feb 8**
Grimaldi, Joseph: Birth Anniv, **Dec 18**

☆ Chase's 2004 Calendar of Events ☆

Grimes, Gary: Birth, Jun 2
Grimke, Sarah: Birth Anniv, Nov 26
Grimm, Jacob: Birth Anniv, Jan 4
Grimm, Wilhelm: Birth Anniv, Feb 24
Grint, Rupert: Birth, Aug 24
Grisham, John: Birth, Feb 8
Grodin, Charles: Birth, Apr 21
Groening, Matt: Birth, Feb 15
Gromyko, Andrei Andreyevich: Birth Anniv, Jul 18
Gross, Mary: Birth, Mar 25
Gross, Michael: Birth, Jun 21
Grotius, Hugo: Birth Anniv, Apr 10
Grouch Day, Natl, Oct 15
Ground Zero Recovery and Cleanup Ends: Anniv, May 30
Groundhog Day, Feb 2
Groundhog Day (Punxsutawney, PA), Feb 2
Groundhog Day (Sun Prairie, WI), Feb 2
Groundhog Days (Woodstock, IL), Jan 31
Groundhog Job Shadow Day, Feb 2
Groundhog Run (Kansas City, MO), Feb 8
Grubstake Days (Yucca Valley, CA), May 27
Grump Out, Great American, May 26
Gruntled Workers Day, Jul 13
Guadalajara Intl Book Fair (Mexico), Nov 27
Guadalcanal, Allies Retake: Anniv, Feb 9
Guadalupe Hidalgo, Treaty of: Anniv, Feb 2
Guadalupe Natl Park Established: Anniv, Sep 30
Guadalupe, Day of Our Lady of, Dec 12
Guam,
  Discovery Day, Mar 1
  Lady of Camarin Day, Dec 8
  Liberation Day, Jul 21
  Magellan Day, Mar 1
  Spanish-American War: Surrender, to US: Anniv, Jun 20
Guatemala,
  Armed Forces Day, Jun 30
  Independence Day, Sep 15
  Kite Fest of Santiago Sacatepequez, Nov 1
  Revolution Day, Oct 20
Guccione, Bob: Birth, Dec 17
Guernica Massacre: Anniv, Apr 26
Guerrero, Vladimir: Birth, Feb 9
Guest, Christopher: Birth, Feb 5
Guest, Edgar A.: Birth Anniv, Aug 20
Guest, Lance: Birth, Jul 21
Guggenheim, Simon: Birth Anniv, Dec 30
Gugliotta, Tom: Birth, Dec 19
Guiding Light TV Premiere: Anniv, Jun 26
Guidry, Ron: Birth, Aug 28
Guilfoyle, Paul: Birth, Jul 12
Guillaume, Robert: Birth, Nov 30
Guillotin, Joseph: Birth Anniv, May 28
Guinea: Anniversary of the Second Republic, Apr 3
Guinea: Independence Day, Oct 2
Guinea-Bissau,
  Colonization Martyr's Day, Aug 3
  Independence Day, Sep 24
  National Holiday, Sep 12
  Natl Heroes Day, Jan 20
  Re-Adjustment Movement's Day, Nov 14
Guinn, Kenny: Birth, Aug 24
Guinness, Sir Alec: Birth Anniv, Apr 2
Guisewite, Cathy Lee: Birth, Sep 5
Gulf of Tonkin Resolution: Anniv, Aug 7
Gumbel, Bryant: Birth, Sep 29
Gumbel, Greg: Birth, May 3
Gumbo Fest (Bridge City, LA), Oct 8
Gumby Show TV Premiere: Anniv, Mar 16
Gun Shows, Sales, Competition,
  Ocean County Decoy/Gun Show (Tuckerton, NJ), Sep 25
  Texas Collectors' Gun & Knife Show (Wichita Falls, TX), Jan 24
  Walsh Invitational Rifle Tourn (Cincinnati, OH), Nov 5
Gunn, Moses: Birth Anniv, Oct 2
Gunpowder Plot Trial: Anniv, Jan 27
Gunsmoke TV Premiere: Anniv, Sep 10
Gutenberg Bible Published: Anniv, Sep 30
Guterson, David: Birth, May 4
Guth, Alan: Birth, Feb 27
Guthrie, Arlo: Birth, Jul 10
Guthrie, Janet: Birth, Mar 7
Guthrie, Woody: Birth Anniv, Jul 14
Guttenberg, Steve: Birth, Aug 24
Guy, Jasmine: Birth, Mar 10
Guyana: National Day, Feb 23
Gwathmey, Charles: Birth, Jun 19
Gwinnett, Button: Death Anniv, May 16
Gwynn, Tony: Birth, May 9
Gwynne, Fred: Birth Anniv, Jul 10
Gymnastics,
  Big Ten Men's Chmpshp (Champaign, IL), Mar 19
  Big Ten Women's Chmpshp (Minneapolis, MN), Mar 20
  Big 12 Women's Chmpshp (Columbia, MO), Mar 20
  NCAA Div I Women's (Los Angeles, CA), Apr 15
Gypsy Rose Lee (Rose L Hovick): Birth Anniv, Feb 9
Haas, Lukas: Birth, Apr 16
Habitat Day, World (UN), Oct 4
Habitat for Humanity Building on the Dream, Jan 16
Habitat for Humanity Intl March Gladness, Mar 1
Habitat for Humanity's Intl Building on Faith Week, Sep 13
Hackman, Gene: Birth, Jan 30

Hadassah: Anniv, Feb 24
Haden, Pat: Birth, Jan 23
Hagar, Sammy: Birth, Oct 13
Hagel, Chuck: Birth, Oct 4
Hagerty, Julie: Birth, Jun 15
Haggard, Merle: Birth, Apr 6
Hagler, Marvelous Marvin: Birth, May 23
Hagman, Larry: Birth, Sep 21
Haid, Charles: Birth, Jun 2
Haig, Alexander: I Am in Control Day: Anniv, Mar 30
Hailey, Arthur: Birth, Apr 5
Haim, Corey: Birth, Dec 23
Hair Broadway Opening: Anniv, Mar 28
Hairball Awareness Day, Natl, Apr 30
Hairstylist Day, Apr 30
Haiti,
  Ancestors' Day, Jan 2
  Army Day, Nov 18
  Discovery Day: Anniv, Dec 5
  Flag and University Day, May 18
  Independence Day, Jan 1
Haitian Heritage Month, May 1
HAL (computer): Birth, Jan 12
Halas, George: Birth Anniv, Feb 2
Halberstam, David: Birth, Apr 10
Halcyon Days, Dec 14
Hale, Barbara: Birth, Apr 18
Hale, Nathan: Birth Anniv, Jun 6
Haleakala Natl Park Established: Anniv, Sep 30
Haley, Alex Palmer: Birth Anniv, Aug 11
Halfway Point of 2004, Jul 1
Halfway Point of Autumn, Nov 6
Halfway Point of Spring, May 5
Halfway Point of Summer, Aug 6
Halfway Point of Winter, Feb 4
Halifax Busker Fest, Intl (Halifax, NS, Canada), Aug 5
Halifax Independence Day (NC), Apr 12
Hall, Anthony Michael: Birth, Apr 14
Hall, Arsenio: Birth, Feb 12
Hall, Daryl: Birth, Oct 11
Hall, Deidre: Birth, Oct 31
Hall, Donald A.: Birth, Sep 20
Hall, Edd: Birth, Dec 7
Hall, Lyman: Birth Anniv, Apr 12
Hall, Monty: Birth, Aug 25
Hall, Tom T.: Birth, May 25
Halley, Edmund: Birth Anniv, Nov 8
Hallmark Hall of Fame TV Premiere: Anniv, Jan 6
Halloween,
  Bloody Brewery in 3-D (Columbus, OH), Oct 1
  Boo at the Zoo (Cleveland, OH), Oct 22
  Bring Your Jack-O-Lantern to Work Day, Oct 29
  Creepy Tales: Haunted History (Staunton, VA), Oct 29
  Devil's Night, Oct 30
  Emma Crawford Fest and Memorial Coffin Race (Manitou Springs, CO), Oct 30
  Family Halloween, A (Woodstock, VT), Oct 24
  Fantasy Fest (Key West, FL), Oct 22
  Frankenstein Friday, Oct 29
  Friendly Forest Halloween Hike (Savannah, GA), Oct 29
  Ghost Tales Around the Campfire (Washington, MS), Oct 29
  Great Pumpkin Carve (Chadds Ford, PA), Oct 21
  Halloween (Arapahoe, NE), Oct 31
  Halloween Haunted Walk and Carnival (Brooklyn, NY), Oct 30
  Hallowe'en or All Hallow's Eve, Oct 31
  Halloween Parade (Toms River, NJ), Oct 30
  Halloween Trail (Worthington, OH), Oct 30
  Haunted Refrigerator Night, Oct 30
  Haute Dog Charity Howl'oween Parade (Long Beach, CA), Oct 31
  Knock-Knock Day, Natl, Oct 31
  Literally, A Haunted House (New Albany, IN), Oct 1
  Magic Day, Natl, Oct 31
  Monster Myths by Moonlight (Milford, KS), Oct 16
  Samhain, Oct 31
  Scare a Friend Day, Oct 1
  Sea Witch Halloween Fest (Rehoboth Beach/Dewey Beach, DE), Oct 29
  Trick or Treat or Beggar's Night, Oct 31
  UNICEF Day, Natl (Pres Proc), Oct 31
  Wisconsin Dells Autumn Harvest Fest (Wisconsin Dells, WI), Oct 23
  WMAS Annual Halloween Ball (Springfield, MA), Oct 29
Halloween Safety Month, Oct 1
Halsey, William "Bull": Birth Anniv, Oct 30
Hamburger Celeb, Home of the (Seymour, WI), Aug 7
Hamburger Hill, Battle of: Anniversary, May 11
Hamburger Month, Natl, May 1
Hamel, Veronica: Birth, Nov 20
Hamill, Mark: Birth, Sep 25
Hamilton, Alexander: Birth Anniv, Jan 11
Hamilton, Alexander: Duel with Aaron Burr: Anniv, Jul 11
Hamilton, Alice: Birth Anniv, Feb 27
Hamilton, George: Birth, Aug 12
Hamilton, Linda: Birth, Sep 26
Hamilton, Scott: Birth, Aug 28
Hamlin, Hannibal: Birth Anniv, Aug 27
Hamlin, Harry: Birth, Oct 30
Hamlisch, Marvin: Birth, Jun 2
Hamm, Mia: Birth, May 17

Hamm, Morgan: Birth, Sep 24
Hamm, Paul: Birth, Sep 24
Hammer, Armand: Birth Anniv, May 21
Hammer, M.C.: Birth, Mar 30
Hammett, Dashiell: Birth Anniv, May 27
Hammon, Jupiter: Birth Anniv, Oct 17
Hampton, James: Birth, Jul 9
Hampton, Lionel: Birth Anniv, Apr 20
Hampton, Mike: Birth, Sep 9
Hancock, Herbie: Birth, Apr 12
Hancock, John: Birth Anniv, Jan 23
Hancock, Winfield Scott: Birth Anniv, Feb 14
Handel, George Frederick: Birth Anniv, Feb 23
Handwriting Analysis Week, Natl, Jan 19
Handwriting Day, Natl, Jan 23
Handy, W.C., Fest (Florence, AL), Jul 25
Handy, William C.: Birth Anniv, Nov 16
Hang Around Victor Day (Victor, NY), Sep 11
Hangul (Korea), Oct 9
Hanks, Tom: Birth, Jul 9
Hanna, William: Birth Anniv, Jul 14
Hannah, Daryl: Birth, Dec 3
Hannukah: See Chanukah, Dec 8
Hansberry, Lorraine: Birth Anniv, May 19
Hansen, Beck: Birth, Jul 8
Hansom, Joseph: Birth Anniv, Oct 26
Hanson, Howard: Birth Anniv, Oct 28
Hanson, Isaac: Birth, Nov 17
Happiness: Hunt for Happiness Week, Jan 18
Happy Birthday to "Happy Birthday to You", Jun 27
Happy Days TV Premiere: Anniv, Jan 15
Happy Mew Year for Cats Day, Jan 2
Harbaugh, Jim: Birth, Dec 23
Hardaway, Penny: Birth, Jul 18
Hardaway, Tim: Birth, Sep 1
Harden, Marcia Gay: Birth, Aug 14
Harding, Florence: Birth Anniv, Aug 15
Harding, Tonya: Birth, Nov 12
Harding, Warren G.: Birth Anniv, Nov 2
Harding, Warren G.: First Radio Broadcast, Jun 14
Hardison, Kadeem: Birth, Jul 24
Hardy, Oliver: Birth Anniv, Jan 18
Harewood, Dorian: Birth, Aug 6
Hargitay, Mariska: Birth, Jan 23
Hari, Mata: Execution Anniv, Oct 15
Harkin, Thomas R.: Birth, Nov 19
Harlem Globetrotters Play First Game: Anniv, Jan 7
Harmon, Angie: Birth, Aug 10
Harmon, Mark: Birth, Sep 2
Harmonic Convergence: Anniv, Aug 16
Harper, Jessica: Birth, Oct 10
Harper, Valerie: Birth, Aug 22
Harrelson, Woody: Birth, Jul 23
Harrington, Pat, Jr: Birth, Aug 13
Harris, Ed: Birth, Nov 28
Harris, Emmylou: Birth, Apr 2
Harris, Franco: Birth, Mar 7
Harris, Joel Chandler: Birth Anniv, Dec 9
Harris, Julie: Birth, Dec 2
Harris, Lou: Birth, Jan 6
Harris, Mel: Birth, Jul 12
Harris, Neil Patrick: Birth, Jun 15
Harris, Patricia Roberts: Birth Anniv, May 31
Harris, Richard: Birth Anniv, Oct 1
Harris, Roy: Birth Anniv, Feb 12
Harrison, Anna: Birth Anniv, Jul 25
Harrison, Benjamin, Christmas at Home (Indianapolis, IN), Nov 22
Harrison, Benjamin: Birth Anniv, Aug 20
Harrison, Benjamin: Birth Celeb (Indianapolis, IN), Aug 20
Harrison, Benjamin: Presidents' Day: Live From Delaware St (Indianapolis, IN), Feb 16
Harrison, Caroline L.S.: Birth Anniv, Oct 1
Harrison, George: Birth Anniv, Feb 25
Harrison, Gregory: Birth, May 31
Harrison, Mary: Birth Anniv, Apr 30
Harrison, Rex: Birth Anniv, Mar 5
Harrison, William Henry: Birth Anniv, Feb 9
Harrold, Kathryn: Birth, Aug 2
Harry (Prince): Birth, Sep 15
Harry, Debbie: Birth, Jul 1
Hart, Charles: Birth, Jun 3
Hart, Gary: Birth, Nov 28
Hart, John: Death Anniv, May 11
Hart, Mary: Birth, Nov 8
Hart, Melissa Joan: Birth, Apr 18
Harte, Bret: Birth Anniv, Aug 25
Hartley, Mariette: Birth, Jun 21
Hartman Black, Lisa: Birth, Jun 1
Hartman, David: Birth, May 19
Hartnett, Josh: Birth, Jul 21
Hartville Annual Fall Fest (Hartville, MO), Oct 16
Haru-No-Yabuiri (Japan), Jan 16
Harvard Univ Founded: Anniv, Oct 28
Harvard, John: Day, Nov 26
Harvest Fest (Hood River, OR), Oct 15
Harvest Moon, Sep 28
Harvest Weekends (Bryan, TX), Jul 23
Harvey, Paul: Birth, Sep 4
Harvey, Steve: Birth, Nov 23
Harvey, William: Birth Anniv, Apr 1
Harwell, Ernie: Birth, Jan 25
Hasek, Dominik: Birth, Jan 29
Hasselhoff, David: Birth, Jul 17
Hastert, Dennis: Birth, Jan 2

707

Index ☆ Chase's 2004 Calendar of Events ☆

Hat—Health

Hat Month, Fall, Sep 1
Hat Month, Straw, Apr 1
Hatch, Orrin: Birth, Mar 22
Hatcher, Teri: Birth, Dec 8
Hate Week, Apr 4
Hatfield-McCoy Feud Erupts: Anniv, Aug 7
Hatsume Fair (Delray Beach, FL), Feb 28
Hauer, Rutger: Birth, Jan 23
Haunted Refrigerator Night, Oct 30
Have a Bad Day Day, Nov 19
Have Gun Will Travel TV Premiere: Anniv, Sep 14
Havel, Vaclav: Birth, Oct 5
Havers, Nigel: Birth, Nov 6
Havlicek, John: Birth, Apr 8
Havoc, June: Birth, Nov 8
Hawaii,
  Admission Day Holiday, Aug 20
  Akaka, Daniel K.: Birth, Sep 11
  Aloha Fest Downtown Ho'olaule'a (Honolulu), Sep 17
  Aloha Fest Floral Parade (Honolulu), Sep 18
  Aloha Fest Opening Ceremony & Royal Pa'ina (Honolulu), Sep 10
  American Psychological Assn Annual Meeting (Honolulu), Jul 28
  Discoverers' Day, Oct 11
  Haleakala Natl Park Established: Anniv, Sep 30
  Hawaii Statehood: Anniv, Aug 21
  Hawaii Volcanoes Natl Park Established: Anniv, Aug 1
  Hula Bowl Maui All Star Classic (Maui), Jan 17
  Inouye, Daniel: Birth, Sep 7
  King Kamehameha I Day, Jun 11
  Lei Day, May 1
  Lingle, Linda: Birth, Jun 4
  Merrie Monarch Fest (Hilo), Apr 11
  Nissan Xterra World Championship (Maui), Oct 24
  Prince Jonah Kuhio Kalanianole Day, Mar 26
  Queen Liliuokalani Deposed: Anniv, Jan 17
  Triple Crown of Surfing (Oahu), Nov 9
  Waikiki Roughwater Swim (Honolulu), Sep 6
Hawaii Annexed by US: Anniv, Jul 7
Hawk, Tony: Birth, May 12
Hawke, Ethan: Birth, Nov 6
Hawking, Stephen: Birth, Jan 8
Hawkins, Hersey: Birth, Sep 29
Hawn, Goldie: Birth, Nov 21
Haworth, Cheryl Ann: Birth, Apr 18
Hawthorne, Nathaniel: Birth Anniv, Jul 4
Hayakawa, Samuel: Birth Anniv, Jul 18
Hayden, Tom: Birth, Dec 11
Haydn, Franz Joseph: Birth Anniv, Mar 31
Hayek, Salma: Birth, Sep 2
Hayes Code: Pre-Will Hayes Movie Day, Feb 14
Hayes, Helen: Birth Anniv, Oct 10
Hayes, Ira Hamilton: Birth Anniv, Jan 12
Hayes, Isaac: Birth, Aug 20
Hayes, Lucy: Birth Anniv, Aug 28
Hayes, Rutherford B.: Birth Anniv, Oct 4
Hayes, Sean P.: Birth, Jun 26
Haymarket Pardon: Anniv, Jun 26
Haymarket Square Riot: Anniv, May 4
Hay-on-Wye Fest of Literature (Hay-on-Wye, Wales), May 28
Hays, Robert: Birth, Jul 24
Haysbert, Dennis: Birth, Jun 2
Hazel TV Premiere: Anniv, Sep 28
Headache Awareness Week, Natl, Jun 6
Headache Fdtn Fundraiser, Natl (New York, NY), Apr 17
Headly, Glenne: Birth, Mar 13
Heald, Anthony: Birth, Aug 25
Health and Welfare,
  Act Happy Day, Mar 15
  Adoption Week, Natl, Nov 21
  Adult Day Services Assn Conference, Natl (New Orleans, LA), Jan 30
  Adult Immunization Awareness Week, Natl, Oct 10
  AIDS Awareness Month, Natl, Nov 1
  AIDS First Noted: Anniv, Jun 5
  Alcohol and Other Drug-Related Birth Defects Week, Natl, May 9
  Alcohol Awareness Month, Apr 1
  Alcohol Screening Day, Natl, Apr 8
  Alcohol-Free Weekend, Apr 2
  Allergy/Asthma Awareness Month, Natl, May 1
  Alzheimer's Disease Month, Natl, Nov 1
  AMA Founded: Anniv, May 5
  AMD/Low Vision Awareness Month, Feb 1
  American Dental Assn: Annual Session (Philadelphia, PA), Sep 30
  American Massage Therapy Assn, Natl Conv (Nashville, TN), Oct 6
  American Red Cross: Founding Anniv, May 21
  Anesthetic First Used in Surgery: Anniv, Mar 30
  Animal Poison Prevention Week, Natl, Mar 14
  Anti-Boredom Month, Natl, Jul 1
  Anxiety Disorders Screening Day, Natl, May 5
  Aphasia Awareness Month, Natl, Jun 1
  Aplastic Anemia Awareness Week, Natl, Dec 1
  Arthritis Month, Natl, May 1
  Artificial Heart Transplant: Anniv, Dec 2
  Assisted Living Week, Natl, Sep 12
  Athletic Training Month, Natl, Mar 1
  Attention Deficit Hyperactivity Disorder Month, Sep 1
  Autism Awareness Month, Natl, Apr 1
  Backpack Safety America Month, Sep 1
  Balance Awareness Week, Sep 19
  Better Hearing and Speech Month, May 1
  Birth Control Clinic Opened, First: Anniv, Oct 16
  Birth Control Pills Sold: Anniv, Aug 18
  Brain Awareness Week, Intl, Mar 15
  Breast Cancer Awareness Month, Natl, Oct 1
  Breast Cancer Awareness Month, Natl (Pres Proc), Oct 1
  Caesarean Section, First: Anniv, Jan 14
  Caffeine Awareness Month, Natl, Mar 1
  Cancer Control Month (Pres Proc), Apr 1
  Cancer from the Sun Month, Jun 1
  Cancer Prevention Month, Natl, Jan 1
  Cancer Survivors Day, Natl, Jun 6
  Cardiac Rehabilitation Week, Feb 8
  Cataract Awareness Month, Aug 1
  Celiac Sprue Awareness Month, Oct 1
  Child Health Day (Pres Proc), Oct 4
  Child Vision Awareness Month, Jun 1
  Childhood Depression Awareness Day, May 4
  Children's Dental Health Month, Natl, Feb 1
  Children's Eye Health and Safety Month, Aug 1
  Children's Miracle Network Celebration, Jun 4
  Christmas Seal Campaign, Sep 1
  Chronic Fatigue Syndrome Awareness Month, Natl, Mar 1
  Cigarettes Reported Hazardous: Anniv, Jan 11
  Clean Air Month, May 1
  Colorectal Cancer Awareness Month, Natl, Mar 1
  Colorectal Cancer Education/Awareness Month, Dec 1
  Condom Week, Natl, Feb 14
  Congenital Heart Defect Awareness Day, Feb 14
  COPD Awareness Month, Natl, Nov 1
  Correct Posture Month, Natl, May 1
  COSAC Annual Conference, May 7
  DAV Day, Natl, Feb 9
  Deaf History Month, Mar 13
  Dental Awareness Month, Intl, May 1
  Dental Hygiene Month, Natl, Oct 1
  Depression Education and Awareness Month, Natl, Oct 1
  Depression Screening Day, Natl, Oct 7
  Diabetes Assn Alert Day, American, Mar 23
  Diabetes Month, American, Nov 1
  Diabetic Eye Disease Month, Nov 1
  Diet Resolution Week, Jan 1
  Doctor-Patient Trust Day, Mar 17
  Doctors' Day, Mar 30
  Dollars Against Diabetes (DAD's) Day, Jun 18
  Donate Life Month, Natl, Apr 1
  Donor Sabbath, Natl, Nov 12
  Down Syndrome Month, Natl, Oct 1
  Eat Better, Eat Together Month, Oct 1
  Eating Disorders Awareness Week, Natl, Feb 22
  Emergency Medical Services Week, Natl, May 16
  Emotional Wellness Month, Oct 1
  Epilepsy Awareness Month, Nov 1
  Eye Donor Month, Natl, Mar 1
  Eye Injury Prevention Month, Jul 1
  Family Fit Lifestyle Month, Jan 1
  Family Health and Fitness Days—USA, Sep 25
  Family Sexuality Education Month, Natl, Oct 1
  Feng Shui Awareness Day, Intl, Apr 8
  Fibromyalgia Education & Awareness Month, May 1
  Fireworks Eye Safety Month, Jun 1
  5-A-Day Month, Natl, Sep 1
  Food Allergy Awareness Month, Sep 1
  Fresh Breath Day, Natl, Aug 6
  Glaucoma Awareness Month, Natl, Jan 1
  Goof-Off Day, Intl, Mar 22
  Graves' Disease Awareness Week, Jan 12
  Great American Low-Cholesterol, Low-Fat Pizza Bake, Sep 1
  Great American Smokeout, Nov 18
  Great American Smokeout Day, Natl (Pres Proc), Nov 18
  Handwriting Analysis Week, Natl, Jan 19
  Have a Heart Day, Natl, Feb 14
  Headache Awareness Week, Natl, Jun 6
  Headache Fdtn Fundraiser, Natl (New York, NY), Apr 17
  Health and Happiness with Hypnosis Day, Jul 27
  Health Care Center Week, Natl (Pres Proc), Aug 15
  Health Care Diversity Month, Mar 1
  Health Education Week, Natl, Oct 18
  Health Literacy Month, Oct 1
  Healthy Vision Month, May 1
  Healthy Weight Week, Jan 18
  Heart Failure Awareness Week, Feb 15
  Heart Month, American, Feb 1
  Heart Month, American (Pres Proc), Feb 1
  Heart Transplant, First: Anniv, Dec 3
  Helen Keller Deaf-Blindness Awareness Week, Jun 27
  Help Someone See Week (Rockford, OH), Mar 7
  Hemochromatosis Screening Awareness Month, Jul 1
  Hepatitis Awareness Month, Natl, May 1
  Herbal/Prescription Awareness Month, Jul 1
  HIV Testing Day, Natl, Jun 27
  Home & Sports Eye Health and Safety Month, Sep 1
  Hospice Month, Natl, Nov 1
  Houston Marathon (Houston, TX), Jan 18
  Hunger Awareness Day, Natl, Jun 5
  Huntington's Disease Awareness Month, May 1
  Hypnotize Yourself Out of Pain Now Day, Dec 1
  Immunization Awareness Month, Natl, Aug 1
  Infection Control Week, Intl, Oct 18
  Infertility Survival Day, Natl, May 2
  Insulin First Isolated: Anniv, Jul 27
  Invisible Chronic Illness Awareness Week, Natl (San Diego, CA), Sep 20
  Jackie Mayer Rehab Center Day, Oct 6
  Jerry Lewis Muscular Dystrophy Association Telethon, Sep 5
  Kidney Month, Natl, Mar 1
  Lee National Denim Day, Oct 8
  Lister, Joseph: Birth Anniv, Apr 5
  Liver Awareness Month, Natl, Oct 1
  Long Term Care Planning Week, Natl, Oct 1
  Lose Weight/Feel Great Week, Natl, Jan 1
  Lung Cancer Awareness Month, Nov 1
  Lupus Alert Day, Apr 1
  Lupus Awareness Campaign, Oct 1
  Mammography Day, Natl, Oct 15
  Marfan Syndrome Awareness Month, Feb 1
  Marrow Awareness Month, Natl, Nov 1
  Massage Therapy Awareness Week, Natl, Oct 24
  Medical Orphans Month, Intl, May 1
  Medical Patient Advocacy Week, Natl, Apr 5
  Medicare: Anniv, Jul 1
  Medication Safety Week, Apr 1
  Melanoma Monday, May 3
  Melanoma/Skin Cancer Detection and Prevention Month, May 1
  Menopause Awareness Month, Sep 1
  Mental Health Month, Natl, May 1
  Mental Illness Awareness Week, Oct 3
  Mental Retardation Awareness Month, Mar 1
  More Herbs, Less Salt Day, Aug 29
  More Than Just a Pretty Face Month, May 1
  MS Walk (San Jose, CA), Apr 17
  Multiple Sclerosis Education & Awareness Month, Natl, Mar 1
  Neurofibromatosis Awareness Month, Natl, May 1
  No Diet Day, May 6
  Nuclear Medicine Week, Oct 3
  Nurse Anesthetists Week, Natl, Jan 25
  Nurses Day and Week, Natl, May 6
  Nursing Assistants Day and Week, Jun 10
  Nursing Conf on Pediatric Primary Care (Dallas, TX), Mar 23
  Nursing Home Week, Natl, May 9
  Nutrition Month, Natl, Mar 1
  Occupational Therapy Month, Natl, Apr 1
  Open-Heart Surgery, First: Anniv, Jul 9
  Organ and Tissue Donor Awareness Week, Natl (Pres Proc), Apr 18
  Orthodonic Health Month, Natl, Oct 1
  Osteoporosis Awareness Month, Natl, May 1
  Ovarian Cancer Awareness Month, Sep 1
  Ovarian Cancer Awareness Month, Natl (Pres Proc), Sep 1
  Pandemic of 1918 Hits US: Anniv, Mar 11
  Parkinson's Awareness Month, Natl, Apr 1
  Pediatric Cancer Awareness Month, Sep 1
  Pediatric Nurse Practitioner Week, Mar 21
  Pediculosis Prevention Month, Natl, Sep 1
  Perioperative (OR) Nurse Week, Nov 14
  Pharmacists Declare War on Alcoholism, Jun 1
  Pharmacists War on Diabetes, Apr 1
  Physical Fitness and Sports Month, Natl, May 1
  Physical Therapy Month, Natl, Oct 1
  Physician Assistant Day, Oct 6
  Poison Prevention Awareness Month, Mar 1
  Poison Prevention Week, Natl, Mar 21
  Polio Vaccine: Anniv, Apr 12
  Pregnancy & Infant Loss Awareness Day, Oct 15
  Prematurity Awareness Day, Nov 18
  Prevent Injuries America, Apr 1
  Prostate Cancer Awareness Week, Sep 12
  Public Health Week, Natl, Apr 5
  Pulmonary Rehabilitation Week, Mar 14
  Purposeful Parenting Month, Natl, Jul 1
  Race for the Cure (Pittsburgh, PA), May 9
  Radon Action Month, Natl, Jan 1
  Rebuild Your Life Month, Jun 1
  Red Cross Month, Mar 1
  Red Cross Month, American (Pres Proc), Mar 1
  Rehabilitation Awareness Celebration, Natl, Sep 19
  Relaxation Day, Natl, Aug 15
  Rett Syndrome Awareness Month, Oct 1
  Rid the World of Fad Diets/Gimmicks Day, Jan 20
  Rosacea Awareness Month, Mar 1
  RSV Awareness Month, Natl, Oct 1
  Running and Fitness Week, Natl, May 16
  Save Your Back Week, Natl, Oct 24
  Save Your Smile Week, Natl, Aug 22
  Save Your Vision Month, Mar 1
  Save Your Vision Week (Pres Proc), Mar 7
  School Breakfast Week, Natl, Mar 8
  Self Day, Apr 9
  Senior Health and Fitness Day, Natl, May 26
  September Is Childhood Cancer Month, Sep 1
  September Is Healthy Aging ® Month, Sep 1
  Sexual Assault Awareness and Prevention Month, Natl, Apr 1
  Sexually Transmitted Diseases (STDs) Awareness Month, Natl, Apr 1
  Sight-Saving/Ultraviolet Awareness Month, Natl, May 1
  Simplify Your Life Week, Aug 1
  Skin Care Awareness Month, Natl, Sep 1
  Sleep Awareness Week, Natl, Mar 29
  Smallpox Vaccine Discovered: Anniv, May 14

☆ Chase's 2004 Calendar of Events ☆ Index

Health (cont'd)—Home

Smokeless Cigarette Withdrawn: Anniv, Feb 28
Social Security Act: Anniv, Aug 14
Social Work Month, Natl Pro, Mar 1
Special Recreation Week, Jul 4
Speech-Language-Hearing Conv, American (Philadelphia, PA), Nov 18
Spina Bifida Awareness Month, Natl, Oct 1
Spinal Cord Injury Awareness Month, Natl, Sep 1
Spinal Health Month, Natl, Oct 1
Spinal Muscular Atrophy Awareness Month, Aug 1
Sports Eye Safety Month, Apr 1
Stay Out of the Sun Day, Jul 3
Stress Awareness Day, Natl, Apr 16
Stress Awareness Month, Apr 1
Strike Out Strokes Day, May 1
Stroke Awareness Month, Natl, May 1
Stuttering Awareness Day, Intl, Oct 22
Stuttering Awareness Week, Natl, May 9
Successful Antirabies Inoculation, First: Anniv, Jul 6
Sudden Infant Death Syndrome Awareness Month, Natl, Oct 1
Suicide Awareness Week, Natl, May 2
Take a New Year's Resolution to Stop Smoking, Jan 1
Talk About Prescriptions Month, Oct 1
Testicular Cancer Awareness Week, Apr 1
Test-Tube Baby: Birth, Jul 25
Therapeutic Recreation Week, Natl, Jul 11
3-A-Day Week, Mar 3
TOPS Club, Inc: Anniv, Jan 21
TOPS Recognition Days, Intl, Jul 15
Tour de Cure (Diabetes), Apr 1
Tuberous Sclerosis Awareness Month, Natl, May 1
UN: Roll Back Malaria in Developing Countries, Particularly in Africa, Decade to, Jan 1
Vegetarian Month, Oct 1
Vision Research Month, Jun 1
Vitamin C Isolated: Anniv, Apr 4
Volunteer Week, Natl, Apr 18
Volunteers Week, Intl, Jun 1
Vulvar Health Awareness Month, Mar 1
Walk Days, Intl, Apr 30
White Cane Safety Day (Pres Proc), Oct 15
Wise Health Care Consumer Month, Feb 1
Women's Eye Health and Safety Month, Apr 1
Women's Health and Fitness Day, Natl, Sep 29
Women's Health Care Month, May 1
Women's Healthy Weight Day, Jan 22
Women's Heart Health Day, Feb 1
Women's Heart Week, Feb 1
Women's Nutrition Week, Natl, Apr 11
Workplace Eye Health and Safety Month, Mar 1
World AIDS Day (Pres Proc), Dec 1
World AIDS Day (UN), Dec 1
World Blindness Awareness Month, Oct 1
World Breastfeeding Week, Aug 1
World Food Day (UN), Oct 16
World Health Day (UN), Apr 7
World Herbal Health Day, Oct 12
World Mental Health Day (UN), Oct 10
World No-Tobacco Day (UN), May 31
World Red Cross Day, May 8
Young Child, Month of the (MI), Apr 1
Youth Sports Safety Month, Natl, Apr 1
Health Care Center Week, Natl (Pres Proc), Aug 15
Health Care Diversity Month, Mar 1
Heard, John: Birth, Mar 7
Hearing and Speech Month, Better, May 1
Hearn, Lafcadio: Birth Anniv, Jun 27
Hearst, William R.: Birth Anniv, Apr 29
Heart Day, Natl Have a, Feb 14
Heart Failure Awareness Week, Feb 15
Heart Month, American (Pres Proc), Feb 1
Heart of America: A Journey Fourth—Lewis and Clark Bicentennial Event (Atchison, Leavenworth and Kansas City, MO), Jul 3
Heatherton, Joey: Birth, Sep 14
Heaton, Patricia: Birth, Mar 4
Hebron Massacre: Anniv, Feb 25
Heche, Anne: Birth, May 25
Hecht, Ben: Birth Anniv, Feb 28
Heckerling, Amy: Birth, May 7
Hee Haw TV Premiere: Anniv, Jun 15
Hefner, Christie: Birth, Nov 8
Hefner, Hugh: Birth, Apr 9
Heiden, Eric: Birth, Jun 14
Heimlich Maneuver Introduced: Anniv, Jun 1
Heine, Heinrich: Birth Anniv, Dec 13
Hejduk, Milan: Birth, Feb 14
Helgenberger, Marg: Birth, Nov 16
Hello Day, World, Nov 21
Hell's Angels: Altamont Concert: Anniv, Dec 6
Helmond, Katherine: Birth, Jul 5
Helms, Edgar J.: Birth Anniv, Jan 19
Helms, Jesse: Birth, Oct 18
Helmsley, Leona: Birth, Jul 4
Heloise: Birth, Apr 15
Helton, Todd: Birth, Aug 20
Hemingway Birthday Celebration (Oak Park, IL), Jul 21
Hemingway, Ernest: Birth Anniv, Jul 21
Hemingway, Ernest: Boxing Day at Birthplace (Oak Park, IL), Dec 26
Hemingway, Mariel: Birth, Nov 22
Hemmings, David: Birth, Nov 21
Hemochromatosis Screening Awareness Month, Jul 1
Hemsley, Sherman: Birth, Feb 1
Henderson, Florence: Birth, Feb 14
Henderson, Rickey: Birth, Dec 25
Henderson, Skitch: Birth, Jan 27
Hendricks, Thomas A: Birth Anniv, Sep 17
Hendrix, Jimi: Birth Anniv, Nov 27
Henie, Sonja: Birth Anniv, Apr 8
Henin-Hardenne, Justine: Birth, Jun 1
Henley, Don: Birth, Jul 22
Henman, Tim: Birth, Sep 6
Henner, Marilu: Birth, Apr 6
Hennessy, Jill: Birth, Nov 25
Henried, Paul: Birth Anniv, Jan 10
Henriksen, Lance: Birth, May 5
Henry, Brad: Birth, Jul 10
Henry, Joseph: Birth Anniv, Dec 17
Henry, Justin: Birth, May 25
Henry, O. (William S. Porter): Birth Anniv, Sep 11
Henry, Patrick: Birth Anniv, May 29
Henson, Jim: Birth Anniv, Sep 24
Henson, John: Birth, Jul 11
Henson, Matthew A.: Birth Anniv, Aug 8
Hentoff, Nat: Birth, Jun 10
Hepatitis Awareness Month, Natl, May 1
Hepburn, Audrey: Birth Anniv, May 4
Hepburn, Katharine: Birth, May 12
Herb Fest (Mattoon, IL), Apr 24
Herbal Health Day, World, Oct 12
Herbal/Prescription Awareness Month, Jul 1
Heritage Day Fest (Lavallette, NJ), Sep 11
Heritage Days Fest (Cumberland, MD), Jun 12
Heritage Days Rendezvous (Kewanee, IL), Jul 2
Heritage Week (New Harmony, IN), Apr 19
Heritagefest (New Ulm, MN), Jul 9
Herman, Alexis: Birth, Jul 16
Herman, Jerry: Birth, Jul 10
Hermit Week, Natl, Jun 13
Hermit, Robert the: Death Anniv, Apr 1
Hernandez, Keith: Birth, Oct 20
Hernandez, Orlando: Birth, Oct 11
Herriman, George: Birth Anniv, Aug 22
Herriot, James: Birth Anniv, Oct 3
Herrmann, Edward: Birth, Jul 21
Hersey, John: Birth Anniv, Jun 17
Hersh, Seymour: Birth, Apr 8
Hershey, Barbara: Birth, Feb 5
Hershiser, Orel: Birth, Sep 16
Herzl, Theodor: Birth Anniv, May 20
Herzog, Chaim: Birth Anniv, Sep 17
Hess, Rudolf: Birth Anniv, Apr 26
Hesseman, Howard: Birth, Feb 27
Heston, Charlton: Birth, Oct 4
Hewes, Joseph: Birth Anniv, Jan 23
Hewitt, Don: Birth, Dec 14
Hewitt, Jennifer Love: Birth, Feb 21
Hewitt, Lleyton: Birth, Feb 24
Heyerdahl, Thor: Birth Anniv, Oct 6
Heyward, Thomas: Birth Anniv, Jul 28
Hiawatha Pageant, Song of (Pipestone, MN), Jul 23
Hickman, Darryl: Birth, Jul 28
Hickok, Wild Bill: Birth Anniv, May 27
Hicks, Catherine: Birth, Aug 6
Higgins, David Anthony: Birth, Dec 9
Higginson, Bobby: Birth, Aug 18
High Tech Month, Natl, Jan 1
Hightower, Jim: Birth, Jan 11
Highway Numbers Introduced: Anniv, Mar 2
Hill Street Blues TV Premiere: Anniv, Jan 15
Hill, Anita: Birth, Jul 30
Hill, Arthur: Birth, Aug 1
Hill, Bernard: Birth, Dec 17
Hill, Dule: Birth, May 3
Hill, Faith: Birth, Sep 21
Hill, Grant: Birth, Oct 5
Hill, Lauryn: Birth, May 25
Hill, Mildred J.: Happy Birthday to "Happy Birthday to You", Jun 27
Hill, Patty Smith: Birth Anniv, Mar 27
Hill, Steven: Birth, Feb 24
Hillary, Sir Edmund: Birth, Jul 20
Hillary, Sir Edmund: Everest Summit Reached: Anniv, May 29
Hillerman, John: Birth, Dec 20
Hillman, Chris: Birth, Dec 4
Hinamatsuri (Japan), Mar 3
Hindemith, Paul: Birth Anniv, Nov 16
Hindenburg Disaster: Anniv, May 6
Hindu: Diwali, Oct 25
Hindu: Holi, Mar 28
Hingis, Martina: Birth, Sep 30
Hinske, Eric: Birth, Aug 5
Hirohito, Emperor: Birth Anniv, Apr 29
Hirohito, Emperor: Death Anniv, Jan 7
Hiroshima Day, Aug 6
Hirsch, Elroy "Crazylegs": Birth, Jun 17
Hirsch, Judd: Birth, Mar 15
Hirschfeld, Al: Birth Anniv, Jun 21
Hispanic,
Cinco de Mayo (Mexico), May 5
Cinco de Mayo Fest (Portland, OR), May 5
Hispanic Heritage Fest (Miami, FL), Oct 1
Hispanic Heritage Month, Natl (Pres Proc), Sep 15
Latino Book & Family Fest (Chicago, IL), Nov 22
League of United Latin American Citizens (LULAC) Founded: Anniv, Feb 17
Mexican Fiesta Internacional (Milwaukee, WI), Aug 27
Viva! Chicago Latin Music Fest (Chicago, IL), Aug 28
Zoot Suit Riots: Anniv, Jun 3
Historic Norwichtown Days (Norwich, CT), Sep 10
Historic Preservation Week, Natl, May 3
Historical Fest, Fort Sisseton (Lake City, SD), Jun 5
Historically Black Colleges and Universities Week, Natl (Pres Proc), Sep 19
History Alive! (Norfolk, VA), Oct 1
History Meets the Arts (Gettysburg, PA), Apr 16
History Month, Black, Feb 1
Hitchcock, Alfred: Birth Anniv, Aug 13
Hite, Shere: Birth, Nov 2
Hitler Celebration, RAF Bombs: Anniv, Jan 30
Hitler Youth Deployed: Anniv, Jan 26
Hitler, Adolf: Birth Anniv, Apr 20
Hitler, Adolf: German Plebiscite: Anniv, Aug 19
Hitler, Adolf: Gersdorff Assassination Attempt: Anniv, Mar 21
Hitler, Adolf: Operation Flash: Anniv, Mar 13
HIV Testing Day, Natl, Jun 27
Ho Chi Minh: Birth Anniv, May 19
Ho, Don: Birth, Aug 13
Hoban, James: Death Anniv, Dec 8
Hobart, Garret A.: Birth Anniv, Jun 3
Hobbit Day, Sep 22
Hobbs, Lucy: First Woman Graduate Dental School: Anniv, Feb 21
Hobby Industry Assn Conv & Trade Show (Anaheim, CA), Feb 5
Hockey, Ice,
First Black Pro Hockey Player: Anniv, Nov 15
Hockey Mask Invented: Anniv, Nov 1
NCAA Div I Men's Chmpshp (Boston, MA), Apr 8
Hockney, David: Birth, Jul 9
Hodge, Patricia: Birth, Sep 29
Hoeven, John: Birth, Mar 13
Hoffa, James: Disappearance Anniv, Jul 30
Hoffman, Abbie: Birth Anniv, Nov 30
Hoffman, Dustin: Birth, Aug 8
Hoffman, Mat: Birth, Jan 9
Hog Capital of the World Fest (Kewanee, IL), Sep 3
Hogan, Ben: Birth Anniv, Aug 13
Hogan, Hulk: Birth, Aug 11
Hogan, Paul: Birth, Oct 8
Hogarth, William: Birth Anniv, Nov 10
Hogg, Ima: Birth Anniv, Jul 10
Hoiby, Lee: Birth, Feb 17
Holbrook, Hal: Birth, Feb 17
Holden, Bob: Birth, Aug 24
Holden, William: Birth Anniv, Apr 17
Holdsclaw, Chamique: Birth, Aug 9
Holi (India), Mar 28
Holiday Bowl Parade/Game, Pacific Life (San Diego, CA), Dec 30
Holiday Day, Make Up Your Own, Mar 26
Holiday, Billie: Birth Anniv, Apr 7
Holiday, First US by Presidential Proclamation: Anniv, Nov 26
Holidays at the Nationality Classrooms (Oakland, PA), Dec 1
Holland Tunnel: Anniv, Nov 13
Holliday, Polly: Birth, Jul 2
Holliger, Heinz: Birth, May 21
Hollings, Ernest F.: Birth, Jan 1
Holloway, Sterling: Birth Anniv, Jan 4
Holly Jolly Weekend (Andrews, TX), Dec 2
Holly, Buddy: Birth Anniv, Sep 7
Holly, Buddy: Day the Music Died: Death Anniv, Feb 3
Holly, Lauren: Birth, Oct 28
Hollyhock Fest (Kyoto, Japan), May 15
Hollywood Magic Day, Sep 20
Hollywood Squares TV Premiere: Anniv, Oct 17
Holm, Celeste: Birth, Apr 29
Holm, Ian: Birth, Sep 12
Holmes, Katie: Birth, Dec 18
Holmes, Oliver W.: Birth Anniv, Aug 29
Holmes, Rupert: Birth, Feb 24
Holmgren, Mike: Birth, Jun 15
Holocaust Day (Israel), Apr 18
Holocaust Museum Opens, US: Anniv, Apr 26
Holtz, Lou: Birth, Jan 6
Holy Humor Month, Apr 1
Holy Innocents Day, Dec 28
Holy See: National Holiday, Oct 22
Holy Thursday, Apr 8
Holy Week, Apr 4
Holyfield, Evander: Birth, Oct 19
Home Comfort Awareness Week, Oct 3
Home Furnishings Week, Protecting Your, Sep 6
Home Improvement Time, Apr 1
Home Improvement TV Premiere: Anniv, Sep 17
Home Inspection Month, Natl, Oct 1
Home Office Safety and Security Week, Jan 11
Home Office, Improve Your, Week, Oct 4
Home Office: Organize Your Home Office Day, Mar 9
Home Office: Work from Home Week, Natl, Oct 3
Home Owners Loan Act: Anniv, Jun 13
Home Run Record: Anniv, Apr 8
Home Sewing Machine Invented: Anniv, Aug 12
Home Shows and Tours,
Candlelight Tours (New Harmony, IN), Dec 4
Fall Maryland Home & Garden Show/Holiday Craft Show (Baltimore, MD), Oct 15
Fest of Houses and Gardens (Charleston, SC), Mar 18

Index ☆ Chase's 2004 Calendar of Events ☆

Home (cont'd)—Humor

Fredericksburg Day (Fredericksburg, VA), **Apr 20**
Galveston Historic Homes Tour (Galveston Island, TX), **May 1**
Great Northeast Home Show (Albany, NY), **Feb 6**
Historic Homes Parlor Tour (Baker City, OR), **Dec 5**
Holiday Tour of Homes (Natchitoches, LA), **Dec 8**
Home and Garden Fest (Wichita Falls, TX), **Feb 28**
Home Furnishings Market, Intl (High Point, NC), **Apr 22**
Home Improvement Show, Milwaukee/NARI (West Allis, WI), **Feb 5**
Home Inspection Month, Natl, **Oct 1**
Lawn Flower & Patio Show (Omaha, NE), **Feb 5**
Litchfield Open House Tour (Litchfield, CT), **Jul 9**
Maryland Home and Garden Show (Baltimore, MD), **Mar 5**
Mother's Day Housewalk (Evanston, IL), **May 9**
Natchez Fall Pilgrimage (Natchez, MS), **Oct 8**
Natchez Spring Pilgrimage (Natchez, MS), **Mar 13**
Natchitoches Historic Pilgrimage (Natchitoches, LA), **Oct 8**
Natl City Cleveland Home and Garden Show (Cleveland, OH), **Feb 7**
New England Home Show (Boston, MA), **Feb 21**
Omaha Home and Garden Expo (Omaha, NE), **Feb 5**
Original Massachusetts Home & Garden Show (West Springfield, MA), **Mar 24**
Quincy Preserves Fall Architectural Tour (Quincy, IL), **Oct 16**
Savannah Tour of Homes and Gardens (Savannah, GA), **Mar 25**
Seashore Open House Tour (Loveladies, NJ), **Aug 4**
Spring Fest (Cape May, NJ), **Apr 23**
Spring Pilgrimage to Antebellum Homes (Columbus, MS), **Mar 30**
Stone House Day (Hurley, NY), **Jul 10**
Victorian Christmas Home Tour (Leadville, CO), **Dec 4**
Wright, Frank Lloyd: Wright Plus (Oak Park, IL), **May 15**
Home: Organize Your Home Day, Jan 5
Home: Prepare Your Home To Be Sold Month, Natl, Mar 1
Home-Based Business Week, Oct 10
Homebirth Week, Natl Unassisted, Jul 1
Homeless Animals Day, Natl/Candlelight Vigils, Aug 21
Homeless Week, Natl, Nov 1
Homeowner's Day, New, May 1
Homer, Louise Dilworth: Birth Anniv, Apr 28
Homer, Winslow: Birth Anniv, Feb 24
Homeschool Month, Natl, Sep 1
Homestead Act: Anniv, May 20
Homestead Days (Beatrice, NE), Jun 16
Homesteader Harvest Fest (Brandon, SD), Sep 12
Hometown Days (Strasburg, CO), Aug 21
Honduras,
Dia De Las Americas, **Apr 14**
Francisco Morazan Holiday, **Oct 3**
Hurricane Mitch: Anniv, **Oct 27**
Independence Day, **Sep 15**
Hone, William: Birth Anniv, Jun 3
Honest Abe Awards: Natl Honesty Day, Apr 30
Honesty Day, Natl, Apr 30
Honey Month, Natl, Sep 1
Honeymoon Weekend, Second, Feb 20
Honeymoon, First Balloon: Anniv, Jun 20
Hong Kong,
Last Hurrah for British, **Jun 30**
Lease Anniv, **Jun 9**
Liberation Day, **Aug 30**
Honor Society Awareness Month, Mar 1
Hood River Valley Blossom Fest (Hood River, OR), Apr 17
Hoodie-Hoo Day, Northern Hemisphere, Feb 20
Hooks, Jan: Birth, Apr 23
Hooks, Kevin: Birth, Sep 19
Hooks, Robert: Birth, Apr 18
Hooper, William: Birth Anniv, Jun 17
Hoover, Herbert: Birth Anniv, Aug 10
Hoover, Herbert: Day (IA), Aug 8
Hoover, J. Edgar: Birth Anniv, Jan 1
Hoover, Lou H.: Birth Anniv, Mar 29
Hopalong Cassidy TV Premiere: Anniv, Jun 24
Hope, Bob: Birth Anniv, May 29
Hope, Bob: Chrysler Golf Classic (La Quinta, CA), Jan 19
Hope, Leslie: Birth, May 6
Hopkins, Bo: Birth, Feb 2
Hopkins, Sir Anthony: Birth, Dec 31
Hopkins, Stephen: Birth Anniv, Mar 7
Hopkins, Telma: Birth, Oct 28
Hopkinson, Francis: Birth Anniv, Sep 21
Hopper, Dennis: Birth, May 17
Hopper, Grace: Birth Anniv, Dec 9
Horn, Paul: Birth, Mar 17
Hornacek, John: Birth, May 3
Horne, Lena: Birth, Jun 30
Horne, Marilyn: Birth, Jan 16
Horowitz, Vladimir: Birth Anniv, Oct 1
Horrocks, Jane: Birth, Jan 18
Horses,
Augusta Futurity (Augusta, GA), **Jan 22**
Badminton Horse Trials (Badminton, England), **Apr 29**
Belmont Stakes (Belmont Park, NY), **Jun 5**
Belmont Stakes, First Running of, **Jun 19**
Block House Steeplechase (Tryon, NC), **Apr 17**
Bonnie Blue Natl Horse Show (Lexington, VA), **May 5**
Britt Draft Horse Show (Britt, IA), **Sep 3**
Central Montana Fair (Lewistown, MT), **Jul 16**
Cheltenham Hunt Fest (Prestbury, England), **Mar 16**
Chincoteague Pony Penning (Chincoteague Island, VA), **Jul 28**
D & G Barrel Race (Wichita Falls, TX), **Nov 28**
Day of the Horse, **Dec 11**
Derby, The (Epsom Downs, England), **Jun 5**
Farrier's Week, Natl, **Jul 11**
First Kentucky Derby: Anniv, **May 17**
Foxfield Races (Charlottesville, VA), **Apr 24**
Gold Cup, Intl (The Plains, VA), **Oct 16**
Horse Expo (Wichita Falls, TX), **Oct 16**
Iron Horse Outraced by Horse: Anniv, **Sep 18**
Iroquois Steeplechase (Nashville, TN), **May 8**
Kentucky Derby (Louisville, KY), **May 1**
Kentucky Derby Fest (Louisville, KY), **Apr 16**
Kentucky State Fair (Louisville, KY), **Aug 19**
Masters (Calgary, AB, Canada), **Sep 8**
Miles City Bucking Horse Sale (Miles City, MT), **May 21**
Missouri State Chmpshp Racking Horse Show (Dexter, MO), **Jun 5**
Natl Tournament (Calgary, AB, Canada), **Jun 9**
North American Tournament (Calgary, AB, Canada), **Jul 7**
Palio (Siena, Italy), **Jul 2**
Point-to-Point (Wilmington, DE), **May 2**
Pony Express Fest (Hanover, KS), **Aug 29**
Pony Express, Inauguration of: Anniv, **Apr 3**
Preakness Stakes (Baltimore, MD), **May 15**
Preakness Stakes: Anniv, **May 27**
Racking World Celebration (Decatur, AL), **Sep 17**
Royal Ascot (Ascot, Berkshire, England), **Jun 15**
Royal Windsor Horse Show (Windsor, England), **May 12**
Sandpoint Saddle Club Horse Show (Sandpoint, ID), **Jun 19**
Steeplechase at Callaway Gardens (Pine Mountain, GA), **Nov 6**
Strawberry Hill Races (Richmond, VA), **Apr 10**
Sussex Farm and Horse Show (Augusta, NJ), **Aug 6**
Taylor Horsefest (Taylor, ND), **Jul 30**
Tennessee Walking Horse Natl Celeb (Shelbyville, TN), **Aug 18**
Trail Ride Gathering, Natl (Live Oak, FL), **Oct 29**
Upperville Colt/Horse Show (Upperville, VA), **Jun 7**
Virginia Gold Cup (Warrenton, VA), **May 1**
West Allis Western Days Family Jamboree (West Allis, WI), **Jun 17**
Horseshoe Tourn, Head-of-the-Mon-River (Fairmont, WV), May 29
Horseshoe Tourn, Silver Valley (Kellogg, ID), Aug 14
Horsley, Lee: Birth, May 15
Hoskins, Bob: Birth, Oct 26
Hospice Month, Natl, Nov 1
Hospital Admitting Clerks Day, Apr 2
Hossa, Marian: Birth, Jan 12
Hostage Released, Last American: Anniv, Dec 4
Hostos, Eugenio Maria: Birth Anniv, Jan 11
Hot Breakfast Month, Natl, Feb 1
Hot Dog Month, Natl, Jul 1
Hot Dog Night (Luverne, MN), Jul 8
Hot Enough For Ya Day, Jul 23
Hot Springs Natl Park Established: Anniv, Mar 4
Houdini, Harry: Birth Anniv, Mar 24
Houdini, Harry: Death Anniv, Oct 31
House of Representatives, First Black Serves in: Anniv, Dec 12
House of Representatives, First Brawl: Anniv, Jan 30
House of Representatives: First Quorum Anniv, Apr 1
Houseman, John: Birth Anniv, Sep 22
Housework Day, No, Apr 7
Houston, Sam: Birth Anniv, Mar 2
Houston, Whitney: Birth, Aug 9
Hovick, Rose L. (Gypsy Rose Lee): Birth Anniv, Feb 9
Howard, Juwan: Birth, Feb 7
Howard, Ken: Birth, Mar 28
Howard, Leslie: Birth Anniv, Apr 3
Howard, Moe: Birth Anniv, Jun 19
Howard, Ron: Birth, Mar 1
Howard, Susan: Birth, Jan 28
Howard, Traylor: Birth, Jun 14
Howard, Trevor: Birth Anniv, Sep 29
Howdy Doody TV Premiere: Anniv, Dec 27
Howe, Elias: Birth Anniv, Jul 9
Howe, Gordie: Birth, Mar 31
Howell, C. Thomas: Birth, Dec 7
Howes, Sally Ann: Birth, Jul 20
Hoyle, Edmund: Death Anniv, Aug 29
Hu, Kelly: Birth, Feb 13
Hubbard, Elbert: Birth Anniv, Jun 19
Hubbard, L. Ron: Birth Anniv, Mar 13
Hubble Space Telescope Deployed: Space Milestone, Apr 25
Hubble, Edwin Powell: Birth Anniv, Nov 20
Huck Finn's Jubilee (Victorville, CA), Jun 18
Huckabee, Mike: Birth, Aug 24
Hudson, Ernie: Birth, Dec 17
Hudson, Kate: Birth, Apr 19
Huerta, Dolores: Birth, Apr 10
Hug a GI Day, Mar 4
Hug a Prom Sponsor Day, Apr 23
Hug a Texas Chef Month, Sep 1
Hug An Australian Day, Apr 26
Hug Holiday Week, Natl, May 2
Hug Your Cat Day, Jun 4
Hugging Day, Natl, Jan 21
Hughes, Barnard: Birth, Jul 16
Hughes, Charles E.: Birth Anniv, Apr 11
Hughes, Finola: Birth, Oct 29
Hughes, Howard: Birth Anniv, Dec 24
Hughes, John: Birth, Feb 18
Hughes, Langston: Birth Anniv, Feb 1
Hughes, Sarah: Birth, May 2
Hughley, D.L.: Birth, Mar 6
Hugo, Victor: Birth Anniv, Feb 26
Hula Bowl Maui All Star Classic (Maui, HI), Jan 17
Hula Dancing: Merrie Monarch Fest & Hula Competition (Hilo, HI), Apr 11
Hulce, Thomas: Birth, Dec 6
Hull House Opens: Anniv, Sep 18
Hull, Bobby: Birth, Jan 3
Hull, Brett: Birth, Aug 9
Hull, Cordell: Birth Anniv, Oct 2
Hull, John: First Mint in America: Anniv, Jun 10
Human Genome Mapped: Anniv, Jun 26
Human Relations. See also Romance,
American Red Cross: Founding Anniv, **May 21**
Be an Angel Day, **Aug 22**
Be Kind to Humankind Week, **Aug 25**
Black History Month, **Feb 1**
Blame Someone Else Day, **Feb 13**
Celebration of Life Day, **Jan 22**
Celebration of Love Week, **Feb 9**
Coaching Week, Intl, **Feb 1**
Day of Prayer and Action for Human Habitat, Intl, **Sep 19**
Decade for Eradication of Poverty (UN), **Jan 1**
Decade for Human Rights Education (UN), **Jan 1**
Diversity Awareness Month, **Oct 1**
Emancipation Proclamation: Anniv, **Sep 22**
Eradication of Poverty, Intl Day for (UN), **Oct 17**
Etiquette Week, Natl, **May 16**
First Natl Convention for Blacks: Anniv, **Sep 15**
First US Breach of Promise Suit: Anniv, **Jun 14**
Fourteen Points Proposed: Anniv, **Jan 8**
Freedom Day, **Jul 4**
Friendship Week, Intl, **Feb 22**
Good Neighbor Day, Natl, **Sep 26**
Good Samaritan Involvement Day, **Mar 13**
Great American Grump Out, **May 26**
Great American Warm-Up, **Nov 5**
Help Someone See Week (Rockford, OH), **Mar 7**
Honesty Day, Natl, **Apr 30**
Hug Holiday Week, Natl, **May 2**
Human Rights Day (Pres Proc), **Dec 10**
Human Rights Day (UN), **Dec 10**
Human Rights Month, Universal, **Dec 1**
Human Rights Week (Pres Proc), **Dec 10**
I Want You to Be Happy Day, **Mar 3**
Intl Week (College Station, TX), **Feb 23**
Joygerm Day, Natl, **Jan 4**
Kindness Day, World, **Nov 13**
Kiss-and-Make-Up-Day, **Aug 25**
Language Week, Intl, **Dec 15**
League of Nations: Anniv, **Jan 10**
Lost Penny Day, **Feb 12**
Lumpy Rug Day, **May 3**
Magic of Differences™ Week, **Oct 3**
Meet a Mate Week, **Jun 14**
Nagging Day, Intl, **Aug 14**
New Friends, Old Friends Week, Natl, **May 16**
Pay-a-Compliment Day, **Feb 6**
Peace Corps Founded: Anniv, **Mar 1**
Peace, Friendship and Good Will Week, **Oct 25**
Pen-Friends Week Intl, **May 1**
Poverty in America Awareness Month, Natl, **Jan 1**
Race Relations Day, **Feb 14**
Race Unity Day, **Jun 13**
Ralph Bunche Awarded Nobel Peace Prize: Anniv, **Dec 10**
Reconciliation Day, **Apr 2**
Red Cross Day, World, **May 8**
Religion Day, World, **Jan 18**
Religious Freedom Week, **Sep 18**
Roots and Branches Month, **Jul 1**
Salvation Army Founder's Day, **Apr 10**
Salvation Army in US: Anniv, **Mar 10**
Spring Fever Week, Natl, **Mar 14**
Swap Ideas Day, **Sep 10**
Thank You Days, Intl, **Jan 11**
Tolerance Week, **Dec 1**
Universal Family Week, **May 11**
Universal Hour of Peace, **Jan 1**
Universal Human Beings Week, **Mar 1**
Volunteer Week, Natl, **Apr 18**
Volunteers Week, Intl, **Jun 1**
World Day of Prayer, **Mar 5**
World Hello Day, **Nov 21**
Human Spirit Day, World, Feb 17
Humbug Day, Dec 21
Hummel, Sister Maria Innocentia: Birth Anniv, May 21
Humor, Comedy,
Alascattalo Day (Anchorage, AK), **Nov 21**
A'phabet Day, **Dec 25**
Bubba Day, Natl, **Jun 2**

710

☆ Chase's 2004 Calendar of Events ☆ Index

Gaines, William M. (Mad magazine): Birth Anniv, **Mar 1**
Holy Humor Month, **Apr 1**
Humor Month, Natl, **Apr 1**
Humorists Are Artists Month (HAAM), **Mar 1**
Just for Laughs Fest (Montreal, QC, Canada), **Jul 15**
Kurtzman, Harvey (Mad magazine): Birth Anniv, **Oct 3**
Love May Make World Go Round but Laughter Keeps Us from Getting Dizzy Week, **Feb 8**
Moment of Laughter Day, **Apr 14**
O. Henry Pun-Off (Austin, TX), **May 1**
Positive Power of Humor, Hope & Healing Conf (Saratoga Springs, NY), **Apr 16**
SCUD Day, **Jul 8**
Someday We'll Laugh About This Week, **Jan 4**
Twit Award Month, Intl, **Apr 1**
HUMOResilience Workshop (Lake George, NY), Oct 22
Humperdinck, Engelbert: Birth, May 3
Humphrey, Hubert: Birth Anniv, May 27
Humphrey, Terin: Birth, Aug 14
Humphries, Barry: Birth, Feb 17
Hungary,
Anniv of 1956 Revolution, **Oct 23**
Anniversary of the 1848 Revolution, **Mar 15**
Hungary Declares Independence: Anniv, **Oct 23**
St. Stephen's Day, **Aug 20**
Hunger Awareness Day, Natl, Jun 5
Hungerford, Margaret Wolf: Duchess Who Wasn't Day, Aug 27
Hunnicutt, Gayle: Birth, Feb 6
Hunt for Happiness Week, Jan 18
Hunt, Bonnie: Birth, Sep 22
Hunt, Helen: Birth, Jun 15
Hunt, Lamar: Birth, Aug 2
Hunt, Linda: Birth, Apr 2
Hunter, Catfish: Birth Anniv, Apr 8
Hunter, David: Hunter Frees the Slaves: Anniv, May 9
Hunter, Holly: Birth, Mar 20
Hunter, Rachel: Birth, Sep 9
Hunter, Tab: Birth, Jul 11
Hunter-Gault, Charlayne: Birth, Feb 27
Hunter's Moon, Oct 27
Hunter's Moon, Feast of (Lafayette, IN), Oct 2
Hunting: Cheltenham Hunt Fest (Prestbury, England), Mar 16
Huntington, Samuel: Birth Anniv, Jul 3
Huntington's Disease Awareness Month, May 1
Huppert, Isabelle: Birth, Mar 16
Hurley, Elizabeth: Birth, Jun 10
Hurricanes, Tornados, Cyclones, Typhoons,
Atlantic, Caribbean and Gulf Hurricane Season, **Jun 1**
Central Pacific Hurricane Season, **Jun 1**
Eastern Pacific Hurricane Season, **May 15**
Galveston, TX: Anniv, **Sep 8**
Hurricane Agnes: Anniv, **Jun 21**
Hurricane Hugo Hits American Coast: Anniv, **Sep 21**
Hurricane Mitch: Anniv, **Oct 27**
Hurricane Supplication Day (Virgin Islands), **Jul 26**
Hurricane Thanksgiving Day (Virgin Islands), **Oct 18**
Port Royal (Jamaica) Hurricane: Anniv, **Aug 28**
Southern Cyclone: Anniv, **Aug 24**
Texas Panhandle Tornado: Anniv, **Apr 9**
Western Pacific Hurricane Season, **Jan 1**
Hurston, Zora Neale: Birth Anniv, Jan 7
Hurston, Zora: Zora Neale Hurston Fest (Eatonville, FL), Jan 28
Hurt, John: Birth, Jan 22
Hurt, Mary Beth: Birth, Sep 26
Hurt, William: Birth, Mar 20
Hus, John: Commemoration Day (Czech), Jul 6
Husband Appreciation Day, Apr 17
Husband Caregiver Day, Jun 20
Husky, Ferlin: Birth, Dec 3
Hussein, King of Jordan: Birth Anniv, Nov 14
Hussein, Saddam: Birth, Apr 28
Hussein, Saddam: Operation Iraqi Freedom: Anniv, Mar 19
Hussey, Olivia: Birth, Apr 17
Huston, Anjelica: Birth, Jul 8
HutchFest (Hutchinson, KS), Jun 27
Hutchins, Robert Maynard: Birth Anniv, Jan 17
Hutchison, Kay Bailey: Birth, Jul 22
Hutton, Betty: Birth, Feb 26
Hutton, Lauren: Birth, Nov 17
Hutton, Timothy: Birth, Aug 16
Huxley, Aldous: Birth Anniv, Jul 26
Huygens, Christiaan: Birth Anniv, Apr 14
Hynde, Chrissie: Birth, Sep 7
Hypnosis: Health and Happiness with Hypnosis Day, Jul 27
I Am in Control Day: Anniv, Mar 30
I Am So Thankful Month, Nov 1
I Love Lucy TV Premiere: Anniv, Oct 15
I Need a Patch for That Day, May 21
I Spy TV Premiere: Anniv, Sep 15
I Want Butterscotch Day, Natl, Feb 15
I Want You to Be Happy Day, Mar 3
Iacocca, Lee: Birth, Oct 15
IBM PC Introduced: Anniv, Aug 12
Ibsen, Henrik: Birth Anniv, Mar 20
Ice Cream Cone: Anniv, Sep 22
Ice Cream Day, Natl, Jul 18
Ice Cream Days (Le Mars, IA), Jul 1
Ice Cream Fest, Old-Fashioned (Utica, OH), May 29
Ice Cream Social (Indianapolis, IN), Jul 4
Ice Fest (Ligonier, PA), Jan 24
Ice T: Birth, Feb 16
Icebox Days XXIII (International Falls, MN), Jan 15
Iced Tea Month, Natl, Jun 1
Iceland,
August Holiday, **Aug 2**
Beer Day, **Mar 1**
Bun Day, **Feb 23**
Bursting Day, **Feb 24**
First Day of Summer, **Apr 22**
Independence Day, **Jun 17**
Laki Volcano Eruption: Anniv, **Jun 8**
Leif Erikson Day, **Oct 9**
University Students' Celebration, **Dec 1**
Iceman Mummy Discovered: Anniv, Sep 19
Idaho,
Admission Day, **Jul 3**
Coeur d'Alene Tribal Pilgrimage (Cataldo), **Aug 15**
Craig, Larry E.: Birth, **Jul 20**
Crapo, Michael: Birth, **May 20**
Dogwood Fest (Lewiston), **Apr 2**
Eastern Idaho State Fair (Blackfoot), **Sep 4**
Festival at Sandpoint (Sandpoint), **Aug 5**
Idaho Fest of Lights (Preston), **Nov 26**
Kempthorne, Dirk: Birth, **Oct 29**
Lionel Hampton Jazz Fest (Moscow), **Feb 25**
Lost in the '50s (Sandpoint), **May 14**
Mountain Man Rendezvous (Cataldo), **Aug 20**
NAIA Baseball World Series (Lewiston), **May 28**
Old Mission Historic Skills Fair (Cataldo), **Jul 11**
Old-Time Fiddlers' Contest and Fest, Natl (Weiser), **Jun 21**
Sacajawea Heritage Days (Salmon), **Aug 20**
Salmon River Days (Salmon), **Jul 1**
Sandpoint Saddle Club Horse Show (Sandpoint), **Jun 19**
Shakespeare Fest (Boise), **Jun 4**
Silver Valley Horseshoe Tourn (Kellogg), **Aug 14**
Simplot Games (Pocatello), **Feb 19**
Snake River Stampede (Nampa), **Jul 20**
That Famous Preston Night Rodeo (Preston), **Jul 29**
Wells Fargo Boulder Mountain Tour (Sun Valley), **Feb 7**
Wells Fargo Winter Games of Idaho, **Feb 1**
Western Idaho Fair (Boise), **Aug 20**
Ideas Month, Intl, Mar 1
Ides Of March, Mar 15
Iditarod Trail Sled Dog Race (Anchorage, AK), Mar 6
Idle, Eric: Birth, Mar 29
Idol, Billy: Birth, Nov 30
Ifans, Rhys: Birth, Jul 22
Ig Nobel Prize Ceremony (Cambridge, MA), Oct 7
Iglesias, Enrique: Birth, May 8
Iglesias, Julio: Birth, Sep 23
Ilitch, Mike: Birth, Jul 20
Illinois,
4th of July Patriotic Concert & Fireworks (Aurora), **Jul 4**
Admission Day, **Dec 3**
Apple Fest (Long Grove), **Oct 1**
Arcola Broom Corn Fest (Arcola), **Sep 10**
Arts/Quincy Riverfest (Quincy), **Sep 19**
Bagelfest (Mattoon), **Jul 28**
Bark in the Park (Chicago), **May 1**
Big Ten Men's Gymnastics Chmpshp (Champaign), **Mar 19**
Big Ten Women's Tennis Chmpshp (Evanston), **Apr 29**
Blagojevich, Rod: Birth, **Dec 10**
Bon Odori Fest of the Lanterns (Chicago), **Jul 10**
BookExpo America (Chicago), **Jun 2**
Boxing Day at the Hemingway Birthplace (Oak Park), **Dec 26**
Bud Billiken Parade (Chicago), **Aug 14**
Carillon Fest, Intl (Springfield), **Jun 6**
Chicago Blues Fest (Chicago), **Jun 10**
Chicago Golf Club: Anniv (Wheaton), **Jul 18**
Chicago Gospel Music Festival (Chicago), **Jun 4**
Chicago Intl Film Fest (Chicago), **Oct 7**
Chicago Jazz Fest (Chicago), **Sep 2**
Chicago Southland's Finest Antiques Show (Tinley Park), **Nov 27**
Chicago Southland's Finest Antiques Show (Tinley Park), **Jun 12**
Chocolate Fest (Galesburg), **Feb 7**
Chocolate Fest (Long Grove), **Apr 30**
Christmas Parade (Woodstock), **Nov 28**
Clarence Darrow Death Commemoration (Chicago), **Mar 13**
Closing of Columbian Exposition: Anniv, **Oct 30**
Columbian Exposition Opening: Anniv, **May 1**
Corps of Discovery Departure: Camp River Dubois—Lewis and Clark Bicentennial Event (Hartford and Wood River), **May 13**
Council of Logistics Mgmt Annual Conf (Chicago), **Oct 3**
Countryside Christmas (Long Grove), **Nov 26**
Decatur Celebration (Decatur), **Aug 6**
Dick Tracy Days (Woodstock), **Jun 16**
Downtown Alive! (Aurora), **Jun 11**
Durbin, Richard J.: Birth, **Nov 21**
Fair in the Square Crafters Show (Woodstock), **Jul 11**
Family, Career and Community Leaders of America Natl Leadership Meeting (Chicago), **Jul 11**
Farmers Market (Woodstock), **May 6**
Fest of the Vine (Geneva), **Sep 10**
Fine Art Fair (Woodstock), **Sep 11**
Fitzgerald, Peter: Birth, **Oct 20**
Frankfort Fall Fest, **Sep 4**
Freedom Fest (Mahomet), **Jul 4**
Friends of Lake Forest Lib Book Sale (Lake Forest), **Sep 16**
Galesburg Railroad Days (Galesburg), **Jun 26**
Gay and Lesbian Pride Parade (Chicago), **Jun 27**
Geneva's Christmas Walk (Geneva), **Dec 3**
Ginza Holiday: Japanese Cultural Fest (Chicago), **Aug 20**
Grand Excursion 2004 (Rock Island, Moline), **Jun 25**
Great Chicago Flood: Anniv, **Apr 13**
Great River Tug Fest (Port Byron), **Aug 13**
Groundhog Days (Woodstock), **Jan 31**
Hankfest (Chicago), **Sep 17**
Harold Washington Elected Chicago's First Black Mayor: Anniv, **Apr 11**
Harvard Milk Days Fest (Harvard), **Jun 4**
Haymarket Pardon: Anniv, **Jun 26**
Haymarket Square Riot: Anniv, **May 4**
Hemingway Birthday Celebration (Oak Park), **Jul 21**
Herb Fest (Mattoon), **Apr 24**
Heritage Days Rendezvous (Kewanee), **Jul 2**
Herrinfesta Italiana (Herrin), **May 27**
Hog Capital of the World Fest (Kewanee), **Sep 3**
Holiday Magic (Aurora), **Nov 26**
Horseradish Fest (Collinsville), **Jun 5**
Illinois Snow Sculpting Competition (Rockford), **Jan 14**
Illinois State Fair (Springfield), **Aug 13**
John Deere Memorabilia Conf (Moline), **Mar 9**
John Deere Tractor & Memorabilia Auction (Moline), **Aug 13**
John Deere's 200th Birthday (Moline), **Feb 7**
Jubilee Days Fest (Zion), **Sep 4**
Knox County Scenic Drive (Galesburg), **Oct 2**
LaSalle Bank Chicago Marathon, The (Chicago), **Oct 10**
Latino Book & Family Fest (Chicago), **Nov 22**
Learning Disabilities Assn Intl Conf (Atlanta), **Mar 17**
Lighting of the Square (Woodstock), **Nov 26**
Little Red School House Annual Art Fair (Willow Springs), **Oct 3**
Lockport Old Canal Days (Lockport), **Jun 19**
Marcie's Place: A Camp for Grieving Children (Ingleside), **Aug 21**
Marigold Fest (Pekin), **Sep 10**
McHenry County Fair (Woodstock), **Aug 4**
Memorial Day Parade (Aurora), **May 31**
Morton Pumpkin Fest (Morton), **Sep 15**
Mother's Day Housewalk (Evanston), **May 9**
Newberry Library's Twentieth Annual Book Fair (Chicago), **Jul 29**
NJCAA Div II Men's Natl Basketball Finals (Danville), **Mar 17**
Northern Illinois Univ Gatherings Powwow (Dekalb), **Nov 6**
Old-Fashioned Harvestfest and Fiddlers Contest (Woodstock), **Sep 19**
On the Waterfront (Rockford), **Sep 2**
Original Raggedy Ann & Andy Fest (Arcola), **May 22**
Party in the Plaza (Aurora), **Jun 17**
Pec Thing (Pecatonica), **May 15**
Pet Parade (LaGrange), **Jun 5**
Printers Row Book Fair (Chicago), **Jun 5**
Quincy Preserves Christmas Candlelight Tour (Quincy), **Dec 12**
Quincy Preserves Fall Architectural Tour (Quincy), **Oct 16**
Radiological Soc of North America Scientific Assembly and Annual Meeting (Chicago), **Nov 28**
Roger Ebert's Overlooked Film Fest (Champaign), **Apr 21**
Scarecrow Fest (St. Charles), **Oct 8**
Shakespeare Fest (Bloomington), **Jun 16**
Special Chefs Blue Ribbon Recipe and Cooking Contest (Chicago), **Oct 16**
Spoon River Valley Scenic Drive (Lewistown), **Oct 2**
Stearman Fly-In Days (Galesburg), **Sep 6**
Strawberry Fest (Long Grove), **Jun 25**
Sunday Architrek Tours (Oak Park), **Apr 4**
Superman Celebration (Metropolis), **Jun 10**
Swedish Days Fest (Geneva), **Jun 22**
Sweetcorn Fest, Natl (Hoopeston), **Sep 2**
Turtle Races (Danville), **Jun 12**
Victorian Christmas Tours at Frank Lloyd Wright Home (Oak Park), **Dec 11**
Viva! Chicago Latin Music Fest (Chicago), **Aug 28**
Winfield Good Old Days (Winfield), **Sep 10**
Woodstock Folk Fest (Woodstock), **Jul 18**
World Chmpshp Old-Time Piano Playing Contest (Peoria), **May 28**
World Freefall Convention (Rantoul), **Aug 6**
Wright, Frank Lloyd: Wright Plus (Oak Park), **May 15**
Wyatt Earp Birthday Celebration (Monmouth), **Aug 8**
I'm Not Going to Take It Anymore Day, Jan 7
Image Improvement Month, Jan 1
Iman: Birth, Jul 25
Imbolc, Feb 2
Immaculate Conception, Feast Of, Dec 8
Immaculate Reception: Anniv, Dec 23
Immigrants' Day (Canada), May 22
Immigration: Ellis Island Opened: Anniv, Jan 1
Immunization Awareness Month, Natl, Aug 1

Humor (cont'd)—Immunization

Index ☆ Chase's 2004 Calendar of Events ☆

Impeachment—Israel

Impeachment: Clinton Proceedings: Anniv, Dec 20
Impeachment: Johnson Proceedings: Anniv, Feb 24
Impeachment: Senate Acquits Clinton: Anniv, Feb 12
Imus, Don: Birth, Jul 23
In Living Color TV Premiere: Anniv, Apr 15
In the Heat of the Night TV Premiere: Anniv, Mar 6
Inane Answering Message Day, Jan 30
Inauguration Day, Old, Mar 4
Incandescent Lamp Demonstarted: Anniv, Oct 21
Income Tax Birthday, Feb 3
Income Tax Due Date, Quarterly Estimated Federal, Sep 15
Income Tax Due Date, Quarterly Estimated Federal, Apr 15
Income Tax Due Date, Quarterly Estimated Federal, Jun 15
Income Tax Due Date, Quarterly Estimated Federal, Jan 15
Income Tax Pay Day, Apr 15
Incredible Hulk TV Premiere: Anniv, Mar 10
Independence Bowl, MainStay (Shreveport, LA), Dec 31
Independence Day (Russia), Jun 12
Independence Day, US (Fourth of July),
  4th of July Patriotic Concert & Fireworks (Aurora, IL), Jul 4
  Aalborg and Rebild Fest (Aalborg and Rebild, Denmark), Jul 2
  Austin Community Fest (Austin, MN), Jul 2
  Boom Box Parade (Willimantic, CT), Jul 4
  Bristol Civic, Military/Firemen's Parade (Bristol, RI), Jul 5
  Calithumpian Parade (Biwabik, MN), Jul 4
  Celebration on the Cane (Natchitoches, LA), Jul 4
  Dam Experience (Warsaw, MO), Jul 3
  Declaration of Independence Approval and Signing: Anniv, Jul 4
  Family Day Celebration (Dahlonega, GA), Jul 4
  Firefall (Springfield, MO), Jul 3
  Firestorm 2004 (Altoona, PA), Jul 4
  Fireworks Celebration (Demopolis, AL), Jul 3
  Fireworks on the Fjord (Poulsbo, WA), Jul 3
  Fourth of July (Winston-Salem, NC), Jul 3
  Fourth of July Celebration (Live Oak, FL), Jul 2
  Fourth of July Extravaganza (Hettinger, ND), Jul 2
  Fourth of July Fireworks (Mackinaw City, MI), Jul 4
  Fredericksburg Heritage Fest (Fredericksburg, VA), Jul 4
  Freedom Days (Farmington, NM), Jul 2
  Freedom Fest (Mahomet, IL), Jul 4
  Haines Stampede and Rodeo (Baker City, OR), Jul 3
  Hometown Family Fourth (Hollywood, FL), Jul 4
  Hood River Old-Fashioned Fourth of July (Hood River, OR), Jul 4
  Independence Day Concert and Fireworks (Wheeling, WV), Jul 4
  Independence Extravaganza (Lavallette, NJ), Jul 4
  Monett Fourth of July (Monett, MO), Jul 4
  Mount Rushmore July 4 Celeb (Mt Rushmore, SD), Jul 3
  Old Glory Jubilee (Elsberry, MO), Jul 3
  Old Vermont Fourth (Woodstock, VT), Jul 4
  Old-Fashioned Fourth of July (Worthington, MN), Jul 4
  Red, White and Boom (Columbus, OH), Jul 2
  Road to Independence (Williamsburg, VA), Jul 3
  Sullivan Freedom Fest (Sullivan, MO), Jul 4
  Sundown Salute (Junction City, KS), Jul 3
  WSB-TV Salute 2 America Parade (Atlanta, GA), Jul 4
Independence Sunday (IA), Jun 27
Independence-from-Meat Day, Jul 4
Independent Retailers Week, Natl, Jul 18
India,
  Baisakhi, Apr 13
  Bhopal Poison Gas Disaster: Anniv, Dec 3
  Children's Day, Nov 14
  Deepavali (Diwali), Oct 25
  Gandhi, Mohandas: Birth Anniv, Oct 2
  Holi, Mar 28
  Independence Day, Aug 15
  Indian Earthquake, Jan 26
  Mohandas Gandhi Assassinated: Anniv, Jan 30
  New Year's Day, Mar 21
  Rajiv Gandhi Assassinated: Anniv, May 21
  Republic Day, Jan 26
  Rohini I: First Satellite Launched, Jul 18
Indian Saint, First: Anniv, Jul 31
Indiana,
  Admission Day, Dec 11
  Amish Acres Arts & Crafts Fest (Nappanee), Aug 12
  Bayh, Evan: Birth, Dec 26
  Benjamin Harrison's Birthday Celeb (Indianapolis), Aug 20
  Berne Swiss Days (Berne), Jul 29
  Big Ten Men's Basketball Tournament (Indianapolis), Mar 11
  Big Ten Men's Swimming/Diving Chmpshp (West Lafayette), Feb 26
  Big Ten Women's Basketball Tournament (Indianapolis), Mar 4
  Big Whopper Liar's Contest (New Harmony), Sep 18
  Candlelight Tours (New Harmony), Dec 4
  Chautauqua of the Arts (Columbus), Sep 18
  Christmas at Benjamin Harrison Home (Indianapolis), Nov 22
  Christmas Gift and Hobby Show (Indianapolis), Nov 10
  Church/Synagogue Library Assn Conf (Indianapolis), Jul 11
  Circus City Fest (Peru), Jul 17
  Colt League Pony Baseball World Series (Lafayette), Aug 3
  Crawfordsville Strawberry Fest (Crawfordsville), Jun 11
  Dean, James, Birthday Celebration (Fairmont), Feb 7
  Elwood Glass Fest (Elwood), Aug 20
  Fairmount Fest/Remembering James Dean (Fairmount), Sep 24
  Feast of the Hunter's Moon (Lafayette), Oct 2
  Fishing Has No Boundaries (Monticello), May 15
  Fulton County Historical Power Show (Rochester), Jun 18
  Germanfest (Fort Wayne), Jun 6
  Heritage Week (New Harmony), Apr 19
  Ice Cream Social (Indianapolis), Jul 4
  Indiana Flower and Patio Show (Indianapolis), Mar 13
  Indy 500-Mile Race (Indianapolis), May 30
  Johnny Appleseed Fest (Fort Wayne), Sep 18
  Literally, A Haunted House (New Albany), Oct 1
  Lugar, Richard G.: Birth, Apr 4
  Marshall County Blueberry Fest (Plymouth), Sep 3
  Mississinewa 1812 (Marion), Oct 8
  Mitchell Persimmon Fest (Mitchell), Sep 18
  O'Bannon, Frank: Birth, Jan 30
  Parke County Covered Bridge Fest (Rockville), Oct 8
  Parke County Maple Fair (Rockville), Feb 28
  Popcorn Fest (Valparaiso), Sep 11
  Presidents' Day: Live from Delaware St (Indianapolis), Feb 16
  Primary Day: Live from Delaware Street (Indianapolis), May 6
  Redbud Trail Rendezvous (Rochester), Apr 24
  Romance & Remembrance (Indianapolis), Feb 14
  Scott County Ugly Woman Contest (Scottsburg), Sep 11
  State Fair (Indianapolis), Aug 11
  Three Rivers Fest (Fort Wayne), Jul 10
  Trail of Courage Living-History Fest (Rochester), Sep 18
  Wizard of Oz Fest (Chesterton), Sep 17
Indiana, Robert: Birth, Sep 13
Indianapolis 500: Anniv, May 30
Indianapolis Sunk: Anniv, Jul 29
Indigenous People, UN Intl Decade of World's, Jan 1
Indonesia,
  Independence Day, Aug 17
  Kartini Day, Apr 21
Infection Control Week, Intl, Oct 18
Infertility Survival Day, Natl, May 2
Informed Woman Month, Apr 1
Ingels, Marty: Birth, Mar 9
Ingram, James: Birth, Feb 16
Inhofe, James M.: Birth, Nov 17
Inkster, Juli: Birth, Jun 24
Innergize Day, Sep 23
Innes, Laura: Birth, Aug 16
Innovation Week Intl, Apr 25
Inouye, Daniel: Birth, Sep 7
INPEX, May 12
Insects: Carpenter Ant Awareness Week, Jun 20
Insulin First Isolated: Anniv, Jul 27
Intergeneration Day, Oct 3
Internal Audit Awareness Month, Intl, May 1
Internet Created: Anniv, Oct 29
Interstate Highway System Born: Anniv, Jun 29
Intimate Apparel Market Week, Jan 12
Intl Week (College Station, TX), Feb 23
Intrepid Media Anniversary Event, Sep 10
Introduce a Girl to Engineering Day, Feb 26
Inventors Congress, Minnesota (Redwood Falls, MN), Jun 11
Inventors Hall of Fame, Woman Inducted to: Anniv, May 18
Inventors' Month, Natl, Aug 1
Iowa,
  Admission Day, Dec 28
  Bald Eagle Appreciation Days (Keokuk), Jan 16
  Balloon Classic, Natl (Indianola), Jul 30
  Big 12 Wrestling Chmpshps (Ames), Mar 6
  Big Ten Men's/Women's Cross Country Chmpshp (Iowa City), Oct 31
  Big Ten Women's Indoor Track/Field Chmpshps (Iowa City), Feb 28
  Big Ten Women's Rowing (Iowa City), May 1
  Bike Van Buren (Van Buren County), Aug 21
  Bix Beiderbecke Mem Jazz Fest (Davenport), Jul 22
  Britt Draft Horse Show (Britt), Sep 3
  Burlington Steamboat Days/Amer Music Fest (Burlington), Jun 15
  Celtic Highland Games of the Quad Cities (Davenport), Aug 28
  Christmas in the Villages (Van Buren County), Dec 4
  Civil War Reenactment (Keokuk), Apr 23
  Creston/Southwest Iowa Balloon Days (Creston), Sep 17
  Donna Reed Performing Arts Fest (Denison), Jun 22
  Dyersville Fest of the Arts (Dyersville), Sep 25
  Forest Craft/Scenic Drive Fest (Van Buren Cnty), Oct 9
  Glenn Miller Birthplace Society Fest (Clarinda), Jun 9
  Grand Excursion 2004 (Davenport, Bettendorf), Jun 25
  Grant Wood Art Fest (Stone City–Anamosa), Jun 13
  Grassley, Charles: Birth, Sep 17
  Great River Tug Fest (LeClaire), Aug 13
  Harkin, Thomas R.: Birth, Nov 19
  Herbert Hoover Day, Aug 8
  Holzfest (Amana), Aug 20
  Ice Cream Days (Le Mars), Jul 1
  Independence Sunday, Jun 27
  Iowa Storytelling Fest (Clear Lake), Jul 23
  Johnson County 4H and FFA Fair (Iowa City), Jul 26
  Jule Fest (Elk Horn), Nov 26
  Marble Meet at Amana (Amana), Jun 12
  Midwest Regional Lawn, Garden and Flower Show (Davenport), Mar 5
  Missisippi Valley Blues Fest (Davenport), Jul 2
  NAIA Wom Div II Basketball Chmpshp Tourn (Sioux City), Mar 10
  No-Tillage Conference, Natl (Des Moines), Jan 7
  Old Threshers Reunion (Mt Pleasant), Sep 2
  Old-Time Country Music Contest, Fest & Expo, Natl (Avoca), Aug 29
  Pella Tulip Time Fest (Pella), May 6
  Perry's "BRR" (Bike Ride to Rippey) (Perry), Feb 7
  Quad City Air Show (Davenport), Jun 25
  Quad City Arts Festival of Trees (Davenport), Nov 18
  Register's Bicycle Ride Across Iowa (Des Moines), Jul 25
  River Rockin' Ribfest (Davenport), Aug 27
  Splinterfest (Amana), Jun 18
  State Fair, Iowa (Des Moines), Aug 12
  Summer Farm Toy Show (Dyersville), Jun 11
  Ten Thousand Crestonians (Creston), Jul 3
  Tivoli Fest (Elk Horn), May 29
  Vilsack, Tom: Birth, Dec 13
Iowa, Explosion on USS: Anniv, Apr 19
Iran,
  Fifteenth of Khordad, Jun 5
  Iran Air Flight 655 Disaster, Jul 3
  Islamic Republic Day, Apr 1
  Khomeini: Death Anniv, Jun 3
  National Day, Feb 11
  Natl Day of Oil, Mar 19
  New Year (Noruz), Mar 21
  Seizure of US Embassy: Anniv, Nov 4
  Teheran Conference: Anniv, Nov 28
  Yalda, Dec 21
Iran-Contra: Oliver North Role: Anniv, Jul 5
Iraq,
  Congress Authorized Force Against Iraq: Anniv, Jan 12
  Desert Shield: Anniv, Aug 7
  Desert Storm: UN Deadline Resolution: Anniv, Nov 28
  Ground War Against Iraq Begins: Anniv, Feb 23
  Invades Kuwait: Anniv, Aug 2
  National Day, Apr 9
  Operation Iraqi Freedom: Anniv, Mar 19
  Persian Gulf War Begins: Anniv, Jan 16
Ireland,
  Bank Holiday, Jun 3
  Bank Holiday, Aug 5
  Bank Holiday, Oct 28
  Bloomsday: Anniv, Jun 16
  Day of the Wren, Dec 26
  Easter Rising, Apr 24
  Ivy Day, Oct 6
  May Day Bank Holiday, May 6
  National Day, Mar 17
  Saint Stephen's Day, Dec 26
Ireland, Kathy: Birth, Mar 8
Ireland, Patricia: Birth, Oct 19
Iris Fest (Sumter, SC), May 27
Irish-American Heritage Month, Mar 1
Iron Curtain Speech: Anniv, Mar 5
Irons, Jeremy: Birth, Sep 19
Ironside TV Premiere: Anniv, Sep 14
Iroquois Steeplechase (Nashville, TN), May 8
Irrational Exuberance Enters Lexicon: Anniv, Dec 5
Irving, Amy: Birth, Sep 10
Irving, Clifford: Fake Howard Hughes Biography: Anniv, Jan 9
Irving, John: Birth, Mar 2
Irving, Washington: Birth Anniv, Apr 3
Irwin Earns 1st Medal of Honor: Anniv, Feb 13
Irwin, Bill: Birth, Apr 11
Irwin, Hale S.: Birth, Jun 3
Irwin, Steve: Birth, Feb 22
Isaak, Chris: Birth, Jun 26
Isherwood, Christopher: Birth Anniv, Aug 26
Ishii, Kazuhiro: Birth, Sep 9
Ising, Rudolf C.: Birth Anniv, Aug 7
Isle of Eight Flags Shrimp Fest (Fernandina Beach, FL), Apr 30
Isle Royale Natl Park Established: Anniv, Apr 3
Isozaki, Arata: Birth, Jul 23
Isra al Mi'raj: Ascent of Prophet Muhammad, Sep 11
Israel,
  Arafat Returns to Palestine: Anniv, Jul 1
  Camp David Accord Signed: Anniv, Mar 26
  Hashoah/Holocaust Day, Apr 18
  Hebron Massacre: Anniv, Feb 25
  Independence Day (Yom Ha'atzma'ut), Apr 26
  Israeli Siege of Suez City Ends: Anniv, Jan 28
  Jerusalem Day (Yom Yerushalayim), May 19
  Remembrance Day (Yom Ha'zikkaron), Apr 25

★ Chase's 2004 Calendar of Events ★ Index

Israeli Olympiad Massacre: Anniv, Sep 5
Issaquah Salmon Days Festival (Issaquah, WA), Oct 2
It Takes a Thief TV Premiere: Anniv, Jan 9
Italian Heritage Fest, West Virginia (Clarksburg, WV), Sep 3
Italy,
 Battle of San Pietro Anniv, **Dec 15**
 Calabria Earthquake: Anniv, **Dec 16**
 Calcio Fiorentino (Florence), **Jun 24**
 Carnival Week (Milan), **Feb 22**
 Epiphany Fair (Rome), **Jan 5**
 Explosion of the Cart (Florence), **Apr 11**
 Feast of the Incappucciati (Gradoli), **Feb 19**
 Feast of the Redeemer (Venice), **Jul 18**
 Fest of St. Efisio (Cagliari), **May 1**
 Gioco Del Ponte (Pisa), **Jun 6**
 Giostra della Quintana (Fcligno), **Sep 12**
 Historical Regatta (Venice), **Sep 5**
 Joust of the Quintana (Ascoli/Piceno), **Aug 1**
 Joust of the Saracen (Arezzo), **Sep 5**
 La Befana, **Jan 6**
 Liberation Day, **Apr 25**
 Mussolini Ousted: Anniv, **Jul 25**
 Palio (Siena), **Jul 2**
 Palio Dei Balestrieri (Gubbio), **May 30**
 Palio del Golfo (La Spezia), **Aug 8**
 Procession of Addolorata and Mysteries (Taranto), **Apr 8**
 Purgatory Banquet (Gradoli), **Feb 25**
 Republic Day, **Jun 2**
 Stresa Music Weeks (Stresa), **Aug 20**
 Venice Film Fest (Venice), **Aug 28**
 Victory Day, **Nov 4**
 Wedding of the Sea (Venice), **May 23**
It's About Time Week, **Dec 25**
Ivanek, Zeljko: Birth, **Aug 15**
I've Got a Secret TV Premiere: Anniv, **Jun 19**
Iverson, Allen: Birth, **Jun 7**
Ives, Burl: Birth Anniv, **Jun 14**
Ivey, Judith: Birth, **Sep 4**
Ivy Day (Ireland), **Oct 6**
Iwo Jima Day: Anniv, **Feb 23**
Jack Benny Program TV Premiere: Anniv, **Oct 28**
Jack the Ripper Letter: Anniv, **Sep 27**
Jackie Mayer Rehab Center Day, **Oct 6**
Jackson, Andrew: Battle of New Orleans: Anniv, **Jan 8**
Jackson, Andrew: Birth Anniv, **Mar 15**
Jackson, Anne: Birth, **Sep 3**
Jackson, Bo: Birth, **Nov 30**
Jackson, Glenda: Birth, **May 9**
Jackson, Jackie: Birth, **May 4**
Jackson, Janet: Birth, **May 16**
Jackson, Jermaine: Birth, **Dec 11**
Jackson, Jesse: Birth, **Oct 8**
Jackson, Joe: Birth, **Aug 11**
Jackson, Jonathan: Birth, **May 11**
Jackson, Joshua: Birth, **Jun 11**
Jackson, Kate: Birth, **Oct 29**
Jackson, Mahalia: Birth Anniv, **Oct 26**
Jackson, Marlon: Birth, **Mar 12**
Jackson, Michael: Birth, **Aug 29**
Jackson, Peter: Birth, **Oct 31**
Jackson, Phil: Birth, **Sep 17**
Jackson, Rachel D.: Birth Anniv, **Jun 15**
Jackson, Randy: Birth, **Oct 29**
Jackson, Reggie: Birth, **May 18**
Jackson, Samuel L.: Birth, **Dec 21**
Jackson, Shirley Ann: Birth, **Aug 6**
Jackson, Stonewall: Birthday Celebration, **Jan 21**
Jackson, Thomas J. "Stonewall": Birth Anniv, **Jan 21**
Jackson, Tito: Birth, **Oct 15**
Jackson, Victoria: Birth, **Aug 2**
Jacob, Irene: Birth, **Jul 15**
Jacobi, Derek: Birth, **Oct 22**
Jacobi, Lou: Birth, **Dec 28**
Jacoby, Scott: Birth, **Nov 19**
Jaeger, Andrea: Birth, **Jun 4**
Jagger, Bianca: Birth, **May 2**
Jagger, Dean: Birth Anniv, **Nov 7**
Jagger, Mick: Birth, **Jul 26**
Jagr, Jaromir: Birth, **Feb 15**
Jahn, Helmut: Birth, **Jan 1**
Jakes, John: Birth, **Mar 31**
Jamaica,
 Abolition of Slavery, **Aug 1**
 Discovery by Columbus: Anniv, **May 4**
 Independence Day, **Aug 2**
 Maroon Fest, **Jan 6**
 Natl Heroes Day, **Oct 18**
 Port Royal Hurricane: Anniv, **Aug 28**
Jamboree in the Hills (St. Clairsville, OH), **Jul 15**
James, Henry: Birth Anniv, **Apr 15**
James, Jesse: Birth Anniv, **Sep 5**
James, John: Birth, **Apr 18**
James, Kevin: Birth, **Apr 26**
James, P.D.: Birth, **Aug 3**
James, Rick: Birth, **Feb 1**
James, Sonny: Birth, **May 1**
James, William: Birth Anniv, **Jan 11**
Jamestown Burned by Bacon's Rebellion: Anniv, **Sep 19**
Jamestown Landing Day (Williamsburg, VA), **May 15**
Jamestown, VA: Founding Anniv, **May 14**
Jamieson, Bob: Birth, **Feb 1**

Jamison, Judith: Birth, **May 10**
Janis, Byron: Birth, **Mar 24**
Janney, Allison: Birth, **Nov 19**
Jansen, Dan: Birth, **Jun 17**
Japan,
 Autumnal Equinox Day, **Sep 22**
 Battle of Bismarck Sea: Anniv, **Mar 2**
 Bean Throwing Fest (Setsubun), **Feb 3**
 Birthday of the Emperor, **Dec 23**
 Bon Fest (Feast of Lanterns), **Jul 13**
 Children's Day, **May 5**
 Chrysanthemum Day, **Sep 9**
 Coming-of-Age Day, **Jan 12**
 Constitution Memorial Day, **May 3**
 Cormorant Fishing Fest, **May 11**
 Culture Day, **Nov 3**
 Day of the Rice God (Chiyoda), **Jun 6**
 Doll Fest (Hinamatsuri), **Mar 3**
 Flower Fest (Hana Matsuri), **Apr 8**
 Foundation Day, Natl, **Feb 11**
 Golden Week Holidays, **Apr 29**
 Greenery Day, **Apr 29**
 Ha-Ri-Ku-Yo (Needle Mass), **Feb 8**
 Haru-No-Yabuiri, **Jan 16**
 Health-Sports Day, **Oct 11**
 Hiroshima Day, **Aug 6**
 Hollyhock Fest (Kyoto), **May 15**
 Japan Agrees to End Use of Drift Nets: Anniv, **Nov 26**
 Japan Bombed: Anniv, **Apr 18**
 Japanese Era New Year, **Jan 1**
 Kakizome, **Jan 2**
 Kanto Earthquake Memorial Day, **Sep 1**
 Labor Thanksgiving Day, **Nov 23**
 Marine Day, **Jul 20**
 Moment of Silence (Nagasaki), **Aug 9**
 Mount Ogura Plane Crash: Anniv, **Aug 12**
 Namahage, **Dec 31**
 Nanakusa, **Jan 7**
 Newspaper Week, **Oct 1**
 Peace Fest (Hiroshima), **Aug 6**
 Respect for the Aged Day, **Sep 15**
 Rice Planting Fest (Osaka), **Jun 14**
 Roughhouse Fest, **Feb 14**
 Ruling Party Loses Majority: Anniv, **Jul 18**
 Shichi-Go-San, **Nov 15**
 Snow Fest, **Feb 8**
 Soma No Umaoi (Wild Horse Chasing), **Jul 23**
 Suffers Major Earthquake: Anniv, **Jan 17**
 Tanabata (Star Fest), **Jul 7**
 Usokae (Bullfinch Exchange Fest), **Jan 7**
 Vernal Equinox Day, **Mar 20**
 Water-Drawing Fest, **Mar 1**
Japanese,
 Bon Odori Fest of Lanterns (Chicago, IL), **Jul 10**
 Ginza Holiday (Chicago, IL), **Aug 20**
 Hatsume Fair (Delray Beach, FL), **Feb 28**
 O-Bon Fest (Delray Beach, FL), **Aug 14**
Japanese Attack on US Mainland: Anniv, **Feb 23**
Japanese Internment (WWII): Anniv, **Feb 19**
Jarman, Claude, Jr: Birth, **Sep 27**
Jarreau, Al: Birth, **Mar 12**
Jarrett, Dale: Birth, **Nov 26**
Jarriel, Thomas Edwin: Birth, **Dec 29**
Jarvik, Robert: Birth, **May 11**
Jarvis, Gregory B.: Birth Anniv, **Aug 24**
Jay, John: Birth Anniv, **Dec 12**
Jazz and Blues,
 Albany Riverfront Jazz Festival (Albany, NY), **Sep 11**
 All That Jazz Weekend (Asheville, NC), **Jan 30**
 Bix Beiderbecke Mem Jazz Fest (Davenport, IA), **Jul 22**
 Charlie Parker at the LA Philharmonic: Anniv, **Mar 25**
 Chicago Blues Fest (Chicago, IL), **Jun 10**
 Chicago Jazz Fest (Chicago, IL), **Sep 2**
 Davis, Miles: Birth Anniv, **May 25**
 Genuine Jazz in Breckenridge (Breckenridge, CO), **Jun 25**
 Guthrie Jazz Banjo Fest (Guthrie, OK), **May 21**
 Jazz Day, Intl, **May 29**
 Jazz Fest, Intl (Pori, Finland), **Jul 17**
 Lionel Hampton Jazz Fest (Moscow, ID), **Feb 25**
 Medford Jazz Jubilee (Medford, OR), **Oct 8**
 Mississippi Valley Blues Fest (Davenport, IA), **Jul 2**
 Monterey Jazz Fest (Monterey, CA), **Sep 17**
 Natchitoches Jazz Festival (Natchitoches, LA), **Apr 2**
 New Orleans Jazz/Heritage Fest (New Orleans, LA), **Apr 22**
 North Sea Jazz Fest (The Hague, Netherlands), **Jul 9**
 Parker, Charlie: Birth Anniv, **Aug 29**
 Ra, Sun: Birth Anniv, **May 22**
 Sacramento Jazz Jubilee (Sacramento, CA), **May 28**
 San Sebastian Jazz Fest (Spain), **Jul 22**
 Satchmo Summer Fest (New Orleans, LA), **Aug 4**
 Snowbird, Utah Jazz & Blues Festival (Snowbird, UT), **Jul 30**
 SunFest (West Palm Beach, FL), **Apr 28**
 Telluride Jazz Celebration (Telluride, CO), **Aug 6**
 Winter Park Jazz Fest (Winter Park, CO), **Jul 10**
 Ziegler Kettle Moraine Jazz Fest (West Bend, WI), **Sep 10**
Jeffers, Robinson: Birth Anniv, **Jan 10**
Jefferson Davis Day (Confederate Memorial Day, KY), **Jun 3**
Jefferson, Joseph: Birth Anniv, **Feb 20**
Jefferson, Martha: Birth Anniv, **Oct 19**
Jefferson, Richard: Birth, **Jun 21**

Jefferson, Thomas, and Adams, John: Death Anniv, **Jul 4**
Jefferson, Thomas: Birth Anniv, **Apr 13**
Jefferson, Thomas: Birth Anniv (Pres Proc), **Apr 13**
Jeffersons TV Premiere: Anniv, **Jan 18**
Jeffords, James M.: Birth, **May 11**
Jeffries, John: Weatherman's Day, **Feb 5**
Jemison, Mae: Birth, **Oct 17**
Jenkins, Stephan: Birth, **Sep 27**
Jenkins's Ear Day, **Apr 9**
Jenner, Bruce: Birth, **Oct 28**
Jenner, Edward: Birth Anniv, **May 17**
Jennings, Jason: Birth, **Jul 17**
Jennings, Peter: Birth, **Jul 29**
Jeopardy TV Premiere: Anniv, **Mar 30**
Jerry Lewis Muscular Dystrophy Association Telethon, **Sep 5**
Jesse James Days, Defeat of (Northfield, MN), **Sep 9**
Jeter, Derek: Birth, **Jun 26**
Jetsons TV Premiere: Anniv, **Sep 23**
Jett, Joan: Birth, **Sep 22**
Jewel: Birth, **May 23**
Jewish Heritage Week (Pres Proc), **Apr 25**
Jewish Observances,
 Asarah B'Tevet, **Dec 22**
 Asarah B'Tevet, **Jan 4**
 Chanukah, **Dec 8**
 Fast of Gedalya, **Sep 19**
 Fast of Tammuz, **Jul 6**
 Hadassah: Anniv, **Feb 24**
 Israel Yom Ha'atzma'ut (Independence Day), **Apr 26**
 Kristallnacht: Anniv, **Nov 9**
 Lag B'Omer, **May 9**
 Liberation of Buchenwald: Anniv, **Apr 11**
 Passover Begins, **Apr 5**
 Pesach (Passover), **Apr 6**
 Purim, **Mar 7**
 Rosh Hashanah (New Year), **Sep 16**
 Rosh Hashanah Begins, **Sep 15**
 Shabbat Across America, **Mar 12**
 Shavuot, **May 26**
 Shavuot Begins, **May 25**
 Shemini Atzeret, **Oct 7**
 Simchat Torah, **Oct 8**
 Sukkot Begins, **Sep 29**
 Sukkot/Succoth/Feast of Tabernacles, **Sep 30**
 Ta'anit Esther (Fast of Esther), **Mar 4**
 Tisha B'Av (Fast cf Ab), **Jul 27**
 Tu B'Shvat, **Feb 7**
 US Holocaust Museum Opens: Anniv, **Apr 26**
 Warsaw Ghetto Revolt: Anniv, **Apr 19**
 Yom Hashoah/Holocaust Day (Israel), **Apr 18**
 Yom Kippur, **Sep 25**
 Yom Kippur Begins, **Sep 24**
Jewison, Norman: Birth, **Jul 21**
Jillette, Penn: Birth, **Mar 5**
Jillian, Ann: Birth, **Jan 29**
Jimmy Durante Show TV Premiere: Anniv, **Oct 2**
Jinnah, Mohammed Ali: Birth Anniv, **Dec 25**
Joan of Arc: Birth Anniv, **Jan 6**
Jobs, Steven: Birth, **Feb 24**
Joe Cain Procession (Mobile, AL), **Feb 22**
Joel, Billy: Birth, **May 9**
Johanns, Mike: Birth, **May 11**
John Deere Tractor & Memorabilia Auction (Moline, IL), **Aug 13**
John Deere's 200th Birthday (Moline, IL), **Feb 7**
John Parker Day, **Apr 19**
John Paul II, Pope: Birth, **May 18**
John, Elton: Birth, **Mar 25**
John, Tommy: Birth, **May 22**
Johnny Appleseed Day, **Mar 11**
Johnny Appleseed Days (Lake City, MN), **Oct 2**
Johnny Appleseed Fest (Fort Wayne, IN), **Sep 18**
Johns, Glynis: Birth, **Oct 5**
Johns, Jasper: Birth, **May 15**
Johnson, Amy: Flight Anniv, **May 5**
Johnson, Andrew, Impeachment Proceedings: Anniv, **Feb 24**
Johnson, Andrew: Birth Anniv, **Dec 29**
Johnson, Arte: Birth, **Jan 20**
Johnson, Ban: Birth Anniv, **Jan 6**
Johnson, Betsy: Birth, **Aug 10**
Johnson, Clark: Birth, **Sep 10**
Johnson, Davey: Birth, **Jan 30**
Johnson, Don: Birth, **Dec 15**
Johnson, Eliza M.: Birth Anniv, **Oct 4**
Johnson, Jimmy: Birth, **Mar 31**
Johnson, John (Jack) Arthur: Birth Anniv, **Mar 31**
Johnson, Kevin: Birth, **Mar 4**
Johnson, Keyshawn: Birth, **Jul 22**
Johnson, Lady Bird: Birth, **Dec 22**
Johnson, Lyndon B.: Birth Anniv, **Aug 27**
Johnson, Lyndon B.: Monday Holiday Law: Anniv, **Jun 28**
Johnson, Lyndon B: Civil Rights Act of 1968: Anniv, **Apr 11**
Johnson, Magic: Birth, **Aug 14**
Johnson, Michael: Birth, **Sep 13**
Johnson, Nick: Birth, **Sep 19**
Johnson, Randy: Birth, **Sep 10**
Johnson, Richard M.: Birth Anniv, **Oct 17**
Johnson, Robert: Birth Anniv, **May 8**
Johnson, Samuel: Birth Anniv, **Sep 18**
Johnson, Tim: Birth, **Dec 28**
Johnson, Virginia: Birth, **Feb 11**

713

Johnson, William H.: Birth Anniv, Mar 18
Johnston, Joseph: Birth Anniv, Feb 3
Johnston, Joseph: Surrender at Durham Station: Anniv, Apr 18
Johnston, Kristen: Birth, Sep 20
Johnstown Flood: Anniv, May 31
Johnstown Folkfest (Johnstown, PA), Sep 3
Join Hands Day, May 1
Joke Day, Presidential, Aug 11
Jolie, Angelina: Birth, Jun 4
Jolson, Al: Birth Anniv, May 26
Jones, Andruw: Birth, Apr 23
Jones, Bobby: Birth Anniv, Mar 17
Jones, Casey: Birth Anniv, Mar 14
Jones, Chipper: Birth, Apr 24
Jones, Chuck: Birth Anniv, Sep 21
Jones, Cobi: Birth, Jun 16
Jones, Davy: Birth, Dec 30
Jones, Dean: Birth, Jan 25
Jones, Eddie: Birth, Oct 20
Jones, Edward "Too Tall": Birth, Feb 23
Jones, George: Birth, Sep 12
Jones, Grace: Birth, May 19
Jones, Howard: Birth, Feb 23
Jones, James Earl: Birth, Jan 17
Jones, Jeffrey: Birth, Sep 28
Jones, Jennifer: Birth, Mar 2
Jones, Jenny: Birth, Jun 7
Jones, John Paul: Birth Anniv, Jul 6
Jones, K.C.: Birth, May 25
Jones, Leroi: See Amiri Baraka: Birth, Oct 7
Jones, Marion: Birth, Oct 12
Jones, Mary H.: Birth Anniv, May 1
Jones, Quincy: Birth, Mar 14
Jones, Ricki Lee: Birth, Nov 8
Jones, Sam J.: Birth, Aug 12
Jones, Shirley: Birth, Mar 31
Jones, Terry: Birth, Feb 1
Jones, Tom: Birth, Jun 7
Jones, Tommy Lee: Birth, Sep 15
Jonestown Massacre: Anniv, Nov 18
Jong, Erica: Birth, Mar 26
Jonson, Ben: Birth Anniv, Jun 11
Joplin, Janis: Birth Anniv, Jan 19
Joplin, Scott: Birth Anniv, Nov 24
Jordan,
 Accession Day, Jun 9
 Great Arab Revolt and Army Day, Jun 10
 Independence Day, May 25
 King Hussein: Birth Anniv, Nov 14
 King's Birthday, Jan 30
Jordan, Michael: Birth, Feb 17
Jordan, Neil: Birth, Feb 25
Jordan, Vernon, Jr: Birth, Aug 15
Joseph, Chief, Surrender: Anniv, Oct 5
Joseph, Chief: Death Anniv, Sep 21
Jouett, Jack: Ride Anniv, Jun 3
Joule, James: Birth Anniv, Dec 24
Journalism,
 All the News That's Fit to Print: Anniv, Feb 10
 Around the World in 72 Days Anniv, Nov 14
 Beginning of the Penny Press: Anniv, Sep 3
 Bolles, Don: Death Anniv, Jun 13
 Brinkley, David: Birth Anniv, Jul 10
 Columnist's Day, Natl, Jun 28
 Dewey Defeats Truman Headline: Anniv, Nov 3
 First American Daily Newspaper Published: Anniv, May 30
 First American Newspaper: Anniv, Sep 25
 First Magazine Published in America: Anniv, Feb 13
 First Newspaper Comic Strip: Anniv, Oct 18
 First Photos Used in a Newspaper Report: Anniv, Jul 1
 First Televised Presidential News Conf: Anniv, Jan 25
 Japan: Newspaper Week, Oct 1
 Life Magazine Debuted: Anniv, Nov 23
 NAB 2004/National Broadcasters Conv (Las Vegas, NV), Apr 17
 New York Times First Published: Anniv, Sep 18
 New York Weekly Journal Anniv First Issue, Nov 5
 New Yorker Published: Anniv, Feb 21
 Newspaper Carrier Day, Sep 4
 Newspaper in Education Week, Mar 1
 Newspaper Week, Natl, Oct 3
 Newspapers Taken to Court: Anniv, Aug 16
 Nixon's Last Press Conf: Anniv, Nov 7
 People Magazine: Anniv, Mar 4
 Pulitzer, Joseph: Birth Anniv, Apr 10
 Pyle, Ernest: Birth Anniv, May 3
 Thomas, Lowell: Birth Anniv, Apr 6
 Time Magazine First Published: Anniv, Mar 3
 UN: World Press Freedom Day, May 3
 USA Today First Published: Anniv, Sep 15
 Zenger, John P.: Arrest Anniv, Nov 17
Journey's End National Art Exhibition (Astoria, OR), Nov 1
Joust of the Quintana (Ascoli/Piceno, Italy), Aug 1
Joy, Robert: Birth, Aug 17
Joyce, James: Birth Anniv, Feb 2
Joygerm Day, Natl, Jan 4
Joyner-Kersee, Jackie: Birth, Mar 3
Juarez, Benito: Birth Anniv, Mar 21
Jubilee Days Fest (Zion, IL), Sep 4
Judd, Ashley: Birth, Apr 19
Judd, Naomi: Birth, Jan 11
Judd, Wynonna: Birth, May 30

Judgment Day, Jan 17
Juggling Day, World, Jun 14
Jule Fest (Elk Horn, IA), Nov 26
Julia, Raul: Birth Anniv, Mar 9
Julian, Percy: Birth Anniv, Apr 11
July Belongs to Blueberries Month, Natl, Jul 1
June Is Perennial Gardening Month, Jun 1
June Is Turkey Lovers' Month, Jun 1
Juneteenth, Jun 19
Junkanoo (Bahamas), Dec 26
Jupiter Effect: Anniv, Mar 10
Jupiter, Comet Crashes into: Anniv, Jul 16
Jurgensen, Sonny: Birth, Aug 23
Jury, First All-Woman: Anniv, Sep 22
Just Do It Day—Make the Connection, Jan 21
Just for Laughs Fest (Montreal, QC, Canada), Jul 15
Just Pray No: Worldwide Weekend Prayer, Apr 17
Just, Ernest E.: Birth Anniv, Aug 14
Justice, David: Birth, Apr 14
Justice, US Dept of: Anniv, Jun 22
Kaczmarek, Jane: Birth, Dec 21
Kahanamoku, Duke: Birth Anniv, Aug 24
Kahlo, Frida: Birth Anniv, Jul 6
Kalb, Marvin: Birth, Jun 9
Kamali, Norma: Birth, Jun 27
Kamehameha Day (HI), Jun 11
Kanakaredes, Melina: Birth, Apr 23
Kanawa, Kiri Te: Birth, Mar 6
Kander, John: Birth, Mar 18
Kane, Carol: Birth, Jun 18
Kansas,
 Admission Day, Jan 29
 Apple Fest (Topeka), Oct 3
 Arkalalah Fest (Arkansas City), Oct 27
 Barbed Wire Swap/Sell (LaCrosse), Apr 29
 Beef Empire Days (Garden City), Jun 8
 Big 12 Men's Golf Chmpshp (Hutchinson), Apr 26
 Brownback, Sam: Birth, Sep 12
 Columbus Day Fest/Hot Air Balloon Regatta (Columbus), Oct 8
 Dalton Defenders Day (Coffeyville), Oct 1
 Dodge City Days (Dodge City), Jul 30
 Eagle Days (Junction City), Jan 17
 Fiesta Bullwhacker (Olathe), Jun 5
 Guitar Flat-Picking Chmpshps/Walnut Valley Fest, Natl (Winfield), Sep 16
 Heritage Christmas (Lindsborg), Dec 4
 Hoisington Celebration (Hoisington), Sep 3
 HutchFest (Hutchinson), Jun 27
 Inter-State Fair/Rodeo (Coffeyville), Aug 7
 Kansas City Renaissance Fest (Bonner Springs), Sep 4
 Kechi Fall Outdoor Antique Swap Meet (Kechi), Sep 25
 Kechi Spring Outdoor Antique Swap Meet & Flea Market (Kechi), May 1
 Kechi's Antique Country Christmas (Kechi), Nov 20
 Leavenworth River Fest (Leavenworth), Jul 1
 Little Balkans Days/Folklife Fest (Pittsburg), Sep 2
 Mennonite Relief Sale (Hutchinson), Apr 16
 Monster Myths by Moonlight (Milford), Oct 16
 NAIA Natl Men's and Women's Swimming and Diving Championships (Lawrence), Mar 3
 NAIA Outdoor Track/Field Chmpshps (Olathe, May 27
 New Beginning Fest (Coffeyville), Apr 23
 Orphan Train Heritage Soc Reunion (Concordia), Sep 30
 Pancake Day, Intl (Liberal), Feb 24
 Pony Express Fest (Hanover), Aug 29
 Powered Parachute Fly-in (Columbus), Sep 16
 Quantrill's Raid on Lawrence, KS: Anniv, Aug 21
 Redbud and Garden Show (Kechi), Apr 24
 Roberts, Pat: Birth, Apr 20
 Salter Elected First Woman Mayor in US: Anniv, Apr 4
 Sibelius, Kathleen: Birth, May 15
 State Fair (Hutchinson), Sep 10
 Sundown Salute (Junction City), Jul 3
 Swap Meet and Tractor Show (Washington), Jun 5
 Twelve Villages of Christmas (Washington County), Dec 4
 Wild West Weekend and Country Music Fest (Clifton), Aug 20
 Winfield Art-in-the-Park Fest (Winfield), Oct 2
 Woofstock (Wichita), Oct 22
 Zoobalee (Garden City), Jul 4
Kansas City Hotel Disaster: Anniv, Jul 17
Kaplan, Gabe: Birth, Mar 31
Kapoor, Shashi: Birth, Mar 18
Karan, Donna: Birth, Oct 2
Karaoke Week, Natl, Apr 18
Kariya, Paul: Birth, Oct 16
Karloff, Boris: Birth Anniv, Nov 23
Karn, Richard: Birth, Feb 17
Karras, Alex: Birth, Jul 15
Kasdan, Lawrence: Birth, Jan 14
Kasem, Casey: Birth, Apr 27
Kasparov, Garry: First Computer Chess Victory: Anniv, Feb 10
Kate Smith Hour TV Premiere: Anniv, Sep 25
Katmai Natl Park: Anniv, Dec 2
Katt, William: Birth, Feb 16
Kauffman, Stanley J.: Birth, Apr 24
Kaufmann, Christine: Birth, Jan 11
Kavner, Julie: Birth, Sep 7
Kaye, Danny: Birth Anniv, Jan 18

Kazakhstan,
 Constitution Day, Aug 31
 Independence Day, Oct 25
Kazan, Elia: Birth, Sep 7
Kazan, Lainie: Birth, May 15
Kazurinsky, Tim: Birth, Mar 3
Keach, Stacy, Jr: Birth, Jun 2
Keane, Bil: Birth, Oct 5
Keaton, Buster: Birth Anniv, Oct 4
Keaton, Diane: Birth, Jan 5
Keaton, Michael: Birth, Sep 9
Keats, John: Birth Anniv, Oct 31
Keegan, Andrew: Birth, Jan 29
Keel, Howard: Birth, Apr 13
Keene, Donald: Birth, Jun 18
Keeshan, Bob (Captain Kangaroo): Birth, Jun 27
Keillor, Garrison: Birth, Aug 7
Keitel, Harvey: Birth, May 13
Keith, David: Birth, May 8
Keller, Helen, Fest (Tuscumbia, AL), Jun 24
Keller, Helen: Birth Anniv, Jun 27
Kellerman, Sally: Birth, Jun 2
Kelley, Kitty: Birth, Apr 4
Kelly, Emmett: Birth Anniv, Dec 9
Kelly, Gene: Birth Anniv, Aug 23
Kelly, Grace: Birth Anniv, Nov 12
Kelly, Walt: Birth Anniv, Aug 25
Kelsey, Linda: Birth, Jul 28
Kemble, Fanny: Birth Anniv, Nov 27
Kemmler, William: First Electrocution for Death Penalty: Anniv, Aug 6
Kemp, Jack: Birth, Jul 13
Kemp, Shawn: Birth, Nov 26
Kempthorne, Dirk: Birth, Oct 29
Kenai Fjords Natl Park: Anniv, Dec 2
Keneally, Thomas: Birth, Oct 7
Kennan, George Frost: Birth, Feb 16
Kennedy Intl Airport Dedication: Anniv, Jul 31
Kennedy, Anthony M.: Birth, Jul 23
Kennedy, Cortez: Birth, Aug 23
Kennedy, Edward Moore: Birth, Feb 22
Kennedy, Ethel: Birth, Apr 11
Kennedy, George: Birth, Feb 18
Kennedy, Jamie: Birth, May 25
Kennedy, John F., Jr: Birth Anniv, Nov 25
Kennedy, John Fitzgerald,
 Assassination Anniv, Nov 22
 Birth Anniv, May 29
 Committee on Assassinations Report, Mar 29
 Cuban Missile Crisis: Anniv, Oct 22
 First Televised Presidential Debate: Anniv, Sep 26
 First Televised Presidential News Conf: Anniv, Jan 25
 Warren Commission Report Anniv, Sep 27
Kennedy, Robert,
 Assassination Anniv, Jun 5
 Birth Anniv, Nov 20
 Committee on Assassinations Report, Mar 29
Kennerly, David Hume: Birth, Mar 9
Kenny G: Birth, Jun 6
Kensit, Patsy: Birth, Mar 4
Kent State Students' Memorial Day, May 4
Kent, Jeff: Birth, Mar 7
Kentucky,
 Admission Day, Jun 1
 American Quilter's Society Show (Paducah), Apr 21
 Barbershop Quartet Singing Intl Conv (Louisville), Jun 27
 Battle of Blue Licks Celebration (Mount Olivet), Aug 21
 Berea Craft Fest (Berea), Jul 9
 Boone Day, Jun 7
 Bunning, Jim: Birth, Oct 23
 Christmas Candlelight Tour (Bardstown), Nov 26
 Confederate Memorial Day, Jun 3
 Corn Island Storytelling Fest (Louisville), Sep 16
 Daniel Boone Pioneer Festival (Winchester), Sep 3
 Everly Brothers/Central City Rock 'n Roll Cruise-In and Concert (Central City), Sep 1
 Fancy Farm Picnic (Fancy Farm), Aug 7
 Fest of the Bluegrass (Lexington), Jun 10
 Great American Brass Band Fest (Danville), Jun 12
 Indian Artifact Show (Owensboro), Aug 6
 Kentucky Apple Fest (Paintsville), Oct 1
 Kentucky Bourbon Fest (Bardstown), Sep 15
 Kentucky Derby (Louisville), May 1
 Kentucky Derby Fest (Louisville), Apr 16
 Lincoln's Birthplace Cabin Wreath Laying (Hodgenville), Feb 12
 Maifest (Covington), May 14
 Mammoth Cave Natl Park Established: Anniv, Jul 1
 Marion County Country Ham Days (Lebanon), Sep 25
 McConnell, Mitch: Birth, Feb 20
 Memory Days (Grayson), May 27
 Mint Julep Scale Meet (Falls of Rough), May 15
 Musical Tribute to Dr. M. L. King (Hodgenville), Jan 18
 Oktoberfest (Covington), Sep 10
 Patton, Paul E.: Birth, May 26
 PGA Seniors' Chmpshp (Louisville), May 24
 Running of the Rodents (Louisville), Apr 5
 Sawyer Triathlon (Louisville), Aug 7
 Send a Kid to Kamp Radiothon (Lexington), May 1
 State Fair (Louisville), Aug 19
 Surrender of Fort Donelson: Anniv, Feb 16
 Swappin' Meetin' (Cumberland), Oct 1

☆ Chase's 2004 Calendar of Events ☆ Index
Kentucky (cont'd)—Lathrop

Williamsburg Old-Fashioned Trading Days (Williamsburg), **Sep 9**
Kentucky Derby, First: Anniv, May 17
Kenya,
Jamhuri Day, **Dec 12**
Kenyatta Day, **Oct 20**
Madaraka Day, **Jun 1**
Kepler, Johannes: Birth Anniv, Dec 27
Kercheval, Ken: Birth, Jul 15
Kern, Jerome: Birth Anniv, Jan 27
Kerns, Joanna: Birth, Feb 12
Kerouac, Jack: Birth Anniv, Mar 12
Kerr, Deborah: Birth, Sep 30
Kerr, Steve: Birth, Sep 27
Kerrigan, Nancy: Birth, Oct 13
Kerry, John F.: Birth, Dec 11
Kerwin, Brian: Birth, Oct 25
Kerwin, Lance: Birth, Nov 6
Kewpie Doll: Rose C. O'Neill: Birth Anniv, Jun 25
Key, Francis Scott: Birth Anniv, Aug 1
Key, Francis Scott: Star-Spangled Banner Inspired: Anniv, Sep 13
Keynes, John Maynard: Birth Anniv, Jun 5
Keys, Alicia: Birth, Jan 25
KGB Founder Statue Dismantled: Anniv, Aug 22
Khachaturian, Aram: Birth Anniv, Jun 6
Khan, Chaka: Birth, Mar 23
Khomeini, Ayatollah: Death Anniv, Jun 3
Kick-Butt Day, Natl, Oct 11
Kidd, Jason: Birth, Mar 23
Kidd, Michael: Birth, Aug 12
Kidder, Margot: Birth, Oct 17
KidFilm® Fest (Dallas, TX), Jan 5
Kidman, Nicole: Birth, Jun 20
Kidnapping, Lindbergh: Anniv, Mar 1
Kidney Month, Natl, Mar 1
Kids' Day, Kiwanis, Natl, Sep 25
Kids' Goal Setting Week, Nov 1
KidsDay, Natl, Aug 1
KidSpree, Jul 17
Kiel, Richard: Birth, Sep 13
Kienzle, William: Birth, Sep 11
Kilborn, Craig: Birth, Aug 24
Killebrew, Harmon: Birth, Jun 29
Killy, Jean-Claude: Birth, Aug 30
Kilmer, Joyce: Birth Anniv, Dec 6
Kilmer, Val: Birth, Dec 31
Kilpatrick, James: Birth, Nov 1
Kim Il Sung: Death Anniv, Jul 8
Kimbrough, Charles: Birth, May 23
Kimmel, Jimmy: Birth, Nov 13
Kind, Richard: Birth, Nov 22
Kindergarten Day, Apr 21
Kindness Day, World, Nov 13
King Family Show TV Premiere: Anniv, Jan 23
King James Bible Published: Anniv, May 2
King, Alan: Birth, Dec 26
King, B.B.: Birth, Sep 16
King, Ben E.: Birth, Sep 28
King, Bille Jean, Wins Battle of Sexes: Anniv, Sep 20
King, Billie Jean: Birth, Nov 22
King, Carole: Birth, Feb 9
King, Coretta Scott: Birth, Apr 27
King, Don: Birth, Aug 20
King, Frank: Birth Anniv, Apr 9
King, Larry: Birth, Nov 19
King, Martin Luther, Jr,
Assassination Anniv, **Apr 4**
Awarded Nobel Peace Prize: Anniv, **Oct 14**
Birth Anniv, **Jan 15**
Birthday Observed, **Jan 19**
Committee on Assassinations Report, **Mar 29**
Habitat for Humanity Building on the Dream, **Jan 16**
March on Washington: Anniv, **Aug 28**
Martin Luther King, Jr, Federal Holiday, **Jan 19**
Musical Tribute to Dr. M. L. King (Hodgenville, KY), **Jan 18**
Opposes Vietnam War: Anniv, **Apr 4**
Stock Exchange Holiday, **Jan 19**
King, Perry: Birth, Apr 30
King, Rodney: Los Angeles Riots: Anniv, Apr 29
King, Stephen: Birth, Sep 21
King, W.L. MacKenzie: Birth Anniv, Dec 17
King, Wayne: Birth Anniv, Feb 16
King, William R.: Birth Anniv, Apr 7
Kingsley, Ben: Birth, Dec 31
Kingston, Alex: Birth, Mar 11
Kinnear, Greg: Birth, Jun 17
Kinney, Kathy: Birth, Nov 3
Kinski, Nastassja: Birth, Jan 24
Kipling, Rudyard: Birth Anniv, Dec 30
Kirby, Bruno: Birth, Apr 28
Kiribati: Independence Day, Jul 12
Kirshner, Don: Birth, Apr 17
Kirtland, Jared: Birth Anniv, Nov 10
Kiss-and-Make-Up-Day, Aug 25
Kissimmee Slough Shootout and Rendezvous (Big Cypress Reservation, FL), Feb 7
Kissinger, Henry: Birth, May 27
Kite, Tom: Birth, Dec 9
Kites, Kite-Flying,
Frankenmuth Skyfest (Frankenmuth, MI), **May 2**
Kite Fest of Santiago Sacatepequez (Guatemala), **Nov 1**
Kite Month, Natl, **Apr 1**
Kitt, Eartha: Birth, Jan 17
Kiwanis,
Kiwanis Intl: Anniv, **Jan 21**
Kiwanis Kids' Day, Natl, **Sep 25**
Kiwanis Prayer Week, **May 9**
Klein, Calvin: Birth, Nov 19
Klein, Robert: Birth, Feb 8
Kliban, B(ernard): Birth Anniv, Jan 1
Kline, Kevin: Birth, Oct 24
Klondike Days (Eagle River, WI), Feb 14
Klondike Eldorado Gold Discovery: Anniv, Aug 31
Klondike Gold Discovery: Anniv, Aug 16
Klugman, Jack: Birth, Apr 27
Knievel, Evel: Birth, Oct 17
Knight Rider TV Premiere: Anniv, Sep 26
Knight, Bobby: Birth, Oct 25
Knight, Gladys: Birth, May 28
Knight, O. Raymond: Birth Anniv, Apr 8
Knight, Shirley: Birth, Jul 5
Knights of Columbus Family Week, Aug 7
Knights of Columbus Founder's Day, Mar 29
Knights of Pythias: Founding Anniv, Feb 19
Knock-Knock Day, Natl, Oct 31
Knotts, Don: Birth, Jul 21
Knox County Scenic Drive (Galesburg, IL), Oct 2
Knuckles Down Month, Natl, Apr 1
Kobuk Valley Natl Park: Anniv, Dec 2
Koch, Edward: Birth, Dec 12
Koenig, Walter: Birth, Sep 14
Koestler, Arthur: Birth Anniv, Sep 5
Kohl, Herb: Birth, Feb 7
Koko the Gorilla: Birth, Jul 4
Kokoschka, Oskar: Birth Anniv, Mar 1
Kolzig, Olaf: Birth, Apr 6
Koop, C. Everett: Birth, Oct 14
Kopell, Bernie: Birth, Jun 21
Koppel, Ted: Birth, Feb 8
Korbut, Olga: Birth, May 16
Korea,
Alphabet Day (Hangul), **Oct 9**
Chusok, **Sep 28**
Constitution Day, **Jul 17**
Independence Day, **Aug 15**
Korea, North and South, End War: Anniv, **Dec 13**
Korean Air Lines Flight 007 Disaster: Anniv, **Sep 1**
Korean War Armistice: Anniv, **Jul 27**
Korean War Began: Anniv, **Jun 25**
Memorial Day, **Jun 6**
National Day, **Sep 9**
National Foundation, **Oct 3**
Samiljol (Independence Movement Day), **Mar 1**
Seoul Recaptured by UN Forces, **Mar 14**
Tano Day, **Jun 22**
Korean War Veterans Armistice Day, Natl (Pres Proc), Jul 27
Korman, Harvey: Birth, Feb 15
Kosar, Bernie: Birth, Nov 25
Kosciusko, Thaddeus: Birth Anniv, Feb 4
Kotto, Yaphet: Birth, Nov 15
Koufax, Sandy: Birth, Dec 30
Kournikova, Anna: Birth, Jun 7
Kovacs, Ernie: Birth Anniv, Jan 23
Kozak, Harley Jane: Birth, Jan 28
Krabbe, Jeroen: Birth, Dec 5
Kraft Television Theatre TV Premiere: Anniv, May 7
Krakatoa Eruption: Anniv, Aug 26
Krantz, Judith: Birth, Jan 9
Krassner, Paul: Birth, Apr 9
Krause, Peter: Birth, Aug 12
Kravitz, Lenny: Birth, May 26
Kreis, Jason: Birth, Dec 29
Kreuk, Kristin: Birth, Dec 30
Kreutzmann, Bill, Jr: Birth, Jun 7
Krige, Alice: Birth, Jun 28
Krim, Mathilde: Birth, Jul 9
Kristallnacht: Anniv, Nov 9
Kristofferson, Kris: Birth, Jun 22
Kroft, Steve: Birth, Aug 22
Krone, Julie: Birth, Jul 24
Krupp, Alfried: Birth Anniv, Aug 13
Kubek, Tony: Birth, Oct 12
Kubrick, Stanley: Birth Anniv, Jul 26
Kudrow, Lisa: Birth, Jul 30
Kuhn, Bowie: Birth, Oct 28
Kuhn, Margaret: Birth Anniv, Aug 3
Kukla, Fran and Ollie TV Premiere: Anniv, Nov 29
Kulongoski, Ted: Birth, Nov 5
Kung Fu TV Premiere: Anniv, Oct 1
Kunis, Mila: Birth, Aug 14
Kunstler, William: Birth Anniv, Jul 7
Kupcinet, Irv: Birth, Jul 31
Kupets, Courtney: Birth, Jul 27
Kuralt, Charles: Birth Anniv, Sep 10
Kurban Bayram: See Eid-al-Adha, Feb 1
Kurosawa, Akira: Birth Anniv, Mar 23
Kurri, Jari: Birth, May 18
Kurtis, Bill: Birth, Sep 21
Kurtz, Swoosie: Birth, Sep 6
Kurtzman, Harvey: Birth Anniv, Oct 3
Kustom Kemps of America Car Show (Biglerville, PA), Jun 11
Kutcher, Ashton: Birth, Feb 7
Kutner, Luis: Birth Anniv, Jun 9
Kuwait,
Iraq Invades Kuwait: Anniv, **Aug 2**
Kuwait Liberated: Anniv, **Feb 27**
National Day, **Feb 25**
Kwan, Michelle: Birth, Jul 7
Kwanzaa, Dec 26
Kyl, Jon: Birth, Apr 25
Kyrgyzstan: Independence Day, Aug 31
Kyser, Kay: Birth Anniv, Jun 18
La Befana (Italy), Jan 6
La Guardia, Fiorello: Birth Anniv, Dec 11
LA Law TV Premiere: Anniv, Oct 3
La Placa, Alison: Birth, Dec 16
La Russa, Tony, Jr: Birth, Oct 4
La Salle, Eriq: Birth, Jul 23
LaBelle, Patti: Birth, May 24
Labonte, Bobby: Birth, May 8
Labor Day Picnic (Live Oak, FL), Aug 28
Labor. See also Careers,
AFL Founded: Anniv, **Dec 8**
AFL-CIO Founded: Anniv, **Dec 5**
Day of the Holy Cross, **May 3**
Five-Dollar-a-Day Minimum Wage: Anniv, **Jan 5**
Haymarket Pardon: Anniv, **Jun 26**
Haymarket Square Riot: Anniv, **May 4**
Jones, Mary H.: Birth Anniv, **May 1**
Labor Day, **Sep 6**
Labor Day, **May 3**
Labor Day (Bahamas), **Jun 4**
Labor Relations Act, Natl: Anniv, **Jul 5**
Ludlow Mine Incident: Anniv, **Apr 20**
Montgomery Ward Seized: Anniv, **Apr 26**
Murray, Philip: Birth Anniv, **May 25**
Nightshift Workers Day, Natl, **May 12**
Schneiderman, Rose: Birth Anniv, **Apr 6**
Lacoste, Rene: Birth Anniv, Jul 2
Lacroix, Christian: Birth, May 17
Ladd, Cheryl: Birth, Jul 12
Ladd, David Alan: Birth, Feb 5
Ladd, Diane: Birth, Nov 29
Ladies' Day Initiated in Baseball: Anniv, Jun 16
Laennec, Rene: Birth Anniv, Feb 17
Laettner, Christian: Birth, Aug 17
Lafayette, Marquis de: Birth Anniv, Sep 6
Laffer, Arthur: Birth, Aug 14
LaFleur, Guy: Birth, Sep 20
Lag B'Omer, May 9
Lagerfeld, Karl: Birth, Sep 10
Lagerlof, Selma: Birth Anniv, Nov 20
Lahti, Christine: Birth, Apr 4
Lailat ul Qadr: (Islamic) Night of Power, Nov 5
Laimbeer, Bill, Jr: Birth, May 19
Laine, Frankie: Birth, Mar 30
Lake Clark Natl Park: Anniv, Dec 2
Lake Fest, Virginia (Clarksville, VA), Jul 16
Lake, Ricki: Birth, Sep 21
Laker, Freddie: Birth, Aug 6
Lalas, Alexi: Birth, Jun 1
Lamas, Lorenzo: Birth, Jan 20
Lamb, Charles: Birth Anniv, Feb 10
Lambert, Christopher: Birth, Mar 29
Lamour, Dorothy: Birth Anniv, Dec 10
Lancaster, Burt: Birth Anniv, Nov 2
Land Mine Ban: Anniv, Mar 1
Landau, Martin: Birth, Jun 20
Landers, Ann: Birth Anniv, Jul 4
Landesberg, Steve: Birth, Nov 3
Landis, Kenesaw: Birth Anniv, Nov 20
Lando, Joe: Birth, Dec 9
Landon, Michael, Jr: Birth, Jun 20
Landon, Michael: Birth Anniv, Oct 31
Landrieu, Mary L.: Birth, Nov 23
Landscape Architecture Month, Natl, Apr 1
Lane, Diane: Birth, Jan 22
Lane, Mark: Birth, Feb 24
Lane, Nathan: Birth, Feb 3
lang, k.d.: Birth, Nov 2
Lang, Stephen: Birth, Jul 11
Lange, Hope: Birth, Nov 28
Lange, Jessica: Birth, Apr 20
Langella, Frank: Birth, Jan 1
Langer, A.J.: Birth, May 22
Langer, Susanne: Birth Anniv, Dec 20
Langley, Samuel Pierpont: Birth Anniv, Aug 22
Langston, Mark: Birth, Aug 20
Language Week, Intl, Dec 15
Lansbury, Angela: Birth, Oct 16
Lansing, Sherry: Birth, Jul 31
Lansky, Aaron: Birth, Jul 17
Lantz, Walter: Birth Anniv, Apr 27
Lanvin, Bernard: Birth, Dec 27
Laos: Natl Holiday, Dec 2
Lappe, Frances Moore: Birth, Feb 10
Lardner, Ring Jr: Birth Anniv, Aug 19
Lardner, Ring: Birth Anniv, Mar 6
Laredo, Ruth: Birth, Nov 20
Largent, Steve: Birth, Sep 28
Larkin, Barry: Birth, Apr 28
Larroquette, John: Birth, Nov 25
Larry King Show TV Premiere: Anniv, Mar 13
Larson, Gary: Birth, Aug 14
Lasek, Bucky: Birth, Dec 3
Laser Patented: Anniv, Mar 22
Lasorda, Tommy: Birth, Sep 22
Lassen Volcanic Natl Park Established: Anniv, Aug 9
Lasser, Louise: Birth, Apr 11
Lassie TV Premiere: Anniv, Sep 12
Late Night with David Letterman TV Premiere: Anniv, Feb 1
Lathrop, Julia C.: Birth Anniv, Jun 29

Index — Chase's 2004 Calendar of Events

Latino Book & Family Fest (Chicago, IL), **Nov 22**
Latino Book & Family Festival (Houston, TX), **Oct 18**
Latvia,
  Baltic States' Independence Recognized: Anniv, **Sep 6**
  Independence Day, **Nov 18**
  John's Day (Midsummer Night Day), **Jun 24**
Lauder, Estee: Birth, **Jul 1**
Lauer, Andy: Birth, **Jun 19**
Lauer, Matt: Birth, **Dec 30**
Laugh and Get Rich Day, **Feb 8**
Laugh at Work Week, **Apr 1**
Laugh-In TV Premiere: Anniv, **Jan 22**
Laundry Workers' Week, Natl, **Jul 4**
Lauper, Cyndi: Birth, **Jun 20**
Laura Ingalls Wilder Pageant (De Smet, SD), **Jul 9**
Laurel and Hardy: Cuckoo Dancing Week, **Jan 11**
Laurel, Stan: Birth Anniv, **Jun 16**
Lauren, Ralph: Birth, **Oct 14**
Lauria, Dan: Birth, **Apr 12**
Laurie, Piper: Birth, **Jan 22**
Laurier, Sir Wilfred: Birth Anniv, **Nov 20**
Lautenberg, Frank: Birth, **Jan 23**
Lauter, Ed: Birth, **Oct 30**
Lavallette Heritage Arts & Crafts Show (Lavallette, NJ), **Jul 25**
Laver, Rod: Birth, **Aug 9**
Laverne and Shirley TV Premiere: Anniv, **Jan 27**
Lavin, Linda: Birth, **Oct 15**
Lavoisier, Antoine: Execution Anniv, **May 8**
Law & Order TV Premiere: Anniv, **Sep 13**
Law Day, USA (Pres Proc), **May 1**
Law Enforcement Appreciation Month in Florida, **May 1**
Law, John Philip: Birth, **Sep 7**
Law, Jude: Birth, **Dec 29**
Law: Mansfield, Arabella: Birth Anniv, **May 23**
Lawless, Lucy: Birth, **Mar 29**
Lawn Mower Race, Sta-Bil Natl Chmpshp (Mansfield, OH), **Sep 4**
Lawnmower Tune-Up Month, Natl, **Mar 1**
Lawrence (of Arabia), T.E.: Birth Anniv, **Aug 16**
Lawrence Welk Show TV Premiere: Anniv, **Jul 2**
Lawrence, Carol: Birth, **Sep 5**
Lawrence, David H.: Birth Anniv, **Sep 11**
Lawrence, Jacob: Birth Anniv, **Sep 7**
Lawrence, James: Birth Anniv, **Oct 1**
Lawrence, Joey: Birth, **Apr 20**
Lawrence, Martin: Birth, **Apr 16**
Lawrence, Sharon: Birth, **Jun 29**
Lawrence, Steve: Birth, **Jul 8**
Lawrence, Vicki: Birth, **Mar 26**
Lawyers: Vote Lawyers Out of Office Day, **Apr 8**
Lazar, Irving ("Swifty"): Birth Anniv, **Mar 28**
Lazarus Saturday, **Apr 3**
Le Mat, Paul: Birth, **Sep 22**
Leach, Robin: Birth, **Aug 29**
Leachman, Cloris: Birth, **Apr 30**
Leacock, Stephen: Birth Anniv, **Dec 30**
Leadership Success Day, **Feb 10**
Leadership Week Intl, **Jan 25**
League of Nations: Anniv, **Jan 10**
League of United Latin American Citizens (LULAC) Founded: Anniv, **Feb 17**
League of Women Voters Formed: Anniv, **Feb 14**
Leahy, Patrick J.: Birth, **Mar 31**
Leakey, Richard E.: Birth, **Dec 19**
Lean, Sir David: Birth Anniv, **Mar 25**
Leap Second Adjustment Time, **Dec 31**
Leap Second Adjustment Time, **Jun 30**
Leap Year Day, **Feb 1**
Leap Year: Bachelors Day, **Feb 1**
Lear, Edward: Birth Anniv, **May 12**
Lear, Evelyn: Birth, **Jan 18**
Lear, Norman: Birth, **Jul 27**
Learn What Your Name Means Day, **Mar 10**
Learned, Michael: Birth, **Apr 9**
Learning Disabilities Assn Intl Conf (Atlanta, GA), **Mar 17**
Leary, Timothy Francis: Birth Anniv, **Oct 22**
Leaud, Jean-Pierre: Birth, **May 5**
Leave It to Beaver TV Premiere: Anniv, **Oct 4**
Leavenworth River Fest (KS), **Jul 1**
Leavitt, Mike: Birth, **Feb 11**
Lebanon,
  Independence Day, **Nov 22**
  Last American Hostage Released: Anniv, **Dec 4**
  Palestinian Massacre: Anniv, **Sep 16**
  St. Maron's Day, **Feb 9**
LeBlanc, Matt: Birth, **Jul 25**
LeBon, Simon: Birth, **Oct 27**
Lebowitz, Fran: Birth, **Oct 27**
LeCarre, John: Birth, **Oct 19**
Ledger, Heath: Birth, **Apr 4**
Lee, Ang: Birth, **Oct 23**
Lee, Ann: Birth Anniv, **Feb 1**
Lee, Brenda: Birth, **Dec 11**
Lee, Bruce: Birth Anniv, **Nov 27**
Lee, Christopher: Birth, **May 27**
Lee, Francis Lightfoot: Birth Anniv, **Oct 14**
Lee, Harper: Birth, **Apr 28**
Lee, Michele: Birth, **Jun 24**
Lee, Peggy: Birth Anniv, **May 26**
Lee, Pinky (Pincus Leff): Birth Anniv, **May 2**
Lee, Richard Henry: Birth Anniv, **Jan 20**
Lee, Robert E.,
  Battle of Spotsylvania: Anniv, **May 12**
  Battle of the Wilderness: Anniv, **May 5**
  Birth Anniv, **Jan 19**
  Defeat at Five Forks: Anniv, **Apr 1**
  Fall of Richmond: Anniv, **Apr 3**
  Lee-Jackson Day, **Jan 16**
  Seven Days Campaign: Anniv, **Jun 25**
Lee, Spike: Birth, **Mar 20**
Leetch, Brian: Birth, **Mar 3**
Leeves, Jane: Birth, **Apr 18**
Legacy Month, Intl, **Apr 1**
Legal Assistants Day, **Mar 26**
Legrand, Michel: Birth, **Feb 24**
LeGuin, Ursula K.: Birth, **Oct 21**
Leguizamo, John: Birth, **Jul 22**
Lehrer, James: Birth, **May 19**
Lehrer, Tom: Birth, **Apr 9**
Lei Day (Hawaii), **May 1**
Leibman, Ron: Birth, **Oct 11**
Leigh, Janet: Birth, **Jul 6**
Leigh, Jennifer Jason: Birth, **Feb 5**
Leigh, Vivian: Gone with the Wind Film Premiere: Anniv, **Dec 15**
Leland, David: Birth, **Apr 20**
Lemieux, Mario: Birth, **Oct 5**
Lemmon, Jack: Birth Anniv, **Feb 8**
Lemon, Meadowlark: Birth, **Apr 25**
LeMond, Greg: Birth, **Jun 26**
LeMoyne House Candlelight Christmas Tours (Washington, PA), **Dec 3**
Lendl, Ivan: Birth, **Mar 7**
L'Enfant, Pierre C: Birth Anniv, **Aug 2**
L'Engle, Madeleine: Birth, **Nov 29**
Lenin, Nikolai: Birth Anniv, **Apr 22**
Lennon, John: Bed-in for Peace: Anniv, **Mar 25**
Lennon, John: Birth Anniv, **Oct 9**
Lennon, John: Lennon-Ono Album Confiscation: Anniv, **Jan 3**
Lennon, Julian: Birth, **Apr 8**
Lennox, Annie: Birth, **Dec 25**
Leno, Jay: Birth, **Apr 28**
Lent, **Feb 25**
Lent, Orthodox, **Feb 23**
Lenz, Kay: Birth, **Mar 4**
Leo Begins, **Jul 23**
Leonard, Elmore: Birth, **Oct 11**
Leonard, Justin: Birth, **Jun 15**
Leonard, Robert Sean: Birth, **Feb 28**
Leonard, Sugar Ray: Birth, **May 17**
Leonardo Da Vinci: Death Anniv, **May 2**
Leoni, Tea: Birth, **Feb 25**
Lerner, Michael: Birth, **Jun 22**
Leroux, Charles: Last Jump: Anniv, **Sep 12**
Leslie, Lisa: Birth, **Jul 7**
Lesotho,
  Army Day, **Jan 20**
  Independence Day, **Oct 4**
  Moshoeshoe's Day, **Mar 12**
  Tree Planting Day, Natl, **Mar 21**
Lester, Mark: Birth, **Jul 11**
Lester, Richard: Birth, **Jan 19**
Let It Go Day, **Jun 23**
Let's Make a Deal TV Premiere: Anniv, **Dec 30**
Letterman, David: Birth, **Apr 12**
Letter-Writing Week, Universal, **Jan 8**
Leutze, Emanuel: Birth Anniv, **May 24**
Levin, Carl: Birth, **Jun 28**
Levine, Charles A.: Death Anniv, **Dec 6**
Levine, David: Birth, **Dec 20**
Levine, Irving R.: Birth, **Aug 26**
Levine, James: Birth, **Jun 23**
Levinson, Barry: Birth, **Apr 6**
Levy, Eugene: Birth, **Dec 17**
Lewis & Clark,
  Clark, William: Birth Anniv, **Aug 1**
  Corps of Discovery Departure: Camp River Dubois (Hartford and Wood River, IL), **May 13**
  Expedition Commissioned: Anniv, **Jan 18**
  Expedition Returns: Anniv, **Sep 23**
  Expedition Sets Out: Anniv, **May 14**
  Heart of America: A Journey Fourth (Atchison, Leavenworth and Kansas City, MO), **Jul 3**
  Journey's End National Art Exhibition (Astoria, OR), **Nov 1**
  Leavenworth River Fest (KS), **Jul 1**
  Lewis & Clark Trad'n Days (Weston, MO), **Jun 26**
  Lewis and Clark Days (Washburn, ND), **Jun 4**
  Lewis, Meriwether: Birth Anniv, **Aug 18**
  Sacagawea: Death Anniv, **Dec 20**
  Sacajawea Heritage Days (Salmon, ID), **Aug 20**
  St. Charles Bicentennial Natl Signature Event (St. Charles, MO), **May 14**
  Three Flags Ceremony (St. Louis, MO), **Mar 10**
Lewis, Anthony: Birth, **Mar 27**
Lewis, C.S.: Birth Anniv, **Nov 29**
Lewis, Carl: Birth, **Jul 1**
Lewis, Clea: Birth, **Jul 19**
Lewis, Emmanuel: Birth, **Mar 9**
Lewis, Francis: Birth Anniv, **Mar 21**
Lewis, Gary: Birth, **Jul 31**
Lewis, Huey: Birth, **Jul 5**
Lewis, Jerry Lee: Birth, **Sep 29**
Lewis, Jerry: Birth, **Mar 16**
Lewis, John L.: Birth Anniv, **Feb 12**
Lewis, Juliette: Birth, **Jun 21**
Lewis, Meriwether: Birth Anniv, **Aug 18**
Lewis, Ramsey: Birth, **May 27**
Lewis, Robert Q.: Birth Anniv, **Apr 25**
Lewis, Sinclair: Birth Anniv, **Feb 7**
Lewis, Sinclair: Sinclair Lewis Days (Sauk Center, MN), **Jul 14**
Lewis, Vicki: Birth, **Mar 17**
Li, Jet: Birth, **Apr 26**
Liar's Contest, Big Whopper (New Harmony, IN), **Sep 18**
Libby, Willard F.: Birth Anniv, **Dec 17**
Liberace Birthday Celebration & Play-A-Like Competition (Las Vegas, NV), **May 15**
Liberace Museum Christmas Tree Lighting (Las Vegas, NV), **Dec 2**
Liberace Show TV Premiere: Anniv, **Jul 1**
Liberace: Birth Anniv, **May 16**
Liberation Day (Poland), **Jan 17**
Liberia,
  Flag Day, **Aug 24**
  J.J. Roberts Day, **Mar 15**
  National Day, **Jul 26**
Liberty Day, **Mar 23**
Libra Begins, **Sep 23**
Library/Librarians,
  American Library Assn Annual Conference (Orlando, FL), **Jun 24**
  Boston Public Library: Anniv, **Apr 3**
  Church/Synagogue Library Assn Conf (Indianapolis, IN), **Jul 11**
  Federation of Library Assns Annual Conference, Intl (Buenos Aires, Argentina), **Aug 21**
  First Presidential Library: Anniv, **Nov 19**
  Freedom of Information Day, **Mar 16**
  Friends of Lake Forest Lib Book Sale (Lake Forest, IL), **Sep 16**
  Library Assn, American: Founding, **Oct 6**
  Library Card Sign-up Month, **Sep 1**
  Library Legislative Day, **May 4**
  Library Lovers' Month, **Feb 1**
  Library of Congress: Anniv, **Apr 24**
  Library Week, Natl, **Apr 18**
  Medical Librarians Month, Natl, **Oct 1**
  New York Public Library: Anniv, **May 23**
  School Library Media Month, **Apr 1**
  Teen Read Week, **Oct 17**
  Thank You, School Librarian Day, **Apr 21**
  Young People's Poetry Week, **Apr 12**
Libya,
  British Bases Evacuation Day, **Mar 28**
  Evacuation Day, **Jun 11**
  Independence Day, **Dec 24**
  Revolution Day, **Sep 1**
License Plates, First: Anniv, **Apr 25**
Lichtenstein, Roy: Birth Anniv, **Oct 27**
Liddy, G. Gordon: Birth, **Nov 30**
Lieberman, Joseph: Birth, **Feb 24**
Liebling, A.J.: Birth Anniv, **Oct 18**
Liechtenstein: National Day, **Aug 15**
Life Balance Month, Intl, **Jan 1**
Life Coach Recognition Week, **May 10**
Life Magazine Debuted: Anniv, **Nov 23**
Life Month, Celebration of, **Jan 1**
Life Week, Celebration of, **Jan 1**
Lifewriting Month, Natl, **Nov 1**
Light the Night for Sight, **May 1**
Light, Judith: Birth, **Feb 9**
Lightfoot, Gordon: Birth, **Nov 17**
Ligonier Highland Games (Ligonier, PA), **Sep 10**
Lil Margaret's Bluegrass and Old-Time Music Fest (Leonardtown, MD), **Aug 12**
Lilac Fest (Mackinac Island, MI), **Jun 4**
Liliuokalani Deposed, Queen: Anniv, **Jan 17**
Lillard, Matthew: Birth, **Jan 24**
Lilly, William: Birth Anniv, **Apr 30**
Limbaugh, Rush, Natl Radio Show Premiere: Anniv, **Aug 1**
Limbaugh, Rush: Birth, **Jan 12**
Limerick Day, **May 12**
Lincoln, Abraham,
  Assassination Anniv, **Apr 14**
  Assassination Conspirators Hanging, **Jul 7**
  Birth Anniv, **Feb 12**
  Birthday Observance (OR), **Feb 2**
  Emancipation Proclamation Takes Effect: Anniv, **Jan 1**
  Emancipation Proclamation: Anniv, **Sep 22**
  Gettysburg Address: Anniv, **Nov 19**
  John Wilkes Booth Escape Route Tour (Clinton, MD), **Apr 17**
  Lincoln Memorial Dedication: Anniv, **May 30**
  Lincoln's Birthplace Cabin Wreath Laying (Hodgenville, KY), **Feb 12**
  Peninsula Campaign Intensified: Anniv, **May 9**
  Signs Income Tax: Anniv, **Jul 1**
Lincoln, Blanche Lambert: Birth, **Sep 30**
Lincoln, Mary Todd: Birth Anniv, **Dec 13**
Lind, Jenny: Birth Anniv, **Oct 6**
Lind, Jenny: US Premiere, **Sep 11**
Linda Dominique Grosvenor Natl Read for Leisure Week, **May 1**
Lindbergh Flight: Anniv, **May 21**
Lindbergh Kidnapping: Anniv, **Mar 1**
Lindbergh, Anne M.: Birth Anniv, **Jun 22**
Lindbergh, Charles A.: Birth Anniv, **Feb 4**
Linden, Hal: Birth, **Mar 20**
Lindros, Eric: Birth, **Feb 28**

716

☆ Chase's 2004 Calendar of Events ☆ Index

Lindsay, Robert: Birth, Dec 12
Lingle, Linda: Birth, Jun 4
Linn-Baker, Mark: Birth, Jun 17
Linney, Laura: Birth, Feb 5
Liotta, Ray: Birth, Dec 18
Lipinski, Tara: Birth, Jun 10
Lippman, Walter: Birth Anniv, Sep 23
Lips Appreciation Day, Mar 16
Lipton, Peggy: Birth, Aug 30
Lisi, Virna: Birth, Nov 8
Listen to Your Inner Critic Month, Oct 1
Listening Awareness Month, Intl, Mar 1
Lister, Joseph: Birth Anniv, Apr 5
Liston, Sonny: Birth Anniv, May 8
Liszt, Franz: Birth Anniv, Oct 22
Litchfield Open House Tour (Litchfield, CT), Jul 9
Literacy Day, Intl (UN), Sep 8
Literacy Decade, UN, Jan 1
Literature,
    American Poet Laureate Establishment: Anniv, Dec 20
    Amis, Kingsley: Birth Anniv, Apr 16
    Anne Bradstreet Day, Sep 16
    Asimov, Isaac: Birth Anniv, Jan 2
    Authors' Day, Natl, Nov 1
    Bad Poetry Day, Aug 18
    Be Kind to Editors and Writers Month, Sep 1
    Beckett, Samuel: Birth Anniv, Apr 13
    Biographers Day, May 16
    Black Poetry Day, Oct 17
    Bollingen Prize Award: Anniv, Feb 19
    Buck, Pearl S.: Birth Anniv, Jun 26
    Child, Lydia Maria: Birth Anniv, Feb 11
    Cooper, James Fenimore: Birth Anniv, Sep 15
    Dickens, Charles: Birth Anniv, Feb 7
    Edgar Allan Poe Fest (Manheim, PA), Oct 29
    Eliot, T.S.: Birth Anniv, Sep 26
    Eliza Doolittle Day, May 20
    Emerson, Ralph Waldo: Birth Anniv, May 25
    First Magazine Published in America: Anniv, Feb 13
    Grapes of Wrath Published: Anniv, Apr 14
    Hay-on-Wye Fest of Literature (Hay-on-Wye, Wales), May 28
    Hobbit Day, Sep 22
    Laura Ingalls Wilder Gingerbread Sociable (Pomona, CA), Feb 7
    Merriam, Eve: Birth Anniv, Jul 19
    Mystery Series Week, Oct 3
    Orwell, George: Birth Anniv, Jun 25
    P.V. Helmerich Distinguished Author Award (Tulsa, OK), Dec 3
    Poe, Edgar Allan: Birth Anniv, Jan 19
    Poetry Month, Natl, Apr 1
    Pulitzer Prizes First Awarded: Anniv, Jun 4
    Silent Spring Publication: Anniv, Apr 13
    Smith, Thorne: Birth Anniv, Mar 27
    Solzhenitsyn Goes Home: Anniv, May 25
    Stowe, Harriett Beecher: Birth Anniv, Jun 14
    Texas Book Festival (Austin, TX), Nov 8
    The Duchess Who Wasn't Day, Aug 27
    Tolkien Week, Sep 19
    Tolkien, J.R.R.: Birth Anniv, Jan 3
    Underdog Day, Dec 17
    Vercors, Jean: Birth Anniv, Feb 26
    Ways With Words Literature Fest (Dartington, England), Jul 9
    Wheatley, Phillis: Death Anniv, Dec 5
    White, E.B.: Birth Anniv, Jul 11
    Whitman, Walt: Birth Anniv, May 31
    Wilde, Oscar: Birth Anniv, Oct 16
    Words by the Water: A Cumbrian Literature Fest (Lake District, England), Mar 9
    Zora Neale Hurston Fest (Eatonville, FL), Jan 28
Lithgow, John: Birth, Oct 19
Lithuania,
    Baltic States' Independence Recognized: Anniv, Sep 6
    Day of Statehood, Jul 6
    Independence Day, Feb 16
    Restitution of Independence Day, Mar 11
Little Bighorn Days (Hardin, MT), Jun 23
Little House on the Prairie TV Premiere: Anniv, Sep 11
Little League Baseball Week, Natl (Pres Proc), Jun 14
Little League Baseball World Series (Williamsport, PA), Aug 20
Little Orphan Annie: see Gray, Harold Lincoln: Birth Anniv, Jan 20
Little Richard: Birth, Dec 5
Little Rock Nine: Anniv, Sep 4
Little, Cleavon: Birth Anniv, Jun 1
Little, Rich: Birth, Nov 26
Liu, Lucy: Birth, Dec 2
Live Aid Concerts: Anniv, Jul 13
Live to Give Week, Feb 16
Liver Awareness Month, Natl, Oct 1
Livermore, Mary: Birth Anniv, Dec 19
Livestock Show, Rio Grande Valley (Mercedes, TX), Mar 20
Livestock Show/Rodeo, Southwestern Expo (Fort Worth, TX), Jan 17
Livingston, Philip: Birth Anniv, Jan 15
Livingston, Robert: Birth Anniv, Nov 27
Livingston, Stanley: Birth, Nov 24
Livingstone, David: Birth Anniv, Mar 19
Livingstone, Stanley Finds: Anniv, Nov 10

Lizard Race, World's Greatest (Lovington, NM), Jul 3
Lloyd Webber, Andrew: Birth, Mar 22
Lloyd, Christopher: Birth, Oct 22
Lloyd, Emily: Birth, Sep 29
Lloyd, Eric: Birth, May 19
Lloyd, Harold: Birth Anniv, Apr 20
Lloyd, Sabrina: Birth, Nov 20
Loan, US Takes Out Its First Loan: Anniv, Sep 18
Lobo, Rebecca: Birth, Oct 6
Lobster Fest, Maine (Rockland, ME), Aug 4
Locke, Gary: Birth, Jan 21
Locke, John: Birth Anniv, Aug 29
Locke, Sondra: Birth, May 28
Lockhart, June: Birth, Jun 25
Lockhart, Keith: Birth, Nov 7
Locklear, Heather: Birth, Sep 25
Lockport Old Canal Days (Lockport, IL), Jun 19
Lockwood, Belva A. Bennett: Birth Anniv, Oct 24
Lockwood, Gary: Birth, Feb 21
Locust Plague of 1874: Anniv, Jul 20
Loewy, Raymond: Birth Anniv, Nov 5
Lofgren, Nils: Birth, Jun 21
Lofton, James: Birth, Jul 5
Lofton, Kenny: Birth, May 31
Log Cabin Day (Michigan), Jun 27
Loggia, Robert: Birth, Jan 3
Logging and Timber Industry; Logger Competition,
    Logger Days (Libby, MT), Jul 16
    Logging Museum Fest Days (Rangeley, ME), Jul 30
    Maynooth Madness (Maynooth, ON, Canada), Sep 4
    Paul Bunyan Show (Nelsonville, OH), Oct 1
    Tupper Lake Woodsmen's Days (Tupper Lake, NY), Jul 10
Loggins, Kenny: Birth, Jan 7
Logistics Mgmt, Council of, Annual Conf (Chicago, IL), Oct 3
Lollobrigida, Gina: Birth, Jul 4
Loloma, Charles: Birth Anniv, Jun 9
Lombardi, Vince: Birth Anniv, Jun 11
Lombroso, Cesare: Birth Anniv, Nov 18
London to Brighton Veteran Car Run (England), Nov 7
London, Jack: Birth Anniv, Jan 12
London, Jeremy: Birth, Nov 7
Lone Ranger TV Premiere: Anniv, Sep 15
Long Beach Bayou Fest (Long Beach, CA), Jun 18
Long Count Day, Sep 22
Long Term Care Planning Week, Natl, Oct 1
Long, Crawford: First Use Anesthetic (Doctor's Day), Mar 30
Long, Howie: Birth, Jan 6
Long, Huey P.: Day, Apr 30
Long, Shelley: Birth, Aug 23
Longest Dam Run (Glasgow, MT), Jun 19
Longest War in History: Ending Anniv, Feb 5
Longfellow, Henry Wadsworth: Birth Anniv, Feb 27
Longwood Gardens Autumn's Colors (Kennett Square, PA), Oct 9
Longwood Gardens Easter Display (Kennett Square, PA), Apr 3
Longwood Gardens Welcomes Spring (Kennett Square, PA), Jan 17
Longyear, John M.: Birth Anniv, Apr 15
Looff Carousel, Santa Cruz Beach: Anniv, Aug 3
Look Up and Live TV Premiere: Anniv, Jan 3
Loomis Day, May 30
Loos, Anita: Birth Anniv, Apr 26
Loosen Up, Lighten Up Day, Nov 14
Lopez, Alfonso Raymond (Al): Birth, Aug 20
Lopez, Javy: Birth, Nov 5
Lopez, Jennifer: Birth, Jul 24
Lopez, Mario: Birth, Oct 10
Lopez, Nancy: Birth, Jan 6
Lopez, Trini: Birth, May 15
Lopiano, Donna: Birth, Sep 11
Lord Mayor's Show (London, England), Nov 13
Lord of the Rings, First Part Published: Anniv, Jul 19
Loren, Sophia: Birth, Sep 20
Loretta Young Show TV Premiere: Anniv, Sep 20
Loring, Gloria: Birth, Dec 10
Los Angeles (CA) Founded: Anniv, Sep 4
Lose Weight/Feel Great Week, Natl, Jan 1
Lost Dutchman Days (Apache Junction, AZ), Feb 27
Lost Penny Day, Feb 12
Lott, Ronnie: Birth, May 8
Lott, Trent: Birth, Oct 9
Lotus 1-2-3 Released: Anniv, Jan 26
Lou Grant TV Premiere: Anniv, Sep 20
Loudon, Dorothy: Birth, Sep 17
Louganis, Greg: Birth, Jan 29
Loughlin, Lori: Birth, Jul 28
Louis v Braddock/Schmeling Fight Anniv, Jun 22
Louis, Joe: Birth Anniv, May 13
Louis-Dreyfus, Julia: Birth, Jan 13
Louise, Tina: Birth, Feb 11
Louisiana,
    Adai Caddo Indian Nation Pow Wow (Marthaville), Oct 16
    Admission Day, Apr 30
    Adult Day Services Assn Conference, Natl (New Orleans), Jan 30
    Breaux, John B.: Birth, Mar 1
    Butler Issues "Woman Order": Anniv, May 16
    Celebration on the Cane (Natchitoches), Jul 4
    Christmas Fest of Lights (Natchitoches), Dec 3

Christmas in Roseland (Shreveport), Nov 19
Christmas-New Orleans Style (New Orleans), Dec 1
Contraband Days (Lake Charles), Apr 27
Creole Heritage Day (Natchitoches), Oct 15
Farragut Captures New Orleans: Anniv, Apr 25
Folklife Festival (Monroe), Sep 11
Foster, Mike: Birth, Jul 11
French Quarter Fest (New Orleans), Apr 16
Gumbo Fest (Bridge City), Oct 8
Holiday in Dixie (Shreveport and Bossier City), Apr 16
Holiday Tour of Homes (Natchitoches), Dec 8
Huey P. Long Day, Aug 30
Landrieu, Mary L.: Birth, Nov 23
Louisiana Purchase Day, Apr 30
Louisiana Yambilee (Opelousas), Oct 27
Lousiana Sportsmen's Show (New Orleans), Mar 3
MainStay Independence Bowl (Shreveport), Dec 31
Marksville Easter Egg Knocking Contest (Marksville), Apr 11
Melrose Plantation Arts/Crafts Fest (Melrose), Jun 12
Miss Louisiana Pageant (Monroe), Jun 17
Mudbug Madness (Shreveport), May 27
Natchitoches Fest of Lights (Natchitoches), Nov 23
Natchitoches Historic Pilgrimage (Natchitoches), Oct 8
Natchitoches Jazz Festival (Natchitoches), Apr 2
Natchitoches/NW State Univ Folk Fest (Natchitoches), Jul 16
New Orleans Boat Show (New Orleans), Feb 4
New Orleans Jazz/Heritage Fest (New Orleans), Apr 22
Nokia Sugar Bowl (New Orleans), Jan 1
Peach Fest, Louisiana (Ruston), Jun 17
Saint Louise de Marillac Louisiana Bar-B-Q Fest (Arabi), Oct 22
Saint Patrick's Day Parade (Baton Rouge), Mar 13
Satchmo Summer Fest (New Orleans), Aug 4
Scrabble Chmpshp, Natl (New Orleans), Aug 7
Shrimp and Petroleum Fest, Louisiana (Morgan City), Sep 2
Spring Fest and Louisiana Fiddler's Chmpnshp (Marthaville), Apr 23
State Fair of Louisiana (Shreveport), Oct 22
Twin Cities Krewe Mardi Gras Parade (Monroe), Feb 14
Veterans Day Celebration (Mamou), Nov 11
Lousma, Jack: Birth, Feb 29
Love a Mensch Week, Sep 13
Love Boat TV Premiere: Anniv, Sep 24
Love Is a Many Splendored Thing TV Premiere: Anniv, Sep 18
Love Litigating Lawyers Day, Aug 31
Love May Make World Go Round but Laughter Keeps Us from Getting Dizzy, Feb 8
Love of Life TV Premiere: Anniv, Sep 24
Love Parade (Berlin, Germany), Jul 10
Love the Children Day, Texas, Mar 29
Love Week, Celebration of, Feb 9
Love, Courtney: Birth, Jul 9
Love, Davis, III: Birth, Apr 13
Love, Mike: Birth, Mar 15
Lovecraft, H.P.: Birth Anniv, Aug 20
Lovejoy, Elijah P.: Birth Anniv, Nov 9
Loveladies Fair (Loveladies, NJ), Jun 5
Lovell, James: Birth, Mar 25
Lovera, Juan: Birth Anniv, Dec 26
Lover's Fair, Book Day and (Spain), Apr 23
Lover's Fair (Belgium), Dec 2
Lovett, Lyle: Birth, Nov 1
Loving v Virginia: Anniv, Jun 12
Lovitz, Jon: Birth, Jul 21
Low Country Shrimp Fest (McClellanville, SC), May 1
Low, Juliet: Birth Anniv, Oct 31
Lowe, Chad: Birth, Jan 15
Lowe, Rob: Birth, Mar 17
Lowell, Amy: Birth Anniv, Feb 9
Lowell, Carey: Birth, Feb 11
Lowell, James R.: Birth Anniv, Feb 22
Lowell, Percival: Birth Anniv, Mar 13
Loy, Myrna: Birth Anniv, Aug 2
Loyalty Day (Pres Proc), May 1
Loyalty Days/Seafair Fest (Newport, OR), Apr 29
Lucas, George: Birth, May 14
Lucas, Josh: Birth, Mar 26
Lucci, Susan: Birth, Dec 23
Luce, Clare Boothe: Birth Anniv, Mar 10
Luce, Henry: Birth Anniv, Apr 3
Lucid, Shannon: Birth, Jan 14
Luckinbill, Laurence: Birth, Nov 21
Ludendorff, Erick: Birth Anniv, Apr 9
Ludington Harbor Fest (Ludington, MI), Jun 18
Luft, Lorna: Birth, Nov 21
Lugar, Richard G.: Birth, Apr 4
Lughnasadh, Aug 1
Lugosi, Bela: Birth Anniv, Oct 20
LULAC (League of United Latin American Citizens) Founded: Anniv, Feb 17
Lully, Jean Baptiste: Birth Anniv, Nov 28
Lumet, Sidney: Birth, Jun 25
Lumiere, Auguste: Birth Anniv, Oct 19
Lumiere, Louis: Birth Anniv, Oct 5
Lumpy Rug Day, May 3
Lunch Prowl Week, Sep 13
Lunden, Joan: Birth, Sep 19

717

Index

Lundgren, Dolph: Birth, Nov 3
Luner, Jamie: Birth, May 12
Lung Assn, American: Christmas Seal Campaign, Sep 1
Lung Cancer Awareness Month, Nov 1
Lunsford, Bascom Lamar: Birth Anniv, Mar 21
Lupercalia, Feb 15
LuPone, Patti: Birth, Apr 21
Lupus Alert Day, Apr 1
Lupus Awareness Campaign, Oct 1
Lusitania Sinking: Anniv, May 7
Luther, Martin: Birth Anniv, Nov 10
Luxembourg,
 Beer Fest, Jul 18
 Blessing of the Wine (Greiveldange), Dec 26
 Bretzelsonndeg (Pretzel Sunday), Mar 21
 Burgsonndeg, Feb 1
 Candlemas, Feb 2
 Emaishen, Apr 12
 Ettelbruck Remembrance Day, Jul 6
 Liberation Ceremony, Sep 9
 National Holiday, Jun 23
 Osweiler, Mar 27
 Schuebermess (Shepherd's Fair), Aug 22
Lydon, Johnny (Rotten): Birth, Jan 31
Lyman, Dorothy: Birth, Apr 18
Lynch, David: Birth, Jan 20
Lynch, Kelly: Birth, Jan 31
Lynch, Thomas: Birth Anniv, Aug 5
Lynley, Carol: Birth, Feb 13
Lynn, Jonathan: Birth, Apr 3
Lynn, Loretta: Birth, Apr 14
Lyon, Mary: Birth Anniv, Feb 28
Lyon, Sue: Birth, Jul 10
M*A*S*H TV Premiere: Anniv, Sep 17
M*A*S*H: Final Episode: Anniv, Feb 28
Ma, Yo-Yo: Birth, Oct 7
Maass, Clara: Birth Anniv, Jun 28
Mabon, Sep 22
Mac, Bernie: Birth, Oct 5
MacArthur Returns: US Landing on Leyte, Philippines: Anniv, Oct 20
MacArthur, Douglas: Birth Anniv, Jan 26
MacArthur, James: Birth, Dec 8
Macau: Reverts to Chinese Control: Anniv, Dec 20
Macaulay, Thomas B.: Birth Anniv, Oct 25
Macchio, Ralph: Birth, Nov 4
MacCorkindale, Simon: Birth, Feb 12
MacDonald, Anne Thompson: Death Anniv, Oct 12
MacDonald, John A.: Birth Anniv, Jan 11
Macdonald, Norm: Birth, Oct 17
MacDowell, Andie: Birth, Apr 21
Macedonia,
 Independence Day, Sep 8
 National Day, Aug 2
Macedonian Uprising: St. Elias Day, Aug 2
MacFadden, Bernarr: Birth Anniv, Aug 16
MacGraw, Ali: Birth, Apr 1
Machias Wild Blueberry Fest (Machias, ME), Aug 20
Machiavelli, Niccolo: Birth Anniv, May 3
MacInnis, Al: Birth, Jul 11
Macintosh Debuts: Anniv, Jan 25
MacKenzie, Alexander: Birth Anniv, Jan 28
Mackenzie, Gisele: Birth, Jan 10
Mackie, Bob: Birth, Mar 24
Mackinac Bridge Walk (St. Ignace, MI), Sep 6
MacLachlan, Kyle: Birth, Feb 22
MacLaine, Shirley: Birth, Apr 24
MacLeish, Archibald: Birth Anniv, May 7
MacLeish, Rod: Birth, Jan 15
MacMurray, Fred: Birth Anniv, Aug 30
MacNeil, Robert: Birth, Jan 19
MacNeil-Lehrer Newshour TV Premiere: Anniv, Sep 5
MacNelly, Jeff: Birth Anniv, Sep 17
MacNicol, Peter: Birth, Apr 10
Macpherson, Elle: Birth, Mar 29
MacRae, Sheila: Birth, Sep 24
Macy, William H.: Birth, Mar 13
Mad magazine: Gaines, William M.: Birth Anniv, Mar 1
Mad magazine: Kurtzman, Harvey: Birth Anniv, Oct 3
Madagascar,
 Commemoration Day, Mar 29
 Independence Day, Jun 26
Madama Butterfly Premiere: Anniv, Feb 17
MADD (Mothers Against Drunk Driving),
 Minimum Legal Drinking Age at 21: Anniv, Jul 17
 New Year's Designate a Driver Campaign, Dec 31
 Tie One On for Safety Campaign, Dec 1
Madden, John: Birth, Apr 10
Maddux, Greg: Birth, Apr 14
Madigan, Amy: Birth, Sep 11
Madison, Dolly: Birth Anniv, May 20
Madison, James: Birth Anniv, Mar 16
Madonna: Birth, Aug 16
Madsen, Michael: Birth, Sep 25
Madsen, Virginia: Birth, Sep 11
Magazine Month, Children's, Oct 1
Magazine, First Published in America: Anniv, Feb 13
Magellan, Ferdinand: Death Anniv, Apr 27
Magic Day, Natl, Oct 31
Magic Days, Michigan (Kalamazoo, MI), May 21
Magic of Differences™ Week, Oct 3
Magna Carta Day, Jun 15
Magnolia Blossom Fest (Magnolia, AR), May 13
Magnum, PI TV Premiere: Anniv, Dec 11

Magnuson, Ann: Birth, Jan 4
Maguire, Tobey: Birth, Jun 27
Maher, Bill: Birth, Jan 20
Mahoney, John: Birth, Jun 20
Maifest (Covington, KY), May 14
Maifest (Hermann, MO), May 15
Mail: Pony Express, Inauguration of: Anniv, Apr 3
Mail: V-Mail Delivery: Anniv, Jun 22
Mailer, Norman: Birth, Jan 31
Mail-Order Catalog: Anniv, Aug 18
Mailorder Gardening Month, Natl, Jan 1
Maiman, Theodore: Birth, Jul 11
Maine,
 Acadia Natl Park Established: Anniv, Jan 1
 Acton Fair (Acton), Aug 26
 Admission Day, Mar 15
 Baldacci, John: Birth, Jan 30
 Bangor State Fair (Bangor), Jul 30
 Blue Hill Fair (Blue Hill), Sep 2
 Chester Greenwood Day Parade (Farmington), Dec 4
 Collins, Susan M.: Birth, Dec 7
 Common Ground Country Fair (Unity), Sep 24
 Eastport "Old Home Week" Celebration (Eastport), Jul 1
 Fryeburg Fair (Fryeburg), Oct 3
 International Fest (Calais, ME/St. Stephen, NB, Canada), Jul 30
 Island Falls Winterfest (Island Falls), Feb 11
 Logging Museum Field Days (Rangeley), Jul 30
 Machias Wild Blueberry Fest (Machias), Aug 20
 Maine Highland Games (Brunswick), Aug 21
 Maine Law: Anniv, Jun 2
 Maine Lobster Fest (Rockland), Aug 4
 Maine Potato Blossom Fest (Fort Fairfield), Jul 9
 Maine State Parade (Lewiston), May 1
 MooseStompers Weekend (Houlton), Jan 30
 Patriot's Day, Apr 19
 Sainte-Croix 1604–2004 (Calais, ME and Bayside, NB, Canada), Jun 25
 Skowhegan State Fair (Skowhegan), Aug 12
 Snowe, Olympia J.: Birth, Feb 21
 Thomas Point Beach Bluegrass Fest (Brunswick), Sep 2
 Windjammer Days (Boothbay Harbor), Jun 22
 Yarmouth Clam Fest (Yarmouth), Jul 16
MainStay Independence Bowl (Shreveport, LA), Dec 31
Majerle, Dan: Birth, Sep 9
Major League Baseball All-Star Game, Jul 13
Major, John: Birth, Mar 29
Majors, Lee: Birth, Apr 23
Make a Difference Day, Oct 23
Make Room for Daddy TV Premiere: Anniv, Sep 29
Make Up Your Mind Day, Dec 31
Make Up Your Own Holiday Day, Mar 26
Makeba, Miriam: Birth, Mar 4
Makepeace, Chris: Birth, Apr 22
Malawi,
 Freedom Day, Jun 14
 John Chilembwe Day, Jan 16
 Martyr's Day, Mar 3
 Republic Day, Jul 6
Malaysia,
 Borneo Rhino Challenge, May 1
 Freedom Day, Aug 31
 Head of State's Official Birthday, Jun 5
Malcolm X: Assassination Anniv, Feb 21
Malcolm X: Birth Anniv, May 19
Malden, Karl: Birth, Mar 22
Maldives,
 National Day, Jul 26
 Republic Day, Nov 11
Maleska, Eugene T.: Birth Anniv, Jan 6
Mali: Independence Day, Sep 22
Malick, Wendie: Birth, Dec 13
Malkovich, John: Birth, Dec 9
Malle, Louis: Birth Anniv, Oct 30
Mallory, George L.: Birth Anniv, Jun 18
Malone, Dorothy: Birth, Jan 30
Malone, Karl: Birth, Jul 24
Malone, Moses: Birth, Mar 23
Maloney, Janel: Birth, Oct 3
Malta,
 Carnival, Feb 21
 Feast of St. Paul's Shipwreck (Valletta), Feb 10
 Independence Day, Sep 21
 Mnarja, Jun 22
 National Day, Jun 7
 Republic Day, Dec 13
 Siege Broken: Anniv, Sep 8
Malthus, Thomas: Birth Anniv, Feb 17
Maltin, Leonard: Birth, Dec 18
Mama TV Premiere: Anniv, Jul 1
Mamet, David: Birth, Nov 30
Mammography Day, Natl, Oct 15
Mammoth Cave Natl Park Established: Anniv, Jul 1
Man Day, Feb 8
Manchester, Melissa: Birth, Feb 15
Manchester, William: Birth, Apr 4
Mancini, Henry: Birth Anniv, Apr 16
Mandan, Robert: Birth, Feb 2
Mandarich, Tony: Birth, Sep 23
Mandel, Howie: Birth, Nov 29
Mandela, Nelson,
 Arrest Anniv, Aug 4
 Birth, Jul 18

Inauguration: Anniv, May 10
Prison Release Anniv, Feb 11
Mandrell, Barbara: Birth, Dec 25
Mandrell, Louise: Birth, Jul 13
Manet, Edouard: Birth Anniv, Jan 23
Mangano, Silvana: Birth Anniv, Apr 21
Mangione, Chuck: Birth, Nov 29
Manheim, Camryn: Birth, Mar 8
Manilow, Barry: Birth, Jun 17
Manistee Natl Forest Fest (Manistee, MI), Jun 30
Mankiewicz, Joseph L.: Birth Anniv, Feb 11
Mankiller, Wilma: Birth, Nov 18
Mann, Horace: Birth Anniv, May 4
Mann, James: Birth Anniv, Oct 19
Mann, Marty: Birth Anniv, Oct 15
Manners, Miss (Judith Martin): Birth, Sep 13
Manning, Danny: Birth, May 17
Manning, Peyton: Birth, Mar 24
Mannix TV Premiere: Anniv, Sep 16
Manoff, Dinah: Birth, Jan 25
Man-Powered Flight, First: Anniv, Aug 23
Mansfield, Arabella: Birth Anniv, May 23
Manson, Patrick: Birth Anniv, Oct 3
Manstein, Erich von: Birth Anniv, Nov 24
Mantegna, Joe: Birth, Nov 13
Mantle, Mickey: Birth Anniv, Oct 20
Mantooth, Randolph: Birth, Sep 19
Mao Tse-Tung: Birth Anniv, Dec 26
Mao Tse-Tung: Death Anniv, Sep 9
Maple Fair, Parke County (Rockville, IN), Feb 28
Maple Fest, Highland County (VA), Mar 13
Maple Leaf Fest (Carthage, MO), Oct 9
Maple Syrup Fest (Beaver, PA), Apr 3
Maple Syrup Saturday (Appleton, WI), Mar 20
Maples, Marla: Birth, Oct 27
Mapplethorpe, Robert: Birth Anniv, Nov 4
Maradona, Diego: Birth, Oct 30
Marathon, Battle of: Anniv, Sep 9
Marathon, Historic Runs: Anniv, Sep 2
Marble Meet at Amana (Amana, IA), Jun 12
Marble Meet, Northeast (Marlborough, MA), Oct 9
Marble Weekend (Millville, NJ), Jun 25
Marbles: Natl Knuckles Down Month, Apr 1
Marbury, Stephon: Birth, Feb 20
Marceau, Marcel: Birth, Mar 22
Marceau, Sophie: Birth, Nov 17
March for Parks (Diamond, MO), Apr 24
March to College Day, Natl, Mar 1
March, Fredric: Birth Anniv, Aug 8
Marchand, Nancy: Birth Anniv, Jun 19
Marciano, Rocky: Birth Anniv, Sep 1
Marconi, Guglielmo: Birth Anniv, Apr 25
Marcos, Ferdinand: Birth Anniv, Sep 11
Marcovicci, Andrea: Birth, Nov 18
Mardi Gras, Feb 24
Mardi Gras in May (Branson, MO), May 27
Marfan Syndrome Awareness Month, Feb 1
Margolin, Stuart: Birth, Jan 31
Margulies, Julianna: Birth, Jun 8
Marie Antoinette: Execution Anniv, Oct 16
Marilyn Monroe's First Screen Test: Anniv, Jul 19
Marin, Cheech: Birth, Jul 13
Marinaro, Ed: Birth, Mar 31
Marine Corps Birthday: Anniv, Nov 10
Marino, Dan: Birth, Sep 15
Mario Day, Mar 10
Marion Popcorn Fest (Marion, OH), Sep 2
Maris Breaks Home Run Record: Anniv, Oct 1
Maris, Roger: Birth Anniv, Sep 10
Maritime Day, Natl, May 22
Maritime Day, Natl (Pres Proc), May 22
Markert, Russell: Birth Anniv, Aug 8
Markham, Monte: Birth, Jun 21
Marley, Bob: Birth Anniv, Feb 6
Maroon Fest (Jamaica), Jan 6
Marquette, Jacques: Birth Anniv, Jun 1
Marriage Day, World, Feb 8
Marriage of Elizabeth and Philip: Anniv, Nov 20
Marriage: Loving v Virginia: Anniv, Jun 12
Married to a Scorpio Support Day, Nov 18
Married With Children TV Premiere: Anniv, Apr 5
Marrow Awareness Month, Natl, Nov 1
Marsalis, Branford: Birth, Aug 26
Marsalis, Wynton: Birth, Oct 18
Marsh, Jean: Birth, Jul 1
Marshall County Blueberry Fest (Plymouth, IN), Sep 3
Marshall Islands: National Day, May 1
Marshall Plan: Anniv, Apr 3
Marshall, Garry: Birth, Nov 13
Marshall, George: Birth Anniv, Dec 31
Marshall, John: Appointed Chief Justice: Anniv, Jan 20
Marshall, John: Birth Anniv, Sep 24
Marshall, Penny: Birth, Oct 15
Marshall, Peter: Birth, Mar 30
Marshall, Thomas Riley: Birth Anniv, Mar 14
Marshall, Thurgood, Resigns from Supreme Court: Anniv, Jun 27
Marshall, Thurgood: Birth Anniv, Jul 2
Marshall, Thurgood: Sworn in to Supreme Court: Anniv, Oct 2
Marti, Jose Julian: Birth Anniv, Jan 28
Martin Z. Mollusk Day (Ocean City, NJ), May 6
Martin, Andrea: Birth, Jan 15
Martin, Ann: Birth, Aug 12

☆ Chase's 2004 Calendar of Events ☆ Index

Martin, Billy: Birth Anniv, May 16
Martin, Curtis: Birth, May 1
Martin, Dean: Birth Anniv, Jun 7
Martin, Dick: Birth, Jan 30
Martin, Jesse L.: Birth, Jan 18
Martin, Judith: Birth, Sep 13
Martin, Kellie: Birth, Oct 16
Martin, Kenyon: Birth, Dec 30
Martin, Mary: Birth Anniv, Dec 1
Martin, Pamela Sue: Birth, Jan 5
Martin, Ricky: Birth, Dec 24
Martin, Steve: Birth, Aug 14
Martinez, Edgar: Birth, Jan 2
Martinez, Jose: Birth, May 14
Martinez, Mel: Birth, Oct 23
Martinez, Pedro: Birth, Oct 25
Martinez, Tino: Birth, Dec 7
Martinique: Mount Pelee Eruption: Anniv, May 8
Martinmas, Nov 11
Martinmas Goose (Switzerland), Nov 11
Martino, Al: Birth, Oct 7
Martyrs Day (Bangladesh), Feb 21
Martyrs' Day (Panama), Jan 9
Martz, Judy: Birth, Jul 28
Marvell, Andrew: Birth Anniv, Mar 31
Marx, Groucho: Birth Anniv, Oct 2
Marx, Harpo: Birth Anniv, Nov 21
Marx, Karl: Birth Anniv, May 5
Marx, Richard: Birth, Sep 16
Mary Tyler Moore Show TV Premiere: Anniv, Sep 19
Mary, Queen of Scots: Execution Anniv, Feb 8
Maryland,
  Adopts Articles of Confederation: Anniv, Jan 30
  Antique Valentine Exhibit (Clinton), Jan 22
  Baltimore Highlands Arts & Crafts Fest, Sep 19
  Boonesborough Days (Boonsboro), Sep 11
  Catoctin ColorFest Arts/Crafts (Thurmont), Oct 9
  Catonsville Arts & Crafts Fest (Catonsville), Sep 12
  Celtic Fest, Southern Maryland (St. Leonard), Apr 24
  Chesapeake Wildfowl Expo (Salisbury), Oct 1
  Chestertown Tea Party Fest (Chestertown), May 29
  Chinese Lunar New Year Fest (Baltimore), Jan 25
  Country Fest and Auction (Deep Creek Lake), Aug 28
  Deep Creek Dunk (McHenry), Feb 21
  Defenders Day, Sep 12
  Delmarva Chicken Fest (Salisbury), Jun 18
  Ehrlich, Robert, Jr: Birth, Nov 25
  Fairmount Academy 1800s Fest (Fairmount), May 29
  Fall Maryland Home & Garden Show/Holiday Craft Show (Baltimore), Oct 15
  Fell's Point Fun Fest (Baltimore), Oct 2
  Frederick Fest of the Arts (Frederick), Jun 5
  Giving Thanks: Hearth and Home in Early Maryland (St. Mary's City), Nov 26
  Grand Militia Muster (St. Mary's City), Oct 16
  Grantsville Days (Grantsville), Jun 25
  Halfway Park Days (Hagerstown), May 29
  Heritage Days Fest (Cumberland), Jun 12
  John Wilkes Booth Escape Route Tour (Clinton), Apr 17
  Jonathan Hager Frontier Craft Days (Hagerstown), Aug 7
  Landon Azalea Garden Fest/Antique Show (Bethesda), Apr 30
  Leitersburg Peach Fest (Leitersburg), Aug 7
  Lil Margaret's Bluegrass and Old-Time Music Fest (Leonardtown), Aug 12
  Margaret Brent Demands a Political Voice: Anniv, Jan 21
  Maryland Constitution Ratification: Anniv, Apr 28
  Maryland Day, Mar 25
  Maryland Day (St. Mary's City), Mar 21
  Maryland Home and Garden Show (Baltimore), Mar 5
  Maryland Renaissance Fest (Annapolis), Aug 28
  Maryland Sheep and Wool Fest (West Friendship), May 1
  Mikulski, Barbara Ann: Birth, Jul 20
  Montgomery County Agricultural Fair (Gaithersburg), Aug 13
  Murder at Ford's Theater: 5th Annual Conf (Clinton), Mar 19
  Museum Open House (Clinton), May 22
  Preakness Stakes (Baltimore), May 15
  Recreational Vehicle Show (Timonium), Feb 20
  Sarbanes, Paul S.: Birth, Feb 3
  Special Olympics Winter Games (McHenry), Feb 22
  St. Mary's County Oyster Fest (Leonardtown), Oct 16
  State Fair (Timonium), Aug 27
  Sugarloaf Crafts Fest (Gaithersburg), Nov 18
  Sugarloaf Crafts Fest (Gaithersburg), Apr 2
  Sugarloaf Crafts Fest (Gaithersburg), Dec 10
  Sugarloaf Crafts Fest (Gaithersburg), Oct 8
  Sugarloaf Crafts Fest (Timonium), Oct 1
  Sugarloaf Crafts Fest (Timonium), Apr 23
  Tidewater Archaeology Dig (St. Mary's City), Jul 31
  Towsontown Spring Fest (Towson), May 1
  Victorian Christmas Celebration (Cumberland), Nov 26
  Victorian Yuletide (Clinton), Dec 11
  Ward World Championship Waterfowl Carving Competition (Ocean City), Apr 23
  Waterfowl Fest (Easton), Nov 12
  Woodland Indian Discovery Day (St. Mary's City), Sep 11
Masih, Iqbal: Death Anniv, Apr 16
Mason, Bobbie Ann: Birth, May 1

Mason, Dave: Birth, May 10
Mason, Jackie: Birth, Jun 9
Mason, Marsha: Birth, Apr 3
Massachusetts,
  American Heroine Rewarded: Anniv, Jun 8
  Amherst's Teddy Bear Rally (Amherst), Aug 7
  Bastille Day Celebration (Boston), Jul 9
  Big E (West Springfield), Sep 17
  Boston Fire: Anniv, Nov 9
  Boston Harborfest (Boston), Jun 29
  Boston Marathon (Boston), Apr 19
  Boston Public Library: Anniv, Apr 3
  Bridge over the Neponset: Anniv, Apr 1
  Bunker Hill Day (Suffolk County), Jun 17
  Catholic Educational Assn Conv/Expo, Natl (Boston), Apr 13
  Children's Day, Jun 13
  Christmas Stroll Weekend (Nantucket Island), Dec 3
  Daffodil Fest Weekend (Nantucket Island), Apr 23
  Deerfield Massacre: Anniv (Feb 29), Feb 1
  Evacuation Day (Boston), Mar 17
  Fall on Nantucket (Nantucket Island), Oct 1
  First Night (Boston), Dec 31
  Haitian Heritage Month, May 1
  Ig Nobel Prize Ceremony (Cambridge), Oct 7
  Kennedy, Edward Moore: Birth, Feb 22
  Kerry, John F.: Birth, Dec 11
  NCAA Div I Men's Ice Hockey Chmpshp (Boston), Apr 8
  New England Home Show (Boston), Feb 21
  Northeast Marble Meet (Marlborough), Oct 9
  Original Massachusetts Home & Garden Show (West Springfield), Mar 24
  Patriot's Day, Apr 19
  Plymouth Plantation Earthquake: Anniv, Jun 1
  Railroad and Hobby Show (West Springfield), Feb 7
  Ratification Day, Feb 6
  Romney, Mitt: Birth, Mar 12
  Sandcastle & Sculpture Day (Nantucket Island), Aug 21
  Student Government Day, Apr 2
  34th St Express (Boston), Dec 11
  US Women's Open Chmpshp (South Hadley), Jul 1
  USA Indoor Track/Field Chmpshps (Boston), Mar 5
  WMAS Annual Halloween Ball (Springfield), Oct 29
  WMAS Valentine's Ball (Springfield), Feb 14
Massacre at Fort Pillow: Anniv, Apr 12
Massage Therapy Awareness Week, Natl, Oct 24
Massey, Anna: Birth, Aug 11
Masterpiece Theatre TV Premiere: Anniv, Jan 10
Masters, Ben: Birth, May 6
Masters, Edgar L.: Birth Anniv, Aug 23
Masterson, Bat: Birth Anniv, Nov 27
Masterson, Christopher: Birth, Jan 22
Masterson, Mary Stuart: Birth, Jun 28
Mastrantonio, Mary Elizabeth: Birth, Nov 17
Mastrioeni, Pablo: Birth, Aug 29
Mastroianni, Marcello: Birth Anniv, Sep 28
Masur, Richard: Birth, Nov 20
Mata Hari: Anniv of Execution, Oct 15
Matanzas Mule Day, Apr 27
Materials Testing Week, Feb 8
Mathers, Jerry: Birth, Jun 2
Mathers, Marshall (Eminem): Birth, Oct 17
Matheson, Tim: Birth, Dec 31
Mathewson, Christy: Birth Anniv, Aug 12
Mathias, Bob: Birth, Nov 17
Mathis, Johnny: Birth, Sep 30
Matisse, Henri: Birth Anniv, Dec 31
Matlin, Marlee: Birth, Aug 24
Matson, Boyd: Birth, Apr 26
Matsui, Hideki: Birth, Jun 12
Matthau, Walter: Birth Anniv, Oct 1
Matthews, Dave: Birth, Jan 9
Matthews, DeLane: Birth, Aug 7
Mattingly, Don: Birth, Apr 20
Maude TV Premiere: Anniv, Sep 12
Maugham, W. Somerset: Birth Anniv, Jan 25
Maundy Thursday (Holy Thursday), Apr 8
Maura, Carmen: Birth, Sep 15
Mauritania: Independence Day, Nov 28
Mauritius: Independence Day, Mar 12
Maury, Matthew Fontaine: Birth Anniv, Jan 14
Maverick TV Premiere: Anniv, Sep 22
Mawlid al Nabi: Birthday of Prophet Muhammad, May 2
Max, Peter: Birth, Oct 19
Maxwell, James Clerk: Birth Anniv, Nov 13
Maxwell, Robert: Death Anniv, Nov 5
May Day, May 1
May Day (Lumpkin, GA), May 7
May Day Bank Holiday (United Kingdom), May 3
May in Montclair (Montclair Township, NJ), May 1
May Ray Day, May 19
May Your Reading Be a Haven Month, Aug 1
May, Elaine: Birth, Apr 21
Mayall, John: Birth, Nov 29
Mayer, Maria Goeppert: Birth Anniv, Jun 28
Mayflower Day, Sep 16
Maymont Flower & Garden Show (Richmond, VA), Feb 19
Maymont's Herbs Galore (Richmond, VA), Apr 24
Mayo, Charles: Birth Anniv, Jul 19
Mayo, Virginia: Birth, Nov 30
Mayo, William J.: Birth Anniv, Jun 29
Mayron, Melanie: Birth, Oct 20

Mays, Willie: Birth, May 6
Mazowiecki, Tadeusz: Poland: Solidarity Founded, Aug 31
Mazursky, Paul: Birth, Apr 25
McAliskey, Bernadette Devlin: Birth, Apr 23
McArdle, Andrea: Birth, Nov 4
McAuliffe, Christa: Birth Anniv, Sep 2
McBride, Brian: Birth, Jun 19
McBride, Martina: Birth, Jul 29
McBride, Patricia: Birth, Aug 23
McCain, John Sidney, III: Birth, Aug 29
McCallum, David: Birth, Sep 19
McCambridge, Mercedes: Birth, Mar 17
McCarthy Silenced by Senate: Anniv, Dec 2
McCarthy, Andrew: Birth, Nov 29
McCarthy, Eugene: Birth, Mar 29
McCarthy, Jenny: Birth, Nov 1
McCarthy, Kevin: Birth, Feb 15
McCartney, Paul: Birth, Jun 18
McCartney, Stella: Birth, Sep 13
McClanahan, Rue: Birth, Feb 21
McClure, Marc: Birth, Mar 31
McClurg, Edie: Birth, Jul 23
McConaughey, Matthew: Birth, Nov 4
McConnell, Mitch: Birth, Feb 20
McCoo, Marilyn: Birth, Sep 30
McCormack, Eric: Birth, Apr 18
McCormick, Cyrus H.: Birth Anniv, Feb 15
McCormick, Pat: Birth, Jul 17
McCoy-Hatfield Feud Erupts: Anniv, Aug 7
McCrea, Joel: Birth Anniv, Nov 5
McDaniel, Hattie: Birth Anniv, Jun 10
McDermott, Dylan: Birth, Oct 26
McDonald's Invades the Soviet Union: Anniv, Jan 31
McDonald's Opens, First : Anniv, Apr 15
McDormand, Frances: Birth, Jun 23
McDowell, Jack Burns: Birth, Jan 16
McDowell, Malcolm: Birth, Jun 13
McEnroe, John Patrick, Jr: Birth, Feb 16
McEntire, Reba: Birth, Mar 28
McEwen, Mark: Birth, Sep 16
McFarland, George (Spanky): Birth Anniv, Oct 2
McFerrin, Bobby: Birth, Mar 11
McGavin, Darren: Birth, May 7
McGillis, Kelly: Birth, Jul 9
McGinley, John: Birth, Aug 3
McGinley, Ted: Birth, May 30
McGoohan, Patrick: Birth, Mar 19
McGovern, Elizabeth: Birth, Jul 18
McGovern, George: Birth, Jul 19
McGovern, Maureen: Birth, Jul 27
McGowan, Rose: Birth, Sep 5
McGrady, Tracy: Birth, May 24
McGrath, Mark: Birth, Mar 15
McGraw, John: Birth Anniv, Apr 7
McGraw, Tim: Birth, May 1
McGreevey, Jim: Birth, Aug 6
McGregor, Ewan: Birth, Mar 31
McGriff, Fred: Birth, Oct 31
McGuffey, William H.: Birth Anniv, Sep 23
McGuinn, Roger: Birth, Jul 13
McGwire Breaks Home Run Record: Anniv, Sep 8
McGwire, Mark: Birth, Oct 1
McHale, Kevin: Birth, Dec 19
McInerney, Jay: Birth, Jan 13
McKay, Jim: Birth, Sep 24
McKean, Michael: Birth, Oct 17
McKean, Thomas: Birth Anniv, Mar 19
McKellar, Danica: Birth, Jan 3
McKellen, Sir Ian: Birth, May 25
McKeon, Doug: Birth, Jun 10
McKeon, Nancy: Birth, Apr 4
McKeon, Philip: Birth, Nov 11
McKinley, Ida Saxton: Birth Anniv, Jun 8
McKinley, Morganfield: see Waters, Muddy, Apr 4
McKinley, William: Birth Anniv, Jan 29
McKinley, William: Death Anniv, Sep 14
McKnight, Brian: Birth, Jun 5
McKuen, Rod: Birth, Apr 29
McLachlan, Sarah: Birth, Jan 28
McLaughlin, John: Birth, Mar 29
McLean, Don: Birth, Oct 2
McLuhan, Marshall: Birth Anniv, Jul 21
McMahon, Ed: Birth, Mar 6
McMahon, Jim: Birth, Aug 21
McNair, Barbara: Birth, Mar 4
McNair, Ronald E.: Birth Anniv, Oct 12
McNamara, Robert S.: Birth, Jun 9
McNichol, Jimmy: Birth, Jul 2
McNichol, Kristy: Birth, Sep 11
McPartland, Marian: Birth, Mar 20
McRae, Carmen: Birth Anniv, Apr 8
McRaney, Gerald: Birth, Aug 19
McShane, Ian: Birth, Sep 29
McTeer, Janet: Birth, May 8
McVie, Christine: Birth, Jul 12
Mead, Margaret: Birth Anniv, Dec 16
Meadows, Jayne: Birth, Sep 27
Meaney, Colm: Birth, May 30
Means, Russell: Birth, Nov 10
Meany, George: Birth Anniv, Aug 16
Meara, Anne: Birth, Sep 20
Mears, Rick: Birth, Dec 3
Meat Loaf: Birth, Sep 27
Mecklenburg Day (NC), May 20
Medal of Honor, First World War II: Anniv, Feb 10

719

Chase's 2004 Calendar of Events — Index

Medal of Honor, Irwin Earns 1st: Anniv, Feb 13
Medical Librarians Month, Natl, Oct 1
Medical Orphans Month, Intl, May 1
Medical Patient Advocacy Week, Natl, Apr 5
Medical School for Women Opened: Anniv, Nov 1
Medicare: Anniv, Jul 1
Medication Safety Week, Apr 1
Medieval Fair (Norman, OK), May 1
Medieval Faire, Hoggetowne (Gainesville, FL), Feb 7
Meditation, Day of, Jan 1
Meditation, World Peace, Annual, Dec 31
Meet a Mate Week, Jun 14
Meet the Press TV Premiere: Anniv, Nov 6
Meeting Planners Appreciation Day, Natl, May 3
Mehta, Zubin: Birth, Apr 29
Meier, Garry: Birth, Dec 2
Meir, Golda: Birth Anniv, May 3
Mekka, Eddie: Birth, Jun 14
Melanoma Monday, May 3
Melanoma/Skin Cancer Detection and Prevention Month, May 1
Mellencamp, John: Birth, Oct 7
Mellon, Andrew W.: Birth Anniv, Mar 24
Meloni, Christopher: Birth, Apr 2
Melville, Herman: Birth Anniv, Aug 1
Melvin, Allan: Birth, Feb 18
Memento Mori, Jan 3
Memoirs, Write Your, Day, Apr 11
Memorial Day (Observed), May 31
Memorial Day (Pres Proc), May 31
Memorial Day (Traditional), May 30
Memorial Day Ceremonies (Andersonville, GA), May 30
Memorial Day Getaway (Live Oak, FL), May 29
Memorial Day Parade and Ceremonies (Gettysburg, PA), May 31
Memory Day, Mar 21
Memory Days (Grayson, KY), May 27
Memphis in May Intl Fest (Memphis, TN), May 1
Men Make Dinner Day, Natl, Nov 4
Mencken, Henry Louis: Birth Anniv, Sep 12
Mendel, Gregor Johann: Birth Anniv, Jul 22
Mendes, Sergio: Birth, Feb 11
Menendez de Aviles, Pedro: Birth Anniv, Feb 15
Menken, Alan: Birth, Jul 22
Menninger, Karl: Birth Anniv, Jul 22
Mennonite Relief Sale (Hutchinson, KS), Apr 16
Mennonite: Pioneer Days (Steinbach, MB, Canada), Jul 30
Menopause Awareness Month, Sep 1
Menopause Day, World, Oct 18
Menotti, Gian Carlo: Birth, Jul 7
Men's Month, Intl, Jun 1
Mensch Week, Love a, May 13
Mental Health Month, Natl, May 1
Mental Illness Awareness Week, Oct 3
Mental Retardation Awareness Month, Mar 1
Mentoring Month, Natl, Jan 1
Menzies, Robert: Birth Anniv, Dec 20
Meramec Community Fair (Sullivan, MO), Jun 24
Mercator, Gerhardus: Birth Anniv, Mar 5
Mercedes-Benz Fashion Week Fall '04 (New York, NY), Feb 6
Mercedes-Benz Fashion Week Spring '05 (New York, NY), Sep 12
Mercedes-Benz Shows LA (Fall Lines) (Los Angeles, CA), Mar 30
Mercedes-Benz Shows LA (Spring Lines) (Los Angeles, CA), Oct 26
Mercer, John Herndon (Johnny): Birth Anniv, Nov 18
Merchant Sailing Ship Preservation Day, Nov 8
Merchant, Natalie: Birth, Oct 26
Mercouri, Melina: Birth Anniv, Oct 18
Meredith (James) Enrolls at Ole Miss: Anniv, Sep 30
Meredith, Burgess: Birth Anniv, Nov 16
Meredith, Don: Birth, Apr 10
Meriwether, Lee: Birth, May 27
Merkerson, S. Epatha: Birth, Nov 28
Mermaids on Parada (Norfolk, VA), Jul 1
Merman, Ethel: Birth Anniv, Jan 16
Merriam, Eve: Birth Anniv, Jul 19
Merrie Monarch Fest & Hula Competition (Hilo, HI), Apr 11
Merrill, Dina: Birth, Dec 9
Merrill, Robert: Birth, Jun 4
Merrimac Destroyed: Anniv, May 11
Merv Griffin Show TV Premiere: Anniv, Oct 1
Mesa Verde Natl Park Established: Anniv, Jun 29
Mesmer, Friedrich: Birth Anniv, May 23
Messier, Mark: Birth, Jan 18
Messina Earthquake Anniv, Dec 28
Messina Hof's Wine Premiere (Bryan, TX), Nov 13
Messina, Jim: Birth, Dec 5
Messing, Debra: Birth, Aug 15
Metaphysical Awareness Month, Sep 1
Metcalf, Laurie: Birth, Jun 16
Meteor Showers, Perseid, Aug 9
Meteorological Day, World (UN), Mar 23
Metheny, Pat: Birth, Aug 12
Metric Conversion Act: Anniv, Dec 23
Metric System Developed: Anniv, Apr 7
Metric Week, Natl, Oct 10
Metropolitan Opera House: Opening Anniv, Oct 22
Metropolitan Opera Radio Broadcasts Premiere: Anniv, Dec 25

Mexican Fiesta Internacional (Milwaukee, WI), Aug 27
Mexican War Declared: Anniv, May 13
Mexico,
 Battle of Puebla: Anniv, May 5
 Benito Juarez : Birth Anniv, Mar 21
 Blessing of Animals at Cathedral, Jan 17
 Cinco de Mayo, May 5
 Constitution Day, Feb 5
 Cortes Conquers Mexico: Anniv, Nov 8
 Day of the Dead, Nov 1
 Day of the Holy Cross, May 3
 Dia de la Candelaria, Feb 2
 Dia de la Raza, Oct 12
 Feast of Our Lady of Solitude, Dec 18
 Feast of the Radishes (Oaxaca), Dec 23
 Flag Day, Feb 24
 Guadalajara Intl Book Fair, Nov 27
 Guadalupe Day, Dec 12
 Independence Day, Sep 16
 Mainly Mozart Fest, May 30
 Mexico City Earthquake: Anniv, Sep 19
 Mexico City Explosion: Anniv, Nov 19
 Posadas, Dec 16
 Postman's Day, Nov 12
 President's State of the Union Address, Sep 1
 Revolution Day, Nov 20
 San Isidro Day, May 15
 Sonora Showcase (Yuma, AZ), Jan 20
 Treaty of Guadalupe Hidalgo (with US): Anniv, Feb 2
 Zapatista Rebellion: Anniv, Jan 1
Mfume, Kweisi: Birth, Oct 24
Miami Intl Boat/Sailboat Show (Miami Beach, FL), Feb 12
Michael, George: Birth, Jun 25
Michaelmas, Sep 29
Michaels, Lorne: Birth, Nov 17
Michelangelo: Birth Anniv, Mar 6
Michele, Michael: Birth, Aug 30
Michelin, Andre: Birth Anniv, Jan 16
Michelson, Albert: First US Scientist Receives Nobel Prize: Anniv, Dec 10
Michener, James: Birth Anniv, Feb 3
Michigan,
 Admission Day, Jan 26
 Alma Highland Fest and Games (Alma), May 29
 Alpenfest (Gaylord), Jul 13
 Ann Arbor Film Fest (Ann Arbor), Mar 16
 Ann Arbor Summer Art Fair (Ann Arbor), Jul 21
 Ann Arbor Winter Art Fair (Ann Arbor), Nov 20
 Antiques by the Bay (St. Ignace), Jun 18
 Arcadia Daze (Arcadia), Apr 23
 Baby Food Fest, Natl (Fremont), Jul 13
 Battle Creek Cereal Fest (with World's Largest Breakfast Table (Battle Creek), Jun 10
 Bay Harbor Summer Art Fair (Bay Harbor), Aug 6
 Big Ten Field Hockey Tourn (East Lansing), Nov 5
 Big Ten Men's Golf Chmpshp (Ann Arbor), May 7
 Big Ten Men's Indoor Track/Field Chmpshps (Ann Arbor), Feb 28
 Big Ten Men's Soccer Chmpnshp (Ann Arbor), Nov 11
 Blissfest (Cross Village), Jul 9
 Blueberry Fest, Natl (South Haven), Aug 12
 Carry Nation Fest (Holly), Sep 11
 Cherry Pit Spitting Contest, Intl (Eau Claire), Jul 3
 Corvette Show (Mackinaw City), Aug 27
 Curwood Fest (Owosso), Jun 3
 Detroit Founded: Anniv, Jul 24
 Dickens Olde-Fashioned Christmas Fest (Holly), Nov 26
 Do-Dah Parade (Kalamazoo), Jun 5
 Fallasburg Fall Fest (Lowell), Sep 25
 Fourth of July Fireworks (Mackinaw City), Jul 4
 Frankenmuth Skyfest (Frankenmuth), May 2
 Grand Rapids Boat Show (Grand Rapids), Feb 17
 Grand Rapids Sport, Fishing & Travel Show (Grand Rapids), Mar 18
 Grandparents and Grandchildren Day, Mar 18
 Granholm, Jennifer: Birth, Feb 5
 Great Fire of 1881: Anniv, Sep 5
 Holland Tulip Time Fest (Holland), May 1
 Isle Royale Natl Park Established: Anniv, Apr 3
 KCQ Country Music Fest (Saginaw), Jun 19
 Lakestride Half-Marathon (Ludington), Jun 19
 Levin, Carl: Birth, Jun 28
 Lilac Fest (Mackinac Island), Jun 4
 Log Cabin Day, Jun 27
 Longhorn Chmpshp Rodeo (Auburn Hills), Feb 13
 Ludington Harbor Fest (Ludington), Jun 18
 Mackinac Bridge Walk (St. Ignace), Sep 6
 Manistee Natl Forest Fest (Manistee), Jun 30
 MiAEYC Early Childhood Conference (Grand Rapids), Mar 25
 Michigan Boat, Sport & Fishing Show (Detroit), Mar 3
 Michigan Camper, Travel & RV Show (Pontiac), Jan 21
 Michigan Fiber Festival (Allegan), Aug 18
 Michigan Home & Garden Show (Pontiac), Mar 4
 Michigan Magic Day (Kalamazoo), May 21
 Michigan Storytellers Fest (Flint), Jul 8
 Midwinter's Day Celebration (Ann Arbor), Feb 6
 Month of the Young Child, Apr 1
 New Year's Fest (Kalamazoo), Dec 31
 On the Waterfront Swap Meet/Car Show (St. Ignace), Sep 10
 Ribfest (Kalamazoo), Aug 5

 Richard Crane Memorial Truck Show (St. Ignace), Sep 10
 Riverwalk Fest (Lowell), Jul 9
 Ryder Cup Matches (Bloomfield Hills), Sep 14
 Saint Johns Mint Fest (St. Johns), Aug 13
 Silver Bells in the City (Lansing), Nov 19
 Snowman Burning (Sault Ste Marie), Mar 19
 Spring Art Fair (Ann Arbor), Mar 27
 St. Ignace Auto Show (St. Ignace), Jun 24
 Stabenow, Debbie: Birth, Apr 29
 State Fair (Detroit), Aug 20
 Sugarloaf Art Fair (Novi), Apr 16
 Sugarloaf Art Fair (Novi), Oct 22
 Summerswap (Frankenmuth), Jul 17
 Tip-Up Town USA (Houghton Lake), Jan 17
 Victorian Christmas Sleighbell Parade (Manistee), Dec 2
 Wayne State Univ: Funeral for Winter (Detroit), Apr 7
 Winterfest (Burton), Jan 17
 Wyandotte Heritage Days (Wyandotte), Sep 10
 Wyandotte Street Art Fair (Wyandotte), Jul 14
 Zehnder's Snowfest (Frankenmuth), Feb 4
Mickelson, Phil: Birth, Jun 16
Mickey Mouse Club TV Premiere: Anniv, Oct 3
Mickey Mouse's Birthday, Nov 18
Micronesia, Federated States of: Independence Day, Nov 3
Micronesia, Federated States of: National Day, May 10
Microsoft Releases Windows: Anniv, Nov 10
Mid-Autumn Fest (China), Sep 28
Middlemark, Marvin: Birth Anniv, Sep 16
Middleton, Arthur: Birth Anniv, Jun 26
Midler, Bette: Birth, Dec 1
Midnight Sun Baseball Game (Fairbanks, AK), Jun 18
Midnight Sun Fest (Nome, AK), Jun 19
Midori: Birth, Oct 25
Mid-South Fair (Memphis, TN), Sep 22
Midsummer (Wiccan), Jun 20
Midsummer Day/Eve Celebrations, Jun 23
Midsummer Nights' Fair (Norman, OK), Jul 16
Midwife's Day (Greece), Jan 8
Midwinter's Day Celebration (Ann Arbor, MI), Feb 6
Mighty Casey Has Struck Out: Anniv, Jun 3
Mighty Mouse Playhouse TV Premiere: Anniv, Dec 10
Migrants Day, Intl (UN), Dec 18
Migratory Bird Day, Intl, May 8
Migratory Bird Day, Intl (Savannah, GA), May 8
Mike Hammer TV Premiere: Anniv, Jan 26
Mikita, Stan: Birth, May 20
Mikulski, Barbara Ann: Birth, Jul 20
Mikulski, Barbara: Polish-American in the House: Anniv, Jan 4
Milano, Alyssa: Birth, Dec 19
Milbrett, Tiffeny: Birth, Oct 23
Miles, Sarah: Birth, Dec 31
Miles, Sylvia: Birth, Sep 9
Miles, Vera: Birth, Aug 23
Military Ban on Homosexuals Eased, Jan 29
Military Dictatorship Ended in Chile: Anniv, Dec 15
MilitaryY Through the Ages (Williamsburg, VA), Mar 20
Milk Days Fest, Harvard (Harvard, IL), Jun 4
Millay, Edna St. Vincent: Birth Anniv, Feb 22
Millennium Summit, UN: Anniv, Sep 6
Miller, Ann: Birth, Apr 12
Miller, Arthur: Birth, Oct 17
Miller, Barry: Birth, Feb 6
Miller, Christa: Birth, May 28
Miller, Dennis: Birth, Nov 3
Miller, Glenn: Birth Anniv, Mar 1
Miller, Glenn: Birthplace Society Fest (Clarinda, IA), Jun 9
Miller, Henry: Birth Anniv, Dec 26
Miller, Jonny Lee: Birth, Nov 15
Miller, Penelope Ann: Birth, Jan 13
Miller, Reggie: Birth, Aug 24
Miller, Roger: Birth Anniv, Jan 2
Miller, Shannon: Birth, Mar 10
Miller, Steve: Birth, Oct 5
Miller, Zell: Birth, Feb 24
Miller's, Joe: Joke Day, Aug 16
Millett, Kate: Birth, Sep 14
Million Man March: Anniv, Oct 16
Million Minute Family Challenge™, Sep 1
Million Mom March: Anniv, May 14
Millionaire TV Premiere: Anniv, Jan 19
Mills, Donna: Birth, Dec 11
Mills, Florence: Birth Anniv, Jan 25
Mills, Hayley: Birth, Apr 18
Mills, Juliet: Birth, Nov 21
Milne, A.A.: Birth Anniv (Pooh Day), Jan 18
Milsap, Ronnie: Birth, Jan 16
Milton Berle Show: Texaco Star Theater, Sep 21
Milton, John: Birth Anniv, Dec 9
Milwaukee Irish Fest (Milwaukee, WI), Aug 19
Mimieux, Yvette: Birth, Jan 8
Mims, Marilyn: Birth, Sep 8
Mind Day, Make Up Your, Dec 31
Mineral Collecting Field Trips (Bancroft, ON, Canada), Jul 3
Mineta, Norman: Birth, Nov 12
Ming, Yao: Birth, Sep 12
Minghella, Anthony: Birth, Jan 6

720

☆ Chase's 2004 Calendar of Events ☆ Index
Mining—Molina

Mining: Boom Days (Leadville, CO), Aug 6
Minnelli, Liza: Birth, Mar 12
Minner, Ruth Ann: Birth, Jan 17
Minnesota,
Admission Day, **May 11**
Aebleskiver Days (Tyler), **Jul 23**
American Nurses Assn Convention (Minneapolis), **Jun 25**
American Soc of Assn Executives Mtg/Expo (Minneapolis), **Aug 14**
Austin Community Fest (Austin), **Jul 2**
Big Island Rendezvous (Albert Lea), **Oct 2**
Blackpowder Historical Fair (Albert Lea), **Feb 14**
Braham Pie Day (Braham), **Aug 6**
Buffalo Days Celebration (Luverne), **Jun 4**
Calithumpian Parade (Biwabik), **Jul 4**
Christmas at Pioneer Village (Worthington), **Dec 2**
Christmas Epiphany Celebration (Isanti), **Jan 4**
Coleman, Norm: Birth, **Aug 17**
Dayton, Mark: Birth, **Jan 26**
Defeat of Jesse James Days (Northfield), **Sep 9**
Edmund Fitzgerald Beacon Lighting (Two Harbors), **Nov 10**
Farm Toy Show & Auction (Sauk Centre), **Feb 14**
Fest of Adventures (Aitkin), **Sep 18**
Festival of Nations (St. Paul), **Apr 29**
Fish House Parade (Aitkin), **Nov 26**
Fishing Has No Boundaries (Bemidji), **Jun 26**
Grand Excursion 2004 (Minneapolis, St. Paul), **Jun 25**
Gymnastics Chmpshp, Big Ten Women's (Minneapolis), **Mar 20**
Halloween Trail (Worthington), **Oct 30**
Heritagefest (New Ulm), **Jul 9**
Hot Dog Night (Luverne), **Jul 8**
Icebox Days XXIII (International Falls), **Jan 15**
Inventors Congress (Redwood Falls), **Jun 11**
Johnny Appleseed Days (Lake City), **Oct 2**
Kanabec Fall Fest (Mora), **Sep 11**
King Turkey Days (Worthington), **Sep 18**
Little Falls Arts/Crafts (Little Falls), **Sep 11**
Minnesota Renaissance Fest (Shakopee), **Aug 14**
Nobel Conference (St. Peter), **Oct 5**
Norwegian Christmas (Brooklyn Park), **Dec 4**
Oktoberfest (New Ulm), **Oct 1**
Old Time School (Cambridge), **Jun 7**
Old-Fashioned Fourth of July (Worthington), **Jul 4**
Paul Bunyan Sled Dog Races, Mutt Races (Bemidji), **Jan 17**
Pawlenty, Tim: Birth, **Nov 1**
Rochesterfest (Rochester), **Jun 19**
Saint Olaf Christmas Fest (Northfield), **Dec 2**
Saint Paul Winter Carnival (St. Paul), **Jan 23**
Scandinavian Hjemkomst Fest (Moorhead), **Jun 25**
Sinclair Lewis Days (Sauk Centre), **Jul 14**
Song of Hiawatha Pageant (Pipestone), **Jul 23**
South St. Paul Kaposia Days (South St. Paul), **Jun 24**
State Fair (St. Paul), **Aug 26**
Swedish Language and Culture Day Camp (Cambridge), **Aug 23**
Take a Kid Fishing Weekend (St. Paul), **Jun 11**
Tall Timber Days Fest (Grand Rapids), **Aug 7**
Tetonkaha Rendezvous (Lake Benton), **Aug 13**
Tri-State Band Fest (Luverne), **Sep 25**
US Amateur Public Links (Golf) Chmpshp (Maple Grove), **Jul 12**
Voyageurs Natl Park Established: Anniv, **Apr 8**
Water Ski Days (Lake City), **Jun 25**
Western Minnesota Steam Thresher's Reunion (Rollag), **Sep 3**
White Oak Rendezvous (Deer River), **Aug 7**
Windsurfing Regatta/Unvarnished Music Fest (Worthington), **Jun 11**
Winterfest (Luverne), **Dec 3**
Women's Big Ten Swimming/Diving Chmpshps (Minneapolis), **Feb 18**
Minority Enterprise Development Week (Pres Proc), Sep 26
Minow, Newton: Birth, Jan 17
Minow, Newton: Vast Wasteland Speech: Anniv, May 9
Mint Julep Scale Meet (Falls of Rough, KY), May 15
Mint, US: Anniv, Apr 2
Miou-Miou: Birth, Feb 22
Miranda Decision: Anniv, Jun 13
Mirra, Dave: Birth, Apr 4
Mirren, Helen: Birth, Jul 26
Mirror of the World Translation: Anniv, Caxton's, Mar 8
Mirth Month, Intl, Mar 1
Mirthday, Jun 22
Mischief Night, Nov 4
Miss America Pageant, First: Anniv, Sep 8
Miss American Rose Day, Oct 20
Missile, First Surface-to-Surface Missile: Anniv, Dec 24
Missing Children's Day, Natl, May 25
Mission Delores Founding: Anniv, Oct 9
Mission San Antonio de Padua: Founding Anniv, Jul 14
Mission San Carlos Borromeo de Carmelo: Founding Anniv, Jun 3
Mission San Diego de Alcala: Founding Anniv, Jul 16
Mission San Gabriel Archangel: Founding Anniv, Sep 8
Mission San Juan Capistrano: Founding Anniv, Nov 1
Mission San Luis Obispo de Tolosa: Founding Anniv, Sep 1
Mission San Luis Rey de Francia: Founding Anniv, Jun 13
Mission Santa Barbara: Founding Anniv, Dec 4
Mission Santa Clara de Asis: Founding Anniv, Jan 12
Mission: Impossible TV Premiere: Anniv, Sep 17
Missionary Fair, Road Church (Stonington, CT), May 15
Mississinewa 1812 (Marion, IN), Oct 8
Mississippi,
Admission Day, **Dec 10**
Chimneyville Crafts Fest (Jackson), **Dec 4**
Choctaw Indian Fair (Philadelphia), **Jul 14**
Civil Rights Workers Found Slain: Anniv, **Aug 4**
Cochran, Thad: Birth, **Dec 7**
Confederate Memorial Day, **Apr 26**
Ghost Tales Around the Campfire (Washington), **Oct 29**
Gum Tree Fest (Tupelo), **May 8**
Lott, Trent: Birth, **Oct 9**
Meredith (James) Enrolls at Ole Miss: Anniv, **Sep 30**
Musgrove, Ronnie: Birth, **Jul 29**
Natchez Fall Pilgrimage (Natchez), **Oct 8**
Natchez Powwow (Natchez), **Mar 27**
Natchez Spring Pilgrimage (Natchez), **Mar 13**
Neshoba County Fair (Philadelphia), **Jul 23**
Pioneer and Indian Fest (Ridgeland), **Oct 23**
Pioneer Days (Washington), **Oct 20**
SPEBSQSA (Barbershop Quartet) Mid-Winter Conv (Biloxi), **Jan 25**
Spring Pilgrimage to Antebellum Homes (Columbus), **Mar 30**
State Fair (Jackson), **Oct 6**
Vicksburg Surrenders: Anniv, **Jul 3**
Mississippi River Arts/Crafts Fest, Great (Hannibal, MO), May 29
Mississippi River Valley Scenic Drive (Cape Girardeau, MO), Apr 24
Missouri,
Adelphian Club Christmas Bazaar (Kennett), **Dec 4**
Admission Day, **Aug 10**
Adoration Parade (Branson), **Dec 5**
American Heritage Bluegrass Fest (Arrow Rock), **Sep 18**
Antique & Collectible Flea Market (Weston), **Apr 24**
Antique Show & Sale (Weston), **Mar 6**
Apple Butter Makin' Days (Mt Vernon), **Oct 8**
Applefest (Weston), **Oct 2**
Arrow Rock Heritage Craft Fest (Arrow Rock), **Oct 9**
Art Fair & Winefest (Washington), **May 21**
Arts & Crafts Fest (Rolla), **Oct 2**
Autumn Historic Folklife Fest (Hannibal), **Oct 16**
Benton Neighbor Day (Benton), **Sep 3**
Big 12 Women's Gymnastics Chmpshp (Columbia), **Mar 20**
Big Muddy Folk Music Fest (Boonville), **Apr 2**
Black Walnut Fest (Stockton), **Sep 22**
Blueberry Hill Open Dart Tourn (St. Louis), **Apr 22**
Bond, Christopher S.: Birth, **Mar 6**
Branson Fest (Branson), **Apr 6**
Carver Day Commemorative Celebration (Diamond), **Jul 17**
Christmas in Weston (Weston), **Dec 4**
Christmas Traditions (St. Charles), **Nov 26**
Coal Miner Days (Novinger), **May 30**
Cow Milked While Flying: Anniv, **Feb 18**
Dam Experience (Warsaw), **Jul 3**
Deaf Conference, Natl Assn of the (Kansas City), **Jul 6**
Deutsch Country Days (Marthasville), **Oct 16**
Dogwood Festival (Camdenton), **Apr 15**
Earth Day Community Fest (St. Louis), **Apr 25**
Earthquakes: Anniv, **Dec 6**
Eldon Turkey Fest (Eldon), **Oct 9**
Elvis Presley Remembered (St. Louis), **Aug 14**
Emmett Kelly Clown Fest (Houston), **Apr 29**
Fall Fest of Arts and Crafts (Washington), **Sep 24**
Farmington Country Days (Farmington), **Jun 4**
Festival of the Little Hills (St. Charles), **Aug 20**
Firefall (Springfield), **Jul 3**
4-Wheel Drive Jamboree (Springfield), **May 8**
Gospel Sing (Arrow Rock), **Apr 25**
Great Mississippi River Arts/Crafts Fest (Hannibal), **May 29**
Greater Springfield Garage Sale (Springfield), **Jan 31**
Groundhog Run (Kansas City), **Feb 8**
Handel's Messiah (Independence), **Nov 20**
Hanging of the Greens (Arrow Rock), **Nov 27**
Hartville Annual Fall Fest (Hartville), **Oct 16**
Heart of America: A Journey Fourth—Lewis and Clark Bicentennial Event (Atchison, Leavenworth and Kansas City), **Jul 3**
Heritage Day (Houston), **Sep 18**
Holden, Bob: Birth, **Aug 24**
Jours de Fete (Ste. Genevieve), **Aug 14**
KRXL Car Cruise (Kirksville), **Aug 7**
Land of Mark Twain Bluegrass Music Fest (Hannibal), **Nov 20**
Lewis & Clark Trad'n Days (Weston), **Jun 26**
Lewis and Clark St. Charles Bicentennial Natl Signature Event (St. Charles), **May 14**
Liberty Fall Festival (Liberty), **Sep 24**
Liberty Spring on the Square Festival (Liberty), **May 15**
Magic Dragon Street Meet Nationals Car Show (Lake Ozark), **Apr 30**
Maifest (Hermann), **May 15**
Maple Leaf Fest (Carthage), **Oct 9**
March for Parks (Diamond), **Apr 24**
Mardi Gras in May (Branson), **May 27**
Mayor's Christmas Tree (Kansas City), **Nov 26**
Meramec Community Fair (Sullivan), **Jun 24**
Mid-America Natl Street Rod Assn Car Show (Springfield), **May 28**
Minority Scientists Showcase (St. Louis), **Jan 17**
Mississippi River Valley Scenic Drive (Cape Girardeau), **Apr 24**
Missouri Day, **Oct 20**
Missouri Day Fest (Trenton), **Oct 15**
Missouri River Fest of Arts (Boonville), **Aug 14**
Missouri State Chmpshp Racking Horse Show (Dexter), **Jun 5**
Monett Fourth of July (Monett), **Jul 4**
NAIA Men's Div I Basketball Chmpshp (Kansas City), **Mar 24**
NAIA Men's Div II Basketball Chmpshp (Branson), **Mar 10**
Natl Soccer Coaches Assn of America Natl Convention (Kansas City), **Jan 14**
NCAA Div I Wrestling Chmpshps (St. Louis), **Mar 18**
North Central Missouri Fair (Trenton), **Jul 27**
Northeast Missouri Triathlon Chmpshp (Kirksville), **Sep 12**
Oktoberfest (Monett), **Oct 23**
Oktoberfest (St. Charles), **Oct 2**
Old Glory Jubilee (Elsberry), **Jul 3**
Orchid Show (St. Louis), **Jan 31**
Osage River Mountain Man Festival and Black Powder Shoot (Lake Ozark), **Sep 17**
Ozark Antique Auto Club Swap Meet (Springfield), **Aug 27**
Ozark Empire Fair (Springfield), **Jul 30**
Ozark Fall Farmfest (Springfield), **Oct 1**
Ozark Mountain Christmas/Branson Fest of Lights (Branson), **Nov 1**
Plaza Lights (Kansas City), **Nov 25**
Prairie Day (Diamond), **Sep 11**
Richmond's Mushroom Fest (Richmond), **Apr 30**
Route 66 Summerfest (Rolla), **Jun 4**
Saint Louis Race Riots: Anniv, **Jul 2**
Saint Louis Variety Club Telethon (St. Louis), **Apr 17**
Saint Louis Walk of Fame Induction (St. Louis), **May 16**
Saint Piran's Day Celeb (Kansas City), **Mar 6**
Santa-Cali-Gon-Days Fest (Independence), **Sep 3**
Show Me State Games (Columbia), **Jul 16**
Southeast Missouri District Fair (Cape Girardeau), **Sep 11**
Southside Fall Fest (St. Joseph), **Sep 17**
State Fair (Sedalia), **Aug 12**
Strawberry Fest (Independence), **Jun 5**
Street Machine Fall Nationals (Springfield), **Sep 17**
Sullivan Freedom Fest (Sullivan), **Jul 4**
Super Scout Sunday (Springfield), **May 15**
Talent, Jim: Birth, **Oct 18**
Texas County Fair/Old Settlers Reunion (Houston), **Aug 3**
Three Flags Ceremony—Lewis and Clark Bicentennial Event (St. Louis), **Mar 10**
Tom Sawyer Days, Natl (Hannibal), **Jul 1**
Trails West! (St. Joseph), **Jul 9**
US Senior Open (Golf) Championship (St. Louis), **Jul 29**
Weston Jaycees' Annual July 4th Celebration (Weston), **Jul 4**
Missouri Compromise: Anniv, Mar 3
Mister Rogers' Neighborhood TV Premiere: Anniv, May 22
Mitchell Persimmon Fest (Mitchell, IN), Sep 18
Mitchell, Andrea: Birth, Oct 30
Mitchell, Chad: Birth, Dec 5
Mitchell, James: Birth, Feb 29
Mitchell, Joni: Birth, Nov 7
Mitchell, Margaret: Birth Anniv, Nov 8
Mitchell, Maria: Birth Anniv, Aug 1
Mitchum, Robert: Birth Anniv, Aug 6
Mix, Tom: Birth Anniv, Jan 6
Mize, Larry: Birth, Sep 23
Mobius Awards (Los Angeles, CA), Feb 20
Mobius, August: Birth Anniv, Nov 17
Moby: Birth, Sep 11
Moceanu, Dominique: Birth, Sep 30
Mochrie, Colin: Birth, Nov 30
Modano, Mike: Birth, Jun 7
Model Airplane: Mint Julep Scale Meet (Falls of Rough, KY), May 15
Model Railroad Show (Wheeling, WV), Jan 17
Model T Introduced: Anniv, Oct 1
Modine, Matthew: Birth, Mar 22
Moffo, Anna: Birth, Jun 27
Mohr, Jay: Birth, Aug 23
Moldova,
Independence Day, **Aug 27**
National Language Day, **Aug 31**
Mole Day, Natl, Oct 23
Moliere Day: Baptism Anniv, Jan 15
Molina, Alfred: Birth, May 24

Index

Molineaux, Tom: First US Heavyweight Defeated: Anniv, Dec 10
Molitor, Paul: Birth, Aug 22
Moll, Richard: Birth, Jan 13
Molson, John: Birth Anniv, Dec 28
Mom and Pop Business Owners Day, Natl, Mar 29
Moment of Frustration Scream Day, Intl, Oct 12
Moment of Laughter Day, Apr 14
Moment of Silence (Nagasaki, Japan), Aug 9
Monaco,
    Circus Festival of Monte Carlo, Intl, Jan 15
    National Holiday, Nov 19
Mondale, Walter Frederick (Fritz): Birth, Jan 5
Monday Holiday Law: Anniv, Jun 28
Monday: Natl Thank God It's Monday! Day, Jan 12
Mondesi, Raul: Birth, Mar 12
Monet, Claude: Birth Anniv, Nov 14
Money, Eddie: Birth, Mar 2
Money, Paper, Issued: Anniv, Mar 10
Mongolia,
    National Holiday, Jul 11
    Republic Day, Nov 26
Monica: Birth, Oct 24
Monitor Sinking: Anniv, Dec 30
Monk, Art: Birth, Dec 5
Monkees TV Premiere: Anniv, Sep 12
Monkey Trial: John T. Scopes Birth Anniv, Aug 3
Monopoly Invented: Anniv, Mar 7
Monroe Doctrine: Anniv, Dec 2
Monroe, Elizabeth K.: Birth Anniv, Jun 30
Monroe, Harriet: Birth Anniv, Dec 23
Monroe, James, Birthday Celebration (Charlottesville, VA), Apr 28
Monroe, James: Birth Anniv, Apr 28
Monroe, Marilyn: Birth Anniv, Jun 1
Monroe, Marilyn: First Screen Test: Anniv, Jul 19
Montagnier, Luc: Birth, Aug 18
Montaigne, Michel de: Birth Anniv, Feb 28
Montalban, Ricardo: Birth, Nov 20
Montana,
    Admission Day, Nov 8
    Arts in the Park (Kalispell), Jul 23
    Bannack Days (Bannack), Jul 17
    Battle of Little Bighorn: Anniv, Jun 25
    Baucus, Max: Birth, Dec 11
    Beartooth Run (Red Lodge), Jun 26
    Big Sky State Games (Billings), Jul 16
    Burns, Conrad: Birth, Jan 25
    Buzzard Day Fest (Glendive), Jun 12
    C.M. Russell Auction Orig Western Art (Great Falls), Mar 17
    Central Montana Fair (Lewistown), Jul 16
    Christmas to Remember (Laurel), Dec 5
    Ennis Rodeo & Parade (Ennis), Jul 3
    Fest of Nations (Red Lodge), Jul 30
    Glacier Natl Park: Anniv, May 11
    Helena Railroad Fair (Helena), Apr 25
    Little Bighorn Days (Hardin), Jun 23
    Livingston Roundup (Livingston), Jul 2
    Logger Days (Libby), Jul 16
    Longest Dam Run (Glasgow), Jun 19
    Martz, Judy: Birth, Jul 28
    Miles City Bucking Horse Sale (Miles City), May 21
    Montana Governor's Cup Walleye Tourn (Fort Peck), Jul 8
    Mountain Man Rendezvous (Red Lodge), Jul 23
    Nordicfest (Libby), Sep 10
    Northeast Montana Threshing Bee/Antique Show (Culbertson), Sep 25
    Northern Intl Livestock Expo (Billings), Oct 20
    NRA/NWRA Rodeo Finals (Billings), Mar 13
    Red Lodge Home of Champions Rodeo/Parade (Red Lodge), Jul 2
    Ski-Joring Finals, Natl (Red Lodge), Mar 13
    State Fair (Great Falls), Jul 31
    Tamarack Time (Bigfork), Oct 16
    Wild Horse Stampede (Wolf Point), Jul 9
    Wildlife Film Fest, Intl (Missoula), May 1
    Winter Carnival (Red Lodge), Mar 6
    Wolf Point's Annual Christmas Parade (Wolf Point), Dec 5
    Wrestling Chmpshps, NAIA (Great Falls), Mar 5
Montana, Joe: Birth, Jun 11
Montand, Yves: Birth Anniv, Oct 13
Monterey Jazz Fest (Monterey, CA), Sep 17
Montessori, Maria: Birth Anniv, Aug 31
Montgolfier, Jacques: Birth Anniv, Jan 7
Montgolfier, Joseph M: Birth Anniv, Aug 26
Montgomery Boycott Arrests: Anniv, Feb 22
Montgomery Bus Boycott Begins: Anniv, Dec 5
Montgomery Bus Boycott Ends: Anniv, Dec 20
Montgomery, Belinda: Birth, Jul 23
Montgomery, Bernard Law: Birth Anniv, Nov 17
Montoya, Carlos: Birth Anniv, Dec 3
Montserrat: Volcano Erupts: Anniv, Jun 25
Monty Python's Flying Circus TV Premiere: Anniv, Oct 5
Moog, Robert: Birth, May 23
Moon, Blue, Jul 31
Moon Day (First Moon Landing), Jul 20
Moon Fest (China), Sep 28
Moon, Harvest, Sep 28
Moon, Hunter's, Oct 27
Moon Phases,
    First Quarter, Jan 29
    First Quarter, Feb 27
    First Quarter, Mar 28
    First Quarter, Apr 27
    First Quarter, May 27
    First Quarter, Jun 25
    First Quarter, Jul 24
    First Quarter, Aug 23
    First Quarter, Sep 21
    First Quarter, Oct 20
    First Quarter, Nov 19
    First Quarter, Dec 18
    Full Moon, Jan 7
    Full Moon, Feb 6
    Full Moon, Mar 6
    Full Moon, Apr 5
    Full Moon, May 4
    Full Moon, Jun 3
    Full Moon, Jul 2
    Full Moon, Jul 31
    Full Moon, Aug 29
    Full Moon, Sep 28
    Full Moon, Oct 27
    Full Moon, Nov 26
    Full Moon, Dec 26
    Last Quarter, Jan 14
    Last Quarter, Feb 13
    Last Quarter, Mar 13
    Last Quarter, Apr 11
    Last Quarter, May 11
    Last Quarter, Jun 9
    Last Quarter, Jul 9
    Last Quarter, Aug 7
    Last Quarter, Sep 6
    Last Quarter, Oct 6
    Last Quarter, Nov 5
    Last Quarter, Dec 4
    New Moon, Jan 21
    New Moon, Feb 20
    New Moon, Mar 20
    New Moon, Apr 19
    New Moon, May 19
    New Moon, Jun 17
    New Moon, Jul 17
    New Moon, Aug 15
    New Moon, Sep 14
    New Moon, Oct 13
    New Moon, Nov 12
    New Moon, Dec 11
Moon, Warren: Birth, Nov 18
Moonlighting TV Premiere: Anniv, Mar 3
Moore, Archie: Birth Anniv, Dec 13
Moore, Clement: Birth Anniv, Jul 15
Moore, Demi: Birth, Nov 11
Moore, Dudley: Birth Anniv, Apr 19
Moore, Garry: Birth Anniv, Jan 31
Moore, Henry: Birth Anniv, Jul 30
Moore, Julia A. Davis: Birth Anniv, Dec 1
Moore, Julianne: Birth, Dec 3
Moore, Lenny: Birth, Nov 25
Moore, Mary Tyler: Birth, Dec 29
Moore, Melba: Birth, Oct 29
Moore, Roger: Birth, Oct 14
Moore, Shemar: Birth, Apr 20
Moore, Terry: Birth, Jan 7
Moose-Dropping Fest (Talkeetna, AK), Jul 10
MooseStompers Weekend (Houlton, ME), Jan 30
Morales, Esai: Birth, Oct 1
Moran, Erin: Birth, Oct 18
Moranis, Rick: Birth, Apr 18
Moravian Easter Resurrection Service (Winston-Salem, NC), Apr 11
Morazan, Francisco: Holiday (Honduras), Oct 3
More Herbs, Less Salt Day, Aug 29
More Than Just a Pretty Face Month, May 1
More, Sir Thomas: Birth Anniv, Feb 7
Moreau, Jeanne: Birth, Jan 23
Moreno, Rita: Birth, Dec 11
Morgan, Harry: Birth, Apr 10
Morgan, Jaye P.: Birth, Dec 3
Morgan, Joe: Birth, Sep 19
Morgan, Joe: Birth, Sep 19
Morgan, John P.: Birth Anniv, Apr 17
Morgan, Michele: Birth, Feb 29
Moriarty, Cathy: Birth, Nov 29
Moriarty, Michael: Birth, Apr 5
Morione's Fest (Marinduque Island, Philippines), Apr 8
Morissette, Alanis: Birth, Jun 1
Morita, Pat: Birth, Aug 28
Morley, Robert: Birth Anniv, May 26
Mormon: Church of Jesus Christ of Latter-day Saints,
    Amnesty for Polygamists: Anniv, Jan 4
    Church of Jesus Christ of Latter-day Saints: Anniv, Apr 6
    Female Relief Society of Nauvoo: Anniv, Mar 17
    Mormon Battalion Arrival in California: Anniv, Jan 29
    Mormon Choir First Performs: Anniv, Aug 22
    Nauvoo Legion Chartered: Anniv, Feb 3
    Pioneer Day, Jul 24
Morning Radio Wise Guy Day, May 28
Morocco,
    Anniv of the Green March, Nov 6
    Independence Day, Jan 11
    Independence Day, Nov 18
    National Day, May 23
    Revolution of the King and the People, Aug 20
    Youth Day, Jul 9
Morrill Land Grant Act Passed: Anniv, Jul 1
Morris, Esther Hobart McQuigg: Birth Anniv, Aug 8
Morris, Garrett: Birth, Feb 1
Morris, Jack: Birth, May 16
Morris, Lewis: Birth Anniv, Apr 8
Morris, Mark: Birth, Aug 29
Morris, Robert: Birth Anniv, Jan 31
Morris, William: Birth Anniv, Mar 24
Morrison, Jim: Birth Anniv, Dec 8
Morrison, Toni: Birth, Feb 18
Morrison, Van: Birth, Aug 31
Morro Bay Harbor Fest (Morro Bay, CA), Oct 2
Morrow, Rob: Birth, Sep 21
Morse, David: Birth, Oct 11
Morse, Robert: Birth, May 18
Morse, Samuel F.: Birth Anniv, Apr 27
Morse, Samuel F.: Opens First US Telegraph Line: Anniv, May 24
Mortensen, Viggo: Birth, Oct 20
Morton, Jelly Roll: Birth Anniv, Sep 20
Morton, Joe: Birth, Oct 18
Morton, Levi P.: Birth Anniv, May 16
Morton, William Thomas Green: Birth Anniv, Aug 9
Moscow Soccer Tragedy: Anniv, Oct 20
Moscow, Nixon First American President to Visit: Anniv, May 22
Moses, Anna: Grandma Moses Day, Sep 7
Moses, Edwin: Birth, Aug 31
Moshoeshoe's Day (Lesotho), Mar 12
Mosquito Fest, Great Texas (Clute, TX), Jul 29
Moss, Randy: Birth, Feb 13
Moth-er Day, Mar 14
Mother Goose Day, May 1
Mother Goose Parade (El Cajon, CA), Nov 21
Mother Language Day, Intl, Feb 21
Mother Ocean Day, May 8
Mother Teresa: Birth Anniv, Aug 27
Mother, Father Deaf Day, Apr 25
Mothering Sunday (England), Mar 21
Mother-in-Law-Day, Oct 24
Mother's Day, May 9
Mother's Day (Pres Proc), May 9
Mother's Day Housewalk (Evanston, IL), May 9
Mothers, Natl Conv American (San Juan, Puerto Rico), Apr 27
Motley, Constance Baker: Birth, Sep 14
Motor Voter Bill Signed: Anniv, May 20
Motorcycle,
    AHRMA Vintage Motorcycle Races (Daytona Beach, FL), Mar 1
    AspenCash Motorcycle Rally (Ruidoso, NM), May 20
    Biketoberfest (Daytona Beach, FL), Oct 21
    Daytona 200 by Arai Superbike Classic (Daytona Beach, FL), Mar 7
    Daytona Supercross by Honda (Daytona Beach, FL), Mar 6
    Fall Cycle Scene Motorcycle Races (Daytona Beach, FL), Oct 21
    Golden Aspen Motorcycle Rally (Ruidoso, NM), Sep 15
    June Jamboree Motorcycle Rally (Lovington, NM), Jun 12
    Motorcycle Safety Month, May 1
    Sturgis Rally (Sturgis, SD), Aug 9
    Trail of Tears Commemoration (Waterloo, AL), Sep 18
    Women's Motorcycle Month, Jul 1
Mott, Lucretia (Coffin): Birth Anniv, Jan 3
Mott, Stewart Rawlings: Birth, Dec 4
Moulin, Jean: Death Anniv, Jul 8
Mount Everest Summit Reached: Anniv, May 29
Mount Everest, First Woman To Climb: Anniv, May 16
Mount Holyoke College Founded: Anniv, Nov 8
Mount Ogura Plane Crash: Anniv, Aug 12
Mount Pelee Eruption: Anniv, May 8
Mount Rainier Natl Park: Anniv, Mar 2
Mount Rushmore Completion: Anniv, Oct 31
Mount Rushmore July 4 Celeb (Mt Rushmore, SD), Jul 3
Mount Saint Helens Eruption: Anniv, May 18
Mountain Craft Days (Somerset, PA), Sep 10
Mountain Dance and Folk Fest (Asheville, NC), Aug 5
Mountain Fair (Hiawassee, GA), Jul 21
Mountain Glory Fest (Marion, NC), Oct 9
Mountain Man Rendezvous (Cataldo, ID), Aug 20
Mountain Man Rendezvous (Red Lodge, MT), Jul 23
Mountbatten, Louis: Assassination Anniv, Aug 27
Mourning, Alonzo: Birth, Feb 8
Move Hollywood & Broadway to Lebanon, PA, Day, Feb 5
Movie Theater Opens, First : Anniv, Apr 23
Moving Month, Natl, May 1
Moya, Carlos: Birth, Aug 27
Moyers, Bill: Birth, Jun 5
Mozambique,
    Armed Forces Day, Sep 24
    Heroes' Day, Feb 3
    Independence Day, Jun 25
Mozart Fest (San Luis Obispo, CA), Jul 16
Mozart Fest, Mainly (San Diego, CA), May 30
Mozart Intl Fest (Bartlesville, OK), Jun 11
Mozart, Wolfgang Amadeus: Birth Anniv, Jan 27
Mr Peepers TV Premiere: Anniv, Jul 3

722

☆ Chase's 2004 Calendar of Events ☆ Index

Mr Wizard—Mystery

Mr Wizard TV Premiere: Anniv, Mar 3
MTV Premiere: Anniv, Aug 1
Mudd Day, Dec 20
Mudd, Roger: Birth, Feb 9
Muddy Frogwater Country Classic Fest (Milton-Freewater, OR), Aug 20
Muffin Wk, Natl, May 3
Muhammad: Isra al Mi'raj: Ascent of Prophet, Sep 11
Muhammad: Mawlid al Nabi: Birth of Muhammad, May 2
Muharram: See Islamic New Year, Feb 22
Muir, John: Birth Anniv, Apr 21
Muldaur, Diana: Birth, Aug 19
Muldaur, Maria: Birth, Sep 12
Mule Day, Oct 26
Mule Day (Columbia, TN), Apr 1
Mulgrew, Kate: Birth, Apr 29
Mulhern, Matt: Birth, Jul 21
Mulholland, Terry: Birth, Mar 9
Mull, Martin: Birth, Aug 18
Mullally, Megan: Birth, Nov 12
Mullen, Larry: Birth, Oct 31
Mulligan, Gerry: Birth Anniv, Apr 6
Mullin, Chris: Birth, Jul 30
Mulroney, Brian: Birth, Mar 20
Mulroney, Dermot: Birth, Oct 31
Multicultural American Child Awareness Day, Jun 13
Multicultural Fest (Dartmouth, NS, Canada), Jun 18
Multiple Sclerosis Education & Awareness Month, Natl, Mar 1
Mummies: Iceman Discovered: Anniv, Sep 19
Mumy, Bill: Birth, Feb 1
Muniz, Frankie: Birth, Dec 5
Munoz-Rivera, Luis: Birth Anniv, Jul 17
Munsel, Patrice: Birth, May 14
Munsters TV Premiere: Anniv, Sep 24
Muppet Show Premiere: Anniv, Sep 13
Muppets: Henson, Jim: Birth Anniv, Sep 24
Mural-in-a-Day (Toppenish, WA), Jun 5
Murder, She Wrote TV Premiere: Anniv, Sep 30
Murdoch, Rupert: Birth, Mar 11
Murkowski, Frank Hughes: Birth, Mar 28
Murkowski, Lisa: Birth, May 22
Murphy Brown TV Premiere: Anniv, Nov 14
Murphy, Audie: Birth Anniv, Jun 20
Murphy, Audie: Spirit of America Awards (Decatur, AL), Jul 3
Murphy, Ben: Birth, Mar 6
Murphy, Dale: Birth, Mar 12
Murphy, Eddie: Birth, Apr 3
Murphy, Michael: Birth, May 5
Murray, Anne: Birth, Jun 20
Murray, Bill: Birth, Sep 21
Murray, Don: Birth, Jul 31
Murray, Eddie: Birth, Feb 24
Murray, Jan: Birth, Oct 4
Murray, Ken: Birth Anniv, Jul 14
Murray, Patty: Birth, Oct 11
Murray, Philip: Birth Anniv, May 25
Musburger, Brent: Birth, May 26
Museum Day, Intl, May 18
Museum Open House (Clinton, MD), May 22
Musgrave, Storey: Birth, Aug 19
Musgrove, Ronnie: Birth, Jul 29
Mushroom Fest (Kennett Square, PA), Sep 11
Mushroom Fest, Richmond's (Richmond, MO), Apr 30
Mushroom Fest, Telluride (CO), Aug 26
Mushroom Month, Natl, Sep 1
Musial, Stan: Birth, Nov 21
Music. See also Bluegrass; Country & Western; Fiddlers; Gospel; Jazz and Blues,
Aberdeen Intl Youth Fest (Aberdeen, Scotland), **Aug 4**
Accordion Awareness Week, Natl, **Jun 1**
Accordion Fest, Sata-Hame (Ikaalinen, Finland), **Jun 29**
Albany Alive at Five (Albany, NY), **Jun 3**
All That Jazz Weekend (Asheville, NC), **Jan 30**
All-Northwest Barbershop Ballad Contest (Forest Grove, OR), **Mar 5**
Altamont Concert: Anniv, **Dec 6**
America the Beautiful Published, **Jul 4**
American Heritage Bluegrass Fest (Arrow Rock, MO), **Sep 18**
Anderson, Marian: Easter Concert: Anniv, **Apr 9**
Ash Lawn Opera Fest (Charlottesville, VA), **Jul 10**
Aspen Music Fest (Aspen, CO), **Jun 24**
Barbershop Quartet Day, **Apr 11**
Barbershop Quartet Singing Intl Conv (Louisville, KY), **Jun 27**
BBC Proms (London, England), **Jul 16**
Beatles Last Concert: Anniv, **Jan 30**
Beethoven by the Beach (Fort Lauderdale, FL), **Jun 26**
Beethoven's Ninth Symphony Premiere: Anniv, **May 7**
Big Band/Swing Dance Weekend (Asheville, NC), **Jan 23**
Big Muddy Folk Music Fest (Boonville, MO), **Apr 2**
Big Valley Jamboree (Camrose, AB, Canada), **Jul 29**
Blast from the Past, A (Manheim, PA), **Jun 12**
Brahms Requiem Premiere: Anniv, **Apr 10**
Branson Fest (Branson, MO), **Apr 6**
Brass Band Festival (Gettysburg, PA), **Jun 18**
Burlington Steamboat Days/Music Fest (Burlington, IA), **Jun 15**
Calgary Folk Fest (Calgary, AB, Canada), **Jul 22**
Canmore Folk Music Fest (Canmore, AB, Canada), **Jul 31**
Cape May Music Fest (Cape May, NJ), **May 23**
Carillon Fest, Intl (Springfield, IL), **Jun 6**
Carry a Tune Wk, Natl, **Oct 3**
Celtic Classic Highland Games & Fest (Bethlehem, PA), **Sep 24**
Celtic Fest, Southern Maryland (St. Leonard, MD), **Apr 24**
Cheltenham Intl Fest of Music (Cheltenham, England), **Jul 2**
Chicago Gospel Music Festival (Chicago, IL), **Jun 4**
Chicago Jazz Fest (Chicago, IL), **Sep 2**
Concert, World's Largest, **Mar 11**
Connecticut Early Music Fest (New London, CT), **Jun 11**
Day the Music Died (Holly, Richardson, Valens Death Anniv), **Feb 3**
Desert Foothills Music Fest (Carefree, AZ), **Feb 6**
Downtown Fest/Art Show (Gainesville, FL), **Nov 6**
Dulcimer Days (Coshocton, OH), **May 14**
Duran Duran Appreciation Day, Natl, **Aug 10**
Eastern Music Fest (Greensboro, NC), **Jun 21**
Edinburgh Intl Fest (Edinburgh, Scotland), **Aug 15**
Edmonton Folk Music Fest (Edmonton, AB, Canada), **Aug 5**
Everly Brothers/Central City Rock 'n Roll Cruise-In and Concert (Central City, KY), **Sep 3**
Exeter Fest (Exeter, England), **Jul 5**
Falcon Ridge Folk Fest (Hillsdale, NY), **Jul 22**
Fall Suwannee River Gospel Jubilee (Live Oak, FL), **Sep 30**
Festival at Sandpoint (Sandpoint, ID), **Aug 5**
Fiddle Fest at Audubon Acres (Chattanooga, TN), **May 22**
Fiddler's Frolics (Hallettsville, TX), **Apr 23**
First Grand Ole Opry Broadcast: Anniv, **Dec 10**
Florida Music Harvest (Live Oak, FL), **Sep 17**
Fredericksburg Music Fest (Fredericksburg, VA), **May 29**
Glenn Miller Birthplace Society Fest (Clarinda, IA), **Jun 9**
God Bless America 1st Performed: Anniv, **Nov 11**
Grammy Awards, **Feb 8**
Grand Teton Music Fest (Teton Village, WY), **Jun 29**
Great American Brass Band Fest (Danville, KY), **Jun 12**
Guelph Spring Fest (Guelph, ON, Canada), **Apr 30**
Guitar Flat-Picking Chmpshps, Natl (Winfield, KS), **Sep 16**
Handel's Messiah (Independence, MO), **Nov 20**
Hankfest (Chicago, IL), **Sep 17**
Happy Birthday to "Happy Birthday to You", **Jun 27**
Harrison Fest of Arts (Harrison Hot Springs, BC, Canada), **Jul 10**
Heritage Craft and Olde-Time Music Fest (Coshocton, OH), **Jun 19**
Hockhocking Folk Fest (Nelsonville, OH), **Jun 5**
Hodag Country Fest (Rhinelander, WI), **Jul 8**
Homeplace Festival (Waretown, NJ), **Nov 20**
Hot August Nights (Reno and Sparks, NV), **Aug 1**
Jamboree in the Hills (St. Clairsville, OH), **Jul 15**
Jazz Day, Intl, **Apr 29**
Joseph Brackett Day, **May 6**
Karaoke Week, Natl, **Apr 18**
Kaustinen Folk Music Fest (Kaustinen, Finland), **Jul 10**
KBCO World-Class Rockfest (Winter Park, CO), **Jul 17**
KCQ Country Music Fest (Saginaw, MI), **Jun 19**
Kingsville Intl Young Performers' Competition (Kingsville, TX), **Apr 1**
Kuopio Dance Fest (Kuopio, Finland), **Jun 17**
Kuumba Fest (Hollywood, FL), **Apr 24**
Ladies of Country Music Show (Waretown, NJ), **Jun 26**
Lahti Organ Fest (Lahti, Finland), **Aug 9**
Lennon-Ono Album Confiscation: Anniv, **Jan 3**
Levitt Pavilion Performing Arts/Music Fest (Westport, CT), **Jun 20**
Liberace Birthday Celebration & Play-A-Like Competition (Las Vegas, NV), **May 15**
Live Aid Concerts: Anniv, **Jul 13**
Llangollen Intl Musical Eisteddfod (Llangollen, Wales), **Jul 6**
Love Parade (Berlin, Germany), **Jul 10**
Lucerne Fest, Ostern (Lucerne, Switzerland), **Mar 27**
Lucerne Fest, Sommer (Lucerne, Switzerland), **Aug 13**
Lucerne Festival, Piano (Lucerne, Switzerland), **Nov 23**
Madrigal Dinner and Concert (Milwaukee, WI), **Dec 4**
Magnolia Fest (Live Oak, FL), **Oct 14**
Mainly Mozart Fest (San Diego, CA), **May 30**
Memorial Day Getaway (Live Oak, FL), **May 29**
Midnight at the Oasis (Yuma, AZ), **Mar 5**
Military Music Fest (Belgium), **Jun 13**
Missouri Day Fest (Trenton, MO), **Oct 15**
Missouri River Fest of Arts (Boonville, MO), **Aug 14**
Mormon Choir First Performs: Anniv, **Aug 22**
Mozart Fest (San Luis Obispo, CA), **Jul 16**
Music Camp, Intl (Dunseith, ND), **Jun 13**
Music in Our Schools Month, **Mar 1**
Music in the Park (Anchorage, AK), **Jun 2**
Musikfest (Bethlehem, PA), **Aug 6**
Natl Eisteddfod of Wales (Newport, Gwent, Wales), **Jul 31**
New World Symphony Premiere: Anniv, **Dec 16**
Newport Music Fest (Newport, RI), **Jul 9**
OK Mozart Intl Fest (Bartlesville, OK), **Jun 11**
Old Stoughton (MA) Musical Society: Anniv, **Nov 7**
Old-Time Country Music Contest, Fest & Expo, Natl (Avoca, IA), **Aug 29**
One-Hit Wonder Day, Natl, **Sep 25**
Opera Fest of New Jersey (Lawrenceville, NJ), **Jun 27**
Oregon Bach Fest (Eugene, OR), **Jun 25**
Oregon Coast Music Fest (Coos Bay, OR), **Jul 17**
Party in the Plaza (Aurora, IL), **Jun 17**
Piano Competition for Outstanding Amateurs, Intl (Fort Worth, TX), **Jun 7**
Piano Month, Natl, **Sep 1**
Piano Playing Contest, World Chmpshp Old-Time (Peoria, IL), **May 28**
Play-the-Recorder Month, **Mar 1**
Polka Fest (Wisconsin Dells, WI), **Apr 16**
Pop Music Chart Introduced: Anniv, **Jan 4**
Porter, Cole: Birth Anniv, **Jun 9**
Prague Autumn Intl Music Festival (Czech Republic), **Sep 12**
Quirky Country Music Song Titles Day, **Mar 27**
Red River Valley Fair (Fargo, ND), **Jun 18**
Rounds Resounding Day, **Aug 1**
Saint Olaf Christmas Fest (Northfield, MN), **Dec 2**
Saint Petersburg Fest/Natl Band Chmpshps (St. Pete, FL), **Apr 2**
Santa Fe Chamber Music Fest (Santa Fe, NM), **Jul 18**
Savonlinna Opera Fest (Savonlinna, Finland), **Jul 8**
Saxophone Day, **Nov 6**
Sea Music Fest (Mystic, CT), **Jun 10**
Sedona Chamber Music Festival (Sedona, AZ), **May 12**
Shrewsbury Intl Music Fest (Shropshire, England), **Jun 25**
Silent Record Week, **Jan 1**
Sing-Out Day, Intl, **Apr 2**
Songwriter's Show (Waretown, NJ), **Mar 20**
South by Southwest (Austin, TX), **Mar 12**
Southern Appalachian Dulcimer Fest (McCalla, AL), **May 1**
Southern Gospel Music Month, **Sep 1**
Space Oddity Song Release: Anniv, **Jun 11**
SPEBSQSA (Barbershop Quartet) Conv (Biloxi, MS), **Jan 25**
Spoleto Festival USA (Charleston, SC), **May 28**
Spring Suwannee River Jubilee (Live Oak, FL), **Jul 7**
Stars and Stripes Forever Day, **May 14**
Strauss, Richard G.: Birth Anniv, **Jun 11**
Stresa Music Weeks (Stresa, Italy), **Aug 20**
Summer Music Fest (Sitka, AK), **Jun 4**
Summerfest (Milwaukee, WI), **Jun 24**
Suwannee Spring Fest (Live Oak, FL), **Mar 18**
Tennessee Fall Homecoming (Norris, TN), **Oct 7**
Time of Music (Viitasaari, Finland), **Jun 29**
Traditional Sousa Concert (Kohler, WI), **Jul 4**
Tri-State Band Fest (Luverne, MN), **Sep 25**
Turku Music Fest (Turku, Finland), **Aug 13**
Vietnam Moratorium Concert: Anniv, **Mar 28**
Vinyl Record Day, **Aug 12**
Viva El Mariachi Fest (Fresno, CA), **Mar 20**
Viva! Chicago Latin Music Fest (Chicago, IL), **Aug 28**
W.C. Handy Fest (Florence, AL), **Jul 25**
Wagner Festspiele (Bayreuth, Germany), **Jul 25**
Willamette Valley Folk Fest (Eugene, OR), **May 21**
Wills, Bob: Birth Anniv, **Mar 6**
Windsurfing Regatta/Unvarnished Music Fest (Worthington, MN), **Jun 11**
Woodstock Folk Fest (Woodstock, IL), **Jul 18**
Zouk Month, **Jun 1**
Muslim Observances,
Ashura: Tenth Day, **Mar 2**
Eid-al-Adha: Feast of the Sacrifice, **Feb 1**
Eid-al-Fitr: Celebrating the Fast, **Nov 14**
Isra al Mi'raj: Ascent of Prophet Muhammad, **Sep 11**
Lailat ul Qadr: The Night of Power, **Nov 5**
Mawlid al Nabi: Birthday of Prophet Muhammad, **May 2**
Muharram (New Year), **Feb 22**
Rabi' I: Month of the Migration, **Apr 21**
Ramadan: Islamic Month of Fasting, **Oct 16**
Yawm Arafat: The Standing at Arafat, **Jan 31**
Mussina, Mike: Birth, Dec 8
Mussolini Ousted: Anniv, Jul 25
Mussolini, Benito: Birth Anniv, Jul 29
Mustang: Intl Ford Mustang Day, Apr 17
Mustard Day, Natl, Aug 7
Mutiny on the Bounty: Anniv, Apr 28
Mutombo, Dikembe: Birth, Jun 25
Muybridge, Eadweard: Birth Anniv, Apr 9
My Friend Flicka TV Premiere: Anniv, Feb 10
My Lai Massacre: Anniv, Mar 16
My Little Margie TV Premiere: Anniv, Jun 15
My Way Day, Feb 17
Myanmar,
Independence Day, **Jan 4**
Resistance Day, **Mar 27**
Union Day, **Feb 12**
Myers, Mike: Birth, May 25
Myers, Russell: Birth, Oct 9
Myerson, Bess: Birth, Jul 16
Mystery Series Week, Oct 3

Index ☆ Chase's 2004 Calendar of Events ☆

NAACP Founded: Anniv, **Feb 12**
NAB 2004/National Broadcasters Conv (Las Vegas, NV), **Apr 17**
Nabisco Championship (Rancho Mirage, CA), **Mar 22**
Nabokov, Evgeni: Birth, **Jul 25**
Nabors, Jim: Birth, **Jun 12**
Nader, Ralph: Birth, **Feb 27**
Nafels Pilgrimage (Canton Glarus, Switzerland), **Apr 1**
NAFTA Signed: Anniv, **Dec 8**
Nagging Day, Intl, **Aug 14**
Nagurski, Bronko: Birth Anniv, **Nov 3**
NAIA Div II Football Chmpshp Game, **Dec 20**
NAIA Men's and Women's Indoor Track/Field Chmpshps (Johnson City, TN), **Mar 4**
NAIA Men's Div I Basketball Chmpshp, **Mar 24**
NAIA Outdoor Track/Field Chmpshps (Olathe, KS), **May 27**
NAIA Women's Div I Basketball Chmpshp (Jackson, TN), **Mar 17**
NAIA Women's Volleyball Chmpshp (San Diego, CA), **Dec 3**
Naismith, James: Birth Anniv, **Nov 6**
Najimy, Kathy: Birth, **Feb 6**
Namath, Joe: Birth, **May 31**
Name That Tune TV Premiere: Anniv, **Jul 6**
Names,
 Get a Different Name Day, **Feb 13**
 Middle Name Pride Day, **Mar 12**
 Name Your PC Day, **Nov 20**
 Namesake Day, **Mar 7**
 Nametag Day, **Mar 11**
 Unique Names Day, **Mar 9**
 Z Day, **Jan 1**
Namibia,
 Heroes' Day, **Aug 26**
 Independence Day, **Mar 21**
Nanakusa (Japan), **Jan 7**
Nanticoke Indian Powwow (Millsboro, DE), **Sep 11**
Napolitano, Janet: Birth, **Nov 29**
Napping Day, Natl Workplace, **Apr 5**
Nash, Graham: Birth, **Feb 2**
Nash, Ogden: Birth Anniv, **Aug 19**
Nast, Thomas: Birth Anniv, **Sep 27**
Nastase, Ilie: Birth, **Jul 19**
Nat King Cole TV Premiere: Anniv, **Nov 5**
Natchez Fall Pilgrimage (Natchez, MS), **Oct 8**
Natchez Spring Pilgrimage (Natchez, MS), **Mar 13**
Natchitoches Historic Pilgrimage (Natchitoches, LA), **Oct 8**
Natchitoches Jazz Festival (Natchitoches, LA), **Apr 2**
Natchitoches/NW State Univ Folk Fest (Natchitoches, LA), **Jul 16**
Nathan Hale Fife and Drum Muster (Coventry, CT), **Jul 24**
Nation, Carry, Fest (Holly, MI), **Sep 11**
Nation, Carry: Birth Anniv, **Nov 25**
National Bank, First Chartered by Congress: Anniv, **Feb 25**
National Park Week (Pres Proc), **Apr 18**
Nations, Fest of (Red Lodge, MT), **Jul 30**
Nations, Festival of (St. Paul, MN), **Apr 29**
Native-American,
 Adai Caddo Indian Nation Pow Wow (Marthaville, LA), **Oct 16**
 American Indian Heritage Day (AL), **Oct 11**
 American Indian Heritage Month, Natl, **Nov 1**
 Apache Wars Began: Anniv, **Feb 4**
 Battle of Little Bighorn: Anniv, **Jun 25**
 Bureau of Indian Affairs Established, **Mar 11**
 Chief Joseph Surrender: Anniv, **Oct 5**
 Choctaw Indian Fair (Philadelphia, MS), **Jul 14**
 Cochise: Death Anniv, **Jun 8**
 Coeur d'Alene Tribal Pilgrimage (Cataldo, ID), **Aug 15**
 Crow Reservation Opened for Settlement: Anniv, **Oct 15**
 Custer Battlefield Becomes Little Bighorn: Anniv, **Nov 26**
 DeSoto Caverns Park Fall Indian Dance Fest (Childersburg, AL), **Sep 25**
 DeSoto Caverns Park Spring Indian Dance Fest (Childersburg, AL), **Apr 3**
 Gift of the Waters Pageant & Art Fest in the Park (Thermopolis, WY), **Aug 6**
 Hayes, Ira Hamilton: Birth Anniv, **Jan 12**
 Heritage Days Rendezvous (Kewanee, IL), **Jul 2**
 Indian Artifact Show (Owensboro, KY), **Aug 6**
 Indian Powwow, Natl Chmpshp (Grand Prairie, TX), **Sep 10**
 Indian Summer Days at Audubon Acres (Chattanooga, TN), **Oct 9**
 Indian Summer Fest (Milwaukee, WI), **Sep 10**
 Iroquois Arts Showcase (Howes Cave, NY), **May 29**
 Iroquois Indian Fest (Howes Cave, NY), **Sep 4**
 Joseph, Chief: Death Anniv, **Sep 21**
 Kiamichi-Owa-Chito Fest of Forest (Broken Bow, OK), **Jun 18**
 Kissimmee Slough Shootout and Rendezvous (Big Cypress Reservation, FL), **Feb 7**
 Last Formal Surrender of Confederate Troops: Anniv, **Jun 23**
 Loloma, Charles: Birth Anniv, **Jun 9**
 Makah Days (Neah Bay, WA), **Aug 27**
 Mescalero Apache Maiden's Puberty Rites (Mescalero, NM), **Jul 1**
 Minority Enterprise Development Week (Pres Proc) **Sep 26**
 Nanticoke Indian Powwow (Millsboro, DE), **Sep 11**
 Natchez Powwow (Natchez, MS), **Mar 27**
 Native American Arts Fest (Grants Pass, OR), **May 8**
 Native American Citizenship Day, **Jun 15**
 Native American Heritage Day (Jonesboro, GA), **Apr 24**
 Native Americans' Day (SD), **Oct 11**
 Northern Illinois Univ Gatherings Powwow (Dekalb, IL), **Nov 6**
 Oconaluftee Indian Village (Cherokee, NC), **May 15**
 Ojibwa Keeshigun (Thunder Bay, ON, Canada), **Aug 14**
 Osceola: Death Anniv, **Jan 30**
 Pioneer and Indian Fest (Ridgeland, MS), **Oct 23**
 Pocahontas: Death Anniv, **Mar 21**
 Red Cloud Indian Art Show (Pine Ridge, SD), **Jun 6**
 Red Cloud: Death Anniv, **Dec 10**
 Red Earth Native American Cultural Fest (Oklahoma City, OK), **Jun 4**
 Sedona Arts Fest (West Sedona, AZ), **Oct 9**
 Seminole Tribe Festival, Powwow and Rodeo (Hollywood, FL), **Feb 12**
 Seminole Tribe of Florida Legally Established: Anniv, **Aug 21**
 Sitting Bull: Death Anniv, **Dec 15**
 Spirit of Wovoka Days Powwow (Yerington, NV), **May 28**
 Tecumseh! Epic Outdoor Drama (Chillicothe, OH), **Jun 11**
 Totah Fest (Farmington, NM), **Aug 27**
 Trail of Courage Living-History Fest (Rochester, IN), **Sep 18**
 Trail of Tears Commemoration (Waterloo, AL), **Sep 18**
 United Tribes Powwow (Bismarck, ND), **Sep 2**
 White Woman Made Indian Chief: Anniv, **Sep 18**
 Woodland Indian Discovery Day (St. Mary's City, MD), **Sep 11**
 Wounded Knee Massacre: Anniv, **Dec 29**
NATO Forces Attack Yugoslavia: Anniv, **Mar 25**
NATO Planes Down Serb Jets: Anniv, **Feb 28**
NATO: Anniv, **Apr 4**
Natural Bridges Natl Monument: Anniv, **Apr 16**
Naughton, David: Birth, **Feb 13**
Naughton, James: Birth, **Dec 6**
Nauru: National Day, **Jan 31**
Nautilus: First Nuclear-Powered Submarine Voyage: Anniv, **Jan 17**
Nauvoo Legion Chartered: Anniv, **Feb 3**
Navratilova, Martina: Birth, **Oct 18**
Navy Birthday, **Oct 13**
Navy Day, **Oct 27**
Navy, US: Fleet Week New York (New York, NY), **May 19**
Neal, Patricia: Birth, **Jan 20**
Nealon, Kevin: Birth, **Nov 18**
Near Miss Day, **Mar 23**
Nearing, Scott: Birth Anniv, **Aug 6**
Neas, Ralph: Birth, **May 14**
Nebraska,
 Admission Day, **Mar 1**
 Applejack Fest (Nebraska City), **Sep 18**
 Arbor Day Fest (Nebraska City), **Apr 30**
 Barn Day (Filley), **Jul 6**
 BCHS Christmas Open House (Ainsworth), **Dec 5**
 Big 12 Men's and Women's Indoor Track Chmpshps (Lincoln), **Feb 27**
 Central Nebraska Ethnic Fest (Grand Island), **Jul 23**
 Christmas at Union Station (Omaha), **Nov 27**
 Christmas on the Prairie (Wahoo), **Dec 4**
 Clarkson Czech Fest (Clarkson), **Jun 24**
 Clearwater Chamber of Commerce Rodeo (Clearwater), **Jun 25**
 Cobblestone Fest (Falls City), **Aug 20**
 Columbus Days (Columbus), **Aug 12**
 Countryside Village Art Fair (Omaha), **Jun 5**
 Crane Watch (Kearney), **Mar 1**
 Curtis Easter Pageant (Curtis), **Apr 4**
 Czechoslovakian Fest, Natl (Wilber), **Aug 6**
 Fairfest (Hastings), **Jul 21**
 Fall Home & Garden Expo (Omaha), **Oct 8**
 Garfield County Fair (Burwell), **Jul 28**
 Gateway Farm Expo (Kearney), **Nov 10**
 Gingerbread on Parade (Omaha), **Nov 20**
 Hagel, Chuck: Birth, **Oct 4**
 Halloween (Arapahoe), **Oct 31**
 Homestead Days (Beatrice), **Jun 16**
 Husker Harvest Days (Grand Island), **Sep 14**
 Industry Day (Beatrice), **Apr 25**
 Johanns, Mike: Birth, **Aug 18**
 Kool-Aid Days (Hastings), **Aug 13**
 Lavitset (Norfolk), **Sep 24**
 Lawn Flower & Patio Show (Omaha), **Feb 5**
 Light of the World Christmas Pageant (Minden), **Nov 27**
 Lisco Old-timers Day (Lisco), **Sep 12**
 Literature Fest (Norfolk), **Jul 31**
 NCAA Div I Men's Baseball Chmpshp (Omaha), **Jun 18**
 Nebraska State Fair (Lincoln), **Aug 28**
 Nebraskaland Days/Buffalo Bill Rodeo (North Platte), **Jun 11**
 Nebraska's Big Rodeo (Burwell), **Jul 29**
 Nelson, Ben: Birth, **May 17**
 Old-Fashioned Danish Christmas (Dannebrog), **Dec 11**
 Omaha Home and Garden Expo (Omaha), **Feb 5**
 Omaha Products Show (Omaha), **Oct 20**
 Oregon Trail Days (Gering), **Jul 8**
 Oregon Trail Rodeo (Hastings), **Sep 3**
 Prairie Pioneer Days (Arapahoe), **Jul 4**
 River City Roundup (Omaha), **Sep 17**
 Scotts Bluff County Fair (Mitchell), **Aug 9**
 Shakespeare on the Green (Omaha), **Jun 24**
 Taste of Omaha (Omaha), **Jun 4**
 Triumph of Ag Expo (Omaha), **Mar 3**
 Ugly Pickup Parade and Contest (Chadron), **Oct 29**
 Wayne Chicken Show (Wayne), **Jul 9**
 Willow Tree Fest (Gordon), **Jul 16**
 Wings Over the Platte Spring Migration Season (Grand Island), **Feb 15**
Neeson, Liam: Birth, **Jun 7**
Nehru, Jawaharlal: Birth Anniv, **Nov 14**
Neighbor Day, **May 23**
Neighbor Day, Natl Good, **Sep 26**
Neill, Sam: Birth, **Sep 14**
Neither Snow Nor Rain Day: Anniv, **Sep 7**
Nelligan, Kate: Birth, **Mar 16**
Nelson, Barry: Birth, **Apr 16**
Nelson, Ben: Birth, **May 17**
Nelson, Bill: Birth, **Sep 29**
Nelson, Cindy: Birth, **Aug 19**
Nelson, Craig T.: Birth, **Apr 4**
Nelson, David: Birth, **Oct 24**
Nelson, Horatio: Birth Anniv, **Sep 29**
Nelson, Judd: Birth, **Nov 28**
Nelson, Thomas: Birth Anniv, **Dec 26**
Nelson, Willie: Birth, **Apr 30**
Nelson: Ozzie and Harriet Show Debut: Anniv, **Oct 8**
Nemec, Corin: Birth, **Nov 5**
Nemerov, Howard: Birth Anniv, **Feb 1**
Nenana Tripod Raising Fest (Nenana, AK), **Mar 6**
Nepal,
 Democracy Day, Natl, **Feb 18**
 King's Birthday National Holiday, **Jul 7**
 National Unity Day, **Jan 11**
Neptune Discovery: Anniv, **Sep 23**
Neptune Fest Boardwalk Weekend (Virginia Beach, VA), **Sep 24**
Nerve Gas Attack on Japanese Subway: Anniv, **Mar 20**
Neshoba County Fair (Philadelphia, MS), **Jul 23**
Nesmith, Michael: Birth, **Dec 30**
Netherlands,
 European Fine Art Fair (Maastricht), **Mar 5**
 Liberation Day, **May 5**
 Midwinter Horn Blowing, **Nov 28**
 National Windmill Day, **May 8**
 Netherlands-United States: Diplomatic Anniv, **Apr 19**
 North Sea Jazz Fest (The Hague), **Jul 9**
 Prinsjesdag (Parliament opening), **Sep 21**
 Queen's Birthday, **Apr 30**
 Relief of Leiden, **Oct 3**
 Scilly Isles Peace Anniv, **Apr 17**
Networking Week, Natl, **Oct 11**
Neuharth, Allen: Birth, **Mar 22**
Neurofibromatosis Awareness Month, Natl, **May 1**
Neutrality Appeal, American: Anniv, **Aug 18**
Neuwirth, Bebe: Birth, **Dec 31**
Nevada,
 ABC (Bowling) Chmpshp Tourn (Reno), **Feb 14**
 ABC (Bowling) Convention (Reno), **Mar 14**
 Admission Day, **Oct 31**
 Armed Forces Day Military Vehicle Rally (Hawthorne), **May 19**
 Artown (Reno), **Jul 1**
 Burning Man (Black Rock Desert), **Aug 30**
 Carson City Library Foundation Oktoberfest (Carson City), **Oct 2**
 Carson City Rendezvous (Carson City), **Jun 11**
 Chmpshp Air Races, Natl (Reno), **Sep 16**
 Cowboy Poetry Gathering, Natl (Elko), **Jan 24**
 Coyote Chase (Wellington), **Jun 19**
 Dietary Managers Assn Mtg/Expo (Reno), **Jul 18**
 Ensign, John: Birth, **Mar 25**
 Family Day, **Nov 26**
 Guinn, Kenny: Birth, **Aug 24**
 Hot August Nights (Reno and Sparks), **Aug 1**
 Liberace Birthday Celebration & Play-A-Like Competition (Las Vegas), **May 15**
 Liberace Memorial Mass (Las Vegas), **Feb 4**
 Liberace Museum Christmas Tree Lighting (Las Vegas), **Dec 2**
 NAB 2004/National Broadcasters Conv (Las Vegas), **Apr 17**
 Nevadapex Coin and Stamp Expo (Laughlin), **Jan 2**
 Nugget Best in the West Rib Cook-Off (Sparks), **Sep 2**
 Reid, Harry: Birth, **Dec 2**
 Reno Birthday, **May 9**
 Spirit of Wovoka Days Powwow (Yerington), **May 28**
 State Fair (Reno), **Aug 25**
 Vegaspex (Las Vegas), **May 21**
Neville, Aaron: Birth, **Jan 24**
Nevis: Independence Day, **Sep 19**
New Beginning Fest (Coffeyville, KS), **Apr 23**
New England Conference on Storytelling for Children (Keene, NH), **Apr 17**
New England Home Show (Boston, MA), **Feb 21**
New England, Dark Day in: Anniv, **May 19**

☆ Chase's 2004 Calendar of Events ☆ Index

New—Nick

New Friends, Old Friends Week, Natl, May 16
New Hampshire,
Artists in the Park (Wolfeboro), **Aug 18**
Benson, Craig: Birth, **Oct 8**
Fine Arts and Crafts Fest (New Ipswich), **Oct 2**
Gregg, Judd: Birth, **Feb 14**
Hopkinton State Fair (Contoocook), **Sep 2**
Jackson Hill Cider Day (Portsmouth), **Sep 11**
League of NH Craftsmen Annual Craftsmen's Fair (Newbury), **Aug 7**
New England Conference on Storytelling for Children (Keene), **Apr 17**
New Hampshire Highland Games (Contoocook), **Sep 24**
Ratification Day, **Jun 21**
Rochester Fair (Rochester), **Sep 10**
Sununu, John: Birth, **Sep 10**
New Jersey,
Apple Festival (Forked River), **Sep 25**
Art Festival (Harvey Cedars), **Jul 18**
Art in the Park (Bay Head), **Jun 12**
Arts & Crafts Fest (Loveladies), **Jul 31**
Barnegat Bay Crab Race and Fest (Seaside Heights), **Aug 29**
Be Nice to New Jersey Week, **Jul 4**
Black Maria Studio: Anniv, **Feb 1**
Blue Claw Crab Craft Show & Crab Race (Harvey Cedars), **Aug 14**
Cape May Food & Wine Fest (Cape May), **Sep 18**
Cape May Music Fest (Cape May), **May 23**
Cattus Island Nature Fest (Toms River), **Oct 3**
Celebrate Earth Day (Point Pleasant Beach), **Apr 17**
Coast Day NJ (Long Beach Island & Cape May), **Oct 9**
Corzine, Jon: Birth, **Jan 1**
Craft Day by the Bay (Harvey Cedars), **Jul 3**
Crustacean Beauty Pageant/Ocean City Creep (Ocean City), **Aug 4**
Day of the Seal Celeb, Intl (Point Pleasant Beach), **Mar 20**
Dickens' Christmas Extravaganza (Cape May), **Dec 3**
Dodge Poetry Fest, **Sep 16**
Eggsibit (Phillipsburg), **Mar 27**
Father's Day Celebration (Point Pleasant Beach), **Jun 20**
Fest of Fine Craft (Millville), **Oct 2**
Fest-in-the-Park (Nutley), **Sep 12**
Festival of the Sea (Point Pleasant Beach), **Sep 18**
First Black Pro Hockey Player: Anniv, **Nov 15**
Fishing Contest (Lakewood), **May 1**
Founders' Day (Toms River), **Jun 12**
Grandparent's Day Celebration (Point Pleasant Beach), **Sep 12**
Halloween Parade (Toms River), **Oct 30**
Heritage Day Fest (Lavallette), **Sep 11**
Hey Rube Get a Tube Ocean Inner Tube Race, **Sep 19**
Holidays at Wheaton Village (Millville), **Nov 27**
Homeplace Festival (Waretown), **Nov 20**
Independence Extravaganza (Lavallette), **Jul 4**
Into the Wood Show (Millville), **Apr 3**
Ladies of Country Music Show (Waretown), **Jun 26**
Lautenberg, Frank: Birth, **Jan 23**
Lavallette Heritage Arts & Crafts Show (Lavallette), **Jul 25**
Long Beach Island Chowder Cook-Off (Beach Haven), **Oct 2**
Long Beach Island Surf Fishing Tournament (Long Beach Island), **Oct 9**
Loveladies Fair (Loveladies), **Jun 5**
Marble Weekend (Millville), **Jun 25**
Martin Z. Mollusk Day (Ocean City), **May 6**
May in Montclair (Montclair Township), **May 1**
McGreevey, Jim: Birth, **Aug 6**
Mid-Summer Antiques & Collectibles Show & Sale (Millville), **Jul 24**
Mid-Winter Antiques Show (Millville), **Feb 7**
Mother's Day Celebration (Point Pleasant Beach), **May 9**
Museum of American Glass Mid-Winter Exhibit (Millville), **Jan 17**
New Jersey State Rowing Chmpshps (Brick), **Jul 8**
Ocean County Bluegrass Fest (Waretown), **Feb 1**
Ocean County Bluegrass Fest (Waretown), **Sep 12**
Ocean County Decoy/Gun Show (Tuckerton), **Sep 25**
Ocean County Wildfowl Art & Decoy Show (Brick), **Feb 14**
Olde-Time Antiques and Collectibles Faire (Toms River), **Sep 4**
Opera Fest of New Jersey (Lawrenceville), **Jun 27**
Penguin Awareness Day (Point Pleasant Beach), **Jan 17**
Picatinny Peak Fall Hawkwatch (Dover), **Sep 1**
Pine Barrens Jamboree (Waretown), **Oct 9**
Ratification Day: Anniv, **Dec 18**
Reptile Awareness Day (Point Pleasant Beach), **Oct 16**
Saint Ann's Italian Street Fest (Hoboken), **Jul 20**
Scandinavian Fest (Stanhope), **Sep 5**
Seashore Open House Tour (Loveladies), **Aug 4**
Shark Awareness Day (Point Pleasant Beach), **Jul 17**
Songwriter's Show (Waretown), **Mar 20**
South Jersey Canoe/Kayak Classic (Lakewood), **Jun 5**
Spring Fest (Cape May), **Apr 23**
State Fair (Augusta), **Aug 6**
Suffragists' Voting Attempt: Anniv, **Nov 19**
Sugarloaf Crafts Fest (Somerset), **Oct 29**
Sugarloaf Crafts Fest (Somerset), **Mar 12**
Sussex Farm and Horse Show/New Jersey State Fair (Augusta), **Aug 6**
Toms River Canoe Race (Toms River), **Oct 2**
Tour of Somerville (Somerville), **May 31**
Victorian Sherlock Holmes Weekend (Cape May), **Mar 5**
Victorian Week (Cape May), **Oct 8**
Weird Contest Week (Ocean City), **Aug 15**
Wings 'n' Water Fest (Stone Harbor), **Sep 18**
New Mexico,
Admission Day, **Jan 6**
Albuquerque Intl Balloon Fiesta (Albuquerque), **Oct 2**
AspenCash Motorcycle Rally (Ruidoso), **May 20**
Bingaman, Jeff: Birth, **Oct 3**
Carlsbad Caverns Natl Park Established: Anniv, **May 14**
Domenici, Pete V.: Birth, **May 7**
Electric Light Parade (Lovington), **Dec 6**
Extraterrestrial Culture Day, **Feb 12**
Farmington Invitational Balloon Fest (Farmington), **May 29**
Freedom Days (Farmington), **Jul 2**
Golden Aspen Motorcycle Rally (Ruidoso), **Sep 15**
June Jamboree Motorcycle Rally (Lovington), **Jun 12**
Lovington Fall Arts/Crafts Fest (Lovington), **Nov 6**
Mescalero Apache Maiden's Puberty Rites (Mescalero), **Jul 1**
New Mexico State Fair (Albuquerque), **Sep 3**
Outdoor Summer Theater (Farmington), **Jun 16**
Richardson, Bill: Birth, **Nov 15**
Santa Fe Chamber Music Fest (Santa Fe), **Jul 18**
Show of Wheels (Lovington), **Feb 7**
Shuttle Camp (Alamogordo), **Jun 7**
Spring Gala (Lovington), **May 1**
Totah Fest (Farmington), **Aug 27**
World Shovel Race Chmpshp (Angel Fire), **Jan 31**
World's Greatest Lizard Race (Lovington), **Jul 3**
New Orleans, Battle of: Anniv, Jan 8
New World Symphony Premiere: Anniv, Dec 16
New Year,
Chinese Lunar New Year Fest (Baltimore, MD), **Jan 25**
Chinese New Year, **Jan 22**
Chinese New Year Fest (San Francisco, CA), **Jan 17**
Ethiopia: New Year's Day, **Sep 11**
First Night (Boston, MA), **Dec 31**
First Night Albany (Albany, NY), **Dec 31**
First Night Asheville (Asheville, NC), **Dec 31**
First Nights (Canada), **Dec 31**
First Nights (US), **Dec 31**
India: New Year's Day, **Mar 21**
Iranian New Year (Persian), **Mar 21**
Japanese Era New Year, **Jan 1**
MADD's New Year's Designate a Driver Campaign, **Dec 31**
Muharram (Islamic New Year), **Feb 22**
Naw-Ruz (Baha'i New Year's Day), **Mar 21**
New Year's Day, **Jan 1**
New Year's Day (Gregorian), **Jan 1**
New Year's Day Observance (Russia), **Jan 1**
New Year's Day Parade (London, England), **Jan 1**
New Year's Dishonor List, **Jan 1**
New Year's Eve, **Dec 31**
New Year's Eve Trail Ride and Party (Live Oak, FL), **Dec 26**
New Year's Fest (Kalamazoo, MI), **Dec 31**
New Year's Resolutions Week, **Jan 1**
Old New Year's Day, **Mar 25**
Rosh Hashanah (Jewish), **Sep 16**
Russia: Old New Year's Eve, **Jan 13**
Sinhala and Tamil New Year (Sri Lanka), **Apr 13**
Stock Exchange Holiday, **Jan 1**
United Kingdom New Year's Holiday, **Jan 1**
New York,
Albany Alive at Five (Albany), **Jun 3**
Albany Riverfest (Albany), **Aug 14**
Albany Riverfront Jazz Festival (Albany), **Sep 11**
Albany Tulip Fest (Albany), **May 7**
Antiques in Schoharie (Schoharie), **Mar 6**
Belmont Stakes (Belmont Park), **Jun 5**
Belmont Stakes, First Running of, **Jun 19**
Brooklyn Bridge Opened: Anniv, **May 24**
Broome County Fair (Whitney Point), **Jul 27**
Clinton, Hillary Rodham: Birth, **Oct 26**
Cohocton Fall Foliage Fest (Cohocton), **Oct 1**
Colton Country Day (Colton), **Jul 17**
Columbia County Fair (Chatham), **Sep 2**
Corn Hill Arts Fest (Rochester), **Jul 10**
Decoy and Wildlife Art Show (Clayton), **Jul 16**
Ellis Island Family History Day (New York), **Apr 17**
Falcon Ridge Folk Fest (Hillsdale), **Jul 22**
Farm Sanctuary's Annual Pignic (Watkins Glen), **Jul 4**
First Night Albany (Albany), **Dec 31**
Fleet Week New York (New York), **May 19**
Great Northeast Home Show (Albany), **Feb 6**
Great NY State Snow & Track Expo (Albany), **Nov 5**
Greenlawn Antiques Show (Greenlawn), **Mar 13**
Halloween Haunted Walk and Carnival (Brooklyn), **Oct 30**
Hang Around Victor Day (Victor), **Sep 11**
Highlights Foundation Writer's Workshop (Chautauqua), **Jul 17**
Holiday Craft Show (Schoharie), **Nov 20**
HUMOResilience Workshop (Lake George), **Oct 22**
Iroquois Arts Showcase (Howes Cave), **May 29**
Iroquois Indian Fest (Howes Cave), **Sep 4**
James Beard Awards Ceremony (New York), **May 10**
Johnson City Field Days (Johnson City), **Sep 3**
Lilac Fest (Rochester), **May 14**
Macy's Thanksgiving Day Parade (New York), **Nov 25**
Mercedes-Benz Fashion Week Fall '04 (New York), **Feb 6**
Mercedes-Benz Fashion Week Spring '05 (New York), **Sep 12**
Model Boat Show (Clayton), **Aug 6**
NCAA Men's Div I Swimming/Diving Chmpshps (East Meadow), **Mar 25**
New York City Marathon (New York), **Nov 7**
New York City Subway: Anniv, **Oct 27**
New York Film Fest (New York), **Oct 1**
New York Public Library: Anniv, **May 23**
New York State Missing Persons Day (Albany), **Apr 6**
New York Subway Accident: Anniv, **Nov 2**
Northeast Great Outdoors Show (Albany), **Mar 19**
Palatine Museum Fall Event (Schoharie), **Sep 25**
Pataki, George: Birth, **Jun 24**
Pickle Festival (Greenlawn), **Oct 3**
Positive Power of Humor, Hope & Healing Conf (Saratoga Springs), **Apr 16**
Prospect Park Fishing Contest (Brooklyn), **Jul 9**
Quilt Show (Clayton), **Jul 23**
Ratification Day, **Jul 26**
Renaissance Fest (Sterling), **Jul 3**
Reopening of 1743 Palatine House Museum (Schoharie), **Jun 6**
Reopening of the Schoharie Valley Railroads Museum (Schoharie), **Jun 5**
Rockefeller Center Christmas Tree Lighting (New York), **Dec 1**
Saint Patrick's Day Parade (Hornell), **Mar 13**
Saint Patrick's Day Parade (New York), **Mar 17**
Saranac Lake Winter Carnival (Saranac Lake), **Feb 6**
Schumer, Charles E.: Birth, **Nov 23**
Stamp & Coin Expo (New York), **Apr 23**
State Fair (Syracuse), **Aug 26**
Stationery Show, Natl (New York), **May 16**
Stone House Day (Hurley), **Jul 10**
Suydam Homestead and Barn Museum (Centerport), **Jun 6**
Toy Tips Executive Toy Test (New York), **Sep 1**
Tupper Lake Woodsmen's Days (Tupper Lake), **Jul 10**
US Amateur (Golf) Chmpshp (Mamaroneck), **Aug 16**
US Open (Golf) Chmpshp (Southampton), **Jun 17**
Valentown Antique Peddler's Market (Victor), **Aug 1**
Westminster Kennel Club Dog Show (New York), **Feb 9**
You Gotta Have Park (Brooklyn), **May 15**
New York Film Fest, Oct 1
New York Stock Exchange Established: Anniv, May 17
New York Times First Published: Anniv, Sep 18
New York Weekly: First Issue Anniv, Nov 5
New Yorker Published: Anniv, Feb 21
New Yorker: Addams, Charles: Birth Anniv, Jan 7
New Zealand,
ANZAC Day, **Apr 25**
Labor Day, **Oct 25**
New Zealand First Sighted by Europeans, **Dec 13**
Otago/Southland Provincial Anniv, **Mar 23**
Waitangi Day, **Feb 6**
Newby, Marcia: Birth, Mar 8
Newcomb, Simon: Birth Anniv, Mar 12
Newhart TV Premiere: Anniv, Oct 25
Newhart, Bob: Birth, Sep 5
Newhouse, Samuel: Birth Anniv, May 24
Newlywed Game TV Premiere: Anniv, Jul 11
Newman, Barry: Birth, Nov 7
Newman, Edwin: Birth, Jan 25
Newman, Laraine: Birth, Mar 2
Newman, Paul: Birth, Jan 26
Newman, Randy: Birth, Nov 28
Newmar, Julie: Birth, Aug 16
Newport Seafood and Wine Fest (Newport, OR), Feb 27
Newspaper Assn of America Convention (Washington, DC), Apr 20
Newspaper Week (Japan), Oct 1
Newspaper Week, Natl, Oct 3
Newspaper, First American: Anniv, Sep 25
Newton, Isaac: Birth Anniv, Jan 4
Newton, Juice: Birth, Feb 18
Newton, Thandie: Birth, Nov 6
Newton, Wayne: Birth, Apr 3
Newton-John, Olivia: Birth, Sep 26
Nez Perce: Chief Joseph Surrender: Anniv, Oct 5
Niagara Falls, Charles Blondin's Conquest of: Anniv, Jun 30
Nicaragua,
Battle of San Jacinto Day, **Sep 14**
Civil War Truce: Anniv, **Apr 19**
Independence Day, **Sep 15**
Natl Liberation Day, **Jul 19**
Nicholas II and Family Executed: Anniv, Jul 17
Nicholas, Denise: Birth, Jul 12
Nichols, Mike: Birth, Nov 6
Nichols, Stephen: Birth, Feb 19
Nicholson, Jack: Birth, Apr 22
Nick at Nite: Anniv, Jul 1

Chase's 2004 Calendar of Events — Index

Nickelodeon Premiere: Anniv, Apr 2
Nickerson, Camille ("Louisiana Lady"): Birth Anniv, Mar 30
Nicklaus, Jack: Birth, Jan 21
Nickles, Don: Birth, Dec 6
Nicks, Stevie: Birth, May 26
Nidetch, Jean: Birth, Oct 12
Nielsen, Arthur Charles: Birth Anniv, Sep 5
Nielsen, Leslie: Birth, Feb 11
Nietzsche, Friedrich Wilhelm: Birth Anniv, Oct 15
Nieuwendyk, Joe: Birth, Sep 10
Niger: Independence Day, Aug 3
Niger: Republic Day, Dec 18
Nigeria: Independence Day, Oct 1
Night Court TV Premiere: Anniv, Jan 4
Night Out, Natl, Aug 3
Night Watch (France), Jul 13
Nightingale, Florence: Birth Anniv, May 12
Nightshift Workers Day, Natl, May 12
Nimoy, Leonard: Birth, Mar 26
Nininger, Alexander, Jr: First WWII Medal of Honor, Feb 10
Nissan Xterra World Championship (Maui, HI), Oct 24
Nixon Birthday Holiday (Yorba Linda, CA), Jan 9
Nixon Pardoned: Anniv, Sep 8
Nixon, Cynthia: Birth, Apr 9
Nixon, John: Death Anniv, Dec 31
Nixon, Pat: Birth Anniv, Mar 16
Nixon, Richard M.,
  Anniv of Trip to China, Feb 21
  Birth Anniv, Jan 9
  Checkers Day, Sep 23
  First American Pres to Visit Moscow, May 22
  First Televised Presidential Debate: Anniv, Sep 26
  Last Press Conf: Anniv, Nov 7
  Moscow Communique: Anniv, May 29
  Nixon's Rejection of Senate Order: Anniv, Jan 4
  Pardoned: Anniv, Sep 8
  Resigns: Anniv, Aug 9
  Saturday Night Massacre, Oct 20
  Shanghai Communique: Anniv, Feb 27
No Diet Day, May 6
No Excuse Sunday, Apr 25
No Homework Day, May 6
No Housework Day, Apr 7
No Interruptions Day, Dec 30
No Socks Day, May 8
Noah, Yannick: Birth, May 18
Nobel Conference (St. Peter, MN), Oct 5
Nobel Prize Ceremonies (Oslo, Norway/Stockholm, Sweden), Dec 10
Nobel Prize, First US Scientist Receives: Anniv, Dec 10
Nobel, Alfred: Birth Anniv, Oct 21
Noiret, Philippe: Birth, Oct 1
Nokia Sugar Bowl (New Orleans, LA), Jan 1
Nolte, Nick: Birth, Feb 8
Nomo, Hideo: Birth, Aug 31
Noone, Kathleen: Birth, Jan 8
Nordicfest (Libby, MT), Sep 10
Norgay, Tensing: Everett Summit Reached: Anniv, May 29
Noriega, Manuel: US Invasion of Panama: Anniv, Dec 20
Norman, Greg: Birth, Feb 10
Norman, Jessye: Birth, Sep 15
Norris, Chuck: Birth, Mar 10
Norskedalen's Midsummer Fest (Coon Valley, WI), Jun 19
Norskedalen's Old-Fashioned Christmas (Coon Valley, WI), Dec 4
North Atlantic Treaty Ratified: Anniv, Apr 4
North Carolina,
  All That Jazz Weekend (Asheville), Jan 30
  Appalachian Potters Market (Marion), Dec 4
  Bald Is Beautiful Convention (Morehead City), Sep 10
  Bele Chere (Asheville), Jul 21
  Big Band/Swing Dance Weekend (Asheville), Jan 23
  Block House Steeplechase (Tryon), Apr 17
  Confederate Memorial Day, May 10
  Craft Fair of the Southern Highlands (Asheville), Jul 15
  Craftsmen's Christmas Classic Arts & Crafts Fest (Greensboro), Nov 26
  Craftsmen's Classic Arts & Crafts Fest (Greensboro), Apr 2
  Dole, Elizabeth: Birth, Jul 29
  Easley, Mike: Birth, Mar 23
  Easter Sunrise Service (Chimney Rock), Apr 11
  Eastern Music Fest (Greensboro), Jun 21
  Edwards, John: Birth, Jun 10
  Everybody's Day Fest (Thomasville), Sep 25
  First Night Asheville (Asheville), Dec 31
  Folkmoot USA: The NC Intl Folk Fest (Waynesville), Jul 12
  Fourth of July (Winston-Salem), Jul 3
  Great Smoky Mountains Natl Park Established: Anniv, Jun 15
  Halifax Independence Day, Apr 12
  Holiday Market (Greensboro), Nov 5
  Home Furnishings Market, Intl (High Point), Apr 22
  Longhorn World Chmpshp Rodeo (Winston-Salem), Feb 27
  Mecklenburg Day, May 20
  Moravian Easter Resurrection Service (Winston-Salem), Apr 11
  Mountain Dance and Folk Fest (Asheville), Aug 5
  Mountain Glory Fest (Marion), Oct 9
  NC RV and Camping Show (Charlotte), Jan 30
  NC RV and Camping Show (Greensboro), Jan 9
  NC RV and Camping Show (Raleigh), Feb 13
  North Carolina Apple Fest (Hendersonville), Sep 3
  North Carolina SweetPotato Month, Feb 1
  Oconaluftee Indian Village (Cherokee), May 15
  Ratification Day, Nov 21
  Seven Days in May (Chapel Hill), May 21
  Singing on the Mountain (Linville), Jun 27
  Soldiers' Reunion Celebration (Newton), Aug 19
  Southern Christmas Show (Greensboro), Nov 10
  State Fair (Raleigh), Oct 15
  Surrender at Durham Station: Anniv, Apr 18
  Whistlers Convention, Intl (Louisburg), Apr 21
  Woolly Worm Fest (Banner Elk), Oct 16
North Cascades Natl Park Established: Anniv, Oct 2
North Dakota,
  Adams County Fair/Rodeo (Hettinger), Jul 29
  Admission Day, Nov 2
  American Legacy (Mandan), Jul 30
  Conrad, Kent: Birth, Mar 12
  Dakota Cowboy Poetry Gathering (Medora), May 29
  Dickens Village Fest (Garrison), Nov 26
  Dorgan, Byron L.: Birth, May 14
  Downtown Art Street Fair (Fargo), Jul 15
  Fort Seward Wagon Trail (Jamestown), Jun 20
  Fort Union Trading Post Rendezvous (Williston), Jun 17
  Fourth of July Extravaganza (Hettinger), Jul 2
  Hoeven, John: Birth, Mar 13
  Killdeer Mountain Roundup Rodeo Days (Killdeer), Jul 3
  Lewis and Clark Days (Washburn), Jun 4
  Makoti Threshing Bee Show (Makoti), Oct 2
  Music Camp, Intl (Dunseith), Jun 13
  Norsk Hostfest (Minot), Oct 5
  North Star Classic (Valley City), Dec 3
  Northern Plains Heritage Fest (Dickinson), Aug 20
  Old-Time Fiddlers' Contest, Intl (Dunseith), Jun 11
  Red River Valley Fair (Fargo), Jun 18
  Rendezvous Fest (Cavalier), Jun 12
  Sheyenne Valley Arts/Crafts Fest (Fort Ransom), Sep 25
  Sodbuster Days (Fort Ransom), Jul 10
  Sodbuster Days—Harvest (Fort Ransom), Sep 11
  State Fair (Minot), Jul 23
  Taylor Horsefest (Taylor), Jul 30
  Theodore Roosevelt Natl Park Established: Anniv, Apr 25
  Ukrainian Fest (Dickinson), Jul 16
  United Tribes Powwow (Bismarck), Sep 2
  Winter Show (Valley City), Mar 5
North Pole Discovered: Anniv, Apr 6
North Pole, Solo Trip to: Anniv, Apr 22
North Sea Oil Rig Disaster: Anniv, Mar 27
North, Oliver Laurence: Birth, Oct 7
North, Oliver, Sentenced: Anniv, Jul 5
North, Sheree: Birth, Jan 17
Northern Exposure TV Premiere: Anniv, Jul 12
Northern Hemisphere Hoodie-Hoo Day, Feb 20
Northern Ireland,
  Belfast Fest at Queen's (Belfast), Oct 31
  Bloody Sunday: Anniv, Jan 30
  Christmas Holiday, Dec 25
  Good Friday Peace Agreement: Anniv, Apr 10
  Orangemen's Day, Jul 12
  Royal Ulster Agri Soc Balmoral Show (Belfast), May 12
  Saint Patrick's Day, Mar 17
Northern Pacific Railroad Completed: Anniv, Sep 8
Northwest Folklife Fest (Seattle, WA), May 28
Northwest Ordinance: Anniv, Jul 13
Norton, Edward: Birth, Aug 18
Norton, Gale: Birth, Mar 11
Norton, Ken: Birth, Aug 9
Norton, Mary: Birth Anniv, Dec 10
Noruz (Iranian New Year), Mar 21
Norville, Deborah: Birth, Aug 8
Norwalk Seaport Oyster Fest (Norwalk, CT), Sep 10
Norway,
  Constitution or Independence Day, May 17
  Edvard Grieg Birth Anniv Celebration, Jun 15
  Midnight Sun at North Cape, May 14
  Nobel Prize Awards Ceremony (Oslo), Dec 10
  Olsok Eve, Jul 29
  Pageantry in Oslo (Oslo), Oct 1
  Tyvendedagen, Jan 13
Norwegian,
  Norsk Hostfest (Minot, ND), Oct 5
  Norwegian Christmas (Brooklyn Park, MN), Dec 4
Nostradamus: Birth Anniv, Dec 14
Noth, Chris: Birth, Nov 13
Nothing Day, Natl, Jan 16
Nouri, Michael: Birth, Dec 9
Nova Scotia Bluegrass/Oldtime Music Fest (Mt Denson, NS), Jul 23
Nova Scotia Intl Tattoo (Halifax, NS, Canada), Jun 29
Nova Scotia's Gem and Mineral Show (Parrsboro, NS, Canada), Aug 20
Novak, Kim: Birth, Feb 13
Novello, Antonia: Birth, Aug 23
Novello, Don: Birth, Jan 1
NOW Founded: Anniv, Jun 30
Nowitzki, Dirk: Birth, Jun 19
Nuclear Chain Reaction, First Self-Sustaining: Anniv, Dec 2
Nuclear Medicine Week, Oct 3
Nuclear Power Plant Accident, Three Mile Island: Anniv, Mar 28
Nuclear-Free World, First Step Toward a: Anniv, Dec 8
Nuclear-Powered Submarine Voyage, First: Anniv, Jan 17
Nude Recreation Week, Jul 5
Nugent, Ted: Birth, Dec 13
Nunavut Independence: Anniv, Apr 1
Nuremberg War Crimes Trial (Germany): Anniv, Nov 20
Nureyev, Rudolf: Birth Anniv, Mar 17
Nurses, Nursing. See also Health,
  American Nurses Assn Convention (Minneapolis, MN), Jun 25
  Delano, Jane: Birth Anniv, Mar 26
  Emergency Nurses Day, Oct 13
  Emergency Nurses Week, Oct 10
  Nurse Anesthetists Week, Natl, Jan 25
  Nurses Day and Week, Natl, May 6
  Nursing Assistants Day and Week, Jun 10
  Nursing Conf on Pediatric Primary Care (Dallas, TX), Mar 23
  Perioperative (OR) Nurse Week, Nov 14
Nursing Home Week, Natl, May 9
Nutrition Month, Natl, Mar 1
Nutrition Week, Natl Women's, Apr 11
Nutt Day, Emma M., Sep 1
Nuyen, France: Birth, Jul 31
Nykvist, Sven Vilhem: Birth, Dec 3
Nylon Stockings: Anniv, May 15
NYPD Blue TV Premiere: Anniv, Sep 21
Nyquist, Ryan: Birth, Mar 6
O. Henry Pun-Off (Austin, TX), May 1
O.K. First Appearance in Print: Anniv, Mar 23
Oakley, Annie: Birth Anniv, Aug 13
Oakley, Charles: Birth, Dec 18
Oates, John: Birth, Apr 7
Oates, Joyce Carol: Birth, Jun 16
Oatmeal Fest (Bertram/Oatmeal, TX), Sep 3
Oatmeal Month, Jan 1
O'Bannon, Frank: Birth, Jan 30
O'Brien, Hugh: Birth, Apr 19
O'Brien, Conan: Birth, Apr 18
O'Brien, Edna: Birth, Dec 15
O'Brien, Margaret: Birth, Jan 15
O'Casey, Sean: Birth Anniv, Mar 30
Occupational Therapy Month, Natl, Apr 1
Ocean Dance (Hollywood, FL), Dec 3
Ocean Fest Sea-Son, Natl Week of (Fort Lauderdale, FL), Mar 6
Ocean, Billy: Birth, Jan 21
Oconaluftee Indian Village (Cherokee, NC), May 15
O'Connell, Daniel: Birth Anniv, Aug 6
O'Connor, Carroll: Birth Anniv, Aug 2
O'Connor, Donald: Birth, Aug 28
O'Connor, Frances: Birth, Jun 12
O'Connor, Glynnis: Birth, Nov 19
O'Connor, Sandra Day: Birth, Mar 26
O'Connor, Sandra Day: First Woman Supreme Court Justice: Anniv, Sep 25
O'Connor, Sinead: Birth, Dec 8
October Frozen Food Fest, Oct 1
October Is Discover America Month, Oct 1
October War (Yom Kippur War), Oct 6
Octoberfest (Appleton, WI), Sep 25
O'Dell, William "Spike": Birth, May 21
Odets, Clifford: Birth Anniv, Jul 18
Odetta: Birth, Dec 31
Odie's Birthday, Aug 8
Odometer Invented: Anniv, May 12
O'Donnell, Chris: Birth, Jun 26
O'Donnell, Rosie: Birth, Mar 21
Ogden, Jonathan: Birth, Jul 31
Oglethorpe Day, Feb 12
Oglethorpe, James: Birth Anniv, Dec 22
O'Grady, Gail: Birth, Jan 23
O'Hara, Catherine: Birth, Mar 4
O'Hara, Maureen: Birth, Aug 17
O'Higgins, Bernardo: Birth Anniv, Aug 20
Ohio,
  Admission Day, Mar 1
  Algonquin Mill Fall Festival (Carrollton), Oct 8
  All-American Soap Box Derby (Akron), Jul 31
  Annie Oakley Days (Greenville), Jul 23
  Antique Power Exhib (Burton), Jul 24
  Anti-Saloon League Founded: Anniv (Oberlin), May 24
  Apple Butter Stirrin' (Coshocton), Oct 15
  Barnesville Pumpkin Fest (Barnesville), Sep 23
  Big Ten Women's Golf Chmpshp (Columbus), Apr 23
  Big Ten Women's Soccer Tournament (Columbus), Nov 4
  Big Ten Wrestling Chmpshps (Columbus), Mar 6
  Bloody Brewery in 3-D (Columbus), Oct 1
  Boo at the Zoo (Cleveland), Oct 22
  Christkindl Market (Canton), Nov 11
  Circleville Pumpkin Show (Circleville), Oct 20
  Civil War Reenactment (Coshocton), Jul 17
  Cleveland Natl Air Show (Cleveland), Sep 4
  Coshocton Canal Fest (Coshocton), Aug 21
  Country Christmas (Coshocton), Dec 4

726

☆ Chase's 2004 Calendar of Events ☆ Index

Ohio (cont'd)—Outhouse

Dandelion May Fest (Dover), **May 7**
DeWine, Mike: Birth, **Jan 5**
Dulcimer Days (Coshocton) **May 14**
Easter Egg Hunt (Rockford), **Apr 10**
Fall Fest of Leaves (Ross County), **Oct 15**
Foothills Art Fest (Jackson), **Oct 15**
Geneva Area Grape Jamboree (Geneva), **Sep 25**
Help Someone See Week (Rockford), **Mar 7**
Heritage Craft and Olde-Time Music Fest (Coshocton), **Jun 19**
Hockhocking Folk Fest (Nelsonville), **Jun 5**
Holiday Happiness (Upper Arlington), **Dec 4**
Jackson County Apple Fest (Jackson), **Sep 21**
Jamboree in the Hills (St. Clairsville), **Jul 15**
Lawn Mower Race, Sta-Bil Natl Chmpshp (Mansfield), **Sep 4**
Longhorn World Chmpshp Rodeo (Cincinnati), **Feb 20**
Longhorn World Chmpshp Rodeo (Columbus), **Feb 6**
Marion Popcorn Fest (Marion), **Sep 2**
Natl City Cleveland Home and Garden Show (Cleveland), **Feb 7**
Ohio River Sternwheel Fest (Marietta), **Sep 10**
Ohio State Fair (Columbus), **Aug 6**
Paul Bunyan Show (Nelsonville), **Oct 1**
Red, White and Boom (Columbus), **Jul 2**
Stokes Becomes First Black Mayor in US: Anniv, **Nov 13**
Storyteller of the Year Contest, Natl (Millersport), **Sep 18**
Swiss Fest (Sugarcreek), **Oct 1**
Taft, Bob: Birth, **Jan 8**
Taste of Cincinnati (Cincinnati), **May 29**
Tecumseh! Epic Outdoor Drama (Chillicothe), **Jun 11**
Twins Day Fest (Twinsburg), **Aug 6**
Utica Old-Fashioned Ice Cream Fest (Utica), **May 29**
Voinovich, George V.: Birth, **Jul 15**
Walsh Invitational Rifle Tourn (Cincinnati), **Nov 5**
Oil Embargo Lifted, Arab: Anniv, Mar 13
Oil Town Fest, Smackover (Smackover, AR), Jun 16
Oil Well, First Commercial: Anniv, Aug 27
Oil: 55 mph Speed Limit: Anniv, Jan 2
O'Keefe, Michael: Birth, Apr 24
O'Keeffe, Georgia: Birth Anniv, Nov 15
Oklahoma,
Admission Day, **Nov 16**
American Rose Society Fall Natl Convention (Tulsa), **Oct 13**
Azalea Fest (Muskogee), **Apr 1**
Big 12 Men's & Women's Outdoor Track/Field Chmpshps (Norman), **Apr 29**
Big 12 Men's & Women's Tennis Chmpshp (Norman), **Apr 29**
Big 12 Women's Softball Chmpshp (Oklahoma City), **Apr 29**
Bullnanza (Guthrie), **Feb 6**
Cherokee Strip Celebration (Perry), **Sep 18**
Cherokee Strip Day, **Sep 16**
Chocolate Fest (Norman), **Feb 7**
Cimarron Territory Celebration (Beaver), **Apr 10**
Eighty-Niner Celebration (Guthrie), **Apr 20**
Garden of Lights (Muskogee), **Nov 25**
Guthrie Jazz Banjo Fest (Guthrie), **May 21**
Henry, Brad: Birth, **Jul 10**
Historical Day, **Oct 10**
Inhofe, James M.: Birth, **Nov 17**
Kiamichi-Owa-Chito Fest of the Forest (Broken Bow), **Jun 18**
Land Rush Begins, **Apr 22**
Last Formal Surrender of Confederate Troops: Anniv, **Jun 23**
Longhorn World Chmpshp Rodeo (Tulsa), **Jan 23**
Medieval Fair (Norman), **Apr 2**
Midsummer Nights' Fair (Norman), **Jul 16**
NCAA Div I Men's Tennis Chmpshp (Tulsa), **May 22**
NCAA Div I Women's Softball Chmpshp (Oklahoma City), **May 27**
Nickles, Don: Birth, **Dec 6**
OK Mozart Intl Fest (Bartlesville), **Jun 11**
Oklahoma City Bombing: Anniv, **Apr 19**
Oklahoma Day, **Apr 22**
Oklahoma Intl Bluegrass Fest (Guthrie), **Sep 30**
Oklahoma State Fair (Oklahoma City), **Sep 17**
Oktoberfest (Tulsa), **Oct 21**
P.V. Helmerich Distinguished Author Award (Tulsa), **Dec 3**
Rattlesnake Derby (Mangum), **Apr 23**
Red Earth Native American Cultural Fest (Oklahoma City), **Jun 4**
Sorghum Day Fest (Wewoka), **Oct 23**
Territorial Christmas Celebration (Guthrie), **Nov 27**
Watermelon Fest (Rush Springs), **Aug 14**
World Cow Chip-Throwing Chmpshp (Beaver), **Apr 17**
Oklahoma City Bombing: Anniv, Apr 19
Oktoberfest (Covington, KY), Sep 10
Oktoberfest (Monett, MO), Oct 23
Oktoberfest (New Ulm, MN), Oct 1
Oktoberfest (Snowbird, UT), Sep 4
Oktoberfest (St. Charles, MO), Oct 2
Oktoberfest (Tulsa, OK), Oct 21
Oktoberfest, Carson City Library Foundation (Carson City, NV), Oct 2
Oktoberfest, Rhinelander's (Rhinelander, WI), Oct 8
Olajuwon, Hakeem: Birth, Jan 21
Old Inauguration Day, Mar 4
Old New Year's Day, Mar 25
Old Stoughton (MA) Musical Society: Anniv, Nov 7
Old Threshers Reunion (Mt Pleasant, IA), Sep 2
Old Time School (Cambridge, MN), Jun 7
Oldenburg, Claes: Birth, Jan 28
Older Americans Month, Natl (Pres Proc), May 1
Oldman, Gary: Birth, Mar 21
Old-Time Country Music Contest, Fest & Expo, Natl (Avoca, IA), Aug 29
Old-Time Fiddlers' Jamboree (Smithville, TN), Jul 2
Olerud, John: Birth, Aug 5
Olin, Ken: Birth, Jul 30
Oliphant, Pat: Birth, Jul 24
Olive Branch Petition: Anniv, Jul 8
Oliver, Jamie: Birth, May 27
Olivier, Laurence: Birth Anniv, May 22
Olmos, Edward James: Birth, Feb 24
Olmsted, Frederick L.: Birth Anniv, Apr 26
O'Loughlin, Gerald: Birth, Dec 23
Olowokandi, Michael: Birth, Apr 3
Olsen, Ashley: Birth, Jun 13
Olsen, Mary-Kate: Birth, Jun 13
Olsen, Merlin: Birth, Sep 15
Olympic Games,
First Modern Olympics Began: Anniv, **Apr 6**
First Perfect Score: Anniv, **Jul 18**
First Winter Olympics: Anniv, **Jan 25**
Games of the XXVIII Olympiad (Athens, Greece), **Aug 13**
Israeli Olympiad Massacre: Anniv, **Sep 5**
Paralympic Games 2004 (Athens, Greece), **Sep 17**
Special Olympics Connecticut 2004 Summer Games (New Haven, CT), **Jun 11**
Special Olympics Day, **Jul 20**
Special Olympics Winter Games (McHenry, MD), **Feb 22**
Olympic Natl Park Established: Anniv, Jun 29
Oman: National Holiday, Nov 18
Omarr, Sydney: Birth Anniv, Aug 5
Omnibus TV Premiere: Anniv, Nov 9
On the Origin of Species Published: Anniv, Nov 22
Onassis, Jacqueline Kennedy: Birth Anniv, Jul 28
One Day at a Time TV Premiere: Anniv, Dec 16
One Life to Live TV Premiere: Anniv, Jul 15
O'Neal, Jermaine: Birth, Oct 13
O'Neal, Ron: Birth, Sep 1
O'Neal, Ryan: Birth, Apr 20
O'Neal, Shaquille: Birth, Mar 6
O'Neal, Tatum: Birth, Nov 5
One-Hit Wonder Day, Natl, Sep 25
O'Neill, Ed: Birth, Apr 12
O'Neill, Eugene: Birth Anniv, Oct 16
O'Neill, Jennifer: Birth, Feb 20
O'Neill, Rose Cecil: Birth Anniv, Jun 25
On-Hold Month, Natl, Mar 1
Onizuka, Ellison S.: Birth Anniv, Jun 24
Ono, Yoko: Bed-in for Peace: Anniv, Mar 25
Ono, Yoko: Birth, Feb 18
Ontkean, Michael: Birth, Jan 24
Open an Umbrella Indoors Day, Natl, Mar 13
Open-Heart Surgery, First: Anniv, Jul 9
Opera,
Aida Premieres: Anniv, **Dec 24**
Donizetti's Lucia Di Lammermoor Premiere: Anniv, **Sep 26**
Madama Butterfly Premiere: Anniv, **Feb 17**
Metropolitan Opera House: Opening Anniv, **Oct 22**
Metropolitan Opera Radio Broadcasts Premiere: Anniv, **Dec 25**
Opera Debut in the Colonies: Anniv, **Feb 8**
Opera Fest of New Jersey (Lawrenceville, NJ), **Jun 27**
Puccini, Giacomo: Birth Anniv, **Dec 22**
Verdi, Giuseppi: Birth Anniv, **Oct 10**
Wagner, Richard: Birth Anniv, **May 22**
Opera Debut in the Colonies: Anniv, Feb 8
Operation Iraqi Freedom: Anniv, Mar 19
Oprah Winfrey Show TV Premiere: Anniv, Sep 8
Optimism Month, Mar 1
Orange Bowl (Miami, FL), Jan 1
Orangemen's Day (Northern Ireland), Jul 12
Orbach, Jerry: Birth, Oct 20
Orchid Show (St. Louis, MO), Jan 31
Ordonez, Reynaldo: Birth, Nov 11
Oregon,
Admission Day, **Feb 14**
All-Northwest Barbershop Ballad Contest (Forest Grove), **Mar 5**
Betty Picnic (Grants Pass), **Jun 12**
Brookings-Harbor Azalea Fest (Brookings), **May 28**
Calico Crafts Bazaar (Gold Beach), **Nov 20**
Catfish Derby (Huntington), **May 29**
Children's Celebration (Springfield), **Jul 10**
Chowder Fest, Flower and Art Show (Gold Beach), **May 1**
Christmas Greens Show (Salem), **Dec 3**
Cinco de Mayo Fest (Portland), **May 5**
Columbia River Cross Channel Swim (Hood River), **Sep 1**
Community Christmas Bazaar (Gold Beach), **Dec 4**
Concours d'Elegance (Forest Grove), **Jul 18**
Crater Lake Natl Park Established: Anniv, **May 22**
Crater Lake Rim Runs and Marathon (Klamath Falls), **Aug 14**
Day on the Farm (Springfield), **Aug 21**
Founder's Day Corn Roast (Forest Grove), **Sep 19**
Haines Stampede and Rodeo (Baker City), **Jul 3**
Hangover Handicap Run (Klamath Falls), **Jan 1**
Historic Homes Parlor Tour (Baker City), **Dec 5**
Hood River County Fair (Hood River), **Jul 28**
Hood River Old-Fashioned Fourth of July (Hood River), **Jul 4**
Hood River Valley Blossom Fest (Hood River), **Apr 17**
Hood River Valley Harvest Fest (Hood River), **Oct 15**
Journey's End National Art Exhibition (Astoria), **Nov 1**
Kulongoski, Ted: Birth, **Nov 5**
Lincoln, Abraham: Birthday Observance (see also DE), **Feb 2**
Loyalty Days/Seafair Fest (Newport), **Apr 29**
Marion County Fair (Salem), **Jul 8**
Medford Cruise (Medford), **Jun 18**
Medford Jazz Jubilee (Medford), **Oct 8**
Megga Hunt (Springfield), **Apr 10**
Miners Jubilee (Baker City), **Jul 16**
Mother's Day Annual Rhododendron Show (Portland), **May 8**
Mt Hood Railroad Season (Mt Hood), **Apr 2**
Muddy Frogwater Country Classic Fest (Milton-Freewater), **Aug 20**
Native American Arts Fest (Grants Pass), **May 8**
Newport Seafood and Wine Fest (Newport), **Feb 27**
Oregon Bach Fest (Eugene), **Jun 25**
Oregon Brewers Fest (Portland), **Jul 23**
Oregon Coast Music Fest (Coos Bay), **Jul 17**
Oregon State Fair (Salem), **Aug 26**
Portland Center Stage (Portland), **Jan 1**
Portland Rose Fest (Portland), **Jun 3**
Portland's Birthday, **Apr 6**
Rhododendron Fest (Florence), **May 21**
Rogue River Jet Boat Marathon (Gold Beach), **Jun 18**
Saint Urho's Day (Hood River), **Mar 16**
Salem Art Fair and Fest (Salem), **Jul 16**
Shakespeare Fest (Ashland), **Feb 27**
Sherwood Robin Hood Fest (Sherwood), **Jul 16**
Smith, Gordon: Birth, **May 25**
South Coast Writer's Conf (Gold Beach), **Feb 13**
State Games of Oregon (Portland), **Jul 9**
Sternwheeler Days (Cascade Locks), **Jun 25**
Turkey Rama (McMinnville), **Jul 8**
Willamette Valley Folk Fest (Eugene), **May 21**
Wyden, Ron: Birth, **May 3**
Oregon Trail: Pony Express Fest (Hanover, KS), Aug 29
Organ and Tissue Donor Awareness Week, Natl (Pres Proc), Apr 18
Organic Act Day (US Virgin Islands), Jun 21
Organization of American States Founded: Anniv, Apr 30
Organization, Organizing,
Clean-Off-Your-Desk Day, Natl, **Jan 12**
Garage Sale Month, Natl, **May 1**
Get Organized Week, **Oct 3**
Love Your Files Week, Natl, **Sep 20**
Organize Your Home Day, **Jan 5**
Organize Your Home Office Day, **Mar 9**
Organizing Week, Natl, **May 3**
Reduce the Clutter Wk, **Aug 15**
Tackle Your Clutter Month, **Apr 1**
Orlando, Tony: Birth, Apr 3
Ormond, Julia: Birth, Jan 4
Orphan Train Heritage Soc Reunion (Concordia, KS), Sep 30
Orr, Bobby: Birth, Mar 20
Orthodontic Health Month, Natl, Oct 1
Orthodox Christian Observances,
Ascension Day, **May 20**
Cheesefare Sunday, **Feb 22**
Dormition of Theotokos, **Aug 15**
Dumb Week (Greece), **Mar 28**
Easter Sunday, **Apr 11**
Festival of All Saints, **Jun 6**
Green Monday (Cyprus), **Feb 23**
Lazarus Saturday, **Apr 3**
Lent, **Feb 23**
Meatfare Sunday, **Feb 15**
Palm Sunday, **Apr 4**
Pentecost, **May 30**
Roman Catholic/Eastern Orthodox Meeting: Anniv, **Jan 5**
Orwell, George: Birth Anniv, Jun 25
Osage River Mountain Man Festival and Black Powder Shoot (Lake Ozark, MO), Sep 17
Osborne, Jeffrey: Birth, Mar 9
Osbourne, Ozzy: Birth, Dec 3
Oscars Presentation, Feb 1
Osceola: Death Anniv, Jan 30
Osgood, Charles: Birth, Jan 8
O'Shea, Milo: Birth, Jun 2
Osment, Haley Joel: Birth, Apr 10
Osmond, Donny: Birth, Dec 9
Osmond, Marie: Birth, Oct 13
Ostara, Mar 20
Osteoporosis Awareness Month, Natl, May 1
Oswalt, Roy: Birth, Aug 29
O'Toole, Annette: Birth, Apr 1
O'Toole, Peter: Birth, Aug 2
Ott, Melvin (Mel): Birth Anniv, Mar 2
Ouimet, Francis DeSales: Birth Anniv, May 8
Our Miss Brooks TV Premiere: Anniv, Oct 3
Outback Bowl (Tampa, FL), Jan 1
Outcault, Richard Felton: Birth Anniv, Jan 14
Outhouse Race, Great Klondike (Dawson City, YT, Canada), Sep 1

Index ☆ Chase's 2004 Calendar of Events ☆

Outlet—Peach Bowl

Outlet Sale, World's Largest (Pigeon Forge, TN), Dec 2
Ovarian Cancer Awareness Month, Sep 1
Ovarian Cancer Awareness Month, Natl (Pres Proc), Sep 1
Overall, Park: Birth, Mar 15
Overlooked Film Fest (Champaign, IL), Apr 21
Overseas Chinese Day (Taiwan), Oct 21
Owen, Michael: Birth, Dec 14
Owen, Robert: Birth Anniv, May 14
Owens, Bill: Birth, Oct 22
Owens, Buck: Birth, Aug 12
Owens, Gary: Birth, May 10
Owens, Jesse: Birth Anniv, Sep 12
Oxenberg, Catherine: Birth, Sep 22
Oyster Fest, St. Mary's County MD (Leonardtown, MD), Oct 16
Oz, Frank: Birth, May 24
Ozark Empire Fair (Springfield, MO), Jul 30
Ozark Jubilee TV Premiere: Anniv, Jan 22
Ozawa, Seiji: Birth, Sep 1
Ozick, Cynthia: Birth, Apr 17
Ozzie and Harriet Show Radio Debut: Anniv, Oct 8
Ozzie and Harriet TV Premiere: Anniv, Oct 3
Paar, Jack: Birth, May 1
Paca, William: Birth Anniv, Oct 31
Pace, Orlando: Birth, Nov 4
Pacific Ocean Discovered: Anniv, Sep 25
Pacific: Eastern Pacific Hurricane Season, May 15
Pacing the Bounds (Liestal, Switzerland), May 17
Pacino, Al: Birth, Apr 25
Paczki Day, Feb 24
Paderewski, Ignace J: Birth Anniv, Nov 6
Paganini, Nicolo: Birth Anniv, Oct 27
Page, Patti: Birth, Nov 8
Pagett, Nicola: Birth, Jun 15
Paglia, Camille: Birth, Apr 2
Paige, Janis: Birth, Sep 16
Paige, Rod: Birth, Jun 17
Paige, Satchel: Birth Anniv, Jul 7
Paine, Robert Treat: Birth Anniv, Mar 11
Paine, Thomas: Birth Anniv, Jan 29
Paine, Thomas: Freethinker's Day, Jan 29
Pak, Se Ri: Birth, Sep 28
Pakistan,
Defense of Pakistan Day, **Sep 6**
Founder's Death Anniv (Qaid-e-Azam), **Sep 11**
Independence Day, **Aug 14**
Jinnah, Mohammed Ali (Qaid-e-Azam): Birth Anniv, **Dec 25**
Republic Day, **Mar 23**
Palance, Jack: Birth, Feb 18
Palatine House Museum, Reopening 1743 (Schoharie, NY), Jun 6
Palatine Museum Fall Event (Schoharie, NY), Sep 25
Palestinian Massacre: Anniv, Sep 16
Palestinian People, Intl Day of Solidarity with (UN), Nov 29
Palffy, Ziggy: Birth, May 5
Palin, Michael: Birth, May 5
Palm Harbor Arts/Crafts/Music Fest (Palm Harbor, FL), Dec 4
Palm Sunday, Apr 4
Palm Sunday, Orthodox, Apr 4
Palme, Olof: Assassination Anniv, Feb 28
Palmeiro, Rafael: Birth, Sep 24
Palmer, Alice Freeman: Birth Anniv, Feb 21
Palmer, Arnold: Birth, Sep 10
Palmer, Betsy: Birth, Nov 1
Palmer, Jim: Birth, Oct 15
Palmer, Lilli: Birth Anniv, May 24
Palminteri, Chazz: Birth, May 15
Palomares Hydrogen Bomb Accident: Anniv, Jan 17
Paltrow, Gwyneth: Birth, Sep 28
Pamper Yourself Day, Natl, Aug 6
Pan Am Circles Earth: Anniv, Jan 6
Pan American Flight 103 Explosion: Anniv, Dec 21
Panama,
Assumes Control of Canal: Anniv, **Dec 31**
First Shout of Independence, **Nov 10**
Flag Day, **Nov 4**
Independence Day, **Nov 3**
Independence from Spain Day, **Nov 28**
Martyrs' Day, **Jan 9**
Panama Canal Opens: Anniv, **Aug 15**
Panama City Foundation Day, **Aug 15**
US Invasion of Panama: Anniv, **Dec 20**
Pan-American Day (Pres Proc), Apr 14
Pan-American Day in Florida, Apr 14
Pan-American Week (Pres Proc), Apr 11
Pancake Day, Intl (Liberal, KS), Feb 24
Pancake Week, Natl, Feb 22
Pandemic of 1918 Hits US: Anniv, Mar 11
Panic Day, Mar 9
Panizzi, Anthony: Birth Anniv, Sep 16
Pankin, Stuart: Birth, Apr 8
Pankow, John: Birth, Apr 18
Panoply (Huntsville, AL), Apr 23
Pantoliano, Joe: Birth, Sep 12
Paper Money Issued: Anniv, Mar 10
Paperback Books Introduced: Anniv, Jul 30
Papp, Joseph: Birth Anniv, Jun 22
Papua New Guinea: Independence Day, Sep 16
Paquin, Anna: Birth, Jul 24
Parachute: Powered Fly-in (Columbus, KS), Sep 16
Parades,
Aloha Fest Floral Parade (Honolulu, HI), **Sep 18**
Arkalahah Fest (Arkansas City, KS), **Oct 27**
Boom Box Parade (Willimantic, CT), **Jul 4**
Bristol Civic, Military/Firemen's Parade (Bristol, RI), **Jul 5**
Bud Billiken Parade (Chicago, IL), **Aug 14**
Calithumpian Parade (Biwabik, MN), **Jul 4**
Canadian Tulip Fest (Ottawa, ON, Canada), **May 6**
Carry Nation Fest (Holly, MI), **Sep 11**
Celebrate France (Paris, France), **Jan 1**
Chester Greenwood Day Parade (Farmington, ME), **Dec 4**
Chinese New Year Golden Dragon Parade (Los Angeles, CA), **Jan 24**
Christmas on the River (Demopolis, AL), **Nov 28**
Christmas Parade (Woodstock, IL), **Nov 28**
Days of '47 Celebration (Salt Lake City, UT), **Jul 19**
Do Dah Day (Birmingham, AL), **May 8**
Do-Dah Parade (Kalamazoo, MI), **Jun 5**
Dodge City Days (Dodge City, KS), **Jul 30**
Dolly's Music on Parade (Pigeon Forge, TN), **Apr 2**
Electric Light Parade (Lovington, NM), **Dec 6**
Ennis Rodeo & Parade (Ennis, MT), **Jul 3**
Fantasy of Light Parade (Wheeling, WV), **Nov 19**
Fish House Parade (Aitkin, MN), **Nov 26**
Fredericksburg Heritage Fest (Fredericksburg, VA), **Jul 4**
Gasparilla Invasion and Parade (Tampa, FL), **Feb 7**
George Washington Birthday (Alexandria, VA), **Feb 16**
Great Circus Parade Week (Milwaukee, WI), **Jul 6**
Halloween Parade (Toms River, NJ), **Oct 30**
Holidays in the City Grand Illumination Parade (Norfolk, VA), **Nov 20**
Hollywood Beach Candy Cane Parade (Hollywood, FL), **Dec 11**
Home of the Hamburger Celeb (Seymour, WI), **Aug 7**
Idaho Fest of Lights (Preston, ID), **Nov 26**
Jersey Battle of Flowers (St. Lawrence, Channel Is), **Aug 12**
Joe Cain Procession (Mobile, AL), **Feb 22**
Love Parade (Berlin, Germany), **Jul 10**
Macy's Thanksgiving Day Parade (New York, NY), **Nov 25**
Maine State Parade (Lewiston, ME), **May 1**
Maple Leaf Fest (Carthage, MO), **Oct 9**
Marigold Fest (Pekin, IL), **Sep 10**
Memorial Day Parade (Aurora, IL), **May 31**
Memorial Day Parade and Ceremonies (Gettysburg, PA), **May 31**
Mother Goose Parade (El Cajon, CA), **Nov 21**
Mummers Parade (Philadelphia, PA), **Jan 1**
New Year's Day Parade (London, England), **Jan 1**
Oktoberfest (Kitchener/Waterloo, ON, Canada), **Oct 8**
Orange Bowl Parade (Miami, FL), **Dec 31**
Pacific Life Holiday Bowl Parade (San Diego, CA), **Dec 30**
Pasadena Doo Dah Parade (Pasadena, CA), **Nov 21**
Pet Parade (LaGrange, IL), **Jun 5**
Pro-Am Snipe Excursion and Parade (Moultrie, GA), **Apr 1**
Pulaski Day Parade (Philadelphia, PA), **Oct 3**
Red Lodge Home Champs Rodeo/Parade (Red Lodge, MT), **Jul 2**
Rhododendron Fest Grand Floral Parade (Florence, OR), **May 21**
Saint Patrick's Day Parade (Baton Rouge, LA), **Mar 13**
Saint Patrick's Day Parade (Hornell, NY), **Mar 13**
Saint Patrick's Day Parade (New York, NY), **Mar 17**
Saint Patrick's Day Parade (Roanoke, VA), **Mar 13**
Saint Urho's Day (Hood River, OR), **Mar 16**
Santa by Stage Coach Parade (El Centro, CA), **Dec 4**
Soldiers' Reunion Celebration (Newton, NC), **Aug 19**
Three Rivers Fest (Fort Wayne, IN), **Jul 10**
Tournament of Roses Parade (Pasadena, CA), **Jan 1**
Twin Cities Krewe/Janus MG Parade (Monroe, LA), **Feb 14**
Ugly Pickup Parade/Contest (Chadron, NE), **Oct 29**
Victorian Christmas Sleighbell Parade (Manistee, MI), **Dec 2**
West Allis Western Days Family Jamboree (West Allis, WI), **Jun 17**
Wild Horse Stampede (Wolf Point, MT), **Jul 9**
Wolf Point's Annual Christmas Parade (Wolf Point, MT), **Dec 5**
WSB-TV Salute 2 America Parade (Atlanta, GA), **Jul 4**
Xcel Energy's Parade of Lights (Denver, CO), **Dec 3**
Paraguay,
Battle of Boqueron Day, **Sep 29**
Independence Day, **May 15**
Natl Heroes' Day, **Mar 1**
Peace with Bolivia Day, **Jun 12**
Paranormal Day, May 3
Paraprofessional Appreciation Day, Apr 7
Parcells, Bill: Birth, Aug 22
Pare, Michael: Birth, Oct 9
Parent Leadership Month, Natl, Feb 1
Parent, Bernie: Birth, Apr 3
Parents as Teachers Day, Natl, Nov 8
Parents' Day (Pres Proc), Jul 25
Paretsky, Sara: Birth, Jun 8
Paris, Treaty of, Ends American Rev, Sep 3
Parish, Robert: Birth, Aug 30
Park Days, Halfway (Hagerstown, MD), May 29
Parker Day, John, Apr 19
Parker, Charlie: at the LA Philharmonic: Anniv, Mar 25
Parker, Charlie: Birth Anniv, Aug 29
Parker, Dave: Birth, Jun 9
Parker, Eleanor: Birth, Jun 26
Parker, Fess: Birth, Aug 16
Parker, George: Death Anniv, Mar 17
Parker, Jameson: Birth, Nov 18
Parker, Mary-Louise: Birth, Aug 2
Parker, Robert Leroy (Butch Cassidy): Birth Anniv, Apr 13
Parker, Sarah Jessica: Birth, Mar 25
Parker, Tony: Birth, May 17
Parker, Trey: Birth, May 30
Parkins, Barbara: Birth, May 22
Parkinson, James: Death Anniv, Dec 21
Parkinson's Awareness Month, Natl, Apr 1
Parkman, Francis: Birth Anniv, Sep 16
Parks Month, Natl Recreation and, Jul 1
Parks, Bert: Birth Anniv, Dec 30
Parks, Gordon: Birth, Nov 30
Parks, Michael: Birth, Apr 4
Parks, Rosa: Birth, Feb 4
Parks, Rosa: Day, Dec 1
Parnell, Charles S.: Birth Anniv, Jun 27
Parry, William: Birth Anniv, Dec 19
Parseghian, Ara: Birth, May 10
Parsons, Estelle: Birth, Nov 20
Particularly Preposterous Packaging Day, Aug 7
Parton, Dolly: Birth, Jan 19
Partridge, John: Death Hoax: Anniv, Mar 29
Pascal, Blaise: Birth Anniv, Jun 19
Pascua Florida Day (FL), Apr 2
Passion Week, Mar 28
Passiontide, Mar 28
Passover, Apr 6
Passover Begins, Apr 5
Passport Presentation (Russia), Jan 2
Pasternak, Boris: Birth Anniv, Feb 10
Pasteur, Louis: Birth Anniv, Dec 27
Pasteur, Louis: First Successful Antirabies Inoculation, Jul 6
Pastoral Care Week, Oct 24
Pastorelli, Robert: Birth, Jun 21
Pat Boone Show TV Premiere: Anniv, Oct 3
Pataki, George: Birth, Jun 24
Patent Issued for First Adding Machine: Anniv, Oct 11
Patent Office Opens, US: Anniv, Jul 31
Paterno, Joe: Birth, Dec 21
Patinkin, Mandy: Birth, Nov 30
Patric, Jason: Birth, Jun 27
Patrick, Dan: Birth, May 15
Patriot Day, Sep 11
Patriot's Day (MA, ME), Apr 19
Patriot's Day in Florida, Apr 19
Patterson, Floyd: Birth, Jan 4
Patton, George S, Jr: Birth Anniv, Nov 11
Patton, Paul E.: Birth, May 26
Patton, Will: Birth, Jun 14
Paul Bunyan Show (Nelsonville, OH), Oct 1
Paul, Adrian: Birth, May 29
Paul, Alexandra: Birth, Jul 29
Paul, Alice: Birth Anniv, Jan 11
Paul, Les: Birth, Jun 9
Pauley, Jane: Birth, Oct 31
Paulus, Friedrich: Birth Anniv, Sep 23
Pause for Pledge (Natl Flag Day USA), Jun 14
Pause the World Day, Sep 16
Pavan, Marisa: Birth, Jun 19
Pavarotti, Luciano: Birth, Oct 12
Pavlova, Anna: Birth Anniv, Feb 12
Pawlenty, Tim: Birth, Nov 1
Pawnbrokers Day, Natl, Dec 6
Paxson, John: Birth, Sep 29
Paxton, Bill: Birth, May 17
Pay-A-Compliment Day, Feb 6
Paymer, David: Birth, Aug 30
Payne, John H.: Birth Anniv, Jun 9
Payroll Week, Natl, Sep 6
Pays, Amanda: Birth, Jun 6
Payton, Gary: Birth, Jul 23
Peña, Elizabeth: Birth, Sep 23
Peabody, Elizabeth Palmer: Birth Anniv, May 16
Peabody, George: Birth Anniv, Feb 18
Peace,
Annual World Peace Meditation, **Dec 31**
Disarmament Week (UN), **Oct 24**
Dream 2004 Day, **Mar 11**
Intl Day of Peace (UN), **Sep 21**
Pause the World Day, **Sep 16**
Peace Corps Proposed: Anniv, **Oct 14**
Peace Fest (Hiroshima, Japan), **Aug 6**
Peace Officer Memorial Day (Pres Proc), **May 15**
Peace, Friendship and Good Will Week, **Oct 25**
UN: Culture of Peace and Non-Violence for the Children of the World, Intl Decade for a, **Jan 1**
Versailles Peace Conference (WWI): Anniv, **Jan 18**
World Hello Day, **Nov 21**
Peace Corps Day, Mar 2
Peace Corps Founded: Anniv, Mar 1
Peace Corps Proposed: Anniv, Oct 14
Peace of Mind Day, Natl, May 1
Peace Rose Introduced to World: Anniv, Apr 29
Peach Bowl, Chick-fil-A (Atlanta, GA), Jan 2

★ Chase's 2004 Calendar of Events ★ Index

Peach Fest, Leitersburg (Leitersburg, MD), Aug 7
Peach Fest, Louisiana (Ruston, LA), Jun 17
Peachtree Road Race (Atlanta, GA), Jul 4
Peale, Anna Claypoole: Birth Anniv, Mar 6
Peale, Charles W.: Birth Anniv, Apr 15
Peale, Norman Vincent: Birth Anniv, May 31
Peanut Butter Lover's Month, Nov 1
Peanuts Debuts: Anniv, Oct 2
Pearl Harbor Day, Dec 7
Pearl Harbor Remembrance Day, Natl (Pres Proc), Dec 7
Pearl, Daniel: Birth Anniv, Oct 10
Pearl, Minnie: Birth Anniv, Oct 25
Pearse, Richard: Flight Anniv, Mar 31
Pearson, Lester B.: Birth Anniv, Apr 23
Peary, Robert E.: Birth Anniv, May 6
Peary, Robert E.: North Pole Discovered: Anniv, Apr 6
Pecan Day, Mar 25
Pecan Month, Natl, Apr 1
Peck, Annie S.: Birth Anniv, Oct 19
Peck, Gregory: Birth Anniv, Apr 5
Peddler's Village Gingerbread House Competition & Display (Lahaska, PA), Nov 19
Peddler's Village Scarecrow Contest and Outdoor Display (Lahaska, PA), Sep 13
Peddler's Village Scarecrow Fest (Lahaska, PA), Sep 18
Peddler's Village Teddy Bear's Picnic (Lahaska, PA), Jul 10
Pediatric Cancer Awareness Month, Sep 1
Pediatric Nurse Practitioner Week, Mar 21
Pediculosis Prevention Month, Natl, Sep 1
Peel, Robert: Birth Anniv, Feb 5
Peet, Amanda: Birth, Jan 11
Peete, Calvin: Birth, Jul 18
Pele: Birth, Oct 23
Pencil Patented: Anniv, Mar 30
Penderecki, Krzysztof: Birth, Nov 23
Pendergrass, Teddy: Birth, Mar 26
Pendleton, Austin: Birth, Mar 27
Pen-Friends Week Intl, May 1
Penguin Awareness Day (Point Pleasant Beach, NJ), Jan 17
Penguin Plunge (Jamestown, RI), Jan 1
Penn, Arthur Heller: Birth, Sep 27
Penn, Irving: Birth, Jun 16
Penn, John: Birth Anniv, May 6
Penn, Sean: Birth, Aug 17
Penn, William: Birth Anniv, Oct 14
Penn, William: Pennsylvania Deeded to: Anniv, Mar 4
Penniman, Little Richard: Birth, Dec 5
Pennsylvania,
 American Dental Assn: Annual Sessions (Philadelphia), Sep 30
 Antique Show (Somerset), Aug 14
 Antiques on the Diamond (Ligonier), Jun 12
 Apple Blossom Fest (Gettysburg), May 1
 Apple Harvest Fest (Gettysburg), Oct 2
 Art in the Garden (Washington), Sep 11
 Battle of Germantown Reenactment (Philadelphia), Oct 2
 Battle of Gettysburg: Anniv, Jul 1
 Belsnickel Craft Show (Boyertown), Nov 26
 Blast from the Past, A (Manheim), Jun 12
 Blueberry Fest (Montrose), Aug 6
 Buhl Day (Sharon), Sep 6
 Celtic Classic Highland Games & Fest (Bethlehem), Sep 24
 Celtic Fling (Manheim), Jun 26
 Chadds Ford Days (Chadds Ford), Sep 11
 Chambersfest (Chambersburg), Jul 17
 Chester Old Fiddlers' Picnic (Coatesville), Sep 11
 Christmas Craft Show (York), Dec 5
 Covered Bridge Fest (Washington County), Sep 18
 Dankfest (Harmony), Aug 28
 Easter Craft Show (York), Feb 8
 Edgar Allan Poe Evermore (Manheim), Oct 29
 Eisenhower Fifties Weekend (Gettysburg), Jun 12
 Eisenhower World War II Weekend (Gettysburg), Sep 18
 Fabulous 1890s Weekend (Mansfield), Sep 24
 Fall State Craft Fest (Richboro), Oct 15
 Farm Show, Jan 10
 Farmers & Threshermens Jubilee (New Centerville), Sep 8
 Festifall (Point Marion), Sep 26
 Fine Art & Crafts Show (Lahaska), Jun 5
 Firestorm 2004 (Altoona), Jul 4
 First American Abolition Soc Founded: Anniv, Apr 14
 First Commercial Oil Well: Anniv, Aug 27
 First Natl Convention for Blacks: Anniv, Sep 15
 First Night Football Game (Mansfield), Sep 28
 First US Zoo: Anniv (Philadelphia), Jul 1
 Flax Scutching Fest (Stahlstown), Sep 11
 Fort Ligonier Days (Ligonier), Oct 8
 Frantic Women Extravaganza (Pittsburgh), Oct 13
 Garden Fair (Chestnut Hill), May 2
 Gardenfest at Longwood Gardens (Kennett Square), Sep 11
 Geographers Annual Meeting, Assn American (Philadelphia), Mar 14
 Gettysburg Address Memorial Ceremony (Gettysburg), Nov 19
 Gettysburg Bluegrass Fest (Gettysburg), May 13
 Gettysburg Brass Band Festival (Gettysburg), Jun 18
 Gettysburg Civil War Heritage Days (Gettysburg), Jun 25
 Gettysburg Fall Bluegrass Fest (Gettysburg), Aug 26
 Gettysburg Outdoor Antique Show (Gettysburg), May 22
 Gettysburg Outdoor Antique Show (Gettysburg), Sep 25
 Gettysburg Yuletide Fest (Gettysburg), Nov 26
 Ghost Tours (New Hope), Jun 5
 Gift Fest, Intl (Fairfield), Nov 4
 Grand Illumination (Lahaska), Nov 19
 Great Flood of 1889 Commemorative Weekend (Johnstown), May 24
 Great Pumpkin Carve (Chadds Ford), Oct 21
 Greater Pittsburgh Arts & Crafts Holiday Spectacular (Greensburg), Nov 5
 Greater Pittsburgh Renaissance Festival (West Newton), Aug 14
 Groundhog Day in Punxsutawney, PA (Punxsutawney), Feb 2
 History Meets the Arts (Gettysburg), Apr 16
 Holiday Craft Fair (Lancaster), Nov 27
 Holiday Craft Show (York), Oct 17
 Holiday Lights on the Lake (Altoona), Nov 20
 Holidays at the Nationality Classrooms (Oakland), Dec 1
 Ice Fest (Ligonier), Jan 24
 INPEX (Pittsburgh), May 12
 Jinglebell Journey (Mt Wolf), Dec 5
 Johnstown Flood: Anniv, May 31
 Johnstown Folkfest (Johnstown), Sep 3
 Keystone Country Fair (Altoona), Sep 10
 Kruisin' Weekend (Altoona), Aug 20
 Kustom Kemps Car Show (Biglerville), Jun 11
 LeMoyne House Candlelight Christmas Tours (Washington), Dec 3
 Ligonier Highland Games (Ligonier), Sep 10
 Little League Baseball World Series (Williamsport), Aug 20
 Longwood Gardens Acres of Spring (Kennett Square), Apr 17
 Longwood Gardens Autumn's Colors (Kennett Square), Oct 9
 Longwood Gardens Christmas Display (Kennett Square), Nov 25
 Longwood Gardens Chrysanthemum Fest (Kennett Square), Oct 23
 Longwood Gardens Easter Display (Kennett Square), Apr 3
 Longwood Gardens Fest of Fountains (Kennett Square), May 29
 Longwood Gardens Welcome Spring (Kennett Square), Jan 17
 Maple Syrup Fest (Beaver), Apr 3
 Memorial Day Parade and Ceremonies (Gettysburg), May 31
 Mifflin-Juniata Arts Fest (Lewistown), May 22
 Mount Pleasant Glass & Ethnic Fest (Mt Pleasant), Sep 24
 Mountain Craft Days (Somerset), Sep 10
 Mummers Parade (Philadelphia), Jan 1
 Mushroom Fest (Kennett Square), Sep 11
 Musikfest (Bethlehem), Aug 6
 New Oxford Outdoor Antique Show (Gettysburg), Jun 19
 North Park's Colonial Arts & Crafts Fest (Pittsburgh), Sep 17
 Peddler's Village Gingerbread House Competition & Display (Lahaska), Nov 19
 Peddler's Village Quilt Competition/Display (Lahaska), Jan 19
 Peddler's Village Scarecrow Contest and Outdoor Display (Lahaska), Sep 13
 Peddler's Village Scarecrow Fest (Lahaska), Sep 18
 Peddler's Village Teddy Bear's Picnic (Lahaska), Jul 10
 Penn State's Agri Progress Days (Rock Springs), Aug 17
 Pennsylvania Arts & Crafts Christmas Fest (Washington), Oct 15
 Pennsylvania Arts & Crafts Colonial Fest (Greensburg), Sep 3
 Pennsylvania Arts & Crafts Country Fest (Uniontown), May 28
 Pennsylvania Deeded to William Penn Anniv, Mar 4
 Pennsylvania Renaissance Faire (Manheim), Aug 21
 Pennsylvania Rib, Wing and Music Fest (Greensburg), Jun 18
 Philadelphia Flower Show (Philadelphia), Mar 7
 Pinchot Lake Festival and Craft Show (Wellsville), May 15
 Pittsburgh Arts & Crafts Spring Fever Fest, Mar 26
 Pocono State Craft Fair (Shawnee-on-the-Delaware), Aug 21
 Polish Christmas Open House (Philadelphia), Dec 12
 Pony League World Series (Washington), Aug 14
 PSFCA East West All-Star Game (Altoona), Jun 26
 Pulaski Day Parade (Philadelphia), Oct 3
 Quilt Odyssey (Gettysburg), Aug 5
 Race for the Cure (Pittsburgh), May 9
 Rain Day (Waynesburg), Jul 29
 Ratification Day, Dec 12
 Remembrance Day (Gettysburg), Nov 20
 Rendell, Ed: Birth, Jan 5
 Rhubarb Fest (Intercourse), May 21
 Santorum, Rick: Birth, May 10
 Seneca Falls Survivor Votes: Anniv (Philadelphia), Nov 2
 Seven Sweets/Seven Sours Fest (Intercourse), Sep 17
 Slow Pitch Softball Tourn (Williamsport), Jul 9
 Snake Hunt (Cross Fork), Jun 26
 Specter, Arlen: Birth, Feb 12
 Speech-Language-Hearing Conv, American (Philadelphia), Nov 18
 Spring Craft Celeb (Richboro), May 15
 Spring Craft Show (York), Apr 18
 Springs Folk Fest (Springs), Oct 1
 State Craft Fair (Lancaster), Jul 23
 Storytelling Historical Walk Around Washington (Washington), May 15
 Strawberry Fest (Lahaska), May 1
 Sugarloaf Crafts Fest (Fort Washington), Oct 15
 Sugarloaf Crafts Fest (Fort Washington), Mar 19
 Summer Craft Show (York), Jul 25
 TOPS Intl Recognition Days (Pittsburgh), Jul 15
 US Women's Amateur (Golf) Chmpshp (Erie), Aug 9
 Victorian Christmas at Mount Hope Mansion (Manheim), Nov 26
 Westmoreland Arts & Heritage Fest (Greensburg), Jul 2
 York Intl Postcard Fair (York), Nov 19
 Zippo/Case Intl Swap Meet (Bradford), Jul 16
Penny Press, Beginning of the: Anniv, Sep 3
Pentagon Completed: Anniv, Jan 15
Pentagon, Vietnam War Protestors Storm Pentagon: Anniv, Oct 21
Pentecost, May 30
People Are Funny TV Premiere: Anniv, Sep 19
People Magazine: Anniv, Mar 4
People Skills Month, Intl, Jun 1
Pepitone, Joe: Birth, Oct 9
Pepper, Barry: Birth, Apr 4
Pepper, Claude Denson: Birth Anniv, Sep 8
Peppercorn Ceremony (Bermuda), Apr 23
Pepys, Samuel: Birth Anniv, Feb 23
Perdue, Sonny: Birth, Dec 20
Perdue, Will: Birth, Aug 29
Perez, Rosie: Birth, Sep 6
Perez, Tony: Birth, May 14
Perigean Spring Tides, Jul 2
Perigean Spring Tides, Dec 11
Perigean Spring Tides, Jun 3
Perihelion, Earth at, Jan 4
Perioperative (OR) Nurse Week, Nov 14
Perkins, Anthony: Birth Anniv, Apr 4
Perkins, Elizabeth: Birth, Nov 18
Perkins, Frances: Appointed to Cabinet, Mar 4
Perkins, Frances: Birth Anniv, Apr 10
Perkins, Millie: Birth, May 12
Perkins, Sam: Birth, Jun 14
Perlman, Itzhak: Birth, Aug 31
Perlman, Rhea: Birth, Mar 31
Perlman, Ron: Birth, Apr 13
Perot, H. Ross: Birth, Jun 27
Perreau, Gigi: Birth, Feb 6
Perrine, Valerie: Birth, Sep 3
Perry Como Show TV Premiere: Anniv, Dec 24
Perry Mason TV Premiere: Anniv, Sep 21
Perry, Gaylord Jackson: Birth, Sep 15
Perry, Jeff: Birth, Aug 16
Perry, Luke: Birth, Oct 11
Perry, Matthew: Birth, Aug 19
Perry, Matthew: Commodore Perry Day: Birth Anniv, Apr 10
Perry, Oliver H.: Birth Anniv, Aug 23
Perry, Rick: Birth, Mar 4
Perry, Steve: Birth, Jan 22
Perry, William "The Refrigerator": Birth, Dec 16
Perseid Meteor Showers, Aug 9
Pershing, John J.: Birth Anniv, Sep 13
Persian Gulf War,
 Begins: Anniv, Jan 16
 Desert Shield: Anniv, Aug 7
 Desert Storm: UN Deadline Resolution: Anniv, Nov 28
 Ground War Begins: Anniv, Feb 23
 Iraq Invades Kuwait: Anniv, Aug 2
 Kuwait Liberated: Anniv, Feb 27
Person, Chuck Connors: Birth, Jun 27
Personal Chef Day, Natl, Sep 19
Personal Self-Defense Awareness Month, Natl, Jan 1
Peru,
 Countryman's Day, Jun 24
 Day of National Honor, Oct 9
 Independence Day, Jul 28
 Saint Rose of Lima Day, Aug 30
Pesach (Passover), Apr 6
Pesach Begins, Apr 5
Pesci, Joe: Birth, Feb 9
Pescow, Donna: Birth, Mar 24
Peshtigo Forest Fire: Anniv, Oct 8
Pet Expo, AFRMA Display at America's Family (Costa Mesa, CA), Apr 2
Pet First Aid Awareness Month, Natl, Apr 1
Pet Owners Independence Day, Apr 18
Pet Parade (LaGrange, IL), Jun 5
Pet Peeve Week, Natl, Oct 11
Pet Sitters Week, Natl Prof, Mar 7
Pet Week, Natl, May 2
Peter and Paul Day, Jun 29
Peter I: Birth Anniv, May 30

Peach Fest—Peter

729

Index ☆ Chase's 2004 Calendar of Events ☆

Peters, Bernadette: Birth, Feb 28
Peters, Roberta: Birth, May 4
Petersen, Paul: Birth, Sep 23
Petersen, William: Birth, Feb 21
Peterson, Cassandra: Birth, Sep 17
Peterson, Roger Tory: Birth Anniv, Aug 28
Peterson, Seth: Birth, Aug 16
Petrified Forest Natl Park Established: Anniv, Dec 9
Petroleum Fest, Louisiana Shrimp and (Morgan City, LA), Sep 2
Pettit, Bob: Birth, Dec 12
Petty, Richard: Birth, Jul 2
Petty, Tom: Birth, Oct 20
Pfeiffer, Michelle: Birth, Apr 29
Phair, Liz: Birth, Apr 17
Pharmacists Declare War on Alcoholism, Jun 1
Pharmacists War on Diabetes, Apr 1
Phil Donahue Show, The: Anniv, Nov 6
Phil Silvers Show TV Premiere: Anniv, Sep 20
Philadelphia Flower Show, Mar 7
Philadelphia Police Bombing: Anniv, May 13
Philbin, Regis: Birth, Aug 25
Philip, King: Assassination Anniv, Aug 12
Philip, Prince: Birth, Jun 10
Philippines,
  Aquino, Benigno: Assassination Anniv, Aug 21
  Ati-Atihan Fest, Jan 17
  Bataan Day: Anniv, Apr 9
  Black Nazarene Fiesta, Jan 1
  Bonifacio Day, Nov 30
  Carabao Fest, May 14
  Christmas Observance, Dec 16
  Earthquake Jolts: Anniv, Jul 16
  Feast of Our Lady of Peace/Good Voyage, May 1
  Feast of the Black Nazarene, Jan 9
  Fil-American Friendship Day, Jul 4
  Holy Week, Apr 4
  Independence Day, Jun 12
  Moriones's Fest (Marinduque Island), Apr 8
  Mount Pinatubo Erupts in Philippines: Anniv, Jun 11
  National Heroes' Day, Aug 29
  Philippine Independence: Anniv, Mar 24
  Rizal Day, Dec 30
  Santacruzan, May 1
  Simbang Gabi, Dec 16
  US Military Leaves, Nov 24
Phillips, Bobbie: Birth, Jan 29
Phillips, Chynna: Birth, Feb 12
Phillips, Julianne: Birth, May 13
Phillips, Lou Diamond: Birth, Feb 17
Phillips, Mackenzie: Birth, Nov 10
Phillips, Michelle: Birth, Jun 4
Phillips, Stone: Birth, Dec 2
Phillips, Wendy: Birth, Jan 2
Phillpotts, Eden: Birth Anniv, Nov 4
Photography,
  Abbott, Berenice: Birth Anniv, Jul 17
  Bourke-White, Margaret: Birth Anniv, Jun 14
  First Photos Used in a Newspaper Report: Anniv, Jul 1
  First Presidential Photograph: Anniv, Feb 14
Physical Fitness and Sports Month, Natl, May 1
Physical Therapy Month, Natl, Oct 1
Physical Wellness Month, Apr 1
Physician Assistant Day, Oct 6
Piano Competition for Outstanding Amateurs, Intl (Fort Worth, TX), Jun 7
Piano Month, Natl, Sep 1
Piano: Kingsville Intl Young Performers' Competition (Kingsville, TX), Apr 1
Piazza, Mike: Birth, Sep 4
Piazzetta, Giovanni Battista: Birth Anniv., Feb 13
Picasso, Pablo: Birth Anniv, Oct 25
Picatinny Peak Fall Hawkwatch (Dover, NJ), Sep 1
Piccard, Auguste: Birth Anniv, Jan 28
Piccard, Jacques: Birth, Jul 28
Piccard, Jean Felix: Birth Anniv, Jan 28
Piccard, Jeannette Ridlon: Birth Anniv, Jan 5
Pickett, Bill: Birth Anniv, Dec 5
Pickett, George: Defeat at Five Forks: Anniv, Apr 1
Pickett, Wilson: Birth, Mar 18
Pickett's Charge: Battle of Gettysburg: Anniv, Jul 1
Pickle Week, Intl, May 21
Pickup Parade and Contest, Ugly (Chadron, NE), Oct 29
Picnic, All States (Yuma, AZ), Jan 7
Pidgeon, Walter: Birth Anniv, Sep 23
Pied Piper of Hamelin: Anniv, Jul 22
Pied Piper: Rat-Catchers Day, Jul 22
Pierce, David Hyde: Birth, Apr 3
Pierce, Franklin: Birth Anniv, Nov 23
Pierce, Jane: Birth Anniv, Mar 12
Pierce, Paul: Birth, Oct 13
Pietz, Amy: Birth, Mar 6
Pig Day, Natl, Mar 1
Piggot-Smith, Tim: Birth, May 13
Pileggi, Mitch: Birth, Apr 5
Pilgrim Landing: Anniv, Dec 21
Pinchbeck, Christopher: Death Anniv, Nov 18
Pinchot, Bronson: Birth, May 20
Pine Barrens Jamboree (Waretown, NJ), Oct 9
Piniella, Lou: Birth, Aug 28
Pinkerton, Allan: Birth Anniv, Aug 25
Pinkett Smith, Jada: Birth, Sep 18
Pinochet, Augusto: Military Dictatorship Ended, Dec 15

Pinter, Harold: Birth, Oct 10
Pinzon, Martin: Arrival Anniv, Mar 1
Pippen, Scottie: Birth, Sep 25
Piquet, Nelson: Birth, Aug 17
Pirate Day, Talk Like a, Sep 19
Pisces Begins, Feb 20
Piscopo, Joe: Birth, Jun 17
Pisier, Marie-France: Birth, May 10
Pitcher, Molly: Birth Anniv, Oct 13
Pitt, Brad: Birth, Dec 18
Pitt, William: Birth Anniv, May 28
Pittsburgh Arts & Crafts Spring Fever Fest (Pittsburg, PA), Mar 26
Piven, Jeremy: Birth, Jul 26
Pizarro, Francesco: Death Anniv, Jun 26
Place, Mary Kay: Birth, Sep 23
Plan Your Epitaph Day, Nov 2
Planck, Max: Birth Anniv, Apr 23
Planet Pluto Discovery: Anniv, Feb 18
Plant the Seeds of Greatness Month, Feb 1
Plant, Robert: Birth, Aug 20
Play Days, Sep 7
Play Presented in North American Colonies, First: Anniv, Aug 27
Playboy First Published: Anniv, Dec 1
Player, Gary: Birth, Nov 1
Playground Safety Week, Natl, Apr 26
Play-the-Recorder Month, Mar 1
Please Take My Children to Work Day, Jun 29
Pleasure Your Mate Month, Sep 1
Pledge of Allegiance Recognized: Anniv, Dec 28
Pledge of Allegiance, Pause for (Natl Flag Day USA), Jun 14
Pledge of Allegiance: School Celebration, Natl, Sep 17
Pleshette, Suzanne: Birth, Jan 31
Plimpton, George: Birth, Mar 18
Plimpton, Martha: Birth, Nov 16
Plimsoll Day, Feb 10
Plough Monday (England), Jan 12
Plumb, Eve: Birth, Apr 29
Plummer, Amanda: Birth, Mar 23
Plummer, Christopher: Birth, Dec 13
Plushenko, Evgeny: Birth, Nov 3
Pluto Discovery, Planet: Anniv, Feb 18
Plutonium First Weighed: Anniv, Aug 20
Plymouth Plantation Earthquake: Anniv, Jun 1
Pocahontas: Death Anniv, Mar 21
Poe, Edgar Allan, Evermore (Manheim, PA), Oct 29
Poe, Edgar Allan: Birth Anniv, Jan 19
Poe, Edgar Allan: Raven Published Anniv, Jan 29
Poetry,
  American Poet Laureate Establishment: Anniv, Dec 20
  Bad Poetry Day, Aug 18
  Cowboy Poetry Gathering, Natl (Elko, NV), Jan 24
  Cullen, Countee: Birth Anniv, May 30
  Dakota Cowboy Poetry Gathering (Medora, ND), May 29
  Dodge Poetry Fest (NJ), Sep 16
  Limerick Day, May 12
  Poetry Contest (El Paso, TX), Jan 1
  Poetry Day in Florida, May 25
  Poetry Month, Natl, Apr 1
  Poet's Day, Aug 21
  Raven Published: Anniv, Jan 29
  Texas Cowboy Poetry Gathering (Alpine, TX), Mar 5
  Wheatley, Phillis: Death Anniv, Dec 5
  Youth Cowboy Poetry Gathering (Boys Ranch, TX), Jun 17
Poinsett, Joel Roberts: Death Anniv, Dec 12
Poinsettia Day, Dec 12
Pointer, Bonnie: Birth, Jul 11
Poison Prevention Awareness Month, Mar 1
Poison Prevention Week, Natl, Mar 21
Poison Prevention Week, Natl (Pres Proc), Mar 21
Poitier, Sidney: Birth, Feb 20
Pol Pot Overthrown: Anniv, Jan 7
Poland,
  Constitution Day, May 3
  Independence Day, Nov 11
  Liberation Day, Jan 17
  Solidarity Founded Anniv, Aug 31
  Solidarity Granted Legal Status: Anniv, Apr 17
Polanski, Roman: Birth, Aug 18
Polar Bear Swim (Nome, AK), Jun 21
Polar Bear Swim (Sheboygan, WI), Jan 1
Police Officers Who Gave Their Lives in the Line of Duty Week, Apr 29
Police Week (Pres Proc), May 9
Police Week, Natl, May 9
Police: Peace Officer Memorial Day (Pres Proc), May 15
Police: Peace Officer Memorial Day, Natl, May 15
Polio Vaccine: Anniv, Apr 12
Polish,
  Polish American Heritage Month, Oct 1
  Polish-American in the House (Mikulski): Anniv, Jan 4
Polito, Jon: Birth, Dec 29
Polk, James: Birth Anniv, Nov 2
Polk, James: First Presidential Photograph: Anniv, Feb 14
Polk, Sarah Childress: Birth Anniv, Sep 4
Poll Tax Outlawed: Anniv, Apr 8
Pollack, Sydney: Birth, Jul 1
Pollak, Kevin: Birth, Oct 30
Pollan, Tracy: Birth, Jun 22

Pollard, Michael J.: Birth, May 30
Polygamists, Amnesty for: Anniv, Jan 4
Pompano Beach Seafood Fest (Pompano Beach, FL), Apr 23
Pompeii Destroyed: Vesuvius Day: Anniv, Aug 24
Ponce de Leon Discovers Florida: Anniv, Apr 2
Ponselle, Rosa: Birth Anniv, Jan 22
Ponti, Carlo: Birth, Dec 11
Pony Express, Inauguration of: Anniv, Apr 3
Pony League World Series (Washington, PA), Aug 14
Pooh Day (A.A. Milne Birth Anniv), Jan 18
Poole, Cecil: First Black US State's Attorney: Anniv, Jul 6
Poor Richard's Almanack: Anniv, Dec 28
Pop Music Chart Introduced: Anniv, Jan 4
Pop, Iggy: Birth, Apr 21
Popcorn Fest (Valparaiso, IN), Sep 11
Popcorn Poppin' Month, Natl, Oct 1
Pope, Alexander: Birth Anniv, May 21
Pope, John: Birth Anniv, Mar 16
Popes, Roman Catholic,
  Benedict XV: Birth Anniv, Nov 21
  John Paul I: Birth Anniv, Oct 17
  John Paul II: Assassination Attempt: Anniv, May 13
  John Paul II: Birth, May 18
  John Paul II: Nixes Ordaining of Women: Anniv, May 30
  John XXIII: Birth Anniv, Nov 25
  Paul VI: Birth Anniv, Sep 26
  Pius XI: Birth Anniv, May 31
  Pius XII: Birth Anniv, Mar 2
  Saint Pius X: Birth Anniv, Jun 2
Popeye Debuts: Anniv, Jan 17
Population Day, World (UN), Jul 11
Population: Day of Five Billion: Anniv, Jul 11
Population: Day of the Six Billion: Anniv, Oct 12
Pork Month, Natl, Oct 1
Porter, Cole: Birth Anniv, Jun 9
Porter, Katherine Anne: Birth Anniv, May 15
Porter, Sylvia: Birth Anniv, Jun 18
Porter, Terry: Birth, Apr 8
Porter, William S. (O. Henry): Birth Anniv, Sep 11
Portman, Natalie: Birth, Jun 9
Portugal,
  Day of Portugal, Jun 10
  Independence Day, Dec 1
  Liberty Day, Apr 25
  Pilgrimage to Fatima, May 12
  Republic Day, Oct 5
  Saint Anthony of Padua: Feast Day, Jun 13
Posey, Parker: Birth, Nov 8
Positive Attitude Month, Oct 1
Post Day, World (UN), Oct 9
Post, Emily: Birth Anniv, Oct 30
Post, Markie: Birth, Nov 4
Post, Wiley: Birth Anniv, Nov 22
Postcard Shows,
  Fun-in-the-Sun Postcard Sale (Orlando, FL), Jan 17
  Postcard Week, Natl, May 2
  York Intl Postcard Fair (York, PA), Nov 19
Postell, Ashley: Birth, Jun 9
Postlethwaite, Pete: Birth, Feb 7
Postman's Day (Mexico), Nov 12
Postmaster General Established, US: Anniv, Sep 22
Poston, Tom: Birth, Oct 17
Posture Month, Natl Correct, May 1
Potato Blossom Fest, Maine (Fort Fairfield, ME), Jul 9
Potato Month, Natl, Sep 1
Potomac Celtic Festival (Leesburg, VA), Jun 12
Potsdam Declaration: Anniv, Jul 26
Potter, Beatrix: Birth Anniv, Jul 28
Potters Market, Appalachian (Marion, NC), Dec 4
Potts, Annie: Birth, Oct 28
Potty Training Awareness Month, Jun 1
Pound, Ezra: Birth Anniv, Oct 30
Pound, Ezra: Bollingen Prize Award, Feb 19
Poundstone, Paula: Birth, Dec 29
Poverty in America Awareness Month, Natl, Jan 1
Poverty, Decade for the Eradication of (UN), Jan 1
Poverty, War on: Anniv, Jan 8
Povich, Maury: Birth, Jan 17
POW/MIA Recognition Day, Natl (Pres Proc), Sep 17
Powell, Colin: Birth, Apr 5
Powell, Cristen: Birth, Mar 22
Powell, Jane: Birth, Apr 1
Powell, John W: Birth Anniv, Mar 24
Powell, Lewis F., Jr: Birth Anniv, Sep 19
Power Show, Fulton County Historical (Rochester, IN), Jun 18
Power, Tyrone: Birth Anniv, May 5
Powers, Francis Gary: Birth Anniv, Aug 17
Powers, Francis Gary: U-2 Incident: Anniv, May 1
Powers, Stefanie: Birth, Nov 2
Prague Autumn Intl Music Festival (Czech Republic), Sep 12
Prairie Day (Diamond, MO), Sep 11
Prairie Dog Chili Cookoff & World Chmpnshp of Pickled Quail-Egg Eating, Apr 3
Prairie Home Companion Premiere, A: Anniv, Feb 17
Prairie Pioneer Days (Arapahoe, NE), Jul 4
Prater's Mill Country Fair (Dalton, GA), Oct 9
Prayer,
  Just Pray No: Worldwide Weekend Prayer, Apr 17
  Kiwanis Prayer Week, May 9
  National Day of Prayer (Pres Proc), May 6

730

☆ Chase's 2004 Calendar of Events ☆   Index

Supreme Court Bans School Prayer: Anniv, Jun 25
World Day of Prayer, **Mar 5**
Preakness Stakes (Baltimore, MD), **May 15**
Preakness Stakes: Anniv, **May 27**
Pregnancy & Infant Loss Awaness Day, Oct 15
Prematurity Awareness Day, Nov 18
Prentiss, Paula: Birth, **Mar 4**
Prepare To Buy a Home Month, Natl, **Apr 1**
Prepare Your Home To Be Sold Month, Natl, **Mar 1**
Preparing Tomorrow's Parents Month, **May 9**
Prescott, William: Birth Anniv, Feb 20
Prescriptions Month, Talk About, **Oct 1**
Presentation of the Lord (Candlemas Day), **Feb 2**
Preservation of the Ozone Layer, Intl Day for (UN), **Sep 16**
Preservation Week, Natl Historic, **May 3**
President Occupies the White House: Anniv, Nov 1
Presidential Debate, First Televised: Anniv, Sep 26
Presidential Inaugural Ball: Anniv, **May 7**
Presidential Inauguration Anniv, George Washington, **Apr 30**
Presidential Inauguration, G. Cleveland's Second: Anniv, **Mar 4**
Presidential Joke Day, **Aug 11**
Presidential Photograph, First: Anniv, Feb 14
Presidential Telecast, First: Anniv, Apr 30
Presidential Visit to Moscow, First American: Anniv, **May 22**
Presidents' Day, **Feb 16**
President's Environmental Youth Award Natl Competition, **Jul 31**
Presley, Elvis,
   Elvis Presley Blvd Named: Anniv, Jun 29
   Elvis Presley Remembered (St. Louis, MO), **Aug 14**
   Elvis Presley's Birthday Celebration (Memphis, TN), **Jan 7**
   Elvis Week (Memphis, TN), **Aug 7**
   First Concert Appearance: Anniv, Jul 30
   First Single Released: Anniv, Jul 19
   Presley, Elvis: Birth Anniv, **Jan 8**
   Presley, Elvis: Death Anniv, **Aug 16**
Presley, Lisa Marie: Birth, **Feb 1**
Presley, Priscilla: Birth, May 24
Press Freedom Day, World (UN), **May 3**
Pressman, Lawrence: Birth, Jul 10
Preston, Billy: Birth, Sep 9
Preston, Kelly: Birth, Oct 13
Pretty Is as Pretty Does Day, Natl, **Aug 2**
Pretzel Month, Natl Soft, **Apr 1**
Prevent Injuries America, **Apr 1**
Prevention of Eye Injuries Awareness Week. Natl, **Jun 27**
Previn, Andre: Birth, Apr 6
Price Is Right TV Premiere: Anniv, Nov 26
Price, Alan: Birth, Apr 19
Price, Leontyne: Birth, Feb 10
Price, Ray: Birth, Jan 12
Price, Vincent: Birth Anniv, May 27
Price, William Mark: Birth, Feb 15
Pride, Charley: Birth, Mar 18
Priesand, Sally: First Woman Rabbi in US: Anniv, **Jun 3**
Priestley, Jason: Birth, Aug 28
Priestly, Joseph: Birth Anniv, Mar 13
Prime Meridian Set: Anniv, Nov 1
Primeau, Keith: Birth, Nov 24
Primetime Live TV Premiere: Anniv, Aug 3
Primus, Barry: Birth, Feb 16
Prince Harry: Birth, Sep 15
Prince Jonah Kuhio Kalanianole Day (HI), Mar 26
Prince William: Birth, Jun 21
Prince: Birth, Jun 7
Princeton, USS, Explosion: Anniv, Feb 28
Principal, Victoria: Birth, Jan 3
Principi, Anthony: Birth, Apr 16
Prine, Andrew: Birth, Feb 14
Printers Row Book Fair (Chicago, IL), **Jun 5**
Printing Week, Intl, **Jan 11**
Prinze, Freddie, Jr: Birth, Mar 8
Prison, Union Officers Escape Libby: Anniv, Feb 9
Prisoner of War Recognition Day, Natl Former (Pres Proc), **Apr 9**
Prisoner TV Premiere: Anniv, Jun 1
Probst, Jeff: Birth, Oct 26
Procession of the Addolorata and Mysteries (Taranto, Italy), **Apr 8**
Procession of the Holy Blood (Belgium), **May 20**
Procrastination Week, Natl, **Mar 1**
Professional Underwriter's Week, Oct 1
Professional Wellness Month, **Jun 1**
Prohibition (18th) Amendment: Anniv, Jan 16
Prohibition Act Veto Overridden, Wilson's: Anniv, **Oct 28**
Prohibition Repealed: 21st Amendment Ratified, **Dec 5**
Prohibition: Maine Law: Anniv, Jun 2
Prom Sponsor Day, Hug a, **Apr 23**
Promotion Month, Shameless, **Sep 1**
Pronger, Chris: Birth, Oct 10
Proposal Day! ®, **Mar 20**
Proposition 13: Anniv, Jun 6
Prosky, Robert: Birth, Dec 13
Prospect Park: You Gotta Have Park (Brooklyn, NY), **May 15**
Prostate Cancer Awareness Week, **Sep 12**
Protecting Your Home Furnishings Week, Sep 6

Proust, Marcel: Birth Anniv, Jul 10
Prout, Mary Ann: Birth Anniv, Feb 14
Prowse, Juliet: Birth Anniv, Sep 25
Pryce, Jonathan: Birth, **Jun 1**
Pryor, Mark: Birth, Jan 10
Pryor, Richard: Birth, Dec 1
Psychic Week, **Aug 2**
PTA Founders' Day, Natl, Feb 17
PTA Teacher Appreciation Week, Natl, **May 3**
Public Health Week, Natl, **Apr 5**
Public Radio, Natl: Anniv, **May 3**
Public Relations: Getting World to Beat Path to Door Week, **Oct 10**
Public Safety and Technology Awareness Week, **May 16**
Public School, First in America: Anniv, Apr 23
Public Television Debuts: Anniv, Nov 3
Publicity for Profit Week, **Feb 1**
Puccini, Giacomo: Birth Anniv, Dec 22
Puccini, Giacomo: Madama Butterfly Premiere: Anniv, Feb 17
Puckett, Kirby: Birth, Mar 14
Pueblo, USS, Seized by North Korea: Anniv, Jan 23
Puente, Tito: Birth Anniv, Apr 20
Puerto Rico,
   American Mothers, Inc, Natl Conv (San Juan), **Apr 27**
   Barbosa, Jose Celso: Birth Anniv, Jul 27
   Carnival de Ponce (Ponce), **Feb 18**
   Constitution Day, **Jul 25**
   Diego, Jose de: Birth Anniv, Apr 16
   Discovery Day, **Nov 19**
   Emancipation Day, **Mar 22**
   Hostos, Eugenio Maria: Birth Anniv, Jan 11
   Las Mananitas, **Dec 12**
   Loiza Aldea Fiesta, **Jul 25**
   Munoz-Rivera Day, **Jul 17**
   Navidades, **Dec 15**
Puff Daddy (Sean Combs): Birth, Nov 4
Pujols, Albert: Birth, Jan 16
Pulaski, Casimir: Birth Anniv, Mar 4
Pulaski, Casimir: Memorial Day (Pres Proc), **Oct 11**
Pulitzer Prizes First Awarded: Anniv, Jun 4
Pulitzer, Joseph: Birth Anniv, Apr 10
Pulliam, Keshia Knight: Birth, Apr 9
Pullman, Bill: Birth, Dec 17
Pullman, George: Birth Anniv, Mar 3
Pulmonary Rehabilitation Week, **Mar 14**
Pumpkin Fest, Morton (Morton, IL), **Sep 15**
Pumpkin Pie Day, **Nov 21**
Pumpkin Show, Circleville (Circleville, OH), **Oct 20**
Punctuation Day, Natl, **Aug 22**
Punsters Day, Abet and Aid, **Nov 8**
Purcell, Henry: Death Anniv, Nov 21
Purcell, Sarah: Birth, Oct 8
Purgatory Banquet (Gradoli, Italy), **Feb 25**
Purim, **Mar 7**
Purl, Linda: Birth, Sep 2
Purple Heart: Anniv, Aug 7
Pursuit of Happiness Week, **Nov 8**
Push-Button Telephone Debuts: Anniv, Nov 18
Pushkin, Alexander: Birth Anniv, Jun 6
Putin, Vladimir: Birth, Oct 7
Pyle, Ernest: Birth Anniv, Aug 3
Pynchon, Thomas: Birth, May 8
Pyramid Fests, **Apr 11**
Qatar: Independence Day, **Sep 3**
Qing Ming Fest or Tomb Sweeping Day, **Apr 4**
Quadrangle Fest (Texarkana, AR and TX), **Sep 11**
Quaid, Dennis: Birth, Apr 9
Quaid, Randy: Birth, Oct 1
Quality of Life Month, Intl, **Jan 1**
Quantrill's Raid on Lawrence, KS: Anniv, Aug 21
Quark, Physicists Discover Top: Anniv, Apr 23
Quayle, Dan: Birth, Feb 4
Quebec Winter Carnival (Quebec City, QC, Canada), **Jan 30**
Queen Elizabeth I: Accession Anniv, Nov 17
Queen Elizabeth I: Birth Anniv, Sep 7
Queen Elizabeth II: Accession Anniv, Feb 6
Queen Elizabeth II: Agrees to Pay Taxes: Anniv, **Nov 26**
Queen for a Day TV Premiere: Anniv, Jan 3
Queen Latifah: Birth, Mar 18
Queen Mary, RMS: Anniv, May 27
Queen Victoria: Death Anniv, Jan 22
Queen's Official Birthday, **Jun 14**
Queen's Official Birthday/Trooping Colours (England), **Jun 12**
Quilt (including quilts, quilting, quilt shows),
   American Quilter's Society Quilt Exposition (Nashville, TN), **Aug 18**
   Mountain Quiltfest (Pigeon Forge, TN), **Mar 10**
   Peddler's Village Quilt Competition/Display (Lahaska, PA), **Jan 19**
   Quilt Odyssey (Gettysburg, PA), **Aug 5**
   Quilt Show (Clayton, NY), **Jul 23**
   Quilt Show (Woodstock, VT), **Jul 29**
   Quilter's Society Show, American (Paducah, KY), **Apr 21**
   Quilting Day, Natl, **Mar 20**
Quincy TV Premiere: Anniv, Oct 3
Quinlan, Karen Ann: Birth Anniv, Mar 29
Quinlan, Kathleen: Birth, Nov 19
Quinn, Aidan: Birth, Mar 8
Quinn, Anthony: Birth Anniv, Apr 21
Quinn, Jane Bryant: Birth, Feb 5

Quirky Country Music Song Titles Day, Mar 27
Quiz Kids TV Premiere: Anniv, Jul 6
Ra, Sun: Birth Anniv, May 22
Rabbi: First Woman Rabbi in US: Anniv, **Jun 3**
Rabe, David: Birth, Mar 10
Rabi' I: Month of the Migration (Islamic), Apr 21
Rabinowitz, Solomon: Birth Anniv, Feb 18
Race for the Cure (Pittsburgh, PA), **May 9**
Race Relations Day, Feb 14
Race Riots, Saint Louis: Anniv, Jul 2
Race Unity Day, **Jun 13**
Race Your Mouse Around the Icons Day, **Aug 28**
Racial Discrimination, Intl Day for Elimination of (UN), **Mar 21**
Racism/Racial Discrimination, Solidarity Against (UN), **Mar 21**
Racking World Celebration (Decatur, AL), **Sep 17**
Radcliffe, Ann: Birth Anniv, Jul 9
Radcliffe, Daniel: Birth, Jul 23
Radio,
   American Top 40: Anniv, **Jul 4**
   Breakfast Club Premiere: Anniv, **Jun 23**
   Car Talk Natl Premiere: Anniv, **Oct 31**
   Federal Communications Commission Created: Anniv, Feb 26
   First Play-by-Play Football Game Broadcast, **Nov 23**
   First Radio Broadcast of a Prizefight: Anniv, **Sep 6**
   First Scheduled Radio Broadcast: Anniv, **Nov 2**
   Howard Stern Show Radio Premiere: Anniv, Nov 18
   Loomis Day, **May 30**
   Metropolitan Opera Radio Broadcasts Premiere: Anniv, Dec 25
   Morning Radio Wise Guy Day, **May 28**
   Ozzie and Harriet Show Debut: Anniv, **Oct 8**
   Prairie Home Companion Premiere, A, Feb 17
   Public Radio, Natl: Anniv, **May 3**
   Radio Broadcast by a President, First, **Jun 14**
   Radio Broadcasting: Anniv, Jan 13
   Radio Commercials: Anniv, **Aug 28**
   Rest of the Story Premiere: Anniv, **May 10**
   Rush Limbaugh Show Natl Radio Premiere: Anniv, **Aug 1**
   Send a Kid to Kamp Radiothon (Lexington, KY), **May 1**
   Transistor Invented: Anniv, **Dec 23**
   War of the Worlds Broadcast: Anniv, **Oct 30**
   Wolfman Jack: Birth Anniv, Jan 21
   Your Hit Parade Radio Premiere: Anniv, **Apr 12**
Radio City Music Hall: Anniv, Dec 27
Radiological Soc of North America Scientific Assembly and Annual Meeting (Chicago, IL), **Nov 28**
Radishes, Feast of (Oaxaca, Mexico), **Dec 23**
Radium Discovered: Anniv, Dec 26
Radner, Gilda: Birth Anniv, Jun 28
Radosavljevic, Predrag: Birth, Jun 24
Radziwill, Lee: Birth, Mar 3
Rae, Charlotte: Birth, Apr 22
Rafalski, Brian: Birth, Sep 28
Raffi: Birth, Jul 8
Raffin, Deborah: Birth, Mar 13
Raffles, Stamford: Birth Anniv, Jul 5
Rafter, Patrick: Birth, Dec 28
Raggedy Ann & Andy Fest, Original (Arcola, IL), **May 22**
Ragsdale, William: Birth, Jan 19
Raid on Entebbe: Anniv, **Jul 3**
Raid on Richmond: Anniv, Mar 1
Railroad,
   America's Subway Day: Anniv, **Mar 29**
   Amtrak: Anniv, **May 1**
   Antique Power Exhib (Burton, OH), **Jul 24**
   Circus Train Wreck: Anniv, **Jun 22**
   Fordyce on the Cotton Belt Fest (Fordyce, AR), **Apr 19**
   Galesburg Railroad Days (Galesburg, IL), **Jun 26**
   Golden Spike Driving: Anniv, **May 10**
   Helena Railroad Fair (Helena, MT), **Apr 25**
   Hometown Days (Strasburg, CO), **Aug 21**
   Hood River Valley Blossom Fest (Hood River, OR), **Apr 17**
   Iron Horse Outraced by Horse: Anniv, Sep 18
   Model Railroad Show (Wheeling, WV), **Jan 17**
   Mt Hood Railroad Season (Mt Hood, OR), **Apr 2**
   New York City Subway: Anniv, **Oct 27**
   Northern Pacific Railroad Completed: Anniv, **Sep 8**
   Railroad and Hobby Show (Springfield, MA), **Feb 7**
   Reopening of the Schoharie Valley Railroads Museum (Schoharie, NY), **Jun 5**
   34th St Express (Boston, MA), **Dec 11**
   Transcontinental US Railway Completion: Anniv, **Aug 15**
Rain Day (Waynesburg, PA), **Jul 29**
Rainbow Warrior Sinking: Anniv, Jul 10
Rainer, Luise: Birth, Jan 12
Raines, Tim: Birth, Sep 16
Rainey, Joseph: First Black in US House of Reps: Anniv, **Dec 12**
Rainey, Ma (Gertrude B.): Birth Anniv, Apr 3
Rainforest Week, World, **Oct 18**
Raitt, Bonnie: Birth, Nov 8
Ram, Jagjivan: Birth Anniv, **Apr 1**
Ramadan: Islamic Month of Fasting, **Oct 16**
Rameau, Jean P.: Birth Anniv, Sep 25
Ramirez, Manny: Birth, May 30

Chase's 2004 Calendar of Events — Index

Ramis, Harold: Birth, Nov 21
Ramo, Roberta Cooper: Birth, Aug 8
Rampling, Charlotte: Birth, Feb 5
Ramses II Unearthed, Statue of: Anniv, Nov 30
Ramson, Feast of the (Richwood, WV), Apr 17
Ranch Roundup, Texas (Wichita Falls, TX), Aug 20
Rand, Sally: Birth Anniv, Apr 3
Randall, Tony: Birth, Feb 26
Randolph, Peyton: Death Anniv, Oct 22
Rankin, Jeannette: Birth Anniv, Jun 11
Raphael, Sally Jessy: Birth, Feb 25
Raphael: Birth Anniv, Apr 6
Rashad, Ahmad: Birth, Nov 19
Rashad, Phylicia: Birth, Jun 19
Rasputin, Grigori: Assassination Anniv, Dec 29
Rat and Mouse Annual Show, Fancy (Riverside, CA), Jan 17
Rat-Catchers Day, Jul 22
Rather, Dan: Birth, Oct 31
Ratification Day, Jan 14
Rattle, Simon: Birth, Jan 19
Rattlesnake Roundup, World's Largest (Sweetwater, TX), Mar 12
Ratzenberger, John: Birth, Apr 6
Rauh, Joseph L., Jr: Birth Anniv, Jan 3
Rauschenberg, Robert: Birth, Oct 22
Raven Published: Anniv, Jan 29
Rawhide TV Premiere: Anniv, Jan 9
Rawlings, Marjorie Kinnan: Birth Anniv, Aug 8
Rawls, Lou: Birth, Dec 1
Ray Day, May, May 19
Ray, Satyajit: Birth Anniv, May 2
Raye, Martha: Birth Anniv, Aug 27
Razor, Electric, First Marketed: Anniv, Mar 18
Rea, Stephen: Birth, Oct 31
Reaching Your Potential Month, Natl, Jan 1
Read Across America Day, Mar 2
Read an E-Book Week, Mar 7
Read Me Week (TN), Mar 1
Read, Allen, Discovers O.K. Origin: Anniv, Mar 23
Read, George: Birth Anniv, Sep 18
Reader's Day, Natl Young, Nov 9
Reading Groups Month, Natl, Oct 1
Reading Is Fun Week, May 2
Reading: Banned Books Week, Sep 18
Reading: Get Caught Reading Month, May 1
Reagan, Nancy: Birth, Jul 6
Reagan, Ronald Prescott: Birth, May 20
Reagan, Ronald Wilson,
 Assassination Attempt On: Anniv, Mar 30
 Birthday, Feb 6
 I Am in Control Day: Anniv, Mar 30
 Presidential Joke Day, Aug 11
 Wedding To Nancy Davis: Anniv, Mar 4
Real Estate Broker Month, Natl Get To Know an Independent, Jan 1
Real Estate: Prepare To Buy a Home Month, Natl, Apr 1
Real Estate: Prepare Your Home To Be Sold Month, Natl, Mar 1
Real McCoys TV Premiere: Anniv, Oct 3
Real People TV Premiere: Anniv, Apr 18
Reasoner, Harry: Birth Anniv, Apr 17
Rebuild Your Life Month, Jun 1
Rebuilding Day, Natl, Apr 24
Receptionists Day, Natl, May 14
Recipe Greetings for the Holidays, Dec 1
Reckell, Peter: Birth, May 7
Reconciliation Day, Apr 2
Recreation and Parks Month, Natl, Jul 1
Recreation Week, Special, Jul 4
Recreational Vehicle Show (Timonium, MD), Feb 20
Red Army Departs Berlin: Anniv, Jun 11
Red Cloud Indian Art Show (Pine Ridge, SD), Jun 6
Red Cloud: Death Anniv, Dec 10
Red Cross Day, World, May 8
Red Cross Month, Mar 1
Red Cross Month, American (Pres Proc), Mar 1
Red Earth Native American Cultural Fest (Oklahoma City, OK), Jun 4
Red Skelton Show TV Premiere: Anniv, Sep 30
Redbud and Garden Show (Kechi, KS), Apr 24
Reddy, Helen: Birth, Oct 25
Redford, Robert: Birth, Aug 18
Redgrave, Lynn: Birth, Mar 8
Redgrave, Vanessa: Birth, Jan 30
Reduce the Clutter Wk, Aug 15
Redwood Natl Park Established: Anniv, Oct 2
Reece, Gabrielle: Birth, Jan 6
Reed, Jack: Birth, Nov 12
Reed, Jerry: Birth, Mar 20
Reed, Pamela: Birth, Apr 2
Reed, Rex: Birth, Oct 2
Reed, Walter: Birth Anniv, Sep 13
Reed, Willis: Birth, Jun 25
Reese, Della: Birth, Jul 6
Reese, Pee Wee: Birth Anniv, Jul 23
Reeve, Christopher: Birth, Sep 25
Reeves, Jim: Birth Anniv, Aug 20
Reeves, Keanu: Birth, Sep 2
Reeves, Martha: Birth, Jul 18
Reformation Day, Oct 31
Reformation Sunday, Oct 31
Refugee Day, World (UN), Jun 20
Register's Bicycle Ride Across Iowa (Des Moines, IA), Jul 25

Rehabilitation Awareness Celebration, Natl, Sep 19
Rehnquist, William: Birth, Oct 1
Reid, Harry: Birth, Dec 2
Reid, Tim: Birth, Dec 19
Reiki, World Day of, Aug 15
Reilly, Charles Nelson: Birth, Jan 13
Reiner, Carl: Birth, Mar 20
Reiner, Rob: Birth, Mar 6
Reinhold, Judge: Birth, May 21
Reinking, Ann: Birth, Nov 10
Reiser, Paul: Birth, Mar 30
Reitman, Ivan: Birth, Oct 26
Rekindle Your Romantic Self Day, Apr 16
Relationship Renewal Day, May 4
Relationship Wellness Month, Feb 1
Relaxation Day, Natl, Aug 15
Religion Day, World, Jan 18
Religion: World Priest Day, Sep 19
Religious Freedom Day, Jan 16
Religious Freedom Day (Pres Proc), Jan 16
Religious Freedom Week, Sep 18
Remar, James: Birth, Dec 31
Rembrandt: Birth Anniv, Jul 15
Remember the Maine Day, Feb 15
Remembrance Day (Canada), Nov 11
Remembrance Day (England), Nov 14
Remembrance Day (Gettysburg, PA), Nov 20
Remick, Lee: Birth Anniv, Dec 14
Remington Steele TV Premiere: Anniv, Oct 1
Remington, Frederic S.: Birth Anniv, Oct 4
Remini, Leah: Birth, Jun 15
Renaissance Fairs,
 Alabama Renaissance Faire (Florence, AL), Oct 23
 Arizona Renaissance Fest (Apache Junction, AZ), Feb 7
 Georgia Renaissance Spring Fest (Atlanta, GA), Apr 17
 Greater Pittsburgh Renaissance Festival (West Newton, PA), Aug 14
 Kansas City Renaissance Fest (Bonner Springs, KS), Sep 4
 Maryland Renaissance Fest (Annapolis, MD), Aug 28
 Minnesota Renaissance Fest (Shakopee, MN), Aug 14
 Pennsylvania Renaissance Faire (Manheim, PA), Aug 21
 Renaissance Fest (Live Oak, FL), Mar 19
 Sterling Renaissance Fest (Sterling, NY), Jul 3
Rendell, Ed: Birth, Jan 5
Rendezvous Fest (Cavalier, ND), Jun 12
Rendezvous, Great (Thunder Bay, ON, Canada), Jul 9
Rendezvous, Mountain Man (Cataldo, ID), Aug 20
Rendezvous, Mountain Man (Red Lodge, MT), Jul 23
Rendezvous, Redbud Trail (Rochester, IN), Apr 24
Renfro, Brad: Birth, Jul 25
Reno, Janet: Birth, Jul 21
Renoir, Pierre: Birth Anniv, Feb 25
Repot Your Plant Day, Natl, Apr 4
Reptile Awareness Day (Point Pleasant Beach, NJ), Oct 16
Republican National Convention (New York, NY), Aug 30
Republican Party Formed: Anniv, Jul 6
Republican Symbol: Anniv, Nov 7
Research Council, Natl: First Meeting: Anniv, Sep 20
Resnik, Judith A.: Birth Anniv, Apr 5
Respect for Parents Day, Aug 1
Respect for the Aged Day (Japan), Sep 15
Respighi, Ottorino: Birth Anniv, Jul 9
Rest of the Story Radio Premiere: Anniv, May 10
Resurrect Romance Wk, Natl, Aug 8
Retrocession Day (Taiwan), Oct 25
Rett Syndrome Awareness Month, Oct 1
Retton, Mary Lou: Birth, Jan 24
Return Day (Georgetown, DE), Nov 4
Return Shopping Carts to the Supermarket Month, Feb 1
Return the Borrowed Books Week, Mar 1
Reuben, Gloria: Birth, Jun 9
Reunification of Germany: Anniv, Oct 3
Reuther, Walter: Birth Anniv, Sep 1
Revere, Anne: Birth Anniv, Jun 25
Revere, Paul: Birth, Jan 7
Revere, Paul: Birth Anniv, Jan 1
Revere, Paul: Ride Anniv, Apr 18
Revolution, American,
 Battle of Blue Licks Celebration (Mount Olivet, KY), Aug 21
 Battle of Brandywine: Anniv, Sep 11
 Battle of Germantown Reenactment (Philadelphia, PA), Oct 2
 Battle of Lexington and Concord: Anniv, Apr 19
 Bennington Battle Day, Aug 16
 Boston Tea Party: Anniv, Dec 16
 Camden, Battle of: Anniv, Aug 16
 Cessation of Hostilities: Anniv, Jan 20
 Chestertown Tea Party Fest (Chestertown, MD), May 29
 Evacuation Day (Boston, MA), Mar 17
 Great Britain-US: Articles of Peace: Anniv, Nov 30
 Hale, Nathan: Birth Anniv, Jun 6
 Henry, Patrick: Birth Anniv, May 29
 Independence Day (US), Jul 4
 John Parker Day, Apr 19
 Liberty Day, Mar 23
 Middleton, Arthur: Birth Anniv, Jun 26
 Nathan Hale Fife and Drum Muster (Coventry, CT), Jul 24
 Olive Branch Petition: Anniv, Jul 8
 Paris, Treaty of: Signing Anniv, Sep 3
 Paul Revere's Ride: Anniv, Apr 18
 Road to Independence (Williamsburg, VA), Jul 3
 Salvador, Francis: Death Anniv, Jul 31
 Sampson, Deborah: Birth Anniv, Dec 17
 Shays Rebellion: Anniv, Aug 29
 Washington, George: Takes Command of Continental Army, Jul 3
 Yorktown Day, Oct 19
 Yorktown Victory Celebration (Yorktown, VA), Oct 16
 Yorktown Victory Day (VA), Oct 11
Revolution, Russian: Anniv, Nov 7
Rex Allen Days (Willcox, AZ), Oct 1
Reyna, Claudio: Birth, Jul 20
Reynolds, Burt: Birth, Feb 11
Reynolds, Debbie: Birth, Apr 1
Reynolds, Joshua: Birth Anniv, Jul 16
Reznor, Trent: Birth, May 17
Rhames, Ving: Birth, May 12
Rhinelander's Oktoberfest (Rhinelander, WI), Oct 8
Rhino Day, Save the, May 1
Rhoda TV Premiere: Anniv, Sep 9
Rhode Island,
 Bristol Civic, Military/Firemen's Parade (Bristol), Jul 5
 Carcieri, Donald: Birth, Dec 16
 Chafee, Lincoln: Birth, Mar 26
 Children's Party at Green Animals (Newport), Jul 14
 Independence Day, May 4
 New England Mid-winter Surfing Chmpshp (Narragansett), Feb 21
 Newport Intl Boat Show (Newport), Sep 16
 Newport Music Fest (Newport), Jul 9
 Newport Winter Fest (Newport), Feb 13
 Penguin Plunge (Jamestown), Jan 1
 Ratification Day, May 29
 Reed, Jack: Birth, Nov 12
 Victory Day, Aug 9
 Voters Reject Constitution: Anniv, Mar 24
Rhodes, Cecil: Birth Anniv, Jul 5
Rhodes, Cynthia: Birth, Nov 21
Rhododendron Fest (Florence, OR), May 21
Rhododendron Fest (Hiawassee, GA), May 7
Rhubarb Fest (Intercourse, PA), May 21
Rhue, Madlyn: Birth, Oct 3
Ricardo, David: Birth Anniv, Apr 19
Ricci, Christina: Birth, Feb 12
Rice Month, Natl, Sep 1
Rice, Anne: Birth, Oct 4
Rice, Condoleezza: Birth, Nov 14
Rice, Glen: Birth, May 28
Rice, Intl Year of, Jan 1
Rice, Jerry Lee: Birth, Oct 13
Rice, Jim: Birth, Mar 8
Rice, Tim: Birth, Nov 10
Rich, Adam: Birth, Oct 12
Richard Crane Memorial Truck Show (St. Ignace, MI), Sep 10
Richard, Rocket: Birth Anniv, Aug 4
Richards, Denise: Birth, Feb 27
Richards, Keith: Birth, Dec 18
Richards, Michael: Birth, Aug 24
Richards, Todd: Birth, Dec 28
Richardson, Bill: Birth Anniv, Nov 15
Richardson, J.P. (Big Bopper): Day the Music Died: Death Anniv, Feb 3
Richardson, Joely: Birth, Jan 9
Richardson, Miranda: Birth, Mar 3
Richardson, Natasha: Birth, May 11
Richardson, Patricia: Birth, Feb 23
Richie, Lionel: Birth, Jun 20
Richmond, Lee: First Perfect Game: Anniv, Jun 12
Richmond, Mitch: Birth, Jun 30
Richter Scale Day, Apr 26
Richter, Andy: Birth, Oct 28
Richter, Mike: Birth, Sep 22
Rickenbacker, Edward V.: Birth Anniv, Oct 8
Rickey, Branch: Birth Anniv, Dec 20
Rickles, Don: Birth, May 8
Rickover, Hyman George: Birth Anniv, Jan 27
Riddles, Libby: Birth, Apr 1
Ride, Sally Kristen: Birth, May 26
Ridge, Thomas J.: Birth, Aug 26
Ridgeley, Andrew: Birth, Jan 26
Ridgway, Matthew Bunker: Birth Anniv, Mar 3
Riefenstahl, Leni: Birth, Aug 22
Riegert, Peter: Birth, Apr 11
Riel, Louis: Hanging Anniv, Nov 16
Rifle Tourn, Walsh Invitational (Cincinnati, OH), Nov 5
Rigby, Cathy: Birth, Dec 12
Rigg, Diana: Birth, Jul 20
Riggs, Bobby: Billie Jean King Wins: Anniv, Sep 20
Right-Brainers Rule Month, Oct 1
Riley, Bob: Birth, Oct 3
Riley, James Whitcomb: Death Anniv, Jul 22
Riley, Pat: Birth, Mar 20
Rimes, LeAnn: Birth, Aug 28
Ringgold, Faith: Birth, Oct 8
Ringwald, Molly: Birth, Feb 18
Rios, Marcelo: Birth, Dec 26
Riot Act: Anniv, Jul 20

★ Chase's 2004 Calendar of Events ★   Index

Riot, Watts: Anniv, Aug 11
Ripa, Kelly: Birth, Oct 2
Ripken, Cal, Jr: Birth, Aug 24
Ripper, Jack the: Letter: Anniv, Sep 27
Ripper, Jack the: Whitechapel Murders Begin: Anniv, Aug 31
Ritt, Martin: Birth Anniv, Mar 2
Ritter, John: Birth, Sep 17
Rivera, Chita: Birth, Jan 23
Rivera, Diego: Birth Anniv, Dec 8
Rivera, Geraldo: Birth, Jul 4
Rivera, Mariano: Birth, Nov 29
Riverbend Fest (Chattanooga, TN), Jun 11
Riverfest (LaCrosse, WI), Jun 30
Riverfront Ribfest (Huntington, WV), Aug 19
Rivers Month, Natl, Jun 1
Rivers, Glenn: Birth, Oct 13
Rivers, Joan: Birth, Jun 8
Rivers, Johnny: Birth, Nov 7
Rizzuto, Phil: Birth, Sep 25
Roach, Hal: Birth Anniv, Jan 14
Roanoke Fest in the Park (Roanoke, VA), May 28
Robards, Jason: Birth Anniv, Jul 26
Robbins, Jerome: Birth Anniv, Oct 11
Robbins, Tim: Birth, Oct 16
Robert the Hermit: Death Anniv, Apr 1
Robert's Rules Day, May 2
Roberts, Cokie: Birth, Dec 27
Roberts, Doris: Birth, Nov 4
Roberts, Eric: Birth, Apr 18
Roberts, Julia: Birth, Oct 28
Roberts, Oral: Birth, Jan 24
Roberts, Pat: Birth, Apr 20
Roberts, Pernell: Birth, May 18
Roberts, Tony: Birth, Oct 22
Robertson, Cliff: Birth, Sep 9
Robertson, Oscar Palmer: Birth, Nov 24
Robertson, Pat: Birth, Mar 22
Robertson, Robbie: Birth, Jul 5
Robeson, Paul: Birth Anniv, Apr 9
Robin Hood Fest, Sherwood (Sherwood, OR), Jul 16
Robinson Crusoe Day, Feb 1
Robinson, Bill "Bojangles": Birth Anniv, May 25
Robinson, Brooks: Birth, May 18
Robinson, Cliff: Birth, Dec 16
Robinson, David: Birth, Aug 6
Robinson, Eddie: Birth, Feb 13
Robinson, Edwin Arlington: Birth Anniv, Dec 22
Robinson, Frank: Birth, Aug 31
Robinson, Glenn: Birth, Jan 10
Robinson, Jackie,
  Birth Anniv, Jan 31
  Breaks Baseball Color Line: Anniv, **Apr 15**
  Named First Black Manager: Anniv, **Oct 3**
Robinson, Roscoe, Jr: Birth Anniv, Oct 11
Robinson, Smokey: Birth, Feb 19
Robinson, Sugar Ray: Birth Anniv, May 3
Robot Homicide, First: Anniv, Jul 21
Rocco, Alex: Birth, Feb 29
Roche, Eugene: Birth, Sep 22
Rochester Fair (Rochester, NH), Sep 10
Rochon, Lela: Birth, Apr 17
Rock Creek Park Nationalized: Anniv, Jun 10
Rock Show, Mineral Capital (Bancroft, ON, Canada), Jul 24
Rock, Chris: Birth, Feb 7
Rockbridge Community Fest (Lexington, VA), Aug 21
Rockefeller, Abby Greene Aldrich: Birth Anniv, Oct 26
Rockefeller, David: Birth, Jun 12
Rockefeller, John D., IV: Birth, Jun 18
Rockefeller, Nelson: Birth Anniv, Jul 8
Rockhound Gemboree (Bancroft, ON, Canada), Jul 29
Rockne, Knute: Birth Anniv, Mar 4
Rockwell, Norman: Birth Anniv, Feb 3
Rockwell, Norman: First Post Cover: Anniv, May 20
Rockwell, Norman: Rockwell's Self-Portrait: Anniv, Oct 8
Rocky and His Friends TV Premiere: Anniv, Nov 19
Rocky Mountain Natl Park Established: Anniv, Jan 26
Roddenberry, Gene: Birth Anniv, Aug 19
Roddick, Andy: Birth, Aug 30
Rodents, Running of the (Louisville, KY), Apr 5
Rodeo,
  Adams County Fair/Rodeo (Hettinger, ND), Jul 29
  Beef Empire Days (Garden City, KS), **Jun 8**
  Black Hills Roundup (Belle Fourche, SD), **Jul 2**
  Black Hills Stock Show and Rodeo (Rapid City, SD), **Jan 30**
  Bullnanza (Guthrie, OK), **Feb 6**
  Cal Farley's Boys Ranch Rodeo (Boys Ranch, TX), **Sep 4**
  Calgary Stampede (Calgary, AB, Canada), **Jul 9**
  Central Montana Fair (Lewistown, MT), **Jul 16**
  Cheyenne Frontier Days (Cheyenne, WY), **Jul 23**
  Cimarron Territory Celebration (Beaver, OK), **Apr 10**
  Clearwater Chamber of Commerce Rodeo (Clearwater, NE), **Jun 25**
  Days of '47 Celebration (Salt Lake City, UT), **Jul 19**
  Dinosaur Roundup Rodeo (Vernal, UT), **Jul 7**
  Eighty-Niner Celebration (Guthrie, OK), **Apr 20**
  Ennis Rodeo & Parade (Ennis, MT), **Jul 3**
  Fiesta De Los Vaqueros (Tucson, AZ), **Feb 25**
  First Intercollegiate Rodeo (Apple Valley, CA), **Apr 8**
  Haines Stampede and Rodeo (Baker City, OR), **Jul 3**
  Houston Livestock Show/Rodeo (Houston, TX), **Feb 26**
  Inter-State Fair/Rodeo (Coffeyville, KS), **Aug 7**
  Killdeer Mountain Roundup Rodeo Days (Killdeer, ND), **Jul 3**
  Livingston Roundup (Livingston, MT), **Jul 2**
  Longhorn Chmpshp Finals Rodeo (Murfreesboro, TN), **Nov 11**
  Longhorn Chmpshp Rodeo (Auburn Hills, MI) **Feb 13**
  Longhorn World Chmpshp Rodeo (Chattanooga, TN), **Mar 5**
  Longhorn World Chmpshp Rodeo (Cincinnati, OH), **Feb 20**
  Longhorn World Chmpshp Rodeo (Columbus, OH), **Feb 6**
  Longhorn World Chmpshp Rodeo (Huntsville, AL), **Mar 12**
  Longhorn World Chmpshp Rodeo (Tulsa, OK), **Jan 23**
  Longhorn World Chmpshp Rodeo (Winston-Salem, NC), **Feb 27**
  Lost Dutchman Days (Apache Junction, AZ), **Feb 27**
  Nebraskaland Days/Buffalo Bill Rodeo (North Platte, NE), **Jun 11**
  Nebraska's Big Rodeo (Burwell, NE), **Jul 29**
  NRA/NWRA Rodeo Finals (Billings, MT), **Feb 13**
  Oregon Trail Rodeo (Hastings, NE), **Sep 3**
  Ranching Heritage Fest, South Texas (Kingsville, TX), **Feb 20**
  Red Lodge Home of Champions Rodeo (Red Lodge, MT), **Jul 2**
  Red River Rodeo (Wichita Falls, TX), **Jun 9**
  River City Roundup (Omaha, NE), **Sep 17**
  Scotts Bluff County Fair (Mitchell, NE), **Aug 9**
  Seminole Tribe Festival, Powwow and Rodeo (Hollywood, FL), **Feb 12**
  Snake River Stampede (Nampa, ID), **Jul 20**
  Southside Fall Fest (St. Joseph, MO), **Sep 17**
  Southwestern Expo Livestock Show/Rodeo (Fort Worth, TX), **Jan 17**
  Texas Ranch Roundup (Wichita Falls, TX), **Aug 20**
  That Famous Preston Night Rodeo (Preston, ID), **Jul 29**
  Utah State Fair (Salt Lake City, UT), **Sep 9**
  Western Stock Show and Rodeo, Natl (Denver, CO), **Jan 10**
  Wichita West Bullfest (Wichita Falls, TX), **Jan 17**
  Wild Horse Stampede (Wolf Point, MT), **Jul 9**
Rodin, Auguste: Birth Anniv, Nov 12
Rodman, Dennis: Birth, May 13
Rodney, Caesar: Birth Anniv, Oct 7
Rodriguez, Alex: Birth, Jul 27
Rodriguez, Ivan "Pudge": Birth, Nov 30
Rodriguez, Juan "Chi-Chi": Birth, Oct 23
Rodriguez, Robert: Birth, Jun 20
Roe v Wade Decision: Anniv, Jan 22
Roentgen, Wilhelm K.: Birth Anniv, Mar 27
Roeper, Richard: Birth, Oct 17
Rogation Sunday, May 16
Roger Ebert's Overlooked Film Fest (Champaign, IL), Apr 21
Rogers, Edith Nourse: Birth Anniv, Mar 19
Rogers, Fred: Birth Anniv, Mar 20
Rogers, Ginger: Birth Anniv, Jul 16
Rogers, Kenny: Birth, Aug 21
Rogers, Mimi: Birth, Jan 27
Rogers, Roy: Birth Anniv, Nov 5
Rogers, Wayne: Birth, Apr 7
Rogers, Will: Birth Anniv, Nov 4
Roget, Peter Mark: Birth Anniv, Jan 18
Roker, Al: Birth, Aug 20
Rolen, Scott: Birth, Apr 4
Roller Coaster: Santa Cruz Beach Giant Dipper: Anniv, May 17
Roller Skating Month, Natl, Oct 1
Rolling Stones: Altamont Concert: Anniv, Dec 6
Rollins, Jimmy: Birth, Nov 27
Roman Catholic/Eastern Orthodox Meeting: Anniv, Jan 5
Roman Catholic: New Catechism: Anniv, Nov 16
Romance (including dating, love, relationships),
  Couple Appreciation Month, **Apr 1**
  Decide to Be Married Day, **Jun 27**
  Dump Your "Significant Jerk" Day, **Feb 3**
  Find Your Soul Mate Day, **May 22**
  Flirting Week, Intl, **Feb 9**
  Love a Mensch Week, **Sep 13**
  Lunch Prowl Week, **Sep 13**
  Pleasure Your Mate Month, **Sep 1**
  Rekindle Your Romantic Self Day, **Apr 16**
  Relationship Renewal Day, **May 4**
  Relationship Wellness Month, **Feb 1**
  Resurrect Romance Wk, Natl, **Aug 8**
  Romance & Remembrance (Indianapolis, IN), **Feb 14**
  Singles Week, Natl, **Sep 19**
  Valentine's Day, **Feb 14**
  Virtual Love Day, **Jul 24**
  Weddings Month, Natl, **Feb 1**
  Wife Appreciation Day, **Sep 18**
  World Marriage Day, **Feb 8**
Romania,
  Ceausescu, Nicolae: Death Anniv, **Dec 25**
  National Day, **Dec 1**
  Surrender to USSR: Anniv, **Aug 23**
Romano, Ray: Birth, Dec 21
Rome Executions: Anniv, Mar 25
Rome Liberated: Anniv, Jun 4
Rome, Sack of: Anniv, May 6
Rome: Birthday (Italy), Apr 21
Romero Barcelo, Carlos: Birth, Sep 4
Romijn-Stamos, Rebecca: Birth, Nov 6
Rommel, Erwin: Birth Anniv, Nov 15
Romney, Mitt: Birth, Mar 12
Ronaldo: Birth, Sep 22
Ronstadt, Linda: Birth, Jul 15
Room of One's Own Day, Jan 25
Rooney, Andy: Birth, Jan 14
Rooney, Mickey: Birth, Sep 23
Roosevelt, Alice: Birth Anniv, Jul 29
Roosevelt, Edith: Birth Anniv, Aug 6
Roosevelt, Eleanor, Day (Willapa, WA), **Aug 7**
Roosevelt, Eleanor: Birth Anniv, Oct 11
Roosevelt, Franklin Delano,
  Bank Holiday: Anniv, **Mar 5**
  Birth Anniv, **Jan 30**
  Christmas Fireside Chat Warning: Anniv, **Dec 25**
  Death Anniv, **Apr 12**
  Elected to Fourth Term: Anniv, **Nov 7**
  FDR Commemorative Ceremony (Warm Springs, GA), **Apr 12**
  First Fireside Chat: Anniv, **Mar 12**
  First Presidential Telecast: Anniv, **Apr 30**
  Unconditional Surrender Statement: Anniv, **Jan 24**
  Warm Springs Thanksgiving (Warm Springs, GA), **Nov 20**
Roosevelt, Theodore: Birth Anniv, Oct 27
Roosevelt, Theodore: First Secret Service Agent to Die in the Line of Duty: Anniv, Sep 3
Roosevelt, Theodore: Wrestling: Anniv, Apr 9
Roots and Branches Month, Jul 1
Rosacea Awareness Month, Mar 1
Rose Bowl Game (Pasadena, CA), Jan 1
Rose Fest, Portland (Portland, OR), Jun 3
Rose Month, Natl, Jun 1
Rose, Billy: Birth Anniv, Sep 6
Rose, Charlie: Birth, Jan 5
Rose, Jalen: Birth, Jan 30
Rose, Pete: Birth, Apr 14
Rose, Peace: Introduced to World: Anniv, Apr 29
Roseanne TV Premiere: Anniv, Oct 18
Roseanne: Birth, Nov 3
Rosenbaum, Michael: Birth, Jul 11
Rosenberg Execution: Anniv, Jun 19
Roses, South Carolina Fest of (Orangeburg, SC), Apr 23
Rosh Hashanah, Sep 16
Rosh Hashanah Begins, Sep 15
Ross, Betsy: Birth Anniv, Jan 1
Ross, Diana: Birth, Mar 26
Ross, George: Birth Anniv, May 10
Ross, Katharine: Birth, Jan 29
Ross, Marion: Birth, Oct 25
Ross, Nellie Tayloe: Birth Anniv, Nov 29
Ross, Nellie Tayloe: Wyoming Inaugurates 1st US Woman Gov: Anniv, Jan 5
Rossellini, Isabella: Birth, Jun 18
Rossner, Judith: Birth, Mar 1
Rossovich, Rick: Birth, Aug 28
Rostropovich, Mstislav Leopoldovich: Birth, Mar 27
Rotary Tiller Race, World Chmpshp/Purplehull Pea Fest (Emerson, AR), Jun 25
Roth, David Lee: Birth, Oct 10
Roth, Philip: Birth, Mar 19
Roth, Tim: Birth, May 14
Roughhouse Fest (Japan), Oct 14
Rounds Resounding Day, Aug 1
Rounds, Mike: Birth, Oct 24
Roundtree, Richard: Birth, Sep 7
Rourke, Mickey: Birth, Sep 16
Rousseau, Henri: Birth Anniv, May 20
Rousseau, Jean J.: Birth Anniv, Jun 28
Route 66 Summerfest (Rolla, MO), Jun 4
Rowan and Martin's Laugh-In, Jan 22
Rowland, John: Birth, May 24
Rowlands, Gena: Birth, Jun 19
Rowling, J.K.: Birth, Jul 31
Roy Rogers Show TV Premiere: Anniv, Dec 30
Roy, Patrick: Birth, Oct 5
Royko, Mike: Birth Anniv, Sep 19
Rozelle, Pete: Birth Anniv, Mar 1
RSV Awareness Month, Natl, Oct 1
Rubens, Paul: Birth, Aug 27
Rubens, Peter P.: Birth Anniv, Jun 28
Rubik, Erno: Birth, Jul 13
Ruble Becomes Convertible: Anniv, Jul 1
Ruck, Alan: Birth, Jul 1
Rucker, Darius: Birth, May 13
Rudd, Paul: Birth, Apr 6
Rudner, Rita: Birth, Sep 17
Rudolph, Wilma: Birth Anniv, Jun 23
Ruffin, Davis Eli (David): Birth Anniv, Jan 18
Ruffin, Edmund: Birth Anniv, Jan 5
Rukeyser, Louis: Birth, Jan 30
Rumsfeld, Donald: Birth, Jul 9
Rundgren, Todd: Birth, Jun 22
Running,
  Al's Memorial Run & Walk (Milwaukee, WI), **Sep 18**
  Anvil Mountain Run (Nome, AK), **Jul 4**
  Atlanta Marathon and Half Marathon (Atlanta, GA), **Nov 25**
  Bay to Breakers Race (San Francisco, CA), **May 14**
  Beartooth Run (Red Lodge, MT), **Jun 26**

733

Index ☆ Chase's 2004 Calendar of Events ☆

Running (cont'd)—Samms

Big Ten Men's/Women's Cross Country Chmpshp (Iowa City, IA), **Oct 31**
Bolder Boulder 10K (Boulder, CO), **May 31**
Borneo Rhino Challenge (Malaysia), **May 1**
Boston Marathon (Boston, MA), **Apr 19**
California Artichoke Festival (Castroville, CA), **May 17**
Coyote Chase (Wellington, NV), **Jun 19**
Crater Lake Rim Runs and Marathon (Klamath Falls, OR), **Aug 14**
Easter Beach Run (Daytona Beach, FL), **Apr 10**
Egg Races (Switzerland), **Apr 12**
59 Min 37 Sec Anvil Mountain Challenge (Nome, AK), **Sep 9**
Groundhog Run (Kansas City, MO), **Feb 8**
Hangover Handicap Run (Klamath Falls, OR), **Jan 1**
Historic Marathon Runs: Anniv, **Sep 2**
Houston Marathon (Houston, TX), **Jan 18**
Jimmy Stewart Relay Marathon (Los Angeles, CA), **Apr 18**
Lakestride Half-Marathon (Ludington, MI), **Jun 19**
LaSalle Bank Chicago Marathon, The (Chicago, IL), **Oct 10**
Leadville Trail 100 Ultramarathon (Leadville, CO), **Aug 21**
Longest Dam Run (Glasgow, MT), **Jun 19**
Mad City Marathon (Madison, WI), **May 31**
Mount Marathon Race (Seward, AK), **Jul 4**
New York City Marathon (New York, NY), **Nov 7**
Peachtree Road Race (Atlanta, GA), **Jul 4**
Romp in the Swamp Fun Walk (Appleton, WI), **Oct 16**
Running and Fitness Week, Natl, **May 16**
San Diego Marathon (Carlsbad, CA), **Jan 18**
Turkey Trot (Parkersburg, WV), **Nov 25**
Runyan, Damon: Birth Anniv, Oct 4
RuPaul: Birth, Nov 17
Rural Life Sunday, May 16
Rush, Barbara: Birth, Jan 4
Rush, Benjamin: Birth Anniv, Jan 4
Rush, Geoffrey: Birth, Jul 6
Rush, William: Death Anniv, Jan 17
Rushdie, Salman, Death Sentence: Anniv, Feb 14
Rushdie, Salman: Birth, Jun 19
Rusk, (David) Dean: Birth Anniv, Feb 9
Russell, Anna: Birth, Dec 27
Russell, Bill: Birth, Feb 12
Russell, Charles M.: Birth Anniv, Mar 19
Russell, Jane: Birth, Jun 21
Russell, Keri: Birth, Mar 23
Russell, Kurt: Birth, Mar 17
Russell, Leon: Birth, Apr 2
Russell, Lillian: Birth Anniv, Dec 4
Russell, Mark: Birth, Aug 23
Russell, Nipsey: Birth, Oct 13
Russell, Theresa: Birth, Mar 20
Russert, Tim: Birth, May 7
Russia,
Army and Navy Day, **Feb 23**
Baltic States' Independence Recognized: Anniv, **Sep 6**
Battle of Stalingrad Begins: Anniv, **Aug 22**
Boris Yeltsin Inaugurated: Anniv, **Jul 10**
Christmas Bells Ring Again: Anniv, **Dec 24**
Christmas Day, **Jan 7**
COMECON and Warsaw Pact Disband: Anniv, **Jun 28**
Constitution Day, **Dec 12**
Czar Nicholas II and Family Executed: Anniv, **Jul 17**
Day of National Reconciliation and Agreement, **Nov 7**
German Surrender at Stalingrad: Anniv, **Feb 2**
Great October Socialist Revolution: Anniv, **Nov 7**
Independence Day, **Jun 12**
Intl Labor Day, **May 1**
KGB Founder Statue Dismantled: Anniv, **Aug 22**
McDonald's Invades the Soviet Union: Anniv, **Jan 31**
New Year's Day Observance, **Jan 1**
October Revolution, **Nov 7**
Old New Year's Eve, **Jan 13**
Passport Presentation, **Jan 2**
Ruble Becomes Convertible: Anniv, **Jul 1**
Saint Petersburg Founded: Anniv, **May 27**
Saint Petersburg Name Restored: Anniv, **Sep 6**
Soviet Communist Party Suspended: Anniv, **Aug 29**
Soviet Cosmonaut Returns to New Country: Anniv, **Mar 26**
Soviet Union Dissolved: Anniv, **Dec 8**
Soviet Union Invaded: Anniv, **Jun 22**
USSR Established: Anniv, **Dec 30**
Victory Day, **May 9**
Women's Day, Intl, **Mar 8**
Russo, Rene: Birth, Feb 17
Rustin, Bayard: Birth Anniv, Mar 17
Ruth, George Herman (Babe),
Babe Ruth Day: Anniv, **Apr 27**
Baseball Hall of Fame's Charter Members: Anniv, **Feb 2**
Birth Anniv, **Feb 6**
Calls His Shot?: Anniv, **Oct 1**
Death Anniv, **Aug 16**
Debut in Majors: Anniv, **Jul 11**
First Major League Home Run: Anniv, **May 6**
First Pro Homer: Anniv, **Sep 5**
House That Ruth Built: Anniv, **Apr 18**
Last Game as Yankee: Anniv, **Sep 30**
Pitching Debut: Anniv, **Apr 22**
Sets Home Run Record: Anniv, **Sep 30**
Rutherford, Ernest: Birth Anniv, Aug 30
Rutledge, Edward: Birth Anniv, Nov 23
Rutledge, John: Death Anniv, Jul 18
Ruttan, Susan: Birth, Sep 16
RV Lifestyle Week, Mar 21
RV Workers and Workampers Day, Jan 9
Rwanda,
Genocide Remembrance Day, **Apr 7**
Independence Day, **Jul 1**
Republic Day, **Sep 25**
Tragedy in Rwanda: Anniv, **Apr 6**
Ryan, Jeri: Birth, Feb 22
Ryan, Meg: Birth, Nov 19
Ryan, Nolan: Birth, Jan 31
Ryan's Hope TV Premiere: Anniv, Jul 7
Rydell, Bobby: Birth, Apr 26
Ryder Cup Matches (Bloomfield Hills, MI), Sep 14
Ryder, Albert Pinkham: Birth Anniv, Mar 19
Ryder, Winona: Birth, Oct 29
Saarinen, Eliel: Birth Anniv, Aug 20
Sabathia, C.C.: Birth, Jul 21
Sabatini, Gabriela: Birth, May 16
Sabato, Antonio, Jr: Birth, Feb 29
Saberhagen, Bret: Birth, Apr 11
Sabin, Albert Bruce: Birth Anniv, Aug 26
Sacagawea: Death Anniv, Dec 20
Sacco-Vanzetti Memorial Day, Aug 23
Sacramento Jazz Jubilee (Sacramento, CA), May 28
Sadat, Anwar El: Assassination Anniv, Oct 6
Sadie Hawkins Day, Nov 6
Safe Boating Week, Natl, May 22
Safe Place Week, Natl, Mar 14
Safer, Morley: Birth, Nov 8
Safety Pin Patented: Anniv, Apr 10
Safety Razor Patented: Anniv, Dec 2
Safety. See also Crime,
Automobile Speed Reduction: Anniv, **Nov 25**
Babysitter Safety Day, **Mar 6**
Cartoonists Against Crime Day, **Oct 25**
Check Your Batteries Day, **Apr 4**
Child Safety Council, Natl: Founding Anniv, **Nov 9**
Childhood Injury Prevention Week, Natl, **Sep 1**
Children and Police Day, Natl, **May 14**
Chimney Safety Wk, Natl, **Sep 26**
Collision Awareness Month, Natl, **Mar 1**
Crime Prevention Month, Natl, **Oct 1**
Day of Natl Concern about Young People and Gun Violence, **Oct 21**
Drunk and Drugged Driving Prevention Month, Natl (Pres Proc), **Dec 1**
Emergency Medical Services Week, Natl, **May 16**
Emergency Preparedness Week, Natl, **Sep 5**
Farm Safety Week, Natl (Pres Proc), **Sep 19**
Fire Prevention Week, **Oct 3**
Fire Prevention Week (Pres Proc), **Oct 3**
Fire Safety Council, Natl: Anniv, **Dec 7**
Firepup's Birthday, **Oct 1**
Fireworks Safety Months, **Jun 1**
Halloween Safety Month, **Oct 1**
Heimlich Maneuver Introduced: Anniv, **Jun 1**
Home & Sports Eye Health and Safety Month, **Sep 1**
Home Office Safety and Security Week, **Jan 11**
Light the Night for Sight, **May 1**
MADD's New Year's Designate a Driver Campaign, **Dec 31**
MADD's Tie One On for Safety, **Dec 1**
Missing Children's Day, Natl, **May 25**
Motorcycle Safety Month, **May 1**
Night Out, Natl, **Aug 3**
Personal Self-Defense Awareness Month, Natl, **Jan 1**
Playground Safety Week, Natl, **Apr 26**
Poison Prevention Week, Natl, **Mar 21**
Poison Prevention Week, Natl (Pres Proc), **Mar 21**
Prevention of Eye Injuries Awareness Week, Natl, **Jun 27**
Safe Boating Week, Natl, **May 22**
Safe Boating Week, Natl (Pres Proc), **May 22**
Safe Kids Week, Natl, **May 1**
Safe Toys and Gifts Month, **Dec 1**
Safety Month, Natl, **Jun 1**
Safetypup's Birthday, **Feb 12**
Sports Eye Safety Month, **Apr 1**
Student Safety Month, **Jun 1**
Workers Memorial Day, **Apr 28**
Youth Sports Safety Month, Natl, **Apr 1**
Safire, William: Birth, Dec 17
Sagal, Katey: Birth, Nov 18
Sagan, Carl: Birth Anniv, Nov 9
Sager, Carole Bayer: Birth, Mar 8
Saget, Bob: Birth, May 17
Sagittarius Begins, Nov 22
Sahl, Mort: Birth, May 11
Sailing Ship Preservation Day, Merchant, Nov 8
Saint Andrew's Day, Nov 30
Saint Ann's Italian Street Fest (Hoboken, NJ), Jul 20
Saint Anthony of Padua: Feast Day (Portugal), Jun 13
Saint Anthony's Day, Jan 17
Saint Apollinaris: Feast Day, Jul 23
Saint Aubin, Helen "Callaghan": Birth Anniv, Mar 13
Saint Augustine of Canterbury, Feast of, May 26
Saint Augustine, Feast of, Aug 28
Saint Barbara's Day, Dec 4
Saint Barthelemy: Patron Saint Day, Aug 24
Saint Bartholomew's Day Massacre: Anniv, Aug 24
Saint Basil's Cathedral: Christmas Bells Again: Anniv, Dec 24
Saint Basil's Day, Jan 1
Saint Bernard of Montjoux: Feast Day, May 28
Saint Catherine of Siena: Feast Day, Apr 29
Saint Catherine's Day, Nov 25
Saint Cecilia: Feast Day, Nov 22
Saint Christopher: Independence Day, Sep 19
Saint Clare of Assisi: Feast Day, Aug 11
Saint Crispin's Day, Oct 25
Saint David's Day (Wales), Mar 1
Saint Edward, The Confessor: Feast Day, Oct 13
Saint Elias Day, Aug 2
Saint Elsewhere TV Premiere: Anniv, Oct 26
Saint Eustatius, West Indies: Statia and America Day, Nov 16
Saint Frances of Rome: Feast Day, Mar 9
Saint Frances Xavier Cabrini: Birth Anniv, Jul 15
Saint Francis of Assisi: Feast Day, Oct 4
Saint Gabriel: Feast Day, Mar 24
Saint George: Feast Day (England), Apr 23
Saint George's Day (Newfoundland, Canada), Apr 26
Saint Gotthard Auto Tunnel: Opening Anniv, Sep 5
Saint Gudula: Feast Day, Jan 8
Saint Ignatius of Loyola, Feast of, Jul 31
Saint James Day: See Spain, Jul 25
Saint James, Susan: Birth, Aug 14
Saint Januarius: Feast Day, Sep 19
Saint Jerome, Feast of, Sep 30
Saint Joan of Arc: Feast Day, May 30
Saint John Nepomucene Neumann: Birth Anniv, Mar 28
Saint John of Capistrano: Death Anniv, Oct 23
Saint John the Baptist Day, Jun 24
Saint John, Apostle-Evangelist: Feast Day, Dec 27
Saint Jude's Day, Oct 28
Saint Lasarus' Day (Bulgaria), Apr 1
Saint Laurent, Yves: Birth, Aug 1
Saint Lawrence Seaway Act: Anniv, May 13
Saint Lawrence Seaway: Dedication Anniv, Jun 26
Saint Lazarus, Procession of Icon of (Cyprus), Apr 3
Saint Lucia: Independence Day, Feb 22
Saint Luke: Feast Day, Oct 18
Saint Nicholas Day, Dec 6
Saint Olaf Christmas Fest (Northfield, MN), Dec 2
Saint Oswald of Worcester Feast Day, Feb 28
Saint Patrick's Day, Mar 17
Saint Patrick's Day (Northern Ireland), Mar 17
Saint Patrick's Day Parade (Hornell, NY), Mar 13
Saint Patrick's Day Parade (New York, NY), Mar 17
Saint Patrick's Day Parade (Roanoke, VA), Mar 13
Saint Paul's Feast (Cyprus), Jun 28
Saint Peter and Paul Day, Jun 29
Saint Peter's Day, Jun 29
Saint Petersburg Founded: Anniv, May 27
Saint Petersburg Name Restored: Anniv, Sep 6
Saint Piran's Day, Mar 5
Saint Piran's Day Celeb (Kansas City, MO), Mar 6
Saint Pius X: Birth Anniv, Jun 2
Saint Stephen's Day, Dec 26
Saint Swithin's Day, Jul 15
Saint Swithun's Celeb (Richmond Hill, ON, Canada), Jul 15
Saint Sylvester's Day, Dec 31
Saint Thomas of Canterbury: Feast Day, Dec 29
Saint Urho's Day (Hood River, OR), Mar 16
Saint Valentine's Day, Feb 14
Saint Vincent and the Grenadines: Independence Day, Oct 27
Saint Vincent De Paul: Feast Day, Sep 27
Saint Vincent De Paul: Old Feast Day, Jul 19
Saint Vincent: Feast Day, Jan 22
Saint, Eva Marie: Birth, Jul 4
Sainte-Croix 1604–2004 (Calais, ME and Bayside, NB, Canada), Jun 25
Sainte-Marie, Buffy: Birth, Feb 20
Saint-Gaudens, Augustus: Birth Anniv, Mar 1
Sajak, Pat: Birth, Oct 26
Sakharov, Andrei Dmitriyevich: Birth Anniv, May 21
Sakic, Joe: Birth, Jul 7
Salaam, Rashaan: Birth, Oct 8
Salad Week, Natl, Jul 25
Salazar, Alberto: Birth, Aug 7
Saldana, Theresa: Birth, Aug 20
Salem Witch Hysteria Begins: Anniv, Mar 1
Salem Witch Trials Begin: Anniv, Jun 2
Sales, Soupy: Birth, Jan 8
Salesperson's Day, Natl, Mar 5
Salinger, J.D.: Birth, Jan 1
Salisbury, Harrison: Birth Anniv, Nov 14
Salk, Jonas: Birth Anniv, Oct 28
Salk, Lee: Birth Anniv, Dec 27
Salmon River Days (Salmon, ID), Jul 1
Salomon, Haym: Death Anniv, Jan 6
Salsa Month, Natl, May 1
Salt, Jennifer: Birth, Sep 4
Salt: No Salt Week, Oct 1
Salter, Susanna, Elected 1st Woman Mayor in US: Anniv, Apr 4
Salvador, Francis: Death Anniv, Jul 31
Salvation Army Founder's Day, Apr 10
Salvation Army in US: Anniv, Mar 10
Salvation Army: Booth, William: Birth Anniv, Apr 10
Salvation Army: Donut Day (Chicago, IL), Jun 4
Sambora, Richie: Birth, Jul 11
Samhain, Oct 31
Samms, Emma: Birth, Aug 28

☆ Chase's 2004 Calendar of Events ☆ Index

Samoa,
  ANZAC Day, **Apr 25**
  Arbor Day, **Nov 5**
  Independence Day, **Jun 1**
  Samoan Fire Dance, **Dec 31**
  White Sunday, **Oct 10**
Samoa, American: Flag Day, **Apr 17**
Sampras, Pete: Birth, **Aug 12**
Sampson, Deborah: Birth Anniv, **Dec 17**
Sampson, Ralph: Birth, **Jul 7**
Samuelson, Joan Benoit: Birth, **May 16**
San Francisco 1906 Earthquake: Anniv, **Apr 18**
San Fransisco 1989 Earthquake: Anniv, **Oct 17**
San Giacomo, Laura: Birth, **Nov 14**
San Isidro Day (Mexico), **May 15**
San Jacinto Day (TX), **Apr 21**
San Marino: National Day, **Sep 3**
San Sebastian's Day (Brazil), **Jan 20**
Sanborn, David: Birth, **Jul 30**
Sand, George: Birth Anniv, **Jul 1**
Sand, Paul: Birth, **Mar 5**
Sanda, Dominique: Birth, **Mar 11**
Sandberg, Ryne: Birth, **Sep 18**
Sandburg, Carl: Birth Anniv, **Jan 6**
Sandcastle Day, **Aug 17**
Sanders, Barry: Birth, **Jul 16**
Sanders, Colonel Harland David: Birth Anniv, **Sep 9**
Sanders, Deion: Birth, **Aug 9**
Sanders, Jay O.: Birth, **Apr 16**
Sanders, Reggie: Birth, **Dec 1**
Sanders, Richard: Birth, **Aug 23**
Sandino, Cesar: Assassination Anniv, **Feb 21**
Sandler, Adam: Birth, **Sep 9**
Sands, Tommy: Birth, **Aug 27**
Sandwich Day: John Montague Birth Anniv, **Nov 3**
Sandy, Gary: Birth, **Dec 25**
Sandys, Edwin: Birth Anniv, **Dec 9**
Sanford and Son TV Premiere: Anniv, **Jan 14**
Sanford, Mark: Birth, **May 28**
Sanger, Margaret (Higgins): Birth Anniv, **Sep 14**
Santa Fe Chamber Music Festival, **Jul 18**
Santa Lucia Day (Sweden), **Dec 13**
Santa-Cali-Gon Days Fest (Independence, MO), **Sep 3**
Santana, Carlos: Birth, **Jul 20**
Santayana, George: Birth Anniv, **Dec 16**
Santiago, Benito: Birth, **Mar 9**
Santiago, Saundra: Birth, **Apr 13**
Santorum, Rick: Birth, **May 10**
Sao Tome and Principe: Independence Day, **Jul 12**
Sarah, Duchess of York: Birth, **Oct 15**
Sarandon, Chris: Birth, **Jul 24**
Sarandon, Susan: Birth, **Oct 4**
Sarazen, Gene: Birth Anniv, **Feb 27**
Sarbanes, Paul S.: Birth, **Feb 3**
Sarcastics Month, Natl, **Oct 1**
Saroyan, William: Birth Anniv, **Aug 31**
Sarrazin, Michael: Birth, **May 22**
Sarto, Andrea Del: Birth Anniv, **Jul 14**
Sartre, Jean-Paul: Birth Anniv, **Jun 21**
Sasaki, Kazuhiro: Birth, **Feb 22**
Sassoon, Vidal: Birth, **Jan 17**
Satisfied Staying Single Day, **Feb 11**
Saturday Night Live TV Premiere: Anniv, **Oct 11**
Saturday Night Massacre, **Oct 20**
Saturnalia, **Dec 17**
Saudi Arabia: Kingdom Unification, **Sep 23**
Sauntering Day, World, **Jun 19**
Savage, Ben: Birth, **Sep 13**
Savage, Fred: Birth, **Jul 9**
Savage, John: Birth, **Aug 25**
Savant, Marilyn vos: Birth, **Aug 11**
Save the Florida Panther Day, **Mar 20**
Save the Rhino Day, **May 1**
Save Your Back Week, Natl, **Oct 24**
Save Your Smile Week, Natl, **Aug 22**
Save Your Vision Month, **Mar 1**
Save Your Vision Week (Pres Proc), **Mar 7**
Savings and Loan: Home Owners Loan Act: Anniv, **Jun 13**
Sawa, Devon: Birth, **Sep 7**
Sawyer, Diane K.: Birth, **Dec 22**
Sax, Adolphe: Birth Anniv (Saxophone Day), **Nov 6**
Saxon, John: Birth, **Aug 5**
Saxophone Day, **Nov 6**
Sayer, Leo: Birth, **May 21**
Sayers, Gale: Birth, **May 30**
SBC Cotton Bowl Classic (Dallas, TX), **Jan 1**
Scacchi, Greta: Birth, **Feb 18**
Scaggs, Boz: Birth, **Jun 8**
Scalia, Antonin: Birth, **Mar 11**
Scaliger, Joseph J: Birth Anniv, **Aug 4**
Scandinavian Hjemkomst Fest (Moorhead, MN), **Jun 25**
Scare a Friend Day, **Oct 1**
Scarecrow and Mrs King TV Premiere: Anniv, **Oct 3**
Scarlatti, Domenico: Birth Anniv, **Oct 26**
Scarry, Richard M.: Birth Anniv, **Jun 5**
Scavullo, Francesco: Birth, **Jan 16**
Scharansky, Natan (Anatoly): Birth, **Jan 20**
Scheider, Roy: Birth, **Nov 10**
Schell, Maximilian: Birth, **Dec 8**
Schembechler, Bo: Birth, **Apr 1**
Schieffer, Bob: Birth, **Feb 25**
Schiff, Richard: Birth, **May 27**
Schiffer, Claudia: Birth, **Aug 25**

Schilling, Curt: Birth, **Nov 14**
Schirra, Wally: Birth, **Mar 12**
Schlafly, Phyllis: Birth, **Aug 15**
Schlatter, Charlie: Birth, **May 1**
Schlesinger, Arthur Meier, Jr: Birth, **Oct 15**
Schmidt, Mike: Birth, **Sep 27**
Schneider, John: Birth, **Apr 8**
Schneider, Maria: Birth, **Mar 27**
Schneider, Rob: Birth, **Oct 31**
Schneiderman, Rose: Birth Anniv, **Apr 6**
Schnitzler, Arthur: Birth Anniv, **May 15**
Scholarship Month, Natl, **May 1**
School Breakfast Week, Natl, **Mar 8**
School Bus Safety Week, Natl, **Oct 17**
School Celebration, Natl, **Sep 17**
School Counseling Week, Natl, **Feb 2**
School Librarian Day, Thank You, **Apr 21**
School Library Media Month, **Apr 1**
School Lunch Week, Natl, **Oct 10**
School Lunch Week, Natl (Pres Proc), **Oct 10**
School Principals' Day, **May 1**
School Spirit Season, Intl, **Apr 30**
School Success Month, Natl, **Sep 1**
Schopenhauer, Arthur: Birth Anniv, **Feb 22**
Schorr, Daniel: Birth, **Aug 31**
Schrempf, Detlef: Birth, **Jan 21**
Schroder, Rick: Birth, **Apr 13**
Schroeder, Gerhard: Birth, **Apr 7**
Schroeder, Patricia: Birth, **Jun 30**
Schubert, Franz: Birth Anniv, **Jan 31**
Schuck, John: Birth, **Feb 4**
Schultz, Charles: Birth Anniv, **Nov 26**
Schultz, Dwight: Birth, **Nov 24**
Schuman Plan Anniv: European Union, **May 9**
Schuman, William Howard: Birth Anniv, **Aug 4**
Schumer, Charles E.: Birth, **Nov 23**
Schurz, Carl: Birth Anniv, **Mar 2**
Schutz, Heinrich: Birth Anniv, **Oct 8**
Schwartzman, Jason: Birth, **Jun 26**
Schwarzenegger, Arnold: Birth, **Jul 30**
Schwarzkopf, Norman H.: Birth, **Aug 22**
Schweitzer, Albert: Birth Anniv, **Jan 14**
Schwenkfelder Thanksgiving, **Sep 24**
Schwikert, Tasha: Birth, **Nov 21**
Schwimmer, David: Birth, **Nov 12**
Schygulla, Hanna: Birth, **Dec 25**
Scialfa, Patty: Birth, **Jul 29**
Science,
  American Assn for the Advancement of Science Annual Meeting (Denver, CO), **Feb 13**
  Astronomy Day, **Apr 24**
  Astronomy Week, **Apr 19**
  Biological Clock Gene Discovered: Anniv, **Apr 28**
  Brain Awareness Week, Intl, **Mar 15**
  Brain Bee, Intl, **Mar 20**
  Bunsen Burner Day, **Mar 31**
  Cellophane Tape Patented: Anniv, **May 27**
  Chemistry Week, Natl, **Oct 17**
  Cloning of an Adult Animal, First: Anniv, **Feb 23**
  CSICOP Annual Superstition Bash, **Feb 13**
  Darwin Day, **Feb 12**
  Diesel Engine Patented: Anniv, **Feb 23**
  Earth's Rotation Proved: Anniv, **Jan 8**
  First Self-Sustaining Nuclear Chain Reaction: Anniv, **Dec 2**
  First US Scientist Receives Nobel Prize: Anniv, **Dec 10**
  Geographers Annual Meeting, Assn American (Philadelphia, PA), **Mar 14**
  Human Genome Mapped: Anniv, **Jun 26**
  Ig Nobel Prize Ceremony (Cambridge, MA), **Oct 7**
  Industry Day (Beatrice, NE), **Apr 25**
  INPEX (Pittsburgh, PA), **May 12**
  Laser Patented: Anniv, **Mar 22**
  Metric Conversion Act: Anniv, **Dec 23**
  Metric System Developed: Anniv, **Apr 7**
  Minority Scientists Showcase (St. Louis, MO), **Jan 17**
  Mole Day, Natl, **Oct 23**
  Nobel Conference (St. Peter, MN), **Oct 5**
  Nuclear Medicine Week, **Oct 3**
  Odometer Invented: Anniv, **May 12**
  Physicists Discover Top Quark: Anniv, **Apr 23**
  Plutonium First Weighed: Anniv, **Aug 20**
  Radiological Soc of North America Scientific Assembly and Annual Meeting (Chicago, IL), **Nov 28**
  Radium Discovered: Anniv, **Dec 26**
  Science Fest, Edinburgh Intl (Edinburgh, Scotland), **Apr 2**
  Sense of Smell Day, Natl, **Apr 17**
  Severe Weather Awareness Week, **Mar 17**
  Sky Awareness Week, **Apr 18**
  Vitamin C Isolated: Anniv, **Apr 4**
  Woman Inducted to Natl Inventors Hall of Fame: Anniv, **May 18**
  X-Ray Discovery Day: Anniv, **Nov 8**
Science Fiction: Asimov, Isaac: Birth Anniv, **Jan 2**
Sciorra, Annabella: Birth, **Mar 24**
Scobee, Francis R.: Birth Anniv, **May 19**
Scofield, Paul: Birth, **Jan 21**
Scoggins, Tracy: Birth, **Nov 13**
Scolari, Peter: Birth, **Sep 12**
Scooby-Doo, Where Are You? TV Premiere: Anniv, **Sep 13**
Scoop the Poop Week, Natl, **Apr 24**
Scopes, John T.: Birth Anniv, **Aug 3**
Scorpio Begins, **Oct 23**

Scorsese, Martin: Birth, **Nov 17**
Scotland,
  Aberdeen Intl Youth Fest (Aberdeen), **Aug 4**
  Bannockburn Day, **Jun 24**
  Braemar Royal Highland Gathering (Braemar), **Sep 4**
  Burns' Nights, **Jan 25**
  Christmas Holiday, **Dec 25**
  Edinburgh Festival Fringe, **Aug 8**
  Edinburgh Intl Book Fest (Edinburgh), **Aug 7**
  Edinburgh Intl Fest (Edinburgh), **Aug 15**
  Edinburgh Intl Science Fest (Edinburgh), **Apr 2**
  Edinburgh Military Tattoo (Edinburgh), **Aug 6**
  Mary, Queen of Scots: Execution Anniv, **Feb 8**
  New Year's Bank Holiday, **Jan 2**
  Open Golf Chmpshp (British Open), **Jul 15**
  Royal Scottish Auto Club Rally, **Jun 11**
  Scottish Intl Badminton Chmpnshp (Edinburgh), **Nov 25**
  Summer Bank Holiday, **Aug 2**
  Tartan Day, **Apr 6**
  Up Helly Aa, **Jan 27**
Scotland Yard First Appearance Anniv, **Sep 29**
Scott County Ugly Woman Contest, **Sep 11**
Scott Thomas, Kristin: Birth, **May 24**
Scott, Campbell: Birth, **Jul 19**
Scott, Robert: Birth Anniv, **Jun 6**
Scott, Ridley: Birth, **Nov 30**
Scott, Sir Walter: Birth Anniv, **Aug 15**
Scott, Willard: Birth, **Mar 7**
Scott, Winfield: Birth Anniv, **Jun 13**
Scottish,
  Alma Highland Fest/Games (Alma, MI), **May 29**
  Braveheart Scottish Weekend (Moultrie, GA), **Feb 13**
  Celtic Fling (Manheim, PA), **Jun 26**
  Celtic Highland Games of the Quad Cities (Davenport, IA), **Aug 28**
  Ligonier Highland Games (Ligonier, PA), **Sep 10**
  Longs Peak Scottish/Irish Highland Fest (Estes Park, CO), **Sep 9**
  Maine Highland Games (Brunswick, ME), **Aug 21**
  New Hampshire Highland Games (Contoocook, NH), **Sep 24**
  Richmond Highland Games/Celtic Fest (Richmond, VA), **Oct 23**
  Southeast Florida Fest & Games (Pembroke Pines, FL), **Mar 6**
Scotto, Renata: Birth, **Feb 24**
Scottsboro Trial: Anniv, **Apr 6**
Scottsdale Culinary Fest (Scottsdale, AZ), **Apr 14**
Scout Sunday, Super (Springfield, MO), **May 15**
Scout Week, Girl, **Mar 7**
Scowcroft, Brent: Birth, **Mar 19**
Scrabble Chmpshp, Natl (New Orleans, LA), **Aug 7**
Scrabble Inventor: Butts, Alfred M.: Birth Anniv, **Apr 13**
Scrapbook Day, Natl, **May 1**
Scrapbooking Industry Day, Intl, **Mar 4**
Scruggs, Earl: Birth, **Jan 6**
Scuba Diving: Seaspace (Houston, TX), **Jun 5**
SCUD Day (Savor the Comic, Unplug the Drama), **Jul 8**
Scully, Vin: Birth, **Nov 29**
Scurry, Briana: Birth, **Sep 7**
Sea Cadet Month, **Sep 1**
Sea Monkey Day, Natl, **May 16**
Seaborg, Glen: Plutonium First Weighed: Anniv, **Aug 20**
Seafair (Seattle, WA), **Jul 3**
Seafood Fest, Grant (Grant, FL), **Feb 28**
Seafood Month, Natl, **Oct 1**
Seagal, Steven: Birth, **Apr 10**
Seal, Intl Day of the, **Mar 22**
Seal: Birth, **Feb 19**
Search for Tomorrow TV Premiere: Anniv, **Sep 3**
Seaspace (Houston, TX), **Jun 5**
Seaver, Tom: Birth, **Nov 17**
Second Day of Christmas, **Dec 26**
Secor, Kyle: Birth, **May 31**
Secret Agent TV Premiere: Anniv, **Apr 5**
Secret Service Agent, First to Die in the Line of Duty: Anniv, **Sep 3**
Secret Storm TV Premiere: Anniv, **Feb 1**
Secretaries Day: See Administrative Professionals Day, **Apr 21**
Secretaries Week: See Administrative Professionals Week, **Apr 18**
Securities and Exchange Commission Created: Anniv, **Jun 6**
Sedaka, Neil: Birth, **Mar 13**
Sedgwick, Kyra: Birth, **Aug 19**
See It Now TV Premiere: Anniv, **Nov 18**
Seeger, Pete: Birth, **May 3**
Seeing Eye Established: Anniv, **Jan 29**
Segal, Erich: Birth, **Jun 16**
Segal, George: Birth, **Feb 13**
Segar, E.C.: Birth Anniv, **Dec 8**
Seger, Bob: Birth, **May 6**
Sehorn, Jason: Birth, **Apr 15**
Seibert, Florence: Birth Anniv, **Oct 6**
Seidelman, Susan: Birth, **Dec 11**
Seikaly, Rony: Birth, **May 10**
Seinfeld TV Premiere: Anniv, **May 31**
Seinfeld, Jerry: Birth, **Apr 29**
Selanne, Teemu: Birth, **Jul 3**
Selby, David: Birth, **Feb 5**
Selena: Birth Anniv, **Apr 16**

Chase's 2004 Calendar of Events

Index — Seles—Slovakia

Seles, Monica: Birth, Dec 2
Self Awareness Month, Intl, Sep 1
Self-Esteem Month, Intl Boost Your, Feb 1
Self-Improvement Month, Sep 1
Self-Promotion Month, Oct 1
Selfridge, Thomas E.: Death Anniv, Sep 17
Self-University Week, Sep 1
Selig, Bud: Birth, Jul 30
Sellecca, Connie: Birth, May 25
Selleck, Tom: Birth, Jan 29
Sellers, Peter: Birth Anniv, Sep 8
Selma Civil Rights March: Anniv, Mar 21
Selznick, David: Gone with the Wind Film Premiere: Anniv, Dec 15
Seminole Tribe of Florida Legally Established: Anniv, Aug 21
Semmes, Raphael: Birth Anniv, Sep 27
Senate Quorum, First: Anniv, Apr 6
Senate: Black Page Appointed: Anniv, Apr 8
Sendak, Maurice: Birth, Jun 10
Senegal: Independence Day, Apr 4
Senior Citizens,
 Adult Day Services Week, Natl, Sep 19
 All States Picnic (Yuma, AZ), Jan 7
 Assisted Living Week, Natl, Sep 12
 Centenarians Day, Natl, Sep 22
 Family Caregivers Month, Natl, Nov 1
 First Social Security Check Issued: Anniv, Jan 31
 Lisco Old-timers Day (Lisco, NE), Sep 12
 Medicare: Anniv, Jul 1
 Older Americans Month, Natl, May 1
 Older Persons, Intl Day of (UN), Oct 1
 Senior Citizens Month, May 1
 Senior Health and Fitness Day, Natl, May 26
 Senior Women's Travel Month, Jan 1
 September Is Healthy Aging® Month, Sep 1
 Shut-In Visitation Day, Natl, Feb 11
 South Florida Senior Games (Hollywood, FL), Jan 21
 Southwest Senior Chmpshp (Yuma, AZ), Jan 20
 Wellderly Day, Mar 15
Senses, Celebration of the, Jun 24
Seoul Recaptured by UN Forces, Mar 14
Separation of Church & State Day, Oct 27
Sequim Irrigation Fest (Sequim), Apr 30
Sequoia and Kings Canyon Natl Park Established: Anniv, Sep 25
Sgt Pepper's Lonely Hearts Club Band Released: Anniv, Jun 1
Serkin, Peter: Birth, Jul 24
Servan-Schreiber, Jean-Claude: Birth, Apr 11
Service Day, Stop the Bad (Customer), Mar 3
Service, Robert William: Birth Anniv, Jan 16
Sesame Street TV Premiere: Anniv, Nov 10
Sessions, Jeff: Birth, Dec 24
Seton, Elizabeth Ann Bayley: Feast Day, Jan 4
Seton, Elizabeth Ann: Canonization Anniv, Sep 14
Setsubun (Japan), Feb 3
Seurat, Georges: Birth Anniv, Dec 2
Seuss, Dr.: Geisel, Theodor: Birth Anniv, Mar 2
Sevareid, Eric: Birth Anniv, Nov 26
Severe Weather Awareness Week, Mar 17
Severinsen, Doc: Birth, Jul 7
Sew Be It! Day, Sep 10
Seward's Day (AK), Mar 29
Sewing Machine: Sew Be It! Day, Sep 10
Sewing Month, Natl, Sep 1
Sex and the City TV Premiere: Anniv, Jun 6
Sex Discrimination, Martha Griffiths Speaks Out Against, Feb 8
Sex Month, Natl Talk With Your Teen About, Mar 1
Sexual Assault Awareness and Prevention Month, Natl, Apr 1
Sexuality Education Month, Natl Family, Oct 1
Sexually Transmitted Diseases (STDs) Awareness Month, Natl, Apr 1
Seychelles,
 Constitution Day, Jun 18
 Independence Day, Jun 29
Seymour, Jane: Birth, Feb 15
Shabbat Across America, Mar 12
Shackleford, Ted: Birth, Jun 23
Shackleton, Ernest: Birth Anniv, Feb 15
Shaffer, Paul: Birth, Nov 28
Shakespeare Fest, Colorado (Boulder, CO), Jun 2
Shakespeare Fest, Illinois (Bloomington, IL), Jun 16
Shakespeare Fest, Oregon (Ashland, OR), Feb 27
Shakespeare, William: Birth and Death Anniv, Apr 23
Shakespeare-on-the-Rocks (El Paso, TX), Sep 3
Shakira: Birth, Feb 9
Shalhoub, Tony: Birth, Oct 9
Shalikashvili: Appointed Chair Joint Chiefs: Anniv, Aug 11
Sham El-Nessim (Egypt), Apr 12
Shamu's Birthday, Sep 26
Shandling, Garry: Birth, Nov 29
Shange, Ntozake: Birth, Oct 18
Shannon, Molly: Birth, Sep 16
Shanty Days (Algoma, WI), Aug 13
Shareware Day, Intl, Dec 11
Sharif, Omar: Birth, Apr 10
Shark Awareness Day (Point Pleasant Beach, NJ), Jul 17
Sharon on the Green Arts and Crafts Fair (Sharon, CT), Aug 7
Shatner, William: Birth, Mar 22
Shaughnessy, Charles: Birth, Feb 9

Shaver, Helen: Birth, Feb 24
Shavuot, May 26
Shavuot Begins, May 25
Shaw, Artie: Birth, May 23
Shaw, George Bernard: Birth Anniv, Jul 26
Shaw, Patty Hearst: Birth, Feb 20
Shawn, Ted: Birth Anniv, Oct 21
Shawn, William: Birth Anniv, Aug 31
Shays Rebellion: Anniv, Aug 29
Sheedy, Ally: Birth, Jun 13
Sheehy, Gail: Birth, Nov 27
Sheen, Charlie: Birth, Sep 3
Sheen, Martin: Birth, Aug 3
Sheep and Wool Fest, Maryland (West Friendship, MD), May 1
Sheep Market, Ho (Denmark), Aug 28
Sheffield, Gary: Birth, Nov 18
Shelby, Richard C.: Birth, May 6
Sheldon, Sidney: Birth, Feb 11
Shelley, Mary Wollstonecraft: Birth Anniv, Aug 30
Shelley, Percy Bysshe: Birth Anniv, Aug 4
Shemini Atzeret, Oct 7
Shenandoah Natl Park Established: Anniv, Dec 26
Shepard, Alan: Birth Anniv, Nov 18
Shepard, Sam: Birth, Nov 5
Shepherd, Cybill: Birth, Feb 18
Shepherd's Fair/Schuebermess (Luxembourg), Aug 22
Sheridan, Jamey: Birth, Jul 12
Sheridan, Nicollette: Birth, Nov 21
Sheridan, Richard B.: Birth Anniv, Oct 30
Sherman Enters Atlanta: Anniv, Sep 2
Sherman, Bobby: Birth, Jul 22
Sherman, James S.: Birth Anniv, Oct 24
Sherman, Roger: Birth Anniv, Apr 19
Sherman, William Tecumseh,
 Birth Anniv, Feb 8
 Surrender at Durham Station: Anniv, Apr 18
 Takes Savannah: Anniv, Dec 21
 War is Hell: Anniv, Jun 19
Sherwood, Brad: Birth, Nov 24
Sherwood, Madeline: Birth, Nov 13
She's Funny That Way Day, Natl, Mar 31
Shields, Brooke: Birth, May 31
Shilts, Randy: Birth Anniv, Aug 8
Shire, Talia: Birth, Apr 25
Shirer, William L.: Birth Anniv, Feb 23
Shirley Temple Theatre TV Premiere: Anniv, Sep 18
Shoemaker, Willie: Birth, Aug 19
Shoemaker-Levy: Comet Crashes into Jupiter: Anniv, Jul 16
Shoes for Orphans Month, Natl, May 1
Shopping Carts to the Supermarket Month, Return, Feb 1
Shopping Reminder Day, Nov 25
Shore, Dinah: Birth Anniv, Mar 1
Shore, Pauly: Birth, Feb 1
Short, Bobby: Birth, Sep 15
Short, Martin: Birth, Mar 26
Shorter, Wayne: Birth, Aug 25
Shostakovich, Dmitri: Birth Anniv, Sep 25
Shovel Race Chmpshp, World (Angel Fire, NM), Jan 31
Show and Tell Day at Work, Jan 8
Show of Wheels (Lovington, NM), Feb 7
Show, Grant: Birth, Feb 27
Shrimp and Petroleum Fest, Louisiana (Morgan City, LA), Sep 2
Shrimp Fest, Isle of Eight Flags (Fernandina Beach, FL), Apr 30
Shriver, Eunice Mary Kennedy: Birth, Jul 10
Shriver, Maria: Birth, Nov 6
Shriver, Pam: Birth, Jul 4
Shrove Monday, Feb 23
Shrove Tuesday, Feb 24
Shrovetide, Feb 22
Shue, Andrew: Birth, Feb 19
Shue, Elisabeth: Birth, Oct 6
Shula, Don: Birth, Jan 4
Shut-In Visitation Day, Natl, Feb 11
Shuttle Camp (Alamogordo, NM), Jun 7
Sibelius, Kathleen: Birth, May 15
Siberian Explosion: Anniversary, Jun 30
Sibling Appreciation Day, May 2
Siblings Day, Natl, Apr 10
Sidney, Philip: Birth Anniv, Nov 30
Siegmeister, Elie: Birth Anniv, Jan 15
Sierra Club Founded: Anniv, May 28
Sierra Leone: Independence Day, Apr 27
Sierra Leone: National Holiday, Apr 19
Sight-Saving/Ultraviolet Awareness Month, Natl, May 1
Sigourney, Lydia: Birth Anniv, Sep 1
Sikh: Baisakhi (India), Apr 13
Sikorsky, Igor: Birth Anniv, May 25
Silent Record Week, Jan 1
Silent Spring Publication: Anniv, Apr 13
Sills, Beverly: Birth, May 25
Silver Bells in the City (Lansing, MI), Nov 19
Silver Spoons TV Premiere: Anniv, Sep 25
Silver, Joel: Birth, Jul 14
Silver, Ron: Birth, Jul 2
Silverman, Fred: Birth, Sep 13
Silverman, Jonathan: Birth, Aug 5
Silverstein, Shel: Birth Anniv, Oct 18
Silverstone, Alicia: Birth, Oct 4

Simchat Torah, Oct 8
Simmons, Gene: Birth, Aug 25
Simmons, J.K.: Birth, Jan 9
Simmons, Jean: Birth, Jan 31
Simmons, Joseph "Run": Birth, Nov 14
Simmons, Richard: Birth, Jul 12
Simms, Hilda: Birth Anniv, Apr 15
Simms, Phil: Birth, Nov 3
Simon, Carly: Birth, Jun 25
Simon, Neil: Birth, Jul 4
Simon, Paul: Birth, Oct 13
Simone, Nina: Birth Anniv, Feb 21
Simplify Your Life Week, Aug 1
Simplon Tunnel Opening: Anniv, May 19
Simpson, O.J.: Birth, Jul 9
Simpsons TV Premiere: Anniv, Dec 17
Sinai Day (Egypt), Apr 25
Sinatra, Frank: Birth Anniv, Dec 12
Sinatra, Nancy: Birth, Jun 8
Sinbad: Birth, Nov 10
Sinclair Lewis Days (Sauk Centre, MN), Jul 14
Sinclair, Upton: Birth Anniv, Sep 20
Sinden, Donald: Birth, Oct 9
Singapore,
 National Day, Aug 9
 Vesak Day, May 10
Singh, Vijay: Birth, Feb 22
Singing Telegram: Anniv, Jul 28
Single Parent Family Day, Sep 25
Single: Satisfied Staying Single Day, Feb 11
Singles Week, Natl, Sep 19
Singletary, Mike: Birth, Oct 9
Singleton, John: Birth, Jan 6
Singleton, Raynoma Gordy: Birth, Mar 8
Sing-Out Day, Intl, Apr 2
Sinise, Gary: Birth, Mar 17
Sinkie Day, Nov 26
Sioux Empire Fair (Sioux Falls, SD), Aug 10
Sioux Empire Farm Show (Sioux Falls, SD), Jan 27
Sirani, Elisabetta: Birth Anniv, Jan 8
Sirica, John: Birth Anniv, Mar 19
Sirk, Douglas: Birth Anniv, Apr 26
Sisley, Alfred: Birth Anniv, Oct 30
Sisters' Day, Aug 1
Sitting Bull: Death Anniv, Dec 15
Six Million Dollar Man TV Premiere: Anniv, Oct 20
$64,000 Question TV Premiere: Anniv, Jun 7
16th Street Baptist Church Bombing: Anniv, Sep 15
Sixty Minutes TV Premiere: Anniv, Sep 24
Skaggs, Ricky: Birth, Jul 18
Skagit Valley Tulip Fest (Burlington, WA), Apr 1
Skating: Natl Roller Skating Month, Oct 1
Skeptics' Day, Intl, Feb 13
Skerritt, Tom: Birth, Aug 25
Skiing,
 American Birkebeiner (Cable to Hayward, WI), Feb 19
 NCAA Skiing Chmpshps (Norden and Soda Springs, CA), Mar 10
 Ski-Joring Finals, Natl (Red Lodge, MT), Mar 13
 Toronto Ski, Snowboard and Travel Show (Toronto, ON, Canada), Oct 14
 Wells Fargo Bank Cup (Winter Park, CO), Feb 6
 Wells Fargo Boulder Mountain Tour (Sun Valley, ID), Feb 7
Skin Care Awareness Month, Natl, Sep 1
Skin: Rosacea Awareness Month, Mar 1
Skinner, B.F.: Birth Anniv, Mar 20
Skowhegan State Fair (Skowhegan, ME), Aug 12
Sky Awareness Week, Apr 18
Sky King TV Premiere: Anniv, Sep 16
Skye, Ione: Birth, Sep 4
Skylab Falls to Earth, Jul 11
Skyscraper, First: Anniv, May 1
Slamdance 2004 (Park City, UT), Jan 17
Slater, Christian: Birth, Aug 18
Slater, Helen: Birth, Dec 15
Slave Revolt, New York: Anniv, Apr 7
Slavery Abolished in District of Columbia: Anniv, Apr 16
Slavery, Abolition of (Jamaica), Aug 1
Slavery: First American Abolition Soc Founded: Anniv, Apr 14
Slavery: Remembrance of the Slave Trade and its Abolition, Intl Day for the (UN), Aug 23
Slayton, Donald "Deke" K.: Birth Anniv, Mar 1
Sled Dog,
 Bancroft Frosty Frolics (Bancroft, ON, Canada), Feb 14
 Iditarod Trail Sled Dog Race (Anchorage, AK), Mar 6
 Klondike Days (Eagle River, WI), Feb 14
 Paul Bunyan Sled Dog Races (Bemidji, MN), Jan 17
 Sled Dogs Save Nome: Anniv, Feb 2
 Yukon Quest Intl 1,000-Mile Sled Dog Race (Whitehorse, YT, Canada), Feb 14
Sleep Awareness Week, Natl, Mar 29
Sleidanus, Johannes: Death Anniv, Oct 31
Slezak, Erika: Birth, Aug 5
Slick, Grace: Birth, Oct 30
Sloane, Hans: Birth Anniv, Apr 16
Slovakia,
 Constitution Day, Sep 1
 Czech-Slovak Divorce: Anniv, Jan 1
 Liberation Day, May 8
 National Uprising Day, Aug 29
 St. Cyril and Methodius Day, Jul 5

☆ Chase's 2004 Calendar of Events ☆ Index

Slovenia—Space Milestones

Slovenia,
Culture Day, **Feb 8**
Independence Day, **Dec 26**
Insurrection Day, **Apr 27**
National Day, **Jun 25**
Slovenian: St. Cyril's Parish Fest (Sheboygan, WI), Jul 18
Slovik, Eddie: Execution Anniv, Jan 31
Slovo, Joe: Birth Anniv, May 23
Slow Pitch Softball Tourn (Williamsport), Jul 9
Slugs Return from Capistrano Day, May 28
Small Business Day, Natl, May 10
Small Business Week, May 12
Smallpox Vaccine Discovered: Anniv, May 14
Smart Sitter Week, Feb 6
Smart, Jean: Birth, Sep 13
Smell Day, Natl Sense of, Apr 17
Smiles, Samuel: Birth Anniv, Dec 23
Smirnoff, Yakov: Birth, Jan 24
Smith Day, Natl, Jan 6
Smith, Adam: Birth Anniv, Jun 5
Smith, Bessie: Birth Anniv, Apr 15
Smith, Bubba: Birth, Feb 28
Smith, Charles Martin: Birth, Oct 30
Smith, Emmitt: Birth, May 15
Smith, Gordon: Birth, May 25
Smith, Holland: Birth Anniv, Apr 20
Smith, Jaclyn: Birth, Oct 26
Smith, James: Death Anniv, Jul 11
Smith, Jedediah Strong: Birth Anniv, Jan 6
Smith, Joseph, Jr, and Hyrum: Death Anniv, Jun 27
Smith, Kate: Birth Anniv, May 1
Smith, Kate: God Bless America 1st Perf: Anniv, Nov 11
Smith, Kurtwood: Birth, Jul 3
Smith, Liz: Birth, Feb 2
Smith, Maggie: Birth, Dec 28
Smith, Margaret: Birth Anniv, Dec 14
Smith, Michael J.: Birth Anniv, Apr 30
Smith, Ozzie: Birth, Dec 26
Smith, Patti: Birth, Dec 30
Smith, Red: Birth Anniv, Sep 25
Smith, Robert: Alcoholics Anonymous: Founding Anniv, Jun 10
Smith, Sammi: Birth, Aug 5
Smith, Steve: Birth, Mar 31
Smith, Taran Noah: Birth, Apr 8
Smith, Thorne: Birth Anniv, Mar 27
Smith, Will: Birth, Sep 25
Smithson, James: Death Anniv, Jun 27
Smithsonian Institution Founded: Anniv, Aug 10
Smitrovich, Bill: Birth, May 16
Smits, Jimmy: Birth, Jul 9
Smits, Rik: Birth, Aug 23
Smokeless Cigarette Withdrawn: Anniv, Feb 28
Smokeout, Great American, Nov 18
Smoking, Take a New Year's Resolution to Stop Smoking, Jan 1
Smoltz, John: Birth, May 15
Smothers Brothers Fired: Anniv, Apr 4
Smothers, Dick: Birth, Nov 20
Smothers, Tom: Birth, Feb 2
Snake Hunt (Cross Fork, PA), Jun 26
Snake River Duck Race (Nome, AK), Sep 6
Snake River Stampede (Nampa, ID), Jul 20
Snead, Sam: Birth Anniv, May 27
Sneak Some Zucchini onto Your Neighbors' Porch Night, Aug 8
Snider, Dee: Birth, Mar 15
Snipe Excursion and Hunt, Pro-Am (Moultrie, GA), Apr 1
Snipes, Wesley: Birth, Jul 31
Snodgrass, W.D.: Birth, Jan 5
Snodgress, Carrie: Birth, Oct 27
Snow Fest (Japan), Feb 8
Snow Plow Mailbox Hockey Day, Jan 23
Snow Sculpting Competition (Rockford, IL), Jan 14
Snow White and the Seven Dwarfs Film Premiere: Anniv, Dec 21
Snow, John: Birth, Aug 2
Snow, Phoebe: Birth, Jul 17
Snowbirds Pancake Breakfast (El Centro, CA), Jan 10
Snowe, Olympia J.: Birth, Feb 21
Snowman Burning (Sault Ste Marie, MI), Mar 19
Snyder, Tom: Birth, May 12
Soap Box Derby, All-American (Akron, OH), Jul 31
Soap TV Premiere: Anniv, Sep 13
Sobieski, Leelee: Birth, Jun 10
Soccer,
Big Ten Men's Soccer Chmpnshp (Ann Arbor, MI), **Nov 11**
Big Ten Women's Soccer Tournament (Columbus, OH), **Nov 4**
Dallas Cup (Dallas, TX), **Apr 4**
NAIA Men's & Women's Natl Chmpshp, **Nov 19**
Natl Soccer Coaches Assn of America Natl Convention (Kansas City, MO), **Jan 14**
Soccer Tragedy (Belgium): Anniv, **May 29**
Soccer Tragedy, Moscow: Anniv, **Oct 20**
World Cup Inaugurated: Anniv, **Jul 13**
Social Security Act: Anniv, Aug 14
Social Security Check Issued, First: Anniv, Jan 31
Social Wellness Month, Jul 1
Social Work Month, Natl Pro, Mar 1
Sodbuster Days (Fort Ransom, ND), Jul 10
Soderbergh, Steven: Birth, Jan 14
Softball. See also Baseball,
Big 12 Women's Softball Chmpshp (Oklahoma City, OK), **Apr 29**
Big Ten Softball Tourn, **May 13**
NAIA Softball Chmpshp (Decatur, AL), **May 21**
NCAA Div I Women's Softball Chmpshp (Oklahoma City, OK), **May 27**
Slow Pitch Softball Tourn (Williamsport, PA), **Jul 9**
365-Inning Softball Game: Anniv, **Aug 14**
Soil Stewardship Sunday: See Rural Life Sunday, May 16
Soldiers' Reunion Celebration (Newton, NC), Aug 19
Solemnity of Mary, Jan 1
Solidarity Granted Legal Status: Anniv, Apr 17
Solidarity with Palestinian People, Intl Day of (UN), Nov 29
Solidarity with the Peoples of Non-Self-Governing Territories, Week of (UN), May 25
Solomon Islands: Independence Day, Jul 7
Solo-Preneuring Week, Jan 25
Solstice, Summer, Jun 20
Solstice, Winter, Dec 21
Solti, Georg: Birth Anniv, Oct 21
Solzhenitsyn Goes Home: Anniv, May 25
Solzhenitsyn, Aleksandr: Birth, Dec 11
Somalia: National Day, Oct 21
Someday, Sep 15
Someday We'll Laugh About This Week, Jan 4
Somers, Suzanne: Birth, Oct 16
Sommer, Elke: Birth, Nov 5
Sondheim, Stephen: Birth, Mar 22
Sonora Showcase (Yuma, AZ), Jan 20
Sontag, Susan: Birth, Jan 16
Sopranos TV Premiere: Anniv, Jan 13
Sorbo, Kevin: Birth, Sep 24
Sorenstam, Annika: Birth, Oct 9
Sorghum Day Fest (Wewoka, OK), Oct 23
Soriano, Alfonso: Birth, Jan 7
Soros, George: Birth, Aug 12
Sorry Charlie Day, Apr 1
Sorvino, Paul: Birth, Apr 13
Sosa, Sammy: Birth, Nov 12
Soul Food Month, Natl, Jun 1
Soul Mate Day, Find Your, May 22
Soul, David: Birth, Aug 28
Sound Barrier Broken: Anniv, Oct 14
Sounds of Season: Holiday Concert (Charlottesville, VA), Dec 26
Soupy Sales TV Premiere: Anniv, Jul 4
Sour Herring Premiere (Sweden), Aug 19
Sourest Day, Oct 25
Sousa, John P.: Birth Anniv, Nov 6
Sousa: Stars and Stripes Forever Day, May 14
Souter, David H.: Birth, Sep 17
South Africa,
African Natl Congress Ban Lifted: Anniv, **Feb 2**
Boer War: Anniv, **Oct 12**
Day of Goodwill, **Dec 26**
Family Day, **Apr 12**
Freedom Day, **Apr 27**
Heritage Day, **Sep 24**
Human Rights Day, **Mar 21**
Mandela Inauguration: Anniv, **May 10**
Multiracial Elections: Anniv, **Apr 26**
National Women's Day, **Aug 9**
New Constitution: Anniv, **Nov 18**
Reconciliation Day, **Dec 16**
Repeals Last Apartheid Law: Anniv, **Jun 17**
Whites Vote to End Minority Rule: Anniv, **Mar 17**
Youth Day, **Jun 16**
South by Southwest (Austin, TX), Mar 12
South Carolina,
Attack on Fort Sumter: Anniv, **Apr 12**
Attack on Fort Wagner: Anniv, **Jul 19**
Charleston Earthquake: Anniv, **Aug 31**
Christmas Craft Show (Aiken), **Dec 3**
Confederate Memorial Day, **May 10**
Craftsmen's Classic Arts & Crafts Fest (Columbia), **Mar 5**
Craftsmen's Classic Arts & Crafts Fest (Myrtle Beach), **Aug 6**
Easter Bunny Bop and Hop (Aiken), **Apr 10**
Fest of Houses and Gardens (Charleston), **Mar 18**
Fort Sumter Returned to Union Control: Anniv, **Feb 17**
Fort Sumter Shelled by North: Anniv, **Aug 17**
Graham, Lindsey: Birth, **Jul 9**
Grand American Coon Hunt (Orangeburg), **Jan 2**
Historic Pendleton Spring Jubilee (Pendleton), **Apr 3**
Hollings, Ernest F.: Birth, **Jan 1**
Iris Fest (Sumter), **May 27**
Jubilee (Bennettsville), **May 8**
Lee County Cotton Festival (Bishopville), **Oct 15**
Low Country Shrimp Fest (McClellanville), **May 1**
Palmetto Sportsmen's Classic (Columbia), **Mar 26**
Ratification Day, **May 23**
Sanford, Mark: Birth, **May 28**
Secession Anniv, **Dec 20**
South Carolina Fest of Roses (Orangeburg), **Apr 23**
South Carolina Festival of Flowers (Greenwood), **Jun 18**
Southeastern Wildlife Expo (Charleston), **Feb 13**
Southern Cyclone: Anniv, **Aug 24**
Spoleto Festival USA (Charleston), **May 28**
Sporting Goods Assn Mgmt Conf, Natl (Hilton Head Island), **May 16**
State Fair (Columbia), **Oct 7**
South Coast Writer's Conf (Gold Beach, OR), Feb 13
South Dakota,
Admission Day, **Nov 2**
Badlands Natl Park Established: Anniv, **Nov 10**
Beach Party (Deadwood), **Mar 13**
Black Hills Passion Play (Spearfish), **Jun 1**
Black Hills Roundup (Belle Fourche), **Jul 2**
Black Hills Stock Show and Rodeo (Rapid City), **Jan 30**
Buffalo Roundup (Custer), **Oct 4**
Buffalo Roundup Arts Fest (Custer), **Oct 2**
Buffalo Wallow Chili Cookoff (Custer), **Oct 3**
Center of Nation All-Car Rally (Belle Fourche), **Jun 12**
Corn Palace Fest (Mitchell), **Sep 1**
Custer State Park Buffalo Auction (Custer), **Nov 20**
Czech Days (Tabor), **Jun 18**
D.C. Booth Day (Spearfish), **May 16**
Dalesburg Midsummer Fest (Vermillion), **Jun 25**
Daschle, Thomas: Birth, **Dec 9**
Fort Sisseton Historical Fest (Lake City), **Jun 5**
Gold Discovery Days (Custer), **Jul 22**
Homesteader Harvest Fest (Brandon), **Sep 12**
Johnson, Tim: Birth, **Dec 28**
Laura Ingalls Wilder Pageant (De Smet), **Jul 9**
Mount Rushmore July 4 Celeb (Mt Rushmore), **Jul 3**
Native Americans' Day, **Oct 11**
Prairie Village Jamboree (Madison), **Aug 27**
Red Cloud Indian Art Show (Pine Ridge), **Jun 6**
Rounds, Mike: Birth, **Oct 24**
Schmeckfest (Freeman), **Apr 1**
Sidewalk Arts Fest (Sioux Falls), **Sep 11**
Sioux Empire Fair (Sioux Falls), **Aug 10**
Sioux Empire Farm Show (Sioux Falls), **Jan 27**
State Fair (Huron), **Jul 26**
Sturgis Rally (Sturgis), **Aug 9**
Wind Cave Natl Park Established: Anniv, **Jan 3**
Armed Forces Day, **Oct 1**
Children's Day, **May 5**
South Pole Discovery: Anniv, Dec 14
South Texas Ranching Heritage Fest (Kingsville, TX), Feb 20
South Texas Wildlife and Birding Festival (Kingsville, TX), Nov 19
Southeast Missouri District Fair (Cape Girardeau, MO), Sep 11
Southeastern Wildlife Expo (Charleston, SC), Feb 13
Southern Fest of Books (Nashville, TN), Oct 8
Southern Hemisphere Hoodie-Hoo Day, Aug 21
Southside Fall Fest (St. Joseph, MO), Sep 17
Soviet Georgia Votes Independence: Anniv, Mar 31
Soviet Union Invaded: Anniv, Jun 22
Sowerby, Leo: Birth Anniv, May 1
Soyfoods Month, Apr 1
Soyinka, Wole: Birth, Jul 13
Space (excluding Space Milestones),
Aerospace Walk of Honor (Lancaster, CA), **Sep 11**
Apollo I: Spacecraft Fire: Anniv, **Jan 27**
Astronomers Find New Solar System: Anniv, **Apr 15**
Challenger Space Shuttle Explosion: Anniv, **Jan 28**
Christmas Greetings from Space: Anniv, **Dec 19**
Closest Approach of a Comet to Earth: Anniv, **Feb 20**
Comet Crashes into Jupiter: Anniv, **Jul 16**
First American Woman in Space: Anniv, **Jun 18**
First Man in Space: Anniv, **Apr 12**
First Woman in Space: Anniv, **Jun 16**
First Woman to Walk in Space, **Jul 17**
Gagarin, Yuri: Birth Anniv, **Mar 9**
Jupiter Effect: Anniv, **Mar 10**
NASA Established: Anniv, **Jul 29**
Near Miss Day, **Mar 23**
Ozark UFO Conf (Eureka Springs, AR), **Apr 9**
Shuttle Camp (Alamogordo, NM), **Jun 7**
Soviet Cosmonaut Returns to New Country: Anniv, **Mar 26**
Space Oddity Song Release: Anniv, **Jun 11**
Space Shuttle Columbia Disaster: Anniv, **Feb 1**
US Natl Commission on Space, **Oct 13**
Windstorms Discovered: Anniv, **Nov 7**
World Space Week (UN), **Oct 4**
Space Milestones,
Year 1 (1957),
Sputnik 1, **Oct 4**
Sputnik 2, **Nov 3**
Year 2 (1958),
Explorer 1, **Jan 31**
Vanguard 1, **Mar 17**
Year 3 (1959),
Luna 1, **Jan 2**
Luna 2, **Sept 12**
Luna 3, **Oct 4**
Year 4 (1960),
Echo 1, **Aug 12**
Sputnik 5, **Aug 19**
Year 5 (1961),
Project Mercury Test, **Jan 31**
Vostok 1, **Apr 12**
Freedom 7, **May 5**
Vostok 2, **Aug 6**
Year 6 (1962),
Friendship 7, **Feb 20**
Aurora 7, **May 24**
Telstar, **July 10**
Vostok 3, **Aug 11**
Year 7 (1963),
Faith 7, **May 15**
Vostok 6, **June 16**

Chase's 2004 Calendar of Events

Index

Space Milestones (cont'd)—Starman

Year 8 (1964),
  Mariner 4, **Nov 28**
Year 9 (1965),
  Voskhod 2, **Mar 18**
  Gemini 4, **June 3**
  Gemini 5, **Aug 21**
  Pegasus 1, **Sept 17**
  Venera 3, **Nov 16**
Year 10 (1966),
  Luna 9, **Jan 31**
  Gemini 8, **Mar 16**
  Gemini 12, **Nov 11**
Year 11 (1967),
  Surveyor 3, **Apr 17**
  Venera 4, **June 12**
  Mariner 5, **June 14**{f1
Year 12 (1968),
  OGO 5, **Mar 4**
  Soyuz 3, **Oct 26**
  Apollo 8, **Dec 21**
Year 13 (1969),
  Soyuz 4, **Jan 14**
  Apollo 10, **May 18**
  Apollo 11, **July 16**
  Moon Day, **July 20**
  Apollo 12, **Nov 14**
Year 14 (1970),
  Osumi, **Feb 11**
  Apollo 13, **Apr 11**
  China 1, **Apr 24**
  Space Rescue Agreement, **Oct 28**
  Luna 17, **Nov 10**
Year 15 (1971),
  Apollo 14, **Jan 31**
  Salyut, **Apr 19**
  Soyuz 10, **Apr 23**
  Mars 2 and Mars 3, **May 19**
  Mariner 9, **May 30**
  Soyuz 11, **June 6**
  Apollo 15, **July 26**
  Intelsat 4 F-3, **Dec 19**
Year 16 (1972),
  Pioneer 10, **Mar 2**
  Venera 8, **Mar 27**
  Apollo 16, **Apr 16**
  Copernicus OAO 4, **Apr 21**
  Apollo 17, **Dec**{Nbs}7
Year 17 (1973),
  Skylab, **May 14**
  Skylab 2, **May 25**
  Skylab 3, **July 28**
  Intelsat-4 F-7, **Aug 23**
  Soyuz 12, **Sept 27**
  Skylab 4, **Nov 16**
Year 19 (1975),
  Soyuz 17, **Jan 10**
  Venera 9 and 10, **June 8**
  Apollo-Soyuz Test Project, **July 17**
  Viking 1 and 2, **Aug 20**
Year 20 (1976),
  Soyuz 21, **July 6**
Year 21 (1977),
  Cosmos 954 Falls, **Jan 24**
  Enterprise, **Aug 12**
  Voyager 2, **Aug 20**
  Voyager 1, **Sept 5**
  Salyut 6, **Sept 29**
  Soyuz 26, **Dec 10**
Year 22 (1978),
  Soyuz 27, **Jan 10**
  Soyuz 28, **Mar 2**
  Pioneer Venus 1, **May 20**
  Pioneer Venus, **Aug 8**
  Soyuz 31, **Aug 26**
Year 23 (1979),
  Soyuz 32, **Feb 25**
  Skylab Falls to Earth, **July 11**
Year 24 (1980),
  SMM, **Feb 14**
  Soyuz 35, **Apr 9**
  Soyuz T-2, **June 5**
  Rohini, **July 18**
  Soyuz 37, **July 23**
  Soyuz 38, **Sept 18**
  Soyuz T-3, **Nov 27**
Year 25 (1981),
  Columbia STS-1, **Apr 12**
  Ariane, **June 19**
  Columbia STS-2, **Nov 12**
Year 26 (1982),
  Salyut 7, **Apr 19**
  Kosmos 1383, **July 1**
  Soyuz T-7, **Aug 19**
  Columbia STS-5, **Nov 11**
Year 27 (1983),
  NOAA 8, **Mar 28**
  Challenger STS-6, **Apr 4**
  Challenger STS-7, **June 18**
  Challenger STS-8, **Aug 30**
  Columbia STS-9, **Nov 28**
Year 28 (1984),
  Challenger STS-10, **Feb 3**
  Soyuz T-12, **July 17**
  Discovery, **Aug 30**
  Challenger STS 41-G, **Oct 5**
  Vega 1, **Dec 15**

Year 29 (1985),
  Discovery, **Jan 24**
  Arabsat-1, **Feb 8**
  Brasilsat 1, **Feb 8**
  Discovery, {fe}Apr 12
  Challenger STS 51-B, **Apr 29**
Year 30 (1986),
  Mir Space Station, **Feb 20**
  Titan 34-D, **Apr 18**
  Delta 3914 Rocket Failure, **May 3**
Year 31 (1987),
  Soyuz TM-3, **July 22**
  Ariane-3, **Sept 15**
Year 32 (1988),
  Phobos 2, **July 12**
  Discovery, **Sept 29**
  Buran, **Nov 15**
Year 33 (1989),
  Atlantis, **May 4**
  Voyager 2, **Aug 24**
Year 34 (1990),
  Hubble Space Telescope, **Apr 25**
  First Soviet Commercial Satellite, **Feb 11**
Year 36 (1992),
  Endeavour, **May 13**
Year 39 (1995),
  Atlantis Docks with Mir, **June 29**
  Record Time, **Mar 22**
  Galileo, **Dec 7**
Year 41 (1997),
  Mars Pathfinder, **July 4**
  Mars Global Surveyor, **Sept 11**
  Cassini, **Oct 15**
Year 42 (1998),
  Lunar Explorer, **Jan 6**
  Columbia Neurolab, **Apr 17**
  Nozomi, **July 4**
  Discovery: Oldest Man in Space, **Oct 29**
  International Space Station Launch, **Dec 4**
Year 43 (1999),
  Stardust, **Feb 7**
  Columbia: First Female Commander, **July 23**
Year 44 (2000),
  Endeavour Mapping Mission, **Feb 11**
  100th Space Shuttle Flight, **Oct 11**
  ISS Inhabited, **Nov 2**
Year 45 (2001),
  100th Spacewalk, **Feb 14**
  Mir Abandoned, **Mar 23**
  Mars Odyssey, **Apr 7**
  First Tourist in Space, **Apr 28**
Spacek, Sissy: Birth, Dec 25
Spacey, Kevin: Birth, Jul 26
Spade, David: Birth, Jul 22
Spader, James: Birth, Feb 7
Spahn, Warren: Birth, Apr 23
Spain,
  Book Day and Lover's Day, **Apr 23**
  Canary Islands Plane Disaster: Anniv, **Mar 27**
  Civil War Begins: Anniv, **Jul 18**
  Constitution Day, **Dec 6**
  Fiesta de Las Fallas (Valencia), **Mar 12**
  La Tomatina, **Aug 25**
  National Holiday, **Oct 12**
  Running of the Bulls, **Jul 7**
  Saint James Day, **Jul 25**
  San Sebastian Jazz Fest, **Jul 22**
  Spain Captures Granada: Anniv, **Jan 2**
Spanish Flu: Pandemic of 1918 Hits US: Anniv, Mar 11
Spanish-American War,
  Maine Memorial Day, **Feb 15**
  Matanzas Mule Day, **Apr 27**
  Remember the Maine Day, **Feb 15**
  Spanish-American War: Surrender of Guam to US: Anniv, **Jun 20**
  Treaty of Paris Signed: Anniv, **Dec 10**
Spank Out Day USA, Apr 30
Spano, Vincent: Birth, Oct 18
Spassky, Boris: Birth, Jan 30
Spay Day USA, Feb 24
Speak Up and Succeed Day, Natl, Jan 27
Spears, Britney: Birth, Dec 2
Special Olympics Connecticut 2004 Summer Games (New Haven, CT), Jun 11
Special Olympics Day, Jul 20
Special Olympics Winter Games (McHenry, MD), Feb 22
Special Recreation Day, Jul 4
Specter, Arlen: Birth, Feb 12
Spector, Phil: Birth, Dec 26
Speech Month, Better Hearing and, May 1
Speech-Language-Hearing Conv, American (Philadelphia, PA), Nov 15
Spelling, Aaron: Birth, Apr 22
Spelling, Tori: Birth, May 16
Spelman College Established: Anniv, Apr 11
Spelvin, George: Day, Nov 15
Spencer, John: Birth, Dec 20
Spengler, Oswald: Birth Anniv, May 29
Spielberg, Steven: Birth, Dec 18
Spillane, Mickey: Birth, May 9
Spina Bifida Awareness Month, Natl, Oct 1
Spinach Lovers Month, Oct 1
Spinal Cord Injury Awareness Month, Natl, Sep 1

Spinal Health Month, Natl, Oct 1
Spinal Muscular Atrophy Awareness Month, Aug 1
Spinks, Leon: Birth, Jul 11
Spinks, Michael: Birth, Jul 13
Spinning and Weaving Week, Oct 4
Spinoza, Baruch: Birth Anniv, Nov 24
Spirit of America (Decatur, AL), Jul 3
Spirit of Freedom Celebration (Florence, AL), Jul 4
Spirit of Wovoka Days Powwow (Yerington, NV), May 28
Spiritual Teachers Month, Feb 1
Spiritual Wellness Month, Mar 1
Spitz, Mark: Birth, Feb 10
Splinterfest (Amana, IA), Jun 18
Splurge Day, Natl, Jun 18
Spock, Benjamin: Birth Anniv, May 2
Spoleto Festival USA (Charleston, SC), May 28
Spoon River Valley Scenic Drive (Lewistown, IL), Oct 2
Spoon River Valley: Knox County Scenic Dr (Galesburg, IL), Oct 2
Spooner, William: Birth Anniv, Jul 22
Spooner's Day, Jul 22
Sporting Goods Assn Mgmt Conf, Natl (Hilton Head Island, SC), May 16
Sports America Kids Month, Jun 1
Sports Eye Safety Month, Apr 1
Sports Show, Milwaukee Journal Sentinel (Milwaukee, WI), Mar 12
Sports, Physical Fitness and, Month, Natl, May 1
Sportsmen's Show, Quebec City (Quebec City, QC, Canada), Mar 11
Sportsmen's Show, Toronto (Toronto, ON, Canada), Mar 17
Spradlin, G.D.: Birth, Aug 31
Sprewell, Latrell: Birth, Sep 8
Spring Begins, Mar 20
Spring Fest, Towsontown (Towson, MD), May 1
Spring Fever Week, Natl, Mar 14
Spring Fling (Wichita Falls, TX), Apr 24
Spring Gala (Lovington, NM), May 1
Spring Pilgrimage to Antebellum Homes (Columbus, MS), Mar 30
Spring Suwannee River Jubilee (Live Oak, FL), Jul 7
Spring, Halfway Point, May 5
Springer, Jerry: Birth, Feb 13
Springfield, Rick: Birth, Aug 23
Springs Folk Fest (Springs, PA), Oct 1
Springsteen, Bruce: Birth, Sep 23
Spruce Goose Flight: Anniv, Nov 2
Spurrier, Steve: Birth, Apr 20
Squirrel Appreciation Day, Jan 21
Squirrel Awareness Week, Oct 3
Sri Lanka,
  Independence Day, Feb 4
  Natl Heroes Day, May 22
  Sinhala and Tamil New Year, Apr 13
St. John, Jill: Birth, Aug 19
St. Laurent, Louis Stephen: Birth Anniv, Feb 1
Stabenow, Debbie: Birth, Apr 29
Stackhouse, Jerry: Birth, Nov 5
Stade, Frederica von: Birth, Jun 1
Stage Days, Butterfield Overland (Benson, AZ), Oct 8
Stagecoach Days (Marshall, TX), May 15
Stagg, Amos Alonzo: Birth Anniv, Aug 16
Stahl, Lesley: Birth, Dec 16
Staley, Dawn: Birth, May 4
Stalin, Joseph: Birth Anniv, Dec 21
Stalingrad, German Surrender at: Anniv, Feb 2
Stallone, Sylvester: Birth, Jul 6
Stamos, John: Birth, Aug 19
Stamp, Terence: Birth, Jul 22
Stamps,
  Nevadapex Coin and Stamp Expo (Laughlin, NV), Jan 2
  Postage Stamps, First US: Anniv, Jul 1
  Stamp & Coin Expo (New York, NY), Apr 23
  Stamp Collecting Month, Natl, Oct 1
  Stamp Expo (Anaheim, CA), May 14
  Stamp Expo (Anaheim, CA), Sep 10
  Stamp Expo (Los Angeles, CA), Apr 2
  Stamp Expo (Pasadena, CA), May 21
  Stamp Expo (Pasadena, CA), Feb 20
  Stamp Expo (Pasadena, CA), Jul 2
  Stamp Expo (Sherman Oaks, CA), Jun 18
  Stamp Expo America (Anaheim, CA), Nov 12
  Stamp Expo USA (Anaheim, CA), Feb 13
  Stamp Expo: Anaheim (Anaheim, CA), Oct 1
  Stamp Expo: California (Pasadena, CA), Nov 19
  Stamp Expo: South (Anaheim, CA), Apr 16
Standard Time Act, US: Anniv, Mar 19
Stanhope, Philip D.: Birth Anniv, Sep 22
Stanley Finds Livingstone: Anniv, Nov 10
Stanley, Henry Morton: Birth Anniv, Jan 28
Stanton, Elizabeth Cady: Birth Anniv, Nov 12
Stanton, Harry Dean: Birth, Jul 14
Stanwyck, Barbara: Birth Anniv, Jul 16
Stapleton, Jean: Birth, Jan 19
Stapleton, Maureen: Birth, Jun 21
Star Fest (Tanabata) (Japan), Jul 7
Star Trek TV Premiere: Anniv, Sep 8
Star Wars Released: Anniv, May 25
Stark, USS Attack: Anniv, May 17
Starker, Janos: Birth, Jul 5
Starman Family-Con 2004 (Hollywood, CA), Apr 23

738

☆ Chase's 2004 Calendar of Events ☆ Index

Starman Month, Intl, Oct 1
Starr, Bart: Birth, Jan 9
Starr, Ringo: Birth, Jul 7
Stars and Stripes Forever Day, May 14
Star-Spangled Banner Inspired: Anniv, Sep 13
State Dept Founded, US: Anniv, Jul 27
State Fairs. See Agriculture, Feb 5
Stationery Show, Natl (New York, NY), May 16
Statue of Liberty: Dedication Anniv, Oct 28
Staub, Rusty: Birth, Apr 1
Staubach, Roger: Birth, Feb 5
Stay Home Because You're Well Day, Nov 30
Stay Home With Your Kids Day, Aug 16
Stay Out of the Sun Day, Jul 3
Stealth Bomber Flight: Anniv, Jul 17
Steel Mills, Fed Govt Seizure: Anniv, Apr 8
Steel, Danielle: Birth, Aug 14
Steele, Tommy: Birth, Dec 17
Steenburgen, Mary: Birth, Feb 8
Steeplechase at Callaway Gardens (Pine Mountain, GA), Nov 6
Steichen, Edward: Birth Anniv, Mar 27
Steiger, Rod: Birth Anniv, Apr 17
Stein, Ben: Birth, Nov 25
Stein, Gertrude: Birth Anniv, Feb 3
Steinberg, David: Birth, Aug 9
Steinbrenner, George: Birth, Jul 4
Steinem, Gloria: Birth, Mar 25
Stella, Frank: Birth, May 12
Stendhal: Birth Anniv, Jan 23
Stengel, Casey: Birth Anniv, Jul 30
Stephens, James: Birth, May 18
Stephenson, George: Birth Anniv, Jun 9
Stephenson, Jan: Birth, Dec 22
Stepmothers Day, May 1
Stepparents' Week, Jun 1
Sterling Renaissance Fest (Sterling, NY), Jul 3
Stern, Daniel: Birth, Aug 28
Stern, Howard: Birth, Jan 12
Stern, Howard: Radio Show Premiere: Anniv, Nov 18
Sterne, Laurence: Birth Anniv, Nov 24
Sternhagen, Frances: Birth, Jan 13
Sternwheel Fest, Ohio River (Marietta, OH), Sep 10
Steve Allen Show TV Premiere: Anniv, Dec 25
Stevens, Cat: Birth, Jul 21
Stevens, Connie: Birth, Aug 8
Stevens, Fisher: Birth, Nov 27
Stevens, John Paul: Birth, Apr 20
Stevens, Stella: Birth, Oct 1
Stevens, Ted: Birth, Nov 18
Stevenson, Adlai: Birth Anniv, Oct 23
Stevenson, Adlai: Birth Anniv, Feb 5
Stevenson, Alexandra: Birth, Dec 15
Stevenson, Parker: Birth, Jun 4
Stevenson, Robert Louis: Birth Anniv, Nov 13
Stewart, Don: Birth, Nov 14
Stewart, Earnie: Birth, Mar 28
Stewart, French: Birth, Feb 20
Stewart, Jackie: Birth, Jun 11
Stewart, Jimmy, Relay Marathon (Los Angeles, CA), Apr 18
Stewart, Jimmy: Birth Anniv, May 20
Stewart, Jon: Birth, Nov 28
Stewart, Kordell: Birth, Oct 16
Stewart, Martha: Birth, Aug 3
Stewart, Patrick: Birth, Jul 13
Stewart, Potter: Birth Anniv, Jan 23
Stewart, Rod: Birth, Jan 10
Stiers, David Ogden: Birth, Oct 31
Stiles, Julia: Birth, Mar 28
Stiles, Ryan: Birth, Apr 22
Still Need To Do Day, Dec 29
Still, Valerie: Birth, May 14
Stiller, Ben: Birth, Nov 30
Stiller, Jerry: Birth, Jun 8
Stills, Stephen: Birth, Jan 3
Stine, R.L.: Birth, Oct 8
Sting (Gordon Sumner): Birth, Oct 2
Stipe, Michael: Birth, Jan 4
Stock Exchange Holiday, Jan 1
Stock Exchange Holiday, Jan 19
Stock Exchange Holiday, Feb 16
Stock Exchange Holiday, Apr 9
Stock Exchange Holiday, May 31
Stock Exchange Holiday, Jul 5
Stock Exchange Holiday, Sep 6
Stock Exchange Holiday, Nov 25
Stock Exchange Holiday, Dec 24
Stock Exchange, NY, Established: Anniv, May 17
Stock Market Crash of 1929: Anniv, Oct 29
Stock Market Crash of 1893: Anniv, May 5
Stock Market Panic: Anniv, Oct 24
Stockholm Syndrome Bank Robbery: Anniv, Aug 23
Stockings, Nylon: Anniv, May 15
Stocks: Dow-Jones Biggest Drop: Anniv, Oct 19
Stocks: Dow-Jones Industrial Average: Anniv, Oct 7
Stocks: Dow-Jones Tops 1,000: Anniv, Nov 14
Stocks: Dow-Jones Tops 5,000: Anniv, Nov 21
Stocks: Dow-Jones Tops 10,000: Anniv, Mar 29
Stocks: Dow-Jones Tops 11,000: Anniv, May 3
Stockton, David: Birth, Nov 2
Stockton, John: Birth, Mar 26
Stockton, Richard: Birth Anniv, Oct 1
Stockwell, Dean: Birth, Mar 5
Stockwell, John: Birth, Mar 25
Stojakovic, Peja: Birth, Jun 9

Stojko, Elvis: Birth, Mar 22
Stokes, Carl: Becomes First Black Mayor in US: Anniv, Nov 13
Stoltz, Eric: Birth, Sep 30
Stone, Dee Wallace: Birth, Dec 14
Stone, Harlan Fiske: Birth Anniv, Oct 11
Stone, Lucy, Married: Anniv, May 1
Stone, Lucy: Birth Anniv, Aug 13
Stone, Oliver: Birth, Sep 15
Stone, Sharon: Birth, Mar 10
Stone, Sly: Birth, Mar 15
Stone, Steve: Birth, Jul 14
Stone, Thomas: Death Anniv, Oct 5
Stonewall Riot: Anniv, Jun 28
Stookey, Noel Paul: Birth, Nov 30
Stoppard, Tom: Birth, Jul 3
Storey, David: Birth, Jul 13
Stories Day, Apr 21
Storm, Gale: Birth, Apr 5
Story, Joseph: Birth Anniv, Sep 18
Storytelling,
    Connecticut Storytelling Fest (New London, CT), Apr 23
    Corn Island Storytelling Fest (Louisville, KY), Sep 16
    Ghost Tales Around the Campfire (Washington, MS), Oct 29
    Iowa Storytelling Fest (Clear Lake, IA), Jul 23
    Michigan Storytellers Fest (Flint, MI), Jul 8
    New England Conference on Storytelling for Children (Keene, NH), Apr 17
    Smoky Mountains Storytelling Fest (Pigeon Forge, TN), Feb 5
    Storyteller of the Year Contest, Natl (Millersport, OH), Sep 18
    Storytelling Fest, Natl (Jonesborough, TN), Oct 1
    Storytelling Historical Walk Around Washington (Washington, PA), May 15
Stotz, Carl E.: Birth Anniv, Feb 20
Stoudamire, Damon: Birth, Sep 3
Stowe, Harriet Beecher: Birth Anniv, Jun 14
Stowe, Madeleine: Birth, Aug 18
Stradivari, Antonio: Death Anniv, Dec 18
Strait, George: Birth, May 18
Straith, Claire: Birth Anniv, Aug 30
Strang, James Jesse: Birth Anniv, Mar 21
Strange, Curtis: Birth, Jan 30
Strassman, Marcia: Birth, Apr 28
Strategic Planning Month, Intl, Oct 1
Strategic Thinking Month, Intl, Sep 1
Stratemeyer, Edward L.: Birth Anniv, Oct 4
Strathairn, David: Birth, Jan 26
Stratton, Dorothy C.: Birth Anniv, Mar 24
Strauss, Levi: Birth Anniv, Feb 26
Strauss, Peter: Birth, Feb 20
Strauss, Richard G.: Birth Anniv, Jun 11
Stravinsky, Igor F.: Birth Anniv, Jun 17
Straw Hat Month, Apr 1
Strawberry Fest (Independence, MO), Jun 5
Strawberry Fest, Poteet (Poteet, TX), Apr 2
Strawberry Fest/Hillsborough County Fair (Plant City, FL), Feb 26
Strawberry Hill Races (Richmond, VA), Apr 10
Strawberry, Darryl: Birth, Mar 12
Streep, Meryl: Birth, Jun 22
Street Machine Fall Nationals (Springfield, MO), Sep 17
Street, Picabo: Birth, Apr 3
Streeter, Ruth Cheney: Birth Anniv, Oct 2
Streisand, Barbra: Birth, Apr 24
Stresa Music Weeks (Stresa, Italy), Aug 20
Stress Awareness Day, Natl, Apr 16
Stress Awareness Month, Apr 1
Stress-Free Family Holidays Month, Natl, Dec 1
Strickland, Rod: Birth, Jul 11
Strike It Rich TV Premiere: Anniv, May 7
Strindberg, August: Birth Anniv, Jan 22
Stringfield, Sherry: Birth, Jun 24
Stritch, Elaine: Birth, Feb 2
Stroke Awareness Month, Natl, May 1
Strokes Day, Strike Out, May 1
Strong, Rider: Birth, Dec 11
Stroud, Don: Birth, Sep 1
Strug, Kerri: Birth, Nov 19
Struthers, Sally: Birth, Jul 28
Stuart, Gilbert: Birth Anniv, Dec 3
Student Government Day (MA), Apr 2
Student Safety Month, Jun 1
Students' Memorial Day, Kent State, May 4
Sturges, John: Birth Anniv, Jan 3
Sturgis Rally and Races, Aug 9
Stuttering Awareness Day, Intl, Oct 22
Stuttering Awareness Week, Natl, May 9
Styron, William: Birth, Jun 11
Subliminal Communications Month, Sep 1
Submarine: First Nuclear-Powered Voyage: Anniv, Jan 17
Substitute Teacher Appreciation Week, Sep 13
Subway Accident, New York: Anniv, Nov 2
Subway, New York City: Subway Anniv, Oct 27
Succoth, Sep 30
Suchet, David: Birth, May 2
Sudan,
    Independence Day, Jan 1
    Revolution Day, Jun 30
Sudden Infant Death Syndrome Awareness Month, Natl, Oct 1

Suez Canal Formal Opening: Anniv, Nov 17
Suez Canal Opens: Anniv, Mar 7
Suez Canal: Evacuation Day (Egypt), Jun 18
Suffrage Parade Attacked, Woman: Anniv, Mar 3
Sugar Bowl, Nokia (New Orleans, LA), Jan 1
Suicide Awareness Week, Natl, May 2
Sukkot, Sep 30
Sukkot Begins, Sep 29
Sullivan, Anne: Birth Anniv, Apr 14
Sullivan, Arthur: Birth Anniv, May 13
Sullivan, Ed: Birth Anniv, Sep 28
Sullivan, Erik Per: Birth, Jul 12
Sullivan, Susan: Birth, Nov 18
Sully, Thomas: Birth Anniv, Jun 19
Sultana Explosion: Anniv, Apr 27
Sulzberger, Arthur O.: Birth, Sep 22
Sumac, Yma: Birth, Sep 10
Summer Arrival: Martin Z. Mollusk Day (Ocean City, NJ), May 6
Summer Begins, Jun 20
Summer Daylight-Saving Time (Europe), Mar 28
Summer Farm Toy Show (Dyersville, IA), Jun 11
Summer Market Fair, Eighteenth-Century (McLean, VA), Jul 17
Summer Music Fest (Sitka, AK), Jun 4
Summer Time (United Kingdom), Mar 29
Summer, Donna: Birth, Dec 31
Summer, Halfway Point, Aug 6
Summerfest (Milwaukee, WI), Jun 24
Summers, Lawrence: Birth, Nov 30
Summitt, Patricia (Pat): Birth, Jun 14
Sumner, Gordon (Sting): Birth, Oct 2
Sun Bowl (El Paso, TX), Dec 31
Sun Yat-Sen: Birth Anniv, Nov 12
Sun Yat-Sen: Death Anniv, Mar 12
Sundance Film Festival (Park City, UT), Jan 15
Sunday Architrek Tours (Oak Park, IL), Apr 4
Sunday School Teacher Appreciation Day, Oct 17
Sunday, Intl Sit-on-the-Front-Pew, Jun 27
Sununu, John: Birth, Sep 10
Super Bowl (Houston, TX), Feb 1
Super Bowl, First: Anniv, Jan 15
Superman Celebration (Metropolis, IL), Jun 10
Supreme Court,
    Abortion Notification Ruling: Anniv, Jun 25
    Bans School Prayer: Anniv, Jun 25
    Brown v Board of Education: Anniv, May 17
    Dred Scott Decision: Anniv, Mar 6
    First Session of: Anniv, Feb 1
    First Woman Justice: Anniv, Sep 25
    Loving v Virginia: Anniv, Jun 12
    Miranda Decision: Anniv, Jun 13
    Roe v Wade Decision: Anniv, Jan 22
    Rules for Bush: Anniv, Dec 12
    Strikes Down Connecticut Law Banning Contraception: Anniv, Jun 7
    Term Begins, Oct 4
    Thurgood Marshall Resigns: Anniv, Jun 27
    Upholds Ban on Abortion Counseling: Anniv, May 23
    Upholds Right to Die: Anniv, Jun 25
    Woman Presides Over: Anniv, Apr 3
Surfing,
    East Coast Surfing Chmpshps/Sports Fest (Virginia Beach, VA), Aug 25
    Kahanamoku, Duke: Birth Anniv, Aug 24
    New England Mid-winter (Narragansett, RI), Feb 21
    Triple Crown of (Oahu, HI), Nov 9
Suriname,
    Independence Day, Nov 25
    Liberation Day, Jul 1
Surratt, Mary: Lincoln Assassination Conspirators Hanging, Jul 7
Survivor TV Premiere: Anniv, May 31
Susskind, David: Birth Anniv, Dec 19
Sutcliffe, Rick: Birth, Jun 21
Sutherland, Donald: Birth, Jul 17
Sutherland, Joan: Birth, Nov 7
Sutherland, Kiefer: Birth, Dec 18
Sutter, John A.: Birth Anniv, Feb 15
Suvari, Mena: Birth, Feb 9
Suzman, Janet: Birth, Feb 9
Suzuki, Ichiro: Birth, Oct 22
Svenson, Bo: Birth, Feb 13
Swallows Depart from San Juan Capistrano (CA), Oct 23
Swallows Return to San Juan Capistrano (CA), Mar 19
Swank, Hilary: Birth, Jul 30
Swanson, Gloria: Birth Anniv, Mar 27
Swanson, Kristy: Birth, Dec 19
Swap Ideas Day, Sep 10
Swappin' Meetin' (Cumberland, KY), Oct 1
Swayze, Patrick: Birth, Aug 18
Swaziland,
    Independence Day, Sep 6
    King's Birthday, Apr 19
    Natl Flag Day, Apr 25
Sweat, Keith: Birth, Jul 22
Sweden,
    All Saints' Day, Nov 6
    Crayfish Premiere, Aug 11
    Feast of Valborg, Apr 30
    Flag Day, Jun 6
    Gustavus Adolphus Day, Nov 6
    Linnaeus Day (Stenbrohult), May 23
    Midsummer, Jun 23

739

Index ☆ Chase's 2004 Calendar of Events ☆

Sweden (cont'd)—Television

Nobel Prize Awards Ceremony (Stockholm), Dec 10
Saint Knut's Day, Jan 13
Saint Martin's Day, Nov 11
Santa Lucia Day, Dec 13
Sour Herring Premiere, Aug 19
Swedenborg, Emanuel: Birth Anniv, Jan 29
Swedish Language and Culture Day Camp (Cambridge, MN), Aug 23
Sweeney, D.B.: Birth, Nov 14
Sweetcorn Fest, Natl (Hoopeston, IL), Sep 2
Sweetest Day, Oct 16
Swift, Jonathan: Birth Anniv, Nov 30
Swimming and Diving,
Big 12 Men's & Women's Swimming Chmpshp (Austin, TX), Feb 25
Big Ten Men's Swimming/Diving Chmpshp (West Lafayette, IN), Feb 26
Columbia River Cross Channel Swim (Hood River, OR), Sep 1
First Woman Swims English Channel: Anniv, Aug 6
Kahanamoku, Duke: Birth Anniv, Aug 24
NAIA Natl Men's and Women's Swimming and Diving Chmpshps (Lawrence, KS), Mar 3
NCAA Men's Div I Swimming/Diving Chmpshps (East Meadow, NY), Mar 25
NCAA Women's Div I Swimming/Diving Chmpshps (College Station, TX), Mar 18
Penguin Plunge (Jamestown, RI), Jan 1
Polar Bear Swim (Nome, AK), Jun 21
Polar Bear Swim (Sheboyan, WI), Jan 1
Swimming School Opens, First US, Jul 23
Waikiki Roughwater Swim (Honolulu, HI), Sep 6
Weissmuller, Johnny: Birth Anniv, Jun 2
Women's Big Ten Swimming/Diving Chmpshps (Minneapolis, MN), Feb 18
Swiss Fest, Ohio (Sugarcreek, OH), Oct 1
Swit, Loretta: Birth, Nov 4
Switzerland,
Berchtoldstag, Jan 2
Chalandra Marz, Mar 1
Confederation Day, Aug 1
Dornach Battle Commemoration, Jul 25
Egg Races, Apr 12
Homstrom (Scuol), Feb 1
Lucerne Fest, Ostern (Lucerne), Mar 27
Lucerne Fest, Sommer (Lucerne), Aug 13
Lucerne Festival, Piano, Nov 23
Martinmas Goose, Nov 11
Meitlisunntig, Jan 11
Morat Battle: Anniv, Jun 22
Nafels Pilgrimage (Canton Glarus), Apr 1
Onion Market (Zibelemarit), Nov 22
Pacing the Bounds (Liestal), May 17
Saint Gotthard Auto Tunnel Opened, Sep 5
Sempach Battle Commemoration, Jul 5
Swoopes, Sheryl: Birth, Mar 25
Synergy Week Intl, Nov 7
Synge, John M.: Birth Anniv, Apr 16
Syrian Arab Republic,
Independence Day, Apr 17
Revolution Day, Mar 8
Szold, Henrietta: Birth Anniv, Dec 21
T, Mr: Birth, May 21
Ta'anit Esther (Fast of Esther), Mar 4
Tabaski: See Eid-al-Adha, Feb 1
Tabei, Junko: Birth, Sep 22
Tabei, Junko: First Woman To Climb Mount Everest, May 16
Tabernacles, Feast of: First Day, Sep 30
Table Manners Wk, Intl, Feb 8
Tabori, Kristoffer: Birth, Aug 4
Taco Day, Chuy's Natl, Jun 8
Tacoma Holiday Food and Gift Fest (Tacoma, WA), Oct 20
Taft, Bob: Birth, Jan 8
Taft, Helen Herron: Birth Anniv, Jan 2
Taft, William H.: Birth Anniv, Sep 15
Taft, William: Opens Baseball Season: Anniv, Apr 14
Tagore, Rabindranath: Birth Anniv, May 6
Tailors Day, Natl, Jun 2
Taiwan,
Birthday of Cheng Huang, Jun 30
Birthday of Kuan Yin, Goddess of Mercy, Mar 9
Cheng Cheng Kung Landing Day, Apr 29
Chiang Kai-Shek Day, Oct 31
Confucius's Birthday and Teachers' Day, Sep 28
Constitution Day, Dec 25
Double Tenth Day, Oct 10
Expelled from UN: Anniv, Oct 25
Foundation Days, Jan 1
Overseas Chinese Day, Oct 21
Retrocession Day, Oct 25
Tomb-Sweeping Day, Natl, Apr 5
Youth Day, Mar 29
Tajikistan: Independence Day, Sep 9
Take a Smart Risk Week, May 2
Take Back Your Time Week, Natl, Jan 26
Take Charge of Change Week, Jul 11
Take Our Daughters and Sons to Work Day, Apr 22
Take Your Houseplants for a Walk Day, Jul 27
Take Your Webmaster to Lunch Day, Jul 6
Talent Scouts TV Premiere: Anniv, Dec 6
Talent, Jim: Birth, Oct 18
Tales of Wells Fargo TV Premiere: Anniv, Mar 18
Talese, Gay: Birth, Feb 7
Talk Like a Pirate Day, Sep 19
Talk With Your Teen About Sex Month, Natl, Mar 1
Tall Timber Days Fest (Grand Rapids, MN), Aug 7
Tallchief, Maria: Birth, Jan 24
Tamale Fiesta (El Centro, CA), Dec 4
Tamarack Time (Bigfork, MT), Oct 16
Tamblyn, Russ: Birth, Dec 30
Tambor, Jeffrey: Birth, Jul 8
Tammuz, Fast of, Jul 6
Tan, Amy: Birth, Feb 19
Taney, Roger B.: Birth Anniv, Mar 17
Tanner, Henry Ossawa: Birth Anniv, Jun 21
Tanzania,
Farmers' Day, Aug 8
Independence and Republic Day, Dec 9
Saba Saba Day, Jul 7
Union Day, Apr 26
Zanzibar Revolution Day, Jan 12
Tap Dance Day, Natl, May 25
Tarantino, Quentin: Birth, Mar 27
Tarbell, Ida M.: Birth Anniv, Nov 5
Tarkenton, Fran: Birth, Feb 3
Tarkington, Booth: Birth Anniv, Jul 29
Tartan Day, Apr 6
Tarzan TV Premiere: Anniv, Sep 8
Tasso, Torquato: Birth Anniv, Mar 11
Tattoo, Nova Scotia Intl (Halifax, NS, Canada), Jun 29
Taurus Begins, Apr 20
Tax Freedom Day, May 3
Tax, Income, Pay Day, Apr 15
Taylor, Billy: Birth, Jul 24
Taylor, Delores: Birth, Sep 27
Taylor, Elizabeth: Birth, Feb 27
Taylor, George: Death Anniv, Feb 23
Taylor, Holland: Birth, Jan 14
Taylor, James: Birth, Mar 12
Taylor, Lawrence: Birth, Feb 4
Taylor, Lili: Birth, Feb 20
Taylor, Lucy Hobbs: Birth Anniv, Mar 14
Taylor, Margaret S.: Birth Anniv, Sep 21
Taylor, Meshach: Birth, Apr 11
Taylor, Paul: Birth, Jul 29
Taylor, Renee: Birth, Mar 19
Taylor, Rod: Birth, Jan 11
Taylor, Zachary: Birth Anniv, Nov 24
Taylor-Young, Leigh: Birth, Jan 25
Tchaikovsky, Peter Ilich: Birth Anniv, May 7
Tea Month, Natl Hot, Jan 1
Tea Party Fest, Chestertown (Chestertown, MD), May 29
Teach Children to Save Day, Natl, Apr 22
Teacher Appreciation Week, May 2
Teacher Appreciation Week, Natl PTA, May 3
Teacher Day, Natl, May 4
Teacher's Day in Florida, May 21
Teachers' Day, Confucius's Birthday and (Taiwan), Sep 28
Teachers' Day, World (UN), Oct 5
Tebaldi, Renata: Birth, Jan 2
Technology Day, Trial, Jun 4
Tecumseh: Death Anniv, Oct 5
Tecumseh: Epic Outdoor Drama (Chillicothe, OH), Jun 11
Ted Mack's Original Amateur Hour TV Premiere: Anniv, Jan 18
Teddy Bear and Doll Classic, American Club (Kohler, WI), Feb 21
Teddy Bear Day, Natl American, Nov 14
Teddy Bear Rally, Amherst's (Amherst, MA), Aug 7
Teddy Bear to Work and School Day, Natl Bring Your, Oct 13
Teen Day, May 1
Teen Read Week, Oct 17
Teflon Invented: Anniv, Apr 6
Teicher, Louis: Birth, Aug 24
Teilhard De Chardin, Pierre: Birth Anniv, May 1
Telecommunication Day, World (UN), May 17
Telecommuter Appreciation Week, Feb 1
Telegram, Singing: Anniv, Jul 28
Telegraph Line, Morse Opens First US: Anniv, May 24
Telegraph, Atlantic Cable Laid: Anniv, Jul 27
Telephone,
Area Codes Introduced: Anniv, Nov 10
AT&T Divestiture: Anniv, Jan 8
Bell, Alexander Graham: Birth Anniv, Mar 3
First Telephone Operator: Emma M. Nutt Day, Sep 1
Inane Answering Message Day, Jan 30
Invention: Anniv, Mar 10
On-Hold Month, Natl, Mar 1
Push-Button Debuts: Anniv, Nov 18
Television,
Abbott and Costello Show TV Premiere: Anniv, Dec 5
Addams Family Premiere: Anniv, Sep 18
Adventures of Ellery Queen Premiere: Anniv, Oct 14
Alfred Hitchcock Presents Premiere: Anniv, Oct 2
Alice Premiere: Anniv, Aug 31
All in the Family Premiere: Anniv, Jan 12
All My Children Premiere: Anniv, Jan 5
Alvin Show Premiere: Anniv, Oct 4
American Bandstand Premiere: Anniv, Aug 5
American Idol Premiere: Anniv, Jun 11
Amos 'n' Andy Premiere: Anniv, Jun 28
Andy Griffith Show TV Premiere: Anniv, Oct 3
Andy Williams Show Premiere: Anniv, Jul 2
Another World Premiere: Anniv, May 4
Arsenio Hall Show Premiere: Anniv, Jan 3
Art Linkletter's House Party Premiere: Anniv, Sep 1
Arthur Murray Party Premiere: Anniv, Jul 20
As The World Turns Premiere: Anniv, Apr 2
Bachelor Father Premiere: Anniv, Sep 15
Ball, Lucille: Birth Anniv, Aug 6
Baretta Premiere: Anniv, Jan 17
Barnaby Jones Premiere: Anniv, Jan 28
Barney & Friends Premiere: Anniv, Apr 6
Barney Miller Premiere: Anniv, Jan 23
Batman Premiere: Anniv, Jan 12
Baywatch Premiere: Anniv, Apr 23
Beat the Clock Premiere: Anniv, Mar 23
Beauty and the Beast Premiere: Anniv, Sep 25
Believe It or Not Premiere: Anniv, Mar 1
Bell Telephone Hour Premiere: Anniv, Jan 12
Benson Premiere: Anniv, Sep 13
Beverly Hillbillies Premiere: Anniv, Sep 26
Bewitched Premiere: Anniv, Sep 17
Big Top Premiere: Anniv, Jul 1
Bob Hope Show Premiere: Anniv, Oct 12
Bob Newhart Show Premiere: Anniv, Oct 10
Bold and the Beautiful Premiere: Anniv, Mar 23
Brady Bunch Premiere: Anniv, Sep 26
Break the Bank Premiere: Anniv, Oct 22
Brothers Premiere: Anniv, Jul 13
Buck Rogers Premiere: Anniv, Apr 15
Buffy the Vampire Slayer Premiere: Anniv, Mar 10
Burns and Allen Show Premiere: Anniv, Oct 12
Cagney & Lacey Premiere: Anniv, Mar 25
Candid Camera Premiere: Anniv, Aug 10
Captain Kangaroo Premiere: Anniv, Oct 3
Captain Midnight Premiere: Anniv, Sep 4
Captain Video and His Video Rangers Premiere: Anniv, Jun 27
Carol Burnett Show Premiere: Anniv, Sep 11
Cathode-Ray Tube Patented: Anniv, Dec 20
Catholic Hour Premiere: Anniv, Jan 4
Cavalcade of Stars Premiere: Anniv, Jun 4
CBS Evening News Premiere: Anniv, May 3
Charlie's Angels Premiere: Anniv, Sep 22
Cheers Premiere: Anniv, Sep 30
Chico and the Man Premiere: Anniv, Sep 13
China Beach Premiere: Anniv, Apr 26
CHiPs Premiere: Anniv, Sep 15
CNN Debuted: Anniv, Jun 1
Columbo Premiere: Anniv, Sep 15
Cosby Show Premiere: Anniv, Sep 20
Court TV Debut: Anniv, Jul 1
CSI: Crime Scene Investigation Premiere: Anniv, Oct 6
Dallas Premiere: Anniv, Apr 2
Daniel Boone Premiere: Anniv, Sep 24
Dark Shadows Premiere: Anniv, Jun 27
Dating Game Premiere: Anniv, Dec 20
David Brinkley's Journal Premiere: Anniv, Oct 11
Davy Crockett Premiere: Anniv, Dec 15
Days of Our Lives Premiere: Anniv, Nov 8
December Bride Premiere: Anniv, Oct 4
Dick Cavett Show Premiere: Anniv, Mar 4
Dick Van Dyke Show Premiere: Anniv, Oct 3
Different World Premiere: Anniv, Sep 24
Dinah Shore Show Premiere: Anniv, Nov 27
Ding Dong School Premiere: Anniv, Dec 22
Doctors Premiere: Anniv, Apr 1
Donny and Marie Premiere: Anniv, Jan 16
Dr. Who Premiere: Anniv, Nov 23
Dragnet Premiere: Anniv, Dec 16
Dukes of Hazzard Premiere: Anniv, Jan 26
Dynasty Premiere: Anniv, Jan 12
Ebert & Roeper and the Movies (Sneak Previews): Anniv, Oct 12
Ed Sullivan Show Premiere: Anniv, Jun 20
Edge of Night Premiere: Anniv, Apr 2
Eight Is Enough Premiere: Anniv, Mar 15
Emergency Premiere: Anniv, Jan 22
ER Premiere: Anniv, Sep 19
Ernie Kovacs Premiere: Anniv, May 14
Evening at Pops Premiere: Anniv, Jul 12
Face the Nation Premiere: Anniv, Nov 7
Facts of Life Premiere: Anniv, Aug 24
Falcon Crest Premiere: Anniv, Dec 4
Family Feud Premiere: Anniv, Jul 12
Family Ties Premiere: Anniv, Sep 22
Fantasy Island Premiere: Anniv, Jan 28
Fat Albert and the Cosby Kids Premiere: Anniv, Sep 9
Fireside Theatre Premiere: Anniv, Apr 5
First Baseball Games Televised: Anniv, Aug 26
First Color TV Broadcast: Anniv, Jun 25
First Presidential Telecast: Anniv, Apr 30
First Scheduled Television Broadcast: Anniv, Jul 1
First Televised Presidential Debate: Anniv, Sep 26
First Televised Presidential News Conf: Anniv, Jan 25
Flintstones TV Premiere: Anniv, Sep 30
Flipper Premiere: Anniv, Sep 19
Flying Nun Premiere: Anniv, Sep 7
48 Hours Premiere: Anniv, Jan 19
Fraggle Rock Premiere: Anniv, Sep 12
Frasier Premiere: Anniv, Sep 16
Fred Waring Show Premiere: Anniv, Apr 17
Friends Premiere: Anniv, Sep 22
Frontline Premiere: Anniv, Jan 17
Fugitive Premiere: Anniv, Sep 17
Gene Autry Show Premiere: Anniv, Jul 23
General Electric Theater Premiere: Anniv, Feb 1

☆ Chase's 2004 Calendar of Events ☆ Index

General Hospital Premiere: Anniv, **Apr 1**
Gentle Ben Premiere: Anniv, **Sep 10**
George Gobel Show Premiere: Anniv, **Oct 2**
Get Smart Premiere: Anniv, **Sep 18**
Gilligan's Island Premiere: Anniv, **Sep 26**
Goldbergs Premiere: Anniv, **Jan 17**
Golden Girls Premiere: Anniv, **Sep 14**
Golden Globe Awards, **Jan 25**
Gong Show Premiere: Anniv, **Jun 14**
Good Morning America Premiere: Anniv, **Nov 6**
Good Sex! with Dr. Ruth Westheimer Premiere: Anniv, **Aug 27**
Good Times Premiere: Anniv, **Feb 1**
Guiding Light Premiere: Anniv, **Jun 26**
Gumby Show Premiere: Anniv, **Mar 16**
Gunsmoke Premiere: Anniv, **Sep 10**
Hallmark Hall of Fame Premiere: Anniv, **Jan 6**
Happy Days Premiere: Anniv, **Jan 15**
Have Gun Will Travel Premiere: Anniv, **Sep 14**
Hazel Premiere: Anniv, **Sep 28**
Hee Haw Premiere: Anniv, **Jun 15**
Hill Street Blues Premiere: Anniv, **Jan 15**
Hollywood Squares Premiere: Anniv, **Oct 17**
Home Improvement Premiere: Anniv, **Sep 17**
Hopalong Cassidy Premiere: Anniv, **Jun 24**
Howdy Doody Premiere: Anniv, **Dec 27**
I Love Lucy Premiere: Anniv, **Oct 15**
I Spy Premiere: Anniv, **Sep 15**
In Living Color Premiere: Anniv, **Apr 15**
In the Heat of the Night Premiere: Anniv, **Mar 6**
Incredible Hulk Premiere: Anniv, **Mar 10**
Ironside Premiere: Anniv, **Sep 14**
It Takes a Thief Premiere: Anniv, **Jan 9**
I've Got a Secret Premiere: Anniv, **Jun 19**
Jack Benny Program Premiere: Anniv, **Oct 28**
Jeffersons Premiere: Anniv, **Jan 18**
Jeopardy Premiere: Anniv, **Mar 30**
Jetsons Premiere: Anniv, **Sep 23**
Jimmy Durante Show Premiere: Anniv, **Oct 2**
Joe Franklin Day, **Mar 9**
Johnny Carson's Final Show, **May 22**
Kate Smith Hour Premiere: Anniv, **Sep 25**
King Family Show Premiere: Anniv, **Jan 23**
Knight Rider Premiere: Anniv, **Sep 26**
Kraft Television Theatre Premiere: Anniv, **May 7**
Kukla, Fran and Ollie Premiere: Anniv, **Nov 29**
Kung Fu Premiere: Anniv, **Oct 1**
LA Law Premiere: Anniv, **Oct 3**
Larry King Show Premiere: Anniv, **Mar 13**
Lassie Premiere: Anniv, **Sep 12**
Late Night with David Letterman Premiere: Anniv, **Feb 1**
Laugh-In Premiere: Anniv, **Jan 22**
Laverne and Shirley Premiere: Anniv, **Jan 27**
Law & Order Premiere: Anniv, **Sep 13**
Lawrence Welk Show Premiere: Anniv, **Jul 2**
Leave It to Beaver Premiere: Anniv, **Oct 4**
Let's Make a Deal Premiere: Anniv, **Dec 30**
Liberace Show Premiere: Anniv, **Jul 1**
Little House on the Prairie Premiere: Anniv, **Sep 11**
Lone Ranger Premiere: Anniv, **Sep 15**
Look Up and Live Premiere: Anniv, **Jan 3**
Loretta Young Show Premiere: Anniv, **Sep 20**
Lou Grant Premiere: Anniv, **Sep 20**
Love Boat Premiere: Anniv, **Sep 24**
Love Is a Many Splendored Thing Premiere: Anniv, **Sep 18**
Love of Life Premiere: Anniv, **Sep 24**
M*A*S*H Premiere: Anniv, **Sep 17**
M*A*S*H: Final Episode: Anniv, **Feb 28**
MacNeil-Lehrer Newshour Premiere: Anniv, **Sep 5**
Magnum, PI Premiere: Anniv, **Dec 11**
Make Room for Daddy Premiere: Anniv, **Sep 29**
Mama Premiere: Anniv, **Jul 1**
Mannix Premiere: Anniv, **Sep 16**
Married With Children Premiere: Anniv, **Apr 5**
Mary Tyler Moore Show Premiere: Anniv, **Sep 19**
Masterpiece Theatre Premiere: Anniv, **Jan 10**
Maude Premiere: Anniv, **Sep 12**
Maverick Premiere: Anniv, **Sep 22**
Meet the Press Premiere: Anniv, **Nov 6**
Merv Griffin Show Premiere: Anniv, **Oct 1**
Mickey Mouse Club Premiere: Anniv, **Oct 3**
Middlemark, Marvin: Birth Anniv, **Sep 16**
Mighty Mouse Playhouse Premiere: Anniv, **Dec 10**
Mike Hammer Premiere: Anniv, **Jan 26**
Millionaire Premiere: Anniv, **Jan 19**
Minow, Newton: Birth, **Jan 17**
Mission: Impossible Premiere: Anniv, **Sep 17**
Mister Rogers' Neighborhood Premiere: Anniv, **May 22**
Monkees Premiere: Anniv, **Sep 12**
Monty Python's Flying Circus: Anniv, **Oct 5**
Moonlighting Premiere: Anniv, **Mar 3**
Mr Peepers Premiere: Anniv, **Jul 3**
Mr Wizard Premiere: Anniv, **Mar 3**
MTV Premiere: Anniv, **Aug 1**
Munsters Premiere: Anniv, **Sep 24**
Muppet Show Premiere: Anniv, **Sep 13**
Murder, She Wrote Premiere: Anniv, **Sep 30**
Murphy Brown Premiere: Anniv, **Nov 14**
My Friend Flicka Premiere: Anniv, **Feb 10**
My Little Margie Premiere: Anniv, **Jun 15**
Name That Tune Premiere: Anniv, **Jul 6**
Nat King Cole Show Premiere: Anniv, **Nov 5**
Newhart Premiere: Anniv, **Oct 25**
Newlywed Game Premiere: Anniv, **Jul 11**
Nick at Nite: Anniv, **Jul 1**
Nickelodeon Premiere: Anniv, **Apr 2**
Nielsen, Arthur Charles: Birth Anniv, **Sep 5**
Night Court Premiere: Anniv, **Jan 4**
Northern Exposure Premiere: Anniv, **Jul 12**
NYPD Blue Premiere: Anniv, **Sep 21**
Omnibus Premiere: Anniv, **Nov 9**
One Day at a Time Premiere: Anniv, **Dec 16**
One Life to Live Premiere: Anniv, **Jul 15**
Oprah Winfrey Show Premiere: Anniv, **Sep 8**
Our Miss Brooks Premiere: Anniv, **Oct 3**
Ozark Jubilee Premiere: Anniv, **Jan 22**
Ozzie and Harriet Premiere: Anniv, **Oct 3**
Pat Boone Show Premiere: Anniv, **Oct 3**
People Are Funny Premiere: Anniv, **Sep 19**
Perry Como Show Premiere: Anniv, **Dec 24**
Perry Mason Premiere: Anniv, **Sep 21**
Phil Donahue Show, The: Anniv, **Nov 6**
Phil Silvers Show Premiere: Anniv, **Sep 20**
Price Is Right Premiere: Anniv, **Nov 26**
Primetime Live Premiere: Anniv, **Aug 3**
Prisoner Premiere: Anniv, **Jun 1**
Public Television Debuts: Anniv, **Nov 3**
Queen for a Day Premiere: Anniv, **Jan 3**
Quincy Premiere: Anniv, **Oct 3**
Quiz Kids Premiere: Anniv, **Jul 6**
Rawhide Premiere: Anniv, **Jan 9**
Real McCoys Premiere: Anniv, **Oct 3**
Real People Premiere: Anniv, **Apr 18**
Red Skelton Show Premiere: Anniv, **Sep 30**
Remington Steele Premiere: Anniv, **Oct 1**
Rhoda Premiere: Anniv, **Sep 9**
Rocky and His Friends Premiere: Anniv, **Nov 19**
Rogers, Fred: Birth Anniv, **Mar 20**
Roseanne Premiere: Anniv, **Oct 18**
Roy Rogers Show Premiere: Anniv, **Dec 30**
Ryan's Hope Premiere: Anniv, **Jul 7**
Saint Elsewhere Premiere: Anniv, **Oct 26**
Sanford and Son Premiere: Anniv, **Jan 14**
Saturday Night Live Premiere: Anniv, **Oct 11**
Scarecrow and Mrs King Premiere: Anniv, **Oct 3**
Scooby-Doo, Where Are You? Premiere: Anniv, **Sep 13**
Search for Tomorrow Premiere: Anniv, **Sep 3**
Secret Agent Premiere: Anniv, **Apr 5**
Secret Storm Premiere: Anniv, **Feb 1**
See It Now Premiere: Anniv, **Nov 18**
Seinfeld Premiere: Anniv, **May 31**
Sesame Street Premiere: Anniv, **Nov 10**
Sex and the City Premiere: Anniv, **Jun 6**
Shirley Temple Theatre Premiere: Anniv, **Sep 18**
Silver Spoons Premiere: Anniv, **Sep 25**
Simpsons Premiere: Anniv, **Dec 17**
Six Million Dollar Man Premiere: Anniv, **Oct 20**
$64,000 Question Premiere: Anniv, **Jun 7**
Sixty Minutes Premiere: Anniv, **Sep 24**
Sky King Premiere: Anniv, **Sep 16**
Smothers Brothers Fired: Anniv, **Apr 4**
Sneak Previews Premiere: Anniv, **Oct 12**
Soap Premiere: Anniv, **Sep 13**
Sopranos Premiere: Anniv, **Jan 13**
Soupy Sales Show Premiere: Anniv, **Jul 4**
Star Trek Premiere: Anniv, **Sep 8**
Starman Month, Intl, **Oct 1**
Steve Allen Show Premiere: Anniv, **Dec 25**
Strike It Rich Premiere: Anniv, **May 7**
Survivor Premiere: Anniv, **May 31**
Talent Scouts Premiere: Anniv, **Dec 6**
Tales of Wells Fargo Premiere: Anniv, **Mar 18**
Tarzan Premiere: Anniv, **Sep 8**
Ted Mack's Original Amateur Hour Premiere: Anniv, **Jan 18**
Television Academy Hall of Fame First Inductees, **Mar 4**
Texaco Star Theater Premiere: Anniv, **Sep 21**
That Girl Premiere: Anniv, **Sep 8**
The X-Files Premiere: Anniv, **Sep 10**
3rd Rock from the Sun Premiere: Anniv, **Jan 9**
Thirtysomething Premiere: Anniv, **Sep 29**
This Is Your Life Premiere: Anniv, **Oct 1**
Three's Company Premiere: Anniv, **Mar 15**
Tiny Tim Weds Miss Vicki on The Tonight Show: Anniv, **Dec 17**
To Tell the Truth Premiere: Anniv, **Dec 18**
Today Premiere: Anniv, **Jan 14**
Tom Corbett, Space Cadet Premiere: Anniv, **Oct 1**
Tonight Show Premiere: Anniv, **Sep 27**
Tony Orlando and Dawn Premiere: Anniv, **Jul 3**
Topper Premiere: Anniv, **Oct 9**
Tracey Ullman Show Premiere: Anniv, **Apr 5**
Truth or Consequences Premiere: Anniv, **Sep 7**
TV Talk-Show Host Day, **Oct 23**
20/20 Premiere: Anniv, **Jun 6**
21 Jump Street Premiere: Anniv, **Apr 12**
Twenty Questions Premiere: Anniv, **Nov 26**
Twilight Zone Premiere: Anniv, **Oct 2**
Ukrainian Famine Film Broadcast: Anniv, **Nov 30**
Upstairs, Downstairs Premiere: Anniv, **Oct 10**
Vast Wasteland Speech: Anniv, **May 9**
Virginian Premiere: Anniv, **Sep 19**
Wagon Train Premiere: Anniv, **Sep 18**
Walt Disney Premiere: Anniv, **Oct 27**
Waltons Premiere: Anniv, **Sep 14**
Welcome Back, Kotter Premiere: Anniv, **Sep 9**
Welk, Lawrence: Birth Anniv, **Mar 11**
What's My Line Premiere: Anniv, **Feb 2**
Wheel of Fortune Premiere: Anniv, **Jan 6**
Wonder Years Premiere: Anniv, **Mar 15**
World Television Day (UN), **Nov 21**
World's Largest Concert, **Mar 11**
Wyatt Earp Premiere: Anniv, **Sep 6**
You Are There Premiere: Anniv, **Feb 1**
You Bet Your Life Premiere: Anniv, **Oct 5**
Young and the Restless Premiere: Anniv, **Mar 26**
Your Hit Parade Premiere: Anniv, **Oct 7**
Your Show of Shows Premiere: Anniv, **Feb 25**
Zane Grey Theater Premiere: Anniv, **Oct 5**
Zoo Parade Premiere: Anniv, **May 28**
Tellabration! An Evening of Storytelling for Grown-Ups (CT), Nov 19
Teller, Edward: Birth, Jan 15
Teller: Birth, Feb 14
Temperance Union, Women's Christian: Anniv, Nov 19
Temperature, North America's Coldest Recorded: Anniv, Feb 3
Temple, Shirley: Birth, Apr 23
Ten Most Wanted List Debuts: Anniv, Mar 14
Ten-Four Day, Oct 4
Tennant, Victoria: Birth, Sep 30
Tennessee,
Admission Day, **Jun 1**
Alexander, Lamar: Birth, **Jul 30**
American Massage Therapy Assn, Natl Conv (Nashville), **Oct 6**
Battle of Chattanooga: Anniv, **Nov 24**
Battle of Nashville: Anniv, **Dec 16**
Battle of Shiloh: Anniv, **Apr 6**
Belle Meade Plantation Fall Fest (Nashville), **Sep 18**
Bredesen, Phil: Birth, **Nov 21**
Celebration of Fine Crafts (Chattanooga), **Oct 2**
Christmas Past at Audubon Acres (Chattanooga), **Dec 4**
Dickens of a Christmas (Franklin), **Dec 11**
Dogwood Arts Fest (Knoxville), **Apr 8**
Dolly's Music on Parade (Pigeon Forge), **Apr 2**
Doodle Soup Days (Bradford), **Sep 10**
1890s Christmas at Belle Meade (Nashville), **Nov 12**
Elvis Presley's Birthday Celebration (Memphis), **Jan 7**
Elvis Week (Memphis), **Aug 7**
Family Day, **Aug 29**
Fiddle Fest at Audubon Acres (Chattanooga), **May 22**
Field Trial Chmpshp (Bird Dogs), Natl (Grand Junction), **Feb 9**
First Grand Ole Opry Broadcast: Anniv, **Dec 10**
Frist, William: Birth, **Feb 22**
Goat Days (Millington), **Sep 10**
Great Egg Caper at Audubon Acres (Chattanooga), **Apr 10**
Great Smoky Mountains Natl Park Established: Anniv, **Jun 15**
Indian Summer Days at Audubon Acres (Chattanooga), **Oct 9**
Iroquois Steeplechase (Nashville), **May 8**
Kroger/St. Jude Intl (Memphis), **Feb 16**
Longhorn Chmpshp Finals Rodeo (Murfreesboro), **Nov 11**
Longhorn World Chmpshp Rodeo (Chattanooga), **Mar 5**
Main Street Fest (Franklin), **Apr 24**
Memphis in May Intl Fest (Memphis), **May 1**
Mid-South Fair (Memphis), **Sep 22**
Mountain Quiltfest (Pigeon Forge), **Mar 10**
Mule Day (Columbia), **Apr 1**
Mustang 40th Anniv Celebration (Nashville), **Apr 15**
NAIA Men's and Women's Indoor Track/Field Chmpshps (Johnson City), **Mar 4**
NAIA Women's Div I Basketball Chmpshp (Jackson), **Mar 17**
Oak Ridge Atomic Plant Begun: Anniv, **Aug 1**
Old-Time Fiddlers' Jamboree (Smithville), **Jul 2**
Polk County Ramp Tramp Fest (Benton), **Apr 24**
Riverbend Fest (Chattanooga), **Jun 11**
Rock of Chickamauga: Anniv, **Sep 20**
Scopes Trial (Dayton), **Jul 15**
Secret City Festival (Oak Ridge), **Jun 18**
Smoky Mountains Storytelling Fest (Pigeon Forge), **Feb 5**
Southern Fest of Books (Nashville), **Oct 8**
State Fair (Nashville), **Sep 10**
Storytelling Fest, Natl (Jonesborough), **Oct 1**
Taca Fall Crafts Fair (Nashville), **Sep 24**
Tennessee Fall Homecoming (Norris), **Oct 7**
Tennessee Walking Horse Natl Celeb (Shelbyville), **Aug 18**
Wilderness Wildlife Week of Nature (Pigeon Forge), **Jan 10**
World's Biggest Fish Fry (Paris), **Apr 18**
World's Largest Outlet Sale (Pigeon Forge), **Dec 2**
Tenney, Jon: Birth, Dec 16
Tenniel, John: Birth Anniv, Feb 28
Tennille, Toni: Birth, May 8
Tennis,
Big 12 Men's & Women's Tennis Chmpshp (Norman, OK), **Apr 29**
Big Ten Men's Tennis Chmpshp, **Apr 29**
Big Ten Women's Tennis Chmpshp (Evanston, IL), **Apr 29**
Kroger/St. Jude Intl (Memphis, TN), **Feb 16**
Lacoste, Rene: Birth Anniv, **Jul 2**

Television (cont'd)—Tennis

Index ☆ Chase's 2004 Calendar of Events ☆

Tennis (cont'd)—Three Stooges

Lawn Tennis Chmpshps at Wimbledon (London, England), **Jun 21**
NAIA Men's & Women's Tennis Chmpshps, **May 17**
NCAA Div I Men's Tennis Chmpshp (Tulsa, OK), **May 22**
NCAA Div I Women's Tennis Chmpshps (Athen, GA), **May 20**
Tennyson, Alfred, Lord: Birth Anniv, Aug 6
Teresa, Mother: Birth Anniv, Aug 27
Tereshkova-Nikolaeva, Valentina: Birth, Mar 6
Terkel, Studs: Birth, May 16
Territorial Christmas Celebration (Guthrie, OK), Nov 27
Terry, Ellen: Birth Anniv, Feb 27
Tesh, John: Birth, Jul 9
Testaverde, Vinny: Birth, Nov 13
Testicular Cancer Awareness Week, Apr 1
Test-Tube Baby: Birth, Jul 25
Tet Offensive Begins: Anniv, Jan 30
Tet: See Chinese New Year, Jan 22
Tetonkaha Rendezvous (Lake Benton, MN), Aug 13
Texaco Star Theater TV Premiere: Anniv, Sep 21
Texas,
Admission Day, **Dec 29**
Aggie Muster (College Station), **Apr 21**
Bayfest (Corpus Christi), **Sep 24**
Big 12 Men's & Women's Swimming Chmpshp (Austin), **Feb 25**
Big 12 Men's Basketball Chmpshp (Dallas), **Mar 11**
Big 12 Women's Basketball Tourn (Dallas), **Mar 9**
Big 12 Women's Golf Chmpshp (College Station), **Apr 23**
Big Bend Natl Park Established: Anniv, **Jun 12**
Bob Wills Day (Turkey), **Apr 24**
Boys Ranch Rodeo (Boys Ranch), **Sep 4**
Branch Davidian Fire at Waco: Anniv, **Apr 19**
CAMEX (San Antonio), **Feb 27**
Charro Days (Brownsville), **Feb 26**
Cherokee Rose Fest (Gilmer), **May 15**
Chili Cookoff/Quail-Egg Eat, Prairie Dog (Grand Prairie), **Apr 3**
Christmas Magic (Wichita Falls), **Nov 5**
Clear Lake Crawfish Fest (Seabrook), **Apr 3**
Clute's Christmas in the Park (Clute), **Dec 7**
Come and Take It Fest (Gonzales), **Oct 2**
Communitywide Garage Sale (Elgin), **May 1**
Confederate Heroes Day, **Jan 19**
Cornyn, John: Birth, **Feb 2**
Cowboy Poetry Gathering (Alpine), **Mar 5**
D & G Barrel Race (Wichita Falls), **Nov 28**
Dallas Cup (Dallas), **Apr 4**
Dia de los Ninos/Dia de los Libros (El Paso), **Apr 24**
Dickens on the Strand (Galveston), **Dec 4**
East Texas Poultry Fest (Center), **Oct 7**
East Texas Yamboree (Gilmer), **Oct 20**
Easter Fete (Austin), **Apr 3**
Electra Goat BBQ Cook-Off (Electra), **May 7**
Elgin Market Days (Elgin), **Feb 7**
Emancipation Day, **Jun 19**
Faith City Kennel Club Dog Show (Wichita Falls), **Feb 27**
Fall Citywide Garage Sale (Electra), **Oct 2**
Fall Fiesta (Andrews), **Sep 25**
Fantasy of Lights (Wichita Falls), **Dec 3**
Fiddler's Frolics (Hallettsville), **Apr 23**
Fiesta San Antonio (San Antonio), **Apr 16**
Fireant Fest (Marshall), **Oct 8**
Fulton Oysterfest (Fulton), **Mar 4**
Galveston Historic Homes Tour (Galveston Island), **May 1**
Galveston Hurricane: Anniv, **Sep 8**
Great Texas Mosquito Fest (Clute), **Jul 29**
Guadalupe Natl Park Established: Anniv, **Sep 30**
Harvest Weekends (Bryan), **Jul 23**
Hogeye Fest (Elgin), **Oct 23**
Holly Jolly Weekend (Andrews), **Dec 2**
Home and Garden Fest (Wichita Falls), **Feb 28**
Horse Expo (Wichita Falls), **Oct 16**
Hotter 'n Hell Hundred Bike Race/Fest (Wichita Falls), **Aug 26**
Houston Livestock Show/Rodeo (Houston), **Feb 26**
Houston Marathon (Houston), **Jan 18**
Hummer/Bird Celebration (Rockport, Fulton), **Sep 16**
Hutchison, Kay Bailey: Birth, **Jul 22**
Independence Day, **Mar 2**
Indian Powwow, Natl Chmpshp (Grand Prairie), **Sep 10**
Intl Week (College Station), **Feb 23**
Josey's World Champion Jr Barrel Race (Marshall), **Apr 30**
Juneteenth, **Jun 19**
KidFilm® Fest (Dallas), **Jan 5**
Kingsville Intl Young Performers' Competition (Kingsville), **Apr 1**
La Posada de Kingsville/Celeb of Lights (Kingsville), **Nov 21**
Latino Book & Family Festival (Houston), **Oct 18**
Marriage of the Port Ceremony (Bryan), **Feb 21**
Messina Hof's Wine Premiere (Bryan), **Nov 13**
Monster Trucks Winter Nationals (Wichita Falls), **Jan 10**
Mustang League World Series (Irving), **Aug 4**
NCAA Div I Men's and Women's Track Chmpshps (Austin), **Jun 9**
NCAA Div I Men's Basketball Chmpshp (San Antonio), **Apr 3**
NCAA Women's Div I Swimming/Diving Chmpshp (College Station), **Mar 18**
North Texas Arts & Crafts Show (Wichita Falls), **Mar 27**
Nursing Conf on Pediatric Primary Care (Dallas), **Mar 23**
O. Henry Pun-Off (Austin), **May 1**
Oatmeal Fest (Bertram/Oatmeal), **Sep 3**
Oil Bowl Football Classic (Wichita Falls), **Jun 19**
Parade of Lights (Kingsville), **Dec 4**
Perry, Rick: Birth, **Mar 4**
Piano Competition for Outstanding Amateurs, Intl (Fort Worth), **Jun 7**
Poetry Contest (El Paso), **Jan 1**
Poteet Strawberry Fest (Poteet), **Apr 2**
Quadrangle Fest (Texarkana), **Sep 11**
Ranch Hand Breakfast (Kingsville), **Nov 20**
Ranching Heritage Fest, South Texas (Kingsville), **Feb 20**
Re/Max Ballunar Liftoff Festival (Houston), **Aug 20**
Red River Rodeo (Wichita Falls), **Jun 9**
Reenactment of Cowtown's Last Gunfight (Fort Worth), **Feb 8**
Rio Grande Valley Livestock Show (Mercedes), **Mar 20**
Rockport Art Fest (Rockport), **Jul 3**
Rockport Seafair (Rockport), **Oct 8**
Sam Rayburn Chili Cook-off (Bonham), **Sep 18**
San Jacinto Day, **Apr 21**
SBC Cotton Bowl Classic (Dallas), **Jan 1**
Seaspace (Houston), **Jun 5**
Shakespeare-on-the-Rocks (El Paso), **Sep 3**
South by Southwest (Austin), **Mar 12**
South Texas Wildlife and Birding Festival (Kingsville), **Nov 19**
Southwestern Expo Livestock Show/Rodeo (Fort Worth), **Jan 17**
Spring Fling (Wichita Falls), **Apr 24**
Spring Swing City Garage Sale (Electra), **Apr 3**
Stagecoach Days (Marshall), **May 15**
State Fair (Dallas), **Sep 24**
Summer Reading Club (El Paso), **Jun 5**
Sun Bowl (El Paso), **Dec 31**
Super Bowl (Houston), **Feb 1**
Taste of the Town (Wichita Falls), **Mar 2**
Texas Book Festival (Austin), **Nov 8**
Texas Collectors' Gun & Knife Show (Wichita Falls), **Jan 24**
Texas Folklife Fest (San Antonio), **Jun 10**
Texas Love the Children Day, **Mar 29**
Texas on the Plate Month, **Oct 1**
Texas Panhandle Tornado: Anniv, **Apr 9**
Texas Ranch Roundup (Wichita Falls), **Aug 20**
Texas-Oklahoma Fair (Wichita Falls), **Sep 14**
Texas-Oklahoma Junior Golf Tournament (Wichita Falls), **Jun 21**
Texoma Farm and Ranch Show (Wichita Falls), **Feb 10**
University Kiwanis Pancake Fest (Wichita Falls), **Jan 31**
USA Film Fest (Dallas), **Apr 22**
Viva El Paso (El Paso), **Jun 10**
Washington's Birthday Celeb (Laredo), **Feb 7**
Watermelon Thump (Luling), **Jun 24**
Westfest (West), **Sep 4**
Wichita West Bullfest (Wichita Falls), **Jan 17**
Wichita West Spring Arts/Crafts Show (Wichita Falls), **Apr 10**
Wine and Garden Fest (Bryan), **Apr 17**
Wonderland of Lights (Marshall), **Nov 24**
World Chmpshp BBQ Goat Cook-off/Crafts Fair (Brady), **Sep 4**
World of Wheels (Wichita Falls), **Jan 30**
World's Largest Rattlesnake Roundup (Sweetwater), **Mar 12**
Wurstfest (New Braunfels), **Oct 29**
Youth Cowboy Poetry Gathering (Boys Ranch), **Jun 17**
Texas City Disaster: Anniv, Apr 16
Texas County Fair/Old Settlers Reunion (Houston, MO), Aug 3
Thackeray, William: Birth Anniv, Jul 18
Thailand,
Birth of the Queen, **Aug 12**
Chakri Day, **Apr 6**
Chulalongkorn Day, **Oct 23**
Constitution Day, **Dec 10**
Coronation Day, **May 5**
Elephant Round-Up at Surin, **Nov 20**
King's Birthday and National Day, **Dec 5**
Midyear Day (Half-Year Day), **Jul 1**
Songkran Fest, **Apr 13**
Thank God It's Monday! Day, Natl, Jan 12
Thank You Days, Intl, Jan 11
Thanks for All the Gifts Week, Aug 8
Thanksgiving Day, Nov 25
Thanksgiving Day (Canada), Oct 11
Thanksgiving Day (Pres Proc), Nov 25
Thanksgiving, Turkey-Free, Nov 25
Thanksgiving: Turkey Trot (Parkersburg, WV), Nov 25
Tharp, Twyla: Birth, Jul 1
That Girl TV Premiere: Anniv, Sep 8
Thatcher, Margaret: Birth, Oct 13
Thatcher, Margaret: First Woman British Prime Minister: Anniv, May 4
Thatcher, Margaret: Resignation: Anniv, Nov 22
Thayer, Ernest L.: Birth Anniv, Aug 14
Thayer, Sylvanus: Birth Anniv, Jun 9
Theater. See also Opera,
Astor Place Riot: Anniv, **May 10**
Black Hills Passion Play (Spearfish, SD), **Jun 1**
Cats Premieres: Anniv, **Oct 7**
Colorado Shakespeare Fest (Boulder, CO), **Jun 2**
Coward, Noel: Birth Anniv, **Dec 16**
Donna Reed Performing Arts Fest (Denison, IA), **Jun 22**
Edinburgh Intl Fest (Edinburgh, Scotland), **Aug 15**
First Actor to Perform in Two Cities Same Day: Anniv, **Feb 10**
First Play Presented in North American Colonies: Anniv, **Aug 27**
First Tony Awards Presented: Anniv, **Apr 6**
Fringe Theatre Fest (Edmonton, AB, Canada), **Aug 12**
George Spelvin Day, **Nov 15**
Hair Broadway Opening: Anniv, **Mar 28**
Harrison Fest of Arts (Harrison Hot Springs, BC, Canada), **Jul 10**
Idaho Shakespeare Fest (Boise, ID), **Jun 4**
Illinois Shakespeare Fest (Bloomington, IL), **Jun 16**
Laura Ingalls Wilder Pageant (De Smet, SD), **Jul 9**
Odets, Clifford: Birth Anniv, **Jul 18**
Outdoor Summer Theater (Farmington, NM), **Jun 16**
Papp, Joseph: Birth Anniv, **Jun 22**
Portland Center Stage (Portland, OR), **Jan 1**
Scopes Trial (Dayton, TN), **Jul 15**
Shakespeare Fest (Ashland, OR), **Feb 27**
Shakespeare on the Green (Omaha, NE), **Jun 24**
Shakespeare-on-the-Rocks (El Paso, TX), **Sep 3**
Song of Hiawatha Pageant (Pipestone, MN), **Jul 23**
Tecumseh! Epic Outdoor Drama (Chillicothe, OH), **Jun 11**
Theater in North America, First Performance: Anniv, **Apr 30**
Viva El Paso (El Paso, TX), **Jun 10**
Walter Plinge Day (England), **Dec 2**
Williams, Tennessee: Birth Anniv, **Mar 26**
Winnipeg Fringe Theatre Fest (Winnipeg, MB, Canada), **Jul 14**
Theisman, Joe: Birth, Sep 9
Theodore Roosevelt Natl Park Established: Anniv, Apr 25
Theodosius I: Birth Anniv, Jan 11
Therapeutic Recreation Week, Natl, Jul 11
Theron, Charlize: Birth, Aug 7
Theroux, Paul: Birth, Apr 10
Theta Nu Xi Multicultural Sorority Founding Day, Apr 11
Thewlis, David: Birth, Mar 20
3rd Rock from the Sun TV Premiere: Anniv, Jan 9
Thible, Marie: First Free Flight by a Woman: Anniv, Jun 4
Thicke, Alan: Birth, Mar 1
Thiessen, Tiffani-Amber: Birth, Jan 23
Thinnes, Roy: Birth, Apr 6
Third Shift Workers Day, Natl, May 12
Third World Day: Anniv, Apr 18
Thirtysomething TV Premiere: Anniv, Sep 29
This Is Your Life TV Premiere: Anniv, Oct 1
Thomas Crapper Day, Jan 27
Thomas, B.J.: Birth, Aug 7
Thomas, Betty: Birth, Jul 27
Thomas, Clarence: Birth, Jun 23
Thomas, Craig: Birth, Feb 17
Thomas, Danny: Birth Anniv, Jan 6
Thomas, Dylan: Birth Anniv, Oct 27
Thomas, Frank: Birth, May 27
Thomas, Heather: Birth, Sep 8
Thomas, Helen: Birth, Aug 4
Thomas, Henry: Birth, Sep 8
Thomas, Isaiah: Birth Anniv, Jan 30
Thomas, Isiah: Birth, Apr 30
Thomas, Jonathan Taylor: Birth, Sep 8
Thomas, Kurt: Birth, Mar 29
Thomas, Lowell: Birth Anniv, Apr 6
Thomas, Marlo: Birth, Nov 21
Thomas, Martha Carey: Birth Anniv, Jan 2
Thomas, Michael Tilson: Birth, Dec 21
Thomas, Philip Michael: Birth, May 26
Thomas, Richard: Birth, Jun 13
Thomas, Robert B.: Birth Anniv, Apr 24
Thomas, Sean Patrick: Birth, Dec 17
Thome, Jim: Birth, Aug 27
Thompson, Emma: Birth, Apr 14
Thompson, Fred: Birth, Aug 19
Thompson, Hunter S.: Birth, Jul 18
Thompson, Jack: Birth, Aug 31
Thompson, John: Birth, Sep 2
Thompson, Lea: Birth, May 31
Thompson, Sada: Birth, Sep 27
Thompson, Tommy G.: Birth, Nov 19
Thomson, Charles: Birth Anniv, Nov 29
Thoreau, Henry David: Birth Anniv, Jul 12
Thorne-Smith, Courtney: Birth, Nov 8
Thornton, Billy Bob: Birth, Aug 4
Thornton, Matthew: Death Anniv, Jun 24
Thorpe, James: Birth Anniv, May 28
3-A-Day Week, Mar 3
Three Flags Ceremony—Lewis and Clark Bicentennial Event (St. Louis, MO), Mar 10
Three Kings Day, Jan 6
Three Stooges: Howard, Moe: Birth Anniv, Jun 19
Three Stooges: De Rita, Joe: Birth Anniv, Jul 12

☆ Chase's 2004 Calendar of Events ☆   Index

Three's Company TV Premiere: Anniv, Mar 15
Threshing Bee Show, Makoti (ND), Oct 2
Threshing Bee, Norskedalen's (Coon Valley, WI), Sep 18
Thumb, Tom: Birth Anniv, Jan 4
Thurber, James: Birth Anniv, Dec 8
Thurman, Uma: Birth, Apr 29
Thurmond, Nate: Birth, Jul 25
Thurmond, Strom: Birth Anniv, Dec 5
Tiananmen Square Massacre: Anniv, Jun 4
Tibet: Dalai Lama Flees Tibet: Anniv, Mar 31
Ticotin, Rachel: Birth, Nov 1
Tides, Perigean Spring, Jul 2
Tides, Perigean Spring, Dec 11
Tides, Perigean Spring, Jun 3
Tidewater Archaeology Dig (St. Mary's City, MD), Jul 31
Tie Month, Natl, Dec 1
Tierney, Gene: Birth Anniv, Nov 20
Tierney, Maura: Birth, Feb 3
Tiffany, Charles L.: Birth Anniv, Feb 15
Tiffany, Louis C.: Birth Anniv, Feb 18
Tiffin, Pamela: Birth, Oct 13
Tighe, Kevin: Birth, Aug 13
Tilbrook, Glenn: Birth, Aug 31
Tilden, Bill: Birth Anniv, Feb 10
Tillis, Mel: Birth, Aug 8
Tilly, Jennifer: Birth, Sep 16
Tilly, Meg: Birth, Feb 14
Time Magazine First Published: Anniv, Mar 3
Time Management Month, Natl, Feb 1
Time Management: Revise Your Work Schedule Month, May 1
Time Management: Take Back Your Time Week, Natl, Jan 26
Time;
  Calendars,
  Ample Time Day, Natl, Nov 8
  Daylight Saving Time Begins, Apr 4
  Daylight Saving Time Ends, Oct 31
  Greenwich Mean Time Begins: Anniv, Sep 25
  Leap Second Adjustment Time, Dec 31
  Leap Second Adjustment Time, Jun 30
  Prime Meridian Set: Anniv, Nov 1
  Summer Daylight-Saving Time (Europe), Mar 28
  Summer Time (United Kingdom), Mar 28
  Time Zone Plan, US Uniform: Anniv, Nov 18
  US Standard Time Act: Anniv, Mar 19
  War Time: Anniv, Feb 9
Tin Can Patent: Anniv, Jan 19
Tinker, Grant: Birth, Jan 11
Tinsley, Jamaal: Birth, Feb 28
Tiny Tim Weds Miss Vicki on The Tonight Show: Anniv, Dec 17
Tip-Up Town USA (Houghton Lake, MI), Jan 17
Tisch, Laurence: Birth, Mar 5
Tisha B'Av (Fast of Ab), Jul 27
Titan II Missile Explosion: Anniv, Sep 19
Titanic (Film) Released: Anniv, Dec 19
Titanic Discovered: Anniv, Sep 1
Titanic, Sinking of the: Anniv, Apr 15
Tito (Josip Broz): Birth Anniv, May 25
Tittle, Y.A.: Birth, Oct 24
Tivoli Gardens Season (Copenhagen, Denmark), May 1
Tivoli-Viking Days at the Nordic Heritage Museum (Seattle, WA), Jul 10
Tkachuk, Keith: Birth, Mar 28
To Tell the Truth TV Premiere: Anniv, Dec 18
Toad Hollow Day of Encouragement, Jan 26
Toad Hollow Day of Thank You, Jun 20
Toad Hollow Week, Natl, Mar 14
Toad Suck Daze (Conway, AR), Apr 30
Tobacco Harvest (McLean, VA), Aug 22
Tobago,
  Emancipation Day, Aug 1
  Independence Day, Aug 31
  Spiritual Baptist Liberation Shouter Day, Mar 30
Tobolowsky, Stephen: Birth, May 30
Today TV Premiere: Anniv, Jan 14
Todd, Beverly: Birth, Jul 11
Toffler, Alvin: Birth, Oct 4
Togo,
  Independence Day, Apr 27
  Liberation Day, Jan 13
Toilet Tank Repair Month, Natl, Oct 1
Tojo Hideki: Execution Anniv, Dec 23
Tolerance Week, Dec 1
Tolerance, Intl Day for (UN), Nov 16
Tolkan, James: Birth, Jun 20
Tolkien Week, Sep 19
Tolkien, J.R.R.: Birth Anniv, Jan 3
Tolkien, J.R.R.: Hobbit Day, Sep 22
Tolkien, J.R.R.: Lord of the Rings, First Part Published: Anniv, Jul 19
Toll Collection Machine, First Automatic: Anniv, Nov 19
Tolstoy, Leo: Birth Anniv, Sep 9
Tom Corbett, Space Cadet TV Premiere: Anniv, Oct 1
Tom Sawyer Days, Natl (Hannibal, MO), Jul 1
Tomatina, La (Spain), Aug 25
Tomato Month, Fresh Florida, Apr 1
Tomb Sweeping Day (China), Apr 4
Tomb-Sweeping Day, Natl (Taiwan), Apr 5
Tomczak, Mike: Birth, Oct 23
Tomei, Concetta: Birth, Dec 30

Tomei, Marisa: Birth, Dec 4
Tomjanovich, Rudy: Birth, Nov 24
Tomlin, Lily: Birth, Sep 1
Tomlinson, LaDanian: Birth, Jun 23
Tompkins, Daniel D.: Birth Anniv, Jun 21
Tonga: Emancipation Day, Jun 4
Tonight Show TV Premiere: Anniv, Sep 27
Tonight Show: Tiny Tim Weds Miss Vicki: Anniv, Dec 17
Tony Awards Presented, First: Anniv, Apr 6
Tony Orlando and Dawn TV Premiere: Anniv, Jul 3
Tools and Skills That Built the Colony (Savannah, GA), Sep 4
Tools of the Trade (Williamsburg, VA), Aug 1
Toomey, William: Birth, Jan 10
Toot Your Flute Day, Intl, Oct 4
Top Spinning at Noon: Worldwide Celebration, Oct 13
Topper TV Premiere: Anniv, Oct 9
TOPS Club, Inc: Anniv, Jan 21
TOPS Intl Recognition Days (Pittsburgh, PA), Jul 15
Tork, Peter: Birth, Feb 13
Torn, Rip: Birth, Feb 6
Torquemada, Tomas de: Death Anniv, Sep 16
Torre, Joe: Birth, Jul 18
Torricelli, Robert G.: Birth, Aug 26
Torture Abolition Day, Feb 4
Toscanini, Arturo: Birth Anniv, Mar 25
Toss Away the Could Haves and Should Haves Day, Jul 17
Tostitos Fiesta Bowl (Tempe, AZ), Jan 2
Totenberg, Nina: Birth, Jan 14
Toulouse-Lautrec, Henri de: Birth Anniv, Nov 24
Tour de France, Jul 3
Tourism Day, World, Sep 27
Tourism Week, Natl, May 8
Tournament of Roses Parade (Pasadena, CA), Jan 1
Town Criers Day, Intl, Jul 12
Town Meeting Day (Vermont), Mar 2
Town Watch: Natl Night Out, Aug 3
Towne, Benjamin: First American Daily Newspaper: Anniv, May 30
Townsend, Robert: Birth, Feb 6
Townshend, Pete: Birth, May 19
Toy Show, Natl Farm (Dyersville, IA), Nov 5
Toy Tips Executive Toy Test (New York, NY), Sep 1
Toynbee, Arnold J.: Birth Anniv, Apr 14
Toys: Farm Toy Show & Auction (Sauk Centre, MN), Feb 14
Tracey Ullman Show TV Premiere: Anniv, Apr 5
Track and Field,
  Bannister Breaks Four-Minute Mile: Anniv, May 6
  Big 12 Men's & Women's Outdoor Track/Field Chmpshps (Norman, OK), Apr 29
  Big 12 Men's and Women's Indoor Track Chmpshps (Lincoln, NE), Feb 27
  Big Ten Men's and Women's Outdoor Track/Field Chmpshps, May 14
  Big Ten Men's Indoor Track/Field Chmpshps (Ann Arbor, MI), Feb 28
  Big Ten Women's Track/Field Chmpshps (Iowa City, IA), Feb 28
  NAIA Men's and Women's Cross Country Natl Chmpshps, Nov 20
  NAIA Men's and Women's Indoor Track/Field Chmpshps (Johnson City, TN), Mar 4
  NAIA Outdoor Track/Field Chmpshps (Olathe, KS), May 27
  NCAA Div I Men's and Women's Track Chmpshps (Austin, TX), Jun 9
  NCAA Indoor Track/Field Chmpshps, Mar 12
  Simplot Games (Pocatello, ID), Feb 19
  USA Indoor Track/Field Chmpshps (Boston, MA), Mar 5
Tracy, Spencer: Birth Anniv, Apr 5
Trade Fair, Canton Autumn (China), Oct 15
Trade Show Image Week, Build a Better, Feb 15
Trade Week, World (Pres Proc), May 16
Trafalgar, Battle of: Anniv, Oct 21
Trail of Courage Living-History Fest (Rochester, IN), Sep 18
Trail of Tears Commemoration (Waterloo, AL), Sep 18
Trails Day, Natl, Jun 5
Transatlantic Flight, First Nonstop: Anniv, Jun 14
Transatlantic Phoning: Anniv, Jan 7
Transcontinental Flight, First Scheduled: Anniv, Jan 25
Transfer Day (US Virgin Islands), Mar 31
Transistor Invented: Anniv, Dec 23
Transit of Venus, Jun 8
Transportation Week, Natl (Pres Proc), May 16
Travalena, Fred: Birth, Oct 6
Travanti, Daniel J.: Birth, Mar 7
Travel Month, Senior Women's, Jan 1
Travelers with Disabilities Awareness Week, Nov 28
Travers, Mary: Birth, Nov 7
Travis, Nancy: Birth, Sep 21
Travis, Randy: Birth, May 4
Travolta, John: Birth, Feb 18
Treasury Dept, US: Anniv, Sep 2
Treaty of Guadalupe Hidalgo: Anniv, Feb 2
Treaty of Paris Ends French and Indian War: Anniv, Feb 10
Trebek, Alex: Birth, Jul 22
Tree Planting Day, Natl (Lesotho), Mar 21

Trelawney, Edward J.: Birth Anniv, Nov 13
Trevino, Lee: Birth, Dec 1
Trial Technology Day, Jun 4
Triangle Shirtwaist Fire: Anniv, Mar 25
Triathlon,
  Northeast Missouri Triathlon Chmpshp (Kirksville, MO), Sep 12
  Sawyer Triathlon (Louisville, KY), Aug 7
Trick or Treat Night, Oct 31
Trillin, Calvin: Birth, Dec 5
Trinidad,
  Carnival (Port of Spain), Feb 23
  Emancipation Day, Aug 1
  Independence Day, Aug 31
  Indian Arrival Day (Port of Spain), May 30
  Spiritual Baptist Liberation Shouter Day, Mar 30
Trinity Sunday, Jun 6
Tripplehorn, Jeanne: Birth, Jun 10
Tritt, Travis: Birth, Feb 9
Triumph Ag Expo (Omaha, NE), Mar 3
Trivia Contest, World's Largest (Stevens Point, WI), Apr 16
Trivia Day, Jan 4
Trollope, Anthony: Birth Anniv, Apr 24
Truancy Law: Anniv, Apr 12
Truck,
  Ugly Pickup Parade/Contest (Chadron, NE), Oct 29
Truck Driver Appreciation Week, Natl, Aug 22
Trudeau, Garry: Birth, Jul 21
Trudeau, Pierre Elliott: Birth Anniv, Oct 18
True Confessions Day, Mar 15
Truffaut, Francois: Birth Anniv, Feb 6
Truman Doctrine: Anniv, May 22
Truman, Bess (Elizabeth): Birth Anniv, Feb 13
Truman, Harry S: Birth Anniv, May 8
Truman, Harry: Dewey Defeats Truman Headline: Anniv, Nov 3
Trumbull, Jonathan: Birth Anniv, Oct 12
Trump, Donald: Birth, Jun 14
Trust Your Intuition Day, May 10
Truth or Consequences TV Premiere: Anniv, Sep 7
Truth, Sojourner: Death Anniv, Nov 26
Tsunami, Highest Recorded in History: Anniv, Jul 9
Tu B'Shvat, Feb 7
Tubb, Ernest: Birth Anniv, Feb 9
Tuberous Sclerosis Awareness Month, Natl, May 1
Tubman, Harriet: Death Anniv, Mar 10
Tucci, Stanley: Birth, Jan 11
Tuchman, Barbara W.: Birth Anniv, Jan 30
Tucker, Chris: Birth, Aug 31
Tucker, Michael: Birth, Feb 6
Tucker, Tanya: Birth, Oct 10
Tulip Fest, Albany (Albany, NY), May 7
Tulip Time Fest, Holland (Holland, MI), May 1
Tulip Time Fest, Pella (Pella, IA), May 6
Tune, Tommy: Birth, Feb 28
Tunie, Tamara: Birth, Mar 14
Tunisia,
  Independence Day, Mar 20
  Martyrs' Day, Apr 9
  Republic Day, Jul 25
  Tree Fest, Nov 14
  Women's Day, Aug 13
Tunney, Gene: Long Count Day, Sep 22
Tunney, James Joseph (Gene): Birth Anniv, May 25
Tupper Lake Woodsmen's Days (Tupper Lake, NY), Jul 10
Turgeon, Pierre: Birth, Aug 29
Turkey,
  Constantinople Falls to the Turks: Anniv, May 29
  National Sovereignty/Children's Day, Apr 23
  Republic Day, Oct 29
  Saint Peter's Day, Jun 29
  Turkish Earthquake: Anniv, Aug 17
  Victory Day, Aug 30
  Youth and Sports Day, May 19
Turkey Days, King (Worthington, MN), Sep 18
Turkey Lovers' Month, June Is, Jun 1
Turkey Rama (McMinnville, OR), Jul 8
Turkey Vultures Return to the Living Sign (Canisteo, NY), Mar 11
Turkey-Free Thanksgiving, Nov 25
Turkmenistan,
  Independence Day, Oct 27
  Neutrality Day, Dec 12
  Revival and Unity Day, May 18
Turkoglu, Hedo: Birth, Mar 19
Turlington, Christy: Birth, Jan 2
Turn Beauty Inside Out Day, May 19
Turner, Ike: Birth, Nov 5
Turner, Janine: Birth, Dec 6
Turner, John Napier: Birth, Jun 7
Turner, Kathleen: Birth, Jun 19
Turner, Ted: Birth, Nov 19
Turner, Tina: Birth, Nov 26
Turner's Frontier Address: Anniv, Jul 12
Turow, Scott: Birth, Apr 12
Turtle Day, World, May 23
Turtle Races (Danville, IL), Jun 12
Turturro, John: Birth, Feb 28
Turturro, Nick: Birth, Jan 29
Tushingham, Rita: Birth, Mar 14
Tuskegee Airmen Activated: Anniv, Mar 22
Tuskegee Institute Opening: Anniv, Jul 4
Tussaud, Marie: Birth Anniv, Dec 7
Tut, King: Tomb Discovery Anniv, Nov 4

743

Index ☆ Chase's 2004 Calendar of Events ☆

Tutor—Upsy

Tutor Appreciation Day, Apr 5
Tutu, Desmond: Birth, Oct 7
Tuvalu: National Holiday, Oct 1
Tuxedo, First Created, Oct 10
TV Turnoff Week, Natl, Apr 19
Twain, Mark (Samuel Clemens): Birth Anniv, Nov 30
Twain, Mark: Natl Tom Sawyer Days (Hannibal, MO), Jul 1
Twain, Shania: Birth, Aug 28
20/20 TV Premiere: Anniv, Jun 6
21 Jump Street TV Premiere: Anniv, Apr 12
Tweed Day, Apr 3
Tweed, Shannon: Birth, Mar 10
Twelfth Day (Epiphany), Jan 6
Twelfth Night, Jan 5
Twellman, Taylor: Birth, Feb 29
Twenty Questions TV Premiere: Anniv, Nov 26
Twiggy: Birth, Sep 19
Twilight Zone TV Premiere: Anniv, Oct 2
Twins Day Fest (Twinsburg, OH), Aug 6
Twit Award Month, Intl, Apr 1
Twitty, Conway: Birth Anniv, Sep 1
2001: A Space Odyssey Premiere: Anniv, Apr 3
Tyler, Anne: Birth, Oct 25
Tyler, John: Birth Anniv, Mar 29
Tyler, Julia G.: Birth Anniv, May 4
Tyler, Letitia Christian: Birth Anniv, Nov 12
Tyler, Liv: Birth, Jul 1
Tyler's Cabinet Resigns: Anniv, Sep 11
Tynwald Day (England), Jul 5
Typewriter, First: Anniv, Jun 23
Tyson, Cicely: Birth, Dec 19
Tyson, Mike: Birth, Jun 30
U-2 Incident: Anniv, May 1
Ueberroth, Peter: Birth, Sep 2
Uecker, Bob: Birth, Jan 26
UFO Days (Elmwood, WI), Jul 23
Uganda,
Independence Day, **Oct 9**
Liberation Day, **Apr 11**
Uggams, Leslie: Birth, May 25
Ukraine,
Chernobyl Reactor Disaster: Anniv, **Apr 26**
Independence Day, **Aug 24**
October Revolution, **Nov 7**
Ukrainian Day, **Jan 22**
Ukraine: Odessa Retaken Anniv, Apr 10
Ukrainian Famine Film Broadcast: Anniv, Nov 30
Ullman, Tracey: Birth, Dec 30
Ullmann, Liv: Birth, Dec 16
Ulrich, Skeet: Birth, Jan 20
Ultraviolet Awareness/Sight-Saving Month, Natl, May 1
Umbrella Month, Natl, Mar 1
Umbrella: Open an Umbrella Indoors Day, Natl, Mar 13
Underdog Day, Dec 17
Underground America Day, May 14
Underwood, Blair: Birth, Aug 25
UNESCO: Anniv, Nov 4
UNICEF (UN): Anniv, Dec 11
Union of Soviet Socialist Republics,
Moscow Communique: Anniv, **May 29**
Saint Petersburg Name Restored: Anniv, **Sep 6**
Soviet Union Dissolved: Anniv, **Dec 8**
Troop Withdrawal/Afghanistan Deadline, **Feb 15**
Unitas, Johnny: Birth Anniv, May 7
United Arab Emirates: Natl Day (Independence), Dec 2
United Kingdom. See also individual countries,
Accession of Queen Elizabeth II: Anniv, **Feb 6**
Battle of Britain Day, **Sep 15**
Battle of Britain Week, **Sep 12**
Boxing Day, **Dec 26**
Boxing Day Bank Holiday, **Dec 26**
Commonwealth Day, **Mar 8**
Coronation Day, **Jun 2**
Easter Monday Bank Holiday, **Apr 12**
Good Friday Bank Holiday, **Apr 9**
Holocaust Memorial Day, **Jan 27**
May Day Bank Holiday, **May 3**
New Year's Holiday, **Jan 1**
Spring Bank Holiday, **May 31**
Summer Bank Holiday, **Aug 30**
Summer Time, **Mar 29**
United Nations,
Abolition of Slavery, Intl Day for the, **Dec 2**
Africa Industrialization Day, **Nov 20**
AIDS Day, World, **Dec 1**
Biological Diversity, Intl Day for, **May 22**
Charter Signed: Anniv, **Jun 26**
Civil Aviation Day, Intl, **Dec 7**
Colonialism, Second Intl Decade for Eradication of, **Jan 1**
Cooperatives, Intl Day of, **Jul 3**
Culture of Peace and Non-Violence for the Children of the World, Intl Decade for a, **Jan 1**
Day for Preventing the Exploitation of the Environment in War and Armed Conflict, Intl, **Nov 6**
Day for Women's Rights & Intl Peace, **Mar 8**
Desert Storm: Deadline Resolution: Anniv, **Nov 28**
Disabled Persons, Intl Day of, **Dec 3**
Disarmament Week, **Oct 24**
Drug Abuse/Illicit Trafficking, Intl Day Against, **Jun 26**
Elimination of Violence against Women, Intl Day for the, **Nov 25**
Eradication of Poverty, Decade for the, **Jan 1**
Eradication of Poverty, Intl Day for, **Oct 17**
Families, Intl Day of, **May 15**
First General Assembly: Anniv, **Jan 10**
General Assembly Opening Day, **Sep 21**
Human Rights Day, **Dec 10**
Human Rights Education, Decade for, **Jan 1**
Indigenous People, Intl Decade of World's, **Jan 1**
Innocent Children Victims of Aggression, Intl Day of, **Jun 4**
Intl Day for Preservation of the Ozone Layer, **Sep 16**
Intl Day for Tolerance, **Nov 16**
Intl Day of Peace, **Sep 21**
Land Mine Ban: Anniv, **Mar 1**
Literacy Day, Intl, **Sep 8**
Literacy Decade: Education for All, **Jan 1**
Migrants Day, Intl, **Dec 18**
Millennium Summit: Anniv, **Sep 6**
Mother Language Day, Intl, **Feb 21**
Natural Disaster Reduction, Intl Day for, **Oct 13**
Older Persons, Intl Day of, **Oct 1**
Racial Discrimination, Intl Day for Elimination of, **Mar 21**
Racism/Racial Discrimination, Solidarity Against, **Mar 21**
Remembrance of the Slave Trade and its Abolition, Intl Day for the, **Aug 23**
Revokes Resolution on Zionism: Anniv, **Dec 16**
Roll Back Malaria in Developing Countries, Particularly in Africa, Decade to, **Jan 1**
Slavery and Its Abolition, Intl Year to Commemorate the Struggle Against, **Jan 1**
Solidarity with Palestinian People, Intl Day of, **Nov 29**
Taiwan Expelled: Anniv, **Oct 25**
Telecommunication Day, World, **May 17**
Torture Abolition Day, **Feb 4**
UNESCO: Anniv, **Nov 4**
UNICEF Day, Natl (Pres Proc), **Oct 31**
UNICEF: Anniv, **Dec 11**
United Nations Day, **Oct 24**
United Nations Day (Pres Proc), **Oct 24**
Universal Children's Day, **Nov 20**
Victims of Torture, Intl Day in Support of, **Jun 26**
Volunteer Day for Economic/Social Dvmt, Intl, **Dec 5**
Water, World Day for, **Mar 22**
Week of Solidarity with the Peoples of Non-Self-Governing Territories, **May 25**
World Book and Copyright Day, **Apr 23**
World Day to Combat Desertification and Drought, **Jun 17**
World Development Information Day, **Oct 24**
World Environment Day, **Jun 5**
World Food Day, **Oct 16**
World Habitat Day, **Oct 4**
World Health Day, **Apr 7**
World Health Organization: Anniv, **Apr 7**
World Mental Health Day, **Oct 10**
World Meteorological Day, **Mar 23**
World No-Tobacco Day, **May 31**
World Population Day, **Jul 11**
World Post Day, **Oct 9**
World Press Freedom Day, **May 3**
World Refugee Day, **Jun 20**
World Space Week, **Oct 4**
World Teachers' Day, **Oct 5**
World Television Day, **Nov 21**
World's Indigenous People, Intl Day of the, **Aug 9**
Year of Rice, Intl, **Jan 1**
Youth Day, Intl, **Aug 12**
United Planet Month, Sep 1
United States (government and history),
Air Force Established: Birth, **Sep 18**
Armed Forces Unified: Anniv, **Jul 26**
Army Established: Anniv, **Jun 14**
Attack on America: Anniv, **Sep 11**
Attack on the USS Liberty: Anniv, **Jun 8**
Bank Bailout Bill: Anniv, **Nov 27**
Bureau of Indian Affairs Established, **Mar 11**
Capitol Cornerstone Laid: Anniv, **Sep 18**
Civil Rights Act of 1964: Anniv, **Jul 2**
Civil Rights Act of 1968: Anniv, **Apr 11**
Clinton Impeachment Proceedings: Anniv, **Dec 20**
Coins Stamped "In God We Trust": Anniv, **Apr 22**
Congress Assembles, **Jan 5**
Congress Authorized Force Against Iraq: Anniv, **Jan 12**
Congress First Meets at Washington: Anniv, **Nov 21**
Congress Passes GATT Treaty: Anniv, **Dec 1**
Congress: First Meeting Anniv, **Mar 4**
Constitution of the US: Anniv, **Sep 17**
Customs: Anniv, **Aug 1**
Daylight Saving Time Begins, **Apr 4**
Daylight Saving Time Ends, **Oct 31**
Death Penalty Banned: Anniv, **Jun 29**
Declaration of Independence Approval and Signing: Anniv, **Jul 4**
Dept of Justice: Anniv, **Jun 22**
Dept of State Founded: Anniv, **Jul 27**
Distinguished Service Medal: Anniv, **Mar 7**
District of Columbia Establishing Legislation: Anniv, **Jul 16**
Dred Scott Decision: Anniv, **Mar 6**
Family-Leave Bill: Anniv, **Feb 5**
Federal Communications Commission Created: Anniv, **Feb 26**
Federal Credit Union Act: Anniv, **Jun 26**
Federal Govt Seizure of Steel Mills: Anniv, **Apr 8**
Female House Page, First Formal: Anniv, **May 14**
55 mph Speed Limit: Anniv, **Jan 2**
First Brawl in US House of Representatives: Anniv, **Jan 30**
First Census: Anniv, **Aug 1**
First Elected Woman Senator: Anniv, **Jan 12**
First Foreign-Born Chair Joint Chiefs: Anniv, **Aug 11**
First Mint in America: Anniv, **Jun 10**
First US Government Building: Anniv, **Jul 31**
First Woman US Ambassador Appointed: Anniv, **Oct 28**
Flag Amendment Defeated: Anniv, **Jun 26**
Flood Victims Relief: Anniv, **Aug 12**
General Election Day, **Nov 2**
Gerald Ford: Assassination Attempts: Anniv, **Sep 5**
Great Seal of the US: Authorization Anniv, **Jan 28**
Great Seal of the US: First Use Anniv, **Sep 16**
Great Seal of the US: Proposed: Anniv, **Jul 4**
Ground War Against Iraq Begins: Anniv, **Feb 23**
Home Owners Loan Act: Anniv, **Jun 13**
Independence Day, **Jul 4**
Invasion of Panama: Anniv, **Dec 20**
Irwin Earns 1st Medal of Honor: Anniv, **Feb 13**
Japan Bombed: Anniv, **Apr 18**
Japanese Internment: Anniv, **Feb 19**
Johnson Impeachment Proceedings: Anniv, **Feb 24**
Justice Thomas Confirmation: Anniv, **Oct 15**
Kuwait Liberated: Anniv, **Feb 27**
Labor Relations Act, Natl: Anniv, **Jul 5**
Lewis & Clark Expedition Commissioned: Anniv, **Jan 18**
Lewis & Clark Expedition Returns: Anniv, **Sep 23**
Lewis and Clark Expedition Sets Out: Anniv, **May 14**
Library of Congress: Anniv, **Apr 24**
Lincoln Signs Income Tax: Anniv, **Jul 1**
Meeting of the Electors, **Dec 13**
Military Ban on Homosexuals Eased: Anniv, **Jan 29**
Moscow Communique: Anniv, **May 29**
Motor Voter Bill Signed: Anniv, **May 20**
NAFTA Signed: Anniv, **Dec 8**
Nuclear-Free World, First Step Toward a: Anniv, **Dec 8**
Operation Iraqi Freedom: Anniv, **Mar 19**
Paper Money Issued: Anniv, **Mar 10**
Peace Corps Founded: Anniv, **Mar 1**
Persian Gulf War Begins: Anniv, **Jan 16**
Philippine Independence: Anniv, **Mar 24**
Pony Express, Inauguration of: Anniv, **Apr 3**
Postmaster General Established: Anniv, **Sep 22**
President Occupies the White House, **Nov 1**
Presidential Succession Act: Anniv, **Jul 18**
Ratification Day, **Jan 14**
Sanctions Against South Africa Lifted: Anniv, **Jul 10**
Securities and Exchange Commission Created: Anniv, **Jun 6**
Senate Acquits Clinton: Anniv, **Feb 12**
Senate Quorum: Anniv, **Apr 6**
Shanghai Communique: Anniv, **Feb 27**
Standard Time Act: Anniv, **Mar 19**
Supreme Court Abortion Notification Ruling: Anniv, **Jun 25**
Supreme Court Bans School Prayer: Anniv, **Jun 25**
Supreme Court Right to Die Ruling: Anniv, **Jun 25**
Supreme Court Upholds Ban on Abortion Counseling: Anniv, **May 23**
Treasury Department: Anniv, **Sep 2**
Treaty of Guadalupe Hidalgo (with Mexico): Anniv, **Feb 2**
Truman Doctrine: Anniv, **May 22**
27th Amendment Ratified: Anniv, **May 7**
Tyler's Cabinet Resigns: Anniv, **Sep 11**
Uniform Time Zone Plan: Anniv, **Nov 18**
US Capital Established at NYC: Anniv, **Sep 13**
US Enters WWI: Anniv, **Apr 6**
US Income Tax: Anniv, **Mar 8**
US Mint: Anniv, **Apr 2**
US Takes Out Its First Loan: Anniv, **Sep 18**
Vietnam Peace Agreement Signed: Anniv, **Jan 27**
Vietnam War Protestors Storm Pentagon: Anniv, **Oct 21**
Voting Rights Act Signed: Anniv, **Aug 6**
WAAC: Anniv, **May 14**
War Department: Establishment Anniv, **Aug 7**
War of 1812: Declaration Anniv, **Jun 18**
War on Poverty: Anniv, **Jan 8**
Water Pollution Control Act: Anniv, **Oct 18**
White House Easter Egg Roll: Anniv, **Apr 2**
Woman Runs the House: Anniv, **Jun 20**
Unity in Diversity Day, May 1
UNIVAC Computer: Anniv, Jun 14
Universal Children's Day (UN), Nov 20
Universal Father's Week, Jun 15
Universal Hour of Peace, Jan 1
Universal Human Rights Month, Dec 1
Universal Letter-Writing Week, Jan 8
Unser, Al, Jr: Birth, Apr 19
Unser, Al: Birth, May 29
Unser, Bobby: Birth, Feb 20
Up Helly Aa (Scotland), Jan 27
Update Your References Week, May 3
Update Your Resume Month, Sep 1
Updike, John: Birth, Mar 18
Upjohn, Richard: Birth Anniv, Jan 22
Uppity Women Day, Mar 8
Upshaw, Gene: Birth, Aug 15
Upstairs, Downstairs TV Premiere: Anniv, Oct 10
Upsy Daisy Day, Jun 8

☆ Chase's 2004 Calendar of Events ☆ Index

Uranus—Virginia

Uranus (planet) Discovery: Anniv, Mar 13
Uris, Leon: Birth Anniv, Aug 3
Urlacher, Brian: Birth, May 25
Uruguay,
Artigas Day, **Jun 19**
Battle of Las Piedras Day, **May 18**
Constitution Day, **Jul 18**
Independence Day, **Aug 25**
Landing of the 33 Patriots, **Apr 19**
US Air Force Academy Established: Anniv, Apr 1
US Amateur (Golf) Chmpshp (Mamaroneck, NY), Aug 16
US Amateur Public Links (Golf) Chmpshp (Maple Grove, MN), Jul 12
US and Vatican Re-establish Diplomatic Relations: Anniv, Jan 10
US House, Black Page Appointed: Anniv, Apr 9
US Income Tax: Anniv, Mar 8
US Junior Amateur (Golf) Chmpship (San Francisco, CA), Jul 27
US Military Academy Founded: Anniv, Mar 16
US Natl Snow Sculpting Competition (Lake Geneva, WI), Feb 4
US Naval Academy Founded: Anniv, Oct 10
US Navy: Authorization Anniv, Oct 13
US Open (Golf) Chmpshp (Southampton, NY), Jun 17
US Senior Open (Golf) Championship (St. Louis, MO), Jul 29
US Virgin Islands,
Danish West Indies Emancipation Day, **Jul 3**
Liberty Day, **Nov 1**
Natl Park Established: Anniv, **Aug 2**
Organic Act Day, **Jun 21**
Transfer Day, **Mar 31**
US Women's Amateur (Golf) Chmpshp (Erie, PA), Aug 9
US Women's Amateur Public Links (Golf) Chmpshp, Jun 15
US Women's Open (Golf) Chmpshp (South Hadley, MA), Jul 1
USA Film Fest (Dallas, TX), Apr 22
USA Today First Published: Anniv, Sep 15
USGA Senior Amateur (Golf) Chmpshp (Los Angeles, CA), Oct 9
USO Birthday, Feb 4
USS Iowa: Explosion on: Anniv, Apr 19
USS Liberty, Attack on: Anniv, Jun 8
USS Princeton Explosion: Anniv, Feb 28
USS Pueblo Seized: Anniv, Jan 23
USS Stark: Attack Anniv, May 17
USSR Established: Anniv, Dec 30
Ustinov, Peter: Birth, Apr 16
Usui, Mikao. See World Day of Reiki, Aug 15
Utah,
Admission Day, **Jan 4**
America's First Department Store (Salt Lake City), **Oct 16**
Arches Natl Park Established: Anniv, **Nov 12**
Bennett, Robert F.: Birth, **Sep 18**
Bryce Canyon Natl Park Established: Anniv, **Jan 1**
Capitol Reef Natl Park Established: Anniv, **Dec 18**
Days of '47 Celebration (Salt Lake City), **Jul 19**
Dinosaur Roundup Rodeo (Vernal), **Jul 7**
Gifted Children Conv, Natl Assn (Salt Lake City), **Nov 3**
Hatch, Orrin: Birth, **Mar 22**
Jell-O Week, **Feb 8**
Leavitt, Mike: Birth, **Feb 11**
Payson Golden Onion Days (Payson), **Sep 3**
Pioneer Day, **Jul 24**
Salt Lake's Family Christmas Gift Show (Salt Lake), **Nov 12**
Slamdance 2004 (Park City), **Jan 17**
Snowbird Jazz & Blues Festival (Snowbird), **Jul 30**
Snowbird Oktoberfest, **Sep 4**
State Fair (Salt Lake City), **Sep 9**
Sundance Film Fest (Park City), **Jan 15**
Utah Women Given Vote: Anniv, **Feb 12**
World Folkfest (Springville), **Jul 10**
Zion Natl Park Established: Anniv, **Nov 19**
Utley, Garrick: Birth, Nov 19
Uzbekistan,
Army Day, **Jan 14**
Constitution Day, **Dec 8**
Day of Memory and Honor, **May 9**
Independence Day, **Sep 1**
Vaccaro, Brenda: Birth, Nov 18
Vachon, Rogie: Birth, Sep 8
Vaisakhi: Baisakhi (India), Apr 13
Valderrama, Carlos: Birth, Sep 2
Valens, Richie: Day the Music Died: Death Anniv, Feb 3
Valentine Exhibit, Antique (Clinton, MD), Jan 22
Valentine, Bobby: Birth, May 13
Valentine, Karen: Birth, May 25
Valentine, Scott: Birth, Jun 3
Valentine's Ball, WMAS's (Springfield, MA), Feb 14
Valentine's Day, Feb 14
Valentine's Day Massacre: Anniv, Feb 14
Valentino (Rudolph) Memorial Service, Aug 23
Valentino, Rudolph: Birth Anniv, May 6
Valenzuela, Fernando: Birth, Nov 1
Vallee, Rudy: Birth Anniv, Jul 28
Valli, Frankie: Birth, May 3
Van Ark, Joan: Birth, Jun 16
Van Brocklin, Norm: Birth Anniv, Mar 15
Van Buren, Abigail: Birth, Jul 4
Van Buren, Hannah Hoes: Birth Anniv, Mar 8
Van Buren, Martin: Birth Anniv, Dec 5
Van Cleef, Lee: Birth Anniv, Jan 9
Van Damme, Jean-Claude: Birth, Oct 18
Van Der Beek, James: Birth, Mar 8
Van Devere, Trish: Birth, Mar 9
Van Doren, Mamie: Birth, Feb 6
Van Dyke, Dick: Birth, Dec 13
Van Dyke, Jerry: Birth, Jul 27
Van Exel, Nick: Birth, Nov 27
Van Fleet, Jo: Birth Anniv, Dec 30
Van Gogh, Vincent: Birth Anniv, Mar 30
Van Gundy, Jeff: Birth, Jan 19
Van Halen, Eddie: Birth, Jan 26
Van Heusen, Jimmy: Birth Anniv, Jan 26
Van Horn, Keith: Birth, Oct 23
Van Patten, Dick: Birth, Dec 9
Van Patten, Joyce: Birth, Mar 9
Van Peebles, Mario: Birth, Jan 15
Van Peebles, Melvin: Birth, Aug 21
Van Slyke, Andy: Birth, Dec 21
Vancouver, George: Birth Anniv, Jun 22
Vanderbilt, Gloria: Birth, Feb 20
Vandross, Luther: Birth, Apr 20
Vanilla Ice: Birth, Oct 31
Vanuatu: Independence Day, Jul 30
Vardalos, Nia: Birth, Sep 24
Vatican and US Re-establish Diplomatic Relations: Anniv, Jan 10
Vatican City: Independence Anniv, Feb 11
Vatican Council II: Anniv, Oct 11
Vaughan Williams, Ralph: Birth Anniv, Oct 12
Vaughan, Sarah: Birth Anniv, Mar 27
Vaughn, Robert: Birth, Nov 22
VCR Introduced: Anniv, Jun 7
V-E Day, May 8
Veblen, Thorstein: Birth Anniv, Jul 30
Veeck, Bill: Birth Anniv, Feb 9
Veep Day, Aug 9
Vega, Suzanne: Birth, Jul 11
Vegan Month, Nov 1
Vegan World Day, Jun 20
Vegetarian Day, World, Oct 1
Vegetarian Month, Oct 1
Vegetarian Resource Group's Essay Contest for Kids, May 1
VelJohnson, Reginald: Birth, Aug 16
Veneman, Ann: Birth, Jun 29
Venezuela,
Battle of Carabobo Day, **Jun 24**
Independence Day, **Jul 5**
Venice Film Fest (Venice, Italy), Aug 28
Ventura, Jesse: Birth, Jul 15
Ventura, Robin: Birth, Jul 14
Venus, Transit of, Jun 8
Vercors, Jean: Birth Anniv, Feb 26
Verdi, Giuseppi: Birth Anniv, Oct 10
Verdon, Gwen: Birth Anniv, Jan 13
Vereen, Ben: Birth, Oct 10
Vermeil, Dick: Birth, Oct 30
Vermont,
Admission Day, **Mar 4**
All About Apples (Woodstock), **Sep 26**
Antique/Classic Car Show (Bennington), **Sep 17**
Brookfield Ice Harvest (Brookfield), **Jan 31**
Champlain Valley Fair (Essex Junction), **Aug 28**
Children's Day (Woodstock), **Aug 21**
Cow Appreciation Day (Woodstock), **Jul 17**
Douglas, Jim: Birth, **Jun 21**
Fall Foliage Fest (Walden), **Sep 27**
Family Halloween, A (Woodstock), **Oct 24**
Harvest Celeb (Woodstock), **Oct 9**
Heirloom Seed Day (Woodstock), **Jun 5**
Jay Peak Annual Arts & Crafts Fair (Jay), **Oct 9**
Jeffords, James M.: Birth, **May 11**
Leahy, Patrick J.: Birth, **Mar 31**
Old Vermont Fourth (Woodstock), **Jul 4**
Pumpkin Day (Woodstock), **Oct 2**
Quilt Show (Woodstock), **Jul 29**
State Fair (Rutland), **Sep 3**
Town Meeting Day, **Mar 2**
Traditional Plowing Match (Woodstock), **May 2**
Vermont Apple Fest (Springfield), **Oct 9**
Vermont Maple Fest (St. Albans), **Apr 23**
Wassail Celebration (Woodstock), **Dec 10**
Wool Day: Sheep to Shawl/Border Collies (Woodstock), **Sep 19**
Verne, Jules: Birth Anniv, Feb 8
Vernon, John: Birth, Feb 24
Verrazano Day, Apr 17
Versailles Peace Conference: Anniv, Jan 18
Vesak, Day of: See Birthday of the Buddha, Apr 8
Vesey, Denmark: Death Anniv, Jul 2
Vespucci, Amerigo: Birth Anniv, Mar 9
Vesuvius Day, Aug 24
Veterans,
Branson Veterans Homecoming, **Nov 5**
Pearl Harbor Remembrance Day, Natl (Pres Proc), **Dec 7**
Remembrance Day (Gettysburg, PA), **Nov 20**
Soldiers' Reunion Celebration (Newton, NC), **Aug 19**
Veterans Bonus Army Eviction: Anniv, **Jul 28**
Veterans Day, **Nov 11**
Veterans Day (Pres Proc), **Nov 11**
Veterans Day Celebration (Mamou, LA), **Nov 11**
Veterans of Foreign Wars Established: Anniv, **Sep 29**
VFW Ladies Auxiliary Organized: Anniv, **Sep 17**
Vietnam Veterans Memorial Statue Unveiling: Anniv, **Nov 9**
Women's War Memorial Dedicated: Anniv, **Nov 11**
Vice Presidential Resignation: Anniv, Dec 28
Vice Presidential Candidate, First Woman: Anniv, Jul 19
Victims of Torture, Intl Day in Support of (UN), Jun 26
Victor Emmanuel III: Birth Anniv, Nov 11
Victor, James: Birth, Jul 27
Victoria Day (Canada), May 24
Victorian Christmas Home Tour (Leadville, CO), Dec 4
Victorian Sherlock Holmes Weekend (Cape May, NJ), Mar 5
Victorian Week (Cape May, NJ), Oct 8
Victory Day (RI), Aug 9
Victory in Europe Day, May 8
Vidal, Gore: Birth, Oct 3
Video Games Day, Sep 12
Vieira, Meredith: Birth, Dec 30
Vietnam,
Ho Chi Minh: Birth Anniv, **May 19**
Liberation Day, **Apr 30**
Natl Holiday, **Feb 3**
Vietnam War (US undeclared),
Battle of Hamburger Hill: Anniv, **May 11**
Cambodia Invaded by US: Anniv, **Apr 30**
Dien Bien Phu Falls: Anniv, **May 7**
Gulf of Tonkin Resolution: Anniv, **Aug 7**
Independence Day, **Sep 2**
King Opposes Vietnam War: Anniv, **Apr 4**
My Lai Massacre: Anniv, **Mar 16**
Saigon Falls to Vietcong: Anniv, **Apr 30**
Tet Offensive Begins, **Jan 30**
Vietnam and US Resume Relations: Anniv, **May 26**
Vietnam Conflict Begins [with French]: Anniv, **Aug 22**
Vietnam Moratorium Concert: Anniv, **Mar 28**
Vietnam Peace Agreement Signed: Anniv, **Jan 27**
Vietnam Veterans Memorial Statue Unveiling: Anniv, **Nov 9**
Vietnam War Protestors Storm Pentagon: Anniv, **Oct 21**
Women's War Memorial Dedicated: Anniv, **Nov 11**
Vigoda, Abe: Birth, Feb 24
Viking Fest (Denmark), Jun 18
Viking Fest (Poulsbo, WA), May 14
Viking: Up Helly Aa (Scotland), Jan 27
Vila, Bob: Birth, Jun 20
Vilas, Guillermo: Birth, Aug 17
Villeneueve, Jacques: Birth, Apr 9
Vilsack, Tom: Birth, Dec 13
Vincent, Fay: Birth, May 29
Vincent, Jan-Michael: Birth, Jul 15
Vinegar Day, Aug 21
Vinson, Fred M.: Birth Anniv, Jan 22
Vinton, Bobby: Birth, Apr 16
Vinyl Record Day, Aug 12
Virchow, Rudolf: Birth Anniv, Oct 13
Virgin Islands,
Hurricane Supplication Day, **Jul 26**
Hurricane Thanksgiving Day, **Oct 18**
Puerto Rico Friendship Day, **Oct 11**
Virginia,
Allen, George: Birth, **Mar 8**
American Business Women's Assn, Natl Conv (Richmond), **Oct 13**
Ash Lawn Opera Fest (Charlottesville), **Jul 10**
Battle of Bull Run: Anniv, **Jul 21**
Battle of Cold Harbor: Anniv, **Jun 3**
Battle of Spotsylvania: Anniv, **May 12**
Battle of the Wilderness: Anniv, **May 5**
Birds & Blossoms Spring Nature Festival (Norfolk), **May 6**
Blue Ridge Folklife Fest (Ferrum), **Oct 23**
Boardwalk Art Show & Fest (Virginia Beach), **Jun 17**
Bonnie Blue Natl Horse Show (Lexington), **May 5**
Bread Riot at Richmond: Anniv, **Apr 2**
Chincoteague Easter Decoy Show (Chincoteague Island), **Apr 9**
Chincoteague Pony Penning (Chincoteague Island), **Jul 28**
Christmas Candlelight Tour (Fredricksburg), **Dec 11**
Civil War Days (Chesapeake), **Sep 11**
Civil War Peace Talks: Anniv, **Feb 3**
Colonial Christmas (Williamsburg), **Dec 18**
Craftsmen's Christmas Classic Arts & Crafts Fest (Richmond), **Nov 5**
Craftsmen's Classic Arts & Crafts Fest (Chantilly), **Mar 26**
Craftsmen's Classic Arts & Crafts Fest (Chantilly), **Oct 15**
Craftsmen's Classic Arts & Crafts Fest (Richmond), **Mar 12**
Craftsmen's Classic Arts & Crafts Fest (Roanoke), **Oct 1**
Creepy Tales: Haunted History (Staunton), **Oct 29**
Cut Your Own Christmas Tree (Charlottesville), **Nov 26**
Defeat at Five Forks: Anniv, **Apr 1**
East Coast Surfing Chmpshps/Sports Fest (Virginia Beach), **Aug 25**
Eighteenth-Century Autumn Market Fair (McLean), **Oct 16**

Index ☆ Chase's 2004 Calendar of Events ☆

Virginia (cont'd)—Washington

Eighteenth-Century Christmas Wassail (McLean), **Dec 12**
Eighteenth-Century Summer Market Fair (McLean), **Jul 17**
Eighteenth-Century Threshing Day (McLean), **Nov 21**
Fall of Richmond: Anniv, **Apr 3**
First US Breach of Promise Suit: Anniv, **Jun 14**
Foods/Feasts of Colonial Virginia (Williamsburg), **Nov 25**
Foxfield Races (Charlottesville), **Apr 24**
Fredericksburg Day (Fredericksburg), **Apr 20**
Fredericksburg Heritage Fest (Fredericksburg), **Jul 4**
Fredericksburg Music Fest (Fredericksburg), **May 29**
Garden of Lights (Norfolk), **Nov 27**
George Washington Birthday Parade (Alexandria), **Feb 16**
Gold Cup, Intl (The Plains), **Oct 16**
Great Peanut Tour (Skippers), **Sep 9**
Highland County Maple Fest (Highland County), **Mar 13**
Historic Garden Week, **Apr 17**
History Alive! (Norfolk), **Oct 1**
Holiday House Tours (Charlottesville), **Dec 11**
Holiday Lantern Tours (Staunton), **Dec 10**
Holidays in the City Grand Illumination Parade (Norfolk), **Nov 20**
James Monroe Birthday Celebration (Charlottesville), **Apr 28**
Jamestown Landing Day (Williamsburg), **May 15**
Lee-Jackson Day, **Jan 16**
Maymont Flower & Garden Show (Richmond), **Feb 19**
Maymont's Herbs Galore (Richmond), **Apr 24**
Mermaids on Parada (Norfolk), **Jul 1**
Migratory Bird Celebration, Intl (Chincoteague), **May 8**
Military Through the Ages (Williamsburg), **Mar 20**
Miss Virginia Pageant (Roanoke), **Jun 24**
NCAA Div I Men's Golf Chmpshp (Hot Springs), **Jun 1**
Neptune Fest Boardwalk Weekend (Virginia Beach), **Sep 24**
Oktoberfest! (Staunton), **Oct 8**
Old Fiddlers' Conv (Galax), **Aug 9**
Oyster Fest (Chincoteague Island), **Oct 9**
Peninsula Campaign Intensified: Anniv, **May 9**
Potomac Celtic Fest (Leesburg), **Jun 12**
Raid on Richmond: Anniv, **Mar 1**
Rappahannock River Waterfowl Show (White Stone), **Mar 20**
Ratification Day, **Jun 25**
Richmond Highland Games/Celtic Fest (Richmond), **Oct 23**
Road to Independence (Williamsburg), **Jul 3**
Roanoke Fest in the Park (Roanoke), **May 28**
Rockbridge Community Fest (Lexington), **Aug 21**
Rockbridge Regional Fair (Lexington), **Jul 20**
Saint Patrick's Day Parade (Roanoke), **Mar 13**
Seed to Stalk (Williamsburg), **Jun 1**
Seven Days Campaign: Anniv, **Jun 25**
Shenandoah Natl Park Established: Anniv, **Dec 26**
Sounds of Season: Holiday Concert (Charlottesville), **Dec 26**
Spring Gardener's Market and Plant Sale (Norfolk), **May 8**
State Chmpshp Chili Cook-off (Roanoke), **May 8**
State Fair (Richmond), **Sep 23**
Stonewall Jackson's Birthday Celebration (Lexington), **Jan 21**
Strawberry Hill Races (Richmond), **Apr 10**
Streetscene (Covington), **Aug 14**
Sugarloaf Crafts Fest (Chantilly), **Apr 30**
Sugarloaf Crafts Fest (Chantilly), **Jan 30**
Sugarloaf Crafts Fest (Manassas), **Sep 10**
Taste of History (Staunton), **Sep 18**
The Present Looks at the Past: Modern Views of the American Revolution (Yorktown), **Jan 1**
Tobacco Harvest (McLean), **Aug 22**
Tools of the Trade (Williamsburg), **Aug 1**
Union Officers Escape Libby Prison: Anniv, **Feb 9**
Upperville Colt/Horse Show (Upperville), **Jun 7**
Virginia Christmas Show (Richmond), **Nov 4**
Virginia Gold Cup (Warrenton), **May 1**
Virginia Lake Fest (Clarksville), **Jul 16**
Virginia Peanut Fest (Emporia), **Sep 24**
Virginia Pork Fest (Emporia), **Jun 9**
Virginia Spring Show (Richmond), **Mar 11**
Virginia Wine Fest (Charlottesville), **May 15**
Warner, John: Birth, **Feb 18**
Warner, Mark: Birth, **Dec 15**
Wheat Harvest, 18th-Century (McLean), **Jun 20**
Yorktown Victory Celebration (Yorktown), **Oct 16**
Yorktown Victory Day, **Oct 11**
Virginia Company Expedition to America: Anniv, Dec 20
Virginia Peanut Fest (Emporia, VA), Sep 24
Virginia Plan Proposed: Anniv, May 29
Virginian TV Premiere: Anniv, Sep 19
Virgo Begins, Aug 23
Virtual Love Day, Jul 24
Vision Research Month, Jun 1
Visit Your Relatives Day, May 18
Visnjic, Goran: Birth, Sep 9
Vitale, Dick: Birth, Jun 9
Vitamin C Isolated: Anniv, Apr 4
Viticulturist's Day (Bulgaria), Feb 14
Vitti, Monica: Birth, Nov 3
Viva El Paso (El Paso, TX), Jun 10
Viva! Chicago Latin Music Fest (Chicago, IL), Aug 28
V-J Day (Announcement), Aug 14
V-J Day (Ratification), Sep 2
V-Mail Delivery: Anniv, Jun 22
Voight, Jon: Birth, Dec 29
Voinovich, George V.: Birth, Jul 15
Volcanoes,
Cameroon: Eruption: Anniv, **Aug 22**
Laki Volcano Eruption: Anniv, **Jun 8**
Montserrat: Volcano Erupts: Anniv, **Jun 25**
Mount Pelee Eruption: Anniv, **May 8**
Mount Pinatubo Erupts in Philippines: Anniv, **Jun 11**
Mount Saint Helens Eruption: Anniv, **May 18**
Vesuvius Day (Pompeii Destroyed: Anniv), **Aug 24**
Volleyball: NAIA Women's Volleyball Chmpshp (San Diego, CA), Dec 3
Voltaire: Birth Anniv, Nov 21
Volunteer Day for Economic/Social Dvmt, Intl (UN), Dec 5
Volunteer Week, Natl, Apr 18
Volunteer Week, Natl (Pres Proc), Apr 18
Volunteers Week, Intl, Jun 1
Volunteers: Make a Difference Day, Oct 23
Von Braun: First Surface-to-Surface Missile: Anniv, Dec 24
Von Furstenberg, Diane: Birth, Dec 31
Von Oy, Jenna: Birth, May 2
Von Richtofen: Red Baron Shot Down: Anniv, Apr 21
Von Steuben, Baron Friedrich: Birth Anniv, Sep 17
Von Sydow, Max: Birth, Apr 10
Vonnegut, Kurt, Jr: Birth, Nov 11
Vote Lawyers Out of Office Day, Apr 8
Vote: Blacks Ruled Eligible to Vote: Anniv, Apr 3
Vote: Motor Voter Bill Signed: Anniv, May 20
Voting Age Changed (26th Amendment): Anniv, Jul 1
Voting Rights Act Signed: Anniv, Aug 6
Vox Populi Day, Nov 11
Voyageurs Natl Park Established: Anniv, Apr 8
Wachowski, Andy: Birth, Dec 29
Wachowski, Larry: Birth, Jun 21
Wade, Virginia: Birth, Jul 10
Wadlow, Robert Pershing: Birth Anniv, Feb 22
Waffle Week, Natl, Sep 5
Waggoner, Lyle: Birth, Apr 13
Wagner, Billy: Birth, Jun 25
Wagner, Honus: Birth Anniv, Feb 24
Wagner, Jack P.: Birth, Oct 3
Wagner, Kurt: Birth, Jun 22
Wagner, Lindsay: Birth, Jun 22
Wagner, Richard: Birth Anniv, May 22
Wagner, Robert: Birth, Feb 10
Wagon Train TV Premiere: Anniv, Sep 18
Wagoner, Porter: Birth, Aug 12
Wahl, Ken: Birth, Dec 11
Wahlberg, Donnie: Birth, Aug 17
Wahlberg, Mark: Birth, Jun 5
Waitangi Day (New Zealand), Feb 6
Waite, Morrison R.: Birth Anniv, Nov 29
Waite, Terry: Birth, May 31
Waits, Tom: Birth, Dec 7
Waitstaff Day, Natl, May 21
Waitz, Grete: Birth, Oct 1
Wald, Lillian D.: Birth Anniv, Mar 10
Walden, Narada Michael: Birth, Apr 23
Walden, Robert: Birth, Sep 25
Waldseemuller, Martin: Remembrance Day, Apr 25
Wales,
Christmas Holiday, **Dec 25**
Hay-on-Wye Fest of Literature (Hay-on-Wye), **May 28**
Llangollen Intl Musical Eisteddfod (Llangollen, Denbighshire), **Jul 6**
Natl Eisteddfod of Wales (Newport, Gwent), **Jul 31**
Saint David's Day, **Mar 1**
Walesa, Lech: Birth, Sep 29
Walesa, Lech: Solidarity Founded Anniv, Aug 31
Walk on Your Wild Side Day, Apr 12
Walk Your Pet Month, Jan 1
Walken, Christopher: Birth, Mar 31
Walker, Alice: Birth, Feb 9
Walker, Ally: Birth, Aug 25
Walker, Antoine: Birth, Aug 12
Walker, Clint: Birth, May 30
Walker, Doak: Birth Anniv, Jan 1
Walker, Herschel: Birth, Mar 3
Walker, Jimmie: Birth, Jun 25
Walker, Larry: Birth, Dec 1
Walker, Mary E.: Birth Anniv, Nov 26
Walker, Mort: Birth, Sep 3
Walking,
Mackinac Bridge Walk (St. Ignace, MI), **Sep 6**
Sauntering Day, World, **Jun 19**
Walk Days, Intl, **Apr 30**
Walkman Debuts: Anniv, Jul 1
Wallace, Chris: Birth, Oct 12
Wallace, George, Shot: Anniv, May 15
Wallace, Henry A.: Birth Anniv, Oct 7
Wallace, Mike: Birth, May 9
Wallace, Rasheed: Birth, Sep 17
Wallace, Rusty: Birth, Aug 14
Wallach, Eli: Birth, Dec 7
Wallenberg, Raoul: Birth Anniv, Aug 5
Wallet, Skeezix: Birth, Feb 14
Walpurgis Night, Apr 30
Walsh, M. Emmet: Birth, Mar 22
Walt Disney TV Premiere: Anniv, Oct 27
Walter Plinge Day (England), Dec 2
Walter, Jessica: Birth, Jan 31
Walters, Barbara: Birth, Sep 25
Walters, Julie: Birth, Feb 22
Walton, Bill: Birth, Nov 5
Walton, George: Death Anniv, Feb 2
Walton, Izaak: Birth Anniv, Aug 9
Walton, Sam: Birth Anniv, Mar 29
Waltons TV Premiere: Anniv, Sep 14
Waltrip, Darrell: Birth, Feb 5
Wambaugh, Joseph: Birth, Jan 22
Wang, Garrett: Birth, Dec 15
Wapner, Joseph: Birth, Nov 15
War is Hell: Anniv, Jun 19
War of 1812: Declaration Anniv, Jun 18
War of the Worlds Broadcast: Anniv, Oct 30
War on Poverty Anniv, Jan 8
War Time: Anniv, Feb 9
Ward, Burt: Birth, Jul 6
Ward, Montgomery, Seized: Anniv, Apr 26
Ward, Rachel: Birth, Sep 12
Ward, Sela: Birth, Jul 11
Ward, Simon: Birth, Oct 19
Warden, Jack: Birth, Sep 18
Warfield, Marsha: Birth, Mar 5
Warhol, Andy: Birth Anniv, Aug 6
Warner Weather Quotation: Anniv, Aug 24
Warner, Charles Dudley: Birth Anniv, Sep 12
Warner, David: Birth, Jul 29
Warner, John: Birth, Feb 18
Warner, Malcolm-Jamal: Birth, Aug 18
Warner, Mark: Birth, Dec 15
Warren Commission Report: Anniv, Sep 27
Warren, Earl: Birth Anniv, Mar 19
Warren, Lesley Ann: Birth, Aug 16
Warren, Michael: Birth, Mar 5
Warren, Robert Penn: Birth Anniv, Apr 24
Warrick, Ruth: Birth, Jun 29
Warwick, Dionne: Birth, Dec 12
Washington,
Admission Day, **Nov 11**
Bumbershoot: The Seattle Arts Fest (Seattle), **Sep 3**
Cantwell, Maria: Birth, **Oct 13**
Christmas in Seattle Holiday Gift Show (Seattle), **Nov 19**
Corvette and High Performance Meet (Puyallup), **Feb 7**
Discovery Walk Festival (Vancouver), **Apr 23**
Eleanor Roosevelt Day (Willapa), **Aug 7**
Everett Salty Sea Days (Everett), **Jun 3**
Fireworks on the Fjord (Poulsbo), **Jul 3**
Issaquah Salmon Days Festival (Issaquah), **Oct 2**
Locke, Gary: Birth, **Jan 21**
Makah Days (Neah Bay), **Aug 27**
Manchester Father's Day Salmon Bake (Manchester), **Jun 20**
Mount Rainier Natl Park: Anniv, **Mar 2**
Mural-in-a-Day (Toppenish), **Jun 5**
Murray, Patty: Birth, **Oct 11**
Nordic Yulefest (Seattle), **Nov 20**
North Cascades Natl Park Established: Anniv, **Oct 2**
Northwest Folklife Fest (Seattle), **May 28**
Olympic Natl Park Established: Anniv, **Jun 29**
Puyallup Spring Fair (Puyallup), **Apr 15**
Seafair (Seattle), **Jul 3**
Seattle Blackout: Anniv, **May 11**
Seattle Boat Show (Seattle), **Jan 16**
Sequim Irrigation Fest (Sequim), **Apr 30**
Skagit Valley Tulip Fest (Burlington), **Apr 1**
Tacoma Holiday Food and Gift Fest (Tacoma), **Oct 20**
Tivoli-Viking Days at the Nordic Heritage Museum (Seattle), **Jul 10**
Viking Fest (Poulsbo), **May 14**
Washington State Apple Blossom Fest (Wenatchee), **Apr 29**
Western Washington Fair (Puyallup), **Sep 10**
Washington, Booker T.: Birth Anniv, Apr 5
Washington, Denzel: Birth, Dec 28
Washington, District of Columbia,
Administrative Professionals Intl Conv, **Aug 1**
African American Holiday Expo, **Dec 18**
American Historical Assn Annual Meeting, **Jan 8**
Cherry Blossom Fest, **Mar 27**
Davidson Fellows Award Reception, **Sep 29**
District-Establishing Legislation: Anniv, **Jul 16**
Education Assn Meeting, Natl, **Jul 2**
Geographic Bee Finals, Natl, **May 25**
Invasion Anniv, **Aug 24**
Newspaper Assn of America Convention, **Apr 20**
Rock Creek Park Nationalized: Anniv, **Jun 10**
Spelling Bee Finals, Natl, **Jun 2**
Vietnam Veterans Memorial Statue Unveiling: Anniv, **Nov 9**
Washington Boat Show, **Feb 18**
Washington Home & Garden Show, **Mar 25**
Washington Monument Dedicated: Anniv, **Feb 21**
White House Easter Egg Roll, **Apr 12**
Women's War Memorial Dedicated: Anniv, **Nov 11**
World Future Society Annual Conference, **Jul 31**
Washington, George,
Address to Continental Army Officers: Anniv, **Mar 15**
Birth Anniv, **Feb 22**
Birthday Observance (Legal Holiday), **Feb 16**
Birthday Parade (Alexandria, VA), **Feb 16**
Presidential Inauguration Anniv, **Apr 30**

★ Chase's 2004 Calendar of Events ★ Index

Takes Command of Continental Army: Anniv, **Jul 3**
Washington's Birthday Celeb (Laredo, TX), **Feb 7**
White House Cornerstone Laid: Anniv, **Oct 13**
Washington, Harold: Birth Anniv, **Apr 15**
Washington, Harold: Elected Chicago's First Black Mayor: Anniv, **Apr 11**
Washington, Martha: Birth Anniv, **Jun 21**
Wasserstein, Wendy: Birth, **Oct 18**
Wasson, Craig: Birth, **Mar 15**
Water Gardening Month, Natl, **Jul 1**
Water Ski Days (Lake City, MN), **Jun 25**
Water, World Day for (UN), **Mar 22**
Water-Drawing Fest (Japan), **Mar 1**
Waterfowl Fest (Easton, MD), **Nov 12**
Waterfront, On the (Rockford, IL), **Sep 2**
Watergate Day, **Jun 17**
Waterloo, Battle of: Anniv, **Jun 18**
Watermelon Fest (Rush Springs, OK), **Aug 14**
Watermelon Fest, Hope (Hope, AR), **Aug 12**
Watermelon Thump (Luling, TX), **Jun 24**
Waters, Ethel: Birth Anniv, **Oct 31**
Waters, John: Birth, **Apr 22**
Waters, Muddy: Birth Anniv, **Apr 4**
Waterston, Sam: Birth, **Nov 15**
Watie, Stand: Birth Anniv, **Dec 12**
Watley, Jody: Birth, **Jan 30**
Watson, Doc: Birth, **Mar 2**
Watson, Emily: Birth, **Jan 14**
Watson, Emma: Birth, **Apr 15**
Watson, James: Birth, **Apr 6**
Watson, Tom: Birth, **Sep 4**
Watt, James: Birth Anniv, **Jan 19**
Wattleton, Alyce Faye: Birth, **Jul 8**
Watts Riot: Anniv, **Aug 11**
Watts, Andre: Birth, **Jun 20**
Watts, Charlie: Birth, **Jun 2**
Watts, Rolonda: Birth, **Jul 12**
Waukesha Riverfest (Waukesha, WI), **Jul 29**
Wave All Your Fingers at Your Neighbor Day, **Feb 7**
Wayans, Damon: Birth, **Sep 4**
Wayans, Keenan Ivory: Birth, **Jun 8**
Wayans, Marlon: Birth, **Jul 23**
Wayans, Shawn: Birth, **Jan 19**
Wayne, John: Birth Anniv, **May 26**
Wayne, Mad Anthony: Birth Anniv, **Jan 1**
Wealth Mentality Month, Intl, **Jan 1**
Wear Your Pajamas To Work Day, Natl, **Apr 16**
Weather,
  Great Blizzard of '88: Anniv, **Mar 12**
  Meteorological Day, World (UN), **Mar 23**
  North America's Coldest Temperature: Anniv, **Feb 3**
  Warmest Year on Record Declared, **Jan 11**
  Warner Quotation: Anniv, **Aug 24**
  Weatherman's Day, **Feb 5**
Weathers, Carl: Birth, **Jan 14**
Weaver, Dennis: Birth, **Jun 4**
Weaver, Fritz: Birth, **Jan 19**
Weaver, Robert C.: First Black US Cabinet Member: Anniv, **Jan 18**
Weaver, Sigourney: Birth, **Oct 8**
Weaving Week, Spinning and, **Oct 4**
Webb, Karrie: Birth, **Dec 21**
Webb, Spud: Birth, **Jul 13**
Webber, Chris: Birth, **Mar 1**
Weber, Carl Maria Von: Birth Anniv, **Nov 18**
Weber, Steven: Birth, **Mar 4**
Webster, Daniel: Birth Anniv, **Jan 18**
Webster, Noah: Birth Anniv, **Oct 16**
Webster-Ashburton Treaty Signed: Anniv, **Aug 9**
Wedding of the Giants (Belgium), **Aug 22**
Wedding of the Sea (Venice, Italy), **May 23**
Wedding: Bill and Hillary Clinton: Anniv, **Oct 11**
Wedding: George H.W. and Barbara Bush: Anniv, **Jan 6**
Wedding: George H. and Laura Bush: Anniv, **Nov 5**
Wedding: Jimmy and Rosalynn Carter: Anniv, **Jul 7**
Wedding: Santa Cruz Bridal Expo (Santa Cruz, CA), **Feb 1**
Weddings Month, Natl, **Feb 1**
Wedgwood, Josiah: Birth Anniv, **Jul 12**
Week of the Ocean, Natl, **Apr 4**
Weems, Mason L. (Parson): Birth Anniv, **Oct 11**
Wegman, William: Birth, **Dec 2**
Weights and Measures Day, **May 20**
Weil, Andrew: Birth, **Jun 8**
Weinberg, Max M.: Birth, **Apr 13**
Weir, Bob: Birth, **Oct 16**
Weir, Peter: Birth, **Aug 21**
Weird Contest Week (Ocean City, NJ), **Aug 15**
Weiskopf, Tom: Birth, **Nov 9**
Weiss, Michael T.: Birth, **Feb 2**
Weiss, Michael: Birth, **Aug 2**
Weissmuller, Johnny: Birth Anniv, **Jun 2**
Weisz, Rachel: Birth, **Mar 7**
Weitz, Bruce: Birth, **May 27**
Weizmann, Chaim: Birth Anniv, **Nov 27**
Welch, Raquel: Birth, **Sep 5**
Welcome Back, Kotter TV Premiere: Anniv, **Sep 9**
Welcomegiving Day, You're, **Nov 26**
Weld, Tuesday: Birth, **Aug 27**
Welfare: See Health and Welfare, **Aug 14**
Welk, Lawrence: Birth Anniv, **Mar 11**
Wellderly Day, **Mar 15**
Weller, Peter: Birth, **Jun 24**
Welles, Orson: Birth Anniv, **May 6**
Welles, Orson: Citizen Kane Premiere: Anniv, **May 1**

Welling, Tom: Birth, **Apr 26**
Wells, H.G.: Birth Anniv, **Sep 21**
Wells, Ida B.: Birth Anniv, **Jul 16**
Wells, Kitty: Birth, **Aug 30**
Wells, Mary: Birth Anniv, **May 13**
Wen, Ming-Na: Birth, **Nov 20**
Wendt, George: Birth, **Oct 17**
Wenner, Jann: Birth, **Jan 7**
Werfel, Franz: Birth Anniv, **Sep 10**
Wesley, John: Birth Anniv, **Jun 17**
West Virginia,
  Admission Day, **Jun 20**
  Apple Butter Fest (Berkeley Springs), **Oct 9**
  Bridge Day (Fayetteville), **Oct 16**
  Byrd, Robert C.: Birth, **Nov 20**
  Fantasy of Light Parade (Wheeling), **Nov 19**
  Feast of the Ramson (Richwood), **Apr 17**
  Head-of-the-Mon-River Horseshoe Tourn (Fairmont), **May 29**
  Hilltop Fest (Huntington), **Sep 11**
  Independence Day Concert and Fireworks (Wheeling), **Jul 4**
  Model Railroad Show (Wheeling), **Jan 17**
  Preston County Buckwheat Fest (Kingwood), **Sep 30**
  Riverfront Ribfest (Huntington), **Aug 19**
  Rockefeller, John D., IV: Birth, **Jun 18**
  State Fair (Lewisburg), **Aug 13**
  Turkey Trot (Parkersburg), **Nov 25**
  West Virginia Italian Heritage Fest (Clarksburg), **Sep 3**
  Wise, Bob: Birth, **Jan 6**
West, Adam: Birth, **Sep 19**
West, Dottie: Birth Anniv, **Oct 11**
West, Rebecca: Birth Anniv, **Dec 25**
Western Idaho Fair (Boise, ID), **Aug 20**
Western Stock Show and Rodeo, Natl (Denver, CO), **Jan 10**
Westheimer, Dr. Ruth: Birth, **Jun 4**
Westinghouse, George: Birth Anniv, **Oct 6**
Westminster Kennel Club Dog Show (New York, NY), **Feb 9**
Westmoreland Arts & Heritage Fest (Greensburg, PA), **Jul 2**
Wettig, Patricia: Birth, **Dec 4**
Whales: Shamu's Birthday, **Sep 26**
Whalin, Justin: Birth, **Sep 6**
Whalley, Joanne: Birth, **Aug 25**
Wharton, Edith: Birth Anniv, **Jan 24**
What Do You Love About America Day, **Nov 24**
What You Think Upon Grows Day, **May 31**
What's My Line TV Premiere: Anniv, **Feb 2**
Wheatley, Phillis: Death Anniv, **Dec 5**
Wheaton, Wil: Birth, **Jul 29**
Wheel of Fortune TV Premiere: Anniv, **Jan 6**
Wheeler, William A.: Birth Anniv, **Jun 30**
Whelchel, Lisa: Birth, **May 29**
Whiner's Day, Natl, **Dec 26**
Whipple, William: Birth Anniv, **Jan 14**
Whiptop Contest, Native American (Burlington, WI), **Jan 31**
Whiskey Flat Days (Kernville, CA), **Feb 13**
Whistler, James: Birth Anniv, **Jul 10**
Whistlers Convention, Intl (Louisburg, NC), **Apr 21**
Whitaker, Forest: Birth, **Jul 15**
White Cane Safety Day (Pres Proc), **Oct 15**
White House Cornerstone Laid: Anniv, **Oct 13**
White House Easter Egg Roll (Washington, DC), **Apr 12**
White House: Pennsylvania Ave Closed: Anniv, **May 20**
White Oak Rendezvous (Deer River, MN), **Aug 7**
White Shirt Day, **Feb 11**
White Sunday (Samoa, American Samoa), **Oct 10**
White, Betty: Birth, **Jan 17**
White, Byron R.: Birth Anniv, **Jun 8**
White, Charles: Birth Anniv, **Apr 2**
White, E.B.: Birth Anniv, **Jul 11**
White, Edward Douglass: Birth Anniv, **Nov 3**
White, Gilbert: Birth Anniv, **Jul 18**
White, Jaleel: Birth, **Nov 27**
White, Reggie: Birth, **Dec 19**
White, Ryan: Death Anniv, **Apr 8**
White, Stanford: Birth Anniv, **Nov 9**
White, Vanna: Birth, **Feb 18**
Whitechapel Murders Begin: Anniv, **Aug 31**
Whitelaw, Billie: Birth, **Jun 6**
Whitfield, Lynn: Birth, **May 6**
Whiting, Margaret: Birth, **Jul 22**
Whitman, Christine T.: Birth, **Sep 26**
Whitman, Slim (Otis): Birth, **Jan 20**
Whitman, Stuart: Birth, **Feb 1**
Whitman, Walt: Birth Anniv, **May 31**
Whitmire, Kathryn: Birth, **Aug 15**
Whitmonday, **May 31**
Whitney, Eli: Birth Anniv, **Dec 8**
Whitsunday, **May 30**
Whittier, John Greenleaf: Birth Anniv, **Dec 17**
Who, Dr., TV Premiere: Anniv, **Nov 23**
Wiccan Observances,
  Beltane, **Apr 30**
  Imbolc, **Feb 2**
  Lughnasadh, **Aug 1**
  Mabon, **Sep 22**
  Midsummer, **Jun 20**
  Ostara, **Mar 20**
  Samhain, **Oct 31**
  Yule, **Dec 21**

Wicker, Tom: Birth, **Jun 18**
Widmark, Richard: Birth, **Dec 26**
Wiesel, Elie: Birth, **Sep 30**
Wiest, Dianne: Birth, **Mar 28**
Wife Appreciation Day, **Sep 18**
Wiggin, Kate Douglas: Birth Anniv, **Sep 28**
Wilbur, Richard: Birth, **Mar 1**
Wilby, James: Birth, **Feb 20**
Wilcox, Dave: Birth, **Sep 29**
Wild West Weekend and Country Music Fest (Clifton, KS), **Aug 20**
Wilde, Oscar: Birth Anniv, **Oct 16**
Wilder Pageant, Laura Ingalls (De Smet, SD), **Jul 9**
Wilder, Billy: Birth Anniv, **Jun 22**
Wilder, Gene: Birth, **Jun 11**
Wilder, L. Douglas: First Black Governor Elected: Anniv, **Nov 7**
Wilder, Laura Ingalls Gingerbread Sociable (Pomona, CA), **Feb 7**
Wilder, Thornton: Birth Anniv, **Apr 17**
Wilderness Wildlife Week of Nature (Pigeon Forge, TN), **Jan 10**
Wildflower Fest of the Arts (Dahlonega, GA), **May 15**
Wildflower Week, Natl, **May 2**
Wildfowl Art & Decoy Show, Ocean County (Brick, NJ), **Feb 14**
Wildfowl Expo, Chesapeake (Salisbury, MD), **Oct 1**
Wildlife Week, Natl, **Apr 19**
Wilkins, Roy: Birth Anniv, **Aug 30**
Wilkinson, Tom: Birth, **Dec 12**
Will Rogers Day, **Nov 4**
Will, George F.: Birth, **May 4**
Willard, Archibald M.: Birth Anniv, **Aug 22**
Willard, Emma Hart: Birth Anniv, **Feb 23**
Willard, Frances E.C.: Birth Anniv, **Sep 28**
William the Conqueror: Death Anniv, **Sep 9**
William, Prince: Birth, **Jun 21**
Williams, Andy: Birth, **Dec 3**
Williams, Archie: Birth Anniv, **May 1**
Williams, Bernie: Birth, **Sep 13**
Williams, Billy Dee: Birth, **Apr 6**
Williams, Cindy: Birth, **Aug 22**
Williams, Clarence, III: Birth, **Aug 21**
Williams, Curtis: Birth, **Dec 11**
Williams, Deniece: Birth, **Jun 3**
Williams, Esther: Birth, **Aug 8**
Williams, Hank, Jr: Birth, **May 26**
Williams, Hank, Sr: Birth Anniv, **Sep 17**
Williams, Jayson: Birth, **Feb 22**
Williams, Jimy: Birth, **Oct 4**
Williams, JoBeth: Birth, **Dec 6**
Williams, John: Birth, **Feb 8**
Williams, Mason: Birth, **Aug 24**
Williams, Matt: Birth, **Nov 28**
Williams, Montel: Birth, **Jul 3**
Williams, Paul: Birth, **Sep 19**
Williams, Robin: Birth, **Jul 21**
Williams, Serena: Birth, **Sep 26**
Williams, Ted: Birth Anniv, **Aug 30**
Williams, Tennessee: Birth Anniv, **Mar 26**
Williams, Treat: Birth, **Dec 1**
Williams, Vanessa: Birth, **Mar 18**
Williams, Venus: Birth, **Jun 17**
Williams, William: Birth Anniv, **Apr 8**
Williamson, Fred: Birth, **Mar 5**
Williamson, Nicol: Birth, **Sep 14**
Willingham, Noble: Birth, **Aug 31**
Willis, Bruce: Birth, **Mar 19**
Willkie, Wendell L.: Birth Anniv, **Feb 18**
Willow Tree Fest (Gordon, NE), **Sep 11**
Wills, Bob: Birth Anniv, **Mar 6**
Wills, Bob: Day (Turkey, TX), **Apr 24**
Wills, Garry: Birth, **May 22**
Willson, Meredith: Birth Anniv, **May 18**
Wilson, Ann: Birth, **Jun 19**
Wilson, August: Birth, **Apr 27**
Wilson, Blaine: Birth, **Aug 3**
Wilson, Brian: Birth, **Jun 20**
Wilson, Cassandra: Birth, **Dec 4**
Wilson, Edith: Birth Anniv, **Oct 15**
Wilson, Elizabeth: Birth, **Apr 4**
Wilson, Ellen L.: Birth Anniv, **May 15**
Wilson, Ellis: Birth Anniv, **Apr 30**
Wilson, Harold: Birth Anniv, **Mar 11**
Wilson, Henry: Birth Anniv, **Feb 16**
Wilson, James: Birth Anniv, **Sep 14**
Wilson, Luke: Birth, **Sep 21**
Wilson, Mary: Birth, **Mar 4**
Wilson, Nancy: Birth, **Feb 20**
Wilson, Owen: Birth, **Nov 18**
Wilson, Tom: Birth, **Aug 1**
Wilson, William G.: Alcoholics Anonymous: Founding Anniv, **Jun 10**
Wilson, William Julius: Birth, **Dec 20**
Wilson, Woodrow: Birth Anniv, **Dec 28**
Wilson, Woodrow: Fourteen Points Proposed: Anniv, **Jan 8**
Wilson's Volstead Prohibition Act Veto Overridden: Anniv, **Oct 28**
Wimbledon: Lawn Tennis Chmpshps at (London, England), **Jun 21**
Winchell, Paul: Birth, **Dec 21**
Winchell, Walter: Birth Anniv, **Apr 7**
Winchell's Donut House Established: Anniv, **Oct 8**
Wind Cave Natl Park Established: Anniv, **Jan 3**
Windjammer Days (Boothbay Harbor, ME), **Jun 22**

747

Index ☆ Chase's 2004 Calendar of Events ☆

Windmill—Woodard

Windmill Day, Natl (Netherlands), May 8
Windom, William: Birth, Sep 28
Window Safety Week, Natl, Apr 18
Windsor, Duke of, Marriage: Anniv, Jun 3
Wine, Blessing of the (Greiveldange, Luxembourg), Dec 26
Winfield, Dave: Birth, Oct 3
Winfield, Paul: Birth, May 22
Winfrey, Oprah: Birth, Jan 29
Winger, Debra: Birth, May 17
Wings 'n' Water Fest (Stone Harbor, NJ), Sep 18
Wings Over the Platte Spring Migration Season (Grand Island, NE), Feb 15
Wings Over Willcox—Sandhill Crane Celebration (Willcox, AZ), Jan 16
Winkler, Henry: Birth, Oct 30
Winningham, Mare: Birth, May 16
Winslet, Kate: Birth, Oct 5
Winston Cup, Daytona 500 NASCAR (Daytona Beach, FL), Feb 15
Winter Begins, Dec 21
Winter Festivals and Celebrations ,
Badger State Winter Games (Wausau, WI), **Feb 6**
Brookfield Ice Harvest (Brookfield, VT), **Jan 31**
Illinois Snow Sculpting Competition (Rockford, IL), **Jan 14**
Newport Winter Fest (Newport, RI), **Feb 13**
Quebec Winter Carnival (Quebec City, QC, Canada), **Jan 30**
Saint Paul Winter Carnival (St. Paul, MN), **Jan 23**
Snowman Burning (Sault Ste Marie, MI), **Mar 19**
Tip-Up Town USA (Houghton Lake, MI), **Jan 17**
US Natl Snow Sculpting Competition (Lake Geneva, WI), **Feb 4**
Winter Carnival (Red Lodge, MT), **Mar 6**
Winter Carnival Bon Soo (Sault Ste. Marie, ON, Canada), **Jan 30**
Winterfest (Flagstaff, AZ), **Feb 1**
Winterfest (Luverne, MN), **Dec 3**
Winterlude (Ottawa, ON, Canada), **Feb 6**
Wisconsin Dells Flake Out Fest (Wisconsin Dells, WI), **Jan 17**
Zehnder's Snowfest (Frankenmuth, MI), **Feb 4**
Winter Solstice: Yalda (Iran), Dec 21
Winter, Alex: Birth, Jul 17
Winter, Edgar: Birth, Dec 28
Winter, Halfway Point, Feb 4
Winter, Johnny: Birth, Feb 23
Winters, Jonathan: Birth, Nov 11
Winters, Shelley: Birth, Aug 18
Winthrop, John: Birth Anniv, Jan 12
Winwood, Steve: Birth, May 12
Wisconsin,
Admission Day, **May 29**
Al's Memorial Run & Walk (Milwaukee), **Sep 18**
American Birkebeiner (Cable to Hayward), **Feb 19**
American Club Teddy Bear and Doll Classic (Kohler), **Feb 21**
Art & Antiques at the American Club (Kohler), **Mar 13**
Art Fair on the Square (Madison), **Jul 10**
Automotion (Wisconsin Dells), **May 22**
Badger State Summer Games Sectionals and Finals, **Jun 17**
Badger State Winter Games (Wausau), **Feb 6**
Baraboo Circus Heritage (Baraboo), **May 14**
Christmas at the Top Museum (Burlington), **Dec 27**
Country Affair (Menomonee Falls), **Oct 16**
Doyle, Jim: Birth, **Nov 23**
Ducktona 500 (Sheboygan Falls), **Jul 4**
EAA Airventure Oshkosh (Oshkosh), **Jul 27**
Faire on the Square Art & Craft Fair (Baraboo), **Oct 9**
Fall in Love with Fond du Lac (Fond du Lac), **Sep 1**
Fashion Show (Milwaukee), **May 14**
Feingold, Russell D.: Birth, **Mar 2**
Fishing Has No Boundaries (Hayward), **May 14**
Grandparent's Day at the Top Museum, Natl (Burlington), **Sep 12**
Great Cardboard Boat Regatta (Sheboygan), **Jul 4**
Great Circus Parade Week (Milwaukee), **Jul 6**
Great Wisconsin Cheese Fest (Little Chute), **Jun 4**
Groundhog Day in Sun Prairie, **Feb 2**
Hodag Country Fest (Rhinelander), **Jul 8**
Holiday Folk Fair Intl (Milwaukee), **Nov 19**
Home Improvement Show, Milwaukee/NARI (West Allis), **Feb 5**
Home of the Hamburger Celeb (Seymour), **Aug 7**
Indian Summer Fest (Milwaukee), **Sep 10**
Intl Tongue Twister Contest (Burlington), **Nov 6**
Kites on Ice (Madison), **Jan 31**
Klondike Days (Eagle River), **Feb 14**
Kohl, Herb: Birth, **Feb 7**
Kohler Arts Center's Outdoor Arts Fest (Sheboygan), **Jul 17**
Ladies' Bliss Weekend (Kohler), **Jan 30**
Mad City Marathon (Madison), **May 31**
Madrigal Dinner and Concert (Milwaukee), **Dec 4**
Maple Syrup Saturday (Appleton), **Mar 20**
Mexican Fiesta Internacional (Milwaukee), **Aug 27**
Milwaukee Boat Show & Wisconsin Sportfishing Expo (Milwaukee), **Feb 11**
Milwaukee Irish Fest (Milwaukee), **Aug 19**
Milwaukee Journal Sentinel Sports Show (Milwaukee), **Mar 12**
Morel Mushroom Fest (Muscoda), **May 14**
Native American Whiptop Contest (Burlington), **Jan 31**
Norskedalen's Midsummer Fest (Coon Valley), **Jun 19**
Norskedalen's Old-Fashioned Christmas (Coon Valley), **Dec 4**
Norskedalen's Threshing Bee (Coon Valley), **Sep 18**
Northeastern Wisconsin Antique Power and Machinery Show Thresheree (Sturgeon Bay), **Aug 20**
Octoberfest (Appleton), **Sep 25**
Oktoberfest (LaCrosse), **Sep 24**
PGA Golf Chmpshp (Kohler), **Aug 9**
Polar Bear Swim (Sheboygan), **Jan 1**
Polka Fest (Wisconsin Dells), **Apr 16**
Prairie Villa Rendezvous (Prairie du Chien), **Jun 17**
Rhinelander's Oktoberfest (Rhinelander), **Oct 8**
Riverfest (LaCrosse), **Jun 30**
Romp in the Swamp Fun Walk (Appleton), **Oct 16**
Saint Cyril's Parish Fest (Sheboygan), **Jul 18**
Shanty Days (Algoma), **Aug 13**
Spring Garden Market (Kohler), **Apr 17**
State Fair (Milwaukee), **Aug 5**
Summerfest (Milwaukee), **Jun 24**
Sun Prairie's Sweet Corn Fest (Sun Prairie), **Aug 19**
Taste of Madison (Madison), **Aug 28**
Traditional Gyroscope and Top Spinning Contest (Burlington), **Aug 14**
Traditional Sousa Concert (Kohler), **Jul 4**
UFO Days (Elmwood), **Jul 23**
US Natl Snow Sculpting Competition (Lake Geneva), **Feb 4**
Waukesha Riverfest (Waukesha), **Jul 29**
West Allis Western Days Family Jamboree (West Allis), **Jun 17**
WI State Yo-Yo Contest (Burlington), **Apr 4**
Wisconsin Cow-Chip Throw (Prairie du Sac), **Aug 27**
Wisconsin Dells Autumn Harvest Fest (Wisconsin Dells), **Oct 23**
Wisconsin Dells Flake Out Fest (Wisconsin Dells), **Jan 17**
Wisconsin Holiday Market (Kohler), **Nov 12**
Wollersheim Winery Grape Stomp Fest (Prairie du Sac), **Oct 2**
World Beef Expo (Milwaukee), **Sep 23**
World's Largest Trivia Contest (Stevens Point), **Apr 16**
Wo-Zha-Wa Fall Fest (Wisconsin Dells), **Sep 17**
Yo-Yo Conv (Burlington), **Apr 3**
Ziegler Kettle Moraine Jazz Fest (West Bend), **Sep 10**
Wise Health Care Consumer Month, Feb 1
Wise, Bob: Birth, Jan 6
Wise, Robert: Birth, Sep 10
Wise, Thomas J.: Birth Anniv, Oct 7
Witches: First in Salem Arrested: Anniv, Feb 1
Witches: Salem Hysteria Begins: Anniv, Mar 1
Witches: Salem Trials Begin: Anniv, Jun 2
Witherspoon, John: Birth Anniv, Feb 5
Witherspoon, Reese: Birth, Mar 22
Witt, Alicia: Birth, Aug 21
Witt, Katarina: Birth, Dec 3
Witt, Paul Junger: Birth, Mar 20
Wizard of Oz Fest (Chesterton, IN), Sep 17
Wizard of Oz Film Released: Anniv, Aug 25
WMAS Annual Halloween Ball (Springfield, MA), Oct 29
Wodehouse, P.G.: Birth Anniv, Oct 15
Wojtyla: Pope John Paul II: Birth, May 18
Wolcott, Oliver: Birth Anniv, Nov 20
Wolf, Peter: Birth, Mar 7
Wolf, Scott: Birth, Jun 4
Wolfe, James: Birth Anniv, Jan 2
Wolfe, Tom: Birth, Mar 2
Wolff, Geoffrey: Birth, Nov 5
Wolff, Josh: Birth, Feb 25
Wolfman Jack: Birth Anniv, Jan 21
Wollersheim Winery Grape Stomp Fest (Prairie du Sac, WI), Oct 2
Wollstonecraft, Mary: Death Anniv, Sept 10
Women,
Abused Women and Children's Awareness Day, **Jun 13**
Alpha Kappa Alpha Sorority Founded: Anniv, **Jan 15**
Amer Business Women's Assn, Natl Conv of (Richmond, VA), **Oct 13**
American Heroine Rewarded: Anniv, **Jun 8**
Around the World in 72 Days: Anniv, **Nov 14**
Aspinwall Crosses US on Horseback: Anniv, **Jul 8**
Billie Jean King Wins Battle of Sexes: Anniv, **Sep 20**
Blackwell, Elizabeth, Awarded MD: Anniv, **Jan 23**
Bloomer, Amelia Jenks: Birth Anniv, **May 27**
Breast Cancer Awareness Month, Natl, **Oct 1**
Business Women's Day, American, **Sep 22**
Business Women's Week, Natl, **Oct 18**
Campbell, Kim, First Woman Prime Minister, **Jun 25**
Canada: Persons Day, **Oct 18**
Day for Women's Rights & Intl Peace (UN), **Mar 8**
Elimination of Violence against Women, Intl Day for the (UN), **Nov 25**
Empowered Women Entrepreneurs Day, **Apr 1**
English Channel, First Woman Swims: Anniv, **Aug 6**
Equal Rights Party Founding: Anniv, **Sep 20**
Female House Page, First Formal: Anniv, **May 14**
Female Relief Society of Nauvoo: Anniv, **Mar 17**
Feminine Mystique Published: Anniv, **Feb 19**
Fibromyalgia Education & Awareness Month, **May 1**
First All-Woman Jury: Anniv, **Sep 22**
First American Woman in Space: Anniv, **Jun 18**
First Doctor of Science Degree Earned by a Woman, **Jun 20**
First Elected Woman Senator: Anniv, **Jan 12**
First Episcopal Bishop: Anniv, **Feb 11**
First Female Congressional Page: Anniv, **Jan 3**
First Female FBI Agents: Anniv, **Oct 25**
First To Climb Mount Everest, **May 16**
First US Woman Governor Inaugurated, **Jan 5**
First Woman in Space: Space Milestone, **Jun 16**
First Woman Rabbi in US: Anniv, **Jun 3**
First Woman to Graduate Dental School: Anniv, **Feb 21**
First Woman to Walk in Space, **Jul 17**
First Woman US Ambassador Appointed: Anniv, **Oct 28**
First Woman Vice-Presidential Candidate: Anniv, **Jul 19**
First Women's Collegiate Basketball Game: Anniv, **Mar 22**
Frantic Women Extravaganza (Pittsburgh, PA), **Oct 13**
Friedan, Betty: Birth, **Feb 4**
Fuller, Margaret: Birth Anniv, **May 23**
Girlfriend's Day, **Aug 1**
Girls and Women in Sports Day, Natl, **Feb 4**
Informed Woman Month, **Apr 1**
Ladies' Bliss Weekend (Kohler, WI), **Jan 30**
Ladies' Day Initiated in Baseball: Anniv, **Jun 16**
League of Women Voters Formed: Anniv, **Feb 14**
Links, Inc: Anniv, **Nov 9**
Lucy Stone Married: Anniv, **May 1**
Mansfield, Arabella: Birth Anniv, **May 23**
Margaret Brent Demands a Political Voice: Anniv, **Jan 21**
Martha Griffiths Speech Against Sex Discrimination, **Feb 8**
Mayer, Maria G.: Birth Anniv, **Jun 28**
Medical School Opened: Anniv, **Nov 1**
Meitlisunntig (Switzerland), **Jan 11**
Merriam, Eve: Birth Anniv, **Jul 19**
Million Mom March: Anniv, **May 14**
National Women's Day (South Africa), **Aug 9**
19th Amendment Ratified, **Aug 18**
NOW Founded: Anniv, **Jun 30**
Perkins, Frances (1st Woman Appointed to US Cabinet), **Mar 4**
Personal Self-Defense Awareness Month, Natl, **Jan 1**
Pocahontas: Death Anniv, **Mar 21**
Pope Nixes Ordaining of Women: Anniv, **May 30**
Queen Liliuokalani Deposed: Anniv, **Jan 17**
Russia: Women's Day, Intl, **Mar 8**
Salter Elected First Woman Mayor in US: Anniv, **Apr 4**
Self Day, **Apr 9**
Seneca Falls Survivor Votes: Anniv, **Nov 2**
Senior Women's Travel Month, **Jan 1**
She's Funny That Way Day, Natl, **Mar 31**
Suffrage Parade Attacked: Anniv, **Mar 3**
Suffragists' Voting Attempt: Anniv, **Nov 19**
Supreme Court Abortion Notification Ruling: Anniv, **Jun 25**
Susan B. Anthony Fined for Voting, **Jun 6**
Tubman, Harriet: Death Anniv, **Mar 10**
Universal Women's Week, **Mar 8**
Uppity Women Day, **Mar 8**
Utah Women Given Vote: Anniv, **Feb 12**
Vulvar Health Awareness Month, **Mar 1**
WAAC: Anniv, **May 14**
White Woman Made Indian Chief: Anniv, **Sep 18**
Woman Inducted to Natl Inventors Hall of Fame: Anniv, **May 18**
Woman Presides Over US Supreme Court: Anniv, **Apr 3**
Woman Runs the House: Anniv, **Jun 20**
Women Denied Vote: Anniv, **Jan 12**
Women's Equality Day, **Aug 26**
Women's Equality Day (Pres Proc), **Aug 26**
Women's Eye Health and Safety Month, **Apr 1**
Women's Friendship Day, **Sep 19**
Women's Hall of Fame, Natl: Dedication Anniv, **Jul 21**
Women's Health and Fitness Day, Natl, **Sep 29**
Women's Health Care Month, **May 1**
Women's Healthy Weight Day, **Jan 22**
Women's Heart Health Day, **Feb 1**
Women's Heart Week, **Feb 1**
Women's History Month (Pres Proc), **Mar 1**
Women's History Month, Natl, **Mar 1**
Women's Motorcycle Month, **Jul 1**
Women's News Day, **Oct 4**
Women's Nutrition Week, Natl, **Apr 11**
Women's Rights Convention Held (Seneca Falls): Anniv, **Jul 19**
Women's Self-Empowerment Week, **Jan 5**
Women's Small Business Month, **Oct 1**
Women's Suffrage Amendment Introduced: Anniv, **Jan 10**
Working Women's Day, Intl, **Mar 8**
World Menopause Day, **Oct 18**
Wonder Years TV Premiere: Anniv, Mar 15
Wonder, Stevie: Birth, May 13
Wonderful Weirdos Day, Sep 9
Wood Pellet BBQ Introduction Day, Jul 5
Wood, Elijah: Birth, Jan 28
Wood, Grant, Art Fest (Stone City–Anamosa, IA), Jun 13
Wood, Grant: Birth Anniv, Feb 13
Wood, Kerry: Birth, Jun 16
Wood, Ron: Birth, Jun 1
Woodard, Alfre: Birth, Nov 8

☆ Chase's 2004 Calendar of Events ☆ Index

Woodcraft: Holzfest (Amana, IA), Aug 20
Woodhull, Victoria C.: Birth Anniv, Sep 23
Woodie Wagon Day, Natl, Jul 21
Woodland Indian Discovery Day (St. Mary's City, MD), Sep 11
Woodruff, Judy: Birth, Nov 20
Woods, Eldrick (Tiger): Birth, Dec 30
Woods, Granville T.: Birth Anniv, Apr 23
Woods, James: Birth, Apr 18
Woodson, Carter Godwin: Birth Anniv, Dec 19
Woodstock Fair (Woodstock, CT), Sep 3
Woodstock: Anniv, Aug 15
Woodward, Bob: Birth, Mar 26
Woodward, Edward: Birth, Jun 1
Woodward, Joanne: Birth, Feb 27
Woodward, Robert B.: Birth Anniv, Apr 10
Woodworking Month, Natl, Apr 1
Woofstock (Wichita, KS), Oct 4
Woolery, Chuck: Birth, Mar 16
Woolf, Virginia: Birth Anniv, Jan 25
Woolly Worm Fest (Banner Elk, NC), Oct 16
Woolworths Opened: Anniv, Feb 22
Wopat, Tom: Birth, Sep 9
Word Origins: O.K.: Anniv, Mar 23
Words by the Water: A Cumbrian Literature Fest (Lake District, England), Mar 9
Wordsmith Day, May 3
Wordsworth, William: Birth Anniv, Apr 7
Work from Home Week, Natl, Oct 3
Work Life Enrichment Month, Intl, Apr 1
Work Like a Dog Day, Aug 6
Work Schedule Month, Revise Your, May 1
Work@Home Father's Day, Jun 18
Workers Memorial Day, Apr 28
Working Women's Day, Intl, Mar 8
Workplace Eye Health and Safety Month, Mar 1
World AIDS Day (Pres Proc), Dec 1
World Breastfeeding Week, Aug 1
World Chmpshp Old-Time Piano Playing (Peoria, IL), May 28
World Communion Sunday, Oct 3
World Cup Inaugurated: Anniv, Jul 13
World Day of Prayer, Mar 5
World Day of Reiki, Aug 15
World Egg Day, Oct 8
World Farm Animals Day, Oct 2
World Food Day, Oct 16
World Future Society Annual Conference (Washington, DC), Jul 31
World Habitat Awareness Month, Apr 1
World Health Organization: Anniv, Apr 7
World Human Spirit Day, Feb 17
World Juggling Day, Jun 14
World Peace Day, Dec 21
World Priest Day, Sep 19
World Smile Day, Oct 1
World Tourism Day, Sep 27
World Trade Center Attack (9-11): Anniv, Sep 11
World Trade Center Bombing of 1993: Anniv, Feb 26
World Trade Center Recovery and Cleanup Ends: Anniv, May 30
World Trade Week (Pres Proc), May 16
World Turtle Day, May 23
World War I,
 Alvin C. York Day, Oct 8
 ANZAC Day, Apr 25
 Armistice: Anniv, Nov 11
 Baseball Declared Non-Essential: Anniv, Jul 20
 Battle of Amiens, Second: Anniv, Aug 8
 Battle of Cambrai–Saint Quentin: Anniv, Sep 27
 Battle of Gallipoli, Apr 25
 Battle of Lys River: Anniv, Apr 7
 Battle of Meuse-Argonne Forest: Anniv, Sep 26
 Battle of Saint-Mihiel: Anniv, Sep 12
 Battle of Somme, Second: Anniv, Mar 21
 Battle of the Marne: Anniv, Jul 15
 Battle of Verdun, Feb 21
 Battle of Vittorio Veneto: Anniv, Oct 24
 Begins: Anniv, Jul 28
 Big Bertha Paris Gun: Anniv, Mar 23
 Campbell Becomes First American Air ACE: Anniv, Apr 14
 Coal Conservation Ordered: Anniv, Jan 16
 Death/Duty Day, Nov 11
 Fourteen Points Proposed: Anniv, Jan 8
 German Revolution of 1918: Anniv, Oct 28
 Ludendorff, Erick: Birth Anniv, Apr 9
 Mata Hari: Execution Anniv, Oct 15
 Neutrality Appeal, American: Anniv, Aug 18
 Red Baron Shot Down: Anniv, Apr 21
 Treaty of Versailles: Anniv, Jun 28
 US Enters WWI: Anniv, Apr 6
 Versailles Peace Conference: Anniv, Jan 18
 Veterans Bonus Army Eviction: Anniv, Jul 28
 Wilhelm II Abdicates: Anniv, Nov 9
World War II,
 Allied Invasion of Sicily: Anniv, Jul 10
 Allied Landing at Anzio: Anniv, Jan 22
 Allied Landings in South of France: Anniv, Aug 15
 Allies Capture Monte Cassino: Anniv, May 18
 Allies Retake Guadalcanal: Anniv, Feb 9
 Allies Take New Guinea: Anniv, Jan 22
 Allies Take Palermo: Anniv, Jul 22
 America Enters World War II, Dec 8
 Arnold, Henry H.: Birth Anniv, Jun 25

Atomic Bomb Delivered: Anniv, Jul 26
Atomic Bomb Dropped on Hiroshima: Anniv, Aug 6
Atomic Bomb Dropped on Nagasaki: Anniv, Aug 9
Atomic Bomb Tested: Anniv, Jul 16
Attempt on Hitler's Life: Anniv, Jul 20
Austria Invaded By Nazi Germany: Anniv, Mar 12
Bataan Death March: Anniv, Apr 10
Battle of Bismarck Sea: Anniv, Mar 2
Battle of Coral Sea: Anniv, May 8
Battle of Kursk: Anniv, Jul 12
Battle of Leyte Gulf: Anniv, Oct 23
Battle of Midway: Anniv, Jun 4
Battle of Okinawa Begins: Anniv, Apr 1
Battle of Okinawa Ends: Anniv, Jun 21
Battle of Philippine Sea, Jun 19
Battle of Salerno: Anniv, Sep 9
Battle of San Pietro: Anniv, Dec 15
Battle of Stalingrad Begins: Anniv, Aug 22
Battle of Tarawa-Makin: Anniv, Nov 20
Battle of the Aleutian Islands: Anniv, May 30
Battle of the Bulge: Anniv, Dec 16
Begins: Germany Invades Poland: Anniv, Sep 1
Bourke-White, Margaret: Birth Anniv, Jun 14
Britain Declares War on Germany: Anniv, Sep 3
British Air Raid on Berlin: Anniv, Jan 16
British Capture Enigma Machine: Anniv, May 9
Christmas Fireside Chat Warning: Anniv, Dec 25
Churchill Enters Germany: Anniv, Mar 25
Civil Air Patrol Founded: Anniv, Dec 1
Clark, Mark: Birth Anniv, May 1
Corsica Liberated: Anniv, Oct 4
Czechoslovakia: Rape of Lidice: Anniv, Jun 10
Davis, Benjamin O., Jr: Birth Anniv, Dec 18
D-Day: Anniv, Jun 6
De Gaulle, Charles: Birth Anniv, Nov 22
Diary of Anne Frank: Last Entry: Anniv, Aug 1
Dresden Firebombing, Feb 13
Dunkirk Evacuated: Anniv, May 26
East Meets West: Anniv, Apr 25
Eisenhower Assumes Command: Anniv, Jan 16
Eisenhower World War II Weekend (Gettysburg, PA), Sep 18
FDR's Unconditional Surrender Statement: Anniv, Jan 24
First Medal of Honor: Anniv, Feb 10
First Surface-to-Surface Missile: Anniv, Dec 24
Four Chaplains Memorial Day, Feb 3
Gasoline Rationing: Anniv, May 15
German 16-Year-Olds Drafted: Anniv, Mar 5
German Surrender at Stalingrad: Anniv, Feb 2
Germany's First Surrender: Anniv, May 7
Germany's Second Surrender: Anniv, May 8
Gersdorff Hitler Assassination Attempt: Anniv, Mar 21
Gilbert Islands Taken: Anniv, Nov 23
Gillars, Mildred E.: Death Anniv, Jun 25
Graham, Calvin ("Baby Vet"): Birth Anniv, Apr 3
Gypsy Condemnation Order: Anniv, Nov 15
Halsey, William "Bull": Birth Anniv, Oct 30
Hamburg Firestorm: Anniv, Jul 28
Hitler Youth Deployed: Anniv, Jan 26
Howard, Leslie: Birth Anniv, Apr 3
Indianapolis Sunk: Anniv, Jul 29
Italy Surrenders: Anniv, Sep 3
Iwo Jima Day: Anniv, Feb 23
Japan Bombed: Anniv, Apr 18
Japanese Attack US Mainland: Anniv, Feb 23
Japanese Internment: Anniv, Feb 19
Japan's Unconditional Surrender: Anniv, Aug 10
Kristallnacht: Anniv, Nov 9
Krupp, Alfried: Birth Anniv, Aug 13
Lady Be Good Lost: Anniv, Apr 4
Leningrad Liberated: Anniv, Jan 27
Liberation of Buchenwald: Anniv, Apr 11
MacArthur Returns: US Landing on Leyte, Philippines: Anniv, Oct 20
Manstein, Erich von: Birth Anniv, Nov 24
Marshall, George C.: Birth Anniv, Dec 31
Montgomery, Bernard Law: Birth Anniv, Nov 17
Moulin, Jean: Death Anniv, Jul 8
Mussolini Executed: Anniv, Apr 28
Mussolini Ousted: Anniv, Jul 25
Napalm Used: Anniv, Jul 11
Nimitz, Chester: Birth Anniv, Feb 24
Oak Ridge Atomic Plant Begun: Anniv, Aug 1
Odessa Retaken: Anniv, Apr 10
Operation Flash: Anniv, Mar 13
Operation Floating Chrysanthemum: Anniv, Apr 6
Operation Overcast, Jul 6
Paris Liberated: Anniv, Aug 25
Paulus, Friedrich: Birth Anniv, Sep 23
Peace Rose Introduced to World: Anniv, Apr 29
Pearl Harbor Day, Dec 7
Potsdam Declaration: Anniv, Jul 26
RAF Bombs Hitler Celebration: Anniv, Jan 30
RAF Bombs Ruhr Dams: Anniv, May 16
RAF Jams Nazi Radar: Anniv, Jul 24
Raising Flag on Iwo Jima: Hayes, Ira: Birth Anniv, Jan 12
Remagen Bridge Capture: Anniv, Mar 7
Ridgway, Matthew Bunker: Birth Anniv, Mar 3
Rogers, Edith Nourse: Birth Anniv, Mar 19
Romania Surrender to USSR: Anniv, Aug 23
Rome Executions: Anniv, Mar 25
Rome Liberated: Anniv, Jun 4
Rommel, Erwin: Birth Anniv, Nov 15

Roosevelt, Franklin D.: Death Anniv, Apr 12
Russia: Victory Day, May 9
Seattle Blackout: Anniv, May 11
Smith, Holland: Birth Anniv, Apr 20
Soviet Union Invaded: Anniv, Jun 22
Stratton, Dorothy C.: Birth Anniv, Mar 24
Suicide Weapon Introduced: Anniv, Mar 18
Teheran Conference: Anniv, Nov 28
Tokyo Blanket Bombing: Anniv, Mar 9
Train for Paris: Anniv, Jan 15
Truman Doctrine: Anniv, May 22
Tunis Campaign Victory: Anniv, May 13
Tuskegee Airmen Activated: Anniv, Mar 22
US Forces Land in Mindoro, Philippines: Anniv, Dec 15
US Landing on Iwo Jima: Anniv, Feb 19
US Landing on Luzon: Anniv, Jan 9
US Landing on Saipan, Jun 15
US Landing on the Admiralty Islands: Anniv, Feb 1
US Troops Enter Germany: Anniv, Sep 15
V-E Day, May 8
V-J Day (Announcement), Aug 14
V-J Day (Ratification), Sep 2
V-Mail Delivery: Anniv, Jun 22
WAAC: Anniv, May 14
War Time: Anniv, Feb 9
Warsaw Ghetto Revolt: Anniv, Apr 19
Warsaw Uprising: Anniv, Aug 1
Yalta Agreement Signed: Anniv, Feb 11
Yamamoto, Isoroku: Birth Anniv, Apr 4
World Wide Web: Anniv, Aug 1
World's End Day, Oct 22
World's Indigenous People, Intl Day of the (UN), Aug 9
Worldwide Celebration: Top Spinning at Noon, Oct 13
Worley, Jo Anne: Birth, Sep 6
Woronov, Mary: Birth, Dec 8
Worthy, James: Birth, Feb 27
Wouk, Herman: Birth, May 27
Wounded Knee Massacre: Anniv, Dec 29
Wozniak, Stephen: Birth, Aug 11
Wrangell-Saint Elias Natl Park: Anniv, Dec 2
Wren, Christopher: Birth Anniv, Oct 20
Wren, Day of the (Ireland), Dec 26
Wrestling,
 Big 12 Chmpshps (Ames, IA), Mar 6
 Big Ten Chmpshps (Columbus, OH), Mar 6
 NCAA Div I Wrestling Chmpshps (St. Louis, MO), Mar 18
 Wrestling Chmpshps, NAIA (Great Falls, MT), Mar 5
 Wrestling President (Theodore Roosevelt): Anniv, Apr 9
 Wristwrestling, World Chmpshp (Petaluma, CA), Oct 9
Wright Brothers Day (Pres Proc), Dec 17
Wright Brothers First Powered Flight: Anniv, Dec 17
Wright Brothers: First Flight 100th Anniv Celeb (Kill Devil Hills, NC), Dec 17
Wright, Amy: Birth, Apr 15
Wright, Frank Lloyd: Birth Anniv, Jun 8
Wright, Frank Lloyd: Wright Plus (Oak Park, IL), May 15
Wright, Gary: Birth, Apr 26
Wright, Orville: Birth Anniv, Aug 19
Wright, Richard: Birth Anniv, Sep 4
Wright, Rick: Birth, Jul 28
Wright, Robin: Birth, Apr 8
Wright, Steven: Birth, Dec 6
Wright, Wilbur: Birth Anniv, Apr 16
Wristwrestling, World Chmpshp (Petaluma, CA), Oct 9
Write a Letter of Appreciation Week, Natl, Mar 1
Write Your Memoirs Day, Apr 11
Writers Appreciation Week, Freelance, Feb 9
Writing: Lifewriting Month, Natl, Nov 1
Wuhl, Robert: Birth, Oct 9
Wurstfest (New Braunfels, TX), Oct 29
Wyatt Earp TV Premiere: Anniv, Sep 6
Wyatt, Jane: Birth, Aug 12
Wyden, Ron: Birth, May 3
Wyle, Noah: Birth, Jun 4
Wyman, Bill: Birth, Oct 24
Wyman, Jane: Birth, Jan 4
Wyoming,
 Admission Day, Jul 10
 Bluegrass Fest (Alta), Aug 13
 Cheyenne Frontier Days (Cheyenne), Jul 23
 Cowboy State Games Sports Fest (Casper), Feb 7
 Enzi, Michael B.: Birth, Feb 1
 First US Woman Governor Inaugurated, Jan 5
 Fort Bridger Rendezvous (Fort Bridger), Sep 3
 Freundenthal, Dave: Birth, Oct 12
 Gift of the Waters Pageant & Art Fest in the Park (Thermopolis), Aug 6
 Grand Teton Music Fest (Teton Village), Jun 29
 Grand Teton Natl Park Established: Anniv, Feb 1
 River Regalia (Thermopolis), Aug 14
 State Fair & Rodeo (Douglas), Aug 14
 Thomas, Craig: Birth, Feb 17
Wythe, George: Death Anniv, Jun 8
Xerox 914 Donated to Smithsonian: Anniv, Aug 20
X-Files TV Premiere: Anniv, Sep 10
X-Ray Discovery Day: Anniv, Nov 8

Index — Chase's 2004 Calendar of Events

Yacht–Zwingli

Yacht Race, Intl: Anniv, Aug 22
Yagudin, Alexei: Birth, Mar 18
Yalda (Iran), Dec 21
Yale Univ Founded: Anniv, Oct 16
Yale, Linus: Birth Anniv, Apr 4
Yalow, Rosalyn: Birth, Jul 19
Yalta Agreement Signed: Anniv, Feb 11
Yamaguchi, Kristi: Birth, Jul 12
Yamamoto, Isoroku: Birth Anniv, Apr 4
Yambilee, Louisiana (Opelousas, LA), Oct 27
Yamboree, East Texas (Gilmer, TX), Oct 20
Yankee Stadium Opens, Apr 18
Yankovic, Weird Al: Birth, Oct 23
Yanni: Birth, Nov 14
Yarborough, Cale: Birth, Mar 27
Yarrow, Peter: Birth, May 31
Yasbeck, Amy: Birth, Sep 12
Yastrzemski, Carl: Birth, Aug 22
Yawm Arafat (Islamic): The Standing at Arafat, Jan 31
Yeager, Chuck: Birth, Feb 13
Yearwood, Trisha: Birth, Sep 19
Yeats, William B: Birth Anniv, Jun 13
Yell "Fudge" at the Cobras in North America Day, Jun 2
Yellow Daisy Fest (Stone Mountain, GA), Sep 9
Yellow Kid: First Newspaper Comic Strip: Anniv, Oct 18
Yellowstone Natl Park Established: Anniv, Mar 1
Yeltsin, Boris, Inaugurated Russian President: Anniv, Jul 10
Yemen: Natl Day, May 22
Yeoh, Michelle: Birth, Aug 6
Yevtushenko, Yevgeny: Birth, Jul 18
YMCA Organized: Anniv, Dec 29
Yoakam, Dwight: Birth, Oct 23
Yom Hashoah (Israel), Apr 18
Yom Kippur, Sep 25
Yom Kippur Begins, Sep 24
Yom Kippur War, Oct 6
York, Alvin C.: Day, Oct 8
York, Michael: Birth, Mar 27
York, Susannah: Birth, Jan 9
Yorktown Day, Oct 19
Yorktown Victory Day (VA), Oct 11
Yosemite Natl Park Established: Anniv, Oct 1
Yothers, Tina: Birth, May 5
You Are There TV Premiere: Anniv, Feb 1
You Bet Your Life TV Premiere: Anniv, Oct 5
You Gotta Have Park (Brooklyn, NY), May 15
Young Achievers Month, May 1

Young and the Restless TV Premiere: Anniv, Mar 26
Young People's Poetry Week, Apr 12
Young, Andrew: Birth, Mar 12
Young, Brigham: Anniv of Last Marriage, Apr 6
Young, Brigham: Birth Anniv, Jun 1
Young, Burt: Birth, Apr 30
Young, Chic: Birth Anniv, Jan 9
Young, Chris: Birth, Apr 28
Young, Cy: American League's First Perfect Game: Anniv, May 5
Young, Cy: Birth Anniv, Mar 29
Young, Loretta: Birth Anniv, Jan 6
Young, Neil: Birth, Nov 12
Young, Paul: Birth, Jan 17
Young, Sean: Birth, Nov 20
Young, Steve: Birth, Oct 11
Yount, Robin: Birth, Sep 16
Your Hit Parade Radio Premiere: Anniv, Apr 12
Your Hit Parade TV Premiere: Anniv, Oct 7
Your Show of Shows TV Premiere: Anniv, Feb 25
You're Welcomegiving Day, Nov 26
Yours, Mine and Ours Month, Natl, Jan 1
Youth Art Month, Mar 1
Youth Cowboy Poetry Gathering (Boys Ranch, TX), Jun 17
Youth Day (Cameroon), Feb 11
Youth Day (People's Republic of China), May 4
Youth Day, Intl (UN), Aug 12
Youth Leadership Month, Feb 1
Youth Service Day, Natl, Apr 16
Youth Sports Safety Month, Natl, Apr 1
Yo-Yo Contest, WI State (Burlington, WI), Apr 4
Yo-Yo Conv (Burlington, WI), Apr 3
Yu, Jessica: Birth, Feb 14
Yugoslavia,
 Civil War: Anniv, Jun 25
 National Day, Apr 27
 NATO Forces Attack: Anniv, Mar 25
 Slovenia and Croatia Independence: Anniv, Jun 25
 Tito (Josip Broz): Birth Anniv, May 25
Yukon Gold Panning (Dawson City, YT, Canada), Jul 1
Yukon Quest Intl 1,000-Mile Sled Dog Race (Whitehorse, YT, Canada), Feb 14
Yukon River Bathtub Race (Whitehorse, YT, Canada), Aug 12
Yule (Wiccan), Dec 21
Yzerman, Steve: Birth, May 9
Z Day, Jan 1
Zadora, Pia: Birth, May 4

Zaharias, Mildred Babe Didrikson: Birth Anniv, Jun 26
Zahn, Paula: Birth, Feb 24
Zaire: Congo (Dem Rep of the): Independence Day, Jun 30
Zambia,
 African Freedom Day, May 25
 Heroes Day, Jul 5
 Independence Day, Oct 25
 Unity Day, Jul 6
 Youth Day, Aug 2
Zane Grey TV Premiere: Anniv, Oct 5
Zane, Billy: Birth, Feb 24
Zanuck, Darryl F.: Birth Anniv, Sep 5
Zappa, Dweezil: Birth, Sep 5
Zappa, Frank: Birth Anniv, Dec 21
Zeffirelli, Franco: Birth, Feb 12
Zellweger, Renee: Birth, Apr 25
Zemeckis, Robert: Birth, May 14
Zenger, John P.: Arrest Anniv, Nov 17
Zerbe, Anthony: Birth, May 20
Zeta-Jones, Catherine: Birth, Sep 25
Zetkin, Clara: Birth Anniv, Jul 5
Ziegler Kettle Moraine Jazz Fest (West Bend, WI), Sep 10
Zimbabwe,
 Book Fair, Intl, Aug 1
 Heroes' Day, Aug 11
 Independence Day, Apr 18
Zimbalist, Efrem, Jr: Birth, Nov 30
Zimbalist, Stephanie: Birth, Oct 6
Zimmer, Don: Birth, Jan 17
Zion Natl Park Established: Anniv, Nov 19
Zionism, UN Revokes Resolution on: Anniv, Dec 16
Zip Codes Inaugurated: Anniv, Jul 1
Zipper Patented: Anniv, Apr 29
Zippo/Case Intl Swap Meetl (Bradford, PA), Jul 16
Zoeller, Fuzzy: Birth, Nov 11
Zola, Emile: Birth Anniv, Apr 2
Zolotow, Charlotte: Birth, Jun 26
Zoo,
 First US Zoo: Anniv (Philadelphia, PA), Jul 1
 Zoobalee (Garden City, KS), Jul 4
Zoo Parade TV Premiere: Anniv, May 28
Zoot Suit Riots: Anniv, Jun 3
Zouk Month, Jun 1
Zucker, David: Birth, Oct 6
Zucker, Jerry: Birth, Mar 11
Zukerman, Pinchas: Birth, Jul 16
Zwingli, Ulrich: Birth Anniv, Jan 1

Yes! Please send me additional copies of *Chase's 2004 Calendar of Events*.

Ship to _____

Address _____

City, State, Zip _____

Phone (___) _____

Please send me _____ copies of the 2004 edition of
CHASE'S CALENDAR OF EVENTS at $54.95 each (0-07-142405-9) $_____

Add applicable sales tax for all states **except** AK, DE, MT, NH, OR $_____

Shipping & Handling: Add $5.00 for the first copy,
$3.50 for each additional copy $_____

Total $_____

☐ Check or money order enclosed payable to: The McGraw-Hill Companies

Charge my ☐ Visa ☐ MasterCard ☐ American Express ☐ Discover Card

Acct. # _____ Exp. Date ___/___

X _____
Signature (if charging to bankcard)

Name (please print) _____

STANDING ORDER AUTHORIZATION

To make sure that I receive each year's new edition, please accept this Standing Order Authorization to ship me ___ copies of Chase's Calendar of Events beginning with the 2004 edition. Bill me at the address shown at the top of this order form. I understand that I may cancel my Standing Order at any time.

X _____
Signature   Date

_____ (___) _____
Name (please print)   Phone

GUARANTEE: Any book you order is unconditionally guaranteed and may be returned within 10 days of receipt for full refund.

Prices subject to change without notice.   9353

Mail to: **McGraw-Hill Customer Service**
P.O. Box 545
Blacklick, OH 43004-0545

Phone: (800) 722-4726 • Fax: (614) 755-5645 • Website: www.chases.com

| HOW TO SUBMIT AN ENTRY | There is no charge for being listed in **Chase's**. Use the form below to submit new entries for forthcoming editions of **Chase's Calendar of Events**. Background information about your entry is also appreciated. Please be sure your dates are confirmed for 2005, or clearly indicate if dates are tentative. Use a separate sheet for each entry submitted. Information selected by the editors may be used and publicized through their books, electronic formats, syndicated services and/or other related products and services. The editors reserve the right to select and edit information received. Please mail all information to: Calendar Editor, Chase's Calendar of Events, Contemporary Books, 130 E. Randolph St., Ste 900, Chicago, IL 60601. |

☞ **DEADLINE FOR 2005 EDITION: APRIL 15, 2004.** PLEASE TYPE OR PRINT VERY CLEARLY.

1. Exact name of entry:
2. Exact INCLUSIVE DATES for 2005:
3. If applicable, estimated attendance (one figure—grand total all days):
4. Location (site [not address], city and state):
5. Brief description:

6. Formula—ONLY if used to set date(s) each year (Example: Annually, the third Monday in May):

7. For public use, complete contact info to be printed in book—name, address, phone, fax, e-mail, web.

8. For Chase's staff use, complete mailing address to send our update form to you next year—name, title or department, organization name, address—as well as a name, phone and e-mail of person we can contact with questions about your entry:

9. Person furnishing information: (print) _____ (sign) _____

10. PLEASE CIRCLE THE EXACT INCLUSIVE DATES FOR YOUR 2005 EVENT ON THE CALENDAR BELOW.

2005 Key dates

M. L. King Birthday, Jan 17
Chinese New Year, Feb 9
Washington's Birthday, Feb 21
Lent begins, Feb 9
Spring, Mar 20

Passover, Apr 24
Easter, Mar 27
Mother's Day, May 8
Memorial Day, May 30
Father's Day, June 19

Summer, June 21
Labor Day, Sept 5
Rosh Hashanah, Oct 4–5
Autumn, Sept 22
Yom Kippur, Oct 13

Columbus Day, Oct 10
Ramadan, Oct 4
Thanksgiving, Nov 24
Chanukah, Dec 26–Jan 2
Winter, Dec 21

Note: This page may be photocopied in order to submit additional event entries to **Chase's 2005 Calendar of Events**

130 E. Randolph St., Ste 900, Chicago, IL 60601 • Phone (312) 233-7560 • Fax (312) 233-7569 • www.chases.com